MW00783145

Koren Talmud Bavli
THE NOÉ EDITION

TA'ANIT · MEGILLA

Shefa

KOREN

תלמוד בבלי

KOREN TALMUD BAVLI

THE NOÉ EDITION

תענית · מגילה

TA'ANIT · MEGILLA

COMMENTARY BY
Rabbi Adin Even-Israel
Steinsaltz

EDITOR-IN-CHIEF
Rabbi Dr Tzvi Hersh Weinreb

EXECUTIVE EDITOR
Rabbi Joshua Schreier

•

SHEFA FOUNDATION
KOREN PUBLISHERS JERUSALEM

MATANEL
FOUNDATION
GRANTED TO GIVE

Supported by the Matanel Foundation

To ***Ira Lipman***

A man of great good will

One who labors to create good deeds that exceed both promises and expectations

A man who is constantly growing as a Jew

My thanks to Ira, who is able to listen and do, who makes the world a bit safer and better.

– Adin Even-Israel Steinsaltz

Koren Talmud Bavli, The Noé Edition
Volume 12: Tractate Ta'anit · Tractate Megilla

Standard Size Color Edition, ISBN 978 965 301 573 9
Daf Yomi Size B&W Edition, ISBN 978 965 301 618 7

First Hebrew/English Edition, 2014

Koren Publishers Jerusalem Ltd.
PO Box 4044, Jerusalem 91040, ISRAEL
PO Box 8531, New Milford, CT 06776, USA
www.korenpub.com

Shefa Foundation

Shefa Foundation is the parent organization of institutions established by Rabbi Adin Even-Israel Steinsaltz

PO Box 45187, Jerusalem 91450 ISRAEL
Telephone: +972 2 646 0900, Fax +972 2 624 9454
www.hashefa.co.il

Talmud Commentary © 1965, 2014 Adin Steinsaltz and Shefa Foundation
Talmud Translation © 2014 Shefa Foundation
Vocalization and punctuation of the Hebrew/Aramaic text © 2014 Shefa Foundation
Koren Tanakh & Siddur Fonts © 1962, 1981, 2014 Koren Publishers Jerusalem Ltd.
Talmud Design © 2014 Koren Publishers Jerusalem Ltd.
Original Illustrations © 1965, 2014 Shefa Foundation
Revised Illustrations © 2014 Koren Publishers Jerusalem Ltd. (except as noted)
Cover image courtesy of the Green Collection: Enamel Megillah Scroll Case (GC.SCR.000614)

Hardcover design by Ben Gasner

Considerable research and expense have gone into the creation of this publication. Unauthorized copying may be considered *geneivat da'at* and breach of copyright law.

No part of this publication (content or design, including use of the Talmud translations and Koren fonts) may be reproduced, stored in a retrieval system or transmitted in any form or by any means electronic, mechanical, photocopying or otherwise, without the prior written permission of the publisher, except in the case of brief quotations embedded in critical articles or reviews.

הִנֵּה יָמִים בָּאִים, נְאֻם אֲדֹנָי יֱהוִֹה, וְהִשְׁלַחְתִּי רָעָב בָּאָרֶץ,
לֹא־רָעָב לַלֶּחֶם וְלֹא־צָמָא לַמַּיִם, כִּי אִם־לִשְׁמֹעַ אֵת דִּבְרֵי יהוה.

Behold, days are coming – says the LORD God –
I will send a hunger to the land, not a hunger for bread
nor a thirst for water, but to hear the words of the LORD.

(AMOS 8:11)

The Noé edition of the Koren Talmud Bavli
with the commentary of Rabbi Adin Even-Israel Steinsaltz
is dedicated to all those who open its cover
to quench their thirst for Jewish knowledge,
in our generation of Torah renaissance.

This beautiful edition is for the young, the aged,
the novice and the savant alike,
as it unites the depth of Torah knowledge
with the best of academic scholarship.

Within its exquisite and vibrant pages,
words become worlds.

It will claim its place in the library of classics,
in the bookcases of the Beit Midrash,
the classrooms of our schools,
and in the offices of professionals and businesspeople
who carve out precious time to grapple with its timeless wisdom.

For the Student and the Scholar

DEDICATED BY LEO AND SUE NOÉ

Shefa

Managing Editor
Rabbi Jason Rappoport

Senior Content Editor
Rabbi Dr. Shalom Z. Berger

Editors
Rabbi Joshua Amaru, *Coordinating Editor*
Tal Avrahami
Aryeh Bernstein
Menucha Chwat
Rabbi Yoel Domb
Rabbi Yehoshua Duker
Rabbi Dov Foxbrunner
Rabbi Yonatan Shai Freedman
Raphael Friedman
Rabbi Uri Goldstein
Nechama Greenberg
Rabbi Alan Haber
Rabbi Tzvi Chaim Kaye
Rabbi Yonatan Kohn
Rabbi Adin Krohn
Catriel Lev
Sholom Licht
Elisha Loewenstern
Adina Luber
Rabbi Avishai Magence, *Content Curator*
Rafi Miller
Rabbi Jonathan Mishkin
Sarit Nagus
Yedidya Naveh
Rabbi Eli Ozarowski
Aharon Rutenberg
Rabbi David Sedley
Shira Shmidman
Rabbi Michael Siev
Avi Steinhart
Rabbi David Strauss
Rabbi Yitzchak Twersky
Rabbi Binyamin Zimmerman

Copy Editors
Aliza Israel, *Coordinator*
Bracha Hermon
Ita Olesker
Debbie Ismailoff
Shira Finson
Ilana Sobel
Deena Nataf
Eliana Kurlantzick Yorav
Nava Wieder

Language Consultants
Dr. Stephanie E. Binder, *Greek & Latin*
Yaakov Hoffman, *Arabic*
Dr. Shai Secunda, *Persian*

KOREN

Design & Typesetting
Raphaël Freeman, *Design & Typography*
Dena Landowne Bailey, *Typesetting*
Rina Ben Gal, *Typesetting*
Tani Bayer, *Jacket Design*

Images
Rabbi Eliahu Misgav, *Illustration*
Yehudit Cohen, *Image Acquisition*

Just as my ancestors planted for me,
I too am planting for my descendants.

(*KOREN TALMUD BAVLI, TA'ANIT* 23A)

Massekhet Ta'anit
is dedicated by a Friend
in honor of

Rav Adin Even-Israel Steinsaltz
A true leader and visionary for Am Yisrael

and

Rav Meni Even-Israel
For conceiving and shepherding
the Koren Talmud Bavli to reality
enabling many new students
to tackle the study of Talmud

יְקוּם פֻּרְקָן מִן שְׁמַיָּא,
חִנָּא וְחִסְדָּא וְרַחֲמֵי וְחַיֵּי אֲרִיכֵי וּמְזוֹנֵי רְוִיחֵי,
וְסִיַּעְתָּא דִשְׁמַיָּא, וּבַרְיוּת גּוּפָא וּנְהוֹרָא מְעַלְיָא, זַרְעָא חַיָּא וְקַיָּמָא,
זַרְעָא דִּי לָא יִפְסֻק וְדִי לָא יִבְטֻל מִפִּתְגָּמֵי אוֹרַיְתָא,
לְמָרָנָן וְרַבָּנָן...וּלְכָל מָאן דְּעָסְקִין בְּאוֹרַיְתָא.

(FROM THE *YEKUM PURKAN* BLESSING)

כָּל יִשְׂרָאֵל יֵשׁ לָהֶם חֵלֶק לָעוֹלָם הַבָּא. שֶׁנֶּאֱמַר:
וְעַמֵּךְ כֻּלָּם צַדִּיקִים, לְעוֹלָם יִירְשׁוּ אָרֶץ
נֵצֶר מַטָּעַי, מַעֲשֵׂה יָדַי לְהִתְפָּאֵר:

All Israel have a share
in the World to Come, as it is said:
"Your people are all righteous;
they shall inherit the land for ever;
they are a shoot of My own planting,
a work of My own hands, that I may be glorified."

(ISAIAH 60:21)

Massekhet Megilla is dedicated by
Boris and Anna Gulko

in memory of
Efraim ben Hilik, Gnesya bat Aaron,
Genya Golda bat Emmanuel,
and Mark ben Alexander

and in honor of our children
David and Chana Michal Shifra

and their children
Sara Nessa, Odelia, and Shylie Efrat

Contents

For the vocalized Vilna Shas layout, please open as a Hebrew book.

Haskama

Rabbi Moshe Feinstein

RABBI MOSES FEINSTEIN
455 F. D. R. DRIVE
New York N. Y. 10002
OREgon 7-1222

משה פיינשטיין
ר"ם תפארת ירושלים
בנוא יארק

בע"ה

הנה ראיתי הפירוש החשוב של הרב הגאון מוהר"ר עדין שטיינזלץ שליט"א מעיה"ק ירושלים, על מסכתות ביצה ור"ה. באמת כבר ידוע לי פירושו של הרה"ג הנ"ל על מסכתות מתלמוד בבלי, וכבר כתבתי מכתב הסכמה עליהם. ובאתי בזה רק להדגיש מחדש איך שהפירושים של הרה"ג הנ"ל, שכולל פירוש חדש על הגמרא עצמו וגם פירוש שיש בו סיכום להלכה מהנידונים שבגמרא, נוסף לעוד כמה חלקים, הם באמת עבודה גדולה, שיכולים להיות לתועלת לא רק לאלו שכבר מורגלים בלמוד הגמרא, ורוצים להעמיק יותר, אלא גם לאלו שמתחילים ללמוד, להדריכם בדרכי התורה איך להבין ולהעמיק בים התלמוד.

והריני מברך להרה"ג הנ"ל שיצליחהו השי"ת בספריו אלו ושיזכה לחבר עוד ספרים, להגדיל תורה ולהאדירה, לתפארת השם ותורתו.

ועל זה באתי על החתום לכבוד התורה ביום ז' לחודש אייר תשמ"ג.

משה פיינשטיין

…These new commentaries – which include a new interpretation of the Talmud, a halakhic summary of the debated issues, and various other sections – are a truly outstanding work; they can be of great benefit not only to those familiar with talmudic study who seek to deepen their understanding, but also to those who are just beginning to learn, guiding them through the pathways of the Torah and teaching them how to delve into the sea of the Talmud.

I would like to offer my blessing to this learned scholar. May the Holy One grant him success with these volumes and may he merit to write many more, to enhance the greatness of Torah, and bring glory to God and His word…

Rabbi Moshe Feinstein
New York, 7 Adar 5743

ר' משה פיינשטיין שליט"א

הנה ראיתי את מסכת אחת מהש"ס שנקד אותה וגם צייר צורות הצמחים וכדומה מדברים שלא ידוע לכמה אנשים הרה"ג ר' עדין שטיינזלץ מירושלים שליט"א וגם הוסיף שם בגליון פירושים וחידושים וניכר שהוא ת"ח וראויין לעיין בהם ת"ח ובני הישיבה וטוב גם לקנותם בבתי כנסיות ובבתי מדרשות שיש שיהיו להם לתועלת. — ועל זה באתי עה"ח ג' אדר ב' תש"ל.

נאם משה פיינשטיין
ר"מ תפארת ירושלים, ניו־יורק, ארה"ב

I have seen one tractate from the Talmud to which the great scholar Rabbi Adin Steinsaltz שליט״א has added *nikkud* (vowels) and illustrations to explain that which is unknown to many people; he has also added interpretations and innovations, and is evidently a *talmid ḥakham*. *Talmidei ḥakhamim* and yeshiva students ought to study these volumes, and synagogues and *batei midrash* would do well to purchase them, as they may find them useful.

Rabbi Moshe Feinstein
New York, Adar 5730

Haskama

Rabbi Menachem Mendel Schneerson

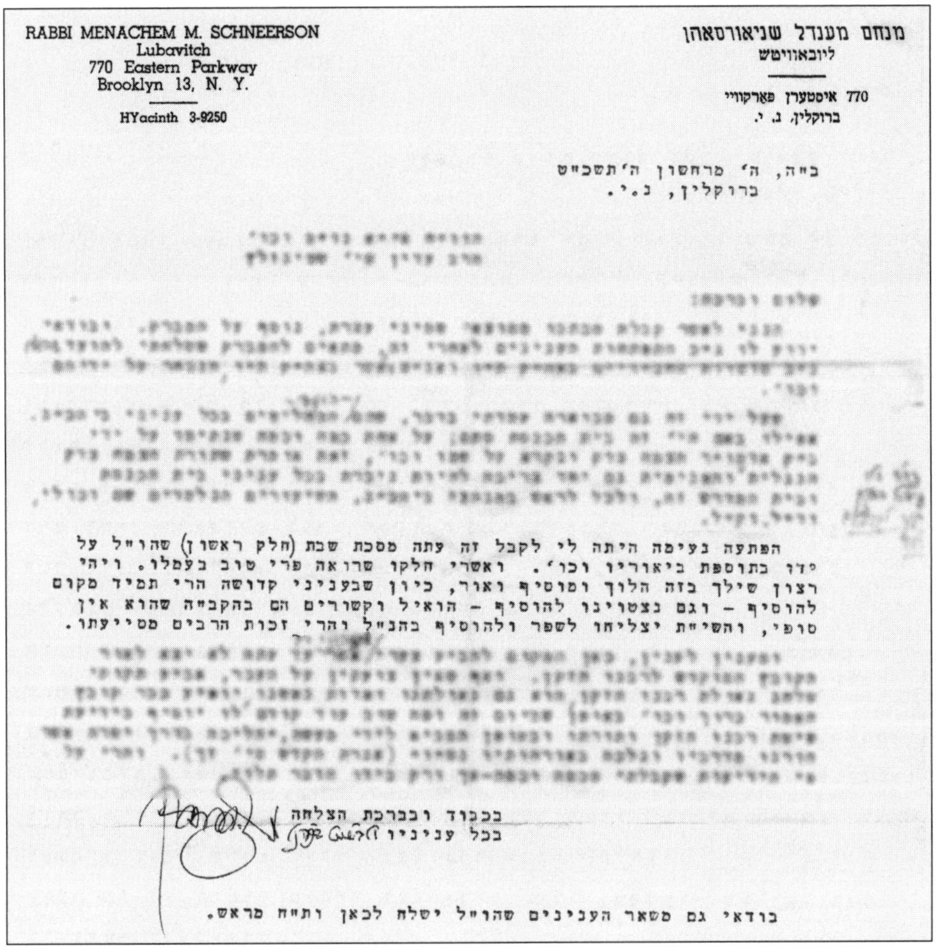

RABBI MENACHEM M. SCHNEERSON
Lubavitch
770 Eastern Parkway
Brooklyn 13, N. Y.

HYacinth 3-9250

מנחם מענדל שניאורסאהן
ליובאוויטש

770 איסטערן פארקוויי
ברוקלין, נ. י.

ב״ה, ה׳ מרחשון ה׳תשכ״ט
ברוקלין, נ.י.

הפתעה נעימה היתה לי לקבל זה עתה מסכת שבת (חלק ראשון) שהו״ל על ידו בתוספת ביאוריו וכו׳. ואשרי חלקו שרואה פרי טוב בעמלו. ויהי רצון שילך בזה הלוך ומוסיף ואור, כיון שבעניני קדושה הרי תמיד מקום להוסיף – וגם נצטוינו להוסיף – הואיל וקשורים הם בהקב״ה שהוא אין סופי, והשי״ת יצליחו לשפר ולהוסיף בהנ״ל והרי זכות הרבים מסייעתו.

בכבוד ובברכת הצלחה
בכל עניניו

בודאי גם משאר הענינים שהו״ל ישלח לכאן ותו״ח מראש.

… I have just had the pleasant surprise of receiving tractate *Shabbat* (part one), which has been published by [Rabbi Steinsaltz] along with his explanations, etc. Happy is the man who sees good fruits from his labors. May he continue in this path and increase light, for in the matters of holiness there is always room to add – and we have been commanded to add – for they are linked to the Holy One, Blessed be He, Who is infinite. And may the Holy One grant him success to improve and enhance this work, since the greater good strengthens his hand …

Rabbi Menachem Mendel Schneerson
The Lubavitcher Rebbe
Brooklyn, 5 Marḥeshvan 5729

Haskama

Rabbi Moshe Zvi Neria

של הרב משה צבי נריה

ב"ה

"ושמעו ביום ההוא החרשים דברי ספר"
(ישעי' כט' יח')

תרגום ספרי קדמונים לשפת דורות אחרונים – היא משימתם של חכמי דור ודור. ובישראל שמצוות "ושננתם לבניך" מקיפה את כל חלקי האומה, ודאי שהיתה זאת המשימה בכל עידן ועידן.

בכל דור כך, ובדורנו אשר רבים בו הקרובים שנתרחקו וחוזרים ומתקרבים – לא כל שכן. כי רבים היום האומרים "מי ישקנו מים מבאר" התלמוד, ומועטים הם הדולים ומשקים.

ראוי אפוא להערכה מיוחדת נסיונו המבורך של הצעיר המופלא, הרב עדין שטיינזלץ, לפרש פרקי-תלמוד בהסברה מורחבת-תמציתית, אשר נוסף על הפרוש המלולי והעניני הוא מעלה גם את ההגיון של הדברים ומתרגמת אותם לשפת-המושגים של בן-דורנו.

דומה שכל הנגשים אל חומר למודי מתוך רצון להבינו – התלמיד החרוץ והמבוגר המשכיל – לא יתקלו בשום קושי בבואם ללמוד סוגיא תלמודית לפי פרוש זה. ולא עוד אלא שיש לקוות כי ההסברה הגיונית תעמידם מיד על טוב-הטעם [redacted] של דף-הגמרא, והם ימשכו יותר ויותר אל הלמוד העיוני הזה אשר טובי המוחות בישראל לנו בעומקו, ואשר ממנו פינה, ממנו יתד לבנין חיינו.

נועם ד' על המפרש הנמרץ להמשיך במפעלו, וברוכים כל העוזרים להוצאתו לאור-עולם.

ביקר אורייתא

(חתימה)

The translation of the books of our past into the language of the present – this was the task of the sages of every generation. And in Israel, where the command to "teach them repeatedly to your children" applies to all parts of the nation, it was certainly the task of every era. This is true for every generation, and in our time – when many of those who have strayed far are once again drawing near – all the more so. For many today say, "Who will let us drink from the well" of Talmud, and few are those who offer up the waters to drink.

We must, therefore, particularly commend the blessed endeavor of Rabbi Adin Steinsaltz to explain the chapters of the Talmud in this extensive yet succinct commentary, which, in addition to its literal interpretation of the text, also explicates the latter's underlying logic and translates it into the language of our generation.

It appears that all those who seek to study Talmud – the diligent student and the learned adult – will have no difficulty understanding when using this commentary. Moreover, we may hope that the logical explanation will reveal to them the beauty of the talmudic page, and they will be drawn deeper and deeper into the intellectual pursuit which has engaged the best Jewish minds, and which serves as the cornerstone of our very lives…

Rabbi Moshe Zvi Neria

Haskama

Rabbi Mordechai Eliyahu

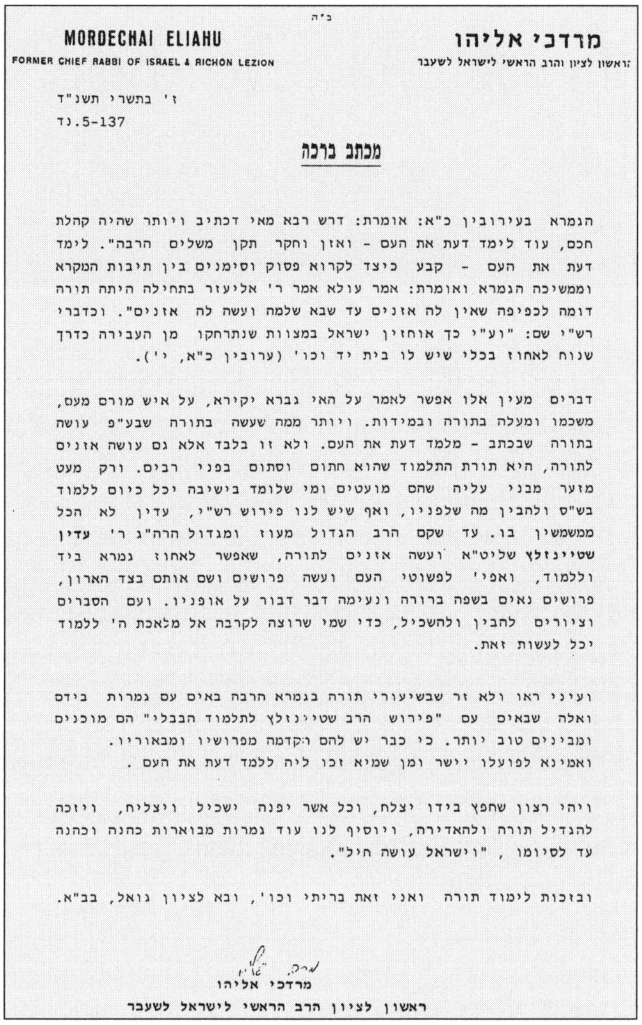

ב"ה

MORDECHAI ELIAHU
FORMER CHIEF RABBI OF ISRAEL & RICHON LEZION

מרדכי אליהו
ראשון לציון והרב הראשי לישראל לשעבר

ז' בתשרי תשנ"ד
נד.5-137

מכתב ברכה

הגמרא בעירובין כ"א: אומרת: דרש רבא מאי דכתיב ויותר שהיה קהלת חכם, עוד לימד דעת את העם - ואזן וחקר תקן משלים הרבה". לימד דעת את העם - קבע כיצד לקרוא פסוק וסימנים בין תיבות המקרא וממשיכה הגמרא ואומרת: אמר עולא אמר ר' אליעזר בתחילה היתה תורה דומה לכפיפה שאין לה אזנים עד שבא שלמה ועשה לה אזנים". וכדברי רש"י שם: "וע"י כך אוחזין ישראל במצוות שנתרחקו מן העבירה כדרך שנוח לאחוז בכלי שיש לו בית יד וכו' (ערובין כ"א, י').

דברים מעין אלו אפשר לאמר על האי גברא יקירא, על איש מורם מעם, משכמו ומעלה בתורה ובמידות. ויותר ממה שעשה בתורה שבע"פ עושה בתורה שבכתב - מלמד דעת את העם. ולא זו בלבד אלא גם עושה אזנים לתורה, היא תורת התלמוד שהוא חתום וסתום בפני רבים. ורק מעט מזער מבני עליה שהם מועטים ומי שלומד בישיבה יכל כיום ללמוד בש"ס ולהבין מה שלפניו, ואף שיש לנו פירוש רש"י, עדין לא הכל ממשמשין בו. עד שקם הרב הגדול מעוז ומגדול הרה"ג ר' **עדין שטיינזלץ** שליט"א ועשה אזנים לתורה, שאפשר לאחוז גמרא ביד וללמוד, ואפי' לפשוטי העם ועשה פרושים ושם אותם בצד הארון, פרושים נאים בשפה ברורה ונעימה דבר דבור על אופניו. ועם הסברים וציורים להבין ולהשכיל, כדי שמי שרוצה לקרבה אל מלאכת ה' ללמוד יכל לעשות זאת.

ועיני ראו ולא זר שבשיעורי תורה בגמרא הרבה באים עם גמרות בידם ואלה שבאים עם "פירוש הרב שטיינזלץ לתלמוד הבבלי" הם מוכנים ומבינים טוב יותר. כי כבר יש להם הקדמה מפרושיו ומבאוריו.
ואמינא לפועלו יישר ומן שמיא זכו ליה ללמד דעת את העם .

ויהי רצון שחפץ בידו יצלח, וכל אשר יפנה ישכיל ויצליח, ויזכה להגדיל תורה ולהאדירה, ויוסיף לנו עוד גמרות מבוארות כהנה וכהנה עד לסיומו , "וישראל עושה חיל".

ובזכות לימוד תורה ואני זאת בריתי וכו', ובא לציון גואל, בב"א.

מרדכי אליהו
ראשון לציון הרב הראשי לישראל לשעבר

The Talmud in *Eruvin* 21b states: Rava continued to interpret verses homiletically. What is the meaning of the verse: "And besides being wise, Kohelet also taught the people knowledge; and he weighed, and sought out, and set in order many proverbs" (Ecclesiastes 12:9)? He explains: He taught the people knowledge; he taught it with the accentuation marks in the Torah, and explained each matter by means of another matter similar to it. And he weighed [*izen*], and sought out, and set in order many proverbs; Ulla said that Rabbi Eliezer said: At first the Torah was like a basket without handles [*oznayim*] until Solomon came and made handles for it. And as Rashi there explains: And thus were Israel able to grasp the mitzvot and distance themselves from transgressions – just as a vessel with handles is easily held, etc.

Such things may be said of this beloved and eminent man, a great sage of Torah and of virtue. And far more than he has done with the Oral Torah, he does with the Written Torah – teaching the people knowledge. And beyond that, he also affixes handles to the Torah, i.e., to the Talmud, which is obscure and difficult for many. Only the intellectual elite, which are a precious few, and those who study in yeshiva, can today learn the Talmud and understand what it says – and even though we have Rashi, still not everyone uses him. But now the great scholar Rabbi Adin Steinsaltz שליט"א has come and affixed handles to the Torah, allowing the Talmud to be held and studied, even by simple men. And he has composed a commentary alongside the text, a fine commentary in clear, comprehensible language, "a word fitly spoken" with explanations and illustrations, so that all those who seek to study the work of God can do so.

Rabbi Mordechai Eliyahu
Former Chief Rabbi of Israel, 7 Tishrei 5754

Message from Rabbi Adin Even-Israel Steinsaltz

The Talmud is the cornerstone of Jewish culture. True, our culture originated in the Bible and has branched out in directions besides the Talmud, yet the latter's influence on Jewish culture is fundamental. Perhaps because it was composed not by a single individual, but rather by hundreds and thousands of Sages in *batei midrash* in an ongoing, millennium-long process, the Talmud expresses not only the deepest themes and values of the Jewish people, but also of the Jewish spirit. As the basic study text for young and old, laymen and learned, the Talmud may be said to embody the historical trajectory of the Jewish soul. It is, therefore, best studied interactively, its subject matter coming together with the student's questions, perplexities, and innovations to form a single intricate weave. In the entire scope of Jewish culture, there is not one area that does not draw from or converse with the Talmud. The study of Talmud is thus the gate through which a Jew enters his life's path.

The *Koren Talmud Bavli* seeks to render the Talmud accessible to the millions of Jews whose mother tongue is English, allowing them to study it, approach it, and perhaps even become one with it.

This project has been carried out and assisted by several people, all of whom have worked tirelessly to turn this vision into an actual set of books to be studied. It is a joyful duty to thank the many partners in this enterprise for their various contributions. Thanks to Koren Publishers Jerusalem, both for the publication of this set and for the design of its very complex graphic layout. Thanks of a different sort are owed to the Shefa Foundation and its director, Rabbi Menachem Even-Israel, for their determination and persistence in setting this goal and reaching it. Many thanks to the translators, editors, and proofreaders for their hard and meticulous work. Thanks to the individuals and organizations that supported this project, chief among them the Matanel Foundation and the Noé family of London. And thanks in advance to all those who will invest their time, hearts, and minds in studying these volumes – to learn, to teach, and to practice.

Rabbi Adin Even-Israel Steinsaltz
Jerusalem 5773

Acknowledgments

We are indeed privileged to dedicate this edition of the *Koren Talmud Bavli* in honor of the generous support of Leo and Sue Noé of London.

The name Noé is synonymous with philanthropy. The family's charitable endeavors span a vast range of educational projects, welfare institutions, and outreach organizations across the globe, with a particular emphasis on the "nurturing of each individual." Among so many other charitable activities, the Noés have been deeply involved with *Kisharon*, which provides the British Jewish community with vital support for hundreds of people with learning difficulties and their families; they provide steadfast support of SEED, which stands at the forefront of adult Jewish education in the UK, and *Kemach*, an organization in Israel that "helps Haredi students sustain themselves in dignity," providing both professional and vocational training for the Haredi community in Israel.

The Noés are not simply donors to institutions. They are partners. Donors think of a sum. Partners think of a cause, becoming rigorously and keenly involved, and giving of their time and energy. We are honored that they have chosen to partner with our two organizations, *Shefa* and *Koren Publishers Jerusalem*, enabling us to further and deepen learning among all Jews.

Leo and Sue are the proud parents and grandparents of five children and their families. The next generation has been taught by example that with life's gifts come the responsibilities to be active within and contribute to society – both Jewish and non-Jewish – as is consistent with the noblest of Jewish values.

Rabbi Adin Even-Israel Steinsaltz
Matthew Miller, Publisher
Jerusalem 5773

Introduction by the Editor-in-Chief

The vastly expanded audience of Talmud study in our generation is a phenomenon of historical proportions. The reasons for this phenomenon are many, and include the availability of a wide array of translations, commentaries, and study aids.

One outstanding example of such a work is the translation of the Talmud into modern Hebrew by Rabbi Adin Even-Israel Steinsaltz. The product of a lifetime of intense intellectual labor, this translation stands out in its uniqueness.

But what can the interested student do if he or she does not comprehend the Hebrew, even in its modern form? Where is the English speaker who wishes to access this instructive material to turn?

The *Koren Talmud Bavli* that you hold in your hand is designed to be the answer to those questions.

This work is the joint effort of Rabbi Steinsaltz himself, his closest advisory staff, and Koren Publishers Jerusalem. It is my privilege to have been designated Editor-in-Chief of this important project, and to have worked in close collaboration with a team of translators and copy editors, artists and graphic designers, scholars and editors.

Together we are presenting to the English-speaking world a translation that has all the merits of the original Hebrew work by Rabbi Steinsaltz, and provides assistance for the beginner of any age who seeks to obtain the necessary skills to become an adept talmudist.

This is the twelfth volume of the project, tractates *Ta'anit* and *Megilla*. It includes the entire original text, in the traditional configuration and pagination of the famed Vilna edition of the Talmud. This enables the student to follow the core text with the commentaries of Rashi, *Tosafot*, and the customary marginalia. It also provides a clear English translation in contemporary idiom, faithfully based upon the modern Hebrew edition.

At least equal to the linguistic virtues of this edition are the qualities of its graphic design. Rather than intimidate students by confronting them with a page-size block of text, we have divided the page into smaller thematic units. Thus, readers can focus their attention and absorb each discrete discussion before proceeding to the next unit. The design of each page allows for sufficient white space to ease the visual task of reading. The illustrations, one of the most innovative features of the Hebrew edition, have been substantially enhanced and reproduced in color.

The end result is a literary and artistic masterpiece. This has been achieved through the dedicated work of a large team of translators, headed by Rabbi Joshua Schreier, and through the unparalleled creative efforts of Raphaël Freeman and the gifted staff at Koren.

The group of individuals who surround Rabbi Steinsaltz and support his work deserve our thanks as well. I have come to appreciate their energy, initiative, and persistence. And I thank the indefatigable Rabbi Menachem Even-Israel, whom I cannot praise highly enough. The quality of his guidance and good counsel is surpassed only by his commitment to the dissemination and perpetuation of his father's precious teachings.

Finally, in humility, awe, and great respect, I acknowledge Rabbi Adin Even-Israel Steinsaltz. I thank him for the inspirational opportunity he has granted me to work with one of the outstanding sages of our time.

Rabbi Tzvi Hersh Weinreb
Jerusalem 5774

Preface by the Executive Editor

Toward the beginning of tractate *Pesaḥim* (3a), the Gemara questions the Mishna's use of the term *or* rather than the standard term *leil* when referring to the evening of the fourteenth of Nisan. The Gemara introduces a discussion of the value of euphemism and refraining from the use of crude language. It concludes that despite the importance of euphemism, if the euphemism comes at the expense of clarity and requires a less succinct formulation, it is preferable to speak concisely. Only when the choice is between equally concise phrases is the euphemism preferred.

In his *peirush*, Rabbi Steinsaltz's language is both concise and aesthetic. While explaining often difficult passages, he avoids the temptation to over-explain, inviting the reader to study the Talmud with him rather than doing all the thinking in the reader's place. We have attempted to follow his path in translating and editing the *Koren Talmud Bavli*.

My involvement in the production of the *Koren Talmud Bavli* has been both a privilege and a pleasure. The Shefa Foundation, headed by Rabbi Menachem Even-Israel and devoted to the dissemination of the wide-ranging, monumental works of Rabbi Adin Even-Israel Steinsaltz, constitutes the Steinsaltz side of this partnership; Koren Publishers Jerusalem, headed by Matthew Miller, with the day-to-day management of the project in the able hands of Dena Landowne Bailey, constitutes the publishing side of this partnership. The combination of the inspiration, which is the hallmark of Shefa, with the creativity and professionalism for which Koren is renowned and which I experience on a daily basis, has lent the *Koren Talmud Bavli* its outstanding quality in terms of both content and form.

I would like to express my appreciation for Rabbi Dr. Tzvi Hersh Weinreb, the Editor-in-Chief, whose insight and guidance have been invaluable. The contribution of my friend and colleague, Rabbi Dr. Shalom Z. Berger, the Senior Content Editor, cannot be overstated; his title does not begin to convey the excellent direction he has provided in all aspects of this project. In addition, I would like to thank Rabbi Jason Rappoport, Managing Editor; Rabbi Joshua Amaru, Coordinating Editor; and Rabbi Avishai Magence, Content Curator, whose tireless devotion to this project has been and continues to be crucial to the continued success of this project. The erudite and articulate men and women who serve as translators, editors, and copy editors have ensured that this project adheres to the highest standards.

There are several others whose contributions to this project cannot be overlooked. On the Steinsaltz side: Meir HaNegbi, Yacov Elbert, and Tsipora Ifrah. On the Koren side, my colleagues at Koren: Rabbi David Fuchs, Rabbi Hanan Benayahu, Efrat Gross, Rachel Hanstater Meghnagi, Rabbi Eliahu Misgav, and Rabbi Yinon Chen. Their assistance in all matters, large and small, is appreciated.

At the risk of being repetitious, I would like to thank Rabbi Dr. Berger for introducing me to the world of Steinsaltz. Finally, I would like to thank Rabbi Menachem Even-Israel, with whom it continues to be a pleasure to move forward in this great enterprise.

Rabbi Joshua Schreier
Jerusalem 5773

Introduction by the Publisher

The Talmud has sustained and inspired Jews for thousands of years. Throughout Jewish history, an elite cadre of scholars has absorbed its learning and passed it on to succeeding generations. The Talmud has been the fundamental text of our people.

Beginning in the 1960s, Rabbi Adin Even-Israel Steinsaltz שליט״א created a revolution in the history of Talmud study. His translation of the Talmud, first into modern Hebrew and then into other languages, as well the practical learning aids he added to the text, have enabled millions of people around the world to access and master the complexity and context of the world of Talmud.

It is thus a privilege to present the *Koren Talmud Bavli*, an English translation of the talmudic text with the brilliant elucidation of Rabbi Steinsaltz. The depth and breadth of his knowledge are unique in our time. His rootedness in the tradition and his reach into the world beyond it are inspirational.

Working with Rabbi Steinsaltz on this remarkable project has been not only an honor, but a great pleasure. Never shy to express an opinion, with wisdom and humor, Rabbi Steinsaltz sparkles in conversation, demonstrating his knowledge (both sacred and worldly), sharing his wide-ranging interests, and, above all, radiating his passion. I am grateful for the unique opportunity to work closely with him, and I wish him many more years of writing and teaching.

Our intentions in publishing this new edition of the Talmud are threefold. First, we seek to fully clarify the talmudic page to the reader – textually, intellectually, and graphically. Second, we seek to utilize today's most sophisticated technologies, both in print and electronic formats, to provide the reader with a comprehensive set of study tools. And third, we seek to help readers advance in their process of Talmud study.

To achieve these goals, the *Koren Talmud Bavli* is unique in a number of ways:

- The classic *tzurat hadaf* of Vilna, used by scholars since the 1800s, has been reset for greater clarity, and opens from the Hebrew "front" of the book. Full *nikkud* has been added to both the talmudic text and Rashi's commentary, allowing for a more fluent reading with the correct pronunciation; the commentaries of *Tosafot* have been punctuated. Upon the advice of many English-speaking teachers of Talmud, we have separated these core pages from the translation, thereby enabling the advanced student to approach the text without the distraction of the translation. This also reduces the number of volumes in the set. At the bottom of each *daf*, there is a reference to the corresponding English pages. In addition, the Vilna edition was read against other manuscripts and older print editions, so that texts which had been removed by non-Jewish censors have been restored to their rightful place.

- The English translation, which starts on the English "front" of the book, reproduces the *menukad* Talmud text alongside the English translation (in bold) and commentary and explanation (in a lighter font). The Hebrew and Aramaic text is presented in logical paragraphs. This allows for a fluent reading of the text for the non-Hebrew or non-Aramaic reader. It also allows for the Hebrew reader to refer easily to the text alongside. Where the original text features dialogue or poetry, the English text is laid out in a manner appropriate to the genre. Each page refers to the relevant *daf*.
- Critical contextual tools surround the text and translation: personality notes, providing short biographies of the Sages; language notes, explaining foreign terms borrowed from Greek, Latin, Persian, or Arabic; and background notes, giving information essential to the understanding of the text, including history, geography, botany, archeology, zoology, astronomy, and aspects of daily life in the talmudic era.
- Halakhic summaries provide references to the authoritative legal decisions made over the centuries by the rabbis. They explain the reasons behind each halakhic decision as well as the ruling's close connection to the Talmud and its various interpreters.
- Photographs, drawings, and other illustrations have been added throughout the text – in full color in the Standard and Electronic editions, and in black and white in the Daf Yomi edition – to visually elucidate the text.

This is not an exhaustive list of features of this edition; it merely presents an overview for the English-speaking reader who may not be familiar with the "total approach" to Talmud pioneered by Rabbi Steinsaltz.

Several professionals have helped bring this vast collaborative project to fruition. My many colleagues are noted on the Acknowledgments page, and the leadership of this project has been exceptional.

RABBI MENACHEM EVEN-ISRAEL, DIRECTOR OF THE SHEFA FOUNDATION, was the driving force behind this enterprise. With enthusiasm and energy, he formed the happy alliance with Koren and established close relationships among all involved in the work.

RABBI DR. TZVI HERSH WEINREB שליט״א, EDITOR-IN-CHIEF, brought to this project his profound knowledge of Torah, intellectual literacy of Talmud, and erudition of Western literature. It is to him that the text owes its very high standard, both in form and content, and the logical manner in which the beauty of the Talmud is presented.

RABBI JOSHUA SCHREIER, EXECUTIVE EDITOR, assembled an outstanding group of scholars, translators, editors, and copy editors, whose standards and discipline enabled this project to proceed in a timely and highly professional manner.

RABBI MEIR HANEGBI, EDITOR OF THE HEBREW EDITION OF THE STEINSALTZ TALMUD, lent his invaluable assistance throughout the work process, supervising the reproduction of the Vilna pages.

RAPHAËL FREEMAN created this Talmud's unique typographic design which, true to the Koren approach, is both elegant and user-friendly.

It has been an enriching experience for all of us at Koren Publishers Jerusalem to work with the Shefa Foundation and the Steinsaltz Center to develop and produce the *Koren Talmud Bavli*. We pray that this publication will be a source of great learning and, ultimately, greater *Avodat Hashem* for all Jews.

Matthew Miller, Publisher
Koren Publishers Jerusalem
Jerusalem 5773

Introduction to **Ta'anit**

Tractate *Ta'anit*, as its name indicates, focuses mainly on the *halakhot* and themes of fast days [*ta'aniyot*], covering both communal fasts and private, individual fasts and addressing both those that have fixed dates and those that are established from time to time in response to various negative events. In the Jerusalem Talmud and certain works of the early authorities, the tractate is called by the plural term, *Ta'aniyot*.

The concept of a fast day as a mitzva in its own right does not appear in the Torah. It is true that the Torah refers to Yom Kippur as an affliction of the soul; see, for example, Leviticus 16:29. However, the Torah's description means that unlike regular fasts, this particular fast is for the purification of the soul. Nevertheless, there is a connection between Yom Kippur and the fasts discussed in this tractate, on both the theoretical and the practical levels.

There are many references to fasts in the Prophets and Writings. Numerous verses teach about the meaning and purpose of fast days, as well as the manner of their observance, both communal and individual, as they were practiced by the Jewish people in ancient times. Consequently, the content of tractate *Ta'anit* is based on oral traditions transmitted to Moses at Sinai, as expressed in practical terms in many books of the Bible.

The fundamental idea of fast days is based on the assumption that events in the world do not happen by chance and for no reason. Rather, just as there are physical causes for occurrences, there are also spiritual and moral explanations. In general terms, reward is bestowed for good deeds and punishment for evil. Human action is scrutinized by Divine Providence, again both on the level of the individual as well as that of the community, or indeed, the entire nation. Therefore, any misfortune visited upon a congregation or an individual has a purpose and a meaning. Sometimes it serves as a warning that one's actions are corrupt and must be amended; on other occasions it is a punishment for sins, as explained at length by the Torah in the chapter of rebuke (Leviticus, chapter 26). Accordingly, in every time of trouble and distress, one should increase his prayers, repent, and make amends for any wrongs he has committed. He should sanctify himself so that his previous transgressions will be forgiven, and pray and beseech God to avert the evil decree.

As indicated by the Hebrew word *ta'anit*, a fast is a time of affliction [*inui*]. As explained in the Gemara and in the books of the Prophets and Writings, on a fast day one abstains from eating and drinking. For the most important fasts, the Sages added the prohibitions against wearing shoes, engaging in conjugal relations, anointing, and bathing. Nevertheless, both the prophets and the Sages stress that the fasting and other suffering that one accepts upon himself are not the purpose and ultimate aim of the fast day. See, for example, Isaiah, chapter 57, which is read on Yom Kippur. The fasting and other suffering are merely a means of achieving atonement and purity of the soul. It is prayer, charity, and repentance, i.e., a reconsideration of past actions and an acceptance of improvement for the future, which constitute the main focus of fast days. For this reason tractate *Ta'anit* does not focus on the detailed *halakhot* of fasting, but on the other aspects of the day: The additional prayers and spiritual awakening through study and action.

The most common misfortune that should stir feelings of repentance is a lack of rain, and therefore most of the tractate deals with this issue. As stated in the Torah (Deuteronomy 11:17), a drought is a sign of God's anger, as both a warning and a punishment. At a time of a dearth of rain, even more than with other disasters, one has no way to improve the situation other than by turning to God and praying. Furthermore, a lack of rain is not simply a local or temporary problem; it can bring catastrophe on the entire country. Much of tractate *Ta'anit*, and indeed many of the *halakhot* of fast days, concern fasts established to entreat God for rainfall.

Since a drought of rain causes increasingly severe difficulties as time goes on, the fasts become correspondingly severe as well. The Sages did not simply establish one fast day, but several complex cycles of fasts, which become more and more stringent as a drought continues.

Any communal fast that does not have a fixed date, i.e., which is neither a response to a current emergency nor commemorates a historical event, is established on a Monday or Thursday, the days on which the Torah is read in public and the courts would convene. The cycle of fast days does not occur on the other days of the week but only on these two days, in consecutive order.

Naturally, there is a gloomy, even mournful, aspect to fasts, as they are declared for sad events and are intended to prevent misfortunes from continuing or becoming worse. One exception to this rule is Yom Kippur, which is classified as a Festival, and which includes the joy of purification. Furthermore, as explained at the end of the tractate, this date was established as a joyful holiday, on which marriageable young girls would go out, dance in the vineyards, and seek husbands.

These apparently negative features of fast days are designed to awaken one's heart to repentance and have the same goal as public gatherings for prayer, readings from the Torah, speeches of moral reproof and instruction, and all other such activities. The aim is for all the participants to correct their errors and shortcomings, both as a community and as individuals.

Although drought is the most common and prolonged cause for fasting, any misfortune that befalls a community should be met with prayers and calling out to God. See, for instance, I Kings, chapter 8. This applies to natural disasters such as flooding and storms, attacks of wild animals or locusts, and infectious diseases, as well as to man-made events, e.g., wars or persecution by the ruling authorities. Under certain circumstances, any of these misfortunes could be a reason for the decreeing of a fast. Furthermore, the purpose of the fast can vary. One might pray that a punishment that has already been imposed be canceled or diminished, or entreat God to avert an impending danger. A fast can even be an act of solidarity with the sufferings of another Jewish community, especially one in Eretz Yisrael. This applies to individual fasts as well.

Sometimes a person will accept a fast upon himself, generally by means of a declaration during the afternoon service of the previous day, as part of a broader effort to achieve atonement for his sins, or as a request that he will not suffer a certain misfortune, e.g., one that appeared in his dreams. Naturally, the status of a fast of an individual, or even a collection of individuals, is unlike that of a communal fast, with regard to both its severity and to the manner of its initiation. In the case of a community these are determined by the events of the day and the needs of the public.

In addition to those fasts, which are a response to current misfortunes and are established in hope of a better future, there are also fixed fast days of memorial which were established to commemorate disasters and occurrences of earlier generations. Yet here too the fast is directed toward the future, as remembering past events is meant to awaken hearts to the general redemption that will be at the end of days. However, these days, which commemorate national disasters, especially those involving the destruction of the First and Second Temples, are not only days of fasting and memorial, but also days of mourning. The most prominent of these dates is the Ninth of Av, which has become a symbol of all the tribulations of the Jewish people, due to the many misfortunes that occurred on this day. Virtually all the mitzvot and prohibitions that apply to someone in mourning for the dead are obligatory for everyone on the Ninth of Av.

With the exception of Yom Kippur, all fast days apply by rabbinic law. Admittedly, the fixed fast dates, i.e., the Ninth of Av, the tenth of Tevet, the seventeenth of Tammuz, and the third of Tishrei, are of ancient origin, as they were instituted by the prophets (see Zechariah, chapter 7). However, as they have no basis in the Torah itself, they are considered to be by rabbinical law.

Since the fasts were established by the Sages, they may not occur on fixed days of delight and rejoicing mandated by Torah law, i.e., Shabbat and Festivals. However, there are other days mentioned in the Torah whose status is not as clear-cut. It must be determined whether fasts can be established on New Moons or the intermediate Festival days, which are days of celebration but not full-fledged Festivals. A similar question applies to festive days established by the Sages over the generations as memorials of happy occasions. When a fast is decreed for a calamity, or when a fast occurs as part of the lengthy cycles of fasts or as a fast of the non-priestly watches, it is possible that it will coincide with one of these days of rejoicing. It is therefore necessary to establish which of these days can be overridden by a fast.

Tractate *Ta'anit* consists of four chapters, each dealing with its own topic:

Chapter One focuses on rainfall, the common dates for the various rainfalls of the year, the significance of rain in general, and the order of the cycles of fasts for rainfall.

Chapter Two addresses the special prayers and customs of fast days, especially those of the major communal fasts.

Chapter Three contains a broad discussion of the events for which fasts are decreed. This chapter focuses on the misfortunes mentioned in the previous chapters, as well as other calamities of various kinds.

Chapter Four primarily addresses days on which fasting is prohibited, due to the fact that those days have been established as permanent days of rejoicing. It also discusses certain fixed communal fasts in memory of general disasters that befell the Jewish people.

Introduction to **Perek I**

And the land, where you are going over to possess it, is a land of hills and valleys, and it drinks water as the rain of heaven comes down; a land which the Lord your God cares for; the eyes of the Lord your God are always upon it, from the beginning of the year until the end of the year.

(Deuteronomy 11:11–12)

And the anger of the Lord will be kindled against you, and He will close up the heavens, and there will be no rain, and the earth will not give its fruit, and you will perish quickly from off the good land which the Lord gives you.

(Deuteronomy 11:17)

When heaven is closed up, and there is no rain, when they sin against You; if they pray toward this place, and confess Your name and turn from their sin, when You afflict them; then You hear in heaven, and forgive the sin of Your servants and of Your people Israel, when You teach them the good way in which they should walk; and send rain upon Your land, which You have given to Your people as an inheritance.

(I Kings 8:35–36)

This chapter deals with the times of fasts decreed for lack of rainfall. Essentially, it addresses two main issues: The appropriate dates for rainfall, and the order of fasts for a drought.

Before discussing the lack of rain, the proper dates of rainfall must be established. The halakhic relevance of this issue involves the times when one mentions and prays for rain, as these formulations are incorporated into the daily prayer service only during the rainy season. It is therefore necessary to establish the start and end of the rainy season. Since the Mishna was composed in Eretz Yisrael and is concerned with life there, the *halakhot* in it are geared primarily toward its climate. Consequently, it remains to be determined how Jews living elsewhere should behave, especially residents of places where the rainy season differs greatly from that of Eretz Yisrael.

A second question is the declaration of fast days for rainfall: When is a lack of rain considered significant and a possible sign of a drought, which necessitates prayer and even a fast? As more time goes by without rain the position of farmers steadily worsens, and the various sets and cycles of fasts that the Sages decreed likewise increase in severity. These sets of fasts differ from each other in number and rigor.

The details of these issues, as well as statements and comments with regard to rain in general, form the subject matter of this chapter.

מתני׳ מֵאֵימָתַי מַזְכִּירִין גְּבוּרוֹת גְּשָׁמִים? רַבִּי אֱלִיעֶזֶר אוֹמֵר: מִיּוֹם טוֹב הָרִאשׁוֹן שֶׁל חַג. רַבִּי יְהוֹשֻׁעַ אוֹמֵר: מִיּוֹם טוֹב הָאַחֲרוֹן שֶׁל חַג.

MISHNA From when, i.e., from which date, **does one begin to mention**[N] **the might of the rains**[H] by inserting the phrase: He makes the wind blow and rain fall, in the second blessing of the *Amida* prayer? **Rabbi Eliezer says:** The phrase is inserted **from the first Festival day of the festival** of *Sukkot*. **Rabbi Yehoshua says: From the last Festival day of the festival** of *Sukkot*.

אָמַר לוֹ רַבִּי יְהוֹשֻׁעַ: הוֹאִיל וְאֵין הַגְּשָׁמִים אֶלָּא סִימַן קְלָלָה בֶּחָג, לָמָּה הוּא מַזְכִּיר? אָמַר לוֹ רַבִּי אֱלִיעֶזֶר: אַף אֲנִי לֹא אָמַרְתִּי לִשְׁאוֹל, אֶלָּא לְהַזְכִּיר מַשִּׁיב הָרוּחַ וּמוֹרִיד הַגֶּשֶׁם בְּעוֹנָתוֹ. אָמַר לוֹ: אִם כֵּן לְעוֹלָם יְהֵא מַזְכִּיר!

Rabbi Yehoshua said to Rabbi Eliezer: **Since rain is nothing other** than **a sign of a curse during the festival**[N] of *Sukkot*, as rainfall forces Jews to leave their *sukkot*, **why** should **one mention** the might of rain during this period? **Rabbi Eliezer said to him: I too did not say** that it is proper **to request** rain at this time, **but** it is proper only **to mention** the phrase: **He makes the wind blow and rain fall, in its due time.**[N] Rabbi Yehoshua **said to him: If so,** i.e., if reciting the phrase does not constitute a request for rain, **one should always mention** rain, even in the summer.

אֵין שׁוֹאֲלִים אֶת הַגְּשָׁמִים אֶלָּא סָמוּךְ לִגְשָׁמִים. רַבִּי יְהוּדָה אוֹמֵר: הָעוֹבֵר לִפְנֵי הַתֵּיבָה בְּיוֹם טוֹב הָאַחֲרוֹן שֶׁל חַג – הָאַחֲרוֹן מַזְכִּיר, הָרִאשׁוֹן אֵינוֹ מַזְכִּיר. בְּיוֹם טוֹב רִאשׁוֹן שֶׁל פֶּסַח – הָרִאשׁוֹן מַזְכִּיר, הָאַחֲרוֹן אֵינוֹ מַזְכִּיר.

The mishna states a general principle: **One requests rain only** immediately **preceding the rainy season.**[B] **Rabbi Yehuda**[P] **says:** With regard to **the one who passes before the ark** as prayer leader **on the concluding Festival day of the festival** of *Sukkot*, the Eighth Day of Assembly: **The last** prayer leader, who leads the additional prayer, **mentions** rain, whereas **the first** prayer leader, for the morning prayer, **does not mention** rain. The opposite is the case at the conclusion of the period for mentioning rain **on the first Festival day of Passover:** Here, **the first** prayer leader, who leads the morning prayer, **mentions** rain, while **the last** prayer leader, who leads the additional prayer, **does not mention** rain.[N]

גמ׳ תַּנָּא הֵיכָא קָאֵי דְּקָתָנֵי ״מֵאֵימָתַי״? תַּנָּא הָתָם קָאֵי,

GEMARA The Gemara asks: **Where does** the ***tanna*** of the mishna **stand, that** he **teaches: From when?** The mishna's opening question indicates that it has already been established that there is an obligation to mention rain at this time of the year. Where is this obligation stated? The Gemara answers: The ***tanna* is standing there,** i.e., he bases himself on a mishna in *Berakhot*.

NOTES

From when does one mention – מֵאֵימָתַי מַזְכִּירִין: Most sources place tractate *Ta'anit* immediately after *Rosh HaShana*. See Meiri, who cites an alternative tradition concerning the arrangement of the tractates. The Rambam, in his introduction to the Commentary on the Mishna, explains that the *tanna* positioned *Ta'anit* right after the tractates that discuss Festivals mandated by Torah law, as the fasts discussed in *Ta'anit* are mentioned by the Prophets, especially those fasts instituted in commemoration of the destruction of the Temple (see Isaiah, chapter 58; Zechariah 8:19). It is logical to list special days mentioned by the Prophets after listing special days mentioned in the Torah. Some add another connection between the two tractates; *Rosh HaShana* discusses the *halakhot* of sounding the *shofar*, and similar blasts are sounded on the fasts days discussed in this tractate. Furthermore, as stated in the Gemara, *Rosh HaShana* mentions the period of judgment for rain, while *Ta'anit* addresses the prayers and the fasting for rain in its proper time (*Melekhet Shlomo*).

A sign of a curse during the festival – סִימַן קְלָלָה בֶּחָג: Rashi and Rav Natronai Gaon explain, based on a statement in tractate *Sukka*, that rainfall during *Sukkot* is considered to be a Divine rebuke to the Jewish people as it indicates that God has rejected their performance of the mitzva of residing in a *sukka*. Others explain that rainfall simply prevents people from fulfilling the mitzva properly (Meiri). Some authorities maintain that it is obligatory to eat in the *sukka* only on the first night of the Festival, which means that rainfall is a curse only on that night. Nevertheless, rainfall at any time during *Sukkot* is not considered to be a blessing. This is particularly true according to Rabbi Eliezer, who maintains that one is obligated to eat two meals in the *sukka* on each of the seven days of *Sukkot*.

He makes the wind blow and rain fall in its due time – מַשִּׁיב הָרוּחַ וּמוֹרִיד הַגֶּשֶׁם בְּעוֹנָתוֹ: Some explain that according to Rabbi Eliezer one must state this entire sentence: He makes wind blow and the rain fall in its due time (see Rabbi Aharon HaLevi). However, most commentaries maintain that the phrase: In its due time, is not part of the text inserted into the *Amida* prayer; rather, it is simply Rabbi Eliezer's interpretation of that insertion. In other words, he maintains that it is appropriate to mention rain anytime throughout the year provided that one intends that the rain should fall in its proper season (see Ritva).

Mentioning rain on *Sukkot* and Passover – הַזְכָּרָה בְּסֻכּוֹת וּבְפֶסַח: In the Jerusalem Talmud, an additional rationale is cited for this *halakha*. As explained in the Gemara (2b), it is preferable to recite the prayer for dew in most of the Festival prayers, as dew is a sign of a reliable blessing that comes without suffering.

HALAKHA

From when does one mention the might of the rains – מֵאֵימָתַי מַזְכִּירִין גְּבוּרוֹת גְּשָׁמִים: One begins to insert the expression: He makes the wind blow and the rain fall, in the additional *Amida* prayer of the last day of *Sukkot*, the Eighth Day of Assembly. One ceases to recite it in the additional *Amida* prayer of the first day of Passover, in accordance with the opinion of Rabbi Yehuda (*Shulḥan Arukh*, *Oraḥ Ḥayyim* 114:1).

BACKGROUND

Immediately preceding the rainy season – סָמוּךְ לִגְשָׁמִים: The details of this mishna and most of the related issues refer to the climate of Eretz Yisrael, as the main themes of communal prayer always refer to Eretz Yisrael, the heart of the Jewish people.

As will be explained at length in this tractate, the rainy season normally begins in Eretz Yisrael in the month of Marḥeshvan, which corresponds to the months of October or November of the Gregorian calendar. If Marḥeshvan occurs relatively early in the solar year, rainfall may begin later than usual. Nevertheless, it is fairly common for scattered showers to fall even during the previous month of Tishrei. As in the other lands of the Mediterranean region, the rainy season lasts throughout the winter, from Marḥeshvan until Nisan. During the summer, no rain falls at all. Indeed, summer rain is likely to cause significant damage to plants and fruit.

PERSONALITIES

Rabbi Yehuda – רַבִּי יְהוּדָה: When the Mishna refers to Rabbi Yehuda without any addition, it means Rabbi Yehuda, son of Rabbi Ilai, one of the greatest of the fourth generation *tanna'im*. He was one of the last five disciples of Rabbi Akiva, while his father, Rabbi Ilai, was a student of Rabbi Eliezer. In his youth, he studied with Rabbi Tarfon, in whose name he cites *halakhot*, in addition to the other Sages of Yavne: Rabbi Eliezer, Rabbi Yehoshua, Rabban Gamliel, Rabbi Elazar ben Azarya, Rabbi Yishmael, and Rabbi Yosei HaGelili. Nevertheless, Rabbi Yehuda's foremost teacher was Rabbi Akiva, and it was in accordance with Rabbi Akiva's opinion that he laid the foundations for the halakhic exegesis of Leviticus known as the *Sifra*, or *Torat Kohanim*. According to tradition, any unattributed statement in the *Sifra* was authored by Rabbi Yehuda.

Rabbi Yehuda was ordained by Rabbi Yehuda ben Bava and is frequently quoted in aggadic statements alongside Rabbi Neḥemya. When there are differences of opinion between Rabbi Yehuda and Rabbi Meir or between Rabbi Yehuda and Rabbi Shimon, the *halakha* is in accordance with the opinion of Rabbi Yehuda. Rabbi Yehuda's disciples included Rabbi Elazar, son of Rabbi Shimon; Rabbi Yishmael, son of Rabbi Yosei; and Rabbi Yehuda HaNasi. His son, known as Rabbi Yosei, son of Rabbi Yehuda, was also a renowned Sage.

דקתני: מזכירים גבורות גשמים בתחיית המתים, ושואלין בברכת השנים, והבדלה בחונן הדעת. וקתני: מאימתי מזכירים גבורות גשמים.

As it teaches (*Berakhot* 33a): **One mentions the might of the rains**[N] and recites: He makes the wind blow and the rain fall **in** the second blessing of the *Amida* prayer, the blessing of **the resurrection of the dead.**[H] **And the request**[B] for rain: And grant dew and rain as a blessing, is recited **in** the ninth blessing of the *Amida* prayer, **the blessing of the years.**[H] **And** the prayer of **distinction** [***havdala***] between the sacred and the profane, recited in the evening prayer following Shabbat and Festivals, is recited **in** the fourth blessing of the *Amida* prayer: **Who graciously grants knowledge.**[H] **And** it is based on that mishna, which establishes the obligation to request for rain, **that** this mishna **teaches: From when does one** begin to **mention the might of the rains.**

וליתני התם, מאי שנא דשבקיה עד הכא?

The Gemara asks: **But** if so, **let** the *tanna* **teach** this *halakha* **there,** in tractate *Berakhot*, at the beginning of the order of *Zera'im*. **What is different** about this case **that he left it until here,** toward the end of the order of *Moed*? In other words, if this issue is indeed a continuation of the mishna in *Berakhot*, why did the *tanna* neglect it until tractate *Ta'anit*?

אלא: תנא מראש השנה סליק, דתנן: ובחג נידונין על המים. ואיידי דתנא ובחג נידונים על המים, תנא מאימתי מזכירין גבורות גשמים.

The Gemara answers: **Rather, the *tanna* interrupted** a discussion **from** tractate ***Rosh HaShana*****. As we learned** in a mishna there: **And on the festival** of *Sukkot* all creatures **are judged for water. Since** the *tanna* **taught: And on the festival** of *Sukkot* all creatures **are judged for water,** from which it can be inferred that one should request rain near the time of this judgment, he **taught** here: **From when does one mention the might of the rains.**

וליתני "מאימתי מזכירים על הגשמי", מאי גבורות גשמים? אמר רבי יוחנן: מפני שיורדין בגבורה, שנאמר "עשה גדלות עד אין חקר ונפלאות עד אין מספר" וכתיב "הנתן מטר על פני הארץ ושלח מים על פני חוצות".

§ The Gemara asks a question with regard to the language of the mishna: **And let** the *tanna* simply **teach: From when does one mention the rains. What is** the meaning of the phrase: **The might of the rains? Rabbi Yoḥanan said: Because** the rains **fall with might.**[B] The might of the rain displays God's power in the world, **as it is stated: "Who does great things beyond comprehension, marvels without number"** (Job 9:10). **And it is also written: "Who gives rain upon the earth, and sends water upon the fields"** (Job 5:10).

מאי משמע? אמר רבה בר שילא: אתיא "חקר" "חקר" מברייתו של עולם.

The Gemara asks: **From where** may it **be inferred** that these verses indicate that rainfall is considered a mighty act of God? **Rabba bar Sheila said:** This is **derived** by means of a verbal analogy between the term **"comprehension"** here and the term **"comprehension"** from a passage that deals with **the creation of the world.**

כתיב הכא "עשה גדלות עד אין חקר" וכתיב התם "הלוא ידעת אם לא שמעת אלהי עולם ה׳ בורא קצות הארץ לא ייעף ולא ייגע אין חקר לתבונתו" וכתיב "מכין הרים בכחו נאזר בגבורה".

Rabba bar Sheila elaborates on this verbal analogy. **It is written here: "Who does great things that are beyond comprehension," and it is written there,** with regard to the creation of the world: **"Have you not known? Have you not heard that the everlasting God, the Lord, the Creator of the ends of the earth, does not grow faint or weary? His discernment is beyond comprehension"** (Isaiah 40:28). This shows that both creation and rainfall are beyond comprehension. **And** concerning the creation of the world, **it is written** elsewhere: **"Who sets firm the mountains with Your strength; Who is girded with might"** (Psalms 65:7). From this verse it can be inferred that rainfall, like the creation of the world, reflects God's might.

NOTES

The might of the rains – גבורות גשמים: Many commentaries elaborate on the connection between rain and the blessing of the resurrection of the dead. They explain that rainfall is a resurrection of the dead in miniature, as plants that appear dead return to life (Rid the Younger; Ritva). Furthermore, rainfall, like the resurrection of the dead, represents a manifestation of God's might and dominion over the world. Another element of similarity shared between rain and the resurrection of the dead is that both emphasize God's loving-kindness since He overrides the established order of nature when He ensures that rain falls at the best time (Ritva). The kabbalists discuss at length the link between rainfall and God's might; they consider rain a manifestation of God's self-contraction and withdrawal [*tzimtzum*], just as it is a manifestation of His loving-kindness (see *Otzar HaKavod*).

HALAKHA

One mentions the might of the rains in the resurrection of the dead – מזכירין גבורות גשמים בתחיית המתים: Throughout the winter, one mentions rain by reciting the phrase: He makes the wind blow and the rain fall, in the second blessing of the *Amida*. During the summer, there are different customs. The practice of Sephardic communities and some Ashkenazic congregations, specifically Hassidic communities and residents of Eretz Yisrael, is to recite during the summer: He brings the dew, whereas Ashkenazic communities outside Eretz Yisrael omit this phrase (*Shulḥan Arukh, Oraḥ Ḥayyim* 114:1–2).

And the request in the blessing of the years – ושואלין בברכת השנים: During the winter, a prayer for rain is inserted in the ninth blessing of the *Amida*: the blessing of the years. One begins to add this prayer from the date fixed by the Gemara later in the discussion (2b). According to Ashkenazic custom, the basic text of the blessing remains the same throughout the year. During the summer, the phrase recited is: And give a blessing, while during the winter it is: And give dew and rain for a blessing. According to Sephardic custom, the text of the ninth blessing recited during the winter differs significantly from that of the summer (*Tur*; *Shulḥan Arukh, Oraḥ Ḥayyim* 117:1).

And the prayer of distinction [*havdala*] in the blessing, Who graciously grants knowledge – והבדלה בחונן הדעת: One recites *havdala* in the evening *Amida* prayer at the conclusion of Shabbat and Festivals in the blessing: Who graciously grants knowledge (*Shulḥan Arukh, Oraḥ Ḥayyim* 294:1).

BACKGROUND

One mentions…and the request – מזכירין...ושואלין: There is a difference in *halakha* between the time when it is appropriate to mention rain and the date when one starts to request rainfall. Naturally, one asks for rain only when he wants it to fall. However, one begins to think about the upcoming year's rainfall before the rainy season begins. Furthermore, as noted in the Gemara, on *Sukkot* the Jewish people are judged with regard to rain; therefore, the appropriate time to begin mentioning rain is during the period of *Sukkot*. Even Rabbi Eliezer agrees that one should not mention a matter at an inappropriate time. This is true even when done in praise of God rather than in the form of a request.

Because they fall with might – מפני שיורדין בגבורה: The issue of rainfall is discussed at great length in *Ta'anit*. The Gemara explains that the might of God is manifested particularly through rain, both due to its power and because of the controlled way in which it falls, as strength and control are both characteristics of might. Nowadays, the force of rainfall can be measured. It is estimated that the energy released in any large rainstorm exceeds that of an atomic bomb.

וּמְנָא לָן דְּבִתְפִלָּה? דְּתַנְיָא: "לְאַהֲבָה אֶת ה׳ אֱלֹהֵיכֶם וּלְעָבְדוֹ בְּכָל לְבַבְכֶם" אֵיזוֹ הִיא עֲבוֹדָה שֶׁהִיא בַּלֵּב – הֱוֵי אוֹמֵר: זוֹ תְּפִלָּה. וּכְתִיב בַּתְרֵיהּ "וְנָתַתִּי מְטַר אַרְצְכֶם בְּעִתּוֹ יוֹרֶה וּמַלְקוֹשׁ".

The Gemara asks: **And from where do we** derive that rain must be mentioned specifically **in the** ***Amida*** **prayer?**[N] The Gemara answers: **As it was taught** in a *baraita* with regard to the verse: **"To love the Lord your God and to serve Him with all your heart"** (Deuteronomy 11:13). **Which is the service** of God **that** is performed **in the heart?**[B] **You must say** that **this** is referring to **prayer. And, afterward, it is written: "And I shall give the rain of your land**[N] **in its due time, the first rain and the last rain"** (Deuteronomy 11:14). This juxtaposition teaches that it is appropriate to request rain while engaged in the service of the heart, i.e., prayer.

אָמַר רַבִּי יוֹחָנָן: שְׁלֹשָׁה מַפְתְּחוֹת בְּיָדוֹ שֶׁל הַקָּדוֹשׁ בָּרוּךְ הוּא שֶׁלֹּא נִמְסְרוּ בְּיַד שָׁלִיחַ, וְאֵלּוּ הֵן: מַפְתֵּחַ שֶׁל גְּשָׁמִים, מַפְתֵּחַ שֶׁל חַיָּה, וּמַפְתֵּחַ שֶׁל תְּחִיַּית הַמֵּתִים.

§ The Gemara cites related statements concerning the idea that rainfall provides evidence of God's might. **Rabbi Yoḥanan said:** There are **three keys**[B] maintained **in the hand of the Holy One, Blessed be He, which were not transmitted to an intermediary,**[N] i.e., God tends to these matters Himself. **And they are: The key of rain, the key of birthing, and the key of the resurrection of the dead.**

מַפְתֵּחַ שֶׁל גְּשָׁמִים – דִּכְתִיב "יִפְתַּח ה׳ לְךָ אֶת אוֹצָרוֹ הַטּוֹב אֶת הַשָּׁמַיִם לָתֵת מְטַר אַרְצְךָ בְּעִתּוֹ". מַפְתֵּחַ שֶׁל חַיָּה מִנַּיִן – דִּכְתִיב "וַיִּזְכֹּר אֱלֹהִים אֶת רָחֵל וַיִּשְׁמַע

Rabbi Yoḥanan cites verses in support of his claim. **The key of rain, as it is stated: "The Lord will open for you His good treasure, the heavens, to give the rain of your land in its due time"** (Deuteronomy 28:12), indicates that rainfall is controlled by God Himself. **From where** is it derived that **the key of birthing** is maintained by God? **As it is written: "And God remembered Rachel and listened**

BACKGROUND

Service [*avoda*] that is in the heart – עֲבוֹדָה שֶׁהִיא בַּלֵּב: The Hebrew word *avoda*, meaning work or service, denotes the worship of God through the Temple service and prayer. It refers to an act by which one expresses his veneration for the Creator. When the term *avoda* appears without qualification in rabbinic sources, it is referring to Temple worship, specifically, the sacrifice of offerings. With regard to the verse: "And to serve Him with all your heart" (Deuteronomy 11:13), the Sages say that this is referring to prayer, which essentially involves directing one's heart to the Creator. This, too, is a form of worship, which is considered one of the most natural ways to serve God.

Three keys – שְׁלֹשָׁה מַפְתְּחוֹת: These three keys all refer to significant changes to reality. Although rainfall and childbirth appear to be natural events to us, they are considered by the Gemara to be departures from the normal course of nature, no less than the resurrection of the dead. Consequently, the control over them is not entrusted to an emissary; God Himself is responsible for them.

NOTES

And from where do we derive that rain must be mentioned in prayer – וּמְנָא לָן דְּבִתְפִלָּה: The Maharsha asks: Why does the Gemara seek a special source for the recital of prayers for rain? This obligation can be derived directly from King Solomon's prayer upon the dedication of the Temple (I Kings 8:35–36). The Maharsha's answer, which is reflected in his commentary to the Gemara, is that Solomon's prayer teaches only that prayers for rain are to be recited in times of drought: "When heaven is closed up" (I Kings 8:35). Here, however, the Gemara is dealing with the obligation to petition for rain on a regular basis in one's daily prayers throughout the rainy season. Alternatively, Solomon's prayer serves as a source for the obligation to request rainfall, whereas here the Gemara wishes to find a supporting verse for the obligation to praise God for His ability to cause rain to fall (*Keren Ora*).

And afterward it is written, And I shall give the rain of your land – וּכְתִיב בַּתְרֵיהּ וְנָתַתִּי מְטַר אַרְצְכֶם: This passage continues: "That you may gather in your grain and your wine and your oil" (Deuteronomy 11:14), which alludes to the *halakha* that the prayers for rain should begin on the festival of *Sukkot* at the time of ingathering of produce from the fields (*Rosh Yosef*).

Which were not transmitted to an intermediary – שֶׁלֹּא נִמְסְרוּ בְּיַד שָׁלִיחַ: Rabbeinu Gershom and Rashi maintain that this means only that all three keys cannot be transmitted to a single intermediary at the same time. This opinion is based on a midrash that Elijah was given two of the three keys but not all three. By contrast, *Tosafot* explain that none of these three keys were transmitted permanently to an intermediary. The Ra'avad likewise states that there is no special angel who is granted the authority to perform these tasks. Although the so-called angel of the interior and the ministering angel of the world perform God's bidding in the world, they have no control over these three keys (Ra'avad; *Shita Mekubbetzet*; *Otzar HaKavod*).

Perek **I**
Daf **2** Amud **b**

אֵלֶיהָ אֱלֹהִים וַיִּפְתַּח אֶת רַחְמָהּ". מַפְתֵּחַ שֶׁל תְּחִיַּית הַמֵּתִים מִנַּיִן – דִּכְתִיב "וִידַעְתֶּם כִּי אֲנִי ה׳ בְּפִתְחִי אֶת קִבְרוֹתֵיכֶם".

to her, and He opened her womb"[N] (Genesis 30:22). **From where** is it derived that **the key of the resurrection of the dead** is maintained by God Himself? **As it is written: "And you shall know that I am the Lord when I have opened your graves"** (Ezekiel 37:13).

NOTES

And He opened her womb – וַיִּפְתַּח אֶת רַחְמָהּ: The Maharsha asks: Why doesn't the Gemara cite the earlier verse: "And when the Lord saw that Leah was hated, He opened her womb" (Genesis 29:31)? He explains that the Gemara cites the verse referring to Rachel because, in that verse, the name of God immediately precedes the expression "and opened her womb." This serves to emphasize that it was God Himself, not an intermediary, who was responsible for opening Rachel's womb. By contrast, in the verse referring to Leah the name of God does not directly precede the expression: "He opened her womb." Consequently, it might have been possible to interpret the verse as follows: And when the Lord saw that Leah was hated, the one entrusted with the key to childbirth opened her womb.

בְּמַעְרְבָא אָמְרִי: אַף מַפְתֵּחַ שֶׁל פַּרְנָסָה, דִּכְתִיב ״פּוֹתֵחַ אֶת יָדֶךָ״ וגו׳. וְרַבִּי יוֹחָנָן מַאי טַעְמָא לֹא קָא חָשֵׁיב לְהָא? אָמַר לָךְ: גְּשָׁמִים הַיְינוּ פַּרְנָסָה.

In the West, Eretz Yisrael, **they say: The key of livelihood** is **also** in God's hand, **as it is written: "You open Your hand**[N] and satisfy every living thing with favor" (Psalms 145:16). The Gemara asks: **And what is the reason** that **Rabbi Yoḥanan did not consider this** key of livelihood in his list? The Gemara answers that Rabbi Yoḥanan could have **said to you: Rain is** the same as **livelihood** in this regard, as rain is indispensable to all livelihoods.

״רַבִּי אֱלִיעֶזֶר אוֹמֵר מִיּוֹם טוֹב הָרִאשׁוֹן שֶׁל חַג״ כו׳. אִיבַּעְיָא לְהוּ: רַבִּי אֱלִיעֶזֶר מֵהֵיכָא גְּמִיר לָהּ, מִלּוּלָב גָּמַר לָהּ אוֹ מִנִּיסּוּךְ הַמַּיִם גָּמַר לָהּ?

§ The mishna taught that **Rabbi Eliezer says:** One mentions rain **from the first Festival day of the festival** of *Sukkot* **etc. A dilemma was raised before** the Sages: **From where did Rabbi Eliezer derive this** *halakha*? He must have learned it from one of the two mitzvot of *Sukkot* that are linked to rain. Did he **derive it from** the mitzva to wave the ***lulav***,[B] **or** did he **derive it from** the obligation of **the water libation?**[B]

מִלּוּלָב גָּמַר לָהּ: מָה לוּלָב בַּיּוֹם – אַף הַזְכָּרָה בַּיּוֹם. אוֹ דִּלְמָא מִנִּיסּוּךְ הַמַּיִם גָּמַר לָהּ: מָה נִיסּוּךְ הַמַּיִם מֵאוּרְתָא, דְּאָמַר מָר ״וּמִנְחָתָם וְנִסְכֵּיהֶם״ אֲפִילּוּ בַּלַּיְלָה, אַף הַזְכָּרָה מֵאוּרְתָא?

The Gemara clarifies the significance of this dilemma: Did he **derive this** *halakha* **from the** ***lulav***, in which case one would say: **Just as** the mitzva to take the ***lulav*** applies **during the day** and not at night, **so too,** the **mention** of rain begins **during the day** of the first Festival day of *Sukkot*. **Or perhaps** he **derives this** *halakha* **from the water libation,** in which case one would say: **Just as the water libation** can be prepared **from the** first **night**[NH] of *Sukkot*, **as the Master said,** with regard to the verse: **"And their meal-offerings and their libations"** (Numbers 29:18), and certain meal-offerings and libations may be brought **even at night, so too,** the **mention** of rain begins **from the evening.**

תָּא שְׁמַע, דְּאָמַר רַבִּי אַבָּהוּ: לֹא לְמָדָהּ רַבִּי אֱלִיעֶזֶר אֶלָּא מִלּוּלָב. אִיכָּא דְּאָמְרִי: רַבִּי אַבָּהוּ גְּמָרָא גְּמִיר לָהּ, וְאִיכָּא דְּאָמְרִי: מַתְנִיתָא שְׁמִיעַ לֵיהּ.

The Gemara seeks to resolve this dilemma: **Come** and **hear** a resolution, **as Rabbi Abbahu**[P] **said** that **Rabbi Eliezer derived this** *halakha* **from nothing other** than the case of ***lulav***. **Some say** that **Rabbi Abbahu learned this** claim **by** way of a **tradition,**[B] which was the source of Rabbi Eliezer's opinion; **and some say** that **he learned it from a** ***baraita***.

BACKGROUND

Lulav – לוּלָב: Referred to by the Torah as "branches of palm trees" (Leviticus 23:40), the *lulav* must be held in one's hand together with three other species on the festival of *Sukkot*: the *etrog*, the myrtle, and the willow. The *lulav* is a young branch of a date palm whose leaves are still pressed tightly against the branch. All four plants must be of high quality; therefore, the *lulav* may not be crooked nor may its top be damaged or broken. The *lulav* must be at least four handbreadths long, roughly 35 cm.

Water libation – נִיסּוּךְ הַמַּיִם: During the festival of *Sukkot*, in addition to the other special offerings brought in the Temple, a water libation was poured. This libation is not mentioned explicitly in the Torah, its source being an oral tradition transmitted to Moses from Mount Sinai. The water libation was accompanied by great festivity and ceremony. The water was drawn from the Siloam pool and poured into a basin placed upon a hole in the southwestern corner of the altar. According to tradition, this hole, and the adjacent hole where wine was poured, descended to the depths of the world. The water libation was offered on all seven days of *Sukkot*, including Shabbat, even though it was not permitted to draw water for this offering on Shabbat.

Reconstruction of basin placed upon the hole on the altar

Dinar coin from the bar Kokheva revolt with depiction of jug for libation

He learned this by way of a tradition – גְּמָרָא גְּמִיר לָהּ: In other words, this matter was derived from a tradition rather than from a verse of the Torah.

HALAKHA

The water libation at night – נִיסּוּךְ הַמַּיִם בַּלַּיְלָה: The wine libations brought together with the offerings are valid only if performed during the day. Conversely, the water libation, which is poured out during *Sukkot*, is brought independently of any offering. The proper time to bring the water libation is together with the morning daily offering. However, if it is performed at night, it is valid, as stated here and in *Sukka* (*Maggid Mishne*; Rambam *Sefer Avoda, Hilkhot Ma'aseh HaKorbanot* 4:5; *Hilkhot Temidin UMusafin* 10:7).

NOTES

You open Your hand – פּוֹתֵחַ אֶת יָדֶךָ: It has been suggested that the inference concerning the key of livelihood is based on a grammatical variation. Throughout Psalm 145, God is referred to in the abstract third person form, whereas in this phrase He is addressed directly, in the second person: "You open Your hand."

The water libation from the night – נִיסּוּךְ הַמַּיִם מֵאוּרְתָא: The early commentaries grapple with this statement, for which they offer different interpretations (see Rashi and Meiri). There are two basic opinions: According to one opinion, the water libation on the altar was not performed at night, as the libations that accompany offerings can be poured out only during the day. Rather, the Gemara is referring to the drawing of the water in preparation for the libation, an act that can take place at night. Consequently, the nighttime can be considered the beginning of the period of the libation (*Tosefot Rid*; Rabbi Elyakim). Similarly, some state that as the sanctification of the water for the libation can occur at night, it is considered as though the time of the libation begins then (Ra'avad; *Shita Mekubbetzet*). A second opinion takes this statement literally, as meaning that the water libation is indeed valid if performed at night, despite the fact that everyone agrees that the proper time for this service is during the day, *ab initio* (see *Tosafot* and Ritva).

PERSONALITIES

Rabbi Abbahu – רַבִּי אַבָּהוּ: A third generation *amora* of Eretz Yisrael, Rabbi Abbahu was the preeminent disciple of Rabbi Yoḥanan. He headed an academy and served as a judge in Caesarea, and also represented the interests of the Jewish people in their dealings with the Romans. He transmitted statements in the name of Reish Lakish, Rabbi Elazar, Rabbi Yosei bar Ḥanina, and others. Rabbi Zeira was a student and colleague of his. His other colleagues included Rabbi Ḥiyya bar Abba, as well as the heads of the Tiberias academy, Rabbi Ami and Rabbi Asi. He counted among his many disciples Rabbi Yona, Rabbi Yosei, and Rabbi Yirmeya. The numerous Sages who gathered around him became known as the Sages of Caesarea.

Rabbi Abbahu taught many statements of *aggada* and was an excellent preacher. He spoke Greek well and taught it to his daughter. His father-in-law was Rabbi Taḥlifa of Caesarea, and his sons were the Sages Rabbi Ḥanina, Avimi, and Rabbi Zeira.

מַאי הִיא – דְּתַנְיָא: מֵאֵימָתַי מַזְכִּירִין עַל הַגְּשָׁמִים – רַבִּי אֱלִיעֶזֶר אוֹמֵר: מִשְּׁעַת נְטִילַת לוּלָב, רַבִּי יְהוֹשֻׁעַ אוֹמֵר: מִשְּׁעַת הַנָּחָתוֹ.

The Gemara asks: **What is the** *baraita* from which Rabbi Abbahu may have derived his statement? The Gemara answers: **As it is taught** in a *baraita*: **From when does one** begin to **mention the rains** in his prayers? **Rabbi Eliezer says: From the time that one takes** the ***lulav***, i.e., the first day of *Sukkot*. **Rabbi Yehoshua says: From the time that one puts** the *lulav* **down,**[NB] i.e., at the conclusion of *Sukkot*.

אָמַר רַבִּי אֱלִיעֶזֶר: הוֹאִיל וְאַרְבַּעַת מִינִין הַלָּלוּ אֵינָן בָּאִין אֶלָּא לְרַצּוֹת עַל הַמַּיִם, וּכְשֵׁם שֶׁאַרְבַּע מִינִין הַלָּלוּ אִי אֶפְשָׁר בָּהֶם בְּלֹא מַיִם – כָּךְ אִי אֶפְשָׁר לָעוֹלָם בְּלֹא מַיִם.

§ The *baraita* cites a discussion of these opinions. **Rabbi Eliezer said:** It is **since these four species,** the *lulav* and the other species taken with it, **come only to offer appeasement for water,** as they symbolize the rainfall of the coming year. **And** this symbolism is as follows: **Just as these four species cannot** exist **without water,** as they need water to grow, **so too, the world cannot** exist **without water.** Therefore, it is proper to mention rain in one's prayers when taking the four species.

אָמַר לוֹ רַבִּי יְהוֹשֻׁעַ: וַהֲלֹא גְּשָׁמִים בֶּחָג אֵינוֹ אֶלָּא סִימַן קְלָלָה! אָמַר לוֹ רַבִּי אֱלִיעֶזֶר: אַף אֲנִי לֹא אָמַרְתִּי לִשְׁאוֹל, אֶלָּא לְהַזְכִּיר. וּכְשֵׁם שֶׁתְּחִיַּית הַמֵּתִים מַזְכִּיר כָּל הַשָּׁנָה כּוּלָּהּ וְאֵינָהּ אֶלָּא בִּזְמַנָּהּ – כָּךְ מַזְכִּירִין גְּבוּרוֹת גְּשָׁמִים כָּל הַשָּׁנָה וְאֵינָן אֶלָּא בִּזְמַנָּן. לְפִיכָךְ, אִם בָּא לְהַזְכִּיר כָּל הַשָּׁנָה כּוּלָּהּ – מַזְכִּיר. רַבִּי אוֹמֵר: אוֹמֵר אֲנִי, מִשָּׁעָה שֶׁמַּפְסִיק לִשְׁאֵלָה כָּךְ מַפְסִיק לְהַזְכָּרָה.

Rabbi Yehoshua said to him in response: **But rain during the festival** of *Sukkot* **is nothing other than a sign of a curse. Rabbi Eliezer said to** Rabbi Yehoshua: **I too did not say** that it is proper **to ask** for rain at this time, **but** only **to mention** it. And **just as** with regard to **the resurrection of the dead, one mentions** it **the entire year and** yet **it** will **come only at its** proper **time,** when God wills the resurrection, **so too, one mentions the might of the rains all the year, and they** fall **only in their season. Therefore, if one seeks to mention** rain **throughout the year, he** may **mention it.**[N] **Rabbi** Yehuda HaNasi **says:** I say that **when one ceases to request** rain, **one also ceases to mention** it.

רַבִּי יְהוּדָה בֶּן בְּתֵירָה אוֹמֵר: בַּשֵּׁנִי בֶּחָג הוּא מַזְכִּיר. רַבִּי עֲקִיבָא אוֹמֵר: בַּשִּׁשִּׁי בֶּחָג הוּא מַזְכִּיר. רַבִּי יְהוּדָה מִשּׁוּם רַבִּי יְהוֹשֻׁעַ אוֹמֵר: הָעוֹבֵר לִפְנֵי הַתֵּיבָה בְּיוֹם טוֹב הָאַחֲרוֹן שֶׁל חַג, הָאַחֲרוֹן מַזְכִּיר, הָרִאשׁוֹן אֵינוֹ מַזְכִּיר. בְּיוֹם טוֹב רִאשׁוֹן שֶׁל פֶּסַח – הָרִאשׁוֹן מַזְכִּיר, הָאַחֲרוֹן אֵינוֹ מַזְכִּיר.

Rabbi Yehuda ben Beteira[P] **says: On the second day of the festival** of *Sukkot* **one mentions** rain, rather than on the first day. **Rabbi Akiva**[P] **says: On the sixth day one mentions** rain. **Rabbi Yehuda says in the name of Rabbi Yehoshua:** With regard to **the one who passes before the ark** as prayer leader **on the concluding Festival day of the festival** of *Sukkot*, the Eighth Day of Assembly, **the last** prayer leader of the additional prayer **mentions** rain, whereas **the first** prayer leader for the morning prayer **does not** mention rain. Conversely, **on the first Festival day of Passover, the first** prayer leader **mentions** rain, while **the last** prayer leader **does not mention** rain.

שַׁפִּיר קָאָמַר לֵיהּ רַבִּי אֱלִיעֶזֶר לְרַבִּי יְהוֹשֻׁעַ! אָמַר לָךְ רַבִּי יְהוֹשֻׁעַ: בִּשְׁלָמָא תְּחִיַּית הַמֵּתִים מַזְכִּיר – דְּכוּלֵּי יוֹמָא זִמְנֵיהּ הוּא,

The Gemara asks: **Rabbi Eliezer is speaking well to Rabbi Yehoshua.** How does Rabbi Yehoshua respond to Rabbi Eliezer's powerful argument that one can mention God's praises at any time of the year? The Gemara answers: **Rabbi Yehoshua** could have **said to you: Granted,** with regard to **the resurrection of the dead,**[B] **one mentions** this daily, **as** although it is not fulfilled every day, **any day is** fit to be **its proper time.**

NOTES

From the time that one puts it down – מִשְּׁעַת הַנָּחָתוֹ: Rashi and *Tosafot* debate the interpretation of the phrase: From the time one puts down the *lulav*. The meaning of this expression is already discussed in the Jerusalem Talmud. It may refer to the seventh day of *Sukkot* after the morning prayers when the *lulav* is usually put down for the last time. Alternatively, as the obligation to take the *lulav* can be fulfilled throughout the day, the time that the *lulav* is put down might refer only to the end of the seventh day of *Sukkot*. According to this interpretation, the time of putting down the *lulav* is at the start of the Eighth Day of Assembly.

The rationales of Rabbi Eliezer and Rabbi Yehoshua – טַעֲמֵי רַבִּי אֱלִיעֶזֶר וְרַבִּי יְהוֹשֻׁעַ: The reasoning of Rabbi Eliezer and Rabbi Yehoshua are explained differently in the Jerusalem Talmud. Rabbi Eliezer contends that it is appropriate to begin mentioning rain on the first day of *Sukkot* because that is when the four species, i.e., the *lulav*, *etrog*, myrtle, and willow, are first taken. Since these species require water for their growth, they serve as suitable advocates for rain. Moreover, when a servant knows that he has obeyed his master faithfully, he can utilize this opportunity to ask for a reward, even if he only wishes to receive it later. It is therefore fitting to begin mentioning rain on the first day of *Sukkot* when God's mitzvot are fulfilled and the four species are first taken. Rabbi Yehoshua counters by pointing out that a servant should not ask for a reward until he has completed his service. Therefore, one should not mention rain until the end of *Sukkot*. Moreover, the proper time to issue a request is just before one wants the request to be granted.

BACKGROUND

From the time that one takes the *lulav*…from the time that one puts it down – מִשְּׁעַת נְטִילַת לוּלָב...מִשְּׁעַת הַנָּחָתוֹ: The *baraita* indicates that both Rabbi Eliezer and Rabbi Yehoshua link the mention of rain with the taking of the *lulav*. The difference is that, in Rabbi Eliezer's opinion, all the actions designed to recall rain should be brought together: The taking of the *lulav*, the water libation, and the mention of rain in the second blessing of the *Amida*. By contrast, Rabbi Yehoshua holds that one must first conclude the symbolic deeds that recall rain and only afterward mention rain explicitly in prayer.

The resurrection of the dead – תְּחִיַּית הַמֵּתִים: This concept is alluded to in various places in the Torah and the Prophets and is mentioned explicitly in Daniel (12:2).

According to the Rambam, the resurrection of the dead will take place after the coming of the Messiah. Many authorities maintain that this will mark the beginning of a new era of life on earth (see Ramban's *Sha'ar HaGemul*). The resurrection of the dead is therefore a unique development that will occur only in the future. Nevertheless, we pray for it and anticipate it at all times.

PERSONALITIES

Rabbi Yehuda ben Beteira – רַבִּי יְהוּדָה בֶּן בְּתֵירָה: The Beteira family produced many renowned Sages over several generations. Some members of the family served as *Nasi* during the time of Hillel, but they transferred the position to him.

There were almost certainly two Sages named Yehuda ben Beteira, the second of whom was possibly the grandson of the first. Both lived in the city of Netzivin, or Nisibis, in Babylonia, one while the Temple was still standing, and the other at the end of the tannaitic period. The Rabbi Yehuda ben Beteira whose teaching is cited here is probably the later of the two. He was one of the greatest Torah scholars of his age, and organized the study of Torah throughout Babylonia before the establishment of the great academies. He was held in great esteem by the Sages of Eretz Yisrael.

Rabbi Akiva – רַבִּי עֲקִיבָא: The greatest of the *tanna'im*, Rabbi Akiva ben Yosef was a third generation tanna who taught many of the fourth generation. He began his Torah education when already an adult and studied under Rabbi Eliezer and Rabbi Yehoshua for many years. Many stories are told in rabbinic literature of his devotion to Torah study, his wife's loyalty to him, and the financial difficulties they had to overcome.

Rabbi Akiva undertook the first systematic arrangement and division of the Oral Law. This work, which was continued by his disciple Rabbi Meir, formed the basis of the final form of the Mishna, as edited by Rabbi Yehuda HaNasi. Rabbi Akiva also founded a new school of Torah interpretation, according to which almost all the regulations of the Oral Law have their basis in the text of the Torah itself. Rabbi Akiva was active in the period between the destruction of the Second Temple and the bar Kokheva revolt, and he played an active role in the preparations for this rebellion. He was brutally martyred by the Romans.

אֶלָּא גְּשָׁמִים כָּל דְּאָתְיָין זִמְנַיְיהוּ הִיא?! וְהָתְנַן: יָצָא נִיסָן וְיָרְדוּ גְּשָׁמִים – סִימַן קְלָלָה הֵם, שֶׁנֶּאֱמַר ״הֲלוֹא קְצִיר חִטִּים הַיּוֹם״ וגו׳.

However, in the case of **rain,** are **all** times **when it falls its proper time? But didn't we learn** in a mishna (12b): **If the month of Nisan has ended and rains** subsequently **fall, they are a sign of a curse, as it is stated: "Is not the wheat harvest today?** I will call to the Lord that He may send thunder and rain, and you will know and see that your wickedness is great, which you have done in the sight of the Lord, in asking you a king" (I Samuel 12:17).

רַבִּי יְהוּדָה בֶּן בְּתֵירָה אוֹמֵר: בַּשֵּׁנִי בֶּחָג הוּא מַזְכִּיר. מַאי טַעְמָא דְּרַבִּי יְהוּדָה בֶּן בְּתֵירָה? דְּתַנְיָא, רַבִּי יְהוּדָה בֶּן בְּתֵירָה אוֹמֵר:

§ The *baraita* states that **Rabbi Yehuda ben Beteira says: On the second day of the festival** of *Sukkot,* **one** begins to **mention** rain. The Gemara asks: **What is the reason for** this ruling of **Rabbi Yehuda ben Beteira?** The Gemara answers: **As it is taught,** in a *baraita* that deals with the source for the water libation on *Sukkot,* that **Rabbi Yehuda ben Beteira says:** The Torah alludes to the water libation in its description of the libations of the additional offerings of *Sukkot.* The Torah uses a slightly different term for the libations of certain days. On most days, it states that the sin-offering must be brought with "its libation [*veniskah*]" (e.g., Numbers 29:16), in the singular form.

נֶאֱמַר בַּשֵּׁנִי ״וְנִסְכֵּיהֶם״ וְנֶאֱמַר בַּשִּׁשִּׁי ״וּנְסָכֶיהָ״ וְנֶאֱמַר בַּשְּׁבִיעִי ״כְּמִשְׁפָּטָם״ –

By contrast, **it is stated on the second day** that one must offer **"their libations [*veniskeihem*]"** (Numbers 29:19). The plural form indicates the presence of multiple offerings. **And** furthermore, **it is stated** concerning the sin-offering libations **on the sixth day: "And its libations [*unsakheha*]"** (Numbers 29:31), which is again a plural form that is referring to many libations. **And** finally, **it is stated,** with regard to the libations of the additional offering **on the seventh day,** that they must apportion the respective animals, i.e., oxen, rams, and sheep: **"According to their laws [*kemishpatam*]"** (Numbers 29:33), using another plural form which differs from the phrase used on the other Festival days: "According to the law [*kamishpat*]" (e.g., Numbers 29:19), in the singular.

הֲרֵי מ״ם יו״ד מ״ם הֲרֵי כָּאן מַיִם. מִכָּאן רֶמֶז לְנִיסּוּךְ הַמַּיִם מִן הַתּוֹרָה.

These variations yield the three superfluous letters ***mem, yod,*** and ***mem,*** from *veniskeiheM, unsakhEha,* and *kemishpataM,* **which** together spell the Hebrew word for **water [*MaYiM*].** The letter *yod* is represented in *unsakhEha* with the letter E and in *MaYiM* with the letter Y. **From here** one learns **an allusion**[B] **to the** mitzva of **the water libation in the Torah.**

וּמַאי שְׁנָא בַּשֵּׁנִי דְּנָקַט – דְּכִי רְמִיזִי לְהוּ בִּקְרָא בַּשֵּׁנִי הוּא דִּרְמִיזִי, הִלְכָּךְ בַּשֵּׁנִי מַדְכְּרִינַן.

The Gemara asks: **And what is different about the second** day **that** Rabbi Yehuda ben Beteira **took** it as the day on which one begins to mention rain? The Gemara answers: The reason is **that when the verse** first **alludes** to the water libation, **it is on the second** day of *Sukkot* **that it alludes** to it (Numbers 29:19). **Therefore, on the second** day one begins to **mention** rain.

רַבִּי עֲקִיבָא אוֹמֵר: בַּשִּׁשִּׁי בֶּחָג הוּא מַזְכִּיר, שֶׁנֶּאֱמַר בַּשִּׁשִּׁי ״וּנְסָכֶיהָ״ – בִּשְׁנֵי נִיסּוּכִין הַכָּתוּב מְדַבֵּר, אֶחָד נִיסּוּךְ הַמַּיִם וְאֶחָד נִיסּוּךְ הַיַּיִן.

The *baraita* stated that **Rabbi Akiva says: On the sixth day one** begins to **mention** rain. The Gemara explains that this ruling is based on the allusion to the water libation in the offering of this day. **As it is stated on the sixth day: "And its libations [*unsakheha*]"**[N] (Numbers 29:31). The allusion is written in the plural, which indicates that **the verse is speaking of two libations: One** is **the water libation and** the other **one** is **the** standard **wine libation.**

אֵימָא תַּרְוַיְיהוּ דְּחַמְרָא! סָבַר לָהּ כְּרַבִּי יְהוּדָה בֶּן בְּתֵירָה, דְּאָמַר: רְמִיזִי מַיָּא.

The Gemara raises an objection: Even if it is accepted that the verse is referring to two libations, one can **say** that **both** libations are **of wine.** The Gemara answers: Rabbi Akiva **holds in accordance with** the opinion of **Rabbi Yehuda ben Beteira, who said** that the superfluous letters of these verses **allude** to **water [*mayim*].** This proves that the additional libation of the sixth day must be a water libation.

BACKGROUND

Allusion – רֶמֶז: The proof offered by Rabbi Yehuda ben Beteira is not regarded as absolute since this method of combining superfluous letters is not included in the hermeneutic principles for the interpretation of the Torah. Nevertheless, this proof provides an allusion to the notion of the water libation in the Torah, which is not mentioned explicitly.

This interpretation of disparate letters is similar to the use of secret codes, which are often based on slight textual deviations. This method was used in many places and generations, especially as a means of highlighting one's name in a well-known text.

The Sages of the Mishna and the Talmud found similar allusions for various *halakhot* elsewhere, and they coined the expression: Although there is no explicit proof of this matter, there is an allusion to the matter. In other words, although the proof from the text is insufficient to establish the *halakha,* it is a hint that provides support for the established *halakha.*

NOTES

As it is stated on the sixth day, and its libations [*unsakheha*] – שֶׁנֶּאֱמַר בַּשִּׁשִּׁי וּנְסָכֶיהָ: The early commentaries ask: Why does Rabbi Akiva say that the allusion to the water libation can be found only in the verse that deals with the sixth day of *Sukkot*: "And its libations [*unsakheha*]" (Numbers 29:31), and not in the verse dealing with the second day of the Festival, which states: "And their libations [*veniskeihem*]" (Numbers 29:19)? Given the plural form in both verses, why does he consider the verse that refers to the sixth day more binding than the verse that speaks of the second day? The *Shita Mekubbetzet* suggests that since the term *veniskeihem* is referring to multiple offerings, that plural form can be understood as referring to all the various libations that accompany the oxen, rams, and lambs mentioned in the previous verse. However, the term *unsakheha* indicates the presence of more than one libation for a single offering; therefore, Rabbi Akiva interprets it as an allusion to an additional libation that accompanies the morning daily offering.

אִי סָבַר לָהּ כְּרַבִּי יְהוּדָה בֶּן בְּתֵירָה נֵימָא כְּוָותֵיהּ! קָסָבַר רַבִּי עֲקִיבָא: כִּי כְּתִיב נִיסּוּךְ יְתֵירָא – בַּשִּׁשִּׁי הוּא דִּכְתִיב.

The Gemara objects: If Rabbi Akiva **holds in accordance with** the opinion of **Rabbi Yehuda ben Beteira** with regard to this derivation, **let** him **say** that it **is in accordance with his** ruling that one begins mentioning rain from the second day of *Sukkot*, not the sixth day. The Gemara answers: **Rabbi Akiva holds** that **when** that **extra** reference to **libation is written** in the verse, it is with regard **to the sixth day that it is written.** In other words, it is the plural phrase: "Its libations [*unsakheha*]" (Numbers 29:31), which appears on the sixth day, that directly indicates that one must perform more than one libation, while the other two superfluous letters merely serve to teach that this second libation must be of water, not wine. Therefore, the additional libation is performed on the sixth day.

תַּנְיָא, רַבִּי נָתָן אוֹמֵר: "בַּקֹּדֶשׁ הַסֵּךְ נֶסֶךְ שֵׁכָר לַה'" – בִּשְׁנֵי נִיסּוּכִין הַכָּתוּב מְדַבֵּר: אֶחָד נִיסּוּךְ הַמַּיִם וְאֶחָד נִיסּוּךְ הַיַּיִן. אֵימָא תַּרְוַיְיהוּ דְּחַמְרָא! אִם כֵּן לִכְתּוֹב קְרָא אוֹ הַסֵּךְ הֶסֵּךְ אוֹ נַסֵּךְ נֶסֶךְ, מַאי "הַסֵּךְ נֶסֶךְ" – שְׁמַעְתְּ מִינָּהּ: חַד דְּמַיָּא וְחַד דְּחַמְרָא.

§ **It is taught** in a *baraita* that **Rabbi Natan says: "In the Sanctuary you shall pour out a libation [*hassekh nesekh*] of strong drink to the Lord"** (Numbers 28:7).[N] The Torah states the term for libation twice, which indicates that **the verse is speaking of two libations: One** is **the water libation and** the other **one** is **the wine libation.** The Gemara asks: Why not **say** that **both** libations are **of wine?** The Gemara answers: **If so, let the verse write either *hassekh hessekh* or *nassekh nesekh*,** with the same prefix each time. **What is** the meaning of the varied formulation: **"*Hassekh nesekh*"? Learn from this** that **one** libation is **of water and** the other **one** is **of wine.**

אֶלָּא הָא דִּתְנַן: נִיסּוּךְ הַמַּיִם כָּל שִׁבְעָה. מַנִּי? אִי רַבִּי יְהוֹשֻׁעַ – נֵימָא חַד יוֹמָא, אִי רַבִּי עֲקִיבָא – תְּרֵי יוֹמֵי, אִי רַבִּי יְהוּדָה בֶּן בְּתֵירָה – שִׁיתָּא יוֹמֵי!

The Gemara asks: **However,** what about **that which we learned** in a mishna (*Sukka* 42b): **The water libation is** performed **all seven days** of *Sukkot*. **Who is** the author of this mishna? **If** you say it is **Rabbi Yehoshua, let us say** that this ritual is performed only **one day,** the Eighth Day of Assembly. **If** it is **Rabbi Akiva,** the mishna should state **two days,** the sixth and the seventh Festival days. **If** it is **Rabbi Yehuda ben Beteira,** the mishna should say that the water libation is performed on **six days,** from the second day of *Sukkot* onward.

לְעוֹלָם רַבִּי יְהוּדָה בֶּן בְּתֵירָה הִיא, וּסְבִירָא לֵיהּ כְּרַבִּי יְהוּדָה דְּמַתְנִיתִין. דִּתְנַן, רַבִּי יְהוּדָה אוֹמֵר: בְּלוֹג הָיָה מְנַסֵּךְ כָּל שְׁמוֹנָה, וּמַפִּיק רִאשׁוֹן וּמְעַיֵּיל שְׁמִינִי.

The Gemara answers: **Actually,** the ruling of the mishna **is** that **of Rabbi Yehuda ben Beteira, and he holds in accordance with** the opinion of **Rabbi Yehuda,** as stated **in a mishna. As we learned** in a mishna (*Sukka* 47a) that **Rabbi Yehuda says: He would pour with** a utensil that held a ***log*** of water **all eight days** of *Sukkot*, which includes the Eighth Day of Assembly. **And** Rabbi Yehuda ben Beteira **removes the first day** from this obligation and **includes the eighth,** which results in seven days of water libations.

וּמַאי שְׁנָא רִאשׁוֹן דְּלָא – דְּכִי רְמִיזִי מַיִם בַּשֵּׁנִי הוּא דִּרְמִיזִי! שְׁמִינִי נַמִי – כִּי רְמִיזִי מַיִם בַּשְּׁבִיעִי הוּא דִּרְמִיזִי!

The Gemara asks: **And what is different** about **the first** day, **that** the water libation **is not** performed on that day, according to the opinion of Rabbi Yehuda ben Beteira? Is the reason **that when** the Torah **alludes** to **water, it is on the second day that it alludes** to this libation? If so, one should not bring the libation on the **eighth** day **either,** because **when** the Torah **alludes** to **water** for the last time, **it is on the seventh day that it alludes** to it.

אֶלָּא, רַבִּי יְהוֹשֻׁעַ הִיא, וְנִיסּוּךְ הַמַּיִם כָּל שִׁבְעָה הִלְכְתָא גְּמִירִי לַהּ.

Rather, the Gemara retracts from the previous explanation in favor of the claim that this mishna **is** in accordance with the opinion of **Rabbi Yehoshua. And** Rabbi Yehoshua maintains that this ruling that **the water libation**[H] **is** performed **all seven days** of *Sukkot* **is a *halakha*** transmitted to Moses from Sinai, **learned through tradition.**[N] In other words, this obligation is not based upon a textual source.

HALAKHA

The water libation – נִיסּוּךְ הַמַּיִם: A water libation was poured on the altar on each of the seven days of the festival of *Sukkot*. This ritual is a *halakha* transmitted to Moses from Sinai (Rambam *Sefer Avoda, Hilkhot Temidin UMusafin* 10:6).

NOTES

In the Sanctuary you shall pour out a libation of strong drink to the Lord – בַּקֹּדֶשׁ הַסֵּךְ נֶסֶךְ שֵׁכָר לַה': The citation of this verse as a scriptural allusion to the water libation brought on *Sukkot* is puzzling because it does not refer to *Sukkot* but to the morning daily offering. One answer offered by Rabbi Nathan is that this verse merely alludes to the general idea of an alternative form of libation, the precise details of which he learns from the allusions in the verses dealing with the offerings of *Sukkot* (*Shita Mekubbetzet*; see *Gevurat Ari*).

Rather, it is Rabbi Yehoshua and…it is learned through tradition – אֶלָּא רַבִּי יְהוֹשֻׁעַ הִיא...הִלְכְתָא גְּמִירִי לַהּ: According to Rashi, this claim that the mishna is in accordance with the opinion of Rabbi Yehoshua corroborates with the opinion of Rabbi Eliezer, that the water libation is a *halakha* transmitted to Moses from Sinai, but excludes the opinions of Rabbi Akiva and Rabbi Yehuda ben Beteira.

Other commentaries assert that, according to all opinions, the water libation is performed on all seven days of *Sukkot*. This *halakha* is learned through tradition, the dispute concerning the allusions from the verses notwithstanding (Rabbi Elyakim; see the lengthy proof to this effect in *Dikdukei Soferim*, as well as in *Sefat Emet*). This is apparently the opinion of the Rambam as well, who states that this is a unanimously accepted *halakha*.

דְּאָמַר רַבִּי אַמִי אָמַר רַבִּי יוֹחָנָן מִשּׁוּם רַבִּי נְחוּנְיָא אִישׁ בִּקְעַת בֵּית חוֹרְתָן: עֶשֶׂר נְטִיעוֹת, עֲרָבָה, וְנִיסּוּךְ הַמַּיִם – הֲלָכָה לְמֹשֶׁה מִסִּינַי.

As Rabbi Ami[P] **said that Rabbi Yoḥanan said in the name of Rabbi Neḥunya of the valley of Beit Ḥortan:**[B] The *halakha* of **ten saplings,**[NH] that if there are ten saplings that require water planted in an area of a *beit se'a*, 2,500 square cubits, it is permitted to plow the entire field in the summer preceding the Sabbatical Year despite the fact that it is prohibited to plow other fields starting from the preceding *Shavuot*; the practice of walking around the altar with **a willow**[NH] and adorning the altar with it on *Sukkot* and taking it on the last day of *Sukkot*; and the obligation of **the water libation**; each of these three is a ***halakha*** transmitted **to Moses from Sinai.**

רַבִּי יְהוּדָה אוֹמֵר מִשּׁוּם רַבִּי יְהוֹשֻׁעַ: הָעוֹבֵר לִפְנֵי הַתֵּיבָה בְּיוֹם טוֹב הָאַחֲרוֹן שֶׁל חַג – הָאַחֲרוֹן מַזְכִּיר, הָרִאשׁוֹן אֵינוֹ מַזְכִּיר. בְּיוֹם טוֹב הָרִאשׁוֹן שֶׁל פֶּסַח – הָרִאשׁוֹן מַזְכִּיר, הָאַחֲרוֹן אֵינוֹ מַזְכִּיר.

It is stated in the same *baraita* cited previously that **Rabbi Yehuda says in the name of Rabbi Yehoshua:** With regard to **the one who passes before the ark** as prayer leader **on the concluding Festival day of the festival** of *Sukkot*, the Eighth Day of Assembly, **the last** prayer leader of the additional prayer **mentions** rain, whereas **the first** prayer leader for the morning prayer **does not mention** rain. Conversely, **on the first Festival day of Passover, the first** prayer leader **mentions** rain, while **the last** prayer leader **does not mention** rain.

הֵי רַבִּי יְהוֹשֻׁעַ? אִילֵימָא רַבִּי יְהוֹשֻׁעַ דְּמַתְנִיתִין – הָא אָמַר בְּיוֹם טוֹב הָאַחֲרוֹן שֶׁל חַג הוּא מַזְכִּיר!

The Gemara asks: To **which** statement of **Rabbi Yehoshua** is Rabbi Yehuda referring? **If we say** that he is referring to the statement of **Rabbi Yehoshua** cited **in the mishna,** this cannot be the case, as Rabbi Yehoshua in our mishna **said** that **one** begins to **mention** rain **on the last Festival day of the festival** of *Sukkot*, the Eighth Day of Assembly. This indicates that one starts to **mention** rain from the beginning of the day, i.e., the evening prayer service.

אֶלָּא רַבִּי יְהוֹשֻׁעַ דְּבָרַיְיתָא – הָאָמַר מִשְּׁעַת הַנָּחָתוֹ!

Rather, you will say that Rabbi Yehuda is referring to the opinion of **Rabbi Yehoshua,** cited **in the *baraita*.** However, this too is untenable, as **didn't** Rabbi Yehoshua **say** there that one begins to mention rain **from the time one puts down** the *lulav*, i.e., from the end of the seventh day of *Sukkot*? This statement also indicates that one begins to mention rain from the evening service of the Eighth Day of Assembly.

וְתוּ, הָא דְּתַנְיָא, רַבִּי יְהוּדָה אוֹמֵר מִשּׁוּם בֶּן בְּתֵירָה: הָעוֹבֵר לִפְנֵי הַתֵּיבָה בְּיוֹם טוֹב הָאַחֲרוֹן שֶׁל חַג הָאַחֲרוֹן מַזְכִּיר, הֵי בֶּן בְּתֵירָה? אִילֵימָא רַבִּי יְהוּדָה בֶּן בְּתֵירָה – הָא אָמַר בַּשֵּׁנִי בֶּחָג הוּא מַזְכִּיר!

The Gemara asks another question: **And, furthermore, that which is taught** in a *baraita* that **Rabbi Yehuda says in the name of ben Beteira:** With regard to **the one who passes before the ark on the concluding Festival day of the festival** of *Sukkot*, the Eighth Day of Assembly, **the last** prayer leader **mentions** rain. To **which** of the *halakhot* of **ben Beteira** is Rabbi Yehuda referring here? **If we say** he is referring to the ruling of **Rabbi Yehuda ben Beteira,** this cannot be the case, **as he said** that **one** begins to **mention** rain **on the second** day of *Sukkot*.

BACKGROUND

The valley of Bet Ḥortan – בִּקְעַת בֵּית חוֹרְתָן: According to parallel sources, Rabbi Neḥunya lived in Hauran, also called Havran, an area partially corresponding to the biblical land of Bashan, a fertile region in the northern part of eastern Transjordan. There are plains and hills in this area, including extinct volcanoes separated by valleys. At one time, many Jewish settlements existed there.

NOTES

Ten saplings – עֶשֶׂר נְטִיעוֹת: It is prohibited to plow a field not only during the Sabbatical Year but also toward the end of the sixth year of the Sabbatical cycle. This is due to the mitzva to add a certain period of non-sacred time to the sacred year, as well as a concern that this plowing will help plants grow on their own during the Sabbatical Year. Consequently, a special leniency was required for plowing around young saplings, which need particular care so that they can survive the Sabbatical Year. The plowing of an entire *beit se'a* is permitted only if there are ten saplings scattered throughout the field, not if they are located in a single row.

Willow – עֲרָבָה: According to most commentaries, this *halakha* is referring to the practice of taking a willow branch in the Temple. There is a requirement to take a willow branch in addition to the willow branches that form part of the four species. Some *ge'onim* maintain that this is referring to the obligation to take the willow in the Temple even on Shabbat.

HALAKHA

Ten saplings – עֶשֶׂר נְטִיעוֹת: If ten saplings are planted in the area of a *beit se'a*, 2,500 square cubits, the entire field may be plowed, on account of the saplings, until Rosh HaShana of the Sabbatical Year. This ruling is a *halakha* transmitted to Moses from Sinai (Rambam *Sefer Zera'im*, *Hilkhot Shemitta VeYovel* 3:5).

Willow – עֲרָבָה: In the Temple, one walks around the altar with a willow branch, on *Sukkot*, based on a *halakha* transmitted to Moses from Sinai. This willow is in addition to the willow branch taken as one of the four species (Rambam *Sefer Zemanim*, *Hilkhot Shofar VeSukka VeLulav* 7:20).

PERSONALITIES

Rabbi Ami – רַבִּי אַמִי: A third generation Eretz Yisrael *amora*, Rabbi Ami bar Natan was a priest and a close friend of Rabbi Asi. They studied with the greatest Sages of Eretz Yisrael and were outstanding disciples of Rabbi Yoḥanan. Rabbi Ami also studied with Rabbi Yoḥanan's preeminent students. In the Jerusalem Talmud, he is usually called Rabbi Immi.

After Rabbi Yoḥanan's death, Rabbi Ami was appointed head of the Tiberias academy in his place. Even Sages from distant Babylonia would consult him about halakhic problems. He is widely quoted in both the Babylonian Talmud and the Jerusalem Talmud, not only when he transmits statements in the name of his teachers, but also for his debates with Rabbi Asi and other Sages of the generation. Most of the *amora'im* of Eretz Yisrael from the following generation received and transmitted his statements. He and Rabbi Asi were also referred to as: The distinguished priests of Eretz Yisrael, and stories are told of their righteousness and sanctity. Rabbi Ami apparently lived a long life as even the Sages of the fourth generation in Babylonia are said to have sent questions to him.

אָמַר רַב נַחְמָן בַּר יִצְחָק: תְּהֵא בְּרַבִּי יְהוֹשֻׁעַ בֶּן בְּתֵירָה; זִמְנִין דְּקָרֵי לֵיהּ בִּשְׁמֵיהּ וְזִימְנִין דְּקָרֵי לֵיהּ בִּשְׁמֵיהּ דְּאַבָּא, וְהָא – מִקַּמֵּי דְּלִיסְמְכוּהוּ, וְהָא – לְבָתַר דְּלִיסְמְכוּהוּ.

Rav Naḥman Bar Yitzḥak said: Let the ben Beteira mentioned by Rabbi Yehuda in the *baraita* **be** understood as a reference **to Rabbi Yehoshua ben Beteira,** and this will resolve all the above difficulties. **At times,** Rabbi Yehuda **calls him by his name,** Rabbi Yehoshua, despite the fact that the name Rabbi Yehoshua generally refers to Rabbi Yehoshua ben Ḥananya. **At** other **times,** Rabbi Yehuda **calls him by his father's name,** e.g., in the second *baraita,* when the ruling is attributed to ben Beteira. **And** the Gemara explains the reason for the different names: **This** *baraita,* where he is called by his father's name, was written **before he was ordained,**[N] **and this** *baraita,* where he is called simply Rabbi Yehoshua, was from **after he was ordained.**

תָּנָא: בְּטַל וּבְרוּחוֹת לֹא חִיְּיבוּ חֲכָמִים לְהַזְכִּיר, וְאִם בָּא לְהַזְכִּיר – מַזְכִּיר. מַאי טַעְמָא? אֲמַר רַבִּי חֲנִינָא: לְפִי שֶׁאֵין נֶעֱצָרִין.

§ It is **taught**[B] in another *baraita*: With regard **to dew**[B] **and** with regard **to wind, the Sages did not obligate one to mention** them[N] by reciting: He makes the wind blow and the dew fall, in the second blessing of the *Amida,* **but if one seeks to mention** them, **he** may **mention**[H] them. The Gemara asks: **What is the reason** that this recitation is optional? **Rabbi Ḥanina**[P] **said: Because** winds and dew **are** consistent and **not withheld,** since the world could not exist without them, their mention is optional.

וְטַל מְנָלַן דְּלָא מִיעֲצַר? דִּכְתִיב "וַיֹּאמֶר אֵלִיָּהוּ הַתִּשְׁבִּי מִתֹּשָׁבֵי גִלְעָד אֶל אַחְאָב חַי ה׳ אֱלֹהֵי יִשְׂרָאֵל אֲשֶׁר עָמַדְתִּי לְפָנָיו אִם יִהְיֶה הַשָּׁנִים הָאֵלֶּה טַל וּמָטָר כִּי אִם לְפִי דְבָרִי" וּכְתִיב "לֵךְ הֵרָאֵה אֶל אַחְאָב וְאֶתְּנָה מָטָר עַל פְּנֵי הָאֲדָמָה". וְאִילּוּ טַל לֹא קָאָמַר לֵיהּ, מַאי טַעְמָא – מִשּׁוּם

The Gemara explains: **And dew, from where do we** derive **that it is not withheld?**[N] **As it is written: "And Elijah the Tishbite, who was of the settlers of Gilead, said to Ahab: As the Lord, the God of Israel, lives, before whom I stand, there shall be no dew or rain in these years**[N] **but according to my word"** (I Kings 17:1), **and it is written: "Go, show yourself before Ahab, and I will send rain upon the land"** (I Kings 18:1). God stated that He will resume rainfall, **whereas He did not say to** Elijah that He will restore **dew. What is the reason? Because** dew

BACKGROUND

Taught – תָּנָא: A term used to introduce quotations from a *baraita.* Usually the *baraitot* introduced by this expression are very short, one or two sentences at most, and they clarify, supplement, or qualify the statements of the mishna.

Dew – טַל: Dew is formed by the condensation of water vapor from the air and the ground. Most objects, including plants, radiate and lose more heat than the air, which means they are cooler than the air. The difference in temperature causes water vapor to form into dew. Although various factors can reduce the formation of dew, e.g., low clouds and strong winds, it is very uncommon for there to be no dew at all, because its formation is the result of local factors, not the general availability of water.

The amount of dew varies according to weather and location. In many areas of Eretz Yisrael, the overall quantity of dew is almost equal to that of rain, and it is only by means of dew that agriculture is possible in those regions.

An excess of dew can damage crops during certain times of the year, which is what the Gemara is referring to when it mentions dew that is not a blessing. Usually, however, dew is a medium of blessing, not only in summer when it is a source of additional water, but also in the rainy season, as it protects against frost at night.

HALAKHA

The mention of dew – הַזְכָּרַת טַל: If one mentions dew in the second blessing of the *Amida* prayer during the rainy season or fails to mention dew during the summer, he is not required to repeat the *Amida.* This is the case even if he has not yet finished reciting the blessing, as there is no obligation to mention dew (*Magen Avraham*). According to Ashkenazic custom, no mention is made of dew in the second blessing, neither in the rainy season nor in the summer (Rema). Members of Sephardic and Hassidic communities, and all Jews living in Eretz Yisrael, insert the expression: He makes the dew fall, in the summer (*Shulḥan Arukh, Oraḥ Ḥayyim* 114:3).

NOTES

This was before he was ordained – הָא מִקַּמֵּי דְּלִיסְמְכוּהוּ: A very young scholar, or one without special status, is regularly referred to as the son of so-and-so. In certain cases, the use of a father's name for a person of status is often considered degrading (see I Samuel 20:27). However, those Sages who did not receive the title of Rabbi would often be referred to in this manner, e.g., ben Azzai, ben Zoma.

With regard to dew and with regard to wind, the Sages did not obligate one to mention them – בְּטַל וּבְרוּחוֹת לֹא חִיְּיבוּ חֲכָמִים לְהַזְכִּיר: Some commentaries explain that the Gemara is discussing whether dew and wind should be mentioned during the rainy season, as during the summer they are certainly not mentioned at all (Rashi; Talmid HaRamban). Others maintain that the Gemara is referring to the custom to mention dew during the summer. In this regard, the Gemara states that even in places where there is a custom to mention dew, it is not obligatory to do so (Ritva; Rav Yehuda ben Binyamin HaRofeh).

That it is not withheld – דְּלָא מִיעֲצַר: See *Tosafot,* who analyze the episode of the miraculous dew of Gideon in light of this claim (Judges 6:36–40). Some commentaries suggest that the Gemara's contention that dew is not withheld does not mean that there are never nights on which dew does not appear, but merely that there are no protracted periods without dew (*Rishon LeTziyyon*).

There shall be no dew or rain in these years – אִם יִהְיֶה הַשָּׁנִים הָאֵלֶּה טַל וּמָטָר: The Gemara here indicates that Elijah did not request that dew be withheld entirely. In the Jerusalem Talmud and the *midrashim* written in Eretz Yisrael, there are opinions that Elijah indeed asked that dew should cease entirely, but God heeded his request only with respect to rain (see Jerusalem Talmud and *Aggadat Bereshit*).

PERSONALITIES

Rabbi Ḥanina – רַבִּי חֲנִינָא: When the plain title Rabbi Ḥanina is used in the Talmud, the reference is to Rabbi Ḥanina bar Ḥama, a first-generation *amora* from Eretz Yisrael. Rabbi Ḥanina originally came from Babylonia, although he emigrated to Eretz Yisrael at a relatively early age. He studied under Rabbi Yehuda HaNasi, who was very fond of him and even remarked that Rabbi Ḥanina was not a human being, but an angel. Rabbi Ḥanina also studied with Rabbi Yehuda HaNasi's preeminent students, especially Rabbi Ḥiyya. Rabbi Yehuda HaNasi, on his deathbed, designated Rabbi Ḥanina as the new head of his academy. However, in his great modesty, Rabbi Ḥanina refused to accept the position as long as his older colleague, Rabbi Efes, was still alive.

Rabbi Ḥanina lived in Tzippori where he earned a living as a honey dealer, from which he grew wealthy and established a large academy. He was renowned for his keenness of mind as well as his righteousness and piety.

Numerous halakhic and aggadic teachings of Rabbi Ḥanina appear in the Babylonian Talmud and the Jerusalem Talmud. He lived a long life and had many students over an extended period, including Rabbi Yehoshua ben Levi, a disciple-colleague of his, and Rabbi Yoḥanan, who studied with him for many years.

His son was the *amora* Rabbi Ḥama, son of Rabbi Ḥanina.

דלא מיעצר. וכי מאחר דלא מיעצר, אליהו אשתבועי למה ליה? הכי קאמר ליה: אפילו טל ברכה נמי לא אתי. וליהדריה לטל דברכה! משום דלא מינכרא מילתא.

is not withheld, and therefore it continued even during this time of drought. The Gemara asks: **And since dew is not withheld, why did Elijah swear**[N] that there would be no dew as well as no rain? The Gemara explains that **this is what** Elijah **said to** Ahab: Not only will there be no rainfall, but **even the dew of blessing,** which helps crops grow, **will not come.** This prediction was indeed fulfilled. The Gemara asks: **But** if so, **let** God **restore** the **dew of blessing** when He ended the drought of rain, in the aforementioned verse. The Gemara answers: This was not necessary, **because the matter is not recognizable,**[N] i.e., people cannot distinguish between dew of blessing and the regular dew which is always present.

אלא, רוחות מנא לן דלא מיעצרי? אמר רבי יהושע בן לוי: דאמר קרא ״כי כארבע רוחות השמים פרשתי אתכם נאם ה׳״ מאי קאמר להו? אילימא הכי קאמר להו הקדוש ברוך הוא לישראל: דבדרתינכו בארבע רוחי דעלמא, אי הכי ״כארבע״? בארבע מיבעי ליה! אלא הכי קאמר: כשם שאי אפשר לעולם בלא רוחות – כך אי אפשר לעולם בלא ישראל.

The Gemara asks: **However,** with regard to **winds,**[B] **from where do we** derive that **it is not withheld** but perpetually blows? **Rabbi Yehoshua ben Levi**[P] **said that the verse states: "For I have spread you abroad as the four winds of the heaven, says the Lord"** (Zechariah 2:10). He clarifies: **What is** God **saying to them? If we say** that **this is what the Holy One, Blessed be He, is saying to the Jewish people: I have scattered you to the four winds of the world; if so,** why did He say **"as the four** winds"? He **should have** said: **To the four** winds. **Rather, this is what** God **is saying: Just as the world cannot** exist **without winds, so too, the world cannot** exist **without the Jewish people.** This interpretation of the verse is based on the claim that the winds never cease.

אמר רבי חנינא: הלכך: בימות החמה, אמר משיב הרוח – אין מחזירין אותו. אמר מוריד הגשם – מחזירין אותו.

Rabbi Ḥanina said: Therefore, since wind and dew are always present, if **during the summer one recited: He makes the wind blow,**[H] **we do not require him to return** and repeat the blessing since the wind blows during the summer as well. However, if **one recited** during the summer: **He makes the rain fall, we require him to return** and repeat the blessing, because rain in the summer is a curse.

בימות הגשמים, לא אמר משיב הרוח – אין מחזירין אותו, לא אמר מוריד הגשם – מחזירין אותו. ולא עוד אלא – אפילו אמר מעביר הרוח ומפריח הטל – אין מחזירין אותו.

Conversely, **in the rainy season,** if **one did not recite: He makes the wind blow, we do not require him to return** to the beginning, because the wind blows regardless. If **one did not recite: He makes the rain fall, we require him to return** and repeat the blessing. **And not only that, but even** if one mistakenly **recited: He removes the wind and lifts the dew,** i.e., that there should be no wind or dew, **we do not require him to return** and repeat the blessing, because wind and dew are always present.

תנא: בעבים וברוחות לא חייבו חכמים להזכיר, ואם בא להזכיר – מזכיר. מאי טעמא – משום דלא מיעצרי.

It was **taught** in a similar *baraita*: With regard **to clouds and** with regard **to wind, the Sages did not obligate one to mention** them, but **if one wishes to mention them, he may mention** them. The Gemara asks: **What is the reason?** The Gemara answers, as above: **Because** clouds and winds are constant and **are not withheld.**

HALAKHA

During the summer one recited, He makes the wind blow – בימות החמה אמר משיב הרוח: If in the second blessing of the *Amida* prayer, during the summer, one recites: He makes the wind blow, without mentioning rain, or if one fails to mention the wind during the rainy season, one is not required to start from the beginning and repeat the blessing. If, during the summer, one recites: He makes the rain fall, one is required to return to the beginning of the blessing; and if he has already completed the blessing, he must return to the beginning of the *Amida*. This mistake must be corrected, even if one recited the prayer in a place where rain is required during the summer months, and even if he mentioned both dew and rain (Rema).

The authorities disagree about whether he must also repeat the introductory verse to the *Amida*: "O Lord, open my lips, and my mouth shall declare Your praise" (Psalms 51:17; see *Sha'arei Teshuva* and *Arukh HaShulḥan*). If, during the rainy season, one fails to mention: He makes the rain fall, he is required to return to the beginning of the *Amida* provided that he did not mention dew. However, if he mentioned dew, he is not required to return and correct the mistake, in accordance with the ruling of the Jerusalem Talmud (*Shulḥan Arukh, Oraḥ Ḥayyim* 114:3–5).

NOTES

Why did he swear – אשתבועי למה ליה: Some commentaries ask why the Gemara doesn't raise a different question: If dew is never withheld, how could Elijah utter an oath that cannot be fulfilled (see *Ein Ya'akov*)? Different answers have been suggested. One explanation is that this is indeed how the Gemara's question is to be understood: If dew is never withheld, why did Elijah pronounce this unworthy oath (*Shita Mekubbetzet*)? Another explanation is that although dew is never withheld by the natural order, a righteous man can request of God that He override the laws of nature. Consequently, the issue at hand is why Elijah saw fit to do so (Maharsha).

The matter is not recognizable – לא מינכרא מילתא: Some commentaries explain that the lack of dew of blessing was in fact recognizable; Ahab could tell that the curse was fulfilled because the dew that was present did not cause the produce to grow. However, the restoration of this dew was not recognizable because the rains returned along with the dew. Therefore, it could have been claimed that the growth was the result of the rain rather than the dew of blessing (Rabbi Yoshiya Pinto).

BACKGROUND

Winds – רוחות: Many different factors lead to the formation of winds, e.g., temperature discrepancies between the ground and the air, between the land and the sea, and between the poles and the equator; and the atmosphere surrounding the globe.

Although the winds that bring rain are linked to intricate systems, the general causes of wind are perpetually in place, therefore there is always some wind factor. In the terms of the Gemara, the wind is never withheld but perpetually blows.

PERSONALITIES

Rabbi Yehoshua ben Levi – רבי יהושע בן לוי: Rabbi Yehoshua ben Levi was one of the preeminent *amora'im* of the first generation in Eretz Yisrael. According to some opinions, Rabbi Yehoshua ben Levi was the son of Levi ben Sisi, an outstanding student of Rabbi Yehuda HaNasi. Apparently, Rabbi Yehoshua ben Levi himself was one of Rabbi Yehuda HaNasi's younger students. Many halakhic disputes are recorded between him and Rabbi Yoḥanan, who was apparently the younger of the two and a disciple-colleague of his. In general, the *halakha* is in accordance with the opinion of Rabbi Yehoshua ben Levi even when he is disputed by Rabbi Yoḥanan, whose authority was very great.

Rabbi Yehoshua ben Levi was also a renowned teacher of *aggada*. Due to the great respect in which he was held, an aggadic statement in his name is presented at the very conclusion of the Mishna.

A great deal is related of his piety and sanctity, and he is regarded as one of the most righteous men who ever lived. It is told that he would sit and study Torah with the most dangerously infected lepers. Rabbi Yehoshua ben Levi was famous as a worker of miracles; according to tradition, Elijah the prophet frequently appeared to him, and his prayers were always answered. According to tradition, he was one of those over whom the Angel of Death had no dominion, and he entered the Garden of Eden alive (*Ketubot* 77b).

Rabbi Yehoshua ben Levi taught many disciples. Virtually all of the Sages of the succeeding generation were his students to some degree, and they quote many statements in his name. His son, Rabbi Yosef, who was also a Sage, married into the family of the *Nasi*.

וְלָא מִיעַצְרִי? וְהָתָנֵי רַב יוֹסֵף: ״וְעָצַר אֶת הַשָּׁמַיִם״ – מִן הֶעָבִים וּמִן הָרוּחוֹת, אַתָּה אוֹמֵר מִן הֶעָבִים וּמִן הָרוּחוֹת, אוֹ אֵינוֹ אֶלָּא מִן הַמָּטָר? כְּשֶׁהוּא אוֹמֵר ״וְלֹא יִהְיֶה מָטָר״ – הֲרֵי מָטָר אָמוּר, הָא מָה אֲנִי מְקַיֵּים ״וְעָצַר אֶת הַשָּׁמַיִם״ – מִן הֶעָבִים וּמִן הָרוּחוֹת.

The Gemara asks: **And are they not withheld? But didn't Rav Yosef**[P] **teach** in a *baraita* that the verse: **"And He will close up the heavens"** (Deuteronomy 11:17), means that God will stop up the heavens **from the clouds and from the winds? Do you say** that "close up the heavens" means **from the clouds and from the winds, or** perhaps **it is only** referring to the absence **of rainfall? When** the same verse **says: "So that there will be no rain," rain** is already **mentioned** explicitly. **How** then **do I uphold** the meaning of the verse: **"And He will close up the heavens"?** This must mean **from the clouds and from the winds.**

קַשְׁיָא רוּחוֹת אַרוּחוֹת, קַשְׁיָא עָבִים אַעָבִים! עָבִים אַעָבִים לָא קַשְׁיָא; הָא – בְּחָרְפֵי, הָא – בְּאַפְלֵי,

The Gemara summarizes its question: This is **difficult** due to the contradiction between the statement about **wind** in the first *baraita* and the statement about **wind** in the second *baraita*, and is similarly **difficult** due to the contradiction between the statement about **clouds** in the first *baraita* and the statement about **clouds** in the second *baraita*. The Gemara answers: The contradiction between one statement about **clouds** and the other statement about **clouds is not difficult,** as **this** first *baraita* is referring to **early** clouds that precede the rain, which come whether or not rain actually falls, whereas **this** second *baraita* is referring to **late** clouds,[N] which materialize after rainfall. These late clouds are sometimes withheld by God as a punishment.

רוּחוֹת אַרוּחוֹת לָא קַשְׁיָא; הָא בְּרוּחַ מְצוּיָה, הָא – בְּרוּחַ שֶׁאֵינָהּ מְצוּיָה. רוּחַ שֶׁאֵינָהּ מְצוּיָה חַזְיָא לְבֵי דָרֵי! אֶפְשָׁר בְּנַפְוָותָא.

Likewise, the contradiction between the first statement about **wind** and the second statement about **wind** is **not difficult,** as **this** first *baraita* is referring to **a typical wind,** which is never withheld, while **this** second *baraita* is referring to **an atypical wind,** which may be withheld. The Gemara asks: **An atypical wind is fit for** winnowing grain on **the threshing floor.** Since this wind is also a necessity, one should pray for it as well. The Gemara answers: Since it is **possible** to winnow grain **with sieves** when there is no wind, there is no great need for these winds.

תָּנָא: הֶעָבִים וְהָרוּחוֹת שְׁנִיּוֹת לַמָּטָר. הֵיכִי דָּמֵי? אָמַר עוּלָּא וְאִיתֵּימָא רַב יְהוּדָה: דְּבָתַר מִיטְרָא. לְמֵימְרָא דְּמַעַלְיוּתָא הִיא? וְהָכְתִיב ״יִתֵּן ה׳ אֶת מְטַר אַרְצְךָ אָבָק וְעָפָר״ וְאָמַר עוּלָּא וְאִיתֵּימָא רַב יְהוּדָה: זִיקָא דְּבָתַר מִטְרָא!

§ It was **taught** in a *baraita*: **Clouds and winds are** so significant that, in terms of their benefit, they are **secondary** only **to rain.**[N] The Gemara asks: **What are the circumstances** in which this claim is correct? **Ulla,**[P] **and some say Rav Yehuda, said:** The *baraita* is referring to the clouds and winds **that** come **after rainfall.** The Gemara asks: **Is this to say that** clouds and winds that come after rain **are beneficial? But isn't it written** in the chapter of the curses: **"The Lord will make the rain of your land powder and dust"** (Deuteronomy 28:24), **and Ulla, and some say Rav Yehuda, said:** This curse is referring to **winds that come after rain,** as they raise up powder and dust?

לָא קַשְׁיָא; הָא – דַּאֲתָא נִיחָא, הָא – דַּאֲתָא רַזְיָא. וְאִי בָּעֵית אֵימָא: הָא – דְּמַעֲלֶה אָבָק, הָא דְּלָא מַעֲלֶה אָבָק.

The Gemara answers: This is **not difficult,** since **this** first statement of Ulla is referring to beneficial wind **that comes gently,**[N] whereas **this** second statement of Ulla is referring to harmful wind **that comes forcefully** [*razya*],[L] raises up powder and dust, and reduces the effectiveness of the rain. **And if you wish, say** instead: **This,** Ulla's second statement, is referring to wind **that raises dust;** whereas **this,** Ulla's first statement, is referring to wind **that does not raise dust.**

PERSONALITIES

Ulla – עוּלָּא: A second-third generation *amora* in Eretz Yisrael, Ulla was the preeminent scholar who transmitted information and halakhic rulings from Eretz Yisrael to the Diaspora. His full name was apparently Ulla, son of Yishmael. Ulla was one of the disciples of Rabbi Yoḥanan and was responsible for conveying the Torah rulings laid down in Eretz Yisrael to the scholars in Babylonia. He would likewise transmit the halakhic teachings of the Babylonian scholars back to Eretz Yisrael.

Ulla apparently undertook regular journeys and would travel from place to place teaching Torah. For this reason Yalta, wife of Rav Naḥman, described him as a peddler (*Berakhot* 51b). In the eyes of the Babylonian scholars, Ulla was particularly important, and the scholars of the second generation of *amora'im* there treated him with great respect. For example, Rav Ḥisda referred to him as: Our teacher who comes from Eretz Yisrael, and Rav Yehuda sent his son to learn practical *halakha* from Ulla's conduct.

In the Jerusalem Talmud, in which he is generally referred to as Rabbi Ulla, son of Yishmael, or Ulla the traveler down to Babylonia, numerous Torah rulings are recorded in his name. Many Sages of the next generation were his pupils.

Of his private life we know nothing. It is possible that the *amora* Rabba, son of Ulla, was his son.

Ulla died in Babylonia on one of his journeys and was brought back to Eretz Yisrael for burial.

PERSONALITIES

Rav Yosef – רַב יוֹסֵף: Rav Yosef, son of Ḥiyya, was one of the greatest of the third generation Babylonian *amora'im*. He was a disciple of Rav Yehuda and a colleague of Rabba, and he headed the Pumbedita academy for two and a half years. He was called Sinai due to his expert knowledge of *baraitot* and the oral traditions of the Torah, as well as the translation of the Torah. His paramount students were Abaye and Rava. An illness caused him to forget all his studies, but Abaye helped him to regain his memory. Rav Yosef also grew blind. After Rav Yosef's death he was succeeded by Abaye as head of the Pumbedita academy.

NOTES

This is referring to early clouds, this is referring to late clouds – הָא בְּחָרְפֵי, הָא בְּאַפְלֵי: The commentary on the text is in accordance with Rashi and most early commentaries, who explain that early and late refer to two types of clouds: The clouds that come before rain, and those that appear in the sky after rain has fallen. The *Shita Mekubbetzet* cites an opposite opinion, i.e., that the term: Early, means clouds that come early after rain, rather than those that precede it. By contrast, some commentaries explain that the terms early and late do not refer to two types of clouds at all, but to two types of crops. Early crops, those that ripen early, are not affected by a lack of clouds following rain; whereas late crops are affected if there are no clouds after the rain, as the ground will dry up and the rain will not help them grow (see *Tosafot* and Ra'avad).

Secondary to rain – שְׁנִיּוֹת לַמָּטָר: Some commentaries explain that the clouds and winds that follow rain benefit the crops like a second rainfall (Rabbeinu Ḥananel).

This is referring to wind that comes gently – הָא דַּאֲתָא נִיחָא: The commentaries dispute the meaning of this answer. Some maintain that it means strong and light winds (Rabbeinu Ḥananel), while others contend that it is referring to the strength of the rain as affected by the wind (Rashi; Rabbi Elyakim). According to the first interpretation, the difference between the two answers is clear, whereas according to Rashi's explanation, the two answers are effectively the same.

LANGUAGE

Forcefully [*razya*] – רַזְיָא: Apparently, derived from the Greek ῥῶσις, *rhosis*, meaning strength or violence.

BACKGROUND

Sunlight that follows after rain – **שִׁימְשָׁא דְּבָתַר מִיטְרָא**: After a considerable amount of rainfall, the sun's heat will cause the water to evaporate into the atmosphere and be absorbed by the fine fibers of the roots of plants. This combination of water and bright sunlight hastens the growth of the plant's leaves.

NOTES

The glow [*gilhei*] of the evening – **גִּילְהֵי דְּלֵילְיָא**: Some commentaries associate *gilhei* with *gilui*, which means to uncover. In other words, the expression is referring to a clear or cloudless evening sky.

For He says to the snow, Fall on the earth – **לַשֶּׁלֶג יֹאמַר הֱוֵא אָרֶץ**: Some commentaries explain this verse as follows: And to the snow that falls in the hills, He shall say: Be as on the plains of the earth, i.e., the snow is compared to that which falls on the plains of the earth (Maharsha).

וְאָמַר רַב יְהוּדָה: זִיקָא דְּבָתַר מִיטְרָא – כְּמִיטְרָא, עִיבָא דְּבָתַר מִיטְרָא – כְּמִיטְרָא, שִׁימְשָׁא דְּבָתַר מִיטְרָא – כִּתְרֵי מִטְרֵי. לְמַעוּטֵי מַאי? לְמַעוּטֵי גִּילְהֵי דְּלֵילְיָא, וְשִׁמְשָׁא דְּבֵינֵי קָרְחֵי.

And on a related topic, **Rav Yehuda said: Wind that** blows **after rain is** as beneficial to the earth **as rain** itself. **Clouds that** appear **after rain are** as beneficial **as rain,** while **sunlight that** follows **after rain**[B] is as beneficial **as two rainfalls.** The Gemara asks: If wind, clouds, and sun are all beneficial after rainfall, **what** does Rav Yehuda's statement serve **to exclude?** The Gemara answers: He comes **to exclude the glow of the evening**[N] **and the sun that** shines **between the clouds,** appearing only in patches. These phenomena are harmful after rain.

אָמַר רָבָא: מַעֲלֵי תַּלְגָּא לְטוּרֵי כְּחַמְשָׁה מִטְרֵי לְאַרְעָא, שֶׁנֶּאֱמַר ״כִּי לַשֶּׁלֶג יֹאמַר הֱוֵא אָרֶץ וְגֶשֶׁם מָטָר וְגֶשֶׁם מִטְרוֹת עֻזּוֹ״.

On a related note, **Rava said: Snow is as beneficial to the mountains as five rainfalls to the earth** of the plains, **as it is stated: "For He says to the snow: Fall on the earth,**[N] **likewise to the shower of rain, and to the showers of His mighty rain"** (Job 37:6). This verse compares snow to rain by means of five allusions to types of rainfall: The word "rain," which appears twice; the word "shower"; and the plural "showers," which indicates two rainfalls. This teaches that snow is as beneficial as five rainfalls.

וְאָמַר רָבָא: תַּלְגָּא – לְטוּרֵי, מִטְרָא רַזְיָא – לְאִילָנֵי, מִטְרָא נִיחָא – לְפֵירֵי,

And on the same topic, **Rava said: Snow** brings benefits **to the mountains; strong rain** provides benefits **to trees; light rain** brings benefit **to fruit;**

Perek **I**
Daf **4** Amud **a**

LANGUAGE

Drizzle [*urpila*] – **עוּרְפִּילָא**: Referring to the finest rain, consisting of drops of mist that have condensed slightly but fall softly and slowly. The earth absorbs this drizzle well. Since this kind of rain fills the air, even places where ordinary rain does not reach are moistened by it.

Seed [*partzida*] – **פַּרְצִידָא**: Phonetically similar to the Arabic فرصد, *firṣid*, which also means seed.

Torah scholar [*tzurva*] – **צוּרְבָא מֵרַבָּנַן**: According to the *ge'onim*, this may be from the word for fire or heat, meaning hot or one who has caught fire; they also suggest it may mean hardened. The Arabic ضرب, *ḍrb*, has all these meanings.

עוּרְפִּילָא אֲפִילּוּ לְפַרְצִידָא דִּתְחוֹתֵי קָלָא מְהַנְיָא לֵיהּ. מַאי עוּרְפִּילָא – עוּרוּ פִּילֵי. וְאָמַר רָבָא: הַאי צוּרְבָא מֵרַבָּנַן דָּמֵי לְפַרְצִידָא דִּתְחוֹתֵי קָלָא, דְּכֵיוָן דְּנָבַט – נָבַט.

and **drizzle** [*urpila*][L] **is even beneficial to a seed** [*partzida*][L] **under a clod** of earth, as it can reach anywhere without causing any harm. The Gemara asks: **What is** the meaning of the word **drizzle?** The Gemara explains: It is a contraction of the phrase: **Arise, furrows** [*uru pilei*].[N] **And** the Gemara cites another saying in which Rava uses the same imagery. **Rava said: This Torah scholar** [*tzurva*][L] **is like a seed under a clod** of earth,[N] **as once he sprouts** and begins to develop, **he** continues to **sprout** and his greatness increases.

וְאָמַר רָבָא: הַאי צוּרְבָא מֵרַבָּנַן דְּרָתַח – אוֹרַיְיתָא הוּא דְּקָא מַרְתְּחָא לֵיהּ, שֶׁנֶּאֱמַר ״הֲלוֹא כֹה דְבָרִי כָּאֵשׁ נְאֻם ה׳״. וְאָמַר רַב אַשִׁי: כָּל תַּלְמִיד חָכָם שֶׁאֵינוֹ קָשֶׁה כְּבַרְזֶל – אֵינוֹ תַּלְמִיד חָכָם, שֶׁנֶּאֱמַר ״וּכְפַטִּישׁ יְפֹצֵץ סָלַע״.

§ **And,** incidentally, the Gemara relates that which **Rava said: This Torah scholar who grows angry,** it can be presumed that **it is his Torah study that angers him.**[N] Therefore, he must be given the benefit of the doubt, **as it is stated: "Is not my word like fire, says the Lord"** (Jeremiah 23:29). **And** similarly, **Rav Ashi said: Any Torah scholar who is not as hard as iron,** but is indecisive and wavers, he **is not a Torah scholar, as it is stated** in the same verse: **"And as a hammer that breaks rock in pieces"** (Jeremiah 23:29).

NOTES

Arise, furrows [*uru pilei*] – **עוּרוּ פִּילֵי**: Some commentaries explain that *uru* is related to *me'arer*, undermines, meaning: Break through the rows (*Arukh*).

Like a seed under a clod of earth – **דָּמֵי לְפַרְצִידָא דִּתְחוֹתֵי קָלָא**: Most commentaries explain that a Torah scholar is initially unknown and he is as obscure as a seed beneath the ground. However, once he begins to develop, he grows significantly. Some explain that the phrase is referring to a seed that sprouts beneath the earth, where it is protected in its initial stages of growth. So too, a Torah scholar will develop his potential best if he is protected when young (Rabbi Elyakim).

It is his Torah study that angers him – **אוֹרַיְיתָא הוּא דְּקָא מַרְתְּחָא לֵיהּ**: Many commentaries are puzzled by these statements, as they apparently praise anger, which is generally considered a problematic trait. One explanation is based on a suggestion of some early commentaries that as the heart of a Sage becomes bound up with the Torah and spiritual matters, he becomes highly sensitive to unseemly and sinful acts and is therefore more susceptible to anger (Meiri; *Shita Mekubbetzet*). Consequently, this rage does not stem from wickedness but from extra sensitivity. Nevertheless, Ravina says that everyone, Torah scholars included, should train themselves to express rebuke appropriately, in a pleasant manner. The reason for this emotional training is that when one grows angry, even when it is justified and motivated by pure intention, one's rage can damage one's own soul. As the Gemara states: When a scholar becomes angry, it causes his studies to be forgotten (*Pesaḥim* 66b). Therefore, it is best to avoid this negative behavior (*Gevurat Ari*; *Ya'arot Devash*).

אֲמַר לֵיהּ רַבִּי אַבָּא לְרַב אַשִׁי: אַתּוּן מֵהָתָם מַתְנִיתוּ לָהּ, אֲנַן מֵהָכָא מַתְנִינַן לָהּ – דִּכְתִיב ״אֶרֶץ אֲשֶׁר אֲבָנֶיהָ בַרְזֶל״, אַל תִּקְרֵי ״אֲבָנֶיהָ״ אֶלָּא בּוֹנֶיהָ. אָמַר רָבִינָא: אֲפִילּוּ הָכִי, מִיבָּעֵי לֵיהּ לְאִינִישׁ לְמֵילַף נַפְשֵׁיהּ בְּנִיחוּתָא, שֶׁנֶּאֱמַר ״וְהָסֵר כַּעַס מִלִּבֶּךָ״ וגו׳.

Rabbi Abba said to Rav Ashi: You learned the proof for this idea **from** that verse **there; we learned it from here, as it is written: "A land whose stones** [*avaneha*] **are iron"** (Deuteronomy 8:9). **Do not read** this phrase as **"whose stones** [*avaneha*]**," rather,** read it as **whose builders** [*boneha*], since Torah scholars build the land spiritually and are as tough as iron. With regard to these statements praising the toughness of a Torah scholar, **Ravina**[P] **said: And even so, one is required to teach himself to act gently,**[H] **as it is stated: "And remove anger from your heart,** and put away evil from your flesh" (Ecclesiastes 11:10).

אָמַר רַבִּי שְׁמוּאֵל בַּר נַחְמָנִי אָמַר רַבִּי יוֹנָתָן: שְׁלֹשָׁה שָׁאֲלוּ שֶׁלֹּא כַּהוֹגֶן, לִשְׁנַיִם הֱשִׁיבוּהוּ כַּהוֹגֶן, לְאֶחָד הֱשִׁיבוּהוּ שֶׁלֹּא כַּהוֹגֶן. וְאֵלּוּ הֵן: אֱלִיעֶזֶר עֶבֶד אַבְרָהָם, וְשָׁאוּל בֶּן קִישׁ, וְיִפְתָּח הַגִּלְעָדִי.

As a preamble to the statement of Rabbi Berekhya, below, the Gemara cites that which **Rabbi Shmuel bar Naḥmani said** that **Rabbi Yonatan said: Three** people **entreated** God in an **unreasonable** manner, i.e., in situations where their requests might have received an unfavorable answer. **To two** of them God **responded reasonably,** with a favorable response to their requests, **and to one** God **responded unreasonably,**[N] i.e., unfavorably, in a manner befitting the unreasonable request. **And they are: Eliezer, servant of Abraham; Saul, son of Kish; and Jephthah the Gileadite.**

אֱלִיעֶזֶר עֶבֶד אַבְרָהָם – דִּכְתִיב ״וְהָיָה הַנַּעֲרָה אֲשֶׁר אֹמַר אֵלֶיהָ הַטִּי נָא כַדֵּךְ״ וגו׳ יָכוֹל אֲפִילּוּ חִיגֶּרֶת אֲפִילּוּ סוּמָא – הֵשִׁיבוֹ כַּהוֹגֶן, וְנִזְדַּמְּנָה לוֹ רִבְקָה.

The Gemara clarifies each of these cases in turn: With regard to **Eliezer, servant of Abraham,** he made a request when he prayed beside the well, **as it is written: "That the maiden to whom I shall say: Please let down your pitcher** that I may drink; and she shall say: Drink, and I will also give your camels to drink; that she be the one whom you have appointed for your servant Isaac" (Genesis 24:14). Eliezer entreated God unreasonably, as his request allowed for the possibility that she **might even** be **lame** or **even blind,** and yet he had promised to take her to Isaac. Nevertheless, God **responded** to him **reasonably and** the eminently suitable **Rebecca happened** to come **to him.**

שָׁאוּל בֶּן קִישׁ – דִּכְתִיב ״וְהָיָה הָאִישׁ אֲשֶׁר יַכֶּנּוּ יַעְשְׁרֶנּוּ הַמֶּלֶךְ עֹשֶׁר גָּדוֹל וְאֶת בִּתּוֹ יִתֶּן לוֹ״ יָכוֹל אֲפִילּוּ עֶבֶד, אֲפִילּוּ מַמְזֵר – הֵשִׁיבוֹ כַּהוֹגֶן, וְנִזְדַּמֵּן לוֹ דָּוִד.

With regard to **Saul, son of Kish,** he made an offer when Goliath the Philistine challenged the Jews, **as it is written: "And it shall be that the man who kills him, the king will enrich him with great riches, and will give him his daughter"** (I Samuel 17:25). The man who killed Goliath **might even** have been **a slave or a *mamzer*,** one born from an incestuous or adulterous union, who would be unfit to marry his daughter. Nevertheless, God **responded** to him **reasonably and David happened** to come **to him.**

יִפְתָּח הַגִּלְעָדִי – דִּכְתִיב ״וְהָיָה הַיּוֹצֵא אֲשֶׁר יֵצֵא מִדַּלְתֵי בֵיתִי״ וגו׳ יָכוֹל אֲפִילּוּ דָּבָר טָמֵא הֵשִׁיבוֹ שֶׁלֹּא כַּהוֹגֶן – נִזְדַּמְּנָה לוֹ בִּתּוֹ.

By contrast, there is the case of **Jephthah the Gileadite.** Upon leaving for battle he issued a statement, **as it is written: "Then it shall be that whatever comes forth from the doors of my house** to meet me when I return in peace… it shall be to the Lord and I will bring it up for a burnt-offering" (Judges 11:31). This **might even** have been **an impure,** non-kosher **animal,** which he had committed himself to sacrifice. In this instance, God **responded** to him **unreasonably, and his daughter happened** to come **to him.**

וְהַיְינוּ דְּקָאָמַר לְהוּ נָבִיא לְיִשְׂרָאֵל: ״הַצֳרִי אֵין בְּגִלְעָד אִם רֹפֵא אֵין שָׁם״.

Regarding the incident of Jephthah, the Gemara remarks: **And this is what the prophet said to the Jewish people: "Is there no balm in Gilead?**[N] **Is there no physician there?** Why then has the health of the daughter of my people not recovered?" (Jeremiah 8:22). This verse alludes to the fact that had he sought a means to do so, Jephthah could have had his vow annulled.

וּכְתִיב ״אֲשֶׁר לֹא צִוִּיתִי וְלֹא דִבַּרְתִּי וְלֹא עָלְתָה עַל לִבִּי״.

And it is written, with regard to human sacrifice: "And they have also built the high places of the Ba'al, to burn their sons in the fire for burnt offerings to Ba'al, **which I did not command, and I did not speak, nor did it come into My heart"** (Jeremiah 19:5).

PERSONALITIES

Ravina – רָבִינָא: A Babylonian *amora* of the fifth and sixth generations, Ravina apparently came from Mata Meḥasya, although some authorities claim that he was from Eretz Yisrael. He was among Rava's students. The Gemara records halakhic discussions between Ravina and Rava, and more frequently records discussions between Ravina and various other students of Rava. Although Ravina was older than Rav Ashi, he accepted him as a teacher and became his disciple-colleague. Apparently, Ravina was also actively involved in editing the Babylonian Talmud, a project that was completed by Rav Ashi. While little information is known about his private life, the Talmud indicates that he had children. Rav Ashi's sons were students of Ravina. Ravina had many other disciples, the most important of whom was Ravina the Younger, his sister's son, who completed the main stages of the final editing of the Talmud.

HALAKHA

Teach himself to act gently – לְמֵילַף נַפְשֵׁיהּ בְּנִיחוּתָא: Anger is an especially problematic trait, and it is proper for one to distance himself from it and train himself not to get angry. If one must instill fear in the members of his household or the community, he should merely act as if he is angry. The Sages therefore commanded that one should distance himself from anger to the point that he is not even stirred by matters that usually cause rage, as stated by Ravina (Rambam *Sefer HaMadda*, *Hilkhot Deot* 2:3).

NOTES

To one He responded unreasonably – לְאֶחָד הֱשִׁיבוּהוּ שֶׁלֹּא כַּהוֹגֶן: Many commentaries discuss the issue of why Jephthah alone received an unfavorable response. Some explain this by pointing out a difference in the nature of the requests. Eliezer and Saul, as well as Caleb (see Rashi and *Tosafot*), were involved in personal or family commitments and were therefore justified in issuing open-ended statements. By contrast, Jephthah uttered a vow to God and should have taken care to do so in an appropriate matter, rather than making his vow dependent on whatever or whomever happened to emerge from his house (*Kli Yakar*; *Iyyun Ya'akov*).

Is there no balm in Gilead – הַצֳרִי אֵין בְּגִלְעָד: Some early commentaries understand the reference to Gilead as a double allusion, since it refers both to Jephthah the Gileadite himself as well as to the one who could have annulled the vow, Pinehas, in accordance with the midrashic tradition that notwithstanding the many years separating them, Pinehas was Elijah, another Gileadite. Indeed, the Sages state elsewhere that the mutual pride of Jephthah and Pinehas, in their refusal to consult one another, prevented Jephthah from learning that his vow was invalid (*Bereshit Rabba* 60:3; Rabbeinu Gershom).

"אֲשֶׁר לֹא צִוִּיתִי" – זֶה בְּנוֹ שֶׁל מֵישַׁע מֶלֶךְ מוֹאָב, שֶׁנֶּאֱמַר "וַיִּקַּח אֶת בְּנוֹ הַבְּכוֹר אֲשֶׁר יִמְלֹךְ תַּחְתָּיו וַיַּעֲלֵהוּ עֹלָה", "וְלֹא דִבַּרְתִּי" – זֶה יִפְתָּח, "וְלֹא עָלְתָה עַל לִבִּי" – זֶה יִצְחָק בֶּן אַבְרָהָם.

The Gemara interprets each phrase of this verse: **"Which I did not command,"** this is referring to **the son of Mesha, king of Moab.** King Mesha sacrificed his son, **as it is stated: "Then he took his firstborn son, who would reign after him, and he offered him as a burnt-offering"** (II Kings 3:27). **"And I did not speak," this** is referring to **Jephthah,** who sacrificed his daughter as an offering. **"Nor did it come into my heart," this** is referring to **Isaac, son of Abraham.** Although God commanded Abraham to sacrifice Isaac, there was no intent in God's heart that he should actually do so; it was merely a test.

אָמַר רַבִּי בֶּרֶכְיָה: אַף כְּנֶסֶת יִשְׂרָאֵל שָׁאֲלָה שֶׁלֹּא כַּהוֹגֶן, וְהַקָּדוֹשׁ בָּרוּךְ הוּא הֱשִׁיבָהּ כַּהוֹגֶן, שֶׁנֶּאֱמַר "וְנֵדְעָה נִרְדְּפָה לָדַעַת אֶת ה׳ כְּשַׁחַר נָכוֹן מוֹצָאוֹ וְיָבוֹא כַגֶּשֶׁם לָנוּ".

§ In light of the above statement, the Gemara returns to the issue of rain. **Rabbi Berekhya**[P] **said: The Congregation of Israel also entreated** God **unreasonably, and** yet **the Holy One, Blessed be He, responded reasonably, as it is stated: "And let us know, eagerly strive to know the Lord. His going forth is sure as the morning, and He will come to us as the rain"** (Hosea 6:3). They compared the revelation of God to the rain.

אָמַר לָהּ הַקָּדוֹשׁ בָּרוּךְ הוּא: בִּתִּי, אַתְּ שׁוֹאֶלֶת דָּבָר שֶׁפְּעָמִים מִתְבַּקֵּשׁ וּפְעָמִים אֵינוֹ מִתְבַּקֵּשׁ, אֲבָל אֲנִי אֶהְיֶה לָךְ דָּבָר הַמִּתְבַּקֵּשׁ לְעוֹלָם, שֶׁנֶּאֱמַר "אֶהְיֶה כַטַּל לְיִשְׂרָאֵל".

In response, **the Holy One, Blessed be He, said to** the Jewish people: **My daughter, you request** the manifestation of My Presence by comparing Me to **a matter,** rain, **that is sometimes desired, but is sometimes undesired,**[N] e.g., during the summer. **However, I will be to you** like **a matter that is always desired,** dew, **as it is stated: "I will be as the dew to Israel"** (Hosea 14:6), since dew appears in all seasons and is invariably a blessing.

וְעוֹד שָׁאֲלָה שֶׁלֹּא כַּהוֹגֶן, אָמְרָה לְפָנָיו: רִבּוֹנוֹ שֶׁל עוֹלָם, "שִׂימֵנִי כַחוֹתָם עַל לִבֶּךָ כַּחוֹתָם עַל זְרוֹעֶךָ". אָמַר לָהּ הַקָּדוֹשׁ בָּרוּךְ הוּא: בִּתִּי, אַתְּ שׁוֹאֶלֶת דָּבָר שֶׁפְּעָמִים נִרְאֶה וּפְעָמִים אֵינוֹ נִרְאֶה, אֲבָל אֲנִי אֶעֱשֶׂה לָךְ דָּבָר שֶׁנִּרְאֶה לְעוֹלָם, שֶׁנֶּאֱמַר "הֵן עַל כַּפַּיִם חַקֹּתִיךְ".

And the Congregation of Israel **further entreated** God **unreasonably** in another context, **saying before Him: Master of the Universe: "Set me as a seal upon Your heart, as a seal upon Your arm"** (Song of Songs 8:6). **The Holy One, Blessed be He, said to her: My daughter, you ask** that I be manifest to you in **a matter that is sometimes visible and sometimes not visible,** as the heart and arm are not covered. **However, I will act** so that I manifest Myself **for you** like **a matter that is always visible, as it is stated: "Behold, I have engraved you on the palms of My hands,** your walls are continually before me" (Isaiah 49:16).

"אֵין שׁוֹאֲלִין אֶת הַגְּשָׁמִים" כו׳. סְבוּרָה: שְׁאֵלָה וְהַזְכָּרָה חֲדָא מִילְּתָא הִיא, מַאן תַּנָּא? אָמַר רָבָא: רַבִּי יְהוֹשֻׁעַ הִיא, דְּאָמַר: מִשְּׁעַת הַנָּחָתוֹ.

§ The Gemara returns to the *halakhot* of the mishna: **One requests rain** only immediately preceding the rainy season. The Sages **assumed that requesting and mentioning are one** and the same **thing,**[N] and consequently they asked: **Who is the** ***tanna*** **who taught** this *halakha*? The Gemara answers that **Rava said: It is** in accordance with the opinion of **Rabbi Yehoshua,**[N] **who said** that one mentions rain **from the time of putting down** the *lulav*, i.e., the Eighth Day of Assembly, which is indeed near the rainy season.

אָמַר לֵיהּ אַבָּיֵי: אֲפִילּוּ תֵּימָא רַבִּי אֱלִיעֶזֶר, שְׁאֵלָה לְחוּד וְהַזְכָּרָה לְחוּד.

Abaye said to him: Even if **you say** that **it is** in accordance with the opinion of **Rabbi Eliezer,** who holds that one mentions rain from the first day of the festival of *Sukkot*, this ruling of the mishna can be explained by distinguishing between the two terms: **Requesting is a discrete** concept **and mentioning is** another **discrete** concept. In other words, even according to the opinion of Rabbi Eliezer, one begins to request rain just before the rainy season, on the Eighth Day of Assembly, whereas one starts to mention rain already on the first day of *Sukkot*.

וְאִיכָּא דְּאָמְרִי: לֵימָא

And some say a different version of this discussion: **Let us say**

NOTES

Sometimes undesired – פְּעָמִים אֵינוֹ מִתְבַּקֵּשׁ: Some commentaries add that excessive rain, even in its proper season, is undesirable, whereas too much dew is not considered a curse (Rabbi Yoshiya Pinto).

Requesting and mentioning are one and the same thing – שְׁאֵלָה וְהַזְכָּרָה חֲדָא מִילְּתָא הִיא: This assumption is puzzling, as the mishna itself apparently distinguishes between the two concepts. Nevertheless, a closer examination of the mishna reveals that although different terminology is used for mentioning and requesting rain, when the term for requesting appears later in the mishna it is used not only in the narrow sense of the request for rain in the ninth blessing but also in reference to the general mention of rain in the second blessing. The two terms are also equated in the Jerusalem Talmud, as well as in Rambam's Commentary on the Mishna.

It is in accordance with the opinion of Rabbi Yehoshua – רַבִּי יְהוֹשֻׁעַ הִיא: There are two basic explanations of this question and answer. Rashi maintains that the question is referring to the discrepancy in days between the beginning of the mention of rain, which occurs at the beginning of *Sukkot*, according to the opinion of Rabbi Eliezer, and the time for the request of rain, which starts just before the rainy season. According to this interpretation, there is a dispute among the early commentaries as to whether this is referring to the seventh day of *Sukkot* (Rabbi Aharon HaLevi), the Eighth Day of Assembly (Rashi; Rabbeinu Yehonatan), or the third or seventh of Marḥeshvan (see Ran and the Ritva). Some explain this question differently: If one says that the mention of rain and the request for rain should begin concurrently, since the request for rain is recited only during weekday services, there must be an opinion that this request begins on a weekday rather than a Festival. See also Rid, who points to textual differences that correspond to the two interpretations (Rabbeinu Ḥananel; Ran; Rabbi Elyakim).

PERSONALITIES

Rabbi Berekhya – רַבִּי בֶּרֶכְיָה: An *amora* of Eretz Yisrael from the fourth generation, Rabbi Berekhya received and transmitted teachings in the names of Sages of previous generations; in particular, he was a student of Rabbi Ḥelbo. He is seldom quoted in the Babylonian Talmud, but his teachings often appear in the Jerusalem Talmud and the *midrashim*. Although there are few halakhic rulings in his name, many of his aggadic statements are recorded. The collections of aggadic midrash from Eretz Yisrael present many of his homiletic interpretations.

We possess almost no information about his personal life. It is stated in the Jerusalem Talmud that his daughter's son, Rabbi Ḥiyya, was also a Torah Sage.

רַבִּי יְהוֹשֻׁעַ הִיא, דְּאָמַר מִשְּׁעַת הַנָּחָתוֹ? אָמַר רָבָא: אֲפִילּוּ תֵּימָא רַבִּי אֱלִיעֶזֶר, שְׁאֵלָה לְחוּד וְהַזְכָּרָה לְחוּד.

that our mishna **is** in accordance with the opinion of **Rabbi Yehoshua, who said** that one mentions rain from **the time of putting** the *lulav* **down,** from the Eighth Day of Assembly, and it is not in accordance with the opinion of Rabbi Eliezer. **Rava said: Even if you say** that the ruling of the mishna **is** in accordance with the opinion of **Rabbi Eliezer,** one can explain this by distinguishing between the terms: **Requesting is a distinct** notion **and mentioning is** another **distinct** notion, even according to the opinion of Rabbi Eliezer.

״רַבִּי יְהוּדָה אוֹמֵר הָעוֹבֵר לִפְנֵי הַתֵּיבָה״ כו׳.

§ The mishna stated that **Rabbi Yehuda says:** With regard to **the one who passes before the ark** as prayer leader on the concluding Festival day of *Sukkot*, the Eighth Day of Assembly, the prayer leader of the additional prayer mentions rain, while the leader of the morning prayer does not. The reverse is the case at the conclusion of the period of mentioning rain, as the leader of the morning prayer mentions rain, while the one who leads the additional prayer[N] does not.

וּרְמִינְהוּ: עַד מָתַי שׁוֹאֲלִין אֶת הַגְּשָׁמִים? רַבִּי יְהוּדָה אוֹמֵר: עַד שֶׁיַּעֲבוֹר הַפֶּסַח, רַבִּי מֵאִיר אוֹמֵר: עַד שֶׁיַּעֲבוֹר נִיסָן!

And the Gemara **raises a contradiction** from a *baraita* (5a): **Until when does one request rain? Rabbi Yehuda says: Until Passover has passed. Rabbi Meir says: Until** the month of **Nisan has passed.** According to the *baraita*, Rabbi Yehuda holds that one prays for rain until the end of Passover, whereas the mishna states that Rabbi Yehuda's opinion is that one prays for rain only until the beginning of the Festival.

אֲמַר רַב חִסְדָּא: לָא קַשְׁיָא, כָּאן – לִשְׁאוֹל, כָּאן – לְהַזְכִּיר. מִישְׁאַל שָׁאֵיל וְאָזֵיל, לְהַזְכִּיר – בְּיוֹם טוֹב הָרִאשׁוֹן פָּסֵיק.

Rav Ḥisda said: This is **not difficult.** The *baraita* **here** is referring to the **request** for rain, which continues until the end of Passover, whereas the mishna **there** rules that one is **to mention** rain only until the first Festival day. In other words, Rabbi Yehuda holds that one **continues requesting rain** until the end of Passover, but with regard **to** the **mention** of rain, already **on the first** day of the **Festival** one **ceases** to do so.

אֲמַר עוּלָּא: הָא דְּרַב חִסְדָּא קַשְׁיָא ״כַּחֹמֶץ לַשִּׁנַּיִם וְכֶעָשָׁן לָעֵינַיִם״. וּמַה בְּמָקוֹם שֶׁאֵינוֹ שׁוֹאֵל – מַזְכִּיר, בְּמָקוֹם שֶׁשּׁוֹאֵל – אֵינוֹ דִּין שֶׁיְּהֵא מַזְכִּיר?!

The Gemara raises a difficulty against this answer. **Ulla said: That which Rav Ḥisda** said is as **difficult** to accept **"as vinegar to the teeth, and as smoke to the eyes"** (Proverbs 10:26).[B] He elaborates: **If when one does not** yet **request** rain, at the beginning of the rainy season, one nevertheless **mentions** rain; **in a case when one requests rain,** i.e., during Passover, according to this explanation, **is it not right that one should** also **mention** rain?

אֶלָּא אָמַר עוּלָּא: תְּרֵי תַנָּאֵי אַלִּיבָּא דְּרַבִּי יְהוּדָה.

Rather, Ulla said an alternative resolution: In fact, **two *tanna'im*** expressed different rulings **in accordance with** the opinion of **Rabbi Yehuda.**[N] According to one *tanna*, Rabbi Yehuda holds that one both mentions and requests rain during Passover, whereas according to the other *tanna*, Rabbi Yehuda holds that one neither mentions nor requests rain after the morning prayer of the first day of Passover.

רַב יוֹסֵף אָמַר: מַאי ״עַד שֶׁיַּעֲבוֹר הַפֶּסַח״ – עַד שֶׁיַּעֲבוֹר שְׁלִיחַ צִבּוּר רִאשׁוֹן הַיּוֹרֵד בְּיוֹם טוֹב רִאשׁוֹן שֶׁל פֶּסַח.

The Gemara cites an additional resolution of the apparent contradiction. **Rav Yosef said: What is** the meaning of the phrase: **Until Passover has passed** [*ya'avor*]? It means: **Until the first prayer leader who descends** to pray has passed before the ark for the morning prayers **on the first Festival** day of **Passover.** According to this explanation, the mishna and *baraita* specify the same time period for the end of the mention and request for rain.

אֲמַר לֵיהּ אַבָּיֵי: שְׁאֵלָה בְּיוֹם טוֹב מִי אִיכָּא?

Abaye said to Rav Yosef: **Is there a request** for rain **on a Festival?** The request for rain is included in the ninth blessing of the *Amida*, the blessing of the years, which is not recited on Shabbat and Festivals. If the term Passover in the *baraita* is referring to the entire Festival, this includes the intermediate Festival days, during which the ninth blessing of the *Amida* is recited. However, according to your interpretation, the *baraita* refers only to the first day of the Festival, and yet the request for rain is not recited on this date.

NOTES

Conclusion of the period in the additional prayers – הַפְסָקָה בִּתְפִלַּת הַמּוּסָפִים: In the Jerusalem Talmud, it is asked why the beginning and cessation of mentioning rain occur specifically in the additional prayers. The answer given there is that in this manner one prays for dew in the morning prayer of the first day of Passover and in the additional prayer and afternoon prayers of *Sukkot*. In this manner a prayer for dew is recited on all of the Festivals, which is fitting, as dew signifies a blessing (Rif). Another reason cited in the Jerusalem Talmud is that the additional prayers are attended even by those who arrive late to the service, and therefore this is the best time to inform the congregation of the change. The transition should not occur in the morning service as some might think that the change was introduced the night before, leading to error in subsequent years. This is particularly true given that there is an opinion that one should not implement this change until after it has been publicly announced by the prayer leader.

Another explanation is that the change is made in the additional service because one's mind is not fully at ease in prayer until that point (Rabbi Zeraḥya HaLevi citing *Pesikta DeRav Kahana*; Ritva).

Two *tanna'im* in accordance with Rabbi Yehuda – תְּרֵי תַנָּאֵי אַלִּיבָּא דְּרַבִּי יְהוּדָה: This expression means that there are two *tanna'im* who dispute the nature of Rabbi Yehuda's opinion. In this case, however, some commentaries explain that one of the two rulings was uttered by Rabbi Yehuda in the name of his teacher, Rabbi Yehoshua ben Beteira, whereas the other statement reflects his own opinion (see *Gevurat Ari* and *Sefat Emet;* Ritva).

BACKGROUND

As vinegar to the teeth and as smoke to the eyes – כַּחֹמֶץ לַשִּׁנַּיִם וְכֶעָשָׁן לָעֵינַיִם: These images refer to an unpleasant, even painful, sensation. In both cases, the sensation becomes harder to bear the longer it continues. Ulla is saying that Rav Ḥisda's explanation aroused similar reactions in him, as the longer he thinks about it the more difficult and less understandable it becomes.

אמר ליה: אין, שואל מתורגמן. וכי מתורגמן שואל דבר שאינו צריך לצבור? אלא, מחוורתא כדעולא.

The Gemara cites the response: Rav Yosef **said to** Abaye: **Yes,** the *baraita* is speaking of the first day of Passover. However, it does not refer to the request for rain recited in the *Amida*. Rather, **the disseminator** and translator of the Torah portion would **recite a request**[N] for rain after the Festival prayers. The Gemara asks: **But would a disseminator request a matter that the community does not need?** As there is no need for rain on Passover, why would the disseminator recite a request for it? **Rather, it is clear, as Ulla** explained, there are two tannaitic versions of Rabbi Yehuda's opinion.

רבה אמר: מאי "עד שיעבור הפסח" – עד שיעבור זמן שחיטת הפסח, וכתחילתו כן סופו, מה תחילתו מזכיר אף על פי שאינו שואל – אף סופו מזכיר אף על פי שאינו שואל.

Rabba said another explanation: **What is** the meaning of the phrase: **Until Passover has passed?** It means **until after the time for the slaughter of the Paschal lamb has passed,**[N] the afternoon of the fourteenth of Nisan, i.e., until the beginning of Passover. **And** according to this opinion, the practice at **the beginning** of the time for praying for rain **is like** that of **the end: Just as at the beginning** of the rainy season **one mentions** rain **although one does not request it, so too,** at **the end,** on the first day of Passover, **one mentions** rain **although one does not request it.** The request for rain ends on the eve of Passover, while the mention of rain continues until the morning service the following day.

אמר ליה אביי: בשלמא תחילתו מזכיר – הזכרה נמי ריצוי שאלה היא, אלא סופו מאי ריצוי שאלה איכא? אלא מחוורתא כדעולא.

Abaye said to Rabba: **Granted,** at **the beginning** of the rainy season **one mentions** rain before requesting it, as **mentioning** rain **is also an appeasement** to God in advance **of** the forthcoming **request.**[B] **However, at the end** of the season, **what appeasement** toward **a request is there** that would necessitate the mention of rain after one has ceased requesting it? The Gemara again concludes: **Rather, it is clear as Ulla** explained.

אמר רבי אסי אמר רבי יוחנן: הלכה כרבי יהודה. אמר ליה רבי זירא לרבי אסי: ומי אמר רבי יוחנן הכי? והתנן: בשלשה במרחשון שואלין את הגשמים, רבן גמליאל אומר: בשבעה בו. ואמר רבי אלעזר: הלכה כרבן גמליאל!

Rabbi Asi said that **Rabbi Yoḥanan said: The *halakha* is in accordance with** the opinion of **Rabbi Yehuda. Rabbi Zeira**[P] **said to Rabbi Asi: And did Rabbi Yoḥanan** actually **say that? But didn't we learn** in a mishna (6a): **On the third of Marḥeshvan** one starts to **request rain.**[H] **Rabban Gamliel**[P] **says:** One starts **on the seventh of** Marḥeshvan. **And** with regard to this mishna, **Rabbi Elazar,** Rabbi Yoḥanan's preeminent student, **said: The *halakha* is in accordance with** the opinion of **Rabban Gamliel.**[N]

NOTES

The disseminator would recite a request – **שואל מתורגמן:** Most commentaries explain that in the course of his explanation and elaboration of the communal prayers, the disseminator would speak of rain. Some hold that it is referring to a specific liturgical poem added to the service (*Shita Mekubbetzet*).

Until after the time for the slaughter of the Paschal lamb has passed – **עד שיעבור זמן שחיטת הפסח:** The commentaries dispute the meaning of this opinion. Some say that one recites the request for rain until the evening service of the first night of Passover. In other words, the recitation continues until the afternoon service of Passover eve, as that is when the Paschal lamb is slaughtered (Rabbeinu Ḥananel; Rabbeinu Gershom). Others explain that the recitation ceases at the time of the slaughter of the Paschal lamb in the afternoon, i.e., one does not recite the request in the afternoon prayer of Passover eve (Rashi; Rabbeinu Yehonatan).

The *halakha* is in accordance with the opinion of Rabban Gamliel – **הלכה כרבן גמליאל:** Based on this statement and the subsequent conclusion of the Gemara, it would appear that when the Temple is not standing in Eretz Yisrael the request for rain is recited starting immediately after *Sukkot*, while in Babylonia it should be first recited on the seventh of Marḥeshvan, and elsewhere in the Diaspora it is recited starting sixty days after the equinox (Rid the Younger; Meiri).

According to the Rambam, in Eretz Yisrael one begins to recite the request for rain on the seventh of Marḥeshvan (Rambam *Sefer Ahava, Hilkhot Tefilla UVirkat Kohanim* 2:16). This ruling is followed in practice today. It is possible that the Rambam's reasoning is that since Rabbi Yoḥanan's opinion that one begins to mention and request rain on the same day is rejected, the two recitations need not commence together and each can start on the most appropriate date. Consequently, the mention of rain begins on the Eighth Day of Assembly, while the request for rain begins on the seventh of Marḥeshvan in Eretz Yisrael and sixty days after the autumnal equinox in the Diaspora (*Leḥem Mishne*).

BACKGROUND

An appeasement in advance of the request – **ריצוי שאלה:** This is describing the proper manner of asking a favor from someone. One does not immediately issue a request. Rather, one first prepares the ground by touching on the subject in a general way, by mentioning it but not yet making the request explicit. Similarly, the mention of rain is similar to a polite beginning, a preamble, later followed by the explicit request for rain.

HALAKHA

From when does one begin to request rain – **ממתי שואלים גשמים:** In Eretz Yisrael, one begins to recite the request for rain on the night of the seventh of Marḥeshvan, in accordance with the opinion of Rabban Gamliel (*Shulḥan Arukh, Oraḥ Ḥayyim* 117:1).

PERSONALITIES

Rabbi Zeira – **רבי זירא:** One of the greatest of the third generation of Babylonian *amora'im*, Rabbi Zeira was educated in the Babylonian tradition and studied mainly with the disciples of Rav and Shmuel. He emigrated to Eretz Yisrael, where he studied under Rabbi Yoḥanan and was a colleague of Rabbi Yoḥanan's foremost disciples. When Rabbi Zeira reached Eretz Yisrael he was extremely impressed by the method of learning he found there, which he adopted in full. Accordingly, he undertook one hundred fasts to help him forget the Babylonian method of learning. He also fasted so that the fires of Gehenna should not rule over him. When he performed tests to see if fire would affect him, the calves of his legs were burned. For this reason he became known as the short man with the scorched calves (*Bava Metzia* 85a). Rabbi Zeira was famous for his great piety, his modesty, and his affable and accommodating nature. He was greatly loved and honored by his peers. Rabbi Zeira had many disciples throughout Eretz Yisrael, and his teachings are widely quoted in both the Babylonian and Jerusalem Talmud. He had a son who was also a Sage, Rabbi Ahava.

Rabban Gamliel II of Yavne – **רבן גמליאל:** Rabban Gamliel was the *Nasi* of the Great Sanhedrin and one of the most important *tanna'im* in the period following the destruction of the Second Temple. Rabban Gamliel moved with the Great Sanhedrin to Yavne at the initiative of Rabban Yoḥanan ben Zakkai after the destruction of the Temple, which is why he is known as Rabban Gamliel of Yavne. After Rabban Yoḥanan ben Zakkai's death, Rabban Gamliel presided over the Great Sanhedrin as Nasi.

Rabban Gamliel sought to create a spiritual center for the Jews that would unite the entire people as the Temple had done until that time. For this reason, he strove to enhance the honor and the central authority of the Great Sanhedrin and its *Nasi*. His strict and vigorous leadership eventually led his colleagues to remove him from his post for a short period, replacing him with Rabbi Elazar ben Azarya (*Berakhot* 27b–28a). However, as everyone knew that his motives and actions were for the good of the people and were not based on personal ambition, they soon restored him to his position.

Although there are not many halakhic rulings in the name of Rabban Gamliel, numerous important decisions were made in his time and under his influence. These included the broad principle that the *halakha* is in accordance with the opinion of Beit Hillel; the rejection of the halakhic system of Rabbi Eliezer; and the establishment of a fixed formulae for prayers. In all decisions attributed to Rabban Gamliel there is an uncompromising approach to *halakha*; he remained faithful to his principles in reaching his conclusions. It is known that two of his sons were Sages: Rabban Shimon ben Gamliel, who served as *Nasi* of the Great Sanhedrin after him, and Rabbi Ḥanina ben Gamliel.

אֲמַר לֵיהּ: גַּבְרָא אַגַּבְרָא קָא רָמֵית?! אִיבָּעֵית אֵימָא: לָא קַשְׁיָא; כָּאן – לִשְׁאוֹל, כָּאן – לְהַזְכִּיר.

Rabbi Asi **said to** Rabbi Zeira: **Are you raising a contradiction** from the statement of **one man against** the statement of another **man?**[N] Although Rabbi Elazar was Rabbi Yoḥanan's student, their opinions need not be consistent with one another. **If you wish, say** instead that this is **not difficult,** as Rabbi Elazar's ruling **here** is referring **to** the **request** for rain, which begins on the seventh of Marḥeshvan, whereas Rabbi Yoḥanan's ruling **there** is referring **to** the **mention** of rain, which begins on the Eighth Day of Assembly.

וְהָאָמַר רַבִּי יוֹחָנָן: בְּמָקוֹם שֶׁשּׁוֹאֵל מַזְכִּיר! הַהוּא לְהַפְסָקָה אִיתְּמַר. וְהָאָמַר רַבִּי יוֹחָנָן: הִתְחִיל לְהַזְכִּיר – מַתְחִיל לִשְׁאוֹל, פָּסַק מִלִּשְׁאוֹל – פּוֹסֵק מִלְּהַזְכִּיר!

The Gemara asks: **But didn't Rabbi Yoḥanan say: At** the same time **when one requests** rain, one **mentions** it. The Gemara answers: **That** ruling **was stated** only with regard **to ceasing** the request and mention of rain. Although Rabbi Yoḥanan maintains that one stops requesting and mentioning rain on the same date, he does not hold that one begins to do both at the same time. The Gemara objects: **But didn't Rabbi Yoḥanan** explicitly **say:** When one **begins to mention** rain, one **begins to request** it; and when one **ceases to request** rain, one **ceases to mention** it. This clearly indicates that, in his opinion, there is no discrepancy between the dates when one begins reciting the two formulations.

אֶלָּא לָא קַשְׁיָא: הָא – לָן, הָא – לְהוּ. מַאי שְׁנָא לְדִידָן – דְּאִית לָן פֵּירֵי בְּדַבְרָא, לְדִידְהוּ נַמִּי – אִית לְהוּ עוֹלֵי רְגָלִים!

The Gemara answers: **Rather,** it is **not difficult. This** statement, where Rabbi Yoḥanan ruled in accordance with the opinion of Rabban Gamliel, **is for us,** who live in Babylonia and start to pray for rain later, whereas **that** statement of the mishna **is for them,** the residents of Eretz Yisrael. The Gemara asks: **What is different** with regard **to us** in Babylonia that we do not request rain immediately after *Sukkot*? The reason is **that we** still **have fruit in the field.** Therefore, we do not want rain to fall. However, **they,** the inhabitants of Eretz Yisrael, **also have pilgrims** who need to travel for a significant time to reach their homes after the Festival, and they do not want it to rain on them.

כִּי קָאָמַר רַבִּי יוֹחָנָן בִּזְמַן שֶׁאֵין בֵּית הַמִּקְדָּשׁ קַיָּים. הָשְׁתָּא דְּאָתֵית לְהָכִי הָא וְהָא לְדִידְהוּ, וְלָא קַשְׁיָא: כָּאן – בִּזְמַן שֶׁבֵּית הַמִּקְדָּשׁ קַיָּים, כָּאן – בִּזְמַן שֶׁאֵין בֵּית הַמִּקְדָּשׁ קַיָּים.

The Gemara answers: **When Rabbi Yoḥanan said** this ruling in the mishna, he was referring to the period **when the Temple is not standing;** therefore, in Eretz Yisrael, one can immediately request rain. The Gemara comments: **Now that you have arrived at this** answer, one can say that both **this** statement **and that** statement **are for them,** i.e., those in Eretz Yisrael. **And** yet, it is **not difficult,** as this statement **here,** that one waits before requesting rain, applies **at the time when the Temple is standing,** while the ruling **there,** that one requests rain right after the Festival, is referring to **the time when the Temple is not standing.**

וַאֲנַן דְּאִית לָן תְּרֵי יוֹמֵי, הֵיכִי עָבְדִינַן? אָמַר רַב: מַתְחִיל בְּמוּסָפִין, וּפוֹסֵק בְּמִנְחָה עַרְבִית וְשַׁחֲרִית, וְחוֹזֵר בְּמוּסָפִין.

The Gemara asks: **And we** in the Diaspora **who have two** Festival **days, how do we act** with regard to beginning the mention of rain, given the uncertainty concerning the Eighth Day of Assembly, which might in reality be the seventh day of *Sukkot*? The Gemara answers that **Rav said: One begins** to mention rain **in the additional prayers** of the eighth day, the first day of the Eighth Day of Assembly. **And one** temporarily **ceases** this practice **on the afternoon prayer** of the eighth day, continuing through **the evening and morning prayers** of the ninth day, the second day of the Eighth Day of Assembly. **And** finally **one again** resumes mentioning rain **in the additional prayers** of the ninth day, *Simḥat Torah*.

אָמַר לְהוּ שְׁמוּאֵל: פּוּקוּ וְאִמְרוּ לֵיהּ לְאַבָּא: אַחַר שֶׁעֲשִׂיתוֹ קוֹדֶשׁ תַּעֲשֵׂהוּ חוֹל?! אֶלָּא אָמַר שְׁמוּאֵל: מַתְחִיל בְּמוּסָפִין וּבְמִנְחָה, וּפוֹסֵק עַרְבִית וְשַׁחֲרִית, וְחוֹזֵר וּמַתְחִיל בְּמוּסָפִין.

Shmuel said to those who reported Rav's explanation to him: **Go out and tell Abba,**[B] referring to Rav by his name, the following objection: **After you have rendered** the first day of the Eighth Day of Assembly **sanctified, shall you defile it** by treating it as though it is not a Festival day? **Rather, Shmuel said** (10a): **One begins** to mention rain **in the additional prayers and** also mentions it **in the afternoon prayer** of the eighth day, the first day of the Eighth Day of Assembly, **and** temporarily **ceases** this practice **on the afternoon prayer** of the eighth day, continuing through **the evening and morning prayers** of the ninth day, *Simḥat Torah*. **And** finally, one **again** resumes mentioning rain **in the additional prayers** of the ninth day, *Simḥat Torah*.

NOTES

Are you raising a contradiction from the statement of one man against the statement of another man – גַּבְרָא אַגַּבְרָא קָא רָמֵית: This objection is so obvious that it is difficult to understand the basis of the question in the first place. Indeed, as indicated in the commentary to the text, the question can be understood only in light of the close connection between Rabbi Yoḥanan and Rabbi Elazar. Although Rabbi Elazar studied with many of the leading Babylonian scholars, it is said of him that his rulings were invariably based on the statements of Rabbi Yoḥanan. If it is assumed that Rabbi Elazar's ruling reflects the opinion of Rabbi Yoḥanan, a difference between a ruling issued by Rabbi Yoḥanan and that of his disciple Rabbi Elazar is indeed a contradiction. Consequently, some commentaries explain that the Gemara answers by saying that there is a dispute among *amora'im* with regard to Rabbi Yoḥanan's opinion (Rabbi Elyakim).

BACKGROUND

And tell Abba – וְאִמְרוּ לֵיהּ לְאַבָּא: According to a geonic tradition, Rav's given name was Abba. Usually people called him by his title, Rav, but since Shmuel was his colleague he referred to him by his given name. Moreover, the name Abba means father, and was used as an honorable epithet for elderly men. Consequently, Shmuel could call Rav by name even in the presence of strangers without appearing disrespectful.

HALAKHA

Once one has started, he no longer stops – כֵּיוָן שֶׁהִתְחִיל, שׁוּב אֵינוֹ פּוֹסֵק: Even in the Diaspora, where two days of each Festival are observed, one begins to insert the expression: He makes the wind blow and the rain fall, in the additional prayers of the Eighth Day of Assembly, from which point one continues to mention rain continuously until the end of the rainy season (*Shulḥan Arukh, Oraḥ Ḥayyim* 114:1).

PERSONALITIES

Rav Ḥananel – רַב חֲנַנְאֵל: A Babylonian *amora* of the second generation, Rav Ḥananel was a disciple of Rav, and most of his teachings are transmitted in the name of his great teacher. He was, apparently, one of Rav's preeminent students; and Rav's successor, Rav Huna, treated Rav Ḥananel with great respect. By profession, he was a scribe who wrote Torah scrolls. It is said of him that he could copy the entire Torah accurately by heart.

BACKGROUND

And the last rain is in Nisan – וּמַלְקוֹשׁ בְּנִיסָן: According to weather observations, only a small amount of rain, one percent of the annual precipitation, falls in Eretz Yisrael in May. Weather observations in the coastal plain, over a period of many years, reveal that the last rain usually falls no later than April 28, around the end of the month of Nisan.

Locust – אַרְבֶּה: The term locust refers to a group of insects that are found worldwide. The common name generally refers to the group of short-horned grasshoppers that often increase greatly in numbers and migrate long distances in destructive swarms. The sporadic appearance and disappearance of locust has bewildered people throughout history and, even today, there are only theories available to explain this phenomenon. Locusts are edible insects and are considered a delicacy in some countries. There have been references to their consumption as food throughout history and some species are permitted for consumption according to Torah law.

Desert locust, a species that is kosher according to some Yemenite traditions

רָבָא אָמַר: כֵּיוָן שֶׁהִתְחִיל – שׁוּב אֵינוֹ פּוֹסֵק וְכֵן אָמַר רַב שֵׁשֶׁת: כֵּיוָן שֶׁהִתְחִיל שׁוּב אֵינוֹ פּוֹסֵק.

Rava said an alternative suggestion: **Once one has started** to mention rain, **he no longer stops,**[H] i.e., he continues the mention of rain consistently until the summer. **And, so too, Rav Sheshet said: Once one has started** to mention rain, **he no longer stops.** In other words, once one has begun to mention rain in his prayers in the additional prayer on the Eighth Day of Assembly, he continues to do so uninterrupted, even in the Diaspora.

וְאַף רַב הֲדַר בֵּיהּ דְּאָמַר רַב חֲנַנְאֵל אָמַר רַב: מוֹנֶה עֶשְׂרִים וְאֶחָד יוֹם כְּדֶרֶךְ שְׁמוֹנֶה עֲשָׂרָה יָמִים מֵרֹאשׁ הַשָּׁנָה עַד יוֹם הַכִּפּוּרִים, וּמַתְחִיל וְכֵיוָן שֶׁהִתְחִיל שׁוּב אֵינוֹ פּוֹסֵק, וְהִלְכְתָא כֵּיוָן שֶׁהִתְחִיל שׁוּב אֵינוֹ פּוֹסֵק.

The Gemara adds: **And even Rav retracted** his previously stated opinion, **as Rav Ḥananel**[P] **said** that **Rav said: One counts twenty-one days** from Rosh HaShana, just **as one counts ten days**[N] **from Rosh HaShana until Yom Kippur. And** after the twenty-one days, **one starts** to mention rain, **and once one has started, he no longer stops.** The Gemara concludes: **And the** ***halakha*** **is in accordance with** the opinion that **once one has started** to mention rain, **he no longer stops.**

מתני׳ עַד מָתַי שׁוֹאֲלִין אֶת הַגְּשָׁמִים? רַבִּי יְהוּדָה אוֹמֵר: עַד שֶׁיַּעֲבוֹר הַפֶּסַח, רַבִּי מֵאִיר אוֹמֵר: עַד שֶׁיֵּצֵא נִיסָן, שֶׁנֶּאֱמַר ״וַיּוֹרֶד לָכֶם גֶּשֶׁם מוֹרֶה וּמַלְקוֹשׁ בָּרִאשׁוֹן״.

MISHNA Until when does one request rain?[N] **Rabbi Yehuda says:** We request rain **until Passover has passed. Rabbi Meir says: Until** the month of **Nisan has ended, as it is stated: "And He causes to come down for you the rain,**[N] **the first rain and** the **last rain, in the first** month" (Joel 2:23). Since the verse states that it rains in Nisan, the first month, this indicates that the entire month is considered part of the rainy season.

גמ׳ אָמַר לֵיהּ רַב נַחְמָן לְרַבִּי יִצְחָק: יוֹרֶה בְּנִיסָן? יוֹרֶה בְּמַרְחֶשְׁוָן הוּא! דִּתְנַן: יוֹרֶה בְּמַרְחֶשְׁוָן וּמַלְקוֹשׁ בְּנִיסָן! אֲמַר לֵיהּ: הָכִי אָמַר רַבִּי יוֹחָנָן: בִּימֵי יוֹאֵל בֶּן פְּתוּאֵל נִתְקַיֵּים מִקְרָא זֶה, דִּכְתִיב בֵּיהּ ״יֶתֶר הַגָּזָם אָכַל הָאַרְבֶּה״ וגו׳. אוֹתָהּ שָׁנָה יָצָא אֲדָר וְלֹא יָרְדוּ גְּשָׁמִים, יָרְדָה לָהֶם רְבִיעָה רִאשׁוֹנָה בְּאֶחָד בְּנִיסָן.

GEMARA Rav Naḥman said to Rabbi Yitzḥak: Is the **first rain in Nisan?** The **first rain is in Marḥeshvan, as we learned** in a *baraita*: **The first rain** is **in Marḥeshvan and the last rain is in Nisan.**[B] Rabbi Yitzḥak **said to** Rav Naḥman that **Rabbi Yoḥanan said as follows: This verse was fulfilled in the days of** the prophet **Joel, son of Pethuel,** in a year **concerning** which **it is written: "That which the palmer-worm has left, the locust**[B] **has eaten** and that which the locust has left, the canker-worm has eaten; and that which the canker-worm has left, the caterpillar has eaten" (Joel 1:4), when no crops remained. In **that year,** the month of **Adar ended and** still **no rain had fallen.** The rain of the **first rainy season fell for them on the first of Nisan.**

אָמַר לָהֶם נָבִיא לְיִשְׂרָאֵל: צְאוּ וְזִרְעוּ. אָמְרוּ לוֹ: מִי שֶׁיֵּשׁ לוֹ קַב חִטִּים אוֹ קַבַּיִם שְׂעוֹרִין יֹאכְלֶנּוּ וְיִחְיֶה, אוֹ יִזְרָעֶנּוּ וְיָמוּת? אָמַר לָהֶם: אַף עַל פִּי כֵן, צְאוּ וְזִרְעוּ. נַעֲשָׂה לָהֶם נֵס וְנִתְגַּלָּה לָהֶם מַה שֶּׁבַּכְּתָלִין וּמַה שֶּׁבְּחוֹרֵי נְמָלִים.

After the first rain fell, **the prophet said to the Jews: Go out and sow. They said to him: One who has one** ***kav*** **of wheat or two** ***kav*** **of barley** left, **should he eat them and live** off them for a while **or sow them and die?** Given the improbability of the crops' growth under these circumstances, it appears wasteful to plant them rather than consume that which remains. The prophet **said to them: Nevertheless, go out and sow. A miracle occurred for them and they discovered** wheat and barley seeds **that** were hidden **in the walls and that** were concealed **in ant holes.**

NOTES

Just as one counts ten days – כְּדֶרֶךְ שְׁמוֹנֶה עֲשָׂרָה יָמִים: The early commentaries offer various explanations of this comparison. The *Shita Mekubbetzet* suggests that just as one counts the ten days from Rosh HaShana to Yom Kippur starting from the first day of Rosh HaShana without taking into account the possibility that Elul might consist of thirty days, in which case one should count only from the second day, so too, with regard to the request for rain, there is no need to entertain the concern that the number of days counted will change based on the length of the month (see also *Gevurat Ari*).

Until when does one request rain – עַד מָתַי שׁוֹאֲלִין אֶת הַגְּשָׁמִים: This mishna is not related to the central topic of this tractate, the fasts for drought. However, as the previous mishna had discussed the date for the beginning of the request for rain, the *tanna* also mentions the date when this request ends (Meiri).

As it is stated, And He causes to come down for you the rain – שֶׁנֶּאֱמַר ״וַיּוֹרֶד לָכֶם גֶּשֶׁם״: The commentaries discuss the nature of this proof. One explanation is that the verse is not cited by Rabbi Meir but by the unattributed author of the mishna, and it is interpreted by each *tanna* in accordance with his respective line of reasoning. Although the verse speaks of the final rain falling in the first month of Nisan, it does not clearly state whether this occurs in the middle or at the end of the month (*Melekhet Shlomo*).

יָצְאוּ וְזָרְעוּ שֵׁנִי וּשְׁלִישִׁי וּרְבִיעִי, וְיָרְדָה לָהֶם רְבִיעָה שְׁנִיָּה בַּחֲמִשָּׁה בְּנִיסָן, הִקְרִיבוּ עוֹמֶר בְּשִׁשָּׁה עָשָׂר בְּנִיסָן, נִמְצֵאת תְּבוּאָה הַגְּדֵילָה בְּשִׁשָּׁה חֳדָשִׁים גְּדֵילָה בְּאַחַד עָשָׂר יוֹם, נִמְצָא עוֹמֶר הַקָּרֵב מִתְּבוּאָה שֶׁל שִׁשָּׁה חֳדָשִׁים קָרֵב מִתְּבוּאָה שֶׁל אַחַד עָשָׂר יוֹם.

They went out and sowed on the second, third, and fourth days of Nisan, **and the** rain of the **second rainy season fell for them on the fifth of Nisan.** The crops grew so quickly that **they** were able to **sacrifice** the *omer* offering in its proper time, **on the sixteenth of Nisan. Consequently, grain that** normally **grows in six months grew in eleven days, and consequently,** the *omer* that is generally **sacrificed from grain** that grows **in six months was sacrificed** that year **from grain** that grew **in eleven days.**

וְעַל אוֹתוֹ הַדּוֹר הוּא אוֹמֵר: ״הַזּוֹרְעִים בְּדִמְעָה בְּרִנָּה יִקְצֹרוּ. הָלוֹךְ יֵלֵךְ וּבָכֹה נֹשֵׂא מֶשֶׁךְ הַזָּרַע״ וגו׳. מַאי ״הָלוֹךְ יֵלֵךְ וּבָכֹה נֹשֵׂא מֶשֶׁךְ״ וגו׳? אָמַר רַבִּי יְהוּדָה: שׁוֹר כְּשֶׁהוּא חוֹרֵשׁ – הוֹלֵךְ וּבוֹכֶה, וּבַחֲזִירָתוֹ אוֹכֵל חָזִיז מִן הַתֶּלֶם. וְזֶהוּ ״בֹּא יָבֹא בְרִנָּה״.

And with regard **to that generation** the verse **says: "They who sow in tears shall reap with** songs of **joy. Though he goes on his way weeping, who bears the measure of seed,** he shall come home with joy, bearing his sheaves" (Psalms 126:6). The Gemara asks: **What is** the meaning of the expression: **"Though he goes on his way weeping, who bears** the measure of seed"? **Rabbi Yehuda said: An ox, when it plowed** at that time, **it went** on its way **weeping** and lamenting its labor; **and** yet **upon its return,** through the same furrow, **it** was able to **eat the young shoots** [*ḥaziz*][L] of crops that had already sprouted **from the furrow. And this is** the meaning of the phrase: **"He shall come home with** songs of **joy."**

מַאי ״נֹשֵׂא אֲלֻמֹּתָיו״? אָמַר רַב חִסְדָּא וְאָמְרִי לָהּ בְּמַתְנִיתָא תָּנָא: קָנֶה – זֶרֶת, שִׁיבּוֹלֶת – זְרָתַיִם.

The Gemara further asks: **What is** the meaning of the expression: **"Bearing his sheaves"? Rav Ḥisda said, and some say this was taught in a** *baraita*: The **stalk** of that crop was one **span,** i.e., the distance between the thumb and the little finger, while the **ear** itself was **two spans,**[B] i.e., the ears were twice as long as the stalk, whereas usually the stalk is three or four times longer than the ear.

אֲמַר לֵיהּ רַב נַחְמָן לְרַבִּי יִצְחָק: מַאי דִּכְתִיב ״כִּי קָרָא ה׳ לָרָעָב וְגַם בָּא אֶל הָאָרֶץ שֶׁבַע שָׁנִים״, בְּהָנָךְ שֶׁבַע שָׁנִים מַאי אֲכוּל?

§ Incidental to the interpretation of these verses, the Gemara cites a series of verses, starting with the topic of hunger, that also involve questions that Rav Naḥman posed to Rabbi Yitzḥak. **Rav Naḥman said to Rabbi Yitzḥak: What is** the meaning of that **which is written: "For the Lord has called upon a famine and it shall also come upon the land seven years"** (II Kings 8:1)? Specifically, **in those seven years, what** did they **eat?**[N]

אֲמַר לֵיהּ: הָכִי אָמַר רַבִּי יוֹחָנָן: שָׁנָה רִאשׁוֹנָה – אָכְלוּ מַה שֶּׁבַּבָּתִּים, שְׁנִיָּה – אָכְלוּ מַה שֶּׁבַּשָּׂדוֹת, שְׁלִישִׁית – בְּשַׂר בְּהֵמָה טְהוֹרָה, רְבִיעִית – בְּשַׂר בְּהֵמָה טְמֵאָה, חֲמִישִׁית – בְּשַׂר שְׁקָצִים וּרְמָשִׂים, שִׁשִּׁית – בְּשַׂר בְּנֵיהֶם וּבְנוֹתֵיהֶם, שְׁבִיעִית – בְּשַׂר זְרוֹעוֹתֵיהֶם, לְקַיֵּים מַה שֶּׁנֶּאֱמַר ״אִישׁ בְּשַׂר זְרֹעוֹ יֹאכֵלוּ״.

Rabbi Yitzḥak **said to** Rabbi Naḥman that **Rabbi Yoḥanan said as follows:** In **the first year they ate** that **which was in their houses;** in **the second** year **they ate** that **which was in their fields;** in **the third** year they ate the **meat of** their remaining **kosher animals;** in **the fourth** year they ate the **meat of** their remaining **non-kosher animals;** in **the fifth** year they ate the **meat of repugnant creatures and creeping animals,** i.e., any insects they found; in **the sixth** year they ate the **flesh of their sons and their daughters;** and in **the seventh** year they ate the **flesh of their** own **arms, to fulfill that which is stated: "Each man shall eat the flesh of his own arm"** (Isaiah 9:19).

וַאֲמַר לֵיהּ רַב נַחְמָן לְרַבִּי יִצְחָק: מַאי דִּכְתִיב ״בְּקִרְבְּךָ קָדוֹשׁ וְלֹא אָבוֹא בְּעִיר״, מִשּׁוּם דִּבְקִרְבְּךָ קָדוֹשׁ לֹא אָבוֹא בָּעִיר? אֲמַר לֵיהּ, הָכִי אָמַר רַבִּי יוֹחָנָן: אָמַר הַקָּדוֹשׁ בָּרוּךְ הוּא לֹא אָבוֹא בִּירוּשָׁלַיִם שֶׁל מַעְלָה עַד שֶׁאָבוֹא לִירוּשָׁלַיִם שֶׁל מַטָּה.

And Rav Naḥman said to Rabbi Yitzḥak: What is the meaning of that **which is written: "It is sacred in your midst, and I will not enter the city"** (Hosea 11:9)? This verse is puzzling: **Because it is sacred in your midst, will** God **not enter the city?** Rabbi Yitzḥak **said to** Rav Naḥman that **Rabbi Yoḥanan said** the verse should be understood **as follows: The Holy One, Blessed be He, said: I shall not enter Jerusalem above,**[N] in heaven, **until I enter Jerusalem** on earth down **below** at the time of the redemption, when it will be sacred in your midst.

וּמִי אִיכָּא יְרוּשָׁלַיִם לְמַעְלָה? אִין, דִּכְתִיב ״יְרוּשָׁלַיִם הַבְּנוּיָה כְּעִיר שֶׁחֻבְּרָה לָּהּ יַחְדָּו״.

The Gemara asks: **And is there** such a place as **Jerusalem above?** The Gemara answers: **Yes, as it is written: "Jerusalem built up, a city unified together"** (Psalms 122:3). The term unified indicates that there are two cities of Jerusalem, a heavenly one and an earthly one, which are bound together.

LANGUAGE

Young shoots [*ḥaziz*] – חָזִיז: According to the *Arukh* and the *ge'onim*, the word is *ḥazin*, which means tender shoots, e.g., bright green stalks of grain.

BACKGROUND

The stalk was one span, the ear two spans – קָנֶה זֶרֶת שִׁיבּוֹלֶת זְרָתַיִם: Normally the stalk and the ear of grain grow to the same length, which complicates the harvesting process. Consequently, in modern times, grain is cultivated with a shorter stalk, by means of various mechanisms. These strains of grain have ears that are longer than those of the taller strains.

NOTES

In those seven years what did they eat – בְּהָנָךְ שֶׁבַע שָׁנִים מַאי אֲכוּל: Although we find other instances of famine in the Bible, including the famous seven year famine in the time of Joseph, Rav Naḥman singled out the famine that afflicted the people in the days of Jehoram, king of Israel, for his question with regard to what people ate during the period of scarcity. One explanation is that the Divine decree concerning this famine was carried out in its full severity and for its entire intended duration, in accordance with the verse: "For the Lord has called upon a famine and it shall also come upon the land seven years" (II Kings 8:1; Maharsha).

I shall not enter Jerusalem above, etc. – לֹא אָבוֹא בִּירוּשָׁלַיִם שֶׁל מַעְלָה וכו׳: One interpretation of the concept of: Jerusalem above, is that Jerusalem and the Temple signify the refined matters of the intellect, as corresponding to the earthly Eretz Yisrael there are spiritual levels located in the lofty worlds (Rashba). With regard to the interpretation of the verse itself, some say that the verse should be read as an expression of wonder: Since your midst shall be sacred, shall I not enter the city? (Maharsha; see *Sefat Emet*). They further explain that the verse is meant as a source of comfort for the Jewish people in exile; that it is almost as if the Almighty Himself is also in exile, and He will not enter Jerusalem up high until the Jews are redeemed on earth (*Iyyun Ya'akov*).

ואמר ליה רבי נחמן לרבי יצחק: מאי דכתיב "ובאחת יבערו ויכסלו מוסר הבלים עץ הוא"? אמר ליה: הכי אמר רבי יוחנן: אחת היא שמבערת רשעים בגיהנם, מאי היא – עבודה זרה. כתיב הכא "מוסר הבלים עץ הוא" וכתיב התם "הבל המה מעשה תעתעים".

§ **And Rav Naḥman said to Rabbi Yitzḥak: What is** the meaning of that **which is written: "And with one they are brutish and foolish, the teaching of their vanity is a stock"** (Jeremiah 10:8)? Rabbi Yitzḥak **said to** Rabbi Naḥman that **Rabbi Yoḥanan said as follows: There is one** transgression **that causes the wicked to burn in Gehenna. What is this** transgression? **Idol worship.** This can be proven by a verbal analogy. **It is written here: "The teaching of their vanity [*hevel*] is a stock," and it is written there,** with regard to idols: **"They are vanity [*hevel*], a work of delusion"** (Jeremiah 10:15).

ואמר ליה רב נחמן לרבי יצחק: מאי דכתיב "כי שתים רעות עשה עמי" תרתין הוא דהוו? עשרין וארבע שביקא להו?! אמר ליה, הכי אמר רבי יוחנן: אחת שהיא

And Rav Naḥman said to Rabbi Yitzḥak: What is the meaning of that **which is written: "For my people have committed two evils"** (Jeremiah 2:13)? **Were there** only **two** evils they performed? Were, then, the **twenty-four** violations listed in the book of Ezekiel **abandoned,**[N] i.e., pardoned? Rabbi Yitzḥak **said to** Rav Naḥman that **Rabbi Yoḥanan said as follows:** They have violated **one** transgression **that is**

NOTES

Were the twenty-four violations abandoned – עשרין וארבע שביקא להו: There are variant textual readings of the number specified here. Some explain that the version that states twenty-two rather than twenty-four is based on a mere semantic difference, as both concur that there are twenty-four violations altogether. Since punishment is meted out for only two of these, the question is raised with regard to the remaining twenty-two. Others suggest that the twenty-two violations are an allusion to the entire Torah, written with the twenty-two letters of the alphabet (Maharsha). Some early commentaries have twenty-six as the number of violations, also based on the list of offenses cited in Ezekiel (Rabbeinu Gershom; *Shita Mekubbetzet*).

As for the significance of these twenty-four offenses, most commentaries explain that they are referring to the twenty-four offenses listed in the book of Ezekiel (chapter 22) as the sins of Jerusalem, as indicated in the midrash. Some *ge'onim* suggest that the twenty-four transgressions can also be found in the continuation of the passage in Jeremiah cited here (Jeremiah 2:13). One commentary cites a tradition that this refers to the twenty-four offenses mentioned in the eleventh chapter of *Sanhedrin* in the Jerusalem Talmud as transgressions for which repentance is particularly difficult (Rabbeinu Ḥananel; see also Rambam *Sefer HaMadda*, *Hilkhot Teshuva*, chapter 4). Rav Hai Gaon suggests that there is no particular significance to the number twenty-four in this context; rather, it merely signifies a large amount.

שקולה כשתים ומאי ניהו – עבודה זרה, דכתיב "כי שתים רעות עשה עמי אותי עזבו מקור מים חיים לחצב להם בארות בארות נשברים". וכתיב בהו "כי עברו איי כתיים וראו וקדר שלחו והתבוננו מאד וגו' ההימיר גוי אלהים והמה לא אלהים ועמי המיר כבודו בלוא יועיל".

equivalent to two.[N] **And what is this sin? Idol worship, as it is written: "For my people have committed two evils; they have forsaken Me, the fountain of living waters, to hew for themselves cisterns, broken cisterns"** (Jeremiah 2:13), **and it is written about** the Jewish people: **"For pass over the isles of the Kittim and see; and send to Kedar and observe carefully, and** see if there has been such a thing. **Has a nation exchanged its gods, although they are no gods? But My people has exchanged its glory for that which does not profit"** (Jeremiah 2:10–11).

תנא: כותיים עובדים לאש, וקדריים עובדין למים. ואף על פי שיודעים שהמים מכבין את האש – לא המירו אלהיהם, "ועמי המיר כבודו בלוא יועיל".

It is **taught** in a *baraita* with regard to this verse: **Kittites,** i.e., the people of the isles of Kittim, **worship fire** and **the people of Kedar worship water, and even though they know that water extinguishes fire,** nevertheless **they have not exchanged their god: "But My people has exchanged its glory for that which does not profit."**

ואמר ליה רב נחמן לרבי יצחק: מאי דכתיב "ויהי כאשר זקן שמואל" ומי סיב שמואל כולי האי? והא בר חמישים ושתים הוה, דאמר מר: מת בחמישים ושתים שנה – זהו מיתתו של שמואל הרמתי!

And Rav Naḥman said to Rabbi Yitzḥak:[P] **What is** the meaning of that **which is written: "And it came to pass when Samuel was old"** (I Samuel 8:1)? **And did Samuel really grow so old? But he was** only **fifty-two years old** when he died, **as the Master said** in a *baraita* that deals with the Divine punishment of *karet*: **One who dies at** the age of **fifty-two years** is not considered to have suffered the premature death of *karet*, as **this is the** age of the **death of Samuel of Rama.** This shows that Samuel died at the relatively young age of fifty-two.

NOTES

One that is equivalent to two – אחת שהיא שקולה כשתים: Some commentaries explain that the phrase: Equivalent to two, is referring to the fire worshippers and the water worshippers mentioned in this passage (Rashi; Rabbeinu Gershom). Others maintain that this is referring to the two aspects of idolatry discussed here, the abandonment of God and the adherence to the vanities of the idolatrous gods (Rabbeinu Ḥananel). Yet others state that as the sin of idolatry is one of the three most severe transgressions, along with forbidden sexual relations and murder, it is considered the equivalent of the other two transgressions (Rabbi Elyakim). Alternatively, idolatry is equivalent to two sins because it constitutes a violation of both the commands: "I am the Lord your God" (Exodus 20:2), and, in the next verse: "You shall have no other gods before Me" (*Ahavat Eitan*).

PERSONALITIES

Rabbi Yitzḥak – רבי יצחק: Two *amora'im* of this name lived in the same period in Eretz Yisrael, both of whom were principal students of Rabbi Yoḥanan. However, one was a renowned halakhic authority, while the other concentrated on *aggada*. Clearly, the Rabbi Yitzḥak mentioned here was the one who dealt in matters of *aggada*. Elsewhere he is called Rabbi Yitzḥak, son of Pineḥas. Rabbi Yitzḥak apparently spent a considerable time in Babylonia, where he taught the Torah he had learned in Eretz Yisrael, particularly the opinions of his teacher, Rabbi Yoḥanan. He was close to Rav Naḥman, who asked him various questions of an aggadic nature. Many aggadic sayings are attributed to him throughout the Babylonian Talmud, and several Babylonia *amora'im* cite statements in his name.

אֲמַר לֵיהּ: הָכִי אָמַר רַבִּי יוֹחָנָן: זִקְנָה קָפְצָה עָלָיו, דִּכְתִיב ״נִחַמְתִּי כִּי הִמְלַכְתִּי אֶת שָׁאוּל״. אָמַר לְפָנָיו: רִבּוֹנוֹ שֶׁל עוֹלָם, שְׁקַלְתַּנִי כְּמֹשֶׁה וְאַהֲרֹן, דִּכְתִיב ״מֹשֶׁה וְאַהֲרֹן בְּכֹהֲנָיו וּשְׁמוּאֵל בְּקֹרְאֵי שְׁמוֹ״, מַה מֹּשֶׁה וְאַהֲרֹן – לֹא בָּטְלוּ מַעֲשֵׂה יְדֵיהֶם בְּחַיֵּיהֶם, אַף אֲנִי לֹא יִתְבַּטֵּל מַעֲשֵׂה יָדַי בְּחַיַּי!

Rabbi Yitzḥak **said to** Rav Naḥman that **Rabbi Yoḥanan said as follows: Old age sprang upon** Samuel,[N] which caused him to appear older than his actual age, **as it is written: "I regret that I made Saul king"** (I Samuel 15:11). Samuel **said before** God: **Master of the Universe, You have** considered **me the equivalent of Moses and Aaron, as it is written: "Moses and Aaron among His priests, and Samuel among those who call upon His Name"** (Psalms 99:6). **Just as** with regard to **Moses and Aaron, their handiwork was not annulled in their lifetimes, so too, let my handiwork not be annulled in my lifetime.** I anointed Saul; please do not annul his reign.

אָמַר הַקָּדוֹשׁ בָּרוּךְ הוּא: הֵיכִי אַעֲבִיד? לֵימוּת שָׁאוּל – לָא קָא שָׁבֵיק שְׁמוּאֵל, לֵימוּת שְׁמוּאֵל אַדְּזוּטָר – מְרַנְּנֵי אַבַּתְרֵיהּ, לָא לֵימוּת שָׁאוּל וְלָא לֵימוּת שְׁמוּאֵל – כְּבָר הִגִּיעָה מַלְכוּת דָּוִד, וְאֵין מַלְכוּת נוֹגַעַת בַּחֲבֶרְתָּהּ אֲפִילּוּ כִּמְלֹא נִימָא.

The Holy One, Blessed be He, said: What shall I do? Shall Saul die now? **Samuel will not allow it,** as he has petitioned that Saul should not die. **Shall Samuel die young,** with Saul passing away immediately afterward? The people **will murmur about him,**[N] and wonder what transgression Samuel committed that caused his early demise. **Shall neither Saul nor Samuel die?** The time of **David's reign has already arrived, and one kingdom does not overlap with another** and subtract from the time allotted to it **even by a hairbreadth** [***nima***].[L]

אָמַר הַקָּדוֹשׁ בָּרוּךְ הוּא: אַקְפִּיץ עָלָיו זִקְנָה, הַיְינוּ דִּכְתִיב ״וְשָׁאוּל יוֹשֵׁב בַּגִּבְעָה תַּחַת הָאֵשֶׁל בָּרָמָה״ וְכִי מָה עִנְיַן גִּבְעָה אֵצֶל רָמָה? אֶלָּא לוֹמַר לְךָ: מִי גָּרַם לְשָׁאוּל שֶׁיֵּשֵׁב בְּגִבְעָה שְׁתֵּי שָׁנִים וּמֶחֱצָה – תְּפִלָּתוֹ שֶׁל שְׁמוּאֵל הָרָמָתִי.

Therefore, **the Holy One, Blessed be He, said: I will spring old age upon him** and everyone will think that Shmuel is elderly. **This is** the meaning of that **which is written: "And Saul dwelled in Gibeah under the tamarisk tree in Rama"** (I Samuel 22:6). **What does Gibeah have to do with Rama;** these are two separate places. **Rather,** the verse comes **to tell you: Who caused Saul to dwell in Gibeah for two and a half years? The prayer of Samuel of Rama.**

וּמִי מִידְּחֵי גַּבְרָא מִקַּמֵּי גַּבְרָא? אִין, דְּאָמַר רַבִּי שְׁמוּאֵל בַּר נַחֲמָנִי אָמַר רַבִּי יוֹחָנָן: מַאי דִּכְתִיב ״עַל כֵּן חָצַבְתִּי בַּנְּבִיאִים הֲרַגְתִּים בְּאִמְרֵי פִי״, בְּמַעֲשֵׂיהֶם לֹא נֶאֱמַר אֶלָּא בְּ״אִמְרֵי פִי״, אַלְמָא: מִידְּחֵי גַּבְרָא מִקַּמֵּי גַּבְרָא.

The Gemara asks: **And is** one **man set aside before** another **man?** In other words, is Samuel's life set aside simply because the time for David's reign has arrived? The Gemara answers: **Yes, as Rabbi Shmuel bar Naḥmani said** that **Rabbi Yoḥanan said: What is** the meaning of that **which is written: "Therefore I have hewn by the prophets, I have slain them by the words of My mouth"** (Hosea 6:5)? **It is not stated: By their deeds, but** rather: **"By the words of My mouth,"** i.e., God sometimes ends the life of an individual simply by virtue of His decree. **Apparently,** one **man is** indeed **set aside before** another **man.**

רַב נַחְמָן וְרַבִּי יִצְחָק הֲווּ יָתְבִי בִּסְעוּדָתָא, אֲמַר לֵיהּ רַב נַחְמָן לְרַבִּי יִצְחָק: לֵימָא מָר מִילְּתָא! אֲמַר לֵיהּ, הָכִי אָמַר רַבִּי יוֹחָנָן: אֵין מְסִיחִין בַּסְּעוּדָּה, שֶׁמָּא יַקְדִּים קָנֶה לַוֵּשֶׁט וְיָבֹא לִידֵי סַכָּנָה.

§ In continuation of Rav Naḥman's questions of Rabbi Yitzḥak, the Gemara relates: **Rav Naḥman and Rabbi Yitzḥak were sitting** and eating together **at a meal. Rav Naḥman said to Rabbi Yitzḥak: Let the Master say a matter,** i.e., share a Torah idea with me. Rabbi Yitzḥak **said to** Rav Naḥman that **Rabbi Yoḥanan said: One may not speak during a meal,**[H] **lest the esophagus will precede the trachea.**[B] Food is meant to enter the trachea, and when one speaks his esophagus opens and the food might enter there. **And** therefore, one should not speak during a meal, as he might **come into the danger** of choking.

NOTES

Old age sprang upon him – זִקְנָה קָפְצָה עָלָיו: Some commentaries are puzzled by this interpretation, as the verse that mentions Samuel's old age precedes Saul's appointment as king (see Maharsha). Apparently, the idea is that God anticipated this situation in advance and caused old age to spring upon Samuel even before Saul was appointed king (Rabbi Yoshiya Pinto; *Ramat Shmuel*).

They will murmur about him – מְרַנְּנֵי אַבַּתְרֵיהּ: Some commentaries explain that people will murmur about Divine justice when they observe the righteous Samuel dying at a young age (*Shita Mekubbetzet*).

LANGUAGE

Hairbreadth [*nima*] – נִימָא: From the Greek νῆμα, *nèma*, meaning thread.

HALAKHA

One may not speak during a meal – אֵין מְסִיחִין בַּסְּעוּדָּה: It is prohibited to converse during a meal, even if the topic is matters of Torah (*Magen Avraham*). Some say that one may converse between courses (*Arukh HaShulḥan*; *Mishna Berura*), whereas others prohibit even this (*Perisha*). In modern times, people are not stringent in this regard, as the stringency was apparently related to the practice of eating while reclining (*Eliyahu Rabba*; *Sha'arei Teshuva*; *Shulḥan Arukh*, *Oraḥ Ḥayyim* 170:1).

BACKGROUND

Lest the esophagus precede the trachea and he come into danger – שֶׁמָּא יַקְדִּים קָנֶה לַוֵּשֶׁט וְיָבֹא לִידֵי סַכָּנָה: Swallowing food consists of three stages. During the first stage food is mixed with saliva for lubrication and is placed on the back of the tongue. Then the mouth closes and the soft palate rises so that the passageway between the nasal and oral cavities is closed off. The tongue then moves backward pushing food into the oral pharynx, a chamber behind the mouth that functions to transport food and air. Once food enters the pharynx, the second stage of swallowing begins. Respiration is temporarily inhibited, as the larynx, or voice box, rises to close the epiglottis, the opening to the air passage, the trachea. At the top of the esophagus there is a muscular constrictor, the upper esophageal sphincter, or UES, which opens when food approaches. Once food is in the esophagus, the final phase of swallowing begins. The larynx lowers, the epiglottis opens, and breathing resumes. Speaking during this process may pose a choking hazard since the larynx may fail to close the epiglottis which prevents food from entering the trachea during the swallowing process.

In the image, the substance being swallowed is represented by the color green.

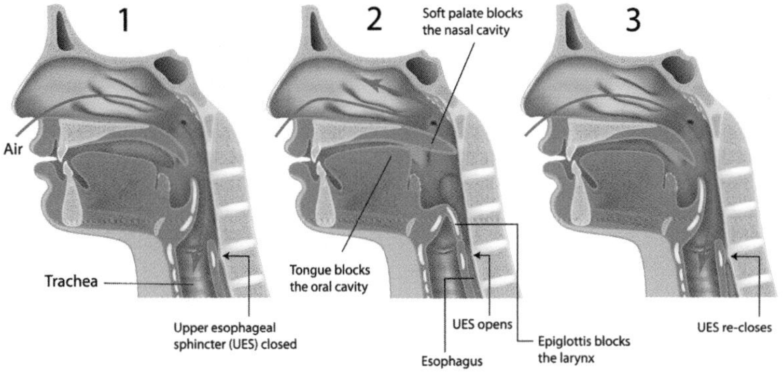

Stages of swallowing

בָּתַר דִּסְעוּד אֲמַר לֵיהּ: הָכִי אָמַר רַבִּי יוֹחָנָן: יַעֲקֹב אָבִינוּ לֹא מֵת. אֲמַר לֵיהּ: וְכִי בִּכְדִי סָפְדוּ סַפְדָנַיָּא וְחָנְטוּ חַנְטַיָּא וְקָבְרוּ קַבְּרַיָּא? אֲמַר לֵיהּ: מִקְרָא אֲנִי דּוֹרֵשׁ, שֶׁנֶּאֱמַר ״וְאַתָּה אַל תִּירָא עַבְדִּי יַעֲקֹב נְאֻם ה׳ וְאַל תֵּחַת יִשְׂרָאֵל כִּי הִנְנִי מוֹשִׁיעֲךָ מֵרָחוֹק וְאֶת זַרְעֲךָ מֵאֶרֶץ שִׁבְיָם״, מַקִּישׁ הוּא לְזַרְעוֹ, מַה זַּרְעוֹ בַּחַיִּים – אַף הוּא בַּחַיִּים.

After they had eaten, Rabbi Yitzḥak **said to** Rav Naḥman that **Rabbi Yoḥanan said as follows: Our patriarch Jacob did not die.**[N] Rav Naḥman **asked him** in surprise: **And was it for naught that the eulogizers eulogized** him and the **embalmers embalmed** him **and the buriers buried** him? Rabbi Yitzḥak **replied to** Rav Naḥman: **I am interpreting a verse,**[N] **as it is stated: "Therefore do not fear, Jacob My servant, says the Lord, neither be dismayed, Israel, for I will save you from afar, and your seed from the land of their captivity"** (Jeremiah 30:10). This verse **juxtaposes Jacob to his seed: Just as his seed is alive** when redeemed, **so too,** Jacob himself **is alive.**

אָמַר רַבִּי יִצְחָק: כָּל הָאוֹמֵר רָחָב רָחָב מִיָּד נִקְרֵי. אֲמַר לֵיהּ רַב נַחְמָן: אֲנָא אָמֵינָא, וְלָא אִיכְפַּת לִי! אֲמַר לֵיהּ: כִּי קָאָמֵינָא – בְּיוֹדְעָהּ וּבְמַכִּירָהּ.

Rabbi Yitzḥak said: Anyone who says: Rahab Rahab, immediately experiences a seminal emission, due to the arousal of desire caused by Rahab's great beauty. **Rav Naḥman said to him: I say** Rahab **and it does not affect me.** Rabbi Yitzḥak **said to** Rav Naḥman: **When I said** this I was specifically referring **to** a man **who knew her and to** one **who recognized her.**[N] With regard to anyone who had met Rahab in person, the mere mention of her name would arouse his lust.

כִּי הָווּ מִיפַּטְרִי מֵהֲדָדֵי אֲמַר לֵיהּ: לִיבָרְכַן מָר! אֲמַר לֵיהּ: אֶמְשׁוֹל לְךָ מָשָׁל, לְמָה הַדָּבָר דּוֹמֶה – לְאָדָם שֶׁהָיָה הוֹלֵךְ בַּמִּדְבָּר וְהָיָה רָעֵב וְעָיֵף וְצָמֵא, וּמָצָא אִילָן שֶׁפֵּירוֹתָיו מְתוּקִין וְצִלּוֹ נָאֶה, וְאַמַּת הַמַּיִם עוֹבֶרֶת תַּחְתָּיו. אָכַל מִפֵּירוֹתָיו, וְשָׁתָה מִמֵּימָיו, וְיָשַׁב בְּצִילּוֹ.

The Gemara relates: **When they were taking leave of one another,** Rav Naḥman **said to** Rabbi Yitzḥak: **Master, give me a blessing.** Rabbi Yitzḥak **said to him: I will tell you a parable. To what is this matter comparable?** It is comparable **to one who was walking through a desert and who was hungry, tired, and thirsty. And he found a tree whose fruits were sweet and whose shade was pleasant, and a stream of water flowed beneath it. He ate from the fruits** of the tree, **drank from the water** in the stream, **and sat in the shade of** the tree.

וּכְשֶׁבִּיקֵּשׁ לֵילֵךְ, אָמַר: אִילָן אִילָן, בַּמָּה אֲבָרֶכְךָ? אִם אוֹמַר לְךָ שֶׁיְּהוּ פֵּירוֹתֶיךָ מְתוּקִין – הֲרֵי פֵּירוֹתֶיךָ מְתוּקִין, שֶׁיְּהֵא צִילְּךָ נָאֶה – הֲרֵי צִילְּךָ נָאֶה, שֶׁתְּהֵא אַמַּת הַמַּיִם עוֹבֶרֶת תַּחְתֶּיךָ – הֲרֵי אַמַּת הַמַּיִם עוֹבֶרֶת תַּחְתֶּיךָ, אֶלָּא: יְהִי רָצוֹן שֶׁכָּל נְטִיעוֹת שֶׁנּוֹטְעִין מִמְּךָ

And when he wished to leave, he said: Tree, tree, with what shall I bless you? If I say to you that your fruits should be sweet, your fruits are already **sweet;** if **I say that your shade should be pleasant, your shade is** already **pleasant;** if I say **that a stream of water should flow beneath you, a stream of water** already **flows beneath you. Rather,** I will bless you as follows: **May it be** God's **will that all saplings which they plant from you**

NOTES

Our patriarch Jacob did not die – יַעֲקֹב אָבִינוּ לֹא מֵת: Many commentaries discuss this puzzling comment. Some explain that Jacob did not die in Egypt, but he merely fainted and all his senses ceased, and that in fact he died in Eretz Yisrael (see Rabbi Yoshiya Pinto and *Ḥokhmat Manoaḥ*). Yet this does not seem to be the main import of this statement. It is more likely that Rabbi Yitzḥak is providing a homiletic interpretation on the level of allusion and hidden ideas, which Rav Naḥman initially understood as addressing the simple meaning of the text. Therefore, Rabbi Yitzḥak cited a proof from another passage, to indicate that he did not mean to offer a straightforward assertion. Rav Naḥman accepted this explanation, despite the fact that the basic claim contradicts explicit statements of the Torah.

As to the deeper meaning of Rabbi Yitzḥak's statement, some commentaries explain that because some of the children of the other patriarchs were not valid successors, i.e., Ishmael and Esau, it cannot be said that Abraham and Isaac continued to live after their death. By contrast, Jacob, whose children will continue along his path until the end of days, is perpetuated by them. Therefore, it is appropriate to say that he never died (Rashba; *Asara Ma'amarot*). Alternatively, the normal progression of death, with the various stages of the descent of the soul and its defilement via the angel of death, only occurs to people whose life was characterized by a struggle with the evil impulse. Jacob, however, had an entirely pure soul, and therefore he did not die in that manner. Rather, his soul passed directly to the life of the World-to-Come (*Otzar HaKavod*). This is similar to the Rambam's description of the death of our teacher Moses.

I am interpreting a verse – מִקְרָא אֲנִי דּוֹרֵשׁ: Rabbi Yitzḥak's statement is apparently based on a close reading of the language of the Torah, as the word death is not mentioned explicitly in connection with Jacob. Since Rabbi Yitzḥak's interpretation appeared strange to Rav Naḥman, Rabbi Yitzḥak noted that it was not based solely on the absence of a single word. Rather, it is connected to the interpretation of various verses which speak of Jacob or of Israel in such a way that the personal, individual denotation of the name and its general, national meaning are not entirely distinguished from each other. Instead, Israel the man and Israel the nation are regarded as a single entity.

To a man who knew her and to one who recognized her – בְּיוֹדְעָהּ וּבְמַכִּירָהּ: See *Tosafot* and the Maharsha in tractate *Megilla*, who suggest that the term: Who knew her, is referring to one who had sexual relations with her, as in the verse: "And no man had known her" (Genesis 24:16).

יִהְיוּ כְּמוֹתְךָ. אַף אַתָּה, בַּמֶּה אֲבָרֶכְךָ? אִם בְּתוֹרָה, הֲרֵי תּוֹרָה. אִם בְּעוֹשֶׁר, הֲרֵי עוֹשֶׁר. אִם בְּבָנִים, הֲרֵי בָּנִים. אֶלָּא, יְהִי רָצוֹן שֶׁיִּהְיוּ צֶאֱצָאֵי מֵעֶיךָ כְּמוֹתְךָ.

be like you. So it is with you. With what shall I bless you? If I bless you **with Torah,** you already have **Torah; if** I bless you **with wealth,** you already have **wealth; if** I bless you **with children,** you already have **children. Rather, may it be** God's **will that your offspring shall be like you.**

תָּנוּ רַבָּנַן: יוֹרֶה שֶׁמּוֹרֶה אֶת הַבְּרִיּוֹת לְהַטִּיחַ גַּגּוֹתֵיהֶן, וּלְהַכְנִיס אֶת פֵּירוֹתֵיהֶן, וְלַעֲשׂוֹת כׇּל צׇרְכֵיהֶן. דָּבָר אַחֵר: שֶׁמַּרְוֶה אֶת הָאָרֶץ וּמַשְׁקֶה עַד תְּהוֹם, שֶׁנֶּאֱמַר: ״תְּלָמֶיהָ רַוֵּה; נַחֵת גְּדוּדֶהָ; בִּרְבִיבִים תְּמֹגְגֶנָּה; צִמְחָהּ תְּבָרֵךְ״. דָּבָר אַחֵר: יוֹרֶה שֶׁיּוֹרֵד בְּנַחַת, וְאֵינוֹ יוֹרֵד בְּזַעַף.

§ The Gemara returns to the topic of rain. **The Sages taught** in a *baraita*: The **first rain [*yoreh*]**[N] is called by this name due to the fact **that it instructs [*moreh*] people to plaster their roofs and to bring in their produce** from the fields to their houses **and to attend to all their needs** in the field before more rain falls. **Alternatively,** *yoreh* is referring to the fact **that it moistens [*marve*] the earth and waters it to the depths, as it is stated: "Watering [*ravvei*] its ridges abundantly, settling down its furrows, You make it soft with showers, You bless its growth"** (Psalms 65:11). **Alternatively,** *yoreh* means **that it falls gently and it does not fall vehemently.**

אוֹ אֵינוֹ יוֹרֶה אֶלָּא שֶׁמַּשִּׁיר אֶת הַפֵּירוֹת, וּמַשְׁטִיף אֶת הַזְּרָעִים, וּמַשְׁטִיף אֶת הָאִילָנוֹת? תַּלְמוּד לוֹמַר: ״מַלְקוֹשׁ״. מַה מַּלְקוֹשׁ לִבְרָכָה, אַף יוֹרֶה לִבְרָכָה. אוֹ אֵינוֹ מַלְקוֹשׁ אֶלָּא שֶׁמַּפִּיל אֶת הַבָּתִּים, וּמְשַׁבֵּר אֶת הָאִילָנוֹת, וּמַעֲלֶה אֶת הַסַּקָּאִין? תַּלְמוּד לוֹמַר: ״יוֹרֶה״. מַה יּוֹרֶה לִבְרָכָה, אַף מַלְקוֹשׁ לִבְרָכָה.

Or perhaps **that is not** the case; rather, *yoreh* means **that** the rain **causes the fruit to drop** from the trees, **washes the seeds** away, **and washes the trees** away in a destructive manner. According to this interpretation, *yoreh* is related to *yeriya*, shooting. Therefore **the verse states: "Last rain [*malkosh*]"** (Deuteronomy 11:14);[N] **just as *malkosh*** refers specifically to rains that are **for a blessing, so too, *yoreh*** is referring to rains that are **for a blessing. Or** perhaps **that is not** the case; rather, ***malkosh*** means **that** the rain falls so hard [*kashe*] and vehemently that **it knocks down the houses, shatters the trees and brings up the locusts?**[N] Therefore, **the verse states: "*Yoreh*,"** from which it may be inferred that **just as *yoreh* is for a blessing, so too, *malkosh* is for a blessing.**

וְיוֹרֶה גּוּפֵיהּ מְנָלַן? דִּכְתִיב: ״וּבְנֵי צִיּוֹן, גִּילוּ וְשִׂמְחוּ בַּה׳ אֱלֹהֵיכֶם, כִּי נָתַן לָכֶם אֶת הַמּוֹרֶה לִצְדָקָה, וַיּוֹרֶד לָכֶם גֶּשֶׁם, מוֹרֶה וּמַלְקוֹשׁ, בָּרִאשׁוֹן״.

And with regard to ***yoreh* itself, from where do we** derive that it is referring to rain that falls for a blessing? **As it is written: "You children of Zion, be glad and rejoice in the Lord your God, for He has given you the first rain [*moreh*] in His kindness, and He caused to come down for you the rain,** the **first rain [*moreh*]** and the **last rain [*malkosh*], in the first** month" (Joel 2:23). This verse clearly states that *yoreh,* also referred to as *moreh,* fall due to God's kindness, for a blessing.

תָּנוּ רַבָּנַן: יוֹרֶה בְּמַרְחֶשְׁוָן וּמַלְקוֹשׁ בְּנִיסָן. אַתָּה אוֹמֵר יוֹרֶה בְּמַרְחֶשְׁוָן וּמַלְקוֹשׁ בְּנִיסָן. אוֹ אֵינוֹ אֶלָּא יוֹרֶה בְּתִשְׁרֵי וּמַלְקוֹשׁ בְּאִיָּיר? תַּלְמוּד לוֹמַר: ״בְּעִתּוֹ״.

The Gemara cites another *baraita* on the same topic. **The Sages taught:** The **first rain** falls **in Marḥeshvan and** the **last rain in Nisan.** Do **you say** that the **first rain is in Marḥeshvan and** the **last rain in Nisan, or** perhaps **it is only** that the **first rain** falls **in Tishrei and** the **last rain in Iyyar?** Therefore, **the verse states:** "I shall give the rain of your land **in its due time**" (Deuteronomy 11:14). Its due time is in Marḥeshvan, when rain is needed for the crops to sprout, and in Nisan, to complete the growth of the crops.

מַלְקוֹשׁ? אָמַר רַב נְהִילַאי בַּר אִידִי אָמַר שְׁמוּאֵל: דָּבָר שֶׁמָּל קַשְׁיוּתֵיהֶן שֶׁל יִשְׂרָאֵל. דְּבֵי רַבִּי יִשְׁמָעֵאל תָּנָא: דָּבָר שֶׁמְּמַלֵּא תְּבוּאָה בְּקַשֶּׁיהָ. בְּמַתְנִיתָא תָּנָא: דָּבָר שֶׁיּוֹרֵד עַל הַמְּלִילוֹת וְעַל הַקַּשִּׁין.

The Gemara clarifies the meaning of the word for the **last rain [*malkosh*]. Rav Nehilai bar Idi said** that **Shmuel said:** It is **a matter that circumcises [*mal*] the stubbornness [*kashyuteihen*] of the Jewish people,** i.e., it penetrates to the hearts of the Jewish people, as when rain does not fall in its time, they turn to God in repentance. **The school of Rabbi Yishmael taught:** The last rain is called *malkosh* because it is **a matter that fills out [*memalle*] produce in its stalks [*bekasheha*].** Although the stalks already exist from earlier in the year, it is this rain that causes the grain within to swell and fill them. **It was taught in a *baraita*:** *Malkosh* is **a matter that comes down on the ears [*melilot*] and on the stalks [*kashin*].**

NOTES

First rain [*yoreh*] – יוֹרֶה: The range of derivations for the word *yoreh* is based on the variety of roots that can be associated with this term, some of which themselves bear multiple meanings. The root *y-r-a*, which represents the straightforward etymology of *yoreh*, can mean tossing, shooting, or instruction. An alternative exposition relates *yoreh* to the root *r-v-a*, meaning satiety, as in the verse: "And he who satisfies others [*marve*] shall himself be sated [*yoreh*]" (Proverbs 11:25).

Last rain [*malkosh*] – מַלְקוֹשׁ: This term is derived from the rare root *l-k-sh*, which apparently means tardy or latter. Rashi notes that in the verse cited by the Gemara (Deuteronomy 11:14) the term *lekesh* is apparently a synonym for locusts.

Locusts [*saka'in*] – סַקָּאִין: Most commentaries hold that this term is referring to locusts, although some maintain that it is referring to a type of worm (Rabbi Elyakim). Similarly, there are various translations for the word *tzelatzal* (Deuteronomy 28:42), which is generally rendered as locust.

תָּנוּ רַבָּנַן: יוֹרֶה בְּמַרְחֶשְׁוָן וּמַלְקוֹשׁ בְּנִיסָן. אַתָּה אוֹמֵר יוֹרֶה בְּמַרְחֶשְׁוָן, אוֹ אֵינוֹ אֶלָּא בְּחֹדֶשׁ כִּסְלֵיו? תַּלְמוּד לוֹמַר: ״בְּעִתּוֹ יוֹרֶה וּמַלְקוֹשׁ״. מַה מַּלְקוֹשׁ בְּעִתּוֹ, אַף יוֹרֶה בְּעִתּוֹ. כֵּיוָן שֶׁיָּצָא נִיסָן וְיָרְדוּ גְּשָׁמִים, אֵינוֹ סִימַן בְּרָכָה.

The Sages taught in a *baraita*: The **first rain** falls **in Marḥeshvan and** the **last rain in Nisan.**[B] Do you say that **the first rain is in Marḥeshvan, or** perhaps **it is only in** the month of **Kislev? The verse states:** "I shall give the rain of your land **in its due time, the first rain and the last rain**" (Deuteronomy 11:14). **Just as the last rain** falls **in its due time, so too,** the **first rain** falls **in its due time.** And, as previously stated, **once Nisan has ended and** the **rains** subsequently **fall,** this **is not a sign of a blessing,** but a curse. Likewise, Marḥeshvan is the best time for the first rains to fall.

תַּנְיָא אִידָךְ: יוֹרֶה בְּמַרְחֶשְׁוָן וּמַלְקוֹשׁ בְּנִיסָן. דִּבְרֵי רַבִּי מֵאִיר. וַחֲכָמִים אוֹמְרִים: יוֹרֶה בְּכִסְלֵיו.

It is taught in **another** *baraita*: The **first rain** is **in Marḥeshvan and** the **last rain** is **in Nisan.** This is **the statement of Rabbi Meir. And the Rabbis say:** The time of the **first rain** is **in Kislev.**

מַאן חֲכָמִים? אָמַר רַב חִסְדָּא: רַבִּי יוֹסֵי הִיא, דְּתַנְיָא: אֵיזוֹ הִיא רְבִיעָה רִאשׁוֹנָה? הַבַּכִּירָה בִּשְׁלֹשָׁה בְּמַרְחֶשְׁוָן. בֵּינוֹנִית בְּשִׁבְעָה בּוֹ. אֲפִילָה בְּשִׁבְעָה עָשָׂר בּוֹ. דִּבְרֵי רַבִּי מֵאִיר. רַבִּי יְהוּדָה אוֹמֵר: בְּשִׁבְעָה, וּבְשִׁבְעָה עָשָׂר, וּבְעֶשְׂרִים וּשְׁלֹשָׁה.

The Gemara asks: **Who are the Rabbis** cited here? **Rav Ḥisda said:** It is the opinion of **Rabbi Yosei,**[P] **as it is taught** in a *baraita*: **When is the first rainfall?**[N] Each opinion cited in the *baraita* provides a range of dates for when this rainfall is expected. **The earliest** date on which the first rainfall might occur is **on the third of Marḥeshvan,** the **intermediate** time is **on the seventh of** the month, **and the latest** is **on the seventeenth of** the month. This is **the statement of Rabbi Meir. Rabbi Yehuda says:** The earliest that it might fall is **on the seventh** of Marḥeshvan, the intermediate date is **on the seventeenth, and** the latest is **on the twenty-third.**

רַבִּי יוֹסֵי אוֹמֵר: בְּשִׁבְעָה עָשָׂר, וּבְעֶשְׂרִים וּשְׁלֹשָׁה, וּבְרֹאשׁ חֹדֶשׁ כִּסְלֵיו. וְכֵן הָיָה רַבִּי יוֹסֵי אוֹמֵר: אֵין הַיְּחִידִים מִתְעַנִּין עַד שֶׁיַּגִּיעַ רֹאשׁ חֹדֶשׁ כִּסְלֵיו.

Rabbi Yosei says: The earliest time for the first rain is **on the seventeenth** of Marḥeshvan, the intermediate date is **on the twenty-third, and** the latest is **on the New Moon of Kislev. And, so too, Rabbi Yosei would say:** The learned **individuals** who would start to fast for rain at an earlier time than the rest of the community **do not** start to **fast** due to a drought **until the New Moon of Kislev.** Until this date arrives it is not considered a drought, as the first rainfall could still fall in its proper time.

אָמַר רַב חִסְדָּא: הֲלָכָה כְּרַבִּי יוֹסֵי. אַמֵּימָר מַתְנֵי לְהָא דְּרַב חִסְדָּא בְּהָא לִישָּׁנָא: בִּשְׁלֹשָׁה בְּמַרְחֶשְׁוָן שׁוֹאֲלִין אֶת הַגְּשָׁמִים. רַבָּן גַּמְלִיאֵל אוֹמֵר: בְּשִׁבְעָה בּוֹ. אָמַר רַב חִסְדָּא: הֲלָכָה כְּרַבָּן גַּמְלִיאֵל.

Rav Ḥisda said: The *halakha* is in accordance with the opinion of **Rabbi Yosei.**[N] **Ameimar** would **teach this** ruling **of Rav Ḥisda in the following language: On the third of Marḥeshvan** one starts to **request rain;**[H] **Rabban Gamliel says: On the seventh.** With regard to this statement, **Rav Ḥisda said: The *halakha* is in accordance with** the opinion of **Rabban Gamliel.**

כְּמַאן אָזְלָא הָא דְּתַנְיָא, רַבָּן שִׁמְעוֹן בֶּן גַּמְלִיאֵל אוֹמֵר: גְּשָׁמִים שֶׁיָּרְדוּ שִׁבְעָה יָמִים זֶה אַחַר זֶה, אַתָּה מוֹנֶה בָּהֶן רְבִיעָה רִאשׁוֹנָה וּשְׁנִיָּה וּשְׁלִישִׁית? כְּמַאן? כְּרַבִּי יוֹסֵי. אָמַר רַב חִסְדָּא: הֲלָכָה כְּרַבִּי יוֹסֵי.

The Gemara asks: **In accordance with whose** opinion **is that which is taught** in a *baraita*. **Rabban Shimon ben Gamliel says:** With regard to **rains that fell** on **seven** consecutive **days, you count them** as two separate rainfalls, either as **the first and second rainfalls** together, or as the second **and third**[N] rainfalls together. **In accordance with whose** opinion is this statement? It is in accordance **with** the opinion of **Rabbi Yosei,** as he alone establishes a set interval of seven days between each of the rainfalls. **Rav Ḥisda said: The *halakha* is in accordance with** the opinion of **Rabbi Yosei.**

BACKGROUND

The times of the first rain and the last rain – זְמַנֵּי יוֹרֶה וּמַלְקוֹשׁ: The establishment of dates concerning rain in the Jewish calendar is complicated, in part because the dates based on the lunar cycle do not always align with the same solar dates.

The first rains generally fall in Eretz Yisrael during the first half of October, which can coincide with the end of Tishrei, while the last rains usually fall at the end of April, which can be in the middle of Iyyar.

NOTES

When is the first rainfall – אֵיזוֹ הִיא רְבִיעָה רִאשׁוֹנָה: The early commentaries cite alternative versions of the text here (see *Rishon LeTziyyon* and *Kesef Mishne*). It stands to reason that the three dates mentioned by each *tanna* do not refer to three possible dates in the same year for the first rainfall. Rather, the early, intermediate, and late dates refer to various years of the leap year cycle. The year following a leap year is called an early year, as the rains can be expected to start at an earlier lunar date. Using similar logic, the year preceding a leap year is labeled a late year, and the intervening year is called an intermediate year.

The *halakha* is in accordance with the opinion of Rabbi Yosei – הֲלָכָה כְּרַבִּי יוֹסֵי: There are different versions of this statement. According to some readings, including the one cited by Rashi, Rav Ḥisda states that the *halakha* is in accordance with the opinion of Rabbi Yehuda. The logic of Ameimar's alternative version of Rav Ḥisda's ruling is clear according to this version: If the time of the first rainfall is the seventh of Marḥeshvan, it stands to reason that one would likewise begin to request rain on this date. With regard to the version of the Gemara here, some commentaries explain that the ruling that one begins to request rain from the seventh of Marḥeshvan can indeed be reconciled with the opinion of Rabbi Yosei, as the idea is that one begins to request rain shortly before the time of the first rainfall, just as one starts to mention rain before it actually falls (Rabbeinu Yehonatan).

The first and second rainfalls, or the second and third – רְבִיעָה רִאשׁוֹנָה וּשְׁנִיָּה וּשְׁלִישִׁית: The explanation here is in accordance with a version of the text which states that these seven days are considered either like the first and second rainfall, or like the second and the third. This is similar to the version of the scholars of Narbonne cited in *Tosafot*. A plain reading of the standard version of the text indicates that the seven days are considered like all three rainfalls. The difficulty with this is that even Rabbi Yosei, who places the rainfalls nearest to each other in time, sets a seven day interval between the various rainfalls, and therefore there is no justification for saying that all three rainfalls have occurred over a period of seven days. One explanation of the version of the *baraita* as it appears here, based on Rabbeinu Ḥananel and the *Arukh*, is that depending on the time of day when the rainfall begins it is indeed possible, according to the opinion of Rabbi Yosei, for the seven days of consecutive rainfall to cover the first two rainfalls and the beginning of the third.

HALAKHA

The time for requesting rain – זְמַן שְׁאִילַת גְּשָׁמִים: In Eretz Yisrael one begins to request rain on the seventh of Marḥeshvan, in accordance with the opinion of Rabban Gamliel, as ruled by Rav Ḥisda (*Shulḥan Arukh, Oraḥ Ḥayyim* 117:1).

PERSONALITIES

Rabbi Yosei – רַבִּי יוֹסֵי: Rabbi Yosei ben Ḥalafta, one of the foremost *tanna'im*, lived in the generation before the completion of the Mishna, and the imprint of his teachings is evident throughout tannaitic literature.

Rabbi Yosei was the son of Abba Ḥalafta who was also a great Sage. He lived in Tzippori, in the Upper Galilee, where he earned his living as a leather worker.

In addition to studying with his father, Rabbi Yosei was a preeminent student of Rabbi Akiva, with the other main disciples of Rabbi Akiva: Rabbi Meir, Rabbi Yehuda, and Rabbi Shimon bar Yoḥai. This group formed the core of scholarly creativity in that generation and their opinions form the backbone of the Mishna. A well-known principle in *halakha* is that Rabbi Yosei's reasoning is with him, i.e., his opinions are always well considered. Rabbi Yosei was so well regarded that the rule was established that the *halakha* is always in accordance with his opinion in a dispute with any of the other leading students of Rabbi Akiva mentioned above. This principle may also be related to the fact that Rabbi Yosei was known for his moderation, both in his rulings and in his lifestyle.

Rabbi Yosei was also renowned for his piety. The Talmud relates many stories about his modesty, humility, and sanctity. It is told that Elijah the Prophet would reveal himself to Rabbi Yosei every day, and several conversations between them are recorded. According to tradition, Rabbi Yosei was the main editor of a series of *baraitot* on the history of the Jewish people known as *Seder Olam*.

Many of the Sages of the following generation were his disciples, including Rabbi Yehuda HaNasi, the redactor of the Mishna. However, his closest students were his five sons, all of whom became Sages. The most famous were Rabbi Eliezer ben Rabbi Yosei, one of the great masters of *aggada*, and Rabbi Yishmael ben Rabbi Yosei.

בִּשְׁלָמָא רְבִיעָה רִאשׁוֹנָה לִשְׁאוֹל, שְׁלִישִׁית לְהִתְעַנּוֹת, שְׁנִיָּה לְמַאי? אָמַר רַבִּי זֵירָא: לִנְדָרִים, דִּתְנַן:

With regard to the mention of three rainfalls in the *baraita*, the Gemara asks: **Granted,** the time of the **first rainfall** is significant, as it is the date when one begins **to request** rain. Likewise, the time of the **third** rainfall is important, so that one knows when to begin **to fast** if no rain has fallen by then. However, **for what** reason is the **second** rainfall mentioned in the *baraita*? **Rabbi Zeira said:** The second rainfall is significant **for** the issue of **vows, as we learned** in a mishna:

Perek **I**
Daf **6** Amud **b**

הַנּוֹדֵר עַד הַגְּשָׁמִים, מִשֶּׁיֵּרְדוּ גְּשָׁמִים, עַד שֶׁתֵּרֵד רְבִיעָה שְׁנִיָּה.

In the case of **one who vows** to prohibit from himself a type of benefit **until the rains,**[H] the vow is in effect **from when the rains** begin to **fall until the second rainfall,** as this is considered the time of the rains.

רַב זְבִיד אָמַר: לְזֵיתִים. דִּתְנַן: מֵאֵימָתַי כָּל אָדָם מוּתָּרִין בְּלֶקֶט, בְּשִׁכְחָה, וּבְפֵאָה? מִשֶּׁיֵּלְכוּ הַנָּמוֹשׁוֹת. בְּפֶרֶט וּבְעוֹלֵלוֹת? מִשֶּׁיֵּלְכוּ עֲנִיִּים בַּכֶּרֶם וְיָבוֹאוּ. בְּזֵיתִים? מִשֶּׁתֵּרֵד רְבִיעָה שְׁנִיָּה.

Rav Zevid said: The time of the second rainfall is also significant with regard to a *halakha* that deals **with olives, as we learned** in a mishna: **From when is any person permitted to** collect **gleanings, forgotten sheaves, and *pe'a*,**[H] produce of the corners of a field, which may normally be taken only by the poor? Any individual is permitted to collect them only **from when the searchers** [***namoshot***], the last of the poor to arrive, **have left** the field. From when may anyone collect yield of the vineyard in the case **of the single grapes and small, incompletely formed clusters of grapes,**[H] likewise reserved for the poor? **From when the poor have left the vineyard and come** back after the second time, an indication that they have collected all that they wish. From when may anyone collect yield of the trees in the case **of** forgotten **olives? From when the second rainfall falls.**

מַאי נָמוֹשׁוֹת? אָמַר רַבִּי יוֹחָנָן: סָבֵי דְּאָזְלִי אַתִּיגְרָא. רֵישׁ לָקִישׁ אָמַר: לָקוֹטֵי בָּתַר לָקוֹטֵי.

Incidentally, the Gemara asks: **What is** the meaning of the term for searchers, ***namoshot*****? Rabbi Yoḥanan said:** It is referring to **elders who walk with a staff** [***atigra***].[N] Since they walk very slowly, they certainly see everything they wish to collect. **Reish Lakish said:** It is referring to the **gleaners** who come **after** all the **gleaners,**[N] i.e., who arrive after two rounds of the poor have passed through the field.

רַב פַּפָּא אָמַר: כְּדֵי לְהַלֵּךְ בִּשְׁבִילֵי הָרְשׁוּת, דְּאָמַר מָר: מְהַלְּכִין כָּל אָדָם בִּשְׁבִילֵי הָרְשׁוּת עַד שֶׁתֵּרֵד רְבִיעָה שְׁנִיָּה.

Rav Pappa said that the time of the second rainfall is significant **so that** one can know until when it is permitted **to walk on the permitted paths**[N] in fields. One may utilize certain paths on private property, provided no damage is caused to the field. **As the Master said: Anyone** may **walk on the permitted paths**[H] **until the second rainfall falls.** One who walks on them at a later point in time is likely to trample the plowed field and damage its crops.

NOTES

With a staff [*atigra*] – **אַתִּיגְרָא**: The correct version of this word is apparently *tigda*, which is used in the Aramaic translations of the Bible to mean a staff, from the root *g-d-d*, meaning cut off, as it is referring to a branch that has been cut off to serve as a staff.

Gleaners who come after gleaners – **לָקוֹטֵי בָּתַר לָקוֹטֵי**: Rashi in *Bava Metzia* (21b) explains that after the first group of poor would pass through the field, a second wave would arrive. Here he explains that the phrase refers to a poor man walking with his son, i.e., there are different types of gleaners collecting simultaneously (see *Gevurat Ari*).

To walk on the permitted paths – **כְּדֵי לְהַלֵּךְ בִּשְׁבִילֵי הָרְשׁוּת**: Aside from public thoroughfares such as main roads, one is allowed to traverse certain other paths, even if they pass through another's private property. Likewise, certain paths serve as temporary shortcuts through fields. The Gemara states elsewhere that when the Jewish people settled Eretz Yisrael, Joshua, son of Nun, instituted various ordinances that declared that anyone could utilize the property of another, provided that no damage was done to the property (*Bava Kamma* 81a).

HALAKHA

One who vows until the rains – **הַנּוֹדֵר עַד הַגְּשָׁמִים**: If one vows to prohibit from himself a certain benefit until the rains, the vow is in effect until the time period of the rains in Eretz Yisrael, which is the first of Kislev. This ruling is in accordance with the opinion of Rabbi Yosei. If rain falls on or after the seventeenth of Marḥeshvan, the vow is no longer in effect. Some authorities maintain that the vow is in effect only until the time period of the first rain according to the opinion of Rabbi Yosei (*Shakh*, citing Ra'avad and Rosh). Others maintain that the correct textual version of the Gemara is that the *halakha* is in accordance with the opinion of Rabbi Yehuda, in which case the vow lapses on the seventh of Marḥeshvan (*Shakh*, citing Rosh). If the vow was formulated as: Until it rains, it remains in effect until rain actually falls after the time of the second rainfall, which is the twenty-third of Marḥeshvan in Eretz Yisrael, in accordance with the opinion of Rabbi Yosei. Others add that in the Diaspora the time of the rains is sixty days after the autumnal equinox. In an ordinary year this is December fourth, while in a Gregorian leap year the date is December fifth. The time of the second rainfall is seventy days after the equinox (*Shulḥan Arukh, Yoreh De'a* 220:18, and in the comment of Rema).

From when is any person permitted to collect gleanings, forgotten sheaves, and *pe'a* – **מֵאֵימָתַי כָּל אָדָם מוּתָּרִין בְּלֶקֶט, בְּשִׁכְחָה, וּבְפֵאָה**: Once the second set of gleaners has finished gleaning, all people are permitted to collect gleanings of grain left over in the field. According to the Rambam, there is no practical difference between the opinions of Rabbi Yoḥanan and Reish Lakish. Rather, they dispute the meaning of the word *namoshot* (*Kesef Mishne*, citing Rashba; Rambam *Sefer Zera'im, Hilkhot Mattenot Aniyyim* 1:11).

In the case of single grapes and small, incompletely formed clusters of grapes – **בְּפֶרֶט וּבְעוֹלֵלוֹת**: Once the poor have passed through the vineyard twice, all people are permitted to collect single grapes and small, incompletely formed clusters of grapes left in the vineyard. With regard to olives forgotten on the tree, anyone may collect them from the first of Kislev (Rambam *Sefer Zera'im, Hilkhot Mattenot Aniyyim* 1:11).

Anyone may walk on the permitted paths – **מְהַלְּכִין כָּל אָדָם בִּשְׁבִילֵי הָרְשׁוּת**: All people are permitted to walk on the paths that pass through privately owned agricultural fields, from the time of the grain harvest until the seventeenth of Marḥeshvan, the date of the second rainfall. The *halakha* is in accordance with the opinion of Rabbi Yehuda, and contrary to the opinion of Rabbi Yosei. After that date, entry into privately owned fields is prohibited, as it may damage the crops (*Tur, Ḥoshen Mishpat* 274).

NOTES

The straw and the hay of the Sabbatical Year – בתבן ובקש של שביעית: According to Rashi, this is referring to straw and hay of the Sabbatical Year itself, when one may derive benefit from the produce and yield of the land only as long as the wild animals of the field can derive benefit from it. *Tosafot* explain that the Gemara is referring to plants that grew of their own accord during the seventh year. These plants retain the sanctity of the Sabbatical Year during the eighth year, and one is allowed to maintain them provided that they are available to the wild animals in the field. Yet others explain, based on an alternative version of the text, that the Gemara is speaking specifically of the eighth year. Up until this time straw and hay are fit for consumption by the wild animals of the field but afterward they are no longer fit as fodder, and consequently may be used for other purposes (Meiri).

Rain that falls prior to, and He will close up – גשמים שירדו קודם ועצר: The *ge'onim* had an alternative version of the text, according to which the best rain is that which falls in the evening after the recitation of *Shema*. They also cite a different version of the folk saying, which refers to rain when the gates are closed, i.e., at the end of the day. Apparently, the statement concerning morning clouds, which follows in the text we have today, is missing from that version.

Donkey-driver, fold your sack – בר חמרא, מוך שקך: Rashi and other commentators explain that early-morning rain is a sign that the entire year will be blessed with bounty and consequently there will be little work for donkey-drivers who transport grain from place to place, as local produce will be plentiful. Conversely, Rabbeinu Ḥananel and most commentaries maintain that rain in the early morning is simply a sign that donkey-drivers should not go out to work that day as it is likely to rain all day.

HALAKHA

The straw and the hay of the Sabbatical Year – בתבן ובקש של שביעית: After the second rainfall in the year after the Sabbatical Year, it is permitted to derive benefit from the straw and hay of the Sabbatical Year or to burn them, as they are no longer fit for animal consumption. The *halakha* is in accordance with the alternative version of the mishna in tractate *Shevi'it* (Rambam *Sefer Zera'im, Hilkhot Shemitta VeYovel* 5:23).

As long as a beast is able to eat in the field – כל זמן שחיה אוכלת בשדה: Produce of the Sabbatical Year that has already been brought into the house may be eaten only as long as there is some produce of that same type remaining in the fields. If this type of produce is no longer available in the fields, the produce must be removed from one's possession (Rambam *Sefer Zera'im, Hilkhot Shemitta VeYovel* 7:1).

BACKGROUND

To seal the opening of a barrel with it – לגוף בה פי חבית: In talmudic times, earthenware casks were commonly used for storing wine. The casks were sealed with a special cover. To preserve the wine, the opening was sealed by smearing mud on the surrounding area.

Morning clouds – ענני דצפרא: The clouds that form over land during the early hours of the morning are usually thin and light. They produce only a small amount of rain, or none at all. Heavy rain clouds form primarily in the afternoon or evening.

רב נחמן בר יצחק אמר: לבער פירות שביעית, דתנן: עד מתי נהנין ושורפין בתבן ובקש של שביעית? עד שתרד רביעה שניה.

Rav Naḥman bar Yitzḥak said that the time of the second rainfall is significant for determining when **to remove the produce of the Sabbatical Year** from one's possession. **As we learned** in a mishna: **Until when may one derive benefit and burn the straw and the hay of the Sabbatical Year?**[N] **Until the second rainfall falls.**[H]

מאי טעמא? דכתיב: "ולבהמתך ולחיה אשר בארצך". כל זמן שחיה אוכלת בשדה, האכל לבהמתך בבית. כלה לחיה מן השדה, כלה לבהמתך מן הבית.

The Gemara asks: **What is the reason** that one must remove the produce of the Sabbatical Year from one's possession? The Gemara answers: **As it is written** with regard to the Sabbatical Year: **"And for your cattle and for the beasts in your land** all its increase shall be for food" (Leviticus 25:7). This verse indicates that **as long as a beast,** i.e., a non-domesticated animal, is able to find and **eat** produce **in the field,**[H] **you** may **feed your cattle,** your domesticated animals, from that type of food **in the house.** However, when a given type of produce **has ceased** to be available **to the beast in the field, cease** providing it to **your cattle in the house.** After the time of the second rainfall there is no longer any straw or hay in the fields.

אמר רבי אבהו: מאי לשון רביעה? דבר שרובע את הקרקע, כדרב יהודה. דאמר רב יהודה: מיטרא בעלה דארעא הוא, שנאמר: "כי כאשר ירד הגשם והשלג מן השמים, ושמה לא ישוב, כי אם הרוה את הארץ, והולידה והצמיחה".

§ The Gemara returns to the subject of rain. **Rabbi Abbahu said: What is** the meaning of the **term** for rainfall, ***revia*?** It is referring to **a matter that penetrates** [*rove'a*], i.e., which causes **the earth** to bear fruit. This is **in accordance with** the opinion of **Rav Yehuda, as Rav Yehuda said: Rain is the husband of the earth, as it is stated: "For as the rain comes down and the snow from heaven, and returns not there, except it waters the earth, and makes it give birth and sprout"** (Isaiah 55:10). This verse indicates that rain fructifies the earth in the manner of a husband and wife.

ואמר רבי אבהו: רביעה ראשונה כדי שתרד בקרקע טפח. שניה כדי לגוף בה פי חבית. אמר רב חסדא: גשמים שירדו כדי לגוף בהן פי חבית אין בהן משום "ועצר".

And Rabbi Abbahu further **said:** For rainfall to be considered the **first rainfall** it must be **sufficient to enter the ground** and saturate it to a depth of one **handbreadth.** The **second** rainfall must be **sufficient** that the soil is moistened enough **to seal the opening of a barrel with its** mud.[B] **Rav Ḥisda said: Rains which fall** and create **sufficient** mud **to seal the opening of a barrel with them** means that the year **does not constitute** a fulfillment of the verse: **"And He will close up** the heavens and there will be no rain" (Deuteronomy 11:17).

ואמר רב חסדא: גשמים שירדו קודם "ועצר" אין בהן משום "ועצר".

And Rav Ḥisda said: Rain that falls early in the day, **prior to** the recitation of *Shema*, which includes the verse: **"And He will close up**[N] the heavens," is enough to ensure that the hour **does not constitute** a fulfillment of the verse: **"And He will close up** the heavens," even if no more rain falls at that time.

אמר אביי: לא אמרן אלא קודם "ועצר" דאורתא, אבל קודם "ועצר" דצפרא יש בהן משום "ועצר". דאמר רב יהודה בר יצחק: הני ענני דצפרא לית בהו מששא, דכתיב: "מה אעשה לך, אפרים? מה אעשה לך, יהודה? וחסדכם כענן בקר" וגו׳.

Abaye said: We said this **only** if the rain fell during the day, **prior to** the recitation of **"and He will close up" of the evening** ***Shema*. However,** if a small amount of rain falls **prior to** the recitation of **"and He will close up" of the morning** ***Shema*, this** rain could still **constitute** an expression of **"and He will close up." As Rav Yehuda bar Yitzḥak said: These morning clouds**[B] **have no substance;** they generally yield minimal or no rain. **As it is written: "What can I do for you, Ephraim, what can I do for you, Judah, for your goodness is like a morning cloud"** (Hosea 6:4). This verse indicates that morning clouds contain little benefit.

אמר ליה רב פפא לאביי: והא אמרי אינשי: במפתח בבי מיטרא, בר חמרא, מוך שקך וגני! לא קשיא. הא דקטיר בעיבא; הא דקטיר בעננֵי.

Rav Pappa said to Abaye: But people say the well-known maxim: **When the gates,** i.e., doors, **are opened** in the morning and **there is rain, donkey-driver, fold your sack**[N] and go to **sleep,** as it is certain to rain all day, which will render the work of donkey-drivers infeasible. This shows that morning clouds are a sign that it will rain all day. The Gemara answers: This is **not difficult. This** statement of Rav Pappa is referring to **when** the sky is **overcast with heavy clouds,** from which rain will fall all day, whereas **that** statement of Rav Ḥisda is referring to a morning **when** the sky is **overcast with light clouds** which will not bring substantial rain.

אָמַר רַב יְהוּדָה: טָבָא לְשַׁתָּא דְּטֵבֵת אַרְמַלְתָּא. אִיכָּא דְּאָמְרִי: דְּלָא בַּיְירִי תַּרְבִּיצֵי. וְאִיכָּא דְּאָמְרִי: דְּלָא שָׁקֵיל שׁוּדְפָנָא. אִינִי? וְהָאָמַר רַב חִסְדָּא: טָבָא לְשַׁתָּא דְּטֵבֵת מְנַוּוּלְתָּא! לָא קַשְׁיָא. הָא דַּאֲתָא מִיטְרָא מֵעִיקָּרָא; הָא דְּלָא אֲתָא מִיטְרָא מֵעִיקָּרָא.

§ **Rav Yehuda said:** It is **good for the year when** the month of **Tevet is a widower,** i.e., when it features no rainfall. The Gemara explains: **Some say** that this is so **that the gardens** [*tarbitzei*][N] should **not be desolate,**[N] as too much rain damages vegetables. **And some say:** The reason is **that it** should **not suffer blight**[N] caused by excessive rain. The Gemara asks: **Is that so? But didn't Rav Ḥisda say:** It is **good for the year when** the month of **Tevet is disgusting,** i.e., muddy from rain. The Gemara answers: This is **not difficult. This** statement of Rav Yehuda is referring to a year **when it rained initially,** i.e., before Tevet, in which case rain during Tevet is not beneficial. **That** statement of Rav Ḥisda is referring to a year **when it did not rain initially,** before Tevet, and therefore rain during Tevet is beneficial.

וְאָמַר רַב חִסְדָּא: גְּשָׁמִים שֶׁיָּרְדוּ עַל מִקְצָת מְדִינָה וְעַל מִקְצָת מְדִינָה לֹא יָרְדוּ אֵין בָּהֶן מִשּׁוּם ״וְעָצַר״. אִינִי? וְהָכְתִיב: ״וְגַם אָנֹכִי מָנַעְתִּי מִכֶּם אֶת הַגֶּשֶׁם בְּעוֹד שְׁלֹשָׁה חֳדָשִׁים לַקָּצִיר, וְהִמְטַרְתִּי עַל עִיר אֶחָת, וְעַל עִיר אַחַת לֹא אַמְטִיר, חֶלְקָה אַחַת תִּמָּטֵר״ וגו׳. וְאָמַר רַב יְהוּדָה אָמַר רַב: שְׁתֵּיהֶן לִקְלָלָה!

And Rav Ḥisda also **said: Rain that fell on** one **part of a country and did not fall on another part of** the **country does not constitute** a fulfillment of the verse: **"And He will close up** the heavens." The Gemara raises an objection: **Is that so? But isn't it written: "And I have also withheld the rain from you, when there were yet three months to the harvest; and I would cause it to rain upon one city, and caused it not to rain upon another city; one piece was rained upon,** and the piece upon which it did not rain withered" (Amos 4:7). **And Rav Yehuda said** that **Rav said: Both** the area that receives rain and the area that does not receive rain **are cursed.** This statement indicates that rain that falls on only part of a country is a curse.

לָא קַשְׁיָא. הָא דַּאֲתָא טוּבָא; הָא דַּאֲתָא כִּדְמִבָּעֵי לֵיהּ. אֲמַר רַב אַשִׁי: דַּיְקָא נַמִי, דִּכְתִיב: ״תִּמָּטֵר״, תְּהֵא מְקוֹם מָטָר. שְׁמַע מִינָּהּ.

The Gemara answers: This is **not difficult. This,** Rav Yehuda's statement, is referring to a case **when excessive** rain **falls** in one part of the country and causes damage; whereas **that,** Rav Ḥisda's statement, is referring to a situation **when the requisite amount** of rain **falls**[N] in one part of the country. In this case, it is not a sign of a curse, but is a blessing for that particular part of the country. **Rav Ashi said:** The language **is also precise** in the verse in Amos that deals with excessive rain in one place, **as it is written: "Was rained upon,"**[N] which indicates that **it shall be a place of rain,** i.e., an area filled with rain and water. The Gemara concludes: Indeed, **learn from it** that this is the correct interpretation.

אָמַר רַבִּי אַבָּהוּ: מֵאֵימָתַי מְבָרְכִין עַל הַגְּשָׁמִים? מִשֶּׁיֵּצֵא חָתָן לִקְרַאת כַּלָּה.

Rabbi Abbahu said: From when does one recite a blessing over rain?[H] **From when the groom goes out to meet the bride,**[N] that is, when there are puddles of water on the ground such that the water below, represented as the bride in this metaphor, is splashed from above by the raindrops, represented as the groom.

HALAKHA

From when does one recite a blessing over rain – מֵאֵימָתַי מְבָרְכִין עַל הַגְּשָׁמִים: If it rains after a drought that caused hardship, a blessing is recited over the rain. The blessing is recited even if no heavy rainfall occurred provided that puddles form, and drops of water splash up from the puddles almost as if they are greeting the falling rain. Some commentaries maintain that it is customary not to recite this blessing in places where rain is generally abundant (Rema, based on *Sefer Mitzvot Gadol*). However, others claim that even in these places, if there is a period of drought followed by rain, the blessing over rain should be recited (*Taz*, citing *Beit Yosef*; *Shulḥan Arukh*, *Oraḥ Ḥayyim* 221:1).

NOTES

Gardens [*tarbitzei*] – תַּרְבִּיצֵי: This Aramaic term means garden. The root *r-v-tz*, meaning to pour out liquid, reflects the fact that plants that need constant watering are commonly grown in a garden. In rabbinic usage, the same term is often used as a poetic epithet for the study hall, which is like a garden in which much water, i.e., Torah, is poured and in which plants, i.e., Torah scholars, can grow.

That the gardens should not be desolate – דְּלָא בַּיְירִי תַּרְבִּיצֵי: Several different interpretations for this expression have been suggested (see Rashi). Some commentaries explain that if it rained during Tevet after it rained in Marḥeshvan, the fields will be too wet to plow again before the spring harvest (*ge'onim*). Others maintain that the courtyards will be emptied of their inhabitants, as people will prefer to stay at home (*Arukh*).

That it should not suffer blight – דְּלָא שָׁקֵיל שׁוּדְפָנָא: The *Arukh* cites an alternative version of the text, according to which he explains that people will prefer to remain in their houses instead of venturing outside. This is similar to his interpretation of the previous phrase: The gardens should not be desolate, as explained in the preceding note. Consequently, he holds that the difference between the two suggestions in the Gemara is stylistic rather than substantive.

That is when the requisite amount of rain falls – הָא דַּאֲתָא כִּדְמִבָּעֵי לֵיהּ: Most commentaries explain that too much rain in a given place is also a curse, whereas an appropriate amount is a blessing. Others explain this distinction in the opposite manner: If an overabundance of rain falls in one part of the country, it is a blessing, as enough can be grown there to provide for the rest of the country that lacks rain. However, if rain falls in only one part of the country, in an amount that suffices for that part of the country alone, the inhabitants of the entire country should view themselves as under a Divine curse. Accordingly, Rav Ashi's interpretation of the verse, that it is referring to a place of rain, means a place where a regular amount of rain falls (Rabbeinu Gershom).

As it is written, was rained upon – דִּכְתִיב תִּמָּטֵר: This homiletic interpretation of the verse is based on its unusual linguistic form. Usually, a verse will speak of the sky or of clouds pouring out water. Here, however, it states that the earth itself will be watered. This can be taken to mean that the earth will become rain, i.e., it will contain much water, as in a flood.

From when the groom goes out to meet the bride – מִשֶּׁיֵּצֵא חָתָן לִקְרַאת כַּלָּה: Rashi and Rav Hai Gaon explain that this expression is a metaphor. The drops of rain, which are described as a groom, fall into the puddles, which are described as a bride; and the water in the puddles splashes up to greet the falling rain. Some commentaries point out that this does not fit with the Gemara's earlier statement, which indicates that the falling rain is comparable to a husband or groom, with respect to the ground. They suggest that while the rain is described as the husband of the ground, the lower drops of rain are compared to a groom. In light of this difficulty, certain commentaries prefer the Rambam's explanation of this phrase: The rain increases the bubbles in the puddles to the point that they greet one another like a groom going out to meet his bride (*Shita Mekubbetzet*; Ritva).

מַאי מְבָרֵךְ? אָמַר רַב יְהוּדָה אָמַר רַב: מוֹדִים אֲנַחְנוּ לָךְ, ה׳ אֱלֹהֵינוּ, עַל כׇּל טִפָּה וְטִפָּה שֶׁהוֹרַדְתָּ לָנוּ. וְרַבִּי יוֹחָנָן מְסַיֵּים בָּהּ הָכִי: אִילּוּ פִּינוּ מָלֵא שִׁירָה כַּיָּם, וּלְשׁוֹנֵנוּ רִנָּה כַּהֲמוֹן גַּלָּיו כו׳, עַד: אַל יַעַזְבוּנוּ רַחֲמֶיךָ, ה׳ אֱלֹהֵינוּ, וְלֹא עֲזָבוּנוּ. בָּרוּךְ רוֹב הַהוֹדָאוֹת.

The Gemara asks: **What blessing** does one recite over rain? **Rav Yehuda said** that **Rav said: We thank you, O Lord our God, for each and every drop that You have made fall for us. And Rabbi Yoḥanan concludes** the blessing **as follows: If our mouth were as full of song as the sea, and our tongue with singing like the multitude of its waves,** etc. And one continues with the formula of the *nishmat* prayer recited on Shabbat morning, **until: May Your mercy not forsake us, O Lord our God, and You have not forsaken us. Blessed** are You, O Lord, to Whom **abundant thanksgivings** are offered.

רוֹב הַהוֹדָאוֹת וְלֹא כׇּל הַהוֹדָאוֹת? אֲמַר רָבָא: אֵימָא: אֵל הַהוֹדָאוֹת. אֲמַר רַב פַּפָּא: הִלְכָּךְ

The Gemara asks: Why does the blessing specify **abundant thanksgivings**[N] **and not all thanksgivings? Rava said:** Emend the formula of the blessing and **say: God of thanksgivings.**[N] **Rav Pappa said: Therefore,** as there are differences of opinion on this,

NOTES

Abundant [*rov*] thanksgivings – רוֹב הַהוֹדָאוֹת: The term *rov* does not mean most, as it is generally used in other contexts. It appears here as an abstract noun meaning abundant, a usage that appears in several places in the Torah (see Genesis 27:28). Consequently, the Gemara's question should be understood as follows: In light of the word's more common meaning, of a majority, which indicates the presence of a contrary minority, perhaps this is not the preferred formulation (Ritva; *Nimmukei Yosef*).

Some commentaries suggest that the term *rov* indeed means a majority of thanksgiving, i.e., man is unable to thank God for all the kindness He bestows upon him, but only for most of His kindness (Rid).

God [*El*] of thanksgivings – אֵל הַהוֹדָאוֹת: In this context, the term *El* is referring not only to God but also bears the secondary meaning of strength and might. Consequently, the phrase can mean: He who is great and worthy of thanksgiving (*Nimmukei Yosef*).

נֵימְרִינְהוּ לְתַרְוַיְיהוּ: אֵל הַהוֹדָאוֹת וְרוֹב הַהוֹדָאוֹת.

we will recite them both:[NH] **God of thanksgivings, and: Abundant thanksgivings.**

אָמַר רַבִּי אַבָּהוּ: גָּדוֹל יוֹם הַגְּשָׁמִים מִתְּחִיַּית הַמֵּתִים. דְּאִילּוּ תְּחִיַּית הַמֵּתִים לַצַּדִּיקִים, וְאִילּוּ גְּשָׁמִים בֵּין לַצַּדִּיקִים בֵּין לָרְשָׁעִים. וּפְלִיגָא דְּרַב יוֹסֵף. דְּאָמַר רַב יוֹסֵף: מִתּוֹךְ שֶׁהִיא שְׁקוּלָה כִּתְחִיַּית הַמֵּתִים, קְבָעוּהָ בִּתְחִיַּית הַמֵּתִים.

§ The Gemara cites statements in praise of rainfall. **Rabbi Abbahu said: The day of rain is greater than the resurrection of the dead.** The reason is that **while the resurrection of the dead** benefits only **the righteous,**[N] **rain** benefits **both the righteous and the wicked.** The Gemara comments: **And** this statement **disagrees with** the opinion of **Rav Yosef, as Rav Yosef said: Since** rainfall **is equivalent to the resurrection of the dead,**[N] the Sages **established** its recitation **in** the second blessing of the *Amida*, the blessing of **the resurrection of the dead.** According to Rav Yosef, rainfall is the equivalent to, but not superior to, the resurrection of the dead.

אָמַר רַב יְהוּדָה: גָּדוֹל יוֹם הַגְּשָׁמִים כַּיּוֹם שֶׁנִּיתְּנָה בּוֹ תּוֹרָה, שֶׁנֶּאֱמַר: ״יַעֲרֹף כַּמָּטָר לִקְחִי״, וְאֵין לֶקַח אֶלָּא תּוֹרָה, שֶׁנֶּאֱמַר: ״כִּי לֶקַח טוֹב נָתַתִּי לָכֶם; תּוֹרָתִי אַל תַּעֲזֹבוּ״. רָבָא אָמַר: יוֹתֵר מִיּוֹם שֶׁנִּיתְּנָה בּוֹ תּוֹרָה, שֶׁנֶּאֱמַר: ״יַעֲרֹף כַּמָּטָר לִקְחִי״. מִי נִתְלָה בְּמִי? הֱוֵי אוֹמֵר: קָטָן נִתְלָה בְּגָדוֹל.

Similarly, **Rav Yehuda said: The day of the rains is as great as the day** on which **the Torah was given, as it is stated: "My doctrine [*likḥi*] shall drop as the rain"** (Deuteronomy 32:2), **and *lekaḥ* means nothing other** than **Torah, as it is stated: "For I give you good doctrine [*lekaḥ*]; do not forsake My Torah"** (Proverbs 4:2). **Rava said:** Rainfall is even **greater than the day on which the Torah was given,**[N] **as it is stated: "My doctrine shall drop as the rain,"** and when one makes a comparison, **which object is made dependent upon which? You must say that the lesser** object **is dependent upon the greater** one. If Torah is compared to rain, it follows that rain is greater than Torah.

רָבָא רָמֵי: כְּתִיב: ״יַעֲרֹף כַּמָּטָר לִקְחִי״, וּכְתִיב: ״תִּזַּל כַּטַּל אִמְרָתִי״! אִם תַּלְמִיד חָכָם הָגוּן הוּא, כַּטַּל, וְאִם לָאו, עוֹרְפֵהוּ כַּמָּטָר.

The Gemara cites another interpretation of the verse from Deuteronomy. **Rava raised a contradiction:** At the beginning of the verse **it is written: "My doctrine shall drop [*ya'arof*] as the rain,"** in a harsh manner, **and** yet later in the verse, **it is written: "My speech shall distill as the dew,"** in a gentle tone. He resolves this apparent contradiction as follows: **If he is a worthy Torah scholar,**[H] the Torah flows through him **like the dew, but if** he is **not** worthy, **it snaps his neck [*orfehu*] like the** powerful **rain.**[N]

NOTES

We will recite them both – נֵימְרִינְהוּ לְתַרְוַיְיהוּ: Some commentaries explain that this refers both to Rav Yehuda's addition and Rabbi Yoḥanan's concluding blessing (Rabbi Zeraḥya HaLevi; Rabbi Yehonatan of Lunel), whereas others reject this opinion and maintain that this is referring to the opinions of Rava and Rav Pappa (Ramban; Rabbi Aharon HaLevi). Although there are variant readings of the text of the blessing, both in the citation here and in *Berakhot*, the accepted version is based on a tradition of the *ge'onim*.

It has been noted that Rav Pappa generally prefers to combine two conflicting opinions rather than decide between them, provided that they are not contradictory (see *Eshel Avraham*).

The resurrection of the dead benefits only the righteous – תְּחִיַּית הַמֵּתִים לַצַּדִּיקִים: Rav Ya'akov Emden explains that the resurrection of the dead will benefit the righteous alone, as the wicked will be revived only to be condemned in judgment.

Equivalent to the resurrection of the dead – שְׁקוּלָה כִּתְחִיַּית הַמֵּתִים: The commentaries write that this is because both events bring life to people and plants that are apparently dead and lifeless.

Greater than the day on which the Torah was given – יוֹתֵר מִיּוֹם שֶׁנִּיתְּנָה בּוֹ תּוֹרָה: One explanation of this claim is that the Torah benefits only the righteous, whereas the rain provides benefit to the wicked, as well (*Keren Ora*). Alternatively, rainfall is greater than the revelation of the Torah because the Torah was given only to the Jewish people, whereas rain is God's gift to the entire world (*Shoḥar Tov*).

It snaps his neck [*orfehu*] like the rain – עוֹרְפֵהוּ כַּמָּטָר: Various explanations for this statement have been suggested (see Rashi). One interpretation is that one should teach a student repeatedly, like a persistent rain (*Shita Mekubbetzet*). Alternatively, *orfehu* means that one should turn one's nape [*oref*] to this person (Maharsha). Yet others maintain that this statement does not refer to a teacher but to how matters of Torah are perceived by its students, i.e., for a worthy student the Torah flows easily like the dew, but for an unworthy student it is as difficult as the rain (*Keren Ora*).

HALAKHA

We will recite them both – נֵימְרִינְהוּ לְתַרְוַיְיהוּ: The blessing recited over rain, as established by the *ge'onim* and by the Rambam, concludes with the formula: Blessed are you, O Lord, God of abundant thanksgivings. This is in accordance with the opinion of Rav Pappa (*Shulḥan Arukh, Oraḥ Ḥayyim* 221:2).

If he is a worthy Torah scholar – אִם תַּלְמִיד חָכָם הָגוּן הוּא: One should not teach Torah to an unworthy student. This student should be helped to mend his ways and only afterward brought into the study hall to begin his studies (*Shulḥan Arukh, Yoreh De'a* 246:7).

תַּנְיָא: הָיָה רַבִּי בְּנָאָה אוֹמֵר: כׇּל הָעוֹסֵק בַּתּוֹרָה לִשְׁמָהּ, תּוֹרָתוֹ נַעֲשֵׂית לוֹ סַם חַיִּים, שֶׁנֶּאֱמַר: ״עֵץ חַיִּים הִיא לַמַּחֲזִיקִים בָּהּ״. וְאוֹמֵר: ״רִפְאוּת תְּהִי לְשׇׁרֶּךָ״. וְאוֹמֵר: ״כִּי מֹצְאִי מָצָא חַיִּים״. וְכׇל הָעוֹסֵק בַּתּוֹרָה שֶׁלֹּא לִשְׁמָהּ, נַעֲשֵׂית לוֹ סַם הַמָּוֶת, שֶׁנֶּאֱמַר: ״יַעֲרֹף כַּמָּטָר לִקְחִי״, וְאֵין עֲרִיפָה אֶלָּא הֲרִיגָה, שֶׁנֶּאֱמַר: ״וְעָרְפוּ שָׁם אֶת הָעֶגְלָה בַּנָּחַל״.

It is taught in a *baraita* that **Rabbi Bena'a**[P] **would say: Anyone who engages in Torah for its own sake, his Torah** study **will be an elixir of life for him, as it is stated: "It is a tree of life to them who lay hold upon it"** (Proverbs 3:18), **and it says: "It shall be health to your navel"** (Proverbs 3:8), **and it says: "For whoever finds Me finds life"** (Proverbs 8:35). **And anyone who engages in Torah not for its own sake,** e.g., for self-aggrandizement, his Torah **will be an elixir of death for him, as it is stated: "My doctrine shall drop [*ya'arof*] as the rain," and *arifa* means nothing other** than **killing, as it is stated: "And they shall break the heifer's neck [*arefu*] there in the valley"** (Deuteronomy 21:4).

אֲמַר לֵיהּ רַבִּי יִרְמְיָה לְרַבִּי זֵירָא: לֵיתֵי מָר לִיתְנֵי! אֲמַר לֵיהּ: חָלֵשׁ לִבַּאי, וְלָא יָכֵילְנָא. לֵימָא מָר מִילְּתָא דְּאַגַּדְתָּא. אֲמַר לֵיהּ: הָכִי אָמַר רַבִּי יוֹחָנָן: מַאי דִּכְתִיב: ״כִּי הָאָדָם עֵץ הַשָּׂדֶה״? וְכִי אָדָם עֵץ שָׂדֶה הוּא?

Rabbi Yirmeya[P] once **said to Rabbi Zeira: Let the Master come and teach** a halakhic discourse. Rabbi Zeira **said to him: My heart is weak and I cannot** strain myself over a halakhic discourse. Rabbi Yirmeya replied to him: In that case, **let the Master tell us a matter of *aggada*,** which does not require as much effort. Rabbi Zeira **said to him** that **Rabbi Yoḥanan said as follows: What is** the meaning of that **which is written: "For man is a tree of the field"** (Deuteronomy 20:19)? **And is man** actually **a tree of the field?**[N]

אֶלָּא מִשּׁוּם דִּכְתִיב: ״כִּי מִמֶּנּוּ תֹאכֵל, וְאֹתוֹ לֹא תִכְרֹת״, וּכְתִיב: ״אֹתוֹ תַשְׁחִית וְכָרָתָּ״. הָא כֵּיצַד? אִם תַּלְמִיד חָכָם הָגוּן הוּא, ״מִמֶּנּוּ תֹאכֵל, וְאֹתוֹ לֹא תִכְרֹת״, וְאִם לָאו, ״אֹתוֹ תַשְׁחִית וְכָרָתָּ״.

Rather, it is **because it is written** earlier in the same verse: **"You may eat of them but you may not cut them down," and it is written** in the next verse: **"Them you may destroy and cut down"** (Deuteronomy 20:20). This indicates that there are certain trees which may be cut down, while others may not be destroyed. **How so? If a Torah scholar is worthy: "You may eat of them but you may not cut them down," but if** he is **not** worthy: **"He you may destroy and cut down."**

אָמַר רַבִּי חָמָא בְּרַבִּי חֲנִינָא: מַאי דִּכְתִיב: ״בַּרְזֶל בְּבַרְזֶל יָחַד״? לוֹמַר לָךְ: מָה בַּרְזֶל זֶה, אֶחָד מְחַדֵּד אֶת חֲבֵירוֹ, אַף שְׁנֵי תַלְמִידֵי חֲכָמִים מְחַדְּדִין זֶה אֶת זֶה בַּהֲלָכָה.

The Gemara cites other expositions that deal with Torah study. **Rabbi Ḥama, son of Rabbi Ḥanina, said: What is** the meaning of that **which is written: "Iron sharpens iron,** so a man sharpens the countenance of his friend" (Proverbs 27:17)? This verse comes **to tell you** that **just as with these iron implements, one sharpens the other** when they are rubbed against each other, **so too,** when **Torah scholars** study together, they **sharpen one another in *halakha*.**

אָמַר רַבָּה בַּר בַּר חָנָה: לָמָּה נִמְשְׁלוּ דִּבְרֵי תוֹרָה כָּאֵשׁ, שֶׁנֶּאֱמַר: ״הֲלֹא כֹה דְבָרִי כָּאֵשׁ? נְאֻם ה׳״? לוֹמַר לָךְ: מָה אֵשׁ אֵינוֹ דּוֹלֵק יָחִיד, אַף דִּבְרֵי תוֹרָה אֵין מִתְקַיְּימִין בְּיָחִידִי.

Rabba bar bar Ḥana said: Why are matters of Torah compared to fire, as it is stated: "Is not My word like fire, says the Lord" (Jeremiah 23:29)? **To tell you: Just as fire does not ignite** in **a lone** stick of wood but in a pile of kindling, **so too, matters of Torah are not retained** and understood properly **by a lone** scholar who studies by himself, but by a group of Sages.

וְהַיְינוּ דְּאָמַר רַבִּי יוֹסֵי בַּר חֲנִינָא: מַאי דִּכְתִיב: ״חֶרֶב אֶל הַבַּדִּים וְנֹאָלוּ״? חֶרֶב עַל שׂוֹנְאֵיהֶן שֶׁל תַּלְמִידֵי חֲכָמִים שֶׁעוֹסְקִין בַּד בְּבַד בַּתּוֹרָה. וְלֹא עוֹד אֶלָּא שֶׁמִּטַּפְּשִׁין, שֶׁנֶּאֱמַר: ״וְנֹאָלוּ״.

And this is what Rabbi Yosei bar Ḥanina said: What is the meaning of that **which is written: "A sword is upon the boasters [*habaddim*], and they shall become fools [*noalu*]"** (Jeremiah 50:36)? This verse can be interpreted homiletically: There is a **sword upon the enemies of Torah scholars,** a euphemism for Torah scholars themselves, **who sit alone [*bad bevad*] and study Torah. And not only that, but** those who study by themselves **grow foolish** from their solitary Torah study, **as it is stated: "And they shall become fools."**

וְלֹא עוֹד אֶלָּא שֶׁחוֹטְאִין. כְּתִיב הָכָא: ״וְנֹאָלוּ״, וּכְתִיב הָתָם: ״אֲשֶׁר נוֹאַלְנוּ וַאֲשֶׁר חָטָאנוּ״. וְאִיבָּעֵית אֵימָא מֵהָכָא: ״נוֹאֲלוּ שָׂרֵי צֹעַן, [וגו׳,] הִתְעוּ אֶת מִצְרַיִם״.

And not only that, but they sin, as it is written here: "And they shall become fools," and it is written there: "For that we have done foolishly [*noalnu*] and for that we have sinned" (Numbers 12:11). **And if you wish, say** instead that it is derived **from here: "The princes of Zoan have become fools [*noalu*]…they have caused Egypt to go astray"** (Isaiah 19:13).

אָמַר רַב נַחְמָן בַּר יִצְחָק: לָמָּה נִמְשְׁלוּ דִּבְרֵי תוֹרָה כָּעֵץ, שֶׁנֶּאֱמַר: ״עֵץ חַיִּים הִיא לַמַּחֲזִיקִים בָּהּ״? לוֹמַר לָךְ: מָה עֵץ קָטָן מַדְלִיק אֶת הַגָּדוֹל, אַף תַּלְמִידֵי חֲכָמִים קְטַנִּים מְחַדְּדִים אֶת הַגְּדוֹלִים. וְהַיְינוּ דְּאָמַר רַבִּי חֲנִינָא: הַרְבֵּה לָמַדְתִּי מֵרַבּוֹתַי, וּמֵחֲבֵירַי יוֹתֵר מֵרַבּוֹתַי, וּמִתַּלְמִידַי יוֹתֵר מִכּוּלָּן.

Rav Naḥman bar Yitzḥak said: Why are Torah matters likened to a tree, as it is stated: "It is a tree of life to them who lay hold upon it" (Proverbs 3:18)? This verse comes **to tell you** that **just as a small** piece of **wood can ignite a large** piece, **so too, minor Torah scholars can sharpen great** Torah scholars and enable them to advance in their studies. **And this is what Rabbi Ḥanina said: I have learned much from my teachers and even more from my friends, but from my students** I have learned **more than** from **all of them.**

PERSONALITIES

Rabbi Bena'a – רַבִּי בְּנָאָה: One of the last of the *tanna'im*, Rabbi Bena'a was not born in Eretz Yisrael, but came from abroad, although his exact place of origin is unknown. We do not know his profession, but in Eretz Yisrael, he marked graves so that priests could avoid ritually impurity. His permanent place of residence was Tiberias, where he founded a large academy. The great *amora* Rabbi Yoḥanan studied Torah from him and it was he who transmitted most of the surviving statements of Rabbi Bena'a. Rabbi Bena'a was famed for his wisdom. He also maintained important relations with the non-Jewish authorities.

Rabbi Yirmeya – רַבִּי יִרְמְיָה: Born in Babylonia, Rabbi Yirmeya was one of the leading *amora'im* of the third and fourth generations. He studied in Babylonia in his youth, but soon thereafter emigrated to Eretz Yisrael, where he became a disciple of some of the greatest Sages of the generation, the students of Rabbi Yoḥanan, Rabbi Zeira and Rabbi Abbahu. Rabbi Yirmeya had a special dialectical method of great acuity, and he would pose provocative questions to his teachers and colleagues. Since these questions gave the impression that Rabbi Yirmeya was seeking to undermine the accepted rules of halakhic dialectic, he was punished and even removed from the study hall for a brief period. Rabbi Yirmeya's statements are quoted extensively in both the Babylonian Talmud and the Jerusalem Talmud, so much so that in the Babylonian Talmud his sayings are often introduced by the expression: They say in the West, i.e., in Eretz Yisrael.

NOTES

And is man a tree of the field – וְכִי אָדָם עֵץ שָׂדֶה הוּא: The connection suggested by Rabbi Yoḥanan between this phrase and a Torah scholar is based on a verse in Psalms (92:13): "The righteous shall flourish like the palm tree; he shall grow like a cedar in Lebanon."

רַבִּי חֲנִינָא בַּר פַּפָּא רָמֵי: כְּתִיב: ״לִקְרַאת צָמֵא הֵתָיוּ מָיִם״, וּכְתִיב: ״הוֹי, כׇּל צָמֵא, לְכוּ לַמַּיִם״! אִם תַּלְמִיד הָגוּן הוּא, ״לִקְרַאת צָמֵא הֵתָיוּ מָיִם״, וְאִי לָא, ״הוֹי, כׇּל צָמֵא, לְכוּ לַמַּיִם״.

Rabbi Ḥanina bar Pappa[P] **raised a contradiction.** In one verse **it is written: "To him who is thirsty bring water"** (Isaiah 21:14), which indicates that the one who has water must bring it to the thirsty person, **and it is written** elsewhere: **"Ho, everyone who thirsts, come for water"** (Isaiah 55:1), from which it may be inferred that the thirsty person must seek out water himself. Rabbi Ḥanina bar Pappa resolves this apparent contradiction by explaining that **if he is a worthy student** the teacher must seek him out, as in **"to him who is thirsty bring water," but if** the student is **not** worthy, then **"Ho, everyone who thirsts, come for water,"** i.e., this student must seek out a teacher himself.

רַבִּי חֲנִינָא בַּר חָמָא רָמֵי: כְּתִיב: ״יָפוּצוּ מַעְיְנֹתֶיךָ חוּצָה״, וּכְתִיב: ״יִהְיוּ לְךָ לְבַדֶּךָ״! אִם תַּלְמִיד הָגוּן הוּא, ״יָפוּצוּ מַעְיְנֹתֶיךָ חוּצָה״, וְאִם לָאו, ״יִהְיוּ לְךָ לְבַדֶּךָ״.

Rabbi Ḥanina bar Ḥama raised another **contradiction.** In one verse **it is written: "Let your springs be dispersed abroad"** (Proverbs 5:16), whereas in the next verse **it is written: "Let them be your own"** (Proverbs 5:17). Rabbi Ḥanina bar Ḥama explains: **If the student** sitting before you **is worthy,** then **"Let your springs be dispersed abroad,"** as you should teach him, but **if** he is **not** worthy, then **"Let them be your own."**

וְאָמַר רַבִּי חֲנִינָא בַּר אִידִי: לָמָּה נִמְשְׁלוּ דִּבְרֵי תוֹרָה לַמַּיִם, דִּכְתִיב: ״הוֹי, כׇּל צָמֵא, לְכוּ לַמַּיִם״? לוֹמַר לְךָ: מַה מַּיִם מַנִּיחִין מָקוֹם גָּבוֹהַּ וְהוֹלְכִין לְמָקוֹם נָמוּךְ, אַף דִּבְרֵי תוֹרָה אֵין מִתְקַיְּימִין אֶלָּא בְּמִי שֶׁדַּעְתּוֹ שְׁפֵלָה.

And Rabbi Ḥanina bar Idi said: Why are matters of Torah likened to water, as it is written: "Ho, everyone who thirsts, come for water" (Isaiah 55:1)? This verse comes **to tell you: Just as water leaves a high place and flows to a low place, so too, Torah matters are retained only by one whose spirit is lowly,**[H] i.e., a humble person.

וְאָמַר רַבִּי אוֹשַׁעְיָא: לָמָּה נִמְשְׁלוּ דִּבְרֵי תוֹרָה לִשְׁלֹשָׁה מַשְׁקִין הַלָּלוּ, בַּמַּיִם, וּבַיַּיִן, וּבֶחָלָב, דִּכְתִיב: ״הוֹי, כׇּל צָמֵא, לְכוּ לַמַּיִם״, וּכְתִיב: ״לְכוּ, שִׁבְרוּ, וֶאֱכֹלוּ; וּלְכוּ, שִׁבְרוּ בְּלוֹא כֶסֶף וּבְלוֹא מְחִיר יַיִן וְחָלָב״? לוֹמַר לְךָ: מַה שְּׁלֹשָׁה מַשְׁקִין הַלָּלוּ אֵין מִתְקַיְּימִין אֶלָּא בַּפָּחוּת שֶׁבַּכֵּלִים, אַף דִּבְרֵי תוֹרָה אֵין מִתְקַיְּימִין אֶלָּא בְּמִי שֶׁדַּעְתּוֹ שְׁפֵלָה.

And Rabbi Oshaya said: Why are matters of Torah likened to these three liquids: To water, wine and milk?[N] **As it is written** with regard to water: **"Ho, everyone who thirsts, come for water," and it is written** in the same verse: **"Come, buy and eat; yea, come, buy wine and milk without money and without price."** This verse comes **to tell you: Just as these three liquids can be retained only in the least of vessels,** e.g., clay pots, but not vessels of silver and gold, as they will spoil, **so too, matters of Torah are retained only by one whose spirit is lowly.**

כִּדְאָמְרָה לֵיהּ בְּרַתֵּיהּ דְּקֵיסָר לְרַבִּי יְהוֹשֻׁעַ בֶּן חֲנַנְיָה: אִי, חׇכְמָה מְפוֹאָרָה בִּכְלִי מְכוֹעָר! אֲמַר לַהּ: אָבִיךְ רָמֵי חַמְרָא בְּמָנֵי דְּפַחְרָא? אֲמַרָה לֵיהּ: אֶלָּא בְּמַאי נִירְמֵי? אֲמַר לַהּ: אַתּוּן דַּחֲשִׁיבִיתוּ רְמוֹ בְּמָאנֵי דַּהֲבָא וְכַסְפָּא.

The Gemara cites a related incident: This **is as the daughter of the** Roman **emperor said to Rabbi Yehoshua ben Ḥananya,** who was an ugly man: **Woe to glorious wisdom** such as yours, which is contained **in an ugly vessel.** Rabbi Yehoshua ben Ḥananya **said to her,** in a seemingly unrelated response: Does **your father keep his wine in** simple **clay vessels?** The emperor's daughter **said to him: Rather, in what,** then, **should he keep it?** Rabbi Yehoshua ben Ḥananya **said to her: You, who are so important,** should **put it in vessels of gold and silver.**

אָזְלָה וַאֲמַרָה לֵיהּ לַאֲבוּהָ. רַמְיָא לְחַמְרָא בְּמָנֵי דַּהֲבָא וְכַסְפָּא, וּתְקֵיף. אֲתוּ וַאֲמַרוּ לֵיהּ. אֲמַר לַהּ לִבְרַתֵּיהּ: מַאן אֲמַר לָךְ הָכִי? אֲמַרָה לֵיהּ: רַבִּי יְהוֹשֻׁעַ בֶּן חֲנַנְיָה. קַרְיוּהוּ. אֲמַר לֵיהּ: אַמַּאי אָמְרַתְּ לַהּ הָכִי? אֲמַר לֵיהּ: כִּי הֵיכִי דַּאֲמַרָה לִי, אֲמַרִי לַהּ. וְהָא אִיכָּא שַׁפִּירֵי דִּגְמִירִי!

The emperor's daughter went and said this **to her father. He put the wine in vessels of gold and silver and it turned sour.** When his advisors **came and told the emperor** that the wine had turned sour,[B] **he said to** his daughter: **Who told you** to do **this?** His daughter **responded: Rabbi Yehoshua ben Ḥananya.** The emperor **summoned him** and **said to him: Why did you say this to her?** Rabbi Yehoshua ben Ḥananya **said to him: Just as she said to me, so I said say to her,** to demonstrate to her that fine material is best preserved in the least of vessels. The emperor said to him: **But there are handsome people who are learned.**

PERSONALITIES

Rabbi Ḥanina bar Pappa – רַבִּי חֲנִינָא בַּר פַּפָּא: A third-generation *amora* of Eretz Yisrael, Rabbi Ḥanina bar Pappa was a colleague of the students of Rabbi Yoḥanan. It is frequently related in the Talmud that Rabbi Ḥanina bar Pappa and his colleagues would sit together and discuss innovative Torah teachings. He was, apparently, a judge in his city, as several halakhic decisions of his are recorded as judgments in civil suits. He was also proficient in *aggada*, and has more aggadic statements than exclusively halakhic statements. He transmitted many aggadic statements in the name of Rabbi Shmuel bar Naḥmani.

Rabbi Ḥanina bar Pappa's was famous for his both his great righteousness in interpersonal matters and his religious piety. It is related that, upon his death, a pillar of fire stood behind his bier.

HALAKHA

Only by one whose spirit is lowly – אֶלָּא בְּמִי שֶׁדַּעְתּוֹ שְׁפֵלָה: Matters of Torah are retained only by people who are humble in spirit, who have no concern for their own honor, and who sit in the dust of the feet of Sages, as stated by Rabbi Ḥanina (Rambam *Sefer HaMadda*, *Hilkhot Talmud Torah* 3:9).

NOTES

To water, wine, and milk – בַּמַּיִם, וּבַיַּיִן, וּבֶחָלָב: The *midrash* explains that these three drinks correspond to the Bible, the Mishna, and the Talmud (see *Iyyun Ya'akov*).

BACKGROUND

Storing wine in metal vessels – יַיִן בִּכְלֵי מַתֶּכֶת: Wine cannot be stored in metal vessels because the acid contained in the wine has a somewhat corrosive effect on most metals, including copper and silver. Furthermore, many compounds of these metals are poisonous, which not only spoils the taste of the wine but also places the drinker's health at risk.

אִי הֲווֹ סָנוּ, טְפֵי הֲווֹ גְּמִירִי. דָּבָר אַחֵר: מָה שְּׁלֹשָׁה מַשְׁקִין הַלָּלוּ אֵין נִפְסָלִין אֶלָּא בְּהֶיסַּח הַדַּעַת, אַף דִּבְרֵי תוֹרָה אֵין מִשְׁתַּכְּחִין אֶלָּא בְּהֶיסַּח הַדַּעַת.

Rabbi Yehoshua replied: **Had they been ugly, they would have been even more learned. Alternatively,** the Torah is likened to water, wine, and milk because **just as these three liquids are spoiled only by diversion of attention, so too, are Torah matters forgotten only through diversion of attention.** If water, wine and milk are guarded, they will not spoil or have dirty objects fall into them.

אָמַר רַבִּי חָמָא בְּרַבִּי חֲנִינָא: גָּדוֹל יוֹם הַגְּשָׁמִים כְּיוֹם שֶׁנִּבְרְאוּ שָׁמַיִם וָאָרֶץ, שֶׁנֶּאֱמַר: ״הַרְעִיפוּ שָׁמַיִם מִמַּעַל, וּשְׁחָקִים יִזְּלוּ צֶדֶק; תִּפְתַּח אֶרֶץ וְיִפְרוּ יֶשַׁע, וּצְדָקָה תַצְמִיחַ יַחַד; אֲנִי ה׳ בְּרָאתִיו״. בְּרָאתִים לֹא נֶאֱמַר, אֶלָּא ״בְּרָאתִיו״.

§ The Gemara returns to the issue of rain. **Rabbi Ḥama, son of Rabbi Ḥanina, said: The day of the rains is as great**[N] **as the day on which the heavens and earth were created, as it is stated: "Drop down, heavens, from above, let the skies pour down righteousness; let the earth open that they may bring forth salvation, and let it cause righteousness to spring up together; I, the Lord, have created it"** (Isaiah 45:8). The Gemara explains that the verse **does not say: I have created them,** in the plural, **but: I have created it.** In other words, the verse is referring to rain, rather than to the heavens and the earth, which indicates that rainfall is as important as the creation of the world.

אָמַר רַב אוֹשַׁעְיָא: גָּדוֹל יוֹם הַגְּשָׁמִים, שֶׁאֲפִילּוּ יְשׁוּעָה פָּרָה וְרָבָה בּוֹ, שֶׁנֶּאֱמַר: ״תִּפְתַּח אֶרֶץ וְיִפְרוּ יֶשַׁע״. אָמַר רַבִּי תַּנְחוּם בַּר חֲנִילַאי: אֵין הַגְּשָׁמִים יוֹרְדִים אֶלָּא אִם כֵּן נִמְחֲלוּ עֲוֹנוֹתֵיהֶן שֶׁל יִשְׂרָאֵל, שֶׁנֶּאֱמַר: ״רָצִיתָ ה׳ אַרְצֶךָ; שַׁבְתָּ שְׁבִית יַעֲקֹב. נָשָׂאתָ עֲוֹן עַמֶּךָ; כִּסִּיתָ כָל חַטָּאתָם. סֶלָה״.

Rabbi Oshaya likewise **said: The day of rain is great, as** rain even facilitates **salvation,** which **is fruitful and multiplies on** that day. It is a time of God's favor, when salvation is brought forth into the world, **as it is stated: "Let the earth open that they may bring forth salvation"** (Isaiah 45:8). **Rabbi Tanḥum bar Ḥanilai said: Rain falls only if the Jewish people's transgressions have been forgiven,**[N] **as it is stated: "Lord, You have been favorable to Your land; You have turned the captivity of Jacob; You have forgiven the iniquity of Your people; You have pardoned all their sin. Selah"** (Psalms 85:2–3). This chapter proceeds to discuss rainfall: "And righteousness has looked down from Heaven" (Psalms 85:12), in the form of rain.

אֲמַר לֵיהּ זְעִירִי מִדִּיהֲבַת לְרָבִינָא: אַתּוּן מֵהָכָא מַתְנִיתוּ לַהּ. אֲנַן מֵהָכָא מַתְנֵינַן לַהּ: ״וְאַתָּה, תִּשְׁמַע הַשָּׁמַיִם, וְסָלַחְתָּ לְחַטַּאת״ וגו׳.

The Sage **Ze'iri from** the town of **Dihavat said to Ravina: You learned this** idea **from here,** whereas **we learned it from here,** a different verse: "When heaven is closed up, and there is no rain, when they sin against You, if they pray toward this place and confess Your name and turn from their sin, when You afflict them, **then You, hear in heaven and forgive the sin of** Your servants and of Your people Israel, when You teach them the good way in which they should walk, and send rain upon Your land, which You have given to Your people as an inheritance" (1 Kings 8:35–36).

אָמַר רַבִּי תַּנְחוּם בְּרֵיהּ דְּרַבִּי חִיָּיא אִישׁ כְּפַר עַכּוֹ: אֵין הַגְּשָׁמִים נֶעֱצָרִין אֶלָּא אִם כֵּן נִתְחַיְּיבוּ שׂוֹנְאֵיהֶן שֶׁל יִשְׂרָאֵל כְּלָיָה, שֶׁנֶּאֱמַר: ״צִיָּה גַם חֹם יִגְזְלוּ מֵימֵי שֶׁלֶג; שְׁאוֹל חָטָאוּ״. אֲמַר לֵיהּ זְעִירִי מִדִּיהֲבַת לְרָבִינָא: אַתּוּן מֵהָכָא מַתְנִיתוּ לַהּ. אֲנַן מֵהָכָא מַתְנֵינַן לַהּ: ״וְעָצַר אֶת הַשָּׁמַיִם... וַאֲבַדְתֶּם מְהֵרָה״.

Rabbi Tanḥum, son of Rabbi Ḥiyya of village of Akko, said: The rains are withheld only if the enemies of the Jewish people, a euphemism for the Jewish people, **have been sentenced to destruction**[N] for their sins, **as it is stated: "Drought and heat will steal the snow waters; to the grave those who have sinned"** (Job 24:19). According to this interpretation, snow water will be stolen by drought, i.e., there will be none available, when people have sinned to the point that they deserve the grave. **Ze'iri from Dihavat said to Ravina: You learned this** idea **from here; we learned it from here:** "And the anger of the Lord will be kindled against you, **and He will close up the heavens,** and there will be no rain, and the earth will not give its fruit, **and you will perish quickly"** (Deuteronomy 11:17).

אָמַר רַב חִסְדָּא: אֵין הַגְּשָׁמִים נֶעֱצָרִין אֶלָּא בִּשְׁבִיל בִּיטּוּל תְּרוּמוֹת וּמַעַשְׂרוֹת, שֶׁנֶּאֱמַר: ״צִיָּה גַם חֹם יִגְזְלוּ מֵימֵי שֶׁלֶג״. מַאי מַשְׁמַע? תָּנָא דְּבֵי רַבִּי יִשְׁמָעֵאל: בִּשְׁבִיל דְּבָרִים שֶׁצִּוִּיתִי אֶתְכֶם בִּימוֹת הַחַמָּה וְלֹא עֲשִׂיתֶם, יִגְזְלוּ מִכֶּם מֵימֵי שֶׁלֶג בִּימוֹת הַגְּשָׁמִים.

Rav Ḥisda said: The rains are withheld only due to the sin of **the nullification of** ***teruma*** **and tithes, as it is stated: "Drought and heat will steal the snow waters"** (Job 24:19). The Gemara asks: **From where** in the verse may this idea **be inferred** from the verse? **The school of Rabbi Yishmael taught: Due to matters that I have commanded you to do in the summer,** e.g., take *teruma* and tithes from the summer produce, **and that you did not do, the snow waters will be stolen from you in the rainy season.**

NOTES

The day of the rains is great – גָּדוֹל יוֹם הַגְּשָׁמִים: Rav Ya'akov Emden points out that these statements about the greatness of rain refer to rainfall after an extended period of drought.

Only if their transgressions have been forgiven – אֶלָּא אִם כֵּן נִמְחֲלוּ עֲוֹנוֹתֵיהֶן: Some commentaries suggest that this is the reason why one does not begin to pray for rain until *Sukkot*, as it is celebrated a few days after Yom Kippur, the day of atonement and forgiveness for all of the sins of Israel (*Sefat Emet*).

Only if the enemies of the Jewish people have been sentenced to destruction – אֶלָּא אִם כֵּן נִתְחַיְּיבוּ שׂוֹנְאֵיהֶן שֶׁל יִשְׂרָאֵל כְּלָיָה: When the Jewish people are condemned to be destroyed, God doesn't carry out the sentence immediately, but first withholds rain in the hope that the people will understand that if they do not repent and forsake their evil ways, they will be destroyed (*Iyyun Ya'akov*).

אָמַר רַבִּי שִׁמְעוֹן בֶּן פָּזִי: אֵין הַגְּשָׁמִים נֶעֱצָרִין אֶלָּא בִּשְׁבִיל מְסַפְּרֵי לְשׁוֹן הָרָע, שֶׁנֶּאֱמַר: ״רוּחַ צָפוֹן תְּחוֹלֵל גָּשֶׁם, וּפָנִים נִזְעָמִים לְשׁוֹן סָתֶר״.

Rabbi Shimon ben Pazi said: The rains are withheld only due to the sin of those **who speak slander, as it is stated: "The north wind brings forth rain, but a backbiting tongue, an angry countenance"**[N] (Proverbs 25:23). This verse indicates that if the countenance of the heavens is angry, with neither clouds nor rain, it is due to slanderous speech.

אָמַר רַב סַלָּא אָמַר רַב הַמְנוּנָא: אֵין הַגְּשָׁמִים נֶעֱצָרִין אֶלָּא בִּשְׁבִיל עַזֵּי פָנִים, שֶׁנֶּאֱמַר: ״וַיִּמָּנְעוּ רְבִבִים, וּמַלְקוֹשׁ לוֹא הָיָה, וּמֵצַח אִשָּׁה זוֹנָה הָיָה לָךְ״ וגו׳. וְאָמַר רַב סַלָּא אָמַר רַב הַמְנוּנָא: כָּל אָדָם שֶׁיֵּשׁ לוֹ עַזּוּת פָּנִים סוֹף נִכְשַׁל בַּעֲבֵירָה, שֶׁנֶּאֱמַר: ״וּמֵצַח אִשָּׁה זוֹנָה הָיָה לָךְ״. רַב נַחְמָן אָמַר: בְּיָדוּעַ שֶׁנִּכְשַׁל בַּעֲבֵירָה שֶׁנֶּאֱמַר: ״הָיָה לָךְ״ וְלֹא נֶאֱמַר ״יִהְיֶה לָךְ״.

Rav Salla said that **Rav Hamnuna said: The rains are withheld only due to impudent** people, **as it is stated: "Therefore the showers have been withheld, and there has been no last rain, yet you had a harlot's forehead,** you refused to be ashamed" (Jeremiah 3:3). **And Rav Salla said** that **Rav Hamnuna said,** with regard to the same verse: **Any man who is insolent will ultimately stumble over** the **transgression** of prostitution, **as it is stated: "Yet you had a prostitute's forehead." Rav Naḥman said:** The verse does not mean that he will commit a sexual transgression in the future; rather, **it is known that he has** already **stumbled over** this **transgression, as it is stated: "You had,"** in the past tense, **and it is not stated: You will.**

אָמַר רַבָּה בַּר רַב הוּנָא: כָּל אָדָם שֶׁיֵּשׁ לוֹ עַזּוּת פָּנִים מוּתָּר לִקְרוֹתוֹ רָשָׁע, שֶׁנֶּאֱמַר: ״הֵעֵז אִישׁ רָשָׁע בְּפָנָיו״. רַב נַחְמָן בַּר יִצְחָק אָמַר: מוּתָּר לִשְׂנְאוֹתוֹ שֶׁנֶּאֱמַר: ״וְעֹז פָּנָיו יְשֻׁנֶּא״. אַל תִּקְרֵי יְשֻׁנֶּא אֶלָּא יִשָּׂנֵא.

Rabba bar Rav Huna said: With regard to **any man who is insolent, it is permitted to call him wicked** to his face, **as it is stated: "A wicked man makes his face insolent"** (Proverbs 21:29). **Rav Naḥman bar Yitzḥak said: It is permitted to hate him, as it is stated: "And the insolence of his face is changed"** (Ecclesiastes 8:1). **Do not read** it as: **"Is changed** [*yeshunne*]"; **rather,** read it as: **Is hated** [*yissane*], as the two words are spelled the same way in Hebrew, albeit with different vocalization and pronunciation.

אָמַר רַב קְטִינָא: אֵין הַגְּשָׁמִים נֶעֱצָרִין אֶלָּא בִּשְׁבִיל בִּיטּוּל תּוֹרָה, שֶׁנֶּאֱמַר: ״בַּעֲצַלְתַּיִם יִמַּךְ הַמְּקָרֶה״ בִּשְׁבִיל עַצְלוּת שֶׁהָיָה בְּיִשְׂרָאֵל שֶׁלֹּא עָסְקוּ בַּתּוֹרָה נַעֲשָׂה שׂוֹנְאוֹ שֶׁל הַקָּדוֹשׁ בָּרוּךְ הוּא מָךְ. וְאֵין ״מָךְ״ אֶלָּא עָנִי, שֶׁנֶּאֱמַר: ״וְאִם מָךְ הוּא מֵעֶרְכֶּךָ״. וְאֵין ״מְקָרֶה״ אֶלָּא הַקָּדוֹשׁ בָּרוּךְ הוּא, שֶׁנֶּאֱמַר: ״הַמְקָרֶה בַמַּיִם עֲלִיּוֹתָיו״.

Rav Ketina said: The rains are withheld only due to the sin of **dereliction in** the study of **Torah, as it is stated: "By slothfulness the rafters** [*hamekare*] **will sink in** [*yimakh*], and through idleness of the hands the house leaks" (Ecclesiastes 10:18). **Due to slothfulness that was** present **amongst the Jewish people, that they did not occupy** themselves **with Torah, the enemy of the Holy One, Blessed be He,** a euphemism for God Himself, **has sunk.**[N] **And sunk** [*makh*] means **nothing other** than **poor, as it is stated: "But if he is too poor** [*makh*] **for your valuation"** (Leviticus 27:8). **And "rafters** [*mekare*]" means **nothing other** than a reference to **the Holy One, Blessed be He, as it is stated: "Who lays the beams** [*hamekare*] **of Your upper chambers in the water"** (Psalms 104:3).

רַב יוֹסֵף אָמַר מֵהָכָא: ״וְעַתָּה לֹא רָאוּ אוֹר, בָּהִיר הוּא בַּשְּׁחָקִים, וְרוּחַ עָבְרָה וַתְּטַהֲרֵם״. וְאֵין ״אוֹר״ אֶלָּא תּוֹרָה, שֶׁנֶּאֱמַר: ״כִּי נֵר מִצְוָה וְתוֹרָה אוֹר״. ״בָּהִיר הוּא בַּשְּׁחָקִים״. תָּנָא דְּבֵי רַבִּי יִשְׁמָעֵאל: אֲפִילּוּ בְּשָׁעָה שֶׁרָקִיעַ נַעֲשָׂה בְּהוֹרִין בְּהוֹרִין לְהוֹרִיד טַל וּמָטָר, ״רוּחַ עָבְרָה וַתְּטַהֲרֵם״.

Rav Yosef said that this idea is derived **from here: "And now that men do not see the light, it is bright in the skies, but the wind passes and cleanses them"** (Job 37:21). **And "light"** means **nothing other** than **Torah, as it is stated: "For a mitzva is a lamp and Torah is a light"** (Proverbs 6:23). According to this interpretation, the verse means that when "men do not see the light," i.e., when they are not occupied with Torah, **"it is bright in the skies,"** as there are no rainclouds. With regard to this verse, **the school of Rabbi Yishmael taught: Even when the sky is comprised of bright clouds** that serve **to bring down dew and rain,** no rain will fall, as **"the wind passes and cleanses them."**

אָמַר רַבִּי אַמִי: אֵין הַגְּשָׁמִים נֶעֱצָרִין אֶלָּא בַּעֲוֹן גָּזֵל, שֶׁנֶּאֱמַר: ״עַל כַּפַּיִם כִּסָּה אוֹר״. בַּעֲוֹן כַּפַּיִם כִּסָּה אוֹר. וְאֵין ״כַּפַּיִם״ אֶלָּא חָמָס, שֶׁנֶּאֱמַר: ״וּמִן הֶחָמָס אֲשֶׁר בְּכַפֵּיהֶם״. וְאֵין ״אוֹר״ אֶלָּא מָטָר, שֶׁנֶּאֱמַר: ״יָפִיץ עֲנַן אוֹרוֹ״.

Rabbi Ami said: The rains are withheld only due to the sin of robbery, as it is stated: "He covers His hands with the light, and He has commanded it due to imploring" (Job 36:32). This means that due **to the sin of** stealing **hands, God has covered the light** and no rain will fall. **And** Rabbi Ami adds that the term **"hand"** means **nothing other** than a sin of **violence, as it is stated:** "And from the violence that is in their hands" (Jonah 3:8). And "light" means **nothing other** than **rain, as it is stated: "He spreads abroad the cloud of His light"** (Job 37:11).

NOTES

But a backbiting tongue an angry countenance – וּפָנִים נִזְעָמִים לְשׁוֹן סָתֶר: According to Rashi and *Tosafot*, Rabbi Shimon ben Pazi interprets the angry countenance mentioned in this verse as referring to God. The lack of rain is not a chance occurrence but a sign that God is angry with His people on account of their slanderous language. Others suggest that, even according to the explanation of Rabbi Shimon ben Pazi, the angry countenance can be understood as a reference to the faces of those who are distressed by the slander spoken against them. God halts the rain when He sees that relations between people are strained on account of the slander that is being circulated (Maharsha).

The enemy of the Holy One, Blessed be He, has sunk – נַעֲשָׂה שׂוֹנְאוֹ שֶׁל הַקָּדוֹשׁ בָּרוּךְ הוּא מָךְ: Rashi explains that when the Jewish people are lazy and fail to study the Torah properly, it is as if God Himself becomes weak, and He is unable to make the rain fall. Others state that when the Jews do not pay sufficient attention to Torah study, God becomes poor in the sense that He is unable to find among the people any merits that would justify bestowing His bounty upon them (Rabbi Elyakim).

מַאי תַּקַּנְתֵּיהּ? יַרְבֶּה בִּתְפִלָּה, שֶׁנֶּאֱמַר: ״וַיְצַו עָלֶיהָ בְמַפְגִּיעַ״. וְאֵין ״פְּגִיעָה״ אֶלָּא ״תְּפִלָּה״, שֶׁנֶּאֱמַר: ״וְאַתָּה, אַל תִּתְפַּלֵּל בְּעַד הָעָם הַזֶּה, וגו׳, וְאַל תִּפְגַּע בִּי״.

What is the remedy of one who has caused the rain to be withheld? He should **increase** his **prayers,**[N] **as it is stated** in the same chapter: **"And He has commanded it due to imploring"** (Job 37:12), **and "imploring"** means **nothing other** than **prayer, as it is stated: "Therefore, do not pray you for this nation,** neither lift up cry nor prayer for them, **neither implore Me"** (Jeremiah 7:16).

וְאָמַר רַבִּי אַמִי: מַאי דִּכְתִיב: ״אִם קֵהָה הַבַּרְזֶל, וְהוּא לֹא פָנִים קִלְקַל״? אִם רָאִיתָ רָקִיעַ שֶׁקֵּיהָה כְּבַרְזֶל מִלְּהוֹרִיד טַל וּמָטָר, בִּשְׁבִיל מַעֲשֵׂה הַדּוֹר שֶׁהֵן מְקוּלְקָלִין, שֶׁנֶּאֱמַר: ״וְהוּא לֹא פָנִים קִלְקַל״.

And Rabbi Ami said: What is the meaning of that **which is written: "If the iron is blunt, and does not whet the edge"** (Ecclesiastes 10:10)? **If you see a sky that is blunt as iron, in that** it does not **bring down dew and rain,** this is **due to** the **deeds of the generation, which are corrupt, as it is stated: "And does not whet [*kilkal*] the edge [*panim*]."** *Panim,* which also means face, is often used in reference to the leaders of a generation, while the term *kilkal* is similar to the word for corrupt, *mekulkalin.*

מַה תַּקַּנְתָּן? יִתְגַּבְּרוּ בְּרַחֲמִים, שֶׁנֶּאֱמַר: ״וַחֲיָלִים יְגַבֵּר, וְיִתְרוֹן הַכְשֵׁיר חָכְמָה״. כׇּל שֶׁכֵּן, אִם הוּכְשְׁרוּ מַעֲשֵׂיהֶן מֵעִיקָּרָא.

What is their remedy? They must **increase** their prayers **for mercy, as it is stated** in the same verse: **"Then must he increase his strength, but wisdom is profitable to direct"** (Ecclesiastes 10:10). This verse hints that rain will fall if one increases his strength, i.e., his prayers for mercy. The last part of the verse means that, **all the more so, if their deeds** had been righteous and **direct from the beginning,** the rains would not have been withheld.

רֵישׁ לָקִישׁ אָמַר: אִם רָאִיתָ תַּלְמִיד

The Gemara cites a different interpretation of the same verse. **Reish Lakish said: If you see a student**

שֶׁלִּמּוּדוֹ קָשֶׁה עָלָיו כְּבַרְזֶל, בִּשְׁבִיל מִשְׁנָתוֹ שֶׁאֵינָהּ סְדוּרָה עָלָיו, שֶׁנֶּאֱמַר: ״וְהוּא לֹא פָנִים קִלְקַל״.

whose studies are hard as iron for him, i.e., difficult to understand, this is **due to his** lack of familiarity with the **Mishna, which is not organized for him.** If the Mishna is unclear, any further study of Gemara is rendered all the more difficult, **as it is stated: "And does not whet [*kilkal*] the edge [*panim*]"** (Ecclesiastes 10:10). As panim can also mean surface, this indicates that the surface, i.e., the basic statements of the Mishna, is corrupted. As stated previously, *kilkal* can also mean corrupted.

מַאי תַּקַּנְתֵּיהּ? יַרְבֶּה בִּישִׁיבָה, שֶׁנֶּאֱמַר: ״וַחֲיָלִים יְגַבֵּר, וְיִתְרוֹן הַכְשֵׁיר חָכְמָה״. כׇּל שֶׁכֵּן אִם מִשְׁנָתוֹ סְדוּרָה לוֹ מֵעִיקָּרָא.

What is his remedy? He must **increase** the time **he sits**[N] and studies, **as it is stated: "Then must he increase his strength"** (Ecclesiastes 10:10). The last part of the verse: **"But wisdom is profitable to direct,"** means that **all the more so, if his** study of the **Mishna is organized for him from the beginning,** he will avoid this trouble.

כִּי הָא דְּרֵישׁ לָקִישׁ הֲוָה מְסַדֵּר מַתְנִיתֵיהּ אַרְבְּעִין זִמְנִין כְּנֶגֶד אַרְבָּעִים יוֹם שֶׁנִּיתְּנָה תּוֹרָה, וְעָיֵיל לְקַמֵּיהּ דְּרַבִּי יוֹחָנָן. רַב אַדָּא בַּר אַהֲבָה מְסַדֵּר מַתְנִיתֵיהּ עֶשְׂרִין וְאַרְבַּע זִמְנִין כְּנֶגֶד תּוֹרָה נְבִיאִים וּכְתוּבִים, וְעָיֵיל לְקַמֵּיהּ דְּרָבָא.

That is **like this** practice **of Reish Lakish,** who **would review his studies forty times, corresponding to** the **forty days in which the Torah was given** to Moses at Sinai, **and** only afterward would he **go before Rabbi Yoḥanan** to study from his teacher. Similarly, **Rav Adda bar Ahava** would **review his learning twenty-four times, corresponding to** the twenty-four books in the **Torah, Prophets, and Writings,** i.e., the Bible, **and** only afterward **go before Rava** to study with him.

רָבָא אָמַר: אִם רָאִיתָ תַּלְמִיד שֶׁלִּמּוּדוֹ קָשֶׁה עָלָיו כְּבַרְזֶל, בִּשְׁבִיל רַבּוֹ, שֶׁאֵינוֹ מַסְבִּיר לוֹ פָּנִים, שֶׁנֶּאֱמַר: ״וְהוּא לֹא פָנִים קִלְקַל״.

With regard to the aforementioned verse from Ecclesiastes, **Rava said: If you see a student whose studies are** as **difficult for him as iron,** this is **due to his teacher, who does not show him a friendly countenance,** but is overly strict with him. This practice inhibits the student's learning, **as it is stated: "And it has not whetted the surface [*panim*]"** (Ecclesiastes 10:10). As explained previously, *panim* can also mean countenance.

NOTES

What is the remedy, he should increase prayers – מַאי תַּקַּנְתֵּיהּ יַרְבֶּה בִּתְפִלָּה: That is, the robber must pray for forgiveness after returning the object that he took by violence. However, if he does not first restore what he took, all of his repentance and prayers are of no avail. As the Gemara states elsewhere (16a), one who confesses to a robbery while the article he has taken is still in his possession is likened to someone undergoing ritual immersion while holding an unclean reptile in his hand. This person remains ritually impure (*Gevurat Ari*).

NOTES

He must increase the time he sits – יַרְבֶּה בִּישִׁיבָה: Rashi explains that a student who finds his studies hard should spend a great deal of time with other students and review with them the material that he has not fully mastered on his own. Others suggest that the student who is struggling with his studies should sit by himself and review the difficult material in an organized manner until he is confident that he knows it thoroughly (Meiri).

LANGUAGE

Corrode [*meshatkhin*] – מְשַׁתְּכִין: Generally means to corrode; its basic meaning is ruin or decay. It is probably related to the Syriac suḥata, which also denotes ruin or decay. In Mandaean, the term shuta, a noun meaning rust, is derived from this root.

מַאי תַּקַּנְתֵּיהּ? יַרְבֶּה עָלָיו רֵעִים, שֶׁנֶּאֱמַר: ״וַחֲיָלִים יְגַבֵּר, וְיִתְרוֹן הַכְשֵׁיר חָכְמָה״. כָּל שֶׁכֵּן אִם הוּכְשְׁרוּ מַעֲשָׂיו בִּפְנֵי רַבּוֹ מֵעִיקָּרָא.

What is the remedy for this student? He must **increase** the number of **friends** he sends to the teacher to intercede **for him, as it is stated: "Then must he increase his strength."** The term used for strength, *ḥayalim*, can also mean soldiers or colleagues. Nevertheless: **"But wisdom is profitable to direct,"** meaning that **all the more so** would he be spared this trouble **if his deeds** were properly **directed before his teacher from the beginning.**

וְאָמַר רַבִּי אַמִי: מַאי דִּכְתִיב: ״אִם יִשּׁךְ הַנָּחָשׁ בְּלוֹא לָחַשׁ, וְאֵין יִתְרוֹן לְבַעַל הַלָּשׁוֹן״? אִם רָאִיתָ דּוֹר שֶׁהַשָּׁמַיִם מְשַׁתְּכִין כִּנְחֹשֶׁת מִלְּהוֹרִיד טַל וּמָטָר, בִּשְׁבִיל לוֹחֲשֵׁי לְחִישׁוֹת שֶׁאֵין בְּדוֹר.

§ The Gemara returns to the topic of rain. **And Rabbi Ami said: What is** the meaning of that **which is written: "If the serpent** [*naḥash*] **bites** [*yishokh*] **before it is charmed** [*laḥash*], **then the charmer has no advantage"** (Ecclesiastes 10:11)? **If you see a generation** for whom **the heavens corrode** [*meshatkhin*][L] **like copper** [*neḥoshet*], which prevents them **from bringing down dew and rain,** this is **due to the lack of those who whisper quiet** [*loḥashei leḥishot*] prayers **in the generation.**

מַאי תַּקַּנְתָּן? יֵלְכוּ אֵצֶל מִי שֶׁיּוֹדֵעַ לִלְחוֹשׁ, דִּכְתִיב: ״יַגִּיד עָלָיו רֵעוֹ״. ״וְאֵין יִתְרוֹן לְבַעַל הַלָּשׁוֹן״. וּמִי שֶׁאֶפְשָׁר לוֹ לִלְחוֹשׁ וְאֵינוֹ לוֹחֵשׁ, מָה הֲנָאָה יֵשׁ לוֹ?

What is their remedy? They should **go to one who knows** how **to whisper** prayers in the proper manner, **as it is written: "Its noise tells concerning it"** (Job 36:33). As for the phrase: **"Then the charmer has no advantage,"** this is referring to **one who is able to whisper** his prayers correctly **and yet does not whisper** them correctly. In this case, of **what benefit to him** is his ability to pray?

וְאִם לָחַשׁ וְלֹא נַעֲנָה, מַאי תַּקַּנְתֵּיהּ? יֵלֵךְ אֵצֶל חָסִיד שֶׁבַּדּוֹר, וְיַרְבֶּה עָלָיו בִּתְפִלָּה, שֶׁנֶּאֱמַר: ״וַיְצַו עָלֶיהָ בְמַפְגִּיעַ״. וְאֵין פְּגִיעָה אֶלָּא תְּפִילָּה, שֶׁנֶּאֱמַר: ״וְאַתָּה, אַל תִּתְפַּלֵּל בְּעַד הָעָם הַזֶּה, וְאַל תִּשָּׂא בַעֲדָם רִנָּה וּתְפִלָּה, וְאַל תִּפְגַּע בִּי״.

And if he whispered his prayers **and** yet **was not answered, what is his remedy?** He should **go to** the most **pious individual of the generation, and** this pious individual will **increase** his **prayers on his behalf, as it is stated** one verse earlier: **"And He has commanded it due to imploring"** (Job 36:32). And **"imploring"** means **nothing other** than **prayer, as it is stated: "Therefore, do not pray you for this nation, neither lift up cry nor prayer for them, neither implore Me"** (Jeremiah 7:16).

וְאִם לָחַשׁ, וְעָלְתָה בְּיָדוֹ, וּמֵגִיס דַּעְתּוֹ עָלָיו, מֵבִיא אַף לָעוֹלָם, שֶׁנֶּאֱמַר: ״מִקְנֶה אַף עַל עוֹלֶה״.

And if he whispered his prayers for rain, **and** his prayers were **successful,** i.e., rain fell as he requested, **and he becomes prideful** as a result, **he brings anger into the world, as it is stated: "The cattle** [*mikne*] **also** [*af*] **concerning the rising storm** [*al oleh*]**"** (Job 36:33). This verse can be read homiletically as: Anger [*af*] is acquired [*mikne*] by one who raises [*al oleh*] his pride.

רָבָא אָמַר: שְׁנֵי תַלְמִידֵי חֲכָמִים שֶׁיּוֹשְׁבִין בְּעִיר אַחַת וְאֵין נוֹחִין זֶה לָזֶה בַּהֲלָכָה, מִתְקַנְּאִין בְּאַף וּמַעֲלִין אוֹתוֹ, שֶׁנֶּאֱמַר: ״מִקְנֶה אַף עַל עוֹלֶה״.

Following the same interpretation of this verse, **Rava said:** If there are **two Torah scholars**[N] **who live in one city, and they are not courteous with one another in** their discussions of ***halakha*****, they arouse anger** upon the world **and cause it to rise up, as it is stated: "Anger is acquired by one who raises his pride."**

אָמַר רֵישׁ לָקִישׁ: מַאי דִּכְתִיב: ״אִם יִשּׁךְ הַנָּחָשׁ בְּלוֹא לָחַשׁ, וְאֵין יִתְרוֹן לְבַעַל הַלָּשׁוֹן״? לֶעָתִיד לָבוֹא, מִתְקַבְּצוֹת וּבָאוֹת כָּל הַחַיּוֹת אֵצֶל הַנָּחָשׁ, וְאוֹמְרִים לוֹ: אֲרִי דּוֹרֵס וְאוֹכֵל, זְאֵב טוֹרֵף וְאוֹכֵל; אַתָּה, מָה הֲנָאָה יֵשׁ לְךָ? אָמַר לָהֶם: ״וְאֵין יִתְרוֹן לְבַעַל הַלָּשׁוֹן״.

The Gemara cites another interpretation of the aforementioned verse. **Reish Lakish said: What is** the meaning of that **which is written: "If the snake bites before it is charmed, then the charmer has no advantage"** (Ecclesiastes 10:11)?[N] **In the future, all the animals will gather together and come to the snake and say to him: A lion mauls** its prey **and eats** it; **a wolf tears apart** its prey **and eats** it; but **you, what pleasure do you have** when you bite a person, as you are incapable of eating him? The snake will **say to them: "The charmer has no advantage."** The Hebrew phrase for snake charmer literally means the master of the tongue, and therefore the snake is saying that he has a more difficult question: What pleasure does a slanderer receive, as he inflicts more harm for which he obtains no physical enjoyment.

NOTES

Two Torah scholars, etc. – שְׁנֵי תַלְמִידֵי חֲכָמִים וכו׳: Some commentaries say that the verse: "Its noise [*reo*] tells concerning it," means: If his colleague [*reo*] speaks harshly to him, and they are discourteous with one another in their discussions of *halakha*, this causes anger to come (Rabbi Elyakim). Rashi presents an opposite reading: They are courteous with one another in *halakha*. In accordance with this version, some explain that if the Sages are too courteous with one another and fail to challenge each other's opinions, the *halakha* will not be fully clarified, and this will bring down anger (*Aggadot HaTalmud*).

Then the charmer has no advantage – וְאֵין יִתְרוֹן לְבַעַל הַלָּשׁוֹן: Rashi here explains that on the Day of Judgment all the creatures of the world will come before God. The snake will argue that although he bites and causes severe harm without deriving any benefit from his actions, nevertheless he is not as bad as slanderers. In his commentary on tractate *Arakhin* (15b) Rashi states that the snake will attempt to justify himself by saying: "If the serpent bites before it is charmed," which can also mean: Unless it is whispered to, i.e., a snake bites only if it commanded to do so by God.

אָמַר רַבִּי אַמִי: אֵין תְּפִלָּתוֹ שֶׁל אָדָם נִשְׁמַעַת אֶלָּא אִם כֵּן מֵשִׂים נַפְשׁוֹ בְּכַפּוֹ, שֶׁנֶּאֱמַר: "נִשָּׂא לְבָבֵנוּ אֶל כַּפָּיִם". אִינִי? וְהָא אוֹקִים שְׁמוּאֵל אָמוֹרָא עֲלֵיהּ וְדָרַשׁ: "וַיְפַתּוּהוּ בְּפִיהֶם, וּבִלְשׁוֹנָם יְכַזְּבוּ לוֹ, וְלִבָּם לֹא נָכוֹן עִמּוֹ, וְלֹא נֶאֶמְנוּ בִּבְרִיתוֹ". וְאַף עַל פִּי כֵן, "וְהוּא רַחוּם, יְכַפֵּר עָוֹן" וגו'.

Rabbi Ami said: A person's prayer is heard only if he places his soul in his palm,[N] i.e., one must submit his entire soul with sincerity in his outstretched hands as he prays, **as it is stated: "Let us lift up our heart with our hands"** (Lamentations 3:41). The Gemara raises an objection: **Is that so? But Shmuel** once **established for himself an interpreter** to teach in public, **and interpreted homiletically** the verse: **"But they beguiled Him with their mouth and lied to Him with their tongue, for their heart was not steadfast with Him, neither were they faithful to His covenant"** (Psalms 78:36–37), **and nevertheless** the psalm continues: **"But He, being full of compassion, forgives iniquity,** and does not destroy" (Psalms 78:38). This indicates that all prayers are accepted, even if they lack sincerity.

לָא קַשְׁיָא. כָּאן בְּיָחִיד, כָּאן בְּצִבּוּר.

The Gemara responds: This is **not difficult,** as **here** Rabbi Ami is referring **to an individual** who prays without sincerity and consequently his prayer goes unheard, whereas **there** Shmuel is saying that when one prays **with** the **community,** even if his prayers are deficient, they are accepted in the merit of the congregation.

אָמַר רַבִּי אַמִי: אֵין גְּשָׁמִים יוֹרְדִין אֶלָּא בִּשְׁבִיל בַּעֲלֵי אֲמָנָה, שֶׁנֶּאֱמַר: "אֱמֶת מֵאֶרֶץ תִּצְמָח, וְצֶדֶק מִשָּׁמַיִם נִשְׁקָף".

Rabbi Ami further **said: Rain falls only due to faithful people, as it is stated: "Truth springs out of the earth, and righteousness has looked down from heaven"** (Psalms 85:12). When "truth springs out of the earth," i.e., if people are faithful, they will find that "righteousness," in the form of rain "has looked down from heaven."

וְאָמַר רַבִּי אַמִי: בֹּא וּרְאֵה כַּמָּה גְּדוֹלִים בַּעֲלֵי אֲמָנָה. מִנַּיִין? מֵחוּלְדָּה וּבוֹר. וּמַה הַמַּאֲמִין בְּחוּלְדָּה וּבוֹר כָּךְ, הַמַּאֲמִין בְּהַקָּדוֹשׁ בָּרוּךְ הוּא עַל אַחַת כַּמָּה וְכַמָּה.

And Rabbi Ami said: Come and see how great the **faithful people are,** and how God assists them. **From where** is it derived? **From** the story of the **marten [*ḥulda*]**[B] **and the pit.**[N] Once a young man saved a girl who had fallen into a pit. After rescuing her they swore to remain faithful to each other, and they declared the pit and a passing marten their witnesses. As time went by the young man forgot his vow and married another woman. They had two children, both of whom died tragically, one by falling into a pit and the other when he was bitten by a marten. Their unusual deaths led the young man to realize his error and he returned to the first woman. **And if this** is the outcome for one **who believes in** signs from **a pit and a marten, all the more so** for **one who has faith in the Holy One, Blessed be He.**

אָמַר רַבִּי יוֹחָנָן: כָּל הַמַּצְדִּיק אֶת עַצְמוֹ מִלְּמַטָּה, מַצְדִּיקִין עָלָיו הַדִּין מִלְּמַעְלָה, שֶׁנֶּאֱמַר: "אֱמֶת מֵאֶרֶץ תִּצְמָח, וְצֶדֶק מִשָּׁמַיִם נִשְׁקָף". רַבִּי חִיָּיא בַּר אָבִין אָמַר רַב הוּנָא: מֵהָכָא: "וּכְיִרְאָתְךָ עֶבְרָתֶךָ".

§ **Rabbi Yoḥanan said: Whoever is exacting with himself,** by striving to act righteously in every way on earth **below,**[NB] **he is judged in an exact manner** in Heaven **above,** in order to improve him further still, **as it is stated: "Truth springs out of the earth, and righteousness has looked down from heaven"** (Psalms 85:12). **Rabbi Ḥiyya bar Avin said** that **Rav Huna**[P] **said** that this idea is derived **from here: "And Your wrath is according to the fear that is due to You"** (Psalms 90:11). The level of God's wrath correlates with the offender's fear of God.

NOTES

He places his soul in his palm – מֵשִׂים נַפְשׁוֹ בְּכַפּוֹ: This means that one must express his innermost thoughts, so that his prayers convey his true feelings (see Rashi; *Shita Mekubbetzet*). Some suggest that Rabbi Ami is alluding to the idea that one must immerse himself in prayer to the point where he strips himself of all materiality, so that his spirit alone communicates with God (see *Nefesh HaḤayyim*).

From the marten and the pit – מֵחוּלְדָּה וּבוֹר: Apparently this story was well known in talmudic times, and did not require retelling. The episode, which is briefly summarized by Rashi and *Tosafot*, is cited by the *Arukh* in a much fuller version, based on a tradition of the *ge'onim*.

Whoever is exacting with himself below – כָּל הַמַּצְדִּיק אֶת עַצְמוֹ מִלְּמַטָּה: According to one interpretation, someone who makes great efforts to act in an exact manner will be treated by God with exacting justice. This individual will be punished in this world for even the slightest infractions, so that he will be entirely cleansed and ready to receive his full reward in the World-to-Come (Rashi; *Shita Mekubbetzet*). Others explain Rabbi Yoḥanan's statement in the opposite manner: One who acts in a particularly righteous manner in this world will be treated by God with special compassion and charity (Rabbi Elyakim).

BACKGROUND

Marten [*ḥulda*] – חוּלְדָּה: The *ḥulda* mentioned in the Talmud has not been clearly identified. Israel Aharoni, an influential early-twentieth-century Israeli zoologist, proposed that it is the brown rat. The brown rat is indeed predatory, and therefore *ḥulda* became the general name for the rat in modern Hebrew. However, we now know that brown rats reached the Middle East from Norway only very recently; in the talmudic era, the only rat in the Middle East was the black rat, a much smaller rodent, which is not predatory. A more viable opinion is that of the medieval European rabbinic tradition, which identifies the *ḥulda* as a member of the weasel family. The weasel itself does not live in the Middle East nowadays, although it did live there in the early biblical era and possibly survived through to talmudic times. However, it is exclusively carnivorous, and would not drag leavened bread, as is mentioned in tractate *Pesaḥim*. As the marten, which belongs to the same family, is found in Israel, it may be the *ḥulda*.

Marten

Whoever is exacting with himself below – כָּל הַמַּצְדִּיק אֶת עַצְמוֹ מִלְּמַטָּה: This idea appears in many statements of the Sages, both by way of interpretations of verses as well as in the form of isolated comments. As a general principle, greatness and righteousness do not exempt one from his duties or from the judgment of Heaven. On the contrary, the greater and more pious the individual, the more is demanded of him and the more severe the punishment for his misdeeds.

PERSONALITIES

Rav Huna – רַב הוּנָא: One of the greatest Babylonian *amora'im* of the second generation, Rav Huna was closely associated with his teacher, Rav. Although Rav Huna was of aristocratic descent and belonged to the house of the Exilarch, he was exceedingly poor for many years. Later he grew wealthy and lived in comfort, while distributing his money for the public good.

Rav Huna was the greatest of Rav's students, so much so that Shmuel, Rav's colleague, treated him with marked respect and sent questions to him. After Rav's death, Rav Huna became the head of the academy of Sura, a position he occupied for about forty years. His eminence in Torah knowledge and his noble character helped turn the Sura academy into the preeminent Torah center for many centuries. Due to Rav Huna's great knowledge of Torah, the *halakha* is almost always decided in accordance with his opinion against that of his colleagues and the other members of his generation, with the exception of monetary cases, in which Rav Naḥman's rulings are accepted.

Rav Huna had many disciples, some of whom received their Torah knowledge directly from him. Moreover, Rav's younger students continued to study with Rav Huna, his disciple. Rav Huna's son, Rabba bar Rav Huna, was one of the greatest Sages of the next generation.

רֵישׁ לָקִישׁ אָמַר: מֵהָכָא: ״פָּגַעְתָּ אֶת שָׂשׂ וְעֹשֵׂה צֶדֶק; בִּדְרָכֶיךָ יִזְכְּרוּךָ; הֵן אַתָּה קָצַפְתָּ וַנֶּחֱטָא; בָּהֶם עוֹלָם וְנִוָּשֵׁעַ״. אָמַר רַבִּי יְהוֹשֻׁעַ בֶּן לֵוִי: כָּל הַשָּׂמֵחַ בַּיִּסּוּרִין שֶׁבָּאִין עָלָיו מֵבִיא יְשׁוּעָה לָעוֹלָם, שֶׁנֶּאֱמַר: ״בָּהֶם עוֹלָם וְנִוָּשֵׁעַ״.

Reish Lakish said that this principle is derived **from here: "You took him away who joyfully performed righteousness, those who remembered You in Your ways, behold You were wroth, and we sinned, upon them have we stayed of old, that we might be saved"** (Isaiah 64:4). This verse also teaches that God displays wrath specifically due to the transgressions of those who are accustomed to acting righteously. **Rabbi Yehoshua ben Levi said** concerning the same verse: **Whoever is joyful in** the **suffering** that comes upon him **brings salvation to the world** [*olam*], **as it is stated: "Upon them have we stayed of old** [*olam*], **that we might be saved."**

אָמַר רֵישׁ לָקִישׁ: מַאי דִּכְתִיב: ״וְעָצַר אֶת הַשָּׁמַיִם״? בְּשָׁעָה שֶׁהַשָּׁמַיִם נֶעֱצָרִין מִלְּהוֹרִיד טַל וּמָטָר, דּוֹמֶה לְאִשָּׁה שֶׁמְּחַבֶּלֶת וְאֵינָהּ יוֹלֶדֶת. וְהַיְינוּ דְּאָמַר רֵישׁ לָקִישׁ מִשּׁוּם בַּר קַפָּרָא: נֶאֶמְרָה עֲצִירָה בִּגְשָׁמִים וְנֶאֶמְרָה עֲצִירָה בְּאִשָּׁה,

§ Returning to the topic of rain, **Reish Lakish said: What is** the meaning of that **which is written: "And He will close up the heavens"** (Deuteronomy 11:17)? This verse teaches that **when the heavens are closed up from bringing down dew and rain,** this is **similar to a woman who has the pangs of labor and** yet **does not give birth,** as the heavens themselves suffer from their inability to bring down rain and dew. **And this is what Reish Lakish said in the name of bar Kappara: Closing up is stated with regard to rains, and closing up is** likewise **stated with regard to a woman.**

Perek **I**
Daf **8** Amud **b**

LANGUAGE

Vault [*kuba*] – קוּבָּה: In the language of the Mishna, this term means a small house or a tent, similar to the Arabic قبة, *qubba*.

נֶאֶמְרָה עֲצִירָה בְּאִשָּׁה, שֶׁנֶּאֱמַר: ״כִּי עָצֹר עָצַר ה׳ בְּעַד כָּל רֶחֶם״. וְנֶאֶמְרָה עֲצִירָה בִּגְשָׁמִים, דִּכְתִיב: ״וְעָצַר אֶת הַשָּׁמַיִם״.

Reish Lakish elaborates: **Closing up is stated with regard to a woman** who cannot give birth, **as it is stated: "For the Lord has fast close up all the wombs"** (Genesis 20:18), **and closing up is stated with regard to rains, as it is written: "And He will close up the heavens"** (Deuteronomy 11:17).

נֶאֱמַר לֵידָה בְּאִשָּׁה וְנֶאֱמַר לֵידָה בִּגְשָׁמִים. נֶאֱמַר לֵידָה בְּאִשָּׁה, דִּכְתִיב: ״וַתַּהַר וַתֵּלֶד בֵּן״. וְנֶאֱמַר לֵידָה בִּגְשָׁמִים דִּכְתִיב: ״וְהוֹלִידָהּ, וְהִצְמִיחָהּ״.

Likewise, an expression of **giving birth is stated with regard to a woman, and** an expression of **giving birth is** also **stated with regard to rain.** Specifically, **giving birth is stated with regard to a woman, as it is written** in the case of Rachel, when God had mercy on her: **"And she conceived and gave birth to a son"** (Genesis 30:23). **And giving birth is stated with regard to rain, as it is written:** "For as the rain comes down, and the snow from heaven, and does not return there, except it waters the earth **and causes it to give birth and bud"** (Isaiah 55:10).

נֶאֱמַר פְּקִידָה בְּאִשָּׁה, וְנֶאֱמַר פְּקִידָה בִּגְשָׁמִים. נֶאֱמַר פְּקִידָה בְּאִשָּׁה, דִּכְתִיב: ״וַה׳ פָּקַד אֶת שָׂרָה״. וְנֶאֱמַר פְּקִידָה בִּגְשָׁמִים, דִּכְתִיב: ״פָּקַדְתָּ הָאָרֶץ וַתְּשֹׁקְקֶהָ; רַבַּת תַּעְשְׁרֶנָּה פֶּלֶג אֱלֹהִים מָלֵא מָיִם״.

Lastly, an expression of **remembering is stated** in connection **with a woman, and** an expression of **remembering is** also **stated** in connection **to rain. Remembering is stated** in connection **with a woman, as it is written: "And the Lord remembered Sarah"** (Genesis 21:1), **and remembering is stated** in connection **to rain, as it is written: "You have remembered the earth and have watered it; greatly enriching it, with the pool of God that is full of water"** (Psalms 65:10).

מַאי: ״פֶּלֶג אֱלֹהִים מָלֵא מָיִם״? תָּנָא: כְּמִין קוּבָּה יֵשׁ בָּרָקִיעַ, שֶׁמִּמֶּנָּה גְּשָׁמִים יוֹצְאִין.

The Gemara asks a question with regard to this verse. **What** is the meaning of the phrase: **"With the pool of God that is full of water"?** The Gemara answers that it was **taught** in a *baraita*: **There is a kind of vault** [*kuba*][L] **in the sky, out of which the rain falls.**

אָמַר רַבִּי שְׁמוּאֵל בַּר נַחְמָנִי: מַאי דִּכְתִיב: ״אִם לְשֵׁבֶט, אִם לְאַרְצוֹ, אִם לְחֶסֶד, יַמְצִאֵהוּ״? ״אִם לְשֵׁבֶט״, בֶּהָרִים וּבִגְבָעוֹת. ״אִם לְחֶסֶד יַמְצִאֵהוּ לְאַרְצוֹ״, בְּשָׂדוֹת וּבִכְרָמִים.

Rabbi Shmuel bar Naḥmani said: What is the meaning of that **which is written:** "Whatever he commands them upon the face of the habitable world, **whether it is for correction, or for His earth, or for mercy that He causes it to come"** (Job 37:12–13)? The phrase **"whether it is for correction"** means that if the people are judged unfavorably, the rain will fall **on the mountains and on the hills.** The phrase "or for His earth" indicates that if they have been judged **"for mercy," He will cause it to come "for His earth," on the fields and on the vineyards.**

"אם לשבט", לאילנות. "אם לארצו", לזרעים. "אם לחסד ימצאהו", בורות, שיחין, ומערות.

Alternatively, the phrase **"whether it is for correction"** means that the rain will provide benefit only **for the trees; "or for His earth"** indicates that rain will fall solely for the benefit **of seeds;** and **"or for mercy that He causes it to come"** means that rain will fill the **cisterns, ditches, and caves** with enough water to last the dry season.

בימי רבי שמואל בר נחמני הוה כפנא ומותנא. אמרי: היכי נעביד? ניבעי רחמי אתרתי? לא אפשר. אלא, ליבעי רחמי אמותנא, וכפנא ניסבול. אמר להו רבי שמואל בר נחמני: ניבעי רחמי אכפנא, דכי יהיב רחמנא שובעא, לחיי הוא דיהיב, דכתיב: "פותח את ידך ומשביע לכל חי רצון".

§ The Gemara relates: **In the days of Rabbi Shmuel bar Naḥmani there was a famine and a plague.** The Sages **said: What** should we **do? Should we pray for mercy for two** troubles, both the famine and the plague? This is **not possible,** as it is improper to pray for the alleviation of two afflictions at once. **Rather, let us pray for mercy for the plague, and** as for the **famine,** we must **bear** it. **Rabbi Shmuel bar Naḥmani said to them:** On the contrary, **let us pray for mercy for the famine, as when the Merciful One provides plenty, He gives it for** the sake of **the living,** i.e., if God answers this prayer then he will certainly bring an end to the plague as well, **as it is written: "You open Your hand and satisfy every living thing with favor"** (Psalms 145:16).

ומנלן דלא מצלינן אתרתי? דכתיב: "ונצומה ונבקשה מאלהינו על זאת". מכלל דאיכא אחריתי. במערבא אמרי משמיה דרבי חגי מהכא: "ורחמין למבעא מן קדם אלה שמיא על רזא דנה". מכלל דאיכא אחריתי.

The Gemara explains: **And from where do we** derive **that** one should not pray **for two** troubles[H] simultaneously? **As it is written: "So we fasted and beseeched our God for this"** (Ezra 8:23). **From the fact** that the verse states: "For this," it may be inferred **that there is another** trouble about which the people did not pray. **In the West,** Eretz Yisrael, **they say in the name of Rabbi Ḥaggai** that this idea comes **from here: "That they might ask mercy of the God of Heaven concerning this secret"** (Daniel 2:18). **From the fact** that the verse states: "This secret," it may be inferred **that there is another** trouble about which they did not pray.

בימי רבי זירא, גזור שמדא, וגזור דלא למיתב בתעניתא. אמר להו רבי זירא: נקבליה עילוון, ולכי בטיל שמדא, ליתביה.

In a similar vein, the Gemara relates: **In the days of Rabbi Zeira a decree of** religious **persecution** was decreed against the Jews. **And** as the **decree** was **that they were not** allowed **to fast,** the Jews were certainly unable to fast and pray for the nullification of the decree itself. **Rabbi Zeira said to** the people: **Let us take** a fast **upon ourselves,**[H] despite the fact that in practice we cannot observe it, **and when** the decree of religious **persecution is annulled we will observe the fast.**

אמרי ליה: מנא לך הא? אמר להו: דכתיב: "ויאמר אלי: אל תירא, דניאל, כי מן היום הראשון אשר נתת את לבך להבין, ולהתענות לפני אלהיך נשמעו דבריך".

They said to him: From where do you know **this,** the fact that one may take a fast upon himself that he cannot observe? Rabbi Zeira **said to them** that the reason is **as it is written: "Then he said to me: Fear not, Daniel, for from the first day that you set your heart to understand, and to fast before your God, your words were heard"** (Daniel 10:12). This verse indicates that from the moment one turns his heart to fast, his prayers are heard.

אמר רבי יצחק: אפילו שנים כשני אליהו, וירדו גשמים בערבי שבתות, אינן אלא סימן קללה. היינו דאמר רבה בר שילא: קשה יומא דמיטרא כיומא דדינא. אמר אמימר: אי לא דצריך לברייתא, בעינן רחמי ומבטלינן ליה.

The Gemara returns to the topic of rain. **Rabbi Yitzḥak said: Even** in **years like the years of Elijah,** when God decreed that no rain would fall, if **rain falls on Shabbat eves it is nothing other** than **a sign of a curse,** as the rain disrupts the preparations for Shabbat. **This is** the same as that **which Rabba bar Sheila said: A rainy day is as difficult as a judgment day.**[N] **Ameimar** even **said:** Were it **not** for the fact **that** rain is needed **by people, we would pray for mercy and** to **annul it,** due to the nuisances that rain causes.

ואמר רבי יצחק: שמש בשבת צדקה לעניים, שנאמר: "וזרחה לכם יראי שמי שמש צדקה ומרפא". ואמר רבי יצחק: גדול יום הגשמים, שאפילו פרוטה שבכיס מתברכת בו, שנאמר: "לתת מטר ארצך בעתו ולברך את כל מעשה ידך".

And Rabbi Yitzḥak said: Sun on Shabbat is charity for the poor,[N] who are then able to enjoy the outdoors without suffering from cold. **As it is stated: "But for you who fear My name, the sun of righteousness shall arise with healing in its wings"** (Malachi 3:20). **And Rabbi Yitzḥak** further **said: The day of the rains is great, as even a *peruta* in** one's **pocket is blessed on it,**[N] **as it is stated: "To give the rain of your land in its due time, and to bless all the work of your hand"** (Deuteronomy 28:12).

HALAKHA

That one should not pray for two troubles – דלא מצלינן אתרתי: If a community is suffering from two afflictions, it should petition for the alleviation of only one of them. The members of the community should recite: Even though we suffer from many afflictions, it is only with respect to this one affliction that we pray before You. If the community suffers from both famine and plague, it should petition for mercy from the famine. The reason is that if God answers their prayers, He will provide them with food that will restore them to good health (*Shulḥan Arukh, Oraḥ Ḥayyim* 576:15).

Let us take upon ourselves – נקבליה עילוון: A single individual who is being pursued by enemies is not permitted to fast, as people under threat must preserve their strength. Likewise, if a city is surrounded by a hostile army, the residents may not fast. Instead, they should take upon themselves the obligation to observe several fasts when they are no longer in danger, in accordance with the opinion of Rabbi Zeira (*Shulḥan Arukh, Oraḥ Ḥayyim* 571:3).

NOTES

As a judgment day – כיומא דדינא: Rashi explains, in accordance with this version of the text, that ordinary activities can be upset by rain, just as they can be disturbed by the noise and tumult emanating from the courthouses on Mondays and Thursdays, when the courts are in session. Rain is all the more disruptive on Fridays, when preparations for Shabbat are underway. Others suggest that the text should be slightly emended so that it reads: A rainy day is difficult on a judgment day (Maharsha). According to this amended version, the Gemara is not providing a comparison but is simply stating that rain causes problems if it falls on a Monday or a Thursday, when the courts are in session. The reason is that on rainy days it is difficult for villagers to travel to the courts, which are found only in the larger cities. Likewise, it is harder to complete one's Shabbat preparations on a rainy Friday.

Sun on Shabbat is charity for the poor – שמש בשבת צדקה לעניים: Some commentators suggest that the poor are especially in need of sunny weather on Shabbat, as they often do not have suitably warm clothing, and on Shabbat they cannot keep themselves warm by engaging in physical labor (*Shita Mekubbetzet*). Others explain that the poor suffer from intestinal pains on Shabbat, because they change their dietary habits on that day and eat much more than during the rest of the week. Therefore, they are in particular need of the healing power of sunny weather (*Iyyun Ya'akov*).

The proof text cited by Rabbi Yitzḥak is somewhat problematic, as the verse does not mention Shabbat at all. Rashi explains that the phrase: You who fear My name, is referring to Shabbat observers. Others point out that the verse in Malachi quoted by Rabbi Yitzḥak alludes to the following verse: "Also the foreigners, who join themselves to the Lord, to minister to Him…to be His servants, every one who keeps Shabbat from profaning it" (Isaiah 56:6). This verse indicates that the proper observance of Shabbat is an essential feature of the fear of God (Rabbi Yoshiya Pinto).

Even a *peruta* in one's pocket is blessed on it – אפילו פרוטה שבכיס מתברכת בו: Rashi notes that rain is a blessing not only for the fields and their produce, but for a person's business pursuits, even those that are not directly dependent on rain. Others add that ample rainfall stimulates the entire economy, even the nonagricultural sector, as when the crops are plentiful food prices fall and more money is available for other business ventures (*Shita Mekubbetzet*).

HALAKHA

One who enters to measure in his granary – **הַנִּכְנָס לָמוֹד אֶת גָּרְנוֹ**: Before measuring the produce in one's granary, one recites: May it be Your will, Lord our God, that You send a blessing upon this pile. Furthermore, while one is actually measuring, one may also recite: Blessed is He who sends a blessing upon this pile. However, one who has completed the measurement may no longer recite a blessing, and if one does so, it is considered a vain prayer (*Shulḥan Arukh, Oraḥ Ḥayyim* 230:2).

וְאָמַר רַבִּי יִצְחָק: אֵין הַבְּרָכָה מְצוּיָה אֶלָּא בְּדָבָר הַסָּמוּי מִן הָעַיִן, שֶׁנֶּאֱמַר: ״יְצַו ה׳ אִתְּךָ אֶת הַבְּרָכָה בַּאֲסָמֶיךָ״. תָּנָא דְּבֵי רַבִּי יִשְׁמָעֵאל: אֵין הַבְּרָכָה מְצוּיָה אֶלָּא בְּדָבָר שֶׁאֵין הָעַיִן שׁוֹלֶטֶת בּוֹ, שֶׁנֶּאֱמַר: ״יְצַו ה׳ אִתְּךָ אֶת הַבְּרָכָה בַּאֲסָמֶיךָ״.

And apropos blessings, **Rabbi Yitzḥak said: A blessing is found only in an object that is hidden** [*samui*] **from the eye,**[N] not in an item visible to all, as public miracles are exceedingly rare. **As it is stated: "The Lord will command His blessing upon you in your barns** [*ba'asamekha*]" (Deuteronomy 28:8). Rabbi Yitzḥak's exposition is based on the linguistic similarity between *samui* and *asamekha*. Likewise, **the school of Rabbi Yishmael taught: A blessing is found only in an object that is not exposed to the eye,**[N] **as it is stated: "The Lord will command His blessing upon you in your barns."**

תָּנוּ רַבָּנַן: הַנִּכְנָס לָמוֹד אֶת גָּרְנוֹ אוֹמֵר: יְהִי רָצוֹן מִלְּפָנֶיךָ, ה׳ אֱלֹהֵינוּ, שֶׁתִּשְׁלַח בְּרָכָה בְּמַעֲשֵׂה יָדֵנוּ. הִתְחִיל לָמוֹד, אוֹמֵר: בָּרוּךְ הַשּׁוֹלֵחַ בְּרָכָה בַּכְּרִי הַזֶּה. מָדַד וְאַחַר כָּךְ בֵּירַךְ, הֲרֵי זוֹ תְּפִלַּת שָׁוְא, לְפִי שֶׁאֵין הַבְּרָכָה מְצוּיָה, לֹא בְּדָבָר הַשָּׁקוּל וְלֹא בְּדָבָר הַמָּדוּד וְלֹא בְּדָבָר הַמָּנוּי אֶלָּא בְּדָבָר הַסָּמוּי מִן הָעַיִן.

The Sages taught: One who enters to measure produce **in his granary**[HN] **recites: May it be Your will, Lord our God, that You send a blessing upon the work of our hands.** After he has **begun to measure, he recites: Blessed** is He **who sends a blessing upon this pile.** If one first **measured and afterward recited the blessing, it is a prayer** in vain, **as a blessing is not found either in an object that is weighed or in an object that is measured or in an object that is counted,** as these would constitute open miracles. **Rather,** a blessing is found only **in an object that is hidden from the eye.**

קִבּוּץ; גְּיָיסוֹת; צְדָקָה; מַעֲשֵׂר; פַּרְנָס; סִימָן. אָמַר רַבִּי יוֹחָנָן: גָּדוֹל יוֹם הַגְּשָׁמִים כְּיוֹם קִבּוּץ גָּלֻיּוֹת, שֶׁנֶּאֱמַר: ״שׁוּבָה ה׳ אֶת שְׁבִיתֵנוּ כַּאֲפִיקִים בַּנֶּגֶב״. וְאֵין ״אֲפִיקִים״ אֶלָּא מָטָר, שֶׁנֶּאֱמַר: ״וַיֵּרָאוּ אֲפִקֵי יָם״.

§ The Gemara cites five statements of Rabbi Yoḥanan, in accordance with the following **mnemonic: Ingathering; armies; charity; tithe; sustainer. Rabbi Yoḥanan said: The day of the rains is as great as the day of the ingathering of the exiles, as it is stated: "Turn our captivity, O Lord, as the streams in the dry land"** (Psalms 126:4), **and "streams"** means **nothing other** than **rain, as it is stated: "And the streams of the sea appeared"** (II Samuel 22:16).

וְאָמַר רַבִּי יוֹחָנָן: גָּדוֹל יוֹם הַגְּשָׁמִים, שֶׁאֲפִילּוּ גְּיָיסוֹת פּוֹסְקוֹת בּוֹ, שֶׁנֶּאֱמַר: ״תְּלָמֶיהָ רַוֵּה; נַחֵת גְּדוּדֶיהָ״. וְאָמַר רַבִּי יוֹחָנָן: אֵין הַגְּשָׁמִים נֶעֱצָרִין אֶלָּא בִּשְׁבִיל פּוֹסְקֵי צְדָקָה בָּרַבִּים וְאֵין נוֹתְנִין, שֶׁנֶּאֱמַר: ״נְשִׂיאִים וְרוּחַ, וְגֶשֶׁם אָיִן, אִישׁ מִתְהַלֵּל בְּמַתַּת שָׁקֶר״.

And Rabbi Yoḥanan said: The day of the rains is great, as **even armies stop fighting on it** due to the rain and mud. **As it is stated: "Watering its ridges abundantly; settling down its furrows** [*gedudeha*]" (Psalms 65:11). As the word *gedudim* can mean both furrows or armies and is spelled identically with each meaning, this alludes to the idea that during the rainy season soldiers become entrenched in place. **And Rabbi Yoḥanan** further **said: Rain is withheld only due to those who pledge charity in public**[N] **but do not give it, as it is stated: "As vapors and wind without rain, so is he who boasts of a false gift"** (Proverbs 25:14).

וַאֲמַר רַבִּי יוֹחָנָן: מַאי דִּכְתִיב:

And Rabbi Yoḥanan said: What is the meaning of that **which is written:**

NOTES

In an object that is hidden from the eye – **בְּדָבָר הַסָּמוּי מִן הָעַיִן**: Some commentaries explain that a divine blessing is considered a miracle, and miracles are generally performed by God in a discreet manner, as He does not want the general public to witness a change in the natural order. Consequently, a blessing is to be found only in an object that is hidden from the eye. Once an item is exposed to the public gaze it is no longer subject to a divine blessing (*Sefat Emet*).

That is not exposed to the eye – **שֶׁאֵין הָעַיִן שׁוֹלֶטֶת בּוֹ**: It is unclear whether there is any substantial difference between Rabbi Yitzḥak's formulation of an object hidden from the eye, and the version of the school of Rabbi Yishmael, who refer to something that is not exposed to the eye. Indeed, some commentaries maintain that these two expressions bear the same meaning (Maharsha). Some note that miracles are normally performed discreetly, as it is considered inappropriate for uninvolved bystanders to observe their occurrence (*Torat Ḥayyim*; see II Kings 4:4). In general, with regard to merchandise that is not exposed to the eye, it has been pointed out that it is unwise to do business with large objects such as barrels, as they attract too much attention (Rosh).

One who enters to measure in his granary – **הַנִּכְנָס לָמוֹד אֶת גָּרְנוֹ**: According to some commentaries, the blessings prescribed here are recited with the full formula beginning with: Blessed are You, Lord our God, King of the Universe (Ritva). The difficulty with this explanation is that formal blessings are normally recited only for definite occurrences, whereas here the farmer is praying for general, unspecified assistance. To resolve this problem, the Ritva quotes the Ramban, who explains that this blessing is recited only when one measures his produce to determine the quantity of tithes to separate, as God promises a blessing to a farmer who tithes his crops (see Malachi 3:10).

Those who pledge charity in public – **פּוֹסְקֵי צְדָקָה בָּרַבִּים**: Rashi explains that Rabbi Yoḥanan refers to people who pledge charity specifically in public, as the pledge might have been stated to impress others and they are liable to neglect it. By contrast, it is unusual for one who pledges charity in private to fail to donate the money, as if he did not intend to fulfill his pledge he would not have said it in the first place. Others suggest that in response to the disappointment suffered by the poor after one has made a public pledge of charity and failed to fulfill his promise, God causes the clouds and wind to disperse, which causes the world a corresponding disappointment when the rain they were promised fails to fall (Maharsha; see also Rashi on Proverbs 25:14).

״עַשֵּׂר תְּעַשֵּׂר״? עַשֵּׂר בִּשְׁבִיל שֶׁתִּתְעַשֵּׁר.

"A tithe shall you tithe [*te'aser*]" (Deuteronomy 14:22)?[N] This phrase can be interpreted homiletically: **Take a tithe [*asser*] so that you will become wealthy [*titasher*],**[H] in the merit of the mitzva.

אַשְׁכַּחֵיהּ רַבִּי יוֹחָנָן לִינוֹקָא דְּרֵישׁ לָקִישׁ. אֲמַר לֵיהּ: אֵימָא לִי פְּסוּקָךְ. אֲמַר לֵיהּ: ״עַשֵּׂר תְּעַשֵּׂר״. אֲמַר לֵיהּ: וּמַאי ״עַשֵּׂר תְּעַשֵּׂר״? אֲמַר לֵיהּ: עַשֵּׂר בִּשְׁבִיל שֶׁתִּתְעַשֵּׁר. אֲמַר לֵיהּ: מְנָא לָךְ? אֲמַר לֵיהּ: זִיל נַסִּי.

Rabbi Yoḥanan found the **young son of Reish Lakish.**[P] **He said to** the boy: **Recite to me your verse,** i.e., the verse you studied today in school. The boy **said to him: "A tithe shall you tithe."** The boy further **said to** Rabbi Yoḥanan: **But** what is the meaning of this phrase: **"A tithe shall you tithe"?** Rabbi Yoḥanan **said to him:** The verse means: **Take a tithe so that you will become wealthy.** The boy **said to** Rabbi Yoḥanan: **From where do you** derive that this is so? Rabbi Yoḥanan **said to him: Go and test**[N] it.

אֲמַר לֵיהּ: וּמִי שָׁרֵי לְנַסּוּיֵיהּ לְהַקָּדוֹשׁ בָּרוּךְ הוּא? וְהָכְתִיב: ״לֹא תְנַסּוּ אֶת ה׳״! אֲמַר לֵיהּ: הָכִי אֲמַר רַבִּי הוֹשַׁעְיָא: חוּץ מִזּוֹ, שֶׁנֶּאֱמַר: ״הָבִיאוּ אֶת כׇּל הַמַּעֲשֵׂר אֶל בֵּית הָאוֹצָר, וִיהִי טֶרֶף בְּבֵיתִי, וּבְחָנוּנִי נָא בָּזֹאת אָמַר ה׳ צְבָאוֹת אִם לֹא אֶפְתַּח לָכֶם אֵת אֲרֻבּוֹת הַשָּׁמַיִם, וַהֲרִיקֹתִי לָכֶם בְּרָכָה עַד בְּלִי דָי״.

The boy **said to him: And is it permitted to test the Holy One, Blessed be He? But isn't it written: "You shall not test the Lord your God"** (Deuteronomy 6:16)? Rabbi Yoḥanan **said to** the boy that **Rabbi Hoshaya said as follows:** It is prohibited to test God in any way, **except in this** case of tithes, **as it is stated: "Bring the whole tithe into the storeroom, that there may be food in My house, and test Me now by this, said the Lord of hosts, if I will not open for you the windows of heaven, and pour out for you a blessing that there shall be more than sufficiency"** (Malachi 3:10).

מַאי: ״עַד בְּלִי דָי״? אָמַר רָמִי בַּר חָמָא אָמַר רַב: עַד שֶׁיִּבְלוּ שִׂפְתוֹתֵיכֶם מִלּוֹמַר: דַּי. אֲמַר לֵיהּ: אִי הֲוַת מָטֵי הָתָם לְהַאי פְּסוּקָא, לָא הֲוֵית צְרִיכְנָא לָךְ וּלְהוֹשַׁעְיָא רַבָּךְ.

In relation to the above verse, the Gemara asks: **What** is the meaning of the phrase: **"That there shall be more than sufficiency [*ad beli dai*]"? Rami bar Ḥama said** that **Rav said:** It means that the abundance will be so great **that your lips will be worn out [*yivlu*],** similar to the word *beli*, **from saying enough [*dai*].** Returning to the above incident, the Gemara adds that the boy **said to** Rabbi Yoḥanan: Your claim appears explicitly in a verse. **If I had arrived there,** at this verse, **I would not have needed you or Hoshaya your teacher,** a I could have understood it on my own.

וְתוּ אַשְׁכְּחֵיהּ רַבִּי יוֹחָנָן לִינוֹקֵיהּ דְּרֵישׁ לָקִישׁ, דְּיָתֵיב וְאָמַר: ״אִוֶּלֶת אָדָם תְּסַלֵּף דַּרְכּוֹ, וְעַל ה׳ יִזְעַף לִבּוֹ״.

The Gemara relates another story about the precociousness of this child. **And furthermore,** on a different occasion **Rabbi Yoḥanan found** the **young son of Reish Lakish, when he was sitting** and studying **and** he was **reciting** the verse: **"The foolishness of man perverts his way, and his heart frets against the Lord"** (Proverbs 19:3). This verse means that when someone sins and every manner of mishap befalls him, he complains and wonders why these things are happening to him.

יָתֵיב רַבִּי יוֹחָנָן וְקָא מַתְמַהּ. אֲמַר: מִי אִיכָּא מִידֵּי דִּכְתִיבִי בִּכְתוּבֵי דְּלָא רְמִיזִי בְּאוֹרַיְיתָא? אֲמַר לֵיהּ: אַטּוּ הָא מִי לָא רְמִיזִי? וְהָכְתִיב: ״וַיֵּצֵא לִבָּם וַיֶּחֶרְדוּ, אִישׁ אֶל אָחִיו לֵאמֹר: מַה זֹּאת עָשָׂה אֱלֹהִים לָנוּ״?

Rabbi Yoḥanan sat down and wondered aloud about this verse, **saying: Is there anything that is written in the Writings that is not alluded to in the Torah** at all? I cannot think of any hint of this idea in the Torah itself. The child **said to him: Is that to say** that **this** idea is really **not alluded to** in the Torah? **But isn't it written,** with regard to Joseph's brothers: **"And their heart failed them and they turned trembling to one to another, saying: What is this that God has done to us?"** (Genesis 42:28). This verse exemplifies the notion that when one sins and encounters troubles, he wonders why it is happening to him.

דַּל עֵינֵיהּ וַחֲזָא בֵּיהּ. אָתְיָא אִימֵּיהּ אַפִּיקְתֵּיהּ. אֲמַרָה לֵיהּ: תָּא מִקַּמֵּיהּ, דְּלָא לִיעֲבַד לָךְ כְּדַעֲבַד לַאֲבוּךְ.

Impressed by the youth's wisdom, Rabbi Yoḥanan **raised his eyes and stared at the boy.** At this point, the boy's **mother came and took him away, saying to him: Come away from** Rabbi Yoḥanan, **so that he does not do to you as he did to your father.** Reish Lakish, the boy's father, died during a heated dispute with Rabbi Yoḥanan over a Torah matter. The argument ended with an offended look from Rabbi Yoḥanan which caused Reish Lakish's death, and the boy's mother was afraid that her son might suffer the same fate.

NOTES

A tithe you shall tithe – עַשֵּׂר תְּעַשֵּׂר: Rabbi Yoḥanan's interpretation of the verse is generally understood as being based on the fact that the Hebrew letters *shin* and *sin* are written with the same character when written without vowels. Accordingly, the second verb can be read with the vowel placement of *shin* as *te'asher*, you will become wealthy, rather than with the vowel placement of *sin* as *te'aser*, you shall tithe. In other words, the verse guarantees that a person who carefully tithes his produce will be blessed with wealth. Alternatively, both verbs are read literally as referring to tithing: Tithe your produce properly so that you may be blessed with plenty and you will be able to tithe your produce many times again (Rabbeinu Ḥananel; see also Maharsha).

From where do you derive it…go test – מְנָא לָךְ...זִיל נַסִּי: Why does Reish Lakish's son ask Rabbi Yoḥanan for a source for his statement that a person who tithes his produce is promised wealth? After all, Rabbi Yoḥanan had just told him that this opinion is based on his interpretation of the expression: A tithe you shall tithe. Moreover, why does Rabbi Yoḥanan respond to the boy that he should go out and tithe to see for himself that he will become wealthy, when he can provide direct support for his opinion by quoting the verse in Malachi that he subsequently cites in response to the boy's next question?

The *Gevurat Ari* explains that Rabbi Yoḥanan does not interpret the expression: A tithe you shall tithe, as a mere promise that one who tithes his produce properly is promised wealth, but as permission for one to tithe his produce for the express purpose of a test as to whether or not God will bless him with wealth. Once he has grasped this point, the boy raises the difficulty that the verse in Deuteronomy indicates that one may not test God, to which Rabbi Yoḥanan answers that the verse in Malachi teaches that the case of tithing is an exception to this principle (*Gevurat Ari*).

HALAKHA

Take a tithe so that you will become wealthy – עַשֵּׂר בִּשְׁבִיל שֶׁתִּתְעַשֵּׁר: Although in general it is prohibited to test God, with regard to charity one may do so by giving charity and waiting to see if he will be rewarded. Some say that this dispensation applies only to tithes (Rema, based on *Beit Yosef*), while others further restrict it to tithes of produce (*Shenei Luḥot HaBerit*), but some authorities do not accept these limitations (*Arukh HaShulḥan*; *Shulḥan Arukh*, *Yoreh De'a* 247:4).

PERSONALITIES

The young son of Reish Lakish – יָנוֹקָא דְּרֵישׁ לָקִישׁ: Reish Lakish married the sister of Rabbi Yoḥanan, who was his principal teacher as well as his regular study partner and disputant. Their frequent disputes and discussions helped broaden and increase their understanding of Torah. Nevertheless, on one occasion Rabbi Yoḥanan grew angry with his student and gazed on him with such a severe countenance that Reish Lakish died. Reish Lakish left behind several children, both boys and girls, and the boy mentioned here was presumably his youngest. Based on the subject matter of the discussion and the style of the exchange, he was probably around seven or eight years old. His comments attest to both his mental acuity and his youthful impudence. Apparently this youth died at an early age, as we find no mention of any sons of Reish Lakish among the Sages of the subsequent generation.

NOTES

Sustenance comes only for the sake of many – פַּרְנָסָה בִּשְׁבִיל רַבִּים: According to Rashi, when Rabbi Yoḥanan says that rain falls even for an individual, he is referring to rain that someone requires so that his crops will not fail or produce yields inferior to those of his neighbors. When he says that sustenance is provided only for the sake of many, he means that a state of prosperity is not granted solely for the sake of an individual. Others explain that rain, which naturally leads to prosperity, falls even for the sake of a single worthy individual, whereas sustenance provided by supernatural means, e.g., manna from Heaven, is provided only when an entire community is considered worthy (Maharsha).

It returned in the merit of both Moses and Aaron – חָזְרָה בִּזְכוּת שְׁנֵיהֶן: Some commentators ask: If the miraculous well from which the Jews drew their water was restored to them due to the merit of Moses and Aaron, their merit should have prevented the well from disappearing in the first place. It has been suggested that although the well returned due to the merit of Moses and Aaron, it did not sustain the people after Miriam's death in the same manner as during Miriam's lifetime (*Ahavat Eitan*). Others state that the well disappeared when Miriam died to demonstrate to the Jews that while she was alive they were blessed with its waters primarily due to her merit (Maharsha).

As Reish Lakish taught – כִּדְדָרֵישׁ רֵישׁ לָקִישׁ: The commentaries struggle to explain the need to apply Reish Lakish's principle here. Most agree that Rabbi Abbahu's interpretation stands on its own but is reinforced by the statement of Reish Lakish (Rosh).

***Ki* has four meanings – כִּי מְשַׁמֵּשׁ בְּאַרְבַּע לְשׁוֹנוֹת:** In his Aramaic translation of the Torah, Onkelos consistently translates the Hebrew term *ki* with the Aramaic word *ari*. However, it can be argued that *ari* has the same wide spectrum of meanings as *ki* itself, so that Onkelos intentionally maintains the ambiguity of the original Hebrew (*Arukh*; Rashi).

It has been further noted that in fact the term *ki* bears other meanings in addition to the four suggested by Reish Lakish. For example, it often means when. Consequently, Reish Lakish is not providing a full list of all possible meanings of the word, but is saying that one should not mistakenly think that *ki* has one uniform meaning.

אָמַר רַבִּי יוֹחָנָן: מָטָר בִּשְׁבִיל יָחִיד. פַּרְנָסָה בִּשְׁבִיל רַבִּים. מָטָר בִּשְׁבִיל יָחִיד, דִּכְתִיב: ״יִפְתַּח ה׳ לְךָ אֶת אוֹצָרוֹ הַטּוֹב... לָתֵת מְטַר אַרְצְךָ״. פַּרְנָסָה בִּשְׁבִיל רַבִּים, דִּכְתִיב: ״הִנְנִי מַמְטִיר לָכֶם לֶחֶם״.

§ After this brief digression, the Gemara turns to the fifth in the series of statements by Rabbi Yoḥanan concerning rain. **Rabbi Yoḥanan said: Rain** falls even **for the sake of an individual,** in response to the petition of a single person in need of rain, whereas a blessing of **sustenance** comes only **for the sake of many.**[N] **Rain** falls even **for the sake of an individual, as it is written: "The Lord will open for you His good treasure,** the heavens, **to give the rain of your land"** (Deuteronomy 28:12). The fact that this verse is written in the second person singular demonstrates that rain can fall even for the sake of an individual. Rabbi Yoḥanan further proves that **sustenance** comes **for the sake of many, as it is written: "Behold I will cause to rain bread from the heavens for you"** (Exodus 16:4). Here, God is referring to the people in the plural form.

מֵיתִיבִי: רַבִּי יוֹסֵי בְּרַבִּי יְהוּדָה אוֹמֵר: שְׁלֹשָׁה פַּרְנָסִים טוֹבִים עָמְדוּ לְיִשְׂרָאֵל, אֵלּוּ הֵן: מֹשֶׁה, וְאַהֲרֹן, וּמִרְיָם. וְשָׁלֹשׁ מַתָּנוֹת טוֹבוֹת נִיתְּנוּ עַל יָדָם, וְאֵלּוּ הֵן: בְּאֵר, וְעָנָן, וּמָן. בְּאֵר בִּזְכוּת מִרְיָם. עַמּוּד עָנָן בִּזְכוּת אַהֲרֹן. מָן בִּזְכוּת מֹשֶׁה. מֵתָה מִרְיָם, נִסְתַּלֵּק הַבְּאֵר. שֶׁנֶּאֱמַר: ״וַתָּמָת שָׁם מִרְיָם״, וּכְתִיב בַּתְרֵיהּ: ״וְלֹא הָיָה מַיִם לָעֵדָה״. וְחָזְרָה בִּזְכוּת שְׁנֵיהֶן.

The Gemara **raises an objection** from a *baraita*: **Rabbi Yosei, son of Rabbi Yehuda,**[P] **says: Three good sustainers rose up for the Jewish people** during the exodus from Egypt, and **they are: Moses, Aaron and Miriam. And three good gifts were given** from Heaven **through their agency, and these are they: The well** of water, the pillar of **cloud, and the manna.** He elaborates: The **well** was given to the Jewish people **in the merit of Miriam;** the **pillar of cloud** was **in the merit of Aaron;** and the **manna in the merit of Moses.** When **Miriam died** the **well disappeared, as it is stated: "And Miriam died there"** (Numbers 20:1), **and it says thereafter** in the next verse: **"And there was no water for the congregation"** (Numbers 20:2). **But** the well **returned in the merit of both** Moses and Aaron.[N]

מֵת אַהֲרֹן, נִסְתַּלְּקוּ עַנְנֵי כָבוֹד, שֶׁנֶּאֱמַר: ״וַיִּשְׁמַע הַכְּנַעֲנִי, מֶלֶךְ עֲרָד״. מַה שְּׁמוּעָה שָׁמַע? שָׁמַע שֶׁמֵּת אַהֲרֹן וְנִסְתַּלְּקוּ עַנְנֵי כָבוֹד, וּכְסָבוּר נִיתְּנָה לוֹ רְשׁוּת לְהִלָּחֵם בְּיִשְׂרָאֵל. וְהַיְינוּ דִּכְתִיב ״וַיִּרְאוּ כָּל הָעֵדָה כִּי גָוַע אַהֲרֹן״.

When **Aaron died** the **clouds of glory disappeared, as it is stated: "And the Canaanite, the king of Arad heard"** (Numbers 33:40). **What report did he hear? He heard that Aaron had died and the clouds of glory had disappeared, and he thought that** the Jewish people were no longer protected by Heaven and therefore **he had been given permission to go to war against the Jewish people. And this** disappearance of the clouds **is** the meaning of that **which is written: "And all the congregation saw that [*ki*] Aaron was dead"** (Numbers 20:29).

אָמַר רַבִּי אַבָּהוּ: אַל תִּקְרֵי: ״וַיִּרְאוּ״, אֶלָּא: וַיֵּרָאוּ, כִּדְדָרֵישׁ רֵישׁ לָקִישׁ. דְּאָמַר רֵישׁ לָקִישׁ: כִּי מְשַׁמֵּשׁ בְּאַרְבַּע לְשׁוֹנוֹת: אִי, דִּלְמָא, אֶלָּא, דְּהָא.

Rabbi Abbahu said: Do not read the verse as: **"And they saw [*va'yiru*]"; rather,** read it as: **And they were seen [*va'yera'u*],** as the clouds which had concealed the Jewish people were temporarily removed. This is **as Reish Lakish taught.**[N] **As Reish Lakish said:** The term ***ki*** actually **has** at least **four** distinct **meanings:**[N] **If; perhaps; but; because,** or that. According to this interpretation, the verse would be rendered: And all the congregation was seen, because [*ki*] Aaron was dead.

חָזְרוּ שְׁנֵיהֶם בִּזְכוּת מֹשֶׁה. מֵת מֹשֶׁה, נִסְתַּלְּקוּ כּוּלָּן, שֶׁנֶּאֱמַר: ״וָאַכְחִד אֶת שְׁלֹשֶׁת הָרֹעִים בְּיֶרַח אֶחָד״. וְכִי בְּיֶרַח אֶחָד מֵתוּ? וַהֲלֹא מִרְיָם מֵתָה בְּנִיסָן, וְאַהֲרֹן בְּאָב, וּמֹשֶׁה בַּאֲדָר? אֶלָּא, מְלַמֵּד שֶׁנִּתְבַּטְּלוּ שָׁלֹשׁ מַתָּנוֹת טוֹבוֹת שֶׁנִּתְּנוּ עַל יָדָן, וְנִסְתַּלְּקוּ כּוּלָּן בְּיֶרַח אֶחָד.

The *baraita* continues: **Both** the well and the clouds of glory **returned in the merit of Moses.** However, when **Moses died all of them disappeared. As it is stated: "And I cut off the three shepherds in one month"** (Zechariah 11:8). **But did** the three shepherds really **die in one month? Didn't Miriam die in** the month of **Nisan, and Aaron in Av and Moses in Adar? Rather,** this verse **teaches** us **that** with the death of Moses the **three good gifts that were given through their agency were annulled, and** all three gifts **disappeared in one month,** which made it seem as though all three leaders had died at the same time.

PERSONALITIES

Rabbi Yosei, son of Rabbi Yehuda – רַבִּי יוֹסֵי בְּרַבִּי יְהוּדָה: Rabbi Yosei, son of Rabbi Yehuda, from the last generation of *tanna'im*, was the son of Rabbi Yehuda bar Il'ai. He was apparently a close disciple of his father, although he occasionally disagreed with him concerning matters of *halakha*. In his work as a halakhic authority he was closely associated with Rabbi Yehuda HaNasi, and his statements are mentioned several times in the Mishna, quite frequently in the *Tosefta*, and elsewhere. Rabbi Yosei, son of Rabbi Yehuda, was also highly prolific in *aggada*, and some well-known sayings are transmitted in his name.

אַלְמָא אַשְׁכְּחַן פַּרְנָסָה בִּשְׁבִיל יָחִיד! שָׁאנֵי מֹשֶׁה. כֵּיוָן דִּלְרַבִּים הוּא בָּעֵי, כְּרַבִּים דָּמֵי.

The Gemara explains the difficulty from this *baraita*. **Apparently, we find** that **sustenance** can come **for the sake of an individual,** as the *baraita* states that sustenance in the form of manna came for the sake of Moses. The Gemara answers: **Moses is different, since he requested** the manna **for many,** and therefore he was considered **like many,** not as an individual.

רַב הוּנָא בַּר מָנוֹחַ וְרַב שְׁמוּאֵל בַּר אִידִי וְרַב חִיָּיא מִוּוסְתָּנְיָא הֲווּ שְׁכִיחִי קַמֵּיהּ דְּרָבָא. כִּי נָח נַפְשֵׁיהּ דְּרָבָא אֲתוֹ לְקַמֵּיהּ דְּרַב פַּפָּא. כׇּל אֵימַת דַּהֲוָה אָמַר לְהוּ שְׁמַעְתָּא וְלָא הֲוָה מִסְתַּבְּרָא לְהוּ, הֲווּ מְרַמְּזִי אַהֲדָדֵי. חֲלַשׁ דַּעְתֵּיהּ.

The Gemara relates a story concerning the aforementioned verse from Zechariah. **Rav Huna bar Manoaḥ, Rav Shmuel bar Idi, and Rav Ḥiyya from Vastanya were** often **found before Rava,** as they were among his most distinguished students. **When Rava died, they came before Rav Pappa** to learn from him. However, as also they were great Sages, **whenever Rav Pappa would say a *halakha* that did not** sound **reasonable to them, they would gesture to each other** that Rav Pappa was not equal in stature to Rava. Rav Pappa **was offended** by their behavior.

Perek **I**
Daf **9** Amud **b**

אַקְרְוֵיהּ בְּחֶלְמֵיהּ: ״וָאַכְחִד אֶת שְׁלֹשֶׁת הָרֹעִים״. לְמָחָר, כִּי הֲווּ מִיפַּטְרוּ מִינֵּיהּ, אֲמַר לְהוּ: לֵיזְלוּ רַבָּנַן בִּשְׁלָמָא.

A verse **was read to** Rav Pappa **in a dream: "And I cut off the three shepherds in one month"** (Zechariah 11:8). **The next day, when they took their leave from him,** Rav Pappa **said to them: May the Rabbis go in peace,**[N] a hint that this would be their final parting. Rav Pappa thought that the three Sages would die as punishment for their behavior and he would never see them again.

רַב שִׁימִי בַּר אַשִׁי הֲוָה שְׁכִיחַ קַמֵּיהּ דְּרַב פַּפָּא. הֲוָה מַקְשֵׁי לֵיהּ טוּבָא. יוֹמָא חַד, חַזְיֵיהּ דְּנָפֵל עַל אַפֵּיהּ. שְׁמַעֵיהּ דְּאָמַר: רַחֲמָנָא לִיצְּלַן מִכִּיסּוּפָא דְשִׁימִי. קַבִּיל עֲלֵיהּ שְׁתִיקוּתָא, וְתוּ לָא אַקְשֵׁי לֵיהּ.

The Gemara relates a similar incident: **Rav Shimi bar Ashi** was often **found before Rav Pappa** and **would raise many objections against** the opinions of Rav Pappa. **One day** Rav Shimi bar Ashi saw Rav Pappa **fall on his face** after prayer. **He heard him say: May the Merciful One save me from the embarrassment of Shimi, and** as a result Rav Shimi bar Ashi **resolved to be silent and not to raise any further objections** against Rav Pappa, as he saw how greatly they pained his teacher.

וְאַף רֵישׁ לָקִישׁ סָבַר מָטָר בִּשְׁבִיל יָחִיד. דְּאָמַר רֵישׁ לָקִישׁ: מִנַּיִן לְמָטָר בִּשְׁבִיל יָחִיד? דִּכְתִיב: ״שַׁאֲלוּ מֵה׳ מָטָר בְּעֵת מַלְקוֹשׁ; ה׳ עֹשֶׂה חֲזִיזִים, וּמְטַר גֶּשֶׁם יִתֵּן לָהֶם; לְאִישׁ עֵשֶׂב בַּשָּׂדֶה״.

§ The Gemara returns to the issue of rain. **And Reish Lakish also maintains** that **rain** can fall **for the sake of an individual, as Reish Lakish said: From where** is it derived **that rain** falls even **for the sake of an individual? As it is written: "Ask of the Lord rain at the time of the last rain; even of the Lord who makes thunderclouds, and He will give them showers of rain; for a man grass in the field"** (Zechariah 10:1).

יָכוֹל לַכֹּל? תַּלְמוּד לוֹמַר: ״לְאִישׁ״. וְתַנְיָא: אִי ״לְאִישׁ״ יָכוֹל לְכׇל שְׂדוֹתָיו? תַּלְמוּד לוֹמַר: ״שָׂדֶה״. אִי שָׂדֶה, יָכוֹל לְכׇל הַשָּׂדֶה? תַּלְמוּד לוֹמַר: ״עֵשֶׂב״.

One **might** have thought that rain falls **for** the sake of **all** the Jewish people. **The verse** therefore **states: "For a man,"** i.e., for the needs of an individual **And it was** further **taught** in a *baraita*: **If** rain falls **"for a man,"** one **might** have thought that the rain is **for all his fields.** Therefore **the verse states: "Field,"** which indicates that at times it rains on only one field. **If** it rains on one **field,** one **might** have thought that the rain is **for the entire field.** This is why **the verse states: "Grass";** rain can fall for the sake of even a single plant in the field.

כִּי הָא דְּרַב דָּנִיאֵל בַּר קְטִינָא. הֲוָה לֵיהּ הַהִיא גִּינְּתָא. כׇּל יוֹמָא, הֲוָה אָזֵיל וְסָיֵיר לַהּ. אֲמַר: הָא מִישְׁרָא בָּעֲיָא מַיָּא, וְהָא מִישְׁרָא לָא בָּעֲיָא מַיָּא. וַאֲתָא מִיטְרָא וְקָמַשְׁקֵי כׇּל הֵיכָא דְּמִיבָּעֵי לֵיהּ מַיָּא.

This is **like** the practice **of Rav Daniel bar Ketina,** who **had a certain garden. Every day he would go and inspect it,** to see what it needed. He **would say: This bed requires water and this bed does not require water, and rain would come and water everywhere that required water,** but nowhere else.

NOTES

May the Rabbis go in peace – לֵיזְלוּ רַבָּנַן בִּשְׁלָמָא: This story can be understood in the light of the statement in tractate *Berakhot* (64a) that someone who bids farewell to a colleague should say: Go to peace, whereas to the dead one says: Go in peace. When Rav Pappa said to the younger Sages: May the Rabbis go in peace, he was using the formula for taking leave of the dead. He felt that this was appropriate, as he interpreted his dream as a divine revelation that the three Sages would soon pass away.

According to a variant reading, found in some texts of the Talmud and in other sources, Rav Pappa actually said: May the Rabbis go to peace, the correct formula used for the living. If so, Rav Pappa understood the quote from the verse in Zechariah as a question: Am I to cut off the three shepherds? Consequently, Rav Pappa told his younger colleagues to go to peace, as he did not want them to be punished on his account (*Shita Mekubbetzet*), or he was hinting to them that it would be safer for them to go and study somewhere else (*Sefat Emet*).

מַאי ״ה׳ עֹשֶׂה חֲזִיזִים״? אָמַר רַבִּי יוֹסֵי בְּרַבִּי חֲנִינָא: מְלַמֵּד שֶׁכָּל צַדִּיק הַקָּדוֹשׁ בָּרוּךְ הוּא עוֹשֶׂה לוֹ חָזִיז בִּפְנֵי עַצְמוֹ. מַאי ״חֲזִיזִים״? אָמַר רַב יְהוּדָה: פּוֹרְחוֹת. אָמַר רַבִּי יוֹחָנָן: סִימָן לְמָטָר פּוֹרְחוֹת. מַאי פּוֹרְחוֹת? אֲמַר רַב פַּפָּא: עֵיבָא קְלִישָׁא תּוּתֵי עֵיבָא סְמִיכְתָּא.

With regard to the aforementioned verse, the Gemara asks: **What** is the meaning of the phrase: **"The Lord** Who **makes thunderclouds"?**[N] **Rabbi Yosei, son of Rabbi Ḥanina, said:** This **teaches** that for **every righteous person, the Holy One, Blessed be He, prepares a separate thundercloud.** The Gemara asks: **What** is the precise meaning of **"thunderclouds"? Rav Yehuda said: Flying** clouds.[B] **Rabbi Yoḥanan said: A sign of** approaching **rain is flying** clouds. The Gemara asks: **What are flying** clouds? **Rav Pappa said:** A flying cloud is **a thin cloud under a thick cloud.**

אֲמַר רַב יְהוּדָה: נְהִילָא מִקַּמֵּי מִיטְרָא אָתֵי מִיטְרָא. בָּתַר מִיטְרָא פָּסֵיק מִיטְרָא. מִקַּמֵּי מִיטְרָא אָתֵי מִיטְרָא, וְסִימָנֵיךְ מְהוֹלְתָא. דְּבָתַר מִיטְרָא פָּסֵיק מִיטְרָא, וְסִימָנֵיךְ חַרְיָא דְעִיזֵּי.

Rav Yehuda said that there is another sign of imminent rain: **Drizzle before rain** means that **rain is coming.** However, drizzle that falls **after rain** is a sign that the **rain is stopping.** Rav Yehuda provides an analogy by way of explanation: Drizzle **before rain** means that **rain is coming, and your mnemonic is a sieve:** Just as small quantities of flour drop from the sieve even before one begins to actively sift it, so too drizzle falls before rain. Conversely, drizzle **that** falls **after rain** signifies that the **rain is stopping, and your mnemonic is goat dung.**[N] A goat's initial droppings are large, whereas its latter droppings are small.

עוּלָּא אִיקְלַע לְבָבֶל. חֲזָא פּוֹרְחוֹת. אֲמַר לְהוּ: פַּנּוּ מָאנֵי, דְּהַשְׁתָּא אָתֵי מִיטְרָא. לְסוֹף לָא אָתֵי מִיטְרָא. אֲמַר: כִּי הֵיכִי דִּמְשַׁקְּרִי בַּבְלָאֵי, הָכִי מְשַׁקְּרִי מִיטְרַיְיהוּ.

The Gemara relates that when **Ulla happened to** come **to Babylonia, he saw flying** clouds. **He said to** the local residents: **Put away** your **vessels, as** the **rain is coming now. Ultimately,** despite the presence of flying clouds, **rain did not fall. He said: Just as Babylonians are liars, so too, their rains are liars,** as flying clouds are a reliable sign of rain in Eretz Yisrael, but not in Babylonia.

עוּלָּא אִיקְלַע לְבָבֶל. חָזֵי מְלָא צַנָּא דְתַמְרֵי בְּזוּזָא. אֲמַר: מְלָא צַנָּא דְּדוּבְשָׁא בְּזוּזָא, וּבַבְלָאֵי לָא עָסְקֵי בְּאוֹרַיְיתָא! בְּלֵילְיָא צַעֲרוּהוּ. אֲמַר: מְלָא צַנָּא דְּסַכִּינָא בְּזוּזָא, וּבַבְלָאֵי עָסְקֵי בְּאוֹרַיְיתָא!

The Gemara recounts another incident that occurred when **Ulla happened to** come **to Babylonia.** He **saw a basket full of dates** on sale **for one dinar, and** he said: One can buy **a basket full of honey dates for a dinar, and** yet these **Babylonians do not occupy themselves with Torah.** In a place where excellent food is so inexpensive, and where there is no need to engage in hard labor for one's material needs, the inhabitants should be able to occupy themselves with Torah. Ulla himself ate many dates, but **during the night they caused him pain** and diarrhea. **He** subsequently **said: A basket full of knives for a dinar, and** yet somehow these **Babylonians** are able to **occupy themselves with Torah,** despite the trouble these dates cause.

תַּנְיָא: רַבִּי אֱלִיעֶזֶר אוֹמֵר: כָּל הָעוֹלָם כּוּלּוֹ מִמֵּימֵי אוֹקְיָינוֹס הוּא שׁוֹתֶה, שֶׁנֶּאֱמַר: ״וְאֵד יַעֲלֶה מִן הָאָרֶץ וְהִשְׁקָה אֶת כָּל פְּנֵי הָאֲדָמָה״. אָמַר לוֹ רַבִּי יְהוֹשֻׁעַ: וַהֲלֹא מֵימֵי אוֹקְיָינוֹס מְלוּחִין הֵן? אָמַר לוֹ: מִמַּתְּקִין בֶּעָבִים.

§ The Gemara discusses the source of rain. It **is taught** in a *baraita* **that Rabbi Eliezer says: The entire world drinks from the waters of the ocean** [*okeyanos*],[L] i.e., evaporated ocean water is the source of rain. **As it is stated: "And there went up a mist from the earth and watered the whole face of the ground"** (Genesis 2:6). **Rabbi Yehoshua said to him: But the waters of the ocean are salty,** whereas rainwater is sweet. Rabbi Eliezer **said to** Rabbi Yehoshua: The waters **are sweetened in the clouds,** before they fall to the earth.

רַבִּי יְהוֹשֻׁעַ אוֹמֵר: כָּל הָעוֹלָם כּוּלּוֹ מִמַּיִם הָעֶלְיוֹנִים הוּא שׁוֹתֶה, שֶׁנֶּאֱמַר: ״לִמְטַר הַשָּׁמַיִם תִּשְׁתֶּה מָּיִם״. אֶלָּא מָה אֲנִי מְקַיֵּים ״וְאֵד יַעֲלֶה מִן הָאָרֶץ״? מְלַמֵּד שֶׁהָעֲנָנִים מִתְגַּבְּרִים וְעוֹלִים לָרָקִיעַ, וּפוֹתְחִין פִּיהֶן כְּנוֹד וּמְקַבְּלִין מֵי מָטָר, שֶׁנֶּאֱמַר: ״יָזֹקּוּ מָטָר לְאֵדוֹ״.

In contrast, **Rabbi Yehoshua says: The entire world drinks from the upper waters,**[N] **as it is stated: "And it drinks water as the rain of heaven comes down"** (Deuteronomy 11:11). The *baraita* asks: **But** according to the opinion of Rabbi Yehoshua, **how do I uphold** the verse: **"And there went up a mist from the earth"?** Rabbi Yehoshua could answer that this verse **teaches that the clouds grow stronger, and rise to the firmament, and open their mouths like** a leather **bottle, and receive the rain waters** from above, **as it is stated:** "For He draws away the drops of water, **which distill rain from His vapor"** (Job 36:27).

וּמְנוּקָּבוֹת הֵן כִּכְבָרָה, וּבָאוֹת וּמְחַשְּׁרוֹת מַיִם עַל גַּבֵּי קַרְקַע, שֶׁנֶּאֱמַר: ״חַשְׁרַת מַיִם, עָבֵי שְׁחָקִים״. וְאֵין בֵּין טִיפָּה לְטִיפָּה אֶלָּא כִּמְלֹא נִימָא, לְלַמֶּדְךָ שֶׁגָּדוֹל יוֹם הַגְּשָׁמִים כְּיוֹם שֶׁנִּבְרְאוּ בּוֹ שָׁמַיִם וָאָרֶץ,

And the clouds **are perforated like a sieve, and they come and sprinkle water onto the ground, as it is stated: "Gathering of waters, thick clouds of the skies"** (II Samuel 22:12). **And between each and every drop**[B] there is **only a hairbreadth,** and yet each drop emerges individually. This serves **to teach you that the day of rains is as great as the day on which Heaven and Earth were created,** i.e., rainfall is as miraculous as creation.

NOTES

Who makes thunderclouds – עֹשֶׂה חֲזִיזִים: This interpretation is based on the fact that "thunderclouds" is plural, whereas all the other words in the verse that refer to rain are in the singular. Rabbi Yosei, son of Rabbi Ḥanina, consequently explains that a separate thundercloud is formed for each and every righteous person.

Goat dung [*ḥarya de'izei*] – חַרְיָא דְעִיזֵּי: The *Arukh* cites a variant reading: *Dadeya de'izei*, goat teats. When one starts to milk a goat the milk gushes out, but as the milking draws to a close, the milk comes out in small drops. Similarly, the light drizzle at the end of a rainstorm is a sure sign that the rain is coming to an end.

Rabbi Eliezer and Rabbi Yehoshua – רַבִּי אֱלִיעֶזֶר וְרַבִּי יְהוֹשֻׁעַ: According to the straightforward understanding of the dispute between Rabbi Eliezer and Rabbi Yehoshua, the two *tanna'im* are debating the scientific question of the source of rainwater, whether rain is recycled water from the ocean, or whether it is derived from some heavenly source (see Maharsha). Other commentators suggest that this dispute is referring to the mutual influences of the heavenly and the mundane worlds. Is the source of all bounty in Heaven, while human endeavor is merely a receptacle for that bounty, or is divine bounty dependent on human activity (see *Otzar HaKavod*)?

BACKGROUND

Flying clouds – פּוֹרְחוֹת: For clouds to produce rain they must possess a significant vertical thickness. Towering clouds of this kind are called cumulonimbus. These clouds can produce thunderstorms and heavy downpours that can even result in flooding.

Cumulonimbus clouds

Between each and every drop – בֵּין טִיפָּה לְטִיפָּה: The details of the process of rain production are an important area of current scientific study. The systems that produce rain, which include the presence of water vapor in sufficient concentration, the temperature at which tiny ice crystals are formed, and the formation and structure of drops, are highly complex and have led to the discipline of a physics of chaos, which investigates the combination of many factors, large and small, into the production of a single event.

The formation of drops, the inner cohesion of the water molecules that form each drop, and the fact that these drops receive a characteristic shape and do not fall in a continuous flow, are all extremely complex matters.

In light of the complexity of rain production, one can understand why the Gemara speaks of the miracle of rain. Although rainfall is a common occurrence, it is very difficult to understand, like other miracles. In its own way, the creation of rainfall can be considered as elaborate and complicated as the creation of the entire universe.

LANGUAGE

The ocean [*okeyanos*] – אוֹקְיָינוֹס: From the Greek ὠκεανός, *okeanos*, one of whose meanings is the Great Sea, or the outer ocean surrounding the world, as opposed to the Mediterranean Sea.

שֶׁנֶּאֱמַר: ״עֹשֶׂה גְדֹלוֹת וְאֵין חֵקֶר״. וּכְתִיב: ״הַנֹּתֵן מָטָר עַל פְּנֵי אָרֶץ״. וּכְתִיב לְהַלָּן: ״הֲלוֹא יָדַעְתָּ? אִם לֹא שָׁמַעְתָּ? אֱלֹהֵי עוֹלָם, ה׳...אֵין חֵקֶר לִתְבוּנָתוֹ״. וּכְתִיב: ״מֵכִין הָרִים בְּכֹחוֹ״ וגו׳.

As it is stated, with regard to the creation of the world: **"Who does great things past finding out"** (Job 9:10), **and** as an example of this **it is written: "Who gives rain upon the earth"** (Job 5:9–10). **And it is written below: "Have you not known? Have you not heard that the everlasting God, the Lord,** the Creator of the ends of the earth, does not faint and is not weary; **His discernment is past finding out"** (Isaiah 40:28). The repetition of "past finding out" indicates that rainfall is as wondrous as the creation of the world. The Gemara adds: **And it is written** in a psalm that deals with rainfall: **"Who by Your strength sets fast the mountains;** Who is girded about with might" (Psalms 65:7).

כְּמַאן אָזְלָא הָא דִּכְתִיב: ״מַשְׁקֶה הָרִים מֵעֲלִיּוֹתָיו״? וְאָמַר רַבִּי יוֹחָנָן: מֵעֲלִיּוֹתָיו שֶׁל הַקָּדוֹשׁ בָּרוּךְ הוּא. כְּמַאן? כְּרַבִּי יְהוֹשֻׁעַ.

The Gemara asks: **In accordance with whose** opinion **is that** verse **which is written: "Who waters the mountains from His upper chambers"** (Psalms 104:13)? **And Rabbi Yoḥanan said:** This phrase indicates that the water comes **from the upper chambers of the Holy One, Blessed be He. In accordance with** whose opinion is this statement? It is **in accordance with** the opinion of **Rabbi Yehoshua,** who maintains that rain falls from above the sky.

וְרַבִּי אֱלִיעֶזֶר? כֵּיוָן דְּסָלְקִי לְהָתָם ״מַשְׁקֶה מֵעֲלִיּוֹתָיו״ קָרֵי לְהוּ. דְּאִי לָא תֵּימָא הָכִי, ״אָבָק וְעָפָר מִן הַשָּׁמַיִם״ הֵיכִי מַשְׁכַּחַת לָהּ? אֶלָּא, כֵּיוָן דְּמִדְּלֵי לְהָתָם, ״מִן הַשָּׁמַיִם״ קָרֵי לֵיהּ. הָכִי נַמִי, דְּסָלְקִי לְהָתָם, ״מֵעֲלִיּוֹתָיו״ קָרֵי לֵיהּ.

The Gemara asks: **And Rabbi Eliezer,** how does he explain this verse? The Gemara answers: According to Rabbi Eliezer, **since** the clouds **ascend there,** to the heavens, the verse **"who waters the mountains from His upper chambers" calls** and describes rainfall as descending from the heavens. **As, if you do not say so,** with regard to the verse: **"Powder and dust from the heavens"** (Deuteronomy 28:24), **where do you find** this phenomenon? Is there powder and dust in Heaven? **Rather,** you must say that **since** dust **rises up there, they are called** dust: **"From the heavens." So too,** as the clouds **ascend there, they are called** and described: "Who waters the mountains **from His upper chambers."**

כְּמַאן אָזְלָא הָא דְּאָמַר רַבִּי חֲנִינָא: ״כֹּנֵס כַּנֵּד מֵי הַיָּם; נֹתֵן בְּאוֹצָרוֹת תְּהוֹמוֹת״. מִי גָּרַם לָאוֹצָרוֹת שֶׁיִּתְמַלְּאוּ בָּר? תְּהוֹמוֹת. כְּרַבִּי אֱלִיעֶזֶר. וְרַבִּי יְהוֹשֻׁעַ? הַהוּא

The Gemara asks: **In accordance with whose** opinion **is that which Rabbi Ḥanina said,** concerning the verse: **"He gathers the waters of the sea together as a heap; he lays up the deep in storerooms"** (Psalms 33:7): **What caused the storerooms to be filled with produce?** It was **the deep,** which is the source of the water that nourishes the produce. The Gemara answers: This explanation is **in accordance with** the opinion of **Rabbi Eliezer. And Rabbi Yehoshua,** how does he explain this verse? Rabbi Yehoshua would say: **That**

Perek **I**
Daf **10** Amud **a**

בִּבְרִיָּיתוֹ שֶׁל עוֹלָם.

verse deals **with the creation of the world,** when all the water was contained in the deep.

תָּנוּ רַבָּנַן: אֶרֶץ יִשְׂרָאֵל נִבְרֵאת תְּחִילָּה וְכָל הָעוֹלָם כּוּלּוֹ נִבְרָא לְבַסּוֹף, שֶׁנֶּאֱמַר: ״עַד לֹא עָשָׂה אֶרֶץ וְחוּצוֹת״. אֶרֶץ יִשְׂרָאֵל מַשְׁקֶה אוֹתָהּ הַקָּדוֹשׁ בָּרוּךְ הוּא בְּעַצְמוֹ, וְכָל הָעוֹלָם כּוּלּוֹ עַל יְדֵי שָׁלִיחַ, שֶׁנֶּאֱמַר: ״הַנֹּתֵן מָטָר עַל פְּנֵי אָרֶץ, וְשֹׁלֵחַ מַיִם עַל פְּנֵי חוּצוֹת״.

The Sages taught in a *baraita*: **Eretz Yisrael was created first and the rest of the entire world was created afterward, as it is stated: "While as yet He had not made the land, nor the fields"** (Proverbs 8:26). Here, and in the following statements, the term "land" is understood as a reference to the Land of Israel, while "the fields" means all the fields in other lands. Furthermore, **Eretz Yisrael is watered by the Holy One, Blessed be He, Himself, and the rest of the entire world** is watered **through an intermediary, as it is stated: "Who gives rain upon the land, and sends water upon the fields"** (Job 5:10).

אֶרֶץ יִשְׂרָאֵל שׁוֹתָה מֵי גְשָׁמִים, וְכָל הָעוֹלָם כּוּלּוֹ מִתַּמְצִית, שֶׁנֶּאֱמַר: ״הַנֹּתֵן מָטָר עַל פְּנֵי אָרֶץ״ וגו׳. אֶרֶץ יִשְׂרָאֵל שׁוֹתָה תְּחִילָּה, וְכָל הָעוֹלָם כּוּלּוֹ לְבַסּוֹף. שֶׁנֶּאֱמַר: ״הַנֹּתֵן מָטָר עַל פְּנֵי אָרֶץ״ וגו׳. מָשָׁל לְאָדָם שֶׁמְּגַבֵּל אֶת הַגְּבִינָה. נוֹטֵל אֶת הָאוֹכֶל וּמַנִּיחַ אֶת הַפְּסוֹלֶת.

Additionally, **Eretz Yisrael drinks rainwater and** the rest of **the entire world** drinks **from** the remaining **residue** of rainwater left in the clouds, **as it is stated** that God is He **"who gives rain upon the land"** and only afterward takes what is left "and sends water upon the fields." **Eretz Yisrael drinks first, and** the rest of **the entire world afterward, as it is stated: "Who gives rain upon the land** and sends water upon the fields." There is **a parable** that illustrates this: **A person** who **kneads** his **cheese** after it has curdled **takes the food and leaves the refuse.**[N]

NOTES

Eretz Yisrael and the entire world – אֶרֶץ יִשְׂרָאֵל וְכָל הָעוֹלָם: Some commentaries write that the comparisons and distinctions drawn here between Eretz Yisrael and the rest of the world are expressions of the idea that the entire world was created for the sake of Eretz Yisrael. Consequently, the most significant events take place in Eretz Yisrael, while the rest of the world plays a secondary role, as the other lands benefit from the divine bounty that is intended primarily for Eretz Yisrael (Rashba).

אָמַר מָר: מְמַתְּקִין הֵן בֶּעָבִים. מְנָלֵיהּ? דְּאָמַר רַב יִצְחָק בַּר יוֹסֵף אָמַר רַבִּי יוֹחָנָן: כְּתִיב: ״חֶשְׁכַת מַיִם, עָבֵי שְׁחָקִים״, וּכְתִיב: ״חַשְׁרַת מַיִם, עָבֵי שְׁחָקִים.״

The Master said above: The ocean waters **are sweetened in the clouds.** The Gemara asks: **From where** does Rabbi Eliezer derive **this?** The Gemara answers **that Rav Yitzḥak bar Yosef said** that **Rabbi Yoḥanan said** that **it is written: "Darkness [*ḥeshkhat*] of waters, thick clouds of the skies"** (Psalms 18:12). **And it is written,** in a similar verse: **"Gathering of [*ḥashrat*] waters, thick clouds of the skies"** (II Samuel 22:12).

שְׁקוֹל כַּף וּשְׁדֵי אַרֵישׁ, וּקְרִי בֵּיהּ חַכְשָׁרַת.

The Gemara explains the significance of this minor variation. These two phrases vary in only one word, which themselves differ by only one letter, a *kaf* for a *reish*. If you join the two versions together, and **take** the letter ***kaf*** from the first version **and** place it **with** the second version of the word, which has **a *reish***, you can **read into** the verse a new word meaning **rendering fit [*ḥakhsharat*].**[N] Accordingly, the verse can be interpreted as: The rendering fit of water is performed in the clouds of the sky.

וְרַבִּי יְהוֹשֻׁעַ, בְּהָנֵי קְרָאֵי מַאי דָּרֵישׁ בְּהוּ? סָבַר לָהּ כִּי הָא: דְּכִי אֲתָא רַב דִּימִי, אֲמַר: אָמְרִי בְּמַעְרְבָא: נְהוֹר עֲנָנֵי, זְעִירִין מוֹהִי; חֲשׁוֹךְ עֲנָנֵי, סַגְיָין מוֹהִי.

The Gemara asks: **And Rabbi Yehoshua,** with regard **to these verses, what** does he learn from **them?** The Gemara answers that Rabbi Yehoshua **holds in accordance with** the opinion of **this** Sage, Rav Dimi. **As when Rav Dimi**[P] **came** from Eretz Yisrael to Babylonia, **he said** that **they say in the West,** Eretz Yisrael: When **clouds are bright,**[B] **they have little water;** when **clouds are dark, they have much water.** Accordingly, Rabbi Yehoshua explains that when there is "a darkness of waters" in the clouds, there is also "a gathering of waters," as rain will fall from them.

כְּמַאן אָזְלָא הָא דְּתַנְיָא: מַיִם הָעֶלְיוֹנִים בְּמַאֲמָר הֵם תְּלוּיִם, וּפֵירוֹתֵיהֶן מֵי גְשָׁמִים, שֶׁנֶּאֱמַר: ״מִפְּרִי מַעֲשֶׂיךָ תִּשְׂבַּע הָאָרֶץ״. כְּמַאן? כְּרַבִּי יְהוֹשֻׁעַ. וְרַבִּי אֱלִיעֶזֶר? הַהוּא בְּמַעֲשֵׂה יָדָיו שֶׁל הַקָּדוֹשׁ בָּרוּךְ הוּא הוּא דִּכְתִיב.

The Gemara asks: **In accordance with whose** opinion **is that which is taught** in a *baraita*: **The upper waters** do not stand in any defined place; rather, they are **suspended by** the **word** of God, **and their fruit is rainwater, as it is stated:** "Who waters the mountains from His upper chambers; **the earth is full of the fruit of Your works"** (Psalms 104:13). **In accordance with whose** opinion is this statement? It is **in accordance with** the opinion of **Rabbi Yehoshua. And Rabbi Eliezer,** how does he explain this verse? Rabbi Eliezer could say: **That** verse from Psalms **is written with regard to the handiwork of the Holy One, Blessed be He,**[N] not the upper waters.

אָמַר רַבִּי יְהוֹשֻׁעַ בֶּן לֵוִי: כָּל הָעוֹלָם כּוּלּוֹ מִתַּמְצִית גַּן עֵדֶן הוּא שׁוֹתֶה, שֶׁנֶּאֱמַר: ״וְנָהָר יֹצֵא מֵעֵדֶן״ וגו׳. תָּנָא: מִתַּמְצִית בֵּית כּוֹר שׁוֹתֶה תַּרְקַב.

Rabbi Yehoshua ben Levi said: The entire world drinks from the runoff of the Garden of Eden, as it is stated: "And a river went out of Eden to water the garden" (Genesis 2:10). It was **taught** in a *baraita*: **From the runoff** of **a *beit kor***, a field in which a *kor* of seed can be planted, which is approximately seventy-five thousand square cubits, a field in which **a half-*se'a* [*tarkav*]**,[L] of seed can be sown, i.e. one-sixtieth the size of a *beit kor*, **can be watered.** If the runoff from a *beit kor* is sufficient for a field one-sixtieth its size, it can be inferred that the rest of the world is one-sixtieth the size of the Garden of Eden.

תָּנוּ רַבָּנַן: אֶרֶץ מִצְרַיִם הָוְיָא אַרְבַּע מֵאוֹת פַּרְסָה עַל אַרְבַּע מֵאוֹת פַּרְסָה. וְהוּא אֶחָד מִשִּׁשִּׁים בְּכוּשׁ. וְכוּשׁ אֶחָד מִשִּׁשִּׁים בָּעוֹלָם. וְעוֹלָם אֶחָד מִשִּׁשִּׁים בַּגַּן. וְגַן אֶחָד מִשִּׁשִּׁים לְעֵדֶן. וְעֵדֶן אֶחָד מִשִּׁשִּׁים לְגֵיהִנָּם. נִמְצָא כָּל הָעוֹלָם כּוּלּוֹ כְּכִיסּוּי קְדֵרָה לְגֵיהִנָּם. וְיֵשׁ אוֹמְרִים: גֵּיהִנָּם אֵין לָהּ שִׁיעוּר. וְיֵשׁ אוֹמְרִים: עֵדֶן אֵין לָהּ שִׁיעוּר.

The Sages taught in a *baraita*: The area of the **land of Egypt is four hundred parasangs [*parsa*] by four hundred parasangs. And** this **is one sixtieth** the size **of Cush,**[B] **and Cush** itself **is one sixtieth** the size **of** the rest of **the world. And the world is one sixtieth of the Garden** of Eden, **and the Garden** of Eden **is one sixtieth of Eden** itself, **and Eden is one sixtieth of Gehenna.** You **find** that **the entire world is like a pot cover for Gehenna,** as Eden, which is far larger than the rest of the world, is only one sixtieth the size of Gehenna. **And some say: Gehenna has no measure. And some say** that **Eden has no measure.**

NOTES

Rendering fit [*ḥakhsharat*] – חַכְשָׁרַת: According to this interpretation, the initial letter *ḥet* is considered the equivalent of the letter *heh*, and therefore this term is similar to *hakhshara*, preparation. This change in letters is accepted without argument, as they are similar both in form and in pronunciation, and in talmudic times there were already a great many people who found it difficult to distinguish between the two. The Sages explicitly say that it is permitted to expound verses by substituting one of these letters for the other (see Jerusalem Talmud, *Shabbat* 7:2).

With regard to the handiwork of the Holy One, Blessed be He – בְּמַעֲשֵׂה יָדָיו שֶׁל הַקָּדוֹשׁ בָּרוּךְ הוּא: In other words, the psalm is referring to the original creation of rain, through which the earth is watered (Rabbi Elyakim).

PERSONALITIES

Rav Dimi – רַב דִּימִי: An *amora* of the third and fourth generations, Rav Dimi lived at various times both in Babylonia and in Eretz Yisrael. He was apparently a Babylonian who moved to Eretz Yisrael in his youth. He returned to Babylonia several times and transmitted the statements of Sages living in Eretz Yisrael. In the Jerusalem Talmud Rav Dimi is called Rav Avdimi Naḥota, or Rav Avduma Naḥota. He was one of the Sages who were given the title *Rabbanan Naḥotei*, the Sages who descend, as they carried the rulings of Eretz Yisrael, primarily the statements of Rabbi Yoḥanan, Reish Lakish, and Rabbi Elazar, to Babylonia. The list of Sages who participated in this task includes Rabba bar bar Ḥana, Ulla, and later, Ravin, Rav Shmuel bar Yehuda, and others. The Talmud reports dozens of halakhic decisions that Rav Dimi transmitted from one Torah center to the other, concerning which he engaged in debates with the greatest Sages of his generation. Toward the end of his life he apparently returned to Babylonia, where he died.

BACKGROUND

Clouds are bright – נְהוֹר עֲנָנֵי: The fact that a cloud is dark is a sign that it is vertically thick and rain-bearing. The darker the cloud, the more drops of water and ice particles it contains. Generally speaking, light-colored clouds either do not produce rain or produce very little rain.

Egypt and Cush – מִצְרַיִם וְכוּשׁ: This map displays the relative sizes of Egypt and Cush, which covered a large proportion of the continent of Africa, and enables a comparison between the two countries and the rest of the world.

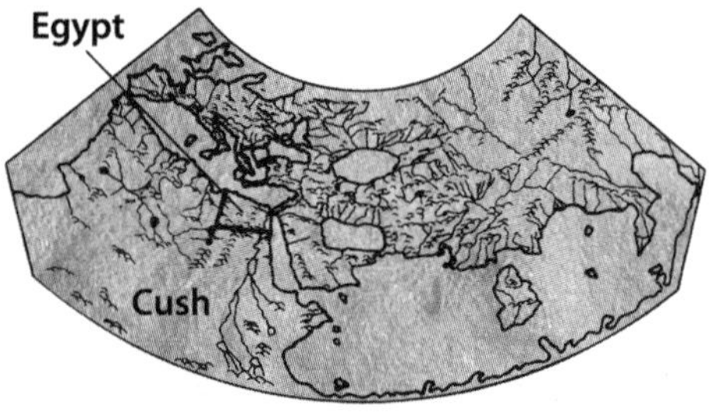

Egypt and Cush, as sketched by Ptolemy of Alexandria

LANGUAGE

A half-*se'a* [*tarkav*] – תַּרְקַב: Of unclear origin. Some authorities maintain that it is from the Greek τρίκαβος, *trikabos*, meaning three *kav*, which are units of volume. However, this etymology is difficult to accept, as generally the Greek letter *tau* becomes the Hebrew letter *tet*. Others claim that it is an abbreviation of *terei ukav*, i.e., two *kav* and another *kav*. Yet others maintain that it was originally a unit of two *kav*, *terei kav*, but the size of the units changed over time. In any event, the Gemara invariably uses the term *tarkav* for a measure of three *kav*, the equivalent of half a *se'a*.

אמר רבי אושעיא: מאי דכתיב: "שכנת על מים רבים, רבת אוצרת"? מי גרם לבבל שיהו אוצרותיה מלאות בר? הוי אומר מפני ששוכנת על מים רבים. אמר רב: עתירה בבל דחצדא בלא מיטרא. אמר אביי: נקיטינן טובעני ולא יובשני.

Rabbi Oshaya said: What is the meaning of that **which is written** about Babylonia: **"You who dwells on many waters, abundant in storehouses"** (Jeremiah 51:13)? **What caused Babylonia to have storehouses full of grain? You must say** that it is **due to** the fact that **it resides on many waters,** the Tigris and the Euphrates Rivers, which render its land easy to irrigate. Similarly, **Rav said: Babylonia is wealthy**[NB] **since** it can **grow crops** for harvest **even without rain. Abaye said: We hold** that it is better for a land to be **swampy** like Babylonia, **and not dry,** as crops in Babylonia grow all year.

מתני׳ בשלשה במרחשון שואלין את הגשמים. רבן גמליאל אומר: בשבעה בו, חמשה עשר יום אחר החג, כדי שיגיע אחרון שבישראל לנהר פרת.

MISHNA On the third of the month of **Marḥeshvan** one starts to **request rain** by inserting the phrase: And give dew and rain, in the blessing of the years, the ninth blessing of the *Amida*. **Rabban Gamliel says:** One starts to request rain **on the seventh of** Marḥeshvan, which is **fifteen days after the festival** of *Sukkot*. Rabban Gamliel explains that one waits these extra four days **so that** the **last** pilgrim **of the Jewish people,** who traveled to Jerusalem on foot for the Festival, **can reach the Euphrates River**[B] without being inconvenienced by rain on his journey home.

גמ׳ אמר רבי אלעזר: הלכה כרבן גמליאל. תניא: חנניה אומר: ובגולה עד ששים בתקופה. אמר רב הונא בר חייא אמר שמואל: הלכה כחנניה.

GEMARA Rabbi Elazar said: The *halakha* is in accordance with the opinion **of Rabban Gamliel,** that one does not begin to request rain until the seventh of Marḥeshvan. **It is taught** in a *baraita* **that Ḥananya**[P] **says: And in the Diaspora**[N] one does not begin to request rain **until sixty** days **into the season,**[NH] i.e., sixty days after the autumnal equinox. **Rav Huna bar Ḥiyya said** that **Shmuel said: The *halakha* is in accordance with** the opinion of **Ḥananya.**

איני? והא בעו מיניה משמואל: מאימת מדכרינן: ותן טל ומטר? אמר להו: מכי מעיילי ציבי לבי טבות רישבא. דילמא אידי ואידי חד שיעורא הוא.

The Gemara asks: **Is that so? But they raised a dilemma before Shmuel: From when does one mention: And give dew and rain? He said to them: From when they bring wood into the house of Tavut the bird hunter [*rishba*].**[L] This is apparently a different date than that mentioned by Ḥananya. The Gemara suggests: **Perhaps this and that are one measure** of time, i.e., Shmuel merely provided a sign of sixty days after the autumnal equinox.

NOTES

Babylonia is wealthy [*atira*] – **עתירה בבל**: According to a variant reading, Rav is stating that in the future [*atida*] Babylonia will be desolate, as its sources of water will dry up and any rainfall will be insufficient to meet its needs (see *Arukh*).

And in the Diaspora – **ובגולה**: When this term is used in the Bible with reference to a specific place, it means the Babylonian exile. See Ezekiel 1:1, and many other instances in that book. Not only was Babylonia the place where the majority of Jews were exiled at the time, but it also became a national spiritual center in its own right. In discussion concerning relations between Eretz Yisrael and the Diaspora, the latter terms refers mainly to the large and important Jewish community in Babylonia.

Sometimes the word has an even more restricted meaning, as it can refer to the city of Pumbedita and its surroundings, the places where Jews apparently first settled upon their exile to Babylonia.

Until sixty days into the season – **עד ששים בתקופה**: The early authorities dispute the meaning of Ḥananya's statement that in the Diaspora one does not insert the request for rain until sixty days after the autumnal equinox. Was he referring only to Babylonia, the principal Diaspora community in the talmudic period, where the land is watered by rivers and rain is not needed until later in the winter, or was he referring to all Jewish communities outside Eretz Yisrael? Many commentators argue that there is no reason why those living in areas where rain is required immediately after *Sukkot* or shortly thereafter should wait until sixty days after the autumnal equinox before inserting the prayer for rain into the *Amida* (see Rosh and Ritva).

In some places it was customary to insert the request for rain immediately after *Sukkot*, in accordance with the opinion of Rabbi Yoḥanan (4b), or on the seventh of Marḥeshvan, as stated by Rabban Gamliel in the mishna. However, in most Diaspora communities the request for rain was not recited until sixty days after the equinox. Some commentaries explain that the Sages instituted two dates on which to begin reciting the request for rain, one for Eretz Yisrael, and one for Babylonia. All other places must follow either the custom of Eretz Yisrael or Babylonia, as there is no third date (Ritva). The *ge'onim* ruled that all Diaspora communities wait until sixty days after the equinox before inserting the prayer for rain into the *Amida*, as in all matters the Diaspora communities follow the practices of Babylonia. Moreover, it is preferable to have a uniform date throughout the Diaspora to begin requesting rain. In any event, the prayer cannot be inserted immediately after *Sukkot*, as in many Diaspora communities there is still grain in the fields that must be harvested before the rains.

PERSONALITIES

Ḥananya – **חנניה**: Ḥananya, a nephew of Rabbi Yehoshua, was from the fourth generation of *tanna'im*. His principal teacher was his uncle, Rabbi Yehoshua, but he also learned Torah from other important Sages of that generation. He apparently went to live in Babylonia before the bar Kokheva revolt. After the war and the ensuing persecutions he was among the remnants of the chief Sages of that generation. This led him to attempt to regulate the Hebrew calendar in Babylonia, as it was difficult to do so in Eretz Yisrael, due to Hadrian's decrees. This effort, which was tantamount to challenging the supreme authority of Eretz Yisrael, led to a sharp response from its Sages, who ultimately were able to persuade Ḥananya to change his mind. However, the results of his action were not entirely undone. The Sages viewed this action in such grave terms that they spoke of a curse upon Ḥananya's descendants due to this sin. Ḥananya lived a long life and died in Babylonia. The great *amora* Shmuel may have been one of his descendants.

HALAKHA

And in the Diaspora until sixty days into the season – **ובגולה עד ששים בתקופה**: Those who live outside Eretz Yisrael begin to insert the request for rain in the ninth blessing of the *Amida* prayer on the night of the sixtieth day after the autumnal equinox. For this purpose, the equinox is determined by the calculations of the *amora* Shmuel, following the tradition of the *ge'onim*. In an ordinary year the request for rain is first inserted on December fourth, while in a Gregorian leap year the date is December fifth.

The later authorities disagree on the *halakha* of a resident of Eretz Yisrael who travels abroad during this period of the year. Some maintain that one inserts the request for rain starting from the seventh of Marḥeshvan, in accordance with the custom in Eretz Yisrael (Rav Ya'akov Castro). Others claim that one follows the practice observed in the Diaspora and does not request rain until sixty days after the equinox (*Mishna Berura*). Some argue that the *halakha* depends on when one intends to return to Eretz Yisrael (*Peri Ḥadash*). In practice, various communities follow different customs in this regard (*Shulḥan Arukh*, *Oraḥ Ḥayyim* 117:1).

LANGUAGE

The bird hunter [*rishba*] – **רישבא**: According to Rashi, *rishba* is identical to the Aramaic *nishba*, which means a net. *Rishba* or *nishba* refers to one who spreads the nets, i.e., one who hunts birds or other animals. However, some explain that *rishba* is an acronym for *reish beit abba*, the head of a paternal household. It is an honorific for the man who is the most prominent member of his family (*ge'onim*; see *Arukh*).

BACKGROUND

Babylonia is wealthy – **עתירה בבל**: The soil of Babylonia is highly fertile, as it is formed from the sediment of rivers. Although only a small amount of rain fell in Babylonia, the rivers and their channels provided plenty of water for the land to produce crops, despite the lack of rain.

So that the last pilgrim can reach…the Euphrates River – **כדי שיגיע אחרון...לנהר פרת**: There were several routes from Eretz Yisrael to Babylonia. The main path was probably via Damascus, through Thapsacus, all the way along the Euphrates to Babylonia. Although this route, which followed inhabited areas, was very long, more than 500 km to Thapsacus, it was the best journey for large convoys, which occasionally included women and children. At a speed of roughly 30 to 40 km a day, the trip would take about fifteen days. A more direct path via the desert, at a quicker pace, offered the traveler a journey of roughly seven days.

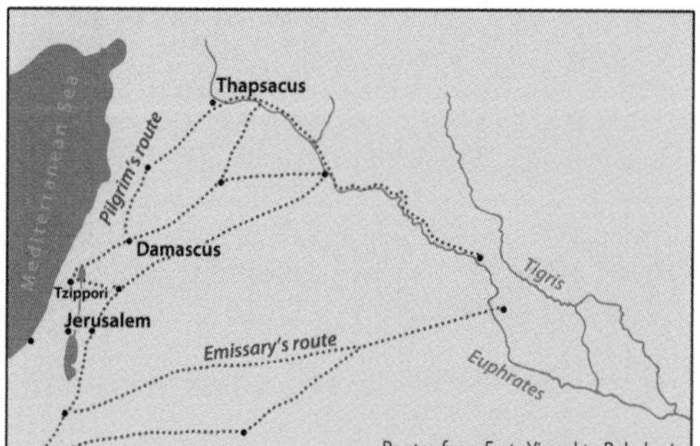

Routes from Eretz Yisrael to Babylonia

איבעיא להו: יום ששים כלפני ששים או כלאחר ששים? תא שמע: רב אמר: יום ששים כלאחר ששים. ושמואל אמר: יום ששים כלפני ששים.

A dilemma was raised before the Sages: Is the **sixtieth day** itself treated as part **of** the period **before** the **sixtieth** day **or** is it included **in** the period **after** the **sixtieth** day? The Gemara answers. **Come** and **hear** that there is a dispute in this regard. **Rav said:** The **sixtieth day** is part **of** the period **after** the **sixtieth** day, **and Shmuel said:** The **sixtieth day** is part **of** the period **before** the **sixtieth.**

אמר רב נחמן בר יצחק: וסימנך: עלאי בעו מיא, תתאי לא בעו מיא. אמר רב פפא: הלכתא: יום ששים כלאחר ששים.

Rav Naḥman bar Yitzḥak said: And your mnemonic to remember the divergent opinions is: **Those above require water; those below**[N] **do not require water.** Since water flows downward, those who live in low places receive their water from above and are generally in less need of additional water. Accordingly, Shmuel, who lived in the lowlands of Babylonia, ruled that one begins to request for rain later, whereas Rav, who studied in Eretz Yisrael, which is higher in elevation and has a greater need for rain, stated an earlier date. **Rav Pappa said: The** ***halakha*** **is** that the **sixtieth day** is part **of** the period **after** the **sixtieth** day, as stated by **Rav,** and therefore one begins to mention the request for rain on the sixtieth day after the autumnal equinox.

מתני׳ הגיע שבעה עשר במרחשון, ולא ירדו גשמים, התחילו היחידים מתענין שלש תעניות. אוכלין ושותין משחשיכה, ומותרין במלאכה, וברחיצה, ובסיכה, ובנעילת הסנדל, ובתשמיש המטה. הגיע ראש חדש כסליו, ולא ירדו גשמים, בית דין גוזרין שלש תעניות על הצבור. אוכלין ושותין משחשיכה, ומותרין במלאכה, וברחיצה, ובסיכה, ובנעילת הסנדל, ובתשמיש המטה.

MISHNA If the **seventeenth of Marḥeshvan arrived**[H] **and rain has not fallen, individuals,** but not the entire community, **begin to fast three fasts** for rain. How are these fasts conducted? As the fast begins in the morning, one **may eat and drink after dark, and one is permitted** during the days of the fasts themselves to engage **in** the performance of **work, in bathing, in smearing oil** on one's body, **in wearing shoes, and in conjugal relations.** If the **New Moon of Kislev arrived**[H] **and rain has** still **not fallen,** the **court decrees three fasts on the** entire **community.** Similar to the individual fasts, everyone **may eat and drink after dark, and they are permitted to** engage in the performance of **work, in bathing, in smearing** one's body **with oil, in wearing shoes, and in conjugal relations.**

גמ׳ מאן יחידים? אמר רב הונא: רבנן. ואמר רב הונא: יחידים מתענין שלש תעניות, שני וחמישי ושני.

GEMARA The Gemara asks: **Who are these individuals** mentioned in the mishna? **Rav Huna said:** This is referring to **the Sages,** who are held to a higher standard and are expected to undertake fasts even when ordinary people do not. **And Rav Huna** further said: The **individuals** who **fast** the **three fasts** do so **on a Monday, and** on the next **Thursday, and** again on the following **Monday.**

מאי קמשמע לן? תנינא: אין גוזרין תענית על הצבור בתחילה בחמישי, שלא להפקיע את השערים. אלא שלש תעניות הראשונות שני וחמישי ושני.

The Gemara asks: **What is** Rav Huna **teaching us? We** already **learned** this (15b):[B] The court **may not decree a fast on the community starting from a Thursday,**[H] **so as not to cause an increase in prices.**[N] **Rather,** the **first three fasts** are established on **Monday, and Thursday, and Monday.** What does Rav Huna's statement add to this ruling?

מהו דתימא: הני מילי צבור, אבל יחיד לא. קמשמע לן. תניא נמי הכי: כשהתחילו היחידים להתענות, מתענין שני וחמישי ושני, ומפסיקין בראשי חדשים

The Gemara answers: Rav Huna's comment is necessary, **lest you say** that **this applies** only to **a community, but** that in the case of **an individual, no,** the series of three fasts does not have to start on a Monday. **This** opinion **is also taught**[B] in a *baraita* with regard to those mentioned in the mishna: **When the individuals begin to fast, they fast on a Monday, a Thursday, and a Monday. And** if one of the fast days occurs on a day with special observances, **they interrupt** the sequence **for New Moons,**[H]

NOTES

Those above…those below – עלאי...תתאי: Rabbeinu Ḥananel, following the *ge'onim*, has an alternate version of the text that states the reverse of the standard text of the Gemara in this instance: Rav said that the sixtieth day is treated as part of the period before the sixtieth day, and Shmuel said that the sixtieth day is part of the period after the sixtieth day. According to this version of the dispute, Shmuel is considered the one who lives above and therefore requires rain, as he lived in Neharde'a, which was situated upstream of the Euphrates River. Rav is viewed as living below and has less need of rain, because after emigrating to Babylonia he established his academy in Sura, a place downstream of the Euphrates from Neharde'a.

So as not to cause an increase in prices – שלא להפקיע את השערים: According to the plain meaning of this mishna, a court may not decree a fast for the first time on a Thursday, as it is already a busy market day when people buy supplies for Shabbat. If the first of a series of fasts were on a Thursday, the demand for food would further increase, as people would go to the market to purchase food for breaking the fast. There is therefore a concern that merchants might take advantage of the sudden rise in demand to raise their prices. Other commentaries add that the villagers who come into town on that day to supply the townspeople with their produce might not hear about the fast in time to bring more than their usual amount of produce. Consequently, food prices will rise on account of the increase in demand (Rabbeinu Gershom). Others suggest that the suppliers might not come into town at all on that day on account of the fast, which will cause a sudden rise in the price of food just before Shabbat (*Sefer HaEshkol*).

HALAKHA

If the seventeenth of Marḥeshvan arrived – הגיע שבעה עשר במרחשון: If the seventeenth of Marḥeshvan arrives and rain has not fallen, Torah scholars begin a series of three fasts, on a Monday, the following Thursday, and the next Monday. These fasts are treated as individual fasts (*Shulḥan Arukh, Oraḥ Ḥayyim* 575:1).

If the New Moon of Kislev arrived – הגיע ראש חדש כסליו: If the New Moon of Kislev arrives and it has still not rained, the court decrees a series of three fasts upon the entire community, on a Monday, the following Thursday, and the next Monday. The prayer services of regular communal fast days are recited during these fasts (*Shulḥan Arukh, Oraḥ Ḥayyim* 575:2).

One may not decree a fast on the community starting from a Thursday – אין גוזרין תענית על הצבור בתחילה בחמישי: In order not to cause a rise in food prices, the court may not decree the first of a series of fasts on a Thursday. Some authorities rule that this *halakha* applies even in places where there is no concern that food prices will rise as a result of the declaration of a fast. Others say that if there is no concern for a sudden rise in food prices, the first of a series of fasts may indeed be decreed on a Thursday (*Magen Avraham*), and this is the accepted practice (*Shulḥan Arukh, Oraḥ Ḥayyim* 572:6).

And they interrupt the sequence for New Moons – ומפסיקין בראשי חדשים: Those who have undertaken a series of fasts, including Torah scholars who are fasting as individuals on account of a drought, must interrupt the series if one of the fast days falls on Hanukkah, Purim, or a New Moon (*Shulḥan Arukh, Oraḥ Ḥayyim* 57:7).

BACKGROUND

We already learned this – תנינא: This phrase introduces an objection that a prior statement or question is superfluous, as it is already covered in a mishna or a *baraita*.

This is also taught – תניא נמי הכי: This phrase introduces a *baraita* that supports the previous statement of the Gemara or an individual *amora*.

וּבְיָמִים טוֹבִים הַכְּתוּבִין בִּמְגִילַּת תַּעֲנִית.

and for commemorative **holidays that are written in** ***Megillat Ta'anit***, which contains a list of dates on which the Sages prohibited fasting.

תָּנוּ רַבָּנַן: אַל יֹאמַר אָדָם: תַּלְמִיד אֲנִי; אֵינִי רָאוּי לִהְיוֹת יָחִיד. אֶלָּא, כָּל תַּלְמִידֵי חֲכָמִים יְחִידִים. אֵיזֶהוּ יָחִיד וְאֵיזֶהוּ תַּלְמִיד? יָחִיד כָּל שֶׁרָאוּי לְמַנּוֹתוֹ פַּרְנָס עַל הַצִּבּוּר. תַּלְמִיד כָּל שֶׁשּׁוֹאֲלִין אוֹתוֹ דְּבַר הֲלָכָה בְּתַלְמוּדוֹ וְאוֹמֵר, וַאֲפִילּוּ בְּמַסֶּכֶת דְּכַלָּה.

The Sages taught in a *baraita*: **A person should not say: I am** only **a student,** and consequently **I am unworthy to be** considered **an individual** who fasts, as stated in the mishna. **Rather,** with regard to the fasts of individuals, **all Torah scholars are individuals.** The *baraita* elaborates: **Who is an individual**[N] **and who is a student?**[H] **An individual** is **anyone who is** learned in Torah **and worthy to be appointed leader** and teacher **over the community. A student** is **any** Torah scholar **who is asked a matter of** ***halakha*** **in his studies and he says** the correct answer, **and** this is the case **even** if he is familiar only **with the tractate of** the ***kalla*** month,[N] i.e., the tractate the community studied that year.

תָּנוּ רַבָּנַן: לֹא כָּל הָרוֹצֶה לַעֲשׂוֹת עַצְמוֹ יָחִיד עוֹשֶׂה; תַּלְמִיד, עוֹשֶׂה. דִּבְרֵי רַבִּי מֵאִיר. רַבִּי יוֹסֵי אוֹמֵר: עוֹשֶׂה, וְזָכוּר לְטוֹב. לְפִי שֶׁאֵין שֶׁבַח הוּא לוֹ, אֶלָּא צַעַר הוּא לוֹ.

The Sages taught in another *baraita*: **Not everyone who wishes to make himself an individual** and conduct himself accordingly **may do** so, and nor may everyone who wants to act like **a student do** so. This is **the statement of Rabbi Meir. Rabbi Yosei says:** One **may do** so, **and** he is even **remembered for good,**[B] as the conduct of a Torah student **is not** a source of **praise for him, but it is** a source of **pain for him.** It is proper for one to take these obligations upon himself and he is not considered to be acting inappropriately.

תַּנְיָא אִידָּךְ: לֹא כָּל הָרוֹצֶה לַעֲשׂוֹת עַצְמוֹ יָחִיד עוֹשֶׂה; תַּלְמִיד, עוֹשֶׂה. דִּבְרֵי רַבִּי שִׁמְעוֹן בֶּן אֶלְעָזָר. רַבָּן שִׁמְעוֹן בֶּן גַּמְלִיאֵל אוֹמֵר: בַּמֶּה דְּבָרִים אֲמוּרִים? בְּדָבָר שֶׁל שֶׁבַח, אֲבָל בְּדָבָר שֶׁל צַעַר עוֹשֶׂה, וְזָכוּר לְטוֹב, שֶׁאֵין שֶׁבַח הוּא לוֹ, אֶלָּא צַעַר הוּא לוֹ.

It **is taught** in **another** *baraita*: **Not everyone who wishes to make himself an individual may do** so, and nor may everyone who wishes to act like **a student do** so. This is **the statement of Rabbi Shimon ben Elazar.**[P] **Rabban Shimon ben Gamliel**[P] **says: In what case is this statement said?** It is said **with regard to a matter of praise,** e.g., adorning oneself with the garments of a Torah scholar. **However, with regard to a matter of pain,** when Torah scholars act strictly, one **may do** so, **and** one who acts strictly is **remembered for good, as it is not** a source of **praise for him, but it is** a source of **pain for him.**

NOTES

Who is an individual – **אֵיזֶהוּ יָחִיד**: It is stated in the Jerusalem Talmud that when the mishna speaks of individuals, it is referring to those Torah scholars who have already been appointed to positions of leadership in the community and found trustworthy. These people are worthy of fasting and reciting prayers on behalf of the entire community in times of trouble.

And even with the tractate of the ***kalla*** **month** – **וַאֲפִילּוּ בְּמַסֶּכֶת דְּכַלָּה**: The early authorities dispute the meaning of this phrase. Some explain that the *baraita* is referring to the tractate studied at the assemblies held twice a year at the talmudic academies during the months of Adar and Elul (Rabbeinu Ḥananel; Ri, cited by *Tosafot* on *Shabbat* 114a). During each of these so-called *kalla* months, one specific tractate was studied, and public lessons were delivered on its topics, which rendered the material familiar even to ordinary people who could not devote their time to Torah study year-round. Accordingly, the *baraita* is stating that one is considered a student of Torah even if he can answer questions only on the tractate studied in a *kalla* month.

Others maintain that the *baraita* is referring to the minor tractate known as tractate *Kalla*, so named because it opens with a discussion of a certain regulation that applies to a bride, a *kalla* (Rashi and *Tosafot* on *Shabbat* 114a; Ritva; Rabbeinu Yehonatan). This tractate is not a part of the Talmud, but is a collection of *baraitot*. The material covered in the tractate is considered intellectually undemanding. Consequently, the *baraita* is saying that if someone can analyze those parts of the Talmud he has studied, even if he has learned only tractate *Kalla*, he is regarded as a student.

This interpretation is somewhat problematic, as the Gemara elsewhere (*Shabbat* 114a) states that a talmudic scholar is deemed worthy of public office only if he can answer halakhic questions on any part of the Talmud, even tractate *Kalla*, which indicates that this was a particularly difficult tractate. The early authorities explain that although this tractate was considered relatively easy, it was not studied regularly in the academies, and therefore one's mastery of it was considered a sign of great erudition.

HALAKHA

Who is a student – **אֵיזֶהוּ תַּלְמִיד**: If one can successfully answer a single question about his studies, even concerning the *halakhot* of a Festival that are taught publicly, one is considered a student. This applies both to the status of an individual for the fasts mentioned in the mishna (*Magen Avraham*), and also with regard to the *halakha* of a man who betroths a woman on condition that he is a Torah student (*Shulḥan Arukh, Even HaEzer* 37:27).

PERSONALITIES

Rabbi Shimon ben Elazar – **רַבִּי שִׁמְעוֹן בֶּן אֶלְעָזָר**: Rabbi Shimon ben Elazar was one of the Sages of the Mishna during the last generation of *tanna'im*. We know almost nothing about his life or family. Furthermore, as he belonged to the generation in which the Mishna was edited, not many of his teachings appear in the Mishna itself, although they are found in *baraitot* and in the Gemara. Rabbi Shimon ben Elazar was a friend of Rabbi Yehuda HaNasi, and several disputes between them appear in the sources. He received most of his Torah knowledge from his teacher, Rabbi Meir, to whom he was devoted and in whose name he cites many rulings.

Rabbi Shimon ben Elazar lived in or near Tiberias, and although he apparently did not have an academy of his own, many statements are attributed to him, concerning both *halakha* and *aggada*.

Rabban Shimon ben Gamliel – **רַבָּן שִׁמְעוֹן בֶּן גַּמְלִיאֵל**: There were two Sages with this name. The first, who lived at the end of the Second Temple period, was executed by the Romans as a leader of the great Jewish revolt. The second was his grandson, son of Rabban Gamliel of Yavne. Here, and in general, the Sage cited in the Talmud is the second of the two, the father and teacher of Rabbi Yehuda HaNasi.

Rabban Shimon ben Gamliel the second was apparently appointed *Nasi* of the Sanhedrin after the bar Kokheva revolt, when the situation of the Jewish people in Eretz Yisrael was extremely dire and a great deal of political acumen was required to restore Jewish life in the country. Rabban Shimon ben Gamliel was one of the youngest of the great Sages of his generation and regarded himself as inferior in status to his contemporaries, the great disciples of Rabbi Akiva: Rabbi Yehuda, Rabbi Yosei, Rabbi Meir, and Rabbi Shimon bar Yoḥai. Nevertheless, he sought to strengthen the position of the *Nasi*. This led to a failed effort to remove him from the office; he ultimately retained his post and those who sought to depose him were severely reprimanded. Few *halakhot* are taught in his name, but the *amora'im* state that in almost every place where he presents a ruling, even against the opinion of an unattributed mishna, the *halakha* is in accordance with him. His most prominent disciple was his eminent son, Rabbi Yehuda HaNasi.

BACKGROUND

And he is remembered for good – **וְזָכוּר לְטוֹב**: If one takes upon himself stringencies that are not required of everyone, this should not be seen as an act of vanity. On the contrary, one is regarded as acting beyond the letter of the law. Throughout the generations the Sages debated the level of stringency an ordinary person may take upon himself and the honors one is permitted to assume if these do not conform to one's general status, one's knowledge of Torah, and one's scrupulousness in the observance of mitzvot.

תנו רבנן: מי שהיה מתענה על הצרה ועברה, על החולה ונתרפא, הרי זה מתענה ומשלים. ההולך ממקום שאין מתענין למקום שמתענין הרי זה מתענה עמהן. ממקום שמתענין למקום שאין מתענין הרי זה מתענה ומשלים.

The Sages taught in a *baraita*: With regard to **one who was fasting for** a certain **trouble and** the trouble **passed,**[H] or if one was fasting **for** the recovery of **a sick person and** that person **was healed,** one may not cease his fast merely because its cause has been removed; rather, **he completes** his **fast.** The *baraita* continues: With regard to **one who goes from a place where they are not fasting to a place where they are fasting,**[HN] **he fasts with them.** Conversely, with regard to one who goes **from a place where they are fasting**[H] **to a place where they are not fasting, he completes his fast**[N] as a resident of his hometown.

שכח ואכל ושתה, אל יתראה בפני הצבור, ואל ינהיג עידונין בעצמו, שנאמר: "ויאמר יעקב לבניו: למה תתראו"? אמר להם יעקב לבניו: אל תראו עצמכם כשאתם שבעין, לא בפני עשו, ולא בפני ישמעאל, כדי שלא יתקנאו בכם.

With regard to one who **forgot** the fast **and ate**[H] **and drank, he should not show himself before the community** while satiated, **and he should not indulge in luxuries.** One should not think that because one has already eaten, his fast is completely nullified, and one may conduct himself as if it were not a fast day at all. Rather, one should minimize one's eating, **as it is stated: "And Jacob said to his sons: Why do you show yourselves?"** (Genesis 42:1). **Jacob said to his sons: Do not show yourselves when you are satiated, not before** the members of the house of **Esau, nor before** those of **Ishmael, so that they not be jealous of you,** as they suffer from hunger. This teaches that one should not show he is full when others are hungry.

"אל תרגזו בדרך". אמר רבי אלעזר: אמר להם יוסף לאחיו: אל תתעסקו בדבר הלכה, שמא תרגזו עליכם הדרך.

§ The Gemara presents another piece of advice related to the story of Joseph and his brothers. Joseph said to them: **"See that you not fall out by the way"** (Genesis 45:24). **Rabbi Elazar said** that **Joseph said to his brothers: Do not become occupied in a matter of *halakha*, lest you fall out on the way.**[N] If you discuss a *halakha* while traveling you might get into an argument, and it is important for travelers to remain on good terms.

איני? והאמר רבי אלעאי בר ברכיה: שני תלמידי חכמים שמהלכים בדרך, ואין ביניהן דברי תורה, ראויין לישרף, שנאמר: "ויהי המה הלכים, הלוך ודבר, והנה רכב אש וסוסי אש ויפרדו בין שניהם". טעמא דאיכא דיבור, הא ליכא דיבור, ראויין לישרף!

The Gemara asks: **Is that so? But didn't Rabbi Elai bar Berekhya say:** With regard to **two Torah scholars who are walking along the road and there are no Torah matters** discussed **between them, they are worthy of being burned, as it is stated: "And it came to pass, as they still went on, and talked, that, behold, there appeared a chariot of fire, and horses of fire, which parted them both asunder"** (II Kings 2:11). The **reason that** the chariot of fire did not harm Elisha is because there **was** a Torah **matter** between them, from which it may be inferred that had they **not** been discussing a Torah **matter, they** would have been **worthy of being burned.**

לא קשיא. הא למיגרס; הא לעיוני.

The Gemara answers: This is **not difficult. This** opinion of Rabbi Elai bar Berekhya is referring to **studying** by rote, by reviewing material one has already learned, which is permitted and even appropriate while traveling, whereas **that** opinion of Rabbi Elazar is referring to **examining** a *halakha* in depth, in which case it is likely that the scholars will come into conflict.

HALAKHA

Fasting for a trouble and it passed – מתענה על הצרה ועברה: If an individual undertakes a fast due to a certain trouble and the trouble passes, or if one fasts for the recovery of an invalid and that person recovers or dies, one must complete the fast or fasts that he has committed to take upon himself. However, if one stipulates at the time of his undertaking the fast that he not have to fast once the cause is removed, he need not do so (see *Shulḥan Arukh, Yoreh De'a*, chapter 220 and *Oraḥ Ḥayyim* 569:1).

One who goes…to a place where they are fasting – ההולך...למקום שמתענין: One who goes from a place where they are not fasting to a place where they are fasting must fast with the people in his destination, even if he already ate earlier in the day (*Eliyahu Rabba*). This is the *halakha* even if he intends to return to his original place of residence. However, since he did not take the fast upon himself, he is permitted to eat if he leaves the city borders. If one arrives before the day of the fast he is required to take the fast upon himself. Even if he neglects to do so explicitly, if he is present when that community takes the fast upon itself, he is obligated to complete the fast with them (*Taz*; *Shulḥan Arukh, Oraḥ Ḥayyim* 574:2).

One who goes from a place where they are fasting – ההולך ממקום שמתענין: With regard to one who goes from a place where the community is fasting to a place where they are not fasting, if he intends to return, he must observe all the fasts of his place of residence. This applies even if he had not taken on this particular fast; if he had expressly taken on the fast the *halakha* is obvious, as he would in any case be obliged to fast for the fulfillment of his vow (*Taz*). However, if he was away from his city when the fast was decreed, he does not have to observe it (*Arukh HaShulḥan*). If the fast was decreed not due to a current calamity, but as a memorial for earlier troubles, he is obligated to fast, even if he did not take it upon himself, as the Sages imposed upon him the stringencies of the place he left, provided that he intends to return there (*Eliyahu Rabba*; *Peri Megadim*; *Shulḥan Arukh, Oraḥ Ḥayyim* 574:1).

Forgot and ate on a fast – שכח ואכל בתענית: One who accidentally eats on a fast day decreed upon the community must not display himself before those who are still fasting as one who has eaten. Even when one is not in the presence of people who are fasting one should not indulge in delicacies. Some claim that one must stop eating as soon as one remembers it is a fast day (*Magen Avraham*; *Shulḥan Arukh, Oraḥ Ḥayyim* 574:3, and in the comment of Rema).

NOTES

One who goes from a place where they are not fasting to a place where they are fasting – ההולך ממקום שאין מתענין למקום שמתענין: The general principle is that one who intends to return home at the end of his journey is not required to adopt the stringencies of the places he is visiting (see *Pesaḥim* 50a). Here, however, the *baraita* obligates the traveler to observe the fast together with the community he is visiting. Some commentaries explain that one must observe this fast even if he plans to return home, as it is prohibited to separate oneself from the distress experienced by the community where he is residing, even if his stay is only temporary (Rabbeinu Yehonatan).

He completes his fast – מתענה ומשלים: A mishna (19a) states that if a fast is observed on account of drought and it begins to rain before noon, the fast need not be completed. Some commentaries distinguish between a fast observed on account of a drought and all other fasts. If it rains on the day of a fast for a drought, there is no longer any reason to continue the fast, as the community is no longer facing danger. However, if the purpose of the fast is to avert some other calamity, the fast must be completed even if the danger has passed, as it may not have been entirely forestalled (Ra'avad, in his note on Rambam *Sefer Zemanim, Hilkhot Ta'anit* 1:15–16). Most other early authorities distinguish between an individual fast and a communal fast (Rambam; Ramban): The *baraita* is concerned with an individual fast, which must be completed even if the calamity has passed, whereas the mishna below speaks of a communal fast, which does not have to be completed if the danger has been averted, so as not to cause the community unnecessary hardship. A communal fast is always considered to have been decreed with the stipulation that it will not have to be completed if the calamity in question is removed.

Lest you fall out on the way – שמא תרגזו עליכם הדרך: Rashi explains: In case you become lost on the way. Others similarly explain that the focus on *halakha* might cause them to become distracted and lose their bearings (Meiri). Yet others maintain that people observing them might suspect them of being quarrelsome (Rabbeinu Gershom).

בְּמַתְנִיתָא תָּנָא: אַל תַּפְסִיעוּ פְּסִיעָה גַּסָּה, וְהַכְנִיסוּ חַמָּה לָעִיר. אַל תַּפְסִיעוּ פְּסִיעָה גַּסָּה, דְּאָמַר מָר: פְּסִיעָה גַּסָּה נוֹטֶלֶת אֶחָד מֵחֲמֵשׁ מֵאוֹת מִמְּאוֹר עֵינָיו שֶׁל אָדָם.

It is taught in a *baraita* that Joseph said to his brothers: **Do not take long strides and bring the sun into the city,** i.e., you should enter the city to spend the night there before the sun has set. The Gemara elaborates: **Do not take long strides, as the Master said: A long stride takes away one five-hundredth of a person's eyesight,** and this loss is not worth the time saved.

וְהַכְנִיסוּ חַמָּה לָעִיר, כִּדְרַב יְהוּדָה אָמַר רַב. דְּאָמַר רַב יְהוּדָה אָמַר רַב: לְעוֹלָם יֵצֵא אָדָם בְּ״כִי טוֹב״ וְיִכָּנֵס בְּ״כִי טוֹב״, שֶׁנֶּאֱמַר: ״הַבֹּקֶר אוֹר, וְהָאֲנָשִׁים שֻׁלְּחוּ״.

The Gemara further explains: **And bring the sun into the city,** this is **in accordance with** a statement that **Rav Yehuda said** that **Rav said. As Rav Yehuda said** that **Rav said: A person** should **always leave** the place where he has spent the night **with "it is good"** (Genesis 1:4), i.e., after sunrise, as the Torah uses the expression "it is good" with regard to the creation of light. This goodness is manifest in the sense of security one feels when it is light. **And** likewise, when one comes into an unfamiliar city **he** should **enter with "it is good,"** before sunset, **as it is stated: "As soon as the morning was light, the men were sent away"** (Genesis 44:3).

אָמַר רַב יְהוּדָה אָמַר רַבִּי חִיָּיא: הַמְהַלֵּךְ בַּדֶּרֶךְ אַל יֹאכַל יוֹתֵר מִשְּׁנֵי רְעָבוֹן. מַאי טַעֲמָא? הָכָא תַּרְגִּימוּ: מִשּׁוּם מַעֲיָינָא. בְּמַעַרְבָא אָמְרִי: מִשּׁוּם מְזוֹנֵי. מַאי בֵּינַיְיהוּ? אִיכָּא בֵּינַיְיהוּ

Similarly, **Rav Yehuda said** that **Rabbi Ḥiyya said: One who is walking along the road** should **not eat more** each day **than** he would normally eat each day **in a year of famine.**[H] The Gemara asks: **What is the reason** for this? **Here** in Babylonia **they interpreted** that the reason is **due to** one's **bowels.**[N] Since the exertion of traveling can damage full bowels, it is preferable to eat less than the normal amount. **In the West,** Eretz Yisrael, they **say** that the reason is **due to food,** i.e., if one eats too much, his food may not last the entire journey, and therefore he should ration his meals. The Gemara asks: **What is** the practical difference **between** these two opinions? The Gemara answers: The practical difference **between them**

HALAKHA

Eating while traveling – אֲכִילָה בַּדֶּרֶךְ: One who is traveling should not eat more than he would during a time of famine, in order to prevent intestinal disease (*Magen Avraham*; *Shulḥan Arukh, Oraḥ Ḥayyim* 110:10).

NOTES

Bowels – מַעֲיָינָא: The commentary on the text follows Rabbeinu Ḥananel, who explains that this is a reference to diarrhea. If a traveler eats in his customary way, he is likely to suffer from stomach problems, which might prevent him from continuing his journey. Others suggest that if one who wishes to set out on a journey eats too much, his full stomach will weigh him down and make it difficult for him to travel as planned (Rabbeinu Gershom).

Perek **I**
Daf **11** Amud **a**

דְּיָתֵיב בְּאַרְבָּא. אִי נַמִי: דְּקָאָזֵיל מֵאַוְונָא לְאַוְונָא.

is in a case **where he is sitting in a boat.** The traveler must be concerned about his food supply, but he need not worry that the jostling of the road might force him to exert himself, which has a tendency to cause digestive problems. **Alternatively,** the practical difference is in a case **where he is traveling from station** [*avna*][L] **to station.** Here the exertion of the road might cause digestive problems, but one need not be concerned about running out of food, as he can resupply along the way.

רַב פַּפָּא כָּל פַּרְסָה וּפַרְסָה אָכֵיל חֲדָא רִיפְתָּא. קָסָבַר: מִשּׁוּם מַעֲיָינָא.

The Gemara relates that when **Rav Pappa** traveled, along **each and every parasang**[N] he would **eat one** loaf of **bread.** Rav Pappa did so because he **maintained** that the prohibition was **due to the bowels,** and as he was healthy he was not concerned that travel by road would irritate his digestion.

אָמַר רַב יְהוּדָה אָמַר רַב: כָּל הַמַּרְעִיב עַצְמוֹ בִּשְׁנֵי רְעָבוֹן נִיצַּל מִמִּיתָה מְשׁוּנָּה, שֶׁנֶּאֱמַר ״בְּרָעָב פָּדְךָ מִמָּוֶת״. מֵרָעָב מִיבָּעֵי לֵיהּ! אֶלָּא, הָכִי קָאָמַר: בִּשְׂכַר שֶׁמַּרְעִיב עַצְמוֹ בִּשְׁנֵי רְעָבוֹן, נִיצּוֹל מִמִּיתָה מְשׁוּנָּה.

Rav Yehuda said that **Rav said: Anyone who** has food for himself but nevertheless **starves himself in years of famine**[H] **will be saved from an unusual death, as it is stated: "In famine, He will redeem you from death"** (Job 5:20).[N] This is derived from the precise wording of the verse. According to its straightforward meaning, instead of "in famine," it **should have** said: **From famine,** as one is delivered from famine. **Rather, this is what** the verse **is saying: As a reward for starving himself in years of famine,** Job **will be saved from an unusual death.**

LANGUAGE

Station [*avna*] – אַוְונָא: From the Syriac word for station or inn, although some associate it with the Greek εὐνή, *eunè*, meaning bed.

NOTES

Each and every parasang – כָּל פַּרְסָה וּפַרְסָה: Some commentators suggest that Rav Pappa maintains that the advice to a traveler to eat sparingly was to help him avoid digestive problems that might result from the consumption of a heavy meal. He therefore divided his rations into small quantities that he ate every parasang, roughly every 4 km. In this way he ate a large number of small meals, rather than a single heavy meal (*Sefat Emet*).

In famine, He will redeem you from death – בְּרָעָב פָּדְךָ מִמָּוֶת: The fact that the verse does not state: He will redeem you from famine, but rather: He will redeem you from death, is an indication that you will be spared all types of unusual deaths (Maharsha).

HALAKHA

Anyone who starves himself in years of famine – כָּל הַמַּרְעִיב עַצְמוֹ בִּשְׁנֵי רְעָבוֹן: In times of famine, one should eat less and allow himself to go hungry, in accordance with the opinion of Rav Yehuda. Furthermore, it is prohibited to engage in marital relations during a famine, except on the night the wife ritually immerses herself. However, couples who are as yet without children may engage in relations even in years of famine. Many authorities rule leniently in this regard, in accordance with the opinion that refraining from sexual relations during years of famine is an act of piety, not a requirement (see *Sha'arei Teshuva*). Others note that these regulations are not limited to times of famine, but they apply whenever the community is faced with an impending calamity (*Shulḥan Arukh, Oraḥ Ḥayyim* 574:4, and in the comment of Rema).

אָמַר רֵישׁ לָקִישׁ: אָסוּר לְאָדָם לְשַׁמֵּשׁ מִטָּתוֹ בִּשְׁנֵי רְעָבוֹן, שֶׁנֶּאֱמַר: ״וּלְיוֹסֵף יֻלַּד שְׁנֵי בָנִים בְּטֶרֶם תָּבוֹא שְׁנַת הָרָעָב״. תָּנָא: חֲסוּכֵי בָנִים מְשַׁמְּשִׁין מִטּוֹתֵיהֶן בִּשְׁנֵי רְעָבוֹן.

Similarly, **Reish Lakish said: It is prohibited for a person to have conjugal relations in years of famine,** so that children not be born during these difficult years. **As it is stated: "And to Joseph were born two sons before the year of famine came"** (Genesis 41:50). It was **taught** in a *baraita*: Nevertheless, **those without children**[N] **may have marital relations in years of famine,** as they must strive to fulfill the mitzva to be fruitful and multiply.

תָּנוּ רַבָּנַן: בִּזְמַן שֶׁיִּשְׂרָאֵל שְׁרוּיִין בְּצַעַר, וּפֵירַשׁ אֶחָד מֵהֶן, בָּאִין שְׁנֵי מַלְאֲכֵי הַשָּׁרֵת שֶׁמְּלַוִּין לוֹ לְאָדָם וּמַנִּיחִין לוֹ יְדֵיהֶן עַל רֹאשׁוֹ וְאוֹמְרִים: פְּלוֹנִי זֶה, שֶׁפֵּירַשׁ מִן הַצִּבּוּר, אַל יִרְאֶה בְּנֶחָמַת צִבּוּר.

Likewise, **the Sages taught** in a *baraita*: **When the Jewish people is immersed in distress, and one of them separates himself**[H] from the community and does not share their suffering, the **two ministering angels who accompany a person come and place their hands on his head,** as though he was an offering, **and say: This** man, **so-and-so, who has separated himself from the community, let him not see the consolation of the community.**

תַּנְיָא אִידָךְ: בִּזְמַן שֶׁהַצִּבּוּר שָׁרוּי בְּצַעַר, אַל יֹאמַר אָדָם: ״אֵלֵךְ לְבֵיתִי וְאוֹכַל וְאֶשְׁתֶּה, וְשָׁלוֹם עָלַיִךְ, נַפְשִׁי״. וְאִם עוֹשֶׂה כֵּן, עָלָיו הַכָּתוּב אוֹמֵר: ״וְהִנֵּה שָׂשׂוֹן וְשִׂמְחָה, הָרֹג בָּקָר וְשָׁחֹט צֹאן, אָכֹל בָּשָׂר וְשָׁתוֹת יָיִן. אָכוֹל וְשָׁתוֹ, כִּי מָחָר נָמוּת״. מַה כְּתִיב בַּתְרֵיהּ? ״וְנִגְלָה בְאָזְנָי ה׳ צְבָאוֹת: אִם יְכֻפַּר הֶעָוֹן הַזֶּה לָכֶם עַד תְּמֻתוּן״.

A similar idea **is taught in another** *baraita*: **When the community is immersed in suffering, a person may not say: I will go to my home and I will eat and drink, and peace be upon you, my soul. And if he does so, the verse says about him: "And behold joy and gladness, slaying oxen and killing sheep, eating flesh and drinking wine; let us eat and drink, for tomorrow we shall die"** (Isaiah 22:13). **And** the prophecy continues with **what is written afterward,** in the following verse: **"And the Lord of hosts revealed Himself in my ears: Surely this iniquity shall not be expiated by you until you die"** (Isaiah 22:14).

עַד כָּאן מִידַּת בֵּינוֹנִים, אֲבָל בְּמִדַּת רְשָׁעִים מַה כְּתִיב? ״אֵתָיוּ, אֶקְחָה יַיִן, וְנִסְבְּאָה שֵׁכָר, וְהָיָה כָזֶה יוֹם מָחָר״. מַה כְּתִיב בַּתְרֵיהּ? ״הַצַּדִּיק אָבָד וְאֵין אִישׁ שָׂם עַל לֵב...כִּי מִפְּנֵי הָרָעָה נֶאֱסַף הַצַּדִּיק״.

The *baraita* comments: Up **to this point** is the **attribute of middling people,** who merely exclude themselves from the suffering of the community. **However,** with regard **to the attribute of wicked people,**[N] **what is written** about those who hope for more of these days? **"Come, I will fetch wine, and we will fill ourselves with strong drink; and tomorrow shall be as this day,** and much more abundant" (Isaiah 56:12). **And what is written afterward? "The righteous perishes, and no man lays it to heart,** and godly men are taken away, none considering **that the righteous is taken away from the evil to come"** (Isaiah 57:1). This verse teaches that righteous people suffer early death to prevent them from witnessing the harm that will befall these evil people.

אֶלָּא, יְצַעֵר אָדָם עִם הַצִּבּוּר. שֶׁכֵּן מָצִינוּ בְּמֹשֶׁה רַבֵּינוּ, שֶׁצִּיעֵר עַצְמוֹ עִם הַצִּבּוּר, שֶׁנֶּאֱמַר: ״וִידֵי מֹשֶׁה כְּבֵדִים וַיִּקְחוּ אֶבֶן וַיָּשִׂימוּ תַחְתָּיו וַיֵּשֶׁב עָלֶיהָ״, וְכִי לֹא הָיָה לוֹ לְמֹשֶׁה כַּר אֶחָד אוֹ כֶּסֶת אַחַת לֵישֵׁב עָלֶיהָ? אֶלָּא, כָּךְ אָמַר מֹשֶׁה: הוֹאִיל וְיִשְׂרָאֵל שְׁרוּיִין בְּצַעַר, אַף אֲנִי אֶהְיֶה עִמָּהֶם בְּצַעַר. וְכָל הַמְצַעֵר עַצְמוֹ עִם הַצִּבּוּר זוֹכֶה וְרוֹאֶה בְּנֶחָמַת צִבּוּר.

The *baraita* continues: **Rather, a person should be distressed together with the community. As we found with Moses our teacher that he was distressed together with the community, as it is stated** during the war with Amalek: **"But Moses' hands were heavy; and they took a stone, and put it under him, and he sat upon it"** (Exodus 17:12). **But didn't Moses have one pillow or one cushion to sit upon;** why was he forced to sit on a rock? **Rather, Moses said as follows: Since the Jewish people are immersed in suffering, I too will be with them in suffering,** as much as I am able, although I am not participating in the fighting. The *baraita* adds: **And anyone who is distressed together with the community will merit seeing the consolation of the community.**

HALAKHA

And one of them separates himself – וּפֵירַשׁ אֶחָד מֵהֶן: One who separates himself from the community at a time of distress, when it is in his power to help the community in some way (*Magen Avraham*), will not merit to see its eventual consolation. Conversely, whoever participates in the community's suffering will merit seeing its consolation (*Shulḥan Arukh*, *Oraḥ Ḥayyim* 574:5).

NOTES

Those without [*ḥasukhei*] children – חֲסוּכֵי בָנִים: Most early authorities maintain that this expression is referring to couples without children, who are permitted to engage in marital relations even during years of famine. The early authorities and the later authorities dispute the precise meaning of the phrase, whether it refers solely to those who have no children at all (Meiri; *Taz*), or whether it includes those who have a son or a daughter, but not both, and who have therefore not yet fulfilled the husband's religious obligation to be fruitful and multiply (Rashi; Ran; Talmid HaRamban).

It is stated in the Jerusalem Talmud that even couples who are without children, whom the Gemara there calls: Those who are desirous of children, may engage in marital relations during years of famine only on the night when the wife ritually immerses herself, when conception is most likely.

The Ritva suggests an entirely different explanation of this passage, which he bases on a variant reading available to many of the early authorities: *Ḥashukhei banim*, those whose children's actions are dark. According to this opinion, those couples whose children are wicked, so-called children of dark deeds, are permitted to engage in marital relations during years of famine.

Middling people…wicked people – בֵּינוֹנִים...רְשָׁעִים: The commentaries suggest various explanations for the difference between those who are considered middling, i.e., neither righteous nor wicked, and those who are classified as wicked. The commentary on the text follows Rashi, who explains that although the members of the middle group refuse to show sympathy toward those who are in distress, they do recognize that they themselves are in danger, whereas the wicked imagine that they are immune to the perils threatening the community.

Others suggest that although the members of the middle group withdraw from the community in its time of need, they do so only in private, whereas the wicked declare publicly that they are unaffected by the problems of others (Rabbi Elyakim). Yet other commentaries argue that although the members of the middle group are indifferent to the troubles suffered by the community, they repent when they themselves are struck by the same afflictions. By contrast, the wicked fail to repent even when suffering reaches their own doors (Ritva).

וְשֶׁמָּא יֹאמַר אָדָם: מִי מֵעִיד בִּי? אַבְנֵי בֵיתוֹ שֶׁל אָדָם וְקוֹרוֹת בֵּיתוֹ שֶׁל אָדָם מְעִידִים בּוֹ, שֶׁנֶּאֱמַר: ״כִּי אֶבֶן מִקִּיר תִּזְעָק, וְכָפִיס מֵעֵץ יַעֲנֶנָּה״. דְּבֵי רַבִּי שֵׁילָא אָמְרִי: שְׁנֵי מַלְאֲכֵי הַשָּׁרֵת הַמְלַוִּין לוֹ לָאָדָם הֵן מְעִידִין עָלָיו, שֶׁנֶּאֱמַר: ״כִּי מַלְאָכָיו יְצַוֶּה לָּךְ״.

The *baraita* further states: **And lest a person say,** I have acted in secret; **who will testify against me**[N] on the Day of Judgment? The *tanna* explains that the **stones of a person's house and the beams of a person's house** will **testify against him, as it is stated: "For a stone shall cry out from the wall, and a beam out of the timber shall answer it"** (Habakkuk 2:11). **In the school of Rabbi Sheila**[P] **they say:** The **two ministering angels who accompany a person** will **testify against him, as it is stated: "For He will give His angels charge over you,** to keep you in all your ways" (Psalms 91:11).

רַבִּי חִידְקָא אוֹמֵר: נִשְׁמָתוֹ שֶׁל אָדָם הִיא מְעִידָה עָלָיו, שֶׁנֶּאֱמַר: ״מִשֹּׁכֶבֶת חֵיקֶךָ שְׁמֹר פִּתְחֵי פִיךָ״. וְיֵשׁ אוֹמְרִים: אֵבָרָיו שֶׁל אָדָם מְעִידִים בּוֹ, שֶׁנֶּאֱמַר: ״אַתֶּם עֵדַי, נְאֻם ה׳״.

Rabbi Ḥidka said: A person's soul will **testify against him, as it is stated: "Keep the doors of your mouth from her who lies in your bosom"** (Micah 7:5). **And some say: A man's limbs** will **testify against him, as it is stated: "You are My witnesses, says the Lord"** (Isaiah 43:10).

״אֵל אֱמוּנָה, וְאֵין עָוֶל״. ״אֵל אֱמוּנָה״: כְּשֵׁם שֶׁנִּפְרָעִין מִן הָרְשָׁעִים לָעוֹלָם הַבָּא אֲפִילּוּ עַל עֲבֵירָה קַלָּה שֶׁעוֹשִׂין. כָּךְ נִפְרָעִין מִן הַצַּדִּיקִים בָּעוֹלָם הַזֶּה עַל עֲבֵירָה קַלָּה שֶׁעוֹשִׂין.

The *baraita* cites another verse that deals with judgment. **"A God of faithfulness and without iniquity,** He is just and righteous" (Deuteronomy 32:4). The *baraita* interprets **"a God of faithfulness"** to mean that **just as punishment is exacted from the wicked in the World-to-Come even for a light transgression that they commit, so too, punishment is exacted from the righteous in this world for a light transgression that they commit.** The righteous suffer their punishment in this world to purify them so they can enjoy the World-to-Come.

״וְאֵין עָוֶל״: כְּשֵׁם שֶׁמְּשַׁלְּמִין שָׂכָר לַצַּדִּיקִים לָעוֹלָם הַבָּא אֲפִילּוּ עַל מִצְוָה קַלָּה שֶׁעוֹשִׂין, כָּךְ מְשַׁלְּמִין שָׂכָר לָרְשָׁעִים בָּעוֹלָם הַזֶּה אֲפִילּוּ עַל מִצְוָה קַלָּה שֶׁעוֹשִׂין.

The *baraita* turns to the second section of the verse: **"And without iniquity."**[N] This teaches that **just as reward is paid to the righteous in the World-to-Come even for a minor mitzva that they fulfill, so too, reward is paid to the wicked in this world for even a minor mitzva that they fulfill,** to give the wicked all the reward they deserve for the performance of mitzvot in this world, and deprive them of any share in the World-to-Come.

״צַדִּיק וְיָשָׁר הוּא״: אָמְרוּ: בִּשְׁעַת פְּטִירָתוֹ שֶׁל אָדָם לְבֵית עוֹלָמוֹ, כָּל מַעֲשָׂיו נִפְרָטִין לְפָנָיו, וְאוֹמְרִים לוֹ: כָּךְ וְכָךְ עָשִׂיתָ בְּמָקוֹם פְּלוֹנִי בְּיוֹם פְּלוֹנִי, וְהוּא אוֹמֵר: הֵן וְאוֹמְרִים לוֹ: חֲתוֹם, וְחוֹתֵם, שֶׁנֶּאֱמַר: ״בְּיַד כָּל אָדָם יַחְתּוֹם״. וְלֹא עוֹד, אֶלָּא שֶׁמַּצְדִּיק עָלָיו אֶת הַדִּין, וְאוֹמֵר לָהֶם: יָפֶה דַּנְתּוּנִי, לְקַיֵּים מַה שֶּׁנֶּאֱמַר: ״לְמַעַן תִּצְדַּק בְּדָבְרֶךָ״.

With regard to the third section of the verse: **"He is just and righteous,"** the Sages **said: At the hour of a person's departure to his eternal home, all his deeds are enumerated before him** and are rendered visible to him once again, **and** the deeds themselves **say to him: You did such and such, in such and such a place, on such and such a day, and he says: Yes,** that is exactly what happened. **And they say to him: Sign** a statement that this is correct, **and he signs it, as it is stated: "He makes the hand of every man sign"** (Job 37:7). **And not only that,** but after a one has been shown all his deeds, **he justifies the judgment upon himself, and says to them: You have judged me well.** This response serves **to fulfill that which is stated: "That You may be justified when You speak and be right when You judge"** (Psalms 51:6).

PERSONALITIES

The school of Rabbi Sheila – דְּבֵי רַבִּי שֵׁילָא: Rabbi Sheila was a Babylonian Sage in the transitional generation between the *tanna'im* and the *amora'im*. His school played an important role in Babylonia, as it was the only important academy there before Rav came. The major *amora'im* Rav and Shmuel, treated Rabbi Sheila with great respect, and when they established Torah centers they did so in other cities, so as not to detract from his honor.

Rabbi Sheila's academy apparently remained active for a considerable time after his passing, which is why there are statements delivered in the name of the school of Rabbi Sheila.

NOTES

Who will testify against me – מִי מֵעִיד בִּי: Some commentaries explain that this testimony should be understood in the sense of the disclosure of the truth (Rashba). The beams of a person's house, the angels who accompany him, his soul, and his very body will reveal his true behavior during those times when the community suffered distress. When the Gemara speaks of the beams of a person's house it is referring to his neighbors, who are aware of his actions in his own home, and who will share their knowledge with the rest of the community. The angels display a person's true character to the public when they withdraw from him the protection that had shielded him from calamity up to that point. A person's soul sheds light on his conduct when it receives fitting punishment in the World-to-Come. Lastly, one's own body reveals his true character when his organs are afflicted in this world.

And without iniquity – וְאֵין עָוֶל: The early authorities cite different versions and interpretations of this passage. According to the standard talmudic text, the first part of the verse: "A God of faithfulness," teaches that punishment is exacted from the righteous in this world even for their slightest transgressions, while the second part of the verse: "And without iniquity," indicates that reward is paid to the wicked in this world for every small mitzva. Rashi explains in his commentary on the verse that both parts promise that one will ultimately be rewarded for his mitzvot. The phrase "a God of faithfulness" teaches that God will reward the righteous in the World-to-Come, while the expression "without iniquity" means that He will reward the wicked in this world.

Others commentaries prefer the version of the *Yalkut Shimoni*, according to which the first part of the verse is referring to all aspects of God's justice, the reward paid to the righteous and to the wicked, as well as the punishment meted out to both the righteous and to the wicked. The second part of the verse teaches the subsequent claim of the *baraita*, that when one dies all his deeds appear before him and remind him of all he did in the course of his lifetime. From the third part of the verse: "He is just and righteous," it is derived that when the deceased receives his punishment he accepts the judgment and confesses his sins (Maharsha).

PERSONALITIES

Rabbi Elazar HaKappar – רַבִּי אֶלְעָזָר הַקַּפָּר: Rabbi Elazar HaKappar was a Sage from the last generation of *tanna'im*. A few of Rabbi Elazar HaKappar's rulings of *halakha* can be found in *baraitot* and halakhic midrash, while many of his moral statements and homiletic expositions of *aggada* are mentioned in the Mishna, the Gemara, and *midrashim*. We do not know any details of Rabbi Elazar HaKappar's life, apart from the fact that he had a son called Rabbi Eliezer. He was apparently active for a time in Lod, and Rabbi Yehoshua ben Levi was his foremost disciple. It is unclear whether the moniker HaKappar is referring to the name of a place, or his occupation, as *fokarin* means wool. There are many theories concerning the relationship between Rabbi Elazar HaKappar and the Sage bar Kappara. An inscription was recently discovered on a doorpost in the Golan Heights that states: This is the study hall of Rabbi Elazar HaKappar.

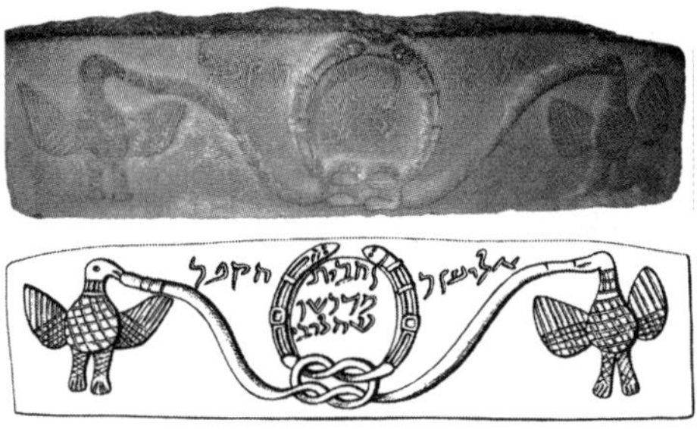

Ancient engraving and sketch. The inscription reads: This is the study hall of Rabbi Elazar HaKappar.

BACKGROUND

The Great [*berabbi*] – בְּרַבִּי: When the epithet *berabbi*, or *beribbi*, appears after the name of a Sage, this means that he was the son of a Rabbi only if a specific Rabbi is named, e.g., Rabbi Yosei *berabbi* Yehuda means Rabbi Yosei, son of Rabbi Yehuda. Here, however, the term *berabbi* is simply an honorific, which literally means the son of great men, of rabbis and great scholars of the generation. Since it is an honorific expression, when *berabbi* appears by itself it does not indicate that the man to whom it is applied is actually the son of great Sages, but rather, that he is himself an important Sage of his generation.

אָמַר שְׁמוּאֵל: כׇּל הַיּוֹשֵׁב בְּתַעֲנִית נִקְרָא חוֹטֵא. סָבַר כִּי הַאי תַּנָּא, דְּתַנְיָא: רַבִּי אֶלְעָזָר הַקַּפָּר בְּרַבִּי אוֹמֵר: מָה תַּלְמוּד לוֹמַר: ״וְכִפֶּר עָלָיו מֵאֲשֶׁר חָטָא עַל הַנָּפֶשׁ״? וְכִי בְּאֵיזֶה נֶפֶשׁ חָטָא זֶה? אֶלָּא, שֶׁצִּיעֵר עַצְמוֹ מִן הַיַּיִן.

§ The Gemara returns return to the primary topic of the tractate, the issue of fasts. **Shmuel said: Whoever sits in** observance of **a fast is called a sinner,**[N] as it is inappropriate to take unnecessary suffering upon oneself. The Gemara comments: Shmuel **holds in accordance with** the opinion of **the following *tanna*, as it is taught** in a *baraita*: **Rabbi Elazar HaKappar**[P] **the Great**[B] **says: What** is the meaning when **the verse states,** with regard to a nazirite: **"And he will atone for him for that he sinned by the soul [*nefesh*]"** (Numbers 6:11). **But with what soul did this** nazirite **sin? Rather,** the nazirite sinned **by** the **distress** he caused **himself when he abstained from wine,** in accordance with the terms of his vow.

וַהֲלֹא דְּבָרִים קַל וָחוֹמֶר? וּמַה זֶּה, שֶׁלֹּא צִיעֵר עַצְמוֹ אֶלָּא מִן הַיַּיִן, נִקְרָא חוֹטֵא, הַמְצַעֵר עַצְמוֹ מִכׇּל דָּבָר וְדָבָר, עַל אַחַת כַּמָּה וְכַמָּה!

And are these **matters not** inferred ***a fortiori*? And if this** nazirite, **who distressed himself** by abstaining **only from wine, is** nevertheless **called a sinner** and requires atonement, then with regard to **one who distresses himself** by abstaining **from each and every matter** of food and drink when he fasts, **all the more so** should he be considered a sinner.

רַבִּי אֶלְעָזָר אוֹמֵר: נִקְרָא קָדוֹשׁ, שֶׁנֶּאֱמַר: ״קָדוֹשׁ יִהְיֶה, גַּדֵּל פֶּרַע שְׂעַר רֹאשׁוֹ״. וּמַה זֶּה, שֶׁלֹּא צִיעֵר עַצְמוֹ אֶלָּא מִדָּבָר אֶחָד, נִקְרָא קָדוֹשׁ, הַמְצַעֵר עַצְמוֹ מִכׇּל דָּבָר, עַל אַחַת כַּמָּה וְכַמָּה!

Conversely, **Rabbi Elazar says:** One who accepts a fast upon himself is **called sacred, as it is stated** with regard to the nazirite: **"He shall be sacred, he shall let the locks of the hair of his head grow long"** (Numbers 6:5). Here too, one can apply an *a fortiori* inference: **And if this** nazirite, **who distressed himself** by abstaining **from only one matter,** wine, is nevertheless **called sacred,** then with regard to **one who distresses himself** by abstaining from **every matter, all the more so** should he be considered sacred.

וְלִשְׁמוּאֵל, הָא אִיקְּרֵי קָדוֹשׁ! הַהוּא אַגִּידּוּל פֶּרַע קָאֵי. וּלְרַבִּי אֶלְעָזָר, הָא נִקְרָא חוֹטֵא! הַהוּא דְּסָאֵיב נַפְשֵׁיהּ.

The Gemara asks: **And according to** the opinion of **Shmuel,** the nazirite **is** indeed **called sacred,** as stated by Rabbi Elazar. The Gemara answers: **That** verse **is referring to** the sanctity of the **growth of the locks,**[N] as the nazirite's hair does possess an element of sanctity, but it does not refer to the nazirite himself. The Gemara reverses the question: **And according to** the opinion of **Rabbi Elazar,** the nazirite **is called a sinner.** The Gemara answers: **That** verse **refers** specifically **to** a nazirite **who rendered himself ritually impure** by coming into contact with a dead body, an act that is prohibited for him. This particular nazirite must bring an offering to atone "for that he sinned by the soul."

וּמִי אֲמַר רַבִּי אֶלְעָזָר הָכִי? וְהָאָמַר רַבִּי אֶלְעָזָר: לְעוֹלָם יָמוֹד אָדָם עַצְמוֹ

The Gemara asks: **And did Rabbi Elazar** actually **say this,** that fasting is a virtuous act? **But didn't Rabbi Elazar say: A person should always consider himself**

NOTES

Whoever sits in observance of a fast is called a sinner – כׇּל הַיּוֹשֵׁב בְּתַעֲנִית נִקְרָא חוֹטֵא: The early and later authorities discuss at length the broader issues of the place of fasting and asceticism in Judaism. *Tosafot* attempt to reconcile the seemingly contradictory talmudic sources and argue that although one who observes a fast is called a sinner, the righteous deed he performs by fasting outweighs the sin he commits by voluntarily undergoing bodily suffering.

Others distinguish between a fast observed as an act of penance and one that serves as a means of attaining sanctity. One who fasts for atonement is called a sinner, not due to the fast, but due to the transgressions that made the fast necessary. When he observes the fast, he acts correctly, but this does not transform him into a sacred or pious man. By contrast, one who fasts to purify his soul is indeed considered a sacred individual, as his purpose is to reach a state of sanctity and closeness to God (Meiri).

Yet others argue that one is called a sinner only if he fails to repent for his sins even after observing his fast. In addition to the sins he committed in the past, he is now guilty of the additional sin of causing his body distress. However, if he sincerely repents he is certainly considered sacred, as he has thereby purified himself of his sins (Rabbi Yoshiya Pinto).

That is referring to the growth of the locks – הַהוּא אַגִּידּוּל פֶּרַע קָאֵי: The commentators disagree over whether this phrase means that the nazirite's hair itself is sacred, or whether the nazirite's act of letting his hair grow is the sacred act of a nazirite, not his abstention from wine. Several early commentaries say that this verse should be read: That is referring to his purification of his soul. A nazirite is called sacred, not because he refrains from drinking wine, but due to the fact that he purifies his soul by avoiding contact with the dead, in accordance with the reading of the verse: "And he will atone for him for that he sinned by the dead [*nefesh*]" (Numbers 6:11), as *nefesh* can mean dead as well as soul (see Rabbeinu Ḥananel and Rabbeinu Gershom).

כְּאִילּוּ קָדוֹשׁ שָׁרוּי בְּתוֹךְ מֵעָיו, שֶׁנֶּאֱמַר ״בְּקִרְבְּךָ קָדוֹשׁ וְלֹא אָבוֹא בְּעִיר״! לָא קַשְׁיָא. הָא דְּמָצֵי לְצַעוּרֵי נַפְשֵׁיהּ; הָא דְּלָא מָצֵי לְצַעוּרֵי נַפְשֵׁיהּ.

as though a sacred object **is immersed in his bowels,** which he may not damage, **as it is stated: "The sacred is in your midst;**[N] **and I will not come into the city"** (Hosea 11:9). This statement indicates that it is prohibited to take a fast upon oneself. The Gemara answers: This is **not difficult. This** first ruling, that one who fasts is sacred, is referring to a case **where he is able to distress himself**[H] without causing bodily harm. **That** second ruling, that one may not overly burden his body, deals with a situation **when he is unable to distress himself** while avoiding all harm, and he proceeds to fast nevertheless.

רֵישׁ לָקִישׁ אָמַר: נִקְרָא חָסִיד, שֶׁנֶּאֱמַר: ״גֹּמֵל נַפְשׁוֹ אִישׁ חָסֶד, וְעֹכֵר שְׁאֵרוֹ״ וגו׳. אָמַר רַב שֵׁשֶׁת: הַאי בַּר בֵּי רַב דְּיָתֵיב בְּתַעֲנִיתָא, לֵיכוֹל כַּלְבָּא לְשֵׁירוּתֵיהּ.

Reish Lakish said: One who fasts is **called pious, as it is stated: "The pious man does good [*gomel*] to his own soul;**[N] **but he who troubles his own flesh** is cruel" (Proverbs 11:17). The verb *gomel* can also mean weaning, or abstaining from unnecessary pleasure. Accordingly, Reish Lakish derives from this verse that one who abstains from food is called pious. Similarly, **Rav Sheshet**[P] **said: This student of a Torah academy who sits in** observance of **a fast** has **let a dog eat his portion.**[N] Since his fast weakens him and prevents him from studying Torah, it is considered as though a dog ate his meal, as the student derived no benefit from it.

אָמַר רַב יִרְמְיָה בַּר אַבָּא: אֵין תַּעֲנִית צִיבּוּר בְּבָבֶל אֶלָּא תִּשְׁעָה בְּאָב בִּלְבַד. אָמַר רַב יִרְמְיָה בַּר אַבָּא אָמַר רֵישׁ לָקִישׁ: אֵין תַּלְמִיד חָכָם רַשַּׁאי לֵישֵׁב בְּתַעֲנִית, מִפְּנֵי שֶׁמְּמַעֵט בִּמְלֶאכֶת שָׁמַיִם.

Rav Yirmeya bar Abba said: There is no completely stringent **communal fast in Babylonia,**[NH] **except for the Ninth of Av alone.** All other fasts, even those which are fixed and routine for the community, are treated as individual fasts, with regard to both the customs of the fast itself and the *halakhot* of who is obligated to fast. **Rav Yirmeya bar Abba said** that **Reish Lakish said: A Torah scholar is not permitted to sit in** observance of **a fast,**[H] **due to** the fact that his fasting **reduces** his strength for the **heavenly service** of Torah study and mitzvot.

NOTES

The sacred is in your midst – בְּקִרְבְּךָ קָדוֹשׁ: Rashi explains that one should always consider himself as though something sacred were immersed in his bowels. According to this interpretation, the verse is to be understood as follows: Since the sacred object inside you is suffering distress because you are fasting, I will not come into the city. Conversely, *Tosafot* explain that the word sacred in the verse is a reference to God Himself. According to this interpretation, the rest of the verse is superfluous in this context, and indeed the phrase: And I will not come into the city, is missing in certain manuscripts.

Does good [*gomel*] to his own soul – גֹּמֵל נַפְשׁוֹ: Rashi explains that Reish Lakish, like Shmuel and Rabbi Elazar, is referring to one who voluntarily observes a fast. This individual, Reish Lakish argues, is pious, as the verse indicates: One who weans his soul by abstaining from food is a pious person. *Tosafot* claim that Reish Lakish is speaking of one who refrains from fasting. According to this interpretation, *gomel* means: One who acts kindly, in this case to his own soul, by sustaining it.

Let a dog eat his portion – לֵיכוֹל כַּלְבָּא לְשֵׁירוּתֵיהּ: Rashi explains that a Torah scholar who observes a fast gains nothing, and therefore he is likened to one who refrains from eating because a dog has consumed his meal. Some commentaries interpret Rav Sheshet's remark as a curse: As for a Torah scholar who observes a fast, may a dog eat his meal (*Shita Mekubbetzet*).

There is no communal fast in Babylonia – אֵין תַּעֲנִית צִיבּוּר בְּבָבֶל: Various reasons have been suggested for this principle. Some say it is because there is no need to pray for rain in Babylonia, where the land is watered by rivers (*Tosafot*). Others claim that as most inhabitants of Babylonia were poor, the Sages did not want to prevent them from working (Ra'avad). Yet others state, based on the Jerusalem Talmud, that a communal fast can be declared only in a place where there is a *Nasi* and a Sanhedrin (Ramban).

HALAKHA

Where he is able to distress himself – דְּמָצֵי לְצַעוּרֵי נַפְשֵׁיהּ: One who observes a fast when he is able to do so without causing himself bodily harm is considered sacred. However, one who does so when he is weak or ill is called a sinner, in accordance with the opinion of Rabbi Elazar. The ruling applies only to one who observes the fast as an act of piety. However, one who knows that he has committed a transgression is required to fast, even if he is weak or ill (*Taz*). The authorities associated with the moralistic *mussar* movement have suggested a variety of alternatives to fasting for those who seek atonement for their sins. These include refraining from eating certain foods, refraining from speech, and secluding oneself for private reflection (see *Shenei Luḥot HaBerit* and *Magen Avraham*; *Shulḥan Arukh, Oraḥ Ḥayyim* 571:1).

Communal fast in Babylonia – תַּעֲנִית צִיבּוּר בְּבָבֶל: All fasts in Babylonia, or anywhere else outside Eretz Yisrael, are treated as individual fasts, apart from the Ninth of Av and Yom Kippur. This means that outside Eretz Yisrael the Ninth of Av and Yom Kippur are the only time when work is prohibited and the fast starts in the evening. Even fasts decreed upon the community are treated as individual fasts outside Eretz Yisrael (*Shulḥan Arukh, Oraḥ Ḥayyim* 568:6, 575:10).

A Torah scholar is not permitted to sit in observance of a fast – אֵין תַּלְמִיד חָכָם רַשַּׁאי לֵישֵׁב בְּתַעֲנִית: It is prohibited for a Torah scholar to accept a fast upon himself, as it diminishes his capacity to study Torah. However, if the entire community is fasting he should do so as well, so as not to separate himself from the community. Whoever spends all his time studying Torah is called a Torah scholar for the purposes of this *halakha*, even nowadays (*Magen Avraham*). Teachers of schoolchildren are also considered Torah scholars, as explicitly stated in the Jerusalem Talmud (*Shulḥan Arukh, Oraḥ Ḥayyim* 571:2).

PERSONALITIES

Rav Sheshet – רַב שֵׁשֶׁת: Rav Sheshet was a famous Babylonian *amora* of the second and third generations, a colleague of Rav Naḥman and Rav Ḥisda. He was outstanding in his knowledge of the Mishna and of *baraitot*, acquiring it through exceptional diligence, despite his blindness. With regard to his disputes with Rav Naḥman, the *ge'onim* rule that the *halakha* is in accordance with Rav Sheshet's opinion in all matters of ritual law. Many *amora'im* of the third and fourth generations were his disciples, including Rava.

״אוֹכְלִין וְשׁוֹתִין מִשֶּׁחָשֵׁיכָה״ כו׳. אָמַר רַבִּי זְעֵירָא אָמַר רַב הוּנָא: יָחִיד שֶׁקִּיבֵּל עָלָיו תַּעֲנִית, אֲפִילּוּ אָכַל וְשָׁתָה כָּל הַלַּיְלָה, לְמָחָר הוּא מִתְפַּלֵּל תְּפִילַּת תַּעֲנִית. לָן בְּתַעֲנִיתוֹ, אֵינוֹ מִתְפַּלֵּל שֶׁל תַּעֲנִית.

§ The mishna taught that during the first set of fasts **they eat and drink from after dark,** and begin fasting in the morning. **Rabbi Zeira said** that **Rav Huna said:** With regard to **an individual who took a fast upon himself,**[N] **even** if **he ate and drank the entire night,**[H] **on the following day he prays** in the *Amida* **the prayer of a fast,** which begins: Answer us on the day of our fast. If after completing his fast he **slept in his fast,**[H] i.e., he continued fasting throughout the night, **he does not pray** the prayer **of a fast** the next morning.

אֲמַר רַב יוֹסֵף: מַאי קָסָבַר רַב הוּנָא? סְבִירָא לֵיהּ אֵין מִתְעַנִּין לְשָׁעוֹת? אוֹ דִּלְמָא, מִתְעַנִּין לְשָׁעוֹת, וְהַמִּתְעַנֶּה לְשָׁעוֹת אֵינוֹ מִתְפַּלֵּל תְּפִלַּת תַּעֲנִית?

Rav Yosef said: What does Rav Huna maintain in this regard? Does **he hold** that **one does not fast for** only a few **hours,**[N] i.e., that fasts that do not last from daybreak until nightfall are not considered fasts at all, and therefore these extra hours of the night are not part of his fast, **or perhaps** he holds that **one does fast for** a few **hours,**[N] **but one who fasts for** a few **hours does not pray the prayer of a fast?**

אֲמַר לֵיהּ אַבַּיֵי: לְעוֹלָם קָסָבַר רַב הוּנָא מִתְעַנִּין לְשָׁעוֹת, וְהַמִּתְעַנֶּה לְשָׁעוֹת מִתְפַּלֵּל תְּפִלַּת תַּעֲנִית. וְשָׁאנֵי הָכָא, דְּאִיכָּא שָׁעוֹת דְּלֵילְיָא דְּלָא קַבֵּיל עֲלֵיהּ מֵעִיקָּרָא.

Abaye said to Rav Yosef: **Actually, Rav Huna holds** that **one does fast for hours, and one who fasts for** a few **hours does pray the prayer of a fast. But** it is **different here, as there are hours of the night that he did not take upon himself at the outset.** Since one must take an individual fast upon himself beforehand, if he merely continues his fast into the night, these extra hours are not part of his obligation, and therefore he does not add the special prayer for a fast, *Aneinu,* on the following morning.

מָר עוּקְבָא אִיקְלַע לְגִינְזַק. בָּעוּ מִינֵּיהּ: מִתְעַנִּין לְשָׁעוֹת, אוֹ אֵין מִתְעַנִּין לְשָׁעוֹת? לָא הֲוָה בִּידֵיהּ. קַנְקַנִּין שֶׁל נׇכְרִים אֲסוּרִין אוֹ מוּתָּרִין? לָא הֲוָה בִּידֵיהּ. בַּמֶּה שִׁימֵּשׁ מֹשֶׁה כׇּל שִׁבְעַת יְמֵי הַמִּלּוּאִים״? לָא הֲוָה בִּידֵיהּ.

§ The Gemara relates: **Mar Ukva**[P] **happened** to come to the city of **Ginzak.**[B] The inhabitants of Ginzak, among other matters, **asked him** three questions to which he did not know the answer: First, **does one fast for hours, or does one not fast for hours?** Mar Ukva **did not have** an answer readily available. Second, are the clay **jars belonging to gentiles,**[H] which have been used for storing wine, permanently **prohibited, or** can they be rendered **permitted?** He **did not have** an answer readily available. Thirdly, **in what** garments did **Moses serve**[N] **all seven days of inauguration,** as the acting priest when Aaron and his sons were initiated into the priesthood? Once again, he **did not have** an answer readily available.

BACKGROUND

Ginzak – **גִּינְזַק**: The commentaries identify Ginzak with the biblical Gozan (I Chronicles 5:26), but the location of this city is unclear. Some maintain that it is the ancient city of Ganzak, which is southeast of Lake Urmia. Others claim that it lies south of the Caspian Sea, while yet others suggest that Ginzak is near Nahrawan. In any case, this Jewish community was apparently isolated from the main Jewish centers of Babylonia, but was important enough for several noteworthy Sages and leaders to visit.

PERSONALITIES

Mar Ukva – **מָר עוּקְבָא**: Mar Ukva was the Exilarch during the first and second generations of *amora'im* in Babylonia. He was famous not only for his elevated position but also for his learning and piety. Mar Ukva was very close to Shmuel, who respected him greatly. He was also renowned for his generous donations to charity and for his great modesty. According to various traditions, Mar Ukva was called Natan Detzutzita, which refers to an incident in which an angel grabbed him by the hair [*tzitzit*] of the head. He was also a famous penitent in his generation. Mar Ukva apparently had two sons who were also Sages.

HALAKHA

An individual who took a fast upon himself, even if he ate and drank the entire night – **יָחִיד שֶׁקִּיבֵּל עָלָיו תַּעֲנִית, אֲפִילּוּ אָכַל וְשָׁתָה כָּל הַלַּיְלָה**: With regard to one who took a fast upon himself in the afternoon service of the previous day, he is permitted to eat during the entire night. Similarly, if one commits to fast for several days in a row, he is permitted to eat and drink on each of the intervening nights. Some authorities add that on each of the days one has committed himself to fast he inserts the *Aneinu* prayer in the afternoon *Amida* (*Shulḥan Arukh, Oraḥ Ḥayyim* 575:7, and in the comment of Rema).

Slept in his fast – **לָן בְּתַעֲנִיתוֹ**: If one obligated himself to fast the following day, and at the conclusion of the fast continued to fast through the next night, the second day is not considered to be a fast for him. This is because he did not take the fast upon himself beforehand. However, the accepted ruling is that he does recite the *Aneinu* prayer, although some authorities disagree (*Magen Avraham*; *Shulḥan Arukh, Oraḥ Ḥayyim* 575:9).

Jars belonging to gentiles – **קַנְקַנִּין שֶׁל נׇכְרִים**: Any vessel that has served for the storage of non-kosher wine may be used after a twelve-month period, as by that time it certainly contains no traces of wine (*Shulḥan Arukh, Yoreh De'a* 135:16).

NOTES

An individual who took a fast upon himself – **יָחִיד שֶׁקִּיבֵּל עָלָיו תַּעֲנִית**: Rashi explains that the Gemara is referring to one who has committed himself to fast for a single day. Rav Huna teaches that he is permitted to eat and drink all night before the fast, and the next day he inserts in the *Amida* the special prayer for a fast, *Aneinu*. However, if he continues his fast the following night, he does not recite that prayer the next day, as he did not declare that day a fast for himself in advance.

Many commentaries have a different reading, according to which the Gemara is referring to a person who commits himself to fast on two successive days (Rif; Rambam). Rav Huna is saying that even if he eats and drinks during the intervening night, he still recites the *Aneinu* prayer on the second day of his fast, as he committed himself to two consecutive fast days from the outset. Conversely, if he obligated himself in only one day of fasting but continued to fast for a second day, he does not recite the prayer for a fast on the second day. Some commentators claim that this dispute has ramifications with respect to the question of whether or not the *Aneinu* prayer is included in the evening *Amida*, which is a matter of dispute between the early authorities.

Does he hold that one does not fast for hours – **סְבִירָא לֵיהּ אֵין מִתְעַנִּין לְשָׁעוֹת**: The Gemara apparently concludes that it is indeed possible to observe a fast that lasts only a few hours. Rashi explains the question as follows: If one undertakes a fast of several hours, is he required to refrain from eating during that period or not? Some commentaries object: Why shouldn't one be required to fulfill a personal obligation, despite its unusual form? After all, the undertaking of a fast is considered a vow, and all vows must be fulfilled (Ritva).

The Ritva explains that although a fast is indeed regarded as a vow, it is not simply a vow by which one renders prohibited something that is ordinarily permitted to him. If a fast is simply a vow to prohibit something that is ordinarily permitted, then it would be obvious that one can render eating prohibited to him, even for no more than a minute. Instead, the acceptance of a fast is considered a vow to perform a meritorious deed, as fasting leads to submission to God and to true contrition. Consequently the Gemara's question is as follows: If someone commits to fast for a few hours, has he vowed to perform a meritorious deed? If so, the vow is binding. Conversely, it is possible that a fast that applies for less than a full day is an insignificant matter and not a meritorious deed, in which case the vow is not binding and he may eat even during those hours in which he had committed to fast.

One does fast for hours – **מִתְעַנִּין לְשָׁעוֹת**: The question with regard to a fast of several hours is whether this vow, which is certainly valid, belongs to the category of fasting, or whether it is considered an act of private self-mortification. In essence, the issue is whether a fast is defined as refraining from food and drink for at least a day, or if a shorter time period is included in the same category. This problem also has bearing on the recital of the *Aneinu* prayer included in the *Amida* on a fast day. If someone is fasting for no more than a few hours, does he recite that prayer?

In what did Moses serve – **בַּמֶּה שִׁימֵּשׁ מֹשֶׁה**: The commentary on the text follows the explanation of Rashi here and in tractate *Avoda Zara* (34a), that Moses could not have worn the priestly garments during the seven days of inauguration, as those garments were designated exclusively for Aaron and his sons, and Moses was not a priest.

Tosafot objects (*Avoda Zara* 34a) that Moses could indeed have worn the priestly garments, as the Gemara states elsewhere (*Zevaḥim* 101b) that during the forty years the Jews spent in the wilderness, Moses had the status of a High Priest. According to *Tosafot*, the Gemara here is asking specifically about Moses' clothes during the seven days of inauguration, as at that time the priestly garments had not yet been consecrated. Some commentaries suggest that even if the priestly garments had already been consecrated, Moses could not have worn them during the seven days of inauguration, as at that time the Tabernacle had the status of an improvised altar, and the priestly garments are not meant to be worn for the service of an altar of this kind (Rabbi Ya'akov of Orleans). Yet others maintain that it is obvious to the Gemara that Moses wore priestly garments during the seven days of inauguration. The question is only whether he wore the eight garments of a High Priest or the four garments of a common priest.

אֲזַל וּשְׁאֵיל בֵּי מִדְרְשָׁא. אֲמַרוּ לֵיהּ: הִלְכְתָא: מִתְעַנִּין לְשָׁעוֹת, וּמִתְפַּלְּלִין תְּפִלַּת תַּעֲנִית. וְהִלְכְתָא: קַנְקַנִּין שֶׁל נׇכְרִים לְאַחַר שְׁנֵים עָשָׂר חֹדֶשׁ מוּתָּרִין. בַּמֶּה שִׁימֵּשׁ מֹשֶׁה כׇּל שִׁבְעַת יְמֵי הַמִּלּוּאִים? בְּחָלוּק לָבָן. רַב כָּהֲנָא מַתְנֵי: בְּחָלוּק לָבָן שֶׁאֵין לוֹ אִימְרָא.

Mar Ukva **went and asked** these questions in the **study hall. They said to him:** The ***halakha*** is: **One fasts for hours, and** he even **prays the prayer of a fast. And the *halakha*** is that the **jars** belonging **to gentiles are permitted after** they have not been used at all for **twelve months.** Finally, **in what** garments did **Moses serve all seven days of inauguration?** He did not serve in his own clothes, nor in the regular priestly garments, **but in a** special **white cloak. Rav Kahana taught:** Moses served **in a white cloak that does not have a hem.**[N]

אֲמַר רַב חִסְדָּא:

Rav Ḥisda said:

NOTES

In a white cloak that does not have a hem [*imra*] – בְּחָלוּק לָבָן שֶׁאֵין לוֹ אִימְרָא: According to most early authorities, the term *imra* is referring to the border of a hem at the bottom of a garment. The white shirt that Moses wore during the seven days of inauguration did not have a border, neither a folded hem nor an additional piece of material sewn to the bottom of the garment. Rashi explains that the shirt was made without a hem so that people could not suspect Moses of illicitly removing money consecrated for the Tabernacle in the folds of his garment. Elsewhere (*Avoda Zara* 34a), Rashi himself rejects this explanation, arguing that by the time the Tabernacle was inaugurated the money donated for its construction had already been spent.

Tosafot (*Avoda Zara* 34a) suggest that Moses' shirt was made without a hem so that it would be clear to all that it was new and had never been worn before. Alternatively, this was to prevent people from thinking that some defect had been found in Moses when they saw that he was replaced by Aaron at the end of the seven days of inauguration. Since the shirt that Moses wore lacked a hem, it would be apparent to all that it had been intended from the outset to be worn for only a short time. *Tosafot* also cite an alternative explanation, that *imra* means wool. The priestly garments were made of wool and linen, a combination that is ordinarily prohibited as diverse kinds. According to this explanation, Rav Kahana is saying that as the cloak worn by Moses was not a priestly garment, it was made of linen without any admixture of wool.

הָא דְּאָמְרַתְּ מִתְעַנִּין לְשָׁעוֹת – וְהוּא שֶׁלֹּא טָעַם כְּלוּם עַד הָעֶרֶב. אֲמַר לֵיהּ אַבָּיֵי: הָא תַּעֲנִית מַעַלְיְיתָא הִיא! לָא, צְרִיכָא דְּאִימְּלַךְ אִימְּלוֹכֵי.

The *halakha* is **that which you said,** that **one may fast for** a few **hours,**[H] provided that one took a fast of a few hours upon himself, **and that he** fasted and **did not taste anything until the evening. Abaye said to** Rav Ḥisda: **This** ruling is obvious, since **it is a full-fledged fast,** as one ultimately fasts the entire day. Rav Ḥisda answered: **No,** it is **necessary** to say this *halakha* in a case **where he changed his mind,** i.e., he began the day without intending to fast, but for various reasons he did not eat, and halfway through the day he decided to continue fasting for another few hours until nightfall. Rav Ḥisda maintains that this kind of fasting for hours is considered a fast.

HALAKHA

One may fast for hours – מִתְעַנִּין לְשָׁעוֹת: One may observe a fast for a few hours, provided that in practice he does not eat the entire day. How so? If one is immersed in his daily activities, and does not eat in the morning, and subsequently decides that he wants to fast for the remainder of the day, he is allowed to do so, and should then insert the *Aneinu* prayer into the *Amida*. However, some authorities maintain that even one who observes a fast for only a few hours needs to have taken it upon himself the previous afternoon. If one obligates himself to fast for the first part of a day, and then eats, or conversely, if he has eaten during the first part of the day and subsequently takes upon himself a fast for the rest of the day, he is not considered to be observing a fast that requires the recital of the *Aneinu* prayer. However, he is required to observe the terms of his obligation (*Shulḥan Arukh*, *Oraḥ Ḥayyim* 571:10–11).

וְאָמַר רַב חִסְדָּא: כׇּל תַּעֲנִית שֶׁלֹּא שָׁקְעָה עָלָיו חַמָּה לָא שְׁמֵיהּ תַּעֲנִית. מֵיתִיבִי: אַנְשֵׁי מִשְׁמָר מִתְעַנִּין, וְלֹא מַשְׁלִימִין. הָתָם לְצַעוּרֵי נַפְשֵׁיהּ בְּעָלְמָא הוּא.

And Rav Ḥisda said: Any fast[N] **upon which the sun does not set,**[H] i.e., when one eats in the middle of the day, it **is not called a fast** at all. The Gemara **raises an objection: The members of the priestly watch,** the priests and Levites who are serving in the Temple that week, **fast** on a communal fast, like the members of the non-priestly watch who are attached to specific groups of priests, **but they do not complete**[N] the fast with the rest of the community. This indicates that even a fast lasting only a few hours is called a fast. The Gemara explains: **There** they abstained from food **merely to cause themselves distress,** as an act of solidarity with the rest of the community, but this was not considered a full-fledged fast.

תָּא שְׁמַע: דְּאָמַר רַבִּי אֶלְעָזָר בְּרַבִּי צָדוֹק: אֲנִי מִבְּנֵי בָנָיו שֶׁל סְנָאָה בֶּן בִּנְיָמִין. וּפַעַם אַחַת חָל תִּשְׁעָה בְּאָב לִהְיוֹת בְּשַׁבָּת, וּדְחִינוּהוּ לְאַחַר הַשַּׁבָּת, וְהִתְעַנֵּינוּ בּוֹ, וְלֹא הִשְׁלַמְנוּהוּ, מִפְּנֵי שֶׁיּוֹם טוֹב שֶׁלָּנוּ הוּא. הָתָם נַמִי לְצַעוּרֵי נַפְשֵׁיהּ בְּעָלְמָא הוּא.

The Gemara cites another proof: **Come and hear, as Rabbi Elazar, son of Rabbi Tzadok, said: I am a descendant of Senaah, son of** the tribe of **Benjamin,**[B] **and once the Ninth of Av occurred on Shabbat, and we postponed** the fast **until after Shabbat,** as Shabbat supersedes the fast of the Ninth of Av. **And we fasted on that** day, **but we did not complete** the fast, **due to** the fact **that** the tenth of Av **is a holiday of ours,**[H] a private holiday for our family (26a), and one does not fast on holidays. This proves that a fast of only a few hours is nevertheless called a fast. The Gemara rejects this claim: **There too,** they did so **merely to cause themselves distress.**

תָּא שְׁמַע, דַּאֲמַר רַבִּי יוֹחָנָן: אֱהֵא בְּתַעֲנִית עַד שֶׁאָבוֹא לְבֵיתִי. הָתָם לְשַׁמּוֹטֵיהּ נַפְשֵׁיהּ מִבֵּי נְשִׂיאָה הוּא דַּעֲבַד.

The Gemara again attempts to disprove the opinion of Rav Ḥisda, this time by citing a custom of Rabbi Yoḥanan: **Come and hear, as Rabbi Yoḥanan** occasionally **said: I shall be in** observance of **a fast until I come to my house.** This indicates that one can take a fast upon himself even for just a few hours. The Gemara rejects this proof as well: **There he did** this **to excuse himself from the household of the** ***Nasi*****.**[N] At times, Rabbi Yoḥanan received an invitation to dine at the house of the *Nasi*, but wanted to decline. To avoid insulting the *Nasi*, he would say that he had taken a fast upon himself, and afterward he would eat at home. Since this was not a real fast, it is not proof of the legitimacy of a partial-day fast.

אָמַר שְׁמוּאֵל: כׇּל תַּעֲנִית שֶׁלֹּא קִיבֵּל עָלָיו מִבְּעוֹד יוֹם לָאו שְׁמֵיהּ תַּעֲנִית. וְאִי יָתֵיב, מַאי? אֲמַר רַבָּה בַּר שֵׁילָא: דָּמֵי לְמַפּוּחָא דְּמַלְיָא זִיקָא.

Shmuel said: Any fast that one did not take upon himself[N] **while it was still day**[H] **is not called a fast.** The Gemara asks: **And if** one happened to **sit** in observance of a fast that day, **what** is that considered? **Rabba bar Sheila said:** He is **likened to a bellows**[N] **that is full of air.** His behavior does not constitute a fast, as he is merely a container full of air, without food.

BACKGROUND

A descendant of Senaah, son of the tribe of Benjamin – מִבְּנֵי בָנָיו שֶׁל סְנָאָה בֶּן בִּנְיָמִין: This statement indicates that the private holidays of families who brought the wood for the Temple were observed by all the members of the family, as Rabbi Elazar, son of Rabbi Tzadok, was a priest whose mother was apparently from the Senaah family.

HALAKHA

Any fast upon which the sun does not set – כׇּל תַּעֲנִית שֶׁלֹּא שָׁקְעָה עָלָיו חַמָּה: A fast that is not observed until nightfall, after the appearance of three medium-sized stars, is not considered a fast. Consequently, if one who is fasting intends to break his fast before that time, he may not recite the *Aneinu* prayer. Certain authorities permit the recitation of the *Aneinu* prayer even if one's fast does not continue until nightfall. These authorities further rule that an individual may insert the *Aneinu* prayer into the sixteenth blessing of the *Amida*, Who listens to prayer, even if one does not intend to continue his fast until nightfall. However, the prayer leader may not recite the *Aneinu* prayer unless a fast taken on by the community will be continued until nightfall (*Shulḥan Arukh, Oraḥ Ḥayyim* 571:1).

That it is a holiday of ours – שֶׁיּוֹם טוֹב שֶׁלָּנוּ הוּא: There were fixed dates for certain families to bring their own wood for the arrangement on the altar. The members of each family would treat the day of their wood offering as a holiday, on which it was prohibited for them to conduct eulogies, fast, or perform work (Rambam *Sefer Avoda, Hilkhot Kelei HaMikdash* 6:9).

Similarly, when the Ninth of Av occurs on a Shabbat and the fast is postponed until Sunday, those involved in a circumcision on Sunday are permitted to pray the afternoon service early on and eat before dark, as it is a holiday for them (*Shulḥan Arukh, Oraḥ Ḥayyim* 559:9).

Any fast that one did not take upon himself while it was still day – כׇּל תַּעֲנִית שֶׁלֹּא קִיבֵּל עָלָיו מִבְּעוֹד יוֹם: If one did not take the obligation of an individual fast upon himself during the afternoon of the day before the proposed fast, it is not considered a fast, whether with respect to the recitation of the *Aneinu* prayer or to the fulfillment of his vow. Some authorities maintain that an individual recites the *Aneinu* prayer even if he did not take the fast upon himself the previous day (Rema). Everyone agrees that one who experiences a disturbing dream during the night may fast the next day to rectify the dream's bad effects, despite the fact that he did not take the fast upon himself the day before (*Shulḥan Arukh, Oraḥ Ḥayyim* 571:5).

NOTES

And Rav Ḥisda said, any fast – וְאָמַר רַב חִסְדָּא כׇּל תַּעֲנִית: The early authorities point out a difficulty. As Rav Ḥisda's first ruling, that one who fasts for hours may not taste anything until evening, is apparently identical to his second statement, that a fast that does not continue until sunset is not considered a fast, one of these statements is apparently superfluous. This difficulty is removed if the reading of Rabbeinu Ḥananel and others is accepted: And Rav Ḥisda follows his own reasoning. According to this version, the Gemara is in fact stating that his two statements amount to the same ruling.

Some commentaries explain that Rav Ḥisda's first statement teaches that one cannot eat in the morning and subsequently observe a fast of hours during the second part of the day. His second statement is that one cannot fast in the morning and proceed to eat in the afternoon (Ritva). Yet others suggest that Rav Ḥisda's first statement is referring to the special *Aneinu* prayer of a fast. One who fasts for hours is considered to be fasting with respect to the recitation of *Aneinu* only if he does not taste any food from the beginning of the day until evening. Rav Ḥisda's second ruling refers to whether or not it is considered a fast that fulfills a vow to observe a fast. If one vowed to observe a fast and fasted for several hours but did not continue until sunset, his vow remains unfulfilled (Ra'avad).

The Rambam (*Sefer Zemanim, Hilkhot Ta'anit* 1:13) rules that if for some reason one neglects to eat in the morning and subsequently decides to observe a fast for the rest of the day, he is considered to be fasting for hours and he recites the *Aneinu* prayer. Even if he eats in the morning and then decides to fast for the rest of the day, he is observing a fast for hours. The early authorities and the later authorities analyze the relationship between this ruling and the two statements of Rav Ḥisda. Some commentaries on the Rambam suggest that he understood Rav Ḥisda's first statement, that one fasting may not eat anything until evening, as referring to the part of the day after he begins his fast. However, if he eats in the morning, before beginning his fast, the remainder of the day is considered a fast (*Maggid Mishne*).

The members of the priestly watch fast but they do not complete – אַנְשֵׁי מִשְׁמָר מִתְעַנִּין וְלֹא מַשְׁלִימִין: Rashi (15b) explains that the members of the priestly watch who serve in the Temple that week observe each fast imposed on the community during periods of drought. However, they do not continue their fast all the way until nightfall, as they must preserve their strength lest the work of the Temple become too difficult for the members of the extended patrilineal family and other priests be called in to help them. Others suggest that they do not complete the fast because they are sometimes required to help eat the offerings sacrificed that day, to ensure that none of the meat is left over after the permitted time for its consumption (Rabbi Elyakim).

To excuse himself from the household of the *Nasi* – לְשַׁמּוֹטֵיהּ נַפְשֵׁיהּ מִבֵּי נְשִׂיאָה: It is inferred in the Jerusalem Talmud (*Nedarim* 8:1) from a similar statement of Rabbi Yoḥanan that one may commit to fast for a period of hours or until a certain event occurs. Apparently, the Gemara there understands that Rabbi Yoḥanan did indeed commit to fast for a few hours, and that one who obligates himself to fast in the morning and eats in the afternoon is considered to have observed a fast. This ruling contradicts the opinion of Rav Ḥisda cited here. Some early authorities attempt to reconcile the opinions of the two passages (see Ritva and Meiri).

Any fast that one did not take upon himself – כׇּל תַּעֲנִית שֶׁלֹּא קִיבֵּל עָלָיו: Some commentaries observe that the *halakha* that on the afternoon prior to a proposed fast one must commit himself to it is derived from the verse: "Sanctify a fast" (Joel 1:14), which indicates that a fast day must be declared and sanctified before it begins (Rif).

Likened to a bellows – דָּמֵי לְמַפּוּחָא: Some commentaries explain that he is similar to a bellows in that the air it contains quickly escapes. Here too, his fast ends after a mere few hours, and therefore it is not considered a proper fast with regard to his prayers.

אֵימַת מְקַבֵּיל לֵיהּ? רַב אָמַר: בְּמִנְחָה. וּשְׁמוּאֵל אָמַר: בִּתְפִלַּת הַמִּנְחָה. אָמַר רַב יוֹסֵף: כְּווֹתֵיהּ דִּשְׁמוּאֵל מִסְתַּבְּרָא, דִּכְתִיב בִּמְגִילַּת תַּעֲנִית: לָהֵן, כָּל אֱינִישׁ דְּיֵיתֵי עֲלוֹהִי מִקַּדְמַת דְּנָא יֵיסַר.

§ The Gemara asks: **When** does one **take** a fast **upon himself? Rav said:** One takes a fast upon himself **in the afternoon**[N] of the day preceding the fast, from midday onward. **And Shmuel said:** One must take a fast upon himself for the following day **at** the end of **the afternoon prayer.**[HN] **Rav Yosef said:** It **stands to reason** that the halakha should be **in accordance with** the opinion of **Shmuel, as it is written in** ***Megillat Ta'anit,*** after a list of all of the Festivals established by the Sages in commemoration of various events throughout Jewish history: **Therefore, whoever has bound himself beforehand** with an obligation to fast on one of these commemorative days, he **will be bound.**

מַאי לָאו יֵיסַר עַצְמוֹ בִּצְלוֹ? לָא. יֵאָסֵר עַצְמוֹ.

The Gemara explains the apparent proof from the text of *Megillat Ta'anit.* **What, is it not** the case that this means that **he binds himself** to the obligation **at** the time of **prayer,**[N] and if he did not do so at that point in time his fast does not go into effect? The Gemara rejects this explanation: **No;** the text should be amended by one letter so that it does not read *yeisar*, he shall bind himself, but *yei'aser*, **he shall render himself prohibited** from transgressing these instructions. In other words, the text is explaining that despite a prior vow to fast, it is prohibited for one to do so on the commemorative days enumerated in *Megillat Ta'anit.*

פְּלִיגִי בָּהּ רַבִּי חִיָּיא וְרַבִּי שִׁמְעוֹן בְּרַבִּי: חַד אָמַר: יֵיסַר, וְחַד אָמַר: יֵאָסֵר. מַאן דְּאָמַר יֵיסַר, כִּדְאָמְרִינַן. לְמַאן דְּאָמַר: יֵאָסֵר, מַאי הִיא?

The Gemara comments: **Rabbi Ḥiyya and Rabbi Shimon, son of Rabbi** Yehuda HaNasi,[P] **disagree** with regard to **this** dispute. **One** of them **said** that the text of *Megillat Ta'anit* reads: He **will be bound, and** the other **one said** that it reads: He **will be prohibited. The one who said:** He **will be bound, this is as we** just **say.** However, **according to the one who said:** He **will be prohibited, what** does **it** mean?

HALAKHA

At the afternoon prayer – בִּתְפִלַּת הַמִּנְחָה: If an individual wishes to observe a fast, he must commit to observing the fast during the afternoon service of the previous day, either during the recitation of the sixteenth blessing or at the conclusion of the *Amida*, in accordance with the opinion of Shmuel. He should explicitly state or mentally verbalize the phrase: Tomorrow I will observe an individual fast. Some commentaries rule that it is preferable to declare one's commitment to the fast after completing the *Amida*, so as not to interrupt the prayer (Rema). If one did not take the fast upon himself during the afternoon service, he may do so later in the afternoon, provided that it is still day (*Baḥ; Magen Avraham; Shulḥan Arukh, Oraḥ Ḥayyim* 571:6).

PERSONALITIES

Rabbi Shimon, son of Rabbi Yehuda HaNasi – רַבִּי שִׁמְעוֹן בְּרַבִּי: Rabbi Yehuda HaNasi's youngest son, Rabbi Shimon, was also his closest disciple. Exchanges between father and son are mentioned several times in the Gemara. This son of Rabbi Yehuda HaNasi became one of the most important Sages of his generation, and the other disciples of Rabbi Yehuda HaNasi, even those who were older than Rabbi Shimon, were his students. He was a particularly close friend of Rabbi Ḥiyya, who was his partner in the silk trade. Rabbi Shimon discussed halakhic issues with other Sages of his generation, and his name is mentioned once in the Mishna. Since he was Rabbi Yehuda HaNasi's youngest son, he did not assume the office of *Nasi*, president of the Sanhedrin, but his father did appoint him to an important position of leadership in his academy after his death, specifically the role of the *Ḥakham*. This was the third most important position in the Sanhedrin.

NOTES

In the afternoon – בְּמִנְחָה: Most early authorities explain that according to the opinion of Rav one who wishes to observe an individual fast is required to take that fast upon himself at some point during the previous afternoon. Rav Hai Gaon states that one must commit to the fast during the second half of the day, from the time of *minḥa gedola*, the earlier afternoon prayer, which begins half an hour after midday. Conversely, Rabbeinu Gershom maintains that one must commit to the fast during the final quarter of the day, from the start of *minḥa ketana*, the later afternoon prayer, nine and a half hours after sunrise.

According to some early authorities, Rav says that one must commit to the fast during the afternoon only to emphasize the difference between his opinion and that of Shmuel, who rules that this must be performed during the afternoon prayer. In fact, Rav maintains that one who wishes to observe an individual fast may take it upon himself well in advance (Ritva; Ran). These commentaries explain the dispute between Rav and Shmuel as follows: According to Rav, the undertaking of a fast is considered a vow to perform a meritorious deed. This vow is binding even if it is uttered well in advance. Shmuel, however, argues that one who undertakes to observe a fast is not vowing to perform a meritorious deed, as his vow will cause him suffering. Consequently, he must take on the fast in the manner in which one accepts Shabbat or a Festival, i.e., in the prayer he recites shortly before the onset of the fast.

At the afternoon prayer – בִּתְפִלַּת הַמִּנְחָה: The early authorities dispute the precise formula of the prayer that signifies taking on a fast, as well as the point in the afternoon when it is recited. According to the Rambam, one who wishes to observe an individual fast must recite the special *Aneinu* prayer in the sixteenth blessing of the afternoon *Amida* the day before the fast (see Rambam *Sefer Zemanim, Hilkhot Ta'anit* 1:10 and *Maggid Mishne* there). Many authorities reject this view, arguing that the sources indicate that the *Aneinu* prayer is recited only on a fast day itself. The Rambam himself apparently changed his opinion, as this ruling does not appear in the standard version of his code.

Most early authorities maintain that a fast must be taken on by reciting the formula: Tomorrow I will observe an individual fast. According to some commentaries, this formula is included in the sixteenth blessing of the afternoon *Amida*. Others claim that it is inserted at the end of the *Amida*, immediately before the last line: May the words of my mouth and the meditation of my heart find favor before You, or immediately after that line, before one takes the three steps backward that signal the conclusion of the *Amida* prayer.

What, is it not the case that he binds himself at the time of prayer – מַאי לָאו יֵיסַר עַצְמוֹ בִּצְלוֹ: Some commentaries ask how the reading: He binds himself, supports the opinion of Shmuel. Even Rav agrees that one who wishes to observe a fast must obligate himself beforehand. Rav can simply explain that one must commit himself at some point during the afternoon before his proposed fast (Ritva).

The Ritva answers that Rav maintains that one is not required to commit to his proposed fast in the afternoon prayer, because he holds that committing to a fast constitutes a vow to perform a meritorious deed. Consequently, it also follows that it is not necessary for him to declare that he is taking the fast on the previous day at all. Instead, he can commit to the fast well in advance, in which case there would be no need for him to mention the fast once again the day before. For this reason, the Gemara claims that this section of *Megillat Ta'anit* is not in accordance with the opinion of Rav. The Gemara answers that the text must be amended to read: He shall render himself prohibited. This means that if one has taken a fast upon himself beforehand, he may not eat on that day, even if it occurs on a day when fasting is prohibited.

דְּתַנְיָא בִּמְגִילַּת תַּעֲנִית: כׇּל אִינִישׁ דְּיֵיתֵי עֲלוֹהִי מִקַּדְמַת דְּנָא יֵאָסֵר. כֵּיצַד? יָחִיד שֶׁקִּיבֵּל עָלָיו שֵׁנִי וַחֲמִישִׁי וְשֵׁנִי שֶׁל כׇּל הַשָּׁנָה כּוּלָּהּ, וְאֵירְעוּ בָּם יָמִים טוֹבִים הַכְּתוּבִין בִּמְגִילַּת תַּעֲנִית, אִם נִדְרוֹ קוֹדֶם לִגְזֵירָתֵנוּ, יְבַטֵּיל נִדְרוֹ אֶת גְּזֵירָתֵנוּ, וְאִם גְּזֵירָתֵנוּ קוֹדֶמֶת לְנִדְרוֹ, תְּבַטֵּל גְּזֵירָתֵנוּ אֶת נִדְרוֹ.

The Gemara explains: This is **as it is taught in *Megillat Ta'anit*: Whoever has taken upon himself beforehand** to fast on one of these Festivals days, he **will be prohibited** to eat and drink. **How so?** With regard to **an individual who took upon himself** to fast on each **Monday, Thursday, and Monday**[H] series **of the entire year, and the** commemorative **holidays** written **in *Megillat Ta'anit* occurred on** these days, **if his vow preceded our decree,**[N] i.e., the decree of the Sages establishing these commemorative days, **his vow annuls our decree** and he must fast, **but if our decree preceded his vow, our decree annuls his vow** and he may not fast on those days.

תָּנוּ רַבָּנַן: עַד מָתַי אוֹכֵל וְשׁוֹתֶה? עַד שֶׁיַּעֲלֶה עַמּוּד הַשַּׁחַר. דִּבְרֵי רַבִּי. רַבִּי אֶלְעָזָר בְּרַבִּי שִׁמְעוֹן אוֹמֵר: עַד קְרוֹת הַגֶּבֶר. אָמַר אַבַּיֵי: לֹא שָׁנוּ אֶלָּא שֶׁלֹּא גָּמַר סְעוּדָתוֹ. אֲבָל גָּמַר סְעוּדָתוֹ אֵינוֹ אוֹכֵל.

The Sages taught in a *baraita*: **Until when may one eat and drink**[H] on communal fasts, when one fasts during the day but not the preceding evening? **Until dawn.** This is **the statement of Rabbi** Yehuda HaNasi. **Rabbi Elazar, son of Rabbi Shimon,**[P] **says: Until the call of the rooster,** which is before dawn. **Abaye said: They taught** this ruling, that one may eat all night, **only if he has not finished his evening meal,** as he may continue eating the same meal all night. **However,** if he has **finished his meal, he may not eat** any more.

אֵיתִיבֵיהּ רָבָא: גָּמַר וְעָמַד, הֲרֵי זֶה אוֹכֵל. הָתָם כְּשֶׁלֹּא סִילֵּק. אִיכָּא דְּאָמְרִי אָמַר רָבָא: לֹא שָׁנוּ אֶלָּא כְּשֶׁלֹּא יָשֵׁן. אֲבָל יָשֵׁן, אֵינוֹ אוֹכֵל. אֵיתִיבֵיהּ אַבַּיֵי: יָשֵׁן וְעָמַד, הֲרֵי זֶה אוֹכֵל. הָתָם בְּמִתְנַמְנֵם.

Rava raised an objection to Abaye from a *baraita*: If **one finished his meal and stood up,** nevertheless, **he may eat** more. This shows that one may in fact eat throughout the night, even if he has finished his meal. Abaye answered: **There** the *baraita* is referring to a situation **where he has not** yet **removed** or cleared the table, and therefore it is as though he has not yet finished his meal. **Some say** a slightly different version of this discussion. **Rava said: They taught** this ruling **only if he did not sleep** after eating, **but if he slept he may not eat** anything else that night. **Abaye raised an objection to** Rava from a *baraita*: If **one slept and arose** from his sleep during the night, **he may eat.** Rava explained: **There** the *baraita* is referring to one who was merely **dozing,** and was not fully asleep.

הֵיכִי דָּמֵי מִתְנַמְנֵם? אָמַר רַב אַשִׁי:

The Gemara asks: **What are the circumstances of dozing? Rav Ashi said:**

HALAKHA

An individual who took upon himself to fast on Monday, Thursday, and Monday – יָחִיד שֶׁקִּיבֵּל עָלָיו שֵׁנִי וַחֲמִישִׁי וְשֵׁנִי: If an individual committed himself to a series of fasts, and one of the days on which he was supposed to fast occurs on a Shabbat, a Festival, a New Moon, Hanukkah, or Purim, then the following *halakha* applies: If he took on the fasts by means of the ordinary formulation, he is not required to fast on those days; however, if he took on the fasts in the form of a vow, his vow is binding and requires annulment (Ramban). The Rambam maintains that if one took the fasts on himself by means of a vow, and one of the days on which he is supposed to fast occurs on a date when fasting is prohibited by Torah law, the vow is binding and requires annulment. Conversely, if that day occurs on Hanukkah or Purim, on which fasting is prohibited by rabbinic decree, the vow is not binding. The accepted custom is in accordance with the opinion of the Ramban (*Shulḥan Arukh, Oraḥ Ḥayyim* 570:1, and in the comment of Rema).

Until when may one eat and drink – עַד מָתַי אוֹכֵל וְשׁוֹתֶה: On any fast that is observed only during the daytime, whether it is an individual or a communal fast, one may eat and drink all night until dawn, in accordance with the opinion of Rabbi Yehuda HaNasi. However, if one falls soundly asleep, he may not eat when he wakes up, unless he stipulated beforehand that he will eat in the event that he awakens. If he merely dozes off, he is permitted to eat until morning. Some authorities maintain that one may drink until morning, even if he falls into a sound sleep without stipulating that he will drink when he wakes up, as he certainly had in mind that he should be permitted to drink until the fast begins (Rema, citing Mordekhai and *Tur*). Some authorities maintain that it is nevertheless preferable to explicitly make a stipulation with regard to drinking as well (*Magen Avraham*). Others argue that nowadays, when all are accustomed to drinking upon awakening, this stipulation is not necessary (*Arukh HaShulḥan*; *Shulḥan Arukh, Oraḥ Ḥayyim* 570:1).

NOTES

If his vow preceded our decree – אִם נִדְרוֹ קוֹדֶם לִגְזֵירָתֵנוּ: The early authorities suggest several interpretations of this passage. Rashi and many other early commentaries explain that this refers to the time when the Sages first instituted the commemorative days recorded in *Megillat Ta'anit*. If the vow preceded that decree, it is valid, but if the decree preceded the vow, the fast is annulled.

Others understand the Gemara differently. In a case in which one has committed himself to a series of fasts, if he has already observed one or more of them and the next fast falls on a day recorded in *Megillat Ta'anit*, then his vow overrules the decree of the Sages. However, if he has not yet observed any of his fasts, and the first of the series falls on a commemorative day listed in *Megillat Ta'anit*, the decree of the Sages cancels his vow, and it is prohibited for him to fast (Ra'avad on Rif).

Yet others explain that if one undertook a series of fasts before the rabbinical court sanctified the New Moon, in which case he could not have known when he vowed that his fasts would fall on days recorded in *Megillat Ta'anit*, his vow overrules the Sages' decree. Conversely, if one vowed after the court had already sanctified the New Moon, so that he should have known that his fasts would occur on days recorded in *Megillat Ta'anit*, the decree of the Sages cancels his vow (Rabbeinu Gershom).

PERSONALITIES

Rabbi Elazar, son of Rabbi Shimon – רַבִּי אֶלְעָזָר בְּרַבִּי שִׁמְעוֹן: A contemporary of Rabbi Yehuda HaNasi, Rabbi Elazar, son of Rabbi Shimon, was a distinguished scholar, like his father, Rabbi Shimon bar Yoḥai. Rabbi Elazar's remarkable personality is the subject of numerous anecdotes. When Rabbi Shimon bar Yoḥai, who was strongly opposed to Roman rule, was betrayed to the authorities by informers, Rabbi Elazar fled with his father and lived with him in a cave for thirteen years. The two subsisted on the barest essentials and spent their time studying Torah. During this period, Rabbi Elazar learned almost everything he knew from his father, who was his principal teacher, though Rabbi Elazar occasionally disagreed with his halakhic rulings. Rabbi Elazar also studied with other scholars of his father's generation, including Rabbi Yehuda, Rabbi Elazar ben Shamua, and Rabbi Meir.

Later, Rabbi Elazar was forced to assume the unpopular position of a law-enforcement officer, and his acceptance of the post aroused opposition among the Sages. His spiritual independence led to friction with other Sages, which cooled his relations with Rabbi Yehuda HaNasi, a friend from his youth.

Nevertheless, all acknowledged his personal piety, asceticism, and greatness in Torah knowledge. His father considered him one of the most pious individuals of all time, and he was apparently considered exceptionally righteous by the common people as well. Rabbi Elazar is also one of the most prominent figures in the *Zohar*. When he died, he was eulogized for his great achievements as a student of the Torah, both Written and Oral, as a preacher, and as a composer of liturgical poetry. The Gemara informs us that he was buried next to his father's grave in Meron.

Rabbi Elazar's teachings are quoted explicitly in several places in the Mishna, while many other rulings of his are apparently stated in the Mishna anonymously. He was therefore referred to as Rabbi Elazar, son of Rabbi Shimon, the Unattributed, i.e., the one whose opinions are often recorded as unattributed *mishnayot*. Some of his statements, which are also quoted by early *amora'im*, are cited in the *Tosefta* and in halakhic midrash.

נִים וְלָא נִים; תִּיר וְלָא תִּיר. דְּקָרוּ לֵיהּ וְעָנֵי. וְלָא יָדַע אַהֲדוּרֵי סְבָרָא, וְכִי מַדְכְּרִי לֵיהּ, מִדְּכַר.

One is asleep but not fully asleep, awake but not fully awake. This means **that if they call him he will answer, but he cannot give** a coherent **reason. And when we remind him** of something that just happened **he remembers** it.

אָמַר רַב כָּהֲנָא אָמַר רַב: יָחִיד שֶׁקִּיבֵּל עָלָיו תַּעֲנִית אָסוּר בִּנְעִילַת הַסַּנְדָּל. חָיְישִׁינַן שֶׁמָּא תַּעֲנִית צִבּוּר קִיבֵּל עָלָיו. הֵיכִי לִיעֲבֵד? אֲמַר רַבָּה בַּר רַב שֵׁילָא: לֵימָא הָכִי: לְמָחָר אֱהֵא לְפָנֶיךָ בְּתַעֲנִית יָחִיד.

Rav Kahana said that **Rav said: An individual who took a fast upon himself is prohibited** to engage **in the wearing of shoes** on the day of his fast. The reason is that **we are concerned** that **perhaps he took a communal fast upon himself,** and wearing shoes is prohibited on communal fast days. The Gemara asks: **How should one act,** to avoid this problem? **Rabba bar Rav Sheila said: Let him recite this** formula: **Tomorrow I shall be before You** in the observance of **an individual fast.**

אֲמַרוּ לֵיהּ רַבָּנַן לְרַב שֵׁשֶׁת: הָא קָא חָזֵינַן רַבָּנַן דִּמְסַיְּימֵי מְסָנַיְיהוּ וְאָתוּ לְבֵי תַּעֲנִיתָא! אִיקְפַּד וַאֲמַר לְהוּ: דִּלְמָא מֵיכַל נַמִי אֲכוּל.

The Gemara relates: **The Sages said to Rav Sheshet,** who was blind: **We see Sages who wear their shoes and go to** the study **house on** a communal **fast** day. This shows that there is no need to be concerned about this prohibition. **Rav Sheshet became angry and said to them: Perhaps they even ate,** if you saw them treating the fast lightly.

אַבַּיֵי וְרָבָא מְעַיְּילִי כִּי מְסַיְּימִי אַפַּנְתָּא. מָרֵימָר וּמָר זוּטְרָא מְחַלְּפִי דִּימִינָא לִשְׂמָאלָא, וְדִשְׂמָאלָא לִימִינָא. רַבָּנַן דְּבֵי רַב אַשִׁי נָפְקִי כִּי אוֹרְחַיְיהוּ. סָבְרִי כִּי הָא דְּאָמַר שְׁמוּאֵל: אֵין תַּעֲנִית צִבּוּר בְּבָבֶל אֶלָּא תִּשְׁעָה בְּאָב בִּלְבַד.

The Gemara further relates: **Abaye and Rava** would **enter** the synagogue **while wearing** sandals on **the leather** [*apanta*][NL] of their shoes, i.e., they would wear their shoes upside down. **Mareimar**[P] **and Mar Zutra**[P] would **switch the right shoe for the left and the left for the right.** By contrast, **the Sages of the school of Rav Ashi** would **go out** wearing shoes **in their usual manner.** They **hold in accordance with that which Shmuel said: The only** completely stringent **communal fast in Babylonia is the Ninth of Av alone.** Therefore, in Babylonia there is no need to be concerned that one might have taken a communal fast upon himself.

אָמַר רַב יְהוּדָה אָמַר רַב: לֹוֶה אָדָם תַּעֲנִיתוֹ וּפוֹרֵעַ. כִּי אָמְרִיתָהּ קַמֵּיהּ דִּשְׁמוּאֵל, אֲמַר לִי: וְכִי נֶדֶר קִבֵּל עֲלֵיהּ דְּלָא סַגִּי דְּלָא מְשַׁלֵּם? לְצַעוּרֵי נַפְשֵׁיהּ קַבֵּיל עֲלֵיהּ. אִי מָצֵי, מְצַעֵר נַפְשֵׁיהּ; אִי לָא מָצֵי, לָא מְצַעֵר נַפְשֵׁיהּ.

The Gemara discusses another topic related to fasts. **Rav Yehuda said** that **Rav said: A person may borrow his fast and repay,**[NH] i.e., if one is unable to fast on the specific day he intended to fast, he may annul his fast for that day and fast on another day instead. Rav Yehuda related: **When I said this** *halakha* **before Shmuel, he said to me: And did he take a vow upon himself,** which would mean **that it is not possible for him not to repay** it? **He took upon himself to cause himself discomfort** on that day. **If he is able,** he must **cause himself discomfort; if he is unable, he does not** need to **cause himself discomfort,** in which case he need not repay the fast.

אִיכָּא דְּאָמְרִי אָמַר רַב יְהוּדָה אָמַר רַב: לֹוֶה אָדָם תַּעֲנִיתוֹ וּפוֹרֵעַ. כִּי אָמְרִיתָהּ קַמֵּיהּ דִּשְׁמוּאֵל, אָמַר לִי: פְּשִׁיטָא! לֹא יְהֵא אֶלָּא נֶדֶר! נֶדֶר מִי לָא מָצֵי בָּעֵי לְשַׁלּוּמֵי וּמֵיזַל לְמָחָר וּלְיוֹמָא אַחֲרִינָא?

Some say a different version of this discussion. **Rav Yehuda said** that **Rav said: One may borrow his fast and repay. When I said this** *halakha* **before Shmuel, he said to me:** This is **obvious. Let it be** considered **only a vow;** even so, **is he not required to repay a vow on the next day or on another day?** Since a commitment to fast is a type of vow, he is obligated to repay it at some point in time.

NOTES

While wearing sandals on the leather [*apanta*] – **כִּי מְסַיְּימִי אַפַּנְתָּא:** The early authorities dispute the precise meaning of the term *apanta*, although they all apparently agree that this is referring to a type of shoe that does not have leather soles. *Tosafot* maintain that *apanta* is referring to a type of footwear consisting only of the upper portion of a shoe, without a sole. Rashi and the *Shita Mekubbetzet* explain that *apanta* is a soft slipper. Others claim that these turned their shoes upside down and walked with their feet touching the soles.

A person may borrow his fast and repay – **לֹוֶה אָדָם תַּעֲנִיתוֹ וּפוֹרֵעַ:** According to the Rambam (*Sefer Hafla'a, Hilkhot Nedarim* 4:15) and several other early authorities, this applies only if one did not specify the date for his fast. However, if he undertook to observe a fast on a specific day, he cannot later transfer his fast to a different date. Conversely, most early authorities maintain that this *halakha* applies even if one undertook to observe a fast on a specific day (Ra'avad; Rashba; Ritva). They argue that support for this opinion is provided by the anecdote cited in the Gemara involving Rav Yehoshua, son of Rav Idi. When Rav Yehoshua explained that he was declining to eat due to his fast, the members of Rav Asi's household suggested that he observe the fast on some other day, without first asking him whether he had specified a particular day.

The early authorities also disagree with regard to the circumstances in which one may cancel his fast and observe it on another day. Some maintain that this *halakha* applies only if he would suffer great distress were he to continue fasting (Rabbeinu Ḥananel). Others rule that it also applies if he is invited to a meal that can be characterized as a religious celebration, or if he wants to participate in a meal as a mark of honor to an important person, or to maintain good social relations with his friends (Rif; Rambam). Yet others claim that the story of Rav Yehoshua, son of Rav Idi, proves that one may postpone his fast even if he cannot provide any special reason for doing so.

LANGUAGE

The leather [*apanta*] – **אַפַּנְתָּא:** The piece of leather on the portion of a shoe that covers the foot. In Syriac, panta means the back of the hand, or the skin covering the foot.

HALAKHA

A person may borrow his fast and repay – **לֹוֶה אָדָם תַּעֲנִיתוֹ וּפוֹרֵעַ:** If one vowed to observe a fast on a particular day, but forgot his vow and ate on that day, he must refrain from eating for the remainder of the day. However, if he vowed to fast without specifying a particular date, and after beginning to fast he forgot and ate, he is required to fast on another day. If one vowed to observe several fasts without specifying the dates, and after starting to fast on a particular day he wants to cancel the fast on account of some other religious obligation, or in honor of an important person, or because he was in a state of distress (Rema), he is permitted to break his fast and repay it on another day (*Shulḥan Arukh, Oraḥ Ḥayyim* 568:1–2).

PERSONALITIES

Mareimar – **מָרֵימָר:** A Babylonian *amora* of the sixth generation, Mareimar was a colleague of Rav Ashi. After Rav Ashi's death, Mareimar is said to have taken his place as head of the Sura academy. Many Sages of the following generation were his students, especially Ravina the younger, his closest disciple. The prefix Mar is possibly an indication that he belonged to the family of the Exilarch. Mareimar's son, Rav Yehuda bar Mareimar, was also a Sage.

Mar Zutra – **מָר זוּטְרָא:** A colleague of Rav Ashi, Mar Zutra was one of the leading Sages of his generation. His teachers Rav Pappa and Rav Naḥman bar Yitzḥak accepted him as their equal. Apart from his greatness in *halakha* and *aggada*, Mar Zutra was a noted preacher, and his sermons are cited in the Gemara. He apparently held an official position as scholar-in-residence and preacher in the household of the Exilarch. In his old age, he was appointed head of the Pumbedita academy.

Some of the meetings between Mar Zutra, Ameimar, and Rav Ashi, which are frequently mentioned in the Talmud, may well have been formal conferences attended by the leaders of Babylonian Jewry.

רַב יְהוֹשֻׁעַ בְּרֵיהּ דְּרַב אִידִי אִיקְּלַע לְבֵי רַב אַסִי. עֲבַדוּ לֵיהּ עֶגְלָא תִּילְתָּא. אֲמַרוּ לֵיהּ: לִיטְעוֹם מָר מִידֵּי. אֲמַר לְהוּ: בְּתַעֲנִיתָא יָתֵיבְנָא. אֲמַרוּ לֵיהּ: וְלוֹזִיף מָר וְלִיפְרַע. לָא סָבַר מָר לְהָא דְּאָמַר רַב יְהוּדָה אָמַר רַב: לֹוֶה אָדָם תַּעֲנִיתוֹ וּפוֹרֵעַ? אֲמַר לְהוּ: תַּעֲנִית חֲלוֹם הוּא.

The Gemara relates: **Rav Yehoshua, son of Rav Idi, happened** to visit **the house of Rav Asi. They prepared a third-born calf,**[N] whose meat is high quality, **for him. They said to him: Let the Master taste something. He said to them: I am sitting in** the observance of **a fast** and may not eat. **They said to him: And let the Master borrow and repay** the fast. **Doesn't the Master hold** in accordance with **this** *halakha* that **Rav Yehuda said** that **Rav said: A person may borrow his fast and repay?** Rav Yehoshua, son of Rav Idi, **said to them: It is a fast for a dream.**[NH] He was fasting to rectify the negative effects of a bad dream he had experienced the night before.

וְאָמַר רַבָּה בַּר מְחַסְיָא אָמַר רַב חָמָא בַּר גּוּרְיָא אָמַר רַב: יָפָה תַּעֲנִית לַחֲלוֹם כָּאֵשׁ לִנְעוֹרֶת. אָמַר רַב חִסְדָּא: וּבוֹ בַּיּוֹם. וְאָמַר רַב יוֹסֵף: וַאֲפִילּוּ בְּשַׁבָּת. מַאי תַּקַּנְתֵּיהּ? לֵיתִיב תַּעֲנִיתָא לְתַעֲנִיתָא.

The Gemara explains the relevance of this last comment. **And Rabba bar Meḥasseya said** that **Rav Ḥama bar Gurya said** that **Rav said: A fast is effective to** neutralize a bad **dream like fire** is effective for burning **chaff. Rav Ḥisda said:** The fast is effective specifically **on that day** that one dreamed. **And Rav Yosef said: And** one suffering from a bad dream is permitted to fast **even on Shabbat.**[NH] The Gemara asks: **What is the remedy** for one who has denigrated Shabbat by fasting? **Let him sit in** observance of another **fast,** on another day, to atone **for** his **fast** on Shabbat.

מתני׳ עָבְרוּ אֵלּוּ וְלֹא נַעֲנוּ, בֵּית דִּין גּוֹזְרִין שָׁלֹשׁ תַּעֲנִיּוֹת אֲחֵרוֹת עַל הַצִּבּוּר. אוֹכְלִין וְשׁוֹתִין מִבְּעוֹד יוֹם, וַאֲסוּרִין בִּמְלָאכָה, וּבִרְחִיצָה, וּבְסִיכָה, וּבִנְעִילַת הַסַּנְדָּל, וּבְתַשְׁמִישׁ הַמִּטָּה, וְנוֹעֲלִין אֶת הַמֶּרְחֲצָאוֹת.

MISHNA **If these** three regular fasts have **passed and they have not been answered** with rain, the **court decrees three other fasts upon the community.** These are severe fasts, in which one **may eat and drink** only **while it is still day,** before the beginning of the night of the fast, **and** on the day of the fast itself **they are prohibited** to engage **in** the performance of **work, in bathing, in smearing with oil, in wearing shoes, and in marital relations; and they lock the bathhouses** so that no one should come to bathe on that day.

עָבְרוּ אֵלּוּ וְלֹא נַעֲנוּ, בֵּית דִּין גּוֹזְרִין עֲלֵיהֶן עוֹד שֶׁבַע, שֶׁהֵן שְׁלֹשׁ עֶשְׂרֵה תַּעֲנִיּוֹת עַל הַצִּבּוּר. הֲרֵי אֵלּוּ יְתֵרוֹת עַל הָרִאשׁוֹנוֹת, שֶׁבָּאֵלּוּ מַתְרִיעִין, וְנוֹעֲלִין אֶת הַחֲנוּיוֹת. בַּשֵּׁנִי מַטִּין עִם חֲשֵׁיכָה, וּבַחֲמִישִׁי מוּתָּרִין מִפְּנֵי כְבוֹד הַשַּׁבָּת.

If these three fasts have **passed and they** still **have not been answered,** the **court decrees on them another seven fasts, which** are a total **of thirteen fasts, upon the community,** not including the first three fasts observed by individuals. **These** seven fast days **are more severe than the first ones, as on these** days, in addition to all the earlier stringencies, they **sound the alarm,** as will be explained in the Gemara, **and they lock the stores.** Although shops must remained closed most of the time on these days, **on Monday** they open them **a little at nightfall** to allow people to purchase food for breaking their fast, **and on Thursday they are permitted** to open the stores all day **in deference to Shabbat,** so that people may purchase food for the sacred day.

עָבְרוּ אֵלּוּ וְלֹא נַעֲנוּ, מְמַעֲטִין בְּמַשָּׂא וּמַתָּן, בְּבִנְיָן וּבִנְטִיעָה, בְּאֵירוּסִין וּבְנִישּׂוּאִין, וּבִשְׁאִילַת שָׁלוֹם בֵּין אָדָם לַחֲבֵירוֹ, כִּבְנֵי אָדָם הַנְּזוּפִין לַמָּקוֹם. הַיְּחִידִים חוֹזְרִין וּמִתְעַנִּין עַד שֶׁיֵּצֵא נִיסָן. יָצָא נִיסָן וְיָרְדוּ גְּשָׁמִים, סִימַן קְלָלָה, שֶׁנֶּאֱמַר: ״הֲלוֹא קְצִיר חִטִּים הַיּוֹם״ וגו׳?

If these fasts have **passed and they have not been answered** the court does not decree additional fasts, but the entire community observes the customs of mourning. **They decrease** their engagement **in business** transactions, **in building and planting, in betrothals and marriages, and in greetings between** each **person and his fellow, like people who have been rebuked by God. The individuals,** i.e., Torah scholars, **resume fasting** every Monday and Thursday **until** the month of **Nisan ends.** After this date they no longer pray for rain, since if **Nisan has ended and rains** subsequently **fall, they are a sign of a curse, as it is stated: "Is not the wheat harvest today?** I will call to the Lord that He may send thunder and rain, and you will know and see that your wickedness is great" (I Samuel 12:17). The wheat harvest is around the time of *Shavuot*, well after Nisan.

גמ׳ בִּשְׁלָמָא כּוּלְּהוּ, אִית בְּהוּ תַּעֲנוּג – רְחִיצָה, וְסִיכָה, וְתַשְׁמִישׁ הַמִּטָּה. אֲבָל מְלָאכָה צַעַר הוּא! אָמַר רַב חִסְדָּא אָמַר רַב יִרְמְיָה בַּר אַבָּא: אָמַר קְרָא: ״קַדְּשׁוּ צוֹם, קִרְאוּ עֲצָרָה, אִסְפוּ זְקֵנִים״. כַּעֲצֶרֶת. מָה עֲצֶרֶת אָסוּר בַּעֲשִׂיַּית מְלָאכָה, אַף תַּעֲנִית אָסוּר בַּעֲשִׂיַּית מְלָאכָה.

GEMARA The Gemara discusses the activities that are prohibited on a communal fast day: **Granted, all of** the other actions are prohibited, **as they** provide **pleasure,** namely, **bathing, smearing, and marital relations. However, working is** a cause of **suffering.** Why was it decreed that one must refrain from working? **Rav Ḥisda said** that **Rav Yirmeya bar Abba said** as that **the verse states: "Sanctify a fast, call a solemn assembly, gather the elders"** (Joel 1:14), this indicates that a fast day is **like** a day of **assembly. Just as** on a day of **assembly,** i.e., a Festival, **it is prohibited** to engage **in working, so too,** on **a fast** it **is prohibited** to engage **in working.**

NOTES

A third-born [*tilta*] calf – עֶגְלָא תִּילְתָּא: Some commentaries on *Shabbat* 11a explain that *tilta* is referring to a calf that reached only a third of its potential size; such a calf has the choicest meat (Rashi). Others say that *meshulash* in the Bible and *tilta* here both mean the best, similar to the term: "And captains [*shalishim*] over them all" (Exodus 14:7), which is referring to the highest ranking soldiers (*Tosafot* in *Shabbat* 11a).

A fast for a dream – תַּעֲנִית חֲלוֹם: This issue of observing a fast for a troubling dream is discussed at length by the commentaries, especially in light of the statement of the Gemara elsewhere (*Sanhedrin* 30a) that dreams do not have any particular significance (Ritva). The Ritva explains that one who has experienced a disturbing dream should take it as a sign from Heaven to examine his ways and repent. Observing a fast is an act that facilitates sincere repentance. The fast should be observed on the day following the dream, even on Shabbat, while the dream is still vivid and likely to lead to repentance. Ordinarily, the obligation to experience joy and pleasure on Shabbat renders it prohibited to fast. However, one who has experienced a disturbing dream is permitted to fast on Shabbat, as he would not enjoy his food anyway. On the contrary, he takes pleasure in fasting, as in this manner he can begin to mend his ways and lessen the anxiety caused by the dream.

And even on Shabbat – וַאֲפִילּוּ בְּשַׁבָּת: Some commentaries explain that this incident involving Rav Yehoshua, son of Rav Idi, occurred on a Shabbat, which is why a third-born calf was prepared for him. This explains the need for him to specify that he was fasting for a bad dream, which is permitted even on Shabbat (*Ramat Shmuel*).

HALAKHA

A fast for a dream – תַּעֲנִית חֲלוֹם: A fast is as beneficial for rectifying the effects of a disturbing dream as fire is powerful against chaff. Therefore, one who has had a bad dream should fast and repent (*Magen Avraham*) on the day following the dream. Nevertheless, fasts for dreams are optional (*Rashba*). In recent times, many authorities have ruled leniently on questions involving fasting for dreams (*Shulḥan Arukh, Oraḥ Ḥayyim* 220:2).

And even on Shabbat – וַאֲפִילּוּ בְּשַׁבָּת: One who is distressed by a bad dream is permitted to observe a fast in order to rectify its negative effects, even on Shabbat. According to some authorities, there are only three types of dreams for which one may fast on Shabbat; others add additional types to the list. Some commentaries add that one should not fast if the suffering caused by his fasting will outweigh the distress caused by the dream (Rivash). In contrast, certain authorities maintain that one should never observe a fast for a disturbing dream on Shabbat (Rav Amram Gaon; *Tur*). One who fasted for a dream on Shabbat is required to observe an additional fast the next day, to atone for fasting on Shabbat. If he is unable to fast on two successive days, or if that Sunday is a day on which fasting is prohibited, he must fast on a different day instead (*Shulḥan Arukh, Oraḥ Ḥayyim* 288:4).

אי מה עצרת מאורתא, אף תענית נמי מאורתא! אמר רבי זירא: לדידי מיפרשא לי מיניה דרבי ירמיה בר אבא: אמר קרא: ״אספו זקנים״. דומיא דאסיפת זקנים. מה אסיפת זקנים ביום, אף צום נמי ביום. ואימא: מטיהרא! אמר רב שישא בריה דרב אידי: מסייע ליה לרב הונא, דאמר מצפרא כינופיא.

The Gemara asks: If so, one could say: **Just as** on a day of **assembly** it is prohibited to work **from** the previous **evening, so too,** on a fast it should be prohibited to work **from** the **evening. Rabbi Zeira said:** This **was explained to me by Rabbi Yirmeya bar Abba himself: The verse states:** "Sanctify a fast, call a solemn assembly, **gather the elders,**" indicating that a fast is **similar to a gathering of elders: Just as the gathering of elders** is performed **by day, so too,** the time for **a fast** is **also by day.** The Gemara asks: **But** if so, one can **say** that the fast should begin **from noon. Rav Sheisha, son of Rav Idi, said:** This **supports** the opinion of[N] **Rav Huna, who said:** The public **gathering** on fast days occurs **in the** hours of **the morning.**

היכי עבדי? אמר אביי: מצפרא עד פלגא דיומא מעיינינן במילי דמתא. מכאן ואילך, רבעא דיומא קרינן בספרא ואפטרתא. מכאן ואילך, בעינן רחמי, שנאמר: ״ויקומו על עמדם, ויקראו בספר תורת ה׳ אלהיהם רבעית היום, ורבעית מתודים, ומשתחוים לה׳ אלהיהם״.

The Gemara asks: **How do they act** on a fast day? **Abaye said: From the morning until the middle of the day**[H] **they examine the affairs of the town**[N] by checking if there are any deficiencies or corruptions in the city, moral or otherwise, and attempt to fix them, as these problems may have been the cause of the Divine punishment. **From this point forward,** for **a quarter of the day they read** a portion **from the Torah and** a portion from **the Prophets** [*haftara*]. **From this point forward, they pray** and petition **for mercy, as it is stated: "And they stood up in their place and they read in the book of the Torah of the Lord their God a fourth part of the day; and another fourth part they confessed, and prostrated themselves before the Lord their God"** (Nehemiah 9:3).

NOTES

This supports the opinion of – מסייע ליה ל: When the Gemara wishes to explore the possibility that the mishna it is analyzing can be cited as proof for the opinion of a Sage, it will typically state: This source supports the statement of that Sage.

They examine the affairs of the town – מעיינינן במילי דמתא: Some commentaries derive this requirement from the following verses: "Is not this the fast that I have chosen? To loosen the fetters of wickedness, to undo the bands of the yoke, and to let the oppressed go free, and that you break every yoke? Is it not to deal your bread to the hungry and that you bring the poor who are cast out to your house? When you see the naked, that you cover him; and that you do not hide yourself from your own flesh?" (Isaiah 58:6–7). These verses teach that God views favorably those fasts on which people examine their behavior and attend to the social injustices they find in their community (Vilna Gaon on *Shulḥan Arukh*, *Oraḥ Ḥayyim* 576:16). Others add that on communal fast days, the leaders gather to attend to the community's problems and requirements, as well as to right any wrongs that the community as a whole may have inflicted on individuals (Rabbi Elyakim).

HALAKHA

From the morning until the middle of the day – מצפרא עד פלגא דיומא: On communal fast days that are decreed to avert an impending calamity, the court judges and the community leaders gather in the synagogues from after the completion of the morning prayers until noon, to examine the conduct of the townspeople. They attempt to rectify any flaws in behavior that they might find, and they admonish wrongdoers and shame those who resort to violence to get their way. During the third quarter of the day, an appropriate section of the Torah is read, as well as a portion from the Prophets related to the occasion. During the last quarter of the day, the congregation recites the afternoon prayer and offers special petitions and supplications. These practices have not been observed in recent generations, either because the courts no longer have the authority to correct the wrongs they find (*Arukh HaShulḥan*), or because in general the customs concerning communal fasts are no longer observed in their entirety (*Shulḥan Arukh*, *Oraḥ Ḥayyim* 576:16).

Perek I
Daf 13 Amud a

איפוך אנא! לא סלקא דעתך, דכתיב: ״ואלי יאספו כל חרד בדברי אלהי ישראל על מעל הגולה״ וגו׳. וכתיב: ״ובמנחת הערב קמתי מתעניתי...ואפרשה כפי אל ה׳״.

The Gemara asks: **I** can **reverse**[N] the order of events, so that the first half of the day is spent in prayer while the second half is focused on the concerns of the community. The Gemara answers: **It should not enter your mind** to say that, **as it is written** elsewhere: **"Then were assembled to me**[N] **everyone who trembled at the words of the God of Israel due to the faithlessness of them of the captivity** and I sat appalled until the evening offering" (Ezra 9:4). **And it is written** in the next verse: **"And at the meal-offering I arose from my fast,** even with my garment and my mantle rent; and I fell on my knees **and I spread out my hands to the Lord"** (Ezra 9:5). These verses indicate that first one must deal with the issues of the community, and only afterward engage in prayer.

NOTES

I can reverse – איפוך אנא: Although it stands to reason that the members of a community should first correct their ways and only afterward petition for mercy, the Gemara argues that there is good reason to reverse the order, as many of the *halakhot* of fasting and repentance are derived from the description of the penitence of the people of Nineveh. The *Ramat Shmuel* points out that the book of Jonah states that the inhabitants of Nineveh first petitioned God for mercy and only then attended to the wrongs committed in their community: "But let them be covered with sackcloth, both man and beast, and let them cry mightily to God; and let them turn every one from his evil way, and from the violence that is in their hands" (Jonah 3:8).

Then were assembled to me, etc. – ואלי יאספו וגו׳: In other words, all those who feared God came to discuss "the faithlessness of the captivity," i.e., the sins of the people of the Babylonian captivity who had ascended to Eretz Yisrael. This is referring to the correction of communal wrongs, as stated in the previous *halakha* (Rabbi Elyakim; Ran).

אמר רפרם בר פפא אמר רב חסדא: כל שהוא משום אבל, כגון תשעה באב, ואבל, אסור בין בחמין בין בצונן. כל שהוא משום תענוג, כגון תענית צבור, בחמין אסור, בצונן מותר.

§ **Rafram bar Pappa**[P] **said that Rav Ḥisda said: Anything that is** prohibited **due to mourning, for example,** bathing on the **Ninth of Av,**[H] **or** prohibited for a private **mourner,** is **prohibited both in hot water and in cold water.**[NH] **Anything that is** prohibited **due to pleasure, for example,** bathing on **a communal fast,** is **prohibited in hot water, but** is **permitted in cold water,**[H] provided one washes for the sake of cleanliness.

אמר רב אידי בר אבין: אף אנן נמי תנינא: "ונועלין את המרחצאות". אמר ליה אביי: ואי בצונן אסור, סוכרין את הנהרות מבעי ליה למיתני?

Rav Idi bar Avin[P] **said: We, too, learn**[B] this in the mishna: **And they lock the bathhouses.** This phrase indicates that only bathing in hot water is prohibited. **Abaye said to** Rav Idi bar Avin: **And if** it were also **prohibited** to wash **in cold water, should** the mishna **have taught: They dam the rivers?** Since it is impossible to dam the rivers to stop people from bathing altogether, the statement of the mishna is insufficient proof that only bathing in hot water is prohibited. Perhaps bathing in cold water is also prohibited but there is no way to prevent it.

אמר רב שישא בריה דרב אידי: אבא הכי קשיא ליה: מכדי תנן: אסור ברחיצה, נועלין את המרחצאות למה לי? אלא לאו שמע מינה: בחמין אסור; בצונן מותר?

Rav Sheisha, son of Rav Idi, said, in explanation of his father's opinion: With regard to my **father, the following** poses **a difficulty to his** ruling: **Since we** already **learned** in the mishna that **one is prohibited** to engage **in bathing, why do I** need the *tanna* to state: **They lock the bathhouses?** Practically speaking, what does this clause add? **Rather, isn't it** correct to **conclude from this** that bathing is **prohibited in hot water** but **permitted in cold water?**

לימא מסייע ליה: כל חייבי טבילות טובלין כדרכן, בין בתשעה באב בין ביום הכפורים. במאי? אילימא בחמין, טבילה בחמין מי איכא? שאובין נינהו!

The Gemara proposes: **Let us say that** the following *baraita* **supports** Rav Ḥisda's ruling that it is prohibited for a mourner to bathe himself even in cold water: **All** who are **obligated in immersions immerse** themselves **in their usual manner,**[H] **both on the Ninth of Av and on Yom Kippur.** The Gemara clarifies this *baraita*: **In what** do they immerse themselves? **If we say** that they immerse themselves **in hot water, is there** such a concept as ritual **immersion in hot water?**[H] Hot water **is** necessarily **drawn water,**[N] as the water has been placed in vessels for heating, and drawn water is invalid for a ritual bath.

PERSONALITIES

Rafram bar Pappa – רפרם בר פפא: Rafram bar Pappa was an *amora* of the third and fourth generations in Babylonia. According to a tradition of the *ge'onim*, Rafram, a name shared by several Sages, is a shortened form of Rav Efrayim. Rafram bar Pappa was a close disciple of Rav Ḥisda, and he is principally mentioned as the transmitter of his great master's statements. Rafram bar Pappa also knew Rav Huna, whose great deeds he related to Rava.

Rav Idi bar Avin – רב אידי בר אבין: Rav Idi bar Avin belonged to the third and fourth generations of Babylonian *amora'im*. It is related that Rav Idi's father, Rav Avin the carpenter, was especially punctilious to observe the mitzva of lighting the Shabbat lamp, a pious practice that led Rav Huna to predict that his sons would become eminent scholars. Indeed, his sons were Rav Ḥiyya bar Avin and Rav Idi bar Avin.

Although Rav Idi bar Avin was Rav Ḥisda's student, he also quotes other Sages from the second generation of Babylonian *amora'im*. He was one of the greatest authorities of his generation, and many of his halakhic discussions with Abaye are recorded in the Gemara. Rav Idi bar Avin was the chief rabbinic authority of his city, Shekhantziv, where he apparently headed an academy. The most eminent scholars of the next generation, Rav Pappa and Rav Huna, son of Rav Yehoshua, were his disciples. Rav Idi bar Avin lived a long life and in his old age he liked to call his students his children. He too had two sons who became Sages, but little else is known of his deeds or his life.

NOTES

Prohibited both in hot water and in cold water – אסור בין בחמין בין בצונן: Elsewhere (*Pesaḥim* 54b), Rabbi Elazar rules that on the Ninth of Av, similar to Yom Kippur, one may not even put his finger into cold water. Some commentaries maintain that Rav Ḥisda agrees with that ruling and that when he says that it is prohibited to bathe in cold water on the Ninth of Av and during the mourning period, he means that one may not wash even his face, hands, or feet in cold water (Ritva). By contrast, Talmid HaRamban argues that according to the opinion of Rav Ḥisda, it is prohibited to bathe only one's entire body in cold water on the Ninth of Av and during a mourning period, but washing one's face, hands, and feet in cold water is permitted. This dispute has ramifications with regard to the Gemara's objections against Rav Ḥisda's opinion below.

Immersion in hot water…it is drawn water – טבילה בחמין...שאובין נינהו: Ritual immersion is performed in a spring, in the sea, or in water that has collected of its own accord, but not in water that has been drawn into vessels. Furthermore, in certain cases a ritual bath can be invalidated when drawn water falls into it.

Water used for bathing was typically heated by the addition of water that had been heated in large containers, as was performed for the benefit of a weak or elderly High Priest on Yom Kippur. Alternatively, the water was placed in a special pool where it could be heated from below, as in the Roman baths. Consequently, hot water could not be used for ritual immersion.

HALAKHA

Bathing on the Ninth of Av – רחיצה בתשעה באב: Bathing on the Ninth of Av is prohibited, both in hot water and cold water, in accordance with the opinion of Rav Ḥisda. One may not even insert his finger into water for the purpose of washing (*Shulḥan Arukh, Oraḥ Ḥayyim* 554:7).

A mourner is prohibited both in hot water and in cold water – אבל אסור בין בחמין בין בצונן: A mourner may not bathe his entire body, even in cold water. It is prohibited for him to wash his face, hands, and feet in hot water; however, he may wash them in cold water. If he is extremely dirty, he is permitted to wash himself in the ordinary manner, in accordance with the opinion of Rav Ḥisda, as explained in the Gemara below. Some commentaries note that strictly speaking, these prohibitions apply only during the first seven days of mourning, although it is customary for mourners to refrain from bathing for thirty days (Rema). In places where this custom prevails, one should not deviate from it (*Shulḥan Arukh, Yoreh De'a* 381:1).

A communal fast is prohibited in hot water but permitted in cold water – תענית צבור בחמין אסור בצונן מותר: On the more severe communal fasts decreed in times of drought, when eating is prohibited from sundown, one may not bathe his entire body in hot water. However, it is permitted to wash one's face, hands, and feet, even in hot water, and it is likewise permitted to wash one's entire body in cold water, in accordance with the opinion of Rav Ḥisda (*Shulḥan Arukh, Oraḥ Ḥayyim* 555:3).

All obligated in immersions immerse themselves in their usual manner – כל חייבי טבילות טובלין כדרכן: If the day designated for one's ritual immersion occurs on the Ninth of Av or on Yom Kippur, he is permitted to immerse himself on that day. Nowadays, however, there is no obligation to immerse on a precise date, and therefore one may not immerse himself on the Ninth of Av or on Yom Kippur (*Shulḥan Arukh, Oraḥ Ḥayyim* 554:8).

Immersion in hot water – טבילה בחמין: Some authorities maintain that it is prohibited to pour hot water into a ritual bath to heat its water, whereas others permit it. In Europe, with its severe winters, it was customary to rule leniently in this regard, especially if hot water was not actually poured into the ritual bath, and only the waters of the ritual bath itself were heated (*Shulḥan Arukh, Yoreh De'a* 201:75).

BACKGROUND

We, too, learn – אף אנן נמי תנינא: This expression is used in the Gemara when proof is adduced for the ruling of an *amora* from a statement of a mishna or a *baraita*. Typically, the tannaitic quotation will not deal directly with the subject at hand, as *amora'im* do not usually issue a halakhic ruling that had already appeared in a mishna. Instead, the proof is usually more complex, i.e., if one were to examine the source closely he would reach the same conclusion as the *amora*, despite the fact that he did not base his ruling on the mishna.

אֶלָּא לָאו בְּצוֹנֵן, וְחַיָּיבֵי טְבִילוֹת, אִין, אִינִישׁ אַחֲרִינָא, לָא? אָמַר רַב חָנָא בַּר קְטִינָא: לָא נִצְרְכָה אֶלָּא לְחַמֵּי טְבֶרְיָא.

Rather, isn't the *baraita* referring **to cold water, and** it teaches that **those obligated in immersions, yes,** they are permitted to use cold water, but **another person,** who is not obligated to immerse, **no,** he may not wash even in cold water. **Rav Ḥana bar Ketina said: This** is no proof, as the ruling of the *baraita* **was necessary only for the hot springs of Tiberias,**[B] which are warm without having been drawn, and in which it is possible to immerse.

אִי הָכִי, אֵימָא סֵיפָא: אָמַר רַבִּי חֲנִינָא סְגַן הַכֹּהֲנִים: כְּדַי הוּא בֵּית אֱלֹהֵינוּ לְאַבֵּד עָלָיו טְבִילָה פַּעַם אַחַת בַּשָּׁנָה. וְאִי אָמְרַתְּ: בְּצוֹנֵן מוּתָּר, יִרְחַץ בְּצוֹנֵן! אָמַר רַב פַּפָּא: בְּאַתְרָא דְּלָא שְׁכִיחַ צוֹנֵן.

The Gemara objects: **If so, say the latter clause** of that same mishna: **Rabbi Ḥanina, the deputy High Priest, said:** The mourning for **the House of our God,** the Holy Temple, **is worthy of the loss of** a ritual **immersion once a year. And if you say** that it is **permitted** to immerse **in cold water,** why does Rabbi Ḥanina the deputy High Priest say that he loses his immersion? **Let him bathe in cold water,** without having to neglect his immersion or transgress the prohibitions of a fast day. **Rav Pappa said:** It could be argued that the *baraita* is referring **to a place where cold water is not available,** but only hot springs. In this case there is no choice but to wait until the following day to immerse.

תָּא שְׁמַע: כְּשֶׁאָמְרוּ אָסוּר בִּמְלָאכָה, לֹא אָמְרוּ אֶלָּא בַּיּוֹם, אֲבָל בַּלַּיְלָה מוּתָּר. וּכְשֶׁאָמְרוּ אָסוּר בִּנְעִילַת הַסַּנְדָּל, לֹא אָמְרוּ אֶלָּא בָּעִיר, אֲבָל בַּדֶּרֶךְ מוּתָּר. הָא כֵּיצַד? יוֹצֵא לַדֶּרֶךְ, נוֹעֵל; נִכְנַס לָעִיר, חוֹלֵץ. וּכְשֶׁאָמְרוּ אָסוּר בִּרְחִיצָה, לֹא אָמְרוּ אֶלָּא כׇּל גּוּפוֹ, אֲבָל פָּנָיו, יָדָיו, וְרַגְלָיו מוּתָּר. וְכֵן אַתָּה מוֹצֵא בִּמְנוּדֶּה וּבְאָבֵל.

The Gemara proposes: **Come and hear: When they said** that one is prohibited **in working** on fast days, **they said** so **only** about working **during the day, but at night** it is **permitted** to work. **And when they said** that one is **prohibited** to engage **in wearing shoes, they said** so **only in a city, but on the road** it is **permitted. How so? When one goes out on the road he wears shoes,** but at the end of his journey, when **he enters the town, he removes** them. **And when they said** that one is **prohibited** to engage **in bathing, they said** this **only** with regard to bathing **his entire body, but** washing **his face, his hands, and his feet** is **permitted. And similarly, you find** that this ruling applies in the case **of one who is ostracized,** i.e., placed under a formal ban, **and** in the case **of a mourner,** who is also prohibited to engage in bathing, smearing, and wearing shoes.

מַאי לָאו אַכּוּלְּהוּ? וּבְמַאי עָסְקִינַן? אִילֵימָא בְּחַמִּין, פָּנָיו, יָדָיו, וְרַגְלָיו מִי שְׁרוּ? וְהָאָמַר רַב שֵׁשֶׁת: אָבֵל אָסוּר לְהוֹשִׁיט אֶצְבָּעוֹ בְּחַמִּין. אֶלָּא לָאו בְּצוֹנֵן?

The Gemara explains the proof from this *baraita*: **What, is it not** the case that all these *halakhot* refer **to all of them,**[N] including one who is ostracized and one who is in mourning? **And with what** form of bathing **are we dealing** here? **If we say** that the *baraita* is referring to bathing **in hot water,** are bathing **his face, his hands, and his feet permitted? But didn't Rav Sheshet say:** It **is prohibited for a mourner to insert** even **his finger into hot water** for the purpose of washing. **Rather, is it not** correct to say that the *baraita* is dealing **with cold water?** If so, it is prohibited on a communal fast to wash one's entire body even in cold water, which contradicts the opinion of Rafram bar Pappa, citing Rav Ḥisda, who permits washing in cold water on those days for the sake of cleanliness.

לָא, לְעוֹלָם בְּחַמִּין. וּדְקָא קַשְׁיָא לָךְ, וְכֵן אַתָּה מוֹצֵא בִּמְנוּדֶּה וּבְאָבֵל, אַשְּׁאָרָא קָאֵי.

The Gemara rejects this argument: **No, actually** the *baraita* is referring **to** bathing in **hot water. And** with regard to **what** posed **a difficulty for you,** the phrase: **And similarly,** that **you find** in the case **of one who is ostracized and** in the case **of a mourner,** does not refer to bathing; rather, **it is referring to the rest** of the prohibitions, e.g., working and wearing shoes. Consequently, it can be claimed that the *baraita* refers specifically to hot water, as this clause does not refer to a mourner but only to a communal fast, and bathing in cold water is permitted on communal fasts.

תָּא שְׁמַע, דְּאָמַר רַבִּי אַבָּא הַכֹּהֵן מִשּׁוּם רַבִּי יוֹסֵי הַכֹּהֵן: מַעֲשֶׂה וּמֵתוּ בָּנָיו שֶׁל רַבִּי יוֹסֵי בֶּן רַבִּי חֲנִינָא, וְרָחַץ בְּצוֹנֵן כׇּל שִׁבְעָה! הָתָם כְּשֶׁתְּכָפוּהוּ אֲבָלָיו הֲוָה. דְּתַנְיָא: תְּכָפוּהוּ אֲבָלָיו בָּזֶה אַחַר זֶה, הִכְבִּיד שְׂעָרוֹ, מֵיקֵל בְּתַעַר, וּמְכַבֵּס כְּסוּתוֹ בְּמַיִם.

The Gemara proposes yet another proof. **Come** and **hear** a statement of a *baraita*, **as Rabbi Abba the priest said in the name of Rabbi Yosei the priest: An incident** occurred in which **the sons of Rabbi Yosei, son of Rabbi Ḥanina, died, and he bathed in cold water all seven** days of mourning. This indicates that a mourner is in fact permitted to bathe. The Gemara rejects this argument: **There it was** a case where **his mourning periods** came **one after the other,** as his sons died in quick succession, and this leniency is **as it is taught** in a *baraita*: **If one's mourning periods** immediately **succeeded**[H] each other **and his hair grew heavy,** then even though it is generally prohibited for a mourner to cut his hair, **he may lighten it with a razor,**[H] **and he may** likewise **wash his garment in water.**[H]

BACKGROUND

The hot springs of Tiberias – חַמֵּי טְבֶרְיָא: The hot springs of Tiberias consist of mineral-rich water heated by geothermal energy. During the Roman period, public baths were erected in Tiberias and the second-largest bath complex in the entire Roman Empire was built in the vicinity. Some baths still function today, e.g., the baths at Ḥamat Gader.

Roman bath in Ḥamat Gader, near Tiberias

NOTES

What, is it not the case that all these *halakhot* refer to all of them – מַאי לָאו אַכּוּלְּהוּ: The early authorities dispute the meaning of the objection raised here. Some commentaries maintain that the Gemara is citing this *baraita* as an objection to Rav Ḥisda's first ruling that it is prohibited to bathe on the Ninth of Av as well as during the week of mourning, whether in hot or cold water (Rabbeinu Gershom; *Tosafot*; Ritva). This is because the *baraita* states that a mourner is governed by the same *halakhot* that apply on a communal fast, when it is prohibited to bathe the entire body, but permitted to wash one's face, hands, and feet. However, the early authorities disagree as to how the *baraita* contradicts Rav Ḥisda's ruling. Some argue that it is because the term bathing generally denotes washing in hot water, which indicates that a mourner is permitted to bathe in cold water (Rabbeinu Gershom). Alternatively, the reason might be that the *baraita* states that washing one's face, hands, and feet is permitted, whereas Rav Ḥisda maintains that this too is prohibited (Ritva).

In contrast, other commentaries claim that the *baraita* is cited to disprove Rav Ḥisda's second ruling, that on communal fasts bathing is prohibited only in hot water, not cold water (Rashi; *Shita Mekubbetzet*; Rabbi Akiva Eiger). This difference in interpretation depends in part on variant readings of this passage, as well as the different interpretations of Rav Ḥisda's opinion.

HALAKHA

If one's mourning periods succeeded – כְּשֶׁתְּכָפוּהוּ אֲבָלָיו: One who observes more than one period of mourning in succession is permitted to wash in cold water, in accordance with the custom of Rabbi Yosei, son of Rabbi Ḥanina (*Shulḥan Arukh, Yoreh De'a* 381:4).

If his hair grew heavy, he may lighten it with a razor – הִכְבִּיד שְׂעָרוֹ, מֵיקֵל בְּתַעַר: If someone is observing two periods of mourning, one immediately after the other, and his hair grows long, he may trim it with a razor, but not with scissors. Furthermore, he may do so only in private (*Shulḥan Arukh, Yoreh De'a* 390:3, and in the comment of Rema).

And he may wash his garment in water – וּמְכַבֵּס כְּסוּתוֹ בְּמַיִם: If one is observing two periods of mourning, one immediately after the other, he may unobtrusively wash his clothes in water. However, he may not use soap or sand, in accordance with the opinion of Rav Ḥisda (*Shulḥan Arukh, Yoreh De'a* 389:1).

BACKGROUND

Natron [*neter*] – נֶתֶר: *Neter* is probably natron which is a naturally occurring mixture of sodium carbonate, $Na_2CO_3 \cdot 10H_2O$, found in desert plains. In antiquity it was produced from algae. Natron is easily soluble in water and has a strong basic reaction that releases Na_2, a substance that breaks up fats. Consequently, it was used as a detergent even in biblical times.

Natural natron deposit

אָמַר רַב חִסְדָּא: בְּתַעַר, אֲבָל לֹא בְּמִסְפָּרַיִם. בְּמַיִם, וְלֹא בְּנֶתֶר וְלֹא בְּחוֹל.

With regard to this *baraita*, **Rav Ḥisda said:** One who is obligated to observe periods of mourning in quick succession may trim his hair **with a razor, but not** in the normal manner, **with scissors.** Likewise, he may wash his garment **in water, but not with natron,**[B] a type of soap, **nor with sand.**

אָמַר רָבָא: אָבֵל מוּתָּר לִרְחוֹץ בְּצוֹנֵן כָּל שִׁבְעָה, מִידֵּי דַּהֲוָה אַבִּשְׂרָא וְחַמְרָא. מֵיתִיבִי:

Rava said: A mourner is permitted to bathe in cold water all seven days of mourning, despite the fact that he derives a certain degree of enjoyment from the cold bath, **just as it is** permitted for him to eat **meat and wine.**[N] The Gemara **raises an objection:**

NOTES

Just as it is permitted to eat meat and wine – מִידֵּי דַּהֲוָה אַבִּשְׂרָא וְחַמְרָא: During the period of acute mourning, which lasts from the time of the death of a close relative until after the funeral, it is prohibited for a mourner to eat meat or drink wine. However, in the period of regular mourning following the funeral, meat and wine are permitted to the mourner. Likewise, Rava maintains that bathing in cold water is permitted during the seven-day period of mourning following burial, despite the fact that it is prohibited during the period of acute mourning (Rabbi Elyakim).

Perek **I**
Daf **13** Amud **b**

NOTES

A grown woman is not permitted – אֵין הַבּוֹגֶרֶת רַשָּׁאָה: *Tosafot* maintain that in this context the term: Not permitted, actually means that she is obligated to wash. Other commentaries provide support for the opinion of *Tosafot* by citing various examples in the Gemara where the term permitted is referring to an obligation (*Gevurat Ari*). In contrast, some commentaries claim that here too, the term is used in its original meaning: A grown woman is not permitted to render herself unattractive when she is in mourning, lest she repel potential suitors. If she renders herself unattractive, she must be admonished (Meiri).

HALAKHA

A grown woman is not permitted – אֵין הַבּוֹגֶרֶת רַשָּׁאָה: It is permitted for a grown woman to paint her eyes and dye her hair when she is in mourning, including the first seven days of mourning (*Arukh HaShulḥan*). However, it is prohibited for a young woman to do so (*Shulḥan Arukh, Yoreh De'a* 381:6).

LANGUAGE

Dyeing [*pirkus*] – פִּירְכּוּס: Of uncertain origin, especially as this term is often exchanged with the root *p-k-s*, although it is spelled with the letter *kuf* rather than a *kaf*; it probably means to apply rouge. Some maintain that *pirkus* is from the Greek root περκάζω, *perkazo*, meaning to dye black, to darken, particularly to darken hair.

אֵין הַבּוֹגֶרֶת רַשָּׁאָה לְנַוֵּול אֶת עַצְמָהּ בִּימֵי אֵבֶל אָבִיהָ. הָא נַעֲרָה רַשָּׁאָה.

A grown woman, i.e., a girl over twelve and a half, who is old enough to be married, **is not permitted**[NH] **to render herself unattractive during the days of mourning for her father,** as this would adversely affect her chances of marriage. The Gemara infers that this *halakha* applies only to a grown woman, whereas **a young woman,** a girl between the ages of twelve and twelve and a half, who is not yet old enough to be married, **is permitted** to render herself unattractive.

מַאי לָאו בִּרְחִיצָה? וּבְמַאי? אִילֵּימָא בְּחַמִּין, אֵין הַבּוֹגֶרֶת רַשָּׁאָה? וְהָאָמַר רַב חִסְדָּא: אָבֵל אָסוּר לְהוֹשִׁיט אֶצְבָּעוֹ בְּחַמִּין! אֶלָּא לָאו בְּצוֹנֵן? לָא. אַכִּיחוּל וּפִירְכּוּס.

The Gemara analyzes this *halakha*: **What, is it not** referring to the prohibition **against bathing? And in what** kind of water may a grown woman bathe? **If we say** that the *baraita* is referring to **hot water,** is **a grown woman not permitted** to render herself unattractive by refraining from washing in hot water? **But didn't Rav Ḥisda say:** It is **prohibited for a mourner to insert** even **his finger into hot water** for the purpose of washing. **Rather, is it not** the case that it is permitted for a grown woman to bathe **in cold water,** from which it may be inferred that it is not permitted for a young woman to bathe even in cold water. The Gemara answers: **No,** the *baraita* is not speaking of bathing at all. Rather it is referring to **painting** the eyes **and dyeing [*pirkus*]**[L] one's hair, which it is permitted for a grown woman to do during mourning.

לֵימָא מְסַיַּיע לֵיהּ: דְּאָמַר רַבִּי אַבָּא הַכֹּהֵן מִשּׁוּם רַבִּי יוֹסֵי הַכֹּהֵן: מַעֲשֶׂה וּמֵתוּ בָּנָיו שֶׁל רַבִּי יוֹסֵי בַּר חֲנִינָא, וְרָחַץ בְּצוֹנֵן כָּל שִׁבְעָה!

The Gemara proposes: **Let say that** the aforementioned *baraita* **supports** Rava's ruling. **As Rabbi Abba the priest said in the name of Rabbi Yosei the priest: An incident** occurred in which **the sons of Rabbi Yosei, son of Rabbi Ḥanina, died, and he bathed in cold water all seven** days of mourning. This ruling apparently indicates that a mourner is permitted to bathe in cold water.

אָמְרִי: הָתָם בְּשֶׁתְּכָפוּהוּ אֲבָלָיו זֶה אַחַר זֶה. דְּתַנְיָא: תְּכָפוּהוּ אֲבָלָיו בָּזֶה אַחַר זֶה, הִכְבִּיד שְׂעָרוֹ, מֵיקֵל בְּתַעַר, וּמְכַבֵּס כְּסוּתוֹ בְּמַיִם. אֲמַר רַב חִסְדָּא: בְּתַעַר, אֲבָל לֹא בְּמִסְפָּרַיִם. בְּמַיִם, וְלֹא בְּנֶתֶר וְלֹא בְּחוֹל וְלֹא בְּאָהָל.

The Gemara responds: This is not a proof, as **they say: There** it is referring to a case where **his mourning periods** came immediately **one after the other, as it is taught** in a *baraita*: **If one's mourning periods** came immediately **one after the other and his hair grew heavy, he may lighten it with a razor, and he may wash his garment in water. And Rav Ḥisda said:** He may trim his hair **with a razor, but not with scissors.** Likewise, he may wash his garment **in water, but not with natron, nor with sand, and nor with iceplant.**[B]

אִיכָּא דְּאָמְרִי אָמַר רָבָא: אָבֵל אָסוּר בְּצוֹנֵן כָּל שִׁבְעָה. מַאי שְׁנָא מִבָּשָׂר וְיַיִן? הָתָם לְפַכּוּחֵי פַּחֲדֵיהּ הוּא דְּעָבֵיד.

The foregoing is one version of Rava's opinion and the ensuing discussion. **Some say** a different version of this debate. **Rava said:** It is **prohibited for a mourner** to bathe **in cold water all seven** days of mourning. The Gemara asks: In **what** way **is** this case **different from** eating **meat and** drinking **wine,**[H] which a mourner is permitted to do? The Gemara responds: **There, he acts to relieve his anxieties.**[N] Since a mourner is typically distressed over the death of a close relative, the Sages permitted him to fortify himself with strong food and drink.

לֵימָא מְסַיַּיע לֵיהּ: אֵין הַבּוֹגֶרֶת רַשָּׁאָה לְנַוּוֹל עַצְמָהּ. הָא נַעֲרָה רַשָּׁאָה. בְּמַאי? אִילֵימָא בְּחַמִּין, אֵין הַבּוֹגֶרֶת רַשָּׁאָה? וְהָאֲמַר רַב חִסְדָּא: אָבֵל אָסוּר לְהוֹשִׁיט אֶצְבָּעוֹ בְּחַמִּין! אֶלָּא לָאו בְּצוֹנֵן? לָא. אַכִּיחוּל וּפִירְכּוּס.

The Gemara proposes: **Let** us **say that** the following *baraita* **supports** Rava's ruling. **A grown woman is not permitted to render herself unattractive** during the days of mourning for her father. As above, the Gemara infers that this *halakha* applies only to a grown woman, but **a young woman is permitted** to render herself unattractive. **In what** kind of water may a grown woman bathe? **If we say** that this is referring to **hot water, is a grown woman not permitted** to refrain from washing in hot water? **But didn't Rav Ḥisda say:** It is **prohibited for a mourner to insert his finger into hot water** for the purpose of washing. **Rather, is it not** the case that the *baraita* is referring **to** bathing **in cold water?** The Gemara answers: **No;** the *baraita* is speaking **of painting** the eyes **and dyeing** the hair.

אָמַר רַב חִסְדָּא: זֹאת אוֹמֶרֶת: אָבֵל אָסוּר בְּתִכְבּוֹסֶת כָּל שִׁבְעָה. וְהִלְכְתָא: אָבֵל אָסוּר לִרְחוֹץ כָּל גּוּפוֹ בֵּין בְּחַמִּין וּבֵין בְּצוֹנֵן כָּל שִׁבְעָה. אֲבָל פָּנָיו, יָדָיו, וְרַגְלָיו בְּחַמִּין אָסוּר, בְּצוֹנֵן מוּתָּר. אֲבָל לָסוּךְ, אֲפִילּוּ כָּל שֶׁהוּא אָסוּר. וְאִם לְעַבֵּר אֶת הַזּוּהֲמָא, מוּתָּר.

Rav Ḥisda said: That is to say, i.e., as the *baraita* states that it is permitted for a grown woman who observes successive periods of mourning to paint and dye her hair, the same *halakha* evidently applies to laundry, from which it may be inferred that in an unexceptional case it is **prohibited for a mourner to** wash **laundry**[H] **all seven** days of mourning.[N] The Gemara concludes: **And the practical *halakha* is:** It is **prohibited for a mourner to bathe his entire body both in hot water and in cold water all seven** days of mourning. **However,** with regard to **his face, his hands, and his feet,** although it is **prohibited** to bathe them **in hot water, in cold water** it is **permitted. However,** with regard **to smearing** with oil, even **any** minimal **amount** of smearing **is prohibited.**[H] **But if** one does so **to remove the dirt,** it is **permitted.**

צְלוֹתָא דְּתַעֲנִיתָא הֵיכִי מַדְכְּרִינַן? אַדְכְּרֵיהּ רַב יְהוּדָה לְרַב יִצְחָק בְּרֵיהּ, וְדָרַשׁ: יָחִיד שֶׁקִּיבֵּל עָלָיו תַּעֲנִית מִתְפַּלֵּל שֶׁל תַּעֲנִית. וְהֵיכָן אוֹמְרָהּ? בֵּין גּוֹאֵל לְרוֹפֵא.

§ The Gemara returns to the discussion of the *Aneinu* prayer, recited on fast days. **The prayer of a fast, how does one mention** it? **Rav Yehuda granted his son Rav Yitzḥak** general **permission** to expound publicly, while instructing him in the substance of what he should say, **and** Rav Yitzḥak **taught: An individual who took a fast upon himself prays** the prayer **of a fast. And where** in the *Amida* **does he recite** this additional prayer? **Between** the seventh blessing of the *Amida*: **Who redeems, and** the eighth blessing: **Who heals.**

מַתְקִיף לָהּ רַב יִצְחָק: וְכִי יָחִיד קוֹבֵעַ בְּרָכָה לְעַצְמוֹ? אֶלָּא אָמַר רַב יִצְחָק: בְּשׁוֹמֵעַ תְּפִלָּה. וְכֵן אָמַר רַב שֵׁשֶׁת: בְּשׁוֹמֵעַ תְּפִלָּה.

Rav Yitzḥak strongly objects to this: But may an individual establish a blessing for himself, in addition to the fixed blessings of the *Amida*? **Rather, Rav Yitzḥak said:** One mentions his fast **in the** blessing: **Who listens to prayer,** in accordance with the general principle that an individual may insert private requests into this general plea for the acceptance of prayers, including matters outside the scope of the established blessings. **And similarly, Rav Sheshet said:** One recites the prayer for a fast day **in the** blessing: **Who listens to prayer.**

BACKGROUND

Iceplant [*ahal*] – אָהָל: There are several plants referred to as *ahal* which are indigenous to Eretz Yisrael. One of them is crystalline iceplant, *Mesembryanthemum crystallinum* L., an annual plant that grows on rocks and walls facing the ocean in the Sharon region and the coastal plain. It is called crystalline iceplant due to its glistening vesicles that resemble crystals. This plant contains a considerable amount of soda, which was used for laundry and bathing.

Crystalline iceplant

HALAKHA

In what way is this different from meat and wine – מַאי שְׁנָא מִבָּשָׂר וְיַיִן: After the deceased is buried, the mourner is permitted to eat meat and drink a small amount of wine during his meal. However, he should not drink heavily (*Shulḥan Arukh*, *Yoreh De'a* 378:8).

It is prohibited for a mourner to wash laundry – אָבֵל אָסוּר בְּתִכְבּוֹסֶת: During the seven-day period of mourning, it is prohibited for a mourner to launder his clothes, both during the day and at night (Rema), in accordance with the opinion of Rav Ḥisda (*Shulḥan Arukh*, *Yoreh De'a* 380:1).

With regard to smearing, even any minimal amount is prohibited – לָסוּךְ אֲפִילּוּ כָּל שֶׁהוּא אָסוּר: During the seven-day period of mourning, it is prohibited for a mourner to smear any of his body with oil, if he does so for pleasure. However, it is permitted to smear oil to remove dirt or for a medicinal purpose (*Shulḥan Arukh*, *Yoreh De'a* 380:2).

NOTES

To relieve his anxieties – לְפַכּוּחֵי פַּחֲדֵיהּ: Eating and drinking helps the mourner cope with his sorrows, whereas washing is a form of pleasure and consequently remains prohibited (*Shita Mekubbetzet*).

That is to say, it is prohibited for a mourner to wash laundry all seven days of mourning – זֹאת אוֹמֶרֶת אָבֵל אָסוּר בְּתִכְבּוֹסֶת כָּל שִׁבְעָה: Rashi explains that Rav Ḥisda derived the *halakha* that it is prohibited for a mourner to launder clothes during the entire seven-day period of mourning from the previous statement that a girl in mourning may not paint her eyes or dye her hair. See Rabbi Akiva Eiger in *Gilyon HaShas*, who notes several difficulties with this explanation. Other commentators connect Rav Ḥisda's statement with the aforementioned *baraita* concerning one who observes two consecutive periods of mourning. Since the *baraita* allows him to wash his soiled clothing in water, it follows that under ordinary circumstances it is prohibited for a mourner to launder his clothes. For this reason, some commentaries transpose Rav Ḥisda's statement so that it appears immediately after the citation of that *baraita*. Others argue that it is common for the Gemara to conclude its discussion of a particular topic and subsequently draw inferences that are not directly related to that issue from one of the sources cited in the course of the discussion (see *Divrei Shlomo*, Rabbi Akiva Eiger, and Rashash).

מֵיתִיבִי: אֵין בֵּין יָחִיד לְצִבּוּר אֶלָּא שֶׁזֶּה מִתְפַּלֵּל שְׁמוֹנֶה עֶשְׂרֵה וְזֶה מִתְפַּלֵּל תְּשַׁע עֶשְׂרֵה. מַאי יָחִיד וּמַאי צִבּוּר? אִילֵימָא: יָחִיד מַמָּשׁ, וְצִבּוּר שְׁלִיחַ צִבּוּר, הָנֵי תְּשַׁע עֶשְׂרֵה? עֶשְׂרִין וְאַרְבַּע הָווּ!

The Gemara **raises an objection** from a *baraita*: **The only** halakhic **difference between an individual and a community**[H] **is that this** one, an individual, **prays eighteen** blessings[N] in his *Amida*, **and that** one, a community, **prays nineteen** blessings. The Gemara analyzes this statement: **What** is **an individual and what is a community** in this context? **If we say** that **an individual** means **an actual** individual, **and community** is referring to the communal **prayer leader,** are **there** really only **nineteen** blessings in the communal *Amida* of a fast? **There are twenty-four** blessings. As will be explained, six additional blessings are added on communal fast days.

אֶלָּא לָאו הָכִי קָאָמַר: אֵין בֵּין יָחִיד דְּקִבֵּל עָלָיו תַּעֲנִית יָחִיד לְיָחִיד שֶׁקִּבֵּל עָלָיו תַּעֲנִית צִבּוּר, אֶלָּא שֶׁזֶּה מִתְפַּלֵּל שְׁמוֹנֶה עֶשְׂרֵה וְזֶה מִתְפַּלֵּל תְּשַׁע עֶשְׂרֵה. שְׁמַע מִינָּהּ: יָחִיד קוֹבֵעַ בְּרָכָה לְעַצְמוֹ!

Rather, is it not the case that **this is what** the *baraita* **is saying: The only** halakhic difference **between an individual who took an individual fast upon himself and an individual who took a communal fast upon himself, is only that this one prays eighteen** blessings, as he mentions his fast in the blessing: Who listens to prayer, **and that one prays nineteen** blessings. **Learn from** this statement that **an individual may establish an individual blessing for himself.**

לָא. לְעוֹלָם אֵימָא לָךְ שְׁלִיחַ צִבּוּר. וּדְקָא קַשְׁיָא לָךְ שְׁלִיחַ צִבּוּר עֶשְׂרִין וְאַרְבַּע מַצְלֵי, בְּשָׁלֹשׁ תַּעֲנִיּוֹת רִאשׁוֹנוֹת דְּלֵיכָּא עֶשְׂרִים וְאַרְבַּע.

The Gemara rejects this contention: **No, actually** I could **say to you** that this mention of a community is referring to the **prayer leader. And** with regard to **what** poses **a difficultly for you,** that the **prayer leader prays twenty-four** blessings, the *baraita* is referring **to the first three fasts,** in **which there are not twenty-four blessings,** but only the usual eighteen blessings, plus one additional blessing for fast days.

וְלָא? וְהָא אֵין בֵּין קָתָנֵי: אֵין בֵּין שָׁלֹשׁ רִאשׁוֹנוֹת לְשָׁלֹשׁ אֶמְצָעִיּוֹת, אֶלָּא שֶׁבְּאֵלּוּ מוּתָּרִין בַּעֲשִׂיַּית מְלָאכָה וּבְאֵלּוּ אֲסוּרִין בַּעֲשִׂיַּית מְלָאכָה. הָא לְעֶשְׂרִים וְאַרְבַּע, זֶה וָזֶה שָׁוִין!

The Gemara questions this resolution: **And** are the six additional blessings **not** recited on the first series of communal fasts? **But** with regard to this issue, a *baraita* **taught** the instructive phrase: **The only** difference between them, as follows: **The difference between** the **first three** fasts **and** the **middle three fasts is only that on these** first fasts it is **permitted** to perform **work, and on these** middle fasts it is **prohibited** to perform **work.** This indicates that with regard **to** reciting all **twenty-four** blessings, both **this and that are identical.**

תָּנָא וְשִׁיֵּיר. מַאי שִׁיֵּיר דְּהַאי שִׁיֵּיר? וְתוּ, וְהָא אֵין בֵּין קָתָנֵי! אֶלָּא, תַּנָּא בְּאִיסּוּרֵי קָא מַיְירֵי, בִּתְפִלּוֹת לָא מַיְירֵי. וְאִי בָּעֵית אֵימָא: בְּאֶמְצָעִיָּיתָא נַמִי לָא מְצַלֵּי עֶשְׂרִים וְאַרְבַּע.

The Gemara rejects this argument: The *tanna* **taught** some of the differences between the fasts, **and omitted**[N] some of them. The Gemara asks: **What** else **did** the *tanna* **omit** that you can justifiably claim **that he omitted this** case? In other words, it is possible for the *tanna* to have omitted a few examples, but he would not have omitted a single case. **And furthermore,** the *baraita* does not merely offer a list of differences, as it **teaches: The** difference **between them is only.** This phrase indicates that this is the only difference. **Rather,** the ***tanna* is speaking of** the various **prohibitions** of fast days, but he is **not speaking of** other differences, such as those that involve the details of **prayers. And if you wish, say** instead that **on** the **middle** three fasts **too,** the prayer leader **does not pray twenty-four** blessings, as the six additional blessings are recited only during the last series of fasts.

וְלָא? וְהָתַנְיָא: אֵין בֵּין שָׁלֹשׁ שְׁנִיּוֹת לְשֶׁבַע אַחֲרוֹנוֹת, אֶלָּא שֶׁבְּאֵלּוּ מַתְרִיעִין וְנוֹעֲלִין אֶת הַחֲנוּיּוֹת. הָא לְכָל דִּבְרֵיהֶן, זֶה וָזֶה שָׁוִין! וְכִי תֵּימָא הָכָא נַמִי תָּנָא וְשִׁיֵּיר, וְהָא אֵין בֵּין קָתָנֵי!

The Gemara expresses surprise at this: **And** does the prayer leader **not** recite all twenty-four blessings during the middle three fasts? **But isn't it taught** in a *baraita*: **The difference between** the **second** set of **three** fasts **and** the **last seven fasts is only that in these they sound the alarm and lock the stores.** This indicates that **with regard to all their** other **matters,** both **this and that are identical. And if you say** that **here, too, he taught and omitted,** but it **teaches: The** difference **between them is only** indicating that there is no other difference.

וְתִסְבְּרָא אֵין בֵּין דַּוְקָא?

The Gemara asks: **And** how can **you understand** it that way? Does the phrase: **The** difference **between them is only, specifically** mean that there is only a single difference between the cases?

HALAKHA

The only difference between an individual and a community – אֵין בֵּין יָחִיד לְצִבּוּר אֶלָּא: An individual who is fasting inserts the *Aneinu* prayer in the blessing: Who listens to prayer, whether he is observing an individual fast or fasting together with the community. Some commentaries note that even when one is observing an individual fast, he should recite the phrase: On the day of our fast. The common practice is that an individual who on a communal fast is not fasting does not recite the *Aneinu* prayer (*Arukh HaShulhan*; *Mishna Berura*; *Shulḥan Arukh*, *Oraḥ Ḥayyim* 565:1).

NOTES

That this one prays eighteen blessings – שֶׁזֶּה מִתְפַּלֵּל שְׁמוֹנֶה עֶשְׂרֵה: Rashi notes that the *Amida* prayer, the main element of the daily service, is also called the *Shemoneh Esreh*, meaning eighteen, despite the fact that it consists of nineteen blessings, as originally only eighteen blessings were included in the prayer. The nineteenth blessing, against heretics, was added at a later stage by Shmuel HaKatan (see *Berakhot* 28b–29a).

Other commentaries discuss the issue at length, and point out that Shmuel HaKatan added the blessing against heretics in the period soon after the destruction of the Second Temple. Consequently, later tannaitic sources would be expected to reflect the fact that the daily *Amida* prayer is comprised of nineteen blessings (Rid). Based on the *Tosefta* and the Jerusalem Talmud, the Rid argues that according to the original custom observed in Eretz Yisrael, the *Amida* prayer consisted of only eighteen blessings even after the addition of the blessing against the heretics, as the request for the reestablishment of the Davidic Kingdom and the prayer for the rebuilding of Jerusalem were originally incorporated into a single blessing.

The *tanna* taught and omitted – תָּנָא וְשִׁיֵּיר: Occasionally, when a conclusion is based on an omission of a certain case from a list in a mishna or a *baraita*, the Gemara will claim that the list is incomplete, as the *tanna* did not see the need to mention all the relevant cases, and therefore no inference can be drawn from the omission of a specific case. Generally, the Gemara will continue with the question: What else did the *tanna* omit that he omitted this case? In other words, the *tanna* of the mishna or *baraita* would not have left out only a single case, and therefore it must be demonstrated that at least one other case was omitted as well.

Several commentators point out that there are in fact other differences between the first three and the middle three fasts. For example, the first three fasts begin at dawn and bathing is permitted, whereas the middle three fasts begin the previous evening and bathing is prohibited for the duration of each fast, as stated in the mishna. If so, it is evident that the *tanna* of the *baraita* left out certain differences. It has been suggested that this *baraita* is not cited in its entirety, and that the differences mentioned in the mishna are also stated in that portion of the *baraita* omitted by the Gemara. It was therefore necessary for the Gemara to find additional differences between the two series of fasts, to justify its claim that there is a difference between them with regard to the number of blessings that must be recited (*Gevurat Ari*; *Keren Ora*).

וְהָא שְׁיֵּיר תֵּיבָה! אִי מִשּׁוּם תֵּיבָה, לָאו שִׁיּוּרָא הוּא. מִילֵּי דִּצְנִעָא קָתָנֵי; מִילֵּי דְּבְפַרְהֶסְיָא לָא קָתָנֵי.

But he omitted any mention of the **ark** and the *halakha* that during the last seven fast days the ark was brought into the streets of the city. The Gemara rejects this argument: **If** the omission is **due to the ark,** that **is not** a real **omission.** The reason is that the *tanna* **teaches** only **matters that are** performed **in private,** whereas he **does not teach matters that are** performed **in public** [*parhesya*].[L]

אָמַר רַב אָשֵׁי: מַתְנִיתִין נַמִי דַּיְקָא, דְּקָתָנֵי: מָה ״אֵלּוּ יְתֵירוֹת עַל הָרִאשׁוֹנוֹת״? אֶלָּא ״שֶׁבְּאֵלּוּ מַתְרִיעִין וְנוֹעֲלִין אֶת הַחֲנוּיוֹת״. אֲבָל בְּכָל דִּבְרֵיהֶן זֶה וָזֶה שָׁוִין. וְכִי תֵּימָא הָכָא נַמִי תָּנָא וְשַׁיֵּיר, וְהָא מָה אֵלּוּ קָתָנֵי!

Rav Ashi said: The wording of **the mishna is also precise,** according to this explanation, **as it teaches: How are these** seven fast days **more stringent than the first ones? Rather,** the difference is **that on these** days, in addition to all the earlier stringencies, they **sound the alarm and they lock the stores. However, in regard to all their** other **matters,** both **this and that are identical. And if you say** that **here too he taught and omitted, but it teaches: How are these** more stringent, an expression that indicates that the mishna states the only difference.

וְתִסְבְּרָא מָה אֵלּוּ דַּוְקָא הוּא? וְהָא שַׁיֵּיר לָהּ תֵּיבָה! אִי מִשּׁוּם תֵּיבָה, לָאו שִׁיּוּרָא הוּא, מִשּׁוּם דְּקָא חָשֵׁיב לָהּ בְּאִידָךְ פִּירְקָא. הַשְׁתָּא דְּאָתֵית לְהָכִי, עֶשְׂרִים וְאַרְבָּעָה נַמִי לָאו שִׁיּוּרָא הוּא, דְּקָתָנֵי לָהּ בְּאִידָךְ פִּירְקָא.

The Gemara asks: **And** how can **you understand** the phrase: **How are these, specifically,** as indicating that there is only one difference between the cases? **But he omitted** the **ark.** The Gemara responds: **If** the omission is **due to the ark,** that **is not** a real **omission, because** the *tanna* **includes it in another chapter** (15a). The Gemara comments: **Now that you have arrived at this**[N] solution, a similar answer can be applied to the earlier difficulties. The matter of the **twenty-four** blessings **is also not an omission, as he teaches** this *halakha* **in another chapter,** also on 15a, where the mishna provides further details of the blessings. Here, however, the *tanna* lists only those matters that are not discussed later.

מַאי הָוֵי עֲלַהּ? אָמַר רַבִּי שְׁמוּאֵל בַּר סַסַרְטַאי, וְכֵן אָמַר רַב חִיָּיא בַּר אָשֵׁי אָמַר רַב: בֵּין גּוֹאֵל לְרוֹפֵא. וְרַב אָשֵׁי אָמַר מִשְּׁמֵיהּ דְּרַבִּי יַנַּאי בְּרֵיהּ דְּרַבִּי יִשְׁמָעֵאל: בְּשׁוֹמֵעַ תְּפִלָּה. וְהִלְכְתָא: בְּשׁוֹמֵעַ תְּפִלָּה.

Since no decisive proof was offered in support of any of the opinions as to where an individual inserts the *Aneinu* prayer, the Gemara asks: **What** halakhic conclusion **was** reached **about** this matter?[N] **Rabbi Shmuel bar Sasretai said, and similarly Rav Ḥiyya bar Ashi said** that **Rav said:** One inserts it **between** the seventh blessing of the *Amida*: **Who redeems, and** the eighth blessing: **Who heals. And Rav Ashi said in the name of Rabbi Yannai, son of Rabbi Yishmael:** One inserts it **in** the blessing: **Who listens to prayer.** The Gemara concludes: **And** the ***halakha*** is that one includes it **in** the blessing: **Who listens to prayer.**

תָּנֵי חֲדָא: עוּבָּרוֹת וּמֵינִיקוֹת מִתְעַנּוֹת בָּרִאשׁוֹנוֹת, וְאֵין מִתְעַנּוֹת בָּאַחֲרוֹנוֹת. וְתַנְיָא אִידָךְ: מִתְעַנּוֹת בָּאַחֲרוֹנוֹת, וְאֵין מִתְעַנּוֹת בָּרִאשׁוֹנוֹת. וְתַנְיָא אִידָךְ: אֵין מִתְעַנּוֹת, לֹא בָּרִאשׁוֹנוֹת וְלֹא בָּאַחֲרוֹנוֹת.

§ It **is taught** in **one** *baraita*: **Pregnant and nursing women fast** with the community **on the first** fasts, **but they do not fast on the last** fasts. **And it was taught** in **another** *baraita*: Pregnant and nursing women **fast on the last** set of fasts **but they do not fast on the first** set of fasts. **And it was taught** in yet **another** *baraita*: **They do not fast either on the first** fast days **or on the last** fast days.

אָמַר רַב אָשֵׁי: נְקוֹט אֶמְצָעִיָּיתָא בִּידָךְ, דְּמִיתָּרְצָן כּוּלְּהוּ.

Rav Ashi said: Take the mention of the **middle** fasts **in your hand**[NH] as the decisive matter, **as** this **resolves all** three *baraitot*. The *halakha* is that pregnant and nursing women fast only on the middle fasts, as they are stricter than the first fasts but less taxing than the last seven fasts. Consequently, when the first *baraita* is referring to the first fasts, it in fact means the middle set, which is the first of the last two sets. Similarly, when the second *baraita* mentions the last fasts, it means the middle set, which is the last of the two sets. In the third *baraita*, the first and last fasts are literally the first three and last seven fasts, respectively. In this manner all three *baraitot* follow the same *halakha*.

LANGUAGE

Public [*parhesya*] – פַּרְהֶסְיָא: From the Greek παρρησία, *parresia*, which originally referred to freedom of speech or a free political regime. As used by the Sages, the word means public or visible to all.

NOTES

Now that you have arrived at this – הַשְׁתָּא דְּאָתֵית לְהָכִי: Sometimes the Sages raise a series of objections to a certain opinion, each of which is met with a different response. Eventually, an answer is suggested to one of the objections that resolves not only that difficulty but all the previous ones as well. At this point the Gemara might use this expression to propose a revision of the solutions first advanced.

What conclusion was reached about this matter – מַאי הָוֵי עֲלַהּ: This question is usually asked at the end of a lengthy discussion of a problem in which different opinions have been expressed and been neither proven nor dismissed. At this point, the Gemara inquires into the final halakhic ruling on the matter.

Take the middle in your hand – נְקוֹט אֶמְצָעִיָּיתָא בִּידָךְ: Most early authorities follow the explanation of Rashi and the Rif, that according to Rav Ashi pregnant and nursing women need observe only the middle three fasts. They are not required to fast on the first three days, as these are not especially stringent, and they are not required to observe the last seven fasts, because those fasts are too numerous and too stringent. Other commentaries add that pregnant and nursing women are not required to observe the last series of fasts because certain practices laden with emotion are observed on those days, e.g., visiting cemeteries and extreme manifestations of crying, which might prove dangerous for them (Rabbeinu Yehonatan).

In contrast, the Rambam rules that pregnant and nursing women fast on the last seven fasts, not on the first or middle series of three fasts (Rambam *Sefer Zemanim*, *Hilkhot Ta'anit* 3:5). Apparently, he understands Rav Ashi as saying: Take the middle *baraita* in your hand, i.e., disregard the first and the last *baraitot*, and rule in accordance with the middle *baraita*, which states that pregnant and nursing women are required to observe only the last fasts. Some commentaries, who accept the Rambam's ruling that pregnant and nursing women fast only on the last series of days, suggest a way in which all three *baraitot* can be reconciled with that opinion (*Shita Mekubbetzet*).

HALAKHA

Take the middle in your hand – נְקוֹט אֶמְצָעִיָּיתָא בִּידָךְ: Pregnant and nursing women are obligated to fast on the middle three fasts imposed upon the community in times of drought, but not the first three fasts or the last seven. However, on fast days that they are not required to observe they may eat only what is necessary for the well-being of the fetus or infant. Some commentaries add that a pregnant or nursing woman may not act stringently and observe a fast from which she is exempt (*Shulḥan Arukh*, *Oraḥ Ḥayyim* 575:5, and in the comment of Rema).

מָה ״אֵלּוּ יְתֵירוֹת עַל הָרִאשׁוֹנוֹת״? אֶלָּא ״שֶׁבְּאֵלּוּ מַתְרִיעִין וְנוֹעֲלִין אֶת הַחֲנוּיוֹת״. בְּמַאי מַתְרִיעִין? רַב יְהוּדָה אָמַר: בְּשׁוֹפָרוֹת. וְרַב יְהוּדָה בְּרֵיהּ דְּרַב שְׁמוּאֵל בַּר שֵׁילַת מִשְּׁמֵיהּ דְּרַב אָמַר: בַּעֲנֵנוּ.

§ The mishna teaches: **How are these** seven fast days **more** stringent **than the first ones? Rather,** the difference is **that on these** days, in addition to all the earlier stringencies, **they sound the alarm and they lock the stores.** The Gemara asks: **With what do they sound the alarm?**[N] **Rav Yehuda said: With *shofarot*. And Rav Yehuda, son of Rav** Shmuel bar Sheilat,[P] **said in the name of Rav: With the *Aneinu*** prayer.

קָא סָלְקָא דַּעְתָּן מַאן דַּאֲמַר: בַּעֲנֵנוּ, לָא אֲמַר: בְּשׁוֹפָרוֹת, וּמַאן דַּאֲמַר: בְּשׁוֹפָרוֹת, לָא אֲמַר: בַּעֲנֵנוּ. וְהָתַנְיָא: אֵין פּוֹחֲתִין מִשֶּׁבַע תַּעֲנִיּוֹת עַל הַצִּבּוּר, שֶׁבָּהֶן שְׁמוֹנֶה עֶשְׂרֵה הַתְרָעוֹת. וְסִימָן לַדָּבָר יְרִיחוֹ. וִירִיחוֹ שׁוֹפָרוֹת הֲוָה. וּתְיוּבְתָּא לְמַאן דַּאֲמַר: בַּעֲנֵנוּ!

The Gemara analyzes the dispute: It might **enter our mind** to say that **the one who said** that the community sounds the alarm **by** reciting ***Aneinu***, i.e., Rav, **did not say** that they cry out **with *shofarot*, and** likewise **the one who said** that they do cry out **with *shofarot***, Rav Yehuda, **did not say** that they sound the alarm **by** reciting ***Aneinu*. But isn't it taught** in a *baraita*: The court **does not** decree **fewer than seven fasts on the community, which include eighteen** acts of **sounding the alarm.**[N] **And a mnemonic for** this **matter is Jericho. And** as **there were** many episodes of sounding the ***shofarot* in Jericho,** this is **a conclusive refutation of the one who said** that according to the opinion of Rav they sound the alarm only **by** reciting ***Aneinu*.**

אֶלָּא, בְּשׁוֹפָרוֹת דְּכוּלֵּי עָלְמָא לָא פְּלִיגִי דְּקָרֵי לַהּ הַתְרָעָה. כִּי פְּלִיגִי בַּעֲנֵנוּ. מָר סָבַר: קָרֵי לַהּ הַתְרָעָה. וּמָר סָבַר: לָא קָרֵי לַהּ הַתְרָעָה.

Rather, the Gemara explains that the dispute must be understood differently: **With regard to *shofarot*, everyone,** i.e., Rav and Rav Yehuda, **agrees** that the mishna **calls this: Sounding the alarm. When they disagree,** it is **with regard to** the ***Aneinu*** prayer. One **Sage,** Rav, **holds** that **this** too **is called sounding the alarm, and** one **Sage,** Rav Yehuda, **holds** that reciting *Aneinu* **is not called sounding the alarm.**

לְמַאן דַּאֲמַר: בַּעֲנֵנוּ – כׇּל שֶׁכֵּן בְּשׁוֹפָרוֹת. וּלְמַאן דַּאֲמַר: בְּשׁוֹפָרוֹת – אֲבָל בַּעֲנֵנוּ לָא.

The Gemara comments: If so, then it follows that **according to the one who said** that they sound the alarm **by** reciting ***Aneinu*, all the more so** they can do so **with *shofarot*,**[N] **but according to the one who said that** they sound the alarm **with *shofarot*,** this is the way they sound the alarm; **however,** they may **not** do so **with *Aneinu***, i.e., the community does not sound the alarm by reciting this prayer. This indicates that the *Aneinu* prayer is recited only in extreme cases, as it is a greater form of petitioning to God than blowing the *shofar*.

PERSONALITIES

Rav Yehuda, son of Rav Shmuel bar Sheilat – רַב יְהוּדָה בְּרֵיהּ דְּרַב שְׁמוּאֵל בַּר שֵׁילַת: Rav Yehuda, son of Rav Shmuel bar Sheilat, was a Babylonian *amora* of the second and third generations. His father, Rav Shmuel bar Sheilat, was a close disciple of Rav, and Rav Yehuda apparently also studied with Rav, as he reports many statements in his name. Rav Yehuda maintained close relations with Rav's important disciples, and the Sages of the subsequent generation often report his teachings.

NOTES

With what do they sound the alarm – בְּמַאי מַתְרִיעִין: A distinction is made between trumpets, which are made of metal, and the *shofar*, which is from an animal horn. The Gemara elsewhere (*Rosh HaShana* 27a) cites a *baraita* that teaches that outside the Temple, at those times when trumpets are sounded, *shofarot* are not sounded, and when *shofarot* are sounded, trumpets are not sounded. Rashi explains that when that *baraita* speaks of a time when trumpets are sounded, it is referring to communal fast days. This indicates that on communal fasts, only trumpets are blown, not *shofarot*.

Rabbi Zeraḥya HaLevi cites the *ge'onim*, who note that by common practice, only *shofarot* are sounded on communal fasts, a practice supported by the Jerusalem Talmud. He further argues that this custom cannot be reconciled with the *baraita* in tractate *Rosh HaShana*. The Ra'avad adds that the Gemara here further strengthens the difficulty with that *baraita*, as Rav Yehuda maintains that the alarm is sounded on communal fasts by means of *shofarot*. He explains that the *baraita* in tractate *Rosh HaShana* is referring to the blasts that follow each of the six additional blessings inserted into the *Amida* recited by the prayer leader. These were performed by trumpets. The Gemara here, in contrast, refers to the blasts of *shofarot* at the conclusion of the *Amida* when the service was extended with additional prayers and supplications.

Others cite an opinion according to which the term *shofar* mentioned by Rav Yehuda actually is referring to trumpets (Ramban; Ritva). According to these two opinions, *shofarot* should not be sounded on communal fasts during the *Amida*, in contradiction to the common practice attested to by the *ge'onim* (see also Rambam *Sefer Zemanim*, *Hilkhot Ta'anit* 1:4, 4:14).

The commentaries suggest several ways in which this passage can be understood in its plain sense, that *shofarot* are sounded after each of the additional blessings recited on communal fasts, and yet the common practice of blowing *shofarot* can be reconciled with the *baraita* in *Rosh HaShana* (Ramban; Rashba; Ritva). One possibility is that when the *baraita* speaks of sounding trumpets, it is not referring to communal fast days but to times of war, when the entire Jewish people gathers together to recite special prayers. Alternatively, the *baraita* may indeed be referring to communal fasts, but it does not mean that only trumpets are sounded. Rather, it merely means that if trumpets are sounded, *shofarot* should not be blown together with them, and vice versa. By common practice, only *shofarot* are blown, as they is generally more available.

Not fewer than seven fasts on the community, which include eighteen acts of sounding the alarm – אֵין פּוֹחֲתִין מִשֶּׁבַע תַּעֲנִיּוֹת עַל הַצִּבּוּר, שֶׁבָּהֶן שְׁמוֹנֶה עֶשְׂרֵה הַתְרָעוֹת: According to the standard text of the Gemara, the *baraita* is teaching that on each of the last seven fasts there are eighteen soundings of the alarm, and, as the Gemara explains, this means *shofarot* blasts. Rashi explains that there are eighteen *shofarot* blasts on each of these fasts, as *shofarot* are sounded three times after each of the six additional blessings inserted into the prayer leader's *Amida*.

Several later authorities point out that there are in fact twenty-one *shofarot* blasts, as *shofarot* are also sounded three times after the prayer leader recites the expanded seventh blessing of: Who redeems the Jewish people (see *Leḥem Mishne*; *Gevurat Ari*; Rashash). However, the *baraita* is referring specifically to the blasts that accompany the special blessings added on these fast days. The Vilna Gaon emends the *baraita* so that it indeed reads: On each of these there are twenty-one soundings of the alarm.

Many early authorities have the version: On which there are seven soundings of the alarm. Some commentaries explain that the *baraita* is referring not to the blasts sounded after each of the additional blessings inserted into the prayer leader's *Amida*, but to the ones sounded at the conclusion of the *Amida* when the service was extended with additional prayers and supplications, with one blast of the *shofar* on each of the seven fasts (Ra'avad). Others explain that all the *shofar* blasts on each of the fasts are called a sounding of the alarm, and the alarm is sounded seven times on each fast day. The alarm is sounded once after the expanded blessing of: Who redeems the Jewish people, and once after each of the six additional blessings inserted into the Amida, with each sounding of the alarm consisting of three *shofar* blasts (see Ramban; Ritva; *Sefer Hashlama*).

All the more so with *shofarot* – כׇּל שֶׁכֵּן בְּשׁוֹפָרוֹת: The meaning of this particular statement depends on how the entire passage is understood: Is the Gemara emphasizing the obligation to sound *shofarot* on the last set of fasts, or is it saying that they recite *Aneinu* and offer special prayers on every major communal fast? Alternative readings of the text suggest a version in which the question is whether the recitation of *Aneinu* is considered to be sounding the alarm at all.

וְהָתַנְיָא: וּשְׁאָר כׇּל מִינֵי פּוּרְעָנִיּוֹת הַמִּתְרַגְּשׁוֹת, כְּגוֹן חִיכּוּךְ, חָגָב, זְבוּב, וְצִירְעָה, וְיַתּוּשִׁין, וְשִׁילּוּחַ נְחָשִׁים וְעַקְרַבִּים, לֹא הָיוּ מַתְרִיעִין, אֶלָּא צוֹעֲקִין. מִדִּצְעָקָה בְּפֶה, הַתְרָעָה בְּשׁוֹפָרוֹת!

The Gemara raises a difficulty against this conclusion. **But isn't it taught** in a *baraita*: **And** with regard to **all other types of calamities** than drought **that break out, for example scabs,**[H] plagues of **locusts,**[H] **flies, or hornets,**[H] **or mosquitoes,**[B] **or infestations of snakes or scorpions, they would not sound the alarm, but they** would **cry out. From** the fact that **crying out** is, according to all opinions, a prayer recited **with** one's **mouth,** it follows that **sounding an alarm** must be **with *shofarot*.**[H] This *baraita* indicates that sounding the alarm with *shofarot* is the response to a serious situation, whereas the *Aneinu* prayer is recited on less worrisome occasions.

תַּנָּאֵי הִיא, דִּתְנַן: עַל אֵלּוּ מַתְרִיעִין בְּשַׁבָּת: עַל עִיר שֶׁהִקִּיפוּהָ גַּיִּיס אוֹ נָהָר, וְעַל סְפִינָה הַמִּטּוֹרֶפֶת בַּיָּם. רַבִּי יוֹסֵי אָמַר: לְעֶזְרָה, אֲבָל לֹא לִצְעָקָה.

The Gemara answers: This **is** a dispute between ***tanna'im*, as we learned** in a mishna: **For the following** calamities **they sound the alarm** even **on Shabbat: For a city that is surrounded by** an enemy **army or** in danger of being flooded by **a river,**[H] **or for a ship tossed about at sea. Rabbi Yosei said:** An alarm may be sounded on Shabbat **to** summon **help, but** it may **not** be sounded **for crying out**[N] to God.

בְּמַאי? אִילֵימָא: בְּשׁוֹפָרוֹת, שׁוֹפָרוֹת בְּשַׁבָּת מִי שָׁרֵי? אֶלָּא לָאו בַּעֲנֵנוּ, וְקָרֵי לַהּ הַתְרָעָה. שְׁמַע מִינָּהּ.

The Gemara clarifies this case. **With what** do they sound the alarm? **If we say with *shofarot*, is** the sounding of ***shofarot* permitted on Shabbat?** Even when Rosh HaShana occurs on Shabbat, one must refrain from sounding the *shofar* on that day. **Rather, is it not** the case that this is referring to the recitation of the ***Aneinu*** prayer, **and** yet the mishna **calls this** recitation: **Sounding the alarm. Conclude from** this that there is a *tanna* who maintains that sounding of the alarm is in fact performed by prayer, as claimed by Rav Yehuda, son of Rav Shmuel bar Sheilat.

בִּשְׁנֵי דְּרַבִּי יְהוּדָה נְשִׂיאָה הֲוָה צַעֲרָא.

§ The Gemara relates: **During the years of Rabbi Yehuda Nesia there was a trouble** that afflicted the community.

HALAKHA

Scabs – חִיכּוּךְ: If the majority of the members of the community are suffering from boils that ooze with pus, they must fast and sound the alarm. However, if they are suffering from dry scabs, they cry out in prayer (*Shulḥan Arukh, Oraḥ Ḥayyim* 576:5).

Locusts [*ḥagav*] – חָגָב: If a community is struck by locusts, its members must fast and sound the alarm. However, if it is plagued by a relatively harmless type of locust called *ḥagav*, they do not fast or sound the alarm. Nowadays, however, when we cannot distinguish between the different types of locusts, the alarm is sounded for all locusts (*Shulḥan Arukh, Oraḥ Ḥayyim* 576:9).

Flies or hornets – זְבוּב וְצִירְעָה: If a community is struck by a plague of flies or hornets, its members do not fast or sound the alarm, but only cry out in prayer (*Shulḥan Arukh, Oraḥ Ḥayyim* 576:7).

Sounding an alarm with *shofarot* – הַתְרָעָה בְּשׁוֹפָרוֹת: In the last set of fasts several blessings are added to the prayers, and in each of those additional blessings *shofarot* are sounded, in accordance with the opinion of Rav Yehuda (*Shulḥan Arukh, Oraḥ Ḥayyim* 575:4).

A city that is surrounded by an army or a river – עִיר שֶׁהִקִּיפוּהָ גַּיִּיס אוֹ נָהָר: If a city is surrounded by an enemy army or threatened by an overflowing river, or if a boat is tossed about at sea, or even if a single individual is in mortal danger, the community cries out and offers special supplications even on Shabbat, but they do not sound the *shofar*. However, they may sound the *shofar* to summon people to assist in the rescue efforts, in accordance with the opinion of the anonymous first *tanna*, who agrees with Rabbi Yosei on this point (*Shulḥan Arukh, Oraḥ Ḥayyim* 576:13).

BACKGROUND

Flies, or hornets, or mosquitoes – זְבוּב, וְצִירְעָה, וְיַתּוּשִׁין: The appearance of a multitude of these insects is caused by particular weather conditions. An increase of flies is a serious nuisance in its own right, so much so that certain nations had a special cult and a god for the removal of flies. Mosquitoes, apart from the irritation they cause, can spread malaria. The hornet, whose sting is mentioned in the Bible as one of the factors that led to the overthrow of the Canaanites (Exodus 23:28; Joshua 24:12), may be identified with the Oriental hornet, *Vespa orientalis*. Similarly, later historians tell of cities that were abandoned due to a plague of mosquitoes or hornets.

Oriental hornet

NOTES

To summon help but not for crying out – לְעֶזְרָה אֲבָל לֹא לִצְעָקָה: Rashi explains Rabbi Yosei's words in two ways. The commentary on the text follows Rashi's first explanation, according to which Rabbi Yosei permits the community to sound the alarm in times of danger to summon people for assistance even on Shabbat, but he does not allow them to cry out to God in prayer on Shabbat. According to Rashi's second explanation, Rabbi Yosei maintains that on Shabbat the people may pray for assistance as individuals, but not as a community.

The Rambam (*Sefer Zemanim, Hilkhot Ta'anit* 1:6) maintains that when Rabbi Yosei permits a community in danger to summon people to its rescue, he even permits the *shofar* to be sounded for that purpose. The anonymous first *tanna* agrees with him on this point, as when it comes to saving lives, all the prohibitions of Shabbat are suspended.

גזר תלת עשרה תעניות, ולא איעני. סבר למיגזר טפי. אמר ליה רבי אמי: הרי אמרו: אין מטריחין את הצבור יותר מדאי.

Rabbi Yehuda Nesia **decreed thirteen fasts, but he was not answered. He considered decreeing more** fasts until they would be answered. **Rabbi Ami said to him** that **they said: One does not trouble the community excessively,** and therefore you should not impose more than thirteen fasts.

אמר רבי אבא בריה דרבי חייא בר אבא: רבי אמי דעבד, לגרמיה הוא דעבד. אלא הכי אמר רבי חייא בר אבא אמר רבי יוחנן: לא שנו אלא לגשמים, אבל לשאר מיני פורענויות מתענין והולכין עד שיענו מן השמים. תניא נמי הכי: כשאמרו שלש וכשאמרו שבע, לא אמרו אלא לגשמים. אבל לשאר מיני פורענויות, מתענין והולכין עד שיענו.

Rabbi Abba, son of Rabbi Ḥiyya bar Abba, said: When Rabbi Ami acted and issued this ruling, **he did** so **on his own** authority,[N] as it went against the majority opinion. **Rather, Rabbi Ḥiyya bar Abba said** that **Rabbi Yoḥanan said as follows: They taught only** that the community observes a maximum of thirteen fasts when they are praying **for rain. However,** with regard **to other types of calamities, they continue to fast until they are answered from Heaven.** The Gemara comments: **This** *halakha* **is also taught** in a *baraita*: **When** the Sages **said three and when they said seven, they spoke only** concerning fasts **for rain. However,** with regard **to other types of calamities, they continue to fast until they are answered.**

לימא תיהוי תיובתיה דרבי אמי? אמר לך רבי אמי: תנאי היא, דתניא: אין גוזרין יותר משלש עשרה תעניות על הצבור, לפי שאין מטריחין את הצבור יותר מדאי. דברי רבי. רבן שמעון בן גמליאל אומר: לא מן השם הוא זה, אלא מפני שיצא זמנה של רביעה.

The Gemara suggests: **Let us say that this** *baraita* **is a conclusive refutation of** the opinion of **Rabbi Ami.** The Gemara answers: **Rabbi Ami** could have **said to you** that this **is** a dispute between *tanna'im*, **as it is taught** in a *baraita*: **One does not decree more than thirteen fasts on the community,**[H] **as one does not trouble the community excessively.** This is **the statement of Rabbi** Yehuda HaNasi. **Rabban Shimon ben Gamliel says: This** *halakha* **is not for** that **reason.** Rather, it is **due to** the fact that after thirteen fasts the **time of the rainfall has** already **passed,** and there is no reason to fast for rain after the rainy season has ended.

שלחו ליה בני נינוה לרבי: כגון אנן, דאפילו בתקופת תמוז בעינן מטרא, היכי נעביד? כיחידים דמינן או כרבים דמינן? כיחידים דמינן, ובשומע תפלה? או כרבים דמינן, ובברכת השנים? שלח להו: כיחידים דמיתו, ובשומע תפלה.

The Gemara relates a story on a similar topic: **The inhabitants of Nineveh**[HB] **sent** a question[N] **to Rabbi** Yehuda HaNasi: People **such as us, who require rain even during the season of Tammuz,** and who live in areas where rain falls all year round, **what** should we **do** when there is a drought during the summer? Are we **likened to individuals or** are we **likened to a community?** The Gemara explains the practical difference between these two options: Are we **likened to individuals and** therefore we pray for rain **in** the blessing: **Who listens to prayer? Or** are we **likened to a community** and we pray for rain **in** the ninth blessing, **the blessing of the years? He sent** his answer **to them: You are likened to individuals and** therefore you pray for rain **in** the blessing: **Who listens to prayer.**

NOTES

He did so on his own authority – לגרמיה הוא דעבד: The translation and commentary follow Rashi's interpretation of this phrase in *Berakhot* 48a. Here, however, Rashi and Rabbeinu Ḥananel offer a different explanation: Rabbi Ami, who issued the ruling that no more than thirteen fasts may be imposed on the community, was speaking on his own behalf, as he personally found fasting difficult.

The question of the inhabitants of Nineveh – שאלת בני נינוה: According to Rashi, their question was whether they should treat the day as an individual fast; the Jerusalem Talmud indicates likewise. However, most early authorities explain that they were inquiring about asking for rain in the blessing of the years. It is possible that the Rambam maintains that their question referred to both issues (*Keren Ora*; see *Sefat Emet*). As for the reason why this request should not be added to the blessing of the years, the commentaries explain that one should not deviate from the formula of blessings established by the Sages. Furthermore, as a blessing of rain in one country can be a curse for others, it is treated as an individual calamity (Ra'avad).

HALAKHA

One does not decree more than thirteen fasts on the community – אין גוזרין יותר משלש עשרה תעניות על הצבור: If the community's prayers have not been answered after thirteen fasts, the court may not decree additional fasts. This ruling applies only if the fasts were decreed on account of drought. However, if they were imposed due to some other calamity, the court may continue to decree fasts until the trouble has passed (*Shulḥan Arukh, Oraḥ Ḥayyim* 575:6).

The inhabitants of Nineveh – בני נינוה: Individuals who are in need of rain during the summer months may not insert the prayer for rain into the blessing of the years; instead they add it in the blessing: Who listens to prayer. Even if an entire city or a whole country is in need of rain, its residents are treated as individuals, in accordance with the opinion of Rabbi Yehuda HaNasi. Some commentaries assert that the prayer for rain is inserted into the blessing: Who listens to prayer, in the silent recitation of the *Amida*, whereas the prayer leader does not recite the prayer for rain when he repeats the *Amida* out loud (*Taz*). In some places it is customary to substitute other forms of petition for rain in the blessing: Who listens to prayer, in place of the usual formula used in the blessing of the years: Give dew and rain (see *Be'er Heitev*; *Shulḥan Arukh, Oraḥ Ḥayyim* 117:2).

BACKGROUND

The inhabitants of Nineveh – בני נינוה: The ancient city of Nineveh was located near modern day Mosul, along the Tigris in northwestern Iraq. Little rain falls in this region, about 400 mm annually, while the summers are invariably extremely dry. It is therefore surprising that the people of Nineveh would pray for rain in the summer. Other versions of the text render this name as differently, e.g., *neve*, dwelling place, and it is possible that this incident occurred in a place that had a different climate, where it usually rained in the summer months.

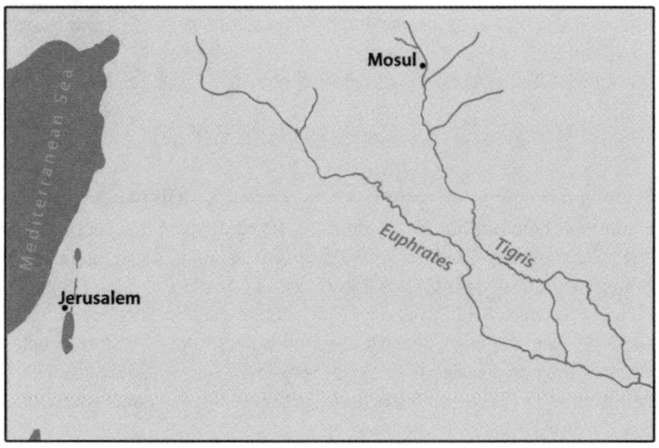

Map showing Mosul in relation to Jerusalem

מיתיבי: אמר רבי יהודה: אימתי? בזמן שהשנים כתיקנן וישראל שרוין על אדמתן. אבל בזמן הזה, הכל לפי השנים, הכל לפי המקומות, הכל לפי הזמן. אמר ליה: מתניתא רמית עליה דרבי? רבי תנא הוא ופליג.

The Gemara **raises an objection** from a *baraita*: **Rabbi Yehuda said: When** do the *halakhot* concerning the times during which the prayer for rain is recited apply? **When the years,** i.e., the climate, **are as they ought to be**[N] **and the Jewish people are living in their land. However, nowadays,**[H] when the Jewish people are dispersed around the world, and the climate is not always as it ought to be, **all is in accordance with the year,** i.e., the local climate, **all is in accordance with the place** in question, and **all is in accordance with** the particular **time,** and therefore one prays for rain in the blessing of the years, as necessary for the local climate. **He said to him: You raise a contradiction from a *baraita* against Rabbi** Yehuda HaNasi? **Rabbi** Yehuda HaNasi himself **is a *tanna*, and** consequently has the authority **to dispute** the opinion of Rabbi Yehuda.

מאי הוי עלה? רב נחמן אמר: בברכת השנים. רב ששת אמר: בשומע תפלה. והלכתא: בשומע תפלה.

The Gemara asks: **What** halakhic conclusion **was** reached **about** this matter? **Rav Naḥman said:** One prays for rain **in the blessing of the years,** in accordance with the opinion of Rabbi Yehuda. **Rav Sheshet said:** One prays **in** the blessing: **Who listens to prayer,** as stated by Rabbi Yehuda HaNasi. The Gemara concludes: **And the *halakha*** is that if rain is required when it is not the rainy season in Eretz Yisrael, one prays for rain **in** the blessing: **Who listens to prayer.**[N]

״בשני מטין עם חשיכה, ובחמישי כל היום מפני כבוד השבת״. איבעיא להו: היכי קתני? בשני מטין עם חשיכה, ובחמישי כל היום מפני כבוד השבת? או דילמא, בשני מטין, ובחמישי פותחין כל היום כולו?

§ The mishna taught: **On Monday** they open the stores **a little at nightfall, and on Thursday** they are permitted to open the stores **all day, in deference to Shabbat. A dilemma was raised before** the Sages: **How is this taught,** i.e., what is the meaning of this ruling? Does it mean that **on Monday** the storeowners open their doors **a little at nightfall, and on Thursday** they likewise open their doors just a little, but do so **all day, in deference to Shabbat? Or perhaps,** the mishna means that **on Monday** they open their doors **a little,** but all day, **and on Thursday they open** their doors wide **the entire day?**

תא שמע, דתניא: בשני מטין עד הערב, ובחמישי פותחין כל היום כולו מפני כבוד השבת. היו לו שני פתחים, פותח אחד ונועל אחד. היה לו אצטבא כנגד פתחו, פותח כדרכו ואינו חושש.

The Gemara answers: **Come and hear** a resolution of this dilemma, **as it is taught** in a *baraita*: **On Monday** they open their doors **a little until the evening, and on Thursday they open** them **the entire day, in deference to Shabbat.** If one's shop **had two entrances,** he **opens one and locks one,** thereby demonstrating that his store is not open in the normal manner. If **he had a platform opposite his entrance**[N] which conceals the door to his store, **he may open in his** usual **manner without concern,** as it is prohibited to open one's store not due to work, but only so that it not appear as though people are eating and drinking on this day.

״עברו אלו ולא נענו, ממעטין במשא ומתן, בבנין ובנטיעה״. תנא: בבנין בנין של שמחה. נטיעה נטיעה של שמחה. אי זהו בנין של שמחה? זה הבונה בית חתנות לבנו. אי זו היא נטיעה של שמחה? זה הנוטע אבוורנקי של מלכים.

§ The mishna taught: **If these** fasts have passed **and they have not been answered, they decrease** their engagement **in** business **negotiations**[H] and **in building and planting.** It was **taught** in the *Tosefta* (*Megilla* 5:2): **Building** means **joyful building,** not building in general. Likewise, **planting** means **joyful planting,** not all planting. The *Tosefta* elaborates: **What is joyful building? This** is referring to **one who builds a wedding chamber for his son.** It was customary upon the marriage of a son to build him a small house where the marriage feast was held and where the newlywed couple would live for a certain period of time. **What is joyful planting? This** is referring to **one who plants a splendid, royal garden** that does not serve practical purposes, but is only for ornamentation.

ובשאילת שלום. תנו רבנן: חברים אין שאילת שלום ביניהן. עמי הארץ ששואלין מחזירין להם בשפה רפה ובכובד ראש. והן מתעטפין ויושבין כאבלים וכמנודין, כבני אדם הנזופין למקום, עד שירחמו עליהם מן השמים.

§ **And** the mishna further taught that they decrease **greetings** between one another. **The Sages taught: *Ḥaverim*,** members of a group dedicated to the precise observance of mitzvot, **do not extend greetings between each other** at all. ***Amei ha'aretz*,** common, uneducated people, **who extend greetings** to *ḥaverim*, do so while unaware that this is inappropriate. The *ḥaverim* **answer them in an undertone and in a solemn manner. And** *ḥaverim* **wrap themselves and sit as mourners and as ostracized ones, like people who have been rebuked by God, until they are shown mercy from Heaven.**

NOTES

When the years are as they ought to be – בזמן שהשנים כתיקנן: Rashi explains that this *baraita* is referring to the order of fasts mentioned in this chapter. The *halakhot* in the mishna for fasts in years of drought apply only when the seasons occur in their regular order, and the Jewish people are living in their land. However, outside Eretz Yisrael, or if the seasons do not occur in their regular manner, fasts are decreed in accordance with the needs of the community in a particular place at a particular time. Conversely, most early authorities maintain that the *baraita* is referring to the prayer for rain in the blessing: Who listens to prayer. The Rambam possibly understands the *baraita* as referring both to the prayer for rain and to the order of the fasts decreed in times of drought (see Rambam's Commentary on the Mishna, *Ta'anit* 1:3; *Sefer Zemanim*, *Hilkhot Ta'anit* 3:10; see *Gevurat Ari*, *Keren Ora*, and *Sefat Emet*.)

And the *halakha* is that one prays in the blessing: Who listens to prayer – והלכתא בשומע תפלה: The Gemara elsewhere (*Avoda Zara* 8a) states that if an individual wishes to offer a private prayer for financial assistance, he should insert his petition in the blessing of the years. Why, then, should those who are in need of rain during the summer months insert the prayer for rain in the blessing: Who listens to prayer, rather than in the blessing of the years?

One answer is that an individual may insert his prayer for financial well-being in the blessing of the years, as his success will not necessarily cause others to suffer, whereas rain will certainly affect everyone. Another explanation is that the insertion of a private prayer for financial well-being is not considered a fundamental change in the blessing of the years, whereas the addition of a private prayer for rain when it is not needed by the entire Jewish people is indeed a deviation from the text of the blessing.

Alternatively, rain during the summer months, while necessary for certain people, is a curse for others (Ra'avad).

If he had a platform opposite his entrance – היה לו אצטבא כנגד פתחו: Rashi and Rabbeinu Gershom explain that the platform somewhat concealed the entrance to the store. Others suggest that it was the usual practice to place one's wares on the platform, and therefore the storeowner would signify his mourning by leaving the platform empty (*Shita Mekubbetzet*).

HALAKHA

However, nowadays – אבל בזמן הזה: In places where the rainy season does not parallel that of Eretz Yisrael, if rain has not fallen when it should, individuals embark on a series of three fasts, after which the court imposes a series of up to thirteen fasts upon the members of the community, in accordance with the opinion of Rabbi Yehuda. Any communal fast decreed outside Eretz Yisrael is considered an individual fast and therefore these fasts begin only at dawn. This is in accordance with the opinion of Shmuel, that there are no communal fasts outside Eretz Yisrael other than the Ninth of Av (*Shulḥan Arukh*, *Oraḥ Ḥayyim* 575:9–10).

If these have passed and they have not been answered, they decrease in business negotiations – עברו אלו ולא נענו ממעטין במשא ומתן: If the thirteen fasts have passed and it has still not rained, no additional fasts are imposed on the community, but business transactions of a joyous nature (*Magen Avraham*) and constructions of a joyous nature must be reduced. Likewise, it is permitted to betroth or marry, only if one has not yet fulfilled his obligation to be fruitful and multiply. Interpersonal greetings must be reduced, and Torah scholars may not extend greetings to each other at all. If an uneducated person greets a Torah scholar, the scholar may answer him in a low and solemn tone. Torah scholars once again begin a series of fasts on Mondays and Thursdays, and continue to do so until the end of the month of Nisan (*Shulḥan Arukh*, *Oraḥ Ḥayyim* 575:7).

אָמַר רַבִּי אֶלְעָזָר: אֵין אָדָם חָשׁוּב רַשַּׁאי לִיפּוֹל עַל פָּנָיו אֶלָּא אִם כֵּן נַעֲנֶה כִּיהוֹשֻׁעַ בִּן נוּן, שֶׁנֶּאֱמַר: ״וַיֹּאמֶר ה׳ אֶל יְהוֹשֻׁעַ קֻם לָךְ, לָמָּה זֶּה אַתָּה נֹפֵל עַל פָּנֶיךָ״?

Rabbi Elazar said: An important person is permitted to fall on his face and humiliate himself in front of the community **only if**[HN] **he** is certain that he **will be answered like Joshua, son of Nun, as it is stated: "And the Lord said to Joshua, Get you up, why are you fallen upon your face?"** (Joshua 7:10). One who is not absolutely certain that he will be answered may not fall on his face in public, as if he is unanswered he will become an object of derision.

וְאָמַר רַבִּי אֶלְעָזָר: אֵין אָדָם חָשׁוּב רַשַּׁאי לַחֲגוֹר שַׂק אֶלָּא אִם כֵּן נַעֲנֶה כִּיהוֹרָם בֶּן אַחְאָב, שֶׁנֶּאֱמַר: ״וַיְהִי, כִשְׁמֹעַ הַמֶּלֶךְ אֶת דִּבְרֵי הָאִשָּׁה, וַיִּקְרַע אֶת בְּגָדָיו, וְהוּא עֹבֵר עַל הַחֹמָה, וַיַּרְא הָעָם, וְהִנֵּה, הַשַּׂק עַל בְּשָׂרוֹ״ וגו׳.

And Rabbi Elazar said: An important person is permitted to gird himself in **sackcloth** as a sign of mourning and to pray for mercy **only if he** is certain that he **will be answered like Jehoram, son of Ahab, as it is stated: "And it came to pass, when the king heard the words of the woman, that he rent his clothes, now he was passing by upon the wall, and the people looked, and, behold, he had sackcloth** within **upon his flesh"** (II Kings 6:30). Although he was wicked, Jehoram was later answered and the suffering of the Jews was alleviated.

וְאָמַר רַבִּי אֶלְעָזָר: לֹא הַכֹּל בִּקְרִיעָה וְלֹא הַכֹּל בִּנְפִילָה. מֹשֶׁה וְאַהֲרֹן בִּנְפִילָה; יְהוֹשֻׁעַ וְכָלֵב בִּקְרִיעָה. מֹשֶׁה וְאַהֲרֹן בִּנְפִילָה, דִּכְתִיב: ״וַיִּפּוֹל מֹשֶׁה וְאַהֲרֹן עַל פְּנֵיהֶם״. יְהוֹשֻׁעַ וְכָלֵב בִּקְרִיעָה, דִּכְתִיב: ״וִיהוֹשֻׁעַ בִּן נוּן, וְכָלֵב בֶּן יְפֻנֶּה...קָרְעוּ בִּגְדֵיהֶם״.

And Rabbi Elazar further **said: Not all** are worthy to petition God **by rending**[N] their garments, **and not all** are worthy **of falling** on their faces in times of trouble. **Moses and Aaron** were worthy of petitioning God **by falling** on their faces, whereas their students **Joshua and Caleb** prayed **by** only **rending** their garments. The Gemara elaborates: **Moses and Aaron** petitioned God **by falling** on their faces, **as it is written: "Then Moses and Aaron fell on their faces"** (Numbers 14:5). **Joshua and Caleb** prayed **by rending** their garments, **as it is written** in the next verse: **"And Joshua, son of Nun, and Caleb, son of Jephunneh,** who were of those who spied out the land, **rent their garments"** (Numbers 14:6).

מַתְקִיף לָהּ רַבִּי זֵירָא, וְאִיתֵּימָא רַבִּי שְׁמוּאֵל בַּר נַחְמָנִי: אִי הֲוָה כְּתִיב, יְהוֹשֻׁעַ, כִּדְקָאָמְרַתְּ. הָשְׁתָּא דִּכְתִיב, ״וִיהוֹשֻׁעַ״, הָא וְהָא עָבֵיד.

Rabbi Zeira strongly objects to this interpretation, **and some say** it was **Rabbi Shmuel bar Naḥmani** who objected: **Had** the verse **written** only: **Joshua** and Caleb, the meaning would be **as you said,** that Moses and Aaron fell upon their faces whereas Joshua and Caleb only rent their garments. However, **now that it is written: "And Joshua,"** it is possible that the connecting word "and" indicates that Moses and Aaron merely fell upon their faces, while Joshua and Caleb **did** both **this and that,** i.e., they rent their clothing in addition to falling upon their faces.

וְאָמַר רַבִּי אֶלְעָזָר: לֹא הַכֹּל בְּקִימָה, וְלֹא הַכֹּל בְּהִשְׁתַּחֲוָיָה. מְלָכִים בְּקִימָה, וְשָׂרִים בְּהִשְׁתַּחֲוָיָה. מְלָכִים בְּקִימָה, דִּכְתִיב: ״כֹּה אָמַר ה׳, גֹּאֵל יִשְׂרָאֵל, קְדוֹשׁוֹ,

And Rabbi Elazar further **said: Not all** dignitaries will worship God in the messianic age **by rising, and not all** will do so **by bowing.** Rather, **kings** will serve God **by rising, and ministers by bowing.** The Gemara elaborates: **Kings by rising, as it is written: "Thus says the Lord, the Redeemer of Israel, his Holy One,**

HALAKHA

An important person is permitted to fall on his face only if – אֵין אָדָם חָשׁוּב רַשַּׁאי לִיפּוֹל עַל פָּנָיו אֶלָּא אִם כֵּן: An important person is not permitted to fall on his face when he prays in public (*Taz*, citing Rosh) on behalf of the community, unless he is certain that he will be answered, like Joshua. Some authorities maintain that one may not fall on his face even if he is praying on his own behalf (*Peri Ḥadash*). Others maintain that it is prohibited for one to fall on his face only when he prays on behalf of the community; however, they add that this stricture applies even if he is praying in private on the community's behalf (*Arukh HaShulḥan*; *Shulḥan Arukh, Oraḥ Ḥayyim* 131:8).

NOTES

An important person is permitted to fall on his face only if – אֵין אָדָם חָשׁוּב רַשַּׁאי לִיפּוֹל עַל פָּנָיו אֶלָּא אִם כֵּן: Rashi states that the reason is so that he does not suffer public humiliation in the event that his prayers go unanswered. Alternatively, if he is not answered after falling on his face, this might constitute a desecration of God's Name (see Jerusalem Talmud and Meiri). Yet others state that this behavior might upset the community (*Nimmukei Yosef*), or that it is a sign of arrogance and pretentiousness, a display of assurance that one's prayers will be answered (*ge'onim*; *Talmid HaRamban*). Some say this *halakha* applies only when an individual is praying in public. However, if one is praying in private or on his own behalf, he is permitted to fall on his face (see Ra'avad on Rambam *Sefer Ahava, Hilkhot Tefilla UVirkat Kohanim* 5:14; see also *Tosafot* on *Megilla* 22b).

Not all are worthy to petition God by rending – לֹא הַכֹּל בִּקְרִיעָה: To illustrate his point that not every person is worthy of falling on his face to elicit divine compassion, Rabbi Elazar cites the example of Joshua and Caleb, who rent their garments but did not fall on their faces. Some commentaries note that at one stage Joshua was in fact answered when he fell on his face in prayer, as Rabbi Elazar also stated (Maharsha). The Maharsha explains that Joshua was not worthy of falling on his face during the lifetimes of Moses and Aaron, as he was not of their stature, and therefore this would have been considered an act of pretentiousness. However, after their death, when Joshua enjoyed the status of king, it was appropriate for him to fall on his face and it was no longer suitable for him to only rend his garments.

לִבְזֹה נֶפֶשׁ, לִמְתָעֵב גּוֹי, לְעֶבֶד מֹשְׁלִים, מְלָכִים יִרְאוּ וָקָמוּ״. וְשָׂרִים בְּהִשְׁתַּחֲוָיָה, דִּכְתִיב: ״שָׂרִים וְיִשְׁתַּחֲווּ״. מַתְקִיף לָהּ רַבִּי זֵירָא, וְאִיתֵּימָא רַבִּי שְׁמוּאֵל בַּר נַחְמָנִי: אִי הֲוָה כְּתִיב, ״וְשָׂרִים יִשְׁתַּחֲווּ״, כִּדְקָאָמְרַתְּ. הָשְׁתָּא דִּכְתִיב, ״שָׂרִים וְיִשְׁתַּחֲווּ״, הָא וְהָא עֲבוּד.

to he who is despised of men, to he who is abhorred of nations, to a servant of rulers: Kings shall see and arise" (Isaiah 49:7); **and ministers by bowing, as it is written,** in the same verse: **"Ministers, and they shall bow." Rabbi Zeira strongly objects to this** interpretation, **and some say** it was **Rabbi Shmuel bar Naḥmani** who objected. **Had** the verse **written: And ministers shall bow,** the meaning would have been **as you said.** However, **now that it is written: "Ministers, and they shall bow,"** this indicates that ministers will **do this and that,** i.e., they will both arise and bow.

אֲמַר רַב נַחְמָן בַּר יִצְחָק: אַף אֲנִי אוֹמֵר: לֹא הַכֹּל לְאוֹרָה, וְלֹא הַכֹּל לְשִׂמְחָה, צַדִּיקִים לְאוֹרָה, וִישָׁרִים לְשִׂמְחָה. צַדִּיקִים לְאוֹרָה, דִּכְתִיב: ״אוֹר זָרֻעַ לַצַּדִּיק״, וְלִישָׁרִים שִׂמְחָה, דִּכְתִיב: ״וּלְיִשְׁרֵי לֵב שִׂמְחָה״.

הדרן עלך מאימתי

Rav Naḥman bar Yitzḥak said: I too say a similar idea. **Not all** are fit **for light, and not all** are fit **for gladness. The righteous** are fit to be rewarded **with light, and the upright** are fit to be rewarded **with gladness. The righteous** are fit to be rewarded **with light,** as it is written: **"Light is sown[N] for the righteous"** (Psalms 97:11), **and the upright** are fit to be rewarded **with gladness, as it is written,** in the same verse: **"And gladness for the upright in heart."**

NOTES

Light is sown, etc. – אוֹר זָרֻעַ וגו׳: According to Rashi, the upright are on a higher spiritual level than the righteous, and their reward is correspondingly greater. Other commentaries maintain that the righteous are on a loftier plane, and that their reward, the Divine light, includes the gladness granted to the upright (Ritva; *Otzar HaKavod*). Similarly, some commentaries state that light, which is a purely spiritual gift, is only for the righteous, while the merely upright are rewarded with gladness, a more material blessing (Maharsha).

Summary of **Perek I**

The prayers for rain can be divided into two time periods. Initially, one merely mentions rain, by means of the statement: He makes the wind blow and the rain fall, in the *Amida* prayer in the second blessing, without actually requesting rainfall. This period begins on the Eighth Day of Assembly immediately following *Sukkot*. During the second period, one also requests rain, adding the phrase: And give dew and rain, in the ninth blessing of the *Amida*. In Eretz Yisrael one first recites this prayer on the seventh of Ḥeshvan, while in Babylonia one starts sixty days after the vernal equinox. The *halakha* for other countries is to act in accordance with the custom of Babylonia, even in places with an entirely different climate.

If no rain has fallen a short while after one starts to request rain, i.e., at the proper time for the first rainfall, marking the beginning of the rainy season, Torah scholars start observing private fasts on behalf of the community. If no rain falls, the entire community observes three fasts that start in the morning, on which they pray for rain. If these fasts have passed and still no rain has fallen, three additional, more severe fasts are declared, again for the entire community. These fasts, which commence at nighttime, involve not only a prohibition against eating and drinking but also against other types of comfort. If the lack of rain continues after this set of three fasts, seven more fast days are decreed. These are even more severe than the previous three, as they include many public displays of mourning, designed to awaken the hearts of the community to prayer.

Incidental to these discussions, the chapter also addressed the *halakhot* of an individual fast. Fast days of this kind must be accepted by the individual in question in the afternoon service of the day before. Private fasts generally start in the morning, and they must be fulfilled like any other vow an individual accepts upon himself.

Introduction to **Perek II**

When heaven is closed up, and there is no rain, when they sin against You; if they pray toward this place, and confess Your name and turn from their sin, when You afflict them; then You hear in heaven, and forgive the sin of Your servants and of Your people Israel, when You teach them the good way in which they should walk; and send rain upon Your land, which You have given to Your people as an inheritance.

(1 Kings 8:35–36)

Blow the horn in Zion, sanctify a fast, call a solemn assembly, gather the people, sanctify the congregation, assemble the elders, gather the children, and those who suck the breasts. Let the bridegroom go forth from his chamber, and the bride out of her pavilion. Let the priests, the ministers of the Lord, weep between the Entrance Hall and the altar, and let them say: Spare Your people, O Lord, and give not Your heritage to reproach, that the nations should make them a byword. Why should they say among the peoples: Where is their God? Then the Lord was jealous for His land, and had pity upon His people. And the Lord answered and said to His people: Behold, I will send you corn, and wine, and oil, and you shall be satisfied with it; and I will no more make you a reproach among the nations.

(Joel 2:15–19)

Since the main aspect of a fast day is not the fast itself but the gathering of the community for prayer and the awakening of the general populace to repentance, the Sages instituted a fixed practice for fast days to further these ends. In addition to abstaining from food and drink, the community recites extra prayers and engages in many rituals to emphasize the importance of the fast and encourage people to amend their behavior and spiritual state. These rituals are an especially prominent feature of the severe fast days, when it is vital to arouse the people's hearts to repentance.

This chapter mainly describes the special order of prayers of the last set of fasts for rain. The details elucidated include the place where the congregation gathers to recite the prayers, as well as other rituals designed to encourage repentance, by stressing the significance of the event and by demonstrating the mourning and suffering experienced by the entire community. Of especial importance are the many additional blessings of these fasts, and the manner of their recitation in public.

Other issues addressed in this chapter are those days on which a fast cannot be declared, and which individuals are exempt from fasting. Apart from Shabbat and Festivals, on which it is prohibited to fast by Torah law, and on which it is even prohibited to display any sign of mourning in public, there are other commemorative days that were established over the course of the generations that are unsuitable for fasts. These holidays came into being either through force of custom or by decree of the Sages. Likewise, there are certain categories of people who do not fast, whether due to weakness or illness or because they are occupied by a sacred service.

Finally, the chapter offers an analysis of the weight of those days on which fasting is prohibited relative to the severity and importance of fast days, as well as the significance of the service performed by those exempt individuals and their obligation to participate in the suffering of the community.

מתני׳ סֵדֶר תַּעֲנִיּוֹת כֵּיצַד? מוֹצִיאִין אֶת הַתֵּיבָה לִרְחוֹבָהּ שֶׁל עִיר, וְנוֹתְנִין אֵפֶר מִקְלֶה עַל גַּבֵּי הַתֵּיבָה, וּבְרֹאשׁ הַנָּשִׂיא, וּבְרֹאשׁ אַב בֵּית דִּין, וְכׇל אֶחָד וְאֶחָד נוֹתֵן בְּרֹאשׁוֹ.

MISHNA What is the customary **order of fast days?**[H] Normally the sacred ark in the synagogue, which was mobile, was kept in a locked room. However, on fast days **they remove the ark to the** main **city square and place burnt ashes**[N] **upon the ark,** as a sign of mourning. **And** they also place ashes **on the head of the** ***Nasi,*** **and on the head of the deputy** ***Nasi,*** **and each and every** member of the community likewise **places** ashes **upon his head.**

הַזָּקֵן שֶׁבָּהֶן אוֹמֵר לִפְנֵיהֶן דִּבְרֵי כִבּוּשִׁין: אַחֵינוּ, לֹא נֶאֱמַר בְּאַנְשֵׁי נִינְוֵה: ״וַיַּרְא אֱלֹהִים אֶת שַׂקָּם וְאֶת תַּעֲנִיתָם״, אֶלָּא: ״וַיַּרְא הָאֱלֹהִים אֶת מַעֲשֵׂיהֶם, כִּי שָׁבוּ מִדַּרְכָּם הָרָעָה״. וּבְקַבָּלָה הוּא אוֹמֵר: ״וְקִרְעוּ לְבַבְכֶם, וְאַל בִּגְדֵיכֶם״.

The eldest member **of the** community **says to** the congregation **statements of reproof,** for example: **Our brothers, it is not stated with regard to the people of Nineveh: And God saw their sackcloth and their fasting. Rather,** the verse says: **"And God saw their deeds, that they had turned from their evil way"** (Jonah 3:10). **And in the Prophets it says:**[N] **"And rend your hearts and not your garments,** and return to the Lord your God" (Joel 2:13). This teaches that prayer and fasting are insufficient, as one must also repent and amend his ways in practice.

עָמְדוּ בִּתְפִלָּה. מוֹרִידִין לִפְנֵי הַתֵּיבָה זָקֵן, וְרָגִיל, וְיֵשׁ לוֹ בָּנִים, וּבֵיתוֹ רֵיקָם, כְּדֵי שֶׁיְּהֵא לִבּוֹ שָׁלֵם בִּתְפִלָּה.

They stood for prayer. The congregation appoints **an elder,** who is **experienced**[H] in leading prayer, **to descend before the ark** as communal prayer leader. **And** this prayer leader must **have children and** must have **an empty house,** i.e., he must be poor, **so that his heart will be fully** concentrated **on the prayer** for the needs of his community.

וְאוֹמֵר לִפְנֵיהֶן עֶשְׂרִים וְאַרְבַּע בְּרָכוֹת, שְׁמוֹנֶה עֶשְׂרֵה שֶׁבְּכׇל יוֹם, וּמוֹסִיף עֲלֵיהֶן עוֹד שֵׁשׁ. וְאֵלּוּ הֵן: זִכְרוֹנוֹת וְשׁוֹפָרוֹת; ״אֶל ה׳ בַּצָּרָתָה לִּי קָרָאתִי, וַיַּעֲנֵנִי״; ״אֶשָּׂא עֵינַי אֶל הֶהָרִים״, וגו׳; ״מִמַּעֲמַקִּים קְרָאתִיךָ, ה׳״; ״תְּפִלָּה לְעָנִי, כִי יַעֲטֹף״.

And he recites twenty-four blessings before the congregation: The **eighteen** blessings **of the everyday** ***Amida*** prayer, **to which he adds another six** blessings, **and they are** as follows: The special series of blessings recited on Rosh HaShana, the **Remembrances and** ***Shofarot;*** and the sections of Psalms that begin with the verses: **"In my distress I called to the Lord and He answered me"** (Psalms 120:1), **"I will lift up my eyes to the mountains;** from where will my help come" (Psalms 121:1), **"Out of the depths I have called You, O Lord"** (Psalms 130:1), and **"A prayer of the afflicted, when he faints"** (Psalms 102:1).

רַבִּי יְהוּדָה אוֹמֵר: לֹא הָיָה צָרִיךְ לוֹמַר זִכְרוֹנוֹת וְשׁוֹפָרוֹת. אֶלָּא אוֹמֵר תַּחְתֵּיהֶן: ״רָעָב כִּי יִהְיֶה בָאָרֶץ, דֶּבֶר כִּי יִהְיֶה״, ״אֲשֶׁר הָיָה דְבַר ה׳ אֶל יִרְמְיָהוּ עַל דִּבְרֵי הַבַּצָּרוֹת״.

Rabbi Yehuda says: The prayer leader **did not need to recite**[N] the **Remembrances and** ***Shofarot*** passages. **Rather, he recites instead of them** the passage beginning with: **"If there be famine in the land, if there be pestilence"** (1 Kings 8:37), followed by the verse **"The word of the Lord that came to Jeremiah concerning the droughts"** (Jeremiah 14:1).

HALAKHA

The order of fast days – סֵדֶר תַּעֲנִיּוֹת: On each of the last seven fasts decreed upon a community in times of drought, the ark is brought out into the open area of the town. All the people congregate there, and cover themselves with sackcloth. Ashes are placed upon the ark, as well as on the Torah scroll it contains. Ashes are also placed on the heads of the *Nasi* and the deputy *Nasi* on the spot where phylacteries are worn, after which everyone else places ashes on his own head. An elder Sage is appointed to reprove the congregation, by reminding them that not sackcloth and fasting, but only repentance and good deeds will save them. When the admonition is completed, everyone rises and the prayer service begins (*Shulḥan Arukh, Oraḥ Ḥayyim* 579:1).

The prayer leader of a fast – בַּעַל תְּפִלָּה בְּתַעֲנִית: The prayer leader on a fast day must be someone who is accustomed to leading prayers and reciting verses. He must also be one who bears the responsibility of children but lacks a steady income, which means he is forced to work hard. Furthermore, neither he nor the members of his household must be guilty of major transgression, nor should he have a bad reputation from his youth. He must be modest and accepted by the community, and have a good voice. Although it is best if he is older, it is preferable to appoint a young man who possesses all these other qualities rather than an older man who does not (*Shulḥan Arukh, Oraḥ Ḥayyim* 579:1).

NOTES

Burnt ashes – אֵפֶר מִקְלֶה: Rashi and many other commentaries explain that burnt ashes are placed on the forehead as a sign of humiliation, as they are more demeaning than dirt. Others add that these ashes are called burnt to differentiate them from the ashes of the red heifer (Meiri; Rashba on *Bava Batra* 60b). *Tosafot* and the *Arukh* cite several interpretations of the term burnt ashes. According to one opinion it refers to ashes from burnt coals, according to another it means ashes from a stove, while a third interpretation is that it refers to ashes formed from a burnt human corpse.

And in the Prophets [*kabbala*] it says – וּבְקַבָּלָה הוּא אוֹמֵר: Several later authorities state that the term *kabbala*, which literally means: Receive, or tradition, is a general reference to the statements of the prophets. Rashi here explains that this expression refers specifically to commands of a prophet to the people. Elsewhere Rashi suggests that statements of *kabbala* are prophecies received in accordance with the requirements of the time, presumably in contrast to the narrative portions of the books of the Prophets and prophecies recorded for future generations. Others explain that actions that the prophets are commanded to perform are called statements of *kabbala*. The reason is that prophets are not permitted to innovate mitzvot of their own, and therefore any mitzva they perform must already have been received on Mount Sinai (*Maḥzor Vitri*).

The prayer leader did not need to recite – לֹא הָיָה צָרִיךְ לוֹמַר: Rabbi Yehuda's wording here is puzzling, as he rules that one does not recite the Remembrances and *Shofarot* at all. One explanation is that Rabbi Yehuda is saying that although the Sages instituted that one must recite lengthy blessings, it is not necessary to include all of the passages of Remembrances and *Shofarot*, as they are not related to the issue of fasts. Others maintain, based on the Rambam, that Rabbi Yehuda does not dispute the basic requirement to recite the Remembrances and *Shofarot* but merely claims that they are not included in these additional blessings (Ritva).

וְאוֹמֵר חוֹתְמֵיהֶן. עַל הָרִאשׁוֹנָה הוּא אוֹמֵר: מִי שֶׁעָנָה אֶת אַבְרָהָם בְּהַר הַמּוֹרִיָּה, הוּא יַעֲנֶה אֶתְכֶם וְיִשְׁמַע בְּקוֹל צַעֲקַתְכֶם הַיּוֹם הַזֶּה. בָּרוּךְ אַתָּה ה׳, גּוֹאֵל יִשְׂרָאֵל. עַל הַשְּׁנִיָּה הוּא אוֹמֵר: מִי שֶׁעָנָה אֶת אֲבוֹתֵינוּ עַל יַם סוּף, הוּא יַעֲנֶה אֶתְכֶם וְיִשְׁמַע קוֹל צַעֲקַתְכֶם הַיּוֹם הַזֶּה. בָּרוּךְ אַתָּה ה׳, זוֹכֵר הַנִּשְׁכָּחוֹת.

And he recites at the end of all of these six blessing **their** unique **conclusions. For** the conclusion of **the first** blessing: Redeemer of Israel, **he recites: He Who answered Abraham on Mount Moriah** (see Genesis 22:11–18), **He will answer you and hear the sound of your cry on this day. Blessed are You, Lord, Redeemer of Israel. For the second** blessing, to which he adds the verses of Remembrances, **he recites: He Who answered our forefathers at the Red Sea** (see Exodus 14:15–31), **He will answer you and hear the sound of your cry on this day. Blessed are You, Lord, Who remembers the forgotten.**

עַל הַשְּׁלִישִׁית הוּא אוֹמֵר: מִי שֶׁעָנָה אֶת יְהוֹשֻׁעַ בַּגִּלְגָּל, הוּא יַעֲנֶה אֶתְכֶם וְיִשְׁמַע בְּקוֹל צַעֲקַתְכֶם הַיּוֹם הַזֶּה. בָּרוּךְ אַתָּה ה׳, שׁוֹמֵעַ תְּרוּעָה״. עַל הָרְבִיעִית הוּא אוֹמֵר: מִי שֶׁעָנָה אֶת שְׁמוּאֵל בַּמִּצְפָּה, הוּא יַעֲנֶה אֶתְכֶם וְיִשְׁמַע בְּקוֹל צַעֲקַתְכֶם הַיּוֹם הַזֶּה. בָּרוּךְ אַתָּה ה׳, שׁוֹמֵעַ צְעָקָה. עַל הַחֲמִישִׁית הוּא אוֹמֵר: מִי שֶׁעָנָה אֶת אֵלִיָּהוּ בְּהַר הַכַּרְמֶל, הוּא יַעֲנֶה אֶתְכֶם וְיִשְׁמַע בְּקוֹל צַעֲקַתְכֶם הַיּוֹם הַזֶּה. בָּרוּךְ אַתָּה ה׳, שׁוֹמֵעַ תְּפִלָּה.

For the third blessing, which includes the verses of *Shofarot*, **he recites: He Who answered Joshua at Gilgal,** when they sounded the *shofar* in Jericho (see Joshua 5:6), **He will answer you and hear the sound of your cry on this day. Blessed are You, Lord, Who hears the *terua*. For the fourth** blessing, **he recites: He Who answered Samuel in Mizpah** (see 1 Samuel, chapter 7), **He will answer you and hear the sound of your cry on this day. Blessed are You, Lord, Who hears cries. For the fifth he recites: He Who answered Elijah on Mount Carmel** (see 1 Kings, chapter 18), **He will answer you and hear the sound of your cry on this day. Blessed are You, Lord, Who hears prayer.**

עַל הַשִּׁשִּׁית הוּא אוֹמֵר: מִי שֶׁעָנָה אֶת יוֹנָה מִמְּעֵי הַדָּגָה, הוּא יַעֲנֶה אֶתְכֶם וְיִשְׁמַע בְּקוֹל צַעֲקַתְכֶם הַיּוֹם הַזֶּה. בָּרוּךְ אַתָּה ה׳, הָעוֹנֶה בְּעֵת צָרָה. עַל הַשְּׁבִיעִית הוּא אוֹמֵר: מִי שֶׁעָנָה אֶת דָּוִד וְאֶת שְׁלֹמֹה בְנוֹ בִּירוּשָׁלַיִם, הוּא יַעֲנֶה אֶתְכֶם וְיִשְׁמַע בְּקוֹל צַעֲקַתְכֶם הַיּוֹם הַזֶּה. בָּרוּךְ אַתָּה ה׳, הַמְרַחֵם עַל הָאָרֶץ.

For the sixth blessing **he recites: He Who answered Jonah from within the innards of the fish** (see Jonah 2:2–11), **He will answer you and hear the sound of your cry on this day. Blessed are You, Lord, Who answers in a time of trouble.** For the conclusion of **the seventh** blessing, which is actually the sixth additional blessing, as the first blessing listed here is an expanded version of a regular weekday blessing, **he recites: He Who answered David and Solomon his son in Jerusalem** (see 1 Kings 8:12–53), **He will answer you and hear the sound of your cry on this day. Blessed are You, Lord, Who has mercy on the Land.**

מַעֲשֶׂה

The mishna relates: **An incident** occurred

Perek **II**
Daf **15** Amud **b**

בִּימֵי רַבִּי חֲלַפְתָּא וְרַבִּי חֲנַנְיָא בֶּן תְּרַדְיוֹן, שֶׁעָבַר אֶחָד לִפְנֵי הַתֵּיבָה וְגָמַר אֶת הַבְּרָכָה כּוּלָּהּ, וְלֹא עָנוּ אַחֲרָיו ״אָמֵן״. ״תִּקְעוּ, הַכֹּהֲנִים, תִּקְעוּ״. ״מִי שֶׁעָנָה אֶת אַבְרָהָם אָבִינוּ בְּהַר הַמּוֹרִיָּה, הוּא יַעֲנֶה אֶתְכֶם וְיִשְׁמַע בְּקוֹל צַעֲקַתְכֶם הַיּוֹם הַזֶּה״. ״הָרִיעוּ, בְּנֵי אַהֲרֹן, הָרִיעוּ״. ״מִי שֶׁעָנָה אֶת אֲבוֹתֵינוּ עַל יַם סוּף, הוּא יַעֲנֶה אֶתְכֶם וְיִשְׁמַע בְּקוֹל צַעֲקַתְכֶם הַיּוֹם הַזֶּה״.

in the days of Rabbi Ḥalafta and Rabbi Ḥananya ben Teradyon, that someone passed before the ark as prayer leader **and finished the entire blessing** of the fast day, **but** the congregation **did not answer amen after him.**[NH] Instead, the attendant of the synagogue said: **Sound** the *shofar* with a long, unwavering sound, **priests, blow**[N] the *shofar*. The prayer leader continued: **He Who answered Abraham on Mount Moriah, He will answer you and hear the sound of your cry on this day.** Once again, the attendant announced: **Blast** the *shofar*, with a wavering sound, **sons of Aaron, blast.** The prayer leader resumed: **He Who answered our forefathers by the Red Sea, He will answer you and hear the sound of your cry on this day,** and continued in this way.

NOTES

But they did not answer amen after him – וְלֹא עָנוּ אַחֲרָיו אָמֵן: The text and commentary follow Rashi's opinion; he explains that the Sages disapproved of the custom of Rabbi Ḥalafta and Rabbi Ḥananya ben Teradyon not to answer amen. The Gemara below (16b) cites a *baraita* that teaches that in areas outside the Temple the congregation responds to the prayer leader's blessings with amen, whereas in the Temple they answer with the formula: Blessed be the name of His glorious kingdom forever and all time. The main difficulty with this explanation is that the texts of the Gemara of most early commentaries actually read the opposite: And they answered after him amen. Moreover, it is difficult to understand how Sages of the stature of Rabbi Ḥalafta and Rabbi Ḥananya ben Teradyon could have made an error of this kind. The early authorities suggest several other possibilities for their error (see 16b).

Sound the *shofar*, priests, blow – תִּקְעוּ, הַכֹּהֲנִים, תִּקְעוּ: Rashi and others maintain that this entire sentence was spoken by the sexton. In other words, he reiterated: Blow, priests, blow, while the actual sounding is not mentioned in the mishna. Others include merely the phrase: Blow, priests, and omit from the text the second mention of blowing (*Melekhet Shlomo*).

HALAKHA

But they did not answer amen after him – וְלֹא עָנוּ אַחֲרָיו אָמֵן: When the special fast day service was conducted in Jerusalem, the people would assemble on the Temple Mount opposite the Eastern Gate. At the conclusion of the passage beginning: He Who answered Abraham, the prayer leader would recite: Blessed is the Lord our God, God of Israel, from everlasting to everlasting. Blessed are You, Lord, Redeemer of Israel. The congregation would respond: Blessed be the name of His glorious kingdom forever and all time (Rambam *Sefer Zemanim*, *Hilkhot Ta'anit* 4:15, 17).

וּכְשֶׁבָּא דָּבָר אֵצֶל חֲכָמִים, אָמְרוּ: לֹא הָיִינוּ נוֹהֲגִין כֵּן אֶלָּא בְּשַׁעַר מִזְרָח וּבְהַר הַבַּיִת.

And when this **matter came before** the **Sages,** and they heard the custom of Rabbi Ḥalafta and Rabbi Ḥananya ben Teradyon, **they said: They would act** in accordance with **this custom only at the Eastern Gate**[B] of the Temple **and on the Temple Mount.** However, this ceremony is never performed outside the Temple.

שָׁלֹשׁ תַּעֲנִיּוֹת הָרִאשׁוֹנוֹת, אַנְשֵׁי מִשְׁמָר מִתְעַנִּין וְלֹא מַשְׁלִימִין, וְאַנְשֵׁי בֵּית אָב לֹא הָיוּ מִתְעַנִּין כְּלָל. שָׁלֹשׁ שְׁנִיּוֹת, אַנְשֵׁי מִשְׁמָר מִתְעַנִּין וּמַשְׁלִימִין, וְאַנְשֵׁי בֵּית אָב מִתְעַנִּין וְלֹא מַשְׁלִימִין. שֶׁבַע אַחֲרוֹנוֹת, אֵלּוּ וָאֵלּוּ מִתְעַנִּין וּמַשְׁלִימִין. דִּבְרֵי רַבִּי יְהוֹשֻׁעַ.

§ On **the first three fasts, the members of the priestly watch,** who are in charge of the Temple service that week, **fast but do not complete** their fast. **And the members of the patrilineal family,**[H] who perform the Temple service on that particular day, **did not fast at all.** On **the second** set of **three** fast days, **the members of the priestly watch fast and complete** the fast, **and the members of the patrilineal family fast but do not complete** their fasts. On **the final seven** fasts, **both** groups **fast and complete** the fasts. This is **the statement of Rabbi Yehoshua.**

וַחֲכָמִים אוֹמְרִים: שָׁלֹשׁ תַּעֲנִיּוֹת הָרִאשׁוֹנוֹת, אֵלּוּ וָאֵלּוּ לֹא הָיוּ מִתְעַנִּין כְּלָל. שָׁלֹשׁ שְׁנִיּוֹת, אַנְשֵׁי מִשְׁמָר מִתְעַנִּין וְלֹא מַשְׁלִימִין, וְאַנְשֵׁי בֵּית אָב לֹא הָיוּ מִתְעַנִּין כְּלָל. שֶׁבַע אַחֲרוֹנוֹת, אַנְשֵׁי מִשְׁמָר מִתְעַנִּין וּמַשְׁלִימִין, וְאַנְשֵׁי בֵּית אָב מִתְעַנִּין וְלֹא מַשְׁלִימִין.

And the Rabbis say: On **the first three fasts,** the members of **both** groups **do not fast at all.** On **the second three** fast days, **the members of the priestly watch fast and do not complete** their fast, **and the members of the patrilineal family do not fast at all.** On **the final seven, the members of the priestly watch fast and complete** the fast, **and the members of the patrilineal family fast but do not complete** their fast.

אַנְשֵׁי מִשְׁמָר מוּתָּרִין לִשְׁתּוֹת יַיִן בַּלֵּילוֹת, אֲבָל לֹא בַּיָּמִים. וְאַנְשֵׁי בֵּית אָב לֹא בַּיּוֹם וְלֹא בַּלַּיְלָה. אַנְשֵׁי מִשְׁמָר וְאַנְשֵׁי מַעֲמָד אֲסוּרִין מִלְּסַפֵּר וּמִלְּכַבֵּס. וּבַחֲמִישִׁי מוּתָּרִין מִפְּנֵי כְבוֹד הַשַּׁבָּת.

The mishna mentions another difference between the members of the priestly watch and the patrilineal family: **The members of the priestly watch** were **permitted to drink wine during the nights, but not during the days,** as they might be called upon to assist in the Temple service, which may not be performed after drinking wine. **And the members of the patrilineal family,** who performed the Temple service, were not permitted to drink wine, **neither at night nor during the day,** as their tasks were performed at night as well. It is **prohibited** for both **the members of the priestly watch and the members of the non-priestly watch to cut their hair or launder** their garments[H] throughout the week, **but on Thursday** it **is permitted** for them to cut their hair and launder their clothes **in deference to Shabbat.**

כָּל הַכָּתוּב בִּמְגִלַּת תַּעֲנִית דְּלָא לְמִסְפַּד – לְפָנָיו אָסוּר, לְאַחֲרָיו מוּתָּר. רַבִּי יוֹסֵי אוֹמֵר: לְפָנָיו וּלְאַחֲרָיו אָסוּר.

§ The mishna returns to the issue of fasting: **Any** day concerning which **it is written in** ***Megillat Ta'anit*** **not to eulogize** on that day, it is also **prohibited** to eulogize on the day **before,** but it is **permitted** to do so on the **following** day. **Rabbi Yosei says:** It is **prohibited** to eulogize both on the day **before and** on the **following** day.

דְּלָא לְהִתְעַנָּאָה – לְפָנָיו וּלְאַחֲרָיו מוּתָּר. רַבִּי יוֹסֵי אוֹמֵר: לְפָנָיו אָסוּר, לְאַחֲרָיו מוּתָּר.

The mishna continues: With regard to those days concerning which it is written only **not to fast,** it is **permitted** to fast on the day **before** and on the **following** day. **Rabbi Yosei says:** Fasting the day **before** is **prohibited,** but on the **following** day it is **permitted** to fast.

אֵין גּוֹזְרִין תַּעֲנִית עַל הַצִּבּוּר בַּתְּחִילָּה בַּחֲמִישִׁי, שֶׁלֹּא לְהַפְקִיעַ הַשְּׁעָרִים. אֶלָּא שָׁלֹשׁ תַּעֲנִיּוֹת הָרִאשׁוֹנוֹת שֵׁנִי וַחֲמִישִׁי וְשֵׁנִי, וְשָׁלֹשׁ שְׁנִיּוֹת חֲמִישִׁי שֵׁנִי וַחֲמִישִׁי. רַבִּי יוֹסֵי אוֹמֵר: כְּשֵׁם שֶׁאֵין הָרִאשׁוֹנוֹת בַּחֲמִישִׁי, כָּךְ לֹא שְׁנִיּוֹת וְלֹא אַחֲרוֹנוֹת.

The mishna continues: **One may not decree a fast on the community starting on a Thursday,**[H] **so as not to cause an increase in prices.** If the first of a series of fasts is on a Thursday, then on Friday everyone will come to purchase their food for after the fast and for Shabbat, which will allow the storeowners to take advantage of the crowds and raise their prices. **Rather, the first** set of **three fasts** is on **a Monday, Thursday,** and the following **Monday, and the second** set of **three** is on **a Thursday, Monday, and** the following **Thursday. Rabbi Yosei says: Just as the first** three fasts do not begin **on Thursday, so too, neither the second** set **nor the last** set starts on a Thursday. Instead, all the series of fasts begin on a Monday.

BACKGROUND

At the Eastern Gate – בְּשַׁעַר מִזְרָח:

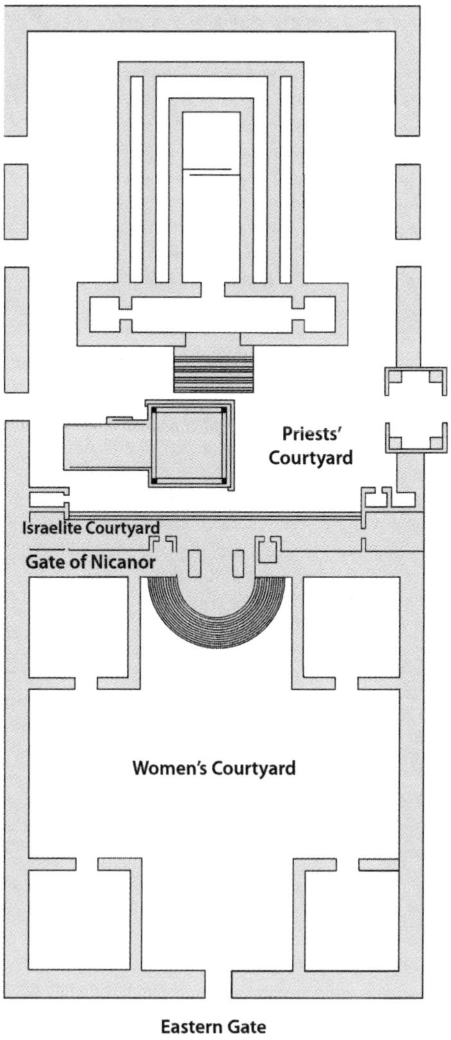

Diagram of the Temple

HALAKHA

The members of the priestly watch…and the members of the patrilineal family – אַנְשֵׁי מִשְׁמָר...וְאַנְשֵׁי בֵּית אָב: On the first three fasts, the members of the priestly watch whose week it was to serve in the Temple did not fast at all. On the second three fasts, they fasted part of the day but did not complete their fasts, while the members of the patrilineal family who were serving in the Temple that day did not fast at all. On the last seven fasts, the members of the priestly watch fasted the entire day, and the members of the patrilineal family fasted part of the day but did not complete their fast. The *halakha* is in accordance with the opinion of the Rabbis (Rambam *Sefer Zemanim, Hilkhot Ta'anit* 3:2, 3, 6).

It is prohibited for the members of the priestly watch and the members of the non-priestly watch to cut their hair or launder their garments – אַנְשֵׁי מִשְׁמָר וְאַנְשֵׁי מַעֲמָד אֲסוּרִין מִלְּסַפֵּר וּמִלְּכַבֵּס: It is prohibited for the members of the priestly watch whose week it is to serve in the Temple, and the members of the non-priestly watch, who are appointed to be present in the Temple that week, to cut their hair or launder their clothes throughout the week of their service. These prohibitions ensure that they will not begin their week of service in soiled clothing or with untrimmed hair (Rambam *Sefer Avoda, Hilkhot Biat HaMikdash* 1:12; *Hilkhot Kelei HaMikdash* 6:11).

One may not decree a fast on the community starting on a Thursday – אֵין גּוֹזְרִין תַּעֲנִית עַל הַצִּבּוּר בַּתְּחִילָּה בַּחֲמִישִׁי: The first of a series of fasts decreed upon the community may not be on a Thursday, so as not to cause a rise in food prices. This ruling applies even in a place where there is no concern that prices will increase (*Shulḥan Arukh, Oraḥ Ḥayyim* 572:1).

אֵין גּוֹזְרִין תַּעֲנִית עַל הַצִּבּוּר בְּרָאשֵׁי חֳדָשִׁים, בַּחֲנוּכָּה, וּבְפוּרִים. וְאִם הִתְחִילוּ, אֵין מַפְסִיקִין. דִּבְרֵי רַבָּן גַּמְלִיאֵל. אָמַר רַבִּי מֵאִיר: אַף עַל פִּי שֶׁאָמַר רַבָּן גַּמְלִיאֵל אֵין מַפְסִיקִין, מוֹדֶה הָיָה שֶׁאֵין מַשְׁלִימִין. וְכֵן תִּשְׁעָה בְּאָב שֶׁחָל לִהְיוֹת בְּעֶרֶב שַׁבָּת.

The mishna further states: **One may not decree a fast on the community on New Moons, on Hanukkah, or on Purim.**[H] **And if they** decreed and **began** a set of fasts, and only afterward realized that one of the fasts would occur on one of these days, **they do not interrupt** the sequence. This is **the statement of Rabban Gamliel. Rabbi Meir said: Although Rabban Gamliel said** that **they do not interrupt** the sequence, he **concedes** that on these days, which are days with special observances, **they do not complete** the fast. **And similarly,** when **the Ninth of Av occurs on Shabbat eve,** the fast is not completed and one eats before the start of Shabbat, so as not to enter Shabbat while fasting.

גמ׳ ״סֵדֶר תַּעֲנִיּוֹת כֵּיצַד מוֹצִיאִין אֶת הַתֵּיבָה״, כו׳. וַאֲפִילּוּ בְּקַמַּיְיתָא? וּרְמִינְהוּ: שָׁלֹשׁ תַּעֲנִיּוֹת רִאשׁוֹנוֹת וּשְׁנִיּוֹת, נִכְנָסִים לְבֵית הַכְּנֶסֶת, וּמִתְפַּלְּלִין כְּדֶרֶךְ שֶׁמִּתְפַּלְּלִין כָּל הַשָּׁנָה כּוּלָּהּ.

GEMARA The mishna teaches: **What is the order of fast days? They remove the ark.** The Gemara asks: **And** is this ritual performed **even on the first** set of fasts? And the Gemara **raises a contradiction** from a *baraita*: On **the first and second** sets of **three fasts,** everyone **enters the synagogue and they pray in the manner that they pray throughout the entire year.**

וּבְשֶׁבַע אַחֲרוֹנוֹת, מוֹצִיאִין אֶת הַתֵּיבָה לִרְחוֹבָהּ שֶׁל עִיר, וְנוֹתְנִין אֵפֶר עַל גַּבֵּי הַתֵּיבָה, וּבְרֹאשׁ הַנָּשִׂיא, וּבְרֹאשׁ אַב בֵּית דִּין, וְכָל אֶחָד וְאֶחָד נוֹטֵל וְנוֹתֵן בְּרֹאשׁוֹ. רַבִּי נָתָן אוֹמֵר: אֵפֶר מִקְלֶה הֵן מְבִיאִין. אָמַר רַב פַּפָּא: כִּי תְּנַן נַמִי מַתְנִיתִין, אַשֶּׁבַע אַחֲרוֹנוֹת תְּנַן.

The *baraita* continues: **And on the final seven** fasts **they remove the ark to the** main **city square and place ashes upon the ark, and on the head of the** ***Nasi*****, and on the head of the deputy** ***Nasi*****, and each and every** member of the community **takes** ashes **and places** them **upon his head. Rabbi Natan says:** They would **bring** specifically **burnt ashes.** This *baraita* indicates that the full ritual is performed only on the final set of fasts. **Rav Pappa said** in explanation: **When we taught the mishna as well,** it was **taught** only with regard **to the final** set of **seven** fasts, not the earlier series of fasts.

״וּבְרֹאשׁ הַנָּשִׂיא״. וַהֲדַר תָּנֵי: ״כָּל אֶחָד וְאֶחָד נוֹתֵן בְּרֹאשׁוֹ״. אִינִי? וְהָתַנְיָא: רַבִּי אוֹמֵר: בִּגְדוּלָּה, מַתְחִילִין מִן הַגָּדוֹל. וּבִקְלָלָה, מַתְחִילִין מִן הַקָּטָן.

§ **And** the mishna further states that ashes are placed **on the head of the** ***Nasi*** and on the head of the deputy *Nasi*. **And then** it **teaches** that **each and every** member of the community **places** ashes **upon his head.** The Gemara asks: **Is that so?** Is this the proper order? **Isn't it taught** in a *baraita* that **Rabbi** Yehuda HaNasi **says:** With regard to matters **of greatness,** where it is a mark of honor and distinction to be treated first, **one begins with the greatest** member of the group, **but** for any matter **involving a curse** or dishonor, **one begins with the least** important member of the group.

בִּגְדוּלָּה, מַתְחִילִין מִן הַגָּדוֹל, שֶׁנֶּאֱמַר: ״וַיֹּאמֶר מֹשֶׁה אֶל אַהֲרֹן, וּלְאֶלְעָזָר וּלְאִיתָמָר״. וּבִקְלָלָה, מַתְחִילִין מִן הַקָּטָן, שֶׁבַּתְּחִלָּה נִתְקַלֵּל נָחָשׁ, וְאַחַר כָּךְ נִתְקַלְּלָה חַוָּה, וְאַחַר כָּךְ נִתְקַלֵּל אָדָם!

The Gemara cites a *baraita* which provides the sources for this principle. With regard to matters **of greatness one begins with the greatest** member, **as it is stated: "And Moses said to Aaron, and to Elazar and to Itamar,** his sons" (Leviticus 10:6). Moses first addresses the most important person, Aaron, and this was a matter of distinction, as the verse continues: "For the anointing oil of the Lord is upon you" (Leviticus 10:7). **And** for any matter **involving a curse, one begins with the least** important member of a group, **as the serpent was cursed first,**[N] **and afterward Eve was cursed and afterward Adam was cursed.**

הָא חֲשִׁיבוּתָא לְדִידְהוּ, דְּאָמְרִי לְהוּ: אַתּוּן חֲשִׁיבִיתוּ לְמִיבְעֵי עֲלַן רַחֲמֵי אַכּוּלֵּי עָלְמָא.

Why, then, are the leaders of the community, its most important members, the first to perform these fast day expressions of mourning, which are a response to a curse? The Gemara answers: The reason is that **this** leadership role in the performance of these acts is considered **a distinction** and an honor **for them, as** it is as though the community is **saying to them: You are worthy of requesting compassion** on behalf **of everyone.**

״כָּל אֶחָד וְאֶחָד נוֹתֵן בְּרֹאשׁוֹ״. נָשִׂיא וְאַב בֵּית דִּין נַמִי נִשְׁקְלוּ אִינְהוּ וְנִינְחוּ בְּרֵאשַׁיְיהוּ! מַאי שְׁנָא דְּשָׁקֵיל אִינִישׁ אַחֲרִינָא וּמַנַּח לְהוּ? אָמַר רַבִּי אַבָּא דְּמִן קֵסָרִי: אֵינוֹ דּוֹמֶה מִתְבַּיֵּישׁ מֵעַצְמוֹ

§ The mishna teaches: **Each and every** member of the community **places** ashes **upon his head.**[N] The Gemara asks: **Let the** ***Nasi*** **and the deputy** ***Nasi*** also take ashes **themselves and place them upon** their own **heads. What is different** with regard to them, **that someone else takes** the ashes **and places them** on their heads? **Rabbi Abba of Caesarea said:** This is done intentionally, as **one who humiliates himself,** in this case by placing ashes upon his own head, **is not similar to**

HALAKHA

One may not decree a fast on the community on New Moons, on Hanukkah, or on Purim – אֵין גּוֹזְרִין תַּעֲנִית עַל הַצִּבּוּר בְּרָאשֵׁי חֳדָשִׁים, בַּחֲנוּכָּה, וּבְפוּרִים: A fast may not be decreed upon the community on New Moons, Hanukkah, or Purim, or on the intermediate days of a Festival. If the community has already started to observe a series of fasts due to an impending calamity, and one fast coincides with one of these days, the fast is observed until nightfall, despite the semi-festive nature of the day. Nowadays, however, when even communal fasts are treated as private fasts, the series is interrupted on days of this kind, and the fast is observed on a different day (*Shulḥan Arukh, Oraḥ Ḥayyim* 572:2; *Magen Avraham*, citing *Beit Yosef*).

NOTES

As the serpent was cursed first – שֶׁבַּתְּחִלָּה נִתְקַלֵּל נָחָשׁ: It can be suggested that the serpent was punished first for an entirely different reason, as it was the one ultimately responsible for the sin since it persuaded Eve to partake of the forbidden fruit. However, as God initially spoke to Adam, followed by Eve, the subsequent punishments should have been announced in that order. The change in order indicates that in matters of dishonor, one starts with the inferior member of the group (*Nezer HaKodesh*).

Each and every member places ashes upon his head – כָּל אֶחָד וְאֶחָד נוֹתֵן בְּרֹאשׁוֹ: In the Jerusalem Talmud it is indicated that the sexton places ashes not only on the heads of the dignitaries but also on the heads of the common people. However, there was a difference between the two, as those people he could not reach would place ashes on their own heads. In the case of the *Nasi* and the deputy *Nasi*, in contrast, particular care was taken that the ashes were placed on their heads by someone else, to maximize their humiliation, as the Gemara explains.

לְמִתְבַּיֵּישׁ מֵאֲחֵרִים. וְהֵיכָא מַנַּח לְהוּ? אָמַר רַבִּי יִצְחָק: בִּמְקוֹם תְּפִילִּין, שֶׁנֶּאֱמַר: ״לָשׂוּם לַאֲבֵלֵי צִיּוֹן, לָתֵת לָהֶם פְּאֵר תַּחַת אֵפֶר״.

one who is humiliated by others. Accordingly, ashes are placed on the heads of the leaders of the community by others, to increase the appearance of their suffering. The Gemara asks: **And where** exactly **are** the ashes **placed** upon their heads? **Rabbi Yitzḥak said: On the place** of the **phylacteries**[HB] of the head, **as it is stated: "To appoint to those who mourn in Zion, to give to them an ornament [*pe'er*] instead of ashes"** (Isaiah 61:3). This verse likens the placement of ashes on one's head to an ornament, and the term *pe'er* is traditionally interpreted as a reference to phylacteries.

רְחוֹב, תֵּיבָה, וְשַׂקִּים, אֵפֶר, אֵפֶר, קְבוּרָה, וּמוֹרִיָּה סִימָן. לָמָּה יוֹצְאִין לָרְחוֹב? רַבִּי חִיָּיא בַּר אַבָּא אָמַר: לוֹמַר: זָעַקְנוּ בִּצְנְעָא וְלֹא נַעֲנֵינוּ. נְבַזֶּה עַצְמֵנוּ בְּפַרְהֶסְיָא.

§ The Gemara provides **a mnemonic** device for the forthcoming statements. **Square; ark; and sackcloth; ashes; ashes; cemetery; and Moriah.** The Gemara asks: **Why do they go out to the square? Rabbi Ḥiyya bar Abba said:** This is a symbolic action, as though **to say: We cried out in private** inside the synagogue **and we were not answered. We will** therefore **disgrace ourselves in public,** so that our prayers will be heard.

רֵישׁ לָקִישׁ אָמַר: גָּלִינוּ. גָּלוּתֵינוּ מְכַפֶּרֶת עָלֵינוּ. מַאי בֵּינַיְיהוּ? אִיכָּא בֵּינַיְיהוּ דְּגָלֵי מִבֵּי כְנִישְׁתָּא לְבֵי כְנִישְׁתָּא.

Reish Lakish said that the move into the square symbolizes exile, as though they are saying: **We have been exiled; may our exile atone for us.** The Gemara asks: **What is** the practical difference **between** these two explanations? The Gemara answers that the practical difference between **them** is in a case **where they are exiled,** i.e., they move, **from** one **synagogue to** another **synagogue.** According to the opinion of Reish Lakish, they have exiled themselves, and therefore this ceremony is adequate. Conversely, Rabbi Ḥiyya bar Abba maintains that as the ritual is performed in private, it is insufficient.

וְלָמָּה מוֹצִיאִין אֶת הַתֵּיבָה לִרְחוֹבָהּ שֶׁל עִיר? אָמַר רַבִּי יְהוֹשֻׁעַ בֶּן לֵוִי: לוֹמַר: כְּלִי צָנוּעַ הָיָה לָנוּ, וְנִתְבַּזָּה בַּעֲוֹנֵינוּ.

The Gemara asks another question concerning the meaning of the ritual. **And why do they remove the ark to the city square? Rabbi Yehoshua ben Levi said:** This is done as though **to say: We had a modest vessel,** which was always kept concealed, **but it has been** publicly **exposed due to our transgressions.**

וְלָמָּה מִתְכַּסִּין בְּשַׂקִּים? אֲמַר רַבִּי חִיָּיא בַּר אַבָּא: לוֹמַר: הֲרֵי אָנוּ חֲשׁוּבִין כִּבְהֵמָה. וְלָמָּה נוֹתְנִין אֵפֶר מִקְלֶה עַל גַּבֵּי תֵיבָה? אָמַר רַבִּי יְהוּדָה בֶּן פָּזִי: כְּלוֹמַר: ״עִמּוֹ אָנֹכִי בְצָרָה״. רֵישׁ לָקִישׁ אָמַר: ״בְּכָל צָרָתָם לוֹ צָר״. אָמַר רַבִּי זֵירָא: מֵרֵישׁ, כִּי הֲוָה חָזֵינָא לְהוּ לְרַבָּנַן דְּיָהֲבֵי אֵפֶר מִקְלֶה עַל גַּבֵּי תֵיבָה, מִזְדַּעֲזַע לִי כּוּלֵּיהּ גּוּפָאִי.

The Gemara further asks: **And why do they cover themselves in sackcloth?**[N] **Rabbi Ḥiyya bar Abba said:** This is as though **to say: We are considered** before You **like animals,** which are likewise covered with hide. **And why do they place burnt ashes on top of the ark? Rabbi Yehuda ben Pazi said:** This is **as though to say** in God's name: **"I will be with him in trouble"** (Psalms 91:15). **Reish Lakish said** that the same idea can be derived from a different verse: **"In all their affliction, He was afflicted"** (Isaiah 63:9).[N] By placing burnt ash on the ark, which is the symbol of the Divine Presence, it is as though God Himself joins the Jews in their pain. **Rabbi Zeira said: At first, when I saw the Sages place burnt ashes upon the ark, my entire body trembled** from the intensity of the event.

HALAKHA

On the place of phylacteries – בִּמְקוֹם תְּפִילִּין: When ashes are placed on the head on public fast days, they are positioned on the spot where the phylacteries are worn (*Shulḥan Arukh*, *Oraḥ Ḥayyim* 579:1).

BACKGROUND

On the place of phylacteries – בִּמְקוֹם תְּפִילִּין: The head phylacteries are to be placed anywhere between one's hairline and the fontanel, the area on the top of a baby's head which is soft.

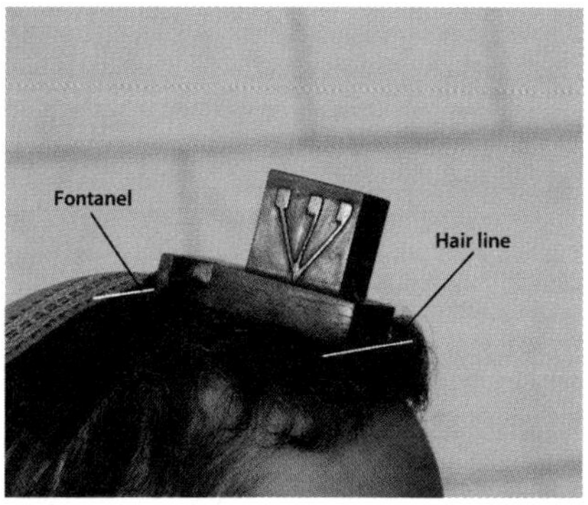

Proper position of head phylacteries

NOTES

And why do they cover themselves in sackcloth – וְלָמָּה מִתְכַּסִּין בְּשַׂקִּים: The early authorities note that some of the practices discussed in the Gemara, e.g., wearing sackcloth and visiting a cemetery, are not explicitly mentioned anywhere in the mishna or the *baraita*. Rashi notes that wearing sackcloth and visiting a cemetery are mentioned in the Jerusalem Talmud. Some commentaries find an allusion to the practice of wearing sackcloth in the message of reproof delivered by the elder that neither sackcloth nor fasting are effective measures for winning divine forgiveness, which indicates that it was indeed customary for people to wear sackcloth on fast days (see the mishna and *baraita*; Meiri; *Mikhtam*). Others maintain that the Gemara is indeed inquiring about practices that do not have a source in the mishna or the *baraita*, but which were nevertheless the prevailing custom (Ritva; Ran).

In all their affliction, He was afflicted – בְּכָל צָרָתָם לוֹ צָר: Some commentaries explain that the sacred ark containing the Torah scroll represents the Ark in the Temple, upon which God's Divine Presence once rested (Maharsha). Placing ashes on the ark is a way of saying that God is with His people in their time of affliction. Just as the people cover themselves with ashes, God acts likewise.

In the Jerusalem Talmud the sacred ark removed from the synagogue is similarly associated with the Ark of the Holy of Holies in the Temple. Ashes are placed on the ark to impress upon the people how different they are from their righteous ancestors, as though to say: Our forefathers covered their Ark with gold, and yet we cover ours with ashes. According to this opinion, the verse should be interpreted as follows: Whenever the Jewish people find themselves in affliction, God too is afflicted, as He participates in their suffering.

Others explain the verse in a slightly different manner: God suffers with the Jewish people, as it were, because His existence and unity are revealed in this world primarily through the Jewish people. Consequently, when the Jews are afflicted, He is afflicted as well (Meiri).

וְלָמָּה נוֹתְנִין אֵפֶר בְּרֹאשׁ כׇּל אֶחָד וְאֶחָד? פְּלִיגִי בָּהּ רַבִּי לֵוִי בַּר חָמָא וְרַבִּי חֲנִינָא. חַד אָמַר: הֲרֵי אָנוּ חֲשׁוּבִין לְפָנֶיךָ כְּאֵפֶר. וְחַד אָמַר: כְּדֵי שֶׁיִּזְכּוֹר לָנוּ אֶפְרוֹ שֶׁל יִצְחָק. מַאי בֵּינַיְיהוּ? אִיכָּא בֵּינַיְיהוּ עָפָר סְתָם.

And why do they place ashes upon the head of each and every individual? **Rabbi Levi bar Ḥama and Rabbi Ḥanina disagree with regard to this** matter. **One said** that this is as though to say: **We are considered like ashes before You. And one said** that these ashes are placed **in order to remind** God of **the ashes of** our forefather **Isaac,**[B] **on our behalf.**[N] The Gemara asks: **What is** the practical difference **between** these two explanations? The Gemara answers that the practical difference **between them** is in a case where one placed **ordinary earth** upon the ark instead of ashes. Although earth does symbolize self-nullification and may be used according to the first explanation, it has no connection to the sacrifice of Isaac, and therefore it does not satisfy the second explanation.

לָמָּה יוֹצְאִין לְבֵית הַקְּבָרוֹת? פְּלִיגִי בָּהּ רַבִּי לֵוִי בַּר חָמָא וְרַבִּי חֲנִינָא. חַד אָמַר: הֲרֵי אָנוּ חֲשׁוּבִין לְפָנֶיךָ כְּמֵתִים. וְחַד אָמַר: כְּדֵי שֶׁיְּבַקְּשׁוּ עָלֵינוּ מֵתִים רַחֲמִים. מַאי בֵּינַיְיהוּ? אִיכָּא בֵּינַיְיהוּ קִבְרֵי נׇכְרִים.

The Gemara further asks: **And why do they go out to the cemetery**[H] on a fast day? Again, **Rabbi Levi bar Ḥama and Rabbi Ḥanina disagree with regard to this** matter. **One said** this is as though to say: **We are like the dead before You. And one said** that one goes out to the cemetery **in order that** the deceased will **request mercy on our behalf.**[N] The Gemara asks: **What is** the practical difference **between them?** The Gemara answers that the practical difference **between them** concerns **graves of gentiles.** If the purpose of going to graves is to say that they stand before God like the dead, graves of gentiles would suffice. However, if they go to the cemetery for the deceased to ask for mercy on their behalf, they should visit specifically Jewish graves.

מַאי הַר הַמּוֹרִיָּה? פְּלִיגִי בָּהּ רַבִּי לֵוִי בַּר חָמָא וְרַבִּי חֲנִינָא. חַד אָמַר: הַר שֶׁיָּצָא מִמֶּנּוּ הוֹרָאָה לְיִשְׂרָאֵל. וְחַד אָמַר: הַר שֶׁיָּצָא מִמֶּנּוּ מוֹרָא לְאוּמּוֹת הָעוֹלָם.

§ Apropos disputes between Rabbi Levi bar Ḥama and Rabbi Ḥanina, the Gemara mentions another dispute between them. **What** is the meaning of the name **Mount** [*Har*] **Moriah,** the Temple Mount? **Rabbi Levi bar Ḥama and Rabbi Ḥanina disagree** with regard to **this** matter. **One said** that the name alludes to the Great Sanhedrin that convened there, as it is the **mountain from which instruction** [*hora'a*] **went out to the Jewish people. And one said** that it is the **mountain from which fear** [*mora*] **went out to the nations of the world,**[N] as this place signifies God's choice of the Jewish people.

״הַזָּקֵן שֶׁבָּהֶן אוֹמֵר לִפְנֵיהֶן דִּבְרֵי כִבּוּשִׁין״. תָּנוּ רַבָּנַן: אִם יֵשׁ זָקֵן, אוֹמֵר זָקֵן. וְאִם לָאו, אוֹמֵר חָכָם. וְאִם לָאו, אוֹמֵר אָדָם שֶׁל צוּרָה. אַטּוּ זָקֵן דְּקָאָמְרִי אַף עַל גַּב דְּלָאו חָכָם הוּא? אֲמַר אַבַּיֵי: הָכִי קָאָמַר: אִם יֵשׁ זָקֵן וְהוּא חָכָם, אוֹמֵר זָקֵן וְהוּא חָכָם. וְאִם לָאו, אוֹמֵר חָכָם. וְאִם לָאו, אוֹמֵר אָדָם שֶׁל צוּרָה.

§ The mishna taught: **The eldest of** the community **says to them statements of reproof.**[NH] **The Sages taught** in a *baraita*: **If there is an elder,** then **the elder says** the admonition, **and if not, a Sage says** the admonition. **And if not, a person of** imposing **appearance**[N] **says** it. The Gemara asks: **Is that to say** that the **elder** of whom **we spoke** is preferred to a scholar simply by virtue of his age, **even though he is not a scholar? Abaye said** that **this is what** the mishna **is saying: If there is an elder, and he is** also **a scholar,** this **elder scholar says** the admonition. **And if not,** even a young **scholar says** the reproof. **And if** there is **no** scholar of any kind available, **a person of** imposing **appearance says** it.

NOTES

In order to remind God of the ashes of Isaac on our behalf – כְּדֵי שֶׁיִּזְכּוֹר לָנוּ אֶפְרוֹ שֶׁל יִצְחָק: In the Jerusalem Talmud an opinion is cited according to which ashes are placed on one's head to recall the merit of Abraham, who said: "I am but dust and ashes" (Genesis 18:27). A second opinion, also cited in the Jerusalem Talmud, is that ashes are placed on the head to symbolize the merit of Isaac, as he is considered burnt to ashes upon the altar. According to the first opinion, ordinary earth can substitute for ashes if necessary, whereas according to the second opinion, only ashes are suitable.

Tosafot explain that as ashes serve as a reminder to God of the ashes of Isaac, the source of the ashes must be human bones. Others reject this opinion, arguing that it is inconceivable that human remains should be burned for this purpose (Rav Ya'akov Emden). On the contrary, the Gemara's association of this custom with the ashes of Isaac proves that human ashes are not required, as Isaac himself was not sacrificed. Rather, the ashes placed on the heads of those fasting serve as a reminder of the ashes of wood burnt on the altar when Isaac was prepared for sacrifice. Yet others explain that the ashes serve as a reminder of the ram that Abraham sacrificed in place of Isaac, which are viewed as equivalent to the ashes of Isaac himself.

In order that the deceased will request mercy on our behalf – כְּדֵי שֶׁיְּבַקְּשׁוּ עָלֵינוּ מֵתִים רַחֲמִים: The Rif refers to both explanations cited here for visiting the cemetery on communal fast days, whereas the Rambam says only that it is a reminder to those fasting that if they fail to repent they will soon join the dead who are buried there (Rambam *Sefer Zemanim*, *Hilkhot Ta'anit* 4:18). It is possible that in this regard the Rambam follows the Jerusalem Talmud, in which only the first reason is mentioned. It has also been suggested that the Rambam rejects the idea that the living appeal to the dead as their intermediaries to petition for mercy (*Sefer HaMeorot*).

From which fear went out to the nations of the world – שֶׁיָּצָא מִמֶּנּוּ מוֹרָא לְאוּמּוֹת הָעוֹלָם: Rashi and *Tosafot* cite an opinion that according to this second explanation, Mount Moriah is identified with Mount Sinai. When the Torah was revealed to the Jewish people on Mount Sinai, the rest of the nations were overcome with fear, as the verse states: "You caused sentence to be heard from heaven; the earth feared, and was still" (Psalms 76:9). Several later commentaries note that this explanation is problematic, as it is traditionally accepted that Mount Moriah is the site upon which the Temple was built in Jerusalem, whereas Mount Sinai is outside Eretz Yisrael (Maharsha; Rabbi Tzvi Hirsch Chajes).

Statements of reproof [*kibbushin*] – דִּבְרֵי כִבּוּשִׁין: Rashi understands *kibbushin* in the sense of pressing, i.e., statements that press against the heart and force repentance. Others explain that it means suppressed, that is, matters that uncover the suppressed emotions in one's heart (*Ein Ya'akov*).

A person of imposing appearance – אָדָם שֶׁל צוּרָה: Several explanations have been suggested for this term. Rashi states that it refers to a tall, imposing person, whose statements of admonition will certainly be heeded. Some claim that it means someone of attractive appearance (commentary on Rif, attributed to Rashi) while others say it is a minor Torah scholar who does not have the status of a Torah Sage (Rosh). Alternatively, it refers to someone fit to be appointed as a communal leader. Some maintain that we are dealing with a man who is known for his fine moral character and piety (Meiri), or even one who is wise in worldly matters (Maharsha).

BACKGROUND

The ashes of Isaac – אֶפְרוֹ שֶׁל יִצְחָק: Although Isaac was not in fact sacrificed, as God provided a ram to be sacrificed in his place, this animal is considered as though it were actually the Patriarch Isaac, as both Abraham and Isaac were entirely willing to offer the supreme sacrifice of their own lives. The binding of Isaac became a model for those Jewish martyrs who actually gave their lives in sanctification of God's name. This is why reference is sometimes made to the ashes of Isaac, as with respect to their willingness and intention it was as though Isaac had truly sacrificed himself in obedience to a divine command, by virtue of which Isaac's descendants became the chosen people.

HALAKHA

They go out to the cemetery – יוֹצְאִין לְבֵית הַקְּבָרוֹת: After prayer services on public fast days, the people go out and visit the cemetery, as a reminder that they will be like the dead unless they repent of their evil ways, in accordance with the first explanation of the Gemara. Consequently, if there are no Jewish cemeteries in the area, they can visit a non-Jewish cemetery (Rema). However, common practice follows the second opinion, according to which only a Jewish cemetery should be visited (*Magen Avraham*). This is the source of the custom followed in many communities to visit a cemetery on the Ninth of Av (see *Tosafot*; *Shulḥan Arukh*, *Oraḥ Ḥayyim* 579:3).

The eldest of the community says to them statements of reproof – הַזָּקֵן שֶׁבָּהֶן אוֹמֵר לִפְנֵיהֶן דִּבְרֵי כִבּוּשִׁין: If an elder who is also a Torah Sage is present, he rebukes the congregation. If there is no elderly Sage present, a young Torah scholar is chosen to reprove the people. If there is no Sage at all, a man of imposing physical appearance delivers the admonition (*Shulḥan Arukh*, *Oraḥ Ḥayyim* 579:1).

אַחֵינוּ, לֹא שַׂק וְתַעֲנִית גּוֹרְמִים. אֶלָּא תְּשׁוּבָה וּמַעֲשִׂים טוֹבִים גּוֹרְמִים. שֶׁכֵּן מָצִינוּ בְּאַנְשֵׁי נִינְוֵה שֶׁלֹּא נֶאֱמַר בָּהֶם: "וַיַּרְא הָאֱלֹהִים אֶת שַׂקָּם וְאֶת תַּעֲנִיתָם", אֶלָּא: "וַיַּרְא הָאֱלֹהִים אֶת מַעֲשֵׂיהֶם, כִּי שָׁבוּ מִדַּרְכָּם הָרָעָה".

What does he say? **Our brothers,** it is **not sackcloth and fasting** that **cause** atonement for our sins. **Rather, repentance and good deeds** will **cause** our atonement. This is **as we find with** regard to **the people of Nineveh, that it is not stated about them: And God saw their sackcloth and their fasting. Rather,** the verse states: **"And God saw their deeds, that they had turned from their evil way"** (Jonah 3:10).

"וְיִתְכַּסּוּ שַׂקִּים הָאָדָם וְהַבְּהֵמָה". מַאי הֲווּ עָבְדִי? אָסְרָא הַבְּהֵמוֹת לְחוּד וְאֶת הַוְּולָדוֹת לְחוּד. אָמְרוּ לְפָנָיו: רִבּוֹנוֹ שֶׁל עוֹלָם! אִם אֵין אַתָּה מְרַחֵם עָלֵינוּ, אֵין אָנוּ מְרַחֲמִים עַל אֵלּוּ.

§ Apropos the repentance of the inhabitants of Nineveh, the Gemara discusses their behavior further. The verse states: **"But let them be covered with sackcloth, both man and beast"** (Jonah 3:8). **What did they do? They confined the** female **animals alone, and** their **young alone,** in a different place. **They** then **said before** God: **Master of the Universe, if You do not have mercy on us, we will not have mercy on these** animals. Even if we are not worthy of Your mercy, these animals have not sinned.

"וְיִקְרְאוּ אֶל אֱלֹהִים בְּחָזְקָה". מַאי אֲמוּר? אָמְרוּ לְפָנָיו: רִבּוֹנוֹ שֶׁל עוֹלָם! עָלוּב וְשֶׁאֵינוֹ עָלוּב, צַדִּיק וְרָשָׁע, מִי נִדְחֶה מִפְּנֵי מִי?

It is further stated with regard to the people of Nineveh: **"And let them cry mightily to God"** (Jonah 3:8). The Gemara asks: **What did they say** that could be described as calling out "mightily"? The Gemara explains that **they said before** God: **Master of the Universe,** if there is a dispute between **a submissive one and an intractable one,** or between **a righteous one and a wicked one, who must yield before whom?** Certainly the righteous forgives the wicked. Likewise, You must have mercy on us.

"וְיָשֻׁבוּ אִישׁ מִדַּרְכּוֹ הָרָעָה, וּמִן הֶחָמָס אֲשֶׁר בְּכַפֵּיהֶם". מַאי "וּמִן הֶחָמָס אֲשֶׁר בְּכַפֵּיהֶם"? אָמַר שְׁמוּאֵל: אֲפִילּוּ גָּזַל מָרִישׁ וּבְנָאוֹ בְּבִירָה, מְקַעֲקֵעַ כָּל הַבִּירָה כּוּלָּהּ וּמַחֲזִיר מָרִישׁ לִבְעָלָיו.

The verse states: **"And let them turn, every one from his evil way, and from the violence that is in their hands"** (Jonah 3:8). **What is** the meaning of the phrase **"and from the violence that is in their hands"? Shmuel said** that the king of Nineveh proclaimed: **Even if one stole a beam**[N] **and built it into** his **building,** he must **tear down the entire building and return the beam to its owner.** Although the Sages decreed that one need only pay financial compensation in a case of this kind, these people wanted to repent completely by removing any remnant of stolen property from their possession.

אָמַר רַב אַדָּא בַּר אַהֲבָה: אָדָם שֶׁיֵּשׁ בְּיָדוֹ עֲבֵירָה, וּמִתְוַדֶּה וְאֵינוֹ חוֹזֵר בָּהּ, לְמָה הוּא דּוֹמֶה? לְאָדָם שֶׁתּוֹפֵס שֶׁרֶץ בְּיָדוֹ, שֶׁאֲפִילּוּ טוֹבֵל בְּכָל מֵימוֹת שֶׁבָּעוֹלָם, לֹא עָלְתָה לוֹ טְבִילָה. זְרָקוֹ מִיָּדוֹ, כֵּיוָן שֶׁטָּבַל בְּאַרְבָּעִים סְאָה מִיָּד עָלְתָה לוֹ טְבִילָה,

§ Similarly, **Rav Adda bar Ahava said: A person who has a transgression in his hand,**[H] **and he confesses but does not repent for** his sin, **to what is he comparable? To a person who holds in his hand** a dead **creeping animal,** which renders one ritually impure by contact. **As** in this situation, **even if he immerses in all the waters of the world, his immersion is ineffective for him,** as long as the source of ritual impurity remains in his hand. However, if he has **thrown** the animal **from his hand, once he has immersed in** a ritual bath of **forty** ***se'a*****, the immersion is immediately effective for him.**

שֶׁנֶּאֱמַר: "וּמוֹדֶה וְעֹזֵב יְרֻחָם". וְאוֹמֵר: "נִשָּׂא לְבָבֵנוּ אֶל כַּפָּיִם אֶל אֵל בַּשָּׁמָיִם".

As it is stated: "He who covers his transgressions shall not prosper, **but whoever confesses and forsakes them shall obtain mercy"** (Proverbs 28:13). That is, confession alone is futile, but one who also abandons his transgressions will receive mercy. **And it states** elsewhere: **"Let us lift up our heart with our hands**[N] **to God in Heaven"** (Lamentations 3:41), which likewise indicates that it is not enough to lift one's hands in prayer; rather, one must also raise his heart and return to God.

"עָמְדוּ בִּתְפִלָּה. מוֹרִידִין לִפְנֵי הַתֵּיבָה זָקֵן", כו'. תָּנוּ רַבָּנַן: עָמְדוּ בִּתְפִלָּה. אַף עַל פִּי שֶׁיֵּשׁ שָׁם זָקֵן וְחָכָם, אֵין מוֹרִידִין לִפְנֵי הַתֵּיבָה אֶלָּא אָדָם הָרָגִיל. רַבִּי יְהוּדָה אוֹמֵר: מְטוּפָּל וְאֵין לוֹ, וְיֵשׁ לוֹ יְגִיעָה בַּשָּׂדֶה, וּבֵיתוֹ רֵיקָם,

§ The mishna teaches: **They stood for prayer,** and the congregation appoints **an elder. The Sages taught** in a *baraita*: **They stood for prayer,** and **even if there is** a man **there who is elderly and a scholar, they** appoint **to descend before the ark** as prayer leader **only a person who is accustomed** to lead in prayer. Who is considered an accustomed prayer leader in this sense? **Rabbi Yehuda says:** One who has financially **dependent** children **but he does not have** the means[H] to support them, **and he has** no choice but to **toil in the field, and whose house is empty,** and who will therefore pray for rain with great devotion.

NOTES

Even if one stole a beam – אֲפִילּוּ גָּזַל מָרִישׁ: In other words, the people of Nineveh went beyond the letter of the law, as they pulled down a building to return a stolen beam that had been incorporated into its structure. By strict Torah law, this action is indeed necessary, but to ease the path to repentance the Sages enacted that the thief could keep the beam and provide financial compensation in its place (see *Gittin* 55a). In their desire to achieve full repentance, the people of Nineveh acted stringently and insisted that the beam itself be returned to its rightful owner.

Some commentaries explain that this *halakha* is derived from the term violence in the verse in Jonah, which is referring to one forcibly paying for and taking an article that does not belong to him. When the people of Nineveh decided to repent, they sought not only to cleanse themselves of the crime of theft, but also to rid themselves of the guilt of violence (*Shita Mekubbetzet*; Meiri). Others maintain that this idea is derived from the verse's expression: "That is in their hands." The people of Nineveh wished to remove all traces of the violence they had incorporated into their constructions with their own hands (Maharsha).

Let us lift up our heart with our hands – נִשָּׂא לְבָבֵנוּ אֶל כַּפָּיִם: Some commentaries explain that this verse indicates that in addition to lifting up one's heart in prayer, one must also purify his hands from violence (Rashi's commentary on Lamentations, and the Aramaic translation of Lamentations).

HALAKHA

A person who has a transgression in his hand – אָדָם שֶׁיֵּשׁ בְּיָדוֹ עֲבֵירָה: One who confesses to a transgression without wholeheartedly committing himself to refrain from sinning again in the future is likened to someone who immerses himself while holding a dead creeping animal in his hand, as he remains ritually impure until he casts the animal away (Rambam *Sefer HaMadda, Hilkhot Teshuva* 2:3).

One who has dependent children but he does not have the means – מְטוּפָּל וְאֵין לוֹ: On a communal fast it is preferable to appoint as prayer leader one who is well versed in the prayers and in reading from the Torah, the Prophets, and the Writings. He should have children who are financially dependent upon him, without enough money to support them. He should have work to do in the field. Also, there should be no major sinners among the members of his household, and he should not have had a bad reputation as a young man. Furthermore, he should be humble and well liked by the congregation. Finally, he should know the proper melodies for the liturgy and have a pleasant voice. It is best if an elder can be found with all these qualities, but if not, a young man should be chosen (*Shulḥan Arukh, Oraḥ Ḥayyim* 579:1).

וּפִרְקוֹ נָאֶה, וּשְׁפַל בֶּרֶךְ, וּמְרוּצֶּה לָעָם, וְיֵשׁ לוֹ נְעִימָה, וְקוֹלוֹ עָרֵב, וּבָקִי לִקְרוֹת בַּתּוֹרָה, וּבַנְּבִיאִים, וּבַכְּתוּבִים, וְלִשְׁנוֹת בַּמִּדְרָשׁ, בַּהֲלָכוֹת, וּבָאַגָּדוֹת, וּבָקִי בְּכָל הַבְּרָכוֹת כּוּלָּן. וְיָהֲבוּ בֵּיהּ רַבָּנַן עֵינַיְיהוּ בְּרַב יִצְחָק בַּר אַמִּי.

Rabbi Yehuda continues with his depiction of the worthy prayer leader. **And his youth was becoming, and** he is **humble and accepted by the people,** as he is likable. **And** furthermore, he must be **familiar with songs and his voice pleasant, and** he is **expert in reading the Torah, the Prophets, and the Writings, and** he knows how **to study midrash,** ***halakha*****, and** ***aggada*****. And** finally, he must be **expert in all of the blessings.** Clearly, it is hard to find someone with all these qualities. **And** the Gemara relates that when this worthy person was described, those **Sages** present **turned their eyes toward Rav Yitzḥak bar Ami,**[P] who possessed all of these virtues.

PERSONALITIES

Rav Yitzḥak bar Ami – רַב יִצְחָק בַּר אַמִּי: A Babylonian *amora* of the third generation, Rav Yitzḥak bar Ami was a student of Rav Ḥisda, in whose name he transmitted statements. Several of Rav Yitzḥak bar Ami's halakhic rulings and interpretations of verses are recorded in the Gemara.

Perek **II**
Daf **16** Amud **b**

הַיְינוּ מְטוּפָּל וְאֵין לוֹ, הַיְינוּ בֵּיתוֹ רֵיקָם. אָמַר רַב חִסְדָּא: זֶהוּ שֶׁבֵּיתוֹ רֵיקָם מִן הָעֲבֵירָה. "וּפִרְקוֹ נָאֶה". אָמַר אַבַּיֵי: זֶה שֶׁלֹּא יָצָא עָלָיו שֵׁם רַע בְּיַלְדוּתוֹ.

The Gemara asks a question concerning the explanation of Rabbi Yehuda: One who has **dependent** children **and does not have** anything with which to support them **is** apparently **the same as** one whose **house is empty.** Why does Rabbi Yehuda list both descriptions? **Rav Ḥisda said: This** expression means **that his house is empty of transgression.**[N] **And** Rabbi Yehuda further said that the prayer leader must be one **whose youth was becoming.** In explanation of this phrase, **Abaye said: This** is **one who did not have a bad reputation** at any time **during his youth.**

"הָיְתָה לִּי נַחֲלָתִי כְּאַרְיֵה בַיָּעַר. נָתְנָה עָלַי בְּקוֹלָהּ; עַל כֵּן שְׂנֵאתִיהָ". מַאי "נָתְנָה עָלַי בְּקוֹלָהּ"? אָמַר מָר זוּטְרָא בַּר טוֹבִיָּה אָמַר רַב, וְאָמְרִי לַהּ אָמַר רַבִּי חָמָא אָמַר רַבִּי אֶלְעָזָר: זֶה שְׁלִיחַ צִבּוּר שֶׁאֵינוֹ הָגוּן הַיּוֹרֵד לִפְנֵי הַתֵּיבָה.

The Gemara cites a verse in relation to the prayer leader: **"My heritage has become to me as a lion in the forest. She has uttered her voice against me; therefore I have hated her"** (Jeremiah 12:8). **What is** the meaning of the phrase: **"She has uttered her voice against me"? Mar Zutra bar Toviyya said** that **Rav said, and some say Rabbi Ḥama said** that **Rabbi Elazar said: This is an unworthy prayer leader who descends before the ark.** When this person calls out to God, He thinks, so to speak: I hate the sound of his prayer.

"וְאוֹמֵר לִפְנֵיהֶם עֶשְׂרִים וְאַרְבַּע בְּרָכוֹת, שְׁמוֹנֶה עֶשְׂרֵה שֶׁבְּכָל יוֹם, וּמוֹסִיף עֲלֵיהֶן עוֹד שֵׁשׁ". הָנֵי שֵׁשׁ? שֶׁבַע הָוְיָין, כְּדִתְנַן: עַל הַשְּׁבִיעִית הוּא אוֹמֵר: בָּרוּךְ מְרַחֵם עַל הָאָרֶץ. אָמַר רַב נַחְמָן בַּר יִצְחָק: מַאי שְׁבִיעִית? שְׁבִיעִית לָאֲרוּכָּה,

§ The mishna teaches: **And** the prayer leader **recites twenty-four blessings before them:** The **eighteen** blessings **of** the **everyday** *Amida* prayer, **to which he adds another six** blessings. The Gemara asks: Are **these six** blessings? In fact, **they are seven, as we learned** in a mishna: **For the seventh he recites,** Blessed are You, Lord, **Who has mercy on the Land. Rav Naḥman bar Yitzḥak said: What** is the meaning of the **seventh** blessing? This is referring to the **seventh for length,** i.e., there were actually six new blessings, but as the prayer leader lengthens the sixth weekday blessing it is considered an additional blessing.

כִּדְתַנְיָא: בְּגוֹאֵל יִשְׂרָאֵל מַאֲרִיךְ, וּבְחוֹתְמָהּ הוּא אוֹמֵר: מִי שֶׁעָנָה אֶת אַבְרָהָם בְּהַר הַמּוֹרִיָּה, הוּא יַעֲנֶה אֶתְכֶם וְיִשְׁמַע בְּקוֹל צַעֲקַתְכֶם הַיּוֹם הַזֶּה. בָּרוּךְ גּוֹאֵל יִשְׂרָאֵל. וְהֵן עוֹנִין אַחֲרָיו אָמֵן. וְחַזַּן הַכְּנֶסֶת אוֹמֵר לָהֶם: תִּקְעוּ, בְּנֵי אַהֲרֹן, תְּקָעוּ.

As it is taught in a *baraita*: **In** the blessing of: **Redeemer of Israel,** the prayer leader **lengthens** the blessing, **and for its conclusion he recites: He Who answered Abraham on Mount Moriah, He will answer you and hear the sound of your cry on this day. Blessed** are You, Lord, **Redeemer of Israel. And** the community **answers amen after him. And the sexton says to them: Blow** a long, unwavering sound, **sons of Aaron, blow.**

וְחוֹזֵר וְאוֹמֵר: מִי שֶׁעָנָה אֶת אֲבוֹתֵינוּ עַל יַם סוּף, הוּא יַעֲנֶה אֶתְכֶם וְיִשְׁמַע בְּקוֹל צַעֲקַתְכֶם הַיּוֹם הַזֶּה. בָּרוּךְ זוֹכֵר הַנִּשְׁכָּחוֹת. וְהֵן עוֹנִין אַחֲרָיו אָמֵן. וְחַזַּן הַכְּנֶסֶת אוֹמֵר לָהֶם: הָרִיעוּ, בְּנֵי אַהֲרֹן, הָרִיעוּ. וְכֵן בְּכָל בְּרָכָה וּבְרָכָה, בְּאַחַת אוֹמֵר, תִּקְעוּ, וּבְאַחַת אוֹמֵר, הָרִיעוּ.

And the prayer leader **resumes and recites** the second blessing, concluding: **He Who answered our forefathers by the Red Sea, He will answer you and hear the sound of your cry on this day. Blessed** are You, Lord, **Who remembers the forgotten. And** the community **answers amen after him. And the sexton says to them: Blast** a wavering sound, **sons of Aaron, blast. And similarly,** this is the procedure **for each and every** additional **blessing: After one** blessing **he says: Blow** a long, unwavering sound, **and after** the next **one he says: Blast** a wavering sound.

NOTES

That his house is empty of transgression – שֶׁבֵּיתוֹ רֵיקָם מִן הָעֲבֵירָה: Rashi explains that the expression: One whose house is empty of transgression, means that his house must be free of stolen property and other ill-gotten gains. If his house is indeed empty of transgression and his youth was becoming, the prayer leader on a fast day is considered to be free of all sin, as the first qualification refers to sins against another, while the second concerns sins against God (*Gevurat Ari*). Others maintain that the term: One whose house is empty of transgression, means that his household must be entirely free of major transgression. Not only must the prayer leader himself be a righteous man, but his children and grandchildren and all his other relatives who are dependent on him must also be free of major sins (Rambam *Sefer Zemanim*, *Hilkhot Ta'anit* 4:4).

בַּמֶּה דְּבָרִים אֲמוּרִים? בִּגְבוּלִין. אֲבָל בַּמִּקְדָּשׁ אֵינוֹ כֵּן, לְפִי שֶׁאֵין עוֹנִין 'אָמֵן' בַּמִּקְדָּשׁ. וּמִנַּיִן שֶׁאֵין עוֹנִין 'אָמֵן' בַּמִּקְדָּשׁ?

The Gemara asks: **In what case is this statement said?** This method applies **in the outlying areas,** i.e., everywhere except in the Temple. **However, in the Temple** itself this **is not** the correct procedure,[HN] **as one does not answer amen in the Temple.** Instead, one responds with a long blessing. The Gemara inquires: **And from where** is it derived **that one does not answer amen in the Temple?**

שֶׁנֶּאֱמַר: "קוּמוּ בָּרְכוּ אֶת ה' אֱלֹהֵיכֶם מִן הָעוֹלָם עַד הָעוֹלָם, וִיבָרְכוּ שֵׁם כְּבֹדֶךָ, וּמְרוֹמַם עַל כָּל בְּרָכָה וּתְהִלָּה". יָכוֹל עַל כָּל בְּרָכוֹת כּוּלָּן לֹא תְּהֵא אֶלָּא תְּהִלָּה אַחַת. תַּלְמוּד לוֹמַר: "וּמְרוֹמַם עַל כָּל בְּרָכָה וּתְהִלָּה" עַל כָּל בְּרָכָה תֵּן לוֹ תְּהִלָּה.

The Gemara answers: **As it is stated: "Stand up and bless the Lord, your God, from everlasting to everlasting, and let them say: Blessed be Your glorious name, that is exalted above all blessing and praise"** (Nehemiah 9:5). One **might** have thought that **for all blessings there should be only one praise,** i.e., all blessings are answered with amen. Therefore, **the verse states: "That is exalted above all [*al kol*] blessing and praise,"** which indicates that **for every [*al kol*] blessing,** you should **give it** its own **praise.**

וְאֶלָּא בַּמִּקְדָּשׁ מַהוּ אוֹמֵר? בָּרוּךְ ה', אֱלֹהֵי יִשְׂרָאֵל, מִן הָעוֹלָם וְעַד הָעוֹלָם. בָּרוּךְ גּוֹאֵל יִשְׂרָאֵל. וְהֵן עוֹנִין אַחֲרָיו: בָּרוּךְ שֵׁם כְּבוֹד מַלְכוּתוֹ לְעוֹלָם וָעֶד. וְחַזַּן הַכְּנֶסֶת אוֹמֵר לָהֶם: תִּקְעוּ, הַכֹּהֲנִים, בְּנֵי אַהֲרֹן, תְּקָעוּ.

But if so, **in the Temple, what** would the prayer leader **recite?** He would conclude the blessing: **Blessed be the Lord, God of Israel, from everlasting to everlasting. Blessed** are You, Lord, **Redeemer of Israel. And** instead of amen, **they answer after him: Blessed be the name of His glorious kingdom forever and all time. And the sexton says to them: Blow, priests, sons of Aaron, blow.**

וְחוֹזֵר וְאוֹמֵר: מִי שֶׁעָנָה אֶת אַבְרָהָם בְּהַר הַמּוֹרִיָּה, הוּא יַעֲנֶה אֶתְכֶם וְיִשְׁמַע בְּקוֹל צַעֲקַתְכֶם הַיּוֹם הַזֶּה. בָּרוּךְ ה', אֱלֹהֵי יִשְׂרָאֵל, זוֹכֵר הַנִּשְׁכָּחוֹת. וְהֵם עוֹנִים אַחֲרָיו: בָּרוּךְ שֵׁם כְּבוֹד מַלְכוּתוֹ לְעוֹלָם וָעֶד. וְחַזַּן הַכְּנֶסֶת אוֹמֵר לָהֶם: הָרִיעוּ, הַכֹּהֲנִים, בְּנֵי אַהֲרֹן, הָרִיעוּ, וכו'. וְכֵן בְּכָל בְּרָכָה וּבְרָכָה, בְּאַחַת אוֹמֵר, תִּקְעוּ, וּבְאַחַת אוֹמֵר, הָרִיעוּ, עַד שֶׁגּוֹמֵר אֶת כּוּלָּן.

And the prayer leader **resumes and recites** the second blessing, concluding: **He Who answered Abraham on Mount Moriah, He will answer you and hear the sound of your cry on this day. Blessed be the Lord, God of Israel, Who remembers the forgotten. And** the community **answers after him: Blessed be the name of His glorious kingdom forever and all time. And the sexton says to them: Blast, priests, sons of Aaron, blast, etc. And similarly,** this is the procedure **for each and every** additional **blessing: After one** blessing **he says: Blow** a long, unwavering sound, **and after** the next **one he says: Blast**[H] a wavering sound, **until he concludes all** the blessings.

וְכָךְ הִנְהִיג רַבִּי חֲלַפְתָּא בְּצִפּוֹרִי וְרַבִּי חֲנַנְיָה בֶּן תְּרַדְיוֹן בְּסִיכְנִי. וּכְשֶׁבָּא דָּבָר לִפְנֵי חֲכָמִים, אָמְרוּ: לֹא הָיוּ נוֹהֲגִין כֵּן אֶלָּא בְּשַׁעֲרֵי מִזְרָח וּבְהַר הַבַּיִת.

§ The Gemara relates: **And this was the custom Rabbi Ḥalafta established in** the city of **Tzippori, and Rabbi Ḥananya ben Teradyon in** the city of **Sikhni. And when** this **matter came before the Sages, they said: They would act** in accordance with **this custom only**[N] **at the Eastern Gate** of the Temple **and on the Temple Mount,** but not outside the Temple.

HALAKHA

However, in the Temple this is not the correct procedure – אֲבָל בַּמִּקְדָּשׁ אֵינוֹ כֵּן: On a fast day service in Jerusalem, the people would congregate on the Temple Mount opposite the Eastern Gate. When the prayer leader reached the passage beginning: He Who answered Abraham, he would say: Blessed are You, Lord, our God, the God of Israel, from everlasting to everlasting. Blessed are You, Lord, Redeemer of Israel. And the congregation would answer after him: Blessed be the name of His glorious kingdom forever and all time (Rambam *Sefer Zemanim, Hilkhot Ta'anit* 4:15).

After one he says blow and after the next one he says blast – בְּאַחַת אוֹמֵר תִּקְעוּ וּבְאַחַת אוֹמֵר הָרִיעוּ: After the first special blessing on a communal fast the sexton announces: Blow a standard blast, a *tekia*, and after the next he says: Blow a *terua*. He alternates these instructions until all seven special blessings are completed (Rambam *Sefer Zemanim, Hilkhot Ta'anit* 4:17).

NOTES

However, in the Temple this is not the correct procedure – אֲבָל בַּמִּקְדָּשׁ אֵינוֹ כֵּן: Some commentaries explain the difference between the congregation's response in the Temple and elsewhere as follows: In the Temple, where the personal name of God is pronounced as it is written, the proper response to a blessing is: Blessed be the name of His glorious kingdom forever and all time. Conversely, in the areas outside of the Temple, where the name is not pronounced as it is written, those who hear a blessing answer amen (Ritva).

They would act in accordance with this custom only – לֹא הָיוּ נוֹהֲגִין כֵּן אֶלָּא: There is a wide range of opinions concerning the mistake committed by Rabbi Ḥalafta and Rabbi Ḥananya ben Teradyon. As explained (15b), Rashi maintains that these Sages instituted that even those assembled for a fast day service outside the Temple should not answer amen after the prayer leader but should say: Blessed be the name of His glorious kingdom forever and all time, as was the custom in the Temple. However, most early authorities reject this explanation. Some early commentaries explain that Rabbi Ḥalafta and Rabbi Ḥananya ben Teradyon adopted the practice of sounding a *shofar* together with the trumpets that are blown on fast days even outside the Temple. The Sages disapproved of this practice, as the two instruments were sounded together only in the Temple itself, whereas outside the Temple the trumpets alone are sounded (see Ritva, Rid, and *Rosh HaShana* 27a). According to others, only on the Temple Mount were the trumpets sounded after each of the seven blessings relating to the special nature of the fast day. In all other places the trumpets were sounded only at the end of the service, after all twenty-four blessings had already been recited (Ritva, citing *Tosafot*; Rambam *Sefer Zemanim, Hilkhot Ta'anit* 4:17). Support for this opinion can be found in the fact that the mishna does not say that the trumpets are sounded after each of the special blessings. Rabbi Ḥalafta and Rabbi Ḥananya ben Teradyon erred by instituting that trumpets must be sounded after each of the seven special blessings outside the Temple as well. The difficulty with this explanation is that the *baraita* here states explicitly that trumpets were sounded after each of the special blessings, even outside the Temple.

Many early commentaries explain that outside the Temple the fast day service was conducted as outlined in the mishna (Rabbeinu Gershom; Ra'avad; Ritva; Ran). The prayer leader recited the entreaty: He Who answered, as part of the concluding formula of each of the special blessings. The congregation answered each blessing with amen, after which the priests sounded the trumpets at the command of the sexton. By contrast, on the Temple Mount the prayer leader did not recite the phrase: He Who answered, etc., as part of the blessing. Instead, he completed the blessing, and the congregation answered: Blessed be the name of His glorious kingdom forever and all time. Next the sexton instructed the priests to sound the trumpets, at which point the prayer leader recited the entreaty that God should answer His people's cry as He did in biblical times, and finally the trumpets were sounded. Alternatively, the prayer leader included the entreaty in the blessing, but he repeated it after the congregation's response. This difference between practice in the Temple and elsewhere is due to the fact that the trumpet blasts are intended to recall the merits of our forefathers, and consequently, they should be sounded immediately after the prayer leader recites each of the entreaties that refer to those merits. The longer response of the congregation to the blessings recited in the Temple separates the entreaty from the sounding of the trumpets. Therefore, the prayer leader's entreaty must either be deferred until after the congregation has responded to the blessing, or it must be repeated, after which the trumpets are sounded immediately. This is not necessary outside the Temple, where the congregation answers with a simple amen. Rabbi Ḥalafta and Rabbi Ḥananya ben Teradyon erred by adopting the Temple practice in their own cities.

וְאִית דְּאָמְרִי כִּדְתַנְיָא: אוֹמֵר לִפְנֵיהֶן עֶשְׂרִים וְאַרְבַּע בְּרָכוֹת, שְׁמוֹנֶה עֶשְׂרֵה שֶׁבְּכָל יוֹם, וּמוֹסִיף עֲלֵיהֶן עוֹד שֵׁשׁ. וְאוֹתָן שֵׁשׁ הֵיכָן אוֹמְרָן? בֵּין גּוֹאֵל לְרוֹפֵא חוֹלֵי. וּמַאֲרִיךְ בִּגְאוּלָּה, וְהֵן עוֹנִין אַחֲרָיו אָמֵן עַל כָּל בְּרָכָה וּבְרָכָה. וְכָךְ הָיוּ נוֹהֲגִין בַּגְּבוּלִין.

And some say that they acted **as it is taught** in a *baraita*: **And he recites twenty-four blessings before them:** The **eighteen** blessings of the **everyday** *Amida* prayer, **to which he adds another six** blessings. **And those** extra **six, where does he recite them? Between** the blessings: **Redeemer** of Israel, **and: Healer of the sick. And he lengthens** the earlier prayer **of redemption,** and the congregation **answers amen after him, for each and every blessing. And this was the custom in the outlying areas,** outside the Temple.

אֲבָל בַּמִּקְדָּשׁ הָיוּ אוֹמְרִים: בָּרוּךְ ה׳, אֱלֹהֵי יִשְׂרָאֵל, מִן הָעוֹלָם וְעַד הָעוֹלָם. בָּרוּךְ גּוֹאֵל יִשְׂרָאֵל. וְלֹא הָיוּ עוֹנִין אַחֲרָיו אָמֵן. וְכָל כָּךְ לָמָּה? לְפִי שֶׁאֵין עוֹנִין אָמֵן בַּמִּקְדָּשׁ. וּמִנַּיִן שֶׁאֵין עוֹנִין אָמֵן בַּמִּקְדָּשׁ? שֶׁנֶּאֱמַר: ״קוּמוּ בָּרְכוּ אֶת ה׳ אֱלֹהֵיכֶם מִן הָעוֹלָם עַד הָעוֹלָם, וִיבָרְכוּ שֵׁם כְּבוֹדֶךָ, וּמְרוֹמַם עַל כָּל בְּרָכָה וּתְהִלָּה״ – עַל כָּל בְּרָכָה וּבְרָכָה תֵּן לוֹ תְּהִלָּה.

However, in the Temple they would recite: Blessed be the Lord, God of Israel, from everlasting to everlasting. Blessed are You, Lord, **Redeemer of Israel, and they would not answer amen after him. And why** did the practice differ so much? **Because one does not answer amen in the Temple. And from where** is it derived **that one does not answer amen in the Temple? As it is stated: "Stand up and bless the Lord, your God, from everlasting to everlasting, and let them say: Blessed be Your glorious Name, that is exalted above all blessing and praise"** (Nehemiah 9:5). As stated above, this verse indicates that **for every blessing,** you should **give it** its own **praise.**

תָּנוּ רַבָּנַן: עַל הָרִאשׁוֹנוֹת הוּא אוֹמֵר: בָּרוּךְ ה׳, אֱלֹהֵי יִשְׂרָאֵל, מִן הָעוֹלָם. וְעַד הָעוֹלָם בָּרוּךְ גּוֹאֵל יִשְׂרָאֵל. וְהֵן עוֹנִין אַחֲרָיו: בָּרוּךְ שֵׁם כְּבוֹד מַלְכוּתוֹ לְעוֹלָם וָעֶד. וְחַזַּן הַכְּנֶסֶת אוֹמֵר: תִּקְעוּ, כֹּהֲנִים, תִּקְעוּ. וְחוֹזֵר וְאוֹמֵר: מִי שֶׁעָנָה אֶת אַבְרָהָם בְּהַר הַמּוֹרִיָּה, הוּא יַעֲנֶה אֶתְכֶם וְיִשְׁמַע בְּקוֹל צַעֲקַתְכֶם הַיּוֹם הַזֶּה. וְהֵן תּוֹקְעִין, וּמְרִיעִין, וְתוֹקְעִין. וְעַל הַשְּׁנִיָּה הוּא אוֹמֵר: בָּרוּךְ ה׳, אֱלֹהֵי יִשְׂרָאֵל, מִן הָעוֹלָם וְעַד הָעוֹלָם. בָּרוּךְ זוֹכֵר הַנִּשְׁכָּחוֹת. וְהֵן עוֹנִין אַחֲרָיו: בָּרוּךְ שֵׁם כְּבוֹד מַלְכוּתוֹ לְעוֹלָם וָעֶד.

The Sages taught: In concluding **the first** blessing **he recites: Blessed be the Lord, God of Israel, from everlasting to everlasting. Blessed** are You, Lord, **Redeemer of Israel, and they would answer after him: Blessed be the name of His glorious kingdom forever and all time. And the sexton says: Blow, priests, blow. And he resumes** the blessings **and recites: He Who answered Abraham on Mount Moriah, He will answer you and hear the sound of your cry on this day. And they blow** a long, unwavering sound, **and blast** a wavering sound, **and blow.**[N] **And for the second** blessing **he recites: Blessed be the Lord, God of Israel, from everlasting to everlasting, who remembers the forgotten, and they would answer after him: Blessed be the name of His glorious kingdom forever and all time.**

וְחַזַּן הַכְּנֶסֶת אוֹמֵר: הָרִיעוּ, בְּנֵי אַהֲרֹן, הָרִיעוּ. וְאוֹמֵר: מִי שֶׁעָנָה אֶת אֲבוֹתֵינוּ עַל יַם סוּף, הוּא יַעֲנֶה אֶתְכֶם וְיִשְׁמַע בְּקוֹל צַעֲקַתְכֶם הַיּוֹם הַזֶּה. וְהֵם מְרִיעִין, וְתוֹקְעִין, וּמְרִיעִין. וְכֵן בְּכָל בְּרָכָה וּבְרָכָה, בְּאַחַת אוֹמֵר, תִּקְעוּ, וּבְאַחַת אוֹמֵר, הָרִיעוּ, עַד שֶׁיִּגְמוֹר אֶת הַבְּרָכוֹת כּוּלָּן. וְכָךְ הִנְהִיג רַבִּי חֲלַפְתָּא בְּצִיפּוֹרִי וְרַבִּי חֲנַנְיָה בֶּן תְּרַדְיוֹן בְּסִיכְנִי. וּכְשֶׁבָּא דָּבָר אֵצֶל חֲכָמִים, אָמְרוּ: לֹא הָיוּ נוֹהֲגִין כֵּן אֶלָּא בְּשַׁעֲרֵי מִזְרָח וּבְהַר הַבַּיִת.

And the sexton says: Blast, sons of Aaron, blast. And he recites: He Who answered our forefathers by the Red Sea, He will answer you and hear the sound of your cry on this day. And they blow, and blast, and blow. And similarly, for each and every blessing: After one he says: Blow, and after the next **one he says: Blast, until he concludes all of them. And this was the custom Rabbi Ḥalafta established in Tzippori, and Rabbi Ḥananya ben Teradyon in Sikhni. And when** this **matter came before the Sages, they said: They would act** in accordance with **this custom only at the Eastern Gate and on the Temple Mount.**

״רַבִּי יְהוּדָה אוֹמֵר: לֹא הָיָה צָרִיךְ לוֹמַר זִכְרוֹנוֹת״, כו׳. אָמַר רַבִּי אַדָּא דְּמִן יָפוֹ: מַאי טַעֲמָא דְּרַבִּי יְהוּדָה? לְפִי שֶׁאֵין אוֹמְרִים זִכְרוֹנוֹת וְשׁוֹפָרוֹת

§ The mishna taught: Rabbi Yehuda says: The prayer leader **did not need to recite** the **Remembrances** and *Shofarot* passages. Instead, he recited verses dealing with famine and suffering. **Rabbi Adda from Jaffa**[P] **said: What is Rabbi Yehuda's reason?** Rabbi Yehuda maintains **that one recites Remembrances and** ***Shofarot***

NOTES

And they blow and blast and blow – וְהֵן תּוֹקְעִין וּמְרִיעִין וְתוֹקְעִין: Some commentaries maintain that after the first blessing the priests blew an unwavering sound [*tekia*], followed by a wavering sound [*terua*], and then a *tekia*; after the second blessing they sounded a *terua*, a *tekia*, and another *terua*, alternating the order of the blasts after each blessing (Rambam *Sefer Zemanim*, *Hilkhot Ta'anit* 4:17). According to other versions of the text, cited by early commentaries, the blasts were sounded in the same order after each blessing, i.e., *tekia*, *terua*, *tekia*. Alternatively, one blessing was followed by a *tekia*, the next by a *terua*, and the following by a *tekia* (see Ritva).

PERSONALITIES

Rabbi Adda from Jaffa – רַבִּי אַדָּא דְּמִן יָפוֹ: An *amora* from Eretz Yisrael, this Sage is seldom mentioned in the Talmud. It is likely that he was from the third generation of *amora'im*. Jaffa is not known to have been an important Torah center, but Rabbi Adda's name shows that there were some Sages of note there. The sources indicate that he was the father of Rabbi Ḥiyya.

אֶלָּא בְּרֹאשׁ הַשָּׁנָה, וּבַיּוֹבְלוֹת, וּבִשְׁעַת מִלְחָמָה.

only on Rosh HaShana, and on Yom Kippur of **Jubilee Years, and in a time of war.**

״עַל הָרִאשׁוֹנָה הוּא אוֹמֵר: מִי שֶׁעָנָה אֶת אַבְרָהָם״, כו׳. תָּנָא: יֵשׁ מַחֲלִיפִין צְעָקָה לְאֵלִיָּהוּ וּתְפִלָּה לִשְׁמוּאֵל. בִּשְׁלָמָא גַּבֵּי שְׁמוּאֵל כְּתִיב בֵּיהּ תְּפִלָּה וּכְתִיב בֵּיהּ צְעָקָה,

§ The mishna teaches: **For the first** blessing **he recites: He Who answered Abraham.** It was **taught** in a *baraita*: **Some reverse** the order of the conclusion of two blessings, by reciting: Who hears **cries,** in the fifth blessing, which deals **with Elijah,** and the conclusion: Who hears **prayer,** in the blessing **of Samuel.** The Gemara asks: **Granted, with regard to Samuel** both options are appropriate, as **it is written concerning him: Prayer, and it is** likewise **written concerning him: Crying.** One verse states: "And Samuel said: Gather all of Israel to Mizpah, and I will pray for you to the Lord" (I Samuel 7:5), while another verse states: "And Samuel cried to the Lord for Israel" (I Samuel 7:9).

אֶלָּא גַּבֵּי אֵלִיָּהוּ תְּפִלָּה כְּתִיב, צְעָקָה לָא כְּתִיב! ״עֲנֵנִי, ה׳, עֲנֵנִי״ לְשׁוֹן צְעָקָה הִיא.

However, with regard to Elijah, although **prayer is written,** as it says: "Elijah the prophet came near and said: Lord, the God of Abraham, of Isaac, and of Israel" (I Kings 18:36), which is referring to a prayer, **crying is not written.** How, then, can one conclude a blessing that deals with Elijah by mentioning crying? The Gemara answers that Elijah's statement: **"Answer me, Lord, answer me"** (I Kings 18:37), **is an expression** of **crying,** even if the term crying does not itself actually appear.

״עַל הַשִּׁשִּׁית הוּא אוֹמֵר: מִי שֶׁעָנָה אֶת יוֹנָה״, כו׳. ״עַל הַשְּׁבִיעִית הוּא אוֹמֵר: מִי שֶׁעָנָה אֶת דָּוִד״, כו׳. מִכְּדֵי יוֹנָה בָּתַר דָּוִד וּשְׁלֹמֹה הֲוָה, מַאי טַעֲמָא מַקְדִּים לֵיהּ בְּרֵישָׁא? מִשּׁוּם דְּבָעֵי לְמֵיחְתַּם: מְרַחֵם עַל הָאָרֶץ. תָּנָא: מִשּׁוּם סוּמָכוֹס אָמְרוּ: בָּרוּךְ מַשְׁפִּיל הָרָמִים.

§ The mishna further teaches: **For the sixth he recites: He Who answered Jonah; for the seventh he recites: He Who answered David.** The Gemara asks: **Since Jonah was after David**[N] **and Solomon, what is the reason** that the *tanna* **mentions** Jonah **first?** The Gemara answers: The reason is **due to** the fact **that he wants to conclude** the series with: Blessed are You, Lord, **Who has mercy on the Land.** Therefore, the last blessing mentions David and Solomon, who were kings of Eretz Yisrael and prayed on its behalf. It was **taught in the name of Sumakhos**[L] that **they said** he concludes the final blessing with: **Blessed** are You, Lord, **Who humbles the exalted.**[N]

״שָׁלֹשׁ תַּעֲנִיּוֹת הָרִאשׁוֹנוֹת, אַנְשֵׁי מִשְׁמָר מִתְעַנִּין וְלֹא מַשְׁלִימִין״ כו׳. תָּנוּ רַבָּנַן: מִפְּנֵי מָה אָמְרוּ אַנְשֵׁי מִשְׁמָר מוּתָּרִין לִשְׁתּוֹת יַיִן בַּלֵּילוֹת, אֲבָל לֹא בַּיָּמִים? שֶׁמָּא תִּכְבַּד הָעֲבוֹדָה עַל אַנְשֵׁי בֵּית אָב, וְיָבוֹאוּ וִיסַיְּיעוּ לָהֶם.

§ The mishna teaches that on **the first three fasts, the members of the priestly watch fast but do not complete** their fasts until nightfall. The mishna then proceeds to cite other *halakhot* that deal with the members of the priestly watch and the patrilineal family. **The Sages taught: For what** reason **did they say** that **the members of the priestly watch are permitted to drink wine at nights but not during the days?**[H] They said this **lest** on a certain day the Temple **service becomes burdensome for the members of the patrilineal family, and** the members of the priestly watch are called to **come and assist them.** Therefore, it is prohibited for them to drink wine during the day, when their help might be needed, so that they do not enter the Temple after drinking wine.

LANGUAGE

Sumakhos – סוּמָכוֹס: From the Greek σύμμαχος, *sumakhos*, meaning an ally.

HALAKHA

At nights but not during the days – בַּלֵּילוֹת אֲבָל לֹא בַּיָּמִים: It is permitted for the members of the priestly watch whose week it is to serve in the Temple to drink wine at night, but not during the day. It is prohibited for the members of the patrilineal family who are responsible for the Temple service that day to drink wine both during the day and during the night (Rambam *Sefer Avoda, Hilkhot Biat HaMikdash* 1:6).

NOTES

Since Jonah was after David – מִכְּדֵי יוֹנָה בָּתַר דָּוִד: The Gemara could equally have asked why Elijah is mentioned before David and Solomon, as he too preceded them (see Maharsha). In the Jerusalem Talmud this question is indeed raised with regard to Elijah, and a similar answer is given as to the inquiry concerning Jonah.

Blessed are You, Lord, Who humbles the exalted – בָּרוּךְ מַשְׁפִּיל הָרָמִים: The early authorities discuss the connection between this concluding formula and David and Solomon. Some commentaries explain that both David and Solomon grew overly proud (Ritva, citing Jerusalem Talmud). David's pride led him to conduct a census of the nation against the advice of his counselor (II Samuel 24:2–4), and Solomon glorified in his achievement of building the Temple (I Kings 8:13). Both of them were subsequently humbled by God, after which they repented and their prayers were answered. This blessing expresses the hope that just as the repentance of David and Solomon was accepted by God, so will the repentance of those who are fasting be accepted, and the calamity threatening the community will be averted.

Others explain this concluding formula in a very different manner. During the reigns of David and Solomon the elevated were humbled, i.e., the nations of the world became subjugated to the Jewish people. Therefore, the series of special blessings recited on account of drought concludes with a general expression of praise to God (*Shita Mekubbetzet*). A variant reading, cited by several early authorities, states: Blessed are You, Lord, Who humbles and exalts.

מפני מה אמרו אנשי בית אב לא ביום ולא בלילה? מפני שהן עסוקין תמיד בעבודה.

The *baraita* continues to explain the reason for the mishna's ruling. **For what** reason **did they say that the members of the patrilineal family** may not drink wine, **neither by day nor by night?**[N] **Because they are constantly engaged in** the Temple **service.**

מכאן אמרו: כל כהן שמכיר משמרתו ומשמרת בית אב שלו, ויודע שבתי אבותיו קבועין שם, אסור לשתות יין כל אותו היום. במכיר משמרתו ואין מכיר משמרת בית אב שלו, ויודע שבתי אבותיו קבועין שם, אסור לשתות יין כל אותה שבת.

From here the Sages **stated:** Even nowadays, after the destruction of the Temple, with regard to **any priest who knows his priestly watch,**[N] in which his family served, **and the watch of his patrilineal family, and he knows that the family of his forefathers was established** as fit for the Temple service **there,**[N] it is **prohibited** for him **to drink wine that entire day,** in the event that the Temple is rebuilt on that day and he will be called to return to the service. In the case of a priest **who knows his priestly watch,** i.e., the week of the year in which his family served, **and does not know the watch of his patrilineal family,** the day of the week that his family served, **but he knows that the family of his forefathers was established there,** it is **prohibited** for him **to drink wine that entire week.**

אינו מכיר משמרתו ומשמרת בית אב שלו, ויודע שבתי אבותיו קבועין שם, אסור לשתות יין כל השנה.

Finally, if he does not know **his priestly watch or the watch of his patrilineal family, but he knows that the family of his forefathers was established there,** he is **prohibited to drink wine that entire year.** When the Temple will be rebuilt, his priestly watch might be called upon to serve, and he is unaware of the appointed time for his Temple service.

רבי אומר: אומר אני: אסור לשתות יין לעולם. אבל מה אעשה? שתקנתו קלקלתו? אמר אביי: כמאן שתו האידנא כהני חמרא? כרבי.

Rabbi Yehuda HaNasi **says: I say** that in accordance with this reasoning it is **prohibited** for any priest **to drink wine at any time,** even if he knows his priestly watch, as the order of the watches might change when the Temple is rebuilt, or perhaps all the watches will participate in the rededication of Temple. **However, what can I do, as his misfortune is his advantage?**[N] The unfortunate fact that so many years have passed since the destruction of the Temple means that this decree prohibiting the priests from drinking cannot be sustained. **Abaye said: In accordance with whose** opinion **do priests drink wine nowadays?**[H] It is **in accordance with** the opinion of **Rabbi** Yehuda HaNasi.

״אנשי משמר ואנשי מעמד אסורים לספר ולכבס. ובחמישי מותרין מפני כבוד השבת״. מאי טעמא? אמר רבה בר בר חנה אמר רבי יוחנן: כדי שלא יכנסו למשמרתם כשהן מנוולין.

§ The mishna teaches: It is **prohibited** for both **the members of the priestly watch and the members of the non-priestly watch to cut their hair or launder** their garments throughout the week, **but on Thursday they are permitted**[H] to cut their hair and launder their clothes **in deference to Shabbat.** The Gemara asks: **What is the reason** for these prohibitions? **Rabba bar bar Ḥana said** that **Rabbi Yoḥanan said:** These prohibitions were enacted **in order to** ensure that the priests will cut their hair and launder their clothes during the week before their service, **so that they will not enter their priestly watch when they are unkempt.**[N]

NOTES

The members of the patrilineal family neither by day nor by night – אנשי בית אב לא ביום ולא בלילה: Most early authorities explain that it is prohibited for the members of the patrilineal family whose turn it is to serve in the Temple to drink wine, not only during the day but also at night, as certain tasks, e.g., the burning of fats and limbs, are carried out at night as well as by day.

Others explain that they may not drink wine at night, lest they rise early in the morning and begin to serve in the Temple before they are entirely sober, thereby violating the prohibition against performing the Temple service in a state of intoxication (Rambam *Sefer Avoda*, *Hilkhot Biat HaMikdash* 1:6).

It has been noted that there is a practical difference between these two explanations: According to the Rambam, it is prohibited for the members of a patrilineal family to drink wine on the night prior to their service in the Temple, whereas according to the other early commentaries they may not drink wine on the night following the day on which they perform their service (*Ḥasdei David*).

Any priest who knows his priestly watch – כל כהן שמכיר משמרתו: Rashi and many other early commentaries maintain that the *baraita* is referring to the period after the destruction of the Temple. Although the Temple is no longer standing, those priests who know that they belong to a certain watch or a patrilineal family are required to abstain from wine at certain times, so that they will be ready to serve if the Temple is suddenly rebuilt. Others indicate that the *baraita* is dealing with the period when the Temple was still standing. During that time, even if a priest was abroad or could not serve in the Temple for some other reason, he was required to abstain from wine during the day or week of the service of his watch or patrilineal family (Rambam *Sefer Avoda*, *Hilkhot Biat HaMikdash* 1:7; see *Gevurat Ari* and *Sefat Emet*).

That the family of his forefathers was established there – שבתי אבותיו קבועין שם: That is, the priest knows that his family was fit to serve in the Temple, as they were never disqualified from participating in the Temple service on account of the personal status of one of the family's ancestors (Rashi).

Some early commentaries explain that there were priests who were not assigned to a particular watch and consequently did not have a set time to serve in the Temple. Rather, they would come to the Temple whenever they wished, and they would assist the members of the watch on duty at the time. According to this interpretation, the expression: He knows that the family of his forefathers was established there, means that he is aware that his family had been attached to a particular priestly watch that had a fixed time to serve in the Temple (see Ramban on *Sefer HaMitzvot*, positive mitzva 36; Ritva).

As his misfortune is his advantage – שתקנתו קלקלתו: Several interpretations have been offered for this expression. Some explain that the fact that the Temple has been destroyed works to the advantage of the priests, as there is no reason to require them to abstain from wine when there is no Temple and no service (*ge'onim*). Rashi and others suggest a slight variation of this interpretation, according to which the misfortune refers to the future, not the present: The fact that the Temple has lain in its ruined state for such a long time benefits the priests, as it is apparently unlikely that it will be rebuilt in the immediate future. Therefore, the restrictions against drinking wine that were once imposed on the priests have been suspended.

Others explain that Rabbi Yehuda HaNasi's comment applies only in the case of a priest who does not know to which priestly watch and patrilineal family he belongs. This priest is permitted to drink wine whenever he wants, as he cannot serve in the Temple until his watch and patrilineal family have been determined. Consequently, the priest's misfortune, i.e., his ignorance, is to his advantage (Rambam *Sefer Avoda*, *Hilkhot Biat HaMikdash* 1:7).

Yet others state an entirely different explanation: It should be prohibited permanently for all priests to drink wine, but this enactment would lead to their downfall, as they would not be able to observe the prohibition. It is therefore preferable to permit them to drink wine, so that they not willfully violate a prohibition (*Mikhtam*; *Kaftor VaFeraḥ*).

That they will not enter their priestly watch when they are unkempt – שלא יכנסו למשמרתם כשהן מנוולין: Some commentaries ask: Since priests are required to cut their hair at least once every thirty days, as stated in the Gemara below, in any case the hair of the priests entering their watch will not be overly long (Ra'avad). Nevertheless, if a priest enters his watch without first trimming his hair, his hair will be somewhat long, even if he has cut it within the last thirty days (Rosh).

HALAKHA

In accordance with whose opinion do priests drink wine nowadays – כמאן שתו האידנא כהני חמרא: If a priest knows the identity of his priestly watch and patrilineal family, and he also knows that his family was established as fit to serve in the Temple, it is prohibited for him to drink wine throughout the day on which his patrilineal family used to serve. If he knows his watch but does not know his patrilineal family, it is prohibited for him to drink wine throughout the week in which his watch served in the Temple. If the priest is unaware of either his priestly watch or his patrilineal family, by right he should be permanently barred from drinking wine. However, his ignorance works to his advantage and he is permitted to drink wine, as he will not be able to serve in the Temple, even when it is rebuilt, until his priestly watch and patrilineal family are established (Rambam *Sefer Avoda*, *Hilkhot Biat HaMikdash* 1:7).

But on Thursday they are permitted – ובחמישי מותרין: It is prohibited for the members of the priestly watch and the patrilineal family on duty in the Temple to cut their hair or launder their clothes during the period of their service, so that they not enter their watch with untrimmed hair or dirty clothing (Rambam *Sefer Avoda*, *Hilkhot Biat HaMikdash* 1:12).

תָּנוּ רַבָּנַן: מֶלֶךְ מִסְתַּפֵּר בְּכָל יוֹם, כֹּהֵן גָּדוֹל מֵעֶרֶב שַׁבָּת לְעֶרֶב שַׁבָּת, כֹּהֵן הֶדְיוֹט אַחַת לִשְׁלֹשִׁים יוֹם. מֶלֶךְ מִסְתַּפֵּר בְּכָל יוֹם. מַאי טַעְמָא? אָמַר רַבִּי אַבָּא בַּר זַבְדָּא: אָמַר קְרָא: ״מֶלֶךְ בְּיָפְיוֹ תֶּחֱזֶינָה עֵינֶיךָ״. כֹּהֵן גָּדוֹל מֵעֶרֶב שַׁבָּת לְעֶרֶב שַׁבָּת. מַאי טַעְמָא? אָמַר רַב שְׁמוּאֵל בַּר יִצְחָק: הוֹאִיל וּמִשְׁמָרוֹת מִתְחַדְּשׁוֹת.

The Sages taught: A king cuts his hair every day,[H] **a High Priest** cuts his hair **every Friday,**[H] and **a common priest once every thirty days.** The Gemara clarifies: **A king cuts his hair every day. What is the reason** for this? **Rabbi Abba bar Zavda said** that **the verse states: "Your eyes shall see the king in his beauty"** (Isaiah 33:17), which indicates that a king must always look his best. **A High Priest cuts his hair every Friday.** The Gemara asks: **What is the reason** for this? **Rav Shmuel bar Yitzḥak**[P] **said: Since the watches are renewed** and changed every Friday, it is fitting for every watch to see the High Priest with his hair perfectly groomed.

״כֹּהֵן הֶדְיוֹט אַחַת לִשְׁלֹשִׁים יוֹם״. מְנָלַן? אָתְיָא ״פֶּרַע״ ״פֶּרַע״ מִנָּזִיר. כְּתִיב הָכָא: ״וְרֹאשָׁם לֹא יְגַלֵּחוּ, וּפֶרַע לֹא יְשַׁלֵּחוּ״, וּכְתִיב הָתָם: ״קָדֹשׁ יִהְיֶה, גַּדֵּל פֶּרַע שְׂעַר רֹאשׁוֹ״. מַה לְּהַלָּן שְׁלֹשִׁים, אַף כָּאן שְׁלֹשִׁים.

§ **A common priest** cuts his hair **once every thirty days.**[H] The Gemara asks: **From where do we** derive this number? It is **derived** by a verbal analogy from the word ***pera*** with regard to priests and ***pera*** in connection **with a nazirite. It is written here,** concerning priests: **"Neither shall they shave their heads, nor suffer their locks [*pera*] to grow long"** (Ezekiel 44:20), **and it is written there,** with regard to a nazirite: **"He shall be sacred, he shall let the locks [*pera*] of the hair of his head grow long"** (Numbers 6:5). **Just as there,** a nazirite who does not specify any other time period cuts his hair after **thirty** days, **so too here,** a priest cuts his hair every **thirty** days.

וְנָזִיר גּוּפֵיהּ מְנָלַן? אָמַר רַב מַתָּנָה: סְתַם נְזִירוּת שְׁלֹשִׁים יוֹם. מְנָלַן? אָמַר קְרָא: ״יִהְיֶה״, בְּגִימַטְרִיָּא תְּלָתִין הָוֵי. אֲמַר לֵיהּ רַב פַּפָּא לְאַבָּיֵי: וְדִלְמָא הָכִי קָאָמַר רַחֲמָנָא: לָא לִירַבּוּ כְּלָל! אֲמַר לֵיהּ: אִי הֲוָה כָּתַב: ״לֹא יְשַׁלְּחוּ פֶּרַע״, כִּדְקָאָמְרַתְּ. הָשְׁתָּא דִּכְתִיב: ״וּפֶרַע לֹא יְשַׁלֵּחוּ״, פֶּרַע לֶיהֱוֵי, שְׁלוּחֵי הוּא דְּלָא לִישַׁלְּחוּ.

The Gemara asks: **And a nazirite himself, from where do we** derive that he may not cut his hair for thirty days? **Rav Mattana**[P] **said:** It is a principle that **an unspecified naziriteship**[H] lasts **thirty days.** The Gemara inquires: **From where do we** derive this principle? The Gemara answers that **the verse states: "He shall be [*yihye*]** sacred" (Numbers 6:5), and **the numerical value [*gimatriya*]**[L] **of *yihye* is thirty. Rav Pappa said to Abaye: But perhaps this is what the Merciful One is saying** in the Torah: They should **not grow** their hair **at all,** as they must cut it every day. Abaye **said to him: If it were written: They shall not grow long their locks,** I might have explained **as you** originally **said. Now that it is written: "Nor suffer their locks to grow long,"** this indicates that they may have locks, but they may not let them grow long.

אִי הָכִי, אֲפִילּוּ הָאִידָּנָא נַמִי! דּוּמְיָא דִּשְׁתוּיֵי יַיִן. מַה שְּׁתוּיֵי יַיִן, בִּזְמַן בִּיאָה הוּא דְּאָסוּר, שֶׁלֹּא בִּזְמַן בִּיאָה שָׁרֵי, אַף הָכָא נַמִי.

The Gemara asks: **If** it is **so** that cutting one's hair is a necessary preparation for the Temple service by Torah law, then **even nowadays** priests should cut their hair every thirty days **as well,** in case the Temple is rebuilt and they must resume their service. The Gemara answers: This issue is **similar** to the prohibition **concerning those who have drunk wine. Just as** with regard to **those who have drunk wine,** it is **when** one **enters** the Temple **that it is prohibited,**[H] whereas **when** one **does not enter** the Temple it is **permitted** to drink wine, **here** the same **also** applies.

וְהָתַנְיָא: רַבִּי אוֹמֵר: אוֹמֵר אֲנִי: כֹּהֲנִים אֲסוּרִים לִשְׁתּוֹת יַיִן לְעוֹלָם. אֲבָל מָה אֶעֱשֶׂה? שֶׁתַּקָּנָתוֹ קַלְקָלָתוֹ. וְאָמַר אַבָּיֵי: כְּמַאן שָׁתוּ הָאִידָּנָא כַּהֲנֵי חַמְרָא

The Gemara questions this conclusion: **But isn't it taught** in the aforementioned *baraita* that **Rabbi** Yehuda HaNasi **says: I say** that it is **prohibited** for all **priests to drink wine at any time. However, what can I do, as his misfortune is his advantage? And Abaye said: In accordance with whose** opinion do **priests drink wine nowadays?**

HALAKHA

A king cuts his hair every day – **מֶלֶךְ מִסְתַּפֵּר בְּכָל יוֹם:** A king must cut his hair and groom himself every day. Furthermore, he must dress in appropriate and splendid garments, in accordance with the verse (Isaiah 33:17) "Your eyes shall see the king in his beauty" (Rambam *Sefer Shofetim, Hilkhot Melakhim UMilḥemoteihem* 2:5).

A High Priest cuts his hair every Friday – **כֹּהֵן גָּדוֹל מֵעֶרֶב שַׁבָּת לְעֶרֶב שַׁבָּת:** A High Priest must never let his hair grow long, even if he does not enter the Temple. Rather, he must cut his hair at least once a week, on Fridays (Rambam *Sefer Avoda, Hilkhot Kelei HaMikdash* 5:6).

A common priest once every thirty days – **כֹּהֵן הֶדְיוֹט אַחַת לִשְׁלֹשִׁים יוֹם:** A common priest who serves in the Temple must cut his hair at least once every thirty days (Rambam *Sefer Avoda, Hilkhot Biat HaMikdash* 1:11).

An unspecified naziriteship – **סְתַם נְזִירוּת:** If one vows to be a nazirite without specifying a time limit, he is a nazirite for a period of thirty days (Rambam *Sefer Hafla'a, Hilkhot Nezirut* 3:1).

It is when one enters that it is prohibited – **בִּזְמַן בִּיאָה הוּא דְּאָסוּר:** Just as it is prohibited for a priest to drink wine only when he enters the Temple, it is likewise prohibited for him to let his hair grow long only when he enters the Temple. Some authorities claim that a priest may not let his hair grow long even when he does not actually enter the Temple. It is only when there is no Temple that he is permitted to let his hair grow long (Ra'avad; Rambam *Sefer Avoda, Hilkhot Biat HaMikdash* 1:10).

LANGUAGE

Numerical value [*gimatriya*] – **גִּימַטְרִיָּא:** From the Greek γεωμετρία, *geometria*, which means measurement or calculation in general, although it later came to refer to a specific type of calculation. In rabbinic literature, it also refers broadly to mathematical calculations, and specifically for tabulating the numerical value of the letters.

PERSONALITIES

Rav Shmuel bar Yitzḥak – **רַב שְׁמוּאֵל בַּר יִצְחָק:** A Babylonian *amora* of the third generation, Rav Shmuel bar Yitzḥak was one of Rav's younger students. He later became a disciple of Rav Huna. Like many of Rav Huna's students, he immigrated to Eretz Yisrael, apparently when he was middle-aged. Although no statements of his in the name of Rabbi Yoḥanan are recorded, he is presented as engaged in discussion with Rabbi Yoḥanan's students, some of whom quote him. Rav Shmuel bar Yitzḥak's aggadic and halakhic statements are found both in the Babylonian Talmud and in the Jerusalem Talmud. While it is unknown what he did for a living, it is known that his daughter married Rabbi Hoshaya. Rav Shmuel bar Yitzḥak conducted himself with humility and deferred to those younger than himself. He used to dance before brides to delight them, as stated in tractate *Ketubot* in the Babylonian Talmud (17a), and in tractate *Pe'a* in the Jerusalem Talmud.

Rav Mattana – **רַב מַתָּנָה:** A second-generation Babylonian *amora*, Rav Mattana studied with first-generation *amora'im* in Babylonia. His name is possibly a shortened form of the biblical name Matanya. He was a disciple of Shmuel, although he also transmitted statements in the name of Rav. Rav Mattana's colleague, Rav Yehuda, was also a disciple of Rav and Shmuel. Many third-generation *amora'im* were Rav Mattana's pupils, and they transmitted statements in his name. Rav Mattana lived in Paphunya, near Pumbedita. He was the rabbi of that town and may also have headed a small academy there. According to a tradition of the *ge'onim*, Rav Mattana was the son of the great *amora* Rabbi Yoḥanan of Eretz Yisrael, who had ten sons that died during his lifetime. He was sent by his father to Babylonia to study with Shmuel.

NOTES

From the fact that the Rabbis prohibit – מִכְּלָל דְּרַבָּנַן אָסְרִי: Some commentaries point out that Abaye himself did not act in accordance with the opinion of Rabbi Yehuda HaNasi, as he was a priest from the house of Eli. It is related that Rava told Abaye's widow that Abaye would never drink wine (*Ketubot* 65a). When Abaye asked how the priests of his day could drink wine, he was simply referring to the prevalent custom, which he himself did not follow (Rabbeinu Ḥananel).

May the Temple be speedily rebuilt – מְהֵרָה יִבָּנֶה בֵּית הַמִּקְדָּשׁ: Some early commentaries claim that one of the reasons that priests act in accordance with the opinion of Rabbi Yehuda HaNasi nowadays, in contradiction to the majority opinion of the Rabbis, is that the decree is based on a very far-fetched concern. Even if the Temple were speedily to be rebuilt, the priestly watches might be completely reorganized, or the entire priesthood might serve together at the rededication ceremonies. Consequently, there is no reason why it should be prohibited for a particular priest to drink wine on a certain day on account of the watch of his ancestors during the Second Temple period (see Meiri).

כְּרַבִּי. מִכְּלָל דְּרַבָּנַן אָסְרִי. מַאי טַעְמָא? מְהֵרָה יִבָּנֶה בֵּית הַמִּקְדָּשׁ, וּבָעֵינַן כֹּהֵן הָרָאוּי לַעֲבוֹדָה, וְלֵיכָּא. הָכָא, אֶפְשָׁר דִּמְסַפֵּר וְעָיֵיל.

It is **in accordance with** the opinion of **Rabbi** Yehuda HaNasi. **From the fact** that Rabbi Yehuda HaNasi permits priests to drink wine, it may be inferred **that the Rabbis prohibit**[N] it even nowadays. Why, then, isn't it prohibited for priests to grow their hair as well? The Gemara explains: **What is the reason** for the prohibition? It is due to the hope: **May the Temple be speedily rebuilt,**[N] **and we will require a priest who is fit for** the Temple **service, and** there will be **none** available, as they have all imbibed wine. The time that it will take for the effects of the wine to wear off will delay the Temple service considerably. **Here,** however, with regard to hair, it is **possible** for a priest **to cut his hair** and be ready **to enter** and perform the Temple service with minimal delay.

אִי הָכִי, שְׁתוּי יַיִן נַמִי, אֶפְשָׁר דְּגָנֵי פּוּרְתָּא וְעָיֵיל, כִּדְרָמֵי בַּר אַבָּא. דְּאָמַר רָמֵי בַּר אַבָּא: דֶּרֶךְ מִיל וְשֵׁינָה כׇּל שֶׁהוּא מְפִיגִין אֶת הַיַּיִן. לָאו מִי אִיתְּמַר עֲלַהּ: אָמַר רַב נַחְמָן אָמַר רַבָּה בַּר אֲבוּהּ: לֹא שָׁנוּ אֶלָּא בְּשֶׁשָּׁתָה שִׁיעוּר רְבִיעִית? אֲבָל שָׁתָה יוֹתֵר מֵרְבִיעִית כׇּל שֶׁכֵּן שֶׁדֶּרֶךְ מַטְרִידַתּוֹ וְשֵׁינָה מְשַׁכַּרְתּוֹ.

The Gemara asks: **If so,** with regard to **those who have drunk wine too,** it is **possible** for him **to sleep a little and** then **enter, in accordance with** the opinion of **Rami bar Abba, as Rami bar Abba said:** Walking **a distance of a** *mil*, **and** similarly, **sleeping** even **a minimal amount,**[H] will **dispel the** effect of **wine** that one has drunk. The Gemara rejects this proof: **Wasn't it stated about this** *halakha* that **Rav Naḥman said** that **Rabba bar Avuh said: They taught** this **only** with regard to one **who has drunk the measure of a quarter-***log* of wine, **but** with regard to **one who has drunk more than a quarter-***log*, walking this distance **will preoccupy** and exhaust **him all the more, and** a small amount **of sleep will** further **intoxicate him.** For this reason, it is prohibited for priests to drink wine, lest no suitable priest will be ready for the Temple service.

רַב אַשִׁי אָמַר: שְׁתוּיֵי יַיִן דִּמְחַלֵּי עֲבוֹדָה, גְּזַרוּ בְּהוּ רַבָּנַן. פְּרוּעֵי רֹאשׁ דְּלָא מְחַלֵּי עֲבוֹדָה, לָא גְּזַרוּ בְּהוּ רַבָּנַן.

Rav Ashi said that there is a different way to distinguish between these two *halakhot*. In the case of **those who have drunk wine,**[H] **who desecrate** the Temple **service, the Sages issued a decree concerning them,** that priests should not drink wine even nowadays. However, with regard to **those who have long hair,**[H] **who do not desecrate** the Temple **service, the Sages did not issue a decree concerning them.**

מֵיתִיבִי: וְאֵלּוּ שֶׁהֵן בְּמִיתָה: שְׁתוּיֵי יַיִן, וּפְרוּעֵי רֹאשׁ. בִּשְׁלָמָא שְׁתוּיֵי יַיִן בְּהֶדְיָא כְּתִיב בְּהוּ: ״יַיִן וְשֵׁכָר אַל תֵּשְׁתְּ״. אֶלָּא פְּרוּעֵי רֹאשׁ מְנָלַן?

The Gemara **raises an objection** from a *baraita*: **And these** are the transgressors who are punished **by death** at the hand of Heaven: Priests who enter the Temple to serve **who have drunk wine, and those** priests **who have long hair** while they serve. The Gemara asks: **Granted, those who have drunk wine** are punished by death, as it is **explicitly written: "Drink no wine nor strong drink,** neither you nor your sons with you, when you enter the Tent of Meeting, that you should not die" (Leviticus 10:9). **However,** with regard to **those** priests **who have long hair, from where do we** derive that they are punishable by death?

דִּכְתִיב: ״וְרֹאשָׁם לֹא יְגַלֵּחוּ, וּפֶרַע לֹא יְשַׁלֵּחוּ״. וּכְתִיב בָּתְרֵיהּ: ״וְיַיִן לֹא יִשְׁתּוּ כׇּל כֹּהֵן, בְּבוֹאָם אֶל הֶחָצֵר הַפְּנִימִית״. וְאִיתְקוּשׁ פְּרוּעֵי רֹאשׁ לִשְׁתוּיֵי יַיִן: מָה שְׁתוּיֵי יַיִן בְּמִיתָה, אַף פְּרוּעֵי רֹאשׁ בְּמִיתָה.

The Gemara answers that this is **as it is written: "Neither shall they shave their heads, nor suffer their locks [*pera*] to grow long"** (Ezekiel 44:20), **and it is written** immediately **afterward: "Neither shall any priest drink wine when they enter the inner courtyard"** (Ezekiel 44:21). **And** in this manner the prohibition concerning **those who have long hair is juxtaposed with** the prohibition concerning **those who have drunk wine,** to teach the following: **Just as those who have drunk wine** and perform the Temple service are subject **to death, so too, those who have long hair** are punishable **by death.**

HALAKHA

Walking a distance of a *mil* and sleeping a minimal amount – דֶּרֶךְ מִיל וְשֵׁינָה כׇּל שֶׁהוּא: A walk of a *mil* or a minimal amount of sleep dissipates the intoxicating effects of wine, provided that only a quarter-*log* or less has been consumed. However, if one has drunk more than a quarter-*log* of wine, sleep merely renders him more intoxicated, and walking makes him more unsteady (*Shulḥan Arukh*, *Oraḥ Ḥayyim* 99:2).

Those who have drunk wine – שְׁתוּיֵי יַיִן: If a priest who is fit for service in the Temple has drunk wine, he is prohibited to go beyond the altar in the Temple courtyard. If he enters and performs the Temple service, his service is disqualified and he is subject to death at the hand of Heaven (Rambam *Sefer Avoda*, *Hilkhot Biat HaMikdash* 1:1).

Those who have long hair – פְּרוּעֵי רֹאשׁ: If a priest has let his hair grow long, it is prohibited for him to go beyond the altar in the Temple courtyard. If he enters and serves, he is subject to death at the hand of Heaven, but his service is not disqualified (Rambam *Sefer Avoda*, *Hilkhot Biat HaMikdash* 1:8–9).

וּמִינָּהּ, אִי מַה שְּׁתוּיֵי יַיִן דִּמְחַלְּלֵי עֲבוֹדָה, אַף פְּרוּעֵי רֹאשׁ דִּמְחַלְּלֵי עֲבוֹדָה! לָא. כִּי אִיתְקוּשׁ, לְמִיתָה הוּא דְּאִתְקוּשׁ. אֲבָל לְאַחוּלֵי עֲבוֹדָה, לָא אִתְקוּשׁ.

The Gemara raises a difficulty: **And from this** comparison one can also argue as follows: If so, **just as those who have drunk wine desecrate** the Temple **service, so too, those who have long hair desecrate the service.** The Gemara rejects this contention: **No, when** the two cases **were juxtaposed,**[N] it was with regard **to death that** they **were juxtaposed. However,** as for **desecrating** the Temple **service,** in this regard they **were not juxtaposed.** Consequently, Rav Ashi's distinction concerning the practical application of these two *halakhot* still applies.

אֲמַר לֵיהּ רָבִינָא לְרַב אַשִׁי: הָא מִקַּמֵּי דַּאֲתָא יְחֶזְקֵאל, מַאן אֲמָרָהּ? אֲמַר לֵיהּ: וּלְטַעְמִיךְ, הָא דְּאָמַר רַב חִסְדָּא: דָּבָר זֶה מִתּוֹרַת מֹשֶׁה לֹא לָמַדְנוּ, וּמִדִּבְרֵי קַבָּלָה לָמַדְנוּ: ״כָּל בֶּן נֵכָר, עֶרֶל לֵב, וְעֶרֶל בָּשָׂר, לֹא יָבוֹא אֶל מִקְדָּשִׁי״. הָא מִקַּמֵּי דַּאֲתָא יְחֶזְקֵאל, מַאן אֲמָרָהּ?

On this issue, **Ravina said to Rav Ashi: Before Ezekiel came** and stated this *halakha*, **who said it?** From where was it derived before Ezekiel that priests may not serve with long hair? This prohibition, which is not mentioned in the Torah, could not have been innovated by Ezekiel, as prophets may not enact new *halakhot*. Rav Ashi **said to him: And according to your reasoning,** there is a similar difficulty with **that which Rabbi Ḥisda said: This matter,** that an uncircumcised priest may not serve in the Temple, **we did not learn it from the Torah of Moses,** but **we learned it from the text of the tradition,** i.e., Prophets and Writings: **"No stranger, uncircumcised in heart or uncircumcised in flesh, shall enter my Temple"** (Ezekiel 44:9). **Before Ezekiel came, who said** that it is prohibited for an uncircumcised priest to serve?

אֶלָּא, גְּמָרָא גְּמִיר לַהּ, וַאֲתָא יְחֶזְקֵאל וְאַסְמְכַהּ אַקְּרָא. הָכָא נַמִי גְּמָרָא גְּמִיר לַהּ, וַאֲתָא יְחֶזְקֵאל וְאַסְמְכַהּ אַקְּרָא. כִּי גְּמִירִי הֲלָכָה, לְמִיתָה. לְאַחוּלֵי עֲבוֹדָה, לָא גְּמִירִי.

Rather, you must say that it **is learned** as a definite **tradition,** like the rest of the Oral Torah, **and Ezekiel came and supported it by** means of **a verse** in his book. He did not, however, teach this *halakha* anew. **Here too,** with regard to a priest with long hair, it **is learned** as a tradition, **and Ezekiel came and supported it by a verse. And when** they **learned** this ***halakha***, they learned only that one is punishable by **death;** however, with regard **to desecrating** the Temple **service, they did not learn** this *halakha*.

״כָּל הַכָּתוּב בִּמְגִילַּת תַּעֲנִית דְּלָא לְמִיסְפַּד, לְפָנָיו אָסוּר, לְאַחֲרָיו מוּתָּר״. תָּנוּ רַבָּנַן: אִלֵּין יוֹמַיָּא דְּלָא לְהִתְעַנָּאָה בְּהוֹן, וּמִקְּצָתְהוֹן דְּלָא לְמִיסְפַּד בְּהוֹן. מֵרֵישׁ יַרְחָא דְּנִיסָן וְעַד תְּמַנְיָא בֵּיהּ, אִיתּוֹקַם תְּמִידָא. דְּלָא לְמִיסְפַּד בְּהוֹן. מִתְּמַנְיָא בֵּיהּ עַד סוֹף מוֹעֲדָא, אִיתּוֹתַב חַגָּא דִּשְׁבוּעַיָּא, דְּלָא לְמִיסְפַּד בְּהוֹן.

§ The mishna teaches: **Any** day concerning which **it is written in *Megillat Ta'anit* not to eulogize** on that day, it is also **prohibited** to fast **on the day before,** but it is **permitted** to do so **on the following day. The Sages taught** in *Megillat Ta'anit*: **These are the days on which fasting is prohibited,**[N] **and on some of them eulogizing is prohibited** as well: **From the New Moon of Nisan until the eighth of** the month, the proper sacrifice of **the daily offering was established,** and therefore it was **decreed not to eulogize on these** dates. **From the eighth** of Nisan **until the end of the festival** of Passover, **the festival of *Shavuot* was restored**[NB] and it was likewise decreed **not to eulogize** during this period.

NOTES

No, when they were juxtaposed – לָא כִּי אִיתְקוּשׁ: The commentary follows the standard text of the Talmud, that this is a rebuttal to the objection raised against Rav Ashi's contention that the service of a priest who has drunk wine is disqualified, whereas the service of a priest with long hair is not. The Gemara suggested that as an analogy is drawn between the punishments for serving in the Temple after imbibing wine and for serving with long hair, a similar analogy can be drawn between the two prohibitions concerning the disqualification of the service, in accordance with the principle that there cannot be juxtaposition halfway, i.e., a comparison must be fully accepted with regard to all relevant *halakhot*. Indeed, in the parallel passage in *Sanhedrin* 22b, the Gemara concludes its objection with the phrase: It is difficult, a reading also found in some manuscripts of the Gemara here, and no resolution of the difficulty is offered. However, in the standard texts of this Gemara the objection is simply met with the unexplained claim that the analogy drawn between the two prohibitions does not extend to the disqualification of the Temple service.

Some commentaries explain that Rav Ashi's comments in the continuation of the passage provide an answer to this objection (Ritva). There it says that Ravina asks: Before Ezekiel, who said that it is prohibited for a priest to let his hair grow long? Rav Ashi explains that there was an oral tradition to this effect going back to Sinai, long before Ezekiel's time. Accordingly, these verses in Ezekiel cannot be viewed as the source of this *halakha* but merely as the prophet's formulation of an established ruling of the Oral Law. If so, the principle that a juxtaposition cannot be applied by half measures has no bearing on this case at all, as the *halakha* of priests who let their hair grow long is not in fact derived from the verse that features the term *pera*.

These are the days on which fasting is prohibited – אִלֵּין יוֹמַיָּא דְּלָא לְהִתְעַנָּאָה בְּהוֹן: According to most early authorities, the prohibition against eulogizing is considered a further stringency than the prohibition against fasting. Consequently, the prohibition against fasting applies on all the days recorded in *Megillat Ta'anit*, whereas the ban against eulogies applies only on the more festive days. Some commentaries add that fasting is a graver violation of a commemorative day than the delivery of a eulogy, as one who fasts suffers throughout the day (Ritva). Others state that as eulogies are delivered in honor of the deceased or those who survive him, the prohibition against eulogizing was instituted only on the more festive days mentioned in *Megillat Ta'anit* (Rabbeinu Yehonatan).

Conversely, some commentaries maintain the opposite, that the prohibition against fasting is a further stringency than that of eulogizing. According to this interpretation, the delivery of a eulogy is regarded as a greater violation of a Festival, as a eulogy is delivered in public (Rabbeinu Efrayim, cited by Rabbi Zeraḥya HaLevi, Ritva, and *Shita Mekubbetzet*). Consequently, the prohibition against eulogizing applies on all the days recorded in *Megillat Ta'anit*, whereas fasting is prohibited on only some of the days. The standard text of the Talmud supports the opinion of the majority of the early commentaries, as the ruling of Rabbeinu Efrayim requires a considerable number of textual emendations.

The daily offering was established…the festival of *Shavuot* was restored – אִיתּוֹקַם תְּמִידָא...אִיתּוֹתַב חַגָּא דִּשְׁבוּעַיָּא: The *ge'onim* were asked about the difference in wording between these two decrees. Indeed, certain variants of the text use identical expressions for the decrees. Nevertheless, the *ge'onim* explained that there is a difference between the daily offering, which was always sacrificed at the proper time and simply had to be properly established as paid by the communal gift-offerings, and the restoration of the festival of *Shavuot*, whose very date the Boethusians tried to change.

BACKGROUND

The daily offering was established…the festival of *Shavuot* was restored – אִיתּוֹקַם תְּמִידָא...אִיתּוֹתַב חַגָּא דִּשְׁבוּעַיָּא: These commemorative days, like the others listed in *Megillat Ta'anit*, are associated with the struggles of the Sages against the Sadducees and the Boethusians. Apparently these cults received significant support from the Hasmonean kings and many important priests who followed them.

The sacrifice of the daily offering refers to the victory over the Sadducees, who claimed that it is permitted to bring this animal from individual gift-offerings. This was a fundamental dispute, as the Sages insisted that the expenses of the Temple sacrificial rites must be taken away from the control of individuals, which in practice meant priests and important persons. Instead, they said, it must be a true communal offering shared by the entire community by means of the universal donation of the half-shekel.

The restoration of the festival of *Shavuot* is connected to a different, long-standing dispute with the Boethusians, who maintained that the phrase "On the morrow after Shabbat" (Leviticus 23:11), which discusses the *omer* offering, refers to the day after Shabbat. Accordingly, they always celebrated *Shavuot* on a Sunday. The Boethusians used every means at their disposal to enforce their opinion, including bribing witnesses and misleading the court (see *Rosh HaShana* 22b). The victory of the Sages in this dispute removed a serious obstacle to the proper observance of the Festival.

NOTES

As the New Moon is itself a holiday – וְרֹאשׁ חוֹדֶשׁ גּוּפֵיהּ יוֹם טוֹב הוּא: Rashi explains that the New Moon is considered a holiday in accordance with the interpretation of the verse: "He has called a solemn assembly [*moed*] against me" (Lamentations 1:15), as a reference to the New Moon (see 29a). The term *moed* is one of the biblical synonyms for a holiday. Others suggest that the verse "And on the day of your rejoicing, and on your appointed seasons, and on your New Moons" (Numbers 10:10) equates New Moons and the other holidays with regard to fasting and eulogizing (Rabbi Elyakim).

אֲמַר מָר: מֵרֵישׁ יַרְחָא דְּנִיסָן עַד תְּמַנְיָא בֵּיהּ, אִיתּוֹקַם תְּמִידָא. דְּלָא לְמִיסְפַּד. לָמָּה לִי מֵרֵישׁ יַרְחָא? לֵימָא מִתְּרֵי בְּנִיסָן, וְרֹאשׁ חוֹדֶשׁ גּוּפֵיהּ יוֹם טוֹב הוּא וְאָסוּר! אָמַר רַב: לֹא נִצְרְכָה אֶלָּא לֶאֱסוֹר יוֹם שֶׁלְּפָנָיו.

The Gemara seeks to clarify these statements by comparing them to the ruling of the mishna. **The Master said** above: **From the New Moon of Nisan until the eighth of** the month, **the daily offering was established,** and therefore it was **decreed not to eulogize on these** dates. The Gemara asks: **Why do I** need *Megillat Ta'anit* to say: **From the New Moon? Let it say: From the second of Nisan, as the New Moon is itself a holiday,**[N] **and** it is already **prohibited** to eulogize on that day. **Rav said: It is necessary** to mention the New Moon of Nisan **only to prohibit** eulogizing on **the day before,** in accordance with the statement in *Megillat Ta'anit* that fasting on the day before any of the specified commemorative days is also prohibited.

וְשֶׁלְּפָנָיו נַמִי – תֵּיפּוֹק לֵיהּ דַּהֲוָה לֵיהּ יוֹם שֶׁלִּפְנֵי רֹאשׁ חֹדֶשׁ! רֹאשׁ חֹדֶשׁ דְּאוֹרַיְיתָא הוּא, וּדְאוֹרַיְיתָא לָא בָּעֵי חִיזּוּק.

The Gemara asks: **And** with regard to the day **before** the New Moon of Nisan **as well,** one can **derive** the prohibition against eulogizing on this day from the fact **that it is the day before the New Moon.** Since it is prohibited to fast on the New Moon, it is likewise prohibited on the day before. The Gemara answers that as **the New Moon is by Torah law and a Torah law requires no reinforcement,** it is permitted to fast on the previous day.

דְּתַנְיָא: הַיָּמִים הָאֵלֶּה הַכְּתוּבִין בִּמְגִילַּת תַּעֲנִית – לִפְנֵיהֶם וּלְאַחֲרֵיהֶם אֲסוּרִין. שַׁבָּתוֹת וְיָמִים טוֹבִים – הֵן אֲסוּרִין, לִפְנֵיהֶן וּלְאַחֲרֵיהֶן מוּתָּרִין. וּמַה הֶפְרֵשׁ בֵּין זֶה לָזֶה? הַלָּלוּ דִּבְרֵי תוֹרָה, וְדִבְרֵי תוֹרָה אֵין צְרִיכִין חִיזּוּק. הַלָּלוּ דִּבְרֵי סוֹפְרִים, וְדִבְרֵי סוֹפְרִים צְרִיכִין חִיזּוּק.

As it is taught in a *baraita*: With regard to **these days that are written in *Megillat Ta'anit*, it is prohibited to fast before them and after them.** However, concerning ***Shabbatot* and Festivals,** fasting on those days **is prohibited,** but **before them and after them** fasting is **permitted. And what is the difference between this and that? These,** Shabbat and Festivals, are **statements of Torah, and statements of Torah do not require reinforcement,** whereas **these** days mentioned in *Megillat Ta'anit* are statements of **rabbinic law,** and statements of **rabbinic law require reinforcement.**

אָמַר מָר: מִתְּמַנְיָא בֵּיהּ עַד סוֹף הַמּוֹעֵד", לָמָּה לִי עַד סוֹף הַמּוֹעֵד? לֵימָא עַד הַמּוֹעֵד, וּמוֹעֵד גּוּפֵיהּ יוֹם טוֹב הוּא וְאָסוּר! אֲמַר רַב פַּפָּא: כְּדַאֲמַר רַב: לָא נִצְרְכָא

§ **The Master said** above: **From the eighth of** Nisan **until the end of the festival** of Passover, the festival of *Shavuot* was restored and it was decreed not to eulogize. The Gemara asks: **Why do I** need *Megillat Ta'anit* to say: **Until the end of the Festival? Let it say: Until the Festival,** as it is anyway **prohibited** to eulogize on the festival of Passover. Rav Pappa said that this, too, should be explained **as Rav said: It is necessary** to mention the first of Nisan

Perek **II**
Daf **18** Amud **a**

NOTES

In accordance with whose opinion, in accordance with the opinion of Rabbi Yosei – כְּמַאן, כְּרַבִּי יוֹסֵי: Some commentaries explain that the Gemara is asking why the *halakha* is in accordance with the minority opinion of Rabbi Yosei (Rashi; *Shita Mekubbetzet*). However, most commentaries maintain that this statement is not a question, but a preamble to the difficulty that results if it is claimed that *Megillat Ta'anit* is in accordance with Rabbi Yosei's opinion.

LANGUAGE

Matron [*matronita*] – מַטְרוֹנִיתָא: From the Aramaic form of the Latin matrona, meaning woman, especially an important woman. In the time of the Mishna, many women of the noble class admired the Jews and their religion, and some even converted to Judaism.

אֶלָּא לֶאֱסוֹר יוֹם שֶׁלְּפָנָיו, הָכָא נַמִי לָא נִצְרְכָה אֶלָּא לֶאֱסוֹר יוֹם שֶׁלְּאַחֲרָיו. כְּמַאן? כְּרַבִּי יוֹסֵי, דְּאָמַר: בֵּין לְפָנָיו וּבֵין לְאַחֲרָיו אָסוּר? אִי הָכִי, בְּעֶשְׂרִים וְתִשְׁעָה נַמִי, מַאי אִירְיָא דְּהָוֵי יוֹמָא דְּמִקַּמֵּי יוֹמָא דְּמִיתּוֹקַם תְּמִידָא? תֵּיפּוֹק לֵיהּ דַּהֲוָה לֵיהּ יוֹמָא דְּבָתַר עֶשְׂרִין וּתְמַנְיָא בֵּיהּ,

only to prohibit eulogizing on **the day before. Here too, it is necessary** to mention Passover **only to prohibit** eulogizing on the **following day.** The Gemara asks: **In accordance with whose** opinion is this ruling? It is **in accordance with** the opinion of **Rabbi Yosei,**[N] **who said** that eulogizing is **prohibited both** on the day **before** the date recorded in *Megillat Ta'anit* **and** on the **following day.** The Gemara asks: **If so,** with regard to **the twenty-ninth** of Adar **too, why** state **specifically** that eulogizing is prohibited then **because it is the day before the day on which the daily offering was established? Let him derive** this prohibition from the fact **that it is the day after the twenty-eighth of** Adar.

דְּתַנְיָא: בְּעֶשְׂרִים וּתְמַנְיָא בֵּיהּ אָתַת בְּשׂוֹרְתָא טַבְתָּא לִיהוּדָאֵי דְּלָא יְעִידוּן מִן אוֹרַיְיתָא. שֶׁפַּעַם אַחַת גָּזְרָה מַלְכוּת הָרְשָׁעָה שְׁמָד עַל יִשְׂרָאֵל שֶׁלֹּא יַעַסְקוּ בַּתּוֹרָה, וְשֶׁלֹּא יָמוּלוּ אֶת בְּנֵיהֶם, וְשֶׁיְּחַלְּלוּ שַׁבָּתוֹת. מֶה עָשָׂה יְהוּדָה בֶּן שַׁמּוּעַ וַחֲבֵרָיו? הָלְכוּ וְנָטְלוּ עֵצָה מִמַּטְרוֹנִיתָא אַחַת שֶׁכָּל גְּדוֹלֵי רוֹמִי מְצוּיִין אֶצְלָהּ.

As it is taught in *Megillat Ta'anit*: **On the twenty-eighth of** Adar **good tidings came to the Jews, that they would not be restricted from Torah** study, and they declared this date a commemorative day. The *baraita* proceeds to describe the events of this day. **As on one occasion the wicked empire,** Rome, **issued a decree of apostasy against the Jews, that they may not occupy themselves with Torah study, and that they may not circumcise their sons, and that they must desecrate Shabbat.** What did **Yehuda ben Shammua and his colleagues do? They went and sought** the **advice of a certain** Roman **matron** [*matronita*][L] **whose** company was kept **by all the prominent** people **of Rome.**

אָמְרָה לָהֶם: עִמְדוּ וְהַפְגִּינוּ בַּלַּיְלָה. הָלְכוּ וְהִפְגִּינוּ בַּלַּיְלָה, אָמְרוּ: אִי שָׁמַיִם! לֹא אַחִים אֲנַחְנוּ, לֹא בְּנֵי אָב אֶחָד אֲנַחְנוּ, לֹא בְּנֵי אֵם אַחַת אֲנַחְנוּ? מַה נִּשְׁתַּנֵּינוּ מִכָּל אוּמָּה וְלָשׁוֹן שֶׁאַתֶּם גּוֹזְרִין עָלֵינוּ גְּזֵירוֹת רָעוֹת! וּבִטְּלוּם. וְאוֹתוֹ יוֹם עֲשָׂאוּהוּ יוֹם טוֹב.

She said to them: Arise and cry out [*hafginu*][L] at night. They went and cried out at night, saying: O Heaven! Are we not brothers? Are we not children of one father? Are we not the children of one mother? How are we different from any other nation and tongue that you single us out and **issue against us evil decrees?** Their cries were effective, **and** the authorities **annulled** the decrees, **and they made that day** a commemorative **holiday.**

אָמַר אַבַּיֵי: לֹא נִצְרְכָה אֶלָּא לְחֹדֶשׁ מְעוּבָּר.

§ Since the twenty-eighth of Adar is also a commemorative day, according to the opinion of Rabbi Yosei, it is also prohibited to fast on the following day. The question therefore remains: Why was it necessary to list the New Moon of Nisan, when the day before was already prohibited? **Abaye said: It is necessary** to include the New Moon of Nisan **only for** the case of **a full,** thirty-day **month.** If the month of Adar is thirty days long, fasting on the thirtieth day would be prohibited only because it is the day preceding the New Moon, not because it follows the twenty-eighth of Adar.

רַב אַשִׁי אָמַר: אֲפִילּוּ תֵּימָא לְחוֹדֶשׁ חָסֵר. כָּל שֶׁלְּאַחֲרָיו, בְּתַעֲנִית אָסוּר בְּהֶסְפֵּד מוּתָּר. וְזֶה, הוֹאִיל וּמוּטָּל בֵּין שְׁנֵי יָמִים טוֹבִים, עֲשָׂאוּהוּ כְּיוֹם טוֹב עַצְמוֹ, וַאֲפִילּוּ בְּהֶסְפֵּד נַמִי אָסוּר.

Rav Ashi said: Even if **you say** that we are dealing **with a deficient month,** with twenty-nine days, the inclusion of the New Moon of Nisan can still be explained. The reason is that with regard to **all** days **that follow** the dates listed in *Megillat Ta'anit*, **fasting is prohibited but eulogizing is permitted.**[N] But in **this** case, **since** the twenty-ninth of Adar **is positioned between two** commemorative **holidays,**[N] the twenty-eighth of Adar and the New Moon of Nisan, the Sages **made it like** a commemorative **holiday in its own right, and** it is therefore **prohibited even to eulogize** on this date.

אֲמַר מָר: מִתְּמַנְיָא בֵּיהּ וְעַד סוֹף מוֹעֲדָא אִיתּוֹתַב חַגָּא דִּשְׁבוּעַיָּא דְּלָא לְמִיסְפַּד. לָמָּה לִי לְמֵימַר מִתְּמַנְיָא בֵּיהּ? לֵימָא מִתִּשְׁעָה בֵּיהּ, וּתְמַנְיָא גּוּפֵיהּ אָסוּר, דַּהֲוָה לֵיהּ יוֹמָא דְּאִיתּוֹקַם בֵּיהּ תְּמִידָא!

§ **The Master said** above, in *Megillat Ta'anit*: **From the eighth of** Nisan **until the end of the festival** of Passover, **the festival of *Shavuot* was restored,** and it was decreed **not to eulogize** during this period. The Gemara asks: **Why do I** need it **to say: From the eighth of** Nisan? **Let** the *tanna* **say: From the ninth of** Nisan, **and the eighth itself** will still be prohibited because, **as** stated earlier, **it is the day on which the daily offering was established.**

כֵּיוָן דְּאִילּוּ מִקְּלַע לֵיהּ מִילְּתָא וּבָטְלִינֵיהּ לְשִׁבְעָה, תְּמַנְיָא גּוּפֵיהּ אָסוּר, דַּהֲוָה לֵיהּ יוֹמָא קַמָּא דְּאִיתּוֹתַב בֵּיהּ חַגָּא דִּשְׁבוּעַיָּא.

The Gemara answers: **Since if** a calamitous **event happened and they canceled**[N] **the seven** days commemorating the establishment of the daily offering, **the eighth** day **itself** will remain **prohibited, as it is the first day on which the festival of *Shavuot* was restored.** Since this date is not merely the last of the series for the daily offering, but it also commemorates the restoration of *Shavuot*, it is not affected by the cancellation of the previous seven days.

הָשְׁתָּא דַּאֲתֵית לְהָכִי, עֶשְׂרִים וְתִשְׁעָה נַמִי, כֵּיוָן דְּאִילּוּ מִיקְּלַע מִילְּתָא וּבָטְלִינֵיהּ לְעֶשְׂרִים וּתְמַנְיָא, עֶשְׂרִין וְתִשְׁעָה גּוּפֵיהּ אָסוּר, דַּהֲוָה לֵיהּ יוֹמָא דְּמִקַּמֵּי יוֹמָא דְּאִיתּוֹקַם תְּמִידָא.

The Gemara notes: **Now that you have arrived at this** conclusion, the same logic can be applied to **the twenty-ninth** of Adar **as well: Since if** a calamitous **event happened and they canceled** the commemoration of **the twenty-eighth** of Adar, nevertheless, **the twenty-ninth** day **itself** will remain **prohibited, as it is the first day on which the daily offering was established.**

אִיתְּמַר: רַב חִיָּיא בַּר אַסִּי אָמַר רַב: הֲלָכָה כְּרַבִּי יוֹסֵי. וּשְׁמוּאֵל אָמַר: הֲלָכָה כְּרַבִּי מֵאִיר.

It was stated that there is a dispute between *amora'im*: **Rav Ḥiyya bar Asi**[P] **said** that **Rav said: The *halakha* is in accordance with** the opinion of **Rabbi Yosei,** that with regard to all the days mentioned in *Megillat Ta'anit* on which eulogizing is prohibited, it is likewise prohibited to eulogize on the day before and the day after. **And Shmuel said: The *halakha* is in accordance with** the opinion of **Rabbi Meir,** the *tanna* of the unattributed mishna, who said that although it is prohibited to eulogize on the day before, it is permitted on the day after.

LANGUAGE

Cry out [*hafginu*] – הַפְגִּינוּ: Possibly related to the Middle Persian verbal stem ābxōn-, meaning cry. The root *p-g-n* is also found in the Aramaic of Targum Yonatan with the same meaning.

NOTES

Fasting is prohibited but eulogizing is permitted – בְּתַעֲנִית אָסוּר בְּהֶסְפֵּד מוּתָּר: This passage is cited in support of the opinion adopted by most early authorities that the prohibition against fasting applies on all the days recorded in *Megillat Ta'anit*, whereas the prohibition against eulogizing applies to only some of them.

Since it is positioned between two commemorative holidays – הוֹאִיל וּמוּטָּל בֵּין שְׁנֵי יָמִים טוֹבִים: As is explained below (19a), the rulings of *Megillat Ta'anit* were later rescinded, which means that fasting and eulogizing are permitted even on the days recorded in the scroll. Consequently, Rav Ashi's statement that a day between two days that have special observances assumes the character of a day with special observances, has no practical significance with respect to those days. Nevertheless, it does have ramifications even today with regard to a different issue. The *taḥanun* prayer, a supplication that is recited after the prayer leader's repetition of the *Amida* in the daily morning and afternoon services and that is omitted on Shabbat, Festivals, and days with special observances, is not recited on the second of Sivan, as that day occurs between the first of Sivan, a New Moon, and the third of Sivan, which is the first of the three days immediately preceding the festival of *Shavuot*. These days are treated in some respects as days with special observances.

Since if an event happened and they canceled – כֵּיוָן דְּאִילּוּ מִקְּלַע לֵיהּ מִילְּתָא וּבָטְלִינֵיהּ: The Jerusalem Talmud also discusses the difficulty that arises from the fact that for various reasons fasting and eulogizing were already prohibited on some of the days recorded in *Megillat Ta'anit*, either because they are Festivals by Torah law, or because they commemorate other events also mentioned in *Megillat Ta'anit*. The Jerusalem Talmud explains that *Megillat Ta'anit* simply provides a list of dates on which miracles occurred for the Jewish people, on account of which fasting, and in some cases eulogizing, are prohibited. The scroll lists all of the dates on which these miracles took place, regardless of the fact that fasting and eulogizing may already be prohibited on some of those dates for other reasons.

PERSONALITIES

Rav Ḥiyya bar Asi – רַב חִיָּיא בַּר אַסִּי: A Babylonian *amora* of the second generation, Rav Ḥiyya bar Asi was a very close disciple of Rav, and he presents statements in his teacher's name in dozens of places in the Talmud. He was also the teacher of Rav's son, and he studied with Shmuel and Zeiri. Rav Ḥiyya bar Asi apparently lived in the city of Korkonya, close to Sura, and seems to have been an artisan, specifically a net maker. He was a colleague of Rav Huna's. Several Sages of his generation and the following one attribute halakhic rulings to Rav Ḥiyya bar Asi. Additionally, the Talmud speaks of his righteousness and piety.

PERSONALITIES

Bali – בָּאלִי: An *amora* of Eretz Yisrael of the third generation, Bali was a student of Rabbi Ḥiyya bar Abba, although he also transmits statements in the name of other Sages. His name is apparently derived from a foreign language; some scholars believe that it is Arabic in origin.

וּמִי אֲמַר שְׁמוּאֵל הָכִי? וְהָתַנְיָא: רַבָּן שִׁמְעוֹן בֶּן גַּמְלִיאֵל אוֹמֵר: וּמַה תַּלְמוּד לוֹמַר בְּהוֹן, בְּהוֹן שְׁתֵּי פְּעָמִים? לוֹמַר לְךָ שֶׁהֵן אֲסוּרִין, לִפְנֵיהֶן וּלְאַחֲרֵיהֶן מוּתָּרִין. וְאָמַר שְׁמוּאֵל: הֲלָכָה כְּרַבָּן שִׁמְעוֹן בֶּן גַּמְלִיאֵל!

The Gemara asks: **And did Shmuel** actually **say this? But isn't it** taught in a *baraita* that **Rabban Shimon ben Gamliel says: And what** is the meaning when *Megillat Ta'anit* **states: On them, on them, twice,** in the phrases: Not to eulogize on them, and: Not to fast on them. This phrase is repeated **to say to you** that fasting and eulogizing **on these** days themselves **is prohibited,** but on the days **before** and on the **following** days it is **permitted. And Shmuel said: The *halakha* is in accordance with** the opinion of **Rabban Shimon ben Gamliel.** How, then, can it be said that Shmuel ruled in accordance with the opinion of Rabbi Meir?

מֵעִיקָּרָא סָבַר כֵּיוָן דְּלֵיכָּא תַּנָּא דְּמֵיקֵל כְּרַבִּי מֵאִיר, אֲמַר הֲלָכָה כְּרַבִּי מֵאִיר. כֵּיוָן דִּשְׁמָעֵיהּ לְרַבָּן שִׁמְעוֹן דְּמֵיקֵל טְפֵי, אֲמַר הֲלָכָה כְּרַבָּן שִׁמְעוֹן בֶּן גַּמְלִיאֵל.

The Gemara answers: **Initially,** Shmuel **maintained** that **since there is no other *tanna* as lenient as Rabbi Meir, he said** that **the *halakha* is in accordance with** the opinion of **Rabbi Meir. When he heard that** the opinion of **Rabban Shimon** ben Gamliel **was more lenient,** he said that **the *halakha* is in accordance with** the opinion of **Rabban Shimon ben Gamliel.** Shmuel consistently ruled in the most lenient manner possible on this issue.

וְכֵן אָמַר בָּאלִי אָמַר רַבִּי חִיָּיא בַּר אַבָּא אָמַר רַבִּי יוֹחָנָן: הֲלָכָה כְּרַבִּי יוֹסֵי. אֲמַר לֵיהּ רַבִּי חִיָּיא לְבָאלִי: אַסְבְּרָא לָךְ. כִּי אֲמַר רַבִּי יוֹחָנָן הֲלָכָה כְּרַבִּי יוֹסֵי, אַדְּלָא לְהִתְעַנָּאָה.

And similarly, the Sage **Bali**[P] **said** that **Rabbi Ḥiyya bar Abba said** that **Rabbi Yoḥanan said: The *halakha* is in accordance with** the opinion of **Rabbi Yosei.** The Gemara relates that **Rabbi Ḥiyya** bar Abba **said to Bali: I will explain** this ruling **to you. When Rabbi Yoḥanan said** that **the *halakha* is in accordance with** the opinion of **Rabbi Yosei,** he was not referring to all matters. Rather, he spoke specifically **with regard to** the day before those dates concerning which *Megillat Ta'anit* said: **Fasting is prohibited.** However, with regard to those days on which it is prohibited to eulogize, he did not rule in accordance with the opinion of Rabbi Yosei, as Rabbi Yoḥanan maintains that eulogizing on the following day is permitted.

וּמִי אֲמַר רַבִּי יוֹחָנָן הָכִי? וְהָאֲמַר רַבִּי יוֹחָנָן: הֲלָכָה כִּסְתַם מִשְׁנָה. וּתְנַן: ״אַף עַל פִּי שֶׁאָמְרוּ מַקְדִּימִין וְלֹא מְאַחֲרִין

The Gemara asks: **And did Rabbi Yoḥanan** actually **say this? But didn't Rabbi Yoḥanan say** as a principle that **the *halakha*** is always in accordance with **an unattributed mishna. And we learned** in a mishna: **Although** the Sages **said,** with regard to reading of the Scroll of Esther, that **one** may read it **earlier but one** may **not** read it **later,**

Perek **II**
Daf **18** Amud **b**

NOTES

The reading of the Scroll of Esther – קְרִיאַת הַמְּגִלָּה: As explained at the beginning of tractate *Megilla*, the Sages instituted that in addition to the official days of Purim, i.e., the fifteenth of Adar for residents of walled cities from the time of Joshua, and the fourteenth for everyone else, sometimes the Scroll of Esther may be read on the eleventh, twelfth, or thirteenth of Adar. The basic principle is that villagers can read the scroll early, on a Monday or Thursday, when they gather together. If Purim occurs on a Tuesday or Friday, they read it one day earlier, on the thirteenth. If Purim occurs on a Wednesday or Shabbat, they read it on the twelfth, and if it occurs on a Sunday they read it even earlier, on the eleventh.

מוּתָּרִין בְּהֶסְפֵּד וְתַעֲנִית. אֵימַת? אִילֵימָא בְּנֵי חֲמֵיסַר וְקָא קָרוּ לֵיהּ בְּאַרְבֵּיסַר, וּמִי שָׁרֵי?

as the Sages decreed that in certain places one may read the Scroll of Esther[N] on the eleventh, twelfth, or thirteenth of Adar, nevertheless, it is **permitted to eulogize and fast** on these days. The Gemara clarifies: **When** does this ruling apply? **If we say** that it applies to **those** in walled cities, who normally read the scroll on the **fifteenth** of Adar **and** yet this year **they read it on the fourteenth,** a day on which they normally are permitted to fast and eulogize, **but** this cannot be the case, as **are they permitted** to fast and eulogize at all on these days?

וְהָכְתִיב בִּמְגִילַּת תַּעֲנִית: יוֹם אַרְבָּעָה עָשָׂר בּוֹ וְיוֹם חֲמִשָּׁה עָשָׂר בּוֹ יוֹמֵי פּוּרַיָּא אִינּוּן, דְּלָא לְמִיסְפַּד בְּהוֹן. וַאֲמַר רָבָא: לָא נִצְרְכָא אֶלָּא לֶאֱסוֹר אֶת שֶׁל זֶה בְּזֶה וְאֶת שֶׁל זֶה בְּזֶה.

But isn't it written in *Megillat Ta'anit*: The day of the fourteenth of Adar **and the day of the fifteenth of** Adar **are the days of Purim, on which eulogizing is prohibited.**[H] **And Rava said:** Since these days are already mentioned in the Bible (Esther 9:18–19), it **is necessary** to state this *halakha* in *Megillat Ta'anit* **only to prohibit** those living **in these** walled cities from fasting and eulogizing **on this** date, the fourteenth, and those living **in these** non-walled cities from fasting and eulogizing **on this date,** the fifteenth.

HALAKHA

These are the days of Purim, on which eulogizing is prohibited – יוֹמֵי פּוּרַיָּא אִינּוּן, דְּלָא לְמִיסְפַּד בְּהוֹן: Eulogizing and fasting are prohibited on the fourteenth and fifteenth of Adar both for those living in walled cities, who celebrate Purim on the fifteenth, and for residents of non-walled cities, who observe Purim on the fourteenth (*Shulḥan Arukh, Oraḥ Ḥayyim* 696:3).

וְאֶלָּא, בְּנֵי אַרְבֵּיסַר וְקָא קָרֵי לֵיהּ בִּתְלֵיסַר. יוֹם נִיקָנוֹר הוּא! וְאֶלָּא, בְּנֵי אַרְבֵּיסַר וְקָא קָרֵי לֵיהּ בִּתְרֵיסַר. יוֹם טוּרְיָינוּס הוּא!

The Gemara continues its explanation of the difficulty. **But rather,** the mishna must be referring to **those** who normally read on the **fourteenth** of Adar, **but who read** the Scroll of Esther early, **on the thirteenth.** However, it is already prohibited to fast on the thirteenth,[N] as **it is Nicanor's Day,** which is a commemorative day in its own right. **But rather,** you will say that the mishna is referring to **those** residents of cities who normally read on **the fourteenth, but who read it** early that year, **on the twelfth;** however, the twelfth of Adar is also a commemorative day, as **it is Trajan's Day.**

אֶלָּא לָאו דְּקָא קָרוּ לֵיהּ בְּחֲדֵיסַר, וְקָתָנֵי: מוּתָּר בְּהֶסְפֵּד וּבְתַעֲנִית!

Rather, isn't the mishna referring to a case **where they read** the Scroll of Esther **on the eleventh** of Adar, **and** nevertheless that mishna **teaches** that it is **permitted to eulogize and fast** on this day, despite the fact that it is the day before Trajan's Day? The opinion in this unattributed mishna is not in accordance with that of Rabbi Yosei, which means that there is a contradiction between the two statements of Rabbi Yoḥanan.

לָא. בְּנֵי אַרְבָּעָה עָשָׂר וְקָא קָרוּ לֵיהּ בִּתְרֵיסַר. וּדְקָאָמְרַתְּ יוֹם טְרָיָינוּס הוּא, יוֹם טְרָיָינוּס גּוּפֵיהּ בַּטּוּלֵי בַּטְלוּהוּ, הוֹאִיל וְנֶהֶרְגוּ בּוֹ שְׁמַעְיָה וַאֲחִיָּה אָחִיו. כִּי הָא דְּרַב נַחְמָן גְּזַר תַּעֲנִיתָא בִּתְרֵיסַר. אֲמַרוּ לֵיהּ רַבָּנַן: יוֹם טוּרְיָינוּס הוּא! אֲמַר לְהוּ: יוֹם טוּרְיָינוּס גּוּפֵיהּ בַּטּוּלֵי בַּטְלוּהוּ, הוֹאִיל וְנֶהֶרְגוּ בּוֹ שְׁמַעְיָה וַאֲחִיָּה אָחִיו.

The Gemara answers: **No;** the mishna is actually referring to **those** who normally read **on the fourteenth, but who read it** that year **on the twelfth** of Adar. **And** with regard to **that which you said,** that **it is Trajan's Day, Trajan's Day itself was annulled** and is no longer celebrated, **since Shemaya and his brother Aḥiya**[B] **were killed on that** day. We learn this **as in** the incident **when Rav Naḥman decreed a fast on the twelfth** of Adar and **the Sages said to him: It is Trajan's Day.**[N] **He said to them: Trajan's Day itself was annulled, since Shemaya and his brother Aḥiya were killed on that** day.

וְתֵיפּוֹק לֵיהּ דַּהֲוָה לֵיהּ יוֹם שֶׁלִּפְנֵי נִיקָנוֹר! אֲמַר רַב אַשִׁי: הָשְׁתָּא אִיהוּ גּוּפֵיהּ בַּטְלוּהוּ, מִשּׁוּם יוֹם נִיקָנוֹר נֵיקוּם וְנִגְזַר?

The Gemara asks: **And let him derive** that fasting on the twelfth is prohibited in any case, **as it is the day before Nicanor's** Day. **Rav Ashi said: Now** that with regard to Trajan's Day **itself, they annulled it, will we** then **arise and issue a decree** not to fast on this date **due to** the following day, **Nicanor's** Day?

מַאי נִיקָנוֹר, וּמַאי טוּרְיָינוּס? דְּתַנְיָא: נִיקָנוֹר אֶחָד מֵאִפַּרְכֵי יְוָונִים הָיָה. וּבְכָל יוֹם וָיוֹם הָיָה מֵנִיף יָדוֹ עַל יְהוּדָה וִירוּשָׁלַיִם, וְאוֹמֵר: אֵימָתַי תִּפּוֹל בְּיָדִי וְאֶרְמְסֶנָּה? וּכְשֶׁגָּבְרָה מַלְכוּת בֵּית חַשְׁמוֹנַאי וְנִצְּחוּם, קִצְּצוּ בְּהוֹנוֹת יָדָיו וְרַגְלָיו וּתְלָאוּם בְּשַׁעֲרֵי יְרוּשָׁלַיִם, וְאָמְרוּ: פֶּה שֶׁהָיָה מְדַבֵּר בְּגַאֲוָה וְיָדַיִם שֶׁהָיוּ מְנִיפוֹת עַל יְרוּשָׁלַיִם – תֵּעָשֶׂה בָּהֶם נְקָמָה.

In relation to the above, the Gemara inquires: **What is** the origin of **Nicanor's Day and what is** the origin of **Trajan's Day? As it is taught** in a *baraita*: **Nicanor**[B] **was one of the generals** [*iparkhei*][L] in the **Greek** army, **and each and every day he would wave his hand over Judea and Jerusalem and say: When will** this city **fall into my hands, and I shall trample it? And when the Hasmonean monarchy overcame** the Greeks **and emerged victorious over them,** they killed Nicanor in battle, **cut off his thumbs and big toes, and hung them on the gates of Jerusalem, saying: The mouth that spoke with pride, and the hands that waved over Jerusalem, may vengeance be taken against them.** This occurred on the thirteenth of Adar.

מַאי טוּרְיָינוּס? אָמְרוּ: כְּשֶׁבִּקֵּשׁ טוּרְיָינוּס לַהֲרוֹג אֶת לוּלְיָנוּס וּפַפּוֹס אָחִיו בְּלוּדְקְיָא, אָמַר לָהֶם: אִם מֵעַמּוֹ שֶׁל חֲנַנְיָה, מִישָׁאֵל, וַעֲזַרְיָה אַתֶּם, יָבֹא אֱלֹהֵיכֶם וְיַצִּיל אֶתְכֶם מִיָּדִי כְּדֶרֶךְ שֶׁהִצִּיל אֶת חֲנַנְיָה, מִישָׁאֵל, וַעֲזַרְיָה מִיַּד נְבוּכַדְנֶצַּר. אָמְרוּ לוֹ: חֲנַנְיָה, מִישָׁאֵל, וַעֲזַרְיָה צַדִּיקִים גְּמוּרִין הָיוּ, וּרְאוּיִין הָיוּ לֵיעָשׂוֹת לָהֶם נֵס, וּנְבוּכַדְנֶצַּר מֶלֶךְ הָגוּן הָיָה, וְרָאוּי לַעֲשׂוֹת נֵס עַל יָדוֹ.

What is the origin of **Trajan's Day? They said** in explanation: **When Trajan**[B] **sought to kill** the important leaders **Luleyanus**[L] **and his brother Pappas in Laodicea, he said to them: If you are from the nation of Hananiah, Mishael, and Azariah, let your God come and save you from my hand, just as He saved Hananiah, Mishael, and Azariah from the hand of Nebuchadnezzar.** Luleyanus and Pappas **said to him: Hananiah, Mishael, and Azariah were full-fledged righteous** people, **and they were worthy that a miracle** should be **performed for them, and Nebuchadnezzar was a legitimate king** who rose to power through his merit, **and it is fitting that a miracle** be performed **through him.**

NOTES

A fast on the thirteenth of Adar – תַּעֲנִית בִּשְׁלֹשָׁה עָשָׂר בַּאֲדָר: There is a fundamental problem here with regard to the fast of Esther, which is a fixed communal fast on the thirteenth of Adar. Since the cancellation of *Megillat Ta'anit* did not include the days of Purim, it should be prohibited to fast as well as to eulogize on the previous day, as accepted by most authorities.

Many resolutions have been offered for this difficulty. Some say that when *Megillat Ta'anit* was rescinded, the prohibition against fasting on the days before all commemorative days was annulled, even if the days of Purim itself were not canceled (Ra'avad, citing Rif). Others say that as Trajan's Day, which was the fixed commemorative day for this date, was annulled, the following day is not significant enough to render it prohibited to fast on the twelfth (Ramban; *Sefer Hashlama*). Yet others maintain that the *halakha* is in accordance with the opinion of Shmuel, that with regard to all of these dates, the day before them is not prohibited (Ritva; *Shita Mekubbetzet*; Meiri).

Another suggestion is that as the days of Purim are written in the Bible, they are considered like statements of Torah, which do not require reinforcement, and therefore it is permitted to fast on the day before (Ran; Rosh). Alternatively, as this fast is merely in commemoration of the events of Purim, its observance is not considered a sign of mourning (Ra'avad).

The Sages said to him, it is Trajan's Day – אֲמַרוּ לֵיהּ רַבָּנַן יוֹם טוּרְיָינוּס הוּא: There is a dispute between the early authorities with regard to the *halakha* that *Megillat Ta'anit* has been rescinded and that all the dates listed there are like regular dates, apart from Hanukkah and Purim. Some maintain that *Megillat Ta'anit* has been canceled only with regard to an individual fast performed in private. A fast of this kind may be performed on the days enumerated in *Megillat Ta'anit*; however, a communal fast may not be declared on those days (Ra'avad). The Ra'avad bases his ruling on the fact that Rav Naḥman justified his decree of a fast on the twelfth of Adar not because *Megillat Ta'anit* had been canceled, but because Shemaya and Aḥiya were killed on that day. Conversely, other authorities reject this proof, claiming that Rav Naḥman merely wanted to provide a more specific reason for fasting on this day (*Sefer Hashlama*).

BACKGROUND

Shemaya and Aḥiya – שְׁמַעְיָה וַאֲחִיָּה: It is unknown who Shemaya and Aḥiya were. According to some opinions, they were the martyrs of Lod (see *Bava Batra* 10b), the pair who accepted responsibility for the murder of the Caesar's daughter in their hometown of Lod in a false confession that spared the rest of the inhabitants from death.

Nicanor – נִיקָנוֹר: Nicanor, Νικάνωρ in Greek, was a general in the army of Antiochus IV Epiphanes. He probably served as the ruler's representative in Judea. On the seventeenth of Adar in the year 161 BCE his army was routed near the town of Ḥadasha, and he himself was killed.

Trajan – טוּרְיָינוּס: The external sources do not fully clarify the events referred to here. Apparently, this episode occurred in the context of the great revolts of the Jews against the Romans toward the end of the reign of the Roman emperor Trajan (98–117 CE). It is likely that the man who ordered the deaths of Luleyanus and Pappas was a captain in Trajan's army, who was later defeated in battle and killed. Luleyanus and Pappas were probably not executed at the time, which is why the date was established as a commemorative day.

LANGUAGE

Generals [*iparkhei*] – אִפַּרְכֵי: From the Greek ἔπαρχος, *eparkhos*, meaning the commander of an important military unit.

Luleyanus – לוּלְיָנוּס: This was the Hebrew pronunciation of the Latin name Julianus.

LANGUAGE

Two officials [*diyoflei*] – דְּיוֹפְלֵי: This word has been explained in various ways, and several readings of the text have been proposed. This particular reading is apparently from the Greek expression διπλοῖ, *diploi*, meaning double.

HALAKHA

One may not decree a fast on New Moons – אֵין גּוֹזְרִין תַּעֲנִית בְּרָאשֵׁי חֳדָשִׁים: One does not decree a fast on the community on a New Moon, on Hanukkah, on Purim, or on the intermediate days of a Festival. However, if the community has already started a series of fasts, even if it has observed only a single one, and the next fast in the series falls on one of these days with special observances, the fast is observed until nightfall (*Shulḥan Arukh, Oraḥ Ḥayyim* 572:2).

NOTES

And how many are a beginning – וְכַמָּה הָוְיָא הַתְחָלָה: The Rambam indicates in his Commentary on the Mishna that this beginning does not refer to the start of a cycle of fasts, but to the beginning of a fast day itself. It is possible that he explains the mentions of one and three in the Gemara as referring not to the number of fasts but to the number of hours that people had already fasted (Rabbi Ovadya MiBartenura).

וְאוֹתוֹ רָשָׁע הֶדְיוֹט הוּא, וְאֵינוֹ רָאוּי לַעֲשׂוֹת נֵס עַל יָדוֹ. וְאָנוּ נִתְחַיַּיבְנוּ כְּלָיָה לַמָּקוֹם. וְאִם אֵין אַתָּה הוֹרְגֵנוּ, הַרְבֵּה הוֹרְגִים יֵשׁ לוֹ לַמָּקוֹם, וְהַרְבֵּה דּוּבִּין וַאֲרָיוֹת יֵשׁ לוֹ לַמָּקוֹם בְּעוֹלָמוֹ שֶׁפּוֹגְעִין בָּנוּ וְהוֹרְגִין אוֹתָנוּ. אֶלָּא לֹא מְסָרָנוּ הַקָּדוֹשׁ בָּרוּךְ הוּא בְּיָדְךָ אֶלָּא שֶׁעָתִיד לִיפָּרַע דָּמֵינוּ מִיָּדְךָ.

But this wicked man, Trajan, **is a commoner,** not a real king, **and it is not fitting that a miracle** be performed **through him.** Luleyanus and Pappas continued: **And** we are not wholly righteous, **and have been condemned to destruction by the Omnipresent** for our sins. **And if you do not kill us, the Omnipresent has many other executioners. And** if men do not kill us, **the Omnipresent has many bears and lions in His world that** can **hurt us and kill us. Instead, the Holy One, Blessed be He, placed us into your hands only so that He will avenge our blood in the future.**

אַף עַל פִּי כֵן, הֲרָגָן מִיָּד. אָמְרוּ: לֹא זָזוּ מִשָּׁם עַד שֶׁבָּאוּ דְּיוֹפְלֵי מֵרוֹמִי וּפָצְעוּ אֶת מוֹחוֹ בִּגְיזְרִין.

Even so, Trajan remained unmoved by their response and **killed them immediately. It is said** that **they had not moved from** the place of execution **when two officials** [*diyoflei*][L] **arrived from Rome** with permission to remove Trajan from power, **and they split his skull with clubs.** This was viewed as an act of divine retribution and was established as a commemorative day.

״אֵין גּוֹזְרִין תַּעֲנִית עַל הַצִּבּוּר בַּתְחִלָּה בַּחֲמִישִׁי״, כו׳. ״אֵין גּוֹזְרִין תַּעֲנִית בְּרָאשֵׁי חֳדָשִׁים״, כו׳. וְכַמָּה הָוְיָא הַתְחָלָה? רַב אַחָא אָמַר: שָׁלֹשׁ. רַבִּי אַסִּי אָמַר: אַחַת.

§ The mishna taught: **One may not decree a fast on the community starting on a Thursday,** so as not to cause prices to rise. Furthermore, **one may not decree a fast on New Moons,**[H] on Hanukkah, or on Purim. However, if one began a set of fasts, one does not interrupt the sequence for these days. The Gemara asks: **And how many** fasts **are** considered **a beginning?**[N] **Rav Aḥa said:** If one fasted **three** fasts before the festive day. **Rabbi Asi said:** Even if one fasted **one** fast before it.

אָמַר רַב יְהוּדָה אָמַר רַב: זוֹ דִּבְרֵי רַבִּי מֵאִיר שֶׁאָמַר מִשּׁוּם רַבָּן גַּמְלִיאֵל. אֲבָל חֲכָמִים אוֹמְרִים: מִתְעַנֶּה וּמַשְׁלִים. דְּרַשׁ מָר זוּטְרָא מִשְּׁמֵיהּ דְּרַב הוּנָא: הֲלָכָה: מִתְעַנֶּה וּמַשְׁלִים.

Rav Yehuda said that **Rav said: This** *halakha* of the mishna that a fast that occurs on a festival is not observed, **is the statement of Rabbi Meir, who said it in the name of Rabban Gamliel. However, the Rabbis say:** If a communal fast occurs on one of these days, one must **fast and complete** the fast until nightfall. **Mar Zutra taught in the name of Rav Huna:** The practical *halakha* is in accordance with the opinion of the Rabbis, that one **fasts and completes** his fast until nightfall.

הדרן עלך סדר תעניות כיצד

Summary of **Perek II**

The important communal fasts, especially the last set of fasts for rain, include two main features designed to emphasize the severity of the trouble and to stir the hearts of the people. The first includes rituals and customs such as the recitation of prayers in the city thoroughfare instead of the synagogue; the placement of ashes on the heads of the people; the removal of the ark, with ashes placed on it, to a public arena; and many other customs all meant to express dread in the face of the developing calamity. Likewise, the second feature was the Sages' institution of seven additional lengthy blessings recited on fast days by the prayer leader. The texts of these blessings are cited in the Mishna and Gemara.

In the Temple, they would add an impressive ritual in which the *shofar* and trumpets were sounded by priests between each blessing. In all places they would recite additional blessings and read passages from the Torah and the Prophets that deal with fasting and prayers for salvation.

With regard to the individuals exempt from fasting, the broad conclusion is that priests assigned to the Temple service, particularly those members of the patrilineal family who are actually involved in the sacred service, are exempt from fasting in practice. However, so as not to separate themselves from the community, they perform symbolic gestures of solidarity with their lay brethren. The more severe the fast, the greater the participation of these exempt individuals, although the members of a ministering patrilineal family never observe a full fast.

Apropos the discussion of these exempt individuals, the chapter also addressed other *halakhot* of the non-priestly watches, the priestly watches, and the patrilineal family. These *halakhot* are designed to prepare the members of these groups for the sacred service, and to prevent them from erring in the performance of their duties. For example, it is prohibited for ministering priests to drink wine or to grow their hair long.

Some dates were established as days of rejoicing to commemorate various happy events that occurred to the Jewish people during the Second Temple period, and on these dates fasting and eulogies were prohibited. The Gemara concludes that none of those dates are in effect nowadays, with the exception of Hanukkah and Purim.

A special halakhic status applies to Hanukkah, Purim, and the New Moon. The court may not decree a fast on these days, *ab initio*. However, if these dates occur in the middle of a sequence of fasts, the order is not changed on their account and the fast is observed as planned.

Introduction to **Perek III**

If there is famine in the land, if there is pestilence, if there is blasting or mildew, locust or caterpillar; if their enemy besiege them in the land of their cities; whatever plague, whatever sickness there be; any prayer and any supplication made by any man of all Your people Israel, who shall know every man the plague of his own heart, and spread forth his hands toward this house. Then may You hear in Heaven, Your dwelling-place, and forgive, and do, and render to every man according to all his ways, whose heart You know, for You, You alone, know the hearts of all the children of men.

(1 Kings 8:37–39)

Up to this point the tractate has discussed the most commonly decreed fast day, i.e., that which is due to a lack of rain. However, it is certainly appropriate to fast and pray concerning any catastrophe that might strike a community. Several issues arise with regard to this. First, the events that warrant a fast must be clarified, as one should fast only over disasters or very serious troubles, not for every problem encountered. Similarly, there are intermediate cases that are not cause for a fast, but for which it is proper to awaken the congregation to repentance by means of prayers and supplications.

In addition to the appropriate conditions for decreeing a fast day, the timing of this declaration is equally important. The order of fasts for rain is more or less fixed, as they depend on the yearly seasons. In contrast, when an event occurs that poses an immediate danger, there is no time to wait before fasting.

An additional question concerns the extent of these fasts. There is a difference between disasters and catastrophes that involve the Jewish people as a whole, and events that affect only a particular place or a small group of people. Sometimes a local occurrence is considered a general threat, and occasionally communities are obligated to participate in the distress of Jews living elsewhere. The clarification of these matters is the main issue of this chapter.

Another issue discussed here is how to proceed when God answers the prayers and rescues the people from the disaster for which a fast was declared. Is it appropriate to conclude the fast as originally planned, or should it be stopped when the reason for its declaration has been removed? Finally, it is necessary to establish how the community should express its gratitude toward God for responding favorably to its prayers.

מתני׳ סֵדֶר תַּעֲנִיּוֹת אֵלּוּ הָאָמוּר בִּרְבִיעָה רִאשׁוֹנָה. אֲבָל צְמָחִים שֶׁשָּׁנוּ, מַתְרִיעִין עֲלֵיהֶן מִיָּד. וְכֵן שֶׁפָּסְקוּ גְּשָׁמִים בֵּין גֶּשֶׁם לְגֶשֶׁם אַרְבָּעִים יוֹם, מַתְרִיעִין עֲלֵיהֶן, מִפְּנֵי שֶׁהִיא מַכַּת בַּצּוֹרֶת.

MISHNA **The order of these fasts** of increasing severity, as explained in Chapter One, **is stated** only **in** a case when **the first rainfall** has not materialized. **However,** if there is **vegetation that** grew and its appearance **changed**[N] due to disease, the court does not wait at all; **they cry out about it immediately.**[NH] **And likewise, if rain ceased** for a period of **forty days** between **one rainfall and another, they cry out about it because it is a plague of drought.**

יָרְדוּ לַצְּמָחִין אֲבָל לֹא יָרְדוּ לָאִילָן, לָאִילָן וְלֹא לַצְּמָחִין, לָזֶה וְלָזֶה אֲבָל לֹא לַבּוֹרוֹת, לַשִּׁיחִין, וְלַמְּעָרוֹת, מַתְרִיעִין עֲלֵיהֶן מִיָּד. וְכֵן עִיר שֶׁלֹּא יָרְדוּ עָלֶיהָ גְּשָׁמִים, דִּכְתִיב: ״וְהִמְטַרְתִּי עַל עִיר אֶחָת, וְעַל עִיר אַחַת לֹא אַמְטִיר, חֶלְקָה אַחַת תִּמָּטֵר״ וגו׳,

If sufficient rain **fell for the vegetation but not** enough **fell for the trees;** or if it was enough **for the trees but not for the vegetation;** or if sufficient rain fell **for both this and that,** i.e., vegetation and trees, **but not** enough **to** fill the **cisterns, ditches, and caves** with water to last the summer, **they cry out about it immediately. And likewise,** if there is a particular **city upon which it did not rain,** while the surrounding area did receive rain, this is considered a divine curse, **as it is written: "And I caused it to rain upon one city, but caused it not to rain upon another city; one piece was rained upon,** and the portion upon which it did not rain withered" (Amos 4:7).

HALAKHA

The dates of communal fasts – זְמַן תַּעֲנִית צִבּוּר: The order of three and seven fasts applies only if no rain fell at all. However, if rain initially fell in the usual manner, and later ceased, or if the vegetation started to dry out, or if not enough rain fell at the right time for seeds, trees, or water caves, in all these cases the court proclaims a fast and the people cry out without delay (*Shulḥan Arukh*, *Oraḥ Ḥayyim* 575:8).

NOTES

Vegetation that changed – צְמָחִים שֶׁשָּׁנוּ: According to most commentaries, this means that the vegetation noticeably changed appearances as it began to wither, or due to disease (Rabbeinu Ḥananel; Rabbeinu Gershom; Rid). Conversely, Rashi and several other commentaries maintain that different plants, i.e., weeds, sprouted in place of the ones that had been sown.

They cry out about it immediately – מַתְרִיעִין עֲלֵיהֶן מִיָּד: The expression: They cry out, is repeated many times in the course of this chapter. Some commentaries explain that this phrase invariably means that the *shofar* is sounded without a fast being proclaimed. If the rain is late, the court proclaims a series of fasts, and the *shofar* is sounded on the last seven of them. In contrast, in the cases discussed in this chapter, the *shofar* is sounded, but fasts are not proclaimed (Ra'avad). This interpretation is based on the argument that the circumstances described in this chapter are less threatening than a delay in the first rain of the season. If the vegetation takes on an unusual appearance or if there is a forty-day interval between the first and second rains of the season, these problems require a less drastic response than if there is no rainfall.

Since the court first decrees a series of less stringent fasts for a lack of rain, and only if the drought persists does it decree the more stringent fasts on which the *shofar* is sounded, it stands to reason that when there is rain but the crops appear unusual, or if there is an interval between rainstorms, the court should not immediately decree a series of severe fasts that include the blowing of the *shofar*.

However, most early authorities maintain that the expression: They cry out, generally means that the court immediately decrees a series of the most severe fasts on which the *shofar* is sounded (Rashi; *Tosafot*; Ramban; Ritva; Ran). This definition is consistently applied unless it is obvious from the context that the *shofar* is sounded without a fast being proclaimed, e.g., if Rabbi Akiva says that they cry out but do not fast, or if the Gemara states that an alarm is sounded for the recitation of special prayers, as in the following case: For these they cry out on Shabbat.

Although the total lack of rain is a greater calamity than the disasters discussed in this chapter, if rain is late the court first proclaims a series of less stringent fasts and then gradually increases their severity. This is because if the month of Kislev has arrived and rain has still not fallen, the situation is not yet calamitous and may yet be rectified. Therefore, the proclaimed fasts are less stringent. It is only after the drought has lasted for some time and the difficulties caused by the failure of rain have become very serious that the most severe fasts are proclaimed and the *shofar* is sounded.

If contrast, if the crops begin to grow strangely, or if there is a forty-day interval between rainstorms, this poses a serious threat, and therefore the court immediately proclaims fasts of the most severe kind.

אוֹתָהּ הָעִיר מִתְעַנָּה וּמַתְרַעַת, וְכׇל סְבִיבוֹתֶיהָ מִתְעַנּוֹת וְלֹא מַתְרִיעוֹת. רַבִּי עֲקִיבָא אוֹמֵר: מַתְרִיעוֹת וְלֹא מִתְעַנּוֹת. וְכֵן עִיר שֶׁיֵּשׁ בָּהּ דֶּבֶר אוֹ מַפּוֹלֶת, אוֹתָהּ הָעִיר מִתְעַנָּה וּמַתְרַעַת, וְכׇל סְבִיבוֹתֶיהָ מִתְעַנּוֹת וְלֹא מַתְרִיעוֹת. רַבִּי עֲקִיבָא אוֹמֵר: מַתְרִיעוֹת וְלֹא מִתְעַנּוֹת.

In a case of this kind, **that city fasts and cries out**[N] by blowing the *shofar*, **and all of its surrounding areas**[H] join them in their **fast, but they do not cry out. Rabbi Akiva** disagrees and **says: They cry out but they do not fast.** The mishna continues: **And likewise,** if a **city** is afflicted **by pestilence**[H] **or collapsing buildings,**[H] **that city fasts and cries out, and all of its surrounding areas fast but they do not cry out. Rabbi Akiva says: They cry out but they do not fast.**

אֵיזֶהוּ דֶּבֶר? עִיר הַמּוֹצִיאָה חֲמֵשׁ מֵאוֹת רַגְלִי, וְיָצְאוּ מִמֶּנָּה שְׁלֹשָׁה מֵתִים בִּשְׁלֹשָׁה יָמִים זֶה אַחַר זֶה – הֲרֵי זֶה דֶּבֶר. פָּחוֹת מִכָּאן, אֵין זֶה דֶּבֶר.

The mishna inquires: **What is** considered a plague of **pestilence?** When is a series of deaths treated as a plague? The mishna answers: **If a city that sends out five hundred infantrymen,** i.e., it has a population of five hundred able-bodied men, **and three dead are taken out of it on three consecutive days, this** is a plague of **pestilence,** which requires fasting and crying out. If the death rate is **lower than that, this is not pestilence.**

עַל אֵלּוּ מַתְרִיעִין בְּכׇל מָקוֹם: עַל הַשִּׁדָּפוֹן, וְעַל הַיֵּרָקוֹן, וְעַל הָאַרְבֶּה, וְעַל הֶחָסִיל, וְעַל הַחַיָּה רָעָה, וְעַל הַחֶרֶב. מַתְרִיעִין עָלֶיהָ, מִפְּנֵי שֶׁהִיא מַכָּה מְהַלֶּכֶת.

For the following calamities **they cry out in every place:**[H] **For blight; for mildew; for locusts; for caterpillars,** a type of locust that comes in large swarms and descends upon a certain place; **for dangerous beasts** that have entered a town; **and for the sword,** i.e., legions of an invading army. The reason that **they cry out about these** misfortunes in every place is **because** these are **calamities that spread.**

מַעֲשֶׂה שֶׁיָּרְדוּ זְקֵנִים מִירוּשָׁלַיִם לְעָרֵיהֶם, וְגָזְרוּ תַּעֲנִית עַל שֶׁנִּרְאָה כִּמְלֹא פִּי תַנּוּר שִׁדָּפוֹן בְּאַשְׁקְלוֹן. וְעוֹד גָּזְרוּ תַּעֲנִית עַל שֶׁאָכְלוּ זְאֵבִים שְׁנֵי תִינוֹקוֹת בְּעֵבֶר הַיַּרְדֵּן. רַבִּי יוֹסֵי אוֹמֵר: לֹא עַל שֶׁאָכְלוּ, אֶלָּא עַל שֶׁנִּרְאוּ.

An incident occurred in **which Elders descended from Jerusalem to their cities** throughout Eretz Yisrael **and decreed a fast** throughout the land **because there was seen in** the city of **Ashkelon** a small amount of **blight,**[H] enough **to fill the mouth of an oven.** This fast was observed throughout Eretz Yisrael, as blight spreads quickly. **And furthermore, they decreed a fast because wolves had eaten two children in Transjordan. Rabbi Yosei says:** This fast was decreed **not because they ate** the children, **but because** these wolves **were** merely **seen** in an inhabited area.

עַל אֵלּוּ מַתְרִיעִין בְּשַׁבָּת: עַל עִיר שֶׁהִקִּיפוּהָ נׇכְרִים אוֹ נָהָר, וְעַל הַסְּפִינָה הַמִּיטָּרֶפֶת בַּיָּם. רַבִּי יוֹסֵי אוֹמֵר: לְעֶזְרָה, וְלֹא לִצְעָקָה. שִׁמְעוֹן הַתִּימְנִי אוֹמֵר: אַף עַל הַדֶּבֶר. וְלֹא הוֹדוּ לוֹ חֲכָמִים.

For the following calamities **they cry out**[N] even **on Shabbat:**[HN] **For a city that is surrounded by gentile** troops, **or** for a place in danger of being flooded by **a river** that has swelled its banks, **or for a ship tossed about at sea. Rabbi Yosei said:** One may cry out on Shabbat **to** summon **help, but** it may **not** be sounded **for crying out** to God. **Shimon the Timnite says:** One may cry out on Shabbat **even for pestilence, but the Rabbis did not agree with him.**

HALAKHA

That city…and all of its surrounding areas – אוֹתָהּ הָעִיר...וְכׇל סְבִיבוֹתֶיהָ: If a specific city is visited by a calamity, the people living there must fast and cry out by blowing the *shofar*. The residents of the surrounding areas must also fast, but they do not cry out, in accordance with the opinion of the first *tanna* of the mishna (*Shulḥan Arukh*, *Oraḥ Ḥayyim* 576:1, 12).

If a city is afflicted by pestilence – עִיר שֶׁיֵּשׁ בָּהּ דֶּבֶר: If a city is struck by a plague of pestilence, its residents must fast and cry out. What is considered a plague of pestilence? If a city has an able-bodied male population of five hundred, and three men die from the disease over a period of three days, one each day, the city is treated as having been struck by a plague. Some commentaries note that fasts were not observed in their day during periods of plague, due to the concern that those who refrain from eating and drinking would weaken themselves and render themselves more susceptible to disease (*Magen Avraham*; *Shulḥan Arukh*, *Oraḥ Ḥayyim* 576:1–2).

Collapsing buildings – מַפּוֹלֶת: If there is an increase in collapsing buildings for no apparent reason in a certain city, or if a place is struck by an earthquake or a storm that causes buildings to collapse, the residents of that city must fast and cry out (*Shulḥan Arukh*, *Oraḥ Ḥayyim* 576:4).

For the following they cry out in every place – עַל אֵלּוּ מַתְרִיעִין בְּכׇל מָקוֹם: If the crops in a certain area are struck by blight or mildew, even if only a small amount of grain is affected, or if the area is struck by locusts or any other type of calamity that can easily spread from one place to another, fasts must be proclaimed and they cry out everywhere. This includes places far from the stricken area, provided that they are in the same country (*Shulḥan Arukh*, *Oraḥ Ḥayyim* 576:8–9, and in the comment of Rema, citing Ran).

Blight – שִׁדָּפוֹן: The court decrees fasts for blight and mildew, even if what appears is enough to fill only the mouth of an oven (*Shulḥan Arukh*, *Oraḥ Ḥayyim* 576:8).

For the following they cry out even on Shabbat – עַל אֵלּוּ מַתְרִיעִין בְּשַׁבָּת: On Shabbat and Festivals, fasts are not observed, there is no crying out, and no special prayers are recited for any type of calamity, with the following exceptions: If the community faces serious difficulties concerning earning a livelihood, they may include special prayers even on Shabbat. Likewise, if a city is threatened by an enemy army or by floodwaters, or if an individual is in a life-threatening situation, special prayers may be recited even on Shabbat. Nevertheless, the *shofar* may not be sounded, except to summon help (*Shulḥan Arukh*, *Oraḥ Ḥayyim* 288:9, 576:12–13).

NOTES

That city fasts and cries out – אוֹתָהּ הָעִיר מִתְעַנָּה וּמַתְרַעַת: Rashi explains that people living in the outlying areas must also fast, as they are indirectly affected by the lack of rain in the neighboring city. If there is no rainfall in the city, its residents will go to purchase food in the outlying areas, causing food shortages and higher prices.

Other commentaries suggest that the residents of surrounding areas must participate in the distress affecting their neighbors in the city and offer prayers on their behalf (Rabbeinu Yehonatan).

In the Jerusalem Talmud, the dispute between the anonymous first *tanna* of the mishna and Rabbi Akiva is explained as follows: The first *tanna* of the mishna derives the regulations that apply to those living outside the stricken city from the *halakhot* of Yom Kippur, on which fasting is required but the *shofar* is not sounded. Conversely, Rabbi Akiva derives these regulations from the *halakhot* of Rosh HaShana, on which the *shofar* is sounded but a fast is not observed.

For the following they cry out – עַל אֵלּוּ מַתְרִיעִין: Some commentaries note that the list in the mishna is incomplete, possibly because it mentions only the more common situations. They cite several talmudic sources that refer to other calamities for which they cry out even on Shabbat (*Gevurat Ari*).

For the following they cry out even on Shabbat – עַל אֵלּוּ מַתְרִיעִין בְּשַׁבָּת: In Chapter One (14a), the Gemara argued that the mishna cannot mean that the *shofar* is sounded on Shabbat over these calamities, as blowing a *shofar* is prohibited on Shabbat. Rather, the first *tanna* of the mishna permits the recitation of the *Aneinu* prayer, recited on fasts, even on Shabbat. Rabbi Yosei disagrees, claiming that although people may cry out for help in times of danger, they may not submit a formal prayer over their distress, as there is no assurance that their prayers will be effective (see Rashi).

Many early authorities maintain that the term cry out usually means that the *shofar* is sounded as part of the observance of a fast. Yet even they agree that in this instance it does not imply the proclamation of a fast, as a fast may not be declared on Shabbat.

However, according to one reading of the Rambam, a fast must be proclaimed even on Shabbat if the community is threatened with one of the calamities listed in the mishna (Rambam *Sefer Zemanim*, *Hilkhot Ta'anit* 1:6).

עַל כׇּל צָרָה שֶׁלֹּא תָּבוֹא עַל הַצִּבּוּר מַתְרִיעִין עֲלֵיהֶן, חוּץ מֵרוֹב גְּשָׁמִים. מַעֲשֶׂה שֶׁאָמְרוּ לוֹ לְחוֹנִי הַמְעַגֵּל: הִתְפַּלֵּל שֶׁיֵּרְדוּ גְשָׁמִים. אָמַר לָהֶם: צְאוּ וְהַכְנִיסוּ תַּנּוּרֵי פְסָחִים בִּשְׁבִיל שֶׁלֹּא יִמּוֹקוּ. הִתְפַּלֵּל, וְלֹא יָרְדוּ גְשָׁמִים.

§ The mishna adds: In general, they cry out **on** account of any **trouble that should not befall the community,** a euphemism for trouble that may befall the community, **except for an overabundance of rain.**[H] Although too much rain may be disastrous, one does not cry out over it, because rain is a sign of a blessing. The mishna relates: **An incident** occurred in **which** the people said **to Ḥoni HaMe'aggel: Pray that rain should fall. He said to them: Go out and bring in** the clay **ovens** used to roast the Paschal lambs, **so that they will not dissolve** in the water, as torrential rains are certain to fall. **He prayed, and no rain fell** at all.

מֶה עָשָׂה? עָג עוּגָה וְעָמַד בְּתוֹכָהּ, וְאָמַר לְפָנָיו: רִבּוֹנוֹ שֶׁל עוֹלָם! בָּנֶיךָ שָׂמוּ פְּנֵיהֶם עָלַי, שֶׁאֲנִי כְּבֶן בַּיִת לְפָנֶיךָ. נִשְׁבָּע אֲנִי בְּשִׁמְךָ הַגָּדוֹל שֶׁאֵינִי זָז מִכָּאן עַד שֶׁתְּרַחֵם עַל בָּנֶיךָ. הִתְחִילוּ גְּשָׁמִים מְנַטְּפִין. אָמַר: לֹא כָּךְ שָׁאַלְתִּי, אֶלָּא גִּשְׁמֵי בוֹרוֹת, שִׁיחִין, וּמְעָרוֹת. הִתְחִילוּ לֵירֵד בְּזַעַף. אָמַר: לֹא כָּךְ שָׁאַלְתִּי, אֶלָּא גִּשְׁמֵי רָצוֹן, בְּרָכָה, וּנְדָבָה.

What did he do? He drew a circle on the ground **and stood inside it and said before** God: **Master of the Universe, Your children have turned their faces toward me, as I am like a member of Your household.** Therefore, **I take an oath by Your great name that I will not move from here until You have mercy upon Your children** and answer their prayers for rain. **Rain began to trickle** down, but only in small droplets. **He said: I did not ask for this, but for rain to** fill the **cisterns, ditches, and caves** with enough water to last the entire year. Rain **began to fall furiously. He said: I did not ask for this** damaging rain either, **but for rain of benevolence, blessing, and generosity.**

יָרְדוּ כְּתִקְנָן, עַד שֶׁיָּצְאוּ יִשְׂרָאֵל מִירוּשָׁלַיִם לְהַר הַבַּיִת מִפְּנֵי הַגְּשָׁמִים. בָּאוּ וְאָמְרוּ לוֹ: כְּשֵׁם שֶׁהִתְפַּלַּלְתָּ עֲלֵיהֶם שֶׁיֵּרְדוּ, כָּךְ הִתְפַּלֵּל שֶׁיֵּלְכוּ לָהֶן. אָמַר לָהֶם: צְאוּ וּרְאוּ אִם נִמְחֵית אֶבֶן הַטּוֹעִין.

Subsequently, the rains **fell in their standard manner** but continued unabated, filling the city with water **until all of the Jews exited** the residential areas of **Jerusalem** and went **to the Temple Mount due to the rain. They came and said to him: Just as you prayed over** the rains **that they should fall, so too, pray that they should stop. He said to them: Go out and see if the Claimants' Stone,** a large stone located in the city, upon which proclamations would be posted with regard to lost and found articles, **has been washed away.**[N] In other words, if the water has not obliterated the Claimants' Stone, it is not yet appropriate to pray for the rain to cease.

שָׁלַח לוֹ שִׁמְעוֹן בֶּן שָׁטַח: אִלְמָלֵא חוֹנִי אַתָּה, גּוֹזְרַנִי עָלֶיךָ נִידּוּי. אֲבָל מָה אֶעֱשֶׂה לְךָ, שֶׁאַתָּה מִתְחַטֵּא לִפְנֵי הַמָּקוֹם, וְעוֹשֶׂה לְךָ רְצוֹנְךָ, כְּבֵן שֶׁהוּא מִתְחַטֵּא עַל אָבִיו, וְעוֹשֶׂה לוֹ רְצוֹנוֹ? וְעָלֶיךָ הַכָּתוּב אוֹמֵר: ״יִשְׂמַח אָבִיךָ וְאִמֶּךָ, וְתָגֵל יוֹלַדְתֶּךָ״.

Shimon ben Shetaḥ,[P] the *Nasi* of the Sanhedrin at the time, **relayed to** Ḥoni HaMe'aggel: **Were you not Ḥoni, I would have decreed that you be ostracized, but what can I do to you? You nag [*mitḥatei*]**[L] **God and He does your bidding, like a son who nags his father and** his father **does his bidding** without reprimand. After all, rain fell as you requested. **About you, the verse states: "Let your father and your mother be glad, and let her who bore you rejoice"** (Proverbs 23:25).

הָיוּ מִתְעַנִּין, וְיָרְדוּ לָהֶם גְּשָׁמִים קוֹדֶם הָנֵץ הַחַמָּה, לֹא יַשְׁלִימוּ. לְאַחַר הָנֵץ הַחַמָּה, יַשְׁלִימוּ. רַבִּי אֱלִיעֶזֶר אוֹמֵר: קוֹדֶם חֲצוֹת, לֹא יַשְׁלִימוּ. לְאַחַר חֲצוֹת, יַשְׁלִימוּ.

The mishna teaches another *halakha* with regard to fast days: If **they were fasting** for rain, **and rain fell for them before sunrise,** they need **not complete** their fast until the evening. However, if it fell **after sunrise, they** must **complete** their fast. **Rabbi Eliezer says:** If rain fell **before midday,** they need **not complete** their fast; but if it rains **after midday, they** must **complete** their fast.

HALAKHA

Except for an overabundance of rain – חוּץ מֵרוֹב גְּשָׁמִים: Fasts are not proclaimed in Eretz Yisrael in times of excessive rainfall, except in places where there is concern that the water might cause buildings to collapse (*Shulḥan Arukh, Oraḥ Ḥayyim* 576:11).

NOTES

If the Claimants' Stone has been washed away – אִם נִמְחֵית אֶבֶן הַטּוֹעִין: This refers to a large stone located in Jerusalem that served as the center for announcements concerning lost property (see *Bava Metzia* 28b). It is called the Claimants' Stone in reference to the claims that were put forward with regard to lost objects.

Some commentaries maintain that the entire phrase means: If the Claimants' Stone has been covered i.e., when this stone is covered with water it is time to cease praying for rain, as this level of water indicates that abundant rain had already fallen (Rashi in *Bava Metzia*; Rambam; Meiri).

Tosafot in *Bava Metzia* cite the Jerusalem Talmud, in which the verb *to'in* means obliteration. According to this interpretation, Ḥoni HaMe'aggel was using hyperbole to inform his listeners that just as water cannot dissolve the Claimants' Stone, I cannot annul the blessed arrival of rain.

LANGUAGE

Nag [*mitḥatei*] – מִתְחַטֵּא: Although many commentaries have argued that the term is derived from the root *ḥ-t-a*, to sin, this interpretation is difficult to accept in this context. Others maintain that it is from the Arabic حظي, *ḥaẓiya*, which means to obtain things by imploring. If so, *mitḥatei* means to beg, implore, and indulge oneself.

PERSONALITIES

Shimon ben Shetaḥ – שִׁמְעוֹן בֶּן שָׁטַח: The *Nasi* of the Sanhedrin during the reign of Alexander Yannai, Shimon ben Shetaḥ was one of the most important Jewish leaders and exponents of the Oral Law. He was an authoritative leader who insisted on observing the minutiae of Torah law. He took vigorous action against anyone who challenged the authority of the accepted *halakha*, whether the challenge came from outside the Jewish community or from sectarians of all kinds within.

In his time, witchcraft was expunged from the land by means of special decrees, and he firmly established the *halakhot* of testimony. He also improved and reinforced marriage contracts. Since he insisted on the overarching power of the Sanhedrin, he even summoned the king to judgment, and demanded that he respect the court like an ordinary citizen.

For this and many other reasons, he came into conflict with Alexander Yannai and was forced to go into hiding on several occasions. However, as evident from the account in *Berakhot* (48a), he did not succumb to threats, honor, or flattery. When people took revenge against him and testified falsely against his son, he and his son accepted punishment so as not to invalidate the established *halakhot*.

Although his sister, Salome Alexandra, was the king's wife, Shimon ben Shetaḥ continued to practice his profession, which was apparently tanning leather. After the death of Alexander Yannai, his widow reigned, and internal affairs were handled by Shimon ben Shetaḥ. This was considered a time of tranquillity in every respect.

BACKGROUND

Where they produced stalks – דְּאַקּוּן: The phenomena described here are connected with various stages in the desiccation of plants. Sometimes a temporary water deficit of 5–10 percent afflicts a plant. This deficit can occur in the summer, in which case it does not impair the plant's growth. However, a water deficit of 30 percent will cause permanent blight, which weakens the plant and causes its leaves to shrivel. If that condition lasts no longer than a short while, the plant will revive if water is supplied. However, if this blight continues for some time, notwithstanding any temporary recovery, the absorptive capacity of the roots will be impaired and the plant will die.

מַעֲשֶׂה שֶׁגָּזְרוּ תַּעֲנִית בְּלוֹד, וְיָרְדוּ לָהֶם גְּשָׁמִים קוֹדֶם חֲצוֹת. אָמַר לָהֶם רַבִּי טַרְפוֹן: צְאוּ, וְאִכְלוּ וּשְׁתוּ, וַעֲשׂוּ יוֹם טוֹב. וְיָצְאוּ, וְאָכְלוּ וְשָׁתוּ, וְעָשׂוּ יוֹם טוֹב. וּבָאוּ בֵּין הָעַרְבַּיִם וְקָרְאוּ הַלֵּל הַגָּדוֹל.

The mishna relates: **An incident** occurred in **which** the court **decreed a fast in Lod** due to a lack of rain, **and rain fell for them before midday. Rabbi Tarfon said to** the people: **Go out, and eat, and drink, and treat** this day as **a Festival. And they went out, and ate, and drank, and treated** the day as **a Festival, and in the afternoon they came** to the synagogue **and recited the great** ***hallel***, to thank God for answering their prayers.

גמ׳ ״סֵדֶר תַּעֲנִיּוֹת הָאֵלּוּ הָאָמוּר בִּרְבִיעָה רִאשׁוֹנָה״. וּרְמִינְהִי: רְבִיעָה רִאשׁוֹנָה וּשְׁנִיָּה, לִשְׁאוֹל; שְׁלִישִׁית, לְהִתְעַנּוֹת.

GEMARA The mishna taught: **The order of these fasts is stated** only when the fast concerns **the first rainfall.**[N] **And** the Gemara **raises a contradiction** between this statement and the following *baraita*: If the periods of **the first and second rainfall** pass without rain, this is the time **to ask** and pray for rain; if **the third** passes without rain, this is the time **to fast.**

אָמַר רַב יְהוּדָה: הָכִי קָאָמַר: סֵדֶר תַּעֲנִיּוֹת הָאָמוּר אֵימָתַי? בִּזְמַן שֶׁיָּצְאָה רְבִיעָה רִאשׁוֹנָה, וּשְׁנִיָּה, וּשְׁלִישִׁית, וְלֹא יָרְדוּ גְּשָׁמִים. אֲבָל יָרְדוּ גְּשָׁמִים בִּרְבִיעָה רִאשׁוֹנָה, וְזָרְעוּ וְלֹא צָמְחוּ, אִי נַמִּי צָמְחוּ וְחָזְרוּ וְנִשְׁתַּנּוּ, מַתְרִיעִין עֲלֵיהֶן מִיָּד.

Rav Yehuda said that **this is what** the mishna **is saying: When** does **the order of** these **fasts** that **is stated** apply? **When** the periods of the **first, second, and third rainfall have passed and rain has not fallen. However, if rain fell in** the time of **the first rainfall, and** the people **sowed but** the plants **did not sprout,** or, **alternatively, if they sprouted** a little, **but** their appearance **changed back** for the worse, as no rain fell after the first rainfall, **they cry out about it immediately.**

אָמַר רַב נַחְמָן: דַּוְקָא נִשְׁתַּנּוּ, אֲבָל יָבְשׁוּ, לֹא. פְּשִׁיטָא, ״נִשְׁתַּנּוּ״ תְּנַן! לָא, צְרִיכָא דְּאַקּוּן. מַהוּ דְּתֵימָא אַקַּנְתָּא מִילְּתָא הִיא. קָמַשְׁמַע לָן.

Rav Naḥman said: This applies **specifically** if their appearance **changed. However,** if they **dried** out entirely, they do **not** cry out, as this condition cannot be improved. The Gemara asks: It **is obvious** that this is the case, because in the mishna **we learned** the word **changed.** The Gemara answers: **No,** it is **necessary** for Rav Naḥman to issue his statement with regard to a case **where they produced stalks**[BN] after they dried out. **Lest you say** that **producing stalks is a matter** of significance, as it is a sign of strengthening, and the crops might be saved through prayer, Rav Naḥman therefore **teaches us** that this is not the case.

״וְכֵן שֶׁפָּסְקוּ גְּשָׁמִים בֵּין גֶּשֶׁם לְגֶשֶׁם״ כו׳. מַאי ״מַכַּת בַּצּוֹרֶת״? אָמַר רַב יְהוּדָה אָמַר רַב: מַכָּה הַמְבִיאָה לִידֵי בַּצּוֹרֶת. אֲמַר רַב נַחְמָן: נַהֲרָא אַנַּהֲרָא

The mishna further taught: **And likewise,** if **rain ceased** for a period of **forty days** between **one rainfall and another,** they cry out about this, because it is a plague of drought. The Gemara asks: **What is** the meaning of the phrase: **A plague of drought?** Isn't this simply a drought? **Rav Yehuda said** that **Rav said:** The mishna means that a period of forty days between one rainfall and the next **is a plague that** may **cause a drought.** In this regard, **Rav Naḥman said:** When crops do not grow in one place due to lack of rain and must be imported by means of one **river to** another **river,**[N]

NOTES

For the first rainfall – בִּרְבִיעָה רִאשׁוֹנָה: Some commentaries explain that the expression: The first rainfall, can be used in two different senses. It might refer to the first rain of the season, which itself can be divided into several separate rainfalls. However, it can also refer to the very first rainfall of the season (Ritva). The Gemara first understood the mishna as referring to the first rainfall according to the second sense, and therefore it raised the objection from another tannaitic source, which states that the fasts do not begin until the time of the third rainfall. Rav Yehuda answered that the mishna is using the term according to the first sense. In other words, the mishna is saying that the fasts do not begin until all the rains of the first rainfall have failed to arrive on time.

No, it is necessary where they produced stalks [*de'akkun*] – לָא צְרִיכָא דְּאַקּוּן: The early commentaries concur that *akkun* refers to some sort of positive development in the growth of plants. However, they disagree over the precise meaning of the term. Some maintain that it is derived from the root *kaneh*, stalk, i.e., the plants produced stalks after (Rashi) or before (Ra'avad) they dried up.

Others derive the term from the root *t-k-n*, improve, explaining that the plants showed some sign of improvement after they had already dried up (Rabbeinu Gershom). Rabbeinu Ḥananel and others similarly suggest that after the plants had already dried up, they once again turned green. Rabbeinu Ḥananel, citing the *ge'onim*, further writes that after the plants had dried up, they became strong again.

Regardless of their precise interpretation of the phrase, most early commentaries understand the Gemara as follows: The ruling of the mishna applies only if the crops have started to grow strangely, in which case they might recover. However, if the crops dried up completely, even if they subsequently produce stalks, improve, turn green, or become stronger, there is no point in crying out, as there is no longer any chance of saving them, and therefore any prayers offered for them would be in vain.

Rashi suggests another interpretation: The mishna's ruling applies if the crops start to grow strangely, in which case they must cry out so that the plants may recover. However, if the crops have dried up, even if they already produced stalks beforehand there is no need to cry out, as they will recover on their own.

River to river – נַהֲרָא אַנַּהֲרָא: Rashi explains that Rav Naḥman distinguishes between drought, when it is possible to transport food from another region by river, and famine, when it is necessary to transport food by land. Rashi suggests a second interpretation, that a drought means that one river has dried up, although water can be diverted from a different river, whereas at a time of famine all the rivers in the region have dried up.

בַּצּוֹרְתָּא; מְדִינְתָּא אַמְּדִינְתָּא, כַּפְנָא. וַאֲמַר רַבִּי חֲנִינָא: סְאָה בְּסֶלַע, וּשְׁכִיחָא, בַּצּוֹרְתָּא; אַרְבָּעָה, וְלָא שְׁכִיחָא, כַּפְנָא.

this is considered **a drought.** If produce must be brought **from** one **province to** another **province,** this is considered **a famine.**[N] **And Rabbi Ḥanina said:** If a *se'a* of grain is sold **for a *sela*, but** it is **available,** this is considered **a drought.** Although prices have risen, there is still grain for those who can afford it. However, if **four *se'a*** of grain is sold **for a *sela*, and** it is **not available,** this is considered **a famine.**

אָמַר רַבִּי יוֹחָנָן: לֹא שָׁנוּ אֶלָּא בִּזְמַן שֶׁהַמָּעוֹת בְּזוֹל וּפֵירוֹת בְּיוֹקֶר. אֲבָל מָעוֹת בְּיוֹקֶר וּפֵירוֹת בְּזוֹל, מַתְרִיעִין עָלֶיהָ מִיָּד. דַּאֲמַר רַבִּי יוֹחָנָן: נְהִירְנָא כַּד הֲווּ קַיְימֵי אַרְבָּעָה סְאִין בְּסֶלַע, וַהֲווּ נְפִישִׁי נְפִיחֵי כָּפָן בִּטְבֶרְיָא, מִדְּלֵית אִיסָּר.

Rabbi Yoḥanan said: They taught this **only** with regard to a time **when money is cheap** and everyone has it, **and produce is expensive.**[N] **However,** when **money is expensive,** i.e., unavailable, **and produce is cheap, they cry out about it immediately,** as this is considered a famine. **As Rabbi Yoḥanan said: I remember when four *se'a*** of produce **were** sold **for one *sela*, and** yet **there were many swollen by famine in Tiberias, as they did not have** even one ***issar*** with which to purchase food.

״יָרְדוּ לַצְּמָחִין אֲבָל לֹא לָאִילָן״. בִּשְׁלָמָא לַצְּמָחִים וְלֹא לָאִילָן – מַשְׁכַּחַת לָהּ דַּאֲתָא נִיחָא, וְלָא אֲתָיָא רַזְיָא. לָאִילָן וְלֹא לַצְּמָחִין – דַּאֲתָיָא רַזְיָא, וְלָא אֲתָיָא נִיחָא.

§ The mishna taught: If sufficient rain **fell for the vegetation but not** enough **fell for the trees;** if it was enough for the trees but not for the vegetation; or if sufficient rain fell for both this and that, i.e., vegetation and trees, but not enough to fill the cisterns, ditches, and caves with water to last the summer, they cry out about it immediately. The Gemara comments: **Granted,** with regard to rain that fell in sufficient quantities **for the vegetation but not for the trees,** this case **can be found,** e.g., **if gentle** rain **fell but heavy** rain **did not fall,** this is insufficient for the trees. Furthermore, it is possible for enough rain to fall **for the trees but** it is **not** effective **for the vegetation, if heavy** rain **fell but gentle** rain **did not fall.**

לָזֶה וְלָזֶה, אֲבָל לֹא לַבּוֹרוֹת, וְלֹא לַשִּׁיחִין וּמְעָרוֹת – מַשְׁכַּחַת לָהּ, דַּאֲתָיָא רַזְיָא וְנִיחָא, מִיהוּ טוּבָא לָא אֲתָיָא. אֶלָּא הָא דְּתַנְיָא: יָרְדוּ לַבּוֹרוֹת, לַשִּׁיחִין, וְלַמְּעָרוֹת, אֲבָל לֹא לָזֶה וְלָזֶה, הֵיכִי מַשְׁכַּחַת לָהּ? דַּאֲתָיָא בִּשְׁפִיכוּתָא.

Likewise, in the case of rain that benefits **both this and that,** trees and vegetation, **but not cisterns, ditches, and caves, you** can **find** this too, **if** both **heavy and gentle** rain **fell, however,** they did **not fall in abundance,** and therefore the water in the cisterns will not last through the summer. **However, that which is taught** in a *baraita*: If sufficient rain **fell for cisterns, ditches, and caves, but not for** either **this or that,** i.e., trees or plants, **how can you find these** circumstances? If the rain is enough to fill cisterns, how could it not be enough for plants and trees? The Gemara answers: **Where rain comes in** a single **downpour,**[B] it will fill the cisterns but will provide no benefit to plants and trees.

תָּנוּ רַבָּנַן: מַתְרִיעִין עַל הָאִילָנוֹת בִּפְרוֹס הַפֶּסַח. עַל הַבּוֹרוֹת, וְשִׁיחִין, וּמְעָרוֹת, בִּפְרוֹס הֶחָג. וְאִם אֵין לָהֶן מַיִם לִשְׁתּוֹת, מַתְרִיעִין עֲלֵיהֶן מִיָּד.

The Sages taught: They cry out about trees that have not received enough rain, until **near Passover,**[NH] as beyond that time any rain will no longer benefit trees. However, they sound the alarm **over cisterns, ditches and caves** that have not been filled until **before the festival** of *Sukkot*.[N] **And** at any time, **if they have no water to drink, they sound the alarm over them immediately.**

וְאֵיזֶהוּ ׳מִיָּד׳ שֶׁלָּהֶן? שֵׁנִי, וַחֲמִישִׁי, וְשֵׁנִי. וְעַל כּוּלָּן אֵין מַתְרִיעִין עֲלֵיהֶן אֶלָּא בְּאִפַּרְכְיָא שֶׁלָּהֶן.

And what exactly is the meaning of **their** use of: **Immediately,** in these cases? **Monday, Thursday, and Monday** of the week in which the court became aware of the crisis, but not necessarily on the very day that it became evident. **And in all of these** cases of interrupted rainfall, **they sound the alarm over them only in their district [*iparkheya*],**[L] but not in other areas where rain is falling normally.

NOTES

From province to province, a famine – מְדִינְתָּא אַמְּדִינְתָּא, כַּפְנָא: Some commentaries explain that this means water has to be brought from one place to another (Rabbeinu Gershom). Others state that as long as produce can be transported by river, it is not called a famine. However, once it has to be carried overland by donkeys and the like, this creates a shortage that leads to famine (Meiri).

When money is cheap and produce is expensive – בִּזְמַן שֶׁהַמָּעוֹת בְּזוֹל וּפֵירוֹת בְּיוֹקֶר: Rabbi Ḥanina's distinction between drought and famine parallels Rabbi Yoḥanan's distinction between a case where money is cheap and produce is expensive and a case where money is expensive and produce is cheap (Ritva). In all these cases, the alarm is sounded immediately, as the mishna indicates that if the alarm is sounded for drought it must also be sounded for the more desperate situation of famine. Consequently, Rabbi Yoḥanan's assertion that the Sages instituted their ordinance only when money is cheap and produce is expensive, but not vice versa, cannot mean that the alarm was not sounded when produce is expensive. Rather, he maintains that the Sages did not need to issue their regulation in that case, as the *halakha* when produce is expensive is obvious.

Near Passover – בִּפְרוֹס הַפֶּסַח: The precise meaning of the term in this context is unclear. The Gemara elsewhere (*Bekhorot* 58a), explains that the expression: Near Passover, refers to the first of Nisan, the midpoint of the thirty-day period before Passover, during which the *halakhot* pertaining to the Festival must be studied (see *Mikhtam* and Meiri). Rashi here states that the alarm is sounded during Passover itself. Others maintain that if Passover has arrived or if it is near the Festival, and rain has not yet fallen in sufficient quantities for the trees, the alarm is sounded immediately (Rambam *Sefer Zemanim, Hilkhot Ta'anit* 2:17).

Before the festival of *Sukkot* – בִּפְרוֹס הֶחָג: Many authorities understand the term Festival in this context in its usual sense, as a reference to the festival of *Sukkot* (Rambam *Sefer Zemanim, Hilkhot Ta'anit* 2:17). However, some commentaries ask: How is it possible that the alarm was not sounded all summer long, when rainfall was most desperately needed, but only at the end of the year, near *Sukkot* (Ritva)? The Ritva explains that although the need for rain is greatest during the summer months, prayers for rain cannot be offered then, as one should not pray for a miracle. However, with the approach of *Sukkot*, prayers may be offered, as at that time the water shortage has already been felt for a long time and the rainy season is now at hand. Others add that the water shortage is really felt only near *Sukkot*, as all summer long there is still some water left in the storage cisterns from the previous winter (Ran). Alternatively, the term Festival means the festival of *Shavuot*, at the start of the summer (Ritva). Indeed, in the Jerusalem Talmud it is stated explicitly that the alarm is sounded for cisterns, ditches, and caves near the festival of *Shavuot*.

BACKGROUND

Downpour – שְׁפִיכוּתָא: Large amounts of heavy rainfall in a short period of time can lead to flooding, which can cause extensive damage to crops and can even wash away much of the topsoil. There are records of over 100 mm of rain falling in an hour and a half in Eretz Yisrael. Although this rainfall fills wells, it is harmful to all forms of vegetation.

LANGUAGE

District [*iparkheya*] – אִפַּרְכְיָא: From the Greek ἐπαρχία, *eparkhia*, a district.

HALAKHA

About trees near Passover – עַל הָאִילָנוֹת בִּפְרוֹס הַפֶּסַח: If Passover is approaching and rain has not fallen in sufficient quantities in order for the trees to produce their fruits, fasts are proclaimed and special prayers recited until adequate rain falls or the rainy season has passed. Likewise, if *Sukkot* is approaching and the storage cisterns contain little water, fasts must be observed until there is adequate rainfall. If there is a shortage of drinking water, fasts are proclaimed at any time of the year, even during the summer months (*Shulḥan Arukh, Oraḥ Ḥayyim* 575:8).

וְאַסְכָּרָא, בִּזְמַן שֶׁיֵּשׁ בָּהּ מִיתָה, מַתְרִיעִין עָלֶיהָ, בִּזְמַן שֶׁאֵין בָּהּ מִיתָה, אֵין מַתְרִיעִין עָלֶיהָ. וּמַתְרִיעִין עַל הַגּוֹבַאי בְּכָל שֶׁהוּא. רַבִּי שִׁמְעוֹן בֶּן אֶלְעָזָר אוֹמֵר: אַף עַל הֶחָגָב.

And with regard to a plague of **diphtheria,**[HB] **when it has** the potential to cause **death they sound the alarm over it,** but **when it does not have** the potential to cause **death they do not sound the alarm over it. And they sound the alarm over** the arrival of **locusts, for any amount,**[H] as it is likely that more locusts are on the way. However, they do not sound the alarm over the arrival of grasshoppers. **Rabbi Shimon ben Elazar says:** They sound the alarm **even over grasshoppers,** as they too can cause a great deal of damage if they swarm in large numbers.

תָּנוּ רַבָּנַן: מַתְרִיעִין עַל הָאִילָנוֹת בִּשְׁאָר שְׁנֵי שָׁבוּעַ. עַל הַבּוֹרוֹת, וְעַל הַשִּׁיחִין, וְעַל הַמְּעָרוֹת, אֲפִילּוּ בַּשְּׁבִיעִית. רַבָּן שִׁמְעוֹן בֶּן גַּמְלִיאֵל אוֹמֵר: אַף עַל הָאִילָנוֹת בַּשְּׁבִיעִית, מִפְּנֵי שֶׁיֵּשׁ בָּהֶן פַּרְנָסָה לַעֲנִיִּים.

The Sages taught in a *baraita*: **They sound the alarm over trees during the other** six **years of the** seven-year Sabbatical **cycle,** when the earth is tilled, but not during the Sabbatical Year, when one must refrain from working the land. However, **for cisterns, ditches, and caves, they sound the alarm even in the Sabbatical Year. Rabban Shimon ben Gamliel says: Even for trees** they sound the alarm **in the Sabbatical Year, because they serve as sustenance for the poor.**[N] Since the poor rely on these trees for their food in the Sabbatical Year, they will lose their means of subsistence if it does not rain.

תַּנְיָא אִידָךְ: מַתְרִיעִין עַל הָאִילָנוֹת בִּשְׁאָר שְׁנֵי שָׁבוּעַ. עַל הַבּוֹרוֹת, עַל הַשִּׁיחִין, וְעַל הַמְּעָרוֹת, אֲפִילּוּ בַּשְּׁבִיעִית. רַבָּן שִׁמְעוֹן בֶּן גַּמְלִיאֵל אוֹמֵר: אַף עַל הָאִילָנוֹת. מַתְרִיעִין עַל הַסְּפִיחִין בַּשְּׁבִיעִית, מִפְּנֵי שֶׁיֵּשׁ בָּהֶן פַּרְנָסָה לַעֲנִיִּים.

It is taught in **another** *baraita*: **They sound the alarm over trees during the other years of the** Sabbatical **cycle,** and **for cisterns, ditches and caves they sound the alarm even in the Sabbatical Year. Rabban Shimon ben Gamliel says: Even for trees.** Furthermore, **they sound the alarm for aftergrowths** of crops that have grown of their own accord **in the Sabbatical Year, because they serve as sustenance for the poor,** as it is permitted to eat aftergrowths.

תַּנְיָא: אָמַר רַבִּי אֶלְעָזָר בֶּן פְּרָטָא: מִיּוֹם שֶׁחָרַב בֵּית הַמִּקְדָּשׁ, נַעֲשׂוּ גְּשָׁמִים צִימּוּקִין לָעוֹלָם. יֵשׁ שָׁנָה שֶׁגְּשָׁמֶיהָ מְרוּבִּין, וְיֵשׁ שָׁנָה שֶׁגְּשָׁמֶיהָ מוּעָטִין. יֵשׁ שָׁנָה שֶׁגְּשָׁמֶיהָ יוֹרְדִין בִּזְמַנָּן, וְיֵשׁ שָׁנָה שֶׁאֵין גְּשָׁמֶיהָ יוֹרְדִין בִּזְמַנָּן.

§ **It is taught** in a *baraita* that **Rabbi Elazar ben Perata said: Since the day that the Temple was destroyed,**[N] **rain has been meager,** i.e., overall, not enough has fallen **in the world. There are years whose rains are abundant, and there are years whose rains are scare. There are years whose rains fall in their proper time,** and **there are years whose rains do not fall in their proper time.**

שָׁנָה שֶׁגְּשָׁמֶיהָ יוֹרְדִין בִּזְמַנָּן – לְמָה הוּא דּוֹמֶה? לְעֶבֶד שֶׁנָּתַן לוֹ רַבּוֹ פַּרְנָסָתוֹ בְּאֶחָד בְּשַׁבָּת. נִמְצֵאת עִיסָּה נֶאֱפֵית כְּתִיקְנָהּ וְנֶאֱכֶלֶת כְּתִיקְנָהּ. שָׁנָה שֶׁאֵין גְּשָׁמֶיהָ יוֹרְדִין בִּזְמַנָּן – לְמָה הוּא דּוֹמֶה? לְעֶבֶד שֶׁנָּתַן לוֹ רַבּוֹ פַּרְנָסָתוֹ בְּעֶרֶב שַׁבָּת. נִמְצֵאת עִיסָּה נֶאֱפֵית שֶׁלֹּא כְּתִיקְנָהּ וְנֶאֱכֶלֶת שֶׁלֹּא כְּתִיקְנָהּ.

With regard to **a year whose rains fall in their proper time, to what may it be compared? To a servant whose master gave him his** weekly **portion on Sunday.** It is thereby **found** that his **dough is baked properly**[B] throughout the week, **and it is eaten properly,** as he has a sufficient amount. Conversely, with regard to **a year whose rains do not fall in their proper time, to what** may **it be compared? To a servant whose master gave him his portion on Shabbat eve,** when there is insufficient time to prepare it fully. It is thereby **found** that his **dough is baked improperly, and it is eaten improperly.**

HALAKHA

Diphtheria – אַסְכָּרָא: If a community is struck by a particular illness, e.g., diphtheria, and people are dying from the disease, the alarm is sounded and fasts are proclaimed (*Shulḥan Arukh, Oraḥ Ḥayyim* 576:5).

Over locusts, for any amount – עַל הַגּוֹבַאי בְּכָל שֶׁהוּא: If even one type of destructive locust is sighted, the alarm is sounded and fasts are proclaimed. If a less devastating type of locust is sighted, special prayers are recited but the alarm is not sounded and fasts are not proclaimed. Nowadays, we are unable to distinguish between the various types of locusts, and therefore the alarm is sounded in all cases (*Shulḥan Arukh, Oraḥ Ḥayyim* 576:9).

BACKGROUND

Diphtheria [*askara*] – אַסְכָּרָא: The translation of *askara* as diphtheria is supported by the descriptions of this illness elsewhere in the Gemara. This disease starts from the mouth and throat. In certain cases, when it spreads to the back of the throat, diphtheria can cause death by strangulation. It can also spread to other areas of the body and even weaken the heart. This disease afflicts mainly children under the age of ten (see 27b).

Baked properly, etc. – נֶאֱפֵית כְּתִיקְנָהּ וכו׳: When there is enough time to prepare and bake dough, it rises at the right temperature and it rises well. However, when bread must be prepared in a hurry, the dough will not be kneaded properly, and it will therefore contain lumps of flour. In an attempt to prepare the bread quicker, it will also be baked at too high a temperature, which will result in bread that is only partially baked or burned. Likewise, periods of rainfall that have long gaps between them and rain that falls after the proper time can prevent plants from sprouting. Even those plants that do sprout often do not flourish due to the shortage of water. Consequently, even if the overall quantity of rain is the same, only the proper distribution of rainfall throughout the season can guarantee adequate growth.

NOTES

Because they serve as sustenance for the poor – מִפְּנֵי שֶׁיֵּשׁ בָּהֶן פַּרְנָסָה לַעֲנִיִּים: The *tanna'im* dispute whether the alarm is sounded in the Sabbatical Year only for trees or even for the aftergrowth of vegetables and grain planted during the previous year. Some commentaries explain that this dispute reflects a more fundamental dispute with regard to the rabbinic prohibition against benefiting from the aftergrowth of crops planted during the sixth year. Did the Sages prohibit the consumption of this produce entirely to people of means, or did they merely prohibit its purchase from one who is suspected of having planted during the Sabbatical Year? (see Rosh on *Shevi'it* 9:1, Rid, and *Gevurat Ari*).

According to the versions of the *baraita* found in the Babylonian Talmud, the alarm is sounded even in the Sabbatical Year if there is no rain, as the produce growing on the trees and the aftergrowths of the previous year's crops, which were supposed to be eaten during the Sabbatical Year, are an important source of sustenance for the poor. However, in the *Tosefta* and the Jerusalem Talmud, the *baraita* states that the alarm is sounded on account of drought even during the Sabbatical Year for the benefit of others. In the Jerusalem Talmud, two explanations of this cryptic term: Others, are cited: Some say that the alarm is sounded for the benefit of gentiles, who are not bound by the restrictions of the Sabbatical Year. Others explain that it is sounded for the benefit of those Jews who are suspected of violating the restrictions and planting during the Sabbatical Year, so that at least the crops should not fail.

Since the day that the Temple was destroyed – מִיּוֹם שֶׁחָרַב בֵּית הַמִּקְדָּשׁ: Some commentaries explain that when the Temple was standing, the High Priest offered a special prayer on Yom Kippur that rain should fall at the appointed time and in abundant amounts. However, after the Temple was destroyed, that prayer was no longer recited, and since then rain has fallen at irregular intervals and in disappointing quantities (Maharsha).

Others have a different reading of this passage: Since the day that the Temple was destroyed, rainfall has become a means of judging the world. While the Temple stood, the generation could see whether it was innocent or guilty by means of the scarlet thread that hung in the Temple. On Yom Kippur, this thread would either turn white, as a sign that the people's sins had been forgiven, or remain scarlet, which indicated that they had not. Since the Temple was destroyed, rain has become the primary test by which a generation can see whether it has been vindicated or found guilty in the eyes of God (*Arukh*).

שָׁנָה שֶׁגְּשָׁמֶיהָ מְרוּבִּין – לְמָה הוּא דּוֹמֶה? לְעֶבֶד שֶׁנָּתַן לוֹ רַבּוֹ פַּרְנָסָתוֹ בְּבַת אַחַת. נִמְצְאוּ רֵיחַיִם טוֹחֲנוֹת מִן הַכּוֹר מַה שֶּׁטּוֹחֲנוֹת מִן הַקַּב, וְנִמְצֵאת עִיסָּה אוֹכֶלֶת מִן הַכּוֹר כְּמוֹ אוֹכֶלֶת מִן הַקַּב.

With regard to **a year whose rains are abundant, to what** may **it be compared? To a servant whose master gave him his portion** for a long period of time all **at once.** He performs all of his milling at one time, and it is therefore **found** that **the mill grinds** and produces waste **from a** ***kor***[B] of produce in the same amount **as it grinds** and produces waste **from** the much smaller *kav* of produce. During each milling process, the same amount of flour goes to waste. Consequently, milling a large amount of flour in a single milling process preserves flour. **And** similarly, it is **found** that **dough is diminished from a** ***kor,***[B] **as it diminishes from a** ***kav.***

שָׁנָה שֶׁגְּשָׁמֶיהָ מוּעָטִין – לְמָה הוּא דּוֹמֶה? לְעֶבֶד שֶׁנָּתַן לוֹ רַבּוֹ פַּרְנָסָתוֹ מְעַט מְעַט. נִמְצְאוּ רֵיחַיִם מַה שֶּׁטּוֹחֲנוֹת מִן הַכּוֹר טוֹחֲנוֹת מִן הַקַּב, נִמְצֵאת עִיסָּה כַּמָּה שֶׁנֶּאֱכֶלֶת מִן הַכּוֹר אוֹכֶלֶת מִן הַקַּב.

In contrast, with regard to **a year whose rains are scarce, to what** may **it be compared? To a servant whose master gave him his portion little by little.** It is thereby **found that** the amount **that the mill** would have **ground from a** ***kor*** of produce is that which in practice **it grinds** and produces **from** each ***kav.*** It is likewise **found** that the **dough** that would have been **diminished from a** ***kor*** is the same amount that is **diminished from a** ***kav.*** In sum, one retains less dough when given his sustenance little by little.

דָּבָר אַחֵר: בִּזְמַן שֶׁגְּשָׁמֶיהָ מְרוּבִּין, לְמָה הוּא דּוֹמֶה? לְאָדָם שֶׁמְּגַבֵּל אֶת הַטִּיט. אִם יֵשׁ לוֹ מַיִם רַבִּים, מַיִם אֵינָן כָּלִין וְהַטִּיט מְגוּבָּל יָפֶה. אִם יֵשׁ לוֹ מַיִם מוּעָטִין, מַיִם כָּלִים וְהַטִּיט אֵינוֹ מִתְגַּבֵּל יָפֶה.

Alternatively, when its rains are abundant, to what may this year **be compared? To a person who kneads clay. If he has a lot of water,** his **water is not used up** and **the clay** will be **well kneaded. If he has** only **a little water,** the **water** will be **used up and the clay will not be well kneaded.**

תָּנוּ רַבָּנַן: פַּעַם אַחַת עָלוּ כׇּל יִשְׂרָאֵל לָרֶגֶל לִירוּשָׁלַיִם, וְלֹא הָיָה לָהֶם מַיִם לִשְׁתּוֹת. הָלַךְ נַקְדִּימוֹן בֶּן גּוּרְיוֹן אֵצֶל הֶגְמוֹן אֶחָד, אָמַר לוֹ: הַלְוֵינִי שְׁתֵּים עֶשְׂרֵה מַעְיָינוֹת מַיִם לְעוֹלֵי רְגָלִים, וַאֲנִי אֶתֵּן לְךָ שְׁתֵּים עֶשְׂרֵה עֵינוֹת מַיִם. וְאִם אֵינִי נוֹתֵן לְךָ, הֲרֵינִי נוֹתֵן לְךָ שְׁתֵּים עֶשְׂרֵה כִּכַּר כֶּסֶף. וְקָבַע לוֹ זְמַן.

§ **The Sages taught: Once all the Jewish people ascended** for **the pilgrimage Festival to Jerusalem and there was not** enough **water for them to drink. Nakdimon**[L] **ben Guryon,**[P] one of the wealthy citizens of Jerusalem, went to **a certain** gentile **officer** [***hegemon***][L] and **said to him: Lend me twelve wells**[N] **of water for the pilgrims, and I will give back to you twelve wells of water. And if I do not give** them **to you, I will give you twelve talents of silver. And** the officer **set him a time** limit for returning the water.

כֵּיוָן שֶׁהִגִּיעַ הַזְּמַן וְלֹא יָרְדוּ גְּשָׁמִים, בְּשַׁחֲרִית שָׁלַח לוֹ: שַׁגֵּר לִי אוֹ מַיִם אוֹ מָעוֹת שֶׁיֵּשׁ לִי בְּיָדְךָ. שָׁלַח לוֹ: עֲדַיִין יֵשׁ לִי זְמַן, כׇּל הַיּוֹם כּוּלּוֹ שֶׁלִּי הוּא. בַּצׇּהֳרַיִים שָׁלַח לוֹ: שַׁגֵּר לִי אוֹ מַיִם אוֹ מָעוֹת שֶׁיֵּשׁ לִי בְּיָדְךָ. שָׁלַח לוֹ: עֲדַיִין יֵשׁ לִי שָׁהוּת בַּיּוֹם. בַּמִּנְחָה שָׁלַח לוֹ: שַׁגֵּר לִי מַיִם אוֹ מָעוֹת שֶׁיֵּשׁ לִי בְּיָדְךָ. שָׁלַח לוֹ: עֲדַיִין יֵשׁ לִי שָׁהוּת בַּיּוֹם. לִגְלֵג עָלָיו אוֹתוֹ הֶגְמוֹן, אָמַר: כׇּל הַשָּׁנָה כּוּלָּהּ לֹא יָרְדוּ גְּשָׁמִים

When the set time arrived and no rain had fallen, in the morning the official **sent** a message **to** Nakdimon: **Send me either** the **water or** the **coins that you owe me.** Nakdimon **sent** a message **to him: I still have time,** as **the entire day is mine. At noontime** the official again **sent** a message **to him: Send me either** the **water or** the **coins that you owe me.** Nakdimon **sent** a message **to him: I still have** time **left in the day.** In the afternoon he **sent** a message **to him: Send me either** the **water or** the **coins that you owe me.** Nakdimon **sent** a message **to him: I still have** time **left in the day. That officer ridiculed him, saying:** Throughout **the entire year rain has not fallen,**

BACKGROUND

The mill grinds from a *kor* – רֵיחַיִם טוֹחֲנוֹת מִן הַכּוֹר: Whenever grain is milled, a certain amount is lost. Some of this loss occurs when the millstones themselves, which must be rough enough to grind the grain, fill with pieces of the ground grain. This wastage can be reduced by the proper adjustment of the space between the millstones, but some very fine flour invariably blows away. Since part of this loss is a constant amount, if only a small quantity of grain is ground, the percentage of the loss is higher, i.e., the loss will be higher in proportion to the total amount of grain milled.

Dough is diminished from a *kor* – עִיסָּה אוֹכֶלֶת מִן הַכּוֹר: In the preparation of dough, some flour is always spilled or scattered, while a certain amount of dough will stick to the sides of the vessel. In this case too, the percentage of loss is greater when a small amount of flour is mixed.

LANGUAGE

Nakdimon – נַקְדִּימוֹן: Apparently from the Greek Νικόδημος, *Nikodemos*, which means the people's victory.

Officer [*hegemon*] – הֶגְמוֹן: From the Greek ἡγεμών, *hègemon*, which means a leader, especially a military leader. It came to refer specifically to Roman prefects. In the Talmud, the term means ruler or high official.

PERSONALITIES

Nakdimon ben Guryon – נַקְדִּימוֹן בֶּן גּוּרְיוֹן: Nakdimon ben Guryon is described in several places in the sources as one of the wealthiest residents of Jerusalem at the time of the destruction of the Temple. He is possibly mentioned in the works of Josephus. As stated in the Gemara, his Hebrew name was apparently Buni, while he also had a Greek name, as was customary at the time. This Greek name was expounded on by the Sages as a way of memorializing this incident.

NOTES

Twelve wells – שְׁתֵּים עֶשְׂרֵה עֵינוֹת מַיִם: Some commentaries write that Nakdimon asked specifically for twelve wells of water, in the hope that the merits of the twelve tribes would help him to repay the loan. If their merits proved insufficient, perhaps the twelve talents of silver would atone for their transgressions (Maharsha).

Perek **III**
Daf **20** Amud **a**

וְעַכְשָׁיו יֵרְדוּ גְּשָׁמִים? נִכְנַס לְבֵית הַמֶּרְחָץ בְּשִׂמְחָה. עַד שֶׁהָאָדוֹן נִכְנָס בְּשִׂמְחָתוֹ לְבֵית הַמֶּרְחָץ, נַקְדִּימוֹן נִכְנַס לְבֵית הַמִּקְדָּשׁ כְּשֶׁהוּא עָצֵב. נִתְעַטֵּף וְעָמַד בִּתְפִלָּה.

and now it will rain? He entered the bathhouse in a state of **joy,** anticipating the large sum of money he was about to receive. **As the master entered the bathhouse**[N] **in his joy, Nakdimon entered the Temple in** a state of **sadness. He wrapped himself** in his prayer shawl **and stood in prayer.**

NOTES

The master entered the bathhouse – נִכְנַס...לְבֵית הַמֶּרְחָץ: The Roman official added insult to injury by entering the bathhouse when the Jews who had arrived in Jerusalem for the Festival did not even have water to drink. In turn, Nakdimon intended to offend the official by demanding payment for the extra rainwater that had been added to his wells (Maharsha).

אָמַר לְפָנָיו: רִבּוֹנוֹ שֶׁל עוֹלָם! גָּלוּי וְיָדוּעַ לְפָנֶיךָ שֶׁלֹּא לִכְבוֹדִי עָשִׂיתִי, וְלֹא לִכְבוֹד בֵּית אַבָּא עָשִׂיתִי. אֶלָּא לִכְבוֹדְךָ עָשִׂיתִי, שֶׁיְּהוּ מַיִם מְצוּיִין לְעוֹלֵי רְגָלִים. מִיָּד נִתְקַשְּׁרוּ שָׁמַיִם בְּעָבִים, וְיָרְדוּ גְּשָׁמִים עַד שֶׁנִּתְמַלְּאוּ שְׁתֵּים עֶשְׂרֵה מַעְיָנוֹת מַיִם וְהוֹתִירוּ.

He said before God: **Master of the Universe, it is revealed and known before You that I did not act for my own honor, nor did I act for the honor of my father's house. Rather, I acted for Your honor, so that there should be water for the Festival pilgrims. Immediately the sky became overcast and rain fell until the twelve cisterns were filled with water, and** there was even more water, so that **they overflowed.**

עַד שֶׁיָּצָא אָדוֹן מִבֵּית הַמֶּרְחָץ נַקְדִּימוֹן בֶּן גּוּרְיוֹן יָצָא מִבֵּית הַמִּקְדָּשׁ. כְּשֶׁפָּגְעוּ זֶה בָּזֶה, אָמַר לוֹ: תֵּן לִי דְּמֵי מַיִם יוֹתֵר שֶׁיֵּשׁ לִי בְּיָדְךָ. אָמַר לוֹ: יוֹדֵעַ אֲנִי שֶׁלֹּא הִרְעִישׁ הַקָּדוֹשׁ בָּרוּךְ הוּא אֶת עוֹלָמוֹ אֶלָּא בִּשְׁבִילְךָ. אֶלָּא עֲדַיִין יֵשׁ לִי פִּתְחוֹן פֶּה עָלֶיךָ שֶׁאוֹצִיא מִמְּךָ אֶת מְעוֹתַיי, שֶׁכְּבָר שָׁקְעָה חַמָּה, וּגְשָׁמִים בִּרְשׁוּתִי יָרְדוּ.

As the master left the bathhouse, Nakdimon ben Guryon left the Temple. When they met one another, Nakdimon **said to him: Give me** the **money you owe me** for **the extra water** you received. The official **said to him: I know that the Holy One, Blessed be He, has shaken His world and caused rain to fall only for you. However, I** still **maintain a claim against you,** by **which I can** legally **take my coins from you,** as you did not pay me on the agreed date, **for the sun had already set, and** therefore **the rain fell onto my property.**

חָזַר וְנִכְנַס לְבֵית הַמִּקְדָּשׁ, נִתְעַטֵּף וְעָמַד בִּתְפִלָּה, וְאָמַר לְפָנָיו: רִבּוֹנוֹ שֶׁל עוֹלָם! הוֹדַע שֶׁיֵּשׁ לְךָ אֲהוּבִים בְּעוֹלָמְךָ. מִיָּד נִתְפַּזְּרוּ הֶעָבִים וְזָרְחָה הַחַמָּה. בְּאוֹתָהּ שָׁעָה אָמַר לוֹ הָאָדוֹן: אִילּוּ לֹא נִקְדְּרָה הַחַמָּה, הָיָה לִי פִּתְחוֹן פֶּה עָלֶיךָ שֶׁאוֹצִיא מִמְּךָ מְעוֹתַיי. תָּנָא: לֹא נַקְדִּימוֹן שְׁמוֹ, אֶלָּא בּוּנִי שְׁמוֹ. וְלָמָּה נִקְרָא שְׁמוֹ נַקְדִּימוֹן? שֶׁנִּקְדְּרָה חַמָּה בַּעֲבוּרוֹ.

Nakdimon **went back and entered the Temple, wrapped himself** in his prayer shawl, **and stood in prayer. He said before** God: **Master of the Universe, let it be known that You have beloved ones in Your world. Immediately, the clouds scattered and the sun shined. At that time, the master said to him: If the sun had not broken through** the clouds, **I would have** had a claim **against you,** by **which I could** have **taken my coins from you.** A Sage **taught: Nakdimon was not his** real **name; rather his name was Buni. And why was** he **called Nakdimon? Because the sun broke through** [*nikdera*] **for him.**[N]

תָּנוּ רַבָּנַן: שְׁלֹשָׁה נִקְדְּמָה לָהֶם חַמָּה בַּעֲבוּרָן: מֹשֶׁה, וִיהוֹשֻׁעַ, וְנַקְדִּימוֹן בֶּן גּוּרְיוֹן. בִּשְׁלָמָא נַקְדִּימוֹן בֶּן גּוּרְיוֹן, גְּמָרָא. יְהוֹשֻׁעַ נַמִי קְרָא, דִּכְתִיב: ״וַיִּדֹּם הַשֶּׁמֶשׁ וְיָרֵחַ עָמָד״ וגו׳. אֶלָּא מֹשֶׁה מְנָלַן?

The Sages taught: With regard to **three** people, **the sun broke through** and shone at an irregular time **for their sake: Moses, Joshua, and Nakdimon ben Guryon.** The Gemara asks: **Granted,** the case of **Nakdimon ben Guryon** is known by the aforementioned **tradition. The case of Joshua too** is derived from **a verse, as it is written: "And the sun stood still, and the moon stayed** until the people had avenged themselves upon their enemies" (Joshua 10:13). **However, from where do we** derive that the sun shined in a supernatural way for **Moses?**

אָמַר רַבִּי אֶלְעָזָר: אָתְיָא ״אָחֵל״, ״אָחֵל״. כְּתִיב הָכָא: ״אָחֵל תֵּת פַּחְדְּךָ״. וּכְתִיב הָתָם: ״אָחֵל גַּדֶּלְךָ״.

Rabbi Elazar said: It is **derived** by verbal analogy between **"I will begin"** and **"I will begin." Here,** with regard to Moses, **it is written:** "This day **I will begin to put the dread of you** and the fear of you upon the peoples that are under all the whole heaven" (Deuteronomy 2:25). **And there,** with regard to Joshua, **it is written:** "On this day **I will begin to magnify you** in the sight of all Israel, that they may know that just as I was with Moses, so I will be with you" (Joshua 3:7). The repeated use of the phrase "I will begin" indicates that all the miracles performed for Joshua were also performed for Moses.[N]

רַבִּי שְׁמוּאֵל בַּר נַחְמָנִי אָמַר: אָתְיָא ״תֵּת״, ״תֵּת״. כְּתִיב הָכָא: ״אָחֵל תֵּת פַּחְדְּךָ״. וּכְתִיב הָתָם: ״בְּיוֹם תֵּת ה׳ אֶת הָאֱמֹרִי״.

Rabbi Shmuel bar Naḥmani said: The fact that the sun stood still for Moses is **derived** by a different verbal analogy, between the terms **"put"** and **"put." Here,** with regard to Moses, **it is written: "I will begin to put the dread of you"** (Deuteronomy 2:25). **And there,** with regard to Joshua, **is it written:** "Then Joshua spoke to the Lord, **on the day when the Lord put the Amorites** before the children of Israel, and he said in the sight of Israel: Sun, stand still upon Gibeon, and you, moon, in the valley of Aijalon" (Joshua 10:12).

רַבִּי יוֹחָנָן אָמַר: אָתְיָא מִגּוּפֵיהּ דִּקְרָא: ״אֲשֶׁר יִשְׁמְעוּן שִׁמְעֲךָ, וְרָגְזוּ וְחָלוּ מִפָּנֶיךָ״. אֵימָתַי רָגְזוּ וְחָלוּ מִפָּנֶיךָ? בְּשָׁעָה שֶׁנִּקְדְּמָה לוֹ חַמָּה לְמֹשֶׁה.

Rabbi Yoḥanan said: This idea is **derived from the verse itself,** as it says with regard to Moses: "This day I will begin to put the dread of you and the fear of you upon the peoples that are under all the whole heaven, **who, when they hear the report of you, shall tremble, and be in anguish due to you"** (Deuteronomy 2:25). **When** did the nations of the world **tremble and** when were they **in anguish due to you? When the sun broke through for Moses.**

NOTES

Because the sun broke through for him – שֶׁנִּקְדְּרָה חַמָּה בַּעֲבוּרוֹ: According to the standard text of the Gemara, the sun broke through the clouds and shone for Nakdimon's sake. However, according to alternative versions found in certain manuscripts and editions, the sun shone for Nakdimon at an hour when it should already have set. This is also consistent with the next *baraita*, which lists Nakdimon together with Joshua, an indication that the sun did not set for Nakdimon, as in the incident of Joshua. Some commentaries explain that the sun did not set at the appointed time for Nakdimon, but remained in the sky until the clouds dispersed, proving to the Roman official that it was still day and that his claim for payment was invalid (Maharsha).

The sun stood for Moses – עֲמִידַת הַחַמָּה לְמֹשֶׁה: In addition to the allusions mentioned in the Gemara, the Sages elsewhere add that the phrase: "Upon the peoples that are under all the whole heaven" (Deuteronomy 2:25), indicates that this was not merely a local victory but an event that affected the entire world (see II Chronicles 32:31).

״וְכֵן עִיר שֶׁלֹּא יָרְדוּ עָלֶיהָ גְּשָׁמִים״ כו׳. אָמַר רַב יְהוּדָה אָמַר רַב: וּשְׁתֵּיהֶן לִקְלָלָה.

§ The mishna taught: **And likewise,** if there is a particular **city upon which it did not rain,** while the surrounding area did receive rain, this is considered a divine curse, as it is written: "And I will cause it to rain on one city, but on one city I will not cause it to rain, one portion will be rained upon, and the portion upon which it did not rain shall wither" (Amos 4:7). **Rav Yehuda said** that **Rav said: And both of** the cities are faced **with a curse,** as one city suffers from drought while the other is afflicted with destructive storms.

״הָיְתָה יְרוּשָׁלַיִם לְנִדָּה בֵּינֵיהֶם״. אָמַר רַב יְהוּדָה אָמַר רַב: לִבְרָכָה. כְּנִדָּה – מָה נִדָּה יֵשׁ לָהּ הֶיתֵּר, אַף יְרוּשָׁלַיִם יֵשׁ לָהּ תַּקָּנָה.

This statement reverses the plain meaning of a verse. The Gemara provides other interpretations that Rav Yehuda attributed to Rav, which also run contrary to the simple meaning of a verse. **"Jerusalem among them was a like a menstruating woman"** (Lamentations 1:17). **Rav Yehuda said** that **Rav said:** Although the simple meaning of this verse is a curse, it can also be understood **as a blessing.** Jerusalem was **like a menstruating woman:**[N] **Just as a menstruating woman** will become **permitted** to her husband after the conclusion of her days of ritual impurity, **so too, Jerusalem** will be **repaired** from its destruction.

״הָיְתָה כְּאַלְמָנָה״. אָמַר רַב יְהוּדָה: לִבְרָכָה. כְּאַלְמָנָה, וְלֹא אַלְמָנָה מַמָּשׁ. אֶלָּא כְּאִשָּׁה שֶׁהָלַךְ בַּעְלָהּ לִמְדִינַת הַיָּם, וְדַעְתּוֹ לַחֲזוֹר עָלֶיהָ.

Similarly, with regard to the verse: **"How she has become like a widow"** (Lamentations 1:1), **Rav Yehuda said:** This too is **for a blessing.** The verse states that Jerusalem is **like a widow, but is not an actual widow. Rather,** Jerusalem is **like a woman whose husband has gone to a country overseas.** Without her husband by her side she is likened to a widow, **and** yet **he intends to return to her.**

״וְגַם אֲנִי נָתַתִּי אֶתְכֶם נִבְזִים וּשְׁפָלִים״. אָמַר רַב יְהוּדָה: לִבְרָכָה, דְּלָא מוֹקְמִי מִינַּן לָא רֵישֵׁי נַהֲרֵי וְלָא גְּזִירִיפְטֵי.

The same manner of explanation is provided for the verse: **"Therefore I have also made you contemptible and base"** (Malachi 2:9). **Rav Yehuda said:** This too can be interpreted **as a blessing,** as meaning that the nations view us as lowly, but nevertheless, they do not assign us unpleasant jobs. **They do not** appoint **from us either river officials**[N] **or government officials** [*geziripatei*].[L]

״וְהִכָּה ה׳ אֶת יִשְׂרָאֵל כַּאֲשֶׁר יָנוּד הַקָּנֶה בַּמַּיִם״. אָמַר רַב יְהוּדָה אָמַר רַב: לִבְרָכָה. דְּאָמַר רַבִּי שְׁמוּאֵל בַּר נַחְמָנִי אָמַר רַבִּי יוֹנָתָן: מַאי דִּכְתִיב: ״נֶאֱמָנִים פִּצְעֵי אוֹהֵב וְנַעְתָּרוֹת נְשִׁיקוֹת שׂוֹנֵא״? טוֹבָה קְלָלָה שֶׁקִּילֵּל אֲחִיָּה הַשִּׁילוֹנִי אֶת יִשְׂרָאֵל יוֹתֵר מִבְּרָכָה שֶׁבֵּרְכָן בִּלְעָם הָרָשָׁע.

The prophet Ahijah the Shilonite cursed Israel in the following terms: **"For the Lord will smite Israel as a reed is shaken in the water"** (I Kings 14:15). **Rav Yehuda said** that **Rav said:** This too is **for a blessing, as Rabbi Shmuel bar Naḥmani said** that **Rabbi Yoḥanan said: What is** the meaning of that **which is written: "Faithful are the wounds of a friend, but the kisses of an enemy are deceitful"** (Proverbs 27:6)? **The curse with which Ahijah the Shilonite cursed the Jewish people is more** effective **than the blessing with which Balaam the wicked blessed them.**

אֲחִיָּה הַשִּׁילוֹנִי קִלְּלָן בְּקָנֶה. אָמַר לָהֶם לְיִשְׂרָאֵל: ״וְהִכָּה ה׳ אֶת יִשְׂרָאֵל כַּאֲשֶׁר יָנוּד הַקָּנֶה״. מָה קָנֶה זֶה עוֹמֵד בִּמְקוֹם מַיִם, וְגִזְעוֹ מַחֲלִיף, וְשָׁרָשָׁיו מְרוּבִּין, וַאֲפִילּוּ כָּל הָרוּחוֹת שֶׁבָּעוֹלָם בָּאוֹת וְנוֹשְׁבוֹת בּוֹ, אֵין מְזִיזוֹת אוֹתוֹ מִמְּקוֹמוֹ, אֶלָּא הוֹלֵךְ וּבָא עִמָּהֶן, דָּמְמוּ הָרוּחוֹת, עָמַד הַקָּנֶה בִּמְקוֹמוֹ.

Rabbi Yoḥanan elaborates: **Ahijah the Shilonite cursed** the Jewish people **by** comparing them to **a reed:**[B] **"For the Lord will smite Israel as a reed is shaken in the water."** Although it seems to be a curse, this verse is actually a blessing. **Just as this reed stands in a place of water, and its shoots replenish** themselves when cut, **and its roots are numerous** for a plant of its size, **and even if all the winds in the world come and blow against it, they cannot move it from its place, rather, it sways with them** until **the winds subside, and the reed** still **stands in its place,** the same applies to the Jewish people. After all the difficulties that they endure, they will ultimately survive and return home.

אֲבָל בִּלְעָם הָרָשָׁע בֵּירְכָן בְּאֶרֶז, שֶׁנֶּאֱמַר: ״כַּאֲרָזִים עֲלֵי מָיִם״ מָה אֶרֶז זֶה אֵינוֹ עוֹמֵד בִּמְקוֹם מַיִם, וְאֵין גִּזְעוֹ מַחֲלִיף, וְאֵין שָׁרָשָׁיו מְרוּבִּין, אֲפִילּוּ כָּל הָרוּחוֹת שֶׁבָּעוֹלָם נוֹשְׁבוֹת בּוֹ, אֵין מְזִיזוֹת אוֹתוֹ מִמְּקוֹמוֹ, כֵּיוָן שֶׁנָּשְׁבָה בּוֹ רוּחַ דְּרוֹמִית, עוֹקַרְתּוֹ וְהוֹפַכְתּוֹ עַל פָּנָיו. וְלֹא עוֹד אֶלָּא שֶׁזָּכָה קָנֶה לִיטּוֹל הֵימֶנּוּ קוּלְמוֹס לִכְתּוֹב בּוֹ סֵפֶר תּוֹרָה, נְבִיאִים, וּכְתוּבִים.

However, Balaam the wicked blessed the Jews **by** comparing them **to a cedar,**[B] **as it is stated: "As cedars beside the waters"** (Numbers 24:6). **Just as this cedar does not stand in a place of water, and its shoots do not replenish** themselves, **and its roots are not numerous,** Balaam wished that the same should apply to the Jewish people. Furthermore, while it is true that **even if all the winds in the world blow** against **it they will not move it from its place, once the southern wind blows** against **it, it uproots** the cedar **and turns it on its face. And not only that, but the reed merited**[H] that **a quill** [*kulmos*][L] **is taken from it to write with it a Torah scroll, the Prophets, and the Writings.** Evidently, the curse comparing Israel to a reed is better than the blessing likening them to a cedar.

NOTES

As a blessing, like a menstruating woman – לִבְרָכָה כְּנִדָּה: Despite the fact that this verse is stated in a the book of Lamentations, there is nevertheless a hint of a blessing within its curse (Rav Yoshiya Pinto).

As they do not appoint from us…river officials – דְּלָא מוֹקְמִי מִינַּן...רֵישֵׁי נַהֲרֵי: Some commentaries explain that it was beneficial for the Jews not to be appointed customs officials or police officers, as this would undoubtedly stir up the anger and jealousy of their gentile neighbors (Rabbeinu Gershom). Others add that since they were not assigned such tasks, they had more time to devote to Torah study (Rabbi Elyakim).

LANGUAGE

Government officials [*geziripatei*] – גְּזִירִיפְטֵי: From the Aramaic *gauzir*, meaning official, and the Iranian suffix pati, meaning lord. This was the title of a Sasanian functionary.

Quill [*kulmos*] – קוּלְמוֹס: From the Greek κάλαμος, *kalamos*, which means reed, as quills were made from reeds.

BACKGROUND

Reed – קָנֶה: This is possibly the common reed, *Phragmites communis*, or the *Arundo donax*. These are species of perennial grasses with straight stems, 2–4 m in height. Normally these reeds grow in dense clumps along the banks of rivers or other bodies of water. Reeds were used to make fences and coarse mats. They were also manufactured into pens, mainly for writing large letters with ink.

Cedar – אֶרֶז: The cedar tree, *Cedrus*, can grow to an enormous height. However, as it grows on mountainous slopes, it does not strike deep roots. Since most of the winds in Eretz Yisrael are from the west or north, the cedar's roots protect it from winds coming from these directions. Consequently, a storm from the south, which can occur on occasion, might uproot a cedar tree entirely.

Lebanon cedar

HALAKHA

The reed merited – זָכָה קָנֶה: According to some authorities, a Torah scroll must be written with a reed quill, not a feather quill (Rema, citing Mordekhai). However, others state that the common custom does not follow this ruling (*Shakh*, citing *Levush*). Nowadays, Ashkenazic scribes write with a feather, while their Sephardic counterparts use a reed (*Shulḥan Arukh*, *Yoreh De'a* 271:7).

תנו רבנן: לעולם יהא אדם רך כקנה ואל יהא קשה כארז. מעשה שבא רבי אלעזר ברבי שמעון ממגדל גדור מבית רבו, והיה רכוב על חמור ומטייל על שפת נהר. ושמח שמחה גדולה, והיתה דעתו גסה עליו מפני שלמד תורה הרבה,

The Sages further **taught** in praise of the reed: **A person should always be soft like a reed, and he should not be stiff like a cedar. An incident** occurred in which **Rabbi Elazar, son of Rabbi Shimon, came from Migdal Gedor,**[B] **from his rabbi's house, and he was riding on a donkey and strolling on the bank of the river. And he was very happy, and his head was swollen with pride because he had studied much Torah.**

Perek **III**
Daf **20** Amud **b**

נזדמן לו אדם אחד שהיה מכוער ביותר. אמר לו: שלום עליך, רבי. ולא החזיר לו. אמר לו: ריקה, כמה מכוער אותו האיש! שמא כל בני עירך מכוערין כמותך? אמר לו: איני יודע, אלא לך ואמור לאומן שעשאני: כמה מכוער כלי זה שעשית! כיון שידע בעצמו שחטא, ירד מן החמור ונשתטח לפניו, ואמר לו: נעניתי לך, מחול לי! אמר לו: איני מוחל לך עד שתלך לאומן שעשאני ואמור לו: כמה מכוער כלי זה שעשית!

He happened upon **an exceedingly ugly person,** who **said to him: Greetings to you, my rabbi, but** Rabbi Elazar **did not return** his greeting. Instead, Rabbi Elazar **said to him: Worthless** [*reika*][L] person, **how ugly is that man.**[N] **Are all the people of your city as ugly as you?** The man **said to him: I do not know, but you** should **go and say to the Craftsman Who made me: How ugly is the vessel you made. When** Rabbi Elazar **realized that he** had **sinned** and insulted this man merely on account of his appearance, **he descended from his donkey and prostrated himself before him, and he said to** the man: **I have sinned against you; forgive me.** The man **said to him: I will not forgive you until you go to the Craftsman Who made me and say: How ugly is the vessel you made.**

היה מטייל אחריו עד שהגיע לעירו. יצאו בני עירו לקראתו, והיו אומרים לו: שלום עליך, רבי, רבי, מורי, מורי. אמר להם: למי אתם קורין: רבי, רבי? אמרו לו: לזה שמטייל אחריך. אמר להם: אם זה רבי, אל ירבו כמותו בישראל! אמרו לו: מפני מה? אמר להם: כך וכך עשה לי. אמרו לו: אף על פי כן, מחול לו, שאדם גדול בתורה הוא.

He walked behind the man, trying to appease him, **until they reached** Rabbi Elazar's **city. The people of his city came out to greet him, saying to him: Greetings to you, my rabbi, my rabbi, my master, my master.** The man **said to them: Who are you calling my rabbi, my rabbi? They said to him: To this man, who is walking behind you. He said to them: If this man is a rabbi, may there not be many like him among the Jewish people. They asked him: For what** reason do you say this? **He said to them: He did such and such to me. They said to him: Even so,** forgive him, **as he is a great Torah scholar.**

אמר להם: בשבילכם הריני מוחל לו, ובלבד שלא יהא רגיל לעשות כן. מיד נכנס רבי אלעזר ברבי שמעון ודרש: לעולם יהא אדם רך כקנה ואל יהא קשה כארז. ולפיכך זכה קנה ליטול הימנה קולמוס לכתוב בו ספר תורה, תפילין, ומזוזות.

He said to them: For your sakes I forgive him, provided that he accepts upon himself **not to become accustomed to behave like this. Immediately, Rabbi Elazar, son of Rabbi Shimon, entered the study hall and taught: A person should always be soft like a reed and he should not be stiff like a cedar,** as one who is proud like a cedar is likely to sin. **And therefore,** due to its gentle qualities, the **reed merited** that **a quill is taken from it to write with it a Torah scroll, phylacteries, and** ***mezuzot.***

"וכן עיר שיש בה דבר או מפולת" כו׳. תנו רבנן: מפולת שאמרו בריאות ולא רעועות; שאינן ראויות ליפול, ולא הראויות ליפול.

§ The mishna taught: **And likewise,** if a **city is** afflicted **by pestilence or collapsing buildings,**[H] that city fasts and sounds the alarm, and all of its surrounding areas fast but they do not sound the alarm. Rabbi Akiva says: They sound the alarm but they do not fast. **The Sages taught:** These collapsing buildings **to which** the Sages **referred** are those of **sturdy and not dilapidated** walls; they have walls **that are not ready to fall, and not those that are ready to fall.**

הי ניהו בריאות הי ניהו שאינן ראויות ליפול; הי ניהו רעועות הי ניהו ראויות ליפול! לא, צריכא דנפלו מחמת גובהייהו. אי נמי, דקיימן אגודא דנהרא.

The Gemara expresses puzzlement with regard to the wording of the *baraita*: **What are sound** walls; **what are** walls **that are not ready to fall; what are dilapidated** walls; **what are those that are ready to fall?**[N] The elements in each pair of walls are apparently the same, and the *baraita* is repetitive. The Gemara answers: **No,** it is **necessary** to specify that in the case of walls **that fell due to their height,** i.e., they are sound but also ready to fall, due to their excessive height. **Alternatively,** the *baraita* is referring to a case **where** the walls **were positioned on a riverbank,** as they are likely to fall despite the fact that they are not dilapidated, as the riverbank itself is unstable.

BACKGROUND

Migdal Gedor – מגדל גדור: The location of Migdal Gedor is unclear. Some contend that it was a small settlement between Ḥamat Gader and Gader. According to this opinion, the river referred to in the Gemara was apparently the Yarmouk.

LANGUAGE

Worthless [*reika*] – ריקה: This term was apparently commonly used at the time, as it is also mentioned in sources outside the Talmud. It is the Aramaic version of the Hebrew *reik*, meaning empty. It is also used to refer to a person void of decent behavior, a worthless individual, e.g., "And there were gathered vain [*reikim*] fellows to Jephthah" (Judges 11:3).

NOTES

How ugly is that man – כמה מכוער אותו האיש: Some commentaries explain that Rabbi Elazar was reacting to the boorishness and moral corruption he thought were expressed in the man's face. When the man responded with his wise retort, Rabbi Elazar realized that he had been mistaken and that the man's ugliness was merely physical, and he immediately expressed his regret for having humiliated him (*Iyyun Ya'akov*).

Dilapidated…ready to fall – רעועות...ראויות ליפול: Apparently, the subsequent incident involving the wall that stood for thirteen years is cited as an example of a shaky wall that is not in danger of imminent collapse but should still be treated as a hazard (see *Dikdukei Soferim*).

HALAKHA

Collpasing buildings – מפולת: If the walls of the buildings in a certain city begin to collapse, and these walls were sound and were not positioned on a riverbank, the people of that city must fast and sound the alarm (*Shulḥan Arukh, Oraḥ Ḥayyim* 576:4).

כִּי הַהִיא אֲשִׁיתָא רְעוּעָה דַּהֲוַאי בִּנְהַרְדְּעָא, דְּלָא הֲוָה חָלֵיף רַב וּשְׁמוּאֵל תּוּתָהּ, אַף עַל גַּב דְּקַיְימָא בְּאַתְרָהּ תְּלֵיסַר שְׁנִין. יוֹמָא חַד אִיקְּלַע רַב אַדָּא בַּר אַהֲבָה לְהָתָם. אֲמַר לֵיהּ שְׁמוּאֵל לְרַב: נֵיתֵי מָר, נַקִּיף. אֲמַר לֵיהּ: לָא צְרִיכְנָא הָאִידָּנָא, דְּאִיכָּא רַב אַדָּא בַּר אַהֲבָה בַּהֲדַן דִּנְפִישׁ זְכוּתֵיהּ, וְלָא מִסְתְּפֵינָא.

The Gemara relates: This is **like that** dilapidated wall **that was in Neharde'a, under which Rav and Shmuel would not pass, although it stood in place thirteen years. One day Rav Adda bar Ahava happened** to come **there** and walked with them. As they passed the wall, **Shmuel said to Rav: Come, Master, let us circumvent** this wall, so that we do not stand beneath it. Rav **said to him:** It is **not necessary** to do so **today, as Rav Adda bar Ahava is with us, whose merit is great,** and therefore **I am not afraid** of its collapse.

רַב הוּנָא הֲוָה לֵיהּ הַהוּא חַמְרָא בְּהַהוּא בֵּיתָא רְעִיעָא, וּבָעֵי לְפַנּוּיֵיהּ. עַיְילֵיהּ לְרַב אַדָּא בַּר אַהֲבָה לְהָתָם, מְשַׁכֵיהּ בִּשְׁמַעְתָּא עַד דְּפַנְּיֵיהּ. בָּתַר דִּנְפַק, נְפַל בֵּיתָא. אַרְגִּישׁ רַב אַדָּא בַּר אַהֲבָה אִיקְּפַד.

The Gemara relates another incident. **Rav Huna had a certain** quantity of **wine in a certain dilapidated house and he wanted to move it,** but he was afraid that the building would collapse upon his entry. **He brought Rav Adda bar Ahava to there,** to the ramshackle house, and **he dragged** out a discussion with **him** concerning a matter of ***halakha*** **until they had removed** all the wine. **As soon as they exited, the building collapsed. Rav Adda bar Ahava realized** what had happened **and became angry.**

סָבַר לָהּ כִּי הָא דְּאָמַר רַבִּי יַנַּאי: לְעוֹלָם אַל יַעֲמוֹד אָדָם בִּמְקוֹם סַכָּנָה וְיֹאמַר: עוֹשִׂין לִי נֵס, שֶׁמָּא אֵין עוֹשִׂין לוֹ נֵס. וְאִם תִּימְצֵי לוֹמַר עוֹשִׂין לוֹ נֵס, מְנַכִּין לוֹ מִזְּכֻיּוֹתָיו. אֲמַר רַב חָנָן: מַאי קְרָא? דִּכְתִיב: ״קָטֹנְתִּי מִכֹּל הַחֲסָדִים וּמִכָּל הָאֱמֶת״.

The Gemara explains: Rav Adda bar Ahava **holds in accordance with this** statement, **as Rabbi Yannai said: A person should never stand in a place of danger and say: A miracle will be performed for me,** and I will escape unharmed, **lest a miracle is not performed for him. And if you say** that **a miracle** will be **performed for him, they will deduct it from his merits. Rav Ḥanan said: What is the verse** that alludes to this idea? **As it is written: "I have become small from all the mercies and all the truth** that You have showed Your servant" (Genesis 32:11). In other words, the more benevolence one receives from God, the more his merit is reduced.

מַאי הֲוָה עוֹבָדֵיהּ דְּרַב אַדָּא בַּר אַהֲבָה? כִּי הָא דְּאִתְּמַר: שָׁאֲלוּ תַּלְמִידָיו לְרַב אַדָּא בַּר אַהֲבָה: בַּמֶּה הֶאֱרַכְתָּ יָמִים? אָמַר לָהֶם: מִיָּמַי לֹא הִקְפַּדְתִּי בְּתוֹךְ בֵּיתִי, וְלֹא צָעַדְתִּי בִּפְנֵי מִי שֶׁגָּדוֹל מִמֶּנִּי,

After recounting stories that reflect Rav Adda bar Ahava's great merit, the Gemara asks: **What were** the exceptional deeds **of Rav Adda bar Ahava?** The Gemara reports that they are **as it is stated:** The students of Rabbi Zeira asked him, and some say that **the students of Rav Adda bar Ahava asked him: To what** do you attribute **your longevity?**[N] **He said to them: In all my days I did not become angry with my household, and I never walked before someone greater than myself;** rather, I always gave him the honor of walking before me.

וְלֹא הִרְהַרְתִּי בַּמְּבוֹאוֹת הַמְטוּנָּפוֹת, וְלֹא הָלַכְתִּי אַרְבַּע אַמּוֹת בְּלֹא תּוֹרָה וּבְלֹא תְּפִילִּין, וְלֹא יָשַׁנְתִּי בְּבֵית הַמִּדְרָשׁ, לֹא שֵׁינַת קֶבַע וְלֹא שֵׁינַת עַרְאַי, וְלֹא שַׂשְׂתִּי בְּתַקָּלַת חֲבֵרִי, וְלֹא קָרָאתִי לַחֲבֵירִי בַּהֲכִינָתוֹ. וְאָמְרִי לַהּ: בַּחֲנִיכָתוֹ.

Rav Adda bar Ahava continued: **And I did not think** about matters of Torah **in filthy alleyways;**[H] **and I did not walk four cubits without** engaging in **Torah and without** donning **phylacteries; and I would not fall asleep in the study hall, neither a deep sleep nor a brief nap; and I would not rejoice in the mishap of my colleague; and I would not call my colleague by his nickname.**[H] **And some say** that he said: I would **not call my colleague by his** derogatory **family name.**[N]

אֲמַר לֵיהּ רָבָא לְרַפְרָם בַּר פַּפָּא: לֵימָא לָן מָר מֵהָנֵי מִילֵּי מְעַלְּיָיתָא דַּהֲוָה עָבֵיד רַב הוּנָא. אֲמַר לֵיהּ: בְּיַנְקוּתֵיהּ לָא דְּכֵירְנָא. בְּסִיבוּתֵיהּ דְּכֵירְנָא: דְּכָל יוֹמָא דְּעֵיבָא הָווּ מַפְּקִין לֵיהּ בְּגוּהַרְקָא דְּדַהֲבָא, וְסָיֵיר לַהּ לְכוּלַּהּ מָתָא. וְכָל אֲשִׁיתָא דַּהֲוַות רְעִיעָתָא הֲוָה סָתַר לַהּ. אִי אֶפְשָׁר לְמָרַהּ, בָּנֵי לַהּ. וְאִי לָא אֶפְשָׁר, בָּנֵי לַהּ אִיהוּ מִדִּידֵיהּ.

§ The Gemara relates another story about the righteous deeds of the Sages involving a dilapidated wall. **Rava said to Rafram bar Pappa: Let the Master tell us some of those fine** deeds **that Rav Huna performed. He said to him: I do not remember** what he did **in his youth, but** the deeds **of his old age I remember. As on every cloudy day they would take him out in a golden carriage** [*guharka*],[L] **and he would survey the entire city. And** he would command **that every unstable wall be torn down,** lest it fall in the rain and hurt someone. **If its owner was able** to build another, Rav Huna would instruct him **to rebuild it. And if he was unable** to rebuild it, Rav Huna would **build it himself with his own money.**

NOTES

To what do you attribute your longevity – **בַּמֶּה הֶאֱרַכְתָּ יָמִים:** *Keren Ora* explains at length that one can live a long life only if his soul finds contentment and pleasure in his body. Each of the righteous acts mentioned here assisted Rav Adda bar Ahava to achieve his long life.

By his nickname…by his family name – **הֲכִינָתוֹ...חֲנִיכָתוֹ:** Rashi and *Tosafot* both explain the distinction between these two terms as follows: A nickname refers to a derogatory epithet applied to a particular person, whereas a family name refers to an insulting moniker applied to an entire family. Others read: My nickname…his nickname, and explain as follows: According to the first version of the story, Rav Adda bar Ahava himself never made up any derogatory nickname, whereas according to the second version, Rav Adda bar Ahava did not even call someone by a nickname used by others (Rabbeinu Ḥananel; *Arukh*). Yet others write that Rav Adda bar Ahava was careful not to call someone even by a nickname that was not intended to be disparaging (*Shita Mekubbetzet*).

HALAKHA

And I did not think about Torah in filthy alleyways – **וְלֹא הִרְהַרְתִּי בַּמְּבוֹאוֹת הַמְטוּנָּפוֹת:** One may not discuss or even meditate upon sacred matters in a toilet, a bathhouse, or any other dirty place (Rambam *Sefer Ahava*, *Hilkhot Keriat Shema* 3:4).

And I would not call my colleague by his nickname – **וְלֹא קָרָאתִי לַחֲבֵירִי בַּהֲכִינָתוֹ:** It is prohibited to call people by derogatory names with the aim of humiliating them, even if they are accustomed to these names (*Shulḥan Arukh*, *Ḥoshen Mishpat* 228:5).

LANGUAGE

Carriage [*guharka*] – **גּוּהַרְקָא:** This word apparently derives from the Middle Iranian juwālak, meaning sack or knapsack.

NOTES

Human food may not be fed to animals – מאכל אדם אין מאכילין לבהמה: It has been pointed out, based on numerous sources, that there is no prohibition against feeding animals food fit for human consumption (Ra'avad). Some commentaries explain that although one may indeed feed animals food fit for humans, it is prohibited to go out and buy this food with the intention of using it as animal fodder. Others suggest that one may feed animals with a small amount of food fit for humans, but not with large quantities of this food. Alternatively, there is a difference between food that is clearly intended for humans and food that is fit for humans but is also commonly given to animals, e.g., carobs and gourds. Lastly, a distinction can be drawn between places where animal fodder is available and places where only food fit for human consumption is available (see Meiri and *Maḥatzit HaShekel*).

The commentaries ask: If it is not permitted to use food fit for human consumption as animal fodder, as this is disrespectful to the food, how could Rav Huna have thrown the vegetables into the river? Rashi explains that Rav Huna intended that the vegetables should drift downstream and be eaten by whoever found them. Others suggest that this was not a recognizable show of disrespect, as those who saw the vegetables in the river would assume that they were already rotten when discarded (*Petaḥ Einayim*, citing Rosh).

HALAKHA

Human food may not be fed to animals – מאכל אדם אין מאכילין לבהמה: One may not feed food that is fit for human consumption to animals, as this is a disrespectful use of the food (*Magen Avraham*; *Shulḥan Arukh*, *Oraḥ Ḥayyim* 171:1).

BACKGROUND

A remedy against Shivta – מילתא דשיבתא: Shivta is mentioned in several places in the Gemara as an evil spirit that rests on the hands of one who neglects to wash his hands at the appropriate times (*Yoma* 77b; *Ḥullin* 107b). In their responsa, the *ge'onim* explain that it is a disease that afflicts young children, causing them to waste away and die.

וכל פניא דמעלי שבתא הוה משדר שלוחא לשוקא, וכל ירקא דהוה פייש להו לגינאי זבין ליה ושדי ליה לנהרא. וליתביה לעניים! זמנין דסמכא דעתייהו, ולא אתו למיזבן. ולשדייה לבהמה! קסבר מאכל אדם אין מאכילין לבהמה.

Rafram bar Pappa further relates: **And every Shabbat eve,** in the **afternoon,** Rav Huna **would send a messenger to the marketplace, and he would purchase all the vegetables that were left with the gardeners** who sold their crops, **and throw** them **into the river.** The Gemara asks: **But** why did he throw out the vegetables? **Let him give them to the poor.** The Gemara answers: If he did this, the poor would **sometimes rely** on the fact that Rav Huna would hand out vegetables, **and they would not come to purchase** any. This would ruin the gardeners' livelihood. The Gemara further asks: **And let him throw them to the animals.** The Gemara answers: **He holds** that **human food** may **not be fed to animals,**[NH] as this is a display of contempt for the food.

ולא ליזבניה כלל! נמצאת מכשילן לעתיד לבא.

The Gemara objects: **But** if Rav Huna could not use them in any way, he should **not purchase** the vegetables **at all.** The Gemara answers: If nothing is done, **you** would have been **found** to have caused **a stumbling block for them in the future.** If the vegetable sellers see that some of their produce is left unsold, the next week they will not bring enough for Shabbat. Therefore, Rav Huna made sure that the vegetables were all bought, so that the sellers would continue to bring them.

כי הוה ליה מילתא דאסותא, הוי מלי כוזא מיניה ותלי ליה בסיפא דביתא ואמר: כל דבעי, ליתי ולישקול. ואיכא דאמרי: מילתא דשיבתא הוה גמיר, והוה מנח כוזא דמיא ודלי ליה ואמר: כל דצריך, ליתי וליעול, דלא לסתכן.

Another custom of Rav Huna was **that when he had** a new **medicine, he would fill** a water **jug** with the medicine **and hang it from the doorpost of his house, saying: All who need, let him come and take** from this new medicine. **And there are** those **say: He had a remedy** against the demon **Shivta**[B] that he knew by **tradition,** that one must wash his hands for protection against this evil spirit. **And** to this end, **he would place a water jug and hang** it by the door, **saying: Anyone who needs, let him come** to the house and wash his hands, so **that he will not be in danger.**

כי הוה כרך ריפתא, הוה פתח לבביה ואמר: כל מאן דצריך, ליתי וליכול. אמר רבא: כולהו מצינא מקיימנא, לבר מהא דלא מצינא למיעבד,

The Gemara further relates: **When** Rav Huna **would eat bread, he would open the doors** to his house, **saying: Whoever needs, let him come in and eat. Rava said: I can fulfill all these** customs of Rav Huna, **except for this one, which I cannot do,**

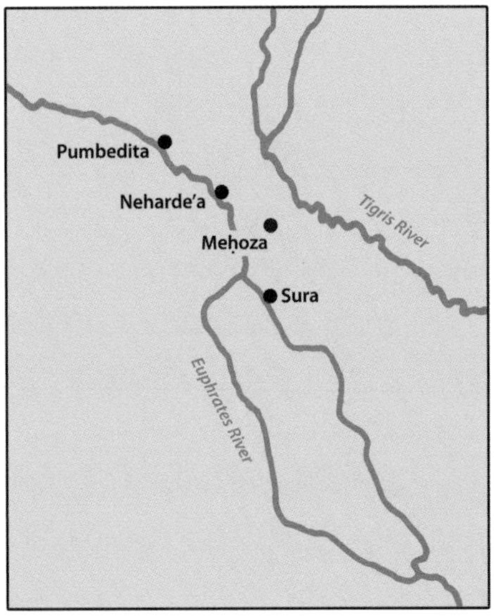

Map of central Babylonia

משום דנפישי בני חילא דמחוזא.

due to the fact that **there are many soldiers in** the city of **Meḥoza,**[B] and if I let them all eat, they will take all the food I own.

BACKGROUND

Meḥoza – מחוזא: A city on the Tigris located near the Malka River, Meḥoza was a large commercial city, and most of its inhabitants were Jews. Unlike most other Jewish communities, Meḥoza's Jews generally earned their living from commerce. Jews from different countries of origin lived in Meḥoza, and many converts lived there as well. After Neharde'a was destroyed in 259 CE, its yeshiva moved to Meḥoza. Meḥoza became the Torah center of leading scholars such as Rav Naḥman; Rav Sheshet; Rava, who later became head of the yeshiva in Meḥoza; Ameimar; and Rav Kahana, Rav Ashi's teacher. After Abaye's death, c. 338 CE, the yeshiva in Pumbedita, then headed by Rava, also moved to Meḥoza for a period of time.

אִילְפָא וְרַבִּי יוֹחָנָן הָווּ גָּרְסִי בְּאוֹרַיְיתָא, דְּחִיקָא לְהוּ מִילְּתָא טוּבָא. אָמְרִי: נֵיקוּם וְנֵיזִיל וְנֶיעֱבַד עִיסְקָא, וּנְקַיֵּים בְּנַפְשִׁין: "אֶפֶס כִּי לֹא יִהְיֶה בְּךָ אֶבְיוֹן". אֲזַלוּ, אוֹתְבֵי תּוּתֵי גּוּדָא רְעִיעָא. הָווּ קָא כָּרְכִי רִיפְתָּא. אָתוּ תְּרֵי מַלְאֲכֵי הַשָּׁרֵת.

§ The Gemara relates another story that involves an unstable wall. **Ilfa**[P] **and Rabbi Yoḥanan studied Torah** together, and as a result **they became very hard-pressed** for money. **They said: Let us get up and go and engage in commerce, and we will fulfill, with regard to ourselves,** the verse: **"Although there should be no needy among you"** (Deuteronomy 15:4), as we will no longer be complete paupers. **They went and sat under a dilapidated wall** and **were eating bread,** when **two ministering angels arrived.**

שְׁמָעֵיהּ רַבִּי יוֹחָנָן דַּאֲמַר חַד לְחַבְרֵיהּ: נִישְׁדֵּי עֲלַיְיהוּ הַאי גּוּדָא וְנִקְטְלִינְהוּ, שֶׁמַּנִּיחִין חַיֵּי עוֹלָם הַבָּא וְעוֹסְקִין בְּחַיֵּי שָׁעָה. אֲמַר לֵיהּ אִידָךְ: שָׁבְקִינְהוּ, דְּאִיכָּא בְּהוּ חַד דְּקַיְימָא לֵיהּ שַׁעְתָּא. רַבִּי יוֹחָנָן שְׁמַע, אִילְפָא לָא שְׁמַע. אֲמַר לֵיהּ רַבִּי יוֹחָנָן לְאִילְפָא: שְׁמַע מָר מִידֵּי? אֲמַר לֵיהּ: לָא. אֲמַר: מִדְּשָׁמְעִי אֲנָא וְאִילְפָא לָא שְׁמַע, שְׁמַע מִינָּהּ לְדִידִי קַיְימָא לִי שַׁעְתָּא.

Rabbi Yoḥanan heard that one angel **said to the other: Let us knock this wall down upon them**[N] **and kill them, as they abandon eternal life** of Torah study **and engage in temporal life** for their own sustenance. **The other** angel **said to him: Leave them, as there is one of them whose time** of achievement **stands before him,** i.e., his time has yet to come. **Rabbi Yoḥanan heard** all this, but **Ilfa did not hear** the angels' conversation. **Rabbi Yoḥanan said to Ilfa: Did the Master hear anything?** Ilfa **said to him: No.** Rabbi Yoḥanan **said** to himself: **Since I heard** the angels **and Ilfa did not hear,** I can **learn from this** that it is **I whose time** of achievement **stands before me.**

אֲמַר לֵיהּ רַבִּי יוֹחָנָן: אִיהֲדַר וְאוֹקֵי בְּנַפְשַׁאי: "כִּי לֹא יֶחְדַּל אֶבְיוֹן מִקֶּרֶב הָאָרֶץ". רַבִּי יוֹחָנָן הֲדַר, אִילְפָא לָא הֲדַר. עַד דַּאֲתָא אִילְפָא, מְלִיךְ רַבִּי יוֹחָנָן.

Rabbi Yoḥanan said to Ilfa: I will return home and **fulfill with regard to myself** the contrary verse: **"For the poor shall never cease out of the land"** (Deuteronomy 15:11). **Rabbi Yoḥanan returned** to the study hall, and **Ilfa did not return,** but went to engage in business instead. **By the time that Ilfa came** back from his business travels, **Rabbi Yoḥanan** had been **appointed** head of the academy, and his financial situation had improved.

אָמְרוּ לוֹ: אִי אֲתֵיב מָר וְגָרֵיס, לָא הֲוָה מָלֵיךְ מָר? אֲזַל תְּלָא נַפְשֵׁיהּ בְּאַסְקַרְיָא דִּסְפִינְתָּא, אֲמַר: אִי אִיכָּא דְּשָׁאֵיל לִי בְּמַתְנִיתָא דְּרַבִּי חִיָּיא וְרַבִּי אוֹשַׁעְיָא וְלָא פָּשְׁטִינָא לֵיהּ מִמַּתְנִיתִין נָפֵילְנָא מֵאַסְקַרְיָא דִּסְפִינְתָּא וְטָבַעְנָא".

His colleagues **said to** Ilfa: **If the Master had sat and studied,** instead of going off to his business ventures, **wouldn't the Master have** been **appointed** head of the academy? Ilfa **went and suspended himself from the mast [*askariya*]**[L] **of a ship, saying: If there is anyone who can ask me** a question **concerning a *baraita* of Rabbi Ḥiyya and Rabbi Oshaya, and I do not resolve his** problem **from a mishna,**[N] **I will fall from the mast of this ship and be drowned.** Ilfa sought to demonstrate that despite the time he had spent in business, he still retained his extensive Torah knowledge.

אֲתָא הַהוּא סָבָא, תְּנָא לֵיהּ: הָאוֹמֵר: תְּנוּ שֶׁקֶל לְבָנַי בְּשַׁבָּת, וְהֵן רְאוּיִין לִתֵּן לָהֶם סֶלַע, נוֹתְנִין לָהֶם סֶלַע. וְאִם אָמַר: אַל תִּתְּנוּ לָהֶם אֶלָּא שֶׁקֶל, אֵין נוֹתְנִין לָהֶם אֶלָּא שֶׁקֶל.

A certain old man came and taught a *baraita* before **him:** If there is a man **who,** upon his deathbed, **says** in his will: **Give a shekel to my sons** every **week,**[H] **but** this is a situation **where,** based on their needs, **they are fit** for the **court to give them a *sela*,** i.e., double the amount, **they give them a *sela*.** When the dying man mentioned a shekel, he presumably meant that they should be given a sum in accordance with their actual requirements, not that specific amount. **But if he said: Give them only a shekel,** the court **gives them only a shekel** and no more.

אִם אָמַר: אִם מֵתוּ, יִרְשׁוּ אֲחֵרִים תַּחְתֵּיהֶם, בֵּין שֶׁאָמַר תְּנוּ, בֵּין שֶׁאָמַר אַל תִּתְּנוּ, אֵין נוֹתְנִין לָהֶם אֶלָּא שֶׁקֶל. אֲמַר לֵיהּ: הָא מַנִּי? רַבִּי מֵאִיר הִיא, דְּאָמַר: מִצְוָה לְקַיֵּים דִּבְרֵי הַמֵּת.

The *baraita* further states that **if one said: If** my sons **die, others should inherit** their portion **in their stead,**[N] regardless of **whether he said: Give them** a shekel, or **whether he said: Give them only** a shekel, then the court **gives** his sons **only a shekel** per week, as their father clearly stated that he wishes to give his sons only a specific stipend and that he intends to leave the bulk of his property to others. Ilfa **said to** the old man: In accordance with **whose** opinion **is this** ruling? **It is** in accordance with the opinion of **Rabbi Meir, who said: It is a mitzva to fulfill the statement of the dead.**[H] This entire *baraita* can be explained based on a principle that appears in a mishna: In all cases, one should try to execute the wishes of the deceased.

PERSONALITIES

Ilfa – אִילְפָא: Ilfa was from the first generation of *amora'im* in Eretz Yisrael. In the Jerusalem Talmud, he is known as Ḥilfai. Apparently, he was a disciple of Rabbi Yehuda HaNasi, and he also studied under some of his rabbi's students. As related here, he was a friend of Rabbi Yoḥanan's. Ilfa was the older of the pair, and indeed Rabbi Yoḥanan and his disciples transmit statements in his name. Still, Ilfa also asked Rabbi Yoḥanan questions. Ilfa had a very sharp mind and was one of the greatest Torah scholars of his generation. Furthermore, he also taught *aggada*, as several statements of *aggada* are attributed to him. Likewise, stories are related of his piety and great righteousness.

NOTES

Let us knock this wall down upon them – נִישְׁדֵּי עֲלַיְיהוּ הַאי גּוּדָא: Some commentaries explain this story in light of the tradition that Satan brings charges against a person specifically in his hour of danger. After Ilfa and Rabbi Yoḥanan put aside their Torah studies, the angels waited until the two men entered a dangerous place before considering what should be done with them (Rav Ya'akov Emden).

And I do not resolve his problem from a mishna – וְלָא פָּשְׁטִינָא לֵיהּ מִמַּתְנִיתִין: The Gemara elsewhere (*Eiruvin* 92a) states a principle in the form of a question: If Rabbi Yehuda HaNasi did not explicitly teach it, from where does his student Rabbi Ḥiyya know it? In other words, any statement included in a *baraita* compiled by Rabbi Ḥiyya and Rabbi Oshaya must be based on traditions they received from Rabbi Yehuda HaNasi, and therefore allusions can be found for these rulings in a mishna.

If one said, if my sons die others should inherit in their stead – אִם אָמַר, אִם מֵתוּ יִרְשׁוּ אֲחֵרִים תַּחְתֵּיהֶם: There is a principle that an inheritance cannot be terminated (*Bava Batra* 129b). In other words, if someone bequeaths his property to his legal heir, saying: This goes to you and afterward to someone else, the property does not pass to the other person upon the heir's death, but to the heir's own heirs. In light of this, the commentaries ask: Why, then, does this *baraita* rule that the father's instructions are effective when he commands that upon his sons' death others will inherit in their place?

Some commentaries explain that the ruling of the *baraita* is restricted to a case where the father explicitly states that his heirs are to receive his property not as an inheritance, but in the form of a gift, as a gift may indeed be terminated (Rambam *Sefer Kinyan*, *Hilkhot Zekhiya UMattana* 12:6). Others maintain that the *baraita* is referring to a situation where the father deposited his assets in the hands of a trustee; if the heirs actually received the property, the inheritance cannot be terminated (Ra'avad; see Meiri).

LANGUAGE

Mast [*askariya*] – אַסְקַרְיָא: Probably from the Greek ἱστοκεραία, *histokeraia*, a mast.

HALAKHA

A man who says, give a shekel to my sons every week – הָאוֹמֵר תְּנוּ שֶׁקֶל לְבָנַי בְּשַׁבָּת: If a man on his deathbed says: Give my sons a shekel a week, or: Give them only a shekel a week, and it turns out that they require a *sela* a week, they are given a *sela* a week, in accordance with the conclusion of the Gemara in *Ketubot* (69b) that there is no practical difference between the two formulations. However, if the father says: When my sons die I wish my estate to pass to other people and not to my grandsons, his sons are given only a shekel a week (*Shulḥan Arukh*, *Ḥoshen Mishpat* 253:17).

It is a mitzva to fulfill the statement of the dead – מִצְוָה לְקַיֵּים דִּבְרֵי הַמֵּת: It is a duty to fulfill the instructions of the deceased, even if he was healthy when the commands were issued. However, this applies only when the deceased deposited the funds for his directives in the hands of a third party; there is no mitzva for anyone to pay from his own funds to fulfill the wishes of the deceased (*Shulḥan Arukh*, *Ḥoshen Mishpat* 252:2; *Even HaEzer* 54:1).

אָמְרוּ עָלָיו עַל נַחוּם אִישׁ גַּם זוֹ שֶׁהָיָה סוּמָא מִשְּׁתֵּי עֵינָיו, גִּדֵּם מִשְּׁתֵּי יָדָיו, קִיטֵּעַ מִשְּׁתֵּי רַגְלָיו, וְכׇל גּוּפוֹ מָלֵא שְׁחִין. וְהָיָה מוּטָּל בְּבַיִת רָעוּעַ וְרַגְלֵי מִטָּתוֹ מוּנָּחִין בְּסִפְלִין שֶׁל מַיִם כְּדֵי שֶׁלֹּא יַעֲלוּ עָלָיו נְמָלִים. פַּעַם אַחַת בִּקְּשׁוּ תַּלְמִידָיו לְפַנּוֹת מִטָּתוֹ וְאַחַר כָּךְ לְפַנּוֹת אֶת הַכֵּלִים. אָמַר לָהֶם: בָּנַי, פַּנּוּ אֶת הַכֵּלִים וְאַחַר כָּךְ פַּנּוּ אֶת מִטָּתִי, שֶׁמּוּבְטָח לָכֶם שֶׁכׇּל זְמַן שֶׁאֲנִי בַּבַּיִת, אֵין הַבַּיִת נוֹפֵל. פִּינּוּ אֶת הַכֵּלִים וְאַחַר כָּךְ פִּינּוּ אֶת מִטָּתוֹ, וְנָפַל הַבַּיִת.

§ The Gemara relates another story about a rundown building. **They said about Naḥum of Gam Zu**[P] **that he was blind in both eyes, both his arms were amputated, both his legs were amputated, and his entire body was covered in boils. And he was lying in a dilapidated house, and legs of his bed were placed in buckets of water so that ants should not climb onto him,** as he was unable to keep them off in any other manner. **Once his students sought to remove his bed** from the house **and afterward remove** his other **vessels. He said to them: My sons, remove the vessels first, and afterward remove my bed, as I can guarantee you that as long as I am in the house, the house will not fall.** Indeed **they removed the vessels and afterward they removed his bed, and** immediately **the house collapsed.**

אָמְרוּ לוֹ תַּלְמִידָיו: רַבִּי, וְכִי מֵאַחַר שֶׁצַּדִּיק גָּמוּר אַתָּה, לָמָּה עָלְתָה לְךָ כָּךְ? אָמַר לָהֶם: בָּנַי, אֲנִי גָּרַמְתִּי לְעַצְמִי. שֶׁפַּעַם אַחַת הָיִיתִי מְהַלֵּךְ בַּדֶּרֶךְ לְבֵית חָמִי, וְהָיָה עִמִּי מַשּׂוֹי שְׁלֹשָׁה חֲמוֹרִים, אֶחָד שֶׁל מַאֲכָל, וְאֶחָד שֶׁל מִשְׁתֶּה, וְאֶחָד שֶׁל מִינֵי מְגָדִים. בָּא עָנִי אֶחָד וְעָמַד לִי בַּדֶּרֶךְ, וְאָמַר לִי: רַבִּי, פַּרְנְסֵנִי! אָמַרְתִּי לוֹ: הַמְתֵּן עַד שֶׁאֶפְרוֹק מִן הַחֲמוֹר. לֹא הִסְפַּקְתִּי לִפְרוֹק מִן הַחֲמוֹר עַד שֶׁיָּצְתָה נִשְׁמָתוֹ.

His students said to him: Rabbi, since you are evidently **a wholly righteous man,** as we have just seen that as long as you were in your house it did not fall, **why has this** suffering **befallen you? He said to them: My sons, I brought it upon myself.** Naḥum of Gam Zu related to them the following: **As once I was traveling along the road to my father-in-law's house, and I had with me a load** distributed among **three donkeys, one of food, one of drink, and one of delicacies. A poor person came and stood** before me **in the road, saying: My rabbi, sustain me. I said to him: Wait until I unload the donkey,** after which I will give you something to eat. However, **I had not managed to unload the donkey before his soul left** his body.

הָלַכְתִּי וְנָפַלְתִּי עַל פָּנָיו, וְאָמַרְתִּי: עֵינַי, שֶׁלֹּא חָסוּ עַל עֵינֶיךָ, יְסוּמוּ. יָדַי, שֶׁלֹּא חָסוּ עַל יָדֶיךָ, יִתְגַּדְּמוּ. רַגְלַי, שֶׁלֹּא חָסוּ עַל רַגְלֶיךָ, יִתְקַטְּעוּ. וְלֹא נִתְקָרְרָה דַּעְתִּי עַד שֶׁאָמַרְתִּי: כׇּל גּוּפִי יְהֵא מָלֵא שְׁחִין. אָמְרוּ לוֹ: אוֹי לָנוּ שֶׁרְאִינוּךָ בְּכָךְ. אָמַר לָהֶם: אוֹי לִי אִם לֹא רְאִיתוּנִי בְּכָךְ.

I went and fell upon his face and said: May my eyes, which had no compassion on your eyes, be blinded; may my hands, which had no compassion on your hands, be amputated; may my legs, which had no compassion on your legs, be amputated. And my mind did not rest until I said: May my whole body be covered in boils. Naḥum of Gam Zu prayed that his suffering might atone for his failure. His students **said to him:** Even so, **woe to us that we have seen you in this state. He said to them: Woe is me if you had not seen me in this** state, as this suffering atones for me.

וְאַמַּאי קָרוּ לֵיהּ נַחוּם אִישׁ גַּם זוֹ? דְּכׇל מִילְּתָא דַּהֲוָה סָלְקָא לֵיהּ, אָמַר: גַּם זוֹ לְטוֹבָה. זִימְנָא חֲדָא בְּעוֹ לְשַׁדּוֹרֵי יִשְׂרָאֵל דּוֹרוֹן לְבֵי קֵיסָר. אָמְרוּ: מַאן יֵיזִיל? יֵיזִיל נַחוּם אִישׁ גַּם זוֹ, דִּמְלוּמָּד בְּנִיסִּין הוּא. שַׁדַּרוּ בִּידֵיהּ מְלֹא סִיפְטָא דַּאֲבָנִים טוֹבוֹת וּמַרְגָּלִיּוֹת. אֲזַל בָּת בְּהַהוּא דִּירָא. בְּלֵילְיָא קָמוּ הָנָךְ דִּיוֹרָאֵי, וְשַׁקְלִינְהוּ לְסִיפְטֵיהּ וּמְלוֹנְהוּ עַפְרָא.

The Gemara inquires: **And why did they call him Naḥum of Gam Zu?**[N] The reason is **that** with regard to **any matter that occurred to him,** he would **say: This too is for the good** [*gam zu letova*]. **Once, the Jews wished to send a gift** [*doron*][L] **to the house of the emperor. They said: Who should go** and present this gift? **Let Naḥum of Gam Zu go, as he is accustomed to miracles. They sent with him a chest** [*sifta*][L] **full of jewels and pearls,** and **he went and spent the night in a certain inn. During the night, these residents** of the inn **arose** and **took all of** the precious jewels and pearls from **the chest, and filled it with earth.** The next day, when he saw what had happened, Naḥum of Gam Zu said: This too is for the good.

כִּי מְטָא הָתָם, שְׁרִינְהוּ לְסִיפְטָא, חֲזַנְהוּ דִּמְלוּ עַפְרָא. בְּעָא מַלְכָּא לְמִקְטְלִינְהוּ לְכוּלְּהוּ. אָמַר: קָא מְחַיְּיכוּ בִּי יְהוּדָאֵי! אָמַר: גַּם זוֹ לְטוֹבָה. אֲתָא אֵלִיָּהוּ, אִדְּמִי לֵיהּ כְּחַד מִינַּיְיהוּ. אָמַר לֵיהּ: דִּלְמָא הָא עַפְרָא מֵעַפְרָא דְּאַבְרָהָם אֲבוּהוֹן הוּא. דְּכִי הֲוָה שָׁדֵי עַפְרָא, הָווּ סַיְיפֵי; גִּילֵי, הָווּ גִּירֵי. דִּכְתִיב: ״יִתֵּן כֶּעָפָר חַרְבּוֹ, כְּקַשׁ נִדָּף קַשְׁתּוֹ״.

When he arrived there, at the ruler's palace, **they opened the chest** and **saw that it was filled with earth. The king wished to put all** the Jewish emissaries **to death. He said: The Jews are mocking me.** Naḥum of Gam Zu **said: This too is for the good. Elijah** the Prophet **came and appeared before** the ruler **as one of** his ministers. He **said to** the ruler: **Perhaps this earth is from the earth of their father Abraham. As when he threw earth, it turned into swords,** and when he threw **stubble, it turned into arrows, as it is written** in a prophecy that the Sages interpreted this verse as a reference to Abraham: **"His sword makes them as the dust, his bow as the driven stubble"** (Isaiah 41:2).

הֲוַאי חֲדָא מְדִינְתָּא דְּלָא מָצוּ לְמִיכְבְּשַׁהּ. בַּדְקוּ מִינֵּיהּ וּכְבַשׁוּהָ. עַיְּילוּ לְבֵי גַנְזֵיהּ, וּמְלוֹהוּ לְסִיפְטֵיהּ אֲבָנִים טוֹבוֹת וּמַרְגָּלִיּוֹת, וְשַׁדְּרוּהוּ בִּיקָרָא רַבָּה.

There was one province that the Romans **were unable to conquer.** They took some of this earth, **tested it** by throwing it at their enemies, **and conquered** that province. When the ruler saw that this earth indeed had miraculous powers, his servants **entered his treasury and filled** Naḥum of Gam Zu's **chest with precious jewels and pearls and sent him off with great honor.**

PERSONALITIES

Naḥum of Gam Zu – נַחוּם אִישׁ גַּם זוֹ: A *tanna* from the end of Second Temple period. Apart from the stories related here, it is known that Rabbi Akiva was his student, whom he taught his hermeneutical principle of amplification and restriction. Apparently, Rabbi Akiva and Rabbi Yishmael's differences of opinion with regard to hermeneutical principles date back to ancient times, as they are based in the principles of Naḥum of Gam Zu and Rabbi Neḥunya ben Hakana, respectively. The system of amplificatory terms is also attributed to Naḥum of Gam Zu.

NOTES

And why did they call him Naḥum of Gam Zu – וְאַמַּאי קָרוּ לֵיהּ נַחוּם אִישׁ גַּם זוֹ: The plain meaning of his name is apparently derived from his town of origin, Gimzo, which is near Lod and is mentioned in the Bible (II Chronicles 28:18). However, due to Naḥum's praiseworthy character, they made a play on words with his name and called him Gam Zu (*Etz Yosef*).

LANGUAGE

Gift [*doron*] – דּוֹרוֹן: From the Greek δῶρον, *doron*, a gift, particularly a gift given in someone's honor.

Chest [*sifta*] – סִיפְטָא: Apparently from the Middle Iranian sapat, which can mean a wicker basket.

כִּי אָתוּ בָּיְתוּ בְּהַהוּא דִּיוֹרָא. אָמְרוּ לֵיהּ: מַאי אַיְיתִית בַּהֲדָךְ דַּעֲבַדִי לָךְ יְקָרָא כּוּלֵּי הַאי? אֲמַר לְהוּ: מַאי דְּשָׁקְלִי מֵהָכָא אַמְטֵי לְהָתָם. סָתְרוּ לְדִירַיְיהוּ וְאַמְטִינְהוּ לְבֵי מַלְכָּא. אָמְרוּ לֵיהּ: הַאי עַפְרָא דְּאַיְיתֵי הָכָא מִדִּידָן הוּא. בְּדַקוּהּ, וְלָא אַשְׁכְּחוּהּ. וְקַטְלִינְהוּ לְהָנָךְ דִּיוֹרָאֵי.

When Naḥum of Gam Zu **came to spend the night at that** same **inn,** the residents **said to him: What did you bring with you** to the emperor **that he bestowed upon you such great honor? He said to them: That which I took from here, I brought there.** When they heard this, the residents of the inn thought that the soil upon which their house stood had miraculous powers. **They tore down their inn and brought** the soil underneath **to the king's palace. They said to him: That earth that was brought here was from our** property. The miracle had been performed only in the merit of Naḥum of Gam Zu. The emperor **tested** the inn's soil in battle, **and it was not found** to have miraculous powers, **and he** had **these residents** of the inn **put to death.**

״אֵי זוֹ הִיא דֶּבֶר? עִיר הַמּוֹצִיאָה חֲמֵשׁ מֵאוֹת רַגְלִי״ כו׳. תָּנוּ רַבָּנַן: עִיר הַמּוֹצִיאָה חֲמֵשׁ מֵאוֹת וְאֶלֶף רַגְלִי, כְּפַר עַכּוֹ, וְיָצְאוּ הֵימֶנָּה תִּשְׁעָה מֵתִים בִּשְׁלֹשָׁה יָמִים זֶה אַחַר זֶה – הֲרֵי זֶה דֶּבֶר.

§ The mishna taught: **What is** considered a plague of **pestilence?** If it is **a city that sends out five hundred infantrymen,** and three dead are removed from it on three consecutive days, one dead per day, this is a plague of pestilence. **The Sages taught:** If **a city that sends out fifteen hundred infantrymen,** i.e., one that has a population of at least fifteen hundred men, e.g., **the village of Akko, and nine dead are removed from it on three consecutive days,** i.e., three dead per day, **this is** considered a plague of **pestilence.**

בְּיוֹם אֶחָד אוֹ בְּאַרְבָּעָה יָמִים – אֵין זֶה דֶּבֶר. וְעִיר הַמּוֹצִיאָה חֲמֵשׁ מֵאוֹת רַגְלִי כְּגוֹן כְּפַר עַמִּיקוֹ, וְיָצְאוּ הֵימֶנָּה שְׁלֹשָׁה מֵתִים בִּשְׁלֹשָׁה יָמִים זֶה אַחַר זֶה – הֲרֵי זֶה דֶּבֶר.

If all nine died **on a single day,** while none died on the other days, **or** if the nine died **over** a period of **four days, this is not** a plague of **pestilence. And a city that sends out five hundred infantrymen, for example, the village of Amiko, and three dead are removed from it on three consecutive days, this is** a plague of **pestilence.**

Perek **III**
Daf **21** Amud **b**

בְּיוֹם אֶחָד אוֹ בְּאַרְבָּעָה יָמִים – אֵין זֶה דֶּבֶר.

If all three died **on one day or over four days,** this is not a plague of **pestilence.**

דְּרוֹקַרְתְּ עִיר הַמּוֹצִיאָה חֲמֵשׁ מֵאוֹת רַגְלִי הֲוָה, וְיָצְאוּ מִמֶּנָּה שְׁלֹשָׁה מֵתִים בְּיוֹם אֶחָד. גְּזַר רַב נַחְמָן בַּר רַב חִסְדָּא תַּעֲנִיתָא. אֲמַר רַב נַחְמָן בַּר יִצְחָק: כְּמַאן? כְּרַבִּי מֵאִיר,

In explanation of the counterintuitive ruling that many deaths in one day is not indicative of a plague, the Gemara relates: **Drokart**[B] was a city that **sent out five hundred infantrymen, and three dead were removed from it on one day. Rav Naḥman bar Rav Ḥisda decreed a fast** on account of the plague. **Rav Naḥman bar Yitzḥak said: In accordance with whose opinion** did you declare this fast? It must be **in accordance with** the opinion of **Rabbi Meir.**

דְּאָמַר: רִיחֵק נְגִיחוֹתָיו חַיָּיב, קֵירֵב נְגִיחוֹתָיו לֹא כׇּל שֶׁכֵּן!

This is related to the definition of a forewarned ox, an animal that has gored enough times to be considered a dangerous beast that requires careful supervision, **as** Rabbi Meir **said:** The owner of an ox is **liable** to pay full damages if **its** acts of **goring were separated,** i.e., if it gored three times on three consecutive days, as claimed by the Rabbis. If **its** acts of **goring were near** each other, performed on a single day, is it **not all the more so** that this animal should be classified as a forewarned ox? However, Rav Naḥman bar Yitzḥak continued, this represents a minority opinion. Just as Rabbi Meir's reasoning is rejected for *halakha* in the case of an ox, so too it is rejected with regard to a plague.

BACKGROUND

Drokart – דְּרוֹקַרְתְּ: The location of Drokart is unclear. Some maintain that it is a city upon which the Arabs later built the city of Wasit in eastern Iraq. Apparently, several important Sages lived inside this city or in the nearby villages, as Rav Huna and Rav Naḥman bar Yitzḥak, among others, resided there.

אֲמַר לֵיהּ רַב נַחְמָן בַּר רַב חִסְדָּא לְרַב נַחְמָן בַּר יִצְחָק: לֵיקוּם מָר, לֵיתֵי לְגַבַּן. אֲמַר לֵיהּ: תָּנֵינָא: רַבִּי יוֹסֵי אוֹמֵר: לֹא מְקוֹמוֹ שֶׁל אָדָם מְכַבְּדוֹ, אֶלָּא אָדָם מְכַבֵּד אֶת מְקוֹמוֹ. שֶׁכֵּן מָצִינוּ בְּהַר סִינַי, שֶׁכׇּל זְמַן שֶׁהַשְּׁכִינָה שְׁרוּיָה עָלָיו, אָמְרָה תּוֹרָה: ״גַּם הַצֹּאן וְהַבָּקָר אַל יִרְעוּ אֶל מוּל הָהָר הַהוּא״. נִסְתַּלְּקָה שְׁכִינָה מִמֶּנּוּ, אָמְרָה תּוֹרָה: ״בִּמְשֹׁךְ הַיֹּבֵל, הֵמָּה יַעֲלוּ בָהָר״.

Upon hearing this impressive argument, **Rav Naḥman bar Rav Ḥisda said to Rav Naḥman bar Yitzḥak: Let the Master arise and come** to live **with us** as our community leader. Rav Naḥman bar Yitzḥak **said to him: We** already **learned** in a *baraita* that **Rabbi Yosei says:** It is **not the place of a person** that **honors him;** rather, the **person honors his place, as we found with regard to Mount Sinai, that as long as the Divine Presence rested upon it, the Torah said: "Neither let the flocks nor the herds feed before that mount"** (Exodus 34:3).[N] Once **the Divine Presence departed from** the mountain, **the Torah said: "When the *shofar* sounds long they shall come up to the mount"** (Exodus 19:13). This indicates that the sanctity was not inherent to the place but was due to the Divine Presence resting there.

וְכֵן מָצִינוּ בְּאֹהֶל מוֹעֵד שֶׁבַּמִּדְבָּר, שֶׁכׇּל זְמַן שֶׁהוּא נָטוּי, אָמְרָה תּוֹרָה: ״וִישַׁלְּחוּ מִן הַמַּחֲנֶה כׇּל צָרוּעַ״. הוּגְלְלוּ הַפָּרוֹכֶת, הוּתְּרוּ זָבִין וְהַמְצוֹרָעִים לִיכָּנֵס שָׁם.

And we likewise found with regard to the Tent of Meeting that was in the wilderness, that whenever it was erected, the Torah said: "That they put out of the camp every leper" (Numbers 5:2). Once **the curtain was rolled up** and the Tent of Meeting was prepared for travel, ***zavim* and lepers were permitted to enter** the place where it had stood. The place itself had no intrinsic sanctity; rather, it was sacred only because the Divine Presence was there. Accordingly, Rav Naḥman bar Yitzḥak maintained that there is no reason for him to move places to receive honor.

אֲמַר לֵיהּ: אִי הָכִי, נֵיקוּם אֲנָא לְגַבֵּי מָר. אֲמַר לֵיהּ: מוּטָב יָבֹא מָנֶה בֶּן פְּרָס אֵצֶל מָנֶה בֶּן מָנֶה, וְאַל יָבֹא מָנֶה בֶּן מָנֶה אֵצֶל מָנֶה בֶּן פְּרָס.

Rav Naḥman bar Rav Ḥisda **said to** Rav Naḥman bar Yitzḥak: **If so, let me arise** and come **to the Master,** to learn Torah from you. Rav Naḥman bar Yitzḥak **said to him:** It is **better** that **one hundred dinars** that is the **son of a *peras*,**[L] fifty dinars, **should come to one hundred dinars** that is the **son of one hundred dinars; but one hundred dinars** that is the **son of one hundred dinars, should not come to one hundred dinars** that is the **son of a *peras*.**[N] In other words, although Rav Naḥman bar Yitzḥak was a learned scholar, comparable to one hundred dinars, it was nevertheless more appropriate for him to come to Rav Naḥman bar Rav Ḥisda. Whereas Rav Naḥman bar Yitzḥak was the son of a *peras*, an ordinary man, Rav Naḥman bar Rav Ḥisda was the son of a scholar.

בְּסוּרָא הֲוָת דְּבַרְתָּא, בְּשִׁיבָבוּתֵיהּ דְּרַב לָא הֲוָת דְּבַרְתָּא. סְבַרוּ מִינֵּיהּ מִשּׁוּם זְכוּתֵיהּ דְּרַב, דְּנָפֵישׁ. אִיתְחֲזִי לְהוּ בְּחֶילְמָא: רַב דִּנְפִישָׁא זְכוּתֵיהּ טוּבָא, הָא מִילְּתָא זוּטְרָא לֵיהּ לְרַב. אֶלָּא מִשּׁוּם הָהוּא גַּבְרָא, דְּשַׁיֵּיל מָרָא וּזְבִילָא לִקְבוּרָה.

The Gemara relates another story involving a plague: Once **there was** a plague of **pestilence in Sura,** but **in the neighborhood of Rav there was no pestilence.** The people **therefore thought** that this was **due to Rav's great merit.** However, **it was revealed to them in a dream** that **Rav's merit was too great** and **this matter too small for** the merit of **Rav**[N] to be involved. **Rather,** his neighborhood was spared **due to** the acts of kindness of **a certain man, who** would **lend his hoe [*mara*]**[L] **and shovel [*zevila*]**[L] to prepare sites **for burial.**

LANGUAGE

Peras – **פְּרָס:** The root of this word is *p-r-s*. Its primary meaning is to cut, break, or count. However, *peras* is often used to mean a half. In this context it means fifty dinars, half of a unit of one hundred dinars.

Hoe [*mara*] – **מָרָא:** From the Latin marra, a hoe.

Roman hoe blade

Shovel [*zevila*] – **זְבִילָא:** This term is apparently related to *zevel*, garbage, and it denotes a tool used for carrying garbage. From the description in the Talmud, it was probably some kind of shovel.

NOTES

Before that mount – אֶל מוּל הָהָר הַהוּא: The maxim that it is the person who bestows honor on the place he occupies, and not vice versa, is derived from the two verses cited here. The word "that" in the expression "that mount" is superfluous, and it teaches that it was prohibited to ascend Mount Sinai only while it remained that mount, i.e., the mount on which the Divine Presence was resting. However, once the Divine Presence withdrew from the mount, it once again became accessible to all, in accordance with the second verse: "When the *shofar* sounds long they shall come up to the mount." According to Rashi, the prohibition against ascending Mount Sinai continued after both sets of tablets were given, as the Divine Presence remained on the mount for almost another full year, until the Tabernacle was erected on the first of Nisan.

Others maintain that the verse: "When the *shofar* sounds long," indicates that the prohibition against ascending the mountain was annulled immediately after the revelation and the first set of tablets of stone were given to Moses. It was therefore necessary for the Torah to again warn the Jewish people that nobody may ascend the mount before the second tablets were given, as access to the mountain in the interim was permitted (Rav Ya'akov Emden).

To one hundred dinars, son of a *peras* – אֵצֶל מָנֶה בֶּן פְּרָס: Rashi and *Tosafot* both note the difference in title between the two scholars featured in this story: Whereas one is called Rav Naḥman bar Rav Ḥisda, the other is Rav Naḥman bar Yitzḥak, and it is not noted that his father was a rabbi. This is because the former scholar was the son of the great Sage Rav Ḥisda, while the father of the latter scholar was not ordained as a rabbi.

Conversely, some commentaries argue that it would have been disrespectful for Rav Naḥman bar Yitzḥak to consider himself his father's superior in Torah knowledge and refer to himself as twice the value of his father in this regard. Rather, Rav Naḥman bar Yitzḥak was speaking not of scholarly accomplishment but material wealth. Rav Naḥman bar Yitzḥak himself was a wealthy man, whereas his father Yitzḥak was not. Rav Naḥman bar Rav Ḥisda, by contrast, was a rich man who was also the son of a rich man (Rav Ya'akov Emden).

This matter is too small for the merit of Rav – הָא מִילְּתָא זוּטְרָא לֵיהּ לְרַב: Some commentaries explain that although it is clear that Rav's great merit contributed to the good fortune of his neighborhood, it was revealed to the people in a dream that they would have been spared even without Rav, by virtue of that righteous man who lent out his grave-digging tools for the benefit of the community. Alternatively, it was not due to Rav's merit that his community was saved, so that he would not have to pay for the miracle performed on the community's behalf with the merits he had accumulated through his righteous behavior in the past (Maharsha).

בִּדְרוֹקַרְתְּ הֲוַאי דְּלֵיקְתָא, וּבְשִׁיבָבוּתֵיהּ דְּרַב הוּנָא לָא הֲוַאי דְּלֵיקְתָא. סְבוּר מִינָּהּ בִּזְכוּתָא דְּרַב הוּנָא, דְּנָפֵישׁ. אִיתְחֲזִי לְהוּ בְּחֶילְמָא: הַאי זוּטְרָא לֵיהּ לְרַב הוּנָא. אֶלָּא מִשּׁוּם הַהִיא אִיתְּתָא דִּמְחַמְּמַת תַּנּוּרָא וּמְשַׁיְּילֵי לְשִׁיבָבוּתֵיהּ.

The Gemara relates a similar incident. **In Drokart there was a fire, but in the neighborhood of Rav Huna there was no fire.** The people **therefore thought** that this was **due to Rav Huna's great merit. It was revealed to them in a dream** that **this** matter was **too small for** the merit of **Rav Huna** to have played a role. **Rather,** it was **due to a certain woman who heats her oven and lends it,** i.e., the use of her oven, **to her neighbors.**

אָמְרוּ לֵיהּ לְרַב יְהוּדָה: אָתוּ קַמְצֵי. גְּזַר תַּעֲנִיתָא. אֲמַרוּ לֵיהּ: לָא קָא מַפְסְדָן. אֲמַר לְהוּ: זְוָודָא אַיְיתוּ בַּהֲדַיְיהוּ?

They said to Rav Yehuda: Locusts have come to our region. Rav Yehuda **decreed a fast. They said to him: They are not destroying** anything, as they are eating only a little. **He said to them: Have they brought provisions with them,** that they have something else to eat? Even if they are not damaging your crops now, they will certainly eat them soon.

אֲמַרוּ לֵיהּ לְרַב יְהוּדָה: אִיכָּא מוֹתָנָא בַּחֲזִירֵי. גְּזַר תַּעֲנִיתָא. נֵימָא קָסָבַר רַב יְהוּדָה מַכָּה מְשׁוּלַּחַת מִמִּין אֶחָד מְשׁוּלַּחַת מִכָּל הַמִּינִין? לָא. שָׁאנֵי חֲזִירֵי, דְּדָמְיָין מֵעַיְיהוּ לִבְנֵי אֱנָשֵׁי.

On another occasion, **they said to Rav Yehuda: There is pestilence among the pigs.**[NH] **Rav Yehuda decreed a fast.** The Gemara asks: **Let us say** that **Rav Yehuda maintains** that **a plague affecting one species** will come to **affect all species,** and that is why he decreed a fast. The Gemara answers: **No,** in other cases there is no cause for concern. However, **pigs are different, as their intestines are similar to** those of **humans.**[B] Consequently, their disease might spread to people.

אֲמַרוּ לֵיהּ לִשְׁמוּאֵל: אִיכָּא מוֹתָנָא בֵּי חוֹזַאי. גְּזַר תַּעֲנִיתָא. אֲמַרוּ לֵיהּ: וְהָא מְרַחַק! אֲמַר: לֵיכָּא מַעְבְּרָא הָכָא דְּפָסֵיק לֵיהּ.

They said to Shmuel: There is pestilence in the region of **Bei Ḥozai,**[HB] which is quite a distance from Babylonia. Shmuel **decreed a fast. They said to him: But it is far** from here. **He said: There is no crossing here that will stop** the pestilence, and therefore there is cause for concern that it will reach us.

אֲמַרוּ לֵיהּ לְרַב נַחְמָן: אִיכָּא מוֹתָנָא בְּאַרְעָא דְּיִשְׂרָאֵל. גְּזַר תַּעֲנִיתָא. אָמַר: אִם גְּבִירָה לוֹקָה, שִׁפְחָה לֹא כָּל שֶׁכֵּן!

They said to Rav Naḥman: There is pestilence in Eretz Yisrael. Rav Naḥman decreed a fast in Babylonia, **saying: If the lady** of the house, i.e., Eretz Yisrael, **is afflicted,** is it **not all the more so** that **the maidservant,** Babylonia, will be afflicted?

טַעֲמָא דִּגְבִירָה וְשִׁפְחָה. הָא שִׁפְחָה וְשִׁפְחָה, לָא. וְהָא אֲמַרוּ לֵיהּ לִשְׁמוּאֵל: אִיכָּא מוֹתָנָא בֵּי חוֹזַאי, גְּזַר תַּעֲנִיתָא! שָׁאנֵי הָתָם, כֵּיוָן דְּאִיכָּא שַׁיָּירָתָא דְּלָווּ וְאָתְיָא בַּהֲדֵיהּ.

The Gemara asks: The **reason** for this ruling is apparently only because Eretz Yisrael is **a lady** in comparison to the Diaspora, which is likened to **a maidservant.** It may be inferred from this that in a case involving **a maidservant and a maidservant,** i.e., two places in the Diaspora, there is no reason to fast. **But** in the previous story, when **they said to Shmuel: There is pestilence in** the region of **Bei Ḥozai, he decreed a fast** in Neharde'a, despite the fact that Neharde'a is not considered a lady with respect to Bei Ḥozai. The Gemara answers: It **is different there. Since there are caravans** that regularly travel from Bei Ḥozai to Neharde'a, the pestilence **will join and accompany** them **in** the caravans.

אַבָּא אוּמָּנָא הֲוָה אָתֵי לֵיהּ שְׁלָמָא מִמְּתִיבְתָּא דִּרְקִיעָא כָּל יוֹמָא, וּלְאַבַּיֵי כָּל מַעֲלֵי יוֹמָא דְּשַׁבְּתָא, לְרָבָא כָּל מַעֲלֵי יוֹמָא דְּכִיפּוּרֵי. הֲוָה קָא חָלְשָׁא דַּעְתֵּיהּ דְּאַבַּיֵי מִשּׁוּם דְּאַבָּא אוּמָּנָא. אֲמַרוּ לֵיהּ: לָא מָצֵית לְמֶיעְבַּד כְּעוֹבָדֵיהּ.

§ Apropos the above stories that deal with the merits of ordinary people, the Gemara relates: **Abba the Bloodletter would receive greetings from the yeshiva on High every day, and Abaye would receive** these greetings **every Shabbat eve, and** Rava would receive greetings only once a year **on Yom Kippur eve.** Abaye **was distressed due to Abba the Bloodletter,** as he did not understand why Abba received greater honor than he did. **They said to him: You are unable to perform what he does,**[N] and therefore you do not merit the same honor.

וּמַאי הָווּ עוֹבָדֵיהּ דְּאַבָּא אוּמָּנָא? דְּכִי הֲוָה עָבֵיד מִילְּתָא, הֲוָה מָחֵית גַּבְרֵי לְחוּד וְנָשֵׁי לְחוּד. וְאִית לֵיהּ לְבוּשָׁא דְּאִית בֵּיהּ קַרְנָא, דַּהֲוַות בְּזִיעָא כִּי כּוּסִילְתָּא. כִּי הֲוַות אָתְיָא לֵיהּ אִיתְּתָא, הֲוָה מַלְבִּישׁ לָהּ, כִּי הֵיכִי דְּלָא נִיסְתַּכֵּל בָּהּ. וְאִית לֵיהּ דּוּכְתָּא דִּצְנִיעָא דְּשָׁדֵי בֵּיהּ פְּשִׁיטֵי דְּשָׁקֵיל. דְּאִית לֵיהּ שָׁדֵי בֵּיהּ; דְּלֵית לֵיהּ לָא מִיכְסִיף.

The Gemara asks: **And what were these** righteous **deeds of Abba the Bloodletter?** The Gemara explains **that when he would perform a matter** of bloodletting, **he would bring in men separately from women,** for reasons of modesty. **And he had** a special **garment** that **had a slit in the place of the incision** [*kusilta*][L] where the bloodletting instrument was inserted. **When a woman came to him, he would** have **her dress in that garment, so that he would not see her** exposed. **And** furthermore, **he had a hidden place** where he worked, **where** customers **would place the coins** [*peshitei*][L] **that he would take** as his fee. In this manner, **one who had** money **would throw** it **there,** while **one who did not have money was not embarrassed.**

NOTES

There is pestilence among the pigs – אִיכָּא מוֹתָנָא בַּחֲזִירֵי: *Tosafot* infer from this incident that if a plague is spreading among the gentile inhabitants of a particular community, their Jewish neighbors must proclaim a fast. If there is concern that a disease afflicting pigs will spread to human beings, as the intestines of a pig are anatomically similar to those of a human being, there is certainly cause for concern that a disease will spread from gentiles to Jews. Others cite a view according to which the Jewish community is not required to proclaim a fast if its gentile neighbors have been struck by disease, because the divine decrees issued against the one group do not necessarily apply to the other (Ritva).

You are unable to perform what he does – לָא מָצֵית לְמֶיעְבַּד כְּעוֹבָדֵיהּ: Some commentaries note that although Abaye certainly engaged in charitable activities, he was first and foremost the head of the academy at Pumbedita. Consequently, he was unable to devote as much of his time and money to charity as did Abba the Bloodletter (Maharsha).

HALAKHA

There is pestilence among the pigs – אִיכָּא מוֹתָנָא בַּחֲזִירֵי: If plague has spread among pigs, a fast must be proclaimed. The intestines of a pig are similar to those of human beings, and therefore there is a concern that the disease will spread to humans. All the more so, a fast must be proclaimed if the plague has reached the Jewish community's gentile neighbors (*Shulḥan Arukh*, *Oraḥ Ḥayyim* 576:3).

There is pestilence in Bei Ḥozai – אִיכָּא מוֹתָנָא בֵּי חוֹזַאי: If a plague has spread across a certain area, and caravans travel regularly between that place and other areas, a fast must be proclaimed in all the locations to which the caravans travel, even if they are far away from the stricken area. This ruling is in accordance with the practice of Shmuel. If a plague breaks out in Eretz Yisrael, a fast must be proclaimed throughout the Diaspora, as stated by Rav Naḥman (*Shulḥan Arukh*, *Oraḥ Ḥayyim* 576:2).

BACKGROUND

As their intestines are similar to those of humans – דְּדָמְיָין מֵעַיְיהוּ לִבְנֵי אֱנָשֵׁי: Although there are parasites that pass from pigs to humans, i.e., trichinae, this generally occurs when the flesh of the pig is eaten, which is not a concern here.

Nevertheless, the resemblance in internal anatomy between pigs and humans, as well as other similarities, are recognized nowadays. For example, pig intestines are often transplanted into human bodies, due to the relatively low rate of rejection. Consequently, Rav Yehuda was concerned that a disease that affects pigs might well be transferable to people.

Bei Ḥozai – בֵּי חוֹזַאי: Bei Ḥozai was a region southeast of the Tigris River, later known as Huzistan. From the perspective of its Jewish inhabitants, it was a distant extension of the main Jewish community in central Babylonia. Due to its great distance from the center of talmudic activity, its inhabitants were said to be ignorant of Torah. Nevertheless, there was strong commercial activity between the residents of central Babylonia and those of Bei Ḥozai, in which many Jews, among them Torah scholars, were involved. Consequently, there was a concern that an infectious disease might be transferred between the two places, albeit after a considerable delay.

LANGUAGE

Incision [*kusilta*] – כּוּסִילְתָּא: A Syrian-Aramaic term meaning an incision in the skin for the purpose of letting blood.

Coins [*peshitei*] – פְּשִׁיטֵי: From the Middle Persian pišīz, a small copper coin.

LANGUAGE

Mats [*bistarkei*] – בִּיסְתַּרְקֵי: Apparently a loanword from the Middle Iranian bistarak, which means bedding, a mattress, or a cover.

כִּי הֲוָה אִתְרַמֵי לֵיהּ צוּרְבָא מֵרַבָּנַן, אַגְרָא מִינֵּיהּ לָא שָׁקֵיל, וּבָתַר דְּקָאֵי, יָהֵיב לֵיהּ פְּשִׁיטֵי, וַאֲמַר לֵיהּ: זִיל בְּרִיא נַפְשָׁךְ. יוֹמָא חַד שְׁדַר אַבַּיֵי זוּגָא דְּרַבָּנַן לְמִיבְדְּקֵיהּ. אוֹתְבִינְהוּ, וְאָכְלִינְהוּ, וְאַשְׁקִינְהוּ, וּמָךְ לְהוּ בִּיסְתַּרְקֵי בְּלֵילְיָא.

When a Torah scholar came to him for bloodletting, **he would take no pay from him, and after** the scholar **arose,** Abba **would give him money and say to him: Go** and purchase food with this money **to heal yourself,** as it is important to eat healthy food after bloodletting. **One day, Abaye sent a pair of Sages to investigate** the extent of Abba the Bloodletter's righteousness. Abba the Bloodletter **sat them down, and gave them** food **to eat, and gave them** something **to drink. And at night he spread out mats** [*bistarkei*][L] **for them** to sleep on.

Perek **III**
Daf **22** Amud **a**

NOTES

I put them out of my mind for charity – אַסַּחְתִּינְהוּ מִדַּעְתָּאִי לִצְדָקָה: Some commentaries conclude from here that although a mental commitment to give charity is not binding unless it is given verbal formulation, it is commendable not to withdraw from a mental stipulation of this kind, even if the commitment was based on an error (Meiri).

You protect your entire city – מַגְנִית אַכּוּלָּא כְּרַכָּא: Some commentaries point out that these words of consolation assume special significance in light of the statement elsewhere that the inhabitants of Meḥoza, Rava's place of residence, were evil people who merited destruction (*Rosh HaShana* 17a). It was only Rava's uncommonly righteous behavior that spared them punishment (Rav Ya'akov Emden).

Worthy of the World-to-Come – בַּר עָלְמָא דְּאָתֵי: Although it is stated elsewhere that with few exceptions all Jews have a share in the World-to-Come (*Sanhedrin* 90a), most people must first pass through Gehenna and receive punishment for the transgressions they committed in this world. Only after they have been purified of sin are they fit to enjoy the delights of the World-to-Come. When Rabbi Beroka met Elijah in the marketplace, he asked if there was a man worthy of entering the World-to-Come directly, without having first to suffer in Gehenna, so that he could learn which righteous behaviors merit that great reward.

לְצַפְרָא כָּרְכִינְהוּ וְשָׁקְלִינְהוּ, וְקָמוּ וּנְפַקוּ לְהוּ לְשׁוּקָא, וְאַשְׁכַּחִינְהוּ. אֲמַרוּ לֵיהּ: לְשַׁיְּימֵיהּ מָר הֵיכִי שָׁווּ. אֲמַר לְהוּ: הָכִי וְהָכִי. אֲמַרוּ לֵיהּ: וְדִלְמָא שָׁווּ טְפֵי. אֲמַר לְהוּ: בְּהָכִי שָׁקְלִינְהוּ. אֲמַרוּ לֵיהּ: דִּידָךְ נִיהוּ, וְשָׁקְלִינְהוּ מִינָּךְ.

In the morning, the Sages **rolled up these rugs and took them, and they arose and went out to the market** with them. **And** when **Abba found them,** the Sages **said to him: Let the Master appraise** these rugs, **how much they are worth. He said to them:** Their value is **such and such. They said to him: But perhaps they are worth more. He said to them: This is what I paid for them. They said to him:** The rugs **are yours and we took them from you.**

אֲמַרוּ לֵיהּ: בְּמָטוּתָא מִינָּךְ, בְּמַאי חֲשַׁדְתִּינַן? אֲמַר לְהוּ: אָמִינָא: פִּדְיוֹן שְׁבוּיִים אִיקְּלַע לְהוּ לְרַבָּנַן, וְאִכְסִיפוּ לְמֵימַר לִי. אֲמַרוּ לֵיהּ: הָשְׁתָּא נִשְׁקְלִינְהוּ מָר! אֲמַר לְהוּ: מֵהַהוּא שַׁעְתָּא אַסַּחְתִּינְהוּ מִדַּעְתָּאִי לִצְדָקָה.

After explaining the reason for their actions, the Sages **said to him: Please** tell us, **what did you suspect of us?** You knew that we had taken your rugs, and yet you did not say anything. **He said to them: I said** to myself, certainly an unexpected opportunity for **a ransom of prisoners became available for the Sages,** and they required immediate funds, **but they were** too **embarrassed to say** so to **me** or to ask for money. Instead, they took the rugs. The Sages **said to him: Now** that we have explained the situation, **let the Master take** back the rugs. **He said to them: From that moment** when I realized they were missing, **I put them out of my mind** and consigned them **for charity.**[N] As far as I am concerned, they are already designated for that purpose, and I cannot take them back.

הֲוָה קָא חָלְשָׁא דַּעְתֵּיהּ דְּרָבָא מִשּׁוּם דְּאַבַּיֵי. אֲמַרוּ לֵיהּ: מִסְתַּיֵּיךְ דְּקָא מַגְנִית אַכּוּלָּא כְּרַכָּא.

Rava was distressed due to the fact **that Abaye** received greetings from Heaven every Shabbat eve, while Rava received such greetings only once a year, on Yom Kippur eve, as stated above. **They said to him: Be content that** through your merit **you protect** your **entire city.**[N]

רַבִּי בְּרוֹקָא חוֹזָאָה הֲוָה שְׁכִיחַ בְּשׁוּקָא דְּבֵי לֶפֶט. הֲוָה שְׁכִיחַ אֵלִיָּהוּ גַּבֵּיהּ. אֲמַר לֵיהּ: אִיכָּא בְּהַאי שׁוּקָא בַּר עָלְמָא דְּאָתֵי? אֲמַר לֵיהּ: לָא. אַדְּהָכִי וְהָכִי, חֲזָא לְהַהוּא גַּבְרָא דַּהֲוָה סַיֵּים מְסָאנֵי אוּכָּמֵי וְלָא רְמֵי חוּטָא דִּתְכֶלְתָּא בִּגְלִימֵיהּ. אֲמַר לֵיהּ: הַאי בַּר עָלְמָא דְּאָתֵי הוּא.

§ The Gemara relates another story about the righteousness of common people. **Rabbi Beroka Ḥoza'a was often found in the market of Bei Lefet,**[B] **and Elijah** the Prophet **would often appear to him.** Once Rabbi Beroka **said to** Elijah: Of all the people who come here, is **there anyone in this market worthy of the World-to-Come?**[N] **He said to him: No. In the meantime,** Rabbi Beroka **saw a man** who was **wearing black shoes,**[B] contrary to Jewish custom, **and who did not place the sky-blue,** dyed **thread** of ritual fringes **on his garment.** Elijah **said to** Rabbi Beroka: **That man is worthy of the World-to-Come.**

BACKGROUND

Bei Lefet – בֵּי לֶפֶט: This city, which was probably known as Bel-apat, the city of Bel, was a large commercial city in the north of Bei Ḥozai. King Shapur, whom the Sages called Shavor Malka, rebuilt Bei Lefet and named it Gunde-sabur after himself. Nevertheless, the name Bei Lefet remained in use for many generations.

Black shoes – מְסָאנֵי אוּכָּמֵי: This was a typical shoe, although there were differences in the number of straps and laces on various shoes. Each social class had shoes of a specific form with straps of a distinctive color, and there were apparently corresponding differences between the shoes worn by Jews and those of gentiles. Jews wore shoes with white straps, while gentiles' shoes had black straps. This enabled people to distinguish immediately between Jews and gentiles, and the Sages were very strict with people who changed the color of their shoes in an effort to resemble gentiles.

רְהַט בָּתְרֵיהּ, אֲמַר לֵיהּ: מַאי עוֹבָדָךְ? אֲמַר לֵיהּ: זִיל הָאִידָּנָא, וְתָא לִמְחָר. לִמְחָר אֲמַר לֵיהּ: מַאי עוֹבָדָךְ? אֲמַר לֵיהּ: זַנְדּוּקְנָא אֲנָא, וְאָסַרְנָא גַּבְרֵי לְחוּד וְנָשֵׁי לְחוּד. וּרְמֵינָא פּוּרְיַאי בֵּין הָנֵי לְהָנֵי כִּי הֵיכִי דְּלָא לֵיתוּ לִידֵי אִיסּוּרָא. כִּי חָזֵינָא בַּת יִשְׂרָאֵל דְּיָהֲבִי נׇכְרִים עֲלַהּ עֵינַיְיהוּ, מָסַרְנָא נַפְשַׁאי וּמַצֵּילְנָא לַהּ. יוֹמָא חַד הֲוָות נַעֲרָה מְאוֹרָסָה גַּבַּן דְּיָהֲבוּ בַּהּ נׇכְרִים עֵינַיְיהוּ. שְׁקַלִי דּוּרְדְּיָיא דְּחַמְרָא וּשְׁדַאי לַהּ בְּשִׁיפּוּלַהּ, וַאֲמַרִי: דַּשְׁתָּנָא הִיא.

Rabbi Beroka **ran after** the man and **said to him: What is your occupation?** The man **said to him: Go away now,** as I have no time, **but come** back **tomorrow** and we will talk. **The next day,** Rabbi Beroka arrived and again **said to him: What is your occupation?** The man **said to him: I am a prison guard [*zandukana*],**[L] **and I imprison the men separately and the women separately, and I place my bed between them so that they will not come to transgression. When I see a Jewish woman upon whom gentiles have set their eyes, I risk my life to save her. One day, there was a betrothed young woman among us, upon whom the gentiles had set their eyes. I took dregs [*durdayya*]**[L] **of red wine and threw them on the lower** part **of her dress, and I said: She is menstruating [*dastana*],**[L] so that they would leave her alone.

אֲמַר לֵיהּ: מַאי טַעְמָא לֵית לָךְ חוּטֵי וְרָמֵית מְסָאנֵי אוּכָּמֵי? אֲמַר לֵיהּ: עָיֵילְנָא וְנָפֵיקְנָא בֵּינֵי נׇכְרִים כִּי הֵיכִי דְּלָא לֵידְעוּ דִּיהוּדָאָה אֲנָא. כִּי הָווּ גָּזְרִי גְּזֵירְתָא, מוֹדַעְנָא לְהוּ לְרַבָּנַן, וּבָעוּ רַחֲמֵי וּמְבַטְּלִי לִגְזֵירְתַיְיהוּ. וּמַאי טַעְמָא כִּי אָמֵינָא לָךְ אֲנָא, מַאי עוֹבָדָךְ? וַאֲמַרְתְּ לִי: זִיל הָאִידָּנָא וְתָא לִמְחָר? אֲמַר לֵיהּ: בְּהַהִיא שַׁעְתָּא גָּזְרִי גְּזֵירְתָא, וְאָמֵינָא: בְּרֵישָׁא אֵיזִיל וְאַשְׁמַע לְהוּ לְרַבָּנַן דְּלִבְעֵי רַחֲמֵי עֲלַהּ דְּמִילְּתָא.

Rabbi Beroka **said to him: What is the reason** that you do not **have threads** of ritual fringes, **and** why **do you wear black shoes?** The man **said to him:** Since **I come and go among gentiles,** I dress this way **so that they will not know that I am a Jew. When they issue a decree, I inform the Sages, and they pray for mercy and annul the decree.** Rabbi Beroka further inquired: **And what is the reason** that **when I said to you: What is your occupation, you said to me: Go away now but come tomorrow?** The man **said to him: At that moment,** they had just **issued a decree, and I said** to myself: **First I** must **go and inform the Sages, so that they will pray for mercy over** this **matter.**

אַדְּהָכִי וְהָכִי, אֲתוּ הָנָךְ תְּרֵי אַחֵי. אֲמַר לֵיהּ: הָנָךְ נָמֵי בְּנֵי עָלְמָא דְּאָתֵי נִינְהוּ. אֲזַל לְגַבַּיְיהוּ אֲמַר לְהוּ: מַאי עוֹבָדַיְיכוּ? אֲמַרוּ לֵיהּ: אֱינָשֵׁי בְּדוּחֵי אֲנַן, מְבַדְּחִינַן עֲצִיבֵי. אִי נָמֵי, כִּי חָזֵינַן בֵּי תְּרֵי דְּאִית לְהוּ תִּיגְרָא בַּהֲדַיְיהוּ, טָרְחִינַן וְעָבְדִינַן לְהוּ שְׁלָמָא.

In the meantime, two brothers came to the marketplace. Elijah **said to** Rabbi Beroka: **These** two **also have a share in the World-to-Come.** Rabbi Beroka **went over to** the men **and said to them: What is your occupation? They said to him: We are jesters, and we cheer up the depressed. Alternatively, when we see two people who have a quarrel between them, we strive to make peace.** It is said that for this behavior one enjoys the profits of his actions in this world, and yet his reward is not diminished in the World-to-Come.

"עַל אֵלּוּ מַתְרִיעִין בְּכׇל מָקוֹם" כו׳. תָּנוּ רַבָּנַן: עַל אֵלּוּ מַתְרִיעִין בְּכׇל מָקוֹם: עַל הַשִּׁדָּפוֹן, וְעַל הַיֵּרָקוֹן, וְעַל אַרְבֶּה וְחָסִיל, וְעַל חַיָּה רָעָה. רַבִּי עֲקִיבָא אוֹמֵר: עַל הַשִּׁדָּפוֹן וְעַל הַיֵּרָקוֹן, בְּכׇל שֶׁהוּא. אַרְבֶּה וְחָסִיל, אֲפִילּוּ לֹא נִרְאָה בְּאֶרֶץ יִשְׂרָאֵל אֶלָּא כָּנָף אֶחָד, מַתְרִיעִין עֲלֵיהֶן.

§ The mishna states: **For the following** calamities **they sound the alarm in every place. The Sages taught: For the following** calamities **they sound the alarm in every place: For blight,**[B] **for mildew, for locusts, for caterpillars,**[H] a type of locust that comes in large swarms and descends upon a certain place, **and for dangerous beasts.**[H] **Rabbi Akiva says: For blight and mildew** they sound the alarm **over any amount. For locusts, and** for **caterpillar, even if only a single wing**[N] of one of these pests **was seen in all of Eretz Yisrael, they sound the alarm over them,** as this is a sign that more are on their way.

"וְעַל חַיָּה" וכו׳. תָּנוּ רַבָּנַן: חַיָּה רָעָה שֶׁאָמְרוּ, בִּזְמַן שֶׁהִיא מְשׁוּלַּחַת, מַתְרִיעִין עָלֶיהָ; אֵינָהּ מְשׁוּלַּחַת, אֵין מַתְרִיעִין עָלֶיהָ. אֵי זוֹ הִיא מְשׁוּלַּחַת וְאֵי זוֹ הִיא שֶׁאֵינָהּ מְשׁוּלַּחַת? נִרְאֵית בָּעִיר, מְשׁוּלַּחַת; בַּשָּׂדֶה, אֵינָהּ מְשׁוּלַּחַת. בַּיּוֹם, מְשׁוּלַּחַת; בַּלַּיְלָה, אֵינָהּ מְשׁוּלַּחַת.

The mishna taught that they sound the alarm **for** dangerous **beasts** that have invaded a town. **The Sages taught** in a *baraita*: The term **dangerous beasts that they said** is referring to a situation **when** there **is** an abnormal **outbreak**[B] of the animals in a populated area (see Leviticus 26:22). In this case, **they sound the alarm over them.** However, if it **is not an outbreak, they do not sound the alarm over them.** The Gemara elaborates: What is considered **an outbreak and what is not an outbreak?** If a dangerous beast is **seen in the city,** this is **an outbreak.** If it is seen **in the field,** where it is usually found, this is **not an outbreak.** If it is seen **during the day,** this is **an outbreak.** If it is seen **at night,** this is **not an outbreak.**

LANGUAGE

Prison guard [*zandukana*] – זַנְדּוּקְנָא: The proper reading of this word is probably *zendankana*. It is probably derived from the Middle Iranian zēndān, prison, with the agent suffix akān.

Dregs [*durdayya*] – דּוּרְדְּיָיא: From the Persian durdī, meaning dregs.

Menstruating [*dastana*] – דַּשְׁתָּנָא: This is the Middle Persian word daštān, meaning menstruation, menstrual blood, or a menstruating woman.

BACKGROUND

Blight – שִׁדָּפוֹן: Blight here probably refers to the disease known nowadays as corn smut, caused by the fungus *Ustilago maydis*. When the plant is first affected, whitish galls are formed. They later rupture to release dark spores that may infect other plants over large distances.

Stalk affected by *Ustilago*

HALAKHA

For locusts, for caterpillar – וְעַל אַרְבֶּה וְחָסִיל: With regard to all kinds of locusts, even if only one specimen is seen in all of Eretz Yisrael, the alarm must be sounded and fasts proclaimed (*Shulḥan Arukh, Oraḥ Ḥayyim* 576:9).

And for dangerous beasts – וְעַל חַיָּה רָעָה: Fasts must be proclaimed and the alarm sounded upon the sighting of wild beasts, provided that they indicate an outbreak. Under what circumstances is there considered to be an outbreak of wild beasts? If a wild beast is seen in the city during the day; if it is spotted by day in a field and it sees two people but does not run away from them; if it sees two people by day in a field close to a marsh and chases after them; or if, in the marsh itself, it not only chases after the two people but attacks them and eats one of them, this is an outbreak. However, if the beast attacks two people in the marsh and eats both of them, this is not considered an outbreak, as the animal was clearly acting out of hunger. Even with regard to a building constructed in an otherwise unpopulated area, if a wild beast climbs onto the roof and removes an infant from its cradle, this is considered an outbreak (*Shulḥan Arukh, Oraḥ Ḥayyim* 576:6–7).

NOTES

Single wing – כָּנָף אֶחָד: Rashi and others explain that this means a single member of that species. Others claim that this means four, or five, members of the species (Rabbeinu Yehonatan).

BACKGROUND

An outbreak of beasts – חַיָּה מְשׁוּלַּחַת: This term: Outbreak, which literally means a dispatch, is based on a biblical expression; see, e.g., "And the teeth of beasts will I send upon them" (Deuteronomy 32:24). Apparently, it refers to the sudden outbreak of wild beasts in human habitations. An outbreak of this kind might be caused by great hunger among these animals, possibly due to overpopulation. When this happens, animals that generally refrain from any contact with people are liable to break into towns and attack them. Several sources indicate that another cause of this phenomenon is an epidemic of rabies among wild animals, which increases their level of aggression. In this case, their bite poses a mortal threat.

רָאֲתָה שְׁנֵי בְנֵי אָדָם וְרָצְתָה אַחֲרֵיהֶן, מְשׁוּלַּחַת; נֶחְבֵּאת מִפְּנֵיהֶן, אֵינָהּ מְשׁוּלַּחַת. טָרְפָה שְׁנֵי בְנֵי אָדָם וְאָכְלָה אֶחָד מֵהֶן, מְשׁוּלַּחַת; אָכְלָה שְׁנֵיהֶן, אֵינָהּ מְשׁוּלַּחַת. עָלְתָה לַגַּג וְנָטְלָה תִּינוֹק מֵעֲרִיסָה, מְשׁוּלַּחַת.

The *baraita* continues: If the beast **saw two people and chased after them,** this is **an outbreak.** If **it hid from them,** this is **not an outbreak.** If **it tore apart two people and ate one of them,** this is **an outbreak,** as it is clear that the animal did not attack merely due to hunger. If **it ate both of them,** this is **not an outbreak,** as the animal was evidently hungry and acted in accordance with its nature. If **it climbed to the roof and took a baby from** its **cradle,** this is **an outbreak.** This concludes the Gemara's citation of the *baraita*.

הָא גּוּפָהּ קַשְׁיָא. אָמְרַתְּ: נִרְאֲתָה בָּעִיר, מְשׁוּלַּחַת. לָא שְׁנָא בַּיּוֹם וְלָא שְׁנָא בַּלַּיְלָה. וַהֲדַר אָמְרַתְּ: בַּיּוֹם, מְשׁוּלַּחַת; בַּלַּיְלָה, אֵינָהּ מְשׁוּלַּחַת!

The Gemara asks: **This** *baraita* **is itself difficult.** Initially, **you said** that if a dangerous beast is **seen in the city,** this is **an outbreak,** which indicates that it **is no different** whether it is seen by day and **it is no different** if it is seen at night. **And then you said:** If the animal is seen **during the day,** this is **an outbreak;** if it is seen **at night,** this is **not an outbreak.**

לָא קַשְׁיָא. הָכִי קָאָמַר: נִרְאֲתָה בָּעִיר בַּיּוֹם, מְשׁוּלַּחַת; בָּעִיר בַּלַּיְלָה, אֵינָהּ מְשׁוּלַּחַת. אִי נַמִי, בַּשָּׂדֶה אֲפִילּוּ בַּיּוֹם, אֵינָהּ מְשׁוּלַּחַת.

The Gemara resolves this difficulty: This is **not difficult,** as **this is what** the *baraita* **is saying:** If it is **seen in the city during the day,** this is **an outbreak;** if it is seen **in the city at night,** this is **not an outbreak. Alternatively,** if it is seen **in the field, even during the day,** this is **not an outbreak.** If it is spotted in the field at night, this is certainly not an outbreak.

רָאֲתָה שְׁנֵי בְנֵי אָדָם וְרָצְתָה אַחֲרֵיהֶן, מְשׁוּלַּחַת. הָא עוֹמֶדֶת, אֵינָהּ מְשׁוּלַּחַת. וַהֲדַר אָמְרַתְּ: נֶחְבֵּאת מִפְּנֵיהֶן, אֵינָהּ מְשׁוּלַּחַת. הָא עוֹמֶדֶת, מְשׁוּלַּחַת!

The Gemara inquires about another apparent contradiction: The *baraita* states that if the beast **saw two people and chased after them,** this is **an outbreak.** This indicates that if **it stands** but does not run away, this is **not an outbreak. And then you said** that if it **hid from them,** this is **not an outbreak,** from which it may be inferred that if **it stands** and does not run away, this is **an outbreak.**

לָא קַשְׁיָא. כָּאן, בְּשָׂדֶה הַסְּמוּכָה לַאֲגַם; כָּאן, בְּשָׂדֶה שֶׁאֵינָהּ סְמוּכָה לַאֲגַם.

The Gemara answers: This is **not difficult,** as the two sections of the *baraita* describe different situations. **Here,** where it is an outbreak, the beast is **standing in a field near a marsh.** It is natural for the animal to stand, for the beast knows that if people attempt to catch it, it can run into the marsh. Conversely, **there,** where it is not an outbreak, the beast is **standing in a field that is not near a marsh.** Since it has nowhere to run, standing demonstrates an unnatural lack of fear.

טָרְפָה שְׁנֵי בְנֵי אָדָם כְּאֶחָד וְאָכְלָה אֶחָד מֵהֶן, מְשׁוּלַּחַת; שְׁנֵיהֶם, אֵינָהּ מְשׁוּלַּחַת. וְהָא אָמְרַתְּ: אֲפִילּוּ רָצְתָה! אָמַר רַב פָּפָּא: כִּי תְּנֵי הַהִיא, בַּאֲגַמָּא.

The *baraita* taught that if the beast **tore apart two people and ate one of them,** this is **an outbreak,** but if it **ate both of them** this is **not an outbreak.** The Gemara asks: **But didn't you say** that **even** if the animal merely **chased after** two people, this is an outbreak? **Rav Pappa said: When that** ruling of a beast that tore apart two people **is taught,** it is referring to an animal **in a marsh.** Since it is in its own habitat, it is natural for a territorial beast to attack.

גּוּפָא: עָלְתָה לַגַּג וְנָטְלָה תִּינוֹק מֵעֲרִיסָה, מְשׁוּלַּחַת. פְּשִׁיטָא! אָמַר רַב פָּפָּא: כְּכוּכֵי דְּצַיָּידֵי.

The Gemara returns to **the** matter of the *baraita* **itself.** If a wild animal **climbed to the roof and took a baby from** its **cradle,** this is **an outbreak.** The Gemara asks: It **is obvious** that this animal is acting unnaturally. Why does the *baraita* mention this case? **Rav Pappa said:** The *baraita* is referring to the roof of **a hunter's hideout.** Since this hut is in a wild area, one might have thought that it is natural for the beast to attack. Therefore, the *baraita* teaches us that this is still considered an outbreak.

״עַל הַחֶרֶב״ וכו׳. תָּנוּ רַבָּנַן: חֶרֶב שֶׁאָמְרוּ, אֵינוֹ צָרִיךְ לוֹמַר חֶרֶב שֶׁאֵינוֹ שֶׁל שָׁלוֹם, אֶלָּא אֲפִילּוּ חֶרֶב שֶׁל שָׁלוֹם. שֶׁאֵין לְךָ חֶרֶב שֶׁל שָׁלוֹם יוֹתֵר מִפַּרְעֹה נְכֹה, וְאַף עַל פִּי כֵן נִכְשַׁל בָּהּ הַמֶּלֶךְ יֹאשִׁיָּהוּ, שֶׁנֶּאֱמַר:

§ The mishna taught that **they sound the alarm for the sword.**[H] **The Sages taught: With** regard to **the sword that they mentioned, it is not necessary to state** that this includes **a sword that is not of peace,** i.e., an enemy army that has come to wage war against the Jews. **Rather, even** in a case of **a sword of peace,**[N] when an army passes through with no intention of waging war against the Jews, but is merely on its way to another place, this is enough to obligate the court to sound the alarm, **as you do not have a greater** example of **a sword of peace than Pharaoh Neco.** He passed through Eretz Yisrael to wage war with Nebuchadnezzar, **and nevertheless King Josiah stumbled in this** matter, **as it is stated:**

HALAKHA

For the sword – עַל הַחֶרֶב: If an enemy army comes to wage war against Israel, or even if it wishes only to pass through the land to fight another country, fasts must be proclaimed and the alarm sounded (*Shulḥan Arukh*, *Oraḥ Ḥayyim* 576:1).

NOTES

A sword of peace – חֶרֶב שֶׁל שָׁלוֹם: Even if the invading army does not wish to attack the Jewish people, but merely to cross its territory to wage war with its true enemy, the court sounds the alarm, as it is likely that the soldiers passing through the country will cause serious damage (Meiri). Moreover, the people's transgressions might cause the foreign army to turn their weapons against the Jews, even if the soldiers had originally planned to pass through the country in peace (Ritva).

״וַיִּשְׁלַח אֵלָיו מַלְאָכִים, לֵאמֹר: מַה לִּי וָלָךְ, מֶלֶךְ יְהוּדָה? לֹא עָלֶיךָ אַתָּה הַיּוֹם, כִּי אֶל בֵּית מִלְחַמְתִּי; וֵאלֹהִים אָמַר לְבַהֲלֵנִי: חֲדַל לְךָ מֵאֱלֹהִים, אֲשֶׁר עִמִּי, וְאַל יַשְׁחִיתֶךָ״.

"But he sent ambassadors to him saying: What have I to do with you, king of Judea? I do not come against you this day, but against the house with which I am at war; and God has commanded me to make haste. Forbear from meddling with God, Who is with me, so that He will not destroy you" (II Chronicles 35:21). This clearly shows that Pharaoh Neco had no intention of engaging Josiah in battle.

מַאי ״אֱלֹהִים, אֲשֶׁר עִמִּי״? אָמַר רַב יְהוּדָה אָמַר רַב: זוֹ עֲבוֹדָה זָרָה אָמַר: הוֹאִיל וְקָא בָּטַח בַּעֲבוֹדָה זָרָה, יָכֵילְנָא לֵיהּ.

The Gemara asks: **What is** the meaning of the phrase **"God, Who is with me"? Rav Yehuda said** that **Rav said: This** is referring to Neco's **idolatry,** which he brought for assistance. In other words, it is a secular reference and should be read as: The god that is with me, in my possession. Josiah **said: Since** he trusts in idolatry, **I will be able** to defeat **him.**

״וַיֹּרוּ הַיֹּרִים לַמֶּלֶךְ יֹאשִׁיָּהוּ, וַיֹּאמֶר הַמֶּלֶךְ לַעֲבָדָיו: הַעֲבִירוּנִי, כִּי הָחֳלֵיתִי מְאֹד״. מַאי ״כִּי הָחֳלֵיתִי מְאֹד״? אָמַר רַב יְהוּדָה אָמַר רַב: מְלַמֵּד שֶׁעָשׂוּ כָּל גּוּפוֹ כִּכְבָרָה.

With regard to Josiah's battle with Pharaoh Neco, the verse states: **"And the archers shot at King Josiah and the king said to his servants: Move me away, for I am seriously wounded"** (II Chronicles 35:23). **What is** the meaning of the phrase: **"For I am seriously wounded"? Rav Yehuda said** that **Rav said:** This **teaches that** the Egyptian archers **made his entire body like a sieve**[N] from the many arrows they shot at him.

אָמַר רַבִּי שְׁמוּאֵל בַּר נַחְמָנִי אָמַר רַבִּי יוֹנָתָן: מִפְּנֵי מָה נֶעֱנַשׁ יֹאשִׁיָּהוּ? מִפְּנֵי שֶׁהָיָה לוֹ לִימָּלֵךְ בְּיִרְמְיָהוּ, וְלֹא נִמְלַךְ. מַאי דָּרַשׁ? ״וְחֶרֶב לֹא תַעֲבֹר בְּאַרְצְכֶם״.

Rabbi Shmuel bar Naḥmani said that **Rabbi Yoḥanan said: For what** reason **was Josiah punished?**[N] **Because he should have consulted with** the prophet **Jeremiah** to find out if he should go to war, **but he did not consult** with him. **How did** Josiah **interpret** the verses of the Torah? How did they lead him to go to war? The verse states: **"Neither shall a sword go through your land"** (Leviticus 26:6).

מַאי ״חֶרֶב״? אִילֵימָא: חֶרֶב שֶׁאֵינָהּ שֶׁל שָׁלוֹם, וְהָכְתִיב: ״וְנָתַתִּי שָׁלוֹם בָּאָרֶץ״! אֶלָּא, אֲפִילּוּ שֶׁל שָׁלוֹם. וְהוּא אֵינוֹ יוֹדֵעַ שֶׁאֵין דּוֹרוֹ דּוֹמֶה יָפֶה.

What is the meaning of the term: **"Sword"? If we say** that it is referring to **a sword that is not of peace, but isn't it written** earlier in the same verse: **"And I will give peace in the land"? Rather,** the verse must mean that **even** a sword **of peace** shall not pass through the land, and Josiah sought to prevent this occurrence, in fulfillment of the blessing. **But he did not know that his generation did not merit** these blessings, and he would therefore not receive divine assistance in this regard.

כִּי הֲוָה נִיחָא נַפְשֵׁיהּ, חֲזָא יִרְמְיָהוּ שִׂפְוָותֵיהּ דְּקָא מְרַחֲשָׁן, אָמַר: שֶׁמָּא, חַס וְשָׁלוֹם, מִילְּתָא דְּלָא מְהַגְּנָא אָמַר אַגַּב צַעֲרֵיהּ. גָּחֵין וּשְׁמָעֵיהּ דְּקָא מַצְדִּיק עֲלֵיהּ דִּינָא אַנַּפְשֵׁיהּ, אֲמַר: ״צַדִּיק הוּא ה׳, כִּי פִיהוּ מָרִיתִי״. פָּתַח עֲלֵיהּ הַהִיא שַׁעְתָּא: ״רוּחַ אַפֵּינוּ, מְשִׁיחַ ה׳״.

The Gemara discusses Josiah's deathbed reflections. **When** Josiah **was dying, Jeremiah saw his lips moving.** Jeremiah **said: Perhaps, Heaven forbid, he is saying something improper** and complaining about God's judgment **on account of his** great **distress.** Jeremiah **bent over and heard that he was justifying** God's **judgment against himself.** Josiah **said: "The Lord is righteous, for I have rebelled against His word"** (Lamentations 1:18). **At that moment,** Jeremiah **began** his eulogy **for** Josiah: **"The breath of our nostrils, the anointed of the Lord,** was trapped in their pits" (Lamentations 4:20).

״מַעֲשֶׂה וְיָרְדוּ זְקֵנִים מִירוּשָׁלַיִם לְעָרֵיהֶם״ כו׳. אִיבַּעְיָא לְהוּ: כִּמְלֹא תַנּוּר תְּבוּאָה, אוֹ דִּלְמָא כִּמְלֹא תַנּוּר פַּת?

§ The mishna taught: **An incident** occurred in **which Elders descended from Jerusalem to their cities** and decreed a fast throughout the land because a small amount of blight was seen in the city of Ashkelon, enough to fill the mouth of an oven. **A dilemma was raised before** the Sages: Did they mean enough **grain to fill** an entire **oven, or perhaps** they meant enough grain to prepare **bread to fill an oven?** This is far less, as bread is stuck to the walls of the oven and does not fill its inner area.

תָּא שְׁמַע: ״כִּמְלֹא פִּי תַנּוּר״. וַעֲדַיִין תִּיבָּעֵי לְהוּ: כְּכִיסּוּיָא דְּתַנּוּרָא, אוֹ דִּלְמָא כִּי דָּרָא דְּרִיפְתָּא דְּהָדַר לֵיהּ לְפוּמָא דְּתַנּוּרָא? תֵּיקוּ.

The Gemara answers: **Come** and **hear** the phrase of the mishna: Enough **to fill the mouth of an oven.**[NH] This indicates that the bread referred to does not fill the entire oven, but rather covers the mouth of the oven. The Gemara further asks: **And still you can raise this dilemma before them:** Is the mishna referring to the bread **of the cover of the oven? Perhaps** it is referring **to a row of bread around the mouth of the oven.** No resolution was found, and the Gemara states that the dilemma **shall stand** unresolved.

NOTES

That the archers made his entire body like a sieve – שֶׁעָשׂוּ כָּל גּוּפוֹ כִּכְבָרָה: Rashi explains that this interpretation is derived from the words "And the archers shot." In Hebrew, the noun archer and the verb shot come from the same root, *y-r-a*. The use of both constitutes repetitive language, which indicates that each archer shot many arrows. Others suggest that it is derived from the word "wounded [*haḥaleiti*]." Rav associates this word with *ḥalal*, a hole. Josiah requested to be taken away because his body had been pierced with holes like a sieve (Rashash).

For what reason was Josiah punished – מִפְּנֵי מָה נֶעֱנַשׁ יֹאשִׁיָּהוּ: In the midrash, the verse "And he did not hearken to the words of Neco from the mouth of God" (II Chronicles 35:22) is interpreted as an allusion to a warning issued by Jeremiah to Josiah, citing Isaiah, that he should not interfere with Pharaoh Neco, as it is stated with regard to the conflicts of Pharaoh Neco: "And I will spur Egypt against Egypt; and they shall fight every one against his brother, and every one against his neighbor; city against city, and kingdom against kingdom" (Isaiah 19:2).

To fill the mouth of an oven – כִּמְלֹא פִּי תַנּוּר: Many commentaries explain that the amount of grain required to fill an oven is greater than the amount needed to make the amount of bread that will fill the same oven (Rashi; Rabbeinu Gershom; *Tosafot*). Others claim the opposite, that more grain is required to produce the amount of bread needed to fill the opening of the oven than is required to fill the opening with the grain itself (Rabbi Elyakim).

HALAKHA

To fill the mouth of an oven – כִּמְלֹא פִּי תַנּוּר: If the crops in a certain area are struck by blight or mildew, even if only a small amount of grain is affected, enough to fill the opening of an oven, fasts must be proclaimed and the alarm must be sounded. The precise definition of this measure has not been determined (*Leḥem Mishne*; *Shulḥan Arukh*, *Oraḥ Ḥayyim* 576:8).

״וְעוֹד גָּזְרוּ תַּעֲנִית עַל שֶׁאָכְלוּ זְאֵבִים״ כּוּ׳. אָמַר עוּלָּא מִשּׁוּם רַבִּי שִׁמְעוֹן בֶּן יְהוֹצָדָק: מַעֲשֶׂה וּבָלְעוּ זְאֵבִים שְׁנֵי תִינוֹקוֹת וֶהֱקִיאוּם דֶּרֶךְ בֵּית הָרְעִי. וּבָא מַעֲשֶׂה לִפְנֵי חֲכָמִים, וְטִיהֲרוּ אֶת הַבָּשָׂר, וְטִמְּאוּ אֶת הָעֲצָמוֹת.

§ The mishna taught: **And furthermore, they decreed a fast because wolves had eaten two children** in Transjordan. **Ulla said in the name of Rabbi Shimon ben Yehotzadak: An incident** occurred in **which wolves**[B] **swallowed**[N] **two children and excreted them. And the incident came before the Sages** for a ruling. They were asked if the remains were ritually impure even after they had passed through the animal's digestive tract, **and they pronounced the flesh ritually pure,**[H] as it had been digested, but they **pronounced** the intact **bones ritually impure.**

״עַל אֵלּוּ מַתְרִיעִין בְּשַׁבָּת״ כּוּ׳. תָּנוּ רַבָּנַן: עִיר שֶׁהִקִּיפוּהָ נׇכְרִים אוֹ נָהָר, וְאֶחָד סְפִינָה הַמִּיטָּרֶפֶת בַּיָּם, וְאֶחָד יָחִיד שֶׁנִּרְדָּף מִפְּנֵי נׇכְרִים אוֹ מִפְּנֵי לִסְטִין, וּמִפְּנֵי רוּחַ רָעָה מַתְרִיעִין בְּשַׁבָּת, וְעַל כּוּלָּן יָחִיד רַשַּׁאי לְסַגֵּף אֶת עַצְמוֹ בְּתַעֲנִית.

§ The mishna further taught: **For the following** calamities **they sound the alarm** even **on Shabbat:** For a city that is surrounded by gentile troops, for a place in danger of being flooded by a river that has swelled its banks, or for a ship tossed about at sea. **The Sages taught:** In the case of **a city that is surrounded by gentile** troops **or a river** that has swelled beyond its banks, and this also applies to **both a ship tossed about at sea and an individual who is being pursued by gentiles, or by thieves, or by an evil spirit,** which may lead him to harm himself, **they sound the alarm** even **on Shabbat. And in all these** cases, **an individual is permitted to afflict himself by fasting**[H] to annul the evil decrees against him.

רַבִּי יוֹסֵי אוֹמֵר: אֵין הַיָּחִיד רַשַּׁאי לְסַגֵּף אֶת עַצְמוֹ בְּתַעֲנִית, שֶׁמָּא יִצְטָרֵךְ לַבְּרִיּוֹת, וְאֵין הַבְּרִיּוֹת מְרַחֲמוֹת עָלָיו. אָמַר רַב יְהוּדָה אָמַר רַב: מַאי טַעְמָא דְּרַבִּי יוֹסֵי? דִּכְתִיב: ״וַיְהִי הָאָדָם לְנֶפֶשׁ חַיָּה״. נְשָׁמָה שֶׁנָּתַתִּי בְּךָ, הַחֲיֵיהָ.

Rabbi Yosei says: An individual is not permitted to afflict himself by fasting, lest he become too weak to work and **be beholden to other beings, and** those **beings will not have mercy on him.**[N] **Rav Yehuda said** that **Rav said: What is the reason of Rabbi Yosei?** It is **as it is written: "And man became a living soul"** (Genesis 2:7). Rabbi Yosei interprets this verse as a command: **The soul I placed within you,** preserve and **sustain it.**

״שִׁמְעוֹן הַתִּימְנִי אוֹמֵר: אַף עַל הַדֶּבֶר״ כּוּ׳. אִיבַּעְיָא לְהוּ: לֹא הוֹדוּ לוֹ חֲכָמִים בְּשַׁבָּת, אֲבָל בְּחוֹל הוֹדוּ לוֹ? אוֹ דִלְמָא לֹא הוֹדוּ לוֹ כְּלָל?

§ The mishna taught that **Shimon the Timnite says:** One may cry out on Shabbat **even for pestilence,**[H] but the Rabbis did not agree with him. **A dilemma was raised before** the Sages: Does this mean that **the Rabbis did not agree with him** with regard to crying out in these cases **on Shabbat,** but if they occur **on a weekday they agreed with him? Or perhaps they did not agree with him at all,**[N] as they maintain that one never cries out over pestilence.

תָּא שְׁמַע, דְּתַנְיָא: מַתְרִיעִין עַל הַדֶּבֶר בְּשַׁבָּת, וְאֵין צָרִיךְ לוֹמַר בְּחוֹל. רַבִּי חָנָן בֶּן פִּיטוֹם, תַּלְמִידוֹ שֶׁל רַבִּי עֲקִיבָא, מִשּׁוּם רַבִּי עֲקִיבָא אוֹמֵר: אֵין מַתְרִיעִין עַל הַדֶּבֶר כָּל עִיקָּר.

The Gemara answers: **Come** and **hear, as it is taught** in a *baraita*: **One cries out for** a plague of **pestilence on Shabbat, and needless to say on weekdays. Rabbi Ḥanan ben Pitom, the student of Rabbi Akiva, says in the name of Rabbi Akiva: One does not cry out for pestilence at all.** This opinion attributed to Rabbi Akiva is the ruling of the Rabbis in the mishna.

BACKGROUND

Wolves – זְאֵבִים: Wolves, even in packs, do not usually attack people. Nevertheless, the wolves in Eretz Yisrael are bigger and stronger than their European counterparts, and cases have been documented of packs of wolves entering inhabited areas and even attacking children.

NOTES

Wolves swallowed – וּבָלְעוּ זְאֵבִים: This does not literally mean that the wolves swallowed them whole; rather, they did not leave behind any physical remains of their bodies (*Gevurat Ari*). The halakhic problem concerns the flesh left on the corpses. Does it still have the status of flesh? Perhaps it no longer confers the ritual impurity of the dead, as it has been partially digested.

And beings will not have mercy on him – וְאֵין הַבְּרִיּוֹת מְרַחֲמוֹת עָלָיו: The commentaries explain that if someone fasts for many days and weakens his body to such an extent that he can no longer work and support himself, he is likely to be viewed as having brought this desperate situation upon himself (Maharsha).

Or perhaps they did not agree with him at all – אוֹ דִלְמָא לֹא הוֹדוּ לוֹ כְּלָל: Many early commentaries pose the following difficulty: Rabbi Ḥanan ben Pitom stated in the name of his teacher, Rabbi Akiva, that the alarm is not sounded for a plague at all, even on weekdays. However, it is stated explicitly in the mishna that according to the opinion of Rabbi Akiva, people living outside a city affected by a plague must sound the alarm but they need not fast. Certainly, then, the residents of the city affected by a plague itself must sound the alarm.

Some commentaries resolve this difficulty by amending the *baraita* to read: Rabbi Ḥanan ben Pitom said in the name of Rabbi Akiva: They do not sound the alarm for a plague on Shabbat (Ra'avad).

However, most early commentaries explain that when Rabbi Akiva said that they do not sound the alarm for a plague at all, he was referring to the communities outside the city affected by the disease and beyond its surrounding areas. Even Rabbi Akiva agrees that the alarm is sounded by the residents of the city afflicted by the plague, as well as by those living in the adjacent areas.

Rabbi Akiva merely disagrees with Shimon the Timnite, who maintains that the alarm is sounded even in other cities, as Rabbi Akiva rules that outside the immediately surrounding areas of a city afflicted by a plague the alarm is not sounded even on weekdays (Ramban; Ritva; Rid).

HALAKHA

And they pronounced the flesh ritually pure – וְטִיהֲרוּ אֶת הַבָּשָׂר: If an animal swallows a child whole, and its remains pass through the creature's excretory channel, the flesh is ritually pure but the bones are impure (Rambam *Sefer Tahara, Hilkhot Tumat Met* 20:4).

An individual is permitted to afflict himself by fasting – יָחִיד רַשַּׁאי לְסַגֵּף אֶת עַצְמוֹ בְּתַעֲנִית: Just as the community must observe fasts and offer special prayers when threatened by calamity, so too must every individual fast when faced with some personal suffering. This is in accordance with the ruling of the *Maggid Mishne* (see *Baḥ* and *Peri Megadim*). The *halakha* is in accordance with the unattributed opinion of the first *tanna* of the *baraita* (*Shulḥan Arukh, Oraḥ Ḥayyim* 578:1).

For pestilence – עַל הַדֶּבֶר: On Shabbat, the alarm is not sounded for a plague of pestilence. During the rest of the week, the alarm is sounded for this reason and fasts are proclaimed (*Shulḥan Arukh, Oraḥ Ḥayyim* 576:2; 288:9).

"עַל כָּל צָרָה שֶׁלֹּא תָּבוֹא עַל הַצִּבּוּר" כו'. תָּנוּ רַבָּנַן: עַל כָּל צָרָה שֶׁלֹּא תָּבוֹא עַל הַצִּבּוּר מַתְרִיעִין עָלֶיהָ, חוּץ מֵרוֹב גְּשָׁמִים. מַאי טַעְמָא? אָמַר רַבִּי יוֹחָנָן: לְפִי שֶׁאֵין מִתְפַּלְּלִין עַל רוֹב הַטּוֹבָה.

§ The mishna further states that they sound the alarm **on** account of any **trouble that should not befall the community,** a euphemism for trouble that may befall the community, except for an overabundance of rain. **The Sages taught** in a *baraita*: **For any trouble that should not befall the community, they sound the alarm for it, except for an overabundance of rain.**[H] The Gemara asks: **What is the reason** for this? **Rabbi Yoḥanan said: Because one does not pray over an excess of good.** Since rain is generally good for the world, it is not appropriate to pray for it to stop, even when it falls in excess.

וְאָמַר רַבִּי יוֹחָנָן: מִנַּיִין שֶׁאֵין מִתְפַּלְּלִין עַל רוֹב הַטּוֹבָה? שֶׁנֶּאֱמַר "הָבִיאוּ אֶת כָּל הַמַּעֲשֵׂר אֶל בֵּית הָאוֹצָר" וגו' מַאי "עַד בְּלִי דָי"? אָמַר רָמִי בַּר חָמָא: עַד שֶׁיִּבְלוּ שִׂפְתוֹתֵיכֶם מִלּוֹמַר: "דַּי".

And Rabbi Yoḥanan said: From where is it derived **that one does not pray over an excess of good?** It **is stated: "Bring the whole tithe into the storeroom,** that there may be food in My house, and test Me now by this, said the Lord of hosts, if I will not open for you the windows of heaven, and pour out for you a blessing that there shall be more than sufficiency" (Malachi 3:10). **What** is the meaning of the phrase: **"That there shall be more than sufficiency [*ad beli dai*]"? Rami bar Ḥama said:** It means that the abundance will be so great **that your lips will be worn out [*yivlu*],** similar to the word *beli,* **from saying enough [*dai*].** In other words, even when a blessing is delivered in gross excess, one should not pray for it to cease, as the verse blesses the people with an excess.

אָמַר רָמִי בַּר רַב יוּד: וּבַגּוֹלָה מַתְרִיעִין עָלֶיהָ. תַּנְיָא נַמִי הָכִי: שָׁנָה שֶׁגְּשָׁמֶיהָ מְרוּבִּין, אַנְשֵׁי מִשְׁמָר שׁוֹלְחִין לְאַנְשֵׁי מַעֲמָד: תְּנוּ עֵינֵיכֶם בַּאֲחֵיכֶם שֶׁבַּגּוֹלָה שֶׁלֹּא יְהֵא בָּתֵּיהֶם קִבְרֵיהֶם.

Rami bar Rav Yud said: This is true in Eretz Yisrael, but in the Diaspora, i.e., Babylonia, **they do sound the alarm over** excessive rain. The reason is that Babylonia is in a low-lying region, where excessive rain poses a real danger. **That** opinion **is also taught** in a *baraita*: In **a year whose rains are abundant, the members of the priestly watch** in the Temple **would send** a message **to the members of the non-priestly watch: Cast your eyes on your brothers in the Diaspora** and have them in mind when you pray, so **that their houses** should not collapse from excessive rain and **become their graves.**

שָׁאֲלוּ אֶת רַבִּי אֱלִיעֶזֶר: עַד הֵיכָן גְּשָׁמִים יוֹרְדִין וְיִתְפַּלְּלוּ שֶׁלֹּא יֵרְדוּ? אָמַר לָהֶם: כְּדֵי שֶׁיַּעֲמוֹד אָדָם בְּקֶרֶן אוֹפֶל, וִישַׁכְשֵׁךְ רַגְלָיו בַּמַּיִם. וְהָתַנְיָא: יָדָיו! רַגְלָיו כְּיָדָיו קָאָמֵינָא.

They asked Rabbi Eliezer: How much rain must fall until **they** should **pray that it should not fall** anymore? **He said to them** by way of exaggeration: Enough rain must fall **so that a person stands at** the colossal cliff **Keren Ophel**[B] **and dips his feet in water.** The Gemara asks: **But isn't it taught** in a *baraita* that Rabbi Eliezer said he must be able to place **his hands** in water? Rabbi Eliezer could answer: When **I said to you** that he must be able to place **his feet,** I meant **like his hands,** i.e., the water must be high enough that he can dip both his hands and feet into the water with ease.

אָמַר רַבָּה בַּר בַּר חָנָה: לְדִידִי חֲזֵיא לִי קֶרֶן אוֹפֶל, דְּקָם הַהוּא טַיָּיעָא כִּי רָכֵיב גַּמְלָא וְנָקֵיט רוּמְחָא בִּידֵיהּ מִיתְחֲזֵי אִינִיבָא.

With regard to the height of this great cliff, **Rabba bar bar Ḥana said: I** personally **saw Keren Ophel,** and when I peered down I saw **that an Arab was positioned** below, and **while riding a camel and** holding **a spear in his hand, he looked like a worm [*iniva*].**[L]

תָּנוּ רַבָּנַן: "וְנָתַתִּי גִשְׁמֵיכֶם בְּעִתָּם". לֹא שִׁכּוֹרָה וְלֹא צְמֵאָה, אֶלָּא בֵּינוֹנִית. שֶׁכָּל זְמַן שֶׁהַגְּשָׁמִים מְרוּבִּין – מְטַשְׁטְשִׁין אֶת הָאָרֶץ, וְאֵינָהּ מוֹצִיאָה פֵּירוֹת. דָּבָר אַחֵר:

The Sages taught: "Then I will give your rains in their season" (Leviticus 26:4). This means that the earth will be **neither drunk nor thirsty; rather, a moderate** amount of rain will fall. **For as long as the rains are abundant, they muddy** the soil of **the land, and it does not give out** its **produce. Alternatively,**

HALAKHA

Except for an overabundance of rain – חוּץ מֵרוֹב גְּשָׁמִים: If there is an excessive amount of rainfall, prayers may be offered for the rain to stop, due to the concern that the water will cause buildings to collapse. In Eretz Yisrael, these prayers are usually not recited, as abundant rain in Eretz Yisrael is considered a blessing and there is no worry that the excessive rainfall will cause buildings to collapse. Even in Eretz Yisrael, however, prayers that the rain should stop must be offered in places such as Safed, where excessive water might cause structural damage (*Shulḥan Arukh, Oraḥ Ḥayyim* 576:11).

BACKGROUND

Keren Ophel – קֶרֶן אוֹפֶל: Some maintain that Keren Ophel is another name for Ophel, the ancient fortress of Jerusalem. The difference in height between Ophel and the nearby Kidron Valley is more than 100 m.

LANGUAGE

Worm [*iniva*] – אִינִיבָא: Probably from a Semitic root. It also appears in Assyrian as nabu, meaning lice or fleas.

בְּעִתָּם בְּלֵילֵי רְבִיעִיּוֹת וּבְלֵילֵי שַׁבָּתוֹת.

“**In their season**” means **on Wednesday eves,**[N] i.e., Tuesday nights, **and on Shabbat eves,** i.e., Friday nights, because at these times people are not out in the streets, either due to fear of demonic forces that were thought to wander on Tuesday nights or due to the sanctity of Shabbat.

שֶׁכֵּן מָצִינוּ בִּימֵי שִׁמְעוֹן בֶּן שֶׁטַח, שֶׁיָּרְדוּ לָהֶם גְּשָׁמִים בְּלֵילֵי רְבִיעִיּוֹת וּבְלֵילֵי שַׁבָּתוֹת, עַד שֶׁנַּעֲשׂוּ חִטִּים כִּכְלָיוֹת וּשְׂעוֹרִים כְּגַרְעִינֵי זֵיתִים וַעֲדָשִׁים כְּדִינְרֵי זָהָב. וְצָרְרוּ מֵהֶם דּוּגְמָא לְדוֹרוֹת, לְהוֹדִיעַ כַּמָּה הַחֵטְא גּוֹרֵם, שֶׁנֶּאֱמַר: ״עֲוֹנוֹתֵיכֶם הִטּוּ אֵלֶּה, וְחַטֹּאתֵיכֶם מָנְעוּ הַטּוֹב מִכֶּם״.

As we found in **the days of Shimon ben Shetaḥ that rain** invariably **fell for them on Wednesday eves and on Shabbat eves, until wheat grew** as big **as kidneys, and barley** as big **as olive pits, and lentils as golden dinars.**[B] **And they tied** up some **of these** crops as **an example** [*dugma*][L] **for** future **generations, to convey** to them **how much** damage **sin causes, as it is stated:** “The Lord our God, Who gives rain, the former rain and the latter rain, in its season that keeps for us the appointed weeks of the harvest. **Your iniquities have turned away these things, and your sins have withheld the good from you**” (Jeremiah 5:24–25).

וְכֵן מָצִינוּ בִּימֵי הוֹרְדוֹס שֶׁהָיוּ עוֹסְקִין בְּבִנְיַן בֵּית הַמִּקְדָּשׁ, וְהָיוּ יוֹרְדִין גְּשָׁמִים בַּלַּיְלָה. לְמָחָר נָשְׁבָה הָרוּחַ, וְנִתְפַּזְּרוּ הֶעָבִים, וְזָרְחָה הַחַמָּה, וְיָצְאוּ הָעָם לִמְלַאכְתָּן, וְיָדְעוּ שֶׁמְּלֶאכֶת שָׁמַיִם בִּידֵיהֶם.

And we likewise found that **in the days of Herod** that **they were occupied in the building of the Temple, and rain would fall at night. And the next day the wind would blow, the clouds would disperse, the sun would shine, and the people would go out to their work. And** as rain would fall only at a time when it would not interfere with their labor, the nation **knew** that **the work of Heaven** was being performed **by their hands.**

״מַעֲשֶׂה שֶׁשָּׁלְחוּ לְחוֹנִי הַמְעַגֵּל״ וכו׳. תָּנוּ רַבָּנַן: פַּעַם אַחַת, יָצָא רוֹב אֲדָר וְלֹא יָרְדוּ גְּשָׁמִים. שָׁלְחוּ לְחוֹנִי הַמְעַגֵּל: הִתְפַּלֵּל וְיֵרְדוּ גְּשָׁמִים. הִתְפַּלֵּל וְלֹא יָרְדוּ גְּשָׁמִים. עָג עוּגָה, וְעָמַד בְּתוֹכָהּ, כְּדֶרֶךְ שֶׁעָשָׂה חֲבַקּוּק הַנָּבִיא, שֶׁנֶּאֱמַר: ״עַל מִשְׁמַרְתִּי אֶעֱמֹדָה, וְאֶתְיַצְּבָה עַל מָצוֹר״ וגו׳.

§ The mishna taught: **An incident** occurred in **which** the people **sent** a message **to Ḥoni HaMe'aggel.** This event is related in greater detail in the following *baraita*. **The Sages taught: Once, most of** the month of **Adar had passed but rain had** still **not fallen. They sent** this message **to Ḥoni HaMe'aggel: Pray, and rain will fall. He prayed, but no rain fell. He drew a circle** in the dust **and stood inside it, in the manner that the prophet Habakkuk did, as it is stated: “And I will stand upon my watch and set myself upon the tower,** and I will look out to see what He will say to me, and what I shall answer when I am reproved” (Habakkuk 2:1). This verse is taken to mean that Habakkuk fashioned a kind of prison for himself where he sat.

אָמַר לְפָנָיו: רִבּוֹנוֹ שֶׁל עוֹלָם! בָּנֶיךָ שָׂמוּ פְּנֵיהֶם עָלַי, שֶׁאֲנִי כְּבֶן בַּיִת לְפָנֶיךָ. נִשְׁבָּע אֲנִי בְּשִׁמְךָ הַגָּדוֹל שֶׁאֵינִי זָז מִכָּאן עַד שֶׁתְּרַחֵם עַל בָּנֶיךָ. הִתְחִילוּ גְּשָׁמִים מְנַטְּפִין. אָמְרוּ לוֹ תַּלְמִידָיו: רַבִּי, רְאִינוּךָ, וְלֹא נָמוּת. כִּמְדוּמִּין אָנוּ שֶׁאֵין גְּשָׁמִים יוֹרְדִין אֶלָּא לְהַתִּיר שְׁבוּעָתְךָ.

Ḥoni **said before** God: **Master of the Universe, Your children have turned their faces toward me, as I am like a member of Your household.**[N] Therefore, **I take an oath by Your great name that I will not move from here until you have mercy upon Your children** and answer their prayers for rain. **Rain began to trickle** down, but only in small droplets. **His students said to him: Rabbi, we have seen** that **you** can perform great wonders, **but** this quantity of rain is not enough to ensure that **we will not die.**[N] **It appears to us that** a small amount of **rain is falling only** to enable you **to dissolve your oath,** but it is not nearly enough to save us.

אָמַר: לֹא כָּךְ שָׁאַלְתִּי, אֶלָּא גִּשְׁמֵי בּוֹרוֹת, שִׁיחִין, וּמְעָרוֹת. יָרְדוּ בְּזַעַף, עַד שֶׁכָּל טִפָּה וְטִפָּה כִּמְלֹא פִּי חָבִית. וְשִׁיעֲרוּ חֲכָמִים שֶׁאֵין טִפָּה פְּחוּתָה מִלּוֹג. אָמְרוּ לוֹ תַּלְמִידָיו: רַבִּי, רְאִינוּךָ, וְלֹא נָמוּת. כִּמְדוּמִּין אָנוּ שֶׁאֵין גְּשָׁמִים יוֹרְדִין אֶלָּא לְאַבֵּד הָעוֹלָם.

Ḥoni **said** to God: **I did not ask for this, but for rain to** fill the **cisterns, ditches, and caves.** Rain **began to fall furiously, until each and every drop** was as big **as the mouth of a barrel, and the Sages estimated that no drop was less than a** *log* **in size. His students said to him: Rabbi, we have seen** that **you** can call on God to perform miracles **and we will not die,** but now **it appears to us that rain is falling only to destroy the world.**

אָמַר לְפָנָיו: לֹא כָּךְ שָׁאַלְתִּי, אֶלָּא גִּשְׁמֵי רָצוֹן, בְּרָכָה, וּנְדָבָה. יָרְדוּ כְּתִיקְנָן, עַד שֶׁעָלוּ כָּל הָעָם לְהַר הַבַּיִת מִפְּנֵי הַגְּשָׁמִים. אָמְרוּ לוֹ: רַבִּי, כְּשֵׁם שֶׁהִתְפַּלַּלְתָּ שֶׁיֵּרְדוּ, כָּךְ הִתְפַּלֵּל וְיֵלְכוּ לָהֶם. אָמַר לָהֶם: כָּךְ מְקוּבְּלַנִי שֶׁאֵין מִתְפַּלְּלִין עַל רוֹב הַטּוֹבָה.

Ḥoni again **said before** God: **I did not ask for this** harmful rain either, **but** for **rain of benevolence, blessing, and generosity.** Subsequently, the rains **fell in their standard manner, until all of the people** sought higher ground and **ascended to the Temple Mount due to the rain. They said to him: Rabbi, just as you prayed that** the rains **should fall, so too, pray that they should stop. He said to them: This is** the tradition that **I received, that one does not pray over an excess of good.**

NOTES

On Wednesday eves [*revi'iyyot*] – בְּלֵילֵי רְבִיעִיּוֹת: Most commentaries explain that this means the nights before the fourth [*revi'i*] day of the week, i.e., Wednesday eves. However, some maintain that it is referring to the nights on which a downpour of rain [*revi'a*] is expected. This interpretation is supported by a version of the text found in some manuscripts and early sources: On the days of *revi'iyyot*.

Like a member of Your household – כְּבֶן בַּיִת לְפָנֶיךָ: Some commentaries maintain that this is as an expression of modesty: Ḥoni HaMe'aggel compared himself to an unimportant member of God's household, who is able to enter his Master's house and submit his requests whenever he wishes, on account of his insignificance (Maharsha).

This is reminiscent of Rabbi Yoḥanan ben Zakkai's explanation as to why he himself did not pray for his son's recovery but asked Rabbi Ḥanina ben Dosa to pray on his behalf instead (*Berakhot* 34b). Rabbi Yoḥanan ben Zakkai viewed himself as the king's officer, while he viewed Rabbi Ḥanina as the king's slave. A slave, who appears regularly before his master, is more suited to submit a request before the king than is an officer, who is not accustomed to addressing him.

We have seen you but this is not enough that we will not die – רְאִינוּךָ וְלֹא נָמוּת: Many commentaries explain this sentence as follows: We have seen that God performs miracles on your behalf. Pray for us now so that we should not die, as we are still in a desperate situation. Others read it as a question: Just because we have seen you, shall we not die? The rain you have brought has not benefited us in any way (Rabbeinu Gershom).

BACKGROUND

As kidneys…as golden dinars – כִּכְלָיוֹת...כְּדִינְרֵי זָהָב: Wheat and barley kernels are roughly 6 mm in size nowadays, while lentils are 3–4 mm. Accordingly, the crops mentioned here were two to three times their regular size.

LANGUAGE

Example [*dugma*] – דּוּגְמָא: From the Greek δεῖγμα, *deigma*, an example or a model.

אף על פי כן, הביאו לי פר הודאה. הביאו לו פר הודאה. סמך שתי ידיו עליו, ואמר לפניו: רבונו של עולם! עמך ישראל שהוצאת ממצרים אינן יכולין לא ברוב טובה ולא ברוב פורענות. כעסת עליהם – אינן יכולין לעמוד. השפעת עליהם טובה – אינן יכולין לעמוד. יהי רצון מלפניך שיפסקו הגשמים ויהא ריוח בעולם. מיד נשבה הרוח, ונתפזרו העבים, וזרחה החמה, ויצאו העם לשדה והביאו להם כמהין ופטריות.

Ḥoni continued: **Nevertheless, bring me a bull.** I will sacrifice it as **a thanks-offering** and pray at the same time. **They brought him a bull** for **a thanks-offering. He placed his two hands on its** head **and said before** God: **Master of the Universe, Your nation Israel, whom You brought out of Egypt, cannot** bear **either an excess of good or an excess of punishment. You grew angry with them** and withheld rain, **and they are unable to bear it. You bestowed upon them** too much **good, and they were** also **unable to bear it. May it be Your will that the rain stop and that there be relief for the world. Immediately, the wind blew, the clouds dispersed, the sun shone, and everyone went out to the fields and gathered for themselves truffles**[B] **and mushrooms** that had sprouted in the strong rain.

שלח לו שמעון בן שטח: אלמלא חוני אתה, גוזרני עליך נידוי. שאילו שנים כשני אליהו שמפתחות גשמים בידו של אליהו, לא נמצא שם שמים מתחלל על ידך?

Shimon ben Shetaḥ relayed to Ḥoni HaMe'aggel: **If you were not Ḥoni, I would have decreed ostracism upon you. For were these years like the years of Elijah,**[N] **when the keys of rain** were entrusted **in Elijah's hands,** and he swore it would not rain, **wouldn't the name of Heaven have been desecrated by your** oath not to leave the circle until it rained? Once you have pronounced this oath, either yours or Elijah's must be falsified.

אבל מה אעשה לך, שאתה מתחטא לפני המקום ועושה לך רצונך, כבן שמתחטא על אביו ועושה לו רצונו. ואומר לו: אבא, הוליכני לרחצני בחמין, שטפני בצונן, תן לי אגוזים, שקדים, אפרסקים, ורמונים, ונותן לו. ועליך הכתוב אומר: "ישמח אביך ואמך ותגל יולדתיך".

However, what can I do to you, as you nag God and He does your bidding, like a son who nags his father and his father **does his bidding. And** the son **says to** his father: **Father, take me to be bathed in hot water; wash me with cold water; give me nuts, almonds, peaches, and pomegranates. And** his father **gives him. About you, the verse states: "Your father and mother will be glad and she who bore you will rejoice"** (Proverbs 23:25).

תנו רבנן: מה שלחו בני לשכת הגזית לחוני המעגל? "ותגזר אמר, ויקם לך, ועל דרכיך נגה אור". "ותגזר אמר" –

The Sages taught: What message did **the members of the Chamber of the Hewn Stone,** the Great Sanhedrin, **send to Ḥoni HaMe'aggel?** About you, the verse states: **"You shall also decree a matter, and it shall be established for you; and the light shall shine upon your ways.** When they cast down, you will say: There is lifting up, for He saves the humble person. He will deliver the one who is not innocent and he will be delivered through the cleanness of your hands" (Job 22:28–30).

אתה גזרת מלמטה, והקדוש ברוך הוא מקיים מאמרך מלמעלה. "ועל דרכיך נגה אור" – דור שהיה אפל הארת בתפלתך.

They interpreted: **"You shall also decree a matter"**; you, Ḥoni, **decree from below, and the Holy One, Blessed be He, fulfills your statement from above. "And the light shall shine upon your ways"; a generation that was in darkness, you have illuminated** it **with your prayer.**

"כי השפילו, ותאמר: גוה" – דור שהיה שפל, הגבהתו בתפלתך. "ושח עינים יושע" – דור ששח בעונו, הושעתו בתפלתך. "ימלט אי נקי" – דור שלא היה נקי, מלטתו בתפלתך. "ונמלט בבר כפיך" – מלטתו במעשה ידיך הברורין.

"When they cast down,[N] **you will say: There is lifting up"; a generation that was cast down, you lifted it up with your prayer. "For He saves the humble person"; a generation that was humble in its transgression, you saved it through your prayer. "He will deliver the one who is not innocent"; a generation that was not innocent, you have delivered it through your prayer. "And he will be delivered through the cleanness of your hands"; you have delivered** an undeserving generation **through the clean work of your hands.**

אמר רבי יוחנן: כל ימיו של אותו צדיק, היה מצטער על מקרא זה: "שיר המעלות: בשוב ה' את שיבת ציון, היינו כחלמים". אמר: מי איכא דניים שבעין שנין בחלמא?

§ The Gemara relates another story about Ḥoni HaMe'aggel. **Rabbi Yoḥanan said: All the days** of the life **of that righteous man,**[N] Ḥoni, **he was distressed over** the meaning of **this verse: "A song of Ascents: When the Lord brought back those who returned to Zion, we were like those who dream"** (Psalms 126:1). **He said** to himself: **Is there** really **a person who can sleep and dream for seventy years?** How is it possible to compare the seventy-year exile in Babylonia to a dream?

BACKGROUND

Truffles – כמהין: Truffles belong to the genus *Tuber*, a special genus of fungi that grows entirely underground, including its fruit. The body of the fruit looks like a slightly rounded mass of various colors, black, brown, and whitish. Truffles generally grow up to 3–5 cm in height. They are up to 10 cm in diameter, and a large truffle can weigh as much as 1 kg. Truffles are harvested by removing the earth from above them, a task sometimes performed by specially trained animals. Most truffles are edible at early stages of their growth and are regarded as a delicacy.

NOTES

For were these years like the years of Elijah – שאילו שנים כשני אליהו: Some commentaries explain that Shimon ben Shetaḥ argued that Ḥoni deserved to be placed under a ban for two reasons: First, he addressed God in a disrespectful manner. Second, he might have created a situation that would have led to the desecration of the divine name. Consequently, this sentence should be read as though it began with the word: And, as it introduces a new reason (*Gevurat Ari*). The Vilna Gaon's version of the Gemara reads explicitly: And moreover.

In the Jerusalem Talmud it is explained that the name of Heaven would have been desecrated if a decree had been issued that rain should be withheld as in the days of Elijah, as in that case everyone would have seen Ḥoni's prayers go unanswered. Some commentaries add that in that case the name of Heaven would have been desecrated because Ḥoni's oath would have been proven false (Maharsha). Rashi writes that in that case, one oath or the other, either Ḥoni's oath not to move from the circle until there was rain or the divine decree withholding rain, would have been falsified, causing a desecration of the name of Heaven.

When they cast down – כי השפילו: In the Jerusalem Talmud, the explanation of this verse in is even more daring: When God said that His people would be cast down, you, Ḥoni, said that they would be lifted up, as God's decree was canceled while Ḥoni's oath was fulfilled.

All the days of that righteous man – כל ימיו של אותו צדיק: According to the Jerusalem Talmud, there were two different Ḥonis, and the Ḥoni who slept for seventy years was an ancestor of the Ḥoni who petitioned God for rain. The first Ḥoni lived at the end of the First Temple period, and slept for the seventy years of the Babylonian captivity. The second Ḥoni lived during the Second Temple period.

Many commentaries see this story, either in whole or in part, as a parable. The exile is viewed as a period of sleep during which there is a pressing need to make adequate preparations for the generations to come (see Maharsha, *Keren Ora*, and *Derash Moshe*).

יומא חד הוה אזל באורחא, חזייה להוא גברא דהוה נטע חרובא. אמר ליה: האי עד כמה שנין טעין? אמר ליה: עד שבעין שנין. אמר ליה: פשיטא לך דחיית שבעין שנין? אמר ליה: האי גברא עלמא בחרובא אשכחתיה. כי היכי דשתלי לי אבהתי, שתלי נמי לבראי.

One day, he was walking along the road when **he saw a certain man planting a carob tree.**[B] Ḥoni **said to him: This** tree, **after how many years** will it **bear** fruit? The man **said to him:** It will not produce fruit **until seventy years** have passed. Ḥoni **said to him: Is it obvious to you that you will live seventy years,** that you expect to benefit from this tree? **He said to him: That man** himself **found a world** full **of carob trees. Just as my ancestors planted for me, I too am planting for my descendants.**

יתיב קא כריך ריפתא. אתא ליה שינתא נים. אהדרא ליה משוניתא איכסי מעינא, ונים שבעין שנין. כי קם, חזייה להוא גברא דהוא קא מלקט מינייהו. אמר ליה: את הוא דשתלתיה? אמר ליה: בר בריה אנא. אמר ליה: שמע מינה דניימי שבעין שנין. חזא לחמריה דאתיילידא ליה רמכי רמכי.

Ḥoni **sat and ate bread. Sleep overcame him and he slept. A cliff formed around him, and he disappeared from sight and slept for seventy years. When he awoke, he saw a certain man gathering** carobs from that tree. Ḥoni **said to him:** Are you **the one who planted** this tree? The man **said to him: I am his son's son.** Ḥoni **said to him:** I can **learn from this that** I have **slept for seventy years,** and indeed **he saw that his donkey had sired several herds** during those many years.

אזל לביתיה אמר להו: בריה דחוני המעגל מי קיים? אמרו ליה: בריה ליתא, בר בריה איתא. אמר להו: אנא חוני המעגל. לא הימנוהו. אזל לבית המדרש שמעינהו לרבנן דקאמרי: נהירן שמעתתין כבשני חוני המעגל, דכי הוי עייל לבית מדרשא כל קושיא דהוו להו לרבנן הוה מפרק להו. אמר להו: אנא ניהו, ולא הימנוהו, ולא עבדי ליה יקרא כדמבעי ליה. חלש דעתיה, בעי רחמי, ומית. אמר רבא, היינו דאמרי אינשי: או חברותא או מיתותא.

Ḥoni **went home and said to** the members of the household: **Is the son of Ḥoni HaMe'aggel alive? They said to him: His son is no** longer with us, **but his son's son is alive. He said to them: I am Ḥoni HaMe'aggel. They did not believe him. He went to the study hall,** where he **heard the Sages say** about one scholar: **His *halakhot* are as enlightening** and as clear **as in the years of Ḥoni HaMe'aggel, for when** Ḥoni HaMe'aggel **would enter the study hall he would resolve for the Sages any difficulty they had.** Ḥoni **said to them: I am he, but they did not believe him and did not pay him proper respect.** Ḥoni **became very upset, prayed for mercy, and died. Rava said:** This explains the folk saying **that people say: Either friendship or death,** as one who has no friends is better off dead.

BACKGROUND

Carob tree – חרובא: Carob trees live for many years. Female carob trees generally produce enough fruit for commercial use only six to eight years after planting. Some commentaries explain that the seventy-year period mentioned here is based on the fact that carob trees are dioecious, meaning that there are female carob trees with pistillate flowers and male carob trees with staminate flowers. At first, the male trees do not bear fruit.

When male trees age, roughly after sixty or seventy years, they become monoecious, or hermaphrodite, and begin to produce fruit. Since the gender of the tree is unclear at the time of planting, it is possible that the tree will begin yielding fruit only seventy years later.

Male carob flowers

Carob fruit and seeds

Female carob flowers

Carob tree

אַבָּא חִלְקִיָּה בַּר בְּרֵיהּ דְּחוֹנִי הַמְעַגֵּל הֲוָה, וְכִי מִצְטְרִיךְ עָלְמָא לְמִיטְרָא הֲווּ מְשַׁדְּרִי רַבָּנַן לְגַבֵּיהּ, וּבָעֵי רַחֲמֵי וְאָתֵי מִיטְרָא. זִימְנָא חֲדָא אִיצְטְרִיךְ עָלְמָא לְמִיטְרָא, שַׁדּוּר רַבָּנַן זוּגָא דְּרַבָּנַן לְגַבֵּיהּ לְמִבְעֵי רַחֲמֵי דְּנֵיתֵי מִיטְרָא. אֲזוּל לְבֵיתֵיהּ וְלָא אַשְׁכְּחוּהוּ. אֲזוּל בְּדַבְרָא וְאַשְׁכְּחוּהוּ דַּהֲוָה קָא רָפֵיק. יְהַבוּ לֵיהּ שְׁלָמָא,

§ The Gemara relates another story, this time about Ḥoni HaMe'aggel's descendants, who were also renowned for their righteous deeds. **Abba Ḥilkiyya was the son of Ḥoni HaMe'aggel's son. And when the world was in need of rain they would send Sages to him, and he would pray for mercy, and rain would fall. Once the world was in need of rain,** and **the Sages sent a pair of Sages to him** so that **he would pray for mercy and rain would fall. They went to his house but they did not find him** there. **They went to the field and found him hoeing** the ground. **They greeted him,**

Perek **III**
Daf **23** Amud **b**

וְלָא אַסְבַּר לְהוּ אַפֵּיהּ. בְּפַנְיָא, כִּי הֲוָה מְנַקֵּט צִיבֵי, דְּרָא צִיבֵי וּמָרָא בְּחַד כַּתְפָּא, וּגְלִימָא בְּחַד כַּתְפָּא. כּוּלַּהּ אוֹרְחָא לָא סַיֵּים מְסָאנֵי. כִּי מָטֵי לְמַיָּא, סַיֵּים מְסָאנֵיהּ. כִּי מָטָא לְהִיזְמֵי וְהִיגֵי, דַּלְּינְהוּ לְמָנֵיהּ. כִּי מָטָא לְמָתָא, נְפַקָה דְּבֵיתְהוּ לְאַפֵּיהּ כִּי מִיקַּשְּׁטָא. כִּי מָטָא לְבֵיתֵיהּ, עָלַת דְּבֵיתְהוּ בְּרֵישָׁא, וַהֲדַר עָיֵיל אִיהוּ, וַהֲדַר עָיְילִי רַבָּנַן. יְתֵיב וְכָרֵיךְ רִיפְתָּא, וְלָא אֲמַר לְהוּ לְרַבָּנַן, תּוּ כְּרוֹכוּ. פְּלַג רִיפְתָּא לִינוּקֵי; לְקַשִּׁישָׁא חֲדָא, וּלְזוּטְרָא תְּרֵי.

but he did not return their greetings. Toward evening, as he was gathering firewood, he placed the wood and hoe on one shoulder and his cloak on the other **shoulder.** Along **the entire way he did not wear his shoes, but when he reached water he put on his shoes. When he reached** an area filled with **shrubs**[B] **and thorns**[B] **he lifted up his clothes. When he reached the city, his wife came out to greet him, adorned** with finery. **When he reached his house, his wife entered first, he entered afterward, and afterward the** two **Sages entered. He sat and ate bread, but he did not say to the Sages: Come** and **eat,** as was customary and polite. **He divided bread to his children; to the elder** child he gave **one piece and to the younger** one he gave **two.**

אֲמַר לַהּ לִדְבֵיתְהוּ: יָדַעְנָא דְּרַבָּנַן מִשּׁוּם מִיטְרָא קָא אָתוּ. נִיסַּק לְאִיגְּרָא, וְנִיבְעֵי רַחֲמֵי. אֶפְשָׁר דְּמִרַצֵּי הַקָּדוֹשׁ בָּרוּךְ הוּא וְיֵיתֵי מִיטְרָא, וְלָא נַחְזֵיק טֵיבוּתָא לְנַפְשִׁין. סְקוּ לְאִיגְּרָא; קָם אִיהוּ בְּחֲדָא זָוִיתָא, וְאִיהִי בְּחֲדָא זָוִיתָא. קַדֵּים סְלוּק עֲנָנֵי מֵהָךְ זָוִיתָא דְּדְבֵיתְהוּ. כִּי נָחֵית, אֲמַר לְהוּ: אַמַּאי אָתוּ רַבָּנַן? אֲמַרוּ לֵיהּ: שַׁדְּרִי לַן רַבָּנַן לְגַבֵּי דְּמָר לְמִיבְעֵי רַחֲמֵי אַמִּיטְרָא. אֲמַר לְהוּ: בָּרוּךְ הַמָּקוֹם שֶׁלֹּא הִצְרִיךְ אֶתְכֶם לְאַבָּא חִלְקִיָּה.

Abba Ḥilkiyya **said to his wife: I know that these Sages have come due to the rain. Let us go up to the roof and pray for mercy. Perhaps the Holy One, Blessed be He, will be appeased, and it will rain, and we will not receive credit ourselves** for the rainfall. **They went up to the roof. He stood in one corner and she stood in** the other **corner. Clouds began to form on that side where his wife** stood. **When he descended, he said** to the Sages: **Why have the Sages come? They said to him: The** other **Sages have sent us to the Master,** so that you should **pray for mercy for rain. He said to them: Blessed is God, Who did not require you to** petition **Abba Ḥilkiyya,** as the sky has filled with clouds and rain is certainly on its way.

אֲמַרוּ לֵיהּ: יָדְעִינַן דְּמִיטְרָא מֵחֲמַת מָר הוּא דְּאָתָא, אֶלָּא לֵימָא לַן מָר הָנֵי מִילֵּי דִּתְמִיהָא לַן: מַאי טַעְמָא כִּי יָהֵיבְנָא לְמָר שְׁלָמָא לָא אַסְבַּר לַן מָר אַפֵּיהּ? אֲמַר לְהוּ: שְׂכִיר יוֹם הֲוַאי, וְאָמֵינָא לָא אִיפַגַּר. וּמַאי טַעְמָא דְּרָא מָר צִיבֵי אַחַד כַּתְפֵּיהּ וּגְלִימָא אַחַד כַּתְפֵּיהּ? אֲמַר לְהוּ: טַלִּית שְׁאוּלָה הָיְתָה. לְהָכִי שְׁאַלִי, וּלְהָכִי לָא שְׁאַלִי.

They said to him: **We know that the rain has come on the Master's account. However, let the Master** please **say** and explain **to us these aspects** of your behavior **that are puzzling to us:**[N] **What is the reason that when we greeted the Master, the Master did not return our greeting? He said to them: I am a day laborer,** hired for the day, **and I said** to myself that I may **not delay** my work to answer you. They further inquired: **And what is the reason** that **the Master carried the firewood on one shoulder and** his **cloak on the other shoulder? He said to them: It was a borrowed robe. I borrowed it for this** purpose, to wear it, **and I did not borrow it for that purpose,** to place wood on it.

מַאי טַעְמָא כּוּלַּהּ אוֹרְחָא לָא סַיֵּים מָר מְסָאנֵיהּ, וְכִי מָטֵי לְמַיָּא סַיֵּים מְסָאנֵיהּ? אֲמַר לְהוּ: כּוּלַּהּ אוֹרְחָא חָזֵינָא; בְּמַיָּא לָא קָא חָזֵינָא. מַאי טַעְמָא כִּי מָטָא מָר לְהִיזְמֵי וְהִיגֵי, דַּלְּינְהוּ לְמָנֵיהּ? אֲמַר לְהוּ: זֶה מַעֲלֶה אֲרוּכָה, וְזֶה אֵינָהּ מַעֲלָה אֲרוּכָה.

The Sages continued to ask Abba Ḥilkiyya about his unusual behavior. **What is the reason** that **the entire way the Master did not wear his shoes, but when he reached water he put on his shoes? He said to them: The entire way I can see** and take care where I walk, and therefore there is no need for me to wear out my shoes, but **in the water I cannot see.** Therefore, I put on my shoes to avoid hurting myself. They asked: **What is the reason** that **when the Master reached shrubs and thorns, he lifted up his clothes? He said to them: This** flesh **will heal** if it is scratched by thorns, **but this** garment **will not heal** if it is torn.

BACKGROUND

Shrubs [*hizmei*] – הִיזְמֵי: *Hizmei* probably refers to the thorny restharrow, *Ononis antiquorum* L., from the Papilinaceae family. It is a thorny bush that grows to a height of 20 cm and is common in fields and near streams. Its leaves are mainly trifoliate, while its lateral branches tend to be thorny and brachiated.

Thorns [*higei*] – הִיגֵי: *Higei* refers to what is probably the thorny restharrow, *Ononis spinosa* L., from the Papilionaceae family. It is a thorny shrub that grows to a height of up to 75 cm, with trifoliolate leaves and thorny side branches. It grows in fields and wadis.

Thorny restharrow

NOTES

Aspects that are puzzling to us – מִילֵּי דִּתְמִיהָא לַן: Not only are the actions of Abba Ḥilkiyya baffling in their own right, but apparently they also conflict with the proper norms of behavior required of a Sage. The Sages taught that one must be careful to extend greetings to all men, avoid all physical harm, and not walk after a woman. Therefore, the visiting Sages sought explanations for his actions.

NOTES

My wife is frequently at home, etc. – אִיתְּתָא שְׁכִיחָא בְּבֵיתָא וכו׳: Rashi explains that Abba Ḥilkiyya provided two reasons here. First, she is always at home when the poor arrive, so she is constantly distributing to the needy. Furthermore, the items she gives provide immediate benefit.

And she prayed that they should repent – וְהִיא בָּעְיָא רַחֲמֵי דְּלִיהַדְרוּ: Elsewhere, the Gemara relates a similar story involving Rabbi Meir and his wife, Berurya (*Berakhot* 10a). When certain hooligans persisted in antagonizing Rabbi Meir, he prayed to God that they should die. However, his wife Berurya chided him, citing the verse "Let sinners cease out of the earth" (Psalms 104:35). Berurya interpreted the word "sinners" to mean sins and argued that God does not desire the disappearance of the sinners themselves, but only of their sin. Rabbi Meir subsequently prayed that the hooligans should repent of their evil ways, and they indeed repented.

He would hide himself in the lavatory – שֶׁהָיָה מַחְבִּיא עַצְמוֹ בְּבֵית הַכִּסֵּא: Rashi and others read: Because he used to hide himself, omitting the last two words found in the standard text of the Talmud. Several explanations of this passage have been suggested. Some maintain that the Sages wanted to appoint Ḥanan to a position of communal leadership, but he refused to accept the appointment and hid himself thereafter from public view (Rabbeinu Ḥananel, citing *ge'onim*). Others explain that when Ḥanan entreated God for rain, he prayed in private for reasons of modesty, so that he would not be credited for causing an end to the drought (Rashi; Rabbeinu Gershom).

The standard reading: Because he used to hide himself in the lavatory, also lends itself to several explanations. Rashi suggests that if these two words are included it means that when Ḥanan entered the lavatory he would conduct himself extremely modestly, by keeping himself covered as much as possible. Alternatively, when the Sages came to ask him to pray for rain, he hid himself in the lavatory to avoid the honor that would be bestowed upon him were his prayers accepted (*ge'onim*). Yet others add that this is the reason why the Sages sent schoolchildren to him, as they would seek him out even in the lavatory (Maharsha).

מַאי טַעְמָא כִּי מְטָא מָר לְמָתָא, נָפְקָא דְּבֵיתְהוּ דְּמָר כִּי מִיקַשְּׁטָא? אֲמַר לְהוּ: כְּדֵי שֶׁלֹּא אֶתֵּן עֵינַי בְּאִשָּׁה אַחֶרֶת. מַאי טַעְמָא עָיְילָא הִיא בְּרֵישָׁא, וַהֲדַר עָיֵיל מָר אַבַּתְרָהּ, וַהֲדַר עָיְילִינַן אֲנַן? אֲמַר לְהוּ: מִשּׁוּם דְּלָא בְּדַקִיתוּ לִי.

They further inquired: **What is the reason** that **when the Master reached the city, the Master's wife came out adorned** in her finery? **He said to them:** She dresses that way **so that** when I walk through the city **I will not set my eyes upon another woman.** They asked: **What is the reason** that **she entered first, and afterward the Master entered, and** only **afterward we entered? He said to them: Because you have not been checked** by me. I cannot be sure how you will act, and therefore I did not want you to be alone with my wife.

מַאי טַעְמָא כִּי כָּרֵיךְ מָר רִיפְתָּא, לָא אֲמַר לָן: אֵיתוּ כְּרוֹכוּ? מִשּׁוּם דְּלָא נְפִישָׁא רִיפְתָּא, וְאָמִינָא לָא אַחֲזִיק בְּהוּ בְּרַבָּנַן טִיבוּתָא בְּחִנָּם. מַאי טַעְמָא יָהֵיב מָר לִינוּקָא קַשִּׁישָׁא חֲדָא רִיפְתָּא וּלְזוּטְרָא תְּרֵי? אֲמַר לְהוּ: הַאי קָאֵי בְּבֵיתָא, וְהַאי יָתֵיב בְּבֵי כְנִישְׁתָּא.

The Sages were not done with their questions. **What is the reason** that **when the Master ate bread,** you **did not say to us: Come and eat?** He replied: **Because there is not enough bread** for guests, **and I said** to myself that **I should not gain credit from the Sages for nothing,** by offering you food I cannot serve you. They asked: **What is the reason** that **the Master gave the older child one piece** of bread **and the younger child two? He said to them: This** older child **stays at home,** and if he is hungry he can eat at any time, **but this** younger child **sits** and studies **in the synagogue,** and therefore he is hungrier.

וּמַאי טַעְמָא קַדִּים סְלוּק עֲנָנֵי מֵהַךְ זָוִיתָא דַּהֲוַות קָיְימָא דְּבֵיתְהוּ דְּמָר לַעֲנָנָא דִּידֵיהּ? מִשּׁוּם דְּאִיתְּתָא שְׁכִיחָא בְּבֵיתָא, וִיהֲבָא רִיפְתָּא לַעֲנִיֵּי, וּמְקָרְבָא הֲנָיָיתָהּ, וַאֲנָא יָהֵיבְנָא זוּזָא, וְלָא מְקָרְבָא הֲנָיָיתֵיהּ. אִי נַמִּי, הָנְהוּ בִּירְיוֹנֵי דַּהֲווֹ בְּשִׁיבָבוּתָן, אֲנָא בְּעֵי רַחֲמֵי דְּלֵימוּתוּ, וְהִיא בָּעְיָא רַחֲמֵי דְּלִיהַדְרוּ בִּתְיוּבְתָּא, וְאַהֲדָרוּ.

The two Sages had one final set of queries for Abba Ḥilkiyya. **And what is the reason** that the **clouds began to form on that side where the Master's wife stood** before your own side? He explained: **Because my wife is frequently at home,**[N] **and she gives bread to the poor, and** therefore **her** provision of **benefit** to the needy is **immediate,** i.e., soon after the rains fall she is able to provide the needy with provisions. Accordingly, her prayers are answered without delay. In contrast, **I give money** to the poor, **and** consequently, **the benefit** of my gift **is not immediate,** i.e., it takes a lot of time before the rainfall results in my ability to give money to the poor. **Alternatively,** her prayers may have been answered first because when **certain hooligans** [*biryonei*][L] **were living in our neighborhood, I prayed that they should die, but she prayed that they should repent.**[N] **And** indeed, **they repented.**

חָנָן הַנֶּחְבָּא בַּר בְּרַתֵּיהּ דְּחוֹנִי הַמְעַגֵּל הֲוָה. כִּי מִצְטְרִיךְ עָלְמָא לְמִיטְרָא, הָווּ מְשַׁדְּרֵי רַבָּנַן יָנוֹקֵי דְּבֵי רַב לְגַבֵּיהּ, וְנָקְטֵי לֵיהּ בְּשִׁיפּוּלֵי גְּלִימֵיהּ וַאֲמַרוּ לֵיהּ: אַבָּא, אַבָּא, הַב לָן מִיטְרָא! אָמַר לִפְנֵי הַקָּדוֹשׁ בָּרוּךְ הוּא: רִבּוֹנוֹ שֶׁל עוֹלָם, עֲשֵׂה בִּשְׁבִיל אֵלּוּ שֶׁאֵין מַכִּירִין בֵּין אַבָּא דְּיָהֵיב מִיטְרָא לְאַבָּא דְּלָא יָהֵיב מִיטְרָא. וְאַמַּאי קָרֵי לֵיהּ חָנָן הַנֶּחְבָּא? מִפְּנֵי שֶׁהָיָה מַחְבִּיא עַצְמוֹ בְּבֵית הַכִּסֵּא.

§ The Gemara relates another story about a descendant of Ḥoni HaMe'aggel. **Ḥanan HaNeḥba was the son of Ḥoni HaMe'aggel's daughter. When the world was in need of rain, the Sages would send schoolchildren to him, and they would grab him by the hem of his cloak and say to him: Father, Father, give us rain. He said before the Holy One, Blessed be He: Master of the Universe, act on behalf of these** children, **who cannot distinguish between** their **Father** in Heaven, **Who can provide rain, and the father who cannot provide rain.** The Gemara asks: **And why was he called Ḥanan HaNeḥba? Because he would hide** [*maḥbi*] **himself in the lavatory**[N] so that people would not bestow honor upon him.

אֲמַר לֵיהּ רַבִּי זְרִיקָא לְרַב סָפְרָא: תָּא חֲזִי מָה בֵּין תַּקִּיפֵי דְּאַרְעָא דְיִשְׂרָאֵל לַחֲסִידֵי דְּבָבֶל. חֲסִידֵי דְּבָבֶל רַב הוּנָא וְרַב חִסְדָּא. כִּי הֲוָה מִצְטְרִיךְ עָלְמָא לְמִיטְרָא, אָמְרִי: נִיכְנִיף הֲדָדֵי וְנִיבְעֵי רַחֲמֵי. אֶפְשָׁר דְּמִירַצֵּי הַקָּדוֹשׁ בָּרוּךְ הוּא דְּיֵיתֵי מִיטְרָא.

The Gemara relates another story about righteous individuals praying for rain. **Rabbi Zerika said to Rav Safra: Come and see what the difference** is between **the powerful men of Eretz Yisrael and the pious men of Babylonia.** This comparison serves to highlight the righteousness of the great men of Eretz Yisrael. By **the pious men of Babylonia,** I mean **Rav Huna and Rav Ḥisda. When the world is in need of rain,** these Sages say: **Let us assemble together and pray for mercy,** and **perhaps the Holy One, Blessed be He, will be appeased and bring rain.** In this manner, the pious men of Babylonia publicized their prayers for rain.

LANGUAGE

Hooligans [*biryonei*] – בִּירְיוֹנֵי: Of unclear origin. Some say it is from the root *b-r*, outside, i.e., savage men outside the boundaries of civilization. However, the word form indicates a non-Hebrew source. Some maintain it is derived from the Latin praetoriani, a member of the imperial guard. Over the years, these men became very powerful and would behave in a coarse and unrestrained manner.

תַּקִּיפֵי דְּאַרְעָא דְּיִשְׂרָאֵל, כְּגוֹן רַבִּי יוֹנָה אֲבוּהּ דְּרַבִּי מָנִי, כִּי הֲוָה מִצְטְרִיךְ עָלְמָא לְמִיטְרָא, הֲוָה עָיֵיל לְבֵיתֵיהּ, וַאֲמַר לְהוּ: הֲבוּ לִי גְּוָאלְקִי, וְאֵיזִיל וְאַיְיתֵי לִי בְּזוּזָא עִיבּוּרָא. כִּי הֲוָה נָפֵיק לְבָרָא, אָזֵיל וְקָאֵי בְּדוּכְתָּא עֲמִיקְתָּא, דִּכְתִיב: ״מִמַּעֲמַקִּים קְרָאתִיךָ, ה׳״. וְקָאֵי בְּדוּכְתָּא צְנִיעָא וּמְכַסֵּי בְּשַׂקָּא, וּבָעֵי רַחֲמֵי, וְאָתֵי מִיטְרָא. כִּי הֲוָה אָתֵי לְבֵיתֵיהּ, אָמְרִי לֵיהּ: אַיְיתֵי מָר עִיבּוּרָא? אֲמַר לְהוּ: אָמִינָא, הוֹאִיל וַאֲתָא מִיטְרָא הָשְׁתָּא, רְוַח עָלְמָא.

By contrast, **the powerful men of Eretz Yisrael, such as Rabbi Yona,**[P] **the father of Rabbi Mani,** acted differently. **When the world was in need of rain, he enters his house and say to** his household: **Give me my sack** [*gevalki*][L] **and I will go and buy myself a dinar of grain. When he went outside, he went and stood in a low place, as it is written: "Out of the depths I have called You, O Lord"** (Psalms 130:1). **And he would stand in a secluded place, and cover** himself **with sackcloth, and pray for mercy, and rain would come. When he would come home, they would say to him:** Did **the Master bring grain? He said to them: I said** to myself, **since rain has** now **come,** there will be **relief in the world** and prices will soon go down. In this manner, he hid his greatness even from his own household.

וְתוּ, רַבִּי מָנִי בְּרֵיהּ הֲווּ קָא מְצַעֲרֵי לֵיהּ דְּבֵי נְשִׂיאָה. יִשְׁתַּטַּח עַל קִבְרָא דַּאֲבוּהּ, אֲמַר לֵיהּ: אַבָּא, אַבָּא, הָנֵי מְצַעֲרוּ לִי. יוֹמָא חַד הֲווּ קָא חָלְפֵי הָתָם, אִינְקוּט כַּרְעָא דְּסוּסָוָתַיְיהוּ, עַד דְּקַבִּילוּ עֲלַיְיהוּ דְּלָא קָא מְצַעֲרוּ לֵיהּ.

And furthermore, the Gemara relates that **Rabbi Mani,** Rabbi Yona's son, **was persecuted by** members **of the house of the** *Nasi*. **He prostrated himself upon his father's grave and said** to him: **Father, Father, these men are persecuting me. One day,** those men **were passing there,** by the grave, and **the legs of their horses became stuck** in the ground **until they accepted upon themselves not to persecute** Rabbi Mani anymore.

וְתוּ, רַבִּי מָנִי הֲוָה שְׁכִיחַ קַמֵּיהּ דְּרַבִּי יִצְחָק בֶּן אֶלְיָשִׁיב. אֲמַר לֵיהּ: עֲתִירֵי דְּבֵי חָמִי קָא מְצַעֲרוּ לִי. אֲמַר: לִיעֲנוּ, וְאִיעֲנוּ. אֲמַר: קָא דָּחֲקוּ לִי. אֲמַר: לִיעַתְרוּ, וְאִיעַתְרוּ.

And furthermore, the Gemara relates that **Rabbi Mani was frequently found before Rabbi Yitzḥak ben Elyashiv,** a well-known miracle worker. Once, Rabbi Mani **said to him: The wealthy members of my father-in-law's house are persecuting me.** Rabbi Yitzḥak **said: May they become poor,** so they will no longer lord over you. **And** indeed, **they became poor.** Some time later, Rabbi Mani **said** to his teacher: Now that they are poor **they are pressuring me** for financial support. Rabbi Yitzḥak **said: May they become rich** again. **And** indeed, **they became rich.**

אֲמַר: לָא מִיקַּבְּלִי עֲלַי אֱינָשֵׁי בֵּיתִי. אֲמַר לֵיהּ: מַה שְּׁמָהּ? חַנָּה. תִּתְיַיפִּי חַנָּה, וְנִתְיַיפַּת. אֲמַר לֵיהּ: קָא מִגַּנְדְּרָא עֲלַי. אֲמַר לֵיהּ: אִי הָכִי, תַּחֲזוֹר חַנָּה לְשַׁחֲרוּרִיתָהּ, וְחָזְרָה חַנָּה לְשַׁחֲרוּרִיתָהּ.

Rabbi Mani **said to** his teacher: **The members of my household,** i.e., my wife, **are not acceptable to me,** as she is not beautiful. Rabbi Yitzḥak **said: What is her name?** Rabbi Mana replied: **Ḥana.** Rabbi Yitzḥak declared: **Let Ḥana grow beautiful, and** indeed **she grew beautiful.** After a while, Rabbi Mani **said** to Rabbi Yitzḥak: **She acts haughtily toward me,** due to her great beauty. **He said to him: If so, let Ḥana return to her homely** appearance, **and she returned to her homely** appearance.

הָנְהוּ תְּרֵי תַּלְמִידֵי דַּהֲווּ קַמֵּיהּ דְּרַבִּי יִצְחָק בֶּן אֶלְיָשִׁיב אֲמַרוּ לֵיהּ: נִיבָּעֵי מָר רַחֲמֵי עֲלַן דְּנִיחְכַּם טוּבָא! אֲמַר לְהוּ: עִמִּי הָיְתָה, וְשִׁלַּחְתִּיהָ.

The Gemara relates: **These two students, who were sitting before Rabbi Yitzḥak ben Elyashiv, said to him: Let the Master pray for mercy on our** behalf, **that we should become very wise. He said to them:** This power **was** indeed **with me** at one stage, as I used to be able to pray for matters of this kind, **but I sent it away.**[N] I took it upon myself never to pray for changes in the world order.

רַבִּי יוֹסֵי בַּר אָבִין הֲוָה שְׁכִיחַ קַמֵּיהּ דְּרַבִּי יוֹסֵי דְּמִן יוֹקֶרֶת. שְׁבַקֵיהּ וַאֲתָא לְקַמֵּיהּ דְּרַב אַשִׁי.

The Gemara cites another story involving a complaint. **Rabbi Yosei bar Avin was frequently found before Rabbi Yosei from Yokrat.** At some point **he left him and came** to study **before Rav Ashi,** who did not recognize him.

PERSONALITIES

Rabbi Yona – רַבִּי יוֹנָה: Rabbi Yona was one of the greatest Sages of the third to fourth generations of *amora'im* in Eretz Yisrael. The youthful Rabbi Yona had the opportunity to study from Rabbi Yoḥanan in his old age. However, he was principally the student of Rabbi Yoḥanan's young disciples, Rabbi Ila and Rabbi Zeira, or Zeira. He even studied Torah from Rabbi Yirmeya. A large number of *halakhot* in the Jerusalem Talmud are attributed to Rabbi Yona, while he himself transmits many statements in the name of various Sages. He apparently lived in Tiberias, where he founded an academy along with his colleague Rabbi Yosei. Although he is cited infrequently in the Babylonian Talmud, he was well known in Babylonia as well.

Rabbi Yona was apparently a wealthy man, as we find several stories that depict his practice of charity. His son Rabbi Mana, or Mani, was one of the greatest *amora'im* of Eretz Yisrael in the following generation.

LANGUAGE

My sack [*gevalki*] – גְּוָאלְקִי: Apparently from the Middle Iranian juwālak, meaning sack or knapsack. The word *guharka*, found previously in the chapter, is also derived from this Middle Iranian term.

NOTES

This power was with me but I sent it away – עִמִּי הָיְתָה וְשִׁלַּחְתִּיהָ: According to Rashi, Rabbi Yitzḥak ben Elyashiv explained to the two students that he had lost the power to have all his prayers answered. However, the expression: I sent it away, indicates that Rabbi Yitzḥak preferred not to submit requests like those of the two students (see Maharsha). Therefore, other commentaries explain that Rabbi Yitzḥak decided not to trouble God with petitions of that kind anymore (Rabbeinu Gershom). Yet others suggests that the only prayer Rabbi Yitzḥak refused to submit was for someone to be endowed with special wisdom, as he recognized the potential danger of this request (*Sefat Emet*).

יוֹמָא חַד שְׁמָעֵיהּ דְּקָא גָּרֵיס: אָמַר שְׁמוּאֵל: הַשּׁוֹלֶה דָּג מִן הַיָּם בְּשַׁבָּת, כֵּיוָן שֶׁיָּבַשׁ בּוֹ כְּסֶלַע, חַיָּיב. אֲמַר לֵיהּ: וְלֵימָא מָר: וּבֵין סְנַפִּירָיו. אֲמַר לֵיהּ: וְלָא סָבַר לָהּ מָר דְּהַהִיא רַבִּי יוֹסֵי בֶּן רַבִּי אָבִין אֲמָרָהּ? אֲמַר לֵיהּ: אֲנָא נִיהוּ.

One day Rabbi Yosei bar Avin **heard** Rav Ashi **studying** and reciting the following statement. **Shmuel said:** With regard to **one who removes a fish from the sea**[NH] on Shabbat, **when** an area **on** the skin of the fish **the size of a *sela*** coin **has dried up,** he is **liable** for violating the prohibition against slaughtering an animal on Shabbat. A fish in that condition cannot survive, and therefore one who removed it from the water is liable for killing it. Rabbi Yosei bar Avin **said to** Rav Ashi: **And let the Master say** that this is the case provided that the skin that dried is **between its fins.**[B] Rav Ashi **said to him: And doesn't the Master maintain that Rabbi Yosei ben Rabbi Avin said this** ruling? Why didn't you state it in his name? Rabbi Yosei bar Avin **said to him: I am he.**

אֲמַר לֵיהּ: וְלָאו קַמֵּיהּ דְּרַבִּי יוֹסֵי דְּמִן יוֹקְרַת הֲוָה שְׁכִיחַ מָר? אֲמַר לֵיהּ: הֵין. אֲמַר לֵיהּ: וּמַאי טַעְמָא שַׁבְקֵיהּ מָר וַאֲתָא הָכָא? אֲמַר לֵיהּ: גַּבְרָא דְּעַל בְּרֵיהּ וְעַל בְּרַתֵּיהּ לָא חַס, עֲלַי דִּידִי הֵיכִי חָיֵיס?

Rav Ashi **said to him: And didn't the Master** sit **before** and **frequent** the study hall **of Rabbi Yosei from Yokrat?** Rabbi Yosei bar Avin **said to him: Yes.** Rav Ashi **said to him: And what is the reason** that **the Master left** him **and came here?** Rabbi Yosei bar Avin **said to him:** I was concerned and departed because he is so severe and unforgiving. He is **a man who has no mercy on his** own **son, and no mercy on his daughter. How,** then, **could he have mercy on me?**

בְּרֵיהּ מַאי הִיא? יוֹמָא חַד הָווּ אָגְרִי לֵיהּ אֲגִירֵי בְּדַבְרָא. נָגַהּ לְהוּ, וְלָא אַיְיתִי לְהוּ רִיפְתָּא. אֲמַרוּ לֵיהּ לִבְרֵיהּ: כָּפִינַן! הָווּ יָתְבִי תּוּתֵי תְּאֵינְתָּא. אֲמַר: תְּאֵנָה, תְּאֵנָה! הוֹצִיאִי פֵּירוֹתַיִךְ, וְיֹאכְלוּ פּוֹעֲלֵי אַבָּא. אַפִּיקוּ, וַאֲכַלוּ.

The Gemara asks: **What is** the incident involving **his son? One day** Rabbi Yosei from Yokrat **hired** day **laborers to** work his **field. It grew late and he did not bring them food.** The workers **said to the son of** Rabbi Yosei from Yokrat: **We are starving. They were sitting under a fig tree,** so the son **said: Fig tree, fig tree. Yield your fruits,** so that my **father's workers may eat.** The fig tree **yielded** fruit, **and they ate.**

אַדְּהָכִי וְהָכִי אֲתָא אֲבוּהּ, אֲמַר לְהוּ: לָא תִּינְקְטוּ בְּדַעְתַּיְיכוּ, דְּהַאי דְּנַגְהָנָא אַמִּצְוָה טָרַחְנָא, וְעַד הָשְׁתָּא הוּא דְּסַגַּאי. אֲמָרוּ לֵיהּ: רַחֲמָנָא לִישְׂבְּעָךְ, כִּי הֵיכִי דְּאַשְׂבְּעָן בְּרָךְ! אֲמַר לְהוּ: מֵהֵיכָא? אֲמַרוּ: הָכִי וְהָכִי הֲוָה מַעֲשֶׂה. אֲמַר לוֹ: בְּנִי, אַתָּה הִטְרַחְתָּ אֶת קוֹנְךָ לְהוֹצִיא תְּאֵנָה פֵּירוֹתֶיהָ שֶׁלֹּא בִּזְמַנָּהּ, יֵאָסֵף שֶׁלֹּא בִּזְמַנּוֹ.

In the meantime, his father came and **said to** the workers: **Do not be angry with me for being late, as I was engaged in a mitzva, and until just now I was traveling** for that purpose and could not get here any sooner. **They said to him:** May **the Merciful One satisfy you just as your son satisfied us** and gave us food. **He said to them: From where** did he find food to give you? **They said: Such-and-such an incident occurred.** Rabbi Yosei from Yokrat **said to** his son: **My son, you troubled your Creator** to cause **the fig to yield its fruit not in its** proper **time,** so too, you will die young. And indeed, his son **died before his time.**

בְּרַתֵּיהּ מַאי הִיא? הֲוְיָא לֵיהּ בְּרַתָּא בַּעֲלַת יוֹפִי. יוֹמָא חַד חֲזְיָא לְהַהוּא גַּבְרָא כַּרְיָא בְּהוּצָא וְקָא חָזֵי לָהּ. אָמַר לוֹ: מַאי הַאי? אֲמַר לֵיהּ: רַבִּי, אִם לְלוֹקְחָהּ לֹא זָכִיתִי, לִרְאוֹתָהּ לֹא אֶזְכֶּה? אָמַר לָהּ: בִּתִּי, קָא מְצַעֲרַתְּ לְהוּ לִבְרְיָיתָא. שׁוּבִי לַעֲפָרֵיךְ, וְאַל יִכָּשְׁלוּ בִּיךְ בְּנֵי אָדָם.

The Gemara asks: **What is** the incident involving **his daughter? He had** a very **beautiful daughter. One day** Rabbi Yosei from Yokrat **saw a certain man piercing a hole in the hedge** surrounding his property **and looking at** his daughter. Rabbi Yosei **said to him: What is this?** The man **said to him: My teacher, if I have not merited taking her** in marriage, shall **I** not at least **merit to look at her? Rabbi Yosei said to her: My daughter, you are causing people distress. Return to your dust, and let people no** longer **stumble** into sin **due to you.**

הֲוְיָא לֵיהּ הַהוּא חֲמָרָא, כִּדְהָווּ אָגְרִי לָהּ כָּל יוֹמָא, לְאוּרְתָּא הָווּ מְשַׁדְּרִי לָהּ אַגְרָהּ אַגַּבָּהּ, וְאָתְיָא לְבֵי מָרָהּ. וְאִי טָפוּ לָהּ אוֹ בָּצְרִי לָהּ, לֹא אָתְיָא. יוֹמָא חַד אִינְשׁוּ זוּגָא דְּסַנְדְּלֵי עֲלָהּ, וְלָא אָזְלָה עַד דְּשָׁקְלוּנְהוּ מִינָּהּ, וַהֲדַר אָזְלָה.

§ The Gemara relates another story involving Rabbi Yosei from Yokrat. **He had a certain donkey that people hired each day** for work. **In the evening they would send it back** with **the money for its hire on its back, and** the animal would **go to its owner's house. But if they added or subtracted from** the appropriate sum, the donkey **would not go. One day** someone **forgot a pair of sandals on** the donkey, **and it did not move until they removed** the sandals **from** its back, **after which it went off.**

NOTES

One who removes a fish from the sea – הַשּׁוֹלֶה דָּג מִן הַיָּם: The early commentaries disagree with regard to the relevant prohibition here. Some explain that according to the opinion of Shmuel, if someone removes a fish from the sea on Shabbat and keeps it out of the water long enough for a portion of the fish's body the size of a *sela* to dry out, he is liable for violating the prohibition against taking the life of a living creature on Shabbat (Rashi; *Tosafot*). Others maintain that he is liable for trapping an animal on Shabbat, whereas he is not liable for violating the prohibition against killing an animal on Shabbat, apparently because he did not kill the fish directly (Rabbi Elyakim). Yet others maintain that he is liable for violating both prohibitions (Rabbeinu Gershom).

HALAKHA

One who removes a fish from the sea – הַשּׁוֹלֶה דָּג מִן הַיָּם: If someone removes a fish from water on Shabbat and leaves it out of the water until it dies, he is liable for slaughtering an animal. Even if the fish has not yet actually died, but an area of the fish's body between its fins the size of a *sela* has become dry, he is liable, as the fish will certainly perish (Rambam *Sefer Zemanim*, *Hilkhot Shabbat* 11:1).

BACKGROUND

Between its fins – בֵּין סְנַפִּירָיו: When a fish is removed from the water its gills and skin cannot provide the oxygen it requires to live. If it is soon returned to the water, the fish will recover by temporarily increasing its breathing, but if it stays out of its natural habitat for a prolonged period it will die of suffocation.

אֶלְעָזָר אִישׁ בִּירְתָּא כַּד הָווּ חָזוּ לֵיהּ גַּבָּאֵי צְדָקָה, הָווּ טָשׁוּ מִינֵּיהּ, דְּכׇל מַאי דַּהֲוָה גַּבֵּיהּ יָהֵיב לְהוּ. יוֹמָא חַד הֲוָה סָלֵיק לְשׁוּקָא לְמִיזְבַּן נְדוּנְיָא לִבְרַתֵּיהּ. חָזְיוּהוּ גַּבָּאֵי צְדָקָה טָשׁוּ מִינֵּיהּ.

The Gemara cites more stories about miracles that occurred to righteous individuals. **Whenever the charity collectors would see Elazar of** the village of **Birta, they would hide from him, as any** money Elazar **had with him he would give them,**[N] and they did not want to take all his property. **One day,** Elazar **went to the market to purchase** what he needed **for his daughter's dowry. The charity collectors saw him and hid from him.**

אֲזַל וּרְהַט בָּתְרַיְיהוּ. אֲמַר לְהוּ: אַשְׁבַּעְתִּיכוּ, בְּמַאי עֲסוּקִיתוּ? אֲמַרוּ לֵיהּ: בְּיָתוֹם וִיתוֹמָה. אֲמַר לָהֶן: הָעֲבוֹדָה! שֶׁהֵן קוֹדְמִין לְבִתִּי. שְׁקַל כׇּל דַּהֲוָה בַּהֲדֵיהּ וִיהַב לְהוּ. פַּשׁ לֵיהּ חַד זוּזָא, זְבַן לֵיהּ חִיטֵּי, וְאַסֵּיק שַׁדְיֵיהּ בְּאַכְלְבָא.

He went and ran after them, saying to them: I adjure you, tell me, **in what** mitzva **are you engaged? They said to him:** We are collecting money for the wedding **of an orphan boy and an orphan girl. He said to them:** I swear **by the Temple service that they take precedence over my daughter. He took everything he had with him and gave it to them. He was left with one** single **dinar,** with which **he bought himself wheat,** and he then **ascended** to his house **and threw it into the granary.**

אֲתַאי דְּבֵיתְהוּ, אֲמַרָה לַהּ לִבְרַתֵּיהּ: מַאי אַיְיתִי אֲבוּךְ? אֲמַרָה לַהּ: כׇּל מַה דְּאַיְיתִי, בְּאַכְלְבָא שְׁדִיתֵיהּ. אָתְיָא לְמִיפְתַּח בָּבָא דְּאַכְלְבָא, חֲזַת אַכְלְבָא דִּמְלְיָא חִיטֵּי, וְקָא נָפְקָא בְּצִינּוֹרָא דְּדַשָּׁא, וְלָא מִיפְתַּח בָּבָא מֵחִיטֵּי. אָזְלָא בְּרַתֵּיהּ לְבֵי מִדְרְשָׁא, אֲמַרָה לֵיהּ: בֹּא וּרְאֵה מַה עָשָׂה לְךָ אוֹהַבְךָ! אֲמַר לַהּ: הָעֲבוֹדָה! הֲרֵי הֵן הֶקְדֵּשׁ עָלַיִךְ, וְאֵין לָךְ בָּהֶן אֶלָּא כְּאֶחָד מֵעֲנִיֵּי יִשְׂרָאֵל.

Elazar's **wife came and said to her daughter: What has your father brought? She said to** her mother: **Whatever he brought he threw into the granary. She went to open the door of the granary,** and **saw that the granary was full of wheat,** so much so that **it was coming out through the doorknob, and the door would not open** due **to the wheat.** The granary had miraculously been completely filled. Elazar's **daughter went to the study hall** and **said to** her father: **Come and see what your He Who loves You,** the Almighty, **has performed for you. He said to her:** I swear **by the Temple service,** as far **as you** are concerned this wheat **is consecrated** property, **and you have** a share **in it only as one of the poor Jews.**[N] He said this because he did not want to benefit from a miracle.

רַבִּי יְהוּדָה נְשִׂיאָה גְּזַר תַּעֲנִיתָא. בְּעָי רַחֲמֵי וְלָא אֲתָא מִיטְרָא. אֲמַר: כַּמָּה אִיכָּא מִשְּׁמוּאֵל הָרָמָתִי לִיהוּדָה בֶּן גַּמְלִיאֵל! אוֹי לוֹ לַדּוֹר שֶׁכֵּן נִתְקַע! אוֹי לוֹ לְמִי שֶׁעָלְתָה בְּיָמָיו כָּךְ! חֲלַשׁ דַּעְתֵּיהּ, וַאֲתָא מִיטְרָא.

The Gemara returns to the topic of fasting for rain. **Rabbi Yehuda Nesia decreed a fast** and **prayed for mercy, but rain did not come. He said,** lamenting: **How great** is the difference **between** the prophet **Samuel of Rama,** for whom rain fell even when he prayed for it in summer, **and** myself, **Yehuda ben Gamliel. Woe to the generation that is stuck** with this leadership; **woe to him in whose days this has occurred. He grew upset, and rain came.**

דְּבֵי נְשִׂיאָה גְּזַר תַּעֲנִיתָא, וְלָא אוֹדְעִינְהוּ לְרַבִּי יוֹחָנָן וּלְרֵישׁ לָקִישׁ. לְצַפְרָא אוֹדְעִינְהוּ. אֲמַר לֵיהּ רֵישׁ לָקִישׁ לְרַבִּי יוֹחָנָן: הָא לָא קַבֵּילְנָא עֲלַן מֵאוּרְתָּא! אֲמַר לֵיהּ: אֲנַן בָּתְרַיְיהוּ גָּרְרִינַן.

The Gemara relates another story involving a *Nasi's* decree of a fast for rain. **In the house of the *Nasi* a fast was declared, but they didn't inform Rabbi Yoḥanan and Reish Lakish** of the fast the day before. **In the they informed them. Reish Lakish said to Rabbi Yoḥanan:** What are we to do? **We did not accept** this fast **upon ourselves the evening before,** and a fast must be accepted in the afternoon service of the day preceding the fast. Rabbi Yoḥanan **said to him: We are drawn after** the community, and therefore, when the *Nasi* declares a public fast there is no need for an individual to accept it upon himself the day before.

דְּבֵי נְשִׂיאָה גְּזַר תַּעֲנִיתָא, וְלָא אֲתָא מִיטְרָא. תְּנָא לְהוּ אוֹשַׁעְיָא זְעֵירָא דְּמִן חֲבֶרַיָּיא: ״וְהָיָה, אִם מֵעֵינֵי הָעֵדָה נֶעֶשְׂתָה לִשְׁגָגָה״.

The Gemara further states that on another occasion, **a fast was declared in the house of the *Nasi*, but rain did not come. Oshaya, the youngest** member **of the group**[P] of Sages, **taught them** a ***baraita***. It is written: **"Then it shall be, if it shall be committed in error by the congregation, it being hidden from their eyes"** (Numbers 15:24). This verse indicates that the leaders are considered the eyes of the congregation.

מָשָׁל לְכַלָּה שֶׁהִיא בְּבֵית אָבִיהָ. כׇּל זְמַן שֶׁעֵינֶיהָ יָפוֹת, אֵין כׇּל גּוּפָהּ צְרִיכָה בְּדִיקָה. עֵינֶיהָ טְרוּטוֹת, כׇּל גּוּפָהּ צְרִיכָה בְּדִיקָה.

Oshaya continued: There is **a parable** that illustrates this, **involving a bride who is in her father's home** and has not yet been seen by her bridegroom. **As long as her eyes are beautiful, her body need not be examined,** as certainly she is beautiful. However, if **her eyes are bleary** [***terutot***],[L] **her entire body requires examination.** So too, if the leaders of the generation are flawed, it is a sign that the entire generation is unworthy.

NOTES

Any money Elazar had with him he would give them – כׇּל מַאי דַּהֲוָה גַּבֵּיהּ יָהֵיב לְהוּ: The later commentaries ask: The Gemara states elsewhere that an ordinance was enacted in Usha that even one who wishes to be liberal in his contributions to charity should not give away more than one-fifth of his assets, lest he himself become financially dependent upon others (*Ketubot* 67b). How, then, could Elazar of Birta give away all he possessed to charity? Some note that there is no difficulty according to the opinion of the Rambam, who writes in his Commentary on the Mishna (*Pe'a* 1:1) that although one is not supposed to donate to the poor more than one-fifth of his assets, he is permitted to do so as an act of piety. It should be noted that elsewhere the Rambam writes that giving away more than one-fifth of one's assets is an act of folly rather than an act of piety (*Sefer Hafla'a*, *Hilkhot Arakhin VaḤaramim* 8:13). Some commentaries suggest that the ordinance of Usha was the subject of a tannaitic dispute, and Elazar of Birta follows the opinion of the *tanna* who maintains that one may give away more than one-fifth of his assets to charity, provided that he keeps a minimal amount for himself (*Gevurat Ari*).

As one of the poor Jews – כְּאֶחָד מֵעֲנִיֵּי יִשְׂרָאֵל: Rashi and others explain that Elazar of Birta did not want his daughter to purchase her dowry with the grain because he did not want to profit from a miracle. However, this entails a difficulty, for in that case, how did he allow himself to derive any sort of benefit from the grain? Some commentaries suggest that Elazar of Birta did not want his daughter to purchase her dowry with the grain because he did not wish to receive a reward for his righteous behavior in this world, as it would diminish his reward in the World-to-Come. Once he dedicated the grain to charity, his daughter, being poor herself, had a right to a portion of it just like any other pauper (*Iyyun Ya'akov*).

PERSONALITIES

Oshaya, the youngest of the group – אוֹשַׁעְיָא זְעֵירָא דְּמִן חֲבֶרַיָּיא: This Sage, who is mentioned on a few occasions, is possibly Rav Oshaya from Babylonia. Even the meaning of his title is unclear, as he might be called Oshaya the Young, perhaps to differentiate from another Oshaya, who came from a place called Ḥavraya. Alternatively, as translated here, he is possibly known as Oshaya, the youngest of the group of Sages.

LANGUAGE

Bleary [*terutot*] – טְרוּטוֹת: Possibly from the Greek δηρός, *dèros*, meaning long or overly long. Alternatively, it is from the Latin teres or teritis, meaning oval, i.e., something elongated with rounded ends. If so, it means very narrow eyes.

NOTES

He also causes us pain – הא נמי מצער לן: Some commentaries explain the argument as follows: When Oshaya said that if a bride's eyes are bleary her entire body requires a careful examination, he insulted not only the *Nasi* but also the rest of the community, i.e., the bride's body. Just as the rest of the community was ready to indulge Oshaya, as they knew he meant everything for the sake of Heaven, the *Nasi*'s men should also allow him to continue preaching (Rabbi Elyakim).

אתו עבדיה ורמו ליה סודרא בצואריה, וקא מצערו ליה. אמרו להו בני מאתיה: שבקיה, דהא נמי מצער לן. כיון דחזינן דכל מיליה לשום שמים, לא אמרי ליה מידי ושבקינן ליה. אתון נמי שבקוהו.

By means of this parable, Oshaya was hinting that rain was withheld from the entire nation due to the evil committed by the household of the *Nasi*. The **servants** of the *Nasi* **came and placed a scarf around his neck and tormented him** as punishment for insulting the house of the *Nasi*. **His townsmen said to them: Let him be, as he also causes us pain**[N] with his harsh reproof, but **since we see that all his actions are for the sake of Heaven we do not say anything to him and let him be. You too** should **let him be.**

רבי גזר תעניתא, ולא אתא מיטרא. נחית קמיה אילפא, (ואמרי לה רבי אילפי). אמר: משיב הרוח, ונשב זיקא. מוריד הגשם, ואתא מיטרא. אמר ליה: מאי עובדך? אמר ליה: דיירנא בקוסטא דחיקא דלית ביה חמרא לקידושא ואבדלתא. טרחנא ואתינא חמרא לקידושא ואבדלתא, ומפיקנא להו ידי חובתייהו.

§ The Gemara relates: **Rabbi** Yehuda HaNasi **declared a fast but rain did not come. Ilfa descended** to lead the service **before him, and some say** it was **Rabbi Ilfi. He recited: He Who makes the wind blow, and the wind** indeed **blew.** He continued to recite: And **Who makes the rain come, and** subsequently, **the rain came.** Rabbi Yehuda HaNasi **said to him: What are your** good **deeds,** in the merit of which your prayers are answered so speedily? **He said to him: I live in an impoverished city, in which there is no wine for *kiddush* or *havdala*. I go to the effort of bringing** the residents **wine for *kiddush* and *havdala*, and I** thereby enable them to **fulfill their duty.** In reward for this mitzva, my prayers for rain were answered.

רב איקלע להוא אתרא. גזר תעניתא, ולא אתא מיטרא. נחית קמיה שליחא דצבורא. אמר: משיב הרוח, ונשב זיקא. אמר: מוריד הגשם, ואתא מיטרא. אמר ליה: מאי עובדך? אמר ליה: מיקרי דרדקי אנא, ומקרינא לבני עניי כבני עתירי. וכל דלא אפשר ליה, לא שקלינא מיניה מידי. ואית לי פירא דכוורי, וכל מאן דפשע, משחדינא ליה מינייהו, ומסדרינן ליה, ומפייסינן ליה, עד דאתי וקרי.

The Gemara relates a similar incident. **Rav happened** to come to **a certain place** where **he decreed a fast but rain did not come. The prayer leader descended** to lead the service **before him** and **recited: He Who makes the wind blow, and the wind blew.** He continued and **said:** And **Who makes the rain fall, and the rain came.** Rav **said to him: What are your** good **deeds? He said to him: I am a teacher of children, and I teach the Bible to the children of the poor as to the children of the rich, and** if there is **anyone who cannot** pay, **I do not take anything from him. And I have a fishpond, and any** child **who neglects** his studies, **I bribe him with** the fish **and calm him, and soothe him until he comes and reads.**

רב נחמן גזר תעניתא. בעא רחמי, ולא אתא מיטרא. אמר: שקלוה לנחמן, חבוטו מן גודא לארעא. חלש דעתיה, ואתא מיטרא.

The Gemara further relates: **Rav Naḥman decreed a fast, prayed for mercy, but rain did not come.** In his misery, he **said: Take Naḥman** and **throw him from the wall to the ground,** as the fast he decreed has evidently had no effect. **He grew upset, and rain came.**

רבה גזר תעניתא. בעי רחמי, ולא אתא מיטרא. אמרו ליה: והא רב יהודה כי הוה גזר תעניתא, אתא מיטרא! אמר להו: מאי אעביד? אי משום תנויי, אנן עדיפינן מינייהו, דבשני דרב יהודה כל תנויי

The Gemara relates: **Rabba decreed a fast. He prayed for mercy, but rain did not come. They said to him: But when** this **Rav Yehuda decreed a fast, rain would come. He said to them: What can I do?** If the difference between us is **due to** Torah **study, we are superior to** the previous generation, **as in the years of Rav Yehuda all of their learning**

Perek **III**
Daf **24** Amud **b**

NOTES

A woman who pickles – האשה שכובשת: The issue discussed in both *mishnayot* is the status of what is called the handles of food. Ordinarily, only the edible portions of food can contract ritual impurity but not the inedible portions, e.g., seed coverings or stems. In some cases, however, the inedible part of the food is used for holding onto the edible part. In these cases, the inedible part is called a handle of food, and it too can contract ritual impurity. Sometimes these handles may even increase the food's volume to the minimum size susceptible to ritual impurity. The leaves of olives and vegetables are generally considered handles that are subject to ritual impurity. If, however, the olives or the vegetables are pickled, their leaves are no longer firm enough to serve as handles, and consequently they are no longer liable to ritual impurity. The complex subject of handles of foods is discussed primarily in tractate *Uktzin*.

בנזיקין הוה, ואנן קא מתנינן בשיתא סדרין. וכי הוה מטי רב יהודה בעוקצין: האשה שכובשת ירק בקדירה, ואמרי לה: זיתים שכבשן בטרפיהן טהורין, אמר: הויות דרב ושמואל קא חזינא הכא!

was connected to the order **of *Nezikin*,** while they were largely unfamiliar with the rest of the Mishna, **and we learn** all **six orders** of the Mishna. **And when Rav Yehuda reached** tractate ***Uktzin*,** which discusses the extent to which various fruits and vegetables are considered an integral part of the produce in terms of becoming ritually impure, which is the basis for the *halakha* that **a woman who pickles**[N] **a vegetable in a pot,** etc. (*Teharot* 2:1), **and some say** that when he reached the *halakha* that **olives that are pickled with their leaves are ritually pure,** etc., as they are no longer considered part of the fruit (*Uktzin* 2:1), **he would say:** Those are **the disputes between Rav and Shmuel that we see here.** He felt it was an extremely challenging passage, as difficult as the most complex arguments between Rav and Shmuel.

וַאֲנַן קָא מַתְנִינַן בְּעוּקְצִין תְּלֵיסַר מְתִיבָתָא. וְאִילּוּ רַב יְהוּדָה כִּי הֲוָה שָׁלֵיף חַד מְסָאנָא, אָתֵי מִיטְרָא וַאֲנַן קָא צָוְוחִינַן כּוּלֵּי יוֹמָא, וְלֵיכָּא דְּאַשְׁגַּח בָּן! אִי מִשּׁוּם עוּבָדָא, אִי אִיכָּא דַּחֲזָא מִידֵי, לֵימָא! אֲבָל מַה יַּעֲשׂוּ גְּדוֹלֵי הַדּוֹר, שֶׁאֵין דּוֹרָן דּוֹמֶה יָפֶה?

And we, in contrast, learn tractate *Uktzin* in thirteen *yeshivot*,[N] while, with regard to miracles, after declaring a fast to pray for a drought to end, when Rav Yehuda would remove one of his shoes as a sign of distress, the rain would immediately come, before he could remove his second shoe. And yet we cry out all day and no one notices us. Rabba continued: If the difference between the generations is due to inappropriate deeds, if there is anyone who has seen me do anything improper, let him say so. I am not at fault, but what can the great leaders of the generation do when their generation is not worthy, and rain is withheld on account of the people's transgressions?

רַב יְהוּדָה חֲזָא הָנְהוּ בֵּי תְּרֵי דְּהָווּ קָא פָּרְצִי בְּרִיפְתָּא, אֲמַר: שְׁמַע מִינָּהּ אִיכָּא שָׂבְעָא בְּעָלְמָא. יְהֵיב עֵינֵיהּ, הֲוָה כַּפְנָא. אֲמַרוּ לֵיהּ רַבָּנַן לְרַב כָּהֲנָא בְּרֵיהּ דְּרַב נְחוּנְיָא שַׁמְּעֵיהּ: מָר, דִּשְׁכִיחַ קַמֵּיהּ, נִיעַשְּׁיֵיהּ דְּלֵיפּוּק בְּפִתְחָא דִּסָמוּךְ לְשׁוּקָא. עַשְּׁיֵיהּ וּנְפַק לְשׁוּקָא. חֲזָא כְּנוּפְיָא.

The Gemara explains the reference to Rav Yehuda's shoe. Rav Yehuda saw two people wasting bread, throwing it back and forth. He said: I can learn from the fact that people are acting like this that there is plenty in the world. He cast his eyes angrily upon the world, and there was a famine. The Sages said to Rav Kahana, son of Rav Neḥunya, the attendant of Rav Yehuda: The Master, who is frequently present before Rav Yehuda, should persuade him to leave[N] by way of the door nearest the market, so that he will see the terrible effects of the famine. Rav Kahana persuaded Rav Yehuda, and he went out to the market, where he saw a crowd.

אֲמַר לְהוּ: מַאי הַאי? אֲמַרוּ לֵיהּ: אַכּוּסְפָּא דְּתַמְרֵי קַיְימֵי דְּקָא מִזְדַּבַּן. אֲמַר: שְׁמַע מִינָּהּ כַּפְנָא בְּעָלְמָא. אֲמַר לֵיהּ לְשַׁמְּעֵיהּ: שְׁלוֹף לִי מְסָאנַיי. שָׁלַף לֵיהּ חַד מְסָאנָא, וַאֲתָא מִיטְרָא. כִּי מְטָא לְמִישְׁלַף אַחֲרִינָא, אֲתָא אֵלִיָּהוּ וְאָמַר לֵיהּ: אֲמַר הַקָּדוֹשׁ בָּרוּךְ הוּא: אִי שָׁלְפַתְּ אַחֲרִינָא, מַחֲרִיבְנָא לְעָלְמָא.

He said to them: What is this gathering? They said to him: We are standing by a container [*kuspa*][L] of dates that is for sale. He said: If so many people are crowding around to purchase a single container of dates, I can learn from this that there is a famine in the world. He said to his attendant: I want to fast over this; remove my shoes as a sign of distress. He removed one of his shoes and rain came. When he began to take off the other shoe, Elijah came and said to him: The Holy One, Blessed be He, said: If you remove your other shoe, I will destroy the entire world[N] so that you will not be further distressed.

אֲמַר רַב מָרִי בְּרָהּ דְּבַת שְׁמוּאֵל: אֲנָא הֲוָה קָאֵימְנָא אַגּוּדָא דִּנְהַר פַּפָּא, חֲזַאי לְמַלְאֲכֵי דְּאִידַּמּוּ לַמַּלָּחֵי דְּקָא מַיְיתֵי חָלָא וּמָלוּנְהוּ לְאַרְבֵּי, וַהֲוָה קִמְחָא דִּסְמִידָא. אָתוּ כּוּלֵּי עָלְמָא לְמִיזְבַּן. אֲמִינָא לְהוּ: מֵהָא לָא תִּיזְבְּנוּן, דְּמַעֲשֵׂה נִסִּים הוּא. לְמָחָר אָתְיָין אַרְבֵי דְחִיטֵּי דְּפָרְזִינָא.

Rav Mari, son of Shmuel's daughter, said: At that moment, I was standing on the bank of the Pappa River. I saw angels[N] who appeared as sailors bringing sand and filling ships with it, and it became fine flour. Everyone came to buy this flour, but I said to them: Do not purchase this flour, as it is the product of miracles. Tomorrow, boats filled with wheat will come from Parzina, and you may purchase that produce.

רָבָא אִיקְּלַע לְהַגְרוֹנְיָא. גְּזַר תַּעֲנִיתָא, וְלָא אֲתָא מִיטְרָא. אֲמַר לְהוּ: בִּיתוּ כּוּלֵּי עָלְמָא בְּתַעֲנִיתַייכוּ. לְמָחָר אֲמַר לְהוּ: מִי אִיכָּא דַּחֲזָא חֶילְמָא, לֵימָא. אֲמַר לְהוּ רַבִּי אֶלְעָזָר מֵהַגְרוֹנְיָא: לְדִידִי אַקְרִיּוּן בְּחֶלְמִי: ״שְׁלָם טָב לְרַב טָב מֵרִיבּוֹן טַב דְּמִטּוּבֵיהּ מֵטִיב לְעַמֵּיהּ״. אֲמַר: שְׁמַע מִינָּהּ עֵת רָצוֹן הִיא מִבָּעֵי רַחֲמֵי. בָּעֵי רַחֲמֵי, וְאָתֵי מִיטְרָא.

§ The Gemara relates another story. Rava happened to come to the city of Hagrunya. He decreed a fast, but rain did not come. He said to the local residents: Everyone, continue your fast and do not eat tonight. The next morning he said to them: Whoever had a dream last night, let him say it. Rabbi Elazar of Hagronya said to them: The following was recited to me in my dream. Good greetings to a good master from a good Lord, Who in His goodness does good for His people. Rava said: I can learn from this that it is a favorable time to pray for mercy. He prayed for mercy and rain came.

הַהוּא גַּבְרָא דְּאִיחַיַּיב נַגְדָּא בְּבֵי דִּינָא דְּרָבָא מִשּׁוּם דְּבְעַל נָכְרִית. נַגְדֵיהּ רָבָא וּמִית. אִשְׁתַּמַּע מִילְּתָא בֵּי שָׁבוּר מַלְכָּא, בְּעָא לְצַעוּרֵי לְרָבָא. אֲמַרָה לֵיהּ אִיפְרָא הוּרְמִיז, אִימֵּיהּ דְּשָׁבוּר מַלְכָּא, לִבְרָהּ: לָא לֶיהֱוֵי לָךְ עֵסֶק דְּבָרִים בַּהֲדֵי יְהוּדָאֵי, דְּכָל מַאן דְּבָעְיָין מִמָּרַיְיהוּ, יָהֵיב לְהוּ.

The Gemara relates another story that deals with prayer for rain. There was a certain man who was sentenced to be flogged by Rava's court because he had relations with a gentile woman. Rava flogged the man and he died as a result. When this matter was heard in the house of the Persian King Shapur, he wanted to punish Rava for imposing the death penalty, as he thought, without the king's permission. Ifra Hormiz,[LP] mother of King Shapur, said to her son: Do not interfere and quarrel with the Jews, as whatever they request from God, their Master, He gives them.

PERSONALITIES

Ifra Hormiz – אִיפְרָא הוּרְמִיז: Queen Ifra Hormiz was the mother of Shapur II, king of Persia (309–379 CE). Since Shapur became king as a child, his mother maintained considerable influence over him for many years. Ifra Hormiz is mentioned on several occasions in the Gemara as an admirer of Judaism and its Sages. She even gave money to several Sages to distribute as charity and for the performance of mitzvot.

NOTES

Thirteen *yeshivot* – תְּלֵיסַר מְתִיבָתָא: Elsewhere Rashi explains that in Rabba's day, thirteen versions of *Uktzin* were being studied, the version of the Mishna as well as the different versions in the collections of *baraitot* transmitted by Rabbi Ḥiyya, Rabbi Oshaya, bar Kappara, and others (*Berakhot* 20a).

Persuade him to leave – נִיעַשְּׁיֵיהּ דְּלֵיפּוּק: Although the Sages could simply have told Rav Yehuda about the famine, they wanted him to see for himself what was happening in the marketplace. They assumed that when Rav Yehuda observed the effects of the famine firsthand, he would certainly petition God that it should come to an end (Maharsha).

I will destroy the world – מַחֲרִיבְנָא לְעָלְמָא: Elsewhere this phrase expresses God's readiness to destroy the world so that a certain righteous man will not have to suffer from its continued existence. Here the meaning of the expression is less clear. Some commentaries suggest that God threatened to destroy the world due to Rav Yehuda's repeated requests, first for a famine and later to bring plenty to the world. If Rav Yehuda was not satisfied with the rain that had already begun to fall as soon as he took off his first shoe, God would destroy the world (Maharsha; see Rabbi Elyakim).

I saw angels, etc. – חֲזַאי לְמַלְאֲכֵי וכו׳: Although the people refused to benefit from the miracle, it had a beneficial effect, as when it became clear that there was plenty of food, prices went down (*Shita Mekubbetzet*).

LANGUAGE

Container [*kuspa*] – כּוּסְפָּא: Some suggest that this is from the κάψα, *kapsa*, or its Latin cognate capsa, meaning a vessel or a box. In Hebrew the letters are inverted. The Aramaic term *kuspa* can also be explained, based on other passages in the Talmud, to mean the material that remains after the juice and moisture have been removed from fruit or seeds. In the context cited in the Gemara, it might refer to the residue of dates after liquor has been made from them.

Ifra Hormiz – אִיפְרָא הוּרְמִיז: Probably from the name Farr Ohrmazd, meaning the splendor of the god Hormiz.

אֲמַר לַהּ: מַאי הִיא? בָּעֵין רַחֲמֵי וְאָתֵי מִיטְרָא. אֲמַר לַהּ: הַהוּא מִשּׁוּם דִּזְימְנָא דְּמִיטְרָא הוּא. אֶלָּא לִבְעוֹ רַחֲמֵי הָאִידָּנָא, בִּתְקוּפַת תַּמּוּז, וְלֵיתֵי מִיטְרָא. שְׁלַחָה לֵיהּ לְרָבָא: כַּוֵּין דַּעְתָּךְ, וּבְעֵי רַחֲמֵי דְּלֵיתֵי מִיטְרָא. בְּעֵי רַחֲמֵי, וְלָא אָתֵי מִיטְרָא.

He said to her: What is this that He grants them? She replied: **They pray for mercy and rain comes. He said to her:** This does not prove that God hears their prayers, **as that** occurs merely **because it is the time for rain,** and it just so happens that rain falls after they pray. **Rather,** if you want to prove that God answers the prayers of the Jews, **let them pray for mercy now,** in the summer **season of Tammuz, and let rain come.** Ifra Hormiz **sent** a message **to Rava: Direct your attention and pray for mercy that rain may come. He prayed for mercy, but rain did not come.**

אֲמַר לְפָנָיו: רִבּוֹנוֹ שֶׁל עוֹלָם! "אֱלֹהִים, בְּאׇזְנֵינוּ שָׁמַעְנוּ, אֲבוֹתֵינוּ סִפְּרוּ לָנוּ, פֹּעַל פָּעַלְתָּ בִימֵיהֶם, בִּימֵי קֶדֶם", וְאָנוּ בְּעֵינֵינוּ לֹא רָאִינוּ. אֲתָא מִיטְרָא עַד דִּשְׁפוּךְ מַרְזְבֵי דְמָחוֹזָא לְדִיגְלַת. אֲתָא אֲבוּהּ אִיתְחֲזִי לֵיהּ בְּחֶלְמֵיהּ, וַאֲמַר לֵיהּ: מִי אִיכָּא דְּמִיטְרַח קַמֵּי שְׁמַיָּא כּוּלֵּי הַאי? אֲמַר לֵיהּ: שַׁנִּי דּוּכְתֵּיךְ. שַׁנִּי דּוּכְתֵּיהּ. לְמָחָר אַשְׁכְּחֵיהּ דִּמְרַשַּׁם פּוּרְיֵיהּ בְּסַכִּינֵי.

He said before God: **Master of the Universe,** it is written: **"O God, we have heard with our ears, our fathers have told us, what work You did in their days, in days of old"** (Psalms 44:2), **but we have not seen it with our** own **eyes.** As soon as he said this, **rain came until the gutters of Meḥoza** overflowed and **poured into the** Tigris River. Rava's **father came** and **appeared to him in a dream and said to him: Is there** anyone **who troubles Heaven so much** to ask for rain out of its season? In his dream, his father further **said to him: Change your place**[N] of rest at night. **He changed his place, and the next day he found that his bed had been slashed by knives.**

רַב פָּפָּא גְּזַר תַּעֲנִיתָא, וְלָא אֲתָא מִיטְרָא. חֲלַשׁ לִיבֵּיהּ, שְׂרַף פִּינְכָּא דְּדַיְיסָא, וּבְעֵי רַחֲמֵי, וְלָא אֲתָא מִיטְרָא. אֲמַר לֵיהּ רַב נַחְמָן בַּר אוּשְׁפַּזְתִּי: אִי שָׂרֵיף מָר פִּינְכָּא אַחֲרִיתִי דְּדַיְיסָא, אָתֵי מִיטְרָא. אִיכְסִיף וַחֲלַשׁ דַּעְתֵּיהּ, וַאֲתָא מִיטְרָא.

The Gemara relates: **Rav Pappa decreed a fast, but rain did not come. His heart became weak** from hunger, so **he swallowed** [*seraf*][L] **a bowl** [*pinka*][L] **of porridge, and prayed for mercy, but rain** still **did not come. Rav Naḥman bar Ushpazti said to him: If the Master swallows another bowl**[N] **of porridge, rain will come.** He was mocking Rav Pappa for eating while everyone else was fasting. Rav Pappa was **embarrassed and grew upset, and rain came.**

רַבִּי חֲנִינָא בֶּן דּוֹסָא הֲוָה קָא אָזֵיל בְּאוֹרְחָא אֲתָא מִיטְרָא. אֲמַר לְפָנָיו: רִבּוֹנוֹ שֶׁל עוֹלָם! כׇּל הָעוֹלָם כּוּלּוֹ בְּנַחַת, וַחֲנִינָא בְּצַעַר? פְּסַק מִיטְרָא. כִּי מְטָא לְבֵיתֵיהּ, אֲמַר לְפָנָיו: רִבּוֹנוֹ שֶׁל עוֹלָם! כׇּל הָעוֹלָם כּוּלּוֹ בְּצַעַר, וַחֲנִינָא בְּנַחַת? אֲתָא מִיטְרָא.

The Gemara tells another story about prayer for rain. **Rabbi Ḥanina ben Dosa**[P] **was traveling along a road** when **it** began **to rain. He said before** God: **Master of the Universe, the entire world is comfortable,** because they needed rain, **but Ḥanina is suffering,** as he is getting wet. **The rain ceased. When he arrived at his home, he said before** God: **Master of the Universe, the entire world is suffering** that the rain stopped, **and Ḥanina is comfortable?**[N] **The rain** began to **come** again.

אֲמַר רַב יוֹסֵף: מַאי אַהֲנְיָא לֵיהּ צְלוֹתָא דְּכֹהֵן גָּדוֹל לְגַבֵּי רַבִּי חֲנִינָא בֶּן דּוֹסָא? דִּתְנַן: הָיָה מִתְפַּלֵּל תְּפִלָּה קְצָרָה בַּבַּיִת הַחִיצוֹן. מַאי מְצַלֵּי? רָבִין בַּר אַדָּא וְרָבָא בַּר אַדָּא דְּאָמְרִי תַּרְוַיְיהוּ מִשְּׁמֵיהּ דְּרַב יְהוּדָה: יְהִי רָצוֹן מִלְּפָנֶיךָ, ה' אֱלֹהֵינוּ, שֶׁתְּהֵא הַשָּׁנָה הַזּוֹ גְּשׁוּמָה וּשְׁחוּנָה. שְׁחוּנָה מַעַלְיוּתָא הִיא? אַדְּרַבָּה, גְּרִיעוּתָא הִיא!

Rav Yosef said, in reaction to this story: **What effect does the prayer of the High Priest have against** that of **Rabbi Ḥanina ben Dosa? As we learned** in a mishna: After leaving the Holy of Holies on Yom Kippur, the High Priest **would recite a brief prayer in the outer chamber.** The Gemara asks: **What would** he **pray? Ravin bar Adda and Rava bar Adda**[P] **both say in the name of Rav Yehuda** that this was his prayer: **May it be Your will, Lord our God, that this year shall be rainy and hot.** The Gemara expresses surprise at this request: **Is heat a good** matter? **On the contrary, it is unfavorable.** Why should he request that the year be hot?

אֶלָּא: אִם שְׁחוּנָה, תְּהֵא גְּשׁוּמָה וּטְלוּלָה. וְאַל יִכָּנֵס לְפָנֶיךָ תְּפִילַּת עוֹבְרֵי דְרָכִים. רַב אַחָא בְּרֵיהּ דְּרָבָא מְסַיֵּים מִשְּׁמֵיהּ דְּרַב יְהוּדָה: לָא יַעֲדֵי עָבֵיד שׁוּלְטָן מִדְּבֵית יְהוּדָה, וְאַל יְהוּ עַמְּךָ יִשְׂרָאֵל צְרִיכִין לְהִתְפַּרְנֵס זֶה מִזֶּה, וְלֹא לְעַם אַחֵר.

Rather, say that he recited the following: **If** the upcoming year is **hot, may it** also **be rainy and moist** with dew, lest the heat harm the crops. The High Priest would also pray: **And let not the prayer of travelers enter Your presence. Rav Aḥa, son of Rava,**[P] **in the name of Rav Yehuda, concluded** the wording of this prayer: **May the rule of power not depart from the house of Judea. And may Your nation Israel not depend upon each other for sustenance, nor upon another nation.**[H] Instead, they should be sustained from the produce of their own land. Evidently, the High Priest's prayer that God should not listen to the prayer of individual travelers was disregarded in the case of Rabbi Ḥanina ben Dosa.

NOTES

Change your place – שַׁנִּי דּוּכְתֵּיךְ: The activities of destructive forces unleashed by God are restricted to a particular place. Consequently, a person against whom a divine decree has been issued might be safe from harm if he moves to a different place (see Maharsha).

If the Master swallows another bowl – אִי שָׂרֵיף מָר פִּינְכָּא אַחֲרִיתִי: Rav Pappa was justified in breaking his fast, as one who takes ill while fasting is permitted to eat. Nevertheless, Rav Naḥman reproached Rav Pappa for breaking his fast before praying for rain (Rashi). Others suggest that Rav Naḥman mocked Rav Pappa for swallowing a whole bowl of cereal. Rav Pappa should have taken the food in small quantities, so as to violate the fast as little as possible (Maharsha).

And Ḥanina is comfortable – וַחֲנִינָא בְּנַחַת: Rashi explains that Rabbi Ḥanina was not troubled with the absence of rain, as he himself did not own any fields. However, other commentaries point out that even those who do not own their own fields should be distressed by a shortage of rain, as they too will feel the results of the drought when food shortages cause prices to rise (*Shita Mekubbetzet*). Rather, the reason Rabbi Ḥanina was not troubled was because he was accustomed to maintaining himself on a *kav* of carobs per week, as stated later in the Gemara, and therefore a drought would have little effect on him.

LANGUAGE

Swallowed [*seraf*] – שְׂרַף: To suck or to sip. It is related to the Arabic verb شرب, *šariba*, meaning to drink.

Bowl [*pinka*] – פִּינְכָּא: Possibly from the Greek πίναξ, *pinax*, which means, among other things, a large dish.

PERSONALITIES

Rabbi Ḥanina ben Dosa – רַבִּי חֲנִינָא בֶּן דּוֹסָא: A *tanna* from the end of the Second Temple period, Rabbi Ḥanina ben Dosa was a disciple of Rabbi Yoḥanan ben Zakkai. Even as a student he was renowned for his righteousness and as a miracle worker, i.e., someone who often had miracles performed for him. Only a very small number of his statements of Torah, mainly of *aggada*, have been preserved. He is primarily known for the many stories concerning his piety and closeness to God, his righteousness, and his ability to make do with little. Throughout the generations he served as the symbol of a wholly righteous man.

Ravin bar Adda and Rava bar Adda – רָבִין בַּר אַדָּא וְרָבָא בַּר אַדָּא: These Sages were brothers, Babylonian *amora'im* of the third generation. They were disciples of Rav Yehuda, in whose name and that of his teacher, Rav, they cite statements. While Ravin bar Adda and Rava bar Adda are often quoted together, they are also mentioned separately in various places in the Babylonian Talmud.

Rav Aḥa, son of Rava – רַב אַחָא בְּרֵיהּ דְּרָבָא: A Babylonian *amora* of the sixth generation, Rav Aḥa, son of Rava, was not related to the famous *amora* Rava. He was a colleague of Rav Ashi and Ravina, and like them was a disciple of Rav Kahana. Rav Aḥa, son of Rava, is cited frequently in the Talmud as engaged in discussions with Rav Ashi and Ravina. Wherever the Gemara states that Rav Aḥa disagrees with Ravina, the commentaries assume that it is referring to Rav Aḥa, son of Rava.

HALAKHA

The High Priest's brief prayer – תְּפִילָּה קְצָרָה שֶׁל כֹּהֵן גָּדוֹל: While in the Sanctuary on Yom Kippur, the High Priest recited this short prayer: May it be Your will, Lord our God, that if this year is hot, may it be rainy. And may the rule of power not depart from the house of Judea, and may Your nation Israel not depend upon each other for sustenance, and let not the prayer of travelers enter Your presence (Rambam *Sefer Avoda*, *Hilkhot Avodat Yom HaKippurim* 4:1).

אָמַר רַב יְהוּדָה אָמַר רַב: בְּכָל יוֹם וָיוֹם בַּת קוֹל יוֹצֵאת וְאוֹמֶרֶת: כָּל הָעוֹלָם כּוּלּוֹ נִיזּוֹן בִּשְׁבִיל חֲנִינָא בְּנִי, וַחֲנִינָא בְּנִי דַּיּוֹ בְּקַב חֲרוּבִים מֵעֶרֶב שַׁבָּת לְעֶרֶב שַׁבָּת. הֲוָה רְגִילָא דְּבֵיתְהוּ לְמֵיחְמָא תַּנּוּרָא כָּל מַעֲלֵי דְּשַׁבְּתָא וְשָׁדְיָיא אַקְטַרְתָּא,

§ The Gemara continues to discuss the righteous Rabbi Ḥanina ben Dosa and the wonders he performed. **Rav Yehuda said** that **Rav said: Each and every day a Divine Voice**[N] **emerges** from Mount Horeb **and says: The entire world is sustained by** the merit of **My son Ḥanina** ben Dosa, **and** yet **for Ḥanina, My son,** ***a kav* of carobs,** a very small amount of inferior food, **is sufficient** to sustain him for an entire week, **from** one **Shabbat eve to** the next **Shabbat eve.** The Gemara relates: Rabbi Ḥanina ben Dosa's **wife would heat the oven every Shabbat eve and create** a great amount of **smoke,**

NOTES

Each and every day a Divine Voice – בְּכָל יוֹם וָיוֹם בַּת קוֹל: Elsewhere Rashi explains that this heavenly voice announcing that the entire world was maintained by the merits of Rabbi Ḥanina ben Dosa issued forth every day during the lifetime of that Sage (*Ḥullin* 86a; see Maharsha). Others suggest that a Divine Voice to this effect is pronounced all the time, as in each and every generation there is a certain person whose merits sustain the entire world (Rav Ya'akov Emden).

מִשּׁוּם כִּיסּוּפָא. הֲוָה לָהּ הָהִיא שִׁיבַבְתָּא בִּישְׁתָּא, אֲמַרָה: מִכְּדִי יָדַעְנָא דְּלֵית לְהוּ וְלָא מִידֵּי. מַאי כּוּלֵּי הַאי? אָזְלָא וְטָרְפָא אַבָּבָא. אִיכְּסְפָא וְעַיְילָא לְאִינְדְּרוֹנָא.

due to embarrassment, to make it appear that she was baking, despite the fact that there was no bread in her house. **She had a certain evil neighbor** who **said** to herself: **Now, I know that they have nothing. What,** then, **is all this** smoke? **She went and knocked on the door** to find out what was in the oven. Rabbi Ḥanina ben Dosa's wife was **embarrassed, and she ascended to an inner room** [*inderona*].[L]

אִיתְעֲבִיד לָהּ נִסָּא דַּחֲזְיָא לְתַנּוּרָא מְלֵא לַחְמָא וְאַגָּנָא מְלֵא לִישָׁא. אֲמַרָה לָהּ: פְּלָנִיתָא, פְּלָנִיתָא! אַיְיתִי מָסָא, דְּקָא חָרִיךְ לַחְמִיךְ. אֲמַרָה לָהּ: אַף אֲנָא לְהָכִי עַיְילִי. תָּנָא: אַף הִיא לְהָבִיא מַרְדֶּה נִכְנְסָה, מִפְּנֵי שֶׁמְּלוּמֶּדֶת בְּנִסִּים.

A miracle was performed for Rabbi Ḥanina ben Dosa's wife, as her neighbor **saw the oven filled with bread and the kneading basin filled with dough. She said to** Rabbi Ḥanina's wife, calling her by name: **So-and-so, so-and-so, bring a shovel, as your bread is burning. She said to** her neighbor: **I too went inside for that** very purpose. A *tanna* **taught: She too had entered** the inner room **to bring a shovel, because** she was **accustomed to miracles** and anticipated that one would occur to spare her embarrassment.

אֲמַרָה לֵיהּ דְּבֵיתְהוּ: עַד אֵימַת נֵיזִיל וְנִצְטַעַר כּוּלֵּי הַאי? אֲמַר לָהּ: מַאי נַעֲבֵיד? בְּעִי רַחֲמֵי דְּנִיתְבוּ לָךְ מִידֵּי. בְּעָא רַחֲמֵי, יָצְתָה כְּמִין פִּיסַּת יָד וְיָהֲבוּ לֵיהּ חַד כַּרְעָא דְּפְתוֹרָא דְּדַהֲבָא. חֲזְיָא בְּחֶלְמָא עֲתִידִי צַדִּיקֵי דְּאָכְלִי אַפְּתוֹרָא דְּדַהֲבָא דְּאִית לֵיהּ תְּלָת כַּרְעֵי, וְאִיהוּ אַפְּתוֹרָא דִּתְרֵי כַּרְעֵי.

The Gemara further relates: Rabbi Ḥanina's **wife said to him: Until when will we continue to suffer this** poverty? **He said to her: What can we do?** She responded: **Pray for mercy that something will be given to you** from Heaven. **He prayed for mercy** and something **like** the **palm of a hand emerged and gave him one leg of a golden table. That** night, **his wife saw in a dream** that in **the future,** i.e., in the World-to-Come, **the righteous will eat at a golden table that has three legs,**[N] **but** she will be eating **on a table that has two legs.**

אֲמַר לָהּ: נִיחָא לָךְ דְּמֵיכָל אָכְלִי כּוּלֵּי עָלְמָא אַפְּתוֹרָא דְּמִשְׁלָם, וַאֲנַן אַפְּתוֹרָא דְּמִיחֲסַר? אֲמַרָה לֵיהּ: וּמַאי נַעֲבֵיד? בְּעֵי רַחֲמֵי דְּנִשְׁקְלִינְהוּ מִינָּךְ. בָּעֵי רַחֲמֵי וּשְׁקָלוּהוּ. תָּנָא: גָּדוֹל הָיָה נֵס אַחֲרוֹן יוֹתֵר מִן הָרִאשׁוֹן. דִּגְמִירִי דְּמֵיהָב יָהֲבִי, מִישְׁקַל לָא שָׁקְלִי.

When she told her husband this story, **he said to her: Are you content that everyone will eat at a complete table and we** will eat **at a defective table? She said to him: But what can we do? Pray for mercy, that** the leg of the golden table should **be taken from you. He prayed for mercy, and it was taken** from him. A *tanna* **taught** in a *baraita*: **The last miracle was greater than the first, as it is learned** as a tradition that Heaven gives but **does not take back.**[N]

חַד בֵּי שִׁמְשֵׁי חַזְיֵיהּ לִבְרַתֵּיהּ דַּהֲוַאת עֲצִיבָא. אֲמַר לָהּ: בִּתִּי, אַמַּאי עֲצִיבַתְּ? אֲמַרָה לֵיהּ: כְּלִי שֶׁל חוֹמֶץ נִתְחַלֵּף לִי בִּכְלִי שֶׁל שֶׁמֶן, וְהִדְלַקְתִּי מִמֶּנּוּ אוֹר לַשַּׁבָּת. אֲמַר לָהּ: בִּתִּי, מַאי אִכְפַּת לָךְ? מִי שֶׁאָמַר לַשֶּׁמֶן וְיִדְלוֹק הוּא יֹאמַר לַחוֹמֶץ וְיִדְלוֹק. תָּנָא: הָיָה דּוֹלֵק וְהוֹלֵךְ כָּל הַיּוֹם כּוּלּוֹ, עַד שֶׁהֵבִיאוּ מִמֶּנּוּ אוֹר לְהַבְדָּלָה.

The Gemara relates that **one** Shabbat **evening,** Rabbi Ḥanina ben Dosa **saw that his daughter was sad. He said to her: My daughter, why are you sad? She said to him: I confused a vessel of vinegar for a vessel of oil and I lit** the **Shabbat** lamp **with** vinegar. Soon the lamp will be extinguished and we will be left in the dark. **He said to her: My daughter, what are you concerned** about? **He Who said to the oil** that it should **burn can say to the vinegar** that it should **burn.** A *tanna* **taught:** That lamp **burned continuously the entire day, until they brought from it light for** ***havdala.***

LANGUAGE

Inner room [*inderona*] – אִינְדְּרוֹנָא: Apparently derived from the Middle Persian andarōn, meaning inside or within.

NOTES

At a golden table that has three legs – אַפְּתוֹרָא דְּדַהֲבָא דְּאִית לֵיהּ תְּלָת כַּרְעֵי: The commentaries have suggested various explanations of this dream. Some say that the three legs of the table allude to the reward that the righteous will receive in the World-to-Come for upholding the three foundations upon which this world rests: Torah, service of God, and acts of charity. When Rabbi Ḥanina ben Dosa asked for an improvement in his financial situation, he was given one of the table legs as a reward for his service of God, i.e., his prayers. When his wife related her dream to him, Rabbi Ḥanina understood that if he accepted the golden leg in this world, his reward in the World-to-Come would be diminished, so he asked for the table leg to be taken back (Maharsha).

Does not take back – מִישְׁקַל לָא שָׁקְלִי: Some commentaries cite the Jerusalem Talmud, where this passage is explained as follows: The hand of the receiver is at the bottom, while the hand of the giver is on top. In other words, man, who is in this lowly world, can receive a gift from Heaven, but under ordinary circumstances he cannot give it back (*Mikhtam*).

רַבִּי חֲנִינָא בֶּן דּוֹסָא הָווּ לֵיהּ הָנָךְ עִיזֵּי. אֲמַרוּ לֵיהּ: קָא מַפְסְדָן. אֲמַר: אִי קָא מַפְסְדָן, נִיכְלִינְהוּ דּוּבֵּי. וְאִי לָא, כָּל חֲדָא וַחֲדָא תֵּיתֵי לְאוּרְתָּא דּוּבָּא בְּקַרְנַיְיהוּ. לְאוּרְתָּא אַיְיתֵי כָּל חֲדָא וַחֲדָא דּוּבָּא בְּקַרְנַיְיהוּ.

Rabbi Ḥanina ben Dosa had some goats. His neighbors **said to him:** Your goats **are damaging** our property by eating in our fields. **He said to them: If they are causing damage, let them be eaten by bears. But if** they are **not** eating your property, let **each of them,** this **evening, bring a bear** impaled **between its horns.** That **evening, each one brought in a bear** impaled **between its horns.**

הֲוָה לֵיהּ הַהִיא שִׁיבַבְתָּא דְּקָא בָּנְיָא בֵּיתָא, וְלָא מָטוּ כְּשׁוּרֵי. אָתְיָא לְקַמֵּיהּ, אֲמָרָה לֵיהּ: בָּנִיתִי בֵּיתִי וְלָא קָמְטוּ כְּשׁוּרַאי! אֲמַר לָהּ: מַה שְּׁמֵךְ? אֲמָרָה לֵיהּ: אִיכּוּ. אֲמַר: אִיכּוּ, נִימְטוּ כְּשׁוּרַיִךְ.

Rabbi Ḥanina ben Dosa **had a certain neighbor who was building a house, but the ceiling beams** were **not** long enough to **reach** from one wall to the other. **She came before** Rabbi Ḥanina ben Dosa and **said to him: I built my house, but my** ceiling **beams do not reach the walls. He said to her: What is your name? She said to him:** My name is **Ikku.** He said: **If so** [*ikku*], **may your beams reach** your walls.

תָּנָא: הִגִּיעוּ, עַד שֶׁיָּצְאוּ אַמָּה לְכָאן וְאַמָּה לְכָאן. וְיֵשׁ אוֹמְרִין: סְנִיפִין עֲשָׂאוּם. תַּנְיָא: פַּלֵּימוֹ אוֹמֵר: אֲנִי רָאִיתִי אוֹתוֹ הַבַּיִת, וְהָווּ קוֹרוֹתָיו יוֹצְאוֹת אַמָּה לְכָאן וְאַמָּה לְכָאן. וְאָמְרוּ לִי: בַּיִת זֶה שֶׁקֵּירָה רַבִּי חֲנִינָא בֶּן דּוֹסָא בִּתְפִלָּתוֹ.

A *tanna* **taught:** The beams were lengthened to such an extent that they not only **reached** the walls, but they continued **until they jutted out a cubit from this side and a cubit from that side. And some say** that **they extended with segments** [*senifin*],[NL] adding new walls at both ends of the beams. **It is taught** in a *baraita* that the Sage **Palaimo**[LP] **says: I saw that house, and its beams jutted out a cubit on this side and a cubit on that side. And they said to me: This is the house that Rabbi Ḥanina ben Dosa roofed by means of his prayer.**

וְרַבִּי חֲנִינָא בֶּן דּוֹסָא מֵהֵיכָן הָווּ לֵיהּ עִזִּים? וְהָא עָנִי הָוֵי! וְעוֹד, אָמְרוּ חֲכָמִים: אֵין מְגַדְּלִין בְּהֵמָה דַּקָּה בְּאֶרֶץ יִשְׂרָאֵל. אָמַר רַב פִּנְחָס: מַעֲשֶׂה וְעָבַר אָדָם אֶחָד עַל פֶּתַח בֵּיתוֹ וְהִנִּיחַ שָׁם תַּרְנְגוֹלִין, וּמְצָאָתָן אִשְׁתּוֹ שֶׁל רַבִּי חֲנִינָא בֶּן דּוֹסָא,

The Gemara asks a question about one of the details of this story. **And Rabbi Ḥanina ben Dosa, from where did he have goats? Wasn't he poor,** as stated above? **And furthermore, the Sages** have **said: One may not raise small, domesticated animals in Eretz Yisrael,**[NH] as they destroy the fields and property of others. How, then, could Rabbi Ḥanina ben Dosa raise goats? **Rav Pineḥas** said that this is how it came to pass: **An incident** occurred in which **a certain man passed by the entrance of** Rabbi Ḥanina's **house and left chickens there. And Rabbi Ḥanina ben Dosa's wife found them** and cared for them.

וְאָמַר לָהּ: אַל תֹּאכְלִי מִבֵּיצֵיהֶן. וְהִרְבּוּ בֵּיצִים וְתַרְנְגוֹלִין, וְהָיוּ מְצַעֲרִין אוֹתָם. וּמְכָרָן, וְקָנָה בִּדְמֵיהֶן עִזִּים. פַּעַם אַחַת עָבַר אוֹתוֹ אָדָם שֶׁאָבְדוּ מִמֶּנּוּ הַתַּרְנְגוֹלִין, וְאָמַר לַחֲבֵירוֹ: בְּכָאן הִנַּחְתִּי הַתַּרְנְגוֹלִין שֶׁלִּי. שָׁמַע רַבִּי חֲנִינָא, אָמַר לוֹ: יֵשׁ לְךָ בָּהֶן סִימָן? אָמַר לוֹ: הֵן. נָתַן לוֹ סִימָן וְנָטַל אֶת הָעִיזִּין. וְהֵן הֵן עִיזֵּי דְּאַיְיתוּ דּוּבֵּי בְּקַרְנַיְיהוּ.

And Rabbi Ḥanina **said her: Do not eat of their eggs,** as they are not ours. **And** the chickens **laid many eggs, and chickens** hatched from the eggs. **And** as the noise and mess of the chickens **were distressing them, they sold them and bought goats with their proceeds. Once that same man who lost the chickens passed by and said to his companion: Here is where I left my chickens.** Rabbi Ḥanina **heard** this and **said to him: Do you have a sign** by which to identify **them? He said to him: Yes. He gave him the sign and took the goats.** The Gemara concludes: **And these are the very goats that brought bears** impaled **between their horns.**

רַבִּי אֶלְעָזָר בֶּן פְּדָת דְּחִיקָא לֵיהּ מִילְּתָא טוּבָא. עֲבַד מִלְּתָא, וְלָא הֲוָה לֵיהּ מִידֵּי לְמִטְעַם. שְׁקַל בָּרָא דְּתוּמָא וְשַׁדְיֵיהּ בְּפוּמֵיהּ. חֲלַשׁ לִבֵּיהּ וְנִים. אֲזוּל רַבָּנַן לְשַׁיּוּלֵי בֵּיהּ, חַזְיוּהוּ דְּקָא בָּכֵי וְחָיֵיךְ, וּנְפַק צוּצִיתָא דְּנוּרָא מֵאַפּוּתֵיהּ.

§ The Gemara relates more stories of desperately poor righteous individuals. **Rabbi Elazar ben Pedat**[N] **was hard-pressed** for money. Once **an act** of bloodletting **was performed on him, but he did not have anything to taste** afterward. **He took a clove of garlic and put it in his mouth. His heart became weak and he fell asleep. The Sages came to inquire** about **his** welfare. They **saw him weeping and laughing, and a ray of light was shining from his forehead.**

כִּי אִתְּעַר, אֲמַרוּ לֵיהּ: מַאי טַעֲמָא קָבָכֵית וְחָיְיכַתְּ? אֲמַר לְהוּ: דַּהֲוָה יָתֵיב עִמִּי הַקָּדוֹשׁ בָּרוּךְ הוּא , וַאֲמַרִי לֵיהּ: עַד מָתַי אֶצְטַעֵר בְּהַאי עָלְמָא? וַאֲמַר לִי: אֶלְעָזָר, בְּנִי, נִיחָא לָךְ דְּאַפְכֵיהּ לְעָלְמָא מֵרֵישָׁא? אֶפְשָׁר דְּמִתְיַלְדַתְּ בְּשַׁעְתָּא דִּמְזוֹנֵי.

When he awoke they said to him: What is the reason that you were laughing and crying? He said to them: The reason is **that** in my dream **the Holy One, Blessed be He, was sitting with me, and I said to Him: Until when will I suffer** such poverty **in this world? And He said to me: Elazar, My son,** is it more **convenient** for **you that I return the world to its** very **beginning? Perhaps you will be born in an hour of sustenance** and not be poor.

אֲמַרִי לְקַמֵּיהּ: כּוּלֵּי הַאי, וְאֶפְשָׁר? אֲמַרִי לֵיהּ: דְּחָיֵי טְפֵי, אוֹ דְּחָיֵינָא? אֲמַר לִי: דְּחָיִית. אֲמַרִי לְקַמֵּיהּ: אִם כֵּן, לָא בָּעֵינָא.

I said before Him: You suggest doing **all this,** to return the world to its beginning, **and** even then is it only **a possibility** that things will be different, not a certainty? **I said to Him:** Are the years **that I have** already **lived more** numerous, **or** are **that I will live** more numerous? **He said to me:** Those years **that you have lived** are greater. **I said before Him: If so, I do not want** You to recreate the world for the sake of a brief few years.

NOTES

They extended with segments – סְנִיפִין עֲשָׂאוּם: Some commentaries explain that small pieces of wood were miraculously added to each of the beams so that they became long enough to reach from one side of the building to the other (Rashi; Rabbeinu Gershom). Others write that the beams became so long that the ends were cut off and used as braces to connect the upper and lower rows of beams supporting the roof (*ge'onim*; *Arukh*).

One may not raise small, domesticated animals in Eretz Yisrael – אֵין מְגַדְּלִים בְּהֵמָה דַּקָּה בְּאֶרֶץ יִשְׂרָאֵל: If it is prohibited to raise domesticated animals in Eretz Yisrael, how could Rabbi Ḥanina ben Dosa have kept the goats in his possession, even if he was looking after them for the owner of the lost chickens?

Some commentaries suggest that Rabbi Ḥanina ben Dosa raised the goats in the desert, where raising domesticated animals is permitted (*Gevurat Ari*). Others maintain that this prohibition applies only to one who wishes to raise his own herd, but the Sages did not prohibit the tending of sheep or goats belonging to someone else (*Ramat Shmuel*).

Rabbi Elazar ben Pedat – רַבִּי אֶלְעָזָר בֶּן פְּדָת: Some commentaries write that Rabbi Elazar ben Pedat's vision of the Holy One, Blessed be He, was merely a dream, whose details may not necessarily bear special significance (*ge'onim*). However, others interpret at length the particulars of Rabbi Elazar ben Pedat's vision. The righteous suffer in this world because God knows that poverty and distress will bring them spiritual benefit. God informs Rabbi Elazar that the spiritual reward in the World-to-Come is superior to material success in this world. The thirteen rivers allude to the thirteen attributes of God (Rashba; see Maharsha). Some explain the alternative reading of twelve rivers as an allusion to the twelve tribes of Israel (*Otzar HaKavod*).

LANGUAGE

Segments [*senifin*] – סְנִיפִין: The Hebrew root *s-n-f* is similar in meaning and is possibly related to the root *a-n-f*. The root *s-n-f* means to join one thing to another. Here it indicates that short pieces of wood were miraculously attached to the ends of the long beams.

Palaimo – פַּלֵּימוֹ: The name Palaimo is apparently derived from the Greek παλαιός, *palaios*, meaning old. Names of this kind, referring to old age, were used in Jewish communities as a sign of good fortune.

PERSONALITIES

Palaimo – פַּלֵּימוֹ: The Sage Palaimo, a disciple of Rabbi Yehuda HaNasi, is sometimes presented as asking his teacher questions of *halakha*, although he also engages in disputes with Rabbi Yehuda HaNasi's colleague, Rabbi Eliezer, son of Rabbi Shimon. Some of his halakhic rulings appear in *baraitot*, while many stories are related about his great piety.

HALAKHA

Small, domesticated animals in Eretz Yisrael – בְּהֵמָה דַּקָּה בְּאֶרֶץ יִשְׂרָאֵל: It is prohibited to raise small, domesticated animals in Eretz Yisrael, as they graze on the property of others and cause considerable damage. One may not raise these animals even inside one's house (*Tur*). However, they may be raised in Syria and in the deserts of Eretz Yisrael (*Shulḥan Arukh*, *Ḥoshen Mishpat* 409:1).

אֲמַר לִי: בְּהַאי אַגְרָא דְּאָמְרַתְּ לָא בָּעֵינָא, יָהֵיבְנָא לָךְ לְעָלְמָא דְּאָתֵי תְּלֵיסְרֵי נַהֲרְוָותָא דְּמִשְׁחָא אֲפַרְסְמוֹן דַּכְיָין כִּפְרָת וְדִיגְלַת, דְּמִעַנְּגַתְּ בְּהוּ. אֲמַרִי לְקַמֵּיהּ: הַאי, וְתוּ לָא? אֲמַר לִי: וּלְחַבְרָךְ מַאי יָהֵיבְנָא? אֲמַרִי לֵיהּ: וַאֲנָא מִגַּבְרָא דְּלֵית לֵיהּ בָּעֵינָא? מַחְיַין בְּאַסְקוּטְלָא אַפּוּתַאי, וַאֲמַר לִי: אֶלְעָזָר, בְּרִי, גִּירַי בָּךְ, גִּירַי!

He said to me: As a reward for saying: I do not want, I will give you in the World-to-Come thirteen rivers of pure balsam oil as large as the Euphrates and the Tigris for you to enjoy. I said before Him: This and no more? He said to me: But if I give you more, what will I give to your colleagues? I said to Him: And do I request this from a person, who does not have enough? You are omnipotent. He playfully snapped His finger [*askutla*][L] on my forehead and said to me: Elazar, my son, My arrows I cast upon you,[N] My arrows. This touch caused the ray of light to shine from his forehead.

רַבִּי חָמָא בַּר חֲנִינָא גְּזַר תַּעֲנִיתָא, וְלָא אֲתָא מִיטְרָא. אָמְרוּ לֵיהּ: וְהָא רַבִּי יְהוֹשֻׁעַ בֶּן לֵוִי גְּזַר תַּעֲנִיתָא, וְאָתֵי מִיטְרָא! אֲמַר לְהוּ: הָא אֲנָא, הָא בַּר לִיוָאֵי! אָמְרוּ לֵיהּ: דְּנֵיתֵי וְנִיכַּוֵּין דַּעְתִּין. אֶפְשָׁר דְּתָבְרִי צִיבּוּרָא לִבַּיְיהוּ, דְּאָתֵי מִיטְרָא. בְּעוֹן רַחֲמֵי, וְלָא אֲתֵי מִיטְרָא.

The Gemara returns to the topic of fasting for rain. **Rabbi Ḥama bar Ḥanina decreed a fast but rain did not come. They said to him: Didn't Rabbi Yehoshua ben Levi decree a fast and rain came? He said to them: This is I; this is a son of a Levite,**[N] i.e., we are two different people of unequal stature. **They said to him: Let us come and focus our minds. Perhaps the hearts of** the members of **the community will break and rain will come. They prayed for mercy, but rain did not come.**

אֲמַר לְהוּ: נִיחָא לְכוּ שֶׁיָּבֹא מָטָר בִּשְׁבִילֵנוּ? אָמְרוּ לֵיהּ: הֵן. אָמַר: רָקִיעַ, רָקִיעַ, כַּסֵּי פָּנֶיךָ! לָא אִיכַּסִּי. אָמַר: כַּמָּה עַזִּין פְּנֵי רָקִיעַ! אִיכַּסִּי, וַאֲתָא מִיטְרָא.

Rabbi Ḥama bar Ḥanina **said to them: Are you content that rain should come on our account,** and through our merit? **They said to him: Yes. He said: Skies, skies, cover your face** with clouds. The sky was **not covered** with clouds. **He said** in rebuke: **How impudent is the face of the sky,** to ignore me. The sky became **covered** with clouds **and rain came.**

לֵוִי גְּזַר תַּעֲנִיתָא, וְלָא אֲתָא מִיטְרָא, אָמַר לְפָנָיו: רִבּוֹנוֹ שֶׁל עוֹלָם! עָלִיתָ וְיָשַׁבְתָּ בַּמָּרוֹם וְאֵין אַתָּה מְרַחֵם עַל בָּנֶיךָ! אֲתָא מִיטְרָא, וְאִיטְּלַע. אָמַר רַבִּי אֶלְעָזָר: לְעוֹלָם אַל יָטִיחַ אָדָם דְּבָרִים כְּלַפֵּי מַעְלָה, שֶׁהֲרֵי אָדָם גָּדוֹל הֵטִיחַ דְּבָרִים כְּלַפֵּי מַעְלָה, וְאִיטְּלַע! וּמַנּוּ? לֵוִי.

The Gemara relates a similar story. **Levi decreed a fast but rain did not come. He said before** God: **Master of the Universe, You have ascended and sat up high, and You do not have mercy upon Your children. Rain came, but** as a punishment for his harsh statement toward God, Levi **became lame.** Consequently, **Rav Elazar said: A person should never cast** harsh **statements toward** God on **High, as a great person cast statements toward** God on **High, and he became lame. And who was** this individual? **Levi.**

הָא גַּרְמָא לֵיהּ? וְהָא לֵוִי אַחְוֵי קִידָּה קַמֵּיהּ דְּרַבִּי וְאִיטְּלַע! הָא וְהָא גַּרְמָא לֵיהּ.

The Gemara asks: **And** did **this** comment of Levi's **cause him** to become lame? **But** it is stated that **Levi demonstrated *kidda*,** a particular type of bowing on one's face, performed by the High Priest, **before Rabbi** Yehuda HaNasi, **and he became lame** as a result (see *Megilla* 22b). The Gemara explains: Both **this and that caused his** lameness. As a punishment for acting improperly, he suffered an injury while he was attempting a difficult physical feat and was vulnerable.

רַבִּי חִיָּיא בַּר לוּלְיָינִי שַׁמְעִינְהוּ לְהָנָךְ עֲנָנֵי דְּקָאָמְרִי: נֵיתוּ וְנִיתְּבֵי מַיָּא בְּעַמּוֹן וּמוֹאָב. אָמַר לְפָנָיו: רִבּוֹנוֹ שֶׁל עוֹלָם! כְּשֶׁנָּתַתָּ תּוֹרָה לְעַמְּךָ יִשְׂרָאֵל, חָזַרְתָּ עַל כׇּל אוּמּוֹת הָעוֹלָם, וְלֹא קִיבְּלוּהָ. וְעַכְשָׁיו אַתָּה נוֹתֵן לָהֶם מָטָר? שְׁדוֹ הָכָא! שַׁדְיוּהָ אַדּוּכְתַּיְהוּ.

The Gemara relates: **Rabbi Ḥiyya bar Lulyani**[P] **heard these clouds saying to one another, let us go and bring water for Ammon and Moab** in Transjordan. **He said before** God: **Master of the Universe, when You gave** Your **Torah to Your nation Israel, You approached all the nations of the world** to see if they would accept the Torah, **and they did not accept it. And** yet **now You are giving them rain. Throw** the water **here.** The clouds **threw the rain in their place** in Eretz Yisrael.

דָּרֵשׁ רַבִּי חִיָּיא בַּר לוּלְיָינִי: מַאי דִּכְתִיב: ״צַדִּיק כַּתָּמָר יִפְרָח, כְּאֶרֶז בַּלְּבָנוֹן יִשְׂגֶּה״? אִם נֶאֱמַר תָּמָר, לָמָּה נֶאֱמַר אֶרֶז, וְאִם נֶאֱמַר אֶרֶז, לָמָּה נֶאֱמַר תָּמָר? אִילּוּ נֶאֱמַר תָּמָר, וְלֹא נֶאֱמַר אֶרֶז, הָיִיתִי אוֹמֵר: מָה תָּמָר

Since the Gemara has mentioned Rabbi Ḥiyya bar Lulyani, it cites a statement in his name. **Rabbi Ḥiyya bar Lulyani taught: What** is the meaning of that **which is written: "The righteous shall flourish like the palm tree; he shall grow like a cedar in Lebanon"** (Psalms 92:13)? **If it is stated "palm tree" why does it state "cedar," and if it is stated "cedar" why does it state "palm tree"?** What is added by this double comparison? He explains: **Were it stated "palm tree" and were it not stated "cedar," I would say** that **just as** in the case **of a palm tree,**

PERSONALITIES

Rabbi Ḥiyya bar Lulyani – רַבִּי חִיָּיא בַּר לוּלְיָינִי: A fifth-generation *amora* from Eretz Yisrael, Rabbi Ḥiyya bar Lulyani is mentioned mainly in the Jerusalem Talmud, where he cites statements in the name of various Sages. He also had students who attributed statements to him. The name Lulyani is an Aramaic form of the Roman name Julianus.

LANGUAGE

Finger [*askutla*] – אַסְקוּטְלָא: From the Greek σκυταλίς, *skutalis*, whose meanings include a bone of a finger, and a finger.

NOTES

My arrows [*girai*] upon you – גִּירַי בָּךְ: Some commentaries read this as a question, an expression of God's dissatisfaction with Rabbi Elazar ben Pedat's repeated requests for additional rewards: Is it your desire that I should shoot My arrows at you? (Rabbi Elyakim). Others interpret it as a blessing, taking the word *girai* to mean converts [*geirim*]. God promised Rabbi Elazar ben Pedat that he would receive his reward in the future when converts would come to learn from him (*ge'onim*; *Arukh*). Alternatively, this response is an expression of joy and amusement, like an adult's reaction when a child answers a question with sharp wit.

This is I; this is a son of a Levite – הָא אֲנָא הָא בַּר לִיוָאֵי: Rashi and others explain that Rabbi Ḥama bar Ḥanina was saying that he recognized Rabbi Yehoshua ben Levi as his superior. Others insist that Rabbi Ḥama bar Ḥanina considered himself Rabbi Yehoshua ben Levi's equal. However, the people who fasted with him were not of the same stature as those who fasted with Rabbi Yehoshua ben Levi. It was subsequently suggested that the entire community should observe a fast, as the merits of the whole congregation might elicit God's compassion. When that too was unsuccessful, Rabbi Ḥama asked the members of the community whether the rain should come for our sake. He wanted them to admit that they were not deserving of rain, and that it should fall on account of their righteous leaders (Maharsha). A similar story is related in the Jerusalem Talmud (*Ta'anit* 3:4), in which Rabbi Ḥama bar Ḥanina's failure to cause rain to fall is attributed to the deficiencies of the community he represented, while Rabbi Yehoshua ben Levi's success was partly due to the merits of his community.

אֵין גִּזְעוֹ מַחֲלִיף, אַף צַדִּיק, חַס וְשָׁלוֹם, אֵין גִּזְעוֹ מַחֲלִיף. לְכָךְ נֶאֱמַר אֶרֶז. אִילּוּ נֶאֱמַר אֶרֶז, וְלֹא נֶאֱמַר תָּמָר, הָיִיתִי אוֹמֵר: מָה אֶרֶז אֵין עוֹשֶׂה פֵּירוֹת, אַף צַדִּיק, חַס וְחָלִילָה, אֵין עוֹשֶׂה פֵּירוֹת. לְכָךְ נֶאֱמַר תָּמָר וְנֶאֱמַר אֶרֶז.

its shoots do not replenish[N] themselves when its stump is cut down, **so too, Heaven forbid,** with regard to **a righteous person, his shoots will not replenish** themselves, i.e., he will be unable to recover from misfortune. **Therefore, it is stated "cedar"** in the verse. Just as the cedar grows new shoots after its stump is cut down, so too, a righteous individual will thrive again. Conversely, **were it stated "cedar" and were it not stated "palm tree," I would say** that **just as** in the case of **a cedar, it does not produce fruit, so too, a righteous man, God forbid, does not produce fruit,** i.e., he will have no reward in the World-to-Come. **Therefore, it is stated "palm tree" and it is also stated "cedar."**

וְאֶרֶז גִּזְעוֹ מַחֲלִיף? וְהָתַנְיָא: הַלּוֹקֵחַ אִילָן מֵחֲבֵירוֹ לָקוּץ, מַגְבִּיהוֹ מִן הַקַּרְקַע טֶפַח וְקוֹצֵץ. בְּסַדַּן הַשִּׁקְמָה, שְׁנֵי טְפָחִים. בִּבְתוּלַת הַשִּׁקְמָה, שְׁלֹשָׁה טְפָחִים. בְּקָנִים וּבִגְפָנִים, מִן הַפְּקָק וּלְמַעְלָה. בִּדְקָלִים וּבַאֲרָזִים, חוֹפֵר לְמַטָּה וּמְשָׁרֵישׁ, לְפִי שֶׁאֵין גִּזְעוֹ מַחֲלִיף.

§ The Gemara asks: **And do a cedar's shoots** really **replenish** themselves? **But isn't it taught** in a *baraita*: With regard to **one who bought a tree from another to chop**[H] it down for wood, without acquiring total ownership of the tree, he must **lift** his ax **a handbreadth and chop** there, so as to allow the tree to grow back? However, **in** a case where he purchased **a large sycamore,** he must leave **two handbreadths. In** the case of **an untrimmed sycamore,**[B] he must leave **three handbreadths. In** a situation where one **bought reeds or grapevines,** he may chop only **from** the first **knot**[B] **and above. In** the case of **palms or cedars,** one may **dig down and uproot**[B] it, **as its shoots** will **not replenish** themselves. This *baraita* indicates that cedars will not grow new shoots after they have been cut down.

הָכָא בְּמַאי עָסְקִינַן? בִּשְׁאָר מִינֵי אֲרָזִים, כִּדְרַבָּה בַּר הוּנָא, דְּאָמַר רַבָּה בַּר הוּנָא: עֲשָׂרָה מִינֵי אֲרָזִים הֵן, שֶׁנֶּאֱמַר: "אֶתֵּן בַּמִּדְבָּר אֶרֶז, שִׁטָּה, וַהֲדַס" וגו׳.

The Gemara answers: **With what are we dealing here? With other species of cedars.** This is **in accordance with** the opinion of **Rabba bar Huna, as Rabba bar Huna said: There are ten species of cedars, as it is stated: "I will plant in the wilderness the cedar, the acacia tree and myrtle** and the oil tree; I will set in the desert cypress, the plane tree and the larch together" (Isaiah 41:19). The seven species mentioned in this verse are all called cedars, as are three additional species.

תָּנוּ רַבָּנַן: מַעֲשֶׂה בְּרַבִּי אֱלִיעֶזֶר שֶׁגָּזַר שְׁלֹשׁ עֶשְׂרֵה תַּעֲנִיּוֹת עַל הַצִּבּוּר, וְלֹא יָרְדוּ גְּשָׁמִים. בָּאַחֲרוֹנָה, הִתְחִילוּ הַצִּבּוּר לָצֵאת. אָמַר לָהֶם: תִּקַּנְתֶּם קְבָרִים לְעַצְמְכֶם? גָּעוּ כׇּל הָעָם בִּבְכִיָּה, וְיָרְדוּ גְּשָׁמִים.

The Sages taught: An incident occurred **involving Rabbi Eliezer, who decreed** a complete cycle of **thirteen fasts upon the congregation, but rain did not fall. At** the end of **the last** fast, **the congregation began to exit** the synagogue. **He said to them: Have you prepared graves for yourselves?** If rain does not fall, we will all die of hunger. **All the people burst into tears, and rain fell.**

שׁוּב מַעֲשֶׂה בְּרַבִּי אֱלִיעֶזֶר שֶׁיָּרַד לִפְנֵי הַתֵּיבָה וְאָמַר עֶשְׂרִים וְאַרְבַּע בְּרָכוֹת, וְלֹא נַעֲנָה. יָרַד רַבִּי עֲקִיבָא אַחֲרָיו, וְאָמַר: אָבִינוּ, מַלְכֵּנוּ, אֵין לָנוּ מֶלֶךְ אֶלָּא אָתָּה. אָבִינוּ, מַלְכֵּנוּ, לְמַעַנְךָ רַחֵם עָלֵינוּ, וְיָרְדוּ גְּשָׁמִים. הָווּ מְרַנְּנִי רַבָּנַן. יָצְתָה בַּת קוֹל וְאָמְרָה: לֹא מִפְּנֵי שֶׁזֶּה גָּדוֹל מִזֶּה, אֶלָּא שֶׁזֶּה מַעֲבִיר עַל מִידּוֹתָיו, וְזֶה אֵינוֹ מַעֲבִיר עַל מִדּוֹתָיו.

There was **another incident involving** Rabbi Eliezer, **who descended** to serve as prayer leader **before the ark** on a fast day. **And he recited twenty-four blessings, but he was not answered. Rabbi Akiva descended before the ark** after him **and said: Our Father, our King, we have no king other** than **You. Our Father, our King, for Your sake, have mercy on us. And rain** immediately **fell. The Sages were whispering** among themselves that Rabbi Akiva was answered while his teacher, Rabbi Eliezer, was not. **A Divine Voice emerged and said:** It is **not because this** Sage, Rabbi Akiva, **is greater than that one,** Rabbi Eliezer, **but that this one is forgiving,**[N] **and that one is not forgiving.** God responded to Rabbi Akiva's forgiving nature in kind by sending rain.

NOTES

Its shoots do not replenish – **אֵין גִּזְעוֹ מַחֲלִיף**: Rashi explains that one who does not renew himself and grow new shoots, so to speak, will not arise in the time of the resurrection, and someone who does not yield fruit, i.e., renew himself, will not receive any reward in the World-to-Come.

Others explain that one who does not grow new shoots refers to one who does not have a son like himself, or else he is unable to stand up again after he stumbles. One who does not yield fruit does not have a share in the World-to-Come, or he does not enjoy the fruit of his actions (Rashbam on *Bava Batra* 80b).

Yet others state that one who does not yield fruit refers to one who fails to leave a Torah legacy that is accepted and studied by later generations (Rabbi Elyakim).

That this one is forgiving – **שֶׁזֶּה מַעֲבִיר עַל מִידּוֹתָיו**: The Gemara elsewhere states that if someone is forgiving and forgoes the opportunity to retaliate against others, God repays him measure for measure, and all of his sins are pardoned (*Rosh HaShana* 17a). Just as such a person does not seek revenge from those who treated him wrongly, God forgives him for the wrongs he himself has committed.

A similar story is related in the Jerusalem Talmud (*Ta'anit* 3:4). Rabbi Eliezer observed a fast but it did not rain, and subsequently Rabbi Akiva fasted and rain began to fall. Rabbi Akiva accounted for the difference by means of a parable. A king had two daughters, one impudent and the other polite. The king wished to be rid of his impudent daughter as quickly as possible, and he would therefore immediately accede to any request she submitted. However, as he desired the company of his polite daughter, he would not answer any of her requests until they were put forward to him repeatedly.

BACKGROUND

A large sycamore…an untrimmed sycamore – **סַדַּן הַשִּׁקְמָה...בְּתוּלַת הַשִּׁקְמָה**: The sycamore tree, *Ficus sycamorus*, is closely related to the fig tree. In ancient times, sycamores were widespread in Eretz Yisrael. Although the fruit of the sycamore, fig mulberries, can be eaten if necessary, the tree mainly served as a source for long, sturdy beams of wood. The wood of the sycamore is light and porous but is relatively unsusceptible to rot. Sycamores were left to grow and develop branches, at which point the so-called virgin or untrimmed sycamore was chopped down for the first time. Its stump would subsequently grow more branches. When these were fully grown, the tree, now a large sycamore, would be chopped once again.

The knot – **הַפְּקָק**: The branches of a grapevine are pruned every year, after which the tree grows new ones. However, care must be taken not to cut the grapevine beneath the knot, as the branches renew themselves from the knot.

In palms…uproot – **בִּדְקָלִים...מְשָׁרֵישׁ**: Unlike most trees, the palm does not have splits or knots in its old leaves or branches. Consequently, if one damages its trunk in the area where new leaves would sprout, and all the more so if one chops down the tree itself, this will cause the palm tree to die, as it will be unable to renew itself.

HALAKHA

One who bought a tree from another to chop – **הַלּוֹקֵחַ אִילָן מֵחֲבֵירוֹ לָקוּץ**: If one buys an olive tree to cut up its trunk for wood, he must leave a stump that is a height of two handbreadths. If he buys a virgin sycamore, he must leave three handbreadths of the stump. If he purchases the trunk of a sycamore that has previously been trimmed, he must leave two handbreadths of the stump. If he buys other trees, he must leave one handbreadth. If he acquires the branches of reeds or grapevines, he may cut them off from the first knot and above. Finally, if he purchases palms or cedars, he may dig down and uproot them completely, as their stumps do not renew themselves (*Shulḥan Arukh*, *Ḥoshen Mishpat* 216:14).

תָּנוּ רַבָּנַן: עַד מָתַי יְהוּ הַגְּשָׁמִים יוֹרְדִין, וְהַצִּבּוּר פּוֹסְקִין מִתַּעֲנִיתָם? כִּמְלֹא בֶּרֶךְ הַמַּחֲרֵישָׁה. דִּבְרֵי רַבִּי מֵאִיר. וַחֲכָמִים אוֹמְרִים: בַּחֲרֵבָה, טֶפַח. בְּבֵינוֹנִית, טְפָחַיִים. בַּעֲבוּדָה, שְׁלֹשָׁה טְפָחִים.

§ **The Sages taught** in a *baraita*: **How much rain must fall for the community to cease their fast**[H] for rain? If the rain penetrates the soil **by the full** depth of the blade of **a plow** until the spot where it **bends,**[BN] they may cease fasting; this is **the statement of Rabbi Meir. And the Rabbis say** a different measurement: If the earth is completely **dry,** the soil must become moist to the depth of a single **handbreadth.** For **average** soil, they must wait until the moisture reaches a depth of **two handbreadths.** If it is **worked**[N] soil, i.e., soil that has been plowed, the moisture must reach to a depth of **three handbreadths.**

תַּנְיָא: רַבִּי שִׁמְעוֹן בֶּן אֶלְעָזָר אוֹמֵר: אֵין לְךָ טֶפַח מִלְמַעְלָה שֶׁאֵין תְּהוֹם יוֹצֵא לִקְרָאתוֹ שְׁלֹשָׁה טְפָחִים. וְהָא תַּנְיָא: טְפָחַיִים! לָא קַשְׁיָא. כָּאן בַּעֲבוּדָה, כָּאן בְּשֶׁאֵינָהּ עֲבוּדָה.

It is taught in a *baraita* that **Rabbi Shimon ben Elazar says: There is no handbreadth** of rain **from above toward which** the water of **the deep does not rise three handbreadths.** The Gemara raises an objection: **But isn't it taught** in another *baraita* that the water of the deep rises **two handbreadths?** The Gemara explains: This is **not difficult. Here,** in first *baraita,* it is referring **to worked** land, which water penetrates faster, whereas **there,** in the second *baraita,* it is referring **to unworked** land,[N] which water does not penetrate as easily, and therefore the water of the deep rises only two handbreadths.

אָמַר רַבִּי אֶלְעָזָר: כְּשֶׁמְּנַסְּכִין אֶת הַמַּיִם בֶּחָג, תְּהוֹם אוֹמֵר לַחֲבֵירוֹ: אַבַּע מֵימֶיךָ, קוֹל שְׁנֵי רֵיעִים אֲנִי שׁוֹמֵעַ, שֶׁנֶּאֱמַר: ״תְּהוֹם אֶל תְּהוֹם קוֹרֵא לְקוֹל צִנּוֹרֶיךָ״ וגו׳.

Rabbi Elazar said: When the water libation **was poured during the festival** of *Sukkot,* these waters of the **deep say to the other** waters of the deep: **Let your water flow, as I hear the voices of two** of our **friends,**[N] the wine libation and the water libation, which are both poured on the altar. **As it is stated: "Deep calls to deep at the sound of your channels,** all Your waves and Your billows are gone over me" (Psalms 42:8), i.e., the upper waters of the deep call to the lower waters of the deep when they hear the sound of the libations.

אֲמַר רַבָּה: לְדִידִי חֲזִי לִי הַאי רִידְיָא דָּמֵי לְעִיגְלָא וּפִירְסָא שִׂפְוָותֵיהּ, וְקַיְימָא בֵּין תְּהוֹמָא תַּתָּאָה לִתְהוֹמָא עִילָּאָה. לִתְהוֹמָא עִילָּאָה אֲמַר לֵיהּ: חֲשׁוֹר מֵימֶיךָ. לִתְהוֹמָא תַּתָּאָה אֲמַר לֵיהּ: אַבַּע מֵימֶיךָ, שֶׁנֶּאֱמַר: ״הַנִּצָּנִים נִרְאוּ בָאָרֶץ״ וגו׳.

Rabba said: I have seen this angel in charge of water, **Ridya,**[L] **in the form of a calf whose lips were parted,**[N] **standing between the lower** waters of the **deep and the upper** waters of the **deep. To the upper** waters of the **deep, he said: Distill your water** and let it rain. **To the lower** waters of the **deep, he said: Let your water flow** from below, **as it is stated: "The flowers appear on the earth;** the time of the singing has come, and the voice of the turtledove [*tur*] is heard in our land" (Song of Songs 2:12). The appearance of flowers in this verse alludes to the libations, as both the blooming of flowers and pouring of these libations are annual events. The time of the singing is referring to the singing of the Festival. Finally, the term *tur* in Aramaic can also mean an ox; in this context, it is interpreted as a reference to the angel Ridya.

HALAKHA

How much rain must fall for the community to cease their fast – עַד מָתַי יְהוּ הַגְּשָׁמִים יוֹרְדִין וְהַצִּבּוּר פּוֹסְקִין מִתַּעֲנִיתָם: If the community is fasting on account of drought, they may stop fasting if the rain has penetrated dry soil to a depth of a handbreadth, average soil to a depth of two handbreadths, or plowed soil to a depth of three handbreadths. The *halakha* is in accordance with the opinion of the Rabbis (*Shulḥan Arukh, Oraḥ Ḥayyim* 575:11).

BACKGROUND

A plow, where it bends [*berekh*] – בֶּרֶךְ הַמַּחֲרֵישָׁה: This apparently refers to the spot where the plow bends. Sometimes, when the blade of the plow plunges deep into the earth, the plow sinks in up to one's knee [*berekh*].

LANGUAGE

Ridya – רִידְיָא: This word has been interpreted in various ways, including derivations from Aramaic and Persian. The most likely explanation is that it is related to the Aramaic *redi*, or *rada*, which can both mean to flow.

NOTES

A plow, where it bends [*berekh*] – בֶּרֶךְ הַמַּחֲרֵישָׁה: Most commentaries concur that the reference is to the depth of the furrow formed by the plow. However, the precise meaning of the term is a matter of dispute. Some explain that *berekh* refers to the furrow itself (Rabbeinu Ḥananel; Rabbeinu Gershom). Others add that the furrow is called *berekh* because water gathers there like in a *bereikha*, a pool (Rav Yehuda ben Binyamin HaRofeh). Yet others contend that *berekh* refers to the bend in the plow that connects the blade with the handle.

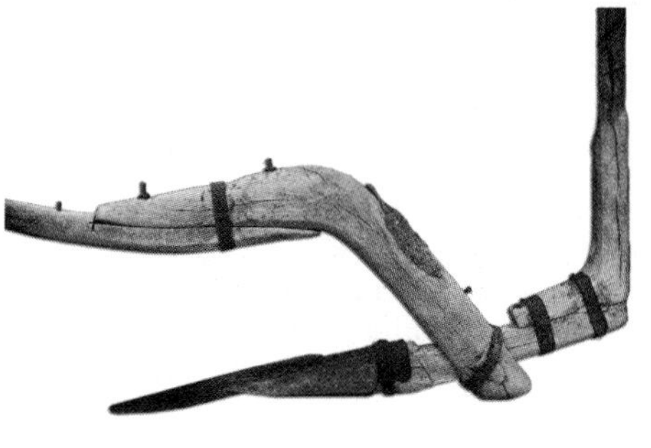

Ancient plow

Dry, average, worked – חֲרֵבָה, בֵּינוֹנִית, עֲבוּדָה: Some commentaries explain that dry soil has not been plowed for a long time, average soil has been plowed in previous years but not this year, and plowed soil has been plowed this year (Rabbeinu Yehonatan). Others maintain that the term dry soil describes soil at the time of the first rainfall, when it is still extremely dry, and the rain can hardly penetrate the ground at all; average soil refers to the second rainfall, when it is already moderately porous; and plowed soil is soil that has already been well plowed, so that rainwater can penetrate deeply (*Mikhtam*).

Here to worked land, there to unworked land – כָּאן בַּעֲבוּדָה כָּאן בְּשֶׁאֵינָהּ עֲבוּדָה: Some commentaries identify the unplowed soil mentioned here with the dry soil mentioned above (*Gevurat Ari*). However, this leads to certain difficulties in reconciling the two passages. Others explain that the unplowed soil referred to here is the same as the aforementioned average soil (Rashash). When rain penetrates average soil by one handbreadth, the same amount of rain penetrates plowed soil by one and a half handbreadths. As stated above, rain penetrates plowed soil 50 percent more deeply than the same amount of rain penetrates average soil, three handbreadths as opposed to two.

Since the water of the deep rises twice as much as the rainwater penetrates, the water of the deep rises two handbreadths to meet the handbreadth of rain that falls on average soil, whereas it rises three handbreadths to meet the same amount of rain that falls on plowed soil, which penetrates one and a half handbreadths.

The voices of two friends, etc. – קוֹל שְׁנֵי רֵיעִים וכו׳: These two friends that call to each other "at the sound of your channels" are the water and wine libations performed on the festival of *Sukkot*. The verse is interpreted as a reference to the mystical meaning of these mitzvot, which correspond to lofty spiritual levels called two friends (see *Otzar HaKavod*).

In the form of a calf whose lips were parted – דָּמֵי לְעִיגְלָא וּפִירְסָא שִׂפְוָותֵיהּ: Some commentaries explain that the angel in charge of rain appears as an ox, as the sign of Iyyar is an ox in the zodiac. Iyyar is the last month of the year in which rainfall is considered a blessing (Maharsha). Others suggest that the angel of rain is compared to an ox because rain leaves its mark on the land like an ox plowing the field (Rav Ya'akov Emden). Both commentaries interpret the calf's parted lips as a symbolic smile, as the angel of rain is glad that he can instruct the upper and lower depths to let their waters flow.

HALAKHA

If they were fasting and rain fell – הָיוּ מִתְעַנִּין וְיָרְדוּ גְּשָׁמִים: If the members of the community are fasting and it begins to rain after midday, they must prolong the fast until the end of the day. If it begins to rain before midday, they do not complete the fast; rather, they eat, drink, and celebrate the day. Toward evening, they gather together and recite *hallel* (*Shulḥan Arukh, Oraḥ Ḥayyim* 575:11).

"הָיוּ מִתְעַנִּין, וְיָרְדוּ גְּשָׁמִים קוֹדֶם הָנֵץ הַחַמָּה", כו'. תָּנוּ רַבָּנַן: הָיוּ מִתְעַנִּין, וְיָרְדוּ לָהֶם גְּשָׁמִים קוֹדֶם הָנֵץ הַחַמָּה, לֹא יַשְׁלִימוּ. לְאַחַר הָנֵץ הַחַמָּה, יַשְׁלִימוּ. דִּבְרֵי רַבִּי מֵאִיר. רַבִּי יְהוּדָה אוֹמֵר: קוֹדֶם חֲצוֹת, לֹא יַשְׁלִימוּ. לְאַחַר חֲצוֹת, יַשְׁלִימוּ.

§ The mishna teaches: If **they were fasting** for rain **and rain fell**[H] **for them before sunrise,** they need not complete their fast until the evening. **The Sages taught:** If **they were fasting** for rain **and rain fell for them before sunrise,** they need **not complete** their fast, as the obligation to fast does not come into effect until sunrise. However, if rain fell **after sunrise, they** must **complete** their fast. This is **the statement of Rabbi Meir. Rabbi Yehuda says:** If rain fell **before midday,**[N] they need **not complete** their fast; however, if it rains **after midday, they** must **complete** their fast.

רַבִּי יוֹסֵי אוֹמֵר: קוֹדֶם ט' שָׁעוֹת, לֹא יַשְׁלִימוּ. לְאַחַר תֵּשַׁע שָׁעוֹת, יַשְׁלִימוּ, שֶׁכֵּן מָצִינוּ בְּאַחְאָב מֶלֶךְ יִשְׂרָאֵל שֶׁהִתְעַנָּה מִתֵּשַׁע שָׁעוֹת וּלְמַעְלָה, שֶׁנֶּאֱמַר: "הֲרָאִיתָ כִּי נִכְנַע אַחְאָב" וגו'.

Rabbi Yosei says: If rain falls **before the ninth hour,** three hours into the afternoon, they need **not complete** their fast; if it rains **after the ninth hour** of the day, they must **complete** their fast, **as we found with regard to Ahab,**[N] **king of Israel, who fasted from the ninth hour and onward,** as it **is stated:** "And it came to pass, when Ahab heard these words, that he rent his clothes, and put sackcloth upon his flesh, and fasted, and lay in sackcloth, and went softly. And the word of the Lord came to Elijah the Tishbite saying: **Do you see how Ahab humbles himself before Me?"** (I Kings 21:27–29). According to tradition, this occurred in the ninth hour.

רַבִּי יְהוּדָה נְשִׂיאָה גְּזַר תַּעֲנִיתָא, וְיָרְדוּ לָהֶם גְּשָׁמִים לְאַחַר הָנֵץ הַחַמָּה. סְבַר לְאַשְׁלוּמִינְהוּ. אֲמַר לֵיהּ רַבִּי אַמִי: קוֹדֶם חֲצוֹת וְאַחַר חֲצוֹת שָׁנִינוּ. שְׁמוּאֵל הַקָּטָן גְּזַר תַּעֲנִיתָא, וְיָרְדוּ לָהֶם גְּשָׁמִים קוֹדֶם הָנֵץ הַחַמָּה. כִּסְבוּרִין הָעָם לוֹמַר שִׁבְחוֹ שֶׁל צִבּוּר הוּא.

Rabbi Yehuda Nesia decreed a fast, and rain fell for them after sunrise. He thought to complete the fast, but **Rabbi Ami said to him** that we learned: **Before noon and after noon,** i.e., the *halakha* is in accordance with the opinion of Rabbi Yehuda. **Shmuel HaKatan decreed a fast, and rain fell for them before sunrise. The people thought to say:** This **is** a sign of **the praiseworthiness of the community,**[N] as we merited rainfall even before we prayed.

אָמַר לָהֶם: אֶמְשׁוֹל לָכֶם מָשָׁל. לְמָה הַדָּבָר דּוֹמֶה? לְעֶבֶד שֶׁמְּבַקֵּשׁ פְּרָס מֵרַבּוֹ. אָמַר לָהֶם: תְּנוּ לוֹ וְאַל אֶשְׁמַע קוֹלוֹ.

He said to them: I will tell you a parable. To what is this matter comparable? To a situation where there is **a slave who requests a reward from his master,** either food or livelihood, **and the** master **says to** his ministers: **Give him** what he asks for **and let me not hear his voice,** as I would rather not have to listen to him. Here, too, evidently God has no desire to hear our prayers.

NOTES

Midday – חֲצוֹת: Rashi explains that according to the opinion of Rabbi Yehuda, the fast must be observed until completion if it rains only after midday, as most people take their main meal at noon. By refraining from that meal, they have determined that it is a fast day. In the Jerusalem Talmud, it is explained that once the greater part of the day has been observed as a fast, it must be completed.

As we found with regard to Ahab – שֶׁכֵּן מָצִינוּ בְּאַחְאָב: The commentaries note that the verse provides no conclusive proof that Ahab did not begin his fast until the end of the ninth hour (Rabbeinu Hananel). However, there is a tradition of the *ge'onim* according to which Naboth's execution, Ahab's entry into Naboth's vineyard, and Elijah's prophecy all took place on the same day. Consequently, it could not have been until late afternoon, the end of the ninth hour, that Ahab rent his clothes and began to fast.

One commentary suggests a novel explanation, according to which the verse: "Do you see how Ahab humbles himself," is not referring to Ahab's repentance for his role in Naboth's execution, but for the episode involving Elijah and the prophets of Baal (I Kings, chapter 18). Elijah caused the rain to fall at the time of the evening sacrifice (I Kings 18:36), after the ninth hour. He subsequently told Ahab to go up and eat and drink (I Kings 18:41), which indicates that until then Ahab had been observing a fast. However, Ahab humbled himself before God, and continued to fast until the end of the day. From this it may be inferred that if a fast is proclaimed on account of drought and it rains after the end of the ninth hour on the day of the fast, the fast must be completed (Rabbi Elyakim).

The people thought to say, this is a sign of the praiseworthiness of the community – כִּסְבוּרִין הָעָם לוֹמַר שִׁבְחוֹ שֶׁל צִבּוּר הוּא: Although the mishna indicates that rain falling on a fast day, whether at the beginning or at the end of the day, is indeed to the community's credit, a pious man such as Shmuel HaKatan would refrain from interpreting rainfall as a sign that God was pleased with His people. Instead, he understood the timing of the rain as an expression of God's displeasure (*HaKotev*).

The Gemara argues that rain can be considered praise to a community only if, as soon as the prayer leader recites: He Who makes the wind blow, a gust of wind indeed blows, and when he recites: And the rain fall, rain immediately begins to fall. Some explains this in light of the verse: "Before they call, I will answer" (Isaiah 65:24). If God is pleased with His people, He will answer their prayers immediately, after they offer Him praise, in this case by means of the phrase: He Who makes the wind blow and the rain fall, even before they actually cry out to Him with their requests (*Keren Ora*).

שׁוּב שְׁמוּאֵל הַקָּטָן גְּזַר תַּעֲנִיתָא, וְיָרְדוּ לָהֶם גְּשָׁמִים לְאַחַר שְׁקִיעַת הַחַמָּה. כִּסְבוּרִים הָעָם לוֹמַר שִׁבְחוֹ שֶׁל צִבּוּר הוּא. אָמַר לָהֶם שְׁמוּאֵל: לֹא שֶׁבַח שֶׁל צִבּוּר הוּא. אֶלָּא אֶמְשׁוֹל לָכֶם מָשָׁל. לְמָה הַדָּבָר דּוֹמֶה? לְעֶבֶד שֶׁמְּבַקֵּשׁ פְּרָס מֵרַבּוֹ, וְאָמַר לָהֶם: הַמְתִּינוּ לוֹ עַד שֶׁיִּתְמַקְמֵק וְיִצְטַעֵר, וְאַחַר כָּךְ תְּנוּ לוֹ.

Again, on another occasion, **Shmuel HaKatan decreed a fast, and rain fell for them after sunset.** Based on his previous response, **the people thought to say:** This **is** a sign of **the praiseworthiness of the community,** as God listened to our prayers all day. **Shmuel** HaKatan **said to them: It is not** a sign of **the praiseworthiness of the community. Rather, I will tell you a parable. To what is this matter comparable? To** a situation where there is **a slave who requests a reward from his master,** and the master **says to** his ministers: **Wait until he pines away and suffers, and afterward give it to him.** Here too, the delay is not to the congregation's credit.

וְלִשְׁמוּאֵל הַקָּטָן, שִׁבְחוֹ שֶׁל צִבּוּר הֵיכִי דָּמֵי? אָמַר: מַשִּׁיב הָרוּחַ, וּנְשַׁב זִיקָא; אָמַר: מוֹרִיד הַגֶּשֶׁם, וַאֲתָא מִיטְרָא.

The Gemara asks: **But** if so, **according to** the opinion of **Shmuel HaKatan,** what is considered **the praiseworthiness of the community; what are the circumstances** in which approval is shown from Heaven? The Gemara explains: When the prayer leader **recites: He Who makes the wind blow, and the wind blows;** and when **he recites:** And **the rain fall, and rain falls.**

"מַעֲשֶׂה וְגָזְרוּ תַּעֲנִית בְּלוֹד" כו׳. וְנֵימָא הַלֵּל מֵעִיקָּרָא? אַבָּיֵי וְרָבָא דְּאָמְרִי תַּרְוַיְיהוּ: לְפִי שֶׁאֵין אוֹמְרִים הַלֵּל

The mishna teaches: **An incident** occurred in **which** the court **decreed a fast in Lod,** and when rain fell they ate and drank, and afterward they recited *hallel.* The Gemara asks: **And let us recite** ***hallel***[N] **at the outset,** without delay. Why did they first go home and eat? **Abaye and Rava both said: Because one recites** ***hallel***

NOTES

Hallel – הַלֵּל: The term *hallel* in this context refers to Psalm 136. Elsewhere, the term is understood as including other psalms, or perhaps it even refers to the regular *hallel* recited on the Festivals, Psalms 113–118 (see *Pesaḥim* 118a; Jerusalem Talmud, *Ta'anit* 3:11). Rashi explains that Psalm 136 was recited after the long-awaited rain because it includes the verse: "Who gives food to all flesh, for His mercy endures forever" (Psalms 136:25). Other commentaries accept the opinion that *hallel* starts with Psalm 135. They explain that this chapter was recited because it includes this verse: "Who causes the vapors to ascend from the ends of the earth; He makes lightnings for the rain; He brings forth the wind out of his treasuries" (Psalms 135:7; see Rabbeinu Ḥananel).

Perek **III**
Daf **26** Amud **a**

אֶלָּא עַל נֶפֶשׁ שְׂבֵעָה וְכָרֵס מְלֵאָה. אִינִי? וְהָא רַב פָּפָּא אִיקְּלַע לְבֵי כְּנִישְׁתָּא דַּאֲבִי גוֹבָר, וּגְזַר תַּעֲנִית, וְיָרְדוּ לָהֶם גְּשָׁמִים עַד חֲצוֹת, וְאָמַר הַלֵּל, וְאַחַר כָּךְ אָכְלוּ וְשָׁתוּ! שָׁאנֵי בְּנֵי מְחוֹזָא, דִּשְׁכִיחִי בְּהוּ שִׁכְרוּת.

only on a satisfied soul[N] **and a full stomach.** Consequently, it is preferable to return home to eat and drink so as to recite *hallel* in the proper frame of mind. The Gemara asks: **Is that so? But Rav Pappa happened** to come to **the synagogue of Avi Govar**[B] in Meḥoza, **and he decreed a fast, and rain fell for them before midday, and** yet **he recited** ***hallel*** immediately, **and** only afterward **they ate and drank.** The Gemara explains: **The inhabitants of** the city of **Meḥoza are different, as drunkenness is common among them.** Had Rav Pappa told them to go home to eat and drink, they would have become drunk and been unable to pray.

הדרן עלך סדר תעניות אלו

NOTES

On a satisfied soul – עַל נֶפֶשׁ שְׂבֵעָה: Rashi explains that *hallel* includes the verse "Who gives food to all flesh, for His mercy endures forever" (Psalms 136:25), and therefore it is improper for a hungry person to recite it.

BACKGROUND

The synagogue of Avi Govar – בֵּי כְּנִישְׁתָּא דַּאֲבִי גוֹבָר: This synagogue was probably located in a small settlement, perhaps in a suburb of Meḥoza, between that city and the town of Mavarkhata. The place itself might have been named after the founder of this synagogue. The synagogue of Avi Govar is mentioned in several points in the Gemara as a location visited by a number of great *amora'im* in different generations. Apparently it served as an important center in that region.

Summary of **Perek III**

It is appropriate to fast over any event that is likely to have serious adverse effects on the livelihood, health, or well-being of the Jewish people. If the danger is immediate, the fast day is decreed as near as possible to the event in question. However, it is not necessary for the event to pose an urgent threat. Even a potential hazard, e.g., an army that is merely passing through the country, is worthy of a fast.

The general principle is that if a misfortune is limited to a certain place, only the residents of that location fast, while Jews living elsewhere pray for them without fasting. However, if the disaster is liable to spread, such as an infectious disease and the like, all those living in that country or region must fast as well. An exception to this rule is a calamity visited upon Eretz Yisrael. In this case, all Jews everywhere must fast, as Eretz Yisrael is considered the center and heart of the nation.

The early commentaries call this chapter: The Chapter of the Pious, as although it contains several halakhic discussions, it is mainly a collection of stories of righteous people who prayed in times of trouble and of how their prayers were answered. These narratives serve an instructional purpose by providing a vivid demonstration that God indeed answers the prayers and requests of the worthy. They also suggest a broad definition of the righteous individual, as they indicate that the identity of the truly righteous is not always known. Furthermore, these narratives teach that anyone who exerts himself in good deeds should pray for assistance on behalf of the community, even if he is not recognized as an especially sacred individual.

Introduction to **Perek IV**

And I will turn your feasts into mourning, and all your songs into lamentation; and I will bring up sackcloth upon all loins, and baldness upon every head; and I will make it as the mourning for an only son, and its end as a bitter day.

(Amos 8:10)

Thus says the Lord of hosts: The fast of the fourth month, and the fast of the fifth, and the fast of the seventh, and the fast of the tenth, shall be to the house of Judah joy and gladness, and cheerful Festivals; therefore love truth and peace.

(Zechariah 8:19)

The fasts discussed in the tractate up until this chapter are those decreed upon the public due to a calamity. These fasts, which include fasts for rain, do not occur on fixed dates but are declared in response to a catastrophe that afflicts the Jewish people. However, there is another category of fast days, those that occur on fixed dates every year.

The fasts discussed in this chapter are of two very different types. One was observed by the members of the non-priestly watch when the Temple was standing. These fasts were not decreed in response to an event that might have occurred at the time, but were designed for general supplications for the continuation of normal life, for health, and for success. This chapter discusses the *halakhot* of these fasts, the special prayers for the non-priestly watches, and the relationship between them and the various holidays throughout the year.

An entirely different type of fast day also discussed in this chapter is the memorial fast, which consists of fasts on dates already decreed following the destruction of the First Temple and reestablished after the Second Temple was destroyed. There are four standard fast days that commemorate general calamities that befell the Jewish people, especially the destruction of the Temple, an event that brought many other catastrophes upon the Jewish people in its wake.

The clarification of the *halakhot* of these memorial days, which are not merely fasts but days of national mourning, especially the Ninth of Av, is the main topic of this chapter. Incidental to this issue, the chapter also addresses the customs of other special dates of the year which were celebrated as days of rejoicing when the Temple was in existence.

מתני׳ בִּשְׁלֹשָׁה פְּרָקִים בַּשָּׁנָה כֹּהֲנִים נוֹשְׂאִין אֶת כַּפֵּיהֶן אַרְבַּע פְּעָמִים בַּיּוֹם, בַּשַּׁחֲרִית, בַּמּוּסָף, בַּמִּנְחָה, וּבִנְעִילַת שְׁעָרִים: בְּתַעֲנִיּוֹת, וּבְמַעֲמָדוֹת, וּבְיוֹם הַכִּפּוּרִים.

MISHNA **At three times in the year priests raise their hands**[H] to recite the Priestly Benediction **four times in** a single **day, in the morning prayer, in the additional prayer, in the afternoon prayer, and** in the evening **in the closing of the gates,**[N] i.e., the *ne'ila* prayer. And these are the three times: **During** communal **fasts**[N] held due to lack of rain, on which the closing prayer is recited; **and during non-priestly watches** [*ma'amadot*],[H] when the Israelite members of the guard parallel to the priestly watch come and read the act of Creation from the Torah, as explained below; **and on Yom Kippur.**

אֵלּוּ הֵן מַעֲמָדוֹת: לְפִי שֶׁנֶּאֱמַר: ״צַו אֶת בְּנֵי יִשְׂרָאֵל. אֶת קָרְבָּנִי, לַחְמִי״. וְכִי הֵיאַךְ קָרְבָּנוֹ שֶׁל אָדָם קָרֵב וְהוּא אֵינוֹ עוֹמֵד עַל גַּבָּיו?

These are the **non-priestly watches: Since it is stated: "Command**[N] **the children of Israel** and say to them: **My offering of food,** which is presented to Me made by a fire, of a sweet savor to Me, you shall guard the sacrifice to Me in its due season" (Numbers 28:2), this verse teaches that the daily offering was a communal obligation that applied to every member of the Jewish people. The mishna asks: **But how can a person's offering**[N] **be sacrificed when he is not standing next to it?**

הִתְקִינוּ נְבִיאִים הָרִאשׁוֹנִים עֶשְׂרִים וְאַרְבָּעָה מִשְׁמָרוֹת. עַל כָּל מִשְׁמָר וּמִשְׁמָר הָיָה מַעֲמָד בִּירוּשָׁלַיִם שֶׁל כֹּהֲנִים, שֶׁל לְוִיִּם, וְשֶׁל יִשְׂרְאֵלִים.

The mishna explains: Since it is impossible for the entire nation to be present in Jerusalem when the daily offering is brought, **the early prophets,** Samuel and David, **instituted** the division of the priests into **twenty-four priestly watches,** each of which served for approximately one week, twice per year. **For each and every priestly watch there was** a corresponding **non-priestly watch in Jerusalem of priests,**[N] **Levites, and Israelites** who would stand by the communal offerings for that day to represent the community.[N]

HALAKHA

Raise their hands – נוֹשְׂאִין אֶת כַּפֵּיהֶן: On a day that includes the closing prayer service, the priests raise their hands to recite the Priestly Benediction only three times, in the morning service, the additional service, and in the closing prayer service (*Shulḥan Arukh, Oraḥ Ḥayyim* 129:1).

Non-priestly watches – מַעֲמָדוֹת: One who brings an offering is required to be present in the Temple when it is sacrificed. Since the communal offerings are brought by the entire Jewish people, but the whole nation cannot be present in the Temple each time those offerings are sacrificed, the early prophets instituted that worthy and sin-fearing people should be selected to represent the nation at the time of the sacrifice. To that end they divided the entire nation into twenty-four watches corresponding to the twenty-four watches of priests and Levites (Rambam *Sefer Avoda, Hilkhot Kelei HaMikdash* 6:1).

NOTES

And in the closing of the gates – וּבִנְעִילַת שְׁעָרִים: In the Jerusalem Talmud two explanations are suggested for this name. Rabbi Yoḥanan states that it refers to the daily closing of the Temple gates, which was performed toward the end of the day. Rav maintains that it refers to the closing at sunset of the heavenly gates, which hide the sun from view until the following morning.

During fasts – בְּתַעֲנִיּוֹת: The mishna is referring to communal fast days proclaimed in times of drought or in the face of other impending calamities, as there is no closing prayer on the fixed fasts that commemorate national calamities. The early commentaries disagree as to whether or not the closing prayer service is conducted on communal fasts proclaimed outside Eretz Yisrael (see Ramban, citing Ra'avad; see Ritva).

Since it is stated, Command – לְפִי שֶׁנֶּאֱמַר צַו: The mishna is apparently claiming that as the verse indicates that the daily offering is brought by the community, the entire nation should ideally be present in the Temple when it is sacrificed. However, as this is a practical impossibility, the system of non-priestly watches was established so that at least representatives of the nation would be present. Some commentaries suggest that the verse itself alludes to the watches, as the continuation of the verse reads: "You shall guard the sacrifice to Me," which indicates that watches must be set up to stand guard around the service and submit prayers that the offering be accepted by God (*Petaḥ Einayim*; see *Tosefot Yom Tov*, whose text of the mishna includes the end of the verse).

But how can a person's offering – וְכִי הֵיאַךְ קָרְבָּנוֹ שֶׁל אָדָם: The later commentaries ask: Why should the entire nation be present in the Temple when the daily offering is sacrificed? Granted, one must be present when his own individual sacrifice is sacrificed, as he must place his hands on the head of the animal before it is slaughtered. However, the daily offering, like most communal offerings, does not require that ceremony. Some suggest that as one who brings an offering is supposed to view himself as though he himself were being sacrificed on the altar, it stands to reason that he should be present in the Temple when any offering that represents him is sacrificed (*Iyyun Ya'akov*).

There was a non-priestly watch in Jerusalem of priests, Levites, and Israelites – הָיָה מַעֲמָד בִּירוּשָׁלַיִם שֶׁל כֹּהֲנִים, שֶׁל לְוִיִּם, וְשֶׁל יִשְׂרְאֵלִים: According to the plain meaning of this sentence, the watch included priests, Levites, and regular Israelites, and several of Rashi's comments on the mishna and Gemara indicate as much. However, others maintain that the watches were comprised exclusively of Israelites (Ritva). They explain that representatives of all three groups were found in Jerusalem when the offerings were sacrificed: Priests to perform the actual sacrificial service, Levites to provide the musical accompaniment, and Israelites who were present when the communal offerings were brought.

Of priests, Levites, and Israelites to represent the community – שֶׁל כֹּהֲנִים, שֶׁל לְוִיִּם, וְשֶׁל יִשְׂרְאֵלִים: The early commentaries ask: Granted, the representatives of the people must be present in the Temple when the communal offerings are sacrificed, but why must ordinary Israelites be included in the watches? Let the priests and Levites, who are in any case in the Temple performing the sacrificial service, also serve as the representatives of the rest of the nation. Some commentaries answer that with regard to certain matters, each tribe is treated as a separate community. Consequently, the members of the tribe of Levi cannot represent the entire nation, but must be joined by representatives of each of the other tribes (*Tosefot HaRosh*, cited by *Petaḥ Einayim*).

הִגִּיעַ זְמַן הַמִּשְׁמָר לַעֲלוֹת, כֹּהֲנִים וּלְוִיִּם עוֹלִים לִירוּשָׁלַיִם, וְיִשְׂרָאֵל שֶׁבְּאוֹתוֹ מִשְׁמָר מִתְכַּנְּסִין לְעָרֵיהֶן וְקוֹרִאין בְּמַעֲשֵׂה בְרֵאשִׁית. וְאַנְשֵׁי הַמַּעֲמָד הָיוּ מִתְעַנִּין אַרְבָּעָה יָמִים בַּשָּׁבוּעַ מִיּוֹם שֵׁנִי וְעַד יוֹם חֲמִישִׁי. וְלֹא הָיוּ מִתְעַנִּין עֶרֶב שַׁבָּת, מִפְּנֵי כְבוֹד הַשַּׁבָּת, וְלֹא בְּאֶחָד בַּשַּׁבָּת, כְּדֵי שֶׁלֹּא יֵצְאוּ מִמְּנוּחָה וָעוֹנֶג לִיגִיעָה וְתַעֲנִית וְיָמוּתוּ.

When the **time arrived** for the members of a certain **priestly watch to ascend,**[H] the **priests and Levites** of that watch would **ascend to Jerusalem** to perform the Temple service. **And** as for **the Israelites** assigned **to that priestly watch,** some of them went up to Jerusalem, while the rest of them **assembled in their towns**[N] **and read the act of Creation. And the members of the non-priestly watch,**[N] who represented the entire community that week, **would fast four days a week, from Monday until Thursday. And they would not fast on Shabbat eve, in deference to Shabbat,** as they did not wish to start Shabbat while fasting. **And** they did **not** fast on Sunday, **so as not to go from rest and delight** immediately **to exertion and fasting,** and run the risk that they might **die** as a result of the abrupt change.

בַּיּוֹם הָרִאשׁוֹן: ״בְּרֵאשִׁית״ וִ״יהִי רָקִיעַ״. בַּשֵּׁנִי, ״יְהִי רָקִיעַ״ וְ״יִקָּווּ הַמַּיִם״. בַּשְּׁלִישִׁי, ״יִקָּווּ הַמַּיִם״ וִ״יהִי מְאֹרֹת״. בָּרְבִיעִי, ״יְהִי מְאֹרֹת״ וְ״יִשְׁרְצוּ הַמַּיִם״. בַּחֲמִישִׁי, ״יִשְׁרְצוּ הַמַּיִם״ וְ״תוֹצֵא הָאָרֶץ״. בַּשִּׁשִּׁי, ״תּוֹצֵא הָאָרֶץ״ ״וַיְכֻלּוּ הַשָּׁמַיִם״.

Which portions of the Torah would the members of the non-priestly watch read on each day? **On Sunday** they would read the portions starting with: **"In the beginning"** and **"Let there be a firmament"** (Genesis 1:1–8). **On Monday** they would read: **"Let there be a firmament"** and **"Let the waters be gathered"** (Genesis 1:9–13). **On Tuesday** they would read: **"Let the waters be gathered"** and **"Let there be lights"** (Genesis 1:14–19). **On Wednesday: "Let there be lights"** and **"Let the waters swarm"** (Genesis 1:20–23). **On Thursday: "Let the waters swarm"** and **"Let the earth bring forth"** (Genesis 1:24–31). **On Friday: "Let the earth bring forth"** and **"And the heaven** and the earth **were finished"** (Genesis 2:1–3).

פָּרָשָׁה גְּדוֹלָה קוֹרִין אוֹתָהּ בִּשְׁנַיִם, וְהַקְּטַנָּה בְּיָחִיד, בַּשַּׁחֲרִית וּבַמּוּסָף. וּבַמִּנְחָה נִכְנָסִין וְקוֹרִין עַל פִּיהֶן כְּקוֹרִין אֶת שְׁמַע. עֶרֶב שַׁבָּת בַּמִּנְחָה לֹא הָיוּ נִכְנָסִין, מִפְּנֵי כְבוֹד הַשַּׁבָּת.

A long passage, consisting of six verses or more, **is read by two**[H] people, **and a short** passage is read **by one,** as one cannot read fewer than three verses from the Torah together. They read from the Torah **in the morning prayer and in the additional prayer. In the afternoon prayer** the members of the non-priestly watch **enter**[N] the synagogue **and read** the daily portion **by heart, just as one recites *Shema*** every day. On **Shabbat eve at the afternoon prayer, they would not enter** the synagogue for the communal Torah readings, **in deference to Shabbat.**

כׇּל יוֹם שֶׁיֵּשׁ בּוֹ הַלֵּל, אֵין מַעֲמָד בַּשַּׁחֲרִית. קׇרְבַּן מוּסָף, אֵין בַּנְּעִילָה. קׇרְבַּן עֵצִים, אֵין בַּמִּנְחָה. דִּבְרֵי רַבִּי עֲקִיבָא.

The mishna states a principle: On **any day that has** the recitation of ***hallel,***[H] but on which the additional offering was not sacrificed, e.g., Hanukkah, **there is no** reading of the Torah by the **non-priestly watch in the morning prayer.** On days that have both *hallel* and **an additional offering,** such as Festivals, the non-priestly watch would also **not** read from the Torah **at the closing prayer.**[N] When **a wood offering**[N] was brought, as explained below, there was **no** non-priestly watch **in the afternoon prayer.** This is **the statement of Rabbi Akiva.**

HALAKHA

When the time arrived for a priestly watch to ascend – הִגִּיעַ זְמַן הַמִּשְׁמָר לַעֲלוֹת: Each week the members of the appointed non-priestly watch would assemble together. Those who lived in or near Jerusalem would enter the Temple together with the watch of priests and Levites who were performing the Temple service that week. Those who lived further away would assemble in their local synagogues. All members of the watch would fast during their week of service, from Monday through Thursday (Rambam *Sefer Avoda, Hilkhot Kelei HaMikdash* 6:2–3).

A long passage is read by two – פָּרָשָׁה גְּדוֹלָה קוֹרִין אוֹתָהּ בִּשְׁנַיִם: The members of the non-priestly watch would read the chapter of the Torah that deals with the Creation. On each day of the week they would read the sections that describe the creation of that day of the week and of the following day. The longer of the two sections was read by two people, while the shorter was read by a single individual. The Torah portion that was read from a scroll in the morning service was read once again from a scroll in the additional service. However, in the afternoon service it was recited by heart (Rambam *Sefer Avoda, Hilkhot Kelei HaMikdash* 6:6–7).

Any day that has *hallel* – כׇּל יוֹם שֶׁיֵּשׁ בּוֹ הַלֵּל: On the eight days of Hanukkah, when *hallel* was recited, there was no non-priestly watch in the morning service. On any day on which an additional offering was brought, there was no watch in the additional service or in the afternoon service, but there was a watch in the morning service and the closing prayer service. On any day on which a wood offering was brought, there was no watch in the closing prayer service, in accordance with the opinion of ben Azzai (Rambam *Sefer Avoda, Hilkhot Kelei HaMikdash* 6:8).

NOTES

There was a non-priestly watch in Jerusalem…and the Israelites assigned to that priestly watch assembled in their towns – הָיָה מַעֲמָד בִּירוּשָׁלַיִם...וְיִשְׂרָאֵל שֶׁבְּאוֹתוֹ מִשְׁמָר מִתְכַּנְּסִין לְעָרֵיהֶן: Some commentaries maintain that those members of the watch who lived in or near Jerusalem would go to the Temple together with the priests and the Levites, while those who resided farther away would assemble in the synagogues in their hometowns (Rambam *Sefer Avoda, Hilkhot Kelei HaMikdash* 6:2). Others suggest that those members of the watch who were able to make the journey to Jerusalem would do so, while the older members of the watch, for whom traveling was difficult, would assemble in their local synagogues (Meiri, citing Ra'avad). Yet others state that some members of each watch were stationed permanently in Jerusalem, so they could enter the Temple and represent the nation when the communal offerings were brought. The rest of the watch remained in their hometowns and assembled in their local synagogues (Rid).

And the members of the non-priestly watch – וְאַנְשֵׁי הַמַּעֲמָד: Some commentaries maintain that although the system of watches included all priests, it did not incorporate all Israelites. Only the most pious and sin-fearing Israelites were chosen to represent the rest of the nation (Rambam).

Enter – נִכְנָסִין: Although the mishna states only that the members of the watch would read the Torah section that describes the act of Creation, it is clear from other sources that they would also read passages that deal with the offerings. Likewise, they would recite special prayers and supplications each time they entered the synagogue. The term: Non-priestly watch, refers not only to the Israelites who served as representatives of the entire nation at the communal offerings, but also to their assembly in the synagogue for the special Torah readings, prayers, and supplications (Rambam *Sefer Avoda, Hilkhot Kelei HaMikdash* 6:6).

On days that have an additional offering, the non-priestly watch would not read at the closing prayer – קׇרְבַּן מוּסָף אֵין בַּנְּעִילָה: As explained in the Gemara below (28b), on days when there was an additional offering, there was no watch in the additional service. The early commentaries note that this apparently contradicts the statement of the mishna that the members of the watch read the story of the Creation in the morning service and again in the additional service.

Rashi and many others explain that on those days when there was an additional offering, there was no watch in Jerusalem for the additional service, as the members of the watch who were in Jerusalem were involved in the sacrificial service in the Temple and did not have the time to conduct the assembly. However, outside Jerusalem there was indeed a watch in the additional service.

Others distinguish between the special supplications offered at the assembly of the watch and the Torah reading they conducted. On those days when there was an additional offering, no special supplications were recited in the additional service, neither in Jerusalem nor outside the capital. Conversely, the act of Creation was indeed read in the additional service even on those days, including in Jerusalem.

Some authorities rule that on each day of the week the members of the watch conducted a special additional service, which was inserted between the morning and the afternoon services. During that additional service, the special Torah reading for the assemblies of the watch was read. The mishna is simply stating that when an additional offering was brought, there were no special prayers of the watch in the closing prayer service, and certainly not in the ordinary additional service conducted on those days (Rambam *Sefer Avoda, Hilkhot Kelei HaMikdash* 6:4).

Wood offering – קׇרְבַּן עֵצִים: In the early years of the Second Temple there was not enough wood to burn the offerings on the altar, and it had to be supplied by various families on a voluntary basis (see 28a). Later, to commemorate their generosity, the day on which each of those families had brought wood for the altar was declared a private holiday for them. They would bring wood for the altar, and it was prohibited for them to fast or to recite eulogies on their special day. According to many early commentaries, the term wood offering refers to the wood itself, which was burned separately on the altar (see Ritva). Others write that it refers to the voluntary burnt-offerings that those families would bring to the Temple together with the wood (Rambam *Sefer Avoda, Hilkhot Kelei HaMikdash* 6:9).

אָמַר לוֹ בֶּן עַזַּאי: כָּךְ הָיָה רַבִּי יְהוֹשֻׁעַ שׁוֹנֶה: קָרְבַּן מוּסָף, אֵין בַּמִּנְחָה. קָרְבַּן עֵצִים, אֵין בַּנְּעִילָה. חָזַר רַבִּי עֲקִיבָא לִהְיוֹת שׁוֹנֶה כְּבֶן עַזַּאי.

Ben Azzai said to Rabbi Akiva that **this is how Rabbi Yehoshua would teach** this *halakha*: On days when **an additional offering** was sacrificed, there was **no** non-priestly watch **in the afternoon prayer.** When **a wood offering** was brought, there was **no** non-priestly watch **in the closing prayer.** Upon hearing this, **Rabbi Akiva retracted** his ruling and began **to teach in accordance with** the opinion of **ben Azzai.**

זְמַן עֲצֵי כֹהֲנִים וְהָעָם תִּשְׁעָה: בְּאֶחָד בְּנִיסָן, בְּנֵי אָרַח בֶּן יְהוּדָה; בְּעֶשְׂרִים בְּתַמּוּז, בְּנֵי דָוִד בֶּן יְהוּדָה; בַּחֲמִשָּׁה בְּאָב, בְּנֵי פַּרְעוֹשׁ בֶּן יְהוּדָה; בְּשִׁבְעָה בּוֹ, בְּנֵי יוֹנָדָב בֶּן רֵכָב; בַּעֲשָׂרָה בּוֹ, בְּנֵי סְנָאָה בֶּן בִּנְיָמִין; בַּחֲמִשָּׁה עָשָׂר בּוֹ, בְּנֵי זַתּוּא בֶּן יְהוּדָה,

The mishna details the **times** for **the wood** offering **of priests and the people.** These were private holidays specific to certain families, on which their members would volunteer a wood offering for the altar. There were **nine** such days and families: **On the first of Nisan, the descendants of Araḥ ben Yehuda; on the twentieth of Tammuz, the descendants of David ben Yehuda; on the fifth of Av, the descendants of Parosh ben Yehuda; on the seventh of Av, the descendants of Jonadab ben Rechab; on the tenth of Av, the descendants of Sena'a ben Binyamin; on the fifteenth of Av, the descendants of Zattu ben Yehuda.**

וְעִמָּהֶם כֹּהֲנִים וּלְוִיִּם, וְכָל מִי שֶׁטָּעָה בְּשִׁבְטוֹ, וּבְנֵי גּוֹנְבֵי עֱלִי וּבְנֵי קוֹצְעֵי קְצִיעוֹת;

And included **with** this group of Zattu ben Yehuda's descendants **were** other **priests; and Levites; and anyone who erred with regard to his tribe,**[N] i.e., Israelites who did not know which tribe they were from, **and the descendants of those who deceived** the authorities **with a pestle; and the descendants of those who packed dried figs.** These last groups and their descriptions are explained in the Gemara.

בְּעֶשְׂרִים בּוֹ, בְּנֵי פַּחַת מוֹאָב בֶּן יְהוּדָה; בְּעֶשְׂרִים בֶּאֱלוּל, בְּנֵי עָדִין בֶּן יְהוּדָה; בְּאֶחָד בְּטֵבֵת, שָׁבוּ בְּנֵי פַּרְעוֹשׁ שְׁנִיָּה. בְּאֶחָד בְּטֵבֵת לֹא הָיָה בּוֹ מַעֲמָד, שֶׁהָיָה בּוֹ הַלֵּל וְקָרְבַּן מוּסָף וְקָרְבַּן עֵצִים.

The mishna resumes its list. **On the twentieth of** Av, **the descendants of Paḥat Moav ben Yehuda; on the twentieth of Elul, the descendants of Adin ben Yehuda; on the first of Tevet, the descendants of Parosh returned** to bring wood for **a second** time; likewise **on the first of Tevet, there was no non-priestly watch,** as it is Hanukkah, **on which *hallel* is** recited, **and** it is the New Moon, on which **an additional offering** is sacrificed, **and** there was also **a wood offering.**

חֲמִשָּׁה דְּבָרִים אֵירְעוּ אֶת אֲבוֹתֵינוּ בְּשִׁבְעָה עָשָׂר בְּתַמּוּז, וַחֲמִשָּׁה בְּתִשְׁעָה בְּאָב. בְּשִׁבְעָה עָשָׂר בְּתַמּוּז

The mishna discusses the five major communal fast days. **Five** calamitous **matters occurred to our forefathers on the seventeenth of Tammuz, and five** other disasters happened **on the Ninth of Av. On the seventeenth of Tammuz**

NOTES

And anyone who erred with regard to his tribe – **וְכָל מִי שֶׁטָּעָה בְּשִׁבְטוֹ:** The fact that the fifteenth of Av was the day on which a large proportion of the Jewish people brought their wood offerings was one more reason, in addition to the justifications listed on 30b–31a, for the celebration of that day as an especially joyous holiday.

נִשְׁתַּבְּרוּ הַלּוּחוֹת, וּבָטֵל הַתָּמִיד, וְהוּבְקְעָה הָעִיר, וְשָׂרַף אַפּוֹסְטְמוֹס אֶת הַתּוֹרָה וְהֶעֱמִיד צֶלֶם בַּהֵיכָל.

the tablets were broken by Moses when he saw that the Jews had made the golden calf; **the daily offering was nullified** by the Roman authorities and was never sacrificed again; **the city** walls of Jerusalem **were breached;** the general **Apostemos**[L] publicly **burned a Torah scroll; and** Manasseh **placed an idol in the Sanctuary.**

בְּתִשְׁעָה בְּאָב נִגְזַר עַל אֲבוֹתֵינוּ שֶׁלֹּא יִכָּנְסוּ לָאָרֶץ, וְחָרַב הַבַּיִת בָּרִאשׁוֹנָה וּבַשְּׁנִיָּה, וְנִלְכְּדָה בֵּיתָר, וְנֶחְרְשָׁה הָעִיר.

On the Ninth of Av it was decreed upon our ancestors that they would all die in the wilderness and **not enter Eretz** Yisrael; **and the Temple was destroyed the first time,** in the days of Nebuchadnezzar, **and the second time,** by the Romans; **and Beitar was captured; and the city** of Jerusalem **was plowed,** as a sign that it would never be rebuilt.

LANGUAGE

Apostemos – אַפּוֹסְטְמוֹס: Postumus in Latin; this is a name given to someone born after his father's death. Several Roman generals were called by this name, but the date and background of this burning of a Torah scroll are unknown.

HALAKHA

From when Av begins – **מִשֶּׁנִּכְנַס אָב**: When the month of Av begins, acts of rejoicing are reduced (*Shulḥan Arukh, Oraḥ Ḥayyim* 551:1).

The week in which the Ninth of Av occurs – **שַׁבָּת שֶׁחָל תִּשְׁעָה בְּאָב לִהְיוֹת בְּתוֹכָהּ**: During the week of the Ninth of Av it is prohibited to cut one's hair or to do laundry. Ashkenazic communities are stringent in this regard from the beginning of the month of Av until after the fast of the Ninth of Av (Rema). Conversely, the Sephardic custom follows the opinion of Rabbi Yosef Karo that these prohibitions need be observed only during the week of the Ninth of Av itself (*Shulḥan Arukh, Oraḥ Ḥayyim* 551:3).

On the eve of the Ninth of Av – **עֶרֶב תִּשְׁעָה בְּאָב**: On the day before the Ninth of Av, one may not eat meat or drink wine during the last meal before the fast, if that meal is taken after midday. This *halakha* is accepted even by those authorities who maintain that it is permitted to partake of meat and wine during the first nine days of Av. Additionally, one may not eat two cooked dishes during that meal (*Shulḥan Arukh, Oraḥ Ḥayyim* 552:1).

מִשֶּׁנִּכְנָס אָב, מְמַעֲטִין בְּשִׂמְחָה. שַׁבָּת שֶׁחָל תִּשְׁעָה בְּאָב לִהְיוֹת בְּתוֹכָהּ, אָסוּר מִלְּסַפֵּר וּמִלְּכַבֵּס. וּבַחֲמִישִׁי מוּתָּרִין מִפְּנֵי כְּבוֹד הַשַּׁבָּת. עֶרֶב תִּשְׁעָה בְּאָב, לֹא יֹאכַל אָדָם שְׁנֵי תַבְשִׁילִין. לֹא יֹאכַל בָּשָׂר וְלֹא יִשְׁתֶּה יַיִן. רַבָּן שִׁמְעוֹן בֶּן גַּמְלִיאֵל אוֹמֵר: יְשַׁנֶּה. רַבִּי יְהוּדָה מְחַיֵּיב בִּכְפִיַּית הַמִּטָּה, וְלֹא הוֹדוּ לוֹ חֲכָמִים.

Not only does one fast on the Ninth of Av, but **from when** the month of **Av begins,**[H] **one decreases** acts of **rejoicing.** During **the week in which the Ninth of Av occurs,**[H] **it is prohibited to cut one's hair and to launder** clothes, **but** if the Ninth of Av occurs on a Friday, **on Thursday** these actions **are permitted in deference to Shabbat.** On **the eve of the Ninth of Av**[H] **a person may not eat two cooked dishes** in one meal. Furthermore, one may **neither eat meat nor drink wine. Rabban Shimon ben Gamliel says:** One must **adjust** and decrease the amount he eats. **Rabbi Yehuda obligates one to overturn the bed** and sleep on the floor like one in a state of mourning, **but the Rabbis did not agree with him.**

אָמַר רַבָּן שִׁמְעוֹן בֶּן גַּמְלִיאֵל: לֹא הָיוּ יָמִים טוֹבִים לְיִשְׂרָאֵל כַּחֲמִשָּׁה עָשָׂר בְּאָב וּכְיוֹם הַכִּפּוּרִים, שֶׁבָּהֶן בְּנוֹת יְרוּשָׁלַיִם יוֹצְאוֹת בִּכְלֵי לָבָן שְׁאוּלִין, שֶׁלֹּא לְבַיֵּישׁ אֶת מִי שֶׁאֵין לוֹ. כָּל הַכֵּלִים טְעוּנִין טְבִילָה.

The mishna cites a passage that concludes its discussion of the month of Av, as well as the entire tractate of *Ta'anit*, on a positive note. **Rabban Shimon ben Gamliel said: There were no days as joyous for the Jewish people as the fifteenth of Av and as Yom Kippur, as on them the daughters of Jerusalem would go out in white clothes,** which each woman **borrowed** from another. Why were they borrowed? They did this **so as not to embarrass one who did not have** her own white garments. **All the garments** that the women borrowed **require immersion,** as those who previously wore them might have been ritually impure.

וּבְנוֹת יְרוּשָׁלַיִם יוֹצְאוֹת וְחוֹלוֹת בַּכְּרָמִים. וּמֶה הָיוּ אוֹמְרוֹת? בָּחוּר! שָׂא נָא עֵינֶיךָ וּרְאֵה מָה אַתָּה בּוֹרֵר לָךְ. אַל תִּתֵּן עֵינֶיךָ בַּנּוֹי. תֵּן עֵינֶיךָ בַּמִּשְׁפָּחָה. ״שֶׁקֶר הַחֵן, וְהֶבֶל הַיֹּפִי, אִשָּׁה יִרְאַת ה׳ הִיא תִתְהַלָּל״. וְאוֹמֵר: ״תְּנוּ לָהּ מִפְּרִי יָדֶיהָ, וִיהַלְלוּהָ בַשְּׁעָרִים מַעֲשֶׂיהָ״.

And the daughters of Jerusalem would go out and dance in the vineyards. And what would they say?[N] **Young man, please lift up your eyes and see what you choose for yourself** for a wife. **Do not set your eyes toward beauty, but set your eyes toward** a good **family,** as the verse states: **"Grace is deceitful and beauty is vain, but a woman who fears the Lord, she shall be praised"** (Proverbs 31:30), **and it** further **says: "Give her the fruit of her hands, and let her works praise her in the gates"** (Proverbs 31:31).

וְכֵן הוּא אוֹמֵר: ״צְאֶינָה וּרְאֶינָה, בְּנוֹת צִיּוֹן, בַּמֶּלֶךְ שְׁלֹמֹה בַּעֲטָרָה שֶׁעִטְּרָה לוֹ אִמּוֹ בְּיוֹם חֲתֻנָּתוֹ, וּבְיוֹם שִׂמְחַת לִבּוֹ״. ״בְּיוֹם חֲתֻנָּתוֹ״ – זֶה מַתַּן תּוֹרָה. ״וּבְיוֹם שִׂמְחַת לִבּוֹ״ – זֶה בִּנְיַן בֵּית הַמִּקְדָּשׁ, שֶׁיִּבָּנֶה בִּמְהֵרָה בְיָמֵינוּ.

And similarly, it says in another verse: **"Go forth, daughters of Zion, and gaze upon King Solomon, upon the crown with which his mother crowned him on the day of his wedding,**[N] **and on the day of the gladness of his heart"** (Song of Songs 3:11). This verse is explained as an allusion to special days: **"On the day of his wedding"; this is the giving of the Torah** through the second set of tablets on Yom Kippur. The name King Solomon in this context, which also means king of peace, is interpreted as a reference to God. **"And on the day of the gladness of his heart"; this is the building of the Temple, may it be rebuilt speedily in our days.**

NOTES

And what would they say – **וּמֶה הָיוּ אוֹמְרוֹת**: In accordance with a *baraita* cited at the end of the tractate, some commentaries divide the statements, attributed here to the young women dancing in the vineyards, between two sets of speakers. The attractive women would say: Young man, lift up your eyes and see what you are choosing for yourself. The women who were unattractive but of distinguished lineage would say: Do not focus on beauty; rather, set your eyes on lineage (Rambam's Commentary on the Mishna).

On the day of his wedding – **בְּיוֹם חֲתֻנָּתוֹ**: The verse from the Song of Songs is cited here together with a homiletic interpretation to teach that the young women's dances on the fifteenth of Av and on Yom Kippur allude to matters of greater spiritual significance, as the giving of the Torah at Sinai is depicted as a wedding celebration. As for the connection between Yom Kippur and the events described here, the early commentaries prove that the second set of tablets was given to Moses at Sinai on Yom Kippur (see 30b). The connection between the building of the Temple and Yom Kippur is less evident. Some commentaries suggest that there is in fact no connection; rather, the building of the Temple is mentioned here only as an interpretation of the rest of the verse. Others argue that on the day after he received the second tablets, which was the day following Yom Kippur, Moses informed the Jews that they were to begin the construction of the Tabernacle in the desert (*Kol Bo*; *Melekhet Shlomo*). Yet others explain that the dedication of the First Temple in the days of King Solomon took place on Yom Kippur (see *Moed Katan* 9a; Rashi on Rif; Rabbi Ovadya MiBartenura).

גמ׳ ״בִּשְׁלֹשָׁה פְּרָקִים בַּשָּׁנָה כֹּהֲנִים נוֹשְׂאִין אֶת כַּפֵּיהֶם״ כו׳. תַּעֲנִיּוֹת וּמַעֲמָדוֹת מִי אִיכָּא מוּסָף? חַסּוּרֵי מִיחַסְּרָא וְהָכִי קָתָנֵי: בִּשְׁלֹשָׁה פְּרָקִים כֹּהֲנִים נוֹשְׂאִין אֶת כַּפֵּיהֶן כׇּל זְמַן שֶׁמִּתְפַּלְּלִין, וְיֵשׁ מֵהֶן אַרְבָּעָה פְּעָמִים בַּיּוֹם, שַׁחֲרִית, וּמוּסָף, מִנְחָה, וּנְעִילַת שְׁעָרִים. וְאֵלּוּ הֵן שְׁלֹשָׁה פְּרָקִים: תַּעֲנִיּוֹת, וּמַעֲמָדוֹת, וְיוֹם הַכִּפּוּרִים.

GEMARA The mishna taught: **At three times in the year priests raise their hands** to recite the Priestly Benediction four times in a single day: On communal fasts, non-priestly watches, and Yom Kippur. The Gemara asks: How do they recite the Priestly Benediction four times on these days? **Do fast days and** gatherings of **non-priestly watches have an additional prayer?**[N] The Gemara explains that the mishna **is incomplete and is teaching the following: At three times in the year priests raise their hands each time they pray, and on some of these** they bless **four times a day,** in **the morning prayer,** in **the additional prayer,** in **the afternoon prayer, and** in **the closing of the gates,** i.e., the *ne'ila* prayer. **And these are** the **three times:** Communal **fasts, non-priestly watches, and Yom Kippur.**

אָמַר רַב נַחְמָן אָמַר רַבָּה בַּר אֲבוּהּ: זוֹ דִּבְרֵי רַבִּי מֵאִיר, אֲבָל חֲכָמִים אוֹמְרִים: שַׁחֲרִית וּמוּסָף יֵשׁ בָּהֶן נְשִׂיאַת כַּפַּיִם; מִנְחָה וּנְעִילָה אֵין בָּהֶן נְשִׂיאַת כַּפַּיִם.

Rav Naḥman said that **Rabba bar Avuh said: This** mishna **is the statement of Rabbi Meir. However, the Rabbis say: The morning prayer and the additional prayer have** the Priestly Benediction of **the raising of the hands,** whereas **the afternoon prayer and the closing prayer** [*ne'ila*] **do not have the raising of the hands.**

מַאן חֲכָמִים? רַבִּי יְהוּדָה הִיא, דְּתַנְיָא: שַׁחֲרִית וּמוּסָף, מִנְחָה וּנְעִילָה – כּוּלָּן יֵשׁ בָּהֶן נְשִׂיאַת כַּפַּיִם. דִּבְרֵי רַבִּי מֵאִיר. רַבִּי יְהוּדָה אוֹמֵר: שַׁחֲרִית וּמוּסָף יֵשׁ בָּהֶן נְשִׂיאַת כַּפַּיִם; מִנְחָה וּנְעִילָה אֵין בָּהֶן נְשִׂיאַת כַּפַּיִם. רַבִּי יוֹסֵי אוֹמֵר: נְעִילָה יֵשׁ בָּהּ נְשִׂיאַת כַּפַּיִם; מִנְחָה אֵין בָּהּ נְשִׂיאַת כַּפַּיִם.

The Gemara asks: **Who are** these **Rabbis,** who disagree with Rabbi Meir? **It is** the opinion of **Rabbi Yehuda, as it is taught** in a *baraita*: **The morning prayer, the additional prayer, the afternoon prayer, and** *ne'ila* **all have** the Priestly Benediction of **the raising of the hands.** This is **the statement of Rabbi Meir. Rabbi Yehuda says: The morning prayer and the additional prayer have** the raising of the hands, whereas **the afternoon prayer and** *ne'ila* **do not have the raising of the hands. Rabbi Yosei says:** *Ne'ila* **has the raising of the hands; the afternoon prayer does not have the raising of the hands.**

בְּמַאי קָמִיפַּלְגִי? רַבִּי מֵאִיר סָבַר: כׇּל יוֹמָא טַעְמָא מַאי לָא פָּרְשִׂי כָּהֲנֵי יְדַיְיהוּ בְּמִנְחָתָא מִשּׁוּם שִׁכְרוּת. הָאִידָּנָא לֵיכָּא שִׁכְרוּת.

The Gemara asks: **With regard to what** principle do they **disagree? Rabbi Meir maintains: What is the reason** that **priests do not spread their hands** to bless the people **every day in the afternoon prayer?** It is **due to** potential **drunkenness,** as people occasionally become intoxicated during their lunch, and it is prohibited for an inebriated priest to bless. However, **now,** on a fast day, **there is no** concern about **drunkenness,** and therefore the priests may recite the Priestly Benediction even in the afternoon prayer.

רַבִּי יְהוּדָה סָבַר: שַׁחֲרִית וּמוּסָף, דְּכׇל יוֹמָא לָא שְׁכִיחַ שִׁכְרוּת, לָא גָּזְרוּ בְּהוּ רַבָּנַן. מִנְחָה וּנְעִילָה, דְּכׇל יוֹמָא שְׁכִיחָא שִׁכְרוּת, גָּזְרוּ בְּהוּ רַבָּנַן.

Conversely, **Rabbi Yehuda maintains** that with regard to **the morning prayer and the additional prayer, when drunkenness is not common on every** ordinary **day, the Sages did not issue a decree** that the Priestly Benediction be omitted **during them.** However, with regard to **the afternoon prayer and** *ne'ila*, **when drunkenness is not common on every day, the Sages issued a decree** that the Priestly Benediction should not be recited **during them,** despite the fact that intoxication is not a concern on a fast day.

רַבִּי יוֹסֵי סָבַר: מִנְחָה, דְּאִיתַהּ בְּכׇל יוֹמָא, גָּזְרוּ בַּהּ רַבָּנַן. נְעִילָה, דְּלֵיתַהּ בְּכׇל יוֹמָא, לָא גָּזְרוּ בַּהּ רַבָּנַן.

Finally, **Rabbi Yosei maintains** that with regard to **the afternoon prayer, which is** recited **every day, the Sages issued a decree concerning it,** whereas with regard to *ne'ila*, **which is not** recited **every day, the Sages did not issue** and apply their **decree to it,** as there is no concern that people might become confused between *ne'ila* and an afternoon prayer of a regular weekday.

אָמַר רַב יְהוּדָה אָמַר רַב: הֲלָכָה כְּרַבִּי מֵאִיר. וְרַבִּי יוֹחָנָן אָמַר: נָהֲגוּ הָעָם כְּרַבִּי מֵאִיר. וְרָבָא אָמַר: מִנְהָג כְּרַבִּי מֵאִיר.

Rav Yehuda said that **Rav said: The** ***halakha*** **is in accordance with** the opinion of **Rabbi Meir. And Rabbi Yoḥanan said: The people act in accordance with** the opinion of **Rabbi Meir. And Rava said: The custom is in accordance with** the opinion of **Rabbi Meir.**

NOTES

Do fast days and non-priestly watches have an additional prayer – **תַּעֲנִיּוֹת וּמַעֲמָדוֹת מִי אִיכָּא מוּסָף**: The Gemara indicates that the additional prayer is recited on Yom Kippur, but not on communal fast days or by non-priestly watches. However, some commentaries maintain that a special additional service was inserted between the morning service and the afternoon service of the gatherings of non-priestly watches, in which the Priestly Benediction was recited and the act of Creation was read from the Torah (Rambam's Commentary on the Mishna 4:1, 4:4; *Sefer Avoda, Hilkhot Kelei HaMikdash* 6:4). Either the Rambam had a different reading of the text, according to which the Gemara inquired only about fast days, or he understood that the Gemara concludes just that the special additional prayer is not recited on days when the additional offering is sacrificed (*Kesef Mishne*). Most early authorities reject the ruling of the Rambam; however, see *Sefat Emet*, who argues that the mishna and the Gemara are best reconciled by the explanation of the Rambam.

Others maintain that on communal fast days a special additional service was conducted, into which the additional blessings discussed in chapter 2 were inserted (Rabbi Zerahya HaLevi in *Sefer HaMaor*, beginning of *Berakhot*). Support for this opinion is found in a statement in *Megilla* (22a), which mentions an additional prayer recited on communal fasts, as well as from a passage in the Jerusalem Talmud (*Berakhot* 1:5). Other commentaries, however, reject this opinion, on the basis of the Gemara here (Ritva; Ran).

HALAKHA

Priests spread their hands in the afternoon prayer of a fast – פָּרְשֵׂי כָּהֲנֵי יְדַיְיהוּ בְּמִנְחָתָא דְּתַעֲנִיתָא: On a day in which the closing prayer is recited, e.g., Yom Kippur, the priests recite the Priestly Benediction in the morning prayer, the additional prayer, and in the closing prayer, but not in the afternoon prayer, in accordance with the opinion of Rabbi Yosei. However, on a fast day that does not include the closing prayer, the Priestly Benediction is recited in the afternoon prayer (*Shulḥan Arukh, Oraḥ Ḥayyim* 129:1).

מַאן דְּאָמַר הֲלָכָה כְּרַבִּי מֵאִיר, דָּרְשִׁינַן לָהּ בְּפִירְקָא. מַאן דְּאָמַר מִנְהָג, מִידְרַשׁ לָא דָּרְשִׁינַן, אוֹרוֹיֵי מוֹרֵינַן. וּמַאן דְּאָמַר נָהֲגוּ, אוֹרוֹיֵי לָא מוֹרֵינַן, וְאִי עָבֵיד, עָבֵיד, וְלָא מְהַדְּרִינַן לֵיהּ.

The Gemara clarifies these statements. **The one who said** that **the** ***halakha*** **is in accordance with** the opinion of **Rabbi Meir** means **that** this ruling **is taught in the** public **lectures** on Shabbat. **The one who said** that **the custom** is in accordance with the opinion of Rabbi Meir means that **one does not teach** this in public, but if someone comes to ask for a practical ruling, **one instructs them** in private that this is the *halakha*. **And the one who said** that the people **act** in accordance with the opinion of Rabbi Meir means that **one does not** even instruct someone that this is the *halakha*, **but** if he **acts** in accordance with Rabbi Meir, he has **acted** in a valid manner **and we do not** require **him to return** and recite the prayer again.[N]

וְרַב נַחְמָן אָמַר: הֲלָכָה כְּרַבִּי יוֹסֵי. וְהִלְכְתָא כְּרַבִּי יוֹסֵי. וְהָאִידָּנָא מַאי טַעֲמָא פָּרְשֵׂי כָּהֲנֵי יְדַיְיהוּ בְּמִנְחָתָא דְּתַעֲנִיתָא? כֵּיוָן דִּבְסָמוּךְ לִשְׁקִיעַת הַחַמָּה קָא פָּרְשֵׂי, כִּתְפִלַּת נְעִילָה דָּמְיָא.

And Rav Naḥman said that **the** ***halakha*** **is in accordance with** the opinion of **Rabbi Yosei.** The Gemara concludes: **And** indeed, **the** ***halakha*** **is in accordance with** the opinion of **Rabbi Yosei.** The Gemara asks: **And nowadays, what is the reason** that **priests spread their hands** to bless the people **in the afternoon prayer of a fast?**[NH] The Gemara explains: **Since they spread** their hands **near sunset,** it is **considered like** ***ne'ila,*** and therefore the decree of the Sages does not apply.

דְּכוּלֵּי עָלְמָא מִיהַת שִׁכּוֹר אָסוּר בִּנְשִׂיאַת כַּפַּיִם. מְנָהָנֵי מִילֵּי? אָמַר רַבִּי יְהוֹשֻׁעַ בֶּן לֵוִי מִשּׁוּם בַּר קַפָּרָא: לָמָּה נִסְמְכָה פָּרָשַׁת כֹּהֵן מְבָרֵךְ לְפָרָשַׁת נָזִיר? לוֹמַר: מָה נָזִיר אָסוּר בְּיַיִן, אַף כֹּהֵן מְבָרֵךְ אָסוּר בְּיַיִן.

In any event, based on the above, **everyone agrees** that **it is prohibited** for **a drunken** priest **to raise his hands** and recite the Priestly Benediction. The Gemara asks: **From where are these matters** derived? **Rabbi Yehoshua ben Levi said in the name of bar Kappara: Why is the portion of the priest who recites the benediction** (see Numbers 6:22–27) **juxtaposed with the portion of the nazirite** (see Numbers 6:1–21)? They are juxtaposed **to say** that **just as it is prohibited** for **a nazirite** to drink **wine, so too, it is prohibited for a priest who recites the benediction** to drink **wine.**

מַתְקִיף לָהּ אֲבוּהּ דְּרַבִּי זֵירָא, וְאָמְרִי לָהּ אוֹשַׁעְיָא בַּר זַבְדָּא: אִי מָה נָזִיר אָסוּר בְּחַרְצָן, אַף כֹּהֵן מְבָרֵךְ אָסוּר בְּחַרְצָן! אָמַר רַבִּי יִצְחָק: אָמַר קְרָא: ״לְשָׁרְתוֹ וּלְבָרֵךְ בִּשְׁמוֹ״. מָה מְשָׁרֵת מוּתָּר בְּחַרְצָן, אַף כֹּהֵן מְבָרֵךְ מוּתָּר בְּחַרְצָן.

Rabbi Zeira's father, and some say it was **Oshaya bar Zavda, strongly objects to this** explanation. **If** you wish to compare these two cases, you can argue as follows: **Just as it is prohibited** for **a nazirite** to eat grape **pits,** as he may not partake of any of the products of a grapevine, **so too,** it should be **prohibited for a priest who recites the benediction** to eat grape **pits.** Certainly a priest is not barred from raising his hands after eating a few grape pits. Rather, **Rabbi Yitzḥak said** that **the verse states: "To minister to Him and to bless in His name"** (Deuteronomy 10:8). **Just as** it is **permitted** for a priest **who ministers** to God in the Temple to partake **of** grape **pits, so too,** it **is permitted** for **a priest who recites the benediction** to partake **of** grape **pits.**

NOTES

The *halakha*, the custom, they act – הֲלָכָה מִנְהָג נָהֲגוּ: The statement that the *halakha* is in accordance with a certain opinion indicates an unambiguous ruling that should be publicized, while those who follow other opinions are censured. If it is stated that the custom is to follow a particular opinion, this means that although no clear-cut ruling has been issued, there is an established custom to follow the opinion of that Sage. Essentially, an accepted custom is as binding as a *halakha*, only it is not taught publicly. Rather, each individual who inquires is informed that he must follow the custom of the people. The phrase: They act in accordance with an opinion, refers to after the fact. In other words, people act this way in practice, but this is not a custom that has been endorsed by the important Sages. Consequently, the practice is not negated, but nor is someone who asks a question instructed to follow that custom (see *ge'onim*).

Priests spread their hands in the afternoon prayer of a fast – פָּרְשֵׂי כָּהֲנֵי יְדַיְיהוּ בְּמִנְחָתָא דְּתַעֲנִיתָא: The early commentaries disagree as to whether the Priestly Benediction is recited in the afternoon prayer even on Yom Kippur and on the other fast days that include the closing prayer, or whether it is recited only on those fast days that do not include the closing prayer. Most early authorities maintain that the Priestly Benediction is not recited in the afternoon prayer of Yom Kippur and other fasts, as on those days the afternoon service is conducted earlier in the day than the time of the closing prayer, and therefore there is a concern that the priests might come to recite the benediction in the afternoon prayer on ordinary days, when they will possibly be drunk (*Tosafot*; Rambam; Ra'avad). The Rambam agrees, however, that if a priest ascends before the congregation to recite the Priestly Benediction in the afternoon prayer of Yom Kippur, he is not ordered to stand down. Conversely, others argue that as the Gemara does not suggest this distinction, the Priestly Benediction is indeed recited in the afternoon prayer of Yom Kippur and the other fasts when the afternoon prayer is immediately followed by the closing prayer (*She'iltot*; Rabbeinu Gershom; Ramban). The sources indicate that there were differences in practice concerning this matter between the communities in Eretz Yisrael and those of Babylonia, as well as differences within Babylonia itself.

אִי מַה מְשָׁרֵת בַּעַל מוּם לֹא, אַף כֹּהֵן מְבָרֵךְ בַּעַל מוּם לֹא! הָא אִיתְקַשׁ לְנָזִיר!

The Gemara asks: **If** so, then **just as** a priest who **ministers** in the Temple may **not** be physically **blemished, so too, a priest who recites the benediction** may **not** be **blemished.**[H] The Gemara rejects this suggestion: The priest who recites the benediction **is** also **juxtaposed to a nazirite,** who is not affected by a blemish.

וּמַאי חָזֵית דִּמַקַּשְׁתְּ לְקוּלָּא? אַקֵּישׁ לְחוּמְרָא! אַסְמַכְתָּא נִינְהוּ מִדְּרַבָּנַן, וּלְקוּלָּא.

The Gemara asks: **And what did you see that you juxtaposed** the cases **in** favor of **a leniency?** Perhaps you should **juxtapose for a stringency,** by comparing the priest who recites the benediction to a nazirite with regard to grape pits, and comparing him to a priest ministering in the Temple in relation to the prohibition against reciting the benediction if he has a physical blemish. The Gemara explains: These proofs **are** cited merely as **support**[N] for *halakhot* that apply **by rabbinic** law, **and** consequently, they are interpreted **as a leniency,** not a stringency.

״אֵלּוּ הֵן מַעֲמָדוֹת: לְפִי שֶׁנֶּאֱמַר ׳צַו אֶת בְּנֵי יִשְׂרָאֵל׳״ כו׳. מַאי קָאָמַר? הָכִי קָאָמַר: אֵלּוּ הֵן מַעֲמָדוֹת. וּמַה טַּעַם תִּיקְּנוּ מַעֲמָדוֹת? לְפִי שֶׁנֶּאֱמַר: ״צַו אֶת בְּנֵי יִשְׂרָאֵל וְאָמַרְתָּ אֲלֵיהֶם: אֶת קָרְבָּנִי, לַחְמִי לְאִשַּׁי״.

§ The mishna taught that **these are** the **non-priestly watches: Since it is stated: "Command the children of Israel."** The Gemara asks: **What is** the mishna **saying** about the non-priestly watches? How does the verse relate to the watches? The Gemara explains that the mishna **is saying as follows:** These are the **non-priestly watches,** which will be explained later. **And what is the reason that they instituted non-priestly watches? Since it is stated: "Command the children of Israel and say to them: My offering of food, which is presented to Me made by a fire,** of a sweet savor to Me, you shall observe to sacrifice to Me in their due season" (Numbers 28:2).

וְהֵיאַךְ קָרְבָּנוֹ שֶׁל אָדָם קָרֵב וְהוּא אֵינוֹ עוֹמֵד עַל גַּבָּיו? הִתְקִינוּ נְבִיאִים הָרִאשׁוֹנִים עֶשְׂרִים וְאַרְבָּעָה מִשְׁמָרוֹת. עַל כָּל מִשְׁמָר וּמִשְׁמָר הָיָה מַעֲמָד בִּירוּשָׁלַיִם שֶׁל כֹּהֲנִים וְשֶׁל לְוִיִּם, וְשֶׁל יִשְׂרְאֵלִים. הִגִּיעַ זְמַן מִשְׁמָר לַעֲלוֹת, כֹּהֲנִים וּלְוִיִּם עוֹלִין לִירוּשָׁלַיִם.

The mishna continues: **But how can a person's offering be sacrificed when he is not standing next to it? The early prophets,** Samuel and David, **instituted twenty-four priestly watches.**[B] **For each and every priestly watch there was a** corresponding **watch in Jerusalem of priests, Levites, and Israelites.** When the **time arrived** for the members of a certain **priestly watch to ascend,** the **priests and Levites** of that watch would **ascend to Jerusalem.**

HALAKHA

Blemished – בַּעַל מוּם: A priest who has a physical blemish on his face or hand may not recite the Priestly Benediction, lest the people are distracted from the benediction by his defect. If the local populace is already accustomed to the priest's defect, or if the priests recite the benediction with their prayer shawls drawn forward to cover their heads and their hands, even a priest with a blemish on his face or hand may recite the benediction (*Shulḥan Arukh*, *Oraḥ Ḥayyim* 128:30–31).

NOTES

Are support, etc. – אַסְמַכְתָּא נִינְהוּ וכו׳: According to many commentaries, the conclusion of the Gemara is that both comparisons, i.e., comparing a priest who recites the benediction to a ministering priest and to a nazirite, are cited merely as support for a rabbinical law. However, some contend that the verse "To minister to Him and to bless in His name" (Deuteronomy 10:8) is an explicit comparison, which cannot be relegated to mere support (Ra'avad). According to this opinion, the prohibition against a drunk priest reciting the benediction is derived from the comparison to a priest who is performing the Temple service in a state of inebriation, a prohibition that is expressly stated in the Torah (Leviticus 10:8). Conversely, the comparison to a nazirite is only a hint that a priest who recites the benediction is not similar to a ministering priest in all regards (see *Mikhtam* and Meiri). Rabbeinu Ḥananel also indicates that only the juxtaposition is rabbinical.

BACKGROUND

Priestly watches – מִשְׁמָרוֹת: The twenty-four priestly watches were apparently centered in specially chosen areas of Eretz Yisrael. Just as when the land was originally distributed among the tribes certain cities were set aside for the priests, the custom continued in the Second Temple period for priests to live in particular locales. Even after the destruction of the Temple, the priests went into exile as families, and each watch lived in a different village in the Galilee, as can be seen from various lists of priestly watches in their towns.

תנו רבנן: עשרים וארבעה משמרות בארץ ישראל, ושתים עשרה ביריחו. שתים עשרה ביריחו?! נפישן להו טובא! אלא: שתים עשרה מהן ביריחו. הגיע זמן המשמר לעלות, חצי המשמר היה עולה מארץ ישראל לירושלים, וחצי המשמר היה עולה מיריחו כדי שיספקו מים ומזון לאחיהם שבירושלים.

The Sages taught: There were **twenty-four priestly watches in Eretz Yisrael, and twelve in Jericho.** The Gemara expresses surprise at this statement: **Twelve in Jericho?** In that case **there are too many of them,** as this makes a total of thirty-six watches. **Rather,** the *baraita* should be read as follows: There were twenty-four in total, **twelve of which were in Jericho.** How so? **When** the **time arrived** for the members of a certain **priestly watch to ascend, half the priestly watch would ascend from** all over **Eretz Yisrael**[B] **to Jerusalem, and half the priestly watch would ascend from Jericho,**[N] **in order to provide water and food to their brothers in Jerusalem** from Jericho.

אמר רב יהודה אמר שמואל: כהנים ולוים וישראלים מעכבין את הקרבן. במתניתא תנא: רבי שמעון בן אלעזר: כהנים, ולוים וכלי שיר מעכבין את הקרבן. במאי קמיפלגי? מר סבר: עיקר שירה בפה. ומר סבר: עיקר שירה בכלי.

Rav Yehuda said that **Shmuel said: Priests, Levites, and Israelites** are all **indispensable for the offering,** and consequently, they all must be present when the daily offering is sacrificed. **It is taught in a *baraita*** that **Rabbi Shimon ben Elazar** says: **Priests, Levites, and musical instruments are indispensable for the offering.** The Gemara asks: **With regard to what** principle do they **disagree? One Sage,** Shmuel, **holds** that **the main** aspect **of** the Levites' **song** that accompanied the offerings is **vocal, and one Sage,** Rabbi Shimon ben Elazar, **holds** that **the main** aspect **of** their **song**[H] is instrumental, performed **with a vessel,** and therefore both the Levites and their instruments must be present for the daily offering.

אמר רב חמא בר גוריא אמר רב: משה תיקן להם לישראל שמונה משמרות, ארבעה מאלעזר וארבעה מאיתמר. בא שמואל והעמידן על שש עשרה. בא דוד והעמידן על עשרים וארבעה, שנאמר: ״בשנת הארבעים למלכות דויד נדרשו, וימצא בהם גבורי חיל ביעזיר גלעד״.

Rav Ḥama bar Gurya said that **Rav said: Moses** initially **instituted for the Jews**[N] **eight priestly watches, four from** the descendants of **Elazar and four from** the descendants of **Itamar. Samuel came and established them as sixteen,** and **David came and established them as twenty-four, as it is stated,** after the watches are listed: **"In the fortieth year**[N] **of the reign of David they were sought for, and there were found among them mighty men of valor at Jazer of Gilead"** (I Chronicles 26:31).

מיתיבי: משה תיקן להם לישראל שמונה משמרות, ארבעה מאלעזר וארבעה מאיתמר. ובא דוד ושמואל והעמידן על עשרים וארבע, שנאמר: ״המה יסד דויד ושמואל הראה באמונתם״! הכי קאמר: מיסודו של דוד ושמואל הרמתי העמידום על עשרים וארבע.

The Gemara **raises an objection** against this opinion from a *baraita*. **Moses instituted for the Jews**[H] **eight priestly watches, four from Elazar and four from Itamar. And David and Samuel came and established them as twenty-four, as it is stated: "Whom David and Samuel the seer ordained in their set office"** (I Chronicles 9:22). This *baraita* indicates that David and Samuel together established the twenty-four watches. The Gemara explains: **This is what** the *baraita* **is saying: Through their ordination by David and Samuel of Rama** the priestly watches incrementally increased in number until **they established them as twenty-four.**

BACKGROUND

Ascend from all over Eretz Yisrael – עולה מארץ ישראל: The list of priestly watches is preserved in memory of the Temple. For many generations, until roughly one thousand years after the destruction of the Temple, there was a custom on each Shabbat to read out the name of the priestly watch for that week, and they would even engrave the names on the walls of synagogues. Here is the list of the watches and their towns in the Galilee:

1. Jehoiarib – Meron
2. Jedaiah – Izippori
3. Harim – Maphshata
4. Seorim – Ithalo
5. Malchijah – Bethlehem
6. Mijamin – Jodfat
7. Hakkoz – Ilbo
8. Abijah – Kfar Uzziah
9. Jeshua – Arbel
10. Shechaniah – Kebul
11. Eliashib – Kanah
12. Jakim – Safed
13. Huppah – Beit Maon
14. Jeshebeab – Shihin
15. Bilgah – Maariah
16. Immer – Jabnit
17. Hezir – Mimlah
18. Happizzez – Nazareth
19. Pethahiah – Arab
20. Jahezkel – Migdal Nuniah
21. Jachin – Kfar Johanah
22. Gamul – Beit Huviah
23. Delaiah – Zalmin
24. Uzziah, aka Maaziah – Hamat Ariah

HALAKHA

The main aspect of their song – עיקר שירה: The musical accompaniment provided by the Levites to the sacrificial services in the Temple was mainly vocal. In addition to the choral singing, there was also instrumental music played by Levites and Israelites (Rambam *Sefer Avoda, Hilkhot Kelei HaMikdash* 3:3).

Moses instituted for the Jews – משה תיקן להם לישראל: Moses divided the priesthood into eight watches, four from the descendants of Elazar and four from the descendants of Itamar. This continued until the days of Samuel, when the prophet and King David divided the priesthood into twenty-four watches (Rambam *Sefer Avoda, Hilkhot Kelei HaMikdash* 4:3).

NOTES

And half the priestly watch would ascend from Jericho – וחצי המשמר היה עולה מיריחו: Some commentaries maintain that when the time came for the members of a particular watch to ascend to Jerusalem for their week of service in the Temple, half would ascend to the capital, while the other half would go to Jericho to bring supplies of water and food for their brothers in Jerusalem. After three days, the two groups would switch roles (Meiri). In the Jerusalem Talmud it is indicated that most of the members of the watches were residents of Jerusalem or Jericho.

Moses instituted for the Jews – משה תיקן להם לישראל: According to the plain meaning of the Gemara, the system of watches originated as an enactment of the prophets, as the different opinions dispute only the precise details of its development. However, some commentaries maintain that the division of the priesthood into watches is a Torah obligation (*Sefer HaMitzvot*, positive mitzva 36; see also *Sefer Avoda, Hilkhot Kelei HaMikdash* 4:3–4). The biblical source for the obligation is the verse: "They shall have like portions to eat, besides that which comes of the sale according to the fathers' houses" (Deuteronomy 18:8), which the *Sifrei* interprets: With the exception of that which the priestly forefathers sold to each other, saying, you have your week and I have my week (see Onkelos on Deuteronomy 18:8).

Others add that it stands to reason that the system of watches applies by Torah law, for had there been no assigned times for the priests to serve in the Temple, but each priest could decide for himself when to serve, there might be occasions when no priests were available for the Temple service (Ritva). However, the number of watches was not fixed by Torah law but by the various enactments issued by Moses, Samuel, and David, with the number growing in accordance with the changing needs of the priests. Yet others conclude that the watch system does not have a scriptural basis. It originated either as an enactment of the prophets or as a *halakha* transmitted to Moses from Sinai (Ramban on *Sefer HaMitzvot*).

As it is stated, In the fortieth year – שנאמר: בשנת הארבעים: This verse is cited to teach us that it was King David, not the prophet Samuel, who expanded the watches so that the total number stood at twenty-four, as Samuel had passed away by the fortieth year of David's reign (Meiri; Maharsha).

תַּנְיָא אִידָךְ: מֹשֶׁה תִּיקֵּן לָהֶם לְיִשְׂרָאֵל שֵׁשׁ עֶשְׂרֵה מִשְׁמָרוֹת, שְׁמוֹנֶה מֵאֶלְעָזָר וּשְׁמוֹנֶה מֵאִיתָמָר. וּכְשֶׁרַבּוּ בְּנֵי אֶלְעָזָר עַל בְּנֵי אִיתָמָר, חִלְּקוּם וְהֶעֱמִידוּם עַל עֶשְׂרִים וְאַרְבַּע, שֶׁנֶּאֱמַר: ״וַיִּמָּצְאוּ בְנֵי אֶלְעָזָר רַבִּים לְרָאשֵׁי הַגְּבָרִים מִן בְּנֵי אִיתָמָר, וַיַּחְלְקוּם. לִבְנֵי אֶלְעָזָר רָאשִׁים לְבֵית אָבוֹת שִׁשָּׁה עָשָׂר וְלִבְנֵי אִיתָמָר לְבֵית אֲבוֹתָם שְׁמוֹנָה״. וְאוֹמֵר: ״בֵּית אָב אֶחָד אָחֻז לְאֶלְעָזָר, וְאָחֻז אָחֻז לְאִיתָמָר״.

It is taught in another *baraita*: **Moses instituted for the Jews sixteen priestly watches, eight from Elazar and eight from Itamar. And when the descendants of Elazar grew more numerous than the descendants of Itamar, he divided** the descendants of Elazar **and established them** together with the descendants of Itamar **as twenty-four** watches, **as it is stated: "And there were more chief men found of the sons of Elazar than of the sons of Itamar, and they were divided thus: Of the sons of Elazar there were sixteen heads of fathers' houses, and of the sons of Itamar, according to their fathers' houses, eight"** (1 Chronicles 24:4). **And it says: "One father's house taken for Elazar, and proportionately for Itamar"** (1 Chronicles 24:6).

מַאי ״וְאוֹמֵר״? וְכִי תֵּימָא כִּי הֵיכִי דִּנְפִישִׁי בְּנֵי אֶלְעָזָר, הָכָא נָמֵי דִּנְפִישִׁי בְּנֵי אִיתָמָר, שְׁמוֹנָה מֵעִיקָּרָא אַרְבָּעָה הָווּ, תָּא שְׁמַע: ״בֵּית אָב אֶחָד אָחֻז לְאֶלְעָזָר, וְאָחֻז אָחֻז לְאִיתָמָר״. תְּיוּבְתָּא דְּרַב חָמָא בַּר גּוּרְיָא!

The Gemara asks: What is: And it says? Why was it necessary to quote a second verse? The Gemara explains: **And if you would say** that **just as the descendants of Elazar increased, so too, the descendants of Itamar increased,** and the **eight** watches **were initially four,** as claimed by Rav Ḥama bar Gurya, then **come and hear: "One father's house taken for Elazar, and proportionately for Itamar,"** which indicates that the descendants of Itamar remained as they were. This verse is an apparently **a conclusive refutation of** the opinion of **Rav Ḥama bar Gurya,** who says that Moses established only eight priestly watches.

אָמַר לָךְ רַב חָמָא בַּר גּוּרְיָא: תַּנָּאֵי הִיא, וַאֲנָא דַּאֲמַרִי כִּי הַאי תַּנָּא דְּאָמַר שְׁמוֹנָה.

The Gemara responds: **Rav Ḥama bar Gurya** could have **said to you** that the initial order of the priestly watches **is** a dispute between ***tanna'im***, as indicated by the previous *baraita*, **and I stated** my opinion **in accordance with that *tanna* who said** that Moses instituted **eight** priestly watches.

תָּנוּ רַבָּנַן: אַרְבָּעָה מִשְׁמָרוֹת עָלוּ מִן הַגּוֹלָה, וְאֵלּוּ הֵן: יְדַעְיָה, חָרִים, פַּשְׁחוּר, וְאִימֵּר. עָמְדוּ נְבִיאִים שֶׁבֵּינֵיהֶם

The Sages taught: Only four **priestly watches ascended from the** Babylonian **exile,**[N] while the other twenty stayed in Babylonia. **And these are** the watches who returned: The descendants of **Jedaiah, Harim, Pashhur, and Immer. The prophets among** those who returned **arose**

Perek **IV**
Daf **27** Amud **b**

וְחִלְּקוּם וְהֶעֱמִידוּם עַל עֶשְׂרִים וְאַרְבָּעָה. בְּלָלוּם וּנְתָנוּם בְּקַלְפֵּי. בָּא יְדַעְיָה וְנָטַל חֶלְקוֹ וְחֵלֶק חֲבֵרָיו – שֵׁשׁ. בָּא חָרִים וְנָטַל חֶלְקוֹ וְחֵלֶק חֲבֵרָיו – שֵׁשׁ. וְכֵן פַּשְׁחוּר, וְכֵן אִימֵּר.

and divided them and established them as twenty-four watches. They achieved this by writing the names of these new twenty-four watches on pieces of paper, **mixing them up, and putting them in a receptacle** [***kalfei***][L] from which lots were drawn. A representative from the family of **Jedaiah came and drew his portion and the lot of** five **other** watches, for a total of **six. Harim came and** also **drew his portion and the lot of** five **other** watches, a total of **six. And likewise Pashhur, and likewise Immer.**

וְכֵן הִתְנוּ נְבִיאִים שֶׁבֵּינֵיהֶם שֶׁאֲפִילּוּ יְהוֹיָרִיב רֹאשׁ מִשְׁמֶרֶת עוֹלֶה, לֹא יִדָּחֶה יְדַעְיָה מִמְּקוֹמוֹ, אֶלָּא יְדַעְיָה עִיקָּר וִיהוֹיָרִיב טָפֵל לוֹ.

And likewise the prophets among them stipulated that even if the descendants of **Jehoiarib,**[N] who originally **headed the priestly watches, ascended** to Eretz Yisrael, **Jedaiah would not be demoted from its place** as the first of the watches. Rather, the watch of **Jedaiah** would retain **precedence, and Jehoiarib** would be **subordinate to it.**

NOTES

Ascended from the exile – עָלוּ מִן הַגּוֹלָה: Rashi asks: Only three of these families, Jedaiah, Harim, and Immer, appear in the list of priestly divisions recorded in 1 Chronicles 24:7–18. Although the family of Pashhur is included among the priestly families that returned from the Babylonian exile in the days of Ezra (Ezra 2:37), nowhere is it mentioned as a separate priestly division. Some commentaries suggest that the watch of Pashhur was comprised of the descendants of Pashhur, son of Immer, who was a priest of importance mentioned in Jeremiah, chapter 20. After his descendants greatly increased in number, the clan of Pashhur separated themselves from the rest of the watch of Immer and set up their own watch (Maharsha; see Rid). Others identify this Pashhur with Pashhur, son of Malchijah, who is mentioned in Jeremiah 38:1, Nehemiah 11:12, and 1 Chronicles 9:12 (*Sefat Emet*). If so, the watch of Pashhur developed from the watch of Malchijah.

LANGUAGE

Receptacle [*kalfei*] – קַלְפֵּי: From the Greek κάλπις, *kalpis*, meaning an urn or a box. It also has the narrower meaning of a receptacle used for ballots, drawing lots, and the like.

NOTES

That even if the descendants of Jehoiarib – שֶׁאֲפִילּוּ יְהוֹיָרִיב: Rashi explains that if the descendants of the priest Jehoiarib were to return to Eretz Yisrael, they would not regain their position as the head of the watches, but would instead take their place after the five watches starting from Jedaiah. However, a simple reading of the Gemara in tractate *Arakhin* 12b and Rashi's commentary on that passage indicate that if the descendants of Jehoiarib were to return, they would not constitute an independent watch at all, but would be subordinated to one of the watches formed from the descendants of Jedaiah (Rid). Several sources, however, suggest that the descendants of Jehoiarib did indeed constitute an independent watch during the Second Temple period. Some commentaries note that at least two other watches from the First Temple period, Bilgah and Jeshebeab, were active as independent watches during the Second Temple period as well.

"וְיִשְׂרָאֵל שֶׁבְּאוֹתוֹ מִשְׁמָר מִתְכַּנְּסִין בְּעָרֵיהֶן וְקוֹרִין בְּמַעֲשֵׂה בְרֵאשִׁית". מְנָהָנֵי מִילֵּי? אָמַר רַבִּי יַעֲקֹב בַּר אַחָא אָמַר רַב אַסִּי: אִלְמָלֵא מַעֲמָדוֹת, לֹא נִתְקַיְּימוּ שָׁמַיִם וָאָרֶץ, שֶׁנֶּאֱמַר: "וַיֹּאמַר: ה׳ אֱלֹהִים, בַּמָּה אֵדַע כִּי אִירָשֶׁנָּה?"

§ The mishna taught: **And the Israelites of that priestly watch assembled in their towns and read the act of Creation.** The Gemara asks: **From where is this matter,** that they must read this specific portion, derived? **Rabbi Ya'akov bar Aḥa said** that **Rav Asi said: Were it not for** the **non-priestly watches** and the Temple service, **heaven and earth would not continue to exist,**[N] **as it is stated: "And he said: Lord God, by what shall I know that I shall inherit it?"** (Genesis 15:8).

אָמַר אַבְרָהָם: רִבּוֹנוֹ שֶׁל עוֹלָם! שֶׁמָּא יִשְׂרָאֵל חוֹטְאִין לְפָנֶיךָ, אַתָּה עוֹשֶׂה לָהֶם כְּדוֹר הַמַּבּוּל וּכְדוֹר הַפַּלָּגָה? אֲמַר לֵיהּ: לָאו. אָמַר לְפָנָיו: רִבּוֹנוֹ שֶׁל עוֹלָם! הוֹדִיעֵנִי, בַּמָּה אִירָשֶׁנָּה? אֲמַר לֵיהּ: "קְחָה לִי עֶגְלָה מְשֻׁלֶּשֶׁת וְעֵז מְשֻׁלֶּשֶׁת," וגו׳.

The Gemara explains this verse. **Abraham said: Master of the Universe, perhaps the Jews will sin before You. Will You treat them as** You did **the generation of the flood and the generation of the dispersion,** and destroy them? God **said to him: No.** Abraham **said before** God: **Master of the Universe, tell me, with what shall I inherit it?** How can my descendants ensure that You will maintain the world? God **said to** Abraham: **"Take for Me a three-year-old heifer, and a three-year-old goat,** and a three-year-old ram, and a turtledove, and a young pigeon" (Genesis 15:9). God was alluding to the offerings, in whose merit the Jewish people, and through them the entire world, will be spared divine punishment.

אָמַר לְפָנָיו: רִבּוֹנוֹ שֶׁל עוֹלָם! תֵּינַח בִּזְמַן שֶׁבֵּית הַמִּקְדָּשׁ קַיָּים. בִּזְמַן שֶׁאֵין בֵּית הַמִּקְדָּשׁ קַיָּים מַה תְּהֵא עֲלֵיהֶם? אָמַר לוֹ: כְּבָר תִּקַּנְתִּי לָהֶם סֵדֶר קָרְבָּנוֹת. בִּזְמַן שֶׁקּוֹרְאִין בָּהֶן לְפָנַי, מַעֲלֶה אֲנִי עֲלֵיהֶם כְּאִילּוּ הִקְרִיבוּם לְפָנַי, וַאֲנִי מוֹחֵל לָהֶם עַל כָּל עֲוֹנוֹתֵיהֶם.

Abraham **said before** God: **Master of the Universe,** this **works out well when the Temple is standing,** but **when the Temple is not standing, what will become of them?** God **said to him: I have already enacted for them the order of offerings. When they read them before Me, I will ascribe them** credit **as though they had sacrificed them before Me and I will pardon them for all their transgressions.** Since the offerings ensure the continued existence of the Jewish people and the rest of the world, the act of Creation is read in their honor.

תָּנוּ רַבָּנַן: אַנְשֵׁי מִשְׁמָר הָיוּ מִתְפַּלְּלִין עַל קָרְבַּן אֲחֵיהֶם שֶׁיִּתְקַבֵּל בְּרָצוֹן. וְאַנְשֵׁי מַעֲמָד מִתְכַּנְּסִין לְבֵית הַכְּנֶסֶת וְיוֹשְׁבִין אַרְבַּע תַּעֲנִיּוֹת: בַּשֵּׁנִי בְּשַׁבָּת, בַּשְּׁלִישִׁי, בָּרְבִיעִי, וּבַחֲמִישִׁי. בַּשֵּׁנִי, עַל יוֹרְדֵי הַיָּם. בַּשְּׁלִישִׁי, עַל הוֹלְכֵי מִדְבָּרוֹת.

§ **The Sages taught: The members of the priestly watch would pray**[N] **for the offerings of their brothers,** the daily offering, **that it should be accepted with favor. And** meanwhile, **the members** of the **non-priestly watch** remained in their towns and would **assemble in the synagogue and observe four fasts:**[N] **On Monday** of that **week, on Tuesday, on Wednesday, and on Thursday. On Monday** they would fast **for seafarers,** that they should be rescued from danger, as the sea was created on Monday. **On Tuesday** they would fast **for those who walk in the desert,** as the dry land was created on Tuesday.

בָּרְבִיעִי, עַל אַסְכָּרָא שֶׁלֹּא תִּיפּוֹל עַל הַתִּינוֹקוֹת. בַּחֲמִישִׁי, עַל עוּבָּרוֹת וּמֵינִיקוֹת. עוּבָּרוֹת, שֶׁלֹּא יַפִּילוּ. מֵינִיקוֹת, שֶׁיֵּינִיקוּ אֶת בְּנֵיהֶם. וּבְעֶרֶב שַׁבָּת לֹא הָיוּ מִתְעַנִּין מִפְּנֵי כְּבוֹד הַשַּׁבָּת, קַל וָחוֹמֶר בַּשַּׁבָּת עַצְמָהּ.

On Wednesday they would fast **over croup,**[N] **that it should not befall the children,** as on the fourth day the bodies of light [*me'orot*] were created, a textual allusion to curses [*me'erot*]. **On Thursday** they would fast **for pregnant women and nursing women,** as living beings were first created on this day. For **pregnant women** they would fast **that they should not miscarry,** while for **nursing women** they would fast **that they** should be able to **nurse their children** properly. **And on Shabbat eve they would not fast, in deference to Shabbat,** and ***a fortiori*** they would not fast **on Shabbat itself.**

NOTES

Heaven and earth would not continue to exist – לֹא נִתְקַיְּימוּ שָׁמַיִם וָאָרֶץ: The Gemara in a parallel passage in *Megilla* 31b cites a different verse to prove that the continued existence of the world depends on the non-priestly watches and the communal offerings that are sacrificed in their presence: "Thus says the Lord: If not for My covenant day and night, I would not have appointed the ordinances of heaven and earth" (Jeremiah 33:25). This verse teaches that were it not for the daily offerings brought in the morning and evening, heaven and earth would cease to exist. The Gemara here derives the connection between the continued existence of the universe and the sacrificial service in the Temple from the conversation between Abraham and God. According to this interpretation of their exchange, Abraham did not ask for a sign that his descendants would inherit Eretz Yisrael, but for a means of atonement that would ensure that his descendants would continue to exist and the land would remain theirs forever (Maharsha).

The members of the priestly watch would pray – אַנְשֵׁי מִשְׁמָר הָיוּ מִתְפַּלְּלִין: Each priestly watch was divided into six or seven sub-groups called patrilineal families, each of which performed the Temple service for one day of the week. While one patrilineal family performed the actual service, the remaining patrilineal families offered prayers that the offerings be accepted by God (Rabbeinu Gershom; Rabbeinu Elyakim).

Four fasts – אַרְבַּע תַּעֲנִיּוֹת: Some commentaries suggest that the groups for which the members of the non-priestly watch fast correspond to those types of people who are obligated to give thanks-offerings and recite special prayers when they are delivered from distress, as derived from Psalm 107: Seafarers, desert travelers, the sick after they have been healed, and those who have been released from prison, as a newborn child may be compared to someone who has been released from confinement (Maharsha). In the Jerusalem Talmud it is inferred from this *baraita* that the same fast may not be proclaimed for more than one impending calamity, as each potential disaster requires a separate fast. In addition, in the Jerusalem Talmud a *baraita* is cited that teaches that the members of the Great Sanhedrin would likewise divide themselves into sub-groups, each of which fasted one day of the week together with the members of the non-priestly watch (see Rabbeinu Ḥananel).

NOTES

On Wednesday they would fast over croup – בָּרְבִיעִי עַל אַסְכָּרָא: Rashi follows the Jerusalem Talmud, where it is explained that the defective spelling of the Hebrew word for lights [*me'orot*], which were created on the fourth day of the week, teaches that Wednesdays are especially susceptible to curses [*me'erot*]. For this reason the members of the non-priestly watch would fast on Wednesdays, so that the disease of croup should not strike children. Others suggest that as the moon was diminished in size on Wednesday and became the smaller of the two celestial lights, small children are especially prone to illness on that day (Rav Yoshiya Pinto). Yet others suggest another explanation: Since croup is a divine punishment for the spreading of gossip, children are especially likely to be attacked by the disease on a Wednesday, as it was on that day that the first gossip was spoken: The moon spoke evil of the sun, as a result of which it was diminished in size (Rashi in *Ein Ya'akov*).

בְּאֶחָד בְּשַׁבָּת מַאי טַעֲמָא לָא? אָמַר רַבִּי יוֹחָנָן: מִפְּנֵי הַנּוֹצְרִים. רַבִּי שְׁמוּאֵל בַּר נַחְמָנִי אָמַר: מִפְּנֵי שֶׁהוּא שְׁלִישִׁי לִיצִירָה.

The Gemara asks: **What is the reason** that they would **not** fast **on Sunday? Rabbi Yoḥanan said: Due to the Christians,**[N] as Sunday is their day of rest, and they would claim that even the Jews ascribe significance to their special day. **Rabbi Shmuel bar Naḥmani said: Because it is the third day after the creation** of man, who was created on Friday, and the third day of recovery from a wound or sickness, in this case one's very creation, is considered the most painful.

רֵישׁ לָקִישׁ אָמַר: מִפְּנֵי נְשָׁמָה יְתֵירָה. דְּאָמַר רֵישׁ לָקִישׁ: נְשָׁמָה יְתֵירָה נִיתְּנָה בּוֹ בְּאָדָם בְּעֶרֶב שַׁבָּת. בְּמוֹצָאֵי שַׁבָּת נוֹטְלִין אוֹתָהּ מִמֶּנּוּ, שֶׁנֶּאֱמַר: "שָׁבַת וַיִּנָּפַשׁ" – כֵּיוָן שֶׁשָּׁבַת, וַי, אָבְדָה נֶפֶשׁ.

Reish Lakish said: They would not fast on Sunday **due to the added soul,**[N] **as Reish Lakish said: An added soul is given to man on Shabbat eve,** and **at the conclusion of Shabbat it is removed it from him, as it is stated: "He ceased from work and rested [*vayinafash*]"** (Exodus 31:17), which he expounds as follows: **Since one has rested** and Shabbat has passed, **woe for the soul [*vai nefesh*]** that is **lost,** the added soul that each individual relinquishes. Consequently, one is still weak from this loss on Sunday.

"בַּיּוֹם הָרִאשׁוֹן: 'בְּרֵאשִׁית', וְ'יְהִי רָקִיעַ'". תָּנָא: "בְּרֵאשִׁית" בִּשְׁנַיִם. "יְהִי רָקִיעַ" בְּאֶחָד. בִּשְׁלָמָא "יְהִי רָקִיעַ" בְּאֶחָד, תְּלָתָא פְּסוּקֵי הָווּ. אֶלָּא "בְּרֵאשִׁית" בִּשְׁנַיִם מַאי טַעֲמָא? חֲמִשָּׁה פְּסוּקֵי הָוְיָין, וְתַנְיָא: הַקּוֹרֵא בַּתּוֹרָה אַל יִפְחוֹת מִשְּׁלֹשָׁה פְּסוּקִים!

The mishna taught that **on Sunday** they would read the portions starting with: **"In the beginning"** (Genesis 1:1–5) **and "Let there be a firmament"** (Genesis 1:6–8). It **is taught** in a *baraita*: The section: **"In the beginning"** is read **by two** people, while **"Let there be a firmament"** is read **by one.** The Gemara asks: **Granted,** the passage **"Let there be a firmament"** is read **by one** individual, as **it is three verses** long, and one who is called to the Torah reads at least three verses. **However, what is the reason** that the section **"In the beginning"** is read **by two** individuals? It is five verses long, **and it is taught** in a mishna (*Megilla* 22a): **One who reads from the Torah** may **not** read **fewer than three**[H] **verses.** How, then, are five verses read by two individuals?

רַב אָמַר: דּוֹלֵג. וּשְׁמוּאֵל אָמַר: פּוֹסֵק. וְרַב, דְּאָמַר דּוֹלֵג, מַאי טַעֲמָא לָא אָמַר: פּוֹסֵק? קָסָבַר: כָּל פְּסוּקָא דְּלָא פַּסְקֵיהּ מֹשֶׁה, אֲנַן לָא פָּסְקִינַן לֵיהּ.

The Gemara cites two answers. **Rav said:** The first reader reads the first three verses, and the second reader **repeats**[H] the last verse read by the first, and continues with the final two verses. **And Shmuel said:** They **split** the middle verse into two, so that each of the pair reads half of it. The Gemara asks: **And** with regard to **Rav, who said** that one **repeats, what is the reason** that **he did not say** they should **split** a verse? The Gemara answers that Rav **maintains** that with regard to **any verse that was not divided by Moses, we do not divide it.**

וּשְׁמוּאֵל אָמַר: פּוֹסֵק. וּמִי פָּסְקִינַן? וְהָאָמַר רַבִּי חֲנִינָא קָרָא: צַעַר גָּדוֹל הָיָה לִי אֵצֶל רַבִּי חֲנִינָא הַגָּדוֹל, וְלֹא הִתִּיר לִי לִפְסוֹק אֶלָּא לְתִינוֹקוֹת שֶׁל בֵּית רַבָּן, הוֹאִיל וּלְהִתְלַמֵּד עֲשׂוּיִן. וּשְׁמוּאֵל: הָתָם טַעֲמָא מַאי מִשּׁוּם דְּלָא אֶפְשָׁר. הָכָא נַמִי לָא אֶפְשָׁר.

And Shmuel said that one **splits** the middle verse into two. The Gemara asks: **And may one split** a single verse? **But didn't Rabbi Ḥanina Kara,**[P] the Bible expert, who taught the Bible to schoolchildren, **say: I had great trouble with Rabbi Ḥanina the Great**[P] when I asked him this question, **and he permitted me to split** long verses into two **only for** the benefit of **schoolchildren, since it is performed to** help them **learn. And Shmuel** can respond that **what is the reason there,** in the case of schoolchildren, that it is permitted to split verses? **Because it is not possible** to proceed in any other way. **Here too, it is not possible** for two people to read five verses other than by splitting one of them into two.

NOTES

Due to the Christians – מִפְּנֵי הַנּוֹצְרִים: Some commentaries explain that according to the opinion of Rabbi Yoḥanan, the members of the non-priestly watch did not fast on Sunday because the day was observed by Christians as a holiday, and there was concern that the Christians would react in a hostile way if the Jews observed a fast on their holiday (Rabbeinu Gershom; see *Soferim* 17:4). Others suggest that as the members of the non-priestly watch would refrain from work whenever they fasted, they did not fast on Sundays, as they did not want anyone to think that they were doing so in deference to the Christian holiday observed on that day (Maharsha). Yet others maintain that the word for Christians, *notzrim*, should be read as *notzarim*, those who are created. In other words, Rabbi Yoḥanan is providing essentially the same explanation as Rabbi Shmuel bar Naḥmani, that the members of the non-priestly watch did not fast on Sunday because it is the third day after the creation of man. An alternative explanation is that the term *notzrim* here is a reference to the Babylonians, as in the verse: "Watchers [*notzrim*] come from a distant country" (Jeremiah 4:16; see Rabbi David Kimḥi's commentary on that verse). Since the Babylonians celebrated Sunday as a holiday, the Sages enacted that the members of the non-priestly watch should not fast on that day.

The added soul – נְשָׁמָה יְתֵירָה: One interpretation of the added soul is that it represents man's ability to enjoy the entirety of creation, which constitutes the soul's rest on Shabbat (Rashba; see *Arukh*).

HALAKHA

One who reads…may not read fewer than three – הַקּוֹרֵא...אַל יִפְחוֹת מִשְּׁלֹשָׁה: One who is called to read from the Torah should read no fewer than three verses (*Shulḥan Arukh, Oraḥ Ḥayyim* 137:2).

Repeats – דּוֹלֵג: On those occasions when the Torah reading cannot be divided in such a way that each person reads a separate section consisting of three verses, e.g., on the New Moon, one of the readers may repeat a verse that has already been read by the previous reader, in accordance with the opinion of Rav (*Shulḥan Arukh, Oraḥ Ḥayyim* 423:2).

PERSONALITIES

Rabbi Ḥanina Kara – רַבִּי חֲנִינָא קָרָא: An *amora* from Eretz Yisrael, from the second generation of *amora'im*. This Rabbi Ḥanina was a student of Rabbi Ḥanina bar Ḥama and Rabbi Yannai. Apparently, he was not only a children's teacher but was also an expert in the Bible, which explains his title. He is presented as engaging in debate with his rabbis concerning matters that pertain to his work, as well as other issues of *halakha*.

Rabbi Ḥanina the Great – רַבִּי חֲנִינָא הַגָּדוֹל: This is Rabbi Ḥanina bar Ḥama, who is labeled this way because he was one of the outstanding Sages of his generation. In the Jerusalem Talmud he is known as Rabbi Ḥanina Rabba, which bears the same meaning. This epithet is generally used when Rabbi Ḥanina is mentioned alongside another Sage of that name, in this case Rabbi Ḥanina Kara, to differentiate between them.

NOTES

And according to the one who said that they split, let them split it – וּלְמַאן דְּאָמַר פּוֹסֵק לִיפְסוֹק: Rashi explains that the opinions of both Rav and Shmuel are contradicted by the clause of the *baraita* that states that a five-verse section should be read by one individual, as according to both of them it is possible for the section to be read by two people, either by repeating or splitting the verse. In a parallel passage in *Megilla* 22a, Rashi says that the following line should be omitted: And according to the one who said that he divides the verse let him divide it. He explains that the difficulty is raised from the last part of the *baraita*, which states that if the first reader read three verses from a five-verse section, the second one should read the next two verses of that section and one or three verses from the subsequent section. That clause is difficult for the opinion of Rav, as it is possible for the second reader to reread the third verse and continue with the next two verses. However, there is no difficulty according to the opinion of Shmuel, as the first reader has already read the third verse, and therefore it is no longer possible to divide that verse between the two readers (see *Tosafot*, Rashba, and Ritva on *Megilla* 22a).

וּשְׁמוּאֵל אָמַר: פּוֹסֵק. מַאי טַעְמָא לָא אָמַר: דּוֹלֵג? גְּזֵירָה מִשּׁוּם הַנִּכְנָסִין, וּגְזֵרָה מִשּׁוּם הַיּוֹצְאִין.

The Gemara questions this last conclusion. **And Shmuel said** that one **splits** the middle verse into two. **What is the reason** that **he did not say** that he **repeats** one of the verses, in accordance with the opinion of Rav? The Gemara explains: It is a rabbinic **decree due to those who enter** the synagogue in the middle of the reading, and **a decree due to those who leave** in the middle. If someone entered or exited in the middle of the reading and heard three full verses, he might think that one of the readers had read fewer than three full verses, which might lead him to conclude that it is permitted to read fewer than three verses.

מֵיתִיבִי: פָּרָשָׁה שֶׁל שִׁשָּׁה פְּסוּקִים קוֹרִין אוֹתָהּ בִּשְׁנַיִם, וְשֶׁל חֲמִשָּׁה בְּיָחִיד. וְאִם הָרִאשׁוֹן קוֹרֵא שְׁלֹשָׁה, הַשֵּׁנִי קוֹרֵא שְׁנַיִם מִפָּרָשָׁה זוֹ, וְאֶחָד מִפָּרָשָׁה אַחֶרֶת. וְיֵשׁ אוֹמְרִים: שְׁלֹשָׁה, לְפִי שֶׁאֵין מַתְחִילִין בְּפָרָשָׁה פָּחוֹת מִשְּׁלֹשָׁה פְּסוּקִין.

The Gemara **raises an objection** from a *baraita*: **A chapter** consisting **of six verses** may **be read by two** individuals, **and** a chapter **of five** verses must be read **by one. And if the first** individual **reads three** verses from the five-verse chapter, **the second** one reads the last **two** verses **of that chapter and one** more from **another chapter. And some say** that **three** verses are read from the next chapter, **as one may not begin to read a chapter** for **fewer than three verses.**

לְמַאן דְּאָמַר דּוֹלֵג לִידְלוֹג וּלְמַאן דְּאָמַר פּוֹסֵק לִיפְסוֹק? שָׁאנֵי הָתָם

The Gemara explains the objection: **According to the one who said** that they **repeat** the middle verse, **let** the second reader **repeat** a verse here as well. **And according to the one who said** that they **split** a verse, here too, **let** them **split** it.[N] Apparently, the *baraita* contradicts the opinions of both Rav and Shmuel. The Gemara answers: **It is different there,**

HALAKHA

And in the afternoon prayer they read by heart – וּבַמִּנְחָה קוֹרִין עַל פִּיהֶן: The same chapters that are read from a Torah scroll in the morning service are again read from a scroll in the additional service. In the afternoon service, they are read by heart (Rambam *Sefer Avoda*, *Hilkhot Kelei HaMikdash* 6:7).

דְּאִית לֵיהּ רַוְוחָא.

as the second reader **has space,** i.e., he has the option to read from the ensuing paragraph.

״פָּרָשָׁה גְּדוֹלָה קוֹרִין אוֹתָהּ בִּשְׁנַיִם בַּשַּׁחֲרִית וּבַמּוּסָף וּבַמִּנְחָה קוֹרִין עַל פִּיהֶן״ כּוּ׳. אִיבַּעְיָא לְהוּ הֵיכִי קָאָמַר בַּשַּׁחֲרִית וּבַמּוּסָף קוֹרִין אוֹתָהּ בַּסֵּפֶר וּבַמִּנְחָה קוֹרִין אוֹתָהּ עַל פֶּה כְּקוֹרִין אֶת שְׁמַע אוֹ דִּלְמָא הָכִי קָתָנֵי בַּשַּׁחֲרִית קוֹרִין אוֹתָהּ בַּסֵּפֶר וּבַמּוּסָף וּבַמִּנְחָה קוֹרִין אוֹתָהּ עַל פֶּה כְּקוֹרִין אֶת שְׁמַע.

§ The mishna taught: **A long passage is read by two** people, and they read from the Torah **in the morning prayer and in the additional prayer. And in the afternoon prayer they read** the daily portion **by heart,**[H] just as one recites *Shema*. **A dilemma was raised before** the Sages: With regard to **what** case **is the** *tanna* **speaking?** Does he mean that **in the morning prayer and in the additional prayer they read** the portion **from** a Torah **scroll, but in the afternoon prayer** each individual **reads by heart, just as one recites *Shema*? Or perhaps this is what is taught: In the morning prayer they read it from** a Torah **scroll, but in the additional prayer and in the afternoon prayer** they read it **by heart, just as one recites *Shema*.**

תָּא שְׁמַע דְּתַנְיָא בַּשַּׁחֲרִית וּבַמּוּסָף נִכְנָסִין לְבֵית הַכְּנֶסֶת וְקוֹרִין כְּדֶרֶךְ שֶׁקּוֹרִין כׇּל הַשָּׁנָה וּבַמִּנְחָה יָחִיד קוֹרֵא אוֹתָהּ עַל פֶּה. אָמַר רַבִּי יוֹסֵי וְכִי יָחִיד יָכוֹל לִקְרוֹת דִּבְרֵי תוֹרָה עַל פֶּה בַּצִּיבּוּר אֶלָּא כּוּלָּן נִכְנָסִין וְקוֹרִין אוֹתָהּ עַל פֶּה כְּקוֹרִין אֶת שְׁמַע.

The Gemara suggests: **Come** and **hear, as it is taught** in a *baraita*: **In the morning prayer and in the additional prayer they** would **enter the synagogue and read** from the Torah **in the manner that they read all year. But in the afternoon prayer,** a single **individual** would **read** the portion for that day **by heart.**[N] **Rabbi Yosei said: But can an individual read matters of Torah by heart in** the presence of **the community? Rather, they all enter and read** that day's portion together, **just as one recites *Shema*.** This *baraita* clearly indicates that they would read by heart only in the afternoon service.

NOTES

An individual reads it by heart – יָחִיד קוֹרֵא אוֹתָהּ עַל פֶּה: This apparently means that a member of the congregation would serve as a kind of prayer leader and read these chapters before the entire community. Rabbi Yosei takes issue with this ritual, as he maintains that the Torah is not read by heart by an individual in public, with the exception of the High Priest on Yom Kippur. Instead, everyone reads the chapter together (see Rid and *Divrei Shlomo*).

״כׇּל יוֹם שֶׁיֵּשׁ בּוֹ הַלֵּל אֵין בּוֹ מַעֲמָד״ כו׳. מַה הֶפְרֵשׁ בֵּין זֶה לָזֶה? הַלָּלוּ דִּבְרֵי תוֹרָה, וְהַלָּלוּ דִּבְרֵי סוֹפְרִים.

The mishna taught: On **any day that has** the recitation of ***hallel***, but on which the additional offering was not sacrificed, **it has no** reading of the Torah by the **non-priestly watch** in the morning service. On days that have both *hallel* and an additional offering, there was no reading in the afternoon prayer. When a wood offering was brought, there was no reading in the closing prayer. The Gemara asks: **What is the difference between this and that,**[N] a day on which an additional offering is sacrificed and a day on which a wood offering is brought? The Gemara explains: **These** days, on which an additional offering is brought, apply **by Torah law, but these** days, on which a wood offering is brought, apply **by rabbinic law,** and therefore it overrides only the closing prayer.

״זְמַן עֲצֵי כֹהֲנִים וְהָעָם״, כו׳. תָּנוּ רַבָּנַן: לָמָּה הוּצְרְכוּ לוֹמַר זְמַן עֲצֵי כֹהֲנִים וְהָעָם? אָמְרוּ: כְּשֶׁעָלוּ בְּנֵי הַגּוֹלָה, לֹא מָצְאוּ עֵצִים בַּלִּשְׁכָּה, וְעָמְדוּ אֵלּוּ וְהִתְנַדְּבוּ מִשֶּׁלָּהֶם.

The mishna continues with a list of the **times** for the **wood offering of priests and the people. The Sages taught: Why was it necessary to state** the **times** for the **wood offering of priests and the people?**[N] **They said** in response that this is what happened: **When the people of the exile ascended** to Jerusalem in the beginning of the Second Temple period, **they did not find** enough wood **in** the Temple **chamber** for the needs of the altar. **And these** families **arose and donated from their own**[N] wood to the Temple.

וְכָךְ הִתְנוּ נְבִיאִים שֶׁבֵּינֵיהֶן שֶׁאֲפִילּוּ לִשְׁכָּה מְלֵאָה עֵצִים, יִהְיוּ אֵלּוּ מִתְנַדְּבִין מִשֶּׁלָּהֶן, שֶׁנֶּאֱמַר: ״וְהַגּוֹרָלוֹת הִפַּלְנוּ עַל קׇרְבַּן הָעֵצִים הַכֹּהֲנִים, הַלְוִיִּם, וְהָעָם, לְהָבִיא לְבֵית אֱלֹהֵינוּ, לְבֵית אֲבוֹתֵינוּ, לְעִתִּים מְזֻמָּנִים שָׁנָה בְשָׁנָה, לְבַעֵר עַל מִזְבַּח ה׳ אֱלֹהֵינוּ, כַּכָּתוּב בַּתּוֹרָה״.

And the prophets among them stipulated as follows, that even if the entire **chamber** were **full of wood,** the descendants of **these** families **would donate wood from their own** property on these specific days, **as it is stated: "And we cast lots, the priests, the Levites and the people, for the wood offering, to bring it into the house of our God, according to our fathers' houses, at appointed times year by year, to burn upon the altar of the Lord our God, as it is written in the Torah"** (Nehemiah 10:35). Although these donations were not always necessary, it was established that all generations would observe these days.

״וְעִמָּהֶם כֹּהֲנִים וּלְוִיִּם וְכׇל מִי״, כו׳. תָּנוּ רַבָּנַן: מָה הָיוּ בְּנֵי גּוֹנְבֵי עֱלִי וּבְנֵי קוֹצְעֵי קְצִיעוֹת?

The mishna further taught that on the fifteenth of Av, wood was brought by the descendants of Zattu ben Yehuda, **and with** this group **were** other **priests and Levites, and anyone** who erred with regard to his tribe, i.e., Israelites who did not know which tribe they were from, and the descendants of those who deceived the authorities with a pestle, and the descendants of those who packed dried figs. **The Sages taught: Who were the descendants of those who deceived** the authorities **with a pestle**[N] **and the descendants of those who packed dried figs?**

אָמְרוּ: פַּעַם אַחַת גָּזְרָה מַלְכוּת הָרְשָׁעָה שְׁמָד עַל יִשְׂרָאֵל שֶׁלֹּא יָבִיאוּ עֵצִים לַמַּעֲרָכָה וְשֶׁלֹּא יָבִיאוּ בִּכּוּרִים לִירוּשָׁלַיִם, וְהוֹשִׁיבוּ פְּרוֹזְדָאוֹת עַל הַדְּרָכִים כְּדֶרֶךְ שֶׁהוֹשִׁיב יָרׇבְעָם בֶּן נְבָט שֶׁלֹּא יַעֲלוּ יִשְׂרָאֵל לָרֶגֶל.

They said in explanation: **Once, the evil kingdom**[B] of Greece **issued** a decree **of apostasy against the Jews, that they may not bring wood for the arrangement** of the altar **and that they** may **not bring first fruits to Jerusalem. And they placed guards** [*prozda'ot*][L] **on the roads, in the manner that Jeroboam, son of Nevat, placed** guards, so **that the Jews** could **not ascend for the** pilgrim **Festival.**

מֶה עָשׂוּ כְּשֵׁרִין וְיִרְאֵי חֵטְא שֶׁבְּאוֹתוֹ הַדּוֹר? הֵבִיאוּ סַלֵּי בִכּוּרִים וְחִיפּוּם בִּקְצִיעוֹת, וּנְטָלוּם וַעֱלִי עַל כִּתְפֵיהֶן. וְכֵיוָן שֶׁהִגִּיעוּ אֵצֶל פְּרוֹזְדָאוֹת, אָמְרוּ לָהֶם: לְהֵיכָן אַתֶּם הוֹלְכִין? אוֹמְרִין לָהֶם: לַעֲשׂוֹת שְׁנֵי עִגּוּלֵי דְבֵילָה בַּמַּכְתֶּשֶׁת שֶׁלְּפָנֵינוּ וּבְעֱלִי שֶׁעַל כְּתֵפֵינוּ. כֵּיוָן שֶׁעָבְרוּ מֵהֶן, עִיטְּרוּם בְּסַלִּים וֶהֱבִיאוּם לִירוּשָׁלַיִם.

What did the worthy and sin-fearing individuals **of that generation do? They brought baskets of first fruits, and covered them with dried figs, and took them with a pestle on their shoulders. And when they reached the guards,** the guards **said to them: Where are you going? They said to them:** We are going **to prepare two round cakes of pressed figs**[B] **with the mortar that is** down the road **before us and with the pestle that** we are carrying on **our shoulders. As soon as they passed** the guards, **they decorated the baskets** of first fruits **and brought them to Jerusalem.**

NOTES

What is the difference between this and that – מַה הֶפְרֵשׁ בֵּין זֶה לָזֶה: Many interpretations have been offered for this obscure statement. Rashi explains the question as follows: Why is the closing prayer treated with less importance than the afternoon service? The Gemara's answer is that there is more of a basis for the afternoon service in the Torah (see Rabbi Tzvi Hirsch Chajes). Alternatively, the Gemara is inquiring about the difference between the two types of offering: Why does the additional offering override the afternoon service whereas the wood offering does not?

According to the Rambam, in his Commentary to the Mishna, the Gemara is asking why the recitation of *hallel* takes precedence over the wood offering. The answer is that *hallel* on Hanukkah applies by rabbinic law, and therefore the status of *hallel* is in need of reinforcement, whereas there is an allusion to the wood offering in the Torah. The Rambam's text of the Gemara apparently included the sentence: A matter of rabbinical law requires reinforcement, but a matter of Torah law does not require reinforcement.

Others understand the answer similarly, but interpret the Gemara's question in a different manner: Why should the wood offering, which applies by rabbinic law, override the non-priestly watch, for which there is more of a basis in the Torah?

Why was it necessary to state the times for the wood offering of priests and the people – לָמָּה הוּצְרְכוּ לוֹמַר זְמַן עֲצֵי כֹהֲנִים וְהָעָם: Some commentaries read: Why was it necessary for the times of the wood of the priests and the people to be counted (Rabbeinu Ḥananel). According to this version, the *baraita* is asking: Why did the mishna need to specify that there are nine dates on which the wood offering is brought? Let it simply list the dates, and each reader can count them for himself. The *baraita* answers that the mishna enumerates the dates so as to emphasize their importance.

And donated from their own – וְהִתְנַדְּבוּ מִשֶּׁלָּהֶם: In the Jerusalem Talmud it is stated that although in later times there was enough ready wood in the Temple, they would still first use the wood brought by these families (see Meiri).

Who were the descendants of those who deceived with a pestle – מָה הָיוּ בְּנֵי גּוֹנְבֵי עֱלִי: The question of the *baraita* is based on the fact that the wood offerings were instituted to commemorate the generosity of those families who donated wood for the altar when the Second Temple was first built, whereas the pestle deceivers did not contribute wood in those early years. The *baraita* explains that the pestle deceivers were granted their own day to bring wood offerings, due to the special efforts they made to ensure that their first fruits would reach Jerusalem so that the sacrificial service would continue without interruption (Rabbi Elyakim).

BACKGROUND

The evil kingdom – מַלְכוּת הָרְשָׁעָה: Although this term is generally a reference to Rome, this incident apparently occurred during the period of Greek reign, and the decree was part of the persecutions that preceded the Hasmonean revolt. The version of the incident that appears in *Megillat Ta'anit* supports this claim.

Fig cakes – עִיגּוּלֵי דְּבֵילָה: In talmudic times, most figs were not eaten fresh. Rather, the major portion of the fig crop was dried in various ways. Typically, after picking the fruit they would cut off its stalk and place it to dry in the sun. At this stage, the fruit is called dry figs [*ketzi'ot*]. A sizeable proportion of the *ketzi'ot* would undergo the further processing stages of preservation and pressing, by being inserted into barrels or circular vessels. These were called *deveilim*. After preservation and a final drying, large and heavy circular fig cakes would be removed from the vessel, and slices would be cut off from these pressed fig cakes as required.

LANGUAGE

Guards [*prozda'ot*] – פְּרוֹזְדָאוֹת: Probably from the Latin praesidia, meaning watches.

תָּנָא: הֵן הֵן בְּנֵי סַלְמַאי הַנְּתוֹפָתִי. תָּנוּ רַבָּנַן: מַה הֵן בְּנֵי סַלְמַאי הַנְּתוֹפָתִי? אָמְרוּ: פַּעַם אַחַת גָּזְרָה מַלְכוּת הָרְשָׁעָה שְׁמָד עַל יִשְׂרָאֵל שֶׁלֹּא יָבִיאוּ עֵצִים לַמַּעֲרָכָה, וְהוֹשִׁיבוּ פְּרוֹזְדָאוֹת עַל הַדְּרָכִים כְּדֶרֶךְ שֶׁהוֹשִׁיב יָרָבְעָם בֶּן נְבָט עַל הַדְּרָכִים שֶׁלֹּא יַעֲלוּ יִשְׂרָאֵל לָרֶגֶל.

A Sage **taught: This** was something that was performed in a similar manner by **the descendants of Salmai**[N] **of Netophat.**[N] The Gemara explains this comment by quoting a *baraita*. **The Sages taught: Who are the descendants of Salmai of Netophat?** They said in explanation: **Once, the evil kingdom** of Greece **issued** a decree **of apostasy against the Jews, that they may not bring wood for the arrangement** of the altar **and that they may not bring first fruits to Jerusalem. And they placed guards on the roads, in the manner that Jeroboam, son of Nevat, placed** guards, so **that the Jews** could **not ascend for the** pilgrim **Festival.**

מֶה עָשׂוּ יִרְאֵי חֵטְא שֶׁבְּאוֹתוֹ הַדּוֹר? הֵבִיאוּ גְּזִירֵיהֶן וְעָשׂוּ סוּלָּמוֹת, וְהִנִּיחוּ עַל כִּתְפֵיהֶם וְהָלְכוּ לָהֶם. כֵּיוָן שֶׁהִגִּיעוּ אֶצְלָן, אָמְרוּ לָהֶם: לְהֵיכָן אַתֶּם הוֹלְכִין? אָמְרוּ לָהֶם: לְהָבִיא גּוֹזָלוֹת מִשּׁוֹבָךְ שֶׁלְּפָנֵינוּ, וּבַסּוּלָּמוֹת שֶׁעַל כְּתֵפֵינוּ. כֵּיוָן שֶׁעָבְרוּ מֵהֶן, פֵּירְקוּם וֶהֱבִיאוּם, וְהֶעֱלוּם לִירוּשָׁלַיִם.

What did the sin-fearing individuals **of that generation do? They brought their pieces of wood and prepared ladders** [*sulamot*], **and they placed** the ladders **on their shoulders and went off** to Jerusalem. **When they reached** the guards, the guards **said to them: Where are you going? They said to them:** We are going **to bring** down **doves from the dovecote that is** located down the road **before us and with these ladders that are on our shoulders. As soon as they had passed** the guards, **they dismantled** the ladders **and took them up to Jerusalem.** The name Salmai alludes to the Hebrew word for ladder, *sulam*.

וַעֲלֵיהֶם וְעַל כַּיּוֹצֵא בָּהֶם הוּא אוֹמֵר: ״זֵכֶר צַדִּיק לִבְרָכָה״, וְעַל יָרָבְעָם בֶּן נְבָט וַחֲבֵרָיו נֶאֱמַר: ״וְשֵׁם רְשָׁעִים יִרְקָב״.

And about these families who provided these donations **and** others **like them,** the verse **says: "The memory of the righteous shall be for a blessing"** (Proverbs 10:7), as they are remembered for the good throughout the generations. **And about Jeroboam, son of Nevat, and his ilk, it is stated: "But the name of the wicked shall rot"** (Proverbs 10:7).

״בְּעֶשְׂרִים בּוֹ, בְּנֵי פַּחַת מוֹאָב בֶּן יְהוּדָה״. תָּנָא: בְּנֵי פַּחַת מוֹאָב בֶּן יְהוּדָה הֵן הֵן בְּנֵי דָוִד בֶּן יְהוּדָה. דִּבְרֵי רַבִּי מֵאִיר. רַבִּי יוֹסֵי אוֹמֵר: הֵן הֵן בְּנֵי יוֹאָב בֶּן צְרוּיָה.

§ The mishna taught: **On the twentieth of** Av, the wood offering was brought by **the descendants of Pahath Moab ben Yehuda.** A *tanna* **taught: The descendants of Pahath Moab ben Yehuda are the descendants of David ben Yehuda.** He is called Moab because Ruth the Moabite was the grandmother of David's father, Yishai. This is **the statement of Rabbi Meir. Rabbi Yosei says: These are the descendants of Joab, son of Zeruiah,** whose mother was the daughter of Yishai and therefore also descended from Ruth.

״בְּעֶשְׂרִים בֶּאֱלוּל, בְּנֵי עָדִין בֶּן יְהוּדָה״, וכו׳. תָּנוּ רַבָּנַן: בְּנֵי עָדִין בֶּן יְהוּדָה הֵן הֵן בְּנֵי דָוִד בֶּן יְהוּדָה. דִּבְרֵי רַבִּי יְהוּדָה. רַבִּי יוֹסֵי אוֹמֵר: הֵן הֵן בְּנֵי יוֹאָב בֶּן צְרוּיָה.

The mishna further taught: **On the twentieth of Elul, the descendants of Adin ben Yehuda** brought their wood offering. **The Sages taught: The descendants of Adin ben Yehuda are the descendants of David**[N] **ben Yehuda,** who was called Adin. This is **the statement of Rabbi Yehuda. Rabbi Yosei says: These are the descendants of Joab, son of Zeruiah.**

״בְּאֶחָד בְּטֵבֵת, שָׁבוּ בְּנֵי פַּרְעוֹשׁ שְׁנִיָּה״, כו׳. מַנִּי מַתְנִי? לָא רַבִּי מֵאִיר, וְלָא רַבִּי יְהוּדָה, וְלָא רַבִּי יוֹסֵי. אִי רַבִּי מֵאִיר, לִיתְנֵי שָׁבוּ בְּנֵי דָוִד בֶּן יְהוּדָה שְׁנִיָּה.

The mishna taught: **On the first of Tevet, the descendants of Parosh returned** to bring wood for **a second** time. The Gemara asks: **Who is** the author of this opinion of **the mishna?** It is **not** the opinion of **Rabbi Meir, nor** that of **Rabbi Yehuda, nor** that of **Rabbi Yosei.** The Gemara elaborates: **If it** represents the opinion of **Rabbi Meir, let him teach,** with regard to the twentieth of Av, that **the descendants of David ben Yehuda returned** for **a second** time. According to Rabbi Meir, the descendants of Pahath Moab are the descendants of David, and consequently they would return for a second time on that date.

אִי רַבִּי יְהוּדָה, לִיתְנֵי שָׁבוּ בְּנֵי דָוִד בֶּן יְהוּדָה שְׁנִיָּה. אִי רַבִּי יוֹסֵי, לִיתְנֵי שָׁבוּ בְּנֵי יוֹאָב בֶּן צְרוּיָה שְׁנִיָּה!

The Gemara continues: **If it** represents the opinion of **Rabbi Yehuda, let him teach** that **the descendants of David ben Yehuda returned** for **a second** time on a different date, the twentieth of Elul, as he contends that the descendants of Adin ben Yehuda are the descendants of David. **And if** the mishna represents the opinion of **Rabbi Yosei, let him teach** that the **descendants of Joab, son of Zeruiah, returned** for **a second** time, as he maintains that the descendants of Pahath Moab and the descendants of Adin ben Yehuda are both the descendants of Joab.

NOTES

This was performed by the descendants of Salmai – הֵן הֵן בְּנֵי סַלְמַאי: Some commentaries explain that those very families who are referred to in the mishna as: Those who deceived the authorities with a pestle and those who pressed dried figs into cakes, were also known as the descendants of Salmai of Netophat, due to another courageous act they performed (see *Tosefta* 3:8; Rabbi Ovadya MiBartenura). Rashi and others indicate that this refers to different people, and the *baraita* merely wishes to compare the efforts of two groups of people to circumvent evil decrees.

Of Netophat – הַנְּתוֹפָתִי: The story related by the *baraita* does not account for the name: Of Netophat, the version of the standard texts of the Gemara. The Jerusalem Talmud, as well as certain manuscripts of the Babylonian Talmud and the *Tosefta*, have the reading: Of Netotzat, which can be understood as referring to the dismantlement, from the root *n-t-tz*, of the ladders, whose wood was brought to the altar. The most plausible reading is: Of Netophat, with the first letter *tav* exchanged for a *tet*. If so, the entire *baraita* is a homiletic interpretation of the verse: "The sons of Salma: Bethlehem, and the Netophathites" (I Chronicles 2:54). Indeed, the *Targum* on that verse interprets the names by citing these two acts of artifice, which were employed to circumvent the decrees against bringing first fruits and wood to the Temple. He explains that the name Netophat means that the acts performed by those people were as good as balm [*netofa*] (see Rabbi Yoshiya Pinto).

The descendants of Adin…are the descendants of David – בְּנֵי עָדִין...הֵן בְּנֵי דָוִד: This is based on a verse that appears in the list of David's mighty men: "Chief of the captains, he was Adino the Eznite" (II Samuel 23:8). The Gemara identifies this individual with David himself (*Moed Katan* 16b), whereas *Midrash Tanḥuma* explains that it is a reference to Joab.

לְעוֹלָם רַבִּי יוֹסֵי, וּתְרֵי תַּנָּאֵי אַלִּיבָּא דְּרַבִּי יוֹסֵי.

The Gemara answers: **Actually,** the mishna represents the opinion of **Rabbi Yosei,**[N] **and** there are **two *tanna'im*** whose opinion is **in accordance with** the opinion of **Rabbi Yosei.** One *tanna* maintains that only the descendants of Pahath Moab are the descendants of Joab, while the other claims that only the descendants of Adin ben Yehuda are the descendants of Joab. According to both opinions, neither group was repeated a second time, and therefore the mishna does not pose a difficulty to either of them.

״בְּאֶחָד בְּטֵבֵת לֹא הָיָה בּוֹ מַעֲמָד״, כּו׳. אֲמַר לֵיהּ מָר קַשִׁישָׁא בְּרֵיהּ דְּרַב חִסְדָּא לְרַב אַשִׁי:

§ The mishna taught that **on the first of Tevet there was no non-priestly watch** at all, as there was an additional offering, *hallel*, and a wood offering. **Mar Kashisha, son of Rav Ḥisda, said to Rav Ashi:**

NOTES

Actually the mishna represents the opinion of Rabbi Yosei – לְעוֹלָם רַבִּי יוֹסֵי: *Tosafot* ask: Why doesn't the Gemara answer that the mishna is in accordance with the opinion of Rabbi Meir, and that two *tanna'im* reported different versions of his view? This answer would apparently be preferable, as there is a principle that an unattributed mishna follows the opinion of Rabbi Meir. *Tosafot* answer that the Gemara chooses to explain the mishna in accordance with the opinion of Rabbi Yosei because, as stated elsewhere, Rabbi Yosei's reasoning is with him, i.e., his opinion is well grounded, and therefore the *halakha* is in accordance with him even against the majority of Sages (see *Eiruvin* 14b).

Others explain simply that it is clear from the *baraitot* that two opinions are ascribed to Rabbi Yosei, whereas there is no basis for the claim that there are conflicting versions of Rabbi Meir's opinion (Maharsha).

Perek **IV**
Daf **28** Amud **b**

מַאי שְׁנָא הַלֵּל דְּדָחֵי דִּידֵיהּ, וּמַאי שְׁנָא מוּסָף דְּלָא דָּחֵי דִּידֵיהּ?

What is different about ***hallel*** **that it overrides its own** watch,[N] i.e., the watch in the morning service, when *hallel* is recited; **and what is different** about **the additional offering, that it does not override its own** watch, of the morning service, but it does override the watch of the afternoon service and the closing prayer?

אֲמַר לֵיהּ רַב אַשִׁי: הָשְׁתָּא דְּלָאו דִּידֵיהּ דָּחֵי, דִּידֵיהּ לֹא כׇּל שֶׁכֵּן! אֲמַר לֵיהּ: הָכִי קָאָמִינָא לָךְ: לָא לִידְחֵי אֶלָּא דִּידֵיהּ!

Rav Ashi said to him: Now, as the additional offering **overrides** the watch of the afternoon service, **which is not its own,** is it **not all the more so** that it should take precedence over **its own** watch? Rav Ḥisda **said to** Rav Ashi: I meant the opposite, as this **is what I am saying to you:** It should not take precedence over another watch, that of the closing prayer; rather, **let it override only its own** watch, the one performed in the additional service.

אֲמַר לֵיהּ: אִיכָּא רַבִּי יוֹסֵי דְּקָאֵי כְּווֹתָךְ. דְּתַנְיָא: רַבִּי יוֹסֵי אוֹמֵר: כׇּל יוֹם שֶׁיֵּשׁ בּוֹ מוּסָף, יֵשׁ בּוֹ מַעֲמָד. מַעֲמָד דְּמַאי? אִילֵימָא מַעֲמָד דְּשַׁחֲרִית, הָא תַּנָּא קַמָּא נַמִי הָכִי קָאָמַר. אֶלָּא מַעֲמָד דְּמוּסָף. דִּידֵיהּ נַמִי לָא דָּחֵי?

Rav Ashi **said to him: There is Rabbi Yosei, who holds in accordance with your** opinion, **as it is taught** in a *baraita* that **Rabbi Yosei says:** On **any day on which there is an additional offering, there is a non-priestly watch.** The Gemara clarifies: **To which non-priestly watch** is he referring? **If we say** that Rabbi Yosei means **the non-priestly watch of the morning prayer, but the first *tanna*** **also said this. Rather,** Rabbi Yosei must mean the **non-priestly watch of the additional prayer.** However, this too is problematic; is it possible that the additional offering does **not override** even **its own** watch, during the additional service itself?

אֶלָּא דְּמִנְחָה. קׇרְבַּן עֵצִים דָּחֵי! אֶלָּא לָאו דִּנְעִילָה. שְׁמַע מִינַּהּ: דִּידֵיהּ דָּחֵי; דְּלָאו דִּידֵיהּ לָא דָּחֵי. שְׁמַע מִינַּהּ.

Rather, Rabbi Yosei must be referring to the watch **of the afternoon prayer.** However, this is also puzzling, for if **the wood offering overrides** the watch of the afternoon service, the additional offering should certainly take precedence over it. **Rather, is it not** the case that Rabbi Yosei is speaking of the watch **in the closing prayer?** One can **learn from this** that the additional offering **overrides its own** watch, but it does **not override** a watch **that is not its own.** The Gemara concludes: Indeed, **learn from this** that this is the case.

NOTES

What is different about *hallel* that it overrides its own watch – מַאי שְׁנָא הַלֵּל דְּדָחֵי דִּידֵיהּ: With regard to the cancellation of the watch assemblies on days of special joy, several fundamental questions arise in connection with this passage. The first issue concerns the correct version of the mishna.

According to the standard texts and most early commentaries, Rabbi Akiva initially maintained that on a day with an additional offering there was no watch in the closing prayer, and when there was a wood offering there was no watch in the afternoon service. Later, Rabbi Akiva reversed his opinion in favor of ben Azzai's ruling. Conversely, according to the *ge'onim* and some early commentaries, Rabbi Akiva's earlier and later opinions were precisely the opposite. The Gemara here assumes that on a day with a wood offering there is no watch in the afternoon service, an opinion that can be reconciled with Rabbi Akiva's final ruling only according to the reading of the *ge'onim*.

The early commentaries disagree as to why *hallel*, the additional offering, and the wood offering affect the various watch gatherings. According to Rashi, *Tosafot*, and others, the watch assemblies were canceled because there was no time to conduct them on those days. For example, on days when *hallel* was recited, it would be too much to conduct watch assemblies in the morning service as well.

The early commentaries further ask: Why should the additional offering sacrificed in Jerusalem cancel the watch gatherings conducted throughout Eretz Yisrael? Moreover, why should the wood offerings brought by specific families interfere with the assemblies conducted by the members of the watch? Some argue that the additional offering canceled the watch only for those members who were present in the Temple for the sacrificial service (Ritva).

Similarly, others maintain that the wood offering negated the watch only for the members of the family who brought the offering (Ra'avad). The *ge'onim* offer an entirely different explanation: The watch assemblies were canceled to grant distinction to those days on which *hallel* was recited, or an additional offering or a wood offering was brought. Consequently, the watch gatherings were canceled even outside of Jerusalem. An extreme opinion is that the watch assemblies were canceled only outside of Jerusalem because these assemblies were conducted only outside the capital (Rid).

The early commentaries further disagree about what exactly was canceled, whether it was the Torah reading, the special supplications, or the entire assembly.

וְלִיתְנֵי נַמִי: בְּאֶחָד בְּנִיסָן לֹא הָיָה בּוֹ מַעֲמָד, מִפְּנֵי שֶׁיֵּשׁ בּוֹ הַלֵּל וְקׇרְבַּן מוּסָף וְקׇרְבַּן עֵצִים! אָמַר רָבָא: זֹאת אוֹמֶרֶת הַלֵּילָא דְּבָרֵישׁ יַרְחָא לָאו דְּאוֹרָיְיתָא.

The Gemara asks: **And let** the mishna **also teach: On the first of Nisan there was no non-priestly watch because** it is a day **on which *hallel* is** recited, **and** it is the New Moon, on which **an additional offering** is sacrificed, and there was also **a wood offering.** Rava said: **That is to say** that **the *hallel*** recited **on a New Moon** is **not** required **by Torah law**[N] but is a custom.

דְּאָמַר רַבִּי יוֹחָנָן מִשּׁוּם רַבִּי שִׁמְעוֹן בֶּן יְהוֹצָדָק: שְׁמוֹנָה עָשָׂר יוֹם בַּשָּׁנָה יָחִיד גּוֹמֵר בָּהֶן אֶת הַהַלֵּל, וְאֵלּוּ הֵן: שְׁמוֹנַת יְמֵי הֶחָג, וּשְׁמוֹנַת יְמֵי חֲנוּכָּה, וְיוֹם טוֹב הָרִאשׁוֹן שֶׁל פֶּסַח, וְיוֹם טוֹב שֶׁל עֲצֶרֶת. וּבַגּוֹלָה, עֶשְׂרִים וְאֶחָד יוֹם, וְאֵלּוּ הֵן: תִּשְׁעַת יְמֵי הֶחָג, וּשְׁמוֹנַת יְמֵי חֲנוּכָּה, וּשְׁנֵי יָמִים הָרִאשׁוֹנִים שֶׁל פֶּסַח, וּשְׁנֵי יָמִים טוֹבִים שֶׁל עֲצֶרֶת.

As Rabbi Yoḥanan said in the name of Rabbi Shimon ben Yehotzadak: On **eighteen days a year,**[H] **the individual completes** the full ***hallel.* And they are: The eight days of the festival** of *Sukkot*, including the Eighth Day of Assembly; **the eight days of Hanukkah; the first Festival** day **of Passover; and the Festival** day **of Assembly,** i.e., *Shavuot.* **And in the Diaspora,** where a second day is added to each Festival due to uncertainty over the correct date, there **are twenty-one days, and they are: The nine days of the festival** of *Sukkot*, including the last day, known as the Celebration of the Torah, **the eight days of Hanukkah, the first two days of Passover, and the two Festival** days **of Assembly.**

רַב אִיקְּלַע לְבָבֶל, חַזְיֵנְהוּ דְּקָא קָרוּ הַלֵּילָא בְּרֵישׁ יַרְחָא. סְבַר לְאַפְסוֹקִינְהוּ. כֵּיוָן דַּחֲזָא דְּקָא מְדַלְּגִי דַּלּוֹגֵי, אָמַר: שְׁמַע מִינַּהּ: מִנְהַג אֲבוֹתֵיהֶם בִּידֵיהֶם. תָּנָא: יָחִיד לֹא יַתְחִיל, וְאִם הִתְחִיל, גּוֹמֵר.

On this topic, the Gemara relates: **Rav happened** to come **to Babylonia,**[N] where **he saw that they were reciting *hallel* on a New Moon.**[H] Unfamiliar with this practice, **he thought to stop them,** as he assumed that they were reciting *hallel* unnecessarily. **Once he saw that they were omitting** portions, **he said:** I can **learn from this** that **they are maintaining the custom of their forefathers,** i.e., they know that it is a custom, not an obligation. It **is taught** in a *baraita*: **An individual should not begin**[N] reciting *hallel* on a New Moon, **but if he has begun he should complete** it.

״חֲמִשָּׁה דְּבָרִים אֵירְעוּ אֶת אֲבוֹתֵינוּ בְּשִׁבְעָה עָשָׂר בְּתַמּוּז״, וכו׳. נִשְׁתַּבְּרוּ הַלּוּחוֹת. מְנָלַן? דְּתַנְיָא: בְּשִׁשָּׁה לַחֹדֶשׁ נִיתְּנוּ עֲשֶׂרֶת הַדִּבְּרוֹת לְיִשְׂרָאֵל. רַבִּי יוֹסֵי אוֹמֵר: בְּשִׁבְעָה בּוֹ. מַאן דְּאָמַר בְּשִׁשָּׁה נִיתְּנוּ, בְּשִׁשָּׁה נִיתְּנוּ וּבְשִׁבְעָה עָלָה מֹשֶׁה.

§ The mishna taught: **Five** calamitous **matters occurred to our forefathers on the seventeenth of Tammuz,** one of which was that **the tablets were broken.** The Gemara asks: **From where do we** derive that the tablets were broken on this day? **As it is taught** in a *baraita*: **On the sixth of the month** of Sivan **the Ten Commandments were given to the Jewish people. Rabbi Yosei says:** It was **on the seventh of that** month. The Gemara comments: According to **the one who said** that **they were given on the sixth** of Sivan, **they were given on the sixth, and on the seventh Moses ascended** to Mount Sinai.

מַאן דְּאָמַר בְּשִׁבְעָה, בְּשִׁבְעָה נִיתְּנוּ וּבְשִׁבְעָה עָלָה מֹשֶׁה, דִּכְתִיב: ״וַיִּקְרָא אֶל מֹשֶׁה בַּיּוֹם הַשְּׁבִיעִי״. וּכְתִיב: ״וַיָּבֹא מֹשֶׁה בְּתוֹךְ הֶעָנָן וַיַּעַל אֶל הָהָר, וַיְהִי מֹשֶׁה בָּהָר אַרְבָּעִים יוֹם וְאַרְבָּעִים לָיְלָה״. עֶשְׂרִים וְאַרְבָּעָה דְּסִיוָן וְשִׁיתְּסַר דְּתַמּוּז מְלוֹ לְהוּ אַרְבְּעִין.

According to **the one who said** that the Ten Commandments **were given on the seventh** of Sivan, **they were given on the seventh, and on the seventh Moses ascended** to Mount Sinai, **as it is written: "And He called to Moses on the seventh day** out of the midst of the cloud" (Exodus 24:16), **and it is written: "And Moses entered into the midst of the cloud, and he went up into the mount, and Moses was on the mount forty days and forty nights"** (Exodus 24:18). The calculation is as follows: There were **twenty-four** days remaining **in Sivan, plus** the first **sixteen days of Tammuz,** which **comes to forty** days.

NOTES

The *hallel* recited on a New Moon is not required by Torah law – הַלֵּילָא דְּבָרֵישׁ יַרְחָא לָאו דְּאוֹרָיְיתָא: One should not infer from this statement that the celebration of Hanukkah is an obligation imposed by Torah law. Rather, the recitation of *hallel* on Hanukkah is a Torah obligation, as there is an obligation to recite *hallel* whenever the Jewish people are miraculously delivered from an impending calamity (see *Pesaḥim* 117a), and the miracle of Hanukkah certainly warrants *hallel*. Conversely, the recitation of *hallel* on the New Moon is a custom, as the New Moon is neither classified as a Festival, nor does it commemorate a miracle performed for the Jewish people (Rabbeinu Yehonatan).

Rav happened to come to Babylonia – רַב אִיקְּלַע לְבָבֶל: According to the plain meaning of this story, Rav was unfamiliar with the custom of reciting *hallel* on the New Moon, which was performed only in Babylonia, not in Eretz Yisrael, Rav's place of origin.

Some suggest that it became customary in Babylonia to recite *hallel* on the New Moon to distinguish between that day and ordinary days. However, in Eretz Yisrael there was no need to take any steps to stress the unique aspects of the day, as the New Moon was proclaimed in Eretz Yisrael, and the additional offering was sacrificed in Jerusalem when the Temple was standing (*Sefer Hashlama*; Meiri).

Others explain that it was customary to recite *hallel* on the New Moon even in Eretz Yisrael; however, different sections of *hallel* were omitted there. When Rav went to Babylonia and observed that the people were reciting *hallel* on the New Moon without making the omissions that were familiar to him, he thought that they were reciting the complete *hallel* and he was about to stop them. But when he saw that the Babylonians also left out certain sections of *hallel*, he withdrew his objection, as he realized that they knew that the recitation of *hallel* on the New Moon was not ordained by Torah law or by rabbinic enactment, but was only a custom.

An individual should not begin – יָחִיד לֹא יַתְחִיל: The early commentaries disagree over the meaning of this *baraita*. Some explain that even in a place where it is customary to recite *hallel* on the New Moon, this applies only to a congregational worship, whereas an individual should not recite *hallel* on the New Moon. However, if he has already recited the blessing, he should finish the abridged form of *hallel*, so that the blessing would not have retroactively been recited in vain (*ge'onim*).

Others maintain that in places where it is customary to recite *hallel* on the New Moon, it may be recited even by an individual. According to the Rif and many other early commentaries, the *baraita* means that an individual should not recite *hallel* on the New Moon with a blessing, but if he began to recite *hallel* with a blessing he should complete his recitation. Opinions differ as to whether one should recite the concluding blessing.

Yet others explain that there is no difference whatsoever between an individual and a congregation with regard to the *hallel* recited on the New Moon, as even an individual recites *hallel* with a blessing. The *baraita* here is not referring to the *hallel* recited on the New Moon, but to the *hallel* recited by an individual in commemoration of a private miracle performed on his behalf. This individual should not recite *hallel* with a blessing, but if he began with a blessing, he should finish his recitation with a blessing (Rabbeinu Tam).

HALAKHA

Eighteen days a year – שְׁמוֹנָה עָשָׂר יוֹם בַּשָּׁנָה: There are eighteen days each year on which there is an obligation to recite the entire *hallel*: The eight days of *Sukkot*, the eight days of Hanukkah, the first day of Passover, and *Shavuot*. In the Diaspora, where a second day of each Festival is observed, *hallel* is completed on twenty-one days per year: The nine days of *Sukkot*, the eight days of Hanukkah, the first two days of Passover, and the two days of *Shavuot* (Rambam *Sefer Zemanim*, *Hilkhot Megilla VaḤanukka* 3:6–7).

***Hallel* on a New Moon – הַלֵּילָא בְּרֵישׁ יַרְחָא:** On a New Moon, an abridged version of *hallel* is recited, both by the congregation and an individual. Some authorities maintain that when this *hallel* is recited by the congregation, it is preceded and followed by blessings, whereas no blessings are recited by an individual (Rif). Others contend that no blessings are recited even by a congregation, in accordance with the opinion of the Rambam, whose ruling is accepted in most Sephardic communities. It is noted that the custom of Ashkenazic communities follows the opinion of the Rosh and Rabbeinu Tam, that even an individual recites blessings before and after *hallel* (Rema; *Shulḥan Arukh*, *Oraḥ Ḥayyim* 422:2).

בְּשִׁיבְסַר בְּתַמּוּז נָחֵית, אֲתָא, וְתַבְרִינְהוּ לַלּוּחוֹת. וּכְתִיב: ״וַיְהִי כַּאֲשֶׁר קָרַב אֶל הַמַּחֲנֶה, וַיַּרְא אֶת הָעֵגֶל. וַיַּשְׁלֵךְ מִיָּדָיו אֶת הַלֻּחֹת, וַיְשַׁבֵּר אֹתָם תַּחַת הָהָר״.

On the seventeenth of Tammuz, Moses **descended, came,** observed the people worshipping the Golden Calf, **and broke the tablets. And it is written: "And it came to pass, as soon as he came near to the camp, that he saw the calf and the dancing, and Moses' anger burned, and he cast the tablets out of his hands, and broke them beneath the mount"** (Exodus 32:19). This shows that the tablets were shattered on the seventeenth of Tammuz.

״בָּטַל הַתָּמִיד״. גְּמָרָא.

§ The mishna taught that on the seventeenth of Tammuz **the daily offering was nullified.**[N] The Gemara explains: It is a **tradition** that this occurred on that date.

״הוּבְקְעָה הָעִיר״. בְּשִׁבְעָה עָשָׂר? וְהָכְתִיב: ״בַּחֹדֶשׁ הָרְבִיעִי, בְּתִשְׁעָה לַחֹדֶשׁ, וַיֶּחֱזַק הָרָעָב בָּעִיר״. וּכְתִיב בַּתְרֵיהּ: ״וַתִּבָּקַע הָעִיר״, וגו׳!

The mishna further taught that on the seventeenth of Tammuz **the city** walls of Jerusalem **were breached.**[N] The Gemara asks: **Was** this tragedy something that occurred **on the seventeenth** of Tammuz? **But isn't it written: "In the fourth month, on ninth of the month, the famine was severe in the city"** (Jeremiah 52:6), **and it is written** immediately **afterward: "Then a breach was made in the city"** (Jeremiah 52:7), which clearly indicates that the city was breached on the ninth.

אֲמַר רָבָא: לָא קַשְׁיָא. כָּאן בָּרִאשׁוֹנָה; כָּאן בַּשְּׁנִיָּה. דְּתַנְיָא: בָּרִאשׁוֹנָה, הוּבְקְעָה הָעִיר בְּתִשְׁעָה בְּתַמּוּז; בַּשְּׁנִיָּה, בְּשִׁבְעָה עָשָׂר בּוֹ.

Rava said: This is **not difficult,** as **here** the verse is referring **to the First** Temple, whereas **there,** in the mishna, it describes the destruction **of the Second** Temple, **as it is taught** in a *baraita*: Upon the destruction **of the First** Temple, **the city** walls **were breached on the ninth of Tammuz;** and at the destruction **of the Second** Temple they were breached **on the seventeenth of** Tammuz.

״שָׂרַף אַפּוֹסְטְמוֹס אֶת הַתּוֹרָה״. גְּמָרָא.

The mishna further taught that on the seventeenth of Tammuz **Apostemos** publicly **burned a Torah scroll.** The Gemara explains: This, too, is **a tradition.**

״הֶעֱמִיד צֶלֶם בַּהֵיכָל״. מְנָלַן? דִּכְתִיב: ״וּמֵעֵת הוּסַר הַתָּמִיד, וְלָתֵת שִׁקּוּץ שֹׁמֵם״.

The mishna also stated that on the seventeenth of Tammuz Manasseh **placed an idol in the Sanctuary.**[N] The Gemara asks: **From where do we** derive that this occurred on the seventeenth of Tammuz? **As it is written: "And from the time that the daily offering shall be taken away and the abomination that causes appallment is set up"** (Daniel 12:11), which indicates that an idol was placed in the Temple on the very day that the daily offering was suspended.

וְחַד הֲוָה? וְהָכְתִיב: ״וְעַל כְּנַף שִׁקּוּצִים מְשֹׁמֵם״! אֲמַר רָבָא: תְּרֵי הָווּ, וְנָפַל חַד עַל חַבְרֵיהּ וּתְבָרֵיהּ לֵיהּ לִידֵיהּ, וְאִשְׁתַּכַּח דַּהֲוָה כְּתִיב:

The Gemara asks: **And was there** only **one** idol placed there? **But isn't it written: "And upon the wing of detestable things shall be that which causes appallment"** (Daniel 9:27)? The plural, "detestable things," indicates the presence of at least two idols. **Rava said: There were** initially **two** idols, **but one fell upon the other and broke its hand.** Since only one idol was whole, the mishna mentions only that one. Rava continues: **And** an inscription was found on the broken idol **that read:**

NOTES

The daily offering was nullified – בָּטַל הַתָּמִיד: Opinions differ with regard to the calamity mentioned here. The Jerusalem Talmud indicates that the seventeenth of Tammuz marks the suspension of the daily offering during the period of the Second Temple. Some commentaries maintain that this occurred during the First Temple period (Rambam *Sefer Zemanim*, *Hilkhot Ta'anit* 5:2). According to Rashi, the daily offering was canceled due to a decree banning its sacrifice, issued by the ruling foreign authorities. Others write that the offering was canceled because the necessary animals were no longer available on account of the siege of Jerusalem (Rabbeinu Yehonatan).

The city walls were breached – הוּבְקְעָה הָעִיר: Contrary to the explanation of the Gemara here, in the Jerusalem Talmud it is stated that the breach in the walls of Jerusalem during the First Temple period also occurred on the seventeenth of Tammuz. However, due to the many calamities that overwhelmed the Jewish people at the time, errors occurred in the calculation of the calendar, and it was mistakenly believed that the breach happened on the ninth of the month. One commentary explains at length that the mistake arose when it became impossible to declare the beginning of the new month on the basis of the testimony of witnesses who had seen the new moon, and the calculations of the calendar were made in accordance with the solar rather than the lunar calendar (Maharsha).

Placed an idol in the Sanctuary – הֶעֱמִיד צֶלֶם בַּהֵיכָל: Some commentaries read: An idol was set up. They explain that the mishna is referring to the idol set up in the First Temple by Manasseh, King of Judah. One problem with this interpretation is that it would mean that the events listed in the mishna are not in chronological order (*Gevurat Ari*). Others read: He set up an idol, and explain that the mishna is speaking of the idol set up in the Second Temple by the same Roman officer, Apostemos, who burned a Torah scroll on the same day.

Perek **IV**
Daf **29** Amud **a**

אַנְתְּ צָבֵית לְחָרוּבֵי בֵּיתָא; יָדָךְ אַשְׁלֵימַת לֵיהּ.

You want[N] **to destroy the Temple; I have given you your hand.** It is as though one idol said to the other: You are seeking to destroy the Temple by causing Israel to pray to you; I, too, give you a hand to assist you.

NOTES

You want, etc. – אַנְתְּ צָבֵית וכו׳: There are numerous readings and interpretations of this cryptic inscription found on the idol. Some understand that the inscription was found on the broken idol, while others suggest that it was found on the idol that remained whole. It is also unclear whether the comment is directed at the other idol or toward God. Most commentaries agree that the idol was suggesting that he will lend a hand in aid of the destruction of the Temple.

NOTES

That day they turned – אוֹתוֹ הַיּוֹם סָרוּ: This comment is apparently based on the juxtaposition of the departure of the Jews and their complaints over the lack of meat (see Meiri and Rashi on *Shabbat* 116a). However, Rashi here writes that it is based on a play on words. With a slight alteration of the vocalization, the verse: "And they departed from the mountain [*mehar*] of the Lord," can be read as: And they departed hastily [*maher*] from the Lord. As explained in a midrash, the Jews departed from Mount Sinai like schoolchildren running away from their master. It is further stated that Moses instructed the Israelites to advance only one day's journey, but they traveled for three days, to distance themselves from the mountain of God (*Yalkut Shimoni*).

For an entire month – עַד חֹדֶשׁ יָמִים: The early commentaries provide several different versions of these calculations, as they dispute whether the three days of travel are included, whether a part of a day is counted as a full day, and whether the months were full or lacking (see *Tosafot*, *Tosefot Rid*, and Maharsha).

He has called an appointed time against me – קָרָא עָלַי מוֹעֵד: Some commentaries explain this proof as follows: Every month that contains a Festival, an appointed time, is a full month of thirty days. Therefore, the verse: "He has called an appointed time against me," alludes to the fact that the month was declared full, as though it included a Festival (Rabbi Elyakim).

"בְּתִשְׁעָה בְּאָב נִגְזַר עַל אֲבוֹתֵינוּ שֶׁלֹּא יִכָּנְסוּ לָאָרֶץ". מְנָלַן? דִּכְתִיב: "וַיְהִי בַּחֹדֶשׁ הָרִאשׁוֹן בַּשָּׁנָה הַשֵּׁנִית, בְּאֶחָד לַחֹדֶשׁ, הוּקַם הַמִּשְׁכָּן". וְאָמַר מָר: שָׁנָה רִאשׁוֹנָה עָשָׂה מֹשֶׁה אֶת הַמִּשְׁכָּן, שְׁנִיָּה הֵקִים מֹשֶׁה אֶת הַמִּשְׁכָּן וְשָׁלַח מְרַגְּלִים. וּכְתִיב: "וַיְהִי בַּשָּׁנָה הַשֵּׁנִית, בַּחֹדֶשׁ הַשֵּׁנִי בְּעֶשְׂרִים בַּחֹדֶשׁ, נַעֲלָה הֶעָנָן מֵעַל מִשְׁכַּן הָעֵדֻת".

§ The mishna taught: **On the Ninth of Av, it was decreed upon our ancestors that they would not enter Eretz** Yisrael. The Gemara asks: **From where do we** derive this? **As it is written: "And it came to pass in the first month in the second year, on the first day of the month, that the Tabernacle was erected"** (Exodus 40:17). **And the Master said:** In the **first year** after leaving Egypt, **Moses built the Tabernacle.** At the beginning of the **second** year, **Moses erected the Tabernacle and sent** the **spies. And it is written: "And it came to pass in the second year in the second month, on the twentieth day of the month, that the cloud was taken up from the Tabernacle of the Testimony"** (Numbers 10:11).

וּכְתִיב: "וַיִּסְעוּ מֵהַר ה' דֶּרֶךְ שְׁלֹשֶׁת יָמִים". אָמַר רַבִּי חָמָא בַּר חֲנִינָא: אוֹתוֹ הַיּוֹם סָרוּ מֵאַחֲרֵי ה'. וּכְתִיב: "וְהָאסַפְסֻף אֲשֶׁר בְּקִרְבּוֹ הִתְאַוּוּ תַּאֲוָה, וַיָּשֻׁבוּ וַיִּבְכּוּ גַּם בְּנֵי יִשְׂרָאֵל", וגו'. וּכְתִיב: "עַד חֹדֶשׁ יָמִים", וגו', דְּהָווּ לְהוּ עֶשְׂרִין וְתַרְתֵּין בְּסִיוָן.

And it is further **written: "And they set forward from the mount of the Lord three days' journey"** (Numbers 10:33). **Rabbi Ḥama bar Ḥanina said: That** very **day, they turned**[N] away from God by displaying their anxiety about leaving Mount Sinai. **And it is written: "And the mixed multitude that was among them fell a lusting, and the children of Israel also wept on their part,** and said: Would that we were given flesh to eat" (Numbers 11:4). **And it is written** that the Jews ate the meat **"for an entire month"** (Numbers 11:20).[N] If one adds to the first twenty days an additional three days' journey, **these are** twenty-three days. Consequently, the subsequent month of twenty-nine days of eating meat ended **on the twenty-second of Sivan.**

וּכְתִיב: "וַתִּסָּגֵר מִרְיָם שִׁבְעַת יָמִים", דְּהָווּ לְהוּ עֶשְׂרִין וְתִשְׁעָה בְּסִיוָן. וּכְתִיב: "שְׁלַח לְךָ אֲנָשִׁים".

After this, the Jews traveled to Hazeroth, where Miriam was afflicted with leprosy, **and it is written: "And Miriam was shut out of the camp for seven days,** and the people did not journey until Miriam was brought in again" (Numbers 12:15). Including **these** seven days, they remained in Hazeroth until **the twenty-ninth of Sivan** before traveling on to Paran, **and it is written** immediately afterward: **"Send you men, that they may spy out the land of Canaan"** (Numbers 13:2).

וְתַנְיָא: "בְּעֶשְׂרִים וְתִשְׁעָה בְּסִיוָן שָׁלַח מֹשֶׁה מְרַגְּלִים". וּכְתִיב: "וַיָּשֻׁבוּ מִתּוּר הָאָרֶץ מִקֵּץ אַרְבָּעִים יוֹם". הָנֵי אַרְבָּעִים יוֹם נְכִי חַד הָווּ!

And this calculation **is taught** in a *baraita*: **On the twenty-ninth of Sivan, Moses sent** the **spies. And it is written: "And they returned from spying out the land at the end of forty days"** (Numbers 13:25), which means that they came back on the Ninth of Av. The Gemara asks: **These are forty days minus one.** The remaining days of the days of Sivan, the entire month of Tammuz, and eight days of Av add up to a total of thirty-nine days, not forty.

אֲמַר אַבַּיֵי: תַּמּוּז דְּהַהִיא שַׁתָּא מַלּוּיֵי מַלְיוּהּ, דִּכְתִיב: "קָרָא עָלַי מוֹעֵד לִשְׁבֹּר בַּחוּרָי".

Abaye said: The month of Tammuz of that year was a full month of thirty days. Accordingly, there are exactly forty days until the Ninth of Av. **And** this is alluded to in the following verse, **as it is written: "He has called an appointed time against me**[N] **to crush my young men"** (Lamentations 1:15). This indicates that an additional appointed day, i.e., a New Moon, was added so that this calamity would fall specifically on the Ninth of Av.

וּכְתִיב: "וַתִּשָּׂא כָּל הָעֵדָה וַיִּתְּנוּ אֶת קוֹלָם, וַיִּבְכּוּ הָעָם בַּלַּיְלָה הַהוּא". אָמַר רַבָּה אָמַר רַבִּי יוֹחָנָן: אוֹתוֹ לַיְלָה לֵיל תִּשְׁעָה בְּאָב הָיָה. אָמַר לָהֶם הַקָּדוֹשׁ בָּרוּךְ הוּא: אַתֶּם בְּכִיתֶם בְּכִיָּה שֶׁל חִנָּם, וַאֲנִי קוֹבֵעַ לָכֶם בְּכִיָּה לְדוֹרוֹת.

And it is further **written: "And all the congregation lifted up their voice and cried and the people wept that night"** (Numbers 14:1). **Rabba said** that **Rabbi Yoḥanan said: That night was the night of the Ninth of Av. The Holy One, Blessed be He, said to them: You wept needlessly** that night, **and I** will therefore **establish for you** a true tragedy over which there will be **weeping in** future **generations.**

"חָרַב הַבַּיִת בָּרִאשׁוֹנָה". דִּכְתִיב: "וּבַחֹדֶשׁ הַחֲמִישִׁי, בְּשִׁבְעָה לַחֹדֶשׁ, הִיא שְׁנַת תְּשַׁע עֶשְׂרֵה שָׁנָה לַמֶּלֶךְ נְבֻכַדְנֶאצַּר, מֶלֶךְ בָּבֶל, בָּא נְבוּזַרְאֲדָן, רַב טַבָּחִים, עֶבֶד מֶלֶךְ בָּבֶל, יְרוּשָׁלָם. וַיִּשְׂרֹף אֶת בֵּית ה'", וגו'. וּכְתִיב: "וּבַחֹדֶשׁ הַחֲמִישִׁי, בֶּעָשׂוֹר לַחֹדֶשׁ, הִיא שְׁנַת תְּשַׁע עֶשְׂרֵה שָׁנָה לַמֶּלֶךְ נְבוּכַדְנֶאצַּר, מֶלֶךְ בָּבֶל, בָּא נְבוּזַרְאֲדָן, רַב טַבָּחִים, עָמַד לִפְנֵי מֶלֶךְ בָּבֶל, בִּירוּשָׁלָם", וגו'.

§ The mishna further taught that on the Ninth of Av **the Temple was destroyed the first time.** The Gemara explains that this is **as it is written: "And in the fifth month, on the seventh day of the month, which was the nineteenth year of King Nebuchadnezzar, king of Babylon, Nebuzaradan, captain of the guard, a servant of the King of Babylon, came to Jerusalem. And he burnt the house of the Lord"** (II Kings 25:8–9). **And it is** also **written: "And in the fifth month, on the tenth day of the month, which was the nineteenth year of King Nebuchadnezzar, king of Babylon, Nebuzaradan, captain of the guard, who served the king of Babylon, came into Jerusalem.** And he burnt the house of the Lord" (Jeremiah 52:12–13).

ותניא: אי אפשר לומר בשבעה, שהרי כבר נאמר בעשור. ואי אפשר לומר בעשור, שהרי כבר נאמר בשבעה. הא כיצד? בשבעה נכנסו נכרים להיכל, ואכלו וקלקלו בו שביעי שמיני,

And it is taught in a *baraita*: **It is impossible to say** that the Temple was burned **on the seventh** of Av, **as it has already been stated,** in Jeremiah, that it was destroyed **on the tenth. And it is** also **impossible to say** that the Temple was burned **on the tenth** of Av, **as it has already been stated** that it was destroyed **on the seventh,** in II Kings 25:8–9. **How so;** what actually occurred? **On the seventh** of Av, **gentiles entered the Sanctuary, and on the seventh and the eighth they ate** there **and desecrated it,** by engaging in acts of fornication.

ותשיעי סמוך לחשיכה הציתו בו את האור, והיה דולק והולך כל היום כולו, שנאמר: "אוי לנו, כי פנה היום, כי ינטו צללי ערב". והיינו דאמר רבי יוחנן: אלמלי הייתי באותו הדור, לא קבעתיו אלא בעשירי, מפני שרובו של היכל בו נשרף. ורבנן? אתחלתא דפורענותא עדיפא.

And on **the ninth, adjacent to nightfall, they set fire to it, and it continuously burned the entire day, as it is stated: "Woe unto us, for the day has declined, for the shadows of the evening are stretched out"** (Jeremiah 4:6). This verse is interpreted as a prophecy about the evening when the Temple was burned. **And this is what Rabbi Yoḥanan** meant when he **said: Had I been** alive **in that generation, I would have established** the fast **only on the tenth**[N] of Av **because most of the Sanctuary was burned on that** day. **And the Sages,** who established the fast on the ninth, how do they respond to that comment? They maintain that it is **preferable** to mark **the beginning of the tragedy.**

"ובשניה". מנלן? דתניא: מגלגלין זכות ליום זכאי, וחובה ליום חייב.

And the mishna further taught that the Temple was destroyed **for the second time** also on the Ninth of Av. The Gemara asks: **From where do we** derive that the Second Temple was destroyed on this date? **It is taught** in a *baraita*: **A meritorious** matter **is brought about on an auspicious day, and a deleterious** matter **on an inauspicious day,** e.g., the Ninth of Av, on which several tragedies had already occurred.

אמרו: כשחרב בית המקדש בראשונה אותו היום תשעה באב היה, ומוצאי שבת היה, ומוצאי שביעית היתה, ומשמרתה של יהויריב היתה, והלוים היו אומרים שירה ועומדין על דוכנם. ומה שירה היו אומרים? "וישב עליהם את אונם, וברעתם יצמיתם". ולא הספיקו לומר: "יצמיתם ה׳ אלהינו", עד שבאו נכרים וכבשום. וכן בשניה.

The Sages **said: When the Temple was destroyed for the first time, that day was the Ninth of Av; and it was the conclusion of Shabbat; and it was the year after a Sabbatical Year; and it was the week of the priestly watch of Jehoiarib; and the Levites were singing** the **song and standing on their platform. And what song were they singing?** They were singing the verse: **"And He brought upon them their own iniquity, and He will cut them off in their own evil"** (Psalms 94:23). **And they did not manage to recite** the end of the verse: **"The Lord our God will cut them off," before gentiles came and conquered them. And likewise,** the same happened **when the Second** Temple was destroyed.

"נלכדה ביתר". גמרא.

The mishna teaches that **Beitar was captured** on the Ninth of Av. The Gemara explains that this is known by **tradition.**

"נחרשה העיר". תניא: כשחרש טורנוסרופוס הרשע את ההיכל, נגזרה גזרה על רבן גמליאל להריגה. בא אותו הגמון ועמד בבית המדרש, ואמר: בעל החוטם מתבקש, בעל החוטם מתבקש. שמע רבן גמליאל. אזל טשא מינייהו.

§ The mishna taught that on the Ninth of Av **the city** of Jerusalem **was plowed. It is taught** in a *baraita*: **When the wicked Turnus Rufus**[P] **plowed the Sanctuary, a decree was issued against Rabban Gamliel for execution. A certain Roman officer came and stood in the study hall and said** surreptitiously: **The man with the nose**[N] **is wanted; the man with the nose is wanted.** This was a hint that Rabban Gamliel, who stood out in his generation like a nose protruding from a face, was sought by the government. Rabban Gamliel **heard and went into hiding.**

NOTES

I would have established it only on the tenth – לא קבעתיו אלא בעשירי: The commentaries discuss at length whether Rabbi Yoḥanan's statement refers specifically to the fast established in the aftermath of the destruction of the First Temple, or whether it includes the fast enacted due to the destruction of the Second Temple (*Gevurat Ari*). The same commentary also discusses the practical ramifications of the aspect of the fast that refers to the First Temple's destruction, bearing in mind that the fast observed nowadays commemorates the destruction of the Second Temple.

The man with the nose – בעל החוטם: Rashi and others explain that this term refers to a prominent man of his generation, just as the nose is the most prominent feature of the face. Some commentaries explain that just as the nose is the most prominent and beautiful feature of the face, the same applies to the leader of the generation (*Sefer Yoḥasin*; also attributed to Rav Tzemaḥ Gaon). Some say that it is a linguistic pun, as Nasotus in Latin means the man with the big nose, and this sounds similar to *Nasi*, indicating that they are looking for the *Nasi* of the Sanhedrin.

PERSONALITIES

Turnus Rufus – טורנוסרופוס: Turnus Rufus refers to the Roman governor Quintus Tineius Rufus, who ruled Judea at the time of the bar Kokheva revolt, which he depressed with great cruelty. For this reason, he was dubbed Turnus Rufus, a deliberate distortion of his name alluding to the phonetically similar Greek word for tyrant, τύραννος, *turannos*. The midrash recounts his debates with Rabbi Akiva, whom he later commanded to be tortured and killed (*Midrash Tanḥuma*, *Tazria* 8). As related here, Turnus Rufus also ordered the plowing of the Sanctuary, as a symbol of its utter destruction.

BACKGROUND

Keys – מפתחות:

Roman key

HALAKHA

When Av begins one decreases rejoicing – משנכנס אב ממעטין בשמחה: From the beginning of the month of Av, expressions of joy are reduced. There is a decline in business activity and a halt in the construction of buildings that will serve joyous purposes. For this reason, some refrain from eating meat and drinking wine from the first of Av. This is the custom of Ashkenazic Jews (*Shulḥan Arukh*, *Oraḥ Ḥayyim* 551:1, 6, 9).

NOTES

When Adar begins one increases rejoicing – משנכנס אדר מרבין בשמחה: Rashi and most early commentaries explain that the joyful character of the month of Adar is due to the miracle of Purim, which was performed on behalf of the Jewish people during that month. Others suggest that just as expressions of gladness are restricted from the beginning of the month of Av as a reminder of the destruction of the Temple, which occurred in that month, so too, rejoicing is increased from the beginning of Adar, as this is when they began to collect the half-shekels for the Temple and the sacrificial service in anticipation of the Temple's new year (*Sefat Emet*).

אזל לגביה בצנעא. אמר ליה: אי מצילנא לך, מייתית לי לעלמא דאתי? אמר ליה: הן. אמר ליה: אשתבע לי. אשתבע ליה. סליק לאיגרא, נפיל, ומית. וגמירי, דכי גזרי גזירתא ומית חד מינייהו, מבטלי לגזרתייהו. יצתה בת קול ואמרה: אותו הגמון מזומן לחיי העולם הבא.

The Roman officer **went to him in private, and said to him: If I save you** from death, **will you bring me into the World-to-Come?** Rabban Gamliel **said to him: Yes.** The officer **said to** Rabban Gamliel: **Swear to me. He swore to him.** The officer **ascended to the roof, fell, and died. And** the Romans had **a tradition that when they issued a decree and one** of their advisors **died, they would cancel the decree.** The officer's sacrifice saved Rabban Gamliel's life. **A Divine Voice emerged and said: That officer is designated for the life of the World-to-Come.**

תנו רבנן: משחרב הבית בראשונה, נתקבצו כיתות כיתות של פרחי כהונה ומפתחות ההיכל בידן. ועלו לגג ההיכל ואמרו לפניו: רבונו של עולם! הואיל ולא זכינו להיות גזברין נאמנים, יהיו מפתחות מסורות לך. וזרקום כלפי מעלה, ויצתה כעין פיסת יד וקיבלתן מהם. והם קפצו ונפלו לתוך האור.

The Sages taught: When the Temple was destroyed for the first time, many groups of young priests gathered together with the Temple keys[B] **in their hands. And they ascended to the roof of the Sanctuary and said before** God: **Master of the Universe, since we did not merit to be faithful treasurers,** and the Temple is being destroyed, **let** the Temple **keys be handed to You. And they threw them upward, and a kind of palm of a hand emerged and received** the keys **from them. And the young priests jumped** from the roof **and fell into the fire** of the burning Temple.

ועליהן קונן ישעיהו הנביא: "משא גיא חזיון. מה לך אפוא, כי עלית כלך לגגות? תשאות מלאה, עיר הומיה, קריה עליזה, חלליך לא חללי חרב, ולא מתי מלחמה". אף בהקדוש ברוך הוא נאמר: "מקרקר קר ושוע אל ההר".

And the prophet Isaiah lamented over them: "The burden of the Valley of Vision. What ails you now that you have all gone up to the roofs? You that were full of uproar, a tumultuous city, a joyous town, your slain are not slain with the sword, nor dead in battle" (Isaiah 22:1–2). This is referring to the young priests who died by throwing themselves off the roof into the fire. **And even with regard to the Holy One, Blessed be He, it is stated:** "For it is a day of trouble, and of trampling, and of confusion for the Lord of hosts, in the Valley of Vision; **a shouting over walls and a cry to the mountain"** (Isaiah 22:5). This verse indicates that even God shouts over the destruction of the Temple.

"משנכנס אב, ממעטין בשמחה", וכו'. אמר רב יהודה בריה דרב שמואל בר שילת משמיה דרב: כשם שמשנכנס אב ממעטין בשמחה, כך משנכנס אדר מרבין בשמחה.

§ The mishna teaches that **from when** the month of **Av begins, one decreases** acts of **rejoicing.**[H] **Rav Yehuda, son of Rav Shmuel bar Sheilat, said in the name of Rav: Just as when Av begins one decreases rejoicing, so too when** the month of **Adar begins, one increases rejoicing.**[N]

Perek **IV**
Daf **29** Amud **b**

NOTES

When his fortune is bad…when his fortune is good – דריע מזליה...דבריא מזליה: Although the Sages have said that there is no constellation that influences the Jewish people, this is a special decree that applies to these dates (Ritva). Other commentaries explain that this is similar to idea mentioned previously in the Gemara that a deleterious matter is brought about on an inauspicious day, when calamities occurred to the Jewish people (Maharsha).

Palm trees and garments of linen – דקלים וכלי פשתן: Rashi explains that palm trees served as the Jewish people's future and hope during their seventy-year exile in Babylonia, as they supported themselves from the fruit of these palms. Several talmudic sources indicate that palm trees served as an important source of income for Babylonian Jewry. Some explain that palm trees and linen garments are singled out as the future and hope of the Jewish people during its exile because both last an especially long time, and therefore they served as a symbol of long-suffering and survival (Maharsha).

אמר רב פפא: הלכך בר ישראל דאית ליה דינא בהדי נכרי לישתמיט מיניה באב, דריע מזליה, ולימצי נפשיה באדר, דבריא מזליה.

Rav Pappa said: Therefore, in the case of **a Jew who has litigation**[H] **with a gentile, let him avoid him in** the month of **Av,** when the Jews' **fortune is bad, and he should make himself available in Adar, when his fortune is good.**[N]

"לתת לכם אחרית ותקוה". אמר רב יהודה בריה דרב שמואל בר שילת משמיה דרב: אלו דקלים וכלי פשתן. "ויאמר: ראה, ריח בני כריח שדה אשר ברכו ה'". אמר רב יהודה בריה דרב שמואל בר שילת משמיה דרב: כריח שדה של תפוחים.

The Gemara mentions a couple of other statements in the name of the same Sages mentioned above. First, it cites a verse that is referring to the Babylonian exile. **"To give to you a future and a hope"** (Jeremiah 29:11). **Rav Yehuda, son of Rav Shmuel bar Sheilat, said in the name of Rav: These are palm trees and garments of linen,**[N] which are long-lasting and bring benefit as long as they exist. With regard to Isaac's comment about Jacob: **"And he said: See, the smell of my son is as the smell of a field which the Lord has blessed"** (Genesis 27:27), **Rav Yehuda, son of Rav Shmuel bar Sheilat, said in the name of Rav:** This smell was like that **of a field of apple trees.**[B]

BACKGROUND

A field of apple trees – שדה של תפוחים: *Tosafot* are puzzled by this comparison. Apparently, this refers to a particular, local type of apple, which ripens to a yellowish-gold and has a sweet and juicy taste and a strong, pleasant odor.

HALAKHA

A Jew who has litigation – בר ישראל דאית ליה דינא: A Jew who has pending litigation with a gentile should try to avoid court proceedings during the month of Av, or at least until after the Ninth of Av (*Korban Netanel*). This ruling is in accordance with the opinion of Rav Pappa (*Shulḥan Arukh*, *Oraḥ Ḥayyim* 551:1).

״שַׁבָּת שֶׁחָל תִּשְׁעָה בְּאָב לִהְיוֹת בְּתוֹכָהּ, אֲסוּרִין לְסַפֵּר וּלְכַבֵּס״. אָמַר רַב נַחְמָן: לֹא שָׁנוּ אֶלָּא לְכַבֵּס וְלִלְבּוֹשׁ, אֲבָל לְכַבֵּס וּלְהַנִּיחַ מוּתָּר. וְרַב שֵׁשֶׁת אָמַר: אֲפִילּוּ לְכַבֵּס וּלְהַנִּיחַ אָסוּר. אֲמַר רַב שֵׁשֶׁת: תֵּדַע, דְּבָטְלִי קָצְרֵי דְּבֵי רַב.

§ The mishna taught: During **the week in which the Ninth of Av occurs, it is prohibited to cut one's hair and to launder** clothes. **Rav Naḥman said: They taught** that it is prohibited **only to launder and to wear** clean clothes before the Ninth of Av; **however,** if one wishes **to launder** garments **and to set** them **aside,** this is **permitted. And Rav Sheshet said: Even to launder** them **and to set** them **aside is prohibited. Rav Sheshet said: Know** that I am correct, **as the launderers of Rav's household were idle**[N] during this week, which shows that laundering in and of itself is prohibited.

מְתִיב רַב הַמְנוּנָא: ״בַּחֲמִישִׁי מוּתָּרִים מִפְּנֵי כְּבוֹד הַשַּׁבָּת״. לְמַאי? אִילֵימָא לְכַבֵּס וְלִלְבּוֹשׁ, מַאי כְּבוֹד שַׁבָּת אִיכָּא?

Rav Hamnuna raised an objection against Rav Naḥman's ruling from the mishna: **On Thursday,** these actions **are permitted in deference to Shabbat.** The Gemara clarifies: **To which** actions is this referring? **If we say** that it is permitted **to launder and to wear** clothing immediately, **what deference to Shabbat is there** in wearing a garment on Thursday?

אֶלָּא, לְהַנִּיחַ. וּבַחֲמִישִׁי הוּא דִּשְׁרֵי, אֲבָל הַשַּׁבָּת כּוּלָּהּ אָסוּר! לְעוֹלָם, לְכַבֵּס וְלִלְבּוֹשׁ, וּכְשֶׁאֵין לוֹ אֶלָּא חָלוּק אֶחָד. דְּאָמַר רַב אַסִי אָמַר רַבִּי יוֹחָנָן: מִי שֶׁאֵין לוֹ אֶלָּא חָלוּק אֶחָד מוּתָּר לְכַבְּסוֹ בְּחוּלּוֹ שֶׁל מוֹעֵד. אִיתְּמַר נַמִי: אָמַר רַבִּי בִּנְיָמִין אָמַר רַבִּי אֶלְעָזָר: לֹא שָׁנוּ אֶלָּא לְכַבֵּס וְלִלְבּוֹשׁ, אֲבָל לְהַנִּיחַ מוּתָּר.

Rather, it must mean that one can wash and **set aside** the garment until Shabbat, **and** this washing **is permitted** only **on Thursday; however,** during the rest of **the entire week it is prohibited.** The Gemara rejects this contention: **Actually,** the mishna permits one **to launder and wear** a garment immediately on Thursday, **and** this ruling is referring **to one who has only one shirt** [*ḥaluk*]. This laundering is also considered in deference to Shabbat because if one does not wash his shirt now, on Thursday, he will not have the opportunity to do so later, as the mishna is referring to a case when the Ninth of Av occurs on a Friday. **As Rabbi Asi said** that **Rabbi Yoḥanan said: One who has only one shirt**[H] **is permitted to launder it on the intermediate days of a Festival,** when it is normally prohibited to do so. **It was also stated** that **Rabbi Binyamin said** that **Rabbi Elazar said: They taught** that it is prohibited **only to launder and to wear** immediately; **however,** if one launders **to set it aside,** this is **permitted.**

מֵיתִיבִי: אָסוּר לְכַבֵּס לִפְנֵי תִּשְׁעָה בְּאָב, אֲפִילּוּ לְהַנִּיחַ לְאַחַר תִּשְׁעָה בְּאָב. וְגִיהוּץ שֶׁלָּנוּ כְּכִיבּוּס שֶׁלָּהֶן. וּכְלֵי פִשְׁתָּן אֵין בָּהֶם מִשּׁוּם גִּהוּץ. תְּיוּבְתָּא.

The Gemara **raises an objection** from a *baraita*: **It is prohibited to launder before the Ninth of Av,**[H] **even** if one intends **to set aside** the clothes **until after the Ninth of Av. And our fine laundering** [*gihutz*][L] in Babylonia **is like their plain laundering**[N] in Eretz Yisrael. But our plain washing in Babylonia is not considered laundering at all, and it is permitted. **And** with regard to **linen garments,** the process **of fine laundry does not apply to them,**[N] as this category applies only to woolen garments.[H] In any case, this *baraita* indicates that laundering clothes and setting them aside is prohibited, which means it is **a conclusive refutation** of the opinion of Rav Naḥman.

HALAKHA

One who has only one shirt – מִי שֶׁאֵין לוֹ אֶלָּא חָלוּק אֶחָד: It is prohibited to launder on the intermediate days of a Festival, but one who has only a single garment may wash it (*Shulḥan Arukh, Oraḥ Ḥayyim* 534:1).

It is prohibited to launder before the Ninth of Av – אָסוּר לְכַבֵּס לִפְנֵי תִּשְׁעָה בְּאָב: During the week of the Ninth of Av, it is prohibited to cut hair or launder. Laundry is prohibited that week even if one does not intend to wear the clean clothing until after the Ninth of Av, and even if he has only one garment. Likewise, it is prohibited to wear freshly washed clothing or use freshly washed linen, even if they were laundered before the week of the Ninth of Av (*Shulḥan Arukh, Oraḥ Ḥayyim* 551:3).

Fine laundering and plain laundering – גִּהוּץ וְכִיבּוּס: Some commentaries say that the prohibition against laundering does not apply to linen garments at all. However, it is customary to prohibit all laundering during the week of the Ninth of Av, even plain washing and even for linen garments. Some authorities maintain that the plain laundering of all countries, with the exception of Babylonia, is considered like the plain laundering of Eretz Yisrael.

Others contend that the plain laundering mentioned in the Gemara refers to washing with water alone, whereas fine laundering refers to washing with water and soap. Consequently, all present-day laundering is prohibited, as it is performed with soap (*Nimmukei Yosef*). The Ashkenazic custom is to refrain from all kinds of laundering from the first of Av (Rema), however, one who has only one garment is permitted to wash it before the week of the Ninth of Av (*Mishna Berura*, citing *Eliya Rabba*; *Shulḥan Arukh, Oraḥ Ḥayyim* 551:3).

LANGUAGE

Fine laundering [*gihutz*] – גִּיהוּץ: In ancient times, at the end of the laundering process garments were provided with a finishing wash in water that contained detergents, and they were scrubbed with soft stones. In Eretz Yisrael, the water was more suitable for laundering and better detergents were available, which meant that the first part of the laundering process in Eretz Yisrael produced garments as clean as the more complex laundering process of Babylonia.

However, linen garments were not finished in this way, as certain types of dirt do not cling to linen and are not absorbed as with woolen garments. Consequently, even if linen garments were given a finishing scrub, it would not greatly improve the results.

NOTES

As the launderers of Rav's household were idle – דְּבָטְלִי קָצְרֵי דְּבֵי רַב: According to a source of the *ge'onim*, the term: Rav's household, which usually refers to a talmudic academy, i.e., the house of the Rabbi, is referring here to house of the *rabba*, the great one, i.e., the Exilarch.

Our fine laundering is like their plain laundering – גִּיהוּץ שֶׁלָּנוּ כְּכִיבּוּס שֶׁלָּהֶן: The early commentaries deal at length with the various aspects of washing clothes mentioned here in the Gemara. Some explain that when the Gemara says that our fine laundering is like their plain laundering, it means that although plain laundering is prohibited in the week of the Ninth of Av in Eretz Yisrael, it is permitted during that period in Babylonia, where only fine laundering is prohibited (Rashi; Ra'avad).

As for the difference between Eretz Yisrael and Babylonia, most explain that either the water in Eretz Yisrael or the process of laundering practiced there was superior to that of Babylonia. In other words, the level of cleanness achieved in Eretz Yisrael through simple washing could be attained in Babylonia only through fine laundering, i.e., by scrubbing the garments with abrasive stones.

The early authorities disagree as to whether plain laundering is permitted in all communities outside Eretz Yisrael or only in Babylonia. Some suggest that plain laundering in Eretz Yisrael achieved the same level of cleanness as fine laundering in Babylonia because the garments in Eretz Yisrael were made of thinner fabrics, which were easier to wash (*Arukh*).

Yet others interpret the statement: Our fine laundering is like their plain laundering, as follows: The fine laundering that we do now, after the initial washing process, is like the plain washing that was performed by earlier generations. Just as their plain washing was prohibited during the week of the Ninth of Av, our fine laundering nowadays is also prohibited.

Consequently, the text is not teaching that plain laundering is permitted anywhere during the week of the Ninth of Av. Instead, it means that our fine laundering is prohibited during the week of the Ninth of Av, even if it is performed on clothing that was laundered in a regular manner the week before (*Sefer Hashlama*; *Mikhtam*).

With regard to linen garments the process of fine laundry does not apply to them – כְּלֵי פִשְׁתָּן אֵין בָּהֶם מִשּׁוּם גִּהוּץ: Some commentaries explain that even fine laundering of linen garments is permitted during the week of the Ninth of Av, as linen garments do not emerge from the fine laundering process as new, unlike woolen garments (Ritva). Others write that linen garments that have been washed by plain laundering before the week of the Ninth of Av may be cleaned in the manner of fine laundering during the week of the Ninth of Av, provided that they will not be worn until after the fast. However, they may not be cleaned by a process of fine laundering during the week of the Ninth of Av if they are to be worn immediately (*Sefer Hashlama*).

שְׁלַח רַב יִצְחָק בַּר גִּיּוֹרֵי מִשְּׁמֵיהּ דְּרַבִּי יוֹחָנָן: אַף עַל פִּי שֶׁאָמְרוּ כְּלֵי פִשְׁתָּן אֵין בָּהֶם מִשּׁוּם גִּהוּץ, אֲבָל אָסוּר לְלוֹבְשָׁן בְּשַׁבָּת שֶׁחָל תִּשְׁעָה בְּאָב לִהְיוֹת בְּתוֹכָהּ.

Rav Yitzḥak bar Giyorei sent in the name of Rabbi Yoḥanan: Although the **Sages** said that with regard to **linen garments,** the process **of fine laundry does not apply to them; still, it is prohibited to wear them** during **the week in which the Ninth of Av occurs.**

אָמַר רַב: לֹא שָׁנוּ אֶלָּא לְפָנָיו, אֲבָל לְאַחֲרָיו מוּתָּר. וּשְׁמוּאֵל אָמַר: אֲפִילּוּ לְאַחֲרָיו נַמִי אָסוּר. מֵיתִיבִי: שַׁבָּת שֶׁחָל תִּשְׁעָה בְּאָב לִהְיוֹת בְּתוֹכָהּ אָסוּר לְסַפֵּר וּלְכַבֵּס. וּבַחֲמִישִׁי מוּתָּרִין מִפְּנֵי כְבוֹד הַשַּׁבָּת. כֵּיצַד? חָל לִהְיוֹת בְּאֶחָד בְּשַׁבָּת, מוּתָּר לְכַבֵּס כָּל הַשַּׁבָּת כּוּלָּהּ.

With regard to these restrictions and prohibitions, which apply during the week of the Ninth of Av, **Rav said: They taught** that these prohibitions apply **only before** the Ninth of Av, **but after** the fast laundering is **permitted.**[H] **And Shmuel said: Even after** the Ninth of Av, laundering is **also prohibited** until the end of the week. The Gemara **raises an objection:** During **the week in which the Ninth of Av occurs,** it is prohibited **to cut one's hair and to launder** clothes, **but on Thursday** these actions **are permitted in deference to Shabbat. How so?** If the Ninth of Av **occurs on a Sunday, it is permitted to launder the entire** preceding **week.**

בְּשֵׁנִי, בִּשְׁלִישִׁי, בִּרְבִיעִי, וּבַחֲמִישִׁי, לְפָנָיו אָסוּר, לְאַחֲרָיו מוּתָּר. חָל לִהְיוֹת בְּעֶרֶב שַׁבָּת, מוּתָּר לְכַבֵּס בַּחֲמִישִׁי, מִפְּנֵי כְבוֹד הַשַּׁבָּת. וְאִם לֹא כִּבֵּס בַּחֲמִישִׁי בְּשַׁבָּת, מוּתָּר לְכַבֵּס בְּעֶרֶב שַׁבָּת מִן הַמִּנְחָה וּלְמַעְלָה. לָיֵיט עֲלָהּ אַבָּיֵי, וְאִיתֵּימָא רַב אַחָא בַּר יַעֲקֹב, אַהָא.

If the Ninth of Av occurs **on a Monday, Tuesday, Wednesday, or Thursday,** on the days **before** the Ninth of Av, laundering is **prohibited,** but **after** the fast it is **permitted.** If the Ninth of Av **occurs on a Friday,**[N] **it is permitted to launder on Thursday in deference to Shabbat. And if,** for whatever reason, **one did not launder on the Thursday of that week, he is permitted to launder on Friday** from *minḥa* time **onward,** despite the fact that it is the Ninth of Av. **Abaye, and some say Rav Aḥa bar Ya'akov, cursed** those who do **this.**[N]

חָל לִהְיוֹת בְּשֵׁנִי וּבַחֲמִישִׁי, קוֹרִין שְׁלֹשָׁה וּמַפְטִיר אֶחָד. בִּשְׁלִישִׁי וּבִרְבִיעִי, קוֹרֵא אֶחָד וּמַפְטִיר אֶחָד. רַבִּי יוֹסֵי אוֹמֵר: לְעוֹלָם קוֹרִין שְׁלֹשָׁה וּמַפְטִיר אֶחָד. תְּיוּבְתָּא דִּשְׁמוּאֵל!

The Gemara resumes its citation of the *baraita*: If the Ninth of Av **occurs on a Monday or on a Thursday, three** people are called to **read** from the Torah, as on a regular week, **and one** of them **recites the portion from the Prophets.**[H] If the Ninth of Av occurs **on a Tuesday or on a Wednesday, one** individual **reads** the Torah **and** the same **one recites the portion from the Prophets. Rabbi Yosei says: Actually, three** people are called to **read,** no matter what day of the week it is, **and one** of them **recites the portion from the Prophets** for the Ninth of Av. In any case, the *baraita* apparently presents **a conclusive refutation of** the opinion of **Shmuel,** as it clearly states that one is permitted to launder during the weekdays following the Ninth of Av.

אָמַר לָךְ שְׁמוּאֵל: תַּנָּאֵי הִיא. דְּתַנְיָא: תִּשְׁעָה בְּאָב שֶׁחָל לִהְיוֹת בְּשַׁבָּת, וְכֵן עֶרֶב תִּשְׁעָה בְּאָב שֶׁחָל לִהְיוֹת בְּשַׁבָּת, אוֹכֵל וְשׁוֹתֶה כָּל צָרְכּוֹ, וּמַעֲלֶה עַל שׁוּלְחָנוֹ אֲפִילּוּ כִּסְעוּדַּת שְׁלֹמֹה בִּשְׁעָתוֹ. וְאָסוּר לְסַפֵּר וּלְכַבֵּס מֵרֹאשׁ חֹדֶשׁ וְעַד הַתַּעֲנִית. דִּבְרֵי רַבִּי מֵאִיר. רַבִּי יְהוּדָה אוֹמֵר: כָּל הַחֹדֶשׁ כּוּלּוֹ אָסוּר. רַבָּן שִׁמְעוֹן בֶּן גַּמְלִיאֵל אוֹמֵר: אֵינוֹ אָסוּר אֶלָּא אוֹתָהּ שַׁבָּת בִּלְבַד.

Shmuel could have **said to you:** This **is** a dispute between *tanna'im*, **as it is taught** in a *baraita*: In the case of **the Ninth of Av that occurs on Shabbat,**[H] **and so too,** on **the eve of the Ninth of Av that occurs on Shabbat,** one need not reduce the amount of food he eats; rather, **he may eat and drink as much as he requires and put on his table a meal even like that of** King **Solomon in his time. And it is prohibited to cut one's hair and to launder from the New Moon until** after **the fast.**[N] This is **the statement of Rabbi Meir. Rabbi Yehuda says:** These activities are **prohibited throughout the entire month. Rabban Shimon ben Gamliel says:** They are **prohibited only** during **that week** of the Ninth of Av.

וְתַנְיָא אִידָּךְ: וְנוֹהֵג אֵבֶל מֵרֹאשׁ חֹדֶשׁ וְעַד הַתַּעֲנִית. דִּבְרֵי רַבִּי מֵאִיר. רַבִּי יְהוּדָה אוֹמֵר: כָּל הַחֹדֶשׁ כּוּלּוֹ אָסוּר. רַבָּן שִׁמְעוֹן בֶּן גַּמְלִיאֵל אוֹמֵר: אֵינוֹ אָסוּר אֶלָּא אוֹתָהּ שַׁבָּת בִּלְבַד.

And it is taught in another *baraita*: **And** one must **observe** the rites of **mourning from the New Moon until** after **the fast;** this is **the statement of Rabbi Meir. Rabbi Yehuda says:** These activities are **prohibited throughout the entire month. Rabban Shimon ben Gamliel says:** They are **prohibited only** during **that week.** These *baraitot* show that there are at least two *tanna'im*, Rabbi Yehuda and Rabban Shimon ben Gamliel, who prohibit certain activities even after the fast, like Shmuel.

אָמַר רַבִּי יוֹחָנָן: וּשְׁלָשְׁתָּן מִקְרָא אֶחָד דָּרְשׁוּ, דִּכְתִיב: ״וְהִשְׁבַּתִּי כָּל מְשׂוֹשָׂהּ, חַגָּהּ, חָדְשָׁהּ, וְשַׁבַּתָּהּ״. מַאן דְּאָמַר מֵרֹאשׁ חֹדֶשׁ וְעַד הַתַּעֲנִית

Rabbi Yoḥanan said: And all three of these *tanna'im* **derived** their opinions from **one verse,** from which they drew different conclusions, **as it is written: "And I will cause all her mirth to cease, her Festival, her New Moon, and her Shabbat"** (Hosea 2:13). **The one who said** that these activities are prohibited **from the New Moon until** after **the fast,** Rabbi Meir,

HALAKHA

After the fast it is permitted – לְאַחֲרָיו מוּתָּר: After the fast of the Ninth of Av has ended, it is immediately permitted to cut one's hair and launder, in accordance with the opinion of Rav. However, the authorities note that it is customary to refrain from engaging in these activities until midday of the tenth of Av (*Mishna Berura*; *Shulḥan Arukh, Oraḥ Ḥayyim* 551:4).

Three read and one recites the portion from the Prophets – קוֹרִין שְׁלֹשָׁה וּמַפְטִיר אֶחָד: On the Ninth of Av, three people are called up to read from the Torah, both in the morning service and in the afternoon service. During the morning prayers the third reader recites the portion from the Prophets (*Tur, Oraḥ Ḥayyim* 559).

The Ninth of Av that occurs on Shabbat – תִּשְׁעָה בְּאָב שֶׁחָל לִהְיוֹת בְּשַׁבָּת: If the Ninth of Av falls on a Sunday or if it is deferred from Shabbat to Sunday, one may eat meat and drink wine during the last meal before the fast, and one may even partake of a lavish meal without any adjustment (*Shulḥan Arukh, Oraḥ Ḥayyim* 551:10).

NOTES

Occurs on a Friday – חָל לִהְיוֹת בְּעֶרֶב שַׁבָּת: Some commentaries note that this *halakha* was applicable only when the New Moon was established on the basis of witness testimony, as only in that period was it possible for the Ninth of Av to occur on a Friday. Nowadays, when a fixed calendar is in use, the Ninth of Av can never occur on a Friday (Rabbeinu Yehonatan).

Abaye cursed…those who did this – לָיֵיט עֲלָהּ אַבָּיֵי...אַהָא: Although the *baraita* expressly permits this practice, Abaye was very strict with those who neglected to wash their clothes earlier and ended up having to do their laundry on the Ninth of Av itself (Rabbeinu Ḥananel; see *Gevurat Ari* and *Sefat Emet*).

And it is prohibited to cut one's hair and to launder from the New Moon until after the fast – וְאָסוּר לְסַפֵּר וּלְכַבֵּס מֵרֹאשׁ חֹדֶשׁ וְעַד הַתַּעֲנִית: The dispute with regard to the prohibitions against laundry and cutting hair continued well beyond the tannaitic period. The Jerusalem Talmud notes that different customs were followed in the various centers of Jewry in Eretz Yisrael, i.e., Tiberias, Tzippori, and the cities of the South. Although the Babylonian Talmud rules that the *halakha* is in accordance with the lenient opinions of Rabban Shimon ben Gamliel and Rabbi Meir, many communities adopted various stringencies of the other tannaitic opinions.

מֵ״חַגָּהּ״. וּמַאן דְּאָמַר כּוּלּוֹ אָסוּר מֵ״חָדְשָׁהּ״. וּמַאן דְּאָמַר כָּל הַשַּׁבָּת כּוּלָּהּ אָסוּר מִ״שַּׁבַּתָּהּ״.

derives **from** the phrase **"her Festival"**[N] that acts of mirth and rejoicing are prohibited from the New Moon, which is considered like a Festival. **And the one who said** that these activities are **prohibited** during **the entire** month learns this **from** the phrase **"her New Moon." And the one who said** that acts of rejoicing are **prohibited** during **the entire week** of the Ninth of Av, derives this **from** the phrase **"her Shabbat,"** which also means a week.

אָמַר רָבָא: הֲלָכָה כְּרַבָּן שִׁמְעוֹן בֶּן גַּמְלִיאֵל. וְאָמַר רָבָא: הֲלָכָה כְּרַבִּי מֵאִיר. וְתַרְוַיְיהוּ לְקוּלָּא, וּצְרִיכָא. דְּאִי אַשְׁמוֹעִינַן הֲלָכָה כְּרַבִּי מֵאִיר, הֲוָה אָמִינָא: אֲפִילּוּ מֵרֹאשׁ חֹדֶשׁ. קָמַשְׁמַע לָן: הֲלָכָה כְּרַבָּן שִׁמְעוֹן בֶּן גַּמְלִיאֵל.

With regard to the *halakha* itself, **Rava said: The *halakha* is in accordance with** the opinion of **Rabban Shimon ben Gamliel. And Rava** also **said** that **the *halakha* is in accordance with** the opinion of **Rabbi Meir.** The Gemara remarks: **And both of** these rulings are intended **as a leniency. And** it is **necessary** for Rava to state both rulings, **for had he taught us** only that **the *halakha* is in accordance with** the opinion of **Rabbi Meir, I would have said** that the mourning practices are obligatory **even from the New Moon,** as maintained by Rabbi Meir. Therefore, Rava **teaches us** that the ***halakha* is in accordance with** the opinion of **Rabban Shimon ben Gamliel,** that the restrictions of mourning do not apply until the week of the Ninth of Av.

וְאִי אַשְׁמוֹעִינַן הֲלָכָה כְּרַבָּן שִׁמְעוֹן בֶּן גַּמְלִיאֵל, הֲוָה אָמִינָא: אֲפִילּוּ לְאַחֲרָיו. קָמַשְׁמַע לָן: הֲלָכָה כְּרַבִּי מֵאִיר.

And had he taught us only that the *halakha* **is in accordance with** the opinion of **Rabban Shimon ben Gamliel, I would have said** that the prohibitions apply **even after** the fast, until the end of the week. Consequently, Rava **teaches us** that the ***halakha* is in accordance with** the opinion of **Rabbi Meir.** The prohibitions apply only until the Ninth of Av itself, not afterward.

״עֶרֶב תִּשְׁעָה בְּאָב, לֹא יֹאכַל אָדָם שְׁנֵי תַבְשִׁילִין״, כו׳. אָמַר רַב יְהוּדָה: לֹא שָׁנוּ אֶלָּא מִשֵּׁשׁ שָׁעוֹת וּלְמַעְלָה, אֲבָל מִשֵּׁשׁ שָׁעוֹת וּלְמַטָּה מוּתָּר. וְאָמַר רַב יְהוּדָה: לֹא שָׁנוּ אֶלָּא בִּסְעוּדָה הַמַּפְסִיק בָּהּ, אֲבָל בִּסְעוּדָה שֶׁאֵינוֹ מַפְסִיק בָּהּ, מוּתָּר.

§ The mishna taught: On **the eve of the Ninth of Av, a person may not eat two cooked dishes**[N] in one meal. **Rav Yehuda said: They taught** that one may not partake of a meal with two dishes **only from six hours** of the day **and onward,** but **from six hours and earlier** it is **permitted. And Rav Yehuda** also **said: They taught** that it is prohibited to eat two dishes **only in the concluding meal**[H] before beginning the fast. **However, in a non-concluding meal** it is **permitted** to eat two cooked dishes.

וְתַרְוַיְיהוּ לְקוּלָּא, וּצְרִיכָא. דְּאִי אַשְׁמְעִינַן בִּסְעוּדָה הַמַּפְסִיק בָּהּ, הֲוָה אָמִינָא: אֲפִילּוּ מִשֵּׁשׁ שָׁעוֹת וּלְמַטָּה. קָמַשְׁמַע לָן: מִשֵּׁשׁ שָׁעוֹת וּלְמַעְלָה. וְאִי אַשְׁמְעִינַן מִשֵּׁשׁ שָׁעוֹת וּלְמַעְלָה, הֲוָה אָמִינָא: אֲפִילּוּ בִּסְעוּדָה שֶׁאֵינוֹ מַפְסִיק בָּהּ. קָמַשְׁמַע לָן בִּסְעוּדָה הַמַּפְסִיק בָּהּ.

The Gemara comments: **And both of** these rulings are intended **as a leniency. And** it is **necessary** for Rav Yehuda to state them both, **for had he taught us** that this *halakha* is referring only **to the concluding meal, I would have said** that this applies **even from six hours and earlier.** Rav Yehuda therefore **teaches us** that it applies only **from six hours and onward. And had he taught us** only that it is prohibited to eat two dishes **from six hours and onward, I would have said** that this applies **even to a meal by which he does not stop** eating. Rav Yehuda therefore **teaches us** that it applies only **to the concluding meal.**

תַּנְיָא כְּלִישָּׁנָא קַמָּא, תַּנְיָא כְּלִישָּׁנָא בַּתְרָא. תַּנְיָא כְּלִישָּׁנָא בַּתְרָא: הַסּוֹעֵד עֶרֶב תִּשְׁעָה בְּאָב, אִם עָתִיד לִסְעוֹד סְעוּדָה אַחֶרֶת, מוּתָּר לֶאֱכוֹל בָּשָׂר וְלִשְׁתּוֹת יַיִן. וְאִם לָאו, אָסוּר לֶאֱכוֹל בָּשָׂר וְלִשְׁתּוֹת יַיִן.

The Gemara comments: **It is taught** in a *baraita* **in accordance with the first version,** and **it is taught** in a *baraita* **in accordance with the second version.** The Gemara elaborates: **It is taught** in a *baraita* **in accordance with the second version,** as follows: With regard to **one who dines on the eve of the Ninth of Av, if he will eat another meal, he is permitted to eat meat and to drink wine** during this first meal. **But if** he does **not** intend to eat another meal, he is **prohibited to eat meat and to drink wine.**

NOTES

From "her Festival" – מֵחַגָּהּ: Rashi explains that the New Moon itself is called a Festival, and therefore the verse is teaching that the mourning rites commemorating the destruction of the Temple begin on the New Moon of Av. Other authorities suggest that the verse means that the Ninth of Av is treated as though it were the final day of the festival of *Sukkot*, which is celebrated for eight days. This indicates that some mourning rites must be observed during the eight days preceding the Ninth of Av.

A person may not eat two cooked dishes – לֹא יֹאכַל אָדָם שְׁנֵי תַבְשִׁילִין: The early commentaries discuss at length the meaning of cooked dishes with regard to this prohibition. This concept is found in several areas of *halakha* and varies in definition. Some argue that whatever is considered a cooked dish for the purposes of the *halakhot* of *eiruvin* or for the Passover Seder is likewise classified as a cooked dish for the prohibition concerning the eve of the Ninth of Av (Rashi on 26b; Ran, citing *ge'onim*). Others maintain that this prohibition depends on the importance of the dish and the enjoyment it provides. Consequently, anything prepared in one pot is considered a single cooked dish, whereas something prepared in two pots is viewed as two cooked dishes (Ramban; Ritva). The early commentaries also disagree as to whether cooked food that could have been eaten raw is excluded from this prohibition, just as it is excluded from the prohibition against eating foods cooked by a gentile (see *Tosafot* and Ritva).

HALAKHA

In the concluding meal – בִּסְעוּדָה הַמַּפְסִיק בָּהּ: On the eve of the Ninth of Av, it is prohibited to eat meat or drink wine during the last meal before the fast, if that meal is taken after midday. During that meal it is also prohibited to eat two cooked dishes. It is even customary to refrain from eating salted meat, fowl, and fish, and from drinking wine that has not yet fermented properly. If a single dish was cooked in two separate pots, the food is considered two cooked dishes. It is proper to act stringently and to refrain from eating even two foods cooked in the same pot, unless those two foods are regularly cooked in the same pot. Food that was cooked but could have been eaten raw is defined as a cooked dish for the purpose of this *halakha*. Some add that for this prohibition there is no difference between boiling and roasting (Rema; *Shulḥan Arukh*, *Oraḥ Ḥayyim* 552:1–3).

תַּנְיָא כְּלִישָּׁנָא קַמָּא: עֶרֶב תִּשְׁעָה בְּאָב, לֹא יֹאכַל אָדָם שְׁנֵי תַבְשִׁילִין. לֹא יֹאכַל בָּשָׂר וְלֹא יִשְׁתֶּה יַיִן. רַבָּן שִׁמְעוֹן בֶּן גַּמְלִיאֵל אוֹמֵר: יְשַׁנֶּה. אָמַר רַבִּי יְהוּדָה: כֵּיצַד מְשַׁנֶּה? אִם הָיָה רָגִיל לֶאֱכוֹל שְׁנֵי תַבְשִׁילִין, יֹאכַל מִין אֶחָד, וְאִם הָיָה רָגִיל לִסְעוֹד בַּעֲשָׂרָה בְּנֵי אָדָם, סוֹעֵד בַּחֲמִשָּׁה. הָיָה רָגִיל לִשְׁתּוֹת עֲשָׂרָה כּוֹסוֹת, שׁוֹתֶה חֲמִשָּׁה כּוֹסוֹת. בַּמֶּה דְּבָרִים אֲמוּרִים? מִשֵּׁשׁ שָׁעוֹת וּלְמַעְלָה, אֲבָל מִשֵּׁשׁ שָׁעוֹת וּלְמַטָּה מוּתָּר.

It is taught in a *baraita* **in accordance with the first version: On the eve of the Ninth of Av, a person may not eat two cooked dishes.** Furthermore, one may **neither eat meat nor drink wine. Rabban Shimon ben Gamliel says:** One must **adjust**[N] and decrease the amount he eats. Rabbi Yehuda said: How should **one adjust** his meal? **If he is accustomed to eat two cooked dishes** at each meal, he should **eat** only **one type** of food; **and if he is accustomed to dine** in the company **of ten people,** he should **dine with** only **five;** and if **he is accustomed to drinking ten cups** of wine, he should **drink** only **five cups. In what** case **is this statement said? From six hours and onward; however, from six hours and earlier** all these practices are **permitted.**

תַּנְיָא אִידָךְ: עֶרֶב תִּשְׁעָה בְּאָב, לֹא יֹאכַל אָדָם שְׁנֵי תַבְשִׁילִין. לֹא יֹאכַל בָּשָׂר וְלֹא יִשְׁתֶּה יַיִן. דִּבְרֵי רַבִּי מֵאִיר. וַחֲכָמִים אוֹמְרִים: יְשַׁנֶּה, וּמְמַעֵט בְּבָשָׂר וּבְיַיִן. כֵּיצַד מְמַעֵט? אִם הָיָה רָגִיל לֶאֱכוֹל לִיטְרָא בָּשָׂר, יֹאכַל חֲצִי לִיטְרָא. הָיָה רָגִיל לִשְׁתּוֹת לוֹג יַיִן, יִשְׁתֶּה חֲצִי לוֹג יַיִן. וְאִם אֵינוֹ רָגִיל כָּל עִיקָּר, אָסוּר. רַבָּן שִׁמְעוֹן בֶּן גַּמְלִיאֵל אוֹמֵר: אִם הָיָה רָגִיל לֶאֱכוֹל צְנוֹן אוֹ מָלִיחַ אַחַר סְעוּדָתוֹ, הָרְשׁוּת בְּיָדוֹ.

It is taught in **another** *baraita*: On **the eve of the Ninth of Av, a person may not eat two cooked dishes,** and he **may neither eat meat nor drink wine;** this is **the statement of Rabbi Meir. And the Rabbis say:** One must **adjust and reduce**[H] his consumption **of meat and wine. How does one reduce** his meat and wine? **If he is accustomed to eating a liter of meat** in his meal, he should **eat half a liter;** if **he is accustomed to drinking a** ***log*** **of wine,** he should **drink half a** ***log*** **of wine; and if he is not accustomed** to eating meat or drinking wine **at all,** it is **prohibited** for him to do so at all. **Rabban Shimon ben Gamliel says: If he is accustomed to eating a radish or a salted** dish **after** his **meal, he has permission** to do so on the eve of the Ninth of Av, as they are not considered an additional dish.

תַּנְיָא אִידָךְ: כָּל שֶׁהוּא מִשּׁוּם תִּשְׁעָה בְּאָב, אָסוּר לֶאֱכוֹל בָּשָׂר וְאָסוּר לִשְׁתּוֹת יַיִן, וְאָסוּר לִרְחוֹץ. כָּל שֶׁאֵינוֹ מִשּׁוּם תִּשְׁעָה בְּאָב, מוּתָּר לֶאֱכוֹל בָּשָׂר וְלִשְׁתּוֹת יַיִן, וְאָסוּר לִרְחוֹץ. רַבִּי יִשְׁמָעֵאל בְּרַבִּי יוֹסֵי אוֹמֵר מִשּׁוּם אָבִיו: כָּל שָׁעָה שֶׁמּוּתָּר לֶאֱכוֹל בָּשָׂר מוּתָּר לִרְחוֹץ.

It is taught in **another** *baraita*: In **any** meal that is eaten **due** to the fast of **the Ninth of Av,** it is **prohibited to eat meat;** and it is **prohibited to drink wine;** and it is likewise **prohibited to bathe**[N] in anticipation of the fast. However, in **any** meal that is **not due to the Ninth of Av,** i.e., one is eating the meal in order that he shouldn't be hungry on the Ninth of Av, it is **permitted to eat meat and to drink wine, but** it is nevertheless **prohibited to bathe** at that time. **Rabbi Yishmael, son of Rabbi Yosei, said in the name of his father:** For the **entire time that one is permitted to eat meat,** he is likewise **permitted to bathe.**

תָּנוּ רַבָּנַן: "כָּל מִצְוֹת הַנּוֹהֲגוֹת בְּאָבֵל נוֹהֲגוֹת בְּתִשְׁעָה בְּאָב: אָסוּר בַּאֲכִילָה וּבִשְׁתִיָּה, וּבְסִיכָה, וּבִנְעִילַת הַסַּנְדָּל, וּבְתַשְׁמִישׁ הַמִּטָּה. וְאָסוּר לִקְרוֹת בַּתּוֹרָה, בַּנְּבִיאִים, וּבַכְּתוּבִים, וְלִשְׁנוֹת בַּמִּשְׁנָה, בַּתַּלְמוּד, וּבַמִּדְרָשׁ, וּבַהֲלָכוֹת וּבָאַגָּדוֹת.

The Sages taught: All mitzvot practiced by a mourner[N] **are** likewise **practiced on the Ninth of Av:**[H] It is **prohibited** to engage **in eating, and in drinking, and in smearing** oil on one's body, **and in wearing shoes, and in conjugal relations.** It is **prohibited** to read **from the Torah, from the Prophets, and from the Writings, or to study from the Mishna, from the Gemara, and from midrash, and from** collections of ***halakhot*****, and from** collections of ***aggadot*****.**

NOTES

One must adjust – יְשַׁנֶּה: The two *baraitot* quoted here indicate that the necessary adjustment is limited to a reduction in the number of cooked dishes, the amount of wine, and the number of people in whose company one dines. Some commentaries suggest that the *baraita* should read: If he is accustomed to eating two cooked dishes, he should eat a different [*aḥer*] type, rather than one [*eḥad*] type.

In other words, in addition to reducing the amount of food one eats and the number of people with whom he dines, one should change his regular eating habits by eating a different type of food.

Prohibited to bathe – אָסוּר לִרְחוֹץ: The text found in many manuscripts, as well as the parallel *baraita* of the *Tosefta*, reads: With regard to any meal that is not being eaten in preparation for the Ninth of Av, it is permitted to eat meat and to drink wine, and it is permitted to bathe. Rabbi Yishmael, son of Rabbi Yosei, says in the name of his father: As long as it is permitted to eat, it is permitted to bathe. According to this version, Rabbi Yishmael, son of Rabbi Yosei, does not mention meat at all.

Some commentaries explain that the expression: Anything that is due to the Ninth of Av, refers to the last meal eaten before that fast, while the phrase: Anything that is not due to the Ninth of Av, refers to a meal eaten earlier in the day (Ramban). Others maintain that the second expression means the last meal eaten before other communal fast days, even those that begin at night like the Ninth of Av (Ra'avad). Rashi cites both interpretations.

The explanation of these two opinions is as follows. According to the Ramban, the first *tanna* maintains that once someone begins to eat his last meal before the fast of the Ninth of Av, it is prohibited for him to eat meat or to drink wine, and it is also prohibited for him to wash himself. Washing is prohibited because the benefit it provides lasts for a significant period of time, and therefore he would appear to be washing for the Ninth of Av itself. However, one is permitted to wear shoes and engage in the other activities that are prohibited on the Ninth of Av. Conversely, during a meal eaten earlier in the day, one is permitted to eat meat and to drink wine, and he may also wash himself at this stage. Rabbi Yishmael, son of Rabbi Yosei, disagrees with the initial ruling of the first *tanna*. Even if one has finished his last meal before the fast of the Ninth of Av, nevertheless, he is permitted to wash as long as he is still permitted to eat, i.e., until sunset.

According to the Ra'avad, the first *tanna* maintains that once someone has completed his last meal before the fast, during which it is prohibited for him to eat meat or to drink wine, it is prohibited for him to eat anything more, as he is considered to have accepted the fast upon himself, and it is for this reason that he is prohibited to wash. However, after eating the last meal before other fasts, during which it is permitted to consume meat and wine, one may not eat anymore at this stage. It is nevertheless permitted to wash. The explanation of the opinion of Rabbi Yishmael, son of Rabbi Yosei, is the same as above.

All mitzvot practiced by a mourner – כָּל מִצְוֹת הַנּוֹהֲגוֹת בְּאָבֵל: One practical ramification of this principle that is not addressed by this *baraita* is the issue of donning phylacteries on the Ninth of Av. According to some early authorities, just as a mourner does not don phylacteries on the first day of mourning, nobody dons phylacteries on the Ninth of Av (Ra'avad). Others argue that only the restrictions that apply to the entire seven days of mourning apply to the Ninth of Av, which means that phylacteries are worn on the Ninth of Av. Moreover, the mourning observed on the Ninth of Av does not override the Torah obligation to wear phylacteries (Ramban; Ritva). In actual practice, customs vary. Most Sephardic Jews don phylacteries on the Ninth of Av in the regular manner. Most Ashkenazic Jews don phylacteries only after midday, when certain leniencies with regard to the mourning restrictions are allowed.

HALAKHA

And reduce – וּמְמַעֵט: In the last meal before the fast of the Ninth of Av, one should adjust his regular habit and eat less than usual. Three adult males should not eat together, so as not to be obligated in the special blessing of *zimmun* (*Shulḥan Arukh*, *Oraḥ Ḥayyim* 552:8).

All mitzvot practiced by a mourner are likewise practiced on the Ninth of Av – כָּל מִצְוֹת הַנּוֹהֲגוֹת בְּאָבֵל נוֹהֲגוֹת בְּתִשְׁעָה בְּאָב: On the Ninth of Av, it is forbidden to wash oneself, to smear one's body with oil, to wear leather shoes, or to engage in conjugal relations. It is likewise prohibited to read from the Torah, Prophets, or the Writings. One may not study Mishna, Gemara, midrash, *halakhot*, or *aggada*. Even schoolchildren must abstain from their studies. However, it is permitted to read from the book of Job, the book of Lamentations, and prophecies of doom in Jeremiah. One may study the midrash on the book of Lamentations and the talmudic sections dealing with the destruction of the Temple. Some authorities render it prohibited for one to even think about the Torah sections that are prohibited for him to read and study. Nevertheless, it is permitted to read the Torah portions that have been incorporated into the daily liturgy, although it is customary to read some of those sections only after midday (*Shulḥan Arukh*, *Oraḥ Ḥayyim* 554:1–4).

אֲבָל קוֹרֵא הוּא בְּמָקוֹם שֶׁאֵינוֹ רָגִיל לִקְרוֹת, וְשׁוֹנֶה בְּמָקוֹם שֶׁאֵינוֹ רָגִיל לִשְׁנוֹת. וְקוֹרֵא בְּקִינוֹת, בְּאִיּוֹב, וּבַדְּבָרִים הָרָעִים שֶׁבְּיִרְמְיָה. וְתִינוֹקוֹת שֶׁל בֵּית רַבָּן בְּטֵלִין, מִשּׁוּם שֶׁנֶּאֱמַר: ״פִּקּוּדֵי ה׳ יְשָׁרִים, מְשַׂמְּחֵי לֵב״.

However, one may read from a place in the Bible **that he is unaccustomed**[N] **to reading,** as it will be difficult for him and he will not derive pleasure from it, **and he** may likewise **study from a place** of the Talmud **that he is unaccustomed to studying. And one may read from** the book of **Lamentations; from** the book of **Job; and from the evil matters in Jeremiah,** i.e., his prophecies of doom. **And schoolchildren interrupt** their studies for the day **because it is stated: "The precepts of the Lord are right, rejoicing the heart"** (Psalms 19:9).

רַבִּי יְהוּדָה אוֹמֵר: אַף אֵינוֹ קוֹרֵא בְּמָקוֹם שֶׁאֵינוֹ רָגִיל לִקְרוֹת, וְאֵינוֹ שׁוֹנֶה בְּמָקוֹם שֶׁאֵינוֹ רָגִיל לִשְׁנוֹת. אֲבָל קוֹרֵא הוּא בְּאִיּוֹב, וּבְקִינוֹת, וּבַדְּבָרִים הָרָעִים שֶׁבְּיִרְמְיָהוּ. וְתִינוֹקוֹת שֶׁל בֵּית רַבָּן בְּטֵלִים בּוֹ, מִשּׁוּם שֶׁנֶּאֱמַר: ״פִּקּוּדֵי ה׳ יְשָׁרִים, מְשַׂמְּחֵי לֵב״.

Rabbi Yehuda says: One may **not even read from a place** in the Bible **that he is unaccustomed to reading, nor** may one **study from a place** of the Talmud **that he is unaccustomed to studying.** However, **one may read from Job, and from Lamentations, and from the evil matters of Jeremiah. And schoolchildren interrupt** their studies **on that** day **because it is stated: "The precepts of the Lord are right, rejoicing the heart"** (Psalms 19:9).

״לֹא יֹאכַל בָּשָׂר וְלֹא יִשְׁתֶּה יַיִן״. תָּנָא: אֲבָל אוֹכֵל הוּא בָּשָׂר מָלִיחַ וְשׁוֹתֶה יַיִן מִגִּתּוֹ. בָּשָׂר מָלִיחַ עַד כַּמָּה? אָמַר רַב חִינְּנָא בַּר כָּהֲנָא מִשְּׁמֵיהּ דִּשְׁמוּאֵל: כָּל זְמַן שֶׁהוּא כִּשְׁלָמִים.

§ The mishna taught that one may **neither eat meat nor drink wine.** A *tanna* **taught** in the *Tosefta*: **However, one may eat** heavily **salted meat and drink wine from his press,**[H] i.e., wine that has not finished fermenting. The Gemara inquires: With regard to **salted meat, how long** must this meat remain in salt before it is permitted? **Rav Ḥinnana bar Kahana said in the name of Shmuel: As long as it is like peace-offerings,**[N] which could be eaten for two days and one night after they were sacrificed. After this time has passed, it is no longer called meat. Therefore, if it was salted for longer than this, it may be eaten on the eve of the Ninth of Av.

וְיַיִן מִגִּתּוֹ עַד כַּמָּה? כָּל זְמַן שֶׁהוּא תּוֹסֵס. תָּנָא: יַיִן תּוֹסֵס אֵין בּוֹ מִשּׁוּם גִּילּוּי. וְכַמָּה תְּסִיסָתוֹ? שְׁלֹשָׁה יָמִים.

The Gemara asks: **And** with regard to **wine from his press, until when** is wine considered from his press? **As long as it is fermenting.**[B] A *tanna* **taught** in a *baraita*: **Wine that is fermenting** does **not have** a problem **with regard to exposed liquids,**[H] as there is no concern that a snake will leave its venom in that wine. **And how long is its fermenting** period? **Three days** from the time the grapes were pressed.

אָמַר רַב יְהוּדָה אָמַר רַב: כָּךְ הָיָה מִנְהָגוֹ שֶׁל רַבִּי יְהוּדָה בְּרַבִּי אִילְעַאי: עֶרֶב תִּשְׁעָה בְּאָב מְבִיאִין לוֹ פַּת חֲרֵבָה בְּמֶלַח, וְיוֹשֵׁב

Rav Yehuda said that **Rav said: This was the custom of Rabbi Yehuda,**[H] **son of Rabbi Ilai. On the eve of the Ninth of Av,** near the evening, **they** would **bring him stale bread with salt, and** he would **sit**

NOTES

From a place that he is unaccustomed – בְּמָקוֹם שֶׁאֵינוֹ רָגִיל: According to Rashi, the first *tanna* of the *baraita* permits one to study a biblical or talmudic section with which he is not familiar, as this study will cause him distress when he arrives at a passage that he does not understand (Rabbi Yehuda bar Natan).

As long as it is like peace-offerings – כָּל זְמַן שֶׁהוּא כִּשְׁלָמִים: There are two versions of this passage: As long as it is like the peace-offerings, and: As long as it is not like the peace-offerings. There is no practical difference between these two readings, as everyone agrees that peace-offerings may be eaten for two days and the intervening night, and that meat that has been heavily salted for that period of time no longer tastes like ordinary meat. According to the first reading, the Gemara is explaining how long heavily salted meat is considered as ordinary meat and is therefore included in the prohibition against eating meat in the last meal before the fast of the Ninth of Av. According to the alternative reading, the Gemara is referring to the time when heavily salted meat ceases to be treated as ordinary meat and is excluded from the prohibition.

BACKGROUND

Fermenting – תּוֹסֵס: After grapes are pressed and preservatives added, the wine begins to ferment, a process that lasts three to four days. During fermentation, the temperature of the wine can rise up to 40°C. The concern for exposure refers to the possibility than a snake might drink from a liquid and inject its venom into it. In this case, however, the heat of the boiling, fermenting wine prevents snakes from tasting it.

HALAKHA

Salted meat and wine from his press – בָּשָׂר מָלִיחַ וְיַיִן מִגִּתּוֹ: During the last meal before the Ninth of Av, it is customary to refrain from eating heavily salted meat and from drinking wine that has not yet fermented properly, despite the fact that the Gemara permits the consumption of these foods (*Shulḥan Arukh, Oraḥ Ḥayyim* 552:2).

Wine that is fermenting does not have a problem with regard to exposed liquids – יַיִן תּוֹסֵס אֵין בּוֹ מִשּׁוּם גִּילּוּי: The prohibition against drinking liquids that have been left exposed to the venom of snakes does not apply to wine that is still fermenting. Wine is considered to be fermenting for three days after the grapes were trodden in the press (Rambam *Sefer Nezikim, Hilkhot Rotze'aḥ UShmirat HaNefesh* 11:8).

This was the custom of Rabbi Yehuda – כָּךְ הָיָה מִנְהָגוֹ שֶׁל רַבִּי יְהוּדָה: During the last meal before the Ninth of Av, one who is able to restrict himself to the consumption of bread with salt and a cup of water should do so. Some cite a custom to dip bread in ashes (Rema), or to eat lentils cooked with eggs, a dish that is often served to mourners. The Rema further adds that some are accustomed to eating hard-boiled eggs, another food eaten by mourners (*Shulḥan Arukh, Oraḥ Ḥayyim* 552:6).

בֵּין תַּנּוּר לַכִּירַיִים, וְאוֹכֵל, וְשׁוֹתֶה עָלֶיהָ קִיתוֹן שֶׁל מַיִם, וְדוֹמֶה כְּמִי שֶׁמֵּתוֹ מוּטָל לְפָנָיו.

between the **oven and the stove,** which was considered the least respectable place in the house. **And he** would **eat** his bread, **and drink a jug** [***kiton***][L] **of water with it, and** in doing so he would **resemble one whose deceased** relative **is laid out** unburied **before him.**[N]

תְּנַן הָתָם: מָקוֹם שֶׁנָּהֲגוּ לַעֲשׂוֹת מְלָאכָה בְּתִשְׁעָה בְּאָב, עוֹשִׂין. מָקוֹם שֶׁנָּהֲגוּ שֶׁלֹּא לַעֲשׂוֹת, אֵין עוֹשִׂין. וּבְכָל מָקוֹם תַּלְמִידֵי חֲכָמִים בְּטֵלִים. רַבָּן שִׁמְעוֹן בֶּן גַּמְלִיאֵל אוֹמֵר: לְעוֹלָם יַעֲשֶׂה כָּל אָדָם עַצְמוֹ כְּתַלְמִיד חָכָם. תַּנְיָא נַמִי הָכִי: רַבָּן שִׁמְעוֹן בֶּן גַּמְלִיאֵל אוֹמֵר: לְעוֹלָם יַעֲשֶׂה אָדָם עַצְמוֹ כְּתַלְמִיד חָכָם, כְּדֵי שֶׁיִּתְעַנֶּה.

§ **We learned** in a mishna **there:** In **a place where** people **were accustomed to perform labor**[H] **on the Ninth of Av, one performs** labor. In **a place where** people **were accustomed not to perform labor,** one does **not perform** labor. **And in all places, Torah scholars are idle** and do not perform labor on the Ninth of Av. **Rabban Shimon ben Gamliel says:** With regard to the Ninth of Av, **a person should always conduct himself** as **a Torah scholar** and refrain from performing labor. **This is also taught** in a *baraita*: **Rabban Shimon ben Gamliel says: A person should always conduct himself** as **a Torah scholar, so that he will** feel the hardship of the **fast.**[N]

תַּנְיָא אִידָךְ: רַבָּן שִׁמְעוֹן בֶּן גַּמְלִיאֵל אוֹמֵר: כָּל הָאוֹכֵל וְשׁוֹתֶה בְּתִשְׁעָה בְּאָב כְּאִילּוּ אוֹכֵל וְשׁוֹתֶה בְּיוֹם הַכִּפּוּרִים. רַבִּי עֲקִיבָא אוֹמֵר: כָּל הָעוֹשֶׂה מְלָאכָה בְּתִשְׁעָה בְּאָב אֵינוֹ רוֹאֶה סִימַן בְּרָכָה לְעוֹלָם.

It is taught in **another** *baraita* that **Rabban Shimon ben Gamliel says: Whoever eats and drinks on the Ninth of Av,** although the prohibition was instituted by the Prophets, it is **as though he eats and drinks on Yom Kippur. Rabbi Akiva says: Whoever performs labor on the Ninth of Av**[H] **never sees a sign of a blessing** from that work.

וַחֲכָמִים אוֹמְרִים: כָּל הָעוֹשֶׂה מְלָאכָה בְּתִשְׁעָה בְּאָב וְאֵינוֹ מִתְאַבֵּל עַל יְרוּשָׁלַיִם אֵינוֹ רוֹאֶה בְּשִׂמְחָתָהּ, שֶׁנֶּאֱמַר: ״שִׂמְחוּ אֶת יְרוּשָׁלַיִם, וְגִילוּ בָהּ, כָּל אֹהֲבֶיהָ: שִׂישׂוּ אִתָּהּ מָשׂוֹשׂ, כָּל הַמִּתְאַבְּלִים עָלֶיהָ״. מִכָּאן אָמְרוּ: כָּל הַמִּתְאַבֵּל עַל יְרוּשָׁלַיִם זוֹכֶה וְרוֹאֶה בְּשִׂמְחָתָהּ, וְשֶׁאֵינוֹ מִתְאַבֵּל עַל יְרוּשָׁלַיִם אֵינוֹ רוֹאֶה בְּשִׂמְחָתָהּ. תַּנְיָא נַמִי הָכִי: כָּל הָאוֹכֵל בָּשָׂר וְשׁוֹתֶה יַיִן בְּתִשְׁעָה בְּאָב, עָלָיו הַכָּתוּב אוֹמֵר: ״וַתְּהִי עֲוֹנוֹתָם עַל עַצְמוֹתָם״.

And the Sages say: Whoever performs labor on the Ninth of Av and does not mourn for Jerusalem will not see her future **joy, as it is stated: "Rejoice with Jerusalem and be glad with her, all who love her; rejoice for joy with her, all who mourn for her"** (Isaiah 66:10). **From here it is stated: Whoever mourns for Jerusalem will merit and see her** future **joy, and whoever does not mourn for Jerusalem will not see her future joy. This is also taught** in a *baraita*: **Whoever eats meat or drinks wine in** the meal before **the Ninth of Av,**[H] **about him the verse states: "And whose iniquities are upon their bones,**[N] because the terror of the mighty was in the land of the living" (Ezekiel 32:27).

LANGUAGE

Jug [*kiton*] – קִיתוֹן: From the Greek κώθων, *kothon*, meaning a vessel used for drinking or a saucer.

NOTES

And he would resemble one whose deceased relative is laid out unburied before him – וְדוֹמֶה כְּמִי שֶׁמֵּתוֹ מוּטָל לְפָנָיו: Rabbi Yehuda, son of Rabbi Ilai, sought to demonstrate that he did not view the Ninth of Av as the commemoration of an event that had taken place in the distant past. Rather, he considered it a day of mourning for a recent loss, as though a deceased relative was lying before him awaiting burial (Maharsha).

So that he will feel the hardship of the fast – כְּדֵי שֶׁיִּתְעַנֶּה: Some commentaries note that this clause explains why it is permitted to act in the manner of a Torah scholar and refrain from working on the Ninth of Av (Rav Tzvi Hirsh Chajes). Elsewhere Rabban Shimon ben Gamliel stated that an ordinary individual may not act like a scholar in a matter that will garner him praise, but only in a matter that will simply cause him pain (10b). Consequently, it is permitted to act as a scholar here because refraining from work on the Ninth of Av is a source of affliction, as he loses money.

Other commentaries offer two explanations for this prohibition: One should refrain from working on the Ninth of Av so as not be involved in work and fail to experience properly the mourning of the day. Alternatively, one should not perform labor so as to preserve enough strength to observe the fast until its conclusion (*Mikhtam*).

And whose iniquities are upon their bones – וַתְּהִי עֲוֹנוֹתָם עַל עַצְמוֹתָם: Some commentaries explain that if one fails to mourn properly for Jerusalem, his punishment will be inflicted on his bones, as they will not take part in the resurrection that will accompany the rebuilding of the Temple (Ritva). This resurrection is promised only to those who mourn for Jerusalem and patiently await its salvation. Others state that the iniquity of eating meat and drinking wine on the eve of the Ninth of Av will leave an imprint on an individual's bones even after he is dead and his flesh has turned to dust (Maharsha).

HALAKHA

A place where people were accustomed to perform labor – מָקוֹם שֶׁנָּהֲגוּ לַעֲשׂוֹת מְלָאכָה: In a place where it is customary for people to perform labor on the Ninth of Av, it is permitted to do so. However, in a place where it is customary for people to refrain from labor, it is prohibited to work. In all places, Torah scholars must abstain from working. Any individual who wishes to act in the manner of a Torah scholar and to refrain from labor is permitted to do so.

Even in a place where it is customary to refrain from working, labor may be performed for a Jew by a gentile. Some authorities add that it is customary to refrain from working only until midday (Rema). Until midday, it is customary not to engage in any type of labor that requires a significant amount of time to complete, even if it does not require professional expertise. However, labor that does not require a significant amount of time, e.g., lighting a candle or tying a knot, is permitted even before midday (*Shulḥan Arukh, Oraḥ Ḥayyim* 554:22).

Whoever performs labor on the Ninth of Av – כָּל הָעוֹשֶׂה מְלָאכָה בְּתִשְׁעָה בְּאָב: Whoever engages in work on the Ninth of Av will not see a blessing from that labor. This applies even if he works after midday (*Magen Avraham*; *Shulḥan Arukh, Oraḥ Ḥayyim* 554:24).

Whoever eats meat or drinks wine in the meal before the Ninth of Av – כָּל הָאוֹכֵל בָּשָׂר וְשׁוֹתֶה יַיִן בְּתִשְׁעָה בְּאָב: One who eats or drinks on the Ninth of Av will not witness the future joy of Jerusalem, whereas those who mourn deeply for Jerusalem will merit seeing this joy. The verse states about those who eat meat or drink wine during the last meal on the eve of the Ninth of Av: "And whose iniquities are upon their bones" (*Shulḥan Arukh, Oraḥ Ḥayyim* 554:24).

"רַבִּי יְהוּדָה מְחַיֵּיב בִּכְפִיַּית הַמִּטָּה, וְלֹא הוֹדוּ לוֹ חֲכָמִים". תַּנְיָא: אָמְרוּ לוֹ לְרַבִּי יְהוּדָה: לִדְבָרֶיךָ, עוּבָּרוֹת וּמֵינִיקוֹת מַה תְּהֵא עֲלֵיהֶן? אָמַר לָהֶם: אַף אֲנִי לֹא אָמַרְתִּי אֶלָּא בְּיָכוֹל.

§ The mishna taught: **Rabbi Yehuda obligates one to overturn the bed, but the Rabbis did not agree with him. It is taught** in a *baraita* that **the Rabbis said to Rabbi Yehuda: According to your statement, pregnant women and nursing women,** who cannot sleep on the floor, **what will become of them?** Rabbi Yehuda **said to them: I, too, spoke only with regard to** those **who are able.**

תַּנְיָא נַמִּי הָכִי: מוֹדֶה רַבִּי יְהוּדָה לַחֲכָמִים בְּשֶׁאֵינוֹ יָכוֹל. וּמוֹדִים חֲכָמִים לְרַבִּי יְהוּדָה בְּיָכוֹל. מַאי בֵּינַיְיהוּ? אִיכָּא בֵּינַיְיהוּ שְׁאָר מִטּוֹת,

This is also taught in another *baraita*: **Rabbi Yehuda concedes to the Rabbis with regard to** one **who is unable** to sleep on the floor, **and the Rabbis concede to Rabbi Yehuda with regard to one who is able** to do so. The Gemara asks: If so, **what is** the practical difference **between them?** The Gemara explains: The practical difference **between them** is the status of **other beds.**

כִּדְתַנְיָא: כְּשֶׁאָמְרוּ לִכְפּוֹת הַמִּטָּה, לֹא מִטָּתוֹ בִּלְבַד הוּא כּוֹפֶה, אֶלָּא כָּל הַמִּטּוֹת כּוּלָּן הוּא כּוֹפֶה. אָמַר רָבָא: הִלְכְתָא כְּתַנָּא דִּידַן, וְלֹא הוֹדוּ לוֹ חֲכָמִים כָּל עִיקָּר.

As it is taught in a *baraita*: **When** the Rabbis **said** that a mourner is required **to overturn the bed,** they meant that **he overturns not only his own bed, but** also that **he** must **overturn all the beds** in the house. Rabbi Yehuda maintains that one must likewise overturn all of the beds of one's house on the Ninth of Av. **Rava said: The *halakha* is in accordance with** the opinion of **the *tanna* of our** mishna, **and the Rabbis did not concede to** Rabbi Yehuda **at all,** even with regard to one who is able. Therefore, there is no requirement to overturn one's bed on the Ninth of Av.

"אָמַר רַבָּן שִׁמְעוֹן בֶּן גַּמְלִיאֵל: לֹא הָיוּ יָמִים טוֹבִים לְיִשְׂרָאֵל כַּחֲמִשָּׁה עָשָׂר בְּאָב וּכְיוֹם הַכִּפּוּרִים". בִּשְׁלָמָא יוֹם הַכִּפּוּרִים, מִשּׁוּם דְּאִית בֵּיהּ סְלִיחָה וּמְחִילָה, יוֹם שֶׁנִּיתְּנוּ בּוֹ לוּחוֹת הָאַחֲרוֹנוֹת.

§ The mishna taught that **Rabban Shimon ben Gamliel said: There were no days as happy for the Jewish people as the fifteenth of Av and as Yom Kippur.** The Gemara asks: **Granted, Yom Kippur** is a day of joy **because it has** the elements of **pardon and forgiveness,** and moreover, it is the **day on which the last** pair of **tablets were given.**[N]

אֶלָּא חֲמִשָּׁה עָשָׂר בְּאָב מַאי הִיא? אָמַר רַב יְהוּדָה אָמַר שְׁמוּאֵל: יוֹם שֶׁהוּתְּרוּ שְׁבָטִים לָבוֹא זֶה בָּזֶה.

However, what is the special joy of the **fifteenth of Av? Rav Yehuda said** that **Shmuel said:** This was the **day on which** the members of different **tribes were permitted**[N] **to enter one another's** tribe, by intermarriage. It was initially prohibited to intermarry between tribes, so as to keep each plot of land within the portion of the tribe that originally inherited it. This *halakha* was instituted by the Torah in the wake of a complaint by the relatives of the daughters of Zelophehad, who were worried that if these women married men from other tribes, the inheritance of Zelophehad would be lost from his tribe (see Numbers 36:1–12).

מַאי דְּרוּשׁ? "זֶה הַדָּבָר אֲשֶׁר צִוָּה ה׳ לִבְנוֹת צְלָפְחָד", וגו׳. דָּבָר זֶה לֹא יְהֵא נוֹהֵג אֶלָּא בְּדוֹר זֶה.

What did they expound, in support of their conclusion that this *halakha* was no longer in effect? The verse states: **"This is the matter that the Lord has commanded concerning the daughters of Zelophehad,** saying: Let them marry whom they think best; only into the family of the tribe of their father shall they marry" (Numbers 36:5). They derived from the verse that **this matter shall be practiced only in this generation,** when Eretz Yisrael was divided among the tribes, but afterward members of different tribes were permitted to marry. On the day this barrier separating the tribes was removed, the Sages established a permanent day of rejoicing.

אָמַר רַב יוֹסֵף אָמַר רַב נַחְמָן: יוֹם שֶׁהוּתַּר שֵׁבֶט בִּנְיָמִין לָבוֹא בַּקָּהָל, שֶׁנֶּאֱמַר: "וְאִישׁ יִשְׂרָאֵל נִשְׁבַּע בַּמִּצְפָּה, לֵאמֹר: אִישׁ מִמֶּנּוּ לֹא יִתֵּן בִּתּוֹ לְבִנְיָמִן לְאִשָּׁה". מַאי דְּרוּשׁ? אָמַר רַב: "מִמֶּנּוּ", וְלֹא מִבָּנֵינוּ.

Rav Yosef said that **Rav Naḥman said:** The fifteenth of Av was the **day on which the tribe of Benjamin was permitted to enter the congregation** of the Jewish people. After the tragic incident at Gibeah, for which the tribe of Benjamin was blamed, the other tribes ostracized them. They took an oath to prohibit themselves from marrying a member of the tribe of Benjamin, **as it is stated: "And the men of Israel had sworn in Mizpah, saying: None of us shall give his daughter to Benjamin as a wife"** (Judges 21:1). The Gemara asks: **What did they expound** that enabled them to dissolve this oath? **Rav said:** They understood the verse literally, as it states: "None **of us," and not:** None **of our children,** i.e., the oath applied only to the generation that took the oath, not their descendants.

NOTES

The day on which the last tablets were given – יוֹם שֶׁנִּיתְּנוּ בּוֹ לוּחוֹת הָאַחֲרוֹנוֹת: The first tablets were broken on the seventeenth of Tammuz, exactly eighty days before Yom Kippur (see Rashi). Some commentaries discuss whether Moses spent the first forty days on the mountain or whether he was sitting in judgment and arranging matters in the camp. In any case, it is stated in many *midrashim* that Moses ascended Mount Sinai for the second time on the first of Elul. This is also the source of the custom to recite special prayers of supplication from the beginning of Elul until Yom Kippur.

The day on which the tribes were permitted – יוֹם שֶׁהוּתְּרוּ שְׁבָטִים: In other words, on this day they expounded the verses and taught this *halakha*. Some add that the celebration was not for the *halakha* itself, but for the novel exposition of the verse, i.e., that the phrase "of us" does not apply to descendants. This exposition gave added weight to the *halakha* (*Gevurat Ari*).

אָמַר רַבָּה בַּר בַּר חָנָה אָמַר רַבִּי יוֹחָנָן: יוֹם שֶׁכָּלוּ בּוֹ מֵתֵי מִדְבָּר. דְּאָמַר מָר: עַד שֶׁלֹּא כָּלוּ מֵתֵי מִדְבָּר, לֹא הָיָה דִּבּוּר עִם מֹשֶׁה, שֶׁנֶּאֱמַר: ״וַיְהִי, כַּאֲשֶׁר תַּמּוּ כׇּל אַנְשֵׁי הַמִּלְחָמָה לָמוּת, וַיְדַבֵּר ה׳ אֵלַי״. אֵלַי הָיָה הַדִּבּוּר.

Rabba bar bar Ḥana said that **Rabbi Yoḥanan said:** The fifteenth of Av was the **day on which the deaths** of the Jews **in the wilderness ceased.**[N] The entire generation that had left Egypt had passed away, **as the Master said:** After the sin of the spies, on account of which the Jews of that generation were sentenced to die in the wilderness, **as long as the death** of the Jews **in the wilderness had not ceased,** God's **speech did not** come **to Moses, as it is stated: "And it came to pass, when all the men of war were consumed and dead from among the people, that the Lord spoke to me, saying"** (Deuteronomy 2:16–17). This indicates that only then, after the last member of that generation had died, was God's **speech** delivered **to me,**[N] i.e., Moses, but not beforehand. When the Jews realized that the decree that God would not speak to Moses had been lifted, they established that day as a permanent day of rejoicing.

עוּלָּא אָמַר: יוֹם שֶׁבִּיטֵּל הוֹשֵׁעַ בֶּן אֵלָה פְּרוֹסְדִיּוֹת שֶׁהוֹשִׁיב יָרׇבְעָם בֶּן נְבָט עַל הַדְּרָכִים, שֶׁלֹּא יַעֲלוּ יִשְׂרָאֵל לָרֶגֶל, וְאָמַר:

Ulla said: The fifteenth of Av was the **day on which** King **Hoshea, son of Ela, canceled** the **guards that Jeroboam, son of Nevat, placed on the roads so that the Jews** would **not ascend** to Jerusalem **for the** pilgrim **Festival. And** Hoshea, son of Ela, **said**

NOTES

The day on which the deaths in the wilderness ceased – יוֹם שֶׁכָּלוּ בּוֹ מֵתֵי מִדְבָּר: Many commentaries cite the following midrash: Every year, on the eighth of Av, a herald proclaimed in the camp of the Jewish people in the wilderness: Let each individual dig his grave. Everyone dug his own grave and spent the night in it. The next day, a second herald proclaimed: Let the living separate themselves from the dead, and whoever was still alive would rise up from his grave. Every year about fifteen thousand Israelites died. However, on the ninth of Av of the fortieth year, all those who had lain in a grave rose up again in the morning. At first, they thought that they had miscalculated, and that it was not yet the ninth of Av. Consequently, they slept in their graves every night for a week. When the fifteenth of Av arrived, the full moon that shone that night convinced them that the Ninth of Av had passed and that all those who were destined to die had already perished (Rashi; *Tosafot*).

The early commentaries disagree as to whether all those who were supposed to die indeed perished in the wilderness or whether some of those who were supposed to die during the fortieth year were pardoned. In commemoration of the end of the punishment, the fifteenth of Av was established as a minor holiday for all generations.

Some explain that the holiday was instituted in commemoration of the resumption of God's direct communication with Moses, which occurred when the generation of the wilderness stopped dying. According to this interpretation, the regular number of Jews died on the Ninth of Av of the fortieth year, after which a seven-day mourning period was then observed. At the conclusion of that period of mourning, on the fifteenth of Av, God's direct communication with Moses resumed, and a holiday was declared (*Tosafot* on *Bava Batra* 121a).

NOTES

The speech delivered to me – אֵלַי הָיָה הַדִּבּוּר: Although God did in fact speak to Moses during the travels of the Jews through the wilderness (see Deuteronomy 2:2), it was only after the last members of the generation of the wilderness had died that the divine revelation took the form of *dibbur*, speech, a more direct form of communication than *amira*, saying (see Rashi, Meiri, and Rabbeinu Beḥaye on Deuteronomy 2:16–17).

לְאֵיזֶה שֶׁיִּרְצוּ יַעֲלוּ.

that **they may ascend to wherever they wish,**[N] i.e., they may go to Jerusalem, Bethel, or Dan.

רַב מַתָּנָה אָמַר: יוֹם שֶׁנִּתְּנוּ הֲרוּגֵי בֵיתָר לִקְבוּרָה. וְאָמַר רַב מַתָּנָה: אוֹתוֹ יוֹם שֶׁנִּתְּנוּ הֲרוּגֵי בֵיתָר לִקְבוּרָה תִּקְּנוּ בְּיַבְנֶה ״הַטּוֹב וְהַמֵּטִיב״. ״הַטּוֹב״ שֶׁלֹּא הִסְרִיחוּ. ״וְהַמֵּטִיב״ שֶׁנִּתְּנוּ לִקְבוּרָה.

Rav Mattana said: There was an additional salvation on this day, as it was the **day that the slain of Beitar**[B] **were brought to burial,**[N] several years after the battle at Beitar (see *Gittin* 57a). **And Rav Mattana said: On the same day that the slain of Beitar were brought to burial, they instituted** the blessing: **Who is good and does good, at Yavne.**[H] **Who is good,** thanking God that the corpses **did not decompose** while awaiting burial, **and does good,** thanking God **that they were** ultimately **brought to burial.**

BACKGROUND

The slain of Beitar – הֲרוּגֵי בֵיתָר: After his final suppression of the bar Kokheva revolt, the Roman emperor Hadrian issued a lengthy series of decrees against Jews and Judaism. These are the so-called decrees of apostasy that are mentioned in many places. One of these decrees was a prohibition against burying those slain in the war. These decrees were in force for at least three years, until Hadrian's death in 138 CE. The decrees were rescinded only in the reign of the following emperor. This dissolution, along with the gradual cancellation of all the decrees, was commemorated for future generations in several ways.

HALAKHA

They instituted, Who is good and does good, at Yavne – תִּקְּנוּ בְּיַבְנֶה הַטּוֹב וְהַמֵּטִיב: The Sages of the Mishna in Yavne instituted the blessing: Who is good and does good, the fourth blessing of Grace after Meals, after those who died at Beitar were brought to burial (Rambam *Sefer Ahava*, *Hilkhot Berakhot* 2:1).

NOTES

They may ascend to wherever they wish – לְאֵיזֶה שֶׁיִּרְצוּ יַעֲלוּ: Hoshea was an evil king, as Rashi notes, as the verse states that Hoshea, son of Ela, "did what was evil in the sight of the Lord, yet not as the kings of Israel who were before him" (II Kings 17:2). Hoshea was not considered as evil as the kings before him because he removed Jeroboam's guards, who were stationed to prevent people from ascending to Jerusalem on the pilgrimage Festivals. However, he was evil nevertheless, as he let the people choose whether to go to Jerusalem or attend the idolatrous sanctuaries in Bethel and Dan. In the Jerusalem Talmud, it is stated that Hoshea was punished for presenting the people of Israel with this choice. During his reign, Shalmaneser, king of Assyria, put an end to the kingdom of Israel.

The day that the slain of Beitar were brought to burial – יוֹם שֶׁנִּתְּנוּ הֲרוּגֵי בֵיתָר לִקְבוּרָה: Some commentaries ask: The fifteenth of Av was evidently celebrated as a holiday during the Second Temple period, as the *baraita* cited below describes how the daughters of the High Priest, his deputy, and the priest anointed for war would each borrow clothing from each other on that day, and these priestly offices ceased with the destruction of the Temple. How, then, could the holiday celebrated on the fifteenth of Av have been instituted to commemorate the interment of the slain of Beitar, a joyous event that took place only after the destruction of the Temple?

The *Gevurat Ari* suggests that the *baraita* is referring to the celebration that accompanied Yom Kippur, whereas the holiday celebrated on the fifteenth of Av was in fact instituted after the Temple was destroyed. Alternatively, the holiday was indeed instituted in the time of the Second Temple, and Rav Mattana is saying that because several joyous events had already occurred on the fifteenth of Av, another joyous event took place on that same date. Moreover, he explains why the day is observed as a semi-holiday even nowadays.

רַבָּה וְרַב יוֹסֵף דְּאָמְרִי תַּרְוַיְיהוּ: יוֹם שֶׁפָּסְקוּ מִלִּכְרוֹת עֵצִים לַמַּעֲרָכָה, דְּתַנְיָא: רַבִּי אֱלִיעֶזֶר הַגָּדוֹל אוֹמֵר: מֵחֲמִשָּׁה עָשָׂר בְּאָב וְאֵילָךְ תָּשַׁשׁ כּוֹחָהּ שֶׁל חַמָּה, וְלֹא הָיוּ כּוֹרְתִין עֵצִים לַמַּעֲרָכָה, לְפִי שֶׁאֵינָן יְבֵשִׁין.

It is **Rabba and Rav Yosef who both say:** The fifteenth of Av was the **day on which they stopped chopping down trees for the arrangement** of wood that burned on the altar, **as it is taught** in a *baraita* that **Rabbi Eliezer the Great says: From the fifteenth of Av[H] onward, the strength of the sun grows weaker,[B]** and from this date **they would not cut** additional **wood for the arrangement, as they** would **not** be properly **dry,** and they would therefore be unfit for use in the Temple.

אֲמַר רַב מְנַשְּׁיָא: וְקָרוּ לֵיהּ יוֹם תְּבַר מַגָּל. מִכָּאן וְאֵילָךְ דְּמוֹסִיף יוֹסִיף, וּדְלָא מוֹסִיף יֶאֱסַף. מַאי יֶאֱסַף? אֲמַר רַב יוֹסֵף: תִּקְבְּרֵיהּ אִימֵּיהּ.

Rav Menashya said: And they called the fifteenth of Av the **day of the breaking of the scythe,** as from this date onward no more trees were cut down, and therefore it was a celebration for the trees. The Gemara adds: **From** the fifteenth of **Av onward,** when the days begin to shorten, **one who adds** to his nightly Torah study **will add** years to his life, **and he who does not add** [*mosif*] **will be gathered** [*ye'asef*].[N] The Gemara asks: **What is** the meaning of the phrase: **He will be gathered? Rav Yosef said:** It means that **his mother will bury him,** as he will be gathered to his grave (see Genesis 49:33).

"שֶׁבָּהֶן בְּנוֹת יְרוּשָׁלַיִם", כו׳. תָּנוּ רַבָּנַן: בַּת מֶלֶךְ שׁוֹאֶלֶת מִבַּת כֹּהֵן גָּדוֹל, בַּת כֹּהֵן גָּדוֹל מִבַּת סְגָן, וּבַת סְגָן מִבַּת מְשׁוּחַ מִלְחָמָה, וּבַת מְשׁוּחַ מִלְחָמָה מִבַּת כֹּהֵן הֶדְיוֹט, וְכָל יִשְׂרָאֵל שׁוֹאֲלִין זֶה מִזֶּה, כְּדֵי שֶׁלֹּא יִתְבַּיֵּישׁ אֶת מִי שֶׁאֵין לוֹ.

§ The mishna taught: **As on them the daughters of Jerusalem** would go out in white clothes, and on the fifteenth of Av they would go out to the vineyards and dance. **The Sages taught** this tradition in greater detail: **The daughter of the king borrows** white garments **from the daughter of the High Priest;[N] the daughter of the High Priest** borrows **from the daughter of the deputy High Priest; the daughter of the deputy High Priest** borrows **from the daughter of** the priest **anointed for war,** i.e., the priest who would read verses of Torah and address the army as they prepared for battle; **the daughter of** the priest **anointed for war** borrows **from the daughter of a common priest; and all the Jewish people borrow from each other.** Why would they all borrow garments? They did this **so as not to embarrass one who did not have** her own white garments.

"כָּל הַכֵּלִים טְעוּנִין טְבִילָה". אָמַר רַבִּי אֶלְעָזָר: אֲפִילּוּ מְקוּפָּלִין וּמוּנָּחִין בְּקוּפְסָא.

The mishna further taught: **All the garments** that the women borrowed **require immersion,[N]** as those who previously wore them before might have been ritually impure. **Rabbi Elazar says: Even** if the garments were **folded and placed in a box** [*kufsa*],[L] an indication that they had not been touched for a long time, they nevertheless require ritual immersion before being worn.

HALAKHA

The fifteenth of Av – חֲמִשָּׁה עָשָׂר בְּאָב: On the fifteenth of Av, it is the custom not to recite the prayers of supplication that usually follow the *Amida*, as is the custom on all days of celebration (*Shulḥan Arukh*, *Oraḥ Ḥayyim* 131:6).

BACKGROUND

The strength of the sun grows weaker – תָּשַׁשׁ כּוֹחָהּ שֶׁל חַמָּה: The fifteenth of Av can occur on various dates of the solar year, between July 30 and August 21. This coincides with the hottest period of the year, when humidity is low in mountainous regions. From August onward, the strength of the sun grows weaker, i.e., the average temperatures decrease and humidity rises.

For wood to dry out sufficiently for use on the altar, a few months of dry climate and low humidity are required. Since moist wood will attract the attention of bugs even after it has been chopped down, during this period the priests would stop cutting down wood for the altar.

LANGUAGE

Box [*kufsa*] – קוּפְסָא: From the Greek κάψα, *kapsa*, or the Latin capsa, meaning a box or container.

NOTES

And he who does not add will be gathered – וּדְלָא מוֹסִיף יֶאֱסַף: Since the Torah is called "your life and the length of your days" (Deuteronomy 30:20), one who neglects its study is effectively proving that he does not seek life (*Mikhtam*).

The daughter of the king borrows from the daughter of the High Priest – בַּת מֶלֶךְ שׁוֹאֶלֶת מִבַּת כֹּהֵן גָּדוֹל: Ordinarily, one borrows from someone of a higher economic and social status. In this case, however, the Sages arranged that the daughter of a man of higher status should borrow from the daughter of someone of lower status, so that nobody would be embarrassed to borrow and everyone would be dressed in similar clothing (*Sefat Emet*).

Require immersion – טְעוּנִין טְבִילָה: Most early commentaries explain that the clothes the young women borrowed from each other required ritual immersion because they might have contracted ritual impurity by being worn by a woman who was ritually impure. Even clothes that had been folded away in boxes required ritual immersion, so as not to embarrass those women who were indeed ritually impure and whose clothes needed to be immersed.

Furthermore, the Sages wished to avoid a situation in which those who were more meticulous about ritual impurity would refrain from borrowing clothes from those who were less scrupulous in this regard (Rashi; Rid; Rabbeinu Yehonatan).

The Jerusalem Talmud, as cited by the Ra'avad and others, explains this regulation differently: The Sages enacted that all clothes must undergo ritual immersion so that the young women would be more willing to lend them. Once the garments had been taken out of storage and immersed (Ritva) they were wet (*Mikhtam*) and no longer pristine. Therefore, women who would otherwise have preferred not to lend their clothes would be ready to exchange them for others.

״בְּנוֹת יִשְׂרָאֵל יוֹצְאוֹת וְחוֹלוֹת בַּכְּרָמִים״. תָּנָא: מִי שֶׁאֵין לוֹ אִשָּׁה נִפְנֶה לְשָׁם.

The mishna also stated that **the daughters of the Jewish people** would **go out and dance**[N] **in the vineyards.** A *tanna* **taught: One who did not have a wife** would **turn to there** to find one.

״מְיוּחָסוֹת שֶׁבָּהֶן הָיוּ אוֹמְרוֹת: בָּחוּר״, וכו׳. תָּנוּ רַבָּנַן: יְפֵיפִיּוֹת שֶׁבָּהֶן מֶה הָיוּ אוֹמְרוֹת? תְּנוּ עֵינֵיכֶם לְיוֹפִי, שֶׁאֵין הָאִשָּׁה אֶלָּא לְיוֹפִי. מְיוּחָסוֹת שֶׁבָּהֶן מֶה הָיוּ אוֹמְרוֹת? תְּנוּ עֵינֵיכֶם לַמִּשְׁפָּחָה, לְפִי שֶׁאֵין הָאִשָּׁה אֶלָּא לְבָנִים. מְכוֹעָרוֹת שֶׁבָּהֶם מֶה הָיוּ אוֹמְרוֹת? קְחוּ מִקַּחֲכֶם לְשׁוּם שָׁמַיִם, וּבִלְבַד שֶׁתְּעַטְּרוּנוּ בִּזְהוּבִים.

It is taught that **those** women **of distinguished lineage among them would say: Young man,** please lift up your eyes and see what you choose for a wife. **The Sages taught** this practice in greater detail in a *baraita*: **What would the beautiful women among them say? Set your eyes toward beauty, as a wife is only for her beauty. What would those of distinguished lineage among them say? Set your eyes toward family, as a wife is only for children,** and the children of a wife from a distinguished family will inherit her lineage. **What would the ugly ones among them say? Acquire your purchase for the sake of Heaven, provided that you adorn us with golden jewelry**[N] after our marriage to beautify us.

אָמַר עוּלָּא בִּירָאָה אָמַר רַבִּי אֶלְעָזָר: עָתִיד הַקָּדוֹשׁ בָּרוּךְ הוּא לַעֲשׂוֹת מָחוֹל לַצַּדִּיקִים, וְהוּא יוֹשֵׁב בֵּינֵיהֶם בְּגַן עֵדֶן, וְכׇל אֶחָד וְאֶחָד מַרְאֶה בְּאֶצְבָּעוֹ, שֶׁנֶּאֱמַר: ״וְאָמַר בַּיּוֹם הַהוּא: הִנֵּה, אֱלֹהֵינוּ זֶה; קִוִּינוּ לוֹ וְיוֹשִׁיעֵנוּ. זֶה ה׳; קִוִּינוּ לוֹ. נָגִילָה וְנִשְׂמְחָה בִּישׁוּעָתוֹ״.

The tractate concludes with a statement related to the topic of dancing. **Ulla** of the city of **Bira'a said** that **Rabbi Elazar said:** In the **future,** in the end of days, **the Holy One, Blessed be He, will arrange a dance of the righteous,**[N] **and He** will **be sitting among them in** the **Garden of Eden, and each and every one** of the righteous will **point** to God **with his finger, as it is stated: "And it shall be said on that day: Behold, this is our God, for whom we waited, that He might save us. This is the Lord; for whom we waited. We will be glad and rejoice in His salvation"** (Isaiah 25:9). God will be revealed, so that every righteous individual will be able to say: This is our God, as though they were pointing at Him with a finger.

הדרן עלך בשלשה פרקים
וסליקא לה מסכת תענית

NOTES

The daughters of the Jewish people would go out and dance – בְּנוֹת יִשְׂרָאֵל יוֹצְאוֹת וְחוֹלוֹת: The commentaries write that this custom is based on the manner by which the daughters of Jabesh-Gilead were permitted to marry the males of the tribe of Benjamin (see Judges 21:13–23; *ge'onim*). The commentaries explain at length that this was a special enactment to help those girls who were having difficulty finding a husband. The men would select potential wives, and later, after the families agreed, they would betroth them (see Ritva).

That you adorn us with golden jewelry – שֶׁתְּעַטְּרוּנוּ בִּזְהוּבִים: The commentaries point out that elsewhere the Sages state: The daughters of Israel are pretty, but poverty makes them ugly (*Nedarim* 66a). Consequently, once they are adorned with finery, their husbands will find them beautiful and come to recognize their other good qualities. An alternative reading is: That you will be adorned with golden jewelry, i.e., if you marry a woman for the sake of Heaven you will earn wealth and honor.

A dance of the righteous – מָחוֹל לַצַּדִּיקִים: As explained by the early and later commentaries, this idea alludes to secret concepts of the Torah. Some write that a dance in the form of a circle signifies an endless activity, comparable to the eternal bounty that will be the portion of the righteous in the World-to-Come (Rabbeinu Beḥaye on the Torah).

Others claim that in the future everyone will attain prophecy, through which it will be possible to point to God, as it were (*Alshikh*). Furthermore, this action hints at the revelation of secrets of the Torah, which is read with a pointed finger (see *Kaftor VaFeraḥ*). In connection with this idea, the commentaries cite the verse: "Then shall the virgin rejoice in the dance, and the young men and the old together; for I will turn their mourning into joy, and I will comfort them, and make them rejoice from their sorrow" (Jeremiah 31:12). This verse links the dance of girls on days of rejoicing to the dance of the righteous in the future (see Maharal).

Summary of **Perek IV**

The common denominator of the non-priestly watches and the dates the wood offerings are brought is that they both are occasions when the Jewish people participate to a certain extent in the Temple service. Although the service itself is performed solely by priests, the entire people, or at least a representative group, symbolically join them in their ministering. In addition to the various details of the non-priestly watches and the wood offerings, the Gemara established that on any commemorative day, whether a fixed Festival from the Torah or a day on which *hallel* is recited, the prayers and fasting of the watches are diminished and the joy of the day is emphasized.

Another topic that was addressed in this chapter was the fixed days of communal fasts. The Mishna and Gemara explained why these dates were chosen for the memorial fasts, and why they were established as permanent fast days. The main focus was on the Ninth of Av which, due to the numerous national disasters that occurred on this date, is not only established as a fixed communal fast, but is equal in severity to the extreme fasts for rain in that it begins at nightfall and requires all five categories of affliction to be observed.

Certain practices of mourning are observed on the Ninth of Av. Essentially, all *halakhot* that apply to an individual mourner are obligatory for everyone on this day, as no actions that gladden the heart may be performed. Moreover, certain periods before the Ninth of Av, specifically the week in which it occurs and the previous eight days of the month, are included in various aspects of the mourning.

The tractate ends on a positive note, as the Mishna mentions the celebratory atmosphere of Yom Kippur and of the fifteenth of Av, on which special festive events were staged for the entire nation with the aim of bringing the Jewish people together and increasing joy among them.

Index of **Background**

Index of **Background**

Index of **Language**

Index of **Personalities**

Image **Credits**

All images are copyright © Koren Publishers Jerusalem Ltd., except:

p10 1st image © **courtesy of the Temple Institute** and Koren Publishers Jerusalem Ltd.; **p10** 2nd image © Dr. David and Jemima Jeselsohn, Zurich; **p24** © AtelierMonpli; **p27** © Alila Medical Images, www.shutterstock.com; **p41** © Herbert Kratky; **p48** © Firo002; **p58** © Ori, Golan Archaeological Museum, Katzrin; **p69** © Dr. Avishai Teicher; **p70** © Stefan Thüngen; **p71** © Dror Melamed, courtesy of *Tzemaḥ HaSadeh*, www.wildflowers.co.il; **p75** © Matti Paavola; **p117** © Patche99z; **p124** © Ancheta Wis; **p127** © Agronom; **p134** top left image © Sarah Gold, courtesy of *Tzemaḥ HaSadeh*, www.wildflowers.co.il; **p134**, bottom left image © Llez; **p134** top right image © Roger Culos; **p134**, bottom right image © Giancarlo Dessi; **p135** © Sarah Gold, courtesy of *Tzemaḥ HaSadeh*, www.wild-flowers.co.il; **p147** © mtsyri, www.shutterstock.com; **p174** © Ab5602

Introduction to **Megilla**

Tractate *Megilla* primarily focuses on explaining all of the *halakhot* that apply to the holiday of Purim. Additionally, it devotes considerable space to the general *halakhot* of synagogues and Torah readings.

The holiday of Purim and its laws are mentioned in the Scroll of Esther but not in the Torah itself, as the events that the holiday commemorates occurred hundreds of years after the giving of the Torah. Although there is a biblical basis for this commemorative holiday, based upon the mitzvot of remembering and defeating Amalek, Purim has a halakhic status in between those of Torah law and rabbinic law, and some of its mitzvot are treated as purely rabbinic enactments.

The Purim story took place during the period of exile between the two Temples and is typical of a time of exile: There was a threat to the very existence of the Jewish people due to the arbitrary decision of a foreign ruler. Even the salvation merely removed the threat, but did not substantially change the living conditions of the Jews at that time. Furthermore, both the threat and the salvation came at a time when the Divine Presence was concealed. This is expressed by the Gemara's statement: From where in the Torah is the name Esther derived? As it is stated: "And I will hide [*haster astir*] My face on that day" (Deuteronomy 31:18).

The fact that the Divine Presence was concealed does not mean that God did not direct the course of events, but that He did so in a way that was not apparent to all, through events that can be seen as random or natural. This makes the miracle of the Purim story different from other miracles described in the Bible, in which the general rules of nature were overridden and the miracle was therefore evident to everyone. Corresponding to the nature of the miracle, the Megilla does not explicitly mention God at all; it simply records the actions and motives of individuals and explains how the events developed as they did. Consequently, one of the basic goals of celebrating Purim is to reveal that which is hidden by publicizing the miracle. There is a greater command to publicize this miracle than to publicize other, more obvious miracles, and Purim is celebrated in a more joyous manner than other holidays.

A further result of the Purim story's taking place during a time of exile relates to the timing of the celebration. Whereas most locations experienced relief on the fourteenth of Adar, the Jews of the capital city of Shushan experienced relief on the fifteenth. In commemoration of this, the Sages declared that Purim must be celebrated on the fifteenth of Adar in Shushan, as well as in any city that was surrounded by a wall in the time of Joshua. The reason that the status of a city is determined by its state at the time of Joshua is in order to emphasize the importance of Eretz Yisrael.

The primary manner in which the miracle of Purim is publicized is through the reading of the Megilla, and this tractate devotes considerable attention to the details of this mitzva. The Sages required that one read the Megilla twice, once at night and once by day. They also established additional days when the Megilla may be read, aside from the days mentioned in the Megilla itself. Similarly, the Gemara delineates how the Megilla must be read in public or by a single individual, the languages in which it may be read, who is obligated to hear the reading of the Megilla, and who may read the Megilla for the entire congregation.

The other mitzvot of Purim were established in order to make the holiday a particularly joyous occasion, based upon the verse: "That they should make them days of feasting and gladness, and of sending portions one to another, and gifts to the poor" (Esther 9:22). The feasting is fulfilled through partaking of a festive meal on Purim. Because it is a day of gladness, it is therefore prohibited to eulogize or to fast on Purim. The phrase "sending portions one to another" is the basis of the requirement for each individual to give gifts of food items to another individual. Furthermore, there is a mitzva to give gifts to the poor so that they too can rejoice fully on Purim. One participates in all of these activities to a greater degree than on other holidays and with a particularly high level of joy.

Since tractate *Megilla* devotes significant attention to issues regarding the reading of the Scroll of Esther, it is the only tractate that addresses the subject of a public reading of the Bible in the synagogue. Furthermore, there are four special Torah portions read on Shabbat over the course of the month of Adar, and therefore the Sages saw fit to expand on these themes and to designate this tractate as the primary source of discussion of the laws of Torah readings, as well as the sanctity of the synagogue and the sacred items therein. This includes a discussion of the days when the Torah is read publicly, a ceremony of ancient origin but one that is not mandated by Torah law. The days on which the Torah is read publically are Shabbat, Festivals and commemorative holidays, the New Moon, public fast days, and every Monday and Thursday. There is also a discussion of how many verses must be read, how many individuals are called to read from the Torah, and how the verses are divided among the different readers. There is a further discussion of the *haftara*, the additional reading from the Prophets upon concluding the Torah reading on certain days.

Additionally, this tractate addresses a synagogue's status and level of sanctity. Because it is a place designated for public prayer gatherings, it is considered like a mini-Temple. Consequently, comparable to the Temple, one must treat a synagogue with reverence while it is functional and even after it has been destroyed. Nonetheless, there are ways to remove the sanctity of a synagogue, either by transferring that sanctity to another item of equal or greater status, or by selling the synagogue with the agreement of the community and its representatives.

Tractate *Megilla* contains four chapters:

Chapter One addresses the days when one may read the Scroll of Esther and contains a section of aggadic exposition of the Megilla. It also discusses a number of unrelated topics, which are cited due to the structural similarity between their presentation in the Mishna and the presentation of one of the laws of the Megilla.

Chapter Two addresses the *halakhot* of how to read the Megilla and who may do so for the public. As an extension of this discussion, this chapter also enumerates mitzvot that must be fulfilled specifically during the day or during the night.

Chapter Three addresses the *halakhot* of reading the Megilla but is primarily devoted to the *halakhot* of public Torah readings, public prayer, the *haftara*, and the Aramaic translation of the Torah reading.

Chapter Four addresses the sanctity of the synagogue and the Torah scroll, and the reading of special Torah portions in honor of particular days during the year.

Introduction to **Perek I**

Therefore the Jews of the villages, who dwell in the unwalled towns, make the fourteenth day of the month of Adar a day of gladness and feasting, and a good day, and of sending portions one to another. And Mordecai wrote these things, and sent letters to all the Jews that were in all the provinces of the king Ahasuerus, both near and far, to enjoin them that they should keep the fourteenth day of the month of Adar and the fifteenth day of the same, in each and every year, as the days on which the Jews rested from their enemies, and the month that was turned for them from sorrow to gladness, and from mourning into a good day; that they should make them days of feasting and gladness, and of sending portions one to another, and gifts to the poor.

(Esther 9:19–22)

The Jews confirmed, and took upon them, and upon their seed, and upon all who joined themselves to them, and it shall not pass, that they would keep these two days according to their writing, and according to their time, in every year; and that these days should be remembered and observed throughout every generation, every family, every province, and every city; and that these days of Purim should not cease from among the Jews, nor the memorial of them perish from their seed.

(Esther 9:27–28)

From the time of its origin, the holiday of Purim has always been celebrated at different times in different locations. As the Megilla itself states, only "the Jews of the villages, that dwell in the unwalled towns" celebrate Purim on the fourteenth of Adar. On the other hand, residents of walled cities celebrate Purim on the fifteenth of Adar. Additionally, in ancient times the Sages instituted that the Megilla may be read by residents of some locations at other times as well. The residents of villages were permitted to advance the reading of the Megilla to the day of ingathering, the Monday or Thursday preceding the fourteenth of Adar. This allowance was made for the benefit of the villagers, who would customarily travel to the larger towns on these days, when the courts were in session, the markets were open, and the Torah was read during the prayer service. Chapter One addresses the details of this institution, as well as related topics, such as when to read the Megilla when Purim occurs on Shabbat.

This chapter will also clarify the criteria for walled and unwalled cities with regard to reading the Megilla. This includes a description of the physical characteristics of a walled city, as well as a discussion of when the city needed to have been surrounded by a wall in order for the Megilla to be read there on the fifteenth of Adar.

As a continuation of its discussion of when to celebrate Purim and read the Megilla, this chapter also includes a summary of the differences between the first and second months of Adar with regard to both the reading of the Megilla and the other mitzvot of Purim and the month of Adar. Following this mishna, the chapter includes several other *mishnayot* that follow a similar structure, which is: There is no difference between A and B except for C. These *mishnayot* are related to the previous mishna in form, although they are not thematically connected to the rest of the chapter or to each other.

Finally, the chapter includes extensive aggadic expositions of numerous verses from the Megilla.

מתני׳ מְגִילָּה נִקְרֵאת בְּאַחַד עָשָׂר, בִּשְׁנֵים עָשָׂר, בִּשְׁלֹשָׁה עָשָׂר, בְּאַרְבָּעָה עָשָׂר, בַּחֲמִשָּׁה עָשָׂר, לֹא פָּחוֹת וְלֹא יוֹתֵר. כְּרַכִּין הַמּוּקָּפִין חוֹמָה מִימוֹת יְהוֹשֻׁעַ בִּן נוּן קוֹרִין בַּחֲמִשָּׁה עָשָׂר, כְּפָרִים וַעֲיָירוֹת גְּדוֹלוֹת קוֹרִין בְּאַרְבָּעָה עָשָׂר, אֶלָּא שֶׁהַכְּפָרִים מַקְדִּימִין לְיוֹם הַכְּנִיסָה.

MISHNA **The Megilla is read**[N] **on the eleventh, on the twelfth, on the thirteenth, on the fourteenth,** or **on the fifteenth** of the month of Adar, **not earlier and not later.**[HN] The mishna explains the circumstances when the Megilla is read on each of these days. **Cities** [***kerakin***][L] **that have been surrounded by a wall since the days of Joshua, son of Nun, read** the Megilla **on the fifteenth** of Adar, whereas **villages and large towns** that have not been walled since the days of Joshua, son of Nun, **read** it **on the fourteenth. However,** the Sages instituted **that the villages may advance** their reading **to the day of assembly,** i.e., Monday or Thursday, when the rabbinical courts are in session and the Torah is read publicly, and the villagers therefore come to the larger towns.[N]

כֵּיצַד? חָל לִהְיוֹת אַרְבָּעָה עָשָׂר בַּשֵּׁנִי, כְּפָרִים וַעֲיָירוֹת גְּדוֹלוֹת קוֹרִין בּוֹ בַּיּוֹם, וּמוּקָּפוֹת חוֹמָה לְמָחָר. חָל לִהְיוֹת בַּשְּׁלִישִׁי אוֹ בָּרְבִיעִי – כְּפָרִים מַקְדִּימִין לְיוֹם הַכְּנִיסָה, וַעֲיָירוֹת גְּדוֹלוֹת קוֹרִין בּוֹ בַּיּוֹם, וּמוּקָּפוֹת חוֹמָה לְמָחָר.

How so? If **the fourteenth** of Adar **occurs on Monday, the villages and large towns read it on that day, and the walled cities** read it **on the next day,** the fifteenth. If the fourteenth **occurs on Tuesday or Wednesday, the villages advance** their reading **to the day of assembly,** i.e., Monday, the twelfth or thirteenth of Adar; **the large towns read** it **on that day,** i.e., the fourteenth of Adar, **and the walled cities** read it **on the next day,** the fifteenth.

חָל לִהְיוֹת בַּחֲמִישִׁי – כְּפָרִים וַעֲיָירוֹת גְּדוֹלוֹת קוֹרִין בּוֹ בַּיּוֹם, וּמוּקָּפוֹת חוֹמָה לְמָחָר. חָל לִהְיוֹת עֶרֶב שַׁבָּת – כְּפָרִים מַקְדִּימִין לְיוֹם הַכְּנִיסָה, וַעֲיָירוֹת גְּדוֹלוֹת וּמוּקָּפוֹת חוֹמָה קוֹרִין בּוֹ בַּיּוֹם.

If the fourteenth **occurs on Thursday, the villages and large towns read** it **on that day,** the fourteenth, **and the walled cities** read it **on the next day,** the fifteenth. If the fourteenth **occurs on Shabbat eve, the villages advance** their reading **to the day of assembly,** i.e., Thursday, the thirteenth of Adar; **and the large towns and the walled cities read** it **on that day,** i.e., the fourteenth of Adar. Even the walled cities read the Megilla on the fourteenth rather than on the fifteenth, as they do not read it on Shabbat.

חָל לִהְיוֹת בַּשַּׁבָּת – כְּפָרִים וַעֲיָירוֹת גְּדוֹלוֹת מַקְדִּימִין וְקוֹרִין לְיוֹם הַכְּנִיסָה, וּמוּקָּפוֹת חוֹמָה לְמָחָר. חָל לִהְיוֹת אַחַר הַשַּׁבָּת – כְּפָרִים מַקְדִּימִין לְיוֹם הַכְּנִיסָה, וַעֲיָירוֹת גְּדוֹלוֹת קוֹרִין בּוֹ בַּיּוֹם, וּמוּקָּפוֹת חוֹמָה לְמָחָר.

If the fourteenth **occurs on Shabbat,** both **the villages and large towns advance** their reading **to the day of assembly,** i.e., Thursday, the twelfth of Adar; **and the walled cities** read it **on the day after** Purim, the fifteenth. If the fourteenth **occurs on Sunday, the villages advance** their reading **to the day of assembly,** i.e., Thursday, the eleventh of Adar; **and the large towns read** it **on that day,** i.e., the fourteenth of Adar; **and the walled cities** read it **on the next day,** the fifteenth.

HALAKHA

Times of reading nowadays – מוֹעֲדֵי הַקְּרִיאָה בִּזְמַנֵּנוּ: In cities that were walled during the days of Joshua, son of Nun, even if they are not surrounded by a wall today, the Megilla is read on the fifteenth of Adar. In all other places, it is read on the fourteenth of Adar (*Shulḥan Arukh, Oraḥ Ḥayyim* 688:1, 3).

LANGUAGE

City [*kerakh*] – כְּרַךְ: A *kerakh* is a large city, and usually walled. Some maintain that the word derives from the Greek χάραξ, *kharax*, which also refers to a place that is fortified with beams. Others suggest that it is of Semitic origin, perhaps Assyrian, and that perhaps it is related to the word *kerakh* meaning circuit or circumference, indicating that that the city is surrounded by a wall.

NOTES

The Megilla is read – מְגִילָּה נִקְרֵאת: The early authorities ask: Why does the mishna state: The Megilla is read, and not: We read the Megilla? The Ritva explains that the mishna uses this formulation because the obligation that applies to each individual is not to read the Megilla, but rather to hear the Megilla being read. Some suggest that this wording is used to teach that there is no obligation to read the Megilla on all of these days; rather, the Megilla is read in each location on only one of these days (*Re'aḥ Duda'im*; *Sefat Emet*).

Not earlier and not later – לֹא פָּחוֹת וְלֹא יוֹתֵר: This phrase literally means not less and not more. The commentators understand that it is referring here to the number of days on which the Megilla is read (Ritva). The author of the *Roke'aḥ* notes that there is an allusion to this in the fact that the word Purim appears five times in the book of Esther, corresponding to the five days established by the Sages for reading the Megilla. The author of *Rishon LeTziyyon* writes that the key elements here are the words: Not later. If the Megilla was not read in its proper time, there is no possibility of making it up afterward.

The days of Purim – יְמֵי הַפּוּרִים: The Ramban asks: Why did the Sages establish the holiday of Purim in such a way that it is celebrated by different sets of Jews on different days rather than by everyone on the same day? He explains that the story of Purim took place after the Jews had already begun their return to Zion. The Jews who returned were, however, still dwelling in towns and villages without walls. They, and others living in similar conditions, were in the greatest danger due to Haman's decree. When these communities were saved from their enemies, they took the initiative to establish a holiday for themselves on the fourteenth of Adar, the day they were able to rest securely. When the Sages formally established Purim as a national holiday, they affirmed its celebration on the fourteenth for those communities who had begun to celebrate it then, and added a day of celebration on the fifteenth for those in walled cities, in commemoration of the day when the Jews of Shushan had rested from battling their enemies.

GEMARA

גמ׳ ״מגילה נקראת באחד עשר״, מנלן? מנלן?! כדבעינן למימר לקמן: חכמים הקילו על הכפרים להיות מקדימין ליום הכניסה כדי שיספקו מים ומזון לאחיהם שבכרכים!

GEMARA We learned in the mishna: **The Megilla is read on the eleventh** of Adar. The Gemara asks: **From where do we** derive this *halakha*? The Gemara expresses surprise at the question: What room is there to ask: **From where do we** derive this *halakha*?[N] The reason is **as we intend to say further on: The Sages were lenient with the villages** and allowed them **to advance** their reading of the Megilla **to the day of assembly, so that they** would be free to **supply water and food to their brethren in the cities** on the day of Purim. Accordingly, the Megilla is read on the eleventh due to a rabbinic enactment.

אנן הכי קאמרינן: מכדי, כולהו אנשי כנסת הגדולה תקנינהו, דאי סלקא דעתך אנשי כנסת הגדולה ארבעה עשר וחמשה עשר תקון – אתו רבנן ועקרי תקנתא דתקינו אנשי כנסת הגדולה? והתנן: אין בית דין יכול לבטל דברי בית דין חבירו אלא אם כן גדול ממנו בחכמה ובמנין.

The Gemara explains: **This is what we said,** i.e., this is what we meant when we asked the question: **Now, all of these** days when the Megilla may be read **were enacted by the members of the Great Assembly**[B] when they established the holiday of Purim itself. **As, if it enters your mind** to say **that the members of the Great Assembly enacted** only **the fourteenth and fifteenth** as days for reading the Megilla, is it possible that **the** later **Sages came and uprooted an ordinance that was enacted by the members of the Great Assembly? Didn't we learn** in a mishna (*Eduyyot* 1:5) that **a rabbinical court cannot rescind the statements of another rabbinical court, unless it is superior to it in wisdom and in number?**[H] No subsequent court was ever greater than the members of the Great Assembly, so it would be impossible for another court to rescind the enactments of the members of the Great Assembly.

אלא פשיטא – כולהו אנשי כנסת הגדולה תקינו, היכא רמיזא?

Rather, it is obvious that **all** these days **were enacted by the members of the Great Assembly,** and the question is: **Where is the allusion** to this in the Bible? The Megilla itself, which was approved by the members of the Great Assembly, mentions only the fourteenth and fifteenth of Adar.

אמר רב שמן בר אבא אמר רבי יוחנן: אמר קרא ״לקיים את ימי הפורים האלה בזמניהם״ זמנים הרבה תקנו להם.

Rav Shemen bar Abba[P] **said** that **Rabbi Yoḥanan said:** It is alluded to when **the verse states: "To confirm these days of Purim in their times"** (Esther 9:31). The phrase "in their times" indicates that **they enacted many times for them** and not only two days.

האי מיבעיא ליה לגופיה! אם כן לימא קרא ״זמן״ מאי ״זמניהם״ – זמנים טובא.

The Gemara objects: **This** verse **is necessary for its own** purpose, to teach that the days of Purim must be observed at the proper times. The Gemara responds: **If so, let the verse say:** To confirm these days of Purim in its **time. What is** the significance of the term **"their times,"** in the plural? It indicates that **many times** were established for the reading of the Megilla.

ואכתי מיבעי ליה: זמנו של זה לא כזמנו של זה! אם כן לימא קרא ״זמנם״, מאי ״זמניהם״ – שמעת מינה כולהו.

The Gemara objects: **But still,** the plural term is **necessary** to indicate that **the time of this** walled city **is not** the same as **the time of that** unwalled town, i.e., Purim is celebrated on different days in different places. The Gemara answers: **If so, let the verse say: Their time,** indicating that each place celebrates Purim on its respective day. **What** is the significance of the compound plural **"their times"? Learn from this** term that although the verse (Esther 9:21) specifies only two days, the Megilla may, at times, be read on **all of** the days enumerated in the mishna.

NOTES

From where do we derive this *halakha* – מנלן: *Tosafot* (*Zevaḥim* 89a) ask: Why is the Gemara astonished about the question: From where do we derive this *halakha*? Even if the derivation is explained in a *baraita*, not all of the *baraitot* were well known, and therefore it is appropriate to ask and to provide an answer from the *baraita*.

The Rashba quotes *Tosafot* as answering that the Gemara's astonishment is based on the fact that the Sages asked for a source for the *halakha* concerning the days on which the Megilla is read but did not ask for a source for the *halakha* in the next clause in the mishna, which states that the villages advance their reading to the day of assembly. The fact that they did not ask for a source for the second *halakha* indicates that they knew that the earlier Sages had allowed the villagers to read the Megilla early, in which case the question about the source for the first clause is unnecessary, as the answer is the same.

Some write that the question: From where do we derive this *halakha*, usually refers to something that is not explicitly written in the Bible but is alluded to in the text. Here, the Gemara asks: Why search for an allusion in the Bible for something that is a rabbinic enactment? (Rabbi Tzvi Hirsch Chajes; see *Kelalei HaTalmud*).

BACKGROUND

The members of the Great Assembly – אנשי כנסת הגדולה: The exact role and composition of the group known as the members of the Great Assembly is unclear. According to the introductory mishna in *Pirkei Avot*, the members of the Great Assembly received the oral tradition from the prophets and served as a link in a chain of transmission of the Torah going back to Moses at Mount Sinai. The assembly served as the religious leadership during the Second Temple period. The last of the prophets, including Haggai, Zechariah, and Malachi, are identified as being part of this group, together with Mordecai of Megillat Esther.

HALAKHA

One court may not annul – אין בית דין יכול לבטל: If a court issued a decree, made an enactment, or established a practice, and it spread throughout the Jewish people, another court cannot cancel the enactment of the first court, unless the latter court is superior in wisdom and in number. Even if the reason for the edict no longer applies, it is not automatically annulled; rather, it must be actively annulled by a court. In the case of earlier and later courts that both consist of seventy-one judges, superiority in number means that the number of Sages who are not members of the court who accept the court's ruling exceeds the number who originally accepted the ruling of the previous court (Rambam *Sefer Shofetim*, *Hilkhot Mamrim* 2:2).

PERSONALITIES

Rav Shemen bar Abba – רב שמן בר אבא: This is Rav Shimon bar Abba HaKohen (Shemen is a version of the name Shimon), a second-generation *amora* in Eretz Yisrael. Rav Shimon bar Abba originally came from Babylonia, where he studied with Shmuel, but he appears to have arrived in Eretz Yisrael at a relatively young age, and there was among the students of Rabbi Ḥanina. His principal teacher, however, was Rabbi Yoḥanan, to whom he attended with great affection. Much has been said in praise of his great righteousness and also of his extensive wisdom. The Sages applied the verse "There is no bread to the wise" (Ecclesiastes 9:11) to Rav Shemen not only due to his poverty, but also due to the fact that although he was certainly one of the leading authorities of his generation, Rabbi Yoḥanan did not succeed in ordaining him.

It is mentioned that Rav Shemen bar Abba married the daughters of his first teacher, Shmuel, after they had been taken captive and were subsequently redeemed in Eretz Yisrael. He married the second one after the first one had passed away. The students of Rabbi Yoḥanan were his colleagues, and the Sages of the next generation report words of Torah in his name. His son, Rav Amram, was also a Torah scholar who reported words of Torah in his father's name.

אֵימָא: זְמַנִּים טוּבָא! ״זְמַנֵּיהֶם״ דּוּמְיָא דִּ״זְמַנָּם״, מַה זְמַנָּם תְּרֵי – אַף ״זְמַנֵּיהֶם״ תְּרֵי.

The Gemara asks: If so, **say** that the plural term indicates **many times**,[N] and the Megilla may be read even earlier than the eleventh of Adar. The Gemara rejects this argument: The compound plural **"their times,"** should be understood as **similar to** the simple plural term, **their time. Just as** the term **their time** can be understood to refer to **two** days, indicating that each location reads the Megilla in its respective time on the fourteenth or the fifteenth of Adar, **so too, "their times"** should be understood as referring to only **two** additional days when the Megilla may be read.

וְאֵימָא תְּרֵיסַר וּתְלֵיסַר! כִּדְאָמַר רַב שְׁמוּאֵל בַּר יִצְחָק: שְׁלֹשָׁה עָשָׂר זְמַן קְהִילָּה לַכֹּל הִיא, וְלָא צְרִיךְ לְרַבּוּיֵי. הָכָא נַמִי שְׁלֹשָׁה עָשָׂר זְמַן קְהִילָּה לַכֹּל הִיא וְלָא צְרִיךְ לְרַבּוּיֵי.

The Gemara asks: **Say** that these two added days are **the twelfth and the thirteenth** of Adar. How is it derived that the Megilla may be read on the eleventh as well? The Gemara answers: It is **as Rav Shmuel bar Yitzḥak said** in a different context: **The thirteenth** of Adar **is a time of assembly for all**,[N] as it was on that day that the Jews assembled to fight their enemies, and the main miracle was performed on that day. Consequently, **there is no need** for a special derivation **to include it** as a day that is fit for reading the Megilla. **Here too,** since **the thirteenth** of Adar **is a time of assembly for all, there is no need** for a special derivation **to include it** among the days when the Megilla may be read.

וְאֵימָא שִׁיתְסַר וְשִׁיבְסַר! ״וְלֹא יַעֲבוֹר״ כְּתִיב.

The Gemara objects: **And say** that the two additional days are **the sixteenth and the seventeenth** of Adar. The Gemara responds: **It is written: "And it shall not pass"** (Esther 9:27), indicating that the celebration of Purim is not delayed until a later date.

וְרַבִּי שְׁמוּאֵל בַּר נַחְמָנִי אָמַר: אָמַר קְרָא ״כַּיָּמִים אֲשֶׁר נָחוּ בָהֶם הַיְּהוּדִים״, ״יָמִים״ ״כַּיָּמִים״ – לְרַבּוֹת אַחַד עָשָׂר, וּשְׁנֵים עָשָׂר.

Having cited and discussed the opinion of Rav Shemen bar Abba, the Gemara cites another answer to the question of where the verses allude to the permissibility of reading the Megilla on the days enumerated in the mishna. **And Rabbi Shmuel bar Naḥmani said:** These dates are alluded to when **the verse states: "As the days on which the Jews rested from their enemies"** (Esther 9:22). The term **"days"** is referring to the two days that are explicitly mentioned in the previous verse, i.e., the fourteenth and the fifteenth. The term **"as the days"** comes **to include** two additional days, i.e., **the eleventh and twelfth** of Adar.

וְאֵימָא תְּרֵיסַר וּתְלֵיסַר! אָמַר רַב שְׁמוּאֵל בַּר יִצְחָק: שְׁלֹשָׁה עָשָׂר זְמַן קְהִילָּה לַכֹּל הִיא, וְלָא צְרִיךְ לְרַבּוּיֵי. וְאֵימָא שִׁיתְסַר וְשִׁיבְסַר! ״וְלֹא יַעֲבוֹר״ כְּתִיב.

The Gemara asks: **And say** that the two additional days are **the twelfth and thirteenth** of Adar. How is it derived that the Megilla may be read on the eleventh as well? In answer to this question, **Rav Shmuel bar Yitzḥak said: The thirteenth** of Adar **is a time of assembly for all, and there is no need** for a special derivation **to include it** as a day fit for reading. The Gemara objects: **Say** that these additional days are **the sixteenth and seventeenth** of Adar. This suggestion is rejected: **It is written: "And it shall not pass."**

רַבִּי שְׁמוּאֵל בַּר נַחְמָנִי מַאי טַעְמָא לֹא אָמַר מִ״בִּזְמַנֵּיהֶם״? זְמַן, זְמַנָּם, זְמַנֵּיהֶם לָא מַשְׁמַע לֵיהּ.

Since two derivations were offered for the same matter, the Gemara asks: **What is the reason** that **Rabbi Shmuel bar Naḥmani did not state** that the days enumerated in the mishna are fit for reading the Megilla **based upon** the term **"in their times,"** in accordance with the opinion of Rav Shemen bar Abba? The Gemara answers: **He does not learn** anything from the distinction between the terms **time, their time,** and **their times.** Therefore, the verse indicates only that there are two days when the Megilla may be read.

וְרַב שֶׁמֶן בַּר אַבָּא, מַאי טַעְמָא לָא אָמַר מִ״כַּיָּמִים״? אָמַר לָךְ: הַהוּא לְדוֹרוֹת הוּא דִּכְתִיב.

The Gemara asks: **And what is the reason** that **Rav Shemen bar Abba did not state** that the days enumerated in the mishna are fit for reading the Megilla **based upon** the term **"as the days,"** in accordance with the opinion of Rabbi Shmuel bar Naḥmani? The Gemara answers: He could have **said to you: That** verse **is written** as a reference **to** future **generations,** and it indicates that just as the Jews rested on these days at that time, they shall rest and celebrate on these days for all generations.

NOTES

Say that the plural term indicates many times – אֵימָא זְמַנִּים טוּבָא: Many ask: Certainly there is a rule that a plural term should be interpreted as implying minimally two. What, then, is the basis for the Gemara's question that the plural should indicate more than two additional days for reading the Megilla? Some answer that since the Megilla states: "The month that was turned for them from sorrow to gladness, and from mourning into a good day; that they should make them days of feasting and gladness, and of sending portions one to another, and gifts to the poor" (Esther 9:22), one might have thought that the Megilla may be read from the beginning of the month (Rashba; Ritva). In fact, according to the Jerusalem Talmud, this verse indicates that one may, in fact, read the Megilla starting from the beginning of the month of Adar.

A time of assembly for all – זְמַן קְהִילָּה לַכֹּל: Rashi explains that the thirteenth of Adar was the day on which the Jews assembled to fight their enemies. Rav Aḥai Gaon, in his *She'iltot*, understands that the term: A time of assembly, alludes to the Fast of Esther, on which all gather in order to fast. If this is the Gemara's intention, this is the earliest reference to the fast, which is not explicitly mentioned in the Talmud (see Rabbeinu Tam, cited in Rosh).

אָמַר רַבָּה בַּר בַּר חָנָה אָמַר רַבִּי יוֹחָנָן: זוֹ דִּבְרֵי רַבִּי עֲקִיבָא סְתִימְתָּאָה, דְּדָרֵישׁ זְמַן, זְמַנָּם, זְמַנֵּיהֶם, אֲבָל חֲכָמִים אוֹמְרִים: אֵין קוֹרִין אוֹתָהּ אֶלָּא בִּזְמַנָּהּ.

§ With regard to the mishna's ruling that the Megilla may be read on the day of assembly, **Rabba bar bar Ḥana said** that **Rabbi Yoḥanan said: This is the statement of Rabbi Akiva the unattributed.**[N] Most unattributed statements of *tanna'im* were formulated by Rabbi Akiva's students and reflect his opinions. **As, he derives** *halakhot* based on the distinction that he draws between the terms **time, their time, and their times. However, the Sages say: One may read** the Megilla **only in its** designated **time,** i.e., the fourteenth of Adar.

מֵיתִיבִי: אָמַר רַבִּי יְהוּדָה אֵימָתַי – בִּזְמַן שֶׁהַשָּׁנִים כְּתִיקְנָן, וְיִשְׂרָאֵל שְׁרוּיִין עַל אַדְמָתָן. אֲבָל בִּזְמַן הַזֶּה, הוֹאִיל וּמִסְתַּכְּלִין בָּהּ – אֵין קוֹרִין אוֹתָהּ אֶלָּא בִּזְמַנָּהּ.

The Gemara **raises an objection** based upon the following *baraita*. **Rabbi Yehuda said: When** is one permitted to read the Megilla from the eleventh to the fifteenth of Adar? One may read on these dates **at a time when the years are established** properly **and the Jewish people dwell** securely **in their** own **land. However, nowadays, since** people **look** to the reading of the Megilla and use it to calculate when Passover begins, **one may read** the Megilla **only in its** designated **time,** so as not to cause confusion with regard to the date of Passover, which is exactly one month from the day after Purim.

רַבִּי יְהוּדָה אַלִּיבָּא דְּמַאן? אִילֵימָא אַלִּיבָּא דְּרַבִּי עֲקִיבָא – אֲפִילּוּ בִּזְמַן הַזֶּה אִיתָא לְהַאי תַּקַּנְתָּא.

The Gemara analyzes this *baraita*: **In accordance with whose** opinion did **Rabbi Yehuda** issue his ruling? **If we say that it is in accordance with** the opinion of **Rabbi Akiva,** whose opinion is expressed in the mishna, there is a difficulty, as Rabbi Akiva holds that **even nowadays**[N] **this ordinance applies.** According to Rabbi Akiva, it is permitted for residents of villages to read the Megilla on the day of assembly even nowadays, as he did not limit his ruling to times when the Jewish people dwell securely in their land.

אֶלָּא לַאו – אַלִּיבָּא דְּרַבָּנַן, וּבִזְמַן שֶׁהַשָּׁנִים כְּתִיקְנָן וְיִשְׂרָאֵל שְׁרוּיִין עַל אַדְמָתָן מִיהָא קָרֵינַן! תְּיוּבְתָּא דְּרַבִּי יוֹחָנָן, תְּיוּבְתָּא.

Rather, is it not in accordance with the opinion of **the Sages,** who disagreed with Rabbi Akiva? **And,** nevertheless, **at least when the years are established** properly **and the Jewish people dwell** securely **in their land,** the Megilla **is read** even prior to the fourteenth, as the Sages disagree only about the *halakha* nowadays. This contradicts the statement of Rabbi Yoḥanan, who holds that the Megilla could never be read earlier than the fourteenth of Adar. The Gemara concludes: **The refutation** of the opinion **of Rabbi Yoḥanan is** indeed **a conclusive refutation.**

אִיכָּא דְּאָמְרִי: אָמַר רַבָּה בַּר בַּר חָנָה אָמַר רַבִּי יוֹחָנָן: זוֹ דִּבְרֵי רַבִּי עֲקִיבָא סְתִימְתָּאָה. אֲבָל חֲכָמִים אָמְרוּ: בִּזְמַן הַזֶּה, הוֹאִיל וּמִסְתַּכְּלִין בָּהּ אֵין קוֹרִין אוֹתָהּ אֶלָּא בִּזְמַנָּהּ.

There are those **who say** a different version of the previous passage. **Rabba bar bar Ḥana said** that **Rabbi Yoḥanan said: This is the statement of Rabbi Akiva, the unattributed. However, the Sages said: Nowadays, since** people **look** to the reading of the Megilla[N] and use it to calculate when Passover begins, **one may read** the Megilla **only in its** designated **time.**

תַּנְיָא נַמִי הָכִי: אָמַר רַבִּי יְהוּדָה: אֵימָתַי – בִּזְמַן שֶׁהַשָּׁנִים כְּתִיקְנָן וְיִשְׂרָאֵל שְׁרוּיִין עַל אַדְמָתָן, אֲבָל בִּזְמַן הַזֶּה הוֹאִיל וּמִסְתַּכְּלִין בָּהּ – אֵין קוֹרִין אוֹתָהּ אֶלָּא בִּזְמַנָּהּ.

The Gemara comments: **This is also taught** in a *baraita*: **Rabbi Yehuda said: When** is one permitted to read the Megilla from the eleventh to the fifteenth of Adar? **At a time when the years are established** properly **and the Jewish people dwell** securely **in their** own **land. However, nowadays, since** people **look** to the reading of the Megilla and use it to calculate when Passover begins, **one may read** the Megilla **only in its** designated **time.**[H] According to this version, Rabbi Yehuda's statement is consistent with the opinion of the Sages, as cited by Rabbi Yoḥanan.

רַב אַשִׁי קַשְׁיָא לֵיהּ דְּרַבִּי יְהוּדָה אַדְּרַבִּי יְהוּדָה,

The Gemara adds: **Rav Ashi** poses **a difficulty** based on an apparent contradiction between the opinion of **Rabbi Yehuda** in the aforementioned *baraita* and a ruling cited in a mishna in the name of **Rabbi Yehuda,**

NOTES

Rabbi Akiva the unattributed – רַבִּי עֲקִיבָא סְתִימְתָּאָה: Rashi explains that many unattributed *mishnayot* reflect the opinion of Rabbi Akiva. Alternatively, most unattributed statements of *tanna'im* were formulated by his students, as explained in tractate *Sanhedrin* (86a). Some suggest that this term simply means that Rabbi Akiva's opinion is cited in this particular mishna anonymously (*Arukh*; Ritva).

In accordance with the opinion of Rabbi Akiva even nowadays – אַלִּיבָּא דְּרַבִּי עֲקִיבָא אֲפִילּוּ בִּזְמַן הַזֶּה: Rashi proves this from the fact that Rabbi Akiva lived after the destruction of the Temple. Note, however, the Rashba, who challenges this assertion, as Rabbi Akiva was also alive when the Temple was still standing, and furthermore, the Sages had much to say about *halakhot* that were no longer practiced in their day.

Since people look [*mistaklin*] to it – הוֹאִיל וּמִסְתַּכְּלִין בָּהּ: According to some, the concern is that people may come to set the date of Passover according to the date on which the Megilla is read (Rashi; Rid). Others explain that the poor look to the time when the Megilla is read and expect to receive the Purim gifts for the needy at the same time. They may become distraught if the Megilla is read and the gifts are not distributed (Rif; Rosh).

Rabbeinu Efrayim explains in similar fashion: If the money is distributed when the Megilla is read in advance of the holiday, the poor might come to squander it and not have any money left with which to celebrate on Purim itself.

Rav Hai Gaon's version of the text read *mistaknin*, they endanger themselves. He explains that nowadays, when the Jews are subject to persecution, it is better not to add to the days of Purim, so as not to intensify the danger. This is also indicated in the Jerusalem Talmud.

HALAKHA

Reading the Megilla early on the day of assembly – הַקְדָּמָה לְיוֹם הַכְּנִיסָה: The enactment that the villages advance their reading of the Megilla to the eleventh, twelfth, and thirteenth of Adar applies only when Israel is sovereign in its land. Today, however, the Megilla is read only on its designated days, the fourteenth and the fifteenth of Adar. This ruling is in accordance with the opinion of Rabbi Yehuda, as the Gemara follows his opinion (Rambam *Sefer Zemanim*, *Hilkhot Megilla* 1:9).

וּמוֹקִים לָהּ לְבָרַיְיתָא כְּרַבִּי יוֹסֵי בַּר יְהוּדָה.

and he establishes the ***baraita*** **in accordance with** the opinion of **Rabbi Yosei bar Yehuda,** rather than Rabbi Yehuda.

וּמִי אָמַר רַבִּי יְהוּדָה בִּזְמַן הַזֶּה הוֹאִיל וּמִסְתַּכְּלִין בָּהּ אֵין קוֹרִין אוֹתָהּ אֶלָּא בִּזְמַנָּהּ? וּרְמִינְהִי, אָמַר רַבִּי יְהוּדָה: אֵימָתַי – מָקוֹם שֶׁנִּכְנָסִין בַּשֵּׁנִי וּבַחֲמִישִׁי, אֲבָל מָקוֹם שֶׁאֵין נִכְנָסִין בַּשֵּׁנִי וּבַחֲמִישִׁי – אֵין קוֹרִין אוֹתָהּ אֶלָּא בִּזְמַנָּהּ.

The Gemara explains the apparent contradiction: **And did Rabbi Yehuda** actually **say** that **nowadays, since** people **look** to the reading of the Megilla and use it to calculate when Passover begins, **one may read** the Megilla **only in its** designated **time?** The Gemara **raises a contradiction** from a mishna (5a): **Rabbi Yehuda said: When** is one permitted to read the Megilla from the eleventh of Adar? In **a place where** the villagers generally **enter** town **on Monday and Thursday.**[H] **However,** in **a place where they do not** generally **enter** town **on Monday and Thursday, one may read** the Megilla **only in its** designated **time,** the fourteenth of Adar.

מָקוֹם שֶׁנִּכְנָסִין בַּשֵּׁנִי וּבַחֲמִישִׁי מִיהָא קָרֵינַן, וַאֲפִילּוּ בִּזְמַן הַזֶּה! וּמוֹקִים לָהּ לְבָרַיְיתָא כְּרַבִּי יוֹסֵי בַּר יְהוּדָה.

The mishna indicates that, **at least** in **a place where** the villagers **enter** town **on Monday and Thursday, one may read** the Megilla from the eleventh of Adar **even nowadays. And** due to this contradiction, Rav Ashi **establishes the** ***baraita*** **in accordance with** the opinion of **Rabbi Yosei bar Yehuda.**

וּמִשּׁוּם דְּקַשְׁיָא לֵיהּ דְּרַבִּי יְהוּדָה אַדְּרַבִּי יְהוּדָה מוֹקִים לָהּ לְבָרַיְיתָא כְּרַבִּי יוֹסֵי בַּר יְהוּדָה?!

The Gemara expresses surprise: **Because** Rav Ashi poses **a difficulty**[N] due to the apparent contradiction between the opinion of **Rabbi Yehuda** in the *baraita* and the opinion cited in a mishna in the name of **Rabbi Yehuda, he establishes the** ***baraita*** **in accordance with** the opinion of **Rabbi Yosei bar Yehuda?** How could he have emended the text just because he had a difficulty that he did not know how to resolve?

רַב אַשִׁי שְׁמִיעַ לֵיהּ דְּאִיכָּא דְּתָנֵי לָהּ כְּרַבִּי יְהוּדָה, וְאִיכָּא דְּתָנֵי לָהּ כְּרַבִּי יוֹסֵי בַּר יְהוּדָה, וּמִדְּקַשְׁיָא לֵיהּ דְּרַבִּי יְהוּדָה אַדְּרַבִּי יְהוּדָה אֲמַר: מַאן דְּתָנֵי לָהּ כְּרַבִּי יְהוּדָה – לָאו דַּוְוקָא, מַאן דְּתָנֵי לָהּ כְּרַבִּי יוֹסֵי בַּר יְהוּדָה – דַּוְוקָא.

The Gemara explains: **Rav Ashi heard that there were those who taught** the *baraita* in the name of **Rabbi Yehuda, and there were those who taught it** in the name of **Rabbi Yosei bar Yehuda. And since he had a difficulty** with the apparent contradiction between one ruling of **Rabbi Yehuda and** another ruling of **Rabbi Yehuda, he said: The one who taught it** in the name of **Rabbi Yehuda is not precise,** whereas **the one who taught it** in the name of **Rabbi Yosei bar Yehuda is precise,** and in this way he eliminated the contradiction.

״כְּרַכִּים הַמּוּקָּפִים חוֹמָה מִימוֹת יְהוֹשֻׁעַ בִּן נוּן קוֹרִין בַּחֲמִשָּׁה עָשָׂר״ וכו׳. מְנָהָנֵי מִילֵּי? אָמַר רָבָא: דְּאָמַר קְרָא ״עַל כֵּן הַיְּהוּדִים הַפְּרָזִים הַיּוֹשְׁבִים בְּעָרֵי הַפְּרָזוֹת״ וגו׳ מִדִּפְרָזִים בְּאַרְבָּעָה עָשָׂר – מוּקָּפִין בַּחֲמִשָּׁה עָשָׂר.

§ We learned in the mishna: **Cities that have been surrounded by a wall since the days of Joshua, son of Nun, read** the Megilla **on the fifteenth** of Adar. The Gemara asks: **From where are these matters** derived, as they are not stated explicitly in the Megilla? **Rava said:** It is **as the verse states: "Therefore the Jews of the villages, who dwell in the unwalled towns,** make the fourteenth day of the month of Adar a day of gladness and feasting" (Esther 9:19). **From** the fact that **the unwalled towns** celebrate Purim **on the fourteenth,** it may be derived that **the walled cities** celebrate Purim **on the fifteenth.**

וְאֵימָא: פְּרָזִים בְּאַרְבָּעָה עָשָׂר – מוּקָּפִין כְּלָל כְּלָל לָא! וְלָאו יִשְׂרָאֵל נִינְהוּ? וְעוֹד, ״מֵהוֹדּוּ וְעַד כּוּשׁ״ כְּתִיב.

The Gemara challenges this answer: **Say** that the **unwalled towns** celebrate Purim **on the fourteenth,** as indicated in the verse, and **the walled cities** do **not** celebrate it **at all.** The Gemara expresses astonishment: **And are they not Jews?**[N] **And furthermore: It is written** that the kingdom of Ahasuerus was **"from Hodu until Cush"** (Esther 1:1), and the celebration of Purim was accepted in all of the countries of his kingdom (Esther 9:20–23).

וְאֵימָא: פְּרָזִים בְּאַרְבֵּיסַר, מוּקָּפִין בְּאַרְבֵּיסַר וּבַחֲמֵיסַר, כְּדִכְתִיב: ״לִהְיוֹת עוֹשִׂים אֵת יוֹם אַרְבָּעָה עָשָׂר לְחֹדֶשׁ אֲדָר וְאֵת יוֹם חֲמִשָּׁה עָשָׂר [בּוֹ] בְּכָל שָׁנָה״!

Rather, the following challenge may be raised: **Say** that **the unwalled towns** celebrate Purim **on the fourteenth** and **the walled cities** celebrate it **on the fourteenth and on the fifteenth, as it is written: "That they should keep the fourteenth day of the month of Adar and the fifteenth day of the same, in every year"** (Esther 9:21). This verse can be understood to mean that there are places where Purim is celebrated on both days.

HALAKHA

A place where they enter on Monday and Thursday – מָקוֹם שֶׁנִּכְנָסִין בַּשֵּׁנִי וּבַחֲמִישִׁי: This provision was enacted on behalf of those villagers who generally go to town on Mondays and Thursdays, in order to allow them to advance their reading of the Megilla to the day of assembly. However, in a place where they do not generally go to town on Mondays and Thursdays, no such enactment was made, in accordance with the opinion of Rabbi Yehuda, following the principle that whenever he says: When, he comes to explain the opinion of the Sages (Rambam *Sefer Zemanim*, *Hilkhot Megilla* 1:6).

NOTES

Because Rav Ashi poses a difficulty – וּמִשּׁוּם דְּקַשְׁיָא לֵיהּ: The Rashba and the Ritva explain that the Gemara's objection to Rav Ashi's reformulation of the *baraita* is based on the fact that it would have been possible to resolve the contradiction in a simpler way by explaining that the conflicting statements of Rabbi Yehuda were stated in accordance with the two different opinions, that of Rabbi Akiva and that of the Sages, and there was no need to attribute one *baraita* to Rabbi Yosei bar Yehuda.

And are they not Jews – וְלָאו יִשְׂרָאֵל נִינְהוּ: Some explain this twofold answer according to the opinion of the Ramban, who states that since the primary danger was to those living in unwalled towns, and especially those in Eretz Yisrael, it was possible to entertain the notion that those living in the walled cities need not celebrate Purim at all. The Gemara answers that, first of all, they too are Jews, and as such they too must celebrate with their brethren. Second, Haman's edict was "from Hodu until Cush" and therefore also included the residents of the walled cities. Even though they were not in immediate danger, they nevertheless shared in the miracle (*Ginzei HaMelekh*).

NOTES

What is the reason for the opinion of Rabbi Yehoshua ben Korḥa – מַאי טַעְמָא דְּרַבִּי יְהוֹשֻׁעַ בֶּן קָרְחָה: The question is not about his basic reasoning. Rather, the question is why was it not enacted that the status of each city be determined by its present situation: A city that is presently walled is a walled city that reads on the fifteenth, and one that is not presently walled is an unwalled town that reads on the fourteenth (*Turei Even*). Indeed, in the Jerusalem Talmud there is a third *tanna*, Rabbi Yosei bar Yehuda, who maintains this opinion as the *halakha*.

From the days of Joshua, son of Nun – מִימוֹת יְהוֹשֻׁעַ בִּן נוּן: The main reason that the status of a city as walled or unwalled depends upon the time of Joshua is to show honor to Eretz Yisrael. In the days of Ahasuerus the cities of Israel were all unwalled cities, yet it would not be fitting to consider them as having the status of unwalled towns for the purposes of reading the Megilla. Therefore, the status of each city is determined based on whether it was walled in the time of Joshua, son of Nun. This is also the understanding in the Jerusalem Talmud, as well as that of the Rambam. Some suggest that since it was Joshua who began the process of wiping out Amalek, the determination of walled and unwalled cities with respect to Purim was made dependent upon his time (Ran; Ritva; Mikhtam; Meiri, citing the midrash).

אִי הֲוָה כְּתַב: ״אֵת יוֹם אַרְבָּעָה עָשָׂר וַחֲמִשָּׁה עָשָׂר״ – כִּדְקָאָמְרַתְּ, הַשְׁתָּא דִּכְתִיב: אֵת יוֹם אַרְבָּעָה עָשָׂר וְאֵת יוֹם חֲמִשָּׁה עָשָׂר – אָתָא ״אֵת״ וּפָסֵיק: הָנֵי בְּאַרְבָּעָה עָשָׂר, וְהָנֵי בַּחֲמִשָּׁה עָשָׂר.

The Gemara rejects this argument: **If it had been written** in the verse: **The fourteenth day and [*ve*] the fifteenth,** it would be **as you** originally **said.** However, **now that it is written: The fourteenth day and [*ve'et*] the fifteenth day,** the particle *et* used here to denote the accusative **comes and interrupts,** indicating that the two days are distinct. Therefore, residents of **these** locations celebrate Purim **on the fourteenth, and** residents of **those** locations celebrate it **on the fifteenth.**

וְאֵימָא: פְּרָזִים בְּאַרְבֵּיסָר, מוּקָפִין – אִי בָּעוּ בְּאַרְבֵּיסָר, אִי בָּעוּ בַּחֲמֵיסָר! אָמַר קְרָא: ״בִּזְמַנֵּיהֶם״ – זְמַנּוֹ שֶׁל זֶה לֹא זְמַנּוֹ שֶׁל זֶה.

The Gemara suggests: **Say** that residents of **unwalled towns** celebrate Purim **on the fourteenth,** as stated in the verse, and with regard to residents of **walled cities, if they wish** they may celebrate it **on the fourteenth,** and **if they wish** they may celebrate it **on the fifteenth.** The Gemara responds: **The verse states: "In their times"** (Esther 9:31), indicating that **the time** when the residents of **this** place celebrate Purim **is not the time** when the residents of **that** place celebrate Purim.

וְאֵימָא בִּתְלֵיסַר! כְּשׁוּשָׁן.

The Gemara raises another challenge: **Say** that the walled cities should celebrate Purim **on the thirteenth** of Adar and not on the fifteenth. The Gemara answers: It stands to reason that the residents of walled cities, who do not celebrate Purim on the fourteenth, celebrate it **as** it is celebrated in **Shushan,** and it is explicitly stated that Purim was celebrated in Shushan on the fifteenth.

אַשְׁכְּחַן עֲשִׂיָּיה, זְכִירָה מְנָלַן? אָמַר קְרָא: ״וְהַיָּמִים הָאֵלֶּה נִזְכָּרִים וְנַעֲשִׂים״, אִיתְקַשׁ זְכִירָה לַעֲשִׂיָּיה.

The Gemara comments: **We found** a source for **observing** the holiday of Purim on the fourteenth of Adar in unwalled towns and on the fifteenth of Adar in walled cities; **from where do we** derive that **remembering** the story of Purim through the reading of the Megilla takes place on these days? The Gemara explains that **the verse states: "That these days should be remembered and observed"** (Esther 9:28), from which it is derived that **remembering is compared to observing.**

מַתְנִיתִין דְּלָא כִּי הַאי תַּנָּא, דְּתַנְיָא, רַבִּי יְהוֹשֻׁעַ בֶּן קָרְחָה אוֹמֵר: כְּרַכִּין הַמּוּקָפִין חוֹמָה מִימוֹת אֲחַשְׁוֵרוֹשׁ קוֹרִין בַּחֲמִשָּׁה עָשָׂר.

§ The Gemara notes that **the mishna is not in accordance with** the opinion of **this *tanna,* as it is taught** in the *Tosefta* (1:1) that **Rabbi Yehoshua ben Korḥa says: Cities that have been surrounded by a wall since the days of Ahasuerus read** the Megilla **on the fifteenth.** According to the *Tosefta,* the status of walled cities is determined based upon whether they were walled in the time of Ahasuerus rather than the time of Joshua.

מַאי טַעְמָא דְּרַבִּי יְהוֹשֻׁעַ בֶּן קָרְחָה? כִּי שׁוּשָׁן, מַה שּׁוּשָׁן מוּקֶּפֶת חוֹמָה מִימוֹת אֲחַשְׁוֵרוֹשׁ וְקוֹרִין בַּחֲמִשָּׁה עָשָׂר – אַף כָּל שֶׁמּוּקֶּפֶת חוֹמָה מִימוֹת אֲחַשְׁוֵרוֹשׁ קוֹרִין בַּחֲמִשָּׁה עָשָׂר.

The Gemara asks: **What is the reason for** the opinion of **Rabbi Yehoshua ben Korḥa?**[N] The Gemara explains that the Megilla is read on the fifteenth in cities that are **like Shushan: Just as Shushan** is a city **that was surrounded by a wall since the days of Ahasuerus, and one reads** the Megilla there **on the fifteenth, so too every** city **that was walled since the days of Ahasuerus reads** the Megilla **on the fifteenth.**

וְתַנָּא דִּידַן מַאי טַעְמָא? יָלֵיף ״פְּרָזִי״ ״פְּרָזִי״, כְּתִיב הָכָא: ״עַל כֵּן הַיְּהוּדִים הַפְּרָזִים״ וּכְתִיב הָתָם: ״לְבַד מֵעָרֵי הַפְּרָזִי הַרְבֵּה מְאֹד״ מַה לְּהַלָּן מוּקֶּפֶת חוֹמָה מִימוֹת יְהוֹשֻׁעַ בִּן נוּן – אַף כָּאן מוּקֶּפֶת חוֹמָה מִימוֹת יְהוֹשֻׁעַ בִּן נוּן.

The Gemara asks: **What is the reason for** the opinion of **the *tanna* of our** mishna? The Gemara explains: It is **derived** through a verbal analogy between one instance of the word **unwalled and** another instance of the word **unwalled. It is written here: "Therefore the Jews of the villages,** who dwell in the unwalled towns" (Esther 9:19), **and it is written there,** in Moses' statement to Joshua before the Jewish people entered Eretz Yisrael: "All these cities were fortified with high walls, gates and bars; **besides unwalled towns, a great many"** (Deuteronomy 3:5). **Just as there,** in Deuteronomy, the reference is to a city **that was surrounded by a wall from the days of Joshua, son of Nun, so too here** it is referring to a city **that was surrounded by a wall from the days of Joshua, son of Nun.**[N]

בִּשְׁלָמָא רַבִּי יְהוֹשֻׁעַ בֶּן קָרְחָה לֹא אָמַר כְּתַנָּא דִּידַן – דְּלֵית לֵיהּ ״פְּרָזִי״ ״פְּרָזִי״ אֶלָּא תַּנָּא דִּידַן מַאי טַעְמָא לֹא אָמַר כְּרַבִּי יְהוֹשֻׁעַ בֶּן קָרְחָה?

The Gemara continues: **Granted** that **Rabbi Yehoshua ben Korḥa did not state** his explanation **in accordance with** the opinion of **the *tanna* of our** mishna **because he did not hold** that a verbal analogy can be established between one verse that employs the word **unwalled** and the other verse that employs the word **unwalled. However, what is the reason** that **the *tanna*** of **our** mishna **did not state** his explanation **in accordance with** the opinion of **Rabbi Yehoshua ben Korḥa?**

מַאי טַעְמָא?! דְּהָא אִית לֵיהּ ״פְּרָזִי״ ״פְּרָזִי״, הָכִי קָאָמַר: אֶלָּא שׁוּשָׁן דַּעֲבְדָא כְּמַאן, לֹא כִּפְרָזִים וְלֹא כְּמוּקָּפִין!

The Gemara expresses astonishment: **What is the reason? Isn't it because he holds** that it is derived from the verbal analogy between one usage of the word **unwalled** and the other usage of the word **unwalled?**[N] The Gemara explains: **This is what he said,** i.e., this was the question: According to the *tanna* of our mishna, **in accordance with whom does Shushan observe** Purim? Shushan is **not like the unwalled towns and not like the walled cities,** as residents of Shushan celebrate Purim on the fifteenth, but the city was not surrounded by a wall since the days of Joshua.

אָמַר רָבָא וְאָמְרִי לָהּ כְּדִי: שָׁאנֵי שׁוּשָׁן הוֹאִיל וְנַעֲשָׂה בָּהּ נֵס.

Rava said, and some say it unattributed to any particular Sage: **Shushan is different since the miracle occurred in it**[N] on the fifteenth of Adar, and therefore Purim is celebrated on that day. However, other cities are only considered walled cities and read the Megilla on the fifteenth of Adar if they were walled since the days of Joshua.[H]

בִּשְׁלָמָא לְתַנָּא דִּידַן – הַיְינוּ דִּכְתִיב: ״מְדִינָה וּמְדִינָה וְעִיר וָעִיר״, ״מְדִינָה וּמְדִינָה״ – לְחַלֵּק בֵּין מוּקָּפִין חוֹמָה מִימוֹת יְהוֹשֻׁעַ בִּן נוּן לְמוּקֶּפֶת חוֹמָה מִימוֹת אֲחַשְׁוֵרוֹשׁ.

The Gemara asks: **Granted, according to the *tanna* of our** mishna, **this is** the meaning of **what is written:** "And these days should be remembered and observed throughout every generation, every family, **every province, and every city**" (Esther 9:28). The phrase "**every province [*medina*]**"[LN] is expressed in the verse using repetition, so that it reads literally: Every province and province, and therefore contains a superfluous usage of the word province, is meant **to distinguish between** cities **that were surrounded by a wall since the days of Joshua, son of Nun,** where the Megilla is read on the fifteenth, **and** a city that **was surrounded by a wall since the days of Ahasuerus,** where the Megilla is read on the fourteenth.

״עִיר וָעִיר״ נַמִי – לְחַלֵּק בֵּין שׁוּשָׁן לִשְׁאָר עֲיָירוֹת. אֶלָּא לְרַבִּי יְהוֹשֻׁעַ בֶּן קָרְחָה, בִּשְׁלָמָא ״מְדִינָה וּמְדִינָה״ – לְחַלֵּק בֵּין שׁוּשָׁן לִשְׁאָר עֲיָירוֹת, אֶלָּא ״עִיר וָעִיר״ לְמַאי אָתָא?

The phrase "**every city,**" which is similarly expressed through repetition and contains a superfluous usage of the word city, **also** serves **to distinguish between Shushan and other cities,** as Purim is celebrated in Shushan on the fifteenth despite the fact that it was not walled since the time of Joshua. **However, according to Rabbi Yehoshua ben Korḥa, granted** that the phrase "**every province**" comes **to distinguish between Shushan and other cities** that were not walled since the days of Ahasuerus; **but what does** the phrase "**every city**" **come** to teach?

אָמַר לָךְ רַבִּי יְהוֹשֻׁעַ בֶּן קָרְחָה: וּלְתַנָּא דִּידַן מִי נִיחָא? כֵּיוָן דְּאִית לֵיהּ פְּרָזִי פְּרָזִי ״מְדִינָה וּמְדִינָה״ לָמָּה לִי? אֶלָּא, קְרָא לִדְרָשָׁה הוּא דַּאֲתָא, וְכִדְרַבִּי יְהוֹשֻׁעַ בֶּן לֵוִי הוּא דַּאֲתָא. דְּאָמַר רַבִּי יְהוֹשֻׁעַ בֶּן לֵוִי: כְּרַךְ וְכָל הַסָּמוּךְ לוֹ וְכָל הַנִּרְאֶה עִמּוֹ נִידּוֹן כִּכְרַךְ.

The Gemara explains that **Rabbi Yehoshua ben Korḥa** could have **said to you: According to the *tanna* of our** mishna, **does it work out well? Since he holds** that it is derived from the verbal analogy between one verse that employs the word **unwalled** and the other verse that employs the word **unwalled, why do I** need the phrase "**every province**"? **Rather, the verse comes for** a midrashic **exposition, and it comes** to indicate that the *halakha* is **in accordance with** the ruling issued by **Rabbi Yehoshua ben Levi. As Rabbi Yehoshua ben Levi said:** A walled **city, and all** settlements **adjacent to it, and all** settlements that can be **seen with it,**[H] i.e., that can be seen from the walled city, are **considered like the** walled **city,** and the Megilla is read there on the fifteenth.

HALAKHA

Reading in Shushan – קְרִיאָה בְּשׁוּשָׁן: Even though the city of Shushan was not walled from the days of Joshua, son of Nun, the Megilla is read there on the fifteenth because the miracle that happened there took place on that day (*Shulḥan Arukh, Oraḥ Ḥayyim* 688:2).

A walled city, and all settlements adjacent to it, and all that can be seen with it – כְּרַךְ וְכָל הַסָּמוּךְ וְכָל הַנִּרְאֶה: A walled city, and all places near it, and all places that can be seen from it, are considered for the purpose of Megilla like the walled city itself, so that the Megilla is read in those places on the fifteenth of Adar, in accordance with the opinion of Rabbi Yehoshua ben Levi (*Shulḥan Arukh, Oraḥ Ḥayyim* 688:2).

LANGUAGE

Province [*medina*] – מְדִינָה: In rabbinic Hebrew, and perhaps also in biblical Hebrew (see Nehemiah 11:3), the term *medina* means a city, and it seems that it is in this sense that the word is understood in the midrashic expositions found here in the Gemara.

NOTES

He holds that it is derived from the verbal analogy between one usage of the word unwalled and the other usage of the word unwalled – אִית לֵיהּ פְּרָזִי פְּרָזִי: This indicates that the book of Esther may be interpreted by way of the hermeneutical rules used for the Torah, such as verbal analogy. This idea is found in the Jerusalem Talmud as well (see Ritva).

Since the miracle occurred in it – הוֹאִיל וְנַעֲשָׂה בָּהּ הַנֵּס: Rashi and others explain that a miracle was performed there during the battles and the people celebrated there on the fifteenth. Others suggest that the central part of the Purim miracle, i.e., all of the actions involving Esther and Mordecai, took place in Shushan, and it is therefore fitting that it should receive special honor and be treated as a walled city for future generations (Rabbeinu Yehonatan; *Turei Even*).

Every province – מְדִינָה וּמְדִינָה: The Rashba explains that according to the *tanna* of the mishna, the words "every family," which are expressed in the verse in the repetitive phrase: Every family and family, is used in order to distinguish between villages that read on the fourteenth and other villages that advance their reading to the day of assembly, or those that are annexed to the walled cities for the purpose of Megilla reading.

עַד כַּמָּה? אָמַר רַבִּי יִרְמְיָה וְאִיתֵימָא רַבִּי חִיָּיא בַּר אַבָּא: כְּמֵחַמְּתָן לִטְבֶרְיָא, מִיל. וְלֵימָא מִיל! הָא קָא מַשְׁמַע לַן: דְּשִׁיעוּרָא דְמִיל כַּמָּה הָוֵי – כְּמֵחַמְּתָן לִטְבֶרְיָא.

The Gemara asks: **Up to what** distance is considered adjacent?[H] **Rabbi Yirmeya said, and some say** that it was **Rabbi Ḥiyya bar Abba** who said: The limit is **like** the distance **from** the town of **Ḥamtan to Tiberias,**[B] a ***mil.*** The Gemara asks: **Let him say** simply that the limit is a ***mil;*** why did he have to mention these places? The Gemara answers that the formulation of the answer **teaches us this: How much** distance comprises **the measure** of a ***mil?*** It is **like** the distance **from Ḥamtan to Tiberias.**

וְאָמַר רַבִּי יִרְמְיָה וְאִיתֵימָא רַבִּי חִיָּיא בַּר אַבָּא: מנצפ״ך צוֹפִים אֲמָרוּם.

§ Having cited a statement of Rabbi Yirmeya, which some attribute to Rabbi Ḥiyya bar Abba, the Gemara cites other statements attributed to these Sages. **Rabbi Yirmeya said, and some say** that it was **Rabbi Ḥiyya bar Abba** who said: **The Seers,** i.e., the prophets, were the ones who **said**[N] that the letters ***mem, nun, tzadi, peh,*** and ***kaf*** [***mantzepakh***],[N] have a different form when they appear at the end of a word.

וְתִסְבְּרָא?! וְהָכְתִיב: ״אֵלֶּה הַמִּצְוֹת״ שֶׁאֵין נָבִיא רַשַּׁאי לְחַדֵּשׁ דָּבָר מֵעַתָּה! וְעוֹד, הָאָמַר רַב חִסְדָּא: מֵ״ם וְסָמֶ״ךְ שֶׁבַּלּוּחוֹת

The Gemara asks: **And** how can **you understand** it that way? **Isn't it written: "These are the commandments** that the Lord commanded Moses for the children of Israel in Mount Sinai" (Leviticus 27:34), which indicates **that a prophet is not permitted to initiate** or change **any matter** of *halakha* **from now on?** Consequently, how could the prophets establish new forms for the letters? **And furthermore, didn't Rav Ḥisda say:** The letters ***mem*** **and *samekh*** **in the tablets** of the covenant given at Sinai

HALAKHA

What is adjacent – אֵיזֶהוּ סָמוּךְ: With regard to reading the Megilla, an adjacent place is a place that is found within a *mil* of the walled city. Some say that in places where there is a train and the like, we do not measure by the distance of a *mil*, but rather the distance one can travel in eighteen minutes (see *Kaf HaḤayyim*; *Shulḥan Arukh, Oraḥ Ḥayyim* 688:2).

BACKGROUND

Like from Ḥamtan to Tiberias – כְּמֵחַמְּתָן לִטְבֶרְיָא: Ḥamtan, also called Ḥamat or Ḥamta, is a city that was built around the hot springs of Tiberias. Although it was close to Tiberias, it was a separate settlement. It was also the seat of one of the priestly watches. Ancient Tiberias was built south of modern-day Tiberias, and the distance between ancient Tiberias and Ḥamtan was a *mil*, approximately 1,000–1,200 m.

Roman bath ruins at Ḥamat Gader and map of area surrounding Geder and Ḥamtan

NOTES

The Seers said – צוֹפִים אֲמָרוּם: The Rashba asks how it is possible that the manner in which these letters are written was forgotten? After all, the Torah scroll written by Moses himself was kept in the Temple in the Ark and could have been checked at any time. He explains that the doubt occurred after King Josiah hid the Ark due to the prophecies predicting the destruction of the Temple. Following Josiah's reign, wicked kings abolished Torah study, and this led to the doubts about how the letters were to be written.

Mem, nun, tzadi, peh, **and *kaf* [*mantzepakh*] – מנצפ״ך:** The *ge'onim* write that the letters were intentionally arranged in this order, and not in alphabetical order [*kemanpatz*], in order to allude to the Seers [*tzofim*] who ordained them.

Perek **I**
Daf **3** Amud **a**

בְּנֵס הָיוּ עוֹמְדִין?

stood by way of a miracle?[N]

אִין, מֶהְוָה הָווּ, וְלָא הָווּ יָדְעִי הֵי בְּאֶמְצַע תֵּיבָה וְהֵי בְּסוֹף תֵּיבָה, וַאֲתוּ צוֹפִים וְתַקִּינוּ: פְּתוּחִין בְּאֶמְצַע תֵּיבָה וּסְתוּמִין בְּסוֹף תֵּיבָה.

The Gemara answers: **Yes,** two forms of these letters **did exist** at that time, **but** the people **did not know which** one of them was to be used **in the middle of the word and which at the end of the word, and the Seers came and established** that **the open** forms are to used be **in the middle of the word and the closed** forms **at the end of the word.**

סוֹף סוֹף ״אֵלֶּה הַמִּצְוֹת״ שֶׁאֵין נָבִיא עָתִיד לְחַדֵּשׁ דָּבָר מֵעַתָּה! אֶלָּא שְׁכָחוּם וְחָזְרוּ וִיסָדוּם.

The Gemara asks: **Ultimately,** however, doesn't the phrase **"these are the commandments"** (Leviticus 27:34) indicate **that a prophet is not permitted to initiate any matter** of *halakha* **from now on? Rather,** it may be suggested that the final letters already existed at the time of the giving of the Torah, but over the course of time the people **forgot them,** and the prophets **then** came and **reestablished them.**

NOTES

Stood by way of a miracle – בְּנֵס הָיוּ עוֹמְדִין: The letters appearing on the tablets of the covenant were engraved into the stone, and there is a tradition that the engraving went completely through the tablet. Most letters are not closed, and therefore the portions of the stone that remained after the engraving were attached to the rest of the stone. However, since the letter *samekh* is closed, the part of the stone inside the letter could only have remained in place by way of a miracle, as it was not attached to the rest of the tablet. The same is true of the letter *mem* when it appears at the end of the word. This statement of Rav Ḥisda indicates that the form of the *mem* as it appears at the end of a word was already established at Sinai.

וְאָמַר רַבִּי יִרְמְיָה וְאִיתֵּימָא רַבִּי חִיָּיא בַּר אַבָּא: תַּרְגּוּם שֶׁל תּוֹרָה – אוּנְקְלוֹס הַגֵּר אֲמָרוֹ מִפִּי רַבִּי אֱלִיעֶזֶר וְרַבִּי יְהוֹשֻׁעַ. תַּרְגּוּם שֶׁל נְבִיאִים – יוֹנָתָן בֶּן עוּזִּיאֵל אֲמָרוֹ מִפִּי חַגַּי זְכַרְיָה וּמַלְאָכִי, וְנִזְדַּעְזְעָה אֶרֶץ יִשְׂרָאֵל אַרְבַּע מֵאוֹת פַּרְסָה עַל אַרְבַּע מֵאוֹת פַּרְסָה. יָצְתָה בַּת קוֹל וְאָמְרָה: מִי הוּא זֶה שֶׁגִּילָּה סְתָרַיי לִבְנֵי אָדָם?

§ The Gemara cites another ruling of Rabbi Yirmeya or Rabbi Ḥiyya bar Abba. **Rabbi Yirmeya said, and some say** that it was **Rabbi Ḥiyya bar Abba** who said: **The** Aramaic **translation of the Torah** used in the synagogues **was composed by Onkelos the convert**[P] **based on** the teachings of **Rabbi Eliezer and Rabbi Yehoshua. The** Aramaic **translation of the Prophets was composed by Yonatan ben Uzziel**[P] **based on** a tradition going back to the last prophets, **Haggai, Zechariah, and Malachi.** The Gemara relates that when Yonatan ben Uzziel wrote his translation, **Eretz Yisrael quaked**[N] over an area of **four hundred parasangs** [*parsa*] **by four hundred parasangs, and a Divine Voice emerged and said: Who is this who has revealed My secrets to mankind?**

עָמַד יוֹנָתָן בֶּן עוּזִּיאֵל עַל רַגְלָיו וְאָמַר: אֲנִי הוּא שֶׁגִּלִּיתִי סְתָרֶיךָ לִבְנֵי אָדָם; גָּלוּי וְיָדוּעַ לְפָנֶיךָ שֶׁלֹּא לִכְבוֹדִי עָשִׂיתִי, וְלֹא לִכְבוֹד בֵּית אַבָּא, אֶלָּא לִכְבוֹדְךָ עָשִׂיתִי שֶׁלֹּא יִרְבּוּ מַחֲלוֹקֶת בְּיִשְׂרָאֵל.

Yonatan ben Uzziel stood up on his feet and said: I am the one who has revealed Your secrets to mankind through my translation. However, **it is revealed and known to You that I did this not for my** own **honor, and not for the honor of the house of** my **father, but rather** it was **for Your honor** that **I did this, so that discord not increase among the Jewish people.** In the absence of an accepted translation, people will disagree about the meaning of obscure verses, but with a translation, the meaning will be clear.

וְעוֹד בִּיקֵּשׁ לְגַלּוֹת תַּרְגּוּם שֶׁל כְּתוּבִים, יָצְתָה בַּת קוֹל וְאָמְרָה לוֹ: דַּיֶּיךָ! מַאי טַעְמָא – מִשּׁוּם דְּאִית בֵּיהּ קֵץ מָשִׁיחַ.

And Yonatan ben Uzziel **also sought to reveal a translation of the Writings,**[NB] but **a Divine Voice emerged and said to him: It is enough for you** that you translated the Prophets. The Gemara explains: **What is the reason** that he was denied permission to translate the Writings? **Because it has in it** a revelation of **the end,** when the **Messiah** will arrive. The end is foretold in a cryptic manner in the book of Daniel, and were the book of Daniel translated, the end would become manifestly revealed to all.

וְתַרְגּוּם שֶׁל תּוֹרָה אוּנְקְלוֹס הַגֵּר אֲמָרוֹ? וְהָא אָמַר רַב אִיקָא בַּר אָבִין אָמַר רַב חֲנַנְאֵל אָמַר רַב, מַאי דִּכְתִיב: "וַיִּקְרְאוּ בַסֵּפֶר תּוֹרַת הָאֱלֹהִים מְפוֹרָשׁ וְשׂוֹם שֶׂכֶל וַיָּבִינוּ בַּמִּקְרָא". "וַיִּקְרְאוּ בַסֵּפֶר תּוֹרַת הָאֱלֹהִים" – זֶה מִקְרָא, "מְפוֹרָשׁ" – זֶה תַּרְגּוּם,

The Gemara asks: **Was the translation of the Torah** really **composed by Onkelos the convert? Didn't Rav Ika bar Avin say** that **Rav Ḥananel said** that **Rav said: What is** the meaning of that **which is written** with respect to the days of Ezra: **"And they read in the book, the Torah of God, distinctly; and they gave the sense, and they caused them to understand the reading"** (Nehemiah 8:8)? The verse should be understood as follows: **"And they read in the book, the Torah of God," this is the** scriptural **text; "distinctly," this is the translation,** indicating that they immediately translated the text into Aramaic, as was customary during public Torah readings.

"וְשׂוֹם שֶׂכֶל" – אֵלּוּ הַפְּסוּקִין, "וַיָּבִינוּ בַּמִּקְרָא" אֵלּוּ פִּיסְקֵי טְעָמִים, וְאָמְרִי לָהּ: אֵלּוּ הַמָּסוֹרֶת. שְׁכָחוּם וְחָזְרוּ וִיסָדוּם.

"And they gave the sense," these are the divisions of the text into separate **verses. "And they caused them to understand the reading," these are the cantillation notes,** through which the meaning of the text is further clarified. **And some say** that **these are the** Masoretic **traditions**[N] with regard to the manner in which each word is to be written. This indicates that the Aramaic translation already existed at the beginning of the Second Temple period, well before the time of Onkelos. The Gemara answers: **The** ancient Aramaic translation **was forgotten and then** Onkelos came and **reestablished it.**

PERSONALITIES

Onkelos the convert – אוּנְקְלוֹס הַגֵּר: There are differing opinions as to whether Onkelos the convert can be identified with Aquila, who translated the Bible into Greek. It is related that Onkelos came from the family of the Roman emperor and subsequently converted and became a student of Rabbi Eliezer and Rabbi Yehoshua. Many stories are told about his conversion process and the powers of persuasion he displayed. According to the theory that Onkelos can be identified with Aquila, he translated the Bible into Greek and then in turn into Aramaic. The translation of Onkelos is considered to be accurate and in line with the Jewish traditions and *halakhot*. Usually the translation presents the literal meaning of the text, with the exception of instances where he thought the simple meaning of the text did not follow the literal translation of the words. In these cases, he would translate the text in a more figurative manner.

Onkelos's Aramaic translation is highly regarded by the Sages, and when they would read from the Torah in synagogue, they would translate the text using this translation. This custom is observed to this day by the Yemenite Jews. At the very least, this translation is recommended in order to fulfill the practice of reading the weekly portion twice in the original and once in translation. Other commentaries elaborate on Onkelos's translation and expound upon its meaning, the most detailed being *Netina LaGer*.

Yonatan ben Uzziel – יוֹנָתָן בֶּן עוּזִּיאֵל: Very little is known of Yonatan ben Uzziel, who was the greatest student of Hillel the Elder. His greatest project, as is related here, was the translation of the books of the Prophets from Hebrew into Aramaic. It is not clear whether the translation that is presently extant is his original one or whether it is merely based on that translation. Clearly, the extant version is a loose translation that includes much interpretation and explanation. Although there were previous translations into Greek, his translation was the first that also served as a type of interpretation and whose methodology was accepted for use by the Sages of Israel. He was a preeminent scholar in his generation, and we find that Shammai the Elder, the president of the court, would discuss *halakha* with him.

BACKGROUND

A translation of the Writings – תַּרְגּוּם שֶׁל כְּתוּבִים: Aramaic translations of the Writings were composed by Sages who lived after Yonatan ben Uzziel. There are actually two such translations of the Scroll of Esther, and it is known that a translation of the book of Job existed already in the time of the Temple. According to the *ge'onim*, however, these translations were not authorized or composed by leading Torah scholars, and consequently they related to them as mere commentaries that do not necessarily always reflect the real meaning of the verse. Furthermore, most of these compositions were composed much later than the time of Yonatan ben Uzziel. They were generally written in Eretz Yisrael and are based on aggadic midrash.

NOTES

Eretz Yisrael quaked – נִזְדַּעְזְעָה אֶרֶץ יִשְׂרָאֵל: It has been suggested that this alludes to the fact that all of the Sages of Eretz Yisrael were greatly disturbed by this translation (*Pardes Rimonim*). Various explanations have been offered for this: Some suggest that it is not proper to reveal something that the Torah has hidden (Rabbeinu Ḥananel); others suggest that there is a concern that people will devote less time and effort to their study of the meaning of the verses and rely instead on the translation (Rid). A third explanation is that they were concerned that people would no longer study the Bible itself, but only the translation (*Penei Yehoshua*).

A translation of the Writings – תַּרְגּוּם שֶׁל כְּתוּבִים: Rashi understands that the revelation of the end is found in the book of Daniel. Others suggest that it is alluded to in other books as well, e.g., the Song of Songs (Rashba). Although Yonatan ben Uzziel did not want to translate Writings if he could not translate it in its entirety, a later Sage translated it with the exception of the book of Daniel, which the Divine Voice indicated should not be translated (Rashba; Ritva).

These are the Masoretic traditions – אֵלּוּ הַמָּסוֹרֶת: This may refer to the tradition [*mesora*] that has come down to us that gathers together and notes linguistic phenomena throughout the Bible, which was arrived at through [*hitbonenut*], careful examination. Alternatively, it is referring to the differences between the ways certain words are written and pronounced, and to instances of extra or missing letters that add to the deeper understanding [*havana*] of the text (Rashash).

מַאי שְׁנָא דְּאוֹרַיְיתָא דְּלָא אִזְדַּעְזְעָה, וַאדִּנְבִיאֵי אִזְדַּעְזְעָה? דְּאוֹרַיְיתָא מִיפָּרְשָׁא מִלְּתָא, דִּנְבִיאֵי אִיכָּא מִילֵּי דְּמִיפָּרְשָׁן, וְאִיכָּא מִילֵּי דְּמִסַּתְּמָן, דִּכְתִיב: "בַּיּוֹם הַהוּא יִגְדַּל הַמִּסְפֵּד בִּירוּשָׁלַיִם כְּמִסְפַּד הֲדַדְרִימּוֹן בְּבִקְעַת מְגִדּוֹן",

The Gemara asks: **What is different** about the translation of Prophets? Why is it that when Onkelos revealed the translation **of the Torah,** Eretz Yisrael **did not quake, and** when he revealed the translation **of the Prophets, it quaked?** The Gemara explains: **The** meaning of **matters** discussed **in the Torah is clear,**[N] and therefore its Aramaic translation did not reveal the meaning of passages that had not been understood previously. Conversely, in **the Prophets, there are matters that are clear and there are matters that are obscure,** and the Aramaic translation revealed the meaning of obscure passages. The Gemara cites an example of an obscure verse that is clarified by the Aramaic translation: **As it is written: "On that day shall there be a great mourning in Jerusalem, like the mourning of Hadadrimmon in the valley of Megiddon"** (Zechariah 12:11).

וַאֲמַר רַב יוֹסֵף: אִלְמָלֵא תַּרְגּוּמָא דְּהַאי קְרָא לָא יָדַעְנָא מַאי קָאָמַר: בְּיוֹמָא הַהוּא יִסְגֵּי מִסְפְּדָא בִּירוּשָׁלֵים כְּמִסְפְּדָא דְּאַחְאָב בַּר עָמְרִי דִּקְטַל יָתֵיהּ הֲדַדְרִימּוֹן בֶּן טַבְרִימּוֹן בְּרָמוֹת גִּלְעָד, וּכְמִסְפְּדָא דְּיֹאשִׁיָּה בַּר אָמוֹן דִּקְטַל יָתֵיהּ פַּרְעֹה חֲגִירָא בְּבִקְעַת מְגִדּוֹ.

And with regard to that verse, **Rav Yosef said: Were it not for the** Aramaic **translation of this verse, we would not have known what it is saying,** as the Bible does not mention any incident involving Hadadrimmon in the valley of Megiddon. The Aramaic translation reads as follows: **On that day, the mourning in Jerusalem will be as great as the mourning for Ahab, son of Omri, who was slain by Hadadrimmon, son of Tavrimon, in Ramoth-Gilead, and like the mourning for Josiah, son of Amon, who was slain by Pharaoh the lame in the valley of Megiddon.** The translation clarifies that the verse is referring to two separate incidents of mourning, and thereby clarifies the meaning of this verse.

"וְרָאִיתִי אֲנִי דָנִיֵּאל לְבַדִּי אֶת הַמַּרְאָה וְהָאֲנָשִׁים אֲשֶׁר הָיוּ עִמִּי לֹא רָאוּ אֶת הַמַּרְאָה אֲבָל חֲרָדָה גְדוֹלָה נָפְלָה עֲלֵיהֶם וַיִּבְרְחוּ בְּהֵחָבֵא". מַאן נִינְהוּ אֲנָשִׁים? אָמַר רַבִּי יִרְמְיָה וְאִיתֵּימָא רַבִּי חִיָּיא בַּר אַבָּא: זֶה חַגַּי זְכַרְיָה וּמַלְאָכִי.

§ The Gemara introduces another statement from the same line of tradition. The verse states: **"And I, Daniel, alone saw the vision, for the men who were with me did not see the vision; but a great trembling fell upon them, so that they fled to hide themselves"** (Daniel 10:7). **Who were these men?** The term "men" in the Bible indicates important people; who were they? **Rabbi Yirmeya said, and some say** that it was **Rabbi Ḥiyya bar Abba** who said: **These are** the prophets **Haggai, Zechariah, and Malachi.**

אִינְהוּ עֲדִיפִי מִינֵּיהּ, וְאִיהוּ עָדִיף מִינַּיְיהוּ. אִינְהוּ עֲדִיפִי מִינֵּיהּ – דְּאִינְהוּ נְבִיאֵי, וְאִיהוּ לָאו נָבִיא. אִיהוּ עָדִיף מִינַּיְיהוּ – דְּאִיהוּ חֲזָא וְאִינְהוּ לָא חֲזוּ.

The Gemara comments: In certain ways **they,** the prophets, **were greater than him,** Daniel, and in certain ways **he,** Daniel, **was greater than them. They were greater than him, as they were prophets and he was not a prophet.**[N] Haggai, Zechariah, and Malachi were sent to convey the word of God to the Jewish people, while Daniel was not sent to reveal his visions to others. In another way, however, **he was greater than them, as he saw** this vision, **and they did not see** this vision, indicating that his ability to perceive obscure and cryptic visions was greater than theirs.

וְכִי מֵאַחַר דְּלָא חֲזוּ מַאי טַעְמָא אִיבְעִיתוּ? אַף עַל גַּב דְּאִינְהוּ לָא חֲזוּ – מַזְּלַיְיהוּ חֲזוּ.

The Gemara asks: **Since they did not see** the vision, **what is the reason that they were frightened?** The Gemara answers: **Even though they did not see** the vision, **their guardian angels saw** it, and therefore they sensed that there was something fearful there and they fled.

NOTES

The meaning of matters discussed in the Torah is clear – דְּאוֹרַיְיתָא מִיפָּרְשָׁא מִלְּתָא: Rabbeinu Ḥananel writes that this is meant as a generalization, i.e., that most of the matters discussed in the Torah are clear (see Rav Ya'akov Emden). Indeed, the language of the Torah itself is generally not obscure, and most verses can be understood in their plain sense. In contrast, the books of the Prophets are often written as parables, and each parable must be explained and its content revealed. A translation, therefore, is not merely a rendering of the material into a different language, but also an explanation. This, in fact, is the nature of the translation attributed to Yonatan ben Uzziel that has come down to us.

He was not a prophet – אִיהוּ לָאו נָבִיא: The *Turei Even* writes that Daniel was not a prophet at all, as we do not find that God Himself spoke to him but only that certain visions were revealed to him by way of an angel. Most of the early authorities, however, maintain that Daniel is counted among the prophets (*Tosefot HaRosh*), as a prophet is one who is sent by God with a message to the Jewish people, regardless of how that message is communicated to him.

אֲמַר רָבִינָא: שְׁמַע מִינָּהּ, הַאי מַאן דְּמִיבְעִית אַף עַל גַּב דְּאִיהוּ לָא חָזֵי מַזָּלֵיהּ חָזֵי. מַאי תַּקַּנְתֵּיהּ? לִיקְרֵי קְרִיאַת שְׁמַע, וְאִי קָאֵים בִּמְקוֹם הַטִּנּוֹפֶת – לִינְשׁוֹף מִדּוּכְתֵּיהּ אַרְבַּע גַּרְמִידֵי, וְאִי לָא – לֵימָא הָכִי: עִיזָּא דְּבֵי טַבָּחֵי שְׁמִינָא מִינַּאי.

Ravina said: **Learn from** this incident that with regard to **one who is frightened**[N] for no apparent reason, **although he does not see** anything menacing, **his guardian angel sees** it, and therefore he should take steps in order to escape the danger. The Gemara asks: **What is his remedy? He should recite *Shema*,** which will afford him protection. **And if he is standing in a place of filth,** where it is prohibited to recite verses from the Torah, **he should distance himself four cubits from his** current **location** in order to escape the danger. **And if** he is **not** able to do so, **let him say the following** incantation: **The goat of the slaughterhouse is fatter than I am,** and if a calamity must fall upon something, it should fall upon it.

וְהַשְׁתָּא דְּאָמְרַתְּ "מְדִינָה וּמְדִינָה" "וְעִיר וָעִיר" לִדְרָשָׁה, "מִשְׁפָּחָה וּמִשְׁפָּחָה" לְמַאי אֲתָא? אָמַר רַבִּי יוֹסֵי בַּר חֲנִינָא: לְהָבִיא מִשְׁפְּחוֹת כְּהוּנָּה וּלְוִיָּה שֶׁמְּבַטְּלִין עֲבוֹדָתָן וּבָאִין לִשְׁמוֹעַ מִקְרָא מְגִילָּה.

§ After this digression, the Gemara returns to the exposition of a verse cited above. **Now that you have said** that the phrases "**every province**" **and** "**every city**" appear **for** the purposes of midrashic **exposition, for what** exposition do the words "**every family**" appear in that same verse (Esther 9:28)? **Rabbi Yosei bar Ḥanina said:** These words come **to include the priestly and Levitical families,** and indicate **that they cancel their service** in the Temple **and come to hear the reading of the Megilla.**

דְּאָמַר רַב יְהוּדָה אָמַר רַב: כֹּהֲנִים בַּעֲבוֹדָתָן, וּלְוִיִּם בְּדוּכָנָן, וְיִשְׂרָאֵל בְּמַעֲמָדָן – כּוּלָּן מְבַטְּלִין עֲבוֹדָתָן וּבָאִין לִשְׁמוֹעַ מִקְרָא מְגִילָּה.

As **Rav Yehuda said** that **Rav said: The priests at their** Temple **service,**[NH] **the Levites on their platform** in the Temple, where they sung the daily psalm, **and the Israelites at their watches,** i.e., the group of Israelites, corresponding to the priestly watches, who would come to Jerusalem and gather in other locations as representatives of the entire nation to observe or pray for the success of the Temple service, **all cancel their service and come to hear the reading of the Megilla.**

תַּנְיָא נַמִּי הָכִי: כֹּהֲנִים בַּעֲבוֹדָתָן, וּלְוִיִּם בְּדוּכָנָן, וְיִשְׂרָאֵל בְּמַעֲמָדָן – כּוּלָּן מְבַטְּלִין עֲבוֹדָתָן וּבָאִין לִשְׁמוֹעַ מִקְרָא מְגִילָּה. מִכָּאן סָמְכוּ שֶׁל בֵּית רַבִּי שֶׁמְּבַטְּלִין תַּלְמוּד תּוֹרָה וּבָאִין לִשְׁמוֹעַ מִקְרָא מְגִילָּה, קַל וָחוֹמֶר מֵעֲבוֹדָה. וּמָה עֲבוֹדָה שֶׁהִיא חֲמוּרָה – מְבַטְּלִינַן, תַּלְמוּד תּוֹרָה – לֹא כׇּל שֶׁכֵּן?!

This is also taught in a *baraita*: **The priests at their service, the Levites on the platform, and the Israelites at their watches, all cancel their service and come to hear the reading of the Megilla.** The Sages of **the house of Rabbi** Yehuda HaNasi **relied upon**[N] the *halakha* stated **here** and determined **that one cancels his Torah study and comes to hear the reading of the Megilla.** They derived this principle by means of **an *a fortiori*** inference **from the** Temple **service: Just as** one who is engaged in performing **service** in the Temple, **which is** very **important, cancels** his service in order to hear the Megilla, is it **not all the more so** obvious that one who is engaged in **Torah study** cancels his study to hear the Megilla?

וַעֲבוֹדָה חֲמוּרָה מִתַּלְמוּד תּוֹרָה? וְהָכְתִיב: "וַיְהִי בִּהְיוֹת יְהוֹשֻׁעַ בִּירִיחוֹ וַיִּשָּׂא עֵינָיו וַיַּרְא וְהִנֵּה אִישׁ עוֹמֵד לְנֶגְדּוֹ [וגו׳] וַיִּשְׁתָּחוּ (לְאַפָּיו)".

The Gemara asks: **Is the** Temple **service more important than Torah study? Isn't it written: "And it came to pass when Joshua was by Jericho that he lifted up his eyes and looked, and behold, a man stood over against him** with his sword drawn in his hand. And Joshua went over to him and said to him: Are you for us, or for our adversaries? And he said, No, but I am captain of the host of the Lord, I have come now. And Joshua fell on his face to the earth, **and bowed down"** (Joshua 5:13–14).

וְהֵיכִי עָבֵיד הָכִי? וְהָאָמַר רַבִּי יְהוֹשֻׁעַ בֶּן לֵוִי: אָסוּר לְאָדָם שֶׁיִּתֵּן שָׁלוֹם לַחֲבֵירוֹ בַּלַּיְלָה, חָיְישִׁינַן שֶׁמָּא שֵׁד הוּא! שָׁאנֵי הָתָם דַּאֲמַר לֵיהּ: "כִּי אֲנִי שַׂר צְבָא ה׳".

The Gemara first seeks to clarify the incident described in the verse. **How did** Joshua **do this,** i.e., how could he bow to a figure he did not recognize? **Didn't Rabbi Yehoshua ben Levi say: It is prohibited for a person to greet his fellow at night**[N] if he does not recognize him, as **we are concerned that perhaps it is a demon?** How did Joshua know that it was not a demon? The Gemara answers: **There it was different,** as the visitor **said to him: But I am captain of the host of the Lord.**

וְדִלְמָא מְשַׁקְּרֵי? גְּמִירִי דְּלָא מַפְּקִי שֵׁם שָׁמַיִם לְבַטָּלָה.

The Gemara asks: **Perhaps** this was a demon **and he lied?** The Gemara answers: It **is learned** as a tradition that demons **do not utter the name of Heaven for naught,** and therefore since the visitor had mentioned the name of God, Joshua was certain that this was indeed an angel.

NOTES

One who is frightened – הַאי מַאן דְּמִיבְעִית: Some explain this figuratively to mean that if one feels a certain weakness in his body, he should recite *Shema*, meaning he should begin with a prayer to God. He should then distance himself from his current location, which means he should change his ways. And he should say: The goat of the slaughterhouse is fatter than I am, which means he should attach less importance to his body and physical needs (*Pardes Rimonim*).

The priests at their Temple service – כֹּהֲנִים בַּעֲבוֹדָתָן: *Tosafot*, and the Rashba in a slightly different manner, explain that the Gemara means to say that the priests may perform their service at a later time than usual. Some write that if for some reason the priests have not yet read the Megilla, and they have insufficient time to both read the Megilla and perform the Temple service, they cancel their service and read the Megilla (*Turei Even*). Others suggest that the members of the priestly watch whose day it is to serve in the Temple may interrupt their service in order to hear the Megilla, and other priests, who have already heard the reading of the Megilla, perform the service in their place (*Sefat Emet*).

The Sages of the house of Rabbi Yehuda HaNasi relied upon – סָמְכוּ שֶׁל בֵּית רַבִּי: The later authorities raise the question: Isn't reading the Megilla also considered Torah study? (*Responsa Beit Efrayim*). Some resolve this by suggesting that if a Torah master did not yet read the Megilla, then even if all of his disciples already did so, he must interrupt his own Torah study and that of his disciples to go and read the Megilla (Rashash).

To greet his fellow at night – שָׁלוֹם לַחֲבֵירוֹ בַּלַּיְלָה: Rashi (on *Sanhedrin* 44a) offers a simple proof that this took place at night from the fact that Joshua did not recognize the figure coming toward him, and so apparently it must have been dark.

HALAKHA

The priests at their Temple service – כֹּהֲנִים בַּעֲבוֹדָתָן: One must be careful not to be negligent about reading the Megilla, for even the priests must interrupt their service in order to hear the reading of the Megilla (*Tur*, *Oraḥ Ḥayyim* 687).

אָמַר לוֹ: אֶמֶשׁ בִּטַּלְתֶּם תָּמִיד שֶׁל בֵּין הָעַרְבַּיִם, וְעַכְשָׁיו בִּטַּלְתֶּם תַּלְמוּד תּוֹרָה! אָמַר לוֹ: עַל אֵיזֶה מֵהֶן בָּאתָ? אָמַר לוֹ: ״עַתָּה בָאתִי״. מִיָּד ״וַיָּלֶן יְהוֹשֻׁעַ בַּלַּיְלָה הַהוּא בְּתוֹךְ הָעֵמֶק״. אָמַר רַבִּי יוֹחָנָן:

As for the angel's mission, the Gemara explains that the angel **said to** Joshua: **Yesterday,** i.e., during the afternoon, **you neglected the afternoon daily offering**[N] due to the impending battle, **and now,** at night, **you have neglected Torah study,** and I have come to rebuke you. Joshua **said to him: For which of these** sins **have you come? He said to him: I have come now,** indicating that neglecting Torah study is more severe than neglecting to sacrifice the daily offering. Joshua **immediately** determined to rectify the matter, as the verses states: **"And Joshua lodged that night"** (Joshua 8:9)[N] **"in the midst of the valley** [*ha'emek*]" (Joshua 8:13), and **Rabbi Yoḥanan said:**

NOTES

You neglected the afternoon daily offering – בִּטַּלְתֶּם תָּמִיד שֶׁל בֵּין הָעַרְבַּיִם: See *Tosafot* for an explanation as to why the offerings were not brought. Some suggest that owing to the journey they did not have time to erect the Tabernacle, and so they were unable to bring the offerings (Rabbeinu Ḥananel; *Arukh*).

And Joshua lodged that night – וַיָּלֶן יְהוֹשֻׁעַ בַּלַּיְלָה הַהוּא: *Tosafot* note that here the Gemara joins together two different verses: "And Joshua lodged that night among the people" (Joshua 8:9), and: "And Joshua went that night into the midst of the valley" (Joshua 8:13). This combination of verses is not uncommon in the Talmud; they are combined because the exposition is based on both of them. The *Rishon LeTziyyon* explains that the entire incident, including the revelation of the angel, took place after the conquering of Jericho, but was written earlier in the text so as not to interrupt the sequence of events with a long digression.

Perek **I**
Daf **3** Amud **b**

מְלַמֵּד שֶׁלָּן בְּעוּמְקָהּ שֶׁל הֲלָכָה. וְאָמַר רַב שְׁמוּאֵל בַּר אוּנְיָא: גָּדוֹל תַּלְמוּד תּוֹרָה יוֹתֵר מֵהַקְרָבַת תְּמִידִין, שֶׁנֶּאֱמַר: ״עַתָּה בָאתִי״!

This **teaches that he spent the night in the depths** [*be'umeka*] **of *halakha*,** i.e., that he spent the night studying Torah with the Jewish people. **And Rav Shmuel bar Unya said:**[N] **Torah study is greater than sacrificing the daily offerings, as it is stated: "I have come now"** (Joshua 5:14), indicating that the angel came to rebuke Joshua for neglecting Torah study and not for neglecting the daily offering. Consequently, how did the Sages of the house of Rabbi Yehuda HaNasi determine that the Temple service is more important than Torah study?

לָא קַשְׁיָא: הָא – דְּרַבִּים, וְהָא – דְּיָחִיד.

The Gemara explains that it is **not difficult. This** statement, with regard to the story of Joshua, is referring to Torah study **by the masses,**[N] which is greater than the Temple service. **That** statement of the Sages of the house of Rabbi Yehuda HaNasi is referring to Torah study **by an individual,** which is less significant than the Temple service.

וּדְיָחִיד קַל? וְהָתְנַן: נָשִׁים בַּמּוֹעֵד מְעַנּוֹת, אֲבָל לֹא מְטַפְּחוֹת. רַבִּי יִשְׁמָעֵאל אוֹמֵר: אִם הָיוּ סְמוּכוֹת לַמִּטָּה – מְטַפְּחוֹת. בְּרָאשֵׁי חֳדָשִׁים בַּחֲנוּכָּה וּבְפוּרִים – מְעַנּוֹת וּמְטַפְּחוֹת בָּזֶה וּבָזֶה אֲבָל לֹא מְקוֹנְנוֹת.

The Gemara asks: Is the Torah study **of an individual a light** matter? **Didn't we learn** in a mishna: **On** the intermediate days of a **Festival, women may lament**[H] the demise of the deceased in unison, **but they may not clap** their hands in mourning?[N] **Rabbi Yishmael says: Those that are close to the bier may clap. On the New Moon, on Hanukkah, and on Purim,** which are not mandated by Torah law, **they may** both **lament and clap** their hands in mourning. However, **on both** groups of days, **they may not wail** responsively, a form of wailing where one woman wails and the others repeat after her.

וְאָמַר רַבָּה בַּר הוּנָא: אֵין מוֹעֵד בִּפְנֵי תַּלְמִיד חָכָם, כָּל שֶׁכֵּן חֲנוּכָּה וּפוּרִים!

And Rabba bar Huna said: All these regulations were said with regard to an ordinary person, but **there are no** restrictions on expressions of mourning on the intermediate days of **a Festival in the presence of a** deceased **Torah scholar.** If a Torah scholar dies on the intermediate days of a Festival, the women may lament, clap, and wail responsively as on any other day, **and all the more so on Hanukkah and Purim.** This indicates that even the Torah study of an individual is of great importance.

כְּבוֹד תּוֹרָה קָאָמְרַתְּ, כְּבוֹד תּוֹרָה דְּיָחִיד – חָמוּר, תַּלְמוּד תּוֹרָה דְּיָחִיד – קַל.

The Gemara rejects this argument: **You speak of the honor** that must be shown **to the Torah,** and indeed, **the honor** that must be shown to **the Torah** in the case of **an individual** Torah scholar **is important;**[N] but **the Torah study of an individual** in itself **is light** and is less significant than the Temple service.

NOTES

And Rav Shmuel bar Unya said – וְאָמַר רַב שְׁמוּאֵל בַּר אוּנְיָא: It was necessary to add this, for if not we might have thought that the angel came because they had transgressed two transgressions and not because the mitzva of Torah study is more important than the Temple service (*Ramat Shmuel*).

Torah study by the masses – תַּלְמוּד תּוֹרָה דְּרַבִּים: Rashi explains that this is referring to the Torah study of the entire Jewish people. He is compelled to explain it in this manner, because the case of the Sages of the house of Rabbi Yehuda HaNasi is also dealing with the Torah study of many people, yet the Gemara does not consider them to be the entire community. This must be due to the fact that in relation to all of Israel they are considered as individuals (*Re'aḥ Duda'im*).

Clap their hands in mourning – מְטַפְּחוֹת: This action involves hands, either clapping the hands together, or clapping the hand against another part of the body, e.g., the face, chest, or thigh (Ritva).

The honor shown to the Torah in the case of an individual Torah scholar is important – כְּבוֹד תּוֹרָה דְּיָחִיד חָמוּר: The reason for this is that the honor that must be shown to a Torah scholar is for all the Torah that he has learned in his life, whereas the honor shown for the Torah study of an individual is only for the Torah he is presently engaged in studying (*Sefat Emet*).

HALAKHA

On the intermediate days of a Festival women may lament – נָשִׁים בַּמּוֹעֵד מְעַנּוֹת: On the intermediate days of a Festival, women are permitted to lament together in unison, but they may not clap their hands in mourning. On the New Moon, Hanukkah, and Purim, they are even permitted to wail responsively, one woman uttering words of lament and the others responding after her. All this applies so long as the deceased has not yet been buried. However, if one hears of the demise of an immediate relative after he has already been buried, the practices mentioned above are permitted on the day one receives the news.

These restrictions are limited to the passing of an ordinary person. However, in the case of the death of a Torah scholar, it is permitted, even on the intermediate days of a Festival, to lament and engage in other mourning practices in the presence of the body of the deceased. Nowadays these customs of mourning are not practiced. However, the *halakhot* mentioned above also apply to eulogies; one is not permitted to eulogize on these days except for when a Torah scholar passes away, and then only in the presence of his body (*Arukh HaShulḥan*; *Shulḥan Arukh*, *Yoreh De'a* 401:5).

אָמַר רָבָא: פְּשִׁיטָא לִי: עֲבוֹדָה וּמִקְרָא מְגִילָּה – מִקְרָא מְגִילָּה עָדִיף, מִדְּרַבִּי יוֹסֵי בַּר חֲנִינָא. תַּלְמוּד תּוֹרָה וּמִקְרָא מְגִילָּה – מִקְרָא מְגִילָּה עָדִיף. מִדְּסָמְכוּ שֶׁל בֵּית רַבִּי,

§ **Rava said:** It **is obvious to me** that if one must choose between Temple **service and reading the Megilla, reading the Megilla** takes **precedence, based upon** the exposition of **Rabbi Yosei bar Ḥanina** with regard to the phrase "every family" (Esther 9:28). Similarly, if one must choose between **Torah study and reading the Megilla, reading the Megilla** takes **precedence, based upon** the fact that the Sages of **the house of Rabbi** Yehuda HaNasi **relied** on Rabbi Yosei bar Ḥanina's exposition to rule that one interrupts Torah study to hear the reading of the Megilla.

תַּלְמוּד תּוֹרָה וּמֵת מִצְוָה – מֵת מִצְוָה עָדִיף, מִדְּתַנְיָא: מְבַטְּלִין תַּלְמוּד תּוֹרָה לְהוֹצָאַת מֵת וּלְהַכְנָסַת כַּלָּה. עֲבוֹדָה וּמֵת מִצְוָה – מֵת מִצְוָה עָדִיף, מִ״וְלַאֲחוֹתוֹ״,

Furthermore, it is obvious that if one must choose between **Torah study and** tending to **a corpse with no one to bury it** [*met mitzva*],[B] the task of burying **the** ***met mitzva*** takes **precedence.** This is derived **from that which is taught** in a *baraita*: **One cancels his Torah study to bring out a corpse** for burial,[H] **and to** join a wedding procession and **bring in the bride.** Similarly, if one must choose between the Temple **service and** tending to **a** ***met mitzva***, tending to the ***met mitzva*** takes **precedence, based upon** the *halakha* derived from the term **"or for his sister"** (Numbers 6:7).[N]

דְּתַנְיָא: ״וְלַאֲחוֹתוֹ״ מַה תַּלְמוּד לוֹמַר? הֲרֵי שֶׁהָיָה הוֹלֵךְ לִשְׁחוֹט אֶת פִּסְחוֹ וְלָמוּל אֶת בְּנוֹ, וְשָׁמַע שֶׁמֵּת לוֹ מֵת, יָכוֹל יִטַּמֵּא –

As it is taught in a *baraita* with regard to verses addressing the laws of a nazirite: "All the days that he consecrates himself to the Lord, he shall not come near to a dead body. For his father, or for his mother, for his brother, or for his sister, he shall not make himself ritually impure for them when they die" (Numbers 6:6–7). **What** is the meaning when **the verse states "or for his sister"?** The previous verse, which states that the nazirite may not come near a dead body, already prohibits him from becoming impure through contact with his sister. Therefore, the second verse is understood to be teaching a different *halakha*: One **who was going to slaughter**[N] **his Paschal** lamb **or to circumcise his son, and he heard that** a relative **of his died,** one **might** have thought that **he** should return and **become ritually impure** with the impurity imparted by a corpse.

אָמַרְתָּ: לֹא יִטַּמָּא. יָכוֹל כְּשֵׁם שֶׁאֵינוֹ מִיטַּמֵּא לַאֲחוֹתוֹ כָּךְ אֵינוֹ מִיטַּמֵּא לְמֵת מִצְוָה – תַּלְמוּד לוֹמַר: ״וְלַאֲחוֹתוֹ״: לַאֲחוֹתוֹ הוּא דְּאֵינוֹ מִיטַּמֵּא, אֲבָל מִיטַּמֵּא לְמֵת מִצְוָה.

You said: He shall not become impure; the death of his relative will not override so significant a mitzva from the Torah. One **might** have thought: **Just as he does not become impure for his sister, so he does not become impure for a corpse with no one to bury it** [***met mitzva***]. **The verse states: "Or for his sister"; he may not become impure for his sister,** as someone else can attend to her burial, **but he does become impure for a** ***met mitzva***.[H]

בָּעֵי רָבָא: מִקְרָא מְגִילָּה וּמֵת מִצְוָה הֵי מִינַּיְיהוּ עָדִיף? מִקְרָא מְגִילָּה עָדִיף מִשּׁוּם פַּרְסוּמֵי נִיסָּא, אוֹ דִּלְמָא מֵת מִצְוָה עָדִיף – מִשּׁוּם כְּבוֹד הַבְּרִיּוֹת? בָּתַר דְּבַעְיָא הֲדַר פַּשְׁטָהּ: מֵת מִצְוָה עָדִיף. דְּאָמַר מָר: גָּדוֹל כְּבוֹד הַבְּרִיּוֹת שֶׁדּוֹחֶה אֶת לֹא תַעֲשֶׂה שֶׁבַּתּוֹרָה.

On the basis of these premises, **Rava raised a dilemma:** If one must choose between **reading the Megilla and** tending to **a** ***met mitzva***,[H] **which of them** takes **precedence?** Does **reading the Megilla** take **precedence due to** the value of **publicizing the miracle, or perhaps** burying **the** ***met mitzva*** takes **precedence due to** the value of preserving **human dignity? After he raised the dilemma,** Rava **then resolved it** on his own and ruled that attending to a ***met mitzva*** takes **precedence, as the Master said: Great is human dignity,**[N] **as it overrides a prohibition in the Torah.** Consequently, it certainly overrides the duty to read the Megilla, despite the fact that reading the Megilla publicizes the miracle.

HALAKHA

Torah study and bringing out a corpse – תַּלְמוּד תּוֹרָה וְהוֹצָאַת הַמֵּת: One is required to interrupt his Torah study in order to bury the deceased (*Shakh*; *Shulḥan Arukh*, *Yoreh De'a* 361:1).

Becoming impure for a *met mitzva* – מִיטַּמֵּא לְמֵת מִצְוָה: Even a High Priest, a nazirite, and one who is on the way to circumcise his son or to slaughter the Paschal lamb is required to abandon the mitzva and become ritually impure in order to bury a *met mitzva*, an unattended corpse (*Shulḥan Arukh*, *Yoreh De'a* 374:1).

Reading the Megilla and tending to a *met mitzva* – מִקְרָא מְגִילָּה וּמֵת מִצְוָה: Although reading the Megilla takes precedence over other mitzvot, burying an unattended corpse overrides reading the Megilla. Some say that this ruling isn't limited to an unattended corpse, but even to one's relative who requires attending. The funeral of a Torah scholar has the same status as that of an unattended corpse (see *Magen Avraham*, citing the *Darkhei Moshe* and *Or Zarua*). There are those who rule that although attending to a *met mitzva* takes precedence over reading the Megilla, if one will not be able to read the Megilla afterward, the reading of the Megilla takes precedence (Rema). Others maintain that even in these circumstances an unattended corpse should be buried first (*Taz*; *Magen Avraham*). This, however, is only true with regard to an unattended corpse; the reading of the Megilla is not completely abandoned in order to bury a regular corpse (*Mishna Berura*; *Shulḥan Arukh*, *Oraḥ Ḥayyim* 687:2).

BACKGROUND

A corpse with no one to bury it [*met mitzva*] – מֵת מִצְוָה: It is an important religious obligation to take part in the burial of the dead. If the deceased has no friends or relatives to bury him, everyone is obligated to assist in his burial. According to *halakha*, a corpse with no one available to bury it acquires his place, i.e., the body must be interred where it was found, provided that it is an honorable location; otherwise, the body must be buried in the nearest cemetery. This religious duty is so important that even priests and nazirites, who are ordinarily prohibited to come in contact with a corpse, may bury a deserted corpse if there is no one else available to bury it. Similarly, the obligation to bury this corpse takes precedence over nearly all other religious obligations.

NOTES

Or for his sister – וְלַאֲחוֹתוֹ: The derivation of this *halakha* may be understood as follows: The verse states with regard to a nazirite: "He shall not come near to a dead body" (Numbers 6:6), teaching that he is forbidden to become ritually impure by coming into contact with a corpse. In the following verse: "For his father, or for his mother, for his brother, or for his sister, he shall not make himself ritually impure for them when they die" (Numbers 6:7), the words "or for his sister" are superfluous, as it would have sufficed to mention his father or his mother in order to teach that this prohibition applies even to close relatives, unlike a priest, who may become ritually impure for his immediate relatives. Therefore one can derive from the language of this verse that "for them," i.e., his relatives, he is forbidden to become ritually impure, but there are other instances in which he is permitted to make himself ritually impure, i.e., for a corpse with no one to bury it [*met mitzva*]. Since the verse mentions four relatives, it may be derived that even in the case of a High Priest, or one who is on his way to slaughter the Paschal lamb, he may nevertheless become ritually impure for the sake of a *met mitzva*.

One who was going to slaughter – הֲרֵי שֶׁהָיָה הוֹלֵךְ לִשְׁחוֹט: Rashi explains that this case refers to anyone who is on his way to perform these mitzvot; just as a nazirite would become ritually impure for a *met mitzva*, so too would someone on his way to perform these mitzvot (see Rashba). However, Rashi (on *Zevaḥim* 100a) explains that the case is where an individual who is both the High Priest and a nazirite is on his way to perform these mitzvot. See the *Tosefot HaRosh* (on *Berakhot* 19b), who addresses the apparent contradiction between Rashi's explanations.

Great is human dignity – גָּדוֹל כְּבוֹד הַבְּרִיּוֹת: The importance of burying a *met mitzva* does not stem from the mitzva to bury the dead, but rather from the principle of human dignity, as it is a disgrace to the deceased if his body is not buried. As for the negative mitzva that is superseded by human dignity, both Rashi and the Rid write that this refers to the cancellation of the positive precept of returning a lost object to its owner when returning the object would cause disgrace to the finder. However, many of the early authorities (see Rabbeinu Yehonatan) understand that the reference is to the negative precept of "Do not deviate" (Deuteronomy 17:11), indicating that the concern for human dignity supersedes rabbinic obligations and prohibitions. Some authorities maintain that human dignity sets aside even Torah commandments, but only in a passive manner, whereas one would be permitted to violate rabbinic prohibitions even actively.

גּוּפָא, אָמַר רַבִּי יְהוֹשֻׁעַ בֶּן לֵוִי: כְּרַךְ וְכׇל הַסָּמוּךְ לוֹ וְכׇל הַנִּרְאֶה עִמּוֹ נִדּוֹן כִּכְרַךְ. תָּנָא: סָמוּךְ אַף עַל פִּי שֶׁאֵינוֹ נִרְאֶה, נִרְאֶה – אַף עַל פִּי שֶׁאֵינוֹ סָמוּךְ.

§ The Gemara examines **the** matter **itself** cited in the course of the previous discussion. **Rabbi Yehoshua ben Levi said: A** walled **city, and all** settlements **adjacent to it, and all** settlements that can be **seen with it,** i.e., that can be seen from the walled city, are **considered like the** walled **city,** and the Megilla is read on the fifteenth.[H] It was **taught** in the *Tosefta*: This is the *halakha* with regard to a settlement **adjacent** to a walled city, **although it cannot be seen** from it, and also a place that **can be seen** from the walled city, **although it is not adjacent** to it.[N]

בִּשְׁלָמָא נִרְאֶה אַף עַל פִּי שֶׁאֵינוֹ סָמוּךְ – מַשְׁכַּחַתְּ לַהּ כְּגוֹן דְּיָתְבָה בְּרֹאשׁ הָהָר. אֶלָּא סָמוּךְ אַף עַל פִּי שֶׁאֵינוֹ נִרְאֶה, הֵיכִי מַשְׁכַּחַתְּ לַהּ? אָמַר רַבִּי יִרְמְיָה: שֶׁיּוֹשֶׁבֶת בְּנַחַל.

The Gemara examines the *Tosefta*: **Granted** that with regard to a place that **can be seen** from the walled city, **although it is not adjacent** to it, **you find it where** the place **is located on the top of a mountain,** and therefore it can be seen from the walled city, although it is at some distance from it. **However,** with regard to a settlement that is **adjacent** to a walled city **although it cannot be seen** from it, **how can you find these** circumstances? **Rabbi Yirmeya said:** You find it, for example, **where** the place **is located in a valley,** and therefore it is possible that it cannot be seen from the walled city, although it is very close to it.

וְאָמַר רַבִּי יְהוֹשֻׁעַ בֶּן לֵוִי: כְּרַךְ שֶׁיָּשַׁב וּלְבַסּוֹף הוּקַּף – נִדּוֹן כִּכְפָר. מַאי טַעְמָא – דִּכְתִיב: ״וְאִישׁ כִּי יִמְכּוֹר בֵּית מוֹשַׁב עִיר חוֹמָה״ שֶׁהוּקַּף וּלְבַסּוֹף יָשַׁב, וְלֹא שֶׁיָּשַׁב וּלְבַסּוֹף הוּקַּף.

And Rabbi Yehoshua ben Levi said: A walled **city that was** initially **settled and** only **later surrounded** by a wall[HN] **is considered a village**[N] rather than a walled city. **What is the reason? As it is written: "And if a man sells a residential house in a walled city"** (Leviticus 25:29).[H] The wording of the verse indicates that it is referring to a place **that was** first **surrounded** by a wall **and** only **later settled, and not** to a place **that was** first **settled and** only **later surrounded** by a wall.[B]

וְאָמַר רַבִּי יְהוֹשֻׁעַ בֶּן לֵוִי: כְּרַךְ שֶׁאֵין בּוֹ עֲשָׂרָה בַּטְלָנִין – נִדּוֹן כִּכְפָר. מַאי קָא מַשְׁמַע לַן? תְּנֵינָא: אֵיזוֹ הִיא עִיר גְּדוֹלָה – כֹּל שֶׁיֵּשׁ בָּהּ עֲשָׂרָה בַּטְלָנִין, פָּחוֹת מִכָּאן – הֲרֵי זֶה כְּפָר. כְּרַךְ אִיצְטְרִיךְ לֵיהּ, אַף עַל גַּב דְּמִיקְּלְעִי לֵיהּ מֵעָלְמָא.

And Rabbi Yehoshua ben Levi said: A walled **city that does not have ten idlers,**[HN] i.e., individuals who do not work and are available to attend to communal needs, **is treated as a village.** The Gemara asks: **What is he teaching us? We** already **learned** in a mishna (5a): **What is a large city? Any** city **in which there are ten idlers;** however, if there are **fewer than that, it is a village.** The Gemara answers: Nevertheless, **it was necessary** for Rabbi Yehoshua ben Levi to teach this *halakha* with regard to a large **city,** to indicate that **even if** idlers **happen to come there from elsewhere,** since they are not local residents, it is still considered a village.

HALAKHA

Nearby and seen – סָמוּךְ וְנִרְאֶה: Anything that is near a walled city, i.e., within the distance of a *mil* from a walled city, is considered to be part of the city with regard to the Megilla reading, even if it cannot be seen from the city, such as if it is in a valley. Anything that can be seen from a walled city is considered to be part of the city. Some say that in order for something to be considered seen, it must also be within the distance of a *mil* (Ritva; *Shulḥan Arukh, Oraḥ Ḥayyim* 688:2).

A city that was settled and only later surrounded by a wall – כְּרַךְ שֶׁיָּשַׁב וּלְבַסּוֹף הוּקַּף: A city that was first settled and then surrounded by a wall has the *halakha* of a village with regard to reading the Megilla. However, a city that was settled with the intention of surrounding it with a wall, as well as a city for which it is not known how it was built, has the *halakha* of a city that was surrounded and then settled (*Shulḥan Arukh, Oraḥ Ḥayyim* 688:1, and in the comment of Rema).

A walled city – עִיר חוֹמָה: A place is not considered a walled city unless it has at least three courtyards, each one consisting of at least two houses. Additionally, it must have been surrounded by a wall and then settled. If it does not fulfill these criteria, its *halakha* is like that of a house in a courtyard. This is in accordance with the opinion of Rabbi Eliezer bar Yosei (Rambam *Sefer Zera'im, Hilkhot Shemitta VeYovel* 12:14).

A walled city that does not have ten idlers – כְּרַךְ שֶׁאֵין בּוֹ עֲשָׂרָה בַּטְלָנִין: A city that does not have ten idlers is considered a village with regard to the Megilla reading, even if it is a large city. However, cities that were surrounded by a wall in the days of Joshua are always considered to be a city, even if they do not have ten idlers. As there are others who dispute this (Ramban), their opinion should be taken into account, and in such a place the Megilla should also be read on the fourteenth (*Mishna Berura*; *Shulḥan Arukh, Oraḥ Ḥayyim* 688:1).

BACKGROUND

Surrounded by a wall and settled – הוּקַּף וְיָשַׁב: For much of history, there was a significant difference between various types of cities. Often a city was designed for the purpose of being a place of shelter and defense for its residents and for the residents of the surrounding villages, and therefore originally built fortified. Other places, however, were first settled, and although they were eventually surrounded by a wall, they are not considered to be as important as cities that were walled from the start. As these cities were not originally planned to provide fortification for the entire area, they are considered open cities that simply had extra defenses added to them at a later time.

NOTES

Can be seen although it is not adjacent – נִרְאֶה אַף עַל פִּי שֶׁאֵינוֹ סָמוּךְ: Some early authorities maintain that a place that can be seen from a walled city is only subordinate to it if it is within a distance of a *mil* from the city (Ritva; some explain that this is the intention of the Rambam and *Tur*; see *Beit Yosef*). If so, one might ask why the settlement is not considered to be adjacent to the city, and what is gained when the place may be seen from the city, as even a location that is not visible from the city is subordinate to it if it is within a *mil*. The answer is that with regard to a settlement that cannot be seen from the walled city, the distance of a *mil* is measured on the road one must travel to get to it; whereas in the case of a settlement that can be seen from the walled city, the distance of a *mil* is measured in a straight line, as the bird flies (see *Beit Peretz*).

That was settled and only later surrounded by a wall – שֶׁיָּשַׁב וּלְבַסּוֹף הוּקַּף: Rashi and the Rambam, according to the *Leḥem Mishne*, explain that this stipulation of Rabbi Yehoshua ben Levi pertains to the *halakhot* of selling a residential house in a walled city. The general principle that property returns to its original owner in the Jubilee Year does not apply to residential houses in walled cities. Furthermore, the original owner may redeem the house for a year after the sale, but if he fails to do so, it becomes the permanent possession of the purchaser. However, many are of the opinion that Rabbi Yehoshua ben Levi's statement here pertains to the reading of the Megilla (*Tosafot*).

Is considered a village – נִדּוֹן כִּכְפָר: The Ramban maintains that such a city is not really treated like a village, but rather like a large town if it is sufficiently large; this seems to be the opinion in the Jerusalem Talmud. Others, however, hold that the city is treated like a village in every respect, even to the extent of advancing the reading of the Megilla to the day of assembly if it is necessary (Rashba).

Ten idlers – עֲשָׂרָה בַּטְלָנִים: Some explain that these ten idlers are ten men who do not have specific work and are consequently always available in the synagogue in order to ensure that there is a quorum for prayer. This appears also to be the opinion in the Jerusalem Talmud. Some authorities, however, understand that the reference is to ten men who are appointed to communal positions: Three judges, three charity collectors, a scribe, a cantor, an officer of the court, and an elementary school teacher (*She'iltot*; see Rashba).

וְאָמַר רַבִּי יְהוֹשֻׁעַ בֶּן לֵוִי: כְּרַךְ שֶׁחָרַב וּלְבַסּוֹף יָשַׁב – נִדּוֹן כִּכְרַךְ. מַאי חָרַב? אִילֵימָא חָרְבוּ חוֹמוֹתָיו, יָשַׁב – אִין לֹא יָשַׁב – לָא? וְהָא תַּנְיָא, רַבִּי אֱלִיעֶזֶר בַּר יוֹסֵי אוֹמֵר: ״אֲשֶׁר לוֹא חוֹמָה״ – אַף עַל פִּי שֶׁאֵין לוֹ עַכְשָׁיו, וְהָיָה לוֹ קוֹדֶם לָכֵן.

And Rabbi Yehoshua ben Levi also **said:** A walled **city that was destroyed and** then **later settled is considered a city.** The Gemara asks: **What is** meant by the term **destroyed? If we say** that the city's **walls were destroyed,** and Rabbi Yehoshua ben Levi comes to teach us that if it was **settled, yes** it is treated as a walled city, but if it was **not settled,** it is **not** treated that way, there is a difficulty. **Isn't it taught** in a *baraita* that **Rabbi Eliezer bar Yosei says:** The verse states: **"Which has** [*lo*] **a wall** (Leviticus 25:30)," and the word *lo* is written with an *alef*, which means no, but in context the word *lo* is used as thought it was written with a *vav*, meaning that it has a wall. This indicates that **even though** the city **does not have** a wall **now,** as the wall was destroyed, if it **had** a wall **before,** it retains its status as a walled city.

אֶלָּא: מַאי חָרַב – שֶׁחָרַב מֵעֲשָׂרָה בַּטְלָנִין.

Rather, what is meant by the term **destroyed? That it was destroyed** in the sense that it no longer has **ten idlers,** and therefore it is treated like a village. However, once it has ten idlers again, it is treated like a city.

וְאָמַר רַבִּי יְהוֹשֻׁעַ בֶּן לֵוִי:

And Rabbi Yehoshua ben Levi said:

Perek **I**
Daf **4** Amud **a**

לוֹד וְאוֹנוֹ וְגֵיא הֶחָרָשִׁים מוּקָּפוֹת חוֹמָה מִימוֹת יְהוֹשֻׁעַ בִּן נוּן הָווּ.

The cities **Lod,**[B] **and Ono,**[N] **and Gei HeḤarashim** are cities **that have been surrounded** by walls **since the days of Joshua, son of Nun.**

וְהָנֵי יְהוֹשֻׁעַ בְּנָנְהִי? וְהָא אֶלְפַּעַל בְּנָנְהִי, דִּכְתִיב: ״[וּ]בְנֵי אֶלְפַּעַל עֵבֶר וּמִשְׁעָם וָשָׁמֶר הוּא בָּנָה אֶת אוֹנוֹ וְאֶת לוֹד וּבְנוֹתֶיהָ״. וּלְטַעֲמִיךְ אָסָא בְּנָנְהִי, דִּכְתִיב: ״וַיִּבֶן (אָסָא אֶת עָרֵי הַבְּצוּרוֹת אֲשֶׁר לִיהוּדָה)״.

The Gemara asks: **Did Joshua, son of Nun,** really **build these** cities? **Didn't Elpaal build them** at a later date, **as it is written: "And the sons of Elpaal: Eber, and Misham, and Shemed, who built Ono and Lod, with its hamlets"** (I Chronicles 8:12)? The Gemara counters: **According to your reasoning,** that this verse proves that these cities were built later, you can also say that **Asa,** king of Judah, **built them, as it is written: "And he,** Asa, **built fortified cities in Judah"** (see II Chronicles 14:5). Therefore, it is apparent that these cities were built more than once.

אָמַר רַבִּי אֶלְעָזָר: הָנֵי מוּקָּפוֹת חוֹמָה מִימוֹת יְהוֹשֻׁעַ בִּן נוּן הָווּ, חֲרוּב בִּימֵי פִילֶגֶשׁ בַּגִּבְעָה וַאֲתָא אֶלְפַּעַל בְּנָנְהִי, הֲדוּר אִינְפּוּל – אֲתָא אָסָא שַׁפְּצִינְהוּ.

Rabbi Elazar said: These cities **were surrounded by a wall since the days of Joshua, son of Nun,** and they **were destroyed in the days of the concubine in Gibea,** as they stood in the tribal territory of Benjamin, and in that war all of the cities of Benjamin were destroyed (see Judges, chapters 19–21). **Elpaal** then **came and built them** again. **They then fell** in the wars between Judah and Israel, and **Asa came and restored them.**

דַּיְקָא נַמִי, דִּכְתִיב: ״וַיֹּאמֶר לִיהוּדָה נִבְנֶה אֶת הֶעָרִים הָאֵלֶּה״ – מִכְּלָל דְּעָרִים הָווּ מֵעִיקָּרָא, שְׁמַע מִינָּהּ.

The Gemara comments: The language of the verse **is also precise** according to this explanation, **as it is written** with regard to Asa: **"And he said to Judah: Let us build these cities"** (II Chronicles 14:6), which proves **by inference that they had** already **been cities at the outset,** and that he did not build new cities. The Gemara concludes: Indeed, **learn from this** that it is so.

NOTES

Lod and Ono – **לוֹד וְאוֹנוֹ:** Rashi explains that Rabbi Yehoshua ben Levi mentioned particularly these cities because their walls had been rebuilt and they did not look ancient enough to have been from the time of Joshua. Alternatively, one could explain that these cities are not mentioned in the book of Joshua among the cities that Joshua conquered, and therefore it was necessary to determine their status. Additionally, Rabbi Yehoshua ben Levi lived in Lod and had to establish the practical *halakha* for the residents of his city.

BACKGROUND

Lod – **לוֹד:** Lod, or Lydda, was one of the oldest towns in Judea. It grew in significance toward the end of the Second Temple period and served as an important cultural center for many generations after the destruction of the Temple. Some of the greatest *tanna'im* lived there, among them Rabbi Eliezer ben Hyrcanus, who was known as Rabbi Eliezer the Great; Rabbi Tarfon; and others. Several important ordinances were instituted in the upper chamber of the house of Nitza in Lod. After the bar Kokheva revolt the town remained an important place of Torah, becoming the center for scholars in the south of Eretz Yisrael. Among the great *amora'im* who lived there were Rabbi Yehoshua ben Levi; Rabbi Simlai; Rabbi Yitzḥak bar Naḥmani; Rabbi Aḥa; Rabbi Shimon ben Pazi; and his son, Rabbi Yehuda.

וְאָמַר רַבִּי יְהוֹשֻׁעַ בֶּן לֵוִי: נָשִׁים חַיָּיבוֹת בְּמִקְרָא מְגִילָּה, שֶׁאַף הֵן הָיוּ בְּאוֹתוֹ הַנֵּס. וְאָמַר רַבִּי יְהוֹשֻׁעַ בֶּן לֵוִי: פּוּרִים שֶׁחָל לִהְיוֹת בְּשַׁבָּת – שׁוֹאֲלִין וְדוֹרְשִׁין בְּעִנְיָנוֹ שֶׁל יוֹם.

§ **And Rabbi Yehoshua ben Levi** also **said: Women are obligated**[N] **in the reading of the Megilla,**[H] **as they too were** significant partners **in that miracle.**[N] **And Rabbi Yehoshua ben Levi** also **said:** When **Purim occurs on Shabbat, one asks** questions **and expounds upon the subject of the day.**[H]

מַאי אִרְיָא פּוּרִים? אֲפִילּוּ יוֹם טוֹב נַמִּי. דְּתַנְיָא: מֹשֶׁה תִּיקֵּן לָהֶם לְיִשְׂרָאֵל שֶׁיְּהוּ שׁוֹאֲלִין וְדוֹרְשִׁין בְּעִנְיָנוֹ שֶׁל יוֹם: הִלְכוֹת פֶּסַח בְּפֶסַח, הִלְכוֹת עֲצֶרֶת בַּעֲצֶרֶת וְהִלְכוֹת חַג בֶּחָג!

The Gemara raises a question with regard to the last *halakha*: **Why** was it necessary to **specify Purim?**[N] The same principle applies **also to the Festivals, as it is taught** in a *baraita*: **Moses enacted for the Jewish people that they should ask** questions about **and expound upon**[N] **the subject of the day:** They should occupy themselves with **the** ***halakhot*** **of Passover on Passover,** with **the** ***halakhot*** **of** ***Shavuot*** **on** ***Shavuot*****, and** with the ***halakhot*** **of the festival** of *Sukkot* **on the festival** of *Sukkot*.[H]

פּוּרִים אִיצְטְרִיכָא לֵיהּ. מַהוּ דְּתֵימָא: נִגְזוֹר מִשּׁוּם דְּרַבָּה, קָא מַשְׁמַע לַן.

The Gemara answers: **It was necessary for** Rabbi Yehoshua ben Levi to mention **Purim, lest you say** that when Purim falls on Shabbat **we should decree** that it is prohibited to expound upon the *halakhot* of the day **due to** the concern of **Rabba,** who said that the reason the Megilla is not read on a Purim that falls on Shabbat is due to a concern that one carry the Megilla in the public domain. Rabbi Yehoshua ben Levi **therefore teaches us** that expounding the *halakhot* of the day is not prohibited as a preventive measure lest one read the Megilla on Shabbat.

וְאָמַר רַבִּי יְהוֹשֻׁעַ בֶּן לֵוִי: חַיָּיב אָדָם לִקְרוֹת אֶת הַמְּגִילָּה בַּלַּיְלָה וְלִשְׁנוֹתָהּ בַּיּוֹם, שֶׁנֶּאֱמַר: ״אֱלֹהַי אֶקְרָא יוֹמָם וְלֹא תַעֲנֶה וְלַיְלָה וְלֹא דוּמִיָּה לִי״.

And Rabbi Yehoshua ben Levi further **said** with regard to Purim: **A person is obligated to read the Megilla at night and** then **to repeat it** [***lishnota***][H] **during the day,**[N] **as it is stated: "O my God, I call by day**[N] **but You do not answer; and at night, and there is no surcease for me"** (Psalms 22:3), which alludes to reading the Megilla both by day and by night.

סְבוּר מִינָּהּ: לְמִקְרְיַיהּ בְּלֵילְיָא, וּלְמִיתְנָא מַתְנִיתִין דִּידַהּ בִּימָמָא. אֲמַר לְהוּ רַבִּי יִרְמְיָה: לְדִידִי מִיפָּרְשָׁא לִי מִינֵּיהּ דְּרַבִּי חִיָּיא בַּר אַבָּא: כְּגוֹן דְּאָמְרִי אִינָשֵׁי: אֶעֱבוֹר פָּרָשְׁתָּא דָּא וְאֶתְנְיַיהּ.

Some of the students who heard this statement **understood from it** that one is obligated **to read** the Megilla **at night and to study its** relevant tractate of **Mishna by day,**[N] as the term *lishnota* can be understood to mean studying Mishna. **Rabbi Yirmeya said to them: It was explained to me** personally **by Rabbi Ḥiyya bar Abba himself** that the term *lishnota* here has a different connotation, **for example, as people say: I will conclude this section and repeat it,** i.e., I will review my studies. Similarly, Rabbi Yehoshua ben Levi's statement means that one must repeat the reading of the Megilla by day after reading it at night.

HALAKHA

Women are obligated in the reading of the Megilla – נָשִׁים חַיָּיבוֹת בְּמִקְרָא מְגִילָּה: All are obligated to read or hear the Megilla: Men, women, converts, and freed slaves. Some say that even Canaanite slaves are obligated in this mitzva (*Magen Avraham*, citing *Beit Yosef*). There is also an obligation to educate the children to read it. A minor who reaches the age of education can discharge a woman's obligation to hear the Megilla. In cases where one who has already read the Megilla reads it is again for a woman to hear, there are some who instruct the woman to make the blessing herself, but it is not fitting to do this; rather, the reader should bless (*Sha'arei Teshuva*; *Shulḥan Arukh, Oraḥ Ḥayyim* 689:1).

A discourse on Purim – דְּרָשָׁה בְּפוּרִים: When Purim occurs on Shabbat, one inquires about and expounds the *halakhot* of Purim on that Shabbat, as a remembrance that it is Purim. Nowadays Purim falls on Shabbat only in walled cities (Rambam *Sefer Zemanim, Hilkhot Megilla* 1:13).

A discourse on a Festival – דְּרָשָׁה בַּמּוֹעֵד: Moses established that one study the laws of the day on every Festival (Rambam *Sefer Ahava, Hilkhot Tefilla* 13:8).

To read the Megilla…and to repeat it – לִקְרוֹת אֶת הַמְּגִילָּה...וְלִשְׁנוֹתָהּ: One is obligated to read the Megilla at night, from the time of the emergence of the stars (*Peri Ḥadash*; Vilna Gaon), and to read it again during the day (*Shulḥan Arukh, Oraḥ Ḥayyim* 687:1).

NOTES

Women are obligated – נָשִׁים חַיָּיבוֹת: Reading the Megilla is a positive, time-bound mitzva, and the general principle is that women are exempt from such mitzvot. Nevertheless, there are some commandments that are exceptions to this principle. In *Ḥavvot Yair* (10–11) there is an extensive discussion as to whether this principle applies to rabbinic commandments (see *She'eilat Yavetz* 1:120).

As they too were partners in that miracle – שֶׁאַף הֵן הָיוּ בְּאוֹתוֹ הַנֵּס: Rashi and most of the commentaries (*ge'onim*; Rabbeinu Yehonatan; Rashba; Ran) explain that women were included in Haman's decree to destroy all of the Jews, and therefore it is fitting for them to take part in giving thanks. This explanation is found in the Jerusalem Talmud as well. Alternatively, Rav Hai Gaon, Rashi (on *Pesaḥim* 108b), and the Rashbam explain that a woman, Esther, was the main catalyst of the miracle. *Tosafot* object to this interpretation of the Gemara's intent, due to the phrase: As they too, which indicates that even women are obligated, but not that they are the main focus of the celebration. The Rashash responds that this phrase is used commonly in the Gemara with regard to items that are of a central role, and not just to refer to items that play a secondary role.

Why specify Purim – מַאי אִרְיָא פּוּרִים: The Gemara initially thought that Rabbi Yehoshua ben Levi's statement is due to the fact that when Purim occurs on Shabbat, the Megilla is not read and there is no practical observance of the holiday; consequently, one should ask questions about and expound upon the subject of the day. The Gemara therefore asks why it is necessary to say this, as there is a general principle that one is supposed to ask questions about and expound the subjects of every holiday on that holiday (Rashba). The Rashba adds that the formulation: Ask questions about and expound, refers to two different things. Within thirty days of a holiday, a student asks his teacher questions about the holiday and the teacher answers, as the questions are not considered to be of immediate practical relevance. Additionally, on the holiday itself, the Sage delivers a discourse related to the holiday.

Ask and expound upon – שׁוֹאֲלִין וְדוֹרְשִׁין: Rashi and the Ritva explain that the intention is that they preach in public and recount the miracle of Purim. However, other commentators maintain that they teach the *halakhot* of Purim (Rashba).

To read the Megilla at night and to repeat it during the day – לִקְרוֹת אֶת הַמְּגִילָּה בַּלַּיְלָה וְלִשְׁנוֹתָהּ בַּיּוֹם: Rabbeinu Tam goes to great lengths to prove that the essence of the mitzva to read the Megilla is specifically during the day, and that the purpose of this teaching is mainly to add the obligation to read at night. Based on this assertion, he determines that there is an obligation to recite the blessing: Who has given us life [*sheheḥeyanu*], during the day. However, the Rambam rules that one recites this blessing prior to the reading of the Megilla only at night.

As it is stated, O my God, I call by day – שֶׁנֶּאֱמַר אֱלֹקַי אֶקְרָא יוֹמָם: Rashi writes that Psalms 22, *Al Ayelet HaShaḥar*, is considered to be a prayer of Esther, and that everything mentioned in it is referring to the days of Purim. From this verse the Sages learn that just as in the time of suffering the Jews prayed night and day, so too during the time of praise and commemoration of the miracle it is fitting to express thanks both at night and during the day (Ran).

Understood from it that one is obligated to study its relevant tractate of Mishna by day – סְבוּר מִינָּהּ לְמִיתְנָא: The commentaries ask how it is possible to entertain this notion, when a mishna further on (20b) states that the mitzva to read the Megilla during the daytime applies all day. This question is answered in various ways: Some explain that the presumption was that only the uneducated are required to read the Megilla by day, whereas learned individuals are required to study the relevant *mishnayot* and *halakhot*. Alternatively, perhaps it was presumed that one is required both to read the Megilla and to study the *mishnayot* (see *Turei Even* and *Sefat Emet*).

אִיתְּמַר נַמִּי, אָמַר רַבִּי חֶלְבּוֹ אָמַר עוּלָּא בִּירָאָה: חַיָּיב אָדָם לִקְרוֹת אֶת הַמְּגִילָּה בַּלַּיְלָה וְלִשְׁנוֹתָהּ בַּיּוֹם, שֶׁנֶּאֱמַר: ״לְמַעַן יְזַמֶּרְךָ כָבוֹד וְלֹא יִדּוֹם ה׳ אֱלֹהַי לְעוֹלָם אוֹדֶךָּ״.

The Gemara notes that this ruling **was also stated** by another *amora*, as **Rabbi Ḥelbo said** that **Ulla Bira'a said: A person is obligated to read the Megilla at night and** then **repeat it during the day, as it is stated: "So that my glory may sing praise to You**[N] **and not be silent; O Lord, my God, I will give thanks to You forever"** (Psalms 30:13). The dual formulation of singing praise and not being silent alludes to reading the Megilla both by night and by day.

״אֶלָּא שֶׁהַכְּפָרִים מַקְדִּימִין לְיוֹם הַכְּנִיסָה״: אָמַר רַבִּי חֲנִינָא: חֲכָמִים הֵקִילּוּ עַל הַכְּפָרִים לִהְיוֹת מַקְדִּימִין לְיוֹם הַכְּנִיסָה כְּדֵי שֶׁיְּסַפְּקוּ מַיִם וּמָזוֹן לַאֲחֵיהֶם שֶׁבַּכְּרַכִּין.

§ We learned in the mishna that residents of unwalled towns read the Megilla on the fourteenth of Adar; **however,** residents of **villages may advance** their reading **to the day of assembly,** the Monday or Thursday preceding Purim. **Rabbi Ḥanina said: The Sages were lenient with the villages** and allowed them **to advance** their reading of the Megilla **to the day of assembly, so that they** could be free to **provide water and food to their brethren in the cities** on the day of Purim. If everyone would be busy reading the Megilla on the fourteenth, the residents of the cities would not have enough to eat.

NOTES

So that my glory may sing praise to You – לְמַעַן יְזַמֶּרְךָ כָבוֹד: The Maharsha adds that the closing words of the verse: "I will give thanks to You forever" (Psalms 30:13), allude to the holiday of Purim, fitting with the words of the Jerusalem Talmud that state that the days of Purim will always exist and will not be annulled even in the World-to-Come.

לְמֵימְרָא דְּתַקַּנְתָּא דִּכְרַכִּין הָוֵי? וְהָתְנַן: חָל לִהְיוֹת בְּשֵׁנִי – כְּפָרִים וַעֲיָירוֹת גְּדוֹלוֹת קוֹרִין בּוֹ בַּיּוֹם, וְאִם אִיתָא – לִיקַדְּמוּ לְיוֹם הַכְּנִיסָה! הָווּ לְהוּ עֲשָׂרָה, וַעֲשָׂרָה לָא תַּקִּינוּ רַבָּנַן.

The Gemara asks: **Is that to say that** this ordinance is **for the benefit of the cities?**[N] **Didn't we learn** in the mishna that if the fourteenth **occurred on a Monday, the** residents of **villages and large towns read it on that very day? If it is so,** that the ordinance allowing the villagers to sometimes advance their reading of the Megilla is for the benefit of the cities, **let** the villagers **advance** their reading **to the** previous **day of assembly** even when the fourteenth occurs on a Monday. The Gemara responds: That would mean that Megilla reading **for them** would take place on **the tenth** of Adar, **and the Sages did not establish the tenth** of Adar as a day that is fit to read the Megilla.

תָּא שְׁמַע: חָל לִהְיוֹת בַּחֲמִישִׁי – כְּפָרִים וַעֲיָירוֹת גְּדוֹלוֹת קוֹרִין בּוֹ בַּיּוֹם. וְאִם אִיתָא – לִיקַדְּמוּ לְיוֹם הַכְּנִיסָה, דְּאַחַד עָשָׂר הוּא! מִיּוֹם הַכְּנִיסָה לְיוֹם הַכְּנִיסָה לָא דָּחֵינַן.

The Gemara continues: **Come** and **hear** a proof from a different statement of the mishna: If the fourteenth **occurs on a Thursday, the villages and large towns read** it **on that day,** the fourteenth, **and the walled cities** read it **on the next day,** the fifteenth. **If it is so,** that the ordinance is for the benefit of the cities, **let** the villagers **advance** their reading of the Megilla **to the** previous **day of assembly,** i.e., the previous Monday, as it is **the eleventh** of Adar. The Gemara responds: **We do not defer** the reading of the Megilla **from** one **day of assembly to** another **day of assembly.**

תָּא שְׁמַע, אָמַר רַבִּי יְהוּדָה: אֵימָתַי – בִּמְקוֹם שֶׁנִּכְנָסִים בַּשֵּׁנִי וּבַחֲמִישִׁי, אֲבָל מְקוֹם שֶׁאֵין נִכְנָסִים בַּשֵּׁנִי וּבַחֲמִישִׁי – אֵין קוֹרִין אוֹתָהּ אֶלָּא בִּזְמַנָּהּ. וְאִי סָלְקָא דַּעְתָּךְ תַּקַּנְתָּא דִּכְרַכִּין הִיא – מִשּׁוּם דְּאֵין נִכְנָסִים בַּשֵּׁנִי וּבַחֲמִישִׁי מַפְסְדִי לְהוּ לִכְרַכִּין?

The Gemara continues: **Come** and **hear** that which was taught in the following mishna (5a): **Rabbi Yehuda said: When** is the Megilla read from the eleventh of Adar and onward? **In a place where** the villagers generally **enter** town **on Monday and Thursday. However,** in a **place where they do not** generally **enter** town **on Monday and Thursday, one may read** the Megilla **only in its** designated **time,** the fourteenth of Adar. The Gemara infers: **If it enters your mind** to say that the ordinance is for **the benefit of the cities,** would it be reasonable to suggest that **because** the villagers **do not enter** town **on Monday and Thursday the** residents of the **cities** should **lose out** and not be provided with food and water?

לָא תֵּימָא: ״כְּדֵי שֶׁיְּסַפְּקוּ מַיִם וּמָזוֹן״, אֶלָּא אֵימָא: מִפְּנֵי שֶׁמְּסַפְּקִים מַיִם וּמָזוֹן לַאֲחֵיהֶם שֶׁבַּכְּרַכִּין.

The Gemara accepts this argument: **Do not say** that the Sages allowed the villages to advance their reading of the Megilla to the day of assembly **so that they** can be free to **provide water and food to their brethren in the cities** on the day of Purim. **Rather, say** that the Sages were lenient with them **because** the villages **supply**[N] **water and food to their brethren in the cities.** This ordinance was established for the benefit of the villagers so that they should not have to make an extra trip to the cities to hear the reading of the Megilla. However, in a place where the villages do not go to the cities, advancing their reading of the Megilla to the day of assembly will not benefit them, and therefore they must read on the fourteenth.

NOTES

Is that to say that this ordinance is for the benefit of the cities – לְמֵימְרָא דְּתַקַּנְתָּא דִּכְרַכִּין הָוֵי: The early authorities wrote that one could have disproven this statement in a different way by citing the case of cities that do not have ten idlers. Even though these are large towns and do not supply food to the cities, nevertheless they have a halakhic status equivalent to the villages. Therefore, it is apparent that this ruling is not for the benefit of the cities. However, it was preferable to disprove the statement from the case of the villages themselves (Rashba; Ritva).

Because the villages supply – מִפְּנֵי שֶׁמְּסַפְּקִים: The Sages were lenient with the villagers and did not require them to make an extra trip to the cities, as reward for the important services they provided to the cities on a regular basis. According to this explanation, it is clear why the reading is not advanced from one day of assembly to another, as doing so would not save the villagers from making an extra trip to the cities (see Rashba). Rabbeinu Ḥananel asked: If the enactment allowing the villages to read the Megilla on the days of assembly was established in the days of Ezra, how is it possible that the Megilla, which was written earlier, refers to this? The resolution of this problem is explained in the Jerusalem Talmud, which states that this enactment is indeed an edict of the Sages, and the verses of the Megilla cited as sources for this enactment are cited merely as an indirect scriptural allusion, rather than as firm halakhic support.

״כֵּיצַד חָל לִהְיוֹת בַּשֵּׁנִי בַּשַּׁבָּת כְּפָרִים וַעֲיָירוֹת גְּדוֹלוֹת קוֹרִין בּוֹ בַּיּוֹם״ וכו׳: מַאי שְׁנָא רֵישָׁא דְּנָקַט סִידּוּרָא דְּיַרְחָא, וּמַאי שְׁנָא סֵיפָא דְּנָקַט סִידּוּרָא דְּיוֹמֵי?

§ We learned in the mishna: **How so?** If the fourteenth of Adar **occurs on Monday, the villages and large towns read** it **on that day.** The mishna continues to explain the days on which the Megilla is read. The Gemara asks: **What is different** about **the first clause** of the mishna, **which employs the order** of the dates **of the month,** i.e., the eleventh of Adar, **and the latter clause, which employs the order of the days** of the week, i.e., Monday?

אַיְּידֵי דְּמִיתְהַפְּכִי לֵיהּ נְקַט סִידּוּרָא דְּיוֹמֵי:

The Gemara answers: **Since** the days of the week **would be reversed**[N] if the latter clause was organized according to the dates of the month, as the mishna would first have to mention a case where the fourteenth occurs on a Sunday, then a case where it occurs on a Wednesday or Shabbat, and then a case where it occurs on a Friday or Tuesday, the mishna **employed the order of the days** of the week in order to avoid confusion.

״חָל לִהְיוֹת בְּעֶרֶב שַׁבָּת״ וכו׳: מַתְנִיתִין מַנִּי? אִי רַבִּי, אִי רַבִּי יוֹסֵי.

§ We learned in the mishna: If the fourteenth **occurs on Shabbat eve,** Friday, the villages advance their reading to the day of assembly, i.e., Thursday, and the large towns and walled cities read it on Friday, the fourteenth of Adar. The Gemara asks: **Whose** opinion is expressed in the **mishna?** It can be **either Rabbi** Yehuda HaNasi **or Rabbi Yosei.**

מַאי רַבִּי – דְּתַנְיָא: חָל לִהְיוֹת בְּעֶרֶב שַׁבָּת – כְּפָרִים וַעֲיָירוֹת גְּדוֹלוֹת מַקְדִּימִין לְיוֹם הַכְּנִיסָה, וּמוּקָּפִין חוֹמָה קוֹרִין בּוֹ בַּיּוֹם. רַבִּי אוֹמֵר: אוֹמֵר אֲנִי, לֹא יִדָּחוּ עֲיָירוֹת מִמְּקוֹמָן, אֶלָּא אֵלּוּ וָאֵלּוּ קוֹרִין בּוֹ בַּיּוֹם.

The Gemara explains: **What is** the opinion of **Rabbi** Yehuda HaNasi? **As it is taught** in a *baraita*: If the fourteenth **occurs on Shabbat eve, villages and large towns advance** their reading **to the day of assembly,** i.e., Thursday, **and walled cities read it on the day** of Purim, Friday. **Rabbi** Yehuda HaNasi disagrees and **says: I say** that **the** readings in the large **towns should not be deferred from their** usual **date,** i.e., the fourteenth of Adar. **Rather, both these,** the large towns **and those,** the walled cities, **read** the Megilla **on the day** of Purim.

מַאי טַעְמָא דְּתַנָּא קַמָּא? דִּכְתִיב: ״בְּכָל שָׁנָה וְשָׁנָה״ מַה כָּל שָׁנָה וְשָׁנָה עֲיָירוֹת קוֹדְמוֹת לְמוּקָּפִין – אַף כָּאן עֲיָירוֹת קוֹדְמוֹת לְמוּקָּפִין.

The Gemara asks: **What is the reason of the first *tanna*?** The Gemara explains that it is **as it is written:** "To keep these two days, according to their writing and according to their time, **in every year**" (Esther 9:27), which indicates that Purim must be celebrated every year in similar fashion. **Just as** in **every** other **year** the large **towns precede the walled cities** by one day, **so too here the** large **towns precede the walled cities** by one day. Consequently, since the walled cities cannot read the Megilla on Shabbat and they are required to advance the reading to Friday, the large towns must also advance their reading a day to Thursday.

וְאֵימָא: ״בְּכָל שָׁנָה וְשָׁנָה״ מַה כָּל שָׁנָה וְשָׁנָה אֵין נִדְחִין עֲיָירוֹת מִמְּקוֹמָן – אַף כָּאן לֹא יִדָּחוּ עֲיָירוֹת מִמְּקוֹמָן! שָׁאנֵי הָכָא דְּלָא אֶפְשָׁר.

The Gemara raises an objection: **Say** that the words "**in every year**" indicate that **just as** in **every** other **year the** Megilla readings in **the** large **towns are not deferred from their** usual **date** and they read the Megilla on the fourteenth, **so too here the** Megilla readings in **the** large **towns should not be deferred from their** usual **date** and they too should read on the fourteenth. The Gemara answers: **Here it is different, as it is not possible** for the large towns to fulfill all of the conditions at the same time, i.e., to read on the fourteenth and to read a day before the walled cities.

וְרַבִּי, מַאי טַעְמֵיהּ? ״בְּכָל שָׁנָה וְשָׁנָה״, מַה כָּל שָׁנָה וְשָׁנָה אֵין עֲיָירוֹת נִדְחִין מִמְּקוֹמָן – אַף כָּאן לֹא יִדָּחוּ עֲיָירוֹת מִמְּקוֹמָן.

The Gemara asks: **And Rabbi** Yehuda HaNasi, **what is** his **reason?** The Gemara explains that it is also based upon the words "**in every year**"; **just as** in **every** other **year the** readings in **the** large **towns are not deferred from their** usual **date** and they read on the fourteenth, **so too here, the** readings in **the** large **towns are not deferred from their** usual **date,** but rather they read on the fourteenth.

וְאֵימָא: ״בְּכָל שָׁנָה וְשָׁנָה״ מַה כָּל שָׁנָה וְשָׁנָה עֲיָירוֹת קוֹדְמוֹת לְמוּקָּפִין אַף כָּאן נַמִּי עֲיָירוֹת קוֹדְמוֹת לְמוּקָּפִין – שָׁאנֵי הָכָא דְּלָא אֶפְשָׁר.

The Gemara raises an objection: **Say** that the words "**in every year**" indicate that **just as every year the** large **towns precede the walled cities** by one day, and read on the fourteenth, **so too here the** large **towns precede the walled cities** by one day, and read on the thirteenth. The Gemara answers: **Here it is different, as it is not possible** to fulfill all of the conditions at the same time, i.e., to read on the fourteenth and to read a day before the walled cities.

NOTES

Since they would be reversed – אַיְּידֵי דְּמִיתְהַפְּכִי: The early authorities explain that for this reason the count in the mishna started with Monday and not with Sunday, for if it would have started with Sunday, the days of the month would be reversed. An additional reason for starting with Monday is that on this day all places are reading at their set times. From there it proceeded to discuss Friday and Wednesday, when the times of reading are changed in the villages (Rid; see Ritva).

מַאי רַבִּי יוֹסֵי – דְּתַנְיָא: חָל לִהְיוֹת בְּעֶרֶב שַׁבָּת – מוּקָּפִין וּכְפָרִים מַקְדִּימִין לְיוֹם הַכְּנִיסָה, וַעֲיָירוֹת גְּדוֹלוֹת קוֹרִין בּוֹ בַּיּוֹם. רַבִּי יוֹסֵי אוֹמֵר: אֵין מוּקָּפִין קוֹדְמִין לַעֲיָירוֹת, אֶלָּא אֵלּוּ וָאֵלּוּ קוֹרִין בּוֹ בַּיּוֹם.

The Gemara asks: **What is the opinion of Rabbi Yosei? As it is taught** in a *baraita*: If the fourteenth **occurs on Shabbat eve, the walled cities and villages advance** their reading of the Megilla **to the day of assembly, and the large towns read** it **on the day** of Purim **itself. Rabbi Yosei says: The walled cities never precede the** large **towns; rather, both these,** the large towns, **and those,** the walled cities, **read on that day,** i.e., Friday, the fourteenth of Adar.

מַאי טַעְמָא דְּתַנָּא קַמָּא? דִּכְתִיב: "בְּכָל שָׁנָה וְשָׁנָה" מַה כׇּל שָׁנָה וְשָׁנָה עֲיָירוֹת בְּאַרְבָּעָה עָשָׂר, וּזְמַנּוֹ שֶׁל זֶה לֹא זְמַנּוֹ שֶׁל זֶה – אַף כָּאן עֲיָירוֹת בְּאַרְבָּעָה עָשָׂר, וּזְמַנּוֹ שֶׁל זֶה לֹא זְמַנּוֹ שֶׁל זֶה.

The Gemara asks: **What is the reason of the first** ***tanna*****? As it is written: "In every year"; just as in every** other **year the** large **towns** read the Megilla **on the fourteenth, and the time for this** type of settlement to read the Megilla **is not the time for that** type of settlement to read the Megilla, as the large towns and walled cities never read the Megilla on the same day, **so too here, the** large **towns** read the Megilla **on the fourteenth, and the time for this** type of settlement to read the Megilla **is not the time for that** type of settlement to read the Megilla. Therefore, the walled cities must advance their reading of the Megilla by two days to the day of assembly, Thursday.

וְאֵימָא: "בְּכָל שָׁנָה וְשָׁנָה" מַה כׇּל שָׁנָה וְשָׁנָה אֵין מוּקָּפִין קוֹדְמִין לַעֲיָירוֹת – אַף כָּאן אֵין מוּקָּפִין קוֹדְמִין לַעֲיָירוֹת! שָׁאנֵי הָכָא דְּלָא אֶפְשָׁר.

The Gemara raises an objection: **Say** that the words **"in every year"** indicate that **just as in every** other **year the walled cities do not precede the** large **towns, so too here, the walled cities do not precede the** large **towns.** The Gemara answers: **Here it is different, as it is not possible** to fulfill all of the conditions at the same time, i.e., that the large towns should read on the fourteenth, the large towns and the walled cities should read on different days, and the walled cities should not precede the large towns.

מַאי טַעְמֵיהּ דְּרַבִּי יוֹסֵי? "בְּכָל שָׁנָה וְשָׁנָה", מַה כׇּל שָׁנָה וְשָׁנָה אֵין מוּקָּפִין קוֹדְמִין לַעֲיָירוֹת אַף כָּאן אֵין מוּקָּפִין קוֹדְמִין לַעֲיָירוֹת.

What is the reason of Rabbi Yosei? It is based upon the words **"in every year"; just as** in **every** other **year the walled cities do not precede the** large towns, **so too here, the walled cities do not precede the** large **towns.**

וְאֵימָא: "בְּכָל שָׁנָה וְשָׁנָה" מַה כׇּל שָׁנָה וְשָׁנָה זְמַנּוֹ שֶׁל זֶה לֹא זְמַנּוֹ שֶׁל זֶה – אַף כָּאן זְמַנּוֹ שֶׁל זֶה לֹא זְמַנּוֹ שֶׁל זֶה! שָׁאנֵי הָכָא דְּלָא אֶפְשָׁר.

The Gemara raises a difficulty: **Say** that the words **"in every year" indicate** that **just as** in **every** other **year, the time for this** type of settlement to read the Megilla **is not the time for that** type of settlement to read the Megilla, **so too here, the time for this** type of settlement to read the Megilla **is not the time for that** type of settlement to read the Megilla. Therefore, since the large towns read on the fourteenth, the walled cities read on the thirteenth. The Gemara answers: **Here it is different, as it is not possible** to fulfill all the conditions. It is clear from these *baraitot* that the *tanna* of the mishna can either be Rabbi Yehuda HaNasi or Rabbi Yosei, but not either of two anonymous *tanna'im*.

וְסָבַר רַבִּי עֲיָירוֹת לָא דָּחֵינַן לְיוֹם הַכְּנִיסָה? וְהָתַנְיָא: חָל לִהְיוֹת בַּשַּׁבָּת – כְּפָרִים מַקְדִּימִין לְיוֹם הַכְּנִיסָה, וַעֲיָירוֹת גְּדוֹלוֹת קוֹרִין בְּעֶרֶב שַׁבָּת וּמוּקָּפוֹת חוֹמָה לְמָחָר. רַבִּי אוֹמֵר: אוֹמֵר אֲנִי, הוֹאִיל וְנִדְחוּ עֲיָירוֹת מִמְּקוֹמָן – יִדָּחוּ לְיוֹם הַכְּנִיסָה!

The Gemara asks: **Does Rabbi** Yehuda HaNasi really **hold that one does not defer** the reading of the Megilla in large towns **to the day of assembly? Isn't it taught** in a *baraita*: If the fourteenth **occurs on Shabbat, the villages advance** their reading of the Megilla **to the day of assembly, the large towns read** it **on Shabbat eve, and the walled cities** read it **the next day,** i.e., on Sunday.[H] **Rabbi** Yehuda HaNasi **says: I say** that **since the** readings in **the** large **towns were** already **deferred from their** usual **date,** i.e., the fourteenth, **they are deferred to the day of assembly,** i.e., to Thursday. Consequently, even Rabbi Yehuda HaNasi agrees that the reading in the large towns can be shifted to the day of assembly. Why doesn't he also hold that large towns read the Megilla on the day of assembly when the fourteenth occurs on a Friday?

הָכִי הָשְׁתָּא?! הָתָם – זְמַנָּם שַׁבָּת הִיא, וְהוֹאִיל דְּנִדְחוּ – יִדָּחוּ. וְהָכָא, זְמַנָּם עֶרֶב שַׁבָּת.

The Gemara responds: **How can these cases be compared? There,** in the second *baraita*, the designated **time for them** to read the Megilla **is Shabbat,** but the Megilla is not read on Shabbat, and therefore they must read it on a different day. Therefore, **since** the readings in the large towns have been **deferred, they are deferred** an additional day, and take place on Thursday, the day of assembly, at the same time as the readings in the villages. **Here, their** designated **time is Shabbat eve,** and there is no reason to move the reading from that day.

HALAKHA

Times of reading – זְמַנֵּי קְרִיאָה: When the Megilla was read on several different days, if the fourteenth occurred on Shabbat, the residents of unwalled cities advanced the reading of the Megilla to the eve of Shabbat, walled cities read the Megilla on Sunday, and the villagers advanced their reading to the day of assembly. This ruling is in accordance with the mishna (Rambam *Sefer Zemanim*, *Hilkhot Megilla* 1:14).

כְּמַאן אָזְלָא הָא דְּאָמַר רַבִּי חֶלְבּוֹ אָמַר רַב הוּנָא: פּוּרִים שֶׁחָל לִהְיוֹת בַּשַּׁבָּת הַכֹּל נִדְחִין לְיוֹם הַכְּנִיסָה. הַכֹּל נִדְחִין סָלְקָא דַּעְתָּךְ?! וְהָא אִיכָּא מוּקָפִין דְּעָבְדִי לְמָחָר! אֶלָּא, כׇּל הַנִּדְחֶה – יִדָּחֶה לְיוֹם הַכְּנִיסָה. כְּמַאן – כְּרַבִּי.

The Gemara asks: **In accordance with whose** opinion **is that which Rabbi Ḥelbo said** that **Rav Huna said:** When **Purim occurs on Shabbat,**[H] the reading of the Megilla in **all** places is **deferred to the day of assembly?** The Gemara corrects the wording of Rav Huna's statement: **Can it enter your mind** to say that the reading of the Megilla in **all** places is deferred to the day of assembly? **Aren't there walled cities that perform** this ceremony **the next day,** i.e., on Sunday? **Rather,** Rav Huna's statement should say as follows: **All** readings **that are deferred are deferred to the day of assembly. In accordance with whose** opinion was this stated? It is **in accordance with** the opinion of **Rabbi** Yehuda HaNasi.

דְּכוּלֵּי עָלְמָא מִיהָא מְגִילָּה בְּשַׁבָּת לָא קָרֵינַן, מַאי טַעְמָא? אָמַר רַבָּה: הַכֹּל חַיָּיבִין בִּקְרִיאַת מְגִילָּה (וּבִתְקִיעַת שׁוֹפָר) וְאֵין הַכֹּל בְּקִיאִין בְּמִקְרָא מְגִילָּה, גְּזֵירָה שֶׁמָּא יִטְּלֶנָּה בְּיָדוֹ וְיֵלֵךְ אֵצֶל בָּקִי לִלְמוֹד, וְיַעֲבִירֶנָּה אַרְבַּע אַמּוֹת בִּרְשׁוּת הָרַבִּים.

In any case, it is apparent from the mishna and the *baraitot* that **everyone agrees that one does not read the** Megilla **on Shabbat.**[H] **What is the reason** for this? **Rabba said: Everyone is obligated** to participate in **reading the Megilla** on Purim[N] **and blowing the** ***shofar*** on Rosh HaShana, **and not everyone is proficient in reading the Megilla.** Therefore, the Sages issued a rabbinic **decree** that the Megilla is not read on Shabbat, **lest one take** the Megilla **in his hand and go to an expert to learn** how to read it or to hear the expert read it, **and,** due to his preoccupation, he will **carry it four cubits**[N] **in the public domain,** and thereby desecrate Shabbat.

וְהַיְינוּ טַעְמָא דְּשׁוֹפָר, וְהַיְינוּ טַעְמָא דְּלוּלָב.

The Gemara comments: **And this** same concern for the sanctity of Shabbat **is the reason** that the Sages decreed **that the** ***shofar*** is not blown when Rosh HaShana occurs on Shabbat. **And this** same concern **is the reason** that the Sages decreed that one may not take **the** ***lulav*** on Shabbat.

רַב יוֹסֵף אָמַר: מִפְּנֵי שֶׁעֵינֵיהֶן שֶׁל עֲנִיִּים נְשׂוּאוֹת בְּמִקְרָא מְגִילָּה. תַּנְיָא נַמִי הָכִי: אַף עַל פִּי שֶׁאָמְרוּ כְּפָרִים מַקְדִּימִין לְיוֹם הַכְּנִיסָה – גּוֹבִין בּוֹ בַּיּוֹם, וּמְחַלְּקִין בּוֹ בַּיּוֹם.

Rav Yosef said that there is another reason the Megilla is not read on Shabbat: **Because the eyes of the poor are raised to the reading of the Megilla.**[N] The poor await the day on which the Megilla is read, because on that day gifts are distributed to the poor. If the Megilla is read on Shabbat, it will not be possible to distribute gifts to the poor, who will be deeply disappointed.[H] The Gemara notes that **this is also taught** in a *baraita*: **Even though** the Sages **said that the villages advance** their reading of the Megilla **to the day of assembly, they** also **collect** the gifts for the poor **on that day, and they distribute** them to the poor **on that day.**

אַף עַל פִּי שֶׁאָמְרוּ? אַדְּרַבָּה, מִשּׁוּם דְּאָמְרוּ הוּא! אֶלָּא: הוֹאִיל וְאָמְרוּ שֶׁכְּפָרִים מַקְדִּימִין לְיוֹם הַכְּנִיסָה – גּוֹבִין בּוֹ בַּיּוֹם וּמְחַלְּקִין בּוֹ בַּיּוֹם, מִפְּנֵי שֶׁעֵינֵיהֶם שֶׁל עֲנִיִּים נְשׂוּאוֹת בְּמִקְרָא מְגִילָּה. אֲבָל

The Gemara is troubled by the wording of this *baraita*. Does the *baraita* read: **Even though** the Sages **said? On the contrary,** it is **because they said** that the villages advance their reading to the day of assembly that the gifts must be collected and distributed to the poor on that very day. **Rather,** the *baraita* should read as follows: **Since** the Sages **said that the villages advance** their reading of the Megilla **to the day of assembly, they collect** the gifts for the poor **on that day and they distribute** them **on that day, because the eyes of the poor are raised to the reading of the Megilla,** and they should not be disappointed. **However,**

HALAKHA

Occurs on Shabbat – חָל לִהְיוֹת בַּשַּׁבָּת: When the fifteenth of Adar occurs on Shabbat, those in walled cities read the Megilla and distribute gifts to the poor on the eve of Shabbat. On Shabbat they take out an additional Torah scroll and read the portion generally read on Purim (Exodus 17:8–16) in addition to the regular weekly Torah portion. They also recite the blessing: On the miracles, during prayers on Shabbat. The sending of gifts and the Purim feast is performed on Sunday. Such a Purim is called a three-part Purim, as residents of walled cities perform various aspects of the Purim celebration over the course of three days. Some say that the feast and the giving of gifts is done both on Shabbat and on Sunday (*Peri Ḥadash*; *Shulḥan Arukh, Oraḥ Ḥayyim* 688:6).

Megilla on Shabbat – מְגִילָּה בְּשַׁבָּת: The Scroll of Esther is never read on Shabbat, due to the decree of Rabba. Some say that it is forbidden to move a Megilla on Shabbat, as it is considered set-aside [*muktze*] because it is not allowed to be read (*Peri Ḥadash*), while some permit it (*Eliyahu Rabba*; *Shulḥan Arukh, Oraḥ Ḥayyim* 688:6).

Gifts for the poor – מַתָּנוֹת לָאֶבְיוֹנִים: On the same day that the Megilla is read, even when the reading is advanced to a different day, gifts for the poor are collected and distributed (*Shulḥan Arukh, Oraḥ Ḥayyim* 688:6).

NOTES

Everyone is obligated to participate in reading the Megilla – הַכֹּל חַיָּיבִין בִּקְרִיאַת מְגִילָּה: Some commentators note that the language: Everyone is obligated, serves to emphasize the reason that the Sages implemented this decree: If the obligation applied only to certain individuals, others would remind them not to carry. However, since the obligation applies to everyone, there is a concern that everyone will be so preoccupied with the mitzva that they will forget they cannot carry, or at least they will not be able to remind others not to carry (*Re'ah Duda'im*; *Zikkaron BaSefer*).

And he will carry it four cubits – וְיַעֲבִירֶנָּה אַרְבַּע אַמּוֹת: The early authorities ask: Why didn't Rabba say that perhaps he will carry it from a private domain to a public domain? Some explain that it is not common for people to mistakenly carry from a private domain to the public domain, since there are noticeable divides between them. However, there may be a Megilla already located in the public domain, and one may then carry within the public domain (*Tosafot*; Meiri). Others suggest the opposite logic: It is clear that the concern for carrying a Megilla from a private domain to a public domain, which is a more likely scenario, would warrant a decree. Rabba adds that even the concern that one might carry within the public domain itself is sufficient grounds for this decree (Ran; Ritva).

Rav Yosef's reason – טַעְמוֹ שֶׁל רַב יוֹסֵף: *Tosafot* explain that Rav Yosef also accepts the reasoning of Rabba, as there is no other reason to prohibit fulfilling the mitzvot of *shofar* and *lulav* on Shabbat. However, he adds this reason, which applies even in the Temple, whereas Rabba's reasoning does not. This is because rabbinic decrees instituted in order to prevent violation of Torah law were not extended to the Temple. Others suggest that Rav Yosef accepts Rabba's reasoning only in the case of *shofar* and *lulav* but not with regard to reading the Megilla. Since the former are required by Torah law, one might think that one is permitted to carry them on Shabbat, whereas in the case of Megilla, no one will err in this regard. The author of *Sefat Emet* adds that according to Rav Yosef, if for whatever reason one did not read the Megilla on the day before Shabbat, he would be required to read it on Shabbat, whereas according to Rabba, there is a prohibition against reading the Megilla on Shabbat.

שִׂמְחָה אֵינָהּ נוֹהֶגֶת אֶלָּא בִּזְמַנָּהּ.

the rejoicing that takes place on Purim **is practiced only in its** designated **time,** the fourteenth of Adar.

אָמַר רַב: מְגִילָּה, בִּזְמַנָּהּ – קוֹרִין אוֹתָהּ אֲפִילּוּ בְּיָחִיד, שֶׁלֹּא בִּזְמַנָּהּ – בַּעֲשָׂרָה. רַב אַסִי אָמַר: בֵּין בִּזְמַנָּהּ בֵּין שֶׁלֹּא בִּזְמַנָּהּ בַּעֲשָׂרָה. הֲוָה עוּבְדָּא וְחָשׁ לֵיהּ רַב לְהָא דְּרַב אַסִי.

§ **Rav said: One may read the Megilla in its** proper **time,** i.e., on the fourteenth of Adar, **even privately.**[H] However, when it is read **not at its** proper **time,**[N] e.g., when the villages advance their reading to the day of assembly, it must be read **with** a quorum of **ten,** because the enactment allowing the Megilla to be read before its proper time was only made for a community. **Rav Asi** disagreed and **said: Both at its** proper **time and not at its** proper **time,** the Megilla must be read **with** a quorum of **ten.** The Gemara relates that **there was an incident** where **Rav** had to read the Megilla on Purim, **and he was concerned for this** opinion **of Rav Asi** and gathered ten men even though he was reading the Megilla in its proper time, on the fourteenth of Adar.

וּמִי אֲמַר רַב הָכִי? וְהָאָמַר רַב יְהוּדָה בְּרֵיהּ דְּרַב שְׁמוּאֵל בַּר שֵׁילַת מִשְּׁמֵיהּ דְּרַב: פּוּרִים שֶׁחָל לִהְיוֹת בַּשַּׁבָּת – עֶרֶב שַׁבָּת זְמַנָּם. עֶרֶב שַׁבָּת זְמַנָּם?! וְהָא שַׁבָּת זְמַנָּם הוּא! אֶלָּא לָאו הָכִי קָאָמַר: שֶׁלֹּא בִּזְמַנָּם – כִּזְמַנָּם, מַה זְּמַנָּם אֲפִילּוּ בְּיָחִיד, אַף שֶׁלֹּא בִּזְמַנָּם – אֲפִילּוּ בְּיָחִיד!

The Gemara asks: **And did Rav** actually **say this,** that when the Megilla is read not at its proper time, it can only be read with a quorum of ten? **Didn't Rav Yehuda, son of Rav Shmuel bar Sheilat, say in the name of Rav:** If **Purim occurs on Shabbat, Shabbat eve is** the proper **time** for reading the Megilla? The Gemara expresses surprise with regard to the wording of Rav's statement: Is **Shabbat eve** the proper **time** for reading the Megilla? **Isn't Shabbat** itself **its** proper **time?**[N] **Rather, is it not** true **that this is what** he **said,** i.e., that this is the way his statement should be understood: Reading the Megilla **not at its** proper **time is like** reading it **at its** proper **time; just as at its** proper **time,** it can be read **even privately, so too, not at its** proper **time,** it can be read **even privately.**

לֹא לְעִנְיַן מִקְרָא מְגִילָּה בַּעֲשָׂרָה. אֶלָּא, מַאי עֶרֶב שַׁבָּת זְמַנָּם – לְאַפּוּקֵי מִדְּרַבִּי, דְּאָמַר: הוֹאִיל וְנִדְחוּ עֲיָירוֹת מִמְּקוֹמָן יִדָּחוּ לְיוֹם הַכְּנִיסָה, הָא קָא מַשְׁמַע לָן דְּעֶרֶב שַׁבָּת זְמַנָּם הוּא.

The Gemara rejects this argument: Rav's statement was **not** made **with regard to reading the Megilla with** a quorum of **ten. Rather, what** is the meaning of Rav's statement that **Shabbat eve is** the proper **time?** It was meant **to exclude** the opinion of **Rabbi** Yehuda HaNasi, **who said: Since** the readings in **the** large **towns were** already **deferred from their** usual **date** and the Megilla was not read on the fourteenth, **they are deferred to the day of assembly. This** statement of Rav **teaches us that Shabbat eve is** the proper **time** for these towns to read the Megilla, as stated in the mishna.

מתני׳ אֵי זוֹ הִיא עִיר גְּדוֹלָה? כָּל שֶׁיֵּשׁ בָּהּ עֲשָׂרָה בַּטְלָנִין. פָּחוֹת מִכָּאן – הֲרֵי זֶה כְּפָר.

MISHNA **What is** considered **a large city,** where the Megilla is read on the fourteenth of Adar? **Any city in which there are ten idlers.**[H] However, if there are **fewer than that, it is** considered **a village,**[N] even if it has many inhabitants.

HALAKHA

Megilla…privately – **מְגִילָּה...בְּיָחִיד:** The Megilla is read in its time even in private, in accordance with the opinion of Rav, who was the teacher of Rav Asi. Rabbi Yoḥanan concurs with Rav's opinion. One should seek out a quorum of ten to read the Megilla *ab initio*, in accordance with the custom of Rav himself, but if it not possible to read it with ten men, it is read privately. If the Megilla was already read in public and an individual was not present, he may read it privately even *ab initio*, as it was already read with a quorum of ten in that same place. In such case the individual needs to recite the blessing (*Shulḥan Arukh, Oraḥ Ḥayyim* 690:18, and in the comment of Rema).

What is considered a large city – **אֵיזֶהוּ עִיר:** A city that does not have ten regular idlers in the synagogue has the *halakha* of a village. During the period when the reading of the Megilla for villagers was advanced to the day of assembly, it was advanced in these places as well (Rambam *Sefer Zemanim, Hilkhot* Megilla 1:8).

NOTES

Not at its proper time – **שֶׁלֹּא בִּזְמַנָּהּ:** Rashi explains this as referring to the villages that advance their reading to the day of assembly. Some find this explanation difficult, because in the time of Rav the villages no longer advanced the time of reading the Megilla. Consequently, they explain that it is discussing a scenario when Purim occurred on Shabbat, and therefore the reading was advanced to Friday (Rashba; Ran). The *ge'onim* explain that this is referring to a situation where one advanced the reading due to unavoidable circumstances, such as one who is traveling in a convoy. This individual is permitted to read before the appointed time like the villages, on the condition that he reads it in a group of ten people (see Rabbi Zeraḥya HaLevi).

Isn't Shabbat itself its proper time – **וְהָא שַׁבָּת זְמַנָּם הוּא:** Some explain this phrase to be referring to the other commandments of the day, like the Purim feast and the sending of portions (see Rabbi Levi ibn Ḥabib).

Fewer than that, it is considered a village – **פָּחוֹת מִכָּאן הֲרֵי זֶה כְּפָר:** Some explain that when there aren't ten regular idlers in the synagogue, the people come to the public prayer service only on Monday and Thursday to hear the Torah reading, and therefore the Megilla is read then as well (Ritva).

בְּאֵלּוּ אָמְרוּ מַקְדִּימִין וְלֹא מְאַחֲרִין. אֲבָל זְמַן עֲצֵי כֹהֲנִים וְתִשְׁעָה בְּאָב, חֲגִיגָה, וְהַקְהֵל – מְאַחֲרִין וְלֹא מַקְדִּימִין.

It was with regard to these times for reading the Megilla that the Sages **said** that **one advances**[N] the reading of the Megilla before the fourteenth of Adar **and one does not postpone** the reading to after its proper time. **However,** with regard to **the time** when families of **priests** donate **wood**[N] for the fire on the altar, which were times those families would treat as Festivals; as well as the fast of the **Ninth of Av;**[H] the **Festival** peace-offering that was brought on the Festivals;[H] **and the** commandment of **assembly** [***hakhel***][HN] of the entire Jewish people in the Temple courtyard on *Sukkot* in the year following the Sabbatical year to hear the king read the book of Deuteronomy; **one postpones** their observance until after Shabbat **and does not advance** their observance to before Shabbat.

אַף עַל פִּי שֶׁאָמְרוּ מַקְדִּימִין וְלֹא מְאַחֲרִין – מוּתָּרִין בְּהֶסְפֵּד וּבְתַעֲנִית וּמַתָּנוֹת לָאֶבְיוֹנִים. אָמַר רַבִּי יְהוּדָה: אֵימָתַי – מָקוֹם שֶׁנִּכְנָסִין בַּשֵּׁנִי וּבַחֲמִישִׁי, אֲבָל מָקוֹם שֶׁאֵין נִכְנָסִין לֹא בַּשֵּׁנִי וְלֹא בַּחֲמִישִׁי – אֵין קוֹרִין אוֹתָהּ אֶלָּא בִּזְמַנָּהּ.

The mishna continues: **Even though** the Sages **said** that **one advances** the time for reading the Megilla **and one does not postpone** the reading, one is **permitted** to **eulogize and fast** on these days, as they are not actually Purim; nevertheless, **gifts for the poor** are distributed on this day.[N] **Rabbi Yehuda said: When** is the Megilla read on the day of assembly, before the fourteenth of Adar? In a **place where** the villagers generally **enter** town **on Monday and Thursday. However,** in **a place where they do not** generally **enter** town **on Monday and Thursday, one may read** the Megilla **only in its** designated **time,** the fourteenth of Adar.[H]

גמ׳ תָּנָא: עֲשָׂרָה בַּטְלָנִין שֶׁבְּבֵית הַכְּנֶסֶת:

GEMARA We learned in the mishna that a large city is one that has ten idlers. It was **taught** in a *baraita*: The **ten idlers** that are mentioned here are ten idlers **that are in the synagogue,** i.e., men who do not have professional responsibilities other than to sit in the synagogue and attend to communal religious needs. The presence of ten such men establishes a location as a prominent city.

״בְּאֵלּוּ אָמְרוּ מַקְדִּימִין וְלֹא מְאַחֲרִין״: מַאי טַעְמָא? אָמַר רַבִּי אַבָּא אָמַר שְׁמוּאֵל: אָמַר קְרָא ״וְלֹא יַעֲבוֹר״.

We learned in the mishna: **It was with regard to these** times for reading the Megilla that the Sages **said** that **one advances** the reading of the Megilla **and one does not postpone** it. The Gemara asks: **What is the reason** for this? **Rabbi Abba said** that **Shmuel said:** The **verse states:** "The Jews ordained, and took upon them, and upon their seed, and upon all who joined themselves to them, **and it shall not pass,** that they should keep these two days" (Esther 9:27), which indicates that the designated time must not pass without the reading of the Megilla.

וְאָמַר רַבִּי אַבָּא אָמַר שְׁמוּאֵל: מִנַּיִן שֶׁאֵין מוֹנִין יָמִים לְשָׁנִים – שֶׁנֶּאֱמַר: ״לְחָדְשֵׁי הַשָּׁנָה״ חֳדָשִׁים אַתָּה מוֹנֶה לְשָׁנִים, וְאִי אַתָּה מוֹנֶה יָמִים לְשָׁנִים.

Having mentioned a teaching of Rabbi Abba in the name of Shmuel, the Gemara cites another of his statements: **And Rabbi Abba said** that **Shmuel said: From where** is it derived **that one does not count days to** make up **years,** i.e., a year is considered to be comprised of either twelve or thirteen lunar months, and not 365 days? **As it is stated: "Of the months of the year"** (Exodus 12:2), which indicates that **you count months to** make up **years,**[H] **but you do not count days** to make up **years.**

HALAKHA

The Ninth of Av is postponed – תִּשְׁעָה בְּאָב מְאַחֲרִין: The Ninth of Av, and the other fast days in particular, when they fall on Shabbat they are postponed until after Shabbat, except for the Fast of Esther, which cannot be postponed and is advanced to Thursday (*Shulḥan Arukh, Oraḥ Ḥayyim* 550:3, 552:10).

The Festival peace-offering is postponed – חֲגִיגָה מְאַחֲרִין: The Festival peace-offering and the burnt-offering of appearance do not override Shabbat. If the Festival occurs on Shabbat, the sacrifice is deferred until after Shabbat (Rambam *Sefer Korbanot, Hilkhot Ḥagiga* 1:8).

The commandment of assembly [*hakhel*] is postponed – הַקְהֵל מְאַחֲרִין: If the day of assembly falls on Shabbat, it is postponed until after Shabbat (Rambam *Sefer Korbanot, Hilkhot Ḥagiga* 3:7).

When did they say that it is advanced – מָתַי אָמְרוּ מַקְדִּימִין: When the reading of the Megilla was advanced to the day of assembly, it was advanced only for the residents of villages who would go to the city on the day of assembly. However, if they would not go into the city on those days, they would read the Megilla on the in its proper time, on the fourteenth of Adar. This ruling is in accordance with the opinion of Rabbi Yehuda, who comes only to explain the opinion of the Sages in the mishna (Rambam *Sefer Zemanim, Hilkhot Megilla* 1:8).

Months to make up years – חֳדָשִׁים לְשָׁנִים: A year is only considered a year when calculated by the number of whole months. Even though the solar year has eleven more days than the lunar year, solitary days are not added; rather, we wait until there is a full month's difference between the calendars and add it in an intercalated year (Rambam *Sefer Zemanim, Hilkhot Kiddush HaḤodesh* 1:2).

NOTES

It was with regard to these that the Sages said that one advances – בְּאֵלּוּ אָמְרוּ מַקְדִּימִין: Rashi and Rabbeinu Yehonatan explain: With regard to these, i.e., the various times for reading the Megilla, one advances the time but does not postpone it. However, the word "these," in plural, is slightly difficult according to this interpretation. Some explain, based on the Jerusalem Talmud and the *Tosefta* (1:4), that the reference is to the reading of the Megilla and the collection of shekels for communal offerings (see Meiri). Others explain that the word "these" refers to the residents of the villages and the small cities (Rashba; Ritva).

The time when families of priests donate wood – זְמַן עֲצֵי כֹהֲנִים: It is explained in tractate *Ta'anit* (28a) that in the time of Ezra and Nehemiah, certain families volunteered to bring the wood offering on set days of the year, since there was a lack of funds in the Temple. Although after a while there was no longer a financial need for this, these families maintained the practice of donating wood and rejoicing on these days. As for the reason why the bringing of the wood is not advanced, some explain that the donation of wood is viewed as a vow that has a specific time that it is supposed to be fulfilled, and therefore donating wood before the appropriate time would not be a fulfillment of the vow (Rashi; Rambam). The Ran and Rashi's commentary that appears with the Rif suggest that if this time were advanced it would interfere with the dates that were set for others to bring the wood offering.

The commandment of assembly [*hakhel*] – הַקְהֵל: The mitzva of *hakhel* is detailed in the Torah (Deuteronomy 31:10–13). This practice took place on the day after the first festival day of *Sukkot*; some say it took place at the conclusion of the last festival day of *Sukkot* (Rashi; Jerusalem Talmud). They would build a stage of wood in the courtyard, and the king would stand upon it and read from the book of Deuteronomy to the entire nation: Men, women, and children. Rashi explains that the reason this is not done on Shabbat is that this ceremony requires that the children be brought as well, and there is concern that the prohibition against carrying and taking out items on Shabbat will be violated (see Rif). A different explanation is cited in the Jerusalem Talmud, which maintains that the reason that *hakhel* did not take place on Shabbat is due to the horn blasts that accompanied the ceremony. Alternatively, it is because they needed to build the stage on that same day.

Gifts for the poor are distributed on this day – וּמַתָּנוֹת לָאֶבְיוֹנִים: From the language of the Rambam it is clear that he understands this phrase to mean that on the day of reading the Megilla, one may bring gifts for the poor and thereby fulfill his obligation. Conversely, some explain that his intention is that on that day one is exempt from giving gifts to the poor (Meiri; see Ran).

וְרַבָּנַן דְּקֵיסָרִי מִשּׁוּם רַבִּי אַבָּא אָמְרוּ: מִנַּיִן שֶׁאֵין מְחַשְּׁבִין שָׁעוֹת לַחֳדָשִׁים – שֶׁנֶּאֱמַר: "עַד חֹדֶשׁ יָמִים" – יָמִים אַתָּה מְחַשֵּׁב לַחֳדָשִׁים, וְאִי אַתָּה מְחַשֵּׁב שָׁעוֹת לַחֳדָשִׁים.

The Gemara adds: **And the Sages of Caesarea said in the name of Rabbi Abba: From where** is it derived **that one does not calculate hours to** reckon the **months?** A lunar cycle takes approximately twenty-nine and a half days, but a calendar month is considered to be twenty-nine or thirty full days and not precisely a lunar cycle. **As it is stated: "Until a month of days"** (Numbers 11:20), which indicates that **you calculate days to** reckon the **months,**[N] **but you do not calculate hours to** reckon the **months.**

"אֲבָל זְמַן עֲצֵי כֹהֲנִים וְתִשְׁעָה בְּאָב וַחֲגִיגָה וְהַקְהֵל מְאַחֲרִין וְלֹא מַקְדִּימִין": תִּשְׁעָה בְּאָב – אַקְדּוּמֵי פּוּרְעָנוּת לָא מַקְדְּמִי, חֲגִיגָה וְהַקְהֵל – מִשּׁוּם דְּאַכַּתִּי לָא מְטָא זְמַן חִיּוּבַיְיהוּ.

§ We learned in the mishna: **However,** with regard to **the time** when families of **priests** donate **wood** for the fire on the altar, the fast of **the Ninth of Av, the Festival** peace-offering, **and the** commandment of **assembly** [*hakhel*], **one postpones** their observance until after Shabbat **and does not advance** their observance to before Shabbat. The Gemara explains the reason for this *halakha* with respect to each item mentioned in the mishna. The fast of **the Ninth of Av** is not advanced because **one does not advance calamity;** since the Ninth of Av is a tragic time, its observance is postponed as long as possible. **The Festival** peace-offering **and the** commandment of **assembly** [*hakhel*] are not advanced **because the time of their obligation has not yet arrived,** and it is impossible to fulfill mitzvot before the designated time has arrived.

תָּנָא: חֲגִיגָה וְכָל זְמַן חֲגִיגָה מְאַחֲרִין. בִּשְׁלָמָא חֲגִיגָה, דְּאִי מִיקְלַע בְּשַׁבְּתָא – מְאַחֲרִינַן לַהּ לְבָתַר שַׁבְּתָא. אֶלָּא זְמַן חֲגִיגָה מַאי הִיא?

It was taught in a *baraita*: **One postpones the Festival** peace-offering **and the entire time** period **of the Festival** peace-offering. The Gemara attempts to clarify this statement: **Granted** that when the *baraita* says that the **Festival** peace-offering is postponed, it means **that if** a Festival **occurs on Shabbat,** when the Festival peace-offering cannot be sacrificed, **one postpones it until after Shabbat** and sacrifices the offering on the intermediate days of the Festival. **However, what is** the meaning of the phrase: **The time** period **of the Festival** peace-offering?

אָמַר רַב אוֹשַׁעְיָא, הָכִי קָאָמַר: חֲגִיגָה בַּשַּׁבָּת, וְעוֹלַת רְאִיָּה אֲפִילּוּ בְּיוֹם טוֹב דִּזְמַן חֲגִיגָה – מְאַחֲרִין.

Rav Oshaya said: This is what the *baraita* **is saying:** One postpones **the Festival** peace-offering if the Festival occurs **on Shabbat, and one postpones the** burnt-offering **of appearance even** due to **the Festival** itself. Despite the fact that a Festival day is **the time** for sacrificing a **Festival** peace-offering, the burnt-offering of appearance may not be sacrificed until after the Festival day.

מַנִּי – בֵּית שַׁמַּאי הִיא, דִּתְנַן: [בֵּית שַׁמַּאי אוֹמְרִים] מְבִיאִין שְׁלָמִים בְּיוֹם טוֹב וְאֵין סוֹמְכִין עֲלֵיהֶן,

The Gemara adds: **Whose** opinion is reflected in the mishna according to Rav Oshaya's explanation? **It is** the opinion of **Beit Shammai, as we learned** in a mishna (*Beitza* 19a) that **Beit Shammai say: One may bring** peace-offerings **on a Festival** day to be sacrificed in the Temple. Most portions of a peace-offering are eaten by the priests and the individual who brought the offering. Consequently, its slaughter is considered food preparation, which is permitted on a Festival day. **And one may not place** his **hands** on the head of the offering, as that includes leaning with all one's might upon the animal, which is prohibited on a Festival.

אֲבָל לֹא עוֹלוֹת, וּבֵית הִלֵּל אוֹמְרִים: מְבִיאִין שְׁלָמִים וְעוֹלוֹת, וְסוֹמְכִין עֲלֵיהֶן.

However, burnt-offerings **may not** be brought at all on the Festival. Since they are not eaten, their slaughter is not considered food preparation, and it therefore constitutes a prohibited labor on the Festival. **Beit Hillel** disagree and **say: One may bring** both peace-offerings **and** burnt-offerings on a Festival day, **and one may** even **place** his **hands on them.**[H]

רָבָא אָמַר: חֲגִיגָה, כָּל זְמַן חֲגִיגָה מְאַחֲרִין, טְפֵי – לָא. דִּתְנַן: מִי שֶׁלֹּא חַג בְּיוֹם טוֹב הָרִאשׁוֹן שֶׁל חַג – חוֹגֵג וְהוֹלֵךְ אֶת כָּל הָרֶגֶל כּוּלּוֹ וְיוֹם טוֹב הָאַחֲרוֹן שֶׁל חָג. עָבַר הָרֶגֶל וְלֹא חַג – אֵינוֹ חַיָּיב בְּאַחֲרָיוּתוֹ.

Rava said that the *baraita* should be understood as follows: **One postpones the Festival** peace-offering **for the entire time** period **of the Festival** peace-offering, i.e., for the entire duration of the Festival. However, it may **not** be postponed for **longer** than this. **As we learned** in a mishna (*Ḥagiga* 9a): **One who did not offer the Festival** peace-offering **on the first Festival day of the festival** of *Sukkot* **may offer the Festival** peace-offering **for the** duration of the **entire pilgrimage Festival,** including the intermediate days **and the last day of the Festival.**[H] If **the pilgrimage Festival has passed and he did not** yet **bring the Festival** peace-offering,[H] **he is not obligated** to pay **restitution for it.** The obligation is no longer in force, and he therefore is not liable to bring another offering as compensation.

NOTES

Days to reckon the months – יָמִים...לַחֳדָשִׁים: These principals are relevant in various ways. They impact the setting of the times of the calendar such that years are only composed of complete months; likewise, months are not counted from the hour of the new moon but rather consist of complete days. The calendar, in turn, impacts the *halakhot* of vows and contracts, which depend upon the months and years.

HALAKHA

Sacrifices of the Festival – קָרְבְּנוֹת הֶחָג: The Festival peace-offering and the burnt-offering of appearance are permitted to be sacrificed on a Festival day. Similarly, the peace-offerings of joy are sacrificed on Festivals. For every offering that is brought, it is permitted for one to place his hands on the head of the offering, in accordance with the opinion of Beit Hillel (Rambam *Sefer Korbanot, Hilkhot Ḥagiga* 1:8–9).

Compensation for the offerings – תַּשְׁלוּמֵי קָרְבָּנוֹת: One who has not brought his Festival peace-offering and the burnt-offering of appearance on the first day of the Festival may bring it on the remaining days of the Festival (Rambam *Sefer Korbanot, Hilkhot Ḥagiga* 1:4).

If the pilgrimage Festival has passed and he did not bring the Festival peace-offering – עָבַר הָרֶגֶל וְלֹא חַג: If the entire Festival has passed and one has not yet brought the offerings of the Festival, he is no longer obligated to bring them. This is a fulfillment of the verse (Ecclesiastes 1:15): "That which is crooked cannot be made straight" (Rambam *Sefer Korbanot, Hilkhot Ḥagiga* 1:6).

רַב אַשִׁי אָמַר: חֲגִיגָה וְכָל זְמַן חֲגִיגָה מְאַחֲרִין – וַאֲפִילּוּ עֲצֶרֶת דְּחַד יוֹמָא מְאַחֲרִין. דִּתְנַן: מוֹדִים, שֶׁאִם חָל עֲצֶרֶת לִהְיוֹת בַּשַּׁבָּת שֶׁיּוֹם טְבוֹחַ אַחַר הַשַּׁבָּת.

Rav Ashi said that the *baraita* should be understood as follows: **The Festival** peace-offering **may be postponed for the entire time** period **of a Festival** peace-offering. This indicates that **even** if ***Shavuot*, which is one day,** occurs on Shabbat, **one postpones** the Festival peace-offering and offers it on one of the six days after *Shavuot*.[H] **As we learned** in a mishna (*Ḥagiga* 17a): Beit Hillel **concede that if *Shavuot* occurs on Shabbat, the day of slaughter is after Shabbat.** Since the Festival peace-offering and the burnt-offering of appearance cannot be sacrificed on Shabbat, they are slaughtered after Shabbat. This indicates that the Festival peace-offering may be slaughtered after the Festival day of *Shavuot*, as is the case on the other Festivals.

HALAKHA

Compensation on *Shavuot* – תַּשְׁלוּמֵי עֲצֶרֶת: One who has not brought the offerings of the Festival on *Shavuot*, may bring them on any of the six days after *Shavuot* (Rambam *Sefer Korbanot, Hilkhot Ḥagiga* 1:7).

אָמַר רַבִּי אֶלְעָזָר אָמַר רַבִּי חֲנִינָא: רַבִּי נָטַע נְטִיעָה בְּפוּרִים,

Rabbi Elazar said that **Rabbi Ḥanina said: Rabbi** Yehuda HaNasi did several unusual things: **He planted a sapling on Purim,** and was not concerned about performing labor and thereby possibly denigrating the day.

Perek **I**
Daf **5** Amud **b**

וְרָחַץ בְּקְרוֹנָה שֶׁל צִפּוֹרִי בְּשִׁבְעָה עָשָׂר בְּתַמּוּז, וּבִקֵּשׁ לַעֲקוֹר תִּשְׁעָה בְּאָב, וְלֹא הוֹדוּ לוֹ.

And he bathed at the time when the **wagons** [***kerona***][L] were traveling through **Tzippori**,[B] i.e., on the market day, when the public would know about it, **on the seventeenth of Tammuz**,[N] to show that bathing is permitted on that day. **And he sought to abolish** the fast of **the Ninth of Av.**[N] **And** with respect to the Ninth of Av, the Sages **did not agree with him.**

אָמַר לְפָנָיו רַבִּי אַבָּא בַּר זַבְדָּא: רַבִּי, לֹא כָּךְ הָיָה מַעֲשֶׂה, אֶלָּא: תִּשְׁעָה בְּאָב שֶׁחָל לִהְיוֹת בַּשַּׁבָּת הֲוָה, וּדְחִינוּהוּ לְאַחַר הַשַּׁבָּת, וְאָמַר רַבִּי: הוֹאִיל וְנִדְחֶה – יִדָּחֶה, וְלֹא הוֹדוּ חֲכָמִים. קָרֵי עֲלֵיהּ: ״טוֹבִים הַשְּׁנַיִם מִן הָאֶחָד״.

Rabbi Abba bar Zavda said to Rabbi Elazar: **My teacher, the incident did not** occur in **this** fashion. Rabbi Yehuda HaNasi never sought to abolish the fast of the Ninth of Av. **Rather, it was** a year when **the Ninth of Av occurred on Shabbat, and they postponed it until after Shabbat. And Rabbi** Yehuda HaNasi **said** about that case: **Since it has** already **been deferred** from its usual time, **let it be** altogether **deferred** this year. **And the Rabbis did not agree with him.** Rabbi Elazar **read** the verse **about** Rabbi Abba bar Zavda: **"Two are better than one"** (Ecclesiastes 4:9), meaning, it is good that you were here to provide an accurate report about that incident.

LANGUAGE

Wagons [*kerona*] – קְרוֹנָה: Apparently from the Greek κρήνη, *krēnē*, meaning a spring or a well of flowing water. This translation is suggested by the *Arukh* as well. Alternatively, the word may be from the Greek κάρρον, *karron*, meaning car.

BACKGROUND

Tzippori – צִפּוֹרִי: Tzippori was a large town in the Upper Galilee and the perennial rival of Tiberias for recognition as the religious capital of Galilee. During the Second Temple period it enjoyed special status among the towns of the Galilee due to its large and learned Jewish community. Among the *tanna'im* who lived there were Rabbi Yoḥanan ben Nuri, Rabbi Ḥalafta, and his famous son Rabbi Yosei. Rabbi Yehuda HaNasi moved to Tzippori toward the end of his life, and it was the seat of the Sanhedrin for about a generation. Rabbi Yehuda HaNasi's leading disciples lived in Tzippori: Rabbi Yishmael, son of Rabbi Yosei; Rabban Gamliel, son of Rabbi, who was later appointed *Nasi*; his brother, Rabbi Shimon; Rabbi Ḥanina bar Ḥama, later the head of the Tzippori yeshiva; and Rabbi Yannai. Even after the Sanhedrin moved to Tiberias, Torah scholars continued to live in Tzippori, among them the important *amora'im* of Eretz Yisrael, Rabbi Ḥanina of Tzippori and Rabbi Mana.

NOTES

Bathed…on the seventeenth of Tammuz – רָחַץ...בְּשִׁבְעָה עָשָׂר בְּתַמּוּז: The Rashba writes that Rabbi Yehuda HaNasi's behavior was in accordance with the principle set forth in tractate *Rosh HaShana* (18b), where it states that in times of peace, one need not observe the fast days of the seventeenth of Tammuz, the Fast of Gedalia, and the tenth of Tevet; in times when there are evil decrees against the Jewish people, these fasts are obligatory; and in times which are neither peaceful nor times of evil decree, these fasts are optional. During the time of Rabbi Yehuda HaNasi, these fasts were optional, yet the Jewish people had accepted upon itself the obligation to fast. Nonetheless, Rabbi Yehuda HaNasi was of the opinion that this voluntary acceptance applied only to actually fasting, but not to other prohibitions of fast days, e.g., bathing. There are those who add that according to the comment of Rabbi Abba bar Zavda, that the Ninth of Av occurred on Shabbat, if the incident of Rabbi Yehuda HaNasi bathing on the seventeenth of Tammuz took place in the same year, it would mean that the seventeenth of Tammuz also occurred on Shabbat and was postponed to Sunday. Perhaps Rabbi Yehuda HaNasi was of the opinion that in such circumstances, the entire fast should not be observed (Rav Ya'akov Emden).

To abolish the fast of the Ninth of Av – לַעֲקוֹר תִּשְׁעָה בְּאָב: *Tosafot* explain that Rabbi Yehuda HaNasi didn't seek to abolish the fast completely, but rather to abolish its severity and make it equivalent to the other fasts. The Ritva expounds upon this idea and explains that according to the original enactment of the fast days by the prophets, there is no difference between the Ninth of Av and other fast days. Consequently, although the Sages did not want to make fasting on the Ninth of Av optional during times when there are no evil decrees against the Jewish people, Rabbi Yehuda HaNasi sought to equate it to the other fast days with regard to other prohibitions, e.g., bathing and wearing leather shoes (Ritva).

וְרַבִּי, הֵיכִי נָטַע נְטִיעָה בְּפוּרִים? וְהָתָנֵי רַב יוֹסֵף: "שִׂמְחָה וּמִשְׁתֶּה וְיוֹם טוֹב", "שִׂמְחָה" – מְלַמֵּד שֶׁאֲסוּרִים בְּהֶסְפֵּד, "מִשְׁתֶּה" מְלַמֵּד שֶׁאָסוּר בְּתַעֲנִית, "וְיוֹם טוֹב" – מְלַמֵּד שֶׁאָסוּר בַּעֲשִׂיַּית מְלָאכָה! אֶלָּא: רַבִּי בַּר אַרְבֵּיסָר הֲוָה, וְכִי נְטַע – בַּחֲמֵיסָר נְטַע.

The Gemara asks: **And how could Rabbi** Yehuda HaNasi **plant a sapling on Purim? Didn't Rav Yosef teach** with regard to the verse: "Therefore the Jews of the villages, who dwell in the unwalled towns, make the fourteenth day of the month of Adar a day of **gladness and feasting, and a good day** [*yom tov*]" (Esther 9:19), that the term **"gladness" teaches that** it is **prohibited** to **eulogize** on Purim; **"feasting" teaches that** it is **prohibited** to **fast; and** the term **"good day"** [*yom tov*] **teaches that** it is **prohibited** to **perform labor,** just as on a Festival, which is also referred to as a *yom tov*? **Rather,** what happened was as follows: **Rabbi** Yehuda HaNasi was in a place that observed Purim **on the fourteenth, and when he planted** the sapling, **he planted** it **on the fifteenth.**

אִינִי? וְהָא רַבִּי בִּטְבֶרְיָא הֲוָה, וּטְבֶרְיָא מוּקֶּפֶת חוֹמָה מִימוֹת יְהוֹשֻׁעַ בִּן נוּן הֲוַאי! אֶלָּא, רַבִּי בַּר חֲמֵיסָר הֲוָה, וְכִי נְטַע – בְּאַרְבֵּיסָר הֲוָה.

The Gemara asks: **Is that so? Wasn't Rabbi** Yehuda HaNasi **in Tiberias, and Tiberias was surrounded by a wall since the days of Joshua, son of Nun.** Consequently, he was obligated to observe Purim on the fifteenth. **Rather,** say just the opposite: **Rabbi** Yehuda HaNasi lived in a place that observed Purim **on the fifteenth, and when he planted** the sapling, **he planted** it **on the fourteenth.**

וּמִי פְּשִׁיטָא לֵיהּ דִּטְבֶרְיָא מוּקֶּפֶת חוֹמָה מִימוֹת יְהוֹשֻׁעַ בִּן נוּן? וְהָא חִזְקִיָּה קָרֵי בִּטְבֶרְיָא בְּאַרְבֵּיסָר וּבַחֲמֵיסָר, מִסַּפְּקָא לֵיהּ אִי מוּקֶּפֶת חוֹמָה מִימוֹת יְהוֹשֻׁעַ בִּן נוּן הִיא אִי לָא! לְחִזְקִיָּה – מִסַּפְּקָא לֵיהּ, לְרַבִּי – פְּשִׁיטָא לֵיהּ.

The Gemara asks: **Wasn't it obvious to** Rabbi Yehuda HaNasi **that** the city of **Tiberias was surrounded by a wall since the days of Joshua, son of Nun? Didn't Hezekiah read** the Megilla **in Tiberias** both **on the fourteenth and on the fifteenth** of Adar, because **he was uncertain if** it had been **surrounded by a wall since the days of Joshua, son of Nun, or not?** The Gemara answers: **Hezekiah was** indeed **uncertain** about the matter, whereas **it was obvious to Rabbi** Yehuda HaNasi that Tiberias had been surrounded by a wall in the time of Joshua.

וְכִי פְּשִׁיטָא לֵיהּ מִי שָׁרֵי? וְהָכְתִיב בִּמְגִילַּת תַּעֲנִית: אֶת יוֹם אַרְבָּעָה עָשָׂר וְאֶת יוֹם חֲמִשָּׁה עָשָׂר יוֹמֵי פוּרַיָּא אִינּוּן, דְּלָא לְמִסְפַּד בְּהוֹן.

The Gemara asks further: **And when it was obvious to** Rabbi Yehuda HaNasi that the Megilla should be read in Tiberias on the fifteenth, **was it permitted** to plant there on the fourteenth? **Isn't it written in *Megillat Ta'anit*[B]** that **the fourteenth day and the fifteenth day of Adar are the days of Purim,** and **one is not** permitted **to eulogize on them?[H]**

וְאָמַר רָבָא: לָא נִצְרְכָא אֶלָּא לֶאֱסוֹר אֶת שֶׁל זֶה בְּזֶה וְאֶת שֶׁל זֶה בְּזֶה! הָנֵי מִילֵּי – בְּהֶסְפֵּד וּבְתַעֲנִית, אֲבָל מְלָאכָה – יוֹם אֶחָד וְתוּ לָא.

And Rava said: This statement **is necessary only to prohibit** those who observe Purim **on this** day to eulogize **on that** day, **and** those who observe Purim **on that** day to eulogize **on this** day. Since the two days are mentioned in the Bible, it was only necessary to mention them in *Megillat Ta'anit* in order to indicate that the prohibition against eulogizing applies to both days. Presumably, the same should apply to the prohibition against performing labor. Consequently, how could Rabbi Yehuda HaNasi plant a sapling on the fourteenth of Adar? The Gemara answers: **That applies** only to **eulogies and fasting. However, labor** is prohibited for only **one day,** either the fourteenth or the fifteenth, **and no more.**

אִינִי? וְהָא רַב חַזְיֵיהּ לְהַהוּא גַּבְרָא דַּהֲוָה קָא שָׁדֵי כִּיתָּנָא בְּפוּרַיָּא, וְלַטְיֵיהּ וְלָא צְמַח כִּיתָּנֵיהּ! הָתָם בַּר יוֹמָא הֲוָה.

The Gemara asks: **Is that so? Didn't Rav see a certain man planting flax on Purim, and cursed him, and** the man's **flax never grew.** The Gemara answers: **There,** the man **was** obligated to observe Purim **on that day** that he planted the flax. Therefore, it was certainly prohibited to perform labor.

רַבָּה בְּרֵיהּ דְּרָבָא אָמַר: אֲפִילּוּ תֵּימָא בְּיוֹמֵיהּ, הֶסְפֵּד וְתַעֲנִית – קַבִּילוּ עֲלַיְיהוּ, מְלָאכָה לָא קַבִּילוּ עֲלַיְיהוּ.

Rabba, son of Rava, said a different answer to the question: **Even if you say** that Rabbi Yehuda HaNasi planted the sapling **on his** own **day** of Purim, i.e., on the day that the Megilla was read in his location, it was still permitted to plant the sapling. This is because the Jewish people **accepted upon themselves** the prohibitions against **eulogizing and fasting** on Purim, but **they did not accept upon themselves the prohibition** against performing **labor.[H]**

BACKGROUND

Megillat Ta'anit – **מְגִילַּת תַּעֲנִית:** Until the Mishna was written, writing down the Oral Torah was prohibited. However, it was standard practice for scholars to write down notes for personal use, known as hidden scrolls. *Megillat Ta'anit* was the first book, apart from the Bible, that was written. This scroll, to which we have access today, includes a list of days on which it is prohibited to eulogize the deceased or fast, due to the miraculous and joyous events that transpired on those days. The scroll is written in two languages: The primary *halakha*, the day, and its legal status is written in Aramaic, while the descriptions of what happened each day are in Hebrew.

Although *Megillat Ta'anit* is attributed to Ḥananya ben Ḥizkiya and his son, they did not author the entire work. Events were added in later generations, continuing until the redaction of the Mishna.

HALAKHA

Mourning on Purim – **אֲבֵלוּת בְּפוּרִים:** During the days of Purim, both the fourteenth and the fifteenth of Adar, in all locations, it is forbidden to eulogize or to visit graves. Additionally, if a funeral takes place on one of those days, neither *Tziduk Hadin* nor *kaddish* is recited next to the grave (*Arukh HaShulḥan*; *Shulḥan Arukh, Oraḥ Ḥayyim* 696:3).

Labor on the days of Purim – **מְלָאכָה בִּימֵי הַפּוּרִים:** Even in places where it is customary on Purim to refrain from performing the labors prohibited on Shabbat, this prohibition applies only on the day of the Megilla reading, and it is not prohibited to perform labor on the day that other cities read. However, some say that one should be strict in this regard (Maharil; Avudraham). It appears the *halakha* in these cases is dependent on the custom of the place (*Mishna Berura*), and in most places it is not the custom to be strict in this regard (*Shulḥan Arukh, Oraḥ Ḥayyim* 696:2).

דְּמֵעִיקָּרָא כְּתִיב: ״שִׂמְחָה וּמִשְׁתֶּה וְיוֹם טוֹב״ וּלְבַסּוֹף כְּתִיב: ״לַעֲשׂוֹת אוֹתָם יְמֵי מִשְׁתֶּה וְשִׂמְחָה״ וְאִילּוּ ״יוֹם טוֹב״ לָא כְּתִיב.

This can be proven from the fact **that initially,** when Mordecai and Esther proposed the celebration of Purim, **it is written:** "A day of **gladness and feasting and a good day** [*yom tov*]" (Esther 9:19), **and at the end,** when it the celebration of Purim was accepted by the Jewish people, **it is written:** "That they should **make them days of feasting and gladness**" (Esther 9:22), **whereas** the term **good day** [*yom tov*], which alludes to a day when it is prohibited to perform labor, **is not written.** The people never accepted upon themselves the prohibition against performing labor on Purim as if it were a Festival, and therefore the prohibition never took effect.

וְאֶלָּא רַב, מַאי טַעְמָא לָטְיֵיהּ לְהַהוּא גַּבְרָא? דְּבָרִים הַמּוּתָּרִין וַאֲחֵרִים נָהֲגוּ בָּהֶן אִיסּוּר הֲוָה, וּבְאַתְרֵיהּ דְּרַבִּי לָא נְהוּג.

The Gemara asks: If labor is permitted on Purim, **what is the reason that Rav cursed that man** who planted the flax? The Gemara answers: **It was** a case of **matters that are permitted** by *halakha*, **but others were accustomed to** treat **them as a prohibition,**[HN] in which case one may not permit these actions in their presence, lest they come to treat other prohibitions lightly. In the place where that man planted his flax, it was customary to abstain from labor on Purim. However, **in Rabbi** Yehuda HaNasi's **place, it was not the custom** to abstain from labor on Purim, and therefore it was permitted for him to plant the sapling even in public.

וְאִיבָּעֵית אֵימָא: לְעוֹלָם נְהוּג, וְרַבִּי נְטִיעָה שֶׁל שִׂמְחָה נְטַע. כִּדְתְנַן: עָבְרוּ אֵלּוּ וְלֹא נַעֲנוּ – מְמַעֲטִין בְּמַשָּׂא וּמַתָּן, בְּבִנְיָן וּבִנְטִיעָה, בְּאֵירוּסִין וּבְנִישּׂוּאִין.

And if you wish, say an alternative answer: **Actually, it was the custom** to abstain from labor on Purim in Rabbi Yehuda HaNasi's place, **and Rabbi** Yehuda HaNasi engaged in a **joyful** act of **planting,** for pleasure rather than for financial benefit. **As we learned** in a mishna with regard to public fasts: If **these** fasts for rain **have passed and** the community's prayers **have** still **not been answered,**[H] and the drought continues, **one decreases his business** activities, as well as **construction, planting, betrothals, and marriages.**

וְתָנָא עֲלַהּ: בִּנְיָן – בִּנְיָן שֶׁל שִׂמְחָה, נְטִיעָה – נְטִיעָה שֶׁל שִׂמְחָה. אֵיזֶהוּ בִּנְיָן שֶׁל שִׂמְחָה – זֶה הַבּוֹנֶה בֵּית חֲתָנוּת לִבְנוֹ. אֵיזוֹ הִיא נְטִיעָה שֶׁל שִׂמְחָה – זֶה הַנּוֹטֵעַ אֲבוּרְנְקִי שֶׁל מְלָכִים.

And it was taught in a *baraita* **about this** mishna: When the Sages said that **construction** must be decreased on public fasts, they were not referring to the construction of homes for people who have nowhere to live, but to **joyful construction.** Similarly, when they said that **planting** must be decreased, they were not referring to planting food crops, but to **joyful planting. What is** meant by **joyful construction? This** is referring to **one who builds a wedding chamber for his son.** It was customary to build a special house where the wedding would take place, and at times the couple would also live there. **What is** meant by **joyful planting? This** is referring to **one who plants** trees for shade and pleasure such as one might find in **a royal garden** [*avurneki*].[L] Rabbi Yehuda HaNasi engaged in joyful planting on Purim, in keeping with the joyous nature of the day.

גּוּפָא, חִזְקִיָּה קָרֵי בְּטִבֶרְיָא בְּאַרְבֵּיסָר וּבַחֲמֵיסָר, מִסַּפְּקָא לֵיהּ אִי מוּקֶּפֶת חוֹמָה מִימוֹת יְהוֹשֻׁעַ בִּן נוּן הִיא אִי לָא. וּמִי מִסַּפְּקָא לֵיהּ מִלְּתָא דְּטִבֶרְיָא? וְהָכְתִיב: ״וְעָרֵי מִבְצָר הַצִּדִּים צֵר וְחַמַּת רַקַּת וְכִנֶּרֶת״ וְקַיְימָא לָן: רַקַּת זוֹ טִבֶרְיָא! הַיְינוּ טַעְמָא דְּמִסַּפְּקָא לֵיהּ: מִשּׁוּם דְּחַד גִּיסָא שׁוּרָא דְּיַמָּא הֲוַת.

§ The Gemara examines **the** matter **itself** cited in the previous discussion. **Hezekiah read** the Megilla **in Tiberias** both **on the fourteenth and on the fifteenth** of Adar, because **he was uncertain**[N] **if it** had been **surrounded by a wall since the days of Joshua, son of Nun, or not.**[H] The Gemara asks: **Was he** really **uncertain about the matter of Tiberias? Isn't it written: "And the fortified cities were Ziddim-zer, and Hammath, Rakkath, and Chinnereth"** (Joshua 19:35), **and we maintain** that **Rakkath is Tiberias?** The Gemara answers: **This is the reason that he was uncertain:** Although Tiberias was surrounded by a wall in the time of Joshua, Hezekiah was uncertain about the *halakha* **due to** the fact **that** on **one side, there was a wall of the sea,** i.e., there was no physical wall, but the city was protected due to the fact that it adjoined the sea.

HALAKHA

The prohibition against performing labor on Purim – אִיסּוּר מְלָאכָה בְּפוּרִים: According to *halakha*, it is permitted to perform labor on Purim, in accordance with the statement of Rabba, son of Rava. However, in a place where the custom is not to perform labor, it is prohibited. In our times it is customary not to perform labor (Rema), and one who does perform labor will not achieve productive results (see Rambam and *Magen Avraham*). However, this custom was not extended to all forms of labor: Festive building and planting is permitted. Additionally, it is permitted to do any work for the sake of fulfilling a mitzva, e.g., writing words of Torah or other matters that involve a mitzva, or something that does not need a lot of consideration (*Magen Avraham*). In order to fill the needs of Purim, even full-fledged labor is permitted (*Shulḥan Arukh, Oraḥ Ḥayyim* 696:1).

If these have passed and the prayers have not been answered – עָבְרוּ אֵלּוּ וְלֹא נַעֲנוּ: When the Sages decree fasts for rain and thirteen fasts pass and yet the prayers have not been answered and rain has not fallen, it is incumbent upon the people to reduce their business transactions that are for the purpose of happiness (*Magen Avraham*), as well as festive building and planting. Similarly, betrothals and other feasts are minimized, as are weddings, unless the mitzva to be fruitful and multiply has not yet been fulfilled (*Shulḥan Arukh, Oraḥ Ḥayyim* 575:7).

Uncertainties with regard to walled cities – סְפֵיקוֹ מוּקָּפִין: With regard to any city in which there is uncertainty as to whether it was surrounded by a wall from the days of Joshua, the custom is like that of Hezekiah in Tiberias, and the Megilla is read on both the fourteenth and the fifteenth, both at night and during the day, and the festivities and the gifts for the poor are observed on both (*Magen Avraham*). However, the blessing is recited only on the fourteenth, and likewise *kaddish* and the *Kedushat HaSeder* are not recited after the reading of the Megilla on the night of the fifteenth, and the Torah is not read during that day (*Kaf HaḤayyim*). There were also cities outside of Eretz Yisrael that followed this protocol for dealing with uncertainty. However, in the more northern European cities there is no need for concern that they may have been walled in the time of Joshua (*Magen Avraham*). The custom in Baghdad was to read on both days. In the ancient cities in Eretz Yisrael, e.g., Hebron, Safed, the custom was to read on both days, and in Tiberias it certainly should be read on both days. This is also the custom in Damascus (*Kaf HaḤayyim*; *Shulḥan Arukh, Oraḥ Ḥayyim* 688:4).

LANGUAGE

Garden [*avurneki*] – אֲבוּרְנְקִי: In the version of the *Arukh* and in the best textual witnesses the reading is *akhvarnka*, which is apparently related to the Middle Persian xwarnak, meaning a lavish building. The *ge'onim* note the usage of the Aramaic word to indicate a pavilion built by kings in a garden.

NOTES

Matters that are permitted but others were accustomed to treat them as a prohibition – דְּבָרִים הַמּוּתָּרִים וַאֲחֵרִים נָהֲגוּ בָּהֶן אִיסּוּר הֲוָה: It is a principle in *halakha* that when something is permitted according to *halakha*, yet people render it prohibited for themselves, one is not allowed to rule that it is permitted or to treat it as permitted in their location. This is the basis for many prohibitions due to custom. However, this principle is limited to scenarios where those who take the prohibition upon themselves know that the action is permitted by *halakha*, and not to cases where they adopt the prohibition due to an error in understanding the law.

Hezekiah…was uncertain – חִזְקִיָּה...מְסַפְּקָא לֵיהּ: The Sages discuss Hezekiah's uncertainty, mainly due to what can be deduced from here with regard to other places where there is uncertainty as to whether a city was surrounded by a wall. It is possible to understand from Hezekiah's actions that whenever there is uncertainty as to whether a particular city was surrounded by a wall from the days of Joshua, the Megilla should be read there on both days. However, this conclusion would contradict the principles normally used to resolve uncertainty. These principles state that in cases such as this, the majority is followed, and similarly that with regard to an uncertainty concerning rabbinic laws, the *halakha* is lenient. Therefore, the *ge'onim* explain that a distinction must be made between the case of Tiberias and other cities whose status is uncertain. With regard to Tiberias, Hezekiah was certain that the city itself existed in the days of Joshua and his uncertainty was whether it was surrounded by a wall. However, with regard to other cities, where the uncertainty is whether the city existed at all during the days of Joshua, there is certainly no reason to be strict. The Ramban writes that when Hezekiah read on two days due to uncertainty, he acted only out of a righteous custom.

אִי הָכִי אַמַּאי מְסַפְּקָא לֵיהּ? וַדַּאי לָאו חוֹמָה הִיא! דְּתַנְיָא: ״אֲשֶׁר לוֹ חוֹמָה״ – וְלֹא שׁוּר אִיגָּר, ״סָבִיב״ פְּרָט לִטְבֶרְיָא שֶׁיָּמָּה חוֹמָתָהּ!

The Gemara asks: **If so, why was he uncertain?** The sea is **certainly not a wall. As it is taught** in a *baraita* with regard to the sale of houses in walled cities, the phrase: **"Which has a wall"** (Leviticus 25:30), indicates that the city has a bona fide wall **and not** merely **a wall of roofs.**[NH] If a city is completely encircled by attached houses but there is no separate wall, it is not considered a walled city. The next verse, which is referring to cities that have no wall **"round about** them" (Leviticus 25:31), **excludes Tiberias** from being considered a walled city, **as the sea is its wall** on one side and it is not fully encircled by a physical wall. Consequently, Tiberias is not considered a walled city.

לְעִנְיַן בָּתֵּי עָרֵי חוֹמָה לָא מְסַפְּקָא לֵיהּ, כִּי קָא מְסַפְּקָא לֵיהּ – לְעִנְיַן מִקְרָא מְגִילָּה: מַאי פְּרָזִים וּמַאי מוּקָּפִין דִּכְתִיבִי גַּבֵּי מִקְרָא מְגִילָּה, מִשּׁוּם דְּהָנֵי מִיגַּלּוּ, וְהָנֵי לָא מִיגַּלּוּ, וְהָא נַמִּי מִיגַּלְיָא, אוֹ דִּלְמָא: מִשּׁוּם דְּהָנֵי מִיגְנוּ וְהָנֵי לָא מִיגְנוּ, וְהָא נַמִּי מִיגַנְיָא. מִשּׁוּם הָכִי מְסַפְּקָא לֵיהּ.

The Gemara answers: **With regard to** the sale of **houses of walled cities,** Hezekiah **was not uncertain. Where he was uncertain was with regard to the reading of the Megilla: What are the unwalled towns and what are the walled cities that are written with regard to the reading of the Megilla?** Is the difference between them **due to** the fact **that these** unwalled towns **are exposed, whereas those** walled cities **are not exposed?** If so, since Tiberias **is also exposed,** as it is not entirely surrounded by a wall, it should be considered unwalled. **Or perhaps** the difference is **due to** the fact **that these** walled cities **are protected, whereas those** unwalled towns **are not protected, and** Tiberias **is also protected** by the sea and should be treated as a walled city. It was **due to that** reason that Hezekiah **was uncertain** when to read the Megilla.

רַב אַסִּי קָרֵי מְגִילָּה בְּהוּצַל בְּאַרְבֵּיסַר וּבַחֲמֵיסַר, מְסַפְּקָא לֵיהּ אִי מוּקֶּפֶת חוֹמָה מִימוֹת יְהוֹשֻׁעַ בִּן נוּן הִיא אִי לָא. אִיכָּא דְּאָמַר, אָמַר רַב אַסִּי: הַאי הוּצַל דְּבֵית בִּנְיָמִין מוּקֶּפֶת חוֹמָה מִימוֹת יְהוֹשֻׁעַ הִיא.

The Gemara relates that **Rav Asi read the Megilla in** the city of **Huzal**[B] in Babylonia on both **the fourteenth and the fifteenth** of Adar, because **he was uncertain if** it had been **surrounded** by a wall **since the days of Joshua, son of Nun, or not.** Huzal was an ancient city, and it was possible that it had been surrounded by a wall in the time of Joshua. **Some say** a different version of this report, according to which there was no uncertainty. **Rav Asi said: This** city of **Huzal of the house of Benjamin was walled since the days of Joshua, son of Nun.**

אָמַר רַבִּי יוֹחָנָן: כִּי הֲוֵינָא טַלְיָא אָמֵינָא מִלְּתָא דְּשָׁאֵילְנָא לְסָבַיָּיא,

Incidental to the previous discussion concerning Tiberias, the Gemara relates that **Rabbi Yoḥanan said: When I was a child I said something that I** later **asked the Elders** about,

NOTES

A wall of roofs – שׁוּר אִיגָּר: Some explain the concept of a wall of roofs as large roofs that reach the ground and encircle the entire city. Others explain that it is an incomplete wall, where only a portion of the city is surrounded by a wall (*Arukh*).

HALAKHA

And not a wall of roofs – וְלֹא שׁוּר אִיגָּר: A city in which the roofs make up the walls, or the sea serves as its wall, does not have the *halakha* of a walled city with regard to *halakhot* of redeeming land. Rather, its status is that of open courtyard cities (Rambam *Sefer Zera'im*, *Hilkhot Shemitta VeYovel* 12:13).

BACKGROUND

Huzal – הוּצַל: Huzal was a small city in Babylonia, south of the city of Neharde'a. This was a very old settlement, and apparently the Jews that resided there belonged to the exiled tribe of Binyamin. In Huzal there was a famous synagogue which was described as a place where the divine spirit rests. A few Sages are known to have lived in that city.

Perek **I**
Daf **6** Amud **a**

וְאִישְׁתַּכַּח כְּוָותִי: חַמַּת זוֹ טְבֶרְיָא, וְלָמָּה נִקְרָא שְׁמָהּ חַמַּת – עַל שׁוּם חַמֵּי טְבֶרְיָא. רַקַּת – זוֹ צִיפּוֹרִי, וְלָמָּה נִקְרָא שְׁמָהּ רַקַּת – מִשּׁוּם דְּמִידַּלְיָיא כְּרַקְתָּא דְנַהֲרָא. כִּנֶּרֶת – זוֹ גִּינוֹסַר, וְלָמָּה נִקְרָא שְׁמָהּ כִּנֶּרֶת – דִּמְתִיקִי פֵּירָא כְּקָלָא דְכִינָּרֵי.

and it was found in accordance with my opinion. I said that **Hammath is Tiberias.**[B] **And why was it called Hammath? On account of the hot springs of** [*ḥammei*] **Tiberias** that are located there. And I said that **Rakkath is Tzippori. And why was it called Rakkath? Because it is raised** above the surrounding areas **like the bank** [*rakta*] **of a river.** And I said that **Chinnereth is Ginosar.**[B] **And why was it called Chinnereth? Because its fruit are sweet like the sound of a harp** [*kinnor*].

אָמַר רָבָא: מִי אִיכָּא לְמַאן דְּאָמַר רַקַּת לָאו טְבֶרְיָא הִיא? וְהָא כִּי שָׁכֵיב אִינִישׁ הָכָא, הָתָם סָפְדִי לֵיהּ הָכִי: גָּדוֹל הוּא בְּשֵׁשַׁךְ, וְשֵׁם לוֹ בְּרַקַּת. וְכִי מַסְּקִי אֲרוֹנָא לְהָתָם סָפְדִי לֵיהּ הָכִי: אוֹהֲבֵי שְׂרִידִים יוֹשְׁבֵי רַקַּת, צְאוּ וְקַבְּלוּ הֲרוּגֵי עוֹמֶק.

Rava said: Is there anyone who says that Rakkath is not Tiberias? Isn't it true that **when a great man dies here,** in Babylonia, **they lament** his demise **there,** in Tiberias, **as follows: Great was he in Sheshakh,** i.e., Babylonia (see Jeremiah 25:26), **and he had a name in Rakkath?** Furthermore, **when they bring up the casket** of an important person **to there,** to Tiberias, **they lament** his demise **as follows:** You **lovers of the remnants** of the Jewish people, **residents of Rakkath, go out and receive the dead from the deep,** i.e., the low-lying lands of Babylonia.

BACKGROUND

Tiberias – טְבֶרְיָא: Herod Antipas founded the city of Tiberias in the year 18 CE and named it after the Roman emperor Tiberias. The city was initially built on the ruins of a previous settlement. The Sages deliberated with regard to the status of the graves that were located in Tiberias, which apparently prevented priests from settling there. As stated in the Gemara here, according to most opinions the city was founded on the ruins of the settlement Rakkath.

Ginosar – גִּינוֹסַר: Ginosar is the name of a beautiful valley that stretches along the western shore of the Sea of Galilee, north of Tiberias. Josephus describes the area as follows: Its nature is wonderful as well as its beauty; its soil is so fruitful that all sorts of trees can grow upon it, and the inhabitants accordingly plant all sorts of trees there. For the temper of the air is so well mixed that it agrees very well with those several sorts, particularly walnuts, which require the coldest air, and flourish there in vast plenty. There are palm trees also, which grow best in hot air; fig trees also and olives grow near them, which yet require an air that is more temperate. It supplies men with the principal fruits, with grapes and figs continually during ten months of the year and the rest of the fruits as they become ripe together through the whole year; for besides the good temperature of the air, it is also watered from a most fertile fountain (*Wars of the Jews*, Book III, 10:8).

כִּי נָח נַפְשֵׁיהּ דְּרַבִּי זֵירָא פְּתַח עֲלֵיהּ הַהוּא סַפְדָּנָא: אֶרֶץ שִׁנְעָר הָרָה וְיָלְדָה אֶרֶץ צְבִי גִּידְּלָה שַׁעֲשׁוּעֶיהָ, אוֹי נָא לָהּ, אָמְרָה רַקַּת, כִּי אִבְּדָה כְּלִי חֶמְדָּתָהּ.

Similarly, the Gemara relates that **when Rabbi Zeira died, a certain eulogizer opened** his eulogy **for him** with these words: **The land of Shinar,** i.e., Babylonia, Rabbi Zeira's birthplace, **conceived and bore** him; **the land of the deer,** i.e., Eretz Yisrael, where Rabbi Zeira lived as an adult and rose to prominence, **raised her delights. Woe unto her, said Rakkath, for she has lost her precious instrument.** It is apparent from these examples that Rakkath is Tiberias.

אֶלָּא אָמַר (רַבָּה): חַמַּת – זוֹ חַמֵּי גְרָר, רַקַּת זוֹ טְבֶרְיָא, כִּינֶּרֶת – זוֹ גִּינוֹסָר, וְלָמָּה נִקְרָא שְׁמָהּ רַקַּת – שֶׁאֲפִילּוּ רֵיקָנִין שֶׁבָּהּ מְלֵאִין מִצְוֹת כְּרִמּוֹן. רַבִּי יִרְמְיָה אָמַר: רַקַּת שְׁמָהּ וְלָמָּה נִקְרָא שְׁמָהּ טְבֶרְיָא – שֶׁיּוֹשֶׁבֶת בְּטַבּוּרָהּ שֶׁל אֶרֶץ יִשְׂרָאֵל. (רָבָא) אָמַר: רַקַּת שְׁמָהּ, וְלָמָּה נִקְרָא שְׁמָהּ טְבֶרְיָא שֶׁטּוֹבָה רְאִיָּיתָהּ.

Rather, Rabba said: Hammath is the hot springs of Gerar that are adjacent to Tiberias; **Rakkath is Tiberias;** and **Chinnereth is Ginosar. And why was** Tiberias **called Rakkath? Because even the empty ones** [*reikanin*] **of** Tiberias[N] **are** as **full of mitzvot as a pomegranate** is full of seeds. **Rabbi Yirmeya said:** In fact, **Rakkath is its** real **name; and why was it called Tiberias? Because it sits in the** very **center** [*tabbur*] **of Eretz Yisrael. Rava said: Rakkath is its** real **name, and why was it called Tiberias?**[N] **Because its appearance is good** [*tova re'iyyata*].[N]

אָמַר זְעֵירָא: קִטְרוֹן זוֹ צִיפּוֹרִי, וְלָמָּה נִקְרָא שְׁמָהּ צִיפּוֹרִי – שֶׁיּוֹשֶׁבֶת בְּרֹאשׁ הָהָר כְּצִפּוֹר.

§ While continuing to identify places that are mentioned in the Bible, **Zeira said:** The city of **Kitron** that is mentioned in the Bible **is** the city of **Tzippori. And why was it called Tzippori? Because it sits on top of a mountain like a bird** [*tzippor*].

וְקִטְרוֹן צִיפּוֹרִי הִיא? וְהָא קִטְרוֹן בְּחֶלְקוֹ שֶׁל זְבוּלוּן הֲוַאי, דִּכְתִיב: "זְבוּלוּן לֹא הוֹרִישׁ אֶת יוֹשְׁבֵי קִטְרוֹן וְאֶת יוֹשְׁבֵי נַהֲלוֹל". וּזְבוּלוּן מִתְרַעֵם עַל מִדּוֹתָיו הֲוָה, שֶׁנֶּאֱמַר: "זְבוּלוּן עַם חֵרֵף נַפְשׁוֹ לָמוּת" מַה טַּעַם – מִשּׁוּם דְּ"נַפְתָּלִי עַל מְרוֹמֵי שָׂדֶה".

The Gemara asks: **Is Kitron** really **Tzippori? Wasn't Kitron in the** tribal **territory of Zebulun, as it is written: "Neither did Zebulun drive out the inhabitants of Kitron, nor the inhabitants of Nahalol"** (Judges 1:30)? **And** the tribe of **Zebulun was resentful of its portion, as it is stated: "Zebulun was a people that jeopardized their lives to the death"** (Judges 5:18).[N] **What is the reason** for their resentfulness? **Because "Naphtali was on the high places of the field"** (Judges 5:18).

אָמַר זְבוּלוּן לִפְנֵי הַקָּדוֹשׁ בָּרוּךְ הוּא: רִבּוֹנוֹ שֶׁל עוֹלָם! לְאַחַיי נָתַתָּ לָהֶם שָׂדוֹת וּכְרָמִים וְלִי נָתַתָּ הָרִים וּגְבָעוֹת, לְאַחַיי נָתַתָּ לָהֶם אֲרָצוֹת וְלִי נָתַתָּ יַמִּים וּנְהָרוֹת. אָמַר לוֹ: כּוּלָּן צְרִיכִין לְךָ עַל יְדֵי חִלָּזוֹן, שֶׁנֶּאֱמַר: "[עַמִּים הַר יִקְרָאוּ] וּשְׂפוּנֵי טְמוּנֵי חוֹל".

The verse should be interpreted as follows: **Zebulun said before the Holy One, Blessed be He: Master of the Universe! To my brothers,** the tribes whose territory is adjacent to mine, **You gave fields and vineyards, whereas to me You gave mountains and hills; to my brothers You gave lands, whereas to me You gave seas and rivers.** God **said** back **to him:** Nevertheless, **all will need you due to the *ḥilazon*,** the small sea creature residing in your territory that is the source of the dye used in the ritual fringes [*tzitzit*]. **As it is stated** in Moses' blessing to Zebulun: **"They shall call the people to the mountain:** There they shall sacrifice offerings of righteousness; for they shall suck of the abundance of the seas, and of the hidden treasures of the sand" (Deuteronomy 33:19).

NOTES

Even the empty ones of Tiberias – אֲפִילּוּ רֵיקָנִין שֶׁבָּהּ: The author of *Turei Even* asked why this is applied specifically to Tiberias here in the Gemara, when elsewhere (see *Berakhot* 57a) this is said of the entire Jewish people. It would appear that Rabba emphasized in this Gemara that this was even more true of Tiberias due to the city's unique position as the religious capital of Eretz Yisrael for many generations. Even during the time of Rav Sa'adia Gaon it was considered an important religious center. Additionally, the vowel notation system for the Hebrew language that is used today was developed in Tiberias.

Why was it called Tiberias – לָמָּה נִקְרָא שְׁמָהּ טְבֶרְיָא: It is certainly well known that the city is named for the Roman emperor Tiberias. Nevertheless, the name of the city was interpreted homiletically in the same manner that other foreign words in Hebrew are interpreted, in order to learn additional ideas.

Because its appearance [*re'iyyata*] is good – שֶׁטּוֹבָה רְאִיָּיתָהּ: *Tosafot* explain that the city was aesthetically pleasing. The Maharsha explains that this phrase should be interpreted to mean that Tiberias was the seat of the Great Sanhedrin for a time, and the Sages who resided there could perceive things that others could not; according to this, the word *re'iyyata* is to be interpreted: Its vision. Others write that since Tiberias did not have a wall on the side that bordered the sea, it offered a view of distant places (see *Ramat Shmuel*).

Jeopardized their lives to the death – חֵרֵף נַפְשׁוֹ לָמוּת: The interpretation of this verse indicates that it was as if the members of the tribe of Zebulun wanted to die because they were angered over the shortcomings of their portion. The Maharsha writes that during the war against enemy forces commanded by Sisera, about which this verse is written, the people of Zebulun passed through Naphtali's portion and compared it to their unfertile land. However, the simple explanation of this verse is that because Zebulun had meager land, and the gentiles did not let them spread out, they fought harder in the war and risked their lives.

תָּנֵי רַב יוֹסֵף: ״שְׂפוּנֵי״ – זֶה חִלָּזוֹן, ״טְמוּנֵי״ – זוֹ טָרִית, ״חוֹל״ – זוֹ זְכוּכִית לְבָנָה. אָמַר לְפָנָיו: רִבּוֹנוֹ שֶׁל עוֹלָם מִי מוֹדִיעֵנִי? אָמַר לוֹ: ״שָׁם יִזְבְּחוּ זִבְחֵי צֶדֶק״ סִימָן זֶה יְהֵא לְךָ: כָּל הַנּוֹטֵל מִמְּךָ בְּלֹא דָמִים – אֵינוֹ מוֹעִיל בְּפַרְקְמַטְיָא שֶׁלּוֹ כְּלוּם.

Rav Yosef teaches about this: **"Treasures"; this is** referring to **the *ḥilazon*,**[B] which is found in the waters of Zebulun. **"Hidden"; this is** referring to the ***tarit*,**[B] a type of sardine, which is also found in Zebulun's coastal waters. **"Sand"; this is** referring to the sand from which **white glass**[B] is made. Zebulun **said to Him:** All of these resources are indeed found in my territory, but **Master of the Universe, who will inform me** if others take them without permission? **He said to** the tribe of Zebulun: **"There they shall sacrifice offerings of righteousness." This shall be a sign for you** that **anyone who takes** these items **from you without** making **payment will not prosper at all in his business.**

וְאִי סָלְקָא דַּעְתָּךְ קִטְרוֹן זוֹ צִיפּוֹרִי, אַמַּאי מִתְרַעֵם עַל מִדּוֹתָיו? וְהָא הָוְיָא צִיפּוֹרִי, מִילְּתָא דַּעֲדִיפָא טוּבָא! וְכִי תֵּימָא דְּלֵית בָּהּ זָבַת חָלָב וּדְבַשׁ – וְהָאָמַר רֵישׁ לָקִישׁ: לְדִידִי חֲזֵי לִי זָבַת חָלָב וּדְבַשׁ דְּצִיפּוֹרִי, וַהֲוָיָא שִׁשָּׁה עָשָׂר מִיל עַל שִׁשָּׁה עָשָׂר מִיל!

It is clear from the exposition of the verse in Judges that the territory of Zebulun did not contain fields and vineyards. **And if it enters your mind** to say that **Kitron is Tzippori, why was** Zebulun **resentful of his portion? Wasn't Tzippori** in his territory, which was land that was **vastly superior** with regard to its produce? **And if you would say that** Zebulun's portion **did not have** quality land **flowing with milk and honey, didn't Reish Lakish say: I myself have seen** the land **flowing with milk and honey** around **Tzippori, and it was sixteen *mil* by sixteen *mil*?**

וְכִי תֵּימָא: דְּלָא נְפִישָׁא דִּידֵיהּ כְּדַאֲחוּהּ – וְהָאָמַר רַבָּה בַּר בַּר חָנָה אָמַר רַבִּי יוֹחָנָן: לְדִידִי חֲזֵי לִי זָבַת חָלָב וּדְבַשׁ דְּכָל אַרְעָא דְּיִשְׂרָאֵל וַהֲוָיָא כְּמִבֵּי כּוֹבֵי עַד אַקְרָא דְּתוּלְבַּקְנִי – עֶשְׂרִין וְתַרְתֵּין פַּרְסֵי אוּרְכָּא, וּפוּתְיָא שִׁיתָּא פַּרְסֵי!

And if you would say that the part of **his** territory that flowed with milk and honey **was not as vast as** that of **his brothers,** the other tribes, **didn't Rabba bar bar Ḥana** say that **Rabbi Yoḥanan said: I myself have seen** the land **flowing with milk and honey** over **all of Eretz Yisrael. And** the size of the fertile land **was like** the distance **from Bei Kovei to the fortress of Tulbakni,** a total of **twenty-two parasangs [*parsa*] in length and six parasangs in width.** A parasang is four *mil*; consequently, the area flowing with milk and honey around Tzippori was four by four parasangs, which is more than the fair share of one tribe among twelve.

אֲפִילּוּ הָכִי שָׂדוֹת וּכְרָמִים עֲדִיפָא לֵיהּ. דַּיְקָא נַמִי, דִּכְתִיב: ״וְנַפְתָּלִי עַל מְרוֹמֵי שָׂדֶה״, שְׁמַע מִינָּהּ.

The Gemara answers: **Even so, fields and vineyards were preferable to** Zebulun. The fertile land in Zebulun's territory is in a mountainous region, which makes it more difficult to cultivate. The Gemara comments: The language of the verse **is also precise** according to this explanation, **as it is written: "And Naphtali was on the high places of the field,"** which indicates that Zebulun's complaint was due to the fact that Naphtali had fields. The Gemara concludes: Indeed, **learn from here** that this is so.

BACKGROUND

Ḥilazon – חִלָּזוֹן: Although there are many opinions as to the identity of the *ḥilazon*, many researchers are of the opinion that it refers to the *Murex trunculus*, a tropical sea snail. Others have suggested the common cuttlefish, *Sepia officinalis*, or the bubble raft snail, *Janthina janthina*. The sky blue [*tekhelet*] dye used for the mitzva to place a sky blue thread on the ritual fringes is extracted from the *ḥilazon*. Purple dye [*argaman*] is also produced from the *ḥilazon*, and both of these dyes were needed for the priestly clothes.

Murex trunculus

Common cuttlefish

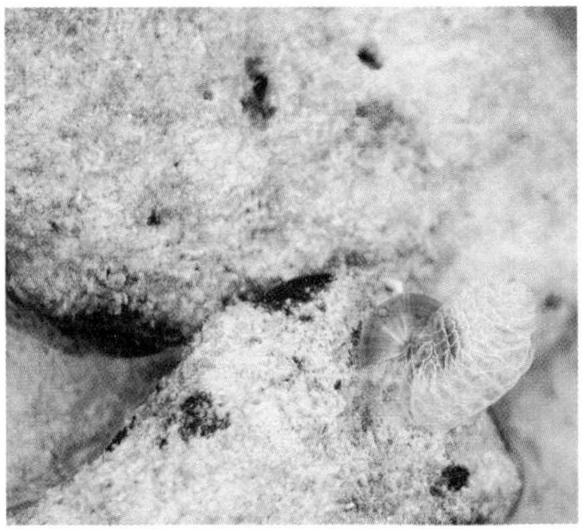

Bubble raft snail

BACKGROUND

Tarit – טָרִית: The *tarit*, *Sardinella aurita*, also known as the round sardinella, is a species of sardine that is commonly eaten salted. It is found in vast numbers in the Mediterranean Sea and is listed among the items with which the coasts of Eretz Yisrael are blessed.

Round sardinella

White glass – זְכוּכִית לְבָנָה: Glass is usually made from a mixture of several silicates, most of which are ubiquitous to sea sand. However, it is difficult to find a suitable mixture of silicates that will be easy to fuse and will not have any metallic substances that give it color. White glass is either completely transparent or white and was very expensive in ancient times.

Ancient glass vessels

אָמַר רַבִּי אַבָּהוּ: ״וְעֶקְרוֹן תֵּעָקֵר״ – זוֹ קֵסָרִי בַּת אֱדוֹם, שֶׁהִיא יוֹשֶׁבֶת בֵּין הַחוֹלוֹת, וְהִיא הָיְתָה יָתֵד תְּקוּעָה לְיִשְׂרָאֵל בִּימֵי יְוָנִים, וּכְשֶׁגָּבְרָה מַלְכוּת בֵּית חַשְׁמוֹנַאי וְנִצְּחוּם הָיוּ קוֹרִין אוֹתָהּ אֲחִידַת מִגְדַּל שִׁיר.

§ The Gemara continues its discussion with regard to identifying places mentioned in the Bible. **Rabbi Abbahu said: "And Ekron shall be uprooted"** (Zephaniah 2:4). **This is** an allusion to **Caesarea,**[B] **daughter of Edom, which is situated among the sands.** Caesarea was primarily populated by Greeks and Romans, and it served as the seat of Roman rule when the Romans, who are identified with Edom in Jewish literature, ruled Eretz Yisrael. **And it was a spike stuck in** the side of **the Jewish people** already **in the days of the Greeks,** as it was an obstacle to the spread of Jewish settlement. **When the Hasmonean monarchy prevailed and triumphed over them, they called it: The captured tower of Shir.**

אָמַר רַבִּי יוֹסֵי בַּר חֲנִינָא, מַאי דִּכְתִיב: ״וַהֲסִירוֹתִי דָמָיו מִפִּיו וְשִׁקּוּצָיו מִבֵּין שִׁנָּיו וְנִשְׁאַר גַּם הוּא לֵאלֹהֵינוּ״, ״וַהֲסִירוֹתִי דָמָיו מִפִּיו״ – זֶה בֵּית בַּמְיָא שֶׁלָּהֶן, ״וְשִׁקּוּצָיו מִבֵּין שִׁנָּיו״ זֶה בֵּית גַּלְיָא שֶׁלָּהֶן,

Rabbi Yosei bar Ḥanina said: What is the meaning of that **which is written: "And I will take away his blood out of his mouth, and his detestable things from between his teeth, and he also shall be a remnant for our God;** and he shall be as a chief in Judah, and Ekron as a Jebusite" (Zechariah 9:7)? The verse should be understood as follows: **"And I will take away his blood out of his mouth"; this is** referring to **their house of altars,** where they sacrifice offerings. **"And his detestable things from between his teeth"; this is** referring to **their house of piles,** where they heap their ritual stones.

״וְנִשְׁאַר גַּם הוּא לֵאלֹהֵינוּ״ – אֵלּוּ בָּתֵּי כְנֵסִיּוֹת וּבָתֵּי מִדְרָשׁוֹת שֶׁבֶּאֱדוֹם. ״וְהָיָה כְּאַלֻּף בִּיהוּדָה וְעֶקְרוֹן כִּיבוּסִי״ – אֵלּוּ תְּרֵאַטְרָיוֹת וְקִרְקְסָיוֹת שֶׁבֶּאֱדוֹם שֶׁעֲתִידִין שָׂרֵי יְהוּדָה לְלַמֵּד בָּהֶן תּוֹרָה בָּרַבִּים.

"And he also shall be a remnant for our God," these words **are** referring to **the synagogues and study halls in Edom. "And he shall be as a chief** [*aluf*] **in Judah,**[N] **and Ekron as a Jebusite,"** these words **are** referring to **the theaters** [*tere'atrayot*][L] **and the circuses** [*kirkesayot*][L] **in Edom where the officers of Judah are destined to teach Torah in public.**

אָמַר רַבִּי יִצְחָק: לֶשֶׁם – זוֹ פַּמְיָיס, עֶקְרוֹן תֵּעָקֵר – זוֹ קֵסָרִי בַּת אֱדוֹם, שֶׁהִיא הָיְתָה מֶטְרוֹפּוֹלִין שֶׁל מְלָכִים. אִיכָּא דְּאָמְרִי: דִּמְרַבֵּי בָּהּ מַלְכֵי, וְאִיכָּא דְּאָמְרִי: דְּמוֹקְמִי מִינָּהּ מַלְכֵי.

Rabbi Yitzḥak said: "And the children of Dan went up and fought against **Leshem"** (Joshua 19:47); **this is** referring to the city that was known in the Talmudic period as **Pamyas. "Ekron shall be uprooted"** (Zephaniah 2:4); **this is** referring to **Caesarea, the daughter of Edom, which was a metropolis** [*metropolin*],[L] i.e., a capital city, **of kings. There are** those **who say** this means **that kings were raised there, and there are** those **who say** it means **that kings were appointed from there,** meaning the kings of Edom were appointed from among the residents of this city.

קֵסָרִי וִירוּשָׁלַיִם, אִם יֹאמַר לְךָ אָדָם: חָרְבוּ שְׁתֵּיהֶן – אַל תַּאֲמֵן, יָשְׁבוּ שְׁתֵּיהֶן – אַל תַּאֲמֵן. חָרְבָה קֵסָרִי וְיָשְׁבָה יְרוּשָׁלַיִם, חָרְבָה יְרוּשָׁלַיִם וְיָשְׁבָה קֵסָרִי – תַּאֲמֵן. שֶׁנֶּאֱמַר ״אִמָּלְאָה הָחֳרָבָה״: אִם מְלֵיאָה זוֹ – חֲרֵבָה זוֹ. אִם מְלֵיאָה זוֹ חֲרֵבָה זוֹ.

The Sages said that the fortunes of **Caesarea,** which represents Rome, **and Jerusalem** are diametric opposites. **If,** therefore, **someone says to you** that **both** cities **are destroyed, do not believe** him. Similarly, if he says to you that **they are both settled** in tranquility, **do not believe** him. If, however, he says to you that **Caesarea is destroyed and Jerusalem is settled,** or that **Jerusalem is destroyed and Caesarea is settled, believe** him. **As it is stated:** "Because Tyre has said against Jerusalem: Aha, the gates of the people have been broken; she is turned to me; **I shall be filled with her that is laid waste"** (Ezekiel 26:2), and Tyre, like Caesarea, represents Rome. Consequently, the verse indicates that **if this** city **is filled, that one is laid waste,** and **if** that city **is filled, this one is laid waste.** The two cities cannot coexist.

BACKGROUND

Caesarea – קֵסָרִי: The city Caesarea was established around the beginning of the Second Temple period by the king of Sidon, Straton, who named it for himself, *Pyrgos Stratonos*, Straton's Tower. In Jewish sources it is referred to as the Tower of Sharshon or the Tower of Shir. Throughout the generations its importance decreased, and Alexander Jannaeus conquered it and annexed it to the land of Judah. In honor of his victory, a holiday was recorded in *Megillat Ta'anit*. From the outset, Caesarea had a very strong gentile and idolatrous character, which remained even after King Herod rebuilt and improved the city.

When the Roman governors started to rule over the land of Israel (6 CE) they turned Caesarea into their administrative center, and the city rapidly developed. The rivalry and animosity that existed between Jerusalem, as the symbol of Jewish independence and rule, and Caesarea, as the center of the gentile government, are apparent in the words of the Sages here. With the destruction of the Temple and Jerusalem, Caesarea became even more prominent and served as the capital of the land until the Moslem conquest. The city continued to be an important and rich city until its destruction in the thirteenth century.

Amphitheater in Caesarea

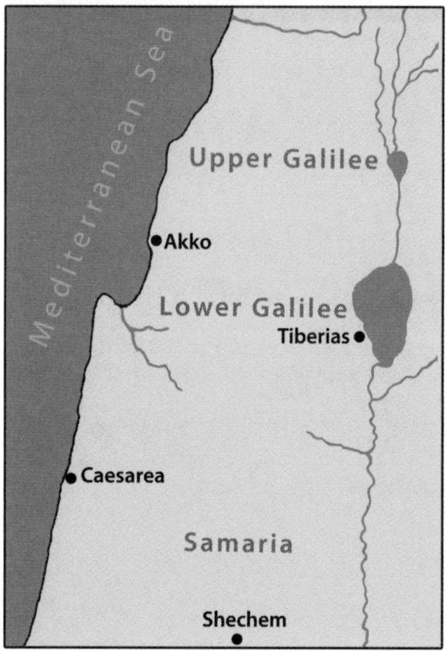

Location of Caesarea

NOTES

As a chief [*aluf*] in Judah – כְּאַלֻּף בִּיהוּדָה: There is a double interpretation of the word *aluf*. In the simple meaning of the verse it refers to the chiefs of Judah, while at the same time there is a play on the Aramaic root *yalaf*, meaning to teach.

LANGUAGE

Theaters [*tere'atrayot*] – תְּרֵאַטְרָיוֹת: This is one of the forms in which the Greek word θέατρον, *theatron*, meaning theater, is written. In the contemporary meaning of the word, it refers to a place for performances and games.

Circus [*kirkesayot*] – קִרְקְסָיוֹת: From the Latin circus, or the Greek κίρκος, *kirkos*, meaning a place in which various competitions take place.

Metropolis [*metropolin*] – מֶטְרוֹפּוֹלִין: From the Greek μητρόπολις, *metropolis*. The literal translation of this word is mother city, meaning the main city or the capital.

רַב נַחְמָן בַּר יִצְחָק אָמַר, מֵהָכָא: ״וּלְאוֹם מִלְאוֹם יֶאֱמָץ״.

Rav Naḥman bar Yitzḥak said: The same idea may be derived **from here,** a verse dealing with Jacob and Esau: **"And the one people shall be stronger than the other people"** (Genesis 25:23), teaching that when one nation rises, the other necessarily falls.

וְאָמַר רַבִּי יִצְחָק, מַאי דִּכְתִיב: ״יוּחַן רָשָׁע בַּל לָמַד צֶדֶק״. אָמַר יִצְחָק לִפְנֵי הַקָּדוֹשׁ בָּרוּךְ הוּא רִבּוֹנוֹ שֶׁל עוֹלָם, יוּחַן עֵשָׂו! אָמַר לוֹ: רָשָׁע הוּא. אָמַר לוֹ: ״בַּל לָמַד צֶדֶק״? אָמַר לוֹ: ״בְּאֶרֶץ נְכוֹחוֹת יְעַוֵּל״. אָמַר לוֹ: אִם כֵּן ״בַּל יִרְאֶה גֵּאוּת ה׳״.

§ Having mentioned Edom, the Gemara cites what **Rabbi Yitzḥak said: What is** the meaning of that **which is written: "Let favor be shown to the wicked, yet will he not learn righteousness;** in the land of uprightness he will deal wrongfully, and will not behold the majesty of the Lord" (Isaiah 26:10)? **Isaac said before the Holy One, Blessed be He: Master of the Universe, let favor be shown to Esau,** my beloved son. God **said to him:** Esau **is wicked.** Isaac **said to** God: **"Yet will he not learn righteousness,"**[N] i.e., is there no one who can find merit in him? God **said to him: "In the land of uprightness he will deal wrongfully,"** meaning that he is destined to destroy Eretz Yisrael. Isaac **said to** God: **If** it is **so** that he is that wicked, **"he will not behold the majesty of the Lord."**

וְאָמַר רַבִּי יִצְחָק, מַאי דִּכְתִיב: ״אַל תִּתֵּן ה׳ מַאֲוַיֵּי רָשָׁע זְמָמוֹ אַל תָּפֵק יָרוּמוּ סֶלָה״. אָמַר יַעֲקֹב לִפְנֵי הַקָּדוֹשׁ בָּרוּךְ הוּא: רִבּוֹנוֹ שֶׁל עוֹלָם, אַל תִּתֵּן לְעֵשָׂו הָרָשָׁע תַּאֲוַת לִבּוֹ. ״זְמָמוֹ אַל תָּפֵק״ – זוֹ

And Rabbi Yitzḥak also **said: What is** the meaning of that **which is written: "Grant not, O Lord, the desires of the wicked; further not his evil device, so that they not exalt themselves. Selah"** (Psalms 140:9)? **Jacob said before the Holy One, Blessed be He: Master of the Universe, grant not to the wicked Esau the desires of his heart,** as he wishes to destroy us. **Further not his evil device** [***zemamo***]; do not remove the muzzle [*zamam*] that constrains him and prevents him from breaking out and gathering further strength. **This is** a reference to

NOTES

Yet will he not learn righteousness – **בַּל לָמַד צֶדֶק**: Some interpret this phrase as a statement, not a question, and explain it as follows: For Esau did not learn righteousness, i.e., Esau did not study Torah. Therefore, perhaps his evil actions were unintentional and he should be forgiven (Rabbi Yoshiya Pinto; Maharsha). In the midrash, this question is explained differently: Did he not learn righteousness? He would certainly diligently observe the commandments of honoring one's father.

Perek **I**
Daf **6** Amud **b**

גֶּרְמַמְיָא שֶׁל אֱדוֹם, שֶׁאִלְמָלֵי הֵן יוֹצְאִין מַחְרִיבִין כָּל הָעוֹלָם כּוּלּוֹ.

Germamya of Edom,[B] i.e., Germany, which is near the land of Edom, i.e., Rome. **As, if** the Germans **would go forth, they would destroy the entire world.**

וְאָמַר רַבִּי חָמָא בַּר חֲנִינָא: תְּלָת מְאָה קְטִירֵי תָּגָא אִיכָּא בְּגֶרְמַמְיָא שֶׁל אֱדוֹם, וּתְלָת מְאָה וְשִׁיתִּין וַחֲמִשָּׁה מַרְזְבָנֵי אִיכָּא בְּרוֹמִי. וּבְכָל יוֹמָא נָפְקִי הָנֵי לְאַפֵּי הָנֵי וּמִקְטִיל חַד מִינַּיְיהוּ וּמִיטַּרְדִי לְאוֹקְמֵי מַלְכָּא.

And Rabbi Ḥama Bar Ḥanina said: There are three hundred young princes with **crowns tied** to their heads **in Germamya of Edom, and there are three hundred and sixty-five chieftains** [***marzavnei***][L] **in Rome. Every day these go out** to battle **against those, and one of them is killed, and they are preoccupied with appointing a** new **king** in his place. Since neither side is united, neither side is able to achieve a decisive victory. It is these wars between Rome and the Germanic tribes that act as a muzzle upon Esau-Edom-Rome and prevent it from becoming too strong.

וְאָמַר רַבִּי יִצְחָק, אִם יֹאמַר לְךָ אָדָם: יָגַעְתִּי וְלֹא מָצָאתִי – אַל תַּאֲמֵן, לֹא יָגַעְתִּי וּמָצָאתִי – אַל תַּאֲמֵן, יָגַעְתִּי וּמָצָאתִי – תַּאֲמֵן.

§ **Rabbi Yitzḥak**[P] **said** in the style of a previous passage: **If a person says to you: I have labored and not found** success,[N] **do not believe** him. Similarly, if he says to you: **I have not labored** but nevertheless **I have found** success,[N] **do not believe** him. If, however, he says to you: **I have labored and I have found** success,[N] **believe** him.

BACKGROUND

Germamya of Edom – **גֶּרְמַמְיָא שֶׁל אֱדוֹם**: In the Gemara's description, there is an indication of one of the essential problems of the Roman Empire: Its relations with the various German tribes. The Germans were divided into a large number of tribes and each one had its own minor king, to whom the Gemara alluded as princes with crowns tied to their heads. The wars with the Germans, which continued intermittently for hundreds of years, depleted the strength of the Roman Empire, until eventually it was conquered by the Germans.

LANGUAGE

Chieftains [*marzavnei*] – **מַרְזְבָנֵי**: From the Middle Persian marzbān, meaning border guard.

PERSONALITIES

Rabbi Yitzḥak – **רַבִּי יִצְחָק**: There were two *amora'im* by this name who lived in Eretz Yisrael at the same time, both of whom were students of Rabbi Yoḥanan. One of these Sages was known for his erudition in Jewish law; while the other, who is, apparently, the individual quoted in our Gemara, focused on *aggada*. It appears that Rabbi Yitzḥak spent significant time in Babylonia and brought many teachings of Eretz Yisrael to the Diaspora community, in particular the teachings of Rabbi Yoḥanan. His aggadic interpretations appear throughout the Babylonian Talmud, and several Babylonian Sages cite teachings in his name.

NOTES

I have labored and not found success – **יָגַעְתִּי וְלֹא מָצָאתִי**: This man claims that he has labored but has not found success. He does not realize that laboring in Torah is success (*Bina Lelttim*).

I have not labored but I have found success – **לֹא יָגַעְתִּי וּמָצָאתִי**: The Torah one attains without effort is certainly lacking. Therefore, one should not believe he has attained true Torah.

I have labored and I have found success – **יָגַעְתִּי וּמָצָאתִי**: The Maharsha writes that this is indicated in the verses: "I trusted even when I spoke, I am greatly afflicted. I said in my haste, all men are liars." (Psalms 116:10–11). "I am greatly afflicted" is an indication of the labor and "I said in my haste" relates to not despairing of the effort.

NOTES

Provoking the wicked – לְהִתְגָּרוֹת בָּרְשָׁעִים: According to the *ge'onim*, it should not be learned from here that one should engage in idle flattery of the wicked. Rather, if one sees a wicked man who is having good fortune, he is permitted to abstain from ruling his case so that he will not be harmed. However, after the trial has started, he may not abstain. See tractate *Berakhot* (7b), where it concludes that one who is not totally righteous should not contend at all with a wicked man who is having good fortune.

הָנֵי מִילֵּי – בְּדִבְרֵי תוֹרָה, אֲבָל בְּמַשָּׂא וּמַתָּן – סִיַּיעְתָּא הוּא מִן שְׁמַיָּא. וּלְדִבְרֵי תוֹרָה לֹא אֲמַרַן אֶלָּא לְחַדּוּדֵי, אֲבָל לְאוֹקְמֵי גִּירְסָא – סִיַּיעְתָּא מִן שְׁמַיָּא הִיא.

The Gemara comments: **This applies** only **to matters of Torah,** as success with respect to Torah study is in accordance with the toil and effort invested. **But with regard to** success in **business, it** all depends upon **assistance from Heaven,** as there is no correlation between success and effort. **And** even **with regard to matters of Torah, we said** this **only with regard to sharpening** one's understanding of Torah, as the more one labors, the deeper the understanding of the material he achieves. **However, to preserve what one has learned,** it is dependent upon **assistance from Heaven.** Not everyone achieves this, even with much effort.

וְאָמַר רַבִּי יִצְחָק: אִם רָאִיתָ רָשָׁע שֶׁהַשָּׁעָה מְשַׂחֶקֶת לוֹ – אַל תִּתְגָּרֶה בּוֹ, שֶׁנֶּאֱמַר: "אַל תִּתְחַר בַּמְּרֵעִים", וְלֹא עוֹד אֶלָּא שֶׁדְּרָכָיו מַצְלִיחִין, שֶׁנֶּאֱמַר: "יָחִילוּ דְרָכָיו בְּכָל עֵת", וְלֹא עוֹד אֶלָּא שֶׁזּוֹכֶה בַּדִּין, שֶׁנֶּאֱמַר: "מָרוֹם מִשְׁפָּטֶיךָ מִנֶּגְדּוֹ", וְלֹא עוֹד אֶלָּא שֶׁרוֹאֶה בְּשׂוֹנְאָיו, שֶׁנֶּאֱמַר: "כָּל צוֹרְרָיו יָפִיחַ בָּהֶם".

And Rabbi Yitzḥak also **said: If you see a wicked man whom the hour is smiling upon,** i.e., who is enjoying good fortune, **do not provoke him,**[N] **as it is stated: "Contend not with evildoers"** (Psalms 37:1). **And not only that, but** if you provoke him, **his undertakings will be successful, as it is stated: "His ways prosper at all times"** (Psalms 10:5). **And not only that, but** even if he is brought to court, **he emerges victorious in judgment, as it is stated: "Your judgments are far above him"** (Psalms 10:5), as though the trial is far removed from him and does not affect him. **And not only that, but he will see his enemies** fall, **as it is stated: "As for all his enemies, he hisses at them"** (Psalms 10:5).

אִינִי? וְהָאָמַר רַבִּי יוֹחָנָן מִשּׁוּם רַבִּי שִׁמְעוֹן בֶּן יוֹחַי: מוּתָּר לְהִתְגָּרוֹת בָּרְשָׁעִים בָּעוֹלָם הַזֶּה, שֶׁנֶּאֱמַר: "עוֹזְבֵי תוֹרָה יְהַלְלוּ רָשָׁע וְשׁוֹמְרֵי תוֹרָה יִתְגָּרוּ בָם". וְתַנְיָא, רַבִּי דּוֹסְתַּאי בַּר מָתוּן אָמַר: מוּתָּר לְהִתְגָּרוֹת בָּרְשָׁעִים בָּעוֹלָם הַזֶּה וְאִם לְחָשְׁךָ אָדָם לוֹמַר: "אַל תִּתְחַר בַּמְּרֵעִים וְאַל תְּקַנֵּא בְּעוֹשֵׂי עַוְלָה" – מִי שֶׁלִּבּוֹ נוֹקְפוֹ אוֹמֵר כֵּן.

The Gemara asks: **Is that so? Didn't Rabbi Yoḥanan say in the name of Rabbi Shimon ben Yoḥai: It is permitted to provoke the wicked in this world, as it is stated: "They that forsake the Torah praise the wicked; but they who keep the Torah contend with them"** (Proverbs 28:4)? **And** furthermore, **it is taught** in a *baraita* that **Rabbi Dostai bar Matun said: It is permitted to provoke the wicked in this world, and if a person whispers to you to say** that this is not so, relying on the verse: **"Contend not with evildoers, nor be envious against the workers of iniquity"** (Psalms 37:1), know that only **one whose heart strikes him** with pangs of conscience over sins that he committed **says this.**

אֶלָּא: "אַל תִּתְחַר בַּמְּרֵעִים" – לִהְיוֹת כַּמְּרֵעִים, "וְאַל תְּקַנֵּא בְּעוֹשֵׂי עַוְלָה" – לִהְיוֹת כְּעוֹשֵׂי עַוְלָה. וְאוֹמֵר: "אַל יְקַנֵּא לִבְּךָ בַּחַטָּאִים" וגו׳!

Rather, the true meaning of that verse is: **"Contend not with evildoers," to be like the evildoers; "nor be envious against the workers of iniquity," to be like the workers of iniquity. And it says** elsewhere: **"Let not your heart envy sinners,** but be in the fear of the Lord all the day" (Proverbs 23:17). In this context, to be envious of sinners means to desire to be like them. Rabbi Yoḥanan and Rabbi Dostai indicate that one is permitted to provoke the wicked, against the opinion of Rabbi Yitzḥak.

לָא קַשְׁיָא: הָא – בְּמִילֵּי דִּידֵיהּ, הָא – בְּמִילֵּי דִּשְׁמַיָּא.

The Gemara explains: This is **not difficult,** as it can be understood that **this,** Rabbi Yitzḥak's statement that one may not provoke the wicked, is referring **to his** personal **matters,** while **that,** the statements of Rabbi Yoḥanan and Rabbi Dostai that it is permitted to provoke them, is referring **to matters of Heaven,** i.e., religious matters.

וְאִיבָּעֵית אֵימָא: הָא וְהָא בְּמִילֵּי דִּידֵיהּ, וְלָא קַשְׁיָא: הָא – בְּצַדִּיק גָּמוּר, הָא – בְּצַדִּיק שֶׁאֵינוֹ גָּמוּר. דְּאָמַר רַב הוּנָא, מַאי דִּכְתִיב: "לָמָּה תַבִּיט בּוֹגְדִים תַּחֲרִישׁ בְּבַלַּע רָשָׁע צַדִּיק מִמֶּנּוּ" – צַדִּיק מִמֶּנּוּ – בּוֹלֵעַ, צַדִּיק גָּמוּר – אֵינוֹ בּוֹלֵעַ.

And if you wish, say: Both **this** statement **and that** statement are stated **with regard to his own affairs, and** still it is **not difficult. This** statement, that it is permitted to provoke the wicked, **applies to a completely righteous** individual; **that** statement, that one may not provoke them, **applies to** an individual **who is not completely righteous. As Rav Huna said: What is** the meaning of that **which is written: "Why do you look upon them that deal treacherously, and remain silent when the wicked devours the man that is more righteous than he"** (Habakkuk 1:13)? This verse indicates that the wicked **devours one who is more righteous than he;** however, **he does not devour one who is completely righteous.**

וְאִי בָּעֵית אֵימָא: שָׁעָה מְשַׂחֶקֶת לוֹ שָׁאנֵי.

And if you wish, say instead: When the **hour is smiling upon him,** i.e., when the wicked individual is enjoying good fortune, it **is different.** He is receiving divine assistance, and even the completely righteous should not provoke him.

אָמַר עוּלָּא: אִיטַלְיָא שֶׁל יָוָן זֶה כְּרַךְ גָּדוֹל שֶׁל רוֹמִי. וְהָוְיָא תְּלָת מְאָה פַּרְסָה עַל תְּלָת מְאָה פַּרְסָה, וְיֵשׁ בָּהּ שְׁלֹשׁ מֵאוֹת שִׁשִּׁים וַחֲמִשָּׁה שְׁווּקִים כְּמִנְיַן יְמוֹת הַחַמָּה, וְקָטָן שֶׁבְּכוּלָּם שֶׁל מוֹכְרֵי עוֹפוֹת, וְהָוְיָא שִׁשָּׁה עָשָׂר מִיל עַל שִׁשָּׁה עָשָׂר מִיל. וּמֶלֶךְ סוֹעֵד בְּכָל יוֹם בְּאֶחָד מֵהֶן.

§ Having mentioned Rome, the Gemara cites what **Ulla said. Greek Italy,**[B] i.e., southern Italy, **is the great city of Rome,**[N] **and it is three hundred parasang [*parsa*] by three hundred parasang. It has three hundred and sixty-five markets, corresponding to the number of days in the solar** year, **and the smallest of them all is** the market **of poultry sellers,** which **is sixteen *mil* by sixteen *mil*. And the king,** i.e., the Roman emperor, **dines every day in one of them.**

וְהַדָּר בָּהּ אַף עַל פִּי שֶׁאֵינוֹ נוֹלָד בָּהּ – נוֹטֵל פְּרָס מִבֵּית הַמֶּלֶךְ וְהַנּוֹלָד בָּהּ אַף עַל פִּי שֶׁאֵינוֹ דָּר בָּהּ – נוֹטֵל פְּרָס מִבֵּית הַמֶּלֶךְ וּשְׁלֹשֶׁת אֲלָפִים בֵּי בָנֵי יֵשׁ בּוֹ, וַחֲמֵשׁ מֵאוֹת חַלּוֹנוֹת מַעֲלִין עָשָׁן חוּץ לַחוֹמָה. צִדּוֹ אֶחָד יָם וְצִדּוֹ אֶחָד הָרִים וּגְבָעוֹת, צִדּוֹ אֶחָד מְחִיצָה שֶׁל בַּרְזֶל, וְצִדּוֹ אֶחָד חוּלְסִית וּמְצוּלָה.

And one who resides in the city, **even if he was not born there, receives an allowance** for his living expenses **from the king's palace. And one who was born there, even if he does not reside there,** also **receives an allowance from the king's palace. And there are three thousand bathhouses in** the city, **and five hundred apertures that let the smoke** from the bathhouses **out beyond the walls** in a way that doesn't blacken the walls themselves. **One side** of the city is bordered by the **sea, one side** by **mountains and hills, one side by a barrier of iron and one side** by **gravel [*ḥulsit*]**[L] **and swamp.**

מתני׳ קָרְאוּ אֶת הַמְּגִילָּה בַּאֲדָר הָרִאשׁוֹן וְנִתְעַבְּרָה הַשָּׁנָה – קוֹרִין אוֹתָהּ בַּאֲדָר שֵׁנִי. אֵין בֵּין אֲדָר הָרִאשׁוֹן לַאֲדָר הַשֵּׁנִי אֶלָּא קְרִיאַת הַמְּגִילָּה וּמַתָּנוֹת לָאֶבְיוֹנִים.

MISHNA If the people **read the Megilla during the first Adar**[H] **and** subsequently **the year was** then **intercalated**[N] by the court and now the following month will be the second Adar, **one reads** the Megilla again **during the second Adar.** The Sages formulated a principle: **The difference between the first Adar and the second Adar** with regard to the mitzvot that are performed during those months **is only** that **the reading of the Megilla and** distributing **gifts to the poor** are performed in the second Adar and not in the first Adar.

גמ׳ הָא לְעִנְיַן סֵדֶר פָּרָשִׁיּוֹת – זֶה וָזֶה שָׁוִין.

GEMARA The Gemara infers **that with regard to the matter of the sequence of** Torah **portions** read each year on two *Shabbatot* before Purim, the portions of *Shekalim* and *Zakhor*, and on two *Shabbatot* after Purim, *Para* and *HaḤodesh*, **this,** the first Adar, **and that,** the second Adar **are equal,** in that reading them during the first Adar exempts one from reading them in the second Adar.

מַנִּי מַתְנִיתִין? לָא תַּנָּא קַמָּא, וְלָא רַבִּי אֱלִיעֶזֶר בְּרַבִּי יוֹסֵי, וְלָא רַבָּן שִׁמְעוֹן בֶּן גַּמְלִיאֵל. דְּתַנְיָא: קָרְאוּ אֶת הַמְּגִילָּה בַּאֲדָר הָרִאשׁוֹן וְנִתְעַבְּרָה הַשָּׁנָה – קוֹרִין אוֹתָהּ בַּאֲדָר הַשֵּׁנִי, שֶׁכָּל מִצְוֹת שֶׁנּוֹהֲגוֹת בַּשֵּׁנִי נוֹהֲגוֹת בָּרִאשׁוֹן חוּץ מִמִּקְרָא מְגִילָּה.

The Gemara asks: If so, **whose** opinion is taught in **the mishna? It is neither** the opinion of **the** anonymous **first *tanna*** of the following *baraita*, **nor** that of **Rabbi Eliezer, son of Rabbi Yosei, nor** that of **Rabban Shimon ben Gamliel, as it is taught** in a *baraita*: If **they read the Megilla during the first Adar and the year was** then **intercalated, they read it during the second Adar, as all mitzvot that are practiced during the second** Adar **are practiced in the first** Adar, **except for the reading of the Megilla.**

רַבִּי אֱלִיעֶזֶר בְּרַבִּי יוֹסֵי אוֹמֵר: אֵין קוֹרִין אוֹתָהּ בַּאֲדָר הַשֵּׁנִי, שֶׁכָּל מִצְוֹת שֶׁנּוֹהֲגוֹת בַּשֵּׁנִי נוֹהֲגוֹת בָּרִאשׁוֹן.

Rabbi Eliezer, son of Rabbi Yosei, says: They do not read it again **during the second Adar, as all mitzvot that are practiced during the second** Adar **are practiced during the first** Adar. Once the Megilla was read during the first Adar, one need not read it again during the second Adar.

רַבָּן שִׁמְעוֹן בֶּן גַּמְלִיאֵל אוֹמֵר מִשּׁוּם רַבִּי יוֹסֵי: אַף קוֹרִין אוֹתָהּ בַּאֲדָר הַשֵּׁנִי, שֶׁכָּל מִצְוֹת שֶׁנּוֹהֲגוֹת בַּשֵּׁנִי אֵין נוֹהֲגוֹת בָּרִאשׁוֹן. וְשָׁוִין בְּהֶסְפֵּד וּבְתַעֲנִית שֶׁאֲסוּרִין בָּזֶה וּבָזֶה.

Rabban Shimon ben Gamliel says in the name of Rabbi Yosei: They even read it again **during the second Adar, as all mitzvot that are practiced during the second** Adar **are not practiced during the first** Adar. **And** they all **agree with regard to eulogy and with regard to fasting that they are prohibited on** the fourteenth and the fifteenth days of **this** month of the first Adar **and on that** month of the second Adar.[H]

HALAKHA

The fourteenth and fifteenth of the first Adar – אַרְבָּעָה עָשָׂר וַחֲמִשָּׁה עָשָׂר בַּאֲדָר הָרִאשׁוֹן: It is prohibited to eulogize and fast on the fourteenth and the fifteenth days of the first Adar, and one does not recite the *taḥanun* prayer. Some maintain that eulogy is permitted, but the custom is to prohibit it (Rema). Some say that one should eat and drink more on these days (Tur, based on the Rif), but that is not the *halakha*, although the Rema writes that one should eat and drink a bit more on these days than he does on a typical day (*Shulḥan Arukh*, *Oraḥ Ḥayyim* 697:1).

BACKGROUND

Greek Italy – אִיטַלְיָא שֶׁל יָוָן: Greek Italy generally refers to southern Italy, since this land was, at that time, a part of Magna Graecia, i.e., Greater Greece; it was ruled by many Greek potentates. However, here, the description of a capital of great dimensions is referring to the city of Rome itself. Some explain this part of the Gemara as referring to Constantinople, which was called, in its day, the new Rome, and which was used as the Roman capital from the beginning of the fourth century; even the description of the place as being between the sea and the hills is fitting. However, this explanation is not historically accurate, as in the time of Ulla, Constantinople was not yet large or important.

NOTES

The great city of Rome – כְּרַךְ גָּדוֹל שֶׁל רוֹמִי: The Maharsha wrote that this passage is cited to underscore that if those who contravene His will, i.e., the Romans, are rewarded, all the more so those who heed His will be rewarded in the future, as it is stated: "For I, says the Lord, will be unto her a wall of fire round about" (Zechariah 2:9). Some commentaries explain in detail that the numbers here are inaccurate, as after analysis it is clear that the calculations do not tally, and this hyperbolic description was stated only to explain the prominence of Rome (*Netzaḥ Yisrael*).

And the year was intercalated – וְנִתְעַבְּרָה הַשָּׁנָה: Some say that this *halakha* applies only when the year was intercalated after the Megilla was already read, or all the more so if it was known in advance that that there will be another month of Adar and they mistakenly read the *Megilla* in the first Adar (see Ritva). The Rosh rules that the fourteenth and fifteenth of the first Adar are days on which eulogy and fasting are prohibited only in the case where the Megilla was read on those days before the year was intercalated.

LANGUAGE

Gravel [*ḥulsit*] – חוּלְסִית: Possibly a hybrid of the Greek κάχληξ, *kakhlèx*, meaning gravel or gravel stones, and the Hebrew *ḥarsit*, which means red soil or clay.

HALAKHA

If the people read the Megilla during the first Adar – קָרְאוּ אֶת הַמְּגִילָּה בַּאֲדָר הָרִאשׁוֹן: If the people read the Megilla during the first Adar and then the year was intercalated, they read it again during the second Adar (*Tur*, *Oraḥ Ḥayyim* 688).

רַבָּן שִׁמְעוֹן בֶּן גַּמְלִיאֵל הַיְינוּ תַּנָּא קַמָּא! אָמַר רַב פַּפָּא: סֵדֶר פָּרָשִׁיּוֹת אִיכָּא בֵּינַיְיהוּ. דְּתַנָּא קַמָּא סָבַר: לְכַתְּחִילָּה בַּשֵּׁנִי, וְאִי עֲבוּד בָּרִאשׁוֹן – עֲבוּד, בַּר מִמִּקְרָא מְגִילָּה דְּאַף עַל גַּב דְּקָרוּ בָּרִאשׁוֹן קָרוּ בַּשֵּׁנִי,

The Gemara analyzes the *baraita*. The opinion of **Rabban Shimon ben Gamliel is** identical to **that of the first *tanna*.** What novel element does he introduce? **Rav Pappa said: There is** a practical difference **between them** with regard to **the sequence of** four Torah **portions,**[H] **as the first *tanna* maintains:** They should read those portions **during the second** Adar, ***ab initio*. However, if they did** so **during the first** Adar, **they did** so; and they fulfilled their obligation and need not read them again during the second Adar, **except for the reading of the Megilla, as even though they** already **read** it **during the first** Adar, **they read it** again **during the second** Adar.

וְרַבִּי אֱלִיעֶזֶר בְּרַבִּי יוֹסֵי סָבַר: אֲפִילּוּ מִקְרָא מְגִילָּה לְכַתְּחִילָּה בָּרִאשׁוֹן. וְרַבָּן שִׁמְעוֹן בֶּן גַּמְלִיאֵל סָבַר: אֲפִילּוּ סֵדֶר פָּרָשִׁיּוֹת, אִי קָרוּ בָּרִאשׁוֹן – קָרוּ בַּשֵּׁנִי.

And Rabbi Eliezer, son of Rabbi Yosei, maintains that **even the reading of the Megilla** may be performed **during the first** Adar, ***ab initio*,** and they need not read it again during the second Adar. **And Rabban Shimon ben Gamliel maintains: Even** with regard to **the sequence of** four Torah **portions, if they read** them **during the first** Adar, **they read** them again **during the second** Adar.

מַנִּי? אִי תַּנָּא קַמָּא – קַשְׁיָא מַתָּנוֹת, אִי רַבִּי אֱלִיעֶזֶר בְּרַבִּי יוֹסֵי – קַשְׁיָא נַמִּי מִקְרָא מְגִילָּה. אִי רַבָּן שִׁמְעוֹן בֶּן גַּמְלִיאֵל – קַשְׁיָא סֵדֶר פָּרָשִׁיּוֹת!

Returning to the original question, according to **whose** opinion is the mishna taught? **If** it is the opinion of **the first *tanna*,** the *halakha* of **gifts** to the poor **is difficult.** The first *tanna* does not mention these gifts, indicating that he maintains that if gifts were distributed during the first Adar one need not distribute gifts to the poor during the second Adar. And **if** the mishna was taught according to the opinion of **Rabbi Eliezer, son of Rabbi Yosei, the reading of the Megilla** is **also difficult.** And **if** it is the opinion of **Rabban Shimon ben Gamliel, the sequence of** Torah **portions** is **difficult.**

לְעוֹלָם תַּנָּא קַמָּא, וּתְנָא מִקְרָא מְגִילָּה וְהוּא הַדִּין מַתָּנוֹת לָאֶבְיוֹנִים, דְּהָא בְּהָא תַּלְיָא.

The Gemara answers: **Actually,** the mishna is according to the opinion of **the first *tanna*, and he taught** the *halakha* with regard to **the reading of the Megilla, and the same is true** with regard to **gifts to the poor, as this** mitzva **is dependent upon that** one. The Gemara already explained that the gifts to the poor are distributed on the day that the Megilla is read.

וְאִיבָּעֵית אֵימָא: לְעוֹלָם רַבָּן שִׁמְעוֹן בֶּן גַּמְלִיאֵל הִיא, וּמַתְנִיתִין חַסּוּרֵי מִיחַסְּרָא, וְהָכִי קָתָנֵי: אֵין בֵּין אַרְבָּעָה עָשָׂר שֶׁבַּאֲדָר הָרִאשׁוֹן לְאַרְבָּעָה עָשָׂר שֶׁבַּאֲדָר הַשֵּׁנִי אֶלָּא מִקְרָא מְגִילָּה וּמַתָּנוֹת, הָא לְעִנְיַן הֶסְפֵּד וְתַעֲנִית – זֶה וָזֶה שָׁוִין. וְאִילּוּ סֵדֶר פָּרָשִׁיּוֹת לָא מַיְירִי.

And if you wish, say instead: **Actually,** the mishna **is** according to the opinion of **Rabban Shimon ben Gamliel, and the mishna is incomplete and is teaching the following: The difference between the fourteenth** day **of the first Adar and the fourteenth** day **of the second Adar is only** with regard to **the reading of the Megilla and** distributing **gifts** to the poor. The Gemara infers **that** with regard to **the matter of eulogy and fasting, this,** the first Adar, **and that,** the second Adar **are equal, while** about **the sequence of** Torah **portions,** the mishna **does not speak** at all. The mishna limits its discussion to the *halakhot* of Purim.

אָמַר רַבִּי חִיָּיא בַּר אָבִין אָמַר רַבִּי יוֹחָנָן: הִלְכְתָא כְּרַבָּן שִׁמְעוֹן בֶּן גַּמְלִיאֵל שֶׁאָמַר מִשּׁוּם רַבִּי יוֹסֵי.

Rabbi Ḥiyya bar Avin said that **Rabbi Yoḥanan said: The *halakha* is in accordance with** the opinion of **Rabban Shimon ben Gamliel, who said** it **in the name of Rabbi Yosei.**

אָמַר רַבִּי יוֹחָנָן: וּשְׁנֵיהֶם מִקְרָא אֶחָד דָּרְשׁוּ: ״בְּכָל שָׁנָה וְשָׁנָה״. רַבִּי אֱלִיעֶזֶר בְּרַבִּי יוֹסֵי סָבַר: ״בְּכָל שָׁנָה וְשָׁנָה״ מָה כָּל שָׁנָה וְשָׁנָה אֲדָר הַסָּמוּךְ לִשְׁבָט – אַף כָּאן אֲדָר הַסָּמוּךְ לִשְׁבָט,

Rabbi Yoḥanan said: And both of them, Rabban Shimon ben Gamliel and Rabbi Eliezer, son of Rabbi Yosei, **interpreted the same verse** differently, leading them to their conclusions. It is written: "To enjoin upon them that they should keep the fourteenth day of the month of Adar and the fifteenth day of the same, **in each and every year**" (Esther 9:21). **Rabbi Eliezer, son of Rabbi Yosei, maintains: "In each and every year"** teaches that Purim must be celebrated the same way each year, even if it is intercalated: **Just as each and every year** Purim is celebrated during **Adar that is adjacent to Shevat, so too here** in an intercalated year Purim is celebrated during **Adar that is adjacent to Shevat.**

HALAKHA

The four Torah portions – אַרְבַּע פָּרָשִׁיּוֹת: The four portions that are read in the Torah around Purim are specifically read in the second Adar. Moreover, the authorities wrote that the *halakha* is in accordance with the opinion of Rabban Shimon ben Gamliel, that even if they were read in the first Adar, they must be repeated in the second (*Shulḥan Arukh, Oraḥ Ḥayyim* 685; *Beit Yosef*; *Darkhei Moshe*).

וְרַבָּן שִׁמְעוֹן בֶּן גַּמְלִיאֵל סָבַר: ״בְּכָל שָׁנָה וְשָׁנָה״, מַה כָּל שָׁנָה וְשָׁנָה אֲדָר הַסָּמוּךְ לְנִיסָן – אַף כָּאן אֲדָר הַסָּמוּךְ לְנִיסָן.

And Rabban Shimon ben Gamliel maintains: "In each and every year" teaches that **just as each and every year** Purim is celebrated in **Adar that is adjacent to Nisan, so too here,** in an intercalated year, Purim is celebrated during **Adar that is adjacent to Nisan.**

בִּשְׁלָמָא רַבִּי אֱלִיעֶזֶר בְּרַבִּי יוֹסֵי – מִסְתַּבֵּר טַעְמָא, דְּאֵין מַעֲבִירִין עַל הַמִּצְוֹת, אֶלָּא רַבָּן שִׁמְעוֹן בֶּן גַּמְלִיאֵל מַאי טַעְמָא?

The Gemara asks: **Granted,** according to **Rabbi Eliezer, son of Rabbi Yosei, the reason** for his opinion **is logical,** based on the principle that **one does not forego** performance of **the mitzvot;** rather, when presented with the opportunity to perform a mitzva, one should do so immediately. **However,** with regard to **Rabban Shimon ben Gamliel, what is the reason** for his opinion?

אָמַר רַבִּי טָבִי: טַעְמָא דְּרַבִּי שִׁמְעוֹן בֶּן גַּמְלִיאֵל מִסְמַךְ גְּאוּלָּה לִגְאוּלָּה עָדִיף.

Rabbi Tavi said: The reason for the opinion **of Rabban Shimon ben Gamliel** is that **juxtaposing** the celebration of one **redemption,** Purim, **to** the celebration of another **redemption,**[N] Passover, **is preferable.**

רַבִּי אֶלְעָזָר אָמַר: טַעְמָא דְּרַבָּן שִׁמְעוֹן בֶּן גַּמְלִיאֵל מֵהָכָא, דִּכְתִיב: ״לְקַיֵּים אֶת אִגֶּרֶת הַפּוּרִים הַזֹּאת הַשֵּׁנִית״.

Rabbi Elazar said: The reason for the opinion **of Rabban Shimon ben Gamliel** is derived **from here, as it is written: "To confirm this second letter of Purim"** (Esther 9:29), indicating that there are circumstances where the Megilla is read a second time (Jerusalem Talmud), i.e., when the year was intercalated after the Megilla was read in the first Adar.

וְאִיצְטְרִיךְ לְמִיכְתַּב

The Gemara comments: **And it was necessary to write**

NOTES

Juxtaposing redemption to redemption – מִסְמַךְ גְּאוּלָּה לִגְאוּלָּה: Some raise the question: As this in no way relates to whether the sequence of four Torah portions should be read in the first Adar or the second Adar, what is the reason for the opinion of Rabban Shimon ben Gamliel? They explain that no special proof was required since three of the four portions relate to Passover: *Shekalim*, because the half-shekel must be collected before the beginning of Nisan; *Para*, because one must undergo purification before the Festival; and *HaHodesh*, to inform the people about the Festival of Passover (see Ritva; *Penei Yehoshua*).

Perek I
Daf 7 Amud a

״הַשֵּׁנִית״ וְאִיצְטְרִיךְ לְמִיכְתַּב ״בְּכָל שָׁנָה וְשָׁנָה״ דְּאִי מִ״בְּכָל שָׁנָה וְשָׁנָה״ הֲוָה אָמִינָא כִּי קוּשְׁיַין, קָא מַשְׁמַע לָן: ״הַשֵּׁנִית״. וְאִי אַשְׁמוּעִינַן ״הַשֵּׁנִית״ הֲוָה אָמִינָא בַּתְּחִילָּה בָּרִאשׁוֹן וּבַשֵּׁנִי, קָא מַשְׁמַע לָן: ״בְּכָל שָׁנָה וְשָׁנָה״.

the term: **The second, and it was** also **necessary to write** the phrase: **In each and every year;** proof from one of the verses would have been insufficient. **As, if** I had derived the *halakha* only **from** the phrase: **In each and every year, I would have said** my conclusion **according to our question** raised earlier: Why not celebrate Purim in the Adar adjacent to Shevat? **Therefore, it teaches us** using the term: **The second. And had it taught us** only the term: **The second, I would have said** that Purim must be celebrated both **in the first** Adar **and in the second** Adar, ***ab initio*. Therefore, it teaches us: In each and every year,** indicating that even in an intercalated year, just as in an ordinary year, Purim is to be celebrated only once.

וְרַבִּי אֱלִיעֶזֶר בְּרַבִּי יוֹסֵי, הַאי ״הַשֵּׁנִית״ מַאי עָבֵיד לֵיהּ? מִיבָּעֵי לֵיהּ לְכִדְרַב שְׁמוּאֵל בַּר יְהוּדָה, דְּאָמַר רַב שְׁמוּאֵל בַּר יְהוּדָה: בַּתְּחִילָּה קְבָעוּהָ בְּשׁוּשַׁן, וּלְבַסּוֹף בְּכָל הָעוֹלָם כּוּלּוֹ.

The Gemara asks: **And Rabbi Eliezer, son of Rabbi Yosei, what does he do with this** term: **The second?** Since he holds that the Megilla is read in the first Adar, what does he derive from the verse? The Gemara answers: **He requires** the term **to** derive **that** statement **of Rav Shmuel bar Yehuda, as Rav Shmuel bar Yehuda said: Initially, they established** the observance of Purim **in** the city of **Shushan**[B] alone, **and ultimately** they established it **throughout the world,** according to the second letter of Purim.

אָמַר רַב שְׁמוּאֵל בַּר יְהוּדָה: שָׁלְחָה לָהֶם אֶסְתֵּר לַחֲכָמִים: קִבְעוּנִי לְדוֹרוֹת! שָׁלְחוּ לָהּ: קִנְאָה אַתְּ מְעוֹרֶרֶת עָלֵינוּ לְבֵין הָאוּמּוֹת. שָׁלְחָה לָהֶם: כְּבָר כְּתוּבָה אֲנִי עַל דִּבְרֵי הַיָּמִים לְמַלְכֵי מָדַי וּפָרַס.

Apropos the statement of Rav Shmuel bar Yehuda with regard to the establishment of the holiday of Purim, the Gemara cites a related statement. **Rav Shmuel bar Yehuda said: Esther sent to the Sages: Establish me for** future **generations.**[N] Esther requested that the observance of Purim and the reading of the Megilla be instituted as an ordinance for all generations. **They sent to her: You will** thereby **arouse the wrath of the nations upon us,** as the Megilla recounts the victory of the Jews over the gentiles, and it is best not to publicize that victory. **She sent** back **to them: I am already written in the chronicles of the kings of Media and Persia,** and so the Megilla will not publicize anything that is not already known worldwide.

BACKGROUND

Shushan – שׁוּשַׁן: The city of Shushan, also referred to as Susa, is identified with the contemporary Iranian city of Shush. The palace of Darius the Great was excavated there.

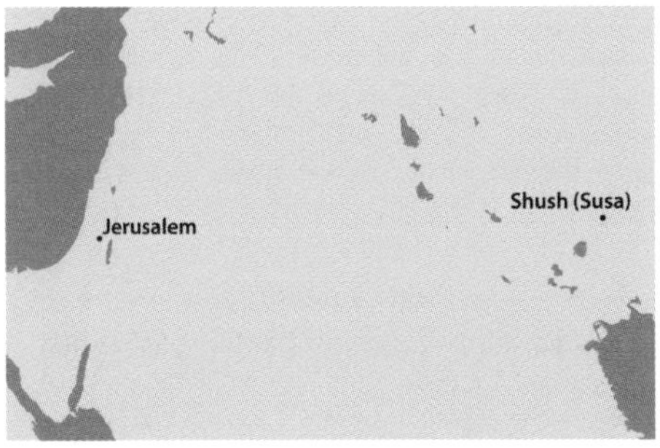

Location of Shush

Ruins of the palace of Darius

NOTES

Establish me for future generations – קִבְעוּנִי לְדוֹרוֹת: Although it was already stated that the Jews accepted upon themselves observance of the days of Purim, that was with regard to feasting and rejoicing. However, they did not want to record the entire story of the miracle (see *Penei Yehoshua*).

NOTES

Write me for future generations – כִּתְבוּנִי לְדוֹרוֹת: There is an allusion to this in the biblical text itself, as it was stated specifically with regard to the second letter of Purim: "And the commandment of Esther confirmed these matters of Purim, and it was written in the book (Esther 9:32). There was an interval after the first letter was dispatched, which included acceptance of the celebratory aspects of Purim. It was only with the dispatch of the second letter that Esther was included as part of the canon (Rabbi Yoshiya Pinto).

Have I not written for you three times – הֲלֹא כָתַבְתִּי לְךָ שָׁלִישִׁים: The understanding here is according to its plain meaning. Even the wisdom of King Solomon, the wisest of men, warranted only three books in the Bible. Apparently then, although the Scroll of Esther may deserve to be canonized, a fourth mention of Amalek should not be added to the canon (Ritva). The *Penei Yehoshua* writes based on the midrash that the term "three times" in this verse refers to the three sections of the Bible: Torah, Prophets, and Writings. Adding the Scroll of Esther to the canon would be adding a fourth category, as its events took place later than the other books of the Bible. Therefore the Sages sought an allusion to indicate that Esther should be categorized as part of the Writings.

Renders the hands ritually impure – מְטַמְּאָה אֶת הַיָּדַיִם: The Sages issued a decree that sacred scrolls shall render hands impure, according hands that come into contact with a sacred scroll second degree ritual impurity status. This decree was issued to encourage greater regard for these scrolls by discouraging casual contact with them, as well as to discourage the practice of storing *teruma* with these scrolls, attracting vermin which gnawed and ruined them. The second degree impurity would disqualify the *teruma* and render its consumption prohibited. The Sages said in the mishna (*Yadayim* 4:6): The greater the significance of an item, the greater its impurity.

Esther was said with the inspiration of the Divine Spirit – אֶסְתֵּר בְּרוּחַ הַקּוֹדֶשׁ נֶאֶמְרָה: A question is raised: From many of these sources, proof may be adduced that Mordecai was inspired by the Divine Spirit, as he was privy to matters that he could not have otherwise known. However, these sources do not prove that the entire book of Esther was divinely inspired. Some answer that it would have been inappropriate to publicize the Divine Spirit in the book of Esther had the book itself not been divinely inspired (*Ye'arot Devash*).

BACKGROUND

Was stated with the inspiration of the Divine Spirit – בְּרוּחַ הַקּוֹדֶשׁ נֶאֶמְרָה: The books of the Bible are divided into three categories: Torah, written by Moses, who enjoyed a direct relationship with God; Prophets, written by the prophets with prophetic insight; and Writings, which were written with divine inspiration. This latter quality, which is on a level below prophecy, distinguishes the books of the Writings from apocryphal books of wisdom such as the book of Ben Sira, which were not included in the biblical canon.

HALAKHA

What is included in the category of sacred writings – מַה נִּכְלָל בְּכִתְבֵי הַקֹּדֶשׁ: Five scrolls are included in the twenty-four books of the Bible: The Scroll of Esther and the books of Ruth, Ecclesiastes, Lamentations, and the Song of Songs. All twenty-four books of the Bible, including these *megillot*, have the legal status of sacred scrolls and render the hands impure, in accordance with the opinion of Rabbi Shimon (Rambam *Sefer Tahara*, *Hilkhot Avot HaTumot* 9:6).

רַב וְרַב חֲנִינָא וְרַבִּי יוֹחָנָן וְרַב חֲבִיבָא מַתְנוּ: בְּכוּלֵּיהּ סֵדֶר מוֹעֵד כׇּל כִּי הַאי זוּגָא חַלּוֹפֵי רַבִּי יוֹחָנָן וּמְעַיֵּיל רַבִּי יוֹנָתָן: שָׁלְחָה לָהֶם אֶסְתֵּר לַחֲכָמִים: כִּתְבוּנִי לְדוֹרוֹת. שָׁלְחוּ לָהּ: ״הֲלֹא כָתַבְתִּי לְךָ שָׁלִישִׁים״ שָׁלִישִׁים וְלֹא רִבֵּעִים.

It was related that **Rav and Rabbi Ḥanina and Rabbi Yoḥanan and Rav Ḥaviva taught** the statement cited below. The Gemara comments: **Throughout the order of *Moed*, wherever this** latter **pair** of Sages is mentioned, **exchange Rabbi Yoḥanan and insert Rabbi Yonatan** in his place. They said: **Esther sent to the Sages: Write me for** future **generations**[N] and canonize my book as part of the Bible. **They sent to her** that it is written: **"Have I not written for you three times"**[N] (Proverbs 22:20), indicating that Israel's battle with Amalek is to be mentioned **three times** in the Bible **and not four times?** Since it is already mentioned three times (Exodus 17:8–16; Deuteronomy 25:17–19; I Samuel 15), there is no need to add a fourth source.

עַד שֶׁמָּצְאוּ לוֹ מִקְרָא כָּתוּב בַּתּוֹרָה: ״כְּתֹב זֹאת זִכָּרוֹן בַּסֵּפֶר״, ״כְּתֹב זֹאת״ מַה שֶּׁכָּתוּב כָּאן וּבְמִשְׁנֵה תוֹרָה, ״זִכָּרוֹן״ – מַה שֶּׁכָּתוּב בַּנְּבִיאִים, ״בַּסֵּפֶר״ – מַה שֶּׁכָּתוּב בַּמְּגִלָּה.

The Sages did not accede to Esther's request **until they found a verse written in the Torah: "Write this for a memorial in the book,** and rehearse it in the ears of Joshua: That I will utterly blot out the remembrance of Amalek from under the heavens" (Exodus 17:14). The Sages interpreted the verse: **"Write this," that which is written** in the Torah **here** in Exodus, **and in Deuteronomy; "a memorial," that which is written in the Prophets,** i.e., in I Samuel, on this matter; **"in the book," that which is written in the Megilla.** The Megilla is the third mention of Amalek and not the fourth, as both mentions in the Torah pertaining to Amalek are considered one; therefore, Esther would be the third, not the fourth source.

כְּתַנָּאֵי: ״כְּתֹב זֹאת״ – מַה שֶּׁכָּתוּב כָּאן, ״זִכָּרוֹן״ – מַה שֶּׁכָּתוּב בְּמִשְׁנֵה תוֹרָה, ״בַּסֵּפֶר״ – מַה שֶּׁכָּתוּב בַּנְּבִיאִים, דִּבְרֵי רַבִּי יְהוֹשֻׁעַ. רַבִּי אֶלְעָזָר הַמּוֹדָעִי אוֹמֵר: ״כְּתֹב זֹאת״ – מַה שֶּׁכָּתוּב כָּאן וּבְמִשְׁנֵה תוֹרָה, ״זִכָּרוֹן״ – מַה שֶּׁכָּתוּב בַּנְּבִיאִים, ״בַּסֵּפֶר״ – מַה שֶּׁכָּתוּב בַּמְּגִילָּה.

The Gemara comments: This matter is **parallel** to a dispute between **the *tanna'im***, as it was taught in a *baraita*: **"Write this," that which is written here,** in the book of Exodus; **"a memorial," that which is written in Deuteronomy; "in the book," that which is written in the Prophets;** this is **the statement of Rabbi Yehoshua. Rabbi Elazar HaModa'i** disagrees and **says: "Write this," that which is written** in the Torah **here** in Exodus, **and in Deuteronomy; "a memorial," that which is written in the Prophets** on this matter; **"in the book," that which is written in the Megilla.** Here too, the *tanna'im* disagreed whether or not the book of Esther has the same force and sanctity as that of the canonized books of the Bible.

אָמַר רַב יְהוּדָה אָמַר שְׁמוּאֵל: אֶסְתֵּר אֵינָהּ מְטַמְּאָה אֶת הַיָּדַיִם.

Rav Yehuda said that **Shmuel said:** The book of **Esther does not render the hands ritually impure.**[N] Although the Sages issued a decree that sacred scrolls render hands ritually impure, the book of Esther was not accorded the sanctity of sacred scrolls.

לְמֵימְרָא דְּסָבַר שְׁמוּאֵל אֶסְתֵּר לָאו בְּרוּחַ הַקּוֹדֶשׁ נֶאֶמְרָה? וְהָאָמַר שְׁמוּאֵל: אֶסְתֵּר בְּרוּחַ הַקּוֹדֶשׁ נֶאֶמְרָה! נֶאֶמְרָה לִקְרוֹת וְלֹא נֶאֶמְרָה לִיכְתּוֹב.

The Gemara asks: **Is this to say that Shmuel maintains** that the book of **Esther was not stated with** the inspiration of **the Divine Spirit? But didn't Shmuel** himself **say** elsewhere that the book of **Esther was stated with** the inspiration of **the Divine Spirit?**[NB] The Gemara answers: **It was stated** with the Divine Spirit that it is **to be read** in public; **however, it was not stated** that it is **to be written.** Therefore, the text was not accorded the sanctity of sacred scrolls.

מֵיתִיבִי: רַבִּי מֵאִיר אוֹמֵר: קֹהֶלֶת אֵינוֹ מְטַמֵּא אֶת הַיָּדַיִם, וּמַחְלוֹקֶת בְּשִׁיר הַשִּׁירִים. רַבִּי יוֹסֵי אוֹמֵר: שִׁיר הַשִּׁירִים מְטַמֵּא אֶת הַיָּדַיִם, וּמַחְלוֹקֶת בְּקֹהֶלֶת. רַבִּי שִׁמְעוֹן אוֹמֵר: קֹהֶלֶת מִקּוּלֵּי בֵּית שַׁמַּאי וּמֵחוּמְרֵי בֵּית הִלֵּל, אֲבָל רוּת וְשִׁיר הַשִּׁירִים וְאֶסְתֵּר – מְטַמְּאִין אֶת הַיָּדַיִם! הוּא דְּאָמַר כְּרַבִּי יְהוֹשֻׁעַ.

The Gemara raises an objection from a *baraita*. **Rabbi Meir says:** The book of **Ecclesiastes does not render the hands ritually impure,** as it was not accorded the sanctity of sacred scrolls; **however, there is a dispute with regard to** whether or not **the Song of Songs** renders the hands impure. **Rabbi Yosei says: The Song of Songs renders the hands ritually impure, but there is a dispute with regard to** the book of **Ecclesiastes. Rabbi Shimon says:** The ruling with regard to **Ecclesiastes is among the leniencies of Beit Shammai and among the stringencies of Beit Hillel,** as according to Beit Hillel it renders the hands impure and according to Beit Shammai it does not. **However,** everyone agrees that the books of **Ruth, and the Song of Songs, and Esther render the hands ritually impure,** contrary to the opinion of Shmuel. The Gemara answers: It was Shmuel **who stated** his opinion **in accordance with** the opinion of **Rabbi Yehoshua** cited earlier that the book of Esther was not accorded the sanctity of sacred scrolls.[H]

תַּנְיָא, רַבִּי שִׁמְעוֹן בֶּן מְנַסְיָא אוֹמֵר: קֹהֶלֶת אֵינוֹ מְטַמֵּא אֶת הַיָּדַיִם, מִפְּנֵי שֶׁחָכְמָתוֹ שֶׁל שְׁלֹמֹה הִיא. אָמְרוּ לוֹ: וְכִי זוֹ בִּלְבַד אָמַר? וַהֲלֹא כְּבָר נֶאֱמַר: ״וַיְדַבֵּר שְׁלֹשֶׁת אֲלָפִים מָשָׁל״ וְאוֹמֵר: ״אַל תּוֹסְףְּ עַל דְּבָרָיו״.

It is taught in a *baraita*: **Rabbi Shimon ben Menasya says:** The book of **Ecclesiastes does not render the hands ritually impure because it is the wisdom of Solomon,** and not divinely inspired. **They said to him:** It was certainly divinely inspired and that is the reason that the book of Ecclesiastes was added to the canon; **as was it this alone that** Solomon **said? Wasn't it already stated: "And he spoke three thousand proverbs,** and his poems were a thousand and five" (I Kings 5:12)? Solomon spoke many proverbs, but only a portion of them were canonized in the Bible. Apparently, what is unique about those in Ecclesiastes is that they were divinely inspired. **And it says: "Add you not unto his words"** (Proverbs 30:6).

מַאי וְאוֹמֵר? וְכִי תֵּימָא: מֵימַר – טוּבָא אֲמַר, דְּאִי בָּעֵי – אִיכְּתִיב וּדְאִי בָּעֵי לָא אִיכְּתִיב. תָּא שְׁמַע ״אַל תּוֹסְףְּ עַל דְּבָרָיו״.

The Gemara asks: **What** is added by the proof introduced with the phrase: **And it says?** Why wasn't the first proof sufficient? The Gemara answers: **And if you would say** that in terms of what **he said, he said a great deal,** with regard to **which, if he** so **desired, it was written, and if he** so **desired, it was not written;** then that is why not all of his statements were preserved. Therefore, **come** and **hear: Add you not unto his words.** Apparently, the reason that it is prohibited to add to the proverbs is that the book of Ecclesiastes was divinely inspired.

תַּנְיָא, רַבִּי אֱלִיעֶזֶר אוֹמֵר: אֶסְתֵּר בְּרוּחַ הַקּוֹדֶשׁ נֶאֶמְרָה, שֶׁנֶּאֱמַר: ״וַיֹּאמֶר הָמָן בְּלִבּוֹ״. רַבִּי עֲקִיבָא אוֹמֵר: אֶסְתֵּר בְּרוּחַ הַקּוֹדֶשׁ נֶאֶמְרָה, שֶׁנֶּאֱמַר: ״וַתְּהִי אֶסְתֵּר נֹשֵׂאת חֵן בְּעֵינֵי כׇּל רֹאֶיהָ״.

It is taught in a *baraita* that **Rabbi Eliezer says:** The book of **Esther was said with** the inspiration of **the Divine Spirit, as it is stated: "And Haman thought in his heart"** (Esther 6:6). If the book of Esther was not divinely inspired, how was it known what Haman thought in his heart? **Rabbi Akiva says:** The book of **Esther was said with** the inspiration of **the Divine Spirit, as it is stated: "And Esther obtained favor in the sight of all those who looked upon her"** (Esther 2:15); this could have been known only through divine inspiration.

רַבִּי מֵאִיר אוֹמֵר: אֶסְתֵּר בְּרוּחַ הַקּוֹדֶשׁ נֶאֶמְרָה, שֶׁנֶּאֱמַר: ״וַיִּוָּדַע הַדָּבָר לְמׇרְדֳּכַי״. רַבִּי יוֹסֵי בֶּן דּוּרְמַסְקִית אוֹמֵר: אֶסְתֵּר בְּרוּחַ הַקּוֹדֶשׁ נֶאֶמְרָה, שֶׁנֶּאֱמַר: ״וּבַבִּזָּה לֹא שָׁלְחוּ אֶת יָדָם״.

Rabbi Meir says: The book of **Esther was said with** the inspiration of **the Divine Spirit, as it is stated** with regard to the conspiracy of Bigtan and Teresh against Ahasuerus: **"And the thing became known to Mordecai"** (Esther 2:22). This too could have been known only through divine inspiration. **Rabbi Yosei ben Durmaskit says:** The book of **Esther was said with** the inspiration of **the Divine Spirit, as it is stated: "But they did not lay their hands on the plunder"** (Esther 9:15). The only way that could have been stated with certainty is through divine inspiration.

אָמַר שְׁמוּאֵל: אִי הֲוַאי הָתָם הֲוָה אָמֵינָא מִלְּתָא דַּעֲדִיפָא מִכּוּלְּהוּ, שֶׁנֶּאֱמַר: ״קִיְּמוּ וְקִבְּלוּ״ קִיְּמוּ לְמַעְלָה מַה שֶּׁקִּיבְּלוּ לְמַטָּה.

Shmuel said: Had I been there among the *tanna'im*, **I would have stated a matter that is superior to them all, as it is stated: "They confirmed, and took upon themselves"** (Esther 9:27), which was interpreted to mean: **They confirmed above** in heaven **what they took upon themselves below** on earth. Clearly, it is only through divine inspiration that this could have been ascertained.

אָמַר רָבָא: לְכוּלְּהוּ אִית לְהוּ פִּירְכָא, לְבַר מִדִּשְׁמוּאֵל דְּלֵית לֵיהּ פִּירְכָא. דְּרַבִּי אֱלִיעֶזֶר – סְבָרָא הוּא, דְּלָא הֲוָה אִינִישׁ דַּחֲשִׁיב לְמַלְכָּא כְּוָותֵיהּ, וְהַאי כִּי קָא מַפִּישׁ טוּבָא וְאָמַר – אַדַּעְתֵּיהּ דְּנַפְשֵׁיהּ קָאָמַר.

Rava said: There is a refutation for all of these proofs, **except for** the proof cited by **Shmuel, for which there is no refutation.** The Gemara elaborates. That which **Rabbi Eliezer** said with regard to knowledge of what Haman was thinking in his heart can be refuted, as **it is** based on **logical reasoning** to conclude that this was his thinking. **There was no** other **person as important to the king as he** was; **and** the fact is **that when he elaborated extensively and said:** "Let the royal apparel be brought" (Esther 6:8), **he said** it **with himself in mind.**

דְּרַבִּי עֲקִיבָא – דִּלְמָא כְּרַבִּי אֶלְעָזָר דְּאָמַר: מְלַמֵּד שֶׁכׇּל אֶחָד וְאֶחָד נִדְמְתָה לוֹ כְּאוּמָּתוֹ.

That which **Rabbi Akiva** said with regard to the knowledge that Esther found favor in the eyes of all, **perhaps** it can be understood and refuted **in accordance with** the opinion of **Rabbi Elazar, who said:** This **teaches that she appeared to each and every one as** one of **his nation,** and they expressed that sentiment aloud.

וְהָא דְּרַבִּי מֵאִיר – דִּלְמָא כְּרַבִּי חִיָּיא בַּר אַבָּא, דְּאָמַר: בִּגְתָן וָתֶרֶשׁ שְׁנֵי טַרְשִׁיִּים הָיוּ.

And that which Rabbi Meir said, i.e., that the divine inspiration of the book of Esther is clear from the fact that Mordecai exposed the conspiracy against Ahasuerus, **perhaps** this can be explained and refuted **in accordance with** the opinion of **Rabbi Ḥiyya bar Abba, who said: Bigtan and Teresh were both** members of the **Tarsi** people[L] and conversed in their own language. Mordecai, who was a member of the Sanhedrin and therefore fluent in many languages, understood what they were saying.

LANGUAGE

Tarsi people – טַרְשִׁיִּים: This refers to people from the city of Tarsus, Ταρσός, in Asia Minor.

והא דרבי יוסי בן דורמסקית – דלמא פריסתקי שדור. דשמואל ודאי לית ליה פירכא. אמר רבינא: היינו דאמרי אינשי: טבא חדא פלפלתא חריפתא ממלי צני קרי.

And that which Rabbi Yosei ben Durmaskit said with regard to the knowledge that no spoils were taken, **perhaps** this can be explained and refuted by the fact that **they dispatched messengers** who informed them of the situation. However, **with regard to Shmuel's** proof from the fact that they confirmed above what they took upon themselves below, **there is certainly no refutation. Ravina said: This** explains the folk saying **that people say: One sharp pepper is better**[N] **than a basketful of pumpkins,** as the quality of the pepper's taste is more significant than the quantity of the pumpkins.

רב יוסף אמר, מהכא: "וימי הפורים האלה לא יעברו מתוך היהודים". רב נחמן בר יצחק אומר, מהכא: "וזכרם לא יסוף מזרעם":

Rav Yosef said: Proof that the book of Esther was divinely inspired may be cited **from here: "And these days of Purim**[N] **shall not cease from among the Jews"** (Esther 9:28), an assertion that could have been made only with divine inspiration. **Rav Naḥman bar Yitzḥak says:** Proof may be cited **from here,** at the end of that verse: **"Nor the memorial of them perish from their seed"** (Esther 9:28).

"ומתנות לאביונים": תני רב יוסף: "ומשלוח מנות איש לרעהו" – שתי מנות לאיש אחד. "ומתנות לאביונים" – שתי מתנות לשני בני אדם.

The mishna mentions: **And gifts** distributed **to the poor. Rav Yosef taught** a *baraita* that the verse states: **"And of sending portions one to another"** (Esther 9:22), indicating **two portions to one person.**[H] The verse continues: **"And gifts to the poor"**[H] (Esther 9:22), indicating **two gifts to two people.**[N]

רבי יהודה נשיאה שדר ליה לרבי אושעיא אטמא דעיגלא תלתא וגרבא דחמרא, שלח ליה:

The Gemara relates that, on Purim, **Rabbi Yehuda Nesia sent to Rabbi Oshaya the leg of a third**-born **calf and a jug of wine.** Rabbi Oshaya **sent him** a message of gratitude:

NOTES

One sharp pepper is better – טבא חדא פלפלתא: It is explained in the *Arukh* that pepper, although it is small, is spicy and preferable to the relatively bland pumpkin. Likewise, although Shmuel was an *amora*, whose standing is less significant than the *tanna'im* who discussed this matter, his statement is more reasonable.

And these days of Purim – וימי הפורים האלה: See *Tosafot*, who explain what Rav Naḥman added to the source cited by Rav Yosef. Some explain that, from the first part of the verse cited by Rav Naḥman, it can be determined only that the Jews took upon themselves to remember the days of Purim. Therefore, Rav Yosef cites the pronouncement in the second part of that verse: "Nor the memorial of them perish from their seed," which was stated with divine inspiration.

Portions and gifts – מנות ומתנות: The early authorities wrote that the obligation to give two portions applies only if the recipient is a person of means, so that he will appreciate that it is a significant gift. However, one is required to give only one portion to a poor person, for whom even one portion is significant.

HALAKHA

Sending portions – משלוח מנות: Every person is obligated to send two portions of food or drink to another person. They must be different types of food. Merely giving a quarter-*log* of drink or an olive-bulk of food is insufficient; rather, it is appropriate to give generous portions. Women are obligated in sending portions just as men are. It is appropriate for a woman to give to a woman and for a man to give to a man (Rema). It is permitted to send money and other non-food items if they can be used on that day to purchase components of the festive meal. Some maintain that even in this case, one fulfills his obligation only with food. Even one who is dependent on another for sustenance, although he is not obligated, should fulfill the mitzva and send portions to another person (*Magen Avraham*). This mitzva is fulfilled during the day of Purim and not at night. It is appropriate to send the portions with a messenger both to display deference to the mitzva and to fulfill the literal meaning of the verse, which uses the term: Sending portions (*Shulḥan Arukh, Oraḥ Ḥayyim* 695:4).

Gifts to the poor – מתנות לאביונים: Every person is obligated on Purim to give at least two gifts to two poor people, one gift to each. One fulfills his obligation with a gift worth a *peruta*. One must give the gifts with his own money, although he may add from the money that he tithes for charity (*Magen Avraham*, citing the Maharil). It is appropriate to give the money on the day of Purim, enabling the poor person to use it on Purim. The Rambam writes that it is preferable to give additional gifts to the poor than to send additional portions (*Shulḥan Arukh, Oraḥ Ḥayyim* 694:1).

קַיַּימְתָּ בָּנוּ רַבֵּינוּ ״וּמִשְׁלוֹחַ מָנוֹת אִישׁ לְרֵעֵהוּ וּמַתָּנוֹת לָאֶבְיוֹנִים״.

You have fulfilled two mitzvot **through us,**[N] **our teacher:** The mitzva of: **"And sending portions one to another,"** and the mitzva of: **"And gifts to the poor,"** as Rabbi Oshaya was poor and this was a substantial gift.

רַבָּה שְׁדַר לֵיהּ לְמָרֵי בַּר מָר בְּיַד אַבַּיֵּי מְלֵא טַסְקָא דְּקַשְׁבָא, וּמְלֵי כָּסָא קִמְחָא דְּאַבְשׁוּנָא. אֲמַר לֵיהּ אַבַּיֵּי: הָשְׁתָּא אָמַר מָרִי: אִי חַקְלָאָה מַלְכָּא לֶיהֱוֵי – דִּיקוּלָא מִצַּוָּארֵיהּ לָא נָחֵית.

The Gemara relates that **Rabba sent** Purim portions from the house of the Exilarch **to Marei bar Mar**[N] **in the hands of Abaye,** who was his nephew and student. The Purim portions consisted of **a sack** [***taska***][L] **full of dates** [***kashva***][L] **and a cupful of roasted flour** [***kimḥa de'avshuna***].[L] **Abaye said to him: Now, Mari will say** the popular expression: Even **if a farmer becomes the king, the basket does not descend from his neck.** Rabba was named the head of the yeshiva in Pumbedita, and nevertheless, he continued to send very plain gifts, because he was impoverished.

הֲדַר שְׁדַר לֵיהּ אִיהוּ מְלֵא טַסְקָא דְּזַנְגְּבִילָא, וּמְלֵא כָּסָא דְּפִלְפַּלְתָּא אֲרִיכָא. אֲמַר אַבַּיֵּי: הָשְׁתָּא אָמַר מָר: אֲנָא שְׁדַרִי לֵיהּ חוּלְיָא וְאִיהוּ שְׁדַר לִי חוּרְפָּא.

Marei bar Mar **sent back to him a sack full of ginger and a cupful of long peppers** [***pilpalta arikha***],[LB] a much more expensive gift. **Abaye said** to him: **The master,** Rabba, **will now say: I sent him sweet** items **and he sent me pungent** ones.

אֲמַר אַבַּיֵּי: כִּי נְפַקִי מִבֵּי מָר הֲוָה שָׂבַעְנָא, כִּי מְטַאי לְהָתָם קְרִיבוּ לִי שִׁיתִּין צָעֵי דְּשִׁיתִּין מִינֵי קְדֵירָה, וַאֲכָלִי בְּהוּ שִׁיתִּין פְּלוּגֵי. וּבִישּׁוּלָא בַּתְרַיְיתָא הָווּ קָרוּ לֵיהּ צְלִי קֵדָר, וּבְעַאי לְמֵיכַס צַעֲא אַבַּתְרָהּ.

In describing that same incident, **Abaye said: When I left** the **house of the master,** Rabba, to go to Marei bar Mar, **I was** already **satiated.** However, **when I arrived there** at Marei bar Mar's house, **they served me sixty plates of sixty kinds of cooked dishes, and I ate sixty portions from** each of **them. The last dish was called pot roast,**[B] **and** I was still so hungry that **I wanted to chew the plate afterward.**

אֲמַר אַבַּיֵּי: הַיְינוּ דְּאָמְרִי אֱינָשֵׁי: כָּפֵין עַנְיָא וְלָא יָדַע. אִי נַמִּי: רַוְוחָא לִבְסִימָא שְׁכִיחַ.

And in continuation **Abaye said: This** explains the folk saying **that people say: The poor** man **is hungry and does not know** it, as Abaye was unaware how hungry he had been in his master's house. **Alternatively,** there is another appropriate, popular expression: **Room** in the stomach **for sweets** can always be **found.**

אַבַּיֵּי בַּר אָבִין וְרַבִּי חֲנִינָא בַּר אָבִין מְחַלְּפִי סְעוּדָתַיְיהוּ לַהֲדָדֵי.

The Gemara relates that **Abaye bar Avin and Rabbi Ḥanina bar Avin would exchange their meals**[HN] **with each other** to fulfill their obligation of sending portions on Purim.

אֲמַר רָבָא: מִיחַיַּיב אִינִישׁ לִבְסוּמֵי בְּפוּרַיָּא עַד דְּלָא יָדַע בֵּין אָרוּר הָמָן לְבָרוּךְ מָרְדֳּכַי.

Rava said: A person is obligated to become intoxicated[HN] with wine **on Purim until he** is so intoxicated **that he does not know** how to distinguish **between cursed is Haman and blessed is Mordecai.**

LANGUAGE

Sack [*taska*] – טַסְקָא: From the late Latin tassa or tasca, meaning small bag or basket.

Dates [*kashva*] – קַשְׁבָא: From the Arabic قسب, *qasb*, meaning dates.

Roasted flour [*kimḥa de'avshuna*] – קִמְחָא דְּאַבְשׁוּנָא: The etymology of the word *avshuna* is unknown. According to Rashi and other commentaries, the term refers to dry, roasted grain. The *ge'onim* disagree and explain that it refers to moist grain or barley.

Long pepper [*pilpalta arikha*] – פִּלְפַּלְתָּא אֲרִיכָא: From the Sanskrit pippali. It was adopted, with variations, by many other languages.

BACKGROUND

Ginger and peppers – זַנְגְּבִיל וּפִלְפֵּל: These spices are extracted from plants that grow in Southeast Asia, South India, and Indonesia. They were greatly valued in ancient times, and due to the need to transport them over great distances, their price was very high.

Pot roast – צְלִי קֵדָר: The *Arukh* explains that pot roast is meat that is roasted without water, inside a pot, in a manner similar to frying.

HALAKHA

Would exchange their meals – מְחַלְּפִי סְעוּדָתַיְיהוּ: One who lacks the means to send portions to another may share a meal with another, and thereby, they both fulfill their obligation (*Shulḥan Arukh, Oraḥ Ḥayyim* 695:4).

A person is obligated to become intoxicated – מִיחַיַּיב אִינִישׁ לִבְסוּמֵי: One is obligated to become intoxicated on Purim until he is unable to distinguish between: Cursed is Haman, and: Blessed is Mordecai, in accordance with the opinion of Rava. Some maintain that in the wake of the incident involving Rava and Rabbi Zeira, the *halakha* is no longer in accordance with Rava's opinion, and one drinks only a bit more than he is accustomed to drink (*Taz*, citing the *Beit Yosef*; Rabbeinu Ephraim). Some maintain that one should drink until he falls asleep, at which point he will no longer be able to distinguish between Haman and Mordecai (*Peri Megadim*; Rambam). If one damages another in the course of the Purim festivities, some hold that he is exempt from the obligation to pay (Rema). If the damages are substantial, the custom is not to exempt him (*Mishna Berura*; *Shulḥan Arukh, Oraḥ Ḥayyim* 695:2).

NOTES

Fulfilled through us – קַיַּימְתָּ בָּנוּ: In the Jerusalem Talmud and the *She'iltot*, a variant reading of the incident is cited. First Rabbi Yehuda Nesia sent a small gift, and Rabbi Oshaya responded that he fulfilled the mitzva: "And gifts to the poor." Therefore, he sent a more substantial gift, and Rabbi Oshaya responded that now he had fulfilled: "And sending portions one to another," i.e., a gift that one sends to another who is his equal. Some explain according to Rashi's reading that this incident comes to teach that one can fulfill both mitzvot by giving to one person (*Turei Even*). Others learn from here that wine, and not only food, is also considered a portion (*Peri Ḥadash*).

Rabba sent to Marei bar Mar – רַבָּה שְׁדַר לֵיהּ לְמָרֵי בַּר מָר: See the *Re'aḥ Duda'im*, which elaborates and explains in detail that this story is not merely a series of lighthearted comments but also teaches several practical *halakhot* concerning the sending of portions on Purim.

Would exchange their meals – מְחַלְּפִי סְעוּדָתַיְיהוּ: The Ran explains simply that the two sons of Rav Avin were poor, and consequently they fulfilled their obligations by exchanging meals. Many later authorities explain that, according to the opinion of Rashi, by eating the Purim feast together they enhanced the joy of Purim.

A person is obligated to become intoxicated – מִיחַיַּיב אִינִישׁ לִבְסוּמֵי: There are many different explanations for this *halakha*. The Rambam explains that one must drink until he falls asleep from the wine and will then be unable to differentiate between Haman and Mordecai (see *Oraḥ Halakha*). *Tosafot*, based on the Jerusalem Talmud, explains that after reading the Megilla, it was customary to recite several passages relating to the characters mentioned in it, and some say that an entire poem was read (Rashash). A person will be unable to recite these texts correctly if he is intoxicated; or he will confuse male and female and singular and plural formulations (*Re'aḥ Duda'im*). The Rema MiPano explains that one will be unable to distinguish between: Cursed is Haman, and: Blessed is Mordecai, when he hears it.

There are several other explanations for this obligation. One is that because the numerological value is equal for the Hebrew terms: Cursed is Haman, and: Blessed is Mordecai, and one is required to drink only until he can no longer make that calculation (*Aguda*; Rav Ya'akov Weil). Another explanation is that this is an allusion to the fact that one should drink until he is unable to distinguish even between diametric opposites. Yet another opinion is that one should drink until he forgets his troubles and the hatred that exists between people, so that it is as if the rancor and struggles between Haman and Mordecai are forgotten as well.

NOTES

Slaughtered Rabbi Zeira – שְׁחַטֵיהּ לְרַבִּי זֵירָא: Both early and later commentaries wonder about this incident. Some explain that slaughtered [*shekhatei*] in this case should be read as squeezed [*sakhtei*]: In his joy, Rava embraced Rabbi Zeira so powerfully that he fainted (Meiri; *Oraḥ Halakha*). The Maharsha explains that Rava forced Rabbi Zeira to drink excessively until he became weak and fainted.

The difference between Festivals and Shabbat is only – אֵין בֵּין יוֹם טוֹב לְשַׁבָּת אֶלָּא: In the Jerusalem Talmud, the question is raised: Aren't there many additional differences between Festivals and Shabbat, e.g., carrying out, as well as several rabbinic prohibitions? The Rambam, in his Commentary on the Mishna in tractate *Beitza*, points out that the Gemara already established that this mishna is according to Beit Shammai, and is therefore not in accordance with the *halakha*. However, the Rashba writes that the mishna can be explained even according to Beit Hillel. Despite the formulation: The difference is only, this mishna and those that follow do not presume to define all the differences between the entities being compared. Rather, the comparison is concerning a specific aspect, and the distinction cited is in accordance with the *halakha*.

רַבָּה וְרַבִּי זֵירָא עֲבַדוּ סְעוּדַת פּוּרִים בַּהֲדֵי הֲדָדֵי, אִיבַּסּוּם, קָם רַבָּה שַׁחְטֵיהּ לְרַבִּי זֵירָא. לְמָחָר בְּעֵי רַחֲמֵי וְאַחֲיֵיהּ. לְשָׁנָה אֲמַר לֵיהּ: נֵיתֵי מָר וְנַעֲבֵיד סְעוּדַת פּוּרִים בַּהֲדֵי הֲדָדֵי! אֲמַר לֵיהּ: לָא בְּכָל שַׁעְתָּא וְשַׁעְתָּא מִתְרְחִישׁ נִיסָּא.

The Gemara relates that **Rabba and Rabbi Zeira prepared a Purim feast with each other,** and **they became intoxicated** to the point that **Rabba arose and slaughtered Rabbi Zeira.**[N] **The next day,** when he became sober and realized what he had done, Rabba **asked** God **for mercy, and revived him. The next year,** Rabba **said to** Rabbi Zeira: **Let the Master come and let us prepare the Purim feast with each other. He said to him: Miracles do not happen each and every hour,** and I do not want to undergo that experience again.

אָמַר רָבָא: סְעוּדַת פּוּרִים שֶׁאֲכָלָהּ בַּלַּיְלָה לֹא יָצָא יְדֵי חוֹבָתוֹ, מַאי טַעְמָא – ״יְמֵי מִשְׁתֶּה וְשִׂמְחָה״ כְּתִיב. רַב אָשֵׁי הֲוָה יָתֵיב קַמֵּיהּ (דְּרַב כָּהֲנָא) נְגַהּ וְלָא אֲתוֹ רַבָּנַן. אֲמַר לֵיהּ: מַאי טַעְמָא לָא אֲתוֹ רַבָּנַן – דִּלְמָא טְרִידִי בִּסְעוּדַת פּוּרִים – אֲמַר לֵיהּ: וְלָא הֲוָה אֶפְשָׁר לְמֵיכְלָהּ בְּאוּרְתָּא? אֲמַר לֵיהּ: לָא שְׁמִיעַ לֵיהּ לְמָר הָא דַּאֲמַר רָבָא: סְעוּדַת פּוּרִים שֶׁאֲכָלָהּ בַּלַּיְלָה לֹא יָצָא יְדֵי חוֹבָתוֹ. אֲמַר לֵיהּ: (אֲמַר רָבָא הָכִי) [אֲמַר לֵיהּ אִין] תְּנָא מִינֵּיהּ אַרְבְּעִין זִימְנִין, וְדָמֵי לֵיהּ כְּמַאן דְּמַנַּח בְּכִיסֵיהּ:

Rava said: A Purim feast[H] **that one ate at night did not fulfill his obligation. What is the reason? "Days of feasting and gladness"** (Esther 9:22) **is written,** i.e., days and not nights. The Gemara relates: **Rav Ashi was sitting before Rav Kahana** his teacher on Purim, and **it grew dark and the Sages** who usually came to study with him **did not come.** Rav Ashi **said to him: What is the reason that the Sages did not come** today? Rav Kahana answered: **Perhaps they are preoccupied with the Purim feast.** Rav Ashi **said to him: Wasn't it possible** for them **to eat** the feast **at night** on Purim, instead of being derelict in their Torah study on Purim day? Rav Kahana **said to him: Didn't the master learn that which Rava said: A Purim feast that one ate at night did not fulfill his obligation?** Rav Ashi **said to him: Did Rava say that?** Rav Kahana **said to him: Yes.** Rav Ashi then **learned it from him forty times until** he remembered it so well that **it seemed to him as if it were placed in his purse.**

מתני׳ אֵין בֵּין יוֹם טוֹב לְשַׁבָּת אֶלָּא אוֹכֶל נֶפֶשׁ בִּלְבַד.

MISHNA The previous mishna concluded with the formula: The difference between… is only, thereby distinguishing between the *halakhot* in two different cases. The following *mishnayot* employ the same formula and distinguish between the *halakhot* in cases unrelated to Purim and the Megilla. The first is: **The difference between Festivals and Shabbat**[H] with regard to the labor prohibited on those days **is only**[N] in **preparing food alone.** It is permitted to cook and bake in order to prepare food on Festivals; however, on Shabbat it is prohibited.

גמ׳ הָא לְעִנְיַן מַכְשִׁירֵי אוֹכֶל נֶפֶשׁ – זֶה וָזֶה שָׁוִין.

GEMARA The Gemara infers **that with regard to the matter of** actions that **facilitate preparation of food,** e.g., sharpening a knife for slaughter, **this,** Shabbat, **and that,** Festivals, **are equal,** in that actions that facilitate preparation of food are prohibited.

מַתְנִיתִין דְּלָא כְּרַבִּי יְהוּדָה, דְּתַנְיָא: אֵין בֵּין יוֹם טוֹב לְשַׁבָּת אֶלָּא אוֹכֶל נֶפֶשׁ, רַבִּי יְהוּדָה מַתִּיר אַף מַכְשִׁירֵי אוֹכֶל נֶפֶשׁ.

The Gemara comments: If so, **the mishna is not in accordance with** the opinion of **Rabbi Yehuda, as it is taught** in a *baraita*: **The difference between Festivals and Shabbat is only** is **preparing food. Rabbi Yehuda permits even** actions that **facilitate preparation of food** on Festivals.

מַאי טַעְמָא דְּתַנָּא קַמָּא – אָמַר קְרָא: ״הוּא״ – וְלֹא מַכְשִׁירָיו, וְרַבִּי יְהוּדָה (אָמַר) ״לָכֶם״ – לָכֶם לְכׇל צׇרְכֵיכֶם.

The Gemara elaborates. **What is the reason** for the opinion **of the first *tanna*?** It is as the **verse states:** "Except that which every person must eat, only that may be done for you" (Exodus 12:16). **"That"** is permitted, **and not** actions that **facilitate** it. **And Rabbi Yehuda says: "For you"** means **for you, for all your needs.**

HALAKHA

Purim feast – סְעוּדַת פּוּרִים: The Purim feast must be eaten on the day of Purim. In accordance with the opinion of Rava, if one eats it at night, he did not fulfill his obligation. The custom is to eat the Purim feast after the afternoon prayer; however, it is appropriate that most of the feast be eaten before nightfall. If Purim occurs on Friday, one eats the Purim feast in the morning. Some hold that the feast should always be before the afternoon prayer (*Shenei Luḥot HaBerit*; *Shulḥan Arukh, Oraḥ Ḥayyim* 695:1).

The difference between Festivals and Shabbat is only, etc. – אֵין בֵּין יוֹם טוֹב לְשַׁבָּת אֶלָּא וכו׳: All labor prohibited on Shabbat is prohibited on Festivals, except for labor performed in the preparation of food. Likewise, in accordance with the opinion of Rabbi Yehuda in tractate *Beitza*, it is permitted to perform labor that facilitates the preparation of food, provided that it was not possible to attend to it prior to the Festival. Some prohibit even the preparation of food itself if the taste of the food is not diminished by preparation prior to the Festival (*Eliya Rabba*; *Peri Ḥadash*), and this is the custom. Nevertheless, if for some reason one failed to perform the labor prior to the Festival and he needs the food on the Festival, the labor is permitted but must be performed in a different manner than it is typically performed (Rema). If he failed to prepare the food before the Festival due to circumstances beyond his control, he may prepare the food on the Festival in the typical manner (*Shulḥan Arukh HaRav*; *Shulḥan Arukh, Oraḥ Ḥayyim* 495:1).

וְאִידָךְ נַמִי, הָכְתִיב ״לָכֶם״! לָכֶם וְלֹא לְגוֹיִם, לָכֶם וְלֹא לִכְלָבִים.

The Gemara asks: **And for the other,** first, *tanna* **too, isn't it written: "For you"?** The Gemara answers: He infers: **For you, and not for gentiles; for you, and not for dogs.**[H] It is forbidden to perform labors for the sake of gentiles, or for animals, even if it is to feed them.

וְאִידָךְ נַמִי, הָא כְּתִיב ״הוּא״! כְּתִיב ״הוּא״ וּכְתִיב ״לָכֶם״, כָּאן – בְּמַכְשִׁירִין שֶׁאֶפְשָׁר לַעֲשׂוֹתָן מֵעֶרֶב יוֹם טוֹב, כָּאן – בְּמַכְשִׁירִין שֶׁאִי אֶפְשָׁר לַעֲשׂוֹתָן מֵעֶרֶב יוֹם טוֹב:

The Gemara asks further: **And for the other** *tanna*, Rabbi Yehuda, **too, isn't it written: "That,"** which is a restrictive term that limits the application of a particular *halakha*? The Gemara answers: **It is written: "That,"** which is restrictive, **and it is written: "For you,"** which is inclusive. Rabbi Yehuda resolves the conflict between the two: **Here,** the word: "That," is referring **to** actions that **facilitate,** in **which it is possible to perform them on the Festival eve** but which are prohibited on the Festival; **there,** the phrase: "For you," is referring **to** actions that **facilitate,** in **which it is impossible to perform them on the Festival eve** and which are permitted even on the Festival.

מתני׳ אֵין בֵּין שַׁבָּת לְיוֹם הַכִּפּוּרִים אֶלָּא שֶׁזֶּה זְדוֹנוֹ בִּידֵי אָדָם וְזֶה זְדוֹנוֹ בְּכָרֵת:

MISHNA **The difference between Shabbat and Yom Kippur** with regard to the labor prohibited on those days **is only that** in **this** case, i.e., Shabbat, **its intentional** desecration is punishable **at the hand of Man,** as he is stoned by a court based on the testimony of witnesses who forewarned the transgressor; **and** in **that** case, i.e., Yom Kippur, **its intentional** desecration is punishable at the hand of God, **with** ***karet***.[HB]

גמ׳ הָא לְעִנְיַן תַּשְׁלוּמִין – זֶה וְזֶה שָׁוִין.

GEMARA The Gemara infers **that with regard to the matter of payment** of damages, both **this,** Shabbat, **and that,** Yom Kippur, **are equal** in that one is exempt in both cases. If one performs an action on Shabbat that entails both a prohibited labor and damage to another's property, since his transgression is punishable by death, he is exempt from paying damages. Apparently, according to the mishna, the same *halakha* applies to Yom Kippur.

מַנִּי מַתְנִיתִין – רַבִּי נְחוּנְיָא בֶּן הַקָּנָה הִיא. דְּתַנְיָא, רַבִּי נְחוּנְיָא בֶּן הַקָּנָה הָיָה עוֹשֶׂה אֶת יוֹם הַכִּפּוּרִים כְּשַׁבָּת לְתַשְׁלוּמִין. מַה שַּׁבָּת מִתְחַיֵּיב בְּנַפְשׁוֹ וּפָטוּר מִן הַתַּשְׁלוּמִין – אַף יוֹם הַכִּפּוּרִים מִתְחַיֵּיב בְּנַפְשׁוֹ וּפָטוּר מִן הַתַּשְׁלוּמִין.

The Gemara asks: According to **whose** opinion is **the mishna** taught? The Gemara answers: **It is** according to the opinion of **Rabbi Neḥunya ben HaKana,**[P] **as it is taught** in a *baraita*: **Rabbi Neḥunya ben HaKana would render Yom Kippur like Shabbat with regard to payment** of damages. **Just as** in the case of one who intentionally desecrates **Shabbat he is liable to** receive the **death** penalty[N] **and** is therefore **exempt from** the obligation of **payment** of damages caused while desecrating Shabbat, **so too,** in the case of one who intentionally desecrates **Yom Kippur, he is liable to** receive the **death** penalty **and** is therefore **exempt from** the obligation of **payment** of damages caused while desecrating Yom Kippur.

תְּנַן הָתָם: כָּל חַיָּיבֵי כְּרֵיתוֹת שֶׁלָּקוּ נִפְטְרוּ מִידֵי כְּרֵיתָתָן, שֶׁנֶּאֱמַר: ״וְנִקְלָה אָחִיךָ לְעֵינֶיךָ״ – כֵּיוָן שֶׁלָּקָה הֲרֵי הוּא כְּאָחִיךָ, דִּבְרֵי רַבִּי חֲנַנְיָה בֶּן גַּמְלִיאֵל. אָמַר רַבִּי יוֹחָנָן: חֲלוּקִין עָלָיו חֲבֵירָיו עַל רַבִּי חֲנַנְיָה בֶּן גַּמְלִיאֵל.

We learned there in a mishna (*Makkot* 23a): **All** those **liable to** receive ***karet*** **who were flogged**[H] in court **were exempted from their** ***karet***, which is imposed by heaven. Most transgressors are liable to receive *karet* for violating prohibitions that are punishable by flogging. If they are flogged, they are exempt from *karet*, **as it is stated** with regard to one liable to receive lashes: **"Then your brother shall be dishonored before you"** (Deuteronomy 25:3), indicating that **once he was flogged he is like your brother,** and his sins have been pardoned; this is **the statement of Rabbi Ḥananya ben Gamliel. Rabbi Yoḥanan said: Rabbi Ḥananya ben Gamliel's colleagues disagree with him** on this issue.

NOTES

Is liable to receive the death penalty – מִתְחַיֵּיב בְּנַפְשׁוֹ: As a rule, one is not liable to receive two punishments for two transgressions violated simultaneously. The principle is: One is liable to receive the greater punishment. There is an additional principle that in the case of a prohibition punishable by death, even if the punishment is not implemented due to lack of testimony or forewarning, the mere fact that the prohibition is associated with the stringent punishment exempts one who violated it from any lesser punishment. The dispute here is with regard to *karet*. Because it is not a punishment administered by the court, perhaps these principles do not apply.

HALAKHA

For you and not for gentiles, for you and not for dogs – לָכֶם וְלֹא לְגוֹיִם, לָכֶם וְלֹא לִכְלָבִים: It is prohibited to perform labor on Festivals, even labor performed in the preparation of food, for the benefit of a gentile. One may not perform labor on a Festival to prepare food for an animal (*Shulḥan Arukh, Oraḥ Ḥayyim* 512:1, 3).

Shabbat and Yom Kippur – שַׁבָּת וְיוֹם הַכִּפּוּרִים: For all labors for which one is liable to be stoned on Shabbat, one is liable to receive *karet* on Yom Kippur. All actions prohibited by rabbinic law on Shabbat are similarly prohibited on Yom Kippur, although one who performs them is exempt from punishment. There is an additional difference between labor performed on Shabbat and labor performed on Yom Kippur with regard to damage caused to the property of another while performing a prohibited labor, e.g., burning another's field. On Yom Kippur, he is obligated to pay for the damage; and on Shabbat, he is exempt, as the *halakha* is ruled contrary to the opinion of Rabbi Neḥunya ben HaKana, who rules that he is exempt from payment on Yom Kippur as well (*Magen Avraham*; *Shulḥan Arukh, Oraḥ Ḥayyim* 611:2).

Those liable to receive *karet* who were flogged – חַיָּיבֵי כְּרֵיתוֹת שֶׁלָּקוּ: All who violated prohibitions and were flogged are rehabilitated. Similarly, one who is liable to receive *karet* and was flogged is exempt from the punishment of *karet*, in accordance with the opinion of Rav Ḥananya ben Gamliel (Rambam *Sefer Shofetim, Hilkhot Sanhedrin* 17:7).

BACKGROUND

***Karet* – כָּרֵת:** *Karet* is a divine punishment administered for serious transgressions. The commentaries dispute its precise parameters. Among the characteristics of *karet* are: Premature or sudden death, no children or death of one's children, excision of the soul from the World-to-Come. In tractate *Kareitot*, thirty-six transgressions punishable with *karet* are enumerated. All are prohibitions, with the exception of two: Failure to sacrifice the Paschal lamb and failure to perform circumcision. *Karet* is administered only to one who commits a transgression intentionally. In many cases, if the transgression was committed in the presence of witnesses, the transgressor is subject to execution administered by the court, or to lashes. Anyone who violates one of the prohibitions punishable by *karet* unwittingly is liable to bring a sin-offering as atonement.

PERSONALITIES

Rabbi Neḥunya ben HaKana – רַבִּי נְחוּנְיָא בֶּן הַקָּנָה: Rabbi Neḥunya ben HaKana was a *tanna* during the generation when the Second Temple was destroyed. It is possible that he is the same *tanna* occasionally referred to as Rabbi Neḥunya the Great. Apparently, he had a close relationship with the students of Rabban Yoḥanan ben Zakkai.

Few of Rabbi Neḥunya ben HaKana's halakhic statements were preserved; however, several aggadic statements are cited in his name. The prayer that he recited upon entering the study hall (*Berakhot* 28b) is widely known. Later in this tractate (28a) his positive attributes and his modesty are recounted. Rabbi Neḥunya is credited with development of the hermeneutical method of generalization and detail, and it is generally attributed to Rabbi Yishmael, his most prominent student. Authorship of *Sefer HaBahir*, a kabbalistic midrash, is also attributed to him, as is the prayer: Please, with the might [*ana bekhoʼaḥ*].

Kana is the name of a city in the tribal territory of Asher (Joshua 19:28). Perhaps his title is attributable to the place where he lived.

אָמַר רָבָא: אָמְרִי בֵּי רַב: תָּנֵינָא אֵין בֵּין יוֹם הַכִּפּוּרִים לְשַׁבָּת אֶלָּא שֶׁזֶּה זְדוֹנוֹ בִּידֵי אָדָם וְזֶה זְדוֹנוֹ בְּהִיכָּרֵת. וְאִם אִיתָא – אִידִי וְאִידִי בִּידֵי אָדָם הִיא!

Rava said that the Sages of **the school of Rav said: We learned: The difference between Yom Kippur and Shabbat is only that** in **this** case, Shabbat, **its intentional** desecration is punishable **at the hand of Man; and** in **that** case, Yom Kippur, **its intentional** desecration is punishable **with *karet*. And if** the statement of Rabbi Ḥananya ben Gamliel **is so,** in both **this** case, Shabbat, **and that** case, Yom Kippur, the punishment **is at the hand of Man.**

אָמַר רַב נַחְמָן: הָא מַנִּי – רַבִּי יִצְחָק הִיא, דְּאָמַר: מַלְקוֹת בְּחַיָּיבֵי כְרִיתוֹת לֵיכָּא. דְּתַנְיָא, רַבִּי יִצְחָק אוֹמֵר: חַיָּיבֵי כְרִיתוֹת בִּכְלָל הָיוּ, וְלָמָּה יָצָאת כָּרֵת בַּאֲחוֹתוֹ – לְדוּנָהּ בְּכָרֵת וְלֹא בְּמַלְקוֹת.

Rav Naḥman said: There is no proof from here that Rabbi Ḥananya ben Gamliel's colleagues disagree with him, as in accordance with **whose** opinion **is this** mishna taught? **It is** according to the opinion of **Rabbi Yitzḥak, who said: There are no lashes in** cases of **those liable** to receive ***karet*, as it is taught** in a *baraita* that **Rabbi Yitzḥak says:** All **those liable** to receive ***karet*** in cases of incest **were included in** the principle: "For whoever shall commit any of these abominations, even the persons that commit them shall be cut off from among their people" (Leviticus 18:29). **And why was *karet*** administered to **one's sister excluded**[N] from this verse and mentioned independently (Leviticus 20:17)? It is **to sentence her to** the punishment of ***karet* and not to** the punishment of **lashes.** This serves as a paradigm; wherever one is liable to receive *karet*, there are no lashes.

רַב אַשִׁי אָמַר: אֲפִילּוּ תֵּימָא רַבָּנַן, זֶה – עִיקַּר זְדוֹנוֹ בִּידֵי אָדָם, וְזֶה – עִיקַּר זְדוֹנוֹ בְּהִיכָּרֵת.

Rav Ashi said: Even if **you say** that the mishna is according to the opinion of **the Rabbis** who disagree with Rabbi Yitzḥak and hold that there are lashes even in cases where there is liability for *karet*, there is no proof that Rabbi Ḥananya ben Gamliel's colleagues disagree with him. The mishna can be understood as follows: In **this** case, Shabbat, the **primary** punishment for **its intentional** desecration is **at the hand of Man; and** in **that** case, Yom Kippur, the **primary** punishment for **its intentional** desecration is **with *karet*.** If, however, he was flogged, he is exempt from *karet.*

NOTES

And why was *karet* administered to one's sister excluded – וְלָמָּה יָצָאת כָּרֵת בַּאֲחוֹתוֹ: The principle here is: A matter that was included in a generalization but was explicitly excluded in order to teach a *halakha*, was not excluded to teach only concerning the specific matter at hand; it was rather excluded in order to teach concerning an entire generalization. In other words, an exception written with regard to one detail applies to the entire generalization. See *Tosafot*, who explain this slightly differently.

Perek **I**
Daf **8** Amud **a**

מתני׳ אֵין בֵּין הַמּוּדָּר הֲנָאָה מֵחֲבֵירוֹ לְמוּדָּר מִמֶּנּוּ מַאֲכָל אֶלָּא דְּרִיסַת הָרֶגֶל, וְכֵלִים שֶׁאֵין עוֹשִׂין בָּהֶן אוֹכֶל נֶפֶשׁ.

MISHNA **The difference between one for whom benefit from another is forbidden by vow and one for whom benefit from** another's **food is forbidden by vow is only** with regard to **stepping foot** on his property, **and** with regard to borrowing **utensils** from him **that one does not use** in the **preparation of food,** but for other purposes; as those two benefits are prohibited to the former, but permitted to the latter.[H]

גמ׳ הָא לְעִנְיַן כֵּלִים שֶׁעוֹשִׂין בָּהֶן אוֹכֶל נֶפֶשׁ – זֶה וָזֶה שָׁוִין.

GEMARA The Gemara infers **that with regard to the matter of utensils that one uses** in **preparation of food,**[N] both **this,** one who vowed that any benefit is forbidden, **and that,** one who vowed that benefit from food is forbidden, **are equal.** It is prohibited for both to derive benefit from utensils used in the preparation of food.

NOTES

Utensils that one uses in preparation of food – כֵּלִים שֶׁעוֹשִׂין בָּהֶן אוֹכֶל נֶפֶשׁ: In the Jerusalem Talmud it is explained that there is a distinction to be made between utensils in which food is prepared, e.g., a sieve and a sifter, which would be prohibited to one who is prohibited by vow from deriving benefit from another's food; and vessels in which food is merely placed, e.g., cups and plates, which are permitted even to that person.

HALAKHA

One prohibited by vow from deriving benefit from another and one prohibited by vow from deriving benefit from another's food – הַמּוּדָּר הֲנָאָה מֵחֲבֵירוֹ לְמוּדָּר מִמֶּנּוּ מַאֲכָל: One for whom it is prohibited to derive benefit from another's possessions is prohibited to pass through his friend's property, even if it does not shorten his path (*Taz*; *Shakh*). He may not even go through his friend's fields during the summer, when people typically overlook trespassing in their fields. Likewise, he may not borrow any vessel from his friend. If he is prohibited by vow from deriving benefit from another's food, it is prohibited to eat his food. If one said: Benefit from your food is prohibited for me, he may not eat the food; however, he may use vessels used in preparation of the food. If he said: Benefit that leads to food is prohibited for me, he may neither eat the food nor benefit from any vessel that is typically rented (*Shulḥan Arukh, Yoreh De'a* 221:1).

"דְּרִיסַת הָרֶגֶל": הָא לָא קָפְדִי אֱינָשֵׁי! אָמַר רָבָא: הָא מַנִּי – רַבִּי אֱלִיעֶזֶר, דְּאָמַר: וִיתּוּר אָסוּר בְּמוּדַּר הֲנָאָה.

The mishna stated that for one for whom benefit from another is forbidden by vow, **stepping foot** on the latter's property is prohibited. The Gemara asks: What benefit is that? **Aren't people not particular**[N] about other people treading on their property? **Rava said:** In accordance with **whose** opinion **is this** mishna taught? It is the opinion of **Rabbi Eliezer, who said: Overlooking is prohibited**[N] in the case **of one for whom benefit is forbidden by vow.** For one for whom benefit from another is forbidden by vow, benefit is forbidden even in matters with regard to which one is typically not particular and overlooks others' use of his property, e.g., stepping foot on it.

מתני׳ אֵין בֵּין נְדָרִים לִנְדָבוֹת אֶלָּא שֶׁהַנְּדָרִים חַיָּיב בְּאַחֲרָיוּתָן, וּנְדָבוֹת אֵינוֹ חַיָּיב בְּאַחֲרָיוּתָן.

MISHNA **The difference between** animals consecrated to the Temple as **vow offerings and** animals consecrated as **gift offerings is only**[N] **that** in the case of **vow offerings,** if they died or were lost before being sacrificed on the altar, one **is obligated in** the **responsibility** to replace **them, and** in the case of **gift** offerings, if they died or were lost, one **is not obligated in** the **responsibility** to replace **them.**[H]

גמ׳ הָא לְעִנְיַן "בַּל תְּאַחֵר" – זֶה וָזֶה שָׁוִין.

GEMARA The Gemara infers **that with regard to the matter of** the prohibition: **Do not be slack**[B] to pay one's pledges, both **this,** a vow offering, **and that,** a gift offering, **are equal.** If one delayed bringing either a vow offering or a gift offering, he violates the prohibition.

תְּנַן הָתָם: אֵי זֶהוּ נֶדֶר – הָאוֹמֵר "הֲרֵי עָלַי עוֹלָה". אֵיזוֹ הִיא נְדָבָה – הָאוֹמֵר "הֲרֵי זוֹ עוֹלָה". וּמָה בֵּין נְדָרִים לִנְדָבוֹת? נְדָרִים, מֵתוּ אוֹ נִגְנְבוּ אוֹ אָבְדוּ – חַיָּיב בְּאַחֲרָיוּתָן, נְדָבוֹת, מֵתוּ אוֹ נִגְנְבוּ אוֹ אָבְדוּ – אֵינוֹ חַיָּיב בְּאַחֲרָיוּתָן,

We learned in a mishna **there: Which is** the case of **a vow** offering? It is **one who says:** It is incumbent **upon me** to bring **a burnt-offering. Which is** the case of **a gift** offering?[H] It is **one who says: This** animal is a **burnt-offering. And what is** the difference **between a vow** offering **and a gift** offering? With regard to **vow** offerings, if the animals **died or were stolen or were lost,** the one who vowed **is obligated in** the **responsibility** to replace **them,** as he undertook to bring a burnt-offering and he is not absolved of his obligation until he brings the offering. With regard to **gift** offerings, however, if the animals **died or were stolen or were lost,** the one who vowed **is not obligated in** the **responsibility** to replace **them.**

מְנָהָנֵי מִילֵּי? דְּתָנוּ רַבָּנַן: "וְנִרְצָה לוֹ לְכַפֵּר עָלָיו" רַבִּי שִׁמְעוֹן אוֹמֵר: אֶת שֶׁעָלָיו חַיָּיב בְּאַחֲרָיוּתוֹ, וְאֶת שֶׁאֵינוֹ עָלָיו אֵינוֹ חַיָּיב בְּאַחֲרָיוּתוֹ.

The Gemara asks: **From where are these matters** derived? The Gemara answers: It is **as the Sages taught** in a *baraita* with regard to a burnt-offering, that the verse states: **"And it shall be accepted for him to make atonement upon him"** (Leviticus 1:4).[N] **Rabbi Shimon says: That which is** incumbent **upon him,** i.e., which he accepted as a personal obligation, **he does not bear responsibility** to replace **it** if it died or was stolen; **however, that which is not** incumbent **upon him,** i.e., that which he did not accept as a personal obligation but which he designated as an offering, he **does not bear responsibility** to replace **it.**

מַאי מַשְׁמַע? אָמַר רַבִּי יִצְחָק בַּר אַבְדִּימִי: כֵּיוָן דְּאָמַר "עָלַי" – כְּמַאן דְּטָעֵין אַכַּתְפֵּיהּ דָּמֵי.

The Gemara asks: **From where may** that conclusion **be inferred** from the verse? **Rabbi Yitzḥak bar Avdimi said: Since he said** it is incumbent **upon me** to bring a burnt-offering, he is **considered as one who bears** it **upon his shoulders.** The expression: Upon me, indicates an assumption of responsibility to bring an offering.

HALAKHA

Vow offerings and gift offerings – נְדָרִים וּנְדָבוֹת: What is the difference between a vow offering and a gift offering? If one designated an animal for an offering by means of a vow, and the animal was lost or died, he is obligated to replace it. If one designated an animal as a gift offering, saying: This is an offering, if the animal dies or is lost, he is not obligated to replace it (Rambam *Sefer Avoda, Hilkhot Ma'aseh HaKorbanot* 14:5).

Which is the case of a vow offering…which is the case of a gift offering – אֵי זֶהוּ נֶדֶר...אֵיזוֹ הִיא נְדָבָה: If one says: It is incumbent upon me to bring an offering, or: It is incumbent upon me to bring the value of a certain object as an offering, that is a vow offering. However, if one says: It is incumbent upon me to bring this animal, or: It is incumbent upon me to bring the value of this object, that is a gift offering (Rambam *Sefer Avoda, Hilkhot Ma'aseh HaKorbanot* 14:4).

BACKGROUND

Do not be slack – בַּל תְּאַחֵר: The source for this prohibition is Deuteronomy 23:22. One violates the prohibition when he fails to fulfill his commitment before three pilgrim Festivals pass from the time it was pledged. The prohibition applies to all obligatory offerings, tithes, gifts, and pledges to the Temple treasury. Moreover, this prohibition also applies to pledges to charity and the like, which must also be honored within the same period of time.

NOTES

Aren't people not particular – הָא לָא קָפְדִי אֱינָשֵׁי: Ostensibly, benefit is limited to situations where, due to friendship, one allows a friend to use his property; he would not allow just anyone to do so. However, stepping foot on one's property, with regard to which people are typically not particular, might not constitute benefit (Rid).

Overlooking is prohibited – וִיתּוּר אָסוּר: Standard cases where people typically overlook benefit accrued by others are when the weight of produce on the scales is slightly more than the amount for which a customer paid, or allowing the customer to keep a *peruta* of change (Meiri).

The difference between vow offerings and gift offerings is only – אֵין בֵּין נְדָרִים לִנְדָבוֹת אֶלָּא: See *Tosafot*, who question why the mishna does not mention other differences between a vow offering and a gift offering. *Tosafot* in tractate *Bava Kamma* (62b) cite additional answers. One is that the mishna is referring to a bird brought as a burnt-offering, with regard to which there are no other differences between the two. A second answer is given according to the Rashba, who explains that despite the formulation: The difference is only, the mishna does not presume to define all of the differences between the items compared. Rather, the comparison is concerning the specific issue of responsibility. That approach solves several comments of later authorities, who noted additional differences.

To make atonement upon him – לְכַפֵּר עָלָיו: Apparently, this is derived from the meaning of the term: Upon him, which is an expression of personal responsibility. The Ritva explains that it is derived from the fact that the term: Upon him, is superfluous in this context.

מתני׳ אֵין בֵּין זָב הָרוֹאֶה שְׁתֵּי רְאִיּוֹת לְרוֹאֶה שָׁלֹשׁ אֶלָּא קׇרְבָּן.

MISHNA **The difference between a *zav* who experiences two emissions**[NH] of a pus-like discharge from his penis **and one who experiences three** emissions **is only**[N] that the *zav* who experienced three emissions is obligated to bring **an offering** after he recovers, in order to complete his purification process.[B]

גמ׳ הָא לְעִנְיַן מִשְׁכָּב וּמוֹשָׁב וּסְפִירַת שִׁבְעָה זֶה וָזֶה שָׁוִין.

GEMARA The Gemara infers **that with regard to the matter of** transmitting ritual impurity to a surface designated for **lying and** a surface designated for **sitting, and** similarly with regard to **the counting of seven** days clean of emissions so that he may immerse in a ritual bath as part of the purification process, both **this,** i.e., one who experienced two emissions, **and that,** one who experienced three emissions, **are equal.**

מְנָהָנֵי מִילֵּי? דְּתָנוּ רַבָּנַן: רַבִּי סִימַאי אוֹמֵר: מָנָה הַכָּתוּב שְׁתַּיִם וּקְרָאוֹ טָמֵא, שָׁלֹשׁ וּקְרָאוֹ טָמֵא. הָא כֵּיצַד? שְׁתַּיִם לְטוּמְאָה, וְשָׁלֹשׁ לְקׇרְבָּן.

The Gemara asks: **From where are these matters** derived? The Gemara answers: It is **as the Sages taught** in a *baraita* that **Rabbi Simai says: The verse enumerated two** emissions: "When any man has an emission out of his flesh, due to his emission he is impure" (Leviticus 15:2), **and it called** the *zav* **impure.** Another verse enumerated **three** emissions: "And this shall be his impurity in his emission: Whether his flesh runs with his emission, or his flesh be stopped from his emission, it is his impurity" (Leviticus 15:3), **and it** too **called him impure. How so?** If he is impure after two emissions, for what purpose does the Torah mention three? It is to teach: **Two** emissions **to** establish **impurity and three to** render him liable to bring **an offering.**

וְאֵימַר: שְׁתַּיִם לְטוּמְאָה וְלֹא לְקׇרְבָּן, שָׁלֹשׁ לְקׇרְבָּן וְלֹא לְטוּמְאָה! אָמְרַתְּ: עַד שֶׁלֹּא רָאָה שָׁלֹשׁ רָאָה שְׁתַּיִם.

The Gemara raises an alternative. **And say** instead: **Two** emissions **to** establish **impurity but not to** render him liable to bring **an offering; three** emissions **to** render him liable to bring **an offering, but not to** establish **impurity.** The Gemara rejects this: That is impossible, as **you** can **say** that **until he experienced three** emissions, **he** already **experienced two,** and therefore he is impure in the case of three emissions as well.

וְאֵימַר: שְׁתַּיִם לְקׇרְבָּן וְלֹא לְטוּמְאָה, שָׁלֹשׁ אַף לְטוּמְאָה! לָא סָלְקָא דַּעְתָּךְ, דְּתַנְיָא: "וְכִפֶּר עָלָיו הַכֹּהֵן לִפְנֵי ה׳ מִזּוֹבוֹ" – מִקְצָת זָבִין מְבִיאִין קׇרְבָּן וּמִקְצָת זָבִין אֵין מְבִיאִין קׇרְבָּן. הָא כֵּיצַד? רָאָה שָׁלֹשׁ – מֵבִיא, שְׁתַּיִם – אֵינוֹ מֵבִיא.

The Gemara raises a different alternative. **And say** instead: **Two** emissions **to** render him liable to bring **an offering, but not to** establish **impurity; three** emissions **to** establish **impurity as well.** The Gemara answers that this suggestion **cannot enter your mind, as it is taught** in a *baraita* that the verse states: **"And the priest shall make atonement for him before the Lord from his emission"** (Leviticus 15:15). The preposition "from" that precedes the words "his emissions" indicates that **some** with the status of a ***zav***[N] **bring an offering and some** with the status of a ***zav*** **do not bring an offering. How so?** If **he experienced three** emissions, **he brings** an offering; if he experienced **two** emissions, **he does not bring** an offering.

אוֹ אֵינוֹ אֶלָּא: רָאָה שְׁתַּיִם – מֵבִיא, רָאָה שָׁלֹשׁ – אֵינוֹ מֵבִיא? אָמְרַתְּ: עַד שֶׁלֹּא רָאָה שָׁלֹשׁ רָאָה שְׁתַּיִם.

The *baraita* suggests: **Or** perhaps, **it** means **nothing other** than that if **one experienced two** emissions, **he brings** an offering; if **he experienced three** emissions, **he does not bring** an offering. The Gemara rejects this: That is impossible, as **you** can **say** that **until he experienced three** emissions, **he** already **experienced two,** and therefore he is obligated to bring an offering in the case of three emissions as well.

וְאִיצְטְרִיךְ דְּרַבִּי סִימָאי, וְאִיצְטְרִיךְ "מִזּוֹבוֹ". דְּאִי מִדְּרַבִּי סִימָאי – הֲוָה אָמִינָא כִּי קוּשְׁיַין, קָמַשְׁמַע לַן "מִזּוֹבוֹ". וְאִי "מִזּוֹבוֹ" – לָא יָדְעֵנָא כַּמָּה רְאִיּוֹת, קָמַשְׁמַע לַן דְּרַבִּי סִימָאי.

The Gemara comments: **It was necessary** to cite the proof **of Rabbi Simai** based on the number of mentions of the word emissions in the two verses, **and it was necessary** to cite the proof from the words: **From his emission. As if** the difference between two and three emissions was derived **from** the statement **of Rabbi Simai, I would have said in accordance with our question:** Perhaps one who experiences two emissions brings an offering, and one who experiences three emissions is impure and brings an offering. Therefore, **it teaches us: From his emission. And if** the difference between two and three emissions was derived from the term: **From his emission, I would not have known how many emissions** render him liable to bring an offering, only that some with the status of a *zav* are not required to bring an offering. Therefore, **it teaches us** the proof cited **by Rabbi Simai.**

NOTES

Emissions of the *zav* – רְאִיּוֹת הַזָּב: The emissions of the *zav* are incidents in which he experienced a discharge, whether on consecutive days, or several times in one day. This is not true regarding a *zava*, where the number of emissions is dependent on the number of days in which there is a blood flow and not the number of times that there is a flow.

The difference between a *zav*…is only – אֵין בֵּין זָב...אֶלָּא: In the Jerusalem Talmud it is noted that there are additional differences between a *zav* who experienced two emissions and one who experienced three emissions. A *zav* who experienced two emissions, unlike one who experienced three emissions, must ascertain whether it was caused by outside circumstances beyond his control. The answer there is that the mishna follows the opinion of Rabbi Eliezer, who requires examination for one who experienced three emissions. See the Jerusalem Talmud for an additional answer that resolves the question according to all opinions.

According to the Rashba this is not difficult, as the mishna here is discussing the difference between the *zav* who experienced two emissions and one who experienced three; it is not defining what is considered an emission (see *Hagahot Porat Yosef*).

From his emission, some with the status of a *zav* – מִזּוֹבוֹ מִקְצָת זָבִין: This is derived from understanding the letter *mem* in the word *mizovo* as meaning from, i.e., limiting the scope of the *halakha*. Therefore, there are certain cases where a *zav* requires atonement and cases where he does not.

HALAKHA

Emissions – רְאִיּוֹת: The status of one who experiences one emission of a *zav* is that of one who experienced a seminal emission. If one experiences two emissions, he is a *zav*, and must count seven days clean of emissions, and immerse in spring water to become pure. If one experiences three emissions, he is obligated to bring an offering in order to complete his purification. The difference between a *zav* who experiences two emissions and one who experiences three emissions is only that the *zav* who experiences three emissions is obligated to bring an offering (Rambam *Sefer Korbanot*, *Hilkhot Meḥusrei Kappara* 2:6).

BACKGROUND

Discharge – זוֹב: The discharge of a *zav* is apparently the discharge of the modern-day condition of gonorrhea. After one contracts the disease, pus begins to discharge from his sexual organ, followed by a discharge of mucous. In the *Tosefta* and the Gemara, the differences between a seminal emission and the emission of a *zav* are delineated.

The severe impurity of the *zav* and his exacting purification process are detailed in the Torah (Leviticus 15:1–15) and in the Mishna (tractate *Zavim*). Although a woman can also contract this disease, a fact acknowledged in the Talmud, only a male becomes impure with the symptoms of a *zav*. A woman becomes impure with the impurity of a *zava* by experiencing a flow of blood not during her menstrual period.

וְהַשְׁתָּא דְּאָמְרַתְּ: ״מִזּוֹבוֹ״ לִדְרָשָׁא, ״וְכִי יִטְהַר הַזָּב מִזּוֹבוֹ״ מַאי דָּרְשַׁתְּ בֵּיהּ?

The Gemara asks: **And now that you said** that the term: **From his emission,** is exclusionary and comes **for derivation, what do you derive from** the verse: **"And when the *zav* is cleansed from his emission"** (Leviticus 15:13)?

הַהוּא מִיבְּעֵי לֵיהּ לְכִדְתַנְיָא: וְכִי יִטְהַר הַזָּב – לִכְשֶׁיִּפְסוֹק, ״מִזּוֹבוֹ״ [מִזּוֹבוֹ] וְלֹא מִזּוֹבוֹ וְנִגְעוֹ. ״מִזּוֹבוֹ וְסָפַר״ – לִימֵּד עַל זָב בַּעַל שְׁתֵּי רְאִיּוֹת שֶׁטָּעוּן סְפִירַת שִׁבְעָה.

The Gemara answers: **That** verse **is needed to** derive **that which was taught** in a *baraita*. It is written: **"And when the *zav* is cleansed** from his emission, then he shall count to himself seven days for his purification" (Leviticus 15:13), **when** his emissions **cease.** The *baraita* infers from the term: **From his emission,** that he needs to be cleansed only **from his emission, but not from his emission and his leprosy.** If one was both a *zav* and also had leprosy, he need not wait until he is asymptomatic of his leprosy before counting seven clean days. Rather, he counts seven clean days, and after the leprosy symptoms cease, he immerses for both impurities. **"From his emission, then he shall count": This teaches concerning a *zav* who experienced two emissions, that he** too **requires a count of seven** clean days.

וַהֲלֹא דִּין הוּא: אִם מְטַמֵּא מִשְׁכָּב וּמוֹשָׁב – לֹא יְהֵא טָעוּן סְפִירַת שִׁבְעָה?!

The *baraita* continues: **But** in order to derive that *halakha*, the verse is unnecessary, as **isn't it** only **logical?** If a *zav* who experienced two emissions **renders** a surface designated for **lying and** a surface designated for **sitting ritually impure** and all strictures of a *zav* apply to him, **wouldn't he require a count of seven** clean days to become purified?

Perek **I**
Daf **8** Amud **b**

״שׁוֹמֶרֶת יוֹם כְּנֶגֶד יוֹם״ תּוֹכִיחַ, שֶׁמְּטַמְּאָה מִשְׁכָּב וּמוֹשָׁב וְאֵינָהּ טְעוּנָה סְפִירַת שִׁבְעָה.

A woman who observes a clean **day for** one **day** or two days that she experiences a discharge **will prove** that this is not the case.[H] This refers to a woman who experienced one or two days of bleeding not during her menstrual period and is required to wait one day without any further discharge of blood before immersion in a ritual bath. This is significant **because she renders** a surface designated for **lying and** a surface designated for **sitting ritually impure, and** nevertheless **she does not require a count of seven** clean days to become purified.

וְאַף אַתָּה אַל תִּתְמַהּ עַל זֶה, שֶׁאַף עַל פִּי שֶׁמְּטַמֵּא מִשְׁכָּב וּמוֹשָׁב לֹא יְהֵא טָעוּן סְפִירַת שִׁבְעָה, תַּלְמוּד לוֹמַר: ״מִזּוֹבוֹ וְסָפַר״ – מִקְצָת זוֹבוֹ וְסָפַר, לִימֵּד עַל זָב בַּעַל שְׁתֵּי רְאִיּוֹת שֶׁטָּעוּן סְפִירַת שִׁבְעָה.

And you too should not then **be surprised that this *zav*, although he renders** a surface designated for **lying and** a surface designated for **sitting ritually impure, he does not require a count of seven** clean days to become purified. Therefore, **the verse states: "From his emission, then he shall count,"** meaning that even **a partial *zav*** is obligated in the mitzva of: **Then he shall count. This teaches concerning a *zav* who experienced two emissions, that he** too **requires a count of seven** clean days.

אֲמַר לֵיהּ רַב פַּפָּא לְאַבַּיֵי: מַאי שְׁנָא הַאי ״מִזּוֹבוֹ״ דִּמְרַבֵּי בֵּיהּ זָב בַּעַל שְׁתֵּי רְאִיּוֹת, וּמַאי שְׁנָא הַאי ״מִזּוֹבוֹ״ דִּמְמַעֵט בֵּיהּ זָב בַּעַל שְׁתֵּי רְאִיּוֹת?

Rav Pappa said to Abaye: What is different about **this** verse that states: **"From his emission," which** is interpreted to **include a *zav* who experienced two emissions** in the obligation to count seven clean days; **and what is different** about **that** verse that states: **"From his emission," which** is interpreted to **exclude**[N] **a *zav* who experienced two emissions** from the obligation to bring an offering? Why is the identical term interpreted once as inclusionary and once as exclusionary?

אֲמַר לֵיהּ: אִי סָלְקָא דַּעְתָּךְ הַאי לְמַעוּטֵי הוּא דַּאֲתָא – לִישְׁתּוֹק קְרָא מִינֵּיהּ. וְכִי תֵּימָא: אָתְיָא מִדִּינָא – שׁוֹמֶרֶת יוֹם כְּנֶגֶד יוֹם תּוֹכִיחַ.

Abaye **said to him: If it enters your mind** to say that **this** instance of the term: "From his emission," **comes to exclude** a *zav* who experienced two emissions from the obligation to count seven clean days, **let the verse remain silent** and omit the term, as there would have been no basis to include a *zav* who experienced two emissions in that *halakha*. **And if you would say** that this **can be inferred logically, a woman who observes a day for a day will prove** that there is no correlation between ritual impurity transmitted to a surface designated for lying and a surface designated for sitting, and the obligation to count seven clean days.

HALAKHA

A woman who observes a clean day for one day or two days that she experiences a discharge – שׁוֹמֶרֶת יוֹם כְּנֶגֶד יוֹם: A lesser *zava*, who observes a clean day for one or two days of discharge, also renders vessels impure through contact, and transmits ritual impurity to a surface designated for lying and a surface designated for sitting, rendering them a primary source of ritual impurity (Rambam *Sefer Tahara, Hilkhot Metamei Mishkav UMoshav* 1:1–2).

NOTES

What is different about this verse…which is interpreted to include…and what is different about that verse…which is interpreted to exclude – מַאי שְׁנָא הַאי...דִּמְרַבֵּי...וּמַאי שְׁנָא הַאי...דִּמְמַעֵט: This does not mean that the term: From his emission, could be understood inclusively or exclusively, as in both possibilities suggested by the Gemara it is exclusionary. According to one possibility, it comes to exclude a *zav*. According to the other possibility, it comes to minimize the number of emissions required, thereby increasing the number of those who enter under the rubric of *zav*.

HALAKHA

A quarantined and a confirmed leper – מְצוֹרָע מוּסְגָּר וּמוּחְלָט: The *halakhot* of a quarantined leper and a confirmed leper are equal with regard to their impurity; however, the quarantined leper is not obligated to let his hair grow wild and to rend his garments. The only difference between the purification process of a quarantined leper and that of a confirmed leper is that the confirmed leper must shave the hair on his entire body and bring the birds (Rambam *Sefer Tahara, Hilkhot Tumat Tzara'at* 10:10).

וְכִי תֵּימָא: הַאי מִיבְּעֵי לֵיהּ "מִזּוֹבוֹ" וְלֹא מִנִּגְעוֹ – אִם כֵּן לִיכְתּוֹב קְרָא "וְכִי יִטְהַר הַזָּב" וְלִישְׁתּוֹק, "מִזּוֹבוֹ" לָמָּה לִי? לִימֵּד עַל זָב בַּעַל שְׁתֵּי רְאִיּוֹת שֶׁטָּעוּן סְפִירַת שִׁבְעָה.

And if you would say that this term: From his emission, **is needed** to derive a different exclusion, i.e., that he counts seven days when he is clean **from his emission and not from his leprosy** and therefore it was necessary to write this term, that is not so. As **if it were so,** then **let the verse write: "And when the *zav* is cleansed" and let** the verse **remain silent** and omit the term, and it would have been clear that even one afflicted with leprosy counts seven clean days once he is cleansed from his emission. **Why** then **do I** need the term: **From his emission?** Rather, it must be understood as an inclusionary term that **teaches concerning a *zav* who experienced two emissions, that he** too **requires a count of seven** clean days.

מתני׳ אֵין בֵּין מְצוֹרָע מוּסְגָּר לִמְצוֹרָע מוּחְלָט אֶלָּא פְּרִיעָה וּפְרִימָה.

MISHNA **The difference between a quarantined leper,** i.e., one examined by a priest who found his symptoms to be inconclusive, and who must therefore remain in isolation for a period of up to two weeks waiting to see if conclusive symptoms develop; **and a confirmed leper,**[HN] i.e., one whose symptoms were conclusive and the priest declared him an absolute leper, **is only** with regard to **letting** the hair on one's head grow **wild and rending** one's garments. A confirmed leper is obligated to let the hair on his head grow wild and rend his garments; a quarantined leper is not.[N]

אֵין בֵּין טָהוֹר מִתּוֹךְ הֶסְגֵּר לְטָהוֹר מִתּוֹךְ הֶחְלֵט אֶלָּא תִּגְלַחַת וְצִפֳּרִים:

The difference between a leper **purified from quarantine,** whose symptoms never became conclusive, **and** a leper **purified from** a state of **confirmed** leprosy **is only** with regard to **shaving** the hair on all his body **and** bringing **birds** as a purification offering, which are obligations incumbent only upon the confirmed leper.

גמ׳ הָא לְעִנְיַן שִׁילּוּחַ [וְטוּמְאָה] – זֶה וָזֶה שָׁוִין.

GEMARA The Gemara infers **that with regard to the matter of expulsion,** from all three camps in the encampment of the Israelites in the desert and from the walled cities in Eretz Yisrael, **and the ritual impurity** of a leper: Both **this,** the quarantined leper, **and that,** the confirmed leper, **are equal.**[N]

מְנָהָנֵי מִילֵּי? דְּתָנֵי רַב שְׁמוּאֵל בַּר יִצְחָק קַמֵּיהּ דְּרַב הוּנָא: "וְטִהֲרוֹ הַכֹּהֵן מִסְפַּחַת הִיא וְכִבֶּס בְּגָדָיו וְטָהֵר" – טָהוֹר מִפְּרִיעָה וּפְרִימָה דְּמֵעִיקָּרָא.

The Gemara asks: **From where are these matters** derived? The Gemara answers: It is **as Rav Shmuel bar Yitzḥak taught** in a *baraita* **before Rav Huna.** It is written with regard to a leper who was purified from quarantine: **"The priest shall pronounce him clean: It is but a scab, and he shall wash his clothes and be purified** [*vetaher*]" (Leviticus 13:6). The word *vetaher* is not in the future tense, which would indicate that from that point he is purified; it is rather in the present tense, indicating **that at the outset,** even before the priest's pronouncement, **he was pure**[N] in the sense that he was exempt **from** the initial obligation of **letting** the hair on his head grow **wild and rending** his garments, as those obligations are incumbent exclusively upon the confirmed leper.

NOTES

A quarantined and a confirmed leper – מְצוֹרָע מוּסְגָּר וּמוּחְלָט: There are additional differences between these two statuses of leper that are not mentioned in the mishna, but are suggested elsewhere. Here too, the opinion of the Rashba and Ritva that despite the phrasing of the mishna, it does not presume to enumerate all of the differences between the categories in question, applies.

The *halakhot* of the leper – דִּינֵי מְצוֹרָע: The *halakhot* of the leper are detailed in the Torah (Leviticus, chapters 13–14) and the Mishna in tractate *Nega'im*. Essentially, one who detects a leprous lesion on his skin goes to a priest, who quarantines him for seven days. If the lesion has grown darker, he is pure, and if it has not, he is quarantined for an additional seven days. If the lesion did not grow, he is pure. If it spread, he is a confirmed leper.

The impurity of the leper is a severe impurity. Not only is it prohibited for him to enter places that are sacred, it is also prohibited for him to enter walled cities, and he must remain outside the three camps. He renders items ritually impure through contact and through lifting, and he renders impure the contents of a house that he enters. When the lesion heals, the leper brings two birds, a cedar branch, and a hyssop, and they slaughter one of the birds and sprinkle its blood. Then the leper shaves all the hair on his body and on the eighth day, he brings a special purification offering.

With regard to the matter of expulsion…both this and that are equal – לְעִנְיַן שִׁילּוּחַ...זֶה וָזֶה שָׁוִין: The Meiri asks: If that is the case, what is the meaning of the term: Quarantined? If it is meant literally, the understanding would be that he must be quarantined in a specific place. The explanation is that perhaps the quarantined leper is required to remain quarantined in a house outside the three camps. The *ge'onim* explain that the term *musgar* does not mean quarantined; it means that they would frame the lesion with paint, in order to ascertain at the end of the week whether or not it had spread.

At the outset he was pure – טָהוֹר מֵעִיקָּרָא: Rashi explains that this is derived from the term *veyit'har*, which is descriptive: After he immerses and washes his clothes, he is pure. In contrast, the term *vetaher* is present perfect, meaning that he remains pure. However, the Rid disagrees, and explains that *vetaher* means from this point forward. Therefore, it would mean that he is completely pure in the sense that he had never been impure at all.

אֲמַר לֵיהּ רָבָא: אֶלָּא מֵעַתָּה, גַּבֵּי זָב דִּכְתִיב: ״וְכִבֶּס בְּגָדָיו וְטָהֵר״ הָתָם מַאי וְטָהֵר מֵעִיקָּרָא אִיכָּא?

Rava said to him: However, if that is **so,** i.e., that *vetaher* means that one is somewhat pure at the outset, then **with regard to a *zav*, as it is written: "And he shall wash his clothes,** and bathe his flesh in running water, **and he shall be clean [*vetaher*]"** (Leviticus 15:13), **there, what** sense **of: And he shall be clean, at the outset is there** in that case? Up until that point, the *zav* was ritually impure in every sense.

אֶלָּא: טָהוֹר הָשְׁתָּא מִלְּטַמֵּא כְּלֵי חֶרֶס בְּהֶיסֵּט, אַף עַל גַּב דְּהָדַר חָזֵי לֹא מְטַמֵּא לְמַפְרֵעַ –

Rather, *vetaher* means that **he is now pure from rendering earthenware vessels impure through movement.**[NH] There is a *halakha* that a *zav* renders a vessel impure if he causes it to be moved, even though he did not come into direct contact with it, even if the opening of the vessel is smaller than a fingerbreadth. The verse teaches that once the *zav* is purified through counting and immersion, he no longer renders vessels impure in that manner. The novelty here is that **even if he then experiences another** emission, **he does not render** the vessels **impure retroactively.** This emission is unrelated to the previous emissions. Therefore, upon experiencing the emission, the *zav* is not retroactively considered to have been ritually impure the entire time, even after immersion. Rather, since he counted seven clean days and immersed, the legal status of this latest emission is that of a new emission.

הָכָא נַמִי טָהוֹר [הָשְׁתָּא מִלְּטַמֵּא בְּבִיאָה לְמַפְרֵעַ]!

Here too, with regard to the leper, *vetaher* means that the quarantined leper **is now pure from retroactively rendering** the contents of a house **impure by** his **entrance** into the house. If someone with inconclusive symptoms of leprosy was quarantined and then declared ritually pure, and subsequently conclusive symptoms of leprosy developed, he is not considered to have been a leper from the time of the original quarantine, in which case the contents of any house he entered from that point would be rendered impure retroactively. Rather, once he was purified, he was absolutely pure. These subsequent conclusive symptoms are unrelated to the previous inconclusive symptoms. Therefore, the proof adduced by Rav Shmuel bar Yitzḥak is no proof.

אֶלָּא אָמַר רָבָא, מֵהָכָא: ״וְהַצָּרוּעַ אֲשֶׁר בּוֹ הַנֶּגַע״ – מִי שֶׁצָּרַעְתּוֹ תְּלוּיָה בְּגוּפוֹ, יָצָא זֶה שֶׁאֵין צָרַעְתּוֹ תְּלוּיָה בְּגוּפוֹ אֶלָּא בְּיָמִים.

Rather, Rava said that the *halakha* that a quarantined leper is exempt from the obligation to let his hair grow and to rend his clothing is derived **from here.** It is written: **"And the leper in whom [*bo*] the plague is,** his clothes shall be rent, and the hair of his head shall grow wild" (Leviticus 13:45), indicating that only **one whose leprosy is dependent on** the state of **his body,** in whom the plague is, is obligated to let his hair grow wild and to rend his garments. This **excludes that** leper **whose leprosy is not dependent** solely **on** the state of **his body, but rather on** the passage of **days,** as he is obligated to wait seven days.

אֲמַר לֵיהּ אַבַּיֵי: אֶלָּא מֵעַתָּה ״כׇּל יְמֵי אֲשֶׁר הַנֶּגַע בּוֹ יִטְמָא״ מִי שֶׁצָּרַעְתּוֹ תְּלוּיָה בְּגוּפוֹ הוּא דְּטָעוּן שִׁילּוּחַ, וְשֶׁאֵין צָרַעְתּוֹ תְּלוּיָה בְּגוּפוֹ – אֵין טָעוּן שִׁילּוּחַ.

Abaye said to him: However, if that is **so,** then also with regard to the verse: **"All the days during which the plague shall be in him [*bo*] he shall be impure"** (Leviticus 13:46), say **one whose leprosy is dependent on** the state of **his body requires expulsion** from the camp, **and one whose leprosy is not dependent** solely **on** the state of **his body,** but rather on the passage of days, **does not require expulsion.**

וְכִי תֵּימָא: הָכִי נַמִי – וְהָא קָתָנֵי: אֵין בֵּין מְצוֹרָע מוּסְגָּר לִמְצוֹרָע מוּחְלָט אֶלָּא פְּרִיעָה וּפְרִימָה, הָא לְעִנְיַן שִׁילּוּחַ וּלְטַמּוּיֵי בְּבִיאָה – זֶה וָזֶה שָׁוִין!

And if you would say: Indeed that is **so, but isn't it taught** in the mishna: **The difference between a quarantined leper and a confirmed leper is only** with regard to **letting** the hair on one's head grow **wild and rending** one's garments? And it is inferred **that with regard to the matter of expulsion and** the capacity of a leper **to render impure** the contents of a house **by entry** into the house, both **this,** the quarantined leper, **and that,** the confirmed leper, **are equal.**

אֲמַר לֵיהּ: ״יְמֵי״ ״כׇּל יְמֵי״ – לְרַבּוֹת מְצוֹרָע מוּסְגָּר לְשִׁילּוּחַ.

Rava **said to him:** There is a different source for the obligation to expel the quarantined leper from the camp. The verse could have stated: **The days** during which the plague shall be upon him. Instead the verse states: **All the days, to include a quarantined leper** in the obligation **of expulsion** from the camp, like a confirmed leper.

NOTES

Now pure from rendering earthenware vessels impure through movement – טָהוֹר הָשְׁתָּא מִלְּטַמֵּא כְּלֵי חֶרֶס בְּהֶיסֵּט: The Rambam rules in accordance with this opinion, meaning that after immersion the *zav* will render impurity retroactively if he again sees an emission on that day. However, the immersion is effective, as it prevents the *zav* from rendering earthenware vessels impure through movement retroactively. Since that form of impurity is unique to the *zav* and is alluded to in the previous verse, it is specifically from that impurity that he is purified. Some question why the Rambam does not issue a similar ruling with regard to the impurity caused to the contents of a house that the leper enters, as that is also impurity unique to the leper (*Rishon LeTziyyon*).

HALAKHA

Now pure from rendering earthenware vessels impure through movement – טָהוֹר הָשְׁתָּא מִלְּטַמֵּא כְּלֵי חֶרֶס בְּהֶיסֵּט: Once a *zav* and a *zava* immerse on the seventh day of their impurity, they no longer render earthenware vessels impure through movement. Even if they experienced an additional emission, they render impurity retroactively only to a surface designated for lying and a surface designated for sitting (Rambam *Sefer Tahara, Hilkhot Metamei Mishkav UMoshav* 5:9).

אִי הָכִי, תִּגְלַחַת וְצִפֳּרִים מַאי טַעְמָא לָא? דִּתְנַן: אֵין בֵּין טָהוֹר מִתּוֹךְ הֶסְגֵּר לְטָהוֹר מִתּוֹךְ הֶחְלֵט אֶלָּא תִּגְלַחַת וְצִפֳּרִים!

The Gemara asks: **If that is so, what is the reason** that a quarantined leper **is not** obligated in **shaving** the hair on all his body **and** bringing **birds** as a purification offering as part of his purification process? **As it teaches** in the mishna: **The difference between** a leper **purified from quarantine,** whose symptoms never became conclusive, **and** a leper **purified from** a state of **confirmed** leprosy, **is only** with regard to **shaving** the hair on all his body **and** bringing **birds** as a purification offering.

אָמַר אַבַּיֵּי, אָמַר קְרָא: ״וְיָצָא הַכֹּהֵן אֶל מִחוּץ לַמַּחֲנֶה וְהִנֵּה נִרְפָּא נֶגַע הַצָּרַעַת״ מִי שֶׁצָּרַעְתּוֹ תְּלוּיָה בִּרְפוּאוֹת, יָצָא זֶה שֶׁאֵין צָרַעְתּוֹ תְּלוּיָה בִּרְפוּאוֹת אֶלָּא בְּיָמִים.

Abaye said that the **verse states: "And the priest shall go out of the camp,** and the priest shall look, **and behold, if the plague of leprosy is healed** in the leper" (Leviticus 14:3), then the purification process that includes shaving and bringing birds commences. This indicates that these *halakhot* apply to a confirmed leper **whose leprosy is dependent on healing,**[N] **to exclude that** leper **whose leprosy is not dependent** solely **on healing but rather on** the passage of **days.** Even if his symptoms are healed, he is pure only at the conclusion of the seven days of quarantine.

מתני׳ אֵין בֵּין סְפָרִים לִתְפִלִּין וּמְזוּזוֹת אֶלָּא שֶׁהַסְּפָרִים נִכְתָּבִין בְּכׇל לָשׁוֹן, וּתְפִלִּין וּמְזוּזוֹת אֵינָן נִכְתָּבוֹת אֶלָּא אַשּׁוּרִית.

MISHNA **The difference between** Torah **scrolls, and phylacteries and *mezuzot*,**[NH] in terms of the manner in which they are written, **is only that** Torah **scrolls are written in any language, whereas phylacteries and *mezuzot* are written only in *Ashurit*,**[B] i.e., in Hebrew and using the Hebrew script.

רַבָּן שִׁמְעוֹן בֶּן גַּמְלִיאֵל אוֹמֵר: אַף בִּסְפָרִים לֹא הִתִּירוּ שֶׁיִּכָּתְבוּ אֶלָּא יְוָנִית.

Rabban Shimon ben Gamliel says: Even with regard to Torah **scrolls,** the Sages **permitted them to be written only** in **Greek.** Torah scrolls written in any other language do not have the sanctity of a Torah scroll.

גמ׳ הָא לְתוֹפְרָן בְּגִידִין וּלְטַמֵּא אֶת הַיָּדַיִם – זֶה וָזֶה שָׁוִין.

GEMARA The Gemara infers **that** with regard **to the matter of stitching** the sheets of parchment **with sinews, and** with regard **to rendering the hands** of one who touches them **impure,** both **this,** Torah scrolls, **and that,** phylacteries and *mezuzot*, are **equal.** The Sages issued a decree rendering the hands of one who touches sacred scrolls impure with second-degree ritual impurity.

״וּסְפָרִים נִכְתָּבִין בְּכׇל לָשׁוֹן״ וכו׳. וּרְמִינְהוּ: מִקְרָא שֶׁכְּתָבוֹ תַּרְגּוּם, וְתַרְגּוּם שֶׁכְּתָבוֹ מִקְרָא, וּכְתָב עִבְרִי – אֵינוֹ מְטַמֵּא אֶת הַיָּדַיִם, עַד שֶׁיִּכְתְּבֶנּוּ בִּכְתָב אַשּׁוּרִית, עַל הַסֵּפֶר, וּבִדְיוֹ!

The mishna stated: Torah **scrolls are written in any language. And** the Gemara **raises a contradiction** from a *baraita*: A Torah scroll containing a Hebrew verse in the **Bible that one wrote in** Aramaic **translation,**[H] or a verse written in Aramaic **translation that one wrote** in the Hebrew of the **Bible,** or either that was written **in** the ancient **Hebrew script** and not in *Ashurit*, **renders the hands impure only if one writes it in *Ashurit* script, on a** parchment **scroll, and in ink.** Apparently, contrary to the mishna, a scroll written in a language other than Hebrew is not sacred.

אָמַר רָבָא: לָא קַשְׁיָא;

Rava said: This is **not difficult.**

NOTES

One whose leprosy is dependent on healing – מִי שֶׁצָּרַעְתּוֹ תְּלוּיָה בִּרְפוּאוֹת: In the Jerusalem Talmud, this is derived from the language of the verse: "This shall be the law of the leper on the day of his purity" (Leviticus 14:2). The obligation to bring an offering is incumbent upon a leper who is purified in one day, one who is healed of his leprosy. A quarantined leper must wait seven days, even if the lesion heals before the conclusion of that period.

The difference between Torah scrolls and phylacteries and *mezuzot* – בֵּין סְפָרִים לִתְפִלִּין וּמְזוּזוֹת: The later authorities (*Rishon LeTziyyon* and others) comment that there are many additional differences between the *halakhot* of phylacteries and the *halakhot* of a Torah scroll. The Rashba and Ritva explain that despite the phrasing of the mishna, it does not presume to enumerate all of the differences between the categories in question (Rabbeinu Yehonatan; Meiri).

HALAKHA

Phylacteries and *mezuzot* – תְּפִלִּין וּמְזוּזוֹת: Phylacteries and *mezuzot* may be written only in *Ashurit* (Rambam *Sefer Ahava, Hilkhot Tefillin* 1:19).

A Hebrew verse in the Bible that one wrote in Aramaic translation – מִקְרָא שֶׁכְּתָבוֹ תַּרְגּוּם: The scroll on which an Aramaic verse is written in Hebrew, or a Hebrew verse is written in Aramaic, or a verse is written in the ancient Hebrew script, does not render the hands impure. It does so only if the scrolls are written in *Ashurit*, on parchment, with ink (Rambam *Sefer Tahara, Hilkhot Avot HaTumot* 9:7).

BACKGROUND

***Ashurit* – אַשּׁוּרִית:** The Hebrew script currently in use is called by the Sages: *Ashurit*, in contrast to the ancient Hebrew script [*Ivrit*] used by the Samaritans. The Sages disagreed as to why the script is called *Ashurit*. Some explained that it is because the Jews brought it with them when they returned from the Babylonian exile, which included Assyria. Others explain that it is from the word happiness [*osher*] or directness [*yosher*], meaning an esthetic, straightforward script. The ancient Hebrew script is still used by Samaritans today. The image depicts a street sign from Holon, Israel, which has a Samaritan community. The top line of the sign is written in *Ashurit* and the bottom line in *Ivrit*.

Street sign with ancient Hebrew script

כָּאן בְּגוּפָן שֶׁלָּנוּ, כָּאן בְּגוּפָן שֶׁלָּהֶן.

Here, the mishna is referring to Torah scrolls written in another language **in our script,** i.e., in Hebrew letters. **There,** the *baraita* is referring to Torah scrolls written in another language **in their script,** in the letters of another alphabet.

אֲמַר לֵיהּ אַבַּיֵי: בְּמַאי אוֹקִימְתָּא לְהַהִיא – בְּגוּפָן שֶׁלָּהֶן, מַאי אִירְיָא מִקְרָא שֶׁכְּתָבוֹ תַּרְגּוּם וְתַרְגּוּם שֶׁכְּתָבוֹ מִקְרָא? אֲפִילּוּ מִקְרָא שֶׁכְּתָבוֹ מִקְרָא וְתַרְגּוּם שֶׁכְּתָבוֹ תַּרְגּוּם נַמִי, דְּהָא קָתָנֵי: ״עַד שֶׁיִּכְתְּבֶנּוּ אַשּׁוּרִית עַל הַסֵּפֶר בִּדְיוֹ״!

Abaye said to Rava: **How did you establish that** *baraita,* i.e., that it is referring to Torah scrolls written in another language **in their script?** If it is so, **why** did the *baraita* **specifically teach** that the legal status of a Hebrew verse in the **Bible that one wrote** in Aramaic **translation, or** a verse written in Aramaic **translation that one wrote** in the Hebrew of the **Bible,** is not that of sacred writings? The legal status of **even** a Hebrew verse in the **Bible that one wrote** in the Hebrew of the **Bible and** a verse written in Aramaic **translation that one wrote in** Aramaic **translation** are **also** not that of sacred writings, **as it is taught** at the end of the *baraita*: A Torah scroll renders the hands impure **only if one writes it in *Ashurit*** script, **on a** parchment **scroll,** and **in ink.**

אֶלָּא, לָא קַשְׁיָא; הָא – רַבָּנַן, הָא – רַבָּן שִׁמְעוֹן בֶּן גַּמְלִיאֵל.

Rather, the matter must be explained differently. This is **not difficult. This** ruling in the mishna is according to **the Rabbis,** who permit writing Torah scrolls in any language, and **that** ruling in the *baraita* is according to **Rabban Shimon ben Gamliel.**

אִי רַבָּן שִׁמְעוֹן בֶּן גַּמְלִיאֵל, הָא אִיכָּא יְוָנִית! אֶלָּא, לָא קַשְׁיָא: כָּאן – בִּסְפָרִים, כָּאן – בִּתְפִלִּין וּמְזוּזוֹת.

The Gemara asks: If the *baraita* is according to **Rabban Shimon ben Gamliel,** in addition to *Ashurit,* **isn't there Greek** in which the Torah may also be written? **Rather,** say this is **not difficult. Here,** the mishna is referring to Torah **scrolls,** which may be written in any language; **there,** the *baraita* is referring to phylacteries and *mezuzot,* which may be written only in Hebrew, using Hebrew script.

תְּפִלִּין וּמְזוּזוֹת מַאי טַעְמָא – מִשּׁוּם דִּכְתִיב בְּהוּ: ״וְהָיוּ״, בַּהֲוָיָיתָן יְהוּ, מַאי תַּרְגּוּם שֶׁכְּתָבוֹ מִקְרָא אִיכָּא? בִּשְׁלָמָא תּוֹרָה – אִיכָּא ״יְגַר שָׂהֲדוּתָא״. אֶלָּא הָכָא, מַאי תַּרְגּוּם אִיכָּא?

The Gemara asks: With regard to **phylacteries and *mezuzot,* what is the reason** that they must be written in Hebrew? The Gemara explains: It is **because it is written with regard to them: "And** these words **shall be"** (Deuteronomy 6:6), indicating that **as they are so shall they be,** without change. The Gemara raises a difficulty: If the *baraita* is referring to phylacteries and *mezuzot,* **what** Aramaic **translation that one wrote** in the Hebrew of the **Bible is there? Granted,** in the **Torah there is** a verse written in Aramaic translation: ***"Yegar sahaduta"*** (Genesis 31:47); **however, here,** in phylacteries and *mezuzot,* **what** verses in Aramaic **translation are there**[N] that could be written in Hebrew?

אֶלָּא לָא קַשְׁיָא; כָּאן – בִּמְגִילָּה, כָּאן – בִּסְפָרִים. מְגִילָּה מַאי טַעְמָא – דִּכְתִיב בָּהּ: ״כִּכְתָבָם וְכִלְשׁוֹנָם״, – מַאי תַּרְגּוּם שֶׁכְּתָבוֹ מִקְרָא אִיכָּא?

Rather, say this is **not difficult. Here,** the *baraita* **is referring to** the **Megilla,** the Scroll of Esther, which must be written in Hebrew; **there,** the mishna **is referring to** Torah **scrolls,** which may be written in any language. The Gemara asks: **What is the reason** that the **Megilla** must be written in Hebrew? It is due to the fact **that it is written with regard to** the Megilla: **"According to their writing, and according to their language"** (Esther 8:9), without change. The Gemara asks: But if the *baraita* is referring to the Megilla, **what** Aramaic **translation that one wrote** in the Hebrew of the **Bible is there?** The entire Megilla is written in Hebrew.

אָמַר רַב פַּפָּא: ״וְנִשְׁמַע פִּתְגָם הַמֶּלֶךְ״. רַב נַחְמָן בַּר יִצְחָק אָמַר: ״וְכָל הַנָּשִׁים יִתְּנוּ יְקָר לְבַעְלֵיהֶן״,

Rav Pappa said that it is written: **"And when the king's decree [*pitgam*] shall be publicized"** (Esther 1:20), and that *pitgam* is essentially an Aramaic word. **Rav Naḥman bar Yitzḥak said** that it is written: **"And all the wives will give honor [*yekar*]**[N] **to their husbands"** (Esther 1:20), and *yekar* is Aramaic for honor.

רַב אַשִׁי אָמַר: כִּי תַּנְיָא הַהִיא בִּשְׁאָר סְפָרִים, וְרַבִּי יְהוּדָה הִיא. דְּתַנְיָא: תְּפִלִּין וּמְזוּזוֹת אֵין נִכְתָּבִין אֶלָּא אַשּׁוּרִית, וְרַבּוֹתֵינוּ הִתִּירוּ יְוָנִית.

Rav Ashi suggested a different explanation and **said: When that** *baraita* **is taught** it is taught **with regard to the rest of** the **books** of the Bible, other than the Torah. **And it is** in accordance with the opinion of **Rabbi Yehuda, as it is taught** in a *baraita*: **Phylacteries and *mezuzot* are written only in *Ashurit*; and our Rabbis permitted** writing them in **Greek** as well.

NOTES

What verses in Aramaic translation are there – מַאי תַּרְגּוּם אִיכָּא: The *Penei Yehoshua* explains that it was possible to say, according to some *tanna'im*, that the word *totafot* (Deuteronomy 6:8) that refers to the phylacteries donned on the head, is in a foreign language, and therefore it would be possible to translate it.

Will give honor [*yekar*] – יִתְּנוּ יְקָר: Some ask: Why doesn't the Gemara cite an earlier verse with the same term: "And the honor [*yekar*] of his excellent majesty" (Esther 1:4)? They answer that in that context, the word could be understood in Hebrew, meaning great value, and not in Aramaic, meaning honor (Responsa *Beit Efrayim*; *Ginzei HaMelekh*).

והכתיב: "והיו"! אלא אימא: ספרים נכתבים בכל לשון, ורבותינו התירו יונית. התירו?! מכלל דתנא קמא אסר!

The Gemara asks: How did our Rabbis permit this? **Isn't it written** with regard to phylacteries and *mezuzot*: **"And** these words **shall be"** (Deuteronomy 6:6), indicating that their language may not be changed. **Rather, say** that this is what the *baraita* is saying: Torah **scrolls are written in any language; and our Rabbis permitted** writing them **in Greek** as well. Once again the Gemara asks: Our Rabbis **permitted? By inference,** apparently **the first** ***tanna*** **prohibits** writing a Torah scroll in Greek. However, he explicitly permits writing a Torah scroll in any language.

אלא אימא: רבותינו לא התירו שיכתבו אלא יונית. ותניא, אמר רבי יהודה: אף כשהתירו רבותינו יונית – לא התירו אלא בספר תורה,

Rather, say in explanation of the *baraita*: **And our Rabbis permitted them to be written only in Greek. And it is taught** in another *baraita* that **Rabbi Yehuda said: Even when our Rabbis permitted Greek, they permitted it only in a Torah scroll,**[N] and not for other books of the Bible, which must be written only in Hebrew.

ומשום מעשה דתלמי המלך, דתניא: מעשה בתלמי המלך שכינס שבעים ושנים זקנים, והכניסן בשבעים ושנים בתים, ולא גילה להם על מה כינסן. ונכנס אצל כל אחד ואחד ואמר להם: כתבו לי תורת משה רבכם. נתן הקדוש ברוך הוא בלב כל אחד ואחד עצה, והסכימו כולן לדעת אחת.

The Gemara continues: **And** this was **due to the incident of King Ptolemy, as it is taught** in a *baraita*: There was **an incident involving King Ptolemy**[P] of Egypt, **who assembled seventy-two Elders**[B] from the Sages of Israel, **and put them into seventy-two** separate **rooms, and did not reveal to them for what** purpose **he assembled them,** so that they would not coordinate their responses. **He entered** and **approached each and every one, and said to** each of **them: Write for me** a translation of **the Torah of Moses your teacher. The Holy One, Blessed be He, placed wisdom in the heart of each and every one, and they all agreed to one** common **understanding.**[B] Not only did they all translate the text correctly, they all introduced the same changes into the translated text.

וכתבו לו: "אלהים ברא בראשית", "אעשה אדם בצלם ובדמות",

And they wrote for him: God created in the beginning [***bereshit***],[N] reversing the order of the words in the first phrase in the Torah that could be misinterpreted as: "*Bereshit* created God" (Genesis 1:1). They did so to negate those who believe in the preexistence of the world and those who maintain that there are two powers in the world: One is *Bereshit*, who created the second, God. And they wrote: **I shall make man**[N] **in image and in likeness,** rather than: "Let us make man in our image and in our likeness" (Genesis 1:26), as from there too one could mistakenly conclude that there are multiple powers and that God has human form.

"ויכל ביום הששי, וישבות ביום השביעי", "זכר ונקבה בראו" ולא כתבו "בראם",

Instead of: "And on the seventh day God concluded His work" (Genesis 2:2), which could have been understood as though some of His work was completed on Shabbat itself, they wrote: **And on the sixth day He concluded** His work, **and He rested on the seventh day.** They also wrote: **Male and female He created him,**[N] **and they did not write** as it is written in the Torah: "Male and female **He created them"** (Genesis 5:2), to avoid the impression that there is a contradiction between this verse and the verse: "And God created man" (Genesis 1:27), which indicates that God created one person.

"הבה ארדה ואבלה שם שפתם" "ותצחק שרה בקרוביה",

Instead of: "Come, let us go down, and there confound their language" (Genesis 11:7), which indicates multiple authorities, they wrote in the singular: **Come, let me go down, and there confound their language.** In addition, they replaced the verse: "And Sarah laughed within herself [*bekirba*]" (Genesis 18:12), with: **And Sarah laughed among her relatives** [***bikroveha***]. They made this change to distinguish between Sarah's laughter, which God criticized, and Abraham's laughter, to which no reaction is recorded. Based on the change, Sarah's laughter was offensive because she voiced it to others.

NOTES

Only in a Torah scroll – אלא בספר תורה: Although the sanctity of the Torah scroll surpasses all the other books, since there was a unique miracle specifically with regard to the translation of the Torah, it is permitted to write the Torah in Greek. However, other books translated into Greek do not have the status of sacred texts.

God created in the beginning [*bereshit*] – אלהים ברא בראשית: See the *Tosefta* where this explanation and the significance of the change are questioned. The believers in two powers explained that *bereshit* refers to the logos, the divine will. Since they took it to the next level and totally separated the logos from God, it was necessary to write that it was God who created this world. See the translation in the Jerusalem *Targum* of the word *bereshit* as: In His wisdom.

I shall make man – אעשה אדם: Some note that this translation resolves an additional problem, as from the original verse one could draw the mistaken conclusion that God has human form. Therefore, they wrote: In image and in likeness. See the explanation in Ibn Ezra's commentary on the Torah (*Korban HaEda*; Rashash; *Sefat Emet*).

Male and female He created him – זכר ונקבה בראו: It is written in the Jerusalem Talmud and elsewhere that the change was that the creation of the female was not mentioned at all.

BACKGROUND

The Septuagint – תרגום השבעים: The Septuagint was the first translation of the Torah into a foreign language. The Sages related to the very translation of the Torah with great concern, to the extent that the day that the Septuagint was completed was designated as a fast in *Megillat Ta'anit*. Over time, the translation was accepted to a large extent as useful and significant, and as mentioned in the mishna it was accorded status of special significance. Among Egyptian Jews the Septuagint was revered and accorded great sanctity.

There is an extended version of this story in Greek, in the ancient letter of Aristeas, which is similar to the account related in the Gemara. It describes the efforts of the king to organize the translation as well as the wisdom of the Elders who came from Eretz Yisrael for that purpose.

The textual changes in the Septuagint – שינויי הנסח בשבעים: The Septuagint was preserved primarily because the Christians adopted it and ascribed greater significance to it than they ascribed to the Hebrew original. Throughout the generations the translation went through several changes, and apparently even Aquila and Symmachus, the Jewish translators, created a version more in line with the approach of the *halakha*. In general, there are many differences between the source text and the Septuagint. The current version contains additional passages, and even entire books, i.e., the Apocrypha. Not all of the changes cited here appear in the current version of the Septuagint, although they did appear in the versions used by the Jews.

PERSONALITIES

King Ptolemy – תלמי המלך: This is the king of Egypt, Ptolemaius II Philadelphus, who ruled over Egypt during the years 246–285 BCE. He inherited his kingdom, which included Eretz Yisrael and parts of North Africa, from his father, Ptolemy I. After his succession to the throne, he worked to establish and organize the kingdom in various ways. He was known as an admirer of culture and science, and during his reign Alexandria developed into the scientific center of the Hellenistic world.

Both the Talmud and the letter of Aristeas attribute the initiative to translate the Torah into Greek to King Ptolemy. Apparently, he showed interest in Eretz Yisrael and had a friendly relationship with the Jews. He renamed the ancient city of Rabat Ammon, which is modern-day Amman, Philadelphia, after himself. The city of Ptolemaius, near Akko, was also named for him.

"כִּי בְאַפָּם הָרְגוּ שׁוֹר וּבִרְצוֹנָם עָקְרוּ אֵבוּס", "וַיִּקַּח מֹשֶׁה אֶת אִשְׁתּוֹ וְאֶת בָּנָיו וַיַּרְכִּבֵם עַל נוֹשֵׂא בְנֵי אָדָם",

They also altered the verse: "For in their anger they slew a man and in their self-will they slaughtered an ox" (Genesis 49:6), to read: **For in their anger they slew an ox**[N] **and in their self-will they uprooted a trough,** to avoid the charge that Jacob's sons were murderers. Instead of: "And Moses took his wife and his sons, and set them upon a donkey" (Exodus 4:20), they wrote: **And Moses took his wife and his sons, and set them upon a carrier of people,**[N] which could be understood as referring to a horse or a camel rather than the lowly donkey.

"וּמוֹשַׁב בְּנֵי יִשְׂרָאֵל אֲשֶׁר יָשְׁבוּ בְּמִצְרַיִם וּבִשְׁאָר אֲרָצוֹת אַרְבַּע מֵאוֹת שָׁנָה", "וַיִּשְׁלַח אֶת זַאֲטוּטֵי בְּנֵי יִשְׂרָאֵל", "וְאֶל זַאֲטוּטֵי בְּנֵי יִשְׂרָאֵל לֹא שָׁלַח יָדוֹ",

Instead of: "And the residence of the children of Israel, who resided in Egypt, was four hundred and thirty years" (Exodus 12:40), which when read literally is imprecise, for they did not dwell in Egypt that long, they wrote: **And the residence of the children of Israel, who resided in Egypt and in other lands, was four hundred years.**[N] Instead of: "And he sent the youth of the children of Israel, who brought burnt-offerings" (Exodus 24:5), which evokes the question of why young men were sent to perform that service, they wrote: **And he sent the elect [*za'atutei*]**[NL] **of the children of Israel.** The same term was substituted again several verses later, rendering the verse: "And upon the nobles of the children of Israel He laid not His hand" (Exodus 24:11), as: **And upon the elect of the children of Israel He laid not His hand.**

NOTES

They slew an ox – הָרְגוּ שׁוֹר: Some point out that had they written man, it could have been misunderstood as saying that Jacob was upset due to the murder of a single individual, Shechem, or, according to certain opinions, due to his sons' intention to kill Joseph. Therefore, they wrote ox to show that Jacob was upset about the wanton slaying of animals, and all the more so over the slaying of people (*Penei Yehoshua*).

A carrier of people – נוֹשֵׂא בְנֵי אָדָם: Some explain that they did not write donkey, so that people would not wonder why Moses did not find a quicker animal, in order to accelerate the redemption of the Jewish people (*Ge'on Ya'akov*). Others explain that it is disrespectful to Moses to mention a donkey, as that would depict him walking on foot alongside the animal (*Gal Naul*).

Four hundred years – אַרְבַּע מֵאוֹת שָׁנָה: Some write that they wrote specifically four hundred years and not 430 so that it would correspond to the number mentioned in the revelation to Abraham during the Covenant of the Pieces (*Yefe Mareh*).

Elect – זַאֲטוּטֵי: Rav Tzemaḥ Gaon explains that *za'atutei* means relatively young men; not youths and not elders, but in between.

LANGUAGE

Elect [*za'atutei*] – זַאֲטוּטֵי: This word does not appear in this form in the Septuagint, and there it is translated as: Young man. It might be a Semitic word, with *zut* meaning small in the sense of youth or young man. In the Jerusalem Talmud it is stated that there is an ancient Torah scroll in which this word appears instead of youth. Some maintain that it is the Greek ζητητής, *zètètès*, meaning seeker or inquirer.

Perek **I**
Daf **9** Amud **b**

"לֹא חֶמֶד אֶחָד מֵהֶם נָשָׂאתִי", "אֲשֶׁר חָלַק ה' אֱלֹהֶיךָ אֹתָם לְהָאִיר לְכֹל הָעַמִּים",

Instead of Moses' assertion: "I have not taken one donkey [*ḥamor*] from them" (Numbers 16:15), they wrote in more general terms: **"I have not taken one item of value [*ḥemed*] from them,"**[N] to prevent the impression that Moses took other items. To the verse that discusses the worship of the sun and the moon, about which it is written: "Which the Lord your God has allotted to all the nations" (Deuteronomy 4:19), they added a word to make it read: **"Which the Lord your God has allotted to give light to all the nations,"** to prevent the potential misinterpretation that the heavenly bodies were given to the gentiles so that they may worship them.

"וַיֵּלֶךְ וַיַּעֲבוֹד אֱלֹהִים אֲחֵרִים אֲשֶׁר לֹא צִוִּיתִי לְעוֹבְדָם",

The verse: **"And has gone and served other gods,** and worshipped them, either the sun, or the moon, or any of the host of heaven, **which I have not commanded"** (Deuteronomy 17:3), could be understood as indicating that God did not command their existence, i.e., these entities created themselves. Therefore, when these Elders translated the verse they added a word to the end of the verse to make it read: Which I have not commanded **to serve them.**

וְכָתְבוּ לוֹ "אֶת צְעִירַת הָרַגְלַיִם" וְלֹא כָתְבוּ לוֹ "אֶת הָאַרְנֶבֶת" מִפְּנֵי שֶׁאִשְׁתּוֹ שֶׁל תַּלְמַי אַרְנֶבֶת שְׁמָהּ, שֶׁלֹּא יֹאמַר: שְׂחֲקוּ בִּי הַיְּהוּדִים וְהֵטִילוּ שֵׁם אִשְׁתִּי בַּתּוֹרָה.

And in the list of unclean animals **they wrote for him: The short-legged beast [*tze'irat haraglayim*].**[L] **And they did not write for him: "And the hare [*arnevet*]"** (Leviticus 11:6), **since the name of Ptolemy's wife was Arnevet, so that he would not say: The Jews have mocked me and inserted my wife's name in the Torah.** Therefore, they did not refer to the hare by name, but by one of its characteristic features.

NOTES

I have not taken one item of value from them – לֹא חֶמֶד אֶחָד מֵהֶם נָשָׂאתִי: The Maharsha writes that the Sages explained the verse: "I have not taken one donkey from them," as follows: Even when Moses needed to travel from Midian to Egypt to take the Jews out of Egypt, he did not take from the children of Israel even the donkey on which he transported his family. Since the seventy-two Elders feared Ptolemy's reaction, they changed the term from donkey to item of value.

LANGUAGE

Short-legged beast [*tze'irat haraglayim*] – צְעִירַת הָרַגְלַיִם: The seventy-two Elders, in their translation of the word hare in the list of non-kosher animals, used the word δασύπους, *dasupous*, which literally means hairy-legged or rough-footed, instead of the standard term for hare, λαγός, *lagos*. They did so because the nickname of the founder of the Ptolemeian kingdom, Ptolemy I, was also named Lagos, and they sought to avoid alluding to him in that context.

NOTES

The beauty of Japheth – יְפִיּוּתוֹ שֶׁל יֶפֶת: It is stated in the Jerusalem Talmud that the Greek language is one of the four beautiful languages in the world, and in Eretz Yisrael, Rabbi Yehuda HaNasi preferred Greek to the spoken Aramaic.

A High Priest anointed with the oil of anointing and one consecrated by donning the multiple garments – כֹּהֵן מָשׁוּחַ בְּשֶׁמֶן הַמִּשְׁחָה לִמְרוּבֵּה בְגָדִים: When the anointing oil was available, until the time of the King Josiah, who sequestered it together with the Ark of the Covenant and the tablets, the High Priests were consecrated by anointment with this oil. However, afterward, the High Priest was appointed by pronouncement (see Jerusalem Talmud) and assumed his position by donning the eight garments of the High Priest and performing the service of the High Priest.

The bull that comes for transgression of any of the mitzvot – פַּר הַבָּא עַל כׇּל הַמִּצְוֹת: There is a special *halakha* with regard to a High Priest, as it is written: "If the anointed priest shall sin so as to bring guilt on the people" (Leviticus 4:3). If he mistakenly issued a lenient ruling with regard to a prohibition punishable by *karet*, and he acted in accordance with his ruling, he is liable to bring a bull as a sin-offering. Based on the phrase "if the anointed priest," it is clear that any other priest is exempt from bringing that offering.

A High Priest currently serving and a former High Priest – כֹּהֵן מְשַׁמֵּשׁ וְכֹהֵן שֶׁעָבַר: Most of the commentaries explain this with regard to a High Priest on Yom Kippur who was rendered unfit and unable to perform the service, requiring the appointment of a different priest in his stead. However, the Rambam and Rabbeinu Yehonatan explain that a former High Priest does not refer specifically to one temporarily replaced. Rather it refers to one who retired due to old age or a permanent blemish, who maintains the legal status of a High Priest. See *Penei Yehoshua* and *Sefat Emet*, who adopt the explanation in the Jerusalem Talmud.

BACKGROUND

Donning the multiple garments – מְרוּבֵּה בְגָדִים: A common priest wore four garments, while the High Priest wore eight.

Garments of a common priest and the High Priest

"רַבָּן שִׁמְעוֹן בֶּן גַּמְלִיאֵל אוֹמֵר אַף בִּסְפָרִים לֹא הִתִּירוּ שֶׁיִּכָּתְבוּ אֶלָּא יְוָנִית". אָמַר רַבִּי אַבָּהוּ אָמַר רַבִּי יוֹחָנָן: הֲלָכָה כְּרַבָּן שִׁמְעוֹן בֶּן גַּמְלִיאֵל וְאָמַר רַבִּי יוֹחָנָן: מַאי טַעְמָא דְּרַבָּן שִׁמְעוֹן בֶּן גַּמְלִיאֵל – אָמַר קְרָא: "יַפְתְּ אֱלֹהִים לְיֶפֶת וְיִשְׁכֹּן בְּאׇהֳלֵי שֵׁם" דְּבָרָיו שֶׁל יֶפֶת יִהְיוּ בְּאׇהֳלֵי שֵׁם.

The mishna cites that **Rabban Shimon ben Gamliel says: Even with regard to** Torah **scrolls,** the Sages **permitted them to be written only** in **Greek.**[H] **Rabbi Abbahu said** that **Rabbi Yoḥanan said: The *halakha* is in accordance with** the opinion **of Rabban Shimon ben Gamliel. And Rabbi Yoḥanan said: What is the reason** for the opinion **of Rabban Shimon ben Gamliel?** He based his opinion on an allusion in the Torah, as the **verse states: "God shall enlarge Japheth, and He shall dwell in the tents of Shem"** (Genesis 9:27), indicating that **the words of Japheth shall be in the tents of Shem.** The language of Javan, who is the forbear of the Greek nation and one of the descendants of Japheth, will also serve as a sacred language in the tents of Shem, where Torah is studied.

וְאֵימָא גּוֹמֶר וּמָגוֹג! אָמַר רַבִּי חִיָּיא בַּר אַבָּא: הַיְינוּ טַעְמָא, דִּכְתִיב: "יַפְתְּ אֱלֹהִים לְיֶפֶת" יָפְיוּתוֹ שֶׁל יֶפֶת יְהֵא בְּאׇהֳלֵי שֵׁם.

The Gemara asks: **And say** that it is the languages of **Gomer and Magog** that serve as sacred languages, as they too were descendants of Japheth (see Genesis 10:2). The Gemara answers that **Rabbi Ḥiyya bar Abba said: This is the reason, as it is written: "God shall enlarge** [*yaft*] **Japheth** [*Yefet*]." *Yaft* is etymologically similar to the Hebrew term for beauty [*yofi*]. The verse teaches that **the beauty of Japheth**[N] **shall be in the tents of Shem,** and Greek is the most beautiful of the languages of the descendants of Japheth.

מתני׳ אֵין בֵּין כֹּהֵן מָשׁוּחַ בְּשֶׁמֶן הַמִּשְׁחָה לִמְרוּבֵּה בְגָדִים אֶלָּא פַּר הַבָּא עַל כׇּל הַמִּצְוֹת.

MISHNA **The difference between a High Priest anointed with the oil of anointing,** which was the method through which High Priests were consecrated until the oil was sequestered toward the end of the First Temple period, **and** one consecrated by donning **multiple garments**[NHB] unique to the High Priest, which was the practice during the Second Temple period, **is only** that the latter does not bring the **bull that comes for** transgression of **any of the mitzvot.**[N] An anointed High Priest who unwittingly issued an erroneous halakhic ruling and acted upon that ruling, and transgressed a mitzva whose unwitting violation renders one liable to bring a sin-offering, is obligated to bring a sin-offering unique to one in his position.

אֵין בֵּין כֹּהֵן מְשַׁמֵּשׁ לְכֹהֵן שֶׁעָבַר אֶלָּא פַּר יוֹם הַכִּפּוּרִים וַעֲשִׂירִית הָאֵיפָה.

The difference between a High Priest currently **serving** in that capacity **and a former** High **Priest,**[NH] who temporarily filled that position when the High Priest was unfit for service, **is only** with regard to **the bull** brought by the High Priest **on Yom Kippur, and the tenth of an ephah** meal-offering brought daily by the High Priest. Each of these offerings is brought only by the current High Priest, and not by a former High Priest.

גמ׳ הָא לְעִנְיַן פַּר יוֹם כִּפּוּרִים וַעֲשִׂירִית הָאֵיפָה – זֶה וָזֶה שָׁוִין.

GEMARA The Gemara infers **that** with regard **to the matter of the bull** brought by the High Priest on **Yom Kippur, and** with regard to **the tenth of an ephah** meal-offering, both **this,** the anointed High Priest, **and that,** the High Priest consecrated by donning multiple garments, are **equal.**

HALAKHA

With regard to Torah scrolls, the Sages permitted them to be written only in Greek – בִּסְפָרִים לֹא הִתִּירוּ שֶׁיִּכָּתְבוּ אֶלָּא יְוָנִית: The *halakha* is in accordance with the opinion of Rabban Shimon ben Gamliel who permitted the Torah to be written in Greek, and it has the sanctity of a Torah scroll. Due to the fact that the modern Greek language is not the Greek discussed in the Gemara, Torah scrolls written in Greek are no longer sacred (Rambam *Sefer Ahava, Hilkhot Tefillin* 1:19).

Anointed with the oil of anointing and donning the multiple garments – מָשׁוּחַ בְּשֶׁמֶן הַמִּשְׁחָה וּמְרוּבֵּה בְגָדִים: The difference between a High Priest anointed with the anointing oil and a High Priest consecrated by donning multiple garments is only with regard to the bull that comes for transgression of any of the mitzvot, which a priest consecrated by donning multiple garments does not bring. In all other respects, they are equal (Rambam *Sefer Avoda, Hilkhot Kelei HaMikdash* 4:14).

A High Priest currently serving and a former High Priest – כֹּהֵן מְשַׁמֵּשׁ וְכֹהֵן שֶׁעָבַר: In the case of an anointed High Priest who left his position, if he sinned unwittingly he brings a bull as a sin-offering, as the only difference between a current High Priest and a former High Priest is with regard to the bull brought by the High Priest on Yom Kippur and the tenth of an ephah meal-offering he brings daily (Rambam *Sefer Korbanot, Hilkhot Shegagot* 15:7).

מַתְנִיתִין דְּלָא כְּרַבִּי מֵאִיר, דְּאִי רַבִּי מֵאִיר, [הָא תַּנְיָא]: מְרוּבֵּה בְגָדִים מֵבִיא פַּר הַבָּא עַל כׇּל הַמִּצְוֹת, דִּבְרֵי רַבִּי מֵאִיר. וַחֲכָמִים אוֹמְרִים: אֵינוֹ מֵבִיא.

The Gemara comments: **The mishna is not in accordance with** the opinion of **Rabbi Meir, as if it** were in accordance with the opinion of **Rabbi Meir,** it would be difficult. **Isn't it taught** in a *baraita*: A High Priest consecrated by donning the **multiple garments** unique to the High Priest **brings the bull brought for** the unwitting violation of **any of the mitzvot;** this is **the statement of Rabbi Meir. And the Rabbis say: He does not bring** that offering.

מַאי טַעְמֵיהּ דְּרַבִּי מֵאִיר – דְּתַנְיָא: ״מָשִׁיחַ״, אֵין לִי אֶלָּא מָשׁוּחַ בְּשֶׁמֶן הַמִּשְׁחָה, מְרוּבֵּה בְגָדִים מִנַּיִן? תַּלְמוּד לוֹמַר: ״הַמָּשִׁיחַ״.

The Gemara asks: **What is the reason** for the opinion **of Rabbi Meir?** It is **as it is taught** in a *baraita* that it is written: "If the anointed priest shall sin" (Leviticus 4:3). From the word **anointed, I have** derived **only** that this *halakha* applies to a High Priest who was actually **anointed with the oil of anointing. From where** do I derive that even a High Priest consecrated by donning the **multiple garments** is also included in this *halakha*? **The verse states: "The anointed,"** with the definite article, indicating that the *halakha* applies to every High Priest.

בְּמַאי אוֹקִימְנָא – דְּלָא כְּרַבִּי מֵאִיר. אֵימָא סֵיפָא: אֵין בֵּין כֹּהֵן מְשַׁמֵּשׁ לְכֹהֵן שֶׁעָבַר אֶלָּא פַּר יוֹם הַכִּפּוּרִים וַעֲשִׂירִית הָאֵיפָה, הָא לְכׇל דִּבְרֵיהֶן – זֶה וָזֶה שָׁוִין. אָתָאן לְרַבִּי מֵאִיר, דְּתַנְיָא: אֵירַע בּוֹ פְּסוּל וּמִינּוּ כֹּהֵן אַחֵר תַּחְתָּיו – רִאשׁוֹן חוֹזֵר לַעֲבוֹדָתוֹ, שֵׁנִי – כׇּל מִצְוֹת כְּהוּנָּה גְּדוֹלָה עָלָיו, דִּבְרֵי רַבִּי מֵאִיר. רַבִּי יוֹסֵי אוֹמֵר: רִאשׁוֹן חוֹזֵר לַעֲבוֹדָתוֹ, שֵׁנִי אֵינוֹ רָאוּי לֹא לְכֹהֵן גָּדוֹל וְלֹא לְכֹהֵן הֶדְיוֹט.

The Gemara asks: **How did we establish** the mishna? We established **that** it is **not in accordance with** the opinion of **Rabbi Meir. Say the latter clause** of the mishna: **The difference between a** High **Priest** currently **serving** in that capacity **and a former** High **Priest is only** with regard to **the bull** brought **on Yom Kippur, and the tenth of an ephah** meal-offering. The Gemara infers **that** with regard **to all** other **matters,** both **this,** a High Priest currently serving, **and that,** a former High Priest, are **equal.**[N] If so **we have arrived at** the opinion of **Rabbi Meir, as it is taught** in a *baraita*: If temporary **disqualification befell** the High Priest,[H] **and they appointed another priest in his stead,** then after the cause of disqualification of **the first** priest passes, he **returns to his service** as High Priest. With regard to **the second** priest, **all of the mitzvot of the High Priest** are incumbent **upon him;** this is **the statement of** Rabbi Meir. **Rabbi Yosei says: The first returns to his service; the second is fit** to serve **neither as a High Priest nor as a common priest.**[N]

וְאָמַר רַבִּי יוֹסֵי: מַעֲשֶׂה בְּרַבִּי יוֹסֵף בֶּן אֵלֶם מִצִּיפּוֹרִי שֶׁאֵירַע בּוֹ פְּסוּל בְּכֹהֵן גָּדוֹל, וּמִינּוּהוּ תַּחְתָּיו, וּבָא מַעֲשֶׂה לִפְנֵי חֲכָמִים וְאָמְרוּ: רִאשׁוֹן חוֹזֵר לַעֲבוֹדָתוֹ, שֵׁנִי אֵינוֹ רָאוּי לֹא לְכֹהֵן גָּדוֹל וְלֹא לְכֹהֵן הֶדְיוֹט.

And Rabbi Yosei said: There was **an incident involving** the priest **Rabbi Yosef ben Elem**[P] **of Tzippori,** who, **when disqualification befell a High Priest,** the priests **appointed him in his stead. And** after the cause of the disqualification was resolved, **the incident came before the Sages** for a ruling with regard to the status of Rabbi Yosef ben Elem. **And the Sages said:** The **original** High Priest **returns to his service,** while the **second is fit** to serve **neither as High Priest nor as a common priest.**

כֹּהֵן גָּדוֹל – מִשּׁוּם אֵיבָה, כֹּהֵן הֶדְיוֹט – מִשּׁוּם ״מַעֲלִין בַּקּוֹדֶשׁ וְלֹא מוֹרִידִין״. רֵישָׁא רַבָּנַן וְסֵיפָא רַבִּי מֵאִיר?!

The Gemara explains: Neither as a **High Priest, due to hatred,** jealousy, and bitterness that would arise if there were two High Priests with equal standing in the Temple; nor as a **common priest, because** the principle is: **One elevates** to a higher level **in** matters of **sanctity and one does not downgrade.** Once he has served as a High Priest he cannot be restored to the position of a common priest. Is that to say that **the first clause** of the mishna is in accordance with the opinion of **the Rabbis,** who disagree with Rabbi Meir, **and the latter clause** is in accordance with the opinion of **Rabbi Meir?**

אָמַר רַב חִסְדָּא: אִין, רֵישָׁא רַבָּנַן וְסֵיפָא רַבִּי מֵאִיר. רַב יוֹסֵף אָמַר: רַבִּי הִיא, וְנָסֵיב לַהּ אַלִּיבָּא דְּתַנָּאֵי.

Rav Ḥisda said: Indeed, the first clause of the mishna is in accordance with the opinion of **the Rabbis, and the latter clause** is in accordance with the opinion of **Rabbi Meir. Rav Yosef said:** The entire mishna **is** according to **Rabbi** Yehuda HaNasi, **and he formulates it according to** the opinions **of** different ***tanna'im***, that is to say, resulting in a third opinion, in accordance with the opinion of the Rabbis with regard to a High Priest consecrated by donning multiple garments, and the opinion of Rabbi Meir with regard to a former High Priest.

NOTES

With regard to all other matters this and that are equal – לכל דבריהן זה וזה שוין: The sanctity, the status, and all the prohibitions of the High Priest continue to apply to a former High Priest. When he serves, he dons eight garments; he may not become impure even when his relatives die; he does not grow his hair or rip his garments when he is in mourning; he sacrifices offerings during his period of acute mourning; it is prohibited for him to marry a widow; he is required to marry a virgin; and one who killed another unwittingly returns home from the city of refuge upon his death.

The second is fit neither as a High Priest nor as a common priest – שני אינו ראוי לא לכהן גדול ולא לכהן הדיוט: This is explicit in the Jerusalem Talmud; see *Oraḥ HaHalakha* with regard to the opinion of the Rambam. Even according to Rabbi Yosei the replacement priest is not fundamentally unfit to be the High Priest; it is merely to prevent animosity and competition that two High Priests cannot serve simultaneously. Although the sanctity and status of the second priest is that of a High Priest, he does not serve as the High Priest. The Ramban writes that when the first priest dies, the priest who temporarily replaced him takes precedence in the choosing of his successor.

HALAKHA

If temporary disqualification befell the High Priest – אירע בו פסול: If a High Priest is rendered temporarily unfit and another priest is appointed in his stead for the Yom Kippur service, the High Priest reassumes his position after Yom Kippur, and his replacement is relieved of his duty. Nevertheless, all the mitzvot of the High Priest remain incumbent upon the temporary replacement, although he does not perform the service of the High Priest. If he does perform the service of the High Priest, the service is valid, in accordance with the opinion of Rav Yosei, as the *halakha* is in accordance with his opinion in tractate *Yoma* (Rambam *Sefer Avoda, Hilkhot Avodat Yom HaKippurim* 1:3).

PERSONALITIES

Yosef ben Elem – יוסף בן אלם: This incident was also related in *Antiquities of the Jews* by Josephus Flavius (Book 17, Chapter 6). When a disqualification befell the High Priest Mattathias, his relative Yosef ben Elem was appointed in his stead for one day.

מתני׳ אֵין בֵּין בָּמָה גְדוֹלָה לְבָמָה קְטַנָּה אֶלָּא פְּסָחִים. זֶה הַכְּלָל: כָּל שֶׁהוּא נִידָּר וְנִידָּב קָרֵב בַּבָּמָה, וְכָל שֶׁאֵינוֹ לֹא נִידָּר וְלֹא נִידָּב – אֵינוֹ קָרֵב בַּבָּמָה.

MISHNA **The difference between a great,** public **altar,** such as the altars established at Nob and Gibeon, which served as religious centers following the destruction of the Tabernacle in Shiloh, **and a small,** personal **altar**[N] on which individuals would sacrifice their offerings, **is only** with regard to **Paschal lambs,** which may not be sacrificed on a small altar. **This is the principle: Any** offering **that is vowed or contributed** voluntarily **is sacrificed on a small altar, and any** offering **that is neither vowed nor contributed** voluntarily, but rather is compulsory, e.g., a sin-offering, **is not sacrificed on a small altar.**

גמ׳ פְּסָחִים וְתוּ לָא? אֵימָא: כְּעֵין פְּסָחִים.

GEMARA The Gemara asks: Is the difference only **Paschal lambs and nothing more?** The continuation of the mishna indicates that there are additional differences. The Gemara answers: **Say** that the difference between them is only with regard to offerings that are **similar to Paschal lambs.**

מַנִּי? רַבִּי שִׁמְעוֹן הִיא. דְּתַנְיָא, רַבִּי שִׁמְעוֹן אוֹמֵר: אַף צִבּוּר לֹא הִקְרִיבוּ אֶלָּא פְּסָחִים וְחוֹבוֹת שֶׁקָּבוּעַ לָהֶם זְמַן, אֲבָל חוֹבוֹת שֶׁאֵין קָבוּעַ לָהֶם זְמַן – הָכָא וְהָכָא לָא קָרֵב.

The Gemara asks: According to **whose** opinion is the mishna taught? The Gemara answers: **It is** according to the opinion of **Rabbi Shimon, as it is taught** in a *baraita* that **Rabbi Shimon says: Even the public sacrificed only Paschal lambs and compulsory** offerings **for which there is a set time,** like fixed communal offerings. **However, compulsory** offerings **for which there is not a set time,** e.g., sin-offerings brought for an unwitting transgression committed by the community, **are sacrificed neither here** on a small altar **nor here** on a great altar; they are sacrificed only in the Temple.

מתני׳ אֵין בֵּין שִׁילֹה לִירוּשָׁלַיִם אֶלָּא שֶׁבְּשִׁילֹה אוֹכְלִין קָדָשִׁים קַלִּים וּמַעֲשֵׂר שֵׁנִי בְּכָל הָרוֹאֶה, וּבִירוּשָׁלַיִם לִפְנִים מִן הַחוֹמָה.

MISHNA **The difference between** the Tabernacle in **Shilo**[B] **and** the Temple in **Jerusalem is only that in Shiloh one eats offerings of lesser sanctity,**[H] e.g., individual peace-offerings, thanks-offerings, and the Paschal lamb, **and** also **the second tithe,**[B] **in any place that overlooks** Shiloh,[N] as Shiloh was not a walled city and any place within its Shabbat boundary was regarded as part of the city. **And in Jerusalem** one eats those consecrated items only **within the walls.**

וְכָאן וְכָאן קָדְשֵׁי קָדָשִׁים נֶאֱכָלִין לִפְנִים מִן הַקְּלָעִים. קְדוּשַּׁת שִׁילֹה

And here, in Shiloh, **and there,** in Jerusalem, **offerings of the most sacred order**[H] **are eaten** only **within the hangings.** The Tabernacle courtyard in Shiloh was surrounded by hangings and the Temple courtyard in Jerusalem was surrounded by a wall. There is another difference: With regard to **the sanctity of Shiloh,**

NOTES

A great public altar and a small personal altar – בָּמָה גְּדוֹלָה וּבָמָה קְטַנָּה: The great altar is the copper altar that stood in the desert Tabernacle, in Nob, and in Gibeon. The reason that the altar there was called the great altar and not the altar of the Tabernacle or Temple is that the Ark of the Covenant was not there; it was at different times taken by the Philistines or stored in Kiriat-je'arim. In tractate *Zevaḥim* several additional differences between a great and small altar are enumerated. However, as explained elsewhere, not all differences are cited in the mishna here.

Small altars were in use during the period when the great altars were functional. Anyone could establish a small altar and sacrifice burnt-offerings and peace-offerings. Service at these altars was not restricted to priests, and many of the other regulations governing the sacrifice of offerings did not apply.

In Shiloh…in any place that overlooks Shiloh – בְּשִׁילֹה...בְּכָל הָרוֹאֶה: The simple reason for this is because Shiloh was open and unwalled, and had no defined boundary. Its domain, similar to the camp of the Israelites in the desert, included all places from which Shiloh or the Tabernacle could be seen (see Jerusalem Talmud). In tractate *Zevaḥim* this is explained homiletically: Since Shiloh was in the tribal territory of Joseph, and because Joseph resisted sinning and did not let his eyes wander inappropriately such as with regard to Potiphar's wife, he was rewarded that in his tribal territory, offerings sacrificed in Shiloh may be eaten anywhere within eyeshot of the town.

HALAKHA

Offerings of lesser sanctity – קָדָשִׁים קַלִּים: Offerings of lesser sanctity and second tithe produce may be eaten only within the walls of Jerusalem (Rambam *Sefer Avoda, Hilkhot Beit HaBeḥira* 7:14).

Offerings of the most sacred order – קָדְשֵׁי קָדָשִׁים: Offerings of the most sacred order are eaten in the Temple courtyard. One who eats an olive-bulk of those offerings outside the courtyard is flogged (Rambam *Sefer Avoda, Hilkhot Ma'aseh HaKorbanot* 11:5).

BACKGROUND

Shiloh – שִׁילֹה: Other than the Temple in Jerusalem, the Divine Presence rested in three places in Eretz Yisrael: Shiloh, where the Tabernacle was erected after the Jewish people entered the land, and Nob and Gibeon, referred to here as great altars. According to the Gemara in tractate *Zevaḥim* (118b), the Tabernacle stood in Shiloh for 369 years and in Nob and Gibeon for a total of fifty-seven years.

The city of Shiloh, which was located in the tribal land of Ephraim (see Judges 21:19), is approximately 35 km north of Jerusalem on the ancient mountain ridge road that traverses the country from north to south, and a bit less than 16 km south of the city of Shechem. In the modern-day settlement of Shiloh, remnants of the Tabernacle were discovered, and a synagogue was built commemorating the Tabernacle.

Second tithe – מַעֲשֵׂר שֵׁנִי: This is the tithe separated after the *teruma* for the priests and the first tithe for the Levites were separated. Second tithe was separated during the first, second, fourth, and fifth years of the Sabbatical cycle. After second tithe was designated, it had to be taken to Jerusalem to be eaten there by its owner. If the journey to Jerusalem was too long, and therefore it was difficult to take the second tithe there, or if the produce became ritually impure, it could be redeemed for an equivalent sum of money. If the owner redeemed his own produce, he was required to add one-fifth of its value. If he redeemed the second tithe produce by selling it to others, there is no need to add one-fifth of its value. The redemption money was then taken to Jerusalem, where it had to be spent on food. Second tithe could be redeemed only with minted coins bearing an imprint; unstamped coins and promissory notes could not be used. Today, second tithe is still redeemed, but for a nominal sum, as in the absence of the Temple it is no longer brought to Jerusalem. The *halakhot* of second tithe are discussed in tractate *Ma'aser Sheni.*

יֵשׁ אַחֲרֶיהָ הֶיתֵּר. וּקְדוּשַּׁת יְרוּשָׁלַיִם אֵין אַחֲרֶיהָ הֶיתֵּר.

after the Tabernacle was destroyed, **there is permission** to sacrifice offerings on improvised altars. **But** with regard to **the sanctity of Jerusalem, after** the Temple was destroyed, **there is no permission** to sacrifice offerings on improvised altars, as the prohibition[H] remains intact.

גמ׳ אָמַר רַבִּי יִצְחָק: שָׁמַעְתִּי שֶׁמַּקְרִיבִין בְּבֵית חוֹנְיוֹ בַּזְּמַן הַזֶּה. קָסָבַר: בֵּית חוֹנְיוֹ לָאו בֵּית עֲבוֹדָה זָרָה הִיא, וְקָא סָבַר: קְדוּשָּׁה רִאשׁוֹנָה – קִידְּשָׁה לִשְׁעָתָהּ וְלֹא קִידְּשָׁה לֶעָתִיד לָבוֹא.

GEMARA Rabbi Yitzḥak said: I heard that one sacrifices offerings **in the temple of Onias** in Egypt **at the present time.** The Gemara cites the basis for the statement of Rabbi Yitzḥak. **He maintains** that **the temple of Onias is not a house of idol worship** but rather a temple devoted to the service of God, **and he maintains** that **the initial consecration sanctified** Jerusalem **for its time and did not sanctify** Jerusalem **forever.** Therefore, after the destruction of the Temple, the sanctity of Jerusalem lapsed and the sacrifice of offerings elsewhere was no longer prohibited. For these reasons it was permitted to sacrifice offerings in the temple of Onias after the Temple was destroyed.

דִּכְתִיב: ״כִּי לֹא בָאתֶם עַד עָתָּה אֶל הַמְּנוּחָה וְאֶל הַנַּחֲלָה״, ״מְנוּחָה״ – זוֹ שִׁילֹה, ״נַחֲלָה״ – זוֹ יְרוּשָׁלַיִם. מַקִּישׁ נַחֲלָה לִמְנוּחָה; מָה מְנוּחָה יֵשׁ אַחֲרֶיהָ הֶיתֵּר – אַף נַחֲלָה יֵשׁ אַחֲרֶיהָ הֶיתֵּר.

The Gemara cites the source of this *halakha*. It is **as it is written: "For you are not as yet come to the rest and to the inheritance"** (Deuteronomy 12:9), which is interpreted: **"Rest," this is Shiloh; "inheritance," this is Jerusalem.** The verse **juxtaposes** and likens **inheritance to rest: Just as** in the place of **rest,** Shiloh, **after** its destruction **there is permission** to sacrifice offerings on improvised altars, **so too** in the place of **inheritance,** Jerusalem, **after** its destruction **there is permission** to sacrifice offerings on improvised altars.

אֲמַרוּ לֵיהּ: אֲמַרְתְּ? אֲמַר לְהוּ: לָא. אָמַר רָבָא: הָאֱלֹהִים! אֲמָרָהּ, וּגְמִירְנָא לַהּ מִינֵּיהּ.

The Gemara reports that the other Sages **said to** Rabbi Yitzḥak: **Did you say** this *halakha* with regard to the temple of Onias? **He said to them: No,** I did not say that.[N] **Rava said,** reinforcing his assertion with an oath: **By God!** Rabbi Yitzḥak **did** in fact **say this, and I** myself **learned it from him,** but he later retracted this ruling.

וּמַאי טַעְמָא קָא הָדַר בֵּיהּ? מִשּׁוּם קוּשְׁיָא דְּרַב מָרִי. דְּמוֹתִיב רַב מָרִי: קְדוּשַּׁת שִׁילֹה יֵשׁ אַחֲרֶיהָ הֶיתֵּר, קְדוּשַּׁת יְרוּשָׁלַיִם אֵין אַחֲרֶיהָ הֶיתֵּר. וְעוֹד תְּנַן: מִשֶּׁבָּאוּ לִירוּשָׁלַיִם נֶאֶסְרוּ הַבָּמוֹת, וְלֹא הָיָה לָהֶם עוֹד הֶיתֵּר, וְהִיא הָיְתָה לְנַחֲלָה.

The Gemara asks: **And what is the reason he retracted** his ruling?[N] The Gemara explains: It is **due to the difficulty** raised **by Rav Mari, as Rav Mari raised an objection** from the mishna: With regard to **the sanctity of Shiloh, after** the Tabernacle was destroyed **there is permission** to sacrifice offerings on improvised altars. But with regard to **the sanctity of Jerusalem, after** the Temple was destroyed **there is no permission** to sacrifice offerings on improvised altars. **And furthermore, we learned** in a mishna (*Zevaḥim* 112b): **Once they came to Jerusalem,** improvised altars **were prohibited, and they did not again have permission** to do so, **and** Jerusalem **became the** everlasting **inheritance.**

HALAKHA

The prohibition against improvised altars – אִיסּוּר בָּמוֹת: After Solomon built the First Temple in Jerusalem, it was prohibited to sacrifice offerings anywhere else. The only Temple to the Lord is the one on Mount Moriah in Jerusalem, with regard to which it is stated: "This is My resting-place forever" (Psalms 132:14; Rambam *Sefer Avoda, Hilkhot Beit HaBeḥira* 1:3).

NOTES

Did you say this? He said to them no – אֲמַרְתְּ? אֲמַר לְהוּ לָא: The Rashba writes that there is no definitive proof from here that Rabbi Yitzḥak completely retracted his opinion. In other places in the Gemara there are cases where one of the Sages learned a certain matter from his teachers. When that matter was challenged from various sources, although he continued to hold in accordance with that which he received from his teacher, rather than enter into a debate over the matter, he attempted to evade the challenge by saying that he never said it.

And what is the reason he retracted his ruling – וּמַאי טַעְמָא קָא הָדַר בֵּיהּ: As is ultimately proven later in the Gemara, there is a tannaitic dispute, as well as a dispute between Rabbi Yoḥanan and Reish Lakish in tractate *Zevaḥim* with regard to this matter. Therefore, there was no need for him to retract his statement. Some explain that he retracted his statement because two unattributed *mishnayot* are very authoritative proofs, and in the face of those proofs, one cannot rely upon the opinion of an individual *tanna* (Rashba). Others write that initially Rav Yitzḥak maintained that this dispute is parallel to the dispute between Rabbi Eliezer and Rabbi Yehoshua. Once that parallel was rejected and there is no proof that they disagreed on this issue, he retracted his statement (*Penei Yehoshua*; *Turei Even*).

תַּנָּאֵי הִיא: (דְּתַנְיָא) אָמַר רַבִּי אֱלִיעֶזֶר: שָׁמַעְתִּי כְּשֶׁהָיוּ בּוֹנִין בַּהֵיכָל עוֹשִׂין קְלָעִים לַהֵיכָל וּקְלָעִים לַעֲזָרָה. אֶלָּא שֶׁבַּהֵיכָל בּוֹנִין מִבַּחוּץ, וּבָעֲזָרָה בּוֹנִין מִבִּפְנִים.

The Gemara comments: **This** matter **is** subject to a dispute between ***tanna'im*****, as it is taught** in a mishna (*Eduyyot* 8:6): **Rabbi Eliezer said: I heard that when they were building the Sanctuary** in the Second Temple, **they fashioned** temporary **hangings for the Sanctuary**[N] **and** temporary **hangings for the courtyard** to serve as partitions until construction of the stone walls was completed. The difference was **only that in** building **the Sanctuary,** the workers **built** the walls **outside** the hangings, without entering, **and in the courtyard,** the workers **built** the walls **inside** the hangings.

וְאָמַר רַבִּי יְהוֹשֻׁעַ: שָׁמַעְתִּי שֶׁמַּקְרִיבִין אַף עַל פִּי שֶׁאֵין בַּיִת, אוֹכְלִין קָדְשֵׁי קָדָשִׁים אַף עַל פִּי שֶׁאֵין קְלָעִים, קָדָשִׁים קַלִּים וּמַעֲשֵׂר שֵׁנִי אַף עַל פִּי שֶׁאֵין חוֹמָה. מִפְּנֵי שֶׁקְּדוּשָּׁה רִאשׁוֹנָה – קִידְּשָׁהּ לְשַׁעְתָּהּ, וְקִידְּשָׁהּ לֶעָתִיד לָבוֹא. מִכְּלָל דְּרַבִּי אֱלִיעֶזֶר סָבַר: לֹא קִידְּשָׁהּ לֶעָתִיד לָבוֹא.

And Rabbi Yehoshua said: I heard that one sacrifices offerings on the altar **even though there is no Temple,**[H] **one eats offerings of the most sacred order** in the Temple courtyard **even if there are no hangings,** and one eats **offerings of lesser sanctity and second tithe** produce in Jerusalem **even if there is no wall** surrounding the city, **due to** the fact **that the initial consecration**[N] **sanctified** Jerusalem **for its time and** also **sanctified** Jerusalem **forever.**[N] Even if the walls do not exist, the sanctity remains intact. The Gemara concludes: From the fact that Rabbi Yehoshua based his opinion on the principle that the initial sanctification sanctified Jerusalem forever, **by inference** one can conclude **that Rabbi Eliezer holds: It did not sanctify** Jerusalem **forever.** Apparently, this issue is subject to a dispute between *tanna'im*.

אֲמַר לֵיהּ רָבִינָא לְרַב אַשִׁי: מִמַּאי? דִּלְמָא דְּכוּלֵּי עָלְמָא קְדוּשָּׁה רִאשׁוֹנָה – קִידְּשָׁהּ לְשַׁעְתָּהּ, וְקִידְּשָׁהּ לֶעָתִיד לָבוֹא. וּמָר מַאי דִּשְׁמִיעַ לֵיהּ קָאָמַר, וּמָר מַאי דִּשְׁמִיעַ לֵיהּ קָאָמַר. וְכִי תֵּימָא קְלָעִים לְרַבִּי אֱלִיעֶזֶר לָמָּה לִי – לִצְנִיעוּתָא בְּעָלְמָא.

Ravina said to Rav Ashi: From where do you draw this inference? **Perhaps everyone maintains that the initial consecration sanctified** Jerusalem **for its time and** also **sanctified** Jerusalem **forever. And** one **Sage,** Rabbi Eliezer, **stated that** tradition, **which he heard** from his teachers, **and** one **Sage,** Rabbi Yehoshua, **stated that** tradition, **which he heard** from his teachers, and there is no dispute between them. **And if you would say: Why** then **do I** need **hangings** at all **according to Rabbi Eliezer?** The original sanctity remained when Jerusalem was not surrounded by walls, and the presence or absence of hangings is irrelevant as well. The Gemara answers: The hangings were established **merely for seclusion,** as it would have been unbecoming for the activity in this most sacred venue to be visible to all.

אֶלָּא, כִּי הָנֵי תַּנָּאֵי. דְּתַנְיָא, אָמַר רַבִּי יִשְׁמָעֵאל בְּרַבִּי יוֹסֵי: לָמָּה מָנוּ חֲכָמִים אֶת אֵלּוּ? שֶׁכְּשֶׁעָלוּ בְּנֵי הַגּוֹלָה מָצְאוּ אֶת אֵלּוּ וְקִידְּשׁוּם, אֲבָל הָרִאשׁוֹנוֹת – בָּטְלוּ מִשֶּׁבָּטְלָה הָאָרֶץ. אַלְמָא קָסָבַר: קְדוּשָּׁה רִאשׁוֹנָה קִידְּשָׁהּ לְשַׁעְתָּהּ וְלֹא קִידְּשָׁהּ לֶעָתִיד לָבוֹא.

Rather, this matter is subject to the dispute between **these** ***tanna'im*****, as it is taught** in a *baraita* that **Rabbi Yishmael, son of Rabbi Yosei, said: Why did the Sages enumerate these** nine cities in tractate *Arakhin* as cities walled since the days of Joshua, son of Nun? Weren't there many more? **As, when the exiles ascended** to Eretz Yisrael from Babylonia, **they discovered these** cities **and consecrated them** as walled cities; **but the** sanctity of the **first** walled cities enumerated in the book of Joshua **was negated when** settlement in **the land was negated** and the Jewish people were exiled. **Apparently,** Rabbi Yishmael, son of Rabbi Yosei, **maintains: The initial consecration sanctified** Jerusalem **for its time** only **and did not sanctify** Jerusalem **forever.**

וּרְמִינְהוּ, אָמַר רַבִּי יִשְׁמָעֵאל בְּרַבִּי יוֹסֵי: וְכִי אֵלּוּ בִּלְבַד הָיוּ? וַהֲלֹא כְּבָר נֶאֱמַר: ״שִׁשִּׁים עִיר כָּל חֶבֶל אַרְגּוֹב״, וּכְתִיב: ״כָּל אֵלֶּה עָרִים בְּצוּרוֹת חוֹמָה גְבוֹהָה״ אֶלָּא לָמָּה מָנוּ חֲכָמִים אֶת אֵלּוּ? שֶׁכְּשֶׁעָלוּ בְּנֵי הַגּוֹלָה מָצְאוּ אֵלּוּ וְקִידְּשׁוּם.

The Gemara **raises a contradiction** from a different *baraita*. **Rabbi Yishmael, son of Rabbi Yosei, said: Were these** cities that were enumerated in tractate *Arakhin* **the only** walled cities? **Wasn't it already stated: "Sixty cities, all the region of Argov"** (Deuteronomy 3:4), **and** concerning these cities **it is written: "All these cities were fortified with high walls,** gates and bars" (Deuteronomy 3:5), indicating that there were a great number of walled cities? **Rather, why then did the Sages enumerate these** specific cities? It is due to the fact **that when the exiles ascended** from Babylonia **they discovered these and consecrated them** as walled cities.

קִידְּשׁוּם?!

The Gemara asks: **Consecrated them?** If their sanctity remained, why was it necessary to consecrate them?

NOTES

Hangings for the Sanctuary – קְלָעִים לַהֵיכָל: Rashi says the Gemara seeks to prove from here that according to Rabbi Eliezer, the initial consecration sanctified Jerusalem for its time only and not forever. Consequently, hangings were necessary to establish barriers around the Temple in order to sanctify it. The hangings were later replaced with walls. Others seek to prove from the statement of Rabbi Eliezer that he maintained that the initial consecration sanctified Jerusalem forever, as otherwise, when they established the hangings they minimized the area of the Sanctuary, and it is prohibited to change its measurements. Therefore, it must be that the hangings were established for seclusion (*Ye'arot Devash*). The Meiri concurs with the first opinion, citing proof from tractate *Ḥagiga*, while Rabbeinu Tam rejects this proof.

First consecration and second consecration – קְדוּשָּׁה רִאשׁוֹנָה וּשְׁנִיָּה: In terms of the Temple, the initial consecration is the establishment of the First Temple, built by Solomon, and the second consecration is the establishment of the Second Temple. However, with regard to the consecration of Eretz Yisrael, the initial consecration is the conquest of the land by Joshua and the second is the return of the exiles, led by Ezra, from Babylonia to Zion.

The initial consecration sanctified Jerusalem for its time and sanctified it forever – קְדוּשָּׁה רִאשׁוֹנָה קִידְּשָׁהּ לְשַׁעְתָּהּ וְקִידְּשָׁהּ לֶעָתִיד לָבוֹא: With regard to this matter there is a fundamental dispute cited by *Tosafot* and the other early authorities here, and it apparently also relates to the dispute between the Rambam and the Ra'avad with regard to the sanctity of the Temple. Based on the Gemara here, there appears to be one question: Was the sanctity of the land abrogated by the destruction of the Second Temple? If it was, then the sanctity of Jerusalem was similarly abrogated.

However, in the opinion of the Rambam and many others, the sanctity of Jerusalem in terms of the prohibition against sacrificing offerings elsewhere and the sanctity of Eretz Yisrael are not interdependent. The sanctity of Jerusalem and the Temple was never abrogated, although the sanctity of Eretz Yisrael was. See the Rashba, who discusses this at length. Others write that Rabbi Yitzḥak retracted his opinion due to those same considerations. Initially, he maintained that there is only one dispute here, basing his opinion on those who said the sanctity of the land was abrogated. However, once he realized that the sanctity of Jerusalem and the sanctity of Eretz Yisrael are not interdependent, and that there is no one who holds that the sanctity of Jerusalem was abrogated, he retracted his opinion (*Zikkaron BaSefer*; *Sefat Emet*).

HALAKHA

One sacrifices offerings even when there is no Temple – מַקְרִיבִין אַף עַל פִּי שֶׁאֵין בַּיִת: It is permitted to sacrifice all of the offerings even although the Temple is not standing. The offerings of the most sacred order may be eaten in the entire courtyard even though its walls are destroyed. Second tithe and offerings of lesser sanctity may be eaten throughout Jerusalem even if its walls are not standing, because the initial consecration sanctified Jerusalem for its time and forever, in accordance with the opinion of Rabbi Yehoshua (Rambam *Sefer Avoda*, *Hilkhot Beit HaBeḥira* 6:15).

הָשְׁתָּא [הָא] אָמְרִי לָא צְרִיכָא לְקִדּוּשֵׁי! אֶלָּא: מָצְאוּ אֶת אֵלּוּ וּמְנָאוּם.

Now, didn't they say later in the same *baraita* that **it is not necessary to consecrate** them? **Rather,** this is what the *baraita* means to say: It is due to the fact that when the exiles ascended from Babylonia **they discovered these and enumerated them.**

וְלֹא אֵלּוּ בִּלְבַד, אֶלָּא כׇּל שֶׁתַּעֲלֶה לְךָ מַסּוֹרֶת בְּיָדְךָ מֵאֲבוֹתֶיךָ שֶׁמּוּקֶּפֶת חוֹמָה מִימוֹת יְהוֹשֻׁעַ בִּן נוּן – כׇּל הַמִּצְוֹת הַלָּלוּ נוֹהֲגִין בָּהּ, מִפְּנֵי שֶׁקְּדוּשָּׁה רִאשׁוֹנָה קִידְּשָׁהּ לִשְׁעָתָהּ וְקִידְּשָׁהּ לֶעָתִיד לָבֹא. קַשְׁיָא דְּרַבִּי יִשְׁמָעֵאל אַדְּרַבִּי יִשְׁמָעֵאל!

The *baraita* continues. **And not only these, but** in **any** city with regard to **which you receive a tradition from your ancestors that it was surrounded by a wall from the days of Joshua, son of Nun, all these mitzvot are observed in it, due to** the fact **that the initial consecration sanctified** Jerusalem **for its time and sanctified** Jerusalem **forever.** This **is difficult,** as there is a contradiction between one statement **of Rabbi Yishmael and** another statement **of Rabbi Yishmael.**

תְּרֵי תַּנָּאֵי אַלִּיבָּא דְּרַבִּי יִשְׁמָעֵאל בְּרַבִּי יוֹסֵי. וְאִיבָּעֵית אֵימָא: הָא – רַבִּי אֶלְעָזָר בַּר יוֹסֵי אֲמָרָהּ. דְּתַנְיָא, רַבִּי אֶלְעָזָר בְּרַבִּי יוֹסֵי אָמַר: ״אֲשֶׁר לוֹא חוֹמָה״ – אַף עַל פִּי שֶׁאֵין לוֹ עַכְשָׁיו וְהָיָה לוֹ קוֹדֶם לָכֵן.

The Gemara answers: This is a dispute between **two** later ***tanna'im*,** who hold **according to** the opinion of **Rabbi Yishmael, son of Rabbi Yosei.** Each transmitted Rabbi Yishmael's opinion in a different manner. **And if you wish, say** instead that one of the traditions is mistaken, as with regard to **this** statement, **Rabbi Elazar bar Yosei said it, as it is taught** in a *baraita*: **Rabbi Elazar, son of Rabbi Yosei,**[P] **said**[N] that the verse states: **"Which has** [*lo*] **a wall"** (Leviticus 25:30). The word *lo* is written with an *alef*, meaning no, that it does not have a wall, but its vocalization is in the sense of its homonym, *lo* with a *vav*, meaning that it has a wall. This indicates that **even though it does not presently have** a wall, as it was destroyed, **but it had a wall previously,** it retains its status as a walled city. It is Rabbi Elazar, son of Rabbi Yosei, who maintains that the first consecration sanctified Jerusalem forever.

״וַיְהִי בִּימֵי אֲחַשְׁוֵרוֹשׁ״. אָמַר רַבִּי לֵוִי וְאִיתֵּימָא רַבִּי יוֹנָתָן: דָּבָר זֶה מַסּוֹרֶת בְּיָדֵינוּ מֵאַנְשֵׁי כְּנֶסֶת הַגְּדוֹלָה: כׇּל מָקוֹם שֶׁנֶּאֱמַר ״וַיְהִי״ אֵינוֹ אֶלָּא לְשׁוֹן צַעַר.

§ The Gemara returns to the primary topic of this chapter, the book of Esther. The Gemara cites various aggadic interpretations of the verses of the Megilla. The opening verse of the Megilla states: **"And it came to pass** [*vayhi*] **in the days of Ahasuerus"** (Esther 1:1). **Rabbi Levi said, and some say** that it was **Rabbi Yonatan** who said: **This matter is a tradition** that **we** received **from the members of the Great Assembly. Anywhere that** the word ***vayhi* is stated, it is** an ominous **term** indicating **nothing other** than impending **grief,** as if the word were a contraction of the words *vai* and *hi*, meaning woe and mourning.

״וַיְהִי בִּימֵי אֲחַשְׁוֵרוֹשׁ״ – הֲוָה הָמָן, ״וַיְהִי בִּימֵי שְׁפוֹט הַשּׁוֹפְטִים״ – הֲוָה רָעָב, ״וַיְהִי כִּי הֵחֵל הָאָדָם לָרוֹב״ – ״וַיַּרְא ה׳ כִּי רַבָּה רָעַת הָאָדָם״.

The Gemara cites several proofs corroborating this interpretation. **"And it came to pass** [*vayhi*] **in the days of Ahasuerus"** led to grief, as there **was Haman. "And it came to pass** [*vayhi*] **in the days when the judges ruled"** (Ruth 1:1) introduces a period when there **was famine. "And it came to pass** [*vayhi*]**, when men began to multiply"** (Genesis 6:1) is immediately followed by the verse: **"And the Lord saw that the wickedness of man was great in the earth"** (Genesis 6:5).

״וַיְהִי בְּנׇסְעָם מִקֶּדֶם״ – ״הָבָה נִבְנֶה לָּנוּ עִיר״. ״וַיְהִי בִּימֵי אַמְרָפֶל״ – ״עָשׂוּ מִלְחָמָה״. ״וַיְהִי בִּהְיוֹת יְהוֹשֻׁעַ בִּירִיחוֹ״ – ״וְחַרְבּוֹ שְׁלוּפָה בְּיָדוֹ״. ״וַיְהִי ה׳ אֶת יְהוֹשֻׁעַ״ – ״וַיִּמְעֲלוּ בְּנֵי יִשְׂרָאֵל״. ״וַיְהִי אִישׁ אֶחָד מִן הָרָמָתַיִם״ – ״כִּי אֶת חַנָּה אָהֵב וַה׳ סָגַר רַחְמָהּ״.

"And it came to pass [*vayhi*] **as they journeyed from the east"** (Genesis 11:2) is followed by: **"Come, let us build us a city"** (Genesis 11:4), which led to the sin of the Tower of Babel. The Gemara cites further examples: **"And it came to pass in the days of Amraphel"** (Genesis 14:1), about whom it is stated: **"These made war"** (Genesis 14:2). Another verse states: **"And it came to pass, when Joshua was by Jericho"** (Joshua 5:13), it was there that he saw an angel **"with his sword drawn in his hand"** as a warning. It is written: **"And the Lord was** [*vayhi*] **with Joshua"** (Joshua 6:27), and immediately afterward: **"But the children of Israel committed a trespass"** (Joshua 7:1). It states: **"And it came to pass that there was a certain man of Ramathaim"** (I Samuel 1:1), and it mentions shortly afterward Hannah's inability to conceive: **"For he loved Hannah, but the Lord had closed up her womb"** (I Samuel 1:5).

PERSONALITIES

Rabbi Elazar, son of Rabbi Yosei – רַבִּי אֶלְעָזָר בְּרַבִּי יוֹסֵי: He was a fifth generation *tanna*, son of the *tanna* Rabbi Yosei ben Ḥalafta. Rabbi Yosei had five sons, all ordained Sages. The most famous among them was Rabbi Yishmael, son of Rabbi Yosei, a disciple-colleague of Rabbi Yehuda HaNasi. Apparently, Rabbi Elazar was significantly older than his brother Rabbi Yishmael, as he participated in a delegation of Sages to Rome together with Rabbi Shimon bar Yoḥai, who was a contemporary of his father's. In several places in the Gemara, there are exchanges between Rabbi Elazar and Rabbi Shimon with regard to both halakhic and aggadic matters. During the visit to Rome, Rabbi Elazar was privileged to see the Temple vessels among the emperor's treasures, and he shared the details of what he saw there with the Sages. He traveled often, was an accomplished conversationalist and debater, and was a man of the world. Several of his halakhic and aggadic statements appear throughout the Talmud.

NOTES

As it is taught in a *baraita*: Rabbi Elazar, son of Rabbi Yosei, said – דְּתַנְיָא רַבִּי אֶלְעָזָר בְּרַבִּי יוֹסֵי אָמַר: The Ramban writes that this *baraita* is not actually dealing with the sanctity of Jerusalem or of Eretz Yisrael. The very existence of a specific verse dealing with the status of walled cities indicates that this is a separate discussion. This statement is cited here only to indicate that Rabbi Elazar, son of Yosei, dealt with a related issue, and it is conceivable that he was the *tanna* of one of the *baraitot* cited earlier.

"וַיְהִי (כִּי) זָקֵן שְׁמוּאֵל" – "וְלֹא הָלְכוּ בָנָיו בִּדְרָכָיו". "וַיְהִי דָוִד לְכָל דְּרָכָו מַשְׂכִּיל [וַה' עִמּוֹ]" – "וַיְהִי שָׁאוּל עוֹיֵן אֶת דָּוִד". "וַיְהִי כִּי יָשַׁב הַמֶּלֶךְ בְּבֵיתוֹ" – "רַק אַתָּה לֹא תִבְנֶה הַבָּיִת".

Similarly, the verse states: **"And it came to pass, when Samuel was old"** (I Samuel 8:1), and then it is written: **"And his sons did not walk in his ways"** (I Samuel 8:3). Also, it states: **"And it came to pass that David was successful in all his ways, and the Lord was with him"** (I Samuel 18:14), and only a few verses prior it is written: **"And Saul viewed David with suspicion"** (I Samuel 18:9). In another instance, the verse states: **"And it came to pass, when the king dwelt in his house"** (II Samuel 7:1). Here King David mentioned his desire to build a temple for God, but it is written elsewhere that he was told: **"Yet you shall not build the house"** (II Chronicles 6:9).

וְהָכְתִיב: "וַיְהִי בַּיּוֹם הַשְּׁמִינִי", וְתַנְיָא: אוֹתוֹ הַיּוֹם הָיְתָה שִׂמְחָה לִפְנֵי הַקָּדוֹשׁ בָּרוּךְ הוּא כְּיוֹם שֶׁנִּבְרְאוּ בּוֹ שָׁמַיִם וָאָרֶץ, כְּתִיב הָכָא: "וַיְהִי בַּיּוֹם הַשְּׁמִינִי" וּכְתִיב הָתָם: "וַיְהִי (בֹקֶר) יוֹם אֶחָד"!

After citing several verses where *vayhi* portends grief, the Gemara mentions a number of verses that seem to indicate otherwise. **But isn't it written: "And it came to pass [*vayhi*] on the eighth day"** (Leviticus 9:1), which was the day of the dedication of the Tabernacle? **And it is taught** in a *baraita* with regard to that day: **On that day there was joy before the Holy One, Blessed be He, similar to** the joy that existed on the **day on which the heavens and earth were created.** The Gemara cites a verbal analogy in support of this statement. **It is written here,** with regard to the dedication of the Tabernacle: **"And it came to pass [*vayhi*] on the eighth day," and it is written there,** in the Creation story: **"And it was [*vayhi*]** evening, and it was **morning, one day"** (Genesis 1:5). This indicates that there was joy on the eighth day, when the Tabernacle was dedicated, similar to the joy that existed on the day the world was created. Apparently, the term *vayhi* is not necessarily a portent of grief.

הָא שְׁכִיב נָדָב וַאֲבִיהוּא.

The Gemara answers: This verse does not contradict the principle. On the day of the dedication of the Tabernacle, a calamity also befell the people, **as Nadav and Avihu died.**

וְהָכְתִיב: "וַיְהִי בִשְׁמוֹנִים שָׁנָה וְאַרְבַּע מֵאוֹת שָׁנָה"! וְהָכְתִיב: "וַיְהִי כַּאֲשֶׁר רָאָה יַעֲקֹב אֶת רָחֵל"! וְהָכְתִיב: "וַיְהִי עֶרֶב וַיְהִי בֹקֶר יוֹם אֶחָד"! וְהָאִיכָּא שֵׁנִי, וְהָאִיכָּא שְׁלִישִׁי, וְהָאִיכָּא טוּבָא!

The Gemara cites additional verses where *vayhi* is not indicative of impending grief: **But isn't it written: "And it came to pass [*vayhi*] in the four hundred and eightieth year"** (I Kings 6:1), which discusses the joyous occasion of the building of the Temple? **And** furthermore, **isn't it written: "And it came to pass [*vayhi*] when Jacob saw Rachel"** (Genesis 29:10), which was a momentous occasion? **And isn't it written: "And it was [*vayhi*] evening, and it was [*vayhi*] morning, one day"** (Genesis 1:5)? **And isn't there the second** day of Creation, **and isn't there the third** day, where the term *vayhi* is used? **And aren't there many** verses in the Bible in which the term *vayhi* appears and no grief ensues? Apparently, the proposed principle is incorrect.

אָמַר רַב אַשִׁי: כָּל "וַיְהִי" – אִיכָּא הָכִי, וְאִיכָּא הָכִי. "וַיְהִי בִּימֵי" אֵינוֹ אֶלָּא לְשׁוֹן צַעַר.

Rather, **Rav Ashi said:** With regard to **every** instance of ***vayhi*** alone, **there are** some that mean **this,** grief, **and there are** some that mean **that,** joy. However, wherever the phrase **"and it came to pass in the days of [*vayhi bimei*]"**[N] is used in the Bible, **it is nothing other** than **a term of** impending **grief.**

חֲמִשָּׁה "וַיְהִי בִּימֵי" הָווּ: "וַיְהִי בִּימֵי אֲחַשְׁוֵרוֹשׁ", "וַיְהִי בִּימֵי שְׁפוֹט הַשּׁוֹפְטִים", "וַיְהִי בִּימֵי אַמְרָפֶל", "וַיְהִי בִּימֵי אָחָז", "וַיְהִי בִּימֵי יְהוֹיָקִים".

The Gemara states that **there are five** instances of ***vayhi bimei*** in the Bible. **"And it came to pass in the days of [*vayhi bimei*] Ahasuerus"; "And it came to pass in the days [*vayhi bimei*] when the judges ruled"; "And it came to pass in the days of [*vayhi bimei*] Amraphel"; "And it came to pass in the days of [*vayhi bimei*] Ahaz"** (Isaiah 7:1); **"And it came to pass in the days of [*vayhi bimei*] Jehoiakim"** (Jeremiah 1:3).[N] In all those incidents, grief ensued.

(אָמַר רַבִּי) לֵוִי: דָּבָר זֶה מָסוֹרֶת בְּיָדֵינוּ מֵאֲבוֹתֵינוּ: אָמוֹץ וַאֲמַצְיָה אַחִים הָווּ. מַאי קָא מַשְׁמַע לַן?

§ Apropos the tradition cited by Rabbi Levi above, the Gemara cites additional traditions that he transmitted. **Rabbi Levi said: This matter is a tradition** that we received **from our ancestors: Amoz,** father of Isaiah, **and Amaziah,** king of Judea, **were brothers.** The Gemara questions: **What** novel element **is this** statement **teaching us?**

NOTES

And it came to pass…And it came to pass in the days of – וַיְהִי...וַיְהִי בִּימֵי: The Gemara explains the basis for associating the term *vayhi*, and it came to pass, with grief by viewing the word as *vai* and *hi*, meaning woe and mourning (see 11a). This explanation is also found in the midrash, which elucidates the term *vayhi* as used to express extremes. In instances of joy and happiness it expresses extreme happiness, while in cases of trouble and grief it refers to overwhelming calamity. There are those who understand Rav Ashi's statement in the Gemara in this manner.

Others explain that when it is written: "And it came to pass," it is possible that the phrase is not indicative of constant misfortune. However, when it is written: "And it came to pass in the days," the verse is referring to an extended period of time, and the expression is always indicative of grief (*Gal Naul*; see *Or Ḥadash*).

And it came to pass in the days of Ahaz, And it came to pass in the days of Jehoiakim – וַיְהִי בִּימֵי אָחָז, וַיְהִי בִּימֵי יְהוֹיָקִים: The Gemara does not state explicitly what form of suffering befell the people during these periods. The Maharsha explains that it is unnecessary to do so, as the passages in the Bible following these verses detail the suffering that occurred to the Jews, including being besieged and defeated in battle.

כִּי הָא דְּאָמַר רַבִּי שְׁמוּאֵל בַּר נַחְמָנִי אָמַר רַבִּי יוֹנָתָן: כׇּל כַּלָּה שֶׁהִיא צְנוּעָה בְּבֵית חָמִיהָ, זוֹכָה וְיוֹצְאִין מִמֶּנָּה מְלָכִים וּנְבִיאִים. מְנָלַן – מִתָּמָר. דִּכְתִיב: ״וַיִּרְאֶהָ יְהוּדָה וַיַּחְשְׁבֶהָ לְזוֹנָה כִּי כִסְּתָה פָּנֶיהָ״. מִשּׁוּם דְּכִסְּתָה פָּנֶיהָ וַיַּחְשְׁבֶהָ לְזוֹנָה?!

The Gemara responds: It is **in accordance with that which Rabbi Shmuel bar Naḥmani said** that **Rabbi Yonatan said: Any bride who is modest**[N] **in the house of her father-in-law merits that kings and prophets** will **emerge from her. From where do we** derive this? **From Tamar, as it is written: "When Judah saw her, he thought her to be a prostitute; for she had covered her face"** (Genesis 38:15). Can it be that **because** Tamar **covered her face he thought her to be a prostitute?** On the contrary, a harlot tends to uncover her face.

אֶלָּא: מִשּׁוּם דְּכִסְּתָה פָּנֶיהָ בְּבֵית חָמִיהָ וְלָא הֲוָה יָדַע לַהּ, זָכְתָה וְיָצְאוּ מִמֶּנָּה מְלָכִים וּנְבִיאִים. מְלָכִים – מִדָּוִד, נְבִיאִים – דְּאָמַר רַבִּי לֵוִי: מָסוֹרֶת בְּיָדֵינוּ מֵאֲבוֹתֵינוּ. אָמוֹץ וַאֲמַצְיָה אַחִים הָיוּ. וּכְתִיב: ״חֲזוֹן יְשַׁעְיָהוּ בֶן אָמוֹץ״.

Rather, because she covered her face in the house of her father-in-law and he was not familiar with her appearance, Judah didn't recognize Tamar, thought she was a harlot, and sought to have sexual relations with her. Ultimately, **she merited that kings and prophets emerged from her. Kings** emerged from her **through David,** who was a descendant of Tamar's son, Peretz. However, there is no explicit mention that she was the forebear of **prophets.** This is derived from that **which Rabbi Levi said:** This matter is **a tradition** that we received **from our ancestors. Amoz,** father of Isaiah, **and Amaziah,** king of Judea, **were brothers,**[N] **and it is written: "The vision of Isaiah the son of Amoz"** (Isaiah 1:1). Amoz was a member of the Davidic dynasty, and his son, the prophet Isaiah, was also a descendant of Tamar.

וְאָמַר רַבִּי לֵוִי: דָּבָר זֶה מָסוֹרֶת בְּיָדֵינוּ מֵאֲבוֹתֵינוּ: מְקוֹם אָרוֹן אֵינוֹ מִן הַמִּדָּה.

And Rabbi Levi said: This matter is a tradition that we received **from our ancestors: The place of the Ark** of the Covenant **is not** included **in the measurement** of the Holy of Holies in which it rested.

תַּנְיָא נַמִּי הָכִי: אָרוֹן שֶׁעָשָׂה מֹשֶׁה יֵשׁ לוֹ עֶשֶׂר אַמּוֹת לְכׇל רוּחַ, וּכְתִיב: ״וְלִפְנֵי הַדְּבִיר עֶשְׂרִים אַמָּה אוֹרֶךְ״, וּכְתִיב: ״כְּנַף הַכְּרוּב הָאֶחָד עֶשֶׂר אַמּוֹת וּכְנַף הַכְּרוּב הָאֶחָד עֶשֶׂר אַמּוֹת״. אָרוֹן גּוּפֵיהּ הֵיכָא הֲוָה קָאֵי? אֶלָּא לָאו שְׁמַע מִינַּהּ: בְּנֵס הָיָה עוֹמֵד.

The Gemara comments: **This is also taught** in a *baraita*: **The Ark crafted by Moses had ten cubits** of empty space **on each side. And it is written** in the description of Solomon's Temple: **"And before the Sanctuary, which was twenty cubits in length,** and twenty cubits in breadth" (I Kings 6:20). The place "before the Sanctuary" is referring to the Holy of Holies. It was twenty by twenty cubits. If there were ten cubits of empty space on either side of the Ark, apparently the Ark itself occupied no space. **And it is written: And the wing of one of the cherubs was ten cubits**[B] **and the wing of the other cherub was ten cubits;** the wings of the cherubs occupied the entire area. If so, **where was the Ark itself standing? Rather,** must one **not conclude from it** that the Ark **stood by means of a miracle** and occupied no space?

רַבִּי יוֹנָתָן פָּתַח לַהּ פִּיתְחָא לְהַאי פָּרָשָׁתָא מֵהָכָא: ״וְקַמְתִּי עֲלֵיהֶם״ וגו׳ ״וְהִכְרַתִּי לְבָבֶל שֵׁם וּשְׁאָר וְנִין וָנֶכֶד נְאֻם ה׳״. ״שֵׁם״ – זֶה הַכְּתָב, ״שְׁאָר״ – זֶה לָשׁוֹן, ״נִין״ – זֶה מַלְכוּת, ״וָנֶכֶד״ – זוֹ וַשְׁתִּי.

§ The Gemara cites prologues utilized by various Sages to introduce study of the Megilla: **Rabbi Yonatan introduced this passage,**[N] the book of Esther, **with an introduction from here: "For I will rise up against them,** says the Lord of hosts, **and cut off from Babylonia name, and remnant, and offspring** [*nin*],[L] **and posterity, says the Lord"** (Isaiah 14:22). This verse may be interpreted homiletically: **"Name," this is** the **writing** of ancient Babylonia that will disappear from the world. **"Remnant," this is** the **language** of ancient Babylonia. **"Offspring," this is** their **kingdom.**[B] And **"posterity," this is Vashti,** who according to tradition was Nebuchadnezzar's granddaughter, and the book of Esther relates how she too was removed from the throne.

BACKGROUND

The wing of one of the cherubs was ten cubits – כְּנַף הַכְּרוּב הָאֶחָד עֶשֶׂר אַמּוֹת:

Cherubs in the First Temple

Writing, language, and kingdom – כְּתָב, לָשׁוֹן, וּמַלְכוּת: After the Babylonian Empire fell to the Persians, many cultural changes occurred. Babylonian cuneiform writing and Akkadian, the Babylonian language, stopped being used and were replaced with the Aramaic alphabet and the Aramaic language. Babylonia as an independent kingdom also ceased to exist, and it remained as a mere district of the great Persian Empire.

LANGUAGE

Offspring [*nin*] – נִין: The exact definition of this word is unclear, and the commentaries offer several opinions as to its meaning. In a number of contexts, it appears to refer to progeny, either a son or a more distant descendant. However, the textual similarity to the verb *yinon* in the verse "May His name endure forever; may His name be continued [*yinon*] as long as the sun" (Psalms 72:17) would seem to indicate that the word *nin* means enduring existence. In that context, *nin* would seem to refer to any form of continued existence or remembrance.

NOTES

Any bride who is modest – כׇּל כַּלָּה שֶׁהִיא צְנוּעָה: Some write that this statement concerning the rewards of a woman who is modest is mentioned in this tractate to connect Rabbi Levi's tradition with the subject of the Megilla. The Gemara relates Esther's modesty and states that various miracles were performed in her merit as a result of it (*Re'ah Duda'im*).

Amoz and Amaziah were brothers – אָמוֹץ וַאֲמַצְיָה אַחִים הָיוּ: The *Ein Ya'akov* explains that, according to tradition, whenever a prophet's name is stated while mentioning his father's name as well, the text is indicating that his father was also a prophet (see 15a). The Maharsha adds that although King David and his son, King Solomon, were prophets, the Gemara did not mention them as proof that one who is modest will merit descendants who are prophets. This is because they were distinguished primarily as monarchs, not prophets. The Gemara is seeking proof of this principle from individuals who were only prophets, and therefore it mentions Isaiah and Amoz, his father.

Introduced this passage – פְּתַח לַהּ פִּיתְחָא: It was a common practice of the Sages of that time to begin teaching a book of the Bible with the aggadic exposition of a verse from another book. These expositions impart a lesson pertinent to the book of the Bible that the Sage is ultimately teaching. These types of introductions are an integral part of aggadic midrash.

The *Penei Yehoshua* explains that although the Talmud rarely includes these forms of aggadic teachings, the numerous introductions here are mentioned in order to support the decision to include the Scroll of Esther in the Bible, by presenting various examples of other books of the Bible alluding to the Scroll of Esther. Others explain that these introductions are intended to prove that the entire Megilla is significant, not only the central part recounting the actual miracle.

The Gemara cites a dispute concerning which sections of the Megilla must be read. These introductions are intended to prove that not only the story of the miracle should be read, but even the first part should be read as well. It appears to be an introduction, but it also has independent importance, as it reveals other miracles that the Holy One, Blessed be He, performed, i.e., how He fulfilled the prophecy to destroy Babylonia and all associated with it (*Ginzei HaMelekh*).

NOTES

And upon all thorns – וּבְכֹל הַנַּעֲצוּצִים: The Maharsha questions the nature of the Gemara's proof, as there seems to be no indication in the verse that it is discussing idolatry, but he leaves his query unanswered. Perhaps the Gemara's understanding relies on the understanding of *Targum Yonatan*. He explains "thorns and brambles" to mean houses that are designated for idolatry.

רַבִּי שְׁמוּאֵל בַּר נַחְמָנִי פְּתַח לַהּ פִּיתְחָא לְהַאי פָּרָשְׁתָּא מֵהָכָא: ״תַּחַת הַנַּעֲצוּץ יַעֲלֶה בְרוֹשׁ וְתַחַת הַסִּרְפַּד יַעֲלֶה הֲדַס״.

Rabbi Shmuel bar Naḥmani introduced this passage with an introduction from here: "Instead of the thorn shall the cypress come up, and instead of the nettle shall the myrtle come up; and it shall be to the Lord for a name, for an everlasting sign that shall not be cut off" (Isaiah 55:13). Rabbi Shmuel bar Naḥmani interpreted the verse homiletically as referring to the righteous individuals who superseded the wicked ones in the book of Esther.

״תַּחַת הַנַּעֲצוּץ״ – תַּחַת הָמָן הָרָשָׁע שֶׁעָשָׂה עַצְמוֹ עֲבוֹדָה זָרָה, דִּכְתִיב: ״וּבְכֹל הַנַּעֲצוּצִים וּבְכֹל הַנַּהֲלוֹלִים״,

"Instead of the thorn"; this means instead of the wicked Haman. He is referred to as a thorn **because he turned himself into an object of idol worship,** as he decreed that all must prostrate themselves before him. The Gemara cites proof that the term thorn is used in connection with idol worship, **as it is written: "And upon all thorns,**[N] **and upon all brambles"** (Isaiah 7:19), which is understood to be a reference to idol worship.

״יַעֲלֶה בְרוֹשׁ״ – זֶה מָרְדְּכַי שֶׁנִּקְרָא רֹאשׁ לְכׇל הַבְּשָׂמִים, שֶׁנֶּאֱמַר: ״וְאַתָּה קַח לְךָ בְּשָׂמִים רֹאשׁ מָר דְּרוֹר״ וּמְתַרְגְּמִינַן: מָרֵי דָּכֵי.

The next section of the verse discusses what will replace the thorns, i.e., Haman: **"Shall the cypress [*berosh*] come up"; this is Mordecai.** Why is he called a cypress [*berosh*]? **Because he was called the chief [*rosh*] of all the spices, as it is stated: "Take you also to yourself the chief spices, of pure myrrh [*mar deror*]"** (Exodus 30:23), **and we translate** "pure myrrh," into Aramaic as ***mari dakhei.*** Mordecai was like *mari dakhi*, the chief [*rosh*] of spices, and therefore he is called *berosh*.

״תַּחַת הַסִּרְפָּד״ – תַּחַת וַשְׁתִּי הָרְשָׁעָה בַּת בְּנוֹ שֶׁל נְבוּכַדְנֶצַּר הָרָשָׁע, שֶׁשָּׂרַף רְפִידַת בֵּית ה׳, דִּכְתִיב: ״רְפִידָתוֹ זָהָב״,

The verse continues: "And **instead of the nettle [*sirpad*],"** this means **instead of the wicked Vashti.** Why is she called a nettle [*sirpad*]? Because she was **the daughter of the son of the wicked Nebuchadnezzar, who burned the ceiling [*saraf refidat*] of the House of God, as it is written: "Its top [*refidato*] of gold"** (Song of Songs 3:10).

״יַעֲלֶה הֲדַס״ – זוֹ אֶסְתֵּר הַצַּדֶּקֶת, שֶׁנִּקְרֵאת הֲדַסָּה, שֶׁנֶּאֱמַר: ״וַיְהִי אוֹמֵן אֶת הֲדַסָּה״. ״וְהָיָה לַה׳ לְשֵׁם״ – זוֹ מִקְרָא מְגִילָּה, ״לְאוֹת עוֹלָם לֹא יִכָּרֵת״ – אֵלּוּ יְמֵי פוּרִים.

The next section of the verse states: **"Shall the myrtle [*hadas*] come up"; this is the righteous Esther, who was called Hadassah** in the Megilla, **as it is stated: "And he had brought up Hadassah;** that is, Esther" (Esther 2:7). The concluding section of the verse states: **"And it shall be to the Lord for a name"; this is the reading of the Megilla. "For an everlasting sign that shall not be cut off"; these are the days of Purim.**

רַבִּי יְהוֹשֻׁעַ בֶּן לֵוִי פְּתַח לַהּ פִּיתְחָא לְהַאי פָּרָשְׁתָּא מֵהָכָא: ״וְהָיָה כַּאֲשֶׁר שָׂשׂ ה׳ עֲלֵיכֶם לְהֵיטִיב אֶתְכֶם, כֵּן יָשִׂישׂ לְהָרַע אֶתְכֶם.

Rabbi Yehoshua ben Levi introduced this passage with an introduction from here: "And it shall come to pass, that as the Lord rejoiced over you to do you good, and to multiply you; so the Lord will rejoice over you to cause you to perish, and to destroy you" (Deuteronomy 28:63). The verse indicates that just as the Lord rejoiced in the good he did on behalf of Israel, so too, the Lord **will rejoice to cause you harm.**

וּמִי חָדֵי הַקָּדוֹשׁ בָּרוּךְ הוּא בְּמַפַּלְתָּן שֶׁל רְשָׁעִים? וְהָא כְּתִיב: ״בְּצֵאת לִפְנֵי הֶחָלוּץ וְאוֹמְרִים הוֹדוּ לַה׳ כִּי לְעוֹלָם חַסְדּוֹ״, וְאָמַר רַבִּי יוֹחָנָן: מִפְּנֵי מָה לֹא נֶאֱמַר ״כִּי טוֹב״ בְּהוֹדָאָה זוֹ – לְפִי שֶׁאֵין הַקָּדוֹשׁ בָּרוּךְ הוּא שָׂמֵחַ בְּמַפַּלְתָּן שֶׁל רְשָׁעִים.

Rabbi Yehoshua ben Levi asked: **Does the Holy One, Blessed be He,** in fact **rejoice over the downfall of the wicked? But it is written: "As they went out before the army, and say: Give thanks to the Lord, for His kindness endures forever"** (II Chronicles 20:21), **and Rabbi Yoḥanan said: For what** reason were the words: **"for He is good" not stated in this** statement of **thanksgiving,** as the classic formulation is: "Give thanks to the Lord; for He is good; for His kindness endures forever" (I Chronicles 16:34)? **Because the Holy One, Blessed be He, does not rejoice over the downfall of the wicked.** Since this song was sung in the aftermath of a military victory, which involved the downfall of the wicked, the name of God was not mentioned for the good.

וְאָמַר רַבִּי יוֹחָנָן, מַאי דִּכְתִיב: ״וְלֹא קָרַב זֶה אֶל זֶה כׇּל הַלָּיְלָה״ – בִּקְּשׁוּ מַלְאֲכֵי הַשָּׁרֵת לוֹמַר שִׁירָה, אָמַר הַקָּדוֹשׁ בָּרוּךְ הוּא: מַעֲשֵׂה יָדַי טוֹבְעִין בַּיָּם וְאַתֶּם אוֹמְרִים שִׁירָה?!

And similarly, **Rabbi Yoḥanan said: What is** the meaning of **that which is written: "And the one came not near the other all the night"** (Exodus 14:20)? **The ministering angels wanted to sing** their **song,** for the angels would sing songs to each other, as it states: "And they called out to each other and said" (Isaiah 6:3), but **the Holy One, Blessed be He, said: The work of My hands,** the Egyptians, are **drowning at sea, and you** wish to **say songs?** This indicates that God does not rejoice over the downfall of the wicked.

אָמַר רַבִּי אֶלְעָזָר: הוּא אֵינוֹ שָׂשׂ, אֲבָל אֲחֵרִים מֵשִׂישׂ. וְדַיְקָא נַמִי, דִּכְתִיב: ״כֵּן יָשִׂישׂ״ וְלָא כְּתִיב ״יָשׂוּשׂ״, שְׁמַע מִינָּהּ.

Rabbi Elazar said that this is how the matter is to be understood: Indeed, God Himself **does not rejoice** over the downfall of the wicked, **but He causes others to rejoice.** The Gemara comments: One can **learn from** the language of the verse **as well, as it is written: "So the Lord will rejoice [*ken yasis*]"** (Deuteronomy 28:63). **And it is not written *yasus*,**[N] the grammatical form of the verb meaning: He will rejoice. Rather, it is written *yasis*. The grammatical form of this verb indicates that one causes another to rejoice. Consequently, these words are understood to mean that God will cause others to rejoice. The Gemara concludes: Indeed, **learn from** it that this is the case.

רַבִּי אַבָּא בַּר כָּהֲנָא פְּתַח לָהּ פִּיתְחָא לְהַאי פָּרָשָׁתָא מֵהָכָא: ״לְאָדָם שֶׁטּוֹב לְפָנָיו נָתַן חָכְמָה וְדַעַת וְשִׂמְחָה״ – זֶה מָרְדֳּכַי הַצַּדִּיק, ״וְלַחוֹטֶא נָתַן עִנְיָן לֶאֱסוֹף וְלִכְנוֹס״ – זֶה הָמָן, ״לָתֵת לְטוֹב לִפְנֵי הָאֱלֹהִים״ – זֶה מָרְדֳּכַי וְאֶסְתֵּר, דִּכְתִיב: ״וַתָּשֶׂם אֶסְתֵּר אֶת מָרְדֳּכַי עַל בֵּית הָמָן״.

Rabbi Abba bar Kahana introduced this passage with an introduction from here. The verse states with regard to God's reward to the righteous: **"He gives to a man that is good in His sight wisdom, and knowledge, and joy"** (Ecclesiastes 2:26). The Gemara explains that **this** verse **is** referring to **the righteous Mordecai.** With regard to the next part of the verse: **"But to the sinner He gives the task of gathering and heaping up," this is** referring to **Haman.** The conclusion of the verse states: **"That he may give it to one who is good before God"** (Ecclesiastes 2:26). **This is Mordecai and Esther, as it is written: "And Esther set Mordecai over the house of Haman"** (Esther 8:2).

רַבָּה בַּר עוֹפְרָן פְּתַח לָהּ פִּיתְחָא לְהַאי פָּרָשָׁתָא מֵהָכָא: ״וְשַׂמְתִּי כִסְאִי בְּעֵילָם וְהַאֲבַדְתִּי מִשָּׁם מֶלֶךְ וְשָׂרִים״. ״מֶלֶךְ״ – זוֹ וַשְׁתִּי, ״וְשָׂרִים״ – זֶה הָמָן וַעֲשֶׂרֶת בָּנָיו.

Rabba bar Oferan introduced this passage with an introduction from here: "And I will set my throne in Elam, and destroy from there the king and the princes, says the Lord" (Jeremiah 49:38). **"The king"** who was destroyed; **this is** referring to **Vashti. "And the princes"; this is** referring to **Haman and his ten sons.**

רַב דִּימִי בַּר יִצְחָק פְּתַח לָהּ פִּיתְחָא לְהַאי פָּרָשָׁתָא מֵהָכָא:

Rav Dimi bar Yitzḥak introduced this passage with an introduction from here:

NOTES

So the Lord will rejoice [*ken yasis*], and it is not written *yasus* – כֵּן יָשִׂישׂ וְלָא כְּתִיב יָשׂוּשׂ: The verb *yasis* can be intransitive or causative, meaning that it can be translated either as: He will rejoice, or: He will cause another to rejoice. However, *yasus* is always causative, and therefore it always implies the latter. For this reason, the Gemara uses the word *yasus* to indicate how *yasis* should be understood (Ḥida; *Maḥzik Berakha*).

Perek **I**
Daf **11** Amud **a**

״כִּי עֲבָדִים אֲנַחְנוּ וּבְעַבְדוּתֵנוּ לֹא עֲזָבָנוּ אֱלֹהֵינוּ וַיַּט עָלֵינוּ חֶסֶד לִפְנֵי מַלְכֵי פָרַס״, אֵימָתַי – בִּזְמַן הָמָן.

"For we are bondmen; yet our God has not forsaken us in our bondage, but has extended mercy unto us in the sight of the kings of Persia" (Ezra 9:9). **When** did this occur? **In the time of Haman.**

רַבִּי חֲנִינָא בַּר פָּפָּא פְּתַח לָהּ פִּתְחָא לְהָא פָּרָשָׁתָא מֵהָכָא: ״הִרְכַּבְתָּ אֱנוֹשׁ לְרֹאשֵׁנוּ בָּאנוּ בָאֵשׁ וּבַמַּיִם״, ״בָּאֵשׁ״ – בִּימֵי נְבוּכַדְנֶצַּר הָרָשָׁע, ״וּבַמַּיִם״ בִּימֵי פַּרְעֹה. ״וַתּוֹצִיאֵנוּ לָרְוָיָה״ – בִּימֵי הָמָן.

Rabbi Ḥanina bar Pappa introduced this passage with an introduction from here: The verse states: **"You have caused men to ride over our heads; we went through fire**[N] **and through water;** but You brought us out into abundance" (Psalms 66:12). **"Through fire";** this was **in the days of the wicked Nebuchadnezzar,** who cast the righteous into the furnace. **"And through water";** this was **in the days of Pharaoh,** who decreed that all newborn males be cast into the water. **"But You brought us out into abundance";** this was **in the days of Haman,** where abundant feasts played a pivotal role in their peril and salvation.

רַבִּי יוֹחָנָן פְּתַח לָהּ פִּתְחָא לְהָא פָּרָשָׁתָא מֵהָכָא: ״זָכַר חַסְדּוֹ וֶאֱמוּנָתוֹ לְבֵית יִשְׂרָאֵל רָאוּ כָל אַפְסֵי אָרֶץ אֵת יְשׁוּעַת אֱלֹהֵינוּ״, אֵימָתַי רָאוּ כָּל אַפְסֵי אָרֶץ אֵת יְשׁוּעַת אֱלֹהֵינוּ – בִּימֵי מָרְדֳּכַי וְאֶסְתֵּר.

Rabbi Yoḥanan introduced this passage with an introduction from here: The verse states: **"He has remembered His mercy and His faithfulness toward the house of Israel: All the ends of the earth have seen the salvation of our God"** (Psalms 98:3). **When did all the ends of the earth see the salvation of our God? In the days of Mordecai and Esther,** for their peril and salvation became known through the letters sent throughout the empire.

NOTES

We went through fire – בָּאנוּ בָאֵשׁ: The Maharsha explains that "through fire" is referring to the burning of the Temple by Nebuchadnezzar. "And you brought us out into abundance" is referring to Purim, primarily because the miracle of Purim relates back to a banquet with an abundance of wine, and Purim is celebrated through the drinking of wine (Rabbi Yoshiya Pinto; Maharsha).

BACKGROUND

Persians – **פַּרְסִיִּים**: Rav Yosef lived among the Persians and was therefore familiar not only with their unique customs with regard to eating and drinking, but also with their layers of flesh and long hair. There is evidence that unlike the Babylonians, the Persians let the hair on their head grow long, at times even braiding it onto their heads. The restlessness attributed here to the Persians may be indicative of their being horseback riders, as their army was based largely on their horses, especially their swiftness and mobility.

And they never rest like a bear – **וְאֵין לָהֶם מְנוּחָה כְּדוֹב**: As opposed to some animals mentioned in the Gemara whose identification is questionable, it is clear that the animal referenced in the Gemara here is in fact a bear. Although bears are heavy, as the Gemara here says that they are coated with flesh, they are known to be restless and can run quite quickly. Consequently, they are said to never rest.

Bear running

רֵישׁ לָקִישׁ פְּתַח לָהּ פִּתְחָא לְהָא פָּרָשָׁתָא מֵהָכָא: ״אֲרִי נוֹהֵם וְדוֹב שׁוֹקֵק מוֹשֵׁל רָשָׁע עַל עַם דָּל״. ״אֲרִי נוֹהֵם״ – זֶה נְבוּכַדְנֶצַּר הָרָשָׁע, דִּכְתִיב בֵּיהּ: ״עָלָה אַרְיֵה מִסֻּבְּכוֹ״, ״דוֹב שׁוֹקֵק״ – זֶה אֲחַשְׁוֵרוֹשׁ, דִּכְתִיב בֵּיהּ: ״וַאֲרוּ חֵיוָה אָחֳרִי תִנְיָנָה דָּמְיָה לְדוֹב״ וְתָנֵי רַב יוֹסֵף: אֵלּוּ פַּרְסִיִּים, שֶׁאוֹכְלִין וְשׁוֹתִין כְּדוֹב, וּמְסוּרְבָּלִין בָּשָׂר כְּדוֹב, וּמְגַדְּלִין שֵׂעָר כְּדוֹב, וְאֵין לָהֶם מְנוּחָה כְּדוֹב.

Reish Lakish introduced this passage with an introduction from here: "As a roaring lion, and a ravenous bear, so is a wicked ruler over a poor people" (Proverbs 28:15). **"A roaring lion"; this is the wicked Nebuchadnezzar, as it is written about him: "The lion has come up from his thicket"** (Jeremiah 4:7). **"A hungry bear"; this is Ahasuerus, as it is written about him: "And behold, another beast, a second one, like a bear"** (Daniel 7:5). **And Rav Yosef taught** that **these** who are referred to as a bear in the verse **are the Persians.**[B] They are compared to a bear, **as they eat and drink** in large quantities **like a bear; and they are coated with flesh like a bear; and they grow their hair** long **like a bear; and they never rest like a bear,**[B] whose manner it is to move about from place to place.

״מוֹשֵׁל רָשָׁע״ – זֶה הָמָן, ״עַל עַם דָּל״ – אֵלּוּ יִשְׂרָאֵל, שֶׁהֵם דַּלִּים מִן הַמִּצְוֹת.

"A wicked ruler"; this is Haman. "Over a poor people"; this is the Jewish people, who are referred to in this manner **because they are poor in** their observance of **the mitzvot.**

רַבִּי אֶלְעָזָר פְּתַח לָהּ פִּתְחָא לְהָא פָּרָשָׁתָא מֵהָכָא: ״בַּעֲצַלְתַּיִם יִמַּךְ הַמְּקָרֶה וּבְשִׁפְלוּת יָדַיִם יִדְלוֹף הַבָּיִת״, בִּשְׁבִיל עַצְלוּת שֶׁהָיָה לָהֶם לְיִשְׂרָאֵל שֶׁלֹּא עָסְקוּ בַּתּוֹרָה, נַעֲשֶׂה שׂוֹנְאוֹ שֶׁל הַקָּדוֹשׁ בָּרוּךְ הוּא מָךְ. וְאֵין מָךְ אֶלָּא עָנִי, שֶׁנֶּאֱמַר: ״וְאִם מָךְ הוּא מֵעֶרְכֶּךָ״, וְאֵין מְקָרֶה אֶלָּא הַקָּדוֹשׁ בָּרוּךְ הוּא, שֶׁנֶּאֱמַר: ״הַמְּקָרֶה בַמַּיִם עֲלִיּוֹתָיו״.

Rabbi Elazar introduced this passage with an introduction from here: "Through laziness the rafters [*hamekare*] sink in [*yimakh*]; and through idleness of the hands the house leaks" (Ecclesiastes 10:18). Rabbi Elazar interprets the verse homiletically: **Through the laziness of the Jewish people, who did not occupy themselves with Torah** study, **the enemy of the Holy One, Blessed be He,** a euphemism for God Himself, **became poor [*makh*],** so that, as it were, He was unable to help them, **as *makh* is nothing other than poor, as it is stated: "But if he be too poor [*makh*] for the valuation"** (Leviticus 27:8). **And the** word ***mekare*** in the verse **is referring** to no one **other than the Holy One, Blessed be He, as it is stated: "Who lays the beams [*hamekare*] of His chambers in the waters"** (Psalms 104:3).

רַב נַחְמָן בַּר יִצְחָק פְּתַח לָהּ פִּתְחָא לְהָא פָּרָשָׁתָא מֵהָכָא: ״שִׁיר הַמַּעֲלוֹת לוּלֵי ה׳ שֶׁהָיָה לָנוּ יֹאמַר נָא יִשְׂרָאֵל לוּלֵי ה׳ שֶׁהָיָה לָנוּ בְּקוּם עָלֵינוּ אָדָם״ – אָדָם וְלֹא מֶלֶךְ.

Rav Naḥman bar Yitzḥak introduced this passage with an introduction from here: "A song of ascents of David. If not for the Lord Who was with us, let Israel now say; if not for the Lord who was with us, when a man rose up against us" (Psalms 124:1–2). The verse speaks of **"a man"** who rose up against us **and not a king.**[N] This occurred in the days of Haman, as he, and not King Ahasuerus, was the chief enemy of the Jewish people.

רָבָא פְּתַח לָהּ פִּתְחָא לְהָא פָּרָשָׁתָא מֵהָכָא: ״בִּרְבוֹת צַדִּיקִים יִשְׂמַח הָעָם וּבִמְשׁוֹל רָשָׁע יֵאָנַח עָם״, ״בִּרְבוֹת צַדִּיקִים יִשְׂמַח הָעָם״ – זֶה מָרְדֳּכַי וְאֶסְתֵּר, דִּכְתִיב: ״וְהָעִיר שׁוּשָׁן צָהֲלָה וְשָׂמֵחָה״, ״וּבִמְשׁוֹל רָשָׁע יֵאָנַח עָם״ – זֶה הָמָן, דִּכְתִיב: ״וְהָעִיר שׁוּשָׁן נָבוֹכָה״.

Rava introduced this passage with an introduction from here: "When the righteous are on the increase, the people rejoice; but when the wicked man rules, the people mourn" (Proverbs 29:2). **"When the righteous are on the increase, the people rejoice"; this is Mordecai and Esther, as it is written: "And the city of Shushan rejoiced and was glad"** (Esther 8:15). **"But when the wicked man rules, the people mourn"; this is Haman, as it is written: "But the city of Shushan was perplexed"** (Esther 3:15).

NOTES

A man and not a king – **אָדָם וְלֹא מֶלֶךְ**: Several explanations are offered for the significance of the distinction between a king and a man. One idea is that because a king is concerned with the stability of his kingdom, he will usually be cautious and therefore resistant to decimating a complete nation from within it. Haman, however, was a regular man, not a king, and therefore he wasn't concerned with threats to the throne and attempted to destroy all of the Jews within the kingdom (*Or Ḥadash*).

רַב מַתָּנָה אָמַר מֵהָכָא: ״כִּי מִי גוֹי גָּדוֹל אֲשֶׁר לוֹ אֱלֹהִים קְרֹבִים אֵלָיו״. רַב אַשִׁי אָמַר מֵהָכָא; ״אוֹ הֲנִסָּה אֱלֹהִים״ וגו׳.

Rav Mattana said his introduction **from here: "For what nation is there so great,**[N] **that has God so near to them"** (Deuteronomy 4:7), as to witness the great miracles in the days of Mordecai and Esther? **Rav Ashi said** his introduction **from here:** The verse states: **"Or has God ventured**[N] to go and take Him a nation from the midst of another nation?" (Deuteronomy 4:34), as in the times of Esther, God saved the Jewish people who were scattered throughout the Persian Empire.

״וַיְהִי בִּימֵי אֲחַשְׁוֵרוֹשׁ״. אָמַר רַב: וַיי וְהִי הֲדָא דִּכְתִיב: ״וְהִתְמַכַּרְתֶּם שָׁם לְאוֹיְבֶיךָ לַעֲבָדִים וְלִשְׁפָחוֹת״ וגו׳.

§ The Gemara returns to its interpretation of the book of Esther. The verse states: **"And it came to pass [*vayhi*] in the days of Ahasuerus"** (Esther 1:1).[N] **Rav said:** The word *vayhi* may be understood as if it said ***vai* and *hi*,** meaning **woe and mourning. This is as it is written: "And there you shall sell yourselves to your enemies for bondsmen and bondswomen,** and no man shall buy you" (Deuteronomy 28:68). The repetitive nature of the verse, indicating that no one will be willing to buy you for servitude, but they will purchase you in order to murder you, indicates a doubly horrific situation, which is symbolized by the dual term *vayhi*, meaning woe and mourning.

וּשְׁמוּאֵל אָמַר: ״לֹא מְאַסְתִּים וְלֹא גְעַלְתִּים לְכַלֹּתָם״, ״לֹא מְאַסְתִּים״ – בִּימֵי יְוָנִים, ״וְלֹא גְעַלְתִּים״ בִּימֵי נְבוּכַדְנֶצַּר, ״לְכַלֹּתָם״ – בִּימֵי הָמָן, ״לְהָפֵר בְּרִיתִי אִתָּם״ – בִּימֵי פַּרְסִיִּים, ״כִּי אֲנִי ה׳ אֱלֹהֵיהֶם״ – בִּימֵי גּוֹג וּמָגוֹג.

And Shmuel said his introduction from here: "And yet for all that, when they are in the land of their enemies, **I will not reject them, nor will I abhor them,** to destroy them utterly, and to break My covenant with them; for I am the Lord their God" (Leviticus 26:44). Shmuel explains: **"I will not reject them";** this was **in the days of the Greeks. "Nor will I abhor them";** this was **in the days of** Vespasian.[N] **"To destroy them utterly";** this was **in the days of Haman. "To break My covenant with them";** this was **in the days of the Persians. "For I am the Lord their God";** this is **in the days of Gog and Magog.**

בְּמַתְנִיתָא תָּנָא: ״לֹא מְאַסְתִּים״ – בִּימֵי כַּשְׂדִּים, שֶׁהֶעֱמַדְתִּי לָהֶם דָּנִיֵּאל חֲנַנְיָה מִישָׁאֵל וַעֲזַרְיָה, ״וְלֹא גְעַלְתִּים״ – בִּימֵי יְוָנִים, שֶׁהֶעֱמַדְתִּי לָהֶם שִׁמְעוֹן הַצַּדִּיק, וְחַשְׁמוֹנַאי וּבָנָיו, וּמַתִּתְיָה כֹּהֵן גָּדוֹל, ״לְכַלֹּתָם״ – בִּימֵי הָמָן, שֶׁהֶעֱמַדְתִּי לָהֶם מָרְדֳּכַי וְאֶסְתֵּר, ״לְהָפֵר בְּרִיתִי אִתָּם״ – בִּימֵי רוֹמִיִּים, שֶׁהֶעֱמַדְתִּי לָהֶם שֶׁל בֵּית רַבִּי וְחַכְמֵי דוֹרוֹת, ״כִּי אֲנִי ה׳ אֱלֹהֵיהֶם״ – לֶעָתִיד לָבוֹא, שֶׁאֵין כָּל אוּמָּה וְלָשׁוֹן יְכוֹלָה לִשְׁלוֹט בָּהֶם.

An alternative understanding **was taught in a *baraita*: "I will not reject them";** this was **in the days of the Chaldeans, when I appointed for them Daniel,**[N] **Hananiah, Mishael, and Azariah** to pray on their behalf. **"Nor will I abhor them";** this was **in the days of the Greeks, when I appointed Shimon HaTzaddik**[P] **for them, and the Hasmonean and his sons,**[B] **and Mattithiah the High Priest. "To destroy them utterly";** this was **in the days of Haman, when I appointed for them** the righteous leaders **Mordecai and Esther. "To break My covenant with them";** this was **in the days of the Romans,**[N] **when I appointed for them** the Sages of **the house of Rabbi** Yehuda HaNasi **and the Sages of** other **generations. "For I am the Lord their God";** this will be **in the future, when no nation or** people of a foreign **tongue will be able** to **subjugate them** further.

רַבִּי לֵוִי אָמַר מֵהָכָא: ״וְאִם לֹא תוֹרִישׁוּ אֶת יוֹשְׁבֵי הָאָרֶץ״.

Rabbi Levi said his introduction **from here: "But if you will not drive out the inhabitants of the land** from before you, then it shall come to pass, that those whom you allow to remain of them shall be as thorns in your eyes" (Numbers 33:55). King Saul's failure to completely annihilate Amalek allowed for the existence of his descendant Haman, who acted as a thorn in the eyes of Israel during the Purim episode.

רַבִּי חִיָּיא אָמַר מֵהָכָא: ״וְהָיָה כַּאֲשֶׁר דִּמִּיתִי לַעֲשׂוֹת לָהֶם אֶעֱשֶׂה לָכֶם״.

Rabbi Ḥiyya said his introduction **from here,** the continuation of the previously cited verse: **"And it shall come to pass, that as I thought to do unto them, so I shall do unto you"** (Numbers 33:56). Prior to the miracle of Purim, the Jewish people were subject to the punishment that the Torah designated for its enemies, because they did not fulfill God's commandments.

NOTES

For what nation is there so great – **כִּי מִי גוֹי גָּדוֹל:** Some explain that this homily is indicating that although the Jews are scattered and divided, they still have "God so near to them" (Maharsha). Others explain that the focus of the statement is the conclusion of that same verse: "As the Lord our God is whenever we call upon Him," for it relates how the Jews called out to God and were answered (*Sefat Emet*).

Or has God ventured, etc. – **אוֹ הֲנִסָּה אֱלֹהִים וגו׳:** The meaning is that the Purim redemption was similar to the redemption from Egypt, which is the subject of this verse. Both were redemptions of "a nation from the midst of another nation," in the sense that both redemptions involved a reversal of fortune for the two nations involved. In Egypt, a body of water that had been the means to drown Jewish babies became the means to drown the Egyptian pursuers of Israel. Similarly, in the case of Purim, lots were cast to pick a day for the destruction of Israel. This day ended up becoming a day of annihilation for many of Israel's enemies (Maharsha).

And it came to pass in the days of Ahasuerus – **וַיְהִי בִּימֵי אֲחַשְׁוֵרוֹשׁ:** Some understand that this explanation of Rav's served as his introduction to the Megilla, connecting it with the verse in Deuteronomy that he cites (*Turei Even*). That verse, which says: "And there you shall sell yourselves to your enemies for bondsmen and bondswomen, and no man shall buy you," correlates with Esther's statement in the Megilla: "But if we had been sold for bondsmen and bondswomen I would have held my peace" (Esther 7:4). The Jews of the time would gladly have sold themselves as slaves to escape death, but there was no buyer (Maharsha).

In the days of Vespasian – **בִּימֵי נְבוּכַדְנֶצַּר:** The Hebrew text reads Nebuchadnezzar, but the English translation reads Vespasian, in order to reflect the original version of the text. To avoid offending the Romans, the censor removed the phrase: In the days of Vespasian, a Roman emperor, and replaced it with the less provocative Nebuchadnezzar.

When I appointed for them Daniel – **שֶׁהֶעֱמַדְתִּי לָהֶם דָּנִיֵּאל:** The Gemara is apparently noting individuals in various generations who were not only righteous but also respected by the gentile governments and thereby awarded a certain measure of authority to defend the Jewish people from their enemies (Rid).

In the days of the Romans – **בִּימֵי רוֹמִיִּים:** The Hebrew text reads: Persians, but the English translation reads Romans, in order to reflect the original version of the text, which was altered by the censor in order to avoid offending the Romans.

PERSONALITIES

Shimon HaTzaddik – **שִׁמְעוֹן הַצַּדִּיק:** There were two High Priests, a grandfather and grandson, who were both named Shimon ben Ḥonyo. It is unclear which one of them is referred to as Shimon HaTzaddik, and it is possible that both shared this epithet. Shimon HaTzaddik was one of the last members of the Great Assembly, and he is the first individual known by name in the chain of transmission of the Oral Law. Many stories of his righteousness appear throughout the Mishna and Talmud. Unique words of praise for him were uttered by his contemporary, Shimon ben Sira, who said that he was: The greatest of his brothers and the splendor of his people; who is concerned for his people and strengthens them in times of trouble…How splendid he is as he looks out from the Temple, and as he emerges from the inner chamber behind the curtain, like a star of light between trees, like a full moon during a Festival (*Sefer Ben Sira* 49).

BACKGROUND

The Hasmonean and his sons – **חַשְׁמוֹנַאי וּבָנָיו:** The source and meaning of the name Hasmonean is unclear. And although the entire dynasty is referred to in Jewish sources as the house of Hasmonean, its origin is unknown. The Gemara here appears to differentiate between Hasmonean and Mattithiah, perhaps indicating that Hasmonean is a nickname for Shimon ben Mattithiah, whose descendants were the Hasmonean kings for generations.

״אֲחַשְׁוֵרוֹשׁ״, אָמַר רַב: אָחִיו שֶׁל רֹאשׁ, וּבֶן גִּילוֹ שֶׁל רֹאשׁ. אָחִיו שֶׁל רֹאשׁ – אָחִיו שֶׁל נְבוּכַדְנֶצַּר הָרָשָׁע שֶׁנִּקְרָא רֹאשׁ, שֶׁנֶּאֱמַר: ״אַנְתְּ הוּא רֵישָׁא דִּי דַהֲבָא״. בֶּן גִּילוֹ שֶׁל רֹאשׁ, הוּא הָרַג – הוּא בִּיקֵּשׁ לַהֲרוֹג, הוּא הֶחֱרִיב – הוּא בִּיקֵּשׁ לְהַחֲרִיב, שֶׁנֶּאֱמַר: ״וּבְמַלְכוּת אֲחַשְׁוֵרוֹשׁ בִּתְחִלַּת מַלְכוּתוֹ כָּתְבוּ שִׂטְנָה עַל יוֹשְׁבֵי יְהוּדָה וִירוּשָׁלִָם״.

The Gemara continues with its explanation of the book of Esther, beginning with a discussion of the name **Ahasuerus.**[N] **Rav said:** The name should be viewed as a contraction: **The brother of the head** [*aḥiv shel rosh*] **and of the same character as the head** [*ben gilo shel rosh*]. Rav explains: **The brother of the head,** i.e., **the brother of the wicked Nebuchadnezzar, who is called "head," as it is stated: "You are the head of gold"** (Daniel 2:38). **Of the same character as the head, for he,** Nebuchadnezzar, **killed** the Jews, and **he,** Ahasuerus, **sought to kill** them. **He destroyed** the Temple, and **he sought to destroy** the foundations for the Temple laid by Zerubbabel, **as it is stated: "And in the reign of Ahasuerus, in the beginning of his reign, they wrote to him an accusation against the inhabitants of Judah and Jerusalem"** (Ezra 4:6), and he ordered that the construction of the Temple cease.

וּשְׁמוּאֵל אָמַר: שֶׁהוּשְׁחֲרוּ פְּנֵיהֶם שֶׁל יִשְׂרָאֵל בְּיָמָיו כְּשׁוּלֵי קְדֵרָה. וְרַבִּי יוֹחָנָן אָמַר: כֹּל שֶׁזּוֹכְרוֹ אָמַר: אָח לְרֹאשׁוֹ. וְרַבִּי חֲנִינָא אָמַר: שֶׁהַכֹּל נַעֲשׂוּ רָשִׁין בְּיָמָיו, שֶׁנֶּאֱמַר: ״וַיָּשֶׂם הַמֶּלֶךְ אֲחַשְׁוֵרוֹשׁ מַס״.

And Shmuel said: The name Ahasuerus should be understood in the sense of black [*shaḥor*], as **the face of the Jewish people was blackened in his days like the bottom of a pot. And Rabbi Yoḥanan said** a different explanation: **Everyone who recalled him said: "Woe upon his head"** [*aḥ lerosho*]. **And Rabbi Ḥanina said:** The name alludes to the fact **that everyone became poor** [*rash*] **in his days,**[B] **as it is stated: "And the king Ahasuerus laid a tribute** upon the land" (Esther 10:1).

״הוּא אֲחַשְׁוֵרוֹשׁ״ – הוּא בְּרִשְׁעוֹ מִתְּחִילָּתוֹ וְעַד סוֹפוֹ. ״הוּא עֵשָׂו״ – הוּא בְּרִשְׁעוֹ מִתְּחִילָּתוֹ וְעַד סוֹפוֹ, ״הוּא דָּתָן וַאֲבִירָם״ – הֵן בְּרִשְׁעָן מִתְּחִילָּתָן וְעַד סוֹפָן, ״הוּא הַמֶּלֶךְ אָחָז״ – הוּא בְּרִשְׁעוֹ מִתְּחִילָּתוֹ וְעַד סוֹפוֹ.

The Gemara continues: **"This is** [*hu*] **Ahasuerus"** (Esther 1:1);[N] the term *hu*, this is, comes to teach that **he** remained as he was **in his wickedness from beginning to end.** Similarly, wherever the words "this is" appear in this manner, the verse indicates that the individual under discussion remained the same from beginning to end, for example: **"This is** [*hu*] **Esau"** (Genesis 36:43); **he** remained **in his wickedness from beginning to end. "This is** [*hu*] **Dathan and Abiram"** (Numbers 26:9); **they** remained **in their wickedness from beginning to end. "This is** [*hu*] **the king Ahaz"** (II Chronicles 28:22); **he** remained **in his wickedness from beginning to end.**

״אַבְרָם הוּא אַבְרָהָם״ – הוּא בְּצִדְקוֹ מִתְּחִילָּתוֹ וְעַד סוֹפוֹ, ״הוּא אַהֲרֹן וּמֹשֶׁה״ – הֵן בְּצִדְקָן מִתְּחִילָּתָן וְעַד סוֹפָן. ״וְדָוִד הוּא הַקָּטָן״ – הוּא בְּקַטְנוּתוֹ מִתְּחִילָּתוֹ עַד סוֹפוֹ, כְּשֵׁם שֶׁבְּקַטְנוּתוֹ הִקְטִין עַצְמוֹ אֵצֶל מִי שֶׁגָּדוֹל מִמֶּנּוּ בְּתוֹרָה – כָּךְ בְּמַלְכוּתוֹ הִקְטִין עַצְמוֹ אֵצֶל מִי שֶׁגָּדוֹל מִמֶּנּוּ בְּחָכְמָה.

The Gemara continues: The word *hu* is also used to recognize sustained righteousness. **"Abram, this is** [*hu*] **Abraham"** (I Chronicles 1:27); this indicates that Abraham didn't change, as **he** remained **in his righteousness from beginning to end.** Similarly, **"This is** [*hu*] **Aaron and Moses"** (Exodus 6:26); **they remained in their righteousness from** the **beginning** of their life **to** the **end** of their life. Similarly, with respect to David: **"And David, this was** [*hu*] **the youngest"** (I Samuel 17:14), indicates that **he remained in his humility from beginning to end. Just as in his youth,** when he was still an ordinary individual, **he humbled himself before anyone who was greater than him in Torah, so too, in his kingship, he humbled himself before anyone who was greater than him in wisdom.**

״הַמּוֹלֵךְ״ אָמַר רַב: שֶׁמָּלַךְ מֵעַצְמוֹ. אָמְרִי לַהּ לְשֶׁבַח, וְאָמְרִי לַהּ לִגְנַאי. אָמְרִי לַהּ לְשֶׁבַח – דְּלָא הֲוָה אִינִישׁ דַּחֲשִׁיב לְמַלְכָּא כְּוָותֵיהּ, וְאָמְרִי לַהּ לִגְנַאי – דְּלָא הֲוָה חֲזֵי לְמַלְכוּתָא, וּמָמוֹנָא יְתֵירָא הוּא דִּיהַב וְקָם.

The next term in the opening verse: **"Who reigned"** (Esther 1:1), is now interpreted. **Rav said:** This comes to teach **that he reigned on his own,**[B] without having inherited the throne. **Some say** this to his **credit, and some say it to his disgrace.** The Gemara explains: **Some say** this **to his credit, that there was no other man as fit as him to be king. And some say it to** his **disgrace, that he was not fit to be king, but he distributed large amounts of money, and** in that way **rose** to the throne.

״מֵהוֹדּוּ וְעַד כּוּשׁ״, רַב וּשְׁמוּאֵל, חַד אָמַר: הוֹדּוּ בְּסוֹף הָעוֹלָם, וְכוּשׁ בְּסוֹף הָעוֹלָם, וְחַד אָמַר: הוֹדּוּ וְכוּשׁ גַּבֵּי הֲדָדֵי הָווּ קָיְימִי, כְּשֵׁם שֶׁמָּלַךְ עַל הוֹדּוּ וְכוּשׁ – כָּךְ מָלַךְ מִסּוֹף הָעוֹלָם וְעַד סוֹפוֹ.

The opening verse continues that Ahasuerus reigned **"from Hodu to Cush."**[B] **Rav and Shmuel** disagreed about its meaning. **One said: Hodu** is a country **at one end of the world, and Cush** is a country **at the other end of the world. And one said: Hodu and Cush are situated next to each other,** and the verse means to say as follows: Just as Ahasuerus **reigned** with ease **over** the adjacent countries of **Hodu and Cush, so too, he reigned** with ease **from one end of the world to the other.**

NOTES

Ahasuerus – אֲחַשְׁוֵרוֹשׁ: The Maharal explains that the homiletic interpretation of the king's name is due to the fact that the Megilla's opening verse states: "And it came to pass in the days of Ahasuerus," without referring to him by his title of king. The impression is that the Megilla is indicating that its purpose is not merely to recount historical events, but to demonstrate that even the name of the king is significant for understanding the unfolding of the story (*Or Ḥadash*).

This is Ahasuerus – הוּא אֲחַשְׁוֵרוֹשׁ: The commentaries note that the Gemara emphasizes that the word *hu* appears in reference to all these wicked individuals to indicate that although there is reason to believe that they changed their ways and improved their character, in truth they remained who they were. For instance, although Ahasuerus ultimately protected the Jews, in truth he essentially remained Ahasuerus the wicked. Similarly, although King Ahaz was in danger and witnessed miracles, he did not change. In a similar vein, the word *hu* used in reference to righteous individuals, such as Abraham, Moses, and David, indicates that they were righteous from beginning to end, as their greatness did not lead them to arrogance (Maharsha).

BACKGROUND

That everyone became poor in his days – שֶׁהַכֹּל נַעֲשׂוּ רָשִׁין בְּיָמָיו: Ahasuerus collected an inordinate amount of taxes to finance his wars and to meet the expenses of his vast building projects, as mentioned by Greek historians from that period.

That he reigned on his own – שֶׁמָּלַךְ מֵעַצְמוֹ: If Ahasuerus is indeed the king referred to by the Greeks as Xerxes I, then the Gemara's intention would seem to be that although he was not the eldest of Darius's sons, he was nevertheless appointed king in place of his older brother.

From Hodu to Cush – מֵהוֹדּוּ וְעַד כּוּשׁ: It appears that the dispute here centers on the meaning of the word Cush. The question is whether it refers to the land of Cush, located in Africa, south of Egypt, or to the nation of the Cushite people, which arose at the time in the western section of India.

כַּיּוֹצֵא בְּדָבָר אַתָּה אוֹמֵר: ״כִּי הוּא רוֹדֶה בְּכָל עֵבֶר הַנָּהָר מִתִּפְסַח וְעַד עַזָּה״, רַב וּשְׁמוּאֵל: חַד אָמַר: תִּפְסַח בְּסוֹף הָעוֹלָם וְעַזָּה בְּסוֹף הָעוֹלָם, וְחַד אָמַר: תִּפְסַח וְעַזָּה בַּהֲדֵי הֲדָדֵי הָווּ קָיְימִי, כְּשֵׁם שֶׁמָּלַךְ עַל תִּפְסַח וְעַל עַזָּה – כָּךְ מָלַךְ עַל כָּל הָעוֹלָם כּוּלּוֹ.

On a similar note, **you say** with regard to Solomon: **"For he had dominion over all the region on this side of the river, from Tiphsah even to Gaza"** (1 Kings 5:4), and also with regard to this **Rav and Shmuel** disagreed. **One said: Tiphsah is at one end of the world, whereas Gaza is at the other end of the world. And one said: Tiphsah and Gaza are situated next to each other,** and the verse means to say as follows: **Just as** Solomon **reigned** with ease **over** the adjacent **Tiphsah and Gaza, so too, he reigned** with ease **over the entire world.**

״שֶׁבַע וְעֶשְׂרִים וּמֵאָה מְדִינָה״ אָמַר רַב חִסְדָּא: בִּתְחִילָּה מָלַךְ עַל שֶׁבַע, וּלְבַסּוֹף מָלַךְ עַל עֶשְׂרִים, וּלְבַסּוֹף מָלַךְ עַל מֵאָה. אֶלָּא מֵעַתָּה, ״וּשְׁנֵי חַיֵּי עַמְרָם שֶׁבַע וּשְׁלֹשִׁים וּמְאַת שָׁנָה״ מַאי דָּרְשַׁתְּ בֵּיהּ? שָׁאנֵי הָכָא דִּקְרָא יְתֵירָא הוּא, מִכְּדִי כְּתִיב: ״מֵהוֹדּוּ וְעַד כּוּשׁ״, ״שֶׁבַע וְעֶשְׂרִים וּמֵאָה מְדִינָה״ לָמָּה לִי? שְׁמַע מִינָּהּ לִדְרָשָׁה.

The opening verse continues, stating that Ahasuerus reigned "over **seven and twenty and a hundred provinces"** (Esther 1:1). **Rav Ḥisda said:** This verse should be understood as follows: **At first he reigned over seven** provinces; **and then he reigned over twenty** more; **and finally he reigned over** another **hundred.** The Gemara asks: **However, if** that is **so,** with regard to the similarly worded verse: **"And the years of the life of Amram**[N] **were seven and thirty and a hundred years"** (Exodus 6:20), **what would you expound** from **it?** The Gemara answers: **It is different here,** in the book of Esther, **as** this part of **the verse is** entirely **superfluous. Since it is** already **written: "From Hodu to Cush,"** why then **do I need "Seven and twenty and a hundred provinces"?** Rather, **learn from here** that these words come **for** this **exposition,** to teach that Ahasuerus did not begin to reign over all of them at the same time.

תָּנוּ רַבָּנַן: שְׁלֹשָׁה מָלְכוּ בְּכִיפָּה, וְאֵלּוּ הֵן: אַחְאָב, וַאֲחַשְׁוֵרוֹשׁ, וּנְבוּכַדְנֶצַּר. אַחְאָב – דִּכְתִיב: ״חַי ה׳ אֱלֹהֶיךָ אִם יֶשׁ גּוֹי וּמַמְלָכָה אֲשֶׁר לֹא שָׁלַח אֲדוֹנִי שָׁם לְבַקֶּשְׁךָ״ וגו׳, וְאִי לָא דַּהֲוָה מָלֵיךְ עֲלַיְיהוּ – הֵיכִי מָצֵי מַשְׁבַּע לְהוּ?

§ Apropos the discussion of the kingdoms of Ahasuerus and Solomon, the Gemara cites a *baraita* in which **the Sages taught: Three** men **ruled over the** entire **world,**[NB] **and they were Ahab, and Ahasuerus, and Nebuchadnezzar.** The Gemara explains: **Ahab, as it is written** in the words of Obadiah, servant of Ahab, to Elijah: **"As the Lord your God lives, there is no nation or kingdom where my master has not sent to seek you,** and they said: He is not there; and he made the kingdom and nation swear, that they had not found you" (1 Kings 18:10). **And if he did not reign over them, how could he have made them swear?** Apparently, then, he reigned over the entire world.

נְבוּכַדְנֶצַּר דִּכְתִיב: ״וְהָיָה הַגּוֹי וְהַמַּמְלָכָה אֲשֶׁר לֹא יִתֵּן אֶת צַוָּארוֹ בְּעוֹל מֶלֶךְ בָּבֶל״ אֲחַשְׁוֵרוֹשׁ – הָא דַּאֲמַרַן.

Nebuchadnezzar also ruled over the whole world, **as it is written: "And it shall come to pass, that the nation and the kingdom** that not serve this same Nebuchadnezzar, the king of Babylonia, and that **will not put their neck under the yoke of the king of Babylonia,** that nation will I visit, says the Lord, with the sword, and with the famine, and with the pestilence, until I have consumed them by his hand" (Jeremiah 27:8). **Ahasuerus** also ruled the world, **as we have said** above.

NOTES

And the years of the life of Amram – וּשְׁנֵי חַיֵּי עַמְרָם: Although, when enumerating the years of the other individuals in the Gemara, the division of years into separate phases could indicate changes that they underwent during different periods in their lives, the Gemara in *Shabbat* (55b) teaches that Amram was completely righteous throughout his lifetime. Therefore, the Gemara proves from the fact that the years of Amram's life were divided in that manner that a phased rendering of one's age is not necessarily indicative of change in the course of one's life (*Haggahot Tiferet LeMoshe*).

Ruled over the entire world – מָלְכוּ בְּכִיפָּה: The Gemara mentions the vast empires of these kings to indicate that the rulers who reigned over the Jewish people were not small kings with limited power. The Gemara teaches that they were great rulers whose reign over the Jewish people does not imply a lessening of Israel's honor. Mentioning the extent of these kings' empires also indicates that their interactions with Israel not only affected the Jewish people but impacted the entire world (*Hatam Sofer*).

BACKGROUND

Ruled over the entire world [*kippa*] – מָלְכוּ בְּכִיפָּה: The term *kippa* refers to *kippat hashamayim*, the celestial sphere. In other words, it refers to those who ruled over the parts of the earth that are found under the celestial sphere.

Perek **I**
Daf **11** Amud **b**

(סִימָן שסד״ך) וְתוּ לֵיכָּא? וְהָא אִיכָּא שְׁלֹמֹה! לָא סְלֵיק מַלְכוּתֵיהּ.

After mentioning three kings who ruled over the world, the Gemara presents **a mnemonic** for the names of other kings that will be discussed below: ***Shin*,** Solomon, i.e., Shlomo; ***samekh*,** Sennacherib; ***dalet*,** Darius; ***kaf*,** Cyrus, i.e., Koresh. The Gemara asks: **But is there no other** king besides those previously mentioned who ruled over the entire world? **But there is** King **Solomon** who ruled over the world and should be added to the list. The Gemara answers: Solomon **did not complete his kingship,**[N] as he left the throne during his lifetime, and therefore, his name doesn't appear on the list.

NOTES

Solomon did not complete his kingship – לָא סְלֵיק מַלְכוּתֵיהּ: The Gemara relates an opinion that King Solomon ceased to rule and went into exile, at which time he wrote the book of Ecclesiastes (*Gittin* 68b). The Rabbis disagree there as to whether he later returned to the throne or whether he remained a commoner the rest of his life.

הָנִיחָא לְמַאן דַּאֲמַר: מֶלֶךְ וְהֶדְיוֹט, אֶלָּא לְמַאן דַּאֲמַר מֶלֶךְ וְהֶדְיוֹט וּמֶלֶךְ, מַאי אִיכָּא לְמֵימַר? שְׁלֹמֹה מִילְּתָא אַחֲרִיתִי הֲוָה בֵּיהּ, שֶׁמָּלַךְ עַל הָעֶלְיוֹנִים וְעַל הַתַּחְתּוֹנִים, שֶׁנֶּאֱמַר: ״וַיֵּשֶׁב שְׁלֹמֹה עַל כִּסֵּא ה׳״.

The Gemara asks: This works out **well according to the one who said** that Solomon was first **a king and** then **a commoner,** never returning to the throne. **But according to the one who said that he was** first **a king and** then **a commoner, and** then afterward he returned again to be **a king, what can be said** to explain why he is not mentioned in the list of kings who ruled over the entire world? The Gemara answers: **There was something else about Solomon** that makes it impossible to compare him to the others, **for he ruled over** the inhabitants of **the heavenly worlds,**[N] i.e., demons and spirits, **as well as** the human inhabitants of **the earthly worlds, as it is stated: "Then Solomon sat upon the throne of the Lord as king"** (I Chronicles 29:23), which indicates that his reign extended even to the heavenly worlds, with King Solomon sitting upon the throne of the Lord, and therefore he cannot be compared to the others, who merely ruled on earth.

וְהָא הֲוָה סַנְחֵרִיב, דִּכְתִיב: ״מִי בְּכָל אֱלֹהֵי הָאֲרָצוֹת הָאֵלֶּה אֲשֶׁר הִצִּילוּ אֶת אַרְצָם מִיָּדִי״! הָא אִיכָּא יְרוּשָׁלַיִם דְּלָא כְּבָשָׁהּ.

The Gemara asks further: **But there was Sennacherib,** who ruled over the entire world, **as it is written: "Who are they among all the gods of these countries, that have delivered their country out of my hand** that the Lord should deliver Jerusalem out of my hand?" (Isaiah 36:20). The Gemara answers: **There is Jerusalem that he did not conquer,** as indicated in the verse.

וְהָא אִיכָּא דָּרְיָוֶשׁ דִּכְתִיב: ״דָּרְיָוֶשׁ מַלְכָּא כְּתַב לְכָל עַמְמַיָּא אוּמַיָּא וְלִשָּׁנַיָּא דִּי דָיְרִין בְּכָל אַרְעָא שְׁלָמְכוֹן יִסְגֵּא״! הָא אִיכָּא שֶׁבַע דְּלָא מָלַךְ עֲלַיְיהוּ, דִּכְתִיב: ״שְׁפַר קֳדָם דָּרְיָוֶשׁ וַהֲקִים עַל מַלְכוּתָא לַאֲחַשְׁדַּרְפְּנַיָּא מְאָה וְעֶשְׂרִין״.

The Gemara continues to ask: **But there is Darius, as it is stated: "Then King Darius wrote to all the peoples, nations, and languages that dwell in all the earth: Peace be multiplied to you"** (Daniel 6:26). The Gemara answers: **There are the seven** provinces **over which he did not rule, as it is written: "It pleased Darius to set over the kingdom a hundred and twenty satraps"** (Daniel 6:2). It is apparent from here that Darius did not rule over the entire world, for his son Ahasuerus ruled over a hundred and twenty-seven provinces, an additional seven.[B]

וְהָא אִיכָּא כּוֹרֶשׁ, דִּכְתִיב: ״כֹּה אָמַר כּוֹרֶשׁ מֶלֶךְ פָּרַס כֹּל מַמְלְכוֹת הָאָרֶץ נָתַן לִי ה׳״! הָתָם אִשְׁתַּבּוּחֵי הוּא דְּקָא מִשְׁתַּבַּח בְּנַפְשֵׁיהּ.

The Gemara raises another question: **But there is Cyrus, as it is written: "Thus says Cyrus, king of Persia: The Lord,** God of heaven, **has given me all the kingdoms of the earth"** (Ezra 1:2). The Gemara answers: This is not proof that he ruled the world, for **there he was** merely **boasting about himself,** although in fact there was no truth to his words.

״בַּיָּמִים הָהֵם כְּשֶׁבֶת הַמֶּלֶךְ״, וּכְתִיב בַּתְרֵיהּ: ״בִּשְׁנַת שָׁלֹשׁ לְמָלְכוֹ״. אָמַר רָבָא: מַאי ״כְּשֶׁבֶת״ – לְאַחַר שֶׁנִּתְיַישְּׁבָה דַּעְתּוֹ. אֲמַר: בֵּלְשַׁצַּר חֵשֵׁב וְטָעָה, אֲנָא חָשֵׁיבְנָא וְלָא טָעֵינָא.

§ The second verse in Esther states: **"In those days when the king** Ahasuerus **sat** on the throne of his kingdom" (Esther 1:2), implying that the events to follow took place during the first year of his reign; **and** one verse **afterward it is written: "In the third year of his reign"** (Esther 1:3), indicating that it was the third year, not the first. **Rava said:** There is no contradiction. **What is** the meaning of **"when he sat"** [*keshevet*]? It is intended to indicate that he acted not immediately upon his rise to the throne, but rather **after his mind was settled**[N] [*shenityasheva*], and he overcame his anxiety and worry with regard to the redemption of the Jewish people. **He said** to himself as follows: **Belshazzar,** the king of Babylonia, **calculated and erred** with regard to the Jewish people's redemption. **I** too **will calculate, but I will not err.**

מַאי הִיא? דִּכְתִיב: ״כִּי לְפִי מְלֹאת לְבָבֶל שִׁבְעִים שָׁנָה אֶפְקוֹד אֶתְכֶם״, וּכְתִיב: ״לְמַלֹּאוֹת לְחָרְבוֹת יְרוּשָׁלַםִ שִׁבְעִים שָׁנָה״. חָשׁוּב אַרְבְּעִין וְחָמֵשׁ דִּנְבוּכַדְנֶצַּר, וְעֶשְׂרִים וּתְלָת דֶּאֱוִיל מְרוֹדַךְ, וְתַרְתֵּי דִּידֵיהּ – הָא שִׁבְעִים. אַפֵּיק מָאנֵי דְּבֵי מַקְדְּשָׁא וְאִשְׁתַּמֵּשׁ בְּהוּ.

The Gemara explains: **What is** this calculation? **As it is written** with regard to Jeremiah's prophecy of a return to Eretz Yisrael: **"After seventy years are accomplished for Babylonia I will remember you** and perform My good word toward you, enabling you to return to this place" (Jeremiah 29:10), **and** elsewhere **it is written** in a slightly different formulation: "In the first year of his reign, I, Daniel, meditated in the books, over the number of the years, which the word of the Lord came to Jeremiah the prophet, **that He would accomplish for the desolations of Jerusalem seventy years"** (Daniel 9:2). **He,** Belshazzar, **calculated** as follows: **Forty-five** years **of Nebuchadnezzar, and twenty-three of Evil-merodach, and two of his** own, for a total of **seventy** years that had passed without redemption. He was therefore certain that Jeremiah's prophecy would no longer be fulfilled, and he therefore said: **I will take out the vessels of the Holy Temple and use them.**

NOTES

He ruled over the heavenly worlds – שֶׁמָּלַךְ עַל הָעֶלְיוֹנִים: Rashi writes that Solomon reigned over spirits and demons (see Maharsha). However, even if Solomon ruled over both the heavenly and earthly worlds, why would that be reason not to mention him among the others who ruled over the entire world? The *Ḥiddushei Aggadot LaRashba* explains that the Gemara is stressing that the kingship of Solomon was of a different nature and therefore cannot be compared with the others. The Rashba elaborates further. He explains that Solomon's rule deserves separate mention, as he did not achieve his reign over the world through victorious battles but rather through his great wisdom. This wisdom also enabled him to reign over the heavenly worlds.

After his mind was settled – לְאַחַר שֶׁנִּתְיַישְּׁבָה דַּעְתּוֹ: Although the simple explanation is that prior to the third year of his reign he was occupied with strengthening his authority and fighting off enemies, nevertheless, he was also worried about the Jewish people's redemption (see *Or Ḥadash*). The Ramban writes that Ahasuerus thought that Cyrus's permitting the return of the Jewish people was sufficient to fulfill the prophecy, but the Temple would not be rebuilt to its former grandeur. Later authorities explain that for this reason Ahasuerus was not punished to the extent that Belshazzar was, since he did not completely deny the prophecy's authenticity.

BACKGROUND

The provinces of Persia – מְדִינוֹת פָּרַס: From the time of Darius, and to an extent even in the days of Cyrus, the Persian Empire was divided into ten regions, each of which was the size of a country. At times, these regions were divided into smaller provinces. For example, Judea, referred to as Yehuda in tractate *Ketubot*, was a province inside the greater region of Transjordan. The division of the provinces and regions within the empire was regularly subject to change. Cyrus was unsuccessful in his conquest of Egypt, and therefore his kingdom was smaller than that of Darius, as it did not include even "all of the kingdoms of the earth" (Ezra 1:2) that had been held in the past by the Persians. Darius succeeded in expanding the empire significantly. However, near the end of his reign several provinces rebelled against him. It would appear that during the early days of Ahasuerus's rule the Persian Empire was at its zenith.

וּנְבוּכַדְנֶצַּר מְנָלַן דְּאַרְבְּעִין וְחָמֵשׁ שְׁנִין מָלַךְ? דְּאָמַר מָר: גָּלוּ בְּשֶׁבַע, גָּלוּ בִּשְׁמוֹנֶה, גָּלוּ בִּשְׁמוֹנֶה עֶשְׂרֵה, גָּלוּ בְּתְשַׁע עֶשְׂרֵה.

The Gemara asks: **From where do we derive that Nebuchadnezzar reigned for forty-five years? As the Master said: They were exiled in the seventh** year;[N] **they were exiled in the eighth** year; **they were exiled in the eighteenth** year; and **they were exiled in the nineteenth** year.

גָּלוּ בְּשֶׁבַע לְכִיבּוּשׁ יְהוֹיָקִים – גָּלוּת יְהוֹיָכִין, שֶׁהִיא שְׁמוֹנֶה לִנְבוּכַדְנֶצַּר. גָּלוּ בִּשְׁמוֹנֶה עֶשְׂרֵה לְכִיבּוּשׁ יְהוֹיָקִים גָּלוּת צִדְקִיָּהוּ שֶׁהִיא תְּשַׁע עֶשְׂרֵה לִנְבוּכַדְנֶצַּר, דְּאָמַר מָר: שָׁנָה רִאשׁוֹנָה כִּיבֵּשׁ נִינְוֵה, שְׁנִיָּה כִּיבֵּשׁ יְהוֹיָקִים, וּכְתִיב: ״וַיְהִי בִּשְׁלֹשִׁים וָשֶׁבַע שָׁנָה לְגָלוּת יְהוֹיָכִין מֶלֶךְ יְהוּדָה בִּשְׁנֵים עָשָׂר חֹדֶשׁ בְּעֶשְׂרִים וַחֲמִשָּׁה לַחֹדֶשׁ נָשָׂא אֱוִיל מְרוֹדַךְ מֶלֶךְ בָּבֶל [בִּשְׁנַת מַלְכוּתוֹ] אֶת רֹאשׁ יְהוֹיָכִין מֶלֶךְ יְהוּדָה וַיּוֹצֵא אוֹתוֹ מִבֵּית הַכֶּלֶא״.

The Gemara explains: **They were exiled in the seventh** year **after** Nebuchadnezzar's **subjugation of Jehoiakim,** in what was known as **the exile of Jehoiachin, which was** actually **the eighth** year **of Nebuchadnezzar's** reign. Then later **they were exiled** a second time **in the eighteenth** year **after the subjugation of Jehoiakim,** in what was known as **the exile of Zedekiah, which was** actually in **the nineteenth** year **of Nebuchadnezzar's** reign, **as the Master said: In the first year** of his reign, Nebuchadnezzar **conquered Nineveh;** in his **second** year **he conquered Jehoiakim. And it is written: "And it came to pass in the thirty-seventh year of the exile of Jehoiachin, king of Judea, in the twelfth month, on the twenty-fifth day of the month, that Evil-merodach, king of Babylonia, in the first year of his reign, lifted up the head of Jehoiachin, king of Judea, and brought him out of prison"** (Jeremiah 52:31).

תְּמָנֵי וּתְלָתִין וְשֶׁבַע – הֲרֵי אַרְבְּעִין וְחָמֵשׁ דִּנְבוּכַדְנֶצַּר. וְעֶשְׂרִין וּתְלָת דֶּאֱוִיל מְרוֹדַךְ – גְּמָרָא, וְתַרְתֵּי דִּידֵיהּ – הָא שִׁבְעִין. אֲמַר: הַשְׁתָּא וַדַּאי תּוּ לָא מִיפַּרְקִי, אַפֵּיק מָאנֵי דְּבֵי מַקְדְּשָׁא וְאֶשְׁתַּמֵּשׁ בְּהוּ.

The Gemara calculates: Since Evil-merodach acted in the first year of his reign, immediately after coming to power, it turns out that Nebuchadnezzar ruled for **eight** years before he sent Jehoiachin into exile, **and thirty-seven** years during which Jehoiachin was in prison. **This** equals **forty-five** years of the reign **of Nebuchadnezzar. And the twenty-three** years **of Evil-merodach** are known through **tradition. And** together with the **two years** of Belshazzar, **this** brings the count of the years of exile to **seventy.** At that point Belshazzar **said** to himself: **Now for sure they will not be redeemed.** Therefore, **I will take out the vessels of the Holy Temple and use them.**

הַיְינוּ דְּקָאָמַר לֵיהּ דָּנִיֵּאל: ״וְעַל מָרֵא שְׁמַיָּא הִתְרוֹמַמְתָּ וּלְמָאנַיָּא דִּי בַיְתֵיהּ הַיְתִיו קָדָמָךְ״, וּכְתִיב: ״בֵּיהּ בְּלֵילְיָא קְטִיל בֵּלְשַׁאצַּר מַלְכָּא [כַשְׂדָּאָי]״, וּכְתִיב: ״וְדָרְיָוֶשׁ מָדָאָה קַבֵּל מַלְכוּתָא כְּבַר שְׁנִין שִׁתִּין וְתַרְתֵּין״.

This is that which **Daniel said to him** with regard to his impending punishment for using the Temple's vessels: **"But you have lifted yourself up against the Lord of heaven; and they have brought the vessels of His House before you"** (Daniel 5:23). **And it is written** further in the chapter: **"In that night Belshazzar, the king of the Chaldeans, was slain"** (Daniel 5:30). This was the description of Belshazzar's mistaken calculation. **And it states** after the fall of Belshazzar: **"And Darius the Mede received the kingdom, being about sixty-two years old"** (Daniel 6:1).[N]

אֲמַר: אִיהוּ מִיטְעָא טָעֵי, אֲנָא חָשֵׁיבְנָא וְלָא טָעֵינָא. מִי כְּתִיב: ״לְמַלְכוּת בָּבֶל״? ״לְבָבֶל״ כְּתִיב. מַאי ״לְבָבֶל״ – לְגָלוּת בָּבֶל. כַּמָּה בְּצִירַן – תְּמָנֵי. חָשֵׁיב וְעָיֵיל חִילּוּפַיְיהוּ. חֲדָא דְּבֵלְשַׁצַּר, וְחָמֵשׁ דְּדָרְיָוֶשׁ וְכוֹרֶשׁ, וְתַרְתֵּי דִּידֵיהּ הָא שִׁבְעִין. כֵּיוָן דַּחֲזֵי דְּמָלוּ שִׁבְעִין וְלָא אִיפְּרוּק, אֲמַר: הַשְׁתָּא וַדַּאי תּוּ לָא מִיפַּרְקִי, אַפֵּיק מָאנֵי דְּבֵי מַקְדְּשָׁא וְאֶשְׁתַּמֵּשׁ בְּהוּ. בָּא שָׂטָן וְרִיקֵּד בֵּינֵיהֶן וְהָרַג אֶת וַשְׁתִּי.

Ahasuerus **said:** He, Belshazzar, **erred.** I too **will calculate, but I will not err,** thinking he understood the source of Belshazzar's mistake. **Is it written:** "Seventy years **for the kingdom of Babylonia**"? **It is written:** "Seventy years **for Babylonia." What is** meant by **"for Babylonia"?** These words are referring to the seventy years **for the exile of Babylonia. How many** years **are** still **lacking** from the seventy years? **Eight** years. **He calculated, and inserted in their stead one** year **of Belshazzar, and five** years **of Darius and Cyrus, and two** years **of his own,** bringing the total to **seventy. Once he saw that seventy** years **had been completed, and** the Jewish people **were** still **not redeemed, he said: Now for sure they will not be redeemed.** Therefore, **I will take out the vessels of the Temple and use them.**[N] What happened to him? As a punishment for what he did, **the Satan came and danced among them, and** brought confusion to his celebration until **he killed Vashti.**

NOTES

They were exiled in the seventh year – גָּלוּ בְּשֶׁבַע: The Maharsha explains that these details are not relevant to the proofs with regard to the period of Nebuchadnezzar's reign. Rather, once the Gemara clarifies the number of years of his rule, it also explains other calculations. Some are calculated from the reign of Nebuchadnezzar, and others from the exile of Jehoiachin, which was concurrent with the conquering of Jehoiakim, as both these incidents took place in the same year.

And Darius the Mede received the kingdom, being about sixty-two years old – וְדָרְיָוֶשׁ מָדָאָה קַבֵּל מַלְכוּתָא כְּבַר שְׁנִין שִׁתִּין וְתַרְתֵּין: The *Turei Even* asks: Why is it necessary to count the number of years of Darius's rule here, as indeed some texts do not mention this? He explains, based on Rashi's commentary to the book of Daniel, that Darius was born in the same year that the exile of Jehoiachin began, and therefore his age is identical to the number of years of that exile.

I will take out the vessels of the Temple and use them – מָאנֵי דְּבֵי מַקְדְּשָׁא וְאֶשְׁתַּמֵּשׁ בְּהוּ: The Ramban explains that the vessels of the Temple were removed twice. At first, some of them were taken out during the exile of Jehoiachin, and these were the vessels that Belshazzar used. Later, after Cyrus allowed the Jews to return to the land to build the Temple, these vessels were returned. Other vessels were taken during the exile of King Zedekiah and remained in the king's treasury even after Cyrus permitted the Jews to return. It was these vessels that Ahasuerus used, and these same vessels were later given to Ezra the Scribe by the king Artaxerxes, to be returned to the Temple upon his return (see Ezra 7:19).

וְהָא שַׁפִּיר חָשֵׁיב? אִיהוּ נַמִּי מִיטְעָא טָעֵי, דְּאִיבָּעֵי לֵיהּ לְמִימְנֵי מֵחָרְבוֹת יְרוּשָׁלַיִם.

The Gemara asks: **But he calculated properly;** why then did this happen? The Gemara answers: **He too erred** in his calculation, **for he should have counted from the destruction of Jerusalem** at the time of the exile of Zedekiah and not from the first exile of Jehoiachin.

סוֹף סוֹף כַּמָּה בְּצֵירַן (חֲדֵיסַר), אִיהוּ כַּמָּה מְלַךְ – אַרְבֵּיסַר, בְּאַרְבֵּיסַר דִּידֵיהּ אִיבָּעֵי לֵיהּ לְמִיבְנֵי בֵּית הַמִּקְדָּשׁ! אַלְמָּה כְּתִיב: ״בֵּאדַיִן בְּטֵילַת עֲבִידַת בֵּית אֱלָהָא דִּי בִּירוּשְׁלֵם״! אָמַר רָבָא: שָׁנִים מְקוּטָּעוֹת הָווּ.

The Gemara asks: **Ultimately, how many** years **were lacking? Eleven,** for the exile of Zedekiah took place eleven years after that of Jehoiachin. **How many** years **did** Ahasuerus **reign** as king? **Fourteen.** Indeed, **in his fourteenth year,** then, **the Temple should have been built.** If so, **why is it written: "Then the work of the House of God, which is in Jerusalem, ceased;** so it ceased until the second year of the reign of Darius, king of Persia" (Ezra 4:24), which indicates that the Temple was not built during the entire reign of Ahasuerus? **Rava said: The years** reckoned **were partial** years. To complete the seventy years, it was necessary to wait until the second year of the rule of Darius II, when indeed the Temple was built.

Perek **I**
Daf **12** Amud **a**

תַּנְיָא נַמִּי הָכִי: וְעוֹד שָׁנָה אַחֶרֶת לְבָבֶל, וְעָמַד דָּרְיָוֶשׁ וְהִשְׁלִימָהּ.

This is also taught in a *baraita*, as an indication that the years counted were only partial years: **And** when Belshazzar was killed, **there was still another year** left **for Babylonia** before the reckoning of the seventy years was completed. **And** then **Darius arose and completed it.** Although seventy years were previously counted according to Belshazzar's count, from the exile of Jehoiakim, because the years were only partial, there was still one year left in order to complete those seventy years.

אָמַר רָבָא: אַף דָּנִיֵּאל טָעָה בְּהַאי חוּשְׁבְּנָא, דִּכְתִיב: ״בִּשְׁנַת אַחַת לְמָלְכוֹ אֲנִי דָּנִיֵּאל בִּינוֹתִי בַּסְּפָרִים״, מִדְּקָאָמַר ״בִּינוֹתִי״ – מִכְּלָל דְּטָעָה.

Rava said: Daniel also erred in this calculation, as it is written: "In the first year of his reign, I, Daniel, meditated in the books over the number of the years, whereof the word of the Lord came to Jeremiah the prophet, that He would accomplish for the desolations of Jerusalem seventy years" (Daniel 9:2). **From** the fact **that he said "I meditated,"** a term indicating recounting and calculating, **it can be inferred that he had** previously **erred.**

מִכָּל מָקוֹם קָשׁוּ קְרָאֵי אַהֲדָדֵי; כְּתִיב: ״מְלֹאות לְבָבֶל״ וּכְתִיב: ״לְחָרְבוֹת יְרוּשָׁלַיִם״!

The Gemara comments: **In any case, the verses contradict each other** with regard to how the seventy years should be calculated. In one verse **it is written:** "After seventy years **are accomplished for Babylonia** I will remember [*efkod*] you, and perform My good word toward you, in causing you to return to this place" (Jeremiah 29:10), which indicates that the seventy years should be counted from the Babylonian exile. **And** in another verse **it is written:** "That he would accomplish **for the desolations of Jerusalem** seventy years" (Daniel 9:2), indicating that the seventy years are calculated from the destruction of Jerusalem.

אָמַר רָבָא: לִפְקִידָה בְּעָלְמָא. וְהַיְינוּ דִּכְתִיב: ״כֹּה אָמַר כּוֹרֶשׁ מֶלֶךְ פָּרַס כֹּל מַמְלְכוֹת הָאָרֶץ נָתַן לִי ה׳ אֱלֹהֵי הַשָּׁמַיִם וְהוּא פָקַד עָלַי לִבְנוֹת לוֹ בַיִת בִּירוּשָׁלַיִם״.

Rava said in response: The seventy years that "are accomplished for Babylonia" were **only for being remembered** [***lifekida***], as mentioned in the verse, allowing the Jews to return to Eretz Yisrael but not to build the Temple. **And this is as it is written** with regard to Cyrus's proclamation permitting the Jewish people's return to Eretz Yisrael, in the seventieth year of the Babylonian exile: **"Thus says Cyrus king of Persia: The Lord, God of heaven, has given me all the kingdoms of the earth; and He has charged [*pakad*] me to build Him a house in Jerusalem"** (Ezra 1:2). The verse makes use of the same root, *peh-kuf-dalet*, heralding the return to Jerusalem to build the Temple, but not its actual completion.

דרש רב נחמן בר רב חסדא, מאי דכתיב: ״כה אמר ה׳ למשיחו לכורש אשר החזקתי בימינו״, וכי כורש משיח היה? אלא אמר ליה הקדוש ברוך הוא למשיח: קובל אני לך על כורש, אני אמרתי ״הוא יבנה ביתי ויקבץ גליותי״. והוא אמר: ״מי בכם מכל עמו...ויעל״.

Apropos its mention of Cyrus, the Gemara states that **Rav Naḥman bar Rav Ḥisda interpreted homiletically** a verse concerning Cyrus: **What is** the meaning of that **which is written: "Thus says the Lord to His anointed, to Cyrus, whose right hand I have held"** (Isaiah 45:1), which seemingly is referring to Cyrus as God's anointed? **Now was Cyrus** God's anointed one, i.e., the **Messiah,** that the verse should refer to him in this manner? **Rather,** the verse should be understood as God speaking to the Messiah with regard to Cyrus: **The Holy One, Blessed be He, said to the Messiah: I am complaining to you about Cyrus,**[N] who is not acting in accordance with what he is intended to do. **I had said: "He shall build My House and gather My exiles"** (see Isaiah 45:13),[N] but he did not carry this out. **Rather, he said: "Whoever is among you of all His people…let him go up** to Jerusalem" (Ezra 1:3). He gave permission to return to Israel, but he did no more than that.

״חיל פרס ומדי הפרתמים״ וכתיב: ״למלכי מדי ופרס״! אמר רבא: אתנויי אתנו בהדדי: אי מינן מלכי – מינייכו איפרכי, ואי מינייכו מלכי מינן איפרכי.

§ The Gemara returns to its interpretations of verses in the Megilla. The Megilla mentions that among those invited to the king's feast were: **"The army of Persia and Media,**[B] **the nobles** and princes of the provinces" (Esther 1:3), **and it is written** near the conclusion of the Megilla: "In the book of chronicles **of the kings of Media and Persia"** (Esther 10:2).[N] Why is Persia mentioned first at the beginning of the Megilla, while later in the Megilla, Media is mentioned first? **Rava said** in response: These two peoples, the Persians and the Medes, **stipulated with each other,** saying: **If the kings** will come **from us, the ministers** will come **from you; and if the kings** will come **from you, the ministers** will come **from us.** Therefore, in reference to kings, Media is mentioned first, whereas in connection with nobles and princes, Persia is given priority.

״בהראותו את עושר כבוד מלכותו״, אמר רבי יוסי בר חנינא: מלמד שלבש בגדי כהונה, כתיב הכא: ״יקר תפארת גדולתו״, וכתיב התם: ״לכבוד ולתפארת״.

The verse states: **"When he showed the riches of his glorious [*kevod*] kingdom** and the honor of his majestic [*tiferet*] greatness" (Esther 1:4). **Rabbi Yosei bar Ḥanina said: This teaches that** Ahasuerus **wore the priestly vestments.** Proof for this assertion may be adduced from the fact that the same terms are written with regard to the priestly vestments, as **it is written here:** "The riches of his glorious [*kevod*] kingdom and **the honor of his majestic [*tiferet*] greatness."** And **it is written there,** with regard to the priestly garments: **"For glory [*kavod*] and for majesty [*tiferet*]"** (Exodus 28:2).

״ובמלאות הימים האלה״ וגו׳, רב ושמואל; חד אמר: מלך פיקח היה, וחד אמר: מלך טיפש היה. מאן דאמר מלך פיקח היה – שפיר עבד דקריב רחיקא ברישא, דבני מאתיה כל אימת דבעי מפייס להו. ומאן דאמר טיפש היה – דאיבעי ליה לקרובי בני מאתיה ברישא, דאי מרדו ביה הנך – הני הוו קיימי שאלו בהדיה.

The verse states: **"And when these days were fulfilled,** the king made a feast for all the people that were present in Shushan the capital" (Esther 1:5). **Rav and Shmuel** disagreed as to whether this was a wise decision. **One said:** Ahasuerus arranged a feast for the residents of Shushan, the capital, after the feast for foreign dignitaries that preceded it, as mentioned in the earlier verses, indicating that **he was a clever king. And** the other **one said:** It is precisely this that indicates that **he was a foolish king. The one who said** that this proves that **he was a clever king** maintains **that he acted well when he first brought close those** more **distant** subjects by inviting them to the earlier celebration, **as he could appease the residents of his** own **city whenever he wished. And the one who said** that **he was foolish** maintains **that he should have invited the residents of his city first, so that if those** faraway subjects **rebelled against him, these** who lived close by **would have stood with him.**[B]

NOTES

I am complaining to you about Cyrus – קובל אני לך על כורש: According Rav Naḥman bar Rav Ḥisda's interpretation, God said to the Messiah: I am complaining with regard to Cyrus, for if he had acted accordingly, the Second Temple would have been built differently, and it would not have been destroyed. There wouldn't have been a last exile, and the coming of the Messiah would have been sooner (*Ḥiddushei Aggadot LaRashba*).

I had said: He shall build My House and gather My exiles – אני אמרתי הוא יבנה ביתי ויקבץ גליותי: This verse appears with different wording later in Isaiah: "He will build My cities and send My exiles" (45:13). This is the text quoted by Rashi, and it appears to be the correct wording of the verse.

Of the kings of Media and Persia – למלכי מדי ופרס: The Maharsha and the *Turei Even* explain, based on *Ester Rabba*, that the essential question is: Why is Persia preceding Media in some verses and vice versa in other verses?

BACKGROUND

Persia and Media – פרס ומדי: Although the Persian Empire began with Cyrus's decisive victory over the Median Empire, in truth Cyrus brought about a situation in which there were two nations sharing the throne. He appointed Medes to prominent positions in the country, even among the ranks of the highest authorities. Statues from the period include soldiers of the king of Persia lined up in pairs, one Persian and one Median.

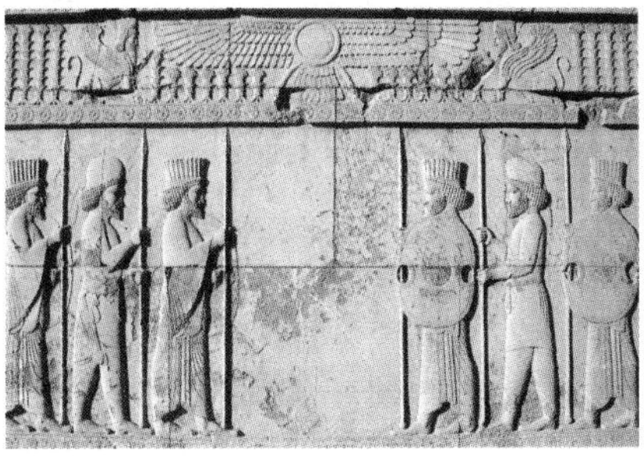

Carving of Persian soldiers

BACKGROUND

Clever or foolish king – מלך פיקח או מלך טיפש: This dispute concerning Ahasuerus's reputation still exists among historians today. His character, as it appears from the lines of the book of Esther, and more so from the midrash, is that of an unbalanced man who is easily influenced by his advisors and chamberlains, unstable and controlled by the women of his palace.

In addition, the Greeks he fought against, and to whom he suffered a number of defeats, vilified him in several ways. Their description of him is quite negative. However, Ahasuerus succeeded in the early years of his rule, until his mind was put at ease, as mentioned earlier (11b). He quelled severe rebellions in Egypt and Babylonia and proved his militaristic abilities in these wars. His grandiose initiative to build Persepolis and other cities with enormous buildings demonstrates his ingenuity and cleverness, although it appears that a large portion of the assets that he amassed through intense taxation were used entirely for this purpose. Therefore, it is difficult to reach a uniformed classification of his character and achievements.

שָׁאֲלוּ תַּלְמִידָיו אֶת רַבִּי שִׁמְעוֹן בַּר יוֹחַאי: מִפְּנֵי מָה נִתְחַיְּיבוּ שׂוֹנְאֵיהֶן שֶׁל יִשְׂרָאֵל שֶׁבְּאוֹתוֹ הַדּוֹר כְּלָיָה? אָמַר לָהֶם: אִמְרוּ אַתֶּם! אָמְרוּ לוֹ: מִפְּנֵי שֶׁנֶּהֱנוּ מִסְּעוּדָּתוֹ שֶׁל אוֹתוֹ רָשָׁע. אִם כֵּן שֶׁבְּשׁוּשָׁן יֵהָרְגוּ, שֶׁבְּכָל הָעוֹלָם כּוּלּוֹ אַל יֵהָרְגוּ! אָמְרוּ לוֹ: אֱמוֹר אַתָּה! אָמַר לָהֶם: מִפְּנֵי שֶׁהִשְׁתַּחֲווּ לְצֶלֶם.

The students of Rabbi Shimon bar Yoḥai[P] **asked him: For what** reason **were the enemies of Jewish people,** a euphemism for the Jewish people themselves when exhibiting behavior that is not in their best interests, **in that generation deserving of annihilation? He,** Rabbi Shimon, **said to them: Say** the answer to your question **yourselves.**[N] **They said to him: It is because they partook of the feast of that wicked one,**[N] Ahasuerus, and they partook there of forbidden foods. Rabbi Shimon responded: **If so, those in Shushan should have been killed** as punishment, but **those in the rest of the world,** who did not participate in the feast, **should not have been killed. They said to him:** Then **you say** your response to our question. **He said to them: It is because they prostrated before the idol** that Nebuchadnezzar had made, as is recorded that the entire world bowed down before it, except for Hananiah, Mishael, and Azariah.

אָמְרוּ לוֹ: וְכִי מַשּׂוֹא פָּנִים יֵשׁ בַּדָּבָר? אָמַר לָהֶם: הֵם לֹא עָשׂוּ אֶלָּא לְפָנִים – אַף הַקָּדוֹשׁ בָּרוּךְ הוּא לֹא עָשָׂה עִמָּהֶן אֶלָּא לְפָנִים, וְהַיְינוּ דִּכְתִיב: ״כִּי לֹא עִנָּה מִלִּבּוֹ״.

They said to him: But if it is true that they worshipped idols and therefore deserved to be destroyed, why was a miracle performed on their behalf? **Is there favoritism** expressed by God **here? He said to them: They did not** really worship the idol, but pretended to **do** so **only for appearance,**[N] acting as if they were carrying out the king's command to bow before the idol. **So too, the Holy One, Blessed be He, did not** destroy them but **did** act angry **with them only for appearance.** He too merely pretended to desire to destroy them, as all He did was issue a threat, but in the end the decree was annulled. **And this is as it is written: "For He does not afflict from His heart** willingly" (Lamentations 3:33), but only for appearances' sake.

״בַּחֲצַר גִּנַּת בִּיתַן הַמֶּלֶךְ״ רַב וּשְׁמוּאֵל; חַד אָמַר: הָרָאוּי לְחָצֵר – לְחָצֵר, הָרָאוּי לְגִינָּה – לְגִינָּה, הָרָאוּי לְבִיתָן – לְבִיתָן. וְחַד אָמַר: הוֹשִׁיבָן בְּחָצֵר – וְלֹא הֶחֱזִיקָתָן, בְּגִינָּה – וְלֹא הֶחֱזִיקָתָן, עַד שֶׁהִכְנִיסָן לְבִיתָן וְהֶחֱזִיקָתָן. בְּמַתְנִיתָא תָּנָא: הוֹשִׁיבָן בְּחָצֵר, וּפָתַח לָהֶם שְׁנֵי פְתָחִים אֶחָד לְגִינָּה וְאֶחָד לְבִיתָן.

The verse states: **"In the court of the garden of the king's palace"** (Esther 1:5). **Rav and Shmuel** disagreed with regard to how to understand the relationship between these three places: Court, garden, and palace: **One said:** The guests were received in different places. **One** who, according to his stature, was **fit for the courtyard** was brought **to the courtyard; one** who was **fit for the garden** was brought **to the garden;** and **one** who was **fit for the palace** was brought **to the palace. And** the other **one said: He** first **sat them in the courtyard, but it did not hold them,** as they were too numerous. He then sat them **in the garden, but it did not hold them** either, **until he brought them into the palace and it held them.** A third understanding **was taught in a** ***baraita*****: He sat them in the courtyard and opened two entranceways for them, one to the garden and one to the palace.**

״חוּר כַּרְפַּס וּתְכֵלֶת״, מַאי חוּר? רַב אָמַר: חֲרֵי חֲרֵי, וּשְׁמוּאֵל אָמַר: מֵילָת לְבָנָה הִצִּיעַ לָהֶם. ״כַּרְפַּס״ אָמַר רַבִּי יוֹסֵי בַּר חֲנִינָא: כָּרִים שֶׁל פַּסִּים.

The verse states: "There were hangings of ***ḥur, karpas,*** **and sky blue"** (Esther 1:6). The Gemara asks: **What is** ***ḥur*****? Rav said:** A fabric fashioned with **many holes** [***ḥarei ḥarei***],[N] similar to lace. **And Shmuel said: He spread out for them** carpets of **white wool,** as the word *ḥavar* means white. And what is ***karpas*****? Rabbi Yosei bar Ḥanina said: Cushions** [***karim***] **of velvet** [***pasim***].

NOTES

He said to them, Say the answer yourselves – אָמַר לָהֶם אִמְרוּ אַתֶּם: Many commentaries question this exchange. Apparently, if the students asked, they did not know the answer. If so, why did Rabbi Shimon ask them for their answer? Some explain that their central question was: Why did the Jewish people deserve to be destroyed? They understood that the people had sinned, yet they couldn't understand why they were punished so severely. For this reason, Rabbi Shimon replied: Say yourselves at least what you do understand; explain the reason you feel that they deserve any punishment (Maharam Schiff; see Rabbi Yoshiya Pinto).

In the work *Ginzei HaMelekh* there is an interesting explanation provided, relating the discussion here to the dispute recorded later (19a) with regard to which part of the Megilla must be read on Purim. Rabbi Shimon maintains that the Megilla is read only from the chapter that begins with "On that night" (Esther, chapter 6), and therefore he is not as concerned with what occurred in the initial chapters of the Megilla. His students, however, maintain that the Megilla should be read in its entirety, as they view the beginning of the Megilla as essential to the unfolding of the story. Therefore, the students asked Rabbi Shimon what is indicated in the latter chapters of the Megilla regarding the cause for Israel's danger. Rabbi Shimon responded to his students, that they who are of the opinion that the beginning of the Megilla is essential, should be the ones to explain what is detailed in the initial chapters as a reason for the impending destruction?

They partook of the feast of that wicked one – מִפְּנֵי שֶׁנֶּהֱנוּ מִסְּעוּדָּתוֹ שֶׁל אוֹתוֹ רָשָׁע: Apparently, the Jewish people ate forbidden foods. Secondly, the Gemara mentions earlier that Ahasuerus held the feast as an act of disbelief in Jeremiah's prophecy, expressing his certainty that the Jews would never return to the Temple. The Jews' participation in the party lent support to Ahasuerus's convictions, and it was therefore a desecration of God's name (Rabbi Yoshiya Pinto).

Only for appearance – אֶלָּא לְפָנִים: The Maharsha explains that the Jewish people's prostration before the idols was only out of fear, and thereby it was an act with only the outer appearance of idol worship. Therefore, the Holy One, Blessed be He, treated them accordingly and only gave the appearance that He would decimate them. In fact, His heart was as true to them as theirs was to Him.

Many holes [*ḥarei ḥarei*] – חֲרֵי חֲרֵי: This explanation of the word *ḥur* indicates that Ahasuerus used porous fabric as partitions, so that the attendees at his party could all see each other. Alternatively, the word *ḥur* come from *ḥerut*, freedom, and it indicated that the partygoers wore clothes worthy of free men (*Arukh*).

PERSONALITIES

Rabbi Shimon bar Yoḥai – רַבִּי שִׁמְעוֹן בַּר יוֹחַאי: Rabbi Shimon bar Yoḥai was one of the greatest *tanna'im* of the generation prior to the redaction of the Mishna. Rabbi Shimon was the preeminent student of Rabbi Akiva, and he considered himself Rabbi Akiva's spiritual heir. Rabbi Akiva had a great deal of respect for his student and said: It is enough for you that I and your Creator recognize your strength. Rabbi Shimon's greatness was manifest in his mastery of both *halakha* and *aggada*, and his statements can be found on all topics in every tractate of the Talmud.

The *halakha* is not always ruled in accordance with Rabbi Shimon bar Yoḥai's opinion, especially in disputes with Rabbi Yosei and Rabbi Yehuda. Nevertheless, the *halakha* follows his opinion with regard to several core issues. He had his own unique method of deriving *halakha* from the Torah, as he factored in the rationale of the verse and inferred halakhic conclusions from the Bible based on the spirit and purpose of the law.

Rabbi Shimon traveled to Rome as an emissary of the people, but he harbored profound enmity toward the Romans. He made no attempt to conceal his feelings of disgust for Rome and was therefore sentenced to death and forced into hiding for many years.

He was an ascetic by nature. He was very exacting, and he was famous in his generation for his righteousness and his performance of miracles. There are many anecdotes related in the Talmud about miraculous acts he performed. The *Sifrei*, a collection of halakhic derivations on Numbers and Deuteronomy, was developed in his study hall. He is also credited with having authored the fundamental kabbalistic work, the *Zohar*. His greatest students were Rabbi Yehuda HaNasi; Rabbi Shimon ben Yehuda; and his son, Rabbi Elazar ben Rabbi Shimon, who was also among the most prominent *tanna'im*.

"עַל גְּלִילֵי כֶסֶף וְעַמּוּדֵי שֵׁשׁ מִטּוֹת זָהָב וָכֶסֶף". תַּנְיָא, רַבִּי יְהוּדָה אוֹמֵר: הָרָאוּי לְכֶסֶף – לְכֶסֶף, הָרָאוּי לְזָהָב – לְזָהָב. אָמַר לוֹ רַבִּי נְחֶמְיָה: אִם כֵּן אַתָּה מַטִּיל קִנְאָה בִּסְעוּדָה, אֶלָּא: הֵם שֶׁל כֶּסֶף וְרַגְלֵיהֶן שֶׁל זָהָב.

The verse states: **"On silver rods and pillars of marble; the couches were of gold and silver"** (Esther 1:6). **It is taught** in a *baraita*: **Rabbi Yehuda says:** Some couches were of gold and others of silver. **One** who, according to his stature, was **fit for silver** sat on a couch of **silver,** and **one** who was **fit for gold** sat on one of **gold. Rabbi Neḥemya said to him:** This was not done. **If so,** you would **cast jealousy into the feast,** for the guests would be envious of each other. **Rather,** the couches **themselves** were made **of silver, and their feet** were made **of gold.**

"בַּהַט וָשֵׁשׁ" אָמַר רַבִּי אַסִי: אֲבָנִים שֶׁמִּתְחוֹטְטוֹת עַל בַּעְלֵיהֶן, וְכֵן הוּא אוֹמֵר "אַבְנֵי נֵזֶר מִתְנוֹסְסוֹת עַל אַדְמָתוֹ".

The verse continues: "Upon a pavement of ***bahat*** **and marble"** (Esther 1:6). **Rabbi Asi said** with regard to the definition of *bahat*: These are **stones that ingratiate themselves**[N] **with their owners,** as they are precious stones that people are willing to spend large amounts of money to acquire. **And similarly, it states** elsewhere that the Jewish people will be likened to precious stones: "And the Lord their God shall save them in that day as the flock of His people; for they shall be as **"the stones of a crown, glittering over His land"** (Zechariah 9:16).

"וְדַר וְסֹחָרֶת" רַב אָמַר: דָּרֵי דָּרֵי וּשְׁמוּאֵל אָמַר: אֶבֶן טוֹבָה יֵשׁ בִּכְרַכֵּי הַיָּם וְדָרָה שְׁמָהּ, הוֹשִׁיבָהּ בְּאֶמְצַע סְעוּדָה וּמְאִירָה לָהֶם כְּצָהֳרַיִם. דְּבֵי רַבִּי יִשְׁמָעֵאל תָּנָא: שֶׁקָּרָא דְּרוֹר לְכָל בַּעֲלֵי סְחוֹרָה.

The verse concludes: **"And *dar* and *soḥaret*"** (Esther 1:6). **Rav said:** *Dar* means **many rows** [***darei darei***] around. Similarly, *soḥaret* is derived from *seḥor seḥor*, around and around, meaning that the floor was surrounded with numerous rows of *bahat* and marble stones. **And Shmuel said:** There is **a precious stone in the seaports, and its name is *dara*,** and Ahasuerus **placed it in the center of** the **feast, and it illuminated** the festivities **for them as** the sun illuminates the world **at midday.** He explains that the word *soḥaret* is derived from *tzohar*, a light. A scholar from **the school of Rabbi Yishmael taught** a *baraita*: This means **that he proclaimed a remission for all the merchants,** absolving them from paying their taxes, understanding that the word *dar* derives from *deror*, freedom, and *soḥaret* from *soḥer*, merchant.

"וְהַשְׁקוֹת בִּכְלֵי זָהָב וְכֵלִים מִכֵּלִים שׁוֹנִים" "מְשׁוּנִּים" מִיבְּעֵי לֵיהּ! אָמַר רָבָא: יָצְתָה בַּת קוֹל וְאָמְרָה לָהֶם: רִאשׁוֹנִים כָּלוּ מִפְּנֵי כֵלִים וְאַתֶּם שׁוֹנִים בָּהֶם?! "וְיֵין מַלְכוּת רָב" אָמַר רַב: מְלַמֵּד שֶׁכָּל אֶחָד וְאֶחָד הִשְׁקֵהוּ יַיִן שֶׁגָּדוֹל הֵימֶנּוּ בְּשָׁנִים.

The verse states: **"And they gave them drink in vessels of gold, the vessels being diverse [*shonim*] from one another"** (Esther 1:7). The Gemara asks: Why does the verse use the term *shonim* to express that they are different? **It should have said** the more proper term ***meshunim.*** **Rava said: A Divine Voice issued forth and said to them: The early ones,** referring to Belshazzar and his people, **were destroyed because** they used **these vessels,** the vessels of the Temple, **and** yet **you use them again [*shonim*]?** The verse continues: **"And royal wine in abundance [*rav*]"** (Esther 1:7). **Rav said: This teaches that each and every** guest at the feast **was poured** well-aged **wine that was older [*rav*] than himself in years.**

"וְהַשְּׁתִיָּה כַדָּת (אֵין אוֹנֵס)" מַאי "כַדָּת"? אָמַר רַבִּי חָנָן מִשּׁוּם רַבִּי מֵאִיר: כְּדָת שֶׁל תּוֹרָה, מַה דָּת שֶׁל תּוֹרָה – אֲכִילָה מְרוּבָּה מִשְּׁתִיָּה, אַף סְעוּדָתוֹ שֶׁל אוֹתוֹ רָשָׁע – אֲכִילָה מְרוּבָּה מִשְּׁתִיָּה.

The verse states: **"And the drinking was according to the law; none did compel"** (Esther 1:8). The Gemara asks: **What is** the meaning of **"according to the law"? Rabbi Ḥanan said in the name of Rabbi Meir:** The drinking was **according to the law of the Torah. Just as,** according to **the law of the Torah,** with regard to offerings, **the food** sacrificed on the altar **is greater** in quantity **than the drink,** for the wine libation is quantitatively much smaller than the sacrificial offerings it accompanies, **so too,** at the **feast of that wicked man, the food was greater** in quantity **than the drink.**

"אֵין אוֹנֵס", אָמַר רַבִּי אֶלְעָזָר: מְלַמֵּד שֶׁכָּל אֶחָד וְאֶחָד הִשְׁקֵהוּ מִיֵּין מְדִינָתוֹ. "לַעֲשׂוֹת כִּרְצוֹן אִישׁ וָאִישׁ", אָמַר רָבָא: לַעֲשׂוֹת כִּרְצוֹן מָרְדֳּכַי וְהָמָן, מָרְדֳּכַי – דִּכְתִיב "אִישׁ יְהוּדִי", הָמָן "אִישׁ צַר וְאוֹיֵב".

The verse states: **"None did compel"** (Esther 1:8). **Rabbi Elazar said: This teaches that each and every** guest at the feast **was poured** a drink **from wine of his** own **country,** so that he would feel entirely free, as if he were in his home country. The verse continues: **"That they should do according to every man's pleasure"** (Esther 1:8). **Rava** commented on the literal meaning of the verse, which is referring to two men, a man and a man [*ish va'ish*], and **said:** The man and man whom they should follow indicates **that they should do according to the wishes of Mordecai and Haman.**[N] The two of them served as butlers at the feast, and they were in charge of distributing the wine. Why is the verse interpreted in this way? **Mordecai** is called "man," **as it is written:** "There was a certain **Jewish man [*ish*]** in Shushan the castle, whose name was Mordecai, the son of Jair" (Esther 2:5). **And Haman** is also called man, as it states: **"A man [*ish*] who is an adversary and an enemy,** this evil Haman" (Esther 7:6).

NOTES

That ingratiate themselves [*shemitḥotetot*] – שֶׁמִּתְחוֹטְטוֹת: This expression is explained in various ways. Some maintain that the Hebrew phrase *shemitḥotetot* connotes pleasure (*Arukh*). Others explain that it means that a man lowers himself before the stones, in that he will do anything to procure them (Rabbeinu Gershom *Maor HaGola*). Perhaps this phrase indicates sin, in the sense that it is prohibited for a private individual to have such precious stones in his possession. He must relinquish them to the monarchy, and if he does not relinquish them, he is executed (Rabbeinu Ḥananel).

According to the wishes of Mordecai and Haman – כִּרְצוֹן מָרְדֳּכַי וְהָמָן: The simple meaning is that the feast was according to everyone's wishes, even two enemies, e.g. Mordecai and Haman. The Maharsha explains that Mordecai intended that all of the feast be in accordance with *halakha*, and Haman wanted the opposite (see Rabbi Yoshiya Pinto and *Ein Ya'akov*).

״גַּם וַשְׁתִּי הַמַּלְכָּה עָשְׂתָה מִשְׁתֵּה נָשִׁים בֵּית הַמַּלְכוּת״, בֵּית הַנָּשִׁים מִיבָּעֵי לֵיהּ! אָמַר רָבָא: שְׁנֵיהֶן לִדְבַר עֲבֵירָה נִתְכַּוְּונוּ. הַיְינוּ דְּאָמְרִי אִינָשֵׁי: אִיהוּ בְּקָרֵי וְאִתְּתֵיהּ

The verse states: **"Also Vashti the queen made a feast for the women, in the royal house,** which belonged to King Ahasuerus" (Esther 1:9). The Gemara questions why she held the feast in the royal house, a place of men, rather than in **the women's house,** where it **should have been. Rava said** in response: **The two of them had sinful intentions.** Ahasuerus wished to fornicate with the women, and Vashti wished to fornicate with the men. **This** explains the folk saying **that people say: He with pumpkins and his wife**

Perek **I**
Daf **12** Amud **b**

בְּבוּצִינֵי.

with zucchinis,[N] indicating that often a man and his wife engage in similar actions.

״בַּיּוֹם הַשְּׁבִיעִי כְּטוֹב לֵב הַמֶּלֶךְ בַּיָּיִן״ אַטּוּ עַד הָשְׁתָּא לָא טַב לִבֵּיהּ בְּחַמְרָא? אָמַר רָבָא: יוֹם הַשְּׁבִיעִי שַׁבָּת הָיָה, שֶׁיִּשְׂרָאֵל אוֹכְלִין וְשׁוֹתִין, מַתְחִילִין בְּדִבְרֵי תוֹרָה וּבְדִבְרֵי תִשְׁבָּחוֹת. אֲבָל אוּמּוֹת הָעוֹלָם שֶׁאוֹכְלִין וְשׁוֹתִין – אֵין מַתְחִילִין אֶלָּא בְּדִבְרֵי תִיפְלוּת.

The verse states: **"On the seventh day,**[N] **when the heart of the king was merry with wine"** (Esther 1:10). The Gemara asks: **Is that to say** that **until now his heart was not merry with wine?** Did it take seven days for him to achieve merriment? **Rava said: The seventh day was Shabbat,** when the difference between the Jewish people and the gentiles is most apparent. On Shabbat, **when the Jewish people eat and drink, they begin** by occupying themselves **with words of Torah and words of praise** for God. **But the nations of the world, when they eat and drink, they begin only with words of licentiousness.**

וְכֵן בִּסְעוּדָּתוֹ שֶׁל אוֹתוֹ רָשָׁע, הַלָּלוּ אוֹמְרִים: מָדִיּוֹת נָאוֹת, וְהַלָּלוּ אוֹמְרִים: פַּרְסִיּוֹת נָאוֹת. אָמַר לָהֶם אֲחַשְׁוֵרוֹשׁ: כְּלִי שֶׁאֲנִי מִשְׁתַּמֵּשׁ בּוֹ אֵינוֹ לֹא מָדַיִי וְלֹא פַּרְסִי אֶלָּא כַּשְׂדִּיי. רְצוֹנְכֶם לִרְאוֹתָהּ? אָמְרוּ לוֹ: אִין, וּבִלְבַד שֶׁתְּהֵא עֲרוּמָּה.

The Gemara continues to detail what occurred at the feast. **So too, at the feast of that wicked man,** Ahasuerus, when the men began to converse, **some said: The Median women are** the most **beautiful, while others said: The Persian women are** the most **beautiful. Ahasuerus said to them: The vessel that I use,** i.e., my wife, **is neither Median nor Persian, but** rather **Chaldean. Do you wish to see her? They said to him: Yes, provided that she be naked,**[N] for we wish to see her without any additional adornments.

שֶׁבְּמִדָּה שֶׁאָדָם מוֹדֵד בָּהּ מוֹדְדִין לוֹ. מְלַמֵּד שֶׁהָיְתָה וַשְׁתִּי הָרְשָׁעָה מְבִיאָה בְּנוֹת יִשְׂרָאֵל וּמַפְשִׁיטָן עֲרוּמּוֹת וְעוֹשָׂה בָּהֶן מְלָאכָה בְּשַׁבָּת, הַיְינוּ דִּכְתִיב ״אַחַר הַדְּבָרִים הָאֵלֶּה כְּשׁוֹךְ חֲמַת הַמֶּלֶךְ אֲחַשְׁוֵרוֹשׁ זָכַר אֶת וַשְׁתִּי וְאֵת אֲשֶׁר עָשָׂתָה וְאֵת אֲשֶׁר נִגְזַר עָלֶיהָ״ כְּשֵׁם שֶׁעָשְׂתָה – כָּךְ נִגְזַר עָלֶיהָ.

The Gemara comments: Vashti was punished in this humiliating way **for it is with the measure that a man measures** to others **that he** himself **is measured.** In other words, God punishes individuals in line with their transgressions, measure for measure. **This teaches that the wicked Vashti would take the daughters of Israel, and strip them naked, and make them work on Shabbat.** Therefore, it was decreed that she be brought before the king naked, on Shabbat. This is **as it is written: "After these things, when the wrath of King Ahasuerus was appeased, he remembered Vashti, and what she had done, and what was decreed against her"** (Esther 2:1). That is to say, **just as she had done** with the young Jewish women, **so it was decreed upon her.**

״וַתְּמָאֵן הַמַּלְכָּה וַשְׁתִּי״, מִכְּדִי פְּרִיצְתָּא הֲוַאי, דַּאֲמַר מָר: שְׁנֵיהֶן לִדְבַר עֲבֵירָה נִתְכַּוְּונוּ, מַאי טַעְמָא לָא אֲתַאי? אָמַר רַבִּי יוֹסֵי בַּר חֲנִינָא: מְלַמֵּד שֶׁפָּרְחָה בָּהּ צָרַעַת. בְּמַתְנִיתָא תָּנָא: [בָּא גַּבְרִיאֵל וְעָשָׂה לָהּ זָנָב.]

The verse states: **"But the queen Vashti refused** to come" (Esther 1:12). The Gemara asks: **Since she was immodest, as the Master said** above: **The two of them had sinful intentions, what is the reason** that **she did not come? Rabbi Yosei bar Ḥanina said: This teaches that she broke out in leprosy,** and therefore she was embarrassed to expose herself publicly. An alternative reason for her embarrassment **was taught in a *baraita*:** The angel **Gabriel came and fashioned her a tail.**[N]

NOTES

He with pumpkins and his wife with zucchinis – אִיהוּ בְּקָרֵי וְאִתְּתֵיהּ בְּבוּצִינֵי: The central point is that a man and his wife usually act in the same fashion. Rashi explains that just as Ahasuerus wished to exhibit his wife's beauty to everyone, she similarly intended to show off her beauty. Others explain the particulars of this idiom, that if a man will have immoral relations under the wide pumpkin leaves, his wife will act similarly, but under zucchinis, in a more observable and public fashion (*HaKotev*; see *Arukh*).

On the seventh day – בַּיּוֹם הַשְּׁבִיעִי: There is nothing distinctive about the seventh day of the feast to make it worthy of special mention, therefore the verse must be discussing the seventh day of the week, Shabbat. On Shabbat, the difference between the feasting of the Jews and the other nations was most apparent (see Maharsha).

Provided that she be naked – וּבִלְבַד שֶׁתְּהֵא עֲרוּמָּה: This interpretation is hinted to in the verse, as it states that Vashti should be brought "wearing the royal crown" (Esther 1:11), which is understood to mean that she should be wearing nothing else (*Re'aḥ Duda'im*).

And fashioned her a tail – וְעָשָׂה לָהּ זָנָב: A number of commentaries explain that the term tail doesn't necessarily indicate an actual tail, as the term is used to refer to numerous forms of abnormal growth. This additional growth was sufficient to convince Vashti that she did not wish to go and expose herself publicly (*Arukh*; *Ḥiddushei Aggadot LaRashba*).

״וַיִּקְצֹף הַמֶּלֶךְ מְאֹד״ אַמַּאי דָּלְקָה בֵּיהּ כּוּלֵּי הַאי? אֲמַר רָבָא: שְׁלַחָה לֵיהּ: בַּר אַהוּרְיָירֵיהּ דְּאַבָּא! אַבָּא לָקֳבֵל אַלְפָּא חַמְרָא שָׁתֵי וְלָא רָוֵי, וְהַהוּא גַּבְרָא אִשְׁתַּטֵּי בְּחַמְרֵיהּ. מִיָּד ״וַחֲמָתוֹ בָּעֲרָה בוֹ״.

The verse continues: "**Therefore the king was very wrathful,** and his anger burned in him" (Esther 1:12). The Gemara asks: **Why did** his anger **burn in him so greatly** merely because she did not wish to come? **Rava said:** Vashti not only refused to come, but she also **sent him** a message by way of a messenger: You, **son of my father's stableman** [*ahuriyyarei*].[L] Belshazzar, **my father, drank wine against a thousand men**[N] **and did not become inebriated,** as the verse in Daniel (5:1) testifies about him: "Belshazzar the king made a great feast to a thousand of his lords, and drank wine before the thousand"; **and that man,** referring euphemistically to Ahasuerus himself, **has become senseless from his wine.** Due to her audacity, **immediately "his anger burned in him"** (Esther 1:12).

״וַיֹּאמֶר הַמֶּלֶךְ לַחֲכָמִים״ מַאן חֲכָמִים – רַבָּנַן, ״יוֹדְעֵי הָעִתִּים״ – שֶׁיּוֹדְעִין לְעַבֵּר שָׁנִים וְלִקְבּוֹעַ חֳדָשִׁים. אֲמַר לְהוּ: דַּיְינוּהָ לִי! אֲמַרוּ: הֵיכִי נַעֲבֵיד? נֵימָא לֵיהּ: קַטְלַהּ – לִמְחַר פָּסֵיק לֵיהּ חַמְרֵיהּ וּבָעֵי לָהּ מִינַּן. נֵימָא לֵיהּ: שְׁבַקַהּ – קָא מְזַלְזְלָה בְּמַלְכוּתָא. אָמְרוּ לוֹ: מִיּוֹם שֶׁחָרַב בֵּית הַמִּקְדָּשׁ וְגָלִינוּ מֵאַרְצֵנוּ נִיטְּלָה עֵצָה מִמֶּנּוּ, וְאֵין אָנוּ יוֹדְעִין לָדוּן דִּינֵי נְפָשׁוֹת. זִיל לְגַבֵּי עַמּוֹן וּמוֹאָב, דְּיָתְבִי בְּדוּכְתַּיְיהוּ כְּחַמְרָא דְּיָתֵיב עַל דּוּרְדְּיֵיהּ.

The following verse states: "**Then the king said to the wise men,** who knew the times" (Esther 1:13). The Gemara asks: **Who are these wise men?** These wise men are **the Sages** of the Jewish people, who are referred to as those **"who knew the times," for they know how to intercalate years and fix the months** of the Jewish calendar. Ahasuerus **said to them: Judge her for me.** The Sages **said** in their hearts: **What should we do? If we say to him: Kill her, tomorrow he will become sober and** then come and **demand her from us.** If **we say to him: Let her be, she has scorned royalty,** and that cannot be tolerated. Consequently, they decided not to judge the matter, and **they said to him** as follows: **From the day that the Temple was destroyed and we have been exiled from our land, counsel** and insight **have been removed from us, and we do not know how to judge capital cases,** as they are exceptionally difficult. **Go to** the people of **Ammon and Moab,**[N] **who have remained** permanently **settled in their places like wine that is settled on its lees,** and so their minds are settled as well.

וְטַעְמָא אֲמַרוּ לֵיהּ: דִּכְתִיב ״שַׁאֲנַן מוֹאָב מִנְּעוּרָיו וְשֹׁקֵט הוּא אֶל שְׁמָרָיו וְלֹא הוּרַק מִכְּלִי אֶל כֶּלִי וּבַגּוֹלָה לֹא הָלָךְ עַל כֵּן עָמַד טַעְמוֹ בּוֹ וְרֵיחוֹ לֹא נָמָר״. מִיָּד ״וְהַקָּרוֹב אֵלָיו כַּרְשְׁנָא שֵׁתָר אַדְמָתָא תַרְשִׁישׁ״.

And they provided a good **reason** when **they spoke to him,** as they proved that one who is settled retains his reasoning: **For it is written: "Moab has been at ease from his youth, and he has settled on his lees, and has not been emptied from vessel to vessel, neither has he gone into exile; therefore his taste has remained in him, and his scent is not changed"** (Jeremiah 48:11). Ahasuerus **immediately** acted on their advice and asked his advisors, as it is written: **"And next to him was Carshena, Shethar, Admatha, Tarshish,** Meres, Marsena, and Memucan" (Esther 1:14).

אָמַר רַבִּי לֵוִי: כָּל פָּסוּק זֶה עַל שׁוּם קָרְבָּנוֹת נֶאֱמַר:

Rabbi Levi said: This entire verse[N] listing the names of the king's advisors **is stated on account of offerings.** Each name alludes to an aspect of the sacrificial service that was unique to the Jewish people, which the ministering angels mentioned as merit for the Jewish people.

״כַּרְשְׁנָא״ אָמְרוּ מַלְאֲכֵי הַשָּׁרֵת לִפְנֵי הַקָּדוֹשׁ בָּרוּךְ הוּא: רִבּוֹנוֹ שֶׁל עוֹלָם, כְּלוּם הִקְרִיבוּ לְפָנֶיךָ כָּרִים בְּנֵי שָׁנָה כְּדֶרֶךְ שֶׁהִקְרִיבוּ יִשְׂרָאֵל לְפָנֶיךָ? ״שֵׁתָר״, כְּלוּם הִקְרִיבוּ לְפָנֶיךָ שְׁתֵּי תוֹרִין? ״אַדְמָתָא״, כְּלוּם בָּנוּ לְפָנֶיךָ מִזְבַּח אֲדָמָה? ״תַּרְשִׁישׁ״, כְּלוּם שִׁימְּשׁוּ לְפָנֶיךָ בְּבִגְדֵי כְהוּנָּה, דִּכְתִיב בְּהוּ ״תַּרְשִׁישׁ וְשֹׁהַם וְיָשְׁפֵה״. ״מֶרֶס״, כְּלוּם מֵירְסוּ בְּדָם לְפָנֶיךָ? ״מַרְסְנָא״, כְּלוּם מֵירְסוּ בִּמְנָחוֹת לְפָנֶיךָ? ״מְמוּכָן״, כְּלוּם הֵכִינוּ שֻׁלְחָן לְפָנֶיךָ?

"**Carshena"; the ministering angels said before the Holy One, Blessed be He: Master of the Universe, did** the gentiles **ever offer before You lambs** [*karim*] **of the first year** [*shana*], **as the Jewish people have offered before You? "Shethar"; have they ever offered before You two turtledoves** [*shetei torim*]? **"Admatha"; have they ever built before You an altar of earth** [*adama*]? **"Tarshish"; have they ever ministered before You in the priestly vestments, as it is written** that on the fourth of the four rows of precious stones contained on the breastplate were: **"A beryl** [*tarshish*], **an onyx, and a jasper"** (Exodus 28:20). **"Meres"; have they ever stirred** [*meirsu*] **the blood of the offerings before You? "Marsena"; have they ever stirred** [*meirsu*] **the meal-offering before You? "Memucan"; have they ever prepared** [*hekhinu*] **the table before You,** on which the shewbread was placed?

״וַיֹּאמֶר מְמוּכָן״, תָּנָא: מְמוּכָן זֶה הָמָן. וְלָמָּה נִקְרָא שְׁמוֹ מְמוּכָן – שֶׁמּוּכָן לְפוּרְעָנוּת. אָמַר רַב כָּהֲנָא: מִכָּאן שֶׁהֶדְיוֹט קוֹפֵץ בָּרֹאשׁ.

The verse states: **"And Memucan said"** (Esther 1:16). A Sage **taught** in a *baraita*: **Memucan is Haman. And why is** Haman **referred to as Memucan? Because he was prepared** [*mukhan*] **to bring calamity**[N] upon the Jewish people. **Rav Kahana said: From here** we see **that the common man jumps to the front** and speaks first, for Memucan was mentioned last of the king's seven advisors, and nevertheless he expressed his opinion first.

LANGUAGE

Stableman [*ahuriyyarei*] – **בַּר אַהוּרְיָירֵיהּ**: From the Middle Persian āxwaryār, as āxwarr means stable, and the suffix -ār acts as an agent, indicating a stableman. It is obvious that Ahasuerus was not actually the stableman of Vashti's father. However, since Vashti belonged to the royal Babylonian family, and Ahasuerus descended from the royal Aḥmanidat dynasty, which was subservient to them, he is referred to as a stableman of the Babylonian king.

NOTES

Drank wine against a thousand men – **לָקֳבֵל אַלְפָּא חַמְרָא שָׁתֵי**: This phrase, which also appears in Daniel 5:1, is difficult to understand literally. It is interpreted to mean that Belshazzar would drink against the greatest of a thousand drinkers. Another interpretation is that the word thousand, *alpa*, being similar to the word *aluf*, an ox, is used here to imply that he would drink large quantities of wine in the way that an ox drinks water (*Tosefot HaRosh*).

Go to Ammon and Moab – **זִיל לְגַבֵּי עַמּוֹן וּמוֹאָב**: The Sages knew that Ahasuerus was an unstable king and therefore feared giving him advice. Consequently, they decided to avoid doing so. Furthermore, they advised him to seek the counsel of Ammon and Moab, who hated the Jews, so that they bear the responsibility for the king's actions (see Rabbi Yoshiya Pinto).

This entire verse – **כָּל פָּסוּק זֶה**: It was not necessary for the text to list the names of the officers and wise men, as it would have been sufficient to mention that Ahasuerus listened to the advice of his counsel. Therefore, the names are interpreted as referring to both the greatness of the Jewish people and their future troubles (see *Gevul Binyamin* and *Re'aḥ Duda'im*).

Prepared to bring calamity – **מוּכָן לְפוּרְעָנוּת**: Rashi explains that it means prepared to be hung. The Maharsha explains that he was ready to cause calamity for all, first for Vashti and later for the Jews.

״לִהְיוֹת כׇּל אִישׁ שׂוֹרֵר בְּבֵיתוֹ״ אָמַר רָבָא: אִלְמָלֵא אִגְּרוֹת הָרִאשׁוֹנוֹת לֹא נִשְׁתַּיֵּיר מִשּׂוֹנְאֵיהֶן שֶׁל יִשְׂרָאֵל שָׂרִיד וּפָלִיט.

The king sent out letters to the people of all his provinces, in which it was written: **"That every man shall wield authority in his own house** and speak according to the language of his people" (Esther 1:22). **Rava said: Were it not for the first letters** sent by Ahasuerus, which everybody discounted, **there would not have been left among the enemies of the Jewish people,** a euphemism for the Jewish people themselves, **a remnant or a refugee.** Since these first letters were the subject of ridicule, people didn't take the king seriously and did not immediately act upon the directive of the later letters, calling for the Jewish people's destruction.

אָמְרִי: מַאי הַאי דְּשַׁדַּיר לַן ״לִהְיוֹת כׇּל אִישׁ שׂוֹרֵר בְּבֵיתוֹ״? פְּשִׁיטָא! אֲפִילּוּ קַרְחָה בְּבֵיתֵיהּ פַּרְדַּשְׁכָּא לֶיהֱוֵי!

The Gemara continues. The reason that the first letters were not taken seriously is that **they** who received them would **say: What is this that he has sent us: "That every man shall wield authority in his own house"?** This is **obvious; even** a lowly **weaver is commander** [*paredashekha*][L] **in his house.** If so, why then did the king find it necessary to make such a proclamation?

״וְיַפְקֵד הַמֶּלֶךְ פְּקִידִים״ אָמַר רַבִּי: מַאי דִּכְתִיב ״כׇּל עָרוּם יַעֲשֶׂה בְדָעַת וּכְסִיל יִפְרֹשׂ אִוֶּלֶת״,

The verse describes Ahasuerus's search for a new wife by stating: **"And let the king appoint officers** in all the provinces of his kingdom, that they may gather together all the fair young virgins unto Shushan the castle" (Esther 2:3). **Rabbi** Yehuda HaNasi **said: What is** the meaning of **that which is written: "In everything a prudent man acts with knowledge, but a fool unfolds his folly"** (Proverbs 13:16)? The verse highlights the difference between two kings' approaches to finding a wife.

״כׇּל עָרוּם יַעֲשֶׂה בְדָעַת״ – זֶה דָּוִד, דִּכְתִיב ״וַיֹּאמְרוּ לוֹ עֲבָדָיו יְבַקְשׁוּ לַאדֹנִי הַמֶּלֶךְ נַעֲרָה בְתוּלָה״ כׇּל מַאן דַּהֲוָה לֵיהּ בְּרַתָּא – אַיְיתַהּ נִיהֲלֵיהּ. ״וּכְסִיל יִפְרוֹשׂ אִוֶּלֶת״ – זֶה אֲחַשְׁוֵרוֹשׁ, דִּכְתִיב ״וְיַפְקֵד הַמֶּלֶךְ פְּקִידִים״. כׇּל מַאן דַּהֲוָה לֵיהּ בְּרַתָּא – אִיטַּמְרַהּ מִינֵּיהּ.

"In everything a prudent man acts with knowledge"; this statement is referring to **David,** who also sought a wife for himself, **as it is written: "And his servants said to him, Let there be sought for my lord the king a young virgin"** (I Kings 1:2). Since he sought one maiden, **whoever had a daughter brought her to him,** for everyone wanted his daughter to be the king's wife. With regard to the continuation of the verse: **"But a fool unfolds his folly"** (Proverbs 13:16), **this** statement **is** referring to **Ahasuerus, as it is written: "And let the king appoint officers"** to seek out many maidens. Since it became clear that the king would have relations with all of them, but in the end he would choose only one as his bride, **whoever had a daughter hid her from him.**

״אִישׁ יְהוּדִי הָיָה בְּשׁוּשַׁן הַבִּירָה״ וגו׳ ״אִישׁ יְמִינִי״. מַאי קָאָמַר? אִי לְיַחוּסֵא קָאָתֵי – לְיַחֲסֵיהּ וְאָזֵיל עַד בִּנְיָמִין! אֶלָּא מַאי שְׁנָא הָנֵי?

The verse that initially describes Mordecai states: **"There was a certain Jew in Shushan the castle,** whose name was Mordecai the son of Jair the son of Shimei the son of Kish, a **Benjamite"** (Esther 2:5). The Gemara asks: **What is it** conveying in the verse by **saying** the names of Mordecai's ancestors? **If** the verse in fact **comes to** trace his **ancestry, it should continue tracing** his lineage **back** all the way **to Benjamin,** the founder of his tribe. **Rather, what is different** about these names that they deserve special mention?

תָּנָא: כּוּלָּן עַל שְׁמוֹ נִקְרְאוּ; ״בֶּן יָאִיר״ – בֵּן שֶׁהֵאִיר עֵינֵיהֶם שֶׁל יִשְׂרָאֵל בִּתְפִלָּתוֹ, ״בֶּן שִׁמְעִי״ – בֵּן שֶׁשָּׁמַע אֵל תְּפִלָּתוֹ, ״בֶּן קִישׁ״ – שֶׁהִקִּישׁ עַל שַׁעֲרֵי רַחֲמִים וְנִפְתְּחוּ לוֹ.

The Gemara answers: A Sage **taught** the following *baraita*: **All of them are names by which** Mordecai **was called.** He was called **"the son of Jair"** because he was **the son who enlightened** [*heir*] **the eyes of** all of **the Jewish people with his prayers; "the son of Shimei"** because he was **the son whom God heard** [*shama*] **his prayers; "the son of Kish" because he knocked** [*hikish*] **on the gates of mercy and they were opened to him.**

קָרֵי לֵיהּ יְהוּדִי – אַלְמָא מִיהוּדָה קָאָתֵי, וְקָרֵי לֵיהּ יְמִינִי – אַלְמָא מִבִּנְיָמִין קָאָתֵי! אָמַר רַב נַחְמָן: מׇרְדֳּכַי מוּכְתָּר בְּנִימוּסוֹ הָיָה.

The Gemara points out a contradiction: Mordecai **is referred to** as a **"Jew** [*Yehudi*]," **apparently** indicating that **he came from** the tribe of **Judah,** but in the continuation of the verse **he is called "Benjamite"** [*Yemini*], **which indicates that he came from** the tribe of **Benjamin. Rav Naḥman said: Mordecai was crowned with** honorary **names.**[N] *Yehudi* is one such honorary epithet, due to its allusion to the royal tribe of Judah, but it is not referring to Mordecai's tribal affiliation.

LANGUAGE

Commander [*paredashekha*] – **פַּרְדַּשְׁכָּא:** The exact etymology of the word is unclear. An alternative form reflected in some manuscripts is *pardakhsha*, which may point to the Middle Persian parda-kaš, meaning one who draws the curtain.

NOTES

Crowned with honorary names – מוּכְתָּר בְּנִימוּסוֹ: Alternative texts, including those of the early authorities, state that he was crowned with his names like an ornament, as he was adorned with numerous titles. The Vilna Gaon explains that Mordecai was called *Yehudi*, although he originated from the tribe of Benjamin, as the small tribe of Benjamin was part of the larger Judean empire, and they were exiled with the tribe of Judah. Mordecai's leadership over both tribes of the exiled Judean empire earned him the title *Yehudi*.

אָמַר רַבָּה בַּר בַּר חָנָה אָמַר רַבִּי יְהוֹשֻׁעַ בֶּן לֵוִי: אָבִיו מִבִּנְיָמִין וְאִמּוֹ מִיהוּדָה. וְרַבָּנַן אָמְרִי: מִשְׁפָּחוֹת מִתְגָּרוֹת זוֹ בְּזוֹ, מִשְׁפַּחַת יְהוּדָה אוֹמֶרֶת: אֲנָא גָּרֵים דְּמִתְיְלֵיד מָרְדֳּכַי, דְּלָא קְטַלֵיהּ דָּוִד לְשִׁמְעִי בֶּן גֵּרָא, וּמִשְׁפַּחַת בִּנְיָמִין אָמְרָה: מִינַּאי קָאָתֵי.

Rabba bar bar Ḥana said that **Rabbi Yehoshua ben Levi said** an alternative explanation: Mordecai's **father was from** the tribe of **Benjamin, and his mother was from** the tribe of **Judah.** Therefore, he was both a *Yemini*, a Benjamite, and a *Yehudi*, from the tribe of Judah. **And the Rabbis say** that the dual lineage is due to a dispute: **The families competed** with **each other** over which tribe could take credit for Mordecai. **The family of Judah** would **say: I caused the birth of Mordecai,** as only **because David did not kill Shimei, the son of Gera,** when he cursed him (see II Samuel, chapter 16) was it possible for Mordecai to be born later from his descendants. **And the family of Benjamin said** in response: In the end **he came from me,** as he in fact was from Benjamin's tribe.

רָבָא אָמַר: כְּנֶסֶת יִשְׂרָאֵל אָמְרָה לְאִידָּךְ גִּיסָא: רְאוּ מֶה עָשָׂה לִי יְהוּדִי וּמַה שִּׁילֵּם לִי יְמִינִי, מֶה עָשָׂה לִי יְהוּדִי –

Rava said: The Congregation of Israel at the time **said** this **from the opposite perspective,** not as a boast, but as a complaint, remarking: **See what a Judean has done to me and how a Benjamite has repaid me. What a Judean has done to me** is referring to

דְּלָא קְטַלֵיהּ דָּוִד לְשִׁמְעִי, דְּאִתְיְלִיד מִינֵּיהּ מָרְדֳּכַי, דְּמִיקַּנֵּי בֵּיהּ הָמָן. וּמַה שִּׁילֵּם לִי יְמִינִי – דְּלָא קְטַלֵיהּ שָׁאוּל לַאֲגַג, דְּאִתְיְלִיד מִינֵּיהּ הָמָן, דִּמְצַעֵר לְיִשְׂרָאֵל.

the responsibility of Judah, **as David did not kill Shimei,** although he was liable to the death penalty. The grave consequences of this failure included **that Mordecai was born from him,**[N] and it was he **against whom Haman was jealous,** leading Haman to issue a decree against all of the Jewish people. **And how a Benjamite has repaid me** is referring to the fact **that Saul,** who was from the tribe of Benjamin, **did not kill** the Amalekite king **Agag** immediately, **from whom Haman was** later **born, and he caused suffering to the Jewish people.**

רַבִּי יוֹחָנָן אֲמַר: לְעוֹלָם מִבִּנְיָמִין קָאָתֵי, וְאַמַּאי קָרֵי לֵיהּ יְהוּדִי – עַל שׁוּם שֶׁכָּפַר בַּעֲבוֹדָה זָרָה. שֶׁכָּל הַכּוֹפֵר בַּעֲבוֹדָה זָרָה נִקְרָא יְהוּדִי, כְּדִכְתִיב ״אִיתַי גּוּבְרִין יְהוּדָאִין״ וגו׳.

Rabbi Yoḥanan said a different explanation of the verse: **Actually,** Mordecai **came from** the tribe of **Benjamin. Why,** then, **was he referred to as *Yehudi*? On account of** the fact **that he repudiated idol worship, for anyone who repudiates idolatry**[N] **is called *Yehudi*.** It is understood here in the sense of *yiḥudi*, one who declares the oneness of God, **as it is written: "There are certain Jews [*Yehuda'in*]**[N] whom thou hast appointed over the affairs of the province of Babylonia, Shadrach, Meshach, and Abed-Nego; these men, O king, have not regarded you: They serve not your gods, nor worship the golden image which you have set up" (Daniel 3:12). These three individuals were in fact Hananiah, Mishael, and Azariah, who were not all from the tribe of Judah but are referred to as *Yehuda'in* because they repudiated idol worship.

NOTES

That Mordecai was born from him – דְּאִתְיְלִיד מִינֵּיהּ מָרְדֳּכַי: The *Rosh Yosef* explains that both the positive and the negative associations concerning Mordecai's lineage were indeed correct. Initially, as the Jewish people were in danger partly due to the actions of Mordecai, they blamed him for their troubles and fought over which tribe should be blamed for Mordecai. After the salvation, the families competed with each other as to who could be credited with Mordecai.

For anyone who repudiates idolatry – שֶׁכָּל הַכּוֹפֵר בַּעֲבוֹדָה זָרָה: This interpretation is derived from the resemblance of the word *Yehudi*, Jew, with *yiḥudi*, one who has complete faith in the unity and singularity of God. For this reason, the midrash calls one who repudiates idolatry a *Yehudi*. The Maharsha adds that the name Yehuda, Judah, contains all the letters of God's explicit, ineffable name, and it is therefore used as a term indicating one's belief in God. The Meiri states further that one who repudiates idolatry acts as a complete Jew and is thereby referred to as a *Yehudi*, based on the established principle that if one repudiates idolatry it is considered as if he accepted the entire Torah.

There are certain Jews – גּוּבְרִין יְהוּדָאִין: According to the text recorded in *Ein Ya'akov*, Hananiah, Mishael, and Azarya were not from the tribe of Judah, as this is a matter of dispute in the Talmud (see *Tosafot*). The Maharsha writes that according to all opinions, the phrase "there are certain Jews" stated here is not meant to associate them with the tribe of Judah, but rather to indicate their commitment to the Jewish faith.

רַבִּי שִׁמְעוֹן בֶּן פָּזִי כִּי הֲוָה פְּתַח בְּדִבְרֵי הַיָּמִים אֲמַר הָכִי: כׇּל דְּבָרֶיךָ אֶחָד הֵם, וַאֲנוּ יוֹדְעִין לְדוֹרְשָׁן. ״וְאִשְׁתּוֹ הַיְהוּדִיָּה יָלְדָה אֶת יֶרֶד אֲבִי גְדוֹר וְאֶת חֶבֶר אֲבִי שׂוֹכוֹ וְאֶת יְקוּתִיאֵל אֲבִי זָנוֹחַ וְאֵלֶּה בְּנֵי בִּתְיָה בַת פַּרְעֹה אֲשֶׁר לָקַח מָרֶד״.

§ Incidental to the exposition of the word *Yehudi* as one who repudiates idolatry, the Gemara relates that **when Rabbi Shimon ben Pazi introduced** his exposition of **the book of Chronicles, he** addressed the book of Chronicles and **said as follows: All of your words are one,**[N] **and we know how to expound them.** This introduction made reference to the fact that the book of Chronicles cannot always be interpreted literally but requires exposition, as the same individual might be called by various different names, as in the following verse: **"And his wife *HaYehudiyya* bore Jered the father of Gedor, and Heber the father of Soco, and Jekuthiel the father of Zanoah. And these are the sons of Bithiah the daughter of Pharaoh, whom Mered took"** (1 Chronicles 4:18).

אַמַּאי קָרֵי לָהּ ״יְהוּדִיָּה״ – עַל שׁוּם שֶׁכָּפְרָה בַּעֲבוֹדָה זָרָה, דִּכְתִיב ״וַתֵּרֶד בַּת פַּרְעֹה לִרְחוֹץ עַל הַיְאוֹר״, וְאָמַר רַבִּי יוֹחָנָן: שֶׁיָּרְדָה לִרְחוֹץ מִגִּילּוּלֵי בֵּית אָבִיהָ.

Why is she, who we are told at the end of the verse was Pharaoh's daughter Bithiah, **referred to as *Yehudiyya*? Because she repudiated idol worship, as it is written: "And the daughter of Pharaoh came down to wash herself in the river"** (Exodus 2:5), **and Rabbi Yoḥanan said: She went down to wash** and purify **herself from the idols of her father's house.**[N]

״יָלְדָה״? וְהָא רַבּוּיֵי רַבִּיתֵיהּ! לוֹמַר לְךָ שֶׁכׇּל הַמְגַדֵּל יָתוֹם וִיתוֹמָה בְּתוֹךְ בֵּיתוֹ מַעֲלֶה עָלָיו הַכָּתוּב כְּאִילּוּ יְלָדוֹ.

The Gemara understands that all the names referred to in the verse as children of Pharaoh's daughter refer to Moses, as it will soon explain. The Gemara asks: Pharaoh's daughter **bore** Moses? **But didn't she** merely **raise him?** Rather, **it is telling you that** with regard to **anyone who raises an orphan boy or girl in his house, the verse ascribes him credit as if he gave birth to him.**

״יֶרֶד״ – זֶה מֹשֶׁה, וְלָמָּה נִקְרָא שְׁמוֹ יֶרֶד – שֶׁיָּרַד לָהֶם לְיִשְׂרָאֵל מָן בְּיָמָיו. ״גְּדוֹר״ – שֶׁגָּדַר פִּרְצוֹתֵיהֶן שֶׁל יִשְׂרָאֵל, ״חֶבֶר״ – שֶׁחִיבֵּר אֶת יִשְׂרָאֵל לַאֲבִיהֶן שֶׁבַּשָּׁמַיִם. ״סוֹכוֹ״ – שֶׁנַּעֲשָׂה לָהֶם לְיִשְׂרָאֵל כְּסוּכָּה. ״יְקוּתִיאֵל״ – שֶׁקִּוּוּ יִשְׂרָאֵל לָאֵל בְּיָמָיו. ״זָנוֹחַ״ – שֶׁהִזְנִיחַ עֲוֹנוֹתֵיהֶן שֶׁל יִשְׂרָאֵל.

The Gemara explains how all the names in fact are referring to Moses: **"Jered"; this is Moses, and why was he called Jered? Because manna came down [*yarad*] for the Jewish people in his days.** He was also called **"Gedor" because he fenced in [*gadar*] the breaches of the Jewish people.** He was called **"Heber" because he connected [*ḥibber*] the Jewish people to their Father in Heaven.** He was called **"Soco" because he was for the Jewish people like a shelter [*sukka*]** and shield. He was called **"Jekuthiel" because the Jewish people trusted in God [*kivu laEl*] in his days.** Lastly, he was called **"Zanoah" because he caused the iniquities of the Jewish people to be disregarded [*hizniaḥ*].**

״אֲבִי אֲבִי אֲבִי״ – אָב בְּתוֹרָה, אָב בְּחָכְמָה, אָב בִּנְבִיאוּת.

The Gemara notes that the words "father of" appear three times in that same verse: "And his wife Hajehudijah bore Jered the **father of** Gedor, and Heber the **father of** Soco, and Jekuthiel the **father of** Zanoah." This teaches that Moses was a father to all of the Jewish people in three respects: **A father in Torah, a father in wisdom,** and **a father in prophecy.**

״וְאֵלֶּה בְּנֵי בִּתְיָה...אֲשֶׁר לָקַח מֶרֶד״ וְכִי מֶרֶד שְׁמוֹ? וַהֲלֹא כָּלֵב שְׁמוֹ! אָמַר הַקָּדוֹשׁ בָּרוּךְ הוּא: יָבֹא כָּלֵב שֶׁמָּרַד בַּעֲצַת מְרַגְּלִים, וְיִשָּׂא אֶת בַּת פַּרְעֹה שֶׁמָּרְדָה בְּגִלּוּלֵי בֵּית אָבִיהָ.

The aforementioned verse stated: **"And these are the sons of Bithiah** the daughter of Pharaoh, **whom Mered took."** The Gemara asks: **Was** Bithiah's husband's **name Mered? Wasn't his name Caleb?** Rather, the verse alludes to the reason that Caleb married Bithiah. **The Holy One, Blessed be He, said: Let Caleb, who rebelled [*marad*] against the advice of the spies, come**[N] **and marry the daughter of Pharaoh, who rebelled against the idols of her father's home.**

״אֲשֶׁר הָגְלָה מִירוּשָׁלַיִם״. אָמַר רָבָא: שֶׁגָּלָה מֵעַצְמוֹ.

§ The Gemara resumes its explanation of the book of Esther. The verse states with regard to Mordecai: **"Who had been exiled from Jerusalem"** (Esther 2:6). **Rava said:** This language indicates **that he went into exile on his own,**[N] not because he was forced to leave Jerusalem. He knew that he would be needed by those in exile, and therefore he consciously left Jerusalem to attend to the needs of his people.

״וַיְהִי אוֹמֵן אֶת הֲדַסָּה״ קָרֵי לָהּ הֲדַסָּה, וְקָרֵי לָהּ אֶסְתֵּר. תַּנְיָא, רַבִּי מֵאִיר אוֹמֵר: אֶסְתֵּר שְׁמָהּ, וְלָמָּה נִקְרָא שְׁמָהּ הֲדַסָּה – עַל שֵׁם הַצַּדִּיקִים שֶׁנִּקְרָאוּ הֲדַסִּים, וְכֵן הוּא אוֹמֵר ״וְהוּא עוֹמֵד בֵּין הַהֲדַסִּים״.

The verse states: **"And he had brought up Hadassah,** that is, Esther" (Esther 2:7). **She is referred to as "Hadassah" and she is referred to as "Esther."** What was her real name? **It is taught** in a *baraita* that the Sages differed in their opinion as to which was in fact her name and which one was a description: **Rabbi Meir says: Esther was her** real **name. Why then was she called Hadassah? On account of the righteous, who are called myrtles [*hadassim*], and so it states: "And he stood among the myrtles [*hahadassim*]"** (Zechariah 1:8).

NOTES

All of your words are one – כׇּל דְּבָרֶיךָ אֶחָד: This is written here primarily to indicate the previously stated idea that the term *Yehudi* is assigned to one who repudiates idolatry. However, there is a secondary indication as well, related to the exegesis of the names, as stated earlier with regard to the exegesis of "the son of Jair, the son of Shimei." In general, as the book of Chronicles provides a large amount of information, specifically with regard to what would seem to be insignificant facts about genealogy, coupled with numerous divergences from the other books of the Bible, the Sages interpreted a large amount of the verses symbolically or euphemistically. This idea goes so far with some commentaries that a number of midrashic works seem to maintain that with regard to the book of Chronicles, homiletic interpretation may take precedence over its simple meaning (see Rabbi Tzvi Hirsch Chajes).

To wash herself from the idols of her father's house – לִרְחוֹץ מִגִּילּוּלֵי בֵּית אָבִיהָ: The *Turei Even* explains that this was not immersion for the sake of conversion; rather, her abandoning her father's idols is symbolically called immersion, for she purified herself from the impurity of idol worship.

Let Caleb who rebelled…come – יָבֹא כָּלֵב שֶׁמָּרַד: The *ge'onim* understood that this midrash interprets the names of Caleb's children as well, for the Caleb mentioned in the book of Chronicles is Caleb, the son of Hezron, while the Caleb who was one of the spies was Caleb, the son of Jephunneh.

That he went into exile on his own – שֶׁגָּלָה מֵעַצְמוֹ: The Maharsha explains that the repetitious language of the verse: "Who had been exiled…with the exiles that had been exiled" (Esther 2:6) indicates that he went into exile alone and later joined up with the other exiles (see *Tosafot*).

רַבִּי יְהוּדָה אוֹמֵר: הֲדַסָּה שְׁמָהּ, וְלָמָּה נִקְרֵאת שְׁמָהּ אֶסְתֵּר – עַל שֵׁם שֶׁהָיְתָה מַסְתֶּרֶת דְּבָרֶיהָ, שֶׁנֶּאֱמַר ״אֵין אֶסְתֵּר מַגֶּדֶת אֶת עַמָּהּ״ וגו׳.

Rabbi Yehuda differs and **says: Hadassah was her** real **name. Why then was she called Esther? Because she concealed** [*masteret*] **the truth** about herself, **as it is stated: "Esther had not yet made known** her kindred nor **her people"** (Esther 2:20).

רַבִּי נְחֶמְיָה אוֹמֵר: הֲדַסָּה שְׁמָהּ, וְלָמָּה נִקְרֵאת אֶסְתֵּר – שֶׁהָיוּ אוּמּוֹת הָעוֹלָם קוֹרִין אוֹתָהּ עַל שׁוּם אִסְתַּהַר. בֶּן עַזַּאי אוֹמֵר: אֶסְתֵּר לֹא אֲרוּכָּה וְלֹא קְצָרָה הָיְתָה אֶלָּא בֵּינוֹנִית, כַּהֲדַסָּה. רַבִּי יְהוֹשֻׁעַ בֶּן קָרְחָה אָמַר: אֶסְתֵּר יְרַקְרוֹקֶת הָיְתָה, וְחוּט שֶׁל חֶסֶד מָשׁוּךְ עָלֶיהָ.

Rabbi Neḥemya concurs and **says: Hadassah was her** real **name. Why then was she called Esther?** This was her non-Hebrew name, **for** owing to her beauty **the nations of the world called her after Istahar,**[L] Venus. **Ben Azzai says: Esther was neither tall nor short, but of average size like a myrtle** tree, and therefore she was called Hadassah, the Hebrew name resembling that myrtle tree. **Rabbi Yehoshua ben Korḥa said: Esther** was called Hadassah because she **was greenish,** having a pale complexion like a myrtle, but **a cord of** Divine **grace was strung around her,** endowing her with a beautiful appearance.

״כִּי אֵין לָהּ אָב וָאֵם״ ״וּבְמוֹת אָבִיהָ וְאִמָּהּ״, לָמָּה לִי? אָמַר רַב אַחָא: עִיבְּרַתָּה – מֵת אָבִיהָ, יְלָדַתָּה – מֵתָה אִמָּהּ.

The verse initially states with regard to Esther: **"For she had neither father nor mother"** (Esther 2:7). **Why do I need** to be told in the continuation of the verse: **"And when her father and mother were dead,** Mordecai took her for his own daughter"? **Rav Aḥa said:** This repetition indicates that **when** her mother **became pregnant** with her, **her father died,** and **when she gave birth** to her, **her mother died,** so that she did not have a mother or a father for even a single day.

״וּבְמוֹת אָבִיהָ וְאִמָּהּ לְקָחָהּ מָרְדֳּכַי לוֹ לְבַת״ תָּנָא מִשּׁוּם רַבִּי מֵאִיר: אַל תִּקְרֵי ״לְבַת״ אֶלָּא לְבַיִת, וְכֵן הוּא אוֹמֵר ״וְלָרָשׁ אֵין כֹּל כִּי אִם כִּבְשָׂה אַחַת קְטַנָּה אֲשֶׁר קָנָה וַיְחַיֶּהָ וַתִּגְדַּל עִמּוֹ וְעִם בָּנָיו יַחְדָּו מִפִּתּוֹ תֹאכַל וּמִכּוֹסוֹ תִשְׁתֶּה וּבְחֵיקוֹ תִשְׁכָּב וַתְּהִי לוֹ כְּבַת״ מִשּׁוּם דִּבְחֵיקוֹ תִּשְׁכַּב הֲוַות לֵיהּ (לְבַת) אֶלָּא (לְבַיִת) – הָכִי נַמִי לְבַיִת.

The verse states: **"And when her father and mother were dead, Mordecai took her for his own daughter"** (Esther 2:7). A *tanna* **taught** a *baraita* **in the name of Rabbi Meir: Do not read** the verse literally as **for a daughter** [*bat*], but **rather** read it as **for a home** [*bayit*].[N] This indicates that Mordecai took Esther to be his wife. **And so it states: "But the poor man had nothing, except one little ewe lamb, which he had bought and reared: And it grew up together with him, and with his children; it did eat of his bread, and drank of his own cup, and lay in his bosom, and was like a daughter** [*kevat*] **to him"** (II Samuel 12:3). The Gemara questions: **Because it lay in his bosom, it "was like a daughter to him"? Rather,** the parable in II Samuel referenced the illicit taking of another's wife, and the phrase should be read: **Like a home** [*bayit*] to him, i.e., a wife. **So too, here,** Mordecai took her **for a home,** i.e., a wife.

״וְאֵת שֶׁבַע הַנְּעָרוֹת״ וגו׳. אָמַר רָבָא: שֶׁהָיְתָה מוֹנָה בָּהֶן יְמֵי שַׁבָּת. ״וַיְשַׁנֶּהָ וְאֶת נַעֲרוֹתֶיהָ״ וגו׳. אָמַר רַב: שֶׁהֶאֱכִילָהּ מַאֲכָל יְהוּדִי.

The verse states: **"And the seven maids** chosen to be given her out of the king's house" (Esther 2:9). **Rava said: She would** have a separate maid attend her each day, and she would **count the days of the week by them,** so she was always aware when Shabbat was. The verse continues: **"And he advanced her and her maids** to the best place in the house of the women." **Rav said:** The advancement in the verse signals **that he fed her food of Jews,** i.e., kosher food.

וּשְׁמוּאֵל אָמַר: שֶׁהֶאֱכִילָהּ קָדְלֵי דַחֲזִירֵי.

And Shmuel said an alternative understanding: The advancement was a well-intentioned act in **that he fed her pig hinds,**[N] thinking she would view it as a delicacy, although in fact they were not kosher.

וְרַבִּי יוֹחָנָן אָמַר: זֵרְעוֹנִים, וְכֵן הוּא אוֹמֵר ״וַיְהִי הַמֶּלְצַר נוֹשֵׂא אֶת פַּת בָּגָם...וְנוֹתֵן לָהֶם זֵרְעוֹנִים״.

And Rabbi Yoḥanan said a third understanding: He gave her **vegetables,** which did not pose a problem with regard to the kosher laws. **And so it states** with regard to the kindness done for Daniel and his associates: **"So the steward took away their food** and the wine that they should drink; **and gave them vegetables"** (Daniel 1:16).

״שִׁשָּׁה חֳדָשִׁים בְּשֶׁמֶן הַמּוֹר״, מַאי שֶׁמֶן הַמּוֹר? רַבִּי חִיָּיא בַּר אַבָּא אָמַר: סְטַכְּת, רַב הוּנָא אָמַר: שֶׁמֶן זַיִת שֶׁלֹּא הֵבִיא שְׁלִישׁ. תַּנְיָא, רַבִּי יְהוּדָה אוֹמֵר: אַנְפַּקִינוֹן – שֶׁמֶן זַיִת שֶׁלֹּא הֵבִיא שְׁלִישׁ, וְלָמָּה סָכִין אוֹתוֹ – שֶׁמַּשִּׁיר אֶת הַשֵּׂיעָר וּמְעַדֵּן אֶת הַבָּשָׂר.

The verse states: **"Six months with oil of myrrh"** (Esther 2:12). The Gemara asks: **What is "oil of myrrh"? Rabbi Ḥiyya bar Abba said:** It is the aromatic oil called ***setakt***.[L] **Rav Huna said:** It is a cosmetic **oil** derived **from olives that have not** yet **reached one-third** of their growth. **It is** similarly **taught** in a *baraita*: **Rabbi Yehuda says:** ***Anpakinon***[L] **is the oil of olves that have not reached one-third** of their growth. **And why is it smeared** on the body? Because **it removes the hair and softens the skin.**

LANGUAGE

Istahar – אִסְתַּהַר: Possibly from the Middle Persian word astar, meaning star. Others explain that Istahar is an Aramaic word meaning moon.

***Setakt* – סְטַכְּת:** From the Greek στακτή, *staktē*, referring to a fragrant oil that is derived from the resin of the myrrh tree, such as the *Commiphora myrrha*.

Common myrrh trees

Resin from a myrrh tree

***Anpakinon* – אַנְפַּקִינוֹן:** From the Greek ὀμφάκινον, *omphakinon*. One meanings of this word is oil from unripe olives.

NOTES

Do not read: For a daughter, but rather: For a home – אַל תִּקְרֵי לְבַת אֶלָּא לְבַיִת: The *Ginzei HaMelekh* explains that this is derived from the words "took her," which indicate that Mordecai took Esther for himself. The *Nezer HaKodesh* and Rabbi Yoshiya Pinto explain that it is derived from the fact that the term took usually indicates taking in marriage. The *Manot HaLevi* explains at length that Esther was not yet Mordecai's actual wife. Mordecai intended to marry her, though, and took her in for her to later become his wife.

Pig [*daḥazirei*] hinds – קָדְלֵי דַחֲזִירֵי: The *Arukh* has a slightly different text, *deḥizri*, meaning heads of radishes and lettuce.

LANGUAGE

Taxes [*karga*] – כַּרְגָּא: From the Middle Persian harg, meaning duty or tribute. In the Talmud it normally refers to a poll tax.

Gifts [*pardishenei*] – פַּרְדִּישְׁנֵי: Apparently from the Middle Iranian pāδ-dāšn. It literally means a gift that is given in exchange for a gift, but it can refer to any type of gift.

NOTES

He went and took advice from Mordecai – אָזֵיל שְׁקַל עֵצָה מִמָּרְדְּכַי: This is derived from the verse "And when the virgins were gathered together the second time and Mordecai sat in the king's gate" (Esther 2:19), indicating that the gathering was done due to Mordecai's advice, as he sat in the king's gate as one of the king's advisors (*Re'aḥ Duda'im*).

"בָּעֶרֶב הִיא בָאָה וּבַבֹּקֶר הִיא שָׁבָה". אָמַר רַבִּי יוֹחָנָן: מִגְּנוּתוֹ שֶׁל אוֹתוֹ רָשָׁע לָמַדְנוּ שִׁבְחוֹ, שֶׁלֹּא הָיָה מְשַׁמֵּשׁ מִטָּתוֹ בַּיּוֹם.

The verse states: **"In the evening she went, and in the morning she returned"** (Esther 2:14). **Rabbi Yoḥanan said: From the** implicit **criticism of that wicked man,** Ahasuerus, who cohabited with many women, **we have** incidentally **learned his praise** as well, **that he would not engage in sexual relations during the day,** but in a more modest fashion at night.

"וַתְּהִי אֶסְתֵּר נֹשֵׂאת חֵן" אָמַר רַבִּי אֶלְעָזָר: מְלַמֵּד שֶׁלְּכָל אֶחָד וְאֶחָד נִדְמְתָה לוֹ כְּאוּמָּתוֹ. "וַתִּלָּקַח אֶסְתֵּר אֶל הַמֶּלֶךְ אֲחַשְׁוֵרוֹשׁ אֶל בֵּית מַלְכוּתוֹ בַּחֹדֶשׁ הָעֲשִׂירִי הוּא חֹדֶשׁ טֵבֵת" – יֶרַח שֶׁנֶּהֱנֶה גּוּף מִן הַגּוּף.

The verse states: **"And Esther obtained favor** in the sight of all those who looked upon her" (Esther 2:15). **Rabbi Elazar said: This teaches that she appeared to each and every one as if** she were a member of **his own nation,** and therefore she obtained favor in the eyes of all. The next verse states: **"So Esther was taken to King Ahasuerus into his royal house in the tenth month, which is the month Tevet"** (Esther 2:16). It was by act of divine providence that Esther was taken to Ahasuerus in a cold winter **month, in which the body takes pleasure in** the warmth of **another body,** and therefore she found favor in his eyes.

"וַיֶּאֱהַב הַמֶּלֶךְ אֶת אֶסְתֵּר מִכָּל הַנָּשִׁים וַתִּשָּׂא חֵן וָחֶסֶד לְפָנָיו מִכָּל הַבְּתוּלוֹת". אָמַר רַב: בִּיקֵּשׁ לִטְעוֹם טַעַם בְּתוּלָה – טָעַם, טַעַם בְּעוּלָה – טָעַם.

The verse states: **"And the king loved Esther more than all the women, and she obtained grace and favor in his sight more than all the virgins"** (Esther 2:17). **Rav said:** This double language indicates that if **he wanted to taste** in her **the taste of a virgin** during intercourse, **he tasted** it, and if he wanted to experience **the taste of a non-virgin, he tasted** it, and therefore he loved her more than all the other women.

"וַיַּעַשׂ הַמֶּלֶךְ מִשְׁתֶּה גָדוֹל" עֲבַד מִשְׁתְּיָא – וְלָא גַּלְיָא לֵיהּ, דָּלֵי כַּרְגָּא – וְלָא גַּלְיָא לֵיהּ, שְׁדַר פַּרְדִּישְׁנֵי – וְלָא גַּלְיָא לֵיהּ,

The verse states: **"Then the king made a great feast** for all his princes and his servants, even Esther's feast" (Esther 2:18). The Gemara explains that this was part of an attempt to have Esther reveal her true identity. **He made** a great **feast** in her honor, **but she did not reveal** her identity **to him. He lowered the taxes** [***karga***][L] in her name, **but** still **she did not reveal** it **to him. He sent gifts** [***pardishenei***][L] to the ministers in her name, **but** even so **she did not reveal** it **to him.**

"וּבְהִקָּבֵץ בְּתוּלוֹת שֵׁנִית" וגו'. אָזֵיל שְׁקַל עֵצָה מִמָּרְדְּכַי. אֲמַר: אֵין אִשָּׁה מִתְקַנְּאָה אֶלָּא בְּיֶרֶךְ חֲבֵירְתָּהּ – וַאֲפִילּוּ הָכִי לָא גַּלְיָא לֵיהּ, דִּכְתִיב "אֵין אֶסְתֵּר מַגֶּדֶת מוֹלַדְתָּהּ" וגו'.

The verse states: **"And when the virgins were gathered together the second time** and Mordecai sat in the king's gate" (Esther 2:19). The Gemara explains: The reason Ahasuerus gathered the women together was that **he went** and **took advice from Mordecai**[N] as to what he should do to get Esther to reveal her identity. Mordecai **said** to him: As a rule, **a woman is jealous only of the thigh of another** woman. Therefore, you should take for yourself additional women. **But even so she did not reveal** her origins **to him, as it is written: "Esther had not yet made known her kindred** nor her people" (Esther 2:20).

אָמַר רַבִּי אֶלְעָזָר: מַאי דִּכְתִיב

§ **Rabbi Elazar said: What is** the meaning of that **which is written:**

Perek **I**
Daf **13** Amud **b**

NOTES

He withdraws not His eyes from the righteous – לֹא יִגְרַע מִצַּדִּיק עֵינָיו: Some explain that this means that the Holy One, Blessed be He, watches over not only the righteous but also their descendants (see *Sefat Emet*).

Was he her father's brother – וְכִי אֲחִי אָבִיהָ הוּא: The *Turei Even* explains that although the term brother is used many times in the Bible to reflect a relationship that isn't necessarily one of a blood brother, the fact that the verse states: "That he was her father's brother, and that he was Rebecca's son" indicates that the term "brother" must be teaching something else here. As the verse explains the exact relationship, i.e., that he is Rebecca's son, the mention of "her father's brother" must be an indication that Jacob is similar to him.

"לֹא יִגְרַע מִצַּדִּיק עֵינָיו" בִּשְׂכַר צְנִיעוּת שֶׁהָיְתָה בָּהּ בְּרָחֵל – זָכְתָה וְיָצָא מִמֶּנָּה שָׁאוּל, וּבִשְׂכַר צְנִיעוּת שֶׁהָיָה בּוֹ בְּשָׁאוּל – זָכָה וְיָצְאת מִמֶּנּוּ אֶסְתֵּר.

"He withdraws not His eyes from the righteous;[N] but with kings upon the throne He establishes them forever, and they are exalted" (Job 36:7)? This teaches that **in reward for the modesty shown by Rachel she merited that Saul,** who was also modest, **should descend from her, and in reward for the modesty shown by Saul, he merited that Esther should descend from him.**

וּמַאי צְנִיעוּת הָיְתָה בָּהּ בְּרָחֵל – דִּכְתִיב "וַיַּגֵּד יַעֲקֹב לְרָחֵל כִּי אֲחִי אָבִיהָ הוּא". וְכִי אֲחִי אָבִיהָ הוּא? וַהֲלֹא בֶּן אֲחוֹת אָבִיהָ הוּא!

The Gemara explains: **What was the modesty shown by Rachel?** It is **as it is written: "And Jacob told Rachel that he was her father's brother,** and that he was Rebecca's son" (Genesis 29:12). It may be asked: **Was he,** Jacob, in fact **her father's brother?**[N] **But wasn't he the son of her father's sister?**

אֶלָּא אֲמַר לָהּ: מִינַּסְבָא לִי? אֲמַרָה לֵיהּ: אִין. מִיהוּ, אַבָּא רַמָּאָה הוּא, וְלָא יָכְלַתְּ לֵיהּ. אֲמַר לָהּ אָחִיו אֲנָא בְּרַמָּאוּת. אֲמַרָה לֵיהּ: וּמִי שָׁרֵי לְצַדִּיקֵי לְסַגּוּיֵי בְּרַמָּיוּתָא? אֲמַר לָהּ: אִין, ״עִם נָבָר תִּתָּבָר וְעִם עִקֵּשׁ תִּתַּפָּל״.

Rather, it must be understood that when Jacob met Rachel, **he said to her: Will you marry me? She said to him: Yes, but my father,** Laban, **is a swindler, and you will not be able to** outwit **him.** Jacob alleviated her fears, as **he said to her** that he is her father's brother, referring not to their familial affiliation but rather to his ability to deal with her father on his level, as if to say: **I am his brother in deception. She said to him: But is it** really **permitted for the righteous to be involved in deception? He said to her: Yes,** it is permitted when dealing with deceptive individuals, as the verse states: **"With the pure you will show yourself pure, and with the perverse you will show yourself subtle"** (II Samuel 22:27), indicating that one should deal with others in the manner appropriate for their personality.

אֲמַר לָהּ: וּמַאי רַמָּיוּתָא? אֲמַרָה לֵיהּ: אִית לִי אַחְתָּא דְּקַשִּׁישָׁא מִינַּאי, וְלָא מִנְסֵיב לִי מִקַּמַּהּ. מָסַר לָהּ סִימָנִים.

Jacob then **said to her: What is the deception** that he will plan to carry out and I should be prepared for? Rachel **said to him: I have a sister who is older than I, and he will not marry me off before her,** and will try to give you her in my place. So Jacob **gave her** certain **distinguishing signs** that she should use to indicate to him that she was actually Rachel and not her sister.

כִּי מְטָא לֵילְיָא, אֲמַרָה: הָשְׁתָּא מִיכַּסְפָא אַחְתַּאי, מְסַרְתִּינְהוּ נִיהֲלָהּ. וְהַיְינוּ דִּכְתִיב ״וַיְהִי בַבֹּקֶר וְהִנֵּה הִיא לֵאָה״, מִכְּלָל דְּעַד הָשְׁתָּא לָאו לֵאָה הִיא?! אֶלָּא: מִתּוֹךְ סִימָנִין שֶׁמָּסְרָה רָחֵל לְלֵאָה לָא הֲוָה יָדַע עַד הָשְׁתָּא. לְפִיכָךְ זָכְתָה וְיָצָא מִמֶּנָּה שָׁאוּל.

When the wedding **night arrived,** and Laban planned to switch the sisters, Rachel **said** to herself: **Now my sister will be embarassed,**[N] for Jacob will ask her for the signs and she will not know them. So **she gave them to her. And this is as it is written: "And it came to pass, that in the morning, behold, it was Leah"** (Genesis 29:25). Does this imply **by inference that until now she was not Leah? Rather, due to the distinguishing signs that Rachel had given to Leah, he did not know until now,** when it was light outside, that she was Leah. **Therefore,** Rachel **merited that Saul should descend from her,** due to her act of modesty in not revealing to Jacob that she had shown the signs to Leah.

וּמַה צְנִיעוּת הָיְתָה בְּשָׁאוּל – דִּכְתִיב ״וְאֶת דְּבַר הַמְּלוּכָה לֹא הִגִּיד לוֹ אֲשֶׁר אָמַר שְׁמוּאֵל״ – זָכָה וְיָצְאָת מִמֶּנּוּ אֶסְתֵּר. וְאָמַר רַבִּי אֶלְעָזָר: כְּשֶׁהַקָּדוֹשׁ בָּרוּךְ הוּא פּוֹסֵק גְּדוּלָּה לְאָדָם – פּוֹסֵק לְבָנָיו וְלִבְנֵי בָנָיו עַד סוֹף כָּל הַדּוֹרוֹת, שֶׁנֶּאֱמַר ״וַיּוֹשִׁיבֵם לָנֶצַח וַיִּגְבָּהוּ״ (וגו׳) וְאִם הִגִּיס דַּעְתּוֹ – הַקָּדוֹשׁ בָּרוּךְ הוּא מַשְׁפִּילוֹ, שֶׁנֶּאֱמַר ״וְאִם אֲסוּרִים בַּזִּקִּים״ וגו׳.

And what was the modesty shown by Saul? As it is written: "But of the matter of the kingdom, of which Samuel spoke, he did not tell him" (I Samuel 10:16). Saul expressed his modesty by not revealing Samuel's promise that he would be king, and thereby **merited that Esther would descend from him.** Similarly, **Rabbi Elazar said: When the Holy One, Blessed be He, assigns greatness to a person, He assigns it to his sons and to his son's sons for all generations, as it is stated:** "He withdraws not his eyes from the righteous; but with kings upon the throne **He establishes them forever, and they are exalted"** (Job 36:7). **And if he becomes arrogant** due to this, **the Holy One, Blessed be He, lowers him** in order to humble him, **as it is stated** in the next verse: **"And if they are bound in chains,** and are held in cords of affliction, then He declares unto them their work, and their transgressions, that they have behaved proudly" (Job 36:8–9).

״וְאֶת מַאֲמַר מָרְדֳּכַי אֶסְתֵּר עוֹשָׂה״. אָמַר רַבִּי יִרְמְיָה: שֶׁהָיְתָה מַרְאָה דַּם נִדָּה לַחֲכָמִים. ״כַּאֲשֶׁר הָיְתָה בְאָמְנָה אִתּוֹ״. אָמַר רַבָּה בַּר לִימָא (מִשְּׁמֵיהּ דְּרַב) שֶׁהָיְתָה עוֹמֶדֶת מֵחֵיקוֹ שֶׁל אֲחַשְׁוֵרוֹשׁ וְטוֹבֶלֶת וְיוֹשֶׁבֶת בְּחֵיקוֹ שֶׁל מָרְדֳּכַי.

§ The Gemara returns to its exposition of the Megilla. The verse states: **"For Esther adhered to the words of Mordecai,**[N] as she did when she was brought up with him" (Esther 2:20). **Rabbi Yirmeya said:** This teaches **that she would show** discharges of her **menstrual blood to the Sages** to inquire whether she was pure or impure. The verse continues: **"As she did when she was brought up with him"** (Esther 2:20). **Rabba bar Lima said in the name of Rav:** This means **that she** maintained a relationship with Mordecai, as she **would arise from the lap of Ahasuerus, immerse herself** in a ritual bath, **and sit in the lap of Mordecai.**

״בַּיָּמִים הָהֵם וּמָרְדֳּכַי יוֹשֵׁב בְּשַׁעַר הַמֶּלֶךְ קָצַף בִּגְתָן וָתֶרֶשׁ״ אָמַר רַבִּי חִיָּיא בַּר אַבָּא אָמַר רַבִּי יוֹחָנָן: הִקְצִיף הַקָּדוֹשׁ בָּרוּךְ הוּא אָדוֹן עַל עֲבָדָיו לַעֲשׂוֹת רְצוֹן צַדִּיק, וּמַנּוּ – יוֹסֵף, שֶׁנֶּאֱמַר ״וְשָׁם אִתָּנוּ נַעַר עִבְרִי״ וגו׳.

The Megilla continues: **"In those days, while Mordecai sat in the king's gate,** two of the king's chamberlains, **Bigthan and Teresh,** of those that guarded the doors, **became angry,** and sought to lay hands on the king Ahasuerus" (Esther 2:21). **Rabbi Ḥiyya bar Abba said** that **Rabbi Yoḥanan said: The Holy One, Blessed be He, caused a master to become angry with his servants** in order **to fulfill the will of a righteous man. And who is this?** It is **Joseph, as it is stated** in the chief butler's account of how Pharaoh had become angry with him and with the chief baker and sent them to jail: **"And there was with us there a young man, a Hebrew"** (Genesis 41:12).

NOTES

Now my sister will be embarrassed – הָשְׁתָּא מִיכַּסְפָא אַחְתַּאי: Many wonder where the modesty is in Rachel's actions, as it seemed that she gave Leah the signs out of a desire to prevent her sister from being embarrassed. One of the many explanations is that her modesty was expressed in her not revealing to her father that Jacob had secretly shown her signs to prevent the switch. Had she done so, Laban may not have tried to have Leah take her place (*Iyyun Ya'akov*).

For Esther adhered to the words of Mordecai – וְאֶת מַאֲמַר מָרְדֳּכַי אֶסְתֵּר עוֹשָׂה: Due to the fact that the verse states: "The words of Mordecai," rather than: The commands of Mordecai, it is understood that she followed the *halakhot* that Mordecai taught in his public lectures with regard to marriage, as well as other *halakhot* (Rabbi Yoshiya Pinto; *Iyyun Ya'akov*; see also *Targum*).

עֲבָדִים עַל אֲדוֹנֵיהֶן לַעֲשׂוֹת נֵס לַצַּדִּיק, וּמַנּוּ – מָרְדֳּכַי, דִּכְתִיב ״וַיִּוָּדַע הַדָּבָר לְמָרְדֳּכַי״ וגו׳.

Similarly, the Holy One, Blessed be He, also caused **servants** to become angry **with their master in order to perform a miracle for** another **righteous man. And who is he?** It is **Mordecai, as** with regard to the plot to kill the king **it is written: "And the matter became known to Mordecai"** (Esther 2:22).

אָמַר רַבִּי יוֹחָנָן: בִּגְתָן וָתֶרֶשׁ שְׁנֵי טַרְסִיִּים הָווּ, וְהָיוּ מְסַפְּרִין בִּלְשׁוֹן טוּרְסִי, וְאוֹמְרִים מִיּוֹם שֶׁבָּאת זוֹ לֹא רָאִינוּ שֵׁינָה בְּעֵינֵינוּ, בֹּא וְנַטִּיל אֶרֶס בַּסֵּפֶל כְּדֵי שֶׁיָּמוּת. וְהֵן לֹא הָיוּ יוֹדְעִין כִּי מָרְדֳּכַי מִיּוֹשְׁבֵי לִשְׁכַּת הַגָּזִית הָיָה וְהָיָה יוֹדֵעַ בְּשִׁבְעִים לָשׁוֹן.

The Gemara explains how the matter became known to him. **Rabbi Yoḥanan said: Bigthan and Teresh were two Tarsians, and they would talk** with one another in the **Tarsian language.**[B] **They said: From the day that** Esther arrived **we have not slept,** as Ahasuerus has been with Esther all night, and he has been busying us with his demands. **Come, let us cast poison in the goblet** from which he drinks **so that he will die. But they did not know that Mordecai was** one **of those who sat** on the Sanhedrin, which convened **in the Chamber of Hewn Stone, and that he knew seventy languages,** a necessity for members of the Sanhedrin.

אָמַר לוֹ: וַהֲלֹא אֵין מִשְׁמַרְתִּי וּמִשְׁמַרְתְּךָ שָׁוָה? אָמַר לוֹ: אֲנִי אֶשְׁמוֹר מִשְׁמַרְתִּי וּמִשְׁמַרְתְּךָ. וְהַיְינוּ דִּכְתִיב ״וַיְבֻקַּשׁ הַדָּבָר וַיִּמָּצֵא״ – שֶׁלֹּא נִמְצְאוּ בְּמִשְׁמַרְתָּן.

While planning their plot, one of them **said to** the other: **But my post and your post are not identical.** How then can one of us leave our position to succeed in our plot to poison the king? The other one **said to him: I will guard** both **my post and your post.**[N] **And this is as it is written** with regard to the king's verifying Mordecai's revelation of the plan to kill the king: **"And when inquiry was made of the matter, it was found to be so"** (Esther 2:23); it was discovered **that they were not** both **found at their posts.**

״אַחַר הַדְּבָרִים הָאֵלֶּה״, (אַחַר מַאי) אָמַר רָבָא: אַחַר שֶׁבָּרָא הַקָּדוֹשׁ בָּרוּךְ הוּא רְפוּאָה לְמַכָּה.

The verse describes when the rest of the events of the Megilla occurred: **"After these events** did King Ahasuerus promote Haman" (Esther 3:1). The Gemara asks: **After what** particular events? **Rava said:** Only **after the Holy One, Blessed be He, created a remedy for the blow**[N] and set in place the chain of events that would lead to the miraculous salvation was Haman appointed, setting the stage for the decree against the Jews to be issued.

דְּאָמַר רֵישׁ לָקִישׁ: אֵין הַקָּדוֹשׁ בָּרוּךְ הוּא מַכֶּה אֶת יִשְׂרָאֵל אֶלָּא אִם כֵּן בּוֹרֵא לָהֶם רְפוּאָה תְּחִילָּה, שֶׁנֶּאֱמַר ״כְּרָפְאִי לְיִשְׂרָאֵל וְנִגְלָה עֲוֹן אֶפְרַיִם״ – אֲבָל אוּמּוֹת הָעוֹלָם אֵינוֹ כֵּן, מַכֶּה אוֹתָן וְאַחַר כָּךְ בּוֹרֵא לָהֶם רְפוּאָה, שֶׁנֶּאֱמַר ״וְנָגַף ה׳ אֶת מִצְרַיִם נָגוֹף וְרָפוֹא״.

Rava explains: **As Reish Lakish said: The Holy One, Blessed be He, does not strike at the Jewish people unless He has** already **created a remedy for them beforehand, as it is stated: "When I would have healed Israel, then the iniquity of Ephraim was uncovered"** (Hosea 7:1). **But** this is **not so** with regard to **the nations of the world.** With them, God first **strikes them and** only **afterward does He create a remedy, as it is stated: "And the Lord shall smite Egypt, smiting and healing"** (Isaiah 19:22).

״וַיִּבֶז בְּעֵינָיו לִשְׁלוֹחַ יָד בְּמָרְדֳּכַי לְבַדּוֹ״ אָמַר רָבָא בִּתְחִילָּה בְּמָרְדֳּכַי לְבַדּוֹ, וּלְבַסּוֹף בְּעַם מָרְדֳּכַי, וּמַנּוּ – רַבָּנַן, וּלְבַסּוֹף בְּכָל הַיְּהוּדִים.

The verse states: **"But it seemed contemptible in his eyes to lay his hand on Mordecai alone;** for they had made known to him the people of Mordecai; wherefore Haman sought to destroy all the Jews that were throughout the whole kingdom of Ahasuerus, even the people of Mordecai" (Esther 3:6). **Rava said: At first** he wanted to lay his hands on **Mordecai alone, and in the end on the people of Mordecai. And who were** the people of Mordecai? They were **the Sages,** i.e., Mordecai's special people. **And ultimately** he sought to bring harm **on all the Jews.**

״הִפִּיל פּוּר הוּא הַגּוֹרָל״ תָּנָא: כֵּיוָן שֶׁנָּפַל פּוּר בְּחוֹדֶשׁ אֲדָר שָׂמַח שִׂמְחָה גְּדוֹלָה, אָמַר: נָפַל לִי פּוּר בְּיֶרַח שֶׁמֵּת בּוֹ מֹשֶׁה. וְלֹא הָיָה יוֹדֵעַ שֶׁבְּשִׁבְעָה בַּאֲדָר מֵת וּבְשִׁבְעָה בַּאֲדָר נוֹלַד.

The verse states: **"They cast *pur*, that is, the lot"** (Esther 3:7). A Sage **taught** the following *baraita*: **Once the lot fell on the month of Adar, he,** Haman, **greatly rejoiced,** for he saw this as a favorable omen for the execution of his plans. **He said: The lot has fallen for me in the month that Moses died,** which is consequently a time of calamity for the Jewish people. **But he did not know that** not only **did** Moses **die on the seventh of Adar,** but **he was** also **born on the seventh of Adar,**[N] and therefore it is also a time of rejoicing for the Jewish people.

BACKGROUND

Tarsians and the Tarsian language – טַרְסִיִּים וּלְשׁוֹן טוּרְסִי: It is not known what language was spoken in Tarsus in that period. However, since it was previously Hittite territory it can be assumed that the Tarsian language was a dialect of the Hittite language. As the Tarsian language is not similar to most of the other languages spoken in the Persian Empire, speakers of Tarsian were able to assume that no one would understand their conversation.

NOTES

My post and your post – מִשְׁמַרְתִּי וּמִשְׁמַרְתְּךָ: Rabbeinu Ḥananel explains simply that they were not at watch at the same hour, as each one took a shift for a different part of the night. Some write that each wanted to assure himself that the other would not betray him, so they changed their shifts in order to cause both to be punished if they were caught (*Rannu LeYa'akov*; see Rashi and Rav Ya'akov Emden).

The Holy One, Blessed be He, created a remedy for the blow – בָּרָא הַקָּדוֹשׁ בָּרוּךְ הוּא רְפוּאָה לְמַכָּה: Although this decree came about only due to the sins of the Jewish people, and God doesn't usually show favoritism by providing unfair benefits for the undeserving, He still prepared a remedy for the Jewish people, as He knows that when the Jews are faced with calamity they repent and return to Him. Therefore, the decree was in fact only a warning and a test to see their reaction, and God took care that they would not be hurt from it by preparing a remedy for the blow (*Gevul Binyamin*).

He did not know that…he was also born on the seventh of Adar – לֹא הָיָה יוֹדֵעַ שֶׁבְּשִׁבְעָה בַּאֲדָר...נוֹלַד: Apparently, Haman was aware of the date of Moses' death, as it can be clearly calculated from the Torah. The Torah states that there were thirty days of mourning for Moses (Deuteronomy 34:8), followed by three days of preparation for the journey into the land of Israel (Joshua 1:13), whereupon the people crossed the Jordan, on the tenth of Nisan (Joshua 4:19). The death of Moses was consequently on the seventh of Adar. Although it is not explicit in the Torah that Moses was born on the same date as he died, it is known through the tradition that the Holy One, Blessed be He, completes the years of the righteous. Therefore, Haman was aware of the date of Moses' death, but not of his birth (Maharsha).

״יֶשְׁנוֹ עַם אֶחָד״ אֲמַר רָבָא: לֵיכָּא דְּיָדַע לִישָּׁנָא בִּישָׁא כְּהָמָן. אֲמַר לֵיהּ: תָּא נִיכְלִינְהוּ! אֲמַר לֵיהּ: מִסְתְּפִינָא מֵאֱלָהָיו, דְּלָא לִיעֲבֵיד בִּי כְּדַעֲבַד בְּקַמָּאֵי. אֲמַר לֵיהּ יָשְׁנוּ מִן הַמִּצְוֹת.

Haman said to Ahasuerus: “**There is** [*yeshno*] **one** people scattered abroad [*mefuzar*] and dispersed [*meforad*] among the peoples in all the provinces of your kingdom; and their laws are diverse from those of every people; nor do they keep the king’s laws; therefore it does not profit the king to tolerate them” (Esther 3:8). **Rava said: There was none who knew how to slander like Haman,** as in his request to the king he included responses to all the reasons Ahasuerus might be reluctant to destroy the Jewish people. **He said to** Ahasuerus: **Let us destroy them.** Ahasuerus **said to him: I am afraid of their God, lest He do to me as He did to those** who stood against them **before me.** Haman **said to him: They have been asleep** [*yashnu*] **with respect to the mitzvot,**[N] having ceased to observe the mitzvot, and, therefore there is no reason to fear.

אֲמַר לֵיהּ: אִית בְּהוּ רַבָּנַן. אֲמַר לֵיהּ: עַם אֶחָד הֵן.

Ahasuerus **said to him: There are the Sages among them** who observe the mitzvot. Haman **said to him: They are one people,**[N] i.e., they are all the same; nobody observes the mitzvot.

שֶׁמָּא תֹּאמַר קָרְחָה אֲנִי עוֹשֶׂה בְּמַלְכוּתְךָ – מְפוּזָּרִין הֵם בֵּין הָעַמִּים, שֶׁמָּא תֹּאמַר אִית הֲנָאָה מִינַּיְיהוּ ״מְפוֹרָד״, כִּפְרֵידָה זוֹ שֶׁאֵינָהּ עוֹשָׂה פֵּירוֹת. וְשֶׁמָּא תֹּאמַר אִיכָּא מְדִינְתָּא מִינַּיְיהוּ – תַּלְמוּד לוֹמַר ״בְּכֹל מְדִינוֹת מַלְכוּתֶךָ״.

Haman continued with his next response as expressed in the verse: **Perhaps you will say that I am making a bald spot in your kingdom,** i.e., you fear that if an entire nation is wiped out there will be a desolate area within the kingdom. There is no need to worry, though, as **they are scattered** [*mefuzarin*] **among the peoples,** and eradicating them will not result in the creation of an unpopulated zone in the area where they had once lived. Furthermore, **perhaps you will say that there is benefit from them;** but this nation is ***meforad*, like this** barren **mule** [*pereida*] **that cannot bear offspring,**[B] and there is no benefit to be gained from them. And **perhaps you will say that there is** at least **a province** that is filled **with them. Therefore the verse states** that they are scattered **“in all the provinces of your kingdom”** (Esther 3:8), and they do not inhabit one place.

״וְדָתֵיהֶם שׁוֹנוֹת מִכָּל עָם״ – דְּלָא אָכְלִי מִינַּן, וְלָא נָסְבִי מִינַּן, וְלָא מַנְסְבִי לַן. ״וְאֶת דָּתֵי הַמֶּלֶךְ אֵינָם עוֹשִׂים״ – דְּמַפְּקִי לְכוּלָּא שַׁתָּא בְּשְׁהִ״י פְּהִ״י. ״וְלַמֶּלֶךְ אֵין שֹׁוֶה לְהַנִּיחָם״ – דְּאָכְלוּ וְשָׁתוּ וּמְבַזּוּ לֵיהּ לְמַלְכוּת. וַאֲפִילּוּ נוֹפֵל זְבוּב בְּכוֹסוֹ שֶׁל אֶחָד מֵהֶן – זוֹרְקוֹ וְשׁוֹתֵהוּ. וְאִם אֲדוֹנִי הַמֶּלֶךְ נוֹגֵעַ בְּכוֹסוֹ שֶׁל אֶחָד מֵהֶן – חוֹבְטוֹ בְּקַרְקַע וְאֵינוֹ שׁוֹתֵהוּ.

Haman continued: **“And their laws are diverse from those of every people”** (Esther 3:8), **as they do not eat from our** food, **nor do they marry from our** women, **nor do they marry off** their women **to us. “Nor do they keep the king’s laws”** (Esther 3:8). **They spend the entire year** in idleness, as they are constantly saying: ***Shehi pehi***, an acronym for: It is Shabbat today [*Shabbat hayom*]; it is Passover today [*Pesaḥ hayom*].[N] The verse continues: **“Therefore it does not profit the king to tolerate them,” as they eat and drink and scorn the throne.** And a proof of this is that **even if a fly falls into the cup of one of them, he will throw** the fly **out and drink** the wine **it** fell into, **but if my master the king were to touch the glass of one of them, he would throw it to the ground, and would not drink it,** since it is prohibited to drink wine that was touched by a gentile.

״אִם עַל הַמֶּלֶךְ טוֹב יִכָּתֵב לְאַבְּדָם וַעֲשֶׂרֶת אֲלָפִים כִּכַּר כֶּסֶף״ וגו׳. אָמַר רֵישׁ לָקִישׁ: גָּלוּי וְיָדוּעַ לִפְנֵי מִי שֶׁאָמַר וְהָיָה הָעוֹלָם שֶׁעָתִיד הָמָן לִשְׁקוֹל שְׁקָלִים עַל יִשְׂרָאֵל, לְפִיכָךְ הִקְדִּים שִׁקְלֵיהֶן לִשְׁקָלָיו.

Therefore, Haman concluded: **“If it please the king, let it be written that they be destroyed, and** I will weigh out **ten thousand talents of silver** into the hands of those who have the charge of the business, to bring it into the king’s treasuries” (Esther 3:9). **Reish Lakish said: It is revealed and known** in advance **to the One Who spoke and the world came into being, that in the future Haman was going to weigh out shekels against the Jewish people; therefore, He** arranged that the Jewish people’s **shekels** that were given to the Temple **preceded**[N] Haman’s **shekels.**

וְהַיְינוּ דִּתְנַן: בְּאֶחָד בַּאֲדָר מַשְׁמִיעִין עַל הַשְּׁקָלִים וְעַל הַכִּלְאַיִם.

And this is as we learned in a mishna (*Shekalim* 2a): **On the first of Adar** the court **makes a** public **announcement about** the contribution to the Temple of half-**shekels**[N] that will soon be due, **and about** the need to uproot forbidden mixtures of **diverse kinds** of seeds from the fields now that they have begun to sprout. Therefore, it turns out that the Jewish people give the shekels on the first of Adar, preceding the date of Haman’s planned destruction of the Jewish people and his own collecting of shekels.

NOTES

They have been asleep [*yashnu*] with respect to the mitzvot – יָשְׁנוּ מִן הַמִּצְוֹת: The fact that the unusual term *yeshno* is used in place of the common form *yesh* is interpreted to indicate *yashnu,* meaning: They have been asleep with respect to their observance (Maharsha).

They are one people – עַם אֶחָד הֵן: Some write that although the Sages were performing the mitzvot, nevertheless, they were faulted for others’ non-observance, as Jews are one people and are responsible for one another (*Manot HaLevi*).

It is Shabbat today, it is Passover today – בְּשְׁהִ״י פְּהִ״י: Most of the commentaries explain this as initials indicating: Today is Shabbat, or *Shavuot*; today is Passover. There is also a secondary meaning in the words themselves, which refer literally to waiting and idleness.

He arranged that the Jewish people’s shekels preceded – הִקְדִּים שִׁקְלֵיהֶן: The shekels are needed for the communal offerings of the upcoming year, which begins on the first of Nisan, and therefore it would be sufficient to begin collecting at the end of the month of Adar. However, the Sages decreed that the collection begin from the beginning of Adar, and in this merit they were saved from Haman’s decree that was to be established with shekels (Maharsha).

Half-shekels – שְׁקָלִים: The half-shekel was an annual contribution to the Temple. All male Jews were required to annually contribute a half-shekel to the Temple before the first day of the month of Nisan, which was the first day of the new Temple year. This money was used to cover the expenses of the Temple, which included buying communal offerings and paying for repairs, and to maintain and repair the walls of Jerusalem. From the beginning of the month of Adar, notice was served to the public that the half-shekel contributions would soon be due. The exact value of the half-shekel changed several times over the course of the generations. Nowadays, toward the end of the Fast of Esther on the thirteenth of Adar, before the beginning of the holiday of Purim, people contribute to charity in commemoration of the half-shekel. The *halakhot* of the half-shekel contributions made to the Temple are discussed in tractate *Shekalim*.

BACKGROUND

Like this barren mule that cannot bear offspring – כִּפְרֵידָה זוֹ שֶׁאֵינָהּ עוֹשָׂה פֵּירוֹת: The offspring of a female horse and a male donkey is a mule, or *Equus mulus*. Horses and donkeys are different species with different numbers of chromosomes. A mule can be either male or female, but even though externally it appears to have fully formed sexual organs, it is infertile because it has sixty-three chromosomes, a mixture of the horse’s sixty-four and the donkey’s sixty-two. The different structure and number usually prevents the chromosomes from pairing up properly and creating viable embryos, rendering most mules infertile.

"וַיֹּאמֶר הַמֶּלֶךְ לְהָמָן הַכֶּסֶף נָתוּן לָךְ וְהָעָם לַעֲשׂוֹת בּוֹ כַּטּוֹב בְּעֵינֶיךָ", אָמַר רַבִּי אַבָּא:

Ahasuerus responded to Haman's request: **"And the king said to Haman: The silver is given to you; the people also, to do with them as it seems good to you"** (Esther 3:11). **Rabbi Abba said:**

Perek **I**
Daf **14** Amud **a**

מָשָׁל דַּאֲחַשְׁוֵרוֹשׁ וְהָמָן לְמָה הַדָּבָר דּוֹמֶה? לִשְׁנֵי בְּנֵי אָדָם, לְאֶחָד הָיָה לוֹ תֵּל בְּתוֹךְ שָׂדֵהוּ, וּלְאֶחָד הָיָה לוֹ חָרִיץ בְּתוֹךְ שָׂדֵהוּ. בַּעַל חָרִיץ אָמַר: מִי יִתֵּן לִי תֵּל זֶה בְּדָמִים! בַּעַל הַתֵּל אָמַר: מִי יִתֵּן לִי חָרִיץ זֶה בְּדָמִים!

The actions of **Ahasuerus and Haman** can be understood with **a parable; to what may they be compared? To two individuals, one** of whom **had a mound in the middle of his field and the other** of whom **had a ditch in the middle of his field,**[N] each one suffering from his own predicament. **The owner of the ditch,** noticing the other's mound of dirt, **said** to himself: **Who will give me this mound** of dirt suitable for filling in my ditch; I would even be willing to pay **for** it with **money,** and **the owner of the mound,** noticing the other's ditch, **said** to himself: **Who will give me this ditch for money,** so that I may use it to remove the mound of earth from my property?

לְיָמִים נִזְדַּוְּגוּ זֶה אֵצֶל זֶה, אָמַר לוֹ בַּעַל חָרִיץ לְבַעַל הַתֵּל: מְכוֹר לִי תִּילְּךָ! אָמַר לוֹ: טוֹל אוֹתָהּ בְּחִנָּם, וְהַלְוַאי!

At a later point, **one day, they** happened to have **met one another. The owner of the ditch said to the owner of the mound: Sell me your mound** so I can fill in my ditch. The mound's owner, anxious to rid himself of the excess dirt on his property, **said to him: Take it for free; if only** you had done so sooner. Similarly, Ahasuerus himself wanted to destroy the Jews. As he was delighted that Haman had similar aspirations and was willing to do the job for him, he demanded no money from him.

"וַיָּסַר הַמֶּלֶךְ אֶת טַבַּעְתּוֹ". אָמַר רַבִּי אַבָּא בַּר כָּהֲנָא: גְּדוֹלָה הֲסָרַת טַבַּעַת יוֹתֵר מֵאַרְבָּעִים וּשְׁמוֹנָה נְבִיאִים וְשֶׁבַע נְבִיאוֹת שֶׁנִּתְנַבְּאוּ לָהֶן לְיִשְׂרָאֵל, שֶׁכּוּלָּן לֹא הֶחֱזִירוּם לְמוּטָב, וְאִילּוּ הֲסָרַת טַבַּעַת הֶחֱזִירָתָן לְמוּטָב.

§ The verse states: **"And the king removed his ring** from his hand" (Esther 3:10). **Rabbi Abba bar Kahana said: The removal of** Ahasuerus's **ring** for the sealing of Haman's decree **was more effective**[N] **than the forty-eight prophets and the seven prophetesses who prophesied on behalf of the Jewish people. As, they were all unable to return** the Jewish people **to the right way, but the removal of** Ahasuerus's **ring returned them to the right way,** since it brought them to repentance.

תָּנוּ רַבָּנַן: אַרְבָּעִים וּשְׁמוֹנָה נְבִיאִים וְשֶׁבַע נְבִיאוֹת נִתְנַבְּאוּ לָהֶם לְיִשְׂרָאֵל, וְלֹא פָּחֲתוּ וְלֹא הוֹתִירוּ עַל מַה שֶּׁכָּתוּב בַּתּוֹרָה, חוּץ מִמִּקְרָא מְגִילָּה.

The Sages taught in a *baraita*: **Forty-eight prophets**[N] **and seven prophetesses prophesied on behalf of the Jewish people, and they neither subtracted from nor added**[N] **onto what is written in the Torah,** introducing no changes or additions to the mitzvot **except for the reading of the Megilla,** which they added as an obligation for all future generations.

NOTES

The parable of a mound and a ditch – מָשָׁל לְתֵל וּלְחָרִיץ: Some commentaries explain the deep meaning of the parable, that it indicates that although both Ahasuerus and Haman hated the Jews, they did so for different reasons. Ahasuerus saw them as a mound, viewing them as too large and successful, and therefore he wanted to destroy them. Haman, however, saw them as inferior, as a ditch that was lower than the other nations. In this way the parable excellently explains their two approaches (*Bina Leittim*; *Gevul Binyamin*; *Ḥatam Sofer*).

The removal of Ahasuerus's ring was more effective – גְּדוֹלָה הֲסָרַת טַבַּעַת יוֹתֵר: Haman's decree alone did not overly concern the Jews, as they were already aware that they had enemies. However, when the king agreed to give Haman his full backing and allowed him to do as he saw fit, the removal of the ring proved to the Jews that they were facing a grave calamity (Maharsha).

Forty-eight prophets – אַרְבָּעִים וּשְׁמוֹנָה נְבִיאִים: Rashi provides a different list of the prophets from that of Rabbeinu Ḥananel, whose opinion is accepted by the *Sefer Halakhot Gedolot* and most later authorities. According to Rabbeinu Ḥananel, the list includes, among others: Moses; Aaron; Assir, Elkana, and Abiasaph, who were sons of Korah; Joshua; Pinehas; Samuel; Elkanah, his father; Gad; Nathan; Asaph; Heman; Jeduthun; David; Ahijah the Shilonite; Shemaiah; Iddo the seer; Azariah, the son of Oded; Hanani; Jehu, the son of Hanani; Elijah; Micaiah, the son of Zephaniah; Jeremiah; Isaiah; Ezekiel; Daniel; Baruch, the son of Neriah; Seraiah; Mordecai; Bilshan; Hosea; Amos; Micah; Joel; Nahum; Haggai; Zechariah; and Malachi.

Furthermore, there are a number of disputes in connection with the actual lists, as Rashi himself mentions that he is certain about only forty six of the prophets, and is unsure who the last two prophets are. Although Rashi mentions David and Solomon in the list, the *Sefer Halakhot Gedolot* does not. There is also a discussion about Daniel, as the Gemara says that he is not counted among the prophets. Others remove Mordecai and Seraiah from the list and in their place some list Shem and Eber (*Asara Ma'amarot*); Eldad and Medad (*Ramat Shmuel*); Elazar the son of Aaron, and Elihu the son of Barachel (*Turei Even*); Chenaniah, chief of the Levites; the elder prophet from Bethel; Zechariah, who had understanding in the vision of God; and Hanan the son of Igdaliah (Rav Ya'akov Emden). In the work *Zikkaron BaSefer* it is suggested to include Bari, the father of Hosea, to whom a prophecy is attributed in the book of Hosea.

Neither subtracted from nor added – לֹא פָּחֲתוּ וְלֹא הוֹתִירוּ: Rashi explains that although there were other rabbinically ordained positive mitzvot, such as the obligation to light Hanukkah candles, they were enacted after prophecy ceased, while Purim was established toward the end of the prophetic era. See the Rambam's discussion with regard to the prohibition against a prophet establishing *halakha* based on prophecy (*Sefer HaMadda*, *Hilkhot Yesodei HaTorah* 9:1–2). The Ran elaborates on Rashi's comment, explaining that although there are numerous other rabbinic enactments, both positive mitzvot and prohibitions, they are all intended to safeguard Torah law, unlike reading the Megilla, which was enacted as an independent mitzva by rabbinic law. Some note that the *Sefer Halakhot Gedolot* lists reading the Megilla as one of the 613 mitzvot, seemingly viewing it as an actual addition to the Torah (*Zikhron Terua*). Conversely, the Rid simply explains that the prophets did not add public readings, other than reading the Megilla.

מַאי דְּרוּשׁ? אָמַר רַבִּי חִיָּיא בַּר אָבִין אָמַר רַבִּי יְהוֹשֻׁעַ בֶּן קָרְחָה וּמַה מֵעַבְדוּת לְחֵירוּת אָמְרִינַן שִׁירָה – מִמִּיתָה לְחַיִּים לֹא כׇּל שֶׁכֵּן?!

The Gemara asks: **What exposition** led them to determine that this was a proper mode of action? On what basis did they add this mitzva? **Rabbi Ḥiyya bar Avin said** that **Rabbi Yehoshua ben Korḥa said** that they reasoned as follows: **If,** when recalling the exodus from Egypt, in which the Jews were delivered **from slavery to freedom, we recite songs** of praise, the Song of the Sea and the hymns of *hallel*, then, in order to properly recall the miracle of Purim and commemorate God's delivering us **from death to life,** is it **not all the more so** the case that we must sing God's praise by reading the story in the Megilla?

אִי הָכִי הַלֵּל נַמִּי נֵימָא לְפִי שֶׁאֵין אוֹמְרִים הַלֵּל עַל נֵס שֶׁבְּחוּצָה לָאָרֶץ. יְצִיאַת מִצְרַיִם דְּנֵס שֶׁבְּחוּצָה לָאָרֶץ, הֵיכִי אָמְרִינַן שִׁירָה?

The Gemara asks: **If so,** our obligation should be at least as great as when we recall the exodus from Egypt, and **let us also recite *hallel*** on Purim. The Gemara answers: *Hallel* is not said on Purim, **because *hallel* is not recited on a miracle** that occurred **outside Eretz** Yisrael. The Gemara asks: If so, with regard to **the exodus from Egypt** as well, **which was a miracle** that occurred **outside Eretz** Yisrael, **how are we able to recite songs** of praise?

כִּדְתַנְיָא: עַד שֶׁלֹּא נִכְנְסוּ יִשְׂרָאֵל לָאָרֶץ הוּכְשְׁרוּ כׇּל אֲרָצוֹת לוֹמַר שִׁירָה. מִשֶּׁנִּכְנְסוּ יִשְׂרָאֵל לָאָרֶץ לֹא הוּכְשְׁרוּ כׇּל הָאֲרָצוֹת לוֹמַר שִׁירָה.

The Gemara answers: **As it is taught** in a *baraita*: **Prior to** the time when **the Jewish people entered Eretz** Yisrael, **all lands were** deemed **fit** for **songs** of praise **to be recited** for miracles performed within their borders, as all lands were treated equally. But **after the Jewish people entered Eretz** Yisrael, that land became endowed with greater sanctity, **and all the** other **lands were no longer** deemed **fit** for **songs** of praise **to be recited** for miracles performed within them.

רַב נַחְמָן אֲמַר: קְרָיָיתָא זוֹ הַלֵּילָא. רָבָא אֲמַר: בִּשְׁלָמָא הָתָם ״הַלְלוּ עַבְדֵי ה׳״ – וְלֹא עַבְדֵי פַרְעֹה, אֶלָּא הָכָא ״הַלְלוּ עַבְדֵי ה׳״ וְלֹא עַבְדֵי אֲחַשְׁוֵרוֹשׁ? אַכַּתִּי עַבְדֵי אֲחַשְׁוֵרוֹשׁ אֲנַן.

Rav Naḥman said an alternative answer as to why *hallel* is not recited on Purim: **The reading of** the Megilla itself **is** an act of reciting ***hallel***.[N] **Rava said** a third reason why *hallel* is not recited on Purim: **Granted** that *hallel* is said **there,** when recalling the exodus from Egypt, as after the salvation there, they could recite the phrase in *hallel*: **"Give praise, O servants of the Lord"** (Psalms 113:1); after their servitude to Pharaoh ended with their salvation, they were truly servants of the Lord **and not servants of Pharaoh. But** can it be said **here,** after the limited salvation commemorated on Purim: **"Give praise, O servants of the Lord,"** which would indicate that after the salvation the Jewish people were only servants of the Lord **and not servants of Ahasuerus?** No, even after the miracle of Purim, **we were still the servants of Ahasuerus,** as the Jews remained in exile under Persian rule, and consequently the salvation, which was incomplete, did not merit an obligation to say *hallel*.

בֵּין לְרָבָא בֵּין לְרַב נַחְמָן קַשְׁיָא: וְהָא תַּנְיָא, מִשֶּׁנִּכְנְסוּ לָאָרֶץ לֹא הוּכְשְׁרוּ כׇּל הָאֲרָצוֹת לוֹמַר שִׁירָה, כֵּיוָן שֶׁגָּלוּ – חָזְרוּ לְהֶכְשֵׁירָן הָרִאשׁוֹן.

The Gemara asks: **Both according to** the opinion of **Rava and according to** the opinion of **Rav Naḥman,** this is **difficult. Isn't it taught** in the *baraita* cited earlier: **After the Jewish people entered Eretz** Yisrael, that land became endowed with greater sanctity, **and all the** other **lands were no longer** deemed **fit** for **songs** of praise **to be recited** for miracles performed within them. Therefore, there should be no *hallel* obligation on Purim for the miracle performed outside of the land of Israel, and Rav Naḥman's and Rava's alternative explanations are incorrect. The Gemara answers: They understood differently, as it can be argued that **when** the people **were exiled** from Eretz Yisrael, the other lands **returned to their initial suitability,** and were once again deemed fit for reciting *hallel* on miracles performed within them.

וְתוּ לֵיכָּא? וְהָכְתִיב ״וַיְהִי אִישׁ אֶחָד מִן הָרָמָתַיִם צוֹפִים״ – אֶחָד מִמָּאתַיִם צוֹפִים שֶׁנִּתְנַבְּאוּ לָהֶם לְיִשְׂרָאֵל!

With regard to the statement that forty-eight prophets and seven prophetesses prophesied on behalf of the Jewish people, the Gemara asks: **Is there no one else? Isn't it written** with regard to Samuel's father, Elkanah: **"And there was a certain** [*eḥad*] **man from Ramathaim-zophim"** (I Samuel 1:1), which is expounded as follows to indicate that Elkanah was a prophet: He was **one** [*eḥad*] **of two hundred** [*mata'im*] **prophets** [*tzofim*] **who prophesied on behalf of the Jewish people.** If so, why was it stated here that there were only forty-eight prophets?

NOTES

The reading of the Megilla is *hallel* – קְרָיָיתָא זוֹ הַלֵּילָא: The Meiri states that according to this opinion, one who does not have a Megilla can fulfill his obligation by reciting *hallel* (see *Birkei Yosef* and *Ḥatam Sofer*).

מִיהֲוָה טוּבָא הֲווּ. כִּדְתַנְיָא: הַרְבֵּה נְבִיאִים עָמְדוּ לָהֶם לְיִשְׂרָאֵל, כִּפְלַיִם כְּיוֹצְאֵי מִצְרַיִם, אֶלָּא, נְבוּאָה שֶׁהוּצְרְכָה לְדוֹרוֹת – נִכְתְּבָה, וְשֶׁלֹּא הוּצְרְכָה – לֹא נִכְתְּבָה.

The Gemara answers: In fact, **there were more** prophets, **as it is taught** in a *baraita*: **Many prophets arose for the Jewish people,** numbering **double the** number of Israelites **who left Egypt.**[N] **However,** only a portion of the prophecies were recorded, because only **prophecy that was needed for** future **generations was written** down in the Bible for posterity, **but that which was not needed,** as it was not pertinent to later generations, **was not written.** Therefore, the fifty-five prophets recorded in the Bible, although not the only prophets of the Jewish people, were the only ones recorded, due to their eternal messages.

רַבִּי שְׁמוּאֵל בַּר נַחְמָנִי אָמַר: אָדָם הַבָּא מִשְּׁתֵּי רָמוֹת שֶׁצּוֹפוֹת זוֹ אֶת זוֹ. רַבִּי חָנִין אָמַר: אָדָם הַבָּא מִבְּנֵי אָדָם שֶׁעוֹמְדִין בְּרוּמוֹ שֶׁל עוֹלָם. וּמַאן נִינְהוּ – בְּנֵי קֹרַח. דִּכְתִיב ״וּבְנֵי קֹרַח לֹא מֵתוּ״. תָּנָא מִשּׁוּם רַבֵּינוּ: מָקוֹם נִתְבַּצֵּר לָהֶם בְּגֵיהִנָּם, וְעָמְדוּ עָלָיו.

Rabbi Shmuel bar Naḥmani said another explanation of the verse "And there was a certain man from Ramathaim-zophim": **A man who comes from two heights** [*ramot*] **that face** [*tzofot*] **one another. Rabbi Ḥanin said** an additional interpretation: **A man who descends from people who stood at the height of** [*rumo*] **the world.**[N] The Gemara asks: **And who are these** people? The Gemara answers: These are the **sons of Korah, as it is written: "But the sons of Korah did not die"** (Numbers 26:11), and with regard to them **it is taught in the name of our teacher,** Rabbi Yehuda HaNasi: A high **place was set aside for them in Gehenna,** as the sons of Korah repented in their hearts, and were consequently not propelled very far down in Gehenna when the earth opened to swallow Korah and his followers; **and they stood on** this high place and sung to the Lord. They alone stood at the height of the lower world.

שֶׁבַע נְבִיאוֹת מַאן נִינְהוּ? שָׂרָה, מִרְיָם, דְּבוֹרָה, חַנָּה, אֲבִיגַיִל, חוּלְדָּה, וְאֶסְתֵּר. שָׂרָה – דִּכְתִיב ״אֲבִי מִלְכָּה וַאֲבִי יִסְכָּה״, וְאָמַר רַבִּי יִצְחָק: יִסְכָּה זוֹ שָׂרָה. וְלָמָּה נִקְרָא שְׁמָהּ יִסְכָּה – שֶׁסָּכְתָה בְּרוּחַ הַקֹּדֶשׁ, שֶׁנֶּאֱמַר ״כֹּל אֲשֶׁר תֹּאמַר אֵלֶיךָ שָׂרָה שְׁמַע בְּקוֹלָהּ״. דָּבָר אַחֵר: יִסְכָּה – שֶׁהַכֹּל סוֹכִין בְּיוֹפְיָהּ.

§ The Gemara asks with regard to the prophetesses recorded in the *baraita*: **Who were the seven prophetesses?** The Gemara answers: **Sarah, Miriam, Deborah, Hannah, Abigail, Huldah, and Esther.** The Gemara offers textual support: **Sarah, as it is written:** "Haran, **the father of Milcah, and the father of Iscah"** (Genesis 11:29). **And Rabbi Yitzḥak said: Iscah is** in fact **Sarah. And why was she called Iscah? For she saw** [*sakhta*] **by means of divine inspiration, as it is stated: "In all that Sarah has said to you, hearken to her voice"** (Genesis 21:12).[N] **Alternatively,** Sarah was also called **Iscah, for all gazed** [*sokhin*] **upon her beauty.**

מִרְיָם – דִּכְתִיב ״וַתִּקַּח מִרְיָם הַנְּבִיאָה אֲחוֹת אַהֲרֹן״ וְלֹא אֲחוֹת מֹשֶׁה? אָמַר רַב נַחְמָן אָמַר רַב: שֶׁהָיְתָה מִתְנַבְּאָה כְּשֶׁהִיא אֲחוֹת אַהֲרֹן, וְאוֹמֶרֶת: עֲתִידָה אִמִּי שֶׁתֵּלֵד בֵּן שֶׁיּוֹשִׁיעַ אֶת יִשְׂרָאֵל. וּבְשָׁעָה שֶׁנּוֹלַד נִתְמַלֵּא כָּל הַבַּיִת כּוּלּוֹ אוֹרָה, עָמַד אָבִיהָ וּנְשָׁקָהּ עַל רֹאשָׁהּ, אָמַר לָהּ: בִּתִּי נִתְקַיְּימָה נְבוּאָתֵיךְ.

Miriam was a prophetess, **as it is written** explicitly: **"And Miriam the prophetess, the sister of Aaron, took** a timbrel in her hand" (Exodus 15:20). The Gemara asks: Was she the sister only of Aaron, **and not the sister of Moses?** Why does the verse mention only one of her brothers? **Rav Naḥman said** that **Rav said: For she prophesied when she was the sister of Aaron,** i.e., she prophesied since her youth, even before Moses was born, **and she would say: My mother is destined to bear a son who will deliver the Jewish people** to salvation. **And at the time when** Moses **was born the entire house was filled with light,** and **her father stood and kissed her on the head,** and **said to her: My daughter, your prophecy has been fulfilled.**

וְכֵיוָן שֶׁהִשְׁלִיכוּהוּ לַיְאוֹר – עָמַד אָבִיהָ וּטְפָחָהּ עַל רֹאשָׁהּ, וְאָמַר לָהּ: בִּתִּי, הֵיכָן נְבוּאָתֵיךְ? הַיְינוּ דִּכְתִיב ״וַתֵּתַצַּב אֲחוֹתוֹ מֵרָחוֹק לְדֵעָה״ – לָדַעַת מַה יְּהֵא בְּסוֹף נְבוּאָתָהּ.

But once Moses **was cast into the river, her father arose and rapped her on the head, saying to her: My daughter, where is your prophecy** now, as it looked as though the young Moses would soon meet his end. **This is** the meaning of **that** which **is written** with regard to Miriam's watching Moses in the river: **"And his sister stood at a distance to know** what would be done to him" (Exodus 2:4), i.e., **to know what would be with the end of her prophecy,** as she had prophesied that her brother was destined to be the savior of the Jewish people.

דְּבוֹרָה – דִּכְתִיב ״וּדְבוֹרָה אִשָּׁה נְבִיאָה אֵשֶׁת לַפִּידוֹת״. מַאי ״אֵשֶׁת לַפִּידוֹת״ – שֶׁהָיְתָה עוֹשָׂה פְּתִילוֹת לַמִּקְדָּשׁ.

Deborah was a prophetess, **as it is written** explicitly: **"And Deborah, a prophetess, the wife of Lappidoth"** (Judges 4:4). The Gemara asks: **What is** the meaning of **"the wife of Lappidoth"?** The Gemara answers: **For she used to make wicks**[N] **for the Sanctuary,** and due to the flames [*lappidot*] on these wicks she was called the wife of Lappidoth, literally, a woman of flames.

NOTES

Double the number of Israelites who left Egypt – כִּפְלַיִם כְּיוֹצְאֵי מִצְרַיִם: To a certain degree it is possible to view as prophets all the Jews who left Egypt, as they witnessed the revelation of God at the Red Sea, and experienced an even greater revelation at Mount Sinai (Rav Ya'akov Emden).

Who stood at the height of the world – שֶׁעוֹמְדִין בְּרוּמוֹ שֶׁל עוֹלָם: Due to the fact that they benefited from this open miracle, as all the others were swallowed up by the ground and they remained in their place, it is stated that they stood at the height of the world (*Ḥiddushei Aggadot LaRashba*).

Hearken to her voice – שְׁמַע בְּקוֹלָהּ: The Gemara's comment is derived from the apparently superfluous term "to her voice" (Maharsha). It is stated in *Bereshit Rabba* that "her voice" also refers to the voice of prophecy, the voice of God that is heard through her mouth.

Make wicks – עוֹשָׂה פְּתִילוֹת: It is written that Deborah would glorify this mitzva by making the wicks the size of torches [*lappidot*], and therefore she was called "the wife of Lappidoth." Since Deborah was more famous than her husband, and the name Lappidoth is unknown, nothing is gained by mentioning it unless it is intended to describe Deborah's deeds (Maharsha).

”וְהִיא יוֹשֶׁבֶת תַּחַת תּוֹמֶר“, מַאי שְׁנָא ”תַּחַת תּוֹמֶר“? אָמַר רַבִּי שִׁמְעוֹן בֶּן אַבְשָׁלוֹם: מִשּׁוּם יִחוּד. דָּבָר אַחֵר: מַה תָּמָר זֶה אֵין לוֹ אֶלָּא לֵב אֶחָד – אַף יִשְׂרָאֵל שֶׁבְּאוֹתוֹ הַדּוֹר לֹא הָיָה לָהֶם אֶלָּא לֵב אֶחָד לַאֲבִיהֶן שֶׁבַּשָּׁמַיִם.

With regard to Deborah, it says: **"And she sat under a palm tree"** (Judges 4:5). The Gemara asks: **What is different** and unique with regard to her sitting **"under a palm tree"** that there is a need for it to be written? **Rabbi Shimon ben Avshalom said:** It is **due to** the prohibition against **being alone together** with a man. Since men would come before her for judgment, she established for herself a place out in the open and visible to all, in order to avoid a situation in which she would be secluded with a man behind closed doors. **Alternatively,** the verse means: **Just as a palm tree has only one heart,**[B] as a palm tree does not send out separate branches, but rather has only one main trunk, **so too, the Jewish people in that generation had only one heart,** directed **to their Father in Heaven.**

חַנָּה – דִּכְתִיב ”וַתִּתְפַּלֵּל חַנָּה וַתֹּאמַר עָלַץ לִבִּי בַּה׳ רָמָה קַרְנִי בַּה׳“, רָמָה קַרְנִי וְלֹא רָמָה פַּכִּי. דָּוִד וּשְׁלֹמֹה שֶׁנִּמְשְׁחוּ בְּקֶרֶן נִמְשְׁכָה מַלְכוּתָן, שָׁאוּל וְיֵהוּא שֶׁנִּמְשְׁחוּ בְּפַךְ – לֹא נִמְשְׁכָה מַלְכוּתָן.

Hannah was a prophetess, **as it is written: "And Hannah prayed and said, My heart rejoices in the Lord, my horn is exalted in the Lord"** (I Samuel 2:1), and her words were prophecy, in that she said: **"My horn is exalted," and not: My pitcher is exalted.**[N] As, with regard to **David and Solomon, who were anointed** with oil **from a horn, their kingship continued,** whereas with regard to **Saul and Jehu, who were anointed** with oil **from a pitcher, their kingship did not continue.** This demonstrates that Hannah was a prophetess, as she prophesied that only those anointed with oil from a horn will merit that their kingships continue.

”אֵין קָדוֹשׁ כַּה׳ כִּי אֵין בִּלְתֶּךָ“ אָמַר רַב יְהוּדָה בַּר מְנַשְּׁיָא: אַל תִּקְרֵי ”בִּלְתֶּךָ“ אֶלָּא ”לְבַלּוֹתֶךָ“. שֶׁלֹּא כְּמִדַּת הַקָּדוֹשׁ בָּרוּךְ הוּא מִדַּת בָּשָׂר וָדָם; מִדַּת בָּשָׂר וָדָם – מַעֲשֵׂה יָדָיו מְבַלִּין אוֹתוֹ, אֲבָל הַקָּדוֹשׁ בָּרוּךְ הוּא – מְבַלֶּה מַעֲשֵׂה יָדָיו.

Apropos the song of Hannah, the Gemara further explains her words: **"There is none sacred as the Lord; for there is none beside You [*biltekha*]"** (I Samuel 2:2). **Rav Yehuda bar Menashya said: Do not read** it as ***biltekha***, "beside You," **but rather** read it as ***levalotekha***, to outlast You. **As the attribute of the Holy One, Blessed be He, is unlike the attribute of flesh and blood.** It is an attribute of man that **his handiwork outlasts him** and continues to exist even after he dies, **but the Holy One, Blessed be He, outlasts His handiwork,** as He exists eternally.

”וְאֵין צוּר כֵּאלֹהֵינוּ“ אֵין צַיָּיר כֵּאלֹהֵינוּ. אָדָם צָר צוּרָה עַל גַּבֵּי הַכּוֹתֶל וְאֵינוֹ יָכוֹל לְהַטִּיל בָּהּ רוּחַ וּנְשָׁמָה קְרָבַיִם וּבְנֵי מֵעַיִם, אֲבָל הַקָּדוֹשׁ בָּרוּךְ הוּא צָר צוּרָה בְּתוֹךְ צוּרָה, וּמַטִּיל בָּהּ רוּחַ וּנְשָׁמָה קְרָבַיִם וּבְנֵי מֵעַיִם.

Hannah further said: **"Neither is there any rock [*tzur*] like our God"** (I Samuel 2:1). This can be understood as saying that **there is no artist [*tzayyar*] like our God.** How is He better than all other artists? **Man fashions a form upon a wall, but is unable to endow it with breath and a soul,** or fill it with **innards and intestines, whereas the Holy One, Blessed be He, fashions a form** of a fetus **inside the form** of its mother, rather than on a flat surface, **and endows it with breath and a soul** and fills it with **innards and intestines.**

אֲבִיגַיִל – דִּכְתִיב ”וְהָיָה הִיא רוֹכֶבֶת עַל הַחֲמוֹר וְיוֹרֶדֶת בְּסֵתֶר הָהָר“. ”בְּסֵתֶר הָהָר“? מִן הָהָר מִיבָּעֵי לֵיהּ!

Abigail was a prophetess, **as it is written: "And it was so, as she rode on the donkey, and came down by the covert of the mountain"** (I Samuel 25:20). The Gemara asks: Why does it say: **"By the covert [*beseter*] of the mountain"? It should have said: From the mountain.**

אֲמַר רַבָּה בַּר שְׁמוּאֵל: עַל עִסְקֵי דָם הַבָּא מִן הַסְּתָרִים. נָטְלָה דָּם וְהֶרְאַתָה לוֹ. אָמַר לָהּ: וְכִי מַרְאִין דָּם בַּלַּיְלָה? אָמְרָה לוֹ: וְכִי דָּנִין דִּינֵי נְפָשׁוֹת בַּלַּיְלָה? אָמַר לָהּ:

The Gemara answers that in fact this must be understood as an allusion to something else. **Rabba bar Shmuel said: Abigail,** in her attempt to prevent David from killing her husband Nabal, came to David and questioned him **on account of** menstrual **blood that comes from the hidden parts [*setarim*]** of a body. How so? **She took** a blood-stained cloth **and showed it to him,** asking him to rule on her status, whether or not she was ritually impure as a menstruating woman. **He said to her: Is blood shown at night?** One does not examine blood-stained cloths at night, as it is difficult to distinguish between the different shades by candlelight. **She said to him:** If so, you should also remember another *halakha*: **Are** cases of **capital law tried at night?** Since one does not try capital cases at night, you cannot condemn Nabal to death at night. David **said to her:**

BACKGROUND

One heart – לֵב אֶחָד: Unlike most trees, the date palm does not have typical branches; its fronds emanate directly from the trunk without being differentiated into secondary branches. For this reason the Jewish people are compared to a date palm, which grows in only one direction and whose center, the heart of palm, is a singular, undifferentiated trunk.

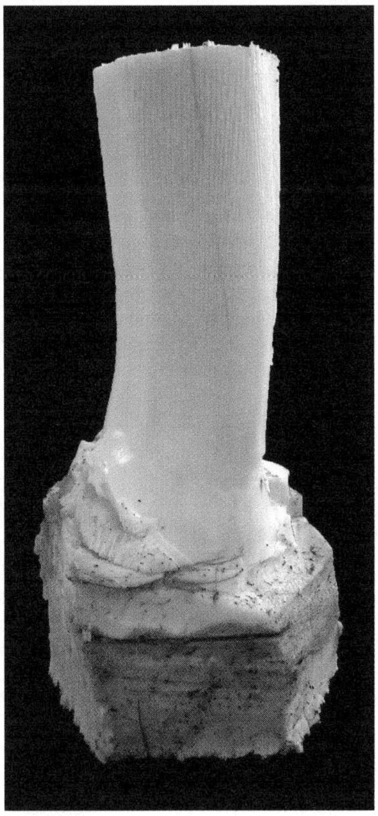

Heart of palm

NOTES

My horn is exalted, and not, My pitcher is exalted – רָמָה קַרְנִי וְלֹא רָמָה פַּכִּי: The simple explanation is that a pitcher is made of earthenware and is therefore breakable, indicating a monarchy that will not last. However, a horn is not easily broken, indicating a prolonged monarchy (Maharsha).

HALAKHA

Is a rebel against the throne – מוֹרֵד בְּמַלְכוּת הוּא: The king may execute anyone who rebels against his authority or does not obey his decrees. The king is permitted to use extra-judicial means to execute the rebel, including punishing him without warning or without the testimony of witnesses (Rambam *Sefer Shofetim, Hilkhot Melakhim UMilḥemoteihem* 3:8, 10).

NOTES

Is a rebel against the throne – מוֹרֵד בְּמַלְכוּת הוּא: See *Tosafot* (s.v. *mored*), who discuss this matter. The *Turei Even* explains at length, similar to the commentary of *Tosafot* in tractate *Sanhedrin*, that even though one who rebels against the throne does not need to be convicted by the usual twenty-three-member court that adjudicates capital offenses, a small court is still required to ascertain the facts and clarify if he rebelled or not. The Radbaz explains in his responsa that from the time David was anointed by Samuel he had the status of king, and therefore he felt that anyone who rebelled against his authority was subject to being executed. Abigail, however, told him that although his rule had begun, his kingship had not been completely established, and therefore he should not execute those who rebelled against his kingship.

Your seal [*tivakha*]…across the world – טִבְעֵךְ בָּעוֹלָם: The word for seal is derived from the Aramaic *tiv'a*, meaning coin. Minting coins with the name of a ruler acts as a public proclamation of independent rule. Furthermore, if the coins are accepted by the society as currency, they indicate that the leader's rule has been accepted as an established fact.

***Damim* indicates two – דָּמִים תַּרְתֵּי מַשְׁמַע:** Rabbi Levi ben Ḥaviv explains that the terminology "coming to bloodguiltiness" is not commonly used to indicate spilling blood, and therefore it was interpreted to indicate that it would involve having relations with a menstruating woman.

Yet the soul of my lord shall be bound in the bond of life – וְהָיְתָה נֶפֶשׁ אֲדוֹנִי צְרוּרָה בִּצְרוֹר הַחַיִּים: The Maharsha and others question why this additional verse is mentioned in the Gemara. Some later commentaries explain, and alternative texts bear out their interpretation, that Abigail said to him that even though he will stumble in the future with regard to the incident of Bathsheba, he will repent, and therefore, "Yet the soul of my lord shall be bound in the bond of life."

מוֹרֵד בְּמַלְכוּת הוּא, וְלָא צְרִיךְ לְמִידַּיְינֵיהּ. אָמְרָה לוֹ: עֲדַיִין שָׁאוּל קַיָּים, וְלֹא יָצָא טִבְעֲךָ בָּעוֹלָם. אֲמַר לָהּ: ״בָּרוּךְ טַעְמֵךְ וּבְרוּכָה אָתְּ אֲשֶׁר כְּלִיתִנִי [הַיּוֹם הַזֶּה] מִבֹּא בְדָמִים״.

Nabal, your husband, **is a rebel against the throne,**[HN] as David had already been anointed as king by the prophet Samuel, and Nabal refused his orders. **And** therefore **there is no need to try him,** as a rebel is not accorded the ordinary prescriptions governing judicial proceedings. Abigail **said to him:** You lack the authority to act in this manner, as **Saul is still alive.** He is the king in actual practice, and **your seal [*tivakha*] has not** yet **spread across the world,**[N] i.e., your kingship is not yet known to all. Therefore, you are not authorized to try someone for rebelling against the monarchy. David accepted her words and **said to her: "And blessed be your discretion and blessed be you who have kept me this day from coming to bloodguiltiness [*damim*]"** (I Samuel 25:33).

דָּמִים תַּרְתֵּי מַשְׁמַע! אֶלָּא מְלַמֵּד שֶׁגִּילְּתָה אֶת שׁוֹקָהּ, וְהָלַךְ לְאוֹרָהּ שָׁלֹשׁ פַּרְסָאוֹת. אָמַר לָהּ: הַשְׁמִיעִי לִי! אָמְרָה לוֹ: ״לֹא תִהְיֶה זֹאת לְךָ לְפוּקָה״, ״זֹאת״ – מִכְּלָל דְּאִיכָּא אַחֲרִיתִי, וּמַאי נִיהוּ – מַעֲשֶׂה דְּבַת שֶׁבַע, וּמַסְקָנָא הָכִי הֲוַאי.

The Gemara asks: The plural term ***damim***, literally, bloods, **indicates two.**[N] Why did David not use the singular term *dam*? **Rather, this teaches that** Abigail **revealed her thigh,** and he lusted after her, **and he went three parasangs by the fire** of his desire for her, and **said to her: Listen to me,** i.e., listen to me and allow me to be intimate with you. Abigail then **said to him: "Let this not be a stumbling block for you"** (I Samuel 25:31). **By inference,** from the word **"this,"** it can be understood that **there is someone else** who will in fact be a stumbling block for him, **and what is** this referring to? **The incident involving Bathsheba. And in the end this is what was,** as indeed he stumbled with Bathsheba. This demonstrates that Abigail was a prophetess, as she knew that this would occur. This also explains why David blessed Abigail for keeping him from being responsible for two incidents involving blood that day: Abigail's menstrual blood and the shedding of Nabal's blood.

״וְהָיְתָה נֶפֶשׁ אֲדֹנִי צְרוּרָה בִּצְרוֹר הַחַיִּים״. כִּי הֲוַת מִיפַּטְרָא מִינֵּיהּ אֲמַרָה לֵיהּ ״וְהֵיטִב ה׳ לַאדֹנִי וְזָכַרְתָּ אֶת אֲמָתֶךָ״.

Apropos Abigail, the Gemara explains additional details in the story. Abigail said to David: **"Yet the soul of my lord shall be bound in the bond of life**[N] with the Lord your God" (I Samuel 25:29), and **when she parted from him she said to him: "And when the Lord shall have dealt well with my lord, and you shall remember your handmaid"** (I Samuel 25:31).

אֲמַר רַב נַחְמָן: הַיְינוּ דְּאָמְרִי אֱינָשֵׁי: אִיתְּתָא בַּהֲדֵי שׁוּתָא פִּילְכָא. אִיכָּא דְּאָמְרִי: שָׁפֵיל וְאָזֵיל בַּר אַוְוזָא וְעֵינוֹהִי מִיטַּיְיפֵי.

Rav Naḥman said that **this** explains the folk saying **that people say: While a woman is engaged in conversation** she also holds **the spindle,** i.e., while a woman is engaged in one activity she is already taking steps with regard to another. Abigail came to David in order to save her husband Nabal, but at the same time she indicates that if her husband dies, David should remember her and marry her. And indeed, after Nabal's death David took Abigail for his wife. **Some say** that Rav Naḥman referred to a different saying: **The goose stoops** its head **as it goes** along,[B] **but its eyes look on from afar** to find what it is looking for. So too, Abigail acted in similar fashion.

חוּלְדָּה – דִּכְתִיב ״וַיֵּלֶךְ חִלְקִיָּהוּ הַכֹּהֵן וַאֲחִיקָם וְעַכְבּוֹר״ וגו׳. וּבִמְקוֹם דְּקָאֵי יִרְמְיָה הֵיכִי מִתְנַבְּיָא אִיהִי? אָמְרִי בֵּי רַב מִשְּׁמֵיהּ דְּרַב: חוּלְדָּה קְרוֹבַת יִרְמְיָה הָיְתָה, וְלָא הֲוָה מַקְפִּיד עֲלֶיהָ.

Huldah was a prophetess, **as it is written: "So Hilkiah the priest and Ahikam and Achbor** and Shaphan and Asaiah went to Huldah the prophetess" (II Kings 22:14) as emissaries of King Josiah. The Gemara asks: **But if Jeremiah was found there, how could she prophesy?** Out of respect for Jeremiah, who was her superior, it would have been fitting that she not prophesy in his presence. The Sages of **the school of Rav say in the name of Rav: Huldah was a** close **relative of Jeremiah, and he did not object to her** prophesying in his presence.

BACKGROUND

The goose stoops its head as it goes along – שָׁפֵיל וְאָזֵיל בַּר אַוְוזָא: The eyes of geese are located far to the sides of their heads. Consequently, although their heads are stooped toward the ground as they seek out food, they remain alert to their surroundings, enabling them to better find food and to be cautious of approaching predators.

וְיֹאשִׁיָּה גּוּפֵיהּ, הֵיכִי שָׁבֵיק יִרְמְיָה וּמְשַׁדַּר לְגַבָּהּ? אָמְרִי דְּבֵי רַבִּי שֵׁילָא: מִפְּנֵי שֶׁהַנָּשִׁים רַחֲמָנִיּוֹת הֵן.

The Gemara asks: **But how could Josiah himself ignore Jeremiah and send** emissaries **to** Huldah? The Sages of **the school of Rabbi Sheila say: Because women are** more **compassionate,** and he hoped that what she would tell them would not be overly harsh.

רַבִּי יוֹחָנָן אָמַר: יִרְמְיָה לָא הֲוָה הָתָם, שֶׁהָלַךְ לְהַחֲזִיר עֲשֶׂרֶת הַשְּׁבָטִים. וּמְנָלַן דְּאַהֲדוּר – דִּכְתִיב ״כִּי הַמּוֹכֵר אֶל הַמִּמְכָּר לֹא יָשׁוּב״, אֶפְשָׁר יוֹבֵל בָּטֵל וְנָבִיא מִתְנַבֵּא עָלָיו שֶׁיִּבָּטֵל? אֶלָּא מְלַמֵּד שֶׁיִּרְמְיָה הֶחֱזִירָן,

Rabbi Yoḥanan said a different answer: **Jeremiah was not there** at the time, because **he went to bring back the ten tribes** from their exile. **And from where do we derive that he brought them back? As it is written: "For the seller shall not return to that which he has sold"** (Ezekiel 7:13), i.e., Ezekiel prophesied that in the future the Jubilee Year would no longer be in effect. Now **is it possible that the Jubilee**[B] **had** already been **annulled?** The *halakhot* of the Jubilee Year apply only when all of the tribes of Israel are settled in their respective places, which could not have happened since the exile of the ten tribes more than a century earlier, **but the prophet is prophesying that it will cease** only in the future. **Rather, this teaches that Jeremiah brought back** the ten tribes from their exile.

וְיֹאשִׁיָּהוּ בֶּן אָמוֹן מָלַךְ עֲלֵיהֶן. דִּכְתִיב ״וַיֹּאמֶר מָה הַצִּיּוּן הַלָּז אֲשֶׁר אֲנִי רוֹאֶה וַיֹּאמְרוּ אֵלָיו אַנְשֵׁי הָעִיר הַקֶּבֶר אִישׁ הָאֱלֹהִים אֲשֶׁר בָּא מִיהוּדָה וַיִּקְרָא אֶת הַדְּבָרִים הָאֵלֶּה אֲשֶׁר עָשִׂיתָ עַל הַמִּזְבֵּחַ בְּבֵית אֵל״. וְכִי מַה טִּיבוֹ שֶׁל יֹאשִׁיָּהוּ עַל הַמִּזְבֵּחַ בְּבֵית אֵל? אֶלָּא מְלַמֵּד שֶׁיֹּאשִׁיָּהוּ מָלַךְ עֲלֵיהֶן. רַב נַחְמָן אָמַר: מֵהָכָא ״גַּם יְהוּדָה שָׁת קָצִיר לָךְ בְּשׁוּבִי שְׁבוּת עַמִּי״.

And Josiah the son of Amon ruled over the ten tribes, **as it is written: "Then he said: What monument is that which I see? And the men of the city told him, It is the tomb of the man of God who came from Judah and proclaimed these things that you have done against the altar of Bethel"** (II Kings 23:17). **Now what connection did Josiah,** king of Judea, **have with the altar at Bethel,** a city in the kingdom of Israel? **Rather, this teaches that Josiah ruled over the** ten tribes of Israel. **Rav Naḥman said:** Proof that the tribes returned may be adduced **from** the verse **here: "Also, O Judah, there is a harvest appointed for you, when I would return the captivity of My people"** (Hosea 6:11), which indicates that they returned to their places.

אֶסְתֵּר – דִּכְתִיב ״וַיְהִי בַּיּוֹם הַשְּׁלִישִׁי וַתִּלְבַּשׁ אֶסְתֵּר מַלְכוּת״, בִּגְדֵי מַלְכוּת מִיבָּעֵי לֵיהּ! אֶלָּא: שֶׁלְּבָשַׁתָּה רוּחַ הַקֹּדֶשׁ. כְּתִיב הָכָא ״וַתִּלְבַּשׁ״ וּכְתִיב הָתָם ״וְרוּחַ לָבְשָׁה אֶת עֲמָשַׂי״ וגו׳.

Esther was also a prophetess, **as it is written: "And it came to pass on the third day that Esther clothed herself in royalty"** (Esther 5:1).[N] **It should have said:** Esther clothed herself in **royal garments. Rather,** this alludes to the fact **that she clothed herself with a divine** spirit of **inspiration. It is written here: "And she clothed herself," and it is written elsewhere: "And the spirit clothed Amasai"** (I Chronicles 12:19). Just as there the reference is to being enclothed by a spirit, so too Esther was enclothed by a spirit of divine inspiration.

אֲמַר רַב נַחְמָן: לָא יָאֶה יְהִירוּתָא לְנָשֵׁי, תַּרְתֵּי נָשֵׁי יְהִירָן הָוְיָין, וְסַנְיָין שְׁמַיְיהוּ, חֲדָא שְׁמָהּ זִיבּוּרְתָּא, וַחֲדָא שְׁמָהּ כַּרְכּוּשְׁתָּא. זִיבּוּרְתָּא – כְּתִיב בָּהּ ״וַתִּשְׁלַח וַתִּקְרָא לְבָרָק״, וְאִילּוּ אִיהִי לָא אָזְלָה לְגַבֵּיהּ. כַּרְכּוּשְׁתָּא כְּתִיב בָּהּ ״אִמְרוּ לָאִישׁ״ וְלֹא אָמְרָה ״אִמְרוּ לַמֶּלֶךְ״.

An additional point is mentioned with regard to the prophetesses. **Rav Naḥman said: Haughtiness is not befitting a woman.** And a proof to this is that **there were two haughty women, whose names were** identical to the names of **loathsome**[N] creatures. **One,** Deborah, **was called a hornet,** as her Hebrew name, Devorah, means hornet; **and one,** Huldah, **was called a marten,** as her name is the Hebrew term for that creature. From where is it known that they were haughty? **With regard to** Deborah, **the hornet, it is written: "And she sent and called Barak"** (Judges 4:6), **but she herself did not go to him.** And **with regard to** Huldah, **the marten, it is written: "Say to the man** that sent you to me" (II Kings 22:15), **but she did not say: Say to the king.**

BACKGROUND

The Jubilee – יוֹבֵל: The fiftieth year, the one following seven Sabbatical cycles of seven years, has a unique status. All the agricultural *halakhot* that are followed in the Sabbatical year must also be observed in the Jubilee Year. In addition, all Jewish slaves, including those who insisted on continuing in servitude beyond their initial obligation, are freed, and fields that have been sold are returned to their original owners (see Leviticus, chapter 25). The liberation of slaves and the restoration of fields take place after Yom Kippur. On Yom Kippur of that year, special prayers are recited and the *shofar* is sounded in a manner similar to that practiced on Rosh HaShana. The Jubilee Year is observed only when the majority of the Jewish people are living in Eretz Yisrael. Consequently, its observance was discontinued during the First Temple period and never renewed.

NOTES

Esther clothed herself in royalty – וַתִּלְבַּשׁ אֶסְתֵּר מַלְכוּת: Divine inspiration and prophecy are often referred to as royalty in the kabbalistic works (see *Otzar HaKavod* and Maharsha). Some question the citation of this verse as proof that Esther was a prophetess, saying that the list of prophets includes only those who had full-fledged prophecy, while this verse may only prove that she, like Amasai, had only divine inspiration. The *Seder Olam*, however, explains that the real proof for her prophecy is the fact that she wrote the Megilla, a prophetic work, together with Mordecai (Rabbi Tzvi Hirsch Chajes).

Whose names were loathsome – וְסַנְיָין שְׁמַיְיהוּ: Having been given these names, they should have realized the need to act with humility despite their important status (*Devash LeFi*).

NOTES

The son of Harhas – בֶּן חַרְחַס: Although the description of Huldah as being married to "the son of Tikvah, the son of Harhas" is really a description of her husband Shallum's lineage, nevertheless the Gemara interprets it to be describing Huldah. The reason for this exposition is that nowhere else does the Bible mention the lineage of a woman who is referred to by the name of her husband. Therefore, mentioning an unknown person like Harhas as a point of lineage for Huldah's husband does not add to the understanding of her husband's background, and the information must be understood as teaching something else, in this case about Huldah's deeds (Maharsha).

Descended from Rahab – יָצְאוּ מֵרָחָב: The fact that priests and prophets descended from Rahab is a matter of interest because it is prohibited for a priest to marry a convert, especially one who was a harlot. A number of commentaries also discuss how Rahab, a member of the Canaanite people, was permitted to marry a Jewish man, albeit a non-priest, after her conversion (see *Tosafot* and *ge'onim*). The *Petah Einayim* and others explain that Joshua married her due to heavenly instruction.

אָמַר רַב נַחְמָן: חוּלְדָּה מִבְּנֵי בָנָיו שֶׁל יְהוֹשֻׁעַ הָיְתָה. כְּתִיב הָכָא ״בֶּן חַרְחַס״ וּכְתִיב הָתָם ״בְּתִמְנַת חֶרֶס״.

Furthermore, **Rav Naḥman said: Huldah was a descendant of Joshua.** An allusion to this **is written here:** "Huldah the prophetess, the wife of Shallum, the son of Tikvah, **the son of Harhas** [*ḥarḥas*]" (II Kings 22:14),[N] **and it says elsewhere** with regard to Joshua: "And they buried him in the border of his inheritance **in Timnath-heres** [*ḥeres*]" (Judges 2:9), therefore intimating that there is a certain connection between them.

אֵיתִיבֵיהּ רַב עֵינָא סָבָא לְרַב נַחְמָן: שְׁמוֹנָה נְבִיאִים וְהֵם כֹּהֲנִים יָצְאוּ מֵרָחָב הַזּוֹנָה, וְאֵלּוּ הֵן: נֵרִיָּה, בָּרוּךְ, וּשְׂרָיָה, מַחְסֵיָה, יִרְמְיָה, חִלְקִיָּה, חֲנַמְאֵל, וְשַׁלּוּם. רַבִּי יְהוּדָה אוֹמֵר: אַף חוּלְדָּה הַנְּבִיאָה מִבְּנֵי בָנֶיהָ שֶׁל רָחָב הַזּוֹנָה הָיְתָה. כְּתִיב הָכָא ״בֶּן תִּקְוָה״ וּכְתִיב הָתָם ״אֶת תִּקְוַת חוּט הַשָּׁנִי״!

Rav Eina the Elder raised an objection from a *baraita* **to Rav Naḥman's** teaching. The *baraita* indicates that Huldah was in fact a descendant of Rahab, and seemingly not of Joshua: **Eight prophets, who were** also **priests, descended from Rahab**[N] **the prostitute, and they are: Neriah;** his son **Baruch; Seraiah; Mahseiah; Jeremiah;** his father, **Hilkiah;** Jeremiah's cousin **Hanamel; and** Hanamel's father, **Shallum. Rabbi Yehuda said: So too, Huldah the prophetess was a descendant of Rahab the prostitute,** as **it is written here** with regard to Huldah: **"The son of Tikvah," and it is written elsewhere** in reference to Rahab's escape from the destruction of Jericho: **"This cord of** [*tikvat*] **scarlet thread"** (Joshua 2:18).

אֲמַר לֵיהּ: עֵינָא סָבָא! וְאָמְרִי לַהּ: פַּתְיָא אוּכָּמָא! מִינִי וּמִינָּךְ תִּסְתַּיֵּים שְׁמַעְתָּא; דְּאִיגַּיְירָא וּנְסָבָהּ יְהוֹשֻׁעַ. וּמִי הָווּ לֵיהּ זַרְעָא לִיהוֹשֻׁעַ? וְהָכְתִיב ״נוֹן בְּנוֹ יְהוֹשֻׁעַ בְּנוֹ״! בָּנֵי – לָא הָווּ לֵיהּ, בְּנָתָן – הָווּ לֵיהּ.

Rav Naḥman responded to Eina the Elder and **said to him: Eina the Elder, and some say** that he said to him: **Blackened pot,** i.e., my colleague in Torah, who has toiled and blackened his face in Torah study, **from me and from you the matter may be concluded,** i.e., the explanation lies in a combination of our two statements. **For** Rahab **converted and married Joshua,** and therefore Huldah descended from both Joshua and Rahab. The Gemara raises a difficulty: **But did Joshua have any descendants? But isn't it written** in the genealogical list of the tribe of Ephraim: **"Nun his son, Joshua his son"** (I Chronicles 7:27)? The listing does not continue any further, implying that Joshua had no sons. The Gemara answers: Indeed, **he did not have sons,** but **he did have daughters.**

Perek **I**
Daf **15** Amud **a**

NOTES

One's name and his father's name – שְׁמוֹ וְשֵׁם אָבִיו: As prophets were well known in their own right, there is no reason to mention a prophet's father other than to indicate that the latter was also a prophet (Maharsha).

It is known that he was from Jerusalem – בְּיָדוּעַ שֶׁהוּא מִירוּשָׁלַיִם: The Maharsha explains that there is an indication to this from a psalm, as it speaks of the praise of Jerusalem: "And of Zion it shall be said: This man and that man was born in her" (Psalms 87:5), signifying that famous people were born there.

בִּשְׁלָמָא אִינְהוּ – מִיפְּרְשִׁי, אֶלָּא אֲבָהֲתַיְיהוּ מְנָלַן?

The Gemara asks in reference to the eight prophets descended from Rahab: **Granted,** with regard to **them, it is explicit,** i.e., the four sons recorded in the list were certainly prophets, as the Bible states this explicitly: Jeremiah was a prophet, his student Baruch was one of the sons of the prophets, his cousin Hanamel came to him at the word of God (see Jeremiah, chapter 32), and Seraiah was his student. **But as for their fathers,** Hilkiah, Neriah, Shallum, and Mahseiah, **from where do we derive** that they were prophets?

כְּדְעוּלָּא. דְּאָמַר עוּלָּא: כָּל מָקוֹם שֶׁשְּׁמוֹ וְשֵׁם אָבִיו בִּנְבִיאוּת – בְּיָדוּעַ שֶׁהוּא נָבִיא בֶּן נָבִיא. שְׁמוֹ וְלֹא שֵׁם אָבִיו – בְּיָדוּעַ שֶׁהוּא נָבִיא וְלֹא בֶּן נָבִיא. שְׁמוֹ וְשֵׁם עִירוֹ מְפוֹרָשׁ – בְּיָדוּעַ שֶׁהוּא מֵאוֹתָהּ הָעִיר, שְׁמוֹ וְלֹא שֵׁם עִירוֹ – בְּיָדוּעַ שֶׁהוּא מִירוּשָׁלַיִם.

The Gemara answers: **As** taught by **Ulla, as Ulla said: Wherever one's name and his father's name**[N] are mentioned **with regard to prophecy, it is known that he was a prophet the son of a prophet,** and therefore his father's name is also mentioned. And wherever **his name** is mentioned **but not his father's name, it is known that he was a prophet but not the son of a prophet.** Similarly, wherever **his name and the name of his city are specified, it is known that he was from that** particular **city,** and wherever **his name** is mentioned **but not the name of his city, it is known that he was from Jerusalem.**[N]

בְּמַתְנִיתָא תָּנָא: כָּל שֶׁמַּעֲשָׂיו וּמַעֲשֵׂה אֲבוֹתָיו סְתוּמִין, וּפֵירֵט לְךָ הַכָּתוּב בְּאֶחָד מֵהֶן לְשֶׁבַח, כְּגוֹן ״דְּבַר ה׳ אֲשֶׁר הָיָה אֶל צְפַנְיָה בֶּן כּוּשִׁי בֶּן גְּדַלְיָה״ – בְּיָדוּעַ שֶׁהוּא צַדִּיק בֶּן צַדִּיק. וְכָל שֶׁפֵּירֵט לְךָ הַכָּתוּב בְּאֶחָד מֵהֶן לִגְנַאי, כְּגוֹן ״וַיְהִי בַּחֹדֶשׁ הַשְּׁבִיעִי בָּא יִשְׁמָעֵאל בֶּן נְתַנְיָה בֶּן אֱלִישָׁמָע״ – בְּיָדוּעַ שֶׁהוּא רָשָׁע בֶּן רָשָׁע.

It was taught in a *baraita*: With regard to **anyone whose actions and the actions of his ancestors are obscured** and not explained, **and the verse mentioned one of them favorably, for example,** the way in which Zephaniah the prophet is introduced: **"The word of the Lord which came to Zephaniah the son of Cushi, the son of Gedaliah"** (Zephaniah 1:1), **it is known that** not only **was he a righteous man,** he was also **the son of a righteous man. And** conversely, **whenever the verse mentioned one of them unfavorably, for example,** in the verse that introduces Ishmael as the one who killed Gedaliah, which states: **"And it came to pass in the seventh month that Ishmael the son of Nethaniah, the son of Elishama"** (Jeremiah 41:1), **it is known that** not only **was he a wicked man,** he was also **the son of a wicked man.**

אָמַר רַב נַחְמָן: מַלְאָכִי זֶה מָרְדֳּכַי, וְלָמָּה נִקְרָא שְׁמוֹ מַלְאָכִי – שֶׁהָיָה מִשְׁנֶה לְמֶלֶךְ. מֵיתִיבִי: בָּרוּךְ בֶּן נֵרִיָּה, וּשְׂרָיָה בֶּן מַעֲשֵׂיָה, וְדָנִיֵּאל, וּמָרְדֳּכַי בִּלְשָׁן, וְחַגַּי, זְכַרְיָה וּמַלְאָכִי – כּוּלָּן נִתְנַבְּאוּ בִּשְׁנַת שְׁתַּיִם לְדָרְיָוֶשׁ! תְּיוּבְתָּא.

Rav Naḥman said: Malachi the prophet **is** in fact **Mordecai, and why was he called Malachi?** To indicate **that he was second to the king** [*melekh*], as Mordecai was appointed such, as is recorded at the end of the Megilla. The Gemara **raises an objection** from the following *baraita*: **Baruch, the son of Neriah; Seraiah, the son of Mahseiah; Daniel; Mordecai; Bilshan; Haggai; Zechariah; and Malachi; all prophesied in the second year of** the reign of **Darius.** The fact that the *baraita* mentions Mordecai and Malachi separately indicates that they were two different people. The Gemara concludes: This is indeed **a conclusive refutation.**

תַּנְיָא, אָמַר רַבִּי יְהוֹשֻׁעַ בֶּן קָרְחָה: מַלְאָכִי זֶה עֶזְרָא, וַחֲכָמִים אוֹמְרִים: מַלְאָכִי שְׁמוֹ. אָמַר רַב נַחְמָן: מִסְתַּבְּרָא כְּמַאן דַּאֲמַר מַלְאָכִי זֶה עֶזְרָא, דִּכְתִיב בִּנְבִיאוּת מַלְאָכִי: ״בָּגְדָה יְהוּדָה וְתוֹעֵבָה נֶעֶשְׂתָה בְיִשְׂרָאֵל וּבִירוּשָׁלָיִם כִּי חִלֵּל יְהוּדָה קֹדֶשׁ ה׳ אֲשֶׁר אָהֵב וּבָעַל בַּת אֵל נֵכָר״,

It is taught in a *baraita*: **Rabbi Yehoshua ben Korḥa said: Malachi is** in fact **Ezra. And the Rabbis say** otherwise: **Malachi was his** real **name,** and it was not merely another name for Ezra or another prophet. **Rav Naḥman said:** It **stands to reason** that indeed, they are one and the same person, **like** the opinion of **the one who said that Malachi is Ezra,** since there is a similarity between them, **as it is stated in Malachi's prophecy: "Judah has dealt treacherously, and a disgusting thing has been done in Israel and in Jerusalem; for Judah has profaned the sanctity of the Lord which he loved, and has married the daughter of a strange god"** (Malachi 2:11).

וּמַאן אַפְרֵישׁ נָשִׁים גּוֹיוֹת – עֶזְרָא, דִּכְתִיב ״וַיַּעַן שְׁכַנְיָה בֶן יְחִיאֵל מִבְּנֵי עֵילָם וַיֹּאמֶר לְעֶזְרָא אֲנַחְנוּ מָעַלְנוּ בֵאלֹהֵינוּ וַנֹּשֶׁב נָשִׁים נָכְרִיּוֹת״.

And who was the one that **removed the foreign women** who were married to Jews? It was **Ezra, as it is written: "And Shecaniah the son of Jehiel, one of the sons of Elam, answered and said unto Ezra: We have broken faith with our God, and have married foreign women** of the peoples of the land" (Ezra 10:2). It therefore appears that Malachi was one of Ezra's names, as the Bible describes them both as confronting an intermarriage epidemic.

תָּנוּ רַבָּנַן: אַרְבַּע נָשִׁים יְפֵיפִיּוֹת הָיוּ בָּעוֹלָם: שָׂרָה (וַאֲבִיגַיִל, רָחָב) וְאֶסְתֵּר. וּלְמַאן דַּאֲמַר אֶסְתֵּר יַרְקְרוֹקֶת הָיְתָה – מַפֵּיק אֶסְתֵּר וּמְעַיֵּיל וַשְׁתִּי.

To complete the discussion about the prophetesses, the Gemara cites a *baraita* in which **the Sages taught: There were four women of extraordinary beauty**[N] **in the world: Sarah, and Abigail, Rahab, and Esther. And according to the one who said** that **Esther was greenish** in color, lacking natural beauty, only that a cord of divine grace was strung around her, **remove Esther** from the list **and insert Vashti** in her place, for she was indeed beautiful.

תָּנוּ רַבָּנַן: רָחָב בִּשְׁמָהּ זִינְּתָה, יָעֵל בְּקוֹלָהּ, אֲבִיגַיִל בִּזְכִירָתָהּ, מִיכַל בַּת שָׁאוּל בִּרְאִיָּיתָהּ. אָמַר רַבִּי יִצְחָק: כׇּל הָאוֹמֵר רָחָב רָחָב – מִיָּד נִיקְרִי. אֲמַר לֵיהּ רַב נַחְמָן: אֲנָא אָמִינָא רָחָב רָחָב וְלָא אִיכְפַּת לִי! אֲמַר לֵיהּ: כִּי קָאָמֵינָא – בְּיוֹדְעָהּ וּבְמַכִּירָהּ.

The Sages taught in a *baraita*: **Rahab aroused impure thoughts by her name,**[N] i.e., the mere mention of her name would inspire lust for her; **Yael, by her voice; Abigail, by remembering her; Michal, the daughter of Saul, by her appearance.** Similarly, **Rabbi Yitzḥak said: Anyone who says Rahab, Rahab, immediately experiences a seminal emission** due to the arousal of desire caused by Rahab's great beauty. **Rav Naḥman said to him: I say: Rahab, Rahab, and it does not affect me.** Rabbi Yitzchak **said to** Rav Naḥman: **When I said this,** I was specifically referring **to one who knows her** personally **and recognizes her** beauty. Only for one who has met Rahab in person is the mere mention of her name capable of arousing lust.

״וּמָרְדֳּכַי יָדַע אֶת כׇּל אֲשֶׁר נַעֲשָׂה״, מַאי אֲמַר? רַב אָמַר: גָּבַהּ הָמָן מֵאֲחַשְׁוֵרוֹשׁ. וּשְׁמוּאֵל אָמַר: גָּבַר מַלְכָּא עִילָּאָה מִמַּלְכָּא תַּתָּאָה.

§ The Gemara returns to its explanation of the verses of the book of Esther. The verse states: **"When Mordecai perceived all that was done,**[N] Mordecai rent his clothes, and put on sackcloth with ashes, and went out into the midst of the city, and cried with a loud and bitter cry" (Esther 4:1). The Gemara asks: **What did** Mordecai **say** when he cried out? **Rav said:** He said that **Haman has risen above Ahasuerus,** for he saw that Haman had become even stronger than Ahasuerus himself, and that he controlled all affairs of the empire. **And Shmuel said: The upper King has prevailed over the lower king,** saying this euphemistically and insinuating just the opposite. In other words, it would appear that Ahasuerus, the lower king, has prevailed over the higher King, God in Heaven, Who desires good for the Jewish people.

״וַתִּתְחַלְחַל הַמַּלְכָּה״, מַאי ״וַתִּתְחַלְחַל״? אָמַר רַב: שֶׁפֵּירְסָה נִדָּה, וְרַבִּי יִרְמְיָה אָמַר: שֶׁהוּצְרְכָה לִנְקָבֶיהָ.

The verse states: **"Then the queen was exceedingly distressed"** [*vatitḥalḥal*] (Esther 4:4). The Gemara asks: **What is** the meaning of *vatitḥalḥal*? **Rav said:** This means **that she began to menstruate**[B] out of fear, as the cavities, *ḥalalim*, of her body opened. **And Rabbi Yirmeya said: Her bowels were loosened,** also understanding the verse as referring to her bodily cavities.

NOTES

There were four woman of extraordinary beauty – אַרְבַּע נָשִׁים יְפֵיפִיּוֹת: Some explain that this is mentioned to indicate how dangerous their beauty was for others, as all who were enticed by their beauty experienced calamity (see *Iyyun Ya'akov* and Maharsha).

Rahab aroused impure thoughts by her name – רָחָב בִּשְׁמָהּ זִינְּתָה: The verses that mention these various women refer to their enticing characteristic. With regard to Rahab, whose name aroused others, it states: "Whose name was Rahab" (Joshua 2:1). With regard to Yael, the verse refers to her speech: "And she said to him, turn in, my lord, turn in to me, fear not" (Judges 4:18). With regard to Abigail, the memory of her was enticing, it states: "Then remember your handmaid" (I Samuel 25:31). With regard to Michal, whose appearance was arousing, it states: "Michal the daughter of Saul appeared through the window" (II Samuel 6:16; see Maharsha). The *Noda Bihuda* explains that this talmudic statement was mentioned in order to teach that each one of these characteristics carries with it potential for arousal, and one must therefore be cautious with regard to them.

All that was done – כׇּל אֲשֶׁר נַעֲשָׂה: According to some interpretations, Mordecai cried out because he was aware of aspects of the decree that others were not. Rashi, in his commentary on the Megilla, explains that Mordecai cried out because it was revealed to him that even Heaven had agreed to this decree (see *Arugot HaBosem*).

BACKGROUND

That she began to menstruate – שֶׁפֵּירְסָה נִדָּה: It is not uncommon for psychological trauma to cause an irregular flow of menstrual blood, even in women with a relatively regular cycle.

NOTES

Hathach is Daniel – הֲתָךְ זֶה דָּנִיאֵל: The Maharsha explains that this is derived from the fact that Hathach appears to be trusted by both Esther and Mordecai, seemingly indicating that he was a Jew. In the book of Daniel (1:18–21), Daniel is mentioned as one of the king's Jewish chamberlains during the time of the Persian Empire.

One does not bring back a sad report – אֵין מְשִׁיבִין עַל הַקַּלְקָלָה: It is generally viewed as proper conduct not to hasten to be the bearer of bad news. Esther's rejection of Mordecai's request to take immediate action was an unfavorable piece of information, and therefore, Hathach did not deliver the news personally (*Manot HaLevi*).

LANGUAGE

An ordinary person [*hedyot*] – הֶדְיוֹט: From the Greek ἰδιώτης, *idiotès*, meaning a simple man who lacks any official position. Here it is used in the context of an ordinary man without any specific spiritual achievement, one not known for his righteousness.

״וַתִּקְרָא אֶסְתֵּר לַהֲתָךְ״ אָמַר רַב: הֲתָךְ זֶה דָּנִיאֵל, וְלָמָּה נִקְרָא שְׁמוֹ הֲתָךְ – שֶׁחֲתָכוּהוּ מִגְּדוּלָּתוֹ. וּשְׁמוּאֵל אָמַר: שֶׁכׇּל דִּבְרֵי מַלְכוּת נֶחְתָּכִין עַל פִּיו.

The verse states: **"Then Esther called for Hathach,** one of the king's chamberlains, whom he had appointed to attend upon her" (Esther 4:5). **Rav said: Hathach is** in fact the prophet **Daniel.**[N] **And why was he called Hathach? Because he was cut down [*ḥatakh*] from his greatness** during Ahasuerus's reign, as he was demoted from his high position. Previously he had served as a senior minister, and now he had become Esther's steward. **And Shmuel** expounded the name Hathach as derived from *ḥatakh* in the opposite sense, as he **said:** Daniel was called Hathach **because all the affairs of the kingdom were decided [*neḥtakhin*] by his word.**

״לָדַעַת מַה זֶּה וְעַל מַה זֶּה״ אָמַר רַבִּי יִצְחָק: שָׁלְחָה לוֹ: שֶׁמָּא עָבְרוּ יִשְׂרָאֵל עַל חֲמִשָּׁה חוּמְשֵׁי תוֹרָה, דִּכְתִיב בָּהֶן ״מִזֶּה וּמִזֶּה הֵם כְּתוּבִים״.

The verse continues to relate that Esther sent Hathach to Mordecai after hearing about the decree: **"To know what this [*zeh*] was, and why it [*zeh*] was"** (Esther 4:5). **Rabbi Yitzḥak said** that Esther **sent** a message **to** Mordecai, saying: **Perhaps the Jews have transgressed the five books of the Torah, as it is written** with regard to the two tablets: **"On this [*zeh*] side and on the other [*zeh*] side were they written"** (Exodus 32:15).

״וַיַּגִּידוּ לְמׇרְדֳּכַי אֵת דִּבְרֵי אֶסְתֵּר״, וְאִילּוּ אִיהוּ לָא אֲזַל לְגַבֵּיהּ – מִכָּאן שֶׁאֵין מְשִׁיבִין עַל הַקַּלְקָלָה.

The verse states: **"And they told Esther's words to Mordecai"** (Esther 4:12), **but he,** Hathach himself, **did not go to tell him** directly. The Gemara explains: **From here** we see that **one does not bring back a sad report.**[N] If one has nothing positive to say, it is best for him to remain silent. This explains why Hathach himself did not report the information to Mordecai, and Esther's words had to be delivered by other messengers.

״לֵךְ כְּנוֹס אֶת כׇּל הַיְּהוּדִים״ וגו׳ עַד ״אֲשֶׁר לֹא כַדָּת״, אָמַר רַבִּי אַבָּא: שֶׁלֹּא כַּדָּת הָיָה, שֶׁבְּכׇל יוֹם וָיוֹם עַד עַכְשָׁיו – בְּאוֹנֶס, וְעַכְשָׁיו – בְּרָצוֹן. ״וְכַאֲשֶׁר אָבַדְתִּי אָבָדְתִּי״ – כְּשֵׁם שֶׁאָבַדְתִּי מִבֵּית אַבָּא כָּךְ אוֹבַד מִמְּךָ.

Esther sent a message to Mordecai: **"Go, gather together all the Jews** who are present in Shushan, and fast for me, and neither eat nor drink for three days, night and day; I also and my maidens will fast likewise, and so will I go in to the king, **not according to the custom"** (Esther 4:16). **Rabbi Abba said: It will not be according to** my usual **custom, for every day until now** when I submitted myself to Ahasuerus it was **under compulsion, but now** I will be submitting myself to him **of my** own free **will.** And Esther further said: **"And if I perish, I perish"** (Esther 4:16). What she meant was: **Just as I was lost to my father's house** ever since I was brought here, **so too, shall I be lost to you,** for after voluntarily having relations with Ahasuerus, I shall be forever forbidden to you.

״וַיַּעֲבֹר מׇרְדֳּכַי״ אָמַר רַב: שֶׁהֶעֱבִיר יוֹם רִאשׁוֹן שֶׁל פֶּסַח בְּתַעֲנִית. וּשְׁמוּאֵל אָמַר: דַּעֲבַר עַרְקוֹמָא דְּמַיָּא.

There is a dispute with regard to the meaning of the verse: **"So Mordecai passed [*vaya'avor*]"** (Esther 4:17). **Rav said:** This means **that he passed the first day of Passover as a fast day,** understanding the word *vaya'avor* in the sense of sin [*aveira*], as by doing so he transgressed the obligation to rejoice on the Festival. **And Shmuel said:** It means **that he crossed over [*avar*] a stream** in order to bring the message to all.

״וַיְהִי בַּיּוֹם הַשְּׁלִישִׁי וַתִּלְבַּשׁ אֶסְתֵּר מַלְכוּת״, בִּגְדֵי מַלְכוּת מִיבְּעֵי לֵיהּ! אָמַר רַבִּי אֶלְעָזָר אָמַר רַבִּי חֲנִינָא: מְלַמֵּד שֶׁלְּבָשַׁתָּה רוּחַ הַקֹּדֶשׁ, כְּתִיב הָכָא ״וַתִּלְבַּשׁ״ וּכְתִיב הָתָם ״וְרוּחַ לָבְשָׁה אֶת עֲמָשַׂי״.

The verse states: **"And it came to pass on the third day, that Esther clothed herself in royalty"** (Esther 5:1). The Gemara asks: **It should have said:** Esther clothed herself in **royal garments. Rabbi Elazar said** that **Rabbi Ḥanina said: This teaches that she clothed herself with** a **divine** spirit of **inspiration,** as **it is written here: "And she clothed herself,"** and **it is written elsewhere: "And the spirit clothed Amasai"** (I Chronicles 12:19). Just as there the reference is to the spirit of divine inspiration, so too here, the term royalty is referring to the spirit of divine inspiration.

וְאָמַר רַבִּי אֶלְעָזָר אָמַר רַבִּי חֲנִינָא: לְעוֹלָם אַל תְּהִי בִּרְכַּת הֶדְיוֹט קַלָּה בְּעֵינֶיךָ, שֶׁהֲרֵי שְׁנֵי גְּדוֹלֵי הַדּוֹר בֵּרְכוּם שְׁנֵי הֶדְיוֹטוֹת וְנִתְקַיְּימָה בָּהֶן, וְאֵלּוּ הֵן: דָּוִד וְדָנִיאֵל. דָּוִד – דְּבָרְכֵיהּ אֲרַוְנָה, דִּכְתִיב ״וַיֹּאמֶר אֲרַוְנָה אֶל הַמֶּלֶךְ״ וגו׳. דָּנִיאֵל – דְּבָרְכֵיהּ דָּרְיָוֶשׁ, דִּכְתִיב ״אֱלָהָךְ דִּי אַנְתְּ פָּלַח לֵיהּ בִּתְדִירָא הוּא יְשֵׁיזְבִנָּךְ״.

Apropos a statement that Rabbi Elazar said that Rabbi Ḥanina said, the Gemara records other such statements: **And Rabbi Elazar** further **said** that **Rabbi Ḥanina said: One should never regard the blessing of an ordinary person [*hedyot*]**[L] **as light in your eyes, as two** of the **great men of** their **generations received blessings from ordinary people and** those blessings **were fulfilled in them. And they were David and Daniel. David, for Araunah blessed him, as it is written: "And Araunah said to the king,** May the Lord your God accept you" (II Samuel 24:23), and it was fulfilled. **Daniel, for Darius blessed him, as it is written: "Your God Whom you serve continually, He will rescue you"** (Daniel 6:17), and this too was fulfilled when Daniel was saved from the lions' den.

וְאָמַר רַבִּי אֶלְעָזָר אָמַר רַבִּי חֲנִינָא: אַל תְּהִי קִלְלַת הֶדְיוֹט קַלָּה בְּעֵינֶיךָ, שֶׁהֲרֵי אֲבִימֶלֶךְ קִלֵּל אֶת שָׂרָה ״הִנֵּה הוּא לָךְ כְּסוּת עֵינַיִם״ וְנִתְקַיֵּים בְּזַרְעָהּ ״וַיְהִי כִּי זָקֵן יִצְחָק וַתִּכְהֶיןָ עֵינָיו״.

And Rabbi Elazar further **said** that **Rabbi Ḥanina said: One should not regard the curse of an ordinary person as light in your eyes, for Abimelech cursed Sarah,** saying: **"Behold, it is to you a covering of the eyes**[N] to all that are with you" (Genesis 20:16), **and** indeed **this was fulfilled in her descendant,** as it is stated: **"And it came to pass, that when Isaac was old, and his eyes were dim,** so that he could not see" (Genesis 27:1). Abimelech's curse of covered eyes was fulfilled through her son Isaac's blindness.

וְאָמַר רַבִּי אֶלְעָזָר אָמַר רַבִּי חֲנִינָא: בֹּא וּרְאֵה שֶׁלֹּא כְּמִדַּת הַקָּדוֹשׁ בָּרוּךְ הוּא מִדַּת בָּשָׂר וָדָם; מִדַּת בָּשָׂר וָדָם אָדָם שׁוֹפֵת קְדֵרָה וְאַחַר כָּךְ נוֹתֵן לְתוֹכָהּ מַיִם, אֲבָל הַקָּדוֹשׁ בָּרוּךְ הוּא – נוֹתֵן מַיִם וְאַחַר כָּךְ שׁוֹפֵת הַקְּדֵרָה, לְקַיֵּים מַה שֶּׁנֶּאֱמַר ״לְקוֹל תִּתּוֹ הֲמוֹן מַיִם בַּשָּׁמַיִם״.

And Rabbi Elazar further **said** that **Rabbi Ḥanina said: Come and see that the attribute of the Holy One, Blessed be He, is unlike the attribute of** a man of **flesh and blood; for** it is **the attribute of flesh and blood** that **a man places the pot on the fire and then puts in the water. However, the Holy One, Blessed be He,** first **puts in the water and then places the pot on the fire, to fulfill that which is stated: "At the sound of His giving a multitude of waters in the heavens"** (Jeremiah 10:13), which he explains as follows: First God set the multitudes of water in place, and afterward He created the heavens to hold the water.

וְאָמַר רַבִּי אֶלְעָזָר אָמַר רַבִּי חֲנִינָא: כׇּל הָאוֹמֵר דָּבָר בְּשֵׁם אוֹמְרוֹ מֵבִיא גְאוּלָּה לָעוֹלָם, שֶׁנֶּאֱמַר: ״וַתֹּאמֶר אֶסְתֵּר לַמֶּלֶךְ בְּשֵׁם מׇרְדֳּכָי״.

And Rabbi Elazar further **said** that **Rabbi Ḥanina said: Whoever reports a saying in the name of he who said it brings redemption to the world. As it is stated** with respect to the incident of Bigthan and Teresh: **"And Esther reported it to the king in the name of Mordecai"** (Esther 2:22), and this eventually brought redemption, as Mordecai was later rewarded for saving the king's life, paving the way for the miraculous salvation.

וְאָמַר רַבִּי אֶלְעָזָר אָמַר רַבִּי חֲנִינָא: צַדִּיק אָבַד – לְדוֹרוֹ אָבַד. מָשָׁל לְאָדָם שֶׁאָבְדָה לוֹ מַרְגָּלִית, כׇּל מָקוֹם שֶׁהִיא – מַרְגָּלִית שְׁמָהּ, לֹא אָבְדָה אֶלָּא לְבַעְלָהּ.

And Rabbi Elazar further **said** that **Rabbi Ḥanina said:** When **a righteous man** passes from this earth and is **lost,**[N] he **is lost** only **for** the rest of **his generation,** who is now deprived of him, not for the righteous individual himself. This is **similar to a man who has lost a pearl.**[B] The pearl does not care if it is lost, as **wherever it is found, it is still a pearl; it is lost only to its owner.**

״וְכׇל זֶה אֵינֶנּוּ שֹׁוֶה לִי״, אָמַר רַבִּי אֶלְעָזָר אָמַר רַבִּי חֲנִינָא: בְּשָׁעָה שֶׁרָאָה הָמָן אֶת מׇרְדֳּכַי יוֹשֵׁב בְּשַׁעַר הַמֶּלֶךְ אָמַר: כׇּל זֶה אֵינוֹ שָׁוֶה לִי כִּדְרַב חִסְדָּא. דְּאָמַר רַב חִסְדָּא: זֶה בָּא בִּפְרוֹזְבּוּלִי וְזֶה בָּא

Haman said: **"Yet all this avails me nothing"** (Esther 5:13). **Rabbi Elazar said** that **Rabbi Ḥanina said: When Haman saw Mordecai sitting at the king's gate he said: Yet all this avails me nothing.** This may be understood **as** was suggested **by Rav Ḥisda, for Rav Ḥisda said: This one,** Mordecai, **came as** one with the heritage of **a rich man** [***perozebuli***],[L] whereas **that one,** Haman, **came**

NOTES

Covering of the eyes – **כְּסוּת עֵינַיִם**: Some explain Abimelech's curse symbolically. Abimelech was angry at Sarah for tricking him, and therefore cursed her that the same should also happen to her descendants. Abimelech's curse came true when Isaac was tricked by his family when blessing his sons (*Yefe Toar*).

When a righteous man is lost – **צַדִּיק אָבַד**: The *Iyyun Ya'akov* explains that this remark was said at Isaac's eulogy, as the essence of the eulogy was not over the death of Isaac, since his soul, like a diamond impervious to damage, was not lost. The purpose of the eulogy was to make known what his loss meant for that generation.

BACKGROUND

Pearl – **מַרְגָּלִית**: A pearl is a hard object produced within the soft tissue of a living shelled mollusk. Just like the shell of a clam, a pearl is made up of calcium carbonate that has been deposited in concentric layers. The ideal pearl is perfectly round and smooth, but many other shapes of pearls occur. The finest-quality natural pearls have been highly valued as gemstones and objects of beauty since antiquity, and because of this the word pearl has become a metaphor for something fine and valuable.

Pearl in oyster

LANGUAGE

A rich man [*perozebuli*] – **פְּרוֹזְבּוּלִי**: The Aramaic usage of this word is a matter of dispute, though it is possibly based on the Greek term used in Egypt, προβολή, *probolh*, meaning producer or originator of a document of indebtedness. However, this explanation does not adequately explain the letter *zayin* in this word.

Perek **I**
Daf **15** Amud **b**

בִּפְרוֹזְבּוּטִי. אָמַר רַב פַּפָּא: וְקָרוּ לֵיהּ עַבְדָּא דְּמִזְדַּבַּן בְּטַלְמֵי.

as one with the heritage of **a poor man** [***perozeboti***],[L] as Mordecai had been Haman's slave master and was aware of Haman's lowly lineage. **Rav Pappa said: And he was called: The slave who was sold for** a loaf of **bread.**[N]

LANGUAGE

Poor man [*perozeboti*] – **פְּרוֹזְבּוּטִי**: From the Greek πρεσβευτής, *presbeutès*, indicating a petitioner. This definition would lead to the opposite understanding of the Gemara, as Haman is the one who has come with his *perozebuli*, his bill of sale, and Mordecai is the petitioner, the one who comes with the claims of the *perozeboti*.

NOTES

The slave who was sold for bread – **עַבְדָּא דְּמִזְדַּבַּן בְּטַלְמֵי**: Both here as well as subsequently (16a), the Talmud makes reference to an aggadic midrash that is not found in the Talmud but appears in several works of *midrashim*. The *aggada* relates that Haman was initially a barber and a bathhouse attendant who later rose to became one of Ahasuerus's ministers. Ahasuerus sent him and Mordecai as army officers to the battlefront. Haman enjoyed himself while away and squandered all of his money. Unable to support himself, and hungry for bread, he was compelled to sell himself as a slave to Mordecai. Although Haman rose to greatness upon his return, he wanted to destroy Mordecai, who held his bill of servitude (see *Manot HaLevi*).

NOTES

To the gate, this is referring to the Torah scholars who arrive early – שָׁעְרָה, אֵלּוּ תַּלְמִידֵי חֲכָמִים שֶׁמַּשְׁכִּימִין: The Maharsha in tractate *Sanhedrin* explains that Torah scholars are like gatekeepers for the synagogues and study halls, as they open and lock the gates.

These also reel through wine – גַּם אֵלֶּה בַּיַּיִן שָׁגוּ: It appears from Rashi that even the Torah scholars had unduly partaken of wine. Others explain that although the Torah scholars did not partake of the wine, the majority of the people did. Nevertheless, the Torah scholars bear communal responsibility and are held responsible for the community's actions (see Rabbi Yoshiya Pinto).

An action done due to circumstances beyond one's control as one done willingly – אוֹנֶס כְּרָצוֹן: The commentaries discuss the various ramifications that stem from this Gemara; see, among others, Responsa *Shevut Ya'akov* and *Noda Bihuda* in their discussion of this issue. They suggest that even though Esther willingly went to Ahasuerus, nevertheless, her actions should still be viewed as having been done under duress, since she did so without any desire other than to save the Jews (see *Iyyun Ya'akov*).

״וְכָל זֶה אֵינֶנּוּ שׁוֶֹה לִי״ – מְלַמֵּד שֶׁכָּל גְּנָזָיו שֶׁל אוֹתוֹ רָשָׁע חֲקוּקִין עַל לִבּוֹ, וּבְשָׁעָה שֶׁרוֹאֶה אֶת מָרְדֳּכַי יוֹשֵׁב בְּשַׁעַר הַמֶּלֶךְ אָמַר: ״כָּל זֶה אֵינֶנּוּ שׁוֶֹה לִי״.

Haman's previously quoted statement: **"Yet all this avails me nothing"** (Esther 5:13), **teaches that all the treasures of that wicked one were engraved on his heart, and when he saw Mordecai sitting at the king's gate, he said:** As long as Mordecai is around, **all this** that I wear on my heart **avails me nothing.**

וְאָמַר רַבִּי אֶלְעָזָר אָמַר רַבִּי חֲנִינָא: עָתִיד הַקָּדוֹשׁ בָּרוּךְ הוּא לִהְיוֹת עֲטָרָה בְּרֹאשׁ כָּל צַדִּיק וְצַדִּיק, שֶׁנֶּאֱמַר: ״בַּיּוֹם הַהוּא יִהְיֶה ה׳ צְבָאוֹת לַעֲטֶרֶת צְבִי״ [וגו׳]. מַאי ״לַעֲטֶרֶת צְבִי וְלִצְפִירַת תִּפְאָרָה״ – לָעוֹשִׂין צִבְיוֹנוֹ וְלַמְצַפִּין תִּפְאַרְתּוֹ. יָכוֹל לַכֹּל – תַּלְמוּד לוֹמַר ״לִשְׁאָר עַמּוֹ״ – לְמִי שֶׁמֵּשִׂים עַצְמוֹ כְּשִׁירַיִם.

And Rabbi Elazar further **said** that **Rabbi Ḥanina said: In the future, the Holy One, Blessed be He, will be a crown on the head of each and every righteous man. As it is stated: "In that day shall the Lord of hosts be for a crown of glory,** and for a diadem of beauty, to the residue of His people" (Isaiah 28:5). **What is** the meaning of **"for a crown of glory [*tzevi*], and for a diadem [*velitzefirat*] of beauty"?** A crown **for those that do His will [*tzivyono*]** and a diadem **for those that await [*velamtzapin*] His glory.** One **might** have thought that this extends **to all** such individuals. Therefore, **the verse states: "To the residue of his people," to whoever regards himself as a remainder,** i.e., small and unimportant like residue. But whoever holds himself in high esteem will not merit this.

״וּלְרוּחַ מִשְׁפָּט״ – זֶה הַדָּן אֶת יִצְרוֹ, ״וּלְיוֹשֵׁב עַל הַמִּשְׁפָּט״ – זֶה הַדָּן דִּין אֱמֶת לַאֲמִתּוֹ. ״וְלִגְבוּרָה״ – זֶה הַמִּתְגַּבֵּר עַל יִצְרוֹ. ״מְשִׁיבֵי מִלְחָמָה״ – שֶׁנּוֹשְׂאִין וְנוֹתְנִין בְּמִלְחַמְתָּהּ שֶׁל תּוֹרָה. ״שָׁעְרָה״ [אֵלּוּ תַּלְמִידֵי חֲכָמִים] שֶׁמַּשְׁכִּימִין וּמַעֲרִיבִין בְּבָתֵּי כְנֵסִיּוֹת וּבְבָתֵּי מִדְרָשׁוֹת.

Apropos the quotation from Isaiah, the Gemara explains the following verse, which states: "And for a spirit of justice to him that sits in judgment and for strength to them that turn back the battle to the gate" (Isaiah 28:6). **"And for a spirit of justice"; this** is referring to **one who brings his** evil **inclination to trial** and forces himself to repent. **"To him that sits in judgment"; this** is referring to **one who judges an absolutely true judgment. "And for strength"; this** is referring to **one who triumphs over his** evil **inclination. "Them that turn back the battle";** this is referring to those **that give and take** in their discussion of *halakha* **in the battle of** understanding **the Torah. "To the gate";** this is referring to **the Torah scholars who arrive early**[N] **and stay late** at the darkened gates **of the synagogues and study halls.**

אָמְרָה מִדַּת הַדִּין לִפְנֵי הַקָּדוֹשׁ בָּרוּךְ הוּא: רִבּוֹנוֹ שֶׁל עוֹלָם! מַה נִּשְׁתַּנּוּ אֵלּוּ מֵאֵלּוּ? אָמַר לָהּ הַקָּדוֹשׁ בָּרוּךְ הוּא: יִשְׂרָאֵל עָסְקוּ בַּתּוֹרָה, אוּמּוֹת הָעוֹלָם לֹא עָסְקוּ בַּתּוֹרָה.

The Gemara continues with an episode associated with a verse in Isaiah. **The Attribute of Justice said before the Holy One, Blessed be He: Master of the Universe, how are these,** referring to the Jewish people, **different from those,** the other nations of the world, such that God performs miracles only on behalf of the Jewish people? **The Holy One, Blessed be He, said to** it: **The Jewish people occupied themselves with Torah,** whereas **the** other **nations of the world did not occupy themselves with Torah.**

אֲמַר לֵיהּ: ״גַּם אֵלֶּה בַּיַּיִן שָׁגוּ וּבַשֵּׁכָר תָּעוּ... פָּקוּ פְּלִילִיָּה״, אֵין ״פָּקוּ״ אֶלָּא גֵּיהִנָּם, שֶׁנֶּאֱמַר ״וְלֹא תִהְיֶה זֹאת לְךָ לְפוּקָה״, וְאֵין ״פְּלִילִיָּה״ אֶלָּא דַּיָּינִין, שֶׁנֶּאֱמַר ״וְנָתַן בִּפְלִלִים״.

The Attribute of Justice **said to Him: "These also reel through wine,**[N] **and stagger through strong drink;** the priest and the prophet reel through strong drink, they are confused because of wine, they stagger because of strong drink; they reel in vision, **they stumble [*paku*] in judgment [*peliliyya*]"** (Isaiah 28:7). The word ***paku*** in this context is referring **only to Gehenna, as it is stated: "That this shall not be a cause of stumbling [*puka*] to you"** (I Samuel 25:31), **and** the word ***peliliyya*** here is referring **only to judges, as it is stated: "And he shall pay as the judges determine [*bifelilim*]"** (Exodus 21:22). The response of the Attribute of Justice was essentially that the Jewish people have also sinned and are consequently liable to receive punishment.

״וַתַּעֲמֹד בַּחֲצַר בֵּית הַמֶּלֶךְ הַפְּנִימִית״. אָמַר רַבִּי לֵוִי: כֵּיוָן שֶׁהִגִּיעָה לְבֵית הַצְּלָמִים – נִסְתַּלְּקָה הֵימֶנָּה שְׁכִינָה, אָמְרָה: ״אֵלִי אֵלִי לָמָה עֲזַבְתָּנִי״ שֶׁמָּא אַתָּה דָּן עַל שׁוֹגֵג כְּמֵזִיד וְעַל אוֹנֶס כְּרָצוֹן?

§ The Gemara returns to its explanation of the verses of the Megilla. The verse states with regard to Esther: **"And she stood in the inner court of the king's house"** (Esther 5:1). **Rabbi Levi said: Once she reached the chamber of the idols,** which was in the inner court, **the Divine Presence left her. She** immediately **said: "My God, my God, why have You forsaken me?"** (Psalms 22:2). **Perhaps** it is because **You judge an unintentional sin as one** performed **intentionally, and** an action **done due to** circumstances **beyond one's control as** one done **willingly.**[N]

אוֹ שֶׁמָּא עַל שֶׁקְּרָאתִיו כֶּלֶב, שֶׁנֶּאֱמַר ״הַצִּילָה מֵחֶרֶב נַפְשִׁי מִיַּד כֶּלֶב יְחִידָתִי״. חָזְרָה וּקְרָאַתּוּ אַרְיֵה, שֶׁנֶּאֱמַר ״הוֹשִׁיעֵנִי מִפִּי אַרְיֵה״.

Or perhaps You have left me **because** in my prayers **I called** Haman **a dog,**[N] **as it is stated: "Deliver my soul from the sword; my only one from the hand of the dog"** (Psalms 22:21). **She** at once **retracted and called him** in her prayers **a lion, as it is stated** in the following verse: **"Save me from the lion's mouth"** (Psalms 22:22).

״וַיְהִי כִרְאוֹת הַמֶּלֶךְ אֶת אֶסְתֵּר הַמַּלְכָּה״ אָמַר רַבִּי יוֹחָנָן: שְׁלֹשָׁה מַלְאֲכֵי הַשָּׁרֵת נִזְדַּמְּנוּ לָהּ בְּאוֹתָהּ שָׁעָה: אֶחָד שֶׁהִגְבִּיהַּ אֶת צַוָּארָהּ, וְאֶחָד שֶׁמָּשַׁךְ חוּט שֶׁל חֶסֶד עָלֶיהָ, וְאֶחָד שֶׁמָּתַח אֶת הַשַּׁרְבִיט.

The verse states: **"And so it was, that when the king saw Esther the queen** standing in the court, that she obtained favor in his sight; and the king held out to Esther the golden scepter that was in his hand" (Esther 5:2). **Rabbi Yoḥanan said: Three ministering angels**[N] **happened to join her at that time: One that raised up her neck,** so that she could stand erect, free of shame; **one that strung a cord** of divine **grace around her,** endowing her with charm and beauty; **and one that stretched the** king's **scepter.**[B]

וְכַמָּה? אָמַר רַבִּי יִרְמְיָה: שְׁתֵּי אַמּוֹת הָיָה וְהֶעֱמִידוֹ עַל שְׁתֵּים עֶשְׂרֵה, וְאָמְרִי לָהּ: עַל שֵׁשׁ עֶשְׂרֵה, וְאָמְרִי לָהּ: עַל עֶשְׂרִים וְאַרְבַּע. בְּמַתְנִיתָא תָּנָא: עַל שִׁשִּׁים. וְכֵן אַתָּה מוֹצֵא בְּאַמָּתָהּ שֶׁל בַּת פַּרְעֹה, וְכֵן אַתָּה מוֹצֵא בְּשִׁינֵּי רְשָׁעִים. דִּכְתִיב ״שִׁינֵּי רְשָׁעִים שִׁבַּרְתָּ״, וְאָמַר רֵישׁ לָקִישׁ: אַל תִּקְרֵי שִׁבַּרְתָּ אֶלָּא שִׁרְיבַּבְתָּ. רַבָּה בַּר עוֹפְרָן אָמַר מִשּׁוּם רַבִּי אֶלְעָזָר, שֶׁשָּׁמַע מֵרַבּוֹ, וְרַבּוֹ מֵרַבּוֹ: מָאתַיִם.

How much was it stretched? **Rabbi Yirmeya said:** The scepter **was two cubits, and he made it twelve** cubits. **And some say** that he made it **sixteen**[N] cubits, and yet **others say twenty-four** cubits. **It was taught in a *baraita*:** He made it **sixty** cubits. **And similarly you find with the arm of Pharaoh's daughter,** which she stretched out to take Moshe. **And so too, you find with the teeth of the wicked, as it is written: "You have broken the teeth of the wicked"** (Psalms 3:8), with regard to which **Reish Lakish said: Do not read** it as **"You have broken [*shibbarta*],"** but as: **You have enlarged [*sheribavta*].**[N] **Rabba bar Oferan said in the name of Rabbi Elazar, who heard it from his teacher,** who in turn heard it **from his teacher:** The scepter was stretched **two hundred** cubits.

״וַיֹּאמֶר לָהּ הַמֶּלֶךְ״ לְאֶסְתֵּר הַמַּלְכָּה ״מַה בַּקָּשָׁתֵךְ עַד חֲצִי הַמַּלְכוּת, וְתֵעָשׂ״ חֲצִי הַמַּלְכוּת וְלֹא כׇּל הַמַּלְכוּת, וְלֹא דָּבָר שֶׁחוֹצֵץ לַמַּלְכוּת, וּמַאי נִיהוּ – בִּנְיַן בֵּית הַמִּקְדָּשׁ.

The verse states: **"Then the king said to her"** (Esther 5:3), to **Esther the queen, "What is your wish, even to half the kingdom, it shall be performed"** (Esther 5:6). The Gemara comments that Ahasuerus intended only a limited offer: Only **half the kingdom, but not the whole kingdom, and not something that would serve as a barrier to the kingdom,** as there is one thing to which the kingdom will never agree. **And what is that? The building of the Temple;** if that shall be your wish, realize that it will not be fulfilled.

״יָבֹא הַמֶּלֶךְ וְהָמָן...אֶל הַמִּשְׁתֶּה״. תָּנוּ רַבָּנַן: מָה רָאֲתָה אֶסְתֵּר שֶׁזִּימְּנָה אֶת הָמָן? רַבִּי אֶלְעָזָר אוֹמֵר: פַּחִים טָמְנָה לוֹ, שֶׁנֶּאֱמַר ״יְהִי שֻׁלְחָנָם לִפְנֵיהֶם לְפָח״,

The verse states that Esther requested: "If it seem good unto the king, **let the king and Haman come this day to the banquet** that I have prepared for him" (Esther 5:4). **The Sages taught** in a *baraita*: **What did Esther see to invite Haman** to the banquet? **Rabbi Elazar says: She hid a snare for him,**[N] **as it is stated: "Let their table become a snare before them"** (Psalms 69:23), as she assumed that she would be able to trip up Haman during the banquet.

BACKGROUND

Scepter – שַׁרְבִיט:

Relief from Persepolis of a Persian king holding his scepter

NOTES

Because I called Haman a dog – עַל שֶׁקְּרָאתִיו כֶּלֶב: The Maharsha explains that Esther at first prayed to be saved from Haman, who is a dog, and afterward she understood that she should also pray for Ahasuerus, the lion, to have a change of heart, as he also hated the Jewish people. Others explain that her whole prayer related to Ahasuerus. At first she referred to him in her heart by the dishonorable title of a dog, but then she realized afterward that she should also refer to his position, and therefore prayed again to be saved from the lion (see *Ya'arot Devash*).

Three ministering angels – שְׁלֹשָׁה מַלְאֲכֵי הַשָּׁרֵת: It has already been pointed out that, as the *Targum* notes, Esther had been fasting for three days and should have been weak and bent over, disheveled, certainly not radiating beauty. The fact that this did not happen was due to a divine miracle that showered her with grace and straightened her posture (see *Gal Naul* and Maharsha).

Twelve…sixteen, etc. – שְׁתֵּים עֶשְׂרֵה...שֵׁשׁ עֶשְׂרֵה וגו׳: The *Ramat Shmuel* explains that each one of these numbers carries with it a certain symbolism (see *Or Ḥadash*). The Maharsha writes that there is a hint to these numbers in the verses, as there are twelve words in this verse from "and the king held out" until the end, there are sixteen words from the beginning of the verse until "the golden scepter," and there are twenty-four words in the entire verse.

You have enlarged the teeth of the wicked – שִׁינֵּי רְשָׁעִים שִׁרְיבַּבְתָּ: Some explain that immediately prior to the downfall of the wicked they have a sudden, unexpected ascent, from the word *shirbuv*, meaning extension, and it is from there that they fall (*Melo HaRo'im*).

She hid a snare for him – פַּחִים טָמְנָה לוֹ: Some explain that she intended to flatter Haman at the party, in order that he would speak her praises in return. She did this so that the disparaging remarks that she would later say about him would not be interpreted as a personal vendetta against him and would provide a greater chance that the king would accept her words (*Manot HaLevi*).

רַבִּי יְהוֹשֻׁעַ אוֹמֵר: מִבֵּית אָבִיהָ לָמְדָה, שֶׁנֶּאֱמַר ״אִם רָעֵב שׂוֹנַאֲךָ הַאֲכִילֵהוּ לָחֶם״ וגו׳, רַבִּי מֵאִיר אוֹמֵר: כְּדֵי שֶׁלֹּא יִטּוֹל עֵצָה וְיִמְרוֹד,

Rabbi Yehoshua says: She learned to do **this from** the Jewish teachings of **her father's house, as it is stated: "If your enemy be hungry, give him bread to eat"** (Proverbs 25:21).[N] **Rabbi Meir says:** She invited him **in order** that he be near her at all times, **so that he would not take counsel and rebel** against Ahasuerus when he discovered that the king was angry with him.

רַבִּי יְהוּדָה אוֹמֵר: כְּדֵי שֶׁלֹּא יַכִּירוּ בָּהּ שֶׁהִיא יְהוּדִית, רַבִּי נְחֶמְיָה אוֹמֵר: כְּדֵי שֶׁלֹּא יֹאמְרוּ יִשְׂרָאֵל אָחוֹת יֵשׁ לָנוּ בְּבֵית הַמֶּלֶךְ וְיַסִּיחוּ דַּעְתָּן מִן הָרַחֲמִים. רַבִּי יוֹסֵי אוֹמֵר: כְּדֵי שֶׁתְּהֵא מְצוּיָה לָהּ בְּכָל עֵת. רַבִּי שִׁמְעוֹן בֶּן מְנַסְיָא אוֹמֵר: אוּלַי יַרְגִּישׁ הַמָּקוֹם וְיַעֲשֶׂה לָנוּ נֵס.

Rabbi Yehuda says: She invited Haman **so that it not be found out that she was a Jew,** as had she distanced him, he would have become suspicious. **Rabbi Neḥemya says:** She did this **so that the Jewish people would not say: We have a sister in the king's house, and** consequently **neglect their** prayers for divine **mercy. Rabbi Yosei says:** She acted in this manner, **so that** Haman would **always be on hand for her,** as that would enable her to find an opportunity to cause him to stumble before the king. **Rabbi Shimon ben Menasya said** that Esther said to herself: **Perhaps the Omnipresent will take notice** that all are supporting Haman and nobody is supporting the Jewish people, **and He will perform for us a miracle.**

רַבִּי יְהוֹשֻׁעַ בֶּן קָרְחָה אוֹמֵר: אַסְבִּיר לוֹ פָּנִים כְּדֵי שֶׁיֵּהָרֵג הוּא וְהִיא. רַבָּן גַּמְלִיאֵל אוֹמֵר: מֶלֶךְ הַפַּכְפְּכָן הָיָה. אָמַר רַבִּי גַּמְלִיאֵל: עֲדַיִין צְרִיכִין אָנוּ לַמּוֹדָעִי. דְּתַנְיָא, רַבִּי אֱלִיעֶזֶר הַמּוֹדָעִי אוֹמֵר: קִנְּאַתּוּ בַּמֶּלֶךְ, קִנְּאַתּוּ בַּשָּׂרִים.

Rabbi Yehoshua ben Korḥa says: She said to herself: **I will act kindly toward him** and thereby bring the king to suspect that we are having an affair; she did so **in order that** both **he and she would be killed.** Essentially, Esther was willing to be killed with Haman in order that the decree would be annulled. **Rabban Gamliel says:** Ahasuerus **was a fickle king,** and Esther hoped that if he saw Haman on multiple occasions, eventually he would change his opinion of him. **Rabban Gamliel said: We still need** the words of Rabbi Eliezer **HaModa'i** to understand why Esther invited Haman to her banquet. **As it is taught** in a *baraita*: **Rabbi Eliezer HaModa'i says: She made the king jealous of him and she made the** other **ministers jealous of him,** and in this way she brought about his downfall.

רַבָּה אָמַר: ״לִפְנֵי שֶׁבֶר גָּאוֹן״, אַבַּיֵי וְרָבָא דְּאָמְרִי תַּרְוַיְיהוּ: ״בְּחוּמָּם אָשִׁית אֶת מִשְׁתֵּיהֶם״ וגו׳, אַשְׁכְּחֵיהּ רַבָּה בַּר אֲבוּהּ לְאֵלִיָּהוּ, אֲמַר לֵיהּ: כְּמַאן חֲזָיָא אֶסְתֵּר וְעָבְדָא הָכִי? אֲמַר לֵיהּ: כְּכוּלְּהוּ תַּנָּאֵי וּכְכוּלְּהוּ אֲמוֹרָאֵי.

Rabba says: Esther invited Haman to her banquet in order to fulfill that which is stated: **"Pride goes before destruction"** (Proverbs 16:18), which indicates that in order to destroy the wicked, one must first bring them to pride. It can be understood according to **Abaye and Rava, who both say** that she invited Haman in order to fulfill the verse: **"When they are heated, I will make feasts for them,** and I will make them drunk, that they may rejoice, and sleep a perpetual sleep" (Jeremiah 51:39). The Gemara relates that **Rabba bar Avuh**[P] once **happened upon Elijah**[P] the Prophet and **said to him: In accordance with whose understanding did Esther see** fit to **act in this manner?** What was the true reason behind her invitation? **He,** Elijah, **said to him:** Esther was motivated by all the reasons previously mentioned and did so **for all** the reasons previously stated by **the *tanna'im* and all** the reasons stated by **the *amora'im*.**

״וַיְסַפֵּר לָהֶם הָמָן אֶת כְּבוֹד עָשְׁרוֹ וְרוֹב בָּנָיו״ וְכַמָּה רוֹב בָּנָיו? אָמַר רַב שְׁלֹשִׁים, עֲשָׂרָה מֵתוּ, וַעֲשָׂרָה נִתְלוּ, וַעֲשָׂרָה מְחַזְּרִין עַל הַפְּתָחִים,

The verse states: **"And Haman recounted to them the glory of his riches, and the multitude of his sons"** (Esther 5:11). The Gemara asks: **And how many** sons did he in fact have that are referred to as **"the multitude of his sons"?**[N] **Rav said:** There were **thirty** sons; **ten** of them **died** in childhood, **ten of them were hanged** as recorded in the book of Esther, **and ten** survived and were forced to **beg at** other people's **doors.**

NOTES

If your enemy be hungry give him bread to eat – אִם רָעֵב שׂוֹנַאֲךָ הַאֲכִילֵהוּ לָחֶם: One explanation understands this statement based on the conclusion of the verse, which is interpreted by some as describing the proper means of coming to peace with one's enemies by choosing to help them rather than mistreat them (see Malbim on Proverbs 25:21). Esther thought that if all else failed, perhaps she would be able to persuade Haman himself to change the decree (see *Manot HaLevi*).

And how many are referred to as the multitude of his sons – וְכַמָּה רוֹב בָּנָיו: The Gemara asks how many sons were in Haman's multitude of sons because ten is not a great number of sons, as several other individuals in the Bible had more. Therefore, the Gemara explains that in fact Haman had more sons but only ten of them were hanged (Maharsha).

PERSONALITIES

Rabba bar Avuh – רַבָּה בַּר אֲבוּהּ: Rabba bar Avuh, a second-generation Babylonian *amora*, was a close student of Rav, whose teachings he often quotes. He lived and taught in the city of Meḥoza. His student, Rav Naḥman, became his son-in-law and continued to teach much of what he learned from his father-in-law. Although Rabba bar Avuh was a member of the Exilarch's family, he remained poor throughout his life, as he did not want to profit from his Torah knowledge. We find a number of stories in the Talmud that describe his interactions with the Elijah the Prophet, to whom he posed various questions. Rabba bar Avuh's son, Rav Ḥama, was also a Sage, and two of his descendants were the great *ge'onim* of Babylonia, Rav Sherira Gaon and Rav Hai Gaon.

Elijah – אֵלִיָּהוּ: In many places in the Talmud and the Midrash, Elijah the Prophet appears to people, especially to Sages, and resolves their dilemmas. As it is stated in the Prophets (II Kings 2:11), Elijah did not die, and he continues to serve as an emissary of God. On the one hand, he is the angel of the covenant. On the other hand, he is an individual who alleviates problems in the world.

וְרַבָּנַן אָמְרִי: אוֹתָן שֶׁמְּחַזְּרִין עַל הַפְּתָחִים שִׁבְעִים הֲוָיָא, דִּכְתִיב ״שְׂבֵעִים בַּלֶּחֶם נִשְׂכָּרוּ״ אַל תִּקְרֵי שְׂבֵעִים אֶלָּא שִׁבְעִים.

And the Rabbis say: Those that begged at other people's **doors** numbered **seventy, as it is written: "Those that were full, have hired themselves out for bread"** (I Samuel 2:5). **Do not read it as: "Those that were full"** [*seve'im*]; **rather,** read it as **seventy** [*shivim*], indicating that there were seventy who "hired themselves out for bread."

וְרָמֵי בַּר אַבָּא אָמַר: כּוּלָּן מָאתַיִם וּשְׁמוֹנָה הָווּ, שֶׁנֶּאֱמַר ״וְרוֹב בָּנָיו״, ״וְרוֹב״ בְּגִימַטְרִיָּא מָאתָן וְאַרְבֵּיסַר הָווּ! אָמַר רַב נַחְמָן בַּר יִצְחָק: ״וְרֹב״ כְּתִיב.

And Rami bar Abba said: All of Haman's sons together numbered **two hundred and eight, as it is stated: "And the multitude** [*verov*] **of his sons."** The numerical value of the word *verov* equals two hundred and eight, alluding to the number of his sons. The Gemara comments: **But** in fact, **the numerical value** [*gimatriyya*][L] **of the** word ***verov*** **equals two hundred and fourteen,** not two hundred and eight. **Rav Naḥman bar Yitzḥak said:** The word ***verov*** **is written** in the Bible without the second *vav*, and therefore its numerical value equals two hundred and eight.

״בַּלַּיְלָה הַהוּא נָדְדָה שְׁנַת הַמֶּלֶךְ״. אָמַר רַבִּי תַּנְחוּם: נָדְדָה שְׁנַת מַלְכּוֹ שֶׁל עוֹלָם. וְרַבָּנַן אָמְרִי: נָדְדוּ עֶלְיוֹנִים, נָדְדוּ תַּחְתּוֹנִים. רָבָא אָמַר: שְׁנַת הַמֶּלֶךְ אֲחַשְׁוֵרוֹשׁ מַמָּשׁ.

The verse states: **"On that night the sleep of the king was disturbed"** (Esther 6:1).[N] **Rabbi Tanḥum said:** The verse alludes to another king who could not sleep; **the sleep of the King of the universe,** the Holy One, Blessed be He, **was disturbed. And the Sages say:** The sleep of **the higher ones,** the angels, **was disturbed, and** the sleep of **the lower ones,** the Jewish people, **was disturbed. Rava said:** This should be understood **literally: The sleep of King Ahasuerus** was disturbed.

נָפְלָה לֵיהּ מִילְּתָא בְּדַעְתֵּיהּ, אָמַר: מַאי דְּקַמָּן דְּזַמִּינְתֵּיהּ אֶסְתֵּר לְהָמָן? דִּלְמָא עֵצָה קָא שָׁקְלִי עִילָּוֵיהּ דְּהַהוּא גַּבְרָא לְמִקְטְלֵיהּ. הָדַר אָמַר: אִי הָכִי לָא הֲוָה גַּבְרָא דְּרָחֵים לִי, דַּהֲוָה מוֹדַע לִי? הָדַר אָמַר: דִּלְמָא אִיכָּא אִינִישׁ דַּעֲבַד בִּי טִיבוּתָא וְלָא פְּרַעְתֵּיהּ, מִשּׁוּם הָכִי מִימְנְעִי אֱינָשֵׁי וְלָא מְגַלּוּ לִי. מִיָּד ״וַיֹּאמֶר לְהָבִיא אֶת סֵפֶר הַזִּכְרוֹנוֹת דִּבְרֵי הַיָּמִים״.

And this was the reason Ahasuerus could not sleep: **A thought occurred to him** and **he said** to himself: **What is this before us that Esther has invited Haman? Perhaps they are conspiring against that man,** i.e., against me, **to kill him. He** then **said again** to himself: **If this is so, is there no man who loves me and would inform me** of this conspiracy? **He** then **said again** to himself: **Perhaps there is some man who has done a favor for me and I have not** properly **rewarded him, and due to that** reason **people refrain from revealing to me** information regarding such plots, as they see no benefit for themselves. **Immediately** afterward, the verse states: **"And he commanded the book of remembrances of the chronicles to be brought"** (Esther 6:1).

״וַיִּהְיוּ נִקְרָאִים״ – מְלַמֵּד שֶׁנִּקְרָאִים מֵאֵילֵיהֶן. ״וַיִּמָּצֵא כָתוּב״, ״כְּתָב״ מִבָּעֵי לֵיהּ! מְלַמֵּד

The verse states: **"And they were read** before the king" (Esther 6:1). The Gemara explains that **this** passive form: "And they were read," **teaches that they were read** miraculously **by themselves.** It further says: **"And it was found written** [***katuv***]**"** (Esther 6:2). The Gemara asks: Why does the Megilla use the word *katuv*, which indicates that it was newly written? **It should have said: A writing** [***ketav***] was found, which would indicate that it had been written in the past. The Gemara explains: This **teaches**

Perek **I**
Daf **16** Amud **a**

שֶׁשִּׁמְשַׁי מוֹחֵק וְגַבְרִיאֵל כּוֹתֵב. אָמַר רַבִּי אַסִּי: דָּרַשׁ רַבִּי שֵׁילָא אִישׁ כְּפַר תְּמַרְתָּא: וּמָה כְּתָב שֶׁלְּמַטָּה שֶׁלִּזְכוּתָן שֶׁל יִשְׂרָאֵל אֵינוֹ נִמְחָק – כְּתָב שֶׁלְּמַעְלָה לֹא כׇּל שֶׁכֵּן?

that Shimshai, the king's scribe who hated the Jews (see Ezra 4:17), **was erasing**[N] the description of Mordecai's saving the king, **and the** angel **Gavriel was writing** it again. Therefore, it was indeed being written in the present. **Rabbi Asi said: Rabbi Sheila, a man of the village of Timarta, taught: If something written** down **below** in this world **that is for the benefit of the Jewish people cannot be erased, is it not all the more so** the case **that something written** up **above** in Heaven cannot be erased?

LANGUAGE

Numerical value [*gimatriyya*] **– גִּימַטְרִיָּא:** Many efforts have been made to find the precise source for this word. It is probably derived from the Greek γεωμετρία, *geometria*, which was understood in the general sense as referring to calculations, and is used in that sense in rabbinic literature. From this it was applied more specifically to calculating the numerical value of the letters of the alphabet.

NOTES

The sleep of the king was disturbed – נָדְדָה שְׁנַת הַמֶּלֶךְ: It has been explained that since no reason is provided for why the king's sleep was disturbed, it must certainly have been brought about by the prayers of the higher ones, i.e., the angels, and the lower ones, i.e., the Jewish people. Similarly, it is understood that anywhere in the Megilla where the word king appears alone, without mentioning Ahasuerus, it refers to the King of all kings, the Holy One, Blessed be He, which would indicate that God's so-called slumber was disturbed due to the decree against the Jewish people. Others explain that the statement: The sleep of the higher ones was disturbed and the sleep of the lower ones was disturbed, indicates that the sleep of both Mordecai, who is known as the higher one, and Haman, who is known as the lower one, were disturbed on that night, each one for a different reason (*Iyyun Ya'akov*).

NOTES

That Shimshai was erasing – שֶׁשִּׁמְשַׁי מוֹחֵק: The book of Ezra states that Shimshai was the scribe who slandered the Jews in order to prevent them from building the Temple. The *Targum* relates that he was Haman's son. The Midrash understands that the account of Mordecai's saving the king was erased because of the language of the verse: "And it was found written," which indicates that the description needed to be found, as it was lost beforehand, having been erased (*Yalkut Shimoni*).

״לֹא נַעֲשָׂה עִמּוֹ דָּבָר״, אָמַר רָבָא: לֹא מִפְּנֵי שֶׁאוֹהֲבִין אֶת מָרְדֳּכַי, אֶלָּא מִפְּנֵי שֶׁשּׂוֹנְאִים אֶת הָמָן.

The verse states that Ahasuerus was told with regard to Mordecai: **"Nothing has been done for him"** (Esther 6:3). **Rava said: It is not because they love Mordecai**[N] that the king's servants said this, **but rather because they hate Haman.**

״הֵכִין לוֹ״, תָּנָא: לוֹ הֵכִין.

The verse states: "Now Haman had come into the outer court of the king's house, to speak to the king about hanging Mordecai on the gallows that he had **prepared for him**" (Esther 6:4). A Sage **taught** in a *baraita*: This should be understood to mean: On the gallows that **he had prepared for himself.**[N]

״וַעֲשֵׂה כֵן לְמָרְדֳּכַי״, אֲמַר לֵיהּ: מַנּוּ מָרְדֳּכַי? אֲמַר לֵיהּ: ״הַיְּהוּדִי״, אֲמַר לֵיהּ: טוּבָא מָרְדֳּכַי אִיכָּא בִּיהוּדָאֵי. אֲמַר לֵיהּ: ״הַיּוֹשֵׁב בְּשַׁעַר הַמֶּלֶךְ״.

The verse relates that Ahasuerus ordered Haman to fulfill his idea of the proper way to honor one who the king desires to glorify by parading him around on the king's horse while wearing the royal garments: "And do so to Mordecai the Jew who sits at the king's gate, let nothing fail of all that you have spoken" (Esther 6:10). The Gemara explains that when Ahasuerus said to Haman: **"And do so to Mordecai,"** Haman **said to him** in an attempt to evade the order: **Who is Mordecai?** Ahasuerus **said to him: "The Jew."** Haman then **said to him: There are several** men named **Mordecai among the Jews.** Ahasuerus then **said to him:** I refer to the one **"who sits at the king's gate."**

אֲמַר לֵיהּ סַגֵּי לֵיהּ בְּחַד דִּיסְקַרְתָּא, אִי נַמִּי בְּחַד נַהֲרָא! אֲמַר לֵיהּ: הָא נַמִּי הַב לֵיהּ, ״אַל תַּפֵּל דָּבָר מִכֹּל אֲשֶׁר דִּבַּרְתָּ״.

Haman **said to him:** Why award him such a great honor? **It would** certainly **be enough for him** to receive **one village** [*disekarta*][L] as an estate, **or one river** for the levy of taxes. Ahasuerus **said to him: This too you must give him. "Let nothing fail of all that you have spoken,"** i.e., provide him with all that you proposed and spoke about in addition to what I had said.

״וַיִּקַּח הָמָן אֶת הַלְּבוּשׁ וְאֶת הַסּוּס״ אֲזַל אַשְׁכְּחֵיהּ דְּיָתְבִי רַבָּנַן קַמֵּיהּ, וּמַחֲוֵי לְהוּ הִלְכוֹת קְמִיצָה לְרַבָּנַן. כֵּיוָן דַּחֲזְיֵיהּ מָרְדֳּכַי דְּאַפֵּיק לְקָבְלֵיהּ, וְסוּסֵיהּ מֵיחַד בִּידֵיהּ, מִירְתַת. אֲמַר לְהוּ לְרַבָּנַן: הַאי רְשִׁיעָא לְמִיקְטַל נַפְשִׁי קָא אָתֵי, זִילוּ מִקַּמֵּיהּ דִּי לָא תִּכָּווּ בְּגַחַלְתּוֹ. בְּהַהִיא שַׁעְתָּא נִתְעַטֵּף מָרְדֳּכַי וְקָם לֵיהּ לִצְלוֹתָא, אֲתָא הָמָן וִיתֵיב לֵיהּ קַמַּיְיהוּ וְאוֹרִיךְ עַד דִּסְלִיק מָרְדֳּכַי לִצְלוֹתֵיהּ.

The Gemara describes what occurred as Haman went to follow the king's orders, as the verse states: **"Then Haman took the apparel and the horse"** (Esther 6:11). When **he went, he found** Mordecai **as the Sages were sitting before him, and he was demonstrating to them the *halakhot* of the handful,**[NB] i.e., the scooping out of a handful of flour from the meal-offering in order to burn it on the altar. **Once Mordecai saw him coming toward him with his horse's** reins **held in his hands, he became frightened,** and **he said to the Sages: This evil man has come to kill me. Go away from him so that you should not get burnt from his coals,** i.e., that you should not suffer harm as well. **At that moment Mordecai wrapped himself** in his prayer shawl **and stood up to pray. Haman came** over to where they were **and sat down before them and waited until Mordecai finished his prayer.**

NOTES

Not because they love Mordecai – לֹא מִפְּנֵי שֶׁאוֹהֲבִין אֶת מָרְדֳּכַי: The idea that they were not fond of Mordecai is indicated in the verse because they did not answer: Nothing of value and greatness was done with him, but rather: "Nothing has been done for him." Essentially they were saying that it is fitting to do something for him, but not necessarily something of value and greatness (Maharsha). Some emphasize that the fact that they refer to Mordecai in that verse as "him" rather than mentioning his name indicates their lack of love for him (*Kol Yehuda*).

That he had prepared for himself – לוֹ הֵכִין: This exposition is derived primarily through the presence of the apparently superfluous term "for him," which is understood to refer to Haman himself, as in the end it was he who was hanged on the tree that he prepared for Mordecai (see Rashi). Similarly, the *midrashim* and the *Targum* explain that from the moment Haman prepared the tree, it was already destined from Heaven to be used to hang Haman (see *Turei Even*).

He was demonstrating to them the *halakhot* of the handful – וּמַחֲוֵי לְהוּ הִלְכוֹת קְמִיצָה: The Midrash explains that as that day was the sixteenth of Nisan, on which the *omer* is offered, they were discussing the *halakhot* of the handful of the *omer* offering, which were pertinent to that day.

LANGUAGE

Village [*disekarta*] – דִּיסְקַרְתָּא: From the Middle Persian dastagird, meaning an inherited plot of land.

BACKGROUND

Handful – קְמִיצָה: This refers to the scooping out of a handful of flour from the meal-offering in order to burn it on the altar. Most meal-offerings require a handful (see, e.g., Leviticus 2:2). This rite, which paralleled the slaughtering of an animal offering, was performed only by a priest. According to many authorities, the priest would scoop out the flour with the three middle fingers of his right hand, using his thumb and little finger to remove any surplus flour. He would then place the flour in a sacred vessel used in the Temple service in order to consecrate it. Since the priest had to scoop out an exact handful of flour, no more and no less, the scooping of the handful was one of the more difficult rites in the Temple.

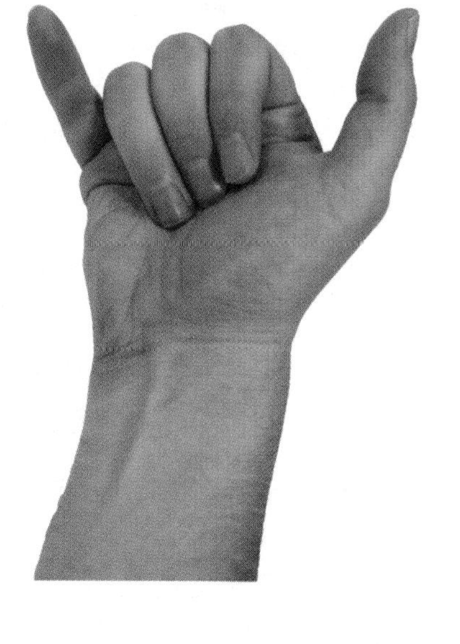

Position of priest's hand after removing surplus flour

אֲמַר לְהוּ: בְּמַאי עָסְקִיתוּ? אֲמַרוּ לֵיהּ: בִּזְמַן שֶׁבֵּית הַמִּקְדָּשׁ קַיָּים, מַאן דִּמְנַדֵּב מִנְחָה מַיְיתֵי מְלֵי קוּמְצֵיהּ דְּסוּלְתָּא וּמִתְכַּפֵּר לֵיהּ. אֲמַר לְהוּ: אֲתָא מְלֵי קוּמְצֵי קִמְחָא דִּידְכוּ, וְדָחֵי עֲשָׂרָה אַלְפֵי כִּכְּרֵי כַּסְפָּא דִּידִי. אֲמַר לֵיהּ: רָשָׁע! עֶבֶד שֶׁקָּנָה נְכָסִים – עֶבֶד לְמִי, וּנְכָסִים לְמִי?

In the interim, as he waited, Haman **said to** the other Sages: **With what were you occupied? They said to him: When the Temple is standing, one who pledges a meal-offering would bring a handful of fine flour and achieve atonement with it. He said to them: Your handful of fine flour has come and cast aside my ten thousand pieces of silver,** which I had pledged toward the destruction of the Jewish people. When Mordecai finished praying, **he said to** Haman: **Wicked man,** when **a slave buys property, to whom belongs the slave and to whom belongs the property?** As I once bought you as a slave, what silver can be yours?

אֲמַר לֵיהּ: קוּם לְבוּשׁ הָנֵי מָאנֵי, וּרְכוֹב הַאי סוּסְיָא, דְּבָעֵי לָךְ מַלְכָּא. אֲמַר לֵיהּ: לָא יָכֵילְנָא עַד דְּעָיֵילְנָא לְבֵי בָנֵי וְאֶשְׁקוֹל לְמַזְיָא, דְּלָאו אוֹרַח אַרְעָא לְאִשְׁתַּמּוּשֵׁי בְּמָאנֵי דְּמַלְכָּא הָכִי.

Haman **said to him: Stand up, put on these garments and ride on this horse, for the king wants you** to do so. Mordecai **said to him: I cannot** do so **until I enter the bathhouse** [*bei vanei*][L] **and trim my hair, for it is not proper conduct to use the king's garments in this state** that I am in now.

שְׁדַרָה אֶסְתֵּר וַאֲסַרְתִּינְהוּ לְכוּלְּהוּ בֵּי בָנֵי, וּלְכוּלְּהוּ אוּמָּנֵי. עַיְילֵיהּ אִיהוּ לְבֵי בָנֵי, וְאַסְחֵיהּ, וְאָזֵיל וְאַיְיתֵי זוּזָא מִבֵּיתֵיהּ, וְקָא שָׁקֵיל בֵּיהּ מַזְיֵיהּ. בַּהֲדֵי דְּקָא שָׁקֵיל לֵיהּ אִינְגַּד וְאִיתְנַח. אֲמַר לֵיהּ: אַמַּאי קָא מִיתְנַחַת? אֲמַר לֵיהּ: גַּבְרָא דַּהֲוָה חֲשִׁיב לֵיהּ לְמַלְכָּא מִכּוּלְּהוּ רַבְרְבָנוֹהִי, הַשְׁתָּא לִישַׁוְּיֵיהּ בַּלָּאנֵי וְסַפָּר? אֲמַר לֵיהּ: רָשָׁע! וְלָאו סַפָּר שֶׁל כְּפַר קַרְצוּם הָיִיתָ? תָּנָא: הָמָן סַפָּר שֶׁל כְּפַר קַרְצוּם הָיָה עֶשְׂרִים וּשְׁתַּיִם שָׁנָה.

In the meantime, **Esther sent** messengers and **closed all the bathhouses and all** the shops of **the craftsmen,** including the bloodletters and barbers. When Haman saw that there was nobody else to do the work, **he** himself **took** Mordecai **into the bathhouse and washed him, and** then **he went and brought scissors** [*zuza*][L] **from his house and trimmed his hair.** While **he was trimming** his hair **he injured himself and sighed.** Mordecai **said to him: Why do you sigh?** Haman **said to him: The man whom the king had** once **regarded above all his** other **ministers is now made a bathhouse attendant** [*balanei*][L] **and a barber.** Mordecai **said to him: Wicked man, were you not** once **the barber of the village of Kartzum?** If so, why do you sigh? You have merely returned to the occupation of your youth. It **was taught** in a *baraita*: **Haman was the barber of the village of Kartzum for twenty-two years.**

בָּתַר דְּשַׁקְלִינְהוּ לְמַזְיֵיהּ לַבְּשִׁינְהוּ לְמָאנֵיהּ, אֲמַר לֵיהּ: סַק וּרְכַב. אֲמַר לֵיהּ: לָא יָכֵילְנָא, דִּכְחִישָׁא חֵילַאי מִימֵי תַעֲנִיתָא. גָּחֵין וּסְלֵיק. כִּי סְלֵיק בְּעַט בֵּיהּ. אֲמַר לֵיהּ: לָא כְּתִיב לְכוּ ״בִּנְפֹל אוֹיִבְךָ אַל תִּשְׂמָח״? אֲמַר לֵיהּ: הָנֵי מִילֵּי – בְּיִשְׂרָאֵל, אֲבָל בְּדִידְכוּ כְּתִיב ״וְאַתָּה עַל בָּמוֹתֵימוֹ תִּדְרוֹךְ״.

After Haman **trimmed his hair,** Haman **dressed** Mordecai in **the** royal **garments.** Haman then **said to him: Mount** the horse **and ride.** Mordecai **said to him: I am unable, as my strength has waned from the days of fasting** that I observed. Haman then **stooped down** before him **and** Mordecai **ascended** on him. **As he was ascending** the horse, Mordecai **gave** Haman **a kick.**[N] Haman **said to him: Is it not written for you: "Do not rejoice when your enemy falls"** (Proverbs 24:17)? Mordecai **said to him: This** statement **applies** only **to Jews, but with regard to you it is written: "And you shall tread upon their high places"** (Deuteronomy 33:29).

״וַיִּקְרָא לְפָנָיו כָּכָה יֵעָשֶׂה לָאִישׁ אֲשֶׁר הַמֶּלֶךְ חָפֵץ בִּיקָרוֹ״. כִּי הֲוָה נָקֵיט וְאָזֵיל בִּשְׁבִילָא דְּבֵי הָמָן חֲזִיתֵיהּ בְּרַתֵּיהּ דְּקַיְימָא אַאִיגְּרָא, סְבָרָה: הַאי דְּרָכֵיב – אֲבוּהּ, וְהַאי דִּמְסַגֵּי קַמֵּיהּ – מָרְדֳּכַי. שְׁקַלָה עֲצִיצָא דְּבֵית הַכִּסֵּא וּשְׁדִיתֵיהּ אַרֵישָׁא דַּאֲבוּהּ. דָּלֵי עֵינֵיהּ וַחֲזַת דַּאֲבוּהּ הוּא, נְפַלָה מֵאִיגְּרָא לְאַרְעָא וּמֵתָה.

The verse states: **"And he proclaimed before him: Thus shall it be done to the man whom the king delights to honor"** (Esther 6:11). **As** Haman **was taking** Mordecai **along the street of Haman's house,** Haman's **daughter was standing on the roof and saw** the spectacle. **She thought** to herself that **the one who is riding** on the horse must be **her father, and the one walking before him** must be **Mordecai. She** then **took a chamber pot** full of feces **and cast its** contents **onto the head of her father,** whom she mistakenly took as Mordecai. When Haman **raised his eyes** in disgust afterward, and looked up at his daughter, **she saw that he was her father.** In her distress, **she fell from the roof to the ground and died.**

וְהַיְינוּ דִּכְתִיב ״וַיָּשָׁב מָרְדֳּכַי אֶל שַׁעַר הַמֶּלֶךְ״ אָמַר רַב שֵׁשֶׁת: שֶׁשָּׁב לְשַׂקּוֹ וּלְתַעֲנִיתוֹ. ״וְהָמָן נִדְחַף אֶל בֵּיתוֹ אָבֵל וַחֲפוּי רֹאשׁ״, ״אָבֵל״ – עַל בִּתּוֹ, ״וַחֲפוּי רֹאשׁ״ – עַל שֶׁאֵירַע לוֹ.

And this is as it is written: "And Mordecai returned to the king's gate" (Esther 6:12). **Rav Sheshet said:** This means **that he returned to his sackcloth and his fasting** over the troubles of the Jewish people. Simultaneously, **"but Haman hastened to his house, mourning, and having his head covered"** (Esther 6:12). **"Mourning"; over** the death of **his daughter. "And having his head covered"; due to what had happened to him,** as his head was full of filth.

LANGUAGE

Bathhouse [*bei vanei*] – בֵּי בָנֵי: Apparently from the Greek βαλανεῖον, *balaneyon*, meaning bathhouse. The letter *lamed* was subsequently dropped from the word.

Scissors [*zuza*] – זוּזָא: From the Greek ζυγόν, *zugon*, meaning yoke or couple. It is similar to *zuga*, and its usage was expanded to other meanings that are connected to pairs, primarily scissors.

Bathhouse attendant [*balanei*] – בַּלָּאנֵי: From the Greek βαλανεύς, *balaneus*, meaning bathhouse attendant.

NOTES

As he was ascending Mordecai gave Haman a kick – כִּי סְלֵיק בְּעַט בֵּיהּ: It is explained that Mordecai tried every possible way to anger Haman, as he hoped that Haman would become angry and hit him, and thereby lose favor in the eyes of the king for failing to fulfill his command of honoring Mordecai (*Yefe Anaf*).

NOTES

Whoever says something wise – כָּל הָאוֹמֵר דְּבַר חָכְמָה: The fact that there are wise men among the nations of the world is not a new idea and is not the novelty in the verse; see, however, the *Ḥatam Sofer*. Rather, the Gemara is explaining that even though they were previously called "his friends," their uttering even one wise statement made them worthy of being called "his wise men" (Rashash). They were wise in that they recognized that there are some Jews before whom if Haman falls even once, it is a sign that he will never again be able to prevail over them (Rabbi Yoshiya Pinto). Others explain that they were wise in that they were indicating to Haman that he should flee to save his life. However, before he was able to do this he was taken to the king (*Iyyun Ya'akov*).

This adversary is not concerned [*eino shoveh*] – צַר זֶה אֵינוֹ שׁוֶֹה: The word *shoveh* is explained here to mean concerned with, or cares about. The same root is used in the verse "which put forth fruit freely [*yeshaveh*]" (Hosea 10:1).

She was pointing toward Ahasuerus – שֶׁהָיְתָה מַחֲוָה כְּלַפֵּי אֲחַשְׁוֵרוֹשׁ: Most of the commentaries explain that she wanted to blame Ahasuerus for his involvement with the decree. However, the *Rishon LeTziyyon* explains that out of emotional excitement she mistakenly pointed her finger at Ahasuerus.

״וַיְסַפֵּר הָמָן לְזֶרֶשׁ אִשְׁתּוֹ וּלְכָל אוֹהֲבָיו״ וגו׳, קָרֵי לְהוּ ״אוֹהֲבָיו״ וְקָרֵי לְהוּ ״חֲכָמָיו״. אָמַר רַבִּי יוֹחָנָן: כָּל הָאוֹמֵר דְּבַר חָכְמָה, אֲפִילּוּ בָּאוּמּוֹת הָעוֹלָם – נִקְרָא חָכָם.

The following verse states: **"And Haman recounted to Zeresh his wife and to all his friends** everything that had befallen him. Then his wise men and Zeresh his wife said to him: If Mordecai, before whom you have begun to fall, be of the seed of the Jews, then you will not prevail over him, but you shall fall before him" (Esther 6:13). The Gemara comments: At the beginning of the verse **it calls them "his friends," and** in the continuation of the verse **it calls them "his wise men." Rabbi Yoḥanan said: Whoever says something wise,**[N] **even if** he is **from the nations of the world, is called** a **wise** man.

״אִם מִזֶּרַע הַיְּהוּדִים מָרְדֳּכַי״ וגו׳, אֲמַרוּ לֵיהּ: אִי מִשְּׁאָר שְׁבָטִים קָאָתֵי – יָכְלַתְּ לֵיהּ, וְאִי מִשֵּׁבֶט יְהוּדָה וּבִנְיָמִין וְאֶפְרַיִם וּמְנַשֶּׁה – לָא יָכְלַתְּ לֵיהּ. יְהוּדָה – דִּכְתִיב ״יָדְךָ בְּעֹרֶף אוֹיְבֶיךָ״, אִינָךְ – דִּכְתִיב בְּהוּ ״לִפְנֵי אֶפְרַיִם וּבִנְיָמִין וּמְנַשֶּׁה עוֹרְרָה אֶת גְּבוּרָתֶךָ״.

The Gemara explains that their wise remark, which earned them their distinction, is contained in their advice: **"If Mordecai be of the seed of the Jews [*Yehudim*],** then you will not prevail over him" (Esther 6:13). The word *Yehudim* can also refer to people from the tribe of Judah. Haman's wise men thereby **said to him: If he descends from the other tribes, you can** still **prevail over him, but if he** descends **from the tribe of** either **Judah, Benjamin, Ephraim, or Manasseh, you cannot prevail over him.** With regard to **Judah,** the proof of this is **as it is written: "Your hand shall be on the neck of your enemies"** (Genesis 49:8), indicating that Judah will emerge victorious over his enemies. And the proof that Haman cannot prevail over **the others** that were mentioned is **as it is written with regard to them: "Before Ephraim and Benjamin and Manasseh, stir up Your might"** (Psalms 80:3).

״כִּי נָפוֹל תִּפּוֹל לְפָנָיו״, דָּרַשׁ רַבִּי יְהוּדָה בַּר אֶלְעַאי: שְׁתֵּי נְפִילוֹת הַלָּלוּ לָמָּה? אָמְרוּ לוֹ: אוּמָּה זוֹ מְשׁוּלָה לְעָפָר וּמְשׁוּלָה לְכוֹכָבִים, כְּשֶׁהֵן יוֹרְדִין – יוֹרְדִין עַד עָפָר, וּכְשֶׁהֵן עוֹלִין – עוֹלִין עַד לַכּוֹכָבִים.

The wise men continued: **"But you shall fall [*nafol tippol*] before him"** (Esther 6:13). **Rabbi Yehuda bar Ilai interpreted** a verse **homiletically: Why are these two fallings,** *nafol* and *tippol*, mentioned here? The wise men **said to** Haman: **This** Jewish **nation is compared** in the Bible **to the dust** of the earth **and it** is also **compared to the stars** in heaven. This teaches you that **when they descend, they descend to the dust, and when they rise, they rise to the stars.** Accordingly, when Mordecai is on the rise, you will be utterly incapable of prevailing over him.

״וְסָרִיסֵי הַמֶּלֶךְ הִגִּיעוּ וַיַּבְהִילוּ״ – מְלַמֵּד שֶׁהֱבִיאוּהוּ בְּבֶהָלָה.

The next verse states: **"The king's chamberlains came, and they hastened [*vayavhilu*]** to bring Haman" (Esther 6:14). **This teaches that they brought him in disarray [*behala*],** not even giving him a chance to wash himself from the filth.

״כִּי נִמְכַּרְנוּ אֲנִי וְעַמִּי״ וגו׳ ״כִּי אֵין הַצָּר שֹׁוֶה בְּנֵזֶק הַמֶּלֶךְ״ אָמְרָה לוֹ: צַר זֶה אֵינוֹ שֹׁוֶה בְּנֵזֶק שֶׁל מֶלֶךְ: אִיקַּנֵּי בָּהּ בְּוַשְׁתִּי – וְקַטְלָהּ, הָשְׁתָּא אִיקַּנֵּי בְּדִידִי – וּמִבָּעֵי לְמִקְטְלִי.

During the banquet Esther said to Ahasuerus: **"For we are sold, I and my people,** to be destroyed, to be slain, and to be annihilated. But if we had been sold merely for bondmen and bondwomen, I would have held my tongue, **since the affliction [*tzar*] would not have been worth [*eino shoveh*] the damage to the king"** (Esther 7:4). The Gemara explains that **she said to him: This adversary [*tzar*] is not concerned [*eino shoveh*]**[N] **about the damage** that he is constantly causing **to the king. First he was jealous of Vashti and killed her,** as it has been explained that Memucan, who suggesting killing Vashti, was Haman; **now he is jealous of me and desires to kill me.**

״וַיֹּאמֶר הַמֶּלֶךְ אֲחַשְׁוֵרוֹשׁ וַיֹּאמֶר לְאֶסְתֵּר הַמַּלְכָּה״, ״וַיֹּאמֶר״ ״וַיֹּאמֶר״ לָמָּה לִי? אֲמַר רַבִּי אַבָּהוּ: בִּתְחִלָּה עַל יְדֵי תוּרְגְּמָן, כֵּיוָן דַּאֲמַרָה לֵיהּ: מִדְּבֵית שָׁאוּל קָאָתֵינָא – מִיָּד ״וַיֹּאמֶר לְאֶסְתֵּר הַמַּלְכָּה״.

The verse states: **"Then said the king Ahasuerus and said to Esther the queen"** (Esther 7:5). The Gemara asks: **Why do I** need it to say **"said"** and again **"said"? Rabbi Abbahu said: At first** he spoke to her **through the translator,** who would interpret on his behalf, because he thought that she was a common woman of lowly ancestry. **Once she told him that she came from the house of Saul, immediately** it says: **"And said to Esther the queen."** Ahasuerus himself spoke to her, as if she had royal lineage, she was a woman befitting his status.

״וַתֹּאמֶר אֶסְתֵּר אִישׁ צַר וְאוֹיֵב הָמָן הָרָע הַזֶּה״ אָמַר רַבִּי אֶלְעָזָר: מְלַמֵּד שֶׁהָיְתָה מַחֲוָה כְּלַפֵּי אֲחַשְׁוֵרוֹשׁ, וּבָא מַלְאָךְ וְסָטַר יָדָהּ כְּלַפֵּי הָמָן.

The next verse states: **"And Esther said: An adversary and enemy is this wicked Haman"** (Esther 7:6). **Rabbi Elazar said:** This **teaches that she was** in fact **pointing toward Ahasuerus,**[N] indicating that in fact he was an adversary and enemy, **and an angel came and pushed her hand toward Haman.**

"וְהַמֶּלֶךְ קָם בַּחֲמָתוֹ" וגו׳ "וְהַמֶּלֶךְ שָׁב מִגִּנַּת הַבִּיתָן" מַקִּישׁ שִׁיבָה לְקִימָה, מָה קִימָה בְּחֵימָה – אַף שִׁיבָה בְּחֵימָה, דַּאֲזַל וְאַשְׁכַּח לְמַלְאֲכֵי הַשָּׁרֵת דְּאִידְּמוּ לֵיהּ כְּגַבְרֵי וְקָא עָקְרֵי לְאִילָנֵי דְבוּסְתָּנֵי, וַאֲמַר לְהוּ: מַאי עוֹבַדַיְיכוּ? אֲמַרוּ לֵיהּ: דְּפַקְדִינַן הָמָן.

The verse states: **"And the king arose** from the banquet of wine **in his wrath** and went into the palace garden" (Esther 7:7), and the next verse states: **"Then the king returned out of the palace garden** to the place of the wine drinking" (Esther 7:8). The Gemara comments: The verses here **compare his returning to his arising: Just as his arising** was **in wrath, so too, his returning** was **in wrath.** And why did he return in wrath? **For when he went out he found ministering angels who appeared to him as people and they were uprooting trees from the garden, and he said to them: What are you doing? They said to him: Haman commanded us** to do this.

אֲתָא לְבֵיתֵיהּ "וְהָמָן נוֹפֵל עַל הַמִּטָּה". "נוֹפֵל"? נָפַל מִיבְּעֵי לֵיהּ! אָמַר רַבִּי אֶלְעָזָר: מְלַמֵּד שֶׁבָּא מַלְאָךְ וְהִפִּילוֹ עָלֶיהָ. אָמַר: וַיי מִבֵּיתָא וַיי מִבָּרָא. "וַיֹּאמֶר הַמֶּלֶךְ הֲגַם לִכְבּוֹשׁ אֶת הַמַּלְכָּה עִמִּי בַּבָּיִת".

And when **he entered his house** he saw that **"Haman was falling upon the bed"** (Esther 7:8). The Gemara asks: Why does it say **"was falling"** [*nofel*] in the present tense, implying that he was currently falling? **It should have said "fell"** [*nafal*] in the past tense. **Rabbi Elazar said: This teaches that an angel came and pushed him down on it,** and every time he would try to stand up, the angel would push him down again. Ahasuerus **said: Woe unto** me **in the house and woe** unto me **outside,** as the verse continues: **"Then the king said: Will he even force the queen before me in the house?"** (Esther 7:8).

"וַיֹּאמֶר חַרְבוֹנָה" וגו׳ אָמַר רַבִּי אֶלְעָזָר: אַף חַרְבוֹנָה רָשָׁע בְּאוֹתָהּ עֵצָה הָיָה, כֵּיוָן שֶׁרָאָה שֶׁלֹּא נִתְקַיְּימָה עֲצָתוֹ – מִיָּד בָּרַח, וְהַיְינוּ דִּכְתִיב "וְיַשְׁלֵךְ עָלָיו וְלֹא יַחְמוֹל מִיָּדוֹ בָּרוֹחַ יִבְרָח".

"And Harbonah, one of the chamberlains, **said** before the king, Behold also, the gallows fifty cubits high, which Haman has made for Mordecai, who spoke good for the king, stands in the house of Haman" (Esther 7:9). **Rabbi Elazar said: Harbonah was also wicked and involved in that plot,**[N] as he too wanted Mordecai executed. **Once he saw that his plot had not succeeded, he immediately fled** and joined Mordecai's side. **And this is** the meaning of **that which is written: "It hurls itself at him, and does not spare; he would fain flee out of its hand"** (Job 27:22), indicating that when God sends calamity upon a wicked person, his friends immediately flee from him.

"וַחֲמַת הַמֶּלֶךְ שָׁכָכָה", שְׁתֵּי שְׁכִיכוֹת הַלָּלוּ לָמָּה? אַחַת שֶׁל מַלְכּוֹ שֶׁל עוֹלָם וְאַחַת שֶׁל אֲחַשְׁוֵרוֹשׁ, וְאָמְרִי לַהּ: אַחַת שֶׁל אֶסְתֵּר וְאַחַת שֶׁל וַשְׁתִּי.

The verse states: **"Then the king's wrath was assuaged** [*shakhakha*]**"** (Esther 7:10). The Gemara asks: **Why are there two assuagings here?** The term *shakhakha* is used rather than *shaka* and indicates doubled wrath. There was **one** assuaging of the wrath **of the King of the universe, and one** of the wrath **of Ahasuerus. And some say:** Ahasuerus's wrath burned within him for two reasons; **one due to** Haman's involvement with **Esther, and one due to** his involvement with **Vashti,** and now they were both assuaged.

"לְכֻלָּם נָתַן לָאִישׁ חֲלִיפוֹת שְׂמָלוֹת וּלְבִנְיָמִן נָתַן... חָמֵשׁ חֲלִיפוֹת", אֶפְשָׁר דָּבָר שֶׁנִּצְטַעֵר בּוֹ אוֹתוֹ צַדִּיק

Before continuing its midrashic interpretation of the rest of the book of Esther, the Gemara expounds a verse concerning Joseph that relates to the Megilla: **"To all of them he gave each man changes of clothing, but to Benjamin he gave** three hundred pieces of silver, and **five changes** of clothing" (Genesis 45:22). The Gemara asks: **Is it possible that in the** very **thing from which that righteous man** Joseph **had suffered,** as his father's show of favoritism toward him aroused the enmity of his brothers,

NOTES

Was also…involved in that plot – בְּאוֹתָהּ עֵצָה הָיָה: The proof that Harbonah was involved in the plot is that otherwise he would not have known that the tree planned for hanging Mordecai was exactly fifty cubits tall (Maharsha; *Yefe Mareh*).

Perek **I**
Daf **16** Amud **b**

יִכָּשֵׁל בּוֹ?! דְּאָמַר רָבָא בַּר מְחַסְיָא אָמַר רַב חָמָא בַּר גּוּרְיָא אָמַר רַב: בִּשְׁבִיל מִשְׁקַל שְׁנֵי סְלָעִים מֵילָת שֶׁהוֹסִיף יַעֲקֹב לְיוֹסֵף מִשְּׁאָר אֶחָיו – נִתְגַּלְגֵּל הַדָּבָר, וְיָרְדוּ אֲבוֹתֵינוּ לְמִצְרַיִם. אָמַר רַבִּי בִּנְיָמִן בַּר יֶפֶת: רֶמֶז רָמַז לוֹ, שֶׁעָתִיד בֵּן לָצֵאת מִמֶּנּוּ שֶׁיֵּצֵא מִלִּפְנֵי הַמֶּלֶךְ בַּחֲמִשָּׁה לְבוּשֵׁי מַלְכוּת, שֶׁנֶּאֱמַר "וּמָרְדֳּכַי יָצָא... בִּלְבוּשׁ מַלְכוּת תְּכֵלֶת" וגו׳.

he himself **should stumble**[N] by showing favoritism to Benjamin? **As Rava bar Meḥaseyya said** that **Rav Ḥama bar Gurya said** that **Rav said: Due to** the weight of **two sela of fine wool that Jacob** gave to Joseph, which he **added to** what he gave **Joseph beyond** what he gave **the rest of his brothers,** as he made him his special coat, **the story progressed and our forefathers went down to Egypt.** How then could Joseph have displayed similar favoritism toward Benjamin? **Rabbi Binyamin bar Yefet said: He** was not showing favoritism. Rather, he **intimated to him that a descendant was destined to issue from him who would go out from the presence of the king** wearing **five royal garments, as it is stated: "And Mordecai went forth** from the presence of the king **in royal apparel of sky blue** and white, and with a great crown of gold, and with a wrap of fine linen and purple" (Esther 8:15).

NOTES

He should stumble – יִכָּשֵׁל בּוֹ: It is explained that the Gemara is indicating that especially since the favoritism Jacob demonstrated toward Joseph involved a preferred garment, it is not fitting that Joseph should single out his brother Benjamin for special treatment with regard to preferred garments (*Shenot Ḥayyim*; see Maharsha). For this reason, the Gemara mentions only the garments and does not comment on the additional three hundred pieces of silver he received. See the later authorities, who explain this at length.

NOTES

On…Benjamin's neck – עַל צַוְּארֵי בִנְיָמִן: The Gemara's comment can be better understood in light of the fact that in several *midrashim* the Temple is referred to as the neck. Most notable in this regard is the Sages' explanation of the blessing that Moses gave to the tribe of Benjamin: "And he dwells between his shoulders" (Deuteronomy 33:17), as referring to the Temple, as the neck, which rests between the shoulders, is indicative of the Temple (Rashash).

Light, this is Torah – אוֹרָה זוֹ תּוֹרָה: One might wonder what is the connection between the salvation of Purim and the light associated with the happiness of Torah, Shabbat, and circumcision. Some commentaries explain, based on the description in tractate *Shabbat* (89a), that during the time of Mordecai, the Jewish people reaccepted the Torah upon themselves. Therefore, the verse refers to the Torah itself and to several mitzvot with which the Jewish people renewed their connection in the aftermath of the miracle (*Zikkaron BaSefer*). Others write, based on the *Targum*, including Rashi, who built his explanation on it, that these mitzvot are singled out because Haman had outlawed their observance, and that when the decree was annulled the Jews once again fulfilled these mitzvot. See the later authorities, who question Rashi's source. Furthermore, the mention of the mitzvot is significant, as the verse indicates that "many from the peoples of the land became Jews" (Esther 8:17), and thereby there was widespread mitzva observance, both new and renewed (Maharsha). Additionally, others understand that since all of the mitzvot mentioned distinguish the Jews from others, during the period of the decree against the Jewish people the Jews observed these mitzvot only in private, so as not to be associated as Jews. After the decree was annulled, they resumed practicing them in public (*Derashot HaRan*).

״וַיִּפּוֹל עַל צַוְּארֵי בִנְיָמִן אָחִיו״ – כַּמָּה צַוָּארִין הָווּ לֵיהּ לְבִנְיָמִין? אָמַר רַבִּי אֶלְעָזָר: בָּכָה עַל שְׁנֵי מִקְדָּשִׁים שֶׁעֲתִידִין לִהְיוֹת בְּחֶלְקוֹ שֶׁל בִּנְיָמִין, וַעֲתִידִין לֵיחָרֵב. ״וּבִנְיָמִין בָּכָה עַל צַוָּארָיו״ – בָּכָה עַל מִשְׁכַּן שִׁילֹה שֶׁעָתִיד לִהְיוֹת בְּחֶלְקוֹ שֶׁל יוֹסֵף, וְעָתִיד לֵיחָרֵב.

The Gemara elaborates on certain elements in the story of Joseph and his brothers. The verse states with regard to Joseph: **"And he fell on his brother Benjamin's neck [*tzavarei*]**[N] **and wept"** (Genesis 45:14). The wording of the verse gives rise to a question, as the word *tzavarei* is plural, meaning necks: **How many necks did Benjamin have,** such that the verse should use the plural *tzavarei* rather than the singular *tzavar*? **Rabbi Elazar said:** This intimates **that** Joseph **cried over the two Temples that were destined to be in the** tribal **territory of Benjamin and were destined to be destroyed.** The same verse continues: **"And Benjamin wept on his neck"** (Genesis 45:14); **he cried over the tabernacle of Shiloh that was destined to be in the** tribal **territory of Joseph and was destined to be destroyed.**

״וְהִנֵּה עֵינֵיכֶם רוֹאוֹת וְעֵינֵי אָחִי בִנְיָמִין״. אָמַר רַבִּי אֶלְעָזָר, אָמַר לָהֶם: כְּשֵׁם שֶׁאֵין בְּלִבִּי עַל בִּנְיָמִין אָחִי שֶׁלֹּא הָיָה בִּמְכִירָתִי – כָּךְ אֵין בְּלִבִּי עֲלֵיכֶם. ״כִּי פִי הַמְדַבֵּר אֲלֵיכֶם״, כְּפִי – כֵּן לִבִּי.

The verse states: **"And behold, your eyes see, and the eyes of my brother Benjamin"** (Genesis 45:12). **Rabbi Elazar said:** Joseph **said to** his brothers as follows: **Just as I** certainly **harbor no** resentment **in my heart toward my brother Benjamin, for he was not** even **present when I was sold, so too, I harbor no** resentment **toward you.** The verse continues: **"That it is my mouth [*ki fi*] that speaks to you"** (Genesis 45:12), i.e., **As my mouth [*kefi*] is, so is my heart.**

״וּלְאָבִיו שָׁלַח כְּזֹאת עֲשָׂרָה חֲמוֹרִים נוֹשְׂאִים מִטּוּב מִצְרָיִם״. מַאי ״מִטּוּב מִצְרָיִם״? אָמַר רַבִּי בִּנְיָמִין בַּר יֶפֶת אָמַר רַבִּי אֶלְעָזָר: שָׁלַח לוֹ יַיִן [יָשָׁן] שֶׁדַּעַת זְקֵנִים נוֹחָה הֵימֶנּוּ.

The verse states: **"And to his father he sent after this manner ten donkeys laden with the good things of Egypt"** (Genesis 45:23). The Gemara asks: **What are "the good things of Egypt"** that are mentioned but not specified here? **Rabbi Binyamin bar Yefet said** that **Rabbi Elazar said: He sent him aged wine, which the elderly find pleasing.**

״וַיֵּלְכוּ גַּם אֶחָיו וַיִּפְּלוּ לְפָנָיו״, אָמַר רַבִּי בִּנְיָמִין בַּר יֶפֶת אָמַר רַבִּי אֶלְעָזָר: הַיְינוּ דְּאָמְרִי אֱינָשֵׁי: תַּעֲלָא בְּעִידָּנֵיהּ סְגִיד לֵיהּ.

Following Jacob's death, it states concerning Joseph: **"And his brothers even went and fell down before him"** (Genesis 50:18). **Rabbi Binyamin bar Yefet said** that **Rabbi Elazar said: This** explains the folk saying **that people say: When the fox is in its hour, bow down to it,** i.e., if a fox is appointed king, one must bow down before and submit oneself to it.

תַּעֲלָא? מַאי בְּצִירוּתֵיהּ מֵאַחֲווֹהִי?! אֶלָּא, אִי אִיתְּמַר הָכִי אִיתְּמַר: ״וַיִּשְׁתַּחוּ יִשְׂרָאֵל עַל רֹאשׁ הַמִּטָּה״, אָמַר רַבִּי בִּנְיָמִין בַּר יֶפֶת אָמַר רַבִּי אֶלְעָזָר: תַּעֲלָא בְּעִידָּנֵיהּ סְגִיד לֵיהּ.

The Gemara expresses astonishment at the use of this parable: Are you calling Joseph **a fox? What, was he inferior to his brothers** such that in relation to them you call him a fox? **Rather, if such a statement was stated, it was stated as follows,** not in connection with this verse, but rather in connection with a different verse. The verse states: **"And Israel bowed himself upon the head of the bed"** (Genesis 47:31). With regard to this, **Rabbi Binyamin bar Yefet said** that **Rabbi Elazar said: When the fox is in its hour, bow down to it,** as Jacob had to bow down before his son Joseph, who had reached greatness.

״וַיְנַחֵם אוֹתָם וַיְדַבֵּר עַל לִבָּם״ אָמַר רַבִּי בִּנְיָמִין בַּר יֶפֶת אָמַר רַבִּי אֶלְעָזָר: מְלַמֵּד שֶׁאָמַר לָהֶם דְּבָרִים שֶׁמִּתְקַבְּלִין עַל הַלֵּב: וּמַה עֲשָׂרָה נֵרוֹת לֹא יָכְלוּ לְכַבּוֹת נֵר אֶחָד – נֵר אֶחָד הֵיאַךְ יָכוֹל לְכַבּוֹת עֲשָׂרָה נֵרוֹת?

It says with regard to Joseph's remarks to his brothers: **"And he comforted them and spoke to their hearts"** (Genesis 50:21). **Rabbi Binyamin bar Yefet said** that **Rabbi Elazar said:** This **teaches that he spoke to them words that are acceptable to the heart,** and alleviated their fears. This is what he said: **If ten lights could not put out one light,** as all of you were unable to do me harm, **how can one light put out ten lights?**

״לַיְּהוּדִים הָיְתָה אוֹרָה וְשִׂמְחָה וְשָׂשׂוֹן וִיקָר״, אָמַר רַב יְהוּדָה: ״אוֹרָה״ זוֹ תּוֹרָה, וְכֵן הוּא אוֹמֵר ״כִּי נֵר מִצְוָה וְתוֹרָה אוֹר״. ״שִׂמְחָה״ – זֶה יוֹם טוֹב, וְכֵן הוּא אוֹמֵר ״וְשָׂמַחְתָּ בְּחַגֶּךָ״, ״שָׂשׂוֹן״ – זוֹ מִילָה, וְכֵן הוּא אוֹמֵר ״שָׂשׂ אָנֹכִי עַל אִמְרָתֶךָ״.

§ The Gemara returns to its explanation of the Megilla. The verse states: **"The Jews had light and gladness, and joy and honor"** (Esther 8:16). **Rav Yehuda said: "Light"; this** is referring to the **Torah**[N] that they once again studied. **And similarly it says: "For the mitzva is a lamp and the Torah is light"** (Proverbs 6:23). **"Gladness" [*simḥa*]; this** is referring to **the Festivals** that they once again observed. **And similarly it says: "And you shall be glad [*vesamakhta*] on your Festival"** (Deuteronomy 16:14). **"Joy" [*sasson*]; this** is referring to **circumcision,** as they once again circumcised their sons. **And similarly it says: "I rejoice [*sas*] at Your word"** (Psalms 119:162), which the Sages understood as referring to David's rejoicing over the mitzva of circumcision.

"וִיקָר" – אֵלּוּ תְּפִלִּין, וְכֵן הוּא אוֹמֵר "וְרָאוּ כׇּל עַמֵּי הָאָרֶץ כִּי שֵׁם ה׳ נִקְרָא עָלֶיךָ וְיָרְאוּ מִמֶּךָּ" וְתַנְיָא, רַבִּי אֱלִיעֶזֶר הַגָּדוֹל אוֹמֵר: אֵלּוּ תְּפִלִּין שֶׁבָּרֹאשׁ.

"Honor"; this is referring to **phylacteries,** which they once again donned. **And similarly it says: "And all peoples of the earth will see that you are called by the name of the Lord; and they will be afraid of you"** (Deuteronomy 28:10). **And it was taught** in a *baraita*: **Rabbi Eliezer the Great said: This is** referring to **the phylacteries worn on the head.** Haman had banned the fulfillment of all the mitzvot mentioned, but upon Haman's demise the Jews returned to their observance.

"וְאֵת פַּרְשַׁנְדָּתָא" וגו׳ "עֲשֶׂרֶת בְּנֵי הָמָן", אָמַר רַב אַדָּא דְּמִן יָפוֹ: עֲשֶׂרֶת בְּנֵי הָמָן וַעֲשֶׂרֶת – צָרִיךְ לְמֵימְרִינְהוּ בִּנְשִׁימָה אַחַת. מַאי טַעְמָא – כּוּלְּהוּ בַּהֲדֵי הֲדָדֵי נָפְקוּ נִשְׁמָתַיְיהוּ. אָמַר רַבִּי יוֹחָנָן: וָיו דְּוַיְזָתָא צָרִיךְ לְמִימְתְּחָהּ בִּזְקִיפָא כְּמוּרְדְּיָא דְּלִבְרוֹת. מַאי טַעְמָא? כּוּלְּהוּ בְּחַד זְקִיפָא אִזְדְּקִיפוּ.

The verse states: "And in Shushan the capital the Jews slew and destroyed five hundred men. **And Parshandatha...** and Vaizatha, **the ten sons of Haman"** (Esther 9:6–10). **Rav Adda from Jaffa said:** When reading the Megilla, the names of **the ten sons of Haman and** the word **"ten" must be said in one breath.**[H] **What is the reason** for this? It is that **their souls all departed together. Rabbi Yoḥanan said:** The letter *vav* **in** the name **"Vaizatha"** is a lengthened *vav*[H] and **must be elongated as a pole,**[N] **like a steering oar of a ship [*liberot*].**[L] **What is the reason** for this? To indicate that **they were all hanged on one pole.**

אָמַר רַבִּי חֲנִינָא בַּר פָּפָּא: דָּרַשׁ רַבִּי שֵׁילָא אִישׁ כְּפַר תְּמַרְתָּא: כׇּל הַשִּׁירוֹת כּוּלָּן נִכְתָּבוֹת אָרִיחַ עַל גַּבֵּי לְבֵנָה וּלְבֵנָה עַל גַּבֵּי אָרִיחַ,

Rabbi Ḥanina bar Pappa said that **Rabbi Sheila, a man of the village of Timarta, interpreted** a verse **homiletically: All of the songs** in the Bible **are written**[HB] in the form of **a half brick arranged upon a whole brick and a whole brick arranged upon a half brick,** i.e., each line of the song is divided into a stitch of text, referred to as a half brick, which is separated by a blank space, referred to as a whole brick, from the concluding stitch of that line of text.

HALAKHA

The ten sons of Haman…in one breath – ...עֲשֶׂרֶת בְּנֵי הָמָן בִּנְשִׁימָה אַחַת: The names of the ten sons of Haman and the word "ten" must be said in one breath, in accordance with the opinion of Rav Adda, and this is specifically *ab initio*. After the fact, however, if the reader paused, he has fulfilled his obligation (see *Tosafot*). The Rema, based on the Maharil and others, says that it is customary to read in one breath from the words "five hundred" until and including the word "ten" (*Shulḥan Arukh*, *Oraḥ Ḥayyim* 690:15).

The *vav* in Vaizatha – וָיו דְּוַיְזָתָא: One must extend the *vav* in the name Vaizatha. The Rema points out that this refers to extending the letter when writing it; he further explains that some say this refers to extending the sound when reading it (*Shulḥan Arukh*, *Oraḥ Ḥayyim* 691:4).

All of the songs in the Bible are written – כׇּל הַשִּׁירוֹת כּוּלָּן נִכְתָּבוֹת: One must write the songs in the Bible, e.g., the Song of the Sea, the Song of David, in a dispersed fashion, with the style of a whole brick on top of a half brick. If a song is written in the form of prose, as the rest of the Torah, it is invalid. If, however, it is written in a dispersed fashion, but in a different style than is traditionally done, for instance, it was written with a whole brick on top of a half brick, then it is valid (*Shulḥan Arukh*, *Yoreh De'a* 275:3).

NOTES

Must be elongated as a pole – צָרִיךְ לְמִימְתְּחָהּ בִּזְקִיפָא: The commentaries disagree as to the exact meaning of this statement. Some write that the letter *vav* here must be extended to be a larger *vav* (Meiri), while others write that the *vav* is written normally but must be read in an extended melody (Rid; Rabbi Aharon HaLevi). Still others understand that both of these explanations are correct and required (Rabbeinu Yehonatan), and some commentaries write that this *vav* must be written in a unique form, with its head raised upward like a pillar (Ran; Ritva).

LANGUAGE

Ship [*liberot*] – לִבְרוֹת: Possibly from the Greek λιβυρνίς, *liburnis*, indicating a Liburnian ship, which was a large ship whose steering oars were understandably very large. Alternatively, *Liberot* is the name of a river or a lake (*Arukh*).

BACKGROUND

Writing the songs – כְּתִיבַת הַשִּׁירוֹת: Usually the text of the Torah and the other books of the Bible is written closely spaced, with virtually no empty spaces in the writing, with the exception of the lengthier empty spaces in the text that are intended to act as breaks between portions or between books of the Torah. Songs in the Torah, on the other hand, are written differently, as blank spaces are placed in the text to differentiate between different sections of the verses. The songs are written in two different forms. One, like the Song of the Sea, is written in the style of a whole brick on top of a half brick and a half brick on top of a whole brick, meaning that the long and short rows are written on top of one another, as in the way a building is built. The second form is like the list of the ten sons of Haman, written as a whole brick on top of a whole brick and a half brick on top of a half brick, meaning that sections of the verses that are similar in length are placed one on top of another.

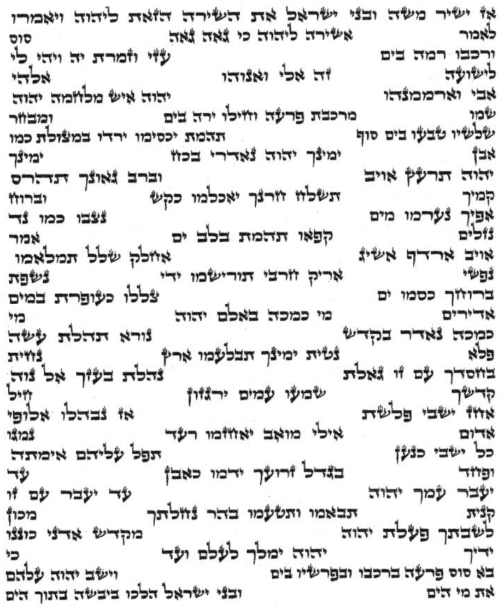

Song of the Sea as it appears in a Torah scroll

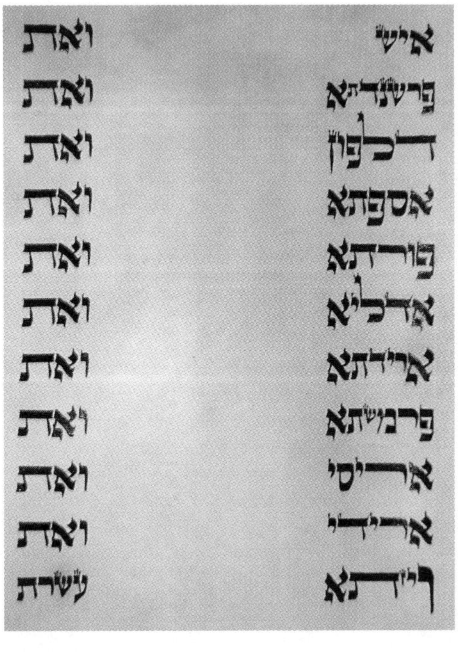

List of the ten sons of Haman as it appears in a Megilla scroll

חוץ משירה זו ומלכי כנען, שאריח על גבי אריח, ולבינה על גבי לבינה. מאי טעמא? שלא תהא תקומה למפלתן.

The next line of the song inverts the sequence. **This is the principle for all songs in the Bible except** for **this song,**[N] referring to the list of Haman's sons, **and** the song listing **the kings of Canaan** who were defeated by Joshua. These two songs are written in the form of **a half brick arranged upon a half brick and a whole brick arranged upon a whole brick,** i.e., one stitch of text over another, and one blank space over another. **What is the reason** that these two songs are written in this anomalous fashion? **So that they should never rise from their downfall.** Just as a wall that is built in this manner will not stand, so too, these individuals should have no resurgence.[H]

"ויאמר המלך לאסתר המלכה בשושן הבירה הרגו היהודים", אמר רבי אבהו: מלמד שבא מלאך וסטרו על פיו.

The verse states: **"And the king said to Esther the queen: The Jews have slain** and destroyed five hundred men **in Shushan the capital,** and also the ten sons of Haman; what have they done in the rest of the king's provinces? Now what is your petition and it shall be granted to you; and what more do you request, and it shall be done" (Esther 9:12). **Rabbi Abbahu said: This teaches that an angel came and slapped him on his mouth,** so that he was unable to finish what he was saying; he started with a complaint about what the Jews were doing, but ended on an entirely different note.

"ובבאה לפני המלך אמר עם הספר" "אמר"? אמרה מיבעי ליה! אמר רבי יוחנן: אמרה לו: יאמר בפה מה שכתוב בספר.

The verse states: **"But when she came before the king, he said with a letter"** (Esther 9:25). Why does it say: **"He said"? It should have said: "She said,"** as it was Esther who changed the decree. **Rabbi Yoḥanan said: She said to** Ahasuerus: **Let it be said by** word of **mouth,**[N] indicating that **that which is written in the letter** should also be ordered verbally.

"דברי שלום ואמת", אמר רבי תנחום, ואמרי לה אמר רבי אסי: מלמד שצריכה שרטוט כאמיתה של תורה.

With regard to what is stated: **"Words of peace and truth"** (Esther 9:30), **Rabbi Tanḥum said, and some say** that **Rabbi Asi** said: This **teaches that** a Megilla scroll **requires scoring,**[H] i.e., that the lines for the text must be scored onto the parchment, **as the Torah itself,**[N] i.e., as is done in a Torah scroll.

"ומאמר אסתר קיים", "מאמר אסתר" – אין, "דברי הצומות" – לא?! אמר רבי יוחנן: "דברי הצומות..." "ומאמר אסתר קיים (את ימי) הפורים האלה".

The verses say: "The matters of the fasts and their cry. **And the decree of Esther confirmed** these matters of Purim" (Esther 9:31–32). The Gemara asks: Should we say that **"the decree of Esther" indeed** confirmed these matters of Purim, but **"the matters of the fasts"** did **not?** But didn't the fasts also contribute to the miracle? **Rabbi Yoḥanan said:** These two verses, **"The matters of the fasts** and their cry. **And the decree of Esther confirmed these matters of Purim,"** should be read as one.

"כי מרדכי היהודי משנה למלך אחשורוש וגדול ליהודים ורצוי לרוב אחיו", "לרוב אחיו" – ולא לכל אחיו, מלמד: שפירשו ממנו מקצת סנהדרין.

The verse states: **"For Mordecai the Jew was second to the king Ahasuerus, and great among the Jews, and accepted by the majority of his brethren"** (Esther 10:3). The Gemara comments: The verse indicates that Mordecai was accepted only **"By the majority of his brethren," but not by all his brethren.** This **teaches that some** members **of the Sanhedrin parted from him,** because he occupied himself with community needs, and was therefore compelled to neglect his Torah study. They felt that this was a mistake and that he should have remained active on the Sanhedrin.

NOTES

Except for this song – חוץ משירה זו: In fact, the song of Ha'azinu (Deuteronomy, chapter 32) is likewise written as a half brick upon a half brick. Still, the Gemara does not mention it, either because the rule stated here is only in reference to songs referring to miracles, such as the death of Haman's sons, or because the song of Ha'azinu also includes the downfall of the wicked and therefore it is fitting for it to be written in this manner (see Meiri and later authorities).

Let it be said by mouth – יאמר בפה: One interpretation of Esther's request is that she asked Ahasuerus for permission to sanction the commemoration of the miracle and the reading of the Megilla aloud, although it could possibly be seen as slightly critical of the king (Ritva; see *Or Ḥadash* and Maharam Schiff). A second understanding is that Esther requested that the announcers should also proclaim this matter out loud for all to hear and not only distribute the letters (Ritva).

As the Torah itself – כאמיתה של תורה: The *ge'onim* cite an alternative version of the text, which reads: As a true Torah; what does this refer to? It is like Elazar, and Moses, and the *Eida*, and the *Nesi'im*. This version of the text also appears in the Jerusalem Talmud (see Meiri). The *ge'onim* explain this version of the text as referring to the episode with the daughters of Zelophehad, who had approached Moses, Elazar, and the princes of the tribes in their efforts to gain a portion of Eretz Yisrael. The message of the Gemara is therefore that even though the incidents recorded in the Megilla are heavily focused on the actions of women, such as Esther and Vashti, it represents the truth and essence of the Torah, and likewise should require scoring the parchment just as does the story of Zelophehad's daughters in the Torah.

However, Rashi and most of the early authorities explain that the intention of the Gemara is simply that the lines of a Megilla must be scored just as the lines of a scroll of the Torah are scored. Rabbeinu Ḥananel and the *Arukh*, as well as Rabbeinu Tam, whose explanation is recorded at length in the *Sefer HaYashar*, explain that in fact a Torah scroll does not need to be scored, and that the Gemara is stating that a Megilla needs to be scored just as a *mezuza* needs to be scored. They explain that a *mezuza* is referred to as a true Torah, as it contains the *Shema*, which declares the essence of faith in the truth of God and of Torah. The Ritva, however, attempts to prove that Rashi is correct based on the parallel passage in the Jerusalem Talmud.

HALAKHA

The ten sons of Haman – עשרת בני המן: The ten sons of Haman must be written in the Megilla as a song, in a manner different from the standard writing. However, the passage is not written like other songs, with blank spaces above the words. Rather, the blank spaces are between the words, and the lines of words are written on top of one another. This is the only valid way to write this portion of the Megilla. It is stated in the Jerusalem Talmud that the word "man" [*ish*] should ideally be written in the beginning of the folio of the Megilla and the word "and" [*ve'et*] at the end of it. Nevertheless, the *Magen Avraham* holds that if it is not written in this manner it is valid, while the *Sheyarei Keneset HaGedola* writes that it is invalid (*Shulḥan Arukh*, *Oraḥ Ḥayyim* 691:3–4).

A Megilla scroll requires scoring – צריכה שרטוט: The Megilla parchment must be scored before it is written, just as is done with a Torah scroll. However, it is enough to score the first line (*Magen Avraham*, citing *Levush*), though the *Ḥakham Tzvi* and the Vilna Gaon disagree, saying that all lines require scoring (*Shulḥan Arukh*, *Oraḥ Ḥayyim* 691:1).

אמר רב יוסף: גדול תלמוד תורה יותר מהצלת נפשות. דמעיקרא חשיב ליה למרדכי בתר ארבעה ולבסוף בתר חמשה. מעיקרא כתיב "אשר באו עם זרובבל ישוע נחמיה שריה רעליה מרדכי בלשן" ולבסוף כתיב "הבאים עם זרובבל ישוע נחמיה עזריה רעמיה נחמני מרדכי בלשן".

Rav Yosef said: Studying Torah is greater than saving lives,[N] **as initially,** when listing the Jewish leaders who came to Eretz Yisrael, **Mordecai was mentioned after four** other people, **but at the end** he was listed **after five.** This is taken to indicate that his involvement in governmental affairs instead of in Torah study lowered his stature one notch. The Gemara proves this: **At first it is written: "Who came with Zerubbabel, Jeshua, Nehemiah, Seraiah, Reelaiah, Mordecai, Bilshan"** (Ezra 2:2); **but in the end** in a later list **it is written: "Who came with Zerubbabel, Jeshua, Nehemiah, Azariah, Raamiah, Nahmani, Mordecai, Bilshan"** (Nehemiah 7:7).

אמר רב ואיתימא רב שמואל בר מרתא: גדול תלמוד תורה יותר מבנין בית המקדש, שכל זמן שברוך בן נריה קיים – לא הניחו עזרא ועלה.

Rav said, and some say that **Rav Shmuel bar Marta** said: **Studying Torah is greater** and more important **that building the Temple.** A proof of this is that **for as long as Baruch ben Neriah was alive**[N] in Babylonia, **Ezra,** who was his disciple, **did not leave him and go up** to Eretz Yisrael to build the Temple.

אמר רבה אמר רב יצחק בר שמואל בר מרתא: גדול תלמוד תורה יותר מכבוד אב ואם, שכל אותן שנים שהיה יעקב אבינו בבית עבר לא נענש. דאמר מר:

Rabba said that **Rav Yitzḥak bar Shmuel bar Marta said: Studying Torah is** greater and **more** important **than honoring one's father and mother,** and a proof of this is **that for all those years that our father Jacob spent in the house of Eber** and studied Torah there **he was not punished** for having neglected to fulfill the mitzva of honoring one's parents. **As the Master said:**

NOTES

Greater than saving lives – יותר מהצלת נפשות: The Gemara is not indicating that saving lives is less important than studying Torah; rather, since Mordecai had already saved the Jews, a number of Sages were angry with him for continuing to be involved in affairs of state with the intention of preventing further danger to Jews, as in this regard the study of Torah should take precedence (*Rishon LeTziyyon*).

For as long as Baruch ben Neriah was alive – כל זמן שברוך בן נריה קיים: A midrash explains that Baruch himself was of advanced age and was consequently unable to go up to Eretz Yisrael (see Maharsha).

למה נמנו שנותיו של ישמעאל – כדי ליחס בהן שנותיו של יעקב. דכתיב "ואלה שני חיי ישמעאל מאת שנה ושלשים שנה ושבע שנים". כמה קשיש ישמעאל מיצחק – ארביסר שנין, דכתיב "ואברם בן שמונים שנה ושש שנים בלדת הגר את ישמעאל לאברם", וכתיב "ואברהם בן מאת שנה בהולד לו את יצחק בנו". וכתיב "ויצחק בן ששים שנה בלדת אותם". בר כמה הוה ישמעאל כדאתיליד יעקב – בר שבעים וארבעה, כמה פיישן משניה – שתין ותלת.

Why were the years of Ishmael mentioned[N] in the Torah? For what purpose were we told the life span of that wicked man? **In order to reckon through them the years of Jacob. As it is written: "And these are the years of the life of Ishmael, a hundred and thirty-seven years"** (Genesis 25:17). **How much older was Ishmael than Isaac? Fourteen years. As it is written: "And Abram was eighty-six years old when Hagar bore Ishmael to Abram"** (Genesis 16:16). **And it is written: "And Abraham was a hundred years old when his son Isaac was born to him"** (Genesis 21:5). **And it is written** with regard to Jacob and Esau: **"And Isaac was sixty years old when she bore them"** (Genesis 25:26). Based on these verses, **how old was Ishmael when Jacob was born? Seventy-four. How many of his years remained** then until his death? **Sixty-three,** as Ishmael died at the age of a hundred and thirty-seven.

ותניא: היה יעקב אבינו בשעה שנתברך מאביו בן ששים ושלש שנה, ובו בפרק מת ישמעאל, דכתיב "וירא עשו כי ברך" וגו' "וילך עשו אל ישמעאל ויקח את מחלת בת ישמעאל אחות נביות" ממשמע שנאמר "בת ישמעאל" איני יודע שהיא אחות נביות? מלמד שקידשה ישמעאל ומת, והשיאה נביות אחיה.

And it was taught in a *baraita*: **Jacob our father was sixty-three years old at the time he was blessed by his father, and at that same time Ishmael died.** How is it known that these two events occurred at the same time? **As it is written: "When Esau saw that Isaac had blessed** Jacob… **then Esau went to Ishmael and took for a wife Mahalath, the daughter of Ishmael,** Abraham's son, **the sister of Nebaioth"** (Genesis 28:6–9). **From the fact that it is stated: "the daughter of Ishmael," do I not know that she was the sister of Nebaioth?** For what purpose then does the verse say this explicitly? **This teaches that Ishmael betrothed her** to Esau[N] **and** in the meantime he **died, and Nebaioth her brother married her off.** Therefore, special mention is made of Nebaioth. Consequently, it is understood that Jacob was sixty-three years old when he received his blessing and left his father's house.

NOTES

Why were the years of Ishmael mentioned – למה נמנו שנותיו של ישמעאל: Rashi explains the Gemara's question as: Why count the life span of a wicked man? The *Turei Even*, however, questions this understanding, as there are opinions that state that Ishmael repented, dying a righteous man (see Maharsha), and according to Rashi's reasoning it would then be worthy of mention. Therefore, he offers an alternative interpretation, explaining simply that there are other righteous men whose life spans are not mentioned in the Torah. Therefore, the Gemara is questioning why Ishmael was singled out for special mention.

This teaches that Ishmael betrothed her to Esau – מלמד שקידשה ישמעאל: This is derived from the language of the verse, as it says: "And Esau went to Ishmael" in order to marry his daughter. Yet when mentioning the actual marriage it states: "The sister of Nebaioth," indicating that it was Nebaioth who actually married her off. Evidently, the verse is meant to teach us that Ishmael betrothed his daughter to Esau, but died before the actual marriage took place, and his son Nebaioth gave her over in marriage (Maharsha).

NOTES

Eber died…two years – עבר מת...שתי שנים: Seemingly, this additional piece of information is not essential to the rest of the story line. However, it is mentioned for a reason, as it indicates that Jacob did not remain studying under Eber until the latter's death sixteen years later, but rather, he completed his studies two years prior to Eber's death (Rabbi Yoshiya Pinto; see *Rosh Yosef*).

He then was in Bethel for six months – ובבית אל עשה ששה חדשים: The Maharsha explains why the Gemara finds it necessary to mention that Jacob brought offerings while in Bethel: Jacob suffered many trials and tribulations during the first eighteen months, including the incident with Dina, which would make it understandable that he would bring offerings upon his arrival in Bethel. Nevertheless, he was faulted for not leaving Bethel earlier and was therefore punished for the entire two years he was not involved in honoring his father.

שתין ותלת, וארביסר עד דמתיליד יוסף – הא שבעין ושבעה. וכתיב "ויוסף בן שלשים שנה בעמדו לפני פרעה" – הא מאה ושבע, שב דשבעא ותרתי דכפנא – הא מאה ושיתסר,

If we calculate these **sixty-three** years **and** the **fourteen until Joseph was born, this** means that Jacob should have been **seventy-seven** at the time of Joseph's birth. **And it is written: "And Joseph was thirty years old when he stood before Pharaoh"** (Genesis 41:46). **This** indicates that Jacob should have then been at least **a hundred and seven** years old when Joseph was thirty. Add the **seven** years **of plenty and** the **two of famine,** and **this** would then indicate that Jacob should have been **a hundred and sixteen** years old when he arrived in Egypt in the second year of the famine.

וכתיב "ויאמר פרעה אל יעקב כמה ימי שני חייך. ויאמר יעקב אל פרעה ימי שני מגורי שלשים ומאת שנה" מאה ושיתסר הויין!

But it is written: "And Pharaoh said to Jacob, How many are the days of the years of your life? And Jacob said to Pharaoh, The days of the years of my sojournings are a hundred and thirty years" (Genesis 47:8–9). Jacob indicated that he was a hundred and thirty-three when he arrived in Egypt, **which is** different from the **hundred and sixteen** years calculated previously. Where are the missing fourteen years from Jacob's lifetime?

אלא שמע מינה: ארבע עשרה שנין דהוה בבית עבר – לא חשיב להו. דתניא: היה יעקב בבית עבר מוטמן ארבע עשרה שנה. עבר מת לאחר שירד יעקב אבינו לארם נהרים שתי שנים. יצא משם ובא לו לארם נהרים. נמצא, כשעמד על הבאר בן שבעים ושבע שנה.

Rather, learn from here that the fourteen years that Jacob spent in the house of Eber are not counted here. **As it is taught** in a *baraita*: **Jacob was** studying **in the house of Eber for fourteen years** while **in hiding** from his brother Esau. If we were to calculate the life spans recorded in the Torah, we would find that **Eber died** when Jacob was seventy-nine years old, **two years**[N] **after Jacob our father went down to Aram-naharaim,** to the house of Laban. When Jacob **left** after completing his studying **there,** he **then went** immediately **to Aram-naharaim.** Therefore, **when** Jacob **stood at the well** upon his arrival in Aram-naharaim, **he was seventy-seven years old.**

ומנלן דלא מיענש – דתניא: נמצא, יוסף שפירש מאביו עשרים ושתים שנה כשם שפירש יעקב אבינו מאביו. דיעקב תלתין ושיתא הויין! אלא: ארביסר דהוה בבית עבר לא חשיב להו.

And from where do we derive **that** Jacob **was not punished** for the fourteen years that he was in the house of Eber, during which time he failed to fulfill the mitzva of honoring one's parents? **As it is taught** in a *baraita*: **It turns out that Joseph was away from his father for twenty-two years, just as Jacob our father was away from his** own **father** for that same period of time. According to the previous calculation, however, the *baraita* is difficult, as **Jacob** was absent for **thirty-six** years. Rather, conclude from here that **the fourteen** years **that he was in the house of Eber are not counted,** as he was not punished for them.

סוף סוף דבית לבן עשרין שנין הויין! אלא, משום דאשתהי באורחא תרתין שנין. דתניא: יצא מארם נהרים ובא לו לסכות, ועשה שם שמונה עשר חודש, שנאמר "ויעקב נסע סכותה ויבן לו בית ולמקנהו עשה סכות". ובבית אל עשה ששה חדשים והקריב זבחים.

The Gemara raises an objection: But **ultimately,** Jacob was in **Laban's house for** only **twenty years.** Why, then, is he faulted for being away from his father for twenty-two years? **Rather,** he was punished **because on his journey** back from Aram-naharaim **he tarried** another **two years** before returning home to his parents, **as it is taught** in a *baraita*: Jacob **left Aram-naharaim and came to Sukkot, and spent eighteen months there, as it is stated: "And Jacob journeyed to Sukkot, built himself a house, and made booths [*sukkot*] for his cattle"** (Genesis 33:17). The Gemara understands this verse to mean that first he made booths [*Sukkot*], to live in during the summer, and then he built a house in the winter, and afterward he again made booths [*sukkot*] during the next summer, indicating that he must have been there for eighteen months. **He then was in Bethel for six months,**[N] **and he brought offerings,** totaling two years in all. In this way, all the various calculations of years are reconciled.

הדרן עלך מגילה נקראת

Summary of **Perek I**

This chapter began with a discussion of the various times that the Megilla is supposed to be read. The two primary days are the fourteenth of Adar for large towns and villages, and the following day, the fifteenth of Adar, for walled cities.

This chapter also discussed the leniency allowing villagers to advance their reading of the Megilla to the day of ingathering, the Monday or Thursday market day prior to the fourteenth of Adar, in order to enable the villagers to supply food and drink to the city dwellers on Purim. This leniency for the villagers was annulled at the end of the period of the Mishna; since then, the villages must read the Megilla as in large towns, on the fourteenth of Adar.

In order for a city to be considered a walled city for the purposes of reading the Megilla on the fifteenth of Adar, it must have an organized Jewish societal apparatus, including the supporting of ten so-called idlers who study Torah on behalf of the community and are designated to take care of communal needs. The wall around the city must also be from the days of Joshua, and be a real wall, not just a fortification.

The Gemara also mentioned that in the event that Purim falls out on Shabbat the Megilla cannot be read on its appropriate day, as the Sages feared that one might transport it in a public domain. Therefore, they decreed that the Megilla may not be read on Shabbat. According to our fixed calendar, however, the fourteenth of Adar can never fall on Shabbat, although the fifteenth can. On years when it does the Megilla is read earlier, on the fourteenth, the same day as in unwalled cities. This is the only extant possibility for the Megilla not being read on its appropriate day.

This chapter dealt with other facets of the holiday of Purim and its unique mitzvot as well, such as the laws of the festive meal, the portions of food given to one's acquaintances, and the unique gifts given to the poor.

Finally, the chapter quoted numerous homiletical explications of various verses of the Megilla, with a focus on revealing some of the hidden miracles that occurred in the Purim story. These aggadic interpretations also express the divine inspiration inherent in the text of the Megilla, as well as indicate the relationship of the miracle of Purim to the fulfillment of the obligation to destroy Amalek.

Introduction to **Perek II**

And that these days shall be remembered and observed throughout every generation, every family, every province, and every city; and that these days of Purim should not cease from among the Jews, nor their memorial perish from their seed. Then Esther the queen, the daughter of Abihail, and Mordecai the Jew, wrote about all the acts of power, to confirm this second letter of Purim. And he sent letters unto all the Jews, to the one hundred and twenty-seven provinces of the kingdom of Ahasuerus, with words of peace and truth, to confirm these days of Purim in their appointed times, as Mordecai the Jew and Esther the queen had enjoined them, and as they had ordained for themselves and for their seed, the matters of the fastings and their cry.

(Esther 9:28–31)

This chapter continues the discussion of the reading of the Scroll of Esther. Here, however, the topic is not the proper time for its reading but the manner in which it is read: How it is read, from what kind of text, from which point in the text, by whom, and at what time of day?

The Scroll of Esther is referred to as a specific document within the Megilla itself. The obligation to read it is learned only from the words: "And that these days shall be remembered" (Esther 9:28), referring to a remembrance read from a written text. Consequently, as we see in this chapter, it is a matter of discussion whether or not the entire scroll must be read to fulfill this obligation.

The Scroll of Esther is referred to both as a book, i.e., a biblical text, and as a letter, i.e., an informal document. Consequently, the Rabbis discuss to what extent the scroll of the Megilla must resemble a Torah scroll, whether it must be written with the full accuracy of a Torah, whether or not there is leeway in terms of its reading, and who may read it for the public.

The time designated for reading the Megilla is Purim day, but no particular time of day is specified for this. Having mentioned this fact, the Mishna tangentially discusses many other mitzvot that are assigned to a specific day but not to any particular time during that day.

מתני׳ הַקּוֹרֵא אֶת הַמְּגִילָּה לְמַפְרֵעַ – לֹא יָצָא. קְרָאָהּ עַל פֶּה, קְרָאָהּ תַּרְגּוּם בְּכׇל לָשׁוֹן – לֹא יָצָא. אֲבָל קוֹרִין אוֹתָהּ לַלּוֹעֲזוֹת בְּלַעַז, וְהַלּוֹעֵז שֶׁשָּׁמַע אַשּׁוּרִית יָצָא.

MISHNA With regard to **one who reads the Megilla out of order,**[NH] reading a later section first, and then going back to the earlier section, **he has not fulfilled** his obligation. If **he read it by heart,**[H] or **if he read it in** Aramaic **translation** or **in** any other **language**[N] that he does not understand, **he has not fulfilled** his obligation. **However, for those who speak a foreign language, one may read** the Megilla **in** that **foreign language. And one who speaks a foreign language who heard** the Megilla read **in** ***Ashurit***, i.e., in Hebrew, **has fulfilled** his obligation.

קְרָאָהּ סֵירוּגִין, וּמִתְנַמְנֵם – יָצָא. הָיָה כּוֹתְבָהּ, דּוֹרְשָׁהּ, וּמַגִּיהָהּ, אִם כִּוֵּון לִבּוֹ – יָצָא, וְאִם לָאו – לֹא יָצָא.

If one **read** the Megilla **at intervals,** pausing and resuming, **or** while **he is dozing off, he has fulfilled his obligation. If one was writing** a Megilla, **or expounding upon it, or correcting it,** and he read all its words as he was doing so, the following distinction applies: **If he had intent** to fulfill his obligation with that reading **he has fulfilled his obligation, but if not, he has not fulfilled** his obligation.

הָיְתָה כְּתוּבָה בְּסַם וּבְסִיקְרָא וּבְקוֹמוֹס וּבְקַנְקַנְתּוֹם, עַל הַנְּיָיר וְעַל הַדִּפְתְּרָא – לֹא יָצָא, עַד שֶׁתְּהֵא כְּתוּבָה אַשּׁוּרִית, עַל הַסֵּפֶר, וּבִדְיוֹ.

If one reads from a Megilla that **was written** not with ink but **with** ***sam*** **or with** ***sikra*** **or with** ***komos*** **or with** ***kankantom***, or from a Megilla that was written not on parchment but **on** ***neyar*** **or on** ***diftera***, a kind of unprocessed leather, **he has not fulfilled** his obligation. He does not fulfill his obligation **unless** he reads from a Megilla that **is written in** ***Ashurit***,[N] i.e., in the Hebrew language and using the Hebrew script, **upon parchment and with ink.**[H]

גמ׳ מְנָא הָנֵי מִילֵּי? אָמַר רָבָא: דְּאָמַר קְרָא ״כִּכְתָבָם וְכִזְמַנָּם״ מָה זְמַנָּם לְמַפְרֵעַ לָא – אַף כְּתָבָם לְמַפְרֵעַ לָא.

GEMARA It was taught in the mishna that one who reads the Megilla out of order has not fulfilled his obligation. The Gemara asks: **From where are these matters** derived? **Rava said: The verse states** concerning Purim: "That they should unfailingly observe these two days **according to their writing, and according to their appointed times**[N] every year" (Esther 9:27), and the word "times" is referring to the two days of Purim, the fourteenth and the fifteenth of Adar. And we learn by way of analogy: **Just as their appointed times cannot be out of order,** as the fifteenth of Adar cannot possibly come before the fourteenth, **so too, their writing must not be out of order.**

מִידֵּי קְרִיאָה כְּתִיבָה הָכָא? עֲשִׂיָּה כְּתִיבָה, דִּכְתִיב ״לִהְיוֹת עוֹשִׂים אֶת שְׁנֵי הַיָּמִים״! אֶלָּא מֵהָכָא: דִּכְתִיב ״וְהַיָּמִים הָאֵלֶּה נִזְכָּרִים וְנַעֲשִׂים״ אִיתְקַשׁ זְכִירָה לַעֲשִׂיָּיה, מָה עֲשִׂיָּיה לְמַפְרֵעַ לָא – אַף זְכִירָה לְמַפְרֵעַ לָא.

The Gemara rejects this derivation: **Is reading written here at all?** It is **"observing"** that **is written** here in this verse, not reading, **as it is written: "That they should unfailingly observe these two days** according to their writing, and according to their appointed times." **Rather,** the proof is **from here, as it is written: "And that these days should be remembered and observed** throughout every generation" (Esther 9:28). **Remembering is juxtaposed to observing,** indicating: **Just as observing cannot be out of order,**[N] as was derived from the words "That they should unfailingly observe these two days according to their writing, and according to their appointed times," **so too, remembering,** by reading the Megilla, **may not be out of order.**

תָּנָא: וְכֵן בְּהַלֵּל, וְכֵן בִּקְרִיאַת שְׁמַע, וּבִתְפִלָּה.

§ The Sages **taught** in a *baraita*: This *halakha* of not reading out of order applies **also to** ***hallel***,[H] **and also to the recitation of** ***Shema***, **and** also **to the** ***Amida*** **prayer,** meaning that to fulfill one's obligation he must recite the text of each of these in order.

NOTES

One who reads the Megilla out of order – הַקּוֹרֵא אֶת הַמְּגִילָּה לְמַפְרֵעַ: Some explain these *halakhot* as being not only derived from the verses cited in the Gemara, but as based on the requirement of reading the Megilla and thereby publicizing the Purim miracle. If one reads the Megilla out of order, the understanding of the events is impaired. Similarly, when one recites the Megilla without reading it from a written text, it appears as the telling of a mere tale, not as reading an incident that is fitting to be publicized with precise wording (*Mikhtam*).

If he read it in Aramaic translation or in any other language – קְרָאָהּ תַּרְגּוּם בְּכׇל לָשׁוֹן: Rashi explains later in the discussion (18a) that the mishna here makes a distinction between Aramaic and other languages, as though to say: The Aramaic translation, which was known, accepted, and used in synagogues, may not be used for reading the Megilla, and all the more so other languages may not be used (see *Turei Even*).

Written in *Ashurit* – כְּתוּבָה אַשּׁוּרִית: Most of the commentaries and halakhic authorities maintain that the term here refers to both the language and the script, i.e., the Megilla must be written in *Ashurit* script and in the Hebrew language. However, some maintain that it is referring specifically to the script and means that even if the Megilla is written in a different language for those who speak that language, it must be transliterated into *Ashurit* script (see *Penei Yehoshua*).

According to their writing and according to their appointed times – כִּכְתָבָם וְכִזְמַנָּם: In the Jerusalem Talmud the words "according to their writing" is adduced as a source for all of the *halakhot* of the mishna, that the Megilla must be read "according to writing" and not out of order, not by heart, and not in a different language.

Just as keeping [*asiyya*] cannot be out of order – מָה עֲשִׂיָּיה לְמַפְרֵעַ לָא: The commentaries disagree in their explanation of this phrase. Some explain that just as it is not possible that the fifteenth of Adar precede the fourteenth, so is it prohibited to change the order of the reading (Rid; Ran). Others, who translate *asiyya* as doing, explain that in general it is impossible, when undertaking a task, to do later that which must, due to the nature of the task, be done first (Rambam's Commentary on the Mishna). The *Turei Even* interprets it to mean that just as people in a walled city celebrate Purim the day after those in an unwalled city, and this order is never reversed, so too, the order of the remembrance of Purim, i.e., the reading of the Megilla, is never reversed.

HALAKHA

Reads the Megilla out of order – קוֹרֵא אֶת הַמְּגִילָּה לְמַפְרֵעַ: One who reads the Megilla out of order, e.g., skips a verse and reads it later, does not fulfill his obligation (*Shulḥan Arukh, Oraḥ Ḥayyim* 690:6).

If he read it by heart – קְרָאָהּ עַל פֶּה: One fulfills his obligation to read the Megilla only if he reads it or hears it being read from the written text but not if he recites it by heart (*Shulḥan Arukh, Oraḥ Ḥayyim* 690:3).

What is a valid Megilla – מַה הִיא מְגִילָּה כְּשֵׁרָה: A Megilla may be written only with ink and on either regular parchment or *gevil* parchment, like a Torah scroll (*Shulḥan Arukh, Oraḥ Ḥayyim* 691:1).

Reading *hallel* out of order – הַלֵּל לְמַפְרֵעַ: One who recites *hallel* out of order does not fulfill his obligation. This pertains to one who changes the order of the verses within the individual paragraphs, not to one who recites an entire paragraph out of its designated place. Some say one should also be stringent if he alters the order of the paragraphs (*Mishna Berura*; *Kaf HaḤayyim*; *Shulḥan Arukh, Oraḥ Ḥayyim* 422:6).

NOTES

From where do we derive that *hallel* may not be recited out of order – הַלֵּל מְנָלַן: The Jerusalem Talmud also offers a proof to this from the verse "From the rising of the sun until its setting"; however, it adds there that the structure of *hallel* itself is written in correspondence to the order of events, as at first it discusses the exodus from Egypt and afterward continues to the present time and to the future redemption.

HALAKHA

Reciting the *Shema* out of order – קְרִיאַת שְׁמַע לְמַפְרֵעַ: One who recites the *Shema* out of order by changing the order of the verses within the individual paragraphs does not fulfill his obligation. However, if he recites an entire paragraph out of order, although one should not do so *ab initio*, he has fulfilled his obligation, because the paragraphs are not written adjacent to one another in the Torah (*Shulḥan Arukh, Oraḥ Ḥayyim* 64:1).

הַלֵּל מְנָלַן? – רַבָּה אָמַר: דִּכְתִיב ״מִמִּזְרַח שֶׁמֶשׁ עַד מְבוֹאוֹ״. רַב יוֹסֵף אָמַר: ״זֶה הַיּוֹם עָשָׂה ה׳״,

The Gemara asks: **From where do we** derive that ***hallel*** may not be recited out of order?[N] **Rabba said: As it is written** in *hallel*: **"From the rising of the sun until its setting** the Lord's name is to be praised" (Psalms 113:3). Just as the sunrise and sunset cannot be reversed, so too, *hallel* may not be recited out of order. **Rav Yosef said:** It is derived from the verse in *hallel* that states: **"This is the day that the Lord has made"** (Psalms 118:24); just as the day follows a certain order, so too, *hallel* must be recited in its proper order.

רַב אָוְיָא אָמַר: ״יְהִי שֵׁם ה׳ מְבוֹרָךְ״, וְרַב נַחְמָן בַּר יִצְחָק, וְאִיתֵּימָא רַב אַחָא בַּר יַעֲקֹב, אָמַר מֵהָכָא: ״מֵעַתָּה וְעַד עוֹלָם״.

Rav Avya said: It is derived from the verse in *hallel*: **"Blessed be the name of the Lord"** (Psalms 113:2), indicating that the blessing of God must "be" just as it is written. **Rav Naḥman bar Yitzḥak said, and some say** that it was **Rav Aḥa bar Ya'akov** who said: It is derived from **here,** the end of the aforementioned verse: **"From now and for evermore"** (Psalms 113:2), i.e., it should be like time, which cannot be reversed.

קְרִיאַת שְׁמַע – דְּתַנְיָא: קְרִיאַת שְׁמַע כִּכְתָבָהּ דִּבְרֵי רַבִּי, וַחֲכָמִים אוֹמְרִים: בְּכָל לָשׁוֹן. מַאי טַעְמָא דְּרַבִּי? אָמַר קְרָא:

From where do we know one has not fulfilled his obligation of **reciting the *Shema*** if he recited it out of order?[H] **As it is taught** in a *baraita*: **The recital of the *Shema* must be as it is written,** i.e., in Hebrew; this is **the statement of Rabbi** Yehuda HaNasi. **But the Rabbis say:** It may be recited **in any language.** The Gemara asks: **What is the reason of Rabbi** Yehuda HaNasi? **The verse states:**

Perek **II**
Daf **17** Amud **b**

NOTES

Hear in any language – שְׁמַע בְּכָל לָשׁוֹן: Some explain that as the word "hear" is in the singular, the implication is that every person in Israel should hear the words in any language that he understands (*Sefat Emet*).

HALAKHA

Hear in any language – שְׁמַע בְּכָל לָשׁוֹן: Although it is preferable to recite the *Shema* in Hebrew (*Baḥ*), the *halakha* is in accordance with the Sages, that it is permitted to read the *Shema* in any language. However, one must take care to avoid making errors in the language he chooses and to read as precisely as in Hebrew. Nowadays, for several reasons, e.g., that we are not confident as to the veracity of the translation into other languages, the *Shema* should be read only in Hebrew (*Arukh HaShulḥan*; *Shulḥan Arukh, Oraḥ Ḥayyim* 62:2).

Making the *Shema* audible – הַשְׁמָעַת קְרִיאַת שְׁמַע: One who reads the *Shema* must hear what his mouth says *ab initio*. However, if he did not recite it audibly he has fulfilled his obligation, as the *halakha* is in accordance with the Sages. Even so, he must enunciate the words, not merely think them (*Shulḥan Arukh, Oraḥ Ḥayyim* 62:3).

״וְהָיוּ״ – בַּהֲוָיָיתָן יְהוּ. וְרַבָּנַן מַאי טַעְמָא? אָמַר קְרָא ״שְׁמַע״ – בְּכָל לָשׁוֹן שֶׁאַתָּה שׁוֹמֵעַ.

"And these words…**shall be"** (Deuteronomy 6:6), teaching that these words, the words of the *Shema*, always **"shall be" as they are,** i.e., in the Hebrew language. The Gemara asks: **And as for the Sages, what is the reason** for their opinion? **The verse states: "Hear,** O Israel" (Deuteronomy 6:4), which could also be translated, "Understand, O Israel," indicating that you may recite these words **in any language**[NH] **that you hear,** i.e., understand.

וְרַבִּי נַמִי, הָא כְּתִיב ״שְׁמַע״! הַהוּא מִיבָּעֵי לֵיהּ: הַשְׁמַע לְאׇזְנֶיךָ מַה שֶּׁאַתָּה מוֹצִיא מִפִּיךָ. וְרַבָּנַן סָבְרִי כְּמַאן דְּאָמַר: הַקּוֹרֵא אֶת שְׁמַע וְלֹא הִשְׁמִיעַ לְאׇזְנוֹ – יָצָא.

The Gemara asks: **And** according to **Rabbi** Yehuda HaNasi **as well, isn't it** indeed **written, "hear"?** What does he learn from this word, if not that the *Shema* may be recited in any language? The Gemara answers: **This** word **is necessary** to teach something else: **Make heard to your ears what your mouth is saying,**[H] i.e., the *Shema* must be recited audibly, not merely thought in one's heart. The Gemara asks: **And** how do **the Sages** know this? The Gemara explains: They **hold like the one who said** that if **one recites the *Shema* but does not make it audible to his ears, he** has nevertheless **fulfilled** his obligation.

וְרַבָּנַן נַמִי, הָכְתִיב ״וְהָיוּ״! הַהוּא מִיבָּעֵי לֵיהּ שֶׁלֹּא יִקְרָא לְמַפְרֵעַ. וְרַבִּי, שֶׁלֹּא יִקְרָא לְמַפְרֵעַ מְנָא לֵיהּ? מִדְּבָרִים ״הַדְּבָרִים״. וְרַבָּנַן ״דְּבָרִים״ ״הַדְּבָרִים״ לָא מַשְׁמַע לְהוּ.

The Gemara asks: **And** according to **the Sages as well, isn't it** indeed **written, "And** these words **shall be"?** What do they learn from this, if not that the *Shema* must be recited in Hebrew? The Gemara answers: **That** word **is necessary** to teach **that one must not recite** the words of the *Shema* **out of order,** but they "shall be" as they are, in the proper order. The Gemara asks: **And from where does Rabbi** Yehuda HaNasi learn **that one must not recite** the *Shema* **out of order?** The Gemara answers: He derives it from the fact that the verse does not say just: **Words,** but **"the words,"** referring to specific words, which teaches that they must be recited in their proper order without any variation. The Gemara asks: **And** what do **the Sages** learn from the phrase "the words"? The difference between **words** and **"the words"** is **inconsequential according to them.**

לֵימָא קָסָבַר רַבִּי כָּל הַתּוֹרָה כּוּלָּהּ בְּכָל לָשׁוֹן נֶאֶמְרָה, דְּאִי סָלְקָא דַּעְתָּךְ בִּלְשׁוֹן הַקּוֹדֶשׁ נֶאֶמְרָה – לָמָּה לִי לְמִכְתַּב ״וְהָיוּ״?

The Gemara analyzes the dispute: **Shall we say that Rabbi** Yehuda HaNasi **maintains** that **the entire Torah may be recited in any language?**[N] **As, if it enters your mind** to say that the entire Torah **may be recited only in the sacred tongue,** Hebrew, and not in any other language, **why do I** need the Torah **to write "and** these words **shall be"** with respect to the *Shema*? Why would I think that the *Shema* is different from the rest of the Torah?

אִצְטְרִיךְ, סָלְקָא דַּעְתָּךְ ״שְׁמַע״ כְּרַבָּנַן – כְּתַב רַחֲמָנָא ״וְהָיוּ״.

The Gemara rejects this argument: There is no proof from here, as even if the Torah must generally be recited in Hebrew **it is** nevertheless **necessary** to specify the matter here, since without such specification **it might have entered your mind** to say that in this context **"hear"** means understand, **as** maintained by **the Sages,** and that the *Shema* may be recited in any language. Therefore **the Merciful One writes** in the Torah, **"and** these words **shall be,"** to teach us that the *Shema* may be recited only in the original Hebrew.

לֵימָא קָסָבְרִי רַבָּנַן כָּל הַתּוֹרָה בִּלְשׁוֹן הַקּוֹדֶשׁ נֶאֶמְרָה, דְּאִי סָלְקָא דַּעְתָּךְ בְּכָל לָשׁוֹן נֶאֶמְרָה – לָמָּה לִי לְמִכְתַּב ״שְׁמַע״?

The Gemara suggests: **Shall we say** then **that the Sages maintain** that **the entire Torah must be recited** specifically **in the sacred tongue,** Hebrew? **As, if it enters your mind** to say that the entire Torah **may be recited in any language, why do I** need the Torah **to write "hear"** with respect to the *Shema*? Why would one think that the *Shema* is different from the rest of the Torah?

אִיצְטְרִיךְ, סָלְקָא דַּעְתָּךְ אָמִינָא ״וְהָיוּ״ כְּרַבִּי – כְּתַב רַחֲמָנָא ״שְׁמַע״.

The Gemara rejects this argument: Even if the Torah may generally be recited in any language, **it was** nevertheless **necessary** to specify the matter here. Without such specification **it could enter your mind to say** that the words **"and** these words **shall be"** teach that the *Shema* may be recited only in Hebrew, **as** asserted by **Rabbi** Yehuda HaNasi. Therefore **the Merciful One writes** the word **"hear"** in the Torah, to teach us that the *Shema* may be recited in any language.

תְּפִלָּה מְנָא לַן? דְּתַנְיָא: שִׁמְעוֹן הַפָּקוּלִי הִסְדִּיר שְׁמוֹנֶה עֶשְׂרֵה בְּרָכוֹת לִפְנֵי רַבָּן גַּמְלִיאֵל עַל הַסֵּדֶר בְּיַבְנֶה. אָמַר רַבִּי יוֹחָנָן, וְאָמְרִי לַהּ בְּמַתְנִיתָא תָּנָא: מֵאָה וְעֶשְׂרִים זְקֵנִים וּבָהֶם כַּמָּה נְבִיאִים תִּיקְנוּ שְׁמוֹנֶה עֶשְׂרֵה בְּרָכוֹת עַל הַסֵּדֶר.

§ The *baraita* cited previously taught that the *halakha* against reciting a text out of order applies to the *Amida* **prayer** as well. The Gemara asks: **From where do we** derive this? **As it is taught** in a *baraita*: **Shimon HaPakuli**[L] **arranged the eighteen blessings** of the *Amida* prayer **before Rabban Gamliel in their** fixed **order in Yavne,**[B] which indicates that there is a specific order to these blessings that must not be changed. **Rabbi Yoḥanan said, and some say that it was taught in a *baraita*: A hundred and twenty Elders,**[N] i.e., the Men of the Great Assembly, and **among them several prophets, established** the **eighteen blessings** of the *Amida* **in their** fixed **order,**[N] which also shows that the order of these blessings may not be changed.

תָּנוּ רַבָּנַן: מִנַּיִן שֶׁאוֹמְרִים אָבוֹת – שֶׁנֶּאֱמַר ״הָבוּ לַה׳ בְּנֵי אֵלִים״, וּמִנַּיִן שֶׁאוֹמְרִים גְּבוּרוֹת – שֶׁנֶּאֱמַר ״הָבוּ לַה׳ כָּבוֹד וָעוֹז״, וּמִנַּיִן שֶׁאוֹמְרִים קְדוּשּׁוֹת – שֶׁנֶּאֱמַר ״הָבוּ לַה׳ כְּבוֹד שְׁמוֹ הִשְׁתַּחֲווּ לַה׳ בְּהַדְרַת קֹדֶשׁ״.

The Gemara proceeds to explain this order: **The Sages taught** in a *baraita*: **From where** is it derived **that one says** the blessing **of the Patriarchs,** the first blessing of the *Amida*? **As it is stated: "Ascribe to the Lord, mighty ones"** (Psalms 29:1), which means that one should mention before the Lord the mighty ones of the world, i.e., the Patriarchs. **And from where** is it derived **that one** then **says** the blessing of **mighty deeds? As it is stated** in the continuation of that verse: **"Ascribe to the Lord glory and strength"** (Psalms 29:1). **And from where** is it derived **that one** then **says** the blessing **of holiness? As it is stated** in the next verse: **"Give to the Lord the glory due to His name; worship the Lord in the beauty of holiness"** (Psalms 29:2).

וּמָה רָאוּ לוֹמַר בִּינָה אַחַר קְדוּשָּׁה – שֶׁנֶּאֱמַר ״וְהִקְדִּישׁוּ אֶת קְדוֹשׁ יַעֲקֹב וְאֶת אֱלֹהֵי יִשְׂרָאֵל יַעֲרִיצוּ״ וּסְמִיךְ לֵיהּ ״וְיָדְעוּ תוֹעֵי רוּחַ בִּינָה״. וּמָה רָאוּ לוֹמַר תְּשׁוּבָה אַחַר בִּינָה – דִּכְתִיב ״וּלְבָבוֹ יָבִין וָשָׁב וְרָפָא לוֹ״.

The Gemara continues: **And why did they see** fit to institute **to say** the blessing of **understanding after** the blessing of **holiness? As it is stated: "They shall sanctify the Holy One of Jacob, and shall revere the God of Israel"** (Isaiah 29:23), and adjacent to that verse it is written: **"They also that erred in spirit shall come to understanding"** (Isaiah 29:24). This shows that it is proper for the theme of understanding to follow the theme of God's holiness. **And why did they see** fit to institute **to say** the blessing of **repentance after** the blessing of **understanding? As it is written: "And they will understand with their heart, repent, and be healed"** (Isaiah 6:10), showing that the theme of repentance properly follows the theme of understanding.

NOTES

The entire Torah may be recited in any language – כָּל הַתּוֹרָה כּוּלָּהּ בְּכָל לָשׁוֹן נֶאֶמְרָה: According to Rashi, as understood by *Tosafot*, this is referring to the public reading of the Torah. *Tosafot* point out, however, that reading the Torah is not mandated by Torah law, except for the remembrance of Amalek, *Parashat Zakhor* (Deuteronomy 25:17–19; see 18a). They therefore explain that the Gemara is referring to various biblical passages that are mandated by Torah law to be recited on certain occasions, such as the passage concerning the *sota*. The Rashba also cites this answer, and adds that it is possible to explain that the Gemara is indeed referring to *Parashat Zakhor*.

In tractate *Sota* (33a), *Tosafot* cite a different explanation in the name of Rabbeinu Ḥananel: The Gemara is referring to the question of whether it is permitted to write a Torah scroll in other languages, an issue that is debated by the *tanna'im* in the first chapter of the tractate. Some explain that the Gemara is in fact referring to reading the Torah and that it is following the opinion that public Torah readings were already instituted by Moses. Moreover, some maintain that there is a mitzva by Torah law to read relevant passages on Shabbat and festivals (see Ritva). Still others explain that the discussion here concerns the prohibition against reciting Torah verses without reading them from a text and addresses the question of whether this applies only to Hebrew or to other languages as well (*Re'ah Duda'im; Sefat Emet*).

A hundred and twenty Elders – מֵאָה וְעֶשְׂרִים זְקֵנִים: This refers to the Men of the Great Assembly, who lived in the early days of the Second Temple, and according to tradition numbered one hundred and twenty. There were several prophets counted in their number, such as Haggai, Zechariah, and Malachi. The question is raised in the Gemara later (18a) that if the *Amida* blessings were already established in ancient times, why was it necessary for Shimon HaPakuli to arrange them again in his day? The answer given there is that the formulation of the blessings of the *Amida* had been forgotten and he arranged them once again. The *ge'onim* write that during the First Temple period only the first three blessings were recited, and this practice was continued in the Temple itself in Second Temple times. The Men of the Great Assembly expanded this into eighteen blessings, and it was further expanded at a later time into nineteen.

In their fixed order – עַל הַסֵּדֶר: There is a midrash that explains that the order of the eighteen blessings was instituted to correspond to incidents that occurred during eighteen progressive generations in the history of the Jewish people. For example, the blessing of the Patriarchs corresponds to events that occurred to Abraham, and so on until the time of the messianic redemption (cited in *Tanya Rabbati*).

LANGUAGE

HaPakuli – הַפָּקוּלִי: From the Greek φάκελος, *fakelos*, meaning bundle or envelope. It appears that this Sage was named after his occupation, and that he was a merchant in balls of linen thread or towels.

BACKGROUND

Yavne – יַבְנֶה: An ancient city, Yavne is identified as the biblical city of Yavne'el in the region of the tribal lands of Judah. It is just over a kilometer from the coast and almost due west of Jerusalem. After the destruction of the Temple, Yavne became an important Torah center and the seat of the Sanhedrin. It appears that Yavne had been a center of Torah study even before the Temple was destroyed, but it attained prominence only after the destruction of the Temple, when Rabban Yoḥanan ben Zakkai reestablished the Sanhedrin there. Until the bar Kokheva revolt, Yavne was the spiritual center of the entire Jewish population in Eretz Yisrael. The Yavne Yeshiva, initially headed by Rabban Yoḥanan ben Zakkai and later by Rabban Gamliel II of Yavne, attracted many of the greatest Torah scholars of that era, and many ordinances were instituted there to maintain Jewish religious and spiritual life after the destruction of the Temple.

אִי הָכִי לֵימָא רְפוּאָה בַּתְרָהּ דִּתְשׁוּבָה! לָא סָלְקָא דַּעְתָּךְ, דִּכְתִיב "וְיָשֹׁב אֶל ה׳ וִירַחֲמֵהוּ וְאֶל אֱלֹהֵינוּ כִּי יַרְבֶּה לִסְלוֹחַ".

The Gemara asks: **If so,** that the sequence of blessings is based on this verse, **let us say** that **the** blessing of **healing should be said after** the blessing of **repentance.** Why, then, is the next blessing in the *Amida* the blessing of forgiveness and not the blessing of healing? The Gemara explains: **This cannot enter your mind, as it is written: "And let him return to the Lord, and He will have compassion upon him; and to our God, for He will abundantly pardon"** (Isaiah 55:7), which shows that the theme of repentance should be followed by that of forgiveness.

וּמַאי חָזֵית דְּסָמְכַתְּ אַהָא, סְמוֹךְ אַהָא! כָּתַב קְרָא אַחֲרִינָא: "הַסֹּלֵחַ לְכָל עֲוֹנֵיְכִי הָרֹפֵא לְכָל תַּחֲלוּאָיְכִי הַגּוֹאֵל מִשַּׁחַת חַיָּיְכִי". לְמֵימְרָא דִּגְאוּלָּה וּרְפוּאָה בָּתַר סְלִיחָה הִיא? וְהָכְתִיב "וָשָׁב וְרָפָא לוֹ"! הַהוּא – לָאו רְפוּאָה דְּתַחֲלוּאִים הִיא, אֶלָּא רְפוּאָה דִּסְלִיחָה הִיא.

The Gemara poses a question: **But what did you see to rely on this** verse? **Rely on the other** verse, which juxtaposes repentance to healing. The Gemara answers: **Another verse,** in which it is **written: "Who forgives all your iniquities, Who heals all your diseases, Who redeems your life from the pit"** (Psalms 103:3–4), proves that the theme of healing should follow that of forgiveness. The Gemara asks: **Is that** verse coming **to say that** the blessings of **redemption and healing** should be placed following the blessing of **forgiveness? But isn't it written: "Repent, and be healed"** (Isaiah 6:10), which suggests that repentance should be followed by healing? The Gemara answers: **That** verse is referring **not** to **the** literal **healing from illness, but rather** to **the** figurative **healing of forgiveness,** and therefore this verse too supports the sequence of forgiveness following repentance.

וּמָה רָאוּ לוֹמַר גְּאוּלָּה בַּשְּׁבִיעִית? אָמַר רָבָא: מִתּוֹךְ שֶׁעֲתִידִין לִיגָּאֵל בַּשְּׁבִיעִית, לְפִיכָךְ קְבָעוּהָ בַּשְּׁבִיעִית. וְהָאָמַר מַר: בַּשִּׁשִּׁית – קוֹלוֹת, בַּשְּׁבִיעִית – מִלְחָמוֹת, בְּמוֹצָאֵי שְׁבִיעִית בֶּן דָּוִד בָּא. מִלְחָמָה נַמִּי אַתְחַלְתָּא דִּגְאוּלָּה הִיא.

The Gemara continues: **And why did they see** fit to institute **to say** the blessing of **redemption as the seventh** blessing? **Rava said: Since** there is a tradition that the Jewish people are **destined to be redeemed in the seventh** year[N] of the Sabbatical cycle, **consequently, they fixed** redemption **as the seventh** blessing. **But didn't the Master say** in a *baraita*: **In the sixth** year of the Sabbatical cycle in the days of the arrival of the Messiah, heavenly **sounds** will be heard; **in the seventh** year there will be **wars; and upon the conclusion of the seventh** year, in the eighth year, **the son of David,** the Messiah, **will come?** The redemption will take place not during the seventh year but after it. The Gemara answers: Nevertheless, the **war** that takes place during the seventh year **is also the beginning of the redemption** process, and it is therefore correct to say that Israel will be redeemed in the seventh year.

וּמָה רָאוּ לוֹמַר רְפוּאָה בַּשְּׁמִינִית? אָמַר רַבִּי אַחָא: מִתּוֹךְ שֶׁנִּתְּנָה מִילָה בַּשְּׁמִינִית, שֶׁצְּרִיכָה רְפוּאָה, לְפִיכָךְ קְבָעוּהָ בַּשְּׁמִינִית.

The Gemara continues: **And why did they see** fit to institute that one **says** the blessing of **healing as the eighth** blessing?[N] **Rabbi Aḥa said: Since circumcision was assigned to the eighth** day of life, and circumcision **requires healing, consequently, they established** healing **as the eighth** blessing.

וּמָה רָאוּ לוֹמַר בִּרְכַּת הַשָּׁנִים בַּתְּשִׁיעִית – אָמַר רַבִּי אֲלֶכְּסַנְדְּרִי: כְּנֶגֶד מַפְקִיעֵי שְׁעָרִים, דִּכְתִיב: "שְׁבוֹר זְרוֹעַ רָשָׁע", וְדָוִד כִּי אֲמָרָהּ – בַּתְּשִׁיעִית אֲמָרָהּ.

And why did they see fit to institute that one **says the blessing of** bountiful **years as the ninth** blessing? **Rabbi Alexandri said:** This blessing was instituted **in reference to those who raise the prices** of food. We pray for rain so that the price of produce will not rise as a result of shortages, **as it is written: "Break the arm of the wicked"** (Psalms 10:15), referring to the wicked, who practice deception and extort the poor. **And when David expressed this** request, **he expressed it in the ninth** psalm. Although today it is considered the tenth psalm, the first and second psalms are actually counted as one, and therefore this is the ninth psalm. Therefore, the blessing of the years was fixed as the ninth blessing.

NOTES

To be redeemed in the seventh year – לִיגָּאֵל בַּשְּׁבִיעִית: Rashi explains that this prayer of redemption is not referring to the Jewish people's complete redemption in the future, but is a request for redemption from all misfortunes that afflict them in any generation. It indeed appears that the blessing of redemption is a general request for salvation from misfortune, both individual and collective, which explains its place in the *Amida* as a general prayer, before the series of blessings relating to the future messianic redemption (*Zikkaron BaSefer*).

And why did they see fit to institute that one says healing as the eighth blessing – וּמָה רָאוּ לוֹמַר רְפוּאָה בַּשְּׁמִינִית: The Ritva writes that although it has been demonstrated that there is no earlier possible place for the blessing of healing, as there are other blessings that must precede it, the Gemara's question is: Why was it not fixed further on, after the blessing of years?

וּמָה רָאוּ לוֹמַר קִיבּוּץ גָּלֻיּוֹת לְאַחַר בִּרְכַּת הַשָּׁנִים – דִּכְתִיב "וְאַתֶּם הָרֵי יִשְׂרָאֵל עַנְפְּכֶם תִּתֵּנוּ וּפֶרְיְכֶם תִּשְׂאוּ לְעַמִּי יִשְׂרָאֵל כִּי קֵרְבוּ לָבוֹא". וְכֵיוָן שֶׁנִּתְקַבְּצוּ גָּלֻיּוֹת – נַעֲשֶׂה דִּין בָּרְשָׁעִים, שֶׁנֶּאֱמַר: "וְאָשִׁיבָה יָדִי עָלַיִךְ וְאֶצְרוֹף כַּבּוֹר סִיגָיִךְ" וּכְתִיב "וְאָשִׁיבָה שׁוֹפְטַיִךְ כְּבָרִאשׁוֹנָה".

The Gemara asks: **And why did they see** fit to institute that one says the blessing of **the ingathering of** the **exiles after the blessing of the years? As it is written: "And you, O mountains of Israel, you shall shoot forth your branches, and yield your fruit to My people Israel; for they will soon be coming"** (Ezekiel 36:8), which indicates that the ingathering of the exiles will follow after Eretz Yisrael is blessed with bountiful produce. **And once the exiles have been gathered, judgment will be meted out to the wicked, as it is stated: "And I will turn my hand against you and purge away your dross as with lye"** (Isaiah 1:25),[N] **and** immediately after **it is written: "And I will restore your judges as at first"** (Isaiah 1:26). For this reason the blessing of the restoration of judges comes after the blessing of the ingathering of the exiles.

NOTES

And I will…purge away your dross as with lye – וְאֶצְרוֹף כַּבּוֹר סִיגָיִךְ: Some write that the Gemara also alludes to the continuation of the verse: "And I will take away all your impurities [*bedilayikh*]," as *bedilayikh* can also mean: Those who separate themselves from you, i.e., sectarians, and the suppression of separatist sects is the central theme of the following blessing.

וְכֵיוָן שֶׁנַּעֲשָׂה דִּין מִן הָרְשָׁעִים – כָּלוּ הַפּוֹשְׁעִים, וְכוֹלֵל זֵדִים עִמָּהֶם, שֶׁנֶּאֱמַר: "וְשֶׁבֶר פּוֹשְׁעִים וְחַטָּאִים יַחְדָּיו (יִכְלוּ)".

And once judgment is meted out to the wicked, the transgressors, i.e., the heretics and sectarians, **will cease to be.** Consequently, the next blessing is that of the heretics, **and one includes evildoers with them, as it is stated: "And the destruction of the transgressors and of the sinners shall be together,** and they that forsake the Lord **shall cease to be"** (Isaiah 1:28). The "transgressors and sinners" are the evildoers, and "they that forsake the Lord" are the heretics.

וְכֵיוָן שֶׁכָּלוּ הַפּוֹשְׁעִים – מִתְרוֹמֶמֶת קֶרֶן צַדִּיקִים, דִּכְתִיב "וְכָל קַרְנֵי רְשָׁעִים אֲגַדֵּעַ תְּרוֹמַמְנָה קַרְנוֹת צַדִּיק", וְכוֹלֵל גֵּירֵי הַצֶּדֶק עִם הַצַּדִּיקִים, שֶׁנֶּאֱמַר "מִפְּנֵי שֵׂיבָה תָּקוּם וְהָדַרְתָּ פְּנֵי זָקֵן" וּסְמִיךְ לֵיהּ "וְכִי יָגוּר אִתְּכֶם גֵּר".

And once the heretics cease to be, the horn, i.e., the glory, **of the righteous will be exalted, as it is written: "All the horns of the wicked will I cut off; but the horns of the righteous shall be exalted"** (Psalms 75:11). Therefore, after the blessing of the heretics, one says the blessing about the righteous. **And he includes the righteous converts along with the righteous, as it is stated: "You shall rise up before the hoary head, and honor the face of the elder"** (Leviticus 19:32), **and adjacent to this** it is stated: **"And if a stranger sojourns with you"** (Leviticus 19:33). An "elder" is one with Torah wisdom and a "stranger" is one who has converted to Judaism.

וְהֵיכָן מִתְרוֹמֶמֶת קַרְנָם – בִּירוּשָׁלַיִם, שֶׁנֶּאֱמַר "שַׁאֲלוּ שְׁלוֹם יְרוּשָׁלָם יִשְׁלָיוּ אוֹהֲבָיִךְ".

And where will the horns of the righteous **be exalted? In Jerusalem, as it is stated: "Pray for the peace of Jerusalem; they who love you shall prosper"** (Psalms 122:6). "They who love you" are the righteous. Therefore, the blessing of the rebuilding of Jerusalem is placed after the blessing of the righteous.

וְכֵיוָן שֶׁנִּבְנֵית יְרוּשָׁלַיִם בָּא דָּוִד, שֶׁנֶּאֱמַר:

And once Jerusalem is rebuilt, the Messiah, scion of the house of **David, will come, as it is stated:**

Perek **II**
Daf **18** Amud **a**

"אַחַר יָשׁוּבוּ בְּנֵי יִשְׂרָאֵל וּבִקְשׁוּ אֶת ה׳ אֱלֹהֵיהֶם וְאֵת דָּוִד מַלְכָּם". וְכֵיוָן שֶׁבָּא דָּוִד – בָּאתָה תְּפִלָּה, שֶׁנֶּאֱמַר "וַהֲבִיאוֹתִים אֶל הַר קָדְשִׁי וְשִׂמַּחְתִּים בְּבֵית תְּפִלָּתִי".

"Afterward the children of Israel shall return, and seek the Lord their God and David their king" (Hosea 3:5), and consequently, the blessing of the kingdom of David follows the blessing of the building of Jerusalem. **And once** the scion of **David comes,** the time for **prayer will come,**[N] **as it is stated: "I will bring them to My sacred mountain and make them joyful in My house of prayer"** (Isaiah 56:7). Therefore, the blessing of hearing prayer is recited after the blessing of the kingdom of David.

וְכֵיוָן שֶׁבָּאת תְּפִלָּה – בָּאת עֲבוֹדָה שֶׁנֶּאֱמַר "עוֹלוֹתֵיהֶם וְזִבְחֵיהֶם לְרָצוֹן עַל מִזְבְּחִי". וְכֵיוָן שֶׁבָּאת עֲבוֹדָה – בָּאתָה תּוֹדָה, שֶׁנֶּאֱמַר "זוֹבֵחַ תּוֹדָה יְכַבְּדָנְנִי".

And after prayer comes, the Temple **service will arrive, as it is stated** in the continuation of that verse: **"Their burnt-offerings and their sacrifices shall be accepted on My altar"** (Isaiah 56:7). The blessing of restoration of the Temple service follows the blessing of hearing prayer. **And when the** Temple **service comes,** with it will also **come thanksgiving,**[N] **as it is stated: "Whoever sacrifices a thanks-offering honors Me"** (Psalms 50:23), which teaches that thanksgiving follows sacrifice. Therefore, the blessing of thanksgiving follows the blessing of restoration of the Temple service.

NOTES

And once the scion of David comes, prayer will come – וְכֵיוָן שֶׁבָּא דָּוִד בָּאתָה תְּפִלָּה: According to the Meiri, this means that the coming of the Messiah is the realization of our most essential prayers.

When the Temple service comes, with it will also come thanksgiving [*toda*] – בָּאת עֲבוֹדָה בָּאתָה תּוֹדָה: Some explain that here thanksgiving refers to the thanks-offering described in Leviticus 7:12, in that it is among the various kinds of sacrifices and services in the Temple (see Meiri). Others explain that here *toda* means confession, not thanksgiving, and the Gemara is saying that the Temple service and confession go hand in hand, as when one brings an offering he also confesses his sins (Maharsha).

NOTES

Why did they see fit that one says grant peace after the Priestly Benediction – וּמָה רָאוּ לוֹמַר שִׂים שָׁלוֹם אַחַר בִּרְכַּת כֹּהֲנִים: Some explain that the Gemara asks why it would not have been more logical to conclude the *Amida* with the Priestly Benediction and to entirely omit the blessing of: Grant peace. The Gemara answers that since the passage in the Torah of the Priestly Benediction concludes with God's blessing, which is peace, the Sages likewise instituted a blessing for peace after the Priestly Benediction (see Ritva).

Only for one who can declare all His praise – לְמִי שֶׁיָּכוֹל לְהַשְׁמִיעַ כָּל תְּהִלָּתוֹ: Rashi explains this to mean that anyone who cannot declare all of God's praises, i.e., any human being, should not even attempt to do so. This concept is explicitly mentioned in tractate *Berakhot* (33b) as well. However, some explain that here the Gemara means something else: One who praises God beyond the set formula runs the risk of erroneously saying something that is not truly praise. Therefore, only one who is a great scholar and who can be certain that he will say only appropriate praises may add to the formula established by the Sages (see Jerusalem Talmud; *Turei Even*).

וּמָה רָאוּ לוֹמַר בִּרְכַּת כֹּהֲנִים אַחַר הוֹדָאָה – דִּכְתִיב ״וַיִּשָּׂא אַהֲרֹן אֶת יָדָיו אֶל הָעָם וַיְבָרְכֵם וַיֵּרֶד מֵעֲשׂוֹת הַחַטָּאת וְהָעוֹלָה וְהַשְּׁלָמִים״.

And why did they see fit to institute that one **says the Priestly Benediction after** the blessing of **thanksgiving? As it is written: "And Aaron lifted up his hand toward the people and blessed them, and he came down from sacrificing the sin-offering, and the burnt-offering, and the peace-offerings"** (Leviticus 9:22), teaching that the Priestly Benediction follows the sacrificial service, which includes the thanks-offering.

אֵימָא קוֹדֶם עֲבוֹדָה! לָא סָלְקָא דַּעְתָּךְ, דִּכְתִיב ״וַיֵּרֶד מֵעֲשׂוֹת הַחַטָּאת״ וְגוֹ׳. מִי כְּתִיב ״לַעֲשׂוֹת״ ״מֵעֲשׂוֹת״ כְּתִיב.

The Gemara asks: But the cited verse indicates that Aaron blessed the people and then sacrificed the offerings. Should we not then **say** the Priestly Benediction **before the** blessing of the Temple **service?** The Gemara answers: **It should not enter your mind** to say this, **as it is written: "And he came down from sacrificing the sin-offering." Is it written** that he came down **to sacrifice** the offerings, implying that after blessing the people Aaron came down and sacrificed the offerings? No, **it is written, "from sacrificing,"** indicating that the offerings had already been sacrificed.

וְלֵימְרָהּ אַחַר הָעֲבוֹדָה! לָא סָלְקָא דַּעְתָּךְ, דִּכְתִיב ״זוֹבֵחַ תּוֹדָה״.

The Gemara asks: If, as derived from this verse, the Priestly Benediction follows the sacrificial service, the Priestly Benediction should be **said** immediately **after** the blessing of restoration of **the** Temple **service,** without the interruption of the blessing of thanksgiving. The Gemara rejects this argument: **It should not enter your mind** to say this, **as it is written: "Whoever sacrifices a thanks-offering** honors Me," from which we learn that thanksgiving follows sacrifice, as already explained.

מַאי חָזֵית דְּסָמְכַתְּ אַהַאי, סְמוֹךְ אַהַאי! מִסְתַּבְּרָא, עֲבוֹדָה וְהוֹדָאָה חֲדָא מִילְּתָא הִיא.

The Gemara asks: **What did you see to rely on this** verse and juxtapose thanksgiving with sacrifice? **Rely** rather **on the other** verse, which indicates that it is the Priestly Benediction that should be juxtaposed with the sacrificial service. The Gemara answers: **It stands to reason** to have the blessing of thanksgiving immediately following the blessing of the sacrificial service, since the sacrificial **service and thanksgiving,** which are closely related conceptually, **are one matter.**

וּמָה רָאוּ לוֹמַר ״שִׂים שָׁלוֹם״ אַחַר בִּרְכַּת כֹּהֲנִים – דִּכְתִיב ״וְשָׂמוּ אֶת שְׁמִי עַל בְּנֵי יִשְׂרָאֵל וַאֲנִי אֲבָרְכֵם״. בְּרָכָה דְּהַקָּדוֹשׁ בָּרוּךְ הוּא – שָׁלוֹם, שֶׁנֶּאֱמַר ״ה׳ יְבָרֵךְ אֶת עַמּוֹ בַשָּׁלוֹם״.

And why did they see fit to institute that one **says** the blessing beginning with the words: **Grant peace, after the Priestly Benediction?**[N] **As it is written** immediately following the Priestly Benediction: **"And they shall put My name upon the children of Israel, and I will bless them"** (Numbers 6:27). The Priestly Benediction is followed by God's blessing, and **the blessing of the Holy One, Blessed be He, is peace, as it is stated: "The Lord blesses His people with peace"** (Psalms 29:11).

וְכִי מֵאַחַר דְּמֵאָה וְעֶשְׂרִים זְקֵנִים, וּמֵהֶם כַּמָּה נְבִיאִים, תִּקְּנוּ תְּפִלָּה עַל הַסֵּדֶר, שִׁמְעוֹן הַפַּקּוֹלִי מַאי הִסְדִּיר? שְׁכָחוּם וְחָזַר וְסִדְּרוּם.

The Gemara returns to the *baraita* cited at the beginning of the discussion: **Now, since** the *baraita* teaches that **a hundred and twenty Elders, including many prophets, established the** *Amida* **prayer in its** fixed **order, what** is it that **Shimon HaPakuli arranged** in a much later period of time, as related by Rabbi Yoḥanan? The Gemara answers: Indeed, the blessings of the *Amida* prayer were originally arranged by the hundred and twenty members of the Great Assembly, but over the course of time the people **forgot them, and** Shimon HaPakuli then **arranged them again.**

מִכָּאן וְאֵילָךְ אָסוּר לְסַפֵּר בְּשִׁבְחוֹ שֶׁל הַקָּדוֹשׁ בָּרוּךְ הוּא, דְּאָמַר רַבִּי אֶלְעָזָר: מַאי דִּכְתִיב ״מִי יְמַלֵּל גְּבוּרוֹת ה׳ יַשְׁמִיעַ כָּל תְּהִלָּתוֹ״, לְמִי נָאֶה לְמַלֵּל גְּבוּרוֹת ה׳ – לְמִי שֶׁיָּכוֹל לְהַשְׁמִיעַ כָּל תְּהִלָּתוֹ.

The Gemara comments: These nineteen blessings are a fixed number, and **beyond this it is prohibited** for one **to declare the praises of the Holy One, Blessed be He,** by adding additional blessings to the *Amida*. As **Rabbi Elazar said: What is** the meaning of that **which is written: "Who can utter the mighty acts of the Lord? Who can declare all His praise?"** (Psalms 106:2)? It means: **For whom is it fitting to utter the mighty acts of the Lord?** Only **for one who can declare all His praise.**[N] And since no one is capable of declaring all of God's praises, we must suffice with the set formula established by the Sages.

אָמַר רַבָּה בַּר בַּר חָנָה אָמַר רַבִּי יוֹחָנָן: הַמְסַפֵּר בְּשִׁבְחוֹ שֶׁל הַקָּדוֹשׁ בָּרוּךְ הוּא יוֹתֵר מִדַּאי – נֶעֱקָר מִן הָעוֹלָם, שֶׁנֶּאֱמַר: ״הַיְסוּפַּר לוֹ כִּי אֲדַבֵּר אִם אָמַר אִישׁ כִּי יְבֻלָּע״.

Rabba bar bar Ḥana said that **Rabbi Yoḥanan said:** With regard to **one who excessively declares the praises of the Holy One, Blessed be He,** his fate **is** to be **uprooted from the world,** as it appears as if he had exhausted all of God's praises. **As it is stated: "Shall it be told to Him when I speak? If a man says** it, **he would be swallowed up"** (Job 37:20). The Gemara interprets the verse as saying: Can all of God's praises be expressed when I speak? If a man would say such a thing, he would be "swallowed up" as punishment.

דְּרַשׁ רַבִּי יְהוּדָה אִישׁ כְּפַר גִּבּוֹרַיָּא, וְאָמְרִי לָהּ אִישׁ כְּפַר גִּבּוֹר חַיִל: מַאי דִּכְתִיב ״לְךָ דוּמִיָּה תְהִלָּה״ – סַמָּא דְכוּלָּה מַשְׁתּוּקָא. כִּי אֲתָא רַב דִּימִי אֲמַר: אָמְרִי בְּמַעַרְבָא: מִלָּה – בְּסֶלַע, מַשְׁתּוּקָא – בִּתְרֵין.

The Gemara relates: **Rabbi Yehuda, a man of Kefar Gibboraya,**[B] **and some say** he was **a man of Kefar Gibboraya, taught: What is** the meaning of that **which is written: "For You silence is praise"** (Psalms 65:2)? **The** best **remedy of all is silence,** i.e., the optimum form of praising God is silence. The Gemara relates: **When Rav Dimi came**[B] from Eretz Israel to Babylonia, **he said: In the West,** Eretz Yisrael, **they say** an adage: If **a word is** worth one ***sela*****, silence is** worth **two.**[N]

״קְרָאָהּ עַל פֶּה לֹא יָצָא״ וכו׳: מְנָלַן? אֲמַר רָבָא: אָתְיָא זְכִירָה זְכִירָה, כְּתִיב הָכָא ״וְהַיָּמִים הָאֵלֶּה נִזְכָּרִים״ וּכְתִיב הָתָם ״כְּתֹב זֹאת זִכָּרוֹן בַּסֵּפֶר״, מַה לְהַלָּן בַּסֵּפֶר – אַף כָּאן בַּסֵּפֶר.

§ It is taught in the mishna: **If one read** the Megilla **by heart he has not fulfilled** his obligation. The Gemara asks: **From where do we** derive this? **Rava said:** This is **derived** by means of a verbal analogy between one instance of the term **remembrance** and another instance of the term **remembrance. It is written here,** with regard to the Megilla: **"That these days should be remembered"** (Esther 9:28), **and it is written elsewhere: "And the Lord said to Moses: Write this for a memorial in the book,** and rehearse it in the ears of Joshua: That I will utterly blot out the remembrance of Amalek from under the heavens" (Exodus 17:14). **Just as there,** with regard to Amalek, remembrance is referring specifically to something written **in a book,** as it is stated, "in the book," **so too here,** the Megilla remembrance is through being written **in a book.**

וּמִמַּאי דְּהַאי זְכִירָה קְרִיאָה הִיא? דִּלְמָא עִיּוּן בְּעָלְמָא! – לָא סָלְקָא דַּעְתָּךְ, (דִּכְתִיב) ״זָכוֹר״ יָכוֹל בַּלֵּב? כְּשֶׁהוּא אוֹמֵר ״לֹא תִשְׁכָּח״ הֲרֵי שִׁכְחַת הַלֵּב אָמוּר, הָא מָה אֲנִי מְקַיֵּים ״זָכוֹר״ – בַּפֶּה.

The Gemara raises a question: **But from where** do we know **that this remembrance** that is stated with regard to Amalek and to the Megilla involves **reading** it out loud from a book? **Perhaps** it requires **merely looking into** the book, reading it silently. The Gemara answers: **It should not enter your mind** to say this, as it was taught in a *baraita*: The verse states: **"Remember** what Amalek did to you" (Deuteronomy 25:17). One **might** have thought that it suffices for one to remember this silently, **in his heart.** But this cannot be, since **when it says** subsequently: **"You shall not forget"** (Deuteronomy 25:19), **it is** already **referring to forgetting from the heart. How,** then, **do I uphold** the meaning of **"remember"?** What does this command to remember add to the command to not forget? Therefore, it means that the remembrance must be expressed out loud, **with the mouth.**

״קְרָאָהּ תַּרְגּוּם לֹא יָצָא״ וכו׳: הֵיכִי דָּמֵי? אִילֵּימָא דִּכְתִיבָה מִקְרָא וְקָרֵי לָהּ תַּרְגּוּם – הַיְינוּ עַל פֶּה! לָא צְרִיכָא, דִּכְתִיבָה תַּרְגּוּם וְקָרֵי לָהּ תַּרְגּוּם.

§ It was taught further in the mishna: **If one read** the Megilla **in** Aramaic **translation he has not fulfilled** his obligation. The Gemara asks: **What are the circumstances** of this case? **If we say that** the Megilla **was written in** the original **biblical text,** i.e., in Hebrew, **and he read it in** Aramaic **translation,** then **this is** the same as reading it **by heart,** as he is not reading the words written in the text, and the mishna has already stated that one does not fulfill his obligation by reading the Megilla by heart. The Gemara answers: **No,** it is **necessary** to teach this case as well, as it is referring to a case in which the Megilla **was written** not in the original Hebrew but **in** Aramaic **translation, and he read it** as written, **in** Aramaic **translation.**

״אֲבָל קוֹרִין אוֹתָהּ לַלּוֹעֲזוֹת בְּלַעַז״ וכו׳: וְהָא אָמַרְתְּ קְרָאָהּ בְּכָל לָשׁוֹן לֹא יָצָא! רַב וּשְׁמוּאֵל דְּאָמְרִי תַּרְוַיְיהוּ: בְּלַעַז יְוָנִי.

§ The mishna continues: **However, for those who speak a foreign language, one may read** the Megilla **in** that **foreign language.** The Gemara raises a difficulty: **But didn't you say** in the mishna: **If he read it in any** other **language he has not fulfilled** his obligation? The Gemara cites the answer of **Rav and Shmuel, who both say:** When the mishna says: A foreign language, it is referring specifically to **the Greek foreign language,** which has a unique status with regard to biblical translation.

BACKGROUND

Kefar Gibboraya – כְּפַר גִּבּוֹרַיָּא: Some claim that the reading should be Kefar Navorayya, or Navor Ḥayil, the name of a place north of Safed, in which the ruins of an ancient synagogue have been found.

When Rav Dimi came – כִּי אֲתָא רַב דִּימִי: Rav Dimi was one of the Sages who would often travel from Eretz Yisrael to Babylonia, primarily to transmit the Torah of Eretz Yisrael to the Torah centers of the Diaspora, although occasionally he traveled on business as well. Consequently, many questions, particularly those concerning the Torah of Eretz Yisrael, remained unresolved, until the messenger would arrive and elucidate the *halakha*, the novel expression, or the unique circumstances pertaining to a particular statement that required clarification.

NOTES

Silence is worth two – מַשְׁתּוּקָא בִּתְרֵין: Some explain that coming up with an appropriate comment to say is worth one *sela*, and refraining from making an inappropriate comment is worth twice as much (*Sefat Emet*).

LANGUAGE

Coptic [*Giptit*] – **גִּיפְּטִית**: From the Greek Αιγύπτιος, *Aigyptios*, meaning Egyptian.

HALAKHA

Coptic to Copts – גִּיפְּטִית לַגִּיפְּטִים: If a Megilla is written in Aramaic or in any other language, only one who knows that language fulfills his obligation by reading it. The Rema states that it is permitted to write the Megilla in any script, but others maintain that it must be written in *Ashurit* script (Rid; *Peri Ḥadash*). The universal custom is to write the Megilla in Hebrew with *Ashurit* script (*Levush*; *Shulḥan Arukh Oraḥ Ḥayyim* 690:9).

הֵיכִי דָּמֵי? אִילֵימָא דִּכְתִיבָה אַשּׁוּרִית וְקָרֵי לָהּ יְוָונִית – הַיְינוּ עַל פֶּה! אָמַר רַבִּי אַחָא אָמַר רַבִּי אֶלְעָזָר: שֶׁכְּתוּבָה בְּלַעַז יְוָונִית.

The Gemara asks: **What are the circumstances** of the case? **If we say that** the Megilla **was written in *Ashurit*,** i.e., in Hebrew, **and he read it in Greek, this is** the same as reading it **by heart,** and the mishna teaches that one does not fulfill his obligation by reading by heart. The Gemara answers: **Rabbi Aḥa said** that **Rabbi Elazar said:** The mishna is dealing with a case in which the Megilla **was written in the Greek foreign language** and was also read in that language.

וְאָמַר רַבִּי אַחָא אָמַר רַבִּי אֶלְעָזָר: מִנַּיִן שֶׁקְּרָאוֹ הַקָּדוֹשׁ בָּרוּךְ הוּא לְיַעֲקֹב ״אֵל״? שֶׁנֶּאֱמַר ״וַיִּקְרָא לוֹ אֵל אֱלֹהֵי יִשְׂרָאֵל״. דְּאִי סָלְקָא דַּעְתָּךְ לַמִּזְבֵּחַ קָרָא לֵיהּ יַעֲקֹב אֵל – ״וַיִּקְרָא לוֹ יַעֲקֹב״ מִיבְּעֵי לֵיהּ, אֶלָּא וַיִּקְרָא לוֹ לְיַעֲקֹב אֵל, וּמִי קְרָאוֹ אֵל – אֱלֹהֵי יִשְׂרָאֵל.

Apropos statements in this line of tradition, the Gemara adds: **And** Rabbi Aḥa further **said** that **Rabbi Elazar said: From where** is it derived **that the Holy One, Blessed be He, called Jacob El,**[N] meaning God? **As it is stated:** "And he erected there an altar, **and he called it El, God of Israel"** (Genesis 33:20). It is also possible to translate this as: And He, i.e., the God of Israel, called him, Jacob, El. Indeed, it must be understood this way, **as if it enters your mind** to say that the verse should be understood as saying that **Jacob called the altar El, it should have** specified the subject of the verb and written: **And Jacob called it** El. **But** since the verse is not written this way, the verse must be understood as follows: **He called Jacob El; and who called him El? The God of Israel.**

מֵיתִיבִי: קְרָאָהּ גִּיפְּטִית, עִבְרִית, עֵילָמִית, מָדִית, יְוָונִית – לֹא יָצָא.

The Gemara returns to discussing languages for reading the Megilla and **raises an objection** against Rav and Shmuel, who said that one may read the Megilla in Greek but not in other foreign languages. It is taught in a *baraita*: **If one read** the Megilla **in Coptic** [***Giptit***],[L] ***Ivrit***,[N] **Elamite, Median, or Greek, he has not fulfilled** his obligation, indicating that one cannot fulfill his obligation by reading the Megilla in Greek.

הָא לָא דָּמְיָא אֶלָּא לְהָא: גִּיפְּטִית לַגִּיפְּטִים, עִבְרִית לָעִבְרִים, עֵילָמִית לָעֵילָמִים, יְוָונִית לַיְּוָונִים – יָצָא.

The Gemara answers: The clause in the mishna that teaches that the Megilla may be read in a foreign language to one who speaks that foreign language **is comparable only to that** which was taught in a different *baraita*: If one reads the Megilla **in Coptic to Copts,**[HN] in ***Ivrit* to *Ivrim*, in Elamite to Elamites, or in Greek to Greeks, he has fulfilled** his obligation. The Megilla may be read in any language, provided the listener understands that language.

אִי הָכִי, רַב וּשְׁמוּאֵל אַמַּאי מוֹקְמִי לָהּ לְמַתְנִיתִין בְּלַעַז יְוָונִית? לוֹקְמָהּ בְּכׇל לַעַז! [אֶלָּא מַתְנִיתִין כִּבְרַיְיתָא] וְכִי אִיתְּמַר דְּרַב וּשְׁמוּאֵל – בְּעָלְמָא אִיתְּמַר. רַב וּשְׁמוּאֵל דְּאָמְרִי תַּרְוַיְיהוּ: לַעַז יְוָונִי לַכֹּל כָּשֵׁר.

The Gemara asks: But **if so,** that one who reads the Megilla in a foreign language that he speaks fulfills his obligation, **why did Rav and Shmuel establish the** ruling of the **mishna as** referring specifically **to Greek? Let them interpret it** as referring **to any foreign language** that one speaks. The Gemara explains: **Rather, the mishna** is to be understood **like the *baraita*,** that one who reads the Megilla in a language that he speaks fulfills his obligation; **and that which was stated** in the name of **Rav and Shmuel was said** as a **general** statement, not relating to the mishna but as an independent ruling, as follows: **Rav and Shmuel both say: The Greek language is acceptable for everyone,**[N] i.e., anyone who reads the Megilla in Greek has fulfilled his obligation, even if he does not understand Greek.

NOTES

From where is it derived that the Holy One, Blessed be He, called Jacob El – מִנַּיִן שֶׁקְּרָאוֹ הַקָּדוֹשׁ בָּרוּךְ הוּא לְיַעֲקֹב אֵל: See *Tosafot*, who note that there are other instances in the Bible in which people call altars by names of God. However, unlike those cases, there was no particular incident at this time that Jacob might have wished to commemorate by giving his altar such a name. The Ritva writes that the Gemara's unconventional interpretation of the verse, that it tells about a name given to Jacob rather than to his altar, is based on the verse's superfluous wording. See Maharsha for a similar idea. As for the concept itself, that Jacob was called El, see Ramban's commentary on the Torah, where he adduces several midrashic statements to the effect that Jacob's image was engraved under God's throne of glory, meaning that Jacob achieved a virtually God-like perfection in this world.

***Ivrit* – עִבְרִית:** Although *Ivrit* usually refers to the Hebrew language, in this context it refers to a different language (Rashba), a language spoken on the other side [*ever*] of the river (Rashi).

Coptic to Copts – גִּיפְּטִית לַגִּיפְּטִים: Many of the commentaries and halakhic authorities discuss this issue, and several varying opinions have been presented with regard to it. It appears that the opinion of the Rambam, and apparently of Rashi as well, is that if one understands a particular foreign language he can fulfill his obligation by hearing the Megilla read in that language. The Ramban, however, basing his opinion on the Jerusalem Talmud, maintains that one is permitted to hear the Megilla in a foreign language only if he does not understand Hebrew at all.

The Greek language is acceptable for everyone – לַעַז יְוָונִי לַכֹּל כָּשֵׁר: The explanation of the various opinions here, as well as the final halakhic decision, is the subject of debate among the commentaries. The Rif's opinion here is unclear and is explained by several commentaries in various ways. Rabbi Zeraḥya HaLevi, the Rambam, and other authorities maintain that although generally one may fulfill his obligation by hearing the Megilla in a foreign language only if he understands that language, one can fulfill his obligation by hearing the Megilla in Greek even if he does not understand Greek, as is the case with Hebrew. Other commentaries rule that that even according to Rabban Shimon ben Gamliel, only one who speaks Greek can fulfill his obligation by hearing the Megilla in Greek (Ramban; Rashba). See the Ritva, Meiri, and Rabbi Zeraḥya HaLevi, who disagree even with regard to the accurate presentation of these opinions. The *Mikhtam* explains that Greek has an exceptional status, because in talmudic times the Greek language was widely used and understood throughout the world. Consequently, it was assigned a special status in *halakha* at that time.

והא קתני יוונית ליוונים - אין, לכולי עלמא - לא! אינהו דאמור כרבן שמעון בן גמליאל - דתנן, רבן שמעון בן גמליאל אומר: אף ספרים לא התירו שיכתבו אלא יוונית.

The Gemara raises a difficulty: **But doesn't** the *baraita* cited above **teach** that if one reads the Megilla in **Greek to Greeks** he has fulfilled his obligation? This implies that reading in Greek, **yes,** this is acceptable for Greeks, but **for everyone** else, **no,** it is not. The Gemara answers: Rav and Shmuel disagree with this statement of the *baraita*, because they **agree with** the opinion of **Rabban Shimon ben Gamliel. As we learned** in a mishna (*Megilla* 8b): **Rabban Shimon ben Gamliel says: Even** for **books** of the Bible, the Sages **did not permit them to be written** in any foreign language **other than Greek,** indicating that Greek has a special status, and is treated like the original Hebrew.

ולימרו הלכה כרבן שמעון בן גמליאל! אי אמרי הלכה כרבן שמעון בן גמליאל הוה אמינא: הני מילי - שאר ספרים, אבל מגילה דכתיב בה "ככתבם" אימא לא - קא משמע לן.

The Gemara asks: But if this was the intention of Rav and Shmuel, **let them state** explicitly: **The** ***halakha*** **is in accordance with** the opinion of **Rabban Shimon ben Gamliel.** Why did Rav and Shmuel formulate their statement as if they were issuing a new ruling? The Gemara answers: **Had they said** simply **that the** ***halakha*** **is in accordance with Rabban Shimon ben Gamliel, I would have said** that **this applies** only **to the other books** of the Bible, **but** with regard to **the Megilla, of which it is written: "According to their writing," I would say** that one does **not** fulfill his obligation if he reads it in Greek. Therefore they stated their own opinion to **teach us** that even in the case of the Megilla one fulfills his obligation if he reads it in Greek.

"והלועז ששמע אשורית יצא" וכו׳: והא לא ידע מאי קאמרי? מידי דהוה אנשים ועמי הארץ.

§ It was taught in the mishna: **And one who speaks a foreign language who heard** the Megilla being read **in** ***Ashurit***, i.e., in Hebrew, **has fulfilled** his obligation.[N] The Gemara asks: **But isn't** it so that **he does not understand what they are saying?** Since he does not understand Hebrew, how does he fulfill his obligation? The Gemara answers: **It is just as it is** with **women and uneducated people;** they too understand little Hebrew, but nevertheless they fulfill their obligation when they hear the Megilla read in that language.

מתקיף לה רבינא: אטו אנן "האחשתרנים בני הרמכים" מי ידעינן? אלא מצות קריאה ופרסומי ניסא - הכא נמי מצות קריאה ופרסומי ניסא.

Ravina strongly objects to the premise of the question raised above, i.e., that someone who does not understand the original, untranslated language of the Megilla cannot fulfill his obligation. **Is that to say** that even **we,** the Sages, who are very well acquainted with Hebrew, **know** for certain the meaning of the obscure words *ha'aḥashteranim benei haramakhim* (Esther 8:10), often translated as: "Used in the royal service, bred from the stud"? **But** nevertheless, we fulfill the **mitzva of reading** the Megilla **and publicizing the miracle** of Purim by reading these words as they appear in the original text. **Here too,** one who speaks a foreign language who hears the Megilla being read in Hebrew fulfills the **mitzva of reading** the Megilla **and publicizing the** Purim **miracle,** even if he does not understand the words themselves.

"קראה סירוגין יצא" וכו׳: לא הוו ידעי רבנן מאי סירוגין, שמעוה לאמתא דבי רבי דקאמרה להו לרבנן דהוי עיילי פסקי פסקי לבי רבי, עד מתי אתם נכנסין סירוגין סירוגין!

§ The mishna continues: **If one reads** the Megilla **at intervals [*seirugin*] he has fulfilled** his obligation. The Gemara relates that **the Sages did not know what is** meant by the word *seirugin*.[N] One day **they heard the maidservant in Rabbi** Yehuda HaNasi's **house saying to the Sages who were entering the house intermittently** rather than in a single group: **How long are you going to enter** ***seirugin seirugin*****?** As she lived in Rabbi Yehuda HaNasi's house and certainly heard the most proper Hebrew being spoken, they understood from this that the word *seirugin* means at intervals.

לא הוו ידעי רבנן מאי חלוגלוגות, שמעוה לאמתא דבי רבי דאמרה ליה לההוא גברא דהוה קא מבדר פרפחיני, עד מתי אתה מפזר חלוגלוגך.

It is similarly related that **the Sages did not know what is** meant by the word *ḥalogelogot,* which appears in various *mishnayot* and *baraitot*. One day **they heard the maidservant in Rabbi** Yehuda HaNasi's **house saying to a certain man who was scattering purslane:**[B] **How long will you go on scattering your** ***ḥalogelogot*****?** And from this they understood that *ḥalogelogot* is purslane.

NOTES

One who speaks a foreign language who heard the Megilla in ***Ashurit*** **has fulfilled his obligation – והלועז ששמע אשורית יצא:** Some explain that as most Jews know some Hebrew, even one who knows no Hebrew can ask other people in the synagogue to explain to him at least the main idea of the Megilla. This, however, is not the case with other languages (Rabbeinu Yehonatan).

What is meant by ***seirugin*** **– מאי סירוגין:** Some explain that they knew the general meaning of the word but were uncertain whether it meant specifically long pauses or if it also included short pauses (see *Penei Yehoshua* and *Sefat Emet*).

BACKGROUND

Purslane – פרפחיני: It appears that this plant is *Portulaca oleracea*, also known as common purslane or pursley. It is a widespread weed, recognizable by its small yellow flowers. It grows in places with ample water sources, and its leaves are eaten fresh in salads or pickled.

Common purslane

LANGUAGE

Arab [*Tayya'a*] – טַיְּיעָא: From the name of an Arab nomadic tribe [*altai*]. Apparently, the members of this tribe were at the time so common in the area close to Babylonia that anyone who was an Arab was called *Tayya'a*.

Your *yehav* – יְהָבִיךְ: It is unclear if that Arab used an Arabic word or a rarely used Aramaic word. However, this root usually means to give or to place one object upon another object in both Aramaic and Hebrew as well as in Arabic: وهب, *wahaba*.

לָא הֲווֹ יָדְעִי רַבָּנַן מַאי ״סַלְסְלֶהָ וּתְרוֹמְמֶךָּ״. שְׁמַעוּהָ לְאַמְתָּא דְּבֵי רַבִּי דַּהֲוָות אָמְרָה לְהַהוּא גַּבְרָא דַּהֲוָה מְהַפֵּךְ בְּמַזְיֵיהּ, אָמְרָה לֵיהּ: עַד מָתַי אַתָּה מְסַלְסֵל בִּשְׂעָרְךָ.

Likewise, **the Sages did not know what is** meant by *salseleha* in the verse: "Get *wisdom*... *salseleha* **and it will exalt you"** (Proverbs 4:7–8). One day **they heard the maidservant in Rabbi** Yehuda HaNasi's **house talking to a certain man who was twirling his hair, saying to him: How long will you go on twirling** [*mesalsel*] **your hair?** And from this they understood that the verse is saying: Turn wisdom around and around, and it will exalt you.

לָא הֲווֹ יָדְעִי רַבָּנַן מַאי ״הַשְׁלֵךְ עַל ה׳ יְהָבְךָ״. אָמַר רַבָּה בַּר בַּר חָנָה: זִימְנָא חֲדָא הֲוָה אָזֵילְנָא בַּהֲדֵי הַהוּא טַיְּיעָא, וְקָא דָּרֵינָא טוּנָא, וַאֲמַר לִי: שְׁקוֹל יְהָבִיךְ וּשְׁדֵי אַגַּמְלַאי.

The Gemara relates additional examples: **The Sages did not know what is** meant by the word *yehav* in the verse: **"Cast upon the Lord your** *yehav*" (Psalms 55:23). **Rabba bar bar Ḥana said: One time I was traveling with a certain Arab** [*Tayya'a*][L] **and I was carrying a load, and he said to me: Take your** *yehav*[L] **and throw it on my camel,** and I understood that *yehav* means a load or burden.

לָא הֲווֹ יָדְעִי רַבָּנַן מַאי ״וְטֵאטֵאתִיהָ בְּמַטְאֲטֵא הַשְׁמֵד״, שְׁמַעוּהָ לְאַמְתָּא דְּבֵי רַבִּי דַּהֲוָות אָמְרָה לַחֲבֶרְתָּהּ: שְׁקוּלִי טָאטִיתָא וְטַאטִי בֵּיתָא.

And similarly, **the Sages did not know what is** meant by the word *matatei* in the verse: **"And I will** ***tatei*** **it with the** ***matatei*** **of destruction"** (Isaiah 14:23). One day **they heard the maidservant in Rabbi** Yehuda HaNasi's **house saying to her friend: Take a** ***tateita*** **and** ***tati*** **the house,** from which they understood that a *matatei* is a broom, and the verb *tati* means to sweep.

תָּנוּ רַבָּנַן: קְרָאָהּ סֵירוּגִין – יָצָא,

On the matter of reading the Megilla with interruptions, **the Sages taught** the following *baraita*: **If one reads the Megilla at intervals,** pausing and resuming at intervals, **he has fulfilled** his obligation.

Perek **II**
Daf **18** Amud **b**

NOTES

Out of order – סֵירוּסִין: It is explained in the Jerusalem Talmud that this refers to skipping verses. The *ge'onim*, however, explain that it is referring to one who reads a verse backward, from the end to the beginning. This appears to be Rashi's interpretation as well.

סֵירוּסִין – לֹא יָצָא. רַבִּי מוֹנָא אוֹמֵר מִשּׁוּם רַבִּי יְהוּדָה: אַף בְּסֵירוּגִין, אִם שָׁהָה כְּדֵי לִגְמוֹר אֶת כּוּלָּהּ – חוֹזֵר לָרֹאשׁ. אָמַר רַב יוֹסֵף: הֲלָכָה כְּרַבִּי מוֹנָא שֶׁאָמַר מִשּׁוּם רַבִּי יְהוּדָה.

But if he reads it **out of order,**[N] i.e., if he changes the order of the words or verses of the Megilla, **he has not fulfilled** his obligation. **Rabbi Mona said in the name of Rabbi Yehuda: Even** when he reads it **at intervals,**[H] **if he pauses** and interrupts his reading long **enough** for one **to finish** reading **the whole** Megilla during that time, **he must go back to the beginning** and start again. **Rav Yosef said: The** ***halakha*** **is in accordance with** the opinion of **Rabbi Mona,** who **stated** his opinion **in the name of Rabbi Yehuda.**

אֲמַר לֵיהּ אַבָּיֵי לְרַב יוֹסֵף: כְּדֵי לִגְמוֹר אֶת כּוּלָּהּ, מֵהֵיכָא דְּקָאֵי לְסֵיפָא, אוֹ דִּלְמָא מֵרֵישָׁא לְסֵיפָא? אֲמַר לֵיהּ: מֵרֵישָׁא לְסֵיפָא, דְּאִם כֵּן נָתַתָּ דְּבָרֶיךָ לְשִׁיעוּרִין.

Abaye said to Rav Yosef: When Rabbi Mona said: Long **enough** for one **to finish** reading **the whole** Megilla, did he mean **from** the verse **where he is** now **until the end? Or perhaps** he meant long enough to read the entire Megilla **from the beginning until the end. He said to him:** Rabbi Mona meant **from the beginning until the end,** as **if** it were **so** that he meant from where he paused until the end of the Megilla, **you would be subjecting your statement to the** varying **circumstances** of each case. There would be no standard principle to determine the length of a permitted pause; in each case, depending on where one stopped, it would take a different amount of time to finish the Megilla until the end. And the Sages did not institute measures that are not standardized.

HALAKHA

At intervals – בְּסֵירוּגִין: If one reads the Megilla with pauses during the reading and continues reading each time from where he left off, he has fulfilled his obligation, even if he pauses long enough to finish reading the entire Megilla. This is in accordance with the final version of the opinion of Rav (*Shulḥan Arukh, Oraḥ Ḥayyim* 690:5). Although it is discouraged to speak during the Megilla reading, one who does so has fulfilled his obligation (Rema). One should not pause repeatedly in the Megilla reading, *ab initio* (*Mishna Berura*, citing Rashba).

אָמַר רַבִּי אַבָּא אָמַר רַבִּי יִרְמְיָה בַּר אַבָּא אָמַר רַב: הֲלָכָה כְּרַבִּי מוֹנָא, וּשְׁמוּאֵל אָמַר: אֵין הֲלָכָה כְּרַבִּי מוֹנָא. בְּסוּרָא מַתְנוּ הָכִי. בְּפוּמְבְּדִיתָא מַתְנוּ הָכִי: אָמַר רַב כָּהֲנָא אָמַר רַב: הֲלָכָה כְּרַבִּי מוֹנָא, וּשְׁמוּאֵל אָמַר: אֵין הֲלָכָה כְּרַבִּי מוֹנָא. רַב בֵּיבָי מַתְנֵי אִיפְּכָא, רַב אָמַר: אֵין הֲלָכָה כְּרַבִּי מוֹנָא, וּשְׁמוּאֵל אָמַר: הֲלָכָה כְּרַבִּי מוֹנָא.

Rabbi Abba said that **Rabbi Yirmeya bar Abba said: Rav said** that **the *halakha* is in accordance with** the opinion of **Rabbi Mona, but Shmuel said** that **the *halakha* is not in accordance with** the opinion of **Rabbi Mona.** The Gemara elaborates: **This is how they taught** the opinions of the Sages **in Sura.**[B] However, **in Pumbedita**[B] **they taught** it slightly differently, **like this: Rav Kahana said** that **Rav said** that **the *halakha* is in accordance with** the opinion of **Rabbi Mona, but Shmuel said** that **the *halakha* is not in accordance with** the opinion of **Rabbi Mona. Rav Beivai taught the opposite: Rav said** that **the *halakha* is not in accordance with** the opinion of **Rabbi Mona, but Shmuel said** that **the *halakha* is in accordance with** the opinion of **Rabbi Mona.**

אָמַר רַב יוֹסֵף: נְקוֹט דְּרַב בֵּיבָי בִּידָךְ, דִּשְׁמוּאֵל הוּא דְּחָיֵישׁ לִיחִידָאָה. דִּתְנַן: שׁוֹמֶרֶת יָבָם שֶׁקִּידֵּשׁ אָחִיו אֶת אֲחוֹתָהּ, מִשּׁוּם רַבִּי יְהוּדָה בֶּן בְּתֵירָה אָמְרוּ: אוֹמְרִים לוֹ הַמְתֵּן עַד שֶׁיַּעֲשֶׂה אָחִיךָ הַגָּדוֹל מַעֲשֶׂה.

Rav Yosef said: Grasp the version of **Rav Beivai in your hand,** i.e., accept it as the most authoritative one. It appears to be correct, as we know that **Shmuel takes into consideration** even an **individual** dissenting opinion when it is more stringent than the majority opinion. The Gemara proves its assertion about Shmuel: **As we learned** in a mishna (*Yevamot* 41a) with regard to a different matter, the case of a widow whose husband died childless and who was waiting for one of his surviving brothers to perform the required levirate marriage with her or, alternatively, to release her with the *ḥalitza* ceremony: In a case where **a woman** was **waiting for her brother-in-law**[N] **and** in the meantime one of her deceased husband's **brothers betrothed** this woman's **sister,**[H] **they said in the name of Rabbi Yehuda ben Beteira: We say to** this brother: **Wait** before marrying your betrothed **until your older brother acts,** performing the levirate marriage or *ḥalitza*.

אָמַר שְׁמוּאֵל: הֲלָכָה כְּרַבִּי יְהוּדָה בֶּן בְּתֵירָה.

The reason for this is that before levirate marriage or *ḥalitza* is performed, all the brothers are considered, by rabbinic decree, to have a quasi-marital connection with the widow. Consequently, just as one may not marry his wife's sister, he may not marry the sister of a woman who is waiting for him to perform levirate marriage. The Sages, however, disagree with Rabbi Yehuda ben Beteira and maintain that only the oldest of the brothers is considered bound to the widow, as he is the primary candidate to perform these acts. Consequently, the widow has no connection at all with the other brothers. And **Shmuel said: The *halakha* is in accordance with** the opinion of **Rabbi Yehuda ben Beteira.** This demonstrates that Shmuel takes into consideration the opinion of a single Sage against the majority when that minority opinion is more stringent than the majority opinion.

תָּנוּ רַבָּנַן: הִשְׁמִיט בָּהּ סוֹפֵר אוֹתִיּוֹת אוֹ פְּסוּקִין, וּקְרָאָן הַקּוֹרֵא כִּמְתוּרְגְּמָן הַמְתַרְגֵּם – יָצָא.

§ **The Sages taught** in a *baraita*: **If the scribe** who wrote the Megilla **omitted letters**[H] or even complete **verses** when he wrote it, **and the reader read** these missing items **as a translator** would do **when translating,**[N] i.e., he recited the missing parts by heart, **he has fulfilled** his obligation.[N] Missing material in a Megilla and reading words or verses by heart do not invalidate the reading.

HALAKHA

A woman was waiting for her brother-in-law [*yavam*] and one of her deceased husband's brothers betrothed her sister – שׁוֹמֶרֶת יָבָם שֶׁקִּידֵּשׁ אָחִיו אֶת אֲחוֹתָהּ: A *yavam*, whether a sole surviving brother or one of several, is prohibited from marrying the close relatives of the widow who is awaiting levirate marriage. Therefore, if one of the brothers betroths a sister of the widow, it is prohibited for him to marry his betrothed until one of the other brothers either marries the widow or performs *ḥalitza*, in accordance with the opinion of Rabbi Yehuda ben Beteira. Some say that if he had already consummated their marriage, the bond between this brother and the widow is dissolved, and it is permitted for him to have relations with his wife even before the levirate marriage or *ḥalitza* takes place.

Some say that nowadays, when Rabbeinu Gershom's strict prohibition against simultaneously having two wives applies, if a man has a sister-in-law who is awaiting levirate marriage it is prohibited for him to marry a different woman until the *ḥalitza* is performed with the widow. However, if the other woman was already betrothed to him it is permitted for him to marry her (*Shulḥan Arukh, Even HaEzer* 159:5, and in the comment of Rema).

If the scribe omitted letters – הִשְׁמִיט בָּהּ סוֹפֵר אוֹתִיּוֹת: A Megilla should be entirely complete when it is read, *ab initio*. However, after the fact, if a Megilla is missing some words in the middle, up to half of the words, it is a valid Megilla and as long as the reader recites the missing words by heart, he has fulfilled his obligation. If the scribe omitted the very beginning or end of the Megilla it is unfit for use (Rashba). Also, if the scribe omitted an entire passage even in the middle of the Megilla it is unfit. If more than half the Megilla is missing or is written with letters that are so blurred that they are not legible, it is unfit (*Shulḥan Arukh, Oraḥ Ḥayyim* 690:3).

BACKGROUND

Sura – סוּרָא: Sura, a town in southern Babylonia, became an important Jewish community only when the great *amora* Rav moved and established the yeshiva there (c. 220 CE). From then until the end of geonic period (c. 1000 CE), Sura was a major Torah center. The yeshiva in Sura, under the leadership of Rav and his closest disciples, was influenced by the halakhic traditions of Eretz Yisrael and was renowned for its unique approach to Torah study. Among the great Sages and leaders of Sura were Rav, Rav Huna, Rav Ḥisda, Ravina, and Rav Ashi. The Babylonian Talmud was redacted primarily in Sura.

Pumbedita – פּוּמְבְּדִיתָא: Pumbedita, a town on the Euphrates River northwest of Neharde'a, was an important center of the Babylonian Jewish community for many generations. As early as the Second Temple period, Pumbedita was referred to simply as the Diaspora. After the destruction of Neharde'a, its yeshiva moved to Pumbedita, and Torah study continued there uninterrupted until the end of the geonic period.

The scholars of Pumbedita were particularly renowned for their acumen. The most famous heads of the yeshiva in Pumbedita were Rav Yehuda, its original founder; Rabba; Rav Yosef; Abaye; Rav Naḥman bar Yitzḥak; Rav Zevid; and Rafram bar Pappa. The yeshiva in Pumbedita was prominent in the geonic period as well, often overshadowing the yeshiva in Sura. The last heads of the yeshiva in Pumbedita were the renowned *ge'onim* Rav Sherira Gaon and his son, Rav Hai Gaon.

NOTES

A woman waiting for her brother-in-law – שׁוֹמֶרֶת יָבָם: A woman whose husband dies without children but with at least one surviving brother has the status of a woman who is waiting for her brother-in-law. It is prohibited for her to marry anyone else until one of the brothers, preferably the eldest, performs levirate marriage or, alternatively, releases her through performing the *ḥalitza* ceremony. Until one of these procedures is done, the widow is bound to her husband's brothers by a bond known as *zika*. The *amora'im* and *tanna'im* debated the type and strength of this bond. The opinion of Rabbi Yehuda ben Beteira is in accordance with those who maintain that the bond is comparable to betrothal. Therefore, until the bond is released it is prohibited for any of the brothers to marry a woman who is a close relative to the widow, just as it is prohibited to marry a close relative of one's actual or betrothed wife.

As a translator would do when translating – כִּמְתוּרְגְּמָן הַמְתַרְגֵּם: The Rif explains this expression: Just as a translator adds words that are not written in the book before him in order to complete and convey the intent of the source he is translating, so too, this reader adds words that are not in the book before him (see Rashi and *Turei Even*).

If the scribe…omitted letters…he has fulfilled his obligation – הִשְׁמִיט בָּהּ סוֹפֵר אוֹתִיּוֹת...יָצָא: The Ran explains, citing the Ramban, that since the Megilla is termed a letter (see 19a), the *halakha* is less demanding than it is concerning the writing of biblical books. Therefore, the Megilla is acceptable even if it is missing material, as long as it is possible to read it understandably. It would seem that the *halakha* is stricter with regard to the Megilla being read out of order than it is with regard to missing words, as a reading that is out of order disrupts the flow of the content (see *Mikhtam*).

HALAKHA

If the reader omitted one verse, etc. – **הַשְׁמִיט בָּהּ הַקּוֹרֵא פָּסוּק וכו׳**: If one reads a verse of the Megilla, skips the next verse, and then continues reading from the third verse, he has not fulfilled his obligation, even if he subsequently returns and reads the skipped verse. He must return to where he erred and read from there, in order, to the end of the Megilla (*Shulḥan Arukh, Oraḥ Ḥayyim* 690:6).

If one enters a synagogue and encounters a congregation that has read half – **מָצָא צִבּוּר שֶׁקָּרְאוּ חֶצְיָהּ**: If one enters a synagogue and finds that the congregation has already read half of the Megilla, he should not listen to the second half with the congregation and later read the first half, as this would be reading out of order. Rather, he should read it from the beginning until the end (Rambam *Sefer Zemanim, Hilkhot Megilla* 2:2).

If one was writing a Megilla or expounding upon it – **כּוֹתְבָהּ, דּוֹרְשָׁהּ**: In the case of one who has a Megilla lying before him and he copies from it verse by verse to another Megilla, if he reads aloud every verse that he writes and intends by this to fulfill his obligation, he has fulfilled his obligation. Likewise, in the case of one who reads the Megilla verse by verse while expounding it as he goes, if he expounds upon only the Megilla itself he has fulfilled his obligation (*Shulḥan Arukh, Oraḥ Ḥayyim* 690:13).

It is prohibited to write…when not copying from a written text – **אָסוּר לִכְתּוֹב...שֶׁלֹּא מִן הַכְּתָב**: One who writes a Torah scroll must have before him another Torah scroll from which he copies, as it is prohibited to write even one letter without referring to the written text. A Torah scroll that is written without copying from a written text may not be used for Torah readings except in exigent circumstances. Some, however, say that once it has already been written it may be used (*Shakh*, citing Ran and Rabbeinu Manoaḥ; *Arukh HaShulḥan*; *Shulḥan Arukh, Yoreh De'a* 274:2).

מֵיתִיבִי: הָיוּ בָּהּ אוֹתִיּוֹת מְטוּשְׁטָשׁוֹת אוֹ מְקוֹרָעוֹת, אִם רִשּׁוּמָן נִיכָּר – כְּשֵׁרָה, וְאִם לָאו – פְּסוּלָה! לָא קַשְׁיָא; הָא בְּכוּלָּהּ, הָא – בְּמִקְצָתָהּ.

The Gemara **raises an objection** from another *baraita*: **If** a Megilla **contains letters that are blurred or torn,** the following distinction applies: **If their imprint is** still **visible,** the Megilla **is fit** for reading, **but if not, it is unfit.** This *baraita* indicates that even the omission of several letters invalidates the Megilla. The Gemara resolves the contradiction between the two *baraitot*: **This** is **not difficult. This** second *baraita*, which says that a Megilla with blurred or torn letters is unfit, is referring to a case where this is so throughout **the whole of** the Megilla; whereas **this** first *baraita*, which says that a Megilla is fit even if whole verses are missing, is referring to a case where the missing material is **in** only **part of it.**

תָּנוּ רַבָּנַן: הִשְׁמִיט בָּהּ הַקּוֹרֵא פָּסוּק אֶחָד לֹא יֹאמַר אֶקְרָא אֶת כּוּלָּהּ וְאַחַר כָּךְ אֶקְרָא אוֹתוֹ פָּסוּק, אֶלָּא קוֹרֵא מֵאוֹתוֹ פָּסוּק וְאֵילָךְ. נִכְנַס לְבֵית הַכְּנֶסֶת וּמָצָא צִבּוּר שֶׁקָּרְאוּ חֶצְיָהּ, לֹא יֹאמַר אֶקְרָא חֶצְיָהּ עִם הַצִּבּוּר, וְאַחַר כָּךְ אֶקְרָא חֶצְיָהּ – אֶלָּא קוֹרֵא אוֹתָהּ מִתְּחִילָּתָהּ וְעַד סוֹפָהּ.

The Sages taught in a *baraita*: **If the reader** of the Megilla **omitted one verse,**[H] **he may not say: I will** continue to **read the whole of** the Megilla in order, **and afterward I will** go back and **read that verse** that I omitted. **Rather, he must** go back and **read from that verse** that he omitted and continue from there to the end of the Megilla. Similarly, **if one enters a synagogue and encounters a congregation that has** already **read half**[H] of the Megilla, **he may not say: I will read** the second **half of** the Megilla with **the congregation,** and **afterward I will** go back and **read** the first **half. Rather, he must** go back and **read it** in its proper order **from the beginning until the end.**

״מִתְנַמְנֵם יָצָא״ וכו׳: הֵיכִי דָּמֵי מִתְנַמְנֵם? אָמַר רַב אַשִׁי: נִים וְלָא נִים, תִּיר וְלָא תִּיר, דְּקָרוּ לֵיהּ וְעָנֵי. וְלָא יָדַע לַאֲהַדּוּרֵי סְבָרָא, וְכִי מַדְכְּרוּ לֵיהּ – מִידְכַּר.

§ It is taught in the mishna: If one read the Megilla **while he is dozing off, he has fulfilled his** obligation. The Gemara asks: **What are the circumstances of** the case of **dozing off? Rav Ashi said:** It is referring to a situation in which one is **asleep yet not** fully **asleep, awake yet not** fully **awake. If someone calls him he answers. And he is** in a mental state in which **he does not know** how **to provide** an answer that requires logical **reasoning, but when people remind him** about something that has happened, **he remembers** it.

״הָיָה כּוֹתְבָהּ, דּוֹרְשָׁהּ, וּמַגִּיהָהּ, אִם כִּוֵּון לִבּוֹ יָצָא״ וכו׳: הֵיכִי דָּמֵי? אִי דְּקָא מְסַדֵּר פְּסוּקָא פְּסוּקָא וְכָתַב לָהּ – כִּי כִּוֵּון לִבּוֹ מַאי הָוֵי? עַל פֶּה הוּא! אֶלָּא דְּכָתַב פְּסוּקָא פְּסוּקָא וְקָרֵי לֵיהּ.

§ The mishna continues: **If one was writing** a Megilla, **or expounding upon it,**[H] **or correcting** it, and he read all its words as he was doing so, **if he had intent** to fulfill his obligation with that reading **he has fulfilled** his obligation.[N] The Gemara asks: **What are the circumstances** of this case? **If he was articulating each verse** of the Megilla and then **writing it down, what of it** that **he intended** to fulfill his obligation with that reading, since he recited those words **by heart? Rather,** it must be that **he** first **wrote each verse** in the Megilla **and** then **read it out.**

וּמִי יָצָא? וְהָאָמַר רַבִּי חֶלְבּוֹ אָמַר רַב חָמָא בַּר גּוּרְיָא אָמַר רַב: הֲלָכָה כְּדִבְרֵי הָאוֹמֵר כּוּלָּהּ. וַאֲפִילּוּ לְמַאן דְּאָמַר ״מֵאִישׁ יְהוּדִי״ צְרִיכָה שֶׁתְּהֵא כְּתוּבָה כּוּלָּהּ!

The Gemara asks: **But does one** really **fulfill** his obligation in this way? **Didn't Rabbi Ḥelbo say** that **Rav Ḥama bar Gurya said** that **Rav said: The *halakha* is in accordance with the statement of the one who says** that the Megilla must be read **in its entirety** in order to fulfill one's obligation. **And** moreover, he said that **even according to the one who said** that one need not read the entire Megilla, but only from **"There was a certain Jew"** (Esther 2:5) and onward, the Megilla itself **must** nevertheless **be written in its entirety.** How, then, can it be suggested that one who is reading each verse as he writes it can fulfill his obligation by reading from a Megilla that is not yet written to the end?

אֶלָּא, דְּמַנְחָה מְגִילָּה קַמֵּיהּ וְקָרֵי לָהּ מִינָּהּ פְּסוּקָא פְּסוּקָא, וְכָתַב לָהּ. לֵימָא מְסַיֵּיע לֵיהּ לְרַבָּה בַּר בַּר חָנָה, דְּאָמַר רַבָּה בַּר בַּר חָנָה אָמַר רַבִּי יוֹחָנָן: אָסוּר לִכְתּוֹב אוֹת אַחַת שֶׁלֹּא מִן הַכְּתָב. דִּלְמָא דְּאִתְרַמֵּי לֵיהּ אִתְרַמּוּיֵי.

The Gemara answers: **Rather,** this is a case in **which a** complete **Megilla is lying before him** and he is copying from it, **and he was reading from** that complete Megilla **verse by verse and** then **writing** each verse **in** his new copy. The Gemara proposes: **Let us say that** this **supports** the opinion of **Rabba bar bar Ḥana, as Rabba bar bar Ḥana said** that **Rabbi Yoḥanan said: It is prohibited to write** even **a single letter** of the Bible when **not** copying **from a written text.**[H] Since it was necessary to explain the mishna as addressing a case in which one was copying a Megilla out of a written text lying before him, this supports Rabbi Yoḥanan's ruling. The Gemara rejects this: This is not a proof, **as perhaps** the mishna is merely dealing with a case **where this is what happened to be** what occurred, that one happened to be copying the text from an existing Megilla, but it is not a requirement to do this.

NOTES

If he had intent he has fulfilled his obligation – **אִם כִּוֵּון לִבּוֹ יָצָא**: According to the opinion mentioned often in the Talmud that one can fulfill a mitzva even without having intent to fulfill that obligation, this line of the mishna would be understood as follows: If the one writing the Megilla or correcting it has intent to pronounce the words correctly he fulfills his obligation; if he does not have this intent, he does not fulfill his obligation (Rabbeinu Yehonatan).

גּוּפָא, אָמַר רַבָּה בַּר בַּר חָנָה אָמַר רַבִּי יוֹחָנָן: אָסוּר לִכְתּוֹב אוֹת אַחַת שֶׁלֹּא מִן הַכְּתָב. מֵיתִיבִי, אָמַר רַבִּי שִׁמְעוֹן בֶּן אֶלְעָזָר: מַעֲשֶׂה בְּרַבִּי מֵאִיר שֶׁהָלַךְ לְעַבֵּר שָׁנָה בְּעַסְיָא, וְלֹא הָיָה שָׁם מְגִילָּה, וּכְתָבָהּ מִלִּבּוֹ וּקְרָאָהּ.

The Gemara examines Rabba bar bar Ḥana's statement. With regard to **the matter itself, Rabba bar bar Ḥana said** that **Rabbi Yoḥanan said: It is prohibited to write** even **a single letter** of the Bible when **not** copying **from a written text.** The Gemara **raises an objection** from a *baraita*: **Rabbi Shimon ben Elazar said:** One Adar there was **an incident involving Rabbi Meir, who went to intercalate the year in Asia** Minor, as, owing to persecutory decrees, he could not do this in Eretz Yisrael. **And there was no** Megilla **there** when Purim arrived, **so he wrote** a Megilla **by heart and read from it.**[N]

אָמַר רַבִּי אַבָּהוּ: שָׁאנֵי רַבִּי מֵאִיר דְּמִיקַּיֵּים בֵּיהּ ״וְעַפְעַפֶּיךָ יַיְשִׁירוּ נֶגְדֶּךָ״. אֲמַר לֵיהּ רָמִי בַּר חָמָא לְרַבִּי יִרְמְיָה מִדִּפְתִּי: מַאי ״וְעַפְעַפֶּיךָ יַיְשִׁירוּ נֶגְדֶּךָ״? אָמַר לוֹ: אֵלּוּ דִּבְרֵי תוֹרָה, דִּכְתִיב בְּהוּ ״הֲתָעִיף עֵינֶיךָ בּוֹ וְאֵינֶנּוּ״ וַאֲפִילּוּ הָכִי - מְיוּשָּׁרִין הֵן אֵצֶל רַבִּי מֵאִיר.

Rabbi Abbahu said: Rabbi Meir is different, as in him is fulfilled the verse: **"And let your eyelids look straight before you"** (Proverbs 4:25), and with regard to this verse, **Rami bar Ḥama said to Rabbi Yirmeya of Difti: What is** the meaning of the phrase **"and let your eyelids** [*afapekha*],"[N] from the root *a-p-p*, **"look straight** [*yaishiru*] **before you"? He said to him: This is referring to the words of the Torah,** which are difficult to remember exactly, **and with regard to which it is written: "Will you glance upon it fleetingly** [*hata'if*], from the root *a-p-p*, **with your eyes? It is already gone"** (Proverbs 23:5), **but nevertheless they remain exact** [*meyusharin*] in the memory of **Rabbi Meir,** since he knows them all by heart.

רַב חִסְדָּא אַשְׁכַּחֵיהּ לְרַב חֲנַנְאֵל דַּהֲוָה כָּתַב סְפָרִים שֶׁלֹּא מִן הַכְּתָב, אֲמַר לֵיהּ: רְאוּיָה כׇּל הַתּוֹרָה כּוּלָּהּ לִיכָּתֵב עַל פִּיךָ, אֶלָּא כָּךְ אָמְרוּ חֲכָמִים: אָסוּר לִכְתּוֹב אוֹת אַחַת שֶׁלֹּא מִן הַכְּתָב. מִדְּקָאָמַר כׇּל הַתּוֹרָה כּוּלָּהּ רְאוּיָה שֶׁתִּיכָּתֵב עַל פִּיךָ - מִכְּלָל דִּמְיוּשָּׁרִין הֵן אֶצְלוֹ, וְהָא רַבִּי מֵאִיר כָּתַב! שְׁעַת הַדְּחָק שָׁאנֵי.

It was related that **Rav Ḥisda** once **found Rav Ḥananel writing** Torah **scrolls,** but he was **not** copying them **from a written text,** as he knew it all by heart. **He said to him: It is fitting** for **the entire Torah to be written by your mouth,** i.e., relying on your memory, **but this is what the Sages said: It is prohibited to write** even **a single letter** of the Bible when **not** copying **from a written text.** The Gemara asks: **Since** Rav Ḥisda **said** to him: **The entire Torah is fitting to be written by your mouth,** it may be concluded **by inference that** the words of the Torah **were exact in his memory,** i.e., that Rav Ḥananel enjoyed total mastery of the text. **But didn't** we say that **Rabbi Meir wrote** a Megilla without copying from a text due to similar proficiency? The Gemara answers: **A time of exigent circumstances is different;** since there was no other option available, he was permitted to rely on his expertise, but otherwise this must not be done.

אַבַּיֵי שָׁרָא לְדְבֵי בַּר חָבוּ לְמִיכְתַּב תְּפִלִּין וּמְזוּזוֹת שֶׁלֹּא מִן הַכְּתָב, כְּמַאן - כִּי הַאי תַּנָּא. דְּתַנְיָא, רַבִּי יִרְמְיָה אוֹמֵר מִשּׁוּם רַבֵּינוּ: תְּפִלִּין וּמְזוּזוֹת נִכְתָּבוֹת שֶׁלֹּא מִן הַכְּתָב, וְאֵין צְרִיכוֹת שִׂרְטוּט.

It was further related that **Abaye permitted** the scribes of **the house of ben Ḥavu to write phylacteries and** *mezuzot* when they were **not** copying **from** a pre-existing **text.** The Gemara asks: **In accordance with whose** opinion did he issue this allowance? The Gemara explains: **In accordance with** the opinion of **the following** ***tanna***, **as it is taught** in a *baraita*: **Rabbi Yirmeya said in the name of our master,** Rabbi Yehuda HaNasi: **Phylacteries and** ***mezuzot*** **may be written** when they are **not** copied **from a written text, and they do not require scoring,** i.e., the parchment is not required to have lines etched in it.

וְהִלְכְתָא: תְּפִלִּין - אֵין צְרִיכִין שִׂרְטוּט, מְזוּזוֹת - צְרִיכִין שִׂרְטוּט. אִידִי וְאִידִי נִכְתָּבוֹת שֶׁלֹּא מִן הַכְּתָב. מַאי טַעְמָא - מִיגְרַס גְּרִיסִין

The Gemara concludes: **And the** ***halakha*** **is** as follows: **Phylacteries do not require scoring,**[H] whereas ***mezuzot*** **require scoring.**[NH] And unlike biblical books, **both these and those,** phylacteries and *mezuzot*, may be **written** when the scribe is **not** copying **from a written text. What is the reason** for this exception? **These** short texts **are well known** to all scribes, and therefore it is permitted to write them by heart.[H]

״הָיְתָה כְּתוּבָה בְּסַם״ כו׳: סַם - סַמָּא, סִקְרָא - אֲמַר רַבָּה בַּר בַּר חָנָה: סִקְרְתָא שְׁמָהּ. קוֹמוֹס - קוֹמָא.

§ The mishna teaches: If one reads from a Megilla that **was written with** ***sam***[L] or with *sikra* or with *komos* or with *kankantom*, he has not fulfilled his obligation. The Gemara identifies these writing materials: ***Sam*** is what is called in Aramaic ***samma***.[B] With regard to ***sikra***, **Rabba bar bar Ḥana said: Its name** in Aramaic **is** ***sikreta***,[B] a type of red paint. ***Komos***[BL] is what is called **koma**, a tree resin.

NOTES

So he wrote a Megilla by heart and read from it – וּכְתָבָהּ מִלִּבּוֹ וּקְרָאָהּ: It is stipulated in the Jerusalem Talmud that a Megilla written by heart may not be used for reading; rather, a second Megilla is copied from it and is read, in order to fulfill the *halakha* that biblical books may not be written unless copied from a pre-existing text.

What is the meaning of…*afapekha* – מַאי וְעַפְעַפֶּיךָ: These Sages did not wish to translate *afapekha* in the usual sense of eyelids, as it is the eyes, not the eyelids that cover them, which see. For this reason they interpreted it homiletically in the sense of that which flies off [*af*] or is fleeting, as in the word *hata'if*.

Mezuzot **require scoring** – מְזוּזוֹת צְרִיכִין שִׂרְטוּט: Some explain that the reason that phylacteries do not require scoring is that the Torah excerpts contained in them are permanently folded and covered. Since they are not intended to be read, the *halakha* does not require scoring to ensure that the lines are perfectly straight. A *mezuza*, however, is sometimes read (Rid; see Ran and Meiri). Others explain that the parchment on which the phylacteries are written is very thin, and would be likely to tear if scoring were required (*Mikhtam*).

HALAKHA

Scoring for phylacteries – שִׂרְטוּט תְּפִלִּין: The body of the passages in the phylacteries do not require scoring, but scoring the top line is required. If a scribe must score each line in order to be able to write in straight lines he should do so; after the fact, even if the lines are written crooked it is valid (*Mishna Berura*, citing *Baḥ*). Some say that scoring should be done on all four sides of the text, and this opinion is accepted in practice. The universal practice nowadays is to score each line of the phylacteries passages (*Mishna Berura*; *Beur Halakha*; *Shulḥan Arukh*, *Oraḥ Ḥayyim* 32:6, and in the comment of Rema).

Scoring for a *mezuza* – שִׂרְטוּט מְזוּזָה: The passages in the *mezuza* require scoring. A *mezuza* written without scoring is invalid (*Shulḥan Arukh*, *Yoreh De'a* 288:8).

Writing the phylacteries passages by heart – כְּתִיבַת תְּפִלִּין בְּעַל פֶּה: It is preferable to copy the phylacteries passages from a written text (*Baḥ*). Moreover, it is fitting that the scribe read each word aloud before writing it, *ab initio*. If he knows the passages well by heart it is permitted for him to write them without copying. In any case, if one writes the passages and does not make any errors, it is valid after the fact (*Mishna Berura*, citing *Beit Yosef*; *Shulḥan Arukh*, *Oraḥ Ḥayyim* 32:29–31).

BACKGROUND

Samma – סַמָּא: It appears that this is an arsenic mineral, perhaps As_2S_3, known as orpiment, which was once used for painting and making dye.

Sikreta – סִקְרְתָא: This is a red pigment used for various purposes, such as dyeing and writing. It appears that it was made from minium, also known as red lead, a type of lead oxide.

Komos – קוֹמוֹס: Apparently this refers to the resin of the tree known as *Acacia arabica* or *Senegalia senegal*. It is not usually used as a writing substance itself, but as a thickener for other dyes. However, it is possible that a colored resin was used for writing as well.

LANGUAGE

Sam – סַם: When it appears in the context of a dyeing substance, the word *sam* is related to the Greek σμῆμα, *smèma*, a soap that is used for smearing or dyeing.

Komos – קוֹמוֹס: From the Latin commis or the Greek κόμμι, *commi*, meaning gum or resin.

HALAKHA

The writing of the Megilla – כְּתִיבַת הַמְּגִילָּה: A Megilla that is written on paper or on untreated parchment is unfit. Moreover, it must be written in ink, as a Torah scroll is written (*Shulḥan Arukh*, *Oraḥ Ḥayyim* 691:1).

קַנְקַנְתּוֹם – חַרְתָּא דְּאוּשְׁכָּפֵי, דִּיפְתְּרָא – דִּמְלִיחַ וּקְמִיחַ וְלָא עֲפִיץ, נְיָיר – מַחֲקָא.

Kankantom is what is called in Aramaic ***ḥarta de'ushkafei***, a black dye used by shoemakers. ***Diftera*** is hide **that was processed with salt and flour,**[B] **but not with gallnuts.** ***Neyar*** is known in Aramaic as ***maḥaka***,[BN] paper made from reeds.

עַד שֶׁתְּהֵא כְּתוּבָה אַשּׁוּרִית: דִּכְתִיב ״כִּכְתָבָם וְכִזְמַנָּם״.

§ It was taught in the mishna: He does not fulfill his obligation **unless** the Megilla **is written in *Ashurit*.** The Gemara explains the reason for this: **As it is written** concerning the Megilla: **"According to their writing and according to their time"** (Esther 9:27), i.e., the way it was originally written.

״עַל הַסֵּפֶר וּבִדְיוֹ״ וכו׳: מְנָלַן? אָתְיָא כְּתִיבָה כְּתִיבָה, כְּתִיב הָכָא ״וַתִּכְתֹּב אֶסְתֵּר הַמַּלְכָּה״ וּכְתִיב הָתָם ״וַיֹּאמֶר לָהֶם בָּרוּךְ מִפִּיו יִקְרָא אֵלַי אֵת כׇּל הַדְּבָרִים הָאֵלֶּה וַאֲנִי כּוֹתֵב עַל הַסֵּפֶר בַּדְּיוֹ״.

The mishna concludes: He does not fulfill his obligation unless the Megilla is written **upon parchment and with ink."** The Gemara asks: **From where do we** derive this? The Gemara answers: It is **derived** by way of a verbal analogy between one instance of **writing** and another instance of **writing.**[N] **It is written here** in the book of Esther: **"Then Esther the queen,** the daughter of Abihail, and Mordecai the Jew, **wrote** all the acts of power, to confirm this second letter of Purim" (Esther 9:29), **and it is written there: "Then Baruch answered them: He pronounced all these words to me with his mouth, and I wrote them with ink on the parchment"** (Jeremiah 36:18). Just as there the writing was with ink on parchment, so too here, a Megilla must be written with ink on parchment.[H]

מתני׳ בֶּן עִיר שֶׁהָלַךְ לִכְרַךְ וּבֶן כְּרַךְ שֶׁהָלַךְ לְעִיר, אִם עָתִיד לַחֲזוֹר לִמְקוֹמוֹ – קוֹרֵא כִּמְקוֹמוֹ, וְאִם לָאו – קוֹרֵא עִמָּהֶן.

MISHNA With regard to **a resident of an** unwalled **town who went to a walled city,** where the Megilla is read on the fifteenth of Adar, and conversely, **a resident of a walled city who went to an** unwalled **town** where it is read on the fourteenth, the following distinction applies: **If he is destined to return to his** original **place, he reads** it **according to the** *halakha* governing **his** own **place, and if not,** i.e., if he is not destined to return to his place, **he reads with them,** the residents of his current location.

וּמֵהֵיכָן קוֹרֵא אָדָם אֶת הַמְּגִילָּה וְיוֹצֵא בָּהּ יְדֵי חוֹבָתוֹ? רַבִּי מֵאִיר אוֹמֵר: כּוּלָּהּ, רַבִּי יְהוּדָה אוֹמֵר: מֵ״אִישׁ יְהוּדִי״. רַבִּי יוֹסֵי אוֹמֵר: מֵ״אַחַר הַדְּבָרִים הָאֵלֶּה״.

Beginning **from where must a person read the Megilla in order to fulfill his obligation? Rabbi Meir says:** He must read **all of it. Rabbi Yehuda says:** He need read only **from** "There was **a certain Jew"** (Esther 2:5). **Rabbi Yosei says: From "After these things"** (Esther 3:1).

BACKGROUND

Processed with salt and flour – דִּמְלִיחַ וּקְמִיחַ: There were several methods used to process hides in ancient times. It appears that hide prepared for writing parchment was first processed with salt and then with a mixture of salt and other substances. The final step was to process it again with gall juice to prevent the ink from fading. *Diftera* is a kind of parchment that was not fully processed.

Maḥaka – מַחֲקָא: According to the opinion that the reference is not to paper, it is apparently referring to what is called in other places *matza*, which is skin that is almost completely crude, meaning that it had its hair removed but was not properly processed with salt and gall.

NOTES

Neyar, maḥaka – נְיָיר, מַחֲקָא: The commentaries disagree as to the meaning of these words. Some say that they are similar to modern paper (Rashi), and others say that it means parchment that was written on and then erased (Rav Natan *Av HaYeshiva*; see Meiri). Still others explain that it is parchment that underwent only partial processing (*Arukh*).

Derived by verbal analogy between writing and writing – אָתְיָא כְּתִיבָה כְּתִיבָה: The Ramban explains the Gemara's discussion as follows: The Gemara later tells us that the Megilla is referred to as a book, meaning that it is similar in its *halakhot* to a Torah scroll, and is also referred to as a letter. Consequently, it has some similarities to the *halakhot* pertaining to Torah scrolls and certain dissimilarities, and the Gemara finds it necessary to offer proofs with regard to various details of *halakhot* for writing a Megilla. The Gemara apparently concludes that with regard to issues relating to writing, such as the requirement for ink and parchment, the *halakhot* of a Torah scroll apply to the Megilla, and with regard to other matters it is considered only a letter, and the stringencies of the Torah scroll do not apply to it.

גמ׳ אָמַר רָבָא: לֹא שָׁנוּ אֶלָּא שֶׁעָתִיד לַחֲזוֹר בְּלֵילֵי אַרְבָּעָה עָשָׂר, אֲבָל אֵין עָתִיד לַחֲזוֹר בְּלֵילֵי אַרְבָּעָה עָשָׂר – קוֹרֵא עִמָּהֶן. אָמַר רָבָא: מְנָא אָמִינָא לָהּ – דִּכְתִיב ״עַל כֵּן הַיְּהוּדִים הַפְּרָזִים הַיּוֹשְׁבִים בְּעָרֵי הַפְּרָזוֹת״, מִכְּדִי כְּתִיב ״הַיְּהוּדִים הַפְּרָזִים״ לָמָּה לִי לְמִיכְתַּב ״הַיּוֹשְׁבִים בְּעָרֵי הַפְּרָזוֹת״? הָא קָא מַשְׁמַע לָן: דִּפְרוּז בֶּן יוֹמוֹ נִקְרָא פָּרוּז.

GEMARA Rava said: **They taught** the mishna that one who is destined to return to his own place reads according to the *halakha* governing his own place **only** with regard to **one who is destined to return**[N] to his own place **on the night of the fourteenth** of Adar. **But if he is not destined to return on the night of the fourteenth, although** he does intend to return to his own place eventually, **he reads with** the residents of his current location.[H] **Rava said: From where do I say this? As it is written: "Therefore the Jews of unwalled towns, who dwell in the unwalled towns,** make the fourteenth day of the month Adar a day of gladness and feasting" (Esther 9:19). **Since it is** already **written: "The Jews of unwalled towns," why do I** need it **to write** further, **"who dwell in the unwalled towns"?** It comes to **teach us this: That one who is in an unwalled town** even **for the day is** also **called one who** lives **in an unwalled town.**

אַשְׁכְּחַן פָּרוּז, מוּקָף מְנָא לָן? סְבָרָא הוּא, מִדִּפְרוּז בֶּן יוֹמוֹ קָרוּי פָּרוּז – מוּקָף בֶּן יוֹמוֹ קָרוּי מוּקָף.

The Gemara asks: **We have found** proof for a resident of a walled city who is temporarily located in **an unwalled town.** But **from where do we** derive the opposite case, that one from an unwalled town who is temporarily in **a walled city** is governed by a similar *halakha*? The Gemara answers: **It is** based on **logical reasoning: Since one who is in an unwalled town for the day is called someone from an unwalled town,** so too conversely, **one who is in a walled city for a day is called someone from a walled city.**

וְאָמַר רָבָא: בֶּן כְּפָר שֶׁהָלַךְ לָעִיר – בֵּין כָּךְ וּבֵין כָּךְ קוֹרֵא עִמָּהֶן. מַאי טַעְמָא? הַאי כִּבְנֵי הָעִיר בָּעֵי לְמִקְרֵי, וְרַבָּנַן הוּא דְּאַקִּילוּ עַל הַכְּפָרִים כְּדֵי שֶׁיְּסַפְּקוּ מַיִם וּמָזוֹן לַאֲחֵיהֶם שֶׁבַּכְּרַכִּין. הָנֵי מִילֵּי – כִּי אִיתֵיהּ בְּדוּכְתֵּיהּ, אֲבָל כִּי אִיתֵיהּ בָּעִיר – כִּבְנֵי עִיר בָּעֵי לְמִקְרֵי.

And Rava said further: **Someone from a village, where** the Megilla is read on the Monday or Thursday prior to Purim (2a), **who went to a town, reads** the Megilla **with** the residents of the town, even if he had already read it in his own place. He does so **in all circumstances,** whether or not he will be returning to his own village. The Gemara explains: **What is the reason** for this ruling? **This** villager **should** actually have **read** at the same time **as the residents of the towns, but the Sages showed leniency toward the** people of the **villages** and allowed them to advance their reading of the Megilla to the previous day of assembly **so that they** would be free to **supply water and food to their brethren in the cities** on the day of Purim. **This,** however, **applies** only **when** the villager **is in his place,** in the village, **but when he is in a town, he is required to read like the residents of the town,** and not like the villagers.

אֵיתִיבֵיהּ אַבַּיֵּי: בֶּן כְּרַךְ שֶׁהָלַךְ לָעִיר – בֵּין כָּךְ וּבֵין כָּךְ קוֹרֵא כִּמְקוֹמוֹ. בֶּן כְּרַךְ סָלְקָא דַּעְתָּךְ? בְּאִם עָתִיד לַחֲזוֹר תַּלְיָא מִילְּתָא! אֶלָּא לָאו – בֶּן כְּפָר!

Abaye raised an objection to Rava from a *baraita*: **A resident of a walled city who went to** an unwalled **town, in all circumstances,** whether or not he will be returning to his own city, **reads** the Megilla **according to** the *halakha* governing **his** permanent **place.** The Gemara first questions the text of the *baraita* as it is currently worded: **Can it enter your mind that the resident of a walled city** always reads in accordance with the *halakha* governing his own place, even if he is currently situated in an unwalled town? But doesn't **the matter depend on whether** or not **he will be returning** on Purim to his hometown, as stated in the mishna? Therefore, it is clear that the *baraita* must be emended. **Rather, is it not** to be changed to: **A resident of a village** who went to an unwalled town? The *baraita* therefore teaches that a resident of a village who is visiting in a town must read the Megilla according to the *halakha* governing his own place, the village, unlike Rava's teaching.

וְלָאו תֵּרוּצֵי מְתָרְצַתְּ? תְּנֵי: קוֹרֵא עִמָּהֶן.

The Gemara rejects this: **But did you not emend** the reading in the *baraita*? Since you admit that the *baraita* in any event requires revision, change it further and **teach: He reads** the Megilla **with** the residents of the town. This wording in the *baraita* would then support the opinion of Rava.

״מֵהֵיכָן קוֹרֵא אָדָם אֶת הַמְּגִילָּה״ וכו׳: תַּנְיָא, רַבִּי שִׁמְעוֹן בַּר יוֹחַאי אוֹמֵר: מִ״בַּלַּיְלָה הַהוּא״.

§ The mishna teaches that three Sages disagree about the question: Beginning **from where must a person read the Megilla** in order to fulfill his obligation? **It is taught** in a *baraita* that there is a fourth opinion as well: **Rabbi Shimon bar Yoḥai says:** One must start to read from **"On that night"** (Esther 6:1).

NOTES

They taught the mishna only with regard to one who is destined to return – לֹא שָׁנוּ אֶלָּא שֶׁעָתִיד לַחֲזוֹר: There are two main approaches to understanding Rava's statement. The discussion revolves around the question of whether or not Rava was specifically discussing residents of walled cities when he mentioned: The night of the fourteenth (Rashi), or referring to residents of both walled cities and unwalled towns (Rosh). Practically speaking, then, according to Rashi, the *halakha* depends on one's intended location at the time they read in his own dwelling place: If he intends to be in his hometown on the day they read, he reads with them. If he intends to be in a different place at that time he should read in accordance with the *halakha* governing that different place. According to the Rosh, however, the *halakha* depends on one's intended location on the fourteenth of Adar. Other early commentaries as well (Ran; Ritva) discuss these two approaches at length, as well as several approaches in between (Rabbi Zeraḥya HaLevi; Ra'avad; Rashba). The opinions of the Rif and the Rambam are unclear, and are subject to much discussion (see *Peri Megadim*).

HALAKHA

A resident of a town who went to a walled city – בֶּן עִיר שֶׁהָלַךְ לִכְרַךְ: With regard to a resident of an unwalled town who went to a walled city or a resident of a walled city who went to an unwalled town, if he intends to return to his original place when the Megilla is read, he reads like the people of his place, even if he did not yet return. And if he does not intend to return by the time the Megilla is read, he should read in accordance with the custom of where he is presently, as the *halakha* is in accordance with the opinion of Rava. There is a fundamental dispute among the early commentaries with regard to the details of this *halakha*, and there are many variations within the main opinions. It appears that most of halakhic authorities follow Rashi's interpretation of the passage (see *Mishna Berura*, *Yemei HaPurim*, and other contemporary sources).

If one leaves an unwalled town for a walled city on the fourteenth of Adar, without intending to return shortly, he must read in both places (*Mishna Berura*, citing Vilna Gaon), though some dispute this (*Kaf HaḤayyim*). Conversely, one who leaves a walled city on the fourteenth of Adar is exempt from Megilla reading in both places (Rema MiPano). All these opinions are based on the Jerusalem Talmud. It is also taught there that one who is traveling in a desert or on a ship reads the Megilla on the fourteenth of Adar, even if he lives in a walled city (*Shulḥan Arukh*, *Oraḥ Ḥayyim* 688:5, and in the comment of Rema).

אָמַר רַבִּי יוֹחָנָן: וְכוּלָּן מִקְרָא אֶחָד דָּרְשׁוּ: ״וַתִּכְתֹּב אֶסְתֵּר הַמַּלְכָּה...וּמָרְדֳּכַי הַיְּהוּדִי אֶת כׇּל תּוֹקֶף״. מַאן דְּאָמַר כּוּלָּהּ – תּוֹקְפּוֹ שֶׁל אֲחַשְׁוֵרוֹשׁ,

Rabbi Yoḥanan said: And all of these *tanna'im*, in arriving at their respective opinions, **were expounding the same verse.** As it is stated: "**Then Esther the queen,** the daughter of Abihail, **and Mordecai the Jew, wrote about all the acts of power** to confirm this second letter of Purim" (Esther 9:29). **The one who said** that the Megilla must be read **in its entirety** interprets "acts of power" as referring to **the power of Ahasuerus,** and so the Megilla must be read from the beginning, where the power of Ahasuerus is recounted.

וּמַאן דְּאָמַר מֵ״אִישׁ יְהוּדִי״ – תּוֹקְפּוֹ שֶׁל מָרְדֳּכַי, וּמַאן דְּאָמַר מֵ״אַחַר הַדְּבָרִים הָאֵלֶּה״ – תּוֹקְפּוֹ שֶׁל הָמָן, וּמַאן דְּאָמַר מִ״בַּלַּיְלָה הַהוּא״ – תּוֹקְפּוֹ שֶׁל נֵס.

And the one who said that it needs to be read **from "There was a certain Jew"** explains that "acts of power" is referring to **the power of Mordecai. And the one who said** that it needs to be read **from "After these things"** maintains that "acts of power" is referring to **the power of Haman. And the one who said** that it needs to be read **from "On that night"** understands that the expression is referring to **the power of the miracle,** which began on that night when Ahasuerus could not sleep, and therefore one must begin reading the Megilla from there.

רַב הוּנָא אָמַר מֵהָכָא: ״וּמָה רָאוּ עַל כָּכָה וּמָה הִגִּיעַ אֲלֵיהֶם״,

Rav Huna said: The four Sages derived their respective opinions **from here:** "Therefore, because of all the words of this letter, **and of that which they saw concerning this matter, and that which had befallen them,** the Jews ordained…that they would keep these two days" (Esther 9:26–27).

מַאן דְּאָמַר כּוּלָּהּ – מָה רָאָה אֲחַשְׁוֵרוֹשׁ שֶׁנִּשְׁתַּמֵּשׁ בַּכֵּלִים שֶׁל בֵּית הַמִּקְדָּשׁ ״עַל כָּכָה״ – מִשּׁוּם דְּחָשֵׁיב שִׁבְעִים שְׁנִין וְלָא אִיפְּרוּק. ״וּמָה הִגִּיעַ אֲלֵיהֶם״ – דִּקְטַל וַשְׁתִּי.

Rav Huna continued: **The one who said** that the Megilla must be read **in its entirety** explains the verse as follows: "They saw" refers to what **Ahasuerus saw, in that he used the vessels of the Temple. "Concerning this matter"** was **because he had calculated seventy years** from the Babylonian exile **and** the Jews **were** still **not redeemed,** and he consequently thought that they would never enjoy deliverance. **"And that which had befallen them"** is referring to the fact **that he had killed Vashti.** Since the Megilla was written and continues to be read in order to inform future generations of all these events and what had happened to the people who were involved, and these are detailed at the beginning of the Megilla, it must be read in its entirety.

וּמַאן דְּאָמַר ״מֵאִישׁ יְהוּדִי״, מָה רָאָה מָרְדֳּכַי דְּאִיקַּנֵּי בְּהָמָן ״עַל כָּכָה״ – דְּשַׁוִּי נַפְשֵׁיהּ עֲבוֹדָה זָרָה, וּמָה הִגִּיעַ אֲלֵיהֶם – דְּאִתְרְחִישׁ נִיסָּא.

And the one who said that the Megilla needs to be read **from "There was a certain Jew"** interprets this verse as follows: **That which Mordecai "saw" in that he acted** so **zealously concerning Haman. "Concerning this matter"** was **because Haman had made himself** an object of **idol worship. "And that which had befallen them"** is referring to the fact **that a miracle took place.** Therefore one must read the Megilla from "There was a certain man," where all this is recounted.

וּמַאן דְּאָמַר ״מֵאַחַר הַדְּבָרִים הָאֵלֶּה״ מָה רָאָה הָמָן שֶׁנִּתְקַנֵּא בְּכׇל הַיְּהוּדִים ״עַל כָּכָה״ מִשּׁוּם דְּ״מָרְדֳּכַי לֹא יִכְרַע וְלֹא יִשְׁתַּחֲוֶה״, ״וּמָה הִגִּיעַ אֲלֵיהֶם״, ״וְתָלוּ אוֹתוֹ וְאֶת בָּנָיו עַל הָעֵץ״.

And the one who said that it needs to be read **from "After these things"** interprets the verse in this way: **That which Haman "saw" in that he became incensed with all the Jews. "Concerning this matter"** was **because "Mordecai did not bow down, nor prostrate himself before him"** (Esther 3:2). **"And that which had befallen them"** is referring to the fact that **"he and his sons were hanged on the gallows"** (Esther 9:25). Accordingly, the Megilla must be read from the first mention of Haman.

וּמַאן דְּאָמַר מִ״בַּלַּיְלָה הַהוּא״, מָה רָאָה אֲחַשְׁוֵרוֹשׁ לְהָבִיא אֶת סֵפֶר הַזִּכְרוֹנוֹת ״עַל כָּכָה״ – דְּזַמִּינְתֵּיהּ אֶסְתֵּר לְהָמָן בַּהֲדֵיהּ, ״וּמָה הִגִּיעַ אֲלֵיהֶם״ – דְּאִתְרְחִישׁ נִיסָּא.

And the one who said that the Megilla must be read **from "On that night"** offers the following explanation: **That which Ahasuerus "saw"** in that he commanded **to bring the book of chronicles** before him. **"Concerning this matter"** was **because Esther had invited Haman** along **with him** to the banquet she made. **"And that which had befallen them"** is referring to the fact **that a miracle took place.** And therefore one must read the Megilla from "On that night the king could not sleep and he commanded to bring the book of chronicles."

אָמַר רַבִּי חֶלְבּוֹ אָמַר רַב חָמָא בַּר גּוּרְיָא אָמַר רַב: הֲלָכָה כְּדִבְרֵי הָאוֹמֵר כּוּלָּהּ. וַאֲפִילּוּ לְמַאן דְּאָמַר ״מֵאִישׁ יְהוּדִי״ – צְרִיכָה שֶׁתְּהֵא כְּתוּבָה כּוּלָּהּ.

Rabbi Ḥelbo[P] **said** that **Rav Ḥama bar Gurya said** that **Rav said: The** *halakha* **is in accordance with the statement of the one who says** that the Megilla must be read **in its entirety.**[H] **And** moreover, **even according to the one who said** that it need be read only from **"There was a certain Jew"** and onward, the Megilla itself **must** nevertheless **be written in its entirety.**

PERSONALITIES

Rabbi Ḥelbo – רַבִּי חֶלְבּוֹ: Rabbi Ḥelbo was a Babylonian *amora* of the third generation who moved to Eretz Yisrael. He was a student of Rav Huna and apparently received most of his Torah education from him; indeed, he often quotes Rav Huna. It appears that he went to Eretz Yisrael near the time of Rav Huna's death and was there when the latter's coffin was brought for burial. In Eretz Yisrael he was a student and colleague of the greatest students of Rabbi Yoḥanan and became one of the leaders of the generation and a halakhic codifier. In the area of *aggada* he was a student of Rabbi Shmuel bar Naḥmani and quotes aggadic traditions in his name. Rabbi Ḥelbo settled in Tiberias and was close to Rabbi Yehuda Nesia. The Talmud relates that he had no children.

HALAKHA

From where does one read the Megilla – מֵהֵיכָן קוֹרְאִים בַּמְּגִילָּה: The Megilla is read in its entirety, as Rav rules in accordance with the opinion of Rabbi Meir (*Shulḥan Arukh, Oraḥ Ḥayyim* 690:3).

וְאָמַר רַבִּי חֶלְבּוֹ אָמַר רַב חָמָא בַּר גּוּרְיָא אָמַר רַב: מְגִילָּה נִקְרֵאת סֵפֶר וְנִקְרֵאת אִגֶּרֶת, נִקְרֵאת סֵפֶר – שֶׁאִם תְּפָרָהּ בְּחוּטֵי פִשְׁתָּן פְּסוּלָה, וְנִקְרֵאת אִגֶּרֶת – שֶׁאִם הִטִּיל בָּהּ שְׁלֹשָׁה חוּטֵי גִּידִין כְּשֵׁרָה, אָמַר רַב נַחְמָן: וּבִלְבַד שֶׁיְּהוּ מְשׁוּלָּשִׁין.

And Rabbi Ḥelbo said further that Rav Ḥama bar Gurya said that Rav said: The Megilla is referred to as a "book" (Esther 9:32), and it is also referred to as a "letter" (Esther 9:29). It is called a book, indicating a comparison to the book of the Torah, i.e., to a Torah scroll, to teach us that if one sewed its parchment sheets together with flax threads the Megilla is unfit, just as a Torah scroll sewn in this manner is unfit. And it is called a letter to teach us that if one stitched the Megilla sheets together with only three threads of sinew,[BH] in the manner of a letter, the Megilla is fit for use, as it does not have to be completely stitched like a Torah scroll. Rav Naḥman said: This is true provided that the stitches are made in three parts.[N]

אָמַר רַב יְהוּדָה אָמַר שְׁמוּאֵל: הַקּוֹרֵא בִּמְגִילָּה הַכְּתוּבָה בֵּין הַכְּתוּבִים – לֹא יָצָא. אָמַר רָבָא: לָא אֲמַרַן אֶלָּא דְּלָא מְחַסְּרָא וּמְיַיתְּרָא פּוּרְתָּא, אֲבָל מְחַסְּרָא וּמְיַיתְּרָא פּוּרְתָּא – לֵית לָן בָּהּ.

Rav Yehuda said that Shmuel said: If one reads from a Megilla that was written together with the rest of the Writings he has not fulfilled his obligation, as it must be evident that one is reading specifically from the Megilla rather than simply reading ordinary passages from the Bible. Rava said: We said this only in a case where the parchment of the Megilla is not a little shorter or longer than the parchment of the other biblical books on the scroll and are consequently not plainly discernible among them. But if it is a little shorter or longer than the other sheets of parchment of the other biblical books, we have no problem with it, and one may read from such a scroll.

לֵוִי בַּר שְׁמוּאֵל הֲוָה קָא קָרֵי קַמֵּיהּ דְּרַב יְהוּדָה בִּמְגִילָּה

It was related that Levi bar Shmuel was once reading before Rav Yehuda from a Megilla

HALAKHA

The stitches of the sheets of a Megilla – תְּפִירַת יְרִיעוֹת הַמְּגִילָּה: A Megilla that is stitched with flax threads is unfit. However, it does not need to be stitched entirely like a Torah scroll; it is sufficient that it be stitched with sinews in threes. Since there are several different interpretations of this expression, one should sew three stitches at the top, three at the bottom and three in the middle, and one stitch at the quarter mark from the top and another at the quarter mark from the bottom. If he has sufficient sinews to do so, he should stitch it entirely (Rema), but he should then leave a small space unstitched (*Arukh HaShulḥan*; *Shulḥan Arukh*, *Oraḥ Ḥayyim* 691:5–6, and in the comment of Rema).

NOTES

In three parts – מְשׁוּלָּשִׁין: There are several opinions with regard to the meaning of this expression. Rashi explains that it means that the stitches should be evenly spaced, i.e., that the distance from the edge of the sheet, both at the top and on the bottom, to the first stitch should equal the length of each stitch. Another opinion is that the page should be divided into three equal parts, with one stitch per part (Rabbeinu Ḥananel). The Rambam's opinion is that the Megilla should be stitched in three places, each stitched area itself consisting of three stitches. See HALAKHA.

BACKGROUND

The stitches of the Megilla – תְּפִירוֹת הַמְּגִילָּה: In most cases one piece of hide is not enough to write an entire Megilla, and therefore several sheets of parchment must be attached together. The Sages taught that like the parchment itself, even the stitches must be from a material that comes from an animal, i.e., thin tendons that are made into strings and used to stitch. Since not all the stringencies of a Torah scroll apply to a Megilla, it is not required that one follow the *halakhot* of stitching a Torah scroll, and it is enough that it be sewn with only three stitches.

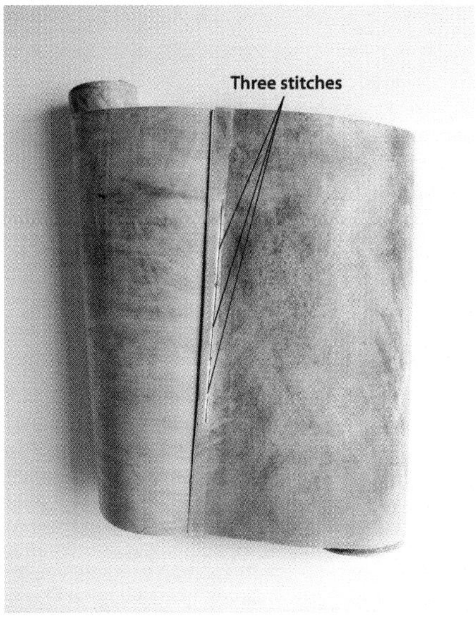

Two pieces of parchment connected by three stitches

Perek **II**
Daf **19** Amud **b**

הַכְּתוּבָה בֵּין הַכְּתוּבִים. אֲמַר לֵיהּ: הֲרֵי אָמְרוּ הַקּוֹרֵא בִּמְגִילָּה הַכְּתוּבָה בֵּין הַכְּתוּבִים לֹא יָצָא.

that was written together with the rest of the Writings.[H] Rav Yehuda said to him: The Sages have said: If one reads from a Megilla that was written together with the rest of the Writings he has not fulfilled his obligation.

HALAKHA

A Megilla that was written together with the rest of the Writings – מְגִילָּה הַכְּתוּבָה בֵּין הַכְּתוּבִים: A Megilla that was written together with the rest of the Writings may not be read for the public, in accordance with the opinion of Rabbi Yoḥanan. Even after the fact, if one has read from such a text, he has fulfilled his obligation only if the parchment of the book of Esther is bigger or smaller than the other parchments of the scroll, so that it is distinguishable as an independent entity. However, a private individual may read from such a text and fulfill his obligation, provided it is written as a scroll, as opposed to bound books, which are common nowadays. Some say that an individual may read from such a scroll even *ab initio* (Vilna Gaon, citing Rosh; *Shulḥan Arukh*, *Oraḥ Ḥayyim* 691:8).

אָמַר רַבִּי חִיָּיא בַּר אַבָּא אָמַר רַבִּי יוֹחָנָן: הַקּוֹרֵא בִּמְגִילָּה הַכְּתוּבָה בֵּין הַכְּתוּבִים – לֹא יָצָא. וּמָחוּ לָהּ אַמּוֹחָא: בְּצִבּוּר שָׁנוּ.

Rabbi Ḥiyya bar Abba said that **Rabbi Yoḥanan said: If one reads from a Megilla that was written together with** the rest of **the Writings he has not fulfilled** his obligation. **But they hit** this *halakha* **on its head,**[N] i.e., immediately after reporting this ruling they added a qualification that removed much of its force: **They taught** this *halakha* only with respect **to** reading the Megilla for **a congregation.**[N] An individual who reads the Megilla in private fulfills his obligation even if the Megilla was written together with the rest of the Writings. Only when it is read in public must it be from a Megilla that is a separate scroll.

וְאָמַר רַבִּי חִיָּיא בַּר אַבָּא אָמַר רַבִּי יוֹחָנָן: שִׁיּוּר הַתֶּפֶר – הֲלָכָה לְמֹשֶׁה מִסִּינַי. וּמָחוּ לָהּ אַמּוֹחָא: וְלֹא אָמְרוּ אֶלָּא כְּדֵי שֶׁלֹּא יִקָּרַע.

Rabbi Ḥiyya bar Abba also **said** that **Rabbi Yoḥanan said:** The *halakha* of **leaving** a space without **stitches,**[H] i.e., that the parchment sheets of a Torah scroll must not be sewn all the way to the edge, but rather a small margin must be left at the top and at the bottom, **is a** ***halakha*** transmitted **to Moses from Sinai,** i.e., it was not written in the Torah but was received in the framework of the Oral Law. **But they** immediately **hit** this *halakha* **on its head,** explaining that this *halakha* is not due to the special sanctity of a Torah scroll; rather, **they said** that it is **only so that it not rip.** If the scroll is wound too forcefully, the sheets of parchment will begin to spread apart since they are not sewn together at their extremities, and the one who is winding will cease to wind it so forcefully. If the stitching went all the way to the end there would be no such warning and the stitches would cause the parchment to rip.

וְאָמַר רַבִּי חִיָּיא בַּר אַבָּא אָמַר רַבִּי יוֹחָנָן: אִלְמָלֵי נִשְׁתַּיֵּיר בַּמְּעָרָה שֶׁעָמַד בָּהּ מֹשֶׁה וְאֵלִיָּהוּ כִּמְלֹא נֶקֶב מַחַט סִדְקִית – לֹא הָיוּ יְכוֹלִין לַעֲמוֹד מִפְּנֵי הָאוֹרָה, שֶׁנֶּאֱמַר "כִּי לֹא יִרְאַנִי הָאָדָם וָחָי".

And Rabbi Ḥiyya bar Abba also **said** that **Rabbi Yoḥanan said: Had there been left** open **a crack** so much as **the size of small sewing needle in the cave**[N] **in which Moses and Elijah stood** when God's glory was revealed to them, as it is written: "And it shall come to pass, while My glory passes by, that I will put you in a cleft of the rock" (Exodus 33:22), and: "And he came there to a cave…and, behold, the Lord passed by" (I Kings 19:9–11), **they would not have been able to endure due to the** intense **light** that would have entered that crack, **as it is stated: "For no man shall see Me and live"** (Exodus 33:20).

וְאָמַר רַבִּי חִיָּיא בַּר אַבָּא אָמַר רַבִּי יוֹחָנָן: מַאי דִּכְתִיב "וַעֲלֵיהֶם כְּכָל הַדְּבָרִים אֲשֶׁר דִּבֶּר ה׳ עִמָּכֶם בָּהָר"? מְלַמֵּד שֶׁהֶרְאָהוּ הַקָּדוֹשׁ בָּרוּךְ הוּא לְמֹשֶׁה דִּקְדּוּקֵי תוֹרָה וְדִקְדּוּקֵי סוֹפְרִים, וּמַה שֶּׁהַסּוֹפְרִים עֲתִידִין לְחַדֵּשׁ, וּמַאי נִיהוּ – מִקְרָא מְגִילָּה.

And Rabbi Ḥiyya bar Abba further **said** that **Rabbi Yoḥanan said: What is** the meaning of that **which is written:** "And the Lord delivered to me two tablets of stone written with the finger of God; **and on them was written according to all the words**[N] **which the Lord spoke with you in the mountain**" (Deuteronomy 9:10)? **This teaches that the Holy One, Blessed be He, showed Moses** on the mountain all **the inferences** that can be derived from the words of **the Torah; and** all **the inferences** that can be derived from the words **of the Scribes,**[N] the early Sages; **and** also **all** the new *halakhot* **that the Scribes were destined to introduce** in the future in addition to the laws of the Torah. **And what is it** specifically that the Scribes would introduce in addition to the laws of the Torah? **The reading of the Megilla.**

NOTES

But they hit this *halakha* on its head – וּמָחוּ לָהּ אַמּוֹחָא: This expression means that the scope and strength of the previously stated *halakha* is diminished, though not invalidated completely. It appears that the mitigation of the *halakha* was stated by a later Sage than the one who had stated the original *halakha* (Rav Ya'akov Emden), although it is also possible to explain that the same Sage who said the first statement subjected it to a more restricted interpretation afterward.

They taught this only with respect to a congregation – בְּצִבּוּר שָׁנוּ: Many commentaries note the difficulty in saying that there is an activity that each individual may do on his own, i.e., read the Megilla from a scroll containing other books of the Bible, whereas if this same act were done in public the reading would be invalid. The *Turei Even* suggests that when the Gemara rules that it may not be done in public, it is referring not to a reading that happens to be done with a congregation, but to those situations in which the Megilla is required to be read with a congregation, as previously discussed (5a; see *Sefat Emet*). However, bearing in mind the reasons given for not reading a Megilla that is written on a scroll with other biblical passages, the Gemara may be understood in its plain sense. Some of these reasons are: (1) Unlearned people may not realize that a special reading is taking place, but will think that it is just an ordinary biblical excerpt being read (Jerusalem Talmud); (2) It is an embarrassment for the congregation that they do not possess a separate Megilla scroll (Ran); and (3) Reading from a Megilla written with other biblical passages diminishes the publicizing of the Purim miracle, but when the reading is done in private there is in any event no publicity (Ritva).

HALAKHA

Leaving a space without stitches – שִׁיּוּר הַתֶּפֶר: When the sheets of a Torah scroll or a Megilla are stitched, an unstitched space must be left at the top and the bottom of the sheet so that it not rip. A minimal margin is sufficient. After the fact, if a margin was not left unstitched, the Torah is fit nevertheless (*Arukh HaShulḥan*; *Shulḥan Arukh, Oraḥ Ḥayyim* 691:7 and *Yoreh De'a* 278:1).

NOTES

Had there been left a crack…in the cave – אִלְמָלֵי נִשְׁתַּיֵּיר בַּמְּעָרָה: When Moses was in the cave, God said, "And I will cover you with My hand until I have passed by" (Exodus 33:22), meaning that God blocked Moses' vision so that nothing would be seen (Maharsha). See Guide of the Perplexed for an explanation of these concepts.

And on them was written according to all the words – וַעֲלֵיהֶם כְּכָל הַדְּבָרִים: The Gemara explains that this expression includes all the inferences that can be derived from the words of the Torah. This is based on the seemingly superfluous word "all." And from the expression "according to all the words," which in Hebrew could also mean "like all the words," the Gemara derives that there are other *halakhot* like the words of the Torah, i.e., the new *halakhot* that the Scribes were destined to introduce in the future, such as the reading of the Megilla, in addition to the laws of the Torah (Maharsha).

The inferences from the words of the Torah and the inferences from the words of the Scribes – דִּקְדּוּקֵי תוֹרָה וְדִקְדּוּקֵי סוֹפְרִים: The early and later commentaries discuss this principle at length. The *Derashot HaRan* explains that not only was the Torah given to Moses, but also all the various approaches of interpretation found in halakhic midrash and aggadic midrash, as well as the questions and dilemmas that the sages of future generations would raise. Although these matters are decided according to the opinion of the majority of sages in those generations, nevertheless all the concepts involved were shown to Moses, along with the stipulation that in all such disputes the majority opinion should be followed.

מתני׳ הַכֹּל כְּשֵׁרִין לִקְרוֹת אֶת הַמְּגִילָּה חוּץ מֵחֵרֵשׁ שׁוֹטֶה וְקָטָן, רַבִּי יְהוּדָה מַכְשִׁיר בְּקָטָן.

MISHNA **Everyone is fit to read the Megilla,**[H] **except for a deaf person,**[N] **an imbecile, and a minor. Rabbi Yehuda** disagrees and **says that a minor is fit** to read the Megilla.

גמ׳ מַאן תְּנָא חֵרֵשׁ דִּיעֲבַד נַמִּי לָא? – אָמַר רַב מַתָּנָה: רַבִּי יוֹסֵי הִיא, דִּתְנַן: הַקּוֹרֵא אֶת שְׁמַע וְלֹא הִשְׁמִיעַ לְאָזְנוֹ – יָצָא, רַבִּי יוֹסֵי אוֹמֵר: לֹא יָצָא.

GEMARA The Gemara asks: **Who is the** ***tanna*** **that taught** that the reading of **a deaf person, even after the fact, no,** it is not valid? **Rav Mattana said: It is Rabbi Yosei,**[N] **as we learned** in a mishna elsewhere (*Berakhot* 15a): **If one recites the** ***Shema*** **but does not make it audible to his ears, he has** nevertheless **fulfilled** his obligation. This is the statement of Rabbi Yehuda. **Rabbi Yosei said: He has not fulfilled** his obligation. Rabbi Yosei's statement implies that one who does not hear what he is saying does not fulfill his obligation. Presumably the *halakhot* for *Shema* recitation and Megilla reading are equivalent.

וּמִמַּאי דְּרַבִּי יוֹסֵי הִיא, וְדִיעֲבַד נַמִּי לָא? דִּלְמָא רַבִּי יְהוּדָה הִיא, וּלְכַתְּחִלָּה הוּא דְּלָא, הָא דִּיעֲבַד – שַׁפִּיר דָּמֵי!

The Gemara questions the assumption on which the previous discussion is based: **But from where** do you know that the mishna, which states that a deaf person may not read the Megilla, reflects the opinion of **Rabbi Yosei,** and that it means to say that **even after the fact, no,** one does not fulfill his obligation if the Megilla is read by a deaf person? **Perhaps** the mishna was taught in accordance with the opinion of **Rabbi Yehuda, and** it should be understood as saying that a deaf person **may not** read ***ab initio*****, but after the fact** his reading **is valid.**

לָא סָלְקָא דַּעְתָּךְ, דְּקָתָנֵי חֵרֵשׁ דּוּמְיָא דְּשׁוֹטֶה וְקָטָן, מָה שׁוֹטֶה וְקָטָן דִּיעֲבַד נַמִּי לָא, אַף חֵרֵשׁ – דִּיעֲבַד נַמִּי לָא.

The Gemara rejects this proposal: **This should not enter your mind, as** the mishna **teaches** the *halakha* of a deaf person, an imbecile, and a minor together, implying that **a deaf person is similar to an imbecile or a minor.** Therefore, it may be inferred that **just as** the readings of **an imbecile and a minor** are **not** valid **even after the fact, so too, even after the fact, no,** the reading of **a deaf person** is not valid.

וְדִלְמָא הָא כִּדְאִיתָא וְהָא כִּדְאִיתָא! – מִדְּקָתָנֵי סֵיפָא: רַבִּי יְהוּדָה מַכְשִׁיר בְּקָטָן – מִכְּלָל דְּרֵישָׁא לָאו רַבִּי יְהוּדָה הִיא.

The Gemara asks: **But perhaps** it is not so that all three cases are equivalent. Perhaps with regard to the imbecile and the minor, **this** *halakha* is **as it is, and** with regard to a deaf person, **that** *halakha* is **as it is.** Although all three cases are taught together, this may be merely because in all three cases he may not read *ab initio*; there may be a difference between them with regard to their status after the fact. It is possible that the mishna means that the reading of a deaf person is valid after the fact, and is citing the opinion of Rabbi Yehuda. The Gemara rejects this: It is impossible to say that the anonymous first *tanna* of the mishna is Rabbi Yehuda, as **from** the fact **that the latter clause teaches: Rabbi Yehuda says that a minor is fit, it may be inferred that the first clause** of the mishna **was not** taught by **Rabbi Yehuda.**

HALAKHA

Everyone is fit to read the Megilla – הַכֹּל כְּשֵׁרִין לִקְרוֹת אֶת הַמְּגִילָּה: Anyone who is obligated to read the Megilla may read it for himself and for others. However, some say a man who hears a woman reading the Megilla does not fulfill his obligation.

Most of the halakhic authorities rule that one cannot fulfill his obligation by hearing the Megilla read by a deaf person, in accordance with the opinion of the first *tanna* (see *Taz*). Others write that after the fact, he has fulfilled his obligation, in accordance with the opinion of Rabbi Yehuda (*Baḥ*, citing Rashba; *Shulḥan Arukh, Oraḥ Ḥayyim* 689:2).

NOTES

Except for a deaf person – חוּץ מֵחֵרֵשׁ: The deaf person mentioned here is different from the standard deaf-mute mentioned in every other place in the Talmud, as usually this term refers to someone who is incapable of both hearing and speaking. Such an individual is often classified along with an imbecile and a minor, under the assumption that his mental capacity is quite low due to his inability to communicate verbally.

The deaf person here, however, is able to speak, since he is capable of reading the Megilla. Consequently, he is considered to be on a par with hearing people. His only disability is that he cannot hear the words he says, as the Gemara discusses in detail.

The early commentaries, and to an even greater extent the later commentaries, distinguish between a hearing individual who did not make his voice heard because he did not speak loudly enough, as in the case of reciting the *Shema*, and a deaf person who does not have the ability to hear himself even if he speaks loudly. Some explain that the essence of the mitzva of Megilla is to read it, not to hear it, but the reading of an individual who cannot hear what he says is considered deficient (*Sefat Emet*).

In the Jerusalem Talmud, a different approach to the term deaf is presented. There it is stated that the deaf person in the mishna is a deaf-mute. Consequently, this term does not belong in the mishna at all, as a deaf-mute by definition cannot possibly read the Megilla (Rid). Despite the word's irrelevance, it is mentioned here along with the imbecile and the minor only because these three terms are so often grouped together throughout the Talmud.

The opinion of Rabbi Yosei – שִׁיטַת רַבִּי יוֹסֵי: In the Jerusalem Talmud it is explained that the opinion of Rabbi Yosei is based on the verse: "And you will give ear to his mitzvot" (Exodus 15:26), indicating that all mitzvot that involve recitation must also include hearing.

וְדִלְמָא כּוּלָּהּ רַבִּי יְהוּדָה הִיא? מִי דָּמֵי? רֵישָׁא לִפְסוּלָה וְסֵיפָא לְכַשֵּׁירָה.

The Gemara continues to ask: **But perhaps** the mishna **in its entirety was** taught by **Rabbi Yehuda** after all, but the first clause of the mishna was taught anonymously, whereas the latter clause was taught explicitly in the name of Rabbi Yehuda. The Gemara rejects this argument: **Are** the two parts of the mishna **comparable,** that they can be associated with a single Sage? **The first clause** of the mishna comes **to disqualify** the reading of a minor, **whereas the latter clause** comes **to declare** a minor **fit.** These two contradictory opinions therefore cannot be understood as the statement of a single Sage.

וְדִלְמָא כּוּלָּהּ רַבִּי יְהוּדָה הִיא, וּתְרֵי גַּוְונֵי קָטָן קָתָנֵי לַהּ, וְחַסּוּרֵי מִיחַסְּרָא וְהָכִי קָתָנֵי: הַכֹּל כְּשֵׁרִין לִקְרוֹת אֶת הַמְּגִילָּה חוּץ מֵחֵרֵשׁ שׁוֹטֶה וְקָטָן, בַּמֶּה דְּבָרִים אֲמוּרִים – בְּקָטָן שֶׁלֹּא הִגִּיעַ לְחִינּוּךְ, אֲבָל בְּקָטָן שֶׁהִגִּיעַ לְחִינּוּךְ – אֲפִילּוּ לְכַתְּחִלָּה, שֶׁרַבִּי יְהוּדָה מַכְשִׁיר בְּקָטָן.

The Gemara asks: **But perhaps** the mishna **in its entirety** expresses the opinion of **Rabbi Yehuda** after all. **And it is teaching** the *halakha* concerning **two** different **types of minors, and** the mishna **is incomplete,** lacking some words of elaboration, **and is teaching the following: Everyone is fit to read the Megilla except for a deaf person, an imbecile, and a minor. In what** case **is this statement said?** Only **with regard to a minor who has not reached** the age of **training** in mitzvot. **But a minor who has reached** the age of **training** in mitzvot may read the Megilla **even *ab initio*, as Rabbi Yehuda says that a minor** who has reached that requisite age **is fit** to read the Megilla.

בְּמַאי אוֹקֵימְתָּא – כְּרַבִּי יְהוּדָה, וְדִיעֲבַד.

The Gemara raises a difficulty with this interpretation of the mishna: **In what** manner **did you establish** the mishna? You established it as being **in accordance with** the opinion of **Rabbi Yehuda,** and you understand the opinion of Rabbi Yehuda to be that a deaf person is disqualified from reading the Megilla *ab initio*, but **after the fact** his reading is valid.

אֶלָּא הָא דְּתָנֵי (רַבִּי) יְהוּדָה בְּרֵיהּ דְּרַבִּי שִׁמְעוֹן בֶּן פָּזִי: חֵרֵשׁ הַמְדַבֵּר וְאֵינוֹ שׁוֹמֵעַ – תּוֹרֵם לְכַתְּחִלָּה, מַנִּי? אִי רַבִּי יְהוּדָה – דִּיעֲבַד אִין, לְכַתְּחִלָּה לָא. אִי רַבִּי יוֹסֵי – דִּיעֲבַד נָמֵי לָא!

But then **that which Rabbi Yehuda, son of Rabbi Shimon ben Pazi, taught** will present a difficulty, as he taught a *baraita*: **A deaf person who can speak but cannot hear may set aside *teruma*** even ***ab initio*,** although he cannot hear himself reciting the blessing that is recited before setting aside *teruma*. Upon **whose** opinion is this *baraita* based? **If** you say it is in accordance with the opinion of **Rabbi Yehuda,** that cannot be, as you have established that Rabbi Yehuda maintains that if one recites something and does not hear it, **after the fact, yes,** his action is valid, but he should **not** do so ***ab initio*. And if** you say it is in accordance with the opinion of **Rabbi Yosei,** this is even more difficult, as he maintains that **even after the fact, no,** his action is not valid. Who, then, is the Sage who would say that a deaf person may set aside *teruma* even *ab initio*?

וְאֶלָּא מַאי – רַבִּי יְהוּדָה וַאֲפִילּוּ לְכַתְּחִלָּה? אֶלָּא הָא דְּתַנְיָא: לֹא יְבָרֵךְ אָדָם בִּרְכַּת הַמָּזוֹן בְּלִבּוֹ, וְאִם בֵּירַךְ – יָצָא, מַנִּי? לָא רַבִּי יְהוּדָה וְלָא רַבִּי יוֹסֵי. אִי רַבִּי יְהוּדָה – אֲפִילּוּ לְכַתְּחִלָּה, אִי רַבִּי יוֹסֵי – אֲפִילּוּ דִּיעֲבַד נָמֵי לָא!

The Gemara rejects this reasoning: **Rather, what** then do you propose to say, that this *baraita* is in accordance with **Rabbi Yehuda and** that Rabbi Yehuda permits a deaf person to read **even *ab initio*,** whereas Rabbi Yosei would disqualify him even after the fact? **But** then **whose is** the opinion that is represented in **that which is taught** in a *baraita*: **A person should not recite the Grace after Meals in his heart,**[H] i.e., inaudibly, **but if he recited** it in this manner, **he has fulfilled** his obligation. It is the opinion of **neither Rabbi Yehuda nor Rabbi Yosei.** As, **if** it follows the opinion of **Rabbi Yehuda,** it should be permitted **even *ab initio*,** and **if** it follows the opinion of **Rabbi Yosei,** then **even after the fact, no,** this should not be valid.

HALAKHA

The Grace after Meals in his heart – בִּרְכַּת הַמָּזוֹן בְּלִבּוֹ: One should recite all blessings loudly enough to hear them himself; however, after the fact, if he did not hear them, he has fulfilled his obligation (Rambam *Sefer Ahava, Hilkhot Berakhot* 1:7).

לְעוֹלָם רַבִּי יְהוּדָה, וַאֲפִילּוּ לְכַתְּחִילָּה. וְלָא קַשְׁיָא; הָא – דִּידֵיהּ, הָא – דְּרַבֵּיהּ.

The Gemara answers: **Actually,** you can indeed say that the *baraita* about *teruma* was taught in accordance with the opinion of **Rabbi Yehuda,** and that Rabbi Yehuda permits a deaf person to read **even *ab initio*,** while Rabbi Yosei disqualifies a deaf person even after the fact. **And** the *baraita* that teaches that one should not recite the Grace after Meals in his heart, but if he did he has fulfilled his obligation, is **not difficult,** as that *baraita* was taught by Rabbi Yehuda as well. The explanation for this is that in **this** *baraita*, about *teruma*, he was teaching **his own** opinion, that it is permitted even *ab initio*, whereas in **that** *baraita*, concerning the Grace after Meals, he was teaching the opinion **of his master,** Rabbi Elazar ben Azarya, that one is required to hear what he is saying when he recites blessings.

דְּתַנְיָא, רַבִּי יְהוּדָה אוֹמֵר מִשּׁוּם רַבִּי אֶלְעָזָר בֶּן עֲזַרְיָה: הַקּוֹרֵא אֶת שְׁמַע צָרִיךְ שֶׁיַּשְׁמִיעַ לְאׇזְנוֹ, שֶׁנֶּאֱמַר: ״שְׁמַע יִשְׂרָאֵל ה׳ אֱלֹהֵינוּ ה׳ אֶחָד״ – הַשְׁמַע לְאׇזְנֶיךָ מַה שֶּׁאַתָּה מוֹצִיא מִפִּיךָ. רַבִּי מֵאִיר אוֹמֵר: ״אֲשֶׁר אָנֹכִי מְצַוְּךָ הַיּוֹם עַל לְבָבֶךָ״ – אַחַר כַּוָּונַת הַלֵּב הֵן הֵן הַדְּבָרִים.

As it is taught in a *baraita*: **Rabbi Yehuda said in the name of Rabbi Elazar ben Azarya: One who recites the *Shema* must make it audible to his ears, as it is stated: "Hear O Israel, the Lord our God; the Lord is One"** (Deuteronomy 6:4), the word "hear" indicating that you should **allow your ears to hear** the words **you are expressing with your mouth. Rabbi Meir** disagrees and **says:** This is not necessary, as it is also stated there: "And these words, **which I command you this day shall be in your heart"** (Deuteronomy 6:6), indicating that "these **words,**" the words of the Shema, go **after the intent of the heart,** as it is unnecessary to pronounce them out loud. We see that according to Rabbi Elazar ben Azarya, as cited by Rabbi Yehuda, the words must be audible to one's ears *ab initio*.

הָשְׁתָּא דְּאָתֵית לְהָכִי, אֲפִילּוּ תֵּימָא רַבִּי יְהוּדָה כְּרַבֵּיהּ סְבִירָא לֵיהּ. וְהָא דְּתָנֵי יְהוּדָה בְּרֵיהּ דְּרַבִּי שִׁמְעוֹן בֶּן פָּזִי – רַבִּי מֵאִיר הִיא.

The Gemara proposes a second solution: **Now that you have arrived at this** point and cited this *baraita*, **you** can **even say that Rabbi Yehuda holds in accordance with his teacher,** Rabbi Elazar ben Azarya, that a deaf person is disqualified *ab initio*, and it is only after the fact that his reading is valid. **And as for that** *baraita* **that Rabbi Yehuda, son of Rabbi Shimon ben Pazi, taught** stating that a deaf person may set aside *teruma* even *ab initio*, this was taught in accordance with the other opinion cited in the *baraita*, i.e., that of **Rabbi Meir,** who maintains that everything depends on the intent of one's heart, and that it is not necessary to pronounce words audibly, even *ab initio*.

רַבִּי יְהוּדָה מַכְשִׁיר בְּקָטָן: (דְּתַנְיָא) אָמַר רַבִּי יְהוּדָה: קָטָן הָיִיתִי וְקָרִיתִיהָ לְמַעְלָה מֵרַבִּי טַרְפוֹן וּזְקֵנִים בְּלוֹד. אָמְרוּ לוֹ: אֵין מְבִיאִין רְאָיָה מִן הַקָּטָן.

§ It was taught in the mishna: **Rabbi Yehuda**[P] **says that a minor is fit** to read the Megilla. **It is taught** in a *baraita*: **Rabbi Yehuda said:** I can offer proof to my opinion, as when **I was a minor** I myself **read** the Megilla **before Rabbi Tarfon and the** other **Elders in Lod. They said to him** in response: **One cannot bring a proof from** the testimony of **a minor.**[N] Since at the time of the supposed incident you were a minor, you are not qualified now to testify about it.

תַּנְיָא, אָמַר רַבִּי קָטָן הָיִיתִי וְקָרִיתִיהָ לְמַעְלָה מֵרַבִּי יְהוּדָה. אָמְרוּ לוֹ: אֵין מְבִיאִין רְאָיָה מִן הַמַּתִּיר.

It is taught in a different *baraita*: **Rabbi** Yehuda HaNasi **said:** When **I was a minor I read** the Megilla **before Rabbi Yehuda. They said to him: One cannot bring a proof** that an act is permitted **from the** behavior of the very **one who permits** it. We know that Rabbi Yehuda maintains that a minor is fit to read the Megilla, and the fact that he acted in accordance with his own opinion does not prove that this is the accepted *halakha*.

וְלֵימְרוּ לֵיהּ: אֵין מְבִיאִין רְאָיָה מִן הַקָּטָן! חֲדָא וְעוֹד קָאָמְרוּ לֵיהּ: חֲדָא – דְּקָטָן הָיִיתָ, וְעוֹד: אֲפִילּוּ גָּדוֹל הָיִיתָ – אֵין מְבִיאִין רְאָיָה מִן הַמַּתִּיר.

The Gemara asks: **And let them say to him,** as the Sages said to Rabbi Yehuda in the previous *baraita*, that **one cannot bring a proof from** the testimony of **a minor.** The Gemara answers: **They said one** thing to him **and** then **another;** i.e., they rejected him with a twofold argument: **One** objection is that **you were a minor** at that time, and therefore your testimony is disqualified. **And furthermore, even** if **you had been an adult** at that time and you had testified that you saw some other minor read the Megilla before Rabbi Yehuda, **one cannot bring a proof** that an act is permitted **from the** behavior of the very **one who permits** it.[N]

PERSONALITIES

Rabbi Yehuda – רַבִּי יְהוּדָה: Rabbi Yehuda bar Ilai was a *tanna* from the fourth generation of *tanna'im*. He was born in Usha in the Galilee and studied under Rabbi Akiva and Rabbi Tarfon. He received rabbinic ordination from Rabbi Yehuda ben Baba, but was then forced to flee due to the Hadrianic persecutions. The Talmud (*Shabbat* 33b) describes a conversation between the Sages with regard to Roman rule in the land of Israel, and Rabbi Yehuda's positive response led the authorities to appoint him to the position of head of the speakers on all occasions.

The Mishna records more than six hundred teachings in the name of Rabbi Yehuda, and he is mentioned in almost every tractate. We find his teachings recorded in the *Tosefta* and *Sifra* more frequently than those of any other *tanna*.

NOTES

One cannot bring a proof from the testimony of a minor – אֵין מְבִיאִין רְאָיָה מִן הַקָּטָן: The early commentaries ask: Reading the Megilla is a mitzva by rabbinic law, and it is taught elsewhere that the testimony of an adult concerning an event that occurred when he was a minor is valid in questions pertaining to rabbinic laws. Some answer that since the Megilla is part of the Bible, it is judged with the severity of a Torah law (Rid). The later commentaries discuss this question at length. Some write that a minor's testimony is accepted in such situations only if he has witnessed a clear, certain fact; however, in this case it is possible that Rabbi Yehuda indeed read the Megilla before these rabbis but they did not consider themselves as having fulfilled their obligation through his reading (*Birkhei Yosef*).

One cannot bring a proof that an act is permitted from the behavior of the one who permits it – אֵין מְבִיאִין רְאָיָה מִן הַמַּתִּיר: It emerges from the Jerusalem Talmud that even a Sage who takes a lenient stance with regard to a particular issue does not generally follow his own opinion if the majority of the Sages disagree with him. This is why the main objection of the Rabbis against Rabbi Yehuda HaNasi's opinion was that the testimony of a minor is invalid, and only after this did they add the secondary objection that one cannot bring a proof from the actions of one who permits that action (*Porat Yosef*).

MISHNA One may not read the Megilla,[H] nor perform a circumcision,[H] nor immerse himself in a ritual bath,[H] nor sprinkle water of purification to purify people and objects that had contracted ritual impurity through contact with a corpse[H] until after sunrise. And also a woman who observes a clean day for each day she experiences a discharge, i.e., a woman who experienced one or two days of non-menstrual bleeding, and must now wait until a day has passed without any discharge of blood before regaining ritual purity, she too may not immerse herself until the sun has risen.[N] And with regard to all these activities that are supposed to be performed during the day, if one did them after daybreak, i.e., after the appearance of the first light of the sun, even before sunrise, they are valid,[N] as at this point it is already considered daytime.

מתני׳ אֵין קוֹרִין אֶת הַמְּגִילָּה, וְלֹא מָלִין, וְלֹא טוֹבְלִין, וְלֹא מַזִּין, וְכֵן שׁוֹמֶרֶת יוֹם כְּנֶגֶד יוֹם – לֹא תִּטְבּוֹל עַד שֶׁתָּנֵץ הַחַמָּה. וְכוּלָּן שֶׁעָשׂוּ מִשֶּׁעָלָה עַמּוּד הַשַּׁחַר – כָּשֵׁר.

GEMARA The Gemara asks: From where do we derive the *halakha* taught in the mishna that the Megilla may be read only during the day? The Gemara answers: As the verse states: "And that these days should be remembered and kept" (Esther 9:28). The word "days" indicates during the day, yes, but at night, no. The Gemara asks: Let us say that this is a conclusive refutation of the opinion of Rabbi Yehoshua ben Levi, as Rabbi Yehoshua ben Levi said: A person is obligated to read the Megilla at night and then repeat it during the day. The Gemara rejects this: There is no proof from here, as when the mishna teaches that the Megilla may be read only during the day, it was referring to the daytime reading, but the nighttime reading is not considered here at all.

גמ׳ מְנָלַן? דְּאָמַר קְרָא ״וְהַיָּמִים הָאֵלֶּה נִזְכָּרִים וְנַעֲשִׂים״, בַּיּוֹם – אִין, בַּלַּיְלָה – לָא. לֵימָא תֶּיהְוֵי תְּיוּבְתָּא דְּרַבִּי יְהוֹשֻׁעַ בֶּן לֵוִי: דְּאָמַר רַבִּי יְהוֹשֻׁעַ בֶּן לֵוִי חַיָּיב אָדָם לִקְרוֹת אֶת הַמְּגִילָּה בַּלַּיְלָה וְלִשְׁנוֹתָהּ בַּיּוֹם! כִּי קָתָנֵי אַדְּיוֹם.

§ The mishna continues: And one may not perform a circumcision until after sunrise, as it is written: "And on the eighth day he shall be circumcised" (Leviticus 12:3).[N] This indicates that the circumcision must be during the day, not at night.

״וְלֹא מָלִין״ וכו׳: דִּכְתִיב ״וּבַיּוֹם הַשְּׁמִינִי יִמּוֹל״.

§ It is further taught in the mishna: And one may not immerse[N] himself in a ritual bath, or sprinkle waters of purification until after sunrise. This too is derived from a verse, as it is written: "And the pure person shall sprinkle upon the impure on the third day and on the seventh day; and on the seventh day he shall purify himself and wash his clothes, and bathe himself in water, and shall be pure at evening" (Numbers 19:19), which teaches that the sprinkling must take place during the day and not at night. And immersion is likened to sprinkling, as it too is mentioned in the verse, "and bathe himself in water," so that whatever is invalid with respect to sprinkling is also invalid with respect to immersion.

וְלֹא טוֹבְלִין וְלֹא מַזִּין וכו׳: דִּכְתִיב ״וְהִזָּה הַטָּהוֹר עַל הַטָּמֵא [וגו׳] בַּיּוֹם הַשְּׁבִיעִי״ וְאִיתְקַשׁ טְבִילָה לַהֲזָיָה.

HALAKHA

Reading the Megilla during the day – קְרִיאַת מְגִילָּה בַּיּוֹם: The time for the daytime reading of the Megilla is after sunrise, but if one reads between daybreak and sunrise, he has fulfilled his obligation after the fact (*Shulḥan Arukh, Oraḥ Ḥayyim* 687:1).

The time for circumcision – זְמַן מִילָה: Circumcision should be performed after sunrise on the eighth day of a baby boy's life. However, if the circumcision was done between daybreak and sunrise, it is valid (*Shulḥan Arukh, Yoreh De'a* 262:1, and in the comment of Rema).

The time for immersion – זְמַן טְבִילָה: All those who must immerse in a ritual bath after a count of days immerse during the day, except for a woman after menstruation and after childbirth, whose immersion takes place at night. All those whose impurity does not entail a count of days may immerse either at night or during the day (Ra'avad; Rambam *Sefer Tahara, Hilkhot Mikvaot* 1:6).

Sprinkling the waters of purification – הַזָּאַת מֵי חַטָּאת: What is the procedure for sprinkling on one who is contaminated by contact with a corpse? Three sprigs of hyssop are taken and bound together. The tips of the sprigs are dipped in a container holding the waters of purification, and the one who is ritually impure is sprinkled with this water on the third and seventh day after he contracts impurity. The time for this sprinkling is after sunrise, but if it was done earlier, between daybreak and sunrise, it is valid. After the sprinkling of the seventh day, the purification takes effect upon the setting of the sun. If the sprigs were dipped at nighttime, even if the sprinkling itself was done during the day, or vice versa, it is invalid (Rambam *Sefer Tahara, Hilkhot Para Aduma* 11:1).

NOTES

One may not read…until the sun has risen – אֵין קוֹרִין...עַד שֶׁתָּנֵץ הַחַמָּה: The Ritva notes that there are many other mitzvot that the mishna does not mention that may be performed only during the day. He states that each case listed in the mishna was recorded because of some remarkable facet of this *halakha*. For instance, since the Megilla is read at night as well as during the day, one might have supposed that the daytime reading may also be done before dawn. Or one might have thought that the requirement to perform circumcision during the daytime applies only when the circumcision is done on the required day, the eighth day of life, but not if it is delayed for some reason. He explains the other cases in the mishna similarly.

All these activities, if one did them after daybreak, they are valid – וְכוּלָּן שֶׁעָשׂוּ מִשֶּׁעָלָה עַמּוּד הַשַּׁחַר כָּשֵׁר: Strictly speaking, daytime begins with dawn, as the Gemara establishes below (20b). However, since the onset of dawn is not easily recognizable, the Sages decreed that all these acts should preferably not be done until the sun rises, when it clearly evident that daytime has arrived (Rabbeinu Yehonatan).

And on the eighth day he shall be circumcised – וּבַיּוֹם הַשְּׁמִינִי יִמּוֹל: *Tosafot* note that this is not the accepted source for this *halakha* elsewhere in the Gemara; see their explanation as to why the Gemara here adduces this verse. The Rashba writes that the verse cited here is the source that a circumcision done after the proper time, i.e., after the eighth day, must also be performed during the daytime, and that the mishna is referring primarily to this kind of circumcision. The Meiri writes that the mishna means that although the circumcision itself is valid even if performed at night, if one performs the circumcision at night he is not considered to have performed a mitzva.

One may not immerse – לֹא טוֹבְלִין: The early commentaries note that there is a dispute with regard to the meaning in this context of the term immerse. Some say it refers to immersing oneself in a ritual bath (Rashi), while others say it means immersing the hyssop into the waters of purification for the purpose of sprinkling it on people who have been rendered impure by contact with a corpse (Rashba).

Rabbeinu Yehonatan connects this dispute with the question of whether the correct reading in the mishna is: One may not immerse or sprinkle, or if it is: One may not sprinkle or immerse. If immersing is mentioned before sprinkling it would appear that the term immerse refers to the hyssop being dipped into the waters of purification rather than to immersion in a ritual bath. According to the opinion that the word immerse refers to immersion in a ritual bath, it should be noted that when the mishna says it may not be done at night, it means only that in the case of an immersion that has to be done after a certain number of days, it cannot be done during the night preceding the required day but only once day has begun; but if the immersion is postponed until after the required day has passed it can certainly take place at night as well (see Rashi and Rid).

"וְכֵן שׁוֹמֶרֶת יוֹם כְּנֶגֶד יוֹם לֹא תִּטְבּוֹל עַד שֶׁתָּנֵץ הַחַמָּה" וכו׳: פְּשִׁיטָא! מַאי שְׁנָא שׁוֹמֶרֶת יוֹם כְּנֶגֶד יוֹם מִכׇּל חַיָּיבֵי טְבִילוֹת?

§ The mishna states: **And also a woman who observes a day for a day**[H] **may not immerse herself until the sun has risen.** The Gemara asks: This **is obvious. What is different about a woman who observes a day for a day,** who must immerse herself in a ritual bath, **from all the others who are obligated to immerse themselves,** as it was already taught that one may not immerse himself in a ritual bath until it is day?

אִיצְטְרִיךְ, סָלְקָא דַּעְתָּךְ אָמִינָא תֶּיהֱוֵי כִּרְאִיָּה רִאשׁוֹנָה שֶׁל זָב, וּרְאִיָּה רִאשׁוֹנָה שֶׁל זָב אִיתְקַשׁ לְבַעַל קֶרִי, דִּכְתִיב "זֹאת תּוֹרַת הַזָּב וַאֲשֶׁר תֵּצֵא מִמֶּנּוּ שִׁכְבַת זֶרַע", מַה בַּעַל קֶרִי טוֹבֵל בַּיּוֹם – הַאי נַמִי לִיטְבּוֹל בְּיוֹמֵיהּ.

The Gemara answers: **It is** nevertheless **necessary** to mention separately the case of a woman who observes a day for a day. As, **it might enter your mind to say that** this woman's bleeding **should be treated like the first emission of a *zav*,** a man who experiences a gonorrhea-like secretion, in that just as a man attains the status of a full-fledged *zav* once he has three such emissions, so too, a woman attains the status of a full-fledged *zava* once she experiences three days of bleeding. **And the first emission of a *zav* is likened to one who experienced a seminal discharge, as it is written: "This is the *halakha* of him that has an issue and of him whose semen goes from him"** (Leviticus 15:32). From this it is learned: **Just as one who experienced a seminal discharge immerses on the** same **day** that he had the discharge, **so too, that one,** the *zav*, **may immerse himself on the** same **day** that he had the emission.

וְהָא בִּימָמָא לָא מָצֵי טָבְלָה דִּכְתִיב "כׇּל יְמֵי זוֹבָהּ כְּמִשְׁכַּב נִדָּתָהּ יִהְיֶה לָּהּ" – בְּלֵילְיָא מִיהַת לִיעֲבֵיד מִקְצָת שִׁימּוּר, וְתִיטְבּוֹל. קָא מַשְׁמַע לָן: כֵּיוָן דְּבָעֲיָא סְפִירָה –

And although **this one,** i.e., a woman who observes a day for a day, **cannot immerse on the** same **day** that she experienced the bleeding, **as it is written: "All the days of her issue shall be to her as the bed of her menstruation"** (Leviticus 15:26), which teaches that she remains the entire day of her issue in her impure state and must wait until the day is over before she can immerse herself, nevertheless, one might have said that **at least during the night** following the day of her issue **she should** be able to **perform a partial observation,** i.e., she should verify that part of the night has gone by without bleeding, **and** then **immerse herself** at night, without waiting until morning. Therefore, the mishna **teaches us** that **since she is required to count** one day of purity after her day of impurity,

HALAKHA

A woman who observes a day for a day – שׁוֹמֶרֶת יוֹם כְּנֶגֶד יוֹם: In the case of a woman who experiences a single day of bleeding outside the time of her menstrual period, if the bleeding stops before nightfall she observes the following night, i.e., she verifies that there is no bleeding during the night, and if there is no further bleeding she may immerse the following day, beginning at daybreak. Her purification is still pending at that point, however, lest there be further bleeding, and therefore she may not yet have intimate relations. If the entire day then passes without any bleeding, she is considered purified. All this is according to Torah law. However, as far back as the time of the early *amora'im*, out of concern for errors that might arise, it has been accepted that a woman who experiences even minimal bleeding, at any time of her cycle, should count seven clean days before immersing, like a full-fledged *zava* (*Tur, Yoreh De'a* 183).

סְפִירָה – בִּימָמָא הִיא.

and **counting** can only be done **during the day** and not at night, as it says: "And she shall count for herself seven days" (Leviticus 15:28), she cannot immerse herself until after sunrise, although here she has to count only one day.

"וְכוּלָּן שֶׁעָשׂוּ מִשֶּׁעָלָה עַמּוּד הַשַּׁחַר כָּשֵׁר": מְנָהָנֵי מִילֵּי? אָמַר רָבָא: דְּאָמַר קְרָא "וַיִּקְרָא אֱלֹהִים לָאוֹר יוֹם" – לַמֵּאִיר וּבָא קְרָאוֹ יוֹם.

§ The mishna concludes: **And** with regard to **all these** things, **if one did them after daybreak they are valid.** The Gemara asks: **From where is this matter** derived, that from daybreak it is already considered daytime? **Rava said: As the verse states: "And God called the light** [*or*] **day"** (Genesis 1:5), meaning: **To that which was becoming lighter and lighter he called day.** The Hebrew word *or* is not to be understood in its usual sense of light, but as a verbal noun: that which is becoming lighter and lighter. It teaches that as soon as light begins to appear in the sky it is called daytime.

אֶלָּא מֵעַתָּה, "וְלַחֹשֶׁךְ קָרָא לָיְלָה" [לַמַּחֲשִׁיךְ וּבָא קָרָא לַיְלָה] הָא קַיְימָא לָן דְּעַד צֵאת הַכּוֹכָבִים לָאו לַיְלָה הוּא!

The Gemara raises a difficulty with this interpretation: **However, if** it is **so** that Rava's interpretation of this phrase is correct, the following phrase: **"And the darkness** [*ḥoshekh*] **He called night"** (Genesis 1:5), should be interpreted in a similar fashion: **That which was becoming darker and darker He called night,** so that immediately after sunset it would be considered nighttime. But don't **we maintain** that **until the stars come out it is not nighttime?** We are forced to say that *ḥoshekh* literally means darkness, and similarly, *or* in the first part of the verse literally means light.

אֶלָּא אָמַר רַבִּי זֵירָא, מֵהָכָא: ״וַאֲנַחְנוּ עוֹשִׂים בַּמְּלָאכָה וְחֶצְיָם מַחֲזִיקִים בָּרְמָחִים מֵעֲלוֹת הַשַּׁחַר עַד צֵאת הַכּוֹכָבִים״, וְאוֹמֵר: ״(וְהָיָה) לָנוּ הַלַּיְלָה (לְמִשְׁמָר)״.

Rather, Rabbi Zeira said: We derive this *halakha* **from here,** as it is stated: **"So we labored in the work; and half of them held the spears from the rising of the morning till the stars appeared"** (Nehemiah 4:15), where "rising of the morning" means daybreak, **and** the next verse **states: "So that in the night they may be a guard to us;** and labor in the day" (Nehemiah 4:16). This demonstrates that the day begins with the dawn.

מַאי ״וְאוֹמֵר״? – וְכִי תֵּימָא ״מִשֶּׁעָלָה עַמּוּד הַשַּׁחַר״ לָאו יְמָמָא, וּמִכִּי עָרְבָא שִׁמְשָׁא לֵילְיָא, וְאִינְהוּ מַקְדְּמִי וּמַחְשְׁכִי – תָּא שְׁמַע ״(וְהָיָה) לָנוּ הַלַּיְלָה מִשְׁמָר וְהַיּוֹם מְלָאכָה״

The Gemara clarifies Rabbi Zeira's statement: **What** need is there for the additional verse introduced by the words **"and it states"?** Why does the first proof-text not suffice? The Gemara explains: The second verse comes to deflect the following possible objection: **You might say that** even **after "the rising of the morning" it is not** yet considered **day, and that from** the time **when the sun sets it is** already considered **night, and** in this particular incident it happened that **they began** their work **early,** before the official beginning of daytime, **and remained** working **late,** after the official end of daytime. Therefore, Rabbi Zeira continued and said: **Come** and **hear that which** is stated in the next verse: **"So that in the night they may be a guard to us; and labor in the day."** The entire time during which they worked is referred to as "day," which proves that the day begins at daybreak.

מתני׳ כָּל הַיּוֹם כָּשֵׁר לִקְרִיאַת הַמְּגִילָּה וְלִקְרִיאַת הַהַלֵּל, וְלִתְקִיעַת שׁוֹפָר, וְלִנְטִילַת לוּלָב, וְלִתְפִלַּת הַמּוּסָפִין, וְלַמּוּסָפִין,

MISHNA Although it is preferable to fulfill a particular day's mitzva at the earliest possible hour, **the entire day is a valid time**[N] **for reading the Megilla;**[H] **for reciting *hallel*;**[H] **for sounding the *shofar***[H] on Rosh HaShana; **for taking the *lulav***[H] and the other species on Sukkot; **for the additional prayer**[H] recited on Shabbat and other occasions; **and for the additional offerings** sacrificed in the Temple on these occasions.[H]

וּלְוִידּוּי הַפָּרִים, וּלְוִידּוּי מַעֲשֵׂר, וּלְוִידּוּי יוֹם הַכִּפּוּרִים,

And the entire day is also a valid time **for the confession over the bulls**[H] brought by the Sanhedrin or by the High Priest to atone for mistakes they had made in their instruction to the people; **for the declaration** made on the last day of Passover in the fourth and seventh year of the Sabbatical cycle, stating that one's obligations **with regard to tithes**[H] have been properly fulfilled (see Deuteronomy 26:12–15); **and for the confession** of sins made by the High Priest **on Yom Kippur** over the special offerings brought on that day.[N]

NOTES

The entire day is a valid time – כָּל הַיּוֹם כָּשֵׁר: The question has been raised: Since the point of this mishna is to list the mitzvot that must be done only during the day, in what way does it differ from the previous mishna, in which a completely different list was given for the same category of mitzvot? Some answer that with regard to the mitzvot listed in the previous mishna, e.g., immersing and sprinkling, although their set time arrives during the day, if they are performed after that set time, the obligation is nevertheless fulfilled. The items listed in this mishna, however, must be performed not only during the day, but on a particular day (Meiri; *Tiferet Yisrael*).

It appears that Rashi alludes to the question as well, as at the beginning of the mishna he mentions the principle that it is proper to perform a daytime mitzva as early in the morning as possible. This is in contrast to those procedures mentioned in the previous mishna, such as immersion, with regard to which it is sometimes preferable to perform them specifically late in the day (see *Penei Yehoshua* and *Turei Even*). Rashba cites Rabbeinu Tam, who also asks why the mishna did not mention the cases in the previous mishna, but the question is left unanswered.

Some early commentaries write that when the mishna begins its list with reading the Megilla, which was enumerated first in the previous mishna, it means: The reading of the Megilla and all the subsequent cases specified along with it in the previous mishna (Ra'avya; Ritva; Meiri). Another question is raised with regard to the mishna as well: Why are certain other procedures that must also be performed during the day, e.g., the observation of signs of leprosy and rendering judgment, omitted from its list? The answer to this appears to be that the mishna relies on the principle stated at the end of the list and consequently did not list each case by name (see Ritva).

The order of the mishna – סֵדֶר הַמִּשְׁנָה: Some commentaries attempt to explain the order of the items on this seemingly random list: The reading of the Megilla is mentioned first because it is the main topic of this tractate. Afterward it lists other mitzvot, such as *shofar* and *lulav*, that, like the Megilla, are performed in the course of the prayers. The additional prayer is listed before the additional offering, although in fact the former is a derivative of the latter, because the *tanna* wanted to give precedence to the item that is a rabbinic enactment rather than an explicit mitzva by Torah law. Some items are arranged in accordance with their appearance in the Torah, such as the confession over the bulls, which precedes the confession of Yom Kippur. The end of the list deals with those actions that are not related to offerings and are not mitzvot, but rather are acts that are undertaken to rectify a defective situation such as ritual impurity. The final item is the purification of the leper, because the *tanna* wanted to end with the subject of purification (*Tosefot Yom Tov*; *Adderet Eliyahu*).

HALAKHA

Reading the Megilla during the day – קְרִיאַת הַמְּגִילָּה בַּיּוֹם: One is obligated to read the Megilla during the day, and its time extends from sunrise until sunset. If one is delayed until after sunset he should read without the blessing (*Arukh HaShulḥan*; *Mishna Berura*; *Shulḥan Arukh, Oraḥ Ḥayyim* 687:1).

The time for *hallel* – זְמַן הַלֵּל: It is permitted to say *hallel* throughout the day (Rambam *Sefer Zemanim, Hilkhot Megilla VaḤanukka* 3:9).

The time for sounding the *shofar* – זְמַן תְּקִיעַת שׁוֹפָר: The time for sounding the *shofar* on Rosh HaShana is during the day, from sunrise to sunset. However, the Sages instituted that the *shofar* should be blown before and during the additional prayer for Rosh HaShana. Even if one blows or hears the *shofar* in private, he should try to arrange for it to be done at the same time the congregation blows the *shofar* in the synagogue (*Mishna Berura*; *Shulḥan Arukh, Oraḥ Ḥayyim* 588:1).

The time for the taking the *lulav* – זְמַן נְטִילַת לוּלָב: One may take the *lulav* anytime during the day. If he does not take the *lulav* on the first day of Sukkot until after sunset, he should take it at that time, without reciting the blessing (*Magen Avraham*). Some say that this should be done on the other the days of Sukkot as well (*Mishna Berura*). On the seventh day of Sukkot and on Friday, however, the *lulav* should not be handled at all after sunset (*Kaf HaḤayyim*; *Shulḥan Arukh, Oraḥ Ḥayyim* 652:1).

The time for the additional prayer – זְמַן תְּפִלַּת הַמּוּסָפִין: The preferred time for the additional prayer is immediately following the morning prayer, and it should not be delayed longer than the seventh hour of the day, i.e., one hour after noon, *ab initio*; however, it may be said at any time during the day if necessary (*Shulḥan Arukh, Oraḥ Ḥayyim* 286:1).

The time for the offerings – זְמַן הַקּוֹרְבָּנוֹת: The entire day is acceptable for many acts associated with offerings: leaning on the offerings, slaughtering, pinching the necks of the bird offerings, burning the fistful of flour on the altar, bringing near a meal-offering to the altar, sprinkling the blood, waving, scooping out a fistful from meal-offerings, and sacrificing the additional offering. Nevertheless, it is preferable to do these mitzvot as early in the day as possible (Rambam *Sefer Avoda, Hilkhot Ma'aseh HaKorbanot* 4:6).

The time for confession over the bulls – זְמַן וִידּוּי הַפָּרִים: The entire day is acceptable for the confession over the Yom Kippur bull as well as for the confession over the sin-offering bulls that are burned (Rambam *Sefer Avoda, Hilkhot Avodat Yom HaKippurim* 2:7).

The time for declaration with regard to tithes – זְמַן וִידּוּי מַעֲשֵׂר: The declaration with regard to the tithes must be done during the day, and may be done at any time throughout the day (Rambam *Sefer Zera'im, Hilkhot Ma'aser Sheni* 11:4).

לִסְמִיכָה, לִשְׁחִיטָה, לִתְנוּפָה, לְהַגָּשָׁה, לִקְמִיצָה, וּלְהַקְטָרָה, לִמְלִיקָה, וּלְקַבָּלָה, וּלְהַזָּיָה,

The entire day is also a valid time **for placing hands** on the head of an offering; **for slaughtering** an offering; **for waving** those offerings that require waving in the Temple; **for bringing** meal-offerings **near** to the altar; **for scooping out a fistful** of flour from a meal-offering in order to burn it on the altar; **and for burning** the fistful of flour on the altar; **for pinching** the necks of the turtledoves and young pigeons sacrificed as offerings in the Temple; **and for receiving** the blood of an offering in a vessel; **and for sprinkling** blood on the altar and on the curtain separating between the Holy and the Holy of Holies.

וּלְהַשְׁקָיַית סוֹטָה, וְלַעֲרִיפַת הָעֶגְלָה, וּלְטָהֳרַת הַמְּצוֹרָע.

And the entire day is also a valid time **for giving a woman suspected by her husband of having been unfaithful** [*sota*] **to drink**[H] from the bitter waters (see Numbers 5:11–31); **for breaking the neck** of the heifer[H] as part of the procedure followed when a corpse is found outside a town and it is not known who caused his death (see Deuteronomy 21:1–9); **and for** all the steps in the **purification process of the leper** (see Leviticus 14:1–20).[H]

כָּל הַלַּיְלָה כָּשֵׁר לִקְצִירַת הָעוֹמֶר, וּלְהֶקְטֵר חֲלָבִים וְאֵבָרִים. זֶה הַכְּלָל: דָּבָר שֶׁמִּצְוָתוֹ בַּיּוֹם - כָּשֵׁר כָּל הַיּוֹם. דָּבָר שֶׁמִּצְוָתוֹ בַּלַּיְלָה - כָּשֵׁר כָּל הַלַּיְלָה.

Correspondingly, all the mitzvot that must be performed at night may be performed anytime during the night: **The entire night is** a valid time for **reaping the *omer***[H] of barley on the night following the first day of Passover, **for burning the fats**[H] of offerings that had been brought during the preceding day, **and** for burning **the limbs** of burnt-offerings. **This is the principle: Something that it is a mitzva** to perform **during the day is valid** if performed anytime during **the entire day;**[N] **something that it is a mitzva** to perform **at night is valid** if performed anytime during **the entire night.**

גמ׳ מְנָלַן - דְּאָמַר קְרָא ״וְהַיָּמִים הָאֵלֶּה נִזְכָּרִים וְנַעֲשִׂים״. לִקְרִיאַת הַהַלֵּל - דִּכְתִיב ״מִמִּזְרַח שֶׁמֶשׁ עַד מְבוֹאוֹ״ (רַבִּי יוֹסֵי) אוֹמֵר: ״זֶה הַיּוֹם עָשָׂה ה׳״.

GEMARA The Gemara asks: **From where do we** derive that these mitzvot were commanded to be performed specifically during the day? With regard to reading the Megilla, **the verse states: "That these days should be remembered**[N] **and kept"** (Esther 9:28). **For reciting the *hallel*,** the proof is from **that which is written** in *hallel*: **"From the rising of the sun to its setting,** the Lord's name is to be praised" (Psalms 113:3). **Rabbi Yosei said:** The proof is from another verse in *hallel*: **"This is the day that the Lord has made"** (Psalms 118:24), implying that it is to be recited during the day and not at night.

וְלִנְטִילַת לוּלָב - דִּכְתִיב ״וּלְקַחְתֶּם לָכֶם בַּיּוֹם הָרִאשׁוֹן״. וְלִתְקִיעַת שׁוֹפָר - דִּכְתִיב ״יוֹם תְּרוּעָה יִהְיֶה לָכֶם״. וּלְמוּסָפִין - דִּכְתִיב ״דְּבַר יוֹם בְּיוֹמוֹ״. וְלִתְפִלַּת הַמּוּסָפִין - כְּמוּסָפִין שַׁוְיוּהּ רַבָּנַן.

And daytime is the time **for taking the *lulav*, as it is written: "And you shall take for yourselves on the first day** the fruit of a beautiful tree, branches of a date palm, and boughs of a dense-leaved tree, and willows of the brook" (Leviticus 23:40). Daytime is also the time **for sounding the *shofar*, as it is written: "It is a day of sounding the *shofar* to you"** (Numbers 29:1). Likewise, the time **for** the **additional offerings**[N] is day, **as it is written** with regard to these offerings: "To sacrifice an offering made by fire to the Lord, a burnt-offering, and a meal-offering, a sacrifice, and libations, **each on its own day"** (Leviticus 23:37). **And** this is also so **for the additional prayer,** because **the Sages made it equivalent to** those **additional offerings.**

וּלְוִידּוּי פָּרִים - דְּיָלֵיף ׳כַּפָּרָה׳ ׳כַּפָּרָה׳ מִיּוֹם הַכִּפּוּרִים, דְּתַנְיָא גַּבֵּי יוֹם הַכִּפּוּרִים: ״וְכִפֶּר בַּעֲדוֹ וּבְעַד בֵּיתוֹ״: בְּכַפָּרַת דְּבָרִים הַכָּתוּב מְדַבֵּר, וְכַפָּרָה בִּימָמָא הוּא, דִּכְתִיב ״בַּיּוֹם הַזֶּה יְכַפֵּר עֲלֵיכֶם״.

And daytime is the time for **the confession over the bulls, as** this is **derived** by way of a verbal analogy between one instance of **atonement** in this context and another instance of **atonement** in the context of **Yom Kippur. As it is taught** in a *baraita* **with regard to Yom Kippur,** the verse states: "And Aaron shall present the bull of the sin-offering that is his, **and atone for himself and for his household"** (Leviticus 16:11). **The verse speaks of atonement** achieved through **words,** i.e., the atonement here is not referring to the sacrifice of offerings and the sprinkling of blood, but rather to atonement achieved through confession. **And the atonement** of Yom Kippur **is only during the day, as it is written: "For on that day will He atone for you"** (Leviticus 16:30). Just as the atonement on Yom Kippur must take place during the day, so must the other cases of atonement, over other bulls brought as sin-offerings, take place during the day.

HALAKHA

The time for giving a woman suspected by her husband of having been unfaithful [*sota*] to drink – זְמַן הַשְׁקָיַית סוֹטָה: The *sota* is given the mixture to drink during the day. This may be done at any time throughout the day (Rambam *Sefer Nashim, Hilkhot Sota* 4:2).

The time for breaking the neck of the heifer – זְמַן עֲרִיפַת הָעֶגְלָה: The breaking of the heifer's neck is done only during the day. It may be done at any time throughout the day (Rambam *Sefer Nezikim, Hilkhot Rotze'aḥ UShmirat HaNefesh* 10:5).

The time for the purification process of the leper – זְמַן טָהֳרַת מְצוֹרָע: The entire day is acceptable for the purification ceremony of the leper; it may be performed at any time throughout the day (Rambam *Sefer Tahara, Hilkhot Tumat Tzara'at* 11:3).

The time for reaping the *omer* – זְמַן קְצִירַת הָעוֹמֶר: It is permitted to reap the *omer* throughout the night; if it was reaped during the day it is also valid (Rambam *Sefer Avoda, Hilkhot Temidin UMusafin* 7:7).

The time for burning the fats – זְמַן הַקְטָרַת חֲלָבִים: The fats of the offerings and the limbs of burnt-offerings may be burned throughout the night (Rambam *Sefer Avoda, Hilkhot Ma'aseh HaKorbanot* 4:6).

NOTES

A mitzva to perform during the day is valid if performed anytime during the entire day – דָּבָר שֶׁמִּצְוָתוֹ בַּיּוֹם כָּשֵׁר כָּל הַיּוֹם: This *halakha* does not apply to those actions to which a specific time of day was set, such as the Paschal offering and the daily offering (Ritva).

That these days should be remembered – וְהַיָּמִים הָאֵלֶּה נִזְכָּרִים: In the Jerusalem Talmud this is derived from a different verse: "On the day that the enemies of the Jews hoped to have rule over them" (Esther 9:1).

The additional offerings – מוּסָפִין: The question may be raised: As the time for the additional offering is after the daily morning offering until the daily afternoon offering, its time is not the entire day. One answer is that theoretically its time is the entire day, but there are external factors that limit the application of this extended time frame. Another possibility is that the additional offering may indeed be valid after the fact if it is brought at any time during the day (Rashba).

NOTES

For placing hands and for slaughtering – לִסְמִיכָה וְלִשְׁחִיטָה: The fact that these two actions, as well as several others, must be done during the day is derived from specific verses, although other sacrificial acts are derived from the verse that states: "On the day that he commanded the children of Israel to present their offerings" (Leviticus 7:38). See *Tosafot*, who explain why this general verse is not used for all actions related to offerings. However, in the Jerusalem Talmud, these actions are indeed derived from the verse that starts: "On the day that he commanded."

וּלְוִידּוּי מַעֲשֵׂר וכו׳: דִּכְתִיב ״וְאָמַרְתָּ לִפְנֵי ה׳ אֱלֹהֶיךָ בִּעַרְתִּי הַקֹּדֶשׁ מִן הַבַּיִת״ וּסְמִיךְ לֵיהּ ״הַיּוֹם הַזֶּה ה׳ אֱלֹהֶיךָ מְצַוְּךָ״.

And daytime is the time **for the declaration with regard to tithes, as it is written** in the formula of this declaration: **"And you shall say before the Lord your God, I have removed the sacred things out of my house"** (Deuteronomy 26:13–15); **and juxtaposed to** that passage it is written: **"This day the Lord your God has commanded you** to do" (Deuteronomy 26:16), implying during the day and not at night.

לִסְמִיכָה וְלִשְׁחִיטָה: דִּכְתִיב ״וְסָמַךְ וְשָׁחַט״, וּכְתִיב בָּהּ בִּשְׁחִיטָה ״בְּיוֹם זִבְחֲכֶם״, וְלִתְנוּפָה – דִּכְתִיב ״בְּיוֹם הֲנִיפְכֶם אֶת הָעוֹמֶר״.

For placing hands on the head of an offering **and for slaughtering**[N] an offering, it is derived **as it is written: "And he shall lay** his hand upon the head of his offering, **and slaughter it"** (Leviticus 3:8), comparing the laying of hands to slaughtering. **And it is written with regard to slaughtering: "On the day that you slaughter"** (Leviticus 19:6), meaning during the day and not at night. **And for waving** the offerings that require waving, it is derived **as it is written: "And on the day you wave the *omer*"** (Leviticus 23:12).

וּלְהַגָּשָׁה – דְּאִיתְקַשׁ לִתְנוּפָה, דִּכְתִיב ״וְלָקַח הַכֹּהֵן מִיַּד הָאִשָּׁה אֵת מִנְחַת הַקְּנָאֹת וְהֵנִיף...וְהִקְרִיב״. וְלִמְלִיקָה וְלִקְמִיצָה וּלְהַקְטָרָה וּלְהַזָּיָה – דִּכְתִיב ״בְּיוֹם צַוֹּתוֹ אֶת בְּנֵי יִשְׂרָאֵל״.

And with regard **to bringing** the meal-offerings **near** the altar, **it is likened to waving, as it is written: "And the priest shall take the meal-offering of jealousy from the woman's hand, and shall wave** the offering before the Lord, **and sacrifice** it upon the altar" (Numbers 5:25). The words "sacrifice it" are referring to bringing the offering near the altar. **And for scooping out a fistful** of flour, **and for pinching** the necks of the bird-offerings, **and for burning** the fistful of flour on the altar, **and for sprinkling** the blood, these are derived **as it is written:** "This is the law of the burnt-offering, of the meal-offering, and of the sin-offering, and of the guilt-offering, and of the consecration-offering, and of the sacrifice of the peace-offering; which the Lord commanded Moses on Mount Sinai on **the day that he commanded the children of Israel** to present their offerings" (Leviticus 7:37–38).

וּלְהַשְׁקָיַית סוֹטָה אָתְיָא ׳תּוֹרָה׳ ׳תּוֹרָה׳; כְּתִיב הָכָא ״וְעָשָׂה לָהּ הַכֹּהֵן אֵת כָּל הַתּוֹרָה הַזֹּאת״ וּכְתִיב הָתָם ״עַל פִּי הַתּוֹרָה אֲשֶׁר יוֹרוּךָ וְעַל הַמִּשְׁפָּט״.

And with regard **to giving the *sota* to drink** from the bitter waters, this **is derived** from a verbal analogy between one instance of the word **"Torah"** and another instance of the word **"Torah." It is written here** with respect to a *sota*: **"And the priest shall execute upon her all this Torah"** (Numbers 5:30), **and it is written there** with regard to judgment: **"According to the Torah, which they shall teach you, and according to the judgment,** which they shall tell you" (Deuteronomy 17:11).

Perek **II**
Daf **21** Amud **a**

מַה מִּשְׁפָּט בַּיּוֹם – אַף כָּאן בַּיּוֹם.

Just as judgment may be done only **by day,**[N] **so too here,** the *sota* is given the bitter waters to drink only **by day.**

״וְלַעֲרִיפַת הָעֶגְלָה״: אָמְרִי דְּבֵי רַבִּי יַנַּאי: כַּפָּרָה כְּתִיב בָּהּ כְּקָדָשִׁים: ״וּלְטָהֳרַת מְצוֹרָע״: דִּכְתִיב – ״זֹאת תִּהְיֶה תּוֹרַת הַמְּצוֹרָע בְּיוֹם טָהֳרָתוֹ״.

And daytime is the time **for breaking the neck of the heifer,** as the Sages of **the school of Rabbi Yannai said: Atonement is written with regard to** the heifer, teaching that it is treated **like sacred** offerings, and it has already been established that all actions relating to offerings must be performed during the day. **And for purifying the leper,** it is derived **as it is written: "This shall be the law of the leper on the day of his cleansing"** (Leviticus 14:2).

NOTES

Just as judgment may be done only by day – מַה מִּשְׁפָּט בַּיּוֹם: How is it known that judgment may be done only by day? Rashi suggests a proof from the verse "Then it shall be in the day that he caused his sons to inherit" (Deuteronomy 21:16); just as matters of inheritance are judged by day, so are all other judgments made by day. *Tosafot* in tractate *Sota* offer a proof from that which is stated with regard to capital punishment: "And hang them…in face of the sun" (Numbers 25:4).

"כל הלילה כשר לקצירת העומר" וכו': דאמר מר: קצירה וספירה בלילה, והבאה ביום: "ולהקטר חלבים ואברים": דכתיב "כל הלילה עד הבוקר.

It was taught in the mishna: **The entire night is a valid** time for **reaping the *omer*,"**[H] **as the Master said** in tractate *Menahot*: The **reaping** of the *omer* **and the counting** of the *omer* must be performed **at night,**[NH] **whereas bringing** the *omer* offering to the Temple must be done **during the day. And for burning the fats and limbs** of the offerings, it is derived **as it is written** with regard to them: "Which shall be burning upon the altar **all night until the morning"** (Leviticus 6:2).

"זה הכלל: דבר שמצותו ביום כשר כל היום": זה הכלל לאתויי מאי? לאתויי סידור בזיכין וסלוק בזיכין.

§ The mishna states: **This is the principle: Something that it is a mitzva** to perform **during the day is valid** if **performed** any time during **the entire day.** The Gemara asks: As the mishna has seemingly mentioned all daytime mitzvot explicitly, the words: **This is the principle, are to add what?** The Gemara answers: This principle comes **to include the arranging of the vessels** of frankincense alongside the shewbread in the Temple, **and the removal of** those **vessels** at the end of the week, as the verse does not specify the time when these procedures should be performed.

וכרבי יוסי. דתניא, רבי יוסי אומר: סילק את הישנה שחרית וסידר את החדשה ערבית – אין בכך כלום.

And this mishna would consequently be **in accordance with** the opinion of **Rabbi Yosei, as it is taught** in a *baraita* that **Rabbi Yosei said: If one removed the old** shewbread and frankincense **in the morning and arranged the new** ones **toward the evening,** i.e., at the end of the day, **there is nothing** wrong **with this,** as it suffices if the changeover is made any time over the course of the same day. The Sages, however, maintain that the new ones must be set in place immediately after the old ones have been removed.

ומה אני מקיים (לפני ה' תמיד) שלא יהא שולחן בלא לחם.

And, according to Rabbi Yosei, **how do I uphold** that which is written with regard to the shewbread: "He shall set it in order **before the Lord continually"** (Leviticus 24:8), implying that the bread must be on the table at all times? It means only **that the table should not be** an entire day **without the bread,** but if there is bread on the table for even a part of the day, it is considered as being there "continually."

"דבר שמצותו בלילה כשר כל הלילה": לאתויי מאי?

§ The mishna concludes: **Something that it is a mitzva** to perform **at night may be performed the entire night.** The Gemara asks: **What** does this principle come **to add**[N] that has not already been mentioned explicitly?

לאתויי אכילת פסחים, ודלא כרבי אלעזר בן עזריה. דתניא, "ואכלו את הבשר בלילה הזה" אמר רבי אלעזר בן עזריה: נאמר כאן "בלילה הזה" ונאמר להלן "ועברתי בארץ מצרים בלילה הזה" מה להלן עד חצות – אף כאן עד חצות.

The Gemara answers: It comes **to include the eating of the Paschal offering,**[H] and consequently this mishna is **not in accordance with** the opinion of **Rabbi Elazar ben Azarya, as it is taught** in a *baraita* that it is written: **"And they shall eat the meat on that night"** (Exodus 12:8). **Rabbi Elazar ben Azarya said: It is stated here: "On that night," and it is stated further on: "And I will pass through the land of Egypt on that night"** (Exodus 12:12). **Just as there,** when God passed through the land of Egypt, it was **until midnight, so too here,** the Paschal offering may be eaten only **until midnight.** The mishna, which asserts that the Paschal offering may be eaten all night, is not in accordance with Rabbi Elazar ben Azarya.

הדרן עלך הקורא למפרע

HALAKHA

The time for reaping the *omer* – זמן קצירת העומר: The time for reaping the *omer* is on the night of the sixteenth of Nisan (Rambam *Sefer Avoda, Hilkhot Temidin UMusafin* 7:6).

Counting the *omer* at night – ספירה בלילה: On the night of the sixteenth of Nisan, after the evening prayer, one begins counting the *omer*. If one forgot to count at the beginning of the night he may count with a blessing at any time throughout the night (*Shulhan Arukh, Orah Hayyim* 489:1).

The time for eating the Paschal offering – זמן אכילת הפסח: By Torah law, the time for eating the Paschal offering is throughout the night; however, the Sages decreed that it should not be eaten beyond midnight, in order to prevent people from transgressing by eating it after sunrise. However, many early authorities maintain that the *halakha* is in accordance with the opinion of Rabbi Elazar ben Azarya, that even by Torah law the Paschal offering may be eaten only until midnight, as there are several *mishnayot* that are in accordance with his opinion (Rabbeinu Hananel; *Tosafot*; Rid). Therefore, the custom with regard to eating the *matza* of the *afikoman*, which is eaten as a remembrance of the Paschal offering, is to finish it before midnight (Rambam *Sefer Korbanot, Hilkhot Korban Pesah* 8:15).

NOTES

Counting the *omer* at night – ספירה בלילה: The halakhic authorities discuss at length whether the counting of the *omer* may be done during the day, without the blessing, if one forgot to count at night. Some compare this situation to the *halakha* that although the reaping of the *omer* barley is supposed to take place at night, if it was reaped by day it is valid after the fact (see Rashba).

The entire night…what does this come to add – כל הלילה לאתויי מאי: A possible answer to this question would seem to be that it comes to include the nighttime reading of the Megilla, which may be done all night. The Gemara does not give this answer, however, because the mishna lists only those *halakhot* that have a biblical basis, and the nighttime reading of the Megilla appears to be a rabbinic enactment.

Summary of **Perek II**

The *halakha* requires that the Scroll of Esther be read in order. Having noted this fact, the Gemara then discussed other texts and formulas that must be recited in their proper order.

Although the Megilla must be written like a book, i.e., like a Torah scroll, when it comes to reading it, it has many characteristics of a less formal letter or document. Some of the *halakhot* established for reading the Torah are not followed for the reading of the Megilla. Someone who is not completely mentally competent may not read the Megilla for others. Although several Sages prescribed shorter or longer excerpts of the Megilla as the minimum to fulfill the obligation of reading, the *halakha* is established that it must be read in its entirety.

The obligation to hear the Megilla during the day extends to the entire day, and similarly the nighttime reading may be done at any time during the night. This is in fact a principle: Any daytime mitzva can be performed at any time during the day, and a nighttime mitzva can be performed at any time during the night. Although there are recommended times for performing some of these mitzvot, these are given only to prevent their being neglected or to encourage alacrity in their performance. Technically, the accepted time frame for their performance is throughout the entire corresponding day or night.

Introduction to **Perek III**

And Ezra the priest brought the Law before the congregation, both men and women, and all that could hear with understanding, upon the first day of the seventh month.

(Nehemiah 8:2)

And Ezra opened the book in the sight of all the people, for he was above all the people; and when he opened it, all the people stood up. And Ezra blessed the Lord, the great God. And all the people answered: Amen, Amen, with the lifting up of their hands; and they bowed their heads, and fell down before the Lord with their faces to the ground.

(Nehemiah 8:5–6)

And they read in the book, in the Law of God, distinctly; and they gave the sense, and caused them to understand the reading.

(Nehemiah 8:8)

The requirement to read the Torah publicly at specific times of the week dates back to the days of Moses. In the time of Ezra, the Men of the Great Assembly added further structure to this enactment, including additional public Torah readings and specific details with regard to how many readers are called to the Torah and how many verses they are required to read.

In the time of the Second Temple, and certainly after that, Hebrew was no longer the spoken language of many Jews, and many individuals needed a translator to aid them in comprehending the public Torah readings. As many individuals could not recite the prayers on their own, it was established that a prayer leader would recite the prayer aloud for them. Consequently, it was necessary to establish guidelines concerning the translation of the Torah readings, which prayers could be recited only in public, and the circumstances under which public prayers could be recited.

Additionally, the formation of various sects with different customs made it necessary to establish clear guidelines as to which customs are acceptable during the prayer service and which are not. The details of these questions form the main concern of this chapter.

מתני׳ הַקּוֹרֵא אֶת הַמְּגִילָּה עוֹמֵד וְיוֹשֵׁב. קְרָאָהּ אֶחָד, קְרָאוּהָ שְׁנַיִם – יָצְאוּ. מְקוֹם שֶׁנָּהֲגוּ לְבָרֵךְ – יְבָרֵךְ. וְשֶׁלֹּא לְבָרֵךְ – לֹא יְבָרֵךְ.

MISHNA **One who reads**[N] **the Megilla** may position himself as he wishes, either **standing or sitting.**[H] Whether **one** person **reads** the Megilla[N] or **two** people **read** it together, **they have fulfilled** their obligation. In **a place where** the people **are accustomed to recite a blessing** over the reading, **one should recite a blessing. And** in a place where it is customary **not to recite a blessing, one should not recite a blessing.**

בְּשֵׁנִי וַחֲמִישִׁי, בְּשַׁבָּת בְּמִנְחָה – קוֹרִין שְׁלֹשָׁה, אֵין פּוֹחֲתִין מֵהֶן וְאֵין מוֹסִיפִין עֲלֵיהֶן, וְאֵין מַפְטִירִין בְּנָבִיא. הַפּוֹתֵחַ וְהַחוֹתֵם בַּתּוֹרָה – מְבָרֵךְ לְפָנֶיהָ וּלְאַחֲרֶיהָ.

The mishna records several laws governing public Torah readings. **On Mondays and Thursdays** during the morning service **and on Shabbat during the afternoon service, three** people **read** from the Torah;[H] **one may neither decrease** the number of readers **nor add to them. And one does not conclude with** a reading from the **Prophets** [*haftara*] on these occasions. Both **the one who begins** the reading **and the one who concludes the** reading from **the Torah recite a blessing;** one recites **before** the beginning of the reading **and** one recites **after its** conclusion, but the middle reader does not recite a blessing.

בְּרָאשֵׁי חֳדָשִׁים וּבְחוּלּוֹ שֶׁל מוֹעֵד – קוֹרִין אַרְבָּעָה, אֵין פּוֹחֲתִין מֵהֶן וְאֵין מוֹסִיפִין עֲלֵיהֶן, וְאֵין מַפְטִירִין בְּנָבִיא. הַפּוֹתֵחַ וְהַחוֹתֵם בַּתּוֹרָה – מְבָרֵךְ לְפָנֶיהָ וּלְאַחֲרֶיהָ.

On the days of the **New Moon**[H] **and on the intermediate days of a Festival,**[H] **four** people **read** from the Torah; **one may neither decrease** the number of readers **nor add to them. And one does not conclude with** a reading from the **Prophets.** Both **the one who begins** the reading **and the one who concludes** the reading from **the Torah recite a blessing.** The first reader recites a blessing **before** the beginning of the reading, **and** the last reader recites a blessing **after its** conclusion, but the middle readers do not recite a blessing.

זֶה הַכְּלָל: כׇּל שֶׁיֵּשׁ בּוֹ מוּסָף וְאֵינוֹ יוֹם טוֹב – קוֹרִין אַרְבָּעָה. בְּיוֹם טוֹב חֲמִשָּׁה. בְּיוֹם הַכִּפּוּרִים – שִׁשָּׁה, בְּשַׁבָּת – שִׁבְעָה. אֵין פּוֹחֲתִין מֵהֶן, אֲבָל מוֹסִיפִין עֲלֵיהֶן, וּמַפְטִירִין בְּנָבִיא. הַפּוֹתֵחַ וְהַחוֹתֵם בַּתּוֹרָה – מְבָרֵךְ לְפָנֶיהָ וּלְאַחֲרֶיהָ.

The mishna formulates a general principle with regard to the number of people who read from the Torah on different occasions. **This is the principle: Any** day **on which there is an additional offering** sacrificed in the Temple **and that is not a Festival,** i.e., the New Moon and the intermediate days of a Festival, **four** people **read** from the Torah; **on a Festival,**[H] **five** people read; **on Yom Kippur, six** people read; and **on Shabbat,**[H] **seven** people read. **One may not decrease** the number of readers, **but one may add to them. And** on these days **one concludes with** a reading from the **Prophets.** Both **the one who begins** the reading **and the one who concludes the** reading[N] from **the Torah recite a blessing;** one recites **before** the beginning of the reading **and** one recites **after its** conclusion, but the middle readers do not recite a blessing.

NOTES

One who reads – הַקּוֹרֵא: In the Mishna, the Jerusalem Talmud, and a version of the Babylonian Talmud used by several early authorities, this chapter comes after the following chapter. It is the fourth chapter in the tractate rather than the third.

Whether one person reads the Megilla – קְרָאָהּ אֶחָד: The commentaries question the necessity of this phrase; isn't it obvious that if one person reads the Megilla, he and his audience have fulfilled their obligation? Some explain that one may have thought that the requirement to publicize the miracle requires multiple people to read the Megilla together, and therefore it was necessary to state that one reader is also acceptable. Alternatively, the mishna is teaching that even if an individual reads the Megilla in private, he has fulfilled his obligation (*Re'ah Duda'im*). With regard to the mishna's statement that two people may read the Megilla, the straightforward interpretation is that two people read it together at the same time. However, the mishna can also be understood as indicating that if one person read part of the Megilla and then another person read the rest of it, the reading is valid (*Sefat Emet*).

The one who begins the reading and the one who concludes the reading – הַפּוֹתֵחַ וְהַחוֹתֵם: *Tosafot* question why it is necessary to repeat this statement three times in the mishna. They answer that one might have thought that when there are more readers, more blessings are required. The Rashba and the Ran expound further: One might have thought that when there are more than three readers, each reader must recite the blessings before and after reading from the Torah. Later authorities explain that since each public Torah reading must have at least three readers, one might have thought that additional readers are considered to be participating in an entirely new Torah reading and must recite additional blessings. Therefore, the mishna states that even when there are four readers, only the first and last readers must recite a blessing. The third time this ruling is stated, it comes to teach that even if they call additional readers beyond those required on a Shabbat, additional blessings are not recited (*Sefat Emet*).

HALAKHA

One who reads the Megilla may position himself either standing or sitting – הַקּוֹרֵא אֶת הַמְּגִילָּה עוֹמֵד וְיוֹשֵׁב: The Megilla may be read either standing or sitting. However, the blessing must be recited while standing (*Magen Avraham*). Still, when one reads in public he should read standing, out of deference to the honor of the congregation. Some say that if the congregation wishes to forgo its honor and allow the reader to sit, they may do so (*Kaf HaHayyim*; *Shulhan Arukh, Orah Hayyim* 690:1).

Reading the Torah on Mondays and Thursdays – קְרִיאַת הַתּוֹרָה בְּשֵׁנִי וּבַחֲמִישִׁי: On Mondays and Thursdays that are regular weekdays, the Torah is read during the morning prayers. Three people read from the Torah; one may neither decrease this number nor call additional readers. One does not conclude with a reading from the Prophets (*Shulhan Arukh, Orah Hayyim* 135:1).

Reading the Torah on the New Moon – קְרִיאַת הַתּוֹרָה בְּרֹאשׁ חוֹדֶשׁ: The Torah is read on the New Moon following the recital of *hallel*. Four people read from the Torah; one may not decrease this number nor call additional readers. One does not conclude with a reading from the Prophets (*Shulhan Arukh, Orah Hayyim* 423:1).

Reading the Torah on the intermediate days of a Festival – קְרִיאַת הַתּוֹרָה בְּחוּלּוֹ שֶׁל מוֹעֵד: Four people read from the Torah on the intermediate days of a Festival. One may neither decrease this number nor add additional readers. One does not conclude with a reading from the Prophets (*Shulhan Arukh, Orah Hayyim* 663:1).

Reading the Torah on a Festival – קְרִיאַת הַתּוֹרָה בְּיוֹם טוֹב: On Festivals, two Torah scrolls are removed from the ark. Five people read from the first scroll and a concluding reader [*maftir*] reads from the second scroll. A *haftara* is read from the Prophets (*Shulhan Arukh, Orah Hayyim* 488:3, 494:1). It is permitted to increase the number of readers on a Festival. However, some say that this should not be done. This is generally the accepted practice. There is an exception on *Simhat Torah*, when it is the universal custom to call many readers to the Torah, and it is common for communities to call every man who is present in the synagogue (*Shulhan Arukh, Orah Hayyim* 282:1, and in the comment of Rema).

Reading the Torah on Shabbat – קְרִיאַת הַתּוֹרָה בְּשַׁבָּת: Generally, one Torah scroll is removed from the ark on Shabbat. On special occasions, when an additional portion is read, two scrolls are removed. Seven people read from the first scroll and one from the second, and a *haftara* is read from the Prophets. It is permitted to increase the number of readers. However, some say that nowadays one should not increase the number. It is proper to abide by this ruling unless it is a situation of need, e.g., there are many guests who have come to celebrate a special occasion (*Magen Avraham*, based on *Tashbetz*). According to some authorities, one should never increase the number of readers (*Tzemah Tzedek, Orah Hayyim* 35; *Shulhan Arukh, Orah Hayyim* 282:1).

גמ׳ תָּנָא: מַה שֶּׁאֵין כֵּן בַּתּוֹרָה. מְנָהָנֵי מִילֵּי? אָמַר רַבִּי אַבָּהוּ: דְּאָמַר קְרָא ״וְאַתָּה פֹּה עֲמֹד עִמָּדִי״. וְאָמַר רַבִּי אַבָּהוּ: אִלְמָלֵא מִקְרָא כָּתוּב אִי אֶפְשָׁר לְאוֹמְרוֹ, כִּבְיָכוֹל אַף הַקָּדוֹשׁ בָּרוּךְ הוּא בַּעֲמִידָה.

GEMARA

We learned in the mishna that one may read the Megilla while sitting. **It was taught** in a *baraita*: This **is not the case with regard to** reading **the Torah,**[N] as one must stand when reading the Torah.[H] The Gemara asks: **From where are these matters** derived? **Rabbi Abbahu said:** It is **as the verse states: "But as for you, stand here with Me,** and I will speak to you all the commandments and the statutes" (Deuteronomy 5:27), which indicates that the Torah must be received while standing. **And Rabbi Abbahu said: Were the verse not written** in this manner, **it would be impossible to utter it,** in deference to God. The phrase "with Me" indicates that, **as it were, even the Holy One, Blessed be He, was standing** at the giving of the Torah.

וְאָמַר רַבִּי אַבָּהוּ: מִנַּיִן לָרַב שֶׁלֹּא יֵשֵׁב עַל גַּבֵּי מִטָּה וְיִשְׁנֶה לְתַלְמִידוֹ עַל גַּבֵּי קַרְקַע – שֶׁנֶּאֱמַר ״וְאַתָּה פֹּה עֲמֹד עִמָּדִי״.

And Rabbi Abbahu also **said: From where** is it derived **that the teacher should not sit on a couch and teach his disciple**[H] while he is sitting **on the ground?** It is **as it is stated: "But as for you, stand here with Me,"** which indicates that the teacher and his disciples should be in the same position.

תָּנוּ רַבָּנַן: מִימוֹת מֹשֶׁה וְעַד רַבָּן גַּמְלִיאֵל לֹא הָיוּ לְמֵדִין תּוֹרָה אֶלָּא מְעוּמָּד, מִשֶּׁמֵּת רַבָּן גַּמְלִיאֵל יָרַד חוֹלִי לָעוֹלָם וְהָיוּ לְמֵדִין תּוֹרָה מְיוּשָּׁב. וְהַיְינוּ דִּתְנַן: מִשֶּׁמֵּת רַבָּן גַּמְלִיאֵל בָּטֵל כְּבוֹד תּוֹרָה.

With regard to Torah study while standing, **the Sages taught: From the days of Moses until** the time of **Rabban Gamliel,**[P] **they would study Torah only while standing,**[N] as learning from one's teacher is comparable to receiving the Torah at Sinai, during which the Jewish people stood. **When Rabban Gamliel died, weakness descended to the world, and they would study Torah while sitting. And this is as we learned** in a mishna (*Sota* 49a): **When Rabban Gamliel died, honor** for **the Torah ceased,** as standing while learning is an expression of honor for the Torah.

כָּתוּב אֶחָד אוֹמֵר ״וָאֵשֵׁב בָּהָר״ וְכָתוּב אֶחָד אוֹמֵר ״וְאָנֹכִי עָמַדְתִּי בָהָר״! אָמַר רַב: עוֹמֵד וְלוֹמֵד, יוֹשֵׁב וְשׁוֹנֶה. רַבִּי חֲנִינָא אָמַר: לֹא עוֹמֵד וְלֹא יוֹשֵׁב אֶלָּא שׁוֹחֶה. רַבִּי יוֹחָנָן אָמַר: אֵין יְשִׁיבָה אֶלָּא לְשׁוֹן עַכָּבָה, שֶׁנֶּאֱמַר ״וַתֵּשְׁבוּ בְקָדֵשׁ יָמִים רַבִּים״. רָבָא אָמַר: רַכּוֹת מְעוּמָּד, וְקָשׁוֹת מְיוּשָּׁב.

The Gemara points out an apparent contradiction with regard to this very issue. **One verse says: "And I sat [*va'eshev*] on the mount"** (Deuteronomy 9:9), **and another verse says: "And I stood on the mount"** (Deuteronomy 10:10). The Gemara cites several possible resolutions. **Rav said:** Moses would **stand and learn** the Torah from God, and then **sit and review** what he had learned. **Rabbi Ḥanina said:** Moses was **not standing or sitting, but rather bowing.**[N] **Rabbi Yoḥanan said:** The term *yeshiva* **is nothing more than an expression of remaining** in one place, **as it is stated: "And you dwelled [*vateshvu*] in Kadesh for many days"** (Deuteronomy 1:46). **Rava said:** Moses studied **easy** material while **standing and difficult** material while **sitting.**

״קְרָאָהּ אֶחָד קְרָאוּהָ שְׁנַיִם יָצְאוּ״ וכו׳.

We learned in the mishna: If **one** person **reads** the Megilla or **two** people **read it** together, **they have fulfilled** their obligation.

HALAKHA

Standing while reading the Torah – עֲמִידָה בִּקְרִיאַת הַתּוֹרָה: The Torah should be read while standing. It is prohibited even to lean on something, unless it is difficult for the reader to stand without leaning (*Magen Avraham*; *Sha'ar Efrayim*). However, if the Torah was read while sitting, the reading is valid after the fact (*Peri Ḥadash*). Nowadays, when there is an official reader, he must stand; the one called to recite the blessings must stand as well. The congregation does not have to stand. However, some have the practice to stand as a sign of honor for the Torah (*Arukh HaShulḥan*, *Shulḥan Arukh*, *Oraḥ Ḥayyim* 141:1).

A master and his disciple – רַב וְתַלְמִידוֹ: A teacher should not sit on a chair while his students are sitting on the ground; rather, the teacher and students should either all be sitting on chairs or all be sitting on the ground. However, some say that this *halakha* applies only to students who have already received rabbinical ordination (Rema). Some have the custom to express honor for the Torah by standing while studying Torah. They should stand while studying easy material and sit while studying difficult material (*Shakh*, citing Ran; *Shulḥan Arukh*, *Yoreh De'a* 246:9).

NOTES

This is not the case with regard to reading the Torah – מַה שֶּׁאֵין כֵּן בַּתּוֹרָה: The Torah may not be read in public while sitting, out of deference to the public or out of deference to the Divine Presence, which is present when there is a quorum (*Tosefot Rid*; see Jerusalem Talmud).

They would study Torah only while standing – לֹא הָיוּ לְמֵדִין תּוֹרָה אֶלָּא מְעוּמָּד: The early commentaries note that it appears from several sources that even before Rabban Gamliel died, people would often study Torah while sitting. They answer that difficult material was studied while sitting and easier material was studied while standing (see Rashba and others).

But rather bowing – אֶלָּא שׁוֹחֶה: This was an expression of honor for the Divine Presence (Maharsha). Bowing can be considered standing, as one is supporting oneself on one's feet, but is also similar to sitting, as one is not standing straight to one's full height. Therefore, different verses use different terms to describe Moses' position.

PERSONALITIES

Rabban Gamliel – רַבָּן גַּמְלִיאֵל: The reference here is to Rabban Gamliel the Elder, and not to his grandson, whose name was also Rabban Gamliel, and who was referred to as Rabban Gamliel of Yavne. Rabban Gamliel the Elder was a grandson of Hillel the Elder and served as the head of the Sanhedrin for many years during the Temple period.

It seems that Rabban Gamliel was the first to receive the honorary title Rabban because he was accepted by all of the Sages of the Jewish people. Many of his rulings were cited in the following generations. He enacted many important decrees, e.g., a woman may remarry based on the testimony of a single witness that her previous husband has died. He enacted other decrees as well, in order to improve the public welfare. During his time, people would still study Torah while standing, and therefore it is said that when Rabban Gamliel died, honor for the Torah ceased.

His son was Rabban Shimon ben Gamliel, who led the Jewish people during the era of the Great Revolt and was later executed by the Romans.

תָּנָא: מַה שֶּׁאֵין כֵּן בַּתּוֹרָה. תָּנוּ רַבָּנַן: בַּתּוֹרָה אֶחָד קוֹרֵא וְאֶחָד מְתַרְגֵּם, וּבִלְבַד שֶׁלֹּא יְהֵא אֶחָד קוֹרֵא וּשְׁנַיִם מְתַרְגְּמִין. וּבַנָּבִיא אֶחָד קוֹרֵא וּשְׁנַיִם מְתַרְגְּמִין, וּבִלְבַד שֶׁלֹּא יְהוּ שְׁנַיִם קוֹרִין וּשְׁנַיִם מְתַרְגְּמִין. וּבְהַלֵּל וּבִמְגִילָּה – אֲפִילּוּ עֲשָׂרָה קוֹרִין וַעֲשָׂרָה מְתַרְגְּמִין.

It was taught: This **is not the case with regard to** reading **the Torah,**[H] which may be read only by a single person. **The Sages taught** (*Tosefta, Megilla* 3:20): When reading from **the Torah, one** person **reads and one may translate**[HB] the reading into Aramaic for the congregation, **provided that there are not one** person **reading and two** people **translating,** because two voices cannot be heard simultaneously. **And** when reading from **the Prophets,**[H] **one** person **reads and two may translate,** as there is less of a need to ensure that everyone hears the precise translation, as the Prophets do not teach *halakha*. This is the case **provided that there are not two** people **reading and two translating. And** when reciting ***hallel***[H] **and** reading **the Megilla,**[H] **even ten** people **may read and ten may translate.**

מַאי טַעְמָא? כֵּיוָן דַּחֲבִיבָה – יָהֲבִי דַּעְתַּיְיהוּ וְשָׁמְעִי.

The Gemara asks: **What is the reason** that the Megilla may be read by several people at once? **Since** the Megilla **is cherished** by the congregation, **they will pay** close **attention and hear it,**[N] and they will not become distracted by the different voices.

"מְקוֹם שֶׁנָּהֲגוּ לְבָרֵךְ יְבָרֵךְ". אָמַר אַבָּיֵי: לֹא שָׁנוּ אֶלָּא לְאַחֲרֶיהָ, אֲבָל לְפָנֶיהָ – מִצְוָה לְבָרֵךְ. דְּאָמַר רַב יְהוּדָה אָמַר שְׁמוּאֵל: כׇּל הַמִּצְוֹת כּוּלָּן מְבָרֵךְ עֲלֵיהֶן עוֹבֵר לַעֲשִׂיָּיתָן.

§ We learned in the mishna: In **a place where** the people **are accustomed to recite a blessing** over the reading, **one should recite a blessing. Abaye said: They taught** that the matter depends upon local custom **only** with regard to the blessing that is recited **after** the reading of the Megilla. **But** as for the blessing that is recited **before** the reading, it is **a mitzva to recite the blessing** according to all opinions, as **Rav Yehuda said that Shmuel said: With regard to all the mitzvot, one recites a blessing over them prior to** [*over*] **their performance.**[NH]

מַאי מַשְׁמַע דְּהַאי "עוֹבֵר" לִישָּׁנָא דְּאַקְדּוּמֵי הוּא? אָמַר רַב נַחְמָן בַּר יִצְחָק, אָמַר קְרָא "וַיָּרׇץ אֲחִימַעַץ דֶּרֶךְ הַכִּכָּר וַיַּעֲבֹר אֶת הַכּוּשִׁי". אַבָּיֵי אָמַר מֵהָכָא: "וְהוּא עָבַר לִפְנֵיהֶם", וְאִיבָּעֵית אֵימָא מֵהָכָא: "וַיַּעֲבֹר מַלְכָּם לִפְנֵיהֶם וַה׳ בְּרֹאשָׁם".

The Gemara asks: **From where** may it **be inferred that** the word *over* **is the language of precedence? Rav Naḥman bar Yitzḥak said that the verse states: "And Ahimaaz ran by the way of the plain, and overran** [*vaya'avor*] **the Cushite"** (II Samuel 18:23), i.e., Ahimaaz overtook the Cushite. **Abaye said:** It is derived **from here: "And he passed** [*avar*] **before them"** (Genesis 33:3). **And if you wish, say** instead that the proof is **from here: "And their king passed** [*vaya'avor*] **before them and the Lord at their head"** (Micah 2:13).

לְפָנֶיהָ מַאי מְבָרֵךְ? רַב שֵׁשֶׁת מִקַּטְרַזְיָא אִיקְּלַע לְקַמֵּיהּ דְּרַב אַשִׁי, וּבָרֵיךְ מנ"ח.

The Gemara asks: **What blessing is recited before** the reading of the Megilla?[H] The Gemara relates that **Rav Sheshet from Katrazya** once **happened** to come **before Rav Ashi, and he recited** three **blessings,** alluded to by the letters *mem, nun, ḥet*: Concerning the reading [*mikra*] of the Megilla; Who has performed miracles [*nissim*] for our fathers; and Who has given us life [*sheheḥeyanu*].

HALAKHA

This is not the case with regard to reading the Torah – מַה שֶּׁאֵין כֵּן בַּתּוֹרָה: Two people should not read the Torah together. Nowadays, one person reads the entire Torah portion aloud and those called to the Torah to recite the blessing do not. However, those who recite the blessing should read along with the reader quietly, so that the congregation will not hear their voice (*Shulḥan Arukh, Oraḥ Ḥayyim* 141:2, and the comment of Rema).

One reads and one may translate – אֶחָד קוֹרֵא וְאֶחָד מְתַרְגֵּם: Two people should not translate the Torah together; rather, one should read and one should translate (Rambam *Sefer Ahava, Hilkhot Tefilla* 12:11).

Reading the Prophets – קְרִיאָה בַּנָּבִיא: One person reads the Prophets, and even two may translate together (Rambam *Sefer Ahava, Hilkhot Tefilla* 12:13).

Reciting *hallel* – קְרִיאַת הַהַלֵּל: Even ten people may read the *hallel* together (*Shulḥan Arukh, Oraḥ Ḥayyim* 488:2).

Reading the Megilla – קְרִיאַת הַמְּגִילָּה: Even ten people may read the Megilla together, and they and those who hear them fulfill their obligation. However, the custom is for only one person to read aloud for the community. One who does not have a valid Megilla should be especially careful to hear the Megilla from the reader and not articulate the words together with him (*Arukh HaShulḥan*; *Shulḥan Arukh, Oraḥ Ḥayyim* 690:2).

Prior to their performance – עוֹבֵר לַעֲשִׂיָּיתָן: Blessings are recited before the performance of a mitzva, in accordance with the statement of Shmuel. However, with regard to washing one's hands and immersing in a ritual bath, the blessing is recited after the performance of the mitzva (*Shulḥan Arukh, Oraḥ Ḥayyim* 25:8).

The blessings over the Megilla – בִּרְכוֹת הַמְּגִילָּה: Before the Megilla is read at night, three blessings are recited: Concerning the reading of the Megilla; Who has performed miracles for our fathers; and Who has given us life. The blessing: Who has given us life, is not repeated before the reading of the Megilla during the day. However, the custom in Ashkenazic communities is to recite this blessing during the day as well (Rema). Some Sephardic communities also have this custom (*Kaf HaḤayyim*). After the reading of the Megilla, it is customary nowadays for each individual to recite the blessing: Who pleads our cause. The blessing is concluded: Who, on behalf of Israel, exacts punishment from all their foes; the God Who brings salvation. This practice is in accordance with the ruling of Rav Pappa (*Shulḥan Arukh, Oraḥ Ḥayyim* 692:1).

BACKGROUND

And one may translate – וְאֶחָד מְתַרְגֵּם: From the time of Ezra the Scribe and through the talmudic period, it was customary to read the Aramaic translation of Onkelos as part of the Torah reading on Shabbat morning. This practice was intended, among other things, to allow even those unfamiliar with biblical Hebrew to understand the reading. This custom is no longer practiced today, with the exception of Yemenite communities, where reading the translation of Onkelos remains part of the service.

NOTES

Since the Megilla is cherished by the congregation, they will pay close attention and hear it – כֵּיוָן דַּחֲבִיבָה יָהֲבִי דַּעְתַּיְיהוּ וְשָׁמְעִי: The Ran and others explain that one will listen carefully and discern one of the voices. Alternatively, one will listen carefully to all of the voices together rather than to one particular voice.

Prior to their performance – עוֹבֵר לַעֲשִׂיָּיתָן: The Gemara proves that *over* means prior to. However, it also indicates that the blessing must be recited immediately before the performance of the mitzva. Perhaps this can be derived from the second verse cited in the Gemara: "And he passed before them," which describes the fact that Jacob went immediately in front of his family members. Similarly, the blessing must be recited immediately before the performance of the mitzva (Ran; Ritva), in order to emphasize that one's intent is to fulfill the mitzva (*Tosefot Rid*).

לְאַחֲרֶיהָ מַאי מְבָרֵךְ? בָּרוּךְ אַתָּה ה׳ אֱלֹהֵינוּ מֶלֶךְ הָעוֹלָם (הָאֵל) הָרָב אֶת רִיבֵנוּ, וְהַדָּן אֶת דִּינֵנוּ, וְהַנּוֹקֵם אֶת נִקְמָתֵנוּ, וְהַנִּפְרָע לָנוּ מִצָּרֵינוּ, וְהַמְשַׁלֵּם גְּמוּל לְכָל אוֹיְבֵי נַפְשֵׁנוּ, בָּרוּךְ אַתָּה ה׳ הַנִּפְרָע לְיִשְׂרָאֵל מִכָּל צָרֵיהֶם. רָבָא אָמַר: הָאֵל הַמּוֹשִׁיעַ. אֲמַר רַב פַּפָּא: הִלְכָּךְ נֵימְרִינְהוּ לְתַרְוַיְיהוּ: בָּרוּךְ אַתָּה ה׳ הַנִּפְרָע לְיִשְׂרָאֵל מִכָּל צָרֵיהֶם הָאֵל הַמּוֹשִׁיעַ.

The Gemara asks: **What blessing is recited after** the reading of the Megilla in places where it is customary to recite such a blessing? The Gemara answers that the following blessing is recited: **Blessed are You, Lord our God, King of the universe, the God Who pleads our cause,**[N] **and Who judges our claim, and Who avenges our vengeance, and Who punishes our foes, and Who and brings retribution to our enemies. Blessed are You, Lord, Who, on behalf of Israel, exacts punishment from all of their foes. Rava said:** The conclusion of the blessing is as follows: Blessed are you, Lord, **the God who brings salvation. Rav Pappa said: Therefore,** since there are two opinions on the matter, **we should say both of them: Blessed are you, Lord, Who, on behalf of Israel, exacts punishment from all their foes; the God Who brings salvation.**[N]

״בְּשֵׁנִי וּבַחֲמִישִׁי, בְּשַׁבָּת בְּמִנְחָה קוֹרִין שְׁלֹשָׁה״ וכו׳. הָנֵי שְׁלֹשָׁה כְּנֶגֶד מִי? אָמַר רַב אַסִי: כְּנֶגֶד תּוֹרָה נְבִיאִים וּכְתוּבִים. רָבָא אָמַר: כְּנֶגֶד כֹּהֲנִים לְוִיִּם וְיִשְׂרְאֵלִים.

We learned in the mishna: **On Mondays and** on **Thursdays** during the morning service **and on Shabbat during the afternoon service, three** people **read** from the Torah. The Gemara asks: **Corresponding to what were these three** readers instituted? **Rav Asi said: They correspond** to the three sections of the Bible: **Pentateuch, Prophets, and Writings. Rava said: They correspond to** the three components of the Jewish people: **Priests, Levites, and Israelites.**

אֶלָּא הָא דְּתָנֵי רַב שִׁימִי: אֵין פּוֹחֲתִין מֵעֲשָׂרָה פְּסוּקִין בְּבֵית הַכְּנֶסֶת. ״וַיְדַבֵּר״ עוֹלֶה מִן הַמִּנְיָן. הָנֵי עֲשָׂרָה כְּנֶגֶד מִי?

The Gemara raises a question: **But** with regard to **this** *baraita* **that Rav Shimi taught: One may not decrease** to fewer than **ten** the number of **verses**[H] read during a public Torah reading **in the synagogue,** and a generic verse, e.g., **"And God spoke** to Moses saying," **is included in the count,**[N] **to what do these ten** verses **correspond?** Why specifically the number ten?

אָמַר רַבִּי יְהוֹשֻׁעַ בֶּן לֵוִי: כְּנֶגֶד עֲשָׂרָה בַּטְלָנִין שֶׁבְּבֵית הַכְּנֶסֶת, רַב יוֹסֵף אָמַר: כְּנֶגֶד עֲשֶׂרֶת הַדִּבְּרוֹת שֶׁנֶּאֶמְרוּ לְמֹשֶׁה בְּסִינַי. (רַבִּי לֵוִי אָמַר: כְּנֶגֶד עֲשָׂרָה הִילּוּלִין שֶׁאָמַר דָּוִד בְּסֵפֶר תְּהִלִּים) וְרַבִּי יוֹחָנָן אָמַר: כְּנֶגֶד עֲשָׂרָה מַאֲמָרוֹת שֶׁבָּהֶן נִבְרָא הָעוֹלָם.

Rabbi Yehoshua ben Levi said: They **correspond to the ten idlers that are in the synagogue,** i.e., ten men who have the leisure not to work, and instead sit in the synagogue and are available to attend to communal needs. **Rav Yosef said:** They **correspond to the Ten Commandments that were spoken to Moses at Sinai. Rabbi Levi said:** They **correspond to the ten** psalms of **praise** that **David said in the book of Psalms. And Rabbi Yoḥanan said: They correspond to the ten utterances**[N] **with which the world was created.**

הֵי נִינְהוּ? ״וַיֹּאמֶר״ דִּבְרֵאשִׁית? הָנֵי תִּשְׁעָה הָווּ! ״בְּרֵאשִׁית״ נַמִי מַאֲמָר הוּא, דִּכְתִיב ״בִּדְבַר ה׳ שָׁמַיִם נַעֲשׂוּ וּבְרוּחַ פִּיו כָּל צְבָאָם״.

The Gemara asks: **What are these** ten utterances? Presumably, they are the utterances introduced by the words **"and God said"** in the story of Creation in the first chapter of **Genesis.** However, **there are** only **nine of these** utterances and not ten. The Gemara answers: The expression: **"In the beginning"** (Genesis 1:1) **is also** considered **an utterance, as it is written: "By the word of the Lord were the heavens made; and all the host of them by the breath of His mouth"** (Psalms 33:6), which indicates that the first utterance of Creation was the general creation of the entire universe.

אָמַר רָבָא: רִאשׁוֹן שֶׁקָּרָא אַרְבָּעָה – מְשׁוּבָּח, שֵׁנִי שֶׁקָּרָא אַרְבָּעָה – מְשׁוּבָּח, שְׁלִישִׁי שֶׁקָּרָא אַרְבָּעָה – מְשׁוּבָּח.

Rava said: Since ten verses must be read, if **the first** of the three readers called to the Torah **read four** verses, **he is praiseworthy;** if **the second one read four** verses, **he is praiseworthy;** and if **the third one read four** verses, **he is praiseworthy.**[H]

רִאשׁוֹן שֶׁקָּרָא אַרְבָּעָה מְשׁוּבָּח – דִּתְנַן: בְּשָׁלֹשׁ קוּפּוֹת שֶׁל שָׁלֹשׁ סְאִין שֶׁבָּהֶן תּוֹרְמִין אֶת הַלִּשְׁכָּה, וְהָיָה כָּתוּב עֲלֵיהֶן אב״ג, לֵידַע אֵיזוֹ מֵהֶן נִתְרְמָה רִאשׁוֹן לְהַקְרִיב מִמֶּנָּה רִאשׁוֹן, שֶׁמִּצְוָה בָּרִאשׁוֹן.

Rava explains: **If the first** of the three readers called to the Torah **read four** verses, **he is praiseworthy** because the first in a series is privileged, **as we learned** in a mishna (*Shekalim* 8a): One **removes** the funds **from the** Temple treasury **chamber,**[H] in order to use them for purchasing communal offerings and attending to other needs of the Temple, **with three** large **baskets,** each measuring **three** ***se'a*****. On** the baskets **is written,** respectively, *alef, beit, gimmel,* in order **to know which of them was removed first,** in order **to sacrifice** offerings purchased with money **from** that basket **first, as it is a mitzva** to use the money collected with **the first** basket before the money collected with the others.

NOTES

Who pleads our cause, etc. – **הָרָב אֶת רִיבֵנוּ וכו׳**: Some early commentaries explain that the five expressions mentioned in this blessing correspond to the five times the Bible mentions that the Jews fought Amalek (*Orḥot Ḥayyim*; *Kol Bo*; *Mikhtam*).

Who on behalf of Israel exacts punishment from all their foes, the God Who brings salvation – **הַנִּפְרָע לְיִשְׂרָאֵל מִכָּל צָרֵיהֶם הָאֵל הַמּוֹשִׁיעַ**: One may not conclude a blessing with two themes; however, in this case the two phrases complement each other and are considered one theme. The reason it was necessary to add: The God Who brings salvation, is so that it not sound as though God exacted punishment from the foes of the Jewish people but did not save the Jews themselves (*Sefer Halakhot Gedolot*). Alternatively, this addition indicates that the Jews were not harmed when they defeated their enemies (Meiri; *Kol Bo*).

And God spoke to Moses saying, is included in the count – **וַיְדַבֵּר, עוֹלֶה מִן הַמִּנְיָן**: Rashi explains the novelty of this ruling: Although nothing is learned from this verse, it nonetheless counts as one of the verses. Later commentaries added that although this verse does teach something, nothing is learned from the fact that it is repeated so many times in the Torah (Rabbi Tzvi Hirsch Chajes). The *Sefat Emet* writes that this *halakha* corresponds to the enumeration of the ten utterances with which the world was created, which is the paradigm for the need to read ten verses. The verse "In the beginning" is a general expression referring to God's utterances, and it is considered one of the ten utterances. Similarly, the generic verse "And God spoke to Moses saying" counts as one of the ten verses in a Torah reading.

Ten utterances – **עֲשָׂרָה מַאֲמָרוֹת**: The commentaries disagree as to which verses are included in this count. All agree that the verse "In the beginning" is inclusive of the entire Creation (see Ramban's Commentary on the Torah).

HALAKHA

Ten verses – **עֲשָׂרָה פְּסוּקִין**: On a day when three readers are called to the Torah, they must read a minimum of ten verses in total. However, if the entire topic being read is concluded in fewer than ten verses, such as the story of the war against Amalek (Exodus 17:8–16), that is sufficient (Jerusalem Talmud; *Shulḥan Arukh, Oraḥ Ḥayyim* 137:1).

He is praiseworthy – **מְשׁוּבָּח**: If three readers are to read a section of ten verses, any one of them can read four verses, and he is considered praiseworthy (*Shulḥan Arukh, Oraḥ Ḥayyim* 137:2).

One removes the funds from the Temple treasury chamber – **תּוֹרְמִין אֶת הַלִּשְׁכָּה**: The small boxes in which the coins are collected from the chamber have the letters *alef, beit,* and *gimmel,* so that the money in the first box will be used first (Rambam *Sefer Zemanim, Hilkhot Shekalim* 2:7).

אֶמְצָעִי שֶׁקָּרָא אַרְבָּעָה מְשׁוּבָּח – דְּתַנְיָא ״אֶל מוּל פְּנֵי הַמְּנוֹרָה יָאִירוּ״ מְלַמֵּד שֶׁמְּצַדֵּד פְּנֵיהֶם כְּלַפֵּי נֵר מַעֲרָבִי, וְנֵר מַעֲרָבִי כְּלַפֵּי שְׁכִינָה. וְאָמַר רַבִּי יוֹחָנָן: מִכָּאן שֶׁאֶמְצָעִי מְשׁוּבָּח.

If **the middle one read four** verses, **he is** also **praiseworthy,** as the middle position is also dignified, **as it is taught** in a *baraita*: "The seven lamps **shall give light in front of the candelabrum**" (Numbers 8:2); **this teaches that** the priest **turns the front** of each lamp **toward** the **western lamp**[B] of the candelabrum, i.e., the middle lamp, **and** the **western lamp** faces **toward the Divine Presence.**[H] **And Rabbi Yoḥanan said:** It is derived **from here that the middle one is** especially **praiseworthy.**

וְאַחֲרוֹן שֶׁקָּרָא אַרְבָּעָה מְשׁוּבָּח – מִשּׁוּם מַעֲלִין בַּקֹּדֶשׁ וְלֹא מוֹרִידִין. רַב פַּפָּא אִיקְלַע לְבֵי כְּנִישְׁתָּא דַּאֲבִי גּוֹבֵר וְקָרָא רִאשׁוֹן אַרְבָּעָה וְשַׁבְּחֵיהּ רַב פַּפָּא.

And if the last one called to the Torah **read four** verses, **he** too **is praiseworthy, due to** the principle that **one elevates** to a higher level of **sanctity**[H] **and does not downgrade.** If the last reader reads more verses than did the first two, this is an elevation in sanctity. The Gemara relates that **Rav Pappa happened** to come **to the synagogue of** the place called **Avi Gover,**[B] **and the first person** called to the Torah **read four** verses, **and Rav Pappa praised him.**[N]

״אֵין פּוֹחֲתִין מֵהֶן וְאֵין מוֹסִיפִין״. תָּנָא: הַפּוֹתֵחַ מְבָרֵךְ לְפָנֶיהָ, וְהַחוֹתֵם מְבָרֵךְ לְאַחֲרֶיהָ.

We learned in the mishna that **one may neither decrease** the number of readers **nor add to them.** The one who begins the reading and the one who concludes the reading from the Torah each recite a blessing. **It is taught** in a *baraita*: **The one who begins** the reading **recites a blessing before** reading from the Torah, **and the one who concludes** the reading **recites a blessing after** the reading.

וְהָאִידָּנָא דְּכוּלְּהוּ מְבָרְכִי לְפָנֶיהָ וּלְאַחֲרֶיהָ – הַיְינוּ טַעְמָא דְּתַקִּינוּ רַבָּנַן: גְּזֵירָה מִשּׁוּם הַנִּכְנָסִין וּמִשּׁוּם הַיּוֹצְאִין.

The Gemara comments: **And now that all** who read from the Torah **recite blessings**[H] both **before and after** reading from the Torah, **this is the reason that the Sages instituted** this policy: It is **a decree due to** both **those who enter**[N] the synagogue in middle of the reading and do not hear the first reader's initial blessing **and due to those who leave** the synagogue early and do not hear the final reader's concluding blessing, lest they come to the erroneous conclusion that one blessing suffices.

״בְּרָאשֵׁי חֳדָשִׁים וּבְחוּלּוֹ שֶׁל מוֹעֵד קוֹרִין אַרְבָּעָה״ וכו׳. בְּעָא מִינֵּיהּ עוּלָּא בַּר רַב מֵרָבָא: פָּרָשַׁת רֹאשׁ חוֹדֶשׁ כֵּיצַד קוֹרִין אוֹתָהּ ״צַו אֶת בְּנֵי יִשְׂרָאֵל וְאָמַרְתָּ אֲלֵיהֶם אֶת קָרְבָּנִי לַחְמִי״ דַּהֲוָיָן תְּמַנְיָא פְּסוּקֵי, הֵיכִי נַעֲבֵיד?

We learned in the mishna: **On the days of the New Moon and on the intermediate days of a Festival, four** people **read** from the Torah. **Ulla bar Rav raised a dilemma before Rava: The** Torah **portion** read **on the New Moon** consists of three short consecutive paragraphs (Numbers 28:1–8, 9–10, 11–15). **How does one read it** in order to divide it among four readers? With regard to the first paragraph, which includes the verse: **"Command the children of Israel and say to them, My offering, the provision** of My sacrifices made by fire" (Numbers 28:2), and **which is eight verses, what shall we do?**

נִיקְרֵי תְּרֵי תְּלָתָא תְּלָתָא פְּסוּקִין – פָּשׁוּ לְהוּ תְּרֵי, וְאֵין מְשַׁיְּירִין בְּפָרָשָׁה פָּחוֹת מִשְּׁלֹשָׁה פְּסוּקִין. נִיקְרֵי אַרְבָּעָה אַרְבָּעָה – פָּשׁוּ לְהוּ שִׁבְעָה. ״וּבְיוֹם הַשַּׁבָּת״ הָוְיָין תְּרֵי, ״וּבְרָאשֵׁי חָדְשֵׁיכֶם״ הָוְיָין חַמְשָׁה, הֵיכִי נַעֲבֵיד? נִיקְרֵי תְּרֵי מֵהָא וְחַד מֵהָנָךְ

If you say that **the first two** readers **should read three verses each, there will remain** only **two** more **verses** until the end of the paragraph, and **one may not leave fewer than three verses** before the end of **a paragraph**[H] at the conclusion of a reading. If you say that the first two readers **should read four** verses **each** and complete the first paragraph, then **seven** verses **will be left** until the end of entire portion; the second paragraph of **"And on Shabbat day"** (Numbers 28:9) **is two** verses, and the third paragraph of **"And on the beginnings of your months"** (Numbers 28:11) **is five** verses. **What shall we do** with them? If the third reader **reads** the **two** verses **from this** paragraph **and one of those** verses in the following paragraph, this is improper due to the principle that

BACKGROUND

Western lamp – **נֵר מַעֲרָבִי**: There was a dispute among the talmudic Sages with regard to the positioning of the candelabrum in the Temple, and accordingly, with regard to the identity of the western lamp. According to the view that the candelabrum was situated on a north-south axis, the western lamp of the candelabrum was actually the middle one. The other lamps were positioned so that their wicks faced the middle lamp.

Candelabrum with wicks facing the middle lamp

The synagogue of Avi Gover – **בֵּי כְּנִישְׁתָּא דַּאֲבִי גּוֹבֵר**: The synagogue of Avi Gover was apparently located in a small town, perhaps a suburb of Meḥoza, between Meḥoza and the town of Mavrakhta. The place may have been named after the founder of this synagogue, which is mentioned several times in the Talmud and was visited by some of the great *amora'im* over a number of generations.

HALAKHA

And the western lamp faces toward the Divine Presence – **וְנֵר מַעֲרָבִי כְּלַפֵּי שְׁכִינָה**: The flames in the six lamps of the branches of the candelabrum all faced the middle lamp, and the flame in the middle lamp faced the Holy of Holies (Rambam *Sefer Avoda*, *Hilkhot Beit HaBeḥira* 3:8).

One elevates to a higher level of sanctity – **מַעֲלִין בַּקֹּדֶשׁ**: A person should be elevated to higher levels of authority and not demoted. Similarly, utensils that are utilized for sacred purposes should be used only for more elevated purposes but not for purposes of lesser sanctity (Rambam *Sefer Avoda*, *Hilkhot Kelei HaMikdash* 4:21 and *Sefer Avoda*, *Hilkhot Beit HaBeḥira* 3:16).

And now that all who read from the Torah recite blessings – **וְהָאִידָּנָא דְּכוּלְּהוּ מְבָרְכִי**: Nowadays all who are called up to the Torah recite a blessing both before and after the reading (*Shulḥan Arukh*, *Oraḥ Ḥayyim* 139:4).

And one may not leave fewer than three verses before the end of a paragraph – **וְאֵין מְשַׁיְּירִין בְּפָרָשָׁה פָּחוֹת מִשְּׁלֹשָׁה פְּסוּקִין**: A reader may not conclude reading the Torah with fewer than three verses left before the end of a paragraph (*Shulḥan Arukh*, *Oraḥ Ḥayyim* 138:1).

NOTES

Rav Pappa praised him – **שַׁבְּחֵיהּ רַב פַּפָּא**: Rav Pappa agreed that it is acceptable for any of the three readers to read four verses. He praised the first reader because he took the initiative to read four verses and thereby demonstrated his zeal to perform mitzvot (Maharsha).

Due to those who enter – **מִשּׁוּם הַנִּכְנָסִין**: Some explain this to mean that the one who comes in late will hear the Torah reading without having heard the blessing recited before the reading, and it is proper for everyone to hear both the Torah reading and the blessings (see *Mikhtam* and Meiri).

אֵין מַתְחִילִין בְּפָרָשָׁה פָּחוֹת מִשְּׁלֹשָׁה פְּסוּקִים. לִיקְרֵי תְּרֵי מֵהָא וּתְלָתָא מֵהָךְ – פָּשׁוּ לְהוּ תְּרֵי!

one may not begin a new **paragraph** and read **fewer than three verses** from it.[H] And if you say **he should read two** verses **from this** paragraph, i.e., the entire second paragraph, **and** then **three** verses **from that** final paragraph, **only two** verses will **remain** from the final paragraph. This is problematic because one may not conclude a reading with fewer than three verses left until the end of a paragraph and because the fourth reader will not have a sufficient number of verses to read.

אָמַר לוֹ: זוֹ לֹא שָׁמַעְתִּי, כַּיּוֹצֵא בָּהּ שָׁמַעְתִּי. דִּתְנַן: בַּיּוֹם הָרִאשׁוֹן ״בְּרֵאשִׁית״ וִ״יְהִי רָקִיעַ״ וְתָנֵי עֲלָהּ: ״בְּרֵאשִׁית״ – בִּשְׁנַיִם, ״יְהִי רָקִיעַ״ – בְּאֶחָד.

Rava **said to him: I have not heard** a solution for **this** problem from my teachers.[N] However, **with regard to a similar** problem **I heard** a solution from them, **as we learned** in a mishna (*Ta'anit* 26a): **On Sunday,** the non-priestly watches would read two paragraphs from the Torah:[H] **"In the beginning"** (Genesis 1:1–5) **and "Let there be a firmament"** (Genesis 1:6–8). **And it is taught in that regard** that the paragraph **"In the beginning"** was read **by two** readers and the paragraph **"Let there be a firmament" by one** reader.

וְהָוֵינַן בָּהּ: בִּשְׁלָמָא ״יְהִי רָקִיעַ״ בְּאֶחָד – דִּתְלָתָא פְּסוּקֵי הָווּ, אֶלָּא ״בְּרֵאשִׁית״ בִּשְׁנַיִם? חֲמִשָּׁה פְּסוּקֵי הָווּ, וְתַנְיָא הַקּוֹרֵא בַּתּוֹרָה לֹא יִפְחוֹת מִשְּׁלֹשָׁה פְּסוּקִים!

And we discussed this ruling and raised difficulties with **it: Granted,** the paragraph **"Let there be a firmament"** was read **by one** reader, **as** it consists of **three verses. But** how was the paragraph **"In the beginning"** read **by two?** It consists of only **five verses, and it was taught** in a mishna (23b): **One who reads from the Torah should not** read **fewer than three verses.**

וְאִיתְּמַר עֲלָהּ: רַב אָמַר: דּוֹלֵג, וּשְׁמוּאֵל אָמַר: פּוֹסֵק.

And it was stated with regard to that mishna that the *amora'im* disagreed about how to divide the verses. **Rav said:** The second reader **repeats** the last verse that the first reader had recited, so that each of them reads three verses. **And Shmuel**[NP] **said:** The first reader **divides** the third verse and reads half of it, and the second reader begins with the second half of that verse, as though each half were its own verse.

רַב אָמַר דּוֹלֵג, מַאי טַעְמָא לָא אָמַר פּוֹסֵק? קָסָבַר: כָּל פְּסוּקָא דְּלָא פַּסְקֵיהּ מֹשֶׁה אֲנַן לָא פָּסְקִינַן לֵיהּ.

The Gemara explains the opinions of Rav and Shmuel. **Rav said** that the second reader **repeats** the last verse that the first reader recited. **What is the reason** that **he did not state** that the first reader **divides** the third verse, in accordance with the opinion of Shmuel? The Gemara answers: **He holds** that **any verse that Moses did not divide, we may not divide.**

וּשְׁמוּאֵל אָמַר: פָּסְקִינַן לֵיהּ. וְהָא אָמַר רַבִּי חֲנַנְיָא קָרָא: צַעַר גָּדוֹל הָיָה לִי אֵצֶל רַבִּי חֲנִינָא הַגָּדוֹל, וְלֹא הִתִּיר לִי לִפְסוֹק אֶלָּא לְתִינוֹקוֹת שֶׁל בֵּית רַבָּן, הוֹאִיל וּלְהִתְלַמֵּד עֲשׂוּיִין!

The Gemara asks: **Does Shmuel say** that **we may divide** a verse into two parts? **Didn't Rabbi Ḥananya Kara,**[P] the Bible expert, **say: I had great distress with Rabbi Ḥanina the Great;** there were many times I had to ask his permission to divide a verse, **and he permitted me to divide** it **only for the** benefit of **schoolchildren, since they** need **to be taught** in this manner, as it is difficult for children to learn long verses all at once? In other cases, however it is prohibited to divide a verse.

HALAKHA

One may not begin a new paragraph and read fewer than three verses from it – אֵין מַתְחִילִין בְּפָרָשָׁה פָּחוֹת מִשְּׁלֹשָׁה פְּסוּקִים: One may not read the beginning of a new paragraph unless one reads at least three verses from it (*Shulḥan Arukh, Oraḥ Ḥayyim* 138:1).

The reading of the non-priestly watches – קְרִיאָה בְּמַעֲמָדוֹת: The non-priestly watches read portions from the story of Creation. On the first day, they read the following paragraphs: "In the beginning" and "Let there be a firmament." After that, on each day of the week they would read the portion relating to what was created on that day and on the following day (Rambam *Sefer Avoda, Hilkhot Kelei HaMikdash* 6:6).

NOTES

I have not heard a solution for this problem from my teachers – זוֹ לֹא שָׁמַעְתִּי: It is difficult to understand how there could have been a doubt about how to read from the Torah on the New Moon, which takes place every month. Perhaps it had been decreed that, on the New Moon, no one may enter or leave the synagogue during Torah reading, and therefore the general prohibitions against beginning a reading fewer than three verses from the beginning of a paragraph or concluding a reading with fewer than three verses remaining in a paragraph had not been enforced (*Ginzei HaMelekh*). Alternatively, there were conflicting customs in this regard and no universal custom had yet been formally established.

Rav and Shmuel – רַב וּשְׁמוּאֵל: The Rashba explains that the dispute between Rav and Shmuel is about whether it is more important to make sure not to divide verses in two or to take precautionary measures with regard to those who enter or leave in the middle of the Torah reading.

According to Rav, it is not common for people to leave in the middle of the Torah reading, and those who enter in the middle will ask those present for an explanation if they see something unusual. Therefore, it is not proper to divide a verse in half in order to ensure that those who enter or leave in the middle of Torah reading do not come to incorrect conclusions.

Shmuel, however, maintains that those who enter in the middle of the reading will not ask but rather they will arrive at their own conclusions (see Meiri), and since it has already been permitted to divide a verse, this solution is preferable.

Conversely, some suggest that Rav's opinion that any verse that Moses did not divide, we may not divide, does not mean that it is prohibited to do so. Rather, a verse that is not whole is not considered a verse with regard to the requirement that each reader must read three verses, and therefore nothing is to be gained by dividing a verse in half (*Sefat Emet*).

PERSONALITIES

Rav and Shmuel – רַב וּשְׁמוּאֵל: When Rav returned to Babylonia from Eretz Yisrael, there were already there several eminent Sages there, including Rav Sheila and Shmuel. However, within a short time, Rav was recognized by all as the greatest Sage of Babylonia. All other Sages were subordinate to him, despite the fact that Rav did not hold any official position of authority. Shmuel was among the first to accept Rav's authority, and he accorded him great honor both in Rav's presence and when he was not present.

However, shortly after Rav came to Babylonia, Shmuel, who was a doctor by profession, tried to heal him of an illness. Rav did not know what Shmuel was doing and thought that Shmuel was needlessly causing him pain. Therefore, he cursed Shmuel. When Rav realized what had happened, he greatly regretted having cursed Shmuel. In order to appease Shmuel, Rav treated him with great honor and gave deference to him whenever they met.

Rabbi Ḥananya Kara – רַבִּי חֲנַנְיָא קָרָא: A second generation *amora* in Eretz Yisrael, Rabbi Ḥananya, who is sometimes called Rabbi Ḥanina, was a disciple of Rabbi Ḥanina bar Ḥama, also known as Rabbi Ḥanina the Great, and Rabbi Yannai. Apparently, Rabbi Ḥananya not only taught young children, but he was also a Bible expert. For this reason, he was called *kara*. In the Talmud and the Midrash, he is mentioned in discussions with his two teachers, both on matters relating to his work and on other halakhic matters.

הָתָם טַעְמָא מַאי – מִשּׁוּם דְּלָא אֶפְשָׁר, הָכָא נַמִּי – לָא אֶפְשָׁר.

The Gemara answers: **There,** in the case of schoolchildren, **what is the reason** that it is permitted to divide a verse? **Because it is not possible** to teach the children without doing so. **Here, too,** when a paragraph of five verses must be divided between two readers, **it is not possible** to divide them without dividing the middle verse.

וּשְׁמוּאֵל אָמַר פּוֹסֵק, מַאי טַעְמָא לָא אָמַר דּוֹלֵג? גְּזֵירָה מִשּׁוּם הַנִּכְנָסִין וּמִשּׁוּם הַיּוֹצְאִין.

The Gemara now examines the opinion of Shmuel. **And Shmuel said:** The first reader **divides** the third verse and reads half of it. The Gemara asks: **What is the reason** that **he did not state** that the second reader **repeats** the last verse recited by the first reader, in accordance with the opinion of Rav? The Gemara answers: It is because of a rabbinic **decree** that was instituted **due to those who enter and those who leave** the synagogue between the readings. These individuals might erroneously conclude that since the reading they heard consisted of three verses, the reading they missed consisted of only two verses. Therefore, the middle verse is divided into two parts, so that all will realize that no reader recites only two verses.

מֵיתִיבִי: פָּרָשָׁה שֶׁל שִׁשָּׁה פְּסוּקִים קוֹרִין אוֹתָהּ בִּשְׁנַיִם, וְשֶׁל חֲמִשָּׁה פְּסוּקִים – בְּיָחִיד. קָרָא רִאשׁוֹן שְׁלֹשָׁה – הַשֵּׁנִי קוֹרֵא שְׁנַיִם מִפָּרָשָׁה זוֹ וְאֶחָד מִפָּרָשָׁה אַחֶרֶת, וְיֵשׁ אוֹמְרִים: שְׁלֹשָׁה, לְפִי שֶׁאֵין מַתְחִילִין בְּפָרָשָׁה פָּחוֹת מִשְּׁלֹשָׁה פְּסוּקִים.

The Gemara **raises an objection** to the opinions of Rav and Shmuel from the following *baraita*: **Two** people may **read a paragraph of six verses, but** a paragraph **of five** verses may be read only by **a single** reader. If **the first** one **read three** verses, **the second** one **reads** the remaining **two** verses **from this paragraph** and then **one** verse **from another,** i.e., the following, **paragraph. And some say** that it does not suffice to read one verse from the next paragraph; rather, he must read **three** verses, as **one may not begin** a new **paragraph** and read **fewer than three verses** from it.

וְאִם אִיתָא, לְמַאן דְּאָמַר דּוֹלֵג – נִדְלוֹג, וּלְמַאן דְּאָמַר פּוֹסֵק – נִפְסוֹק!

And if it is so, if it is permissible to do as Rav and Shmuel suggested, **according to the one who said** that the second reader **repeats** a verse that the previous reader recited, i.e., Rav, **let him repeat** the verse in this case as well. **And according to the one who said** that the second reader **divides** the verse, i.e., Shmuel, **let him divide** the verse in this case as well.

שָׁאנֵי הָתָם, דְּאֶפְשָׁר בְּהָכִי.

The Gemara answers: **There,** in the case of the *baraita,* **it is different, as it is possible to** solve the problem **in this** manner by reading additional verses. On the New Moon, however, the next paragraph deals with an entirely different subject, and consequently it cannot be included in the Torah reading. Therefore, Rav and Shmuel presented alternate solutions.

אָמַר רַבִּי תַּנְחוּם אָמַר רַבִּי יְהוֹשֻׁעַ בֶּן לֵוִי: הֲלָכָה כְּיֵשׁ אוֹמְרִים. וְאָמַר רַבִּי תַּנְחוּם אָמַר רַבִּי יְהוֹשֻׁעַ בֶּן לֵוִי: כְּשֵׁם שֶׁאֵין מַתְחִילִין בְּפָרָשָׁה פָּחוֹת מִשְּׁלֹשָׁה פְּסוּקִים – כָּךְ אֵין מְשַׁיְּירִין בְּפָרָשָׁה פָּחוֹת מִשְּׁלֹשָׁה פְּסוּקִים.

With regard to the dispute cited in the *baraita,* **Rabbi Tanḥum said that Rabbi Yehoshua ben Levi said: The** ***halakha*** **is in accordance with** the opinion introduced by the phrase: **Some say,** which maintains that at least three verses must be read from the next paragraph. **And** furthermore, **Rabbi Tanḥum said that Rabbi Yehoshua ben Levi said: Just as one may not begin** a new **paragraph** and read **fewer than three verses** from it, **so too, one may not leave fewer than three verses** before the end of **a paragraph** at the conclusion of a reading.

פְּשִׁיטָא! הַשְׁתָּא וּמָה אַתְחַלְתָּא, דְּקָא מֵקִיל תַּנָּא קַמָּא – מַחְמִירִי יֵשׁ אוֹמְרִים, שִׁיּוּר דְּמַחְמִיר תַּנָּא קַמָּא, לֹא כָּל שֶׁכֵּן דְּמַחְמִירִי יֵשׁ אוֹמְרִים?!

The Gemara challenges this statement: This **is obvious. Now,** if with regard to **the beginning** of a paragraph, where **the first** ***tanna*** **is lenient** and holds that it is sufficient to read one verse from the next paragraph, the opinion introduced with the phrase: **Some say, is stringent,** then with regard to **leaving** verses at the end of a paragraph, where even **the first** ***tanna*** **is stringent** and holds that one may not conclude a reading with fewer than three verses remaining until the end of a paragraph, is it **not all the more so** obvious that the opinion introduced with: **Some say, is stringent?**

מַהוּ דְּתֵימָא: נִכְנָסִין – שְׁכִיחִי, יוֹצְאִין – לָא שְׁכִיחִי דְּמַנְחִי סֵפֶר תּוֹרָה וְנָפְקִי, קָא מַשְׁמַע לָן.

The Gemara answers: **Lest you say: Entering** in the middle of the Torah reading **is common,** and therefore one should not conclude a reading after having read fewer than three verses of a paragraph, but **leaving** in the middle of the Torah reading, whereby one **abandons a Torah scroll and leaves, is not common,** and therefore one may conclude a reading with fewer than three verses left in the paragraph, Rabbi Yehoshua ben Levi **teaches us** that the second opinion cited in the mishna is also concerned that people may leave in the middle of the Torah reading, and consequently one may not conclude a reading with fewer than three verses left in the paragraph.

וְתַנָּא קַמָּא מַאי שְׁנָא שִׁיּוּרֵי דְּלָא – מִשּׁוּם יוֹצְאִין, אַתְחוּלֵי נַמִּי – גְּזֵירָה מִשּׁוּם הַנִּכְנָסִין! אָמְרִי: מַאן דְּעָיֵיל – שַׁיּוּלֵי שָׁיֵיל.

The Gemara asks: **And** according to **the first *tanna*, what is different** about **leaving** fewer than three verses at the end of a paragraph, **which** is **not** permitted **due to** concern about **those who leave** the synagogue in the middle of the Torah reading? In the case of **beginning** a paragraph without reading at least three verses, he should **also** hold that there is a rabbinic **decree due to those who enter,**[N] lest the latecomer think that the previous reader read fewer than three verses. The Gemara responds: **Say** in answer to this question that **one who enters** in the middle of the Torah reading **asks** how the Torah was read until then, and those present will explain to him that the reader started in the previous paragraph. Therefore, he will not erroneously think that the reader recited fewer than three verses.

שְׁלַח לֵיהּ רַבָּה בְּרֵיהּ דְּרָבָא לְרַב יוֹסֵף: הִלְכְתָא מַאי? שְׁלַח לֵיהּ: הִלְכְתָא דּוֹלֵג, וְאֶמְצָעִי דּוֹלְגָן.

Rabba, son of Rava, sent a messenger **to** ask **Rav Yosef: What is the *halakha*** with regard to dividing a small Torah portion? Rav Yosef **sent him** the following answer: **The *halakha*** is that **one repeats** a verse, in accordance with the opinion of Rav, **and** it is **the middle** reader who **repeats** it,[NH] and not the last reader, so that it will not be necessary to leave fewer than three verses until the end of the paragraph.

״זֶה הַכְּלָל כָּל שֶׁיֵּשׁ בּוֹ מוּסָף״ וכו׳. אִיבַּעְיָא לְהוּ: תַּעֲנִית צִבּוּר בְּכַמָּה? רֹאשׁ חֹדֶשׁ וּמוֹעֵד דְּאִיכָּא קׇרְבַּן מוּסָף – אַרְבָּעָה, אֲבָל הָכָא דְּלֵיכָּא קׇרְבַּן מוּסָף – לָא, אוֹ דִּלְמָא: הָכָא נַמִּי אִיכָּא מוּסָף תְּפִלָּה?

§ We learned in the mishna: **This is the principle: Any** day **on which there is an additional offering** sacrificed in the Temple and that is not a Festival, four people read from the Torah. **A dilemma was raised before** the Sages: On **a public fast, how many** people read from the Torah?[N] Does the mishna mean to say that only on **the New Moon and** the intermediate days of **a Festival, when there is an additional offering, four** people read; **but here,** on a public fast day, **when there is no additional offering, no,** only three people read? **Or perhaps here, too, there is an additional prayer,**[N] as on public fast days the prayer: *Aneinu*, is inserted into the *Amida* prayer, and so too an additional reader is called to read from the Torah.

תָּא שְׁמַע: בְּרָאשֵׁי חֳדָשִׁים וּבְחוּלּוֹ שֶׁל מוֹעֵד קוֹרִין אַרְבָּעָה, הָא בְּתַעֲנִית צִבּוּר – שְׁלֹשָׁה! אֵימָא רֵישָׁא: בְּשֵׁנִי וּבַחֲמִישִׁי, וּבְשַׁבָּת בְּמִנְחָה קוֹרִין שְׁלֹשָׁה, הָא תַּעֲנִית צִבּוּר – אַרְבָּעָה! אֶלָּא, מֵהָא לֵיכָּא לְמִישְׁמַע מִינַּהּ.

The Gemara attempts to adduce a proof: **Come** and **hear that** which we learned in the mishna: **On** the days of the **New Moon and on the intermediate days of a Festival, four** people **read** from the Torah. **Doesn't** this indicate that **on a public fast,** only **three** people read? The Gemara responds: **Say the first clause** of the mishna: **On Mondays and Thursdays** during the morning service **and on Shabbat during the afternoon service, three** people **read** from the Torah. **Doesn't** this indicate that on **a public fast, four** people read from the Torah? **Rather,** it must be concluded that **nothing can be derived from this** mishna with regard to a public fast day, as the mishna does not mean to indicate the *halakha* in every possible case.

תָּא שְׁמַע, דְּרַב אִיקְּלַע לְבָבֶל בְּתַעֲנִית צִבּוּר, קָם קְרָא בְּסִיפְרָא, פְּתַח בְּרִיךְ, חֲתִים וְלָא בְּרִיךְ. נְפוּל כּוּלֵּי עָלְמָא אַאַנְפַּיְיהוּ. וְרַב לָא נְפַל עַל אַפֵּיהּ.

A different proof is now suggested. **Come** and **hear** the following incident: **Rav** once **happened** to come **to Babylonia on a public fast. He stood and read from** a Torah **scroll.** When **he began** to read, **he recited a blessing,** but when **he concluded, he did not recite a blessing. Everyone** else **fell on their faces,** i.e., bowed down on the floor, during the *Taḥanun* supplication, as was the custom, **but Rav did not fall on his face.**

NOTES

Due to those who enter – מִשּׁוּם הַנִּכְנָסִין: Most of the commentaries explain that the concern is that someone will enter between readings. When the next reader begins his reading fewer than three verses from the beginning of a paragraph, the latecomer will mistakenly assume that the previous reader had begun from the beginning of the paragraph and had read fewer than three verses. The Ritva adds that there is also a concern that someone will enter in the middle of the previous reading, and when the reader concludes after having read fewer than three verses from the beginning of a paragraph, the latecomer will assume that he had begun from the beginning of the paragraph and read fewer than three verses.

The *halakha* is that one repeats a verse, and it is the middle reader who repeats it – הִלְכְתָא דּוֹלֵג וְאֶמְצָעִי דּוֹלְגָן: The early commentaries disagree with regard to this statement. Rashi explains that this applies to the readings of the non-priestly watches; however, the Gemara does not come to a conclusion with regard to the reading on the New Moon. Others question this explanation, as it is unusual for the Gemara to state: The *halakha* is, etc., with regard to a matter that has not been observed since the destruction of the Temple, such as the non-priestly watches. Conversely, the Rif and *ge'onim* explain that the Gemara's ruling is referring to the Torah reading on the New Moon. The *ge'onim* further explain that the middle reader is the second reader. Others have noted that this is difficult, as there are four readers, and therefore none of them is the middle reader (*Re'ah Duda'im*). In fact, some hold that it is the third reader who repeats verses, as he can also be considered a middle reader (Ramban; Vilna Gaon, based on tractate *Soferim*). However, some argue that the Gemara is referring to the first of the middle readers. There are other instances in which the second in a group or series is referred to as the middle (*Turei Even*).

On a public fast, how many people read from the Torah – תַּעֲנִית צִבּוּר בְּכַמָּה: Rabbeinu Tam asks: Can't it be proven from the Torah readings of the non-priestly watches, who would also fast, that there are three readers on a fast day? A possible answer is that three readers would read the portion of the day relating to the watch, and an additional reader would read a portion pertaining to the fast.

An additional prayer – מוּסָף תְּפִלָּה: Rashi and others explain that this addition is the prayer: *Aneinu*. Some say that it is referring to the twenty-four blessing *Amida* that was customarily recited on certain fasts. Others explain that it is referring to the *ne'ila* prayer that was recited at the end of the day on public fast days (Ritva, based on Ramban).

HALAKHA

One repeats a verse, and it is the middle reader who repeats it – דּוֹלֵג וְאֶמְצָעִי דּוֹלְגָן: On the New Moon, the Torah reading is divided up among the readers in the following manner: The priest reads the first three verses (Numbers 28:1–3) of the paragraph. The Levite repeats verse 3 and reads the following two verses. The Israelite then reads the final three verses of the paragraph (Numbers 28:6–8), as well as the next paragraph, which consists of two verses (Numbers 28:9–10). The fourth reader then reads the next paragraph, which is the portion that relates to the New Moon (Numbers 28:11–15). However, some have the custom for the Levite to read from where the priest left off until the end of the paragraph (Numbers 28:4–8), and for the Israelite to repeat the last two verses of that paragraph and to read the two verses of the following paragraph (Vilna Gaon, based on tractate *Soferim*; *Shulḥan Arukh*, *Oraḥ Ḥayyim* 423:2).

מִכְּדֵי רַב בְּיִשְׂרָאֵל קְרָא, מַאי טַעְמָא חָתַם וְלָא בְּרֵיךְ? לָאו מִשּׁוּם דְּבָעֵי לְמִיקְרֵי אַחֲרִינָא בָּתְרֵיהּ?

The Gemara attempts to clarify the *halakha* based upon Rav's conduct. **Now,** Rav must have **read** the portion that is designated for **an Israelite,** as he was neither a priest nor a Levite, and therefore he was the third person to read from the Torah. **What,** then, **is the reason** that when **he concluded** his reading **he did not recite a blessing? Was it not because another** person **was to read after him,** and since only the last reader recites a blessing, Rav did not recite a blessing upon completion of his portion? This would indicate that four readers are called to the Torah on public fasts.

לָא, רַב בְּכָהֲנֵי קְרָא, דְּהָא רַב הוּנָא קָרֵי בְּכָהֲנֵי.

The Gemara rejects this proof: **No, Rav read** the first reading, which is generally designated for **priests.** He was the leading Torah authority of his generation, and one who holds this position is called to read from the Torah even before a priest, **as Rav Huna**[P] **would read** the first reading, which is generally designated for **priests,**[N] and Rav would do the same.

בִּשְׁלָמָא רַב הוּנָא קָרֵי בְּכָהֲנֵי – דְּהָא אֲפִילּוּ רַב אַמִּי וְרַב אַסִּי, דְּכָהֲנֵי חֲשִׁיבֵי דְּאַרְעָא יִשְׂרָאֵל, מֵיכָּף כַּיְיפִי לֵיהּ לְרַב הוּנָא. אֶלָּא רַב, הָא אִיכָּא שְׁמוּאֵל, דְּכָהֲנָא הֲוָה וּדְבַר עֲלֵיהּ!

The Gemara raises a difficulty: **Granted, Rav Huna read** the portion designated for **priests, as even Rav Ami and Rav Asi,** who were **the most esteemed priests in Eretz Yisrael, were subordinate to Rav Huna,** and he was considered the undisputed rabbinic leader of the Jewish people. **However,** in the case of **Rav, there was Shmuel, who was a priest, and** Rav had **elevated** him **above himself,** showing Shmuel deference in all matters of honor. Consequently, Rav was not the singular leader of his generation and would not have read the first reading in place of a priest.

שְׁמוּאֵל נַמִי מֵיכָּף הֲוָה כַּיֵּיף לֵיהּ לְרַב, וְרַב הוּא דַּעֲבַד לֵיהּ כָּבוֹד. וְכִי עָבֵיד לֵיהּ – בְּפָנָיו, שֶׁלֹּא בְּפָנָיו – לָא עָבֵיד לֵיהּ.

The Gemara answers: In fact, **Shmuel was also subordinate to Rav,** as Rav was indeed the leading authority in Babylonia, **and it was Rav who showed** Shmuel **honor** of his own volition, in order to appease him for having cursed him. **And he did this** only when Shmuel was **in his presence,** but **when he was not in his presence,** Rav **did not do this,** and therefore Rav would read first from the Torah when Shmuel was not present.

הָכִי נַמִי מִסְתַּבְּרָא דְּרַב בְּכָהֲנֵי קְרָא, דְּאִי סָלְקָא דַּעְתָּךְ בְּיִשְׂרָאֵל קְרָא – לְפָנֶיהָ מַאי טַעְמָא בָּרֵיךְ? לְאַחַר תַּקָּנָה.

The Gemara comments: **So too, it is reasonable** to assume that **Rav read** first **from** the portion that is generally designated for **priests, because if it enters your mind to say** that **he read** third, **from** the portion designated for **an** ordinary **Israelite, what is the reason he recited a blessing before** reading his portion? Only the first reader recites a blessing before reading from the Torah. The Gemara rejects this argument: This incident took place **after it was instituted** that all those called to read from the Torah recite a blessing.

אִי הָכִי לְאַחֲרֶיהָ נַמִי לִבְרֵיךְ? שָׁאנֵי הֵיכָא דְּיָתֵיב רַב, דְּמֵיעַל עָיְילִי

The Gemara asks: **If so, he should also have recited a blessing after** his reading, as the rabbinic enactment requires those who read from the Torah to recite blessings both before and after their reading. The Gemara answers: The reason that the Sages required all the readers to recite blessings both before and after their readings was to prevent misunderstandings on the part of both those who enter the synagogue in the middle of the reading and those who leave early. But **it was different where Rav was present, as** people **would enter** the synagogue in the middle of the reading,

PERSONALITIES

Rav Huna – רַב הוּנָא: Rav Huna was one of the great second-generation Babylonian *amora'im*. He succeeded his teacher, Rav, as the head of the yeshiva of Sura. After the death of Shmuel, Rav Huna was considered by all to be the greatest Sage in Babylonia. His colleagues, Rav's other students, accepted his rulings, and even Shmuel asked him questions on several occasions.

Under his tenure, the yeshiva of Sura experienced significant growth, both in the number of its students and in their quality. Almost all of the Sages of the next generation were considered Rav Huna's students to a certain degree. This included Rav Ami and Rav Asi, who studied from Rav Huna in Babylonia. Even after they moved to Eretz Yisrael and were recognized as the leading Sages there, they considered themselves subordinate to Rav Huna.

According to a tradition recorded by the *ge'onim*, Rav Huna was from the family of the Exilarch. Nonetheless, he was very poor in his youth, but he studied Torah despite his poverty. He became wealthy later in life (see 27b). The Talmud recounts numerous anecdotes about Rav Huna's piety (see *Ta'anit* 20b), and his wisdom was legendary.

Rav Huna lived for over eighty years, and after his death he was brought with great honor to Eretz Yisrael, where he was buried next to the great Sage Rabbi Ḥiyya.

Rav Huna's son, Rabba bar Rav Huna, was among the most prominent *amora'im* of the next generation.

NOTES

Rav Huna would read the first reading, which is generally designated for priests – רַב הוּנָא קָרֵי בְּכָהֲנֵי: Although there is a mitzva to honor priests by allowing them to take precedence over non-priests, the honor of the Torah supersedes the honor of priests. The mishna in tractate *Horayot* (13a) states that a Torah scholar of illegitimate lineage [*mamzer*] takes precedence over a High Priest who is an ignoramus. The law of honoring the priest applies only when the people involved are of equal stature in Torah knowledge (see Rambam *Sefer HaMadda, Hilkhot Talmud Torah* 3:1–2). However, the universal custom is to honor the priest with the first reading from the Torah, in order to avoid strife (see Meiri and *Beit Peretz*).

Perek **III**
Daf **22** Amud **b**

מֵיפַּק לָא נָפְקִי.

but **they would not leave** early, out of deference to Rav, and therefore it was not necessary for him to recite a blessing after he finished his portion. In any event, the incident with Rav does not provide conclusive proof as to the number of readers on a public fast day.

תָּא שְׁמַע: זֶה הַכְּלָל: כׇּל שֶׁיֵּשׁ בּוֹ בִּיטּוּל מְלָאכָה לָעָם, כְּגוֹן תַּעֲנִית צִבּוּר וְתִשְׁעָה בְּאָב – קוֹרִין שְׁלֹשָׁה,

The Gemara tries to adduce another proof: **Come** and **hear** the following *baraita*: **This is the** general **principle: Any** day **on which** labor is permitted and prolonging the prayer service would constitute **a deprivation of labor for the masses, for example, a public fast day**[H] **and the Ninth of Av,** only **three** people **read** from the Torah, so as not to lengthen the prayer service unnecessarily.

HALAKHA

Torah reading on a fast day – קְרִיאַת הַתּוֹרָה בְּתַעֲנִית: On fast days, three people read from the Torah during both the morning and afternoon prayer services (Rambam *Sefer Ahava, Hilkhot Tefilla* 12:16).

NOTES

Any day on which prolonging the prayer service would not constitute a deprivation of labor for the masses, for example, the New Moon – וְשֶׁאֵין בּוֹ בִּיטּוּל מְלָאכָה לָעָם, כְּגוֹן רָאשֵׁי חֳדָשִׁים: The early commentaries attempt to clarify the meaning of this sentence in light of the fact that it is not halakhically prohibited to perform labor on the New Moon. Rashi and others explain that the Gemara is referring to the custom for women to refrain from labor on the New Moon, as though it were the intermediate days of a Festival. Other commentaries argue that there are indications in the Bible that the original custom was for even men to refrain from labor, and this custom has been preserved with regard to women (see Rabbeinu Yehonatan). Some suggest that men should refrain from engaging in hard labor on the New Moon (see Responsa of the Maharit). The *Turei Even* maintains that during the time of the Temple it was halakhically prohibited to perform labor on the New Moon.

Reading from the Torah and concluding with a reading from the Prophets – קוֹרִין וּמַפְטִיר: The *Turei Even* asks: If more readers were not called up to the Torah out of a concern not to deprive the masses from time to work, why did the Sages institute a *haftara* on public fast days, despite the fact that this also prolongs the service? Some explain that since the *haftara* includes words of encouragement to repent, it is an integral part of the prayers on fast days (*Sefat Emet*).

It merely gives a mnemonic – סִימָנָא בְּעָלְמָא יָהֵיב: Rav Ashi originally assumed that the principle was meant to include a *halakha* that was not mentioned explicitly in the mishna. The conclusion is that the principle is merely a mnemonic device to remember what is mentioned in the mishna, and it is not intended to allude to any *halakhot* that are not mentioned in the mishna.

וְשֶׁאֵין בּוֹ בִּיטּוּל מְלָאכָה לָעָם, כְּגוֹן רָאשֵׁי חֳדָשִׁים וְחוּלּוֹ שֶׁל מוֹעֵד – קוֹרִין אַרְבָּעָה, שְׁמַע מִינָּהּ.

But any day **on which** prolonging the prayer service would **not** constitute **a deprivation of labor for the masses, for example,** the days of **the New Moon,**[N] when it is customary for women to refrain from work, **and on the intermediate days of a Festival,** when one may not perform labor unless refraining from labor will cause him to lose money, **four** people **read** from the Torah. The Gemara concludes: Indeed, **learn from here** that on a public fast day three people read from the Torah.

אָמַר רַב אַשִׁי: וְהָא אֲנַן לָא תְּנַן הָכִי: זֶה הַכְּלָל: כׇּל יוֹם שֶׁיֵּשׁ בּוֹ מוּסָף וְאֵינוֹ יוֹם טוֹב – קוֹרִין אַרְבָּעָה, לְאַתּוֹיֵי מַאי – לָאו לְאַתּוֹיֵי תַּעֲנִית צִיבּוּר וְתִשְׁעָה בְּאָב!

Rav Ashi said: Didn't we learn in the mishna as follows: This is the principle: Any day on which there is an additional offering sacrificed in the Temple **and it is not a Festival, four** people **read** from the Torah? **What is added** by the formulation of this principle? **Does it not** come **to add a public fast and the Ninth of Av,** when there is an addition to the prayer service, and therefore four people read from the Torah?

וּלְרַב אַשִׁי מַתְנִיתִין מַנִּי? לָא תַּנָּא קַמָּא וְלָא רַבִּי יוֹסֵי. דְּתַנְיָא: חָל לִהְיוֹת בַּשֵּׁנִי וּבַחֲמִישִׁי – קוֹרִין שְׁלֹשָׁה וּמַפְטִיר אֶחָד. בַּשְּׁלִישִׁי וּבָרְבִיעִי קוֹרֵא אֶחָד וּמַפְטִיר אֶחָד. רַבִּי יוֹסֵי אוֹמֵר: לְעוֹלָם קוֹרִין שְׁלֹשָׁה וּמַפְטִיר אֶחָד.

The Gemara asks: **But according to Rav Ashi, who is** the *tanna* of **the mishna? It is not the first** *tanna* of the following *baraita* **and not Rabbi Yosei. As it is taught** in a *baraita*: If the Ninth of Av **occurs on a Monday or a Thursday,** days on which there is always a Torah reading, **three** people **read** from the Torah. **And** the last **one** of them **concludes** with a reading from the Prophets[N] [*haftara*]. If it falls **on a Tuesday or a Wednesday, one** person **reads** from the Torah, **and** the same **one concludes** with a reading from the Prophets. **Rabbi Yosei said: Three** people **always read** from the Torah on the Ninth of Av, **and** the last **one concludes** with a reading from the Prophets. All agree that no more than three people read from the Torah on the Ninth of Av and other public fast days.

וְאֶלָּא קַשְׁיָא ״זֶה הַכְּלָל״! לָא, לְאַתּוֹיֵי רֹאשׁ חוֹדֶשׁ וּמוֹעֵד.

The Gemara responds: **However,** if only three people read from the Torah on these days, the statement: **This is the principle,** is **difficult,** as the mishna has already specifically mentioned every case included in the principle. The Gemara explains: **No,** it is not difficult; it comes **to add the New Moon and** the intermediate days of **a Festival.**

הָא בְּהֶדְיָא קָתָנֵי לַהּ: בְּרָאשֵׁי חֳדָשִׁים וּמוֹעֵד קוֹרִין אַרְבָּעָה!

The Gemara challenges this explanation: **Aren't these** days **taught explicitly** in the mishna: **On the New Moon and on** the intermediate days of **a Festival, four** people **read** from the Torah?

סִימָנָא בְּעָלְמָא יָהֵיב, דְּלָא תֵּימָא יוֹם טוֹב וְחוּלּוֹ שֶׁל מוֹעֵד כִּי הֲדָדֵי נִינְהוּ, אֶלָּא נְקוֹט הַאי כְּלָלָא בִּידָךְ: כׇּל דְּטָפֵי לֵיהּ מִילְּתָא מֵחַבְרֵיהּ – טָפֵי לֵיהּ גַּבְרָא יְתֵירָא.

The Gemara answers: The principle was not intended to add to what is stated explicitly in the mishna. The mishna **merely gives a mnemonic**[N] by which to remember the number of readers on each day. It expresses the following: **Do not say that a Festival and the intermediate days of the Festival are the same** with regard to their sanctity, and therefore the same numbers of readers are called to the Torah on these days. **Rather, hold this rule** firmly **in your hand:** On any day **when there is an additional element** of the laws of the day, **an extra person is added** to the number of those who read from the Torah.

הִלְכָּךְ, בְּרֹאשׁ חוֹדֶשׁ וּמוֹעֵד דְּאִיכָּא קׇרְבַּן מוּסָף – קוֹרִין אַרְבָּעָה, בְּיוֹם טוֹב דְּאָסוּר בַּעֲשִׂיַּית מְלָאכָה – חֲמִשָּׁה, בְּיוֹם הַכִּפּוּרִים דַּעֲנוּשׁ כָּרֵת – שִׁשָּׁה. שַׁבָּת דְּאִיכָּא אִיסּוּר סְקִילָה – שִׁבְעָה.

Therefore, on the New Moon and the intermediate days of a **Festival,** when **there is an additional offering, four** people **read** from the Torah. **On a Festival, when** it is **prohibited** to **perform labor, five** people read from the Torah. **On Yom Kippur, when** performance of prohibited labor **is punishable by** *karet*, **six** people read from the Torah. On **Shabbat, when there is a prohibition** to perform labor that is punishable by **stoning, seven** people read.

גּוּפָא, רַב אִיקְּלַע לְבָבֶל בְּתַעֲנִית צִבּוּר. קָם קְרָא בְּסִפְרָא, פְּתַח בְּרֵיךְ, חֲתַם וְלָא בְּרֵיךְ. נְפוּל כּוּלֵּי עָלְמָא אַאַנְפַּיְיהוּ – וְרַב לָא נְפַל עַל אַנְפֵּיהּ. מַאי טַעְמָא רַב לָא נָפֵיל עַל אַפֵּיהּ?

The Gemara cited an incident involving Rav, and now it returns to examine **the** matter **itself. Rav** once **happened** to come **to Babylonia on a public fast. He stood and read from a** Torah **scroll.** When **he began** to read, **he recited a blessing,** but when **he concluded, he did not recite a blessing. Everyone** else **fell on their faces,** i.e., bowed down on the floor, during the *taḥanun* supplication, as was the custom, **but Rav did not fall on his face.** The Gemara asks: **What is the reason that Rav did not fall on his face?**

רִצְפָּה שֶׁל אֲבָנִים הָיְתָה. וְתַנְיָא: "וְאֶבֶן מַשְׂכִּית לֹא תִתְּנוּ בְּאַרְצְכֶם, לְהִשְׁתַּחֲוֺת עָלֶיהָ", עָלֶיהָ אִי אַתָּה מִשְׁתַּחֲוֶה בְּאַרְצְכֶם אֲבָל אַתָּה מִשְׁתַּחֲוֶה עַל אֲבָנִים שֶׁל בֵּית הַמִּקְדָּשׁ. כִּדְעוּלָּא, דְּאָמַר עוּלָּא: לֹא אָסְרָה תּוֹרָה אֶלָּא רִצְפָּה שֶׁל אֲבָנִים בִּלְבָד.

The Gemara answers: **It was a stone floor, and it was taught** in a *baraita* with regard to the verse: **"Nor shall you install any figured stone**[H] **in your land,**[N] **to bow down upon it"** (Leviticus 26:1), that, **upon it,** i.e., any type of figured stone, **you shall not bow down in your land,** i.e., anywhere in your land other than in the Temple; **but you shall bow down upon the stones of the Temple.** This is **in accordance with** the opinion of **Ulla,** as **Ulla said: The Torah prohibited** bowing down **only** upon **a stone floor.**[H]

אִי הָכִי מַאי אִירְיָא רַב? אֲפִילּוּ כּוּלְּהוּ נַמִי! קַמֵּיהּ דְּרַב הֲוַאי.

The Gemara asks: **If so, why** was it **specifically Rav** who did not bow down? **All of** the other people present were **also** prohibited from bowing down on the stone floor. The Gemara answers: The stone section of the floor was only **in front of Rav,** as the rest of the floor was not paved.

וְלֵיזִיל לְגַבֵּי צִיבּוּרָא, וְלִינְפּוֹל עַל אַפֵּיהּ! לָא בָּעֵי לְמִיטְרַח צִיבּוּרָא. וְאִיבָּעֵית אֵימָא: רַב פִּישׁוּט יָדַיִם וְרַגְלַיִם הֲוָה עָבֵיד, וְכִדְעוּלָּא, דְּאָמַר עוּלָּא: לֹא אָסְרָה תּוֹרָה אֶלָּא פִּישׁוּט יָדַיִם וְרַגְלַיִם בִּלְבָד.

The Gemara comments: If so, Rav **should have gone to** where the rest of **the congregation** was standing **and fallen on his face** there. The Gemara responds: **He did not want to trouble the congregation** to make room for him. **And if you wish, say** the following: **Rav would stretch out his arms and legs** and fully prostrate himself on the ground, whereas the others would merely bend their bodies as a symbolic gesture but would not prostrate themselves on the ground. **And** this is **in accordance with** the opinion of **Ulla, as Ulla said: The Torah prohibited** bowing down upon a stone floor **only** when it is done with **outstretched arms and legs.**

וְלִיפּוֹל עַל אַפֵּיהּ וְלָא לֶיעֱבִיד פִּישׁוּט יָדַיִם וְרַגְלַיִם! לָא מְשַׁנֵּי מִמִּנְהֲגֵיהּ.

The Gemara challenges this response: Rav **should have fallen on his face without stretching out his arms and legs.** The Gemara answers: **He did not** want to **change his** usual **custom** of full prostration, and where he was standing he could not fully prostrate himself in his usual manner because there the floor was of stone.

וְאִיבָּעֵית אֵימָא: אָדָם חָשׁוּב שָׁאנֵי, כִּדְרַבִּי אֶלְעָזָר, דְּאָמַר רַבִּי אֶלְעָזָר, אֵין אָדָם חָשׁוּב רַשַּׁאי לִיפּוֹל עַל פָּנָיו אֶלָּא אִם כֵּן נַעֲנֶה כִּיהוֹשֻׁעַ בִּן נוּן, דִּכְתִיב "וַיֹּאמֶר ה׳ אֶל יְהוֹשֻׁעַ קֻם לָךְ" [וגו׳].

And if you wish, say a different reason as to why Rav did not fall on his face: **An important person is different, in accordance with** the opinion of **Rabbi Elazar, as Rabbi Elazar said: An important person is not permitted to fall on his face** in public[NH] **unless** he knows that **he will be answered like Joshua bin Nun**[N] in his time, **as it is written: "And the Lord said to Joshua: Get up;** why do you lie upon your face?" (Joshua 7:10). It is a disgrace for a distinguished person to fall on his face and have his prayers unanswered. Consequently, Rav did not prostrate himself in public.

HALAKHA

Figured stone – אֶבֶן מַשְׂכִּית: The term figured stone refers to a stone designated for bowing upon. It is prohibited to bow upon a stone even if one is bowing to God. If one fully prostrates oneself on stone, he is flogged. This prohibition applies outside of the Temple; in the Temple, it is permitted to fully prostrate oneself on stone (Rambam *Sefer HaMadda, Hilkhot Avoda Zara* 6:6–7).

Bowing down upon a stone floor – הִשְׁתַּחֲוָאָה עַל אֲבָנִים: It is prohibited by Torah law to prostrate oneself with outstretched arms and legs on a stone floor. It is prohibited by rabbinic decree to prostrate oneself even where there is no stone floor, or to bow with one's head touching the ground on a stone floor even if one does not lie down with outstretched arms and legs. However, if one leans to his side or places something on the floor, it is permitted, and this is what is done on Yom Kippur (*Shulḥan Arukh, Oraḥ Ḥayyim* 131:8, and in the comment of Rema).

An important person is not permitted to fall on his face in public – אֵין אָדָם חָשׁוּב רַשַּׁאי לִיפּוֹל עַל פָּנָיו: An important person who is praying for the public is not permitted to fall on his face, unless he is certain that his prayers will be answered. However, this is prohibited only if he is praying in public; it is not prohibited if he is praying in his home for the public (*Taz*, citing Mordekhai). The type of falling on one's face that is customarily practiced nowadays during the daily prayers, which consists merely of lowering one's head and covering it, is permitted everywhere (Rivash; *Shulḥan Arukh, Oraḥ Ḥayyim* 131:8).

NOTES

Nor shall you install any figured stone in your land – וְאֶבֶן מַשְׂכִּית לֹא תִתְּנוּ בְּאַרְצְכֶם: It was necessary for the Gemara to cite the *baraita* in addition to the verse itself because the verse could have been interpreted as stating that the prohibition of prostrating oneself on stone applies only in Eretz Yisrael. The *baraita* indicates that the reason the verse states "in your land" is to exclude the Temple from the prohibition, but not to exclude lands outside of Eretz Yisrael. This is in accordance with the principle that non-agricultural mitzvot apply equally outside of Eretz Yisrael (*Turei Even*).

The Rambam writes that the reason for this prohibition is because the gentiles would prostrate themselves on stone floors as part of their pagan rituals. In order to distance the Jewish people from these practices, prostration was prohibited outside of the Temple.

An important person is not permitted to fall on his face in public – אֵין אָדָם חָשׁוּב רַשַּׁאי לִיפּוֹל עַל פָּנָיו: The commentaries discuss at length the reason for this policy. The widely accepted explanation is that if an important person falls on his face, which is an act of submission and self-nullification, and his prayers are not answered, he will be humiliated in the presence of the congregation (Rabbeinu Yehonatan). Some explain that if he is praying as an individual on behalf of the community, he appears haughty, and this is permitted only for someone whose prayers will certainly be answered (see *Mikhtam*).

Answered like Joshua bin Nun – נַעֲנֶה כִּיהוֹשֻׁעַ בִּן נוּן: The commentaries question why the Gemara specifically mentions Joshua. Some explain that other Elders also fell on their face in prayer, but since God said only to Joshua: "Get up; why do you lie upon your face?" (Joshua 7:10), it is clear that only Joshua acted properly by doing so (*Re'aḥ Duda'im*). Conversely, Rashi explains that God's comment to Joshua indicates that Joshua should not have prostrated himself. The commentary of the Rashash on tractate *Ta'anit* (14b) points out that, according to the Jerusalem Talmud (*Ta'anit* 2:6), Joshua's prayer was answered. He adds that Rashi in tractate *Megilla* disagrees.

תָּנוּ רַבָּנַן: קִידָּה – עַל אַפַּיִם, שֶׁנֶּאֱמַר: "וַתִּקֹּד בַּת שֶׁבַע אַפַּיִם אֶרֶץ". כְּרִיעָה – עַל בִּרְכַּיִם, וְכֵן הוּא אוֹמֵר: "מִכְּרוֹעַ עַל בִּרְכָּיו". הִשְׁתַּחֲוָאָה – זוֹ פִּישׁוּט יָדַיִם וְרַגְלַיִם, שֶׁנֶּאֱמַר: "הֲבוֹא נָבוֹא אֲנִי וְאִמְּךָ וְאַחֶיךָ לְהִשְׁתַּחֲוֹת לְךָ אָרְצָה".

Apropos Rav's practice of prostrating himself, the Gemara continues with a discussion of different forms of bowing. **The Sages taught** in a *baraita*: The term ***kidda*** indicates falling **upon** one's **face,**[N] with one's face toward the ground, **as it is stated: "Then Bathsheba bowed [*vatikod*] with her face to the ground"** (I Kings 1:31). ***Keria*** means bowing **upon one's knees, as it is stated** with regard to Solomon: He finished praying and **"he rose from before the altar of the Lord, from kneeling [*mikkeroa*] upon his knees"** (I Kings 8:54). Finally, ***hishtaḥava'a,***[N] **that is** bowing with one's **arms and legs spread** in total submission, **as it is stated** that Jacob asked, in response to Joseph's dream: **"Shall I and your mother and your brothers indeed come to bow down [*lehishtaḥavot*] to you to the ground?"** (Genesis 37:10).

לֵוִי אַחְוֵי קִידָּה קַמֵּיהּ דְּרַבִּי וְאִיטְלַע.

The Gemara relates that **Levi**[P] once **demonstrated** the form of ***kidda*** that was performed by the High Priest **before Rabbi** Yehuda HaNasi. This bowing was especially difficult, as it involved bending from the waist until his head reached the ground, supporting his body with his thumbs, and then rising at once. In the course of his demonstration, Levi dislocated his hip and **became lame.**

וְהָא קָא גָּרְמָא לֵיהּ? וְהָאָמַר רַבִּי אֶלְעָזָר: לְעוֹלָם אַל יַטִּיחַ אָדָם דְּבָרִים כְּלַפֵּי מַעְלָה, שֶׁהֲרֵי אָדָם גָּדוֹל הֵטִיחַ דְּבָרִים כְּלַפֵּי מַעְלָה וְאִיטְלַע, וּמַנּוּ – לֵוִי! הָא וְהָא גָּרְמָא לֵיהּ.

The Gemara asks: Was it **this that caused** Levi to become lame? **Didn't Rabbi Elazar say: A person should never speak impertinently toward** God **on High, as a great man** once **spoke impertinently toward** God **on High and he became lame? And who was he? Levi.** The reason Levi became lame was because of the way he spoke to God (see *Ta'anit* 25a), not due to having performed *kidda*. The Gemara answers: Both **this and that caused** Levi to become lame. Since he spoke impertinently toward God, he was worthy of punishment, and he therefore suffered an injury while exerting himself to perform *kidda*.

אֲמַר רַב חִיָּיא בַּר אָבִין: חָזֵינָא לְהוּ לְאַבָּיֵי

On the topic of bowing, **Rav Ḥiyya bar Avin said: I saw Abaye**

NOTES

The term *kidda* indicates falling upon one's face – קִידָּה, עַל אַפַּיִם: *Tosafot* question the Gemara's biblical proofs, as there are other verses that seem to give alternate descriptions of these types of bowing. They conclude that the meaning of these different terms was known through oral tradition. The Maharsha answers the questions of *Tosafot* by explaining that *kidda* means bowing with only one's face touching the ground; *keria* is *kidda* with the addition that one's knees also touch the ground; and *hishtaḥava'a* is *keria* with the rest of one's body also on the ground.

Kidda, *keria*, and *hishtaḥava'a* – קִידָּה, כְּרִיעָה, וְהִשְׁתַּחֲוָאָה: The act of bowing before God expresses three levels of submission before Him. The first, *kidda*, or falling on one's face, conveys the nullification of human wisdom and intelligence, which are nothing in comparison with Godly intellect. The second, *keria*, or falling on one's knees, communicates that human urges and impulses are subjugated to the will of God. The third, *hishtaḥava'a*, bowing with outspread arms and legs, indicates the recognition that all human action and activity are in the hands of God and the individual is merely a tool wielded by Him. Although God grants many freedoms to human beings, the religious person recognizes that everything he does pales in comparison with God's actions, which are directed by an intelligence that is beyond human comprehension (Rabbi Avraham Yitzḥak Kook, *Ein Aya*).

PERSONALITIES

Levi – לֵוִי: This is Levi ben Sisi, who lived in Eretz Yisrael during the transitional generation from *tanna'im* to *amora'im*. Levi was one of the foremost students of Rabbi Yehuda HaNasi, the redactor of the Mishna, and he participated, along with the other prominent students, in halakhic deliberations in the presence of Rabbi Yehuda HaNasi. Rabbi Yehuda HaNasi was particularly fond of Levi, and when he sent Levi to serve as a rabbi and rabbinical judge, he wrote that Levi was: A man like me.

It is known that Levi was tall. The Gemara relates that during his attempt to show Rabbi Yehuda HaNasi the *kidda* performed by the High Priest, he became lame. A few years after Rabbi Yehuda HaNasi's death, Levi was unable to remain in Eretz Yisrael due to personal considerations. He immigrated to Babylonia and renewed his friendship with his old friend, Rav. He also became a close friend of Abba bar Abba, the father of Shmuel. Shmuel became Levi's disciple-colleague. Levi also engaged in organizing collections of *baraitot*.

It is not known with certainty whether Levi had any sons; however, some maintain that Rabbi Yehoshua ben Levi, the great *amora*, was his son.

וְרָבָא דְּמַצְלֵי אַצְלוּיֵי.

and Rava, who would bend their heads[N] and not actually prostrate themselves on the ground.

״בְּיוֹם טוֹב חֲמִשָּׁה בְּיוֹם הַכִּפּוּרִים שִׁשָּׁה״ כו׳. מַתְנִיתִין מַנִּי? לֹא רַבִּי יִשְׁמָעֵאל וְלֹא רַבִּי עֲקִיבָא, דְּתַנְיָא: בְּיוֹם טוֹב – חֲמִשָּׁה, וּבְיוֹם הַכִּפּוּרִים – שִׁשָּׁה, וּבְשַׁבָּת – שִׁבְעָה, אֵין פּוֹחֲתִין מֵהֶן וְאֵין מוֹסִיפִין עֲלֵיהֶן, דִּבְרֵי רַבִּי יִשְׁמָעֵאל. רַבִּי עֲקִיבָא אוֹמֵר: בְּיוֹם טוֹב – חֲמִשָּׁה, וּבְיוֹם הַכִּפּוּרִים – שִׁבְעָה, וּבְשַׁבָּת – שִׁשָּׁה, אֵין פּוֹחֲתִין מֵהֶן אֲבָל מוֹסִיפִין עֲלֵיהֶן.

We learned in the mishna: **On a Festival, five** people read; **on Yom Kippur, six** people read; and on Shabbat, seven people read. One may not decrease the number of readers, but one may add to them. The Gemara asks: **Who is the** *tanna* **of the mishna?** It is **not Rabbi Yishmael**[P] **and not Rabbi Akiva, as it is taught** in a *baraita*: **On a Festival, five** people read from the Torah; **and on** Yom Kippur, **six** people read; **and on Shabbat, seven** people read. **One may not decrease or add to** the required number of readers. This is **the statement of Rabbi Yishmael. Rabbi Akiva** disagrees and **says: On a Festival, five** people read from the Torah; **and on Yom Kippur, seven** people read;[N] **and on Shabbat, six** people read. **One may not decrease** these numbers, **but one may add to them.**

מַנִּי? אִי רַבִּי יִשְׁמָעֵאל – קַשְׁיָא תּוֹסֶפֶת, אִי רַבִּי עֲקִיבָא – קַשְׁיָא שִׁשָּׁה וְשִׁבְעָה!

Who is the *tanna* of the mishna? **If** you say it is **Rabbi Yishmael,** it is **difficult** due to the ruling with regard to **adding,** as the mishna states that one may add additional readers but Rabbi Yishmael holds that one may not do so. **If** you say it is **Rabbi Akiva,** it is **difficult** due to the ruling concerning the days on which there are **six and seven** readers.

אֲמַר רָבָא: תַּנָּא דְּבֵי רַבִּי יִשְׁמָעֵאל הִיא, דְּתָנָא דְּבֵי רַבִּי יִשְׁמָעֵאל: בְּיוֹם טוֹב – חֲמִשָּׁה, בְּיוֹם הַכִּפּוּרִים – שִׁשָּׁה, בְּשַׁבָּת – שִׁבְעָה, אֵין פּוֹחֲתִין מֵהֶן אֲבָל מוֹסִיפִין עֲלֵיהֶן, דִּבְרֵי רַבִּי יִשְׁמָעֵאל.

Rava said: It is **the** *tanna* **of the school of Rabbi Yishmael, as it was taught in the school of Rabbi Yishmael: On a Festival, five** people read from the Torah; **on Yom Kippur, six** people read; **on Shabbat, seven** people read. **One may not decrease these** numbers **but one may add to them.** This is **the statement of Rabbi Yishmael.**

קַשְׁיָא דְּרַבִּי יִשְׁמָעֵאל אַדְּרַבִּי יִשְׁמָעֵאל! תְּרֵי תַּנָּאֵי אַלִּיבָּא דְּרַבִּי יִשְׁמָעֵאל.

The Gemara comments: If so, **there is a contradiction** between the opinion of **Rabbi Yishmael,** as expressed in the mishna, and the opinion of **Rabbi Yishmael** himself, as recorded in the *baraita*. The Gemara responds: **Two** ***tanna'im***, students of Rabbi Yishmael, expressed different opinions **in accordance with** the opinion of **Rabbi Yishmael.**

מַאן תְּנָא לְהָא דְּתַנְיָא: בְּיוֹם טוֹב מְאַחֲרִין לָבוֹא וּמְמַהֲרִין לָצֵאת, בְּיוֹם הַכִּפּוּרִים מְמַהֲרִין לָבוֹא וּמְאַחֲרִין לָצֵאת, וּבְשַׁבָּת מְמַהֲרִין לָבוֹא וּמְמַהֲרִין לָצֵאת – לֵימָא רַבִּי עֲקִיבָא, דְּאִית לֵיהּ גַּבְרָא יְתֵירָא? אֲפִילּוּ תֵּימָא רַבִּי יִשְׁמָעֵאל, דְּנָפֵישׁ סִידּוּרָא דְּיוֹמָא.

The Gemara asks: **Who is the** *tanna* **who taught that which is taught** in a *baraita*: **On a Festival, one is slow to arrive** at the synagogue[H] because one is busy preparing for the festive meal, **and one is quick to leave** in order to eat; **on Yom Kippur, one is quick to arrive**[N] at the synagogue **and slow to leave; and on Shabbat, one is quick to arrive,** as the meal has been prepared before Shabbat, **and quick to leave**[H] in order to eat the Shabbat meal? **Let us say** it is **Rabbi Akiva, who holds** that **an additional man** reads from the Torah on Yom Kippur,[N] which prolongs the service on that day. The Gemara rejects this suggestion: **Even if you say** it is **Rabbi Yishmael,** one leaves the synagogue late because **the order of the day,** i.e., the prayer service, **is very long,** as it includes many supplications and confessions.

NOTES

Who would bend their heads – דְּמַצְלֵי אַצְלוּיֵי: There is a dispute as to why Abaye and Rava did not completely prostrate themselves. Some explain that the prohibition against prostrating oneself on a stone floor was extended by rabbinic decree to include prostration on other surfaces as well, and that is the reason that Abaye and Rava did not prostrate themselves. Conversely, Rashi explains that they did not prostrate themselves because an esteemed person is prohibited to fall on his face in public. According to this explanation, the Gemara does not indicate that it is prohibited to prostrate oneself on a floor that is not made from stone.

On Yom Kippur, seven people read – בְּיוֹם הַכִּפּוּרִים, שִׁבְעָה: The *Turei Even* wonders why Rabbi Akiva accords Yom Kippur greater honor than Shabbat. He considers it improbable that the reason is due to the prohibition against eating. Perhaps the unique service in the Temple on Yom Kippur indicates that the sanctity of the day is greater than the sanctity of any other day.

One is quick to arrive – מְמַהֲרִין לָבוֹא: There is an alternate version of this *baraita* in tractate *Soferim*, which states that on Shabbat people are quick to arrive and slow to leave. They are quick to arrive in order to recite the *Shema* in its proper time, and slow to leave because they stay and listen to a halakhic discourse. On the Festivals, however, it was not customary for there to be public discourses about *halakha*, and therefore congregants were quick to leave.

Who holds that an additional man reads from the Torah on Yom Kippur – דְּאִית לֵיהּ גַּבְרָא יְתֵירָא: The Rashba questions why calling an additional reader to the Torah would cause the Yom Kippur service to take longer than the service on Shabbat, when the Torah portion that is read is longer than that of Yom Kippur. He explains that the Gemara suggests that this *baraita* is in accordance with the opinion of Rabbi Akiva. The *baraita* mentions Shabbat before Yom Kippur, just as Rabbi Akiva mentions Shabbat before Yom Kippur, due to the fact that there is an additional reader on Yom Kippur. The reason that the prayer service on Yom Kippur takes longer is for a different reason: During the prayer service, they recited the service of the day that was performed in the Temple, as is customary nowadays. This answer is based on the Rashba's version of the text of the Gemara, in which the *baraita* does mention Shabbat before Yom Kippur.

HALAKHA

On a Festival, one is slow to arrive at the synagogue – בְּיוֹם טוֹב מְאַחֲרִין לָבוֹא: On Festivals, the prayer service in the synagogue starts late in order for people to be able to prepare the meal, and one is quick to leave, due to the obligation to rejoice on the Festivals. However, on Rosh HaShana, it is customary to arrive early at the synagogue (*Magen Avraham*). In a place where liturgical poems are added to the prayer service on Festivals, it is fitting to start early, so that the time for saying the *Shema* does not pass (*Magen Avraham*; *Shulḥan Arukh HaRav*; *Shulḥan Arukh, Oraḥ Ḥayyim* 529:1, and in the comment of Rema).

And on Shabbat one is quick to arrive and quick to leave – וּבְשַׁבָּת מְמַהֲרִין לָבוֹא וּמְמַהֲרִין לָצֵאת: On Shabbat, the evening prayers are started earlier than on weekdays. The morning prayers begin earlier on Shabbat morning than on the morning of a Festival, but it is permitted to begin the prayer service later than it begins on a weekday. On Shabbat and Festivals, it is best not to extend the prayer service to the point that people will not be able to eat before midday (*Shulḥan Arukh, Oraḥ Ḥayyim* 267:2; 281:1 in the comment of Rema).

PERSONALITIES

Rabbi Yishmael – רַבִּי יִשְׁמָעֵאל: Rabbi Yishmael ben Elisha II was the grandson of Rabbi Yishmael ben Elisha the High Priest, who served at the end of the Second Temple period. The grandson is the *tanna* who is usually referred to simply as Rabbi Yishmael throughout the Talmud. As a young man he was imprisoned by the Romans and was redeemed by Rabbi Yehoshua, whose student he ultimately became. After a time, he became one of the renowned scholars in Yavne, where he was a close friend and intellectual adversary of Rabbi Akiva. Each of them developed a unique system of biblical hermeneutics. The thirteen principles of interpretation formulated by Rabbi Yishmael serve as the foundation for halakhic midrash that derives Jewish law from the Torah. Many of his teachings are found throughout the Mishna, and many more are found in the Talmud, taught by his students under the rubric: It was taught in the school of Rabbi Yishmael.

It appears that Rabbi Yishmael passed away prior to the bar Kokheva revolt. The Talmud mentions his sons and daughters; it is likely that the *tanna* Rabbi Eliezer, son of Rabbi Yishmael, was his son.

הָנֵי שְׁלֹשָׁה, חֲמִשָּׁה וְשִׁבְעָה כְּנֶגֶד מִי? פְּלִיגִי בָּהּ רַבִּי יִצְחָק בַּר נַחְמָנִי וְחַד דְּעִמֵּיהּ, וּמַנּוּ – רַבִּי שִׁמְעוֹן בֶּן פָּזִי, וְאָמְרִי לָהּ: רַבִּי שִׁמְעוֹן בֶּן פָּזִי וְחַד דְּעִמֵּיהּ, וּמַנּוּ – רַבִּי יִצְחָק בַּר נַחְמָנִי, וְאָמְרִי לָהּ רַבִּי שְׁמוּאֵל בַּר נַחְמָנִי. חַד אָמַר: כְּנֶגֶד בִּרְכַּת כֹּהֲנִים, וְחַד אָמַר: כְּנֶגֶד שְׁלֹשָׁה שׁוֹמְרֵי הַסַּף, חֲמִשָּׁה מֵרוֹאֵי פְּנֵי הַמֶּלֶךְ, שִׁבְעָה רוֹאֵי פְּנֵי הַמֶּלֶךְ.

A question is raised with regard to the number of readers on different days. **Corresponding to what** were **these three, five, and seven,** readers[N] instituted? **Rabbi Yitzḥak bar Naḥmani and one** other Sage **who was with him disagree about this. And who was** that other scholar? **Rabbi Shimon ben Pazi. And some say** that this was a matter of dispute between **Rabbi Shimon ben Pazi and one** other scholar **who was with him. And who was** that other scholar? **Rabbi Yitzḥak bar Naḥmani, and some say** it was **Rabbi Shmuel bar Naḥmani. One said:** These numbers **correspond** to the number of Hebrew words in the three verses of **the Priestly Benediction. And one said:** These numbers **correspond to the three guards of the door** (II Kings 25:18), **five of** the officers **who saw the king's face** (II Kings 25:19), **and the seven** officers **who saw the king's face** (Esther 1:14).[N]

תָּנֵי רַב יוֹסֵף: שְׁלֹשָׁה, חֲמִשָּׁה וְשִׁבְעָה: שְׁלֹשָׁה שׁוֹמְרֵי הַסַּף, חֲמִשָּׁה מֵרוֹאֵי פְּנֵי הַמֶּלֶךְ, שִׁבְעָה רוֹאֵי פְּנֵי הַמֶּלֶךְ. אָמַר לֵיהּ אַבַּיֵי: עַד הָאִידָּנָא מַאי טַעְמָא לָא פָּרֵישׁ לַן מָר? אֲמַר לֵיהּ: לָא הֲוָה יָדַעְנָא דִּצְרִיכְתּוּ לֵיהּ, וּמִי בְּעֵיתוּ מִינַּאי מִילְּתָא וְלָא אֲמַרִי לְכוּ?

Similarly, **Rav Yosef taught** a *baraita*: The **three, five, and seven** people who read from the Torah correspond to the **three guards of the door, five of** the officers **who saw the king's face,** and **the seven** officers **who saw the king's face.** When Rav Yosef taught this, **Abaye said to him: What is the reason that until now the Master did not explain** the matter **to us** in this way? Rav Yosef **said to him: I did not know that you needed this** information, as I thought that you were already familiar with the *baraita*. **Have you** ever **asked me something and I did not tell you?**

אֲמַר לֵיהּ יַעֲקֹב מִינָאָה לְרַב יְהוּדָה: הָנֵי שִׁשָּׁה דְּיוֹם הַכִּפּוּרִים כְּנֶגֶד מִי? אֲמַר לֵיהּ: כְּנֶגֶד שִׁשָּׁה שֶׁעָמְדוּ מִימִינוֹ שֶׁל עֶזְרָא וְשִׁשָּׁה מִשְּׂמֹאלוֹ, שֶׁנֶּאֱמַר "וַיַּעֲמֹד עֶזְרָא הַסּוֹפֵר עַל מִגְדַּל עֵץ אֲשֶׁר עָשׂוּ לַדָּבָר וַיַּעֲמֹד אֶצְלוֹ מַתִּתְיָה וְשֶׁמַע וַעֲנָיָה וְאוּרִיָּה וְחִלְקִיָּה וּמַעֲשֵׂיָה עַל יְמִינוֹ וּמִשְּׂמֹאלוֹ פְּדָיָה וּמִישָׁאֵל וּמַלְכִּיָּה וְחָשֻׁם וְחַשְׁבַּדָּנָה זְכַרְיָה מְשֻׁלָּם".

Ya'akov of Mina said to Rav Yehuda: Corresponding to whom were these six readers **on Yom Kippur** instituted? Rav Yehuda **said to him:** The number six **corresponds to the six** people **who stood to Ezra's right and the six** people who **stood to his left, as it is stated: "And Ezra the Scribe stood upon a platform of wood, which they had made for the purpose, and beside him stood Mattithiah, and Shema, and Anaiah, and Uriah, and Hilkiah, and Maaseiah, on his right hand, and on his left hand, Pedaiah, and Mishael, and Malchiah, and Hashum, and Hashbadanah, Zechariah, Meshullam"** (Nehemiah 8:4).

הָנֵי שִׁבְעָה הָווּ! הַיְינוּ זְכַרְיָה הַיְינוּ מְשֻׁלָּם, וְאַמַּאי קָרוּ מְשֻׁלָּם דְּמִישְׁלַם בְּעוֹבָדֵיהּ.

The Gemara challenges this answer: **Those** that stood to his left **were seven** and not six. The Gemara responds: **Zechariah is** the same as **Meshullam,**[N] that is to say, they are not two separate people, but rather one person with two names. **And why was he called Meshullam? Because he was perfect** [*mishlam*] **in his actions.**

תָּנוּ רַבָּנַן: הַכֹּל עוֹלִין לְמִנְיַן שִׁבְעָה, וַאֲפִילּוּ קָטָן וַאֲפִילּוּ אִשָּׁה. אֲבָל אָמְרוּ חֲכָמִים: אִשָּׁה לֹא תִּקְרָא בַּתּוֹרָה, מִפְּנֵי כְּבוֹד צִבּוּר.

§ **The Sages taught** in a *Tosefta* (*Megilla* 3:11): **All** people **count toward the quorum of seven** readers,[H] **even a minor and even a woman. However, the Sages said** that **a woman should not read the Torah, out of respect for the congregation.**

אִיבַּעְיָא לְהוּ: מַפְטִיר מַהוּ שֶׁיַּעֲלֶה לְמִנְיַן שִׁבְעָה? רַב הוּנָא וְרַבִּי יִרְמְיָה בַּר אַבָּא, חַד אָמַר: עוֹלֶה, וְחַד אָמַר: אֵינוֹ עוֹלֶה. מַאן דְּאָמַר עוֹלֶה – דְּהָא קָרֵי.

A dilemma was raised before the Sages: With regard to the reader who **concludes** [*maftir*] the Torah reading and reads from the Prophets [*haftara*], **what is** the *halakha*; does he **count toward the quorum**[H] **of seven** readers? **Rav Huna and Rabbi Yirmeya bar Abba** disagreed about this matter. **One said: He counts, and one said: He does not count. The one who said** that **he counts** toward the seven readers holds that opinion **because he reads** from the Torah.

וּמַאן דְּאָמַר אֵינוֹ עוֹלֶה – כְּדְעוּלָּא, דְּאָמַר עוּלָּא: מִפְּנֵי מָה הַמַּפְטִיר בַּנָּבִיא צָרִיךְ שֶׁיִּקְרָא בַּתּוֹרָה תְּחִלָּה – מִפְּנֵי כְּבוֹד תּוֹרָה, וְכֵיוָן דְּמִשּׁוּם כְּבוֹד תּוֹרָה הוּא – לְמִנְיָינָא לָא סָלֵיק.

And the one who said that **he does not count** holds **in accordance with** the opinion **of Ulla, as Ulla said: For what** reason **must** the one **who concludes** with a reading from **the Prophets read from the Torah first?** It is **due to respect for the Torah,** so that those present should not conclude that he was called up only to read from the Prophets because the honor due the Torah and the honor due the Prophets are equal. **And since** he reads only **out of respect for the Torah, he is not included in the quorum** of seven readers.

NOTES

These three, five, and seven readers – הָנֵי שְׁלֹשָׁה חֲמִשָּׁה וְשִׁבְעָה: The Ritva explains that the Gemara's explanations are merely textual allusions, but they are not the main reasons for the institutions of these numbers of readers. The main reason is that the greater the level of a day's sanctity, as indicated by the *halakhot* of the day, the greater the number of people called to read from the Torah. This is essentially the answer that the *Tosafot* and the Rid give to explain why the Gemara did not provide a source for the practice of calling four readers to the Torah on the New Moon and the intermediate days of the Festival. Since there is an additional offering on these days, it is obvious that they have a greater level of sanctity than regular weekdays.

The seven who saw the king's face – שִׁבְעָה רוֹאֵי פְּנֵי הַמֶּלֶךְ: Rashi explains that these are the seven advisors of King Ahasuerus (Esther 1:14), five of whom were more prominent than the others. *Tosafot* express astonishment that the number of people called to the Torah would be established to correspond to the number of advisors of a gentile king. It has been suggested in defense of Rashi's explanation that since the Gemara is referring to those who saw the king's face, which is an expression based upon the verse in Esther, it is clear that the Gemara is alluding to the advisors of King Ahasuerus. Later commentaries have added that just as Ahasuerus had seven advisors, Jewish kings also had seven primary advisors (*Ramat Shmuel*). It has also been suggested, based upon the Jerusalem Talmud, that the number of readers from the Torah corresponds to the number of advisors to a gentile king in order to nullify the evil decrees of gentile governments. The Ritva and *Otzar HaKavod* explain that the number of advisors to earthly kings merely parallels the number of angelic ministers in heaven.

Zechariah is the same as Meshullam – הַיְינוּ זְכַרְיָה הַיְינוּ מְשֻׁלָּם: The Maharsha wrote that this is indicated in the verse itself, as the letter *vav*, indicating the word "and," appears between most of the names but not between the names Zechariah and Meshullam.

HALAKHA

All people count toward the quorum of seven readers – הַכֹּל עוֹלִין לְמִנְיַן שִׁבְעָה: All people count toward the quorum of seven readers, including women. However, on days when fewer than seven readers are called to the Torah, this is not the case (*Magen Avraham*; *Olat Shabbat*). The Sages said that a woman should not read the Torah in public out of deference to the congregation. A minor who understands the concept of a blessing may also read from the Torah. However, nowadays the custom is to call up a minor only for *maftir* (*Magen Avraham*; *Shulḥan Arukh*, *Oraḥ Ḥayyim* 282:3).

The reader who concludes the Torah reading…does he count toward the quorum – מַפְטִיר...לְמִנְיַן: The Gemara did not provide a final ruling with regard to this debate. Some hold that the reader who concludes the Torah reading and reads the *haftara* is included in the quorum (Rif; Ran), while others disagree (Rid). Some say that the issue remains unresolved (*ge'onim*). In practice, the custom is to call seven readers to the Torah without the *maftir*. *Kaddish* is then recited, and then the *maftir* reads some verses that the previous reader already read, and then he reads the *haftara*. This is the practice on Shabbat and Festivals. However, when a *haftara* is read on public fasts, when it is prohibited to add additional readers, the third reader also reads the *haftara* (*Shulḥan Arukh*, *Oraḥ Ḥayyim* 282:4).

מֵיתִיבִי: הַמַּפְטִיר בַּנָּבִיא לֹא יִפְחוֹת מֵעֶשְׂרִים וְאֶחָד פְּסוּקִין כְּנֶגֶד שִׁבְעָה שֶׁקָּרְאוּ בַּתּוֹרָה. וְאִם אִיתָא, עֶשְׂרִים וְאַרְבָּעָה הָוְיָין! כֵּיוָן דְּמִשּׁוּם כְּבוֹד תּוֹרָה הוּא,

The Gemara **raises an objection** based upon the following *baraita*: **The one who concludes with** a reading from **the Prophets may not** read **fewer than twenty-one verses,**[H] **corresponding to the seven who read from the Torah.** Each one who reads from the Torah must read at least three verses, for a total of at least twenty-one verses. **And if it is so,** that the one who reads the *haftara* does not count toward the quorum of seven readers, and he is an eighth reader, the minimum number of verses that must be read from the Torah **is twenty-four** and not twenty-one. The Gemara answers: **Since** the one who reads the *haftara* reads from the Torah first only **due to respect for the Torah,**

HALAKHA

May not read fewer than twenty-one verses – לֹא יִפְחוֹת מֵעֶשְׂרִים וְאֶחָד פְּסוּקִין: The *haftara* is read from the Prophets on Shabbat, and no fewer than twenty-one verses are read. However, if one concludes an entire topic, he need not continue even if he has read fewer than twenty-one verses. On Festivals, when only five readers are called to the Torah, the *haftara* need not be longer than fifteen verses (*Shulḥan Arukh*, *Oraḥ Ḥayyim* 284:1, and in the comment of Rema).

Perek **III**
Daf **23** Amud **b**

כְּנֶגְדּוֹ נַמִּי לָא בָּעֵי.

it is not necessary to also add corresponding verses in the *haftara*.

מַתְקִיף לַהּ רָבָא: וַהֲרֵי ״עוֹלוֹתֵיכֶם סְפוּ״ דְּלָא הָוְיָין עֶשְׂרִין וְחַד, וְקָרֵינַן! שָׁאנֵי הָתָם דִּסְלִיק עִנְיָינָא.

Rava strongly objects to this *baraita*: **But** there is the *haftara* that begins with the words: **"Add your burnt offerings"** (Jeremiah 7:21–28), **which does not have twenty-one verses, and** nevertheless **we read it.** The Gemara answers: **There it is different, as the topic is completed** in fewer than twenty-one verses, and it is not necessary to begin another topic merely to complete the number of verses.

וְהֵיכָא דְּלָא סָלִיק עִנְיָינָא לָא? וְהָאָמַר רַב שְׁמוּאֵל בַּר אַבָּא: זִמְנִין סַגִּיאִין הֲוָה קָאֵימְנָא קַמֵּיהּ דְּרַבִּי יוֹחָנָן, וְכִי הֲוָה קָרֵינַן עֲשָׂרָה פְּסוּקֵי אֲמַר לַן: אַפְסִיקוּ! מָקוֹם שֶׁיֵּשׁ תּוּרְגְּמָן שָׁאנֵי. דְּתָנֵי רַב תַּחְלִיפָא בַּר שְׁמוּאֵל: לֹא שָׁנוּ אֶלָּא בְּמָקוֹם שֶׁאֵין תּוּרְגְּמָן, אֲבָל מָקוֹם שֶׁיֵּשׁ תּוּרְגְּמָן – פּוֹסֵק.

The Gemara asks: **But** is it true that **where the topic is not completed,** we do **not** read fewer than twenty-one verses? **Didn't Rav Shmuel bar Abba say: Many times I stood before Rabbi Yoḥanan** as a translator, **and when we had read ten verses he would say to us: Stop.** This indicates that a *haftara* need not be twenty-one verses. The Gemara answers: **In a place where there is a translator,**[NHB] who translates each verse into Aramaic and adds additional explanation, **it is different.** In that case, it is not necessary for the *haftara* to consist of twenty-one verses, so as not to overburden the congregation, **as Rav Taḥalifa bar Shmuel taught: They taught** that twenty-one verses must be read from the *haftara* **only** in **a place where there is no translator; but in a place where there is a translator, one may stop** even before that.

NOTES

In a place where there is a translator – מָקוֹם שֶׁיֵּשׁ תּוּרְגְּמָן: The Meiri explains that since the translator translates every verse, the ten verses and their translations are counted as twenty. The reader then repeats the last verse for a total of twenty-one. Alternatively, Rashi and others explain that the reason one need not read twenty-one verses is so that the congregation not be overly burdened. This is also mentioned explicitly in the Jerusalem Talmud. According to this explanation, it is possible to suggest that since the Torah reading itself was very lengthy, it is not necessary to read twenty-one verses, and it is possible that one may conclude after even fewer than ten verses.

HALAKHA

In a place where there is a translator – מָקוֹם שֶׁיֵּשׁ תּוּרְגְּמָן: In a place where there is a translator, it is sufficient to read and translate ten verses from the Prophets, even if the topic has not been concluded (Rambam *Sefer Ahava*, *Hilkhot Tefilla* 12:13).

BACKGROUND

Translator – תּוּרְגְּמָן: During the talmudic era, it was customary to read the Aramaic translation of the Torah, written by Onkelos, as part of the Torah reading on Shabbat morning. The purpose of this was to allow those unfamiliar with biblical Hebrew to understand the reading. The translation would greatly extend the time of the reading. If the translation of the *haftara* was also recited, that would extend the time even more, especially since the translation of the Prophets incorporates more explanation of the text than the translation of the Torah itself. Therefore, it was necessary to shorten the *haftara* so that the congregation would not be overly burdened.

מתני׳ אֵין פּוֹרְסִין עַל שְׁמַע, וְאֵין עוֹבְרִין לִפְנֵי הַתֵּיבָה, וְאֵין נוֹשְׂאִין אֶת כַּפֵּיהֶם, וְאֵין קוֹרִין בַּתּוֹרָה, וְאֵין מַפְטִירִין בַּנָּבִיא,

MISHNA One does not recite the introductory prayers and **blessing** [***poresin***] before ***Shema***;[NH] **nor does one pass before the ark**[H] to repeat the *Amida* prayer; **nor do the** priests **lift their hands** to recite the Priestly Benediction;[NH] **nor is the Torah read** in public;[H] **nor does one conclude with** a reading from **the Prophets** [*haftara*][NH] in the presence of fewer than ten men.

וְאֵין עוֹשִׂין מַעֲמָד וּמוֹשָׁב, וְאֵין אוֹמְרִים בִּרְכַּת אֲבֵלִים וְתַנְחוּמֵי אֲבֵלִים, וּבִרְכַּת חֲתָנִים, וְאֵין מְזַמְּנִין בַּשֵּׁם פָּחוֹת מֵעֲשָׂרָה. וּבַקַּרְקָעוֹת – תִּשְׁעָה וְכֹהֵן, וְאָדָם כַּיּוֹצֵא בָּהֶן.

And one does not observe the practice of **standing up and sitting down** for the delivery of eulogies at a funeral service; **nor does one recite the mourners' blessing or comfort mourners** in two lines after the funeral; **or** recite the **bridegrooms' blessing; and one does not invite** others to recite Grace after Meals, i.e., conduct a *zimmun*, **with the name** of God, **with fewer than ten** men present. If one consecrated **land** and now wishes to redeem it, the land must be assessed by **nine** men **and one priest,** for a total of ten. **And similarly,** assessing the value of **a person** who has pledged his own value to the Temple must be undertaken by ten people, one of whom must be a priest.

גמ׳ מְנָא הָנֵי מִילֵּי? אָמַר רַבִּי חִיָּיא בַּר אַבָּא אָמַר רַבִּי יוֹחָנָן: דְּאָמַר קְרָא ״וְנִקְדַּשְׁתִּי בְּתוֹךְ בְּנֵי יִשְׂרָאֵל״ – כׇּל דָּבָר שֶׁבִּקְדוּשָּׁה לֹא יְהֵא פָּחוֹת מֵעֲשָׂרָה.

GEMARA The Gemara asks: **From where are these matters,** i.e., that ten people are needed in each of these cases, derived? **Rabbi Ḥiyya bar Abba said that Rabbi Yoḥanan said:** It is **as the verse states: "And I shall be hallowed among the children of Israel"** (Leviticus 22:32), which indicates that **any expression of sanctity may not be** recited in a quorum of **fewer than ten** men.[H]

מַאי מַשְׁמַע? דְּתָנֵי רַבִּי חִיָּיא: אָתְיָא ״תּוֹךְ״ ״תּוֹךְ״, כְּתִיב הָכָא ״וְנִקְדַּשְׁתִּי בְּתוֹךְ בְּנֵי יִשְׂרָאֵל״ וּכְתִיב הָתָם ״הִבָּדְלוּ מִתּוֹךְ הָעֵדָה״,

The Gemara asks: **From where** in the verse may this **be inferred?**[N] The Gemara responds that it must be understood **as Rabbi Ḥiyya taught: It is inferred** by means of a verbal analogy [*gezera shava*] between the words **"among," "among." Here, it is written: "And I shall be hallowed among the children of Israel," and there,** with regard to Korah's congregation, **it is written "Separate yourselves from among this congregation"** (Numbers 16:21). Just as with regard to Korah the reference is to ten men, so too, the name of God is to be hallowed in a quorum of ten men.

וְאָתְיָא ״עֵדָה״ ״עֵדָה״, דִּכְתִיב הָתָם ״עַד מָתַי לָעֵדָה הָרָעָה הַזֹּאת״ מַה לְּהַלָּן עֲשָׂרָה – אַף כָּאן עֲשָׂרָה.

The connotation of ten associated with the word "among" in the portion of Korah is, in turn, **inferred** by means of another verbal analogy between the word **"congregation"** written there and the word **"congregation"** written in reference to the ten spies who slandered Eretz Yisrael, **as it is written there: "How long shall I bear with this evil congregation?"** (Numbers 14:27). Consequently, **just as there,** in the case of the spies, it was a congregation of **ten** people, as there were twelve spies altogether, and Joshua and Caleb were not included in the evil congregation, **so too, here,** in the case of Korah, the reference is to a congregation of **ten** people. The first several items mentioned in the mishna are expressions of sanctity, and they consequently require a quorum of ten.

NOTES

Recite the blessing [*poresin*] before *Shema* – פּוֹרְסִין עַל שְׁמַע: The commentaries debate the meaning of the word *poresin* and, therefore, the meaning of this statement in the mishna. The Ran and others quote the *ge'onim*, who explain that *poresin* connotes beginning. Consequently, this phrase means that one begins to recite the blessings of the *Shema*. Rashi, the Ra'avad, and others explain that *poresin* means to divide. In these cases, one would divide the two blessings before *Shema* and recite only the first one. Others cite the Aramaic *Targum* to the book of Samuel as proof that the word *poresin* can mean reciting a blessing (see I Samuel 9:13; *Arukh*; Rid; *Mikhtam*). The Rambam, in his Commentary on Mishna, explains that *poresin* means to organize or arrange the blessings before *Shema*.

The commonly accepted interpretation is that this is referring to reciting *kaddish*, *barekhu*, and the first of the blessings before *Shema*. Since *kaddish* and *barekhu* are expressions of sanctity, they may be recited only in the presence of ten men. However, many early commentaries (*ge'onim*) explained that ten men are required for the first blessing before *Shema*, which contains *kedusha*, the responsive prayer of praise that parallels the praises offered to God by the angels. Nonetheless, common practice accords with the opinion of the Ra'avad, who maintains that the verses recited during this blessing are not considered a true recitation of *kedusha*. Consequently, it is permitted to recite this blessing without a quorum of ten men.

Nor do the priests lift their hands to recite the Priestly Benediction – וְאֵין נוֹשְׂאִין אֶת כַּפֵּיהֶם: The Rashba explains that the reason this is recited only in the presence of ten men is because the blessings mention the name of God (see *Turei Even*). The Ran explains that it is because the Torah states: "In this way shall you bless the children of Israel" (Numbers 6:23), and the term "children of Israel" refers only to a group of at least ten.

Nor does one conclude with a reading from the Prophets [*haftara*] – וְאֵין מַפְטִירִין בַּנָּבִיא: The Rashba wonders why there is no *haftara* in the presence of fewer than ten men, and he does not suggest an answer. The Meiri explains that since the reader of the *haftara* first reads from the Torah, he must begin the blessing over the Torah with *barekhu*, which is an expression of sanctity. The Ran explains that the *haftara* is a rabbinic decree, and it was instituted that it be read only in public.

From where in the verse may this be inferred – מַאי מַשְׁמַע: Several of the early commentaries cite an answer that does not appear in the Gemara but is mentioned in the Jerusalem Talmud (*Megilla* 4:4). There is a verse that states: "And the children of Israel came to buy among those that came" (Genesis 42:5). The children of Israel [*benei Yisrael*] referred to in the verse are ten of Jacob's sons. Therefore, wherever a verse states *benei Yisrael*, it is referring to a group of at least ten (Rabbeinu Baḥya in his Commentary on the Torah).

HALAKHA

One does not recite the introductory prayers and blessing before *Shema* – אֵין פּוֹרְסִין עַל שְׁמַע: If there are individuals who prayed privately and did not hear *kaddish*, one of them may recite *kaddish*, *barekhu*, and the first of the blessings before *Shema*. This is permitted only in the presence of ten men. Preferably, one should attempt to ensure that there are six men present who have not yet heard *kaddish*, but this procedure may be done even if there is only one who has not yet heard *kaddish*. Nowadays, the custom is to say only *kaddish* and *barekhu*, but not the first of the blessings before *Shema*. In the evening, individuals who already prayed privately do not recite *barekhu*; however, one who has not yet recited the evening prayers at all may do so (*Mishna Berura*; *Shulḥan Arukh, Oraḥ Ḥayyim* 69:1 and the comment of Rema).

Nor does one pass before the ark – וְאֵין עוֹבְרִין לִפְנֵי הַתֵּיבָה: One may go before the ark to recite the communal *Amida* prayer only in the presence of ten men. If there are those who have already prayed but did not hear *kedusha*, the sanctification prayer, one of them may recite the first two blessings of the *Amida* aloud, followed by *kedusha* and the third blessing (*Shulḥan Arukh, Oraḥ Ḥayyim* 69:1).

Nor do the priests lift their hands to recite the Priestly Benediction – וְאֵין נוֹשְׂאִין אֶת כַּפֵּיהֶם: The priests may recite the Priestly Benediction only in a quorum of ten, and the priests are included as part of the quorum (*Shulḥan Arukh, Oraḥ Ḥayyim* 128:1).

Nor is the Torah read in public – וְאֵין קוֹרִין בַּתּוֹרָה: The Torah is read only in the presence of a quorum of ten. However, if they began to read the Torah with a quorum and some individuals left, they may continue the reading (*Shulḥan Arukh, Oraḥ Ḥayyim* 143:1).

Nor does one conclude with a reading from the Prophets [*haftara*] – וְאֵין מַפְטִירִין בַּנָּבִיא: The *haftara* may be read only with a quorum of ten (Rambam *Sefer Ahava, Hilkhot Tefilla* 8:4).

Any expression of sanctity may not be recited in a quorum of fewer than ten men – כׇּל דָּבָר שֶׁבִּקְדוּשָּׁה לֹא יְהֵא פָּחוֹת מֵעֲשָׂרָה: Expressions of sanctity may be recited only in the presence of a quorum of ten men. However, if they began with a quorum and some individuals left, they may continue (Rambam *Sefer Ahava, Hilkhot Tefilla* 8:6).

״וְאֵין עוֹשִׂין מַעֲמָד וּמוֹשָׁב פָּחוֹת מֵעֲשָׂרָה״. כֵּיוָן דְּבָעֵי לְמֵימַר: עִמְדוּ יְקָרִים, עֲמוֹדוּ! שְׁבוּ יְקָרִים, שְׁבוּ! בְּצִיר מֵעֲשָׂרָה לָאו אוֹרַח אַרְעָא.

§ We learned in the mishna: **And one does not observe** the practice of **standing up and sitting down** for the delivery of eulogies at a funeral service **with fewer than ten** men present.[H] As this is not an expression of sanctity, it is therefore necessary to explain why a quorum is required. The Gemara explains: **Since** the leader of the funeral procession **is required to say: Stand, dear** friends, **stand; sit down, dear** friends, **sit down,** when there are **fewer than ten it is not proper conduct** to speak in such a dignified style.

״וְאֵין אוֹמְרִים בִּרְכַּת אֲבֵלִים וּבִרְכַּת חֲתָנִים״ (וכו׳). מַאי בִּרְכַּת אֲבֵלִים? בִּרְכַּת רְחָבָה. דְּאָמַר רַבִּי יִצְחָק אָמַר רַבִּי יוֹחָנָן: בִּרְכַּת אֲבֵלִים בַּעֲשָׂרָה, וְאֵין אֲבֵלִים מִן הַמִּנְיָן. בִּרְכַּת חֲתָנִים בַּעֲשָׂרָה – וַחֲתָנִים מִן הַמִּנְיָן.

We also learned in the mishna that **one does not recite the mourners' blessing and the bridegrooms' blessing** with fewer than ten men present. The Gemara asks: **What is the mourners' blessing? The blessing** recited **in the square** next to the cemetery. Following the burial, those who participated in the funeral would assemble in the square and bless the mourners that God should comfort them, **as Rabbi Yitzḥak said that Rabbi Yoḥanan said: The mourners' blessing** is recited only **with ten** men present, **and mourners** themselves **are not included in the count.**[N] **The bridegrooms' blessing** is also recited only **with ten** men present,[H] **and bridegrooms** themselves **are included in the count.** Consequently, only nine other men are needed.

״וְאֵין מְזַמְּנִין עַל הַמָּזוֹן בַּשֵּׁם פָּחוֹת מֵעֲשָׂרָה״ (וכו׳). כֵּיוָן דְּבָעֵי לְמֵימַר נְבָרֵךְ לֵאלֹהֵינוּ – בְּצִיר מֵעֲשָׂרָה לָאו אוֹרַח אַרְעָא.

We learned further in the mishna: **And one does not invite** others to recite Grace after Meals, i.e., conduct a *zimmun*, in order to thank God **for** one's **nourishment, with the name** of God, **with fewer than ten** men present.[H] **Since one is required to say: Let us bless our Lord,** in the presence of **fewer than ten** it is **not proper conduct** to mention the name of God.

״וְהַקַּרְקָעוֹת תִּשְׁעָה וְכֹהֵן וְאָדָם כַּיּוֹצֵא בָּהֶן״ (וכו׳). מְנָא הָנֵי מִילֵּי?

§ If one consecrated **land** and now wishes to redeem it, the land must be assessed by **nine** Israelites **and one priest,**[H] for a total of ten. **And similarly,** assessing the value of **a person** who has pledged his own value to the Temple must be undertaken by ten people, one of whom must be a priest. The Gemara asks: **From where are these matters,** that consecrated land must be assessed by ten people, one of whom is a priest, derived?

אָמַר שְׁמוּאֵל: עֲשָׂרָה כֹּהֲנִים כְּתוּבִים בַּפָּרָשָׁה, חַד לְגוּפֵיהּ, (וְחַד לְמַעוּטֵי) וְאִידָךְ הָוֵי מִיעוּט אַחַר מִיעוּט וְאֵין מִיעוּט אַחַר מִיעוּט אֶלָּא לְרַבּוֹת: תִּשְׁעָה יִשְׂרְאֵלִים וְחַד כֹּהֵן.

Shmuel said: The word **priest** is **written ten** times[N] **in the** Torah **portion** that addresses the redemption of consecrated property, indicating that ten people are required to assess the value of such property (Leviticus, chapter 27). **One** instance of the word is needed **for itself,** to indicate that a priest must participate in the assessment. **And one** instance is needed **to exclude** all non-priests from fulfilling that role. **And** all **the other** instances of the word **are restrictions following** other **restrictions,** and there is a general hermeneutical principle that **one restriction after another** serves **only to amplify.** Therefore, each additional time the word priest is repeated, it extends the criteria applied to appraisers, so as to allow non-priests to participate. Consequently, the assessment may be carried out by **nine** ordinary **Israelites and one priest.**

וְאֵימָא חֲמִשָּׁה כֹּהֲנִים וַחֲמִשָּׁה יִשְׂרְאֵלִים! קַשְׁיָא.

The Gemara asks: **And** on the basis of this principle, **say** that the first usage of the term is restrictive and requires a priest for the assessment; the second usage amplifies and allows for a non-priest; the third usage again requires a priest; the fourth usage allows for a non-priest; and so on. Consequently, the assessment must be carried out by **five priests**[N] **and five** ordinary **Israelites.** The Gemara concludes: Indeed, it is **difficult,** as the derivation has not been sufficiently explained.

״וְאָדָם כַּיּוֹצֵא בָּהֶן״. אָדָם מִי קָדוֹשׁ?

We learned in the mishna: **And similarly,** assessing the value of **a person**[H] who has pledged his own value to the Temple must be undertaken by ten people, one of whom must be a priest. The Gemara asks: **Can a person become consecrated** and thereby require redemption?

HALAKHA

And one does not observe the practice of standing up and sitting down with fewer than ten men present – וְאֵין עוֹשִׂין מַעֲמָד וּמוֹשָׁב פָּחוֹת מֵעֲשָׂרָה: The practice of standing up and sitting down for eulogies is practiced only with a quorum of ten. However, nowadays this custom is no longer observed at all (Rambam *Sefer Shofetim, Hilkhot Evel* 12:4; *Shulḥan Arukh, Yoreh De'a* 376:3).

The bridegrooms' blessing is recited only with ten men present – בִּרְכַּת חֲתָנִים בַּעֲשָׂרָה: The bridegrooms' blessing is recited only with ten men present, and the bridegroom may be considered one of the ten (*Shulḥan Arukh, Even HaEzer* 62:4).

And one does not invite others to thank God for one's nourishment with the name of God with fewer than ten men present – וְאֵין מְזַמְּנִין עַל הַמָּזוֹן בַּשֵּׁם פָּחוֹת מֵעֲשָׂרָה: The invitation to say Grace after Meals is recited with the name of God only in the presence of ten men (*Shulḥan Arukh, Oraḥ Ḥayyim* 192:1).

Land must be assessed by nine Israelites and one priest – וְהַקַּרְקָעוֹת תִּשְׁעָה וְכֹהֵן: If one consecrated land and wants to redeem it, the assessment of the value of the land is conducted by a group of ten, one of whom must be a priest (Rambam *Sefer Hafla'a, Hilkhot Arakhin* 8:2).

And similarly, assessing the value of a person – וְאָדָם כַּיּוֹצֵא בָּהֶן: If an individual pledges to donate his own value to the Temple treasury, his value is assessed as though he were being sold as a slave. The assessment is conducted by a group of ten, one of whom must be a priest (Rambam *Sefer Hafla'a, Hilkhot Arakhin* 8:2).

NOTES

Mourners themselves are not included in the count – אֵין אֲבֵלִים מִן הַמִּנְיָן: Rashi and many others explain that this is because the consolers would recite a blessing of consolation to the mourner, and the mourner would recite a separate blessing for those who had come to console him. Therefore, the quorum of ten must be in addition to the mourner himself. The Rid explains that since mourners are preoccupied in their mourning, they do not pay close attention to the blessing and therefore do not count for the quorum. This is not the case with regard to bridegrooms.

The word priest is written ten times – עֲשָׂרָה כֹּהֲנִים כְּתוּבִים: *Tosafot* question why an even number of people would participate in this formal appraisal of value, as it seems to contradict the general rule that a court may not be composed of an even number of judges. The Rashba explains that since the number of appraisers is derived from a verse, it need not follow general court procedures. Others explain that an appraisal of value is not equivalent to a court case, and the appraisers are not considered a court (see Ritva and *Turei Even*).

Say that the assessment must be carried out by five priests – וְאֵימָא חֲמִשָּׁה כֹּהֲנִים: This question has been explained in the commentary to the Gemara based upon the interpretation of Rashi. The Ran offers another explanation based upon the general principle: It is sufficient for the conclusion that emerged from the inference to be like the inference, which means that the conclusion of an inference cannot be applied more broadly than the source of that inference. In this case, since it is derived from the term "priest" that even non-priests may participate, it can be derived only that the number of non-priests who may participate is equal to the number of priests who must be included; it cannot be derived that the number of non-priests may exceed the number of priests.

The Gemara concluded by stating that it is indeed difficult to understand why there may be more than five non-priests in the group that performs the assessment. As an explanation of this point, some say that in a series of multiple restrictive expressions, all the expressions after the first one are considered amplifications (*Panim Meirot*).

אָמַר רַבִּי אַבָּהוּ: בְּאוֹמֵר דָּמַי עָלַי. דְּתַנְיָא: הָאוֹמֵר דָּמַי עָלַי – שָׁמִין אוֹתוֹ כְּעֶבֶד. וְעֶבֶד אִיתְקַשׁ לְקַרְקָעוֹת, דִּכְתִיב ״וְהִתְנַחַלְתֶּם אוֹתָם לִבְנֵיכֶם אַחֲרֵיכֶם לָרֶשֶׁת אֲחוּזָּה״.

Rabbi Abbahu said: The mishna is referring **to one who says: My assessment** is incumbent **upon me,** and thereby pledges to donate a sum of money equivalent to his own monetary value to the Temple treasury, **as it is taught** in a *baraita*: With regard to **one who says: My assessment** is incumbent **upon me,** the court **assesses him as** though he were **a slave** in order to determine the amount he is obligated to donate to the Temple treasury. **And a slave is compared to land, as it is written** with regard to slaves: **"And you shall take them as an inheritance for your children after you, to inherit them for a possession"** (Leviticus 25:46). Consequently, the same criteria that apply to assessing consecrated land apply to assessing the monetary value of an individual.

מתני׳ הַקּוֹרֵא בַּתּוֹרָה לֹא יִפְחוֹת מִשְּׁלֹשָׁה פְּסוּקִים, וְלֹא יִקְרָא לַמְתוּרְגְּמָן יוֹתֵר מִפָּסוּק אֶחָד.

MISHNA **One who reads from the Torah** in the synagogue **should not read fewer than three verses.**[H] **And** when it is being translated, **he should not read to the translator more than one verse** at a time, so that the translator will not become confused.

HALAKHA

One who reads from the Torah should not read fewer than three verses – הַקּוֹרֵא בַּתּוֹרָה לֹא יִפְחוֹת מִשְּׁלֹשָׁה פְּסוּקִים: Three verses are the minimal number that can be publically read from the Torah. If there is a translator, the reader should read one verse at a time before the translator translates it for the congregation (*Shulḥan Arukh, Oraḥ Ḥayyim* 137:2, 145:1).

וּבַנָּבִיא שְׁלֹשָׁה. הָיוּ שְׁלָשְׁתָּן שָׁלֹשׁ פָּרָשִׁיּוֹת – קוֹרִין אֶחָד אֶחָד.

And with regard to the Prophets, one may read to the translator **three** verses at a time.[H] With respect to the Torah, an incorrect translation might lead to an error in practice, but this concern does not apply to the Prophets. **If the three** verses **constitute three** separate **paragraphs,**[N] that is to say, if each verse is a paragraph in itself, **one must read** them to the translator **one by one.**

מְדַלְּגִין בַּנָּבִיא, וְאֵין מְדַלְּגִין בַּתּוֹרָה. וְעַד כַּמָּה הוּא מְדַלֵּג? עַד כְּדֵי שֶׁלֹּא יִפְסוֹק הַמְתוּרְגְּמָן.

One may skip from one place to another while reading **the Prophets, but one may not skip** from one place to another while reading **the Torah.**[H] **How far may he skip? As far as** he can, provided that **the translator will not conclude** his translation while the reader is still rolling the scroll to the new location. The reader may not cause the congregation to wait for him after the translator has finished, as that would be disrespectful to the congregation.

גמ׳ הָנֵי שְׁלֹשָׁה פְּסוּקִין כְּנֶגֶד מִי? אָמַר רַב אַסִי: כְּנֶגֶד תּוֹרָה נְבִיאִים וּכְתוּבִים.

GEMARA The Gemara asks: **Corresponding to what were these three verses,** i.e., the minimal Torah reading, instituted? **Rav Asi said:** They **correspond to the Torah, Prophets, and Writings.**

וְלֹא יִקְרָא לַמְתוּרְגְּמָן יוֹתֵר מִפָּסוּק אֶחָד וּבַנָּבִיא שְׁלֹשָׁה פְּסוּקִים, וְאִם הָיוּ שְׁלָשְׁתָּן שָׁלֹשׁ פָּרָשִׁיּוֹת – קוֹרֵא אֶחָד אֶחָד, כְּגוֹן ״כִּי כֹה אָמַר ה׳ חִנָּם נִמְכַּרְתֶּם״; ״כִּי כֹה אָמַר ה׳ אֱלֹהִים מִצְרַיִם יָרַד עַמִּי בָרִאשׁוֹנָה״; ״וְעַתָּה מַה לִּי פֹה נְאֻם ה׳״.

We learned in the mishna: **And** when it is being translated, **one should not read to the translator more than one verse** at a time. **And with regard to the Prophets,** he may read to the translator **three** verses at a time. **If the three** verses **constitute three** separate **paragraphs, he must read** them to the translator **separately, for example,** the verses: **"For thus says the Lord, You were sold for naught"** (Isaiah 52:3); **"For thus says the Lord God, at first My people went down to Egypt"** (Isaiah 52:4); **"Now therefore what have I here, says the Lord"** (Isaiah 52:5). These are three adjacent verses, each one constituting an independent paragraph.

״מְדַלְּגִין בַּנָּבִיא וְאֵין מְדַלְּגִין בַּתּוֹרָה״. וּרְמִינְהִי: קוֹרֵא ״אַחֲרֵי מוֹת״ וְ״אַךְ בֶּעָשׂוֹר״. וְהָא קָא מְדַלֵּג!

§ We learned further in the mishna: **One may skip** from one place to another while reading **the Prophets, but one may not skip** from one place to another while reading **the Torah.** The Gemara **raises a contradiction** from a mishna (*Yoma* 68b): On Yom Kippur, the High Priest **reads** the section beginning with the verse: **"After the death"** (Leviticus 16:1), and then he reads the section beginning with the verse: **"Only on the tenth day"** (Leviticus 23:27). **Doesn't he skip** from the first section to the second section?

אֲמַר אַבַּיֵי: לָא קַשְׁיָא: כָּאן בִּכְדֵי שֶׁיִּפְסוֹק הַתּוּרְגְּמָן, וְכָאן – בִּכְדֵי שֶׁלֹּא יִפְסוֹק הַתּוּרְגְּמָן.

Abaye said: This is not difficult. Here, where it says that one may not skip in the Torah, **the translator will conclude** his translation before the reader is ready to continue reading. **There, where** it is permitted to skip, **the translator will not conclude** his translation before the reader is ready to continue reading.

HALAKHA

And with regard to the Prophets, three verses at a time – וּבַנָּבִיא שְׁלֹשָׁה: If there is a translator in the synagogue, it is permitted to read three verses at once from the Prophets and then the translator recites the translation of all three verses. If the verses are from three distinct paragraphs, one should read the verses one at a time and allow the translator to translate each one separately (Rambam *Sefer Ahava, Hilkhot Tefilla* 12:14).

One may skip while reading the Prophets, but one may not skip while reading the Torah – מְדַלְּגִין בַּנָּבִיא וְאֵין מְדַלְּגִין בַּתּוֹרָה: It is permitted to skip from one section to another while reading the Torah, as long as both sections address the same topic. Conversely, while reading the Prophets, it is permitted to skip from one section to another within one book of the Prophets even if they address different topics. However, one should not cause the congregation to have to wait for the reading to continue. It is prohibited to skip from one book of the Prophets to another; unless the sections address the same topic, in which case it is permitted (*Peri Ḥadash*). Within the twelve books of Prophets that are grouped together, it is permitted to skip from one book to another, but only if one skips ahead to a section that comes later (*Shulḥan Arukh, Oraḥ Ḥayyim* 144:1).

NOTES

If the three verses constitute three separate paragraphs – הָיוּ שְׁלָשְׁתָּן שָׁלֹשׁ פָּרָשִׁיּוֹת: The Ran adds that even if the verses do not constitute three separate paragraphs, if they address different topics, they should not be read together. Rabbeinu Yehonatan explains that the reason the mishna specifically cited the example of verses that constitute distinct paragraphs is to allude to the prophecies of consolation that these verses express.

וְהָא עֲלַהּ קָתָנֵי: מְדַלְּגִין בַּנָּבִיא וְאֵין מְדַלְּגִין בַּתּוֹרָה, וְעַד כַּמָּה הוּא מְדַלֵּג – עַד כְּדֵי שֶׁלֹּא יִפְסוֹק הַתּוּרְגְּמָן, מִכְּלָל דְּבַתּוֹרָה כְּלָל כְּלָל לָא!

The Gemara asks: **Wasn't it taught** in the mishna **with regard to that** issue: **One may skip while** reading **the Prophets, but one may not skip while** reading **the Torah. How far may he skip? As far as** he can, provided that **the translator will not conclude** his translation before the reader is ready to continue reading. This applies to reading the Prophets; it therefore proves **by inference that** while reading **the Torah** one may **not** skip **at all.**

אֶלָּא אֲמַר אַבָּיֵי: לָא קַשְׁיָא: כָּאן – בְּעִנְיָן אֶחָד, כָּאן – בִּשְׁתֵּי עֲנְיָינוֹת. וְהָתַנְיָא: מְדַלְּגִין בַּתּוֹרָה בְּעִנְיָן אֶחָד, וּבְנָבִיא בִּשְׁנֵי עֲנְיָינִין. כָּאן וְכָאן בִּכְדֵי שֶׁלֹּא יִפְסוֹק הַתּוּרְגְּמָן.

Rather, Abaye said it is **not difficult** for a different reason: **Here,** where it says that the High Priest skipped from one section to another, it was permitted because the two sections address **one topic. There,** where the mishna says one may not skip while reading the Torah, it is where the two sections address **two** distinct **topics. And so it is** explicitly **taught** in a *baraita*: **One may skip** from one section to another while reading **the Torah** if the two sections address **one topic, and in** the **Prophets** one may skip even if the two sections address **two** distinct **topics.** Both **here and there,** with regard to the Torah and the Prophets, one may skip only if **the translator will not conclude** his translation before the reader is ready to continue reading.

תַּנְיָא אִידָךְ: אֵין מְדַלְּגִין מִנָּבִיא לְנָבִיא, וּבְנָבִיא שֶׁל שְׁנֵים עָשָׂר – מְדַלֵּג, וּבִלְבַד שֶׁלֹּא יְדַלֵּג מִסּוֹף הַסֵּפֶר לִתְחִילָּתוֹ.

It is taught in **another** *baraita*: **One may not skip from prophet to prophet,** i.e., from one book of Prophets to another, even if the selections address the same topic. **However, one may skip** from one **prophet** to another **among the twelve** books of Prophets,[N] which are grouped together, **provided that he does not skip from the end of the book to the beginning,** i.e., that he does not read a later section and then an earlier section.

מתני׳ הַמַּפְטִיר בַּנָּבִיא הוּא פּוֹרֵס עַל שְׁמַע, וְהוּא עוֹבֵר לִפְנֵי הַתֵּיבָה, וְהוּא נוֹשֵׂא אֶת כַּפָּיו. וְאִם הָיָה קָטָן – אָבִיו אוֹ רַבּוֹ עוֹבְרִין עַל יָדוֹ.

MISHNA **The one who concludes with** a reading from **the Prophets** [*haftara*] **is** also **the one** who is honored to **recite the** introductory prayers and **blessing** before *Shema*,[N] **and he passes before the ark** to repeat the *Amida* prayer, **and** if he is a priest **he lifts his hands** to recite the Priestly Benediction.[N] **And if** the one who reads the *haftara* **is a minor,** who may read the *haftara* but is not qualified to lead the congregation in prayer, **his father or teacher** is honored to **pass** before the ark **in his place.**

NOTES

The twelve books of Prophets – שְׁנֵים עָשָׂר: In several of the methods in which the Bible is divided, including the Gemara's method in *Bava Batra* 14a, there are twenty-four books of the Bible. In that case, the twelve books of Hosea, Joel, Amos, Obadiah, Jonah, Micah, Nahum, Habakkuk, Zephaniah, Haggai, Zechariah, and Malachi are seen as one book.

The one who concludes with a reading from the Prophets [*haftara*] is also the one to recite the introductory prayers and blessing before *Shema* – הַמַּפְטִיר בַּנָּבִיא הוּא פּוֹרֵס עַל שְׁמַע: Rashi explains that this is referring to one who regularly reads the *haftara*. This resolves a difficulty with regard to the sequence of the prayer service, as the *Shema* is recited before the reading of the *haftara*. Since this individual agrees to regularly read the *haftara*, he is compensated in the form of other honorific tasks (Ritva). The reason the reader of the *haftara* needed to be compensated was because he was not counted for the quorum of readers from the Torah but rather was called to supplement the Torah reading. Furthermore, it was common for a minor to be appointed to read the *haftara*, and therefore an adult who accepts the responsibility of regularly reading the *haftara* lowers his stature. However, over the course of the generations, since they would grant numerous honors to the one who read the *haftara*, reading the *haftara* became an honorable position, and it is generally viewed as an honor in its own right.

And he lifts his hands to recite the Priestly Benediction – וְהוּא נוֹשֵׂא אֶת כַּפָּיו: This phrase is difficult to understand, as every priest recites the Priestly Benediction, regardless of whether he read the *haftara*. The commentaries suggested various answers to this question. Some say that it is referring to a synagogue where all the congregants were priests, in which case they do not all recite the Priestly Benediction (*Turei Even*). Alternatively, when a priest serves as the prayer leader, he generally does not recite the Priestly Benediction, due to a concern that he will become confused and will not be able to continue reciting the prayers. In this case, however, he would be permitted to recite the Priestly Benediction (Rashash). Others explain that the Gemara means to say that even if his beard has yet to grow, he may regularly recite the Priestly Benediction (*Sefat Emet*). The *Tosefot Yom Tov* explains that this phrase is inserted merely to ensure consistent phraseology between the beginning and end of the mishna.

HALAKHA

He may not pass before the ark – אֵינוֹ עוֹבֵר לִפְנֵי הַתֵּיבָה: Only one whose beard has fully grown should be appointed as the regular prayer leader. This does not refer to growing an actual beard; rather, it indicates that one must have reached the age when this usually occurs (*Arukh HaShulḥan*). Some say that since this is out of respect for the congregation, the congregation may forgo its honor in this matter (see *Magen Avraham*). Others disagree (*Baḥ*; *Taz*). However, it is permitted for anyone who has reached adulthood to lead the prayers on a temporary basis. On public fast days and the High Holidays, however, even one who serves as the prayer leader on a temporary basis must be one whose beard has fully grown (*Mishna Berura*; *Shulḥan Arukh*, *Oraḥ Ḥayyim* 53:6).

He may not lift his hands to recite the Priestly Benediction – אֵינוֹ נוֹשֵׂא אֶת כַּפָּיו: One who has not reached physical maturity, signified by the growth of two pubic hairs, may not recite the Priestly Benediction on his own, i.e., if there are no other priests in the synagogue. Some say that once he turns thirteen, it can be assumed that he has grown two hairs and this need not be verified (*Eliya Rabba*), while others disagree (*Magen Avraham*). However, if other priests are reciting the Priestly Benediction, even a minor may join them in order to learn how to perform this mitzva. Once he has reached maturity, a priest may recite the benediction even if no other priests are present. However, he should not do this on a regular basis until his beard has grown in (*Shulḥan Arukh*, *Oraḥ Ḥayyim* 128:34).

One whose limbs are exposed [*poḥe'aḥ*] – פּוֹחֵחַ: A *poḥe'aḥ* is one whose garments are torn so that his arms and shoulders are bare (Vilna Gaon). He may not serve as the prayer leader or read from the Torah, but he is permitted to lead the congregation in reciting the introductory prayers and blessing before *Shema*. It is proper for the prayer leader to wear clothes that cover his legs, and if his garments are not long enough, he should wear socks that go up to his knees (Rambam *Sefer Ahava*, *Hilkhot Tefilla* 8:12; *Shulḥan Arukh*, *Oraḥ Ḥayyim* 53:13; *Kaf HaḤayyim*).

One who is blind may recite the introductory prayers and blessing before *Shema* – סוּמָא פּוֹרֵס אֶת שְׁמַע: One who is blind may recite the introductory prayers and blessing before *Shema*, even if he has been blind his entire life. He may also serve as the prayer leader for the duration of the prayer service (*Mishna Berura*). The *halakha* is in accordance with the first view cited in the mishna (*Shulḥan Arukh*, *Oraḥ Ḥayyim* 69:2).

קָטָן קוֹרֵא בַּתּוֹרָה וּמְתַרְגֵּם, אֲבָל אֵינוֹ פּוֹרֵס עַל שְׁמַע וְאֵינוֹ עוֹבֵר לִפְנֵי הַתֵּיבָה, וְאֵינוֹ נוֹשֵׂא אֶת כַּפָּיו.

A minor may read the Torah in public **and** also **translate** the text for the congregation into Aramaic, **but he may not recite the** introductory prayers and **blessing** before ***Shema*, and he may not pass before the ark** to lead the congregation in prayer,[H] **and he may not lift his hands** to recite the Priestly Benediction.[H]

פּוֹחֵחַ פּוֹרֵס אֶת שְׁמַע וּמְתַרְגֵּם, אֲבָל אֵינוֹ קוֹרֵא בַּתּוֹרָה, וְאֵינוֹ עוֹבֵר לִפְנֵי הַתֵּיבָה, וְאֵינוֹ נוֹשֵׂא אֶת כַּפָּיו.

One whose limbs are exposed [*poḥe'aḥ*][NH] **may recite the** introductory prayers and **blessing** before ***Shema* and translate** the Torah reading into Aramaic, **but he may not read from the Torah** out of respect for the Torah; **he may not pass before the ark** to lead the congregation in prayer; **and he may not lift his hands** to recite the Priestly Benediction out of respect for the congregation.

סוּמָא פּוֹרֵס אֶת שְׁמַע וּמְתַרְגֵּם, רַבִּי יְהוּדָה אוֹמֵר: כָּל שֶׁלֹּא רָאָה מְאוֹרוֹת מִיָּמָיו – אֵינוֹ פּוֹרֵס עַל שְׁמַע.

One who is **blind may recite the** introductory prayers and **blessing** before ***Shema*,**[H] **and he may** also **translate** the Torah reading into Aramaic. **Rabbi Yehuda says: Anyone who has not seen the luminaries,** the sun, moon, and stars, **in his life,** i.e., he was blind from birth, **may not recite the** introductory prayers and **blessing** before ***Shema*.** The first of the blessings before *Shema* is the blessing over the luminaries, and one who has never seen them cannot recite the blessing at all.

גמ׳ מַאי טַעְמָא? רַב פָּפָּא אָמַר: מִשּׁוּם כָּבוֹד, רַבָּה בַּר שִׁימִי אָמַר: מִשּׁוּם דְּאָתֵי לְאִינְצוּיֵי.

GEMARA The Gemara asks: **What is the reason** that the one who reads the *haftara* is honored with these other roles? **Rav Pappa said:** It is **due to** a desire to grant him **honor.** Since even minors are qualified to read the *haftara*, it was considered an insult for a person to be called up to read the *haftara* rather than be called up as one of those needed to read the Torah. Since he was willing to serve in this role, he is granted other, more honorable roles in the synagogue. **Rabba bar Shimi said** a different reason: It is **due to** a concern that **they will come to quarrel,** as the individual who read the *haftara* will quarrel with the individual honored to lead the congregation in prayer.

מַאי בֵּינַיְיהוּ? אִיכָּא בֵּינַיְיהוּ דְּעָבֵיד בְּחִנָּם.

The Gemara asks: **What is** the practical difference **between them?** The Gemara explains: **There is** a practical difference **between them where** the one who passes before the ark **does so free of** charge.[N] In that case, there is still a need to grant the one who read the *haftara* honor, but it is not likely that they will quarrel.

תְּנַן: וְאִם הָיָה קָטָן – אָבִיו אוֹ רַבּוֹ עוֹבְרִין עַל יָדוֹ. אִי אָמְרַתְּ מִשּׁוּם נִצּוּיֵי – קָטָן בַּר נִצּוּיֵי הוּא?

We learned in the mishna: **And if** the one who reads the *haftara* **is a minor, his father or teacher** is honored to **pass** before the ark **in his place. If you say** that the reason the reader of the *haftara* passes before the ark is **due to** a concern that they will **quarrel, will a minor engage in quarreling?** He has no valid claim to the right to pass before the ark. Consequently, the concern for strife must not be the reason for the *halakha* stated in the mishna.

אֶלָּא מַאי מִשּׁוּם כָּבוֹד – קָטָן בַּר כָּבוֹד הוּא?! אֶלָּא: אִיכָּא כְּבוֹד אָבִיו וּכְבוֹד רַבּוֹ,

The Gemara rejects this argument: **Rather, what** is the reason; is it **due to honor? Does a minor have honor** that is slighted when he reads the *haftara* and therefore must be assuaged? **Rather,** according to Rav Pappa **it is** a display of **honor** to **his father and his teacher.**

NOTES

One whose limbs are exposed [*poḥe'aḥ*] – פּוֹחֵחַ: Many explanations have been suggested for the term *poḥe'aḥ*, which indicates someone who is not properly dressed, and parts of his body are therefore exposed. Some explain that it refers to one who is wearing only a sash around his hips and waist (*Sefer Halakhot Gedolot*). Others hold that it refers to one whose garment does not have sleeves (*Arukh*), one whose arms and shoulders are bare (Rosh), or one whose chest is bare (Meiri; Rid the Younger). It appears that the term is used in tractate *Soferim* to refer to one whose legs are bare. Some of these interpretations are based upon the verse: "Like as my servant Isaiah has walked naked [*paḥiaḥ*] and barefoot" (Isaiah 20:3). The previous verse states: "Loosen the sackcloth from off your loins" (Isaiah 20:2), indicating that removing certain garments causes one to be a *paḥiaḥ* (see Rashi and Rosh).

Where he does so free of charge – דְּעָבֵיד בְּחִנָּם: According to most commentaries, it was customary for those leading the prayer service to be paid for their services. Alternately, some explain that this means that one reads the *haftara* without the desire to receive another honor in return (*Sefat Emet*).

הָכָא נַמִי אִיכָּא נְצוּיֵי אָבִיו וּנְצוּיֵי רַבּוֹ.

Here, also, according to Rabba bar Shimi, **it is** to prevent **his father or teacher** from **quarreling.**

״פּוֹחֵחַ פּוֹרֵס עַל שְׁמַע״ וכו׳. בְּעָא מִינֵּיהּ עוּלָּא בַּר רַב מֵאַבַּיֵי: קָטָן פּוֹחֵחַ מַהוּ שֶׁיִּקְרָא בַּתּוֹרָה?

§ We learned in the mishna: **One whose limbs are exposed** [*poḥe'aḥ*] **may recite the** introductory prayers and **blessing** before ***Shema*** and translate the Torah reading into Aramaic, but he may not read from the Torah. **Ulla bar Rav raised a dilemma before Abaye: What is** the *halakha* with regard to whether **a minor whose limbs are exposed** may **read from the Torah?** Can it be argued that a minor's bare limbs do not fall under the category of nakedness, and therefore it is permitted for him to read the Torah despite the fact that parts of his body are exposed?

אֲמַר לֵיהּ: וְתִיבְּעֵי לָךְ עָרוֹם? עָרוֹם מַאי טַעְמָא לָא – מִשּׁוּם כְּבוֹד צִבּוּר, הָכָא נַמִי – מִשּׁוּם כְּבוֹד צִבּוּר.

Abaye **said to him: And** according to this reasoning, **raise the dilemma** with regard to a minor who is totally **naked. What is the reason that** a minor who is **naked may not** read the Torah?[N] It is **due to respect for the public. Here, too,** a *poḥe'aḥ* may not read from the Torah **due to respect for the public.**

״סוּמָא פּוֹרֵס עַל שְׁמַע״ וכו׳. תַּנְיָא, אָמְרוּ לוֹ לְרַבִּי יְהוּדָה: הַרְבֵּה צָפוּ לִדְרוֹשׁ בַּמֶּרְכָּבָה וְלֹא רָאוּ אוֹתָהּ מִימֵיהֶם.

The mishna continues: One who is **blind may recite the** introductory prayers and **blessing** before ***Shema*, and he may** also **translate** the Torah reading into Aramaic. Rabbi Yehuda says: Anyone who has not seen the luminaries in his life may not recite the first of the blessings before *Shema*, which is the blessing over the luminaries. **It is taught** in a *baraita* that **they said to Rabbi Yehuda: Many have seen** enough with their mind **to expound upon the** Divine **Chariot, although they have never** actually **seen it.** Similarly, even one who has never seen the luminaries may recite the blessing.

וְרַבִּי יְהוּדָה: הָתָם בְּאַבַנְתָּא דְּלִיבָּא תַּלְיָא מִילְּתָא, וְהָא קָא מִיכַּוֵּין וְיָדַע. הָכָא – מִשּׁוּם הֲנָאָה הוּא, וְהָא לֵית לֵיהּ הֲנָאָה.

And how does **Rabbi Yehuda** counter this argument? He can say that **there,** with regard to the Chariot, **the matter depends upon the heart's comprehension, and one can concentrate** his mind **and understand** the Chariot even if he has never actually seen it. But **here,** with regard to the luminaries, the blessing is recited **due to the benefit** one derives from them, **and** one who is blind **does not derive** any **benefit** from them, and therefore he may not recite a blessing over them.

וְרַבָּנַן: אִית לֵיהּ הֲנָאָה, כְּרַבִּי יוֹסֵי. דְּתַנְיָא, אָמַר רַבִּי יוֹסֵי: כׇּל יָמַי הָיִיתִי מִצְטַעֵר עַל מִקְרָא זֶה ״וְהָיִיתָ מְמַשֵּׁשׁ בַּצׇּהֳרַיִם כַּאֲשֶׁר יְמַשֵּׁשׁ הָעִוֵּר בָּאֲפֵלָה״, וְכִי מָה אִכְפַּת לֵיהּ לְעִוֵּר בֵּין אֲפֵילָה לְאוֹרָה?

And the Rabbis maintain that even a blind man **derives benefit** from the luminaries, **in accordance with** the opinion **of Rabbi Yosei, as it is taught** in a *baraita* that **Rabbi Yosei said: All of my life I was troubled by this verse,** which I did not understand: **"And you shall grope at noon as the blind man gropes in the darkness"** (Deuteronomy 28:29).[N] I was perplexed: **What** does it **matter to a blind** person **whether** it is **dark or light?** He cannot see in any event, so why does the verse speak about a blind man in the darkness?

עַד שֶׁבָּא מַעֲשֶׂה לְיָדִי. פַּעַם אַחַת הָיִיתִי מְהַלֵּךְ בְּאִישׁוֹן לַיְלָה וַאֲפֵלָה, וְרָאִיתִי סוּמָא שֶׁהָיָה מְהַלֵּךְ בַּדֶּרֶךְ וַאֲבוּקָה בְּיָדוֹ. אָמַרְתִּי לוֹ: בְּנִי, אֲבוּקָה זוֹ לָמָּה לָךְ? אָמַר לִי: כׇּל זְמַן שֶׁאֲבוּקָה בְּיָדִי – בְּנֵי אָדָם רוֹאִין אוֹתִי, וּמַצִּילִין אוֹתִי מִן הַפְּחָתִין וּמִן הַקּוֹצִין וּמִן הַבַּרְקָנִין.

I continued to ponder the matter **until** the following **incident occurred to me. I was once walking in the absolute darkness of the night, and I saw a blind man who was walking on** his **way with a torch in his hands. I said to him: My son, why do you** need **this torch** if you are blind? **He said to me: As long as I have a torch in my hand, people see me and save me from the pits and the thorns and the thistles.** Even a blind man derives at least indirect benefit from the light, and therefore he may recite the blessing over the heavenly luminaries.

NOTES

What is the reason that a minor who is naked may not read the Torah – עָרוֹם מַאי טַעְמָא לָא: It is generally prohibited for one who is naked to read the Torah. However, the male organ is only considered nakedness when it is fit for sexual activity. Therefore, the general prohibition against reading the Torah while unclothed does not apply to a minor. If he is prohibited from reading the Torah, it must be due to another factor (see *Turei Even*).

NOTES

As the blind man gropes in the darkness – כַּאֲשֶׁר יְמַשֵּׁשׁ הָעִוֵּר בָּאֲפֵלָה: As Rabbi Yosei explains, during the daytime the blind man is seen by others who can direct him to safety. At night, when he is unable to see and others do not see him, he is more likely to become injured. The plain meaning of the verse is that a blind man constantly gropes in the darkness due to his blindness.

LANGUAGE

Satis – סָטִיס: From the Greek word ἰσάτις, *isatis*, which is the woad plant.

BACKGROUND

Satis – סָטִיס: *Satis* is referring to *Isatis tinctoria* L., also known as dyer's woad, a plant from the *Brassicaceae* family that can be annual or perennial. It grows to a height of 1 m and has smooth leaves and yellow flowers. A blue dye, indigo, can be produced from material extracted from the leaves of this plant. Indigo is a very stable dye, and it is therefore difficult to clean from one's hands. Nowadays, this plant is generally not used for dying, as synthetic indigo is cheaper to manufacture than indigo from woad. However, it grows wild in many places in Eretz Yisrael.

Woad flowers

Old woad mill

Indigo from woad

מתני׳ כֹּהֵן שֶׁיֵּשׁ בְּיָדָיו מוּמִין לֹא יִשָּׂא אֶת כַּפָּיו. רַבִּי יְהוּדָה אוֹמֵר: אַף מִי שֶׁהָיוּ יָדָיו צְבוּעוֹת סָטִיס לֹא יִשָּׂא אֶת כַּפָּיו מִפְּנֵי שֶׁהָעָם מִסְתַּכְּלִין בּוֹ.

MISHNA **A priest who has blemishes on his hands**[NH] **may not lift his hands** to recite the Priestly Benediction. Because of his blemish, people will look at his hands, and it is prohibited to look at the hands of the priests during the Priestly Benediction. **Rabbi Yehuda says: Even one whose hands were colored**[H] **with *satis*,**[LB] a blue dye, **may not lift his hands** to recite the Priestly Benediction **because the congregation will look at him.**[N]

גמ׳ תָּנָא: מוּמִין שֶׁאָמְרוּ – בְּפָנָיו, יָדָיו וְרַגְלָיו. אָמַר רַבִּי יְהוֹשֻׁעַ בֶּן לֵוִי: יָדָיו בּוֹהֲקָנִיּוֹת – לֹא יִשָּׂא אֶת כַּפָּיו. תַּנְיָא נָמֵי הָכִי: יָדָיו בּוֹהֲקָנִיּוֹת – לֹא יִשָּׂא אֶת כַּפָּיו. עֲקוּמוֹת, עֲקוּשׁוֹת – לֹא יִשָּׂא אֶת כַּפָּיו.

GEMARA It is **taught** in a *baraita*: **The blemishes that** the Sages **said** disqualify a priest from reciting the Priestly Benediction include any blemishes found **on his face, hands, and feet,** but not blemishes that are not visible to others. **Rabbi Yehoshua ben Levi said:** If **his hands are spotted** with white blotches, **he may not lift his hands** to recite the Priestly Benediction. The Gemara notes that **this is also taught** in a *baraita*: If a priest's **hands are spotted, he may not lift his hands** to recite the Priestly Benediction. Similarly, if his hands are **curved** inward **or bent** sideways,[N] **he may not lift his hands** to recite the Priestly Benediction.

NOTES

Who has blemishes on his hands – שֶׁיֵּשׁ בְּיָדָיו מוּמִין: Most commentaries explain that the reason he cannot recite the Priestly Benediction is because people will look at him. However, the Rid explains that the reason is because it is not respectful to the congregation for a deformed man to bless them.

Because the congregation will look at him – מִפְּנֵי שֶׁהָעָם מִסְתַּכְּלִין בּוֹ: Rashi explains that the reason it is prohibited to look at the priests during the Priestly Benediction is because the Divine Presence rests on their hands. However, *Tosafot* (*Ḥagiga* 16a) and other commentaries point out that this is true only in the Temple. They explain, based on the Jerusalem Talmud, that the reason it is prohibited to look at the priests during the Priestly Benediction outside the Temple is because one will be distracted from focusing on the blessings themselves.

Bent sideways – עֲקוּשׁוֹת: Some explain this term as indicating that his hands are clenched and he cannot open them (Ran).

HALAKHA

A priest who has blemishes on his hands – כֹּהֵן שֶׁיֵּשׁ בְּיָדָיו מוּמִין: A priest who has a blemish on his face or hands may not lift his hands to recite the Priestly Benediction because the people will look at him during the Priestly Benediction. The same applies to one who has a blemish on his feet, in a place where the priests recite the Priestly Benediction without socks. This also applies to one whose saliva drools from his mouth, or whose eyes constantly tear, or if he is blind in one of his eyes and it is a noticeable condition (*Mishna Berura*). In all of these cases, if the priest is a familiar figure in his community and people are accustomed to seeing his blemish and no longer gaze at it, he may recite the Priestly Benediction, even if he is blind in both eyes.

Anyone who is a permanent resident of a city, or who moves to a new city and has been there for thirty days, is considered a familiar figure. If one visits another city, some hold that after thirty days he is considered a familiar figure (*Magen Avraham*, citing *Baḥ*), while others hold that he is not a familiar figure until he has been there for twelve months (*Shulḥan Arukh HaRav*).

If it is customary in a particular location for priests to cover their hands with their *tallit* during the Priestly Benediction, even a priest who has multiple blemishes may recite the Priestly Benediction; this is so as long as his blemishes are not noticeable from under his *tallit* (*Kaf HaḤayyim*, citing Radvaz) and he does not uncover his hands (Rema). Some permit him to recite the Priestly Benediction even in a place where this is not the custom, if it is the custom for the members of the congregation to cover their faces with a *tallit* (*Taz*). However, common custom is not in accordance with this opinion (*Shulḥan Arukh HaRav*; *Shulḥan Arukh*, *Oraḥ Ḥayyim* 128:30–31).

One whose hands were colored – מִי שֶׁהָיוּ יָדָיו צְבוּעוֹת: A priest whose hands are colored may not recite the Priestly Benediction. However, if the majority of the residents of the town work in a profession that causes their hands to become colored, he may recite the Priestly Benediction. Similarly, a priest may recite the Priestly Benediction if he is a familiar figure in town (*Shulḥan Arukh HaRav*) or if he is in a place where the priests cover their hands with a *tallit* (*Mishna Berura*; *Shulḥan Arukh*, *Oraḥ Ḥayyim* 128:32).

אָמַר רַב אַסִי: חֵיפָנֵי (וּבֵשָׁנֵי) לֹא יִשָּׂא אֶת כַּפָּיו. תַּנְיָא נַמִּי הָכִי: אֵין מוֹרִידִין לִפְנֵי הַתֵּיבָה לֹא אַנְשֵׁי בֵית שְׁאָן, וְלֹא אַנְשֵׁי בֵית חֵיפָה, וְלֹא אַנְשֵׁי טִבְעוֹנִין, מִפְּנֵי שֶׁקּוֹרִין לְאָלְפִין עַיְינִין וּלְעַיְינִין אָלְפִין.

Apropos the previous discussion, **Rav Asi said:** A priest **from Haifa or Beit She'an**[H] **may not lift his hands** to recite the Priestly Benediction, as he does not know how to properly pronounce the guttural letters. **This is also taught** in a *baraita*: **One may not allow the people of Beit She'an,**[B] **nor the people of Beit Haifa, nor the people of Tivonin to pass before the ark** in order to lead the service **because they pronounce *alef* as *ayin* and *ayin* as *alef*,**[NH] and they thereby distort the meaning of the prayers.

אֲמַר לֵיהּ רַבִּי חִיָּיא לְרַבִּי שִׁמְעוֹן בַּר רַבִּי: אִלְמָלֵי אַתָּה לֵוִי פָּסוּל אַתָּה מִן הַדּוּכָן, מִשּׁוּם דַּעֲבֵי קָלָךְ. אֲתָא אֲמַר לֵיהּ לַאֲבוּהּ. אֲמַר לֵיהּ: זִיל אֵימָא לֵיהּ: כְּשֶׁאַתָּה מַגִּיעַ אֵצֶל ״וְחִכִּיתִי לַה׳״ לֹא נִמְצֵאתָ מְחָרֵף וּמְגַדֵּף?

The Gemara relates that **Rabbi Ḥiyya**[P] once **said to Rabbi Shimon, son of Rabbi** Yehuda HaNasi:[P] **If you were a Levite, you would be disqualified from** singing on **the platform** in the Temple courtyard **because your voice is thick.** Offended by this remark, Rabbi Shimon **went and told his father,** Rabbi Yehuda HaNasi, what Rabbi Ḥiyya had said. Rabbi Yehuda HaNasi **said to him: Go and say to him:**[N] **When you** study and **reach** the verse: **"And I will wait upon [*veḥikkiti*] the Lord"** (Isaiah 8:17), **will you not be a maligner and a blasphemer?** Rabbi Ḥiyya, who was from Babylonia, was unable to differentiate between the letters *ḥet* and *heh*, and he would therefore pronounce the word *veḥikkiti* as *vehikkiti*, which means: And I will strike.

אָמַר רַב הוּנָא: זַבְלְגָן לֹא יִשָּׂא אֶת כַּפָּיו. וְהָא הַהוּא דַּהֲוָה בְּשִׁיבָבוּתֵיהּ דְּרַב הוּנָא, וַהֲוָה פָּרֵיס יְדֵיהּ! הַהוּא דָּשׁ בְּעִירוֹ הֲוָה. תַּנְיָא נַמִּי הָכִי: זַבְלְגָן לֹא יִשָּׂא אֶת כַּפָּיו, וְאִם הָיָה דָּשׁ בְּעִירוֹ – מוּתָּר.

Rav Huna said: A priest **whose eyes** constantly **run** with tears **may not lift his hands** to recite the Priestly Benediction. The Gemara asks: **Wasn't there a certain** priest with this condition **in the neighborhood of Rav Huna, and he would spread his hands** and recite the Priestly Benediction? The Gemara answers: **That** priest **was a familiar** figure **in his town.** Since the other residents were accustomed to seeing him, he would not draw their attention during the Priestly Benediction. **This is also taught** in a *baraita*: **One whose eyes run should not lift his hands** to recite the Priestly Benediction, **but if he is a familiar** figure **in his town,**[N] **he is permitted** to do so.

PERSONALITIES

Rabbi Ḥiyya – רַבִּי חִיָּיא: Rabbi Ḥiyya, son of Abba from the Babylonian city of Kafri, was one of the last of the *tanna'im* and a contemporary of Rabbi Yehuda HaNasi. Rabbi Ḥiyya was born to an important family that traced its roots to King David and included many important Jewish Sages. Rabbi Ḥiyya was recognized as a leading Torah scholar even while living in Babylonia. Many credited his efforts with saving the Torah from oblivion. Upon moving to Eretz Yisrael, Rabbi Ḥiyya became a close friend and colleague of Rabbi Yehuda HaNasi. He also became a close friend of Rabbi Yehuda HaNasi's son, Rabbi Shimon, with whom he became partners in trade. A powerful force in his generation, Rabbi Ḥiyya also worked closely with Rav, who was recognized as the leader of the Jewish people but still learned from Rabbi Ḥiyya.

Rabbi Ḥiyya's greatest work was his compilation of oral traditions that were not included in the Mishna of Rabbi Yehuda HaNasi. This collection, which was assembled with the assistance of Rabbi Ḥiyya's disciple-colleague, Rabbi Oshaya, was viewed as authoritative, to the extent that there are statements of *amora'im* that assert that any *baraita* that was not found in his work should not be discussed in the study hall. Some believe that Rabbi Ḥiyya edited the version of the *Tosefta* that is extant today.

While it appears that Rabbi Ḥiyya received financial support when he first came to Eretz Yisrael, ultimately he became a successful merchant. He dealt in international business ventures, particularly the silk trade. He had a set of twin daughters, Pazi and Tavi, as well as twin sons, Yehuda and Ḥizkiyya, who were leading Sages in the generation between the *tanna'im* and *amora'im*. Apparently, they took over Rabbi Ḥiyya's yeshiva in Tiberias after his passing.

Rabbi Shimon, son of Rabbi Yehuda HaNasi – רַבִּי שִׁמְעוֹן בַּר רַבִּי: Rabbi Shimon was the youngest son of Rabbi Yehuda HaNasi and his close student. He was one of the great students of Rabbi Yehuda HaNasi and discussed various halakhic issues with Rabbi Yehuda HaNasi's other prominent students. He was especially close to Rabbi Ḥiyya, who was also his partner in the silk business. In many places, it is noted that Rabbi Shimon was very meticulous about his honor, which he saw as related to the honor of the *Nasi*. In particular, he was careful to ensure that nothing he did would imply offense to his great father. At least one of his sayings is found in the Mishna itself, although he actually lived in the transition generation between the *tanna'im* and *amora'im*. His sayings are often introduced by the word: *Itmar*, it was stated, which commonly introduces statements of *amora'im*.

Rabbi Yehuda HaNasi considered Rabbi Shimon to be a great scholar, and before his death he appointed Rabbi Shimon as the *Ḥakham*, the third-highest position in the Sanhedrin after the *Nasi* and the president of the court. However, he appointed Rabbi Shimon's older brother, Rabban Gamliel, to be his replacement as *Nasi*.

HALAKHA

A priest from Haifa or Beit She'an – חֵיפָנֵי וּבֵשָׁנֵי: One who does not pronounce certain letters properly, e.g., *ayin* like *alef*, *ḥet* like a *heh* (*Magen Avraham*, citing Radvaz), or *shin* like a *samekh* (Rambam), may recite the Priestly Benediction only in a place where most people pronounce the letters in this manner (*Shulḥan Arukh*, *Oraḥ Ḥayyim* 128:33; *Shulḥan Arukh HaRav*).

Because they pronounce *alef* as *ayin* and *ayin* as *alef* – מִפְּנֵי שֶׁקּוֹרִין לְאָלְפִין עַיְינִין וּלְעַיְינִין אָלְפִין: One who does not pronounce certain letters properly may not serve as the prayer leader. However, in a place where most people pronounce the letters in this manner, it is permitted (*Magen Avraham*, citing Radvaz). Some say that if he is the one who is most fit to lead the prayers, he may do so even if he does not pronounce certain letters properly (*Peri Ḥadash*). Others prohibit this unless he can pronounce the letters properly when he exerts himself to do so (*Shulḥan Arukh*, *Oraḥ Ḥayyim* 53:12; *Peri Megadim*).

BACKGROUND

The people of Beit She'an – אַנְשֵׁי בֵית שְׁאָן: Whereas residents of Judea, including the family of Rabbi Yehuda HaNasi, had a rich vocabulary and clear pronunciation, the residents of the Galilee had difficulty pronouncing the guttural letters properly and hardly differentiated between the letters *alef* and *ayin*. This was particularly true in certain cities in the Galilee, especially those with large gentile populations. Similarly, Babylonian Jews, perhaps due to the influence of the Babylonian language, which had eliminated guttural letters in ancient times, also had difficulty pronouncing these letters. It is therefore not surprising that Rabbi Ḥiyya, who was Babylonian, had difficulty pronouncing the letter *ḥet* and would pronounce it as a *heh*.

NOTES

Because they pronounce *alef* as *ayin* and *ayin* as *alef* – מִפְּנֵי שֶׁקּוֹרִין לְאָלְפִין עַיְינִין וּלְעַיְינִין אָלְפִין: Although most modern Hebrew speakers pronounce these letters the same way, the *ayin* is actually a more guttural sound than the *alef*.

Go and say to him – זִיל אֵימָא לֵיהּ: The *Ḥatam Sofer* (*Nidda* 49b) offers the following explanation of this conversation: Rabbi Ḥiyya was of the opinion that Rabbi Shimon, son of Rabbi Yehuda HaNasi, was unfit to succeed his father as *Nasi* because one who has a blemish that would disqualify a Levite from singing on the platform in the Temple is disqualified from serving on the Sanhedrin. Rabbi Yehuda HaNasi responded that just as Rabbi Ḥiyya himself was fit to serve on the Sanhedrin despite his own speech defect, Rabbi Shimon was also fit to serve on the Sanhedrin.

A familiar figure in his town – דָּשׁ בְּעִירוֹ: This is generally interpreted to mean that the residents of the town are used to seeing this priest. However, the *ge'onim* interpreted this expression to mean that if the priest is used to reciting the blessings, he may continue to do so, even in a different city.

אָמַר רַבִּי יוֹחָנָן: סוּמָא בְּאַחַת מֵעֵינָיו לֹא יִשָּׂא אֶת כַּפָּיו. וְהָא הַהוּא דַּהֲוָה בְּשִׁיבָבוּתֵיהּ דְּרַבִּי יוֹחָנָן, דַּהֲוָה פָּרֵיס יְדֵיהּ! הַהוּא דָּשׁ בְּעִירוֹ הֲוָה. תַּנְיָא נַמִּי הָכִי: סוּמָא בְּאַחַת מֵעֵינָיו לֹא יִשָּׂא אֶת כַּפָּיו, וְאִם הָיָה דָּשׁ בְּעִירוֹ – מוּתָּר.

Rabbi Yoḥanan said: One who is blind in one eye may not lift his hands to recite the Priestly Benediction because people will gaze at him. The Gemara asks: **Wasn't there a certain** priest who was blind in one eye **in the neighborhood of Rabbi Yoḥanan, and he would lift his hands** and recite the Priestly Benediction? The Gemara answers: **That** priest **was a familiar** figure **in his town,** and therefore he would not attract attention during the Priestly Benediction. **This is also taught** in a *baraita*: **One who is blind in one eye may not lift his hands** and recite the Priestly Benediction, **but if he is a familiar** figure **in his town, he is permitted** to do so.

״רַבִּי יְהוּדָה אוֹמֵר מִי שֶׁהָיוּ יָדָיו צְבוּעוֹת לֹא יִשָּׂא אֶת כַּפָּיו״. תָּנָא: אִם רוֹב אַנְשֵׁי הָעִיר מְלַאכְתָּן בְּכָךְ – מוּתָּר.

We learned in the mishna that **Rabbi Yehuda said: One whose hands are colored should not lift his hands** to recite the Priestly Benediction. It was **taught** in a *baraita*: **If most of the townspeople are engaged in this occupation,** dyeing, **he is permitted** to recite the Priestly Benediction, as the congregation will not pay attention to his stained hands.

מתני׳ הָאוֹמֵר אֵינִי עוֹבֵר לִפְנֵי הַתֵּיבָה בִּצְבוּעִין – אַף בִּלְבָנִים לֹא יַעֲבוֹר. בְּסַנְדָּל אֵינִי עוֹבֵר – אַף יָחֵף לֹא יַעֲבוֹר.

MISHNA **One who says: I will not pass before the ark** to lead the prayer service **in colored garments,**[HB] **may not pass** before the ark to lead the prayer service **even in white** garments. There is concern that one who insists on wearing clothing of a specific color during his prayers is a heretic and therefore unfit to lead the service. Similarly, if one says: **I will not pass** before the ark **wearing sandals, he may not pass** before it **even barefoot,** as he is not acting in accordance with the teachings of the Sages.

הָעוֹשֶׂה תְּפִלָּתוֹ עֲגוּלָּה – סַכָּנָה וְאֵין בָּהּ מִצְוָה. נְתָנָהּ עַל מִצְחוֹ אוֹ עַל פַּס יָדוֹ – הֲרֵי זוֹ דֶּרֶךְ הַמִּינוּת. צִיפָּן זָהָב וּנְתָנָהּ עַל בֵּית אוּנְקְלִי שֶׁלּוֹ – הֲרֵי זוֹ דֶּרֶךְ הַחִיצוֹנִים.

One who constructs his phylacteries in **a round** shape exposes himself to **danger**[N] during times of persecution, when foreign governments impose a ban on the mitzva of phylacteries, **and** yet he does **not** fulfill the **mitzva**[HB] to don phylacteries, as phylacteries must be square. **If one placed** the phylacteries worn on the head **on his forehead,** and not in its proper place above his hairline, **or** if he placed the phylacteries worn on the arm **on his palm,** and not on his bicep, **this is the way of the heretics,** i.e., those who reject the tradition of the Sages with regard to the proper placement of the phylacteries. If **one plated** his phylacteries **with gold**[H] **or placed** the phylacteries worn on the arm **on** the outside **of his sleeve** [***unkeli***],[L] **this is the way of the outsiders,**[N] i.e., those who do not take part in the traditions of the Jewish people.

גמ׳ מַאי טַעְמָא? חָיְישִׁינַן שֶׁמָּא מִינוּת נִזְרְקָה בּוֹ.

GEMARA **What is the reason** that one who wishes to pray only with white clothes or barefoot is not permitted to lead the prayer? **We are concerned that perhaps he has been imbued with heresy,** as these are the practices of idolaters. He is therefore barred from leading the service.

״הָעוֹשֶׂה תְּפִלָּתוֹ עֲגוּלָּה סַכָּנָה וְאֵין בָּהּ מִצְוָה״. לֵימָא תְּנֵינָא לְהָא דְּתָנוּ רַבָּנַן: תְּפִלִּין מְרוּבָּעוֹת הֲלָכָה לְמֹשֶׁה מִסִּינַי! וְאָמַר רָבָא: בְּתִפְרָן וּבַאֲלַכְסוֹנָן.

We learned in the mishna: **One who constructs his phylacteries** in **a round** shape exposes himself to **danger and** does **not** fulfill the **mitzva** to don phylacteries. The Gemara comments: **Let us say** that **we** already **learned** in this mishna **that which the Sages taught** in a *baraita*: The requirement that **phylacteries** must be **square**[H] **is a *halakha*** transmitted **to Moses from Sinai. And Rava said** about this: Square means **along their seams and their diagonals** [***alakhsonan***],[NL] i.e., they must be perfectly square. It would seem that all this was already stated in the mishna, which says that round phylacteries are disqualified.

LANGUAGE

Sleeve [*unkeli*] – **אוּנְקְלִי**: From the Greek ἀνάκωλος, *anakolos*, meaning a short garment, like a short tunic with sleeves. According to this interpretation, one who places his phylacteries there does not fulfill the mitzva because he has placed it on his garment rather than directly on his body. Conversely, some explain that *unkeli* is from the Greek ἀγκάλη, *ankalè*, meaning a bent arm or elbow. According to this interpretation, the problem is that one has placed the phylacteries on the wrong part of his arm.

Their diagonals [*alakhsonan*] – **אֲלַכְסוֹנָן**: From the Greek λοξόν, *loxon*, meaning slanting or crosswise. This term is generally used in talmudic parlance to refer to the hypotenuse of a triangle.

HALAKHA

I will not pass before the ark in colored garments – אֵינִי עוֹבֵר לִפְנֵי הַתֵּיבָה בִּצְבוּעִין: One who says that he will not lead the prayers while he is dressed in colored clothes or wearing shoes may not serve as the prayer leader for prayer at all, due to a concern that he has been affected by heretical beliefs. This applies even if he gives a different reason for his actions (*Shulḥan Arukh, Oraḥ Ḥayyim* 53:18 and in the comment of Rema).

And he does not fulfill the mitzva – וְאֵין בָּהּ מִצְוָה: One who placed his phylacteries on his palm instead of on his bicep or on his forehead instead of above his hairline is following the practices of the Sadducees. Additionally, one who constructs his phylacteries to be round like a nut does not fulfill a mitzva (Rambam *Sefer Ahava, Hilkhot Tefillin* 4:3).

If one plated his phylacteries with gold – צִיפָּן זָהָב: If one plates his phylacteries with gold, the phylacteries are disqualified (*Shulḥan Arukh, Oraḥ Ḥayyim* 32:48).

The requirement that phylacteries must be square – תְּפִלִּין מְרוּבָּעוֹת: There is a *halakha* transmitted to Moses from Sinai that requires both the phylacteries worn on the arm and those worn on the head to be square. This applies both to the base of the phylacteries as well as to the box that sits on the base. However, they do not need to be a perfect cube, and therefore the height of the box does not need to be the same dimension as its length and width (Rema). Some say that even if the phylacteries were originally square, if they become damaged and are no longer square, they must be repaired (*Shulḥan Arukh, Oraḥ Ḥayyim* 32:39).

BACKGROUND

I will not pass before the ark in colored garments – אֵינִי עוֹבֵר לִפְנֵי הַתֵּיבָה בִּצְבוּעִין: There are sources in the Torah that identify white clothes as a symbol of sanctity, e.g., the priestly vestments, particularly the High Priest's vestments on Yom Kippur. However, insisting on wearing white clothes for prayer was apparently a custom of heretics. The Essenes insisted on this, and it is possible that some of their sects were considered outsiders. Additionally, early Christian priests wore white robes as part of their ritual service.

One who constructs his phylacteries in a round shape exposes himself to danger and does not fulfill the mitzva – הָעוֹשֶׂה תְּפִלָּתוֹ עֲגוּלָּה סַכָּנָה וְאֵין בָּהּ מִצְוָה: In point of fact, there is evidence that phylacteries worn on the arm were made round throughout history, inasmuch as such phylacteries were found in the Cairo Geniza and in various illustrations of Jewish practice. The Mordekhai, writing in the thirteenth century, relates that this tradition still existed in his time, although he rejects it entirely.

NOTES

He exposes himself to danger – סַכָּנָה: Rashi and many others explain that the danger here is due to the phylacteries themselves: Were they to be spherical, if one bumped into something, the phylacteries could cause him injury. Since phylacteries are square, the force of the collision gets spread through the entire bottom side; whereas if they were circular, the impact of the force would be at a single point, where the circle meets his head.

The way of the outsiders – דֶּרֶךְ הַחִיצוֹנִים: It is not considered heresy, as he does accept the traditions of the Sages; however, he transgresses the details pertaining to this mitzva (Ran).

Along their seams and their diagonals – בְּתִפְרָן וּבַאֲלַכְסוֹנָן: This means that one must be careful to sew the stitches in a way that will not ruin the square shape of the phylacteries. Additionally, the phylacteries must be a perfect square, with the appropriate relative lengths of the sides and diagonals; it is not sufficient for the phylacteries to merely be a rectangle (Rabbeinu Yehonatan).

אֲמַר רַב פַּפָּא: מַתְנִיתִין דַּעֲבִידָא כִּי אַמְגּוּזָא.

Rav Pappa said: It is possible to understand that **the mishna** is referring to phylacteries **that one constructed** to be round **like a nut,** i.e., in the shape of a ball. However, the mishna does not indicate that the phylacteries must be square, as it does not address the case of phylacteries that are rounded but not a true sphere.

מתני׳ הָאוֹמֵר

MISHNA If **one says** in his prayers:

Perek **III**
Daf **25** Amud **a**

יְבָרְכוּךָ טוֹבִים – הֲרֵי זוֹ דֶּרֶךְ הַמִּינוּת. עַל קַן צִפּוֹר יַגִּיעוּ רַחֲמֶיךָ, וְעַל טוֹב יִזָּכֵר שְׁמֶךָ, מוֹדִים מוֹדִים – מְשַׁתְּקִין אוֹתוֹ.

May the good bless You,[N] **this is a path of heresy,** as heretics divide the world into two domains, good and evil. If one says the following in his prayers: Just as **Your mercy is extended to a bird's nest,**[H] as You have commanded us to send away the mother before taking her chicks or eggs (see Deuteronomy 22:6–7), so too extend Your mercy to us; **or: May Your name be mentioned with the good;** or: **We give thanks, we give thanks,** twice,[H] he is suspected of heretical beliefs and they **silence him.**

הַמְכַנֶּה בַּעֲרָיוֹת – מְשַׁתְּקִין אוֹתוֹ, הָאוֹמֵר: "וּמִזַּרְעֲךָ לֹא תִתֵּן לְהַעֲבִיר לַמֹּלֶךְ", לֹא תִּתֵּן לְאַעְבָּרָא בַּאֲרָמִיּוּתָא – מְשַׁתְּקִין אוֹתוֹ בִּנְזִיפָה.

If **one modifies** the text while reading the laws of **forbidden sexual relations,** i.e., he introduces euphemisms out of a sense of propriety, **they silence him.** Similarly, if **one says** while translating the verse: **"And you shall not give any of your seed to set them apart to Molekh"** (Leviticus 18:21): And **you shall not give** any of your seed **to impregnate an Aramean woman, he is silenced with rebuke.**

גמ׳ בִּשְׁלָמָא מוֹדִים מוֹדִים – דְּמִיחֱזֵי כִּשְׁתֵּי רְשׁוּיוֹת. וְעַל טוֹב יִזָּכֵר שְׁמֶךָ נַמִי, דְּמַשְׁמַע: עַל טוֹב – אִין, וְעַל רַע – לָא, וּתְנַן: חַיָּיב אָדָם לְבָרֵךְ עַל הָרָעָה כְּשֵׁם שֶׁהוּא מְבָרֵךְ עַל הַטּוֹבָה. אֶלָּא, עַל קַן צִפּוֹר יַגִּיעוּ רַחֲמֶיךָ, מַאי טַעְמָא?

GEMARA The mishna cites three instances where the communal prayer leader is silenced. The Gemara clarifies: **Granted,** they silence one who repeats: **We give thanks, we give thanks, as it appears like** he is acknowledging and praying to **two authorities. And,** granted, **they also** silence one who says: **May Your name be mentioned with the good,** as this formulation **indicates** one is thanking God only **for the good and not for the bad, and we learned** in a mishna (*Berakhot* 54a): **One is obligated to bless** God **for the bad**[H] **just as he blesses** Him **for the good. However,** in the case of one who recites: Just as **Your mercy is extended to a bird's nest, what is the reason** that they silence him?

פְּלִיגִי בָּהּ תְּרֵי אָמוֹרָאֵי בְּמַעַרְבָא: רַבִּי יוֹסֵי בַּר אָבִין וְרַבִּי יוֹסֵי בַּר זְבִידָא, חַד אָמַר: מִפְּנֵי שֶׁמַּטִּיל קִנְאָה בְּמַעֲשֵׂה בְרֵאשִׁית, וְחַד אָמַר: מִפְּנֵי שֶׁעוֹשֶׂה מִדּוֹתָיו שֶׁל הַקָּדוֹשׁ בָּרוּךְ הוּא רַחֲמִים, וְאֵינָן אֶלָּא גְּזֵירוֹת.

Two *amora'im* **in the West,** Eretz Yisrael, **disagree** about **this** question, **Rabbi Yosei bar Avin and Rabbi Yosei bar Zevida. One said** that this was **because** one who says this **engenders jealousy**[N] **among God's creations,** as it appears as though he is indicating that God favored one creature over all others. **And one said** that saying this is prohibited **because one transforms the attributes of the Holy One, Blessed be He, into** expressions of **mercy, and they are nothing but decrees** of the King[N] that must be fulfilled without inquiring into the reasons behind them.

HALAKHA

Just as Your mercy is extended to a bird's nest – **עַל קַן צִפּוֹר יַגִּיעוּ רַחֲמֶיךָ:** One who says in his prayers: Just as You have shown mercy to birds, as expressed through the mitzva to chase away the mother bird before taking eggs from its nest, have mercy and pity upon us, or: You have shown mercy to animals, as reflected in the prohibition of slaughtering an animal and its offspring on the same day, have mercy and pity upon us, is silenced. These mitzvot are not due to mercy, but they are decrees of God (Rambam *Sefer Ahava, Hilkhot Tefilla* 9:7).

We give thanks, we give thanks – **מוֹדִים מוֹדִים:** One who says this twice is silenced (*Shulḥan Arukh, Oraḥ Ḥayyim* 121:2).

One is obligated to bless God for the bad – **חַיָּיב אָדָם לְבָרֵךְ עַל הָרָעָה:** One is obligated to recite the blessing: The true judge, when bad things occur. The blessing should be recited with full sincerity, just as when one recites a blessing over good tidings (*Shulḥan Arukh, Oraḥ Ḥayyim* 222:3).

NOTES

May the good bless You – **יְבָרְכוּךָ טוֹבִים:** There are several explanations as to why this expression is heretical. Rashi and others explain that one who says this phrase includes only the righteous among those who praise God, whereas this category must include the entire Jewish people. Conversely, many commentaries explain this *halakha* based on the verse: "For then we had plenty of food and were well [*tovim*]" (Jeremiah 44:17), which indicates that *tovim* means satiated (Rid; Rabbeinu Yehonatan). Therefore, those who insert the phrase: May the *tovim* bless You, indicate that only one who is fully satiated must recite Grace after Meals. The *halakha*, however, is that anyone who has eaten an olive-bulk of bread must recite Grace after Meals. Similarly, the Ra'avad and Rabbeinu Yona explain that the implication is that only those who are satiated and happy bless God. The Meiri cites an explanation that *tovim* refers to the angels. Consequently, one who says this phrase removes God's glory from the earthly world and confines it to the upper realms. This constitutes heresy.

This engenders jealousy, etc. – **מַטִּיל קִנְאָה וכו׳:** In the Jerusalem Talmud, it is explained that the problem is that the individual limits God's mercy by implying that it is applied only to birds.

And they are nothing but decrees of the King – **וְאֵינָן אֶלָּא גְּזֵירוֹת:** The great thinkers and philosophers have debated the meaning of this statement; they especially discussed its implications with regard to suggesting reasons for the mitzvot. According to the Rambam, presenting reasons for the mitzvot is problematic when one assumes that he has completely understood the full significance of a mitzva. This is an assumption that human beings have no right to make. Some explain that with regard to the mitzva of chasing away a bird, mercy is indeed a reason for the mitzva; however, the mitzva is not due to God's mercy toward the birds, but rather by God's interest in training mankind to be merciful (Meiri; see Maharal, *Tiferet Yisrael*).

הַהוּא דִּנְחֵית קַמֵּיהּ דְּרַבָּה, אֲמַר: אַתָּה חַסְתָּ עַל קַן צִפּוֹר אַתָּה חוּס וְרַחֵם עָלֵינוּ, (אַתָּה חַסְתָּ עַל אוֹתוֹ וְאֶת בְּנוֹ אַתָּה חוּס וְרַחֵם עָלֵינוּ) אֲמַר רַבָּה: כַּמָּה יָדַע הַאי מֵרַבָּנַן לְרַצּוּיֵי לְמָרֵיהּ! אֲמַר לֵיהּ אַבַּיֵי: וְהָא מְשַׁתְּקִין אוֹתוֹ תְּנַן!

The Gemara relates that **a particular** individual **descended** before the ark as prayer leader **in the presence of Rabba,**[P] and **said** in his prayers: **You have shown mercy to birds,** as expressed through the mitzva to chase away the mother bird before taking eggs from its **nest; have mercy and pity upon us. You have shown mercy** to animals, as expressed through the prohibition against slaughtering an animal **and its offspring** on the same day; **have mercy and pity upon us. Rabba said: How much does this rabbi know to appease** the Lord, **his Master! Abaye**[P] **said to him: Didn't we learn** in the mishna that **they silence him?**

וְרַבָּה לְחַדּוּדֵי לְאַבַּיֵי הוּא דִּבְעָא.

The Gemara explains: **And Rabba,** too, held in accordance with this mishna but merely acted this way because **he wanted to hone Abaye's** intellect.[N] Rabba did not make his statement to praise the rabbi, but simply to test his nephew and student, Abaye, and to encourage him to articulate what he knows about the mishna.

הַהוּא דִּנְחֵית קַמֵּיהּ דְּרַבִּי חֲנִינָא, אֲמַר: הָאֵל הַגָּדוֹל הַגִּבּוֹר וְהַנּוֹרָא הָאַדִּיר וְהֶחָזָק וְהָאַמִּיץ.

With regard to additions to prayers formulated by the Sages, the Gemara relates that **a particular** individual **descended** before the ark as prayer leader **in the presence of Rabbi Ḥanina.** He extended his prayer and **said: God, the great, the mighty, and the awesome, the powerful, and the strong, and the fearless.**

אֲמַר לֵיהּ: סַיֵּימְתִּינְהוּ לְשִׁבְחֵיהּ דְּמָרָךְ?! הָשְׁתָּא הָנֵי תְּלָתָא, אִי לָאו דִּכְתַבִינְהוּ מֹשֶׁה בְּאוֹרַיְיתָא וְאָתוּ כְּנֶסֶת הַגְּדוֹלָה וְתַקְּנִינְהוּ, אֲנַן לָא אָמְרִינַן לְהוּ, וְאַתְּ אָמְרַתְּ כּוּלֵּי הַאי? מָשָׁל לְאָדָם שֶׁהָיוּ לוֹ אֶלֶף אַלְפֵי אֲלָפִים דִּינָרֵי זָהָב, וְהָיוּ מְקַלְּסִין אוֹתוֹ (בְּאֶלֶף) דִּינָרֵי כֶסֶף. לֹא גְּנַאי הוּא לוֹ?

When he finished, Rabbi Ḥanina **said to him: Have you concluded** all of **the praises of your Master? Even these three** praises **that we recite:** The great, the mighty, and the awesome, **had Moses our teacher not written them in the Torah** (Deuteronomy 10:17), **and had the members of the Great Assembly not come and incorporated them** into the *Amida* prayer (see Nehemiah 9:32), **we would not** be permitted to **recite them. And you went on and recited all of these. It is comparable to a man who possessed many thousands of golden dinars, yet they were praising him for** owning **a thousand silver** ones. **Isn't that deprecatory toward him?** All of the praises one can lavish upon the Lord are nothing but a few silver dinars relative to many thousands of gold dinars. Reciting a litany of praise does not enhance God's honor.[H]

אָמַר רַבִּי חֲנִינָא: הַכֹּל בִּידֵי שָׁמַיִם, חוּץ מִיִּרְאַת שָׁמַיִם, שֶׁנֶּאֱמַר ״וְעַתָּה יִשְׂרָאֵל מָה ה׳ אֱלֹהֶיךָ שׁוֹאֵל מֵעִמָּךְ כִּי אִם לְיִרְאָה״.

Tangentially, the Gemara cites an additional statement by Rabbi Ḥanina, concerning principles of faith. **Rabbi Ḥanina said: Everything is in the hands of Heaven, except for fear of Heaven.**[H] Man has free will to serve God or not, **as it is stated: "And now, Israel, what does the Lord your God ask of you other than to fear** the Lord your God" (Deuteronomy 10:12). The fact that God asks man to fear Him indicates that it is in man's ability to do so.

מִכְּלָל דְּיִרְאָה מִילְּתָא זוּטַרְתִּי הִיא? אִין, לְגַבֵּי מֹשֶׁה רַבֵּינוּ מִילְּתָא זוּטַרְתִּי הִיא, מָשָׁל לְאָדָם שֶׁמְּבַקְּשִׁין הֵימֶנּוּ כְּלִי גָּדוֹל וְיֵשׁ לוֹ – דּוֹמֶה עָלָיו כִּכְלִי קָטָן, קָטָן וְאֵין לוֹ – דּוֹמֶה עָלָיו כִּכְלִי גָּדוֹל.

The Gemara notes: This proves **by inference that fear** of Heaven **is a minor matter,** as the verse is formulated as though God is not asking anything significant. Can it in fact be maintained that fear of Heaven is a minor matter? The Gemara responds: **Indeed, for Moses our teacher,** fear of Heaven **is a minor matter. It is comparable to one who is asked for a large vessel and he has** one; **it seems to him like a small vessel** because he owns it. However, one who is asked for just **a small** vessel and he does not have one, **it seems to him like a large vessel.** Therefore, Moses could say: What does the Lord your God ask of you other than to fear, because in his eyes it was a minor matter.

PERSONALITIES

Rabba – רַבָּה: Rav Abba bar Naḥmani HaKohen, popularly referred to as Rabba throughout the Babylonian Talmud, was a third-generation Babylonian *amora*. Rabba was a student of Rav Huna, who himself was a student of Rav. Consequently, Rabba's approach to *halakha* was in concert with Rav's teachings. Rabba was considered the sharpest among his peers, to the extent that he was referred to as: One who uproots mountains, in contrast with his colleague, Rav Yosef, whose breadth of knowledge earned him the nickname: Sinai. With regard to disagreements between Rabba and Rav Yosef, the *halakha* is almost always in accordance with the opinion of Rabba.

Rabba had many students, and virtually all of the Sages of the following generation studied with him. His personal life was one of great tragedy. It appears that his children died during his lifetime. He was poverty stricken his entire life, eking out a living from agricultural work. When his nephew, Abaye, became orphaned at a young age, Rabba took him in and raised him.

Abaye – אַבַּיֵי: Abaye was one of the most famous of the Babylonian *amora'im*. The disagreements between Abaye and his colleague Rava, recorded in the Gemara, are so essential that the Talmud itself is sometimes referred to as: The discussions of Abaye and Rava. Among those hundreds of discussions, the ruling follows Abaye in only six cases.

Abaye was orphaned at the time of his birth and was raised by his paternal uncle, Rabba. The woman who raised him impressed upon him many life lessons, which he quotes in the Gemara in her name. The Gemara records numerous incidents that illustrate Abaye's sharp intellect even as a child, including a number where his adoptive father, Rabba, tests him with questions.

Abaye was chosen to head the academy in Pumbedita. He celebrated the study of Torah and would announce a holiday for the scholars whenever one of them completed a tractate. Growing up in his uncle's home, he was aware of the difficulties of scholars who were without financial means. The Gemara in tractate *Berakhot* (35b) relates that he testified that many were successful following the path of Rabbi Yishmael, who instructed his students to plow, plant, and harvest in the appropriate time; only very few were successful following the path of Rabbi Shimon bar Yoḥai, who taught that one should devote himself entirely to Torah study and ignore worldly concerns.

NOTES

To hone Abaye's intellect – לְחַדּוּדֵי לְאַבַּיֵי: Many have questioned how Rabba intended to hone Abaye's intellect by saying something that contradicts an explicit mishna. Additionally, why did the Sage who served as the prayer leader act in a way that contradicts this mishna? Some explain that since the prayer leader mentioned both birds and animals, he reasoned that it was clear that he intended to state general praises of God. Abaye, however, understood that it is nonetheless prohibited.

HALAKHA

One should not recite too many praises – לֹא יַרְבֶּה בִּשְׁבָחִים: One should not use too many adjectives to praise God during his prayer. He should say only: God, the great, the mighty, and the awesome. This is the formula said by Moses and established by the Sages as part of the daily prayer. Since man is unable to fully articulate God's greatness, adding additional superlatives is deprecatory (Rambam *Sefer Ahava*, *Hilkhot Tefilla* 9:7).

Everything is in the hands of Heaven except for fear of Heaven – הַכֹּל בִּידֵי שָׁמַיִם חוּץ מִיִּרְאַת שָׁמַיִם: God does not decree in advance whether one will be righteous or wicked. Each individual may choose whether to be righteous or wicked and he is not forced in either direction (Rambam *Sefer Madda*, *Hilkhot Teshuva* 5:2).

אָמַר רַבִּי זֵירָא: הָאוֹמֵר שְׁמַע שְׁמַע כְּאוֹמֵר מוֹדִים מוֹדִים דָּמֵי.

Rabbi Zeira said: One who repeats himself while reciting *Shema* and **says: Listen** Israel, **listen** Israel,[HN] **is like one who says: We give thanks, we give thanks.**

מֵיתִיבִי: הַקּוֹרֵא אֶת שְׁמַע וְכוֹפְלָהּ – הֲרֵי זֶה מְגוּנֶּה. מְגוּנֶּה הוּא דְּהָוֵי, שַׁתּוֹקֵי לָא מְשַׁתְּקִינַן לֵיהּ! לָא קַשְׁיָא: הָא – דְּאָמַר מִילְּתָא מִילְּתָא וְתָנֵי לָהּ, הָא – דְּאָמַר פְּסוּקָא פְּסוּקָא וְתָנֵי לָהּ.

The Gemara **raises an objection:** It was taught in a *baraita*: **One who recites *Shema* and repeats it, it is reprehensible.** One may infer: **It is reprehensible,** but **they do not silence him.** The Gemara answers: **This is** not **difficult. This** case, where one repeats *Shema* and it is reprehensible but they do not silence him, is referring to **one who recites and repeats each individual word.** In so doing, he ruins the recitation of *Shema*. However, **that** case, where Rabbi Zeira holds that they silence one who repeats *Shema*, is referring to **one who recites and repeats an entire verse,** as it appears that he is worshipping separate authorities.

אָמַר לֵיהּ רַב פָּפָּא לְרָבָא – וְדִלְמָא מֵעִיקָּרָא לָא כַּיֵּין דַּעְתֵּיהּ וְהַשְׁתָּא כַּיֵּין דַּעְתֵּיהּ? אָמַר לֵיהּ: חֲבָרוּתָא כְּלַפֵּי שְׁמַיָּא?! אִי לָא מְכַוֵּין דַּעְתֵּיהּ – מָחֵינָא לֵיהּ בְּאַרְזַפְתָּא דְּנַפָּחָא עַד דִּמְכַוֵּין דַּעְתֵּיהּ.

Rav Pappa said to Rava with regard to this *halakha*: **And perhaps initially he did not focus his attention** on the recitation of *Shema* and therefore had to repeat it, **and now he focused his attention.** Rava **said to him: Can one have** that degree of **familiarity with Heaven,** to the extent that he can take his words lightly and say them however he likes? **If he did not focus his attention, we beat him with a blacksmith's hammer until he focuses his attention,** as conduct of that sort is unacceptable.

״הַמְכַנֶּה בַּעֲרָיוֹת מְשַׁתְּקִין אוֹתוֹ״. תָּנָא רַב יוֹסֵף: קְלוֹן אָבִיו וּקְלוֹן אִמּוֹ.

We learned in the mishna: If **one modifies** the text while reading the laws of **forbidden sexual relations, they silence him. Rav Yosef taught** that this is referring to one who says: **The shame of his father and the shame of his mother,**[N] instead of: "The nakedness of your father and the nakedness of your mother you shall not uncover" (Leviticus 18:7).

״הָאוֹמֵר וּמִזַּרְעֲךָ לֹא תִתֵּן לְהַעֲבִיר״ וכו׳. תָּנָא דְּבֵי רַבִּי יִשְׁמָעֵאל: בְּיִשְׂרָאֵל הַבָּא עַל הַגּוֹיָה וְהוֹלִיד מִמֶּנָּה בֵּן לַעֲבוֹדָה זָרָה הַכָּתוּב מְדַבֵּר.

We learned in the mishna: If **one says,** while translating the verse: **"And you shall not give any of your seed to set them apart to Molekh"** (Leviticus 18:21): And you shall not give any of your seed to impregnate an Aramean woman, he is silenced with rebuke. A Sage **from the school of Rabbi Yishmael taught:**[N] One who translates the verse in this manner maintains that **the verse speaks of a Jew who has relations with a gentile woman and fathered from her a son** who will be raised to engage in **idol worship.**

מתני׳ מַעֲשֵׂה רְאוּבֵן נִקְרָא וְלֹא מִתַּרְגֵּם, מַעֲשֵׂה תָמָר נִקְרָא וּמִתַּרְגֵּם, מַעֲשֵׂה עֵגֶל הָרִאשׁוֹן נִקְרָא וּמִתַּרְגֵּם וְהַשֵּׁנִי נִקְרָא וְלֹא מִתַּרְגֵּם. בִּרְכַּת כֹּהֲנִים, מַעֲשֵׂה דָּוִד וְאַמְנוֹן נִקְרָאִין וְלֹא מִתַּרְגְּמִין.

MISHNA The incident of Reuben, about which it says: "And Reuben went and lay with Bilhah, his father's concubine" (Genesis 35:22), **is read** from the Torah in public **but not translated,** so that the uneducated not come to denigrate Reuben. **The incident of Tamar** (Genesis, chapter 38) **is read** in public **and** also **translated. The first** report of the **incident of the** Golden **Calf,** i.e., the Torah's account of the incident itself (Exodus 32:1–20), **is read and translated, but the second** narrative, i.e., Aaron's report to Moses of what had taken place (Exodus 32:21–24) **is read but not translated.** The verses constituting **the Priestly Benediction** (Numbers 6:24–26) **and the incident of David and Amnon** (II Samuel, chapter 13) are **read, but not translated.**

אֵין מַפְטִירִין בַּמֶּרְכָּבָה, וְרַבִּי יְהוּדָה מַתִּיר. רַבִּי אֱלִיעֶזֶר אוֹמֵר: אֵין מַפְטִירִין בְּ״הוֹדַע אֶת יְרוּשָׁלַםִ״.

One may not conclude the Torah reading **with** by reading from the Prophets **the** account of the Divine **Chariot** (Ezekiel, chapter 1), so as not to publicize that which was meant to remain hidden. **And Rabbi Yehuda permits** it. **Rabbi Eliezer says: One may not conclude with** section from the Prophets beginning with: **"Make known to Jerusalem** her abominations" (Ezekiel 16:2), because it speaks derogatively of the Jewish people.

גמ׳ תָּנוּ רַבָּנַן: יֵשׁ נִקְרִין וּמִתַּרְגְּמִין, וְיֵשׁ נִקְרִין וְלֹא מִתַּרְגְּמִין, וְיֵשׁ לֹא נִקְרִין וְלֹא מִתַּרְגְּמִין. אֵלּוּ נִקְרִין וּמִתַּרְגְּמִין: בל״ת עק״ן נשפ״ה סִימָן.

GEMARA The Sages taught in the *Tosefta* (3:31): **There are** portions of the Bible that are **read and translated; there are** portions that **are read but not translated; and there are** portions that **are neither read nor translated. The following are read and translated:** The Hebrew acronym ***bet, lamed, tav*; *ayin, kuf, nun*; *nun, shin, peh, heh*** comprise a **mnemonic** for the sections included in this category, as the Gemara will explain.

HALAKHA

One who says: Listen Israel, listen Israel – הָאוֹמֵר שְׁמַע שְׁמַע: It is prohibited to repeat the *Shema*, whether one repeats the entire verse or any individual word. If one was not focused while reciting the verse, he should repeat it quietly (*Taz*). However, when one reviews the weekly Torah portion by reciting each verse twice and then the *Targum*, he may read the verse of *Shema* twice as well (*Shulḥan Arukh, Oraḥ Ḥayyim* 61:9).

NOTES

One who says: Listen Israel, listen Israel – הָאוֹמֵר שְׁמַע שְׁמַע: Most of the commentaries maintain that one who says the complete verse and then repeats it is silenced, whereas one who says any word twice is denounced because it is foolishness. Conversely, Rabbeinu Ḥananel and others explain that one who repeats the verse is denounced and one who repeats a word is silenced (see Ritva).

The shame of his father and the shame of his mother – קְלוֹן אָבִיו וּקְלוֹן אִמּוֹ: Most commentaries explain that out of respect to the listeners, he does not say: The nakedness of your father, but rather: The nakedness of his father, in the third person (see Rav Hai Gaon; Rabbeinu Ḥananel; *Arukh*; Rambam). This is the implication of the Jerusalem Talmud as well. Conversely, Rashi, as well as the Rid and Ran, explain that one is giving a different meaning to the verse, explaining it to mean that one may not reveal embarrassing information about one's relatives. It is also possible that one does not even pronounce the word nakedness, but instead says: Shame.

A Sage from the school of Rabbi Yishmael taught – תָּנָא דְּבֵי רַבִּי יִשְׁמָעֵאל: It would seem that this Sage interprets the verse precisely as the mishna states one may not interpret it. Some explain that the Sage was merely explaining the mistaken interpretation that the mishna was referring to. However, this explanation is difficult.

The *Arukh* and others explain that the mishna is referring to one who interprets the verse as relating only to Arameans. One might infer from this that it is permissible to marry women from other nations who do not worship Molekh. The Sage from the school of Rabbi Yishmael explained that the verse is referring to all gentile women. It can also be suggested that the interpretation of the verse as referring to fathering a child with a gentile woman is a valid homiletic approach, but it may not be presented as the literal meaning of the verse (*Re'ah Duda'im*). This also explains why the *Targum Yonatan* interprets the verse in this manner, as it is a homiletic work.

מַעֲשֵׂה בְרֵאשִׁית נִקְרָא וּמִתַּרְגֵּם. פְּשִׁיטָא! מַהוּ דְּתֵימָא: אָתוּ לְשַׁיּוּלֵי מַה לְּמַעְלָה מַה לְּמַטָּה,

The Gemara enumerates the sections indicated by the letters of the mnemonic. The section **of the act of Creation** [***bereshit***], alluded to by the letter *bet*, **is read and translated.** The Gemara comments: This **is obvious.** Why might one think otherwise? The Gemara answers: **Lest you say** that if the story of the Creation is read in public people **will come to ask** questions that should not be asked, for instance: **What is above and what is below,**

Perek **III**
Daf **25** Amud **b**

וּמַה לְּפָנִים וּמַה לְּאָחוֹר, קָא מַשְׁמַע לָן.

what was before Creation **and what is after,** i.e., what will be at the end of time, **therefore** the *Tosefta* **teaches us** that the act of Creation is read in public.

״מַעֲשֵׂה לוֹט וּשְׁתֵּי בְנוֹתָיו נִקְרָא וּמִתַּרְגֵּם״. פְּשִׁיטָא! מַהוּ דְּתֵימָא: נֵיחוּשׁ לִכְבוֹדוֹ דְּאַבְרָהָם, קָא מַשְׁמַע לָן.

The *Tosefta* continues: **The incident of Lot and his two daughters is read and translated.** The name Lot begins with a *lamed*, the second letter of the mnemonic. The Gemara comments: This **is obvious.** Why might one think otherwise? The Gemara answers: **Lest you say** that **one should be concerned for the honor of Abraham,** as Lot was his nephew, and therefore the incident casts shame upon Abraham as well, **therefore** the *baraita* **teaches us** that this is not a concern.

״מַעֲשֵׂה תָמָר וִיהוּדָה נִקְרָא וּמִתַּרְגֵּם״. פְּשִׁיטָא! מַהוּ דְּתֵימָא: לֵיחוּשׁ לִכְבוֹדוֹ דִּיהוּדָה, קָא מַשְׁמַע לָן: שְׁבָחֵיהּ הוּא דְּאוֹדֵי.

The *Tosefta* continues: **The incident of Tamar,** beginning with a *tav*, **and Judah**[N] **is read and translated.** The Gemara comments: This **is obvious.** The Gemara answers: **Lest you say** that **one should be concerned for the honor of Judah, therefore** the *Tosefta* **teaches us** that there is no such concern. On the contrary, the story **is to his credit, as he confessed** to his sin.

״מַעֲשֵׂה עֵגֶל הָרִאשׁוֹן נִקְרָא וּמִתַּרְגֵּם״. פְּשִׁיטָא! מַהוּ דְּתֵימָא: לֵיחוּשׁ לִכְבוֹדָן שֶׁל יִשְׂרָאֵל. קָא מַשְׁמַע לָן: כָּל שֶׁכֵּן דְּנִיחָא לְהוּ דְּהָוְיָא לְהוּ כַּפָּרָה.

The *Tosefta* continues: **The first** report **of the incident of the** Golden **Calf** [***egel***] **is read and translated.** *Egel* begins with the letter *ayin*, the next letter of the mnemonic. The Gemara comments: This **is obvious.** The Gemara answers: **Lest you say** that **one should be concerned for the honor of the Jewish people, therefore** the *Tosefta* **teaches us that all the more so is it amenable to them** that the matter be publicized, so that they will achieve atonement through their shame.

״קְלָלוֹת וּבְרָכוֹת נִקְרִין וּמִתַּרְגְּמִין״. פְּשִׁיטָא! מַהוּ דְּתֵימָא: נֵיחוּשׁ דִּלְמָא פַּיְיגָא דַּעֲתַיְיהוּ דְּצִבּוּרָא, קָא מַשְׁמַע לָן.

The *Tosefta* states: **The curses** [***kelalot***] **and blessings are read and translated.** The Gemara comments: This **is obvious.** The Gemara answers: **Lest you say** that **one should be concerned that perhaps the congregation will become dismayed** by the many curses, **therefore** the *Tosefta* **teaches us** that this is not a concern.

״אַזְהָרוֹת וְעוֹנָשִׁין נִקְרִין וּמִתַּרְגְּמִין״. פְּשִׁיטָא! מַהוּ דְּתֵימָא: נֵיחוּשׁ דִּלְמָא אָתוּ לְמֶעֱבַד מִיִּרְאָה, קָא מַשְׁמַע לָן.

The *Tosefta* continues: **The warnings and punishments** [***onashin***], alluded to in the first *nun* of the mnemonic mentioned above, **are read and translated.** The Gemara comments: This **is obvious.** The Gemara answers: **Lest you say** that if this section is read aloud, people **will come to act out of fear** and keep the mitzvot due to the fear of punishment rather than love of God, **therefore** the *Tosefta* **teaches us** that this is not a concern.

״מַעֲשֵׂה אַמְנוֹן וְתָמָר נִקְרָא וּמִתַּרְגֵּם״, [״מַעֲשֵׂה אַבְשָׁלוֹם נִקְרָא וּמִתַּרְגֵּם״]. פְּשִׁיטָא! מַהוּ דְּתֵימָא: לֵיחוּשׁ לִיקָרֵיהּ דְּדָוִד, קָא מַשְׁמַע לָן.

It is further taught: **The incident of Amnon and Tamar,** alluded to in the second *nun* in the mnemonic mentioned above, **is read and translated.** Additionally, **the incident of Absalom is read and translated,** alluded to in the *shin* of the mnemonic, the third letter of his name. The Gemara comments: This **is obvious.** The Gemara explains: **Lest you say** that **one should be concerned for the honor of David, therefore** the *Tosefta* **teaches us** that this section is read and translated.

״מַעֲשֵׂה פִּילֶגֶשׁ בַּגִּבְעָה נִקְרָא וּמִתַּרְגֵּם״. פְּשִׁיטָא! מַהוּ דְּתֵימָא: לֵיחוּשׁ לִכְבוֹדוֹ דְּבִנְיָמִין, קָא מַשְׁמַע לָן.

The *Tosefta* continues: **The incident of the concubine** [***pilegesh***] **in Gibeah is read and translated.** The Gemara comments: This **is obvious.** The Gemara explains: **Lest you say** that **one should be concerned for the honor of** the tribe of **Benjamin, therefore** the *Tosefta* **teaches us** that this section is read and translated.

NOTES

The incident of Tamar and Judah – מַעֲשֵׂה תָמָר וִיהוּדָה: It is explained in *Otzar HaKavod* that an additional reason why this section should be read is to indicate that Judah performed a mitzva. Before the giving of the Torah, perpetuating the legacy of the deceased through levirate marriage [*yibbum*] applied to the closest relative and not just to the brother of the deceased.

״הוֹדַע אֶת יְרוּשָׁלַיִם אֶת תּוֹעֲבוֹתֶיהָ״ נִקְרָא וּמִתַּרְגֵּם. פְּשִׁיטָא! לְאַפּוֹקֵי מִדְּרַבִּי אֱלִיעֶזֶר. דְּתַנְיָא: מַעֲשֶׂה בְּאָדָם אֶחָד שֶׁהָיָה קוֹרֵא לְמַעְלָה מֵרַבִּי אֱלִיעֶזֶר ״הוֹדַע אֶת יְרוּשָׁלַיִם אֶת תּוֹעֲבוֹתֶיהָ״, אָמַר לוֹ: עַד שֶׁאַתָּה בּוֹדֵק בְּתוֹעֲבוֹת יְרוּשָׁלַיִם – צֵא וּבְדוֹק בְּתוֹעֲבוֹת אִמְּךָ. בָּדְקוּ אַחֲרָיו וּמָצְאוּ בּוֹ שֶׁמֶץ פְּסוּל.

The *Tosefta* continues: The section of: **"Make known [*hoda*] to Jerusalem her abominations"** (Ezekiel 16:2) **is read and translated.** The Gemara comments: This **is obvious.** The Gemara answers: This is needed **to exclude** the opinion of **Rabbi Eliezer,** who held that this chapter may not be read as a *haftara,* **as it is taught** in a *baraita*: There was **an incident with regard to a certain man who was reading** the *haftara* **in the presence of Rabbi Eliezer,** and he read the section of: **"Make known to Jerusalem**[N] **her abominations."** Rabbi Eliezer **said to him: Before you examine the abominations of Jerusalem, go and examine the abominations of your** own **mother.** The Gemara relates that **they examined his** lineage **and found him to have a stain of illegitimacy.** His mother had engaged in illicit sexual relations, and therefore he was of questionable lineage.

״וְאֵלּוּ נִקְרִין וְלֹא מִתַּרְגְּמִין״ (רעבד״ן סִימָן) ״מַעֲשֵׂה רְאוּבֵן נִקְרָא וְלֹא מִתַּרְגֵּם״. וּמַעֲשֶׂה בְּרַבִּי חֲנִינָא בֶּן גַּמְלִיאֵל שֶׁהָלַךְ לְכָבוּל, וְהָיָה קוֹרֵא חַזַּן הַכְּנֶסֶת ״וַיְהִי בִּשְׁכּוֹן יִשְׂרָאֵל״ וְאָמַר לוֹ לַמְתוּרְגְּמָן: (הַפְסֵק) אַל תְּתַרְגֵּם אֶלָּא אַחֲרוֹן, וְשִׁיבְּחוּהוּ חֲכָמִים.

The *Tosefta* also states: **And these** sections are **read but are not translated.** The acrostic composed of the letters ***reish, ayin, bet, dalet, nun*** is a **mnemonic** for the sections included in this category, as the Gemara will explain. The *Tosefta* states that **the incident of Reuben**[N] **is read but not translated.** The name Reuben begins with a *reish*, the first letter of the mnemonic. And there was **an incident involving Rabbi Ḥanina ben Gamliel, who went to** the village of **Kavul, and the sexton of the synagogue was reading: "And it came to pass, while Israel dwelt** in that land, that Reuben went and lay with Bilhah, his father's concubine; and Israel heard of it" (Genesis 35:22). Rabbi Ḥanina **said to the translator: Stop, translate only the end** of the verse. **And the Sages praised him** for this.

״מַעֲשֵׂה עֵגֶל הַשֵּׁנִי נִקְרָא וְלֹא מִתַּרְגֵּם״. אֵיזֶה מַעֲשֵׂה עֵגֶל הַשֵּׁנִי? מִן ״וַיֹּאמֶר מֹשֶׁה״ עַד ״וַיַּרְא מֹשֶׁה״.

The *Tosefta* continues: **The second** narrative of the **incident of the** Golden **Calf**[N] **is read but not translated.** *Egel,* the Hebrew word for calf, begins with an *ayin,* the second letter in the mnemonic. The Gemara explains: **What is the second** narrative of the **incident of the** Golden **Calf?** Aaron's account of what had taken place, **from "And Moses said** to Aaron" (Exodus 32:21) **until "And Moses saw"** (Exodus 32:25).

תַּנְיָא, רַבִּי שִׁמְעוֹן בֶּן אֶלְעָזָר אוֹמֵר: לְעוֹלָם יְהֵא אָדָם זָהִיר בִּתְשׁוּבוֹתָיו, שֶׁמִּתּוֹךְ תְּשׁוּבָה שֶׁהֵשִׁיבוֹ אַהֲרֹן לְמֹשֶׁה פָּקְרוּ הַמְעַרְעֲרִים, שֶׁנֶּאֱמַר ״וָאַשְׁלִיכֵהוּ בָאֵשׁ וַיֵּצֵא הָעֵגֶל הַזֶּה״.

With regard to Aaron's account, the Gemara cites that which **is taught** in a *baraita*: **Rabbi Shimon ben Elazar says: A person should always be careful in** the way he formulates **his responses,** as sometimes the explanation that a person provides for his actions is worse than the original action itself, **as,** for example, **based on Aaron's response to Moses, the skeptics renounced** their religious beliefs. **It is stated** in Aaron's response: **"And I cast it into the fire and this calf came forth"** (Exodus 32:24). This formulation implies that the calf came from the fire by itself, suggesting that it had divine power and substance.

״בִּרְכַּת כֹּהֲנִים נִקְרִין וְלֹא מִתַּרְגְּמִין״. מַאי טַעְמָא? מִשּׁוּם דִּכְתִיב ״יִשָּׂא״.

We learned in the mishna: The verses constituting **the Priestly Benediction [*birkat kohanim*]** are **read but not translated.** The Gemara asks: **What is the reason** for this? The Gemara explains that it is **because it is written:** "May the Lord **lift up** His countenance to you" (Numbers 6:26). Listeners may understand this to mean that God shows unfair favoritism to the Jewish people.

״מַעֲשֵׂה דָּוִד וְאַמְנוֹן לֹא נִקְרִין וְלֹא מִתַּרְגְּמִין״, וְהָא אָמְרַתְּ מַעֲשֵׂה אַמְנוֹן וְתָמָר נִקְרָא וּמִתַּרְגֵּם! לָא קַשְׁיָא: הָא – דִּכְתִיב אַמְנוֹן בֶּן דָּוִד, הָא – דִּכְתִיב אַמְנוֹן סְתָמָא.

We also learned in the mishna: **The incident of David and Amnon**[N] **is neither read nor translated.**[N] David's name begins with a *dalet*, the next letter in the mnemonic; *nun*, the last letter of the mnemonic, is the third letter in Amnon's name. The Gemara asks: **Didn't you say** in the *Tosefta* that **the incident of Amnon and Tamar is** both **read and translated?** The Gemara explains that **this is not difficult. This** statement of the mishna applies **where** Amnon's name **is written: Amnon, son of David. That** statement of the *Tosefta* applies **where it is written** simply as **Amnon.**[H]

NOTES

Make known to Jerusalem – הוֹדַע אֶת יְרוּשָׁלַיִם: The reason Rabbi Eliezer took issue with the reader despite the fact that he acted in accordance with the opinion of other Sages was because the reader should not have read this *haftara* in Rabbi Eliezer's town without his permission (Ran). The author of the *Levush* wrote that the accepted *halakha* does not prohibit reading this section as a *haftara*, and it was read as the *haftara* for *Parashat Shemot*. However, it is no longer customary to read it as a *haftara* because it speaks in a derogatory fashion about the Jewish people.

The incident of Reuben – מַעֲשֵׂה רְאוּבֵן: Reuben also admitted his guilt, as Judah did; however, since this is not explicitly mentioned in the verses or the translation, there was concern for Reuben's honor (Maharsha). Some say that the section is not translated due to concern for Jacob's honor.

The second narrative of the incident of the Golden Calf – מַעֲשֵׂה עֵגֶל הַשֵּׁנִי: Rashi and many others explain that the reason that this section is not translated is because a listener might think that the calf emerged from the fire on its own and possessed real power. However, *Tosafot* and the Rif explain that it is not translated due to Aaron's honor. The first narrative of the incident of the Golden Calf does not accentuate Aaron's role in the affair, while the second narrative does.

The incident of David and Amnon – מַעֲשֵׂה דָּוִד וְאַמְנוֹן: Some explain that this is referring to two separate incidents: The incident of David and Bathsheba and the incident of Amnon and Tamar (Rabbeinu Yehonatan; *Kesef Mishne*). Some commentaries accepted a version of the text that states that these sections are not read at all. Whereas the Torah is read in public in its entirety, not every section of Prophets is read as a *haftara*; therefore, it is possible to skip these sections entirely (*Tosefot Yom Tov*).

The incident of David and Amnon is neither read nor translated – מַעֲשֵׂה דָּוִד וְאַמְנוֹן לֹא נִקְרִין וְלֹא מִתַּרְגְּמִין: The version of the mishna printed in the Vilna Talmud actually states: The incident of David and Amnon is read but not translated. Commentaries dispute whether the correct version of the mishna is as stated here in the Gemara, or whether the text of the Gemara should be adjusted to remain consistent with the version of the mishna printed on 25a.

HALAKHA

What is translated and what is not translated – מַה מְתַרְגְּמִים וּמַה אֵין מְתַרְגְּמִים: Not all of the Bible is translated in public. The incident of Reuben; the Priestly Benediction; the incident of the Golden Calf from: "And Moses said to Aaron" (Exodus 32:21) until: "And Moses saw" (Exodus 32:25); as well as the verse: "And the Lord smote the people" (Exodus 32:35), are read but are not translated. Additionally, with regard to the incident of Amnon and Tamar, verses that mention Amnon, son of David, are not translated (Rambam *Sefer Ahava, Hilkhot Tefilla* 12:12).

תָּנוּ רַבָּנַן: כׇּל הַמִּקְרָאוֹת הַכְּתוּבִין בַּתּוֹרָה לִגְנַאי קוֹרִין אוֹתָן לְשֶׁבַח, כְּגוֹן "יִשְׁגָּלֶנָּה" – יִשְׁכָּבֶנָּה, "בַּעְפוֹלִים" – בַּטְּחוֹרִים, "חִרְיוֹנִים" – דִּבְיוֹנִים, "לֶאֱכוֹל אֶת חוֹרֵיהֶם וְלִשְׁתּוֹת אֶת מֵימֵי שִׁינֵיהֶם" – לֶאֱכוֹל אֶת צוֹאָתָם וְלִשְׁתּוֹת אֶת מֵימֵי רַגְלֵיהֶם,

§ **The Sages taught** in a *baraita*: **All of the verses that are written in the Torah in a coarse manner**[B] **are read in a refined manner. For example,** the term **"shall lie with her** [*yishgalena*]**"** (Deuteronomy 28:30) is read as though it said ***yishkavena***, which is a more refined term. The term **"with hemorrhoids** [***bafolim***]**"** (Deuteronomy 28:27) is read ***bateḥorim***. The term **"doves' dung** [***ḥiryonim***]**"** (II Kings 6:25) is read ***divyonim***. The phrase **"to eat their own excrement** [***ḥoreihem***] **and drink their own urine** [***meimei shineihem***]**"** (II Kings 18:27) is read with more delicate terms: **To eat their own excrement** [***tzo'atam***] **and drink their own urine** [***meimei ragleihem***].

"לְמַחֲרָאוֹת" – לְמוֹצָאוֹת. רַבִּי יְהוֹשֻׁעַ בֶּן קׇרְחָה אוֹמֵר: לְמַחֲרָאוֹת – כִּשְׁמָן, מִפְּנֵי שֶׁהוּא גְּנַאי לַעֲבוֹדָה זָרָה.

The term **"into latrines** [***lemoḥra'ot***]**"** (II Kings 10:27) is read as the more refined ***lemotza'ot***. **Rabbi Yehoshua ben Korḥa says:** ***Lemoḥara'ot*** is read **as it is written because it is** used here as an expression of **contempt for idol worship**, and it is therefore permissible to use an indelicate term.

אָמַר רַב נַחְמָן: כׇּל לֵיצָנוּתָא אֲסִירָא בַּר מִלֵּיצָנוּתָא דַּעֲבוֹדָה זָרָה דִּשְׁרֵיָא, דִּכְתִיב "כָּרַע בֵּל קֹרֵס נְבוֹ" וּכְתִיב "קָרְסוּ כָּרְעוּ יַחְדָּיו לֹא יָכְלוּ מַלֵּט מַשָּׂא" וגו׳. רַבִּי יַנַּאי אָמַר מֵהָכָא: "לְעֶגְלוֹת בֵּית אָוֶן יָגוּרוּ שְׁכַן שׁוֹמְרוֹן כִּי אָבַל עָלָיו עַמּוֹ וּכְמָרָיו עָלָיו יָגִילוּ עַל כְּבוֹדוֹ כִּי גָלָה מִמֶּנּוּ", אַל תִּקְרֵי "כְּבוֹדוֹ" אֶלָּא כְּבֵידוֹ.

Similarly, **Rav Naḥman said: All mockery** and obscenity **is forbidden except for mockery of idol worship,**[H] **which is permitted, as it is written: "Bel bows down, Nevo stoops"** (Isaiah 46:1). The prophet mocks these idols by describing them as crouching in order to defecate. Additionally, **it is written: "They stoop, they bow down together; they could not deliver the burden"** (Isaiah 46:2). **Rabbi Yannai said:** This principle that one is permitted to mock idol worship is derived **from here: "The inhabitants of Samaria shall be in dread for the calves of Beth-aven; for its people shall mourn over it, and its priests shall tremble for it, for its glory, because it is departed from it"** (Hosea 10:5). **Do not read** it is as **"its glory** [*kevodo*]**,"** rather read it as **its burden** [*keveido*], meaning that it is unable to restrain itself from defecating.

אָמַר רַב הוּנָא בַּר מָנוֹחַ מִשְּׁמֵיהּ דְּרַב אַחָא בְּרֵיהּ דְּרַב אִיקָא: שָׁרֵי לֵיהּ לְבַר יִשְׂרָאֵל לְמֵימַר לֵיהּ לְגוֹי שְׁקַלֵיהּ לַעֲבוֹדָה זָרָה וְאַנְחֵיהּ בְּשִׁין תָּיו שֶׁלּוֹ. אֲמַר רַב אַשִׁי: הַאי מַאן דִּסְנַאי שׁוּמְעָנֵיהּ שָׁרֵי לֵיהּ לְבַזּוּיֵיהּ בְּגִימ״ל וְשִׁי״ן. הַאי מַאן דְּשַׁפִּיר שׁוּמְעָנֵיהּ – שָׁרֵי לְשַׁבּוּחֵיהּ, וּמַאן דְּשַׁבְּחֵיהּ יָנוּחוּ לוֹ בְּרָכוֹת עַל רֹאשׁוֹ.

Rav Huna bar Manoaḥ said in the name of Rav Aḥa, son of Rav Ika: It is permitted for a Jew to say to a gentile: Take your idol and put it in your *shin tav*, i.e., *shet*, buttocks. **Rav Ashi said: One whose reputation is tarnished,** i.e., he is known as a philanderer, **it is permitted to humiliate him** by calling him ***gimmel sin***,[N] an acronym for *girta sarya*, son of a putrid harlot. **One whose reputation is commendable, it is permitted to** publicly **praise him,**[N] **and one who praises him, blessings will rest upon his head.**

הדרן עלך הקורא את המגילה עומד

BACKGROUND

Written in the Torah in a coarse manner – כְּתוּבִין בַּתּוֹרָה לִגְנַאי: The words mentioned in the Gemara are written in the Torah scroll, but when the Torah is read, these words are not pronounced. Instead, other words are verbalized in their place. The Rambam explains that the written words that are replaced are not obscene; they are merely blunt, and therefore when the Torah is read, they are replaced with words that are more delicate. However, the majority of the commentaries agree with the Ramban that these words are indeed coarse, and for that reason they are replaced with more dignified words when the Torah is read.

HALAKHA

Mockery of idol worship – לֵיצָנוּתָא דַּעֲבוֹדָה זָרָה: Although mockery in general is forbidden, it is permitted to mock idol worship (*Shulḥan Arukh, Yoreh De'a* 147:5).

NOTES

Gimmel sin – גימ״ל שי״ן: The Gemara itself did not explain clearly the meaning of this in order to avoid writing coarse language. The commentaries dispute the meaning of this acronym. Rashi explains in the name of his teachers that it stands for *gaifa shatya*, foolish harlot. Some explain that it means: Son of a gentile [*goya*] maidservant [*shifḥa*]. Others explain that it stands for rebuke [*ga'ara*] and excommunication [*shamta*]. The Gemara in tractate *Sanhedrin* (63b) derives from here that it is permitted to mock the parents of a wicked individual, even if the parents themselves are not wicked (see *Nimmukei Yosef*).

It is permitted to praise him – שָׁרֵי לְשַׁבּוּחֵיהּ: It is not advisable to praise others in public, as it may lead to mentioning the individual's faults. Therefore, it was necessary for the Gemara to mention that it is permitted to do so in this case because praising the individual increases the honor of Heaven (Maharsha).

Summary of **Perek III**

Although divergent customs exist even nowadays with regard to prayer and public Torah readings, this chapter addressed aspects of these areas where clear halakhic guidelines were established.

Concerning Torah readings, it was determined that seven readers are called to the Torah on Shabbat; six on Yom Kippur; five on Festivals; four on the intermediate days of Festivals and on New Moons; and three on Monday and Thursday mornings, during the afternoon prayer on Shabbat, and on public fast days. Regular Torah portions have been established for Shabbat mornings. In Eretz Yisrael it was customary to read the entire Torah once every three or three and a half years, whereas in Babylonia it was customary to read the entire Torah every year, a practice that has become adopted universally. On Monday and Thursday mornings and during the afternoon prayer on Shabbat, the beginning of the next week's Torah portion is read. On Festivals, even when they occur on Shabbat, a portion that is related to the Festival is read.

This chapter also established procedures that apply while reading the Torah. It is prohibited to begin or conclude a reading within three verses of the beginning or end of a paragraph. Blessings are recited before and after the reading. In the time of the *tanna'im*, only the first and last readers recited blessings, but in the time of the *amora'im* it was established that each reader recites blessings both before and after reading from the Torah.

Public prayer services, and any ritual that is performed only in public, must be performed in the presence of ten adult males. The main reason for this is that sanctification of God's name must be performed in a dignified manner.

In addition to concern for the honor of God, the honor of the congregation must be taken into account as well. Therefore, the Sages issued decrees to ensure that the prayer leader is someone who represents the congregation in a dignified manner. Similarly, there are requirements that govern whether a priest may recite the Priestly Benediction in public.

The Sages also instituted guidelines due to other reasons. They instituted procedures governing the distribution of honors during the prayer service in order to prevent strife. They prohibited individuals who act in particular ways that indicate they might hold heretical views from serving as prayer leaders, in order to distance the community from these views. And they decreed that certain portions of the Bible not be read or translated publicly, as these portions may reflect poorly on the leaders of the nation when they are not accompanied by a proper explanation, which it is not always possible to provide in the context of a public Torah reading.

Introduction to **Perek IV**

Therefore say: So says the Lord God, Although I have removed them far off among the nations, and although I have scattered them among the countries, yet I have been to them as a little sanctuary in the countries where they have come.

(Ezekiel 11:16)

The concept of a synagogue as a fixed place of prayer had already been established during the Second Temple period. Indeed, in the Temple complex itself, a synagogue existed for those visiting the Temple, in order for them to be able to participate in the communal prayers that were held there.

The primary use of a synagogue was for the daily prayers that were instituted in parallel to the communal sacrifices, and for the public reading of the Torah from the regular weekly portion. In addition, many synagogues were also used as study houses for children and eventually as a place where people would gather to hear words of Torah from the Sages. With this, the synagogue became a so-called little sanctuary that was endowed with its own sanctity in addition to the sanctity it gained by virtue of the Torah scrolls it housed.

This chapter deals with the issues relating to the sanctity of the synagogue. What level of decorum is required inside a synagogue, how does one treat the synagogue structure and place after it has been destroyed, what happens to its sanctity when it is sold, and under what circumstances is it permitted to do so? Closely related to this, the chapter also discusses the status of other items that are also endowed with differing degrees of sanctity due to their use and association with the Torah and various mitzvot.

Another issue dealt with at length in this chapter is the reading of the special Torah portions at various points throughout the year. First discussed are the four special Torah portions read on the *Shabbatot* during and immediately prior to the month of Adar. Which passages of the Torah are selected for those portions, and what are the determining factors regarding which portion is read on which Shabbat? Following this, the chapter focuses on which portions are read on the various Festivals and other special days throughout the year.

מתני׳ בְּנֵי הָעִיר שֶׁמָּכְרוּ רְחוֹבָהּ שֶׁל עִיר – לוֹקְחִין בְּדָמָיו בֵּית הַכְּנֶסֶת, בֵּית הַכְּנֶסֶת – לוֹקְחִין תֵּיבָה, תֵּיבָה – לוֹקְחִין מִטְפָּחוֹת, מִטְפָּחוֹת –

MISHNA **Residents of a town**[N] **who sold the town square,**[N] which was at times used for public prayer and therefore attained a certain degree of sanctity, may use the proceeds of the sale only to purchase something of a greater degree of sanctity.[H] They may therefore **purchase a synagogue with the proceeds** of the sale. If they sold **a synagogue, they may purchase an ark** in which to house sacred scrolls. If they sold **an ark, they may purchase wrapping cloths**[B] for the sacred scrolls. If they sold **wrapping cloths,**

NOTES

Residents of a town – בְּנֵי הָעִיר: While in the standard version of the Babylonian Talmud this chapter appears as the fourth and final chapter in the tractate, in the Mishna and in the Jerusalem Talmud it appears at the third chapter of the tractate. Furthermore, many of the early commentaries appear to have that order in their versions of the Babylonian Talmud. See *Tosefot Yom Tov*, who explains the ordering of the chapters.

Who sold the town square – שֶׁמָּכְרוּ רְחוֹבָהּ שֶׁל עִיר: The mishna discusses a case in which the items of sanctity had already been sold. The commentaries discuss whether such a sale is permitted *ab initio*. Furthermore, the mishna mentions only that it is permitted to purchase an item of greater sanctity. The commentaries debate whether it is also permitted to purchase an item of equal sanctity if one wishes to replace an old item (see Rashba, Ra'avad, and *Rishon LeTziyyon*).

HALAKHA

Selling sacred items – מְכִירַת תַּשְׁמִישֵׁי קְדוּשָּׁה: When selling sacred items, the proceeds may be used only to purchase other items of a greater degree of sanctity. Therefore, residents of a town who sold a synagogue are permitted to purchase an ark or the table on which the Torah is placed. Similarly, if they sold an ark, they may use the proceeds to purchase wrapping cloths for the Torah (*Shulḥan Arukh, Oraḥ Ḥayyim* 153:2).

BACKGROUND

Wrapping cloths – מִטְפָּחוֹת: It would appear that in the period of the Mishna, scrolls of the Torah and other sacred texts were not covered in mantles, as is the Ashkenazic custom today. Rather, they were wrapped in pieces of cloth, which the mishna refers to as wrapping cloths. Alternatively, the wrapping cloths mentioned were attached to the back of scrolls in order to protect them from any damage or wear.

יִקְחוּ סְפָרִים, סְפָרִים – לוֹקְחִין תּוֹרָה.

they may purchase scrolls[N] of the Prophets and the Writings. If they sold **scrolls** of the Prophets and Writings, **they may purchase a Torah** scroll.

אֲבָל אִם מָכְרוּ תּוֹרָה – לֹא יִקְחוּ סְפָרִים, סְפָרִים – לֹא יִקְחוּ מִטְפָּחוֹת, מִטְפָּחוֹת – לֹא יִקְחוּ תֵּיבָה, תֵּיבָה – לֹא יִקְחוּ בֵּית הַכְּנֶסֶת, בֵּית הַכְּנֶסֶת – לֹא יִקְחוּ אֶת הָרְחוֹב,

However, the proceeds of a sale of a sacred item may not be used to purchase an item of a lesser degree of sanctity. Therefore, **if they sold a Torah** scroll, **they may not** use the proceeds to **purchase scrolls** of the Prophets and the Writings. If they sold **scrolls** of the Prophets and Writings, **they may not purchase wrapping cloths.** If they sold **wrapping cloths, they may not purchase an ark.** If they sold **an ark, they may not purchase a synagogue.** If they sold **a synagogue, they may not purchase a town square.**

וְכֵן בְּמוֹתְרֵיהֶן.

And similarly, the same limitation applies **to** any **surplus funds** from the sale of sacred items, i.e., if after selling an item and purchasing something of a greater degree of sanctity there remain additional, unused funds, the leftover funds are subject to the same principle and may be used to purchase only something of a degree of sanctity greater than that of the original item.[H]

NOTES

Scrolls – סְפָרִים: Some explain that the reference is to scrolls of the Prophets and the Writings (Rashi). Others suggest that the term includes other sacred texts, such as scrolls of the Mishna (Meiri). A third opinion maintains that the reference is to scrolls of the individual books of the Torah. Since they only contained a single book, they had a lesser degree of sanctity that an entire Torah scroll (Rambam).

HALAKHA

Selling sacred items – מְכִירַת תַּשְׁמִישֵׁי קְדוּשָּׁה: If the wrapping cloths of scrolls were sold, the proceeds may be used to purchase scrolls of individual books of the Torah, scrolls of the Prophets, or scrolls of the Writings. Whether there is a distinction between different types of scrolls is a matter of debate: Some suggest that a scroll of an individual book of the Torah has a greater degree of sanctity than a scroll of the Prophets or the Writings (*Magen Avraham*). Others assert that scrolls of all sacred books have the same degree of sanctity, apart from a scroll of the entire Torah (*Ḥatam Sofer*). Some suggest further that if the texts are printed together in a book then all authorities would agree that they will all have the same degree of sanctity, even if one of them is an individual book of the Torah and the other is a book of the Prophets or the Writings (*Arukh HaShulḥan*). If the scrolls are sold, the only item that may be purchased with the proceeds is a scroll of the entire Torah. In the event that after the purchase there are still surplus funds, they should also be used to purchase only items of greater sanctity than the original one (*Shulḥan Arukh, Oraḥ Ḥayyim* 153:2).

HALAKHA

The town square – רחובה של עיר: Although prayers are held in the town square on public fast days, town squares do not have any sanctity. This is in accordance with the opinion of the Rabbis. Likewise, houses in which prayers are held irregularly have no sanctity; the same is true for a place where there are regular prayers but its main purpose is for other uses (*Mishna Berura*). Some say that even an ark is endowed with sanctity only if its purpose is to provide an honored place in which to house the Torah scroll; however if it is used only to protect the scroll, it is not considered a sacred item (*Shulḥan Arukh, Oraḥ Ḥayyim* 154:1, 3, and in the comment of Rema).

Selling a synagogue – מכירת בית כנסת: It is permitted to sell the synagogue only of a village, since it is built exclusively for the local residents. This is true even if it was built with funds brought from outside the village (Rema). Similarly, a synagogue built by a group of individuals to be used exclusively by them may be sold by that group, even if it is located in a city. However, a synagogue built in a city for public use, even if it was funded exclusively by the residents, may be sold only if there is already another synagogue available (*Taz*), or if it has already fallen into disuse (*Magen Avraham*, citing Mabit). Even with regard to a synagogue in a city, if there is an individual with the sole authority to make decisions about it, he is also allowed to sell it. This ruling is in accordance with the opinion of Rav Ashi (*Shulḥan Arukh, Oraḥ Ḥayyim* 153:7).

LANGUAGE

Bronze workers [*tursiyyim*] – טורסיים: Some suggest that the word is derived from Ταρσός; *Tarsus*, the name of the historic city of Tarsus. The city was a major center of trade and its residents were craftsmen. The term was then borrowed to refer to other craftsmen, such as weavers. Alternatively, it is possible that the word is from the Greek τορευτής, *toreutès*, which means a craft that uses metal. In this vein, Rashi explains that it refers to bronze workers.

גמ׳ בני העיר שמכרו רחובה של עיר. אמר רבה בר בר חנה אמר רבי יוחנן: זו דברי רבי מנחם בר יוסי סתומתאה, אבל חכמים אומרים: הרחוב אין בו משום קדושה.

GEMARA The mishna states: **Residents of a town who sold the town square**[H] may purchase a synagogue with the proceeds. Concerning this mishna, **Rabba bar bar Ḥana said** that **Rabbi Yoḥanan said: This is the statement of Rabbi Menaḥem bar Yosei, cited unattributed.**[N] **However, the Rabbis say: The town square does not have any sanctity.** Therefore, if it is sold, the residents may use the money from the sale for any purpose.

ורבי מנחם בר יוסי מאי טעמיה? הואיל והעם מתפללין בו בתעניות ובמעמדות. ורבנן: ההוא אקראי בעלמא.

And Rabbi Menaḥem bar Yosei, what is his reason for claiming that the town square has sanctity? **Since the people pray in** the town square **on** communal **fast days and on** non-priestly **watches,**[N] it is defined as a place of prayer and as such has sanctity. **And the Rabbis,** why do they disagree? They maintain **that** use of the town square **is merely an irregular occurrence.** Consequently, the town square is not to be defined as a place of prayer, and so it has no sanctity.

״בית הכנסת לוקחין תיבה״: אמר רבי שמואל בר נחמני אמר רבי יונתן: לא שנו אלא בית הכנסת של כפרים, אבל בית הכנסת של כרכין, כיון דמעלמא אתו ליה – לא מצו מזבני ליה, דהוה ליה דרבים.

§ The mishna states: If they sold **a synagogue, they may purchase an ark.**[H] The Gemara cites a qualification to this *halakha*: **Rabbi Shmuel bar Naḥmani said** that **Rabbi Yoḥanan said: They taught** this **only** with regard to **a synagogue of a village,** which is considered the property of the residents of that village. **However,** with regard to **a synagogue of a city,**[N] **since** people **come to it from the** outside **world,** the residents of the city **are not able to sell it, because it is** considered to be the property **of the public** at large and does not belong exclusively to the residents of the city.

אמר רב אשי: האי בי כנישתא דמתא מחסיא. אף על גב דמעלמא אתו לה, כיון דאדעתא דידי קאתו – אי בעינא מזבנינא לה.

Rav Ashi said: This synagogue of Mata Meḥasya,[N] **although** people **from the** outside **world come to it, since they come at my discretion,** as I established it, and everything is done there in accordance with my directives, **if I wish, I can sell it.**

מיתיבי, אמר רבי יהודה: מעשה בבית הכנסת של טורסיים שהיה בירושלים שמכרוה לרבי אליעזר, ועשה בה כל צרכיו. והא התם דכרכים הוה! ההיא בי כנישתא זוטי הוה, ואינהו עבדוה.

The Gemara **raises an objection** to Rabbi Shmuel bar Naḥmani's statement, from a *baraita*: **Rabbi Yehuda said:** There was **an incident involving a synagogue of bronze workers** [*tursiyyim*][L] **that was in Jerusalem, which they sold to Rabbi Eliezer, and he used it for all his own needs.** The Gemara asks: **But wasn't** the synagogue **there** one **of cities,** as Jerusalem is certainly classified as a city; why were they permitted to sell it? The Gemara explains: **That** one **was a small synagogue, and** it was the bronze workers **themselves** who **built it.** Therefore, it was considered exclusively theirs, and they were permitted to sell it.

NOTES

This is the statement of Rabbi Menaḥem bar Yosei, cited unattributed – זו דברי רבי מנחם בר יוסי סתומתאה: Generally, the *halakha* is in accordance with unattributed *mishnayot*. However, in certain cases the Gemara identifies an unattributed mishna as being in accordance with a minority opinion. In such a case, the *halakha* often follows the majority opinion that opposes the opinion in the mishna (see *Rishon LeTziyyon*, Rid, and *Sefat Emet*).

On fast days and on non-priestly watches – בתעניות ובמעמדות: Many note that normally the non-priestly watches would meet and pray in the synagogue and not in the town square. Therefore, mention of the town square as a place for prayer is imprecise (Rid). However, others suggest that at times, if the synagogue was unable to contain such a large congregation, even the prayers of the non-priestly watches would be held in the town square (Meiri; see Rashi).

However, a synagogue of a city – אבל בית הכנסת של כרכין: Why is it prohibited to sell such a synagogue? Some suggest, and it is similarly explained in the Jerusalem Talmud, that since the wider public would use the synagogue, they would also financially contribute to its upkeep. Consequently, they shared monetary ownership of the synagogue. Since all of an item's owners must agree to its sale for the sale to be valid, the residents of the city did not have the right to unilaterally sell the synagogue. Others suggest that the issue is not the monetary ownership of the wider public. Rather, since the synagogue was dedicated to the use of the wider public, its sanctity could not be removed by the decision of the city's residents alone (Rambam; see Rashba).

Mata Meḥasya – מתא מחסיא: Mata Meḥasya was merely a village that was situated near the city of Sura. The village did not have particular significance and was not generally visited by the wider public until Rav Ashi settled there, at which point, due to his fame, it became a major center (Rabbeinu Yehonatan).

מֵיתִיבִי: ״בְּבֵית אֶרֶץ אֲחוּזַּתְכֶם״ – אֲחוּזַּתְכֶם מִיטַּמֵּא בִּנְגָעִים, וְאֵין יְרוּשָׁלַיִם מִיטַּמֵּא בִּנְגָעִים. אָמַר רַבִּי יְהוּדָה: אֲנִי לֹא שָׁמַעְתִּי אֶלָּא מְקוֹם מִקְדָּשׁ בִּלְבָד.

The Gemara **raises an objection** from another *baraita*: The verse states with regard to leprosy of houses:[B] "And I put the plague of leprosy **in a house of the land of your possession**" (Leviticus 14:34), from which it may be inferred: **"Your possession,"** i.e., a privately owned house, **can become ritually impure with leprosy,**[H] **but** a house in **Jerusalem cannot become ritually impure with leprosy,** as property there belongs collectively to the Jewish people and is not privately owned. **Rabbi Yehuda said: I heard** this distinction stated **only** with regard to **the site of the Temple alone,** but not with regard to the entire city of Jerusalem.

הָא בָּתֵּי כְנֵסִיּוֹת וּבָתֵּי מִדְרָשׁוֹת מִיטַּמְּאִין, אַמַּאי? הָא דִּכְרַכִּין הָווּ! אֵימָא: אָמַר רַבִּי יְהוּדָה: אֲנִי לֹא שָׁמַעְתִּי אֶלָּא מָקוֹם מְקוּדָּשׁ בִּלְבָד.

The Gemara explains: From Rabbi Yehuda's statement, it is apparent that only the site of the Temple cannot become ritually impure, **but synagogues and study halls** in Jerusalem **can become ritually impure. Why** should this be true given **that they are** owned by the **city?** The Gemara answers: Emend the *baraita* and **say** as follows: **Rabbi Yehuda said: I heard** this distinction stated **only** with regard to **a sacred site,**[N] which includes the Temple, synagogues, and study halls.

בְּמַאי קָמִיפַּלְגִי? תַּנָּא קַמָּא סָבַר: לֹא נִתְחַלְּקָה יְרוּשָׁלַיִם לִשְׁבָטִים, וְרַבִּי יְהוּדָה סָבַר: נִתְחַלְּקָה יְרוּשָׁלַיִם לִשְׁבָטִים,

With regard to what principle do the first *tanna* and Rabbi Yehuda **disagree? The first *tanna* holds that Jerusalem was not apportioned to the tribes,**[N] i.e., it was never assigned to any particular tribe, but rather it belongs collectively to the entire nation. **And Rabbi Yehuda holds: Jerusalem was apportioned to the tribes,** and it is only the site of the Temple itself that belongs collectively to the entire nation.

וּבִפְלוּגְתָּא דְּהָנֵי תַּנָּאֵי,

The Gemara notes: They each follow a different opinion **in the dispute** between **these *tanna'im*:**

דְּתַנְיָא: מֶה הָיָה בְּחֶלְקוֹ שֶׁל יְהוּדָה – הַר הַבַּיִת, הַלְּשָׁכוֹת וְהָעֲזָרוֹת. וּמֶה הָיָה בְּחֶלְקוֹ שֶׁל בִּנְיָמִין – אוּלָם וְהֵיכָל וּבֵית קָדְשֵׁי הַקֳּדָשִׁים.

One *tanna* holds that Jerusalem was apportioned to the tribes, **as it is taught** in a *baraita*: **What** part of the Temple **was in the** tribal **portion of Judah? The Temple mount, the** Temple **chambers, and the** Temple **courtyards. And what was in the** tribal **portion of Benjamin? The Entrance Hall, the Sanctuary, and the Holy of Holies.**[B]

וּרְצוּעָה הָיְתָה יוֹצֵאת מֵחֶלְקוֹ שֶׁל יְהוּדָה וְנִכְנֶסֶת בְּחֶלְקוֹ שֶׁל בִּנְיָמִין, וּבָהּ מִזְבֵּחַ בָּנוּי, וְהָיָה בִּנְיָמִין הַצַּדִּיק מִצְטַעֵר עָלֶיהָ בְּכׇל יוֹם לְבוֹלְעָהּ, שֶׁנֶּאֱמַר ״חוֹפֵף עָלָיו כׇּל הַיּוֹם״, לְפִיכָךְ זָכָה בִּנְיָמִין וְנַעֲשָׂה אוּשְׁפִּיזְכָן לַשְּׁכִינָה.

And a strip of land **issued forth from the portion of Judah and entered into the portion of Benjamin, and upon** that strip **the altar was built, and** the tribe of **Benjamin, the righteous, would agonize over it every day** desiring **to absorb it** into its portion, due to its unique sanctity, **as it is stated** in Moses' blessing to Benjamin: **"He covers it throughout the day,** and he dwells between his shoulders" (Deuteronomy 33:12). The phrase "covers it" is understood to mean that Benjamin is continually focused upon that site. **Therefore, Benjamin was privileged by becoming the host** [*ushpizekhan*][L] **of the** Divine Presence, as the Holy of Holies was built in his portion.

HALAKHA

Your possession can become ritually impure with leprosy – אֲחוּזַּתְכֶם מִיטַּמֵּא בִּנְגָעִים: Leprosy of houses applies only in territory in Eretz Yisrael that was apportioned to one of the tribes. As such, houses outside of Eretz Yisrael and houses in Jerusalem, which was never apportioned to any specific tribe, can never become ritually impure with leprosy (Rambam *Sefer Tahara, Hilkhot Tumat Tzara'at* 14:11).

NOTES

Only with regard to a sacred site – מָקוֹם מְקוּדָּשׁ בִּלְבָד: Rashi explains that all sacred sites are considered to be consecrated to God. As such, even if a sacred site is privately owned, it does not fully match the Torah's prescription that only "a house that is his" (Leviticus 14:35) can become ritually impure with leprosy of houses. *Turei Even* notes that the Gemara in tractate *Yoma* explains that according to all opinions, the site of the Temple was bought with funds collected from all the tribes, and therefore it was certainly not considered to be privately owned.

Jerusalem was not apportioned to the tribes – לֹא נִתְחַלְּקָה יְרוּשָׁלַיִם לִשְׁבָטִים: The book of Joshua states that the city of Jerusalem was given to the tribe of Benjamin. According to the opinion that Jerusalem was not apportioned, the reference in the book of Joshua must be referring only to the outskirts of the city, whereas the city proper was never given to one tribe. Alternatively, the city was initially allotted to the tribe of Benjamin, but later Jericho was given to them in exchange for Jerusalem. From that point it became a nationally owned city.

BACKGROUND

Leprosy of houses – נִגְעֵי בָתִּים: By Torah law (Leviticus 14:33–57), if leprous spots appear in a house, all the objects in the house must be removed in order to prevent them from becoming ritually impure in the event that the house is declared leprous. A priest is then brought to examine the house. If he confirms that the spots are leprous, the house is left uninhabited for a week, after which it is reexamined. If the leprous spots darken or disappear, the house is declared ritually pure. If the spots are unchanged, the house is isolated for a second week, after which it is reexamined. If by that point the spots have darkened, the house is declared ritually impure and must undergo a purification process involving birds, cedar wood, and red thread, much parallel to the purification process through which a leprous person is purified. If, however, the spots remained unchanged, the affected parts of the house are removed and replaced with new construction materials, after which the house is isolated a third time. If the spots reappear, the entire house must be destroyed, and its stones are disposed of in a ritually impure place.

There are many halakhic restrictions on the applicability of the laws pertaining to leprosy of houses, including limiting its application in Jerusalem.

The apportionment of Jerusalem to the tribes – חֲלֻקַּת יְרוּשָׁלַיִם לִשְׁבָטִים: The image depicts the area of the Temple as it was divided between the tribes of Benjamin and Judah. Rashi and other commentaries explain that only a small portion of the altar was within the portion of Judah, while the majority of the altar was in the portion of Benjamin.

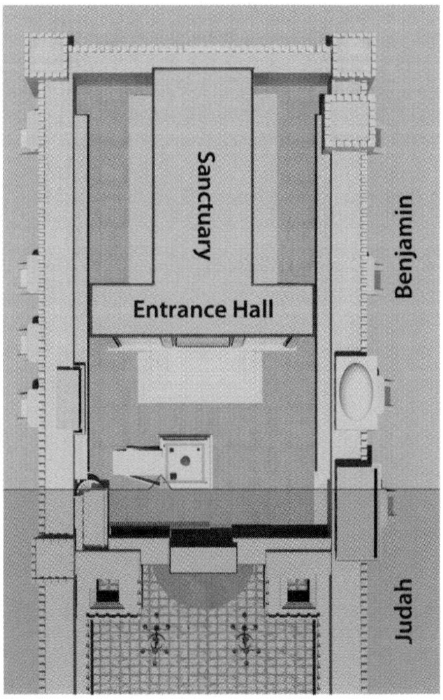

Temple divided between Benjamin and Judah

LANGUAGE

Host [*ushpizekhan*] – אוּשְׁפִּיזְכָן: From the Latin hospes, meaning hospital, or the Middle Persian aspinj, meaning hospital or inn.

וְהַאי תַּנָּא סָבַר: לֹא נִתְחַלְּקָה יְרוּשָׁלַיִם לִשְׁבָטִים. דְּתַנְיָא: אֵין מַשְׂכִּירִים בָּתִּים בִּירוּשָׁלַיִם, מִפְּנֵי שֶׁאֵינָן שֶׁלָּהֶן. רַבִּי אֶלְעָזָר (בַּר צָדוֹק) אוֹמֵר: אַף לֹא מִטּוֹת. לְפִיכָךְ עוֹרוֹת קָדָשִׁים בַּעֲלֵי אוּשְׁפִּיזִין נוֹטְלִין אוֹתָן בִּזְרוֹעַ.

And this other ***tanna* holds** that **Jerusalem was not apportioned to the tribes, as it is taught** in a *baraita*: **One may not rent out houses in Jerusalem,**[H] **due to** the fact **that** the houses **do not belong to** those occupying them. Rather, as is true for the entire city, they are owned collectively by the nation. **Rabbi Elazar bar Tzadok says: Even beds may not** be hired out. **Therefore,** in the case of the **hides of** the renter's **offerings** that the innkeepers take in lieu of payment, the **innkeepers** are considered to be **taking them by force,** as they did not have a right to demand payment.

אָמַר אַבָּיֵי: שְׁמַע מִינַּהּ אוֹרַח אַרְעָא לְמִישְׁבַּק אִינַשׁ גּוּלְפָּא וּמַשְׁכָּא בְּאוּשְׁפִּיזֵיהּ.

Apropos the topic of inns, the Gemara reports: **Abaye said: Learn from** this *baraita* that **it is proper etiquette** for **a person to leave** his wine **flask and** the **hide** of the animal that he slaughtered **at his inn,** i.e., the inn where he stayed, as a gift for the service he received.

אָמַר רָבָא לֹא שָׁנוּ אֶלָּא שֶׁלֹּא מָכְרוּ שִׁבְעָה טוֹבֵי הָעִיר בְּמַעֲמַד אַנְשֵׁי הָעִיר אֲבָל מָכְרוּ שִׁבְעָה טוֹבֵי הָעִיר בְּמַעֲמַד אַנְשֵׁי הָעִיר – אֲפִילּוּ

§ The Gemara returns its discussion of the mishna: **Rava said: They taught** that there is a limitation on what may be purchased with the proceeds of the sale of a synagogue **only when the seven representatives of the town**[HN] who were appointed to administer the town's affairs **had not sold** the synagogue **in an assembly of the residents of the town. However,** if **the seven representatives of the town had sold** it **in an assembly of the residents of the town,** then **even**

HALAKHA

Renting out houses in Jerusalem – הַשְׂכָּרַת בָּתִּים בִּירוּשָׁלַיִם: Houses may not be rented out in Jerusalem, because Jerusalem was not apportioned to the tribes and consequently the houses there do not belong to those who ostensibly possess them. Some claim that this applies only to renting houses to pilgrims ascending to Jerusalem on the pilgrimage Festivals (Rashi). However the Rambam implies that the prohibition applies in all cases. Some of the early authorities note that this *halakha* is no longer practiced (*Kaftor VaFeraḥ*; Rambam *Sefer Avoda*, *Hilkhot Beit HaBeḥira* 7:14).

The seven representatives of the town – שִׁבְעָה טוֹבֵי הָעִיר: When a synagogue is sold by the residents of the town, the proceeds retain the sanctity of the synagogue. However, if it is sold by the seven representatives of the town in an assembly of the residents of the town, for which it is sufficient that the sale be fully publicized even if not all of the residents are physically present at the time of the sale (Rema), or if an individual is given the authority to perform the sale in the residents' name, then the proceeds do not have any sanctity and the community may use them for any purpose. Likewise, the place itself does not retain any sanctity and may be used for any purpose. This ruling is in accordance with the opinion of Rava (*Shulḥan Arukh*, *Oraḥ Ḥayyim* 153:7).

NOTES

The seven representatives of the town – שִׁבְעָה טוֹבֵי הָעִיר: The Meiri explains that these seven men were not appointed by the residents. Rather, they were the seven people who generally ran the town's affairs. He adds, however, that if the residents were to appoint even a single individual to be their representative to make the sale, he would have the full authority to do so, just like the seven representatives.

Perek **IV**
Daf **26** Amud **b**

לְמִישְׁתָּא בֵּיהּ שִׁיכְרָא שַׁפִּיר דָּמֵי.

to drink beer with the proceeds[N] **seems well** and is permitted. The seven representatives have the authority to annul the sanctity of the synagogue, and therefore the proceeds of its sale do not retain any sanctity.

רָבִינָא הֲוָה לֵיהּ הַהוּא תִּילָּא דְּבֵי כְנִישְׁתָּא אֲתָא לְקַמֵּיהּ דְּרַב אַשִׁי, אֲמַר לֵיהּ: מַהוּ לְמִיזְרְעַהּ? אֲמַר לֵיהּ: זִיל זַבְנֵיהּ מִשִּׁבְעָה טוֹבֵי הָעִיר בְּמַעֲמַד אַנְשֵׁי הָעִיר, וּזְרַעָהּ.

The Gemara relates: **Ravina had a certain** piece of land on which stood **a mound** of the ruins **of a synagogue.**[N] **He came before Rav Ashi** and **said to him: What is** the *halakha* with regard **to sowing** the land? **He said to him: Go, purchase it from the seven representatives of the town in an assembly of the residents of the town, and** then you may **sow it.**

NOTES

To drink beer with the proceeds – לְמִישְׁתָּא בֵּיהּ שִׁיכְרָא: Some explain that this means to drink beer with it, i.e., the proceeds can even be used to purchase beer (Rabbeinu Ḥananel; Rashi). Others explain that the intention is to drink beer in it, i.e., the synagogue building itself may be used for any purpose, even as a tavern (see Rabbeinu Yehonatan and Ran).

Ravina had a certain mound of the ruins of a synagogue – רָבִינָא הֲוָה לֵיהּ הַהוּא תִּילָּא דְּבֵי כְנִישְׁתָּא: Some explain that the property belonged to Ravina, and he originally thought that in order to remove its sanctity it was sufficient to redeem it with money equal to the value of the synagogue ruins. Rav Ashi therefore told him that this could be achieved only by completing the sale before the seven representatives of the town (Ramban). Others explain that Ravina was concerned that the residents of the town would not direct the funds they received for the synagogue appropriately, and as such the sanctity would not transfer from the synagogue (Ra'avad). Alternatively, he thought that as long as a new item is not bought with the funds, the sanctity of the synagogue is retained (Ran).

רָמִי בַּר אַבָּא הֲוָה קָא בָנֵי בֵּי כְנִישְׁתָּא, הֲוָה הַהִיא כְנִישְׁתָּא עַתִּיקָא הֲוָה בָּעֵי לְמִיסְתְּרֵיהּ וּלְאַתּוֹיֵי לִיבְנֵי וְכָשׁוּרֵי מִינַּהּ, וְעַיּוֹלֵי לְהָתָם. יָתֵיב וְקָא מִיבַּעְיָא לֵיהּ הָא דְּרַב חִסְדָּא. דְּאָמַר רַב חִסְדָּא: לָא לִיסְתּוֹר בֵּי כְנִישְׁתָּא עַד דְּבָנֵי בֵּי כְנִישְׁתָּא אַחֲרִיתִי, הָתָם – מִשּׁוּם פְּשִׁיעוּתָא, כִּי הַאי גַּוְונָא מַאי? אֲתָא לְקַמֵּיהּ דְּרַב פָּפָּא – וַאֲסַר לֵיהּ, לְקַמֵּיהּ דְּרַב הוּנָא – וַאֲסַר לֵיהּ.

Rami bar Abba was once **building a synagogue. There was a certain old synagogue** that **he wished to demolish, and bring bricks and beams from it, and bring them to there,** to construct a new synagogue. **He sat and considered that which Rav Ḥisda** said, **as Rav Ḥisda said: One should not demolish a synagogue until one has built another synagogue.** Rami bar Abba reasoned that Rav Ḥisda's ruling **there** is **due to** a concern of **negligence,** as perhaps after the first synagogue is demolished, people will be negligent and a new one will never be built. However, in **a case like this,** where the new synagogue is to be built directly from the materials of the old one, **what** is the *halakha*? **He came before Rav Pappa** to ask his opinion, **and he prohibited him** from doing so. **He** then came **before Rav Huna, and he** also **prohibited him** from doing so.[H]

אָמַר רָבָא: הַאי בֵּי כְנִישְׁתָּא, חֲלוּפַהּ וְזַבּוּנַהּ – שָׁרֵי, אוֹגוּרַהּ וּמַשְׁכּוּנַהּ – אָסוּר. מַאי טַעְמָא – בִּקְדוּשְּׁתַהּ קָאֵי.

Rava said: With regard to **this synagogue, exchanging it** for a different building **or selling it** for money **is permitted,**[H] but **renting it** out **or mortgaging it is prohibited. What is the reason** for this? When a synagogue is rented out or mortgaged, **it remains in its sacred state.** Therefore, it is prohibited to rent it out or mortgage it, because it will then be used for a non-sacred purpose. However, if it is exchanged or sold, its sanctity is transferred to the other building or to the proceeds of the sale, and therefore the old synagogue building may be used for any purpose.

לִיבְנֵי נָמֵי, חֲלוּפִינְהוּ וְזַבּוּנִינְהוּ – שָׁרֵי, אוֹזוּפִינְהוּ – אָסוּר. הָנֵי מִילֵּי – בְּעַתִּיקָתָא, אֲבָל בַּחֲדָתָא – לֵית לַן בַּהּ.

The same *halakha* is **also** true of the **bricks** of a synagogue; **exchanging them or selling them is permitted,** but **renting them out is prohibited.**[N] The Gemara comments: **This applies to old** bricks that have already been part of a synagogue, **but as for new** bricks that have only been designated to be used in a synagogue, **we have no** problem **with it** if they are rented out for a non-sacred purpose.

וַאֲפִילּוּ לְמַאן דְּאָמַר הַזְמָנָה מִילְּתָא הִיא – הָנֵי מִילֵּי כְּגוֹן הָאוֹרֵג בֶּגֶד לְמֵת, אֲבָל הָכָא כְּטָווּי לְאָרִיג דָּמֵי, וְלֵיכָּא לְמַאן דְּאָמַר.

And even according to the one who said that mere **designation is significant,** i.e., although a certain object was not yet used for the designated purpose, the halakhic ramifications of using it for that purpose already take hold, **this applies** only in a case where it was created from the outset for that purpose, **for example, one who weaves a garment** to be used as shrouds **for a corpse. However, here** the bricks are **comparable to** already **spun** thread that was then designated to be used **to weave** burial shrouds. Concerning such designation, where nothing was specifically created for the designated purpose, **there is no one who said** that the designation is significant.

מַתָּנָה, פְּלִיגִי בָּהּ רַב אַחָא וְרָבִינָא, חַד אָסַר וְחַד שָׁרֵי. מַאן דְּאָסַר בְּהַאי תִּפְקַע קְדוּשְּׁתַהּ? וּמַאן דְּשָׁרֵי: אִי לָאו דַּהֲוָה לֵיהּ הֲנָאָה מִינֵּיהּ – לָא הֲוָה יָהֵיב לֵיהּ, הֲדַר הֲוָה לֵיהּ מַתָּנָה כִּזְבִינֵי.

Rav Aḥa and Ravina disagree about whether it is permitted to give away a synagogue as **a gift** to then be used for a non-sacred purpose. **One** of them **prohibited** it, **and the other one permitted** it. **The one who prohibits** it says: Is it possible that **with this** act of giving alone **its sanctity is removed?** This cannot be the case. Since the synagogue was not exchanged for anything else, there is nothing to which the sanctity may be transferred. Consequently, the synagogue remains sacred. **And the one who permitted** it does so because he reasons that **if** the donor **did not** receive any **benefit from** giving the synagogue, **he would not have given it.** Therefore, **the gift has reverted to being like a sale,** and the sanctity is transferred to the benefit received.

HALAKHA

Demolishing a synagogue – סְתִירַת בֵּית כְּנֶסֶת: A synagogue may not be demolished, even if one intends to build another one. Some prohibit this even when there are two synagogues in the city (*Magen Avraham*), while others are lenient in such a case (*Taz*). The majority of authorities follow this leniency (*Arukh HaShulḥan*). In cases where it is prohibited, one must first build the new synagogue and only then may the old one be demolished. This is also the custom when a wall in a synagogue is to be moved.

All this applies only in a case where there is no concern that the synagogue may collapse. If there is such a concern, it should be demolished immediately and the rebuilding done rapidly through day and night. It is prohibited even to remove stones from an existing synagogue in order to build a new one. In general, it is prohibited to demolish any part of a synagogue unless one does so for the sake of improving that synagogue (*Shulḥan Arukh, Oraḥ Ḥayyim* 152:1, and in the comment of Rema).

Transferring ownership of a synagogue – הַעֲבָרַת בַּעֲלוּת עַל בֵּית כְּנֶסֶת: It is permitted to transfer the ownership of a synagogue or its wood and stones either by sale, exchange, or gift. Some say this may be done only by the representatives of the town in an assembly of the residents of the town (*Magen Avraham*, citing Rif and Rosh). Others, permit the transfer of ownership even if it is not done in front of all the residents of the town (*Peri Megadim* and *Mishna Berura*, citing Ramban and Rashba). These halakhot apply in villages but not in cities (*Magen Avraham*).

It is prohibited to mortgage, rent out, or lend a synagogue, as in such cases its sanctity does not transfer to anything else. However, it is permitted to lend a Torah scroll to another for the purpose of reading it, and one may lend a synagogue to be used for prayer. This is true even in the case of lending a synagogue that belongs to the public to an individual, because it retains its original sanctity (*Shulḥan Arukh, Oraḥ Ḥayyim* 153:11, and in the comment of Rema).

NOTES

The sanctity of a synagogue – קְדוּשַּׁת בֵּית הַכְּנֶסֶת: The Ramban discusses at length the nature of the sanctity of the synagogue and how it may be removed or redeemed. His conclusion is that a synagogue does not have intrinsic sanctity akin to articles used for items of sanctity, such as the wrapping cloths of a Torah scroll. Rather, its sanctity is akin to that of articles used in the fulfillment of a mitzva, such as a *lulav*, since the building is used to pray inside it. Therefore, when a synagogue falls into disuse, it does not truly retain any sanctity.

תנו רבנן: תשמישי מצוה – נזרקין, תשמישי קדושה – נגנזין. ואלו הן תשמישי מצוה: סוכה, לולב, שופר, ציצית. ואלו הן תשמישי קדושה: דלוסקמי ספרים, תפילין ומזוזות, ותיק של ספר תורה, ונרתיק של תפילין ורצועותיהן.

§ **The Sages taught** in a *baraita*: **Articles** used in the performance **of a mitzva**[H] **may be thrown out** after use.[N] Although these items were used in the performance of a mitzva, they are not thereby sanctified. However, **articles** associated with the **sanctity** of God's name,[H] i.e. articles on which God's name is written, and articles that serve an article that has God's name written on it, even after they are no longer used, **must be interred** in a respectful manner. **And these** items **are** considered **articles of a mitzva: A** ***sukka*****;** a ***lulav*****;** a ***shofar*****;** and **ritual fringes. And these** items **are** considered **articles of sanctity: Cases of scrolls,** i.e. of Torah scrolls; **phylacteries; and** ***mezuzot*****; and a container for a Torah scroll; and a cover for phylacteries; and their straps.**

אמר רבא: מריש הוה אמינא האי כורסיא תשמיש דתשמיש הוא, ושרי. כיון דחזינא דמותבי עלויה ספר תורה, אמינא: תשמיש קדושה הוא, ואסור.

Rava said: Initially, I used to say that **this lectern** in the synagogue upon which the Torah is read **is** only **an article of an article** of sanctity, as the Torah scroll does not rest directly upon the lectern but rather upon the cloth that covers it. **And** the *halakha* is that once an article of an article of sanctity is no longer used, **it is permitted** to throw it out. However, **once I saw that the Torah scroll** is sometimes **placed** directly **upon** the lectern without an intervening cloth. **I said** that **it is an article** used directly for items **of sanctity, and** as such **it is prohibited** to simply discard it after use.

ואמר רבא: מריש הוה אמינא האי פריסא תשמיש דתשמיש הוא, כיון דחזינא דעייפי ליה ומנחי סיפרא עלויה אמינא: תשמיש קדושה הוא, ואסור.

And Rava similarly **said: Initially, I used to say** that **this curtain,** which is placed at the opening to the ark as a decoration, **is** only **an article of an article** of sanctity, as it serves to beautify the ark but is not directly used for the Torah scroll. However, **once I saw that** sometimes the curtain **is folded over and a Torah scroll is placed upon it. I said** that **it is an article** used directly for items **of sanctity and** as such **it is prohibited** to simply discard it after use.

ואמר רבא: האי תיבותא דאירפט, מיעבדה תיבה זוטרתי – שרי, כורסייא – אסיר. ואמר רבא: האי פריסא דבלה, למיעבדיה פריסא לספרי – שרי, לחומשין – אסיר.

And Rava further **said:** With regard to **this ark that has fallen apart, constructing a smaller ark** from its materials **is permitted,** as both have the same level of sanctity, but to use the materials to construct **a lectern is prohibited** because the lectern has a lesser degree of sanctity. **And Rava** similarly **said:** With regard to **this curtain** used to decorate an ark **that has become worn out, to fashion it** into **a wrapping cloth for** Torah **scrolls is permitted,** but to fashion it into a wrapping cloth **for** a scroll of **one of the five** books of the Torah **is prohibited.**[H]

ואמר רבא: הני זבילי דחומשי, וקמטרי דספרי – תשמיש קדושה נינהו, ונגנזין. פשיטא! מהו דתימא: הני לאו לכבוד עבידן, לנטורי בעלמא עבידי, קא משמע לן.

And Rava also **said:** With regard to **these cases for** storing scrolls of **one of the five** books of the Torah **and sacks for** storing Torah **scrolls, they are** classified as **articles of sanctity.** Therefore, **they are to be interred** when they are no longer in use. The Gemara asks: **Isn't** that **obvious?** The Gemara answers: **Lest you say** that since **these** items **are not made for the honor** of the scrolls but rather **are made merely to** provide **protection,** they should not be classified as articles of sanctity, Rava therefore **teaches us** that although they are indeed made to protect the scrolls, they also provide honor and are therefore to be classified as articles of sanctity.

ההוא בי כנישתא דיהודאי רומאי דהוה פתיח לההוא אידרונא, דהוה מחית ביה מת, והוו בעו כהני למיעל לצלויי התם. אתו אמרו ליה לרבא, אמר להו: דלו תיבותא, אותבוה, דהוה ליה כלי עץ העשוי לנחת, וכלי עץ העשוי לנחת – אינו מקבל טומאה, וחוצץ בפני הטומאה.

The Gemara relates: There was **a certain synagogue of the Jews of Rome that opened out into a room in which a corpse was lying,** thereby spreading the ritual impurity of the corpse throughout the synagogue. **And the priests wished to enter** the synagogue **in order to pray there.** However, it was prohibited for them to do so because a priest may not come in contact with ritual impurity of a corpse. **They came and spoke to Rava,** about what to do. **He said to them: Lift up the ark and put it down** in the opening between the two rooms, **as it is a wooden utensil that is designated to rest**[HN] in one place and not be moved from there, **and the** *halakha* is that **a wooden utensil that is designated to rest is not susceptible to ritual impurity, and** therefore it **serves as a barrier to** prevent **ritual impurity** from spreading.[H]

HALAKHA

Articles used in the performance of a mitzva – תשמישי מצוה: Articles that were used in the performance of a mitzva but are no longer needed, such as the strings of ritual fringes that were ripped, do not need to be interred, and it is permitted to dispose of them. Nevertheless, it is fitting to treat them with respect, and one who takes upon himself to store them will receive a blessing (Rema). It is preferable to use them for a different mitzva (*Magen Avraham*; *Taz*). This is the custom also for the roofing of the *sukka* and other objects that are used to perform mitzvot (*Taz*; *Shulḥan Arukh*, *Oraḥ Ḥayyim* 21:1).

Articles of sanctity – תשמישי קדושה: Articles of sanctity have inherent sanctity and therefore should not be disposed of; rather they must be interred. This includes items such as a Torah scroll; *mezuzot*; straps of the phylacteries; an ark; a lectern on which the Torah scroll is directly placed and read; and in certain cases, the curtain of an ark. A curtain of an ark only has sanctity if the Torah scroll is sometimes placed directly upon it (*Magen Avraham*). Therefore, nowadays, when Torah scrolls are never placed directly on the curtain, they are not considered articles of sanctity (*Taz*). Only items that have God's name written on them, or that directly serve such an item, whether functionally or by giving honor to them, are classified as articles of sanctity. However, an item that serves only to protect an article of sanctity is not considered an article of sanctity and is referred to as an article of an article of sanctity (*Shulḥan Arukh*, *Oraḥ Ḥayyim* 154:3).

Changing the use of articles of sanctity – שינוי תשמישי קדושה: An ark may not be made into a lectern for reading from the Torah. However, a small ark may be constructed from a larger one, and a small lectern may be made from a larger one. It is permitted to make a small wrapping cloth for a Torah scroll from a larger one, but it is not permitted to make it into a wrapping cloth that will be used for the scroll of an individual book of the Torah. The curtain of the ark has the sanctity of the synagogue, not the sanctity of the ark. The pointer that is used to show the place that is being read is considered an article of sanctity, since it is customarily placed on the Torah scroll for the splendor of the Torah (*Magen Avraham*; *Shulḥan Arukh*, *Yoreh De'a* 282:13).

A wooden utensil that is designated to rest – כלי עץ העשוי לנחת: A wooden utensil that is made to remain unmoved in one set place is not susceptible to ritual impurity (Rambam *Sefer Tahara*, *Hilkhot Kelim* 3:1).

Serves as a barrier to prevent ritual impurity from spreading – חוצץ בפני הטומאה: A large wooden utensil, more than four *se'a*, that is not moved when it is both empty and full is not susceptible to ritual impurity. Therefore, it is an effective barrier to prevent ritual impurity from spreading (Rambam *Sefer Tahara*, *Hilkhot Tumat Met* 13:3).

NOTES

Articles used in the performance of a mitzva may be thrown out after use – תשמישי מצוה נזרקין: The *She'iltot* writes that articles used in the performance of a mitzva are considered dedicated to that mitzva until they are destroyed. Therefore, one is not allowed to throw them out or use them for any other purpose. Rather, they must be burned. This is indeed the custom with the remainders of the wicks used to light the Hanukkah lamps.

A wooden utensil that is designated to rest – כלי עץ העשוי לנחת: A wooden utensil is susceptible to ritual impurity only if can be moved both when filled and when empty. A very large utensil that can be moved only when it is empty is not considered a utensil and is not susceptible to ritual impurity.

אָמְרוּ לֵיהּ רַבָּנַן לְרָבָא: וְהָא זִמְנִין דִּמְטַלְטְלֵי לֵיהּ כִּי מָנַח סֵפֶר תּוֹרָה עִלָּוֵיהּ, וַהֲוָה לֵיהּ מִיטַּלְטֵל מָלֵא וְרֵיקָם! אִי הָכִי לָא אֶפְשָׁר.

The Rabbis said to Rava: But isn't the ark **sometimes moved when** a Torah scroll is still **resting inside it, and** therefore **it is** a utensil that **is moved** both **when it is full and when it is empty;** such a utensil is susceptible to ritual impurity and cannot prevent ritual impurity from spreading. He said to them: **If so,** if it is as you claim, then **it is not possible** to remedy the situation.

אָמַר מָר זוּטְרָא: מִטְפָּחוֹת סְפָרִים שֶׁבָּלוּ עוֹשִׂין אוֹתָן תַּכְרִיכִין לְמֵת מִצְוָה, וְזוֹ הִיא גְּנִיזָתָן.

Mar Zutra said: With regard to **wrapping cloths of** Torah **scrolls that have become worn out, they may be made into shrouds for a corpse with no one to bury it [*met mitzva*], and this is their** most appropriate manner for being **interred.**[H]

וְאָמַר רָבָא: סֵפֶר תּוֹרָה שֶׁבָּלָה גּוֹנְזִין אוֹתוֹ אֵצֶל תַּלְמִיד חָכָם, וַאֲפִילּוּ שׁוֹנֶה הֲלָכוֹת. אָמַר רַב אַחָא בַּר יַעֲקֹב: וּבִכְלִי חֶרֶס, שֶׁנֶּאֱמַר ״וּנְתַתָּם בִּכְלִי חָרֶשׂ לְמַעַן יַעַמְדוּ יָמִים רַבִּים״.

And Rava said: A Torah scroll that became worn out is interred and buried **next to a Torah scholar,**[N] **and** in this regard, a Torah scholar is defined **even** as **one who** only **studies the *halakhot*** in the Mishna and the *baraitot* but is not proficient in their analysis. **Rav Aḥa bar Ya'akov said: And** when it is buried, it is first placed **in an earthenware vessel, as it is stated: "And put them in an earthenware vessel, that they may last for many days"** (Jeremiah 32:14).[H]

(וְאָמַר) רַב פַּפִּי מִשְּׁמֵיהּ דְּרָבָא: מִבֵּי כְנִישְׁתָּא לְבֵי רַבָּנַן – שָׁרֵי, מִבֵּי רַבָּנַן לְבֵי כְנִישְׁתָּא – אָסִיר. וְרַב פָּפָּא מִשְּׁמֵיהּ דְּרָבָא מַתְנֵי אִיפְּכָא, אָמַר רַב אַחָא:

§ **And Rav Pappi said in the name of Rava:** To convert a building **from a synagogue into a study hall is permitted,** but **from a study hall into a synagogue is prohibited,** as he holds that a study hall has a higher degree of sanctity than a synagogue. **And Rav Pappa in the name of Rava teaches the opposite,** as he holds that a synagogue has a higher degree of sanctity than a study hall. **Rav Aḥa said:**

HALAKHA

Wrapping cloths of Torah scrolls – מִטְפְּחוֹת סְפָרִים: It is permitted to make burial shrouds from wrapping cloths of a Torah scroll that have become worn out. This is considered their interment. However, worn-out wrapping cloths of a Torah scroll may not be used as a covering for phylacteries (*Eshel Avraham*; *Shulḥan Arukh*, *Oraḥ Ḥayyim* 154:4).

The storing away of a Torah scroll – גְּנִיזַת סֵפֶר תּוֹרָה: It is prohibited to burn a Torah scroll, sacred books, and articles of sanctity (*Magen Avraham*; see *Responsa Shevut Ya'akov* and *Sedei Ḥemed*). Instead, they are placed in an earthenware utensil and interred in a Torah scholar's grave. For this purpose, the scholar is not required to be a great Sage. Rather, it is sufficient even if he studied only *halakhot*. This ruling is in accordance with the opinion of Rava and Rav Aḥa (*Shulḥan Arukh*, *Oraḥ Ḥayyim* 154:5).

NOTES

A Torah scroll that became worn out is interred and buried next to a Torah scholar – סֵפֶר תּוֹרָה שֶׁבָּלָה גּוֹנְזִין אוֹתוֹ אֵצֶל תַּלְמִיד חָכָם: This *halakha* is based on the principle that the honor of a Torah scholar is greater than the honor of a Torah scroll. The Gemara here indicates that this principle is true even of a scholar who studied only *halakhot*.

Perek **IV**
Daf **27** Amud **a**

כְּווֹתֵיהּ דְּרַב פַּפִּי מִסְתַּבְּרָא, דְּאָמַר רַבִּי יְהוֹשֻׁעַ בֶּן לֵוִי: בֵּית הַכְּנֶסֶת מוּתָּר לַעֲשׂוֹתוֹ בֵּית הַמִּדְרָשׁ, שְׁמַע מִינַּהּ.

It stands to reason to rule **in accordance with** the opinion of **Rav Pappi, as Rabbi Yehoshua ben Levi said: It is permitted** for a **synagogue to be made** into **a study hall.**[H] The Gemara concludes: Indeed, **learn from it** that the opinion of Rav Pappi is correct.

דָּרַשׁ בַּר קַפָּרָא: מַאי דִּכְתִיב ״וַיִּשְׂרֹף אֶת בֵּית ה׳ וְאֶת בֵּית הַמֶּלֶךְ וְאֵת כָּל בָּתֵּי יְרוּשָׁלַ͏ִם וְאֶת כָּל בֵּית גָּדוֹל שָׂרַף בָּאֵשׁ״. ״בֵּית ה׳״ – זֶה בֵּית הַמִּקְדָּשׁ, ״בֵּית הַמֶּלֶךְ״ – אֵלּוּ פַּלְטְרִין שֶׁל מֶלֶךְ, ״וְאֵת כָּל בָּתֵּי יְרוּשָׁלַ͏ִם״ – כְּמַשְׁמָעָן, ״וְאֶת כָּל בֵּית גָּדוֹל שָׂרַף בָּאֵשׁ״ רַבִּי יוֹחָנָן וְרַבִּי יְהוֹשֻׁעַ בֶּן לֵוִי, חַד אָמַר: מָקוֹם שֶׁמְּגַדְּלִין בּוֹ תּוֹרָה, וְחַד אָמַר: מָקוֹם שֶׁמְּגַדְּלִין בּוֹ תְּפִלָּה.

§ **Bar Kappara interpreted** a verse **homiletically: What is** the meaning of that **which is written: "And he burnt the house of the Lord, and the king's house, and all the houses of Jerusalem, and every great house he burnt with fire"** (II Kings 25:9)? He explained: **"The house of the Lord"; this is the Holy Temple. "The king's house"; these are the king's palaces [*palterin*].**[L] **"And all the houses of Jerusalem";** as understood **in its literal sense.** With regard to the final phrase: **"And every great house**[N] **he burnt with fire," Rabbi Yoḥanan and Rabbi Yehoshua ben Levi** disagree about the meaning of "great house": **One** of them **said:** It is referring to **a place where the Torah is made great,** i.e., the study hall; **and** the other **one said:** It is referring to **a place where prayer is made great,** i.e., the synagogue.

מַאן דְּאָמַר תּוֹרָה, דִּכְתִיב ״ה׳ חָפֵץ לְמַעַן צִדְקוֹ יַגְדִּיל תּוֹרָה וְיַאְדִּיר״. וּמַאן דְּאָמַר תְּפִלָּה דִּכְתִיב ״סַפְּרָה נָּא... הַגְּדוֹלוֹת אֲשֶׁר עָשָׂה אֱלִישָׁע״. וֶאֱלִישָׁע דַּעֲבַד – בְּרַחֲמֵי הוּא דַּעֲבַד.

The Gemara explains their respective opinions: **The one who said** that the reference is to where the **Torah** is made great bases his opinion on a verse that describes Torah study as great, **as it is written: "The Lord was pleased, for His righteousness' sake, to make Torah great and glorious"** (Isaiah 42:21). **And the one who said** that the reference is to where **prayer** is made great bases his opinion on a verse that describes prayer as great, **as it is written: "Tell me,** I pray you, all **the great things that Elisha has done"** (II Kings 8:4), **and that which Elisha did,** i.e., restored a boy to life, **he did through prayer.**

HALAKHA

A synagogue and a study hall – בֵּית כְּנֶסֶת וּבֵית מִדְרָשׁ: It is permitted to convert a synagogue into a study hall or to sell a synagogue in order to buy a study hall. However, a study hall may not be converted into a synagogue. This ruling is in accordance with the opinion of Rav Pappi. Nowadays, as synagogues are also used for Torah study, they have the sanctity of a study hall (see *Mishna Berura*; *Shulḥan Arukh*, *Oraḥ Ḥayyim* 153:1).

LANGUAGE

Palaces [*palterin*] – פַּלְטְרִין: From the Latin palatinum and the Greek παλάτιον, *palation*, meaning palace or temple.

NOTES

Every great house – כָּל בֵּית גָּדוֹל: The verse makes a distinction between "all the houses of Jerusalem," which are grouped together, and "every great house," which is different. The Gemara understands this to imply that the significance of a "great house" is such that it must always remain distinct from the other houses of Jerusalem. It may not be used for any purpose other than what it was designated for. However, see the Jerusalem Talmud, in which "all the houses of Jerusalem" is expounded in a different manner.

NOTES

What is the *halakha* with regard to whether it is permitted to sell an old Torah scroll – מַהוּ לִמְכּוֹר סֵפֶר תּוֹרָה יָשָׁן: The solution to this dilemma cannot be inferred from the mishna. This is because if the first clause of the mishna is assumed to be precise, it would imply that it is prohibited to sell an item if its sanctity will not be elevated. However, the opposite conclusion is reached if one reads that latter clause of the mishna precisely. As such, a proof cannot be derived from the mishna (Rabbi Zeraḥya HaLevi, citing Rabbeinu Efrayim; see *Turei Even*).

Scrolls of one of the five books of the Torah may be rolled up in wrapping cloths used for the Prophets or Writings – וְחוּמָּשִׁין בְּמִטְפְּחוֹת נְבִיאִים וּכְתוּבִים: Rabbeinu Yehonatan explains that the verse: "And there has not risen a prophet since in Israel like Moses" (Deuteronomy 34:10) expresses the supremacy of Moses' prophecy and consequently proves that although the individual books of the Torah do not have the sanctity of a full Torah scroll, they have a greater degree of sanctity than the other books of the Bible.

תִּסְתַּיֵּים דְּרַבִּי יְהוֹשֻׁעַ בֶּן לֵוִי הוּא דַּאֲמַר מָקוֹם שֶׁמְּגַדְּלִין בּוֹ תּוֹרָה, דְּאָמַר רַבִּי יְהוֹשֻׁעַ בֶּן לֵוִי: בֵּית הַכְּנֶסֶת מוּתָּר לַעֲשׂוֹתוֹ בֵּית הַמִּדְרָשׁ, שְׁמַע מִינַּהּ.

The Gemara comments: **Conclude that Rabbi Yehoshua ben Levi is the one who said** that "great house" is referring to **a place where the Torah is made great, as Rabbi Yehoshua ben Levi said** elsewhere: **It is permitted** for **a synagogue to be made** into **a study hall.** This ruling indicates that he holds that a study hall has a higher degree of sanctity than a synagogue. It is therefore reasonable that he assumes that "great house" is referring specifically to a study hall. The Gemara concludes: Indeed, **learn from it** that he was the one who said the term is referring to a place where the Torah is made great.

״אֲבָל מָכְרוּ תּוֹרָה לֹא יִקְחוּ סְפָרִים״ וכו׳: אִיבַּעְיָא לְהוּ: מַהוּ לִמְכּוֹר סֵפֶר תּוֹרָה יָשָׁן לִיקַּח בּוֹ חָדָשׁ? כֵּיוָן דְּלָא מַעֲלֵי לֵיהּ – אָסוּר, אוֹ דִּלְמָא כֵּיוָן דְּלֵיכָּא לְעִלּוּיֵי עִילּוּיָיא אַחֲרִינָא – שַׁפִּיר דָּמֵי?

§ The mishna states: **However, if they sold a Torah** scroll, **they may not** use the proceeds to **purchase scrolls** of the Prophets and the Writings. Similarly, the proceeds of the sale of any sacred item may not be used to purchase an item of a lesser degree of sanctity. **A dilemma was raised before** the Sages: **What is** the *halakha* with regard to whether it is permitted **to sell an old Torah scroll**[N] in order **to purchase a new one?** The Gemara explains the sides of the dilemma: On the one hand, **since** the proceeds **are not raised** to a higher degree of sanctity by doing so, maybe **it is prohibited; or, perhaps** in this case, **since there is no** possibility of **raising** it to **another, higher** degree of sanctity, it **seems well** and should be permitted?

תָּא שְׁמַע: אֲבָל מָכְרוּ תּוֹרָה – לֹא יִקְחוּ סְפָרִים. סְפָרִים הוּא דְּלָא, הָא תּוֹרָה בְּתוֹרָה – שַׁפִּיר דָּמֵי! מַתְנִיתִין דִּיעֲבַד, כִּי קָא מִיבַּעְיָא לַן – לְכַתְּחִלָּה.

Come and **hear** a resolution to this dilemma from the mishna: **However, if they sold a Torah** scroll, **they may not** use the proceeds to **purchase scrolls** of the Prophets and the Writings. One may infer: **It is** only **scrolls** of the Prophets and the Writings **that may not** be purchased with the proceeds, **but** to purchase a new **Torah** scroll **with** the proceeds of an old **Torah** scroll **seems well** and is permitted. The Gemara rejects this proof: **The mishna** discusses the *halakha* that applies only **after the fact** that a Torah scroll was sold. Perhaps it is only in that case where the proceeds may be used to purchase another Torah scroll. **When the dilemma was raised to us,** it was with respect to permitting the sale of one Torah scroll in order to purchase another ***ab initio***.

תָּא שְׁמַע: גּוֹלְלִין סֵפֶר תּוֹרָה בְּמִטְפְּחוֹת חוּמָּשִׁין, וְחוּמָּשִׁין בְּמִטְפְּחוֹת נְבִיאִים וּכְתוּבִים, אֲבָל לֹא נְבִיאִים וּכְתוּבִים בְּמִטְפְּחוֹת חוּמָּשִׁין, וְלֹא חוּמָּשִׁין בְּמִטְפְּחוֹת סֵפֶר תּוֹרָה.

Come and **hear** a resolution to this dilemma from a *baraita*: **A Torah scroll may be rolled up in wrapping cloths** that are used for scrolls of **one of the five** books of the Torah. **And** scrolls of **one of the five** books of the Torah may be rolled up **in wrapping cloths** that are used for scrolls **of the Prophets or Writings,**[N] since in each case the wrapping cloths are being used for something with a greater degree of sanctity. **However,** a scroll of **the Prophets or Writings may not** be rolled up **in wrapping cloths** that are used for scrolls **of one of the five** books of the Torah, and scrolls of **one of the five** books of the Torah **may not** be rolled up **in wrapping cloths** that are used **for a Torah scroll.**

קָתָנֵי מִיהַת: גּוֹלְלִים סֵפֶר תּוֹרָה בְּמִטְפְּחוֹת חוּמָּשִׁין, מִטְפְּחוֹת חוּמָּשִׁין – אִין, מִטְפְּחוֹת סֵפֶר תּוֹרָה – לָא.

The Gemara explains the proof: **In any event,** the *baraita* **is teaching: A Torah scroll may be rolled up in wrapping cloths** that are used for scrolls **of one of the five** books of the Torah. One may infer: A Torah scroll may be rolled up only in **wrapping cloths** that are used for scrolls **of one of the five** books of the Torah; but to roll it up in **wrapping cloths of** another **Torah scroll, no,** it is not permitted. By extension, one Torah scroll may certainly not be sold in order to purchase another.

אֵימָא סֵיפָא: וְלֹא חוּמָּשִׁין בְּמִטְפְּחוֹת סֵפֶר תּוֹרָה. הָא תּוֹרָה בְּתוֹרָה – שַׁפִּיר דָּמֵי! אֶלָּא, מֵהָא לֵיכָּא לְמִישְׁמַע מִינַּהּ.

The Gemara rejects the proof: If this inference is valid, one should be able to **say the latter clause** and make a similar inference from it. The latter clause teaches: **And** scrolls of **one of the five** books of the Torah **may not** be rolled up **in wrapping cloths** that are used for **a Torah scroll.** It may be inferred from this that it is prohibited only to roll up scrolls of one of the five books of the Torah in wrapping cloths that are used for a Torah scroll, **but** to roll up one **Torah** scroll **in** the wrapping cloths of another **Torah** scroll **seems well.** By extension, one should be permitted to sell a Torah scroll to purchase another. **Rather,** perforce one must conclude that **no** inference beyond its basic meaning **can be deduced from** the *baraita*, as the inferences are contradictory.

תָּא שְׁמַע: מַנִּיחִין סֵפֶר תּוֹרָה עַל גַּבֵּי תוֹרָה, וְתוֹרָה עַל גַּבֵּי חוּמָּשִׁין, וְחוּמָּשִׁין עַל גַּבֵּי נְבִיאִים וּכְתוּבִים. אֲבָל לֹא נְבִיאִים וּכְתוּבִים עַל גַּבֵּי חוּמָּשִׁין, וְלֹא חוּמָּשִׁין עַל גַּבֵּי תוֹרָה.

Come and **hear** a resolution to this dilemma from the *Tosefta* (*Megilla* 3:12): **A Torah scroll may be placed upon** another **Torah** scroll, **and a Torah** scroll may be placed **upon** scrolls of **one of the five** books of the Torah, **and** scrolls of **one of the five** books of the Torah may be placed **upon** scrolls of **the Prophets or Writings. However,** scrolls of **the Prophets or Writings may not** be placed **upon** scrolls of **one of the five** books of the Torah, **and** scrolls of **one of the five** books of the Torah **may not be placed upon a Torah** scroll.[H] From the first clause, it is apparent that one Torah scroll may be used for the sake of another. By extension, it should be permitted to sell one Torah scroll to purchase another.

הַנָּחָה קָאָמְרַתְּ? שָׁאנֵי הַנָּחָה דְּלָא אֶפְשָׁר. דְּאִי לָא תֵּימָא הָכִי – מִיכְרַךְ הֵיכִי כָּרְכִינַן? וְהָא קָא יָתֵיב דַּפָּא אַחַבְרֵיהּ! אֶלָּא, כֵּיוָן דְּלָא אֶפְשָׁר – שָׁרֵי, הָכָא נַמִי כֵּיוָן דְּלָא אֶפְשָׁר – שָׁרֵי.

The Gemara rejects this proof: Can **you say** a proof from the *halakha* **of placing** one Torah scroll upon another? The *halakha* of **placing** scrolls upon one another **is different, because it is impossible** to place them in any other way, as they must be laid one atop the other when placed in the ark. **As, if you do not say so,** that it is indeed permitted when in an unavoidable situation, **how** could we **furl** a Torah scroll at all? **Does** one **sheet** of parchment **not rest upon another? Rather, since it is impossible** to furl the scroll in any other way, **it is permitted. Here too, since it is impossible** to place the scrolls in the ark in any other way, **it is permitted.**

תָּא שְׁמַע: דְּאָמַר רַבָּה בַּר בַּר חָנָה אָמַר רַבִּי יוֹחָנָן מִשּׁוּם רַבָּן שִׁמְעוֹן בֶּן גַּמְלִיאֵל: לֹא יִמְכּוֹר אָדָם סֵפֶר תּוֹרָה יָשָׁן לִיקַּח בּוֹ חָדָשׁ.

Come and **hear** a resolution to this dilemma from a *baraita*: **As Rabba bar bar Ḥana said** that **Rabbi Yoḥanan said in the name of Rabban Shimon ben Gamliel: A person may not sell an old Torah scroll** in order **to purchase a new one.**[H]

הָתָם מִשּׁוּם פְּשִׁיעוּתָא, כִּי קָאָמְרִינַן – כְּגוֹן דִּכְתִיב וּמַנַּח לְאִיפְּרוּקֵי, מַאי?

The Gemara rejects this proof. **There,** in the case of the *baraita*, it is prohibited **because of** a concern for **negligence.** The old one might be sold and a new one never bought. However, **when we speak,** it is of a case **where** the new scroll **is** already **written and waiting to be redeemed** immediately with the proceeds of the sale. Therefore, the question remains: **What** is the *halakha* in this case?

תָּא שְׁמַע דְּאָמַר רַבִּי יוֹחָנָן מִשּׁוּם רַבִּי מֵאִיר: אֵין מוֹכְרִין סֵפֶר תּוֹרָה אֶלָּא לִלְמוֹד תּוֹרָה, וְלִישָּׂא אִשָּׁה.

Come and **hear** a resolution to this dilemma from a *baraita*: **As Rabbi Yoḥanan said in the name of Rabbi Meir: A Torah scroll may be sold only** if the seller needs the money in order **to study Torah or to marry a woman.**

שְׁמַע מִינָּהּ: תּוֹרָה בְּתוֹרָה שַׁפִּיר דָּמֵי. דִּלְמָא שָׁאנֵי לִמּוּד, שֶׁהַלִּמּוּד מֵבִיא לִידֵי מַעֲשֶׂה. אִשָּׁה נַמִי ״לֹא תֹהוּ בְרָאָהּ לָשֶׁבֶת יְצָרָהּ״, אֲבָל תּוֹרָה בְּתוֹרָה – לָא.

Learn from this *baraita* that exchanging one entity of **Torah,** i.e., a Torah scroll, **for** another entity of **Torah,** i.e., Torah study, **seems well,** and by extension, it should be permitted to sell one Torah scroll to purchase another. The Gemara rejects the proof: **Perhaps** Torah **study is different, as the study** of Torah **leads to action,** i.e., the fulfillment of the mitzvot, and perhaps it is only due to its great importance of Torah study that it is permitted to sell a Torah scroll for it. Similarly, marrying **a woman is also** of utmost importance, as it is stated with regard to Creation: **"He created it not a waste; He formed it to be inhabited"** (Isaiah 45:18). This indicates that marrying and having children fulfills a primary goal of Creation. **But** selling an old **Torah** in order to buy a new **Torah** might **not** be permitted.

תָּנוּ רַבָּנַן: לֹא יִמְכּוֹר אָדָם סֵפֶר תּוֹרָה אַף עַל פִּי שֶׁאֵינוֹ צָרִיךְ לוֹ, יָתֵר עַל כֵּן אָמַר רַבָּן שִׁמְעוֹן בֶּן גַּמְלִיאֵל: אֲפִילּוּ אֵין לוֹ מַה יֹּאכַל וּמָכַר סֵפֶר תּוֹרָה אוֹ בִּתּוֹ – אֵינוֹ רוֹאֶה סִימָן בְּרָכָה לְעוֹלָם.

On the same topic, **the Sages taught** in a *baraita*: **A person may not sell a Torah scroll,**[N] **even if he does not need it. Furthermore, Rabban Shimon ben Gamliel said: Even** if a person **has nothing to eat, and** out of his need **he sold a Torah scroll or** he sold **his daughter** to be a maidservant, **he never sees a sign of blessing** from the proceeds of either sale. Clearly, it is never appropriate to sell a Torah scroll for any purpose.

HALAKHA

The placing of one scroll upon another – הַנָּחַת סֵפֶר עַל סֵפֶר: A Torah scroll may be placed upon another Torah scroll, and individual books of the Torah may be placed upon scrolls of the Prophets, the Writings, the Mishna, and the Talmud (Responsa of Rabbi Yosef Migash). However a scroll of the Prophets or Writings may not be placed upon individual books of the Torah, and individual books of the Torah may not be placed upon a full Torah scroll. However, scrolls of the Writings may be placed upon scrolls of the Prophets. These *halakhot* apply when the texts are written in distinct scrolls, but when they appear in the same scroll it does not matter if the text of the Prophets lies upon the text of the Torah when the scroll is rolled (*Shulḥan Arukh, Yoreh De'a* 282:19, and in the comments of Rema).

Selling a Torah scroll – מְכִירַת סֵפֶר תּוֹרָה: It is prohibited to sell a Torah scroll. This *halakha* applies only to scrolls that were made to be read to the public, but it is permitted to sell scrolls that were written for individuals (*Shakh*, citing Rabbeinu Manoaḥ). However, even in such a case, one will not see any blessing from the proceeds (*Arukh HaShulḥan*, citing *Beit Yosef*). This applies even if one has many Torah scrolls, and even if he has almost no food to eat (Rema).

It is also prohibited to sell a Torah scroll to buy a new one. However, it is permitted to sell a Torah scroll in order to use the proceeds for the study of Torah, if one has nothing else to sell. It is also permitted to sell a Torah scroll in order to free captives (Rema) and in order to get treatment for a dangerous illness (*Arukh HaShulḥan*). In these cases, selling a Torah scroll is permitted not only when the people in need are one's family, but to help anyone who has these needs, and doing so is indeed a great mitzva (*Shulḥan Arukh, Yoreh De'a* 270:1).

NOTES

A person may not sell a Torah scroll – לֹא יִמְכּוֹר אָדָם סֵפֶר תּוֹרָה: The early commentaries record two different versions of the Gemara here: The first version states: Even if he does not need it, meaning that he already has another Torah scroll in his possession. The other version has: Even if he has a need for it, meaning he has no money and needs the proceeds from the sale of the Torah scroll to buy necessities (*Mikhtam*).

״וְכֵן בְּמוֹתְרֵיהֶן״: אָמַר רָבָא: לֹא שָׁנוּ אֶלָּא שֶׁמָּכְרוּ וְהוֹתִירוּ, אֲבָל גָּבוּ וְהוֹתִירוּ מוּתָּר.

The mishna states: **And similarly,** the same limitation applies **to** any **surplus funds** from the sale of sacred items. **Rava said: They taught** that the surplus funds have sanctity **only** in a case **where** the community **sold** a sacred object and then used the proceeds to purchase something with a greater degree of sanctity, **and there was** money **left over. However, if** the community **collected** money from its members in order to purchase a sacred object, **and there was** extra money **left over**[H] beyond the price of the object, that extra money **is permitted**[N] to be used for any purpose, as the money was never sanctified.

אֵיתִיבֵיהּ אַבָּיֵי: בַּמֶּה דְּבָרִים אֲמוּרִים שֶׁלֹּא הִתְנוּ, אֲבָל הִתְנוּ – אֲפִילּוּ לְדוּכְסוּסְיָא מוּתָּר.

Abaye raised an objection to Rava from a *baraita*: **In what** case **is this statement** of the mishna **said? When they did not** explicitly **stipulate** that they would do with the surplus funds as they see fit. **However,** if **they made** such **a stipulation,** then **even** to use the money **for a** *dukhsusya* **is permitted.** The Gemara will explain the meaning of the term *dukhsusya*.

הֵיכִי דָמֵי? אִילֵימָא שֶׁמָּכְרוּ וְהוֹתִירוּ – כִּי הִתְנוּ מַאי הָוֵי? אֶלָּא שֶׁגָּבוּ וְהוֹתִירוּ, טַעְמָא – דְּהִתְנוּ, הָא לָא הִתְנוּ – לָא!

Abaye explains the challenge: **What are the circumstances** of this stipulation? **If we say that they sold** a sacred object **and** after using the proceeds to purchase another sacred object **there was** money **left over,** then even **when they made a stipulation, of what** avail **is it?** How can a stipulation desanctify the money? **Rather,** the mishna must be referring to a case **where they collected** money to purchase a sacred object **and there was** money **left over** after they made the purchase. In such a case, **the reason** that it is permitted to use the extra money for any purpose is **that they made** an explicit **stipulation. However, if they did not make a stipulation, no,** it would not be permitted.

לְעוֹלָם שֶׁמָּכְרוּ וְהוֹתִירוּ, וְהָכִי קָאָמַר: בַּמֶּה דְּבָרִים אֲמוּרִים – שֶׁלֹּא הִתְנוּ שִׁבְעָה טוֹבֵי הָעִיר בְּמַעֲמַד אַנְשֵׁי הָעִיר, אֲבָל הִתְנוּ שִׁבְעָה טוֹבֵי הָעִיר בְּמַעֲמַד אַנְשֵׁי הָעִיר – אֲפִילּוּ לְדוּכְסוּסְיָא נַמִי מוּתָּר.

Rava rejects this argument: **Actually,** you can explain that the mishna is referring to a case **where they sold** a sacred object **and there was** money **left over** after purchasing a new one, **and this is what** the *baraita* **is saying: In what** case **is this statement** of the mishna **said?** In a case **where the seven representatives of the town did not** explicitly **stipulate** that they could use the money as they see fit, **in an assembly of the residents of the town. However, if the seven representatives of the town made** such **a stipulation in an assembly of the residents of the town,** then **even** to use the money **for a** ***dukhsusya*** **would also be permitted.**

אֲמַר לֵיהּ אַבָּיֵי לְהַהוּא מֵרַבָּנַן דַּהֲוָה מְסַדֵּר מַתְנִיתָא קַמֵּיהּ דְּרַב שֵׁשֶׁת: מִי שְׁמִיעַ לָךְ מֵרַב שֵׁשֶׁת מַאי דּוּכְסוּסְיָא? אֲמַר לֵיהּ: הָכִי אֲמַר רַב שֵׁשֶׁת: פָּרָשָׁא דְּמָתָא.

Abaye said to one of the Sages who would arrange the Mishna before Rav Sheshet: Did you hear anything **from Rav Sheshet** with regard to **what** the meaning of the term ***dukhsusya***[L] is? **He said to him: This is what Rav Sheshet said:** It is **the town horseman** who would serve the townspeople as a sentry and for public dispatches.

אֲמַר אַבָּיֵי: הִלְכָּךְ, הַאי צוּרְבָא מֵרַבָּנַן דִּשְׁמַע לֵיהּ מִילְּתָא וְלָא יָדַע פֵּירוּשָׁא – לִישַׁיְילָה קַמֵּיהּ דִּשְׁכִיחַ קַמֵּיהּ רַבָּנַן, דְּלָא אֶפְשָׁר דְּלָא שְׁמִיעַ לֵיהּ מִן גַּבְרָא רַבָּה.

The Gemara introduces a parenthetical comment: **Abaye said: Accordingly,** one can learn from this incident that with regard to **this young Torah scholar who has heard something and does not know the meaning** of it, **he should inquire** of its meaning **before** somebody **who is frequently before the Sages, as it is impossible that** such a person **did not hear** something about it **from** some **great man.**

אָמַר רַבִּי יוֹחָנָן: מִשּׁוּם רַבִּי מֵאִיר: בְּנֵי הָעִיר שֶׁהָלְכוּ לְעִיר אַחֶרֶת וּפָסְקוּ עֲלֵיהֶן צְדָקָה – נוֹתְנִין, וּכְשֶׁהֵן בָּאִין מְבִיאִין אוֹתָהּ עִמָּהֶן, וּמְפַרְנְסִין בָּהּ עֲנִיֵּי עִירָן.

§ **Rabbi Yoḥanan said in the name of Rabbi Meir:** In the case of **residents of a town who** collectively **went to another town and,** while there, the charity collectors in that town **made them pledge** a certain sum for **charity,**[H] **they must give** the promised sum to the town's charity collector, so as not to be suspected of reneging. **But when they go** home, their money is returned to them, and **they bring it** back **with them, and with it they finance the poor of their** own **town.**

HALAKHA

If they collected and there was money left over – גָּבוּ וְהוֹתִירוּ: If money is collected in order to buy a sacred object, and the community wishes to use the money for something else, they may use it only in order to purchase something of a similar or greater degree of sanctity. The exception to this is when the funds were collected by the seven representatives of the town in an assembly of the residents of the town (*Magen Avraham*). If money was collected and there is money left over from the purchase, some say that the community may purchase with those funds whatever they see fit (*Magen Avraham*) and others say that they are allowed to purchase only items used in the fulfillment of mitzvot or for public needs (*Taz*). If it was stipulated when the money was collected that it may be used as the community sees fit, then even if they used the funds to purchase a sacred object, it is permitted for them to sell that object and purchase another object, even if the new object has a lower degree of sanctity than the first one. However, some prohibit this (*Shulḥan Arukh, Oraḥ Ḥayyim* 153:5).

One who pledged money in a different town – מִי שֶׁנָּדַר צְדָקָה בְּעִיר אַחֶרֶת: An individual who goes to a different town and pledges a sum to charity should give it to that town. If many people come together, they should give the sum to the town's collector, so that they are not suspected of reneging. When they are ready to return home, the town collector should return the money to them and they should take it home with them and then distribute it to the poor of their own town. However, if there is a Torah scholar in the town they go to, under all circumstances they should give the money to him and he decides to whom the money should be given. Money that is collected from villagers who come to the town to pray should be distributed in their village (*Shakh*, citing *Beit Yosef*). However one who purchased the right to perform a mitzva in a synagogue is required to give what he promised to that synagogue (*Shakh*; *Shulḥan Arukh, Yoreh De'a* 256:6).

NOTES

If they collected and there was money left over it is permitted – גָּבוּ וְהוֹתִירוּ מוּתָּר: When there are surplus funds after money is raised for charity for the poor or for redeeming captives, the *halakha* is that those funds must also be put to the same purpose for which they were raised. Why, then, does the Gemara state here that surplus funds do not need to be put to the same purpose for which they were collected? Some explain that since there are always poor people, any money that is collected is automatically dedicated to that cause. However, the Gemara here concerns a collection toward the purchase of a specific object. In such a case, only the sum that is necessary for that purchase is consecrated, since there was never any intention to buy similar objects with any surplus (Rashba).

LANGUAGE

Dukhsusya – **דּוּכְסוּסְיָא:** Rashi and others explain that this word is a composite of the words *dukh*, meaning place, and *sus*, meaning horse. Consequently, it refers to the horse and rider who serve a certain place. However, this explanation appears to be a homily. The source of the word is not clear, although some maintain that it is related to the Greek ταξεώτης, *taxeotès*, meaning a clerk who works for a municipality.

תַּנְיָא נַמִּי הָכִי: בְּנֵי הָעִיר שֶׁהָלְכוּ לְעִיר אַחֶרֶת וּפָסְקוּ עֲלֵיהֶן צְדָקָה – נוֹתְנִין, וּכְשֶׁהֵן בָּאִין מְבִיאִין אוֹתָהּ עִמָּהֶן. וְיָחִיד שֶׁהָלַךְ לְעִיר אַחֶרֶת וּפָסְקוּ עָלָיו צְדָקָה תִּנָּתֵן לַעֲנִיֵּי אוֹתָהּ הָעִיר.

The Gemara comments: **That is also taught** in a *baraita*: In the case of **residents of a town who** collectively **went to another town and,** while there, the local charity collectors **made them pledge** a certain sum for **charity, they must give** the promised sum to the town's charity collector. **But when they go** home, their money is returned to them, and **they bring it** back **with them. But** in the case of **an individual who went** from his hometown **to another town and,** while there, the local charity collectors **made him pledge** a certain sum for **charity, he should give it to the poor of that town.**

רַב הוּנָא גְּזַר תַּעֲנִיתָא, עָל לְגַבֵּיהּ רַב חָנָה בַּר חֲנִילַאי וְכָל בְּנֵי מָתֵיהּ, רָמוּ עֲלַיְיהוּ צְדָקָה וִיהַבוּ. כִּי בָּעוּ לְמֵיתֵי, אֲמַרוּ לֵיהּ: נוֹתְבַהּ לַן מָר, וְנֵיזוֹל וּנְפַרְנֵס בָּהּ עֲנִיֵּי מָאתִין!

The Gemara relates: **Rav Huna** once **decreed a fast day.** On the day of the fast, **Rav Ḥana bar Ḥanilai**[P] **and all the people of his town came to** Rav Huna. A certain sum of **charity was imposed upon them and they gave it. When they wanted to go** home, **they said to** Rav Huna: **May our Master give to us** the charity that we gave, **and we will go** back, **and with it we will finance the poor of our own town.**

אֲמַר לְהוּ: תַּנְיָא, בַּמֶּה דְּבָרִים אֲמוּרִים – בְּשֶׁאֵין שָׁם

He said to them: It was taught in a *baraita*: **In what** case **is this statement,** that the money is returned when the people leave, **said? When there is no**

PERSONALITIES

Rav Ḥana bar Ḥanilai – רַב חָנָא בַּר חֲנִילַאי: A second-generation Babylonian *amora*, Rav Ḥana bar Ḥanilai was probably the leader of a Jewish community near the town of Sura. On several occasions, he is presented as a disciple of Rav Huna, who in all probability was his primary teacher. He is also cited in discussions of *halakha* with Rav Ḥisda.

Rav Ḥana was apparently a wealthy man, as he was renowned for his charity and hospitality. Not only would he assist the poor, but he would do so in a manner that would allow the recipient to maintain his dignity and avoid shame.

Perek **IV**
Daf **27** Amud **b**

חָבֵר עִיר אֲבָל יֵשׁ שָׁם חָבֵר עִיר – תִּינָּתֵן לְחָבֵר עִיר. וְכָל שֶׁכֵּן דַּעֲנִיֵּי דִּידִי וְדִידְכוּ עֲלַי סְמִיכִי.

town scholar[N] supervising the handling of the community's needs, in the town in which the charity was collected. **However,** if **there is a town scholar there,** the money **should be given to the town scholar,** and he may use it as he sees fit. Since, in this case, the money had been given to Rav Huna, the use of the money should be up to his discretion. Rav Huna added: **And all the more so** in this instance, **as both my poor** in my town **and your** poor in your town **rely upon me** and my collections of charity. Rav Huna was also in charge of distributing charity for the surrounding area. It was certainly proper to leave the money with him, so that he could distribute it among all those in need.

מתני׳ אֵין מוֹכְרִין אֶת שֶׁל רַבִּים לְיָחִיד מִפְּנֵי שֶׁמּוֹרִידִין אוֹתוֹ מִקְּדוּשָּׁתוֹ, דִּבְרֵי רַבִּי מֵאִיר. אָמְרוּ לוֹ: אִם כֵּן אַף לֹא מֵעִיר גְּדוֹלָה לְעִיר קְטַנָּה.

MISHNA They may not sell a sacred object **belonging to the community to an individual,**[N] even if the object will still be used for the same purpose, **due to** the fact **that** by doing so **they downgrade its** degree of **sanctity,** as an item used by fewer people is considered to have a lower degree of sanctity than one used by many; this is **the statement of Rabbi Meir.** The Rabbis **said to him: If so,** by your logic, it should **also not** be permitted to sell a sacred object **from a large town to a small town.** However, such a sale is certainly permitted, and therefore it must also be permitted to sell such an object to an individual.

גמ׳ שַׁפִּיר קָאָמְרִי לֵיהּ רַבָּנַן לְרַבִּי מֵאִיר! וְרַבִּי מֵאִיר: מֵעִיר גְּדוֹלָה לְעִיר קְטַנָּה – מֵעִיקָּרָא קַדִּישָׁא, הָשְׁתָּא נַמִּי קַדִּישָׁא, מֵרַבִּים לְיָחִיד – לֵיכָּא קְדוּשָּׁה.

GEMARA The Gemara asks: **The Rabbis are saying well to Rabbi Meir,** as they provided a rational argument for their opinion. How could Rabbi Meir counter their claim? The Gemara answers: **Rabbi Meir** holds that when a sacred object is transferred **from a large town to a small town,** there is no significant downgrade in the degree of sanctity, **as at the outset it was sacred** for a community and **now too it is sacred** for a community. But when it is transferred **from a community to an individual,** there is a significant downgrade in the degree of sanctity, as **there is no** longer **the** degree of **sanctity** that existed beforehand.

NOTES

Town scholar – חָבֵר עִיר: The *ge'onim* deliberate on the meaning of this Hebrew expression, whether it should be read as *ḥaver ir*, referring to a Torah scholar who was appointed to oversee and take care of the town's needs, or as *ḥever ir*, referring to the town council.

They may not sell a sacred object belonging to the community – אֵין מוֹכְרִין אֶת שֶׁל רַבִּים לְיָחִיד: In the Jerusalem Talmud, there is a discussion about the opinion of Rabbi Meir. It concludes that his ruling pertains not to the sale of a synagogue, but rather to the sale of a Torah scroll that is used by the community. The Ra'avad explains in *Temim De'im* that the sanctity of a synagogue is to be viewed in some aspects as though it were inherent; the Ramban explains similarly. As such, even when its sanctity is transferred though a sale, it nevertheless retains a certain degree of sanctity. In a different vein, Rashi explains that according to Rabbi Meir the sale is itself considered disrespectful of the synagogue's sanctity.

וְרַבָּנַן: אִי אִיכָּא לְמֵיחַשׁ – כִּי הַאי גַּוְונָא נַמִּי אִיכָּא לְמֵיחַשׁ, מִשּׁוּם "בְּרׇב עָם הַדְרַת מֶלֶךְ".

And the Rabbis, how could they respond to Rabbi Meir's claim? **If there is** cause **to be concerned** about the decrease in the number of people who will use the object when it is transferred from a community to an individual, then **in a case like this as well,** where the object is transferred to a smaller community, **there** should be cause **to be concerned** about this **due to** the principle expressed in the verse: **"In the multitude of people is the king's glory"** (Proverbs 14:28). The verse teaches that the larger the assembly involved in a mitzva, the greater the honor to God. However, it is apparent that this principle does not prevent the sale of a synagogue to a smaller community, and therefore it should not prevent the selling of a synagogue to an individual.

מתני׳ אֵין מוֹכְרִין בֵּית הַכְּנֶסֶת אֶלָּא עַל תְּנַאי שֶׁאִם יִרְצוּ יַחֲזִירוּהוּ, דִּבְרֵי רַבִּי מֵאִיר. וַחֲכָמִים אוֹמְרִים: מוֹכְרִין אוֹתוֹ מִמְכַּר עוֹלָם, חוּץ מֵאַרְבָּעָה דְּבָרִים: לְמֶרְחָץ, וּלְבוּרְסְקִי, לִטְבִילָה, וּלְבֵית הַמַּיִם. רַבִּי יְהוּדָה אוֹמֵר: מוֹכְרִין אוֹתָהּ לְשֵׁם חָצֵר, וְהַלּוֹקֵחַ מַה שֶּׁיִּרְצֶה יַעֲשֶׂה.

MISHNA They may sell a synagogue only with a stipulation that if the sellers so **desire it,** the buyers **will return it** to them; this is **the statement of Rabbi Meir. And the Rabbis say: They may sell a synagogue with a permanent sale** for any usage, **except** the following **four things,** which would be an affront to the synagogue's previous sanctity: **For a bathhouse,** where people stand undressed; **or for a tannery** [***burseki***],[LB] due to the foul smell; **for immersion,** i.e., to be used as a ritual bath, where people also stand undressed; **or for a lavatory. Rabbi Yehuda says: They may sell** a synagogue **for** the generic purpose of **serving as a courtyard, and** then **the buyer may** then **do** with it **as he wishes,**[N] even if that is one of the above four purposes.[H]

גמ׳ וּלְרַבִּי מֵאִיר הֵיכִי דָּיְירִי בָּהּ? הָא הָוְיָא לָהּ רִבִּית!

GEMARA The Gemara asks: **But according to Rabbi Meir, how may** those who purchased the synagogue **live in it? Isn't** living there **tantamount** to taking **interest?** If the sellers demand the synagogue's return, the payment given for it would be returned to the buyers. Accordingly, in a broad view of things, that sum of money may be considered as a loan that was given from the buyers to the sellers, until the synagogue was demanded back. The buyers benefited from giving that loan by being able to live in the synagogue building. However, gaining any benefit from a loan is prohibited as interest.

אָמַר רַבִּי יוֹחָנָן: רַבִּי מֵאִיר בְּשִׁיטַת רַבִּי יְהוּדָה אֲמָרָהּ, דְּאָמַר: צַד אֶחָד בְּרִבִּית – מוּתָּר.

Rabbi Yoḥanan said: Rabbi Meir stated his opinion **in** accordance with **the opinion of Rabbi Yehuda, who said: Uncertain interest,**[N] i.e., a transaction that will not certainly result in a situation of interest, **is permitted.**

דְּתַנְיָא: הֲרֵי שֶׁהָיָה נוֹשֶׁה בַּחֲבֵירוֹ מָנֶה וְעָשָׂה לוֹ שָׂדֵהוּ מֶכֶר, בִּזְמַן שֶׁמּוֹכֵר אוֹכֵל פֵּירוֹת – מוּתָּר, לוֹקֵחַ אוֹכֵל פֵּירוֹת – אָסוּר.

In the case of the mishna, the sale might never be undone, and then there would be no loan to speak of. It should therefore be permitted as a case of uncertain interest, **as it is taught** in a *baraita*: If **one had a debt of one hundred dinars against his fellow, and** the borrower **made** a conditional **sale of his field** because he did not have any money to repay the loan, stipulating that if he later comes into the possession of money with which to repay the loan, the field reverts back to his ownership, then **as long as the seller** of the field **consumes the produce** of that field, such an arrangement **is permitted.** If the **buyer consumes the produce,** the arrangement is **prohibited,** as if the sale were to be reverted, then the money given for it would be considered a loan from the buyer to the seller, and therefore any benefit the buyer gains due to that loan should be prohibited as interest.

NOTES

And the buyer may do with it as he wishes – וְהַלּוֹקֵחַ מַה שֶּׁיִּרְצֶה יַעֲשֶׂה: Even Rabbi Yehuda agrees that it is not correct to sell the synagogue if one is aware that it will be used for an inappropriate purpose. The novelty of his ruling is that one need not inquire what the buyer intends, and the buyer may then use the place that was originally used as a synagogue for one of those four purposes, and there is no need to prevent him doing so (Rabbeinu Yehonatan).

Uncertain interest – צַד אֶחָד בְּרִבִּית: A case of uncertain interest occurs when the lender's chance of receiving any return on his loan is dependent on various circumstances and is not guaranteed. The case in the mishna is similar to this in that it is not certain that the transaction will involve a loan with interest. If the sale is never revoked, then the original payment for the field was indeed a payment and not a loan at all.

LANGUAGE

Tannery [*burseki*] – בּוּרְסְקִי: From the Greek βυρσική, *bursikè*. It means relating to the tanning of hides.

BACKGROUND

Tannery – בּוּרְסְקִי: Since tanning by ancient methods emits a foul smell, this trade was relegated to the outskirts of town, among the poor. Skins typically arrived at the tannery dried stiff and dirty with soil and blood. First, the tanners would soak the skins in water to clean and soften them. Then they would pound and scour the skin to remove any remaining flesh and fat. Next, the tanner needed to remove the hair fibers from the skin. This was done by soaking the skin in urine, painting it with an alkaline lime mixture, or allowing the skin to putrefy for several months before dipping it in a salt solution. Once the hair fibers were loosened, the tanners would scrape them off with a knife and then bate the material by pounding dung, usually from dogs or pigeons, into the hide. It was this combination of urine, animal feces and decaying flesh that made ancient tanneries so malodorous.

Old-fashioned leather tanning vats in Fez, Morocco

HALAKHA

How is a synagogue sold – כֵּיצַד מוֹכְרִים בֵּית כְּנֶסֶת: When the residents of a town sell a synagogue, they may sell it with a permanent sale. This ruling is in accordance with the Rabbis. The buyer may do with the building as he wishes, but he should not use it as a bathhouse, a tannery, a place for immersion, or a lavatory.

If it was sold by the seven representatives of the town in an assembly of the residents of the town, then the buyer may use it for any purpose. However, some suggest that the buyer may do so only if he was explicitly given permission at the time of the sale (*Peri Megadim*). Others suggest that this is permitted only in the case of a ruin of a synagogue that was sold (Ra'avad). Therefore, ideally the buyer should always avoid using the synagogue for any of these four uses (*Mishna Berura*; *Shulḥan Arukh*, *Oraḥ Ḥayyim* 153:9).

רַבִּי יְהוּדָה אוֹמֵר אֲפִילּוּ לוֹקֵחַ אוֹכֵל פֵּירוֹת מוּתָּר. וְאָמַר רַבִּי יְהוּדָה: מַעֲשֶׂה בְּבַיְתּוֹס בֶּן זוֹנִין שֶׁעָשָׂה שָׂדֵהוּ מֶכֶר עַל פִּי רַבִּי אֶלְעָזָר בֶּן עֲזַרְיָה, וְלוֹקֵחַ אוֹכֵל פֵּירוֹת הָיָה. אָמְרוּ לוֹ: מִשָּׁם רְאָיָה?! מוֹכֵר אוֹכֵל פֵּירוֹת הָיָה, וְלֹא לוֹקֵחַ.

Rabbi Yehuda says: Even if the **buyer consumes the produce, it is permitted.** Since it is possible that the sale might never be undone, in which case there would be no loan to speak of, it is a case of uncertain interest, which is permitted. **And Rabbi Yehuda said:** There was **an incident involving Baitos ben Zunen,**[LP] **who made** a conditional **sale of his field** in a similar arrangement **under the direction of Rabbi Elazar ben Azarya, and the buyer was consuming the produce** in accordance with Rabbi Yehuda's ruling. The Rabbis **said to him:** Do you seek to bring **a proof from there?** In that case, it was actually **the seller who was consuming the produce and not the buyer.**

מַאי בֵּינַיְיהוּ? צַד אֶחָד בְּרִבִּית אִיכָּא בֵּינַיְיהוּ. מָר סָבַר: צַד אֶחָד בְּרִבִּית – מוּתָּר, וּמָר סָבַר: צַד אֶחָד בְּרִבִּית – אָסוּר.

The Gemara analyses the dispute: **What is** the practical difference **between them?** The permissibility of **an uncertain interest** agreement **is the** practical difference **between them.** One **Sage,** Rabbi Yehuda, **holds** that **uncertain interest is permitted and** one **Sage,** i.e., the Rabbis, **holds** that **uncertain interest is prohibited.**

רָבָא אָמַר: דְּכוּלֵּי עָלְמָא צַד אֶחָד בְּרִבִּית אָסוּר, וְהָכָא רִבִּית עַל מְנָת לְהַחֲזִיר אִיכָּא בֵּינַיְיהוּ. מָר סָבַר: רִבִּית עַל מְנָת לְהַחֲזִיר – מוּתָּר, וּמָר סָבַר: אָסוּר.

Rava said a different explanation of the dispute: **According to everyone, uncertain interest is prohibited, and here** it is the question of the permissibility of **interest** given **on the condition that it will be returned** that is the practical difference **between them.** In addition to the arrangement described in the *baraita*, the parties in this case agreed that the buyer would consume the produce; if the sale would later be reverted, then the buyer would reimburse the seller for the value of the produce. One **Sage,** Rabbi Yehuda, **holds** that **interest** that is given **on condition that it will be returned is permitted;** this is because even if the sale is reverted and the sale becomes a loan retroactively, the buyer-lender will not benefit from that loan since he reimbursed the seller-borrower for the value of the produce. **And** one **Sage,** i.e., the Rabbis, **holds** that **it is prohibited.**

״וַחֲכָמִים אוֹמְרִים מוֹכְרִין אוֹתוֹ מִמְכַּר עוֹלָם״ וכו׳: אָמַר רַב יְהוּדָה אָמַר שְׁמוּאֵל: מוּתָּר לְאָדָם לְהַשְׁתִּין מַיִם בְּתוֹךְ אַרְבַּע אַמּוֹת שֶׁל תְּפִלָּה.

§ The mishna states: **And the Rabbis say: They may sell a synagogue with a permanent sale.** However, it may not be sold if it will be used for activities that would be an affront to the synagogue's previous sanctity. The Gemara considers a related *halakha*: **Rav Yehuda said** that **Shmuel said: It is permitted for a person to urinate within four cubits of** where one has just offered **a prayer,**[H] i.e., one may urinate even in the same place as he prays.

אָמַר רַב יוֹסֵף: מַאי קָא מַשְׁמַע לָן? תָּנֵינָא, רַבִּי יְהוּדָה אוֹמֵר: מוֹכְרִין אוֹתָהּ לְשׁוּם חָצֵר, וְלוֹקֵחַ מַה שֶּׁיִּרְצֶה יַעֲשֶׂה. וַאֲפִילּוּ רַבָּנַן לָא קָאָמְרִי אֶלָּא בֵּית הַכְּנֶסֶת דִּקְבִיעַ קְדוּשָּׁתֵיהּ, אֲבָל אַרְבַּע אַמּוֹת דְּלָא קְבִיעַ קְדוּשַּׁתַיְיהוּ – לָא.

Rav Yosef said: What is he teaching us? We already **learned** this in the mishna: **Rabbi Yehuda says: They may sell** a synagogue for the generic purpose of serving **as a courtyard, and the buyer may** then **do with it as he wishes,** even if he wishes to make it into a lavatory. **And even the Rabbis,** who disagree with Rabbi Yehuda, **say** their ruling **only** with regard to **a synagogue whose sanctity is permanent. However,** with regard to the **four cubits** of where one happened to stand in prayer, **whose sanctity is not permanent, no,** even the Rabbis would be lenient.

תָּנֵי תַּנָּא קַמֵּיהּ דְּרַב נַחְמָן: הַמִּתְפַּלֵּל מַרְחִיק אַרְבַּע אַמּוֹת וּמַשְׁתִּין, וְהַמַּשְׁתִּין מַרְחִיק אַרְבַּע אַמּוֹת וּמִתְפַּלֵּל.

A *tanna* **taught** a *baraita* **before Rav Naḥman: One who prayed should distance himself four cubits** from where he was standing, and only then **may he urinate. And one who urinated should distance himself four cubits, and** only then **may he pray.**

אֲמַר לֵיהּ: בִּשְׁלָמָא הַמַּשְׁתִּין מַרְחִיק אַרְבַּע אַמּוֹת וּמִתְפַּלֵּל תָּנֵינָא: כַּמָּה יַרְחִיק מֵהֶן וּמִן הַצּוֹאָה – אַרְבַּע אַמּוֹת,

Rav Naḥman **said to him: Granted,** the second clause of the *baraita*, that **one who urinated should distance himself four cubits and** only then **may he pray,** makes sense, as **we** already **learned** in a mishna (*Berakhot* 22b): **How far must one distance** oneself **from** urine **and excrement? Four cubits.**

אֶלָּא הַמִּתְפַּלֵּל מַרְחִיק אַרְבַּע אַמּוֹת וּמַשְׁתִּין לָמָּה לִי? אִי הָכִי, קִדַּשְׁתִּינְהוּ לְכוּלְּהוּ שְׁבִילֵי דִּנְהַרְדְּעָא! תְּנֵי: יְשַׁהֶה.

But the first clause of the *baraita*, that **one who prayed should distance** himself **four cubits** from where he was standing **and** only then **may he urinate, why should I** require this? How could there be such a *halakha*? **If that is so, you have sanctified all the streets of the city of Neharde'a,** for people have certainly prayed on every one of its streets. According to this *halakha*, it should be prohibited to urinate everywhere. The Gemara answers: Emend and **teach** the *baraita* as saying not that one should distance himself four cubits, but that **one should wait the time** it takes to walk four cubits.

LANGUAGE

Baitos ben Zunen – בַּיְתּוֹס בֶּן זוֹנִין: The name Baitos, Boëthus in Greek, is from the Greek word βοηθός, *boēthus*, meaning assistant. It is possible that it is a translation of the Hebrew name Ezra, meaning help. Zunen is from the Greek name Ζήνων, Zeno, and may derive from the word ζιζάνιον, *zizanion*, meaning darnel.

PERSONALITIES

Baitos ben Zunen – בַּיְתּוֹס בֶּן זוֹנִין: Baitos was a man of means and stature. He resided in Lod during the days of Rabban Gamliel of Yavne. From many sources in the Gemara, it appears that he was a major importer and exporter of goods, and he possessed large amounts of real estate. It appears that he was closely associated to the house of the *Nasi*, and he was careful to ensure that all of his actions were carried out according to opinions of the Sages. As such, proofs of a particular *halakha* are often adduced from his actions. It may be that Zunen, Baitos's father, was the same Zunen who served as Rabban Gamliel's assistant. Alternatively, the Gemara also mentions another Zunen who was a man of significance during the days of Rabbi Yehuda HaNasi.

HALAKHA

Distancing from urine – הַרְחָקָה מִמֵּי רַגְלַיִים: If one is reciting the *Shema* and urine falls on the ground near him, he should distance himself four cubits from it or wait until it is absorbed into the ground before continuing (Rema). If urine falls during his recitation of the *Amida*, when it is prohibited for him to move his feet, and consequently he is unable to distance himself from the urine, he should spill water on it. If he has none, he may continue praying (see *Taz*, citing *Beit Yosef*). Some say that even during the *Amida* one may move to distance oneself from urine (*Arukh HaShulḥan*; *Shulḥan Arukh*, *Oraḥ Ḥayyim* 78:1).

בשלמא משתין ישהה כדי הילוך ארבע אמות – משום ניצוצות, אלא מתפלל ישהה כדי הילוך ארבע אמות למה לי? אמר רב אשי: שכל ארבע אמות תפלתו סדורה בפיו ורחושי מרחשן שפוותיה.

The Gemara addresses the emended version of the *baraita*: **Granted,** its second clause, that **one who urinated waits the time it takes to walk four cubits**[H] and only then may he pray, makes sense. This is **due to the droplets** of urine that may still be issuing from him; he should wait until they cease entirely. **However,** with regard to the first clause, that **one who prayed should wait the time it takes to walk four cubits** and only then may he urinate, **why should I** require this? **Rav Ashi said: Because** for **all** the time it takes to walk **four cubits, his prayer is** still **arranged in his mouth, and his lips are** still **articulating** them.

זלפ״ן סימן.

§ The Gemara cites a series of Sages who explained the reasons they were blessed with longevity and provides **a mnemonic** device, indicating the order in which the Sages are cited: ***Zayin, lamed, peh, nun.*** *Zayin* for Rabbi Zakkai; *lamed* for Rabbi Elazar; *peh* for Rabbi Perida; *nun* for Rabbi Neḥunya.

שאלו תלמידיו את רבי זכאי: במה הארכת ימים? אמר להם: מימי לא השתנתי מים בתוך ארבע אמות של תפלה, ולא כניתי שם לחבירי, ולא ביטלתי קידוש היום. אמא זקינה היתה לי, פעם אחת מכרה כפה שבראשה והביאה לי קידוש היום.

The Gemara presents the first incident: **Rabbi Zakkai was** once **asked by his disciples: In** the merit of **which** virtue **were you** blessed with **longevity?**[N] **He said to them: In all my days, I never urinated within four cubits of** a place that had been used for **prayer. Nor did I** ever **call my fellow by a nickname.**[N] **And I never neglected** the mitzva of **sanctifying the day** of Shabbat over wine.[N] I was meticulous about this mitzva to the extent that **I had an elderly mother,** and **once,** when I did not have wine, **she sold the kerchief that was on her head, and** from the proceeds **she brought me** wine upon which to do the mitzva of **sanctifying the day.**

תנא: כשמתה הניחה לו שלוש מאות גרבי יין, כשמת הוא הניח לבניו שלשת אלפים גרבי יין.

It was taught concerning Rabbi Zakkai: **When** his mother **died, she left him three hundred barrels of wine. When he died,** he **left his sons three thousand barrels of wine.** Since they were so meticulous in the mitzva of sanctifying the day of Shabbat with wine, God rewarded them with wealth and an abundance of wine.

רב הונא הוה אסר ריתא וקאי קמיה דרב, אמר ליה: מאי האי? אמר ליה: לא הוה לי קידושא, ומשכנתיה להמיינאי, ואתאי ביה קידושא. אמר ליה: יהא רעוא דתיטום בשיראי.

In a related incident, it once happened that **Rav Huna was girded with** a piece of **straw** [*rita*][L] **and was standing before Rav.** Rav **said to him: What is this?** Why are you dressed in this way? **He said** to him: **I had no** wine for **sanctifying** the day of Shabbat, **so I pawned my belt** [*hemyanai*],[L] **and with** the proceeds **I brought** wine for **sanctifying** the day. Rav **said to him: May it be** God's **will** that **you be enveloped in silk** [*shira'ei*][L] in reward for such dedication.

כי איכלל רבה בריה, רב הונא איניש גוצא הוה, גנא אפוריא, אתיין בנתיה וכלתיה שלחן ושדיין מנייהו עליה, עד דאיטום בשיראי. שמע רב ואיקפד, אמר: מאי טעמא לא אמרת לי כי ברכתיך וכן למר?

When Rabba, his son, was married, Rav Huna, who **was a short man, was lying on** his **bed,** and owing to his diminutive size he went unnoticed. **His daughters and daughters-in-law came** into the room and **removed and threw their** silk **garments upon him until he was** entirely **enveloped in silk.** With this, Rav's blessing was fulfilled to the letter. When **Rav heard** about this, **he became angry** with Rav Huna, and **said: What is the reason** that **when I blessed you, you did not** respond in kind and **say to me: And likewise to the Master?** Had you done so, I would have also benefitted from the blessing.

HALAKHA

One…waits the time it takes to walk four cubits – ישהה כדי הילוך ארבע אמות: After urinating, it is prohibited to pray until the time it takes to walk four cubits has passed. Similarly, one who prayed should not urinate until he has waited the time it takes to walk four cubits, as the words of prayer are still on his lips. It is permitted to urinate in a place where one prayed; nevertheless, refraining from doing so is a righteous custom (*Magen Avraham*; *Shulḥan Arukh*, *Oraḥ Ḥayyim* 92:8).

LANGUAGE

Straw [*rita*] – **ריתא:** Possibly related to the New Persian rišta, meaning thread.

My belt [*hemyanai*] – **המיינאי:** Originally from the Iranian hamyān, meaning a belt apparently worn by priests. This word was adapted to Hebrew during the time of the Mishna.

Silk [*shira'ei*] – **שיראי:** Apparently from the Greek σηρικόν, *sērikon*, meaning silk or silk garment.

NOTES

In the merit of which virtue were you blessed with longevity – במה הארכת ימים: As a general principle, reward for the fulfillment of mitzvot is not given in this world, only in the World-to-Come. Nevertheless, it is clear from the Gemara here that someone who is meticulous in his observance of certain practices may be blessed with longevity. The commentaries assume this is true only when a person does more than what is required by *halakha*. They explain all of the Gemara's examples in this vein (see Maharsha).

Nor did I ever call my fellow by a nickname – ולא כניתי שם לחבירי: Rabbeinu Yehonatan explains that he was careful not to use a derogatory nickname even if it had been long established in a family or even if the person was not bothered by it (see *Tosafot*).

And I never neglected the mitzva of sanctifying the day of Shabbat over wine – ולא ביטלתי קידוש היום: The Rashba explains that it is in fact perfectly permitted to sanctify the day on bread. Reciting *kiddush* over wine is considered a more beautiful way to fulfill the mitzva, but strictly speaking it is unnecessary. Rabbi Zakkai went beyond the normative requirement by always striving to sanctify the day over wine, and he was therefore blessed for doing so.

Most commentaries, however, disagree with the Rashba and assume that sanctifying the day on wine is not simply a praiseworthy practice but a rabbinic requirement. Even so, when wine is not available, one is not required to seek it out, and one may use bread instead. Nevertheless, Rabbi Zakkai always ensured he had wine and was blessed for his behavior.

שָׁאֲלוּ תַּלְמִידָיו אֶת רַבִּי אֶלְעָזָר בֶּן שַׁמּוּעַ: בַּמֶּה הֶאֱרַכְתָּ יָמִים? אָמַר לָהֶם: מִיָּמַי לֹא עָשִׂיתִי קַפֶּנְדַּרְיָא לְבֵית הַכְּנֶסֶת, וְלֹא פָּסַעְתִּי עַל רָאשֵׁי עַם קָדוֹשׁ, וְלֹא נָשָׂאתִי כַּפַּי בְּלֹא בְּרָכָה.

The Gemara discusses the second occasion where a Sage explained his longevity: **Rabbi Elazar ben Shammua**[P] **was** once **asked by his disciples: In** the merit of **which** virtue **were you** blessed with **longevity? He said to them: In all my days, I never made a shortcut**[N] **through a synagogue. Nor did I** ever **stride over** the **heads of** the **sacred people**, i.e., I never stepped over people sitting in the study hall in order to reach my place, so as not to appear scornful of them. **And I never raised my hands** in the Priestly Benediction **without** reciting **a blessing** beforehand.[N]

שָׁאֲלוּ תַּלְמִידָיו אֶת רַבִּי פְּרִידָא: בַּמֶּה הֶאֱרַכְתָּ יָמִים? אָמַר לָהֶם: מִיָּמַי לֹא קְדָמַנִי אָדָם לְבֵית הַמִּדְרָשׁ

On the third occasion, **Rabbi Perida was** once **asked by his disciples: In** the merit of **which** virtue **were you** blessed with **longevity? He said to them: In all my days, no person** ever arrived **before me to the study hall**, as I was always the first to arrive.

PERSONALITIES

Rabbi Elazar ben Shammua – רַבִּי אֶלְעָזָר בֶּן שַׁמּוּעַ: Rabbi Elazar ben Shammua was a *tanna* in the generation prior to the redaction of the Mishna and was among the greatest of Rabbi Akiva's students. Rabbi Elazar was among the leaders of the Jewish people in the years following the persecution in the wake of the failure of the bar Kokheva rebellion. Despite the dire situation, many students studied with him. One of his primary students was Rabbi Yehuda HaNasi, the redactor of the Mishna. Not many of Rabbi Elazar's *halakhot* are cited in the Mishna; however, he was held in high esteem by the Sages of the following generations. Rav, an *amora*, referred to him as the happiest of the Sages, and Rabbi Yoḥanan said of him: The hearts of the early Sages were like the Entrance Hall to the Sanctuary. In the Mishna and in *baraitot*, he is called simply Rabbi Elazar.

Rabbi Elazar ben Shammua lived a long life. According to one tradition he was 105 years old when he was killed. He is listed among the ten martyrs executed by the Romans.

NOTES

I never made a shortcut – לֹא עָשִׂיתִי קַפֶּנְדַּרְיָא: Generally, it is prohibited to take a shortcut through a synagogue. Therefore, some explain that Rabbi Elazar ben Shammua was particular about this even in cases where it was permitted to do so, such as in cases where the shortcut predated the synagogue. Similarly, a person who is needed by the community may stride over the people's heads. However, even in such a case, Rabbi Elazar ben Shammua was careful not to do so (see *Ramat Shmuel* and *Turei Even*).

And I never raised my hands without a blessing – וְלֹא נָשָׂאתִי כַּפַּי בְּלֹא בְּרָכָה: The raising of one's hands in the Priestly Benediction and reciting a blessing upon doing so is an obligation upon every priest. What was unique here about Rabbi Elazar ben Shammua's behavior? Some explain that he would make a blessing even in cases where he could have relied on the blessing of his peers, since he had already fulfilled the mitzva once that day. Others suggest that Rabbi Elazar ben Shammua was referring to various additional blessings that were customary for priests to say following the Priestly Benediction (see Rabbi Yoshiya Pinto, Ritva, and Meiri).

Perek **IV**
Daf **28** Amud **a**

וְלֹא בֵּרַכְתִּי לִפְנֵי כֹּהֵן, וְלֹא אָכַלְתִּי מִבְּהֵמָה שֶׁלֹּא הוּרְמוּ מַתְּנוֹתֶיהָ.

And I never recited Grace after Meals **in the presence of a priest**, but rather I gave him the privilege to lead. **And I never ate from an animal whose** priestly **portions**,[N] i.e., the foreleg, the jaw, and the maw, **had not** already **been set aside.**

דְּאָמַר רַבִּי יִצְחָק אָמַר רַבִּי יוֹחָנָן: אָסוּר לֶאֱכוֹל מִבְּהֵמָה שֶׁלֹּא הוּרְמוּ מַתְּנוֹתֶיהָ. וְאָמַר רַבִּי יִצְחָק: כָּל הָאוֹכֵל מִבְּהֵמָה שֶׁלֹּא הוּרְמוּ מַתְּנוֹתֶיהָ – כְּאִילּוּ אוֹכֵל טְבָלִים. וְלֵית הִלְכְתָא כְּוָותֵיהּ.

Another example of Rabbi Perida's meticulous behavior is based on that **which Rabbi Yitzḥak said** that **Rabbi Yoḥanan said: It is prohibited to eat** meat **from an animal whose** priestly **portions have not been set aside.**[H] **And Rabbi Yitzḥak said: Anyone who eats** meat **from an animal whose** priestly **portions have not been set aside is** regarded **as if he were eating untithed produce.** The Gemara comments: **And the *halakha* is not in accordance with his** opinion. Rather, it is permitted to eat meat from such an animal. Nevertheless, Rabbi Perida acted stringently and did not eat from it.

וְלֹא בֵּרַכְתִּי לִפְנֵי כֹּהֵן,

The Gemara considers another of Rabbi Perida's actions: He said: **And I never blessed** Grace after Meals **in the presence of a priest,** but rather I gave him the privilege to lead.

לְמֵימְרָא דְּמַעַלְיוּתָא הִיא? וְהָא אָמַר רַבִּי יוֹחָנָן: כָּל תַּלְמִיד חָכָם שֶׁמְּבָרֵךְ לְפָנָיו, אֲפִילּוּ כֹּהֵן גָּדוֹל עַם הָאָרֶץ – אוֹתוֹ תַּלְמִיד חָכָם חַיָּיב מִיתָה, שֶׁנֶּאֱמַר ״כָּל מְשַׂנְאַי אָהֲבוּ מָוֶת״. אַל תִּקְרֵי ״מְשַׂנְאַי״ אֶלָּא מַשְׂנִיאַי!

Is this to say that doing so is especially **virtuous? But** hasn't **Rabbi Yoḥanan said: Any Torah scholar who** allows someone else **to bless** Grace after Meals **in his presence,** i.e., to lead for him, **even if** that person is **a High Priest who is an ignoramus,** then **that Torah scholar is liable to** receive the **death penalty** for belittling his own honor? This is **as it is stated: "All those who hate me, love death"** (Proverbs 8:36). **Do not read** it as **"those who hate Me [*mesan'ai*],"** rather read it as though it said: **Those who make Me hated [*masni'ai*].** The honor due to a Torah scholar is representative of the honor of God in the world. Therefore, by belittling his own honor, he causes others to fail to respect God, which can ultimately develop into hate. If so, why did Rabbi Perida consider his behavior to be so deserving of praise?

NOTES

Priestly portions – מַתְּנוֹתֶיהָ: The Torah specifies that the foreleg, the jaw, and the maw of an animal should be given to a priest (Deuteronomy 18:3). These gifts differ from the priestly tithes separated from grain and produce of the land in two ways: First, from the outset these gifts are distinct and defined parts of the animals, unlike the tithes, which are taken as a portion of the grain as a whole. Second, unlike the tithes, the foreleg, the jaw, and the maw have no sanctity, and therefore the priest who receives them may give them to a non-priest to consume. For these reasons, it is permitted to consume those parts of the animal that do not have to be given to a priest, even before one has given the parts that do have to be so given (Ritva).

HALAKHA

An animal whose priestly portions have not been set aside – בְּהֵמָה שֶׁלֹּא הוּרְמוּ מַתְּנוֹתֶיהָ: The *halakha* is not in accordance with the opinion of Rabbi Yitzḥak. It is permitted to eat from an animal whose priestly portions have not been set aside (Rambam *Sefer Zera'im*, *Hilkhot Bikkurim* 9:14).

כִּי קָאָמַר אִיהוּ – בְּשָׁוִין.

The Gemara answers: **When** Rabbi Perida **says this,** he was speaking **of** people of **equal** stature. He was particular to honor the priesthood only when the priest was also a Torah scholar.

שָׁאֲלוּ תַּלְמִידָיו אֶת רַבִּי נְחוּנְיָא בֶּן הַקָּנָה: בַּמֶּה הֶאֱרַכְתָּ יָמִים? אָמַר לָהֶם: מִיָּמַי לֹא נִתְכַּבַּדְתִּי בִּקְלוֹן חֲבֵרִי, וְלֹא עָלְתָה עַל מִטָּתִי קִלְלַת חֲבֵרִי, וַוְתְּרָן בְּמָמוֹנִי הָיִיתִי.

The Gemara discusses the fourth Sage who was blessed with longevity: **Rabbi Neḥunya ben HaKana was** once **asked by his disciples: In** the merit of **which** virtue **were you** blessed with **longevity? He said to them: In** all **my days, I never attained veneration at** the expense of **my fellow's degradation. Nor did my fellow's curse** ever **go up with me upon my bed.** If ever I offended someone, I made sure to appease him that day. Therefore, when I went to bed I knew that no one had any grievances against me. **And I was** always **openhanded with my money.**

לֹא נִתְכַּבַּדְתִּי בִּקְלוֹן חֲבֵרִי – כִּי הָא דְּרַב הוּנָא דְּרֵי מָרָא אַכַּתְפֵּיהּ, אֲתָא רַב חָנָא בַּר חֲנִילָאִי וְקָא דָּרֵי מִינֵּיהּ. אֲמַר לֵיהּ: אִי רְגִילַתְּ דְּדָרֵית בְּמָאתִיךְ – דְּרֵי, וְאִי לָא – אִתְיַיקּוּרֵי אֲנָא בְּזִילוּתָא דִּידָךְ, לָא נִיחָא לִי.

The Gemara clarifies the meaning of his statement: Rabbi Neḥunya said: **I never attained veneration at** the expense of **my fellow's denigration.**[N] This is referring to conduct **such as that of Rav Huna, who was carrying a hoe over his shoulder** as he returned from his work. **Rav Ḥana bar Ḥanilai came and,** out of respect for his teacher, **took the hoe from him** to carry it for him. Rav Huna **said to him: If you are accustomed to carry** such objects **in your own city,** you may **carry it; but if not,** then **for me to be venerated through your denigration is not pleasing for me.**

וְלֹא עָלְתָה עַל מִטָּתִי קִלְלַת חֲבֵרִי – כִּי הָא דְּמָר זוּטְרָא, כִּי הֲוָה סָלֵיק לְפוּרְיֵיהּ אֲמַר: שְׁרֵי לֵיהּ לְכָל מַאן דְּצַעֲרָן.

Rabbi Neḥunya also said: **Nor did** I ever allow the resentment caused by **my fellow's curse** to **go up with me upon my bed.** This is referring to conduct **such as that of Mar Zutra. When he would go to bed** at night, **he would** first **say: I forgive anyone who has vexed me.**

וַוְתְּרָן בְּמָמוֹנִי הָיִיתִי – דַּאֲמַר מָר: אִיּוֹב וַוְתְּרָן בְּמָמוֹנֵיהּ הֲוָה, שֶׁהָיָה מַנִּיחַ פְּרוּטָה לַחֶנְוָנִי מִמָּמוֹנֵיהּ.

Lastly, Rabbi Neḥunya said: **And I was** always **openhanded with my money.** This is referring to conduct such as **that which the Master said: Job was openhanded with his money, as he would** always **leave** at least **a** *peruta* **of his money with the shopkeeper.** He never demanded the change from his transactions.

שָׁאַל רַבִּי עֲקִיבָא אֶת רַבִּי נְחוּנְיָא הַגָּדוֹל, (אָמַר לוֹ) בַּמֶּה הֶאֱרַכְתָּ יָמִים? אָתוּ גַּוְוזֵי וְקָא מָחוּ לֵיהּ. סְלֵיק יְתֵיב אַרֵישָׁא דְּדִיקְלָא, אֲמַר לֵיהּ: רַבִּי, אִם נֶאֱמַר ״כֶּבֶשׂ״ לָמָּה נֶאֱמַר ״אֶחָד״? אֲמַר לְהוּ: צוּרְבָא מִדְּרַבָּנַן הוּא, שְׁבַקוּהוּ.

On a similar occasion, **Rabbi Akiva asked Rabbi Neḥunya the Great; he said to him: In** the merit of **which** virtue **were you** blessed with **longevity?** Rabbi Neḥunya's **attendants** [*gavzei*][L] **came and** started **beating** Rabbi Akiva, for they felt that he was acting disrespectfully by highlighting Rabbi Neḥunya's old age. Rabbi Akiva ran away from them, and **he climbed up and sat upon the top of a date palm.** From there, **he said to** Rabbi Neḥunya: **My teacher,** I have a question about the verse concerning the daily offering that states "one lamb" (Numbers 28:4). **If it is stated "lamb"** in the singular, **why is it** also **stated "one";**[N] isn't this superfluous? Upon hearing Rabbi Akiva's scholarly question, Rabbi Neḥunya **said to** his attendants: **He is** clearly **a young Torah scholar, let him be.**

אֲמַר לֵיהּ: ״אֶחָד״ מְיוּחָד שֶׁבְּעֶדְרוֹ.

Rabbi Neḥunya then addressed Rabbi Akiva's questions. With regard to the second question, **he said to him:** The word **"one"** teaches that the lamb should be **the unique one of its flock,** i.e., only the best quality lamb should be used.

אֲמַר לֵיהּ: מִיָּמַי לֹא קִבַּלְתִּי מַתָּנוֹת, וְלֹא עָמַדְתִּי עַל מִדּוֹתַי, וַוְתְּרָן בְּמָמוֹנִי הָיִיתִי.

With regard to the original question, Rabbi Neḥunya **said to him: In** all **my days I never accepted gifts. Nor was I** ever **inflexible** by exacting **a measure** of retribution[H] against those who wronged me. **And I was** always **openhanded with my money.**

NOTES

I never attained veneration at the expense of my fellow's denigration – לֹא נִתְכַּבַּדְתִּי בִּקְלוֹן חֲבֵרִי: To pursue honor through degrading one's fellow is certainly prohibited. Rabbi Neḥunya ben HaKana was praiseworthy because he would not accept veneration even in cases where other people wished to do so at their own expense, such as in the case of Rav Huna, cited by the Gemara.

If it is stated lamb why is it also stated one – אִם נֶאֱמַר כֶּבֶשׂ לָמָּה נֶאֱמַר אֶחָד: It would appear that the question is relatively simple. How, then, did it prove to Rabbi Neḥunya that Rabbi Akiva was a Torah scholar? Some note that in the *Sifrei* there is an extended discussion with regard to the repeated appearances in the Torah of the mitzva to bring the daily offering. They explain that Rabbi Akiva demonstrated his scholarship by referring to that discussion (*Gan Naul*; see *Noda Bihuda*). Others explain that Rabbi Akiva was hinting to his first question. He knew that the meaning of "one lamb" was that only the unique animal in the flock is chosen to be used as an offering to God. With this he hinted that his original question was to be understood as follows: What unique virtue of Rabbi Neḥunya was responsible for his longevity? (*Re'aḥ Duda'im*).

LANGUAGE

Attendants [*gavzei*] – גַּוְוזֵי: This word also means a eunuch. It would appear that the root is *g-o-z*, or *g-z-z*, both of which mean cut. Kings would often use eunuchs as their servants, and the term eventually came to be used to refer to a servant in general.

HALAKHA

Nor was I inflexible by exacting a measure of retribution – וְלֹא עָמַדְתִּי עַל מִדּוֹתַי: One should not be merciless when it comes to forgiving an injustice that has been done to him. However, if one's intention in not forgiving is ultimately for the benefit of the person who wronged him, it is permitted to refuse forgiveness (*Magen Avraham*). In all cases, one must certainly banish any feelings of hate from his heart (*Mishna Berura*). One does not have to forgive another who slandered him; however, a humble person will do so (*Magen Avraham*, citing *Yam Shel Shlomo*). One is required to forgive the the person who wronged him if he publicly states his remorse (*Arukh HaShulḥan*; *Shulḥan Arukh*, *Oraḥ Ḥayyim* 606:1, and in the comment of Rema).

לֹא קִבַּלְתִּי מַתָּנוֹת, כִּי הָא דְּרַבִּי אֶלְעָזָר, כִּי הָווּ מְשַׁדְּרִי לֵיהּ מַתָּנוֹת מִבֵּי נְשִׂיאָה לָא הֲוָה שָׁקֵיל, כִּי הֲוָה מְזַמְּנִי לֵיהּ – לָא הֲוָה אָזֵיל, אֲמַר לְהוּ: לָא נִיחָא לְכוּ דְּאֶחְיֶה? דִּכְתִיב ״שׂוֹנֵא מַתָּנוֹת יִחְיֶה״. רַבִּי זֵירָא, כִּי הָווּ מְשַׁדְּרִי לֵיהּ מִבֵּי נְשִׂיאָה – לָא הֲוָה שָׁקֵיל, כִּי הֲוָה מְזַמְּנִי לֵיהּ – אָזֵיל, אֲמַר: אִתְיַיקּוּרֵי דְּמִתְיַיקְּרִי בִּי.

The Gemara explains: **I never accepted gifts;** this is referring to conduct **such as that of Rabbi Elazar. When they would send him gifts from the house of the *Nasi*, he would not take** them, **and when they would invite him, he would not go** there, as he considered hospitality to be a type of gift. **He would say to them: Is it not pleasing to you that I should live, as it is written: "He that hates gifts shall live"** (Proverbs 15:27)? In contrast, it was reported about **Rabbi Zeira**[P] that **when they would send him** gifts **from the house of the *Nasi*, he would not accept** them, **but when they would invite him, he would go** there. **He said: They are honored by my** presence; therefore my visiting is not considered like I am taking a gift from them.

וְלֹא עָמַדְתִּי עַל מִדּוֹתַי – דְּאָמַר רָבָא: כׇּל הַמַּעֲבִיר עַל מִדּוֹתָיו מַעֲבִירִין מִמֶּנּוּ כׇּל פְּשָׁעָיו, שֶׁנֶּאֱמַר ״נוֹשֵׂא עָוֹן וְעוֹבֵר עַל פֶּשַׁע״ לְמִי נוֹשֵׂא עָוֹן – לְמִי שֶׁעוֹבֵר עַל פֶּשַׁע.

He also said: **Nor was I** ever **inflexible** in exacting **a measure** of retribution against those who wronged me. This is referring to conduct such as that **which Rava said: Anyone who overlooks** exacting **a measure** of retribution against those who wronged him, **all his transgressions are removed from him, as it is stated: "He pardons iniquity and overlooks transgression"** (Micah 7:18), which is homiletically read as saying: **For whom does He pardon iniquity? For he who overlooks transgressions** that others have committed against him.

שָׁאַל רַבִּי אֶת רַבִּי יְהוֹשֻׁעַ בֶּן קׇרְחָה: בַּמֶּה הֶאֱרַכְתָּ יָמִים? אֲמַר לֵיהּ: קַצְתָּ בְּחַיַּי? אָמַר לוֹ: רַבִּי, תּוֹרָה הִיא וְלִלְמוֹד אֲנִי צָרִיךְ, אֲמַר לֵיהּ: מִיָּמַי לֹא נִסְתַּכַּלְתִּי בִּדְמוּת אָדָם רָשָׁע. דְּאָמַר רַבִּי יוֹחָנָן: אָסוּר לְאָדָם לְהִסְתַּכֵּל בְּצֶלֶם דְּמוּת אָדָם רָשָׁע, שֶׁנֶּאֱמַר ״לוּלֵא פְּנֵי יְהוֹשָׁפָט מֶלֶךְ יְהוּדָה אֲנִי נוֹשֵׂא אִם אַבִּיט אֵלֶיךָ וְאִם אֶרְאֶךָּ״.

In a similar incident, **Rabbi Yehuda HaNasi** once **asked Rabbi Yehoshua ben Korḥa:**[P] **In** the merit of **which** virtue **were you** blessed with **longevity? He said to him:** Why do you ask me, **are you wearied of my** long **life?** Rabbi Yehuda HaNasi **said to him: My teacher, it is Torah and** so **I must learn** it. Rabbi Yehoshua ben Korḥa **said to him: In all my days I never gazed at the likeness of a wicked man, as Rabbi Yoḥanan said: It is prohibited for a person to gaze in the image of the likeness of a wicked man,**[N] **as it is stated** that the prophet Elisha said to Jehoram king of Israel: **"Were it not that I regard the presence of Jehoshaphat, the king of Judea, I would not look toward you, nor see you"** (II Kings 3:14).

רַבִּי אֶלְעָזָר אָמַר: עֵינָיו כֵּהוֹת, שֶׁנֶּאֱמַר ״וַיְהִי כִּי זָקֵן יִצְחָק וַתִּכְהֶיןָ עֵינָיו מֵרְאֹת״, מִשּׁוּם דְּאִסְתַּכֵּל בְּעֵשָׂו הָרָשָׁע.

Rabbi Elazar said: One who gazes at the likeness of an evil man, **his eyes become dim, as it is stated: "And it came to pass, that when Isaac was old, and his eyes were dim so that he could not see"** (Genesis 27:1). This happened **because he gazed at the wicked Esau.**

וְהָא גָּרְמָא לֵיהּ? וְהָאָמַר רַבִּי יִצְחָק: לְעוֹלָם אַל תְּהִי קִלְלַת הֶדְיוֹט קַלָּה בְּעֵינֶיךָ, שֶׁהֲרֵי אֲבִימֶלֶךְ קִלֵּל אֶת שָׂרָה וְנִתְקַיֵּים בְּזַרְעָהּ, שֶׁנֶּאֱמַר ״הִנֵּה הוּא לָךְ כְּסוּת עֵינַיִם״, אַל תִּקְרֵי ״כְּסוּת״ אֶלָּא כְּסִיַּית עֵינַיִם!

The Gemara asks: **Did this cause** Isaac's blindness? **Didn't Rabbi Yitzḥak say: A curse of an ordinary person should not be lightly regarded in your eyes, because Abimelech cursed Sarah, and** although he was not a righteous man, his curse **was** nevertheless **fulfilled,** albeit **in her descendant. As it is stated** that Abimelech said to Sarah with regard to the gift that he gave to Abraham: **"Behold, it is for you a covering of the eyes"** (Genesis 20:16). **Do not read** it as **"a covering [*kesut*]** of the eyes," but **rather** read it as: **A blindness [*kesiat*] of the eyes.** Abimelech's words were a veiled curse for Sarah to suffer from blindness. While she herself did not suffer, the curse was apparently fulfilled in the blindness of her son, Isaac.

הָא וְהָא גָּרְמָא לֵיהּ. רָבָא אֲמַר מֵהָכָא: ״שְׂאֵת פְּנֵי רָשָׁע לֹא טוֹב״.

According to Rabbi Yitzḥak, Abimelech's curse was the cause of Isaac's blindness, and it was not, as Rabbi Elazar suggested, the fact he gazed at Esau. The Gemara explains: Both **this and that** jointly **caused it. Rava said:** The prohibition against gazing at the likeness of a wicked person is derived **from here: "It is not good to raise the face of the wicked"** (Proverbs 18:5).

NOTES

In the image of the likeness of a wicked man – בְּצֶלֶם דְּמוּת אָדָם רָשָׁע: This is prohibited because when one gazes at the likeness of another, one is drawn to him and begins to feel closer to him (*Pardes Rimonim*). Therefore, only extended gazing and study of the image is prohibited, but not a casual glance (*Gilyon HaShas*). Furthermore, some suggest that the phrase: The image of the likeness, which appears repetitious, is intended to extend the prohibition to looking at even a picture of an evil man and not just the person in the flesh and blood (*Ramat Shmuel*).

PERSONALITIES

Rabbi Zeira – רַבִּי זֵירָא: Born in Babylonia, Rabbi Zeira, known in the Jerusalem Talmud as Rabbi Ze'ira, was one of the great third-generation *amora'im* in Eretz Yisrael. His father was a tax collector for the Persian government, who was praised as one of the few who filled that position with honesty. Rabbi Zeira ascended to Eretz Yisrael, where he entirely identified with the style of Torah study there. The Gemara relates that he fasted one hundred fasts in order to forget the Torah that he had studied in Babylonia.

Rabbi Zeira was famous for his sharp intellect, and he was the author of incisive *halakhot*. He was also known as an extremely God-fearing man. There are several stories related to his distinction in this area. His modesty was such that he did not even want to be ordained with the title rabbi. He relented only after he was told that with ordination comes atonement for one's sins.

The Gemara relates that he fasted one hundred additional fasts so that the fire of Gehenna would not harm him. He would test himself by entering a fiery furnace. On one occasion, his legs were scorched, and from then on he was called: The little man with the scorched legs. He was a contemporary of Rav Ḥisda, Rav Sheshet, and Rabba in Babylonia, and of the disciples of Rabbi Yoḥanan in Eretz Yisrael, and he engaged in extensive halakhic discourse with all of them.

Apparently, he was a flax merchant in Eretz Yisrael, and it is conceivable that he had occasion in the course of his business to return to Babylonia several times.

The text of the beginning of Rabbi Zeira's eulogy is preserved in the Talmud: The land of Shinar, Babylonia, conceived and gave birth; the land of splendor, Eretz Yisrael, raised her plaything. Woe unto her, said Reket, Tiberias, for she has lost her beloved vessel.

He had a son, Rabbi Ahava, who was a Sage in the following generation.

Rabbi Yehoshua ben Korḥa – רַבִּי יְהוֹשֻׁעַ בֶּן קׇרְחָה: Little is known about the life of Rabbi Yehoshua ben Korḥa. From the list of Sages with whom he deliberated, it appears that he was one of the students of Rabbi Akiva. Some even suggest that Korḥa is a nickname for Rabbi Akiva himself, and thereby identify him as Rabbi Yehoshua, son of Rabbi Akiva, who is mentioned elsewhere. However, there is little evidence for this. As mentioned in the Gemara, Rabbi Yehoshua lived a long life, and therefore it seems that he must have been born around the time of the destruction of the Second Temple, although he mainly taught during the years after Rabbi Akiva was executed. Rabbi Yehoshua ben Korḥa's teachings on *halakha* and *aggada* are found in the Mishna and in *baraitot*. It appears that he was a gifted debater and would often debate against the heretics and the gentiles of his day.

בִּשְׁעַת פְּטִירָתוֹ אֲמַר לֵיהּ: [רַבִּי] בָּרְכֵנִי! אֲמַר לֵיהּ: יְהִי רָצוֹן שֶׁתַּגִּיעַ לַחֲצִי יָמַי. וּלְכוּלְּהוּ לָא? אֲמַר לוֹ: הַבָּאִים אַחֲרֶיךָ בְּהֵמָה יִרְעוּ?

At the time of Rabbi Yehoshua ben Korḥa's **departure** from this world, Rabbi Yehuda HaNasi **said to him: My teacher, bless me. He said to him: May it be** God's **will that you** live to **reach to half of my days.** When Rabbi Yehuda HaNasi heard this, he asked in astonishment: Are you saying that **to the entirety of** your days I should **not** reach? Why? Rabbi Yehoshua ben Korḥa **said to him: Shall those who come after you** just **tend cattle?** If you live as long as me, your sons will never be able to succeed you in the position of Nasi. As such, they will never achieve greatness in Torah, and it will be as if they just tended cattle throughout their lives. It is therefore better that your life not be so prolonged, so that they have the opportunity to rise to eminence.

אֲבוּהּ בַּר אִיהִי וּמִנְיָמִן בַּר אִיהִי, חַד אֲמַר: תֵּיתֵי לִי דְּלָא אִסְתַּכַּלִי בְּגוֹי, וְחַד אֲמַר: תֵּיתֵי לִי דְּלָא עֲבַדִי שׁוּתָּפוּת בַּהֲדֵי גּוֹי.

Avuh bar Ihi and Minyamin bar Ihi both spoke on this topic: **One** of them **said: May** a blessing **come to me for I never gazed at** a wicked **gentile. And** the other **one said: May** a blessing **come to me for I never formed a partnership with** a wicked **gentile,**[N] so as not to have any association with a wicked person.

שָׁאֲלוּ תַּלְמִידָיו אֶת רַבִּי זֵירָא: בַּמֶּה הֶאֱרַכְתָּ יָמִים? אָמַר לָהֶם: מִיָּמַי לֹא הִקְפַּדְתִּי בְּתוֹךְ בֵּיתִי, וְלֹא צָעַדְתִּי בִּפְנֵי מִי שֶׁגָּדוֹל מִמֶּנִּי, וְלֹא הִרְהַרְתִּי בַּמְּבוֹאוֹת הַמְטוּנָּפוֹת, וְלֹא הָלַכְתִּי אַרְבַּע אַמּוֹת בְּלֹא תּוֹרָה וּבְלֹא תְּפִילִּין, וְלֹא יָשַׁנְתִּי בְּבֵית הַמִּדְרָשׁ לֹא שֵׁינַת קֶבַע וְלֹא שֵׁינַת עֲרַאי, וְלֹא שַׂשְׂתִּי בְּתַקָּלַת חֲבֵירִי, וְלֹא קָרָאתִי לַחֲבֵירִי (בַּחֲנִיכָתוֹ) וְאָמְרִי לָהּ (בַּחֲכִינָתוֹ).

The Gemara presents a similar incident: **Rabbi Zeira was** once **asked by his disciples: In** the merit of **which** virtue **were you** blessed with **longevity? He said to them: In** all **my days, I was never angry inside my house** with members of my household who acted against my wishes. **Nor did I** ever **walk ahead of someone who was a greater** Torah scholar **than me. Nor did I** ever **meditate** upon words of Torah **in filthy alleyways,**[NH] as doing so is a disgrace to the Torah. **Nor did I** ever **walk four cubits without** meditating on words of **Torah or without** wearing **phylacteries. Nor did I** ever **sleep in a study hall,**[H] **neither a deep sleep or a brief nap. Nor did I** ever **rejoice when my fellow stumbled.**[N] **Nor did I ever call my fellow by his derogatory nickname** [***ḥanikhato***].[N] **And some say** that he said: I never called my fellow by **his nickname** [***ḥakhinato***], i.e., even one that is not derogatory.

NOTES

For I never formed a partnership with a gentile – דְּלָא עֲבַדִי שׁוּתָּפוּת בַּהֲדֵי גּוֹי: *Tosafot* note that entering into a partnership with a gentile can lead to an actual prohibition: If there is a dispute between the parties and the gentile is required to attest under oath to the truth of his claim, he will probably swear on his idol, and it is prohibited for a Jew to cause this. Since the Gemara is speaking of a Sage performing a righteous act that is not strictly required, one must explain that the Gemara here is referring to a case where they agreed from the outset that if an oath will be required, the gentile will not make it on an idol (Rashba).

Nor did I meditate in filthy alleyways – וְלֹא הִרְהַרְתִּי בַּמְּבוֹאוֹת: The *halakha* is that meditating upon words of Torah in a filthy alleyway is prohibited. Why, then, was Rabbi Zeira praiseworthy for doing that which he was required to do? Some suggest that Rabbi Zeira himself ruled in accordance with the opinion of Rabbi Yoḥanan, that it is permitted to meditate upon words of Torah even in a filthy alleyway, but that out of righteousness he refrained from doing so. He therefore considered his action to be particularly virtuous (Rashba). Others suggest that since Rabbi Zeira was always deep in thought of Torah, it was particularly hard for him to clear his mind. He was praiseworthy for nevertheless exercising control over his mind when he walked through such places (*Rishon LeTziyyon*).

Nor did I rejoice when my fellow stumbled – וְלֹא שַׂשְׂתִּי בְּתַקָּלַת חֲבֵירִי: It would appear that such practice is not just virtuous but required, as the verse states: "Do not rejoice over your enemies' downfall" (Proverbs 24:17). Some suggest that verse is referring only to enemies but not one's fellow. When one rejoices over his enemies' downfall it is an expression of his hatred towards them and is therefore prohibited. However, if a person rejoices over his fellow's downfall it is clearly not an expression of his hatred towards him; rather, it is certainly due to the benefit he derived from the situation. For example, if one purchased something from another at a low price, even though the other certainly lost out, one may still rejoice over his own gain. To refrain from such rejoicing is only a righteous custom (Maharsha; see *Rishon LeTziyyon*). Others explain that his statement should be understood differently: Rabbi Zeira so empathized with his colleagues that if they stumbled he would not rejoice even when he was involved in celebrating a joyous occasion such as a wedding or Festival (*Dagan Shamayim*).

His derogatory nickname [*ḥanikhato*] – חֲנִיכָתוֹ: The intention is to a nickname that although it is somewhat derogatory, one has come to terms with it and doesn't mind being referred to by it. Some explain that the root of the word is *k-n-h*, similar to the word *kinui*, which means a nickname. Although it would appear the root should be *ḥ-n-k*, meaning educate, if that is the case it is hard to understand what the connection is with its meaning here.

HALAKHA

Meditating on words of Torah in a filthy place – הִרְהוּר תּוֹרָה בְּמָקוֹם מְטוּנָּף: It is prohibited even to think about words of Torah in a filthy place, i.e., a place that has excrement or urine (*Shulḥan Arukh, Oraḥ Ḥayyim* 85:2).

Sleeping in a study hall – שֵׁינָה בְּבֵית הַמִּדְרָשׁ: It is prohibited to sleep in a study hall. This *halakha* is in accordance with the opinion of Rabbi Zeira. A brief nap is permitted, but it is a righteous custom not to sleep there at all (*Shulḥan Arukh, Yoreh De'a* 246:16; *Shakh*).

מתני׳ וְעוֹד אָמַר רַבִּי יְהוּדָה: בֵּית הַכְּנֶסֶת שֶׁחָרַב אֵין מַסְפִּידִין בְּתוֹכוֹ, וְאֵין מַפְשִׁילִין בְּתוֹכוֹ חֲבָלִים, וְאֵין פּוֹרְשִׂין לְתוֹכוֹ מְצוּדוֹת, וְאֵין שׁוֹטְחִין עַל גַּגּוֹ פֵּירוֹת, וְאֵין עוֹשִׂין אוֹתוֹ קַפֶּנְדַּרְיָא,

MISHNA And Rabbi Yehuda said further:[N] **A synagogue that fell into ruin** still may not be used for a mundane purpose. Therefore, **one may not eulogize in it. And nor may one stretch out** and repair **ropes in it.** The wide expanse of the synagogue would have been particularly suitable for this. **And nor may one spread** animal **traps within it. And nor may one spread out produce upon its roof** to dry. **And nor may one make it** into **a shortcut.**

שֶׁנֶּאֱמַר ״וַהֲשִׁמּוֹתִי אֶת מִקְדְּשֵׁיכֶם״, קְדוּשָּׁתָן אַף כְּשֶׁהֵן שׁוֹמְמִין.

The *halakha* that a synagogue in disrepair still may not be used for mundane purposes is derived from a verse, **as it is stated: "And I will bring desolation to your sanctuaries"**[N] (Leviticus 26:31). The fact that the word "sanctuaries" appears after the word "desolation" indicates that **their sanctity** remains upon them **even when they are desolate.**

עָלוּ בוֹ עֲשָׂבִים – לֹא יִתְלוֹשׁ, מִפְּנֵי עַגְמַת נֶפֶשׁ.

However, if **grass sprang up** of its own accord **in** the ruined synagogue, although it is not befitting its sanctity, **one should not pick** it, **due to** the **anguish** that it will bring to those who see it. It will remind them of the disrepair of the synagogue and the need to rebuild it.

גמ׳ תָּנוּ רַבָּנַן: בָּתֵּי כְנֵסִיּוֹת אֵין נוֹהֲגִין בָּהֶן קַלּוּת רֹאשׁ: אֵין אוֹכְלִין בָּהֶן, וְאֵין שׁוֹתִין בָּהֶן,

GEMARA The Sages taught in a *baraita*: With regard **to synagogues: One may not act inside them with frivolity.** Therefore, **one may not eat in them; nor may one drink in them;**

NOTES

And Rabbi Yehuda said further – וְעוֹד אָמַר רַבִּי יְהוּדָה: In the previous mishna, Rabbi Yehuda rules that even though a synagogue may not be sold to someone who wishes to use it for inappropriate purposes, it may be sold to be used as a courtyard, and the buyer may then do with it as he wishes. *Tosafot* ask: The fact Rabbi Yehuda's statement is introduced in the mishna as: And he said further, suggests that his statement in this mishna is a progression of his statement in the previous mishna. However, it is difficult to understand how that could be when in the previous mishna he is lenient and in this mishna he is stringent. See their answer, as well as *Tosefot Yom Tov*.

This question is based on the standard text of the Mishna. However, many early commentaries had a different text of the mishna. According to that version it is Rabbi Yehuda, and not Rabbi Meir, who prohibits the sale of the synagogue from a community to an individual. If so, this statement of Rabbi Yehuda is a continuation of that ruling and presents another *halakha* based on the stringency that Rabbi Yehuda attaches to the sanctity of a synagogue.

As it is stated, And I will bring desolation to your sanctuaries – שֶׁנֶּאֱמַר וַהֲשִׁמּוֹתִי אֶת מִקְדְּשֵׁיכֶם: The *Sefat Emet* suggests that the words "your sanctuaries," as opposed to: Your houses of sanctuary, indicates that the sanctity of a synagogue does not depend on its being a house, i.e., a sound structure. Rather, even in a state of desolation it retains its sanctity. Other suggestions can be found in *Tosefot Yom Tov* and the Responsa of Maharit (222).

Perek **IV**
Daf **28** Amud **b**

וְאֵין נֵיאוֹתִין בָּהֶם, וְאֵין מְטַיְּילִין בָּהֶם, וְאֵין נִכְנָסִין בָּהֶן בַּחַמָּה מִפְּנֵי הַחַמָּה וּבַגְּשָׁמִים מִפְּנֵי הַגְּשָׁמִים, וְאֵין מַסְפִּידִין בָּהֶן הֶסְפֵּד שֶׁל יָחִיד. אֲבָל קוֹרִין בָּהֶן, וְשׁוֹנִין בָּהֶן, וּמַסְפִּידִין בָּהֶן הֶסְפֵּד שֶׁל רַבִּים.

and one may not adorn oneself[N] **inside them; nor may one wander about inside them; nor may one enter them in the sun** for protection **from the sun, or in the rain** to find shelter **from the rain; nor may one offer a eulogy inside them for an individual,** which is a private event. **However, one may read** the Bible **inside them, and one may study** *halakhot* **inside them,**[N] **and one may offer a eulogy inside them for** a Torah scholar, if **the public** attends the eulogy.[H]

אָמַר רַבִּי יְהוּדָה: אֵימָתַי – בְּיִשּׁוּבָן, אֲבָל בְּחוּרְבָּנָן – מַנִּיחִין אוֹתָן וְעוֹלִין בָּהֶן עֲשָׂבִים, וְלֹא יִתְלוֹשׁ מִפְּנֵי עַגְמַת נֶפֶשׁ.

Rabbi Yehuda said: When does this apply? **When** the synagogues are **occupied** by the people using them. **But when they are in a** state of **ruin, they should be left alone** so that **grass will sprout up inside them. And** that grass **should not be picked** and removed, **due to** the **anguish** that it will bring to those who see it. It will remind them of the disrepair of the synagogue and the need to rebuild it.

NOTES

Adorn oneself [*nei'otin*] – נֵיאוֹתִין: Rashi and many others understand that this word is derived from the word *noi*, meaning beauty. They therefore explain that the prohibition is to adorn oneself inside a synagogue. The Meiri assumes the word is derived from *naveh*, meaning an abode, and therefore explains that there is a prohibition to use a synagogue as one's dwelling place. Rashi suggests in tractate *Shabbat* (42b) that the word is derived from the *hana'a*, meaning pleasure or benefit, and therefore there is a prohibition to use the synagogue for one's private affairs.

One may read the Bible inside them and one may study *halakhot* inside them – קוֹרִין בָּהֶן וְשׁוֹנִין בָּהֶן: It is not immediately obvious that it should be permitted to study and perform mitzvot other than prayer inside a synagogue. The synagogue is a place designated uniquely for prayer, and therefore one might have deemed it inappropriate to do anything else there, even actions of religious value. Furthermore, the Gemara cites an opinion that the sanctity of the synagogue, i.e., of prayer, is greater than that of a study hall, i.e., of Torah study. Therefore, it is necessary for the *baraita* to teach that these activities are indeed permitted (*Rishon LeTziyyon*).

HALAKHA

How one should act in a synagogue – כֵּיצַד נוֹהֲגִים בְּבֵית הַכְּנֶסֶת: One should not act with frivolity in a synagogue or jest or engage in idle talk there. This applies even if the activity is for the sake of one's livelihood (*Magen Avraham*). One who frequently talks idly in the synagogue should repent in the following way: He should fast for forty days, receive lashes every day, and accept upon himself to no longer speak at all when in a synagogue (*Kaf HaḤayyim*, citing *Roke'aḥ*).

One may not eat or drink in a synagogue, nor may one do labor there (*Mishna Berura*). One may not adorn oneself or wander about, and it is prohibited to enter in order to shelter oneself from the sun or the rain. Business calculations may not be done there, except calculations for the fulfillment of a mitzva, such as for the sake of charity or redeeming captives.

Only a leader of the generation, or the relatives of a leader if the public gathers for them, may be eulogized in a synagogue. Rabbi Yitzḥak Luria would be cautious not to speak even words of ethics in a synagogue, in order to avoid the speech digressing into common talk (*Magen Avraham*). And one should not kiss one's children in a synagogue, to show that there is no love like the love of the Holy One, Blessed be He (*Agudda*). However, one may kiss the hand of a scholar or of his father or teacher when he descends from being called up to the Torah, as this demonstrates one's respect for the mitzvot (*Shulḥan Arukh*, *Oraḥ Ḥayyim* 151:1).

עֲשָׂבִים – מַאן דְּכַר שְׁמַיְיהוּ? חַסּוּרֵי מִיחַסְּרָא וְהָכִי קָתָנֵי: וּמְכַבְּדִין אוֹתָן, וּמַרְבִּיצִין אוֹתָן כְּדֵי שֶׁלֹּא יַעֲלוּ בָּהֶן עֲשָׂבִים. אָמַר רַבִּי יְהוּדָה: אֵימָתַי – בְּיִשּׁוּבָן, אֲבָל בְּחוּרְבָּנָן – מַנִּיחִין אוֹתָן לַעֲלוֹת. עָלוּ בָּהֶן עֲשָׂבִים – לֹא יִתְלוֹשׁ, מִפְּנֵי עַגְמַת נֶפֶשׁ.

The Gemara asks: Why did Rabbi Yehuda discuss the *halakha* about **grass? Who mentioned** anything **about it?** The Gemara explains: The text of the *baraita* **is incomplete and is teaching the following:**[B] **And** among the other things that may be done in synagogues, **they should** also be sure to **sweep them and** to **sprinkle** their floors with water, **in order that grass not sprout up in them. Rabbi Yehuda said: When** does this apply? **When** the synagogues are **occupied** by the people using them, **but when they are in** a state of **ruin, they should be left alone** so that grass **will sprout up inside them.** If **grass did sprout up, it should not be removed, due to** the **anguish** that this will bring to those who see it.

אָמַר רַב אַסִי: בָּתֵּי כְנֵסִיּוֹת שֶׁבְּבָבֶל עַל תְּנַאי הֵן עֲשׂוּיִין, וְאַף עַל פִּי כֵן אֵין נוֹהֲגִין בָּהֶן קַלּוּת רֹאשׁ. וּמַאי נִיהוּ – חֶשְׁבּוֹנוֹת.

Rav Asi said: Synagogues in Babylonia are built from the outset **with a stipulation**[N] that they not have the full sanctity of a synagogue, in order that it be permitted to use them for the community's general needs.[H] **But nevertheless,** one **should not act inside them with frivolity.** The Gemara explains: **What is** meant by **this?** One should not make business **calculations** in a synagogue.

אָמַר רַב אַסִי: בֵּית הַכְּנֶסֶת שֶׁמְּחַשְּׁבִין בּוֹ חֶשְׁבּוֹנוֹת – מַלִּינִין בּוֹ אֶת הַמֵּת. מַלִּינִין סָלְקָא דַּעְתָּךְ? לָא סַגִּי דְּלָאו הָכִי?! אֶלָּא: לַסּוֹף שֶׁיַּלִּינוּ בּוֹ מֵת מִצְוָה.

Rav Asi said: With regard to **a synagogue in which** people **make** business **calculations, they will** eventually **keep a corpse inside it overnight.** The Gemara questions the wording of this dictum: **Can** it really **enter your mind** to say that **they will** ever actually **keep a corpse inside it overnight?** Could it really be that **there will not be any other alternative? Rather,** Rav Asi means that as a punishment for acting with frivolity people in the community will die, including those who have no family, and so **ultimately they will** have to **keep a corpse with no one to bury it** [*met mitzva*] **overnight** in the synagogue.

וְאֵין נֵיאוֹתִין בָּהֶן: אָמַר רָבָא: חֲכָמִים וְתַלְמִידֵיהֶם מוּתָּרִין. דַּאֲמַר רַבִּי יְהוֹשֻׁעַ בֶּן לֵוִי: מַאי בֵּי רַבָּנַן – בֵּיתָא דְּרַבָּנַן.

§ The *baraita* taught: **And one may not adorn oneself inside them. Rava said:** The prohibition applies only to laypeople, but **Torah scholars and their disciples are permitted**[N] to do so,[H] **as Rabbi Yehoshua ben Levi said: What** is the meaning of the term: ***Bei* of the Sages,** which is used to describe a study hall? It is a shortened form of **house** [***beita***] **of the Sages.** In order to facilitate the constant presence of the Torah scholars in the study hall, it is permitted for them to use the hall as though it were their home.

וְאֵין נִכְנָסִין בָּהֶן בַּחַמָּה מִפְּנֵי הַחַמָּה וּבַגְּשָׁמִים מִפְּנֵי הַגְּשָׁמִים: כִּי הָא דְּרָבִינָא וְרַב אַדָּא בַּר מַתָּנָה הָווּ קָיְימִי וְשָׁאֲלִי שְׁאֵילְתָא מֵרָבָא, אֲתָא זִילְחָא דְּמִיטְרָא. עָיְילִי לְבֵי כְנִישְׁתָּא. אָמְרִי: הַאי דְּעָיְילִינַן לְבֵי כְנִישְׁתָּא – לָאו מִשּׁוּם מִיטְרָא, אֶלָּא מִשּׁוּם דִּשְׁמַעְתָּא בְּעָא צִילּוּתָא כְּיוֹמָא דְּאִסְתְּנָא.

The *baraita* continued: **And nor may one enter them in the sun** for protection **from the sun, or in the rain** to find shelter **from the rain.** The Gemara explains: This **is similar to that** case of **Ravina**[P] **and Rav Adda bar Mattana. They were standing and asking a question of Rava, when a shower** [***zilḥa***][L] **of rain began** to fall upon them. **They** all **entered the synagogue, saying: Our having entered the synagogue is not due to the rain,** that we stay dry; **rather, it is due to** the fact that **the** ***halakha*** we were discussing **requires clarity like the day the north wind** [***istena***][L] blows and the sky is perfectly clear. Therefore, we are entering the synagogue for the sake of studying Torah, which is certainly permitted.

BACKGROUND

The text of the *baraita* is incomplete and is teaching the following – חַסּוּרֵי מִיחַסְּרָא וְהָכִי קָתָנֵי: This method of explanation, which is commonly used by the Gemara, does not suggest an actual emendation of the text of the *baraita*. Rather, the addition introduced by the Gemara is an elaboration upon that which is written in the *baraita*, which is insufficiently clear in its current form. The addition provides the necessary clarification.

NOTES

Are built with a stipulation – עַל תְּנַאי הֵן עֲשׂוּיִין: Some suggest that the stipulation is effective only to permit the use of a synagogue for other purposes once it has been abandoned or has fallen into disrepair. At that point, due to the stipulation, it automatically loses its sanctity and may be used even for mundane purposes (*Tosafot*). However, others claim that the stipulation is effective even while the synagogue is still in use (Rashi). Therefore, some authorities rule that a synagogue may be used even to house guests, based on the stipulation (Rid the Younger; Rashba).

Torah scholars and their disciples are permitted – חֲכָמִים וְתַלְמִידֵיהֶם מוּתָּרִין: The commentaries are divided on how to relate to this permission. Some suggest that it is permitted for scholars to use the synagogue for their own needs only out of necessity; if the scholars were forced to return home to eat and drink, it would interrupt their study. Therefore, a special dispensation was provided for them (*Tur*). However, others suggest that because the scholars are constantly present in the study hall, it becomes a home for them. As such, it is no longer inappropriate for them to eat and drink there. In the Jerusalem Talmud, this issue is discussed at length.

HALAKHA

Synagogues in the Diaspora – בָּתֵּי כְנֵסִיּוֹת שֶׁבְּחוּצָה לָאָרֶץ: If a stipulation was made during the construction of a synagogue that it will be permitted to use the synagogue for all purposes, then it is permitted to use it for these purposes once it falls into ruin. However, while it is still standing, it is prohibited to do so. Even when the synagogue is falls into ruin, the stipulation does not permit use of the synagogue for disrespectful purposes, e.g., sowing plants or business calculations of the community. This stipulation is effective only in the Diaspora, but not in Eretz Yisrael. However, some claim that even in Eretz Yisrael a stipulation can be made to permit the use of a synagogue for non-frivolous behavior (*Magen Avraham*) and one may rely on the lenient opinions (*Mishna Berura*). Some say that if the intention from the outset was to use the place for prayer for only a limited time, then once it is no longer used for prayer, it may be used for any purpose (*Arukh HaShulḥan*, citing *Baḥ*; *Shulḥan Arukh*, *Oraḥ Hayyim* 151:11).

Torah scholars in a study hall – תַּלְמִידֵי חֲכָמִים בְּבֵית מִדְרָשׁ: Torah scholars and their disciples are allowed to eat and drink in a synagogue when absolutely necessary. Some say that it is permitted in a study hall even when there is no pressing need, provided that those doing so are studying there (*Magen Avraham*; *Shulḥan Arukh*, *Oraḥ Hayyim* 151:1 and in the comment of Rema).

LANGUAGE

Shower [*zilḥa*] – זִילְחָא: A root used in the Semitic languages, prominent in Assyrian and used in Syriac to mean to pour or throw.

North wind [*istena*] – אִסְתְּנָא: This is the Syriac name for the north wind. The day of the *istena* is the day when the north wind is strongest. It clears the sky of its clouds, and consequently it is a sign that the coming year will be bright and clear.

PERSONALITIES

Ravina – רָבִינָא: Ravina was a sixth-generation Babylonian Sage whose major work was assisting Rav Ashi in editing the Babylonian Talmud. In his youth, he studied under Rava. Ravina and Rav Ashi are found discussing matters of *halakha* in many places throughout the Talmud. He passed away in 422 CE.

There is an expression found in the Talmud that Ravina and Rav Ashi are the last decisors, which credits them both with the editing of the Talmud. However, Ravina and Rav Ashi were not the first to edit the oral traditions, as there are many discussions in the Talmud whose language and style show that they were prepared long before their time. Their contribution was that they arranged the material that they received from previous generations, which emanated from different academies and were written in different styles, to produce an organized and uniform Talmud.

אמר ליה רב אחא בריה דרבא לרב אשי: אי אצטריך ליה לאיניש למיקרי גברא מבי כנישתא, מאי? אמר ליה: אי צורבא מרבנן הוא לימא הלכתא, ואי תנא הוא – לימא מתניתין, ואי קרא הוא, לימא פסוקא. ואי לא – לימא ליה לינוקא: אימא לי פסוקיך. אי נמי, נישהי פורתא וניקום.

Rav Aḥa, son of Rava, said to Rav Ashi: If a person needs to summon an individual from inside a synagogue, what should he do, since it is not permitted to enter a synagogue just for that purpose?[H] Rav Ashi **said to him: If he is a young Torah scholar, let him recite a *halakha*** upon entering the synagogue; **and if he is a *tanna*** who memorizes large numbers of *mishnayot*, **let him recite** various ***mishnayot*; and if he is an expert in** the **Bible, let him recite a verse; and if** he is **not** able to do even this, **let him say to a child: Recite for me a verse** that you have learned today. **Alternatively, he should remain** in the synagogue **for a short time**[N] **and** only afterward **stand up** and leave.

ומספידין בהן הספד של רבים: היכי דמי הספידא דרבים? מחוי רב חסדא: כגון הספידא דקאי ביה רב ששת, מחוי רב ששת: כגון הספידא דקאי ביה רב חסדא.

The *baraita* continues: **And one may offer a eulogy inside them** for a Torah scholar if **the public** attends the eulogy. The Gemara asks: **What are the circumstances of a eulogy for the public? Rav Ḥisda depicted** a case: **For example, a eulogy** for a Torah scholar **at which Rav Sheshet is present.** Owing to his presence, many people will come. **Rav Sheshet** himself **depicted** another case: **For example, a eulogy at which Rav Ḥisda is present.**

רפרם אספדה לכלתיה בבי כנישתא, אמר: משום יקרא דידי ודמיתא אתו כוליה עלמא. רבי זירא ספדיה לההוא מרבנן בבי כנישתא, אמר: אי משום יקרא דידי, אי משום יקרא דידיה, דמיתא, אתו כולי עלמא.

The Gemara offers another example: **Rafram** once **eulogized his daughter-in-law inside a synagogue. He said: Due to my honor and** the honor **of the deceased, everyone will come** to the eulogy. It will consequently be a public event, and it is therefore permitted to hold it in a synagogue. Similarly, **Rabbi Zeira** once **eulogized a certain Sage inside a synagogue. He said: Whether due to my honor, or whether due to the honor of the deceased, everyone will come** to the eulogy.

ריש לקיש ספדיה לההוא צורבא מרבנן דשכיח בארעא דישראל, דהוי תני הלכתא בעשרים וארבע שורתא, אמר: ווי, חסרא ארעא דישראל גברא רבה.

Reish Lakish[P] once **eulogized a certain young Torah scholar who was frequently** present **in Eretz Yisrael**[N] **and who used to study *halakha* in the twenty-fourth row**[NB] of the study hall. He sat so far back because he was not one of the principal scholars. Nevertheless, when he died, Reish Lakish **said: Alas, Eretz Yisrael has lost a great man.**

ההוא דהוי תני הלכתא סיפרא וסיפרי ותוספתא, ושכיב. אתו ואמרו ליה לרב נחמן: ליספדיה מר! אמר: היכי נספדיה? הי צנא דמלי סיפרי דחסר!

In contrast, there was **a certain man who used to study *halakha*, the *Sifra*, and the *Sifrei*, and the *Tosefta*, and he died.** People **came and said to Rav Naḥman: Let the Master eulogize him. He said** to them: **How can I eulogize him?** Should I say: **Alas, a basket filled with books is lost?** This would not be true. Although the man studied many areas of Torah, he was not proficient in them.

תא חזי מה בין תקיפי דארעא דישראל לחסידי דבבל.

The Gemara compares the conduct of Reish Lakish in Eretz Yisrael to that of Rav Naḥman in Babylonia. **Come** and **see what** the difference is **between the harsh** scholars **of Eretz Yisrael and the saintly ones of Babylonia.** Although Reish Lakish was known for his harsh nature, he was still more respectful than Rav Naḥman, who was known for his saintliness.

תנן התם: ודאשתמש בתגא חלף, תני ריש לקיש: זה המשתמש במי ששונה הלכות, כתרה של תורה,

We learned in a mishna **there** (*Avot* 1:13): **And one who makes use of the crown** [*taga*][L] of Torah learning **will perish**[H] from the world. **Reish Lakish taught: This is referring to one who** allows himself to be **served by one who studies *halakhot*,** which is **the crown of the Torah.**

HALAKHA

Summoning a person from a synagogue – קריאת אדם מבית כנסת: When one must enter a synagogue in order to summon another, he should enter and engage in Torah study or read a verse of Torah. If he does not know how, he should stay in the synagogue for a short time, the amount of time it takes to walk through two four-handbreadth-wide doors (*Shulḥan Arukh*, *Oraḥ Ḥayyim* 151:1, and in the comment of Rema).

One who makes use of the crown will perish – ודאשתמש בתגא חלף: One who studies Torah in order to gain wealth or honor does not merit the crown of Torah. Some say that this is referring to the prohibition against reciting the sacred names of God as incantations. Others say that also included in this prohibition is taking advantage of someone who studies *halakhot* (*Shakh*, citing Rif; Rosh; *Shulḥan Arukh Yoreh De'a* 246:21, and in the comment of Rema).

NOTES

He should remain for a short time – נישהי פורתא: The early commentaries cite Rabbeinu Moshe, who explains that doing so is permitted because being present in a synagogue and in other sacred places is itself a mitzva, based on the verse: "Praiseworthy are those that dwell in Your house" (Psalms 84:5).

Who was frequently present in Eretz Yisrael – דשכיח בארעא דישראל: Maharsha explains that this detail is mentioned to emphasize the great affection that Reish Lakish held for this Torah scholar. Although the Torah scholar did not live in Eretz Yisrael and so was not a fellow countryman of Reish Lakish, Reish Lakish nevertheless showed him great respect.

In the twenty-fourth row – בעשרים וארבע שורתא: Some suggest that this scholar would sit in the twenty-fourth row of the study hall, due to his low status as a scholar, and Reish Lakish nevertheless held him in high esteem (Maharsha). This is the explanation in the commentary of the Gemara. Others suggest that the eulogy was delivered in the presence of twenty-four rows of disciples (Rashba, citing *Tosafot*).

BACKGROUND

Twenty-fourth row – בעשרים וארבע שורתא: During the period of the Mishna and Talmud, and especially in Eretz Yisrael when the Sanhedrin still sat, the scholars would sit in the study hall in an order that was set according to their greatness in Torah. The scholar who was teaching would sit at the front and face the students. At times, people of distinguished lineage would also sit at the front. The students listening would sit in rows. In the first row would be the greatest scholars, and it appears that even they sat in a specific order defined by their greatness. The next row had the next greatest scholars, and so on. Consequently, one's row and seat was a mark of the degree of his greatness in Torah study.

LANGUAGE

Crown [*taga*] – תגא: The word originates from the Iranian word tāg, meaning crown. It was then adopted into the Semitic languages. The word *tahg* is still used in Hebrew to refer to the crowns drawn on top of letters.

PERSONALITIES

Reish Lakish – ריש לקיש: Reish Lakish is a contraction of Rabbi Shimon ben Lakish. A disciple-colleague of Rabbi Yoḥanan, he was one of the greatest of the first generation of *amora'im* in Eretz Yisrael. It appears that he was from an important family, and in his youth he strived in his Torah study. However, due to his poverty he was forced to find a means to earn a living. To this end and due to his great physical strength and prowess, he became a gladiator. Only later, under the influence of Rabbi Yoḥanan, he returned to studying Torah. The halakhic decisions of Rabbi Yoḥanan and Reish Lakish form a large part of the Jerusalem and Babylonian Talmuds.

Reish Lakish was well known for his sharp rebukes. He lived a very harsh life. It is recounted that a laugh was never seen on his face, and he chose his friends very carefully. All of the Sages in Eretz Yisrael in the second generation of the *amora'im* were his students, and they passed on his teachings.

HALAKHA

Jewish women were strict upon themselves – בְּנוֹת יִשְׂרָאֵל הֵן הֶחְמִירוּ עַל עַצְמָן: If a woman sees blood, even a small drop the size of a mustard seed, she must wait for seven clean days before purifying herself (*Shulḥan Arukh*, *Yoreh De'a* 183:1).

וְאָמַר עוּלָּא: לִשְׁתַּמֵּשׁ אִינִישׁ בְּמַאן דְּתָנֵי אַרְבָּעָה וְלָא לִשְׁתַּמֵּשׁ בְּמַאן דְּמַתְנֵי אַרְבָּעָה. כִּי הָא דְּרֵישׁ לָקִישׁ הֲוָה אָזֵיל בְּאוֹרְחָא, מְטָא עוּרְקְמָא דְּמַיָּא, אֲתָא הַהוּא גַּבְרָא אַרְכְּבֵיהּ אַכַּתְפֵּיהּ, וְקָא מַעְבַּר לֵיהּ. אֲמַר לֵיהּ: קְרֵית? אֲמַר לֵיהּ: קְרֵינָא. תְּנֵית? תְּנֵינָא אַרְבָּעָה סִידְרֵי מִשְׁנָה. אֲמַר לֵיהּ: פְּסַלְתְּ לָךְ אַרְבָּעָה טוּרֵי, וְטָעֲנַתְּ בַּר לָקִישׁ אַכַּתְפָּךְ?! שְׁדֵי בַּר לָקִישָׁא בְּמַיָּא!

And Ulla said: It is better that **a person should be served by one who studies four** orders of the Mishna,[N] **and he should not** allow himself to **be served by one who teaches**[N] to others **four** orders of the Mishna, **as in that** case **of Reish Lakish. He was traveling along the road** when **he reached** a deep **puddle of water. A certain man came** and **placed him upon his shoulders and** began **transferring him** to the other side. Reish Lakish **said to him: Have you read** the Bible? **He said to him: I have read** it. He then asked: **Have you studied** the Mishna? He answered him: **I have studied four orders of the Mishna.** Reish Lakish then **said to him: You have hewn** these **four mountains and** yet **you bear the weight of the son of Lakish upon your shoulders?** It is inappropriate for you to carry me; **throw the son of Lakish into the water.**

אֲמַר לֵיהּ: נִיחָא לִי דְּאֲשַׁמְּעִינַן לְמָר. אִי הָכִי גְּמוֹר מִינִּי הָא מִלְּתָא דַּאֲמַר רַבִּי זֵירָא: בְּנוֹת יִשְׂרָאֵל הֵן הֶחְמִירוּ עַל עַצְמָן, שֶׁאֲפִילּוּ רוֹאוֹת טִיפַּת דָּם כְּחַרְדָּל יוֹשְׁבוֹת עָלָיו שִׁבְעָה נְקִיִּים.

The man **said to** Reish Lakish: **It is pleasing for me to serve the Master** in this way. Reish Lakish said to him: **If so, learn from me this matter**[N] **that Rabbi Zeira said.** In this way you will be considered my disciple, and it will then be appropriate for you to serve me. **Jewish women were strict upon themselves**[HN] **in that even if they see a spot of** menstrual **blood** that is only the size **of a mustard seed they wait on its account seven clean** days before immersing themselves in a ritual bath to purify themselves.

תָּנָא דְּבֵי אֵלִיָּהוּ: כָּל הַשּׁוֹנֶה הֲלָכוֹת מוּבְטָח לוֹ שֶׁהוּא בֶּן עוֹלָם הַבָּא, שֶׁנֶּאֱמַר ״הֲלִיכוֹת עוֹלָם לוֹ״ אַל תִּקְרֵי הֲלִיכוֹת אֶלָּא הֲלָכוֹת.

The school of Eliyahu taught: Anyone who studies ***halakhot*** every day,[N] **he is guaranteed that he is destined for the World-to-Come, as it is stated: "His ways [*halikhot*] are eternal"** (Habakkuk 3:6): **Do not read** the verse as ***halikhot*** [**ways**]; **rather,** read it as ***halakhot*.**[N] Consequently, the verse indicates that the study of the *halakhot* brings one to eternal life.

תָּנוּ רַבָּנַן:

The Sages taught in a *baraita*:

NOTES

Four orders – אַרְבָּעָה סִידְרֵי: Although there are six orders of the Mishna, not all of them had the same prominence, and not all were studied to the same degree. The orders of *Moed*, *Nashim*, and *Nezikin* were studied even in the diaspora of Babylonia, due to their practical relevance, in contrast to the orders of *Zera'im*, *Kodashim*, and *Teharot*, the *halakhot* of which did not apply to the situation in Babylonia. Nevertheless, the order of *Kodashim* continued to be studied since the study of the laws of offerings is considered to be of particular value. This reality is highlighted by the fact that only these four orders are significantly represented by the Babylonian Talmud. In the extended version of the Jerusalem Talmud, there is no Gemara on *Kodashim* or *Teharot* at all.

Who studies…who teaches [*dematnei*] – דְּתָנֵי...דְּמַתְנֵי: Some explain that Ulla is highlighting the superior status of one who studies and teaches as compared to one who studies only for himself (Rashi on Rif). Others explain the word *dematnei* refers not to one who teaches but rather to one who studies the *halakhot* of the Mishna as well as the Talmud, i.e., the explanations of the *mishnayot* and *baraitot* (Rif).

Learn from me this matter – גְּמוֹר מִינִּי הָא מִלְּתָא: Ostensibly, Reish Lakish's actions would seem to contradict Ulla's teaching above. The commentaries explain that this is not the case. According to the opinion that Ulla made a distinction between one who only studied and one who also taught, some explain that Reish Lakish assumed that this man also taught, and therefore Reish Lakish did not want to be served by him; however, Reish Lakish claimed that this prohibition does not apply to one's disciple. According to the opinion that Ulla made a distinction between one who studies the *halakhot* and one who also studies the Talmud, Reish Lakish wished to teach the man something from the Talmud in order for him to deepen his study (Maharsha). Some suggest that Reish Lakish wished to teach him this *halakha* because it was from the order of *Teharot*, which the man had not yet studied (*Zikkaron BaSefer*).

Jewish women were strict upon themselves – בְּנוֹת יִשְׂרָאֵל הֵן הֶחְמִירוּ עַל עַצְמָן: According to Torah law, a woman who experiences a flow of uterine blood becomes ritually impure. If she experiences the flow during the time of her regular menses, she is classified as a *nidda* and may immerse seven days later, even if she has additional discharges during that week. However, if she experiences discharges on three consecutive days when it is not the time of her menses, she is classified as a *zava*. She must then observe seven clean days without any discharge before she is able to immerse and ritually purify herself. Rabbi Zeira reports that Jewish women were stringent in that they essentially ignored the distinctions between these two categories. In all cases, even for a single drop of blood, they accepted upon themselves the observance of seven clean days.

Anyone who studies *halakhot* every day – כָּל הַשּׁוֹנֶה הֲלָכוֹת: Some suggest that this teaching is specifically mentioned here to counterbalance Rabbi Zeira's teaching. Once Jewish women accepted upon themselves this stringency, much of the *halakhot* discussed in tractate *Nidda*, which discusses the differences between the status of a *nidda* and a *zava*, became irrelevant. Nevertheless, the Gemara emphasizes that there is still value in learning the *halakhot* pertaining to them.

Halikhot, *halakhot* – הֲלִיכוֹת, הֲלָכוֹת: The word *halakha* is itself derived from the word *halikhot*, ways, because *halakha* provides the path in which the Jewish people have walked and will continue to walk throughout the generations (*Arukh*).

מְבַטְּלִין תַּלְמוּד תּוֹרָה לְהוֹצָאַת הַמֵּת וּלְהַכְנָסַת הַכַּלָּה. אָמְרוּ עָלָיו עַל רַבִּי יְהוּדָה בְּרַבִּי אֶילְעַאי שֶׁהָיָה מְבַטֵּל תַּלְמוּד תּוֹרָה לְהוֹצָאַת הַמֵּת וּלְהַכְנָסַת הַכַּלָּה. בַּמֶּה דְּבָרִים אֲמוּרִים – בְּשֶׁאֵין שָׁם כׇּל צוֹרְכּוֹ, אֲבָל יֵשׁ שָׁם כׇּל צוֹרְכּוֹ – אֵין מְבַטְּלִין.

One interrupts his **Torah study**[N] **to carry out the dead** for burial[H] **and to escort a bride** to her wedding. **They said about Rabbi Yehuda, son of Rabbi Elai, that he would interrupt** his **Torah study to carry out the dead** for burial **and to escort a bride** to her wedding. The Gemara qualifies this ruling: **In what** case **is this statement said?** Only **where there are not sufficient** numbers of other people available to perform these mitzvot and honor the deceased or the bride appropriately. **However,** when **there are sufficient** numbers, additional people **should not interrupt** their Torah study to participate.

וְכַמָּה כׇּל צוֹרְכּוֹ? אֲמַר רַב שְׁמוּאֵל בַּר אִינְיָא מִשְּׁמֵיהּ דְּרַב: תְּרֵיסַר אַלְפֵי גַּבְרֵי וְשִׁיתָּא אַלְפֵי שִׁיפּוּרֵי. וְאָמְרִי לַהּ: תְּרֵיסַר אַלְפֵי גַּבְרֵי, וּמִינַּיְיהוּ שִׁיתָּא אַלְפֵי שִׁיפּוּרֵי. עוּלָּא אֲמַר: כְּגוֹן דְּחָיְיצִי גַּבְרֵי מֵאַבּוּלָּא עַד סִיכְרָא.

The Gemara asks: **And how many** people **are** considered **sufficient? Rav Shmuel bar Inya said in the name of Rav: Twelve thousand men**[N] and another **six thousand** men to blow **horns** as a sign of mourning. **And some say** a different version: **Twelve thousand men, among whom are six thousand** men with **horns. Ulla said: For example,** enough **to make a procession of people** all the way **from the** town **gate** [*abbula*][L] **to the place of burial.**[N]

רַב שֵׁשֶׁת אָמַר: כִּנְתִינָתָהּ כָּךְ נְטִילָתָהּ. מַה נְּתִינָתָהּ בְּשִׁשִּׁים רִיבּוֹא – אַף נְטִילָתָהּ בְּשִׁשִּׁים רִיבּוֹא. הָנֵי מִילֵּי – לְמַאן דְּקָרֵי וְתָנֵי, אֲבָל לְמַאן דְּמַתְנֵי – לֵית לֵיהּ שִׁיעוּרָא.

Rav Sheshet said: As the Torah **was given, so it** should be **taken away,** i.e., the same honor that was provided when the Torah was given at Mount Sinai should be provided when the Torah is taken through the passing away of a Torah scholar. **Just as** the Torah **was given in the presence of six hundred thousand** men, **so too its taking** should be done **in the presence of six hundred thousand** men. The Gemara comments: **This applies to someone who read** the Bible **and studied** *halakhot* for himself. **But for someone who taught** others, **there is no limit** to the honor that should be shown to him.

תַּנְיָא, רַבִּי שִׁמְעוֹן בֶּן יוֹחַי אוֹמֵר: בּוֹא וּרְאֵה כַּמָּה חֲבִיבִין יִשְׂרָאֵל לִפְנֵי הַקָּדוֹשׁ בָּרוּךְ הוּא. שֶׁבְּכׇל מָקוֹם שֶׁגָּלוּ – שְׁכִינָה עִמָּהֶן. גָּלוּ לְמִצְרַיִם – שְׁכִינָה עִמָּהֶן, שֶׁנֶּאֱמַר: ״הֲנִגְלֹה נִגְלֵיתִי לְבֵית אָבִיךָ בִּהְיוֹתָם בְּמִצְרַיִם״ וגו׳, גָּלוּ לְבָבֶל – שְׁכִינָה עִמָּהֶן, שֶׁנֶּאֱמַר: ״לְמַעַנְכֶם שֻׁלַּחְתִּי בָבֶלָה״. וְאַף כְּשֶׁהֵן עֲתִידִין לִיגָּאֵל שְׁכִינָה עִמָּהֶן, שֶׁנֶּאֱמַר: ״וְשָׁב ה׳ אֱלֹהֶיךָ אֶת שְׁבוּתְךָ״, וְהֵשִׁיב לֹא נֶאֱמַר אֶלָּא ״וְשָׁב״, מְלַמֵּד שֶׁהַקָּדוֹשׁ בָּרוּךְ הוּא שָׁב עִמָּהֶן מִבֵּין הַגָּלֻיּוֹת.

§ **It is taught** in a *baraita*: **Rabbi Shimon ben Yoḥai says: Come and see how beloved the Jewish people are before the Holy One, Blessed be He. As every place they were exiled, the Divine Presence** went **with them.**[N] **They were exiled to Egypt,** and **the Divine Presence** went **with them, as it is stated: "Did I reveal myself**[N] **to the house of your father when they were in Egypt?"** (I Samuel 2:27). **They were exiled to Babylonia,** and **the Divine Presence** went **with them, as it is stated: "For your sake I have sent to Babylonia"** (Isaiah 43:14). **So too, when, in the future, they will be redeemed, the Divine Presence will be with them,**[N] **as it is stated: "Then the Lord your God will return with your captivity"** (Deuteronomy 30:3). **It does not state: He will bring back,** i.e., He will cause the Jewish people to return, **but rather** it says: **"He will return," which teaches that the Holy One, Blessed be He, will return** together **with them from among the** various **exiles.**

NOTES

One interrupts his Torah study – מְבַטְּלִין תַּלְמוּד תּוֹרָה: Torah study is interrupted in this case because, as is stated in the beginning of the tractate (3b), the honor of those who study Torah is greater than the honor due to the Torah itself (*Rishon LeTziyyon*; see *Turei Even*).

Twelve thousand men – תְּרֵיסַר אַלְפֵי גַּבְרֵי: Some suggest that this number is based on a precedent, which is either the size of the Jewish army that went to battle at Midian (Maharsha) or the number of angels that were revealed at the giving of the Torah at Sinai (*Ramat Shmuel*).

From the town gate to the place of burial – מֵאַבּוּלָּא עַד סִיכְרָא: The *Arukh* interprets this differently, as: From the place of mourning to the grave.

As every place they were exiled, the Divine Presence went with them – שֶׁבְּכׇל מָקוֹם שֶׁגָּלוּ שְׁכִינָה עִמָּהֶן: The Divine Presence accompanies the Jewish people in order to protect them and ensure that they will not be assimilated among the nations (Alsheikh).

Did I reveal myself – הֲנִגְלֹה נִגְלֵיתִי: Although this is stated rhetorically, in many cases rhetorical statements are made based on facts that are actually true (see commentaries on I Samuel 2:27 and *Targum Yonatan* there).

When in the future they will be redeemed, the Divine Presence will be with them – כְּשֶׁהֵן עֲתִידִין לִיגָּאֵל שְׁכִינָה עִמָּהֶן: The *baraita* omits the fact that the Divine Presence is also with the Jewish people in the current exile. The Ritva explains that the omission is out of respect for the Divine Presence. *Re'aḥ Duda'im* suggests that the omission is because the accompaniment of the Divine Presence in exile is noticed only at the time of the redemption.

HALAKHA

Interrupting Torah study to carry out the dead for burial – בִּיטּוּל תּוֹרָה לְהוֹצָאַת הַמֵּת: Torah study is interrupted, and one is obligated to interrupt it (*Shakh*), in order to take out the dead for burial. If the deceased used to teach Torah to others, there is no limit to the honor that should be afforded to him, and even if thousands are already accompanying him, one should interrupt one's Torah study to accompany him to the grave.

If the deceased studied but did not teach, then it is fitting that six hundred thousand people accompany him. If the deceased did not study Torah, then as long as there are ten men to accompany him, it is not necessary to interrupt one's Torah study.

Nowadays, it is rare that someone has not studied at all, and therefore Torah study is interrupted for any commoner (Rema). The custom is to be lenient for a woman and a child and to act as one would for a man who did study. The Torah study of children is not interrupted under any circumstances (*Shulḥan Arukh*, *Yoreh De'a* 361:1).

LANGUAGE

Gate [*abbula*] – אַבּוּלָא: If the Gemara's intention is to the town gate, this word is likely from the Greek ἐμβολή, *embolè*, one of whose meanings is gate, or the structure in which a gate is built.

NOTES

That was destroyed and rebuilt – דשף ויתיב: The *ge'onim* record a tradition that the synagogue was known as the one that was destroyed and rebuilt because when the Jews were exiled they took stones and materials from the Temple and used them to build the synagogue in Neharde'a.

Once I heard – כיון דשמעית להא: Abaye was certainly familiar with this verse. His intention was that he had not yet studied its full meaning (Rashba). Alternatively, he had assumed that the verse is referring to the Temple, but after hearing that synagogues are also considered miniature sanctuaries, he realized that in Psalms 90:1 as well, "dwelling place" is referring to the synagogues and study halls, and therefore it is especially valuable to study in them (Maharsha).

Why do you seek to enter into a legal dispute – למה תרצו דין: The midrash describes that all the mountains desired for the Torah to be given upon them. They debated among themselves who was the tallest and therefore the most worthy of the privilege. God responded that their great height, an allegorical reference to their arrogance, was in fact the very reason they were considered unfit for the task (Maharsha).

BACKGROUND

Neharde'a – נהרדעא: A city on the Euphrates, near the Malka River, Neharde'a was one of the oldest Jewish communities in Babylonia. According to tradition, Jews lived in Neharde'a as early as First Temple period, in the sixth century BCE, beginning with the exile of King Jehoiachin of Judea. Neharde'a was one of the most important Jewish communities in Babylonia. It was a center of Torah learning from an early period, and its yeshiva was the oldest in Babylonia. Many of the greatest *tanna'im* visited Neharde'a, among them Rabbi Akiva, who intercalated the calendar there (*Yevamot* 122b). During Rav's time, the first half of the third century CE, the yeshiva in Neharde'a was headed by Rav Sheila, and after him by Shmuel. Since the city lay near the border between the Roman and the Persian Empires, it frequently suffered from the wars between the two, and Papa ben Nazer Odonathus, king of Tadmor, destroyed it completely in 259 CE. Later, however, Jews resettled there, and many Torah scholars remained in Neharde'a even after its yeshiva split and was reestablished in Meḥoza and Pumbedita.

PERSONALITIES

Rav Sheshet – רב ששת: A prominent third-generation Babylonian *amora*, Rav Sheshet was the primary student of Rav Huna, although he also served and studied under the rest of the Sages of that generation. Even in his generation, Rav Sheshet was famous for his unsurpassed expertise in *baraitot*. Due to his comprehensive familiarity with even the most obscure areas of Oral Law, he was nicknamed Sinai. Many of the Sages of the generation came to study from him, as they knew that his teachings were always based on early sources. In his later years, Rav Sheshet became blind, but he remained involved in all aspects of life and was a frequent visitor to the house of the Exilarch. He was characteristically extremely forceful, hard as steel, and did not defer even to eminent world leaders. Apparently, Rav Sheshet supported himself as a garment merchant and earned enough to live comfortably.

בבבל היכא? אמר אביי: בבי כנישתא דהוצל, ובבי כנישתא דשף ויתיב בנהרדעא. ולא תימא הכא והכא, אלא: זמנין הכא, וזמנין הכא. אמר אביי: תיתי לי, דכי מרחיקנא פרסה – עיילנא ומצלינא התם. אבוה דשמואל [ולוי] הוו יתבי בכנישתא דשף ויתיב בנהרדעא, אתיא שכינה, שמעו קול ריגשא. [קמו ונפקו.

The Gemara asks: **Where in Babylonia** does the Divine Presence reside? **Abaye said: In the** ancient **synagogue of Huzal and in the synagogue that was destroyed and rebuilt**[N] **in Neharde'a.**[B] **And do not say** that the Divine Presence resided **here and there,** i.e., in both places simultaneously. **Rather, at times** it resided **here** in Huzal **and at times there** in Neharde'a. **Abaye said: I have** a blessing **coming to me, for whenever I am** within **a distance of a parasang** from one of those synagogues, **I go in and pray there,** due to the special honor and sanctity attached to them. It was related that **the father of Shmuel and Levi were** once **sitting in the synagogue that was destroyed and rebuilt in Neharde'a. The Divine Presence came** and **they heard a loud sound,** so **they arose and left.**

רב ששת הוה יתיב בבי כנישתא דשף ויתיב בנהרדעא אתיא שכינה] ולא נפק. אתו מלאכי השרת וקא מבעתו ליה, אמר לפניו: רבונו של עולם! עלוב ושאינו עלוב מי נדחה מפני מי? אמר להו: שבקוהו.

It was further related that **Rav Sheshet**[P] **was** once **sitting in the synagogue that was destroyed and rebuilt in Neharde'a,** and **the Divine Presence came but he did not go out. The ministering angels came and were frightening him** in order to force him to leave. Rav Sheshet turned to God and **said before Him: Master of the Universe,** if one is **wretched and** the other is **not wretched, who should defer to whom?** Shouldn't the one who is not wretched give way to the one who is? Now I am blind and wretched; why then do you expect me to defer to the angels? God then turned to the angels and **said to them: Leave him.**

"ואהי להם למקדש מעט", אמר רבי יצחק: אלו בתי כנסיות ובתי מדרשות שבבבל. ורבי אלעזר אמר: זה בית רבינו שבבבל.

The verse states: **"Yet I have been to them as a little sanctuary** in the countries where they have come" (Ezekiel 11:16). **Rabbi Yitzḥak said: This** is referring to **the synagogues and study halls in Babylonia. And Rabbi Elazar said: This** is referring to **the house of our master,** i.e., Rav, **in Babylonia,** from which Torah issues forth to the entire world.

דרש רבא: מאי דכתיב "ה' מעון אתה היית לנו" – אלו בתי כנסיות ובתי מדרשות. אמר אביי: מריש הואי גריסנא בביתא ומצלינא בבי כנשתא, כיון דשמעית להא דקאמר דוד "ה' אהבתי מעון ביתך" – הואי גריסנא בבי כנישתא.

Rava interpreted a verse **homiletically: What is** the meaning of that **which is written: "Lord, You have been our dwelling place** in all generations" (Psalms 90:1)? **This** is referring to **the synagogues and study halls. Abaye said: Initially, I used to study** Torah **in** my **home and pray in the synagogue. Once I heard**[N] and understood **that which** King **David says: "Lord, I love the habitation of Your house"** (Psalms 26:8), **I would** always **study** Torah **in the synagogue,** to express my love for the place in which the Divine Presence resides.

תניא, רבי אלעזר הקפר אומר: עתידין בתי כנסיות ובתי מדרשות שבבבל שיקבעו בארץ ישראל, שנאמר "כי כתבור בהרים וככרמל בים יבא", והלא דברים קל וחומר: ומה תבור וכרמל שלא באו אלא לפי שעה ללמוד תורה – נקבעים בארץ ישראל, בתי כנסיות ובתי מדרשות שקורין ומרביצין בהן תורה – על אחת כמה וכמה.

It is taught in a *baraita*: **Rabbi Elazar HaKappar says: In the future, the synagogues and the study halls in Babylonia will be** transported and **reestablished in Eretz Yisrael, as it is stated: "Surely, like Tabor among the mountains, and like Carmel by the sea, so shall he come"** (Jeremiah 46:18). There is a tradition that these mountains came to Sinai at the giving of the Torah and demanded that the Torah should be given upon them. **And are these matters not** inferred through an ***a fortiori*** argument: **Just as Tabor and Carmel, which came only momentarily to study Torah, were** relocated and **established in Eretz Yisrael** in reward for their actions, **all the more so** should **the synagogues and study halls** in Babylonia, **in which the Torah is read and disseminated,** be relocated to Eretz Yisrael.

דרש בר קפרא: מאי דכתיב "למה תרצדון הרים גבנונים", יצתה בת קול ואמרה להם: למה תרצו דין עם סיני? כולכם בעלי מומים אתם אצל סיני. כתיב הכא "גבנונים" וכתיב התם "או גבן או דק", אמר רב אשי: שמע מינה האי מאן דיהיר – בעל מום הוא.

Bar Kappara interpreted a verse **homiletically: What is** the meaning of that **which is written: "Why do you look askance [*teratzdun*], O high-peaked mountains,** at the mountain that God has desired for His abode" (Psalms 68:17)? **A Divine Voice issued forth and said to** all the mountains that came and demanded that the Torah be given upon them: **Why do you seek [*tirtzu*]** to enter into **a legal dispute**[N] **[*din*]** with **Mount Sinai? You are all blemished in comparison to Mount Sinai,** as **it is written here: "High-peaked [*gavnunnim*]" and it is written there,** with regard to the blemishes that disqualify a priest: **"Or crookbacked [*gibben*] or a dwarf"** (Leviticus 21:20). **Rav Ashi said: Learn from** this that **one who is arrogant is** considered **blemished.** The other mountains arrogantly insisted that the Torah should be given upon them, and they were therefore described as blemished.

אֵין עוֹשִׂין אוֹתוֹ קַפֶּנְדַּרְיָא: מַאי קַפֶּנְדַּרְיָא? אֲמַר רָבָא: קַפֶּנְדַּרְיָא כִּשְׁמָהּ – מַאי כִּשְׁמָהּ? כְּמַאן דְּאָמַר: אַדְּמַקִּיפְנָא אַדָּרֵי אֵיעוֹל בְּהָא.

§ The mishna teaches that even if a synagogue fell into ruin, **it may not be made** into a *kappendarya*.[L] The Gemara asks: **What is** meant by ***kappendarya*? Rava said: A shortcut,**[H] **as** implied by **its name.** The Gemara clarifies: **What** do you mean by adding: **As** implied by **its name?** It is **like one who said: Instead of going around the** entire row of **houses** [*makkifna addari*] to get to the other side, thereby lengthening my journey, **I will enter this** house and walk through it to the other side. The word *kappendarya* sounds like a contraction of *makkifna addari*. This is what Rava meant by saying: As implied by its name.

אָמַר רַבִּי אַבָּהוּ: אִם הָיָה שְׁבִיל מֵעִיקָּרָא – מוּתָּר.

Rabbi Abbahu said: If a public **path had initially** passed through that location, before the synagogue was built, **it is permitted** to continue to use it as a shortcut, for the honor due to a synagogue cannot annul the public's right of access to the path.

אָמַר רַב נַחְמָן בַּר יִצְחָק: הַנִּכְנָס עַל מְנָת שֶׁלֹּא לַעֲשׂוֹת קַפֶּנְדַּרְיָא מוּתָּר לַעֲשׂוֹתוֹ קַפֶּנְדַּרְיָא. וְאָמַר רַבִּי חֶלְבּוֹ אָמַר רַב הוּנָא: הַנִּכְנָס לְבֵית הַכְּנֶסֶת לְהִתְפַּלֵּל מוּתָּר לַעֲשׂוֹתוֹ קַפֶּנְדַּרְיָא, שֶׁנֶּאֱמַר ״וּבְבֹא עַם הָאָרֶץ לִפְנֵי ה׳ בַּמּוֹעֲדִים הַבָּא דֶּרֶךְ שַׁעַר צָפוֹן לְהִשְׁתַּחֲווֹת יֵצֵא דֶּרֶךְ שַׁעַר נֶגֶב״.

Rav Naḥman bar Yitzḥak said: With regard to **one who enters** a synagogue **without intending to make it** into **a shortcut,** when he leaves **he is permitted to make it** into **a shortcut** for himself, by leaving through the exit on the other side of the building. **And Rabbi Ḥelbo said** that **Rav Huna said:** With regard to **one who enters a synagogue to pray, he is permitted to make it** into a **shortcut** for himself[N] by leaving through a different exit, and it is fitting to do so, **as it is stated: "And when the people of the land shall come before the Lord in the appointed seasons, he that enters by way of the north gate to bow down shall go forth by the way of the south gate"** (Ezekiel 46:9). This indicates that it is a show of respect not to leave through the same entrance through which one came in; it is better to leave through the other side.

״עָלוּ בּוֹ עֲשָׂבִים לֹא יִתְלוֹשׁ מִפְּנֵי עַגְמַת נֶפֶשׁ״. וְהָתַנְיָא: אֵינוֹ תּוֹלֵשׁ וּמַאֲכִיל, אֲבָל תּוֹלֵשׁ וּמַנִּיחַ! כִּי תְּנַן נַמִי מַתְנִיתִין – תּוֹלֵשׁ וּמַאֲכִיל תְּנַן.

§ The mishna teaches: If **grass sprang up**[H] **in** a ruined synagogue, although it is not befitting its sanctity, **one should not pick** it, **due to** the **anguish** that it will cause to those who see it. It will remind them of the disrepair of the synagogue and the need to rebuild it. The Gemara asks: **But isn't it taught** in a *baraita*: **One may not pick** the grass **and feed** it to one's animals, **but he may pick** it **and leave** it there? The Gemara answers: **When we learned** the prohibition against picking the grass in **the mishna as well, we learned** only that it is prohibited to **pick** it and **feed** it to one's animals, but it is permitted to leave it there.

תָּנוּ רַבָּנַן: בֵּית הַקְּבָרוֹת אֵין נוֹהֲגִין בָּהֶן קַלּוּת רֹאשׁ: אֵין מַרְעִין בָּהֶן בְּהֵמָה, וְאֵין מוֹלִיכִין בָּהֶן אַמַּת הַמַּיִם, וְאֵין מְלַקְּטִין בָּהֶן עֲשָׂבִים, וְאִם לִיקֵּט – שׂוֹרְפָן בִּמְקוֹמָן מִפְּנֵי כְּבוֹד מֵתִים.

The Sages taught in a *baraita*: In **a cemetery, one may not act with frivolity; one may not graze an animal** on the grass growing **inside it; and one may not direct a water channel** to pass **through it;**[N] **and one may not gather grass inside it** to use the grass as feed for one's animals; **and if one gathered** grass for that purpose, **it should be burnt on the spot, out of respect for the dead.**[H]

אַהַיָּיא? אִילֵימָא אַסֵּיפָא – כֵּיוָן שֶׁשּׂוֹרְפָן בִּמְקוֹמָן מַאי כְּבוֹד מֵתִים אִיכָּא? אֶלָּא אַרֵישָׁא.

The Gemara clarifies: With regard to the phrase: Out of respect for the dead, **to which** clause of the *baraita* does it refer? **If we say** it is referring **to the last clause,** that if one gathered grass that it should be burnt out of respect for the dead, then one could ask: **Since** the grass **is burnt on the spot,** and not publicly, **what respect for the dead is there** in this act? **Rather,** the phrase must be referring **to the first clause** of the *baraita*, and it explains why it is prohibited to act with frivolity.

מתני׳ רֹאשׁ חֹדֶשׁ אֲדָר שֶׁחָל לִהְיוֹת בְּשַׁבָּת – קוֹרִין בְּפָרָשַׁת שְׁקָלִים. חָל לִהְיוֹת בְּתוֹךְ הַשַּׁבָּת – מַקְדִּימִין לְשֶׁעָבַר, וּמַפְסִיקִין לְשַׁבָּת אַחֶרֶת,

MISHNA On four *Shabbatot* during and surrounding the month of Adar, a Torah portion of seasonal significance is read. When **the New Moon of Adar occurs on Shabbat,** the congregation **reads the portion of *Shekalim*** on that Shabbat. If the New Moon **occurs during** the middle of **the week, they advance** the reading of that portion **to the previous** Shabbat, **and,** in such a case, **they interrupt** the reading of the four portions **on the following Shabbat,** which would be the first Shabbat of the month of Adar, and no additional portion is read on it.

LANGUAGE

Shortcut [*kappendarya*] – קַפֶּנְדַּרְיָא: Apparently from the Latin phrase, via compendria, meaning a short route. Rava's explanation was not providing the source of the word but rather for remembering it by the similar sounding Aramaic phrase *makkif dara*.

HALAKHA

Using a synagogue as a shortcut – קַפֶּנְדַּרְיָא בְּבֵית הַכְּנֶסֶת: It is prohibited to pass through a synagogue in order to shorten one's journey. However, if one reads or learns a little in the synagogue, it is permitted (*Mishna Berura*). If the path existed before the synagogue was built, it remains permitted to use it. It appears that this prohibition applies only to the synagogue building itself. However, it is permitted to use the synagogue courtyard and even the hallway of a synagogue as a shortcut (*Arukh HaShulḥan*). If one enters a synagogue in order to pray, it is a mitzva for him to leave through an entrance different from the one through which he entered (*Shulḥan Arukh, Oraḥ Ḥayyim* 151:5).

If grass sprang up – עָלוּ בּוֹ עֲשָׂבִים: One must continue to show respect to a synagogue even if it falls into disrepair, even in the Diaspora (*Mishna Berura*). If grass sprung up inside it, it may be picked. However, there is no obligation to do so (*Mishna Berura*). Even if the grass is picked, it should be left on the ground where it was picked in order that those who see it feel anguish over the synagogue's state that will lead them to rebuild it. If it has been decided not to rebuild that synagogue and a different synagogue has already been built, this *halakha* does not apply. Nevertheless, according to the opinion of the *Taz*, even in such a case, it is fitting to place a boundary around the ruins, in order that people will not act disrespectfully when inside them (*Shulḥan Arukh, Oraḥ Ḥayyim* 151:10).

Respect for a cemetery – כְּבוֹד בֵּית הַקְּבָרוֹת: One should not act with frivolity in a cemetery. One should not eat or drink there, nor may one read, learn, or make calculations there. One may not graze animals there. Water canals may not be directed through a cemetery, nor may a cemetery be used as a shortcut. Grass should not be picked from a cemetery. If it is picked, for instance, in order to maintain the graves, it should be burned on the spot (*Shulḥan Arukh, Yoreh De'a* 368:1, and in the comment of Rema).

NOTES

He is permitted to make it into a shortcut for himself – מוּתָּר לַעֲשׂוֹתוֹ קַפֶּנְדַּרְיָא: Many of the commentaries suggest that because of the verse in Ezekiel, it is not only permitted in this instance to use the synagogue as a shortcut, but it is a mitzva to do so. Although the Gemara states only that it is permitted and does not state that it's a mitzva, it could be referring to a case where there are multiple alternative exits; specifically selecting the one that is more convenient is permitted although not a mitzva.

One may not direct a water channel to pass through it – אֵין מוֹלִיכִין בָּהֶן אַמַּת הַמַּיִם: Most of the prohibitions in a cemetery exist in order to defend the honor of the dead. Although they are now but dust of the earth, they were once great people. However, the prohibition against directing a water channel to pass through a cemetery is due to the concern that it may break its banks and flood the graves (Rabbeinu Yehonatan).

NOTES

They resume the regular order of readings – חוֹזְרִין לְכִסְדְרָן: Although the return to the regular weekly cycle is ostensibly an obvious fact, some suggest that one might have mistakenly suggested that since it so close to Passover, portions from the Torah relating to that Festival should be read instead (*Penei Yehoshua*).

HALAKHA

The four portions – אַרְבַּע פָּרָשִׁיּוֹת: During the month of Adar and just prior to it, four special Torah portions are read, as explained in the Gemara (*Shulḥan Arukh*, *Oraḥ Ḥayyim* 685).

They make a public announcement concerning the half-shekels – מַשְׁמִיעִין עַל הַשְּׁקָלִים: When the Temple stood, the requirement to donate the half-shekels was publicly announced on the first of Adar, in order that people give it during that month (Rambam *Sefer Zemanim*, *Hilkhot Shekalim* 1:9).

בַּשְּׁנִיָּה ״זָכוֹר״, בַּשְּׁלִישִׁית ״פָּרָה אֲדוּמָּה״, בָּרְבִיעִית ״הַחוֹדֶשׁ הַזֶּה לָכֶם״, בַּחֲמִישִׁית חוֹזְרִין לְכִסְדְרָן.

On the second Shabbat, the Shabbat prior to Purim, they read the portion: "**Remember** what Amalek did" (Deuteronomy 25:17–19), which details the mitzva to remember and destroy the nation of Amalek. **On the third** Shabbat, they read the portion of **the Red Heifer** [*Para*] (Numbers 19:1–22), which details the purification process for one who became ritually impure through contact with a corpse. **On the fourth** Shabbat, they read the portion: "**This month** [*haḥodesh*] **shall be for you**" (Exodus 12:1–20), which describes the offering of the Paschal lamb. **On the fifth** Shabbat, **they resume the** regular weekly **order** of readings[N] and no special portion is read.[H]

לַכֹּל מַפְסִיקִין, בְּרָאשֵׁי חֳדָשִׁים, בַּחֲנוּכָּה, וּבְפוּרִים, בְּתַעֲנִיּוֹת, וּבְמַעֲמָדוֹת, וּבְיוֹם הַכִּפּוּרִים.

For all special days, the congregation **interrupts** the regular weekly order of readings, and a special portion relating to the character of the day is read. This applies **on the New Moons, on Hanukkah, and on Purim, on fast days, and on the** non-priestly **watches, and on Yom Kippur.**

גמ׳ תְּנַן הָתָם בְּאֶחָד בַּאֲדָר מַשְׁמִיעִין עַל הַשְּׁקָלִים

GEMARA **We learned** in a mishna **there** (*Shekalim* 1:1): **On the first of Adar they make** a public **announcement concerning** the forthcoming collection of half-**shekels.**[H] The money is used for the communal offerings in the Temple in the coming year.

Perek **IV**
Daf **29** Amud **b**

HALAKHA

And concerning diverse kinds – וְעַל הַכִּלְאַיִם: On the first of Adar, an announcement is made concerning diverse kinds, and everyone goes out and uproots any instances of diverse kinds in his fields (Rambam *Sefer Zera'im*, *Hilkhot Kilayim* 2:15).

Offering from the new collections – קׇרְבָּן מִתְּרוּמָה חֲדָשָׁה: From the New Moon of Nisan, offerings may be brought only from animals purchased with the new collections. However, in the event that the collection was not yet made, money from the old collection may be used (Rambam *Sefer Zemanim*, *Hilkhot Shekalim* 4:11).

וְעַל הַכִּלְאַיִם.

And a public announcement is made **concerning** the need to uproot any instances of **diverse kinds**[H] that have grown in the fields.

בִּשְׁלָמָא עַל הַכִּלְאַיִם – דִּזְמַן זְרִיעָה הִיא, אֶלָּא עַל הַשְּׁקָלִים מְנָלַן?

The Gemara asks: **Granted,** an announcement is made **concerning** the need to uproot **diverse kinds, as** the beginning of the month of Adar **is a time of sowing.** Instances of diverse kinds are already noticeable, and therefore it is a fitting time to deal with the matter. **But** with regard to the announcement **concerning the** half-**shekels, from where do we** derive that it should be made at this point in the year?

אָמַר רַבִּי טָבִי אָמַר רַבִּי יֹאשִׁיָּה: דְּאָמַר קְרָא ״זֹאת עוֹלַת חוֹדֶשׁ בְּחָדְשׁוֹ״, אָמְרָה תּוֹרָה: חַדֵּשׁ וְהָבֵא קׇרְבָּן מִתְּרוּמָה חֲדָשָׁה.

Rabbi Tavi said that **Rabbi Yoshiyya said:** It is **as the verse states: "This is the burnt-offering of each New Moon in its renewal** throughout the months of the year" (Numbers 28:14). **The Torah says:** There is a month in which you must begin to **renew and bring the** daily and additional **offering from** animals purchased with **the new collections**[H] of half-shekels collected that year. Each year a collection is made with which to finance the purchase of communal offerings for the following year. Offerings during that year may be purchased only from collections made for that year.

וְכֵיוָן דְּבְנִיסָן בָּעֵי אַקְרוּבֵי מִתְּרוּמָה חֲדָשָׁה, קָדְמִינַן וְקָרֵינַן בְּאֶחָד בַּאֲדָר, כִּי הֵיכִי דְּלֵיתוּ שְׁקָלִים לַמִּקְדָּשׁ.

Elsewhere it is derived through a verbal analogy that the yearly cycle begins with the month of Nisan. **And since** starting from and **during** the month of **Nisan** the offerings **must be brought from the new collections** of half-shekels, it is necessary to make the collection in the preceding month, i.e., in Adar. Therefore, **they advance** the reading of *Shekalim*, **and they read** it **on the first of Adar, in order that** the people **will** be reminded to **bring** the half-**shekels to the Temple** in good time.

כמאן – דלא כרבן שמעון בן גמליאל. דאי רבן שמעון בן גמליאל – האמר שתי שבתות, דתניא: שואלין בהלכות הפסח קודם לפסח שלשים יום, רבן שמעון בן גמליאל אומר: שתי שבתות.

The Gemara asks: **In accordance with whose** opinion is the mishna taught? It is **not in accordance with** the opinion of **Rabban Shimon ben Gamliel, for if** someone would suggest that it is in accordance with the opinion of **Rabban Shimon ben Gamliel,** one could counter: **Didn't he say** that **two weeks** is a sufficient period of preparation? **As it is taught** in a *baraita*: **We** begin to **inquire into the *halakhot* of Passover**[HN] **thirty days before Passover. Rabban Shimon ben Gamliel says:** We begin to inquire only **two weeks** before Passover. As such, it should be sufficient to announce the collection of half-shekels from two weeks before Nisan, and there should be no need to advance the announcement to the beginning of Adar, as stated in the mishna.

אפילו תימא רבן שמעון בן גמליאל, כיון דאמר מר: בחמשה עשר בו שולחנות יושבין במדינה, ובעשרים וחמשה יושבין במקדש – משום שולחנות קדמינן וקרינן.

Even if **you say** that the mishna is in accordance with the opinion of **Rabban Shimon ben Gamliel,** it is possible that even he agrees that the announcement concerning the collection of the half-shekels should be made on the first of Adar, **since the Master said: On the fifteenth** of Adar money-changing **tables**[B] for collecting the half-shekels **are set up throughout the country, and on the twenty-fifth** of Adar **they are set up in the Temple.**[HN] **Because of** the possibility to donate the half-shekels at **the tables** already from the fifteenth, **they advance** the reading of *Shekalim* to inform people of that possibility **and read it** two weeks earlier, on the first of Adar.

מאי פרשת שקלים? רב אמר: "צו את בני ישראל ואמרת אליהם את קרבני לחמי". ושמואל אמר: "כי תשא".

§ The Gemara clarifies which passage is read: **What is this portion of *Shekalim*?**[HN] **Rav said:** It is the portion of **"Command the children of Israel, and say to them: My offering, the provision** of My offerings made by fire" (Numbers 28), which details the daily and additional offerings. **And Shmuel said:** It is the portion of **"When you take the count"** (Exodus 30:11–16).

בשלמא למאן דאמר "כי תשא" היינו דקרי לה פרשת שקלים, דכתיב בה שקלים. אלא למאן דאמר "את קרבני לחמי", הכא מידי שקלים כתיבי התם? אין, טעמא מאי – כדרבי טבי.

Granted, according to the one who said that it is the portion of **"When you take the count," this is** the reason **that it is called the portion of *Shekalim*, for** the obligation to give half-**shekels is written in** that portion. **However, according to one who said** that it is the portion of **"My offering, the provision** of My offerings," why should that portion be read? **Is there anything written** about the half-**shekels here?** The Gemara answers: **Yes. What is the reason** that they are collected in Adar? **As per** the explanation **of Rabbi Tavi,** the half-shekels are collected to be used for the coming year's daily and additional offerings. Therefore, reading the portion concerning those offerings will serve well as a reminder for people to donate.

HALAKHA

We begin to inquire into the *halakhot* of Passover – שואלין בהלכות הפסח: Queries are made with regard to the laws of Passover from thirty days beforehand. This is in accordance with the opinion of the Rabbis who dispute the opinion of Rabbi Shimon ben Gamliel. Some say this *halakha* applies also to the other Festivals (*Magen Avraham*, citing *Baḥ*). However, others claim that a three-day period before *Shavuot* is sufficient (Vilna Gaon). Others limit the *halakha* to Passover (*Mishna Berura*, citing *Beit Yosef*). Nowadays, when there are no offerings, the custom is limited to delivering a halakhic discourse on the Shabbat before Passover. However, some claim that even nowadays the thirty-day period still applies (*Tosafot*; see *Taz*). For all Festivals, during the Festival itself, there is an obligation to study the *halakhot* of the day (*Magen Avraham*; *Shulḥan Arukh*, *Oraḥ Ḥayyim* 429:1).

The collection of half-shekels – גביית מחצית השקל: On the fifteenth of Adar, the money changers sit in every city and request the half-shekel. However, they do not force the people to contribute. On the twenty-fifth of Adar, the money changers sit in the Temple, and they then begin to demand the contribution of the half-shekel (Rambam *Sefer Zemanim*, *Hilkhot Shekalim* 1:9).

This portion of *Shekalim* – פרשת שקלים: *Shekalim* is the portion of Exodus 30:11–16. This is in accordance with the opinion of Rav. Although the *halakha* is normally decided in accordance with Shmuel, in this case there is a *baraita* in accordance with Rav's opinion, and the Gemara discusses his opinion, which suggests that it rules in accordance with him. The story involving Jehoiada the priest is read as the *haftara* (*Shulḥan Arukh*, *Oraḥ Ḥayyim* 685:1).

BACKGROUND

Money-changing tables – שולחנות: Every adult male, both in Eretz Yisrael and in the Diaspora, was obligated to donate a half-shekel toward the purchase of the public offerings and the maintenance of the Temple. Through this, the entire Jewish people became partners in the Temple service. The key issue was not the amount that was given, but the fact that each person gave the same amount. Therefore, it is understandable that the amount to be donated was changed throughout the generations. For example, toward the end of the Temple period, the amount was fixed at two dinars, which is half a *sela* and is referred to as the sacred shekel. The donation was not always made in the exact amount and the money changers would provide change. Therefore, to ensure the right amount was given and to pay the money changers for their efforts, a small coin was paid in addition to the half-shekel.

NOTES

We begin to inquire into the *halakhot* of Passover – שואלין בהלכות הפסח: This is referring neither to the announcement of the upcoming Festival nor to the delivery of sermons concerning it. Rather, it is referring to the point at which it is deemed appropriate to begin analyzing the pertinent *halakhot* in the study hall. As such, it is possible that even the Sages, who dispute Rabban Shimon ben Gamliel here, would agree that two weeks prior to an event is sufficient time for a public announcement. They dispute only that the analysis of the *halakhot* requires a longer time (Ritva).

And on the twenty-fifth they are set up in the Temple – ובעשרים וחמשה יושבין במקדש: Rashi explains that from this date, tables were set up in the Temple in order to inform people that those who had still not fulfilled their obligation to donate a half-shekel would be forced to do so. The Ritva and the Meiri add that by this date the majority of people had certainly already paid their dues, and therefore it was no longer necessary to have tables set up in the rest of the country. With regard to the choice of this date, some suggest it is based on the opinion of Rabbi Yehoshua that the world was created on the twenty fifth-of Adar, which makes it a fitting time for a beginning (Rav Yitzḥak Ḥaver). The *Turei Even* discusses at length the need to prepare the offerings for the New Moon of Nisan from four days prior to it, which is the twenty-fifth of Adar.

What is this portion of *Shekalim* – מאי פרשת שקלים: It is difficult to understand how this matter could be subject to a dispute. Wasn't it consistently practiced each and every year, and the choice of portion well known? Some suggest that the dispute relates only to the choice of portion when the New Moon of Adar occurs on a Shabbat, something that did not occur often (*Penei Yehoshua*; see *Sefat Emet*).

בִּשְׁלָמָא לְמַאן דְּאָמַר "צַו אֶת בְּנֵי יִשְׂרָאֵל" – מִשּׁוּם דִּכְתִיבִי קׇרְבָּנוֹת הָתָם, כִּדְרַבִּי טָבִי. אֶלָּא לְמַאן דְּאָמַר "כִּי תִשָּׂא", קׇרְבָּנוֹת מִי כְּתִיבִי? שְׁקָלִים לַאֲדָנִים כְּתִיבִי!

Granted, according to the one who said that it is the portion of **"Command the children of Israel:** My offering, the provision of My offerings," it is logical to read that portion, **because the offerings** that will be purchased with the half-shekels **are written there, as per** the explanation **of Rabbi Tavi. However, according to one who said** that it is the portion of **"When you take the count,"** why should that portion be read? **Is** anything about **the offerings written** in that portion? The collection of half-**shekels for** use in the construction of **the sockets**[B] of the Tabernacle **are** the only thing **written** in that portion. What does that have to do with the collection of half-shekels for the purchase of offerings that is held in the month of Adar?

כִּדְתָנֵי רַב יוֹסֵף: שָׁלֹשׁ תְּרוּמוֹת הֵן, שֶׁל מִזְבֵּחַ לַמִּזְבֵּחַ, וְשֶׁל אֲדָנִים לַאֲדָנִים, וְשֶׁל בֶּדֶק הַבַּיִת לְבֶדֶק הַבַּיִת.

The Gemara answers: The selection of that portion is **in accordance with** the explanation of the portion **that Rav Yosef taught:** The three instances of the word: Contribution, in that portion teach that **there were three contributions** of half-shekels:[N] The contribution **of the altar** is **for** the purchase of communal offerings to be sacrificed on **the altar; and** the contribution **of the sockets** is **for** constructing **the sockets; and** the contribution **of the Temple maintenance** is **for the Temple maintenance.** Therefore, according to Rav Yosef, it is understandable why the portion of "When you take the count" is read. It deals explicitly with the collection of half-shekels.

בִּשְׁלָמָא לְמַאן דְּאָמַר "כִּי תִשָּׂא" הַיְינוּ דְּשָׁנֵי הַאי רֹאשׁ חֹדֶשׁ מִשְּׁאָר רָאשֵׁי חֳדָשִׁים,

The Gemara asks further: **Granted, according to the one who said** that it is the portion of **"When you take the count," this is what is different** about **this New Moon** of Adar **and other New Moons** when they occur on Shabbat. On the New Moon of Adar, "When you take the count" is read because it describes the collection of half-shekels. On other New Moons, when they occur on Shabbat, the portion of "Command the children of Israel" is read because it mentions the additional offerings brought on Shabbat and the New Moon.

אֶלָּא לְמַאן דְּאָמַר "צַו...אֶת קׇרְבָּנִי" מַאי שָׁנֵי? שָׁנֵי, דְּאִילּוּ רָאשֵׁי חֳדָשִׁים – קָרוּ שִׁיתָּא בְּעִנְיָינָא דְּיוֹמָא, וְחַד בְּדְרֹאשׁ חוֹדֶשׁ. וְאִילּוּ הָאִידָּנָא כּוּלְּהוּ בִּדְרֹאשׁ חוֹדֶשׁ.

However, according to the one who said that **"Command** the children of Israel, and say to them: **My offering," what is different** about the portion read on the New Moon of Adar and the portion read on other New Moons when they occur on Shabbat, for the same portion is read in all cases? The Gemara answers: They are **different: For** on other **New Moons,** when they occur on Shabbat, **six** people **read from** the regular weekly portion **of the matter of the day and one** reads **from** the portion for **the New Moon, whereas now,** on the New Moon of Adar, if it occurs on Shabbat, **all** seven read from the portion of **the New Moon.**

הָנִיחָא לְמַאן דַּאֲמַר לְסֵדֶר פָּרָשִׁיּוֹת הוּא חוֹזֵר,

The Gemara asks: This answer **works out well according to the one who said that** when the mishna states that on the fifth Shabbat, we resume the regular order of readings. The intention is that **one resumes the** regular weekly **order** of Torah **portions.** This implies that on the previous four *Shabbatot*, the regular portion was not read at all. Rather, only the special portions delineated in the mishna were read. Therefore, it makes sense to say that all seven people read from the special portion.

אֶלָּא לְמַאן דַּאֲמַר לְסֵדֶר הַפְטָרוֹת הוּא חוֹזֵר, וּפָרָשָׁתָא דְּיוֹמָא קָרֵינַן, מַאי שָׁנֵי?

However, according to the one who says that the mishna's intention is that **one resumes the** regular **order of concluding** readings from the Prophets [*haftarot*], **and** on the previous *Shabbatot* **one also reads from** the regular portion **of the matter of the day, then** the original question stands: **What is different** about the portion read on the New Moon of Adar and the portion read on other New Moons when they occur on Shabbat?

שָׁנֵי, דְּאִילּוּ רָאשֵׁי חֳדָשִׁים קָרוּ שִׁיתָּא בְּעִנְיָינָא דְּיוֹמָא, וְחַד קָרֵי בִּדְרֹאשׁ חוֹדֶשׁ, וְאִילּוּ הָאִידָּנָא קָרוּ תְּלָתָא בְּעִנְיָינָא דְּיוֹמָא וְאַרְבָּעָה קָרוּ בִּדְרֹאשׁ חוֹדֶשׁ.

The Gemara answers: They are **different: For whereas** on other **New Moons,** when they occur on Shabbat, **six** people **read from** the regular weekly portion **of the matter of the day and one** reads **from** the portion for **the New Moon, now,** on the New Moon of Adar, if it occurs on Shabbat, **three** people read from the regular weekly portion **of the matter of the day and four read from** the portion for **the New Moon.**

BACKGROUND

Sockets – אֲדָנִים:

Depiction of sockets used in the construction of the Tabernacle

NOTES

There were three contributions of half-shekels – שָׁלֹשׁ תְּרוּמוֹת הֵן: The first mention: "A half-shekel, a contribution to the Lord" (Exodus 30:13), is referring to the contribution for the sockets. The mention in the verse "Every one that passes among them that are numbered…shall give a contribution of the Lord" (Exodus 30:14) is referring to the contribution for Temple maintenance. The final mention: "The rich shall not give more, and the poor shall not give less, than a half-shekel, when they give the contribution of the Lord, to make atonement for your souls" (Exodus 30:15), is referring to the contribution for the altar (Rabbeinu Yehonatan).

מֵיתִיבִי: רֹאשׁ חֹדֶשׁ אֲדָר שֶׁחָל לִהְיוֹת בְּשַׁבָּת קוֹרִין בְּפָרָשַׁת שְׁקָלִים, וּמַפְטִירִין בִּיהוֹיָדָע הַכֹּהֵן. בִּשְׁלָמָא לְמַאן דְּאָמַר "כִּי תִשָּׂא" – הַיְינוּ דְּמַפְטִירִין בִּיהוֹיָדָע הַכֹּהֵן", דְּדָמֵי לֵיהּ, דִּכְתִיב "כֶּסֶף נַפְשׁוֹת עֶרְכּוֹ",

The Gemara **raises an objection** from the *Tosefta* (*Megilla* 3:1): When **the New Moon of Adar occurs on Shabbat, they read the** Torah **portion of** ***Shekalim*****, and they read as the** ***haftara*** the story involving **Jehoiada the priest** (II Kings 12:1–17). **Granted, according to the one who said** that *Shekalim* is the portion of **"When you take the count," this is** the reason **that they read as the** ***haftara*** the story involving **Jehoiada the priest: Because it is comparable** in content **to** the Torah reading, **as it is written** in the story of Jehoiada: **"The money of his assessment of persons"** (II Kings 12:5), which is referring to his collection of the half-shekels, and the *haftara* should always contain a theme similar to the Torah reading.

אֶלָּא לְמַאן דְּאָמַר "אֶת קָרְבָּנִי לַחְמִי" מִי דָּמֵי? דָּמֵי, כִּדְרַבִּי טָבִי.

However, according to the one who said that **"My offering, the provision** of My offerings" is read as the portion of *Shekalim*, **is** the *haftara* **comparable** to that portion? **It is comparable, as per** the explanation of **Rabbi Tavi:** It is appropriate to read the portion about offerings because the collection of half-shekels is for that purpose.

מֵיתִיבִי: חָל לִהְיוֹת בַּפָּרָשָׁה הַסְּמוּכָה לָהּ, בֵּין מִלְּפָנֶיהָ וּבֵין מִלְּאַחֲרֶיהָ – קוֹרִין אוֹתָהּ, וְכוֹפְלִין אוֹתָהּ.

The Gemara **raises an objection** from a *baraita*: If the New Moon of Adar **occurs on** the Shabbat on which **the portion** to be read for the regular weekly reading **is adjacent to** the portion read as *Shekalim*, **whether** on the Shabbat **preceding** the Shabbat on which *Shekalim* will be read as part of the weekly reading **or following it,** then **they read and repeat** *Shekalim* on both *Shabbatot*, one time as the special portion *Shekalim* and the other as part of the regular order.

בִּשְׁלָמָא לְמַאן דְּאָמַר "כִּי תִשָּׂא" – הַיְינוּ דְּמִתְרַמֵּי בְּהַהוּא זִימְנָא,

Granted, according to the one who said that the portion of **"When you take the count"** is read as *Shekalim*, **this is** how it is possible: **That** portion **could occur at that time** in the yearlong cycle of the order of readings. In the regular order of reading, "When you take the count" is often read during the beginning of Adar.

אֶלָּא לְמַאן דְּאָמַר "צַו אֶת קָרְבָּנִי", מִי מִתְרַמֵּי בְּהַהוּא זִימְנָא? אִין, לִבְנֵי מַעַרְבָא דְּמַסְּקֵי לִדְאוֹרַיְיתָא בִּתְלָת שְׁנִין.

However, according to the one who said that the portion of **"Command** the children of Israel, and say to them, **My offering"** is read as *Shekalim*, **does** that portion **ever occur at that time** of the year? That portion usually occurs much later in the year, in the summer. The Gemara answers: **Yes,** it sometimes occurs that this portion is read during the beginning of Adar, **for the people of the West,** i.e., Eretz Yisrael, **who complete** the cycle of reading **the Torah** not in one year but **in three years.**[BH]

תַּנְיָא כְּוָותֵיהּ דִּשְׁמוּאֵל: רֹאשׁ חֹדֶשׁ אֲדָר שֶׁחָל לִהְיוֹת בְּשַׁבָּת קוֹרִין "כִּי תִשָּׂא" וּמַפְטִירִין בִּיהוֹיָדָע הַכֹּהֵן.

It is taught in a *baraita* **in accordance with** the opinion of **Shmuel: When the New Moon of Adar occurs on Shabbat, they read** the portion of **"When you take the count," and they read as the** ***haftara*** the story involving **Jehoiada the priest.**

אָמַר רַבִּי יִצְחָק נַפָּחָא: רֹאשׁ חֹדֶשׁ אֲדָר שֶׁחָל לִהְיוֹת בְּשַׁבָּת מוֹצִיאִין שָׁלֹשׁ תּוֹרוֹת וְקוֹרִין בָּהֶן, אֶחָד בְּעִנְיָינוֹ שֶׁל יוֹם, וְאֶחָד בְּשֶׁל רֹאשׁ חֹדֶשׁ, וְאֶחָד בְּ"כִי תִשָּׂא". וְאָמַר רַבִּי יִצְחָק נַפָּחָא: רֹאשׁ חֹדֶשׁ טֵבֵת שֶׁחָל לִהְיוֹת בְּשַׁבָּת מְבִיאִין שָׁלֹשׁ תּוֹרוֹת וְקוֹרִין בָּהֶן: אֶחָד בְּעִנְיָינוֹ שֶׁל יוֹם, וְאֶחָד בְּרֹאשׁ חוֹדֶשׁ, וְאֶחָד בַּחֲנוּכָּה.

§ **Rabbi Yitzḥak Nappaḥa said:** When **the New Moon of Adar occurs on Shabbat,**[H] the congregation **takes out three Torah scrolls**[N] from the ark **and reads from them.** From the first **one,** they read the portion of the regular weekly reading **of the matter of the day;**[N] **and** from the second **one** they read the portion **for the New Moon; and** from the third **one** they read *Shekalim*, which begins with **"When you take the count." And Rabbi Yitzḥak Nappaḥa** further **said:** When **the New Moon of Tevet,** which always falls during Hanukkah, **occurs on Shabbat,**[H] **they bring three Torah scrolls and read from them.** From the first **one,** they read **the** portion of the regular cycle of reading **of the matter of the day; and** from the second **one,** they read the portion **for the New Moon; and** from the third **one,** they read the portion **for Hanukkah.**

BACKGROUND

For the people of the West who complete the cycle of the Torah in three years – לִבְנֵי מַעַרְבָא דְּמַסְּקֵי לִדְאוֹרַיְיתָא בִּתְלָת שְׁנִין: The triennial cycle of completing the Torah reading on Shabbat was commonplace in ancient Eretz Yisrael, and there is testimony of the traveler, Benjamin MiTudela, that even in the twelfth century this was the practice in some communities. According to the traditional Masoretic division of the Torah, the text is divided into 154 sections of at least twenty-one verses each. It is likely that the Torah readings in the triennial cycle were based on this system. Maimonides, who was familiar with this tradition, nevertheless ruled that the annual cycle is the accepted practice (see HALAKHA).

HALAKHA

Who complete the Torah in three years – דְּמַסְּקֵי לִדְאוֹרַיְיתָא בִּתְלָת שְׁנִין: The standard custom is to complete the reading of the entire Torah each year. There are also those who complete it only every three years (Rambam *Sefer Ahava, Hilkhot Tefilla* 13:1).

When the New Moon of Adar occurs on Shabbat – רֹאשׁ חֹדֶשׁ אֲדָר שֶׁחָל לִהְיוֹת בְּשַׁבָּת: When the New Moon of Adar, or, in a leap year, of the second Adar occurs on a Shabbat, three Torah scrolls are taken out. Six people read the regular portion of the week from the first scroll. In places where the custom on a regular Shabbat is to call additional people to read, they may also do so on this Shabbat (*Magen Avraham*). The portion of the New Moon is read from the second scroll, and *Shekalim* is read as *maftir* from the third scroll. This ruling is in accordance with the opinion of Rabbi Yitzḥak Nappaḥa (Rambam *Sefer Ahava, Hilkhot Tefilla* 13:23).

When the New Moon of Tevet occurs on Shabbat – רֹאשׁ חֹדֶשׁ טֵבֵת שֶׁחָל לִהְיוֹת בְּשַׁבָּת: When the New Moon of Tevet, which always occurs during Hanukkah, occurs on Shabbat, three Torah scrolls are taken out. Six people read the entire portion of the week from the first scroll. It would also be permitted to call up only five, even seven, or more (*Mishna Berura*). The portion of the New Moon is read from the second scroll, and the portion for Hanukkah is read from the third scroll (*Shulḥan Arukh, Oraḥ Ḥayyim* 684:3).

NOTES

The congregation takes out three Torah scrolls – מוֹצִיאִין שָׁלֹשׁ תּוֹרוֹת: Although it is possible to use a single scroll and then to roll it from one passage to the next, this would take a long time. It is therefore preferable to use three scrolls in order not to burden the community and keep them waiting. Although the Gemara in tractate *Yoma* (70a) mentions the concern that using additional scrolls will raise suspicions among the members of the congregation that the first scroll is flawed, that concern does not exist when different people read from each scroll (Ritva).

From the first one they read of the matter of the day – אֶחָד בְּעִנְיָינוֹ שֶׁל יוֹם: The order of the readings is based on the principle that a frequent practice takes precedence over an infrequent practice (Ritva).

HALAKHA

When the New Moon of Tevet occurs on a weekday – רֹאשׁ חֹדֶשׁ טֵבֵת שֶׁחָל לִהְיוֹת בְּחוֹל: When the New Moon of Tevet occurs on a weekday, two Torah scrolls are taken out. From the first scroll, three read the portion for the New Moon and the fourth reads from the second scroll the portion for Hanukkah. This ruling is in accordance with the opinion of Rava (*Shulḥan Arukh, Oraḥ Ḥayyim* 684:3).

NOTES

What caused the fourth to come – מִי גָּרַם לָרְבִיעִי שֶׁיָּבֹא: An additional reason to give preference to the portion for Hanukkah is that since there is a mitzva on Hanukkah to publicize the miracle, the reading for Hanukkah should be given greater prominence (*Penei Yehoshua*).

וּצְרִיכָא: דְּאִי אִיתְּמַר בְּהָא – בְּהָא קָאָמַר רַבִּי יִצְחָק, אֲבָל בְּהָךְ – כְּרַב סְבִירָא לֵיהּ, דְּאָמַר פָּרָשַׁת שְׁקָלִים "אֶת קָרְבָּנִי לַחְמִי", וּבִשְׁתֵּי תוֹרוֹת סַגִּי, קָא מַשְׁמַע לָן.

The Gemara comments: **And** it is **necessary** for Rabbi Yitzḥak Nappaḥa to state the *halakha* in both cases, **as, if it had been stated** only **with regard to** the New Moon of Tevet, one could have mistakenly thought that only **with regard to that** case **does Rabbi Yitzḥak** Nappaḥa **state** that three Torah scrolls are used. **But with regard to** the New Moon of Adar, one might think that **he holds in accordance with** the opinion of **Rav, who said** that **the portion of *Shekalim* is** the portion of **"My offering, the provision** of My offerings," **and two Torah** scrolls will therefore **suffice,** since the same portion is used both for the portion for the New Moon and for the portion of *Shekalim*. Therefore, he **teaches us** that three Torah scrolls are used even on the New Moon of Adar.

וְלֵימָא הָא וְלָא בָּעֵיָא הָךְ! חֲדָא מִכְּלַל חֲבֶירְתָּהּ אִיתְּמַר.

The Gemara asks: **But,** based on that logic, **let** Rabbi Yitzḥak just **say** the *halakha* **with respect to this** case of the New Moon of Adar, **and there would be no need** to state **that** case of the New Moon of Tevet. The Gemara answers: Indeed, **one was stated from the other by inference,** i.e., Rabbi Yitzḥak Nappaḥa stated the *halakha* explicitly only with regard to the New Moon of Adar, and it was inferred that the same is true of the New Moon of Tevet.

אִיתְּמַר, רֹאשׁ חֹדֶשׁ טֵבֵת שֶׁחָל לִהְיוֹת בְּחוֹל, אָמַר רַבִּי יִצְחָק: קָרוּ תְּלָתָא בְּרֹאשׁ חֹדֶשׁ וְחַד בַּחֲנוּכָּה. וְרַב דִּימִי דְּמִן חֵיפָא אֲמַר: קָרוּ תְּלָתָא בַּחֲנוּכָּה וְחַד בְּרֹאשׁ חֹדֶשׁ.

§ An amoraic dispute **was stated:** When **the New Moon of Tevet occurs on a weekday,**[H] what Torah portion is read? **Rabbi Yitzḥak** Nappaḥa **said: Three** people **read** from the portion **for the New Moon, and one** reads from the portion **for Hanukkah. And Rav Dimi of Haifa said: Three read** from the portion **for Hanukkah, and one** reads from the portion **for the New Moon.**

אֲמַר רַבִּי מָנִי: כְּוָותֵיהּ דְּרַבִּי יִצְחָק נַפָּחָא מִסְתַּבְּרָא, דְּתָדִיר וְשֶׁאֵינוֹ תָּדִיר – תָּדִיר קוֹדֵם.

Rabbi Mani said: It stands to reason to rule **in accordance with** the opinion of **Rabbi Yitzḥak Nappaḥa, for** it is already an established principle that when **a frequent** practice **and an infrequent** practice conflict, the **frequent** practice **takes precedence** over the infrequent practice. Since the portion for the New Moon is read more frequently than the portion for Hanukkah, it should be given greater prominence.

אָמַר רַבִּי אָבִין: כְּוָותֵיהּ דְּרַב דִּימִי מִסְתַּבְּרָא, מִי גָּרַם לָרְבִיעִי שֶׁיָּבֹא – רֹאשׁ חֹדֶשׁ, הִלְכָּךְ רְבִיעִי בְּרֹאשׁ חֹדֶשׁ בָּעֵי מִיקְרֵי.

Rabbi Avin said: It stands to reason to rule **in accordance with** the opinion of **Rav Dimi,** for the following reason: **What caused the fourth** person **to come**[N] and read from the Torah? **The New Moon,** as on the other days of Hanukkah only three people read from the Torah. **Therefore,** it is only logical that **the fourth person should read** from the portion **for the New Moon.**

מַאי הָוֵי עֲלָהּ? רַב יוֹסֵף אָמַר: אֵין מַשְׁגִּיחִין בְּרֹאשׁ חוֹדֶשׁ. וְרַבָּה אָמַר: אֵין מַשְׁגִּיחִין בַּחֲנוּכָּה. וְהִלְכְתָא: אֵין מַשְׁגִּיחִין בַּחֲנוּכָּה, וְרֹאשׁ חֹדֶשׁ עִיקָּר.

The Gemara asks: **What** halakhic conclusion **was** reached **about** this matter? **Rav Yosef said: We do not concern ourselves** with making the portion for **the New Moon** the primary reading. Rather, three people read from the portion for Hanukkah, and only the fourth reads the portion for the New Moon. **And Rabba said: We do not concern ourselves with** making the portion for **Hanukkah** the primary reading. Rather, three people read from the portion for the New Moon, and only the fourth reads the portion for Hanukkah. The Gemara concludes: **And the *halakha*** is that **we do not concern ourselves with** making the portion for **Hanukkah** the primary reading, **and** therefore the portion for **the New Moon is primary.**

אִיתְּמַר, חָל לִהְיוֹת בִּ"וְאַתָּה תְּצַוֶּה", אֲמַר רַבִּי יִצְחָק נַפָּחָא: קָרוּ שִׁיתָּא מִ"וְאַתָּה תְּצַוֶּה" עַד "כִּי תִשָּׂא", וְחַד מִ"כִּי תִשָּׂא" עַד "וְעָשִׂיתָ". אֲמַר אַבָּיֵי:

§ An amoraic dispute **was stated:** If the Shabbat on which the portion of *Shekalim* is to be read **occurs on** the Shabbat in which the regular weekly portion is **"And you shall command"** (Exodus 27:20–30:10), what should be done? **Rabbi Yitzḥak Nappaḥa said: Six** people **read from** the portion **"And you shall command," until** but not including the weekly portion of **"When you take the count"** (Exodus 27:20–30:10), **and one** person reads the portion of *Shekalim* **from "When you take the count," until** but not including the verse: **"And you shall make** a copper laver" (Exodus 30:11–16). **Abaye said:**

אָמְרִי: אוֹקוֹמֵי הוּא דְּקָא מוֹקְמִי הָתָם.

Since *Shekalim* is read from the portion in the Torah immediately following the regular weekly Torah reading, people **will** mistakenly **say** that **they** merely extended the regular reading and then **halted there,** and they will not realize that the last reading was actually for the sake of *Shekalim.*

אֶלָּא אֲמַר אַבָּיֵי: קָרוּ שִׁיתָּא מִ״וְאַתָּה תְּצַוֶּה״ עַד ״וְעָשִׂיתָ״, וְחַד תָּנֵי וְקָרֵי מִ״כִּי תִשָּׂא״ עַד ״וְעָשִׂיתָ״,

Rather, Abaye said: Six people **read from "And you shall command" until** but not including **"And you shall make** a copper laver," which concludes with the portion used for *Shekalim.* **And** then **one** person **repeats and reads** *Shekalim* **from "When you take the count" until** but not including **"And you shall make** a copper laver." The repetition of this portion serves to highlight the fact it was read for the sake of *Shekalim.*

מֵיתִיבִי: חָל לִהְיוֹת בַּפָּרָשָׁה הַסְּמוּכָה לָהּ, בֵּין מִלְּפָנֶיהָ בֵּין מִלְּאַחֲרֶיהָ – קוֹרִין אוֹתָהּ וְכוֹפְלִין אוֹתָהּ.

The Gemara **raises an objection** from a *baraita*: If the Shabbat on which *Shekalim* is to be read **occurs on** the Shabbat on which **the portion** to be read for the regular weekly reading **is adjacent to** *Shekalim,* **whether** on the Shabbat **preceding** that Shabbat **or following it,** then **they read and repeat** *Shekalim.*

בִּשְׁלָמָא לְאַבָּיֵי – נִיחָא, אֶלָּא לְרַבִּי יִצְחָק נַפָּחָא קַשְׁיָא!

Granted, according to the opinion of **Abaye, it works out well,** for the conclusion of the *baraita,* that we repeat *Shekalim,* supports his opinion. **But according to** the opinion of **Rabbi Yitzḥak Nappaḥa,** it is **difficult.**

אָמַר לָךְ רַבִּי יִצְחָק נַפָּחָא: וּלְאַבָּיֵי מִי נִיחָא? תֵּינַח לְפָנֶיהָ, לְאַחֲרֶיהָ הֵיכִי מַשְׁכַּחַתְּ לַהּ?

The Gemara answers: **Rabbi Yitzḥak Nappaḥa** could have **said to you: And according to Abaye, does it** really **work out well?** The reference of the *baraita* to a case where the Shabbat on which *Shekalim* is read **precedes** the Shabbat on which that portion will be read as part of the weekly reading **works out well,** since it can indeed occur. However, with regard to the reference to that Shabbat **following** the Shabbat on which that portion is read as part of the weekly reading, under **what circumstances** can this case **be found?** It never occurs like that.

אֶלָּא מַאי אִית לָךְ לְמֵימַר – כּוֹפְלָהּ בְּשַׁבָּתוֹת, הָכָא נַמִי – כּוֹפְלָהּ בְּשַׁבָּתוֹת.

Rather, perforce, **what have you to say?** That when the *baraita* refers to repeating *Shekalim* when the Shabbat on which *Shekalim* is read follows the Shabbat on which it is read as the regular weekly reading, it means that **one repeats it** by reading it **on** two successive ***Shabbatot.*** Similarly, **here too,** when the *baraita* refers to repeating *Shekalim* when the Shabbat on which *Shekalim* is read precedes the Shabbat on which it is read as the regular weekly reading, it means that **one repeats it** by reading it **on** two successive ***Shabbatot.***

חָל לִהְיוֹת בְּ״כִי תִשָּׂא״ עַצְמָהּ, אָמַר רַבִּי יִצְחָק נַפָּחָא: קָרוּ שִׁיתָּא מִן ״וְעָשִׂיתָ״ עַד ״וַיַּקְהֵל״ וְחַד קָרֵי מִ״כִּי תִשָּׂא״ עַד ״וְעָשִׂיתָ״.

The Gemara considers a similar case: If the Shabbat on which *Shekalim* is to be read **occurs on** the Shabbat on which the regular portion **itself** begins with **"When you take the count,"** what should be done? **Rabbi Yitzḥak Nappaḥa said: Six** people **read from "And you shall make** a copper laver" **until** but not including the portion of **"And he assembled"** (Exodus 30:17–34:35). This is the entire regular weekly portion of "When you take the count" without the opening passage, which is also the portion of *Shekalim.* **And** then **one** person goes back and **reads** the portion of *Shekalim* **from "When you take the count" until** but not including **"And you shall make** a copper laver."

מַתְקִיף לַהּ אַבָּיֵי: הַשְׁתָּא אָמְרִי: לְמַפְרֵעַ הוּא דְּקָרֵי! אֶלָּא אֲמַר אַבָּיֵי: קָרוּ שִׁיתָּא עַד ״וַיַּקְהֵל״ וְחַד תָּנֵי וְקָרֵי מִ״כִּי תִשָּׂא״ עַד ״וְעָשִׂיתָ״.

Abaye strongly objects to this: Now people **will** mistakenly **say** that **they are reading** the regular weekly portion **out of sequence,** and they will not realize that the last reading was actually for the sake of the portion of *Shekalim.* **Rather, Abaye said: Six** people **read** the entire portion of "When you shall count" **until** but not including the portion of **"And he assembled"** (Exodus 30:11–34:35), **and** then **one** person **repeats and reads** the portion of *Shekalim* **from "When you take the count" until** but not including **"And you shall make** a copper laver."

תַּנְיָא כְּוָותֵיהּ דְּאַבַּיֵי: חָל לִהְיוֹת בְּ״כִי תִשָּׂא״ עַצְמָהּ – קוֹרִין אוֹתָהּ וְכוֹפְלִין אוֹתָהּ.

The Gemara notes: **It is taught** in a *baraita* **in accordance with** the opinion **of Abaye:** If the Shabbat on which *Shekalim* is to be read **occurs on** the Shabbat on which the regular portion **itself** is **"When you take the count,"** the first part of that portion **is read** once as part of the weekly reading **and** then **repeated** as the portion of *Shekalim*.[H]

״חָל לִהְיוֹת בְּתוֹךְ הַשַּׁבָּת מַקְדִּימִין לְשַׁבָּת שֶׁעָבְרָה״: אִיתְּמַר, רֹאשׁ חֹדֶשׁ אֲדָר שֶׁחָל לִהְיוֹת בְּעֶרֶב שַׁבָּת, רַב אָמַר: מַקְדִּימִין, וּשְׁמוּאֵל אָמַר: מְאַחֲרִין.

§ The mishna states: If the New Moon of Adar **occurs during** the middle of **the week,**[H] the congregation **advances** the reading of *Shekalim* **to the previous week.** With regard to this, an amoraic dispute **was stated:** With regard to when **the New Moon of Adar occurs on Friday, Rav said:** The congregation **advances** the reading of the portion to the previous week. **And Shmuel said: They defer** the reading of the portion to the following day, and it is read on the coming Shabbat.

רַב אָמַר: מַקְדִּימִין, דְּאִם כֵּן – בָּצְרִי לְהוּ יוֹמֵי שׁוּלְחָנוֹת, וּשְׁמוּאֵל אָמַר: מְאַחֲרִין, אָמַר לָךְ: סוֹף סוֹף חֲמֵיסַר בְּמַעֲלֵי שַׁבְּתָא מִיקְלַע, וְשׁוּלְחָנוֹת לָא נָפְקֵי עַד חַד בְּשַׁבָּא, הִלְכָּךְ מְאַחֲרִין.

The Gemara explains the two opinions: **Rav said: They advance** the reading to the previous week, **as, if** one would read the portion only on the following day, **there will be less than the** required number **of days,** i.e., two weeks, that the announcement needs to precede the setting up of **the** money-changing **tables** on the fifteenth. **And Shmuel said: They defer** the reading of the portion to the following day. As for Rav's argument, Shmuel could have **said to you: Ultimately,** in such a year **the fifteenth** of Adar also **occurs on a Friday, and** therefore **the** money-changing **tables will not be brought out**[N] **until Sunday.** Consequently, there will still be a full two weeks between the announcement and the setting of the tables. **Therefore, they** can **defer** the reading to the following day.[B]

תְּנַן: חָל לִהְיוֹת בְּתוֹךְ הַשַּׁבָּת מַקְדִּימִין לְשֶׁעָבַר, וּמַפְסִיקִין לְשַׁבָּת אַחֶרֶת. מַאי לָאו – אֲפִילּוּ בְּעֶרֶב שַׁבָּת! לָא, בְּתוֹךְ הַשַּׁבָּת דַּוְקָא.

The Gemara offers various proofs for Rav's opinion: **We learned** in the mishna: If the New Moon **occurs during** the middle of **the week, they advance** the reading of that portion **to the previous** Shabbat, **and** in such a case **they interrupt** the reading of the four portions **on the following Shabbat.** The Gemara explains the proof: **What; is it not** that this is referring **even** to a case when the New Moon occurs **on Friday?** This would prove Rav's opinion. **No;** it is referring **specifically** to a case where it occurs **during** the middle **of the week.**

תָּא שְׁמַע: אֵיזוֹ הִיא שַׁבָּת רִאשׁוֹנָה – כָּל שֶׁחָל רֹאשׁ חֹדֶשׁ אֲדָר לִהְיוֹת בְּתוֹכָהּ, וַאֲפִילּוּ בְּעֶרֶב שַׁבָּת. מַאי לָאו – אֲפִילּוּ בְּעֶרֶב שַׁבָּת דּוּמְיָא דְּתוֹכָהּ, מַה תּוֹכָהּ – מַקְדִּימִין, אַף עֶרֶב שַׁבָּת – מַקְדִּימִין!

Come and **hear** another proof from a *baraita*: **Which is the first Shabbat** of the four *Shabbatot* on which the special portions are read? The Shabbat of **whichever** week **during which the New Moon of Adar occurs, and** this is the case **even** if it occurs **on Friday.** The Gemara explains the proof: **What, is it not** that the *baraita* teaches that the case when it occurs **even on Friday**[N] **is similar to** the case where it occurs **during** the middle of the week, and **just as** when it occurs **during** the middle of the week, **they advance** the reading to the previous Shabbat, **so too,** when it occurs on **Friday, they advance** the reading to the previous Shabbat? This would therefore prove Rav's opinion.

אָמַר שְׁמוּאֵל: בָּהּ, וְכֵן תָּנָא דְּבֵי שְׁמוּאֵל: בָּהּ.

Shmuel said: The *baraita* should be emended, and instead of saying: During which the New Moon occurs, it should say: **On which** the New Moon occurs, i.e., on Shabbat itself. **And so the school of Shmuel taught: On which** the New Moon occurs.

HALAKHA

When the reading of *Shekalim* occurs on the Shabbat when the regular portion is "And you shall command" or "When you take the count" – פָּרָשַׁת שְׁקָלִים בִּתְצַוֶּה וְכִי תִשָּׂא: When the New Moon of Adar occurs on the Shabbat on which the regular weekly portion is "And you shall command," six read from "And you shall command," until but not including "And you shall make a copper laver," and the seventh reads *Shekalim* by going back and repeating the last section from "When you take the count" until "And you shall make a copper laver." This ruling is in accordance with the opinion of Abaye.

When the New Moon of Adar occurs on the Shabbat on which the regular weekly portion is "When you take the count," six read the entire portion, and the seventh goes back and repeats the last section from "When you take the count" until "And you shall make a copper laver," in accordance with the opinion of Abaye. However, nowadays, the order of the weekly portions are set so that the New Moon of Adar never coincides with the portions of "When you take the count" or "And you shall command" (Rambam *Sefer Ahava*, *Hilkhot Tefilla* 13:22).

If the New Moon of Adar occurs during the middle of the week – חָל לִהְיוֹת בְּתוֹךְ הַשַּׁבָּת: If the New Moon of Adar occurs during the middle of the week, and even if it occurs on Friday, *Shekalim* is read on the previous Shabbat. Similarly, if Purim occurs on Friday, the portion of *Zakhor* is read on the previous Shabbat. This ruling is in accordance with the opinion of Rav, for whenever he disputes ritual matters with Shmuel, the *halakha* is ruled in accordance with the former's opinion (*Shulḥan Arukh*, *Oraḥ Ḥayyim* 685:5).

NOTES

And the tables will not be brought out – וְשׁוּלְחָנוֹת לָא נָפְקֵי: The money changers would not sit on Friday, out of respect for Shabbat. Consequently, no days were lost.

What, is it not even on Friday – מַאי לָאו, אֲפִילּוּ בְּעֶרֶב שַׁבָּת: The Rashba notes that in the same way that the mishna poses a challenge to Shmuel's opinion, it also poses a challenge to Rav's opinion. Nevertheless, the Gemara only presents it as a challenge to Shmuel's opinion. The Rashba explains that the Gemara does so because, in general, when the Gemara analyzes an issue, it does not explore all possible questions when doing so will not highlight any new issues.

BACKGROUND

The order of the reading of the four portions – סִדְרֵי קְרִיאַת אַרְבַּע פָּרָשִׁיּוֹת: Today, when there is a fixed calendar, the *Shabbatot* on which each of the special portions are read and the *Shabbatot* on which none are read are fixed. The early commentaries provided mnemonics with which to remember the order using letters corresponding to the numeric values of the days of the week, e.g., *alef* represents day 1, i.e., Sunday, and the days of the month.

The New Moon of Adar can occur only on **זבד״ו**, i.e., day 7, 2, 4, or 6 of the week. The mnemonics indicate on which *Shabbatot* no special portion is read:

זט״ו – *Zatu*, i.e., *zayin*, *tet-vav*, the numeric value of 7 and 15, respectively. If the New Moon occurs on Shabbat, represented by 7, then the Shabbat that occurs on the fifteenth of the month will have no special reading.

ב״ו – *Bo*, i.e., *bet*, *vav*, the numeric value of 2 and 6, respectively. If the New Moon occurs on Monday, represented by 2, then the Shabbat that occurs on the sixth of the month will have no special reading.

ד״ד – *Dad*, i.e., *dalet*, *dalet*, the numeric value of 4 and 4. If the New Moon occurs on Wednesday, represented by 4, then the Shabbat that occurs on the fourth of the month will have no special reading.

ובי״ו – *Ubiyav*, i.e., *vav*, *bet*, *yud-vav*, the numeric value of 6, 2, and 16. If the New Moon occurs on Friday, represented by 6, then the *Shabbatot* that occur on the second and sixteenth of the month will have no special reading.

כְּתַנָּאֵי: מַסְרְגִין לְשַׁבָּתוֹת, דִּבְרֵי רַבִּי יְהוּדָה הַנָּשִׂיא. רַבִּי שִׁמְעוֹן בֶּן אֶלְעָזָר אוֹמֵר: אֵין מַסְרְגִין. אָמַר רַבִּי שִׁמְעוֹן בֶּן אֶלְעָזָר: אֵימָתַי אֲנִי אוֹמֵר אֵין מַסְרְגִין – בִּזְמַן שֶׁחָל לִהְיוֹת בְּעֶרֶב שַׁבָּת, אֲבָל בִּזְמַן שֶׁחָל לִהְיוֹת בְּתוֹךְ הַשַּׁבָּת – מַקְדִּים וְקוֹרֵא מִשַּׁבָּת שֶׁעָבְרָה אַף עַל פִּי שֶׁהוּא שְׁבָט.

The Gemara suggests: This dispute between the *amora'im* is **like** a dispute between ***tanna'im***, as it is taught in a *baraita*: With regard to the reading of the four special portions, **they interrupt the flow**[N] **of *Shabbatot*,** i.e., there is a Shabbat in which no special portion is read; this is **the statement of Rabbi Yehuda HaNasi. Rabbi Shimon ben Elazar said: They do not interrupt the flow** of *Shabbatot*. **Rabbi Shimon ben Elazar said: When do I say that they do not interrupt the flow** of *Shabbatot*? **When** the New Moon of Adar **occurs on Friday,** since I hold that in that case *Shekalim* is read on the following day, and therefore the four portions are read on four consecutive weeks. **However, when** the New Moon of Adar **occurs during the week, one advances and reads** *Shekalim* **on the previous Shabbat, although it is** still the month of **Shevat,** and therefore on one of the *Shabbatot* in Adar there will be no reading. It would appear, then, that Shmuel holds in accordance with the opinion of Rabbi Shimon ben Elazar, whereas Rav holds in accordance with the opinion of Rabbi Yehuda HaNasi.

״בַּשְּׁנִיָּה זָכוֹר״ וכו׳: אִיתְּמַר, פּוּרִים שֶׁחָל לִהְיוֹת בְּעֶרֶב שַׁבָּת, רַב אָמַר: מַקְדִּימִין פָּרָשַׁת זָכוֹר, וּשְׁמוּאֵל אָמַר: מְאַחֲרִין.

§ The mishna states: **On the second** Shabbat of Adar, the Shabbat prior to Purim, they read the portion of **"Remember [*zakhor*]** what Amalek did" (Deuteronomy 25:17–19). The portion of *Zakhor* is associated with Purim because according to tradition, Haman was a descendant of Amalek, and so the victory over him and his supporters was a victory against Amalek. With regard to this, an amoraic dispute **was stated:** With regard to when **Purim occurs on a Friday,**[N] **Rav said:** The congregation **advances** the reading of **the portion of *Zakhor*** to the previous Shabbat. **And Shmuel said: They defer** it to the Shabbat following Purim.

רַב אָמַר: מַקְדִּימִין, כִּי הֵיכִי דְּלָא תִּיקְדּוֹם עֲשִׂיָּה לִזְכִירָה. וּשְׁמוּאֵל אָמַר: מְאַחֲרִין, אָמַר לָךְ: כֵּיוָן דְּאִיכָּא מוּקָּפִין דְּעָבְדִי בַּחֲמֵיסַר – עֲשִׂיָּה וּזְכִירָה בַּהֲדֵי הֲדָדֵי קָא אָתְיָין.

The Gemara explains the two opinions: **Rav said: They advance** it to the previous Shabbat, **in order that the observance** of Purim **should not precede the remembrance** of the destruction of Amalek, which is achieved through reading the portion of *Zakhor*. **And Shmuel said: They defer** its reading. And as for Rav's argument, Shmuel could have **said to you: Since there are the walled** cities **that observe** Purim **on the fifteenth,** at least with regard to them, **the observance and the remembrance come together** on the same day, and that is sufficient.

תְּנַן: בַּשְּׁנִיָּה זָכוֹר. וְהָא כִּי מִיקְּלַע רֵישׁ יַרְחָא בְּשַׁבָּת מִיקְּלַע פּוּרִים בְּעֶרֶב שַׁבָּת, וְקָתָנֵי: בַּשְּׁנִיָּה זָכוֹר! אָמַר רַב פָּפָּא: מַאי שְׁנִיָּה – שְׁנִיָּה לְהַפְסָקָה.

The Gemara offers various proofs for Rav's opinion: **We learned** in the mishna: **On the second** Shabbat they read the portion of ***Zakhor***.[H] The Gemara suggests: **Is it not** the case that **when the New Moon** of Adar **occurs on Shabbat, Purim occurs on Friday, and** yet the mishna **teaches: On the second** Shabbat they read the portion of ***Zakhor***? This supports Rav's opinion that in all cases the portion is read before Purim. **Rav Pappa said:** There is no proof, because one could argue as follows: **What is** the intention of the mishna when it is referring to **the second** Shabbat? It could mean **the second** Shabbat on which a special portion is read, which, if Purim occurs on Friday, occurs only **after the interruption**[N] of the previous Shabbat, during which no portion was read.

תָּא שְׁמַע: אֵיזוֹ שַׁבָּת שְׁנִיָּה – כֹּל שֶׁחָל פּוּרִים לִהְיוֹת בְּתוֹכָהּ, וַאֲפִילּוּ בְּעֶרֶב שַׁבָּת. מַאי לָאו עֶרֶב שַׁבָּת דּוּמְיָא דְּתוֹכָהּ, מָה תּוֹכָהּ – מַקְדִּימִין, אַף עֶרֶב שַׁבָּת מַקְדִּימִין!

Come and **hear** another proof from a *baraita*: **Which is the second Shabbat** on which a special portion is read? The Shabbat of **whichever** week **during which Purim occurs, and** this is the case **even** if it occurs **on Friday.** The Gemara explains the proof: **What, is it not** that the *baraita* teaches that **even** if Purim occurs **on Friday,** the case **is similar to** the case when it occurs **during** the middle of the week, and therefore, **just as** when it occurs **during** the middle of the week **we advance** the reading to the previous Shabbat, **so too,** when it occurs on **Friday, we** should **advance** the reading to the previous Shabbat? This *baraita* would therefore prove Rav's opinion.

אָמַר שְׁמוּאֵל: בָּהּ, וְכֵן תָּנָא דְּבֵי שְׁמוּאֵל: בָּהּ.

Shmuel said: The *baraita* should be emended, and instead of saying: During which Purim occurs, it should say: **On which** Purim occurs, i.e., on Shabbat itself. **And so the school of Shmuel taught: On which** Purim occurs.

NOTES

They interrupt the flow – מַסְרְגִין: In practice, there is usually at least one Shabbat in Adar, and at times even two *Shabbatot*, on which no special portion is read. However, based on the ruling of the Jerusalem Talmud, there is never an interruption between *Para* and *HaHodesh*. An mnemonic provided for this is that there an interruption is not allowed between the third and fourth cups of wine at the Passover seder. The early halakhic authorities delineated exactly when each portion should be read and which *Shabbatot* will have no special reading, based on the various days on which the New Moon of Adar can occur (see BACKGROUND, previous page).

When Purim occurs on a Friday – פּוּרִים שֶׁחָל לִהְיוֹת בְּעֶרֶב שַׁבָּת: Several of the early commentaries' manuscripts read: When Purim occurs on Shabbat (see Rid and Ritva). This change also affects the text of the Gemara later on (see *Noda Bihuda*). It would appear that many preferred the version that currently appears in the Gemara because, according to the set calendar, Purim never occurs on Shabbat, except for in Jerusalem and other historically walled cities.

What is the second Shabbat? The second Shabbat after the interruption – מַאי שְׁנִיָּה, שְׁנִיָּה לְהַפְסָקָה: In truth, even Rav Pappa's explanation is not entirely precise, for the *Shabbatot* are not counted in relation to the month of Adar. Rather, the count is generally made from the first of the *Shabbatot* on which a special portion is read. Counting in this way, the portion of *Zakhor* is always read on the second Shabbat, and this was probably the intention of the *tanna* of the mishna (Ritva).

HALAKHA

On the second Shabbat they read the portion of *Zakhor* – בַּשְּׁנִיָּה זָכוֹר: On the Shabbat immediately preceding Purim, two Torah scrolls are removed from the ark. From the first, the regular weekly portion is read, and from the second the portion of *Zakhor* is read as the *maftir*. The *haftara* is read from the account of the battle against Amalek in the book of I Samuel, chapter 15. Some begin from the first verse of that chapter (*Arukh HaShulhan*). Some hold that the obligation to read the portion of *Zakhor* is a biblical requirement, and therefore everyone must be particularly careful to hear it. The *Magen Avraham* states that if one did not hear it then, one may rely on the Torah reading on Purim, which also mentions the destruction of Amalek (*Shulhan Arukh*, *Orah Hayyim* 685:2, 7).

NOTES

The portions of *Para* and *HaḤodesh* – פָּרָשַׁת פָּרָה וְהַחוֹדֶשׁ: In the Jerusalem Talmud, the ruling is set that although *HaḤodesh* should really be read before *Para*, both because the portion of *HaḤodesh* was given to the Jewish people first, and because its fulfillment is on the New Moon of Nisan, whereas the first ashes of the red heifer were prepared only on the second of Nisan, nevertheless, it was considered fitting to advance the reading of *Para*, because it concerns the purity of the Jewish people.

חָל לִהְיוֹת בְּשַׁבָּת עַצְמָהּ, אָמַר רַב הוּנָא: לְדִבְרֵי הַכֹּל אֵין מַקְדִּימִין. וְרַב נַחְמָן אָמַר: עֲדַיִין הִיא מַחְלוֹקֶת. אִיתְּמַר נַמִי, אָמַר רַבִּי חִיָּיא בַּר אַבָּא אָמַר רַבִּי אַבָּא אָמַר רַב: פּוּרִים שֶׁחָל לִהְיוֹת בְּשַׁבָּת – מַקְדִּים וְקוֹרֵא בְּשַׁבָּת שֶׁעָבְרָה ״זָכוֹר״.

With regard to when Purim **occurs on Shabbat itself, Rav Huna said: Everyone agrees,** i.e., both Rav and Shmuel, that **they do not advance** the reading of the portion of *Zakhor* to the previous Shabbat, but it is read on that Shabbat. **And Rav Naḥman said:** Even in this case there **is still a dispute,** for Rav maintains that in all cases the remembrance of the destruction of Amalek, which is achieved through reading the portion of *Zakhor*, must always precede the observance of Purim. **It was also stated** that **Rabbi Ḥiyya bar Abba said** that **Rabbi Abba said** that **Rav said:** If **Purim occurs on Shabbat, one advances and reads** the portion of ***Zakhor*** **on the previous Shabbat,** as Rav Naḥman understood Rav's opinion.

״בִּשְׁלִישִׁית פָּרָה אֲדוּמָּה״ וכו׳: תָּנוּ רַבָּנַן: אֵיזוֹ הִיא שַׁבָּת שְׁלִישִׁית – כׇּל שֶׁסְּמוּכָה לְפוּרִים מֵאַחֲרֶיהָ. אִיתְּמַר: רַבִּי חָמָא בְּרַבִּי חֲנִינָא אָמַר: שַׁבָּת הַסְּמוּכָה לְרֹאשׁ חֹדֶשׁ נִיסָן.

§ The mishna states: **On the third** Shabbat, they read the portion of **the Red Heifer** [***Para***] (Numbers 19:1–22).[H] **The Sages taught** in a *baraita*: **Which is the third Shabbat? Whichever** Shabbat occurs **immediately after Purim.** It was also **stated: Rabbi Ḥama, son of Rabbi Ḥanina, said: The Shabbat that is immediately** after **the New Moon of Nisan.**

וְלָא פְּלִיגִי; הָא – דְּאִיקְּלַע רֹאשׁ חֹדֶשׁ נִיסָן בְּשַׁבָּת, הָא דְּאִיקְּלַע בְּאֶמְצַע שַׁבָּת.

The Gemara comments: **And** these two statements **do not disagree,** as they refer to different cases: **This** statement of Rabbi Ḥama, son of Rabbi Ḥanina, is referring to a case **where the New Moon of Nisan occurs on Shabbat** itself. In that case, the portion of *HaḤodesh* is read then, and therefore the reading of *Para* is deferred to the following Shabbat. **And that** statement of the *baraita* is referring to a case **where** the New Moon of Nisan **occurs during the middle of the week.** Therefore, *HaḤodesh* is read on the Shabbat immediately preceding the New Moon, and *Para* is read on the Shabbat before that one, which is the Shabbat that is adjacent to Purim and after it.[N]

״בִּרְבִיעִית הַחֹדֶשׁ הַזֶּה לָכֶם״: תָּנוּ רַבָּנַן: ״רֹאשׁ חֹדֶשׁ אֲדָר שֶׁחָל לִהְיוֹת בְּשַׁבָּת – קוֹרִין ״כִּי תִשָּׂא״ וּמַפְטִירִין בִּיהוֹיָדָע וְאֵי זוֹ הִיא שַׁבָּת רִאשׁוֹנָה – כׇּל שֶׁחָל רֹאשׁ חֹדֶשׁ אֲדָר לִהְיוֹת בְּתוֹכָהּ, וַאֲפִילּוּ בְּעֶרֶב שַׁבָּת. בַּשְּׁנִיָּה ״זָכוֹר״ וּמַפְטִירִין ״פָּקַדְתִּי״, וְאֵי זוֹ הִיא שַׁבָּת שְׁנִיָּה – כׇּל שֶׁחָל פּוּרִים לִהְיוֹת בְּתוֹכָהּ, וַאֲפִילּוּ בְּעֶרֶב שַׁבָּת.

§ The mishna states: **On the fourth** Shabbat, they read the portion of **"This month [*haḥodesh*] shall be for you"** (Exodus 12:1–20).[H] **The Sages taught** in a *baraita*: When **the New Moon of Adar occurs on Shabbat, they read "When you take the count"** as the portion of *Shekalim*. **And they read as the *haftara*** the story involving **Jehoiada** the priest (II Kings 12:1–27). **And which is the first Shabbat?** The Shabbat of **whichever** week **during which the New Moon of Adar occurs, and** this is the case **even** if it occurs **on Friday. On the second** Shabbat, they read the portion of ***Zakhor*, and they read as the *haftara*** of **"I remembered** that which Amalek did" (I Samuel 15:1–34). **And which is the second Shabbat?** The Shabbat of **whichever** week **during which Purim occurs, and** this is the case **even** if it occurs **on Friday.**

בַּשְּׁלִישִׁית – פָּרָה אֲדוּמָּה, וּמַפְטִירִין ״וְזָרַקְתִּי עֲלֵיכֶם״, וְאֵי זוֹ הִיא שַׁבָּת שְׁלִישִׁית – כׇּל שֶׁסְּמוּכָה לְפוּרִים מֵאַחֲרֶיהָ. בָּרְבִיעִית ״הַחֹדֶשׁ הַזֶּה״ וּמַפְטִירִין ״כֹּה אָמַר ה׳ [אֱלֹהִים] בָּרִאשׁוֹן בְּאֶחָד לַחֹדֶשׁ״.

On the third Shabbat, they read the portion of **the Red Heifer** [***Para***], **and they read as the *haftara*** the portion of **"Then will I sprinkle** clean water **upon you"** (Ezekiel 36:25–38). **And which is the third Shabbat? That which is adjacent to Purim and after it. On the fourth** Shabbat, they read the portion of **"This month** [***haḥodesh***] shall be for you," **and they read as the *haftara*** the portion of **"Thus says the Lord God: In the first month, on the first day of the month"** (Ezekiel 45:18–46:18).

HALAKHA

On the third Shabbat they read the portion of *Para* – בַּשְּׁלִישִׁית פָּרָה: When the New Moon of Adar occurs on Shabbat, no portion is read on the third Shabbat, and *Para* is read on the fourth Shabbat. When the New Moon of Adar occurs during the week, *Para* is read on the third Shabbat. Two Torah scrolls are removed from the ark: From the first, the regular weekly portion is read; from the second, *Para* is read as the *maftir*. The *haftara* is Ezekiel 36:16–36. However, Sephardic Jews and members of other communities conclude two verses later, at verse 38 (*Arukh HaShulḥan*; *Shulḥan Arukh, Oraḥ Ḥayyim* 685:3, 5)

On the fourth Shabbat they read the portion of: This month shall be for you – בָּרְבִיעִית הַחוֹדֶשׁ הַזֶּה לָכֶם: The week within which the New Moon of Nisan occurs is the fourth week on which a special portion is read. Two Torah scrolls are removed from the ark: From the first, the regular weekly portion is read; from the second, *HaḤodesh* is read. The *haftara* is taken from Ezekiel. The Sephardic custom is to read Ezekiel 45:18–46:15, while the Ashkenazic custom is to read 45:16–46:18.

If the New Moon of Nisan occurs on Shabbat, three Torah scrolls are removed from the ark: From the first scroll, six or more people read the regular weekly portion; from the second scroll, a seventh person reads the portion of the New Moon; and from the third, *HaḤodesh* is read. Even in this case, the *haftara* is the one normally read with *HaḤodesh*, not the *haftara* normally read when the New Moon occurs on Shabbat (see *Taz*, citing *Levush*). However, some add the first and last verses of that *haftara* (*Shulḥan Arukh, Oraḥ Ḥayyim* 685:4).

וְאֵיזוֹ הִיא שַׁבָּת רְבִיעִית – כׇּל שֶׁחָל רֹאשׁ חֹדֶשׁ נִיסָן לִהְיוֹת בְּתוֹכָהּ, וַאֲפִילּוּ בְּעֶרֶב שַׁבָּת.

And which is the fourth Shabbat?[H] The Shabbat of **whichever** week **during which the New Moon of Nisan occurs, and** this is the case **even** if it occurs **on Friday.**

״בַּחֲמִישִׁית חוֹזְרִין לְכִסְדְּרָן״ וכו׳: לְסֵדֶר מַאי? רַבִּי אַמִּי אָמַר: לְסֵדֶר פָּרָשִׁיּוֹת הוּא חוֹזֵר, רַבִּי יִרְמְיָה אָמַר: לְסֵדֶר הַפְטָרוֹת הוּא חוֹזֵר.

§ The mishna states: **On the fifth** Shabbat, **we resume the** regular weekly **order.** The Gemara clarifies the mishna's intent: **To the order of what** does one resume? **Rabbi Ami said: One resumes the** regular weekly **order of** Torah **portions.**[N] Rabbi Ami holds that on the weeks on which the special portions are read, the regular weekly Torah portion is not read at all, and therefore the cycle is resumed only on the fifth Shabbat. **Rabbi Yirmeya said: One resumes the** regular weekly **order of the *haftarot*.**[H] Rabbi Yirmeya holds that even on the *Shabbatot* on which the special portions are read, the regular weekly portion is still read; the special portion is read by the last reader as the *maftir*. However, the *haftara* of the regular cycle is entirely replaced with a portion from the Prophets that parallels the special portion. As such, it is the cycle of *haftarot* that is resumed on the fifth Shabbat.

אָמַר אַבָּיֵי: כְּוָותֵיהּ דְּרַבִּי אַמִּי מִסְתַּבְּרָא. דִּתְנַן: לַכֹּל מַפְסִיקִין: לְרָאשֵׁי חֳדָשִׁים, לַחֲנוּכָּה וּלְפוּרִים, לְתַעֲנִיּוֹת וּלְמַעֲמָדוֹת, וּלְיוֹם הַכִּפּוּרִים.

Abaye said: It stands to reason that one should rule **in accordance with** the opinion **of Rabbi Ami, as we learned** in the mishna: **For all** special days, **we interrupt** the regular order of readings, and a special portion relating to the character of the day is read. This applies **to the New Moons, to Hanukkah, and to Purim, to fast days, and to** non-priestly **watches, and to Yom Kippur.**

בִּשְׁלָמָא לְמַאן דְּאָמַר לְסֵדֶר פָּרָשִׁיּוֹת הוּא חוֹזֵר – הַיְינוּ דְּאִיכָּא פָּרָשָׁה בַּחוֹל, אֶלָּא לְמַאן דְּאָמַר לְסֵדֶר הַפְטָרוֹת הוּא חוֹזֵר – הַפְטָרָה בַּחוֹל מִי אִיכָּא?

Abaye explains his proof: **Granted, according to the one who said that one resumes the** regular weekly **order of** Torah **portions, this** statement in the mishna **is** referring to the fact **that there is** a reading of the weekly Torah **portion on weekdays.** If one of the special days listed in the mishna occurs on Monday or Thursday, the weekly Torah reading is replaced by the special portion for that day. **However, according to one who said** that **one resumes the** regular weekly **order of *haftarot*,** what could the mishna mean when it says that the regular cycle is interrupted? **Is there a *haftara* on weekdays?** The mishna therefore supports Rabbi Ami's opinion.

וְאִידָךְ: הָא כִּדְאִיתָא, וְהָא כִּדְאִיתָא.

And the other one, Rabbi Yirmeya, would counter: **This** case is **as it is, and that** case is **as it is.** On days when there is a *haftara*, the reference in the mishna is to the order of the *haftarot*. On weekdays, when there is no *haftara*, the reference is to the order of the Torah readings. Therefore, no proof can be deduced from the mishna.

וּבְתַעֲנִיּוֹת לָמָּה לִי הַפְסָקָה? לִיקְרֵי מְצַפְרָא בְּעִנְיָינָא דְּיוֹמָא, וּבְמִנְחָה – בְּתַעֲנִיתָא! מְסַיֵּיעַ לֵיהּ לְרַב הוּנָא, דְּאָמַר רַב הוּנָא: מְצַפְרָא כְּינוּפְיָא.

The Gemara asks: **But on fast days, why do I** need to have any **interruption** of the regular order of Torah readings? **Let us read in the morning** the regular weekly portion **of the matter of the day, and in the afternoon** service let us read the portion **of a fast day.** The Gemara comments: This **supports** the statement of **Rav Huna, for Rav Huna said: From the morning** of communal fasts, **a gathering** is held[N] in the synagogue. The community leaders examine the conduct of the townspeople and admonish those whose behavior is found wanting. Therefore, there is no time in the morning to read the Torah portion for fast days.

הֵיכִי עָבְדִינַן? אָמַר אַבָּיֵי: מְצַפְרָא לְפַלְגֵיהּ דְּיוֹמָא מְעַיְּינִינַן בְּמִילֵּי דְמָתָא, מִפַּלְגֵיהּ דְּיוֹמָא לְפַנְיָא – רִיבְעָא דְּיוֹמָא קָרֵו וּמַפְטְרִי, וְרִיבְעָא דְּיוֹמָא בָּעוּ רַחֲמֵי, שֶׁנֶּאֱמַר ״וַיִּקְרְאוּ בְּסֵפֶר תּוֹרַת ה׳ אֱלֹהֵיהֶם רְבִיעִית הַיּוֹם וּרְבִיעִית (הַיּוֹם) מִתְוַדִּים וּמִשְׁתַּחֲוִים״.

The Gemara asks: **What does** the community **do** on a public fast day? **Abaye said: From the morning until the middle of the day,** the community gathers in the synagogue, and the leaders **examine the affairs of the town** to determine whether and how the people's conduct needs to be improved. **From the middle of the day until the evening, a quarter of the day** is spent **reading** from the Torah **and reading the *haftara*, and a quarter of the day** is spent **praying, as it is stated: "And they read in the book of the Torah of the Lord their God one quarter of the day, and a quarter of the day they confessed, and they prostrated themselves** before the Lord their God" (Nehemiah 9:3).[H]

HALAKHA

The fourth Shabbat – שַׁבָּת רְבִיעִית: The fourth Shabbat is the Shabbat that follows the week during which the New Moon of Nisan occurs, even if it occurs on Friday (Rambam *Sefer Ahava, Hilkhot Tefilla* 13:20).

One resumes the order of the *haftarot* – לְסֵדֶר הַפְטָרוֹת הוּא חוֹזֵר: When the four portions are read, they are read only in place of the *maftir*. The regular weekly portion is read beforehand, but the *haftara* is entirely replaced. Consequently, on the following week one resumes the regular weekly order of *haftarot*. This ruling is in accordance with Rabbi Yirmeya (*Shulḥan Arukh, Oraḥ Ḥayyim* 685).

The order on a public fast day – סֵדֶר תַּעֲנִיּוֹת צִיבּוּר: The proceedings of a fast day, as delineated by the Gemara, are as follows: After the morning prayers, the court convenes together with the community leaders in the synagogue. They examine the actions of the townspeople and make amends wherever necessary. From midday the Torah portion and the *haftara* are read. Then, during the last quarter of the day, the community prays the afternoon prayer, including additional pleas as necessary. Nowadays, the custom does not follow this order (see *Magen Avraham*). This may be because the court no longer has the power to compel sinners to amend their ways (*Arukh HaShulḥan*; *Shulḥan Arukh, Oraḥ Ḥayyim* 576:15).

NOTES

One resumes the regular weekly order of Torah portions – לְסֵדֶר פָּרָשִׁיּוֹת הוּא חוֹזֵר: It is clear from the Gemara here that Rabbi Ami assumes that when the special portions were read, the regular weekly portion was not. Although this poses the problem that the special portions are not long enough to provide for seven readers, it must be assumed that the portion would be repeated over and over again until seven people had read, as is the custom today on the intermediate days of *Sukkot* (*Turei Even*).

From the morning a gathering is held – מְצַפְרָא כְּינוּפְיָא: Since nowadays the public is not gathered in this way on a fast day, it seems that the custom was adjusted to read from the Torah during the morning prayers as well.

BACKGROUND

Non-priestly watches – מַעֲמָדוֹת: In the Temple era, priests and Levites were divided into twenty-four watches. Each watch served in the Temple for one week, two or three times a year. The entire nation was also divided into twenty-four watches, with each watch attached to a specific group of priests. During the week when the priestly watch was on duty in the Temple, some members of the corresponding non-priestly watch were dispatched to Jerusalem to be present in the Temple. The remainder of the non-priestly watch would stay at home, and during that week they would fast for several days. Vestiges of the customs of the non-priestly watch are found in various prayer books.

וְאֵיפוֹךְ אֲנָא! לָא סָלְקָא דַּעְתָּךְ דִּכְתִיב ״וְאֵלַי יֵאָסְפוּ כֹּל חָרֵד בְּדִבְרֵי אֱלֹהֵי יִשְׂרָאֵל עַל מַעַל הַגּוֹלָה וַאֲנִי יוֹשֵׁב מְשׁוֹמֵם עַד לְמִנְחַת הָעָרֶב״ וּכְתִיב ״וּבְמִנְחַת הָעֶרֶב קַמְתִּי מִתַּעֲנִיתִי״.

The Gemara objects: **But** perhaps **I should reverse** the order, and the first half of the day should be spent reading from the Torah and praying, and the second half of the day should be spent examining the affairs of the townspeople. The Gemara answers: **It should not enter your mind** to say this, **as it is written: "Then everyone who trembled at the words of the God of Israel due to the transgression of the exiles gathered around me, and I sat appalled until the evening offering"** (Ezra 9:4), **and it is written** in the next verse: **"And at the evening offering I arose from my fast,** and having rent my garment and my mantle; I fell on my knees, and I spread out my hands to the Lord my God" (Ezra 9:5). This indicates that the first half of a public fast should be dedicated to an inspection of the community's behavior, and the rest of the day should be devoted to prayer.

מתני׳ בְּפֶסַח קוֹרִין בְּפָרָשַׁת מוֹעֲדוֹת שֶׁל תּוֹרַת כֹּהֲנִים, בָּעֲצֶרֶת ״שִׁבְעָה שָׁבוּעוֹת״, בְּרֹאשׁ הַשָּׁנָה ״בַּחֹדֶשׁ הַשְּׁבִיעִי בְּאֶחָד לַחֹדֶשׁ״, בְּיוֹם הַכִּפּוּרִים ״אַחֲרֵי מוֹת״. בְּיוֹם טוֹב הָרִאשׁוֹן שֶׁל חַג קוֹרִין בְּפָרָשַׁת מוֹעֲדוֹת שֶׁבְּתוֹרַת כֹּהֲנִים, וּבִשְׁאָר כׇּל יְמוֹת הֶחָג בְּקׇרְבְּנוֹת הֶחָג.

MISHNA **On** the first day of **Passover,** the congregation **reads**[N] **from the portion of the Festivals of Leviticus** (Leviticus 22:26–23:44). **On** ***Shavuot*** they read the portion of **"Seven weeks"** (Deuteronomy 16:9–12). **On Rosh HaShana** they read the portion of "And **on the seventh month on the first of the month"** (Leviticus 23:23–25). **On Yom Kippur** they read the portion of **"After the death"** (Leviticus 16). **On the first Festival day of *Sukkot* they read from the portion of the Festivals of Leviticus** (Leviticus 22:26–23:44), **and on the other days of *Sukkot*** they read selections **from** the portion of **the offerings of *Sukkot*** (Numbers 29:12–39).[N]

בַּחֲנוּכָּה בַּנְּשִׂיאִים, בְּפוּרִים ״וַיָּבֹא עֲמָלֵק״, בְּרָאשֵׁי חֳדָשִׁים ״וּבְרָאשֵׁי חׇדְשֵׁיכֶם״. בַּמַּעֲמָדוֹת בְּמַעֲשֵׂה בְרֵאשִׁית, בַּתַּעֲנִיּוֹת

On each day of **Hanukkah** they read selections **from** the portion of the dedication of the altar by **the** tribal **princes** (Numbers 7).[N] **On Purim** they read the portion of **"And Amalek came"** (Exodus 17:8–16). **On the New Moon** they read the portion of **"And in the beginnings of your months"** (Numbers 28:11–15). **And in the** non-priestly **watches**[B] they read **the act of Creation** (Genesis 1:1–2:3). The Jewish people were divided into twenty-four watches. Each week, it would be the turn of a different watch to send representatives to Jerusalem to be present in the Temple to witness the sacrificial service. Those remaining behind would fast during the week, from Monday to Thursday, offer special prayers, and read the account of Creation from the Torah. **On fast days,**

NOTES

On Passover the congregation reads – בְּפֶסַח קוֹרִין: The order of the days listed in the mishna follows the order presented in the portion of Festivals in Leviticus, chapters 22–23. Afterward, the non-biblical holidays are listed, first those with fixed dates and then those that have no specific date (*Tosefot Yom Tov*).

From the portion of the offerings of *Sukkot* – בְּקׇרְבְּנוֹת הֶחָג: *Tosafot* note that there is no mention in the Talmud of the now-established custom to take out a second Torah scroll on Festivals and read *maftir* from the portion of the offerings of the Festival. The custom is first recorded in the Prayer Book of Rav Amram Gaon.

Some maintain that this custom is post-talmudic and began during the savoraic period (Rid). However, others claim that the custom was already practiced during the talmudic period, and the fact that it is not explicitly recorded in the Talmud does not prove otherwise. They point to the fact that the complete order of prayers and many other daily rituals are also not explicitly or fully recorded in the Talmud. Nevertheless, they note that various *halakhot* in the Talmud do seem to indicate the existence of this custom, e.g., the way in which the reading for Hanukkah and the New Moon were established and the reading for Yom Kippur (see Rashba).

On Hanukkah they read from the portion of the tribal princes – בַּחֲנוּכָּה בַּנְּשִׂיאִים: This portion was selected because the gifts of the tribal princes were presented in honor of the dedication of the Tabernacle, which closely parallels the holiday of Hanukkah, a holiday that was established following the rededication of the Temple during the Hasmonean period. Additionally, some early commentaries found an allusion to Hanukkah in this portion. Aaron, the High Priest, was distressed that he and his tribe had not presented a gift in the manner of the other tribal princes. God comforted him that he and his descendants would be able to light the candelabrum as long as the Tabernacle or the Temple stood, and even following its destruction the mitzva would continue through the lighting of the Hanukkah candles (see *Tur* and Ramban on Numbers 8:2).

בְּרָכוֹת וּקְלָלוֹת. אֵין מַפְסִיקִין בִּקְלָלוֹת, אֶלָּא אֶחָד קוֹרֵא אֶת כּוּלָּן.

they read the portion of **blessings and curses** (Leviticus, chapter 26). **One should not interrupt** the reading of the **curses** by having two different people read them. **Rather, one person reads all of them.**

בַּשֵּׁנִי וּבַחֲמִישִׁי, בְּשַׁבָּת בַּמִּנְחָה – קוֹרִין כְּסִדְרָן, וְאֵין עוֹלִים לָהֶם מִן הַחֶשְׁבּוֹן,

On Mondays, and on Thursdays, and **on Shabbat during the afternoon** service, **they read in accordance** with the regular weekly **order,** i.e., they proceed to read the first section of the Torah portion that follows the portion that was read on the previous Shabbat morning. **However,** these readings **are not counted** as a progression **in the reckoning** of reading the Torah portions, i.e., they do not proceed on Monday to read the section that immediately follows the section read on Shabbat during the afternoon, and then the following section on Thursday. Rather, until the reading on the following Shabbat morning, they return to and read the same first section of the Torah portion that follows the portion that was read on the previous Shabbat morning.

שֶׁנֶּאֱמַר: ״וַיְדַבֵּר מֹשֶׁה אֶת מוֹעֲדֵי ה׳ אֶל בְּנֵי יִשְׂרָאֵל״ – מִצְוָתָן שֶׁיְּהוּ קוֹרִין כָּל אֶחָד וְאֶחָד בִּזְמַנּוֹ.

On Festivals and holidays, they read a portion relating to the character of the day, **as it is stated: "And Moses declared to the children of Israel the appointed seasons of the Lord"** (Leviticus 23:44), which indicates that part of **the mitzva** of the Festivals is **that** the people **should read** the portion relating to them, **each one in its** appointed **time.**[N]

גמ׳ תָּנוּ רַבָּנַן: בְּפֶסַח קוֹרִין בְּפָרָשַׁת מוֹעֲדוֹת, וּמַפְטִירִין בְּפֶסַח גִּלְגָּל. וְהָאִידָּנָא דְּאִיכָּא תְּרֵי יוֹמֵי, יוֹמָא קַמָּא בְּפֶסַח גִּלְגָּל, וּלְמָחָר – בְּפֶסַח יֹאשִׁיָּהוּ.

GEMARA **The Sages taught** in a *baraita*: **On** the first day **of Passover,** the congregation **reads from the portion of the Festivals** (Leviticus 22:26–23:44), **and they read as the *haftara*** the account of the **Passover** celebrated at **Gilgal** (Joshua 5:2–14).[H] The Gemara comments: **And nowadays,** in the Diaspora, **when there are two** Festival **days of Passover, on the first day** they read as the *haftara* the account of the **Passover** celebrated **at Gilgal, and on the next day** they read **from** the account of the **Passover** observed **by Josiah** (II Kings 23).[H]

וּשְׁאָר יְמוֹת הַפֶּסַח מְלַקֵּט וְקוֹרֵא מֵעִנְיָנוֹ שֶׁל פֶּסַח. מַאי הִיא? אָמַר רַב פַּפָּא: מאפ״ו סִימָן.

The *baraita* continues: **And on the other days of Passover, one collects and reads** from various Torah portions of **matters** relating **to Passover.** The Gemara asks: **What are these** portions? **Rav Pappa said: A mnemonic** for them is ***mem, alef, peh vav.*** Each letter stands for a different reading: *Mem* for the portion of: "Draw out [*mishkhu*] and take your lambs" (Exodus 12:21–51); *alef* for the portion of "If [*im*] you lend money to any of My people" (Exodus 22:24–23:19); *peh* for the portion of "Hew [*pesol*] for yourself" (Exodus 34:1–26); and *vav* for the portion "And the Lord spoke [*vaydabber*]" (Numbers 9:1–14).

יוֹם טוֹב הָאַחֲרוֹן שֶׁל פֶּסַח קוֹרִין ״וַיְהִי בְּשַׁלַּח״, וּמַפְטִירִין ״וַיְדַבֵּר דָּוִד״. וּלְמָחָר ״כָּל הַבְּכוֹר״, וּמַפְטִירִין ״עוֹד הַיּוֹם״.

The *baraita* continues: **On the last Festival day of Passover, they read** the portion of **"And it came to pass, when** Pharaoh **let** the people **go"** (Exodus 13:17–15:26), because it includes the account of the splitting of the Red Sea, **and they read as the *haftara*** the portion **"And David spoke"** (II Samuel 22), which is the song of David. **And** in the Diaspora, **on the next day,** the eighth day of Passover, they read the portion **"All the firstborns"** (Deuteronomy 15:19–16:17), **and they read as the *haftara*** the portion of **"This very day"** (Isaiah 10:32–12:6), because it discusses the downfall of Sennacherib, which occurred on the night of Passover.

אָמַר אַבַּיֵי: וְהָאִידָּנָא נְהוּג עָלְמָא לְמִיקְרֵי: מְשַׁךְ תּוֹרָא, קַדֵּשׁ בְּכַסְפָּא, פְּסֹל בְּמַדְבְּרָא, שַׁלַּח בּוּכְרָא.

Abaye said: And nowadays, on the eight days of Passover in the Diaspora, **everyone is accustomed to read** portions that are indicated by the mnemonic phrase: **Draw the bull, sanctify with money, hew in the wilderness, send the firstborn.** This alludes to the following portions: "Draw out and take your lambs" (Exodus 12:21–51) and "A bull or a sheep" (Leviticus 22:26–23:44); "Sanctify to Me all the firstborn" (Exodus 13:1–16) and "If you lend money to any of My people" (Exodus 22:24–23:19); "Hew for yourself" (Exodus 34:1–26) and "And the Lord spoke to Moses in the wilderness of Sinai" (Numbers 9:1–14); "And it came to pass, when Pharaoh let the people go" (Exodus 13:17–15:26) and "All the firstborns" (Deuteronomy 15:19–16:17).[H]

NOTES

The order of reading from the Torah – סִדְרֵי הַקְּרִיאָה בַּתּוֹרָה: The order of readings presented in the mishna was not fully practiced, even in the talmudic period, as is evident from the ensuing Gemara. Even the order established by the Gemara was later changed in accordance with the order set by tractate *Soferim* and the customs established by the *ge'onim*. Essentially, the precise selection of the portions was never absolute *halakha*, and the *ge'onim* already established that each place should follow its own customs in this regard.

HALAKHA

The Torah reading on the first day of Passover – קְרִיאָה בְּיוֹם רִאשׁוֹן שֶׁל פֶּסַח: On the first day of Passover, two Torah scrolls are removed. From the first scroll, five people read the portion of "Draw out and take your lambs" (Exodus 12:21–51). From the second scroll, the portion of the offering of the day is read as *maftir* (Numbers 28:16–25). The *haftara* is the account of the observance of Passover in Gilgal. The Ashkenazic custom is to read from Joshua 3:5–6:1, while the Sephardic custom is to read from Joshua 5:2–6:1 (*Shulḥan Arukh, Oraḥ Ḥayyim* 488:3).

The Torah reading on the second day of Passover – קְרִיאָה בְּיוֹם שֵׁנִי שֶׁל פֶּסַח: In the Diaspora, on the second Festival day of Passover, the portion of "A bull or a sheep" (Leviticus 22:26–23:44) is read. The *maftir* is the same as on the first day. The *haftara* is taken from the account of the Passover of Isaiah (II Kings 23:1–25; *Shulḥan Arukh, Oraḥ Ḥayyim* 490:1).

The Torah reading during the days of Passover – קְרִיאָה בִּימֵי פֶּסַח: During the days of Passover, the Torah reading follows the order delineated by Abaye with the mnemonic phrase: Draw the bullock, sanctify with money, hew in the wilderness, send the firstborn. This order is fixed, except when the first day of Passover occurs on Thursday. In such a case, since the third day of Passover is a Shabbat, the portion of "Hew for yourself" (Exodus 34:1–26) is read then rather than on the fifth day (see *Tosafot*; *Shulḥan Arukh, Oraḥ Ḥayyim* 490:5).

בַּעֲצֶרֶת ״שִׁבְעָה שָׁבוּעוֹת״ וּמַפְטִירִין בַּחֲבַקּוּק, אֲחֵרִים אוֹמְרִים: ״בַּחֹדֶשׁ הַשְּׁלִישִׁי״ וּמַפְטִירִין בַּמֶּרְכָּבָה. וְהָאִידָּנָא דְּאִיכָּא תְּרֵי יוֹמֵי – עָבְדִינַן כִּתְרַוַיְיהוּ, וְאִיפְּכָא.

The *baraita* continues: **On *Shavuot*** they read the portion of **"Seven weeks," and they read as the *haftara* from Habakkuk,** chapter 2, since it mentions the giving of the Torah at Sinai. **Others say:** They read the portion of **"In the third month"** (Exodus 19:1–20:23), which describes the giving of the Torah, **and they read as the *haftara* from** the account of **the** Divine **Chariot** (Ezekiel 1). The Gemara comments: **And nowadays,** in the Diaspora, **when there are two days** of *Shavuot*, **we act in accordance with both** opinions, **but in the reverse order.** On the first day they read the portion of "In the third month," and on the second day they read the portion of "Seven weeks."[H]

בְּרֹאשׁ הַשָּׁנָה ״בַּחֹדֶשׁ הַשְּׁבִיעִי״ וּמַפְטִירִין ״הֲבֵן יַקִּיר לִי אֶפְרַיִם״, וְיֵשׁ אוֹמְרִים ״וַה׳ פָּקַד אֶת שָׂרָה״ וּמַפְטִירִין בְּחַנָּה.

The *baraita* continues: **On Rosh HaShana** they read the portion of **"On the seventh month** on the first of the month" (Numbers 29:1–6) **and they read as the *haftara* "Is Ephraim My dear son?"** (Jeremiah 31:1–20), as it contains the verse: "I earnestly remember him still," which recalls God's love for His people. **And some say** that they read **"And the Lord visited Sarah"** (Genesis 21), which describes how God blessed her that she should have a child, and, according to tradition, God blessed her on Rosh HaShana. **And they read as the *haftara* from** the account of **Hannah** (1 Samuel 1:1–2:10), who, according to tradition, was also blessed on Rosh HaShana that she should have a child.

וְהָאִידָּנָא דְּאִיכָּא תְּרֵי יוֹמֵי, יוֹמָא קַמָּא – כְּיֵשׁ אוֹמְרִים, לְמָחָר ״וְהָאֱלֹהִים נִסָּה אֶת אַבְרָהָם״ וּמַפְטִירִין ״הֲבֵן יַקִּיר״.

The Gemara comments: **And nowadays, when there are two days** of Rosh HaShana, on **the first day** they read Genesis 21 **in accordance** with the opinion cited as: **Some say. And on the next day** they read **"And God tested Abraham"** (Genesis 22), in order to mention the merit of the binding of Isaac on the day of God's judgment, **and they read as the *haftara* "Is Ephraim My dear son?"**[H]

בְּיוֹם הַכִּפּוּרִים קוֹרִין ״אַחֲרֵי מוֹת״ וּמַפְטִירִין ״כִּי כֹה אָמַר רָם וְנִשָּׂא״, וּבְמִנְחָה קוֹרִין בָּעֲרָיוֹת וּמַפְטִירִין בְּיוֹנָה.

The *baraita* continues: **On Yom Kippur they read** the portion of **"After the death"** (Leviticus 16), **and they read as the *haftara*** the portion of **"For thus says the High and Lofty One"** (Isaiah 57:14–58:14), which deals with fasting and repentance.[H] **And during the afternoon** service they **read from** the portion detailing **forbidden sexual relations** (Leviticus 18)[N] to convey the severity of these transgressions, so that if anyone transgressed any of these prohibitions he will repent on Yom Kippur. **And they read as the *haftara*** the book of **Jonah,** which mentions the repentance of the people of Nineveh.[H]

אָמַר רַבִּי יוֹחָנָן: כׇּל מָקוֹם שֶׁאַתָּה מוֹצֵא גְּבוּרָתוֹ שֶׁל הַקָּדוֹשׁ בָּרוּךְ הוּא אַתָּה מוֹצֵא עַנְוְותָנוּתוֹ; דָּבָר זֶה כָּתוּב בַּתּוֹרָה וְשָׁנוּי בַּנְּבִיאִים וּמְשׁוּלָּשׁ בַּכְּתוּבִים.

Having mentioned the *haftara* read on Yom Kippur, the Gemara cites that which **Rabbi Yoḥanan said: Wherever you find** a reference in the Bible to **the might of the Holy One, Blessed be He, you** also **find** a reference to **His humility** adjacent to it.[N] Evidence of **this fact is written in the Torah, repeated in the Prophets, and stated a third time in the Writings.**

כָּתוּב בַּתּוֹרָה ״כִּי ה׳ אֱלֹהֵיכֶם הוּא אֱלֹהֵי הָאֱלֹהִים וַאֲדוֹנֵי הָאֲדוֹנִים״ וּכְתִיב בַּתְרֵיהּ ״עוֹשֶׂה מִשְׁפַּט יָתוֹם וְאַלְמָנָה״. שָׁנוּי בַּנְּבִיאִים ״כֹּה אָמַר רָם וְנִשָּׂא שׁוֹכֵן עַד וְקָדוֹשׁ״ וגו׳ וּכְתִיב בַּתְרֵיהּ ״וְאֶת דַּכָּא וּשְׁפַל רוּחַ״. מְשׁוּלָּשׁ בַּכְּתוּבִים דִּכְתִיב ״סוֹלּוּ לָרוֹכֵב בָּעֲרָבוֹת בְּיָהּ שְׁמוֹ״ וּכְתִיב בַּתְרֵיהּ ״אֲבִי יְתוֹמִים וְדַיַּן אַלְמָנוֹת״.

It is written in the Torah: "For the Lord your God is the God of gods and the Lord of lords" (Deuteronomy 10:17), **and it is written** immediately **afterward: "He executes the judgment of the fatherless and widow"** (Deuteronomy 10:18), displaying his humility in caring for even the weakest parts of society. **It is repeated in the Prophets: "For thus says the High and Lofty One that inhabits eternity, Whose name is sacred"** (Isaiah 57:15), **and it is written** immediately **afterward:** "In the high and holy place I dwell **with him that is of a contrite and humble spirit,** to revive the spirit of the humble, and to revive the heart of the contrite ones" (Isaiah 57:15). **It is stated a third time in the Writings, as it is written: "Extol Him Who rides upon the clouds, Whose name is the Lord"** (Psalms 68:5), **and it is written** immediately **afterward: "A father of the fatherless, and a judge of widows"** (Psalms 68:6).

HALAKHA

The Torah reading on *Shavuot* – קְרִיאָה בַּעֲצֶרֶת: On *Shavuot*, the portion of "In the third month" (Exodus 19–20) is read. The Ten Commandments, which are part of that portion, is read using the special, higher trop, which breaks up the commandments into ten distinct parts (*Magen Avraham)*.

In Ashkenazic communities, the liturgical poem *Akdamot* is recited. Some are accustomed to recite it after completing the first verse of the Torah reading. While one should not oppose such a custom, it is more correct to recite it before the Torah reading (*Taz*; see *Shulḥan Arukh HaRav*). Sephardic communities have the custom to recite the liturgical poem *Ketuba LeShavuot*.

For the *maftir*, the portion of "And on the day of the first fruits" (Numbers 28:26–31) is read from a second Torah scroll. The *haftara* is the description of God's Chariot (Ezekiel 1). In the Diaspora, on the second day, the portion of "All the firstborns" (Deuteronomy 15:19–16:18) is read from the first scroll, and the *maftir* is read from the second scroll, as on the first day. The *haftara* is taken from Habakkuk. The Ashkenazic custom is to read chapter 3, while the Sephardic custom is to read 2:20–3:19 (*Shulḥan Arukh*, *Oraḥ Ḥayyim* 494:1–2).

The Torah reading on Rosh HaShana – קְרִיאָה בְּרֹאשׁ הַשָּׁנָה: On the first day of Rosh HaShana, the portion of "And the Lord visited Sarah" (Genesis 21) is read. The *maftir* is the portion of "In the seventh month" (Numbers 29:1–6), and the *haftara* is the story of Hannah (1 Samuel 1:1–2:10). On the second day, the account of the binding of Isaac is read (Genesis 22). The *maftir* is the same as on the first day, and the *haftara* (Jeremiah 31:1–20) is the portion of "Is Ephraim My dear son?" (*Shulḥan Arukh*, *Oraḥ Ḥayyim* 584:2, 601:1).

The Torah reading on Yom Kippur – קְרִיאָה בְּיוֹם הַכִּפּוּרִים: On Yom Kippur, during the morning service, the portion of "After the death" (Leviticus 16) is read. The *maftir* is the portion of "On the tenth of the month" (Numbers 29:7–11), and the *haftara*, is the portion of Isaiah (57:14–58:14): "For thus says the High and Lofty One" (*Shulḥan Arukh*, *Oraḥ Ḥayyim* 621:1).

The Torah reading of the afternoon service on Yom Kippur – קְרִיאָה בְּמִנְחַת יוֹם הַכִּפּוּרִים: In the afternoon service on Yom Kippur, three people read the portion detailing forbidden sexual relations (Leviticus 18). The last person who reads is considered to be the *maftir*, and then the book of Jonah is read as the *haftara* (*Shulḥan Arukh*, *Oraḥ Ḥayyim* 622:2).

NOTES

They read from the portion detailing forbidden sexual relations – קוֹרִין בָּעֲרָיוֹת: Given the solemnity and holiness of the day, this choice of Torah portion is quite surprising. Various suggestions for the choice have been offered. Some suggest that the selection was made in order to mention the merit of the Jewish people on this day, for they always distance themselves from these relationships (*Gan Naul*). See also Rashi and *Tosafot* here.

God's might and humility – גְּבוּרָתוֹ וְעַנְוְותָנוּתוֹ: Some connect this concept with the previous Gemara concerning the selection of the Torah reading. The selection was made in order to stir one to improve his ways. So too, this teaching is designed to humble a person (*Zikkaron BaSefer*). The scholars of ethics explain that in essence God's might and His humility are functions of each other: His might is that He reveals His splendor to mankind, but that itself is an expression of humility, for in comparison to God man is of insignificance (*Bina LeIttim*; *Ya'arot Devash*).

יוֹם טוֹב הָרִאשׁוֹן שֶׁל חַג קוֹרִין בְּפָרָשַׁת מוֹעֲדוֹת שֶׁבְּתוֹרַת כֹּהֲנִים, וּמַפְטִירִין "הִנֵּה יוֹם בָּא לַה'", וְהָאִידָּנָא דְּאִיכָּא תְּרֵי יוֹמֵי, לְמָחָר מִיקְרָא הָכִי נַמִי קָרֵינַן, אַפְטוֹרֵי מַאי מַפְטִירִין? "וַיִּקָּהֲלוּ אֶל הַמֶּלֶךְ שְׁלֹמֹה".

The *baraita* continues: On **the first Festival day of *Sukkot*, they read from the portion of the Festivals found in Leviticus** (Leviticus 22:26–23:44), **and they read as the *haftara*** the portion **of "Behold the day of the Lord comes"** (Zechariah 14), which mentions the festival of *Sukkot*.[H] The Gemara comments: **And nowadays,** in the Diaspora, **when there are two** Festival **days** of *Sukkot*, **on the next day, they read the same** Torah portion. But **what do they read as the *haftara*?** They read the portion of **"And** all the men of Israel **assembled themselves to King Solomon"** (1 Kings 8:2–21), which describes events that took place on the festival of *Sukkot*.[H]

וּשְׁאָר כָּל יְמוֹת הֶחָג. קוֹרִין בְּקָרְבְּנוֹת הֶחָג יוֹם טוֹב הָאַחֲרוֹן קוֹרִין "כָּל הַבְּכוֹר" מִצְוֹת וְחוּקִּים וּבְכוֹר, וּמַפְטִירִין "וַיְהִי כְּכַלּוֹת שְׁלֹמֹה", לְמָחָר קוֹרִין "וְזֹאת הַבְּרָכָה" וּמַפְטִירִין "וַיַּעֲמֹד שְׁלֹמֹה".

The *baraita* continues: **And on all the other days of *Sukkot*, they read** selections **from** the portion of **the offerings of *Sukkot*** found in the book of Numbers, chapter 29. **On the last Festival day** of *Sukkot*, i.e., the Eighth Day of Assembly, **they read** the portion of **"All the firstborns,"** starting with the portion of "You shall tithe," since it includes many **mitzvot and statutes** relating to gifts for the poor, who should be helped during this period of rejoicing, and it concludes with the *halakhot* governing **firstborns** (Deuteronomy 14:22–16:17). **And they read as the *haftara*** the portion of **"And it was so, that when Solomon had made an end** of praying" (1 Kings 8:54–9:1), which occurred on that day.[H] **On the next day,** the second day of the Eighth Day of Assembly in the Diaspora, **they read** the portion of **"And this is the blessing"** (Deuteronomy, chapters 33–34) until the end of the Torah, **and they read as the *haftara* "And Solomon stood"** (1 Kings 8:22–53).[H]

אָמַר רַב הוּנָא אָמַר רַב: שַׁבָּת שֶׁחָל לִהְיוֹת בְּחוּלּוֹ שֶׁל מוֹעֵד, בֵּין בְּפֶסַח בֵּין בְּסוּכּוֹת, מִקְרָא קָרֵינַן "רְאֵה אַתָּה", אַפְטוֹרֵי, בְּפֶסַח "הָעֲצָמוֹת הַיְבֵשׁוֹת", וּבְסוּכּוֹת "בְּיוֹם בֹּא גוֹג".

Rav Huna said that **Rav said:** When **Shabbat occurs on** one of **the intermediate days** of a Festival, **whether on Passover or on *Sukkot*, they read the Torah** portion of **"See, You** say to me" (Exodus 33:12–34:26), as it includes the *halakhot* of the Festivals and the intermediate days. **They read as the *haftara*, on Passover,** from the portion of **the dry bones** (Ezekiel 37:1–14), which portrays redemption from servitude, **and on *Sukkot*** they read "And it shall come to pass **on that day when Gog shall come"** (Ezekiel 38:18–39:16), which speaks of the future redemption.[NH]

NOTES

The *haftarot* of Shabbat of the intermediate days – הַפְטָרוֹת שַׁבָּת חוֹל הַמּוֹעֵד: Rav Hai Gaon records a tradition that the revival of the dead will occur on the intermediate days of Passover, and the battle of Gog will occur on the intermediate days of *Sukkot*. This explains the respective selection of these portions for the *haftarot*.

HALAKHA

The Torah reading of the first Festival day of *Sukkot* – קְרִיאָה בְּיוֹם טוֹב הָרִאשׁוֹן שֶׁל סֻכּוֹת: On the first Festival day of *Sukkot*, the portion of the Festivals is read (Leviticus 22:26–23:44). The *maftir* is the portion detailing the additional offering of the day (Numbers 29:11–16), and the *haftara* is from Zechariah, chapter 14 (*Shulḥan Arukh, Oraḥ Ḥayyim* 659:1).

The Torah reading of the second day of *Sukkot* – קְרִיאָה בְּיוֹם שֵׁנִי שֶׁל סֻכּוֹת: In the Diaspora, where the second day of *Sukkot* is also a Festival day, the Torah reading is the same as the first day, and the *haftara* is the portion of "And all the men of Israel assembled themselves to King Solomon" (I Kings 8:2–21). In Eretz Yisrael, the second day is already one of the intermediate days, and the reading is as on the rest of the days: Four read the portion detailing the additional offering of that day (*Shulḥan Arukh, Oraḥ Ḥayyim* 662:3).

The Torah reading of the Eighth day of Assembly – קְרִיאָה בִּשְׁמִינִי עֲצֶרֶת: In Eretz Yisrael, where the Eighth Day of Assembly is also *Simḥat Torah*, three Torah scrolls are removed. From the first, the portion of "And this is the blessing," the final portion of the Torah, is read in its entirety. From the second scroll, the opening portion of Genesis (1:1–2:3) is read. From the third scroll, the *maftir* is read from "And on the eighth day" (Numbers 29:35–30:1). The *haftara* is from the opening chapter of Joshua (1:1–18). This is in accordance with the custom of the *ge'onim*.

In the Diaspora, where *Simḥat Torah* will occur only on the following day, only two Torah scrolls are removed. From the first, five people read from the portion of "All the firstborns" (Deuteronomy 15:19–16:17), and if it occurs on Shabbat, then seven read, and the reading begins slightly earlier, from the verse "You will tithe" (Deuteronomy 14:22). The Ashkenazic custom is to always begin from "You will tithe" (*Magen Avraham*). The *maftir* is from the portion of "And on the eighth day" (Numbers 29:35–30:1). The *haftara*, from I Kings (8:54–61), is the portion of "And it was so, that when Solomon had made an end of praying" (*Shulḥan Arukh, Oraḥ Ḥayyim* 662:14, 22, 868:2).

The Torah reading of *Simḥat Torah* – קְרִיאָה בְּשִׂמְחַת תּוֹרָה: In Eretz Yisrael, where there is only one Festival day of the Eighth Day of Assembly, *Simḥat Torah,* i.e., the completion of the cycle of reading the entire Torah and the accompanying celebration, is held then. However, in the Diaspora, where there are two Festival days of the Eighth Day of Assembly, the celebration of *Simḥat Torah* is reserved exclusively for the second day. The reading with which the Torah is completed is considered a special honor, and the person who reads it is designated as the groom of the Torah. Similarly, the one privileged to read the opening portion is designated as the groom of Genesis. Various others customs and honors exist in this regard. Generally, the honors are given to important members of the community. It is a day of great joy. The established customs are based on those described in the writings of the *ge'onim*. Although these customs are not mentioned in the Talmud, they have been universally accepted by all communities in varying forms (*Shulḥan Arukh, Oraḥ Ḥayyim* 669:1).

The Torah reading of the intermediate days – קְרִיאָה בְּחֻלּוֹ שֶׁל מוֹעֵד: On the Shabbat of the intermediate days, two Torah scrolls are removed. From the first, the portion of "See, You say to me" (Exodus 33:12–34:26) is read, both on Passover and *Sukkot*. The *maftir* is the same as for the rest of the intermediate days: The portion of the additional offerings of that day is read. On Passover, the *haftara* is the portion of the dry bones (Ezekiel 37:1–14), and on *Sukkot* it is the portion from Ezekiel (38:18–39:9): "On the day Gog comes" (*Shulḥan Arukh, Oraḥ Ḥayyim* 663:3).

בַּחֲנוּכָּה – בַּנְּשִׂיאִים, וּמַפְטִירִין בְּנֵרוֹת דִּזְכַרְיָה. וְאִי מִיקַּלְעִי שְׁתֵּי שַׁבָּתוֹת, קַמַּיְיתָא – בְּנֵרוֹת דִּזְכַרְיָה, בַּתְרַיְיתָא בְּנֵרוֹת שְׁלֹמֹה.

The *baraita* continues: **On** each day of **Hanukkah** they read a selection **from** the portion of the dedication of the altar by **the** tribal **princes** (Numbers 7), **and they read as the *haftara* from** the portion of **the lamps of Zechariah** (Zechariah 2:14–4:7). The Gemara comments: **And if it occurs that there are two *Shabbatot*** during Hanukkah, **on the first** Shabbat they read **from** the portion of **the lamps of Zechariah, and on the latter one** they read **from** the portion of **the lamps of Solomon**[N] (I Kings 7:40–50), which discusses the lamps in the Temple.[H]

בְּפוּרִים "וַיָּבֹא עֲמָלֵק". בְּרָאשֵׁי חֳדָשִׁים "וּבְרָאשֵׁי חָדְשֵׁיכֶם". רֹאשׁ חֹדֶשׁ שֶׁחָל לִהְיוֹת בְּשַׁבָּת מַפְטִירִין "וְהָיָה מִדֵּי חֹדֶשׁ בְּחָדְשׁוֹ". חָל לִהְיוֹת בְּאֶחָד בְּשַׁבָּת, מֵאֶתְמוֹל מַפְטִירִין "וַיֹּאמֶר לוֹ יְהוֹנָתָן מָחָר חֹדֶשׁ".

The *baraita* continues: **On Purim** they read the portion of **"And Amalek came"** (Exodus 17:8–16).[H] **On the New Moon** they read the portion of **"And in the beginnings of your month"** (Numbers 28:11–15). When **the New Moon occurs on Shabbat, they read as the *haftara*** the portion that concludes with **"And it shall come to pass that every New Moon,** and every Shabbat, shall all flesh come to bow down on the ground before Me" (Isaiah 66), as it mentions both Shabbat and the New Moon.[H] When the New Moon **occurs on Sunday, on the previous day,** i.e., Shabbat, **they read as the *haftara*** the portion of **"And Jonathan said to him: Tomorrow is the New Moon"** (I Samuel 20:18–42), which describes events that took place on the eve of the New Moon.[H]

אָמַר רַב הוּנָא:

Rav Huna said:

NOTES

And on the latter one they read from the portion of the lamps of Solomon – בַּתְרַיְיתָא בְּנֵרוֹת שְׁלֹמֹה: The commentaries explain that the portion of the lamps of Zechariah is read first because it occurred during the Second Temple period, which is when the miracle of Hanukkah took place.

HALAKHA

The Torah reading on the Shabbat of Hanukkah – קְרִיאָה בְּשַׁבַּת חֲנֻכָּה: On the Shabbat of Hanukkah, two Torah scrolls are removed: From the first, the regular weekly Torah portion is read, and from the second scroll the account of the gifts of the tribal princes for that day is read as *maftir*. The *haftara* is the portion of the lamps of Zechariah (Zechariah 2:14–4:7). If there are two *Shabbatot* in Hanukkah, the portion of the lamps of Solomon (I Kings 7:40–50) is read on the second Shabbat (*Shulḥan Arukh*, *Oraḥ Ḥayyim* 684:2).

The Torah reading on Purim – קְרִיאָה בְּפוּרִים: On Purim, three people read from the portion of "And Amalek came" (Exodus 17:8–16). Since there are only nine verses, the portion is split into three sections of three verses. Sephardic communities are accustomed to repeat the last verse, so that the minimum of ten verses for a portion will have been read (*Kaf HaḤayyim*). Ashkenazic Jews do not follow this custom (Rema). When Shushan Purim occurs on Shabbat, the regular weekly portion is read, and then the portion of "And Amalek came" is read as *maftir* (*Shulḥan Arukh*, *Oraḥ Ḥayyim* 693:4).

The Torah reading when the New Moon occurs on Shabbat – קְרִיאָה בְּרֹאשׁ חֹדֶשׁ בְּשַׁבָּת: When the New Moon occurs on Shabbat, the *maftir*, which is read from a second scroll, is the portion that combines both the sections of Shabbat, i.e., "And on the day of Shabbat" (Numbers 28:9–10) and of the New Moon, i.e., "And on the New Moons" (Numbers 28:11–15). The *haftara* is the portion "The heaven is My throne" (Isaiah 66). On the *Shabbatot* leading up to the Ninth of Av, a series of *haftarot* describing the destruction of the Temple are read, and then on the *Shabbatot* following the Ninth of Av a series of *haftarot* with prophecies of conciliation are read. Various customs exist with regard to which *haftara* is read when the New Moon occurs on one of these *Shabbatot* (*Shulḥan Arukh*, *Oraḥ Ḥayyim* 425:1).

The Torah reading when the New Moon occurs on Sunday – קְרִיאָה בְּרֹאשׁ חֹדֶשׁ בְּיוֹם רִאשׁוֹן: If the New Moon occurs on Sunday, the *haftara* on the Shabbat immediately beforehand is "Tomorrow is the New Moon" (I Samuel 20:18–42). In the event that there are two days of the New Moon, and Shabbat is the first day, the *haftara* is "The heaven is My throne," and the first and last verses of the portion "Tomorrow is the New Moon" are also read. Some disagree and say that in such a case only the portion "The heaven is My throne" is read (*Shulḥan Arukh*, *Oraḥ Ḥayyim* 424:2, and in the comment of Rema).

רֹאשׁ חֹדֶשׁ אָב שֶׁחָל לִהְיוֹת בְּשַׁבָּת מַפְטִירִין ״חׇדְשֵׁיכֶם וּמוֹעֲדֵיכֶם שָׂנְאָה נַפְשִׁי הָיוּ עָלַי לָטוֹרַח״. מַאי ״הָיוּ עָלַי לָטוֹרַח״? אָמַר הַקָּדוֹשׁ בָּרוּךְ הוּא: לֹא דַּיָּין לָהֶם לְיִשְׂרָאֵל שֶׁחוֹטְאִין לְפָנַי, אֶלָּא שֶׁמַּטְרִיחִין אוֹתִי לֵידַע אֵיזוֹ גְּזֵירָה קָשָׁה אָבִיא עֲלֵיהֶם.

When the **New Moon of Av occurs on Shabbat, they read as the** ***haftara*** the portion that includes the verse **"Your New Moons and your Festivals,**[N] **My soul hated; they were a burden to Me"** (Isaiah 1:14). The Gemara asks: **What is** the meaning of: **"They were a burden to Me"?** The Gemara explains: **The Holy One, Blessed be He, said: It is not enough for the Jewish people that they sin before Me, but** in addition, **they burden Me to reconsider what harsh decree I shall bring upon them,** for they are petitioning Me to annul those decrees.

בְּתִשְׁעָה בְּאָב גּוּפֵיהּ מַאי מַפְטְרִינַן? אָמַר רַב: ״אֵיכָה הָיְתָה לְזוֹנָה״, מִקְרָא מַאי? תַּנְיָא, אֲחֵרִים אוֹמְרִים: ״וְאִם לֹא תִשְׁמְעוּ לִי״ רַבִּי נָתָן בַּר יוֹסֵף אוֹמֵר: ״עַד אָנָה יְנַאֲצוּנִי הָעָם הַזֶּה״, וְיֵשׁ אוֹמְרִים ״עַד מָתַי לָעֵדָה הָרָעָה הַזֹּאת״. אָמַר אַבַּיֵי: הָאִידָּנָא נְהוּג עָלְמָא לְמִיקְרֵי ״כִּי תוֹלִיד בָּנִים״ וּמַפְטִירִין ״אָסֹף אֲסִיפֵם״.

The Gemara asks: **On the Ninth of Av itself, what do we read as the** ***haftara*****? Rav said:** The portion containing the verse **"How did the faithful city become a harlot?"** (Isaiah 1:21). The Gemara asks: **What Torah portion** do they read? **It is taught** in a *baraita* that **others say:** They read the portion containing the verse **"But if you will not hearken to me"** (Leviticus 26:14). **Rabbi Natan bar Yosef said:** They read the portion containing the verse: **"How long will this people provoke me?"** (Numbers 14:11). **And some say:** They read the portion containing the verse: **"How long shall I bear with this evil congregation?"** (Numbers 14:27). The Gemara comments that **Abaye said: Nowadays, everyone is accustomed to read** the portion of **"When you shall beget children"** (Deuteronomy 4:25–40), **and they read as the** ***haftara*** the portion of **"I will utterly consume them"** (Jeremiah 8:13–9:23).[H]

״[בַּמַּעֲמָדוֹת] בְּמַעֲשֵׂה בְרֵאשִׁית״ וכו׳: מְנָהָנֵי מִילֵּי? אָמַר רַבִּי אַמִי: אִלְמָלֵא מַעֲמָדוֹת לֹא נִתְקַיְּימוּ שָׁמַיִם וָאָרֶץ, שֶׁנֶּאֱמַר ״אִם לֹא בְרִיתִי יוֹמָם וָלָיְלָה חוּקּוֹת שָׁמַיִם וָאָרֶץ לֹא שָׂמְתִּי״,

§ The mishna states: **In the** non-priestly **watches** they read **the act of Creation.** The Gemara asks: **From where are these matters** derived, i.e., why do they read the account of Creation? **Rabbi Ami said:** To allude to the fact that **were it not for** the non-priestly **watches, heaven and earth would not endure, as it is stated: "Were it not for My covenant day and night, I would not have set the statutes of heaven and earth"** (Jeremiah 33:25). God's covenant is referring to the offerings sacrificed in the Temple, which sustain the world.

וּכְתִיב ״וַיֹּאמַר ה׳ אֱלֹהִים בַּמָּה אֵדַע כִּי אִירָשֶׁנָּה״ אָמַר אַבְרָהָם לִפְנֵי הַקָּדוֹשׁ בָּרוּךְ הוּא: רִבּוֹנוֹ שֶׁל עוֹלָם! שֶׁמָּא חַס וְשָׁלוֹם יִשְׂרָאֵל חוֹטְאִים לְפָנֶיךָ וְאַתָּה עוֹשֶׂה לָהֶם כְּדוֹר הַמַּבּוּל וּכְדוֹר הַפַּלָּגָה? אָמַר לוֹ: לָאו.

And with regard to Abraham **it is written: "And he said, O Lord God, by what shall I know that I shall inherit it?"** (Genesis 15:8). **Abraham said before the Holy One, Blessed be He: Master of the Universe, perhaps, Heaven forbid, the Jewish people will sin before You, and You will do to them as** You did to the **generation of the Flood and as** You did to the **generation of the Dispersion,** i.e., You will completely destroy them? God **said to him: No,** I will not do that.

אָמַר לְפָנָיו: רִבּוֹנוֹ שֶׁל עוֹלָם, בַּמָּה אֵדַע? אָמַר לוֹ: ״קְחָה לִי עֶגְלָה מְשׁוּלֶּשֶׁת״ וגו׳. אָמַר לְפָנָיו: רִבּוֹנוֹ שֶׁל עוֹלָם, תֵּינַח בִּזְמַן שֶׁבֵּית הַמִּקְדָּשׁ קַיָּים, בִּזְמַן שֶׁאֵין בֵּית הַמִּקְדָּשׁ קַיָּים מַה תְּהֵא עֲלֵיהֶם? אָמַר לוֹ: כְּבָר תִּקַּנְתִּי לָהֶם סֵדֶר קׇרְבָּנוֹת, כׇּל זְמַן שֶׁקּוֹרְאִין בָּהֶן מַעֲלֶה אֲנִי עֲלֵיהֶן כְּאִילּוּ מַקְרִיבִין לְפָנַי קׇרְבָּן, וּמוֹחֵל אֲנִי עַל כׇּל עֲוֹנוֹתֵיהֶם.

Abraham then **said before Him: Master of the Universe: "By what shall I know this?"** God **said to him: "Take Me a heifer of three years old"** (Genesis 15:9). With this, God intimated to Abraham that even if his descendants will sin, they will be able to achieve atonement through sacrificing offerings. Abraham **said before Him: Master of the Universe,** this **works out well when the Temple is standing** and offerings can be brought to achieve atonement, but **when the Temple will no** longer **be standing, what will become of them?** God **said to him: I have already established for them the order of offerings,** i.e., the verses of the Torah pertaining to the *halakhot* of the offerings. **Whenever they read those** portions, **I will deem it as if they sacrificed an offering before Me, and I will pardon them for all of their iniquities.**

NOTES

Your New Moons and your Festivals – חׇדְשֵׁיכֶם וּמוֹעֲדֵיכֶם: Why does the verse emphasize specifically "your," i.e., the Jewish people's, Festivals? The Maharsha explains that the verse is referring to the Festivals that the Jewish people improperly established for themselves, similar to those established by Jeroboam. It is therefore understandable that they are considered a burden to God. Others explain that the reference is to the fast days instituted following the destruction of the Temple, which express the Jewish people's mourning. Why, then, were they a burden to God? They are an expression of the decrees that God, so to speak, has to exert Himself in imposing upon the Jewish people.

HALAKHA

The Torah reading on the Ninth of Av – קְרִיאָה בְּתִשְׁעָה בְּאָב: Nowadays, the custom is in accordance with the opinion of Abaye. Three people read from the portion "When you shall beget children" (Deuteronomy 4:25–40), and the *haftara* is the portion (Jeremiah 8:13–9:23) "I will utterly consume them" (*Shulḥan Arukh, Oraḥ Ḥayyim* 559:4, and in the comment of Rema).

"בְּתַעֲנִיּוֹת בְּרָכוֹת וּקְלָלוֹת וְאֵין מַפְסִיקִין בַּקְּלָלוֹת": מְנָא הָנֵי מִילֵּי? אָמַר רַבִּי חִיָּיא בַּר גַּמְדָּא אָמַר רַבִּי אַסִּי: דְּאָמַר קְרָא "מוּסַר ה׳ בְּנִי אַל תִּמְאָס".

§ The mishna states: **On fast days** the congregation reads the portion of **blessings and curses** (Leviticus, chapter 16),[NH] **and one may not interrupt** the reading of the **curses**[H] by having two different people read them. Rather, one person reads all of them. The Gemara asks: **From where are these matters** derived? Why does one not interrupt the reading of the curses? **Rabbi Ḥiyya bar Gamda said** that **Rabbi Asi said: For the verse states: "My son, do not despise the chastening of the Lord,** nor be weary of His correction" (Proverbs 3:11). If one makes a break in the middle of the curses, it appears as if he loathes rebuke.

רֵישׁ לָקִישׁ אָמַר: לְפִי שֶׁאֵין אוֹמְרִים בְּרָכָה עַל הַפּוּרְעָנוּת. אֶלָּא הֵיכִי עָבֵיד? תָּנָא: כְּשֶׁהוּא מַתְחִיל – מַתְחִיל בַּפָּסוּק שֶׁלִּפְנֵיהֶם, וּכְשֶׁהוּא מְסַיֵּים – מְסַיֵּים בַּפָּסוּק שֶׁלְּאַחֲרֵיהֶן.

Reish Lakish said a different answer: It is **because one does not say a blessing over a calamity.**[N] If a second person were to begin to read in the middle of the portion of the curses, the blessing upon his reading would be considered a blessing over a calamity. **Rather,** what **does one do?** It is **taught** in a *baraita*: **When one begins** the reading, **one begins with the verse before** the curses, **and when one concludes** the reading, **one concludes with the verse after them.** In this way, neither the blessing before the reading nor after it relates directly to verses of calamity.

אָמַר אַבַּיֵי: לֹא שָׁנוּ אֶלָּא בַּקְּלָלוֹת שֶׁבְּתוֹרַת כֹּהֲנִים, אֲבָל קְלָלוֹת שֶׁבְּמִשְׁנֵה תוֹרָה – פּוֹסֵק. מַאי טַעְמָא? הַלָּלוּ – בִּלְשׁוֹן רַבִּים אֲמוּרוֹת, וּמֹשֶׁה מִפִּי הַגְּבוּרָה אֲמָרָן. וְהַלָּלוּ – בִּלְשׁוֹן יָחִיד אֲמוּרוֹת, וּמֹשֶׁה מִפִּי עַצְמוֹ אֲמָרָן.

Abaye said: They taught this **only with regard to the curses that are** recorded **in Leviticus, but with regard to the curses that are** recorded **in Deuteronomy, one may interrupt** them by having two different people read them. **What is the reason** for this distinction? **These** curses in Leviticus **are stated in the plural, and Moses pronounced them from the mouth of the Almighty.** As such, they are more severe. However, **these** curses in Deuteronomy **are stated in the singular, and Moses said them on his own,**[N] like the rest of the book of Deuteronomy. They are therefore less harsh and may be interrupted.

לֵוִי בַּר בּוּטֵי הֲוָה קָרֵי וְקָא מְגַמְגֵּם קַמֵּיהּ דְּרַב הוּנָא בְּאָרוּרֵי אָמַר לוֹ: אַכְּנַפְשָׁךְ, לֹא שָׁנוּ אֶלָּא קְלָלוֹת שֶׁבְּתוֹרַת כֹּהֲנִים, אֲבָל שֶׁבְּמִשְׁנֵה תוֹרָה – פּוֹסֵק.

It was related that **Levi bar Buti was** once **reading the** portion of the **curses before Rav Huna, and he was stammering** in his reading, as it was difficult for him to utter such harsh pronouncements. Rav Huna **said to him: If you wish,** you may stop where you are and a different reader will continue, for **they taught** one may not have two people read the curses **only with regard to the curses that are** recorded **in Leviticus. But with regard to the curses that are** recorded **in Deuteronomy, one may interrupt** them by having two different people read them.

תַּנְיָא, רַבִּי שִׁמְעוֹן בֶּן אֶלְעָזָר אוֹמֵר: עֶזְרָא תִּיקֵּן לָהֶן לְיִשְׂרָאֵל שֶׁיְּהוּ קוֹרִין קְלָלוֹת שֶׁבְּתוֹרַת כֹּהֲנִים קוֹדֶם עֲצֶרֶת, וְשֶׁבְּמִשְׁנֵה תוֹרָה קוֹדֶם רֹאשׁ הַשָּׁנָה. מַאי טַעְמָא? אָמַר אַבַּיֵי וְאִיתֵּימָא רֵישׁ לָקִישׁ: כְּדֵי שֶׁתִּכְלֶה הַשָּׁנָה וְקִלְלוֹתֶיהָ.

It is taught in a *baraita*: **Rabbi Shimon ben Elazar said: Ezra enacted**[N] **for the Jewish people that they should read** the portion of **the curses that are** recorded **in Leviticus before *Shavuot* and** the portion of the curses **that are** recorded **in Deuteronomy before Rosh HaShana.**[H] The Gemara asks: **What is the reason** for this? **Abaye said, and some say** that it was **Reish Lakish** who said: **In order that the year may conclude** together with **its curses,** and the new year may begin without the ominous reading of the curses.

NOTES

On fast days the congregation reads the portion of blessings and curses – בְּתַעֲנִיּוֹת בְּרָכוֹת וּקְלָלוֹת: The *ge'onim* write that already in their time the custom on fast days was to read only the portion of "And he assembled" (Exodus 22:11). However, Rav Hai Gaon and others explain that the fast days referred to in the Gemara here are those instituted in response to crisis, such as a lack of rain. Only on those occasions would the portion of the blessings and the curses be read.

Because one does not say a blessing over a calamity – לְפִי שֶׁאֵין אוֹמְרִים בְּרָכָה עַל הַפּוּרְעָנוּת: In the Jerusalem Talmud and tractate *Soferim* additional reasons are recorded: God states: It should not be that My children are being cursed while I am being blessed. Also, it is fitting for the one who reads the Torah to start and finish with something positive. Accordingly, nowadays the custom is to always ensure that when portions are divided between multiple readers, each section begins and ends on a positive note.

And Moses said them on his own – וּמֹשֶׁה מִפִּי עַצְמוֹ אֲמָרָן: This does not mean that the covenant was forged by Moses, for the Torah states explicitly that the covenant was between God and the Jewish people. Rather, the language and formulation of the rebuke was from Moses, delivered through his Divine Spirit (Rid). Despite this, the entire Torah certainly has equal sanctity. The Gemara argues here that since the curses in Deuteronomy were formulated by Moses, when one interrupts this portion one is not breaking up something that is called God's direct rebuke.

Ezra enacted – עֶזְרָא תִּיקֵּן: This enactment is not listed as one of the ten enactments of Ezra. This may be because it is included in the enactment to regularly read the Torah for the public (Rid).

HALAKHA

The Torah reading on a fast day – קְרִיאָה בְּתַעֲנִית: Nowadays, the custom is not to read the portion of the blessing and curses on a public fast day (*Soferim* 17:5; see *Tosafot*). Instead, "And he beseeched" is read, skipping over the mentions of the Golden Calf in Exodus 33:11–14 and 34:1–10 (*Dagul MeRevava*; *Tur*, *Oraḥ Ḥayyim* 579).

One may not interrupt the reading of the curses – אֵין מַפְסִיקִין בַּקְּלָלוֹת: The curses in Leviticus should not be broken up by being read by two people. Rather, one person should read the entire portion. The first person should start reading from the verses immediately preceding the portion of the curses. This is in accordance with the opinion of Reish Lakish. The custom is to begin three verses beforehand (*Magen Avraham*, citing *Beit Yosef* and *Tosafot*).

It is permitted to break up the curses in Deuteronomy. However, the custom is to have a single person read all of them (Rema). In certain places, there is a custom not to call a person to the reading by his name. Rather, it is announced: Arise whoever wishes. This custom was not fully embraced (see Rema and *Arukh HaShulhan*). There are some places where the rabbi is called up, so that it is as if he were rebuking his community, and it is not considered an affront to the rabbi's honor (*Shulḥan Arukh*, *Oraḥ Ḥayyim* 428:6).

The times when the portions of rebuke are read – זְמַנֵּי קְרִיאַת הַתּוֹכֵחוֹת: Ezra enacted that the curses in Leviticus be read before *Shavuot*. In practice, this occurs naturally as part of the regular cycle of Torah readings, in which the end of Leviticus, which contains the curses, is always read in the weeks preceding *Shavuot*. Usually it is read two weeks, and sometimes three weeks, before *Shavuot*, which means the first and sometimes second Torah portions of the book of Numbers are read on the intervening *Shabbatot*. So too, the portion of the curses in Deuteronomy is always read before Rosh HaShana (*Shulḥan Arukh*, *Oraḥ Ḥayyim* 428:4).

בִּשְׁלָמָא שֶׁבְּמִשְׁנֵה תּוֹרָה אִיכָּא כְּדֵי שֶׁתִּכְלֶה שָׁנָה וְקִלְלוֹתֶיהָ, אֶלָּא שֶׁבְּתוֹרַת כֹּהֲנִים, אַטּוּ עֲצֶרֶת רֹאשׁ הַשָּׁנָה הִיא? אִין, עֲצֶרֶת נַמִּי רֹאשׁ הַשָּׁנָה הִיא, דִּתְנַן: וּבַעֲצֶרֶת עַל פֵּירוֹת הָאִילָן.

The Gemara asks: **Granted,** with regard to the curses **that are** recorded **in Deuteronomy, there is** relevance to the reason: **In order that the year may conclude** together with **its curses,** for Rosh HaShana is clearly the beginning of a new year. **However,** with regard to the curses **that are** recorded **in Leviticus,** what relevance does that reason have? **Is that to say *Shavuot* is a new year?** The Gemara answers: **Yes,** indeed, ***Shavuot* is also a new year, as we learned** in a mishna (*Rosh HaShana* 16a): **And on *Shavuot*,** divine judgment is made **concerning the fruit of the trees,** which indicates that *Shavuot* also has the status of a new year.

תַּנְיָא, רַבִּי שִׁמְעוֹן בֶּן אֶלְעָזָר אוֹמֵר: אִם יֹאמְרוּ לְךָ זְקֵנִים סְתוֹר, וִילָדִים בְּנֵה – סְתוֹר וְאַל תִּבְנֶה, מִפְּנֵי שֶׁסְּתִירַת זְקֵנִים – בִּנְיָן, וּבִנְיַן נְעָרִים – סְתִירָה, וְסִימָן לַדָּבָר: רְחַבְעָם בֶּן שְׁלֹמֹה.

It is taught in a *baraita*: **Rabbi Shimon ben Elazar says: If old men say to you: Demolish,**[N] **and children** say to you: **Build,** then **demolish and do not build, because the demolishing of old men is** ultimately as constructive as **building,** despite the fact that it appears destructive, **and the building of children is** as destructive as **demolishing. An indication of this matter** is **Rehoboam, son of Solomon.** He ignored the advice of the Elders and did not lower himself before his people, which ultimately led to the people rebelling against him.

תָּנוּ רַבָּנַן: מָקוֹם שֶׁמַּפְסִיקִין בַּשַּׁבָּת שַׁחֲרִית שָׁם קוֹרִין בַּמִּנְחָה, בַּמִּנְחָה – שָׁם קוֹרִין בַּשֵּׁנִי, בַּשֵּׁנִי – שָׁם קוֹרִין בַּחֲמִישִׁי, בַּחֲמִישִׁי – שָׁם קוֹרִין לַשַּׁבָּת הַבָּאָה, דִּבְרֵי רַבִּי מֵאִיר. רַבִּי יְהוּדָה אוֹמֵר: מָקוֹם שֶׁמַּפְסִיקִין בַּשַּׁבָּת שַׁחֲרִית – שָׁם קוֹרִין בַּמִּנְחָה, וּבַשֵּׁנִי וּבַחֲמִישִׁי וְלַשַּׁבָּת הַבָּאָה.

The Sages taught in a *baraita*: With regard to **the place** in the Torah **where** the congregation **concludes**[H] the reading **on Shabbat morning,** it is from **there** that **they** continue to **read in the afternoon** service on Shabbat. Where they conclude **in the afternoon** service on Shabbat, from **there they** continue to **read on Monday** morning. Where they conclude **on Monday,** from **there they** continue to **read on Thursday** morning. Where they conclude **on Thursday,** from **there they** continue to **read on the coming Shabbat.** This is **the statement of Rabbi Meir. Rabbi Yehuda says:** With regard to **the place** in the Torah **where they conclude** the reading **on Shabbat morning,** it is from **there** that **they** continue to **read in the afternoon** service on Shabbat. **And** from that same place **they** continue to **read on Monday** morning, **and on Thursday** morning, **and on the coming Shabbat.**

אָמַר רַבִּי זֵירָא: הֲלָכָה, מָקוֹם שֶׁמַּפְסִיקִין בַּשַּׁבָּת שַׁחֲרִית – שָׁם קוֹרִין בַּמִּנְחָה וּבַשֵּׁנִי וּבַחֲמִישִׁי וְלַשַּׁבָּת הַבָּאָה. וְלֵימָא: הֲלָכָה כְּרַבִּי יְהוּדָה!

The Gemara notes that **Rabbi Zeira said: The *halakha*** is that with regard to **the place where they conclude** the reading **on Shabbat morning,** it is from **there** that **they** continue to **read in the afternoon** service on Shabbat. **And** from that same place **they** continue to **read on Monday** morning, **and on Thursday** morning, **and on the coming Shabbat.** The Gemara asks: If so, **let him** simply **say: The *halakha* is in accordance with** the opinion of **Rabbi Yehuda.** Why did he have to explicitly state the whole *halakha*?

Perek **IV**
Daf **32** Amud **a**

מִשּׁוּם דְּאַפְכִי לְהוּ.

The Gemara answers: **Because there are those who reversed** the names[N] in the *baraita* and attributed the position of Rabbi Yehuda to Rabbi Meir, and vice versa. Therefore, in order to avoid any lack of clarity, Rabbi Zeira stated the *halakha* explicitly.

NOTES

If old men say to you: Demolish – אִם יֹאמְרוּ לְךָ זְקֵנִים סְתוֹר: What is the connection between this teaching and the previous Gemara? Some suggest that the Gemara here warns: Even if one's judgment tells him that it would be better not to read the curses so near to the new year, nevertheless, he should rely on the old men, i.e., Ezra and the Men of the Great Assembly who enacted these readings, and act based on their wisdom and experience (*Re'aḥ Duda'im*).

HALAKHA

The place in the Torah where the congregation concludes – מָקוֹם שֶׁמַּפְסִיקִין: It is from the place in the Torah where the congregation concludes the reading on Shabbat morning that they read in the afternoon service on Shabbat, on Monday morning, on Thursday morning, and on the coming Shabbat (*Tur*, *Oraḥ Ḥayyim* 292).

NOTES

Because there are those who reversed the names – מִשּׁוּם דְּאַפְכִי לְהוּ: Why didn't Rabbi Zeira simply state that the *halakha* is in accordance with the mishna, which also expresses Rabbi Yehuda's opinion? Some explain that even this would be insufficient, because the mishna itself is somewhat ambiguous. From the formulation of the mishna, one could have understood that the reading on Monday continues from where the reading on Shabbat afternoon concluded, and then the reading on Thursday continues from where the reading on Monday concluded. Therefore, it was necessary for him to state the *halakha* explicitly (Ran).

תָּנוּ רַבָּנַן: פּוֹתֵחַ וְרוֹאֶה, גּוֹלֵל וּמְבָרֵךְ, וְחוֹזֵר וּפוֹתֵחַ וְקוֹרֵא, דִּבְרֵי רַבִּי מֵאִיר. רַבִּי יְהוּדָה אוֹמֵר: פּוֹתֵחַ וְרוֹאֶה וּמְבָרֵךְ וְקוֹרֵא.

The Sages taught in a *baraita*: When a person reads from the Torah, **he should open** the scroll **and see** the place from where he will read, **furl** it so that it is closed, **and recite the blessing, and** then **he should again open** the scroll, **and read.** This is **the statement of Rabbi Meir. Rabbi Yehuda said: He should open** the scroll, **and see** the place from where he will read, **and,** without closing it again, **he should recite the blessing,**[H] **and read.**

מַאי טַעְמָא דְּרַבִּי מֵאִיר – כִּדְעוּלָּא, דְּאָמַר עוּלָּא: מִפְּנֵי מָה אָמְרוּ הַקּוֹרֵא בַּתּוֹרָה לֹא יְסַיֵּיעַ לַמְתוּרְגְּמָן – כְּדֵי שֶׁלֹּא יֹאמְרוּ תַּרְגּוּם כָּתוּב בַּתּוֹרָה, הָכָא נַמִי – כְּדֵי שֶׁלֹּא יֹאמְרוּ בְּרָכוֹת כְּתוּבִין בַּתּוֹרָה.

The Gemara asks: **What is the reason for Rabbi Meir's** opinion that the blessing is not recited over an open scroll? The Gemara answers: His reasoning is **in accordance with** the statement **of Ulla, as Ulla said: For what** reason **did** the Sages **say** that **one who reads from the Torah should not assist the translator,** but rather the translation should be exclusively said by the translator? **In order that** people **should not say** that **the translation is written in the Torah. Here too,** the scroll should be closed when reciting the blessings, **in order that** people **should not say** that **the blessings are written in the Torah.**

וְרַבִּי יְהוּדָה: תַּרְגּוּם אִיכָּא לְמִיטְעֵי, בְּרָכוֹת – לֵיכָּא לְמִיטְעֵי.

And Rabbi Yehuda is not concerned about this, as he claims that with regard to the **translation, there is** the possibility of people **erring** in this way, but with regard to **the blessings, there is no** concern about people **erring.** People will realize the blessings are not actually part of the Torah's text because they are recited by each person who reads.

אָמַר רַבִּי זֵירָא אָמַר רַב מַתָּנָה: הֲלָכָה, פּוֹתֵחַ וְרוֹאֶה וּמְבָרֵךְ וְקוֹרֵא. וְלֵימָא הֲלָכָה כְּרַבִּי יְהוּדָה! מִשּׁוּם דְּאָפְכִי לְהוּ.

Rabbi Zeira said that **Rav Mattana said:** The ***halakha*** is that **he should open** the scroll, **see** the place from which he will read, **and,** without closing it again, **he should recite the blessing and read.** The Gemara asks: If so, **let him** simply **say: The *halakha* is in accordance with** the opinion of **Rabbi Yehuda.** Why did he have to explicitly state the whole *halakha*? The Gemara answers: **Because there are those who reversed** the names in the *baraita* and attributed the position of Rabbi Yehuda to Rabbi Meir and vice versa. In order to avoid any lack of clarity, Rabbi Zeira stated the *halakha* explicitly.

אָמַר רַבִּי זֵירָא אָמַר רַב מַתָּנָה: הַלּוּחוֹת וְהַבִּימוֹת אֵין בָּהֶן מִשּׁוּם קְדוּשָּׁה.

Rabbi Zeira said that **Rav Mattana said: The boards,**[HN] i.e., the empty margins of a Torah scroll, **and the platforms**[HN] from which the Torah is read **do not have any sanctity.**

אָמַר רַבִּי שְׁפַטְיָה אָמַר רַבִּי יוֹחָנָן: הַגּוֹלֵל סֵפֶר תּוֹרָה צָרִיךְ שֶׁיַּעֲמִידֶנּוּ עַל הַתֶּפֶר.

§ **Rabbi Shefatya said** that **Rabbi Yoḥanan said: When one furls a Torah scroll, he needs to position it** so that it closes **on the seam**[H] between two sheets of parchment. Once closed, the seam should be between the two rolls of the scroll, so that if it is mishandled or overly tightened, it will come apart along the seam and not be torn across the writing.

וְאָמַר רַבִּי שְׁפַטְיָה אָמַר רַבִּי יוֹחָנָן: הַגּוֹלֵל סֵפֶר תּוֹרָה – גּוֹלְלוֹ מִבַּחוּץ וְאֵין גּוֹלְלוֹ מִבִּפְנִים,

And Rabbi Shefatya said that **Rabbi Yoḥanan said: When one rolls a Torah scroll** from one section to another, **he should roll it from the outside,**[H] i.e., he should position the scroll so the two rollers are parallel to him and then roll the scroll by rotating the roller farthest away from him by rotating it toward himself, **and he should not roll it from the inside,** by rotating the roller nearest to him away from himself. If one does this and loses control, the scroll could roll away from him onto the floor.

HALAKHA

He should open the scroll, and see the place, and he should recite the blessing – פּוֹתֵחַ וְרוֹאֶה וּמְבָרֵךְ: The *halakha* is in accordance with Rabbi Yehuda. One should open the scroll, see the place from which one will read, and then, without necessarily closing the scroll again, recite the blessing. However, some hold that even Rabbi Yehuda agrees that ideally one should first close the scroll (*Magen Avraham*, citing *Tosafot*). This is the custom in Hasidic communities.

Some say that one should leave the scroll open and turn one's face to the side when reciting the blessing. Some say that one should turn one's face to the left (Rema), others say one should turn one's face to the right (*Arukh HaShulḥan*). Sephardic communities are accustomed to following this practice. Many even cover the scroll with a cloth during the blessings. Some say that one should rely on the many authorities who hold that one should leave the scroll open, and there is no need to turn one's face away at all (Rambam; *Baḥ*). Many follow this custom, especially in Ashkenazic communities (*Shulḥan Arukh*, *Oraḥ Ḥayyim* 139:4).

The boards – הַלּוּחוֹת: Boards upon which children have written words of Torah as part of their study do not have the sanctity of a Torah scroll, but they do have the sanctity of a synagogue. Some understand that the Gemara is referring to the boards upon which the translator and the person reading *maftir* stand (Rambam *Sefer Ahava*, *Hilkhot Sefer Torah* 10:4, and in the comment of Ra'avad).

The platforms – הַבִּימוֹת: The platform upon which the reader or prayer leader stands does not have the sanctity of a Torah scroll, but it does have the sanctity of a synagogue (*Shulḥan Arukh*, *Oraḥ Ḥayyim* 154:7).

He needs to position it so that it closes on the seam – צָרִיךְ שֶׁיַּעֲמִידֶנּוּ עַל הַתֶּפֶר: One who furls a Torah scroll should position it upon the seam, so that if it tears, it will tear only upon the seam (*Shulḥan Arukh*, *Oraḥ Ḥayyim* 147:3).

He should roll it from the outside – גּוֹלְלוֹ מִבַּחוּץ: When tying a Torah scroll closed, the wrapping cloth should first be placed on the underside of the scroll and then wrapped around and tucked in or tied on the text side. When one person both holds the scroll and rolls it, the text should face the person furling it and tying it up. However, in Ashkenazic communities, where one person raises the scroll and then another person furls it, the text should face the one who raises it (*Shulḥan Arukh*, *Oraḥ Ḥayyim* 147:4, and in the comment of Rema).

NOTES

Boards – לוּחוֹת: Rashi explains that these are boards on which the children would write during their Torah study. The *Arukh* explains that the boards are the empty margins of a Torah scroll.

Platforms – בִּימוֹת: Rashi and the Rambam understand that this is referring to the stage that would be constructed for the king to stand upon when reading the Torah in the Assembly held during the Festival of *Sukkot* of the year following the Sabbatical year (Deuteronomy 31:10–13). Others explain that the reference is to the table in the synagogue upon which the Torah is read and where the prayer leader sometimes stands (Rabbeinu Yehonatan; Ritva). The *Arukh* offers that it is the empty margins of the Torah scroll, above and below the text. Others explain that it is referring to the holders on which the Torah scroll is rolled (Rid).

וּכְשֶׁהוּא מְהַדְּקוֹ – מְהַדְּקוֹ מִבִּפְנִים, וְאֵינוֹ מְהַדְּקוֹ מִבַּחוּץ.

And when one tightens the scroll, after he has found the new section, **he should tighten it from the inside,**[N] by rotating the roller nearest to him, **and not from the outside,** by rotating the roller furthest away from him, in order not to extend his arms over the text of the Torah and obscure the view of the community, for it is a mitzva for them to be able to see the text.

וְאָמַר רַבִּי שְׁפַטְיָה אָמַר רַבִּי יוֹחָנָן: עֲשָׂרָה שֶׁקָּרְאוּ בַּתּוֹרָה – הַגָּדוֹל שֶׁבָּהֶם גּוֹלֵל סֵפֶר תּוֹרָה. הַגּוֹלְלוֹ נוֹטֵל שְׂכַר כּוּלָּן, דְּאָמַר רַבִּי יְהוֹשֻׁעַ בֶּן לֵוִי: עֲשָׂרָה שֶׁקָּרְאוּ בַּתּוֹרָה – הַגּוֹלֵל סֵפֶר תּוֹרָה קִיבֵּל שְׂכַר כּוּלָּן. שְׂכַר כּוּלָּן סָלְקָא דַּעְתָּךְ? אֶלָּא אֵימָא: קִיבֵּל שָׂכָר כְּנֶגֶד כּוּלָּן.

And Rabbi Shefatya said that **Rabbi Yoḥanan said: If ten** people **read from the Torah,**[N] **the greatest among them**[H] **should furl the Torah scroll,** for this is the most distinguished honor. **And the one who furls it takes the reward of all of them, as Rabbi Yehoshua ben Levi said: If ten** people **read from the Torah, the one who furls it receives the reward of all of them.**[N] The Gemara asks: **Can it enter your mind** to say that he actually receives **the reward of all of them?** Why should all the others forfeit their reward? **Rather, say** instead: **He receives a reward equivalent to** that of **all of them.**

וְאָמַר רַבִּי שְׁפַטְיָה אָמַר רַבִּי יוֹחָנָן: מִנַּיִן שֶׁמִּשְׁתַּמְּשִׁין בְּבַת קוֹל – שֶׁנֶּאֱמַר ״וְאָזְנֶיךָ תִּשְׁמַעְנָה דָבָר מֵאַחֲרֶיךָ לֵאמֹר״. וְהָנֵי מִילֵּי – דְּשָׁמַע קַל גַּבְרָא בְּמָתָא, וְקַל אִיתְּתָא בְּדַבְרָא. וְהוּא דְּאָמַר הֵין הֵין, וְהוּא דְּאָמַר לָאו לָאו.

And Rabbi Shefatya said that **Rabbi Yoḥanan said:** If one was deliberating about whether to do a certain action, and a Divine Voice indicated what he should do, **from where** is it derived **that one may make use of a Divine Voice**[N] and rely upon it? **As it is stated: "And your ears shall hear a word behind you saying:** This is the way, walk in it" (Isaiah 30:21). The Gemara comments: **This applies** only **when one heard a male voice in the city,** which is unusual, for men are usually found in the fields, **or** when one heard **a female voice in the fields,** for women are generally not found there. Since the voice is unusual, one need not doubt it and may rely upon it. **And that** applies **when** the voice repeated its message and **said: Yes, yes.**[N] **And that** also applies **when** the voice **said: No, no.**

וְאָמַר רַבִּי שְׁפַטְיָה אָמַר רַבִּי יוֹחָנָן: כָּל הַקּוֹרֵא בְּלֹא נְעִימָה וְשׁוֹנֶה בְּלֹא זִמְרָה – עָלָיו הַכָּתוּב אוֹמֵר ״וְגַם אֲנִי נָתַתִּי לָהֶם חוּקִים לֹא טוֹבִים״ וגו׳.

And Rabbi Shefatya said that **Rabbi Yoḥanan said: Concerning anyone who reads** from the Torah **without a melody or studies** the Mishna **without a song, the verse states: "So too I gave them statutes that were not good,** and judgments whereby they should not live" (Ezekiel 20:25), as one who studies Torah through song demonstrates that he is fond of his learning. Furthermore, the tune helps him remember what he has learned.

מַתְקִיף לַהּ אַבָּיֵי: מִשּׁוּם דְּלָא יָדַע לְבַסּוּמֵי קָלָא ״מִשְׁפָּטִים לֹא יִחְיוּ בָּהֶם״ קָרֵית בֵּיהּ?! אֶלָּא כִּדְרַב מְשָׁרְשִׁיָּא, דְּאָמַר: שְׁנֵי תַלְמִידֵי חֲכָמִים הַיּוֹשְׁבִים בְּעִיר אַחַת וְאֵין נוֹחִין זֶה אֶת זֶה בַּהֲלָכָה – עֲלֵיהֶם הַכָּתוּב אוֹמֵר ״וְגַם אֲנִי נָתַתִּי לָהֶם חוּקִים לֹא טוֹבִים וּמִשְׁפָּטִים לֹא יִחְיוּ בָּהֶם״.

Abaye strongly objects to this: Just **because one does not know** how **to make** his **voice pleasant, you read concerning him: "And judgments whereby they should not live"? Rather,** the verse should be understood **in accordance** with the statement of **Rav Mesharshiyya, who said: Concerning two Torah scholars who dwell in the same city and are not pleasant to one other in** matters of ***halakha,*** and they quarrel and stir up controversy, **the verse states: "So too I gave them statutes that were not good, and judgments whereby they should not live."**

HALAKHA

The greatest among them – הַגָּדוֹל שֶׁבָּהֶם: The greatest of the people who read from the Torah should furl it. The term furling here refers both to raising it up and then furling it (*Mishna Berura*). Some say that the most important person in the synagogue should do this (*Magen Avraham*). This is indeed the custom (*Mishna Berura*). Many communities are accustomed to sell the honor for significant sums. In more recent times, the custom is not to be particular that only the most important people receive the honor. Some even give the honor to a minor who is already aware of the concepts of sanctity (*Mishna Berura*, citing *Sha'arei Efrayim*; *Shulḥan Arukh*, *Oraḥ Ḥayyim* 147:1).

NOTES

He should roll it from the outside…and tighten it from the inside – גּוֹלְלוֹ מִבַּחוּץ...וּמְהַדְּקוֹ מִבִּפְנִים: Many explanations have been offered for this directive. The commentary here follows the opinion of Rashi. *Tosafot* and the Rosh, however, cite Rabbeinu Ḥananel, who says the Gemara refers to the furling of the Torah scroll after one has used it. They explain that after the scroll has been lifted up, the person designated to furl it and tie it up should begin by placing on the outside, i.e., the underside, of the scroll the wrapping cloth used to tie the scroll and then wrap it around the scroll. The wrapping cloth is then tightened by tying it or tucking it into the inside, i.e., the text side, of the scroll. In this way, when the scroll is next opened, one will be able to untie it without needing to turn it over. This is how the *Shulḥan Arukh* rules (see HALAKHA).

Another interpretation is offered by Rav Palti Gaon. He explains that typically, when one wishes to tighten a regular scroll, he holds it by one end, entirely unravels it, and then begins to furl it again, tightly. This is what the Gemara objects to. Instead, the scroll should be tightened with both sides rolled at all times, loosening one side to allow the other to be tightened (see *ge'onim*).

If ten people read from the Torah – עֲשָׂרָה שֶׁקָּרְאוּ בַּתּוֹרָה: Some explain that this is referring to the quorum of ten men required for reading the Torah (Rashba). Others explain that the reference is to the seven people who read the main portion, the one who reads the *maftir*, the translator, and the leader of the prayers (see *Beit Peretz*).

The one who furls it receives the reward of all of them – הַגּוֹלֵל סֵפֶר תּוֹרָה קִיבֵּל שְׂכַר כּוּלָּן: The Rambam explains that the greatest one in the congregation reads last from the scroll. Therefore, he is the one to furl the scroll. Since he concludes the mitzva, he receives all of the merit.

That one may make use of a Divine Voice – שֶׁמִּשְׁתַּמְּשִׁין בְּבַת קוֹל: It would appear that the reference to a Divine Voice does not have the same meaning as in other places in the Talmud, where it refers to a heavenly voice, which is a form of prophecy. The reference here is to an echo, the origin of which is unknown. The novelty of this ruling is that it is permitted to follow an auspicious sign particularly in cases where one who is undecided about what to do hears a voice indicating which path to take (Maharsha), despite the fact that it is prohibited to use any form of sorcery (see *Tosafot* and Ritva).

Yes, yes – הֵין הֵין: In many instances, the repetition of a message is an indicator that it is a sign from Heaven (see Genesis 41:32; *Ramat Shmuel*). Furthermore, the Gemara elsewhere states that repeating the word: Yes, is a formulation used for making an oath, which would therefore suggest the seriousness of the message (Maharsha).

אָמַר רַבִּי פַּרְנָךְ אָמַר רַבִּי יוֹחָנָן: כָּל הָאוֹחֵז סֵפֶר תּוֹרָה עָרוֹם נִקְבַּר עָרוֹם. עָרוֹם סָלְקָא דַּעְתָּךְ? אֶלָּא אֵימָא: נִקְבַּר עָרוֹם בְּלֹא מִצְוֹת.

Rabbi Parnakh said that **Rabbi Yoḥanan said: Anyone who holds onto an uncovered Torah scroll,**[NH] i.e., holds the parchment directly without anything intervening, **will be** punished by being **buried uncovered.** The Gemara asks: **Can it enter your mind to say** that he will be actually be buried **uncovered?** Why should he be buried in such a disgraceful manner? **Rather, say** that **he will be buried** metaphorically **uncovered,** i.e., **without** the merit of having performed **mitzvot.**

בְּלֹא מִצְוֹת סָלְקָא דַּעְתָּךְ?! אֶלָּא אָמַר אַבַּיֵי: נִקְבַּר עָרוֹם בְּלֹא אוֹתָהּ מִצְוָה.

The Gemara again asks: **Can it enter your mind to say** that he will be buried **without** the merit of having performed **mitzvot?** Why should he forfeit the merit of all the mitzvot that he performed during his lifetime? **Rather, Abaye said: He will be buried** metaphorically **uncovered,** i.e., **without** the merit of **that mitzva.** He forfeits the reward of the mitzva he performed while holding directly onto the parchment.

אָמַר רַבִּי יַנַּאי בְּרֵיהּ דְּרַבִּי יַנַּאי סָבָא מִשְּׁמֵיהּ דְּרַבִּי יַנַּאי רַבָּה: מוּטָב תִּיגָּלֵל הַמִּטְפַּחַת וְאַל יִגָּלֵל סֵפֶר תּוֹרָה.

Rabbi Yannai, son of Rabbi Yannai the Elder, said in the name of Rabbi Yannai the Great: It is proper that **the cloth** cover of a Torah scroll **be rolled**[NH] around the scroll, while holding the scroll stationary, **and one should not roll the Torah scroll** itself in the cloth in order to cover it.

"וַיְדַבֵּר מֹשֶׁה אֶת מוֹעֲדֵי ה׳ אֶל בְּנֵי יִשְׂרָאֵל" מִצְוָתָן שֶׁיְּהוּ קוֹרִין אוֹתָן כָּל אֶחָד וְאֶחָד בִּזְמַנּוֹ: תָּנוּ רַבָּנַן: מֹשֶׁה תִּיקֵּן לָהֶם לְיִשְׂרָאֵל שֶׁיְּהוּ שׁוֹאֲלִין וְדוֹרְשִׁין בְּעִנְיָנוֹ שֶׁל יוֹם, הִלְכוֹת פֶּסַח בְּפֶסַח, הִלְכוֹת עֲצֶרֶת בַּעֲצֶרֶת, הִלְכוֹת חַג בֶּחָג.

§ The mishna states: The verse **"And Moses declared**[N] **to the children of Israel the appointed seasons of the Lord"** (Leviticus 23:44) indicates that part of **the mitzva** of the Festivals is **that they should read** the portion relating to them, **each one in its** appointed **time. The Sages taught** in a *baraita*: **Moses enacted for the Jewish people that they should make** halakhic **inquiries and expound upon the matter of the day.** They should occupy themselves with **the *halakhot* of Passover on Passover,** with **the *halakhot* of *Shavuot* on *Shavuot*, and** with the ***halakhot* of *Sukkot* on *Sukkot*.**

הדרן עלך בני העיר
וסליקא לה מסכת מגילה

NOTES

Anyone who holds onto an uncovered Torah scroll – כָּל הָאוֹחֵז סֵפֶר תּוֹרָה עָרוֹם: A different explanation is cited in name of the Ra'avad: One who is not clothed should not hold onto a Torah scroll. Doing so is an affront to the sanctity of the scroll.

It is proper that the cloth be rolled – מוּטָב תִּיגָּלֵל הַמִּטְפַּחַת: Some explain that the cloth must be rolled around the scroll, and not the scroll rolled around in the cloth (Rashi; Meiri). Others explain that the intention is that when the scroll is rolled, one should not touch the parchment with one's bare hands. Rather, one should use a cloth to do so. Rav Hai Gaon found difficulty with the current version of the text and offered various emendations. According to one of them, the intention is that the Torah scroll be rolled from place to place in private, and it is better that it remain in its covers than be rolled in public. Alternatively, even if the scroll is rolled in public, it should be covered while doing so. If this is not possible, it is better not to roll it at all.

And Moses declared – וַיְדַבֵּר מֹשֶׁה: This verse appears at the very conclusion of the portion of Festivals. As such, its very position indicates that even after Moses delineated everything contained in that portion, it was then that he began to expound to the Jewish people about those Festivals (*Melekhet Shlomo*).

HALAKHA

Anyone who holds onto an uncovered Torah scroll – כָּל הָאוֹחֵז סֵפֶר תּוֹרָה עָרוֹם: It is prohibited to hold onto a Torah scroll directly, without using a cloth or the like. Some say that one should not even hold the rollers upon which the scroll is wrapped without an interposition (*Magen Avraham*, citing *Baḥ*). However, others permit this (*Taz*), and this is the accepted custom (*Arukh HaShulḥan*). Nevertheless, some people are particular to act stringently in this regard (*Shulḥan Arukh, Oraḥ Ḥayyim* 147:1).

It is proper that the cloth be rolled – מוּטָב תִּיגָּלֵל הַמִּטְפַּחַת: It is proper that the cloth cover of a Torah scroll be rolled around the scroll while holding the scroll stationary, and one should not roll the Torah scroll itself in the cloth in order to cover it. This ruling is in accordance with Rabbi Yannai (*Shulḥan Arukh, Oraḥ Ḥayyim* 147:5).

Summary of **Perek IV**

This chapter opened with a discussion of the sanctity of the synagogue and other sacred items. There is a scale of varying degrees of sanctity for each of them. A Torah scroll is considered to have the highest degree of sanctity. Then, as a general rule, the more similar to, or more closely associated an item is with a Torah scroll, the greater its degree of sanctity. Therefore, items that are used with or for a Torah scroll, such as its wraps or the ark, and similarly other sacred scrolls, all have a high degree of sanctity, albeit not as great as a Torah scroll itself. The synagogue, which merely houses the Torah scroll and provides a place of prayer, has the least degree of sanctity. The Gemara explains that it is permitted to sell or exchange an item of sanctity only in order to procure an item of greater sanctity.

Despite its relatively low degree of sanctity, a synagogue is nevertheless afforded the status of a "little sanctuary" (Ezekiel 11:16), and as such one is required to treat it with great reverence. This applies both when the synagogue is still used by the community and even after it has become desolate. Furthermore, even when it is permitted to sell the synagogue, it is permitted to do so only with the consent of the whole community.

The second major topic of this chapter is the special Torah portions that are read at various occasions during the year. Initially, this chapter focused on the four special portions that are read immediately prior to and during the month of Adar. The goal of these portions is to publicly mention the mitzvot that apply in that month, i.e., the collection of shekels for the Temple and the obligation to recall the destruction of Amalek, as well as to begin to prepare for the upcoming festival of Passover though the reading of the portion beginning "this month" (Exodus 12:2) and that of the Red Heifer. The Gemara established that each portion is to be read before the fulfillment of that mitzva it relates to, in order that the reading may serve as a reminder for the community.

The chapter then discussed the portions to be read on the special days and Festivals throughout the year. With regard to this, the Gemara pointed out that already in the period of the *amora'im*, the custom of which portions to read had veered from that which is recorded in the Mishna. And indeed, in the post-talmudic period, the customs changed and developed beyond that which was decided by the Gemara. Nevertheless, this was not considered a breach of authority. Rather, each community with its customs was ultimately seeking to achieve the similar goal of choosing a portion that appropriately expressed the unique character of the day. As such, there is room for variation, and each community should continue to follow the practice of its forebears.

Index of **Background**

Index of **Background**

Index of **Language**

Index of **Personalities**

Image **Credits**

All images are copyright © Koren Publishers Jerusalem Ltd., except:

p202 photograph © Josh Hochman; **p223** 1st image © H. Zell; **p223** 2nd image © Hans Hillewaert; p 223 bottom left © NOAA Photo Library; **p223** bottom right © Clara Amit, Yoram Lehman, Yael Yolovitch, Miki Koren, and Mariana Salzberger, courtesy of the Israel Antiquities Authority; **p224** © Government Press Office; **p229** 2nd image © Pentocelo; **p246** © courtesy of the Temple Institute; **p253** © courtesy of the Temple Institute; **p256** © Malene Thyssen; **p263** © Arad; **p271** 2nd image © Vladimir Melnik, www.shutterstock.com; **p279** © Dr. Miriam Aharoni, Zemach Tissue Culture, Ltd.; **p285** © ZoneFatal, www.shutterstock.com; **p295** left image © Elihu Shanun; **p295** right image © Daniel Tzvi; **p311** © Didier Descouens; **p339** © courtesy of the Temple Institute; **p356** 1st image © H. Zell; **p356** 2nd image © CTHOE; **p356** 3rd image © H. Zell; **p371**© HaRav Menachem Makover, courtesy of Harenu Bevinyano; **p380** Bernard Gagnon; **p396** © HaRav Menachem Makover, courtesy of Harenu Bevinyano

תלמוד בבלי

— מהדורת נאה —

תענית · מגילה

Shefa

ירושלים

KOREN

תלמוד בבלי

הוצאת קורן ירושלים

— מהדורת נאה —

תענית · מגילה

COMMENTARY BY

Rabbi Adin Even-Israel Steinsaltz

EDITOR-IN-CHIEF

Rabbi Dr Tzvi Hersh Weinreb

EXECUTIVE EDITOR

Rabbi Joshua Schreier

•

SHEFA FOUNDATION
KOREN PUBLISHERS JERUSALEM

מאימתי

מזכירין גבורות גשמים? רבי אליעזר אומר: מיום טוב הראשון של חג. ר' יהושע אומר: מיום טוב האחרון של חג. אמר לו ר' יהושע: הואיל ואין הגשמים אלא סימן קללה בחג, למה הוא מזכיר? אמר לו ר' אליעזר: אף אני לא אמרתי לשאול, אלא להזכיר "משיב הרוח ומוריד הגשם" בעונתו. אמר לו: א"כ לעולם יהא מזכיר! אין שואלין את הגשמים אלא סמוך לגשמים. ר' יהודה אומר: [א]העובר לפני התיבה ביו"ט האחרון של חג – האחרון מזכיר, הראשון אינו מזכיר. [ב]ביו"ט הראשון של פסח – הראשון מזכיר, האחרון אינו מזכיר. §

גמ' *תנא היכא קאי דקתני: "מאימתי"? תנא התם קאי, דקתני: *[ג]"מזכירין גבורות גשמים ב'תחיית המתים', [ד]ושואלין ב'ברכת השנים', [ה]והבדלה ב'חונן הדעת'". וקתני: "מאימתי מזכירין 'גבורות גשמים'". וליתני התם! מ"ש דשבקיה עד הכא? אלא, תנא מראש השנה סליק. דתנן: *"ובחג נידונין על המים". ואיידי דתנא: "ובחג נידונין על המים", תנא: "מאימתי מזכירין 'גבורות גשמים'". וליתני: "מאימתי מזכירין על הגשמים", מאי גבורות גשמים? א"ר יוחנן: מפני שיורדין בגבורה, שנאמר *°"עושה גדולות (א) עד אין חקר, ונפלאות עד אין מספר". וכתיב °"הנותן מטר על פני ארץ, ושולח מים על פני חוצות". מאי משמע? אמר רבה בר שילא: אתיא "חקר", "חקר", מברייתו של עולם. כתיב הכא: "עושה גדולות עד אין חקר", וכתיב התם °"הלא ידעת אם לא שמעת אלהי עולם, ה', בורא קצות הארץ, לא ייעף ולא ייגע אין חקר לתבונתו".(ב) וכתיב °"מכין הרים בכחו נאזר בגבורה". ומנא לן דבתפלה? דתניא: °"לאהבה את ה' אלהיכם ולעבדו בכל לבבכם". איזו היא עבודה שהיא בלב – הוי אומר זו תפלה. וכתיב בתריה °"ונתתי מטר ארצכם בעתו, יורה ומלקוש". אמר ר' יוחנן: *ג' מפתחות בידו של הקב"ה שלא נמסרו ביד שליח, ואלו הן: מפתח של(ג) גשמים, ומפתח של חיה, ומפתח של תחיית המתים. מפתח של גשמים – דכתיב °"יפתח ה' לך את אוצרו הטוב, את השמים, לתת מטר ארצך בעתו". מפתח של חיה מנין – דכתיב °"ויזכור אלהים את רחל, וישמע אליה

רש"י

מאימתי מזכירין גבורות גשמים. שאומר "משיב הרוח ומוריד הגשם". ובגמרא מפרש טעמא אמאי קרי ליה גבורות גשמים – מפני שיורדין בגבורה, שנאמר "עושה גדולות" וגו': סימן קללה בחג הן. כדאמרינן במס' סוכה בפרק "הישן" (דף כח:): מאימתי מותר לפנות – משתסרח המקפה, משל לעבד שבא למזוג כוס לרבו ושפך לו קיתון על פניו, וא"ל אי אפשי בשמושך. כלומר: כשהגשמים יורדין לסוכה הכל יוצאין, ונראה שאין הקב"ה חפץ בשמושם לפניו. ואמאי מתחילין להזכיר גבורות גשמים בחג, ונראה שהוא מתפלל שיבא מטר בחג? **לא אמרתי** לשאול. שיתפלל על הגשמים בחג, כגון "ותן טל ומטר": **אלא** להזכיר. שמתחיל להזכיר בחג גבורות של מקום שמוריד גשמים: בעונתו. כלומר: בזמנו: **אם** כן. ואמאי פוסק בפסח מלהזכיר? **גמ'** תנא היכא קאי. כלומר, מדקתני "מאימתי", מכלל דפשיטא ליה להאי תנא דחייבים להזכיר, והיכא חזינן דמחייב להזכיר? התם קאי. "מזכירין גבורות גשמים" כו', במסכת ברכות: (וליתני התם. במסכת ברכות. סמוך דתני מזכירין, ליתני מאימתי): מ"ש דשבקיה עד הכא. כלומר, האי דקתני הכא בסדר מועד מאימתי – ליתני התם, (ד) דקתני מזכירין, במסכת ברכות היינו סדר זרעים: עד הכא. עד סדר מועד: **אלא**. לא תימא דהא דקתני "מאימתי" דהתם קאי, דתנא מראש השנה סליק, ששניהן בסדר אחד הן, להכי לא מצי למימר מאי שנא דשבקיה עד הכא: (בחג. הוי דין על המים, ומשום דתני מאימתי הוי דין על המים – קתני נמי אימתי זמן הזכרה) (ה): **ואיידי** דתני בחג נידונין. כלומר, אגב דתנא בחג נידונין על המים, קסבר בנפשיה הואיל ונידונין בחג על המים – ש"מ בעינן להזכיר עניינא דמיא, לרצויי על המים דליתו לברכה, להכי קתני מאימתי מזכירין: כתיב עושה גדולות (ו) עד אין חקר. אלמא דכתיב "חקר" בגשמים, וכתיב "חקר" בברייתו של עולם. מה ברייתו של עולם כתיב ביה גבורה – אף גשמים הוי כמאן דכתיב ביה גבורה: **ואמר** רבי יוחנן שלש מפתחות. היינו שלא נמסרו לשליח אחד ביחד (ז): יפתח ה'. ולא שליח: כי

תוספות

מאימתי. מיום טוב האחרון של חג. שמיני, דלא יתבון בסוכה. ואפילו האידנא אינו אלא מדרבנן, משום ספיקא. ואע"ג דבקיאינן בקביעא דירחא – גזרה שמא יחזור הדבר לקלקולו, או משום מנהג אבותינו בידינו, כדאי' פ"ק דביצה (דף ד:), ולכן מדכרינן. אבל כל שבעה – לא, שהגשמים בימי סוכה סימן קללה הן, כדתנן פרק שני דסוכה (דף כח:): משל לעבד וכו':

אם כן. אם אתה אומר מזכירין אע"פ שאין שואלין, הואיל ומשמע בעונתו – אף בקיץ יזכירו, ומה אתה נותן סימן מי"ט הראשון? ור' אליעזר אומר בברייתא בגמרא: כל הקיץ, אם בא להזכיר – מזכיר, דלעולם בעונתו משמע. מיהו, עד השתא לא רמי עליה חובה, אבל בי"ט ראשון – חובה לרצות לפני שאלה, שכל הבא לבקש מקדים ומרצה. ואסימן קללה לא קפדינן, ורבי יהושע קפיד:

התם קאי. פירוש: בסדר זרעים, בברכות, פרק "אין עומדין" (דף לג.) וליתני התם מאי שנא כו'. כלומר, אמאי תנא הכא במועד מאי דתני התם בסדר זרעים:

אלא תנא מראש השנה קא סליק. פירוש: ור"ה הויא בסדר מועד. ואם תאמר: ואכתי ליתני בסדר זרעים! וי"ל: דהכא עיקר, דאמר בחג נידונין על המים, ואורחא דמילתא לרצות לפני שאלה, לכך שביק עד הכא. אבל בסדר זרעים(ח) אומרים מזכירין גבורות גשמים – אפשר דמשמע לעולם. כמו תחיית המתים, או הבדלה בחונן הדעת:

וליתני מאימתי מזכירין(ט) גשמים מאי גבורות גשמים אמר ר' יוחנן שיורדין בגבורה. תימה: התם בברכות פ' "אין עומדין" (שם) קתני כי הכא: מזכירין גבורות גשמים ושואלין הגשמים וכו', אמאי לא קא מקשה כמו הכא: וליתני מזכירין על הגשמים, מאי גבורות? ויש לומר: שאני הכא, דהוי עיקר סדר של גשמים באיזה זמן מתחילין לאומרו, ומאימתי פוסקין מלאומרו, ומשום הכי פריך הכא טפי מהתם:

וכתיב מכין הרים בכחו נאזר בגבורה. וזה גבי בריאת עולם, וכי היכי דהאי "חקר" בבריאת העולם, רוצה לומר בגבורות. כמו כן הכא גבי גשמים, האי "חקר" נמי רוצה לומר גבורות. אכן, יש להקשות: אמאי נקט גבורות טפי מכח? וכמו כן הוה ליה למימר: מאימתי מזכירין כח גשמים, או ליתני גדולות גשמים! וי"ל: דמן הדין נקט גבורות, משום טעמא דאיכא כח ואיכא גדולה. אי נמי, משום דהברכה מתחלת בגבורה, להכי נקט גבורות:

שלשה מפתחות שלא נמסרו לשליח. וא"ת: והא אמרינן (סנהדרין דף קיג.) דמפתח הגשמים(י) נמסרין לאליהו, וכן מפתח של תחיית המתים. וכן לאלישע, דכתיב (מלכים א יז) "ויאמר אליהו חי ה'" וגו' דה"נ אומר בפירקין דלקמן (דף כג.)! וי"ל: דהא דקאמר שלא שנמסרו לשליח אינו ר"ל שלא נמסרו מעולם, דהא של תחיית המתים ושל גשמים נמסרו, אלא לא נמסרו לשליח להיות לעולם ממונה עליהם:

וישמע אליה אלהים ויפתח את רחמה. פירוש: שהוא בעצמו עשה. וא"ת: מהכא משמע דליכא אלא שלשה מפתחות, וא"כ יש להקשות: והא כתיב (ירמיה נ) "פתח ה' את אוצרו ויוצא את כלי זעמו" ומשמע נמי שלא נמסרו לשליח, וכמו ההיא "וישמע אליה אלהים" וגו', וא"כ אמאי לא חשיב להו? וי"ל: דלא חשיב כי אם אותן מפתחות של טובה, ולהכי לא קא חשיב מפתח של זעם. וא"ת: דמשמע מהאי קרא ד"פתח ה'" שלא נמסר מפתח של זעם לשליח, והא אמרינן (פסחים דף קיח.): יורקמי שר של ברד הוי! וי"ל: מכלי זעם אחרינא קאמר, שלא נמסרו לשליח. אבל משום ברד – לא, דאותו של ברד נמסרו: איבעיא

עין משפט נר מצוה

א א ב ג מיי' פ"ב מהלכות תפלה הלכה טו סמג עשין יט טוש"ע א"ח סי' קיד סעיף א:
ב ד מיי' שם הלכה טז וסמ"ג שם טוש"ע א"ח סי' קיז סעיף א:
ג ה מיי' שם הלכה יב וסמג שם טוש"ע א"ח סי' רצד סעיף א:

מסורת הש"ס

רש"א מ"ז
[ברכות ב.]
שם לג.
ר"ה טז.
רש"א מ"ז
איוב ט
שם ה
[נ"ל עושה גדולות ואין חקר נפלאות עד אין מספר (איוב ה פ"ט) וכן בח"א למהרש"א ע"ש וגם לקמן ט: ונדה לא. ובפי' הרע"ב מ"ב פ"ה דברכות צריכין אנו להגיה על דרך הנ"ל]
ישעיהו מ
תהלים סה
דברים יא
שם
סנהדרין קיג.
דברים כח
בראשית ל

רבינו חננאל

(אידי) [אהדא] דתנן במתניתין מאימתי מזכירין גבורות גשמים מקשי תנא היכא קאי דקתני מאימתי כלומר מי הזכיר שנזכיר גבורות גשמים עד שיאמר מאימתי. ושנינן תנא מר"ה סליק דתנן ובחג נידונין על המים. ולפיכך תנא הכא מאימתי מזכירין גבורות גשמים. ואמאי תני גבורות כלומר מה גבורה יש בגשמים. וא"ר יוחנן שיורדין בגבורה שנאמר בענין המטר עושה גדולות עד אין חקר וגמר חקר חקר מברייתו של עולם שנאמר בורא קצות הארץ אין חקר לתבונתו. וכתיב מכין הרים בכחו נאזר בגבורה. מיכן סמכו לומר גבורות גשמים ופריש במתני' בתפלה ואמרי' ומנא לן שלא תהא הזכרה זו אלא בתפלה. ופשטנא מדכתיב [ולעבדו] בכל לבבכם וגו' ונתתי מטר ארצכם בעתו יורה ומלקוש וגו'. ודייקינן איזו היא [עבודה] בלב שבשבילה המטר יורד הוי אומר זו תפלה. וא"ר יוחנן שלשה מפתחות לא נמסרו לשליח אלא הם בידו של הקב"ה. מפתח גשמים שנאמר יפתח ה' לך את אוצרו הטוב את השמים וגו'. מפתח של חיה

רבינו גרשום

מאימתי מזכירין גבורת גשמים. שאומ' מוריד הגשם: מאחר שהגשמים סימן קללה הוא בחג כדאמרן בסוכה משל לעבד שמשמש לרבו והפך לו רבו קיתון על פניו כלומר שאינו חפץ בו אף כך כשיורדין גשמים בחג יוצאין הכל מן הסוכה ונראה שאין חפץ הקב"ה שישבו בסוכה ואמאי מתחיל להזכיר גבורות גשמים ונראה שהוא מתפלל שירדו גשמים בחג: לא אמרתי לישאל שיתפלל על הגשמים בחג אלא להזכיר. שמתחיל להזכיר בחג *) גבורות של גשמים מקום שמוריד גשמים בעונתם לאחר החג כשצריכין: אם כן לעולם יהא מזכיר אפי' בימות החמה שמוריד גשמים בעונתן: גמ' התם קאי מזכירין כו' במס' ברכות: וליתני התם במס' [ברכות] סמוך לדתני מזכירין כו' ליתני מאימתי מ"ש דשבקיה עד הכא כלומר מי קתני הכא בסדר מועד מאימתי אמאי דתני מזכירין במס' ברכות דהיינו בסדר זרעים. תנא מר"ה סליקי ששניהם בסדר אחד הן להכי לא מצי למימר מ"ש דשבקיה עד הכא. כתיב עושה גדולות עד אין חקר אלמא דכתיב חקר בגשמים וכתיב חקר בברייתו של עולם מה בברייתו של עולם כתיב ביה גבורה אף בגשמים הוי כמו דכתיב גבורה: שלא נמסרו שלשתן ביחד ביד שליח. יפתח ה' ולא שליח כי

*) נראה דצ"ל גבורות של מקום שמוריד גשמים וכו'.

הגהות הב"ח

(א) גמ' שנאמר עושה גדולות ואין חקר נפלאות כו' כצ"ל ותיבת עד נמחק ונ"ב (איוב ה): (ב) שם אין חקר לתבונתו נותן ליעף כח וכתיב מכין הרים: (ג) שם ואלו הן מפתח של חיה ומפתח של גשמים ומפתח של תחיית המתים מפתח של חיה מנין דכתיב ויזכור אלהים את רחל וישמע אליה אלהים ויפתח את רחמה מפתח של גשמים מנין דכתיב יפתח ה' לך גו' מטר ארצך בעתו מפתח של תחיית המתים וכו' כצ"ל: (ד) רש"י ד"ה מאי שנא כו' ליתני התם היכא דתני כו' סדר זרעים אמאי שבקיה עד הכא כו' כצ"ל: (ה) ד"ה בחג כו' זמן הזכרה ליכנא אחרינא ואיידי דתני כו' כצ"ל והד"א: (ו) ד"ה כתיב עושה גדולות ואין חקר כו': (ז) ד"ה ואמר כו' ביחד. נ"ב דקא קשיא ליה קושיית התוס': (ח) תום' ד"ה אלא כו' אבל בסדר זרעים דתני מזכירין כצ"ל: (ט) ד"ה וליתני מאימתי מזכירין על הגשמים כו' פרק אין עומדין דקתני כי הכא מזכירין גבורות גשמים ושואלין וכו' אמאי לא כו' כצ"ל ותיבת הגשמים נמחק: (י) ד"ה שלשה כו' דמפתח הגשמים נמסר לאליהו:

ד א מיי' פ"ד מהלכות מעשה הקרבנות הלכה ה:

לפנינו איתא ר' אבא ואי תימא רמי בר חמא ואי תימא ר' יוחנן

אליה אלהים ויפתח את רחמה". מפתח של תחיית המתים מנין — דכתיב °"וידעתם כי אני ה', בפתחי את קברותיכם". [יחזקאל לז] במערבא אמרי: אף מפתח של פרנסה, דכתיב °"פותח את ידך" וגו'. [תהלים קמה] ור' יוחנן מאי טעמא לא קא חשיב להא? אמר לך: גשמים (א) היינו פרנסה. § "ר' אליעזר אומר: מיום טוב הראשון של חג" כו'. § איבעיא להו: ר' אליעזר מהיכא גמיר לה, מלולב גמר לה או מניסוך המים גמר לה? מלולב גמר לה: מה לולב ביום — אף הזכרה ביום. או דלמא מניסוך המים גמר לה? מה ניסוך המים מאורתא — *דאמר מר: א°"ומנחתם ונסכיהם" [במדבר כט] אפילו בלילה — אף הזכרה מאורתא? תא שמע, דאמר רבי אבהו: לא למדה ר' אליעזר אלא מלולב. איכא דאמרי ר' אבהו גמרא גמיר לה, ואיכא דאמרי מתניתא שמיע ליה. מאי היא? דתניא: "מאימתי מזכירין על הגשמים? *רבי אליעזר אומר: משעת נטילת לולב. *ר' יהושע אומר: משעת הנחתו. א"ר אליעזר: הואיל וארבעת מינין הללו אינן באין אלא לרצות על המים, וכשם שארבע מינין הללו אי אפשר בהם בלא מים — כך אי אפשר לעולם בלא מים. אמר לו ר' יהושע: והלא גשמים בחג אינו אלא סימן קללה? אמר לו ר' אליעזר: אף אני לא אמרתי 'לשאול', אלא 'להזכיר'. וכשם שתחיית המתים מזכיר כל השנה כולה, ואינה אלא בזמנה — כך מזכירים גבורות גשמים כל השנה, ואינן אלא בזמנן. לפיכך, אם בא להזכיר כל השנה כולה — מזכיר. רבי אומר: אומר אני משעה שמפסיק לשאלה כך מפסיק להזכרה. ר' יהודה בן בתירה אומר: בשני בחג הוא מזכיר. ר' עקיבא אומר: בששי בחג הוא מזכיר. ר' יהודה משום ר' יהושע אומר: העובר לפני התיבה ביום טוב האחרון של חג — האחרון מזכיר, הראשון אינו מזכיר. ביום טוב ראשון של פסח — הראשון מזכיר, האחרון אינו מזכיר. שפיר קאמר ליה ר"א לרבי יהושע! אמר לך רבי יהושע: בשלמא תחיית המתים מזכיר — דכולי יומא זמניה הוא. אלא גשמים כל אימת דאתיין, זמנייהו היא? והתנן: *"יצא ניסן וירדו גשמים — סימן קללה הם, שנאמר °"הלא קציר [ש"א יב] חטים היום" וגו'. ר' יהודה בן בתירה אומר: בשני בחג הוא מזכיר. מ"ט דרבי יהודה בן בתירה? דתניא: *"רבי יהודה בן בתירה אומר: נאמר בשני °'ונסכיהם', [במדבר כט] ונאמר בששי: 'ונסכיה', ונאמר בשביעי: 'כמשפטם' — הרי מ"ם יו"ד מ"ם. הרי כאן 'מים'. מכאן רמז לניסוך המים מן התורה. ומאי שנא בשני דנקט? דכי רמיזי להו בקרא, בשני הוא דרמיזי. הלכך בשני מדכרינן. רבי עקיבא אומר: בששי בחג הוא מזכיר. שנאמר בששי: 'ונסכיה'. *בשני ניסוכין הכתוב מדבר, [זבחים קי:] אחד ניסוך המים ואחד ניסוך היין. ואימא תרוייהו דחמרא! סבר לה כר' יהודה בן בתירה, דאמר: רמיזי מיא.
אי

כי אני ה'. ולא שליח: פותח את ידך. ולא שליח: גשמים נמי היינו פרנסה. (ב) וכבר חשבנא ליה: מלולב גמר ליה. שדומה ללולב, שכשם שאי אפשר לאלו ארבע מינין בלא גשמים, ובאין לרצות על המים, כדאמרינן בסוכה, *כך אי אפשר לעולם בלא מים: [דף לז: ע"י תוס' שם ד"ה כדי] מה לולב ביום. שמתחילין ליטול ביום ראשון, אף הזכרה נמי ביום. כלומר, שאין מזכירין בלילי יום טוב הראשון, עד למחר: מה ניסוך המים מאורתא. כדאשכחן במס' סוכה (דף מח:) שממלאין הכלי מים לניסוך המים בלילה. ויש ספרים דכתיב בהו: דאמר מר: ומנחתם ונסכיהם בלילה, (ג) שמקריבין הקרבנות ביום יכולין להביא המנחות והנסכים בלילה. אף האי, ניסוך המים, נמי יכול לנסך בלילה: אף הזכרה נמי מאורתא. שבלילי י"ט הראשון קאמר ר' אליעזר שמתחילין להזכיר גבורות גשמים: גמרא גמיר לה. [תמורה יד. [זבחים ח. פד.] מנחות מד: נב.] רבי אבהו, דרבי אליעזר לא למדה אלא מלולב: *)מתניתין שמיע ליה. דרבי אליעזר גמר מלולב: משעת הנחתו. מיום שמברכין בו באחרונה, דהיינו בשביעי א]: ארבעה מינין הללו. שבלולב ואתרוג: כך גשמים. [לקמן ז.] יהא מזכיר כל השנה, אפילו בימות החמה, [שם] אם הוא רוצה — יהא מזכיר: משעה שפוסק מלשאול. שבפסח פוסק מלומר "ותן טל ומטר" פוסק מלהזכיר גבורות גשמים. והשתא לא מצית למימר אם בא להזכיר כל השנה כולה מזכיר, אלא בימות החמה אינו מזכיר — הואיל ואין זמנו, אף בחג אינו מזכיר — הואיל ולא סימן ברכה הן: האחרון. המתפלל תפלת מוסף: הראשון. המתפלל תפלת יוצר: אינו מזכיר. ושוב אין מזכירין: שפיר קאמר ליה ר' אליעזר לר' יהושע. דקאמר: כי היכי דמזכירין תחיית המתים כל השנה, ואף על גב דלא מטא זימנייהו — כך מזכירין גבורות גשמים, אם רוצה, כל השנה. ובחג נמי, אע"ג דלאו סימן ברכה הן — מזכירין, הואיל ואין שואלין: כל אימת דאתיין זימנייהו הוא. וכיון דלאו זימניה הוא — אין מזכירין, והוא הדין בחג: בשני ונסכיהם. דסגי בנסכה, וכיון דבשני אייתר מ"ם לדרשה — להכי מתחילין להזכיר בשני: בשני ניסוכין הכתוב מדבר. שני ניסוכין על קרבן אחד. אבל "ונסכיהם" (ד) משמע הרבה, דבקרבנות [לקמן יב:] הרבה. לכן לא הוה דריש רבי עקיבא מ"ונסכיהם": סבר לה כרבי יהודה. דמ"ם יו"ד מ"ם מרבה ניסוך המים: [שבת קג:]
אי

*) נ"ל מתניתא

איבעיא להו רבי אליעזר מהיכא גמיר לה מלולב גמיר מה לולב ביום וכו'. פי': ולולב הוי רצוי דמים, וגדל על המים. או דלמא מניסוך גמר לה, פי': ונפקא מינה(ה), אי מלולב גמר לה, אבל ניסוך המים סבירא ליה דלאו ביום ראשון הוא. או מניסוך המים קא גמר לה, דסבירא ליה דניסוך המים ביום ראשון הוא. אי נמי: דאי מלולב גמר — הוה דווקא ביום, שנאמר (ויקרא כג) "ולקחתם לכם ביום". אבל אי מנסוך — הוה אפילו בלילה. ולענין זה אהני דאמר מר "ומנחתם ונסכיהם"(ו) בלילה, אף וכו'. פירוש: דאע"ג דניסוך קרבנות לא הוי עד לאחר הקרבת קרבנותיהם, ואם כן היאך קריבי נסכים בלילה — רוצה לומר בלילה שניה. והניסוך החג דהוי ממים מצי למהוי בלילה ראשונה. ואע"ג דאמרינן במסכת יומא בפ' "בראשונה" (דף כו:): *אמר רב ואיתימא ר' יוחנן אין מנסכים מים בחג אלא בתמיד של שחר. וא"כ לא הוי בלילה ראשונה, דהא אינה אלא ביום! יש לומר: דאינו חייב לנסך אלא בתמיד של שחר, מכל מקום, אי בעי — עביד ליה בליליא:

דאמר רבי אבהו לא למדה רבי **אליעזר אלא** מלולב. פירוש: וסבירא ליה דניסוך לא הוי עד בשני: **משעת** נטילת לולב. פירוש, דהיינו: תחילת יום ראשון של סוכות. ורבי יהושע אומר: משעת הנחתו, פירוש: לאורתא דמוצאי שביעי של סוכות, שמניחין בו את הלולב:

משעה שמפסיקין לישאל. "ותן טל ומטר" בברכת השנים פוסקין מלהזכיר "מוריד הגשם" בתחיית המתים: **העובר** לפני התיבה בי"ט של חג האחרון מזכיר וכו'. פי': האחרון — שמתפלל תפלת מוסף. הראשון אינו מזכיר — פירוש: שמתפלל שחרית אינו מזכיר. ובירושלמי קאמר: אמאי אינו מזכיר מאורתא? פירוש: מתפלת ערבית. ומשני: דלית תמן כל עמא, ולדכרו בצפרא, פירוש: בתפלת שחרית! ומשני: דהוו סברי דהוו מדכרו ליה מאורתא:

מים. מ"ם מנסכיהם דכתיב בשני, ויו"ד דכתיב בששי ונסכיה, ומ"ם שבשביעי כתיב כמשפטם, והוי מים(ז). טעמא דרבי עקיבא בששי — ונסכיה, דמשמע תרי נסכים, הלכך בששי בחג הוא מזכיר גבורות גשמים:
אי

רבינו חננאל

שנאמר וישמע אליה אלהים ויפתח את רחמה. מפתח של תחיית המתים שנאמר וידעתם כי אני ה' בפתחי את קברותיכם וגו'. גשמים היינו פרנסה ומשום שהגשמים חשובים כתחיית המתים קבעו ברכה זו בתחיית המתים: **פיסקא** ר' אליעזר אומר מיו"ט הראשון של חג מזכיר. [איבעיא להו אי מלילי יו"ט הראשון מזכיר] וגמר לה מניסוך דאתקש ניסוך המים לניסוך היין דאמר מר ומנחתם ונסכיהם (מליל"י יו"ם טו"ב הראשו"ן מזכי"ר) אפילו בלילה. פירושו בתמורה בתחלת פרק יש בקרבנות. או מלולב גמר לה דכתיב ולקחתם לכם ביום ולא בלילה ופשטנא מהא דתניא מאימתי מזכירין על הגשמים. ר' אליעזר אומר משעת נטילת לולב. ר' יהושע אומר משעת הנחתו. א"ר אליעזר הואיל וארבעת מינים הללו אינם באין [אלא] לרצות המים כו'. שפיר קאמר ליה רבי אליעזר לר' יהושע אני לא אמרתי לשאל אלא להזכיר כשם שתחיית המתים מזכיר כל השנה ואינה אלא בזמנה כך גשמים מזכיר ואינן אלא בזמנן. ואמרינן ר' יהושע פריך הכי מה לתחיית המתים שמזכיר בכל יום דכל יומא זמניה היא אלא גשמים אטו כל יומא זמנייהו הוא. והתנן יצא ניסן וירדו גשמים סימן קללה היא ר' יהודה בן בתירה אומר בשני של חג הוא מזכיר. וגמר לה מניסוך דכתיב בשני ונסכיהם מדכתיב מ"ם יתירה דהוה ליה למכתב ונסכה וכתיב ונסכיהם. ובששי כתיב יוד יתירה דכתיב ונסכיה. ובשביעי כמשפטם. כתיב מ' יתירה. מיכן לניסוך המים מן התורה. וכי רמיזי מיום שני רמיזי הלכך מיום שני מזכיר. ר' עקיבא אומר בששי בחג הוא מזכיר. ר' עקיבא נמי אית ליה מיכן לניסוך המים. מיהו דייק מדכתיב ביום הששי. ונסכיה. בשני ניסוכין הכתוב מדבר ניסוך מים וניסוך יין

רבינו גרשום

כי אני ה' ולא שליח פותח את ידך ולא שליח. גשמים נמי היינו פרנסה וכבר חשיבנא ליה: **פיסקא** מלולב גמר לה שדומה ללולב שכשם שאי אפשר לאילו בלא מים כך אי אפשר לעולם בלא מים מה לולב ביום שמתחיל ליטול ביום ראשון אף הזכרה ביום (בו' צ"ל כלומר) שאינו מתחיל להזכיר בלילי יו"ט ראשון עד למחר. מה ניסוך המים מאורתא כדאשכחן במס' סוכה שממלאין המים לניסוך המים בלילה ויש ספרים שכתוב בהן [דאמר מר] מנחתם ונסכיהם בלילה שמקריבין קרבן ביום יכולין להביא המנחה והנסכים בלילה אף האי ניסוך המים יכולין לנסך בלילה. אף הזכרה נמי מאורתא שבלילי יו"ט הראשון קאמר ר' אליעזר שמזכירין להזכיר גבורות גשמים. גמרא גמיר לה ר' אבהו דר' אליעזר לא למדה אלא מלולב. ממתניתין שמיעה ליה דר' אליעזר גמר מלולב: משעת הנחתו מיום שמברכין בו באחרונה דהיינו בשביעי. ארבעת מינין הללו שבלולב ואתרוג: כך גשמים יהא מזכיר כל השנה אפי' בימות החמה אם הוא רוצה אף בחג נמי אם הוא רוצה יהא מזכיר. משעה שפוסק מלשאל שבפסח פוסק מלומר ותן טל ומטר פוסק מלהזכיר גבורת הגשמים ועכשיו לא מצית למימר אם בא להזכיר כל השנה מזכיר אלא בימות החמה אינו מזכיר הואיל ואין זמנו אף בחג אינו מזכיר הואיל ולאו זמן ברכה הוא. האחרון המתפלל תפלת מוסף. הראשון המתפלל (תפלת) יוצר: מזכיר ושוב אינו מזכיר. שפיר קאמר ליה ר' אליעזר לר"י דכי היכי דמזכירין תחיית המתים כל השנה אע"ג דלא זמניה כך מזכירין גבורות גשמים אם רוצה כל השנה ובחג נמי אע"ג דלאו סימן ברכה הוא מזכירין. סימן קללה הוא וכיון דלאו זמנה אין מזכירין וה"ה בחג: נאמר בשני ונסכיהם דסגי בנסכה וכיון דבשני אתרבי מ' לדרשה דמים לפיכך מתחיל להזכיר בשני: בשני ניסוכין הכתוב מדבר שני ניסוכין על קרבן אחד ונסכיהם משמע ניסוכין הרבה הקרבנות הרבה. סבר לה כר"י דמרבה ניסוך המים
אי

הגהות הב"ח

(א) גמ' אמר לך גשמים נמי היינו פרנסה: (ב) רש"י ד"ה גשמים נמי היינו פרנסה שזורעים ופירות גדלים מהם לפרנסת העולם וכבר חשבנא ליה: (ג) ד"ה מה ניסוך כו' ונסכיהם בלילה אפילו בלילה דלאע"ש שמקריבין הקרבנות: (ד) ד"ה בשני ניסוכין כו' אבל ונסכיהם משמע הרבה ניסוכין בקרבנות הרבה: (ה) תוס' ד"ה איבעיא כו' ונפקא מינה כו' אי מלולב גמר לה כו' או מניסוך כו' דסבירא ליה דניסוך המים ביום ראשון הוא: (ו) בא"ד ומנחתם ונסכיהם אפילו בלילה כו' וא"כ האיך קריבי נסכים בלילה [illegible] בלילה שניה כו' מ"מ הניסוך דחג דהוי ממים כו' נ"ל: (ז) ד"ה מים כו' וטעמא דר"ע דכתיב בששי ונסכיה:

הגהות מהר"ב רנשבורג

א] רש"י ד"ה משעת הנחתו וכו' דהיינו בשביעי. נ"ב וכן פרש"י לקמן דף ג ע"ב בד"ה אלא ר' יהושע היא וכו' דהיינו בשביעי וכו' עכ"ל. וע"ע לקמן דף ה סע"א בד"ה ר' יהושע היא וכו' דהיינו יום שמיני וכו' ע"ל. וכן משמע מדברי הש"ס שם ודו"ק. שוב ראיתי [illegible] משעת נטילה וכן נלמד ממהרש"א לקמן דף ג ע"ב ד"ה גמ' יהושע:

אי סבר לה כרבי יהודה בן בתירה, נימא כוותיה! קסבר רבי עקיבא: כי כתיב ניסוך יתירא — בששי הוא דכתיב. תניא, ר' נתן אומר: "בקדש הסך נסך שכר לה'". בשני ניסוכין הכתוב מדבר, אחד ניסוך המים ואחד ניסוך היין". אימא תרוייהו דחמרא! אם כן, ליכתוב קרא או 'הסך הסך' או 'נסך נסך'. מאי 'הסך נסך'? שמעת מינה: חד דמיא וחד דחמרא. אלא הא דתנן: *א"ניסוך המים כל ז' מני? אי ר' יהושע, נימא חד יומא. אי ר"ע — תרי יומי. אי ר' יהודה ב"ב — שיתא יומי! לעולם ר' יהודה ב"ב היא, וס"ל כר' יהודה דמתני' דתנן, *רבי יהודה אומר: בלוג היה מנסך כל שמונה. ומפיק ראשון ומעייל שמיני. ומאי שנא ראשון דלא? דכי רמיזי מים, בשני הוא דרמיזי? שמיני נמי, כי רמיזי מים, בשביעי הוא דרמיזי! אלא רבי יהושע היא, וניסוך המים כל שבעה הלכתא גמירי לה. *דאמר ר' אמי א"ר יוחנן משום ר' נחוניא איש בקעת בית חורתן: בעשר נטיעות, געבה, דוניסוך המים — הלכה למשה מסיני.§ רבי יהודה אומר משום רבי יהושע: העובר לפני התיבה ביום טוב האחרון של חג — האחרון מזכיר, הראשון אינו מזכיר. ביום טוב הראשון של פסח — הראשון מזכיר, האחרון אינו מזכיר".§ הי רבי יהושע? אילימא רבי יהושע דמתניתין, הא אמר ביום טוב האחרון של חג הוא מזכיר! אלא ר' יהושע דברייתא? האמר: "משעת הנחתו"! ותו, הא דתניא: "ר' יהודה אומר משום בן בתירה: העובר לפני התיבה ביום טוב האחרון של חג — האחרון מזכיר", הי בן בתירה? אילימא רבי יהודה בן בתירה, הא אמר: 'בשני בחג הוא מזכיר'! אמר רב נחמן בר יצחק: (א) תהא ברבי יהושע בן בתירה. זמנין דקרי ליה בשמיה וזמנין דקרי ליה בשמיה דאבא. והא — מקמי דליסמכוהו, והא — לבתר דליסמכוהו. התנא: 'בטל וברוחות לא חייבו חכמים להזכיר, ואם בא להזכיר, מזכיר'. מ"ט? א"ר חנינא: לפי שאין נעצרין. וטל מנלן דלא מיעצר? דכתיב "ויאמר אליהו התשבי, מתושבי גלעד, אל אחאב: חי ה' אלהי ישראל, אשר עמדתי לפניו, אם יהיה השנים האלה טל ומטר כי אם לפי דברי". וכתיב "לך הראה אל אחאב, ואתנה מטר על פני האדמה". ואילו טל, לא קאמר ליה. מאי טעמא? משום דלא

במדבר כח | מ"א יז | שם יח

רש"י

אי סבר לה כר' יהודה לימא כר"י. שמזכיר בשני: ניסוך יתירא בששי כתיב. כלומר "ונסכיה" דמרבי תרי ניסוכין כתיב בששי, להכי אמר בששי מתחיל להזכיר. והאי מ"ם יו"ד מ"ם – מים, דלא מצינו למימר תרוייהו דיין: או הסך הסך או נסך נסך. מדשני קרא בדיבוריה – ש"מ תרתי: אי ר"ע תרי יומי הוו. ותו לא, דהא אמר (ב) "ונסכיה" דהיינו בששי מרבה ניסוך המים: וסבר לה כר' יהודה דמתניתין. דאמר: בלוג היה מנסך כל שמנה, לא סבר כוותיה במה דאמר כל שמונה מנסך, אלא במה דאמר בשמיני מנסך. וכיון דבשמיני מנסך – משכחת לה לרבי יהודה [ב"ב] דאמר: בשני מתחילין לניסוך המים כל שבעה: (ג) דמפיק ראשון ומעייל שמיני. משיב בעל הגמרא: מי מצי אמר רבי יהודה דבשמיני מנסך? מאי שנא. דקאמר דבראשון אינו מזכיר, דכי רמיזי מיא – בשני הוא דרמיזי, דמ"ונסכיהם" מרבה ניסוך המים, שמיני נמי, מי מצי אמר דמנסך? הא שביעי אמר רחמנא, דמ"ם יו"ד מ"ם מים כתיב בשביעי, דסיום קראי דניסוך המים בשביעי כתיב "כמשפטם", ולא בשמיני: אלא ר' יהושע היא. דאמר משעת הנחתו (ד) [דהיינו בשביעי] מזכיר, ואעפ"כ סבר דניסוך המים כל שבעה, דגמרא גמיר לה הלכה למשה מסיני דניסוך המים כל שבעה. ודאי כר"א אתי שפיר. אבל כרבי יהודה בן בתירה וכר"ע לא מיתוקמא, אלא להכי לא מוקי לה כר' אליעזר – דהא לא מיבעי אי ר' אליעזר סבירא ליה הכי, דודאי לרבי אליעזר אתי שפיר. והא דקא מוקים כר' יהושע – רבותא קמשמע לן. אבל כר"י בן בתירה וכר"ע – לא מיתוקמא. דרבי יהודה יליף מונאמר בשני "ונסכיהם" כו' אלמא דסבר דניסוך המים לא הוו אלא ו' ימים, דאיהו לא מפיק ראשון ומעייל שמיני. משום הני פירכא דפריך לעיל – לא אתי כרבי יהודה. ורבי עקיבא יליף מ"ונסכיה" שנאמר בששי, אלמא דסבר דניסוך המים לא הוו אלא תרי יומי, אבל כרבי יהושע מיתוקמא. לפיכך אין מזכירין אלא ביו"ט האחרון, דגשמים בחג סימן קללה, אבל ניסוך המים – הוי כל שבעה, דגמרא גמיר לה: עשר נטיעות. המפוזרות בתוך בית סאה חורשין כל בית סאה ערב שביעית עד ר"ה. אע"ג דשאר שדות אין חורשין לפני שביעית ל' יום – זה חורשין, דהואיל אם אין חורשין סביבן – מפסידין: וניסוך המים. כל שבעה: ר' יהודה אומר משום רבי יהושע העובר לפני התיבה בי"ט האחרון של חג כו'. כעין אמר מר הוא, כלומר: אמרינן לעיל ר' יהודה אומר: הי רבי יהושע אילימא רבי יהושע דמתני' (ה) מיו"ט האחרון הוא מזכיר. דראשון נמי, המתפלל תפלת יוצר מזכיר. ואילו הכא תני: הראשון אינו מזכיר: האמר משעת הנחתו. דהיינו בשביעי. והכא קתני יו"ט האחרון של חג, דהיינו בשמיני: ותו הא דתניא. במכילתא אחריתי: ר' יהודה אומר משום בן בתירה: העובר לפני התיבה בי"ט אחרון של חג – האחרון מזכיר, הראשון אינו מזכיר: (אלא) אמר רב נחמן בר יצחק תהא. תרוייהו, הא דבעית הי ר' יהושע, והא דבעית הי בן בתירה – ר' יהושע בן בתירה היא. דהאי דקאמר רבי יהודה לעיל משום ר' יהושע, והדר קאמר משום בן בתירה – תהא תרוייהו רבי יהושע בן בתירה, ולא קשיא: זמנין קרו ליה בשמיה דאבוה בן בתירה, וזמנין דקרו ליה בשמיה דידיה – ר' יהושע: מקמי דליסמכוהו. לא הוה חשוב, וקרו ליה בשמיה דאבוה. והאי דקרו ליה בשמיה דנפשיה, ר' יהושע – היינו לבתר דסמכוהו: בטל וברוחות. "משיב הרוח ומוריד הטל" לא חייבוהו חכמים להזכיר, אפילו בימות הגשמים: לפי שאינן נעצרין. שאלמלא(ו) הן אין העולם מתקיים. והאי דאמרינן בתפלה "משיב הרוח ומוריד הגשם" – לאו משום חיוב אלא חוק גשם הוא מזכיר[א], דטל ורוחות מועילות לארץ לתקנה ולנגבה, כדכתיב: זיקא דבתר מיטרא כמיטרא: ואילו טל לא קאמר. ואתנה טל ומטר, אלא מטר בלבד: ולא

תוספות

אי רבי יהודה בן בתירה. דאמר בשני בחג הוא מזכיר – שית יומי הוו, א"כ לא יהיה הניסוך כי אם ששה ימים: עשר נטיעות. פירש"י: (ז) נטיעות מפוזרות בבית סאה חורש כל בית סאה בשבילן, דכל נטיעה יונקת. ודווקא מבית סאה היה צריך להם יכול לחרוש עד ר"ה של שביעית, דהוו שפיר אוקמי אילנא – שרי. אבל יותר מבית סאה – אינו חורש אלא כדי צורכן. דהואיל ומפוזרות ביותר מבית סאה – קיימי שפיר. ובפחות מיכן למה קיימי, וליעקר קיימי. ודוקא נטיעות אמר דחורשין בשבילן עד ראש השנה, אבל אילנות – אסור דאורייתא כל אלול, ומדרבנן *פסח ועצרת תקון. בשדה הלבן עד פסח – מותר, אבל מפסח ולהלן – אסור. ושדה אילן, עד עצרת – מותר, מכאן ואילך – אסור: ערבה. שמקיפין את המזבח, וניסוך המים – הלכה למשה מסיני כולהו: ויאמר אליהו התשבי מתושבי גלעד. לכך נקרא "מתושבי גלעד" לפי שהרגו ישראל אנשי יבש גלעד על מעשה פילגש בגבעה, ולא נשאר ביבש גלעד כי אם מעט אנשים מן המיושבים בעיר, כי כל השאר היו עם אספסוף. לכך מעיד כי אליהו מן התושבים. כך שמעתי מהר"י טרוט"י משם הר"י בה"ר יצחק ממלאון: בטל וברוחות לא חייבו חכמים להזכיר. "משיב הרוח ומוריד הטל" כו' לפיכך אין קפידא לומר "מוריד הטל" אפילו בימות החמה, אך שלא יאמר מוריד הגשם. והכי הלכתא. ואם לא אמר בימות הגשמים כי אם "מוריד הגשם" ודילג "משיב הרוח ומוריד הטל" – אין מחזירין: ואילו טל לא מיעצר. ומ"ה נראה דגבי גדעון (שופטים ו) כשאמר (ח) "על הארץ יהיה טל ועל הגיזה יהיה חורב" כתיב "ויעש כן", אבל כשאמר "על הארץ יהיה חורב ועל הגיזה יהיה טל" כתיב "ויהי כן" כלומר: דעל הגיזה היה הטל, אבל לא כתיב "ויעש כן", משמע דעל הארץ היה טל, דטל לא מיעצר. ע"כ בנוסח שלפני. ועוד מצאתי: כשאמרו "על כל הארץ יהיה טל" כתיב "ויעש אלהים כן" וכשאמר "טל יהיה על הגיזה לבדה (ט) ועל כל הארץ יהיה חרב" כתיב "ויהי כן" ולא הזכיר בזה הש"י, וטעמו אשר אומר כי הוא זה, כי אין הש"י מזכיר שמו על הרעה. כי אם יהיה חורב על כל הארץ היתה רעת יושבי בה, וכתיב (שמות כ) "בכל המקום אשר אזכיר את שמי אבוא אליך וברכתיך". אבל כשאמר "על כל הארץ (י) יהיה טל" כתיב "ויעש אלהים". וכדומה לזה (בראשית א) "ויקרא אלהים לאור יום ולחשך קרא לילה" וגבי חשך לא הזכיר השם יתברך. וכן בחמשה דברות אחרונות (שמות כ) מ"לא תרצח" ואילך לא הזכיר הש"י – הכל הולך אל מקום אחד. משל למלך שבנה דירה נאה והניח לצייר מגינו לפני כל חדרי הבית, זולתי בית הכסא, מקום הטינוף:

עין משפט נר מצוה

ה א מיי' פ"י מהלכות תמידין הלכה ו סמג עשין קצה:
ו ב מיי' פ"ג מהלכות שמיטה ויובל הלכה ה:
ז ג מיי' פ"ז מהלכות לולב הלכה כב:
ח ד מיי' פ"י מהלכות תמידין הלכה ו:
ט ה מיי' פ"ב מהלכות תפלה הלכה ח סמג עשין יט טוש"ע א"ח סי' קיד סעיף ג:

[שביעית פ"ב מ"א ומו"ק דף ג:]

מסורת הש"ס

סוכה מב: | שם מח: | מו"ק ג: ע"ש סוכה לד. מד. ע"ש זבחים קי:

הגהות הגר"א

[א] רש"י ד"ה לפי כו'. מזכיר לרוחות מועילות כו' כצ"ל:

גליון הש"ס

גמ' לכתוב קרא או הסך וכו' בכ"ק דף סה ע"א ודף פה ע"ב ובמנחות דף יז ע"ב:

רבינו חננאל

יין. דכי כתיב ניסוך יתירה בששי כתי' הלכך בששי מזכיר. ואקשינן אלא הא דתנן ניסוך המים שבעה מני אי ר' יהודה בן בתירה האמר ניסוך המים מיום שני של חג מתחיל משעה שמזכיר ולא משכחת אלא ששה אי ר' עקיבא תרי יומי הוו כו' כל אחד משעה שאומ' פי' מזכיר מאותה שעה מתחיל ימי הניסוך ואסיקנא הא דתנן ניסוך המים ז' גמרא היא דאמר משמיה דר' יוחנן ערבה ביום השביעי של חג. וניסוך המים שבעת ימי החג. ועשר נטיעות (מעודרות) [מפוזרות] בבית סאה חורשין כל בית סאה בשבילן כבר פירשנוהו. ואלו כולן גמרא בידינו כי הל"מ הם. ותריצנה הכי א"ר יהודה משום ר' יהושע בן בתירה העובר לפני התיבה ביו"ט אחרון של חג האחרון מזכיר. פי' המתפלל במוסף הוא מזכיר בתחיית המתים מוריד הגשם. [והמתפלל שחרית אינו מזכיר וביו"ט הראשון של פסח] המתפלל שחרית מזכיר מוריד הגשם ופוסק. והמתפלל במוסף אינו מזכיר כלל. וכן הלכתא (ד)גרסינן בירושלמי א"ר יוחנן הלכה כר' יהודה שאמר משום ר' יהודה בן בתירה. ומ"ט דר' יהודה [כדי שיצאו] המועדות בטל. מפני שהטל סימן יפה לעולם. אם לא הזכיר גשמים בתחיית המתים ולא שאלה בברכת השנים מחזירין אותו. היכן הוא חוזר בו ויהיה כמו שא' בר"ח אם עקר את רגלו חוזר בתחלה. ואם לאו חוזר לעבודה. והכא אם עקר את רגליו חוזר בתחלה ואם לאו חוזר לשומע תפלה *) (וכן

א"ר יהודה קודם שיסמך בישיבה היו קורין אותו בן בתירה). מתוך ה' דברים נגאלו ישראל ממצרים. מתוך צרה שנאמר ויאנחו בני ישראל מן העבודה. מתוך צווחה שנאמר וישמע אלהים את נאקתם. מתוך זכות אבות שנאמר ויזכור אלהים את בריתו וגו'. מתוך תשובה שנאמר וירא אלהים את בני ישראל וגו'. מתוך הקץ שנאמר וידע אלהים. וכך הם מפורשים בענין בצר לך ומצאוך. וכן בענין וירא בצר להם בשמעו את רנתם. אסור ליחיד להזכיר עד שיזכיר ש"צ ויאמר מוריד הגשם קמון לצלותא כמו שיזכיר ש"צ דמי ומזכירין הצבור ביחיד אע"פ שלא מקמי ש"צ: תנא בטל וברוחות לא חייבו חכמים להזכיר שאינן נעצרין כמו המטר דכתיב חי ה' אם יהיה טל ומטר כי אם לפי דברי. וכתיב לך הראה אל אחאב ואתנה מטר על פני האדמה. ואלו טל לא אדכר. למימרא דלא

*) נראה שהסגור שייך למעלה וכצ"ל ותריצנה הכי אמר ר"י משום ריב"ב וקודם שנסמך בישיבה היו קורין אותו בן בתירה.

רבינו גרשום

אי סבר כר"י [לימא כר"י] שיזכיר בשני. ניסוך יתירה בשני כתיב כלומר ונסכיה דמרבה תרי ניסוכין כתיב בששי להכי אמר בששי מתחיל להזכיר ואהני מים דלא מצי למימר תרווייהו דיין: אי ר"ע תרי יומי הוו ותו לא דהא אמר ונסכיה דכתיב בששי מרבה ניסוך המים. אי ר' יהודה (בן בתירה) שתא הוי ותו לא דהא אמר מ"י'ם מים דהיינו בשני מרבה ניסוך המים: וסבר לה כר' יהודה דמתניתין דאמר בלוג היה מנסך כל שמונה ולא אמר דסבר כוותיה במה דאמר מנסך כל שמונה אלא במה דאמר בשמיני מנסך וכיון דבשמיני מנסך משכחת לה לר' יהודה [ב"ב] דאמר בשני מתחיל לנסך ניסוך המים כל שבעה דאפיק ראשון ועייל שמיני: משיב בעל התלמוד מי מצי אמר ר' יהודה דבשמיני מנסך מ"ש דקאמר דבראשון אינו מזכיר דכי רמיזי מיא בשני רמיזי דמונסכיהם מרבה ניסוך המים: שמיני נמי מי מצי אמר דמנסך ביה מיא שביעי אמר רחמנא דמים כתיב בשביעי ולא בשמיני אלא ר' יהושע היא דאמר משעת הנחתו דהיינו בשביעי מזכיר ואעפ"כ סבר דניסוך המים כל שבעה דגמרא גמיר לה הלכה למשה מסיני דניסוך המים כל ז' ודאי כר"א אתי אלא להכי לא מוקים לה כר' אליעזר דהוא לא בעי אי ר' אליעזר [היא] דודאי כר"א אתי שפיר: אי ר' יהושע חדא יומא ותו לא דאמר משעת הנחתו בשביעי מזכיר וה"ה דמתחיל לנסך: עשר נטיעות מפוזרות בתוך

י א מיי' פ"י מהלכות תפלה הלכה ח סמג עשין יט טוש"ע א"ח סימן קיד סעיף ג ד ה:

דְּלָא מִיעֲצַר, וְכִי מֵאַחַר דְּלָא מִיעֲצַר, אֵלִיָּהוּ אִשְׁתַּבּוּעֵי לָמָּה לֵיהּ? הָכִי קא"ל: אֲפִילּוּ טַל דִּבְרָכָה נַמִי לָא אָתֵי. וְלִיהַדְרֵיהּ לְטַל דִּבְרָכָה! מִשּׁוּם דְּלָא מִינְכְּרָא מִילְּתָא. (*אֶלָּא) רוּחוֹת מְנָא לַן דְּלָא מִיעַצְרִי? *א"ר יְהוֹשֻׁעַ בֶּן לֵוִי: דַּאֲמַר קְרָא °"כִּי כְּאַרְבַּע רוּחוֹת הַשָּׁמַיִם פֵּרַשְׂתִּי אֶתְכֶם, נְאֻם ה'". מַאי קָאָמַר לְהוּ? אִילֵימָא הָכִי קָאָמַר לְהוּ הקב"ה לְיִשְׂרָאֵל: דְּבַדַּרְתִּינְכוּ בְּאַרְבַּע רוּחֵי דְּעָלְמָא, אִי הָכִי, "כְּאַרְבַּע"? "בְּאַרְבַּע" מִיבָּעֵי לֵיהּ! אֶלָּא הָכִי קָאָמַר: כְּשֵׁם שֶׁאִי אֶפְשָׁר לָעוֹלָם בְּלֹא רוּחוֹת — כָּךְ א"א לָעוֹלָם בְּלֹא יִשְׂרָאֵל. א"ר חֲנִינָא: אהִלְכָּךְ, בִּימוֹת הַחַמָּה אָמַר: "מַשִּׁיב הָרוּחַ" — אֵין מַחֲזִירִין אוֹתוֹ. אָמַר: "מוֹרִיד הַגֶּשֶׁם" — מַחֲזִירִין אוֹתוֹ. בִּימוֹת הַגְּשָׁמִים לֹא אָמַר: "מַשִּׁיב הָרוּחַ" — אֵין מַחֲזִירִין אוֹתוֹ. לֹא אָמַר: "מוֹרִיד הַגֶּשֶׁם" — מַחֲזִירִין אוֹתוֹ. וְלֹא עוֹד אֶלָּא אֲפִילּוּ אָמַר: "מַעֲבִיר הָרוּחַ וּמַפְרִיחַ הַטַּל" — אֵין מַחֲזִירִין אוֹתוֹ. תָּנָא: "בְּעָבִים וּבְרוּחוֹת לֹא חִיְּיבוּ חֲכָמִים לְהַזְכִּיר, וְאִם בָּא לְהַזְכִּיר — מַזְכִּיר. מ"ט — מִשּׁוּם דְּלָא מִיעַצְרִי. וְלָא מִיעַצְרִי? וְהָתָנֵי רַב יוֹסֵף: °"וְעָצַר אֶת הַשָּׁמַיִם" מִן הֶעָבִים וּמִן הָרוּחוֹת. אַתָּה אוֹמֵר מִן הֶעָבִים וּמִן הָרוּחוֹת. אוֹ אֵינוֹ אֶלָּא מִן הַמָּטָר? כְּשֶׁהוּא אוֹמֵר: "וְלֹא יִהְיֶה מָטָר" — הֲרֵי מָטָר אָמוּר. הָא מָה אֲנִי מְקַיֵּים "וְעָצַר אֶת הַשָּׁמַיִם" — מִן הֶעָבִים וּמִן הָרוּחוֹת. קַשְׁיָא רוּחוֹת אַרוּחוֹת, קַשְׁיָא עָבִים אַעָבִים! עָבִים אַעָבִים לָא קַשְׁיָא; הָא — בְּחָרְפֵּי, הָא — בְּאַפְלֵי. רוּחוֹת אַרוּחוֹת לָא קַשְׁיָא; הָא — בְּרוּחַ מְצוּיָה, הָא — בְּרוּחַ שֶׁאֵינָהּ מְצוּיָה. רוּחַ שֶׁאֵינָהּ מְצוּיָה חַזְיָא לְבֵי דָרֵי! אֶפְשָׁר בְּנַפְוָותָא. תָּנָא: הֶעָבִים וְהָרוּחוֹת שְׁנִיּוֹת לְמָטָר. הֵיכִי דָּמֵי? אֲמַר עוּלָּא וְאִיתֵימָא רַב יְהוּדָה: דְּבָתַר מִיטְרָא. לְמֵימְרָא דְּמַעַלְיוּתָא הִיא? וְהָכְתִיב °"יִתֵּן ה' אֶת מְטַר אַרְצְךָ אָבָק וְעָפָר". וַאֲמַר עוּלָּא וְאִיתֵימָא רַב יְהוּדָה: זִיקָא דְּבָתַר מִטְרָא! לָא קַשְׁיָא; הָא — דַּאֲתָא נִיחָא, הָא — דַּאֲתָא רַזְיָא. (וְאִי בָּעֵית אֵימָא:) הָא — דְּמַעֲלֶה אָבָק, הָא — דְּלָא מַעֲלֶה אָבָק. וַאֲמַר רַב יְהוּדָה: זִיקָא דְּבָתַר מִיטְרָא — כְּמִיטְרָא. עִיבָא דְּבָתַר מִיטְרָא — כְּמִיטְרָא. שִׁימְשָׁא דְּבָתַר מִיטְרָא — כִּתְרֵי מִטְרֵי. לְמַעוּטֵי מַאי? לְמַעוּטֵי גִּילְהֵי דְּלֵילְיָא, וְשִׁמְשָׁא דְּבֵינֵי קַרְחֵי. אֲמַר רָבָא: מְעַלֵּי תַּלְגָּא לְטוּרֵי כְּחַמְשָׁה מִטְרֵי לְאַרְעָא, שֶׁנֶּאֱמַר: °"כִּי לַשֶּׁלֶג יֹאמַר, 'הֱוֵא אָרֶץ', וְגֶשֶׁם מָטָר, וְגֶשֶׁם מִטְרוֹת עֻזּוֹ". וַאֲמַר רָבָא: תַּלְגָּא — לְטוּרֵי, מִטְרָא רַזְיָא — לְאִילָנֵי, מִטְרָא נִיחָא — לְפֵירֵי, עוּרְפִילָא

(מסורת: זכריה ב; דברים יא; שם כח; איוב לז)

רש"י

דְּלָא מִיעֲצַר. לְעוֹלָם, אֲפִילּוּ בְּאוֹתָן שָׁנִים: אִישְׁתַּבּוּעֵי לָמָּה לֵיהּ. (א) "אִם יִהְיֶה הַשָּׁנִים הָאֵלֶּה טַל וּמָטָר כִּי אִם לְפִי דְבָרִי" — הָא לֹא נֶעֱצַר: אֲפִילּוּ טַל דִּבְרָכָה. שֶׁיַּצְמִיחַ שׁוּם צֶמַח: וְלִיהַדְרֵיהּ לְטַל דִּבְרָכָה. וְלֵימָא: וְאֶתְּנָה טַל וּמָטָר: דְּלָא מִינְכְּרָא מִילְּתָא. דְּהָא טַל הֲוָה מֵעִיקָּרָא, וְלֹא הָיָה אַחְאָב הָרָשָׁע מוֹדֶה בַּחֲזָרָה דְּטַל שֶׁל בְּרָכָה, דְּאִי הֲוָה אוֹמֵר וְאֶתְּנָה טַל וּמָטָר — הָיָה אַחְאָב מְקַנְטְרוֹ וְאוֹמֵר לוֹ שֶׁלֹּא נֶעֱצַר: אֶלָּא דְּמַכְנִיפְנָא לְכוּ מד' רוּחֵי עָלְמָא. לֹא גָּרְסִינַן. דְּהָא "פֵּרַשְׂתִּי אֶתְכֶם" כְּתִיב בִּקְרָא. וְאִיכָּא לְמֵימַר דְּגָרֵס לֵיהּ, וְהָכִי מַשְׁמַע קְרָא: כִּי מד' רוּחוֹת הַשָּׁמַיִם שֶׁפֵּרַשְׂתִּי אֶתְכֶם — מִשָּׁם אֲקַבֶּצְכֶם. וַאֲרִיכוּת לָשׁוֹן בְּעָלְמָא הוּא, דְּלָא כְּתִיב קִיבּוּץ בִּקְרָא: כְּשֵׁם שֶׁא"א לָעוֹלָם בְּלֹא רוּחוֹת. שֶׁלֹּא יִתְקַיֵּים מֵרוֹב הֶבֶל וַחֲמִימוּת: בְּלֹא יִשְׂרָאֵל. שֶׁאֵין הָעוֹלָם מִתְקַיֵּים אֶלָּא בִּשְׁבִיל יִשְׂרָאֵל. וְהָכִי אָמַר קְרָא: כִּי כְּד' רוּחוֹת הַשָּׁמַיִם פֵּרַשְׂתִּי אֶתְכֶם לְרוּחוֹת הָעוֹלָם, כְּדֵי שֶׁיִּתְקַיֵּים. שֶׁנֶּאֱמַר (ירמיהו לג) "אִם לֹא בְרִיתִי יוֹמָם וָלַיְלָה חֻקּוֹת שָׁמַיִם וָאָרֶץ לֹא שָׂמְתִּי": בִּימוֹת הַחַמָּה. מִנִּיסָן עַד הֶחָג: מַשִּׁיב הָרוּחַ אֵין מַחֲזִירִין אוֹתוֹ. דְּבִלָּאו הָכִי לָא מִיעֲצַר: מוֹרִיד הַגֶּשֶׁם מַחֲזִירִין אוֹתוֹ. דְּמִיעֲצַר. וְכֵיוָן דִּבְעָא אַמִּיטְרָא — לֹא הִתְפַּלֵּל תְּפִלָּתוֹ כַּהוֹגֶן, וְחוֹזֵר לְרֹאשׁ הַבְּרָכָה, וְאוֹמְרָהּ בְּלֹא "מוֹרִיד הַגֶּשֶׁם", לְפִי שֶׁהַגְּשָׁמִים בַּקַּיִץ סִימַן קְלָלָה הֵן, מִפְּנֵי הַקָּצִיר: מַעֲבִיר הָרוּחַ. שֶׁלֹּא יְנַשֵּׁב: וּמַפְרִיחַ הַטַּל. שֶׁלֹּא יֵרֵד: אֵין מַחֲזִירִין אוֹתוֹ. דְּלָא מִיעַצְרֵי: בְּעָבִים. מְקַשֵּׁר עָבִים: לְמֵימְרָא דְּלָא מִיעַצְרִי. לְפִיכָךְ לֹא חִיְּיבוּהוּ לְהַזְכִּיר: בְּחָרְפֵּי. עָבִים בְּכִירוֹת, הַבָּאִים לִפְנֵי הַמָּטָר, אֵינָן עֲצוּרוֹת: בְּאַפְלֵי. הַבָּאוֹת מְאוּחָרוֹת לְאַחַר הַמָּטָר, דִּשְׁנִיּוֹת לַמָּטָר הֵן, כִּדְלְקַמָּן. וּבְהָנְהוּ כְּתִיב "וְעָצַר", וְכֵיוָן דְּאֵין כּוּלָּם נֶעֱצָרוֹת — לֹא חִיְּיבוּ לְהַזְכִּיר: שֶׁאֵינָהּ מְצוּיָה. כְּתִיב "וְעָצַר", וְאַפ"ה לֹא חִיְּיבוּהוּ לְהַזְכִּיר, דְּסַגֵּי לֵיהּ בִּמְצוּיָה, רוּחוֹת לָא מָצֵי לְתָרוֹצֵי: הָא בְּחָרְפֵּי הָא בְּאַפְלֵי, דְּרוּחַ בֵּין בְּמָטָר בֵּין בְּלֹא מָטָר לֹא מִיעֲצַר, כְּגוֹן רוּחַ מְצוּיָה: רוּחַ שֶׁאֵינָהּ מְצוּיָה נַמִי חַזְיָא לְבֵי דָרֵי. לַגּוֹרֶן, לִזְרוֹת הַקַּשִּׁין מִן הַתְּבוּאָה, וְנִחַיֵּיב לְהַזְכִּיר: אֶפְשָׁר בְּנַפְוָותָא. וו"ן בְּלַעַ"ז, בְּנָפָה וּכְבָרָה: שְׁנִיּוֹת. כִּמְעַט שֶׁמּוֹעִילוֹת כַּמָּטָר עַצְמוֹ: מַאי הִיא. (ב) אֵי זֶה עָבִים וְרוּחוֹת קָאָמַר דִּשְׁנִיּוֹת לַמָּטָר? אָמַר עוּלָּא וְאִיתֵימָא רַב יְהוּדָה דְּבָתַר מִיטְרָא. עָבִים וְרוּחוֹת שֶׁלְּאַחַר הַמָּטָר: זִיקָא. ל"ג הָכָא: יִתֵּן ה' אֶת מְטַר אַרְצְךָ אָבָק וְעָפָר וגו': זִיקָא דְּבָתַר מִיטְרָא. שֶׁהָרוּחַ מַעֲלֶה אָבָק אַחַר הַגְּשָׁמִים, וְנִדְבָּק בַּתְּבוּאָה: ה"ג: הָא דַּאֲתָא נִיחָא הָא דַּאֲתָא רַזְיָא. כְּשֶׁיֵּרֵד בְּנַחַת אֵינוֹ מַעֲלֶה אָבָק: רַזְיָא. בְּכֹחַ. וְלֹא גָּרְסִינַן וְאִי בָּעֵית אֵימָא הָא וְהָא כו', אֶלָּא ה"ג: הָא דְּמַעֲלֶה אָבָק הָא דְּלֹא מַעֲלֶה אָבָק, וְהַיְינוּ הַךְ: כְּמִיטְרָא. שְׁנִיּוֹת לַמָּטָר, כִּדְקָתָנֵי בַּתּוֹסֶפְתָּא: לְמַעוּטֵי מַאי. מֵאַחַר דְּכוּלְּהוּ כְּמִיטְרָא, מַאי קָמְמַעֲטִינַן דַּהֲוֵי בַּתְרֵיהּ, וְלָא הָוֵי כְּמִיטְרָא? גִּילְהֵי דְּלֵילְיָא. אִישְׁלוּשְׁטר"א בְּלַעַ"ז. בְּגִילְהֵי הֲוָה קָאֵי בְּמַסֶּ' (פסחים דף יג.), וְרוֹב גִּילְהֵי בְּלֵילְיָא שְׁכִיחַ: וּבְיוֹמָא שִׁמְשָׁא דְּבֵינֵי קַרְחֵי. שֶׁבֵּין הֶעָבִים, שֶׁנִּרְאֶה בְּמָקוֹם אֶחָד אוֹרָה וּבְמָקוֹם אַחֵר מְעוּנָּן, כְּקֵרֵחַ שֶׁיֵּשׁ לוֹ שְׂעָרוֹת בְּמָקוֹם אֶחָד וְקָרְחָה בְּמָקוֹם אַחֵר: מְעַלֵּי תַּלְגָּא לְטוּרֵי. וְכ"ש לְבִקְעָה, אֶלָּא הָרִים אֵין לָהֶם גְּשָׁמִים אֶלָּא שֶׁלֶג, שֶׁהַגְּשָׁמִים יוֹרְדִין לְמַטָּה וְאֵין הָהָר שׁוֹתֶה מֵהֶן. וְעוֹד, שֶׁלֶג שֶׁבָּעֲמָקִים נָמֵס וְהוֹלֵךְ מִפְּנֵי הַחוֹם שֶׁשּׁוֹלֵט שָׁם — כְּמַיִם הוּא, אֲבָל בֶּהָרִים קָרוּי שֶׁלֶג: כְּחַמְשָׁה מִטְרֵי לְאַרְעָא. דְּהָכִי מַשְׁמַע קְרָא "כִּי לַשֶּׁלֶג יֹאמַר הֱוֵא אָרֶץ", כְּשֶׁיֹּאמַר לַשֶּׁלֶג הֱוֵה אָרֶץ — הֲרֵי הוּא כְּגֶשֶׁם מָטָר וְגֶשֶׁם מִטְרוֹת, וַהֲרֵי יֵשׁ כָּאן חֲמִשָּׁה: מִטְרָא נִיחָא. שֶׁיּוֹרֵד בְּנַחַת יָפֶה לְפֵירוֹת הַתְּבוּאָה: עוּרְפִילָא

תוספות

בימות החמה אמר משיב הרוח אין מחזירין אותו מוריד הגשם מחזירין אותו. אבל אם דילג, שלא אמר לא גשם ולא טל — אין מחזירין. ובימות הגשמים, לא אמר "משיב הרוח" — אין מחזירין אותו, לא אמר "מוריד הגשם" — מחזירין אותו. אבל, אם אמר "מוריד הטל" בימות הגשמים — אין מחזירין, ואם ספק אם הזכיר אם לאו, אם אינו זכור(ג) שלא אמר שום דבר בימות הגשמים — כל ל' יום חזקה מה שהוא למוד הוא אומר, ומחזירין מספק כל ל' יום. וכן "זכרנו" ו"מי כמוך", "וכתוב לחיים" שאומרים מן הכסה עד יום הכפורים — מספק מחזירין. ירושלמי בשם רבי חנינא: היה שייך בגשם והזכיר טל — אין מחזירין אותו, בטל והזכיר של גשמים — מחזירין אותו. והתניא: בטל וברוחות לא חייבו חכמים להזכיר, ואם בא להזכיר מזכיר! לא דמי ההוא דמצלי ומיקל להוא דלא מצלי ולא מיקל. ומפרש רבינו נתנאל(ד): טוב כשאינו מזכיר לא גשם ולא טל מכשהוא מזכיר גשם, לפי שהגשמים סימן קללה בימות החמה. היה שייך בטל לא הזכיר לא טל ולא גשם — אין מחזירין אותו. והדין להפך ב"מוריד הגשם", דאמר בירושלמי: בגשם והזכיר של טל — אין מחזירין אותו. והתניא: אם לא שאל בברכת השנים, או שלא אמר גבורות גשמים מחזירין! בההוא דלא הזכיר כלל לא טל ולא מטר. ומשם הר"ס: שאין לומר בימות החמה "משיב הרוח" דהא אמר רבי חנינא: בימות החמה אמר "משיב הרוח" — אין מחזירין אותו, מכלל דלכתחילה אין לאומרו. ומשום הכי אמר הר"י בשם א"ז: לעולם, בין בימות החמה בין בימות הגשמים "מוריד הטל". דלעולם לא אתי לידי ספק אמר ספק לא אמר. והיכא דלא מזכיר בגבורות — מזכיר בשומע תפלה. דהכי קאמר בירושלמי: ומה שאלה שהיא מדוחק — אומר בש"ת, הזכרה שהיא מרווח — לא כ"ש! וכי היכי דשואלין בש"ת — הוא מזכיר בש"ת. ואפילו (ה) הזכיר קודם שומע תפלה — אינו אומר עד שיגיע לש"ת. והיכא דלא אמר בשומע תפלה, אי נזכר קודם שעקר רגליו — חוזר לש"ת. ואי לא — חוזר לראש, בין לא אמר "מוריד הגשם" ובין לא אמר "ותן טל ומטר" (ומחזירין). וכן הפסק. והני מילי — ביחיד, אבל שליח צבור — פסק רבינו יהודה דאין מחזירין, לפי דאין מחזירין שליח צבור אלא משום ג' דברים: מתחיית המתים, ומבונה ירושלים, ומברכת ולמלשינים, משום דנראה ככופר. שמעתי מפי רבי שלמה: לא דמי (ו) מצלי ומיקל למאן דלא מצלי ולא מיקל, פירוש: מיקל — כמו מקלל. כלומר: שאין מחזירין אם לא אמר "ותן טל ומטר":

הא בחרפי. פי': הא דאמר נעצרים — היינו בחריפי, כלומר בפירות המתבכרות וכו'. אבל באפלי, במאוחרות — לא מיעצרי:

רוחות ארוחות לא קשיא הא ברוח וכו'. וה"ה דמצי לשנויי הא בחריפי הא באפלי, אלא שפיר קא משני ליה: הא ברוח מצויה וכו':

שניות למטר. שניות במעלה, כדאמרי אינשי משנה למלך:

הא דאתא ניחא. פי': כשיורדות בנחת — חשובה, כאן ברזיא — כלומר בחוזק, ואז אינה טובה:

גילהי דליליא. פי': זריחת הלילה, שקורין לניסו"ר בלע"ז:

ושמשא דביני קרחי. פי': כמו דבר קרחה, שמכאן ומכאן יורדין הגשמים והשמש זורח באמצע, זה דשמש לא מעלי:

עורפילא

רבינו חננאל

דלא מיעצרי. וכן הרוחות לא מיעצרי. דכתיב כי כארבע רוחות השמים פרשתי אתכם. א"ר חנינא בימות החמה אמר משיב הרוח אין מחזירין אותו. אמר מוריד הגשם מחזירין אותו בימות הגשמים לא אמר משיב הרוח אין מחזירין אותו. לא אמר מוריד הגשם מחזירין אותו ולא עוד אלא אפילו אמר מעביר הרוח ומפריח הטל אין מחזירין אותו לפי שאינן נעצרין. תנא בעבים וברוחות לא חיבו חכמים להזכיר. ואם בא להזכיר מזכיר. איני והא תני רב יוסף ועצר את השמים מן העבים ומן הרוחות ושנינן [עבים אעבים ל"ק] חרפי אין נעצרים. אפלי נעצרים משום דמעלי כדבעינן למימר קמן. רוחות ארוחות נמי [ל"ק] רוח מצויה לא מיעצרא. רוח גדולה שאינה מצויה בכל עת נעצרת. ולמה אין מזכירין. וצריכין אותה לזרות בגרנות. ושנינן אפשר בנפוותא פי' יכולין להבר בלא רוח לכבור בכברה ולהסיר התבן מן הבר. תנא עבים ורוחות שניות למטר. פי' מיטרא ובתריה זיקא בניחותא או עיבא מעלי כאילו מטרא תניינא. שמשא בתר מטרא כתרי מטרי והני מילי שימשי בגלויא אבל גלוהי דליליא ושמשי דביני קרחי לא השלג מועיל לארץ מה' מטרות שנאמר כי לשלג יאמר הוי ארץ. וגשם א' מטר ב' וגשם ג' מטרות ב' הרי כאן חמשה. השלג מועיל להרים. המטר הגדול לאילנות מטר בניחותא

רבינו גרשום

בתוך בית סאה חורשין כל השדה כולה בשבילן ערב שביעית עד ר"ה אע"ג דשאר שדות אין חורשין לפני שביעית שלשים יום זה חורשין דהואיל דילדות הן אם אין חורשין סביבן מפסידין: וניסוך המים כל שבעה: ר"י משום ר' יהושע יו"ט האחרון של חג וכו' הי רבי יהושע אילימא ר' יהושע דמתניתין דאמר ביו"ט האחרון הוא מזכי' (מיו"ט האחרון מזכיר) דראשון נמי המתפלל יוצר אור מזכיר ואלו הכא תני הראשון אינו מזכיר האמר משעת הנחתו דהיינו בשביעי והכא קתני יו"ט האחרון דהיינו בשמיני. ותו הא דתניא במכילתא אחריתי ר' יהודה [אומר] משום בן בתירה העובר לפני התיבה ביו"ט האחרון [אחרון] מזכיר ראשון אינו מזכיר: אלא אמר רב נחמן בר יצחק תהא תרווייהו הא דבעית הי ר' יהושע

והא דבעית הי בן בתירה ר' יהושע בן בתירה. זימנין קרי ליה בשמיה דאבוה [ר"ל בן בתירה] וזימנין קרי ליה בשמיה דידיה ר' יהושע. מקמי דליסמכיה לא הוי חשוב וקרי ליה משמיה דאבוה: בטל וברוחות לא חייבו. משיב הרוח ומוריד הטל: מ"ט לא חייבו חכמים להזכיר דלא מיעצרי כלומר שמעולם ירד טל ומנשב רוח ולא צדיכי (שאין ברכה מ"ט דלא מיעצר כלומר שלעולם יורד ואין בו) ברכה: ה"ק ליה אפי' טל שיורד לברכה לא ליהוי: וליהדריה נמי לטל דברכה כלומר אמאי לא אמר ליה ואתנה מטר וטל על פני האדמה: משום דלא מינכרא: דכיון דבכל יומא הוי נחית טל שאינו של ברכה כי א"ל האידנא נחית טל דברכה לא מינכר בין טל דעד השתא [ר"ל דעד השתא נמי] הוי נחית טל: דמכניפנא לכו והכי משמע כי מארבע רוחות אשר פרשתי אתכם אקבץ אתכם כשם שאי אפשר לעולם בלא רוח שבכל יום משיב הרוח: אמר משיב הרוח אין מחזירין אותו. אע"ג דלא זמניה הוא: אמר מעביר הרוח אין בכך כלום ואפ"ה לא מיעצר: בעבים וברוחות משיב הרוח ומביא עבים: למימרא דלא מיעצרי שתדיר באין עבים ומנשב הרוח ואין בהם לא קללה ולא ברכה. בעבים וברוחות הכתוב מדבר. אלמא דאית בהו ברכה וקללה ואמאי אמרת לא חיובו חכמים להזכיר: קשיא עבים אעבים כו' חרפי שלפני המטר אין בהן משום ברכה. אפלי שלאחר המטר יש בהן משום ברכה. רוח מצויה. שאינה מצויה אינה ברכה: מיבעי לבי דרי. וכיון שצריכין הן אלמא דמיעצרי דיש בהן משום ברכה: אפשר בנפוותא. וכיון שאין צריכין אין בהן משום ברכה ולא מיעצרי: שניות למטר כלומר טובים הם כמטר כמו שני למלך: דאתיא ניחא הוה שני למטר כמטר: דאתיא רזיא כתיב ביה יתן ה' מטר ארצך אבק וגו': גלוהי דליליא ברק: שמשא דביני קרחי שזורח כאן ואין זורח כאן: מעלי חד תלגא לטורי להכי אמר לטורי שתדיר השלג בהרים: גשם מטר וגשם מטרות הרי ה': אמר רבא תלגא לטורי מעלי עורפילא

הגהות הב"ח

(א) רש"י ד"ה אישתבועי למה ליה דקאמר אם יהיה: (ב) ד"ה מאי היא כצ"ל ... עבים: (ג) תוס' ד"ה בימות כו' אם אינו זכור שאמר שום דבר כו' כל"ל ותיבת שלא נמחק: (ד) בא"ד ומפרש רבינו נתנאל יותר טוב כשאינו מזכיר כו' בימות החמה הלכך היה שייך בטל ולא הזכיר כו' גבורות גשמים בתחיית המתים מחזירין כו' ולא מטר (ומשם הר"ס) שאין לומר כו' לכתחלה אין לאומרו: (ה) בא"ד הוא מזכיר בש"ת ואפילו נזכר קודם ש"ת: (ו) בא"ד מפי ר' שלמה לא דמי ההוא דמצלי ומיקל למאן:

[בע"י ליתא]

ע"ז י: ע"ש

עורפילא אפילו לפרצידא דתותי קלא מהניא ליה. מאי עורפילא? עורו פילי. ואמר רבא: האי צורבא מרבנן דמי לפרצידא דתותי קלא, דכיון דנבט — נבט. ואמר רבא: האי צורבא מרבנן דרתח — אורייתא הוא דקא מרתחא ליה, שנאמר °"הלא כה דברי כאש נאם ה'". ואמר רב אשי: *כל ת"ח שאינו קשה כברזל — אינו ת"ח, שנא' °"וכפטיש יפוצץ סלע". א"ל רבי אבא לרב אשי: אתון מהתם מתניתו לה, אנן מהכא מתנינן לה — דכתיב °"ארץ אשר אבניה ברזל". אל תקרי "אבניה" אלא "בוניה". אמר רבינא: אפ"ה, מיבעי ליה לאיניש למילף נפשיה בניחותא, שנאמר °"והסר כעס מלבך" וגו'. א"ר שמואל בר נחמני אמר רבי יונתן: שלשה שאלו שלא כהוגן. לשנים *השיבוהו כהוגן, לאחד השיבוהו שלא כהוגן. ואלו הן: אליעזר עבד אברהם, ושאול בן קיש, ויפתח הגלעדי. אליעזר עבד אברהם — דכתיב (א) °"והיה הנערה אשר אומר אליה הטי נא כדך" וגו'. יכול אפי' חיגרת, אפי' סומא — השיבו כהוגן, ונזדמנה לו רבקה. שאול בן קיש — דכתיב °"והיה האיש אשר יכנו, יעשרנו המלך עושר גדול ואת בתו יתן לו". יכול אפי' עבד, אפילו ממזר — השיבו כהוגן, ונזדמן לו דוד. יפתח הגלעדי — דכתיב °"והיה היוצא אשר יצא מדלתי ביתי" וגו'. יכול אפילו דבר טמא — השיבו שלא כהוגן — נזדמנה לו בתו. והיינו דקאמר להו נביא לישראל °"הצרי אין בגלעד? אם רופא אין שם?". וכתיב °"אשר לא צויתי, ולא דברתי, ולא עלתה על לבי". "אשר לא צויתי" — זה בנו של מישע מלך מואב, שנאמר *°"ויקח את בנו הבכור אשר ימלך תחתיו ויעלהו עולה". "ולא דברתי"(ב) — זה יפתח. "ולא עלתה על לבי" — זה יצחק בן אברהם. אמר רבי ברכיה: אף כנסת ישראל שאלה שלא כהוגן, והקב"ה השיבה כהוגן, שנא' °"ונדעה, נרדפה לדעת את ה'. כשחר נכון מוצאו, ויבוא כגשם לנו". אמר לה הקב"ה: בתי, את שואלת דבר שפעמים מתבקש ופעמים אינו מתבקש. אבל אני אהיה לך דבר המתבקש לעולם, שנאמר °"אהיה כטל לישראל". ועוד שאלה שלא כהוגן. אמרה לפניו: רבש"ע °"שימני כחותם על לבך כחותם על זרועך". א"ל הקב"ה: בתי, את שואלת דבר שפעמים נראה ופעמים אינו נראה. אבל אני אעשה לך דבר שנראה לעולם, שנאמר °"הן על כפים חקותיך". § "אין שואלין את הגשמים" כו'. § סברוה: שאלה והזכרה חדא מילתא היא. מאן תנא? אמר רבא: ר' יהושע היא, דאמר: *"משעת הנחתו". א"ל אביי: אפילו תימא רבי אליעזר. שאלה לחוד והזכרה לחוד. ואיכא דאמרי: לימא רבי

(ירמיהו כג; שם; דברים ח; קהלת יא; בראשית כד; ש"א יז; שופטים יא; ירמיהו ח; שם יט; מ"ב ג; הושע ו; שם יד; שיר ח; ישעיהו מט)

רש"י

עורפילא. גשמים דקים, כך שמן כדלקמן: אפי' לפרצידא דתותי קלא. הגרעין שתחת גושה של קרקע: מהניא. שמתחיל לבלבן ולעלות מיד: עורו פילי. שפותח סדקי הארץ. ל"א: שמגדלת ומצמחת הגרעינין העומדין בסדקי הקרקע: צורבא מרבנן. בחור חריף. כמו ביעי דצריבן במסכת ביצה (דף ז.). תלמיד חכם זקן לא קרי צורבא, אלא "ההוא מרבנן" קרי ליה: כיון דנבט נבט. שמתחיל לבלבן ולעלות — עולה למעלה. כך תלמיד חכם, כיון שיצא שמו — הולך וגדל למעלה: אורייתא מרתחא ליה. שיש לו רוחב לב מתוך תורתו, ומשים ללבו יותר משאר בני אדם. וקמ"ל דחייבין לדונו לכף זכות: כאש. שמחמם כל גופו: בוניה. תלמידי חכמים מקיימי עולם בבנייניהו: ברזל. קפדנים וקשים כברזל: שלשה שאלו כו'. משום דרבי ברכיה מיירי בגשמים לקמן, נקט לה: ובנות אנשי העיר יוצאות והיה הנערה. משמע: הנערה היוצאה תחילה מן העיר, ויאמר לה השקיני, (ג) לה היה מנחש: אפי' חיגרת אפי' סומא. לפי שלא פירש בשאילתו, ואפשר שתהיה בעלת מום, ולא יבין בה אליעזר ויקחנה: (אלא) השיבוהו כהוגן. וזימנו לו רבקה: דבר טמא. כלב או חזיר: והיינו דאמר להו נביא כו'. מדגלי ביה קרא ואמר "הצרי אין בגלעד" [אלמא דלא הוי ניחא קמי שמיא, כדאמרינן "הצרי אין בגלעד"] פנחס היה שם, והיה יכול להתיר נדרו. אלא שלא רצה יפתח לילך אצלו(ד), והוא לא רצה לבוא אצל יפתח, בבראשית רבה*: וכתיב אשר לא צויתי. בירמיה כתיב בפרשת בקבוק: "ובנו את במות (*התופת אשר בגיא בן הנם) לשרוף את (בנותיהם ואת) בניהם באש אשר לא [צויתי ולא] דברתי ולא עלתה על לבי". שלא תאמרו: הלא צוה כמו כן הקב"ה ליפתח ומישע ואברהם, כי מעולם לא צויתי למישע לשרוף את בנו באש, דכתיב "ויקח את בנו הבכור אשר ימלך תחתיו ויעלהו עולה על החומה", ולשמים נתכוון, כסבור היה לרצות להקב"ה. והאי דכתיב* "על שרפו עצמות מלך אדום לשיד" — מילתא אחריתא הוא. ו"לא דברתי" — ליפתח(ה), "מימים ימימה ותהי חק בישראל". ובתרגום מזכיר פנחס לגנאי ויפתח לגנאי, אלמא: לא היה הקב"ה רוצה בבתו, שהרי מזכירם לגנאי, לפי שלא הלכו זה אצל זה לבטל הנדר. ה"ג: "ולא עלתה על לבי" — זה יצחק בן אברהם. כלומר, שאע"פ שצויתי לו — מעולם לא עלתה על לבי לשחוט בנו, אלא לנסותו, מפני קטיגורו היינו שטן. כדאמר בסנהדרין ב"הנחנקין" (דף פט:): "ויהי אחר הדברים האלה" — אחר דבריו של שטן וכו'. ואית דלא גרסינן האי "ולא עלתה על לבי", *דטעי בקרא אחרינא, דלא כתב אלא "אשר לא צויתי ולא דברתי" (ירמיהו ז פסוק כא), ובפרשת בקבוק כתיב כל הני תלתא "אשר לא צויתי ולא דברתי ולא עלתה על לבי". בתנחומא: "אשר לא צויתי" — זו בתו של יפתח. אע"פ שצויתי לו תורה ומצות — מצוה זו לא צויתי עליו. "ולא דברתי" — זה בנו של מישע מלך מואב. והלא מישע נכרי הוא, ולא חולין הוא לי לדבר עמו אפילו דיבור בעלמא? ובאגדה קא חשיב כלב בהדייהו, "אשר יכה את קרית ספר ולכדה" וגו'. ורבי יונתן דלא חשיב ליה, דבגמרא פשיט ליה להאי קרא בהלכות שנשתכחו בימי אבלו של משה, כדאמרינן בתמורה (דף טז.), ואין לחוש שתשרה רוח הקודש על עבד ועל ממזר, כדאמרינן בנדרים (דף לח.): שאין שכינה שורה כו'. מפי רבי. וגדעון ששאל למנוע טל מעל הארץ ובגיזה לבדה יהיה — אין זה שלא כהוגן, ומה תקלה יש אם יחסר העולם טל לילה אחת לבדה? מפי רבי: ויבוא כגשם לנו. פעמים אינו מתבקש, שהוא סימן קללה בקיץ:(ו) דבר המתבקש לעולם. טל אפילו בימות החמה: פעמים נראה. כשהוא ערום נראה זרועו וכנגד לבו ואינו נראה כשהוא לבוש, והכף נראית כל שעה שהיד נראית לעינים. וי"ל: על כפים(ז) — על השמים — צורת אדם שהוא בכסא, וכן "נשא לבבנו אל כפים" (איכה ג), מפי רבי:(ח) ה"ג: סברוה שאלה והזכרה חדא מילתא היא. כלומר הא דקתני "אין שואלין את הגשמים" היינו "אין מזכירין את הגשמים": ומאן תנא. דקאמר סמוך לימות הגשמים מזכירין אבל לא קודם לכן: רבי יהושע היא. דקאמר משעת הנחת לולב הוא מזכיר, דהיינו יום שמיני וזהו סמוך לגשמים, דמן החג ואילך הוא זמן גשמים:

[עי' תוספות סוכה נב. ד"ה אם ברזל] [נ"ל השיבום יעב"ץ] [פ' חיי שרה] נ"ל הבעל [סנהדרין לט:] [עמוס ב] [לעיל ב:] [נ"ל משום דטעו וכ"ה ברש"י שבע"י]

תוספות

עורפילא. היינו גשם דק. אפילו לפרצידא דתותי קלא מהניא. פי' פרצידא — זו גרעין שהוא מתחת האבן, היינו כמו חטה שמתחת הקרקע: מאי עורפילא עורו פילי. פי': מעוררן ומצמיחן. פילי — פי': אותן העומדים בסדקי הארץ:

שלשה שאלו שלא כהוגן. אליעזר שאול ויפתח. וא"ת: אמאי לא חשיב כלב בן יפונה, שאמר "אשר יכה את קרית ספר ולכדה ונתתי לו את עכסה בתי לאשה", אמאי לא פריך כמו הכא: יכול ממזר או עבד! וי"ל: דהא דקאמר כלב שיתן לו(ט) הקב"ה כל מי שיכול לחזור אותן הלכות ששכחו בימי אבלו של משה — אתן לו עכסה בתי. וי"מ דלכך נקראת *עכסה, שכל הרואה אותה כועס על אשתו, וזהו ודאי משום צניעות יתירה דקא חזו בה. והיה סומך דזכותה וזכות דידיה מסייע, דלא מזווגין לה אלא כפי מעשיה, כדאיתא בסוטה (דף ב.) דאין מזווגין וכו': יכול אפי' חיגרת או סומא. תימה: אמאי לא נקט הכא גבי אליעזר עבד אברהם כמו דקאמר גבי שאול בסמוך: יכול אפי' ממזרת או שפחה וכו'. ואמר רש"י: משום דגבי אליעזר לא שייך עדיין ממזרת, דהא לא נתנה תורה. אי נמי: דגבי אשה לא דייק עלמא אלא ליופי. וא"ת: היכי קאמר דשאל אליעזר שלא כהוגן? והא לא אמר אלא "אשר אומר אליה הטי נא כדך" ואם יראה שתהא חיגרת או סומא — לא יאמר לה! וי"ל, דה"פ: יכול אפילו חיגרת ואפילו סומא, יכול אפי' חיגרת שיהיה לה אפילו רגל של עץ והוא לא יהא רואה, או סומא כגון שיש לה עינים יפים ואינה רואה כלל: והיינו דקאמר להו נביא לישראל הצרי אין בגלעד אם רופא אין שם. כלומר, להתיר נדרו ליפתח. והא הוה פנחס, ואמאי לא הלך יפתח אצלו להתיר נדרו? אלא מתוך גסות רוחו אמר: לא אלך אצלו, שאני שופט ונגיד. ופנחס אמר: ליתי גבאי, דאנא נביא ועל ידי תהא פטורה, שהייתי(י) שורה ומתיר הנדר ופוטר אותה. ולבסוף נענשו שניהם; יפתח נענש שנפלו אבריו קודם מיתה, כדכתיב "ויקבר בערי גלעד" ופנחס נענש דכתיב "לפנים היה ה' עמו"*:

[כל זה איתא במ"ר סוף סדר בחקותי]

רבינו חננאל

לפירות: עורו פילי. פי' הטפה היורדת בכח מערערת פילא כמו פילחא כדכתיב כמו פולח ובוקע בארץ. אפי' לפרצידא דתותי קלא. פי' שתחת האבן צומח *) וכן ת"ח דומה לפרי תחת האבן (ששואב שואב) וכיון שצומח [צומח] בבת אחת. צורבא מרבנן דמרתח אורייתא מרתחא ליה שנאמר הלא כה דברי כאש: אמר רב שמואל בר נחמני א"ר יונתן ג' שאלו שלא כהוגן אליעזר שאול ויפתח. ומצינו בבראשית רבה ד' הן ששאלו שלא כהוגן אליעזר שאול ויפתח וכלב ופשטיה כיון דשאול וכלב שוין דתרווייהו נתינת [בתם חשיב] להו כאחד. לפיכך תני הכא שלשה: אין שואלין הגשמים כיון ששנינו כאן שאילת הגשמים סמוך לגשמים היא הוצרכנו לומר סברוה שאלה והזכרה ביום אחד הן הניחא לר' יהושע דאמר משעת הנחתו מזכיר ומיד שואל כי אין שאלה אלא בתפלת החול בי"ח בברכת השנים אלא לר' אליעזר קשיא ושנינן הזכרה לחוד ושאלה לחוד לזמן אחר ולאו כי הדדי:

*) עי' מ"ש בפירוש רבינו לקמן ריש פ"ג וצ"ע כאן.

רבינו גרשום

עורפילא. מיטרא דקה. פרצידא גרגר: דתותי קלא. תחת קרקע קשה: עורו פילי התעוררו בקעים כלומר שמכנים המטר דקה בבקעים ומוציא התבואה שבהם: כיון דנבט שבקע ויוצא אף ת"ח כיון שיוצא שמו בעולם שוב הולך וגדול בכל שעה: שאינו קשה כברזל. שאינו קשה לרצות. הצרי אין בגלעד כלומר שהיה יכול לילך אצל אליהו ומתיר לו נדרו: על לבי זה יצחק שלא היה בלבו של הקב"ה שישחטהו אלא בפה כדי לנסותו: על כפים חקותיך. וידים נראין לעולם: אין שואלין את הגשמים. ותן טל ומטר: ר' יהודה אמר האחרון מזכיר. גבורת גשמים וה"ה דשואלין ותן טל ומטר: מאן תנא דהתחלת שאלה והזכרה מצי למיהוי ביום אחד: דאמר משעת הנחתו דהיינו בשביעי מתחילין להזכיר שהוא חולו של מועד מצי להתחיל לשאול בברכת השנים שהרי מתפללין אתה חונן. דאי ר' אליעזר כיון דאמר בראשון מתחיל להזכיר לא מצי למיהוי התחלת הזכרה והתחלת שאלה ביום אחד דביו"ט ראשון ליכא שאלה שהרי אין מתפללין בו אתה חונן ולא מצי למישאל אלא בברכת השנים אפי' תימא דקתני אין שואלין ר' אליעזר היא ולא תימא שאלה והזכרה כהדדי.

הגהות הב"ח

(א) גמ' אליעזר עבד אברהם דכתיב ובנות אנשי העיר יוצאות וגו' והיה הנערה אשר: (ב) שם ולא דברתי זו בתו של יפתח:

גליון הש"ס

גמ' ר"י היא דאמר משעת הנחתו. תמוה לי אמאי נקט ר"י דברייתא ולא נקט ר"י דמתני' מיו"ט האחרון אח"כ מצאתי בעז"ה בספר המכריע לריא"ז דמחק זה וכצ"ל סתם מני ר"י היא:

(ג) רש"י ד"ה ובנות כו' השקיני בה היה מנחש: (ד) ד"ה והיינו כו' יפתח לילך אצלו מתוך גסות רוחו אמר לא אלך אצלו שאני שופט ונגיד ופנחס לא היה רוצה לבא אצל יפתח שהוא נביא בב"ר: (ה) ד"ה וכתיב כו' ולא דברתי ליפתח שנאמר מימים ימימה כו' ואית דלא גרסי האי: (ו) ד"ה ויבוא כו' קללה בקיץ הס"ד ואח"כ מה"ד טל דבר המתבקש לעולם אפילו בימות: (ז) ד"ה פעמים כו' ויש לומר על כפים השמים כו' כצ"ל ותיבת על נמחק: (ח) בא"ד מפי רבי הס"ד ואח"כ מה"ד שאלה והזכרה כו' ותיבות ה"ג סברוה נמחק ונ"ב זהו פי' למאי דקאמר שאלה וכו': (ט) תום' ד"ה שלשה וכו' שיתן לו בתו הכי קאמר כל מי וכו': (י) שם ד"ה והיינו וכו' שהייתי מורה ומתיר:

יא א מיי' פ"ב מהל' תפלה הל' יז סמג עשין יט טוש"ע א"ח סי' קיז סעיף א:

תורה אור

רַבִּי יְהוֹשֻׁעַ הִיא, דְּאָמַר: מִשְּׁעַת הֲנָחָתוֹ? אָמַר רָבָא: אֲפִילּוּ תֵּימָא רַבִּי אֱלִיעֶזֶר, שְׁאֵלָה לְחוּד וְהַזְכָּרָה לְחוּד. § "רַבִּי יְהוּדָה אוֹמֵר: הָעוֹבֵר לִפְנֵי הַתֵּיבָה" כו'. § וּרְמִינְהוּ: *עַד מָתַי שׁוֹאֲלִין אֶת הַגְּשָׁמִים? (א) ר' יְהוּדָה אוֹמֵר: עַד שֶׁיַּעֲבוֹר הַפֶּסַח. ר' מֵאִיר אוֹמֵר: עַד שֶׁיַּעֲבוֹר נִיסָן! אָמַר רַב חִסְדָּא: לָא קַשְׁיָא, כָּאן – לִשְׁאוֹל. כָּאן – לְהַזְכִּיר. מִישְׁאַל – שָׁאֵיל וְאָזֵיל, לְהַזְכִּיר – בְּיו"ט הָרִאשׁוֹן פָּסֵיק. אָמַר עוּלָּא: הָא דְּרַב חִסְדָּא קַשְׁיָא *°"כַּחוֹמֶץ לַשִּׁינַּיִם וְכֶעָשָׁן לָעֵינַיִם". וּמַה בְּמָקוֹם שֶׁאֵינוֹ שׁוֹאֵל – מַזְכִּיר, בְּמָקוֹם שֶׁשּׁוֹאֵל – אֵינוֹ דִּין שֶׁיְּהֵא מַזְכִּיר! אֶלָּא אָמַר עוּלָּא: תְּרֵי תַּנָּאֵי אַלִּיבָּא דְּר' יְהוּדָה. רַב יוֹסֵף אָמַר: מַאי "עַד שֶׁיַּעֲבוֹר הַפֶּסַח"? עַד שֶׁיַּעֲבוֹר שְׁלִיחַ צִבּוּר רִאשׁוֹן הַיּוֹרֵד בְּיו"ט רִאשׁוֹן שֶׁל פֶּסַח. א"ל אַבַּיֵי: שְׁאֵלָה בְּיו"ט מִי אִיכָּא? א"ל: אִין, שׁוֹאֵל מְתוּרְגְּמָן. וְכִי מְתוּרְגְּמָן שׁוֹאֵל דָּבָר שֶׁאֵינוֹ צָרִיךְ לַצִּבּוּר? אֶלָּא, מְחַוַּורְתָּא כִּדְעוּלָּא. רַבָּה אָמַר: מַאי "עַד שֶׁיַּעֲבוֹר הַפֶּסַח"? עַד שֶׁיַּעֲבוֹר זְמַן שְׁחִיטַת הַפֶּסַח. וְכִתְחִילָּתוֹ, כֵּן סוֹפוֹ. מַה תְּחִילָּתוֹ מַזְכִּיר אע"פ שֶׁאֵינוֹ שׁוֹאֵל – אַף סוֹפוֹ מַזְכִּיר אע"פ שֶׁאֵינוֹ שׁוֹאֵל. א"ל אַבַּיֵי: בִּשְׁלָמָא תְּחִילָּתוֹ מַזְכִּיר – (ב) הַזְכָּרָה נַמִי רִיצּוּי שְׁאֵלָה הִיא. אֶלָּא סוֹפוֹ מַאי רִיצּוּי שְׁאֵלָה אִיכָּא? אֶלָּא מְחַוַּורְתָּא כִּדְעוּלָּא. *)א"ר אַסִי א"ר יוֹחָנָן: הֲלָכָה כְּר' יְהוּדָה. א"ל ר' זֵירָא לְר' אַסִי: וּמִי אָמַר רַבִּי יוֹחָנָן הָכִי? וְהָתְנַן: *בִּשְׁלֹשָׁה בְּמַרְחֶשְׁוָון שׁוֹאֲלִין אֶת הַגְּשָׁמִים. רַבָּן גַּמְלִיאֵל אוֹמֵר: בְּשִׁבְעָה בּוֹ. *וְא"ר אֶלְעָזָר: *אהֲלָכָה כְּרַבָּן גַּמְלִיאֵל! א"ל: **)גַּבְרָא אַגַּבְרָא קָא רָמֵית?! אִיבָּעֵית אֵימָא: לָא קַשְׁיָא. כָּאן – לִשְׁאוֹל. כָּאן – לְהַזְכִּיר. וְהָאָמַר ר' יוֹחָנָן: בְּמָקוֹם שֶׁשּׁוֹאֵל מַזְכִּיר! הַהוּא לְהַפְסָקָה אִיתְּמַר. וְהָאָמַר ר' יוֹחָנָן: הִתְחִיל לְהַזְכִּיר – מַתְחִיל לִשְׁאוֹל. פָּסַק מִלִּשְׁאוֹל – פּוֹסֵק מִלְּהַזְכִּיר! אֶלָּא, לָא קַשְׁיָא. *הָא – לָן. הָא – לְהוּ. מַאי שְׁנָא לְדִידַן – דְּאִית לָן פֵּירֵי בְּדַבְרָא, לְדִידְהוּ נַמִי אִית לְהוּ עוֹלֵי רְגָלִים! כִּי קא"ר יוֹחָנָן, בִּזְמַן שֶׁאֵין בֵּית הַמִּקְדָּשׁ קַיָּים. הַשְׁתָּא דְּאָתֵית לְהָכִי, הָא וְהָא לְדִידְהוּ, וְלָא קַשְׁיָא. כָּאן – בִּזְמַן שֶׁבֵּית הַמִּקְדָּשׁ קַיָּים. °כָּאן – בִּזְמַן שֶׁאֵין בֵּית הַמִּקְדָּשׁ קַיָּים. וַאֲנַן דְּאִית לָן תְּרֵי יוֹמֵי, הֵיכִי עָבְדִינַן? אָמַר רַב: מַתְחִיל בְּמוּסָפִין, וּפוֹסֵק בְּמִנְחָה, עַרְבִית, וְשַׁחֲרִית, וְחוֹזֵר בְּמוּסָפִין. אָמַר לְהוּ שְׁמוּאֵל: פּוּקוּ וְאִמְרוּ לֵיהּ לְאַבָּא: אַחַר שֶׁעֲשִׂיתוֹ קוֹדֶשׁ, תַּעֲשֵׂהוּ חוֹל? אֶלָּא אָמַר שְׁמוּאֵל: מַתְחִיל בְּמוּסָפִין וּבְמִנְחָה, וּפוֹסֵק עַרְבִית וְשַׁחֲרִית, וְחוֹזֵר וּמַתְחִיל בְּמוּסָפִין.

רָבָא

*) גי' הרא"ש א"ר יוסי בר חנינא הלכה כו' **) [ב"ק מג: סנהדרין כה. ל: חולין נב:]

(משלי י)

הָכִי גָּרְסִינַן: וְאִיכָּא דְּאָמְרִי לֵימָא ר' יְהוֹשֻׁעַ הִיא אֲפִי' תֵּימָא רַבִּי אֱלִיעֶזֶר כו'. וְלָא גָּרְסִינַן סַבְרוּהָ שְׁאֵלָה לְחוּד וְהַזְכָּרָה לְחוּד, דְּהָא לָא מִשְׁתַּמַּע מִמַּתְנִי': עַד אֵימָתַי שׁוֹאֲלִין אֶת הַגְּשָׁמִים. בְּסוֹף יְמוֹת הַגְּשָׁמִים: עַד שֶׁיַּעֲבוֹר הַפֶּסַח. דְּאָמְרִינַן כָּל חוּלּוֹ שֶׁל מוֹעֵד "וְתֵן טַל וּמָטָר": עַד שֶׁיֵּצֵא נִיסָן. וְכִדְמַפֵּיק טַעְמָא בְּמַתְנִי': הָכִי גָּרְסִינַן: אָמַר רַב חִסְדָּא כָּאן לִשְׁאוֹל כָּאן לְהַזְכִּיר מִישְׁאִיל שָׁאֵיל וְאָזֵיל וְהַזְכָּרָה בְּיו"ט רִאשׁוֹן פּוֹסֵק. לִשְׁאוֹל – שׁוֹאֵל וְהוֹלֵךְ עַד שֶׁיַּעֲבוֹר הַפֶּסַח, כִּדְקָתָנֵי עַד מָתַי שׁוֹאֲלִין כו'. לְהַזְכִּיר – אֵינוֹ מַזְכִּיר אֶלָּא בִּתְפִלַּת יוֹצֵר שֶׁל יו"ט רִאשׁוֹן: בְּמָקוֹם שֶׁאֵינוֹ שׁוֹאֵל. בְּיו"ט הָאַחֲרוֹן שֶׁל חַג, שֶׁאֵינוֹ מִתְפַּלֵּל תְּפִלָּתוֹ תְּפִלַּת חוֹל, דְּאֵין שְׁאֵלָה אֶלָּא בְּבִרְכַּת הַשָּׁנִים: מַזְכִּיר. גְּבוּרוֹת גְּשָׁמִים כִּדְאָמַר רַבִּי יְהוּדָה: הָאַחֲרוֹן מַזְכִּיר: בְּמָקוֹם שֶׁהוּא שׁוֹאֵל. בְּחוּלּוֹ שֶׁל מוֹעֵד שֶׁל פֶּסַח: תְּרֵי תַּנָּאֵי. חַד אָמַר עַד שֶׁיַּעֲבוֹר הַפֶּסַח שׁוֹאֲלִין – כָּל שֶׁכֵּן שֶׁמַּזְכִּירִין, וְחַד אָמַר שְׁאֵלָה עַד הַפֶּסַח, וְהַזְכָּרָה, שֶׁיָּכוֹל לְהַזְכִּיר בְּיו"ט – מַזְכִּיר בְּיו"ט הָרִאשׁוֹן שֶׁל פֶּסַח בִּתְפִלַּת יוֹצֵר, וּבְמוּסָפִין פּוֹסֵק: רַב יוֹסֵף אָמַר. הַאי דְּקָתָנֵי עַד אֵימָתַי שׁוֹאֲלִין עַד שֶׁיַּעֲבוֹר כו' – ה"ק: עַד שֶׁיַּעֲבוֹר שְׁלִיחַ צִבּוּר כו'. וְהַיְינוּ כְּאִידָךְ רַבִּי יְהוּדָה דְּמַתְנִי', דְּאָמַר: הָרִאשׁוֹן מַזְכִּיר הָאַחֲרוֹן אֵינוֹ מַזְכִּיר: שְׁאֵלָה בְּיו"ט מִי אִיכָּא. וְכִי מִתְפַּלֵּל הוּא תְּפִלַּת חוֹל, שֶׁאַתָּה אוֹמֵר עַד שֶׁיַּעֲבוֹר הַפֶּסַח? דְּהַיְינוּ (ג) זְמַן שְׁלִיחַ צִבּוּר שֶׁל תְּפִלַּת יו"ט הָרִאשׁוֹן שֶׁל פֶּסַח: אָמַר לֵיהּ אִין שְׁאֵלָה דִּמְתוּרְגְּמָן. בִּדְרָשָׁה שֶׁהוּא דּוֹרֵשׁ אוֹמֵר בִּרְכַּת שְׁאֵלָה לְבַדָּהּ: דָּבָר שֶׁאֵינוֹ צָרִיךְ לַצִּבּוּר דְּכֵיוָן דִּזְמַן הַפְסָקָה הוּא – לָאו אוֹרַח אַרְעָא לְמִישְׁאַל בַּצִּבּוּר דָּבָר שֶׁאֵינוֹ צָרִיךְ: עַד שֶׁיַּעֲבוֹר זְמַן שְׁחִיטַת פֶּסַח. (ד) חֲצוֹת יוֹם דְּאַרְבָּעָה עָשָׂר, עַד שֶׁיַּעֲבוֹר חֲצוֹת – דְּהַיְינוּ כָּל תְּפִלַּת יוֹצֵר. וְאַשְׁמְעִינַן ר' יְהוּדָה דִּבְמִנְחָה דְּעַרְבֵי פְּסָחִים, אע"ג דִּמְצַלֵּינַן תְּפִלַּת חוֹל מַפְסִיקִינַן, וְלֹא יֹאמַר "וְתֵן טַל וּמָטָר". וְאע"ג דְּמַדְכְּרִינַן עַד לְאַחַר בְּמוּסָפִין – פּוֹסֵק הַשְּׁאֵלָה בִּתְפִלַּת מִנְחָה שֶׁל עֶרֶב יו"ט הָרִאשׁוֹן. וְהַזְכָּרָה, שֶׁיָּכוֹל לְהַזְכִּיר בְּיוֹם טוֹב – מַזְכִּיר עַד תְּפִלַּת מוּסָף שֶׁל יוֹם טוֹב הָרִאשׁוֹן: כִּתְחִילָּתוֹ. שֶׁהוּא מַזְכִּיר תְּחִלָּה בְּיוֹם טוֹב אַחֲרוֹן שֶׁל חַג, וְאֵינוֹ שׁוֹאֵל עַד לְאַחַר הֶחָג (ה) – כָּךְ בְּסוֹפוֹ אֵינוֹ שׁוֹאֵל בְּמִנְחָה עֶרֶב יו"ט הָרִאשׁוֹן, וּמַזְכִּיר עַד מוּסָף שֶׁל יו"ט רִאשׁוֹן. וְהָכָא לֵיכָּא לְמִיפְרַךְ: שְׁאֵלָה בְּיו"ט מִי אִיכָּא: דְּהַזְכָּרָה נַמִי צוֹרֶךְ שְׁאֵלָה הִיא. שֶׁמְּרַצֶּה תְּחִלָּה לִפְנֵי שֶׁא"א לוֹ לִשְׁאוֹל בְּיו"ט, וְכֵיוָן דְּאִיכָּא שְׁאֵלָה אֲבַתְרֵיהּ מַזְכִּיר הוּא לְרַצּוּיֵי בְּעָלְמָא: אֲבָל סוֹפוֹ. לָמָּה הוּא מַזְכִּיר הוֹאִיל וְאֵינוֹ צָרִיךְ לִשְׁאוֹל מִכָּאן וָאֵילָךְ. הָא כֵּיוָן דְּהִפְסַקְתָּ מֵאֶתְמוֹל – גָּלֵית אַדַּעְתָּךְ דְּלָא נִיחָא לָךְ בְּהוּ, וְאַמַּאי מַזְכִּיר? הֲלָכָה כְּרַבִּי יְהוּדָה. דְּאָמַר: הָעוֹבֵר לִפְנֵי הַתֵּיבָה וכו': מִי אָמַר רַבִּי יוֹחָנָן הָכִי. דַּהֲלָכָה כְּרַבִּי יְהוּדָה, דְּמַזְכִּיר בְּיו"ט הָאַחֲרוֹן: בִּשְׁלֹשָׁה בְּמַרְחֶשְׁוָן. הָכִי קִים לְהוּ דַּהֲוָה זְמַן גְּשָׁמִים כו': הֲלָכָה כְּרַבָּן גַּמְלִיאֵל. דְּאֵינוֹ שׁוֹאֵל עַד שִׁבְעָה בְּמַרְחֶשְׁוָן. וְקָא ס"ד דִּבְמָקוֹם שֶׁהוּא שׁוֹאֵל מַזְכִּיר, עַד דִּמְשַׁנֵּי לְקַמָּן: כָּאן לִשְׁאוֹל. בְּשִׁבְעָה בְּמַרְחֶשְׁוָן: כָּאן לְהַזְכִּיר. מִיו"ט הָאַחֲרוֹן. וְר' יוֹחָנָן אִית לֵיהּ דְּרַבִּי אֶלְעָזָר: וְהָא א"ר יוֹחָנָן בְּמָקוֹם שֶׁשּׁוֹאֵל מַזְכִּיר. (ו) בְּמָקוֹם שֶׁאֵינוֹ שׁוֹאֵל אֵינוֹ מַזְכִּיר. וְהֵיכִי א"ר יוֹחָנָן דַּהֲלָכָה כְּר' יְהוּדָה שֶׁמַּזְכִּיר בְּיו"ט הָאַחֲרוֹן? הָא לֵיכָּא שְׁאֵלָה, דְּאֵין אוֹמֵר בִּרְכַּת הַשָּׁנִים בְּיו"ט: לְהַפְסָקָה אִיתְּמַר. דִּכְשֶׁהוּא מַפְסִיק לִשְׁאֵלָה בְּעֶרֶב הַפֶּסַח – פּוֹסֵק נַמִי לְהַזְכָּרָה, דְּהָכִי מַשְׁמַע "בְּמָקוֹם שֶׁשּׁוֹאֵל מַזְכִּיר": וְהָא תַּרְוַיְיהוּ אִיתְּמַר. הַתְחָלָה וְהַפְסָקָה: יַתְחִיל לִשְׁאוֹל. דְּהַיְינוּ בְּחוֹל, שֶׁיָּכוֹל לִשְׁאוֹל: פָּסַק מִלִּשְׁאוֹל. בְּעֶרֶב הַפֶּסַח, פּוֹסֵק מִלְּהַזְכִּיר. אַלְמָא לָא סְבִירָא לֵיהּ כְּרַבִּי יְהוּדָה, וְהֵיכִי אָמַר הֲלָכָה כְּמוֹתוֹ? הָא לָן וְהָא לְהוּ. לִבְנֵי בָּבֶל, שֶׁיֵּשׁ לָנוּ תְּבוּאָה וּפֵירוֹת בַּשָּׂדֶה כָּל תִּשְׁרֵי – אֵין מַזְכִּירִין עַד שִׁבְעָה בְּמַרְחֶשְׁוָן, וְאָז שׁוֹאֲלִים, כִּדְאָמַר רַבִּי יוֹחָנָן: מַתְחִיל לְהַזְכִּיר מַתְחִיל לִשְׁאוֹל: וְהָא לְהוּ. לִבְנֵי אֶרֶץ יִשְׂרָאֵל דְּקוֹצְרִין בְּנִיסָן וְאוֹסְפִין בְּתִשְׁרֵי – מַזְכִּירִין בְּי"ט הָאַחֲרוֹן, כְּרַבִּי יְהוּדָה, דְּאָמַר רַב אַסִי הֲלָכָה כְּמוֹתוֹ: בְּדַבְרָא. מִדְבָּר, כְּלוֹמַר בַּשָּׂדוֹת: אִית לְהוּ עוֹלֵי רְגָלִים. וְאִם יֵרְדוּ לָהֶן גְּשָׁמִים – קָשֶׁה לָהֶן בַּחֲזִירָתָן: אֶלָּא כִּי א"ר יוֹחָנָן. הֲלָכָה כְּר' יְהוּדָה, דְּמַזְכִּיר מִיו"ט הָאַחֲרוֹן כו', בִּזְמַן שֶׁאֵין בהמ"ק קַיָּים, וְלֵיכָּא עוֹלֵי רְגָלִים – מַזְכִּיר: כָּאן בִּזְמַן שֶׁבֵּית הַמִּקְדָּשׁ קַיָּים. דְּאִיכָּא עוֹלֵי רְגָלִים, אֵינוֹ מַזְכִּיר עַד ז' בְּמַרְחֶשְׁוָן: אֲנַן דְּאִית לָן תְּרֵי יוֹמֵי. שְׁנֵי יָמִים טוֹבִים אַחֲרוֹנִים, שְׁמִינִי סָפֵק שְׁבִיעִי, וּתְשִׁיעִי סָפֵק שְׁמִינִי. לְרַבִּי יְהוּדָה דְּאָמַר מִיו"ט הָאַחֲרוֹן, בְּאֵיזֶה מֵהֶן מַזְכִּיר. מַתְחִיל בְּמוּסָף. שֶׁל שְׁמִינִי סָפֵק שְׁבִיעִי, דְּשֶׁמָּא שְׁבִיעִי חוֹל הוּא, וְאֵין זְמַן הַזְכָּרָה עַד מוּסָף שֶׁל מָחָר: וּפוֹסֵק בְּמִנְחָה. שֶׁמָּא יו"ט הָאַחֲרוֹן הוּא: וּפוֹסֵק נַמִי בְּעַרְבִית וְשַׁחֲרִית. שֶׁל תְּשִׁיעִי סָפֵק שְׁמִינִי: לְאַבָּא. חֲבֵרִי: לְאַחַר שֶׁעֲשִׂיתוֹ קוֹדֶשׁ. לִשְׁמִינִי סָפֵק שְׁבִיעִי, שֶׁהִזְכַּרְתָּ בּוֹ גְּבוּרוֹת גְּשָׁמִים כְּרַבִּי יְהוּדָה מִיו"ט הָאַחֲרוֹן: תַּעֲשֵׂהוּ חוֹל. בִּתְמִיָּה: שֶׁמַּפְסִיק בְּמִנְחָה שֶׁל אוֹתוֹ הַיּוֹם: וּפוֹסֵק עַרְבִית וְשַׁחֲרִית. דְּלָאו הַיְינוּ תְּפִלָּה שֶׁל אוֹתוֹ הַיּוֹם:

רָבָא

ואמר ר' אלעזר הלכה כר"ג דאמר דאין שואלין עד שבעה וכו'. פירוש: ולא אמרת הלכה כר' יהודה בהא דקאמר במתני': רבי יהודה אומר העובר לפני התיבה בי"ט האחרון של חג, האחרון מזכיר והראשון אינו מזכיר. ומדמינן לעיל שאלה להזכרה, דפריך: ורמינהו עד מתי שואלין את הגשמים עד שיעבור וכו', ומשני: גברא אגברא וכו': **והא** אמר רבי יוחנן במקום ששואלין הגשמים מזכיר. ומשני: ההוא להפסקה. פי': דבמקום שמפסיק מלשאול מפסיק מלהזכיר, אבל מתחיל קודם להזכיר. וטעמא הוי דהזכרה הוה ריצוי שאלה, ומש"ה ליכא חששא אם מזכיר קודם: **הא** לן. פירוש: לבני בבל (ז) [א] עד לאחר שבעה במרחשון, דאית להו פירי בדברא. ובארץ ליכא חששא, דהא יכולים פירותיהן להיות יבשים בלא הולכה למדבר: **והא** להו. כי המתחיל להזכיר יתחיל לשאול:

רבא

רבינו חננאל

פיסקא ר' יהודה אומר העובר לפני התיבה ורמינן עלה עד מתי שואלין את הגשמים ר' יהודה אומר עד שיעבור הפסח ומשני רב חסדא פוסק מלהזכיר מיום הראשון של פסח ושואל עד שיעבור הפסח. וזהו כחומץ לשינים (וכעשן) שמקהה לשינים וכעשן לעינים. ומשני עולא תרי תנאי ואליבא דר' יהודה [רב יוסף אמר כו'] ואקשינן ושאלה ביו"ט מי איכא ופריק אין לשאול מתורגמן ומדלא דחי לה ואמר מי איכא תורגמן בצלותא שמעינן מינה דבי דינא הוו מוקמי מתורגמן לישאל מלתא דהוה צריכא להו לפיכך אמר אפשר לההוא לשאל בערבית ושחרית של יו"ט יהי רצון מלפניך ה' אלהינו שתתן טל ומטר על פני האדמה: רבה אמר מאי עד שיעבור הפסח עד שיעבור זמן שחיטת הפסח. פי' שואלין את הגשמים עד ערב הפסח זמן שחיטת הפסח ופוסק ומזכיר עד מנחה ואע"פ שפוסק מלישאל עדיין מזכיר ליל ט"ו ושחרית ביו"ט ופוסק נמצא מזכיר מאחרי שפסק מלשאל כתחלתו מה תחלתנו מזכיר אע"פ שאינו [שואל] כן בסוף ודחה לה אביי בשלמא תחלתו מזכיר כי הוא ריצוי לשאלה. כלומר להבא עוד צריך לשאל. אלא סיפא הזכרה בלא שאלה למה כו' אלא מחוורתא כדעולא. דאמר תרי תנאי אליבא דר' יהודה: א"ר אסי א"ר יוחנן הלכה כר' יהודה דקתני העובר לפני התיבה ביו"ט האחרון של חג האחרון מזכיר. פירוש ש"ץ המתפלל מוסף הוא מזכיר מוריד הגשם ומזכיר והולך עד יו"ט הראשון של פסח בתפלת שחרית ואח"כ פוסק. ואקשינן איני דהלכתא כר' יהודה והאמר ר' אלעזר הלכתא כר"ג דתני בשבעה במרחשון שואלין את הגשמים ושנינן רבי אלעזר קא רמית אר' יוחנן. איבעית אימא הלכה כר' יהודה להזכיר כלומר מזכירין מיו"ט (הראשון) [האחרון] של (פסח) [חג] והלכתא כר"ג לשאל שאין שואלין את הגשמים ואין אומרים ותן טל ומטר אלא בז' במרחשון ונדחת זו דהא בהדיא לית ליה לר' יוחנן הפסקה בין הזכרה לשאלה דאמר ר' יוחנן התחיל להזכיר ישאל פסק מלשאל יפסוק מלהזכיר. אלא לא קשיא הא דר' יוחנן לבני ארץ ישראל והא דאמר רבי אלעזר עד ז' במרחשון לבני בבל משום דאית להו פירא בדברא והמטר מפסידם ואקשינן בני ארץ ישראל נמי יש להם עולי רגלים. ואם ישאלו מיום טוב (הראשון) [האחרון] של חג וירד המטר נמצא המטר מעכבן בחזירתן ואוקימנא בזמן הזה דליכא בית המקדש ושקלי

רבינו גרשום

אלא שאלה לחוד והזכרה לחוד דמזכירין ביום ראשון ושואלין בחולו של מועד. אמר רבא [אפילו תימא] ר' אליעזר היא דאמר הזכרה ביו"ט הראשון ולא מצי למישאל ביה שהרי אין מתפלל אתה חונן. דראשון מזכיר וה"ה שואל. ר"י אמר עד שיעבור הפסח והיכי אמר במתני' שאינו שואל אלא עד יום ראשון של פסח כאן לשאול כאן להזכיר. הא דאמר ר' יהודה במתניתין הראשון מזכיר ביו"ט ראשון של פסח היינו להזכיר אבל לשאול יכול לשאול עד שיעבור הפסח: במקום שאינו שואל מזכיר. שהרי מתחיל להזכיר בחג ואינו שואל עד ששים בתקופה: מקום שהוא שואל דקאמרת דשואל עד שיעבור הפסח: על אחת כמה וכמה שיזכיר (ומתרץ) [והיכי תריץ] רב חסדא דרבי יהודה קאמר שאינו מזכיר אלא עד יום ראשון של פסח וה"ה לשאלה *) דפרכת האמר ר' יהודה ששואל עד שיעבור הפסח תרי תנאי ואליבא דר"י: עד שיעבור ש"ץ ראשון של יו"ט ראשון היינו נמי כדאמר ר' יהודה במתניתין הראשון [מזכיר האחרון] אינו מזכיר וה"ה לשאלה: שאלה ביו"ט מי איכא דקאמרת דקאמר ר' יהודה ביו"ט ראשון שואל והא אינו מתפלל אתה חונן והיאך אמר שאלה בברכת השנים. שואל במתורגמן המתורגמן המתרגם דרשה ביו"ט של פסח אומר שאלה בדרשה: דבר שאינו צריך לצבור כלומר שאין הצבור שואלין בתפלתן היאך ישאל המתורגמן אלא כדעולא דלא תריץ ליה עד שיעבור ש"ץ אלא לאחר הפסח ממש: עד שיעבור זמן שחיטת פסח דהיינו י"ד אבל ביו"ט ראשון אינו שואל והאי דקאמר ר' יהודה במתניתין עד יו"ט הראשון היינו להזכרה ולא לשאלה מה תחלתו מזכיר אע"פ שאינו שואל שמזכיר בחג ואינו שואל עד ששים בתקופה: אף סופו מזכיר. עד יום ראשון ואינו שואל אלא עד י"ד: דהזכרה נמי ריצוי שאלה היא כלומר להכי מזכיר בחג הואיל ועתיד לשאול בששים בתקופה שלפניו. מאי ריצוי שאלה איכא והא **) עדיין הוא עתיד לשאול אלא מכיון שפסק מלשאול שוב אינו מזכיר אלא כדעולא דתריץ עד שיעבור הפסח ממש והא דא"ר יהודה במתני' עד יום ראשון של פסח ***) היינו להזכרה ולא לשאלה. הלכה כר' יהודה דאמר מזכיר ביום אחרון של חג וה"ה לשאלה כאן לשאול כאן להזכיר הא דאמר ר' יוחנן הלכה

*) נראה דל"ל אלא אמר עולא הא דפרכת וכו'. **) נראה דל"ל והא תו אינו עתיד לשאול וכו'. ***) הדבר תמוה דהא תי' זה כבר דחי הגמ' לעיל ועולא הא מתרץ דתרי תנאי אליבא דר"י וצ"ע.

לקמן ה.

[קידושין מה:]

[לקמן י. וש"נ]

[שם]

[עי' תוספות יומא יג. ד"ה הלכה]

ברכות ה: מד. שבת ע: סוכה לו. מח: יומא כח: ביצה ה. יד: קידושין כט: [ב"מ קז. ב"ב קמז.]

הגהות הגר"א

[א] תום' ד"ה הא לן פי' לבני בבל אין שואלין עד שבעה. כצ"ל (ועמ"ש רבינו בא"ח ריש סימן קי"ז):

גליון הש"ס

גמ' כאן בזמן שאין בית המקדש קיים. עי' יומא דף יג ע"א תוס' ד"ה הלכה:

הגהות הב"ח

(א) גמרא ורמינהו עד מתי שואלין את הגשמים ר"מ אומר עד שיצא ניסן רבי יהודה אומר כו': (ב) שם בשלמא תחלתו מזכיר הזכרה נמי ריצוי: (ג) רש"י ד"ה שאלה כו' שיעבור הפסח היינו עד שיעבור זמן הפסח קודם שליח צבור: (ד) ד"ה עד שיעבור זמן שחיטת פסח עד שיעבור חצות יום י"ד היינו כל זמן תפלת יוצר כו' עד לאחר במוספין ל"א פוסק השאלה בתפלת ערבית של ערב יו"ט: (ה) ד"ה כתחלתו כו' לאחר החג הס"ד ואח"כ מה"ד כך בסופו אינו שואל בלילי יו"ט: (ו) ד"ה והא אמר כו' במקום: (ז) תוס' ד"ה הא לן פי' לבני בבל אין מזכירין עד שבעה במרחשון דאית להו פירי בדברא לכך יתחיל כו' המתחיל להזכיר יתחיל לשאול ולהו פי' לבני א"י ליכא חששא דהא יכולים להיות נמחק.

גמרא

רָבָא אָמַר: כֵּיוָן שֶׁהִתְחִיל — שׁוּב אֵינוֹ פּוֹסֵק. וְכֵן אָמַר רַב שֵׁשֶׁת: כֵּיוָן שֶׁהִתְחִיל, שׁוּב אֵינוֹ פּוֹסֵק. וְאַף רַב הֲדַר בֵּיהּ, דְּאָמַר רַב חֲנַנְאֵל אָמַר רַב: מוֹנֶה עֶשְׂרִים וְאֶחָד יוֹם, כְּדֶרֶךְ שֶׁמּוֹנֶה עֲשָׂרָה יָמִים מֵר"ה עַד יוה"כ [א]וּמַתְחִיל. וְכֵיוָן שֶׁהִתְחִיל — שׁוּב אֵינוֹ פּוֹסֵק. [ב]וְהִלְכְתָא: כֵּיוָן שֶׁהִתְחִיל, שׁוּב אֵינוֹ פּוֹסֵק.§ **מתני'** *עַד מָתַי שׁוֹאֲלִין אֶת הַגְּשָׁמִים? ר' יְהוּדָה אוֹמֵר: עַד שֶׁיַּעֲבוֹר הַפֶּסַח. ר' *מֵאִיר אוֹמֵר: עַד שֶׁיֵּצֵא נִיסָן, שֶׁנֶּאֱמַר °"וַיּוֹרֶד לָכֶם גֶּשֶׁם, יוֹרֶה וּמַלְקוֹשׁ, בָּרִאשׁוֹן".§ **גמ'** א"ל רַב נַחְמָן לְר' יִצְחָק: יוֹרֶה בְּנִיסָן? (א) יוֹרֶה בְּמַרְחֶשְׁוָן הוּא! (*דִּתְנַן: *יוֹרֶה בְּמַרְחֶשְׁוָן וּמַלְקוֹשׁ בְּנִיסָן.) א"ל הָכִי אָמַר רַבִּי יוֹחָנָן: בִּימֵי יוֹאֵל בֶּן פְּתוּאֵל נִתְקַיֵּים מִקְרָא זֶה. דִּכְתִיב בֵּיהּ °"יֶתֶר הַגָּזָם אָכַל הָאַרְבֶּה" וגו'. אוֹתָהּ שָׁנָה יָצָא אֲדָר וְלֹא יָרְדוּ גְּשָׁמִים. יָרְדָה לָהֶם רְבִיעָה רִאשׁוֹנָה בְּאֶחָד בְּנִיסָן. אָמַר לָהֶם נָבִיא לְיִשְׂרָאֵל: "צְאוּ וְזִרְעוּ". אָמְרוּ לוֹ: מִי שֶׁיֵּשׁ לוֹ קַב חִטִּים אוֹ קַבַּיִם שְׂעוֹרִין, יֹאכְלֶנּוּ וְיִחְיֶה, אוֹ יִזְרָעֶנּוּ וְיָמוּת? אָמַר לָהֶם: אעפ"כ צְאוּ וְזִרְעוּ. נַעֲשָׂה לָהֶם נֵס, וְנִתְגַּלָּה לָהֶם מַה שֶּׁבַּכְּתָלִין וּמַה שֶּׁבְּחוֹרֵי נְמָלִים. יָצְאוּ וְזָרְעוּ שֵׁנִי וּשְׁלִישִׁי וּרְבִיעִי, וְיָרְדָה לָהֶם רְבִיעָה שְׁנִיָּה בַּחֲמִשָּׁה בְּנִיסָן. הִקְרִיבוּ עוֹמֶר בְּשִׁשָּׁה עָשָׂר בְּנִיסָן. נִמְצֵאת תְּבוּאָה הַגְּדֵילָה בְּשִׁשָּׁה חֳדָשִׁים גְּדֵילָה בְּאַחַד עָשָׂר יוֹם. נִמְצָא עוֹמֶר הַקָּרֵב מִתְּבוּאָה שֶׁל שִׁשָּׁה חֳדָשִׁים קָרֵב מִתְּבוּאָה שֶׁל אַחַד עָשָׂר יוֹם. וְעַל אוֹתוֹ הַדּוֹר הוּא אוֹמֵר: °"הַזּוֹרְעִים בְּדִמְעָה בְּרִנָּה יִקְצֹרוּ. הָלוֹךְ יֵלֵךְ וּבָכֹה, נֹשֵׂא מֶשֶׁךְ הַזָּרַע" וגו'. מַאי: "הָלוֹךְ יֵלֵךְ וּבָכֹה, נוֹשֵׂא מֶשֶׁךְ" וגו'? א"ר יְהוּדָה: שׁוֹר כְּשֶׁהוּא חוֹרֵשׁ — הוֹלֵךְ וּבוֹכֶה, וּבַחֲזִירָתוֹ אוֹכֵל חָזִיז מִן הַתֶּלֶם. וְזֶהוּ: "בֹּא יָבֹא בְרִנָּה". מַאי: "נוֹשֵׂא אֲלֻמּוֹתָיו"? א"ר חִסְדָּא, וְאָמְרִי לָהּ בְּמַתְנִיתָא תָּנָא: "קָנֶה — זֶרֶת, שִׁיבּוֹלֶת — זֶרְתַּיִם". א"ל רַב נַחְמָן לְר' יִצְחָק: מַאי דִּכְתִיב °"כִּי קָרָא ה' לָרָעָב, וְגַם בָּא אֶל הָאָרֶץ שֶׁבַע שָׁנִים", בְּהָנָךְ שֶׁבַע שָׁנִים מַאי אֲכוּל? א"ל: הָכִי אָמַר רַבִּי יוֹחָנָן: שָׁנָה רִאשׁוֹנָה — אָכְלוּ מַה שֶּׁבַּבָּתִּים. שְׁנִיָּה — אָכְלוּ מַה שֶּׁבַּשָּׂדוֹת. שְׁלִישִׁית — בְּשַׂר בְּהֵמָה טְהוֹרָה. רְבִיעִית — בְּשַׂר בְּהֵמָה טְמֵאָה. חֲמִישִׁית — בְּשַׂר שְׁקָצִים וּרְמָשִׂים. שִׁשִּׁית — בְּשַׂר בְּנֵיהֶם וּבְנוֹתֵיהֶם. שְׁבִיעִית — בְּשַׂר זְרוֹעוֹתֵיהֶם, לְקַיֵּים מַה שֶּׁנֶּאֱמַר °"אִישׁ בְּשַׂר זְרֹעוֹ יֹאכֵלוּ". וא"ל רַב נַחְמָן לְר' יִצְחָק: מַאי דִּכְתִיב °"בְּקִרְבְּךָ קָדוֹשׁ, וְלֹא אָבוֹא בְּעִיר", מִשּׁוּם דִּבְקִרְבְּךָ קָדוֹשׁ, לֹא אָבוֹא בָּעִיר? א"ל, הָכִי א"ר יוֹחָנָן: אָמַר הקב"ה: לֹא אָבוֹא בִּירוּשָׁלַיִם שֶׁל מַעְלָה עַד שֶׁאָבוֹא לִירוּשָׁלַיִם שֶׁל מַטָּה. וּמִי אִיכָּא יְרוּשָׁלַיִם לְמַעְלָה? אִין, דִּכְתִיב °"יְרוּשָׁלַיִם הַבְּנוּיָה כְּעִיר שֶׁחֻבְּרָה לָּהּ יַחְדָּיו". וא"ל רַב נַחְמָן לְר' יִצְחָק: מַאי דִּכְתִיב °"וּבְאַחַת יִבְעֲרוּ וְיִכְסָלוּ, מוּסַר הֲבָלִים עֵץ הוּא"? א"ל: הָכִי א"ר יוֹחָנָן: אַחַת הִיא שֶׁמְּבַעֶרֶת רְשָׁעִים בְּגֵיהִנָּם. מַאי הִיא? ע"ז. כְּתִיב הָכָא "מוּסַר הֲבָלִים עֵץ הוּא", וּכְתִיב הָתָם °"הֶבֶל הֵמָּה, מַעֲשֵׂה תַּעְתֻּעִים". וא"ל רַב נַחְמָן לְר' יִצְחָק: מ"ד °"כִּי שְׁתַּיִם רָעוֹת עָשָׂה עַמִּי", תַּרְתֵּין הוּא דַּהֲווֹ? עֶשְׂרִין *וְאַרְבַּע שְׁבִיקָא לְהוּ?! א"ל, הָכִי א"ר יוֹחָנָן: אַחַת שֶׁהִיא

שְׁקוּלָה

רש"י

רבא אמר כיון שהתחיל. בשמיני ספק שביעי שוב אינו פוסק: **הדר ביה.** מהאי דאמר פוסק: **מונה כ"א יום.** מראש השנה עד שמיני ספק שביעי של חג, כדרך שמונה מר"ה ועד יוה"כ י' ימים, שמתחיל למנות מיום ראשון של ר"ה, ומזכיר מכאן ואילך. והוו שמזכיר בשמיני ספק שביעי שהוא כ"ב — שוב אינו פוסק. והא דמתחילין אנו למנות מיום א' — דהא דאנו עושין ב' ימים לאו משום ספק דשמא עיברו לאלול, דהא אנן בקיאינן בקביעא דירחא. אלא משום דמנהג אבותינו בידינו. ל"א: מונה כ"א יום כדרך שמונה כו'. כלומר, אם עיברו אלול — לא יחשוב מיום ראשון של ר"ה כ"א יום — שאם כן לא ימלאו בידו אלא כ', וכלים (ב) ביום טוב שביעי, יום נטילת ערבה. אלא מיום שמתחילין למנות עשרה ימים, לעשות בעשירי יוה"כ — יתחיל למנות באלו, שבכך לא יטעה, שיום הכפורים יום אחד לבד, וידע מהיכן התחילו למנות לו. ובאיום שכלין כ"א (ג), דהיינו ביום טוב אחרון — מתחיל להזכיר, וכיון שהתחיל — שוב אינו פוסק: **א"ל רב נחמן לר' יצחק יורה בניסן הוא.** דכתיב "ויורד לכם גשם מורה ומלקוש בראשון" בתמיה: **והא במרחשון הוא.** כדתניא לקמן, ובספרי הוא: **יורה ומלקוש.** מפרש לקמן: **אמר ליה.** ודאי במרחשון הוא, ומקרא זה בימי יואל בן פתואל נתקיים, שיורה ומלקוש היה בראשון על ידי נס. שהיה רעב שבע שנים, דכתיב "כי קרא ה' לרעב וגם בא אל הארץ שבע שנים", וכתיב "יתר הגזם אכל הארבה" וגו': **הכי גרסינן: יצא אדר ולא ירדו גשמים.** ולא זרעו רוב אדר לא גרסינן: **רביעה ראשונה.** התחלת גשמים. ולקמן (דף ו:) מפרש: רביעה — שמרביע את הארץ: **או יזרענו וימות.** ברעב, קודם שתגדל התבואה החדשה, שלא יהיה לו מה יאכל: **נעשה להם נס כו'.** והיינו דכתיב "ושלמתי לכם את השנים אשר אכל הארבה" וגו': **נתגלה להם תבואה שבחורי נמלים ומה שבכתלים.** שאכלו העכברים: **יצאו וזרעו.** (ד) וזרעו מה שבידם: **שני.** בניסן, ושלישי ורביעי, ומה שמלאו אכלו. ולאחר שזרעו — ירדו להם גשמים בה' בניסן, והקריבו עומר בט"ז בניסן מאותה תבואה חדשה: **הגדילה בששה חדשים.** מתשרי ועד ניסן: **בי"א יום.** מחמשה בניסן עד ט"ז בו: **הזורעים בדמעה ברנה יקצורו.** שלא היה להן מה לאכול: **מאי הלך ילך ובכה.** אם לבני אדם — כבר נאמר "הזורעים בדמעה ברנה יקצורו", אלא על השור הכתוב אומר: **בהליכתו.** לחרוש התלם: **ובחזירתו אוכל חזיז.** שחת, מן התלם שזרעו בהליכתן. שכשהוא זורע — מיד מתחלת ליגדל: **מאי בא יבוא ברנה נושא אלומותיו.** אם מפני התבואה שיש להם לאכול — הרי כבר אמור "ברנה יקצורו": **שבולת זרתים.** זהו נס גדול, מה שאין כן דרך כל תבואה, שהקנה פי שלשה וארבעה בשבולת: **כי קרא ה' לרעב.** בימי יהורם בן אחאב נאמר: **מה שבשדות.** ספיחים, ומה שנשתייר בשדות: **אכלו בשר בניהם.** מקלסם: **משום דבקרבך קדוש.** *שאתה מטיב מעשיך — לא יבא הקב"ה בעיר?! **לא אבא בירושלים כו'.** והכי קאמר: עד שיהא בקרבך קדוש למטה, דהיינו ירושלים, לא אבוא בעיר שלמעלה: **ירושלים הבנויה כעיר שחוברה לה יחדיו.** ירושלים שלמטה תהא בנויה כעיר שחוברה לה, שהיא כיוצא בה, חבירתה ודוגמתה. מכלל דאיכא ירושלים אחריתי, והיכן אם לא למעלה? **ובאחת יבערו ויכסלו מוסר הבלים עץ הוא.** אי לאו גזרה שוה היה משמע: קטומים כעץ לקבל מוסר, ולשוא היו לוקין: **באחת.** עבירה שהן עושין יתבערו הכסילים — רשעים: **עשרים *וארבע שביקא להו.** בתמיה. בפרשת "התשפוט" (יחזקאל כב) כ"ד עבירות שעברו. ל"א: שעברו על כ"ד ספרים:

תוספות

רבא אמר כיון שהתחיל שוב אינו פוסק. כלומר: כיון שהתחיל ביום ראשון של (ה) אחרונים — שוב אינו פוסק, וכן הפסק:

יורה במרחשון הוא. פי': אקרא דכתיב "ויורד לכם גשם מורה ומלקוש בראשון" פריך. דמתני' אפשר לתרץ דאמלקוש קסמיך, אבל ביורה — מודה דמברחשון:

ובחזירתו אוכל חזיז מן התלם וכו'. וקשיא: הא דקאמר לעיל נמצא הגדילה בששה חדשים גדילה באחד עשר יום — הוה ליה למימר גדילה בתליסר *ובי"ד יומי, שהרי מיד מתחלת ליגדל! ושמא י"ל דלכל המאוחרת שנזרעה בשלישית קאמר, נמצא גדילה בי"א יום. ול"ע:

לא אבוא בעיר. פירוש בעיר: ר"ל בעיר ממש. וי"מ: פשטיה דקרא בעיר = בשנאה, כלומר: לא אבוא בשנאה. ועיר הוי ל' שנאה, כמו "ומלאו פני תבל ערים" (ישעיה יד): ומי

רבינו חננאל

ואסקוה [מונה] כ"א יום מר"ה ועד יו"ט האחרון של חג ומתחיל להזכיר ביו"ט האחרון כדרך שמונה י' ימים מר"ה ועד יוה"כ והעשירי הוא יוה"כ. ומתחיל להזכיר וכיון שמתחיל שוב אינו פוסק וכן הלכה: **מתני'** עד מתי שואלין את הגשמים כו' א) הא אסיק' לשמעתא כי ש"ץ היורד לפני התיבה ביו"ט הראשון של פסח מזכיר מוריד הגשם ופוסק מלהזכיר והיורד במוסף אינו מזכיר ב) כיון שא"ר מאיר עד שיצא ניסן שנא' ויורד לכם גשם מורה ומלקוש בראשון ואקשינן והא מורה במרחשון הוא ומלקוש בניסן ושנינן בימי יואל בן פתואל ג) (ש"מ) [נאמר] מורה בניסן שיצא אדר ולא ירדו גשמים. ירד רביעה ראשונה באחד בניסן אמר להם הנביא צאו וזרעו נעשה להן נס ונתגלה להם החטים שאוגרין הנמלין בחורין ובכתלים ולקחו אותן וזרעו ירדה להן רביעה שנייה בחמשה בניסן וצמחו זרעים והקריבו העומר בי"ו בניסן. נמצאת תבואה הגדילה בו' חדשים גידלה בי"א יום על אותו דור נאמר הזורעים בדמעה ברנה יקצורו השור שהיה בהליכתו הולך כמו בוכה. בחזירתו היה אוכל חזיז. בא יבא ברנה [נושא] אלומותיו קנה זרת שבולת שתים. א"ל רב נחמן לר' יצחק הא דכתיב כי קרא ה' לרעב וגו' אותן ז' שנים מאי אכול א"ל הכי א"ר יוחנן שנה ראשונה אכלו מה שבבתים שניה אכלו מה שבשדות כו'. ותוב בעא מיניה בקרבך קדוש ולא אבוא בעיר א"ל הקדוש ברוך הוא לישראל שאינו בא בירושלים של מעלה עד שיבנה להם ירושלים של מטה וישרה שכינתו הקדושה בקרבם. ותוב בעא מיניה מ"ד ובאחת יבערו ויכסלו וגו'. א"ל אחת היא שמבערת הרשעים לגיהנם ומאי ניהי ע"ז. ותוב בעא מיניה מ"ד כי שתים רעות עשה עמי וגו' תרתי בלחוד הוא דעבוד. כ"ב שביקא להו יש מי שמפרש וכי יש עבירה הכתובה בכ"ד ספרים כלומר במקרא שלא עשו אותה ואמאי כתיב כי שתים רעות (וכ"ב דמתמה. כלומר וכי הניחו כ"ד ספרים עבירה הכתובה בהם שלא עשו אותה) ואנו קבלנו מרבותינו כי אלו הן כ"ד חטאות בכאן הם המפורשים בתלמוד א"י בפרק אלו שאין להם חלק ד) יש מן החכמים המפרשים שהיו אומרים כ"ד רעות אלו הן הנדברות באזני קרא אותי עזבו מקור מים חיים. לחצוב להם. עזבך את ה' אלהיך. רעתך ומשובותיך ולא פחדתי אליך לא אעבור צועה זונה נהפכת נכתם עונך לא נטמאתי דרכך בגיא אהבתי זרים ואחריהם אלך הובישו המה מלכיהם שריהם כהניהם ונביאיהם אומרים לעץ אבי אתה ולאבן את ילדתנו כי פנו אלי עורף מספר עריך היו אלהיך אלו כ"ד רעות א"ר יוחנן לא גלו ישראל עד שנעשו כ"ד כתות של מינים שנאמר בן אדם שולח אני אותך וגו' אל גוי המורד לא נאמר אלא גוי המורדים ומצאנו במדרש חזית א"ר יוחנן כ"ד חטאות הוכיח יחזקאל הנביא את ישראל בפרשת התשפוט את עיר הדמים אלו הן עיר שופכת דם ועשתה גלולים טמאת השם רבת המהומה איש לזרועו היו בך למען שפוך דם ה) אב ואם הקלו בך לגר עשו בעושק בתוכך יתום ואלמנה הונו בך קדשי בזית ואת שבתותי חללת אנשי רכיל היו בך ואל ההרים אכלו בך זמה עשו בתוכך ערות אב גלה בך טמאת הנדה ענו בך ואיש את אשת רעהו עשה תועבה ואיש את כלתו טמא בזמה ואיש את אחותו בת אביו ענה בך שוחד לקחו בך נשך ותרבית לקחת ותבצעי רעיך בעשק ואותי שכחת נאם ה' ועל כולם לא חתם אלא על הגזל והנה הכיתי כפי אל בצעך אשר עשית ועל דמך אשר היו בתוכך. היעמוד לבך אם תחזקנה ידיך לימים אשר אני עושה אותך

א) נראה דר"ל דאיסקופא לעיל דלאו הלכה כר"י דהך מתני' רק כאידך דר"י דש"ץ היורד וכו'. ב) נראה דל"ל ר"מ אומר עד שיצא וכו'. ג) אולי צ"ל בימי יואל בן פתואל ירד מורה בניסן. ד) כאן צ"ל מ"ש למטה אר"י לא גלו ישראל וכו'. ה) אב ואם נתקבים לב' וכן יתום ואלמנה כ"ה בערוך.

הגהות הב"ח

(א) גמ' יורה בניסן הוא יורה במרחשון הוא: (ב) רש"י ד"ה מונה כו' אלא כו' וכלים ביום שביעי יום כו' כצ"ל ותיבת טוב נמחק: (ג) בא"ד דהיינו ביו"ט אחרון. נ"ב כלומר עד ליל יו"ט ולא ליל יו"ט בכלל: (ד) ד"ה וזרעו וחרעו מה שבידם שני מה כצ"ל ותיבת וחרעו נמחק: (ה) תוס' ד"ה רבא כו' ביום ראשון של שני ימים אחרונים שוב:

עין משפט נר מצוה

יב א ב מיי' פ"ב מהל' תפלה הל' טו טוש"ע א"ח סימן קיד סעיף ה:

רבינו גרשום

כו' יהודה היינו להזכיר שמתחיל להזכיר בחג והא דאמר ר' אלעזר הלכה כר"ג היינו לשאלה. והאמר ר' יוחנן במקום שהוא שואל מזכיר אלמא הא דאמר ר' יוחנן הלכה כר' יהודה היינו בין לשאול בין להזכיר דכי הדדי נינהו וקשיא הלכתא אהלכתא: ההוא להפסקה. כלומר הא דאמר מקום שהוא שואל הוא מזכיר היינו להפסקה כלומר שפוסק מלשאול ומלהזכיר ביום ראשון של פסח אבל להתחלה מתחיל בחג ושואל בשבעה במרחשון: הא לן והא להו הא דאמר הלכה כר"ג דאינו שואל עד שבעה במרחשון היינו לן באר"י דלית לן פירי בדברא: איכא להו פירי בדברא ואין צריכין לגשמים עד ז' במרחשון והא דאמר הלכה כר' יהודה בחג באר"י דלית לן פירי בדברא: איכא להו עולי רגלים ואם יורדין גשמים בג' *) אינן יכולין לחזור מפני הגשמים: כי קאמר ר' יוחנן הלכה כר' יהודה דשואל ומזכיר בחג בזמן שאין בית המקדש קיים דליכא עולי רגלים והא דאמר הלכה כר"ג בזמן שביהמ"ק קיים ובז' במרחשון כבר חזרו. ומנא ידעת הלכה היכי עבדינן הא אחד מהן חול הוא ובאיזה יום יתחיל לשאול. מתחיל במוספין של יום ראשון מימים האחרונים ופוסק במנחה דשמא חול הוא וערבית ושחרית מיום האחרון לגמרי. לאחר שעשיתו קדש ששאלת במוסף אלמא דקדש הוא תעשהו חול שאין אתה מזכיר במנחה: ופוסק ערבית שהרי היא הכנסה דיום אחרון ושחרית ושואל במוסף כמו שעשה אתמול דקדש הוא ואמר דאחרון שואל: כיון שהתחיל לשאול במוסף דיום ראשון שוב אינו פוסק אלא שואל במנחה בשחרית ובערבית ומוסף וכו' ואף רב הדר ביה ואמר כיון שהתחיל שוב אינו פוסק. מונה כ"א בתשרי דהיינו ראשון של אחרון ויתחיל לשאול ושוב אינו פוסק: כדרך שמונה מר"ה ועד יוה"כ. יורה ומלקוש בראשון האי ראשון היינו ניסן. בימי יואל נתקיים מקרא הזה יורה בראשון ולעולם יורה במרחשון הוא: שני ושלישי ורביעי בניסן נמצא תבואה שרגילה להתגדל בו' חדשים גדילה בי"א יום מרביעי דניסן עד יום י"ו בו שמקריבין בו העומר: כשהשור הולך לזרוע בוכה שרעב. מהו אלומותיו דמשמע תרי דקנה זרת ושיבולת שתי זרתות: אמר הקב"ה לא אכנס בירושלים של מעלה דהכי משמע עד שבקרבך קדוש שיבנה ירושלים למטה לא אכנס לירושלים של מעלה: יחדיו משמע תרי ירושלים. ומנלן דהאי אחת משמע ע"ז כתיב הכא מוסר הבלים עץ הוא. עשרים וארבעה שביקא להו כלומר והלא עברו על עשרים וארבעה ספרים ע"א

*) אולי צ"ל בג' במרחשון או לצ"ל בחג אינן יכולין לחזור וכו'.

רבינו חננאל

אני ה' דברתי ועשיתי. והפיצותי אותך בגוים וזריתיך בארצות והתימותי טומאתך ממך ונחלת בך לעיני גוים וידעת כי אני ה'. א"ל הכי אמר ר' יוחנן עבירה אחת שיש בה שתי רעות ומאי ניהו ע"ז שנאמר כי שתים רעות עשה עמי אותי עזבו והלכו אל הגלולים כי עברו איי כתיים גו' עד ועמי המיר כבודו בלא יועיל. ותוב בעא מיניה כתיב ויהי כי זקן שמואל מי קא סיב כולי האי והאמר מר במסכת מועד במשקין מת בן חמשים שנה זו היא מיתתו של שמואל הרמתי א"ל הכי אמר ר' יוחנן זקנה הקפיץ הקב"ה עליו שנאמר (ויהי כי זקן שמואל) נחמתי כי המלכתי את שאול למלך. ויחר לשמואל ויזעק אל ה' כל הלילה אמר לפניו רבש"ע שקלתני כמשה ואהרן כו'. עד מי גרם לשאול לישב שתי שנים ומחצה בגבעה תפלתו של שמואל הרמתי. וכי מידחי גברא מקמי גברא אין שנאמר חצבתי בנביאים הרגתים באמרי פי במעשיהם לא נאמר אלא באמרי פי אלמא מדחי גברא מקמי גברא. אין אומרים דבר הלכה בסעודה שמא יקדים קנה לושט ויבא לידי סכנה (ותתקל הסעודה) בתר דסעיד א"ל הכי אמר ר' יוחנן יעקב אבינו לא מת שנאמר כי הנני מושיעך מרחוק ואת זרעך מארץ שבים וגו' מקיש יעקב לזרעו מה זרעו בחיים אף הוא בחיים.

ומי סיב שמואל והא בר נ"ב שנין הוה וכו'. ועתה: (*אפי') חיי [נ"ל אפרכן] שמואל נ"ב שנה, שהרי בשנה ראשונה שהיה עלי ממונה לכ"ג נולד שמואל, כדכתיב (שמואל א א) "ועלי יושב" כלומר: אותו יום נתיישב ונתמנה. ועלי היה נביא ושופט ארבעים שנה, כדמפרש בקרא. ושמואל היה נביא ושופט י' שנים קודם מלכות שאול, כדאיתא בסדר עולם. נמצא שהיה שמואל בן מ"ט שנה כשפסק מלהיות שופט. ותלי שנה שבשנה ראשונה שהיה עלי נביא נולד, ותרתין שנין ופלגא דשאול המלך – הרי נ"ב שנין. ולהכי קא פריך: ומי סיב? ומורי ש"י השיב הני ארבעים שנה דעלי קודם שנשבה הארון, ובאותו יום שנשבה מת, כדכתיב "ויהי כהזכירו ארון האלהים ויפול אחורנית ותשבר מפרקתו וגו'". והארון היה בבית אבינדב בגבעה עשרים שנה, כדכתיב (שמואל א ז) "וירבו הימים ויהיו עשרים שנה וינהו כל בית ישראל אחרי ה'". ומיד כשמלך דוד בירושלים, דהיינו לאחר כשמלך בחברון שבע שנים ומחצה – הביאו לשם. לא וחשוב: ארבעים שחיה עלי, עם עשרים שנה שהיה הארון בבית אבינדב – היינו ששים, נמצא שהיה ששים שנה משנולד שמואל עד שבא הארון בירושלים. אע"ג דנולד בשנה הראשונה – א"כ נכי לפחות חלי שנה *דהריון, אותן שבעה חדשים(ג) היה הארון בשדה פלשתים דלא קא חשיב, ומלי' להנהו דשעת הריון, נמצא שהיה שמונה שנים ממיתת שמואל עד שבא הארון לירושלים, שהרי היה ששה חדשים ממיתת שמואל קודם שמשחו דוד למלך בחברון, ומלך שם שבע שנים ומחצה, ומיד מלך בירושלים והביא הארון. ועתה הסר שמונה שנים מן ששים שנים, שהיה משנולד שמואל עד הבאת הארון – וישאר נ"ב שנים: **יעקב** אבינו לא מת. וכן משמע(ד) דכתיב "ויגוע" ולא כתיב "וימת", כדמפרש בסוטה (דף יג.) גבי מעשה דחושים: [פי' בפ"ק דר"ה דף יא. מהרב"א]

ביודעה ומכירה קאמינא. פי': ביודעה – שבא עליה, ומכירה – שראה אותה: מלקוש

תורה אור

שְׁקוּלָה כִּשְׁתַּיִם. וּמַאי נִיהוּ — ע"ז, דִּכְתִיב °"כִּי שְׁתַּיִם רָעוֹת עָשָׂה עַמִּי. אוֹתִי עָזְבוּ, מְקוֹר מַיִם חַיִּים, לַחְצוֹב לָהֶם בֹּארוֹת, בֹּארוֹת נִשְׁבָּרִים". וּכְתִיב בְּהוּ °"כִּי עִבְרוּ אִיֵּי כִתִּיִּים וּרְאוּ וְקֵדָר שִׁלְחוּ וְהִתְבּוֹנְנוּ מְאֹד, וגו'. הַהֵימִיר גּוֹי אֱלֹהִים, וְהֵמָּה לֹא אֱלֹהִים? וְעַמִּי הֵמִיר כְּבוֹדוֹ בְּלוֹא יוֹעִיל". תָּנָא: כּוּתִּיִּים עוֹבְדִים לָאֵשׁ, וְקֵדָרִיִּים עוֹבְדִין לַמַּיִם. וְאע"פ שֶׁיּוֹדְעִים שֶׁהַמַּיִם מְכַבִּין אֶת הָאֵשׁ — לֹא הֵמִירוּ אֱלֹהֵיהֶם, "וְעַמִּי הֵמִיר *כְּבוֹדִי בְּלֹא יוֹעִיל". וְא"ל רַב נַחְמָן לְר' יִצְחָק: מ"ד °"וַיְהִי כַּאֲשֶׁר זָקֵן שְׁמוּאֵל", וּמִי סִיב שְׁמוּאֵל כּוּלֵּי הַאי? וְהָא בַּר נ"ב הֲוָה, דְּאָמַר מָר: *מֵת בְּנ"ב שָׁנָה — זֶהוּ מִיתָתוֹ שֶׁל שְׁמוּאֵל הָרָמָתִי! א"ל: הָכִי א"ר יוֹחָנָן: *זִקְנָה קָפְצָה עָלָיו, דִּכְתִיב °"נִחַמְתִּי כִּי הִמְלַכְתִּי אֶת שָׁאוּל". אָמַר לְפָנָיו: רבש"ע שְׁקַלְתַּנִי כְּמֹשֶׁה וְאַהֲרֹן, *דִּכְתִיב °"מֹשֶׁה וְאַהֲרֹן בְּכֹהֲנָיו, וּשְׁמוּאֵל בְּקוֹרְאֵי שְׁמוֹ". מַה מֹשֶׁה וְאַהֲרֹן — לֹא בָּטְלוּ מַעֲשֵׂה יְדֵיהֶם בְּחַיֵּיהֶם, אַף אֲנִי לֹא יִתְבַּטֵּל מַעֲשֵׂה יָדַי בְּחַיַּי. אָמַר הקב"ה: הֵיכִי אַעֲבִיד? לֵימוּת שָׁאוּל — לָא קָא שָׁבֵיק שְׁמוּאֵל. לֵימוּת שְׁמוּאֵל אַדְּזוּטַר — מְרַנְּנֵי אַבַּתְרֵיהּ. לָא לֵימוּת שָׁאוּל וְלָא לֵימוּת שְׁמוּאֵל — כְּבָר הִגִּיעָה מַלְכוּת דָּוִד, *וְאֵין מַלְכוּת נוֹגַעַת בַּחֲבֶרְתָּהּ אֲפִילּוּ כְּמְלֹא נִימָא. אָמַר הקב"ה: אַקְפִּיץ עָלָיו זִקְנָה. הַיְינוּ דִּכְתִיב °"וְשָׁאוּל יוֹשֵׁב בַּגִּבְעָה תַּחַת הָאֶשֶׁל בָּרָמָה". *וְכִי מָה עִנְיַן גִּבְעָה אֵצֶל רָמָה? אֶלָּא לוֹמַר לְךָ: מִי גָּרַם לְשָׁאוּל שֶׁיֵּשֵׁב בַּגִּבְעָה שְׁתֵּי שָׁנִים וּמֶחֱצָה — תְּפִלָּתוֹ שֶׁל שְׁמוּאֵל הָרָמָתִי. וּמִי מִידְּחֵי גַּבְרָא מִקַּמֵּי גַּבְרָא — אִין, דְּא"ר שְׁמוּאֵל בַּר נַחְמָנִי א"ר (*יוֹחָנָן): מ"ד °"עַל כֵּן חָצַבְתִּי בַּנְּבִיאִים הֲרַגְתִּים בְּאִמְרֵי פִי", 'בְּמַעֲשֵׂיהֶם' לֹא נֶאֱמַר, אֶלָּא: "בְּאִמְרֵי פִי". אַלְמָא: מִידְּחֵי גַּבְרָא מִקַּמֵּי גַּבְרָא. רַב נַחְמָן וְר' יִצְחָק הֲווּ יָתְבִי בִּסְעוּדְתָא. אָמַר לֵיהּ רַב נַחְמָן לְר' יִצְחָק: "לֵימָא מָר מִילְּתָא!" א"ל "הָכִי א"ר יוֹחָנָן: אֵין מְסִיחִין בִּסְעוּדָה, שֶׁמָּא יַקְדִּים קָנֶה לַוֶּשֶׁט, וְיָבֹא לִידֵי סַכָּנָה. בָּתַר דִּסְעוּד, א"ל: הָכִי א"ר יוֹחָנָן: יַעֲקֹב אָבִינוּ לֹא מֵת. א"ל: וְכִי בִּכְדִי סָפְדוּ סַפְדָנַיָּא וְחָנְטוּ חַנְטַיָּא וְקָבְרוּ קַבְּרַיָּא? א"ל: מִקְרָא אֲנִי דּוֹרֵשׁ, שֶׁנֶּאֱמַר °"וְאַתָּה, אַל תִּירָא, עַבְדִּי יַעֲקֹב, נְאֻם ה', וְאַל תֵּחַת, יִשְׂרָאֵל, כִּי הִנְנִי מוֹשִׁיעֲךָ מֵרָחוֹק, וְאֶת זַרְעֲךָ מֵאֶרֶץ שִׁבְיָם". מַקִּישׁ הוּא לְזַרְעוֹ. מַה זַּרְעוֹ בַּחַיִּים — אַף הוּא בַּחַיִּים. א"ר יִצְחָק: *כָּל הָאוֹמֵר, "רָחָב רָחָב", מִיָּד נִקְרֵי. א"ל: רַב נַחְמָן: אֲנָא אָמִינָא, וְלָא אִיכְפַּת לִי! א"ל: כִּי קָאָמִינָא — בְּיוֹדְעָהּ וּבְמַכִּירָהּ *(וּבְמַזְכִּיר אֶת שְׁמָהּ.) כִּי הֲווּ מִיפַּטְרִי מֵהֲדָדֵי, א"ל: "לִיבָרְכַן מָר"! אֲמַר לֵיהּ: אֶמְשׁוֹל לְךָ מָשָׁל, לְמה"ד — לְאָדָם שֶׁהָיָה הוֹלֵךְ בַּמִּדְבָּר, וְהָיָה רָעֵב וְעָיֵף וְצָמֵא, וּמָצָא אִילָן שֶׁפֵּירוֹתָיו מְתוּקִין, וְצִילּוֹ נָאֶה, וְאַמַּת הַמַּיִם עוֹבֶרֶת תַּחְתָּיו. אָכַל מִפֵּירוֹתָיו, וְשָׁתָה מִמֵּימָיו, וְיָשַׁב בְּצִילּוֹ. וּכְשֶׁבִּיקֵּשׁ לֵילֵךְ, אָמַר: אִילָן, אִילָן, בַּמֶּה אֲבָרֶכְךָ? אִם אוֹמַר לְךָ שֶׁיְּהוּ פֵּירוֹתֶיךָ מְתוּקִין — הֲרֵי פֵּירוֹתֶיךָ מְתוּקִין. שֶׁיְּהֵא צִילְּךָ נָאֶה — הֲרֵי צִילְּךָ נָאֶה. שֶׁתְּהֵא אַמַּת הַמַּיִם עוֹבֶרֶת תַּחְתֶּיךָ — הֲרֵי אַמַּת הַמַּיִם עוֹבֶרֶת תַּחְתֶּיךָ. אֶלָּא, יְהִי רָצוֹן שֶׁכָּל נְטִיעוֹת שֶׁנּוֹטְעִין מִמְּךָ יִהְיוּ

(ירמיהו ב; שם; ש"א ח; שם טו; תהלים צט; ש"א כב; הושע ו; ירמיהו ל; מגילה טו. [ליקוט שם])

שֶׁשְּׁקוּלָה כִּשְׁתַּיִם. דְּכוּתִּיִּים וְקֵדָרִיִּים, כִּדְמְפָרֵשׁ שֶׁהֵרֵעוּ מִשְּׁנֵיהֶן, לֹא הֵבִינוּ מֵהֶן, דְּכוּתִּיִּים וְקֵדָרִיִּים (א) אע"פ שֶׁיִּרְאָתָם פְּחוּתָה לֹא רָצוּ לְהָמִיר – וְעַמִּי הֵמִירוּ בְּאַחֵר, וְלֹא עוֹד אֶלָּא בְּלֹא יוֹעִיל: וְהָאָמַר מָר. בְּמוֹעֵד קָטָן (דף כח.): זוֹ מִיתָתוֹ שֶׁל שְׁמוּאֵל הָרָמָתִי (ב). וְלֹא *כָּרֵת הִיא. בְּמַסֶּכֶת שְׂמָחוֹת (פ"ג) מְפָרֵשׁ: מֵת בְּכָךְ שָׁנִים – זוֹ הִיא מִיתַת כָּרֵת. בְּכָךְ וְכָךְ – זוֹ הִיא מִיתַת אַסְכָּרָה: יָמָיו שֶׁל שְׁמוּאֵל נ"ב שָׁנָה. דִּכְתִיב "עַד יִגָּמֵל הַנַּעַר" וגו' – דְּשִׁירֵי"ר בְּלַעַ"ז. וְכ"ד חֳדָשִׁים נִקְרָא תִּינוֹק, וּכְתִיב (שמואל א א) "וְיָשַׁב שָׁם עַד עוֹלָם", עוֹלָמוֹ שֶׁל לֵוִי חֲמִשִּׁים שָׁנָה, שֶׁנֶּאֱמַר (במדבר ח) "וּמִבֶּן חֲמִשִּׁים שָׁנָה יָשׁוּב מִצְּבָא הָעֲבוֹדָה". (*בְּבִכּוּרוֹת) יְרוּשַׁלְמִי וּבְסֵדֶר עוֹלָם תִּמְצָא כִּשְׁנֵי דַפִּין תּוֹסֶפֶת עַל זֶה: קָפְצָה. הִלְבִּין שְׂעָרוֹ: נִחַמְתִּי. וְרָצָה הקב"ה לְהוֹרְגוֹ מִיָּד: שְׁקַלְתַּנִי כְּמֹשֶׁה וְאַהֲרֹן דִּכְתִיב מֹשֶׁה וְאַהֲרֹן בְּכֹהֲנָיו וּשְׁמוּאֵל בְּקוֹרְאֵי שְׁמוֹ וגו'. שָׁוִין הֵן: מַעֲשֵׂה יְדֵיהֶן. יְהוֹשֻׁעַ אַף הוּא הָיָה תַּלְמִידוֹ שֶׁל אַהֲרֹן, כִּדְאָמְרִי' בְּעֵירוּבִין (דף נד:): יָצָא מֹשֶׁה וְשָׁנָה לָהֶן אַהֲרֹן פִּירְקוֹ: כִּי זוּטַר. בָּחוּר: מְרַנְּנֵי כּוּלֵּי עָלְמָא אַבַּתְרֵיהּ. דְּאָמְרִי: מִדְּמִית זוּטַר שְׁמָא ח"ו עֲבֵירָה הָיְתָה בּוֹ: וְכִי מָה עִנְיַן גִּבְעַת בִּנְיָמִין אֵצֶל רָמָה. בְּהַר אֶפְרַיִם: שֶׁיֵּשֵׁב ב' שָׁנִים וּמֶחֱצָה. כִּדְמְפָרֵשׁ בְּסֵדֶר עוֹלָם: שֶׁמָּלַךְ מֵחֲלִית שְׁנַת עַשְׁתֵּי עֶשְׂרֵה וּשְׁנֵים עֶשְׂרֵה וּשְׁלֹשָׁה עָשָׂר, וּשְׁמוּאֵל מֵת בְּתוֹךְ שְׁנַת שְׁלֹשׁ עֶשְׂרֵה לְסוֹף שְׁמוֹנָה חֳדָשִׁים: מִי מִידְחֵי גַּבְרָא כו'. דְּאִידַּחִי שְׁמוּאֵל מִקַּמֵּי דָּוִד: בְּמַעֲשֵׂיהֶם לֹא נֶאֱמַר. דְּמַשְׁמַע בַּעֲבוּר חֵטְא: אֶלָּא בְּאִמְרֵי פִּי. מִפְּנֵי דָּבָר שֶׁגָּזַרְתִּי, כְּגוֹן הַאי מַעֲשֶׂה דִּשְׁמוּאֵל: שֶׁמָּא יַקְדִּים קָנֶה. כְּשֶׁיּוֹצִיא הַקּוֹל נִפְתָּח אוֹתוֹ כּוֹבַע שֶׁעַל פִּי הַקָּנֶה, וְנִכְנָס בּוֹ הַמַּאֲכָל וּמִסְתַּכֵּן. וּלְפִיכָךְ לֹא אוֹמַר לְךָ כְּלוּם. מַאֲכָל וּמַשְׁקֶה הוֹלֵךְ דֶּרֶךְ הַוֶּשֶׁט: ה"ג: לֵימָא לָן מָר מִידֵי. וְלָא גָּרְסִינַן חַד לַחֲבְרֵיהּ: לֹא מֵת. אֶלָּא חַי הוּא לְעוֹלָם: בִּכְדִי. וְכִי בְּחִנָּם סָפְדוּ סַפְדַיָּא וְחָנְטוּ חַנְטַיָּא? דִּכְתִיב בֵּיהּ (בראשית נ) "וַיַּחַנְטוּ (אוֹתוֹ) וַיִּסְפְּדוּ (לוֹ)": מִקְרָא אֲנִי דּוֹרֵשׁ. וְהַאי דְּחָנְטוּ חַנְטַיָּא סְבוּרִים הָיוּ שֶׁמֵּת: מַה זַּרְעוֹ בַּחַיִּים. כְּשֶׁהוּא מְקַבֵּץ אֶת יִשְׂרָאֵל מֵאֶרֶץ שִׁבְיָם – הַחַיִּים הוּא מְקַבֵּץ, שֶׁהֵן בַּשְּׁבִי, שֶׁהַמֵּתִים אֵינָן בַּשְּׁבִי: אַף הוּא בַּחַיִּים. שֶׁיְּבִיאֶנּוּ בַּגּוֹלָה כְּדֵי לִגְאוֹל אֶת בָּנָיו לְעֵינָיו, כְּמוֹ שֶׁמָּלְיָנוּ בְּמִצְרַיִם: "וַיַּרְא יִשְׂרָאֵל" וגו', וְדָרְשִׁינַן: יִשְׂרָאֵל סָבָא. וּדְחָנְטוּ חַנְטַיָּא – נִדְמֶה לָהֶם שֶׁמֵּת, אֲבָל חַי הָיָה: כָּל הָאוֹמֵר רָחָב רָחָב מִיָּד נִקְרִי. נַעֲשֶׂה בַּעַל קֶרִי: לָא אִיכְפַּת לִי. אֵינִי חוֹשֵׁשׁ: בְּיוֹדְעָהּ. הַיְינוּ נַמִּי מַכִּירָהּ: כִּי הֲוָה מִיפַּטַר. רַב נַחְמָן מֵרַב יִצְחָק: וְהָיָה צִילּוֹ נָאֶה. שֶׁזֶּה צָרִיךְ לָאָדָם עָיֵף לָנוּחַ תַּחְתָּיו: וּפֵירוֹתָיו מְתוּקִין. לְרָעֵב: וְאַמַּת הַמַּיִם. לְצָמֵא: יִהְיוּ

מסורת הש"ס

[נ"ל מיתת כרת]

[נ"ל בכורים פ"ב ע"ש]

[נ"ל כבודו]

מו"ק כח.

[שבת קנב.]

[עמ"ש תוס' גיטין סח. ד"ה וכתיב]

[ברכות מח: וש"נ]

[תוספתא דסוטה פי"א]

[נ"ל יונתן]

הגהות הב"ח

(א) רש"י ד"ה ששקולה כו'. נ"ב מלשון רש"י משמע שהיה גורס כותיים עובדים למים וקדריים עובדין לאש וכ"ה בילקוט ע"ש: (ב) ד"ה והאמר מר כו' של שמואל הרמתי כרת היא במס' שמחות מפרש מת בכך וכך שנים כו' כנ"ל ותיבת ולא נמחק: (ג) תום' ד"ה ומי כו' אותן שבעה חדשים שהיה הארון כו' דשעת הריון ונמצא שהיו שמונה: (ד) ד"ה יעקב כו' וכן משמע מדכתיב ויגוע:

רבינו גרשום

ע"א עשרים ושש עבירות כתיבי באותה פרשה התשפט: ומאי ניהו ע"ז דכתיב פן תשחיתון ועשיתם פסל ואמר כל מקום שנאמר השחתה אינו אלא דבר ערות וע"ז. ע"א. מאי ניהו ע"ז כלומר כשהוא עובד הני תרי ע"ז דקדריים וכותיים ומנלן דהאי קרא כי שתים רעות משמע ע"ז כתיב הכא כו': לא בטלו מעשה ידיהן בחייהן. משכן: מרנני כל עם אבתריה. דאמרי לפי שחטא מת בחור. קפצה עליו זקנה דלא רנני עליה דסבר זקן הוא. אלא באמרי פי כגון שמואל: ביודעה ומכירה: שמורה הבריות לפי שהוא מטר הראשון: שיורד בנחת כמו עושה הוראה לבניו בנחת: ששוטף את הגרנות. דמשמע יורה כחץ: שמפיל אילנות. דמשמע *) מחתך מלקושה: סקאין. צלצל: שמל קשיותן. שכשאינו יורה מתענין ומתפללין: או אינו יורה אלא בכסליו: בעתו. היינו י"ז במרחשון: בבירה גרסינן. עד שיגיע ר"ח כסליו כדאמר דאין מתענין אלא עד השלישית שאינה

*) אולי נ"ל דכן משמע לשון מלקוש.

יְהִיוּ כְּמוֹתְךָ. אַף אַתָּה, בַּמֶּה אֲבָרֶכְךָ? אִם בְּתוֹרָה — הֲרֵי (א) תוֹרָה. אִם בְּעוֹשֶׁר — הֲרֵי עוֹשֶׁר. אִם בְּבָנִים — הֲרֵי בָּנִים. אֶלָּא, יְהִי רָצוֹן *שֶׁיִּהְיוּ צֶאֱצָאֵי מֵעֶיךָ כְּמוֹתְךָ.§ ת"ר: יוֹרֶה — שֶׁמּוֹרֶה אֶת הַבְּרִיּוֹת לְהַטִּיחַ גַּגּוֹתֵיהֶן, וּלְהַכְנִיס אֶת פֵּירוֹתֵיהֶן, וְלַעֲשׂוֹת כָּל צָרְכֵיהֶן. (ב) דָּבָר אַחֵר: שֶׁמַּרְוֶה אֶת הָאָרֶץ וּמַשְׁקֶה עַד תְּהוֹם, שֶׁנֶּאֱמַר: (תהלים סה) °"תְּלָמֶיהָ רַוֵּה נַחֵת גְּדוּדֶיהָ בִּרְבִיבִים תְּמוֹגְגֶנָּה צִמְחָהּ תְּבָרֵךְ". דָּבָר אַחֵר: יוֹרֶה — שֶׁיּוֹרֵד בְּנַחַת, וְאֵינוֹ יוֹרֵד בְּזַעַף. אוֹ אֵינוֹ יוֹרֶה אֶלָּא שֶׁמַּשִּׁיר אֶת הַפֵּירוֹת, וּמַשְׁטִיף אֶת הַזְּרָעִים, וּמַשְׁטִיף אֶת הָאִילָנוֹת — ת"ל "מַלְקוֹשׁ". מַה מַּלְקוֹשׁ לִבְרָכָה — אַף יוֹרֶה לִבְרָכָה. אוֹ אֵינוֹ מַלְקוֹשׁ אֶלָּא שֶׁמַּפִּיל אֶת הַבָּתִּים, וּמְשַׁבֵּר אֶת הָאִילָנוֹת, וּמַעֲלֶה אֶת הַסְּקָאִין — ת"ל "יוֹרֶה". מַה יוֹרֶה לִבְרָכָה — אַף מַלְקוֹשׁ לִבְרָכָה. וְיוֹרֶה גּוּפֵיהּ מְנָלַן? דִּכְתִיב (יואל ב) °"וּבְנֵי צִיּוֹן, גִּילוּ וְשִׂמְחוּ בַּה' אֱלֹהֵיכֶם, כִּי נָתַן לָכֶם אֶת הַמּוֹרֶה לִצְדָקָה, וַיּוֹרֶד לָכֶם גֶּשֶׁם, מוֹרֶה וּמַלְקוֹשׁ, בָּרִאשׁוֹן".§ ת"ר: *יוֹרֶה בְּמַרְחֶשְׁוָן וּמַלְקוֹשׁ בְּנִיסָן. אַתָּה אוֹמֵר יוֹרֶה בְּמַרְחֶשְׁוָן וּמַלְקוֹשׁ בְּנִיסָן. אוֹ אֵינוֹ אֶלָּא יוֹרֶה בְּתִשְׁרֵי וּמַלְקוֹשׁ בְּאִיָּיר? ת"ל: "בְּעִתּוֹ". מַלְקוֹשׁ, אָמַר רַב נְהִילַאי בַּר אִידִי אָמַר שְׁמוּאֵל: דָּבָר שֶׁמָּל קַשְׁיוּתֵיהֶן שֶׁל יִשְׂרָאֵל. דְּבֵי ר' יִשְׁמָעֵאל תָּנָא: דָּבָר שֶׁמְּמַלֵּא תְבוּאָה בְּקַשֶּׁיהָ. בְּמַתְנִיתָא תָּנָא: דָּבָר שֶׁיּוֹרֵד עַל הַמְּלִילוֹת וְעַל הַקַּשִּׁין. ת"ר: יוֹרֶה בְּמַרְחֶשְׁוָן וּמַלְקוֹשׁ בְּנִיסָן. אַתָּה אוֹמֵר יוֹרֶה בְּמַרְחֶשְׁוָן. אוֹ אֵינוֹ אֶלָּא בְּחֹדֶשׁ כִּסְלֵיו? ת"ל (דברים יא) °"בְּעִתּוֹ יוֹרֶה וּמַלְקוֹשׁ". מַה מַּלְקוֹשׁ בְּעִתּוֹ — אַף יוֹרֶה בְּעִתּוֹ. (*כֵּיוָן שֶׁיָּצָא נִיסָן וְיָרְדוּ גְּשָׁמִים, אֵינוֹ סִימַן בְּרָכָה.) תַּנְיָא אִידָךְ: יוֹרֶה בְּמַרְחֶשְׁוָן וּמַלְקוֹשׁ בְּנִיסָן, דִּבְרֵי ר"מ. וַחֲכָמִים אוֹמְרִים: יוֹרֶה בְּכִסְלֵיו. *מַאן חֲכָמִים? אָמַר רַב חִסְדָּא: ר' יוֹסֵי הִיא, דְּתַנְיָא: *)אֵיזוֹ הִיא רְבִיעָה רִאשׁוֹנָה? הַבַּכִּירָה — בִּשְׁלֹשָׁה בְּמַרְחֶשְׁוָן. בֵּינוֹנִית — בְּשִׁבְעָה בּוֹ. אֲפִילָה — בְּשִׁבְעָה עָשָׂר בּוֹ. דִּבְרֵי ר"מ. ר' יְהוּדָה אוֹמֵר: בְּשִׁבְעָה, וּבְי"ז וּבְעֶשְׂרִים וּשְׁלֹשָׁה. [א]ר' יוֹסֵי אוֹמֵר: בְּי"ז וּבְעֶשְׂרִים וּשְׁלֹשָׁה, וּבְרֹאשׁ חֹדֶשׁ כִּסְלֵיו. וְכֵן הָיָה ר' יוֹסֵי אוֹמֵר: אֵין הַיְחִידִים מִתְעַנִּין עַד שֶׁיַּגִּיעַ רֹאשׁ חֹדֶשׁ כִּסְלֵיו. אָמַר רַב חִסְדָּא: הֲלָכָה כְּר' יוֹסֵי. אַמֵימָר מַתְנֵי לְהָא דְּרַב חִסְדָּא בְּהָא לִישָּׁנָא: *בִּשְׁלֹשָׁה בְּמַרְחֶשְׁוָן שׁוֹאֲלִין אֶת הַגְּשָׁמִים. רַבָּן גַּמְלִיאֵל אוֹמֵר: בְּשִׁבְעָה בּוֹ. אָמַר רַב חִסְדָּא: [ב]הֲלָכָה כְּרַבָּן גַּמְלִיאֵל. כְּמַאן *אָזְלָא הָא דְּתַנְיָא, "ר"ש בֶּן גַּמְלִיאֵל אוֹמֵר: גְּשָׁמִים שֶׁיָּרְדוּ שִׁבְעָה יָמִים זֶה אַחַר זֶה, אַתָּה מוֹנֶה בָּהֶן רְבִיעָה רִאשׁוֹנָה וּשְׁנִיָּה וּשְׁלִישִׁית"? כְּמַאן — כְּר' יוֹסֵי. אָמַר רַב חִסְדָּא: הֲלָכָה כְּר' יוֹסֵי. בִּשְׁלָמָא רְבִיעָה רִאשׁוֹנָה — לִשְׁאוֹל, שְׁלִישִׁית — לְהִתְעַנּוֹת, שְׁנִיָּה לְמַאי? אָמַר ר' זֵירָא: לִנְדָרִים, דִּתְנַן: הַנּוֹדֵר

רש"י

יהיו כמותך. בתורה, ולעושר וכבוד: יורה. "ונתתי מטר ארצכם בעתו יורה ומלקוש" (דברים יא): יורה. רביעה ראשונה היורדת במרחשון, כדלקמן: למה נקרא יורה — שמורה להן להטיח גגותיהן בטיח של טיט, שלא יטפו גשמים בבית: ולהכנים פירותיהן. שהניחו בשדות לייבשן עד עכשיו: כל צרכיהן. שאר דברים הצריכים לימות הגשמים: שיורד בנחת. והכי משמע: יורה — כאדם שמורה לתלמידיו בנחת, דכתיב (קהלת ט): "דברי חכמים בנחת נשמעים". אי נמי: לשון חץ יורה, ההולך ביושר ואינו נוטה לכאן ולכאן. לשון אחר: שמתכוין לארץ, ואינו יורד בזעף, בספרי: תלמיה רוה. כשאתה מרוה תלמי חרישה של ארץ ישראל: נחת הוא לגדודיה. בני אדם. היינו פשט המקרא. ולקמיה *דריש שאפי' גייסות פוסקות בו: ה"ג: או אינו אלא ששוטף את הזרעים. כלומר, דעד השתא אמרינן יורה לברכה, או אינו אלא יורה לשון קללה כמו "ירה יירה" (שמות יט) — ששובר הכל, או לשון חץ היורה, והכי משמע קרא: "והיה אם שמוע תשמעו אל מצותי" וגו', ואם לאו — ונתתי מטר ארצכם יורה לרעה. מלתא בעלמא הוא, ואורחא דברייתא למתני כי האי גוונא: משיר פירותיהן. שעודן באילן, כגון אתרוגים או רמונים, או סופי תאנים. ולא גרסינן שוטף את הגרנות — דגרנות (ג) במרחשון ליכא: מה מלקוש לברכה. שא"א לדורשו לשבר גרנות ולהשיר פירות, שאינם מצויים באותו הפרק. ואי אתה יכול לדורשו אלא לטובה, שיורד על המלילות ועל הקשין, וממלא את התבואה בקשיה. הדר אמר: דלמא מלקוש קללה הוא, והכי משמע: שמל וקשה, כלומר: מל את הבתים והאילנות, שמפילן ומשברן, וקשה לתבואה: שמעלה סקאים. וברכה דקרא למילוי מים בורות שיחין ומערות. גימגום: שמפיל את הבתים. ומשמעו כדלקמן, שמל קשיותן של ישראל. אי נמי: שמל דבר הקשה — חותך ומשבר את הבתים. כלומר, אין בו תקלת גרנות והשרת פירות, לפי שא"א לו: סקאי. מין ארבה, כדמתרגם "הצלצל" (דברים כח) — סקאה. ומלקוש לשון ארבה, כמו "והנה לקש אחר גזי המלך" (עמוס ז): את המורה לצדקה. אלמא: יורה לטובה: ה"ג: או אינו אלא יורה בתשרי ומלקוש באייר. שיש עדין מלילות וקשין: ת"ל בעתו. יורה במרחשון ומלקוש בניסן, שכך היא העת והזמן, ויפה הוא. כדלקמן דזמן רביעה ראשונה במרחשון הוא. אית ספרים דכתוב בהו: או אינו אלא בכסליו דזמן יורה בכסליו הוא, וכרבנן דפליגי עליה דר"מ לקמן, ת"ל "בעתו" יורה ומלקוש, מה מלקוש בעתו — אף יורה בעתו, דמלקוש זהו שיורד על המלילות ועל הקשין, וזהו ניסן שיש בו קשין ומלילות: דבר שמל קשיותן של ישראל. שכשאינו יורד חוזרין ישראל בתשובה, ומתענין ועושין צדקות: מלילות. ראשי שיבולות שאדם מולל בידו, כדכתיב (דברים כג) "וקטפת מלילות בידך": וקשין. קנה: שממלא תבואה בקשיה. ומשלימה: (ד) הי רביעה. איזה זמן רביעה: בכירה. ראשונה. ולקמן מפרש למאי הלכתא ניהו. יורה יש בו ג' זמני גשמים: אפילה. אחרונה, כמו "כי אפילות הנה" (שמות ט): רבי יהודה אומר. בכירה בז' במרחשון, ובינונית בי"ז, ואפילה בכ"ג. וכולהו הני תלתא "יורה" קרי להו: אין היחידים מתענין כו'. דאמרי' בסמוך: שלישית להתענות, והואיל וזמן שלישית בראש חדש הוא — אין ליחידים להתענות (ה): יחידים. חסידים, והכי אמרי' במתני' לקמן (דף י.): הגיע י"ז במרחשון ולא ירדו גשמים — התחילו היחידים להתענות, שמכאן ואילך זמן רביעה אפילה לר"מ, דקתם מתני' ר"מ. וה"נ אמר ר' יוסי דאין מתענין עד ר"ח כסליו — דהיינו רביעה אפילה, והיינו כחכמים דאמרי יורה בכסליו: אמר רב חסדא הלכה כרבי יוסי. ואמימר תני להא דאמר רב חסדא הלכה כרבן גמליאל, דאינו שואל עד ז' במרחשון: ז' ימים בזה אחר זה. שירדו גשמים (ו) עכשיו א], ופסקו עד יום שביעי, וירדו ז' ימים זה אחר זה — אתה מונה בהן ראשונה ושניה ושלישית: כרבי יוסי. דאליבא דר' יוסי הכי הוו בין רביעה ראשונה ושניה, או שניה ושלישית. דראשונה בי"ז, ושניה בכ"ג — דהיינו ז' ימים עם שני ימי רביעה, ומכ"ג עד ל' — ז' ימים בלא יום רביעה אחרונה. דלכולהו תנאי לא הוי הכי, דלר"מ דאמר ראשונה בג' ושניה בז' — ליכא בין זו לזו אלא ארבעה ימים, בין שניה לשלישית יש י' ימים. ולר' יהודה בין ראשונה לשניה י' ימים, אבל בין שניה לשלישית יש ב] *) יותר: נראה לרבי דהכי גרסינן: אמר רב חסדא הלכה כרבי יהודה דאמר בכירה בז' במרחשון, ואז מתחילין לשאול כדלקמן (דף י.): ראשונה לשאול. מכאן ואילך "ותן טל ומטר": שלישית להתענות. שאם לא ירדו גשמים עד זמן רביעה שלישית אפילו פעם אחת — מתענין היחידים שני וחמישי ושני:

*) ס"א ז' ימים

תוספות

מלקוש לברכה או אינו אלא שמפיל הבתים ומשבר האילנות וכו'. נ"ע אמאי לא קאמר ומשבר הגרנות ומשיר את הפירות כדלעיל: גשמים שירדו ז' ימים זה אחר זה ולא פסקו אתה מונה בהן רביעה ראשונה ושניה. כיון דלא פסקו ז' ימים: דאין בין י"ז לכ"ג אלא ז' ימים: י"ז, י"ח, י"ט, כ', כ"א, כ"ב, כ"ג, אבל לא גרסינן ושלישית, שהרי אם יתחיל בכ"ג וירדו ז' ימים רצופים (ז) אכתי לא תמלא רביעה שלישית דאיכא ח' ימים מכ"ג עד ר"ח כסליו. ואנשי נרבונ"א גורסין: גשמים שירדו ז' ימים זה אחר זה אתה מונה בהם רביעה שניה ושלישית. כילד? הגשמים התחילו באמצע היום וירדו ז' ימים רצופים, א"כ ירדו עד חצי יום של ר"ח מעט לעט: דאזלי

מסורת הש"ס

[ב"מ קז.] — דף ח: — [לעיל ה.] — [עירובין סג. וש"נ] *) נדרים סג. [ע"ש תוספת' פ"א] — לקמן י. [וש"נ] — [נדרים סג. ע"ש תוספתא פ"א]

עין משפט נר מצוה

יג א מיי' פ"י מהלכות נדרים הל' יא ופ"א מהלכות מתנות עניים הלכה יא סמג לאוין רמב טוש"ע י"ד סי' רכ סעיף יח:

יד ב מיי' פ"ב מהלכות תפלה הלכה טז סמג עשין יט טוש"ע א"ח סי' קיז סעיף א:

גליון הש"ס

גמ' לנדרים דתנן. תמוה לי אמאי לא נקט נמי לשכירות בתים דקתני ברישא דמתני' שם המשכיר בית לחבירו עד הגשמים עד שתרד רביעה שניה:

הגהות מהר"ב רנשבורג

א] רש"י ד"ה שבעה ימים וכו' שירדו גשמים עכשיו ופסקו נ"ב ולא פסקו: ב] ד"ה כר' יוסי וכו' אבל בין שניה לשלישית יש יותר נ"ל אין יותר:

רש"א מ"ז ועי' בילקוט ולעיל גבי או אינו אלא מלקוש באייר ת"ל בעתו שייך למיתני בתר הכי כיון שיצא ניסן כו'

רבינו גרשום

שאינה יורדת: כמאן כר' יוסי דאמר ראשונה בי"ז ושניה בכ"ג הרי ראשונה ושניה בז' ימים: עד שתרד רביעה ראשונה אינה חשובה כלום:

הגהות הב"ח

(א) גמ' אם בתורה הרי יש לך תורה ואם לגדולה הרי יש לך גדולה ואם לכבוד הרי יש לך כבוד ואם בעושר הרי יש לך עושר אם בבנים הרי יש לך בנים אלא יהי רצון שיהו כל צאצאי מעיך: (ב) שם ולעשות כל צרכיהן ד"א יורה שיורד בנחת ואינו יורד בזעף ד"א שמרוה את הארץ כו' נמחה תברך או אינו יורה כו' את הזרעים ומשבר את הגרנות ת"ל יורה ומלקוש מה מלקוש לברכה: (ג) רש"י ד"ה משיר כו' לגרנות במרחשון ליכא וברכה דקרא למילוי מים בורות שיחין ומערות גימגו"ס הס"ד ואח"כ מה"ד יורה ומלקוש אם מלקוש לטובה יורה נמי לטובה ליתנא אחרינא מה מלקוש לברכה אף א"ח כו' התבואה בקשיה ומה"ד הדר אמר וכו' וקשה לתבואה שמעלה סקאים הס"ד ואח"כ מה"ד שמפיל את כו' ומשבר את הבתים ואילנות ואין בו תקלת כו' כצ"ל ותיבת כלומר נמחק: (ד) ד"ה הי רביעה נ"ל איזוהי רביעה: (ה) ד"ה אין היחידים כו' אין ליחידים להתענות אלא משלישית ואילך והכי אמרינן במתני' לקמן וכו' דאמרי יורה בכסליו הס"ד ואח"כ מה"ד ואמימר תני להא דאמר כו' כצ"ל ותיבות אמר רב חסדא הלכה כר' יוסי נמחק: (ו) ד"ה ז' ימים כו' שירדו הגשמים עכשיו ולא פסקו עד: (ז) תום' ד"ה גשמים כו' ז' ימים רצופים אח"כ ירדו עד חצי יום אכתי לא תמלא:

רבינו חננאל

מורה ומלקוש. מורה שמורה את הבריות להטיח גגותיהן ולהכנים פירותיהן מלקוש שמל קשיותיהן של ישראל. תנא דבר שיורד על המלילות ועל הקשין וממלא התבואה בקשיה: ת"ר מורה במרחשון ומלקוש בניסן דברי ר' מאיר וחכמים אומרים מורה בחדש כסלו. מאן חכמים אמר רב חסדא ר' יוסי היא. דתניא מאימתי זמן רביעה. ר' מאיר אומר בבירה בשלשה בינונית בשבעה אפילה בי"ז. ר' יהודה אומר בשבעה ובשבעה עשר ובעשרים ושלשה. ר' יוסי אומר בי"ז ובכ"ג ובר"ח כסלו וכן היה ר' יוסי אומר אין היחידים מתענין עד שיגיע ר"ח כסלו. כמאן אזלא הא דתניא ר"ש בן גמליאל אומר גשמים שירדו ז' ימים זה אחר זה אתה מונה רביעה ראשונה ושניה ושלישית כמאן כר' יוסי פי' כגון שהתחילו הגשמים לירד ביום הראשון מחצי יום וכשתחשוב ז' ימים מעת לעת אתה מוצא מקצת מיום השמיני להשלמת ז' ימים ולא תמצא מאלו התנאים בז' ימים למנות בהן רביעה ראשונה ושניה או שניה ושלישית אלא לר' יוסי בלבד דאי ר"מ ראשונה ושניה משכחת לה שניה ושלישית לא משכחת לה דהא בין שניה ושלישית י' ימים ואי לר' יהודה שניה ושלישית הוא משכחת לה ראשונה ושניה לא משכחת לה דהא לדבריו י' ימים בין הראשונה לשניה אבל ר' יוסי דאמר ראשונה בי"ז שניה בכ"ג הנה ז' ימים ביניהם. אתה מונה בהן ראשונה ושניה ואם התחילו הגשמים בחצי היום בכ"ג יום למרחשון נמצאו עד ר"ח כסליו ז' ימים ומקצת היום של יום ראשון אתה משלימן מיום ראשון של חדש כסלו נמצאת מונה להן שניה ושלישית והוא שהיה (ר' א') [ר"ח] מרחשון חסר כי בשלשה איתא בפיר' בתוספתא שהיה ר' יוסי אומר בבירה בי"ז בינונית בכ"ג. אפילה בל'. אמר רב חסדא הלכה כר' יוסי ואמרינן בשלמא רביעה ראשונה לשאול ותן טל ומטר כר' מאיר דאמר בבירה בג' במרחשון דתנן בג' במרחשון שואלין את הגשמים שלישית להתענות כדתנן הגיע י"ז במרחשון ולא ירדו גשמים התחילו היחידים מתענין אלא רביעה שניה למאי פירוש כיון דמרביעה ראשונה מתחילין לשאול עד רביעה שלישית ובשלישית מתחילין להתענות שניה למה לי הלא מתחלת רביעה ראשונה עד שלישית כולן ימי שאלה הן למה נקראת שניה והביאו טעם ר' זירא ורב זביד

*א הנודר 'עד הגשמים',(א) — *משירדו גשמים עד שתרד רביעה שניה. רב זביד אמר: לזיתים. דתנן: *במאימתי כל אדם מותרין בלקט, בשכחה, ובפאה — משילכו הנמושות. בפרט ובעוללות — משילכו עניים בכרם ויבואו. בזיתים — משתרד רביעה שניה. מאי נמושות? אמר ר' יוחנן: סבי דאזלי *אתיגרא. ר"ל אמר: לקוטי בתר לקוטי. רב פפא אמר: כדי להלך בשבילי הרשות, דאמר מר: *גמהלכין כל אדם בשבילי הרשות עד שתרד רביעה שניה. רב נחמן בר יצחק אמר: לבער פירות שביעית, *דתנן: *עד מתי נהנין ושורפין בתבן ובקש של שביעית — עד שתרד רביעה שניה. מאי טעמא — דכתיב °"ולבהמתך ולחיה אשר בארצך". דכל זמן שחיה אוכלת בשדה — האכל לבהמתך בבית. כלה *לחיה מן השדה — כלה לבהמתך מן הבית. אמר רבי אבהו: מאי לשון רביעה — דבר שרובע את הקרקע, כדרב יהודה. דאמר רב יהודה: מיטרא בעלה דארעא הוא, שנאמר °"כי כאשר ירד הגשם והשלג מן השמים, ושמה לא ישוב, כי אם הרוה את הארץ, והולידה והצמיחה". ואמר רבי אבהו: רביעה ראשונה — כדי שתרד בקרקע טפח. שניה — כדי לגוף בה פי חבית. אמר רב חסדא: גשמים שירדו כדי לגוף בהן פי חבית — אין בהן משום "ועצר". ואמר רב חסדא: גשמים שירדו קודם "ועצר" אין בהן משום "ועצר". אמר אביי: לא אמרן אלא קודם "ועצר" דאורתא, אבל קודם "ועצר" דצפרא יש בהן משום "ועצר". דאמר רב יהודה בר יצחק: *הני ענני דצפרא לית בהו משָשא, דכתיב °"מה אעשה לך, אפרים? מה אעשה לך, יהודה? וחסדכם כענן בקר" וגו'. א"ל רב פפא לאביי: והא אמרי אינשי: "במפתח בבי מיטרא — בר חמרא מוך שקך וגני"! לא קשיא. הא — דקטיר בעיבא, הא — דקטיר בעננא. אמר רב יהודה: טבא לשתא דטבת ארמלתא. איכא דאמרי: דלא ביירי תרביצי. ואיכא דאמרי: דלא שקיל שודפנא. איני? והאמר רב חסדא: טבא לשתא דטבת מנוולתא! לא קשיא. הא — דאתא מיטרא מעיקרא, הא — דלא אתא מיטרא מעיקרא. ואמר רב חסדא: גשמים שירדו על מקצת מדינה ועל מקצת מדינה לא ירדו — אין בהן משום "ועצר". איני? והכתיב °"וגם אנכי מנעתי מכם את הגשם בעוד שלשה חדשים לקציר, והמטרתי על עיר אחת, ועל עיר אחת לא אמטיר, חלקה אחת תמטר" וגו'. *ואמר רב יהודה אמר רב: שתיהן לקללה! לא קשיא. הא — דאתא טובא, הא — דאתא כדמבעי ליה. אמר רב אשי: דיקא נמי, דכתיב: "תמטר" — תהא מקום מטר, ש"מ. א"ר אבהו: *המאימתי מברכין על הגשמים — משיצא חתן לקראת כלה. ומאי מברך? אמר רב יהודה אמר רב: *"מודים אנחנו לך, ה' אלהינו, על כל טפה וטפה שהורדת לנו". ור' יוחנן מסיים בה הכי: "אילו פינו מלא שירה כים, ולשוננו רנה כהמון גליו" כו', עד:[א] "אל יעזבונו רחמיך, ה' אלהינו, ולא עזבונו. ברוך רוב ההודאות". "רוב ההודאות" ולא "כל ההודאות"? אמר רבא, אימא: "אל ההודאות". אמר רב פפא: זהלכך נימרינהו

תורה אור: ויקרא כה | ישעיהו נה | הושע ו | עמוס ד | [לקמן כ:] | [ע"ז ה: ב"מ קכט:]

רש"י

הנודר עד הגשמים. דאמר: קונם אם אהנה מדבר זה עד הגשמים: עד שתרד רביעה שניה. בנדרים הולכין אחר לשון בני אדם, ואין קורין גשמים לראשונה, עד שתרד שניה. שמכאן ואילך מקולקלות הדרכים ומאוסות מפני הגשמים. ל"א: עד הגשמים משמע תרי, דהיינו רביעה שניה: כל אדם. אפילו העשירים: *) פרט. "לא תפאר אחריך" (דברים כד) – לא תטול תפארתו ממנו: משילכו הנמושות. בשדה, דמכאן ואילך נתייאשו שאר העניים, לפי שיודעין אם נשאר לקט שכחה ופאה – נמושות נטלום: נמושות. לשון ממשש: משילכו עניים בכרם ויבואו. כלומר: שלקטו וחזרו ובאו פעם שניה, והשתא מסחי דעתייהו עניים: משתרד רביעה שניה. דעד ההיא שעתא לקטו הכל: דאזלי אתיגרא. הולכין בנחת, ומעייני טפי. "מחזיק בפלך" (שמואל ב ג) מתרגמא: אתיגרא: לקוטי בתר לקוטי. עני מוליך בנו אחריו, שמכאן ואילך פוסקין שאר עניים מללקוט: ה"ג: רב פפא אמר לשבילי הרשות. כלומר, שיש רשות מב"ד לעוברי דרכים לקצר שבילן לילך בשדות: עד שתרד רביעה שניה. שמכאן ואילך גדלה התבואה, וקשה לה דישת הרגל. דאמר מר בפרק "מרובה"* בתנאים שהתנה יהושע: מהלכין בשבילי הרשות וכו': בתבן וקש של שביעית. ספיחים שגדלו בשביעית, דיש בהן איסור שביעית. או תבואה שגדלה בשביעית לאחר שנכנסה: כלה לחיה מן השדה. לשון זכר, כמו (בראשית יח) "עשו כלה", כלומר: כלה האוכל: כלה לבהמתך. כמו "כלה בחימה כלה ואינימו" (תהלים נט), ומשירדה רביעה שניה מכאן ואילך אין תבן וקש בשדות, שהגשמים עושין אותן זבל: והולידה. כאדם שמוליד: גשמים ברביעה ראשונה. אם באין כל כך שנימס הקרקע (ב) – יפין הן ואין צריך להתענות: לגוף בה פי חבית. שהשוחת מן המים עד שנעשה טיחוח כל כך שיכול לעשות מגופת חבית בלא תוספת מים: אין בהם משום ועצר. אין זו קללה של "ועצר את השמים": קודם ועצר. קודם זמן ק"ש, דכתיב ביה "ועצר את השמים", אף על פי שלא יהיה רוב גשמים: אבל ירדו קודם ועצר דצפרא יש בהן משום ועצר. הואיל ולא ירדו ביום, ואין יפין לעולם: לית בהו משָשא. ואין שנתן מתברכת: וחסדכם כענן בקר. שאין בו ממש: מיטרא במיפתח בבי. אם יורדין בבקר, כשפותחין הפתחים – יקפל החמר שמוכר תבואה את שקו ליכנס לישן, מפני שהשנה מתברכת, ויהיה שובע בעולם ולא *ישתכר במכירת תבואתו. אלמא: יפין הן: דקטיר בעיבא. אם נתקשרו שמים בעננים עבים, ולא קלושים – אין בהם משום ועצר: דקטיר בעננא. שהיא קלושה מעט – אין בו ממש: טבא לשתא. אחריה. כלומר, טובה יש לשנה דטבת ארמלתא – שאין גשמים יורדין בה להרביע את הארץ: איכא דאמרי דלא ביירי תרביצי. אותן מקומות שמרביצין בהן תורה אינן בורות, מפני שהדרכים יפין הן, והולכין התלמידים ממקום למקום ללמוד תורה. ל"א: לא ביירי תרביצי – גנות, שאינן גדילין על רוב מים, כגון כרשינין: לא שקיל שודפנא. אין השדפון נאחז ומתדבק בתבואה: מנוולתא. שהדרכים מנוולים בטיט מפני הגשמים: הא דאתא מיטרא מעיקרא. שירדו הגשמים בזמנן במרחשון, וירדו אף בטבת – רעים הן, שכבר די לעולם בגשמים של מרחשון: דלא אתא מיטרא מעיקרא. טבא לשתא, דטבת מנוולתא. לשון אחר: הא דאתא מיטרא מעיקרא – טבא, דמנוולתא: אין בהם משום ועצר. דאותן של קצת מדינה שירדו להן גשמים מוכרין לאחרים: ואמר רב יהודה אמר רב שתיהן לקללה. אותן שירדו ואותן שלא ירדו, מפני שרוב גשמים קלקלו את תבואתם: הא דאיכא מיטרא טובא. יותר מדאי, שתיהן לקללה: כדמבעי ליה. אין בהם משום "ועצר", שקצת מדינה מספק לקצת מדינה: תמטר תהא מקום מטר. כלומר יותר מדאי: מאימתי מברכין על הגשמים. בפרק "הרואה" (ברכות דף נד.) אמרינן: על הגשמים אומר "הטוב והמטיב", והתם (דף נט.) פרכינן הך ברכה דתקון לה רבנן, ומשנינן לה: הא – דחזא מיחזא, והא – דשמע משמע: חתן לקראת כלה. שירדו כל כך, שכשהטפה נופלת יוצאה אחרת ועולה כנגדה, מפי מורי. ל"א: שהשלוליקין מקלחין מים, שוק מקלח וזה מקלח כנגדו: רוב ההודאות. כלומר: רוב ההודאות אתה קורא להקב"ה, ולא כל ההודאות. והכי משמע: ברוך אתה ברוב ההודאות, ולא בכל. אלא כך חותם: בא"י אמ"ה אל ההודאות, דמשמע כל ההודאות: למימרינהו:

תוספות

דאזלי אתיגרא. פי': שהולכים במקלות ונשענים עליהם. ואמר דתרגומא "מחזיק בפלך" דכתיב *גבי יואב: היי באתיגרא: בשבילי הרשות. פי': בדרך שעשוי דרך השדות והכרמים: עד שתרד רביעה שניה. מכאן ואילך מזקי להו: עד מתי נהנין ושורפין בתבן ובקש של שביעית. פירוש: בשנה שמינית וכו'. וס"ל כמ"ד ספיחי זרעים מותרים. ולר' עקיבא דאמר ספיחי זרעים אסורים, מקרא ד"הן לא נזרע ולא נאסוף" כדמפרש במסכת פסחים פרק "מקום שנהגו" (דף נא:) – צ"ל דמוקי לה ולבהמתך ולחיה וגו' בספיחי אילנות, ולאו דוקא תבואה קאמר, אלא כגון תבואת הכרם דהיינו אילנות, אבל ספיחי זרעים – אסורים: לא אמרן אלא קודם ועצר דאורתא. כלומר: שירדו גשמים קודם ק"ש של ערבית. אבל קודם של שחרית – יש בהם משום "ועצר", כדאמר רב שמואל בר רב יצחק: איכא דאמרי לא ביירי תרביצי. שאין הגנות ריקים מזרעים: וכל

עין משפט נר מצוה

[שמואל ב ג]

טו א מיי' פ"י מהלכות נדרים הלכה יא סמג לאוין רמב טוש"ע י"ד סימן רכ סעיף יח:

נדרים סב: שביעית פ"ט מ"ז

פאה פ"ח מ"א ב"מ כא:

טז ב מיי' פ"א מהלכות מתנות עניים הלכה יא:

[הערוך בערך גד ובערך נמש גרס אתיגדא ע"ש שמביא ראיה מתרגום]

יז ג מיי' פ"ה מהלכות נזקי ממון הלכה ד טור ח"מ סי' רעד:

[במשנה דשביעית איתא מאימתי כו' משתרד רביעה כו' עי' ר"ש שם וברא"ש כתב דשניהם אמת]

יח ד מיי' פ"ז מהלכות שמטה ויובל הל' א סמג עשין קמח:

יט ה מיי' פ"י מהלכות ברכות הלכה ו סמג עשין כז טוש"ע א"ח סי' רכא סעיף א:

כ ו ז מיי' שם הלכה ה טוש"ע שם סעיף ב:

מסורת הש"ס

[נ"ל עד שיהו כך איתא במשנה נדרים סב: ועי' במשנה ז פ"ט דשביעית]

*) [נ"ל פאה ר"ל בזית עי' חולין קלא:]

ב"ק פא.

[פסחים נב. נדה נא:]

[ב"ק דף פא.]

ברכות נט. ע"ש

ברכות נט: וע"ש

[גי' רי"ף אר"י מודים וגי' רא"ש א"ר הונא]

[שם בברכות פרש"י בע"א ע"ש]

הגהות הב"ח

(א) גמ' הנודר עד הגשמים עד שיהו גשמים עד שתרד: (ב) רש"י ד"ה גשמים שנימס הקרקע בעומק טפח יפין הן:

הגהות הגר"א

[א] גמ' כהמון גליו כו' עד כ"ב וימליכו את שמך מלכנו כ"ה גירסת הרי"ף וש"פ:

גליון הש"ס

רש"י ד"ה מאימתי מברכים כו' ומשנין לה הא דחזי מחזי. ק"ל הא לחינן שם כך תירוצא ומסקינן אידי ואידי דמחזי כאן לאתא טובא וכו' וצ"ע:

רבינו חננאל

למאי הלכתא. (למאי הלכתא) נקראת שניה. ובפרק ג' פירש כי רביעה א' וב' לשאול ג' להתענות וכן הלכתא. וא"ר זירא שניה לנודר דתניא הנודר עד הגשמים עד שתרד רביעה שניה רב זביד אמר לזיתים. דתניא מאימתי כל אדם מותרין בלקט שכחה ופאה משילכו הנמושות בפרט ובעוללות משילכו עניים בכרם ויבאו. בזיתים עד שתרד רביעה שניה. סבי דאזלו אתגרא. זקנים המהלכים במשענת בנתיבי בני רה"ר. מאי לשון רביעה שרובע לקרקע כדרב יהודה דאמר מטרא בעלה דארעא היא שנאמר והולידה והצמיחה. רביעה [ראשונה] כדי שתרד בקרקע טפח. שניה כדי לגוף בה פי חבית: אמר רב חסדא גשמים שירדו כדי לגוף בה פי חבית אין בהם משום ועצר. וכן גשמים שירדו קודם ועצר. פי' קודם ק"ש שכתוב בה ועצר את השמים. אמר אביי לא אמרן אלא קודם קרית של ערב אבל קודם שמע דצפרא יש בהן משום ועצר כלומר המטר היורד בשחר אינו כלום ועובר הוא כדכתיב חסדכם כענן בקר והני מילי במטר דקטיר בעננא. והוא שעמד והולך. אבל אם נתקשרו שמים בעבים בבקר אינו פוסק אותו היום מטר וזהו האמור בר חמרא מוך שקיך וגני. הצע השק שלך ושכב שאין לך היום הליכה. וטוביא דשתא דטבת ארמלתא דלא ביירא תרביצי. כגון הא דגרסי' (כ"ג ז.) חד מטיא תרביצא וחד מטיא אספלידא. וי"א דלא ביירי תרביצי ביירי מלשון בורה כדכתיב והאדמה לא תשם ומתרגמינן וארעא לא תבור כלומר שהשקה ונשאר בה לחלוחית עדיין (משתיב) חורשין אותה וזורעין אותה היינו דלא ביירי תרביצי. פי' טבת ארמלתא שלא ירדו גשמים בטבת שהגשמים הם בעל לארץ שנאמר והולידה והצמיחה (הן) [אין] מניחין *) האכסדרא בורא (שדה) בור שוכנין בה מפני שלא באו גשמים ליכנס בבית אלא יושבין באכסדראות כמו אלמנה שאין לה ישיבת בית איכא דאמרי דלא שקיל שיבתנא כלומר לא נסתלק החום אלא ישנים בפתחים פתוחים מפני חוק החום איני כי טוב היא כאשר לא יבא המטר בטבת והאמר רב חסדא טבא דטבת מטולתא כלומר בעת שיהו בני אדם מטונפים את רגליהם ובבגדיהם בטיט בזה טובת השנה ושנינן אם היו גשמים במרחשון וכסלו הטוב שלא יהיו בטבת גשמים ואם לא היו גשמים במרחשון וכסלו (הוו ביה תשתא) [טוביא דשתא] דטבת מטולתא. ועוד א' גשמים שירדו על מקצת מדינה אין בהם משום ועצר איני והכתיב חלקה אחת תמטר וחלקה אשר לא תמטיר עליה תיבש ואמר רב שתיהן לקללה ושנינן אי אתא טובא ומתכנשין תמן מיא לקללה. כדכתיב [תמטר] שם יהיה המטר כנוס כלומר נקוים שם המים כגון

*) זהו פי' ב' ומ"ש למעלה כגון הא דגרסי' כו' על אספלידא שייך לכאן.

רבינו גרשום

מאימתי כל אדם מותרין בלקט בשכחה ובפאה של בעה"ב המוציא לקט שכחה ופאה יכול ליקח. משילכו הנמושות שכבר הסיחו עניים מדעתן. אתיגדא בטורח שכבר לא השאירו כלום: שבילי הרשות דרכים שהם ברשות היחיד בשדות: ברביעה *) שניה כבר כלה לחיה: שניה אין צריך אלא כדי שיכול ללוש מהן עפר לגוף פי החבית. אין בהן משום ועצר. כלומר דיש בהן משום ברכה. קודם ועצר דק"ש. מוך קפל. ודמוך כלומר שכל היום יורד מטר: עיבא עבים עבות הן של ברכה ובהכי אמרו מוך שקך וגני: ענני קטנים. ארמלתא שאין יורד גשמים. לא ביירי תרביצי אין חריבין בתי מדרשות שיכולין תלמידים לבוא שאין מעכבין להן גשמים ובטבת יש להם פנאי יותר מכל ימות השנה ע"א שאין מפסידין הגנות: דאתא מיטרא מעיקרא. קודם טבת ובטבת (נמי אתי טוביה אי ומוקפין) הוי ארמלתא: הא כתיב והמטרתי **) לפורענות: הא דאתא טובא אין בהן משום ועצר דברכה הוי. דאתא כדבעי כלומר זעיר הוי קללה דיקא נמי דקרא בזעיר מיטרא כתיב: תמטר תהא מקום מטר כל דהו: משיצא חתן לקראת כלה. משיצאו מים

*) נראה דל"ל עד מתי נהנין וכו' עד שתרד רביעה שניה שאז כבר כלה לחיה. **) נ"ל ואר"י אמר רב שתיהן לפורענות.

*נימרינהו לתרוייהו: "אל ההודאות" ו"רוב ההודאות". אמר ר' אבהו: גדול יום הגשמים מתחיית המתים. דאילו תחיית המתים לצדיקים, ואילו גשמים — בין לצדיקים בין לרשעים. ופליגא דרב יוסף, דאמר רב יוסף: *מתוך שהיא שקולה כתחיית המתים — קבעוה בתחיית המתים. אמר רב יהודה: גדול יום הגשמים כיום שניתנה בו תורה, שנא' °"יערף כמטר לקחי", ואין לקח אלא תורה, שנא' °"כי לקח טוב נתתי לכם תורתי אל תעזובו". רבא אמר: יותר מיום שניתנה בו תורה, שנאמר: "יערף כמטר לקחי". *מי נתלה במי — הוי אומר: קטן נתלה בגדול. רבא רמי, כתיב: "יערף כמטר לקחי", וכתיב: "תזל כטל אמרתי"! אם תלמיד חכם הגון הוא — כטל, ואם לאו — עורפהו כמטר. תניא: היה ר' בנאה אומר: כל העוסק בתורה לשמה, תורתו נעשית לו סם חיים, שנאמר °"עץ חיים היא למחזיקים בה". ואומר: °"רפאות תהי לשרך". ואומר: °"כי מוצאי מצא חיים". וכל העוסק בתורה שלא לשמה, נעשית לו סם המות, שנאמר: "יערף כמטר לקחי", ואין 'עריפה' אלא הריגה, שנאמר °"וערפו שם את העגלה בנחל". א"ל ר' ירמיה לר' זירא: "ליתי מר ליתני"! א"ל: חלש לבאי, ולא יכילנא. לימא מר מילתא דאגדתא. א"ל: "הכי אמר ר' יוחנן: מאי דכתיב °"כי האדם עץ השדה", וכי אדם עץ שדה הוא? אלא משום דכתיב °"כי ממנו תאכל, ואותו לא תכרת", וכתיב: "אותו תשחית וכרת". הא כיצד? אם ת"ח הגון הוא — "ממנו תאכל, ואותו לא תכרת", ואם לאו — "אותו תשחית וכרת".

אמר רבי חמא (*אמר רבי) חנינא: מאי דכתיב °"ברזל בברזל יחד"? לומר לך: מה ברזל זה, אחד מחדד את חבירו — אף שני תלמידי חכמים מחדדין זה את זה בהלכה. אמר רבה בר בר חנה: למה נמשלו דברי תורה כאש, שנאמר °"הלא כה דברי כאש נאם ה'"? לומר לך: מה אש אינו דולק יחידי — אף דברי תורה אין מתקיימין ביחידי. והיינו דאמר רבי יוסי בר חנינא: *מאי דכתיב °"חרב אל הבדים ונואלו" — חרב על שונאיהן של תלמידי חכמים שעוסקין בד בבד בתורה. ולא עוד אלא שמטפשין, שנאמר: "ונואלו". ולא עוד אלא שחוטאין. כתיב הכא: "ונואלו", וכתיב התם °"אשר נואלנו ואשר חטאנו". ואיבעית אימא מהכא °"נואלו שרי צוען, [וגו'] והתעו את מצרים". אמר רב נחמן בר יצחק: למה נמשלו דברי תורה כעץ, שנאמר: °"עץ חיים היא למחזיקים בה"? לומר לך: מה עץ קטן מדליק את הגדול — אף תלמידי חכמים קטנים מחדדים את הגדולים. והיינו דאמר ר' חנינא: *הרבה למדתי מרבותי, ומחבירי יותר מרבותי, ומתלמידי יותר מכולן. רבי חנינא בר פפא רמי: כתיב °"לקראת צמא התיו מים", וכתיב °"הוי, כל צמא, לכו למים"! אם תלמיד הגון הוא — "לקראת צמא התיו מים", ואי לא — "הוי, כל צמא, לכו למים". רבי חנינא בר חמא רמי: כתיב °"יפוצו מעינותיך חוצה", וכתיב: °"יהיו לך לבדך"! [א]אם תלמיד הגון הוא — "יפוצו מעינותיך חוצה", ואם לאו — "יהיו לך לבדך". (*ואמר) רבי חנינא בר אידי: [ב]למה נמשלו דברי תורה למים, דכתיב: "הוי, כל צמא, לכו למים" — לומר לך: מה מים מניחין מקום גבוה והולכין למקום נמוך, אף דברי תורה אין מתקיימין אלא במי שדעתו שפלה. *ואמר רבי אושעיא: למה נמשלו דברי תורה לשלשה משקין הללו: במים, וביין, ובחלב, דכתיב: "הוי, כל צמא, לכו למים", וכתיב °"לכו, שברו, ואכלו, ולכו, שברו בלא כסף ובלא מחיר יין וחלב"? לומר לך: מה שלשה משקין הללו אין מתקיימין אלא בפחות שבכלים, אף דברי תורה אין מתקיימין אלא במי שדעתו שפלה. (א) כדאמרה ליה *ברתיה דקיסר לר' יהושע בן חנניה: אי, *חכמה מפוארה בכלי מכוער! אמר לה: אביך רמי חמרא במני דפחרא? אמרה ליה: אלא במאי נירמי? אמר לה: אתון דחשביתו — רמו במאני דהבא וכספא. אזלה ואמרה ליה לאבוה. רמייא לחמרא במני דהבא וכספא, ותקיף. אתו ואמרו ליה. אמר לה לברתיה: מאן אמר לך הכי? אמרה ליה: רבי יהושע בן חנניה. קריוהו. אמר ליה: אמאי אמרת לה הכי? אמר ליה: כי היכי דאמרה לי, אמרי לה. והא איכא שפירי דגמירי! אי

מקורות המקראות: דברים לב; משלי ד; משלי ג; שם; שם ח; דברים כא; דברים כ; שם; משלי כז; ירמיהו כג; שם כג; במדבר יב; ישעיהו יט; משלי ג; ישעיהו כא; שם נה; משלי ה; שם; ישעיהו נה

רש"י

למימרינהו לתרוייהו. "ברוך אתה ברוב ההודאות" — במרבית ההודאות, האל של כל ההודאות משמע. ומתחלה היה משמע רוב ממש, ולא מרובות. וכמו כן בישתבח, "אל מלך גדול בתשבחות אל ההודאות". מפי רבי: (ב) רשעי עובדי כוכבים אינן חיין, "כי תולעתם לא תמות ואשם לא תכבה" (ישעיה סו): ופליגא דרב יוסף. דאיהו אמר כתחיית המתים ולא יותר, שבה חיים בני אדם, שהתבואה גדילה בו: כמטר לקחי. השוה לקח למטר: יערף. כמו "אף שמיו יערפו טל" (דברים לג), "ושחקים ירעפו טל" (משלי ג) — שהיא מרבה הפירות: כתיב תזל כטל. דמשמע נחת: ערפיהו כמטר. הרגהו: לשמה. משום "כאשר צוני ה' אלהי", ולא כדי להקרות רבי: לא יכילנא. למיגמר: וכי אדם עץ השדה. אלא מקיש אדם לעץ השדה: מה עץ השדה, אם עץ מאכל הוא — ממנו תאכל ואותו לא תכרות, כך תלמידי חכמים: אם הגון הוא — ממנו תאכל, למוד הימנו. ואם לאו — אותו תשחית, סור מעליו: ברזל בברזל יחד. "ואיש יחד פני רעהו". מה ברזל זה, אחד מחדד את חבירו, כגון סכין על גבי חבירתה: אינה דולקת יחידי. עץ אחד אינה דולקת, אלא ב' או ג' כיחד: יחידי. בלא חבר שיחדדנו: שמוסיפין טפשות דכתיב (ג) נואלנו. "אשר נואלנו" מתרגם: דאיטפשנא: שחוטאין. דכתיב "נואלו" גבי חטאנו: ואיבעית אימא מהכא נואלו שרי צוען וגו' והתעו את מצרים. ותועה היינו חוטא: תורה בעץ. דכתיב "עץ חיים היא למחזיקים בה", כשמדליק את האור מצית את העצים דקין תחלה: קטנים מחדדין. ששואלין כל שעה: התיו. משמע: להוליך לו מים: וכתיב לכו למים. ילך הוא עצמו: אם תלמיד (חכם) הגון. שרוצה ללמוד ממך — מצוה לרב לילך אצלו במקומו: ואם לאו. ילך הוא אל הרב: יפוצו מעינותיך חוצה. אם הגון הוא — אמור לו (ד) סתרי תורה: ואם לאו יהיו לך לבדך. "ואין לזרים אתך": שלשה משקים הללו. מים יין וחלב (ה), זו התורה שאינו נותן בה כלום ויודעה ולומדה: בפחות שבכלים. במאני דפחרא (ו) במאני דפחרא. בדרך שחוק אמר, ומרמז: מה את אומרת לי? והלא אביך נותן יין בכלים מכוערין של חרס: ואלא במאי נירמיה. אם לא בשל חרס, הא כולי עבדי הכי! ותקיף. החמיץ: כי היכי דאמרה לי. אי חכמה מפוארה בכלי מכוער, הכי אמרי לה (ז) דיין משתמר בכלי מכוער — אף התורה מתקיימת בי יותר משאילו הייתי נאה: אי

תוספות

וכל העוסק בתורה שלא לשמה תורתו נעשית לו סם המות. וקשה: והלא אמרינן (פסחים דף נ:): לעולם יעסוק אדם בתורה אע"ג שאינה לשמה, שמתוך שלא לשמה בא לשמה! ויש לומר: דתרי שלא לשמה הוי, דמה שאמרינן לעולם יעסוק בתורה אפילו שלא לשמה — היינו כלומר כדי שיקרא רבי, או כדי שיכבדוהו. ומה שאמרינן הכא כל העוסק בתורה שלא לשמה נעשה לו סם המות — היינו מי שלומד לקנטר*: אם תלמיד חכם הגון ממנו תאכל. פירוש: למוד לפניו. ואותו לא תכרות — כלומר לא תפרד ממנו לילך לפני רב אחר, ואם לאו — לא תלמוד לפניו. והא דאמרינן דלומדים מת"ח, אע"פ שאינו הגון, כר"מ שהיה לומד לפני אחר במסכת חגיגה (דף טו.) — היינו דוקא תלמיד חכם (אחר) יכול ללמוד לפניו, לפי שלא ילמוד ממעשיו. אבל אם אינו תלמיד חכם — אינו רשאי ללמוד לפניו:

אף דברי תורה וכו'. וכן נמי אמרינן בעירובין פ' "כילד מעברין" (דף נה.) "לא בשמים היא ולא מעבר לים היא" כלומר: לא תמצא התורה במי שמגביה עצמו כשמים שדעתו גבוה, ולא בסוחרים ההולכים במדינת הים בעבר הים. *דאי ספרא לא סייפא, ואי סייפא לא ספרא. והכי נמי איתא התם: לא בסחרנין ולא בתגרין ולא *באיסטרולוגין — כלומר באותן שרואין בכוכבים. אמרו ליה לשמואל: והא מר איסטרולוגוס הוא! אמר להו: תיתי לי דלא מעיינא בהו אלא בעידן דנפקא *למיא. פירוש: להטיל מים, ולא אני מבטל לעצמי:

*אי הוו סנו הוו חכימי טפי. (ח) פי': אם היו שונאים היופי הוו תלמידי חכמים ביותר: בראתים

עין משפט נר מצוה

כא א מיי' פ"ד מהל' ת"ת הל' א טוש"ע י"ד סימן רמו סעיף ז:
כב ב מיי' שם פ"ג הלכה ט:

רבינו חננאל

שנתון במקום האשבורן. אבל אם באו כדבעו לה לברכה: משיצא חתן לקראת כלה. כשתרד הטיפה על הקרקע שכבר ירד בו מטר מעלת כמין אבעבועין היו מברכין ברכת גשמים: א"ר אבהו גדול יום הגשמים כיום שנתנה בו תורה כו'. כל העוסק בתורה לשמה נעשית לו סם חיים שנאמר עץ חיים היא למחזיקים בה והמתעסק שלא לשמה נעשית לו סם המות שנאמר יערוף כמטר לקחי ואין עריפה אלא הריגה א"ר יוחנן כתיב כי האדם עץ השדה אם ת"ח הוא הגון ממנו תאכל ואותו לא תכרות. ואם אינו הגון אותו תשחית וכרת. דברי תורה אין מתקיימין ביחידי שנאמר חרב על הבדים ונואלו. והקטנים מחדדים את הגדולים כו'. ומתלמידי יותר מכולם. (למה)

רבינו גרשום

מים התחתונים לקראת מים העליונים כדרך שיבא חתן לקראת כלה: ששקולה כתחיית המתים ששניהם חיים לעולם. אלא להכי כתיב כי האדם [עץ השדה] שת"ח נמשל בו וממנו תאכל. כלומר שיכול להבין בתורה: אותו תשחית וכרת שהתורה משחתת בו. נואלו שדי צוען. והרי הן היו חוטאין: בפחות שבכלים.

הגהות הב"ח

(א) גמ' אלא במי שדעתו שפלה עליו כדאמרה ליה כו' בכלי מכוער אמר לה אי בת מלכא אבוך במאי רמי חמרא אמרה ליה במאני דפחרא אמר לה כ"ע במאני דפחרא ואבוך במאני דפחרא אמרה ליה אלא במאי נירמי אמר לה כגון אתון דחשביתון רמו: (ב) רש"י ד"ה (רשעי עובדי כוכבים) תא"מ ונ"ב ס"א רשעים: (ג) ד"ה שמוסיפין טפשות דכתיב אשר נואלנו מתרגם כו' כצ"ל: (ד) ד"ה יפוצו כו' אמור לו (סתרי תורה) תא"מ ונ"ב ס"א דברי תורה: (ה) ד"ה שלשה כו' מים יין וחלב בלא כסף זו התורה מי שאינו נותן:

גליון הש"ס

תוס' ד"ה אף ד"ת וכו' וה"ג איתא התם במדרש דברים רבה פ"ח:

ברכות נט: מגילה כח:
[ברכות לג.]
[ב"ב יב.]
[נ"ל ברבי]
ברכות סג: מכות י. ע"ש
[מכות י. ע"ש]
[נ"ל אמר]
נ"ל אמר
נדרים נ: ע"ש
[עי' פרש"י בע"ז טז: סד"ה פתיא אוכמא]
[ואין זה בעירובין אלא במדרש פ' נצבים איתא קלת מזה]
[במדרש הנ"ל איתא לבית המים]
שייך לע"ב

(ו) ד"ה בפחות כו' דפחרא הס"ד ואח"כ מה"ד א"ל אי בת מלכא את כו' בשחוק אמר: (ז) ד"ה כי היכי כו' הכי אמרי לה כי היכי דיין משתמר: (ח) תוס' ד"ה אי הוו כו' פי' אם היו שונאים. נ"ב ולהאי פירושא ניחא משופריה דיעקב ודרבי אבהו אבל לפרש"י קשיא:

רבינו חננאל

אין הגשמים יורדין בעולם אא"כ נמחלו עונותיהם של ישראל שנאמר רצית ה' ארצך וגו' נשאת עון עמך וגו' ואתה תשמע השמים וסלחת לחטאת עבדיך ועמך ישראל כי תורם את הדרך הטובה אשר ילכו בה ונתת מטר על ארצך אשר נתת לעמך לנחלה. אין הגשמים נעצרים אא"כ נתחייבו שונאי ישראל כלייה כו' או בשביל תרומות ומעשרות. ובשביל מספרי לשה"ר. ובשביל עזי פנים. וכל מי שיש לו עזות פנים ודאי נכשל בעבירה. ומותר לקרותו רשע שנאמר העז איש רשע בפניו ומותר לשנאותו [שנאמר] ועוז פניו ישונא א"ת ישונה אלא ישנא. אין הגשמים נעצרים אלא בעון גזל שנאמר על כפים כסה אור ואין כפים אלא גזל שנאמר ומן החמס אשר בכפיהם. וכן נמי נעצרים בשביל ישראל שמעשיהם מקולקלין. והוא לא פנים קלקל

תוספות

בראתים לא נאמר אלא בראתיו. פי': דמשמע דמהדר אגשם. ואם כן, משום דגדול יום הגשמים כיום שנברא בו שמים וארץ משתבח ביה הקב"ה. אי הוה כתיב "בראתים" הוה משמע דאהדר אשמים וארץ: **פנים** נזעמים לשון סתר. פירוש: בשביל לשון שקר, שאומר לשון הרע – "הרוח צפון תבטל הגשם", והיינו פנים נזעמים: **מותר** לקרותו רשע. אף על גב דאמרי' בקדושין (דף כח.): הקורא לחבירו רשע יורד עמו לחייו – לזה מותר, דודאי נכשל בעבירה ועומד במורדו, דהכרת פניו ענתה בו: **בהורין.** לשון בהרות, טרוק"ש בלע"ז:

אם

גמרא

אִי הָווּ סְנוּ – טְפֵי הָווּ גְּמִירֵי. דָּבָר אַחֵר: מַה שְּׁלֹשָׁה מַשְׁקִין הַלָּלוּ אֵין נִפְסָלִין אֶלָּא בְּהֶיסַּח הַדַּעַת, אַף דִּבְרֵי תוֹרָה – אֵין מִשְׁתַּכְּחִין אֶלָּא בְּהֶיסַּח הַדַּעַת. אָמַר רַבִּי חָמָא בְּר' חֲנִינָא: גָּדוֹל יוֹם הַגְּשָׁמִים (א) כַּיּוֹם שֶׁנִּבְרְאוּ שָׁמַיִם וָאָרֶץ, שֶׁנֶּאֱמַר °"הַרְעִיפוּ שָׁמַיִם מִמַּעַל וּשְׁחָקִים יִזְּלוּ צֶדֶק תִּפְתַּח אֶרֶץ וְיִפְרוּ יֶשַׁע וּצְדָקָה תַצְמִיחַ יַחַד אֲנִי ה' בְּרָאתִיו". "בְּרָאתִים" לֹא נֶאֱמַר, אֶלָּא "בְּרָאתִיו". אָמַר רַב אוֹשַׁעְיָא: גָּדוֹל יוֹם הַגְּשָׁמִים, שֶׁאֲפִי' יְשׁוּעָה פָּרָה וְרָבָה בּוֹ, שֶׁנֶּאֱמַר: "תִּפְתַּח אֶרֶץ וְיִפְרוּ יֶשַׁע". אָמַר רַבִּי תַּנְחוּם בַּר חֲנִילַאי: אֵין הַגְּשָׁמִים יוֹרְדִים אֶלָּא א"כ נִמְחֲלוּ עֲוֹנוֹתֵיהֶן שֶׁל יִשְׂרָאֵל, שֶׁנֶּאֱמַר °"רָצִיתָ ה' אַרְצֶךָ שַׁבְתָּ שְׁבוּת יַעֲקֹב נָשָׂאתָ עֲוֹן עַמֶּךָ כִּסִּיתָ כָל חַטָּאתָם סֶלָה". א"ל זְעֵירִי מִדִּיהֲבַת לְרָבִינָא: אַתּוּן מֵהָכָא מַתְנִיתוּ לַהּ, אֲנַן מֵהָכָא מַתְנֵינַן לַהּ °"וְאַתָּה, תִּשְׁמַע הַשָּׁמַיִם, וְסָלַחְתָּ לְחַטַּאת" וגו'. אָמַר ר' תַּנְחוּם בְּרֵיהּ דְּרַבִּי חִיָּיא אִישׁ כְּפַר עַכּוֹ: אֵין הַגְּשָׁמִים נֶעֱצָרִין אא"כ נִתְחַיְּיבוּ שׂוֹנְאֵיהֶן שֶׁל יִשְׂרָאֵל כְּלָיָה, שֶׁנֶּאֱמַר °"צִיָּה גַם חֹם יִגְזְלוּ מֵימֵי שֶׁלֶג שְׁאוֹל חָטָאוּ". א"ל זְעֵירִי מִדִּיהֲבַת לְרָבִינָא: אַתּוּן מֵהָכָא מַתְנִיתוּ לַהּ, אֲנַן מֵהָכָא מַתְנֵינַן לַהּ °"וְעָצַר אֶת (ב) הַשָּׁמַיִם וַאֲבַדְתֶּם מְהֵרָה". אָמַר רַב חִסְדָּא: אֵין הַגְּשָׁמִים נֶעֱצָרִין אֶלָּא בִּשְׁבִיל בִּיטּוּל תְּרוּמוֹת וּמַעַשְׂרוֹת, שֶׁנֶּאֱמַר: "צִיָּה גַם חֹם יִגְזְלוּ מֵימֵי שֶׁלֶג". מַאי מַשְׁמַע? *תָּנָא דְּבֵי רַבִּי יִשְׁמָעֵאל: בִּשְׁבִיל דְּבָרִים שֶׁצִּוִּיתִי אֶתְכֶם בִּימוֹת הַחַמָּה וְלֹא עֲשִׂיתֶם – יִגְזְלוּ מִכֶּם מֵימֵי שֶׁלֶג בִּימוֹת הַגְּשָׁמִים. אָמַר רַבִּי שִׁמְעוֹן בֶּן פָּזִי: אֵין הַגְּשָׁמִים נֶעֱצָרִין אֶלָּא בִּשְׁבִיל מְסַפְּרֵי לָשׁוֹן הָרָע, שֶׁנֶּאֱמַר °"רוּחַ צָפוֹן תְּחוֹלֵל גָּשֶׁם, וּפָנִים נִזְעָמִים לְשׁוֹן סָתֶר". אָמַר רַב סַלָּא אָמַר רַב הַמְנוּנָא: אֵין הַגְּשָׁמִים נֶעֱצָרִין אֶלָּא בִּשְׁבִיל עַזֵּי פָנִים, שֶׁנֶּאֱמַר °"וַיִּמָּנְעוּ רְבִיבִים, וּמַלְקוֹשׁ לוֹא הָיָה, וּמֵצַח אִשָּׁה זוֹנָה הָיָה לָךְ" וגו'. וְאָמַר רַב סַלָּא אָמַר רַב הַמְנוּנָא: כָּל אָדָם שֶׁיֵּשׁ לוֹ עַזּוּת פָּנִים סוֹף נִכְשָׁל בַּעֲבֵירָה שֶׁנֶּאֱמַר: "וּמֵצַח אִשָּׁה זוֹנָה הָיָה לָךְ". רַב נַחְמָן אָמַר: בְּיָדוּעַ שֶׁנִּכְשַׁל בַּעֲבֵירָה שֶׁנֶּאֱמַר: "הָיָה לָךְ" וְלֹא נֶאֱמַר "יִהְיֶה לָךְ". אָמַר רַבָּה בַּר רַב הוּנָא: כָּל אָדָם שֶׁיֵּשׁ לוֹ עַזּוּת פָּנִים מוּתָּר לְקוֹרְתוֹ רָשָׁע, שֶׁנֶּאֱמַר °"הֵעֵז אִישׁ רָשָׁע בְּפָנָיו". רַב נַחְמָן בַּר יִצְחָק אָמַר: מוּתָּר לְשׂנְאוֹתוֹ שֶׁנֶּאֱמַר °"וְעֹז פָּנָיו יְשׁוּנֶּא". אַל תִּקְרֵי "יְשׁוּנֶּא" אֶלָּא יִשָּׂנֵא. אָמַר רַב קְטִינָא: אֵין הַגְּשָׁמִים נֶעֱצָרִין אֶלָּא בִּשְׁבִיל בִּיטּוּל תּוֹרָה, שֶׁנֶּאֱמַר °"בַּעֲצַלְתַּיִם יִמַּךְ הַמְּקָרֶה" *בִּשְׁבִיל עַצְלוּת שֶׁהָיָה בְּיִשְׂרָאֵל שֶׁלֹּא עָסְקוּ בַּתּוֹרָה נַעֲשָׂה שׂוֹנְאוֹ שֶׁל הקב"ה מָךְ. וְאֵין "מָךְ" אֶלָּא "עָנִי", שֶׁנֶּאֱמַר °"וְאִם מָךְ הוּא מֵעֶרְכֶּךָ". וְאֵין "מְקָרֶה" אֶלָּא הקב"ה שֶׁנֶּאֱמַר °"הַמְקָרֶה בַמַּיִם עֲלִיּוֹתָיו". רַב יוֹסֵף אָמַר מֵהָכָא: °"וְעַתָּה לֹא רָאוּ אוֹר, בָּהִיר הוּא בַּשְּׁחָקִים, וְרוּחַ עָבְרָה וַתְּטַהֲרֵם". וְאֵין "אוֹר" אֶלָּא תּוֹרָה, שֶׁנֶּאֱמַר °"כִּי נֵר מִצְוָה וְתוֹרָה אוֹר". "בָּהִיר הוּא בַּשְּׁחָקִים". תָּנָא דְּבֵי ר' יִשְׁמָעֵאל: אֲפִילּוּ בְּשָׁעָה שֶׁרָקִיעַ נַעֲשָׂה בְּהוֹרִין בְּהוֹרִין לְהוֹרִיד טַל וּמָטָר, 'רוּחַ עָבְרָה וַתְּטַהֲרֵם'. אָמַר ר' אַמִי: אֵין הַגְּשָׁמִים נֶעֱצָרִין אֶלָּא בַּעֲוֹן גָּזֵל, שֶׁנֶּאֱמַר °"עַל כַּפַּיִם כִּסָּה אוֹר", בַּעֲוֹן כַּפַּיִם כִּסָּה אוֹר. וְאֵין "כַּפַּיִם" אֶלָּא "חָמָס", שֶׁנֶּאֱמַר °"וּמִן הֶחָמָס אֲשֶׁר בְּכַפֵּיהֶם". וְאֵין "אוֹר" אֶלָּא "מָטָר", שֶׁנֶּאֱמַר °"יָפִיץ עֲנַן אוֹרוֹ". מַאי תַּקַּנְתֵּיהּ? יַרְבֶּה בִּתְפִלָּה, שֶׁנֶּאֱמַר °"וַיְצַו עָלֶיהָ בְמַפְגִּיעַ". *וְאֵין "פְּגִיעָה" אֶלָּא "תְּפִלָּה", שֶׁנֶּאֱמַר °"וְאַתָּה, אַל תִּתְפַּלֵּל בְּעַד הָעָם הַזֶּה, [וגו',] וְאַל תִּפְגַּע בִּי". וא"ר אַמִי: מַאי דִּכְתִיב °"אִם קֵהָה הַבַּרְזֶל, וְהוּא לֹא פָנִים קִלְקַל"? אִם רָאִיתָ רָקִיעַ שֶׁקֵּיהָה כְּבַרְזֶל מִלְּהוֹרִיד טַל וּמָטָר, בִּשְׁבִיל מַעֲשֵׂה הַדּוֹר שֶׁהֵן מְקוּלְקָלִין, שֶׁנֶּאֱ' "וְהוּא לֹא פָנִים קִלְקַל". מַה תַּקַּנְתָּן? יִתְגַּבְּרוּ בְּרַחֲמִים, שֶׁנֶּאֱ' °"וַחֲיָלִים יְגַבֵּר, וְיִתְרוֹן הַכְשֵׁיר חָכְמָה". כָּל שֶׁכֵּן, אִם הוּכְשְׁרוּ מַעֲשֵׂיהֶן מֵעִיקָּרָא. רֵישׁ לָקִישׁ אָמַר: אִם רָאִיתָ תַּלְמִיד

שֶׁלִּמּוּדוֹ

תורה אור: ישעיהו מה; תהלים פה; מ"א ח; איוב כד; דברים יא; משלי כה; ירמיהו ג; משלי כח; קהלת ח; שם י; ויקרא כז; תהלים קד; איוב לז; משלי ו; איוב לו; יונה ג; איוב לו; שם לו; ירמיהו ז; קהלת י; שם

רש"י

אִי הָווּ סְנוּ. אוֹתָם נָאִים שֶׁהֵם חֲכָמִים: טְפֵי הָווּ גְּמִירֵי. שֶׁאִי אֶפְשָׁר לְנָאֶה לְהַשְׁפִּיל דַּעְתּוֹ, וּבָא לִידֵי שִׁכְחָה: בְּהֶיסַּח הַדַּעַת. שֶׁאִם לֹא יִשְׁמְרֵם יָפֶה יְהוּ נִשְׁפָּכִין אוֹ נוֹפֵל לְתוֹכָן דָּבָר מָאוּס, וְנִפְסָלִים מִלִּשְׁתּוֹת בְּדָבָר קַל, יוֹתֵר מִשֶּׁמֶן וּדְבַשׁ שֶׁמִּתּוֹךְ שֶׁהֵן עָבִים צָפָה הַפְּסוֹלֶת לְמַעְלָה, וְאֶפְשָׁר אָדָם נוֹטֵל הָעֶלְיוֹן וְזוֹרְקוֹ לַחוּץ, וְהַתַּחְתּוֹן בַּר וְנָקִי. מַה שֶּׁאֵין כֵּן בְּמַשְׁקֶה צָלוּל שֶׁאֵינוֹ עָב, קליי"ר בְּלַעַ"ז: בְּהֶיסַּח הַדַּעַת. אִם אֵינוֹ מַחֲזִירָם תָּמִיד: שֶׁנֶּאֱמַר הַרְעִיפוּ שָׁמַיִם מִמַּעַל וּשְׁחָקִים יִזְּלוּ צֶדֶק תִּפְתַּח אֶרֶץ וְיִפְרוּ יֶשַׁע וּצְדָקָה תַצְמִיחַ יַחַד אֲנִי ה' בְּרָאתִיו בְּרָאתִים לֹא נֶאֱמַר. דְּמַשְׁמַע הַשְּׁחָקִים יִזְּלוּ קָאֵי, אֶלָּא "אֲנִי ה' בְּרָאתִיו" לְטַל וּמָטָר, שְׁמַע מִינָּהּ שֶׁמִּשְׁתַּבֵּחַ וּמִתְפָּאֵר (ג) הקב"ה בִּמְטַר הַשָּׁמַיִם: יְשׁוּעָה פָּרָה וְרָבָה בּוֹ. מְלִיצֵי זְכוּת נִכְנָסִין לְפָנָיו בְּיוֹם הַגְּשָׁמִים, שֶׁנִּזְכָּר לִישׁוּעָה מִתּוֹךְ שְׁעַת רָצוֹן. הוּא לִישְׁנָא דִּקְרָא "וְיִפְרוּ יֶשַׁע", וְאֵימָתַי – בִּזְמַן שֶׁהַשְּׁחָקִים יִזְּלוּ צֶדֶק: רָצִיתָ ה' אַרְצֶךָ. בְּמַיִם: נָשָׂאתָ עֲוֹן עַמֶּךָ. מִיָּד: ה"ג: אֲמַר לֵיהּ מָר זְעִירִי מִדִּיהֲבַת לְרָבִינָא כו'. זְעִירִי קָדַם הָיָה מִן הָרִאשׁוֹנִים, וְרָבִינָא סוֹף הוֹרָאָה, לֹא רָאוּ זֶה אֶת זֶה: וְאַתָּה תִּשְׁמַע הַשָּׁמַיִם וגו'. וְאוֹמֵר "וְנָתַתָּ מָטָר עַל אַרְצְךָ" בִּתְפִלָּה דִּשְׁלֹמֹה: צִיָּה גַם חֹם יִגְזְלוּ מֵימֵי שֶׁלֶג. כְּשֶׁצִּיָּה גַּם חוֹם גּוֹזְלִין מֵימוֹת הַשֶּׁלֶג, שֶׁאֵינָן יוֹרְדִין מָטָר כְּמִשְׁפָּטָם – בְּיָדוּעַ שֶׁשְּׁאוֹל חָטְאוּ: וְלֹא יִהְיֶה מָטָר. וְסָמִיךְ לֵיהּ "וַאֲבַדְתֶּם": צִיָּה. דָּרֵישׁ לְשׁוֹן צִוּוּי, דְּבָרִים שֶׁצִּוִּיתִי אֶתְכֶם בִּימוֹת הַחַמָּה – תְּרוּמוֹת וּמַעַשְׂרוֹת, גָּזְלוּ מֵימֵי שֶׁלֶג אֶת הַמָּטָר: רוּחַ צָפוֹן תְּחוֹלֵל גֶּשֶׁם וּפָנִים נִזְעָמִים לְשׁוֹן *שֶׁקֶר. תְּחוֹלֵל – תְּבַטֵּל, כְּמוֹ "לֹא יַחֵל דְּבָרוֹ" (במדבר ל), כִּדְאָמְרִי' בִּיבָמוֹת (דף עב.) דְּרוּחַ צָפוֹן בָּרוּר הוּא, וּמֵבִיא אוֹרָה לָעוֹלָם. מַה שֶּׁגְּשָׁמִים נֶעֱצָרִין וּפָנִים נִזְעָמִין שֶׁמַּרְאֶה הקב"ה, שֶׁאֵינוֹ מֵבִיא מָטָר לָעוֹלָם, מִפְּנֵי לְשׁוֹן שֶׁקֶר – רְכִילוּת. וּפְשַׁט הַמִּקְרָא: כְּשֵׁם שֶׁרוּחַ צָפוֹן תְּחוֹלֵל גֶּשֶׁם, כָּךְ פָּנִים נִזְעָמִים מִפְּנֵי לְשׁוֹן שֶׁקֶר: וַיִּמָּנְעוּ רְבִיבִים. מִשּׁוּם דְּמֵחֲנֶפֶת הַכַּלָּה, שֶׁהָיָה בָּךְ עַזּוּת: הָיָה. מַשְׁמַע כְּבָר נִכְשַׁל: הֵעֵז אִישׁ. שֶׁיֵּשׁ בּוֹ עַזּוּת פָּנִים, אָמוּר לוֹ "רָשָׁע" בְּפָנָיו, וְאֵין בּוֹ מִשּׁוּם מַלְקוֹת, כִּדְאָמְרִי' בְּמַסֶּכֶת קִדּוּשִׁין (דף כח.). וּמִשּׁוּם דָּבָר זֶה בִּלְבַד מוּתָּר לְקוֹרְתוֹ רָשָׁע: מוּתָּר לְשׂנְאוֹתוֹ. אע"ג דִּכְתִיב "וְאָהַבְתָּ לְרֵעֲךָ כָּמוֹךָ": וְעֹז פָּנָיו יְשׁוּנֶּא. וְעֹז כְּתִיב חָסֵר ו', מִי שֶׁהוּא עַז פָּנִים – יִשָּׂנֵא בְּשִׁי"ן*): יִמַּךְ. כְּמִי שֶׁאֵין בּוֹ כֹּחַ לְהוֹרִיד טַל וּמָטָר: וְעַתָּה לֹא רָאוּ אוֹר. מִפְּנֵי שֶׁלֹּא רָאוּ אוֹר שֶׁל תּוֹרָה: אֲפִילּוּ כְּשֶׁהַשָּׁמַיִם בְּהוֹרִין. כְּמוֹ בַּהֶרֶת, מְנוּמָּר בְּעָבִים, וְרוֹצֶה לְהוֹרִיד גְּשָׁמִים – רוּחַ עָבְרָה וַתְּטַהֲרֵם, מְפַזֶּרֶת הֶעָבִים: (ד) הַמַּלְאָךְ אַף בְּרִי שְׁמוֹ – יָפִיץ עֲנַן אוֹרוֹ, גֶּשֶׁם שֶׁלּוֹ: וַיְצַו. הַקָּדוֹשׁ בָּרוּךְ הוּא: עָלֶיהָ. עַל הַגֶּשֶׁם שֶׁתֵּרֵד: בְּמַפְגִּיעַ. כְּשֶׁיִּתְפַּלֵּל עָלֶיהָ, כְּמוֹ "וְאַל תִּפְגַּע בִּי": קֵהָה הַבַּרְזֶל. כְּמוֹ "הַקְהֵה אֶת שִׁנָּיו"* וְ"שִׁנֵּי בָנִים תִּקְהֶינָה" (ירמיהו לא): וְהוּא לֹא פָנִים קִלְקַל. שֶׁקִּלְקְלוּ הַדּוֹר: וכ"ש אִם הוּכְשְׁרוּ מַעֲשֵׂיהֶן. קוֹדֶם לָכֵן. וְהָכִי מַשְׁמַע: וְיִתְרוֹן הַכְשֵׁיר – וְיִתְרוֹן שֶׁהִכְשִׁיר לַחָכְמָה, אִם הִכְשִׁירוּ מַעֲשֵׂיהֶן מִתְּחִלָּה, שֶׁיָּבוֹאוּ הַגְּשָׁמִים – יוֹתֵר מִבַּתְחִילִּים יְגַבֵּר, שֶׁהֵן מַגְבִּירִין חֲיָלִים וְעוֹמְדִין בִּתְפִלָּה בִּזְמַן שֶׁקִּלְקְלוּ:

שֶׁלִּמּוּדוֹ

*) [נ"ל בשי"ן שמאלית וע' מהרש"א בח"א]

רבינו גרשום

כלי חרס: נפסלין בהיסח הדעת. כלומר מפסידין כשאין משתמרין. אלא בראתיו. דהיינו בריית עולם: שצויתי אתכם בימות החמה היינו תרומות ומעשרות: שנאמר ומצח שהוא עז פנים מיד אשה זונה היה לך ועוז פניו שמעיז פניו ישונא: ימוך שאינו נותן מטר: בהרים גדודים:

הגהות הב"ח

(א) גמרא גדול יום הגשמים כיום שנבראו ס"א מיום: (ב) שם ועצר את השמים ולא יהיה מטר ואבדתם: (ג) רש"י ד"ה שנאמר כו' ומתפאר בו הקב"ה (ומניח שמים תא"מ ונ"ב ס"א אין זה ולספרים דגרסי גדול יום הגשמים מיום שנבראו הי' ניחא ומכריח ממה שמניח שמים אלמא דגדול מיום: (ד) ד"ה אפי' כו' המלאך אף ברי. נ"ב לשון רש"י באיוב אף ברי שם מלאך הממונה על העננים והוא יפיץ ענן מטרו של המקום:

מסורת הש"ס

שבת לב:

[נ"ל סתר]

[מגילה יח.]

[לקמן ח. ברכות כו: סוטה יד. סנהדרין לה:]

[בהגדה של פסח]

שֶׁלִּמּוּדוֹ קָשֶׁה עָלָיו כְּבַרְזֶל — בִּשְׁבִיל מִשְׁנָתוֹ שֶׁאֵינָהּ סְדוּרָה עָלָיו, שֶׁנֶּאֱמַר °"וְהוּא לֹא פָנִים קִלְקַל". מַאי תַּקַּנְתֵּיהּ — יַרְבֶּה בִּישִׁיבָה, שֶׁנֶּאֱמַר °"וַחֲיָלִים יְגַבֵּר וְיִתְרוֹן הַכְשֵׁיר חָכְמָה". כ"ש אִם מִשְׁנָתוֹ סְדוּרָה לוֹ מֵעִיקָּרָא. כִּי הָא דְּרֵישׁ לָקִישׁ הֲוָה מְסַדֵּר מַתְנִי' אַרְבְּעִין זִמְנִין כְּנֶגֶד מ' יוֹם שֶׁנִּיתְּנָה תּוֹרָה, וְעָיֵיל לְקַמֵּיהּ דְּר' יוֹחָנָן. רַב אַדָּא בַּר אַהֲבָה מְסַדֵּר מַתְנִי' עֶשְׂרִין וְאַרְבַּע זִמְנִין כְּנֶגֶד תּוֹרָה נְבִיאִים וּכְתוּבִים, וְעָיֵיל לְקַמֵּיהּ דְּרָבָא. רָבָא אָמַר: אִם רָאִיתָ תַּלְמִיד שֶׁלִּמּוּדוֹ קָשֶׁה עָלָיו כְּבַרְזֶל, בִּשְׁבִיל רַבּוֹ, שֶׁאֵינוֹ מַסְבִּיר לוֹ פָּנִים, שֶׁנֶּאֱמַר "וְהוּא לֹא פָנִים קִלְקַל". מַאי תַּקַּנְתֵּיהּ? יַרְבֶּה עָלָיו רֵעִים, שֶׁנֶּאֱמַר: "וַחֲיָלִים יְגַבֵּר, וְיִתְרוֹן הַכְשֵׁיר חָכְמָה". כ"ש אִם הוּכְשְׁרוּ מַעֲשָׂיו בִּפְנֵי רַבּוֹ מֵעִיקָּרָא. וְאָמַר ר' אַמִי: מַאי דִּכְתִיב °"אִם יִשֹּׁךְ הַנָּחָשׁ בְּלוֹא לָחַשׁ, וְאֵין יִתְרוֹן לְבַעַל הַלָּשׁוֹן"? אִם רָאִיתָ דּוֹר שֶׁהַשָּׁמַיִם מִשְׁתַּכִּין (א) כִּנְחֹשֶׁת מִלְּהוֹרִיד טַל וּמָטָר — בִּשְׁבִיל לוֹחֲשֵׁי לְחִישׁוֹת שֶׁאֵין בַּדּוֹר. מַאי תַּקַּנְתָּן? יֵלְכוּ אֵצֶל מִי שֶׁיּוֹדֵעַ לִלְחוֹשׁ, דִּכְתִיב °"יַגִּיד עָלָיו רֵעוֹ". "וְאֵין יִתְרוֹן לְבַעַל הַלָּשׁוֹן", וּמִי שֶׁאֶפְשָׁר לוֹ לִלְחוֹשׁ וְאֵינוֹ לוֹחֵשׁ, מָה הֲנָאָה יֵשׁ לוֹ? וְאִם לָחַשׁ וְלֹא נַעֲנָה, מַאי תַּקַּנְתֵּיהּ? יֵלֵךְ אֵצֶל חָסִיד שֶׁבַּדּוֹר, וְיַרְבֶּה עָלָיו בִּתְפִלָּה, שֶׁנֶּאֱמַר °"וַיְצַו עָלֶיהָ בְמַפְגִּיעַ". *וְאֵין פְּגִיעָה אֶלָּא תְּפִלָּה, שֶׁנֶּאֱמַר °"וְאַתָּה, אַל תִּתְפַּלֵּל בְּעַד הָעָם הַזֶּה, וְאַל תִּשָּׂא בַעֲדָם רִנָּה וּתְפִלָּה, וְאַל תִּפְגַּע בִּי". וְאִם לָחַשׁ, וְעָלְתָה בְּיָדוֹ, וּמֵגִיס דַּעְתּוֹ עָלָיו — מֵבִיא אַף לָעוֹלָם, שֶׁנֶּאֱמַר °"מִקְנֶה אַף עַל עוֹלֶה". רָבָא אָמַר: שְׁנֵי ת"ח שֶׁיּוֹשְׁבִין בְּעִיר אַחַת וְאֵין נוֹחִין זֶה לָזֶה בַּהֲלָכָה — מִתְקַנְּאִין בְּאַף וּמַעֲלִין אוֹתוֹ, שֶׁנֶּאֱמַר "מִקְנֶה אַף עַל עוֹלֶה". *אָמַר ר"ל: מַאי דִּכְתִיב "אִם יִשֹּׁךְ הַנָּחָשׁ בְּלוֹא לָחַשׁ, וְאֵין יִתְרוֹן לְבַעַל הַלָּשׁוֹן"? לֶעָתִיד לָבֹא, מִתְקַבְּצוֹת וּבָאוֹת כָּל הַחַיּוֹת אֵצֶל הַנָּחָשׁ, וְאוֹמְרִים לוֹ: אֲרִי דּוֹרֵס וְאוֹכֵל, זְאֵב טוֹרֵף וְאוֹכֵל, אַתָּה, מָה הֲנָאָה יֵשׁ לְךָ? אָמַר לָהֶם: "וְאֵין יִתְרוֹן לְבַעַל הַלָּשׁוֹן". אָמַר רַבִּי אַמִי: אֵין תְּפִלָּתוֹ שֶׁל אָדָם נִשְׁמַעַת אֶלָּא אִם כֵּן מֵשִׂים נַפְשׁוֹ בְּכַפּוֹ, שֶׁנֶּאֱמַר °"נִשָּׂא לְבָבֵנוּ אֶל כַּפָּיִם". [*אִינִי? וְהָא] אוֹקִים שְׁמוּאֵל אָמוֹרָא עֲלֵיהּ וְדָרַשׁ: °"וַיְפַתּוּהוּ בְּפִיהֶם, וּבִלְשׁוֹנָם יְכַזְּבוּ לוֹ, וְלִבָּם לֹא נָכוֹן עִמּוֹ, וְלֹא נֶאֶמְנוּ בִּבְרִיתוֹ". וְאַף עַל פִּי כֵן — °"וְהוּא רַחוּם, יְכַפֵּר עָוֹן" וגו'! *לָא קַשְׁיָא. כָּאן — בְּיָחִיד, כָּאן — בְּצִבּוּר. אָמַר ר' אַמִי: אֵין גְּשָׁמִים יוֹרְדִין אֶלָּא בִּשְׁבִיל בַּעֲלֵי אֲמָנָה, שֶׁנֶּאֱמַר °"אֱמֶת מֵאֶרֶץ תִּצְמָח, וְצֶדֶק מִשָּׁמַיִם נִשְׁקָף". וְא"ר אַמִי: בֹּא וּרְאֵה כַּמָּה גְּדוֹלִים בַּעֲלֵי אֲמָנָה. מִנַּיִן? מֵחוּלְדָּה וּבוֹר. וּמָה הַמַּאֲמִין בְּחוּלְדָּה וּבוֹר — כָּךְ, הַמַּאֲמִין בְּהקב"ה — עאכ"ו. אָמַר רַבִּי יוֹחָנָן: כָּל הַמַּצְדִּיק אֶת עַצְמוֹ מִלְּמַטָּה — מַצְדִּיקִין עָלָיו הַדִּין מִלְּמַעְלָה, שֶׁנֶּאֱמַר "אֱמֶת מֵאֶרֶץ תִּצְמָח, וְצֶדֶק מִשָּׁמַיִם נִשְׁקָף". רַבִּי חִיָּיא בַּר אָבִין אָמַר רַב הוּנָא, מֵהָכָא: °"וּכְיִרְאָתְךָ עֶבְרָתֶךָ". רֵישׁ לָקִישׁ אָמַר מֵהָכָא: °"פָּגַעְתָּ אֶת שָׂשׂ וְעֹשֵׂה צֶדֶק בִּדְרָכֶיךָ יִזְכְּרוּךָ הֵן אַתָּה קָצַפְתָּ וַנֶּחֱטָא בָּהֶם עוֹלָם וְנִוָּשֵׁעַ". אָמַר ריב"ל: כָּל הַשָּׂמֵחַ בַּיִּסּוּרִין שֶׁבָּאִין עָלָיו — מֵבִיא יְשׁוּעָה לָעוֹלָם, שֶׁנֶּאֱמַר "בָּהֶם עוֹלָם וְנִוָּשֵׁעַ". אָמַר רֵישׁ לָקִישׁ: מַאי דִּכְתִיב °"וְעָצַר אֶת הַשָּׁמַיִם"? בְּשָׁעָה שֶׁהַשָּׁמַיִם נֶעֱצָרִין מִלְּהוֹרִיד (*טַל וּמָטָר) — דּוֹמֶה לְאִשָּׁה שֶׁמְּחַבֶּלֶת וְאֵינָהּ יוֹלֶדֶת. וְהַיְינוּ דְּאָמַר רֵישׁ לָקִישׁ מִשּׁוּם בַּר קַפָּרָא: נֶאֶמְרָה עֲצִירָה בִּגְשָׁמִים וְנֶאֶמְרָה עֲצִירָה בְּאִשָּׁה. נֶאֶמְרָה

(מראי מקומות בגליון: קהלת י; שם; שם; איוב לו; שם; ירמיהו ז; איוב לו; איכה ג; תהלים עח; שם; שם פה; שם ל; ישעיהו סד; דברים יא)

תורה אור

רש"י

שֶׁלִּמּוּדוֹ קָשֶׁה עָלָיו כְּבַרְזֶל. שֶׁקָּשֶׁה לוֹ מֵרוֹב קוּשְׁיוֹת — בִּשְׁבִיל מִשְׁנָתוֹ שֶׁאֵינָהּ סְדוּרָה לוֹ, וְאֵינוֹ זוֹכֵר מַה כְּתִיב בָּהּ. וּלְפִיכָךְ אֵינוֹ יוֹדֵעַ לְפָרֵק. אִי נַמִּי שֶׁגּוֹרְסָהּ בְּטָעוּת, פּוֹטֵר עַל הַחִיּוּב וּמְחַיֵּיב עַל הַפְּטוּר, וּמַקְשֵׁי עֲלָהּ מִדּוּכְתָּא אַחֲרִיתִי. וְהָכִי מַשְׁמַע קְרָא: וְהוּא לֹא (ב), שֶׁאֵינוֹ יוֹדֵעַ שְׁמוּעָתוֹ — מִפְּנֵי שֶׁפָּנִים קִלְקַל, שֶׁקִּלְקֵל בַּמִּשְׁנָה שֶׁהִיא קוֹדֶם לַגְּמָרָא: יַרְבֶּה בִּישִׁיבָה. שֶׁיַּסְדִּירוּ בְּנֵי הַיְשִׁיבָה מִשְׁנָתָם, שֶׁנֶּאֱמַר "וַחֲיָלִים" — בֵּין תַּלְמִידִים, שֶׁהֵן חַיָּילוֹת חַיָּילוֹת: וְיִתְרוֹן הַכְשֵׁיר. כְּשֶׁסִּידֵּר מִשְׁנָתוֹ מִתְּחִילָּה: כְּנֶגֶד מ' יוֹם שֶׁנִּיתְּנָה הַתּוֹרָה. שֶׁתִּתְקַיֵּים בְּיָדוֹ, וְהָדַר עָיֵיל קַמֵּיהּ דְּר' יוֹחָנָן, לְמִיגְמַר גְּמָרָא: כְּנֶגֶד תַּנַ"ךְ. שֶׁהֵן כ"ד סְפָרִים: שֶׁפָּנִים קִלְקַל. שֶׁהֶרְאָה לוֹ פָּנִים רָעוֹת: יַרְבֶּה עָלָיו רֵעִים. לְפַיֵּיס הֵימֶנּוּ, שֶׁיַּסְבִּיר לוֹ פָּנִים: מִשְׁתַּכִּין עָלָיו כִּנְחֹשֶׁת. מַאֲדִימִין פָּנִים, כְּעֵין רודילי"א, כִּדְאָמְרִי' בְּבָבָא מְצִיעָא (דף כו.): דִּשְׁתִיךְ טְפֵי — שֶׁהֶעֱלָה חֲלוּדָה. שֶׁנֶּעֱצָרִין (*מִלְּהוֹלִיד) טַל וּמָטָר: לוֹחֲשֵׁי לְחִישׁוֹת. בִּשְׁבִיל שֶׁאֵין מִתְפַּלְּלִים תְּפִלָּה בְּלַחַשׁ: יַגִּיד עָלָיו רֵעוֹ. יִתְפַּלֵּל עָלָיו חֲבֵירוֹ. וְגַבֵּי גְּשָׁמִים כְּתִיב, בְּאִיּוֹב: וְאֵין יִתְרוֹן לְבַעַל הַלָּשׁוֹן. כְּלוֹמַר: מָה הֲנָאָה יֵשׁ לְבַעַל הַלָּשׁוֹן שֶׁיּוֹדֵעַ לִלְחוֹשׁ וְאֵינוֹ לוֹחֵשׁ: מִקְנֶה אַף עַל עוֹלֶה. מִקְנֶה אַף — מִי שֶׁמֵּגִיס דַּעְתּוֹ וְעוֹלֶה: וְאֵין נוֹחִין זֶה לָזֶה כו'. וְהָכִי מַשְׁמַע: בִּשְׁבִיל שֶׁצָּרִיךְ לְהַגִּיד זֶה לָזֶה וְלִהְיוֹת נוֹחִין בַּהֲלָכָה, וְאֵינָן עוֹשִׂין, מִקְנֶה — מִתְקַנְּאִים מִתְגָּרִים בְּאַף, וּמַעֲלִים אוֹתוֹ וּמְבִיאִים אוֹתוֹ עֲלֵיהֶן. וְיֵשׁ גּוֹרְסִין: וְנוֹחִין זֶה לָזֶה בַּהֲלָכָה — מִתְקַנְּאִים בְּאַף וכו' מִשֶּׁיַּגִּיד עָלָיו רֵעוֹ שֶׁנּוֹחִין זֶה לָזֶה מִתְקַנְּאִים בְּאַף וּמַעֲלִים אוֹתוֹ מֵעֲלֵיהֶם: אֲרִי דּוֹרֵס וְאוֹכֵל. מִיָּד, וְאֵינוֹ מִתְיָרֵא: טוֹרֵף וְאוֹכֵל. שֶׁמּוֹלִיךְ לַחוֹרָיו וְאוֹכֵל שָׁם, שֶׁמְּפַחֵד מִן הַבְּרִיּוֹת, וּלְכוּלָּן יֵשׁ לָהֶם הֲנָאָה: וּלְךָ מָה הֲנָאָה יֵשׁ לְךָ. שֶׁאַתָּה נוֹשֵׁךְ בְּנֵי אָדָם וְהוֹרְגָן? וְהוּא אוֹמֵר: מַה יִּתְרוֹן לְבַעַל הַלָּשׁוֹן שֶׁמְּסַפֵּר לָשׁוֹן הָרַע, אע"פ שֶׁאֵין לוֹ הֲנָאָה. וּלְפִיכָךְ מְבִיאוֹ (ג) הקב"ה בַּדִּין אֵצֶל נָחָשׁ, כְּדֵי שֶׁיִּתְבַּיֵּישׁ, מִפְּנֵי שֶׁהִשִּׂיא אָדָם הָרִאשׁוֹן, וּמִתְבַּיְּישִׁין עִמּוֹ מְסַפְּרֵי לָשׁוֹן הָרַע: וְלִבָּם לֹא נָכוֹן עִמּוֹ. עִם הקב"ה: וְאעפ"כ. כָּתוּב בְּסָמוּךְ "וְהוּא רַחוּם יְכַפֵּר עָוֹן" וְשׁוֹמֵעַ תְּפִלָּתָם. וְהֵיכִי אָמְרַתְּ שֶׁאֵין תְּפִלָּתָם נִשְׁמַעַת אא"כ מֵשִׂים נַפְשׁוֹ בְּכַפּוֹ? כְּלוֹמַר, שֶׁנַּפְשׁוֹ מְכוּוֶּנֶת בְּכַפּוֹ (ד): בְּצִבּוּר. תְּפִלָּתָם נִשְׁמַעַת, וְאע"פ שֶׁאֵין לֵב כּוּלָּם שָׁלֵם, כִּדִכְתִיב "וַיְפַתּוּהוּ בְּפִיהֶם" בִּדְבָרִים, ל' רַבִּים: בְּיָחִיד. אֵינוֹ אֶלָּא א"כ לִבּוֹ מְכוּוָּן: בִּזְמַן שֶׁאֱמֶת מֵאֶרֶץ תִּצְמָח. שֶׁיֵּשׁ אֱמוּנָה בְּמַשָּׂא וּמַתָּן — אָז "צֶדֶק מִשָּׁמַיִם נִשְׁקָף", דְּהַיְינוּ גְּשָׁמִים, שֶׁהֵן צְדָקָה: מֵחוּלְדָּה וּבוֹר. שֶׁהֵמִיתוּ שְׁנֵי בְּנֵי אָדָם. מָצוּי הוּא בָּאַגָּדָה (ה): מַעֲשֶׂה בְּבָחוּר אֶחָד שֶׁנָּתַן אֱמוּנָתוֹ לְרִיבָה אַחַת שֶׁיִּשָּׂאֶנָּה, אָמְרָה: מִי מֵעִיד? וְהָיָה שָׁם בּוֹר אֶחָד וְחוּלְדָּה, אָמַר הַבָּחוּר: בּוֹר וְחוּלְדָּה עֵדִים בַּדָּבָר. לְיָמִים עָבַר עַל אֱמוּנָתוֹ וְנָשָׂא אַחֶרֶת, וְהוֹלִיד שְׁנֵי בָּנִים. אֶחָד נָפַל לְבוֹר וָמֵת, וְא' נְשָׁכַתּוּ חוּלְדָּה וָמֵת. אָמְרָה לוֹ אִשְׁתּוֹ: מַה מַּעֲשֶׂה הוּא זֶה שֶׁבָּנֵינוּ מֵתִים בְּמִיתָה מְשׁוּנָּה? וְאָמַר לָהּ: כָּךְ וְכָךְ הָיָה הַמַּעֲשֶׂה: הַמַּאֲמִין בְּהַקָּדוֹשׁ בָּרוּךְ הוּא. שֶׁמְּשִׂימוֹ עֵד בֵּינוֹ לְבֵין חֲבֵירוֹ — עַל אַחַת כַּמָּה וְכַמָּה: הַמַּצְדִּיק עַצְמוֹ. שֶׁמַּכְשִׁיר וּמְקַשֵּׁט מַעֲשָׂיו: מַצְדִּיקִין עָלָיו. מְדַקְדְּקִין עִמּוֹ אֲפִילּוּ כְּחוּט הַשַּׂעֲרָה, יוֹתֵר מִשֶּׁאִילּוּ מְקַלְקֵל מַעֲשָׂיו כְּדֵי לְמָרֵק עֲוֹנוֹתָיו: שֶׁנֶּאֱמַר אֱמֶת מֵאֶרֶץ תִּצְמָח. אָז "צֶדֶק מִשָּׁמַיִם נִשְׁקָף", צְדָקָה אֵין כְּתִיב כָּאן, אֶלָּא צֶדֶק — דְּמַשְׁמַע דִּין: וּכְיִרְאָתְךָ עֶבְרָתֶךָ. עַל מִי שֶׁהוּא יְרֵא אוֹתְךָ אַתָּה מַחֲזִיק עֶבְרָתְךָ, כְּדֵי לְמָרֵק עֲוֹנוֹתָיו. וּפְשַׁט הַמִּקְרָא: מִי יוֹדֵעַ עוֹז אַפֶּךָ — מִי יוֹדֵעַ עוֹז וְכֹחַ לִמְצוֹא אוֹתוֹ לָנוּס מִפָּנֶיךָ בְּיוֹם אַפֶּךָ, וּכְיִרְאָתְךָ עֶבְרָתֶךָ — כְּשֵׁם שֶׁאַתָּה יָרְאוּי וּמְפוּחָד, כָּךְ יֵשׁ לְהִתְיָירֵא וּלְהִתְפַּחֵד מֵעֶבְרָתֶךָ: פָּגַעְתָּ אֶת שָׂשׂ וְעוֹשֵׂה צֶדֶק. בְּמִי שֶׁשָּׂמֵחַ וְעוֹשֶׂה צֶדֶק, שֶׁהֵן הָעוֹשִׂים כָּךְ — בִּדְרָכֶיךָ יִזְכְּרוּךָ, אַתָּה פּוֹגֵעַ בּוֹ אִם חוֹטֵא כְּלוּם, כְּמוֹ "וַיִּפְגַּע בּוֹ וַיָּמֹת". קְרָא הָכִי הוּא: פָּגַעְתָּ אֶת שָׂשׂ וְעוֹשֶׂה צֶדֶק — וְהֵן הָעוֹשִׂין כָּךְ — בִּדְרָכֶיךָ יִזְכְּרוּךָ, בְּאוֹתָם דְּרָכִים שֶׁאַתָּה מְיַיסְּרָן בְּיִסּוּרִין יַזְכִּירוּךְ לְטוֹבָה, וְאוֹמְרִים הֵן: אַתָּה קָצַפְתָּ בִּשְׁבִיל שֶׁחָטָאנוּ בָּהֶם, עוֹלָם וְנִוָּשֵׁעַ — בִּשְׁבִילָם נִוָּשַׁע לָעוֹלָם הַבָּא: שֶׁמְּחַבֶּלֶת. כְּמוֹ חֶבְלֵי יוֹלֵדָה, אַף הַשָּׁמַיִם עוֹשִׂין כֵּן, וְקָשֶׁה לָעוֹלָם. וְעַל חֵטְא הוּא: נֶאֶמְרָה

תוספות

אם ראית דור שהשמים משתכין עליו כנחושת מלהוריד גשם עליו וכו'. מכאן מוכיח ר"ת דהא דאמרי' בבבא בתרא (דף יט. ושם) אין טומנין בסלעים, מ"ט משום דמשתכי ליה לקדירה — ר"ל משתכי — מקלקלים המאכל שבקדירה, ובלע"ז אורמשי"ר. והא דאמר לקדירה — לאו דוקא לקדירה, אלא למאכל שבקדירה. דהכי נמי קאמר (שבת דף יח:) האי קדרה חייתא שרי. ואין לפרש כפרש"י שפי' התם: משתכי — משברים הקדירה, דא"כ מאי קאמר הכא שהשמים משתכין (ו) ר"ל שהשמים משתברין? אלא ודאי משתכים — ר"ל מעלין חלודה, כמו דבר שבטל ממלאכתו ימים רבים ומחליד, ובלע"ז ראולי"ר: **ואי** לוחש ועלתה בידו ומגים דעתו מביא אף לעולם שנאמר יגיד עליו ריעו וגו'. כלומר: אם יגיד עליו ריעו שעל ידו באו הגשמים, והוא מגים דעתו — מקנה אף עולה. כלומר: הוא קונה אף ועולה, כלומר אם עולה שמגים דעתו עליו — הוא מקנה האף:

בחולדה ובור כך בהקב"ה על אחת כמה וכמה. פי': מאמין בחולדה ובור. מעשה היה בנערה אחת, היתה רוצה לילך לבית אביה, והיה בור בדרך ונפלה. ובא בחור אחד, ואמר: אם אני אעליך תנשאי לי? אמרה לו: הן. ונשבעו ביניהן שהוא לא ישא אשה אחרת, והיא לא תנשא לאיש אחר. ואמרו: מי מעיד בינינו? והיתה חולדה אחת הולכת לפני הבור, ואמרו: אלו שניס, בור וחולדה יהיו עדים בינינו. והלכו לדרכם. והיא עמדה בשבועתה, והוא נשא אשה אחרת וילדה בן, באת חולדה ונשכתו ומת. וילדה לו בן שני — ונפל לבור ומת. אמרה לו אשתו: מה זה המעשה שהגיע לנו שלא כשאר בני אדם? נזכר השבועה, וסיפר לאשתו כל המעשה. אמרה לו: א"כ חזור וקחנה. וכתב לה גט, והלך ונשא את הבתולה. והיינו דאמרי: המאמין בבור וחולדה — שהעמידו עדותן:

ונאומה

רבינו חננאל

תלמיד שתלמודו קשה עליו מפני שאין רבו מסביר לו פנים בהלכה: אם ראית הגשמים נעצרים ומתכסין שאין בדור לוחש לחישות כראוי כו'. ואין הגשמים יורדין אלא בשביל בעלי אמונה שנאמר אמת מארץ תצמח א"ר יוחנן כל המצדיק עצמו מלמטה ומחזיק דרך החסידות אפילו מעט אם יטה מדקדקין עליו מלמעלה ולוקחין הדין ממנו שנאמר אמת מארץ תצמח וצדק משמים נשקף ועוד מהכא וכיראתך עברתך. לפי דקדוקן ביראתך כן מדקדקין עליהם בעברתך ועוד מהכא בדרכיך יזכירוך. כפי דרכך מזכירין אותך מלמעלה. אריב"ל כל ששמח ביסורין הבאין עליו מביא ישועה לעולם שנאמר הן אתה קצפת ונחטא בהם עולם ונושע. הן קצפת והכית אותנו בשביל חטאתינו שחטאנו שמחנו בהן כלומר הודינו כי הכאה זו בשביל עונותינו היא עולם ונושע ראויה זו להיות ישועה לעולם. א"ר שמעון בן לקיש נאמרה עצירה

רבינו גרשום

וכ"ש היכא דהוכשרו מעשיהם מעיקרא דהיינו יתרון הכשר והוא לא פנים קלקל שלא הראה פנים במשנה קלקל בתלמוד: והוא לא פנים. שאין רבו מסביר לו פנים ירבה עליו רעים. לרצות את רבו שיסביר לו פנים: משתכין. מחליד: לוחשי לחישות. שיודעין להתפלל ואין מתפללין: מקנה שמגים דעתו אף על עולה מעלה כעס על העולם: ומעלי אותו שמסלקין אותו מן העולם: מה הנאה יש לך. שאתה נושך ואינך אוכל. כאן ביחיד. נשא לבבנו: כאן בצבור. ויפתוהו בפיהם: מצדיקים עליו מלמעלה כדכתיב וסביביו נשערה מאד:

הגהות הב"ח

(א) גמ' דור שהשמים משתכין עליו כנחשת מלהוריד כו' לחישות שאין באותו הדור מאי: (ב) רש"י ד"ה שלמודו כו' משמע קרא והוא לא פנים קלקל שאינו יודע: (ג) ד"ה ולך כו' מביאו הקב"ה בדין (אצל נחש) תא"מ ונ"ב ס"א אינו ולגירסא שלפנינו נ"ל מביאן: (ד) ד"ה ואעפ"כ כו' מכוונת בכפו מבחוץ הס"ד נ"ב כלומר עם כפו: (ה) ד"ה מחולדה כו' מעשה בבחור אחד. נ"ב עי' בערוך ערך חלד מבאר המעשה באריכות: (ו) תום' ד"ה אם כו' קאמר הכא שהשמים משתכין שאין ר"ל שהשמים:

מסורת הש"ס

[נ"ל מלהוריד]
[לעיל ז: וש"נ]
ערכין טו:
גי' רש"א
[בשאלתות ס"ס קכג איתא קשין אהדדי לא קשיא כאן ביחיד כאן בציבור וכו' וכ"א בע"י ומעתה אין צורך להגהת רש"א לעיל בסמוך איני והא]
[ילקוט איתא מטר]

נֶאֶמְרָה "עֲצִירָה" בְּאִשָּׁה, שֶׁנֶּאֱמַר "כִּי עָצֹר עָצַר ה' בְּעַד כָּל רֶחֶם". וְנֶאֶמְרָה "עֲצִירָה" בִּגְשָׁמִים, דִּכְתִיב "וְעָצַר אֶת הַשָּׁמַיִם". נֶאֱמַר "לֵידָה" בְּאִשָּׁה וְנֶאֱמַר "לֵידָה" בִּגְשָׁמִים. נֶאֱמַר "לֵידָה" בְּאִשָּׁה, דִּכְתִיב "וַתַּהַר וַתֵּלֶד בֵּן". וְנֶאֱמַר "לֵידָה" בִּגְשָׁמִים דִּכְתִיב "וְהוֹלִידָהּ, וְהִצְמִיחָהּ". נֶאֱמַר "פְּקִידָה" בְּאִשָּׁה, וְנֶאֱמַר "פְּקִידָה" בִּגְשָׁמִים. נֶאֱמַר "פְּקִידָה" בְּאִשָּׁה, דִּכְתִיב "וַה' פָּקַד אֶת שָׂרָה". וְנֶאֱמַר "פְּקִידָה" בִּגְשָׁמִים, דִּכְתִיב "פָּקַדְתָּ הָאָרֶץ וַתְּשֹׁקְקֶהָ רַבַּת תַּעְשְׁרֶנָּה פֶּלֶג אֱלֹהִים מָלֵא מָיִם". מַאי: "פֶּלֶג אֱלֹהִים מָלֵא מָיִם"? תָּנָא: "כְּמִין קוּבָּה יֵשׁ בָּרָקִיעַ, שֶׁמִּמֶּנָּה גְּשָׁמִים יוֹצְאִין. אָמַר רַבִּי שְׁמוּאֵל בַּר נַחְמָנִי: מַאי דִּכְתִיב: "אִם לְשֵׁבֶט, אִם לְאַרְצוֹ, אִם לְחֶסֶד, יַמְצִיאֵהוּ"? "אִם לְשֵׁבֶט" — בֶּהָרִים וּבִגְבָעוֹת. "אִם לְחֶסֶד יַמְצִיאֵהוּ לְאַרְצוֹ" — בְּשָׂדוֹת וּבִכְרָמִים. "אִם לְשֵׁבֶט" — לְאִילָנוֹת. "אִם לְאַרְצוֹ" — לִזְרָעִים. "אִם לְחֶסֶד יַמְצִיאֵהוּ" — בּוֹרוֹת, שִׁיחִין, וּמְעָרוֹת. בִּימֵי רַבִּי שְׁמוּאֵל בַּר נַחְמָנִי הֲוָה כַּפְנָא וּמוֹתָנָא. אָמְרִי: הֵיכִי נַעֲבֵיד? [א]נִיבְעֵי רַחֲמֵי אַתַּרְתֵּי — לָא אֶפְשָׁר. אֶלָּא: לִיבְעֵי רַחֲמֵי אַמּוֹתָנָא, וְכַפְנָא נִיסְבּוֹל. אֲמַר לְהוּ ר' שְׁמוּאֵל בַּר נַחְמָנִי: [ב]נִיבְעֵי רַחֲמֵי אַכַּפְנָא, דְּכִי יָהֵיב רַחֲמָנָא שׂוֹבְעָא — לְחַיֵּי הוּא דְּיָהֵיב, דִּכְתִיב "פּוֹתֵחַ אֶת יָדֶךָ וּמַשְׂבִּיעַ לְכָל חַי רָצוֹן". וּמְנָלַן דְּלָא מְצַלֵּינַן אַתַּרְתֵּי? דִּכְתִיב "וַנָּצוּמָה וַנְּבַקְשָׁה מֵאֱלֹהֵינוּ עַל זֹאת", מִכְּלָל דְּאִיכָּא אַחֲרִיתֵי. בְּמַעַרְבָא אָמְרִי מִשְּׁמֵיהּ דְּר' חַגַּי מֵהָכָא: "וְרַחֲמִין לְמִבְעֵא מִן קֳדָם אֱלָהּ שְׁמַיָּא עַל רָזָא דְנָא" — מִכְּלָל דְּאִיכָּא אַחֲרִיתֵי. בִּימֵי ר' זֵירָא, גְּזוּר שְׁמָדָא, וּגְזוּר דְּלָא לְמֵיתַב בְּתַעֲנִיתָא. אֲמַר לְהוּ ר' זֵירָא: [ג]נְקַבְּלֵיהּ עִילָּוָון, וְלִכִי בָּטֵיל הַגְּזֵירָה — לִיתְבֵיהּ. אָמְרִי לֵיהּ: מְנָא לָךְ הָא? אֲמַר לְהוּ: דִּכְתִיב "וַיֹּאמֶר אֵלַי אַל תִּירָא דָנִיֵּאל כִּי מִן הַיּוֹם הָרִאשׁוֹן אֲשֶׁר נָתַתָּ אֶת לִבְּךָ לְהָבִין וּלְהִתְעַנּוֹת לִפְנֵי אֱלֹהֶיךָ נִשְׁמְעוּ דְבָרֶיךָ". אָמַר רַבִּי יִצְחָק: אֲפִילּוּ שָׁנִים כִּשְׁנֵי אֵלִיָּהוּ, וְיָרְדוּ גְּשָׁמִים בְּעַרְבֵי שַׁבָּתוֹת — אֵינָן אֶלָּא סִימַן קְלָלָה. הַיְינוּ *דַּאֲמַר רַבָּה בַּר שֵׁילָא: *קָשֶׁה יוֹמָא דְּמִיטְרָא כְּיוֹמָא דְּדִינָא. אֲמַר אַמֵּימָר: אִי לָא דִּצְרִיךְ לְבִרְיָיתָא — בָּעֵינַן רַחֲמֵי וּמְבַטְּלִינַן לֵיהּ. וְאָמַר רַבִּי יִצְחָק: שֶׁמֶשׁ בְּשַׁבָּת — צְדָקָה לַעֲנִיִּים, שֶׁנֶּאֱמַר "וְזָרְחָה לָכֶם יִרְאֵי שְׁמִי שֶׁמֶשׁ צְדָקָה וּמַרְפֵּא". וְאָמַר רַבִּי יִצְחָק: גָּדוֹל יוֹם הַגְּשָׁמִים, שֶׁאֲפִילּוּ פְּרוּטָה שֶׁבַּכִּיס מִתְבָּרֶכֶת בּוֹ, שֶׁנֶּאֱמַר "לָתֵת מְטַר אַרְצְךָ בְּעִתּוֹ וּלְבָרֵךְ אֵת כָּל מַעֲשֵׂה יָדֶךָ". וְאָמַר רַבִּי יִצְחָק: *אֵין הַבְּרָכָה מְצוּיָה אֶלָּא בְּדָבָר הַסָּמוּי מִן הָעַיִן, שֶׁנֶּאֱמַר "יְצַו ה' אִתְּךָ אֶת הַבְּרָכָה בַּאֲסָמֶיךָ". תָּנָא דְּבֵי ר' יִשְׁמָעֵאל: אֵין הַבְּרָכָה מְצוּיָה אֶלָּא בְּדָבָר שֶׁאֵין הָעַיִן שׁוֹלֶטֶת בּוֹ, שֶׁנֶּאֱמַר: "יְצַו ה' אִתְּךָ אֶת הַבְּרָכָה בַּאֲסָמֶיךָ". ת"ר: [ד]הַנִּכְנָס לָמוֹד אֶת גָּרְנוֹ אוֹמֵר: יר"מ ה' אֱלֹהֵינוּ, שֶׁתִּשְׁלַח בְּרָכָה בְּמַעֲשֵׂה יָדֵינוּ. הִתְחִיל לָמוֹד, אוֹמֵר: בָּרוּךְ הַשּׁוֹלֵחַ בְּרָכָה בַּכְּרִי הַזֶּה. מָדַד וְאח"כ בֵּירַךְ — הֲרֵי זוֹ תְּפִלַּת שָׁוְא. לְפִי שֶׁאֵין הַבְּרָכָה מְצוּיָה, לֹא בְּדָבָר הַשָּׁקוּל וְלֹא בְּדָבָר הַמָּדוּד וְלֹא בְּדָבָר הַמָּנוּי אֶלָּא בְּדָבָר הַסָּמוּי מִן הָעַיִן.§ קִיבּוּץ גָּיְיסוֹת צְדָקָה, (*מַעֲשֶׂה) פַּרְנָס, סִימָן.§ אָמַר רַבִּי יוֹחָנָן: גָּדוֹל יוֹם הַגְּשָׁמִים כְּיוֹם קִבּוּץ גָּלֻיּוֹת, שֶׁנֶּאֱמַר "שׁוּבָה ה' אֶת שְׁבִיתֵנוּ כַּאֲפִיקִים בַּנֶּגֶב". וְאֵין "אֲפִיקִים" אֶלָּא "מָטָר", שֶׁנֶּאֱמַר "וַיֵּרָאוּ אֲפִיקֵי יָם". וְאָמַר רַבִּי יוֹחָנָן: גָּדוֹל יוֹם הַגְּשָׁמִים, שֶׁאֲפִילּוּ גָּיְיסוֹת פּוֹסְקוֹת בּוֹ, שֶׁנֶּאֱמַר "תְּלָמֶיהָ רַוֵּה נַחֵת גְּדוּדֶיהָ". וְאָמַר רַבִּי יוֹחָנָן: אֵין הַגְּשָׁמִים נֶעֱצָרִין אֶלָּא בִּשְׁבִיל פּוֹסְקֵי צְדָקָה בָּרַבִּים וְאֵין נוֹתְנִין, שֶׁנֶּאֱמַר "נְשִׂיאִים וְרוּחַ, וְגֶשֶׁם אָיִן, אִישׁ מִתְהַלֵּל בְּמַתַּת שָׁקֶר". וְא"ר יוֹחָנָן: מַאי דִּכְתִיב
עַשֵּׂר

רש"י

נֶאֶמְרָה עֲצִירָה בְּאִשָּׁה כו'. כְּלוֹמַר, עַל כּוּלָּן מְבַקְּשִׁים רַחֲמִים: פֶּלֶג. בְּרֵיכָה: כְּמִין קוּבָּה. אֹהֶל מָלֵא מַיִם: אִם לְשֵׁבֶט. אִם גָּזַר הקב"ה רוֹב גְּשָׁמִים לְרָעָה — אָז יוֹרְדִים בְּכֹחַ כְּשֵׁבֶט שֶׁמַּכֶּה בְּכֹחַ. וְחָזְרוּ בִּתְשׁוּבָה — הקב"ה מוֹרִידָן עַל הָרִים וּגְבָעוֹת, מָקוֹם שֶׁאֵין שָׁם אִישׁ: אֲבָל אִם לְחֶסֶד. שֶׁיּוֹרְדִין בְּנַחַת — יַמְצִיאֵהוּ לְאַרְצוֹ, לְאֶרֶץ יִשְׂרָאֵל: אַתַּרְתֵּי. לָא בָּעֵינַן רַחֲמֵי אַהֲדָדֵי, כִּדְלְקַמָּן: נִבְעֵי רַחֲמֵי אַכַּפְנָא. דְּלֵיתִיב שׂוֹבְעָא, וּמוֹתָנָא לִיבָּטֵל מֵמֵילָא: דְּכִי יָהֵיב רַחֲמָנָא שׂוֹבְעָא לְחַיֵּי הוּא דְּיָהֵיב. לְחַיִּים וְלֹא לְמֵתִים, דְּאֵינוֹ מֵבִיא שׂוֹבְעָא כְּדֵי לְהָמִית בְּנֵי אָדָם, אֶלָּא כְּדֵי שֶׁיִּחְיוּ: מַשְׂבִּיעַ לְכָל חַי רָצוֹן. שׂוֹבַע נוֹתֵן לִבְנֵי אָדָם חַיִּים: עַל זֹאת. עַל אַחַת מַשְׁמַע. בְּעֶזְרָא כְּתִיב: עַל רָזָא דְנָא. בְּדָנִיֵּאל כְּתִיב: דְּלָא לֵיתְבוּ בְּתַעֲנִיתָא. דְּלָא בָּעוּ דְּלֵיתֵי בְּרָכָה לָעוֹלָם בִּשְׁבִילָן: נִיקַבֵּל עִילָּוָון. יוֹמֵי תַּעֲנִיתָא. דְּמִשּׁוּם קַבָּלָה מְהַנֵּי לָן כְּתַעֲנִיתָא, וְכִי בָּטֵיל גְּזֵרָה — עָבְדִין לְהוּ: וּמְנָלַן דְּעָבְדִינַן הָכִי. כְּלוֹמַר, דִּמְהַנֵּי אִי עָבְדִינַן הָכִי: אֲשֶׁר נָתַתָּ לִבְּךָ לְהִתְעַנּוֹת לִפְנֵי אֱלֹהֶיךָ נִשְׁמְעוּ דְבָרֶיךָ. אַלְמָא: מִשֶּׁקִּיבֵּל עָלָיו נִשְׁמְעוּ דְבָרָיו: כִּשְׁנֵי אֵלִיָּהוּ. בִּימֵי אַחְאָב, שֶׁהָיָה הָעוֹלָם צָרִיךְ לִגְשָׁמִים, דִּכְתִיב (מלכים א יז) "אִם יִהְיֶה הַשָּׁנִים הָאֵלֶּה טַל וּמָטָר כִּי אִם לְפִי דְבָרִי": סִימַן קְלָלָה. שֶׁבְּנֵי אָדָם צְרִיכִים לַחֲזֹר בַּשּׁוּק לִקְנוֹת סְעוּדַּת שַׁבָּת(א): קָשֵׁי יוֹמֵי דְּמִיטְרָא. שֶׁאֵין בְּנֵי אָדָם יְכוֹלִין לַעֲשׂוֹת צָרְכֵיהֶן: כְּיוֹמָא דְּדִינָא. שֵׁנִי וַחֲמִישִׁי, שֶׁמִּתְקַבְּלִין בְּנֵי אָדָם לָדוּן עִם חַבְרֵיהֶן, כְּתַקָּנַת עֶזְרָא. שֶׁיֵּשׁ הוֹמוֹת וְקוֹלוֹת וְאַוְושׁוֹת בְּיוֹם הַגְּשָׁמִים כְּיוֹם הַדִּין. וּבְעֶרֶב שַׁבָּת כָּל שֶׁכֵּן דְּקָשֵׁי מִיטְרָא: וְהַיְינוּ. דְּאָמַר ר' שֵׁילָא: וּמְבַטְּלִינְהוּ לִירִידַת גְּשָׁמִים שֶׁטּוֹרְחִין בְּנֵי אָדָם, וְאֵינָן יְכוֹלִין לָצֵאת וְלָבֹא: צְדָקָה לַעֲנִיִּים. שֶׁמִּתְעַדְּנִין בָּהּ, וְנוֹחַ לָהֶן יוֹם בָּרוּר, וּמִתְחַמְּמִין בָּהּ בְּיוֹם הַלַּיְנָה: יִרְאֵי שְׁמִי. שׁוֹמְרֵי שַׁבָּת: פְּרוּטָה שֶׁבַּכִּיס. אֲפִי' מַעֲשֵׂה יָדַיִם שֶׁאֵינָן צְרִיכִים לִגְשָׁמִים מִתְבָּרְכִין: בָּרוּךְ הַשּׁוֹלֵחַ בְּרָכָה. (*שִׁיפּוּעַ) וּמַזְכִּיר בָּהּ מַלְכוּת וְאַזְכָּרָה כְּכָל הַבְּרָכוֹת כּוּלָּן: הֲרֵי זוֹ תְּפִלַּת שָׁוְא. (ב) וְשׁוּב אֵין בְּרָכָה נִכְנֶסֶת בָּהּ: בְּדָבָר הַסָּמוּי מִן הָעַיִן. שֶׁאֵינוֹ יוֹדֵעַ הַסְּכוּם: כַּאֲפִיקִים. כַּאֲפִיקֵי נְחָלִים: בַּנֶּגֶב.(ג) יַבָּשָׁה. "וְהִנֵּה חָרְבוּ" מְתַרְגְּמִינַן נְגִיבוּ: אֲפִיקֵי יָם. מוֹצָאֵי (ד)יָם. אַלְמָא: אָפִיק לְשׁוֹן מַיִם, וַאֲפִיקִים בַּנֶּגֶב נַמִי לְשׁוֹן גְּשָׁמִים: גָּיְיסוֹת. חַיָּלוֹת. כְּשֶׁהַמָּטָר מְרַוֶּה תַּלְמֵי הָאָרֶץ בַּגֶּשֶׁם מִיָּד גְּדוּדִים נוֹחִין, כִּדְלְקַמָּן: פּוֹסְקֵי צְדָקָה בָּרַבִּים. לְשֵׁם וּלְפָנִים. וְאוֹרְחָא דְּמִילְּתָא נָקַט, שֶׁאֵין אָדָם עָשׂוּי לִפְסוֹק צְדָקָה בֵּינוֹ לְבֵין עַצְמוֹ וְאֵינוֹ נוֹתֵן: נְשִׂיאִים וְרוּחַ. דּוֹמִין לָעוֹלָם כְּאִילּוּ גְּשָׁמִים יוֹרְדִין — וְאֵינָן יוֹרְדִין, בִּשְׁבִיל הָאִישׁ הַמִּתְהַלֵּל בְּמַתַּת שֶׁקֶר. דִּכְשֶׁם שֶׁהוּא עוֹשֶׂה לְפָנִים וּמַחֲנִיף אֶת הָעֲנִיִּים — אַף שָׁמַיִם מַחֲנִיפִין אֶת הָאָרֶץ, שֶׁמַּרְאִין נְשִׂיאִים וְרוּחַ — וְגֶשֶׁם אָיִן. אִי נַמִי: אַיִן קָאֵי אַשְׁלָשְׁתָּם, דְּמִכָּל אֵלּוּ נֶעֱצָרִין:
לֵינוּקָא

תוספות

ונצומה ונבקשה מאלהינו. ויעתר לנו. פירוש: מדקאמר על [זאת] — משמע דאיכא מילתא אחריתא. וכן פירש בסמוך "על דנא": **אלא** בדבר הסמוי מן העין שנאמר יצו ה' וגו'. תימה: דאמרינן פרק "כל הבשר" (חולין דף קה:) גבי הני שקולאי דדרו חביתא דחמרא, בעו לאתפושי אותבוהו תותי מרזיבא, פקע חביתא. ומפרש התם: בשביל השד שהיה שם, עד דאכפייה מר בר רב אשי לשד לשלם, אמר ליה שידא למר בר רב אשי: ליקבע לי מר זימנא דאיזיל ואשלם. קבע ליה זימנא, כי מטא זימניה איעכב. ואמר ליה: אמאי לא אתית בזמנך? אמר ליה: כל מידי דצייר וחתים וכייל ומני — לית לן רשות למישקל מיניה אלמא בדבר המדוד והמנוי לית ליה רשות למשקל מיניה. ובדבר הסמוי אית ליה רשות, אלמא אין ברכה בדבר הסמוי! וי"ל: דלא קשה מידי, דהא דקאמר התם (ה)היינו טעמא דלית להו אלא בדבר הפקר, ולא דבר דכייל ומנוי או צייר וחתים — היינו בשביל דאין ברכה מלויה בהני, ולית בהו דבר הפקר, והאי דבעלים ניניהו. אלא בדבר הסמוי, והיינו מטעם דהברכה מלויה בדבר הסמוי, ומה שמתברכה בשביל הברכה — אית להו רשות למישקל בסמוי, דהיינו כמו הפקר שאין לשום אדם זכות בו. אי נמי, הכא איירי בדבר המנוי והמדוד בלא צייר וחתים, ובהא אית להו רשותא, והתם איירי במדוד ומנוי וכייל וצייר וחתים — ובהא לית להו רשותא: **גדול** יום גשמים כיום קיבוץ גליות שנאמר שובה ה' את שביתנו כאפיקים בנגב וגו'. ואם תאמר: אמאי לא קאמר גדול יום הגשמים יותר מקיבוץ גליות, דהא "כאפיקים בנגב" כתיב, ומי נתלה במי — קטן נתלה בגדול, שאפיקים גדולים מיום קיבוץ גליות! דהכי נמי אמר (לעיל דף ז.): "יערוף כמטר לקחי" מי נתלה במי — קטן נתלה בגדול! וי"ל, דה"פ: אנו מתפללים הכי: שובה ה' את שביתנו כאפיקים היורדין בנגב, שגדול יום קיבוץ כאפיקים בנגב. א"כ עשה עמנו לטובה אות בקבוץ גליות, בהיות כי זה כמו זה, ואפיקים בנגב תחדש בכל יום — כיום קיבוץ גליות, אבל יותר לא:
עשר

עין משפט נר מצוה

כג א ב טוש"ע א"ח סי' תקעו סעיף טו:
כד ג שם סימן תקעא סעיף ג:
כה ד מיי' פ"י מהל' ברכות הלכה כב סמג עשין כו טוש"ע א"ח סימן רל סעיף ב:

רבינו חננאל

ולידה ופקידה באשה וכנגדן ברקיע ובארץ. פקידה שנאמר פקדת ארץ ותשוקקה. לידה שנאמר והולידה והצמיחה עצירה שנא' ועצר את השמים תנא כמין קובה יש ברקיע ומשם גשמים יורדים שנאמר פלג אלהים מלא מים: הוה כפנא ומותנא אמרי לא אפשר למבעי רחמי אתרתי דכתיב ונצומה ונבקשה מאלהינו על זאת. במערבא אמרי ורחמין למיבעי מן קדם אלהא על רזא דנא. מכלל דאיכא (אחד) אחריתי: אלא מיבעי רחמי אכפנא (ומותנא נסבול) דכי יהב רחמנא שובעא לחיי הוא דיהיב שנאמר פותח את ידך ומשביע לכל חי רצון. בימי רבי זירא גזור שמדא ומנעום מלקבוע תענית א"ר זירא ניקבליה עלוון מהשתא ולכי בטיל שמדא ניתוב בתעניתא שנאמר ויאמר אלי אל תירא דניאל כי מן היום אשר נתת לבך להבין ולהתענות וגו'. גשמים (בלילי) [בערבי] שבתות אפילו שנים כשני אליהו סימן קללה הן. אין הברכה מצויה לא בדבר המדוד ולא בדבר המנוי ולא בדבר השקול אלא בדבר הסמוי מן העין שנאמר יצו ה' אתך את הברכה באסמיך וגו'. א"ר יוחנן אין הגשמים נעצרין אלא בשביל פוסקי צדקה ברבים ואינם נותנים שנאמר נשיאים ורוח וגשם אין וגו'.

רבינו גרשום

אם לשבט דאתי ברזיא: להרים שילך על ההרים: אם לחסד שיורד בנחת ימציאהו ליישוב: צדקה לעניים. שמתחממין שהן ערומים: בערבי שבתות סימן קללה הוא שאין יכולין לטרוח לכבוד שבת. *) כדעבד לאבוך. שנעשה גל של עצמות:
*) שייך לדף ט.

הגהות הב"ח

(א) רש"י ד"ה סימן כו' סעודת שבת הס"ד ואחר כך מה"ד והיינו דאמר ר' שילא קשי יומי דמיטרא שאין כו' עד כ"ש דקשי מיטרא מה"ד ומבטלינהו לירידת גשמים כו': (ב) ד"ה הרי זו תפלת שוא. דשוב אין ברכה: (ג) ד"ה בנגב. לשון יובש והנה חרבו: (ד) ד"ה אפיקי ים. מוצאי מים אלמא כו' כצ"ל: (ה) תוס' ד"ה אלא כו' דהא דקאמר התם הכי היינו טעמא:

"עשר תעשר"? *עשר בשביל שתתעשר. אשכחיה ר' יוחנן לינוקא דריש לקיש. אמר ליה: אימא לי פסוקיך. א"ל: "עשר תעשר". א"ל: ומאי "עשר תעשר"? א"ל: עשר בשביל שתתעשר. אמר ליה: מנא לך? א"ל: זיל נסי. אמר ליה: ומי שרי לנסוייה להקב"ה? והכתיב "לא תנסו את ה'"! א"ל: הכי אמר רבי הושעיא: חוץ מזו, שנאמר: "הביאו את כל המעשר אל בית האוצר, ויהי טרף בביתי, ובחנוני נא בזאת אמר ה' צבאות אם לא אפתח לכם את ארובות השמים, והריקותי לכם ברכה עד בלי די" *מאי "עד בלי די"? אמר רמי בר חמא אמר רב: עד שיבלו שפתותיכם מלומר "די". א"ל: אי הות מטי התם להאי פסוקא, לא הוית צריכנא לך ולהושעיא רבך. ותו אשכחיה ר' יוחנן לינוקיה דריש לקיש, דיתיב ואמר: "אולת אדם תסלף דרכו, ועל ה' יזעף לבו". יתיב רבי יוחנן וקא מתמה; אמר: מי איכא מידי דכתיבי בכתובי דלא רמיזי באורייתא? א"ל: אטו הא מי לא רמיזי? והכתיב "ויצא לבם ויחרדו, איש אל אחיו לאמר מה זאת עשה אלהים לנו"?! דל עיניה וחזא ביה. אתיא אימיה אפיקתיה. אמרה ליה: תא מקמיה, דלא ליעבד לך כדעבד לאבוך. (*א"ר) יוחנן: מטר — בשביל יחיד. פרנסה — בשביל רבים. מטר בשביל יחיד — דכתיב "יפתח ה' לך את אוצרו הטוב לתת מטר ארצך". פרנסה בשביל רבים — דכתיב "הנני ממטיר לכם לחם". מיתיבי, ר' יוסי בר' יהודה אומר: שלשה פרנסים טובים עמדו לישראל, אלו הן: משה, ואהרן, ומרים. וג' מתנות טובות ניתנו על ידם, ואלו הן: באר, וענן, ומן. באר — בזכות מרים. עמוד ענן — בזכות אהרן. מן — בזכות משה. מתה מרים — נסתלק הבאר. שנאמר "ותמת שם מרים" וכתיב בתריה: "ולא היה מים לעדה". וחזרה בזכות שניהן. מת אהרן — נסתלקו ענני כבוד, שנאמר "וישמע הכנעני, מלך ערד". *מה שמועה שמע? שמע שמת אהרן ונסתלקו ענני כבוד, וכסבור ניתנה לו רשות להלחם בישראל. והיינו דכתיב "ויראו כל העדה כי גוע אהרן". אמר ר' אבהו: אל תקרי "ויראו" אלא "וייראו", כדדריש ר"ל. *דאר"ל: "כי" משמש בארבע לשונות: "אי", "דלמא", "אלא", *"דהא". חזרו שניהם בזכות משה. מת משה — נסתלקו כולן, שנאמר "ואכחיד את שלשת הרועים בירח אחד". וכי בירח אחד מתו? והלא מרים מתה בניסן, ואהרן באב, ומשה באדר? אלא, מלמד שנתבטלו ג' מתנות טובות שניתנו על ידן, ונסתלקו כולן בירח אחד. אלמא אשכחן פרנסה בשביל יחיד! שאני משה. *כיון דלרבים הוא בעי — כרבים דמי. רב הונא בר מנוח ורב שמואל בר אידי ורב חייא מווסתניא הוו שכיחי קמיה דרבא. כי נח נפשיה דרבא אתו לקמיה דרב פפא. כל אימת דהוה אמר להו שמעתא ולא הוה מסתברא להו, הוו מרמזי אהדדי. חלש דעתיה. אקרויה

רש"י

לינוקא דריש לקיש. בן אחותו של ר' יוחנן. ולאחר מיתתו של ריש לקיש, כדמוכח לקמן: אמר. ינוקא לר' יוחנן: מאי "עשר תעשר"? אמר ליה ינוקא. והכתיב "לא תנסו": שיבלו. כלומר: שייגעו — דולורא"ט בלע"ז: אי הוה מטינא להתם. להאי קרא ד"הביאו את כל המעשר" הוה ידעית ליה מילתא: לר' הושעיא רבך. דאמרית לי משמיה: אולת אדם תסלף דרכו ועל ה' יזעף לבו. כשאדם חוטא מסלף דרכו, שבאין עליו פגעים — ועל השם יזעף לבו, שכועס ואומר: מפני מה אירע לי פגע זה? ולא רמזה. משה באורייתא? שהחומש הוא יסוד נביאים וכתובים, וכולן יש סמך למצוא מן התורה: דלי עיניה. רבי יוחנן, שהיו עפעפיו מכסין את עיניו, ומגביהן במזלגי דכספא, כדאמר קמא בפ' אחרון (דף קיז.). שהיה רוצה לראותו, מפני שהוא חריף: דלא ליעביד לך כדעבד לאבוך. שלא יתן עיניו בך כמו שנתן באביך והמיתו, כדאמר מליעא (דף פד.): מטר בשביל יחיד. שאם א"צ מטר אלא לאדם אחד, כגון שזרע אחר זמן זריעת בני אדם, או שדר בעיר שכולה נכרים וצריך למטר — בא בזכותו (א). ופרנסה שפע טובה ומחיה לכל העולם אינו בא לעולם בזכות אחד אלא בשביל רבים. שאם רבים צריכין שובע, שתשלח ברכה בתבואה — הקב"ה עושה, אם זכו. אבל יחיד הצריך שיתברכו תבואותיו — אין הקב"ה משנה בעבורו דין השנה, אלא כפי ברכותיה. ואע"פ שמוריד*) בשביל יחיד מטר זה להשביח תבואותיו, שלא יהו גרועות משל אחרים — אבל לעשות שדהו כשדה שובע — לא: מטר ארצך. של אחד משמע: ממטיר לכם. לשון רבים: בארה של מרים. סלע, וזבין ממנו מים, והיה מתגלגל והולך עם ישראל. והוא הסלע שבו הכה משה, שלא היה רוצה להזיל מימיו בשבילו, לפי שמתה מרים: ונסתלקו ענני כבוד. ענני רקיע וענני עשן. ושאר עננים אינן של כבוד: חזרה בזכות שניהן. שכן כתיב "ודברתם שניכם אל הסלע ונתן מימיו": כי משמש ארבע לשונות אי דלמא אלא דהא. כל מקום שצריך לדרוש 'כי', בין לענין דרשה בין למשמעות המקרא — תוכל לשנותו באחד מהני ארבע לשונות. דלשון 'כי' משמע בכולם. וכן 'וכד' 'וברם' 'ואדי' בכלל הני ד' הן. והאי ד"כי גוע אהרן" משתמש בלשון דהא, ושמעינן מינה טעמא דקרא: דמה טעם נתראו — דהא מית, שהרי מת אהרן. וריש לקיש לא אתי למימר דלא מתרגמין שום כי בעולם אלא (ב) מהני לשונות, אלא אפי' מתרגמא] דלמא אדי — דרשינן משמעותיה כמשמעות "דהא". ומאן דמתרגם "וחזיאו כל כנישתא דהא מית" — טועה הוא, דאם כן "ואתחזיאו" מיבעי ליה. "ויראו כל העדה" במשקל "ויראו ראשי הבדים" "וירפו המים" "ויעלו מעל משכן קרח": חזרו שניהם בזכות משה. מדכתיב "ואכחיד את שלשת הרועים" פשיטא לן דבדידהו משתעי, שלא מצינו פרנסים לישראל שלשה כאחד אלא הם: מתה בניסן. שנאמר (במדבר כ) "ויבואו בני ישראל כל העדה מדבר צין בחדש הראשון וישב העם בקדש ותמת שם מרים ותקבר שם" (*בפרה) אדומה: אהרן מת. באחד לחדש*: מווסתניא. מאותו מקום: אחוו להדדי. מראין ומביטין זה לזה, דלא סלקא להו שמעתא כרבא: אקרויה

*) בשביל זה מטר להשביח רש"א.

תוספות

עשר תעשר. הכי איתא בסיפרי: "עשר תעשר את כל תבואת זרעך היוצא השדה שנה שנה". אין לי אלא תבואת זרעך שחייב במעשר, רבית ופרקמטיא וכל שאר רווחים מנין — ת"ל "את כל". דהוה מצי למימר "את תבואתך", מאי "כל"? לרבות רבית ופרקמטיא וכל דבר שמרויח בו. והכי נמי איכא בהגדה: *"היוצא השדה שנה [שנה]". כלומר, אם לא תעשר שדך כהוגן — לא יהיה לך אלא היוצא מן השדה, כלומר לא יעשה שדך אלא כפי מעשרות שהיו קודם לכן. דהיינו "היוצא מן השדה" כלומר: מה שהיית רגיל להוציא למעשר מן השדה. ומעשה באדם אחד שהיה עשיר, והיה לו שדה שעשתה אלף כור, והיה אותו עשיר נוטל ק' כורין למעשר ומפריש כל שנה ושנה, וכן עשה כל ימיו. כשחלה למות קרא לבנו ואמר לו: בני, דע שדה זו שאני מוריש לך עושה בכל שנה ושנה אלף כורין, הזהר שתפריש ק' כורין כאשר עשיתי ומת אותו האיש. ועמד הבן במקומו, ועשה השדה אלף כורין כאשר היה עושה בחיי האב, והפריש ממנה ק' כורין. בשנה שניה נסתכל וראה הבן שמעשר היה דבר גדול, ואמר שלא יפריש. לשנה אחרת נתמעט השדה ולא עשה כי אם מאה כורין. נצטער עליו, ושמעו קרוביו שכך מיעט ולא הפריש מעשר — באו כולם אצלו מלובשים לבנים ושמחים. אמר להם: כמדומה לי שאתם שמחים בקלקלתי! אמרו לו: נצטער עליך כי גרמת לך כל הרעה הזאת, ומפני מה לא הפרשת מעשר כראוי היטב! בא וראה כי מתחלה כשבא השדה לידך היית בעל הבית והקב"ה כהן, שהיה המעשר חלקו, ליתן לעניים. ועכשיו שלא הפרשת חלקו לו — היה הקב"ה בעל הבית ואתה כהן, שאין שדך עושה (ג) מה שהיה עושה מתחלה, אלף כורין, והפריש לך מאה כורין. והיינו דכתיב (במדבר ה) "ואיש את קדשיו לו יהיו" כלומר, *כשאינו מפריש כהוגן — לא יהיה לו אלא הקדשים, כלומר המעשר. ועל זה אמרו חכמים: המעכב מעשרותיו — לסוף בא שלא יהיה לו אלא אחד מעשר, כדכתיב (ישעיה ה) "וזרע חומר יעשה איפה" דהיינו המעשר, דאיפה ג' סאין ובחומר יש (לו) ל' סאין. וכן כתיב *"כי עשרת צמדי כרם יעשו בת אחת". וה"ר נתן האופניא"ל פי': *היוצא מן השדה כלומר: ואם לאו, שאין אתה מפריש — העישור יהיה לאותו היוצא לשדה, דהיינו עשו הרשע, כלומר שיקחוהו הנכרים:

תלמוד

מסורת הש"ס

[שבת קיט.]

[לקמן כב:] שבת לב: מכות כג:

[נ"ל ואמר רבי]

ר"ה ג.

גיטין ל. שבועות מט:

[פסחים לג:]

ס"א כיון דאלים זכותו כרבים דמי

[נ"ל בפרשת פרה]

[נ"ל באחד לחדש בחדש החמישי בפ' אלה מסעי]

תורה אור

דברים יד; שם ו; מלאכי ג; משלי יט; בראשית מב; דברים כח; שמות טז; במדבר כ; שם כא; שם כ; זכריה יא

הגהות מהר"ב רנשבורג

[א] רש"י ד"ה כי משמש וכו' אלא אפי' מתורגם אדי כצ"ל:

[עי' ילקוט רמז תתלב וכן איתא בתנחומא פ' ראה]

[גם זה איתא בילקוט רמז תתלג וכן בתנחומא]

רבינו חננאל

עשר תעשר כלומר עשר כדי שירבה קניינך ותעשר עוד פעמים אחרים. ואמרינן מי שרי למימר הכי והכתיב לא תנסו את ה' אלהיכם ושנינן חוץ מזו שנאמר הביאו וגו' ובחנוני נא בזאת וגו' כתיב אולת אדם תסלף דרכו ועל ה' יזעף לבו. כיוצא בו בתורה דכתיב ויחרדו איש אל אחיו לאמר מה זאת עשה אלהים לנו: א"ר יוחנן מטר בזכות יחיד שנאמר לתת מטר ארצך בעתו ר"ל אמר מהכא שאלו מה' מטר וגו' ותניא ומטר גשם יתן להם לאיש יכול לכל השדות שלו ת"ל בשדה. יכול לכל השדה ת"ל עשב השדה וכדר' דניאל בר רב קטינא דהוה סייר גינתיה ואמר האי משרא בעי מיא והאי משרא לא בעי מיא ואתי מטרא להאי משרא דאמר בעי מיא. פרנסה בשביל רבים שנאמר הנני ממטיר לכם לחם מן השמים וגו'. ואקשינן והא משה רבינו יחידי הוה (וקמא) [וקאמר] כי המן ירד בזכותו. והענן בזכות אהרן והבאר בזכות מרים. וכולן כיון שמתו נסתלקו כל אחד ואחד הדבר שהיה בזכותו. וחזרו בשביל מרע"ה. וכיון שמת נסתלקו הכל שנאמר ואכחיד שלשת הרועים בירח אחד. ושנינן שאני משה רבינו כיון דאלים זכותיה כרבים דמי. ג' פרנסים טובים עמדו לישראל. ואלו הן משה ואהרן ומרים וג' מתנות נתן להם הקב"ה על ידם ואלו הן מן ובאר ועמוד הענן כו': תלמידי דרבא כד נח נפשיה אתו לקמיה דרב פפא לא הוו מסתברי להו שמעתתיה הוה מרמזי להדדי חזנהו

הגהות הב"ח

(א) רש"י ד"ה מטר כו' בא בזכותו הס"ד ומה"ד ופרנסה כו' ואף על פי שמוריד בשביל זה מטר להשביח: (ב) ד"ה כי משמש כו' שום כי בעולם אלא באחד מהני לשונות: (ג) תום' ד"ה עשר כו' ואתה כהן שאין שדך עושה עתה מה שהיה עושה:

תורה אור

אַקְרוּיֵהּ בְּחֶלְמֵיהּ °"וָאַכְחִד אֶת שְׁלֹשֶׁת הָרֹעִים". זכריה יא
לְמָחָר, כִּי הָווּ מִיפַּטְרוּ מִינֵּיהּ, אֲמַר לְהוּ: לֵיזְלוּ רַבָּנַן *בִּשְׁלָמָא.§ רַב שִׁימִי בַּר אַשִׁי הֲוָה שְׁכִיחַ קַמֵּיהּ דְּרַב פָּפָּא, הֲוָה מַקְשֵׁי לֵיהּ טוּבָא. יוֹמָא חַד, חַזְיֵיהּ דְּנָפַל עַל אַפֵּיהּ. שְׁמָעֵיהּ דַּאֲמַר: רַחֲמָנָא לִיצְּלַן מִכִּיסּוּפָא דְשִׁימִי. קַבֵּיל עֲלֵיהּ שְׁתִיקוּתָא, וְתוּ לָא אַקְשֵׁי לֵיהּ. וְאַף ר"ל סָבַר מָטָר בִּשְׁבִיל יָחִיד. דְּאָמַר ר"ל: מִנַּיִן לְמָטָר בִּשְׁבִיל יָחִיד — דִּכְתִיב °"שַׁאֲלוּ מֵה' מָטָר בְּעֵת מַלְקוֹשׁ, ה' עֹשֶׂה חֲזִיזִים, וּמְטַר גֶּשֶׁם יִתֵּן לָהֶם לְאִישׁ עֵשֶׂב בַּשָּׂדֶה". יָכוֹל לַכֹּל? תַּלְמוּד לוֹמַר "לְאִישׁ". וְתַנְיָא: אִי לְאִישׁ — יָכוֹל לְכָל שְׂדוֹתָיו? ת"ל "שָׂדֶה". אִי שָׂדֶה, יָכוֹל לְכָל הַשָּׂדֶה — ת"ל "עֵשֶׂב". כִּי הָא דְּרַב דָּנִיֵּאל בַּר קְטִינָא הֲוָה לֵיהּ הַהִיא גִּינְּתָא. כָּל יוֹמָא, הֲוָה אָזֵיל וְסָיֵיר לַהּ. אֲמַר: הָא מִישְׁרָא בָּעֲיָא מַיָּא, וְהָא מִישְׁרָא לָא בָּעֲיָא מַיָּא. וַאֲתָא מִיטְרָא וְקָמַשְׁקֵי כָּל הֵיכָא דְּמִיבָּעֵי לֵיהּ מַיָּא. מַאי "ה' עֹשֶׂה חֲזִיזִים"? א"ר יוֹסֵי (*בַּר) חֲנִינָא: מְלַמֵּד שֶׁכָּל צַדִּיק וְצַדִּיק הקב"ה עוֹשֶׂה לוֹ חָזִיז בִּפְנֵי עַצְמוֹ. מַאי "חֲזִיזִים"? אָמַר רַב יְהוּדָה: פּוֹרְחוֹת. אָמַר רַבִּי יוֹחָנָן: סִימָן לְמָטָר — פּוֹרְחוֹת. מַאי "פּוֹרְחוֹת"? אָמַר רַב פָּפָּא: עֵיבָא קְלִישָׁא תּוּתֵי עֵיבָא סְמִיכְתָּא. אָמַר רַב יְהוּדָה: נְהִילָא מַקַּמֵּי מִיטְרָא — אָתֵי מִיטְרָא. בָּתַר מִיטְרָא — פָּסֵיק מִיטְרָא. מִקַּמֵּי מִיטְרָא אָתֵי מִיטְרָא, וְסִימָנֵיךְ: מְהוּלְתָּא. דְּבָתַר מִיטְרָא פָּסֵיק מִיטְרָא, וְסִימָנֵיךְ: חַרְיָא דְעִיזֵּי.§ עוּלָּא אִיקְּלַע לְבָבֶל. חֲזָא פּוֹרְחוֹת. אֲמַר לְהוּ: "פַּנּוּ מָאנֵי, דְּהַשְׁתָּא אָתֵי מִיטְרָא". לְסוֹף לָא אָתֵי מִיטְרָא. אֲמַר: "כִּי הֵיכִי דְּמִשַּׁקְּרִי בַּבְלָאֵי, הָכִי מְשַׁקְּרִי מִיטְרַיְיהוּ". *עוּלָּא אִיקְּלַע לְבָבֶל, חֲזֵי מְלָא צַנָּא דְּתַמְרֵי בְּזוּזָא. אֲמַר: מְלָא צַנָּא דְּדוּבְשָׁא בְּזוּזָא, וּבַבְלָאֵי לָא עָסְקֵי בְּאוֹרַיְיתָא! בְּלֵילְיָא צַעֲרוּהוּ. אֲמַר: מְלָא צַנָּא דְּסַכִּינָא בְּזוּזָא, וּבַבְלָאֵי עָסְקֵי בְּאוֹרַיְיתָא! תַּנְיָא:* ר' אֱלִיעֶזֶר אוֹמֵר: כָּל הָעוֹלָם כּוּלּוֹ מִמֵּימֵי אוֹקְיָינוֹס הוּא שׁוֹתֶה, שֶׁנֶּאֱמַר: °"וְאֵד יַעֲלֶה מִן הָאָרֶץ וְהִשְׁקָה אֶת כָּל פְּנֵי הָאֲדָמָה". בראשית ב
אָמַר לוֹ רַבִּי יְהוֹשֻׁעַ: וַהֲלֹא מֵימֵי אוֹקְיָינוֹס מְלוּחִין הֵן? אָמַר לוֹ: *מְמַתְּקִין בֶּעָבִים. ר' יְהוֹשֻׁעַ אוֹמֵר: כָּל הָעוֹלָם כּוּלּוֹ מִמַּיִם הָעֶלְיוֹנִים הוּא שׁוֹתֶה, שֶׁנֶּאֱמַר: °"לִמְטַר הַשָּׁמַיִם תִּשְׁתֶּה מָּיִם". אֶלָּא מָה אֲנִי מְקַיֵּים "וְאֵד יַעֲלֶה מִן הָאָרֶץ" — מְלַמֵּד שֶׁהֶעָנָנִים מִתְגַּבְּרִים וְעוֹלִים לָרָקִיעַ, וּפוֹתְחִין פִּיהֶן כְּנוֹד וּמְקַבְּלִין מֵי מָטָר, שֶׁנֶּאֱמַר: °"יָזֹקּוּ מָטָר לְאֵדוֹ". וּמְנוּקָּבוֹת הֵן כִּכְבָרָה, וּבָאוֹת וּמְחַשְּׁרוֹת מַיִם עַל גַּבֵּי קַרְקַע, שֶׁנֶּאֱמַר: °"חַשְׁרַת מַיִם, עָבֵי שְׁחָקִים". וְאֵין בֵּין טִיפָּה לְטִיפָּה אֶלָּא כִּמְלֹא נִימָא, לְלַמֶּדְךָ שֶׁגָּדוֹל יוֹם הַגְּשָׁמִים כְּיוֹם שֶׁנִּבְרְאוּ בּוֹ שָׁמַיִם וָאָרֶץ, *)שֶׁנֶּאֱמַר *°"עֹשֶׂה גְדֹלוֹת עַד אֵין חֵקֶר". וּכְתִיב °"הַנֹּתֵן מָטָר עַל פְּנֵי אָרֶץ". וּכְתִיב לְהַלָּן: °"הֲלוֹא יָדַעְתָּ אִם לֹא שָׁמַעְתָּ, אֱלֹהֵי עוֹלָם ה'... אֵין חֵקֶר לִתְבוּנָתוֹ".[א] **) (וּכְתִיב °"מֵכִין הָרִים בְּכֹחוֹ" וגו'). כְּמַאן אָזְלָא הָא דִּכְתִיב °"מַשְׁקֶה הָרִים מֵעֲלִיּוֹתָיו" — וְא"ר יוֹחָנָן: מֵעֲלִיּוֹתָיו שֶׁל הקב"ה, כְּמַאן — כְּרַבִּי יְהוֹשֻׁעַ. וְר' אֱלִיעֶזֶר? כֵּיוָן דְּסָלְקֵי לְהָתָם "מַשְׁקֶה מֵעֲלִיּוֹתָיו" קָרֵי לְהוּ. דְּאִי לָא תֵּימָא הָכִי, °"אָבָק וְעָפָר מִן הַשָּׁמַיִם" הֵיכִי מַשְׁכַּחַתְּ לַהּ? אֶלָּא, כֵּיוָן דְּמִדְּלֵי לְהָתָם — "מִן הַשָּׁמַיִם" קָרֵי לֵיהּ. הָכָא נַמִי, כֵּיוָן דְּסָלְקֵי לְהָתָם, "מֵעֲלִיּוֹתָיו" קָרֵי לֵיהּ. כְּמַאן אָזְלָא [הָא] דְּא"ר חֲנִינָא: °"כֹּנֵס כַּנֵּד מֵי הַיָּם נֹתֵן בְּאוֹצָרוֹת תְּהוֹמוֹת". מִי גָּרַם לָאוֹצָרוֹת שֶׁיִּתְמַלְּאוּ בָּר — תְּהוֹמוֹת,(א) כְּרַבִּי אֱלִיעֶזֶר. וְר' יְהוֹשֻׁעַ — הַהוּא בִּבְרִיָּיתוֹ

(מראי מקומות בגליון: זכריה יא; שם י; בראשית ב; דברים יא; איוב לו; שמואל ב כב; איוב ט; שם ה; ישעיהו מ; תהלים סה; שם קד; דברים כח; תהלים לג)

*) [לעיל ב.] **) [לא גרסינן הכא עי' רש"י ד"ה ללמדך אלא לעיל ב. גרס לזה שפיר]

רש"י

אַקְרוּיֵהּ. הָיוּ מַקְרִין אוֹתוֹ מִקְרָא זֶה בַּחֲלוֹם: "וָאַכְחִיד אֶת שְׁלֹשֶׁת הָרוֹעִים בְּיֶרַח אֶחָד", שֶׁרוֹצִין לְעוֹנְשָׁן בַּשָּׁמַיִם, מִשּׁוּם דְּמַכְסְפֵי לֵיהּ: קַבֵּל עָלָיו. רַב שִׁימִי שְׁתִיקוּתָא מִלְּהַקְשׁוֹת עוֹד: יָכוֹל לַכֹּל. כְּלוֹמַר, יָכוֹל אֵין נוֹתֵן מָטָר אא"כ הַכֹּל צְרִיכִין לוֹ: ת"ל לְאִישׁ. אֲפִילּוּ בִּשְׁבִיל אֶחָד: אִי לְאִישׁ יָכוֹל לְכָל שְׂדוֹתָיו. כְּלוֹמַר, אֵינוֹ יוֹרֵד עַד שֶׁהוּא צָרִיךְ לְכָל שְׂדוֹתָיו: ת"ל שָׂדֶה. אֲפִי' אֵינוֹ צָרִיךְ אֶלָּא בְּשָׂדֶה אֶחָד: אִי בְּשָׂדֶה יָכוֹל עַד שֶׁיִּצְטָרֵךְ לְכָל הַשָּׂדֶה ת"ל עֵשֶׂב. אֲפִילּוּ אֵינוֹ צָרִיךְ אֶלָּא לְעֵשֶׂב אֶחָד, (עֵשֶׂב) בִּשְׁבִיל יָרָק אֶחָד יוֹרֵד עָלָיו מָטָר: וְסָיֵיר. מְעַיֵּין: מִישְׁרָא. עֲרוּגָה: עוֹשֶׂה לוֹ חָזִיז. לְכָל צַדִּיק הַבָּא בָּעוֹלָם הַזֶּה, לְהָרִיק לוֹ גְּשָׁמִים עַל שְׂדוֹתָיו. בְּרֵישָׁא בָּעֵי: מַאי "חֲזִיזִים" לְשׁוֹן רַבִּים, וְהָדַר בָּעֵי: וּמַאי נִינְהוּ חֲזִיזִים, מַאי נִינְהוּ דְּקָרֵי חֲזִיזֵי? ה"ג: עֵיבָא קְלִישְׁתָּא דְּתוּתֵי עֵיבָא סְמִיכְתָּא. דְּתוּתֵי עֵיבָא — כְּלַפֵּי הָאָרֶץ: נְהִילָא. (ב)כְּמוֹ קִיטְמָא נְהִילָא (חולין דף נא:) שֶׁהִיא דַּקָּה, גְּשָׁמִים דַּקִּים כְּקִמְחָא נְהִילָא, שֶׁהִיא דַּקָּה, הַבָּאִין תְּחִילָּה לְמָטָר, וְאח"כ בָּא מָטָר: אָתֵי מִיטְרָא. גְּשָׁמִים יוֹרְדִין לָרוֹב, וְאֵין פּוֹסְקִין מַהֵר. אֲבָל בָּא מָטָר תְּחִילָּה וּמַתְחִילִין דַּקִּין לָבֹא — פּוֹסְקִין מִיָּד: מְהוּלְתָּא. שֶׁמִּתְּחִילָּה יוֹצֵא קֶמַח דַּק, וּלְבַסּוֹף סוּבִּין גַּסִּין: חַרְיָא דְעִיזֵּי. רֵיעִי שֶׁל עִזִּים. בִּתְחִילָּה יוֹצְאָה גַּסָּה, וּלְבַסּוֹף דַּקָּה, וּפוֹסֵק: דְּתַמְרֵי. דְּבַשׁ עוֹשִׂין מֵהֶן: וּבַבְלָאֵי לָא עָסְקֵי. כְּלוֹמַר, יְכוֹלִין הֵן לַעֲסוֹק תָּמִיד, שֶׁיֵּשׁ לָהֶן מְזוֹנוֹת בְּזוֹל וּבְלֹא טוֹרַח:(ג) מְצַעֲרִים. בְּשִׁלְשׁוּל, דְּאָמְרוּ (גיטין דף ע.): תַּמְרֵי מְשַׁחֲנָן וּמְשַׁלְשְׁלָן: מְלָא צַנָּא דְּסַכִּינֵי בְּזוּזָא. שֶׁמִּתּוֹךְ שֶׁלּוֹקְחִין אוֹתוֹ בְּזוֹל אוֹכְלִין מֵהֶן הַרְבֵּה, וּמְצַעֲרִים אוֹתָן: מִמֵּימֵי אוֹקְיָינוֹס. כְּלוֹמַר: מִמַּיִם שֶׁל מַטָּה, וְלֹא מִמַּיִם שֶׁל מַעְלָה, שֶׁנֶּאֱמַר "וְאֵד יַעֲלֶה מִן הָאָרֶץ", שֶׁשָּׁתָה בָּאָרֶץ וְעָלָה: מְלוּחִין הֵן. וְאֵין תְּבוּאָה גְּדֵילָה מֵהֶן: יָזֹקּוּ מָטָר לְאֵדוֹ. רְקִיעִין מוֹלִיכִין מַיִם לֶעָבִים: יָזֹקּוּ. כְּמוֹ "יָלוֹקוּ", "לַק לָעָם וַיֹּאכֵלוּ" (מלכים ב ז): חַשְׁרַת מַיִם עָבֵי שְׁחָקִים. הֶעָבִים מְחַשְּׁרִין, כְּלוֹמַר: מַשִּׁירִין הַמַּיִם לָאָרֶץ: לְלַמֶּדְךָ. מִקְרָא דִּלְקַמָּן קָאֵי. וְאוֹמֵר מֵכִין הָרִים — לָא גָּרְסִינַן הָכָא: *כְּרַבִּי יְהוֹשֻׁעַ. דְּאָמַר מִמַּיִם הָעֶלְיוֹנִים: וְאָמַר רַבִּי יוֹחָנָן מֵעֲלִיּוֹתָיו שֶׁל מַעְלָה. כְּלוֹמַר מִמַּיִם הָעֶלְיוֹנִים. וְרַבִּי יוֹחָנָן מַיִם הָעֶלְיוֹנִים אָתָא לְאַשְׁמוּעִינַן, דְּאִי לָאו רַבִּי יוֹחָנָן — הֲוֵי אָמֵינָא דְּהָכִי קָאָמַר: מֵעֲלִיּוֹת שֶׁהַקָּדוֹשׁ בָּרוּךְ הוּא עוֹמֵד בָּהֶם הוּא מַשְׁקֶה אוֹתָן לְמַטָּה, וּלְעוֹלָם הַמַּיִם מֵאוֹקְיָינוֹס: וְר' אֱלִיעֶזֶר. אָמַר לְעוֹלָם מֵעֲלִיּוֹתָיו שֶׁל הקב"ה, כְּרַבִּי יוֹחָנָן וכו': תְּהוֹמוֹת. מַיִם שֶׁל מַטָּה, כִּדְכְתִיב "תְּהוֹמוֹת יְכַסְיֻמוּ" (שמות טו): בִּבְרִיָּיתוֹ

תוספות

תלמוד לומר עשב. פי': שאם לא יהיו צריכים אלא לעשב אחד — ירד על אותו עשב, ועל שאר כל השדה לא ירדו:

נהילא מקמי מיטרא. פי': גשם דק. וסימנך מהולתא. פירוש: שמתחילה יוצא הפסולת, ואח"כ הסולת. פירוש: שלא היו עושין כמו דעבדינן האידנא(ג), היו כותשין החטין במכתשת עד שנקלף כל הסובין מעל החטים, וכי הוו מרקדין על גבי נפה היה הפסולת הסובין שעליו יוצא לכתחילה, ואחר כך היה יוצא הסולת:

חריא דעיזי. פי': ריעי של עזים, שבתחילה ריעי גדול, וכשהיא פוסקת מתרזת ובא דק:

ואמר רבי יוחנן מעליותיו של הקב"ה כמאן כר' יהושע. פי': כרבי יהושע, דאמר: כל העולם כולו ממים העליונים הם שותים. דאי כרבי אליעזר — הא אמר: מימי אוקיינוס הוא שותה:

קרי

רבינו חננאל

חלש דעתיה אקריות בחלמא ואכחיד את שלשת הרועים וגו'. כי הוה מפטרי מיניה אמר להו ניזולו רבנן בשלום: רב שימי בר אשי הוה מקשי לרב פפא טובא יומא חד חזייה דנפל על אפיה ובעי רחמי ואמר רחמנא שזבן מכיסופא דשימי קביל עליה שתיקותא ותו לא אקשיה ליה. עבים הדקים נקראים חזיזים אמר רב פפא עיבא קלישתא דתותי עיבא סמיכתא ונקראות פורחות: אמר רב יהודה נהילא פי' מטר היורד דק כמו קמח. אם הם תחלת ירידת המטר ירד מטר וסימנא נפה שכיון שמתחלת לפלוט הדק פולטת סולת וצריד וכיוצא. אבל אם זו נהילא באחרית מטר דע דפסק מטרא וזהו תמצית המטר וסימנך חריא דעיזא כיון שאינו בא בקילוח אלא כעין שותת טפה לא נשאר בו כלום: תניא רבי אליעזר אומר כל העולם כולו מימי אוקינוס שותה שנאמר ואד יעלה מן הארץ והשקה וגו' ואע"פ שמלוחין מתמתקים הם בעבים. ר' יהושע אומר כל העולם כולו ממים העליונים הוא שותה שנאמר למטר השמים תשתה מים והאי דכתיב ואד יעלה מן הארץ מלמד שענני כבוד מתגברות ועולות לרקיע ופותחות פיהם כנוד ומקבלות מטר שנאמר יזוקו מטר לאדו ומנוקבות ככברה ומחשרות על הארץ. שנאמר חשרת מים עבי שחקים ובין טפה לטפה כמלא נימא כו'.

[נ"ל מתמתקין]

רבינו גרשום

מטר אתי בשביל תפלת יחיד ולברך את מעשה ידיך שבשביל יחיד אתי מטר: יכול לכל כלומר שאינו יורד גשם אלא בשביל כולם ת"ל לאיש שמוריד לו מטר בשביל תפלתו: נהילא. מטר דקה סימן דאתי מיטרא: מהולתא. שבתחלה מוציא קמח דקה ולבסוף מוציא עבה: חריא דעיזי. ריעי של עזים שמוציא ריעי לבסוף דק:

הגהות הב"ח

(א) גמ' לאוצרות שיתמלאו בר תהומות כמאן כר"א: (ב) רש"י ד"ה נהילא כמו קיטמא נהילא. נ"ב בפ"ק דברכות איתא האי ליטנא אבל כאן צריך לפרש דמדמה ליה לקמח שיש בו דק וגס כמו גשמים וכמ"ש וסימניך מהולתא: (ג) ד"ה מצערים. נ"ל נערוה: (ד) תוס' ד"ה נהילא כו' כמו דעבדינן האידנא אלא היו כותשין:

מסורת הש"ס

[בע"י הגיר' לשלמא ועי' ברכות סד. ומ"ק כט.]

[נ"ל בר']

פסחים פח. ע"ש

עירובין מה:

[נ"ל עושה גדולות ואין חקר (איוב ה פסוק ט)]

[דיבור זה שייך בסמוך לאחר דיבור המתחיל ואמר ר' יוחנן]

הגהות הגר"א

[א] גמ' (וכתיב מכין הרים בכחו וגו') תא"מ:

גליון הש"ס

רש"י ד"ה מלוחים ואין תבואה גדילה מהן. לא ידעתי למאי צריך לזה ולא כפשוטו שאנו רואים שאינם מלוחים:

עין משפט נר מצוה

כו א ב ג מיי' פ"ב מהלכות תפלה הלכה טז סמג עשין יט טור ש"ע א"ח סי' קיז סעיף א:
כז ד ה מיי' פ"ג מהל' תענית הלכה א והלכה ב טוש"ע א"ח סי' תקעה סעיף א ב:
כח ו מיי' שם פ"א הלכה ה טוש"ע א"ח סי' תקעב סעיף א:
כט ז מיי' שם הלכה ט ופ"ג הלכה י וטוש"ע שם סי' תקעה סעיף ז:

קרי ביה חכשרת. פי': קטל הכ"ף מן חשכת, ושדי עם חשרת – ויהיה חכשרת. כלומר: שהמים בעננים מתכשרים, שהעננים שותים לבסוף הם ממתקים בעבים: **טובעני** ולא יובשני. פי': מוטב להיות בארץ שהיא לחה, מכשהיא יבשה:

הלכתא יום ס' כלאחר ס'. וכן עמא דבר, ויום תקופה מתחיל: **אין** גוזרין תענית על הצבור בתחילה בחמישי שלא להפקיע השערים. פי': שע"י שעשו הצבור תענית – יקנו מזון של חמישי ושל שבת, וכסבורים העם יוקר היא – ויפקיעו השערים:

איזהו

בברייתו שֶׁל עוֹלָם. ת"ר: א"י נִבְרֵאת תְּחִילָּה וְכָל הָעוֹלָם כּוּלּוֹ נִבְרָא לְבַסּוֹף, שֶׁנֶּאֱמַר: "עַד לֹא עָשָׂה אֶרֶץ וְחוּצוֹת". א"י (א) מַשְׁקֶה אוֹתָהּ הקב"ה בְּעַצְמוֹ, וְכָל הָעוֹלָם כּוּלּוֹ ע"י שָׁלִיחַ, שֶׁנֶּאֱמַר: "הַנּוֹתֵן מָטָר עַל פְּנֵי אָרֶץ, וְשׁוֹלֵחַ מַיִם עַל פְּנֵי חוּצוֹת". א"י שׁוֹתָה מֵי גְשָׁמִים, וְכָל הָעוֹלָם כּוּלּוֹ מִתַּמְצִית, שֶׁנֶּאֱמַר "הַנּוֹתֵן מָטָר עַל פְּנֵי אָרֶץ" וגו'. א"י שׁוֹתָה תְּחִילָּה, וְכָל הָעוֹלָם כּוּלּוֹ לְבַסּוֹף, שֶׁנֶּאֱמַר "הַנּוֹתֵן מָטָר עַל פְּנֵי אָרֶץ" וגו'. מָשָׁל לְאָדָם שֶׁמְּגַבֵּל אֶת הַגְּבִינָה. נוֹטֵל אֶת הָאוֹכֶל וּמַנִּיחַ אֶת הַפְּסוֹלֶת. אָמַר מָר: מְמַתְּקִין הֵן בְּעָבִים. מְנָלֵיהּ? דְּא"ר יִצְחָק בַּר יוֹסֵף א"ר יוֹחָנָן: כְּתִיב "חֶשְׁכַת מַיִם עָבֵי שְׁחָקִים", וּכְתִיב "חַשְׁרַת מַיִם עָבֵי שְׁחָקִים". שְׁקוֹל כַּף וּשְׁדֵי אַרֵישׁ, וּקְרִי בֵּיהּ *"חַכְשָׁרַת". וְר' יְהוֹשֻׁעַ, בְּהָנֵי קְרָאֵי מַאי דָּרֵישׁ בְּהוּ? סָבַר לָהּ כִּי הָא, דְּכִי אֲתָא רַב דִּימִי אֲמַר: אָמְרִי בְּמַעַרְבָא: נְהוֹר עֲנָנֵי – זְעִירִין מוֹהִי; חֲשׁוֹךְ עֲנָנֵי – סַגְיָין מוֹהִי. כְּמַאן אָזְלָא הָא דְּתַנְיָא: מַיִם הָעֶלְיוֹנִים בְּמַאֲמָר הֵם תְּלוּיִם, וּפֵירוֹתֵיהֶן מֵי גְשָׁמִים, שֶׁנֶּאֱמַר "מִפְּרִי מַעֲשֶׂיךָ תִּשְׂבַּע הָאָרֶץ". כְּמַאן? כְּר' יְהוֹשֻׁעַ. וְר' אֱלִיעֶזֶר: הַהוּא בְּמַעֲשֵׂה יָדָיו שֶׁל הקב"ה הוּא דִּכְתִיב. אריב"ל: כָּל הָעוֹלָם כּוּלּוֹ מִתַּמְצִית גַּן עֵדֶן הוּא שׁוֹתֶה, שֶׁנֶּאֱמַר "וְנָהָר יוֹצֵא מֵעֵדֶן" וגו'. תָּנָא: מִתַּמְצִית בֵּית כּוֹר שׁוֹתֶה *תַּרְקַב.§ ת"ר: *אֶרֶץ מִצְרַיִם הָוְיָא ד' מֵאוֹת פַּרְסָה עַל ד' מֵאוֹת פַּרְסָה. וְהוּא אֶחָד מִשִּׁשִּׁים בְּכוּשׁ. וְכוּשׁ אֶחָד מִשִּׁשִּׁים בָּעוֹלָם. וְעוֹלָם א' מִשִּׁשִּׁים בַּגַּן. וְגַן אֶחָד מִשִּׁשִּׁים לְעֵדֶן. וְעֵדֶן אֶחָד מִס' לְגֵיהִנָּם. נִמְצָא כָּל הָעוֹלָם כּוּלּוֹ כְּכִיסּוּי קְדֵרָה לְגֵיהִנָּם. וְי"א: גֵּיהִנָּם אֵין לָהּ שִׁיעוּר. וְי"א: עֵדֶן אֵין לָהּ שִׁיעוּר. א"ר אוֹשַׁעְיָא: מַאי דִּכְתִיב "שׁוֹכַנְתְּ עַל מַיִם רַבִּים רַבַּת אוֹצָרוֹת". מִי גָּרַם לְבָבֶל שֶׁיְּהוּ אוֹצְרוֹתֶיהָ מְלֵיאוֹת בָּר – הֱוֵי אוֹמֵר מִפְּנֵי שֶׁשּׁוֹכֶנֶת עַל מַיִם רַבִּים. אָמַר רַב: עֲתִירָה בָּבֶל דְּחָצְדָא בְּלָא מִיטְרָא. אָמַר אַבַּיֵי: נְקִיטִינַן *טוֹבְעָנֵי וְלָא יוֹבְשָׁנֵי.§

מתני' *בְּג' בְּמַרְחֶשְׁוָן שׁוֹאֲלִין אֶת הַגְּשָׁמִים. רַבָּן גַּמְלִיאֵל אוֹמֵר: א בְּשִׁבְעָה בּוֹ, ט"ו יוֹם אַחַר הֶחָג, כְּדֵי שֶׁיַּגִּיעַ אַחֲרוֹן שֶׁבְּיִשְׂרָאֵל לִנְהַר פְּרָת.§ **גמ'** *א"ר אֶלְעָזָר: הֲלָכָה כְּרַבָּן גַּמְלִיאֵל. תַּנְיָא, חֲנַנְיָה אוֹמֵר: ב וּבַגּוֹלָה עַד שִׁשִּׁים בַּתְּקוּפָה. אָמַר רַב הוּנָא בַּר חִיָּיא אָמַר שְׁמוּאֵל: הֲלָכָה כַּחֲנַנְיָה. אִינִי? וְהָא בְּעוֹ מִינֵּיהּ מִשְּׁמוּאֵל: מֵאֵימַת מַדְכְּרִינַן: "וְתֵן טַל וּמָטָר"? אֲמַר לְהוּ: מִכִּי מְעַיְּילִי צִיבֵי לְבֵי טָבוּת *רִישְׁבָּא. דִּילְמָא אִידֵי וְאִידֵי חַד שִׁיעוּרָא הוּא. אִיבַּעְיָא לְהוּ: יוֹם שִׁשִּׁים כְּלִפְנֵי שִׁשִּׁים אוֹ כִּלְאַחַר שִׁשִּׁים? ת"ש; רַב אָמַר: יוֹם שִׁשִּׁים כִּלְאַחַר שִׁשִּׁים. וּשְׁמוּאֵל אָמַר: יוֹם שִׁשִּׁים כְּלִפְנֵי שִׁשִּׁים. א"ר נַחְמָן בַּר יִצְחָק: וְסִימָנָךְ: עִילָּאֵי בָּעוּ מַיָּא, תַּתָּאֵי לָא בָּעוּ מַיָּא. אָמַר רַב פָּפָּא: ג הִלְכְתָא: יוֹם שִׁשִּׁים כִּלְאַחַר שִׁשִּׁים.§

מתני' ד הִגִּיעַ י"ז בְּמַרְחֶשְׁוָן, וְלֹא יָרְדוּ גְשָׁמִים – הִתְחִילוּ הַיְּחִידִים מִתְעַנִּין ג' תַּעֲנִיּוֹת. אוֹכְלִין וְשׁוֹתִין מִשֶּׁחָשֵׁיכָה, וּמוּתָּרִין בִּמְלָאכָה, וּבִרְחִיצָה, וּבְסִיכָה, וּבִנְעִילַת הַסַּנְדָּל, וּבְתַשְׁמִישׁ הַמִּטָּה. ה הִגִּיעַ ר"ח כִּסְלֵיו, וְלֹא יָרְדוּ גְשָׁמִים – ב"ד גּוֹזְרִין שָׁלֹשׁ תַּעֲנִיּוֹת עַל הַצִּבּוּר. אוֹכְלִין וְשׁוֹתִין מִשֶּׁחָשֵׁיכָה, וּמוּתָּרִין בִּמְלָאכָה, וּבִרְחִיצָה, וּבְסִיכָה, וּבִנְעִילַת הַסַּנְדָּל, וּבְתַשְׁמִישׁ הַמִּטָּה.§ **גמ'** מַאן "יְחִידִים"? אָמַר רַב הוּנָא: רַבָּנַן. וְאָמַר רַב הוּנָא: יְחִידִים מִתְעַנִּין שָׁלֹשׁ תַּעֲנִיּוֹת, שֵׁנִי וַחֲמִישִׁי וְשֵׁנִי. מַאי קָמַשְׁמַע לָן? תְּנֵינָא: *ו"אֵין גּוֹזְרִין תַּעֲנִית עַל הַצִּבּוּר בַּתְּחִלָּה בַּחֲמִישִׁי – שֶׁלֹּא לְהַפְקִיעַ אֶת הַשְּׁעָרִים. אֶלָּא שָׁלֹשׁ תַּעֲנִיּוֹת הָרִאשׁוֹנוֹת שֵׁנִי וַחֲמִישִׁי וְשֵׁנִי. מַהוּ דְּתֵימָא: הָנֵי מִילֵּי – צִבּוּר, אֲבָל יָחִיד – לָא, קָמַשְׁמַע לָן. תַּנְיָא נַמִּי הָכִי: כְּשֶׁהִתְחִילוּ הַיְּחִידִים לְהִתְעַנּוֹת – מִתְעַנִּין שֵׁנִי וַחֲמִישִׁי וְשֵׁנִי, ז וּמַפְסִיקִין בְּרָאשֵׁי חֳדָשִׁים וּבְיָמִים

בברייתו שֶׁל עוֹלָם. כְּתִיב, שֶׁהָיָה כָּל הָעוֹלָם שָׁטוּף בַּמַּיִם, וְהקב"ה כּוֹנְסָן בְּמָקוֹם אֶחָד כְּמַכְנִיס מַיִם בְּנֹאד (ב), שֶׁנְּתָנָם בְּאוֹצָרוֹת, דִּכְתִיב "נוֹתֵן בְּאוֹצָרוֹת תְּהוֹמוֹת", שָׂם חוֹל גְּבוּלוֹ וְאוֹצָר לַיָּם: מִשְּׁיוּרֵי תַמְצִית. מַה שֶּׁנִּשְׁאָר בֶּעָבִים אַחַר שְׁתִיָּיתָהּ: עַל פְּנֵי אָרֶץ. א"י: בַּתְּחִילָּה שׁוֹתָה. שָׁם יוֹרְדִין הַגְּשָׁמִים תְּחִילָּה, כָּךְ שָׁמַעְתִּי: חַשְׁרַת מַיִם וְחֶשְׁכַת מַיִם. שְׁנֵי מִקְרָאוֹת הֵן, חַד בִּתְהִלִּים וְחַד בִּשְׁמוּאֵל, בְּ"וַיְדַבֵּר דָּוִד": ה"ג: שְׁקוֹל כַּף וּשְׁדֵי אַרֵישׁ. כְּלוֹמַר: קַח כַּף שֶׁבְּמִלַּת חֶשְׁכַת, וְצָרְפוֹ עִם מִלַּת חַשְׁרַת, וּקְרֵי בֵּיהּ (ג) חַכְשָׁרַת – שֶׁמְּמַתְּקִין וּמַכְשִׁירִין בֶּעָבִים: חֲשׁוֹךְ עֲנָנֵי סַגִּיאִין מֵימוֹהִי. וְהַיְינוּ דִּכְתִיב חֶשְׁכַת מַיִם: נְהוֹר עֲנָנֵי. כְּשֶׁהֶעָנָן קָלִישׁ זְעִירָן מֵימוֹהִי, וּמִכְּלָל חֲשׁוֹךְ סַגִּיאִין, אַתָּה לָמֵד: אֲבָל נְהוֹר זְעִירִין. וְחַשְׁרַת – לְשׁוֹן הַשָּׁרָה, כְּמוֹ "אֵין שׁוֹרִין דְּיוֹ" (שבת דף יז:) כו' כִּדְדָרֵישׁ לֵיהּ רַבִּי יְהוֹשֻׁעַ לְעֵיל, אֲבָל חֶשְׁכַת מִיבָּעֵי לֵיהּ לְהָכִי וּלְהָכִי: בְּמַאֲמָר הֵן תְּלוּיִן. אֵינָן נָחוֹת עַל שׁוּם דָּבָר, אֶלָּא מְכוּנָּסוֹת וְעוֹמְדוֹת כְּמִין בְּרֵיכָה, וּתְלוּיוֹת בְּמַאֲמָרוֹ שֶׁל הקב"ה: וּפֵירוֹתֵיהֶן מֵי גְשָׁמִים. מִשּׁוּם לִישְׁנָא דִּקְרָא נָקַט הָכִי, מִשּׁוּם דִּכְתִיב "מִפְּרִי מַעֲשֶׂיךָ תִּשְׂבַּע הָאָרֶץ". וּפֵירוֹתֵיהֶם, כְּלוֹמַר מְזִיעַת הַמַּיִם, שֶׁאֵין נֶחְסָרִין כְּלוּם, כִּדְכְתִיב (תהלים סה) "פֶּלֶג אֱלֹהִים מָלֵא מַיִם" כָּל שָׁעָה, וְהַקֶּרֶן קַיֶּימֶת, וּפֵירוֹתֵיהֶן מֵי גְשָׁמִים. וְכֵן מְפוֹרָשׁ בִּבְרֵאשִׁית רַבָּה: וְנָהָר יוֹצֵא מֵעֵדֶן. (ד) סִימָן לְדָבָר שֶׁגַּן עֵדֶן שׁוֹתֶה מִן הַגְּשָׁמִים תְּחִילָּה, דִּכְתִיב "וְנָהָר יוֹצֵא מֵעֵדֶן לְהַשְׁקוֹת אֶת הַגָּן" וגו': תָּנָא מִתַּמְצִית בֵּית כּוֹר. כְּלִי שֶׁמַּשְׁקִין בְּמֵימָיו בֵּית כּוֹר יְכוֹלִין לְהַשְׁקוֹת בְּתַמְצִיתוֹ שִׁיעוּר זְרִיעַת תַּרְקַב, שֶׁהוּא אֶחָד מִשִּׁשִּׁים בְּבֵית כּוֹר. וְהָכִי נַמִּי, עוֹלָם אֶחָד מִשִּׁשִּׁים בְּגַן עֵדֶן, וְדַי לוֹ בְּתַמְצִית הָעֲנָנִים הַמַּשְׁקִין אֶת הַגָּן (ה). גַּן לִפְנֵי כָּל הָעוֹלָם כּוּלּוֹ כְּעֵדֶן לַגָּן: נִמְצָא כָּל הָעוֹלָם כְּכִיסּוּי קְדֵרָה. הַקָּטָן כְּנֶגֶד הַקְּדֵרָה: "שׁוֹכַנְתְּ עַל מַיִם רַבִּים. רַבַּת אוֹצָרוֹת בָּא קִצֵּךְ אַמַּת בִּצְעֵךְ": שֶׁרַבּוּ אוֹצְרוֹתֶיהָ. שֶׁקָּנוּ עוֹשֶׁר: מַיִם רַבִּים. שֶׁמַּשְׁקִין שְׂדוֹתֵיהֶן, דְּבָבֶל עֲמוּקִים מִכָּל הָאֲרָצוֹת, וּגְשָׁמִים מְטַפְטְפִין וְיוֹרְדִין שָׁם: עֲתִירָה בָּבֶל. עֲשִׁירָה הִיא בָּבֶל, שֶׁקּוֹצְרִין בָּהּ תְּבוּאָה בְּלֹא מָטָר, שֶׁאֵינָן צְרִיכִים לִגְשָׁמִים: נְקִיטִינַן. דְּהָכִי (ו) חָלְדָא בָּבֶל בְּלָא מִיטְרָא: דְּטוֹבְעָנֵי. הִיא מָקוֹם מְצוּלָה וְרָקָק: וְלֹא יוֹבְשָׁנֵי. שֶׁאֵינָהּ יְבֵשָׁה:

מתני' בִּשְׁלֹשָׁה בְּמַרְחֶשְׁוָן שׁוֹאֲלִין אֶת הַגְּשָׁמִים וכו' רַבָּן גַּמְלִיאֵל אוֹמֵר בְּשִׁבְעָה בּוֹ בְּט"ו יוֹם אַחַר הֶחָג. כְּלוֹמַר, בְּשִׁבְעָה בְּמַרְחֶשְׁוָן הוּא ט"ו אַחַר הֶחָג: כְּדֵי שֶׁיַּגִּיעַ הָאַחֲרוֹן. כְּלוֹמַר, קוֹדֶם בִּיאַת מַיִם לִנְהַר פְּרָת, שֶׁהוּא רָחוֹק יוֹתֵר: **גמ'** וּבַגּוֹלָה שִׁשִּׁים. וּבַגּוֹלָה אֵין שׁוֹאֲלִין עַד שִׁשִּׁים בַּתְּקוּפָה, לְפִי שֶׁהוּא מָקוֹם נָמוּךְ, וְאֵין צְרִיכִים מָטָר כָּל כָּךְ: מִכִּי מְעַיְּילִי צִיבֵי לְבֵי טָבוּת רִישְׁבָּא. מִשָּׁעָה שֶׁמַּכְנִיסִין עֵצִים לָאוֹצָר לְאוֹרֶךְ יְמוֹת הַגְּשָׁמִים. שֶׁכֵּן הָיוּ נוֹהֲגִין, לְפִי שֶׁהָיוּ יוֹדְעִין שֶׁזְּמַן גְּשָׁמִים הוּא מִשָּׁם וְאֵילָךְ, וְלֹא הָיוּ יְכוֹלִין לַחֲטוֹב עֵצִים בַּיַּעַר: רִישְׁבָּא. צַיַּיד עוֹפוֹת, כְּמוֹ "אֵין פּוֹרְשִׂין *רְשָׁתִים לַיּוֹנִים" (ב"ק דף עט:). טָבוּת – שֵׁם אָדָם: כְּלִפְנֵי ס'. וְלֹא מַדְכְּרִינַן: כִּלְאַחַר ס'. וּמַדְכְּרִינַן: עִילָּאֵי בָּעוּ מַיִם. הָעוֹמְדִים בֶּהָרִים צְרִיכִין יוֹתֵר מַיִם, מִפְּנֵי שֶׁהַגְּשָׁמִים מִתְגַּלְגְּלִים וְיוֹרְדִין לְמַטָּה: תַּתָּאֵי לָא בָּעוּ מַיִם. שֶׁמִּתְכַּנְּסִין כָּל מֵימֵי הֶהָרִים לַבִּקְעָה. ה"נ, רַב שֶׁהָיָה מֵאֶרֶץ יִשְׂרָאֵל, כִּדְאָמְרִינַן בְּעָלְמָא (גיטין דף ו.) מִכִּי אָתָא רַב לְבָבֶל, וְאֶרֶץ יִשְׂרָאֵל גְּבוֹהָה מִכָּל הָאֲרָצוֹת, מִשּׁוּם הָכִי אָמַר כִּלְאַחַר שִׁשִּׁים. וּבְבָבֶל, בַּגּוֹלָה מִתּוֹךְ שֶׁאֵינָן צְרִיכִין לִגְשָׁמִים – אֵין שׁוֹאֲלִין עַד ס' לִתְקוּפַת תִּשְׁרֵי, וְכֵן אָנוּ נוֹהֲגִים, שֶׁכָּל מִנְהָגֵינוּ אַחַר בְּנֵי בָבֶל:

מתני' הִגִּיעַ שִׁבְעָה עָשָׂר וכו'. אוֹכְלִין וְשׁוֹתִין מִשֶּׁחָשֵׁיכָה, שֶׁאֵין אוֹכְלִין מִבְּעוֹד יוֹם כְּיוֹם הַכִּפּוּרִים וְתִשְׁעָה בְּאָב: **גמ'** מַאי קָא מַשְׁמַע לָן. הַאי דְּקָאָמַר שֵׁנִי וַחֲמִישִׁי וְשֵׁנִי: תְּנֵינָא. בְּפִירְקִין דִּלְקַמָּן (דף טו:): אֵין גּוֹזְרִין תַּעֲנִית כו' שֶׁלֹּא לְהַפְקִיעַ אֶת הַשְּׁעָרִים, שֶׁאִם הָיוּ מַתְחִילִין לְהִתְעַנּוֹת בַּחֲמִישִׁי הָיוּ קוֹנִין לְמוֹצָאֵי הַתַּעֲנִית שְׁתֵּי סְעוּדוֹת גְּדוֹלוֹת, אֶחָד לַתַּעֲנִית וְאֶחָד לַשַּׁבָּת, וּכְסָבוּר הַמּוֹכֵר שֶׁרָעָב בָּא לָעוֹלָם וְאָתֵי לְאַפְקוּעֵי שְׁעָרִים: אַפְקוּעֵי. מְבַטֵּל שִׁיעוּר מִדָּה הָרִאשׁוֹנָה, וּמְמַעֲטָהּ: אֲבָל יְחִידִים לֹא. שָׁלֹשׁ תַּעֲנִיּוֹת שֶׁהַיְּחִידִין עוֹשִׂין קוֹדֶם לַצִּבּוּר – אֵינָן זְקוּקִין לְהַתְחִיל בַּשֵּׁנִי, דְּלֵיכָּא אַפְקִיעַת שְׁעָרִים מִשּׁוּם יְחִידִים לְחוּדַיְיהוּ. וְהַלָּלוּ ג' תַּעֲנִיּוֹת דִּיחִידִים אֵינָן בִּכְלַל י"ג תַּעֲנִיּוֹת דְּצִבּוּר, תֵּדַע דְּקָא חָשֵׁיב בְּמַתְנִי' שָׁלֹשׁ וְשָׁלֹשׁ וָשֶׁבַע: וּמַפְסִיקִין בְּרָאשֵׁי חֳדָשִׁים. שֶׁאִם חָל ר"ח בַּשֵּׁנִי וּבַחֲמִישִׁי לְאַחַר שֶׁהִתְחִילוּ לְהִתְעַנּוֹת – פּוֹסְקִין תַּעֲנִיתָם:

וְכֵן

מסורת הש"ס: [כלומר נכשרין ומתמתקין ערוך] | [פי' תרי וקב והיינו חצי סאה ערוך] | [כלומר מוטב שיהיה מטר הרבה מהיות חורב בלי מטר. ערוך] | [פי' הגאון כאשר כתיב נשיא בית אב תרגומו רב בית אבא זה ראש בית אב. ערוך ערך רשבא א] | לקמן טו: | [ובנוסחאות דיקן כתוב ניסבין ועיין בערוך ערך רשבא ב] | ש"ב כב | פסחים צד. | [לעיל ז:] | לעיל ו. ב"מ כח.

(משלי ח; איוב ה; תהלים יח; תהלים קד; בראשית ב; ירמיהו נא)

רבינו חננאל

ארץ ישראל נבראת תחלה שנאמר עד לא עשה ארץ וחוצות א"י הקב"ה משקה אותה [בעצמו] וכל העולם כולו ע"י שליח. שנאמר הנותן מטר על פני ארץ ושולח מים על פני חוצות. א"י שותה מי גשמים וכל העולם שותה תמצית שנאמר הנותן מטר וגו' משל לאדם מגבל גבינה. נוטל מאכל ומניח הפסולת: ת"ר מצרים ד' מאות פרסה על ד' מאות פרסה. ואחד מס' בכוש. וכוש אחד מס' בעולם. והעולם אחד מס' בגן. וגן אחד מס' בעדן. ועדן אחד מס' בגיהנם. נמצא כל העולם כולו ככיסוי קדירה לגיהנם. אריב"ל כל העולם מתמצית הגן הוא שותה שנאמר ונהר יוצא מעדן להשקות את הגן. תנא מתמצית בית כור שותה. תרקב. פי' התרקב הוא חצי סאה. והכור יש בו ל' סאין. נמצא א' מס' בכור. וכיון ששנה בחיצונה והעולם א' מס' בגן. נמצא העולם כולו חלק א' מס' חלקים בגן ומתמציתו שותה כל העולם. דקדק התנא שמתמצית בית כור שותה תרקב שהרי זה התרקב א' מס' בכור כמו שהוא העולם א' מס' בגן ושותה תמציתו: **מתני'** בג' מרחשון שואלין הגשמים ר"ג אומר (בשמונה) [בשבעה] בו. א"ר אלעזר הלכה כר"ג. תנא חנניה אומר ובגולה עד ס' יום בתקופה. אמר שמואל הלכתא כחנניה. וזמן הכנסת עצים דבי טיבות רישבא מן השדה הוה ס' בתקופה. ואיבעיא לן יום ס' כלפני ס' ואינו שואל או כלאחר ס' ושואל. רב אמר כלפני ס' ושמואל אמר כלאחר ס' וסימניך עילאי בעי מיא תתאי לא בעו מיא. פי' נהרדעא אתריה דשמואל והיא גבוהה והן מבקשים מים. וסורא אתריה דרב והיא לגבי נהרדעא תתאה. והן אינן מבקשין מים כלומר כיון שהן תחתיין נקוין המים בהן ומתקיימין אצלם. אמר רב פפא הלכתא יום ס' כלאחר ס': **מתני'** הגיע י"ז במרחשון ולא ירדו גשמים התחילו היחידים מתענים. ואוקים רב הונא להני יחידים רבנן ומתענין ב' וה' וב'. ומפסיקין בר"ח וביו"ט

הגהות הב"ח

(א) גמ' שנאמר עד לא עשה ארץ וחוצות א"י משקה אותה הקב"ה בעצמו וכו' מתמצית וכו' על פני ארץ וגו' משל לאדם שמגבן את הגבינה: (ב) רש"י ד"ה בברייתו כו' כמכניס מים בנאד ונתנם באוצרות כו' ואוצר לים מה"ד שותה תחלה שם יורדין הגשמים תחלה כך שמעתי ומה"ד מתמצית משיורי מים שנשאר בעבים כו' א"י מה"ד חשרת כו': (ג) ד"ה ה"ג שקול כו' חכשרת. נ"ב ולהכי נקט רי"ש ולא נקט שי"ן דשי"ן הכא והכא כתיב: (ד) ד"ה ונהר יוצא מעדן כלומר סימן לדבר כו' דכתיב קרא ונהר יוצא מעדן תחילה להשקות הגן: (ה) ד"ה תנא כו' להשקות את הגן הס"ד ואח"כ מה"ד גן לפני כל עולם כולו כגן עדן לעולם: (ו) ד"ה נקיטינן דהכי הוא דחלדא בבל בלא מיטרא דטובעני כו' הד"א:

רבינו גרשום

כמאן כר' יהושע דאמר ממים העליונים הם. כמאן כר' אליעזר דאמר מן הארץ עולה מטר. מתמצית כור שותה תרקב. מתמצית גן עדן שותה כל העולם דכל העולם לגבי גן עדן כתרקב לפני כור תרקב תרי קבין. כור ל' סאין ותרקב חצי סאה נמצא תרקב אחד מששים בכור וכל העולם אחד מששים בגן עדן: דחצדא בלא מטרא כלומר שקוצרת בלא מטר כלומר שאינה צריכה מטר שיושבת בין ביצעי המים. ע"א אצדא: טובעני ולא יובשני כלומר מיתרמי שטובעין הזרעים אבל לעולם אין מתייבשין: ר"ג אומר בשבעה בו בחמשה עשר יום אחר החג כלומר דז' במרחשון הוא ט"ו אחר החג כדי שיגיע האחרון כו' קודם הגשמים: ובגולה אין שואלין את הגשמים עד ששים בתקופה. לפי שהן במקום נמוך ואין צריכין למטר כל כך: ציבי דטבות רישבא. דהוה עשיר והיו עצים שלו מונחים ליבש בשדה עד שיכנסם במרחשון: כלפני ששים. ואין שואלין בו: או כלאחר ששים. ושואלין בו: עילאי בעו מיא רב דהוה מא"י בעי מים בששים. תתאי לא בעי מיא שמואל דהוה מבבל עד לבסוף לא בעי מיא עד ששים ואחד: אוכלין ושותין משחשכה. שאין אוכלין מבעוד יום כיוה"כ וכתשעה באב: שלא להפקיע את השערים. דבני כפרים הבאים ליום הכניסה מספקים מים ומזון לאחיהן שבכרכין

גמרא

ובימים טובים הכתובין במגילת תענית. תנו רבנן: אל יאמר אדם: תלמיד אני, איני ראוי להיות יחיד. אלא, [א]כל תלמידי חכמים יחידים. אי זהו יחיד ואיזהו תלמיד? יחיד — כל שראוי למנותו פרנס על הצבור. תלמיד — *כל ששואלין אותו דבר הלכה בלמודו ואומר, ואפילו במסכת דכלה. תנו רבנן: לא כל הרוצה לעשות עצמו יחיד — עושה, תלמיד — עושה, דברי ר' מאיר. רבי *יוסי אומר: [ב]עושה, וזכור לטוב. לפי שאין שבח הוא לו, אלא צער הוא לו. תניא אידך: לא *כל הרוצה לעשות עצמו יחיד — עושה, תלמיד — עושה, דברי רבי שמעון בן אלעזר. רבן שמעון בן גמליאל אומר: במה דברים אמורים? בדבר של שבח, אבל בדבר של צער — עושה, וזכור לטוב, שאין שבח הוא לו, אלא צער הוא לו. [ג]ת"ר: *מי שהיה מתענה על הצרה ועברה, על החולה ונתרפא — הרי זה מתענה ומשלים. [ד]ההולך ממקום שאין מתענין למקום שמתענין — הרי זה מתענה עמהן. [ה]ממקום שמתענין למקום שאין מתענין — הרי זה מתענה ומשלים. [ו]שכח ואכל ושתה — אל יתראה בפני הצבור, ואל ינהיג עידונין בעצמו, שנאמר: °"ויאמר יעקב לבניו למה תתראו"? אמר להם יעקב לבניו: אל תראו עצמכם כשאתם שבעין, לא בפני עשו, ולא בפני ישמעאל, כדי שלא יתקנאו בכם. °"אל תרגזו בדרך". אמר רבי אלעזר: אמר להם יוסף לאחיו: אל תתעסקו בדבר הלכה, שמא תרגזו עליכם הדרך. איני? והאמר ר' אלעאי בר ברכיה: *שני תלמידי חכמים שמהלכים בדרך, ואין ביניהן דברי תורה, ראויין לישרף, שנאמר °"ויהי המה הולכים, (*הולך) ודבר והנה רכב אש וסוסי אש ויפרדו בין שניהם". טעמא — דאיכא דיבור, הא ליכא דיבור — ראויין לישרף! לא קשיא. הא — למיגרס, הא — לעיוני. במתניתא תנא: אל תפסיעו פסיעה גסה, והכניסו חמה לעיר. אל תפסיעו פסיעה גסה — דאמר מר: *פסיעה גסה נוטלת *אחד מחמש מאות ממאור עיניו של אדם. והכניסו חמה לעיר — כדרב יהודה אמר רב. *דאמר רב יהודה אמר רב: לעולם יצא אדם ב"כי טוב" ויכנס ב"כי טוב", שנאמר °"הבקר אור, והאנשים שלחו". אמר רב יהודה אמר רבי חייא: ⊕המהלך בדרך אל יאכל יותר משני רעבון. מאי טעמא? הכא תרגימו: משום מעיינא. במערבא אמרי: משום מזוני. מאי בינייהו? איכא בינייהו דיתיב

תורה אור: בראשית מב | שם מה | מ"ב ב | בראשית מד

רש"י

וכן בימים טובים. הכתובים במגילת תענית: תלמיד אני. ואיני חשוב כל כך כיחידים, כלומר: איני ראוי להתחיל תענית עם היחידים: לא כל הרוצה לעשות עצמו יחיד. לענין תענית: עושה. דנראה מגסי הרוח, ותנן (אבות פ"ג משנה י): כל שרוח הבריות נוחה הימנו כו': הכי גרסינן: התלמידים עושין עצמן. כדאמרינן לעיל, שכל התלמידים ראויין לכך, ואין בהם משום גסות הרוח: רבי יוסי אומר כל אדם. ואפילו שאינו תלמיד, עושה עצמו יחיד להתענות, וזכור לטוב, דצער הוא לו ולא גסות. לישנא אחרינא גרסינן: לא כל הרוצה לעשות עצמו יחיד עושה, תלמיד עושה. כלומר: ולא כל הרוצה נמי לעשות עצמו תלמיד, להתנהג עצמו במדת *תלמיד בחלוקו ובמטתו, ולהתנאות בסודר של תלמידי חכמים ושאר דברים עושה, דכל הרוצה ליטול לו את השם לא יטול. ורבי יוסי אחרישא. ומסתבר כי האי לישנא, מדקא מהדר רבן שמעון בן גמליאל: דבר של שבח — אינו עושה, מכלל דאיירי בשבח: על החולה ונתרפא. הוא הדין אם מת החולה, בעי לקיומי נדרו: על הצרה ועברה. מתענה ומשלים. ואם לאו — נראה כמתנה עם קונו: אם תעבור (*אתענה), ואם לאו — (לא) אתענה: למקום שאין מתענין הרי זה מתענה ומשלים. כל התעניות שקבלו עליהן בני עירו, דנותנין עליו חומרי המקום שיצא משם: אכל ושתה. דיעבד: אל יתראה בפניהן. שנראה כחתן בין אבלים, ויתקנאו בו: ואל ינהיג עדונים בעצמו. שלא יאמר: הואיל ואכלתי כל שהוא — אוכל הרבה: אל תראו עצמכם. שיש לכם חטים הרבה. ולא הלכו אלא בשביל דבר זה, שלא להתראות בפני בני עשו, שהיו לעורים ורעבים: תרגזו עליכם הדרך. תתעו: לישרף באש. דכתיב "והנה סוסי אש", וכתיב בההוא ענינא "הלוך ודבר", והכי כתביה, לאשמועינן דאי לאו שהיו הולכין (א) בעומקה של הלכה — לא [היו ניצולין]: הא למגרס. מבעי ליה באורחא, אבל במלתא דמבעי ליה לעיוני — לא: במתניתא תנא. מאי "אל תרגזו בדרך" — אל תזיקו עצמכם בפסיעה גסה: והכניסו חמה לעיר. כשאתם לנין ושוכבין בדרך בעיירות, הכניסו לעיר בעוד שהחמה זורחת: יצא אדם בכי טוב. שימתין עד שיאור, כמו "וירא אלהים את האור כי טוב" (בראשית א): ויכנס בכי טוב. בערב בעוד שהחמה זורחת, שאין ליסטין מצויין. אי נמי: שלא יפול בבורות ובקעים שבעיר, שלא יעלילו עליו עלילות מרגל אתה או גנב: הבוקר אור והאנשים שולחו המה וחמוריהם. מיכן שיצאו בכי טוב. והוא הדין ליכנס בכי טוב. יש ספרים דלא כתיב בהו האי קרא, אלא מילתא דרב יהודה סברא הוא, ולא בעי' קרא: לא יאכל יותר ממה שאוכל בשני רעבון. דאמר לקמן (דף יא.) שצריך להרעיב עצמו בשני רעבון: (הכא(ב). תלמיד זה בבלי הוא, וכי משתעי בבבל קאמר הכא, וכל הא לן והא להו בבבל קאמר): משום מעיינא. שלא יתחלחלו מעיו של אדם ברוב אכילתו מפני טורח הדרך. יש אומרים: יהיו מעיו של אדם שופכין זה לזה כעין מעיין: משום מזוני. שמא(ג) אין לו לאח"כ:

תוספות

איזהו יחיד כו' שראוי למנותו פרנס על הצבור (ד) להיות פרנס ואיזהו תלמיד כל ששואלין דבר הלכה בכל מקום וכו'. וקשה: דהכא משמע דקרי יחיד אותו שיודע להשיב כששואלין לו דבר הלכה בכל מקום ואומרה, והתם אמרינן במס' שבת פרק "ואלו קשרים" (דף קיד.): איזהו תלמיד — הראוי למנותו פרנס על הצבור, כשיודע להשיב כל ששואלין (ה) דבר הלכה, ואפילו במסכת כלה. אלמא: הראוי למנותו פרנס על הצבור הוי כשיודע להשיב, והכא משמע דאותו הראוי למנותו פרנס — הוי מילתא אחריתי. ועוד: דהכא משמע דיחיד עדיף, מדקאמר בסמוך: לא כל הרוצה לעשות עצמו יחיד עושה, אבל הרוצה לעשות עצמו תלמיד — עושה! ויש לומר: דיש חילוק בתלמיד, דדוקא כשהרב בא אל מקום אחד וכל התלמידים אצלו, זה שואל אל הרב ממה שהוא לומד וזה שואל ממקום אחר, ואותו הרב יודע להשיב לכל התלמידים, לכל אחד ואחד כפי שאלתו, ואפילו במס' כלה — זהו יחיד דעדיף מתלמיד דהכא, ונקרא תלמיד התם בפרק "אלו קשרים" — אותו ודאי ראוי למנותו פרנס על הצבור. אבל אם אינו יודע להשיב אלא במסכת שלו — נקרא גם כן תלמיד, ומזה איירי הכא:

ההולך ממקום שמתענין למקום שאין מתענין הרי מתענה ומשלים. ל"ש דעתו לחזור ל"ש אין דעתו לחזור, הואיל וקבל עליו התענית: **למה** תתראו. כמו שמפרש: אל תראו עצמכם בפני בני עשו וכו'. ויש במדרש: למה תתראו, פירוש: למה תהיו כחושין:

אל תרגזו בדרך. ויש מדרש: אל תפסיקו מדבר הלכה:

ואין ביניהם דברי תורה ראוים לישרף דכתיב ויהי המה הולכים הלוך ודבר וגו' טעמא דאיכא דבור וכו'. ויש מדרש: שהם היו מדברים דברים בטלים, ומש"ה ראוין לישרף: **פסיעה** גסה נוטלת אחת מחמש מאות ממאור עיניו של אדם. ואין להקשות: אם כן בחמש מאות פסיעות גסות יהיה ניטל כל מאור עיניו של אדם, והא קא חזינן דלאו הכי הוה! ונראה לפרש: דהפסיעה ראשונה נוטל אחת מחמש מאות, והפסיעה שניה נוטל פחות מן הראשונה, ששניה אינה נוטלת אלא אחד מחמש מאות הנשארים, כמו בעישורייתא דבי רבי (כתובות דף סח.) — ר"ל: העישור ממה שנשאר. אבל עדיין קשה, דמ"ש פסיעה ראשונה דנוטלת יותר מן השניה? אלא יש לומר: דלא נוטלת אלא פסיעה ראשונה דוקא, ומכאן ואילך — כיון דדש דש, אי נמי: פסיעה ראשונה נוטלת טפי, משום *)דכל התחלות קשות: **לעולם** יצא אדם בכי טוב. פי' בפרק קמא דפסחים (דף ב.) [וע"ע תוס' ב"ק ס:]: **משום** מעיינא. פירוש: משום שהבני מעיין הוי קשה להו: אסור

*) [מכילתא הביאו רש"י פ' יתרו יט פ"ה]

עין משפט נר מצוה

ל א ב מיי' פ"ג מהלכות תעניות הלכה א טוש"ע א"ח סי' תקעה סעיף א:
לא ג מיי' פ"ק מהלכות תעניות הלכה טו טוש"ע א"ח סי' תקסט סעיף א:
לב ד מיי' שם טוש"ע א"ח סי' תקעד סעיף ב:
לג ה מיי' שם וטוש"ע שם סעיף א:
לד ו מיי' שם וטוש"ע שם סעיף ג:

[גי' רי"ף יהודה]

רבינו חננאל

וביו"ט הכתובים במגלת תענית: ת"ר לא יאמר זה איני ראוי לכך. אלא כל התלמידים ראוין לכך. איזהו יחיד כל שראוי למנותו פרנס על הצבור. ואיזה תלמיד כל ששואלין אותו הלכה בכל מקום ואומרה. פי' בכלום מקום כלומר מקום מן התלמוד. ואפי' במס' דכלה. שמתעסקין בה כל תלמיד חכם שרוצים לשנותה בכלה של אדר תניא לא כל הרוצה לעשות עצמו יחיד עושה שנראה כיהירות התלמידים עושין דברי ר' שמעון בן אלעזר. רשבג"א דבר של שבח אינו עושה. דבר של צער עושה עצמו יחיד וכן ר' יוסי אומר עושה וזכור לטוב. שאינו שבח לו התענית אלא צער הוא לו: ת"ר הרי שהיה מתענה על החולה ונתרפא על צער צרה ועברה מתענה ומשלים ההולך ממקום שמתענין למקום שאין מתענין וכו'. זה שאמר יוסף לאחיו אל תרגזו בדרך. אל תתעסקו בדבר הלכה שלא תתגר עליהם הדרך ואוקימנא לעיוני אבל במגרס לא. דא"מ ב' ת"ח המהלכים בדרך ואין ביניהם דברי תורה ראוין לישרף שנאמר ויהי המה הולכים הלוך ודבר והנה רכב אש וסוסי אש ויפרידו בין שניהם. במתניתא תנא אל תפסיעו פסיעה גסה שנוטלת אחד מחמש מאות ממאור עיניו של אדם. והכניסו חמה לעיר. כדרב יהודה אמר רב לעולם יכנס אדם בכי טוב ויצא בכי טוב כלומר באור היום כדכתיב וירא אלהים את האור כי טוב. וכתיב הבקר אור והאנשים שלחו. משום מעיינא פי' אם יאכל הרבה יקחהו שלשול ויבא להתאחר מן השיירא.

מסורת הש"ס

שבת קיד. קדושין מט:
[ב"ב ח:]
[תוספתא פ"א]
[תוספ' פ"ב]
[נ"ל לא תתענה]
סוטה מט.
[נ"ל הלוך]
[פסחים מב.]
פסחים ב. ב"ק ס: ע"ש

הגהות הב"ח

(א) רש"י ד"ה לישרף באש כו' שהיו הולכין בדבר של הלכה: (ב) ד"ה הכא תרגימו. בבבל תלמוד זה כו': (ג) ד"ה משום מזוני שמא לא יהי' לו לאח"כ: (ד) תוס' ד"ה איזהו כו' פרנס על הצבור ואיזהו תלמיד כו' כנ"ל ותיבות להיות פרנס נמחק: (ה) בא"ד כל ששואלין אותו דבר הלכה ואפילו:

גליון הש"ס

גמ' המהלך בדרך אל יאכל כו'. עי' מג"א סי' קי ס"ק י:

רבינו גרשום

שבכרכין וכשהן באין בחמישי לא ידעו שקבלו עליהם תענית ואין מביאין מזון אלא לצורך השבת ולוקחין הכל לצורך ליל חמישי לפי שהתענו בו ומתייקר המזון לצורך השבת אבל כשגוזרין בשני כשבאין בשני לעיר שומעין כשגוזרין תענית וכשבאין בחמישי מביאין מזון כדי למכור ללילי חמישי ולשבת: מפסיקין בראשי חדשים אם אירעו בחמישי ושני הכתוב במגילת תענית דלא להתענאה בהון: אל יאמר תלמיד [אני] איני ראוי לכך להתענות. ר' יוסי אומר כל אדם נמי עושה עצמו וזכור לטוב: אפילו במס' כלה שאין רגילין להתעסק בו שאין שבח הוא לו שמתענה: דבר של שבח אינו עושה כגון חתן קורא ק"ש בלילה הראשון. של צער מתענה. ות"ח עושה. בין של שבח בין של צער: הרי זה מתענה ומשלים שנותנין עליו חומרי מקום שהלך לשם וחומרי מקום שיצא משם: אל יתראה בפניהם. כשהוא שבע. אל ינהיג בעצמו עידונין. שלא יאמר הואיל שאכלת כל שהוא אוכל הרבה: והן רעיבין מפני הרעב: שמא ירגז עליכם הדרך. שהרואה אתכם שאתם חולקין בדבר הלכה סבור נלחמים אתם ומתרגזים

דיתיב בארבא. אי נמי: דקאזיל מאוונא לאוונא. רב פפא כל פרסה ופרסה אכיל חדא ריפתא. קסבר: משום מעיינא. אמר רב יהודה אמר רב: [א]כל המרעיב עצמו בשני רעבון ניצל ממיתה משונה, שנאמר °"ברעב פדך ממות". 'מרעב' מיבעי ליה! אלא, הכי קאמר: בשכר שמרעיב עצמו בשני רעבון, ניצול ממיתה משונה. אמר ריש לקיש: [ב]אסור לאדם לשמש מטתו בשני רעבון, שנאמר °"וליוסף ילד שני בנים בטרם תבוא שנת הרעב". תנא: *חסוכי בנים משמשין מטותיהן בשני רעבון. תנו רבנן: [ג]בזמן שישראל שרויין בצער, ופירש אחד מהן, באין שני מלאכי השרת שמלוין לו לאדם ומניחין לו ידיהן על ראשו ואומרים: פלוני זה, שפירש מן הצבור, אל יראה בנחמת צבור. תניא אידך: בזמן שהצבור שרוי בצער, אל יאמר אדם: אלך לביתי ואוכל ואשתה, ושלום עליך, נפשי. ואם עושה כן — עליו הכתוב אומר °"והנה ששון ושמחה, הרוג בקר ושחוט צאן, אכול בשר ושתות יין. אכול ושתו, כי מחר נמות". מה כתיב בתריה? "ונגלה באזני ה' צבאות אם יכופר העון הזה לכם עד תמותון". עד כאן מדת בינונים, אבל במדת רשעים מה כתיב — °"אתיו, אקחה יין, ונסבאה שכר, והיה כזה יום מחר". מה כתיב בתריה — "הצדיק אבד ואין איש שם על לב... כי מפני הרעה נאסף הצדיק". *אלא, יצער אדם עם הצבור. שכן מצינו במשה רבינו, שציער עצמו עם הצבור, שנאמר °"וידי משה כבדים ויקחו אבן וישימו תחתיו וישב עליה", וכי לא היה לו למשה כר אחת או כסת אחת לישב עליה? אלא, כך אמר משה: הואיל וישראל שרויין בצער, אף אני אהיה עמהם בצער. וכל המצער עצמו עם הצבור — זוכה ורואה בנחמת צבור. *ושמא יאמר אדם: מי מעיד בי? אבני ביתו של אדם וקורות ביתו של אדם מעידים בו, שנאמר °"כי אבן מקיר תזעק, וכפים מעץ יעננה". דבי רבי שילא אמרי: שני מלאכי השרת המלוין לו לאדם הן מעידין עליו, שנאמר °"כי מלאכיו יצוה לך". רבי חידקא אומר: *נשמתו של אדם היא מעידה עליו, שנאמר °"משוכבת חיקך שמור פתחי פיך". ויש אומרים: אבריו של אדם מעידים בו, שנאמר °"אתם עדי, נאם ה'". °"אל אמונה, ואין עול". "אל אמונה" — כשם שנפרעין מן הרשעים לעולם הבא אפילו על עבירה קלה שעושין, כך נפרעין מן הצדיקים בעולם הזה על עבירה קלה שעושין. "ואין עול" — כשם שמשלמין שכר לצדיקים לעולם הבא אפילו על מצוה קלה שעושין, כך משלמין שכר לרשעים בעולם הזה אפילו על מצוה קלה שעושין. "צדיק וישר הוא" *) (אמרו: בשעת) פטירתו של אדם לבית עולמו, כל מעשיו (*נפטרין) לפניו, ואומרים לו: כך וכך עשית במקום פלוני ביום פלוני, והוא אומר: (*היין) ואומרים לו: חתום! וחותם, שנאמר °"ביד כל אדם יחתום". ולא עוד, אלא שמצדיק עליו את הדין, ואומר להם: יפה דנתוני, לקיים מה שנאמר °"למען תצדק בדברך". אמר שמואל: כל היושב בתענית נקרא חוטא. (א) סבר כי האי תנא, דתניא: *ר' אלעזר הקפר ברבי אומר: מה תלמוד לומר °"וכפר עליו מאשר חטא על הנפש"? וכי באיזה נפש חטא זה? אלא, שציער עצמו מן היין. והלא דברים קל וחומר; ומה זה, שלא ציער עצמו אלא מן היין, נקרא חוטא, המצער עצמו מכל דבר ודבר — על אחת כמה וכמה! ר' אלעזר אומר: נקרא קדוש, שנאמר: °"קדוש יהיה, גדל פרע שער ראשו". ומה זה, שלא ציער עצמו אלא מדבר אחד, נקרא קדוש, המצער עצמו מכל דבר — על אחת כמה וכמה. ולשמואל, הא איקרי קדוש! ההוא אגידול פרע קאי. ולר' אלעזר, הא נקרא חוטא! ההוא דסאיב נפשיה. ומי אמר רבי אלעזר הכי? והאמר ר' אלעזר: לעולם ימוד אדם עצמו

כאילו

*) [נ"ל מלמד שבשעת כך אי' בשאלתות]

(מסורת הש"ס: איוב ה; בראשית מא; ישעיהו כב; שם נו; שמות יז; חבקוק ב; תהלים צא; מיכה ז; ישעיהו מג; דברים לב; איוב לז; תהלים נא; במדבר ו; שם)

רש"י

דיתיב בארבא. שהולך בספינה. משום מזוני — איכא, משום מעיינא — ליכא: מאוונא לאוונא. מקום מלון התגרים מכפר לכפר, דמשתכחי מזוני, וליכא למיחש למזוני. ולמעיינא איכא למיחש: כל פרסה ופרסה אכיל ריפתא. קסבר רב פפא: הא דאמור רבנן לא ליכול טפי — משום מעיינא, ואיהו לא מיספפי ממעיינא, דבעל *בטן הוה. ענין אחר: כריסו רחבה, כדאיתא בבבא מציעא (דף פד.) דקא חשיב אבריה דרב פפא, וכאיש גבורתו, ולפיכך יכול לאכול הרבה ואינו מזיק לו: מיתה משונה. מת בחרב וברעב. וכל מיתה שאינה בידי מלאך המות כדרך כל אדם על מטתו: בשכר שמצער עצמו. כשישראל בצער: אסור לשמש מטתו בשני רעבון. דצריך אדם לנהוג צער בעצמו: חסוכי בנים. חסירי בנים(ב). דגרסינן במנחות (דף כט.) לגבי מנורה: ומי חסיכי כולי האי. *שלא קיימו פריה ורביה: שני מלאכי שרת(ג) מלוין לו לאדם. אחד מימינו ואחד משמאלו, דכתי' (תהלים צא) "כי מלאכיו יצוה לך": הנה ששון ושמחה הרוג בקר ושחוט צאן אכול בשר ושתות יין כי מחר נמות ונגלה באזני ה' צבאות אם יכופר העון הזה לכם עד תמותון: זו מדת בינונים. שיראין מן המיתה, כדכתיב בהו "כי מחר נמות": אתיו אקחה יין ונסבאה שכר והיה כזה יום מחר. גדול יותר מאד: הצדיק אבד ואין איש שם על לב. מפני מה הוא מת — מפני הרעה נאסף הצדיק, מפני שלא יצטער הוא ברעה. ואחר שהיא גזרה מלפניו, כי מפני הרעה נאסף הצדיק. ל"א: מפני רעות של אלו הוא נאסף, שאין הקב"ה רוצה שיבקש עליהם רחמים: כפים. חלי לבינה, ורגילין לתתה בין שתי נדבכי העצים: הכי גרסינן: אבריו של אדם הן מעידין בו, שנאמר "ואתם עדי" לשון רבים "נאם ה'": מאי דכתיב אל אמונה ואין עול כשם שמשלם כו'. כך משלם לרשעים בעולם הזה, כדי לטורדן מן העולם הבא, וכדכתיב (דברים ז) "ומשלם לשונאיו אל פניו להאבידו": ואין עול. שאין עושה (ד)דין בלא דין אמת וצדק: צדיק וישר. מצדיק הדין על הצדיקים לפרוע מהם, ועושה טובה וישרות עם הרשעים לפרוע כל זכותם בעולם הזה, כדי לטורדן: ביד כל אדם יחתום. כותב מעשה כל אדם, ומחתים(ה) יד על כל מעשיו: למען תצדק בדברך. שהוא מצדיק עליו בדבריך, שאתה מראה לו(ו): לשמואל קדוש יהיה אגדל פרע קאי. ששערו אסור בהנאה, אבל הוא עצמו לא נקרא קדוש. ולר' אלעזר חוטא, דסאיב כתרגומו "מאשר חטא על הנפש". פשט המקרא — על שנטמא במת: וכי באיזה נפש חטא זה. מי הרג שנקרא חוטא? שאין מצוה לצער עצמו, כדאמרינן: צדיקי (*מי) אכלי האי עלמא (והאיך) מי סני להו, במסכת הוריות (פ"ג דף י:): נקרא קדוש. רישיה דקרא קא דריש, בשביל שמתוך כך מתמרקין עונותיו שמתענה:

כאילו

(גי' רש"א בשר; [לשון חוסר כמו לא חשכת. ערוך]; עי' בהגהות מהרי"ף שם; חגיגה טז. [ע"ש כמה שינויים]; ג"ז שם; [נ"ל נפרטין וכ"ה בשאלתו']; [נ"ל הן]; [שבועות ח. סוטה טו. כריתות כו. ב"ק צא: נזיר יט. כב. נדרים י.]; [נ"ל אי])

תוספות

אסור לאדם לשמש מטתו בשני רעבון. ואם תאמר: הרי יוכבד *נולדה בין החומות, ואותו העת עת רעב היה, וע"כ שימשו מטותיהן בשני רעבון! ויש לומר: דלכ"ע לא הוי אסור, אלא למי שרוצה לנהוג עצמו בחסידות, ויוסף לא שימש, אבל שאר בני אדם שימשו:

אמר שמואל כל היושב בתענית נקרא חוטא. וקשיא: דאמרינן בפ' "החובל" (ב"ק דף צא: ושם): החובל בעצמו — רשאי, אבל אחרים שחבלו בו — חייבים. ומפרש התם: הא דקאמר החובל בעצמו רשאי — אמר שמואל: ביושב בתענית. אלמא משמע דשמואל קאמר דיושב בתענית לא נקרא חוטא! ויש לומר: דודאי הוי חוטא, כדאמרינן הכא, מקל וחומר מנזיר: ומה נזיר שלא ציער עצמו אלא מיין וכו'. אבל מכל מקום, המצוה שהוא עושה התענית — גדול יותר מן העבירה, ממה שהוא מצער נפשו. דמצוה לנדור, כדאמרינן (סוטה דף ב.): הרואה סוטה בקלקולה, יזיר עצמו מן היין. ומכל מקום יש קצת חטא, מידי דהוה *אמתענה תענית חלום בשבת, דקורעין גזר דינו ונפרעין ממנו תענית של שבת, ומאי תקנתיה — ליתב תעניתא לתעניתיה*:

כאילו

([תוספות ישנים] ; [ברכות לא: ולקמן יב:]; [וע"ע תוס' ב"ק נט: ד"ה אלא ותוס' נזיר ב: ד"ה ולמאי]; [ואף לצדיק גמור לריך לצער עצמו עם הצבור שכן מצינו במשה רבינו שציער עצמו וכו' כך אי' בשאלתות פ' האזינו סימן קסג])

עין משפט נר מצוה

לה א ב מיי' פ"ג מהל' תענית הלכה ח טוש"ע א"ח סי' תקעד סעיף ד:

לו ג שם סעיף ה:

רבינו חננאל

והמרעיב עצמו בשני רעבון ניצל ממיתה משונה שנאמר ברעב פדך ממות. אסור לאדם לשמש מטתו בשני רעבון. תנא חשוכי בנים משמשין מטותיהן בשני רעבון. חייב אדם לצער עצמו עם הצבור שבזמן שפורש עצמו מן הצבור ב' מלאכי השרת המלוין אותו מניחין ידיו על ראשו ואומרים פלוני שפירש מן הצבור אל יראה בנחמת ישראל. אלא מיבעי ליה לצעורי עם הצבור שכן מצינו במרע"ה שציער עצמו עם הצבור שנאמר וידי משה כבדים וגו'. וכי לא היה לו כר או כסת לישב בה אלא רצה להצטער בצער צבור. ושמא תאמר מי מעיד בו. אבני ביתו. שנאמר כי אבן מקיר תזעק. ומלאכים השומרים אותו שנאמר כי מלאכיו יצוה לך וגו'. כתיב אל אמונה ואין עול. כשם שנפרעים מן הרשעים לעוה"ב אפילו בעבירה קלה כך נפרעין מן הצדיקים בעוה"ז וכשם שמשלמין שכר טוב בעוה"ב לצדיקים [אפי' על מצוה קלה] כך משלמין שכר טוב לרשעים אפילו על מצוה קלה בעוה"ז. בשעת פטירתו של אדם. כל מעשיו נפרטין לפניו. אומרים לו עשית במקום פלוני והוא אומר הן. אומרים לו חתום. וחותם שנאמר ביד כל אדם יחתום. ולא עוד אלא שמצדיק עליו את הדין ואומר יפה דנתוני שנא' למען תצדק בדברך וגו': אמר שמואל היושב בתענית נקרא חוטא. סבר לה כר' אלעזר הקפר בר' [דאמר] בשביל שציער עצמו מן היין קראו הכתוב חוטא שנאמר וכפר עליו מאשר חטא על הנפש המצער עצמו מכל מאכל ומשתה לא כ"ש. ומפני מה כתיב בו קדוש יהיה משום (דמרבי) [דמדכי] נפשיה מטומאה*). ור' אלעזר פליג עליה דאמר המצטער עצמו לשם שמים כגון הנזיר וכיוצא

*) נראה מזה דרבינו היה לו גי' אחרת בכאן ההוא דמדכי נפשי' וכ"ה גי' רבינו גרשום כאן.

רבינו גרשום

ומתרגמים עליכם. בעיוני. לא עייני באורחא: משום מעיינא. שאם אוכל הרבה מתכבד במיעיו ואין יכול לילך. משום מזוני דלא שכיחי באורחא: דיתיב בארבא. ליכא משום מעיינא ואיתא משום מזוני. דאזיל מאונא לאונא. דשכיחי מזוני. משום מזוני ליכא משום מעיינא איכא: רב פפא הוי אכיל סגי: חסוכי בנים ולא כולי עלמא: זו מדה בינונית שהרי מזכירין יום המיתה כדכתיב כי מחר נמות: ההוא דמדכי בנפשיה. כלומר שנזיר שמצער עצמו מן הטומאה קרוי קדוש ולא ליושב בתענית. ההוא אשר חטא על הנפש דמסאב נפשיה על המת: כאילו קדוש שרוי בתוך מיעיו ולא יתענה ר"ל

הגהות הב"ח

(א) גמ' כל היושב בתענית נקרא חוטא (סבר כי האי תנא) תא"מ ונ"ב ס"א שנאמר וכפר עליו מאשר חטא על הנפש וכי באיזה נפש חטא זה אלא שציער נפשו מן היין דתניא וכו' ולשמואל הא איקרי קדוש. נ"ב פירוש מדפליג אדשמואל אלמא דלשמואל לא נקרא קדוש אבל לר' אלעזר הקפר לא קשיא דלמא מודה דנקרא קדוש אלא דנקרא ג"כ חוטא אבל לשמואל קשיא דמשמע לדידיה לא נקרא קדוש ואע"פ דמודה שמואל דעושה מצוה בנזירתו מ"מ לא נקרא קדוש ובתר הכי פריך אר' אלעזר הא נקרא חוטא דמפליג אשמואל אלמא דס"ל דלא נקרא חוטא: (ב) רש"י ד"ה חסוכי בנים חסירי בנים כמו דגרסינן במנחות: (ג) ד"ה שני וכו' שמלוין: (ד) ד"ה ואין עול שאין עושה דבר בלא דין: (ה) ד"ה ביד כל כו' ומחתים יד כל אדם על כל: (ו) ד"ה למען כו' שאתה מראה לו מה"ד וכי באיזה נפש חטא זה מי הרג שנקרא חוטא הס"ד ואח"כ מה"ד אלא שציער עצמו וכו' שאין מצוה לצער עצמו כדאמרינן אטו צדיקי אי אכלי תרי עלמא וכו' עד עונותיו שמתענה מה"ד לשמואל קדוש יהיה וכו' לא נקרא קדוש הס"ד ואח"כ מה"ד ולר' אלעזר וכו' שנטמא במת הס"ד:

עין משפט נר מצוה

לז א טוש"ע א"ח סי' תקעא סעיף א:
לח ב מיי' פ"ג מהלכות תענית הלכה יא טוש"ע א"ח סי' תקסח סעיף ו:
לט ג טוש"ע א"ח סי' תקעא סעיף ב:
מ ד מיי' פ"א מהלכות תענית הלכה י סמג עשין יג טוש"ע א"ח סי' תקסב סעיף ז:
מא ה מיי' שם הלכה יא סמג שם טור ש"ע א"ח שם סעיף ט:
מב ו מיי' שם הלכה יג טוש"ע שם סעיף י:
מג ז מיי' פי"א מהלכו' מאכלות אסורות הלכה טו סמג לאוין קמח טוש"ע י"ד סי' קלה סעיף טז:

גמרא

כאילו קדוש שרוי בתוך מעיו, שנאמר "בקרבך קדוש ולא אבוא בעיר"! לא קשיא. הא — דמצי לצעורי נפשיה, הא — דלא מצי לצעורי נפשיה. ר"ל אמר: נקרא חסיד, שנאמר "גומל נפשו איש (א) (*חסיד,) ועוכר שארו" וגו'. אמר רב ששת: האי בר בי רב דיתיב בתעניתא — ליכול כלבא לשירותיה. אמר רבי ירמיה בר אבא: *אין תענית ציבור בבבל אלא תשעה באב בלבד. (*אמר) ר' ירמיה בר אבא אמר ריש לקיש: אין תלמיד חכם רשאי לישב בתענית, מפני שממעט במלאכת שמים. § "אוכלין ושותין משחשיכה" כו'. אמר רבי זעירא אמר רב הונא: יחיד שקיבל עליו תענית, אפילו אכל ושתה כל הלילה — למחר הוא מתפלל תפלת תענית. לן בתעניתו — (ב) אינו מתפלל של תענית. אמר רב יוסף: מאי קסבר רב הונא? סבירא ליה אין מתענין לשעות? או דלמא, מתענין לשעות, והמתענה לשעות אינו מתפלל תפלת תענית? אמר ליה אביי: לעולם קסבר רב הונא מתענין לשעות, והמתענה לשעות מתפלל תפלת תענית. ושאני הכא — דאיכא שעות דליליא דלא קביל עליה מעיקרא. *מר עוקבא איקלע לגינזק. בעו מיניה: מתענין לשעות, או אין מתענין לשעות? לא הוה בידיה. קנקנין של נכרים אסורין או מותרין? לא הוה בידיה. *במה שימש משה כל שבעת ימי המלואים? לא הוה בידיה. אזל ושאיל בי מדרשא. אמרו ליה, הלכתא: מתענין לשעות, ומתפללין תפלת תענית. והלכתא: קנקנין של נכרים לאחר שנים עשר חדש מותרין. במה שימש משה כל ז' ימי המלואים — בחלוק לבן. רב כהנא מתני: בחלוק לבן שאין לו אימרא. אמר רב חסדא:
הא

תורה אור השלם — הושע יא; משלי יא

רש"י

כאילו קדוש שרוי בתוך מעיו. כאילו כל מעיו קדוש, ואסור להכחישן. דהכי משמע: בקרבך קדוש, כלומר: דאסור להתענות(ג). בקרבך קדוש רישיה דקרא קדריש, בשביל שקדוש שרוי בקרבך — לא אבוא בעיר של מעלה, עד שתבנה ירושלים של מטה. ורמיזא בעלמא הוא: הא דמצי מצער נפשיה. שיכול לסבול התענית — משבחו הקב"ה, אבל מי שאינו יכול להתענות נקרא חוטא: נקרא חסיד. המתענה, דכתיב "גומל נפשו איש חסד" — מפריש עצמו ממאכל ומשתה, כמו "ביום הגמל את יצחק" (בראשית כא) — שברי"ר בלע"ז. מפי מורי. אי נמי: גומל — לשון תגמול, שמשלים נפשו לקונו (ד): ועוכר שארו. המתענה ומכחיש בשרו נקרא אכזר: שממעט במלאכת שמים. חלש הוא, ואינו יכול ללמוד: שירותיה. סעודתו. כלבא ליכול סעודתו. ולכך המתענה אינו מועיל לו, אלא כמי שמתענה מפני שאין לו מה יאכל: אין תענית צבור בבבל. לענין איסורי חומרי תענית אמר ר' ירמיה למילתיה, שהיו נוהגין בו כעין אבילות, שהיו אוכלין מבעוד יום ואסורין בנעילת הסנדל, אלא תשעה באב בלבד: יחיד שקיבל עליו תענית. מאתמול(ה): הרי אני יושב בתענית למחר, אפילו אכל ושתה כל הלילה עד עמוד השחר — למחר מתפלל תפלת תענית "עננו": לן בתעניתו. באותו תענית שקיבל עליו, שלא אכל במוצאי תעניתו, ולן כל אותו הלילה לשם תענית עד הבקר: למחר אין מתפלל תפלת תענית. אינו יכול להתפלל(ו) "עננו" קודם שיאכל, כדי לצאת ידי חובת תענית של לילה, אע"פ שהוא יום אחד כדכתיב (בראשית א) "ויהי ערב ויהי בוקר יום אחד". ולקמן מפרש ואזיל מאי קסבר רב הונא, מאי טעמא אין מתפלל למחר עננו: והכי גרסינן: מאי קסבר רב הונא מיסבר קסבר אין מתענין לשעות או דלמא קסבר מתענין לשעות והמתענה לשעות אינו מתפלל תפלת תענית אמר אביי לעולם קסבר מתענין לשעות (*ומתפלל) תפלת תענית כו'. פירוש: מאי קסבר רב הונא אין מתענין לשעות. כלומר, האי דקאמר למחר אין מתפלל תפלת תענית — לכך אינו מתפלל, דקבלת תענית זה אינו קבלה, ואינו תענית כלל. ואם רוצה לאכול ולסעוד בתוך התענית — הרשות בידו, דאין מקבלין תענית לשעות, כגון זה שלא קיבל תענית של לילה זה מאתמול(ז), כדקתני: לן בתעניתו, דמשמע: מאליו, כשהחשיך ובא לסעוד עמד ולא אכל. כלומר, שהיה בדעתו לאכול עד שעבר מקצת הלילה שעה אחת או שתי שעות, ואחר כך נמלך ולן בתעניתו. או דלמא האי דקאמר רב הונא למחר אין מתפלל תפלת תענית — לאו משום דאין מתענין לשעות, דשם תענית עליו, ואם רוצה לחזור בו ולטעום אחר שהתחיל בתענית — אינו יכול, אלא להכי אינו מתפלל תפלת תענית, דסבר: אין תענית של שעות חשוב וחמור כל כך שיהא צריך להתפלל עליו "עננו": לעולם קסבר. בעלמא דמתענין לשעות, והמתענה לשעות מתפלל תפלת תענית. והכא מאי טעמא אין מתפלל תפלת תענית, דשאני הכא היכא דהתענה אתמול ובלילה לן בתעניתו דלא קיבלה עילויה(ח), שלא קיבל עליו תענית זה בפני עצמו מאתמול כדרך שאר מתענין לשעות, ואינו חשוב להתפלל עליו "עננו": מר עוקבא איקלע לגינזק. גרסינן. דאילו ר' עקיבא לא היה מסתפק לו הנך בעיי. ועוד, דבלשון ברייתא הוה משתעי ביה: מעשה ברבי עקיבא כו', ולא בגמרא*: קנקנים של חרס. שמכניסין בהן יין לקיום — אסור להשתמש בהן: במה שימש משה. דאילו באהרן כתיב בגדי כהונה, דכתיב (שמות כט) "והלבשתם", שבשעה שהיה משה עובד, אהרן היה לבוש בגדי כהונה. ועבודה דמשה גזירת הכתוב הוא, ובגדי כהונה לא מלינו בו. ומסתמא אין הדבר כשר שהיה עובד בבגדיו של חול, שיוצא בהן לשוק: לאחר שנים עשר חדש. הולך טעם יין נסך, ומותרים בלא עירוי מים. אבל תוך י"ב חדש — צריך עירוי שלשה ימים מעת לעת: בחלוק לבן. של פשתן, עשוי לשם כך: רב כהנא מתני. כי האי לישנא: בחלוק לבן שאין בו אימרא. 'שפה' מתרגמינן אימרא (שם כח)(ט) כלומר, *תחוב היה מחוט אחד כל החלוק. ולא כבגדים שלנו שבתי הידים מדובקין בבגד הגוף בתפירה, כדי שלא יחשדוהו שמא באותה שפה הוציא מעות הקודש, משום שנאמר (במדבר לב) "והייתם נקיים מה' ומישראל":
הא

תוספות

כאילו קדוש. הקב"ה(י). פירוש: והא אמר לעיל שנקרא קדוש כלומר: שהיושב בתענית נקרא קדוש! ומשני: לא קשיא: גומל נפשו. פירוש: שגומל חסד לנפשו, שאינו מתענה, נקרא חסיד: אין תענית צבור בבבל אלא תשעה באב בלבד. פירוש: שהיה להם הרבה גשמים: יחיד שקיבל עליו תענית אע"פ שאכל ושתה כל הלילה מתפלל תפלת תענית. תימה: אמאי נקט יחיד? לצבור נמי, דאמרינן במתני' (לעיל דף י.) דעושין שלשה תעניות ואוכלים משחשיכה! וצ"ע: לן בתעניתו. פירוש: שהתענה היום, ובלילה לא אכל, ולן בתעניתו. אע"ג שהלינה היא מכח תענית שקיבל עליו — אינו מתפלל תפלת תענית. ובה"ג יש: אוכל ומתפלל תפלת תענית. ומפרש כמו הכא, דבשחרית אומר תפלת תענית, אע"פ שאכל כל הלילה. ויש מתענה שאינו מתפלל, כמו בערבית אע"פ שלא אכל. ומפרש בהלכות גדולות: דאין אומרין "עננו" בתפלת שחרית, שמא נמצא שקרן בתפלתו. דשמא לא יסיים התענית. ולי נראה דלא נקרא שקרן, כיון שהיה בדעתו להתענות, אפילו אקרי אונס אחר כך ולא מצי לצער נפשיה — לא גרע ממתענין לשעות. וכן משמע מהא דתנן (לקמן דף יט.): ירדו להם גשמים קודם חצות — אינן משלימין. ומסתמא משמע שאמרו תפלת תענית. מכל מקום אין זה ראיה גמורה, דשמא לא אמרוה. ומהא דלקמן (דף יב:) גבי רב הונא בריה דרב יהושע בריה דרב אידי *דיתיב בתעניתא מדאמרו ליה ליזוף מר וליפרע, ואמר להו: תענית חלום הוא. אמאי לא אמר מפני שאמר תפלת תענית? אין זה ראיה(כ) לדברי ה"ג, דלא היה דעתו להתענות מבעוד יום, ולא קבל עליו. וכתב הר"מ: מי שלא קבל עליו מבעוד יום דאין אומר עננו, אי לאו דתענית חלום הוא. ונוהגים שש"צ לצבור אומרו בשחרית כדי להודיע לעולם ולהזכיר התענית, אבל יחיד אינו אומר עד המנחה. [ובטור אורח חיים (סי' תקסה) אומר: שליח צבור אומר בכל פעם, שאי אפשר שלא יתענו קצת מקהל, עכ"ל]:

רבינו חננאל

וכיוצא בו [נקרא] קדוש כדכתי' קדוש יהיה. א"כ מה ת"ל מאשר חטא על הנפש בנזיר שנטמא הכתוב מדבר ומפני שנטמא נקרא חוטא. ור"ל אמר המונע עצמו מן התענית הוא חסיד שנאמר גומל נפשו איש חסד. הגומל טוב לנפשו איש חסד: א"ר ירמיה אין ת"ח רשאי לסגף עצמו בתענית מפני שממעט (עצמו) במלאכת שמים. אמר רב הונא יחיד שקבל עליו תענית ב' ימים זה אחר זה אפילו אוכל ושותה כל הלילה כו'. הדין במי שקבל עליו יום אחד או ב' ימים תענית דינם אחד מיהו נוח להתלמד להבין פירושו בשני ימים מיום אחד. וכן פירושו. אדם שקבל עליו להתענות שני ושלישי והתענה יום ב' ובערב אכל ושתה למחר *) עוד ביום ג' מתענה ומתפלל תפלת תענית **) אע"פ שמתענה רוב יום ג' מפני שלא קבל עליו מיום ב' להתענות יום ג' ונמצא תעניתו ביום ג' תענית שעות דהא לא קיבל תענית מאתמול. ועל זה מדקדק רב יוסף מ"ט דרב הונא. מי אמרינן קסבר רב הונא מתענה לשעות. והמתענה לשעות אינו מתפלל תפלת תענית. או דלמא קסבר רב הונא אין מתענין לשעות ואינם תענית כלל. לפיכך אינו מתפלל תפלת תענית. ואמר אביי לעולם קסבר רב הונא מתענין לשעות והמתענה לשעות מתפלל תפלת תענית. ושאני הכא דלא קביל עליה מעיקרא. ועוד לא היה בדעתו להשלים תעניתו עד הערב. וקיי"ל כל תענית שלא שקעה עליו חמה לאו שמיה תענית לפיכך ***) תמצא תענית שעות. ומסתברא דמי שנזדמן לו ולא אכל עד שעבר רוב היום וכיון שראה כך הסכים לצום ולהשלימו אותו יום בתענית זהו תענית שעות ומתפלל באותה שעה שהסכים להשלימו תענית שעות תפלת תענית עננו בשומע תפלה. ודווקא אחר שקבל עליו לעצמו ****) שמתפלל תפלת תענית אבל מקודם לא: ר"ע אקלע לגינזק בעו מיניה מתענין לשעות כו' ואסיקנא הלכתא המתענה לשעות מתפלל תפלת תענית וקנקנים (שלמים) [ישנים] ששימשו בהן גוים ביין שלהן לאחר שישפכו היין מהן אם ישארו ריקים י"ב חודש מותר לישראל להטיל בהן יין להשתמש בהן.
אמר

*) דברי רבינו כמו שהם לפנינו אין לו שום ביאור כלל ועי' ברא"ש כאן ואולי כצ"ל לן בתעניתו כלו' אם לא קבל עליו תענית אלא יום ב' בלבד והתענה אותו היום ובלילה נמלך ולן בתעניתו למחר אין מתפלל תפלת תענית אע"פ שמתענה יום ב' ויום ג' כו' ועי' ברי"ף ובמלחמות בשם רבינו. **) חסר כאן ותמצא גי' רבינו ז"ל ופירושו באר היטב. ***) אולי צ"ל לא נקרא תענית שעות. ****) אולי צ"ל לעצמו להשלים התענית מתפלל תפלת תענית.

מסורת הש"ס

[נ"ל חסיד]
[לקמן יב: ע"ש פסחים נד: ע"ש]
[נ"ל ואמר]
[לפנינו איתא שזה היה רב יהושע בריה דרב אידי]
ע"ז לד. [ע"ש בתוס' ד"ה ר' עקיבא]
[עי' תוס' חגיגה ו: ד"ה מאי נ"מ ותוס' סנהדרין טו: ד"ה שור סיני]
[נ"ל מתענין לשעות והמתענה לשעות מתפלל]
[ועמ"ש תוס' כט"ב לד. ד"ה ר"ע וכו' על דברי רש"י דהכא]
[נ"ל ארוג יעב"ץ]

רבינו גרשום

ר"ל אמר יושב בתענית נקרא חסיד שנא' גומל נפשו איש חסד שפירש עצמו מליכל כמו ויגמל: ממעט במלאכת שמים. שאינו יכול לעסוק בתורה: יחיד שקיבל עליו תענית. כראוי מבעוד יום. לן בתענית. ה"ק אם לא קבל מבעוד יום אלא בצפרא קבל עליה להתענות חצי היום ובחצי היום קביל עליה עד לאורתא ולן בלילה בתעניתו ולא קבל עליה כלום והתענה אף למחר אין מתפלל תפלת תענית שכבר יצא בתפלת תענית דאתמול. ושאני הכא דלא קביל עליה מאורתא כלומר באותו יום שמתענה לשעות מתפלל תפלת תענית אבל הכא דלן בתעניתו עבדיה להאי תענית שני כתענית אריכא שהוא מאתמול שעדיין לא אכל וכיון שהתפלל אתמול תפלת תענית אין צריך להתפלל היום: מתענין לשעות שמקבלין תענית ביום אע"ג דלא קביל עליה מאורתא: קנקנים של גוים שנשתמש בהן יין. לאחר שנים עשר חודש. לאחר שנשתמשו בו גוים: חלוק לבן שאין לו אימרא. שאין לו שפה כדי שלא יחשדוהו שמא באותה שפה הכנים מעות הקדש שגנב משום שנאמר והייתם נקיים

גליון הש"ס

גמ' הא דמצי לצעורי. עי' לקמן דף כב ע"ב תוד"ה ר' יוסי: שם למחר הוא מתפלל תפלת תענית. מדברי רש"י שבת כד ע"א ד"ה ערבית נראה שלא היה לרש"י שם הגי' כאן תיבת למחר:

הגהות הב"ח

(א) גמ' שנאמר גומל נפשו איש חסד אמר ר' ירמיה בר אבא אמר ריש לקיש אין ת"ח וכו' שממעט במלאכת שמים אמר רב ששת האי בר בי רב וכו' אלא תשעה באב בלבד אוכלין כו': (ב) שם לן בתעניתו למחר אינו מתפלל: (ג) רש"י ד"ה כאילו כו' לאסור להתענות הס"ד ומה"ד בקרבך קדוש כו': (ד) ד"ה נקרא כו' שמשלים נפשו לקונו חסיד ועוכר שארו כו' כצ"ל והד"א: (ה) ד"ה יחיד כו' מאתמול שאמר הרי אני יושב: (ו) ד"ה למחר כו' אינו יכול להתפלל. נ"ב פי' אינו יכול אע"פ שרוצה להתפלל בלא חיוב ונראה דלא פירש כן אלא למאי דקס"ד דאין מתענין לשעות ס"ל לרב הונא דלאו תענית הוא אבל למסקנא דמתענין לשעות שם תענית עליו אפי' לן בתעניתו דאינו חשוב וחמור להתפלל עננו בתורת חיוב מ"מ הרשות בידו להתפלל עננו שהרי שם תענית עליו שאסור לו לאכול: (ז) ד"ה וה"ג מאי כו' תענית של לילה זה מאתמול. נ"ב פירוש מאתמול מזמן המנחה: (ח) ד"ה לעולם כו' דלא קיבלה עילויה. נ"ב ר"ל דלא קיבלו כלל מאתמול דאף בלילה לא קיבלו: (ט) ד"ה רב כהנא כו' (כלומר תחוב) תא"מ ונ"ב ס"א כלי חשוב: (י) תוס' ד"ה כאילו קדוש הקב"ה שרוי בתוך מעיו ואסור להכחישן פי' והא אמרינן לעיל: (כ) ד"ה לן כו' אין זה ראיה דלדברי ה"ג איכא למימר דלא היה דעתו:

הא דאמרת מתענין לשעות — והוא שלא טעם כלום עד הערב. א"ל אביי: הא תענית מעלייתא היא! לא צריכא דאימלך אימלוכי. ואמר רב חסדא: *כל תענית שלא שקעה עליו חמה לאו שמיה תענית. מיתיבי: *אנשי משמר מתענין, ולא משלימין! התם לצעורי נפשיה בעלמא הוא. תא שמע: *דא"ר אליעזר (*בן) צדוק: אני מבני בניו של *סנאב בן בנימין. ופעם אחת חל ט' באב להיות בשבת, ודחינוהו לאחר השבת, והתענינו בו, ולא השלמנוהו, מפני שיו"ט שלנו הוא! התם נמי לצעורי נפשיה בעלמא הוא. תא שמע, *דאמר רבי יוחנן: אהא בתענית עד שאבוא לביתי! התם לשמוטיה נפשיה מבי נשיאה הוא דעבד. אמר שמואל: כל תענית שלא קיבל עליו מבעוד יום — לאו שמיה תענית. ואי יתיב, מאי? אמר רבה בר שילא: דמי למפוחא דמליא זיקא. אימת מקביל ליה? רב אמר: במנחה. ושמואל אמר: בתפלת המנחה. אמר רב יוסף: כוותיה דשמואל מסתברא, דכתיב במגילת תענית: "להן, כל איניש דייתי עלוהי מקדמת דנא ייסר". מאי לאו ייסר עצמו בצלו? לא, יאסר עצמו. פליגי בהא רבי חייא ורבי שמעון ברבי: חד אמר: "ייסר", וחד אמר: "יאסר". (א) מ"ד "ייסר" — כדאמרינן. למאן דאמר: "יאסר", מאי היא? דתניא במגילת תענית: כל איניש דייתי עלוהי מקדמת דנא יאסר. כיצד? יחיד שקיבל עליו שני וחמישי (ושני) של כל השנה כולה, ואירעו בהם ימים טובים הכתובין במגילת תענית, אם נדרו קודם לגזרתנו — יבטיל נדרו את גזרתנו ואם גזרתנו קודמת לנדרו — תבטל גזרתנו את נדרו. תנו רבנן: *עד מתי אוכל ושותה — עד שיעלה עמוד השחר. דברי רבי. *רבי אליעזר בר שמעון אומר: עד קרות הגבר. אמר *אביי: לא שנו אלא שלא גמר סעודתו. אבל גמר סעודתו — אינו אוכל. איתיביה *רבא: גמר ועמד, הרי זה אוכל! התם כשלא סילק. איכא דאמרי אמר רבא: לא שנו אלא כשלא ישן — אבל ישן — אינו אוכל. איתיביה אביי: (ב) ישן ועמד, הרי זה אוכל! התם במתנמנם. *היכי דמי מתנמנם? אמר רב אשי:
נים

רש"י

הא דאמרת מתענין לשעות והוא שלא טעם כלום כל אותו היום. כלומר, לא אמרו במתענה שאכל בו ביום כגון שהתחיל להתענות עד חצי היום ואח"כ אכל — דאין זה עינוי. ואם אכל קודם חצות — אין בכך כלום, דאינו תענית של כלום, אלא כשהשלים כל היום, אע"פ שלא קיבלו עליו מאתמול. ופריך: אי דקבל עליו להתענות עד חצי יום, והדר מתענה כל היום — האי תעניתא מעלי' הוא, ופשיטא דתענית גמור הוא, ואפילו תפלת תענית נמי מתפלל עליו. ולא איצטריך לאוקומי הלכה בהכי, דזהו תענית גמור. והאי מקשה סבר, דהאי הלכה מתענין לשעות — כמשמעו, דיכול להתענות עד חצי היום — מתענה קרינא ביה: לא צריכנא דממליך אימלוכי. כלומר, לא היה בדעתו כלל להתענות, אלא אתא ליה טרדא ולא אכל עד חצי היום, וכי מטא חצי יום ממליך, אמר: הואיל והתעניתי עד חצי היום — אתענה כל היום: שלא שקעה עליו חמה. שלא התענה עד אותה שעה: אנשי משמר. כהנים ולוים העובדין מתענין, כדלקמן בפרק "סדר תעניות": ולא משלימין. לפי שהן עסוקין בעבודה, ואין יכולים להשלים. אלמא, אע"ג דאינו משלים — מתענה קרי ליה: לצעורי נפשייהו. עם הצבור, אבל אינו תענית לא להתפלל תפלת "עננו" ולא לקובעו עליו חובה כלל, וכל שעה שהוא רוצה לאכול — אוכל: מבני *(סנאב) בן בנימין. משבט בנימין: שיו"ט שלנו היה. כדלקמן: בשלשה פרקים (דף כו.) זמן עצי כהנים והעם כו', עד בחמשה באב בני פרעוש בן יהודה, בעשרה בו בני (*סנאב) בן בנימין. שעל ידי מעשה קבעו להן חכמים להתנדב עצים ולהביא למערכה, וכשמגיע זמנו מביאין אותן ומדליקין אותן על גבי המזבח, אע"פ שהיו שם שאר עצים הרבה. מפא"כ בשאר מתנדבי עצים, דאין מבערין אותן בזמן שיש עצים אחרים. במסכת מנחות (דף קו:) אמרינן: המתנדב עצים לא יפחות משני גזירין, ועצים טעונין קמיצה, טעונים הגשה כו': דאמר רבי יוחנן. פעמים שהיה אומר אהא בתענית עד שאבוא לביתי, ואי מטי לביתיה בשתים או בג' שעות ביום — הוה אכיל, וקרי ליה מתענה: לשמוטיה נפשיה מבי נשיאה. דלא ליטרחוהו למיכל בהדייהו, שהיה מבקש הימנו שיאכל עמו, היה אומר כן, שלא יטריחנו לאכול עמו. ומיהו לא הוי תענית, שאם היה רוצה — היה אוכל מיד, ואין בנדרו כלום: ואי יתיב מאי. מי סליק לתענית אי לא: למפוחא. הוא המפוח שנופחין בו הנפחין את האור, המתמלא ברוח, אף זה נתמלא רוח — שלא אכל בחנם: במנחה. בזמן המנחה. ואפילו בשוק אומר: הריני מחר בתענית: בתפלת המנחה. בסופה(ג), תוספת ריצוי ותחנונים, עד שאומר: הריני מחר בתענית. ודוקא נקט מנחה, משום דסמוך לתחלת יום תעניתו. לאפוקי תפלת יוצר. ודיקא נמי, מדפסיק שמואל ופליג אדרב דאמר בזמן המנחה, שיעורא יתירא: כדכתיב במגילת תענית. לסוף ימים טובים הכתובים במגילת תענית כתיב בה: מקדמת דנא ייסר. לעיל מיניה תני, אילין יומיא די לא להתענאה בהון, להן כל איניש דייתי עלוהי תענית מן קדמת דנא, לפני אלו ימים טובים. כגון שקיבל עליו עשרה תעניות או עשרים, ונכנסו אלו הימים בהם: ייסר בצלו. בתפלה. ואי לא קבליה עליה בתפלת המנחה — לא דחי להנך ימים טובים. אלמא: דעיקר תענית בעי לקבולי בתפלת המנחה עילויה, ואי לא קבליה עילויה בתפלת המנחה — לא עשה כלום: ייסר. לשון "ואסרה אסר" (במדבר ל): בצלו. צלותא. איכא דאמרי: לשון נדר, שקבל עליו להתענות, כמו "הרימותי ידי אל ה'" (בראשית יד) דמתרגמינן: ארימית ידי בצלו. ואין רבי מודה. האי דקתני "דכתיב" — משום דמגילת תענית היתה נכתבת לבד, לזכרון נסים: וחד אמר יאסר. דלא הוי תני ייסר(ד) בצלו, דמשמע דוקא כדאמרינן אי מקבל בתפלת המנחה — אין, ואי לא — לא. אלא יאסר, דמשמע: יהא אסור לאכול אי אתי עליה תענית מן קדמת דנא. בין בתפלה בין שלא בתפלה: מאי היא. מאי קסבר? ומשני: כדתניא, יחיד שקבל עליו תענית שני וחמישי של כל השנה כולה. כלומר, כדמפרש בהדיא אם נדרו קודם לגזרתנו כו' ולא שנא בין בתפלה בין שלא בתפלה: קודם גזרתנו. קודם שגזרו חכמים ימים טובים הללו. אבל משגזרו, אע"פ שהתחיל תעניותיו קודם הזמנים הללו — לא דחו: עד מתי אוכל ושותה. בלילה, כשמתענה למחר, בכל תעניות שהוא אוכל משתחשך, ואפילו בתענית יחיד קא מיירי: עד קרות הגבר. אפילו פעם ראשונה קאמר, מדקאמר גבי יולא יחידי בלילה בסדר יומא (דף כא.): עד שישלש: שלא גמר סעודתו. אבל גמר דברי הכל אינו אוכל: אבל ועמד. אע"פ שבירך ועמד משולחנו — חוזר ואוכל, ואין בכך כלום: שלא סילק. את הטבלא, דלאו עקירה היא, ולא אסח דעתיה מאכילה, וכסעודה אריכתא דמיא: איכא דאמרי אמר רבא כו'. והלכה כאיכא דאמרי: אוכל ושותה עד שיישן קבע, ועד שיעלה עמוד השחר, כרבי: אבל ישן. הפסקה היא, ושוב אינו אוכל: התם. לאו ישן ממש, אלא מתנמנם — סומליי"ר בלע"ז:
תיר

תוספות

כל תענית שלא שקעה עליו חמה לא שמיה תענית. פי' במסכת ע"ז פרק "אין מעמידין" (דף לד.). וכן בחלוק שאין לו אימרא, פירש התם. וכל הפסק דמתענין לשעות דכל תענית צריך לקבלו מבערב בתפלת המנחה ב"שומע תפלה", ואם הוא שבת — ב"אלהי נצור". וצריך שיאמר למחר אהיה בתענית יחיד, כי היכי דליכא למטעי בתענית צבור: **התם** לצעורי נפשיה בעלמא. ואע"ג דאמרינן (ר"ה דף יח:) משחרב בית המקדש בטלה מגילת תענית, והאי עובדא דרבי אליעזר בר צדוק היה לאחר חורבן, דאי קודם החורבן אמרינן: (שם) (ה) כיון שיש שלום — אין שם גזירות המלכות, האי תנא סבר דלא בטלה:
יאסר. פי': יאסר באל"ף הוי לשון אסור, שאסר עצמו. וייסר — הוי לשון הסרה, כלומר: יסור מן הנדר, (ו) יהיה מותר לאכול למחר, שיהיה יום טוב ואין להתענות:
ואם גזרתנו קודם לנדרו ידחה נדרו מפני גזרתנו. אומר רש"י: ידחה נדרו מכל וכל, ולא ישלים אותו תענית. והר"י מסופק בדבר. ויש להחמיר, דדוקא אותו יום לא יתענה, אבל ישלים אותו ליום(ז) מחר. וכן יש ליזהר שלא להתענות בראש חדש ובחנוכה ובפורים, דמאלו ודאי לא בטלה מגילת תענית:
ניס

מד א ב מיי' פ"א מהל' תענית הלכה יג סמג עשין ג טוש"ע א"ח סי' תקסב סעיף ז:
מה ג שם סעיף ח:
מו ד מיי' פ"ו מהלכות כלי מקדש הלכה ט:
מז ה מיי' פ"א מהלכות תענית הלכה י טור שו"ע שם סעיף ו:
מח ו מיי' שם וטוש"ע שם סעיף ו:
מט ז ח מיי' שם הלכה ח סמג עשין ג טוש"ע שם סי' תקסד סעיף א:

[עי' תוס' ע"ז לד. ד"ה מתענין ותוס' מנחות כ: ד"ה נפסל]
[ג"ל ברבי]
[ג"ל סנאה עי' תוס' עירובין מא. ד"ה מבני]
[תוספ' פ"א] פסחים ב ע"ש [עי' תוס' שבת קיח ד"ה לפי שאין]
ס"י רבא וכן הוא ברא"ש
ס"י אביי

לקמן טו:
עירובין מא.
[מכות כד.]
[ג"ל סנאה]
[ג"ל סנאה]
[גי' רא"ש ר' אלעזר אומר]
[פסחים קב: מגילה יח: יבמות נד. נדה סג.]

רבינו חננאל

אמר רב חסדא הא דאמרת מתענין לשעות ומתפלל תפלת תענית והוא שלא טעם כלום עד הערב ואע"ג דאמליך אמלוכי. רב חסדא לטעמיה דאמר כל תענית שלא שקעה עליו חמה לא שמיה תענית. ואותבינן עליה הא דתנן אנשי משמר מתענין ולא משלימין. והא דאמר ר' אלעזר בר צדוק והתענו בו ולא השלמנוהו הנה תעניותם תענית אף על פי שלא שקעה עליו חמה. ומשני התם אינה תענית אלא רצו להצטער גם הם בצער צבור. ולא משום דתורת דין תענית עליהם ור' יוחנן לא הוה מסכים תענית בלבו ולא היה אומר אלא להשתמט מבי נשיאה שלא היה רוצה לסעוד אצלם: אמר שמואל כל תענית שלא קבלה מבע"י אינה תענית אימת מקבל לה רב אמר במנחה משעה *) שיסכן לתפלת המנחה. ואפי' מתעסק במלאכתו אומר מחר אהיה בתענית. יהי רצון שתהא תפלתי ביום תעניתי מקובלת. ושמואל אמר בתפלת המנחה כלומר צריך להיות כולל אלו הדברים בשומע תפלה וגו'. אמר רב יוסף כשמואל מסתברא דכתיב במגלת תענית להן כל איניש דייתי עלייהו מן קדמת דנא יאסר. מאי יאסר עצמו בצלו מקודם שיקבל עליו בתפלתו תענית שנמצא אוסר עצמו באכילה ובשתיה בקבלתו תענית בתפלתו: פליגו בה ר' חייא ור' שמעון בר' חד תני ייסר וחד תני יאסר. מאן דתני ייסר כלומר ייסר עצמו בצלו בתפלת המנחה ואיסור אוסר על עצמו בתפלתו. ומאן דתני יאסר כדתניא להן כל אינש דייתי עלוהי [מקדמת דנא] יאסר. כיצד יחיד שקיבל עליו תענית ב' וה' (וב') של כל השנה ואירעו בהן י"ט הכתובים במגלת תענית כגון שמונת ימים שמראש חדש ניסן וכיוצא בהן דלא להתענאה בהן. אם נדרו קודם לגזרתנו ידחה נדרו את גזרתנו כו'. פי' כל איניש דייתי עלייהו נדר תענית מקדמת גזרה דנא להיות היום י"ט ושיהיה אסור בתענית יאסר באכילה ובשתייה ומקיים נדרו. הגיע ר"ח כסלו ולא ירדו גשמים ב"ד גוזרין ג' תעניות על הצבור אוכלין ושותין משחשכה ומותרין במלאכה כו': ת"ר עד מתי אוכלין ושותין עד שיעלה עמוד השחר דברי רבי ר"ש בן אלעזר אומר עד קרות הגבר. אמר רבה לא שנו עד שיעלה עמוד השחר אלא אם לא ישן
שנת

*) שיתכוין כצ"ל וכ"ה בערוך.

הגהות הב"ח

(א) גמ' וחד אמר יאסר בשלמא מ"ד ייסר כדאמרינן אלא למאן דאמר יאסר מאי היא כדתני' במגילת תענית: (ב) שם איתיביה אביי אכל ועמד הרי זה אוכל: (ג) רש"י ד"ה בתפלת המנחה בסופה אומר תוספת ריצוי: (ד) ד"ה וחד אמר יאסר דלא הוה תני ייסר דמשמע בצלו דוקא: (ה) תום' ד"ה התם כו' קודם החורבן אמרינן בזמן שיש שלום אין שם נוס האי תנא סבר: (ו) ד"ה יאסר כו' ויהיה מותר: (ז) ד"ה ואם כו' אבל ישלים אותו ליום אחר וכן יש ליזהר:

רבינו גרשום

נקיים מה' ומישראל. דקא מימלך מימלוכי. שקיבל עליו תענית בשחרית עד הצהרים ובצהרים קבל עליו להתענות עד לאורתא. שלא שקעה עליו חמה כלומר שלא התענה כל היום עד לאורתא: לצעורי נפשייהו מיכוונו אבל תענית לא מיקרו אלא א"כ משלים כל היום: מפני שיו"ט שלהם היה. שמביאין בו עצים למערכה: התם לצעורי נפשייהו בעלמא מיכוונו ולא לתענית שהרי יו"ט שלהן היה: עד שאבא לביתי אלמא דאין משלימין: התם לשמוטיה נפשיה מבי נשיאה שהיה מבקש ממנו שיאכל עמו היה אומר כן כדי שלא יטריחו לאכול עמו: במנחה. בט' שעות ומחצה: כל איניש דאתי עליהון שקיבל עליו תענית. מקדמת דנא קודם שהגיעו אותן ימים שאמרו חכמים במגילת תענית שלא להתענות בהן ואירע התענית באותן ימים: מאי לאו ייסר עצמו בצלו. כלומר שייסר עצמו בתענית ממה שקבל עליו בתפלת המנחה. מאן דאמר ייסר כדאמרן דאפי' קיבל עליו התענית לאחר שנתקנו אותן ימים טובים שלא להתענות בהן אלא שקיבל עליו קודם שהגיעו שייך נפשיה בתענית ממה שקיבל עליו תענית בתפלת המנחה: אם נדרו קודמת לגזירתנו אם קיבל עליו תענית קודם שתיקנו חכמים אותן ימים טובים: תדחה גזירתנו מפני נדרו דאסור באכילה הואיל שקיבל עליו בתפלת המנחה: אם גזירתנו קודמת לנדרו שתיקנו אותן ימים טובים קודם שקיבל זה עליו אלו תעניות תדחה נדרו מפני גזירתנו שאינו מתענה מפני אילו ימים טובים. ועוד הורה ששמע משום אב ב"ד שבירוני' אם נדרו קודמת לגזירתנו קודם שקבעו ב"ד את החדש שבו אלו ימים טובים היינו גזירתנו קיבועה חדש תדחה גזירתנו מפני נדרו דהואיל כשקיבל עליו תענית לא ידע באיזה יום יארע ימים טובים אלו אבל קדם גזירתנו לנדרו שקבעו ב"ד את החדש קודם זה שקיבל עליו תענית וכשקיבל כבר ידע באיזה יום יארע ימים טובים אלו ואעפ"כ קבל לפיכך ידחה נדרו דאינו מתענה באילו ימים טובים
עד

גמרא

תורה אור

*נים ולא נים; תיר ולא תיר, דקרו ליה וְעָנֵי. ולא ידע אהדורי סברא, וכי מדכרי ליה — מדכר. אמר רב כהנא אמר רב: יחיד שקיבל עליו תענית — אסור בנעילת הסנדל. חיישינן שמא תענית צבור קיבל עליו. היכי ליעבד? אמר רבה בר רב שילא: לימא הכי: [א]למחר אהא לפניך בתענית יחיד. אמרו ליה רבנן לרב ששת: הא קא חזינן רבנן דמסיימי מסנייהו ואתו לבי תעניתא! איקפד ואמר להו: דלמא מיכל נמי אכול. אביי ורבא מעיילי כי מסיימי אפנתא. מרימר ומר זוטרא מחלפי דימינא לשמאלא, ודשמאלא לימינא. רבנן דבי רב אשי נפקי כי אורחייהו. סברי כי הא דאמר שמואל: *אין תענית צבור בבבל אלא תשעה באב *בלבד. אמר רב יהודה אמר רב: [ב]לוה אדם תעניתו ופורע. כי אמריתה קמיה דשמואל, אמר לי: וכי נדר קבל עליה א] דלא סגי דלא משלם? לצעורי נפשיה קביל עליה. אי מצי — מצער נפשיה, אי לא מצי — לא מצער נפשיה. איכא דאמרי, אמר רב יהודה אמר רב: לוה אדם תעניתו ופורע. כי אמריתה קמיה דשמואל, אמר לי: פשיטא, לא יהא אלא נדר! נדר מי לא מצי בעי לשלומי ומיזל למחר וליומא אחרינא? *רב יהושע בריה דרב אידי איקלע לבי רב אסי, עבדו ליה עגלא תילתא. אמרו ליה: ליטעום מר מידי! א"ל: בתעניתא יתיבנא. אמרו ליה: ולוזיף מר וליפרע. לא סבר מר להא דאמר רב יהודה אמר רב: לוה אדם תעניתו ופורע? אמר להו: תענית חלום הוא. ואמר רבה בר מחסיא אמר רב חמא בר גוריא אמר רב: [ג]יפה תענית לחלום כאש לנעורת. (*אמר) רב חסדא: [ד]ובו ביום. ואמר רב יוסף: [ה]ואפילו בשבת. *מאי תקנתיה? [ו]ליתיב תעניתא לתעניתא.§

מתני' [ז]עברו אלו ולא נענו — בית דין גוזרין ג' תעניות אחרות על הצבור. *אוכלין ושותין מבעוד יום, ואסורין במלאכה, וברחיצה, ובסיכה, ובנעילת הסנדל, ובתשמיש המטה, ונועלין את המרחצאות. [ח]עברו אלו ולא נענו — ב"ד גוזרין עליהן עוד שבע, שהן י"ג תעניות על הצבור. *הרי אלו יתרות על הראשונות, שבאלו מתריעין, ונועלין את החנויות. *)בשני מטין עם חשיכה, ובחמישי מותרין מפני כבוד השבת. *[ט]עברו אלו ולא נענו — ממעטין במשא ומתן, בבנין ובנטיעה, באירוסין ובנישואין, *ובשאילת שלום בין אדם לחבירו, כבני אדם הנזופין למקום. היחידים חוזרין ומתענין עד שיצא ניסן. *יצא ניסן וירדו גשמים — סימן קללה, שנא' °"הלא קציר חטים היום" וגו'.§

גמ' בשלמא כולהו — אית בהו תענוג: רחיצה, וסיכה, ותשמיש המטה. אבל מלאכה — צער הוא! אמר רב חסדא אמר רב ירמיה בר אבא: אמר קרא °"קדשו צום, קראו עצרה, אספו זקנים" — כעצרת. מה עצרת אסור בעשיית מלאכה — אף תענית אסור בעשיית מלאכה. אי מה עצרת מאורתא — אף תענית נמי מאורתא! אמר רבי זירא: לדידי מיפרשא לי מיניה דר' ירמיה בר אבא: אמר קרא: "אספו זקנים". דומיא דאסיפת זקנים. מה אסיפת זקנים ביום — אף צום נמי ביום. ואימא: *מטיהרא! אמר רב ששא בריה דרב אידי: מסייע ליה לרב הונא, דאמר **)מצפרא כינופיא. היכי עבדי? אמר אביי: מצפרא עד פלגא דיומא מעיינינן במילי דמתא. מכאן ואילך, ריבעא דיומא קרינן בספרא ואפטרתא. מכאן ואילך, בעינן רחמי, שנא' °"ויקומו על עמדם, ויקראו בספר תורת ה' אלהיהם רביעית היום, ורביעית מתודים, ומשתחוים לה' אלהיהם".

*) [פרש"י על זה לקמן דף יד:]

רש"י

תיר. ער, כדמתרגמינן (בראשית מא) ויקץ — ואיתער: אהדורי סברא. אם צריך ממנו דבר שצריך הרהור — אינו יודע לומר בעוד שמתנמנם: וכי מדכרו ליה מדכר. כזה שמעת — מדכר: יחיד שקבל עליו תענית. סתם, ואינו יודע איזה תענית קבל עליו, אם של(א) יחיד אם של צבור: ואסור בנעילת כו'. שמא תענית צבור, כג' *ראשונות או כז' אחרונות, קיבל עליו: קאתו רבנן לתעניתא כו'. בתענית צבור. וסברי לה כשמואל, דאמר: אין תענית צבור בבבל, בפרק "מקום שנהגו" (פסחים דף נד:)(ב), דאסור בנעילת הסנדל ובכל הני: איקפד רב ששת דלמא מיכל נמי אכלי. ופורשים מדרכי צבור, ולית ליה דשמואל. ואנן הא ידנא נהגינן כשמואל: אפנתא. אישקריפי"ט: מחלפי. ביומא דתעניתא: לצעורי בעלמא. אי מצי מצער נפשיה, ואי לא(ג) — לא יהא אלא (*ליומא) אחרינא: ואפילו בשבת. יכול להתענות, כדי שיתבטל צער גופו: "קדשו צום קראו עצרה אספו זקנים. כל יושבי הארץ בית ה' אלהיכם וזעקו אל ה'": מה עצרת. שבועות ושמיני עצרת: אי מה עצרת. איסור מלאכתו מאורתא: דומיא דאסיפת זקנים ביום. דבלילה כל אחד בביתו, ואינן נאספין: מסייע ליה לרב הונא. הא דפשיטא לך דאסיפת זקנים ביום: דאמר מצפרא כינופיא. ביום תענית צבור מתקבלין ובאין לבית הכנסת מן הבקר: מעיינין במילי דמתא. דרישה וחקירה, לבדוק במעשיהם בעסקי בני העיר, אם גזל וחמס ביניהן, ומפייסין אותן:(ד) היכי עבדי. מאי עבדי בכינופיא דמצפרא ובכוליה יומא דתעניתא: ריבעא דיומא. מחלות ואילך עושין ב' חלקים: בפלגא. דהיינו ריבעא דיומא, קרו "ויחל משה" ומפטירין "דרשו את ה' בהמצאו":

תוספות

נים ולא נים תיר ולא תיר. *אומר רבי: *נים ולא נים — בתוך השינה, כשיעור משנתו, תיר ולא תיר — בתחילת השינה. *אך לא נראה(ה) ב"ערבי פסחים" (דף קכ:) דקאמר: נתנמנמו — יאכלו, נרדמו — לא יאכלו. ואמר רב אשי: ה"ד נתנמנמו? נים ולא נים וכו', והתם מיירי בתחילת השינה, בין נים ולא נים בין תיר ולא תיר. *לכנ"ל כפירוש רש"י. דאי הוה אמר נים ולא נים — הוה אמינא דתיר הוי טפי מניס, ואי הוה אמר תיר ולא תיר — ה"א דניס הוי טפי מתיר, הלכך איצטריך תרווייהו. וכולהו בתחילת השינה, כדמפרש התם(ו). ובירושלמי מפורש גבי הך ברייתא: עד כמה אוכל ושותה — עד קרות הגבר. וה"ה עד שיעלה עמוד השחר. ובד"א — שהתנה, אבל לא התנה וישן — אינו יכול לאכול:

אביי ורבא סיימי אפנתא. פירוש: במנעל שאין (ו) סוליים, שול"א בלע"ז: **דאי** מצי מצער נפשיה עביד אי לא מצי מצער נפשיה לא עביד. ומשום הכי קאמר שמואל דלוה תעניתו ופורע — דוקא היכי דלא מצי מצער נפשיה, אבל היכי דמצי מצער נפשיה — לא מצי ללוות תעניתו. והכי מסקנא: אם אמר הריני בתענית למחר — צריך לצעוריה נפשיה, ואינו יכול ללוות ופורע בחנם, ואפילו אכל בשוגג — ישלים אותו. והר"י מסופק בדבר אם יכול ללוותו ולפרוע היכי דקביל עליה כבר להתענות, והתענה עד חצי היום או רביע יום, ואפילו לא מצי לצעורי נפשיה. אבל לא התענה — ודאי דיכול ללוות אחר בשבילו. או אם טעה ואכל בשוגג — יאכל וישלים יום אחר. ואם התענה בשבת, כגון תענית חלום, דצריך לפרוע, כדאמר ובלבד דיתיב תעניתא לתעניתא, אם אירע שיהיה ר"ח אותו יום — אז ידחה לתעניתו עד יום אחר בשבוע, וכן נראה למ"ר שי':

מה אסיפת זקנים ביום אף צום ביום. אבל בלילה לא. תימה: אמאי אוכלים ושותים מבעוד יום? כל הלילה נמי היו יכולין לאכול ולשתות, מה אסיפת זקנים ביום — אף צום ביום, אבל בלילה — לא! ויש לומר: דלא יליף צום מאסיפה אלא לענין עשיית מלאכה, דדוקא מלאכה גמרינן מאסיפה, דהא לא כתיב בקרא אלא "אספו זקנים וקדשו צום", אבל אכילה — לא כתיב בקרא:

רבינו חננאל

שנת תרדמה אלא נים ולא נים כגון זה אע"פ שמתנמנם אוכל. (אלא) [אבל] אם ישן שנת קבע ונרדם (לא היא אלא ישן) לגמרי אינו אוכל: **ירושלמי** ישן ועמד אסור לא שנו אלא שלא התנה אבל התנה מותר. קי"ל דלגבי תענית דאכיל בלילה ומפסיק. אם גמר וסלק לא יאכל. אבל אם לא סילק ודעתו עוד ליכל אע"פ שישן עומד ואוכל. אבל בתעני' שפוסק בו מבע"י אע"פ שפוסק חוזר ואוכל עד שיבא השמש כי הא דאיתא באגדת איכה. ר' יהודה בן בתירה אזל לנציבין בערובת צומא רבה אתא ריש כנשתא לזמוניה. א"ל כבר אכלי ופסקי לי. א"ל אשגח עלי דלא לימא ההוא ר' לא אשגח עליו אזל עמיה ובסיפא אמרין אכל מן כל עיגול חד פתית ואכל מן כל תבשיל חד פת ושתה מן כל (כום וכום) (חבית וחבית] חד כום. ש"מ דאע"ג דפסק אכיל. ולענין מישתו מיא היכא דאית ליה למיכל. אית ליה למשתי כו'. וכן כתב ופירש רבינו הגאון זצ"ל*). אמר רב יחיד שקבל עליו תענית אמר רבה בר רב שילא לימא הכי מחר אהא בתענית יחיד דאי לא חיישינן שמא תענית צבור קביל עליה ואסור בנעילת הסנדל כו'. ואסיקנא רבנן דבי רב אשי באלו התעניות השנויות במשנתנו הוו מסיימי. מסאנייהו כי אורחייהו ואתו לבי תענית. סברי לה כשמואל דאמר אין תענית צבור בבבל אלא ט' באב בלבד. וכך הלכה: אמר רב יהודה אמר רב לווה אדם תעניתו ופורע. פי' היכא דאיכא צערא או אונס וכיוצא בו. לווה תעניתו ופורע דאמרי לא יהא אלא נדר מי לא פרע למחר וליום אחרא כ"ש תענית. ושמעינן הא סברא מדברי שמואל דאמר צערא קבל עליה אי מצי מצער נפשיה כו'. מכלל דרב במצטער הוא דאמר: יפה תענית לחלום כאש בנעורת ובו ביום אפילו בשבת. וכן הלכתא. ויתיב תעניתא לתעניתא ומפורש בשבת בפ' א': [מתני'] עברו אלו ולא נענו ב"ד גוזרין ג' תעניות כו'. ואקשינן בשלמא רחיצה וסיכה ונעילת הסנדל וכיוצא בהן משום תענוג אלא מלאכה אמאי צערא הוא ומשנינן אמר קרא קדשו צום קראו עצרה. פי' קראו עצרה לקידוש (היום) [הצום]. מה עצרת אסור במלאכה אף צום אסור במלאכה. ומאימתי איסורו משעת אסיפת זקנים ואימתי אסיפת זקנים ביום. שנאמר תקעו שופר בציון הריעו בהר קדשי ירגזו כל יושבי ארץ כי בא יום ה'. אמר רב כהנא כינופיא מצפרא. היכי עבדינן. אמר אביי מצפרא עד פלגיה יומא מעיינינן ולפניא ריבעא דיומא. קרינן בספרא ובאפטרתא. ורבעא בתרא

*) עי' ברא"ש כאן שהביא כל דברי רבינו בכאן וכתב ראיה לדבריו ע"ש.

עין משפט נר מצוה

[עמ"ש הטו"ז א"ח סי' תרל"ט ס"ק ח הגיה הכא קנת בהלכות]

נ א מיי' פ"א מהלכות תענית הלכה י טוש"ע א"ח סי' תקסח סעיף ג:

[ועי' תוס' נדה סג: ד"ה נים]

נא ב מיי' פ"ד מהלכות נדרים הלכה טז סמג עשין רמב טוש"ע שם סעיף ב:

נב ג מיי' פ"א מהלכות תענית הלכה יב סמג עשין מד"ס ג טור וש"ע שם סי' רכ סעיף ג:

נג ד מיי' שם טוש"ע שם סי' תקסח סעיף ב:

נד ה ו מיי' וסמג שם טוש"ע שם סי' רפח סעיף ד:

נה ז מיי' פ"ג מהלכות תענית הלכה ג והלכה ד טוש"ע א"ח סי' תקעה סעיף ג:

נו ח מיי' שם הלכה ה טוש"ע שם סעיף ד:

נז ט מיי' שם הלכה ח וטוש"ע שם סעיף ז:

נח י טוש"ע א"ח סי' תקעו סעיף טז:

מסורת הש"ס

[נ"ל חמנעלות] פסחים קב: מגילה יח: יבמות נד. נדה סג.

[נ"ל כיומא אם לא דמלת אלא היא כטעות]

לעיל יא: פסחים נד: ע"ש

[גיר' הרא"ש בסו' יט אלא ט"ב וכו"ב]

שבת יא. ע"ש

[נ"ל ואמר]

[ברכות לא:]

פסחים נד:

[לקמן יד. וכס איתא מה אלו יש הוא גיר' ירושלמי]

מגילה ה: [וע' תוס' שם]

[מועד קטן טו.]

[לעיל ב:]

שמואל א יב

יואל א

[תרגום של ממעט בלורביס בטיהרה לדבריס כה כלו]

**) מגילה ל:

נחמיה ט

רבינו גרשום

עד מתי אוכל והולך. מי שיש לו להתענות למחר: שלא סילק השלחן: היכי עביד כשקיבל עליו שיהא למחר מותר בנעילת הסנדל דאמר למחר הריני בתענית יחיד: דילמא מיכל נמי אכיל כלומר כי היכי דסיימי סנדל ה"נ יכולין לאכול: סיימי אפנתא שנועלין עליונו של סנדל העור שעל הרגל אבל העץ שתחת הרגל לא היו מניחין. סברי לה כשמואל דאמר אין תענית צבור בבבל לפיכך אין אסורין בנעילת הסנדל שהן י"ג

גליון הש"ס

תום' ד"ה נים וכו' אומר רבי נים ולא נים בתוך השינה. בתחלת השינה. תיר ולא תיר בסוף השינה כצ"ל: **בא"ד** אך לא נראה בע"פ. כאן ובע"פ כצ"ל ע"ז א"ח סי' תרל ס"ק ח:

הגהות הב"ח

(א) רש"י ד"ה יחיד כו' אם של צבור אסור כו' הס"ד ואח"כ מה"ד שמא ת"צ בשלש אחרונות או בשבע כו': (ב) ד"ה קאתו כו' בפ' מקום שנהגו דליאסר בנעילת הסנדל: (ג) ד"ה לצעורי כו' ואי לא מצי לא מצער נפשיה הס"ד ואח"כ מה"ד לא יהא אלא נדר וכי אינו משלם את נדרו ליומא אחרינא: (ד) ד"ה היכי עבדי נ"ל קודם ד"ה מעיינין: (ה) תום' ד"ה נים כו'. אך לא נראה הכי בערבי פסחים: (ו) בא"ד ובירושלמי מפורש גבי הך ברייתא. נ"ב פי' דתני בה ישן ועמד ה"ז אוכל: (ז) ד"ה אביי כו' שאין לו סוליים שול"א:

הגהות מהר"ב רנשבורג א] גמ' דלא סגי דלא משלם. עי' ר"ן וריטב"א ומשמע דלא הוי זה בגירסתם וכן בפסיקתות אתי שפיר פרש"י ותוס' וא"ל למ"ש בעל אהבת עולם ושער המלך:

אֵיפוּךְ אֲנָא! לָא סָלְקָא דַּעְתָּךְ, דִּכְתִיב °"וְאֵלַי יֵאָסְפוּ כֹּל חָרֵד בְּדִבְרֵי אֱלֹהֵי יִשְׂרָאֵל עַל מַעַל הַגּוֹלָה" וגו'. וּכְתִיב °"וּבְמִנְחַת הָעֶרֶב קַמְתִּי מִתַּעֲנִיתִי... וָאֶפְרְשָׂה כַפַּי אֶל ה'". אָמַר רַפְרָם בַּר פַּפָּא אָמַר רַב חִסְדָּא: כָּל שֶׁהוּא מִשּׁוּם אֵבֶל, (א) כְּגוֹן [א]תִּשְׁעָה בְּאָב [ב]וְאָבֵל — אָסוּר בֵּין בְּחַמִּין בֵּין בְּצוֹנֵן. [ג]כָּל שֶׁהוּא מִשּׁוּם תַּעֲנוּג, כְּגוֹן תַּעֲנִית צִבּוּר, בְּחַמִּין — אָסוּר, בְּצוֹנֵן — מוּתָּר. אֲמַר רַב אִידִי בַּר אָבִין: אַף אֲנַן נַמִּי תָּנֵינָא: וְנוֹעֲלִין אֶת הַמֶּרְחֲצָאוֹת. א"ל אַבַּיֵי: וְאִי בְּצוֹנֵן אָסוּר, "סוֹכְרִין אֶת הַנְּהָרוֹת" מִבָּעֵי לֵיהּ לְמִיתְנֵי? אֲמַר רַב שֵׁישָׁא בְּרֵיהּ דְּרַב אִידִי: אַבָּא הָכִי קַשְׁיָא לֵיהּ: מִכְּדִי תְּנַן אָסוּר בִּרְחִיצָה, נוֹעֲלִין אֶת הַמֶּרְחֲצָאוֹת לָמָּה לִי? אֶלָּא לָאו ש"מ: בְּחַמִּין — אָסוּר, בְּצוֹנֵן — מוּתָּר? לֵימָא מְסַיַּיע לֵיהּ: *[ד]כָּל חַיָּיבֵי טְבִילוֹת טוֹבְלִין כְּדַרְכָּן, בֵּין בְּט' בְּאָב בֵּין בְּיוה"כ. בְּמַאי? אִילֵימָא בְּחַמִּין, *טְבִילָה בְּחַמִּין מִי אִיכָּא? [א] שְׁאוּבִין נִינְהוּ! אֶלָּא לָאו — בְּצוֹנֵן, וְחַיָּיבֵי טְבִילוֹת — אִין, אִינִישׁ אַחֲרִינָא — לָא? אֲמַר רַב חָנָא בַּר קְטִינָא: לֹא נִצְרְכָה אֶלָּא לְחַמֵּי טְבֶרְיָא. אִי הָכִי, אֵימָא סֵיפָא: א"ר חֲנִינָא סְגַן הַכֹּהֲנִים: כְּדַי הוּא בֵּית אֱלֹהֵינוּ לְאַבֵּד עָלָיו טְבִילָה פַּעַם אַחַת בַּשָּׁנָה. וְאִי אָמְרַתְּ בְּצוֹנֵן מוּתָּר — יִרְחַץ בְּצוֹנֵן! אָמַר רַב פַּפָּא: בְּאַתְרָא דְּלָא שְׁכִיחַ צוֹנֵן. תָּא שְׁמַע: *[ה]כְּשֶׁאָמְרוּ אָסוּר בִּמְלָאכָה — לֹא אָמְרוּ אֶלָּא בַּיּוֹם, אֲבָל בַּלַּיְלָה — מוּתָּר. *[ו]וּכְשֶׁאָמְרוּ אָסוּר בִּנְעִילַת הַסַּנְדָּל, לֹא אָמְרוּ אֶלָּא בָּעִיר, אֲבָל בַּדֶּרֶךְ — מוּתָּר. הָא כֵּיצַד? יוֹצֵא לַדֶּרֶךְ — נוֹעֵל, נִכְנָס לָעִיר — חוֹלֵץ. *[ז]וּכְשֶׁאָמְרוּ אָסוּר בִּרְחִיצָה — לֹא אָמְרוּ אֶלָּא כָּל גּוּפוֹ, אֲבָל פָּנָיו, יָדָיו, וְרַגְלָיו מוּתָּר. וְכֵן אַתָּה מוֹצֵא בִּמְנוּדֶּה וּבְאָבֵל. מַאי לָאו — אַכּוּלְּהוּ? וּבְמַאי (ב) עָסְקִינַן? אִילֵימָא בְּחַמִּין, — פָּנָיו, יָדָיו, וְרַגְלָיו מִי שָׁרוּ? וְהָאָמַר רַב שֵׁשֶׁת: [ח]אָבֵל אָסוּר לְהוֹשִׁיט אֶצְבָּעוֹ בְּחַמִּין. אֶלָּא לָאו בְּצוֹנֵן? לָא, לְעוֹלָם בְּחַמִּין. וּדְקָא קַשְׁיָא לָךְ, "וְכֵן אַתָּה מוֹצֵא בִּמְנוּדֶּה וּבְאָבֵל" — אַשְּׁאָרָא קָאֵי. תָּא שְׁמַע, דְּאָמַר ר' אַבָּא הַכֹּהֵן מִשּׁוּם ר' יוֹסֵי הַכֹּהֵן: מַעֲשֶׂה וּמֵתוּ בָּנָיו שֶׁל ר' יוֹסֵי בֶּן רַבִּי חֲנִינָא, וְרָחַץ בְּצוֹנֵן כָּל שִׁבְעָה! הָתָם כְּשֶׁתְּכָפוּהוּ אֲבָלָיו הֲוָה. דְּתַנְיָא: *[ט]תְּכָפוּהוּ אֲבָלָיו זֶה אַחַר זֶה, הִכְבִּיד שְׂעָרוֹ — מֵיקֵל בְּתַעַר, [י]וּמְכַבֵּס כְּסוּתוֹ בְּמַיִם. אָמַר רַב חִסְדָּא: [כ]בְּתַעַר — אֲבָל לֹא בְּמִסְפָּרַיִם. [ל]בְּמַיִם — וְלֹא בְּנֶתֶר וְלֹא בְחוֹל. אָמַר רָבָא: אֲבָל מוּתָּר לִרְחוֹץ בְּצוֹנֵן כָּל שִׁבְעָה, מִידֵי דַּהֲוָה אַבִּשְׂרָא וְחַמְרָא. מֵיתִיבֵי: אֵין

אֵיפוּךְ אֲנָא. דְּפַלְגָא דְיוֹמָא קַמָּא הָווּ קָרוּ וּמַפְטְרִי וּבָעוּ רַחֲמֵי, וּבְאִידָךְ פַּלְגָא מְעַיְּינֵי: עַל מַעַל הַגּוֹלָה. "וַאֲנִי יוֹשֵׁב מְשׁוֹמֵם עַד מִנְחַת הָעֶרֶב וּבְמִנְחַת הָעֶרֶב קַמְתִּי מִתַּעֲנִיתִי וּבְקָרְעִי בִגְדִי וּמְעִילִי וָאֶכְרְעָה עַל בִּרְכַּי וָאֶפְרְשָׂה כַפַּי אֶל ה' אֱלֹהָי": וּבְמִנְחַת הָעֶרֶב קַמְתִּי. אַלְמָא בְּאִידָךְ פַּלְגָא בָּעוּ רַחֲמֵי עַד פַּנְיָא, מִכְּלָל דְּפַלְגָא קַמָּא – מְעַיְּינֵי בְּמִילֵּי דְמָתָא: בִּנְחֶמְיָה בֶּן חֲכַלְיָה כְּתִיב בְּעֶזְרָא וְאֵלַי יֵאָסְפוּ. לִי הָיוּ מִתְאַסְּפִין וּבָאִין טוֹבִים שֶׁבָּהֶן, לְהַגִּיד לְפָנַי עַל מַעַל וְחֵטְא הַגּוֹלָה, לְהַפְרִישָׁם: מְשׁוֹמֵם. אישתורדי"ן בְּלַעַ"ז. עַל מַעֲלָם שֶׁמִּתְוַודִּין עַד מִנְחַת הָעֶרֶב מֵחֲצוֹת וְאֵילָךְ, שֶׁהַצֵּל נוֹטֶה, כִּדְאָמְרִינַן בְּמַסֶּ' יוֹמָא (דף כח:): צְלוֹתֵיהּ דְּאַבְרָהָם מִכִּי מַשְׁחֲרֵי כּוֹתְלֵי: קַמְתִּי מִתַּעֲנִיתִי. לֹא שֶׁמִּתְעַנֶּה עַד הַמִּנְחָה וְאַחַ"כ אוֹכֵל, אֶלָּא כְּלוֹמַר מְצַעֵר נַפְשֵׁיהּ. "וּבְקָרְעִי" – וְאִם שֶׁאֲנִי קוֹרֵעַ בְּגָדַי וּמְעִילִי הָיִיתִי מִתְפַּלֵּל, כְּדֵי שֶׁאֶתְרַצֶּה: כָּל שֶׁהוּא מִשּׁוּם אֵבֶל. כָּל תַּעֲנִית שֶׁאָסְרוּ חֲכָמִים רְחִיצָה מִשּׁוּם אֵבֶל, כְּגוֹן ט' בְּאָב שֶׁהוּא מִשּׁוּם אֲבֵילוּת חוּרְבָּן, וְכָל שֶׁכֵּן אָבֵל מַמָּשׁ שֶׁמֵּתוֹ לְפָנָיו, דְּאִית לֵיהּ צַעֲרָא טוּבָא – אָסוּר בֵּין בְּחַמִּין וכו': מִשּׁוּם תַּעֲנוּג. שֶׁמְּצַטַּעֲרִין, וְאוֹסְרִין עַצְמָן בְּתַעֲנוּג: ה"ג: אָמַר רַב אִידִי בַּר אָבִין אַף אֲנַן נַמִּי תָּנֵינָא וְנוֹעֲלִין אֶת הַמֶּרְחֲצָאוֹת וְא"ל אַבַּיֵי: וְאִי בְּצוֹנֵן אָסוּר, סוֹכְרִין אֶת הַנְּהָרוֹת מִיבָּעֵי לֵיהּ לְמִיתְנֵי. בִּתְמִיָּה. אַף אֲנַן נַמִּי תָּנֵינָא בְּמַתְנִיתִ', דְּקָתָנֵי גַּבֵּי תַּעֲנִית צִבּוּר: וְנוֹעֲלִין אֶת הַמֶּרְחֲצָאוֹת – דְּהַיְינוּ חַמִּין, אֲבָל צוֹנֵן מוּתָּר. אָמַר לֵיהּ אַבַּיֵי: כְּלוֹמַר, וְאִי הֲוָה סְבִירָא לֵיהּ לְתַנָּא דִּידַן דִּבְצוֹנֵן אָסוּר – הֵיכִי הֲוָה בָּעֵי לְמִיתְנֵי סוֹכְרִין אֶת הַנְּהָרוֹת? הֵיכִי מָצֵי לְמִיסְכְּרִינְהוּ? אַבָּא. רַב אִידִי, הָכִי קָא קַשְׁיָא לֵיהּ בְּמַתְנִיתִין, דְּקָאָמַר שְׁמַע מִינָּהּ דְּלָא אָסַר אֶלָּא חַמִּין. מִכְּדִי קָתָנֵי מַתְנִי' אֲסוּרִין בִּרְחִיצָה, וּסְתָם רְחִיצָה בֵּין חַמִּין בֵּין צוֹנֵן – לָמָּה לִי תּוּ לְמִיהְדַר וּמִיתְנָא וְנוֹעֲלִין? אֶלָּא לְמֵימְרָא דְּדַוְקָא חַמִּין וכו': לֵימָא מְסַיַּיע לֵיהּ. לְרַב חִסְדָּא, דְּאָמַר כָּל שֶׁהוּא מִשּׁוּם אֵבֶל – אָסוּר אֲפִילּוּ בְּצוֹנֵן: כָּל חַיָּיבֵי טְבִילוֹת. נִדָּה וְיוֹלֶדֶת טוֹבְלִים כְּדַרְכָּן: טְבִילָה בְּחַמִּין מִי אִיכָּא. חַמֵּי הָאוּר, הָא שְׁאוּבִין נִינְהוּ: אֶלָּא לָאו בְּצוֹנֵן. וְחַיָּיבֵי טְבִילוֹת – אִין מִשּׁוּם דִּטְבִילָה בִּזְמַנָּהּ מִצְוָה, שֶׁמְּמַהֵר לְטַהֵר עַצְמוֹ: ה"ג: כּוּלֵּי עָלְמָא לֹא (ג) בְּחַמִּין וְלֹא בְּצוֹנֵן: לֹא נִצְרְכָה אֶלָּא לְחַמֵּי טְבֶרְיָא. וְהִלְכָּךְ: חַיָּיבֵי טְבִילוֹת – אִין, כּוּלֵּי עָלְמָא – לָא. אֲבָל בְּצוֹנֵן שָׁרוּ: כְּדַי. רָאוּי הוּא בֵּית אֱלֹהֵינוּ כו': וְאִם אִיתָא. כִּדְמוֹקְמַתְּ לָהּ דִּבְצוֹנֵן שָׁרֵי, מַאי קָא מְהַדַּר לֵיהּ רַבִּי חֲנִינָא לְתַנָּא קַמָּא מֵאִיבּוּד טְבִילָה? נְהִי דְּלָא טָבְלֵי בְּחַמִּין מִשּׁוּם כְּבוֹד בֵּית אֱלֹהֵינוּ, הָא מָצוּ טָבְלֵי בְּצוֹנֵן! אֶלָּא לָאו – בְּצוֹנֵן נַמִּי אָסִירִי, וְהַיְינוּ דְּקָאָמַר לְאַבֵּד: אָמַר רַב פַּפָּא. לְעוֹלָם חַמֵּי טְבֶרְיָא, וְהַיְינוּ דְּקָאָמְרִי' חַיָּיבֵי טְבִילוֹת – אִין, כּוּלֵּי עָלְמָא – לָא, וּבְצוֹנֵן כ"ע שָׁרֵי, וּמַאי לְאַבֵּד דְּקָאָמַר ר' חֲנִינָא, כְּגוֹן בְּאַתְרָא דְּלָא שְׁכִיחַ צוֹנֵן: כְּשֶׁאָמְרוּ אָסוּר (ד) [בִּמְלָאכָה]. גַּבֵּי תַּעֲנִית צִבּוּר, לֹא אָמְרוּ אֶלָּא בַּיּוֹם, אֲבָל בַּלַּיְלָה מוּתָּר. מֵהָכָא *מַשְׁמַע דִּבְלֵילֵי תִּשְׁעָה בְּאָב מוּתָּר בִּמְלָאכָה וְאֵין בִּיטּוּל אֶלָּא בַּיּוֹם, אֲבָל אֵין מְפַרְסְמִין הַדָּבָר: יָצָא לַדֶּרֶךְ. חוּץ לָעִיר: וְכֵן אַתָּה מוֹצֵא בִּמְנוּדֶּה וְאָבֵל. הָכִי גָּרְסִינַן: בְּמַאי? אִילֵימָא בְּחַמִּין – מִי שָׁרֵי, וְהָאָמַר רַב שֵׁשֶׁת: אָבֵל אָסוּר לְהוֹשִׁיט אֶצְבָּעוֹ בְּחַמִּין. אֶלָּא לָאו – בְּצוֹנֵן. מַאי לָאו אַכּוּלְּהוּ כו' הָא דְּקָתָנֵי וְכֵן אַתָּה מוֹצֵא בִּמְנוּדֶּה וְאָבֵל – אַכָּל הָנֵי קָאֵי, וַאֲפִילּוּ אַרְחִיצָה. וּשְׁמַע מִינָּהּ דִּבְתַעֲנִית צִבּוּר אָסוּר לִרְחוֹץ כָּל גּוּפוֹ, וַאֲפִילּוּ בְּצוֹנֵן, וּתְיוּבְתָּא לְרַפְרָם בַּר פַּפָּא: לֹא אַשְּׁאָרָא קָאֵי. אַנְּעִילָה (ה) וְסִיכָה, וּלְעוֹלָם הַךְ רְחִיצָה – בְּחַמִּין הִיא, אֲבָל בְּצוֹנֵן – שָׁרֵי לִרְחוֹץ כָּל גּוּפוֹ. וְהָשְׁתָּא דְּאָמְרַתְּ בִּמְנוּדֶּה וְאָבֵל, לָאו אַרְחִיצָה קָיְימִי – לֵיכָּא לְאַקְשׁוּיֵי כִּדְפָרְכַתְּ לְעֵיל: אִילֵימָא בְּחַמִּין מִי שָׁרֵי: וְרָחַץ בְּצוֹנֵן בְּתוֹךְ שִׁבְעָה. גָּרְסִינַן. אַלְמָא: בְּצוֹנֵן שָׁרֵי: שֶׁתְּכָפוּהוּ אֲבָלָיו. בָּזֶה אַחַר זֶה. כִּדְקָתָנֵי: שֶׁמֵּתוּ בָּנָיו, שְׁנֵיהֶם, וּלְפִיכָךְ הִתִּירוּ לוֹ, כִּדְאַשְׁכְּחַן גַּבֵּי שֵׂיעָר: מֵיקֵל בְּתַעַר. דְּשָׁקֵיל פּוּרְתָּא מִינַּיְיהוּ: וּבְתַעַר. דֶּרֶךְ שִׁינּוּי: נֶתֶר. קַרְקַע הוּא, אוֹ אֶבֶן, כְּעֵין שֶׁקּוֹרִין קרי"א בְּלַעַ"ז: בְּנֶתֶר וְחוֹל. דֶּרֶךְ לְכַבֵּס שֶׁיִּתְלַבֵּן: מִידֵי דַּהֲוָה אַבִּשְׂרָא וְחַמְרָא. דְּתַעֲנוּג הֵן כְּצוֹנֵן:

איפוך אנא. פי': דנימא פלגא קמייתא דיומא מצלו ובעו רחמי, ואידך פלגא מעייני במילי דמתא, ומשני לא ס"ד:

אמר רב חסדא כל שהוא משום אבל כגון תשעה באב (ו) אסור אפילו בצונן ואבל אסור בין בחמין בין בצונן וכו'. ירושלמי: יוסף בריה דרבי יהושע בן לוי בתשעה באב וביוה"כ מרחיץ ידיו ומקנח במפה ומעבירה על גבי עיניו. רבי יונה תרי סמרטוטי ויהיב תותי כרעיה, פי': היה מניח סמרטוט תחת הכר כדי ללחלחו. ומעבירו על גבי עיניו: **וכל** שהוא משום תענוג וכו'. ועכשיו שאין תענית צבור בבבל אלא תשעה באב – מותרין אפילו בחמין אפילו י"ז בתמוז וצום גדליה, כך פסק ראבי"ה. ור' יואל אביו: אסר לרחוץ בחמין:

ונועלין המרחצאות. פי': שהן חמין: **אטו** סוכרין נהרות כו'. כלומר: אי הוה אסור בצונן מי איכא למיתני סוכרים נהרות? פשיטא דלא מצי למסכר. כלומר, כמו כן לא תידוק מהא דקתני "ונועלין המרחצאות": **טבילה** בחמין מי איכא. הא שאובים נינהו. מדלא קאמר משכחת לה טבילה (בחמין) דכשירה בחמין כגון שהוחמו והומשכו לבריכה, אלא שאמר בחמי טבריא – יש להוכיח דכולו שאוב, אפילו ע"י המשכה, לא מהניא טבילה. והא דאמר* דהמשכה כולה כשירה – ר"ל לענין שאינה פוסלת את המקוה כשאר מים שאובים, אבל טבילה ודאי אינו עולה בהם:

וכן אתה מוצא במנודה ואבל מאי לאו אכולהו. פי': (ז) אהא דקאמרינן ובצונן מותר, דאבל נמי מותר בצונן. וקשיא לרב חסדא, דאמר אבל אסור בין בחמין בין בצונן. ומשני: אשארא. כלומר, אשאר דינין (ח), אנעילה וסיכה. אבל לא קאי אהא דבצונן:

הכביד שערו מיקל בתער. פי': דרך חתיכה. אבל לא כדרכו דרך גילוח, מדקאמר מיקל, ולא קאמר מגלח:

עזרא ט | שם

שבת קיא. ביצה יח: יומא פח.

[ברכות כב.]

מו"ק טו:

[תוספ' פ"א]

[מו"ק שם פסחים נד:]

מו"ק יז:

[עי' רש"י פסחים נד: ד"ה בין השמשות וכו' והמג"א סי' תקנד ס"ק כב הניחו בצ"ע]

נט א מיי' פ"ה מהלכות תעניות הלכה י סמג עשין מד"ס ג טוש"ע א"ח סי' תקנד סעיף ז:

ס ב מיי' פ"ה מהלכות אבל הלכה ד סמג שם טוש"ע י"ד סי' שפא סעיף א:

סא ג מיי' פ"ג מהלכות תענית הלכה ד טוש"ע א"ח סי' תקעה סעיף ג:

סב ד מיי' פ"ג מהלכות שביתת עשור הלכה ב טוש"ע שם סי' תקנד סעיף ח:

סג ה ו ז מיי' פ"ג מהלכות תענית הלכה ד טור ש"ע שם סימן תקעה סעיף ג:

סד ח מיי' פ"ה מהלכות אבל הלכה ד סמג עשין ב טוש"ע י"ד סי' שפא סעיף א:

סה ט מיי' שם פ"ו הלכה יג טוש"ע י"ד סי' של סעיף ג:

סו י מיי' שם טוש"ע שם סי' שפט סעיף א:

סז כ מיי' שם טוש"ע שם סי' של סעיף ג:

סח ל מיי' שם טוש"ע שם סי' שפט סעיף א:

הגהות הגר"א

[א] גמ' (שאובין נינהו) תא"מ (ועמ"ש רבינו ביו"ד סי' רא ס"ק קכה וצ"ע):

רבינו חננאל

בתרא מצלינן ומתודינן [אבל] תפלת התענית בשחרית לא יכלינן למימר דכתיב ואלי יאספו כל חרד בדברי אלהי ישראל על מעל הגולה ואני יושב משומם עד למנחת הערב ובמנחת הערב קמתי מתעניתי ובקרעי בגדי ומעילי [ואכרעה על] ברכי ואפרשה כפי אל ה' אלהי. ש"מ דתפלת התענית באחרית היום הוא ברביעית האחרון אמר רב חסדא כל שהוא משום אבל כגון ט' באב ואבל אסור ברחיצה בין בחמין בין בצונן. אבל כל שהוא משום תענוג כגון תענית צבור בחמין אסור ובצונן מותר. ודייק רב אידי ממתני' מאחר דקתני אסורים ברחיצה למה לי למתנא (כתב) ונועלין את המרחצאות אלא [ה"ק] רחיצה דאסרנא רחיצה במרחץ בחמין הוא דאסור אבל בצונן שרי ואתינן לסיועיה לר' חסדא מהא דתניא כל חייבי טבילות טובלין כדרכן בין בט' באב בין ביוה"כ ואמרי' [בחמין] ליכא לאוקומה דשאובין נינהו אלא בצונן ואי אמרינן לכ"ע רחיצה בט' באב בצונן שרי אצטריך לאשמעינן טבילה בצונן שהיא מצוה בזמנה דשרי אלא ש"מ רחיצה אפי' בצונן אסור ובטבילה דמצוה שרי ולכ"ע אסור ואדחי' לעולם בצונן לכ"ע שרי והא ברייתא בחמין היא. וא"ת מים שאובין הן כגון חמי טבריא דמים חמין הן.

ואקשינן אי הכי סיפא דקתני ר' חנניא סגן הכהנים אומר כדי הוא בית אלהינו לאבד עליו טבילה אחת בשנה. לטבול בצונן דשרי וליכא עבירה. ודחי באתרא דליכא צונן. ורחיצה בחמין אסור משום כבוד בית אלהינו שחרב כדי הוא בית אלהינו לאבד מצות טבילה אחת בזמנה פעם אחת: ת"ש כשאמרו בתענית אסור ברחיצה לא אמרו אלא כל גופו אבל פניו ידיו ורגליו מותר. וכשאמרו אסור במלאכה לא אמרו אלא ביום אבל בלילה מותר. וכשאמרו אסור בנעילת הסנדל לא אמרו אלא בעיר אבל בדרך מותר הא כיצד יצא לדרך נועל. הגיע לעיר חולץ הסנדל מרגלו ומהלך יחף. וכן אתה אומר במנודה ובאבל.

רבינו גרשום

י"ג ו' ראשונים ז' אחרונים. בשלמא רחיצה וסיכה ונעילת הסנדל ותשמיש המטה. מה אסיפת זקנים ביום. כנופיא מצפרא ולא מאורתא. איפוך אנא דמצפרא מצלי ולאורתא קרו ומפטרו. במנחת הערב ואכרעה על ברכי אלמא דרביעית בתרא הוו מצלי: אף אנן נמי תנינא דבתענית צבור אינו אסור אלא בחמין דקתני נועלין את המרחצאות *) אבל היכי איבעי ליה למיתני מי מצי למיתני סוכרין את הנהרות א"ר שישא בר אבא רב אידי בר אבין הכי קשיא ליה מכדי קתני אסורין ברחיצה דרחיצה משמע בחמין למה לי למתני נועלין את המרחצאות דמשמע נמי חמין לאו למימר דבחמין אסור ובצונן מותר והיינו דקאמר אף אנן נמי תנינא כרב חסדא דבתענית צבור בצונן מותר. נימא מסייע ליה לאביי דשמעינן ליה דאמר תענית צבור אסור בין בחמין בין בצונן: לכולי עלמא לא הרי לך תשעה באב **) שהוא תענית צבור ודייקינן דאפי' בצונן אסור אמר רב חנא מהכא לא תסייעי' לאביי דלא נצרכא הא דקתני טובלין כדרכן אלא לחמי טבריא דמצי למיטבל בהו והכי קאמר טובלין כדרכן בחמין אבל כ"ע לא אבל בצונן אפי' לכ"ע שרי: כדיי הוא בית אלהינו לאבד עליו טבילה אחת שלא יהיה טובל עליו בת"ב כלל. א"א בשלמא דת"ק אמר כל חייבי טבילות טובלין כדרכן בצונן בת"ב אבל כ"ע לא היינו דקא פליג רב חנינא עליה דת"ק דחייבי טבילות אין טובלין בצונן דכדיי הוא בית אלהינו לאבד עליו טבילה אחת אלא אי אמרת בצונן שרי לת"ק והכי קתני חייבי טבילות טובלין כדרכן בחמין אבל כ"ע לא אבל בצונן מותר לכ"ע וקפליג רב חנינא עליה דת"ק דלא מצי למיטבל בחמין א"כ ליכא איבוד טבילה דהא טביל בצונן אע"פ שאינו טובל בחמין דהא שרי בצונן לכ"ע אלא לאו לעולם אמר ת"ק בצונן טובלין אבל כ"ע לא ומסייעא. לאביי א"ר פפא לעולם אמר ת"ק טובלין כדרכן בחמין אבל לכ"ע אסור וצונן שרי לכ"ע ודאמר א"כ טבילה בצונן איכא וליכא איבוד טבילה ר' חנינא הוה קאי בדוכתא דלא שכיחא צונן ולעולם מהכא לא תסייעיה לאביי. (כל) אמרו אסור ברחיצה כו' באלו תעניות. מאי לאו הא דקתני וכן אתה מוצא באבל אכולהו אהאי נמי דקתני בסיפא דמילתא בהאי מסכתא באידך פירקא כשאמרו אסור ברחיצה וכו' ורחיצה לא משמע אלא בחמין וקשיא למאן דאמר כל שהוא משום אבל אסור בין בחמין ובין בצונן. לא אשארא לבד מרחיצה קאמר וכן אתה מוצא באבל אבל

*) אולי צ"ל א"ל אביי אלא היכי וכו'. **) לכאורה תמוה דהא גם לר"ח בת"ב אסור בצונן ומאי מייתי מינה ראיה לאביי ואולי דרבינו לא היה גורס בדברי ר"ח כגון ת"ב ועדיין צ"ע.

הגהות הב"ח

(א) גמ' כל שהוא משום אבל כגון תשעה באב. נ"ב פי' בדרבנן אית לפלוגי בין שהוא משום אבל ובין שהוא משום תענוג אבל ביוה"כ שהוא דאורייתא אע"פ שהוא משום תענוג אסור בין בחמין בין בצונן: (ב) שם מאי לאו אכולהו ובמאי אילימא בחמין כו' כצ"ל ותיבת עסקינן נמחק: (ג) רש"י ד"ה ה"ג כ"ע לא לא בחמין: (ד) ד"ה כשאמרו אסור ברחילה גבי תענית: (ה) ד"ה לא אשארא קאי אנעילה ומלאכה ולעולם הך: (ו) תום' ד"ה אמר ר"ח כו' כגון תשעה באב ואבל אסור בין כו' כצ"ל ותיבות אסור אפילו בצונן נמחק: (ז) ד"ה וכן כו' פירוש דקאי אהא דקאמרינן דבצונן מותר: (ח) בא"ד כלומר אשאר דינין קאי אנעילה ומלאכה אבל לא:

גליון הש"ס

תום' ד"ה וכן. מותר בצונן וקשי' לר"ח. ק' לי הא אדרבה כיון דמיירי בצונן ואפ"ה תני כל גופו אסור א"ו דהקושיא בהיפוך דמוכח דבתענית ג"כ אסור בצונן כל גופו וקשיא לר"ח וכמ"ש רש"י:

אין הבוגרת רשאה לנוול את עצמה בימי אבל אביה. הא נערה — רשאה. מאי לאו ברחיצה? ובמאי? אילימא בחמין, אין הבוגרת רשאה? והאמר רב חסדא: אבל אסור להושיט אצבעו בחמין! אלא לאו — בצונן לא, אכיחול ופירכוס. לימא מסייע ליה: דא"ר אבא הכהן משום רבי יוסי הכהן: מעשה ומתו בניו של ר' יוסי בר חנינא, ורחץ בצונן כל שבעה! אמרי: התם בשתכפוהו אבליו זה אחר זה. דתניא: תכפוהו אבליו זה אחר זה, הכביד שערו — מיקל בתער, ומכבס כסותו במים. אמר רב חסדא: בתער — אבל לא במספרים. במים — ולא בנתר ולא בחול ולא באהל. איכא דאמרי אמר רבא: אבל אסור בצונן כל שבעה. מאי שנא מבשר ויין? התם *לפכוחי פחדיה הוא דעביד. לימא מסייע ליה: אין הבוגרת רשאה לנוול עצמה. הא נערה — רשאה. במאי? אילימא בחמין, אין הבוגרת רשאה, והאמר רב חסדא: אבל אסור להושיט אצבעו בחמין! אלא לאו בצונן לא, אכיחול ופירכוס. אמר רב חסדא, זאת אומרת: [א]אבל אסור בתכבוסת כל שבעה. [ב]והלכתא: אבל אסור לרחוץ כל גופו בין בחמין בין בצונן כל שבעה. אבל פניו, ידיו, ורגליו, בחמין — אסור, בצונן — מותר. [ג]אבל לסוך — אפילו כל שהוא אסור. ואם לעבר את הזוהמא — מותר. צלותא דתעניתא היכי מדכרינן? אדבריה רב יהודה לרב יצחק בריה, ודרש: יחיד שקיבל עליו תענית מתפלל של תענית. והיכן אומרה? בין "גואל" ל"רופא". מתקיף לה רב *יצחק: וכי יחיד קובע ברכה לעצמו? אלא אמר רב יצחק: [ד]ב"שומע תפלה". וכן אמר רב ששת: ב"שומע תפלה". מיתיבי: אין בין יחיד לצבור אלא שזה מתפלל שמונה עשרה וזה מתפלל תשע עשרה. מאי יחיד ומאי צבור? אילימא: יחיד — ממש, וצבור — ש"צ, הני תשע עשרה? עשרין וארבע הוו! אלא לאו ה"ק: אין בין יחיד דקבל עליו תענית יחיד, ליחיד שקבל עליו תענית צבור, אלא שזה מתפלל שמונה עשרה וזה מתפלל תשע עשרה. ש"מ: יחיד קובע ברכה לעצמו! לא, לעולם אימא לך שליח צבור. ודקא קשיא לך שליח צבור עשרין וארבע מצלי (א) — בג' תעניות ראשונות, [ה]דליכא עשרים וארבע. ולא? והא "אין בין" קתני: "אין בין ג' ראשונות לג' אמצעיות, אלא שבאלו מותרין בעשיית מלאכה ובאלו אסורין בעשיית מלאכה". הא לכ"ד — זה וזה שוין! *תנא ושייר. מאי שייר דהאי שייר? (ב) ותו, והא "אין בין" קתני! אלא, תנא באיסורי קא מיירי, בתפלות לא מיירי. ואי בעית אימא: [ו]באמצעייתא נמי לא מצלי כ"ד. ולא? והתניא: *אין בין ג' שניות לשבע אחרונות, אלא שבאלו מתריעין ונועלין את החנויות. הא לכל דבריהן — זה וזה שוין! וכי תימא הכא נמי תנא ושייר — והא "אין בין" קתני! ותסברא "אין בין" דוקא? והא

[גי' רא"ש יוסף]

*) [וע"ע תוספות מגילה ח. ד"ה אין ותוס' ב"ק סב: ד"ה מי קתני ותוס' חגיגה ח. ד"ה אמאי ותוספות שבת סג. ד"ה אין]

רש"י

אין הבוגרת. שהביאה שתי שערות, רשאה לנוול את עצמה, אלא מתקשטת כדי שיקפצו עליה (ג). הא נערה, שאינה ראויה להינשא עדיין עד שתבגר – רשאה, דבת חיוב אבילות היא. וקטנה אינה חייבת ולא כלום: בימי אבל אביה. אפילו אירע אבילות לאביה, שמת בנו. אי נמי: שמת אביה ממש, אע"פ שהיא בת חיוב אבילות – אינה רשאה לנוול: אלא לאו בצונן. ואפ"ה נערה אינה רוחצת בצונן, אלמא: דאבל אף בצונן אסור: אכיחול ואפירכוס. ולא קא מיירי ברחיצה כלל. פירכוס – בשיער, כבוס – בבגדים, רחיצה – בגוף: זאת אומרת. מדמוקמינן לה בכיחול ופירכוס, הוא הדין לתכבוסת: תפלת תענית. עננו: בין גואל לרופא. ברכה בפני עצמה: וכי יחיד. חשוב כל כך שיהו מתקנין לו ברכה בפ"ע, להוסיף בתפלתו?! בשומע תפלה. שכוללה בתוך הברכה, וחותם ב"שומע תפלה", דאותה ברכה וחתימתה משמע בין לתענית בין לכל מילי: אין בין יחיד לצבור. גבי תענית: שזה. יחיד מתפלל ביום תעניתו שמונה עשרה, וכולל תפלת תענית בשומע תפלה: תשע עשרה. דקבע ליה בין גואל לרופא. סתם תפלה קרי שמונה עשרה, דברכת "ולמלשינים" ביבנה תקנוה, כדאמרינן בברכות (דף כח:): כ"ד הויין. (ד) בפירקין דלקמן (דף טו.), דכ"ד ברכות הוו ביומא דתעניתא, והכא קתני י"ט ותו לא! וצבור. יחיד שקיבל עליו תענית צבור. אלמא: יחיד קובע ברכה לעצמו כשקיבל תענית צבור: בקמייתא. בג' תעניות ראשונות (ה) דליכא כ"ד, כדאמרינן בפרק "סדר תעניות כיצד" בגמ' (בראשית): דאלו מותרין בעשיית מלאכה וכו'. ראשונות דלא חמירי כולי האי (ו). הא לכ"ד ברכות – זה וזה שוין. וקס"ד דאיתנהו לכ"ד באמצעיות, מדקמתרץ קמייתא דליכא כ"ד – מכלל דבאמצעייתא איתנהו. ולא היא, דליתנהו אלא באחרונות, כדקתני התם. ומשום דהא מילתא קמייתא, מש"ה פריך ליה מכ"ד דליתנהו באמצעיות: תנא ושייר. תנא מילי דאיתנהו בין אמצעיות לראשונות, ושייר. "אין בין" לאו דוקא הוא, כדמוכח לקמן גבי אידך: ה"ג: מאי שייר דהאי שייר, אלא באיסורי קא מיירי בתפלות לא קא מיירי. ומאן דגריס שייר תיבה מוציאין את התיבה כו' – שיבוש הוא, דאינה אלא באחרונות, כדבסמוך. ומיפשט פשיטא ליה דאינה אלא באחרונות: מאי שייר דהאי שייר. דלא אורחא דתנא למתני כל מילי ולשיורי חדא. אלא לעולם כ"ד בקמייתא ליתנהו, ולהכי לא חשיב להו ב"אין בין", דבתפלה לא קמיירי: באמצעיות נמי ליכא כ"ד. אלא באחרונות, כדאמרינן התם: שבאלו. האחרונות מתריעים ונועלין, כדתנן נמי במתני'.* הא לכ"ד – זה וזה שוין, דבתרוייהו איתנהו: והא

[ז"ל רש"י ב"מ סו: ד"ה לפכוחי פחדיה להפיג דאגתו וכו']
[סוכה נג. וש"נ]
[תוספתא מגילה פ"א]
[לעיל יב:]

תוספות

אין הבוגרת רשאה לטול עצמה. אומר ר"י: דהא רשאה – לאו דוקא. *אלא ה"ק: אין הבוגרת חייבת, הא נערה – חייבת:

אלא (ז) בצונן. וקאמר נערה רשאה, כלומר דאסורה ואת אמרת דבצונן מותר. וקשה לרבא, דאמר דבצונן מותר! ומשני: כי קתני "אכיחול ואפירכוס":

אלא אמר רב יצחק בשומע תפלה. והכי פסק בשמעתא דתפלת תענית: בשומע תפלה, ואין יחיד קובע ברכה לעצמו. לכך צריך כשאומר "עננו" בש"ת (דצריך) לאומרו קודם שאומר הברכה, כשמגיע לעננו קודם שיתחיל לומר "כי אתה ש"ת עמך ישראל ברחמים" יאמר עננו ולא יחתום, אלא יאמר "כי אתה ה' עונה בעת צרה ומושיע" ואח"כ "כי אתה ש"ת עמך ישראל ברחמים בא"י שומע תפלה". אבל שליח צבור אומר "גואל ישראל" וקובע ברכה, וחותם:

תנא ושייר. פי': תנא עשיית מלאכה, ושייר כ"ד ברכות. פי': כ"ד ברכות: שבתענית היו מוסיפין ו' ברכות, כדמפרש לקמן ברפ"ב (דף טו.):

מאי שייר דהאי שייר כו'. פי': דמשום חדא מילתא לא הוי (ח) לתנא לשייר. וא"ת: הכא קאמר דלא תנא ושייר, דהא "אין בין" קאמר, דמשמע: דאין בין זה לזה אלא אלו בלבד, וקשה: דהא במגילה (דף ח.) קתני אין בין נדרים לנדבות אלא שהנדרים חייב באחריותן ונדבות אינו חייב באחריותן, ואנו יודעין דיש (ט) חילוק אחר: דנדרים אינן באים אלא מן החולין, דכל דבר שבחובה אינו בא אלא מן החולין, ונדבות באות מן המעשר, כדאמר (דברים כז) "וזבחת שלמים ואכלת" דכתיב גבי מעשר! וי"ל: דהתם נמי דזה וזה שוה, והני מילי גבי שלמים יש חילוק, והא דקתני אין בין – מיירי בעולות, דאין בין עולות דנדרים לעולות דנדבה אלא שהנדרים חייב באחריותן, מה שאין כן בנדבה. דהא אין בין עולות דנדרים לעולות דנדבות אלא חילוק זה, דהא כל עולות אינן באין אלא מן החולין*):

ותסברא והא שייר תיבה. פי': (י) מפרש לקמן (דף טו:) שמוציאין התיבה ברחוב העיר (באמצעיות) באחרונות. ותסברא דהא שייר תיבה! פי': וליכא למימר דבאיסורא קמיירי, דהא דמתריעין ונועלין – מאי איסור איכא? לאו

[ועי' תוס' קידושין לג. ותוס' חולין נד: ד"ה אין ותוס' ערכין כח: ד"ה אומדין]

עין משפט נר מצוה

סט א מיי' פ"ה מהלכות אבל הלכה א סמג עשין מד"ס ג טוש"ע י"ד סי' ש"פ סעיף א וסי' שפט סעיף א:

ע ב מיי' שם הלכה ד טוש"ע שם סי' שפא סעיף א:

עא ג מיי' שם טוש"ע שם סעיף ב:

עב ד מיי' פ"ב מהלכות תפלה הלכה יד סמג עשין יט טוש"ע א"ח סי' תקסה סעיף א:

עג ה מיי' פ"ג מהלכות תענית הלכה ב טוש"ע א"ח סי' תקעה סעיף ב:

עד ו מיי' שם הלכה ג טוש"ע שם סעיף ג:

רבינו חננאל

ודחינן לא כי קא קתני וכן באבל אנעילת סנדל ואמלאכה קאי אבל (רחיצה לא) [לא ארחיצה] ולעולם בחמין. אמר רבא אבל אסור כל ז' אפי' בצונן ומ"ש מבשר ויין דשרי ליה. ודחי בשר ויין שרינן ליה כדי לפכוחי פחדיה אבל רחיצה דמשום תענוג היא לא התירו. לימא מסייעא ליה אין הבוגרת רשאה לנוול עצמה בימי אבל בית אביה. אבל הנערה שרי לנוול עצמה ושלא לרחוץ אפילו בצונן. וש"מ אבל אפי' בצונן אסור. ודחי לא הבוגרת התירו לכחול ולפרכס. תניא תכפוהו אבליו זה אחר זה שערו מיקל בתער ומכבס כסותו במים. אמר רב חסדא בתער ולא במספרים. במים ולא בנתר. ולא בחול. אמר רב חסדא זאת אומרת אבל אסור בתכבוסת. והלכתא אסור לרחוץ כל גופו כל ז' בין בחמין בין בצונן אבל פניו ידיו ורגליו בחמין אסור ובצונן מותר. ולסוך אפי' כל שהוא אסור. ואם לעבר הזוהמא מות' לסוך שמן טוב. דרש רב יצחק יחיד שקבל עליו תענית מתפלל עננו בין גואל לרופא ואקשינן עליה וכי יחיד קובע ברכה לעצמו אלא מתפלל עננו בשומע תפלה בכלל הברכה ואינו מתפלל אותה ברכה בפ"ע. ומותבינן עליה מהא דתניא מה בין יחיד לצבור אלא שזה מתפלל שמ"ע ואלו מתפללין י"ט היכי דמי אילימא יחיד המתפלל בינו לבין עצמו עם הצבור וצבור דקתני ש"ץ היורד לפני התיבה האי י"ט ברכות מתפלל בתענית כ"ד מתפלל כדתנן עמדו בתפלה מורידין לפני התיבה זקן ורגיל כו' ואומר לפניהם כ"ד ברכות. ושנינן הכי קתני אין בין יחיד דקאי בצבור כדאמרן ליחיד המתפלל חוץ לביהכ"נ אלא שזה היחיד העומד בחוץ מתפלל י"ח ויחיד המתפלל בכנסת מתפלל י"ט ברכות. אלמא יחיד קובע ברכה לעצמו. ושנינן לעולם יחיד. יחיד דקאי בצבור וצבור ש"ץ ממש. וזה ש"ץ המתפלל י"ט ברכות בתעניות ראשונות הוא שאין בה כ"ד ברכות לפיכך זה מתפלל י"ח וזה מתפלל י"ט. ואקשינן והא תעניות אמצעיות דקתני בהו ואסור במלאכה וברחיצה כו'. ולא קתני כ"ד. ושנינן האי תנא באיסורא קמיירי. כלומר אסור במלאכה וברחיצה כו' הוא דמיירי בתפלות לא קמיירי. אי בעי תימא כ"ד ברכות באמצעייתא נמי ליכא. ואקשינן והא תניא אין בין ג' אמצעיות לז' אחרונות. אלא שבאלו מתריעין ונועלין את החנויות הא לכ"ד זה וזה שוין. לעולם אימא לך באמצעיות נמי אין כ"ד ברכות בהן. ותנא מקצת מה שיש בשבע האחרונות ואינם בג' אמצעיות ושייר

גליון הש"ס

רש"י ד"ה זאת אומרת. מדמוקמינן לה בכיחול כו'. [illegible]

רבינו גרשום

ברחיצה מוחלקין דאילו בתענית קתני ברחיצה דמשמע בחמין אבל לא בצונן ואילו באבל אסור בין בחמין בין בצונן. אין הבוגרת רשאי לנוול עצמה לפי שעומדת על פרקה וראויה לינשא. אילימא בחמין אין הבוגרת רשאי לנוול עצמה כלומר דיכולה לרחוץ בחמין: אלא לאו בצונן קאמר אין הבוגרת רשאה לנוול עצמה אלא רוחצין בצונן הא נערה רשאה לנוול עצמה דאפי' בצונן אינה רוחצת וקשיא לרבא דאמר אבל בצונן מותר. לא כי קתני אין הבוגרת רשאי לנוול הא נערה רשאה אכיחול אבל בצונן מותר אפי' בנערה. התם בבשרא וחמרא ליכא אלא לפכוחי פחדא אבל ליכא תענוג לפיכך שרי. הכא בצונן איכא תענוג לפיכך אסור. אלא לאו בצונן קאמר דנערה רשאה לנוול עצמה [ש"מ] דאבל אסור בין בחמין בין בצונן והוי סיועא לא כי קתני נערה רשאה לנוול בכיחול ופירכוס אבל בצונן מותר ולא הוי סיועא: וכי יחיד קובע ברכה לעצמו. *) יש מברך העונה בעת צרה: בשומע תפלה. שכולל בשומע תפלה ואינו מברך ברכה לעצמו. הני דש"ץ כ"ד הויין כדמפרש לקמן וקתני שזה מתפלל תשע עשרה. אלמא דקובע ברכה לעצמו שמברך העונה בעת צרה: [ודקא קשיא לך דהא] הויין כ"ד ברכות בדקמייתא בשלש תעניות ראשונות קא מיירי דליכא בהו כ"ד ולא הוי אלא י"ט ולעולם אין היחיד קובע ברכה לעצמו: אלא שבאלו אמצעיות אסורין במלאכה וראשונות מותרין במלאכה הא לעשרים וארבעה זה וזה שוין כי היכי דבאמצעיות איכא עשרים וארבעה הכא נמי איכא בראשונות כ"ד ולא מצית לתרוצי דצבור מתפלל י"ט בש"ץ דהא איכא כ"ד אלא ביחיד שקיבל תענית צבור ותיפשוט דיחיד קובע ברכה לעצמו. ה"נ תנא באיסור קא מיירי כלומר לעולם בראשונות ליכא כ"ד והא דלא קתני שבאלו יש כ"ד ובאלו אין כ"ד משום דבאיסורי קא מיירי דהוי אסור בעשיית מלאכה ובתפלה לא מיירי בברכות ולעולם הא דקתני דצבור מתפלל י"ט מוקמינן בש"ץ אבל לא ביחיד דאין יחיד קובע ברכה לעצמו. ואיב"א לעולם בראשונות ליכא כ"ד ולהכי לא קתני שבאלו יש כ"ד ובאלו אין כ"ד דבאמצעיות נמי אין כ"ד: **) ה"נ תנא ושייר ולא נמי כלומר שייר כ"ד דבשבע איכא ובאמצעיות ליכא: והא אין בין קתני דמשמע דהוי דוקא כי היכי דאמרינן דאין בין קמא דוקא אלמא דליכא ביניהו אלא מתריעין ונועלין אבל לכ"ד שוין אלמא דבאמצעיות איכא כ"ד

*) אולי צ"ל וכי יכול לברך וכו'. **) נראה דצ"ל ה"ג וכ"ת תנא ושייר ולא גרסינן נמי כלומר וכו'.

הגהות הב"ח

[illegible]

והא שייר תיבה! אי משום תיבה — לאו שיורא הוא. מילי דצינעא — קתני, מילי דבפרהסיא — לא קתני. אמר רב אשי: מתני' נמי דיקא, דקתני: *מה אלו יתירות על הראשונות? אלא שבאלו מתריעין ונועלין את החנויות. אבל בכל דבריהן זה וזה שוין. וכ"ת הכא נמי *תנא ושייר — והא "מה אלו" קתני! ותסברא "מה אלו" דווקא הוא? והא שייר לה תיבה! אי משום תיבה — לאו שיורא הוא, משום דקא חשיב לה באידך פרקא. השתא דאתית להכי — עשרים וארבעה נמי לאו שיורא הוא, דקתני לה באידך פירקא. מאי הוי עלה? אמר רב שמואל בר ססרטאי, וכן אמר רב חייא בר אשי אמר רב: בין "גואל" ל"רופא". ורב אשי אמר משמיה דרבי ינאי בריה דרבי ישמעאל: ב"שומע תפלה". והלכתא: ב"שומע תפלה".§ תני חדא: עוברות ומיניקות — מתענות בראשונות, ואין מתענות באחרונות. ותניא אידך: מתענות באחרונות, ואין מתענות בראשונות. ותניא אידך: אין מתענות, לא בראשונות ולא באחרונות. אמר רב אשי: [א]נקוט אמצעייתא בידך, דמיתרצון כולהו.§ "מה אלו יתירות על הראשונות? אלא שבאלו מתריעין ונועלין את החנויות".§ במאי מתריעין? רב יהודה אמר: [ב]בשופרות. ורב יהודה בריה דרב שמואל בר שילת משמיה דרב אמר: ב"עננו". קס"ד מאן דאמר ב"עננו", לא אמר בשופרות, ומאן דאמר בשופרות, לא אמר ב"עננו". והתניא: "אין פוחתין משבע[א] תעניות על הצבור, שבהן י"ח התרעות. וסימן לדבר יריחו. ויריחו שופרות הוה, ותיובתא למאן דאמר: ב"עננו"! אלא, בשופרות — דכולי עלמא לא פליגי דקרי לה התרעה. כי פליגי — ב"עננו". מר סבר: קרי לה התרעה. ומר סבר: לא קרי לה התרעה. למ"ד ב"עננו" — כל שכן בשופרות. ולמ"ד בשופרות — אבל ב"עננו" לא. והתניא: *ושאר כל מיני פורענויות המתרגשות, כגון [ג]חיכוך, [ד]חגב, [ה]זבוב, וצירעה, ויתושין, ושילוח נחשים ועקרבים — לא היו מתריעין, אלא צועקין. (א) מדצעקה בפה — התרעה בשופרות! תנאי היא, *דתניא: *[ו]על אלו מתריעין בשבת: על עיר שהקיפוה גיים או נהר, ועל ספינה המטורפת בים. ר' יוסי אמר: לעזרה, אבל לא לצעקה. במאי? אילימא: בשופרות — שופרות בשבת מי שרי? אלא לאו ב"עננו", וקרי לה התרעה. ש"מ.§ בשני דר' יהודה נשיאה הוה צערא. גזר

רש"י

והא שייר תיבה. דבאחרונות איתא והכא ליתא, כדקתני לקמן (דף טו.): סדר תעניות כיצד? מוציאין את התיבה כו'. ומותבינן בגמרא בהדיא מתיבה דליתא אלא באחרונות! ומשני: כי קתני נמי מתניתין — *בקמייתא: מילי דצינעא. מתריעין בבית הכנסת, וכ"ד נמי בבית הכנסת: בפרהסיא. תיבה ברחובה של עיר: דיקא נמי. דלכ"ד זה וזה שוין, דקתני מתניתין: מה אלו יתירות על הראשונות כו', ואלו כ"ד לא קא חשיב גבי אחרונות: והא מה אלו קתני. דמשמע דווקא: דהא קתני לה באידך פירקין. דמי ששנה מתניתין דהכא תנא נמי דהתם, והאי דלא תנא בהאי — סמיך אהתם, דקתני: באחרונות מוציאין התיבה, מה שאין כן באמצעיות: השתא דאתית להכי. דמשום דקתני לה באידך פירקין דאמרת דלא הוי שיור, כ"ד נמי דאמרת דשוין נינהו — איכא למימר דלא הוי שוין. דהא אפי' שיורא נמי לא הוי, דבהדיא קתני לה באידך פירקין דבאחרונות איתנהו, באמצעיות לא, ואיכא לתרוצי כתירוצא קמא: בקמייתא דליכא כ"ד: מאי הוי עלה. היכן אומרה יחיד: נקוט מציעתא בידך. כלומר: תרין דבשלש אמצעיות היו מתענין, ומתרצא לכולהו הנך מתנייתא. הא דקתני בראשונות ולא באחרונות — הנך ראשונות לאו ראשונות ממש נינהו, אלא אמצעיות, דאינהו הוו ראשונות לאחרונות. אבל בשבע אחרונות — לא מיתענו, דכיון דשבע נינהו לא מצו עוברות ומיניקות למיקם בהו. והא דקתני באחרונות ולא בראשונות — הנך אחרונות אמצעיות נינהו, והראשונות ראשונות ממש. ואין מתענין בהן — דלא תקיף רוגזא כולי האי. ונחות לשון הוא לתנא למיקרי לאמצעיות ראשונות לאחרונו', ואחרונו' לראשונות: בשופרות. היו עושין התרעות. ולשון התרעה כמו תרועה, וסתם תרועה פשוטה לפניה ולאחריה, במסכת ראש השנה (דף לג.). ואהכי מתריעין בשופרות, כדכתיב (במדבר י) "ותקעתם בחצוצרות" וגו'. תוקעין בשופרות כדי שיכניעו לבם לקול השופר, ויהיו נרתעים מחטאתם. ואשש ברכות שהיו מוסיפין ביום התענית היו תוקעין על כל ברכה יבבא אחת, שהן י"ח התרעות: רב יהודה אמר. מתריעין "עננו" בקול רם היו צועקים: עננו אבינו עננו, עננו אלהי אברהם עננו, עננו אלהי יצחק עננו, עננו אלהי יעקב עננו. הכל כפי שאומרים בסוף הסליחות. אבל עננו דתפלת תענית — אומר אפי' בראשונות, ואפי' יחיד אוקימנא דאומרה ב"שומע תפלה". ותפלה קרי ליה התרעה, דאי בשופרות — מריעין מיבעי ליה. ומאן דמפרש "עננו" של תפלת תענית — משבש, דהא קתני בסמוך שהן י"ח התרעות, וקא פריך מן וסימן לדבר יריחו, ואם איתא — ליפריך בהדיא: י"ח תפלות של שמונה עשרה ברכות מי איכא בשבע תעניות? אין פוחתין מז' תעניות. באחרונות: שמונה עשרה התרעות. שהן מוסיפין ו' ברכות מי"ח עד כ"ד, ולכל אחת שלש תרועות: וסימן לדבר. שלא תטעה אם התרעה הזו תרועה או תפלה: יריחו. דכתיב בה שופרות. לישנא אחרינא: סימן לדבר, כלומר לכך מתריעין — כדי שיענו כדרך שנענו ביריחו על ידי שופרות, דכתיב (יהושע ו) "ויתקעו בשופרות" וגו', וכתיב (בראשית) "ותפול החומה תחתיה": אלא בשופרות כולי עלמא וכו'. דהא מתריעין דקתני הכא במתניתין, דעבדינן בתעניות בשופרות: כי פליגי בעננו. כי פליגי במתריעין דאמרינן בעלמא על שאר פורענויות, מ"ס "עננו" נמי התרעה, והאי דקתני בעלמא מתריעין — ב"עננו". ומאן דאמר בשופרות — אבל ב"עננו" לא: חגב. ארבה, כתרגומו: צירעה. עוקצת את האדם: יתושין. נכנסין בעיניו ובחוטמו: חיכוך. כמו נתחכך בכותל: הא צעקה בפה היא. אלמא דצעקת פה לא קרי ליה התרעה: תנאי היא. האי תנא דשאר מיני פורעניות סבר: צעקת פה לאו שמה התרעה, ואידך סבר כו': גיים. וקרין עליה: נהר. המתפשט ויוצא לחוץ לשטוף את השדה ואת הבתים: המטורפת. כמו בילים טרופות (חולין דף סד.) — שהולכת ונדה, ועתידה להיטבע במים: לעזרה. צועקין לבני אדם שיבואו לעזרם: ולא לצעקה. תפלה, שאין אנו בטוחין כל כך שתועיל תפלתנו לצעוק עליהן בשבת. אלמא: צעקת פה קרי התרעה, מפי מורי. ל"א: לעזרה דקאמר תנא קמא מתריעין, דמשמע בקול רם. ואמר ליה רבי יוסי: לעזרה — שיהו מתפללין כל אחד בביתו לעזרה בעלמא:

תוספות

לאו שיורא הוא דהא קתני לה באידך פירקא. והוא הדין דהוה מצי לתרוצי כדלעיל: מילי דפרהסיא לא קתני:

תני חדא מתענות בראשונות ולא באחרונות ותנא אידך מתענין באחרונות ולא בראשונות ותני אידך לא מתענין לא בראשונות ולא באחרונות (ב) נקוט מציעתא בידך. פירש הקונטרס: השלש תעניות אמצעיות בידך, דבאותן תעניות עוברות ומיניקות מתענות. וה"ק: מתענות בראשונות, פי' 'בראשונו' ר"ל אמצעיות, דהם ראשונות לאחרונו' שהיו חמורות — אבל לא באחרונות, דנפישי ולא מצו עבדי להו. והא דקתני באחרונות ולא בראשונות — האי אחרונו' היינו אמצעיות, וקרי להו אחרונות — שהם אחרונות מן הראשונות. בתחלה גוזרין שלש תעניות, וכן בשניה שלש, אבל אין מתענות בראשונות שהם קלות. והא דקתני לא בראשונות ולא באחרונות, כלומר לא בשלש הראשונות ממש, ולא בשבע האחרונות ממש, אלא דווקא באמצעיות:

ורב יהודה בריה דרב שמואל בר שילת משמיה דרב אמר עננו. אומר הר"י(ג): והאי "עננו" לא ר"ל עננו שבתפלת תענית, אלא עניינו שאומרים בסליחות וביום הכפורים: עננו אבינו עננו. אבל עננו דתפלה — לא קאמר, דהא בשלש ראשונות נמי אמר לה:

ובהן י"ח תרועות וסימן לדבר יריחו. פירוש: שבריחו עשו כן, שהקיפוה ז' ימים והיו תוקעין בכל יום — כמו כן תקנו בתעניות. ובכל תענית מוסיפין שש ברכות, ועל כל ברכה תוקעין מריעין ותוקעין, א"כ היינו י"ח תרועות:

מתריעין לעזרה. פי': שיבואו לעזור העיר וכו'. ומתריעין בפה — פירוש: והאי תרועה ר"ל מתריעין בפה, דאין להתיר תרועה בשופר בשבת:

רבי

רבינו חננאל

אחרונות כגון הני כ"ד וכיוצא בהן אמר רב אשי הא דדייקת מתנייתא דייק ממתני' דקתני מה אלו יתירות על הראשונות אלא שבאלו מתריעין ונועלין החנויות הא לכל דבריהן זה וזה שוין. תנא מקצת ושייר מקצת מאי שייר דהאי שייר [שייר] תיבה דלא קתני ומוציאין התיבה אלא אמרינן תנא ושייר כשם ששייר התיבה שייר כ"ד ברכות ולעולם [אין] מתפללין באמצעיות כ"ד ברכות ודחינן תיבה לאו שיור הוא דקתני באידך פרקין: סדר תעניות כיצד מוציאין התיבה הנה מפרש אכולהו תעניות מוציאין את התיבה. ואמרינן השתא דאתית להכי גם זה השינוי תשני בהא נמי ואימא מדקתני סדר תעניות כיצד וקא מפרש כ"ד ברכות ש"מ אכולהו תעניות קמיירי וזו שנויה היא ולא סמכינן עליה דהא באידך פרקין *) דאין מוציאין התיבה אלא בז' אחרונות: מאי הוה עלה ואסיקנא הלכתא יחיד מתפלל עננו ל"ש יחיד קאי בצבור ול"ש יחיד דקאי בעלמא וקיי"ל דכל יחיד מזכיר עננו בשומע תפלה. תני חדא עוברות ומיניקות מתענות בראשונות ואין מתענות באחרונות ותניא אידך מתענות באחרונות ואין מתענות בראשונות. ותניא אידך אין מתענות לא באחרונות ולא בראשונות אמר רב ששת נקיט אמצעייתא בידך כי מתענין בהן דמתרצין כולהו פי' הא דקתני בראשונה מתענות בראשונות בשלש אמצעיות [מיירי] ולגבי שבע אחרונות (הני אחרונות) הני שלש אמצעיות ראשונות להני ז' נינהו ואמצעיות דקתני מתענין באחרונות הן ג' אמצעיות דלגבי שלש הראשונות האמצעיות אחרונות מקרו. ובריית' דקתני אין מתענות לא בראשונות [בראשונות] ממש שהן שלש ראשונות ולא באחרונות [באחרונות ממש] שהן ז' האחרונות מכלל דג' הראשונות מתענות לדברי שלשתן ויש לומר דכלהו מודו באמצעיות

ירושלמי

ירושלמי: עוברות ומיניקות מתענות בט' באב ובג' שניות ולא בז' אחרונות: מתני' אין גוזרין תענית בתחלה בחמישי כו' עד ר' יוסי אומר כשם שאין הראשונות בחמישי כך לא השניות ולא האחרונות: מתני' עברו אלו ולא נענו ב"ד גוזרין עוד כו'. מתריעין דתני במתני' כיצד הוא רב יהודה אמר התרעה בשופר משמיה דרב אמרו התרעה בעננו ומותבינן [עלה] דרב אין פוחתין מז' תעניות על הצבור ובהן ז' התרעות וסימן לדבר יריחו והתרעות דירחו בשופר הוו. ושנינן בשופר דברי הכל התרעה היא כי פליגי בעננו רב יהודה סבר עננו לאו התרעה היא ורב סבר עננו נמי התרעה היא. ותוב מותבינן עליה ושאר כל מיני פורעניות המתרגשות על העולם כגון חיכוך חגב זבוב צרעה ויתושין ושילוח נחשים ועקרבים לא היו מתריעין אלא צועקין. והנה עננו צעקה היא ואם תאמר שגם עננו התרעה היא נמצא עננו התרעה והיא הצעקה היכי קתני צועקין ולא מתריעין ושנינן תנאי היא יש תנא (שקירא) [שקורא] עננו התרעה דתנן בפירקין [דחסידא] (קרא) על אלו מתריעין בשבת על עיר שהקיפוה גיים או נהר

*) אולי צ"ל דהא באידך פרקין אמרינן דאין מוציאין וכו'.

רבינו גרשום

הא שייר תיבה דבאחרונות איכא ובאמצעיות ליכא אי משום תיבה לאו שיורא הוא דמילי בצינעא קתני כגון מתריעין ונועלין מילי דפרהסיא כגון תיבה שמוציאין לרחוב לא קתני ולעולם איכא תיבה באחרונות ולא באמצעיות אבל כ"ד דהוי בצנעא אם איתא דליכא באמצעיות הוה קתני שבאילו מתפללין כ"ד ובאילו אין מתפללין כ"ד אלא ש"מ דבאמצעיות איכא כ"ד ולא מצית לתרוצי אב"א באמצעיות ליכא כ"ד ולעולם אמרינן הא דקתני אין בין ג' ראשונות לג' אמצעיות כו' הא לכ"ד שוין דהיכי דבאמצעיות איכא כ"ד ה"נ איכא בראשונות ולא מצית לתרוצי הא דתני שצבור מתפלל י"ט דהא איכא כ"ד אלא מוקמינן ליה ביחיד שקיבל עליו תענית צבור ותפשוט דיחיד קובע ברכה לעצמו מתניתין נמי דיקא דבאמצעיות איכא כ"ד מה אילו אחרונות יתירות על הראשונות דהיינו אמצעיות שבאלו אחרונות מתריעין ונועלין אבל לכל דבריהם זה וזה שוין אלמא דכי היכי דאיכא כ"ד באחרונות איכא נמי באמצעיות וכי תימא ה"נ תנא ושייר כלומר דה"נ איכא בראשונות ובאמצעיות אלא שאין כ"ד ובאילו יש כ"ד ואלא אין כ"ד אלא ששיירו הא מה אילו קתני דמשמע דהוי דוקא דליכא בינייהו אלא להני דתני בהדיא אבל לכ"ד זה וזה שוין דכי היכי דאיכא כ"ד באחרונות איכא נמי באמצעיות. אי משום תיבה לאו שיורא הוא אלא כיון דשייר כ"ד אלמא ש"מ דכי היכא דבאחרונות איכא כ"ד ה"נ איכא כ"ד באמצעיות השתא דאתית להכי דתרצית דקתני באידך פרקין דכ"ד לא הוי שיורא כלומר לעולם באחרונות איכא כ"ד ובאמצעיות לא והא דלא קתני שבאילו יש כ"ד ובאילו אין כ"ד משום דקתני לה באידך פירקא דבאחרונות איכא כ"ד ולא באמצעיות והא דקתני אין בין שלש ראשונות לשלש אמצעיות וכו' אמר הא לכל דבריהם זה וזה שוין דכי היכי דבאמצעות ליכא כ"ד ה"נ בראשונות ומצינו לאוקמי הא דקתני שצבור מתפללין י"ט בש"צ בקמייתא דליכא כ"ד ולא ביחיד דאין יחיד קובע ברכה לעצמו: נקוט אמצעייתא בידך כלומר כולהי אמרו דבאמצעייתא מתענות ולא בראשונות ולא באחרונות בראשונות לא דאכתי לא תקיף רוגזא ובאחרונות דקשי עלה להתענות שבעת ימים ומתרצו כולהי הא דקתני מתענות

מסורת הש"ס / עין משפט / הגהות

נ"ל שנ"ל באחרונות

[לעיל יב: ע"ש]

[סוכה נג. וש"נ]

עה א מיי' פ"ג מהל' תעניות הלכה ה טוש"ע א"ח סימן תקעה סעיף ה:
עו ב מיי' שם הלכה ז טוש"ע שם סעיף ז:
עז ג מיי' שם פ"ב הל' יג טוש"ע שם סימן תקעו סעיף א:
עח ד מיי' שם הלכה ו טוש"ע שם סעיף ט:
עט ה מיי' שם הלכה ט טוש"ע שם סעיף ט:
פ ו מיי' פ"א שם הל' ו טוש"ע שם סימן תקעו סעיף יג:

הגהות הב"ח

(א) גמ' לא הוו מתריעין אלא צועקין הא צעקה בפה הוא ומלצעקה בפה התרעה: (ב) תוס' ד"ה תני כו' לא ברשונות ולא באחרונות אמר רב אשי נקוט מציעתא בידך פירש הקונטר' השלש תעניות: (ג) ד"ה ורב יהודה כו' אומר הר"י דהאי עננו:

הגהות הגר"א

[א] גמ' אין פוחתין משבע. שבכן כ"ה בתוספ' כל"ל (ועי' לחם משנה פ"ג מהלכות תענית הלכה יז):

ב"ק פ:

[צ"ל דתנן] לקמן יט.

גליון הש"ס

גמרא אמר רב אשי נקוט אמצעייתא. כעין זה נדה דף כ ע"ב:

גזר תלת עשרה תעניות, ולא איעני. סבר למיגזר טפי. אמר ליה ר' אמי: הרי אמרו אין מטריחין את הצבור יותר מדאי. אמר ר' אבא בריה דרבי חייא בר אבא: רבי אמי *דעבד — לגרמיה הוא דעבד. אלא הכי אמר ר' חייא בר אבא אמר ר' יוחנן: לא שנו אלא לגשמים, אבל לשאר מיני פורענויות — מתענין והולכין עד שיענו מן השמים. תניא נמי הכי: כשאמרו שלש וכשאמרו שבע — לא אמרו אלא לגשמים, אאבל לשאר מיני פורעניות, מתענין והולכין עד שיענו. לימא תיהוי תיובתיה דר' אמי? אמר לך רבי אמי: תנאי היא, דתניא: אין גוזרין יותר משלש עשרה תעניות על הצבור, לפי שאין מטריחין את הצבור יותר מדאי. דברי רבי. רשב"ג אומר: לא מן השם הוא זה, אלא מפני שיצא זמנה של רביעה. שלחו ליה בני נינוה לרבי: כגון אנן, דאפילו בתקופת תמוז בעינן מיטרא, היכי נעביד? כיחידים דמינן או כרבים דמינן? כיחידים דמינן — וב"שומע תפלה"? או כרבים דמינן — ובברכת השנים? בשלח להו: כיחידים דמיתו, וב"שומע תפלה". מיתיבי, אמר רבי יהודה: *גאימתי? — בזמן שהשנים כתיקנן וישראל שרוין על אדמתן. אבל בזמן הזה — הכל לפי השנים, הכל לפי המקומות, הכל לפי הזמן. אמר ליה: מתניתא רמית עליה דרבי? רבי תנא הוא ופליג. מאי הוי עלה? רב נחמן אמר: בברכת השנים. רב ששת אמר: ב"שומע תפלה". והלכתא: ב"שומע תפלה". § "בשני מטין עם חשיכה, ובחמישי כל היום מפני כבוד השבת". § איבעיא להו: היכי קתני? בב' מטין עם חשיכה, ובה' כל היום מפני כבוד השבת? או דילמא: בשני מטין, ובחמישי פותחין כל היום כולו? תא שמע, דתניא: דבשני מטין עד הערב, ובחמישי פותחין כל היום כולו מפני כבוד השבת. היו לו שני פתחים, פותח אחד ונועל אחד. היה לו אצטבא כנגד פתחו — פותח כדרכו ואינו חושש. § "עברו אלו ולא נענו, ממעטין במשא ומתן, ובבנין ובנטיעה". § תנא: *ה"בבנין — בנין של שמחה. נטיעה — נטיעה של שמחה. אי זהו בנין של שמחה — זה הבונה בית חתנות לבנו. אי זו היא נטיעה של שמחה — זה הנוטע *אבוורנקי של מלכים". § "ובשאילת שלום". § תנו רבנן: וחברים אין שאילת שלום ביניהן. עמי הארץ ששואלין מחזירין להם בשפה רפה ובכובד ראש. *והן מתעטפין ויושבין כאבלים וכמנודין, כבני אדם הנזופין למקום, עד שירחמו עליהם מן השמים. *אמר ר' אלעזר: זאין אדם חשוב רשאי ליפול על פניו אלא אם כן נענה כיהושע בן נון, שנאמר °"ויאמר ה' אל יהושע קום לך, למה זה אתה נופל על פניך" ואמר ר' אלעזר: אין אדם חשוב רשאי לחגור שק אלא אם כן נענה כיהורם בן אחאב, שנאמר °"ויהי, כשמוע המלך את דברי האשה, ויקרע את בגדיו, והוא עובר על החומה, וירא העם, והנה, השק על בשרו" וגו'. ואמר ר' אלעזר: לא הכל בקריעה ולא הכל בנפילה. משה ואהרן בנפילה, יהושע וכלב בקריעה. משה ואהרן בנפילה, דכתיב °"ויפל משה ואהרן על פניהם". יהושע וכלב בקריעה, דכתיב °"ויהושע בן נון, וכלב בן יפנה... קרעו בגדיהם". מתקיף לה ר' זירא, ואיתימא ר' שמואל בר נחמני: אי הוה כתיב "יהושע", כדקאמרת, השתא דכתיב, "ויהושע", הא והא עביד. ואמר ר' אלעזר: לא הכל בקימה, ולא הכל בהשתחויה. מלכים — בקימה, ושרים — בהשתחויה. מלכים בקימה, דכתיב: °"כה אמר ה', גואל ישראל, קדושו, לבזה

רבי יהודה נשיאה גזר תליסר תעניות. על שאר פורעניות. (ג)ומיהו קאמר ליה רבי אמי דאין מטריחין, דהכי נמי משמע דהוה אשאר מיני פורעניות, מדמייתי עלה הא דקאמר רבי יוחנן: ל"ש אלא לגשמים אבל לשאר מינים וכו':

שיצאה זמנה של רביעה. דזמן רביעה דיורה הוי במרחשון, ויצא מרחשון:

שלח להו כיחידים דמיתו. פירוש: ובשומע תפלה תאמרו תפלת(ד) תענית. והא דיחיד אומר "ותן טל ומטר" בברכת השנים, אע"ג שמתפלל בעצמו — הואיל וזמן לצבור הוא. אבל בני נינוה הוו יחידים, אפי' בתקופת תמוז צריכין למטרא:

הכל לפי השנים. אם צריכים אותה שנה גשמים שהיא שחונה, ואם צריכים גשמים כבני נינוה — שואלין "ותן טל ומטר" בברכת השנים:

תורה אור

גזר תליסר תעניתא. כדאמרינן במתניתין (דף טו:): שלש ראשונות ושלש אמצעיות ושבע אחרונות. ולשאר פורעניות עביד להו ולא לגשמים: **לגרמיה.** לעצמו דרש, שלא אמר אלא לפי שהוא לא היה רוצה להתענות: **לא שנו.** דאין גוזרים יותר משלש עשרה: **כשאמרו.** להתענות שלש ראשונות ושלש אמצעיות ושבע אחרונות: **לא מן השם הוא זה.** שאין זה (א) טעם, שאין מניחין בשביל טורח, אלא שכבר יצא זמנה של רביעה של יורה. שהרי מרחשון עבר על כולן לסוף התעניות, שמקצתן היו בכסליו, כדקתני מתניתין. ואיכא למשמע מדרבי שמעון דבשאר מיני פורעניות, דכל שעתא הוי זימנייהו למיבטלי — אפילו טפי גזרינן. ורבי דאמר אין מטריחין — סתמא אכולהו קאמר, ואנא דאמרי כרבי: **ובשומע תפלה.** אמרינן לשאילת מטר כיחיד השואל צרכיו בשומע תפלה. דהא דאמרינן שאלה בברכת השנים אפי' ביחיד — משום דזמן צבור הוא. אבל במילתא אחריתי, דהוי ליחיד ולא לצבור, כהכא דבתקופת תמוז לאו זמן שאילת צבור הוא — בשומע תפלה הוא דמדכר ליה, ולא בברכת השנים, כדאמרינן במסכת ע"ז (דף ח.) ובברכות (דף לא.): אם היה לו חולה בתוך ביתו — מזכיר עליו בברכת החולים, ולבסוף מוקמינן: והלכתא בשומע תפלה, כך שמעתי: **אימתי.** הוא סדר תעניות: **בזמן שהשנים כתיקנן.** שהיא קציר בניסן, וזריעה במרחשון, ואין סדר השנים משתנה: **וישראל שרוין על אדמתן.** שמנהג ארץ ישראל בכך: **הכל לפי השנים.** אם צריכה אותה שנה למטר, כגון שנה שחונה שצריכה לגשמים הרבה: **לפי המקומות.** כגון נינוה, דאפי' בתקופת תמוז בעו מטרא — לא גרסינן לפי הזמן, שלא ירדו עדיין גשמים: ***בשני מטין עם חשיכה.** ולא נועלין ולא פותחין, הואיל ולאו *)לכבוד שבת הוה. ובחמישי מותרין לפתוח לגמרי: **מטין.** שלא יראו בני אדם ויצטערו, אלא לעת ערב פותחין מקצתן, כדי שיהא להם מה לאכול בלילה: **או דילמא.** פותחין כל היום, והכי משמע מתניתין: בשני מטין ובה' היה פתוח כדרכו כל היום לגמרי, מפני כבוד השבת: **איצטבא.** כסא. דהשתא אין החנות פתוחה לרשות הרבים, ואם הוא פתוח — אינו נראה כל כך: **פותח כדרכו.** אפי' בשני (ג): ה"ג: **תנא** בבנין בנין של שמחה נטיעה נטיעה של שמחה. בנין דקתני מתניתין לא בנין הצריך לו, אלא בנין הצריך לשמחה, דדבר שמחה ממעטינן: **בית חתנות.** לעשות חופתו: **אבוורנקי של מלכים.** שכך היו נוהגין: כשנולד בן למלך היו נוטעין אילן לשמו, ויום שממליכין אותו עושין לו כסא ממנו. לישנא אחרינא: אילן גדול המיסך על הארץ לטייל המלך תחתיו, ודומה לו בעירובין (דף כה:): ההוא אבוורנקא דהוה ליה לריש גלותא בבוסתניה: **של מלכים.** דרך מלכים נוטעין אותו לצל, הוא נוטעו כמו כן לצל היא והיא נטיעה של שמחה: **ששאל בשלום.** תלמיד חכם מחזיר לו משום איבה, ובשפה רפה: **אבל ומנודה חייבין בעטיפה.** ⁰דכתיב "ועל שפם יעטה" במועד קטן (דף טו.): **רשאי ליפול על פניו.** לבזות עצמו בפני הצבור, שאם לא יענה יחרפוהו, כך שמעתי. אלא אם כן יודעין בו שהוא חשוב כיהושע, שאמר לו הקב"ה: "קום לך, למה זה אתה נופל על פניך": **אלא אם כן נענה.** שיודעין הן שנענה כיהורם. יהורם רשע היה, אלא שהתענה על רעב שהיה בימיו ונענה, דכתיב (מלכים ב ז) "ויהי סאה סולת בשקל וסאתים שעורים בשקל": **לא הכל.** נענין (*בתפלה) ולא הכל נענין בקריעה. דיהושע וכלב שלא היו חשובין כמשה ואהרן לא זכו ליענות אלא בקריעה. ומקרא בעלמא קא דריש: ויהושע בן נון. כתיב בתריה דההוא ד"ויפל", וי"ו מוסיף על ענין ראשון:

[נ"ל בנפילה]

*) ולאו לכבוד שבת הוא לא מטין כל היום שיראו בני אדם ויצטערו אלא לעת ערב כנ"ל וכל זה עד לאכול בלילה הוא דיבור אחד:

עין משפט נר מצוה

פא א מיי' פ"ב מהל' תענית הלכה ב טור ש"ע א"ח סימן תקעו סעיף א:

פב ב מיי' פ"ב מהלכות תפלה הלכה יז טוש"ע א"ח סימן קיז סעיף ב:

פג ג מיי' פ"ג מהל' תענית הלכה י טור ש"ע א"ח סימן תקעה סעיף ט:

פד ד מיי' שם הלכה ז טוש"ע שם סעיף ד:

פה ה ו מיי' שם הל' ח טוש"ע שם סעיף ז:

פו ז מיי' פ"ה מהלכות תפלה הלכה יז טוש"ע א"ח סימן קלא סעיף ח:

רבינו חננאל

נהר ועל הספינה המטרפת בים ר' יוסי אומר לעזרה אבל לא לצעקה והא הכא התרעה בשופר ליכא למימר דהא שבת היא ושופר בשבת אסור אלא לאו בעננו וקתני מתריעין בשבת ש"מ דקרי לעננו התרעה ש"מ הא דא"ר אמי אין מטריחין על הצבור יותר מדאי ואמרינן לגרמיה הוא דעביד כלומר לא היה יכול להתענות ובשביל עצמו אמר אין מטריחין דתניא כשאמרו י"ג תעניות לפי שאין מטריחין על הצבור לא אמרו אלא לגשמים בלבד אבל לשאר מיני פורעניות מתענין והולכין עד שיענו. ומשני ר' אמי תנאי היא דתניא אין גוזרין על הצבור יותר מי"ג תעניות לפי שאין מטריחין על הצבור יותר מדאי דברי רבי רשב"ג אומר לא מן השם הוא זה אלא מפני שיצא זמנה של רביעה. בני נינוה בעו מר' אנן דאפילו בתקופת תמוז בעי' מטרא אנה נזכיר ותן טל ומטר בברכת השנים או בשומע תפלה כיחיד ששואל צרכיו בשומע תפלה אמר להו בשומע תפלה כיחידים ואותבינן עליה א"ר יהודה אימתי שואלין הגשמים בפרקים הללו בזמן שהשנים כתיקונן וישראל שרוין על אדמתם אבל בזמן הזה הכל לפי השנים הכל לפי המקומות הכל לפי הזמן קשיא לרבי ודחי רבי תנא הוא וחולק על התנאים. מאי הוה עלה ואסיקנא רב ששת אמר בשומע תפלה וקיי"ל כוותיה. ותוב לגבי איסורא הלכתא כרב ששת וזו איסורא היא: **פיסקא** בשני מטין עם חשכה ומיבעיא לן ופשטנא ממתני' דתניא בשני מטין לעת ערב ובחמישי פותחין כל היום מפני כבוד השבת היו לו ב' פתחים פותח אחד ונועל א' היתה לו איצטבא כנגד פתחו פותח ונועל כדרכו ואינו חושש עברו אלו [י"ג תעניות] ולא נענו ממעטין במשא ומתן כו' בנין זה בנין של שמחה: **ירושלמי** אריב"ל ל"ש אלא בנין של שמחה ממעטין אבל אם היה נוהה סותרו ובונה: ת"ר חבירין אין שאילת שלום ביניהן עמי הארץ ששאלו מחזירין להן בשפה רפה ובכובד ראש. והן מתעטפין ויושבין כמנודין וכאבלים כבני ניזופין עד שירחמו

הגהות הב"ח

(א) רש"י ד"ה לא מן השם וכו' שאין זה הטעם: (ב) ד"ה פותח כדרכו אפילו בשני מה"ד הלא קציר חטים וגו' ודעו וראו כי רעתכם רבה אלמא סימן קללה הוי הס"ד וכ"ב זהו פי' לסוף המשנה דלעיל בדף יב ע"ב: (ג) תוס' ד"ה ר' יהודה כו' שאר פורענות והאי קאמר ליה כו' והכי נמי משמע: (ד) ד"ה שלח כו' תאמרו תפלת מטר והא דיחיד אומר כו' הוו יחידים דאפילו בתקופת תמוז:

גליון הש"ס

רש"י ד"ה אבל ומנודה דכתיב ועל שפם יעטה. תמוה לי הא הך קרא במצורע כתיב ואבל נפקא לן במו"ק מדאזהר ליחזקאל לא תעטה ע"ש הא אחר צריך עיטוף. ובמנודה לא מייתי קרא כלל והוא איבעיא דלא אפשיטא שם ועע"ג:

מסורת הש"ס

[ברכות מח. וש"נ]

מגילה ה:

[דיבור זה שייך לעיל במשנה יב:]

מו"ק טו.

מגילה כב:

רבינו גרשום

מתענות בראשונות ולא באחרונות היינו אמצעיתא שהן ראשונות לאחרונות ולא באחרונות ממש והאי דקתני מתענות באחרונות היינו אמצעות שהן אחרונות לראשונות ולא בראשונות ממש והאי דקתני אין מתענות לא בראשונות ולא באחרונות היינו ראשונות ממש היינו אחרונות ממש שהן שלש עשרה דהאי שלש שהיחידים מתענין לא חשיב כלום: בעננו והיינו התרעה דהוו בכינופיא ובהן י"ג תרועות כדאמרן בפירקין דלקמן דבברכה ראשונה אמר להם קודם הברכה תקעו ולאחר הברכה תקעו ותוקעין ומריעין ותוקעין וקודם ברכה שניה אומר להם הריעו ומריעין ולאחר ברכות אומר להם הריעו ומריעין ותוקעין ומריעין נמצא בברכה ראשונה מריע אחת ובשניה ג' וכן בכל אלו ז' ברכות בראשונה תרועה אחת ובשניה ג' תרועות נמצא לז' ברכות י"ג תקיעות וסימן לדבר דעבדינן תרועה יריחו הא יריחו בשופרות הוות ומדנקט סימן יריחו ש"מ דתרועה בשופר: החיכוך שחין היה צעקה בפה ומדקתני לא דיו מתריעין אלא צועקין אלמא דצעקה בפה ותרועה בשופר: לעזרה ולא לצעקה כל אחד מתפלל בפני עצמו אבל אין עושין כנופיא. ר' יהודה גזר תליסר תעניתא הני דקתני במתניתין רב אמי דאמר אין מתענין יותר מי"ג לגרמיה עבד לא הורה כהלכה: לא שנו שאין מטריחין יותר מדאי אלא לגשמים אבל לשאר פורעניות מתענין והולכין עד שיענו והאי דר' יהודה נשיאה שאר מיני פורעניות הוה: שאין מטריחין את הצבור יותר מדאי דברי רבי אפילו בשאר מיני פורעניות ור' אמי דאמר כר' לא מן השם הוא זה כלומר לאו להכי הוא דבשאר מיני פורעניות אין מטריחין יותר מי"ג אלא לגשמים אין מתענין יותר מי"ג כבר יצאה זמנה של רביעה דבר"ח כסלו הוה ביום ראשון וגזרו תענית בשני ובחמישי ושני דהיינו ט"ו יום בכסליו ומתחיל השניות בשני וחמישי ושני הרי כבר יצא כל כסליו ועכשיו בר"ח טבת מתחילין הז' תעניות חמישי ושני בכל שבוע הרי יצאו בו' תעניות ג' שבועות וגוזרין בשביעי ביום שני בשבוע רביעי הרי יצא כל טבת וי"ג תעניות ואם היו גוזרין עוד תעניות לא היו יכולין לגזור בטבת דאין גוזרין בתחלה אלא ביום שני ושני דטבת כבר עבר אלא היה להם לגזור ביום שני שבשבט וכבר עבר מקצת שבט ובר"ח כבר יצא זמן רביעה וכבר יצאו רוב גשמי שנה דלהכי הוי *) אמר בשבט ר"ה לאילן דכבר יצאו רוב גשמי שנה: כיחידים דמין ובשומע תפלה ושואלים מטר כיחיד ששואל צרכיו בשומע תפלה א"ר יהודה אימתי סדר כל אילו התעניות הכל לפי השנים דשנה שחונה צריכה לרוב גשמים ושאינה שחונה אינה צריכה גשמים מרובים הכל לפי המקומות כגון נינוה שואלין הגשמים [בתקופת תמוז] ומדכולל הכי ש"מ דשואלין בצבור: מטין עם חשכה לא נועלין ולא פותחין לא נועלין משום בני כפרים שבאין להספיק מים ומזון לאחיהם שבכרכין ולא פותחין הואיל דלאו לכבוד שבת הוא: ובחמישי מותרין לפתוח לגמרי: יש לו שני פתחים בשני פותח אחד לגמרי הואיל ונועל אחר ואם אין לו אלא פתח אחד ולפניו אצטבה פותח [ונועל] כדרכו לגמרי אפילו בשני הואיל ויש לפניו איצטבא דיש היכר. ה"ג תנא

*) אולי צ"ל אחד בשבט אבל צ"ע דא"כ שנה משנתו כב"ש ואפשר דצ"ל ט"ו בשבט וצ"ע.

לבזה נפש, למתעב גוי, לעבד מושלים, מלכים יראו וקמו". ושרים בהשתחויה, דכתיב: "שרים וישתחוו". מתקיף לה רבי זירא, ואיתימא רבי שמואל בר נחמני: אי הוה כתיב, "ושרים ישתחוו", כדקאמרת. השתא דכתיב, "שרים וישתחוו", הא והא עבוד. אמר רב נחמן בר יצחק: אף אני אומר: לא הכל לאורה, ולא הכל לשמחה, צדיקים לאורה, וישרים לשמחה. תהלים צז צדיקים לאורה, דכתיב: °"אור זרוע לצדיק", ולישרים שמחה, דכתיב: "ולישרי לב שמחה".§

הדרן עלך מאימתי

סדר [א]תעניות כיצד? מוציאין את התיבה לרחובה של עיר, *ונותנין אפר מקלה על גבי התיבה, ובראש הנשיא, ובראש אב בית דין, וכל אחד ואחד נותן בראשו. הזקן שבהן אומר לפניהן דברי כבושין: אחינו! יונה ג לא נאמר באנשי נינוה: "וירא אלהים את שקם ואת תעניתם", אלא °"וירא יואל ב אלהים את מעשיהם, כי שבו מדרכם הרעה". ובקבלה הוא אומר °"וקרעו לבבכם, ואל בגדיכם" עמדו בתפלה. מורידין לפני התיבה זקן, ורגיל, ויש לו בנים, וביתו ריקם, כדי שיהא לבו שלם בתפלה. [ב]ואומר לפניהן עשרים וארבעה ברכות, י"ח שבכל יום, ומוסיף עליהן עוד שש. ואלו הן: זכרונות תהלים קכ ושופרות; °"אל ה' בצרתה לי קראתי, ויענני"; °"אשא עיני אל ההרים" וגו' שם קכא °)"ממעמקים קראתיך, ה'"; °°)"תפלה לעני, כי יעטוף". ר' יהודה אומר: לא היה צריך לומר זכרונות ושופרות. אלא אומר תחתיהן °°°)"רעב כי יהיה בארץ, ירמיהו יד דבר כי יהיה", °"אשר היה דבר ה' אל ירמיהו על דברי הבצרות". ואומר חותמיהן. על הראשונה הוא אומר: "מי שענה את אברהם בהר המוריה, הוא יענה אתכם וישמע בקול צעקתכם היום הזה. ברוך אתה ה', גואל ישראל". על השניה הוא אומר: "מי שענה את אבותינו על ים סוף, הוא יענה אתכם וישמע קול צעקתכם היום הזה. ברוך אתה ה', זוכר הנשכחות". על השלישית הוא אומר: "מי שענה את יהושע בגלגל, הוא יענה אתכם וישמע בקול צעקתכם היום הזה. ברוך אתה ה', שומע תרועה". על הרביעית הוא אומר: "מי שענה את שמואל במצפה, הוא יענה אתכם וישמע בקול צעקתכם היום הזה. ברוך אתה ה', שומע צעקה". על החמישית הוא אומר: "מי שענה את אליהו בהר הכרמל, הוא יענה אתכם וישמע בקול צעקתכם היום הזה. ברוך אתה ה', שומע תפלה". על הששית הוא אומר: "מי שענה את יונה ממעי הדגה, הוא יענה אתכם וישמע בקול צעקתכם היום הזה. ברוך אתה ה', העונה בעת צרה". על השביעית הוא אומר: "מי שענה את דוד ואת שלמה בנו בירושלים, הוא יענה אתכם וישמע בקול צעקתכם היום הזה. ברוך אתה ה', המרחם על הארץ".§ מעשה בימי

°) תהלים קל °) שם קב °) מ"א ח

לבזה נפש למתעב גוי לעבד מושלים. לישראל הבזוים ומתועבים ועבדים מושלין בהן: ולא הכל בקימה. לקראת ישראל לעתיד לבא "מלכים יראו וקמו שרים וישתחוו": ה"ג: לא הכל לאורה ולא הכל לשמחה דכתיב אור זרוע לצדיק ולישרי לב שמחה. ישרים לשמחה, דישרים עדיפי מצדיקים: תורה אור

הדרן עלך מאימתי

סדר תעניות כיצד כו': אפר מקלה. אפר ממש ולא עפר. אפר סתם הוא עפר, דכשם שאפר קרוי עפר, דכתיב (במדבר יט) "מעפר שרפת החטאת", כך עפר קרוי אפר סתם, והיינו דקתני אפר מקלה – אפר שריפה. אי הוה תני אפר סתם – הוה משמע עפר. ואפר מקלה גנאי יותר מעפר סתם. ובגמרא מפרש מאי טעמא נותנין אותו: כבושין. לשון עבירה. כמו מכבש, בלע"ז פריש"א (א)– שכובשין את הלבבות להחזירם למוטב, ואלו הן דברי כבושין: אחינו כו': ובקבלה. שהנביא מצוה לישראל (עמדו בתפלה). והקשה תוספות מאן דהו: מאי שנא בהאי קרא דכתיב ביונה "וירא האלהים את מעשיהם" וגו' °ולא קרי ליה דברי קבלה, ובהאי קרא ד"וקרעו לבבכם" קרי ליה קבלה? ופריק איהו: כל מקום שהנביא מצוה ומודיע ומזהיר את ישראל – קרי ליה קבלה, ובכל דוכתא דלא איתפקד נביא כי האי "וירא האלהים", שהוא כמספר והולך, דיליף מיניה אגב אורחיה מילתא – לא קרינן ליה קבלה: (ב) ברחובה של עיר. בגלוי. וכי הך דאמרינן במסכת מגילה (דף כה:): בני העיר שמכרו רחובה של עיר. והתם מפרש בהדיא, *אמר ר' זירא: הואיל והעם מתפללים בו בתעניות ובמעמדות: ורגיל. רגיל להתפלל, ותפלתו שגורה בפיו ולא יטעה, שכל (ג) חזן שטועה סימן רע לשולחיו*: וביתו ריקם. משמע דהוא עני, ואין לו מחיה בביתו, ובגמרא מפרש טעמא אחרינא: וגופו נקי מעבירות, שלא חטא, ולא יצא עליו שום שם רע בשום עבירה כו': זכרונות ושופרות. כל הפסוקים שאומרים בראש השנה: אל ה' בצרתה לי כו'. כולן הן מזמורים: ואומר חותמיהן. על כל פרשה ופרשה, אחר זכרונות – חתימת זכרונות, ואחר שופרות – חתימת שופרות, וכן אחר כולם מעין הפרשה, כדמפרש ואזיל: על הראשונה. בפעם ראשונה הוא אומר: מי שענה לאברהם כו'. בגואל ישראל היה מתחיל להאריך, והולך ואומר לכולן שש ברכות: על השניה. זו היא ברכה ראשונה של שש ברכות, כדאמרינן בגמ'. והיאך דגואל ישראל – זו היא ברכה עצמה של שמונה עשרה, ואינה מאותן שש, אלא שבה היה מתחיל להוסיף ולהאריך. על הזכרונות הוא אומר "זוכר הנשכחות", ועל השופרות "שומע תרועה", והיא שניה למנינה, ועל "אל ה' בצרתה לי", והיא שלישית למנין שש, "שומע צעקה" (ד) שלישית, וכן כולן: ומי שענה את אבותינו על ים סוף. לפיכך אומרה בזכרונות, לפי שהיו ישראל נשכחים במצרים כמה שנים, ונתייאשו מן הגאולה, וזכרם המקום וגאלם, דכתיב (שמות ו) "ואזכור את בריתי": ובשופרות היה אומר מי שענה את יהושע בגלגל. לפי שנענה בשופרות ביריחו, וזהו בעוד שהיו ישראל בגלגל: ואליהו בהר הכרמל. כנגד "אשא עיני אל ההרים", וכן כולן לפי ענין המזמורים, אליהו נענה בהר הכרמל מעין "אשא עיני אל ההרים", ושמואל במצפה דכתיבי קראי ומעין "אל ה' בצרתה לי": ממעי הדגה. מעין "ממעמקים קראתיך ה'" ועונה בעת צרה, שכן כתיב ביונה "קראתי מצרה לי" (יונה ב). ובשמואל כתיב "ויזעק אל ה'" (שמואל א ז) ובאליהו כתיב (מלכים א יח) "עננו" – זו תפלה: ועל השביעית. מפרש בגמרא מאי שביעית. מי שענה דוד "ויהי רעב בימי דוד שלש שנים שנה אחר שנה" (שמואל ב כא): ושלמה. כשהכניס הארון לבית קדש הקדשים. אי נמי "רעב כי יהיה בארץ" וגו' (מלכים א ח), ולפיכך חותם "מרחם על הארץ", שהן התפללו על ארץ ישראל. ו"תפלה לעני כי יעטוף" – על דוחק גשמים נופל, וכתיב ביה (בראשית) "בהעצר שמים": *בימי רבי חלפתא בצפורי. אביו של רבי יוסי, דאמרינן בסנהדרין (דף לב:): אחר רבי יוסי לצפורי, [אחר ר' חנניה בן תרדיון] בסיכני: וגומר

אור זרוע לצדיק ולישרי לב שמחה. פירוש: ואין לומר כדלעיל ולישרים האי והאי שמחה ואורה (ה), א"כ דאמרינן דלישרי לב קאי אהא דלעיל – כמו כן אמרינן דלדיקים קאי אהא דלאבתריה, כיון דסמוך לדיק לישרי לב, ובודאי יש הפרש בין זה לזה. דאם לא כן – לערבינהו ולכתוב "לצדיקים ולישרי לב אורה ושמחה". אבל ההיא דלעיל לא הוו מלכים ושרים כי הדדי, אלא יראו וקמו בינייהו, וכמו יראו וקמו, דהוי קודם שרים, קאי על מלכים דלעיל, – קאי נמי אשרים דכתיב אבתריה. אבל הכא אין לפרש אלא אור זרוע לצדיקים ולישרי לב שמחה*:

הדרן עלך מאימתי

א א מיי' פ"ד מהלכות תענית הלכה א ב ג טוש"ע א"ח סימן תקעט סעיף א:

ב ב מיי' שם ה"ז טור א"ח סימן תקעט:

[ועי' תוספו' מנחות יט. ד"ה במקרא]

רבינו חננאל

שירחמו עליהם מן השמים. א"ר אלעזר אין אדם חשוב רשאי ליפול על פניו א) [יחיד בצבור וכן מפורש בתלמוד ירושלמי] [בפ"ב ה"ו] אא"כ נענה כיהושע בן נון שנאמר ויאמר ה' אל יהושע קום לך למה זה אתה נופל על פניך וכן אין אדם חשוב רשאי לחגור שק על בשרו אא"כ נענה כיהורם שנאמר ויהי כשמוע המלך את דברי האשה ויקרע את בגדיו וירא העם והנה השק על בשרו. וא"ר אלעזר משה ואהרן בנפילה. יהושע וכלב בקריעה. ומסקנא יהושע הא והא קא עבד ועוד אמר מלכים בקימה שרים בהשתחויה ואני ב) אומר צדיקים וישרים בשמחה שנא' אור זרוע לצדיק ולישרי לב שמחה:

הדרן עלך מאימתי מזכירין

סדר תעניות כיצד מוציאין את

רבינו גרשום

תנא בנין בנין של שמחה כלומר הא דקתני ממעטין בבנין היינו בבנין של שמחה ג) אבוורנקי של מלכים שכשנולד בן נוטעין אילן אחד לשמו וכשמעמידין אותו למלך עושין ממנו כסא מלכות. ומנא לן דיהושע נענה דכתיב ויאמר ה' אל יהושע וגו' ויהושע ו' מוסיף על ענין ראשון דהא והא עבד בנפילה כמשה ובקריעה. לא הכל בקימה כלומר לעתיד לבוא שעומדין כנגד ישראל והא והא עביד קימה והשתחויה. ה"ג הכל לאורה ולא הכל לשמחה צדיקים לאורה ולזו לשמחה ישרים אף לשמחה דישרים עדיפי מצדיקים:

הדרן עלך מאימתי

סדר תעניות כו' ואפי' בקמייתא כלומר

א) נראה דצ"ל פי' יחיד בציבור וכו'. ב) נראה דחסר כאן וצ"ל אמר רנב"י אף אני אומר צדיקים לאורה וישרים לשמחה שנאמר וכו'. ג) אולי צ"ל ובנטיעה היינו נטיעה של שמחה כגון אבורנקי וכו'.

עי' תוספות לקמן ע"ב ד"ה ונותנין

[לפנינו שם סתמא דגמרא הוא ולא ר' זירא אמרה]

[ברכות לד.]

סייך לע"ב

הגהות הב"ח

(א) רש"י ד"ה כבושין כו' (שכובשין את הלבבות להחזירם למוטב) תא"מ ונ"ב ס"א שכובשין ודוחקין את הלב לעשות תשובה. תו' ענין אחר שמגלה להם סתרי מעשיהם כמו בהדי כבשי דרחמנא כו' פר"ח ז"ל: (ב) ד"ה ובקבלה כו' לישראל והקשה כצ"ל ותיבות עמדו בתפלה נמחק לא קרינן ליה קבלה מה"ד עמדו בתפלה ברחובה של עיר: (ג) ד"ה ורגיל כו' שכל ש"ל שטועה: (ד) ד"ה על השניה כו' שומע לעקה וכן כולם כצ"ל ותיבת שלישית נמחק והד"א עם ד"ה מי שענה וד"ה ובשופרות וד"ה ואליהו וכו' ושמואל במצפה כדכתיבי קראי וכו' והד"א עד בימי רבי חלפתא: (ה) תוספות ד"ה אור כו' שמחה ואורה דאם כן אמרינן דלישרי לב כו' כמו כן אמרינן דלדיק קאי אהא דלאבתריה כו' ולכתוב לצדיק ולישרי לב אורה ושמחה אבל בההיא דלעיל לא הוו מלכים ושרים כתובים אהדדי אלא כו' אור זרוע לצדיק ולישרי לב שמחה:

גליון הש"ס

רש"י ד"ה ובקבלה וכו' ולא קרי ליה דברי קבלה. עיין חולין דף קלז ע"א רש"י ד"ה תורת משה:

ג א מיי' פ"ד מהלכות תענית הלכה יז טור א"ח סימן תקעט:
ד ב מיי' שם פ"ג ה"ב:
ה ג מיי' שם הלכה ג:
ו ד מיי' שם הלכה ו:
ז ה ו מיי' פ"א מהלכות ביאת מקדש הלכה ו:
ח ז מיי' שם הלכה יב:
ט ח מיי' פ"ו מהלכות כלי המקדש הל' יא:
י ט מיי' פ"א מהלכות תענית הלכה ה טוש"ע א"ח סי' תקעב סעי' א:
יא י מיי' שם פ"ג הל' ג והל' ה טוש"ע שם סי' תקעה סעיף ג ד:
יב כ מיי' שם פ"א הל' ז טוש"ע שם סימן תקעב סעיף ב:
יג ל מיי' פ"ד שם הלכה א טוש"ע שם סימן תקעט סעיף א:

תורה אור

בימי רבי חלפתא ור' חנניא בן תרדיון, שעבר אחד לפני התיבה וגמר את הברכה כולה, ולא ענו אחריו "אמן". 'תקעו, הכהנים [א] ותקעו'. "מי שענה את אברהם אבינו בהר המוריה, הוא יענה אתכם וישמע בקול צעקתכם היום הזה". 'הריעו, בני אהרן הריעו'. "מי שענה את אבותינו על ים סוף, הוא יענה אתכם וישמע בקול צעקתכם היום הזה". (א) [א]וכשבא דבר אצל חכמים, אמרו: לא היינו נוהגין כן אלא בשער מזרח ובהר הבית. שלש תעניות הראשונות, *אנשי משמר מתענין ולא משלימין, ואנשי בית אב לא היו מתענין כלל. שלש שניות, אנשי משמר מתענין ומשלימין, ואנשי בית אב מתענין ולא משלימין. שבע אחרונות – אלו ואלו מתענין ומשלימין. דברי רבי יהושע. וחכמים אומרים: [ב]שלש תעניות הראשונות, אלו ואלו לא היו מתענין כלל. [ג]שלש שניות, – אנשי משמר מתענין ולא משלימין, ואנשי בית אב לא היו מתענין כלל. [ד]שבע אחרונות, – אנשי משמר מתענין ומשלימין, ואנשי בית אב מתענין ולא משלימין. [ה]אנשי משמר מותרין לשתות יין בלילות, אבל לא בימים. [ו]ואנשי בית אב לא ביום ולא בלילה *[ז]אנשי משמר [ח]ואנשי מעמד אסורין מלספר ומלכבס. *ובחמישי מותרין מפני כבוד השבת. כל הכתוב במגילת תענית "דלא למספד", לפניו אסור, לאחריו מותר. רבי יוסי אומר: לפניו ולאחריו אסור. "דלא להתענאה" – לפניו ולאחריו מותר. ר' יוסי אומר: לפניו אסור, לאחריו מותר. *[ט]אין גוזרין תענית על הצבור בתחילה בחמישי, שלא להפקיע השערים, אלא שלש תעניות הראשונות שני וחמישי ושני, ושלש שניות חמישי שני וחמישי. ר' יוסי אומר: [י]כשם שאין הראשונות בחמישי, כך לא שניות ולא אחרונות. *[כ]אין גוזרין תענית על הצבור בראשי חדשים, בחנוכה, ובפורים. ואם התחילו – אין מפסיקין, דברי רבן גמליאל. אמר רבי מאיר: אף על פי שאמר רבן גמליאל אין מפסיקין – מודה היה שאין משלימין. וכן תשעה באב שחל להיות בערב שבת.§ **גמ'** "סדר תעניות כיצד? מוציאין את התיבה" כו'. ואפילו בקמייתא?! ורמינהו: שלש תעניות ראשונות ושניות, נכנסים לבית הכנסת, ומתפללין כדרך שמתפללין כל השנה כולה. ובשבע אחרונות, מוציאין את התיבה לרחובה של עיר, ונותנין אפר על גבי התיבה, ובראש הנשיא, ובראש אב בית דין, וכל אחד ואחד [ב] נוטל ונותן בראשו. רבי נתן אומר: אפר מקלה הן מביאין. אמר רב פפא: [ל]כי תנן נמי מתניתין – אשבע אחרונות תנן.§ "ובראש הנשיא".§ והדר תני "כל אחד ואחד [ג] (*נוטל ונותן) בראשו". איני?! (*והתנן) *רבי אומר: בגדולה – מתחילין מן הגדול. *ובקללה – מתחילין מן הקטן. בגדולה, מתחילין מן הגדול – שנאמר "ויאמר משה אל אהרן, ולאלעזר ולאיתמר". ויקרא י ובקללה, מתחילין מן הקטן – (*דאמר מר) *בתחלה נתקלל נחש, ואחר כך נתקללה חוה, ואח"כ נתקלל אדם"! הא חשיבותא לדידהו, דאמרי להו: אתון חשיביתו למיבעי עלן רחמי אכ"ע.§ (*"כל אחד ואחד [ד] (*נוטל ונותן) בראשו".§ אמר רב אדא) וכל אחד ואחד (*נוטל ונותן) בראשו, נשיא ואב בית דין נמי נשקלו אינהו ונינחו בראשייהו! מאי שנא דשקיל איניש אחרינא ומנח להו? אמר רבי *אבא דמן קסרי: *אינו דומה מתבייש מעצמו למתבייש

[שייך לע"א במשנה]
[נ"ל והתניא] [נ"ל נותן]
[ליתא בברכות והם מסוללי הכנה]
רש"א מוחק זה והפיסקא מתחיל מן אילך וכל אחד ואחד וכו'
[גי' רי"ף אדא וגי' רא"ש זירא]

ואפילו בקמייתא. כלומר ואפי' בג' תעניות הראשונות ובג' שניות קאמר במתני' דמוציאין את התיבה לרחובה של עיר ואומר כ"ד ברכות כו'. ורמינהו, והתניא: ראשונות ושניות נכנסין כו', פי': ומתפללין בה כדרך כל השנה כולה, כלומר: שיאמר י"ח ברכות כדרך שמתפללין כל השנה. וקשה: דהא לעיל(ד) בפ"ק (דף יג:) קאמרינן אין בין ג' תעניות שניות לשלש ראשונות אלא שבאלו (ה)מתפללין ומותרין בעשיית מלאכה ובאלו אסורין בעשיית מלאכה. הא לענין עשרים וארבעה – זה וזה שוין, דבין בראשונות בין באמצעיות היו אומרים כ"ד! ועוד קשה, דאמרינן לעיל: ואיבעית אימא באמצעיות נמי לא מצלו כ"ד, ואמאי לא מייתי לה סיועא מהא דהכא? וי"ל: דהא דקאמר הכא ומתפללין כדרך כל השנה לאו בעשרים וארבע ברכות קאמר, אלא קאמר שמתפללין כדרך כל השנה, שלא היו מוציאין את התיבה לרחובה של עיר:

***ונותנין** אפר על גבי כו'. ואותו אפר הוי מעצם אדם, שהרי (ו) הוא האפר הוי לזכרון העקידה, ובעקידה היה עצמות: במקום

וגומר כל הברכה. כל אותה ברכה עצמה: ה"ג: ולא ענו אחריו אמן תקעו בני אהרן תקעו. חזן הכנסת אומר להן על כל ברכה וברכה, והוא השמש, ולא שליח צבור: לא היינו נוהגין. שלא לענות אמן: אלא בשער מזרח ובהר הבית. כלומר, בזמן שבית המקדש קיים כשמתפללין בהר הבית נכנסין בדרך שער המזרח. לפי שלא היו עונין אמן במקדש, כדאמרינן בגמרא (דף טז:). ואין לומר לא היו נוהגין כן לתקוע אלא במקדש – דודאי תוקעין בגבולים, כדמוכח בכולה הך מסכת ומסכת ראש השנה (דף כו: כז.): אנשי משמר. של אותה שבת: ולא משלימין. שעדיין אינן חמורין כל כך. ובגמרא (דף יז.) מפרש שמא תכבד העבודה על אנשי בית אב, שהיו עובדין אותו היום, ובאים הן לסייעם. ואם היו מתענים(ב) – לא היה להם כח לעמוד בעבודה: אנשי בית אב. המשמרה מתחלקת לשבעה בתי אבות, כנגד שבעת ימי השבוע, בית אב ליום: אנשי [מעמד]. אחד כהנים ולוים וישראלים הקבועים ועומדין ומתפללין על קרבן אחיהם שיתקבל לרצון, ועומדים לשם בשעת עבודה. דהיאך קרבנו של אדם קרב והוא אינו עומד על גביו? וכולהו מפרש בפרק אחרון (דף כו.): מותרין לשתות יין. לאו גבי תענית איתמר, אלא אגב דמיירי בבני משמר מייתי לה: בלילות. אין לחוש שמא תכבד העבודה, שהרי לאו מבערב שפסקו הקרבנות ולא כבדה העבודה. *שיביאו רוב קרבנות ולא יספיקו בני בית אב של אותו היום, וצריכין אלו לסייען, והרי אינן ראויין לעבודה משום שכרות: אנשי בית אב אסורין בין ביום ובין בלילה. לפי שהיו מעלין כל הלילה אברים ופדרים שפקעו מעל המזבח. א"נ: לא גמרו ביום – גומרים בלילה. אבל אנשי משמר אינן צריכין לסייע בלילה להפך במזלג, דבית אב יכול להספיק לבדו היפוך המערכה: אסורים לספר ולכבס. משנכנסו למשמרתם, כל אותה שבת, אלא מסתפרין קודם לכן. וטעמא מפרש בגמרא: ובחמישי. של משמרתן מותרים. דרך רוב בני אדם להסתפר בחמישי, ולא בערב שבת, מפני הטורח: כל הכתוב במגילת תענית דלא למיספד. דאית יומא דלא להתענאה, ומקצתהון דחמירי טפי דלא למיספד. ואותן שהן חמורים ואסורים בהספד – לפניו אסור בהספד, דילמא אתי למיעבד ביו"ט גופיה: ולאחריו מותר. דכיון שעבר יום לא חיישינן. ואותן שאינן חמורין ליאסר בהספד, אלא דלא להתענאה בין לפניו כו': שלא להפקיע את השערים. כשרואין בעלי חניות שקונין למוצאי יום חמישי שתי סעודות גדולות, אחת(ג) לליל חמישי ואחת לשבת, סבורים שבא רעב לעולם ומייקרים ומפקיעים השער. אבל משהתחילו להתענות – יודעין שאינו אלא מפני התענית: בראשי חדשים. דאיקרי מועד: ואם התחילו. שקיבלו תענית מקודם לכן, ונכנס בהן ראש חדש – אין מפסיקין. דאף על גב דאיקרי מועד – לא כתיב ביה יום משתה ושמחה*: שאין משלימין. להתענות כל היום, אלא אוכלין סמוך לערב: מגילת תענית נכתבה בימי חכמים, אע"פ שלא היו כותבין הלכות. והיינו דקתני "כל הכתוב במגילת תענית", כאילו היה מקרא: **גמ'** אפילו בקמייתא. מוציאין את התיבה?! בתמיה: כי קתני נמי מתני'. סדר תעניות כיצד – בסדר תעניות אחרונות קא מיירי: ה"ג בגמרא: ונותנין אפר על גבי התיבה. ולא גרסינן אפר מקלה*. אפר שריפה עדיף, משום אפרו של יצחק, כדלקמן: בגדולה. מנוה בעצמא שלא לפורענות "וידבר משה אל אהרן ואל אלעזר" וגו'. הא נמי דיהבינן בראשייהו דנשיא ואב ב"ד ברישא חשיבותא הוא, דאמרי להו אתון חשיביתו טפי כו': דשקיל איניש אחרינא כו'. דקתני: ונותנין ע"ג התיבה כו' ועל ראש הנשיא כו' – דמשמע על ידי אחר. וגבי שאר כל אדם לא תני נותנין, אלא כל אחד ואחד (*נוטל) כו':

[לעיל יב.]
[מו"ק יז.]
[לקמן כט:]
[בימים שיביאו רוב כו' והוא דיבור בפ"ע]
עירובין מח.
ברכות סא.
[בסי' ובקלקלה וכן בסמוך]
[שם. עירובין יח.]
[נ"ל נותן]
[נ"ל נותן]
[סנהדרין מב.]
[עי' תוי"ט]
הס"ד ואח"כ מד"א אפר מקלה אפר כו' כנ"ל
[נ"ל נותן]

רבינו חננאל

התיבה כו'. ואקשינן סדר תעניות מכלל דבכולהו מוציאין את התיבה והתניא שלשה תעניות הראשונות נכנסין לבתי כנסיות ומדרשות ומתפללין כדרך שמתפללין כל השנה שבע אחרונות מוציאין את התיבה לרחובה של עיר כו'. ושני רב פפא כי תנן מוציאין את התיבה בז' אחרונות תנן. ואקשינן אמאי אין מתחילין מן הקטן דתניא ר' אומר בגדולה מתחילין מן הגדול שנאמר ויאמר משה אל אהרן. *) ואל אלעזר ואל איתמר בניו ובקללה מתחילין מן הקטן דאמר מר בתחלה נתקלל הנחש ואחריו חוה ואחריה אדם ושנינן נתינת אפר על ראש הנשיא חשיבות היא לו דאמרינן ליה חשיבת קמיה דקב"ה למבעי

*) נ"ל ולאלעזר ולאיתמר או נ"ל וידבר משה וכו'.

רבינו גרשום

דתני בסתם מוציאין את התיבה דמשמע אפילו בראשונות. פאר זו תפילין דכתיב פארך חבוש עליך

גליון הש"ס

רש"י ד"ה מגילת תענית נכתבה. עיין לעיל דף יב ע"א רש"י ד"ה בלנו:

הגהות הגר"א

[א] במשנה ותקעו. נ"ל תקעו (וכ"ה במשניות): [ב] גמ' וכל אחד ואחד נותן כנ"ל ובשבתיים מוקף: [ג] שם כל או"א נותן כנ"ל: [ד] שם כל או"א נותן בראשו אמר כו' כנ"ל ובשבתיים מוקף:

הגהות הב"ח

(א) גמ' את אבותינו על ים סוף כו' היום הזה וכן בכל ברכה וברכה וכשבא הדבר אצל חכמים: (ב) רש"י ד"ה ולא משלימין כו' ואם היו מתענים ומשלימין לא היה להם: (ג) ד"ה שלא להפקיע כו' סעודות גדולות אחת ליום התענית לליל חמישי: (ד) תוספות ד"ה ואפילו כו' וקשה דהא לעיל. נ"ב פירוש המקשה קאמר הכי לעיל ואם כן סתרי דברי המקשה אהדדי דהכא אלא י"ח: (ה) בא"ד אלא שבאלו מותרין בעשיית מלאכה כו' כנ"ל ותיבת מתפללין נמחק: (ו) ד"ה ונותנין כו' שהרי האפר הוי כו' כנ"ל ותיבת הוא נמחק:

גמרא

לְמִתְבַּיֵּישׁ מֵאֲחֵרִים. וְהֵיכָא מַנַּח לְהוּ אָמַר רַבִּי יִצְחָק: בִּמְקוֹם תְּפִילִּין, שֶׁנֶּאֱמַר "לָשׂוּם לַאֲבֵלֵי צִיּוֹן, לָתֵת לָהֶם פְּאֵר תַּחַת אֵפֶר". § רְחוֹב, תֵּיבָה, וְשַׂקִּים, אֵפֶר, קְבוּרָה, וּמוֹרִיָּה סִימָן. § לָמָּה יוֹצְאִין לִרְחוֹב? ר' חִיָּיא בַּר אַבָּא אָמַר, לוֹמַר: זָעַקְנוּ בְּצִנְעָא וְלֹא נַעֲנֵינוּ. נְבַזֶּה עַצְמֵנוּ בְּפַרְהֶסְיָא. רֵישׁ לָקִישׁ אָמַר: גָּלִינוּ. גָּלוּתֵינוּ מְכַפֶּרֶת עָלֵינוּ. מַאי בֵּינַיְיהוּ? אִיכָּא בֵּינַיְיהוּ דְּגָלֵי מִבֵּי כְּנִישְׁתָּא לְבֵי כְּנִישְׁתָּא. וְלָמָּה מוֹצִיאִין אֶת הַתֵּיבָה לִרְחוֹבָהּ שֶׁל עִיר? אָמַר ר' יְהוֹשֻׁעַ בֶּן לֵוִי, לוֹמַר: כְּלִי צָנוּעַ הָיָה לָנוּ, וְנִתְבַּזָּה בַּעֲוֹנֵינוּ. וְלָמָּה מִתְכַּסִּין בְּשַׂקִּים? אָמַר ר' חִיָּיא בַּר אַבָּא, לוֹמַר: הֲרֵי אָנוּ חֲשׁוּבִין כִּבְהֵמָה. וְלָמָּה נוֹתְנִין אֵפֶר מִקְלֶה עַל גַּבֵּי תֵיבָה? אָמַר רַבִּי יְהוּדָה בֶּן פָּזִי, כְּלוֹמַר "עִמּוֹ אָנֹכִי בְצָרָה". רֵישׁ לָקִישׁ אָמַר "בְּכָל צָרָתָם לוֹ צָר". אָמַר ר' זֵירָא: מֵרֵישׁ, כִּי הֲוָה חָזֵינָא לְהוּ לְרַבָּנַן דְּיָהֲבֵי אֵפֶר מִקְלֶה עַל גַּבֵּי תֵיבָה — מִזְדַּעְזַע לִי כּוּלֵּיהּ גּוּפַאי. וְלָמָּה נוֹתְנִין אֵפֶר בְּרֹאשׁ כָּל אֶחָד וְאֶחָד? פְּלִיגִי בָּהּ ר' לֵוִי בַּר חָמָא וְר' חֲנִינָא. חַד אָמַר: הֲרֵי אָנוּ חֲשׁוּבִין לְפָנֶיךָ כְּאֵפֶר. וְחַד אָמַר: כְּדֵי שֶׁיִּזְכּוֹר לָנוּ אֶפְרוֹ שֶׁל יִצְחָק. מַאי בֵּינַיְיהוּ? אִיכָּא בֵּינַיְיהוּ עָפָר סְתָם. לָמָּה יוֹצְאִין לְבֵית הַקְּבָרוֹת? פְּלִיגִי בָּהּ ר' לֵוִי בַּר חָמָא וְר' חֲנִינָא. חַד אָמַר: הֲרֵי אָנוּ חֲשׁוּבִין לְפָנֶיךָ כְּמֵתִים. וְחַד אָמַר: כְּדֵי שֶׁיְּבַקְּשׁוּ עָלֵינוּ מֵתִים רַחֲמִים. מַאי בֵּינַיְיהוּ? אִיכָּא בֵּינַיְיהוּ קִבְרֵי נָכְרִים. מַאי "הַר הַמּוֹרִיָּה"? פְּלִיגִי בָּהּ ר' לֵוִי בַּר חָמָא וְר' חֲנִינָא. חַד אָמַר: הַר שֶׁיָּצָא מִמֶּנּוּ הוֹרָאָה לְיִשְׂרָאֵל. וְחַד אָמַר: הַר שֶׁיָּצָא מִמֶּנּוּ מוֹרָא לְאוּמּוֹת הָעוֹלָם. § "הַזָּקֵן שֶׁבָּהֶן אוֹמֵר לִפְנֵיהֶן דִּבְרֵי כִבּוּשִׁין". § ת"ר: אִם יֵשׁ זָקֵן — אוֹמֵר זָקֵן. וְאִם לָאו — אוֹמֵר חָכָם. וְאִם לָאו — אוֹמֵר אָדָם שֶׁל צוּרָה. אַטּוּ זָקֵן דְּקָאָמְרִי אַף עַל גַּב דְּלָאו חָכָם הוּא? אָמַר אַבָּיֵי: הָכִי קָאָמַר: אִם יֵשׁ זָקֵן וְהוּא חָכָם — אוֹמֵר זָקֵן וְהוּא חָכָם. וְאִם לָאו — אוֹמֵר חָכָם. וְאִם לָאו — אוֹמֵר אָדָם שֶׁל צוּרָה: אַחֵינוּ, לֹא שַׂק וְתַעֲנִית גּוֹרְמִים. אֶלָּא תְּשׁוּבָה וּמַעֲשִׂים טוֹבִים גּוֹרְמִים. שֶׁכֵּן מָצִינוּ בְּאַנְשֵׁי נִינְוֵה שֶׁלֹּא נֶאֱמַר בָּהֶם: 'וַיַּרְא הָאֱלֹהִים אֶת שַׂקָּם וְאֶת תַּעֲנִיתָם', אֶלָּא "וַיַּרְא הָאֱלֹהִים אֶת מַעֲשֵׂיהֶם, כִּי שָׁבוּ מִדַּרְכָּם הָרָעָה". "וְיִתְכַּסּוּ שַׂקִּים הָאָדָם וְהַבְּהֵמָה". מַאי הֲווֹ עָבְדִי? אָסְרָא הַבְּהֵמוֹת לְחוּד וְאֶת הַוְּלָדוֹת לְחוּד. אָמְרוּ לְפָנָיו: רִבּוֹנוֹ שֶׁל עוֹלָם! אִם אֵין אַתָּה מְרַחֵם עָלֵינוּ, אֵין אָנוּ מְרַחֲמִים עַל אֵלּוּ. "וְיִקְרְאוּ אֶל אֱלֹהִים בְּחָזְקָה". מַאי אָמוּר? אָמְרוּ לְפָנָיו: רִבּוֹנוֹ שֶׁל עוֹלָם! עָלוּב וְשֶׁאֵינוֹ עָלוּב, (א) צַדִּיק וְרָשָׁע, מִי נִדְחֶה מִפְּנֵי מִי? "וְיָשֻׁבוּ אִישׁ מִדַּרְכּוֹ הָרָעָה, וּמִן הֶחָמָס אֲשֶׁר בְּכַפֵּיהֶם". מַאי "וּמִן הֶחָמָס אֲשֶׁר בְּכַפֵּיהֶם"? אָמַר שְׁמוּאֵל: אֲפִילּוּ גָּזַל מָרִישׁ וּבְנָאוֹ בְּבִירָה — מְקַעְקֵעַ כָּל הַבִּירָה כּוּלָּהּ וּמַחֲזִיר מָרִישׁ לִבְעָלָיו. אָמַר רַב אַדָּא בַּר אַהֲבָה: אָדָם שֶׁיֵּשׁ בְּיָדוֹ עֲבֵירָה, וּמִתְוַדֶּה וְאֵינוֹ חוֹזֵר בָּהּ, לְמָה הוּא דּוֹמֶה? לְאָדָם שֶׁתּוֹפֵס שֶׁרֶץ בְּיָדוֹ, שֶׁאֲפִי' טוֹבֵל בְּכָל מֵימוֹת שֶׁבָּעוֹלָם — לֹא עָלְתָה לוֹ טְבִילָה. זְרָקוֹ מִיָּדוֹ, כֵּיוָן שֶׁטָּבַל בְּאַרְבָּעִים סְאָה — מִיָּד עָלְתָה לוֹ טְבִילָה, שֶׁנֶּאֱמַר "וּמוֹדֶה וְעוֹזֵב יְרוּחָם". וְאוֹמֵר "נִשָּׂא לְבָבֵנוּ אֶל כַּפָּיִם אֶל אֵל בַּשָּׁמָיִם". § "עָמְדוּ בִּתְפִלָּה. מוֹרִידִין לִפְנֵי הַתֵּיבָה זָקֵן" כו'. § תָּנוּ רַבָּנַן: עָמְדוּ בִּתְפִלָּה. אע"פ שֶׁיֵּשׁ שָׁם זָקֵן וְחָכָם, אֵין מוֹרִידִין לִפְנֵי הַתֵּיבָה אֶלָּא אָדָם הָרָגִיל. (*אֵיזֶהוּ רָגִיל) ר' יְהוּדָה אוֹמֵר: מְטוּפָּל וְאֵין לוֹ, וְיֵשׁ לוֹ יְגִיעָה בַּשָּׂדֶה, וּבֵיתוֹ רֵיקָם, וּפִרְקוֹ נָאֶה, וּשְׁפַל בֶּרֶךְ, וּמְרוּצֶּה לָעָם, וְיֵשׁ לוֹ נְעִימָה, וְקוֹלוֹ עָרֵב, וּבָקִי לִקְרוֹת בַּתּוֹרָה, וּבַנְּבִיאִים, וּבַכְּתוּבִים, וְלִשְׁנוֹת בַּמִּדְרָשׁ, בַּהֲלָכוֹת, וּבָאַגָּדוֹת, וּבָקִי בְּכָל הַבְּרָכוֹת כּוּלָּן. וְיָהֲבוּ בֵּיהּ רַבָּנַן עֵינַיְיהוּ בְּר' יִצְחָק בַּר אַמִי, הַיְינוּ

רש"י

לְמִתְבַּיֵּישׁ מֵאֲחֵרִים. דְּאִיכָּא עָגְמַת נֶפֶשׁ טְפֵי. וּמִשּׁוּם חֲשִׁיבוּתָם הֵם מִתְבַּיְּישִׁים מֵאֲחֵרִים. אֲבָל שְׁאָר בְּנֵי אָדָם דְּלָא חֲשִׁיבִי — לָא מִתְבַּיְּישִׁי בִּנְתִינַת אֲחֵרִים, וְסַגִּי לְהוּ בִּנְתִינַת עַצְמָן: פְּאֵר תַּחַת אֵפֶר. ש"מ בִּמְקוֹם תְּפִילִּין, דִּכְתִיב בְּהוּ (יחזקאל כד) "פְּאֵרְךָ חֲבוֹשׁ עָלֶיךָ", וְאָמְרִינַן (ברכות דף יא.) אֵלּוּ תְּפִילִּין. וּמְתַרְגְּמִינַן נַמִי: טוֹטֶפְתָּךְ הָוְיָין עֲלָךְ. וְהֵיכָא מַנִּיחִין תְּפִילִּין — בְּמָקוֹם שֶׁמּוֹחוֹ שֶׁל תִּינוֹק רוֹפֵף: בְּצִינְעָא. בְּבֵית הַכְּנֶסֶת: גָּלִינוּ. שֶׁיָּצָאנוּ מִכְּנִיסָתֵנוּ: (ב) גָּלוּתֵינוּ. תְּהֵא מְכַפֶּרֶת עָלֵינוּ: דְּגָלוּ מִבֵּי כְּנִישְׁתָּא לְבֵי כְּנִישְׁתָּא אַחֲרִיתָא. גָּלוּת — אִיכָּא, פַּרְהֶסְיָא — לֵיכָּא: נִתְבַּזָּה בַּעֲוֹנֵינוּ. וִידּוּי: [וְלָמָּה מִתְכַּסִּין]. חוֹגְרוֹת שַׂקִּין. תָּנֵינַן בִּירוּשַׁלְמִי: שֶׁהָיוּ חוֹגְרוֹת שַׂקִּין וְיוֹצְאִין לְבֵית הַקְּבָרוֹת וְתוֹקְעִין בִּקְרָנוֹת, וּבָעֵי לֵיהּ מִיבַּעְיָא: שַׂקִּין לָמָּה, וּבֵית הַקְּבָרוֹת לָמָּה, וּתְקִיעַת שׁוֹפָר לָמָּה? כִּבְהֵמָה. דְּמִשְּׂעַר בְּהֵמָה נִינְהוּ, מְנוּלָּה שֶׁל עִזִּים: עָפָר סְתָם. שֶׁאֵינוֹ אֵפֶר מִקְלֶה. זְכִירַת אֶפְרוֹ שֶׁל יִצְחָק — לֵיכָּא. סְתָם לָא גָּרְסִינַן, אֶלָּא אִיכָּא בֵּינַיְיהוּ עָפָר: קִבְרֵי נָכְרִים. בְּמָקוֹם שֶׁאֵין קִבְרֵי יִשְׂרָאֵל, לְבַקֵּשׁ רַחֲמִים אֲפִי' עַל עַצְמָן לֵיכָּא, כָּל שֶׁכֵּן עָלֵינוּ: מַאי הַר הַמּוֹרִיָּה וכו'. אַיְּידֵי דְּאַיְירֵי בִּפְלוּגְתָּא דְּרַבִּי לֵוִי וְר"ח תָּנָא נַמִי הָא פְּלוּגְתָּא מַאי הַר מוֹרִיָּה. דְּאַבְרָהָם קָרָא לִמְקוֹם הָעֲקֵידָה "הַר יִרְאֶה", וּכְתִיב (בראשית כב) *"אֶל אֶרֶץ הַמּוֹרִיָּה": חַד אָמַר הַר שֶׁיָּצָא (ג) הוֹרָאָה. תּוֹרָה לְיִשְׂרָאֵל "כִּי מִצִּיּוֹן תֵּצֵא תוֹרָה" (ישעיה ב), "יוֹרוּ מִשְׁפָּטֶיךָ לְיַעֲקֹב" (דברים לג), וְלִשְׁכַּת הַגָּזִית שֶׁבָּהּ עָמְדוּ הַנְּבִיאִים הַמּוֹכִיחִים לְיִשְׂרָאֵל: מוֹרָא לְאוּמּוֹת הָעוֹלָם. שֶׁשּׁוֹמְעִין גְּדוּלּוֹת יִשְׂרָאֵל וִירוּשָׁלַיִם וּמִתְפַּחֲדִים עֲלֵיהֶם, שְׁמַעְתִּי. לִישָּׁנָא אַחֲרִינָא: הַר הַמּוֹרִיָּה — הַר סִינַי, מוֹרָא לְאוּמּוֹת הָעוֹלָם — בְּמַתַּן תּוֹרָה, דִּכְתִיב (תהלים עו) "אֶרֶץ יָרְאָה וְשָׁקָטָה": אע"ג דְּלָאו חָכָם. אֶלָּא עַם הָאָרֶץ. בִּתְמִיָּה: הָא וַדַּאי חָכָם עָדִיף! אִם יֵשׁ זָקֵן וְהוּא חָכָם. אוֹמֵר זָקֵן וְהוּא חָכָם: אָדָם שֶׁל צוּרָה. בַּעַל קוֹמָה, שֶׁיִּשְׁמְעוּ וִיקַבְּלוּ דְבָרָיו לְהַמְרִיךְ אֶת הַלֵּב: מַאי אָמוּר. אַנְשֵׁי נִינְוֵה, דִּכְתִיב "בְּחָזְקָה", דְּמַשְׁמַע כֹּחַ וְנִיצּוּחַ דִּין: מִי נִדְחֶה מִפְּנֵי מִי. הֱוֵי אוֹמֵר צַדִּיק מִפְּנֵי רָשָׁע: אִם אֵין אַתָּה מְרַחֵם כו'. כְּלוֹמַר: כְּשֵׁם שֶׁאַתָּה אוֹמֵר לְרַחֵם עַל אֵלּוּ, דִּכְתִיב (תהלים קמה) "וְרַחֲמָיו עַל כָּל מַעֲשָׂיו" — כֵּן תְּרַחֵם עָלֵינוּ: מָרִישׁ. קוֹרָה: בִּירָה. מִגְדָּל: שֶׁיֵּשׁ בְּיָדוֹ עֲבֵירָה. גָּזֵל: וְאֵינוֹ חוֹזֵר בּוֹ. לְשַׁלֵּם אֶת הַגָּזֵל, לְמָה הוּא דּוֹמֶה וכו': נִשָּׂא לְבָבֵנוּ אֶל כַּפָּיִם. עִם הַכַּפַּיִם צָרִיךְ לִישָּׂא הַלֵּב לַשָּׁמַיִם, כְּלוֹמַר: שֶׁיַּחֲזוֹר מִקִּלְקוּלוֹ: מְטוּפָּל וְאֵין לוֹ. יֵשׁ לוֹ טְפָלִים, וְאֵין לוֹ בַּמֶּה לְהִתְפַּרְנֵס. שֶׁלִּבּוֹ דּוֹאֵג עָלָיו, [וְהוּא צָרִיךְ לִקְרוֹת מִקִּירוֹת לִבּוֹ עֲלֵיהֶן]: וְיֵשׁ לוֹ יְגִיעָה. שֶׁמִּתְכַּוֵּין יוֹתֵר בִּתְפִלַּת הַגְּשָׁמִים: וּפִרְקוֹ נָאֶה. מְפָרֵשׁ לְקַמָּן: וּשְׁפַל בֶּרֶךְ. עָנָיו: וּמְרוּצֶּה לָעָם. נוֹחַ לַבְּרִיּוֹת, וּמַסְכִּימִין לִתְפִלָּתוֹ: נְעִימָה. בְּסוּמֵי קָלָא, שֶׁמּוֹשֵׁךְ הַלֵּב: וְרָגִיל לִקְרוֹת כו'. שֶׁיְּהוּ הַפְּסוּקִים שֶׁל תְּפִלָּה סְדוּרִין בְּפִיו: הַיְינוּ

תוספות

במקום תפילין. פירוש: לתת האפר במקום הפאר דאילו התפילין נקראו פאר, כדכתיב "לשום לאבילי ציון לתת להם פאר" וגו': **איכא** בינייהו דגלו מבי כנישתא לבי כנישתא. פירוש: למ"ד משום גלות — איכא, ולמ"ד משום פרהסיא — ליכא, דהא בי כנישתא הוי כמו בצנעא:

אפר מקלה. פירוש: אותו אפר הוא מדבר הנשרף מעצמות אדם, כדי לזכור עקידת יצחק דאלמלא שלא היה בא אלא כדי לומר שהרי אנו לפניך כאפר — כמו כן מהני עפר סתם. והיינו פירוש איכא בינייהו עפר סתם:

יוצאין לבית הקברות. מכאן נוהגין בכל מקום לילך לבית הקברות בט' באב, שהרי ט"ב הוי תענית צבור כמו שהיו עושין מפני הגשמים:

הר שיצאה ממנו הוראה לישראל. י"מ: *דזה ירושלם, שנקרא על שם אברהם שקראוהו הר ה' יראה (בראשית כב) (ד). והעיר היה נקרא כבר שלם, כדכתיב (שם יד) "ומלכי צדק מלך שלם", ונקרא ירושלם על שם יראה ועל שם שלם. לכך אין אנו נותנין יו"ד בירושלם בין למ"ד למ"ם, על שם שלם. וההר נקרא מוריה על שם תורה, כדכתיב (ישעיה ב) "כי מציון תצא תורה" וכתיב (דברים לג) "יורו משפטיך ליעקב" — והוא לשכת הגזית. המוריה — זה סיני, ונקרא מוריה על שם שממנו יצא מורא לאומות העולם במתן תורה, כדכתיב (תהלים עו): "ארץ יראה ושקטה". אי נמי, רצה לומר דירושלם נקרא מוריה — על שם שיש מורא לאומות העולם על גדולתה, ומתפחדים:

אדם שיש לו צורה. פירוש: בעל קומה, כדי שישמעו דבריו ויקבלו ממנו להמריך הלב. ופרקו נאה — פירוש: כשעמד על פרקו, אפילו כשהיה בחור, היה בלא שם רע:

מאי

רבינו חננאל

רחמי אכולי עלמא. ולמה אינו נותן הנשיא ואב ב"ד הן בעצמן על ראשיהם שהמתבייש מן אחרים גדול הוא מהמתבייש עצמו. כלומר בושה גדולה היא כדי שיכוין כל לבו והיכן מחית ליה לאפר זה בראשו במקום תפילין שנאמר לתת להם פאר תחת אפר: יוצאין לרחובה כדי לשבר הצבור לבם. כלומר צעקנו בצנעא ולא ענינו נבזה עצמנו בפרהסיא ור"ל אמר שתחשב לנו גלות כי הגלות מכפרת עון. ולמה מוציאין את התיבה לרחובה אריב"ל כלי צנוע היה לנו ונתבזה. נתינת אפר על גבי התיבה משום שנאמר בכל צרתם לו צר ולמה מתכסים בשקים לומר כי נחשבנו כבהמה וכל אחד נותן אפר בראשו לומר הנה אנו כאפר (אולי יזכור) [וי"א להזכר] זכות אפרו של יצחק (ופעמים) [וטעם] שיוצאין לבית הקברות כלומר הרי אנו כמתים וי"א שיבקשו מתים עלינו רחמים מאי הר המוריה הר שיצא ממנו הוראה לישראל. וי"א שיצא ממנו מורא לגוים: **ירושלמי** ונותנין אפר בראש נשיא. ר' אבהו ורבנן חד אמר חטא הנשיא הגדולה במקומה (כל ישראל נשאים) חטא הצבור נדחית הגדולה וחד אמר לפי שחטא הלמד והמלמד לפיכך יצאו ויתפרסמו על שם והוציא את הפר מחוץ למחנה שידעו הכל חטאתו של כ"ג: נשא לבבנו אל כפים אל אל בשמים נשוה לבבנו לכף ידינו כשם שכף ידינו נקיה כך ניקה לבנו ואח"כ אל אל בשמים. ג' דברים מבטלין רוע גזרה תפלה תשובה צדקה. ושלשתן בפסוק אחד נאמרו [דה"ב ז'] ויכנעו עמי אשר נקרא שמי עליהם ויתפללו ויבקשו פני. ויתפללו זו תפלה. ויבקשו פני זו צדקה שנא' אני בצדק אחזה פניך. וישובו מדרכיהם הרעים זו תשובה. מה כתוב תמן ואני אשמע (מן) השמים ולמה יוצאין בין הקברות אם נתחייבנו רעב הרי אנו רעבים ומתענים. ואם נתחייבנו גלות הרי גלינו ממקום למקום. ואם נתחייבנו מיתה הרי אנו בבית הקברות כמתים וקרעו לבבכם ואל בגדיכם אם קרעתם לבבכם בתשובה אינכם קורעין בגדיכם על בניכם כי חנון ורחום הוא מאריך *) חמיה: ת"ר אם יש שם זקן חכם אומר זקן חכם ואם לאו אומר אדם של צורה אחינו לא שק ותענית גורמין אלא תשובה ומע"ט גורמין שלא נאמר באנשי נינוה וירא אלהים את שקם ואת תעניתם אלא וירא אלהים את מעשיהם כי שבו מדרכם הרעה אפילו מי שגזל מריש ובנאו בבירה היה מקעקע הבירה כולה ומחזיר המריש לבעליו: ת"ר אדם שיש בו עבירה ומתודה ואינו חוזר בו דומה למי שיש בידו שרץ שאפילו הוא טובל בכל מימות שבעולם אין טהרה שנאמר מכסה פשעיו לא יצליח זרקו כיון שטובל במ' סאה כו' שנאמר ומודה ועוזב ירוחם: **מתני'** עמדו בתפלה מורידין לפני התיבה זקן ורגיל: ת"ר אע"פ שאמרו אם יש שם זקן חכם אין מורידין לפני התיבה אלא רגיל רבי יהודה אומר דל שיש לו טף ויש לו יגיעה בשדה

*) ט"ס כאן עיין בירושלמי.

עין משפט נר מצוה

יד א מיי' פ"ד מהלכות תענית הלכה א טוש"ע א"ח סימן תקעט סעיף א:
טו ב מיי' שם הלכה יז טוש"ע שם ס"ג:
טז ג מיי' שם הלכה ד טוש"ע שם ס"ה:
יז ד מיי' פ"ב מהל' תשובה הלכה ג:
יח ה מיי' פ"ד מהל' תענית הלכה ג טוש"ע א"ח סימן תקעט סעיף א [וסימן נג סעיף ד]:

מסורת הש"ס / הגהות בצד

[גי' רא"ש אמר רבי לומר כו']

[גי' רי"ף ורא"ש ר' לוי בר לחמא ור' חמא בר חנינא]

[פי' אחרים אגדות]

[ילקוט שם"ב ד' אלך לי אל הר המור כו' הר המור פליגי בה כו']

[מגילה כט.]

[תוספתא פ"א]

[ליתא ברב אלפסי וגם ברא"ש ע"ש]

[וכל זה נתבאר במדרש רבה בראשית פ' נ"ו והביא הערוך ערך ירושלם]

רבינו גרשום

דגלו מבי כנישתא [לבי כנישתא] למ"ד גלות הא איכא למ"ד פרהסיא ליכא: הרי אנו חשובין לפניו כבהמה שהרי לובשין שק שהן של שיער בהמה: א"ב עפר סתם למ"ד הרי אנו חשובין לפניו כעפר בעפר סתם סגי למ"ד כדי שיזכור אפרו של יצחק מיבעי ליה אפר מקלה: קברי גוים למ"ד הרי אנו חשובין כמתים ה"נ מצי למיפק לך לקברי אבות של גוים ומ"ד כדי שיבקשו עלינו רחמים איבעי להו למיפק לקברי ישראל: מאי הר המוריה למה נקרא שמה הר המוריה *) דאברהם קראו יראה ומלכי צדק קראו שלם ועשה הקב"ה פשרה ביניהם וקראו ירושלם: הר המוריה שיצאה ממנו הוראה לישראל שכן יושבין סנהדרין בלשכת הגזית ומורין הוראות. דברי כיבושין דברים שאדם מכבש ללבו: מי נדחה מפני מי כלומר דחה גזירתם מלפנינו: מריש. קורה: ועוזב שחוזר בו: ורגיל להתפלל שצ"ל זכרונות ושופרות לפי שאין זכרונות ושופרות אלא בר"ה:

הגהות הב"ח

(א) גמ' עלוב ושאינו עלוב יכול צדיק ורשע כו' ומחזיר מריש לבעליו נ"ב תמסן יהיב דמי ולא רצו ליפטר במעות: (ב) רש"י ד"ה גלינו כו' וד"ה גלותינו כו' הס"א: (ג) ד"ה חד אמר הר שיצא ממנו הוראה לישראל תורה שנאמר כי מציון: (ד) תוס' ד"ה הר כו' הר ה' יראה וה"פ מתחלה היה נקרא כך שלם כדכתיב ומלכי צדק מלך שלם ואח"כ נקרא ירושלים:

גליון הש"ס

גמרא כדי שיבקשו עלינו רחמים. עיין סוטה דף לד ע"ב תוס' ד"ה אבותי:

יט א ב מיי׳ פ"ד מהל׳ תענית הלכה ג טוש"ע א"ח סימן תקעט סעיף א [וסימן נג סעיף ד]:
כ ג מיי׳ שם הלכה ו טור א"ח סי׳ תקעט:
כא ד ה מיי׳ שם הלכה טו:

מאי שביעית שביעית לארוכה. פירוש: שמתחילין להאריך ולומר בקשות ותחינות בתוך ברכה של גואל ישראל. אבל מ"מ אינה בכלל הנוספות בימי תענית. דלא היו מוסיפין רק ששה. ועל כל הברכות יש טעם על מה הם חותמות בכך. הראשונה של גואל אינה מן המנין, ובה אומרים "מי שענה לאברהם" – לפי שהיה ראשון לנגאלין, שניצול מנמרוד. ובשניה שהיא ראשונה מן הששה הנוספות אמר "מי שענה לאבותינו על ים סוף" וחותם "ברוך זוכר הברית" ולפיכך אומרה בזכרונות, לפי שהיו במצרים ונתייאשו מן הגאולה, ועליו נאמר (שמות ו) "ואזכור את בריתי". וכן בשלישית, שהיא שניה מן המנין "שומע תרועה" ביהושע שנענה ביריחו, דהיינו בעוד ישראל בגלגל, בשופרות היה אומר "מי שענה ליהושע בגלגל" – לפי שנענה בשופרות. על הרביעית והיא שלישית מן המנין "מי שענה לשמואל" וכו׳, ובשמואל כתיב צעקה ותפלה, וגבי אליהו כתיב תפלה "ענני ה׳ ענני" ואמרינן בגמרא: לצעקה גבי שמואל, ותפלה גבי אליהו. וי"א: תפלה גבי שמואל וצעקה גבי אליהו. דהא דכתיב ענני גבי אליהו – הוא צעקה. שמואל במצפה מעין "אל ה׳ בצרתה לי". לאליהו בהר הכרמל – כנגד "אשא עיני אל ההרים" וכן כולם:

ברוך מרחם על הארץ. דגבי דוד ושלמה שייך לומר על הארץ. דדוד ושלמה התפללו על הארץ, דוד גבי מלאך המות בגורן ארונה, ושלמה בתפלה, דקאמר "רעב כי יהיה בארץ". ועוד יש לומר: משום דאתקין בהמ"ק בארץ. ולא קשיא הא דחשיב יונה מקמי דוד, אע"ג שהיה קודם – משום דבעי למיחתם "על הארץ", כדמפרש בגמרא:

ויודע

הַיְינוּ מְטוּפָּל וְאֵין לוֹ הַיְינוּ בֵּיתוֹ רֵיקָם! אָמַר רַב חִסְדָּא: [א]זֶהוּ שֶׁבֵּיתוֹ רֵיקָם מִן הָעֲבֵירָה.§ "וּפִרְקוֹ נָאֶה".§ אָמַר אַבַּיֵי: [ב]זֶה שֶׁלֹּא יָצָא (*לוֹ) שֵׁם רַע בְּיַלְדוּתוֹ. °"הָיְתָה לִּי נַחֲלָתִי כְּאַרְיֵה בַיָּעַר. נָתְנָה עָלַי בְּקוֹלָהּ עַל כֵּן שְׂנֵאתִיהָ". מַאי "נָתְנָה עָלַי בְּקוֹלָהּ"? אָמַר מָר זוּטְרָא בַּר טוֹבִיָּה אָמַר רַב, וְאָמְרִי לָהּ אָמַר רַבִּי חָמָא אָמַר רַבִּי אֶלְעָזָר: זֶה שְׁלִיחַ צִבּוּר (*הַיּוֹרֵד לִפְנֵי הַתֵּיבָה. שֶׁאֵינוֹ הָגוּן)§ "וְאוֹמֵר לִפְנֵיהֶם עֶשְׂרִים וְאַרְבַּע בְּרָכוֹת, שְׁמוֹנֶה עֶשְׂרֵה שֶׁבְּכָל יוֹם, וּמוֹסִיף עֲלֵיהֶן עוֹד שֵׁשׁ".§ הָנֵי שֵׁשׁ?! שֶׁבַע הָוְיָין! כִּדְתְנַן: עַל הַשְּׁבִיעִית הוּא אוֹמֵר: בָּרוּךְ מְרַחֵם עַל הָאָרֶץ. אָמַר רַב נַחְמָן בַּר יִצְחָק: מַאי שְׁבִיעִית? שְׁבִיעִית לָאֲרוּכָּה, כִּדְתַנְיָא: [ג]בְּ׳גוֹאֵל יִשְׂרָאֵל׳ מַאֲרִיךְ, וּבְחוֹתְמָהּ הוּא אוֹמֵר: מִי שֶׁעָנָה אֶת אַבְרָהָם בְּהַר הַמּוֹרִיָּה, הוּא יַעֲנֶה אֶתְכֶם וְיִשְׁמַע בְּקוֹל צַעֲקַתְכֶם הַיּוֹם הַזֶּה. בָּרוּךְ גּוֹאֵל יִשְׂרָאֵל. וְהֵן עוֹנִין אַחֲרָיו אָמֵן. וְחַזַּן הַכְּנֶסֶת אוֹמֵר לָהֶם: תִּקְעוּ, בְּנֵי אַהֲרֹן, תִּקְעוּ! [א] וְחוֹזֵר וְאוֹמֵר: מִי שֶׁעָנָה אֶת אֲבוֹתֵינוּ עַל יַם סוּף, הוּא יַעֲנֶה אֶתְכֶם וְיִשְׁמַע בְּקוֹל צַעֲקַתְכֶם הַיּוֹם הַזֶּה. בָּרוּךְ זוֹכֵר הַנִּשְׁכָּחוֹת. וְהֵן עוֹנִין אַחֲרָיו אָמֵן. וְחַזַּן הַכְּנֶסֶת אוֹמֵר לָהֶם: 'הָרִיעוּ, בְּנֵי אַהֲרֹן, הָרִיעוּ'. וְכֵן בְּכָל בְּרָכָה וּבְרָכָה, בְּאַחַת אוֹמֵר, 'תִּקְעוּ', וּבְאַחַת אוֹמֵר 'הָרִיעוּ'.§ בַּמֶּה דְּבָרִים אֲמוּרִים – בַּגְּבוּלִין. אֲבָל בַּמִּקְדָּשׁ אֵינוֹ כֵּן, [ד]לְפִי *שֶׁאֵין עוֹנִין אָמֵן בַּמִּקְדָּשׁ. וּמִנַּיִן שֶׁאֵין עוֹנִין אָמֵן בַּמִּקְדָּשׁ? שֶׁנֶּאֱמַר °"קוּמוּ בָּרְכוּ אֶת ה׳ אֱלֹהֵיכֶם מִן הָעוֹלָם עַד הָעוֹלָם, וִיבָרְכוּ שֵׁם כְּבוֹדֶךָ, וּמְרוֹמַם עַל כָּל בְּרָכָה וּתְהִלָּה". יָכוֹל עַל כָּל בְּרָכוֹת כּוּלָּן לֹא תְהֵא אֶלָּא תְּהִלָּה אַחַת – ת"ל: "וּמְרוֹמַם עַל כָּל בְּרָכָה וּתְהִלָּה" – עַל כָּל בְּרָכָה תֵּן לוֹ תְּהִלָּה. וְאֶלָּא בַּמִּקְדָּשׁ מַהוּ אוֹמֵר? בָּרוּךְ ה׳, [ב] אֱלֹהִים אֱלֹהֵי יִשְׂרָאֵל, מִן הָעוֹלָם וְעַד הָעוֹלָם. בָּרוּךְ גּוֹאֵל יִשְׂרָאֵל. וְהֵן עוֹנִין אַחֲרָיו: 'בָּרוּךְ שֵׁם כְּבוֹד מַלְכוּתוֹ לְעוֹלָם וָעֶד'. וְחַזַּן הַכְּנֶסֶת אוֹמֵר לָהֶם: תִּקְעוּ, הַכֹּהֲנִים, בְּנֵי אַהֲרֹן, תִּקְעוּ. וְחוֹזֵר וְאוֹמֵר: מִי שֶׁעָנָה אֶת אַבְרָהָם בְּהַר הַמּוֹרִיָּה, הוּא יַעֲנֶה אֶתְכֶם וְיִשְׁמַע בְּקוֹל צַעֲקַתְכֶם הַיּוֹם הַזֶּה. בָּרוּךְ ה׳, אֱלֹהֵי יִשְׂרָאֵל, [ג] זוֹכֵר הַנִּשְׁכָּחוֹת. וְהֵם עוֹנִים אַחֲרָיו: בשכמל"ו. וְחַזַּן הַכְּנֶסֶת אוֹמֵר לָהֶם: הָרִיעוּ, הַכֹּהֲנִים בְּנֵי אַהֲרֹן, הָרִיעוּ וכו׳. וְכֵן בְּכָל בְּרָכָה וּבְרָכָה, בְּאַחַת אוֹמֵר, 'תִּקְעוּ', וּבְאַחַת אוֹמֵר, 'הָרִיעוּ', עַד שֶׁגּוֹמֵר אֶת כּוּלָּן. וְכָךְ הִנְהִיג ר׳ חֲלַפְתָּא בְּצִפּוֹרִי וְר׳ חֲנַנְיָה בֶּן תְּרַדְיוֹן בְּסִיכְנִי. וּכְשֶׁבָּא דָּבָר לִפְנֵי חֲכָמִים, אָמְרוּ: לֹא הָיוּ נוֹהֲגִין כֵּן אֶלָּא בְּשַׁעֲרֵי מִזְרָח, וּבְהַר הַבַּיִת. וְאִית דְּאָמְרִי כִּדְתַנְיָא: אוֹמֵר לִפְנֵיהֶן עֶשְׂרִים וְאַרְבַּע בְּרָכוֹת, שְׁמוֹנֶה עֶשְׂרֵה שֶׁבְּכָל יוֹם, וּמוֹסִיף עֲלֵיהֶן עוֹד שֵׁשׁ. וְאוֹתָן שֵׁשׁ הֵיכָן אוֹמְרָן? בֵּין 'גּוֹאֵל' לְ'רוֹפֵא חוֹלֵי'. וּמַאֲרִיךְ בִּגְאוּלָּה, וְהֵן עוֹנִין אַחֲרָיו אָמֵן עַל כָּל בְּרָכָה וּבְרָכָה. וְכָךְ הָיוּ נוֹהֲגִין בַּגְּבוּלִין. אֲבָל בַּמִּקְדָּשׁ הָיוּ אוֹמְרִים: בָּרוּךְ ה׳, אֱלֹהֵי יִשְׂרָאֵל, מִן הָעוֹלָם וְעַד הָעוֹלָם. בָּרוּךְ גּוֹאֵל יִשְׂרָאֵל. וְלֹא הָיוּ עוֹנִין אַחֲרָיו אָמֵן. וְכָל כָּךְ לָמָּה? לְפִי שֶׁאֵין עוֹנִין אָמֵן בַּמִּקְדָּשׁ. וּמִנַּיִן שֶׁאֵין עוֹנִין אָמֵן בַּמִּקְדָּשׁ? שֶׁנֶּאֱמַר "קוּמוּ בָּרְכוּ אֶת ה׳ אֱלֹהֵיכֶם מִן הָעוֹלָם וְעַד הָעוֹלָם, וִיבָרְכוּ (אֶת) שֵׁם כְּבוֹדֶךָ, וּמְרוֹמַם עַל כָּל בְּרָכָה וּתְהִלָּה" – עַל כָּל בְּרָכָה וּבְרָכָה תֵּן לוֹ תְּהִלָּה.§ תָּנוּ רַבָּנַן: [ה]'עַל הָרִאשׁוֹנוֹת הוּא אוֹמֵר בָּרוּךְ ה׳ אֱלֹהֵי יִשְׂרָאֵל. מִן הָעוֹלָם וְעַד הָעוֹלָם בָּרוּךְ גּוֹאֵל יִשְׂרָאֵל. וְהֵן עוֹנִין אַחֲרָיו: בָּרוּךְ שֵׁם כְּבוֹד מַלְכוּתוֹ לְעוֹלָם וָעֶד. וְחַזַּן הַכְּנֶסֶת אוֹמֵר: 'תִּקְעוּ כֹּהֲנִים תִּקְעוּ'. וְחוֹזֵר וְאוֹמֵר: מִי שֶׁעָנָה אֶת אַבְרָהָם בְּהַר הַמּוֹרִיָּה, הוּא יַעֲנֶה אֶתְכֶם וְיִשְׁמַע בְּקוֹל צַעֲקַתְכֶם הַיּוֹם הַזֶּה (וְהֵן תּוֹקְעִין, וּמְרִיעִין, וְתוֹקְעִין). וְעַל הַשְּׁנִיָּה הוּא אוֹמֵר: בָּרוּךְ ה׳, אֱלֹהֵי יִשְׂרָאֵל, מִן הָעוֹלָם וְעַד הָעוֹלָם. בָּרוּךְ זוֹכֵר הַנִּשְׁכָּחוֹת. וְהֵן עוֹנִין אַחֲרָיו: 'בָּרוּךְ שֵׁם כְּבוֹד מַלְכוּתוֹ לְעוֹלָם וָעֶד'. וְחַזַּן הַכְּנֶסֶת אוֹמֵר: 'הָרִיעוּ בְּנֵי אַהֲרֹן הָרִיעוּ'. וְאוֹמֵר: מִי שֶׁעָנָה אֶת אֲבוֹתֵינוּ עַל יַם סוּף, הוּא יַעֲנֶה אֶתְכֶם וְיִשְׁמַע בְּקוֹל צַעֲקַתְכֶם הַיּוֹם הַזֶּה. וְהֵם מְרִיעִין, וְתוֹקְעִין, וּמְרִיעִין. וְכֵן בְּכָל בְּרָכָה וּבְרָכָה, בְּאַחַת אוֹמֵר, 'תִּקְעוּ', וּבְאַחַת אוֹמֵר, 'הָרִיעוּ', עַד שֶׁיִּגְמוֹר אֶת הַבְּרָכוֹת כּוּלָּן. וְכָךְ הִנְהִיג ר׳ חֲלַפְתָּא בְּצִפּוֹרִי וְר׳ חֲנַנְיָה בֶּן תְּרַדְיוֹן בְּסִיכְנִי. וּכְשֶׁבָּא דָּבָר אֵצֶל חֲכָמִים, אָמְרוּ: לֹא הָיוּ נוֹהֲגִין כֵּן אֶלָּא בְּשַׁעֲרֵי מִזְרָח וּבְהַר הַבַּיִת".§ "ר׳ יְהוּדָה אוֹמֵר: לֹא הָיָה צָרִיךְ לוֹמַר זִכְרוֹנוֹת" כו׳.§ א"ר אַדָּא דְּמִן יָפוֹ: מַאי טַעֲמָא דְּר׳ יְהוּדָה? לְפִי שֶׁאֵין אוֹמְרִים זִכְרוֹנוֹת וְשׁוֹפָרוֹת אֶלָּא

הַיְינוּ מְטוּפָּל וְאֵין לוֹ הַיְינוּ בֵּיתוֹ רֵיקָן. הַיְינוּ כְּמוֹ (*אֵיזֶהוּ): **בֵּיתוֹ** רֵיקָם מִן הָעֲבֵירָה. שֶׁאֵין חָמָס וְגָזֵל בְּבֵיתוֹ: **וּפִרְקוֹ נָאֶה.** אֲפִילּוּ כְּשֶׁעָמַד עַל בַּחֲרוּתוֹ הָיָה נָאֶה, בְּלִי שֵׁם רָע: **זֶה הַמַּעֲמִיד** חַזָּן שֶׁאֵינוֹ הָגוּן לִפְנֵי הַתֵּיבָה. רָשָׁע, שֶׁהקב"ה שׂוֹנֵא אוֹתוֹ יוֹתֵר מִכּוּלָּן, וְהוּא נוֹתֵן בְּקוֹלוֹ לְפָנָיו: **שְׁבִיעִית לָאֲרוּכָּה.** שְׁבִיעִית לְאוֹתָהּ בְּרָכָה שֶׁהִתְחִיל לְהַאֲרִיךְ בָּהּ. וְאוֹתָהּ אֵינָהּ מִן הַתּוֹסֶפֶת, אֶלָּא מִי"ח בְּרָכוֹת הִיא, כִּדְתַנְיָא: **בְּגוֹאֵל יִשְׂרָאֵל הוּא מַאֲרִיךְ: הוּא אוֹמֵר** לִפְנֵיהֶן. אוֹתוֹ הַזָּקֵן הָרָגִיל וּמַאֲרִיךְ בִּגְאוּלָּה, כִּדְקָתָנֵי מַתְנִי׳: **בד"א.** דְּהֵן עוֹנִין אַחֲרָיו אָמֵן, בַּגְּבוּלִין: **אֲבָל** בַּמִּקְדָּשׁ. אוֹמֵר אוֹתוֹ הַזָּקֵן לְאַחַר הַפָּרָשִׁיּוֹת: מִי שֶׁעָנָה אֶת אַבְרָהָם הוּא יַעֲנֶה אֶתְכֶם וְיִשְׁמַע קוֹל צַעֲקַתְכֶם בַּיּוֹם הַזֶּה בא"י אֱלֹהֵי יִשְׂרָאֵל מִן הָעוֹלָם וְעַד הָעוֹלָם בָּרוּךְ גּוֹאֵל יִשְׂרָאֵל, וְהֵן עוֹנִים אַחֲרָיו בשכמל"ו. **וְכֵן בְּכָל בְּרָכוֹת שֶׁבַּמִּקְדָּשׁ: לְפִי שֶׁאֵין עוֹנִין אָמֵן בַּמִּקְדָּשׁ.** כִּדְיָלֵיף לְקַמָּן מִקְּרָא: **מִנַּיִין שֶׁאֵין** עוֹנִין אָמֵן בַּמִּקְדָּשׁ. דִּכְתִיב בִּתְפִלַּת עֶזְרָא בְּבַיִת שֵׁנִי "קוּמוּ *וּבָרְכוּ אֶת ה׳ אֱלֹהֵיכֶם" – וְהַיְינוּ בָּרוּךְ ה׳ אֱלֹהֵי יִשְׂרָאֵל כו׳: **וִיבָרְכוּ שֵׁם כְּבוֹדֶךָ.** הַיְינוּ שֶׁעוֹנִין אַחֲרָיו בשכמל"ו. כָּךְ הוּא הַפָּסוּק: "וִיבָרְכוּ שֵׁם כְּבוֹדֶךָ וּמְרוֹמַם עַל כָּל בְּרָכָה וּתְהִלָּה": ה"ג: יָכוֹל עַל כָּל הַבְּרָכוֹת כּוּלָּן תְּהִלָּה אַחַת – ת"ל "עַל כָּל בְּרָכָה", עַל כָּל בְּרָכָה תֵּן לוֹ תְּהִלָּה: **חַזַּן הַכְּנֶסֶת.** לֹא אוֹתוֹ זָקֵן נִיהוּ, וְחוֹזֵר חַזַּן הַכְּנֶסֶת וְאוֹמֵר לָהֶן: מִי שֶׁעָנָה כו׳, אע"פ שֶׁאֲמָרוֹ אוֹתוֹ זָקֵן: **כְּשֶׁמְּרִיעִין.** תְּחִלָּה הוּא אוֹמֵר לָהֶן: הָרִיעוּ בְּנֵי אַהֲרֹן! וּכְשֶׁתּוֹקְעִין תְּחִלָּה הוּא אוֹמֵר לָהֶן: תִּקְעוּ בְּנֵי אַהֲרֹן כו׳: **וְכָךְ הִנְהִיג.** כָּל מִנְהָג זֶה רַבִּי חֲלַפְתָּא בְּצִפּוֹרִי: **לֹא הָיוּ** נוֹהֲגִין כֵּן. שֶׁיְּהוּ עוֹנִין אַחֲרָיו בָּרוּךְ שֵׁם כְּבוֹד מַלְכוּתוֹ לְעוֹלָם וָעֶד, אֶלָּא עוֹנִין אָמֵן בַּגְּבוּלִין: **וְאִית דְּאָמְרִי** כִּדְתַנְיָ׳ כו׳. כְּלוֹמַר, וְאִיכָּא דְּמַתְנֵי הָכִי: **וְכֵן הִנְהִיג.** מִנְהָג זֶה הַמִּקְדָּשׁ קָאֵי: אֶלָּא

תורה אור: ירמיהו יב | נחמיה ט

[נ"ל זהו וכ"א ברש"י שבע"י וכ"א בריי"ף וברא"ש]
[נ"ל עליו כך גי׳ הערוך ערך פרק]
[נ"ל שאינו הגון היורד לפני התיבה וכ"א ברש"י ד"ה זה]
נ"ל ברכו
ברכות סג. סוטה מ:
רש"א מותק זה

רבינו חננאל

בשדה וביתו ריקם מעבירה ופרקו נאה שלא יצא עליו שם רע בילדותו שפל ברך ומרוצה לעם ויש לו נעימה וקולו ערב ובקי לקרות בתורה ובנביאים ובכתובים ולשנות במדרש בתלמוד בהלכות ובאגדות ובקי בכל הברכות כולן. יהבי ביה רבנן עינייהו בר׳ יצחק בר אמי: **היתה** לי נחלתי כאריה ביער א"ר אלעזר זה ש"ץ היורד לפני התיבה שאינו הגון: **ירושלמי** ר׳ אחא בשם רב אמר אין תענית עכשיו א"ר יוסי הדא אמרה אלין תעניתא דאנן עבדין לית קריין תעניתא. א"ל כן אמור רבנן כל תענית שאינה נעשית (כמצותה) [כתיקונה] עליו הכתוב אומר נתנה עלי בקולה על כן שנאתיה: **אומר** לפניהם כ"ד ברכות י"ח שבכל יום מוסיף עוד שש. ואלו הן זכרונות ושופרות כו׳. ואקשינן והתנן על השביעית הוא אומר כו׳. הנה ז׳ ברכות מוסיף ואמאי תנינן ומוסיף עוד שש ושנינן שביעית לארוכות כלומר מוסיף ומאריך בגואל ישראל. נמצאת ברכה גואל ישראל ארוכה שהיא מכלל י"ח ברכות ושש מוסיפין היינו ז׳ ארוכות ועלה תנן על השביעית הוא אומר וכדתניא בגואל ישראל הוא מאריך ובחותמה אומר מי שענה את אברהם אבינו בהר המוריה ה׳ י׳ ע׳ א׳ ו׳ ק׳ צ׳ ב׳ ה׳ ב׳ (ר"ת הוא יענה אתכם וישמע קול צעקתכם ביום הזה ברוך) גואל ישראל. והן עונין אחריו אמן. וחזן הכנסת אומר תקעו בני אהרן תקעו ותוקעין ומריעין ותוקעין וכן בכל ברכה וברכה באחת אומר תקעו בני אהרן תקעו ובא׳ אומר הריעו בני אהרן הריעו במה דברים אמורים בגבולים אבל במקדש אינו אומר אלא ברוך ה׳ אלהי ישראל מן העולם ועד העולם ברוך גואל ישראל והן עונין אחריו בשכמל"ו לפי שאין עונין אמן במקדש שנא׳ קומו ברכו את ה׳ אלהיכם ואומר ויברכו שם כבודך ומרומם וגו׳ על כל ברכה תן לו תהלה וכן הנהיג רבי חלפתא בצפורי וכשבא דבר אצל חכמים אמרו לא היו עושין כן אלא בשערי מזרח ובהר הבית בלבד. תניא אומרים לפניהם כ"ד ברכות י"ח שבכל יום ומוסיף עליהן עוד שש והיכן אמרו הני שש ברכות בין גואל לרופא ועונין אמן אחר כל ברכה ותוקעין על כל אחת ואחת כו׳ על הראשונה הוא אומר מי שענה את אברהם אבינו בהר המוריה כו׳. בשניה מי שענה את משה ואבותינו על ים סוף כו׳ בשלישית מי שענה את יהושע בגלגל ברביעית מי שענה את שמואל במצפה. בחמישית מי שענה את אליהו בהר הכרמל כו׳

הגהות הגר"א

[א] גמרא (וחוזר ואומר) תא"מ: [ב] שם (אלהים) תז"מ: [ג] שם ברוך ה׳ אלהי ישראל. נ"ב מן העולם ועד העולם:

רבינו גרשום

ואומר חותמיהן שחותם בברכה לכל פסוק: מיטפל (ובנין) [ואין] לו כלומר שיש לו טיפול בנים ואין לו עושר: ויש לו יגיעה בשדה ששדותיו זרועות שצריכין לגשמים: וביתו ריקם שאין לו עושר: שפל ברך עניו: ויש לו נעימה שיודע לבסם קולו: שבע לארוכות כלומר ודאי אין מוסיפין על שש אלא הא דקתני שבע דארוכות הן שבע דגואל ישראל שבתפלה הוא מאריך ומכאן ואילך אמר אילו שש שהן כמו ארוכות: בד"א שעונין אמן *) קומו וברכו את ה׳ מן העולם ועד העולם כלומר במקום אמן יש לענות אחר (ברכו) [הברכה] (אמרו) [ולומר] ברוך ה׳ מן העולם ועד העולם יכול על כל הברכות אין עונה אמן אלא פעם אחת [ת"ל וכו׳]: וכן הנהיג ר׳ חלפתא בצפורי. לומר שלאחר ברכה זו מי שענה כו׳: לא היו נוהגין כן אלא בשערי מזרח. במקדש אבל בגבולין אומר העניות קודם ברכות כדאמרן לעיל: משום דבעי למיחתם במרחם על הארץ ועיקר א"י בימי דוד ושלמה: ואמר כל הברכות כולן על הסדר וענו אחריו אמן אחר כל ברכה וברכה: וכשבא דבר לפני חכמים שאמרו הענייה אחר הברכה אמרו לא היו נוהגין כן אלא בשערי מזרח במקדש אבל בגבולין

*) נראה דחסר כאן וצ"ל בד"א שעונין אמן בגבולין אבל במקדש אינו כן שנאמר קומו כו׳.

אֶלָּא בְּרֹאשׁ הַשָּׁנָה, וּבַיּוֹבְלוֹת, וּבִשְׁעַת מִלְחָמָה.§ "עַל הָרִאשׁוֹנָה הוּא אוֹמֵר מִי שֶׁעָנָה אֶת אַבְרָהָם" כו'.§ תָּנָא: יֵשׁ מַחֲלִיפִין 'צְעָקָה' לְאֵלִיָּהוּ וּ'תְפִלָּה' לִשְׁמוּאֵל. בִּשְׁלָמָא גַּבֵּי שְׁמוּאֵל כְּתִיב בֵּיהּ 'תְּפִלָּה' וּכְתִיב בֵּיהּ 'צְעָקָה', אֶלָּא גַּבֵּי אֵלִיָּהוּ 'תְּפִלָּה' כְּתִיב, 'צְעָקָה' לָא כְּתִיב! "עֲנֵנִי, ה', עֲנֵנִי" לְשׁוֹן צְעָקָה הִיא.§ עַל הַשִּׁשִּׁית הוּא אוֹמֵר: מִי שֶׁעָנָה אֶת יוֹנָה כו'. עַל הַשְּׁבִיעִית הוּא אוֹמֵר: מִי שֶׁעָנָה אֶת דָּוִד כו'.§ מִכְּדִי יוֹנָה בָּתַר דָּוִד וּשְׁלֹמֹה הֲוָה, מַאי טַעֲמָא מַקְדִּים לֵיהּ בְּרֵישָׁא? מִשּׁוּם דְּבָעֵי לְמִיחֲתַם: 'מְרַחֵם עַל הָאָרֶץ'. תָּנָא: מִשּׁוּם סוּמָכוֹס אָמְרוּ: 'בָּרוּךְ מַשְׁפִּיל הָרָמִים'.§ "שָׁלֹשׁ תַּעֲנִיּוֹת הָרִאשׁוֹנוֹת, אַנְשֵׁי מִשְׁמָר מִתְעַנִּין וְלֹא מַשְׁלִימִין" כו'.§ תָּנוּ רַבָּנַן: א"מִפְּנֵי מָה אָמְרוּ אַנְשֵׁי מִשְׁמָר מוּתָּרִין לִשְׁתּוֹת יַיִן בַּלֵּילוֹת, אֲבָל לֹא בַּיָּמִים — שֶׁמָּא תִּכְבַּד הָעֲבוֹדָה עַל אַנְשֵׁי בֵּית אָב, וְיָבוֹאוּ וִיסַיְּיעוּ לָהֶם. מִפְּנֵי מָה אָמְרוּ אַנְשֵׁי בֵּית אָב לֹא בַּיּוֹם וְלֹא בַּלַּיְלָה — מִפְּנֵי שֶׁהֵן עֲסוּקִין תָּמִיד בַּעֲבוֹדָה. במִכָּאן אָמְרוּ: כָּל כֹּהֵן שֶׁמַּכִּיר מִשְׁמַרְתּוֹ וּמִשְׁמֶרֶת בֵּית אָב שֶׁלּוֹ, וְיוֹדֵעַ שֶׁבָּתֵּי אֲבוֹתָיו קְבוּעִין שָׁם — אָסוּר לִשְׁתּוֹת יַיִן כָּל אוֹתוֹ הַיּוֹם. גבְּמַכִּיר מִשְׁמַרְתּוֹ וְאֵין מַכִּיר מִשְׁמֶרֶת בֵּית אָב שֶׁלּוֹ, וְיוֹדֵעַ שֶׁבָּתֵּי אֲבוֹתָיו קְבוּעִין שָׁם — אָסוּר לִשְׁתּוֹת יַיִן כָּל אוֹתָהּ שַׁבָּת. אֵינוֹ מַכִּיר מִשְׁמַרְתּוֹ וּמִשְׁמֶרֶת בֵּית אָב שֶׁלּוֹ, וְיוֹדֵעַ שֶׁבָּתֵּי אֲבוֹתָיו קְבוּעִין שָׁם — אָסוּר לִשְׁתּוֹת יַיִן כָּל הַשָּׁנָה. *רַבִּי אוֹמֵר, אוֹמֵר אֲנִי: אָסוּר לִשְׁתּוֹת יַיִן לְעוֹלָם. דאֲבָל מָה אֶעֱשֶׂה שֶׁתַּקָּנָתוֹ קַלְקָלָתוֹ. אָמַר אַבָּיֵי: כְּמַאן שָׁתוּ הָאִידָּנָא כָּהֲנֵי חַמְרָא — כְּרַבִּי.§ "אַנְשֵׁי מִשְׁמָר וְאַנְשֵׁי מַעֲמָד אֲסוּרִים לְסַפֵּר וּלְכַבֵּס. וּבַחֲמִישִׁי מוּתָּרִין מִפְּנֵי כְּבוֹד הַשַּׁבָּת".§ מַאי טַעְמָא? *אָמַר רַבָּה בַּר בַּר חָנָה אָמַר ר' יוֹחָנָן: הכְּדֵי שֶׁלֹּא יִכָּנְסוּ לְמִשְׁמַרְתָּם כְּשֶׁהֵן מְנוּוָּלִין. ת"ר: *ו"מֶלֶךְ מִסְתַּפֵּר בְּכָל יוֹם, זכֹּהֵן גָּדוֹל מֵעֶרֶב שַׁבָּת לְעֶרֶב שַׁבָּת, חכֹּהֵן הֶדְיוֹט אַחַת לִשְׁלֹשִׁים יוֹם". "מֶלֶךְ מִסְתַּפֵּר בְּכָל יוֹם". מ"ט? אָמַר רַבִּי אַבָּא בַּר זַבְדָּא: אָמַר קְרָא "מֶלֶךְ בְּיָפְיוֹ תֶּחֱזֶינָה עֵינֶיךָ". כֹּהֵן גָּדוֹל מֵע"ש לְעֶרֶב שַׁבָּת — מ"ט? אָמַר רַב שְׁמוּאֵל בַּר יִצְחָק: הוֹאִיל וּמִשְׁמָרוֹת מִתְחַדְּשׁוֹת. כֹּהֵן הֶדְיוֹט אַחַת לִשְׁלֹשִׁים יוֹם — מְנָלַן? אָתְיָא "פֶּרַע" "פֶּרַע" מִנָּזִיר. כְּתִיב הָכָא "וְרֹאשָׁם לֹא יְגַלֵּחוּ, וּפֶרַע לֹא יְשַׁלֵּחוּ", וּכְתִיב הָתָם "קָדֹשׁ יִהְיֶה, גַּדֵּל פֶּרַע שְׂעַר רֹאשׁוֹ". מָה לְהַלָּן שְׁלֹשִׁים — אַף כָּאן שְׁלֹשִׁים. וְנָזִיר גּוּפֵיהּ מְנָלַן? אָמַר רַב מַתָּנָה: *טסְתָם נְזִירוּת שְׁלֹשִׁים יוֹם. מְנָלַן? אָמַר קְרָא: "יִהְיֶה", בְּגִימַטְרִיָּא תְּלָתִין הָוֵי. א"ל רַב פַּפָּא לְאַבָּיֵי: וְדִילְמָא ה"ק רַחֲמָנָא: לָא לִירַבּוּ כְּלָל! אֲמַר לֵיהּ: אִי הֲוָה כָּתַב: "לֹא יְשַׁלְּחוּ פֶּרַע" — כִּדְקָאָמְרַתְּ. הָשְׁתָּא דִּכְתִיב "וּפֶרַע לֹא יְשַׁלֵּחוּ" — פֶּרַע לֶיהֱוֵי, שִׁלּוּחֵי הוּא דְּלָא לִישַׁלְּחוּ. אִי הָכִי, אֲפִילּוּ הָאִידָּנָא נַמִי! ידּוּמְיָא דִּשְׁתוּיֵי יַיִן. מָה שְׁתוּיֵי יַיִן — בִּזְמַן בִּיאָה הוּא דְּאָסוּר, שֶׁלֹּא בִּזְמַן בִּיאָה שָׁרֵי. אַף הָכָא נַמִי. וְהָתַנְיָא: *רַבִּי אוֹמֵר אוֹמֵר אֲנִי: כֹּהֲנִים אֲסוּרִין לִשְׁתּוֹת יַיִן לְעוֹלָם. אֲבָל מָה אֶעֱשֶׂה שֶׁתַּקָּנָתוֹ קַלְקָלָתוֹ. וַאֲמַר אַבָּיֵי: כְּמַאן שָׁתוּ הָאִידָּנָא כָּהֲנֵי חַמְרָא? כְּרַבִּי

(מ"א יח) (ישעיהו לג) (יחזקאל מד) (במדבר ו)

רש"י

אֶלָּא בְּרֹאשׁ הַשָּׁנָה. כִּדְאָמְרִינַן בְּר"ה (דף טז.): אִמְרוּ לְפָנַי מַלְכֻיּוֹת וְזִכְרוֹנוֹת וכו': וּבַיּוֹבֵל. בְּיוֹם הַכִּפּוּרִים שֶׁל יוֹבֵל, כִּדְתְנַן הָתָם (דף כו:): שָׁוֶה הַיּוֹבֵל לְר"ה לִתְקִיעָה וְלִבְרָכוֹת כו': וּבִשְׁעַת מִלְחָמָה. דִּכְתִיב (במדבר י) "וְכִי תָבֹאוּ מִלְחָמָה בְּאַרְצְכֶם עַל הַצַּר הַצּוֹרֵר אֶתְכֶם" וגו'. וְלָא יָדְעִינַן מְנָא אִיתְפָּרֵישׁ דְּאוֹמֵר בְּרָכוֹת וּפְסוּקֵי מַלְכֻיּוֹת זִכְרוֹנוֹת וְשׁוֹפָרוֹת בִּשְׁעַת מִלְחָמָה: צְעָקָה לְאֵלִיָּהוּ. עַל מִי שֶׁעָנָה אֶת אֵלִיָּהוּ חוֹתֵם "שׁוֹמֵעַ צְעָקָה", וּבִשְׁמוּאֵל "שׁוֹמֵעַ תְּפִלָּה" דִּכְתִיב בֵּיהּ תְּפִלָּה (שמואל א ז): "קִבְצוּ אֶת כָּל יִשְׂרָאֵל הַמִּצְפָּתָה וְאֶתְפַּלֵּל בַּעַדְכֶם": צְעָקָה. דִּכְתִיב (בראשית טו) "וַיִּחַר לִשְׁמוּאֵל וַיִּזְעַק אֶל ה' כָּל הַלָּיְלָה". וְאִיכָּא לְמֵימַר בַּמִּצְפָּה הֲוָה הַהִיא זְעָקָה, דְּבָתַר פָּרָשַׁת "קִבְצוּ כָּל יִשְׂרָאֵל הַמִּצְפָּתָה" כְּתִיב, בְּפָרָשַׁת *"נִחַמְתִּי כִּי הִמְלַכְתִּי אֶת שָׁאוּל" וגו'. כָּךְ שָׁמַעְתִּי: גַּבֵּי אֵלִיָּהוּ. בְּמַעֲשֵׂה דְּהַר הַכַּרְמֶל כְּתִיב תְּפִלָּה, דִּכְתִיב "עֲנֵנִי ה' עֲנֵנִי", דְּמַשְׁמַע לְשׁוֹן בַּקָּשָׁה וּתְפִלָּה, וְלֹא לְשׁוֹן זְעָקָה. וּמְשַׁנֵּי: "עֲנֵנִי ה' עֲנֵנִי" — לְשׁוֹן זְעָקָה הוּא. כָּךְ שָׁמַעְתִּי: יוֹנָה בָּתַר דָּוִד וּשְׁלֹמֹה. דַּהֲוָה בִּימֵי אֲמַצְיָהוּ, בְּסֵדֶר עוֹלָם: דְּבָעֵי לְמִחְתַּם. בְּסוֹף כָּל בְּרָכוֹת "בָּרוּךְ מְרַחֵם עַל הָאָרֶץ", וּלְהָכִי בָּעֵי בְּאוֹתָהּ חֲתִימָה דָּוִד וּשְׁלֹמֹה, שֶׁהֵן הִתְפַּלְּלוּ עַל אֶרֶץ יִשְׂרָאֵל(א), כָּךְ שָׁמַעְתִּי. אִי נַמִי: מִשּׁוּם דְּאִינְהוּ תִּקּוּן בֵּית הַמִּקְדָּשׁ, דְּהוּא עִיקַּר הָאָרֶץ. כָּךְ שָׁמַעְתִּי: בָּרוּךְ מַשְׁפִּיל הָרָמִים. הָיוּ אוֹמְרִים בִּמְקוֹם בָּרוּךְ מְרַחֵם, שֶׁהִכְנִיעַם בַּמָּטָר שֶׁשָּׁבוּ בִּתְשׁוּבָה: מִכָּאן אָמְרוּ. מִדְּקָתָנֵי הָכָא, דַּאֲפִילּוּ אַנְשֵׁי מִשְׁמָר שֶׁלֹּא הָיוּ עוֹבְדִין בְּאוֹתוֹ הַיּוֹם כְּלָל — אֲפִילּוּ הָכִי אֲסוּרִין לִשְׁתּוֹת יַיִן: כֹּהֵן. בַּזְּמַן הַזֶּה: הַמַּכִּיר מִשְׁמַרְתּוֹ. הַיּוֹדֵעַ מֵאֵיזוֹ מִשְׁמֶרֶת הוּא, מִיהוֹיָרִיב אוֹ מִידַעְיָה, אוֹ אַחַת מִכ"ד מִשְׁמָרוֹת. שֶׁיּוֹדֵעַ שְׁמוֹת אֲבוֹתָיו וַאֲבוֹת אֲבוֹתָיו עַד יְהוֹיָרִיב, וְיוֹדֵעַ אֵיזֶה יוֹם וְאֵיזֶה שַׁבָּת הָיוּ עוֹבְדִים: קְבוּעִין. שֶׁיּוֹדֵעַ וַדַּאי שֶׁבֵּית אָב שֶׁלּוֹ עוֹבֵד בַּמִּקְדָּשׁ, לְפִי שֶׁהַרְבֵּה הָיוּ מִבָּתֵּי אֲבוֹת הַכֹּהֲנִים שֶׁלֹּא הוּקְבְּעוּ. שׁוּב אָמַר לִי רַבִּי: קְבוּעִין — שֶׁלֹּא נִתְחַלֵּל בֵּית אָב שֶׁלּוֹ לִהְיוֹת מְגוֹאָל מִן הַכְּהוּנָּה, וְיוֹדֵעַ שֶׁרָאוּי בֵּית אָב שֶׁלּוֹ לַעֲבוֹד: אָסוּר לִשְׁתּוֹת יַיִן כָּל אוֹתוֹ הַיּוֹם. [א] וְתוּ לָא, שֶׁמָּא יִבָּנֶה בֵּית הַמִּקְדָּשׁ וְתִכְבַּד הָעֲבוֹדָה, וְיִהְיֶה זֶה צָרִיךְ לַעֲבוֹד: מַכִּיר מִשְׁמַרְתּוֹ. שֶׁיּוֹדֵעַ אֵיזֶה שַׁבָּת בַּשָּׁנָה עוֹבְדִין: וְאֵינוֹ יוֹדֵעַ מֵאֵיזֶה בֵּית אָב. דְּעַכְשָׁיו אֵינוֹ מַכִּיר בְּאֵיזֶה יוֹם בַּשַּׁבָּת עוֹבְדִין, וְיוֹדֵעַ שֶׁבָּתֵּי אֲבוֹתָיו קְבוּעִין — אָסוּר כָּל אוֹתָהּ שַׁבָּת מִסְּפֵיקָא. בְּכוּלְּהוּ גָּרְסִינַן: וְיוֹדֵעַ שֶׁבָּתֵּי אֲבוֹתָיו קְבוּעִין הֵן, דְּאִם אֵינוֹ יוֹדֵעַ שֶׁבָּתֵּי אֲבוֹתָיו קְבוּעִין לַעֲבוֹד — מוּתָּר הוּא לִשְׁתּוֹת יַיִן כָּל הַשָּׁנָה, וְלָא חָיְישִׁינַן שֶׁמָּא יִבָּנֶה, וְשֶׁמָּא בֵּית אָב שֶׁלּוֹ יַעַבְדוּ הַיּוֹם: רַבִּי אוֹמֵר אוֹמֵר אֲנִי כֹּהֵן אָסוּר כו'. כְּלוֹמַר, אִי חָיְישִׁינַן לְשֶׁמָּא יִבָּנֶה — יְהֵא אָסוּר לְעוֹלָם, אֲפִי' הַמַּכִּיר מִשְׁמַרְתּוֹ וּמִשְׁמֶרֶת בֵּית אֲבוֹתָיו, דְּחָיְישִׁינַן שֶׁמָּא יִשְׁתַּנֶּה סֵדֶר מִשְׁמָרוֹת, וְשֶׁמָּא יַעַבְדוּ כּוּלָּם לַחֲנוּכַּת הַבַּיִת בְּבַת אַחַת, וְנִמְצָא זֶה צָרִיךְ לַעֲבוֹד. אֲבָל מָה אֶעֱשֶׂה(ב) שֶׁתַּקָּנָתוֹ קַלְקָלָתוֹ. דַּהֲוֵי כַּמָּה שָׁנִים שֶׁלֹּא חָזְרָה בִּירָה, וְקַלְקָלָה זוֹ תַּקָּנָתוֹ לִשְׁתּוֹת יַיִן בְּהֶדְיָא, וּלְשֶׁמָּא יִבָּנֶה לָא חָיְישִׁינַן: כְּשֶׁהֵן מְנוּוָּלִין. שֶׁלֹּא יְהוּ סוֹמְכִין עַל יוֹם אֶחָד מִימֵי שַׁבָּת, וְאֵין מִסְתַּפְּרִין בַּשַּׁבָּת שֶׁעָבְרָה: מִסְתַּפֵּר בְּכָל יוֹם. מִצְוָה: מֵעֶרֶב שַׁבָּת לְעֶרֶב שַׁבָּת. וְלֹא יִשְׁהֶה מְגֻלָּח יוֹתֵר: וּמִשְׁמָרוֹת מִתְחַדְּשׁוֹת. בְּכָל שַׁבָּת וְשַׁבָּת, וּמִשְׁמָרָה שֶׁלֹּא רָאַתְהוּ עַד עַכְשָׁיו וְנָאֶה לִרְאוֹתוֹ — הַדָּבָר נָאֶה שֶׁתִּרְאֵהוּ בְּיוֹפְיוֹ: לָא לִירַבּוּ כְּלָל. [ב] אֶלָּא יִסְתַּפְּרוּ בְּכָל יוֹם. דְּהָכִי מַשְׁמַע "וּפֶרַע", דְּהַיְינוּ שְׁלֹשִׁים לֹא יְשַׁלֵּחוּ, אֶלָּא יְגַלְּחוּ: שִׁלּוּחֵי לָא מְשַׁלְּחֵי. הָכִי מַשְׁמַע פֶּרַע שֶׁגִּדְּלוּ — אֵינָן רַשָּׁאִין לְגַדֵּל עוֹד: אִי הָכִי. כֵּיוָן דְּמִקְּרָא מַפְּקַתְּ לַהּ, הָאִידָּנָא נַמִי לָא לִישַׁלְּחוּ! וּמְשַׁנֵּי: כְּיַיִן, דּוּמְיָא דְּיַיִן, דִּכְתִיב בְּסָמוּךְ לְהַאי "וּפֶרַע לֹא יְשַׁלֵּחוּ", "וְיַיִן לֹא יִשְׁתּוּ כָּל כֹּהֵן": מַה יַּיִן בִּזְמַן בִּיאָה הוּא דְּאָסוּר. דִּכְתִיב (יחזקאל מד) "בְּבוֹאָם אֶל הֶחָצֵר" וגו', בִּזְמַן שֶׁבֵּית הַמִּקְדָּשׁ קַיָּים, שֶׁבָּאִין שָׁם לַעֲבוֹד: שֶׁלֹּא בִּזְמַן בִּיאָה. כְּגוֹן הָאִידָּנָא, שֶׁהַבַּיִת חָרֵב, וְלָא זְמַן בִּיאָה הִיא: וְהָתַנְיָא רַבִּי אוֹמֵר אֲנִי כו' וְאָמַר אַבָּיֵי כו'. מִכְּלָל דְּרַבָּנַן אָסְרִי, דְּחָיְישִׁינַן לְשֶׁמָּא יִבָּנֶה. וּמָלֵי נַמִי מַיְיתִי רֵישָׁא דְּבָרַיְיתָא, מִפְּנֵי מָה אָמְרוּ אַנְשֵׁי מִשְׁמָר כו', וְאַיְיתִי סֵיפָא בִּלְשׁוֹן קְלָרָה וְדַיֵּיק מִינָּהּ מִכְּלָל דְּרַבָּנַן אָסְרִי:

תוספות

וְיוֹדֵעַ שבתי אבותיו קבועין לשם אסור לשתות יין וכו'. פירוש: אסור לשתות יין חוץ לסעודתו. אבל בסעודתו – מותר, דיין שבתוך הסעודה אינו משכר:

וּבַחֲמִישִׁי מותרין מפני כבוד השבת מאי טעמא. פי': מאי טעמא אין הכהנים מותרין להסתפר אלא דווקא בחמישי בשבת – כדי שלא יכנסו למשמר כשהן מנוולין. פי': ולא ימתינו עד יום אחד מימי השבוע הבא ויסתפרו קודם שיכנסו למשמרת, דאם לא יסתפרו קודם – יהיו אסורין כל השבוע הבא עד יום החמישי. ומתוך זה שאסרו לספר כל השבוע הבא יסתפרו קודם שיכנסו למשמרתם, ולא יהיו מנוולים:

כֹּהֵן גדול מסתפר מע"ש לערב שבת וכהן הדיוט אחד לשלשים יום. פירוש: שאינו יכול להשהות יותר. והאי דקאמר בסמוך: השתא דכתיב פרע לא ישלחו פרע ליהוי פי': פרע ליהוי – עד שלשים יום, אם ירצה:

לֹא לירבו כלל. פירוש: ואפילו עד ל' יום. וקשה: דאם כן ג"ש דפרע למה לי(ג)? וי"ל: דשמא ר"ל לא לירבו עד ל' יום, אלא יגלח בכ"ט:

שִׁלּוּחֵי לא משלחו. יותר משלשים יום:

עין משפט נר מצוה

כב א מיי' פ"א מהל' ביאת מקדש הלכה ב סמג עשין קצו:

כג ב ג ד מיי' שם הלכה ה:

כד ה מיי' שם הלכה יב ופ"ו מהלכות כלי המקדש הלכה יא:

כה ו מיי' פ"ב מהלכות מלכים הלכה ה:

כו ז מיי' פ"ה מהלכות כלי המקדש הל' ו:

כז ח מיי' פ"א מהלכות ביאת מקדש הלכה יא סמג עשין קעב:

כח ט מיי' פ"ג מהל' נזירות הלכה א ופ"א מהלכות ביאת מקדש הלכה יא סמג עשין רב:

כט י מיי' פ"א מהלכות ביאת מקדש הל' ו:

מסורת הש"ס

[נ"ל ויזעק שמואל אל ה' בעד ישראל]

סנהדרין כב:

[מו"ק יז.]

סנהדרין כב: וכל הסוגיא עד סופו וע"ש כמה וכמה שינוים

נזיר ה. לט. סנהדרין שם ע"ש מו"ק יט:

סנהדרין שם

הגהות הב"ח

(א) רש"י ד"ה בסוף דבעי למחתם כו' על א"י וכן שמעתי) תא"מ וע"ב נ"ל דזה טעות: (ב) ד"ה רבי אומר כו' אבל מה אעשה שתקנתן קלקלתן דהוי כמה שנים שלא חזרה עבודה וקלקלה זו תקנתן: (ג) תום' ד"ה לא לירבו כו' וי"ל. נ"ב לפי זה לא גרס מלת כלל:

הגהות מהר"ב רנשבורג

[א] רש"י ד"ה אסור לשתות יין וכו' ותו לא שמא וכו'. נ"ב פי' לא אסור משום שמא יבנה וכו' ותכבד עבודה לטולי האי לא גרסינן כמ"ש רש"י כד"ה ואינו יודע וכו' ולא חיישינן אבל ר"ל ולפיכך אסור רק אותו יום לחוד ולק"מ קושית מהרש"א ודו"ק: [ב] שם ד"ה לא לירבו כלל. בכ"ם ליתא כן לירבו כו' אלא יסתפרו בכל יום. נ"ב ע"ע לדף טז מה שעינה לקושי' התוס' ד"ה לא לירבו וביותר יפלא דסוף לשון רש"י הוא כמעט כתירוץ התוספות ונמצאו דברי רש"י סותרים תוך כדי דיבור:

רבינו חננאל

כו'. על הששית מי שענה את יונה במעי הדגה על השביעית מי שענה את דוד ושלמה בנו בירושלים תנא יש שמחליפין צעקה לאליהו וחותמין בברכה החמישית ברוך שומע צעקה ובברכה רביעית שהיא מי שענה את שמואל חותמים ברוך שומע תפלה. ואסיקנא ענני ה' ענני דכתיב ביה באליהו לשון צעקה הוא. ואמאי חתים לדוד ושלמה בנו בסוף והלא אינהו קדימי ליונה משום דבעי למחתם ברוך מרחם על הארץ תנא סומכוס אומר בשביעית הוא אומר ברוך משפיל רמים: מתני' שלש תעניות הראשונות אנשי משמר כו' פי' הכהנים היו חלוקים כ"ד חלקים משמש שבוע ומתחלף יוצא זה נכנס אחר ואותו החלק המשמש שבוע נקרא משמר וכל המשמר היו חולקין ז' חלקים כל אחד משמש יומו ויצא ונכנס אחר משמש למחר ונקרא חלק שהוא אחד משבעה במשמר בית אב. וכן הוא מפורש בתוספתא (דמכילתין) משמר שיש בו ד' בתי אבות או ז' בתי אבות או ח' או ט' משמר שיש בו ד' בתי אבות ג' מהן מקריבין כל אחד ב' ימים והרביעי מקריב יום אחד ומשמר שיש בו ח' בתי אבות כו'. משמר שיש בו ז' בתי אבות כל אחד משמר יומו והן כל אחד ואחד ועל זה הסדר שנו בחיצונה אנשי משמר מותרין לשתות יין בלילות אבל לא בימים שמא יזדמנו אותו היום זבחים הרבה ותכבד העבודה על אנשי (בתי דין) בית אב ויסייעו אותן אבל אנשי בית אב אסורין לשתות יין בין ביום בין בלילה מפני שהן תדירין בעבודה ויש באלו כ"ד משמרות שהפילו גורלות מי שעלה גורלו ביום ראשון *) נקבע במשמרתו להיות היא משמש ביום ראשון לעולם ומי שנקבע ביום שני כמוהו כגון שהיא משמרת יהויריב בתחלת ניסן בית אב פלוני באחד בשבת. בית אב פלוני בשני בשבת. וכן כולן לפיכך אמרו [המכיר] משמרתו באיזה חדש ובאיזה שבוע זמנו ובית אב שלו באיזה היום מן השבוע זמנו והוא מן הקבועים לעולם אסורין לשתות יין בו ביום מ"ט אמרינן שמא יבנה הבית ויהיה שתוי ואינו יכול לשמש בו ביום ומי שאינו מכיר בית אב שלו אבל מכיר באיזה שבוע זמן משמרתו אסור לשתות יין כל אותו שבוע ומי שאינו מכיר [לא] זה ולא זה אבל יודע שבתי אבותיו קבועין בעבודה אסור לשתות יין לעולם דבכל יום חיישנן שמא יומו הוא ר' אומר אומר אני כגון זה אסור לשתות יין לעולם **) אסור דרבנן וכדאמרין (אצל) [אבל] תקנתו קלקלתו זה השמועה כולה בסנהדרין בסוף פ' כ"ג פי' כיון שנתקלקלה בבית אב שלו הותר שאפילו אם יבנה הבית אינו משמש עד שישב ב"ד של כהונה ויקבעוהו באיזה יום ישמש לפיכך עכשיו מותר וכן כל כהן שאינו בר עבודה ביום ידוע מותר ועל זה אמר אביי כמאן שתי האידנא כהני חמרא כרבי מכלל רבנן סברי

רבינו גרשום

בגבולין אומר העניה ואח"כ אומר הברכה כדאמר' לעיל: אנשי משמר מתענין ולא משלימין מתענין הואיל ואין עצמן עוסקין בקרבנות ולא משלימין דכיון דמשמר שלהן עוסקין בקרבן היום יו"ט הוא להם לפיכך אין משלימין: אנשי בית אב שמקריבין קרבן היום לא היו מתענין כלל הואיל ועוסקין בקרבן: שלש שנים. שכבר תקפה הגזירה: אנשי משמר מותרין לשתות יין בלילות הואיל ואין עוסקין בקרבן היום: אנשי בית אב שעובדין היום לא ביום ולא בלילה הואיל דבלילות מקריבין נמי אברים ופדרים שלא נתעכלו מבערב: כל כהן שמכיר משמרתו ויודע מאיזה משמרה הוא ומשמרת בית אב שלו שיודע באיזה בית אב הוא ויודע שבתי אבותיו קבועין ביהמ"ק אסור לשתות יין כל אותו היום אע"פ שאינו בירושלים אלא הואיל וידוע שהיום עובדין בית אב שלו ואסורין ביין הוא נמי אסור: מכיר משמרתו שיודע מאיזה משמרה הוא ואינו מכיר משמרת בית אב שלו שאינו יודע מאיזה בית אב הוא: ויודע שבתי אבותיו קבועין שיודע שמשמרה שלו קבועין ועובדין בשבת [זו] אבל אינו יודע באיזה יום עובד בית אב שלו אסור לשתות יין כל השבת דשמא היום עובד בית אב שלו: ויודע שבתי אבותיו קבועין שיודע שבית אב שלו עובדין יום אחד בשנה שהרי כהנים הן *) ובית המקדש קיים רבי אומר אומר אני אם היה כהן בזמן ביהמ"ק קיים שאין מכיר משמרתו ומשמרת בית אב שלו היה אסור לשתות יין לעולם אבל מה אעשה שתקנתו קלקלתו כלומר חרבן ביהמ"ק שהיא קלקלתם תקנתם לשתות יין כרבי דאמר שתקנתו קלקלתו אבל חכמים אומרים אין מותרין לעולם כדי שלא יכנסו למשמרתם כשהן מנוולין שכשיודעין שאין יכולין לספר ולכבס במשמרתן מספרין ומכבסין קודם שיכנסו למשמרתם

*) והיו עובדין עבודה בזמן שבהמ"ק היה קיים כנ"ל.

גמרא

כְּרַבִּי, מִכְּלָל דְּרַבָּנַן אָסְרִי. מ"ט? מְהֵרָה יִבָּנֶה בֵּית הַמִּקְדָּשׁ, וּבָעֵינַן כֹּהֵן הָרָאוּי לַעֲבוֹדָה, וְלֵיכָּא. הָכָא, אֶפְשָׁר דִּמְסַפֵּר וְעָיֵיל. אִי הָכִי, שְׁתוּיֵי יַיִן נַמִי, אֶפְשָׁר דְּגָנֵי פּוּרְתָּא וְעָיֵיל, *כִּדְרָמִי בַּר אַבָּא. דְּאָמַר רָמִי בַּר אַבָּא: [א]דֶּרֶךְ מִיל וְשֵׁינָה כָּל שֶׁהוּא מְפִיגִין אֶת הַיַּיִן! לָאו מִי אִיתְּמַר עֲלָהּ, אָמַר רַב נַחְמָן אָמַר רַבָּה בַּר אֲבוּהּ: *[ב]לֹא שָׁנוּ — אֶלָּא כְּשֶׁשָּׁתָה שִׁיעוּר רְבִיעִית? אֲבָל שָׁתָה יוֹתֵר מֵרְבִיעִית — כָּל שֶׁכֵּן שֶׁדֶּרֶךְ מַטְרִידָתוֹ וְשֵׁינָה מְשַׁכַּרְתּוֹ. רַב אַשִׁי אָמַר: [ג]שְׁתוּיֵי יַיִן דִּמְחַלֵּי עֲבוֹדָה — גָּזְרוּ בְּהוּ רַבָּנַן. [ד]פְּרוּעֵי רֹאשׁ דְּלָא מְחַלֵּי עֲבוֹדָה — לָא גָּזְרוּ בְּהוּ רַבָּנַן. מֵיתִיבֵי: *"וְאֵלּוּ שֶׁהֵן בְּמִיתָה: [ה]שְׁתוּיֵי יַיִן, [ו]וּפְרוּעֵי רֹאשׁ. בִּשְׁלָמָא שְׁתוּיֵי יַיִן — בְּהֶדְיָא כְּתִיב בְּהוּ °"יַיִן וְשֵׁכָר אַל *תֵּשְׁתְּ". (ויקרא י) אֶלָּא פְּרוּעֵי רֹאשׁ מְנָלַן? דִּכְתִיב °"וְרֹאשָׁם לֹא יְגַלֵּחוּ, וּפֶרַע לֹא יְשַׁלֵּחוּ". (יחזקאל מד) וּכְתִיב בַּתְרֵיהּ "וְיַיִן לֹא יִשְׁתּוּ כָּל כֹּהֵן, בְּבֹאָם אֶל הֶחָצֵר הַפְּנִימִית". וְאִיתְקוּשׁ פְּרוּעֵי רֹאשׁ לִשְׁתוּיֵי יַיִן: מַה שְׁתוּיֵי יַיִן בְּמִיתָה — אַף פְּרוּעֵי רֹאשׁ בְּמִיתָה. וּמִינַּהּ, אִי מַה שְׁתוּיֵי יַיִן דִּמְחַלֵּי עֲבוֹדָה — אַף פְּרוּעֵי רֹאשׁ דִּמְחַלֵּי עֲבוֹדָה! (*לָא. כִּי אִיתְקוּשׁ — לְמִיתָה הוּא דְּאִיתְקוּשׁ. אֲבָל לְאַחוּלֵי עֲבוֹדָה — לָא אִיתְקוּשׁ.) א"ל רָבִינָא לְרַב אַשִׁי: הָא מִקַּמֵּי דַּאֲתָא יְחֶזְקֵאל, מַאן אֲמָרָהּ? א"ל: וְלִיטַעֲמִיךְ, הָא דְּאָמַר רַב חִסְדָּא: *)דָּבָר זֶה מִתּוֹרַת מֹשֶׁה לֹא לָמַדְנוּ, וּמִדִּבְרֵי קַבָּלָה לָמַדְנוּ °"כָּל בֶּן נֵכָר, עֶרֶל לֵב, וְעֶרֶל בָּשָׂר, לֹא יָבוֹא אֶל מִקְדָּשִׁי (לְשָׁרְתֵנִי)" (שם) הָא מִקַּמֵּי דַּאֲתָא יְחֶזְקֵאל, מַאן אֲמָרָהּ? אֶלָּא, גְּמָרָא גְּמִיר לָהּ, וַאֲתָא יְחֶזְקֵאל וְאַסְמְכַהּ אַקְּרָא. הָכָא נַמִי גְּמָרָא גְּמִיר לָהּ, וַאֲתָא יְחֶזְקֵאל וְאַסְמְכַהּ אַקְּרָא. (*כִּי גְּמִירִי הֲלָכָה — לְמִיתָה. לְאַחוּלֵי עֲבוֹדָה — לָא גְּמִירִי). § כָּל הַכָּתוּב בִּמְגִילַּת תַּעֲנִית 'דְּלָא לְמִיסְפַּד', לְפָנָיו — אָסוּר, לְאַחֲרָיו — מוּתָּר". § תָּנוּ רַבָּנַן: *"אִלֵּין יוֹמַיָּא דְּלָא לְהִתְעַנָּאָה בְּהוֹן, וּמִקְצָתְהוֹן דְּלָא לְמִיסְפַּד בְּהוֹן. מֵרֵישׁ יַרְחָא דְּנִיסָן וְעַד תְּמָנְיָא בֵּיהּ, אִיתּוֹקַם תְּמִידָא, דְּלָא לְמִיסְפַּד בְּהוֹן. מִתְּמַנְיָא בֵּיהּ עַד סוֹף מוֹעֲדָא, אִיתּוֹתַב *חַגָּא דִשְׁבוּעַיָּא, דְּלָא לְמִיסְפַּד בְּהוֹן. אָמַר מָר: מֵרֵישׁ יַרְחָא דְּנִיסָן עַד תְּמָנְיָא בֵּיהּ, אִיתּוֹקַם תְּמִידָא, דְּלָא לְמִיסְפַּד. לָמָּה לִי מֵרֵישׁ יַרְחָא? לֵימָא מִתְּרֵי בְּנִיסָן, וְר"ח גּוּפֵיהּ יו"ט הוּא וְאָסוּר! אָמַר רַב: לֹא נִצְרְכָה אֶלָּא לֶאֱסוֹר יוֹם שֶׁלְּפָנָיו. וְשֶׁלְּפָנָיו נַמִי — תֵּיפּוֹק לֵיהּ דַּהֲוָה לֵיהּ יוֹם שֶׁלִּפְנֵי רֹאשׁ חֹדֶשׁ! ר"ח דְּאוֹרַיְיתָא הוּא, וּדְאוֹרַיְיתָ' לָא בָּעֵי חִיזּוּק. דְּתַנְיָא: *הַיָּמִים הָאֵלֶּה הַכְּתוּבִין בִּמְגִילַּת תַּעֲנִית — לִפְנֵיהֶם וּלְאַחֲרֵיהֶם אֲסוּרִין. שַׁבָּתוֹת וְיָמִים טוֹבִים — הֵן אֲסוּרִין, לִפְנֵיהֶן וּלְאַחֲרֵיהֶן — מוּתָּרִין. וּמַה הֶפְרֵשׁ בֵּין זֶה לָזֶה? הַלָּלוּ דִּבְרֵי תוֹרָה, *וְדִבְרֵי תוֹרָה אֵין צְרִיכִין חִיזּוּק. הַלָּלוּ דִּבְרֵי סוֹפְרִים, *וְדִבְרֵי סוֹפְרִים צְרִיכִין חִיזּוּק. אָמַר מָר: מִתְּמַנְיָא בֵּיהּ עַד סוֹף מוֹעֲדָא אִיתּוֹתַב חַגָּא דִשְׁבוּעַיָּא דְּלָא לְמִיסְפַּד. לָמָּה לִי עַד סוֹף מוֹעֵד? לֵימָא עַד הַמּוֹעֵד, וּמוֹעֵד גּוּפֵיהּ יוֹם טוֹב הוּא וְאָסוּר! אָמַר רַב פָּפָּא: כִּדְאָמַר רַב: לָא נִצְרְכָא אֶלָּא

*) [במסקנא דגמ' זבחים יח. אלטריך ולהבדיל בין הקודש לדרשא אחרינא ושתויי יין דמחלי עבודה יליף התם מג"ש לחוקה חוקה ממחוסר בגדים וקל"ע] **) [וכ"ה בגמרא מנחות סה. להדיא]

רש"י

מכלל דרבנן אסרי. פי': מכלל דרבנן אסרי לשתות יין משום דשמא יבנה ביהמ"ק, ובעינן כהן ראוי לעבוד וליכא! ומשני: אפשר דמספר ועייל:

בעינן כהנים הראויים לעבודה וליכא. וא"ת: והלא בלא יין נמי אסורין בעבודה, דטמאי מתים נינהו וצריכין הזאה ג' [וז'] ואמאי אסרי להו יין! וי"ל: דמ"מ מותרין בעבודת צבור, דטומאה הותרה בצבור:

פרועי ראש דלא מחלי עבודה. פי' (ה): דלא כתיב בסמוך ולהבדיל וגו': (דבר תורה):

דבר זה מתורת משה לא למדנו. וא"ת: נילף מק"ו, ומה בעל מום שמותר באכילת קדשים, כדדרשינן במסכת קדושין פרק "האיש מקדש" (דף נג.) "וכל מנחה מחבת וכל מרחשת לכהנים יהיה איש כאחיו" ואפ"ה – בעל מום אסור לעבוד עבודה, ערל שאסור באכילת קדשים, דדרשינן פרק "הערל" (יבמות דף ע.) בג"ש תושב ושכיר מפסח, דערל אסור בו – אינו דין שאסור לעבודה? וי"ל: דחלל יוכיח, שאינו אוכל בקדשים – ואפ"ה כשר לעבודה. וכדאמר פרק "האומר" (קדושין דף סו:) מדכתיב "ברך ה' חילו ופועל ידיו תרצה" דמשמע אפילו [חולין שבו] הוא רוצה בעבודתו. אי (רש"א) נמי, מבעל מום לא מצי יליף, דאיכא למיפרך מה לבעל מום שכן עשו בו קריבין כמקריבים, שכל הקריבין פסולים (ו) שהם בעלי מומים כמו המקריב, תאמר בערל – שלא עשה בו קריבין כמקריבין, דמה ערלות שייך בבהמה:

שתויי יין דמחללי עבודה. פי': דכתיב "יין ושכר אל תשת וגו' ולהבדיל בין הקודש ובין *)החול":

מריש ירחא דניסן ועד תניא (דהא) [ביה] איתוקם תמידא. פי': כדמפרש במגילת תענית [פ"א], **)שהיו הבייתוסים אומרים שיחיד מתנדב תמיד, משום דכתיב "תעשה" "את הכבש אחד תעשה בבקר", "תעשה" – משמע יחיד, והדרי להו "את קרבני לחמי לאשי תשמרו להקריב" – לשון רבים: הלכו

תוספות

כְּרַבִּי הָא רַבָּנַן מֵיסַר אָסְרִי. אֲפִילוּ שֶׁלֹּא בִּזְמַן בִּיאָה. וּמְשַׁנֵּי: מַאי טַעְמָא כו' וְהָכָא כו'. מַאי טַעְמָא תֵּירוּצָא הוּא. כְּלוֹמַר, דְּטַעְמָא מַאי גְּזוּר רַבָּנַן בְּיַיִן – שֶׁמָּא יִבָּנֶה כו'. אֲבָל גַּבֵּי פְּרוּעֵי רֹאשׁ – לֹא גָּזְרוּ. דְּאֶפְשָׁר דְּמִסְתַּפֵּר מִיָּד, וְהָדַר עָיֵיל לְבֵית הַמִּקְדָּשׁ לַעֲבוֹדָה: דֶּרֶךְ מִיל וְשֵׁינָה כָּל שֶׁהוּא כו': וְשֵׁינָה מְשַׁכַּרְתּוֹ. וְהַאי שִׁינּוּי אִיכָּא בְּהַךְ מִיהָא: שְׁתוּי יַיִן דִּמְחַלֵּי עֲבוֹדָה. דִּכְתִיב "יַיִן וְשֵׁכָר אַל תֵּשְׁתְּ", וּסְמִיךְ לֵיהּ "וּלְהַבְדִּיל בֵּין הַקֹּדֶשׁ וּבֵין הַחוֹל", בֵּין עֲבוֹדָה קְדוֹשָׁה לִמְחוּלֶּלֶת, דְּאִי עָבִיד עֲבוֹדָה שְׁתוּי יַיִן – חִילֵּל: פְּרוּעֵי רֹאשׁ. דְּלָא כְּתִיב בֵּיהּ חִלֵּל, דְּלֹא נִרְאֶה חִילּוּל: וְאֵילוּ שֶׁבְּמִיתָה. בִּידֵי שָׁמַיִם, בְּמַסֶּכֶת סַנְהֶדְרִין בְּ"אֵלּוּ הֵן הַנִּשְׂרָפִין" (דף פג.) שְׁתוּיֵי יַיִן. בְּמִיתָה, דִּכְתִיב "יַיִן וְשֵׁכָר אַל תֵּשְׁתְּ בְּבוֹאֲכֶם אֶל אֹהֶל מוֹעֵד וְלֹא תָמוּתוּ" – דְּהַיְינוּ מִיתָה בִּידֵי שָׁמַיִם, מִדְּלָא כְּתִיב "יוּמַת", וְאָמַר בִּשְׁלָמָא כו': ה"ג: וּמִינַּהּ מַה שְׁתוּיֵי יַיִן מְחַלֵּי עֲבוֹדָה אַף פְּרוּעֵי רֹאשׁ מְחַלֵּי עֲבוֹדָה. קַשְׁיָא לָא גָּרַס: כִּי גְּמִירִי הֲלָכָה לְמִיתָה. לְאַחוּלֵי עֲבוֹדָה לָא גְּמִירִי: מְחַלֵּי עֲבוֹדָה. חוּלִּין הִיא כָּל עֲבוֹדָתוֹ שֶׁעָבַד: אַף פְּרוּעֵי רֹאשׁ. עֲבוֹדָתָם מְחוּלֶּלֶת, דִּלְכָל מִילֵּי אִיתְקוּשׁ. וּתְיוּבְתָּא דְּרַב אַשִׁי דְּאָמַר: פְּרוּעֵי רֹאשׁ לֹא מְחַלֵּי עֲבוֹדָה: דְּרַב חִסְדָּא. (א) בְּפֶרֶק שְׁנִי דִּזְבָחִים, וְקָא בָּעֵי הָתָם: כֹּהֵן עָרֵל שֶׁמֵּתוּ אֶחָיו מֵחֲמַת מִילָה מַהוּ? וְאָמַר רַב חִסְדָּא כו': עֶרֶל לֵב וְעֶרֶל בָּשָׂר: הִלְכְתָא גְּמִירֵי לָהּ. מַתְנִי': (ב) מֵרֵישׁ יַרְחָא דְּנִיסָן עַד תְּמָנְיָא בֵּיהּ. דְּכָל שְׁמוֹנָה יָמִים נָשְׂאוּ וְנָתְנוּ בַּדָּבָר, עַד שֶׁנִּצְּחוּ אֶת הַצְּדוֹקִין, וְעָשׂוּ אוֹתָם יוֹם טוֹב. וְדָבָר זֶה מְפוֹרָשׁ בִּמְנָחוֹת בְּפֶרֶק "רַבִּי יִשְׁמָעֵאל" וּבִמְגִילַּת תַּעֲנִית הַמְּלוּיָה אֶצְלֵנוּ: דְּלָא לְהִתְעַנָּאָה בְּהוֹן. שֶׁכּוּלָּן אֲסוּרִין בְּתַעֲנִית, וּמִקְצָתְהוֹן שֶׁיֵּשׁ בָּהֶן קְצָת חֲמוּרִין כָּל כָּךְ שֶׁבְּהֶסְפֵּד נַמִי אֲסוּרִין: (ג) אִיתּוֹקַם תְּמִידָא וְאִיתּוֹתַב חַגָּא דִשְׁבוּעַיָּא. בְּעִנְיָנִים רַבִּים חָלְקוּ בַּיְיתוֹסִין עִם חֲכָמִים, וּמְפוֹרָשִׁין בִּמְנָחוֹת וּבִמְגִילַּת תַּעֲנִית [פ"א]. וְה"ג הָתָם בְּפֶ' "ר' יִשְׁמָעֵאל" [ס"ה.], ת"ר: אִלֵּין יוֹמַיָּא דְּלָא לְהִתְעַנָּאָה בְּהוֹן, וּמִקְצָתְהוֹן דְּלָא לְמִיסְפַּד בְּהוֹן. מֵרֵישׁ יַרְחָא דְּנִיסָן עַד תְּמַנְיָא בֵּיהּ אִיתּוֹקַם תְּמִידָא, דְּלָא לְמִיסְפַּד. וּמִתְּמַנְיָא בֵּיהּ עַד סוֹף מוֹעֲדָא אִיתּוֹתַב חַגָּא דִשְׁבוּעַיָּא, דְּלָא *)לְמִיסְפַּד: מֵרֵישׁ יַרְחָא דְּנִיסָן וְעַד תְּמַנְיָא בֵּיהּ אִיתּוֹקַם תְּמִידָא דְּלָא לְמִיסְפַּד. שֶׁהָיוּ הַצְּדוֹקִים אוֹמְרִים יָחִיד מִתְנַדֵּב וּמֵבִיא תָּמִיד, מַאי דָּרוּשׁ – "אֶת הַכֶּבֶשׂ אֶחָד תַּעֲשֶׂה בַבֹּקֶר וְאֵת הַכֶּבֶשׂ הַשֵּׁנִי תַּעֲשֶׂה בֵּין הָעַרְבָּיִם". מַאי אַהְדְּרוּ לְהוּ – "אֶת קָרְבָּנִי לַחְמִי לְאִשַּׁי תִּשְׁמְרוּ לְהַקְרִיב" לְשׁוֹן רַבִּים הוּא, שֶׁיְּהוּ כּוּלָּן בָּאִין מִתְּרוּמַת הַלִּשְׁכָּה: מִתְּמַנְיָא בֵּיהּ כו' עַד דְּלָא לְמִיסְפַּד. שֶׁהָיוּ בַּיְיתוֹסִים אוֹמְרִים עֲצֶרֶת אַחַר הַשַּׁבָּת הוּא, שֶׁהָעוֹמֶר מַתְחִיל אֶחָד בַּשַּׁבָּת שֶׁנֶּאֱמַר "וּסְפַרְתֶּם לָכֶם מִמָּחֳרַת הַשַּׁבָּת". נִיטַפַּל לָהֶן רַבָּן יוֹחָנָן בֶּן זַכַּאי וְא"ל: שׁוֹטִים, מִנַּיִן לָכֶם? וְלֹא הָיָה אָדָם שֶׁהֶחֱזִירוּ דָּבָר, חוּץ מִזָּקֵן אֶחָד שֶׁהָיָה מְפַטְפֵּט כְּנֶגְדּוֹ, וְאָמַר: מֹשֶׁה רַבֵּינוּ אוֹהֵב יִשְׂרָאֵל הָיָה, וְיוֹדֵעַ שֶׁעֲצֶרֶת יוֹם אֶחָד הוּא, עָמַד וְתִיקְנָהּ אַחַר שַׁבָּת, כְּדֵי שֶׁיִּהְיוּ מִתְעַנְּגִים שְׁנֵי יָמִים וכו'. וְדָחוּ אוֹתָן, וְהָלְכוּ לָהֶן בַּיְיתוֹסִים מִכָּל הַפְּסוּקִין עַל כָּרְחָן, וְחָזְרוּ בָּהֶן. (ע"כ הַגָּ'). אִיתּוֹקַם תְּמִידָא דְּלָא לְמִיסְפַּד גָּרְסִינַן. וְלָא גָּרְסִינַן לְהִתְעַנָּאָה, כִּדְמוּכַח בְּסָמוּךְ דְּקָתָנֵי: לֹא נִצְרְכָה אֶלָּא לֶאֱסוֹר אֶת שֶׁלְּפָנָיו. וְאִי גָּרְסִינַן לְהִתְעַנָּאָה – א"כ הַיְינוּ רַבִּי יוֹסֵי, דְּאָמַר: לְפָנָיו אָסוּר. וְהָא לֵיכָּא לְמֵימַר דְּרַבִּי יוֹסֵי הִיא. דְּקָא פָּרֵיךְ, כְּמַאן – כְּרַבִּי יוֹסֵי? בִּתְמִיהָה. מִכְּלָל דִּכְרַבָּנַן פְּסִיקָא לֵיהּ: עַד סוֹף מוֹעֲדָא. פֶּסַח: חַגָּא דִשְׁבוּעַיָּא דְּלָא לְמִיסְפַּד. בִּמְגִילַּת תַּעֲנִית [פ"א] מְפָרֵשׁ מַאי אִיתּוֹקַם: וְר"ח יו"ט הוּא. דִּכְתִיב "קָרָא עָלַי מוֹעֵד", וְהָוֵי רֹאשׁ חוֹדֶשׁ חַג (ד), בְּהַאי מַסֶּכְתָּא לְקַמָּן (דף כט.): לֶאֱסוֹר

*) גי' רש"י במנחות להתענאה.

שלפניו: (ד) ד"ה ולאו חדש כו' והוי ר"ח אב כלאיתא בהאי מסכת: (ה) תוספות ד"ה פרועי כו' פי' דבר תורה דלא כתיב: (ו) ד"ה דבר כו' כשהן בעלי מומין:

רבינו חננאל

כשמעתייהו ואביי דהוא כהן מבני עלי לא הוה שתי חמרא דהא אמר רבא לדביתהו דאביי ידענא בית בנחמני דלא הוה שתי חמרא (כתובות סה ע"א) ונהגו הכהנים לשתות יין עכשיו כרבי. הכהנים והלוים אנשי משמר וישראל אנשי מעמד בשבוע המשמשין בעבודה אסורין לספר ולכבס כדי שלא יכנסו במשמרתם מנוולים כיון שיודעין שאסורים (אף) [אז] מקדימין ומתקנים את עצמן ובחמישי מותרין לכבס ולספר מפני כבוד השבת: ת"ר מלך מסתפר בכל יום כ"ג מע"ש לע"ש הואיל ומשמרות מתחדשים כהן הדיוט אחד לשלשים יום. שנאמר וראשם לא יגלחו יכול לא יגלחו לעולם אלא יגדלו שערם ת"ל ופרע לא ישלחו לא יתנו שלוח לשער כלו' לא יאריכו שער להיות משלח לפניהם ולאחריהם כסום יכסמו את ראשיהם אין להם לגדל אלא כשיעור כסוי הראש והוא שלשים יום כנזירות דכתיב ביה יהיה יהיה בגימטריא ל' וגמרינן פרע פרע מנזיר ואמאי לא גזרו בפרע כמו שגזרו ביין אמר רב אשי שתויי יין דמחלל עבודה גזרו בהו רבנן פרע ראש דלא מחללי עבודה לא גזרו בהו רבנן מיתיבי אלו שבמיתה שתויי יין ופרועי ראש כו'. ואסיקנא דאתקוש פרועי ראש לשתויי יין במיתה ומינה מה שתויי יין מחלי עבודה אף פרועי ראש מחלי עבודה ושקלו וטרו ואמרינן האי עד דלא אתא יחזקאל וכתב ופרע לא ישלחו וכתיב בתריה ויין לא ישתו כל כהן וגו' דגמרינן מינייהו דאתקוש לשתויי יין [אלא גמרא גמירי להו] ואתא יחזקאל ואסמכא אקראי וכי גמרא גמירי לה דפרועי ראש במיתה אבל לאחולי עבודה לא גמירי גמרא: **מתני'** כל הכתוב במגלת תענית די לא למספד כו'. ת"ר אלין יומא דלא להתענאה בהון ומקצתהון כו'. אמר מר ריש ירחא דניסן עד תמניא ביה אתוקם תמידא די לא להתענאה *) ואקשינן אמאי לא תני מתרי בניסן דהא ר"ח גופא לא אצטריך ושני רב לאסור באדר ביום שלפניו ותניא ימים הכתובים במגלת תענית לפניהם ולאחריהם אסור. ואי משום ר"ח דאורייתא איסוריה ואין דברי תורה צריכין חיזוק וכן אקשי אסיפא דקתני מתמניא ביה ועד סוף מועדא איתותב חגא דשבועיא דלא למספד

*) גי' רבינו כמו שהיתה הגי' לפני התוס' במנחות סה ע"ש.

עין משפט נר מצוה

ל א ב מיי' פ"א מהל' ביאת מקדש הלכה ה ופ"ד מהלכות תפלה הל' יז סמג עשין מ ולאוין לט טוש"ע א"ח סימן קנ סעיף ב:

לא ג מיי' פ"א מהל' ביאת מקדש הלכה א סמג לאוין סג:

לב ד מיי' שם הל' ח:

לג ה מיי' שם הל' א:

לד ו מיי' שם הלכה יד:

מסורת הש"ס

[עירובין סד: סנהדרין כב: ע"ש]

עירובין סד: סנהדרין כב:

סנהדרין שם [פג. שבועות לו:]

[נ"ל אל תשת אתה ובניך ולא תמותו]

[כל זה ליתא בסנהדרין אלא מסיק שם קשיא ע"ש ותוספות שם] [וגם רש"א מוחק כל זה וגרס דמחלי עבודה קשיא]

*) יומא עא: מו"ק ה. סנהדרין כב. פג: זבחים יח: כב:

[כל אלו מוחק הרש"ל בסנהדרין כב:]

[מנחות סה. ע"ש גירסת הספרים בתוס' ד"ה מריש]

[נתישב על דינו שבאותן ימים נלחו חכמים את הבייתוסים רש"י שם במנחות]

ר"ה יט.

[יבמות פה:]

[שם]

גליון הש"ס

גמרא ואתא יחזקאל ואסמכה אקרא. עיין יומא דף לה ע"ב וברש"י שם ד"ה מיתיבי:

הגהות הב"ח

(א) רש"י ד"ה דרב חסדא בזבחים פרק שני דקא בעי התם: (ב) ד"ה מריש ירחא כו' נ"ל אחר ד"ה דלא להתענאה כו': (ג) ד"ה איתוקם תמידא כו' וד"ה מריש ירחא כו' וד"ה מתמניא כו' עד על כרחן וחזרו בהן הד"א ואח"כ מה"ד ה"ג איתוקם תמידא וכו' אלא לאסור את יום

רבינו גרשום

למשמרתם כשהן מנוולין הואיל ומשמרות מתחדשות שיראו אותו ביפיותו: ראשם לא יגלחו פרע לא ישלחו ראשם לא יגלחו משמע לא יגלחו כל שעריהם לגמרי ופרע לא ישלחו משמע שלא יגדלו שעריהם: ודילמא הכי אמרה רחמנא ופרע לא ישלחו דלא לירבו כלל אלא מסתפרין בכל יום: פרע להביא שיגדילו שערם כל שהוא דהיינו ל' יום שלוחי לא ישלחו יותר מדאי: אי הכי הואיל וילפת פרע פרע מנזיר אפילו האידנא נמי יהו אסורין בפרוע ראש נמי שהרי נזירות נוהג בזמן הזה: דומיא דיין דהא איתקש פרוע ראש ליין דכתיב ויין לא ישתו כל כהן וגו' בזמן ביאה למקדש אסור דכתיב יין ושכר אל תשת אתה ובניך אתך בבואכם אל אהל מועד: מכלל דרבנן אסרי בזמן הזה ביין ונימא דפרוע ראש בזמן הזה נמי אסור. תריץ מ"ט אסרי רבנן בזמה"ז מהרה יבנה ביהמ"ק וכו' אבל פרוע ראש לא אסרי: כש"כ ששינה משכרתו ולהכי אסרי בשתויי יין דאי אפשר בתקנה אבל פרוע ראש דאפשר בתקנה לא אסרי: רב אשי אמר להכי אסרי רבנן שתויי יין בזמה"ז הואיל דחמור דהרי מחלל עבודה דאמרינן התם במס' זבחים כתיב בשתויי יין חוקה דכתיב יין ושכר אל תשת וגו' וכתיב בבגדי כהונה חוקה דכתיב (וחבשת) [וחגרת אתם] אבנט אהרן ובניו וגו' מה בגדי כהונה שאינו לובשן ועובד מחל עבודה כדאמרינן בגדיהם עליהם כהונתם

אלא לאסור יום שלפניו, ה"נ לא נצרכה אלא לאסור יום שלאחריו. כמאן? כרבי יוסי, דאמר: בין לפניו בין לאחריו אסור; אי הכי, בעשרים ותשעה נמי, מאי איריא דהוי יומא דמקמי יומא דמיתוקם תמידא? תיפוק ליה דה"ל יומא דבתר עשרין ותמניא ביה, דתניא: *בעשרים ותמני' ביה אתת בשורתא טבתא ליהודאי דלא יעידון מן אורייתא, (א) שפעם אחת גזרה מלכות הרשעה שמד על ישראל שלא יעסקו בתורה, ושלא ימולו את בניהם, ושיחללו שבתות. מה עשה יהודה בן שמוע וחביריו? הלכו ונטלו עצה ממטרוניתא אחת שכל גדולי רומי מצויין אצלה. אמרה להם: עמדו והפגינו בלילה. הלכו והפגינו בלילה, אמרו: אי שמים! לא אחים אנחנו, לא בני אב אחד אנחנו, לא בני אם אחת אנחנו? מה נשתנינו מכל אומה ולשון שאתם גוזרין עלינו גזירות רעות! ובטלום. ואותו היום עשאוהו יו"ט. אמר אביי: לא נצרכה אלא לחדש מעובר. רב אשי אמר: אפילו תימא לחדש חסר. א) כל שלאחריו, בתענית אסור בהספד מותר. וזה, הואיל ומוטל בין שני ימים טובים — עשאוהו כיו"ט עצמו, ואפילו בהספד נמי אסור. אמר מר: מתמניא ביה ועד סוף מועדא איתותב חגא דשבועיא דלא למיספד. למה לי למימר מתמניא ביה? לימא מתשעה ביה, ותמניא גופיה אסור, דה"ל יומא דאיתוקם ביה תמידא! כיון דאילו מקלע (ליה) מילתא ובטליניה לשבעה — תמניא גופיה אסור, דה"ל יומא קמא דאיתותב ביה חגא דשבועיא. השתא דאתית להכי — עשרים ותשעה נמי, כיון דאילו מיקלע מילתא ובטליניה לעשרים ותמניא, עשרין ותשעה גופיה אסור, דה"ל יומא דמקמי יומא דאיתוקם תמידא. איתמר, ר' חייא בר אסי אמר רב: הלכה כר' יוסי. ושמואל אמר: הלכה כר' מאיר. ומי אמר שמואל הכי? והתניא, רשב"ג אומר: ומה תלמוד לומר 'בהון', 'בהון' שתי פעמים — לומר לך שהן אסורין, לפניהן ולאחריהן מותרין. ואמר שמואל: הלכה כרבן שמעון בן גמליאל! מעיקרא סבר כיון דליכא תנא דמיקל כרבי מאיר — אמר הלכה כרבי מאיר. כיון דשמעיה לרבן שמעון (ג) דמיקל טפי — אמר הלכה כרבן שמעון בן גמליאל. וכן אמר באלי אמר רבי חייא בר אבא א"ר יוחנן: הלכה כרבי יוסי. א"ל רבי חייא לבאלי: אסברא לך, *כי אמר ר' יוחנן הלכה כרבי יוסי — אדלא להתענאה. ומי אמר רבי יוחנן הכי? והאמר ב) ר' יוחנן: הלכה כסתם משנה. ותנן: ג) *אע"פ שאמרו מקדימין [א] ולא מאחרין, מותרין

א) עי' תוס' מנחות סה. ד"ה אלין יומא ב) [שבת מו. וש"נ] ג) מגילה ה.

רש"י

לאסור את שלפניו. להכי נקט מריש ירחא דניסן, לאסור את יום שלפני ר"ח בתענית, כדתניא בסמוך: לפניהן אסורין. דאי משום ר"ח לא היה נאסר, כדמפרש: דדברי תורה אין צריכין חיזוק: כמאן כר' יוסי. דמתני', דאמר אף לאחריו בתמיה, ושבקת רבנן. אי הכי, דאליבא דר' יוסי מוקמת לה למגילת תענית — כ"ט באדר נמי, דקתרצת לעיל דאדהכי נקט ריש ירחא דניסן, דהיינו יום שלשים, דאדר הסמוך לניסן לעולם חסר, מכ"ט יום הוא, משום דקא בעי למיסר יום כ"ט — תיפוק ליה דבלאו הכי הוי אסור יום כ"ט, דה"ל יום דבתר כ"ח, שהוא י"ט כו' ואסור יום שלאחריו כרבי יוסי, ואמאי נקט ריש ירחא, לאסור את שלפניו? דלא יעידון. שלא יהו צריכין ליבטל מתלמוד תורה, שנגזר עליהן שלא יעסקו בתורה: הפגינו. צעקו. כך מתרגמינן בתהלים כל לשון שועה וצעקה — לשון פגינה: אי שמים גרסינן. אהה ה', להקב"ה היו צועקים, על אותם שגזרו עליהם גזרות קשות, והיו אומרים להם לפני הקב"ה: וכי לא אחיכם וכו': לא נצרכה אלא לחדש מעובר. בשנה מעוברת, שיש בה שני (ג) אדר והאחד חסר. *דהשתא, כי הוה אדר שני מלא — הוה יום שלשים לפני ר"ח ניסן. א"נ, דעברוה לאדר, כגון שלא נראה החדש יום ל'. דמשום יו"ט דר"ח לא מיתסר אלא כ"ט: (ד) רבא אמר אפילו תימא חדש חסר. ואהכי נקט מריש ירחא, דאי הוה חסר ליה ליום כ"ט משום בתר כ"ח — לא הוה חסר ליה אלא בתענית לחודיה: דכל שלאחריו כו'. כלומר, כל שאסור משום אחר י"ט — בתענית הוא דאסור, הא בהספד — מותר. ואהכי נקט מריש ירחא, דלהוי האי כ"ט דנקט מוטל בין שני ימים, משום דאי מיתסר משום דלפני יו"ט — אימור לא איתסר בהספד, דהאי דנקט כל שלאחריו כו' — לאו משום דלפניו נמי אסור בהספד, אלא איידי דפריך דליתסר יום כ"ט משום בתר כ"ח הוא דמיהדר ליה, כל שלאחריו כו': לימא מתשעה (ה) ותמניא גופיה. י"ט הוא, דהא הוה ליה מהנך ימים טובים דאיתוקם בהו תמידא, כדכתיב ביה: מריש ירחא עד תמניא: ה"ג: דאי איקלע מילתא ובטליני' לשבעה תמניא גופיה אסור דהוה ליה יומא (ו) דאיתותב חגי דשבועיא. דאי איקלע מילתא, שאם נגזר גזירה וצריכין להתענות תוך אלו ימים טובים דתמיד, ובטלו אותן להתענות בכולן, שאין לבטלה לחלאין: אכתי יומא תמניא אסור משום חגא דשבועיא. ואי קשיא: אכתי לימא תשעה, ואפילו אם אירע מילתא דבטלי — אכתי הוא אסור, תמניא גופיה, משום קמא יומא דחג שבועיא, דהוה יום שלפניו! לאו פירכא הוא, דהא יו"ט גופיה בטיל, ואנא ליקום וליגזור קמיה יומא דאיתותב חגא דשבועיא?! וכה"ג מתרץ לקמן ביום טוריינוס: כ"ט נמי. דקתרצת לה לעיל לא נצרכה כו', להכי נקט בריש ירחא דאי מיקלע כו': כרבי יוסי. דאמר בין לפניו בין לאחריו אסור: כר"מ. סתם מתניתין, דקתני: לאחריו מותר: מה ת"ל בהון בהון. דלא להתענאה בהון, ומקצתהון דלא למספד בהון. וקא דריש לה כדדייק לקמן 'בהון' משמע מיעוט: ואמר שמואל. גרס: הלכה כרבי שמעון. (ז) דמדרבנן ניהו, ולא מחמרינן כולי האי: באלי. שם חכם: ה"ג: כי אמר רבי יוחנן הלכה אדלא להתענאה. דימים הכתובים במגילת תענית דלא להתענאה — לפניהן אסורים ולאחריו מותרין, כר' יוסי ולא כר"מ, דאמר: אף לפניהם מותר. אבל אדלא למספד — דאין הלכה כרבי יוסי [דאמר] לפניו ולאחריו אסור, אלא כר"מ, דאמר: לפניו — אסור לאחריו — מותר: ומי א"ר יוחנן הכי. דלפניו מיהא אסור, כרבי יוסי: מקדימין. שקראו קודם זמנו:

תוספות

הלכו והפגינו. הפיגו — לשון נהי וצעקה. "אי שמים" גרסינן, פירוש שמים: להקב"ה היו צועקין: למה יאמרו הגוים איה אלהיכם, ולהם אמרו — וכי לאו אחיכם אנחנו וכו': לא נצרכה אלא לחדש מעובר. פירוש: דעברוה לאדר, שלא נראה הלבנה עד יום ל' והוי ר"ח ניסן יום ל"א. פירוש: וא"כ האי כ"ט לא מצינו לאוסרו *משום יום שלפני ר"ח ניסן, דיום ל' מפסיק בינתים — משום הכי איצטריך לאוסרו משום יום שלאחר עשרים ותמניא: דאילו אי איקלע וכו'. שום גזרה מריש ירחא וכו' תמניא גופיה אסור דה"ל וכו'. והקשה הקונטרס: אכתי לימא תשעה, ואפילו אי מיקלע שום גזרה ובטלינא לז' ימים וכו' — אכתי אסור תמניא גופיה משום דהוי יומא דמקמי יומא דאיתותב חגא דשבועיא! ותירץ הקונטרס: הא לאו פירכא, דהא מיו"ט גופיה דתמיד מבטלינן ליה, ואנא ניקום ונגזור משום קמי יומא דאיתותב? חגא דשבועיא (ח) וכי האי מתרלינן לקמן ביום טוריינוס: רב אמר הלכה כר' יוסי דאמר לפניו אסור אבל לאחריו מותר. וא"ת: כיון דאמר הלכה כר' יוסי, היאך אנו מתענין לפני הפורים? דאי משום דבטלה מגילת תענית — מ"מ אחנוכה ואפורים לא בטלו! וי"ל: דהא דאמר חנוכה ופורים לא בטלו — ר"ל הדינין שלהם, לעשותן י"ט, ודלא להתענאה בהון. אבל בדינים דלפניהם — בטלו. עוד י"ל (ט): דכיון דיום שלפני הפורים שנתבטל מיו"ט דידהו, שהיו רגילין לעשות בהן ונתבטלו יו"ט שלהם — ה"נ יש לנו לומר שיבטלו משום טעם לפני הפורים, דה"נ אמרינן בסמוך גבי יום שלפני נקנור וכו' וכן גבי יו"ט טוריינוס, דכיון דבטלו מיום (י) שלהם — לא יאסרו משום יו"ט הבא אחריהם, דאסורים משום יום שלפניהם — כמו כן ה"נ: דכיון דיום שלפני הפורים נתבטל משום עצמו ומותר להתענות — לא יאסר משום יום שלפני הפורים: הלכה

רבינו חננאל

לימא עד המועד. ומועד גופיה יום טוב הוא ולא צריך. ושנינן לאסור שלאחריו כר' יוסי דאמר ימים הללו בין לפניהם בין לאחריהם אסורין. אי הכי רישא דתני מריש ירחא דניסן. ואוקימנא דלא תנא ר"ח אלא לאסור יום כ"ט באדר. למה לי תיפוק דהוה לי' יום שלאחר כ"ח באדר ועשאוהו יו"ט. משום דבו בטל שמדא ואתא בשרתא טבא ליהודאי דלא יעידון מן אורייתא. ושני אביי לא נצרכה זו וזו אלא אם יזדמן להתעבר יהיה יום כ"ט אסור בו משום שהוא יום אחר כ"ח בו ויום ל' נמי יהיה אסור משום שהוא יום דמקמי יומא דאיתוקם ביה תמידא. ואקשינן נמי למה לי למימר מתמניא בניסן מימים טובים משום דקבעי דאיתותב חגא דשבועיא. תיפוק ליה דהוה ליה מן הימים טובים דאיתוקם בהו תמידא ושנינן לא נצרכא אלא דאי הדרי ביה רבנן ובטלי להני יומי דקבעו משום דאיתוקם תמידא דלא בטלי מנייהו אלא ז' יומי ויום ח' אסור מכלל יומא דאיתותב בהו חגא דשבועיא. השתא דאתית להכי כ"ט נמי דאי מקלעא כו' איתוקם תמידא ואיתותב חגא דשבועיא. מפורש במנחות בפרק רבי ישמעאל אומר עומר היה כו' איתוקם תמידא שהיו הצדוקים אומרים יחיד מתנדב ומביא תמיד דהוו דרשי את הכבש תעשה לשון יחיד ואהדרו להו רבנן את קרבני לחמי [תשמרו] שיהיו באין מתרומת הלשכה. ודחו דבריהם. ונתקיימו דברי רבותינו שלא יהיה תמיד בא אלא משל צבור. וכן הוו חולקים ואמרין אין עצרת חלה אלא לאחר שבת. ואהדרו להו רבנן ונדחו החזירו הדבר ליושנו שיהיו סופרים נ' יום ממחרת יו"ט של פסח. ולפי שנדחו דברי צדוקים ונתקיימו דברי חכמים עשאום אותם הימים טובים כימי גאולה מידי צורריהם. רב אמר הלכה כר' יוסי דאמר כל הכתוב במגלת תענית די לא למספד בין לפניו בין לאחריו אסור. [די לא להתענאה לפניו אסור] לאחריו מותר. ושמואל אמר הלכה כת"ק והוא ר"מ. וסתמא דמתני' דיליה היא דא' בדי לא למספד לפניו אסו' לאחריו מותר ובדלא לאתענאה בין לפניו ובין לאחריו מותר איני והא' שמואל הלכה כרשב"ג דאמר לפניהם ולאחריהם מותרים.

ומשנינן שמואל הלכה לקולא גמירי. מעיקרא סבר ליכא תנא דמיקל טפי מת"ק דמתני' דהוא ר' מאיר. ואמר הלכתא כת"ק. כיון דחזא רשב"ג דמיקל טפי אמר הלכתא כרשב"ג. אמר באלי א"ר יוחנן

רבינו גרשום

כהונתם עליהם אין בגדיהם עליהם אין כהונתם עליהם אף פרועי ראש מחלי עבודה וכי היכי דאסרי רבנן שתויי יין בזמה"ז הכי ליסרו פרועי ראש. ותריצן הא דדייקת מינה לא כלום הוא דא"כ הוא עד שאתי יחזקאל מאן אמרה. בן נכר ערל לב זה כהן משומד בן שנתנכרו מעשיו לאביו שבשמים ערל בשר כהן שמתו אחיו מחמת מילה הכא נמי פרועי ראש מחלי עבודה גמרא גמירי לה ואמאי לא אסרי רבנן פרועי ראש כבשתויי יין תריצן כי גמירי מה שתויי יין במיתה וכו' לאחולי עבודה לא גמירי לה דייקינן האי ומינה אלא לעולם פרועי ראש לא מחלי עבודה להכי לא אסרי רבנן בזמנו"ז אע"ג דאסרי בשתויי יין: ה"ג מריש ירחא דניסן עד תמניא ביה איתוקם תמידא דלא למיספד שהיו אומרים מנין מתנדב יחיד תמיד שהיו דורשין את הכבש אחד תעשה שהוא לשון יחיד וחכמים היו אומרים אינו בא אלא מתרומת הלשכה שהרי כתיב ביה לאשי דמשמע שבא ממקום ששאר קרבנות באין דהיינו מתרומת הלשכה. ומריש ירחא דניסן עד תמניא ביה נשאו ונתנו בדבר והודו מינין לחכמים: איתותב חגא דשבועייא דלא למספד שהיו מינין אומרין אין עצרת בא אלא [באחד] בשבת שהיו דורשין ממחרת השבת תספרו חמשים כלומר לאחר שבת בראשית הוי עצרת וחכ"א כתיב חמשים יום דמשמע בכל יום שבא חמשים יום קובע עצרת וכתיב שבע שבתות תמימות תהיינה דמשמע תמימות ממש מאחד בשבת לאחר בשבת הא כאן שחל עצרת באמצע שבת הויין חמשים יום בלא שבע שבתות תמימות מאחד בשבת [כאן שחל עצרת באחד בשבת]: לא נצרכא לאסור שלפניו להכי קאמר דריש ירחא הוי יו"ט לאסור כ"ט דאדר בתענית ובהספד דאי משום מועד לא הוי אסור דדברי תורה אין צריכין חיזוק. כמאן כר' יוסי דאמר למספד בין לפניו בין לאחריו אסור בהספד דאי דרבנן הא אמרו לאחריו מותר. אי הכי כיון דר' יוסי עשרין ותשעה באדר נמי מאי איריא דהוה יומא מקמי דאיתוקם תמידא דקאמר להכי קאמר מריש ירחא דניסן לאסור כ"ט באדר שלפניו תיפוק ליה דלהכי הוה אסור דהוה ליה יומא דבתר כ"ח דהוי יו"ט דאסור למספד והוי כ"ט אסור דהא אמר ר' יוסי בין לאחריו אסור ועדיין פריכנא למה לי למימר מריש ירחא דניסן לימא מתרי דניסן: והפגינו בלילה כדי שישמע קולם: אמר אביי להכי קאמר מריש ירחא לאסור שלפניו לחדש מעובר דהוי *) ל"א כ"ח קאסר ל' שלפניו דאילו משום כ"ח לא הוי אסור אלא כ"ט: ה"ג רב אשי אמר אפי' תימא בחדש חסר ודפרכת כיון דמוקים לה כר' יוסי למה לי למימר מריש ירחא דניסן משום כ"ט כדי לאסור [לכ"ט] לאדר שלפניו תיפוק ליה דהוי יומא דבתר כ"ח תריץ כל שלאחריו בתענית אסור בהספד מותר כלומר האי דאמר ר' יוסי בין לפניו בין לאחריו אסור לא אמר לאחריו אסור אלא להתענאה אבל בהספד מותר ולהכי איצטריך מריש ירחא דניסן כדי שיהא כ"ט מוטל בין שני ימים טובים **) בין כ"ח לכ"ח דליהוי כיו"ט עצמו דאסור אפי' בהספד וכ"ש בתענית. נפרש מתניתין שלא פי' לעיל כך הורה המורה כל הכתוב במגילת תענית דלא למספד כלומר אותם ימים טובים הכתובים במג"ת שמותרין כל כך דאסור להו למספד וכ"ש להתענאה לפניו אסור ***) בהספד ובתענית הואיל וחמור הרבה שביו"ט עצמו אסור אפי' בהספד לאחריו מותר בהספד ובתענית ר' יוסי אומר הואיל וחמור כך שאסור אפי' בהספד נחמיר נמי שבין לפניו ובין לאחריו אסור בין בהספד בין בתענית ודלא להתענאה כלומר ואותן ימים טובים דמג"ת שאינו חמור כל כך שאינן אסורין אלא בתענית אבל בהספד מותרין בין לפניו בין לאחריו הואיל וקל כ"כ [מותרין] ר' יוסי מחמיר מכ"מ אע"פ שקל כ"כ לפניו אסור: ת"ר אלין יומיא דלא להתענאה כלומר כל ימים טובים הכתובים במג"ת אסורין בתענית אבל יש בהן שאין אסורין בהספד ומקצתהון די לא למספד בהון יש מהן שחמורין הרבה שאפי' בהספד אסורין עכשיו נחזור ונפרש ההלכה כסדרה. מתמניא ביה עד סוף מועדיא איתוקם ביה חגא דשבועיא למה לי למימר מתמניא ביה לימא מט' ביה ותמניא גופיה אסור דהא אמרינן לעיל מריש ירחא עד תמניא ביה איתוקם תמידא תריץ להכי אצטריך למימר מתמניא דאי מקלע מילתא להוא יו"ט דתמידא

*) נראה דצ"ל דהוי ל' יום דנאסר ל' שלפניו וכו'. **) נ"ל בין כ"ח לריש ירחא דניסן. ***) הדבר צ"ע דהרי בהדיא אמר הש"ס לעיל דכל שלפניו או לאחריו אינו אסור רק בתענית.

עין משפט נר מצוה

לה א מיי' פ"ב מהלכות מגילה הלכה יג:

מסורת הש"ס

ר"ה יט.

הגהות הב"ח

(א) גמ' דלא יעידון מן אורייתא דלא למספד שפעם אחת כו' ואמרו אי שמים לא אחיכם אנחנו: (ב) שם כיון דשמעיה לרבן שמעון בן גמליאל דמיקל: (ג) רש"י ד"ה לא נצרכה כו' שני אדרים והראשון חסר והשני מלא דהשתא כי הוה: (ד) ד"ה רבא אמר כו' הד"א עם ד"ה דכל שלאחריו וכו' מוטל בין שני ימים והא דלא קאמר לאסור בהספד משום דהוי יום שלפניו משום דלא מיתסר כו' והאי דנקט כל שלאחריו: (ה) ד"ה לימא מתשעה ביה ותמניא: (ו) ד"ה ה"ג דאי כו' דהוה ליה יומא קמא דאיתותב ביה חגא כצ"ל והד"א עם ד"ה אכתי וכו' אסור תמניא גופיה ולגזור משום קמיה יומא דחג: (ז) ד"ה הלכה כר"ש ב"ג דמדרבנן: (ח) תום' ד"ה דאילו כו' וכה"ג נמי מתרלינן: (ט) ד"ה רב כו' ועוד י"ל דכיון דימים שלפני הפורים נתבטלו: (י) בא"ד דכיון דבטלו מיום טוב שלהם כו' הבא אחריהם דלהוי אסורים משום:

גליון הש"ס

גמ' כי אמר רבי יוחנן הלכה כר' יוסי אדלא להתענאה. וכעין זה פסחים יג ע"א מנחות לב ע"ב: רש"י ד"ה לא נצרכה וכו' דהשתא כי הוה אדר שני. עי' מג"א סי' תקמ"ח ס"ק כ: תוס' ד"ה לא נצרכה. משום יום שלפני ר"ח ניסן. הלשון מגומגם דהא עיקר מה [illegible] משום יום ל' שלאחריו [illegible] כ"ח:

הגהות הגר"א

[א] גמ' (ולא מאחרין) תא"מ:

לו א מיי' פ"ב מהלכות מגילה הלכה יג טור ש"ע א"ח סי' תרצו סעיף ב:
לז ב ג מיי' פ"א מהל' תעניות הלכה ז סמג עשין ג טוש"ע א"ח סי' תקעב סעיף ב:
א ד מיי' פ"ב מהלכות תעניות הלכה טז יז יח טוש"ע א"ח סי' תקעה סעיף ח:

הלכה מתענה ומשלים. פי': הא דקפסק הלכה מתענה ומשלים – אר"ח קאי, דאי אחנוכה ואפורים – אינו יכול להתענות, ד"יום משתה ושמחה" כתיב:

הדרן עלך סדר תעניות קמא

מתריעין עליהם מיד ומתענין כמו כן. ואפילו בראשונות, שחומר האחרונות נוהגין בו. ואם תאמר (ז): הא דמתריעין משמע דמתריעין ומתענין, אמאי צריך לפרש במתני' בסמוך אותה העיר מתענה ומתרעת? כיון דסתם מתריעות משמע תרוייהו! ויש לומר: משום דבעי לאפלוגי ר' עקיבא בסיפא, דקאמר: מתריעות ולא מתענות:

מוּתָּרִין בְּהֶסְפֵּד וְתַעֲנִית. אֵימַת? אִילֵימָא בְּנֵי חֲמֵיסַר וְקָא קָרוּ לֵיהּ בְּאַרְבֵּיסַר – וּמִי שָׁרֵי? וְהָכְתִיב בִּמְגִילַּת תַּעֲנִית: *יוֹם אַרְבָּעָה עָשָׂר בּוֹ וְיוֹם חֲמִשָּׁה עָשָׂר בּוֹ יוֹמֵי פוּרַיָּא אִינּוּן, דְּלָא לְמִיסְפַּד בְּהוֹן. וַאֲמַר רָבָא: *[א]לָא נִצְרְכָא אֶלָּא לֶאֱסוֹר אֶת שֶׁל זֶה בָּזֶה וְאֶת שֶׁל זֶה בָּזֶה. וְאֶלָּא, בְּנֵי אַרְבֵּיסַר וְקָא קָרֵי לֵיהּ בִּתְלֵיסַר. יוֹם נִיקָנוֹר הוּא! וְאֶלָּא, בְּנֵי אַרְבֵּיסַר וְקָא קָרֵי לֵיהּ בִּתְרֵיסַר. יוֹם טוּרְיָינוּס הוּא! אֶלָּא לָאו – דְּקָא קָרוּ לֵיהּ בַּחֲדֵיסַר, וְקָתָנֵי: מוּתָּר בְּהֶסְפֵּד וּבְתַעֲנִית! לָא. בְּנֵי אַרְבָּעָה עָשָׂר וְקָא קָרוּ לֵיהּ בִּתְרֵיסַר. וּדְקָאָמְרַתְּ יוֹם טְרְיָינוּס הוּא, יוֹם טְרְיָינוּס גּוּפֵיהּ בַּטּוּלֵי בַּטְלוּהוּ, הוֹאִיל וְנֶהֶרְגוּ בּוֹ *שְׁמַעְיָה וַאֲחִיָּה אָחִיו. כִּי הָא דְּרַב נַחְמָן גְּזַר תַּעֲנִיתָא בִּתְרֵיסַר. אֲמַרוּ לֵיהּ רַבָּנַן: יוֹם טוּרְיָינוּס הוּא! אֲמַר לְהוּ: יוֹם טוּרְיָינוּס [א] גּוּפֵיהּ בַּטּוּלֵי בַּטְלוּהוּ, הוֹאִיל וְנֶהֶרְגוּ בּוֹ שְׁמַעְיָה וַאֲחִיָּה אָחִיו. וְתֵיפּוֹק לֵיהּ דַּהֲוָה לֵיהּ יוֹם שֶׁלִּפְנֵי נִיקָנוֹר! אֲמַר רַב אַשִׁי: הַשְׁתָּא אִיהוּ גּוּפֵיהּ בַּטְלוּהוּ, מִשּׁוּם יוֹם נִיקָנוֹר נֵיקוּם וְנִגְזַר? מַאי נִיקָנוֹר, וּמַאי טוּרְיָינוּס? דְּתַנְיָא: נִיקָנוֹר אֶחָד מֵאַפַּרְכֵי יְוָונִים הָיָה. וּבְכָל יוֹם וָיוֹם הָיָה מֵנִיף יָדוֹ עַל יְהוּדָה וִירוּשָׁלַיִם, וְאוֹמֵר: אֵימָתַי תִּפּוֹל בְּיָדִי וְאֶרְמְסֶנָּה? וּכְשֶׁגָּבְרָה מַלְכוּת בֵּית חַשְׁמוֹנַאי וְנִצְּחוּם, קִצְּצוּ בְּהוֹנוֹת יָדָיו וְרַגְלָיו וּתְלָאוּם בְּשַׁעֲרֵי יְרוּשָׁלַיִם, וְאָמְרוּ: פֶּה שֶׁהָיָה מְדַבֵּר בְּגַאֲוָה וְיָדַיִם שֶׁהָיוּ מְנִיפוֹת עַל יְרוּשָׁלַיִם – תֵּעָשֶׂה בָּהֶם נְקָמָה. מַאי *טוּרְיָינוּס? אָמְרוּ: כְּשֶׁבִּקֵּשׁ טוּרְיָינוּס לַהֲרוֹג אֶת לוּלְיָינוּס וּפַפּוֹס אָחִיו בְּלוּדְקִיָּא, אָמַר לָהֶם: אִם מֵעַמּוֹ שֶׁל חֲנַנְיָה, מִישָׁאֵל, וַעֲזַרְיָה אַתֶּם, יָבֹא אֱלֹהֵיכֶם וְיַצִּיל אֶתְכֶם מִיָּדִי כְּדֶרֶךְ שֶׁהִצִּיל אֶת חֲנַנְיָה, מִישָׁאֵל, וַעֲזַרְיָה מִיַּד נְבוּכַדְנֶצַּר. אָמְרוּ לוֹ: חֲנַנְיָה, מִישָׁאֵל, וַעֲזַרְיָה צַדִּיקִים גְּמוּרִין הָיוּ, וּרְאוּיִין הָיוּ לֵיעָשׂוֹת לָהֶם נֵס, וּנְבוּכַדְנֶצַּר מֶלֶךְ הָגוּן הָיָה, וְרָאוּי לֵיעָשׂוֹת נֵס עַל יָדוֹ. וְאוֹתוֹ רָשָׁע הֶדְיוֹט הוּא, וְאֵינוֹ רָאוּי לֵיעָשׂוֹת נֵס עַל יָדוֹ. וְאָנוּ נִתְחַיַּיבְנוּ (א) כְּלָיָה לַמָּקוֹם. וְאִם אֵין אַתָּה הוֹרְגֵנוּ, הַרְבֵּה הוֹרְגִים יֵשׁ לוֹ לַמָּקוֹם, וְהַרְבֵּה דּוּבִּין וַאֲרָיוֹת יֵשׁ לוֹ לַמָּקוֹם בְּעוֹלָמוֹ שֶׁפּוֹגְעִין בָּנוּ וְהוֹרְגִין אוֹתָנוּ. אֶלָּא לֹא מְסָרָנוּ הַקָּדוֹשׁ בָּרוּךְ הוּא בְּיָדְךָ אֶלָּא שֶׁעָתִיד לִיפָּרַע דָּמֵינוּ מִיָּדְךָ. אעפ"כ הֲרָגָן מִיָּד. אָמְרוּ: לֹא זָזוּ מִשָּׁם עַד שֶׁבָּאוּ דְּיוֹפְלֵי מֵרוֹמִי וּפָצְעוּ אֶת מוֹחוֹ בִּגְיזִרִין.§ "אֵין גּוֹזְרִין תַּעֲנִית עַל הַצִּבּוּר בַּתְּחִלָּה בַּחֲמִישִׁי, כו'. אֵין גּוֹזְרִין תַּעֲנִית בְּרָאשֵׁי חֳדָשִׁים" כו'.§ וְכַמָּה הָוְיָא הַתְחָלָה? א)רַב אַחָא אָמַר: שָׁלֹשׁ. רַבִּי אַסִּי אָמַר: באַחַת. אָמַר ב)רַב יְהוּדָה אָמַר רַב: זוֹ דִּבְרֵי רַבִּי מֵאִיר שֶׁאָמַר מִשּׁוּם רַבָּן (שִׁמְעוֹן בֶּן) גַּמְלִיאֵל. אֲבָל חֲכָמִים אוֹמְרִים: גמִתְעַנֶּה וּמַשְׁלִים. ג)דָּרַשׁ מָר זוּטְרָא מִשְּׁמֵיהּ דְּרַב הוּנָא: הֲלָכָה: מִתְעַנֶּה וּמַשְׁלִים.§

תורה אור [בעמוד הזה]: מגילה ה:; [שם]; [תמורה פ"ח]; [ב"ב י:]; [פסחים נ.]

הדרן עלך סדר תעניות כיצד

סֵדֶר דתַּעֲנִיּוֹת אֵלּוּ ד)הָאָמוּר בִּרְבִיעָה רִאשׁוֹנָה. אֲבָל צְמָחִים שֶׁשָּׁנוּ, מַתְרִיעִין עֲלֵיהֶן מִיָּד. וְכֵן שֶׁפָּסְקוּ גְּשָׁמִים בֵּין גֶּשֶׁם לְגֶשֶׁם אַרְבָּעִים יוֹם – מַתְרִיעִין עֲלֵיהֶן, ה)מִפְּנֵי שֶׁהִיא מַכַּת בַּצּוֹרֶת. יָרְדוּ לַצְּמָחִין אֲבָל לֹא יָרְדוּ לָאִילָן, לָאִילָן וְלֹא לַצְּמָחִין, לָזֶה וְלָזֶה אֲבָל לֹא לַבּוֹרוֹת, לַשִּׁיחִין, וְלַמְּעָרוֹת – מַתְרִיעִין עֲלֵיהֶן מִיָּד. וְכֵן עִיר שֶׁלֹּא יָרְדוּ עָלֶיהָ גְּשָׁמִים, דִּכְתִיב: °"וְהִמְטַרְתִּי עַל עִיר אֶחָת, וְעַל עִיר אַחַת לֹא אַמְטִיר, חֶלְקָה אַחַת תִּמָּטֵר" וגו', עמוס ד אוֹתָהּ

א) גי' רי"ף רש"י ורא"ש ר' אחא כו' ר' יוסי כו' ועי' מ"מ מהל' תענית פ"א הלכה ז ב) [עירובין מא.]
ג) [שם מא:] ד) גי' הרא"ש האמורים וכ"ה ברש"י שברי"ף וכר"ן ה) מיד כ"ה במשנה שבמשניות וברי"ף ורא"ש

רש"י

מוּתָּרִין בְּהֶסְפֵּד וּבְתַעֲנִית. בְּנֵי ט"ו (ב) קְרִיאַת מְגִילָּה דִּכְרַכִּין קוֹדֶם זְמַנָּהּ, כִּדְמְפָרֵשׁ הָתָם: בְּי"א, בְּי"ב, בְּי"ג, בְּי"ד, בְּט"ו, שֶׁהַכְּפָרִים מַקְדִּימִין לְיוֹם הַכְּנִיסָה – מוּתָּרִין, אוֹתָן יָמִים שֶׁקְּרָאוּהָ קוֹדֶם זְמַנָּהּ, בְּהֶסְפֵּד וְתַעֲנִית: בְּנֵי חֲמֵיסַר. דְּהַיְינוּ כְּרַכִּים הַמּוּקָּפִין חוֹמָה מִימוֹת יְהוֹשֻׁעַ בִּן נוּן, וְקָא קָרֵי בְּאַרְבֵּיסַר – כְּגוֹן שֶׁהָלַךְ לִכְפָר וְקָרָא עִמָּהֶן, דְּפָרוּז בֶּן יוֹמוֹ נִקְרָא פָּרוּז, כִּדְאָמְרִינַן בִּמְגִילָּה (דף יט.): מִי שָׁרֵי. י"ד אֲפִילּוּ לִבְנֵי ט"ו בְּהֶסְפֵּד וְתַעֲנִית: וְאָמַר רָבָא לֹא נִצְרְכָה. לִכְתּוֹב בִּמְגִילַּת תַּעֲנִית לִגְזוֹר הַהֶסְפֵּד וְתַעֲנִית לִבְנֵי י"ד בְּי"ד וְלִבְנֵי ט"ו בְּט"ו – דְּהָא קְרָא כְּתִיב בְּהֶדְיָא "לִהְיוֹת עוֹשִׂים אֶת יְמֵי הַפּוּרִים הָאֵלֶּה" וגו': אֶלָּא לֶאֱסוֹר אֶת שֶׁל זֶה בָּזֶה. כְּגוֹן בְּנֵי ט"ו (דְּקָרוּ) בְּי"ד וּבְנֵי י"ד בְּט"ו: בְּנֵי אַרְבֵּיסַר. נִינְהוּ, כְּפָרִים וַעֲיָירוֹת: וְקָא קָרֵי בְּי"ג. כְּגוֹן שֶׁחָל י"ד בְּג' בְּשַׁבָּת, וּמַקְדִּימִין לְיוֹם הַכְּנִיסָה: יוֹם נִיקָנוֹר הוּא. לְקַמָּן מְפָרֵשׁ, וְאָסוּר בְּהֶסְפֵּד וְתַעֲנִית: אֶלָּא בְּנֵי י"ד וְקָרוּ בְּי"ב. שֶׁחָל י"ד בִּרְבִיעִי בְּשַׁבָּת, וְהִקְדִּימוּ לְיוֹם הַכְּנִיסָה דְּהַיְינוּ י"ב: טוּרְיָינוּס. בְּסָמוּךְ מְפָרֵשׁ: בַּחֲדֵיסַר. שֶׁחָל לִהְיוֹת י"ד בְּאֶחָד בְּשַׁבָּת, וּכְפָרִים מַקְדִּימִין לְיוֹם הַכְּנִיסָה דְּהָווּ י"א. וּשְׁמַע מִינַּהּ, דְּאַע"ג שֶׁהוּא יוֹם שֶׁלִּפְנֵי טוּרְיָינוּס – שָׁרֵי בְּהֶסְפֵּד וְתַעֲנִית: שְׁמַעְיָה וַאֲחִיָּה. חֲסִידִים הָיוּ, וְלֹא פֵּירֵשׁ מִי הֵם. דְּאוֹתוֹ שֶׁאֲכָלוֹ הָאֲרִיֵה – עִידּוֹ *הָיָה וְלֹא שְׁמַעְיָה: אִיפַּרְכֵי. דּוּכוּס: לוּלְיָינוּס וּפַפּוֹס אָחִיו. צַדִּיקִים גְּמוּרִים הָיוּ: בְּלוּדְקִיָּא. הִיא לוּד. וְהַיְינוּ דְּאָמְרִינַן בְּכָל דּוּכְתָּא (ב"ב דף י:)*: הֲרוּגֵי לוּד אֵין כָּל בְּרִיָּה יְכוֹלָה לַעֲמוֹד בִּמְחִיצָּתָן בְּגַן עֵדֶן. וְיֵשׁ אוֹמְרִין שֶׁנֶּהֶרְגוּ עַל בִּתּוֹ שֶׁל מֶלֶךְ שֶׁנִּמְצֵאת הֲרוּגָה, וְאָמְרוּ הַיְּהוּדִים הֲרָגוּהָ, וְגָזְרוּ גְּזֵרָה עַל שׂוֹנְאֵיהֶן שֶׁל יִשְׂרָאֵל, וְעָמְדוּ אֵלּוּ וּפָדוּ אֶת יִשְׂרָאֵל, וְאָמְרוּ: אָנוּ הֲרַגְנוּהָ, וְהָרַג הַמֶּלֶךְ לְאֵלּוּ בִּלְבָד: אִם מֵעַמּוֹ כו': נִתְחַיַּיבְנוּ הֲרִיגָה. עַל חֵטְא חַיָּיבֵי מִיתוֹת בֵּית דִּין: דְּיוֹפְלִין. שְׁנֵי שָׂרִים. וְכֵן מֶטְרוֹפּוֹלִין שֶׁל מְלָכִים – לְשׁוֹן שָׂרִים: בִּגְזִירִין. מַקְלוֹת, כְּמוֹ גְּזִירֵי עֵצִים: (ג) שָׁלֹשׁ. תַּעֲנִיּוֹת שֵׁנִי וַחֲמִישִׁי וְשֵׁנִי: וְכַמָּה הַוְיָא הַתְחָלָה. שֶׁאֵינוֹ מַפְסִיק לְאַחַר מִכָּאן: רַבִּי אַחָא וְרַבִּי יוֹסֵי. (ד) אֲמוֹרָאֵי נִינְהוּ, דְּלָאו אוֹרְחָא דְּתַנָּאֵי לְאִשְׁתַּעוּיֵי בַּגְּמָרָא כִּי הַאי גַּוְונָא: זוֹ דִּבְרֵי ר"מ. וְאַדִּבְרֵי ר"מ דְּמַתְנִי' קָאֵי, דְּקָתָנֵי אֵין מַשְׁלִימִין: מִתְעַנֶּה וּמַשְׁלִים. עַד חֲשֵׁיכָה:

הדרן עלך סדר תעניות קמא

סֵדֶר תַּעֲנִיּוֹת אֵלּוּ. הָאָמוּר בְּפֶ' רִאשׁוֹן (דף י.), שֶׁבַּתְּחִילָּה יְחִידִים מִתְעַנִּין (ה) סֵדֶר תַּעֲנִיּוֹת, וְאַחַר כָּךְ צִבּוּר הוֹלְכִין וּמִתְעַנִּין עַד י"ג, אִם לֹא נַעֲנוּ: בִּרְבִיעָה רִאשׁוֹנָה. אִם עָבַר זְמַן רְבִיעָה רִאשׁוֹנָה שֶׁל יוֹרֶה, וְלֹא יָרְדוּ גְּשָׁמִים – מִתְעַנִּין וְהוֹלְכִין כַּסֵּדֶר הַזֶּה: אֲבָל צְמָחִים שֶׁשָּׁנוּ. שֶׁנִּשְׁתַּנּוּ מִמִּנְהָגָן, תַּחַת חִטָּה יָצָא חוֹחַ, תַּחַת שְׂעוֹרָה בָּאְשָׁה (ו), שֶׁלֹּא הָיוּ חִטִּים בַּשִּׁבּוֹלִים אוֹ שִׁינּוּי אַחֵר – מַתְרִיעִין עֲלֵיהֶן מִיָּד, אֲפִילּוּ בָּרִאשׁוֹנוֹת, שֶׁכָּל חוֹמֶר הָאַחֲרוֹנוֹת נוֹהֵג בָּהֶן: בֵּין גֶּשֶׁם לְגֶשֶׁם. בֵּין רְבִיעָה רִאשׁוֹנָה לַשְּׁנִיָּה – סִימָן בַּצּוֹרֶת הִיא: יָרְדוּ לִצְמָחִים אֲבָל לֹא לָאִילָן. מְפָרֵשׁ בַּגְּמָ': לְבוֹרוֹת שִׁיחִין וּמְעָרוֹת. *בְּבָבָא בַּתְרָא מְפָרֵשׁ מַאי בּוֹר וּמַאי שִׁיחַ וּמַאי מְעָרָה, וְכוּלָּן בֵּית כְּנִיסִיּוֹת מֵי גְשָׁמִים לִשְׁתִיָּה: שֶׁלֹּא יָרְדוּ עָלֶיהָ גְּשָׁמִים דִּכְתִיב וְהִמְטַרְתִּי עַל עִיר אֶחָת וְעַל עִיר אַחַת לֹא אַמְטִיר וגו'. כְּגוֹן שֶׁהִמְטִיר בְּעִיר זוֹ, וּבַחֲבֵירְתָּהּ לֹא הִמְטִיר, דִּקְלָלָה הִיא: [נ"ל בב"ק נ:]

ה"ג

תוספות (ראו לעיל: הלכה מתענה ומשלים; מתריעין)

הגהות הב"ח

(א) גמ' ואנו נתחייבנו הריגה למקום ואם אין אתה הורגנו כו' יש לו למקום הרבה דובין ואריות: (ב) רש"י ד"ה מותרין וכו' בני ט"ו דכרכין ובני י"ד לכפרים ועיירות שקראו מגילה קודם זמנם כדמפרש התם מגילה נקראת בי"א בי"ב בי"ג בי"ד בט"ו לא פחות ולא יותר כרכין המוקפין חומה מימות יהושע בן נון קורין בט"ו כפרים ועיירות גדולות קורין בי"ד אלא שהכפרים מקדימין ליום הכניסה: (ג) ד"ה שלש וכו' כצ"ל אחר ד"ה וכמה הויא: (ד) ד"ה רבי אחא וכו' יוסי אמוראי נינהו. נ"ב לפי הגירסא שלפנינו דגרס רבי אסי לא הוצרך לפרש דפשיטא דאמוראי נינהו: (ה) רש"י ד"ה סדר תעניות כו' בתחלה יחידים מתענין ואחר כך צבור הולכין ומתענין עד י"ג תעניות כו' כצ"ל ותיבות סדר תעניות נמחק: (ו) ד"ה שנשתנו כו' תחת שעורה באשה [illegible] נמחק: (ז) תוס' ד"ה מתריעין כו' א"כ כיון דהא דמתריעין משמע:

הגהות הגר"א

[א] גמ' אמר להו יום טוריינוס (גופיה) תז"מ:

[בערוך ערך הרג מפרש לשמעיה ואחיה בן המה הרוגי לוד הנזכרים בפסחים נ. וב"ב י: ע"ש]

רבינו חננאל

הלכה כר' יוסי אדילא להתענאה דלפניו אסור איני והאמר ר' יוחנן הלכה כסתם משנה. ותנן במס' מגילה אע"פ שאמרו מקדימין כפרים ליום הכניסה ולא מאחרין. מותרין בהספד ובתענית בו ביום שקורין בו. וליכא לאוקומא להא מתני' בי"ד ובט"ו דקי"ל אע"פ שאין קורין בהן אסורין דתניא בהדיא ארביסר וחמיסר פוריא אינון די לא למספד בהון. ואמר רבא לא נצרכא אלא לאסור את זה בזה ואת של זה בזה. ואפילו מי שאינו יומו ואינו קורא בו אסור בתליסר ובתריסר נמי ליכא לאוקומא דהא יום נקנור ויום טוריינוס אינון וימים טובים נינהו. ליכא לאוקומא אלא כגון שהיה יום הכניסה בי"א וקורין בו ביום. ואע"פ שהוא יום לפני טוריינוס מותר בהספד ובתענית קשיא לר' יוחנן דאמר הלכתא כר' יוסי דאוסר לפניהם ושנינן יום טוריינוס בטולי בטלוה כו'. ושאר השמועה פשוטה היא: **מתני'** אין גוזרין תענית על הצבור בתחלה בחמישי כו'. אין גוזרין תענית בראשי חדשים בחנוכה ובפורים ואם התחילו כו'. כמה הוא התחלה. ר' אחא אמר ג' ר' יוסי אומר אחת וקיי"ל כר' יוסי. ואסיקנא אם התחילו כו'. ט' באב שחל להיות ע"ש. פי' הא דתנינן בסוף בכל מערבין ומשתתפין ט' באב שחל להיות בע"ש כו'. קבלה בידינו כי פסח של אותה שנה היה ביום ה'. ומלאי תמוז דההיא שתא וחל ר"ח אב בחמישי. וחל ט' באב להיות בע"ש וחסרו אב ואלול חל להיות ע"ש ור"ה בשבת. דבר ברור הוא שיש לסנהדרין לקבוע חסירין זה אחר זה כפי המסורת שבידם. ובפירוש שנו בענין עצרת (ר"ה ו ע"ב) שניהן מלאין ה' חסרין ו' והם ניסן ואייר *) ור' עקיבא שגמע ביצה שגמע ביצה מגולגלת מסוכן היה משום שהיה חולה ואמרו לו הרופאים כי גמיעת ביצה מיד בלא מלח באחרית היום היא רפואתו. וכיון שראהו ר' יהודה נדמה לו דסבר המתענה בע"ש אינו משלים **) ט' באב שחל להיות בע"ש. כגון דאקלע פסח דההיא שתא בחמישי בשבת וחל ט' באב בע"ש לפי שהיה תמוז מלא וחיסרו (עוד לחדש) [אב ואלול] וחל ר"ה להיות בשבת: **ירושלמי** אפי' יחיד שקבל על עצמו תענית מתענה ומשלים. ירושלמי (ברכות פ"ד) י"ח ברכות שבכל יום כנגד י"ח מזמורים שמראש תהלים עד יענך ולמה רגשו גוים אינו מן המנין. דברכת המינים ביבנה תקנוה. וכנגד י"ח פעמים שכתוב בתורה אברהם יצחק ויעקב. גם ויקרא בהם שמי ושם אבותי בכלל. וכנגד י"ח צוויים שכתוב בתורה בפרשת המשכן שני מן ואתו אהליאב עד סוף הספר. ז' ברכות של שבת כנגד ז' קולות שכתוב בהבו לה' בני אלים וכנגד ז' אזכרות שכתוב במזמור שיר ליום השבת. ט' ברכות של ר"ה כנגד ט' אזכרות הכתובים בפרש' חנה ובסוף כתיב ה' ידין אפסי ארץ. כ"ד ברכות של תענית צבור כנגד כ"ד רנה תחנה תפלה שכתובים בפרשת שלמה. ר' זירא אמר יחיד בתענית צבור צריך להזכיר עננו ה' עננו כו'. ואסיקנא איכן אמרה כלילי שבת וכיומו. וקיי"ל ש"צ אומר בין גואל לרופא חולי. יחיד בשומע תפלה. ר' אחא אמר יחיד בט' באב צריך להזכיר מעין המאורע והוא רחם ה' עלינו ועל ישראל עמך ועל ירושלים עירך ועל ציון משכן כבודך. ועל העיר האבלה ההרוגה כו' עד ואני אהיה לה נאם ה' חומת אש סביב ולכבוד אהיה בתוכה. והיכן אומרה הכי ר' ירמיה כל דבר שהוא להבא אומרו בעבודה לשעבר אמרו בהודאה כדתנן (פ"ט דברכות) ונותן הודאה לשעבר וצועק לעתיד לבוא. כל הברכות כולן אחר חותמיהן. ואינו אומר בברכה פסוק כלומר אינו מזכיר פסוק לבדו וחותם ברכה. ואלין דאמרי צהלי ורוני יושבת ציון וחותם בברכה אין בו משום ברכת פסוק. ר' זעירא צם תת"ק תענית ולא חשש למגלת תענית. ר' יעקב בר מפקיד לספריא ***) אין אתת בך אנשי שאיל לכון אמרון ליה (הכל) [בכל] מתענין חוץ משבתות וי"ט ור"ח וחוש"מ וחנוכה ופורים. והלכתא אפילו יחיד שקיבל עליו תענית בע"ש מתענה ומשלים (עירובין מא:): הדרן עלך סדר תעניות כיצד

*) מכאן ועד וחל ר"ה להיות בשבת הובא בתוס' עירובין דף מ"א ד"ה בילה בשם רבינו ע"ש היטב. **) זה נכלל במ"ש למעלה ואולי ט"ס כאן. ***) בירושל' לפנינו הגי' אין אתת איתא מישאל נכון אמרון לה וכו' וע"ש במפרש.

סדר

רבינו גרשום

דתמידא דלא ניבטיל אלא שבעה אבל תמניא אסור משום דאיתותב ביה חגא דשבועיא. השתא דאתת להכי דתרצת משום דאי איקלע מילתא ובטיל ליה עשרין ותשעה נמי דפרכת למה לי' למימר מריש ירחא דניסן משום לאסור כ"ט באדר תיפוק ליה דהוה יומא דבתר כ"ח לעולם להכי אמר מריש ירחי' דניסן כדי לאסור כ"ט באדר שלפניו דאי איקלע מילתא ובטליניה לכ"ח כו': אמר רב הלכה כר' יוסי דאמר דאי לא למספד בין לפניו ובין לאחריו אסור: ושמואל אמר הלכה כר"מ ת"ק דר' יוסי דסתם מתני' ר"מ וקאמר לפניו אסור לאחריו מותר: מי אמר שמואל הכי דאמר לפניו אסור מעיקרא דשמעיה לר"מ דמיקל יותר מר' יוסי דר"מ אינו אוסר אלא לפניו ור' יוסי אוסר בין לפניו בין לאחריו. אדלא להתענאה דקאמר [illegible]

יום טוריינוס ומי אמר ר' יוחנן הלכה כר' יוסי דלפניו אסור לעולם בני ארביסר דקרו בתריסר ולהכי מותרין דלא הוי יומא טבא: תיפוק ליה דתריסר הוי יומא דמקמיה יום ניקנור ולא ליהוי מותר בהספד ובתענית: דיופלי. שלוחים: בגיזירין. קופיץ: וכן בת"ב שחל להיות בע"ש אין משלימין: וכמה הויא התחלה דקאמר אם התחילו אין מפסיקין רב אחא אמר שלש שאם היו ג' תעניות קודם ר"ח ורביעי בר"ח אין מפסיקין זו דברי ר"ג דאמר אם התחילו אין מפסיקין אבל אין משלימין:

הדרן עלך סדר תעניות כיצד

סדר תעניות האמור כל אלו תעניות דאמרן לעיל דאין גוזרין לאלתר ברביעה ראשונה ולא ירדו גשמים אבל צמחים ששנו שנשתנה מראה שלהן מתריעין עליהן מיד קודם רביעה שלישית להתענות ומי אמרת לאלתר ברביעה ראשונה מתענין. אבל יבשו לא דכיון שיבשו לית להו תקנתא כלל ואי מתריען עליהן

אאוֹתָהּ הָעִיר מִתְעַנָּה וּמַתְרַעַת, וְכָל סְבִיבוֹתֶיהָ מִתְעַנּוֹת וְלֹא מַתְרִיעוֹת. רַבִּי עֲקִיבָא אוֹמֵר: מַתְרִיעוֹת וְלֹא מִתְעַנּוֹת. בוְכֵן עִיר שֶׁיֵּשׁ בָּהּ דֶּבֶר אוֹ מַפּוֹלֶת, אוֹתָהּ הָעִיר מִתְעַנָּה וּמַתְרַעַת, וְכָל סְבִיבוֹתֶיהָ מִתְעַנּוֹת וְלֹא מַתְרִיעוֹת. רַבִּי עֲקִיבָא אוֹמֵר: מַתְרִיעוֹת וְלֹא מִתְעַנּוֹת. גאֵיזֶהוּ דֶּבֶר? עִיר הַמּוֹצִיאָה חֲמֵשׁ מֵאוֹת רַגְלִי, וְיָצְאוּ מִמֶּנָּה ג' מֵתִים בְּג' יָמִים זֶה אַחַר זֶה (א) — הֲרֵי זֶה דֶּבֶר. פָּחוֹת מִכָּאן — אֵין זֶה דֶּבֶר. דעַל אֵלּוּ מַתְרִיעִין בְּכָל מָקוֹם: עַל הַשִּׁדָּפוֹן, וְעַל הַיֵּרָקוֹן, וְעַל הָאַרְבֶּה, וְעַל הֶחָסִיל, הוְעַל הַחַיָּה רָעָה, וְעַל הַחֶרֶב. מַתְרִיעִין עָלֶיהָ, מִפְּנֵי שֶׁהִיא מַכָּה מְהַלֶּכֶת. מַעֲשֶׂה שֶׁיָּרְדוּ זְקֵנִים מִירוּשָׁלַיִם לְעָרֵיהֶם, ווְגָזְרוּ תַּעֲנִית עַל שֶׁנִּרְאָה כִּמְלֹא פִּי תַנּוּר שִׁדָּפוֹן בְּאַשְׁקְלוֹן. וְעוֹד גָּזְרוּ תַּעֲנִית עַל שֶׁאָכְלוּ זְאֵבִים שְׁנֵי תִינוֹקוֹת בְּעֵבֶר הַיַּרְדֵּן. רַבִּי יוֹסֵי אוֹמֵר: לֹא עַל שֶׁאָכְלוּ, אֶלָּא עַל שֶׁנִּרְאוּ.§ *זעַל אֵלּוּ מַתְרִיעִין בְּשַׁבָּת: עַל עִיר שֶׁהִקִּיפוּהָ נָכְרִים אוֹ נָהָר, וְעַל הַסְּפִינָה הַמִּיטָּרֶפֶת בַּיָּם. ר' יוֹסֵי אוֹמֵר: (ב) חלְעֶזְרָה, וְלֹא לִצְעָקָה. שִׁמְעוֹן הַתֵּימְנִי אוֹמֵר: אַף עַל הַדֶּבֶר. וְלֹא הוֹדוּ לוֹ חֲכָמִים.§ עַל כָּל צָרָה שֶׁלֹּא תָּבֹא עַל הַצִּבּוּר מַתְרִיעִין עֲלֵיהֶן, טחוּץ מֵרוֹב גְּשָׁמִים. מַעֲשֶׂה שֶׁאָמְרוּ לוֹ לְחוֹנִי *הַמְעַגֵּל: הִתְפַּלֵּל שֶׁיֵּרְדוּ גְּשָׁמִים. אָמַר לָהֶם: צְאוּ וְהַכְנִיסוּ תַנּוּרֵי פְסָחִים בִּשְׁבִיל שֶׁלֹּא יִמּוֹקוּ. הִתְפַּלֵּל, וְלֹא יָרְדוּ גְּשָׁמִים. מֶה עָשָׂה? *עָג עוּגָה וְעָמַד בְּתוֹכָהּ, וְאָמַר לְפָנָיו: רבש"ע! בָּנֶיךָ שָׂמוּ פְּנֵיהֶם עָלַי, שֶׁאֲנִי כְּבֶן בַּיִת לְפָנֶיךָ. נִשְׁבָּע אֲנִי בְּשִׁמְךָ הַגָּדוֹל שֶׁאֵינִי זָז מִכָּאן עַד שֶׁתְּרַחֵם עַל בָּנֶיךָ. הִתְחִילוּ גְּשָׁמִים מְנַטְּפִין. אָמַר: לֹא כָּךְ שָׁאַלְתִּי, אֶלָּא גִּשְׁמֵי בוֹרוֹת, שִׁיחִין, וּמְעָרוֹת. הִתְחִילוּ לֵירֵד בְּזַעַף. אָמַר: לֹא כָּךְ שָׁאַלְתִּי, אֶלָּא גִּשְׁמֵי רָצוֹן, בְּרָכָה, וּנְדָבָה. יָרְדוּ כְּתִקְנָן, עַד שֶׁיָּצְאוּ יִשְׂרָאֵל מִירוּשָׁלַיִם לְהַר הַבַּיִת מִפְּנֵי הַגְּשָׁמִים. בָּאוּ וְאָמְרוּ לוֹ: כְּשֵׁם שֶׁהִתְפַּלַּלְתָּ עֲלֵיהֶם שֶׁיֵּרְדוּ, כָּךְ הִתְפַּלֵּל שֶׁיֵּלְכוּ לָהֶן. אָמַר לָהֶם: *צְאוּ וּרְאוּ אִם נִמְחֵית אֶבֶן *הַטּוֹעִין. *שָׁלַח לוֹ שִׁמְעוֹן בֶּן שָׁטָח: אִלְמָלֵא חוֹנִי אַתָּה, גּוֹזְרַנִי עָלֶיךָ (ג) נִידּוּי. אֲבָל מָה אֶעֱשֶׂה לְךָ, שֶׁאַתָּה מִתְחַטֵּא לִפְנֵי הַמָּקוֹם, וְעוֹשֶׂה לְךָ רְצוֹנְךָ, כְּבֵן שֶׁהוּא מִתְחַטֵּא עַל אָבִיו, וְעוֹשֶׂה לוֹ רְצוֹנוֹ? וְעָלֶיךָ הַכָּתוּב אוֹמֵר: (משלי כג) "יִשְׂמַח אָבִיךָ וְאִמֶּךָ, וְתָגֵל יוֹלַדְתֶּךָ".§ (*מתני') הָיוּ מִתְעַנִּין, וְיָרְדוּ לָהֶם גְּשָׁמִים *קוֹדֶם הָנֵץ הַחַמָּה — לֹא יַשְׁלִימוּ. לְאַחַר הָנֵץ הַחַמָּה — יַשְׁלִימוּ. ר"א אוֹמֵר: יקוֹדֶם חֲצוֹת — לֹא יַשְׁלִימוּ, לְאַחַר חֲצוֹת — יַשְׁלִימוּ. מַעֲשֶׂה שֶׁגָּזְרוּ תַּעֲנִית בְּלוֹד, וְיָרְדוּ לָהֶם גְּשָׁמִים קוֹדֶם חֲצוֹת. אָמַר לָהֶם ר' טַרְפוֹן: צְאוּ, וְאִכְלוּ וּשְׁתוּ, וַעֲשׂוּ יו"ט. וְיָצְאוּ, וְאָכְלוּ וְשָׁתוּ, וְעָשׂוּ יוֹם טוֹב. וּבָאוּ בֵּין הָעַרְבַּיִם כוְקָרְאוּ הַלֵּל הַגָּדוֹל.§ **גמ'** "סֵדֶר תַּעֲנִיּוֹת הָאֵלּוּ הָאָמוּר בִּרְבִיעָה רִאשׁוֹנָה". וּרְמִינְהִי: רְבִיעָה רִאשׁוֹנָה וּשְׁנִיָּה — לִשְׁאוֹל, שְׁלִישִׁית — לְהִתְעַנּוֹת! אָמַר רַב *יְהוּדָה: ה"ק: סֵדֶר תַּעֲנִיּוֹת הָאָמוּר אֵימָתַי? בִּזְמַן שֶׁיָּצְאָה רְבִיעָה רִאשׁוֹנָה, וּשְׁנִיָּה, וּשְׁלִישִׁית, וְלֹא יָרְדוּ גְּשָׁמִים. אֲבָל יָרְדוּ גְּשָׁמִים בִּרְבִיעָה רִאשׁוֹנָה, וְזָרְעוּ וְלֹא צָמְחוּ, אִי נַמִּי צָמְחוּ וְחָזְרוּ וְנִשְׁתַּנּוּ — מַתְרִיעִין עֲלֵיהֶן מִיָּד. אָמַר רַב נַחְמָן: דַּוְקָא נִשְׁתַּנּוּ, לאֲבָל יָבְשׁוּ — לֹא. פְּשִׁיטָא, "נִשְׁתַּנּוּ" תְּנַן! לָא, צְרִיכָא (ד) *דְּאַקּוּן. מַהוּ דְּתֵימָא אַקַּנְתָּא מִילְּתָא הִיא, קָמַשְׁמַע לָן.§ "וְכֵן שֶׁפָּסְקוּ גְּשָׁמִים בֵּין גֶּשֶׁם לְגֶשֶׁם" כו'.§ מַאי "מַכַּת בַּצּוֹרֶת"? אָמַר רַב יְהוּדָה אָמַר רַב: מַכָּה הַמְבִיאָה לִידֵי בַּצּוֹרֶת. אָמַר רַב נַחְמָן: נַהֲרָא אַנַּהֲרָא — בַּצּוֹרְתָא

תורה אור

רש"י

ה"ג: **אוֹתָהּ הָעִיר מִתְעַנָּה וּמַתְרַעַת וְכָל סְבִיבוֹתֶיהָ מִתְעַנּוֹת וְלֹא מַתְרִיעוֹת.** וּלְפִיכָךְ מִתְעַנּוֹת, (ה) שֶׁאוֹתָהּ הָעִיר שֶׁלֹּא יָרְדוּ עָלֶיהָ גְּשָׁמִים תֵּלֵךְ לִקְנוֹת הַתְּבוּאָה בְּאוֹתָהּ הָעִיר וְיִהְיֶה בָּהּ רָעָב: **אוֹ מַפּוֹלֶת.** שֶׁחוֹמוֹתֶיהָ וְהַבָּתִּים נוֹפְלִין בָּרוּחַ: **מַתְרִיעִים בְּכ"מ.** אִם (ו) יֵרָאוּ בְּאַסְפַּמְיָא — מַתְרִיעִין בְּבָבֶל, בְּבָבֶל — מַתְרִיעִין בְּאַסְפַּמְיָא כִּדְקָתָנֵי טַעְמָא בְּסֵיפָא: מִפְּנֵי שֶׁהִיא מַכָּה מְהַלֶּכֶת, אִם בְּמָקוֹם אֶחָד הִיא — מַתְרִיעִין עָלֶיהָ כָּל הַשּׁוֹמְעִין, כְּדֵי שֶׁלֹּא תָּבֹא עֲלֵיהֶן: **שִׁדָּפוֹן.** בַּתְּבוּאוֹת: **יֵרָקוֹן.** חוֹלִי: **חַיָּה רָעָה.** מְשַׁכֶּלֶת בְּנֵי אָדָם: **חֶרֶב.** חַיָּילוֹת הַהוֹלְכִין לַהֲרוֹג וּלְהַשְׁחִית בְּכָל מָקוֹם: **מְלֹא תַּנּוּר.** מְפָרֵשׁ בַּגְּמָ': **לְעָרֵיהֶם.** בְּא"י: **בְּאַשְׁקְלוֹן.** בְּאֶרֶץ פְּלִשְׁתִּים: **וְעַל שֶׁאָכְלוּ זְאֵבִים.** שֶׁהִיא חַיָּה רָעָה, וּמַכָּה מְהַלֶּכֶת הִיא: **שֶׁנִּרְאוּ.** וּבָאוּ בָּעִיר: **מַתְרִיעִין.** בַּגְּ' "עֲנֵנוּ": **הַמְטוֹרֶפֶת.** מִלְּשׁוֹן טָרַף בְּכַדָּא (ברכות דף כח.), וּמִלְּשׁוֹן בֵּיצָה טְרוּפָה (עדיות פ"ב מ"ד) כו'. כִּדְמְפָרֵשׁ בַּפֶּרֶק שֶׁלְּמַעְלָה (דף יד.): **שִׁמְעוֹן הַתֵּימָנִי.** מִתְּמְנָה הָיָה: **שֶׁלֹּא תָבֹא.** לִישָּׁנָא מְעַלְּיָא נָקַט: **מֵרוֹב גְּשָׁמִים.** לָאו כְּגוֹן שֶׁיָּרְדָה עַל עִיר אַחַת וְעַל עִיר אַחַת לֹא יָרְדָה, שֶׁשָּׁם וַדַּאי שְׁתֵּיהֶן לִקְלָלָה, כִּדְאָמַר רַב יְהוּדָה (לעיל ו:) "תִּמָּטֵר" * — מְקוֹם מָטָר, שֶׁמְּקַלְקֵל תְּבוּאָה. אֶלָּא כְּבָר יָרְדוּ, וְטוֹרַח הֵם לִבְנֵי אָדָם, אֲבָל אֵינָן מְקַלְקְלִין תְּבוּאוֹת. וְטַעְמָא מְפָרֵשׁ בַּגְּמָרָא לָמָּה אֵין מַתְרִיעִין: **תַּנּוּרֵי פְּסָחִים.** שֶׁהֵם בַּחֲצֵרוֹת, וְשֶׁל חֶרֶס הֵן, וּמְטַלְטְלִין אוֹתָן שֶׁלֹּא יִמּוֹקוּ בַּגְּשָׁמִים: **גִּשְׁמֵי בּוֹרוֹת.** שִׁיפּוּעַ גְּשָׁמִים לְמַלְאוֹת בּוֹרוֹת: **וּנְדָבוֹת.** רָצוֹן וְעַיִן יָפָה: **אֶבֶן הַטּוֹעִין.** אֶבֶן טוֹעִין הָיְתָה בִּירוּשָׁלַיִם, וְכָל מִי שֶׁאָבְדָה לוֹ אֲבֵדָה כו'. בְּבָבָא מְצִיעָא (דף כח:): **לְנַדּוֹת.** (ז) עַל כְּבוֹד הָרַב: **מִתְחַטֵּא.** פורפיי"ש בְּלַעַ"ז "יִשְׂמַח אָבִיךָ וְאִמֶּךָ וְתָגֵל יוֹלַדְתֶּךָ": **גְּמָ' רְבִיעָה רִאשׁוֹנָה וּשְׁנִיָּה לִשְׁאוֹל.** שֶׁאַף עַל פִּי שֶׁלֹּא יָרְדוּ גְּשָׁמִים לֹא בָּרִאשׁוֹנָה וְלֹא בַּשְּׁנִיָּה — לֹא הָיוּ מִתְעַנִּין אֶלָּא שׁוֹאֲלִין. וְקַשְׁיָין מַתְנִי', דְּקָתָנֵי: סֵדֶר תַּעֲנִיּוֹת אֵלּוּ הָאָמוּר בִּרְבִיעָה רִאשׁוֹנָה, וּבָרַיְתָא — אַהֲדָדֵי: **הָכִי קָאָמַר כו'.** (ח) וּכְגוֹן רְבִיעָה רִאשׁוֹנָה שְׁנִיָּה וּשְׁלִישִׁית דְּכוּלֵּי יוֹרֶה קָרֵי לֵיהּ רְבִיעָה [א], כָּךְ שָׁמַעְתִּי: **דַּוְקָא נִשְׁתַּנּוּ.** דְּכִי נִשְׁתַּנּוּ וַדַּאי הוּא דְּמַתְרִיעִין מִיָּד, דְּצָרִיךְ לְהִתְפַּלֵּל עָלֶיהָ (ט) שֶׁיַּחֲזִיר יוֹפִי כְּתִקְנָן: **אֲבָל יָבְשׁוּ.** לֹא צָרִיךְ, דְּמִכָּאן וְאֵילָךְ לֹא יוֹעִיל. וְהוּא תְּפִלַּת שָׁוְא. אֲפִילּוּ יָבְשׁוּ כְּשֶׁהֵן חִטִּין עֲדַיִין דַּקִּין — אֲפִילּוּ הָכִי לֹא מַתְרִיעִין: הָכִי גָּרְסִינַן: **פְּשִׁיטָא** (י) **שְׁנוּ תְּנַן לָא צְרִיכָא דְּאַקּוּן מַהוּ דְּתֵימָא כו':** **דְּאַקּוּן.** שֶׁעָלוּ בַּקָּנֶה, שֶׁנִּתְקְנוּ מְעַט לְאַחַר שֶׁנִּתְיַיבְּשׁוּ: **מַהוּ דְּתֵימָא אַקַּנְתָּא מִילְּתָא הִיא.** דְּהוֹאִיל וְנִתְקְנוּ מְעַט, אִם יִתְפַּלֵּל — מוֹעִיל לָהֶם. קָא מַשְׁמַע לָן רַב נַחְמָן דְּאַקְנָא לָאו מִילְּתָא. ל"א: **אֲבָל יָבְשׁוּ לֹא** — דְּמִמֵּילָא חוֹזְרִין: **לָא צְרִיכָא דְּאַקּוּן.** שֶׁעָלוּ בַּקָּנֶה. **מַהוּ דְּתֵימָא אַקַּנְתָּא מִילְּתָא הִיא,** דְּכֵיוָן שֶׁעָלוּ בַּקָּנֶה וַעֲדַיִין לֹא בָּשְׁלוּ כָּל צָרְכָּן — וַדַּאי, אִי לֹא מַתְרִיעִין — תּוּ לָא גָּדְלֵי, קָמַשְׁמַע לָן דְּלָאו מִילְּתָא הִיא, דְּאַף עַל גַּב דְּאַקּוּן אַכַּתִּי גָּדְלֵי טְפֵי: **נַהֲרָא אַנַּהֲרָא בַּצּוֹרְתָא.** כְּשֶׁאֵין תְּבוּאָה בְּעִיר אַחַת, וְיֵשׁ בַּעֲיָירוֹת אֲחֵרוֹת, וְאֶפְשָׁר לְהָבִיא מִזֶּה לָזֶה דֶּרֶךְ נָהָר בִּסְפִינָה: בַּצּוֹרְתָא

תוספות

לא צריכא דאקון. פי': לאחר שעלו בקנה נתייבשו. מהו דתימא: אקנתא מילתא היא, פי': דהואיל ועלו בקנה ולא נתבשלו כל צורכם — ליבעי התרעה, קמ"ל דלאו מילתא היא: **נהרא אנהרא בצורתא.** פי' (כ) (*הכי): בשאין תבואה בעיר, ויש הרבה בשאר עיירות, ויכולין להביא מזו לזו — היינו מקרי בצורת, ולא מקרי רעב (ל), ומאחר שיכולין להביא ע"י הנהר, דליכא אלא טרחא זעירא. ומהאי, כלומר: מדבר מועט כזה — אין מתריעין. מדינתא אמדינתא — פירוש: שצריך להוליא ממדינה למדינה אחרת ע"י חמורים וסוסים — ואז מתריעין, דאי אפשר להביא בשפע כ"כ כמו בספינות. ל"א: נהרא אנהרא. כלומר אם יבש הנהר זה, וצריך להסב נהר אחר לכאן. אי נמי: צריך להמתין עד שיגדל הנהר האחר ויבא בכאן — זה בצורת, ולא מתריעין. מדינתא אמדינתא, אם יבשו כל הנהרות שבזו העיר, וצריכין להביא מים מעיר אחרת — כפנא. וקשה: דבמתני' משמע דאבצורת (מ) מתענין, דקתני מתריעין עליהן מפני שהיא מכת בצורת! ויש לומר: דמכת בצורת דמתני' הוי כמו דכפנא, כאשר פירשתי שתחת חטה יצא חוח, ומשום הכי מתריעין, אע"ג דעדיין אינו רק בצורת — הואיל וסופו רעב מתריעין, אע"ג דאכתי לא הוו כפנא. אבל לעולם אין מתריעין על מכת בצורת, אי לא מצי לבא לידי רעב. ולהכי קאמר הכא דנהרא אנהרא, דלא הוי אלא כי בצורתא, ולא מתריעין:

נהירנא

עין משפט נר מצוה

ב א מיי' פ"ב מהלכות תענית ה"ב טוש"ע א"ח סי' תקעו סעיף יא וסעיף יב:

הקונטרס כל"ל

ג ב ג מיי' שם הל' ב וה"ל ה טוש"ע שם סעיף ב:

ד ד מיי' שם הל' יא טוש"ע שם סעיף ח ט:

ה ה מיי' שם הלכה ז טוש"ע שם סעיף ו:

ו ו מיי' שם הלכה יח טוש"ע שם סעיף יא:

ז ז מיי' שם הלכה ה ופ"ב מהלכות שבת הלכה כב סמג עשין ג טוש"ע שם סעיף יג וסי' רפח סעיף ט:

ח ח מיי' פ"ב הלכה טו טוש"ע א"ח סי' תקעו סעיף יא:

ט ט מיי' פ"א הלכה טז טור ש"ע א"ח סימן תקסט סעיף א וסי' תקעה סעיף יא:

י י מיי' שם טוש"ע א"ח סי' תקעה סעיף יא:

יא ל מיי' שם פ"ב הלכה טו טוש"ע א"ח סי' תקעה סעיף ח:

מסורת הש"ס

לעיל יד.

[ז"ל רש"י מנחות לב: ד"ה דעגיל וכו' לדקרינן חוני המעגל על שם עוגה]

[עי' פירש"י לקמן כג: ד"ה עוגה]

ב"מ כח.

[ברכות יט.]

[עי' אותה הטוען וע"ש תוס' מ"ק בשם הירושלמי]

טעות הדפוס

[רש"י ע"ז לקמן כה:]

[גי' רה"ש הונא]

[גיטין ל. ע"ש ג"ע על לשון אחרון שכתב רש"י וכן תוס' ד"ה לא צריכא]

הגהות הגר"א

[א] רש"י ד"ה הכי קאמר כו' ליה רביעה. נ"ב ראשונה.

גליון הש"ס

גמ' כבן שהוא מתחטא. עי' מנחות דף סו ע"ב תד"ה כנף רננים:

רבינו חננאל

סדר תעניות האלו האמור ברביעה ראשונה כו'. תרצה רב יהודה הכי סדר תעניות האלו בזמן שיצתה רביעה ראשונה ושניה ולא ירדו גשמים. אבל אם ירדו גשמים וצמחו זרעים וחזרו ושנו. כלומר כמשו מתריעין עליהן מיד ודוקא שנו כעין כמוש אבל יבשו לגמרי אע"ג דחדור אקון אין מתריעין עליהן פי' אקון שחזרו לירוקתן כלומר חזרו לחיותן. ורבותינו הגאונים ז"ל אמרו האי אקון אקנתא לשון חזקה בלשון ארמית ובלשון הזה הוא בגטין (בפרק מי שאחזו קורדייקום) [כל הגט דף ל ע"א] *) (פי' פרצידא דתותי קלא. זרע תבואה שהיא תחת אבן צומחת. פי' קלא מלשון (פסחים סב: וש"מ) שקל קלא פתק ביה). מכת בצורת. פי' רב יהודה מכה הבאה לידי בצורת. [אר"נ נהרא אנהרא] הוצרכו האנשים המסתפקין מים מזה הנהר לילך לנהר אחר בצורת

*) כל הסגור שייך לעיל בגמרא ריש דף ד'.

רבינו גרשום

עליהן הוי תפלת שוא: דאקון שנראה להן קצת תקנה: נהרא אנהרא בצורתא כשצריכין להביא מים מנהר זה להשקות שדות שעל נהר אחר לפי שאין באותו נהר אחר מים כדי סיפוק להשקות שדותיו זהו סימן בצורת:

הגהות הב"ח

(א) גמ' ג' מתים בג' ימים זה אחר זה (הרי זה דבר פחות מכאן אין זה דבר) תא"מ ונ"ב ס"א אין זה: (ב) שם ר' יוסי אומר לעזרה ולא לצעקה. נ"ב עי' פירושו בדף יד ע"א: (ג) שם אלמלא חוני אתה גוזרני עליך לנדות אבל מה אעשה: (ד) שם לא צריכא דהדר אקון מהו דתימא: (ה) רש"י ד"ה ה"ג אותה כו' לפיכך מתענות מפני שאותה העיר וכו' התבואה באותה שסביבותיה ויהיה בה רעב: (ו) ד"ה מתריעים בכ"מ אם נראו באספמיא כו' שהיא מכה מהלכת ולפיכך אף אם במקום אחד: (ז) ד"ה לנדות שמנדין על כבוד הרב שהטיח דברים כלפי מעלה לאמר לא כך שאלתי הס"ד: (ח) ד"ה הכי קאמר כו' כלומר סדר תעניות אלו אמור בשביל רביעה ראשונה כשעברה מכל וכל כגון רביעה ראשונה: (ט) ד"ה דוקא כו' להתפלל עליהן שיחזרו ביופי כתקנן אבל יבשו לא צריך כו' והוא תפלת שוא הס"ד ומה"ד אבל יבשו. כשהן חטין עדיין כו': (י) ד"ה ה"ג פשיטא נשתנו תנן לא צריכא דהדר אקון מהו דתימא כו' דאקון שעלו כו' שנתייבשו מהו דתימא כו' דאקנתא לאו מילתא הס"ד: (כ) תוס' ד"ה נהרא כו' כשאין כל"ל ותיבת הכי נמחק: (ל) בא"ד ולא מיקרי רעב דמאחר שיכולין כו' זעירא ומהאי מילתא כלומר כו' ע"י חמורים וסוסים כפנא פי' ואז מתריעין: (מ) בא"ד דבמתני' משמע דאבצורת מתריעין דקתני מתריעין כו' כאשר פירש"י שתחת חטה כו' אע"ג דעדיין אינו בא רעב כ"א בצורת הואיל:

יב א מיי' פ"ב מהלכות תענית הלכה טו טוש"ע א"ח סי' תקעה סעיף ח:

יג ב מיי' שם הלכה יג טוש"ע א"ח סי' תקעה סעיף ו:

[נ"ל זוכר]

יד ג מיי' שם הלכה י טוש"ע שם סעיף ח:

בצורתא. בצורת היא זו ולא רעב, הואיל ויכולין לישא בספינות: **מדינתא אמדינתא.** (ה) וצריכין להוליך ממדינה למדינה על ידי חמרים: **כפנא.** רעב. ורעב קשה מבצורת, לפי שאי אפשר להביא בשופי, מ"ר (ו). לשון אחר: נהרא אנהרא, אם יבש מעיין זה וצריך להסב מעיין אחר בכאן, אי נמי להמתין עד שיגדל נהר אחרת ויבא כאן — בצורת הוא זה: **מדינתא אמדינתא.** אם יבשו כל הנהרות שבתוך העיר, וצריכין להביא מים מעיר אחרת, כפנא — רעב הוא זה, תקיפא מבצורתא: **סאה בסלע ושכיחא.** כי זבני סאה של חיטין בסלע דהיינו יוקר ומצויה לקנות בכל עת — בצורתא: **מעות ביוקר.** אין מעות מצויות להן: **נהירנא.** אני זוכר: **מדלית איסר.** מאין מעות: **דאתיא ניחא.** ואמרינן בפירקא דלעיל (דף ג:): מיטרא ניחא לפירי ולתבואה, ומיטרא רזיא לאילני (ז), דאתיא ניחא לפירי ואתיא רזא לאילנות: **בשפיכתא.** בכח גדול יותר מדאי, דאינה טובה לא לזה ולא לזה. שוב אמר רבי: שפיכותא — מטר דק ועבה יותר מדאי, לאילני לא מהניא — דלאו רזיא היא, לצמחים נמי לא — שהגשמים מרובין באין ושוטפין אותן: (ח) **בפרום הפסח.** בימי הפסח [א], על בורות שיחין ומערות אם לא ירדו להן גשמים: [ב]**אפילו בפרום החג.** להשקות זרעים ואת בהמתם: **אם אין להם** (ט) **לשתות מתריעין וכו'.** אפילו[ג] בפרום החג, דימות החמה נינהו, אפילו הכי — מתריעין, משום דכולן צריכות לשתות: **וכולן.** כל אלו: **בהיפרכיא שלהן.** באותו מלכות שכלו שם מי בורות שיחין ומערות: **ואסכרא.** בולמ"ע בלע"ז. פעמים שנקבע בתוך פיו של אדם ומת, לשון "כי יסכר פי דוברי שקר" (תהלים סג), והיא סרונכה, מיתה משונה: **בזמן שיש בה מיתה.** שהיא (י) משולחת — מהלכת, ומתים בה: **על הגובאי.** שמכלה את התבואה, כל שהוא — אפילו לא נראה אלא קנת, בידוע שעתידין לבוא לרוב. אבל חגב כל שהוא מצוי הוא, ואינו מכלה כל כך כארבה: **בשאר שני שבוע.** דשמיטה. אבל בשמיטה — לא, דהפקר נינהו: **אפילו בשביעית.** כל שעה צריכין לשתיה, ואע"פ שהגשמים מועילין לקרקע בשביעית: **רבן שמעון בן גמליאל אומר.** מתריעין על האילנות, ואף על הספיחין של שביעית שאינן חשובין כל כך: **צמוקין.** שיורדין בקושי, מלשון "ושדיים צומקים" (הושע ט): **למה הוא דומה.** פרנסתו של כל (כ) השבת כולה: **נאפית כתקנה.** שיש לו פנאי לאפותה: **פרנסתו בבת אחת.** פרנסת כל השנה, וטוחן אותה ביחד: **נמצאת רחיים כמה שאוכלת מן הכור כו'.** שכן דרך שמשתייר מן הקמח ברחיים. וכן כשהגשמים יורדין מרובים ומרביעין את הארץ, ומה שהיו טרשים בולעים מן (ל) הרוב — בולעין מן המיעוט, ומה שהרוח מנשבת ובולעת מן הרוב — בולעת מן המיעוט: **נמצאת עיסה.** עריבה שלשין בה את הבצק, שמשתייר בשוליה מן העיסה (מ). אף גשמים, כשיורדין מעט מעט — נבלעין בטרשין ואין מרביעין את הארץ: ה"ג: מימיו מרובין (נ) אינו כלין, וטיט מתגבל יפה. מימיו מועטין הטיט אינו מתגבל יפה. מים אינן כלין, ויוכלו לגבל טיט הרבה כמה שירצה: **נקדימון בן גוריון.** עשיר גדול היה: **ואני אתן לך י"ב מעיינות מים.** כלומר, שירדו גשמים ויתמלאו כל המעיינות מים. אותן מעיינות לא היו נובעין מים כל כך, ואינן מתמלאין מאיליהן כשאר מעיינות: **ועכשיו**

נהירנא. פירוש: (*זכור) אני: **בהפרכיא** שלהן. פי': באותו מלכות:

רבן שמעון בן גמליאל אומר אף על האילנות בשביעית מפני שיש בהם פרנסה לעניים. פי': הס הספיחים היוצאין מהן. וצ"ל: דסבר כמ"ד (פסחים דף נא:) ספיחי זרעים אסור. דהיינו ר' עקיבא, מדקאמר: על האילנות, ולא קאמר על הספיחים:

נקדרה

בצורתא, מדינתא אמדינתא — כפנא. וא"ר חנינא: סאה בסלע, ושכיחא — בצורתא, ארבעה,(א) ולא שכיחא — כפנא. א"ר יוחנן: לא שנו אלא בזמן שהמעות בזול ופירות ביוקר. אבל מעות ביוקר ופירות בזול — מתריעין עליה מיד. דא"ר יוחנן: *נהירנא כד הוו קיימי ד' סאין בסלע, והוו נפישי נפיחי כפן בטבריא, מדלית איסר.§ "ירדו לצמחין אבל לא לאילן".§ בשלמא לצמחים ולא לאילן — משכחת לה, דאתא ניחא, ולא אתיא רזיא. לאילן ולא לצמחין — דאתיא רזיא, ולא אתיא ניחא. לזה ולזה, אבל לא לבורות, ולא לשיחין ומערות — משכחת לה, דאתיא רזיא וניחא, *מיהו טובא לא אתיא. אלא הא דתניא "ירדו לבורות, לשיחין, ולמערות, אבל לא לזה ולזה", היכי משכחת לה? דאתיא בשפיכותא. ת"ר: א"מתריעין על האילנות בפרום הפסח. על הבורות, ושיחין,[א] ומערות (ב) — אפילו בפרום החג. ועל כולן, אם אין להן מים לשתות — מתריעין עליהן מיד. ואיזהו 'מיד' שלהן — שני, וחמישי, ושני. (ג) ועל כולן אין מתריעין עליהן אלא באפרכיא שלהן. בואסכרא, בזמן שיש בה מיתה — מתריעין עליה, בזמן שאין בה מיתה — אין מתריעין עליה. גומתריעין על הגובאי בכל שהוא. רבי שמעון בן אלעזר אומר: אף על החגב. ת"ר: מתריעין על האילנות בשאר שני שבוע. על הבורות, ועל השיחין, ועל המערות, אפילו בשביעית. רשב"ג אומר: אף על האילנות בשביעית, מפני שיש בהן פרנסה לעניים. תניא אידך: מתריעין על האילנות בשאר שני שבוע. על הבורות, על השיחין, ועל המערות, אפילו בשביעית. רבן שמעון בן גמליאל אומר: אף על האילנות. מתריעין על הספיחין בשביעית, מפני שיש בהן פרנסה לעניים. תניא, א"ר אלעזר בן פרטא: מיום שחרב בית המקדש, נעשו גשמים *צימוקין לעולם. יש שנה שגשמיה מרובין, ויש שנה שגשמיה מועטין. יש שנה שגשמיה יורדין בזמנן, ויש שנה שאין גשמיה יורדין בזמנן. שנה שגשמיה יורדין בזמנן למה הוא דומה — לעבד שנתן לו רבו פרנסתו בא' בשבת, נמצאת עיסה נאפית כתיקנה ונאכלת כתיקנה. שנה שאין גשמיה יורדין בזמנן למה הוא דומה — לעבד שנתן לו רבו פרנסתו בע"ש נמצאת עיסה נאפית שלא כתיקנה ונאכלת שלא כתיקנה. שנה שגשמיה מרובין למה הוא דומה — לעבד שנתן לו רבו פרנסתו בבת אחת. נמצאו ריחים טוחנות מן הכור (ד) מה שטוחנות מן הקב, ונמצאת עיסה אוכלת מן הכור כמו אוכלת מן הקב. שנה שגשמיה מועטין — למה הוא דומה? לעבד שנתן לו רבו פרנסתו מעט מעט. נמצאו ריחיים מה שטוחנות מן הכור טוחנות מן הקב, נמצאת עיסה כמה שנאכלת מן הכור אוכלת מן הקב. ד"א: בזמן שגשמיה מרובין, למה הוא דומה — לאדם שמגבל את הטיט. אם יש לו מים רבים — מים אינן כלין והטיט מגובל יפה. אם יש לו מים מועטין, מים כלים והטיט אינו מתגבל יפה. ת"ר: פעם אחת עלו כל ישראל לרגל לירושלים, ולא היה להם מים לשתות. הלך נקדימון בן גוריון אצל הגמון, אחד, אמר לו: הלויני שתים עשרה *מעיינות מים לעולי רגלים, ואני אתן לך שתים עשרה עינות מים. ואם איני נותן לך — הריני נותן לך שתים עשרה ככר כסף. וקבע לו זמן. כיון שהגיע הזמן ולא ירדו גשמים, בשחרית שלח לו: שגר לי או מים או מעות שיש לי בידך. שלח לו: עדיין יש לי זמן, כל היום כולו שלי הוא. בצהרים שלח לו: שגר לי או מים או מעות שיש לי בידך. שלח לו: עדיין יש לי שהות ביום. במנחה שלח לו: שגר לי או מים או מעות שיש לי בידך. שלח לו: עדיין יש לי שהות ביום. לגלג עליו אותו הגמון, אמר: כל השנה כולה לא ירדו גשמים, ועכשיו

ס"א מעלות

כ"ב נה:

[רי"ף ורא"ש ל"ג הני ד' תיבות]

[ע' בערוך ערך סקמיון]

רבינו חננאל

בצורת כלומר עצירת מטר מדינה להביא ממדינה אחרת רעב. א"ר יוחנן ל"ש אלא שהמעות בזול ופירות ביוקר כלומר המשא ומתן מצוי ומרויחין בני אדם. אבל מעות ביוקר מתריעין מיד. וא"ר יוחנן נהירנא דהוו ד' סאין בסלע במבריא והוו נפישי נפיחי כפן מדלית איסר. גשמי צמחים הבאים בניחותא. גשמי אילן היורדין ברזיא. לא לאילן ולא לזרעים אלא לבורות. כגון דנחתי בשפיכותא שוטפים ויורדין בבורות: ת"ר מתריעין על האילנות בפרום הפסח ועל מי בורות שיחין ומערות בפרום החג ועל כולן אינן מתריעין עליהן אלא באיפרכיא שלהן כלומר אנשי מקום בלבד. ואם אין להם מים לשתות מתריעין עליהן מיד ב' וה' וב'. ועל האסכרה כל זמן שהיא ממיתה. ומתריעין על הגובאי ועל החגב [ועל האילנות ועל הספיחין] ובאילנות ובספיחי' בשביעית מפני שיש בהן פרנסה לעניים. ר' אלעזר בן פרטא אומר מיום שחרב ביהמ"ק לא ירדו גשמי ברכה ונעשו צמוקים לעולם. שנה שגשמיה ירדו בזמנן דומה לעבד שנתן לו רבו פרנסתו באחד בשבת כו'. נמצאו טוחנין מן הכור כו'. מדה אחת נשארת בפי הריחיים בכור כמה שנשארת מן הקב. וכך נדבקת מן העיסה בסדקי העריבה ובסביבותיה מן המעט כמו מן הרב. וכן בהגבלת הטיט. אם יש לו מים בבת אחת כדי גיבול שופך ומגביל ואם אין לו אלא מעט שופך מה שבידו ועד שיבואו אחרים יבשו הללו וכאלו לא שפך בהן כלום. *) כך סוגיא כו': ת"ר פעם אחת עלו ישראל לחג ולא היה [להם] מים לשתות הלך נקדימון כו'

*) אולי צ"ל כולה סוגיא פשוטה.

הגהות מהר"ב רנשבורג

[א] רש"י ד"ה בפרום הפסח. בימי הפסח הוא סס"ד:

הגהות הגר"א

[א] גמ' ומערות בפרום החג. ואם אין כו' כצ"ל (וכ"ה ברי"ף ורא"ש ובתוספתא ומלת אפי' ליתא גם בגמ' דפוס ישן): [ב] רש"י ד"ה אפילו. רשום קו על מלה זו למחקה: [ג] שם ד"ה אף אין כו' אפי' קודם לפרום החג. כצ"ל:

הגהות הב"ח

(א) גמ' ושכיחא בצורתא ארבעה ולא שכיחא כפנא: (ב) שם ת"ר כו' ושיחין ומערות בפרום החג ואם אין להם מים

כצ"ל ותיבות אפילו ותיבת על כולן נמחק: (ג) שם שני וחמישי ושני וכולן אין מתריעין עליהן ותיבת ועל כולן נמחק: (ד) שם רחיים טוחנות מן הכור כמה שטוחנות מן כו' אוכלת מן הכור כמה שאוכלת מן הקב: (ה) רש"י ד"ה מדינתא אמדינתא לצריכין להוליך: (ו) ד"ה כפנא כו' מ"ר הס"ד: (ז) ד"ה לאתיא כו' לאילני הס"ד: (ח) ד"ה בפרום הפסח בימי הפסח הס"ד ואח"כ מה"ד על בורות וכו' גשמים הס"ד ואח"כ מה"ד בפרום ותיבת אפילו נמחק: (ט) ד"ה אם אין להם מים לשתות מתריעין אפילו בפרום החג: (י) ד"ה בזמן כו' שהיא מכה משולחת דמתים בה: (כ) ד"ה למה הוא דומה פרנסתו של כל השנה כולה: (ל) ד"ה וכן שהיו טרשים בולעין מן המיעוט בולעין מן הרוב ומה שהרוח מנשבת ובולעת מן המיעוט בולעת מן הרוב: (מ) ד"ה נמצאת עיסה כו' מן העיסה הס"ד ומה"ד טוחנות מן הקב אף גשמים כו': (נ) ד"ה ה"ג מימיו מרובין מים אינן כלין כו' מימיו מועטין כלין והטיט אינו מתגבל:

רבינו גרשום

מדינתא אמדינתא כפנא כשצריכין להביא מים ממדינה למדינה זו הוא סימן רעב: סאה בסלע ושכיחא בצורתא ד' סאין בסלע ולא שכיחא אע"ג דלא הוה יוקר הואיל ולא שכיחא הוי כפנא דאתיא הכי והכי ניחא ורזיא מיהו טובא לא אתא דליהוי לבורות לשיחין ולמערות היכי משכחת לה כיון דאתא לבורות היינו רזיא היינו לאילן: דאתיא בשפיכותא דהוי טפי מרזיא דלא ניחא לאילן אלא לבורות. באיפרכיא שלהן ... צריכין להן בשאר שני שבוע אבל לא בשביעית הואיל ואין אוכלין פירות הגדילין בשביעית: מפני שיש בהן צדקה לעניים דעניים אוכלין פירות הגדילין בשביעית. נעשו מי גשמים מצומצמין שאין באין בשפע: נמצא ריחים שאוכלות מן הקב אוכלות מן הכור כלומר שאין קולטין הריחים מן הכור קמח יותר מן הקב דהיינו תקנתו: נמצאת עיסה שאין העריבה אוכלת מן העיסה מן הכור יותר מן הקב: וכן עיר שלא ירדו עליה גשמים ועל האחרת ירדה ואותה העיר שלא ירדה

וְעַכְשָׁיו יֵרְדוּ גְּשָׁמִים? (א) נִכְנַס לְבֵית הַמֶּרְחָץ בְּשִׂמְחָה. עַד שֶׁהַהֶגְמוֹן נִכְנַס בְּשִׂמְחָתוֹ לְבֵית הַמֶּרְחָץ, נַקְדִּימוֹן נִכְנַס לְבֵית הַמִּקְדָּשׁ כְּשֶׁהוּא עָצֵב. נִתְעַטֵּף וְעָמַד בִּתְפִלָּה. אָמַר לְפָנָיו: רִבּוֹנוֹ שֶׁל עוֹלָם! גָּלוּי וְיָדוּעַ לְפָנֶיךָ שֶׁלֹּא לִכְבוֹדִי עָשִׂיתִי, וְלֹא לִכְבוֹד בֵּית אַבָּא עָשִׂיתִי. אֶלָּא לִכְבוֹדְךָ עָשִׂיתִי, שֶׁיְּהוּ מַיִם מְצוּיִין לְעוֹלֵי רְגָלִים. מִיָּד נִתְקַשְּׁרוּ שָׁמַיִם בְּעָבִים, וְיָרְדוּ גְּשָׁמִים עַד שֶׁנִּתְמַלְּאוּ שְׁתֵּים עֶשְׂרֵה מַעְיָנוֹת מַיִם וְהוֹתִירוּ. עַד שֶׁיָּצָא הֶגְמוֹן מִבֵּית הַמֶּרְחָץ נַקְדִּימוֹן בֶּן גּוּרְיוֹן יָצָא מִבֵּית הַמִּקְדָּשׁ. כְּשֶׁפָּגְעוּ זֶה בָּזֶה, אָמַר לוֹ: תֵּן לִי דְּמֵי מַיִם יוֹתֵר שֶׁיֵּשׁ לִי בְּיָדְךָ. אָמַר לוֹ: יוֹדֵעַ אֲנִי שֶׁלֹּא הִרְעִישׁ הקב"ה אֶת עוֹלָמוֹ אֶלָּא בִּשְׁבִילְךָ. אֶלָּא עֲדַיִין יֵשׁ לִי פִּתְחוֹן פֶּה עָלֶיךָ שֶׁאוֹצִיא מִמְּךָ אֶת מְעוֹתַיי, שֶׁכְּבָר שָׁקְעָה חַמָּה, וּגְשָׁמִים בִּרְשׁוּתִי יָרְדוּ. חָזַר וְנִכְנַס לְבֵית הַמִּקְדָּשׁ, נִתְעַטֵּף וְעָמַד בִּתְפִלָּה, וְאָמַר לְפָנָיו: רִבּוֹנוֹ שֶׁל עוֹלָם! הוֹדַע שֶׁיֵּשׁ לְךָ אֲהוּבִים בְּעוֹלָמְךָ. מִיָּד נִתְפַּזְּרוּ הֶעָבִים וְזָרְחָה הַחַמָּה. בְּאוֹתָהּ שָׁעָה אָמַר לוֹ הַהֶגְמוֹן: אִילּוּ לֹא נִקְדְּרָה הַחַמָּה, הָיָה לִי פִּתְחוֹן פֶּה עָלֶיךָ שֶׁאוֹצִיא מִמְּךָ מְעוֹתַיי. תָּנָא: לֹא נַקְדִּימוֹן שְׁמוֹ, אֶלָּא בּוּנִי שְׁמוֹ. וְלָמָּה נִקְרָא שְׁמוֹ נַקְדִּימוֹן? (ב) שֶׁנִּקְדְּרָה חַמָּה בַּעֲבוּרוֹ. תָּנוּ רַבָּנַן: *שְׁלֹשָׁה נִקְדְּמָה לָהֶם חַמָּה בַּעֲבוּרָן: מֹשֶׁה, וִיהוֹשֻׁעַ, וְנַקְדִּימוֹן בֶּן גּוּרְיוֹן. בִּשְׁלָמָא נַקְדִּימוֹן בֶּן גּוּרְיוֹן, גְּמָרָא. (יהושע י) יְהוֹשֻׁעַ נַמִּי קְרָא, דִּכְתִיב °"וַיִּדֹּם הַשֶּׁמֶשׁ וְיָרֵחַ עָמָד" וגו'. אֶלָּא מֹשֶׁה מְנָלַן? אֲמַר (דברים ב) רַבִּי אֶלְעָזָר: אָתְיָא "אָחֵל", "אָחֵל". כְּתִיב הָכָא: °"אָחֵל תֵּת פַּחְדְּךָ". וּכְתִיב הָתָם (יהושע ג) °"אָחֵל גַּדֶּלְךָ". רַבִּי שְׁמוּאֵל בַּר נַחְמָנִי אָמַר: אָתְיָא "תֵּת", "תֵּת". כְּתִיב הָכָא "אָחֵל תֵּת פַּחְדְּךָ". וּכְתִיב הָתָם (שם י) °"בְּיוֹם תֵּת ה' אֶת הָאֱמֹרִי". רַבִּי יוֹחָנָן אָמַר: אָתְיָא מִגּוּפֵיהּ (דברים ב) דִּקְרָא °"אֲשֶׁר יִשְׁמְעוּן שִׁמְעֲךָ, וְרָגְזוּ וְחָלוּ מִפָּנֶיךָ". אֵימָתַי רָגְזוּ וְחָלוּ מִפָּנֶיךָ? [illegible] שֶׁנִּקְדְּמָה לוֹ חַמָּה לְמֹשֶׁה. § "וְכֵן עִיר שֶׁלֹּא יֵרְדוּ עָלֶיהָ [illegible] בֵּינֵיהֶם". אָמַר רַב (איכה א) יְהוּדָה אָמַר רַב: וּשְׁתֵּיהֶן לִקְלָלָה. °"הָיְתָה [illegible] יֵשׁ לָהּ הֶיתֵּר, אַף יְרוּשָׁלַיִם יֵשׁ לָהּ יְהוּדָה אָמַר רַב: לִבְרָכָה. [illegible] רַב יְהוּדָה: לִבְרָכָה. *כְּאַלְמָנָה — וְלֹא אַלְמָנָה מַמָּשׁ. (שם) תַּקָּנָה. °"הָיְתָה [illegible] שֶׁהָלַךְ בַּעְלָהּ לִמְדִינַת הַיָּם, וְדַעְתּוֹ לַחֲזוֹר עָלֶיהָ. °"וְגַם אֲנִי נָתַתִּי (מלאכי ב) אֶתְכֶם נִבְזִים וּשְׁפָלִים". אָמַר רַב יְהוּדָה: לִבְרָכָה, דְּלָא מוֹקְמִי מִינַּן לָא רֵישֵׁי נַהֲרֵי (מ"א יד) וְלָא *גַּזִּירִפַּטֵי. °"וְהִכָּה ה' אֶת יִשְׂרָאֵל כַּאֲשֶׁר יָנוּד הַקָּנֶה בַּמַּיִם". אָמַר רַב יְהוּדָה אָמַר רַב: לִבְרָכָה. דְּאָמַר רַבִּי שְׁמוּאֵל בַּר נַחְמָנִי אָמַר רַבִּי יוֹנָתָן: *)מַאי דִּכְתִיב (משלי כז) °"נֶאֱמָנִים פִּצְעֵי אוֹהֵב וְנַעְתָּרוֹת נְשִׁיקוֹת שׂוֹנֵא" — טוֹבָה קְלָלָה שֶׁקִּילֵּל אֲחִיָּה הַשִּׁילוֹנִי אֶת יִשְׂרָאֵל יוֹתֵר מִבְּרָכָה שֶׁבֵּירְכָן בִּלְעָם הָרָשָׁע. אֲחִיָּה הַשִּׁילוֹנִי קִלְּלָן בְּקָנֶה. אָמַר לָהֶם לְיִשְׂרָאֵל "וְהִכָּה ה' אֶת יִשְׂרָאֵל כַּאֲשֶׁר יָנוּד *הַקָּנֶה". מַה קָּנֶה זֶה עוֹמֵד בִּמְקוֹם מַיִם, וְגִזְעוֹ מַחֲלִיף, וְשָׁרָשָׁיו מְרוּבִּין, וַאֲפִילּוּ כׇּל הָרוּחוֹת שֶׁבָּעוֹלָם בָּאוֹת וְנוֹשְׁבוֹת בּוֹ, (ג) אֵין מְזִיזוֹת אוֹתוֹ מִמְּקוֹמוֹ, אֶלָּא הוֹלֵךְ וּבָא עִמָּהֶן, דָּמְמוּ הָרוּחוֹת, עָמַד הַקָּנֶה בִּמְקוֹמוֹ. אֲבָל בִּלְעָם הָרָשָׁע בֵּירְכָן בְּאֶרֶז, שֶׁנֶּאֱמַר (במדבר כד) °"כַּאֲרָזִים *(עֲלֵי מָיִם") מָה אֶרֶז זֶה אֵינוֹ עוֹמֵד בִּמְקוֹם מַיִם, וְאֵין גִּזְעוֹ מַחֲלִיף, וְאֵין שָׁרָשָׁיו מְרוּבִּין, אֲפִילּוּ כׇּל הָרוּחוֹת שֶׁבָּעוֹלָם נוֹשְׁבוֹת בּוֹ, אֵין מְזִיזוֹת אוֹתוֹ מִמְּקוֹמוֹ, כֵּיוָן שֶׁנָּשְׁבָה בּוֹ רוּחַ דְּרוֹמִית — עוֹקַרְתּוֹ וְהוֹפַכְתּוֹ עַל פָּנָיו. וְלֹא עוֹד אֶלָּא שֶׁזָּכָה קָנֶה לִיטּוֹל הֵימֶנּוּ קוּלְמוֹס לִכְתּוֹב בּוֹ סֵפֶר תּוֹרָה, נְבִיאִים, וּכְתוּבִים. תָּנוּ רַבָּנַן: לְעוֹלָם יְהֵא אָדָם רַךְ כְּקָנֶה וְאַל יְהֵא קָשֶׁה כְּאֶרֶז. *מַעֲשֶׂה שֶׁבָּא רַבִּי אֶלְעָזָר **(בֶּן ר') שִׁמְעוֹן מִמִּגְדַּל גְּדוֹר מִבֵּית רַבּוֹ, וְהָיָה רָכוּב עַל הַחֲמוֹר וּמְטַיֵּיל עַל שְׂפַת נָהָר. וְשָׂמַח שִׂמְחָה גְּדוֹלָה, וְהָיְתָה דַּעְתּוֹ גַּסָּה עָלָיו מִפְּנֵי שֶׁלָּמַד תּוֹרָה הַרְבֵּה.
נִזְדַּמֵּן

*) סנהדרין קה: **) [נ"ל ברבי]

וְעַכְשָׁיו יֵרְדוּ גְּשָׁמִים. בִּתְמִיָּה: בּוּנִי שְׁמוֹ: נִקְדְּרָה. זָרְחָה. לְשׁוֹן מַקְדִּיר, שֶׁהָיְתָה חַמָּה קוֹדֶרֶת בָּרָקִיעַ וְזוֹרַחַת, פירטול"ר בְּלַעַ"ז: הָכִי גַּרְסִינַן. נַקְדִּימוֹן בֶּן גּוּרְיוֹן הָא דַּאֲמַרַן: אָתְיָא אָחֵל אָחֵל. כְּתִיב בְּמִלְחֶמֶת יְהוֹשֻׁעַ (יהושע ג) "אָחֵל גַּדֶּלְךָ", וּבְמִלְחֶמֶת מֹשֶׁה כְּתִיב (דברים ב) "אָחֵל תֵּת פַּחְדְּךָ". מַה יְהוֹשֻׁעַ (ד) נִקְדְּמָה לוֹ חַמָּה בְּמִלְחַמְתּוֹ, כְּדִכְתִיב בְּהֶדְיָא — אַף מֹשֶׁה כֵּן. שֶׁכֵּן דֶּרֶךְ הַכְּתוּבִין, לָמַד סָתוּם מִן הַמְפוֹרָשׁ בְּרֶמֶז בְּדִיבּוּר דּוֹמֶה לַחֲבֵירוֹ. וּגְזֵירָה שָׁוָה אַחַת מִן י"ג מִדּוֹת שֶׁנִּיתְּנוּ לוֹ לְמֹשֶׁה מִסִּינַי, וּבִתְחִילַּת סִיפְרָא מְפוֹרָשׁ: שְׁתֵּיהֶן לִקְלָלָה. אַקְּרָא קָאֵי, הַאי דִּכְתִיב "עַל עִיר אֶחָת אַמְטִיר וְעַל עִיר אַחַת לֹא אַמְטִיר" — שְׁנֵיהֶם לִקְלָלָה, אוֹתָהּ שֶׁיַּמְטִיר עָלֶיהָ — רוֹב גְּשָׁמִים שֶׁמְּקַלְקְלִין אֶת הַתְּבוּאָה. וְאֶת שֶׁלֹּא יַמְטִיר — אֵין גְּשָׁמִים וְאֵין תְּבוּאָה גְּדֵילָה. "אֲשֶׁר לֹא תַמְטִיר עָלֶיהָ" מוּסָב הַדָּבָר עַל הֶעָב, שֶׁהֶעָב בִּלְשׁוֹן נְקֵיבָה, דִּכְתִיב (מלכים א יח) "הִנֵּה עָב קְטַנָּה כְּכַף אִישׁ עוֹלָה מִיָּם": וְלֹא אַלְמָנָה גְּמוּרָה. דְּהָא לָא כְּתִיב "אַלְמָנָה" אֶלָּא "הָיְתָה כְּאַלְמָנָה" — כְּאִשָּׁה הָעוֹמֶדֶת בְּאַלְמְנוּת חַיּוּת עַל בַּעְלָהּ שֶׁהָלַךְ וְעָתִיד לַחֲזוֹר: דְּלָא מוּקְמִי מִינַּן רֵישֵׁי נַהֲרֵי. מוֹכְסִין: גַּזִּירִפַּטֵי. סַרְדְּיוֹטִין, מֵרוֹב בִּזָּיוֹן: וְנַעְתָּרוֹת נְשִׁיקוֹת שׂוֹנֵא. נַעְתָּרוֹת לְשׁוֹן הֶפֶךְ, כִּדְאָמְרִינַן בְּמַסֶּכֶת סוּכָּה (דף יד.): "וַיֵּעָתֶר לוֹ", מָה עֶתֶר זֶה מְהַפֵּךְ אֶת הַתְּבוּאָה — פורק"א בְּלַעַ"ז. אִי נַמִּי: נַעְתָּרוֹת — לְשׁוֹן רִבּוּי וְיִיתּוּר, אינקרי"ש בְּלַעַ"ז, כְּמוֹ "הַעְתַּרְתֶּם עָלַי דִּבְרֵיכֶם" (יחזקאל לה): בֵּירְכָן בְּאֶרֶז. "כַּאֲרָזִים עֲלֵי מָיִם" (במדבר כד): אֶרֶז זֶה אֵינוֹ עוֹמֵד בִּמְקוֹם מַיִם כו'. וְאַע"ג דִּכְתִיב בִּקְרָא "כַּאֲרָזִים עֲלֵי מָיִם" — הַהוּא לָאו בִּלְעָם קָאָמַר לֵיהּ, דְּבִלְעָם אָמַר "כַּאֲרָזִים" וְהַמַּלְאָךְ הֱשִׁיבוֹ "עֲלֵי מָיִם", וְכֵן כּוּלְּהוּ, דְּבִלְעָם אָמַר "כִּנְחָלִים" דִּזְמִינִין מִתְיַיבְּשִׁין — וְקָאָמַר לֵיהּ הַמַּלְאָךְ "נִטָּיוּ", דְּאֵין יְבֵשִׁין לְעוֹלָם. וְהַיְינוּ דִּכְתִיב "וַיַּהֲפֹךְ ה' אֱלֹהֶיךָ לְּךָ אֶת הַקְּלָלָה לִבְרָכָה" עַל יְדֵי מַלְאָךְ, שֶׁהֱשִׁיבוֹ עַל יְדֵי מַלְאָךְ: וַאֲפִילּוּ כׇּל הָרוּחוֹת. שֶׁאֵינָן קָשׁוֹת: רוּחַ דְּרוֹמִית. הִיא קָשָׁה, כִּדְאָמְרִינַן (ב"ב ד' כה:): אִילְמָלֵא בֶּן נֵץ [illegible] עֲמוֹד מִפָּנֶיהָ, — אֵין כׇּל בְּרִיָּה יְכוֹלָה [illegible] שֶׁנֶּאֱמַר "[illegible] יַאֲבֶר נֵץ יִפְרֹשׂ כְּנָפָיו לְתֵימָן": וּמְטַיֵּיל. לִשְׂמוֹחַ:
נִזְדַּמֵּן

נקדרה. כמו "מקדר בהרים" (עירובין נח.) כלומר: שמנקב הרקיע: גזיריפטי. פירוש: סרדיוטין ושוטרי העס במקל: ונעתרות נשיקות שונא. פירוש(ה): כלומר, נאמנים פצעי אוהב, וחילופיהן בשונא. ונעתרות — לשון *הפוך בעתר, פורק"א בלע"ז, שמהפכין בה את התבואה. והכי פשטיה דקרא: פצעי אוהב נאמנים, שהוא עושה לטובה, אפילו כשמכה חבירו — מתכוין לטובה. ונשיקות שונא הם להיפך, שעושה הכל לרעה. וי"מ פשטיה דקרא הכי: "נאמנים פצעי אוהב ונעתרות נשיקות שונא". כלומר, ונעתרות — לשון ריבוי. כלומר, נשיקות שונא — דומים הם למשא, כלומר, הם מרובות ולמשא לעולם. וי"מ הכי: כשאוהבים עושים מריבה ושונאים זה את זה — השנאה נאמנה. והכי פירוש: נאמנים פצעי אוהב — הפצעים זהו השנאה שבין אוהבים, הם נאמנות. ונעתרות נשיקות שונא, פי': דכששונאים עושים שלום זה לזה — השלום והפשרה שביניהן אמנה וקיימת. והיינו נעתרות נשיקות שונא — כלומר, נשיקות שונא נעתרות:
מה ארז זה. פירוש: דאע"ג דכתיב ביה בקרא "עלי מים" — ההוא לאו בלעם קאמר ליה, אלא מלאך. וכן כולהו, בלעם אמר כנחלים ומלאך אמר נטיו דאינן מתייבשים, וכן "עלי נהר":
נזדמן

[סוכה יד. יבמות סד.]

ע"ז כה.

לעיל ו:

סנהדרין קה. ע"ש

[גיר' ערוך ערך גז ז' גאוז דפטאי]

[ע"ע הקנה במים]

במדבר כד

[בילקוט ליתא וכן משמע מדברי תוספות ד"ה מה ארז וכו' וכ"מ מרש"י]

[אבות דר"נ פמ"א מס' ד"א פ"ד ובכניהס אי' ר"ש בן אלעזר]

רבינו חננאל

תנא לא נקדימון שמו אלא בוני שמו. ומפני שנקדמה לו חמה נקרא נקדימון. והמטרתי על עיר אחת ועל עיר אחת לא אמטיר. אמרו שתיהן לקללה. זו שגשמיה מרובין יותר מראי מטשטשין הארץ ואינה עושה פירות. ומי שגשמיה נעצרים אינה מצמחת. היתה ירושלם לנדה. לברכה שיש לה היתר לבעל כנדה. היתה כאלמנה שגער בה בעלה. לא אלמנה ממש. נבזים ושפלים לברכה שאין מהן שרים למלחמה ולהשתמש אותם לעבודת המלך. קנה במים שרשיו מרובים וגזעו מחליף הולך ובא עם הרוחות כו'. ת"ר מעשה בר' שמעון בן אלעזר

רבינו גרשום

עליו מתענה: שתיהן לקללה. אותה שלא ירדה עליה ואותה שירדה עליה ושתיהן מתענות. דלא מוקמי מינן גזי ריפטי ולא מיגרו (פי) [בן]: כארזים עלי מים הוא [illegible]
*) עי' תוס' ד"ה מה ארז.

הגהות הב"ח

(א) [illegible] גשמים מיד נכנס לבית המרחץ בשמחה ובעוד שהאדון נכנס כו' מעיינות מים והותירו בעוד שילא האדון כו' חזר ונכנס נקדימון בן גוריון לבית המקדש כו' אהובים בעולמך וכשם שעשית נס כן עשה מיד נשבה הרוח ונתפזרו העבים: (ב) שם ולמה נקרא שמו נקדימון שעמדה [אולי צ"ל שנקדמה] לו חמה: (ג) שם באות ונושבות בו (אין מזיזות אותו ממקומו) תא"מ ונ"ב ס"א אינו הולך ובא עמהן: (ד) רש"י ד"ה אתיא כו' מה יהושע נקדרת לו חמה: (ה) תוס' ד"ה ונעתרות כו' פירוש כו' ותיבת נאמנים כו' כל"ל ותיבת כלומר נמחק:

נִזְדַּמֵּן לוֹ אָדָם אֶחָד שֶׁהָיָה מְכוֹעָר בְּיוֹתֵר. אָמַר לוֹ: שָׁלוֹם עָלֶיךָ, רַבִּי! וְלֹא הֶחֱזִיר לוֹ. אָמַר לוֹ: רֵיקָה, כַּמָּה מְכוֹעָר אוֹתוֹ הָאִישׁ! שֶׁמָּא כָּל בְּנֵי עִירְךָ מְכוֹעָרִין כְּמוֹתְךָ? אָמַר לוֹ: אֵינִי יוֹדֵעַ, אֶלָּא לֵךְ וֶאֱמוֹר לָאוּמָּן שֶׁעֲשָׂאַנִי "כַּמָּה מְכוֹעָר כְּלִי זֶה שֶׁעָשִׂיתָ"! כֵּיוָן שֶׁיָּדַע בְּעַצְמוֹ שֶׁחָטָא, יָרַד מִן הַחֲמוֹר וְנִשְׁתַּטַּח לְפָנָיו, וְאָמַר לוֹ: *נַעֲנֵיתִי לְךָ, מְחוֹל לִי! אָמַר לוֹ: אֵינִי מוֹחֵל לְךָ עַד שֶׁתֵּלֵךְ לָאוּמָּן שֶׁעֲשָׂאַנִי וֶאֱמוֹר לוֹ: "כַּמָּה מְכוֹעָר כְּלִי זֶה שֶׁעָשִׂיתָ"! הָיָה מְטַיֵּיל אַחֲרָיו עַד שֶׁהִגִּיעַ לְעִירוֹ. יָצְאוּ בְּנֵי עִירוֹ לִקְרָאתוֹ, וְהָיוּ אוֹמְרִים לוֹ: שָׁלוֹם עָלֶיךָ, רַבִּי, רַבִּי, מוֹרִי, מוֹרִי. אָמַר לָהֶם: לְמִי אַתֶּם קוֹרִין "רַבִּי, רַבִּי"? אָמְרוּ לוֹ: לָזֶה שֶׁמְּטַיֵּיל אַחֲרֶיךָ. אָמַר לָהֶם: אִם זֶה רַבִּי, אַל יִרְבּוּ כְּמוֹתוֹ בְּיִשְׂרָאֵל! אָמְרוּ לוֹ: מִפְּנֵי מָה? אָמַר לָהֶם: כָּךְ וְכָךְ עָשָׂה לִי. אָמְרוּ לוֹ: אעפ"כ מְחוֹל לוֹ, שֶׁאָדָם גָּדוֹל בַּתּוֹרָה הוּא. אָמַר לָהֶם: בִּשְׁבִילְכֶם הֲרֵינִי מוֹחֵל לוֹ, וּבִלְבַד שֶׁלֹּא יְהֵא רָגִיל לַעֲשׂוֹת כֵּן. מִיָּד נִכְנַס רַבִּי אֶלְעָזָר (א) בֶּן רַבִּי שִׁמְעוֹן וְדָרַשׁ: לְעוֹלָם יְהֵא אָדָם רַךְ כְּקָנֶה וְאַל יְהֵא קָשֶׁה כְּאֶרֶז. וּלְפִיכָךְ זָכָה קָנֶה לִיטּוֹל הֵימֶנָּה קוּלְמוֹס לִכְתּוֹב בּוֹ סֵפֶר תּוֹרָה, תְּפִילִּין, וּמְזוּזוֹת.§ "וְכֵן עִיר שֶׁיֵּשׁ בָּהּ דֶּבֶר אוֹ מַפּוֹלֶת" כו'.§ תָּנוּ רַבָּנַן: מַפּוֹלֶת שֶׁאָמְרוּ בְּרִיאוֹת וְלֹא רְעוּעוֹת. שֶׁאֵינָן רְאוּיוֹת לִיפּוֹל, וְלֹא הָרְאוּיוֹת לִיפּוֹל. הֵי נִיהוּ בְּרִיאוֹת – הֵי נִיהוּ שֶׁאֵינָן רְאוּיוֹת לִיפּוֹל, הֵי נִינְהוּ רְעוּעוֹת – הֵי נִיהוּ רְאוּיוֹת לִיפּוֹל! לָא צְרִיכָא, דְּנָפְלוּ מֵחֲמַת גּוֹבְהַיְיהוּ. אִי נַמִּי, דְּקַיְימָן אַגּוּדָּא דְּנַהֲרָא. כִּי הַהִיא אֲשִׁיתָא רְעוּעָה דַּהֲוַאי בִּנְהַרְדְּעָא, דְּלָא הֲוָה חָלֵיף רַב וּשְׁמוּאֵל תּוּתַהּ, אע"ג דְּקַיְימָא בְּאַתְרַהּ תְּלֵיסַר שְׁנִין. (ב) יוֹמָא חַד אִיקְּלַע רַב אַדָּא בַּר אַהֲבָה לְהָתָם. אֲמַר לֵיהּ שְׁמוּאֵל לְרַב "נֵיתֵי מָר, נַקִּיף". אֲמַר לֵיהּ: "לָא צְרִיכְנָא [illegible] דְּאִיכָּא רַב אַדָּא בַּר אַהֲבָה בַּהֲדַן דִּנְפִישׁ זְכוּתֵיהּ, וְלָא מִסְתְּפֵינָא". רַב אַדָּא בַּר אַהֲבָה [illegible] חַמְרָא בְּהַהוּא בֵּיתָא רְעִיעָא, וּבָעֵי לְפַנּוּיֵיהּ. עַיְילֵיהּ לְרַב אַרְגִּישׁ רַב אַדָּא בַּר אַהֲבָה [illegible] בִּשְׁמַעְתָּא עַד דְּפַנְּיֵיהּ. בָּתַר דִּנְפַק, נְפַל בֵּיתָא. [illegible] אַל יַעֲמוֹד אָדָם בִּמְקוֹם סַכָּנָה וְיֹאמַר: עוֹשִׂין [illegible] כִּי הָא *דְּאָמַר רַבִּי יַנַּאי: לְעוֹלָם לוֹמַר עוֹשִׂין לוֹ נֵס, מְנַכִּין לוֹ מִזְּכֻיּוֹתָיו. אֲמַר רַב חָנָן: מַאי [illegible] לוֹ נֵס. וְאִם תִּימְצֵי לוֹמַר עוֹשִׂין לוֹ נֵס, מְנַכִּין לוֹ מִזְּכֻיּוֹתָיו. אָמַר רַב חָנָן: מַאי קְרָא? °"קָטֹנְתִּי מִכֹּל הַחֲסָדִים וּמִכָּל הָאֱמֶת". מַאי הֲוָה עוֹבָדֵיהּ דְּרַב אַדָּא בַּר אַהֲבָה? דְּאִתְּמַר: *שָׁאֲלוּ תַּלְמִידָיו (*אֶת רַבִּי זֵירָא וְאָמְרִי לָהּ) לְרַב אַדָּא בַּר אַהֲבָה: בַּמֶּה הֶאֱרַכְתָּ יָמִים? אָמַר לָהֶם: מִיָּמַי לֹא הִקְפַּדְתִּי בְּתוֹךְ בֵּיתִי, וְלֹא צָעַדְתִּי בִּפְנֵי מִי שֶׁגָּדוֹל מִמֶּנִּי, (ג) וְלֹא הִרְהַרְתִּי בַּמְּבוֹאוֹת הַמְטוּנָּפוֹת, וְלֹא הָלַכְתִּי ד' אַמּוֹת בְּלֹא תּוֹרָה וּבְלֹא תְּפִילִּין, וְלֹא יָשַׁנְתִּי בְּבֵית הַמִּדְרָשׁ, לֹא שֵׁינַת קֶבַע וְלֹא שֵׁינַת עֲרַאי, וְלֹא שַׂשְׂתִּי בְּתַקָּלַת חֲבֵרִי, וְלֹא קָרָאתִי לַחֲבֵירִי *בַּהֲכִינָתוֹ. וְאָמְרִי לָהּ: *)בַּחֲנִיכָתוֹ. אֲמַר לֵיהּ רָבָא לְרַפְרָם בַּר פַּפָּא: לֵימָא לָן מָר מֵהָנֵי מִילֵּי מְעַלְּיָיתָא דַּהֲוָה עָבֵיד רַב הוּנָא. אֲמַר לֵיהּ: בְּיַנְקוּתֵיהּ לָא דְּכִירְנָא. בְּסִיבוּתֵיהּ דְּכִירְנָא: דְּכָל יוֹמָא דְּעֵיבָא הָווּ מַפְּקִין לֵיהּ בְּגוּהַרְקָא דְּדַהֲבָא, וְסָיֵיר לָהּ לְכוּלָּהּ מָתָא. וְכָל אֲשִׁיתָא דַּהֲוַות רְעִיעָתָא הֲוָה סָתַר לָהּ. *אִי אֶפְשָׁר לְמָרַהּ, בָּנֵי לָהּ. וְאִי לָא אֶפְשָׁר, בָּנֵי לָהּ אִיהוּ מִדִּידֵיהּ. וְכָל פַּנְיָא דְּמַעֲלֵי שַׁבְּתָא הֲוָה מְשַׁדַּר שְׁלוּחָא לְשׁוּקָא, וְכָל יַרְקָא דַּהֲוָה פָּיֵישׁ לְהוּ לְגִינָּאֵי זָבֵין לֵיהּ וְשָׁדֵי לֵיהּ לְנַהֲרָא. וְלֵיתְבֵיהּ לַעֲנִיִּים! זִמְנִין דְּסָמְכָא דַּעְתַּיְיהוּ, וְלָא אָתוּ לְמִיזְבַּן. וְלִשְׁדְּיֵיהּ לִבְהֵמָה! °קָסָבַר מַאֲכַל אָדָם אֵין מַאֲכִילִין לִבְהֵמָה. וְלָא לִיזְבְּנֵיהּ כְּלָל! נִמְצֵאת מַכְשִׁילָן לֶעָתִיד לָבֹא. כִּי הֲוָה [א] לֵיהּ מִילְּתָא דְּאָסוּתָא, הֲוֵי מָלֵי כּוּזָא (ד) דְּמַיָּא וְתָלֵי לֵיהּ בְּסִיפָּא דְּבֵיתָא וְאָמַר: כָּל דְּבָעֵי, לֵיתֵי וְלִישְׁקוֹל. וְאִיכָּא דְּאָמְרִי: מִילְּתָא דְּשִׁיבְתָּא הֲוָה גְּמִיר, וַהֲוָה מַנַּח כּוּזָא דְּמַיָּא וְדָלֵי לֵיהּ וְאָמַר: כָּל דִּצְרִיךְ, לֵיתֵי וְלֵיעוּל, דְּלָא לִסְתַּכַּן. כִּי הֲוָה כָּרֵךְ רִיפְתָּא, הֲוָה פָּתַח לְבָבֵיהּ וְאָמַר: כָּל מַאן דִּצְרִיךְ, לֵיתֵי וְלֵיכוּל. אֲמַר רָבָא: כּוּלְּהוּ מָצֵינָא מְקַיְּימְנָא, לְבַר מֵהָא דְּלָא מָצֵינָא לְמֶיעְבַּד, מִשּׁוּם

רש"י

נִזְדַּמֵּן לוֹ אָדָם. יֵשׁ סְפָרִים שֶׁכָּתוּב בָּהֶן: אֵלִיָּהוּ זָכוּר לַטּוֹב, וְהוּא נִתְכַּוֵּון לְהוֹכִיחוֹ שֶׁלֹּא יַרְגִּיל בַּדָּבָר: ה"ג: מַפּוֹלֶת שֶׁאָמְרוּ בְּרִיאוֹת וְלֹא רְעוּעוֹת שֶׁאֵינָן רְאוּיוֹת לִיפּוֹל וְלֹא שֶׁרְאוּיוֹת לִיפּוֹל הֵי נִיהוּ בְּרִיאוֹת וְהֵי נִיהוּ שֶׁאֵינָן רְאוּיוֹת לִיפּוֹל הֵי נִיהוּ רְעוּעוֹת וְהֵי נִיהוּ רְאוּיוֹת לִיפּוֹל לָא צְרִיכָא דְּקַיְימָן אַגּוּדָא דְּנַהֲרָא. מַפּוֹלֶת שֶׁיֵּשׁ שָׁם רוּחַ חָזָק שֶׁמַּפִּיל הַחוֹמוֹת (ה). מַפּוֹלֶת שֶׁאָמְרוּ מַתְרִיעִין עֲלֵיהֶן – בִּבְרִיאוֹת קָאָמְרִינַן, שֶׁיְּהוּ הַחוֹמוֹת בְּרִיאוֹת וְאַף עַל פִּי כֵן נוֹפְלוֹת מִכֹּחַ נְשִׁיבַת הָרוּחַ. אֲבָל אִם הָיוּ הַחוֹמוֹת הַנּוֹפְלוֹת רְעוּעוֹת – אֵין מַתְרִיעִין עֲלֵיהֶן. וּכְשֶׁאֵינָן רְאוּיוֹת לִיפּוֹל – מַתְרִיעִין עֲלֵיהֶן, וְלֹא בִּרְאוּיוֹת לִיפּוֹל: לָא צְרִיכָא. הָא דְּקָתָנֵי שֶׁאֵינָן רְעוּעוֹת וּרְאוּיוֹת לִיפּוֹל אֶלָּא כְּגוֹן דְּקָאֵי אַגּוּדָא דְּנַהֲרָא, עַל שְׂפַת הַנָּהָר, שֶׁאע"פ שֶׁהִיא בְּרִיאָה – רְאוּיָה הִיא לִיפּוֹל, שֶׁהַמַּיִם מַפִּילִין אוֹתָהּ, שֶׁמְּקַלְקְלִין אֶת הַקַּרְקַע וְשׁוֹחֲקִין אֶת הַיְּסוֹד: כִּי הַהִיא אֲשִׁיתָא רְעוּעָה כו': בְּאַתְרָהּ. בִּמְקוֹמָהּ, אַף עַל גַּב דְּאֵינָהּ רְאוּיָה לִיפּוֹל, דְּהָא קָמָה בְּאַתְרָהּ כּוּלֵּי הַאי – אֲפִילּוּ הָכִי, כֵּיוָן דִּרְעוּעָה הִיא – לָא הָווּ חָלְפֵי תּוּתָהּ, אֶלָּא הָיָה מַקִּיף סְבִיבוֹתֶיהָ: מְנַכִּין. מְמַעֲטִין: ה"ג: לֹא הִקְפַּדְתִּי בְּתוֹךְ בֵּיתִי (ו) וְלֹא הָלַכְתִּי בְּלֹא תּוֹרָה. דְּכָל שַׁעְתָּא הֲוָה גָּרֵיס: בַּהֲכִינָתוֹ. שֶׁמְּכַנִּים לוֹ בְּנֵי אָדָם (ז), כְּגוֹן שֵׁם לְוַאי: חֲנִיכָתוֹ. כְּמוֹ: חֲנִיכַת אָבוֹת בְּגִיטִּין עַד י' דּוֹרוֹת (גיטין דף פח.): בְּיוֹמָא דְּעֵיבָא. יוֹם הַמְעוּנָּן, דַּהֲוֵי רוּחַ מְנַשֶּׁבֶת, וּמִסְתְּפֵי דְּלָא תַּפִּיל חוֹמוֹת: בְּגוּהַרְקָא. תֵּיבָה תְּלוּיָה בַּעֲגָלָה, וְשָׂרוֹת יוֹשְׁבוֹת בָּהֶן: וְסָיֵיר. בּוֹדֵק. תַּרְגּוּם פּוֹקֵד (שמות לד) – מְסָעֵר, כְּמוֹ: הַאי טַבָּחָא דְּלָא סָר סַכִּינָא קַמֵּיהּ חָכָם*: כִּי הֲוָה לֵיהּ מִילְּתָא דְּאָסוּתָא רָמֵי לֵיהּ אַכּוּזָא דְּמַיָּא כו' לָא גָּרְסִינַן: זָבֵין לֵיהּ וְשָׁדֵי לֵיהּ בְּנַהֲרָא. לְהָכִי זָבֵין לְהוּ, דְּאִי הֲוָה מִשְׁתַּיֵּיר מִידֵי לַגַּנָּנִין – אָזְלָא לְאִיבּוּד דְּמִכַּמְּשָׁא בְּשַׁבָּת, וְנִמְצָא מַכְשִׁילָן לֶעָתִיד לָבֹא, דְּלָא מַיְיתֵי יַרְקֵי לִסְעוּדַת שַׁבָּת: דְּסָמְכָא דַּעְתַּיְיהוּ. שֶׁנִּסְמָכִין עֲנִיִּים [illegible] יָרָק, וְאוֹמְרִים: אֵין אָנוּ צְרִיכִין לִקְנוֹת, [illegible] לֹא יִשְׁתַּיֵּיר שָׁם כְּלוּם וְאֵין לָהֶן מַה [illegible] בְּשַׁבָּת: אֵין מַאֲכִילִין אוֹתָן לִבְהֵמָה. [illegible] אוֹכָלִין (ח), וּמֶחֱזֵי כְּבוֹעֵט בַּטּוֹבָה שֶׁהִשְׁפִּיעַ הקב"ה בָּעוֹלָם. אִי נַמִּי: מִשּׁוּם דְּחָסָה תּוֹרָה עַל מָמוֹנָן שֶׁל יִשְׂרָאֵל. וְזָרֵק לַנָּהָר, וְהוֹלְכִין לְמָקוֹם אַחֵר, וּמוֹצְאִין אוֹתָם בְּנֵי אָדָם וְאוֹכְלִין אוֹתָן, כָּךְ שָׁמַעְתִּי: מִילְּתָא דְּשִׁיבְתָּא. מִנְהַג שֵׁדִים, שֶׁמַּזִּיקִין לְמִי שֶׁיֹּאכַל וְאֵינוֹ נוֹטֵל יָדָיו. דְּשִׁיבְתָּא כְּהַךְ דְּגָרְסִינַן בְּמַסֶּכֶת יוֹמָא (דף עז:): אָמַר אַבַּיֵּי מִשּׁוּם שִׁיבְתָּא. וַהֲוָה תָּלֵי לֵיהּ לְהַהוּא כּוּזָא דְּמַיָּא, כִּי הֵיכִי דְּלִימְשׁוּ יְדַיְיהוּ מִינֵּיהּ: בַּר מֵהָא. חוּץ מִזּוֹ, דְּכָל מַאן דְּבָעֵי הֲוָה עָיֵיל וְאָכַל:
מִשּׁוּם

תוספות

נזדמן לו אדם אחד שהוא מכוער ביותר. – במסכת דרך ארץ *מפרש דאותו אדם היינו אליהו, ולטוב נתכוין, כדי שלא ירגיל בדבר: לא צריכא דנפלי מחמת גובהייהו. פי': דהוו בריאות, ולא היו ראויות ליפול אלא מחמת גובהן: אמר ליה דאיכא רב אדא בהדן דנפיש זכותיה. וה"ל דתרי רב אדא הוו. דהא רב אדא בר אהבה הוה בימי רבא, דמצינו בכמה מקומות: אמר רב אדא בר אהבה אמר רבא(ט), והא רב אדא בר אהבה דהכא משמע דהוה חבר לרב ולשמואל, מדקאמר ליה שמואל לרב, וקאמר ליה: הא איכא רב אדא בהדן. ואנן ידענא דרב יהודה היה תלמיד דרב ושמואל, ורבא *הוה נולד ביום שמת רב יהודה, ורב אדא היה תלמיד דרבא – א"כ ע"כ צ"ל דתרי רב אדא הוו*: בהכינתו. פירוש בכינוי שמכנין אותו (י) בני אדם לגנאי. בחניכתו, פי': כינוי שם משפחתו, שם לווי, כמו שם חניכת אבות בגיטין עד עשרה דורות (גיטין דף פח.), כגון רבי אברהם אבן עזרא, שכל בני משפחתו היו נקראים כך. ודוקא לגנאי, אבל לשבח – מותר:
אמרו

עין משפט נר מצוה

[אפשר דבנוסחאות שהיה לפני תוס' היה כך אבל לפנינו ליתא]

טו א מיי' פ"ב מהלכות תענית הלכה יב טוש"ע א"ח סי' תקעו סעיף ז:

[קידושין עב:]

[וע"ע תוספות קידושין עב: ד"ה היום ותוס' ב"ב כב. ד"ה אמר]

רבינו חננאל

שפגע באחד ואמר כמה מכוער כלי זה שמא כל בני עירך מכוערים כמותך. כיון שידע שחטא התחיל לבקש מחילה. נפק ודרש לעולם יהא אדם רך כקנה ואל יהא קשה כארז: מלתא דשיבתא פי' משקה של רפואה:

רבינו גרשום

בריאות נופלות. מתענין: דקמו אגודא דנהרא וה"ק (רעועות) [בריאות] ולא ראויות ליפול [illegible] דקאי אגודא ליפול דאבלה [illegible] אין מתענין עליהן והויא לה *) נמי בריאות ראויות ליפול דקאי באתרא לאחר שהיתה רעועה דהא כיון דקם באתרא הויא כבריאה וכיון דהויא רעועה הויא ראויה ליפול. קטנתי מכל החסדים כלומר נתמעטו הזכיות בשביל נסים כי במקלי וגו'. בהכינתו שכבר קוראין לו ולא **) בחכינתי שאני קריתי לו שם. ביומא דעיבא ודזיקא ***) זבין להו דאי יתרי ומפסדי לא הוו מייתי בערב שבת אחר: ולא אתו למיזבן וזימנין דלא יתרי להו כלום וסמכו עליה ולא הוה להן מאכל. לשיבתא מילתא דשיבתא הוה גמיר שהיה יודע שרוח רעה שורה (על המים) [על הידים]. ותלי כוזא דמיא (נמי) [כלי] שנוטלין בה את ידיהן ונכנסין. בר מהא דהוה פתח לבבא:

*) נראה מזה דרבינו היה גורס אי נמי כההיא אשיתא וכו' והוא נמי פירוש על בריאות וראויות ליפול ולא כפרש"י.

**) גי' רבינו בחניכתי ביו"ד לבסוף וכ"ה בערוך ערך חנך ולפיכך פי' רבינו שאני קריתי וכו' ובערוך כתוב שלא כניתי לו שם ואולי דגם בדברי רבינו צריך להגיה כן וצ"ע.

***) נראה דחסר כאן וצ"ל ודזיקא הוה סייר לכלהו מתא וכו' וכל ירקא דהוו פייש להו לגינאי זבין להו וכו'.

מסורת הש"ס

תורה אור

[ברכות כח. וע"ש פרש"י כתובות סז:]

חולין יח.

שבת לב.

בראשית לב

מגילה כח.

[בע"י ליתא]

[גירס' הערוך בחניכתו פי' שלא כניתי לו שם]
*) [פי' הערוך ערך חנך אפי' שם שכינו לו אחרים לא קראתיו]

[פי' אם ובע"י גרס אם]

גליון הש"ס

גמ' קסבר מאכל אדם אין מאכילים לבהמה. מג"א סימן קעא ס"ק א:

הגהות הגר"א

[א] גמ' כי הוה ליה. רשום קו על מלת ליה:

הגהות הב"ח

(א) גמ' ברבי שמעון: (ב) דקיימא באתרה תליסר שנין ולא נפלה יומא חד כו' ניתי מר ונקיף א"ל: (ג) שם בפני מי שגדול ממני בחכמה ולא הרהרתי: (ד) שם הוי מלי כוזא מיניה ותלי ליה: (ה) רש"י ד"ה ה"ג מפולת כו' לנהרא הס"ד ואח"כ מה"ד מפולת וכו' החומות הס"ד ומה"ד מפולת שאמרו כו' עליהן הס"ד ומה"ד בבריאות כו' עליהן הס"ד ומה"ד וכשאינן ראויות כו': (ו) ד"ה ה"ג לא כו' ביתי הס"ד ומה"ד ולא הלכתי כו': (ז) ד"ה בהכינתו כו' בני אדם לגנאי כגון: (ח) ד"ה אין מאכילין כו' ביזוי אוכלין דמיחזי כבועט: (ט) תוס' ד"ה א"ל כו' אמר רבא והאי רב אדא: (י) ד"ה בהכינתו כו' שמכנין אותו בני אדם לגנאי כגון שם לווי בחניכתו פי' כינוי בשם משפחתו דיש משפחה שמכנין בני אדם לכל המשפחה וקוראין בחניכת שם לווי כמו שם חניכת:

משום דנפישי בני חילא דמחוזא. אילפא ור' יוחנן הוו גרסי באורייתא, דחיקא להו מילתא טובא. אמרי: ניקום וניזיל וניעבד עיסקא, ונקיים בנפשין °"אפס כי לא יהיה בך אביון". אזלו, (א) אותבי תותי גודא רעיעא. הוו קא כרכי ריפתא. אתו תרי מלאכי השרת. שמעיה רבי יוחנן דאמר חד לחבריה: נישדי עלייהו האי גודא ונקטלינהו, *שמניחין חיי עולם הבא ועוסקין בחיי שעה. אמר ליה אידך: שבקינהו, דאיכא בהו חד דקיימא ליה שעתא. רבי יוחנן שמע, אילפא לא שמע. אמר ליה ר' יוחנן לאילפא: שמע מר מידי? אמר ליה: לא. אמר: מדשמעי אנא ואילפא לא שמע, ש"מ לדידי קיימא לי שעתא. אמר ליה רבי יוחנן: איהדר ואוקי בנפשאי °"כי לא יחדל אביון מקרב הארץ". ר' יוחנן הדר, אילפא לא הדר. עד דאתא אילפא – מליך רבי יוחנן. אמרו לו: אי אתיב מר וגרים, לא הוה מליך מר? *אזל *תלא נפשיה באסקריא דספינתא, אמר: אי איכא דשאיל לי במתניתא דר' חייא ורבי אושעיא ולא פשטינא ליה ממתני' נפילנא מאסקריא דספינתא וטבענא. אתא ההוא סבא, תנא ליה: *האומר: 'תנו שקל לבניי בשבת', והן ראויין לתת להם סלע – נותנין להם סלע. ואם אמר: 'אל תתנו להם אלא שקל' – אין נותנין להם אלא שקל. [א]אם אמר: *'מתו, ירשו אחרים תחתיהם', בין שאמר, 'תנו', בין שאמר, 'אל תתנו', אין נותנין להם אלא שקל. א"ל: הא מני – ר"מ היא, דאמר: [ב]מצוה לקיים דברי המת. אמרו עליו על נחום איש גם זו שהיה סומא משתי עיניו, גידם משתי ידיו, קיטע משתי רגליו, וכל גופו מלא שחין. והיה מוטל בבית רעוע ורגלי מטתו מונחין בספלין של מים כדי שלא יעלו עליו נמלים. פעם אחת [היתה מטתו מונחת בבית רעוע] בקשו תלמידיו לפנות מטתו ואח"כ לפנות את הכלים. אמר להם: בניי, פנו את הכלים ואח"כ פנו את מטתי, שמובטח לכם שכל זמן שאני בבית, אין הבית נופל. פינו את הכלים ואחר כך פינו את מטתו, ונפל הבית. אמרו לו תלמידיו: רבי, וכי מאחר שצדיק גמור אתה, למה עלתה לך כך? אמר להם: בניי, אני גרמתי לעצמי. שפעם אחת הייתי מהלך בדרך לבית חמי, והיה עמי משוי ג' חמורים, אחד של מאכל, ואחד של משתה, ואחד של מיני מגדים. בא עני אחד ועמד לי בדרך, ואמר לי: רבי, פרנסני! אמרתי לו: המתן עד שאפרוק מן החמור. לא הספקתי לפרוק מן החמור עד שיצתה נשמתו. הלכתי ונפלתי על פניו, ואמרתי: עיני, שלא חסו על עיניך, יסומו. ידיי, שלא חסו על ידיך, יתגדמו. רגליי, שלא חסו על רגליך, יתקטעו. ולא נתקררה דעתי עד שאמרתי: כל גופי יהא מלא שחין. אמרו לו: אוי לנו שראינוך בכך. אמר להם: אוי לי אם לא ראיתוני בכך. *ואמאי קרו ליה נחום איש גם זו? דכל מילתא דהוה סלקא ליה, אמר: "גם זו לטובה". *זימנא חדא בעו לשדורי ישראל דורון לבי קיסר. אמרו: מאן ייזיל? ייזיל נחום איש גם זו, דמלומד בניסין הוא. שדרו בידיה מלא סיפטא דאבנים טובות ומרגליות. אזל, בת בההוא דירה. בליליא קמו הנך דיוראי, ושקלינהו לסיפטיה ומלונהו עפרא. (למחר כי חזנהו אמר: גם זו לטובה.) כי מטא התם, [שרינהו לסיפטא, חזנהו דמלו עפרא.] בעא מלכא למקטלינהו לכולהו. אמר: קא מחייכו בי יהודאי! [אמר: גם זו לטובה.] אתא אליהו, אדמי ליה כחד מינייהו. א"ל: דלמא הא עפרא מעפרא דאברהם אבוהון הוא. דכי הוה שדי עפרא – הוו סייפיה, גילי – הוו גירי. דכתיב °"יתן כעפר חרבו, כקש נדף קשתו". הויא חדא מדינתא דלא מצו למיכבשה. בדקו מיניה וכבשוה. עיילו לבי גנזיה, ומלוהו לסיפטיה אבנים טובות ומרגליות, ושדרוהו ביקרא רבה. כי אתו ביתו בההוא דיורא. אמרו ליה: מאי אייתית בהדך דעבדי לך יקרא כולי האי? אמר להו: מאי דשקלי מהכא אמטי להתם. סתרו לדירייהו ואמטינהו לבי מלכא. אמרו ליה: האי עפרא דאייתי הכא מדידן הוא. בדקוה, ולא אשכחוה. וקטלינהו להנך דיוראי. § "אי זו היא דבר? עיר המוציאה חמש מאות רגלי" כו'. § ת"ר: [ג]"עיר (ב) המוציאה חמש מאות ואלף רגלי, כגון כפר עכו, ויצאו הימנה תשעה מתים בשלשה ימים זה אחר זה – הרי זה דבר. ביום אחד או בד' ימים – אין זה דבר. *ועיר המוציאה חמש מאות רגלי כגון כפר עמיקו, ויצאו ממנה שלשה מתים בג' ימים זה אחר זה – הרי זה דבר, ביום

תורה אור: דברים טו | שם | ישעיהו מא

רש"י

משום דנפישי בני מחוזא. דאיכא עניי טפי, וקא מיכלי קרנא: דחיקא להו. עניות: כי לא יהיה בך אביון. בך בעצמך: חיי העולם הבא. תורה: חיי שעה. עולם הזה, זה סחורה: קיימא ליה שעתא. עתיד להתגדל, ואין זמנו למות: שמע מינה. מדאנא שמעתיה – איהדר איזיל לתורתי: עד דאתא אילפא. ממקום שהלך שם לסחורה: מלך רבי יוחנן. מינוהו ראש ישיבה עליהן. מנהג הוא: מי שהוא ראש ישיבה היו מגדלין אותו משלהן, ומעשירין אותו, כדאמרינן לגבי כהן גדול בספרא וביומא (דף יח.): "והכהן הגדול מאחיו" – גדלוהו משל אחיו: אמרו לו. אנשי המקום לאילפא: אי (ג) אתיב מר וגרים. אם היית יושב ועוסק בתורה, היינו ממליכין אותך כמו שעשינו לר' יוחנן. דאילפא הוי גמיר טפי מר' יוחנן: תלא נפשיה באסקריא. כלונס עץ ארוך תקוע בלב הספינה, שמניחין עליה מכסה, וילו"ן בלע"ז: דשאיל לי כו'. כלומר, אף על גב דעבדי עיסקא – גריסנא אנא טפי מינייהו: דבי ר' חייא ודבי ר' אושעיא. דהוו מסדרי מתניתא על פי רבינו הקדוש, שהיה רבם: ולא פשיטנא ליה ממתני'. דמשכחנא משנה כוותיה דההיא ברייתא: תנא ליה. שנה לפניו, כלומר: בעא מיניה: האומר תנו שקל לבניי. מי שמת, והניח ממונו ביד איש נאמן, ואמר: תנו שקל, חצי סלע, לבניי להוצאה בשבוע: וראויין לתת להן סלע. שיש לו בנים הרבה, ואין מסתפקין לשבת בפחות מסלע: נותנין להן סלע. דאי הוה בדעתיה דלא למיתן להו אלא שקל – הוה מצוה: אל תתנו להן אלא שקל, והאי דקאמר תנו להן שקל ולא אמר תנו סלע – משום דבעי לזרוזינהו, כדאמרן בכתובות (דף ע.): כדי לזרזן במשא ובמתן, כדי שיטרחו וילמדו דרך ארץ וירויחו: אם מתו ירשו אחרים תחתיהן. אף על גב דאמר תנו שקל, ולא אמר אל תתנו אלא שקל – גלי בדעתיה דלא בעי למיתב להו אלא שקל בשבת, כי היכי דאי מתו – ירשו אחרים תחתיהן: אמר ליה. אילפא: הא מני. דקתני אע"ג דלא ספקי בצריך מסלע לא יהבינן להו אלא שקל (ד) – ר"מ היא, דאמר במסכת כתובות במתני' (דף סט:): מצוה לקיים דברי המת. דאי לאו מצוה – מן הדין נותנין להן כל הראוי להן, שהרי כל הממון שלהן הוא, ואין בו לאותן אחרים כלום. אלא לאחר מיתתן, אם יש מותר – יש להן, ואם לאו – לא יטלו. ומתוך שרולין אנו לקיים דבריו שירשו אחרים תחתיהם – אנו מקמצין את הממון, כדי שיהא שם מותר: והיה מטתו מונחת כו'. רגלי המטה מונחין בספלים מלאים מים, שלא יעלו אליו נמלים דרך רגלי המטה. מפני שהיה גידם, ואם היו עולים – אינו יכול ליטלם בידיו ולזורקן: דסלקי ליה. כל המאורע לו, אפילו רעה: בת בההיא דיורא. לן לילה אחת באותו המלון: לסיפטיה. ארגז שלו: לכולהו. שונאיהן של ישראל: כחד מינייהו. כאחד משרי קיסר: מעפרא דאברהם הוא. כשנלחם עם המלכים: גילי. קשין: ביתו. לנו במלון: (ה) כפר עמיקו שלשה מתים בשלשה ימים. מת אחד בכל יום: ביום

תוספות

אמרו ליה לאילפא אי יתיב מר לא הוה מלך מר. פי': (ו) כלומר לא היית מולך לראש ישיבה. וי"מ: בניחותא, דמר קאי אר' יוחנן, כלומר: אי – יתיב מר לא הוה מליך ר' יוחנן:

יבא

מסורת הש"ס

[שבת י. לג: ביצה טו:]

[כתובות סט:]

[עי' רש"י גיטין לב: ד"ה דקלי פי' נשען וכן בפסחים סח: פרש"י ד"ה ותלי נשען ובפרש"י חגיגה טו: תלי נשען]

ב"ב קכט. כתובות סט: [תוספתא כתובות פ"ו]

[נ"ל אם מתו]

סנהדרין קח: ע"ש

עי' ברכות ס:

[בכי"ף ובהרא"ש גרס ברישא עיר המוציאה ת"ק וכו' וכסיפא אלף ות"ק וכו']

עין משפט נר מצוה

טז א מיי' פ"ב מהלכות זכיה ומתנה הלכה ו טוש"ע ח"מ סי' רנג סעיף יז:

יז ב מיי' פ"ב מהלכות אישות הלכה יד סמג עשין מח טוש"ע אה"ע סי' נד וטוש"ע ח"מ סי' רנב סעיף ב:

יח ג מיי' פ"ב מהלכות תעניות הלכה ה טוש"ע א"ח סי' תקעו סעיף ב:

רבינו חננאל

אילפא ור' יוחנן דחיק להו עלמא אמרי ניקום ונעביד עסקא עד דהדר אילפא מלך ר"י. אתא אלפא תלא נפשיה. אמר אי איכא דשאיל לי מתנייתא מדבי ר' חייא ודבי ר' אושעיא ולא פשטנא ליה ממתני'. כלומר כל מה שיש במשניות החיצונות עיקר שלהן במשנתנו ואין כל חכם יודעו לפיכך אני גדול מר"י. ולמה זכה לישב בראש ולא זכיתי אני ושאליה ההוא סבא הא דתניא. האומר תנו לבניי שקל בשבת וצוה ומת וראויין לתת להן סלע. כי השקל הוא חצי סלע. אם אינו מספיק להן נותן להן סלע. אם אמר בלשון הזה אל תתנו להן אלא שקל אע"פ שאינו מספיק להן אינו נותן להן אלא שקל ואם אמר אם מתו יירשו אחרים תחתיהן כו'. שמעינן מינה דאין אדם רשאי לשנות מדברי המת. ופשט אילפא הא מתניתא אליבא דר' מאיר היא ששנינו במשנתנו בכתובות בפרק מציאת האשה המשליש מעות לבתו והיא אומרת נאמן עלי בעלי יעשה שליש מה שהושליש בידו דברי ר' מאיר. ואוקימנא התם טעמא דר' מאיר משום דמצוה לקיים דברי המת ואין לשנות מדבריו: אמרו עליו על נחום איש גם זו. שם מקום הוא ראיה על אמתת הדבר בדברי הימים (ב' כ"ח) הוא שנקרא לשם שם אחת העיירות גמזו והוא האמת (א) ירושלמי א"ר יוסי בר אבין בזכות ג' דברים גשמים יורדים. בזכות הארץ. ובזכות החסד ובזכות יסורין וכולן בפסוק אחד נאמרו. אם לשבט אם לארצו אם לחסד. מצאנו שבט אלו יסורין. מפני (ג') ד' דברים גשמים יורדין מלמעלה מפני טללים הרעים ומפני בעלי זרוע ושיהא שותה העליון כתחתון ושיהו עיני הכל נשואות לשמים. בעון (ג') ד' דברים גשמים נעצרים בעון ע"ז שנאמר ועבדתם שם אלהים אחרים וכתיב בתריה ועצר את השמים. בעון ג"ע שנאמר ותחניפי ארץ בזנותייכי וכתיב וימנעו רביבים וגו'. בעון ש"ד שנאמר כי הדם הוא יחניף את הארץ. פי' יחן אף על הארץ. (וכתיב וחרה אף ה' בכם ועצר את השמים)ב) בעון פוסקי צדקה ברבים ואינן נותנים דכתיב נשיאים ורוח וגשם אין איש מתהלל במתת שקר. [חמשה] שמות נקרא אד [עב] ענן חזיז ונשיא א"ר חנינא מה יעשו גדולי הדור. ואין הצבור נידון אלא אחר רובו. שכן מצינו שכל ל"ח שנים שהיו ישראל כמנודים לשמים לא היה הדבור עם משה. שנאמר ויהי כאשר תמו כל אנשי המלחמה וגו' וכתיב וידבר ה' אלי לאמר. ר' אליעזר עבד תענית ולא נחית מטרא עבד ר' עקיבא תלמידי' ונחית מטרא. עאל ר"ע ואמר מלה"ד למלך שהיו לו ב' בנות אחת חצופה וכיון שהיתה נכנסת אצלו בבקשה הוא אומר תנו לה בקשתה ותצא ואחרת היתה צנועה. וכשהיתה נכנסת אצלו היה מאריך רוחו עמה כדי שישמע שיחתה שהיה מתאוה לשמוע שיחתה. עשה כן ר"ע בשביל ר' אליעזר רבו כדי שלא יאמרו כי אינו הגון ונמצא חלול שמים. (בירושלמי פ"ג ה"ה) כתיב ויקבצו המצפתה וישאבו מים וישפכו לפני ה' וכי מים שפכו אלא לבם שפכו כמים. ויאמרו שם חטאנו לה' לבש שמואל חלוקו של ישראל אמר לפניו רבש"ע כלום אתה דן את האדם ג) על אמרך לא חטאתי. ואלו אומרים לפניך חטאנו: מתני' איזו היא דבר. עיר המוציאה ת"ק רגלי עיר גדולה המוציאה אלף ת"ק רגלי יוצאי צבא כגון כפר עכו. ויצאו הימנה ט' מתים בג' ימים (בג' ימים אנשים ממש) [זא"ז] הרי דבר בד'

א) עי' בערוך השלם ערך גם זו. ב) בירושלמי לפנינו ליתא זה אך רבינו היה גורס כן בירושלמי ומביא ראיה מהך קרא דהך אף לאידך קרא היינו שיהיה עצירת גשמים.
ג) אלא על שהוא אומר לפניך לא חטאתי הנני נשפט אותך על אמרך לא חטאתי (ירמיה ב').

רבינו גרשום

באסקריא דספינתא: מֶשֶׁט: נותנין להם סלע דאזלינן בתר אומדין דעתי' דלהכי אמר שקל אם אפשר להם לצמצם אבל אם אי אפשר להם נותנין להם סלע *) כיון שאמר תנו אין נותנים להם אלא שקל דאזלינן בתר אומדין דעתיה דכיון דבעי דלירשו אחרים ודאי הוה ליה צר עין על בניו א"ל הא מני ר"מ דמתניתין: מונחת על ארבעה ספלים שלא יעלו עליו הרחש: ביום אחד

*) נ"ל ואם אמר אם מתו ירשו אחרים תחתיהם בין שאמר תנו ובין שאמר אל תתנו אין נותנין להם וכו'.

הגהות הב"ח

(א) גמ' אזלו אותיבו תותי גודא וכו' אי יתיב מר וגרים: (ב) שם ת"ר עיר גדולה המוציאה חמש מאות כו' ועיר קטנה המוציאה כו': (ג) רש"י ד"ה אי יתיב מר וגרים: (ד) ד"ה הא מני כו' אלא שקל הס"ד ומה"ד ר"מ היא וכו' שיהא שם מותר הס"ד ומה"ד ורגלי מטתו מונחין כו': (ה) ד"ה ביתו לנו במלון הס"ד ואח"כ מה"ד כגון כפר עמיקו ויצאו ממנה שלשה מתים: (ו) תוס' ד"ה אמרו כו'. פי' בתמיה כלומר וכי לא היית:

יבא מנה בן פרס. כלומר: מוטב שיבא גדול בן הדיוט. דפרס לא הוה אלא חצי מנה, ואל יבא מנה בן מנה דהיינו רב חסדא דהיה מנה, כלומר שהיה חשוב. ופרס היינו יצחק אבוה דרב נחמן, דלא מיקרי רב יצחק: *אמר ליה זוודא אייתי בהדייהו. פירוש: וכי לידה הביאו עמהם שיהו אוכלות? כלומר, אי אפשר שלא יאכלו התבואה והזרעים: **אמרו** ליה לרב יהודה איכא מותנא בחזירי גזר תעניתא וכו' עד שאני חזירי דדמו מעייהו לבני אינשי. פירוש: שבני מעיו של חזיר דומין למעים של בני אדם, ויש לחוש שיבא (ט) על בני אדם. מכאן נראה שאם יהיה דבר על נכרים שיש לחוש ויש להתענות, דהא הכא חזינן דגזר תעניתא (י) מדבר שהיה בחזירין משום דדמו מעייהו לבני אדם, וכל שכן דנכרים דדמו לישראל: **גבירה** לוקה. פי': זו ארץ ישראל:

טרפה

ביום אחד או בארבעה ימים – אין זה דבר. דרוקרת עיר המוציאה חמש מאות רגלי הוה, ויצאו ממנה שלשה מתים ביום אחד. גזר רב נחמן בר רב חסדא תעניתא. אמר רב נחמן בר יצחק: כמאן? כר"מ, דאמר: *ריחק נגיחותיו – חייב, קירב נגיחותיו – לא כ"ש? א"ל רב נחמן בר רב חסדא לרב נחמן בר יצחק: ליקום מר, ליתי לגבן! א"ל: תנינא, רבי יוסי אומר: לא מקומו של אדם מכבדו, אלא אדם מכבד את מקומו. שכן מצינו בהר סיני, שכל זמן שהשכינה שרויה עליו, אמרה תורה °"גם הצאן והבקר אל ירעו אל מול ההר ההוא". נסתלקה שכינה ממנו – אמרה תורה °"במשוך היובל, המה יעלו בהר". וכן מצינו באהל מועד שבמדבר, שכל זמן שהוא נטוי, אמרה תורה °"וישלחו מן המחנה כל צרוע". *הוגללו הפרוכת – הותרו זבין והמצורעים ליכנס שם. אמר ליה: אי הכי (א) – ניקום אנא לגבי מר. אמר ליה: מוטב יבא מנה בן פרס אצל מנה בן מנה, ואל יבא מנה בן מנה אצל מנה בן פרס. בסורא הוות דברתא, בשיבבותיה דרב לא הוות דברתא. סברו מיניה משום זכותיה דרב, דנפיש. איתחזי להו בחילמא: רב דנפישא זכותיה טובא, הא מילתא זוטרא ליה לרב. אלא משום ההוא גברא, דשייל מרא וזבילא לקבורה. בדרוקרת הוות דליקתא, ובשיבבותיה דרב הונא לא הוות דליקתא. סבור מינה בזכותא דרב הונא, דנפיש. איתחזי להו בחילמא: האי זוטרא ליה לרב הונא. אלא משום ההיא איתתא דמחממת תנורא (ב) ומשיילי לשיבבותיה. אמרו ליה לרב יהודה: אתו קמצי. גזר תעניתא. אמרו ליה: לא קא מפסדן. אמר להו: זוודא אייתו בהדייהו? אמרו ליה לרב יהודה: איכא מותנא בחזירי. גזר תעניתא. נימא קסבר רב יהודה מכה משולחת (ג) ממין אחד משולחת מכל המינין? לא. אשאני חזירי, דדמיין מעייהו לבני אינשי. אמרו ליה לשמואל: איכא מותנא בי חוזאי. גזר תעניתא. א"ל: והא מרחק! אמר: ליכא מעברא הכא דפסיק ליה. אמרו ליה לרב נחמן: באיכא מותנא בארעא דישראל. גזר תעניתא. אמר: אם גבירה לוקה, שפחה לא כל שכן! טעמא דגבירה ושפחה, הא שפחה ושפחה – לא. והאמרו ליה לשמואל: איכא מותנא בי חוזאי, גזר תעניתא! גשאני התם, כיון דאיכא שיירתא דלווי ואתיא בהדיה. אבא אומנא הוה אתי ליה שלמא ממתיבתא דרקיעא כל יומא, ולאביי כל מעלי יומא דשבתא, לרבא כל מעלי יומא דכיפורי. הוה קא חלשא דעתיה דאביי משום דאבא אומנא. אמרו ליה: לא מצית למיעבד כעובדיה. (ד) ומאי הוו עובדיה דאבא אומנא? דכי הוה עביד מילתא, הוה מחית גברי לחוד ונשי לחוד. ואית ליה לבושא דאית ביה קרנא, דהוות בזיעא כי כוסילתא. כי הוות אתיא ליה איתתא, הוה מלביש לה, כי היכי דלא ניסתכל בה. ואית ליה דוכתא *דצניעא דשדי ביה פשיטי דשקיל. דאית ליה – שדי ביה, דלית ליה – *)לא מיכסיף. כי הוה אתרמי ליה צורבא מרבנן, אגרא מיניה לא שקיל, *ובתר דקאי – יהיב ליה פשיטי, ואמר ליה: זיל בריא נפשך. יומא חד שדר אביי זוגא דרבנן למיבדקיה. אותבינהו, ואכלינהו, ואשקינהו, ומך להו ביסתרקי בליליא. לצפרא

*) ס"א הוה אתי ויתיב ולא

תורה אור: שמות לד · שם יט · במדבר ה

ביום אחד אין זה דבר. דאקראי בעלמא הוא: ה"ג: עיר גדולה המוציאה אלף וחמש מאות רגלי יצאו הימנה תשעה מתים וכו'. אלף וחמש מאות איש דהיינו פי שלשה בעיר קטנה (ה): כפר עכו דרוקרת. נ"א: דיוקרא, עיר ששמה יו"ד, והיא קטנה, על שם שיו"ד קטנה באותיות: ה"ג. יצאו הימנה ג' מתים *בג' ימים: ריחק נגיחותיו. בשור מועד קאי, בבבא קמא, בפרק "כיצד הרגל מועדת", אי זהו תם ואי זהו מועד? כל שהעידו בו ג' ימים – דברי ר' יהודה. ר' מאיר אומר: כל שהעידו בו שלש פעמים ביום אחד. ר' יהודה סבר: כתיב "או נודע כי שור נגח הוא מתמול שלשום", מתמול – תרי, שלשום – תלת, הרי ג' ימים. ור"מ סבר: ריחק נגיחותיו, כשנגח בג' ימים זה אחר זה – חייב, קירב נגיחותיו שנגח ג' פעמים – ביום אחד לא כל שכן? ליקום מר להכא. דרב נחמן בר יצחק הוה יתיב בין גברי דלא חשיבי כולי האי, וקאמר ליה רב נחמן בר רב חסדא ליקום מר מהתם וליתי ליתיב גבאי: תנינא. תני אנא, שונה אני ברייתא זו: רבי יוסי אומר כו': לא מקומו של אדם מכבדו. ואם אלך ואשב שם – אין המקום מכבדני: גם הצאן והבקר אל ירעו. דמשום שכינה היה הר סיני מכובד ומקודש: אל מול ההר ההוא. מדכתיב "ההוא" משמע: כל זמן שהוא בגדולתו, שהשכינה עליו (ו). נסתלקה השכינה במשוך היובל וגו'. ואע"ג דהאי קרא בלוחות הראשונות כתיב – לא נסתלקה שכינה עד לוחות האחרונות שניתנו ביום הכפורים. וגם כל ימות החורף שעסקו במלאכת המשכן שהתה שכינה בהר, ומשם ניתנו כל המצות בקולי קולות ולפידים ביום קבלת עשרת הדברות, עד אחד בניסן שהוקם המשכן. ונסעה וחזה שכינה מן ההר וישבה לה על *הכפורת, ושם באהל מועד נשנית התורה כללותיה ופרטותיה. ועל אותה שעה היה מתיר להם בלוחות הראשונות לעלות, כדאמרינן במסכת ביצה (דף ה.): כל דבר שבמנין – צריך מנין אחר להתירו. ובראש קונטרס רומי חתה מולא תשובת *רבים בכך: במשוך היובל. בסיום השופר, כשמסתלק השכינה. דרך הוא להאריך ולמשוך התקיעה בשעת סיום: הוגללו הפרוכת. שהיו נגללין בשעת נסיעתן (ז) היו נוסעין כולן, ובאין זבים ומצורעים ונכנסין במחנה: פרס. חצי מנה, ולשון פרוסה. כמו "פרס פריסת מלכותך" (דניאל ה). שאביו של רב נחמן בר רב חסדא גדול מיצחק אביו של רב נחמן, מדמיתקרי בר רב חסדא ואידך רב נחמן בר יצחק, מכלל שלא נסמך: דברתא. דבר: בשיבבותיה. בשכונתו: איתחזי להו בחילמא. להנך אינשי דסברי (ח) משום זכותיה דרב הוא: הא זוטר ליה לרב. נס זה קטן הוא לפי גדולת רב: מרא. פוסוי"ר בלע"ז: זבילא. פלי"א בלע"ז: לקבורה. ומשום זכותיה דקבורה מדדו בו מדה כנגד מדה: ומשיילא לשיבבותיה. ומשאלתו לשכנותיה לאחר שהסיקתו משלה, לפיכך נמדדת השכר בה במדה: קמצא. ארבה שמכלה את התבואה: לא קא מפסדא. לא בעינן למיגזר תעניתא: זוודא אייתו בהדייהו. בתמיה: וכי לידה הביאו עמם שלא יפסידו את התבואה? מעייהו. בני מעיין שלהן. שאין להן כרס הפנימי כשאר בהמה, וסימן רע הוא: בי חוזאי. מקום במלכות בבל: גזר תעניתא. בעירו: הא מרחק. ואין לחוש שמא יבא עד כאן: אמר להו וכי מעברא פסיק להו. וכי מעברות ושאר מחיצות מפסיקין לפני הדבר שלא יבא? שפחה לא כל שכן. ויש לחוש שמא ישתלח עד כאן: הא שפחה ושפחה. שתי עיירות של חוצה לארץ, כגון בי חוזאי ונהרדעא דאתריה דשמואל: שיירתא. דאזלי מבי חוזאי לנהרדעא: דלווי. מתלוה ובא עמהן: שלמא מרקיעא. בת קול אומרת לו: שלום עליך: אבא אומנא. מקיז דם: כי הוה עביד מילתא. כשהיה מקיז דם לבני אדם: ודנשים לחודייהו. לצניעותא: דאית ביה קרנא. וינטוז"א, שהיה תקוע בו הקרן שהוא מקיז בו, ולנשים הוי מלביש לה: ולא מכסיף. דלאחר *שהכה לא הוה ידע מאן רמי (בכסילתיה) פשיטי להתם, ומאן דלא רמי: בריא נפשך. תבריא עצמך: למיבדקיה. לבדקו במעשיו: ומך להו בסתרקי. קיפל תחתיהן תכשיטי צמר, טפיד"ו בלע"ז, לישן בהן: לצפרא

יט א טוש"ע א"ח סי' תקעו סעיף ג:

[נ"ל אמר להו]

כ ב ג מיי' פ"ב מהלכות תענית הלכה ו טוש"ע שם סעיף ב:

רבינו חננאל

בד' ימים או ביום אחד אינו דבר. א"ל רב נחמן בר רב חסדא לרב נחמן בר יצחק ליתי מר יקום הכא. א"ל תנינא לא המקום מכבד את האדם אלא אדם מכבד את מקומו. שכן מצינו בסיני כ"ז שהשכינה עליו כתיב גם הצאן והבקר אל ירעו. נסתלקה שכינה כתיב במשוך היובל המה יעלו בהר. וכן באהל מועד כ"ז שהיה נטוי כתיב וישלחו מן המחנה כל צרוע וגו' הוגללו הפרוכת הותרו הזבים והמצורעים להכנס. א"ל אבוא אני אצלך. א"ל מוטב יבא מנה בן פרס. פי' חכם בן מי שלא היה אביו חכם אצל חכם בן חכם. בסורא הוה מותנא בשיבבותיה דרב לא הות וכן הות דלקת בדיוקרתא ובשיבבותיה דרב הונא לא הות. ואסיקנא דלאו בזכותייהו דהני אלא בשביל ההוא גברא דמושיל מרא לאינשי לקבורה. ובדיל ההיא אתתא דמחממא תנורא ומושלא לשביבתא. אמרו לר"י איכא מותנא בחזירי אמר כיון דדמיין מעייהו לבני אדם גזרינן תעניתא

רבינו גרשום

אחד אין זה דבר דאקראי בעלמא הוא: או בארבעה מרוחקין: ט מתים דהיינו נמי ג' מתים לג' ימים: ריחק נגיחותיו שנגח בג' ימים הוי מועד. קירב נגיחותיו שנגח ג' ביום אחד לא כ"ש. מעברי מפסקי כלומר שיירות מצויין שעוברין במעברות מבי חוזאי להכא כיון דשכיחי שיירתא מבי חוזאי להכא גזר אבל מא"י לבבל דלא שכיחי שיירתא אי לאו משום גבירתה לא הוה גזר. אתי ליה שלמא מכרזי עליה שלמא מרקיעא: דאית ביה קרני כלומר אתרא לקרני.

הגהות הב"ח

(א) גמ' א"ל אי הכי איקום אנא ואיזול לגבי מר: (ב) שם ההיא איתתא דמחממת תנורא מע"ש לע"ש ומשיילא לשיבבותה: (ג) שם מכה משולחת במין אחד משולחת בכל המינין: (ד) שם למיעבד כעובדיה דאבא אומנא ומאי הוו כו' כי כוסילתא דכי הוות כו' דלא ליסתכיל בה והוה ליה דוכתא לצניעה: (ה) רש"י ד"ה ה"ג עיר כו' ויצאו הימנה ט' מתים וכו' כגון כפר עכו אלף וחמש מאות וכו' בעיר קטנה הס"ד ואח"כ מה"ד דרוקרת נ"א יו"ד קרת עיר ששמה יו"ד והיא עיר קטנה על שם כו' כצ"ל ותיבות כפר עכו נמחק: (ו) ד"ה אל מול כו' שהשכינה עליו הס"ד ומה"ד נסתלקה וכו' ובראש קונטרס תשובת רומי: (ז) ד"ה הוגללו וכו' והיו נוסעין וכו' במחנה שכינה הס"ד: (ח) ד"ה איתחזי וכו' דמשום זכותיה: (ט) תוס' ד"ה אמרו כו' ויש לחוש שיבא דבר על בני אדם:
(י) בא"ד אדבר שהיה בחזירין. נ"ב וקשה דאמרינן דקטנה בתרי אומי לא שלטא:

נ"ל ביום אחד. רש"א

ב"ק כד. ב"ב כח:

[מנחות לה.]

הכפורת באהל מועד ושם נשנית התורה כצ"ל. רש"א

[ורבינו ברוך ס"א]

ס"א מאבראי

ס"א וכי הוי חזי אינש דלא אפשר ליה הוה יהיב ליה כו'

נ"ל שנ"ל שסקיז

לצפרא ברכינהו. רבנן לדיספרקי דאבא אומנא, ואייתינהו לשוקא לזבנינהו: אמרו ליה. לאבא אומנא: לשיימינהו מר, והב לן דמייהו. והיו בודקין אותו אם יחשדם כגזלנין, או אם יהא שם אותם פחות מכדי דמיהם: במאי חשדתינן. כשלקחנום: ובסיפא. לכו מילתא למימר לי לאלתר ליתן אותם, והשכי אתו למיגבי גבאי, למיעבד כולי האי: לשקלינהו מר. שלא היינו רוצין אלא לנסותך: חלשא דעתיה דרבא אדאביי. דלרבא לא אתי שלמא אלא ממעלי יומא דכיפורי למעלי יומא דכיפורי, ולאביי כל מעלי שבתא: אבולא כרבא. על כל בני עירך: רב ברוקא חוזאה. שהיה מבני חוזאי: דבי לפט. מקום: א"ל. רב ברוקא לאליהו: מי איכא בהאי שוקא כו': מסאני אוכמי. מנעלים שחורים(ד), שלא כמנהג היהודים: ולא רמי חוטא. לא הטיל ציצית בטליתו: אמר ליה. אליהו לרב ברוקא: האי בר עלמא דאתי הוא: קרא ליה. רב ברוקא להווא גברא: זנדוקנא. שומר בית האסורין(ה): רמינא פורייאי כו'. מטיל אני מטתי בין אנשים לנשים: דיהבי נכרים עינייהו עלה. בעלי בית האסורים: איתרמי נערה כו'. דהויא בבית הסוהר: דורדיא דחמרא. שמרים של יין, האדומים כדם: בשיפולה. בשולי בגדיה: דיסתנא. דרך נשים לה, ומאוסה היא. והוא לשון פרסי*: אמר ליה. אליהו לרב ברוקא: הני נמי בני עלמא דאתי נינהו: בדוחי. שמחים, ומשמחים בני אדם: טרחינן. במילי דבדיחותא ביניהו: עד דעבדי שלמא.(ו) שהן דברים שאדם אוכל פירותיהן בעולם הזה והקרן קיימת וכו': הבאת שלום בין אדם לחבירו: שדפון וירקון. כיון שנראה כל שהוא מתריעין. ומלא תנור דמתניתין להתענות. אי נמי, מעשה(ז) היה כך: כנף אחד. עוף אחד של אותו מין, כעין "לפור כל כנף" (בראשית ז): משולחת. מן השמים: בשדה אינה משולחת. דהיינו אורחה: טרפה שני בני אדם. ולא אכלה אלא אחד מהם — ודאי משולחת, דכיון דלא היתה רעבה אלא לאחד — מאי טעמא קטלה ליה לאידך? שניהן אינה משולחת. שמפני הרעב אכלתם: עלתה לגג. רגילין היו להשתמש כל תשמישיהן בגגות, שלא היו משופעים אלא חלקים ושוין, והוא הדין לבית שתחתיו: עריסה. ברש"ל בלע"ז: הכי קאמר. האי דקתני נראתה בעיר כו' הכי קאמר: נראתה בעיר, כגון שנראתה ביום, דסתם נראתה — ביום משמע. אבל בלילה — אינה משולחת והאי דקתני נראתה ביום (ח) א] — אשדה קאי, דאם נראתה בשדה ביום — אינה משולחת: הא עמדה. בשדה, דלא רצתה ולא נחבאת: בשדה הסמוכה לאגם. עמדה אינה משולחת, דכיון דסמוכה לאגם — היינו רביתה. ולא ברחה — סברה: אי אתי בתראי — עריקנא לאגם מיד: בשדה שאינה סמוכה לאגם. עמדה — משולחת, דכיון דלאו מקום רביתה הוא וקיימא — ודאי משולחת גזירה היא: אגם. מרש"ק בלע"ז. הסמוך לעיר, והוא מלא קולים: כי תניא ההיא. דאכלה אין, רצתה — לא, באגם(ט), דכיון דהיינו דוכתה — סמכה אדעתה ורהטא אבתרייהו: כוכא דציידי. כוך קטן של ציידין, שמסתפרו למארב העופות. ואף על גב דלאו בנין קבוע הוא, ולא הוה כיישוב — הויא משולחת: אין צריך לומר חרב שאינו של שלום. שמתריעין עליה:(י) אלא אפילו חרב של שלום. העוברת דרך אותו מלכות לילך להלחם במקום אחרת: וישלח

לצפרא ברכינהו ושקלינהו, וקמו ונפקו להו לשוקא, ואשכחינהו. א"ל: לשיימיה מר היכי שוו? א"ל: הכי והכי. א"ל: ודלמא שוו טפי. א"ל: בהכי שקלינהו. אמרו ליה: דידך ניהו, ושקלינהו מינך. אמרו ליה: במטותא מינך, במאי חשדתינן? א"ל: אמינא; פדיון שבויים איקלע להו לרבנן, ואכסיפו למימר לי. אמרו ליה: השתא נשקלינהו מר! אמר להו: מההוא שעתא אסחתינהו מדעתאי לצדקה. הוה קא חלשא דעתיה דרבא משום דאביי. (א) אמרו ליה: מסתייך דקא מגנית אכולה כרכא. ר' ברוקא חוזאה הוה שכיח בשוקא דבי לפט. הוה שכיח אליהו גביה. א"ל: *איכא בהאי שוקא בר עלמא דאתי? א"ל: לא. אדהכי והכי, חזא לההוא גברא דהוה סיים מסאני אוכמי, ולא רמי חוטא דתכלתא בגלימיה. א"ל: האי בר עלמא דאתי הוא. (ב) רהט בתריה, א"ל: מאי עובדך? א"ל: זיל האידנא, ותא למחר. למחר א"ל: מאי עובדך? א"ל: *זנדוקנא אנא, ואסרנא גברי לחוד ונשי לחוד. ורמינא פורייאי בין הני להני כי היכי דלא ליתו לידי איסורא. כי חזינא בת ישראל דיהבי נכרים עלה עינייהו, מסרנא נפשאי ומצילנא לה. יומא חד הוות נערה מאורסה גבן דיהבו בה נכרים עינייהו. שקלי דורדייא דחמרא ושדאי לה בשיפולה, ואמרי: *דיסתנא היא. א"ל: מאי טעמא לית לך חוטי (ג) ורמית מסאני אוכמי? א"ל: עיילנא ונפיקנא ביני נכרים כי היכי דלא לידעו דיהודאה אנא. כי הוו גזרי גזירתא, מודענא להו לרבנן, ובעו רחמי ומבטלי לגזירתייהו. ומאי טעמא כי אמינא לך אנא, מאי עובדך? ואמרת לי: זיל האידנא ותא למחר? א"ל: בההיא שעתא גזרי גזירתא, ואמינא: ברישא איזיל ואשמע להו לרבנן דלבעי רחמי עלה דמילתא. אדהכי והכי, אתו הנך תרי *אתי. א"ל: הנך נמי בני עלמא דאתי נינהו. אזל לגבייהו אמר להו: מאי עובדייכו? אמרו ליה: אינשי בדוחי אנן, מבדחינן עציבי. אי נמי, כי חזינן בי תרי דאית להו תיגרא בהדייהו — טרחינן ועבדינן להו שלמא.§ "על אלו מתריעין בכל מקום" כו'.§ ת"ר: על אלו מתריעין בכל מקום: על השדפון, ועל הירקון, ועל ארבה וחסיל, ועל חיה רעה. *ר' עקיבא אומר: על השדפון ועל הירקון — בכל שהוא. אארבה וחסיל — אפילו לא נראה בא"י אלא כנף אחד, מתריעין עליהן.§ "ועל חיה" וכו'.§ ת"ר: חיה רעה שאמרו, בזמן שהיא משולחת — מתריעין עליה, אינה משולחת — אין מתריעין עליה. באי זו היא משולחת ואי זו היא שאינה משולחת? נראית בעיר — משולחת, בשדה — אינה משולחת. ביום — משולחת, בלילה — אינה משולחת. ראתה שני בני אדם ורצתה אחריהן — משולחת, *נחבאת מפניהן — אינה משולחת. טרפה שני בני אדם ואכלה אחד מהן — משולחת, אכלה שניהן — אינה משולחת. עלתה לגג ונטלה תינוק מעריסה — משולחת. הא גופה קשיא. אמרת: נראתה בעיר — משולחת. לא שנא ביום ולא שנא בלילה; והדר אמרת: ביום — משולחת, בלילה — אינה משולחת! לא קשיא. גהכי קאמר: נראתה בעיר ביום — משולחת, בעיר בלילה — אינה משולחת. אי נמי, בשדה — [אפילו] ביום [אינה] משולחת. (בשדה בלילה אינה משולחת.) ראתה שני בני אדם ורצתה אחריהן — משולחת, הא עומדת — אינה משולחת! והדר אמרת: נחבאת מפניהן — אינה משולחת, הא עומדת — משולחת! לא קשיא. דכאן — בשדה הסמוכה לאגם, כאן — בשדה שאינה סמוכה לאגם. טרפה שני בני אדם כאחד ואכלה אחד מהן — משולחת, שניהם — אינה משולחת. והא אמרת: אפילו רצתה! אמר רב פפא: הכי תני ההיא — באגמא.§ גופא, עלתה לגג ונטלה תינוק מעריסה — משולחת. פשיטא! אמר רב פפא: וכבוכי דציידי.§ על החרב וכו'.§ ת"ר: ז"חרב שאמרו, אינו צריך לומר חרב שאינו של שלום, אלא אפילו חרב של שלום. שאין לך חרב של שלום יותר מפרעה נכה, ואעפ"כ נכשל בה המלך יאשיהו, שנאמר

וישלח

טרפה שני בני אדם אכלה אחד מהן משולחת. והוא הדין לא אכלה אחד מהם משולחת, שהרי אם אכלה שניהם – אינה משולחת, דהא דאכלה שניהם לא הוי מטעם משולחת, אלא מטעם דהיא רעיבה. והא דנקט אכלה אחד מהם – רבותא הוי, דאע"ג דאכלה אחד מהן – הוי משולחת:

כמלא

רבינו חננאל

רבא מגנא זכותיה אכולא כרכא: א"ל ר' ברוקה לאליהו הראיני אדם שהוא מבני העוה"ב א"ל זה הלך אחריו שאלו אמר לו שומר האסירים אני ואסרנא גברי לחוד ונשי לחוד ולא רמינא ציצית כי היכי דלא לרגשו דאנא יהודאי. וכי שמענא דגזרה על ישראל מהודענא להון ובעו רחמי ומבטלי. דורדיא שמרים של יין. דשתנא נדה. וזה הנראה בבגדיה ככתם דמיה הן. תוב א"ל אליהו הני נמי בני עלמא דאתי נינהו ושאלינהו ואמרו ליה משמחי לב עציבי אנן כלומר יש לנו חן שפה ודברים המסירים עצב מן הלב וכי חזינן נמי צערא בין גברא לחבריה אי בין גברא לאתתיה טרחינן ועבדינן שלמא בינייהו: על אלו מתריעין בכל מקום על השדפון ועל הירקון כו' וקי"ל כר' עקיבא דברייתא דתני על השדפון ועל [הירקון] (הארבה) בכל שהוא ואוקימנא למתני' לקמן דנראה. באשקלון שדפון כמלא פי תנור תבואה כלומר כשיעור פי תנור נשדפה תבואה בשדה וגזרו תענית ואיבעיא לן האי שדפון דמשערינן ליה בשדה שיעור ככיסוי פי התנור הוא. אי כשיעור דרא רפתא דהדר לפומא דתנורא ועלתה בתיקו. וכן נמי א"ר עקיבא וכן בארבה ובחסיל אפילו לא נראה אלא כנף אחד בא"י מתריעין עליהן מיד: **פיסקא** ועל חיה רעה ת"ר חיה רעה בזמן שהיא משולחת כו' ואוקימנא איזו היא משולחת שנראתה בעיר בלילה אי נמי נראתה בשדה ביום אינה משולחת. ראתה שנים ורצתה אחריהן משולחת אבל ראתה אותם ונחבאת מפניהם אי נמי לא נחבאת אלא עמדה בשדה הסמוכה לאגם אינה משולחת טרפה שנים באגם ואכלה אחד מהם משולחת ואם לא אכלה ולא אחד מהם אינה משולחת והני מילי באגם אבל שלא במקום אגם אע"פ שלא אכלה אלא רצתה אליהם משולחת: **פיסקא** ועל החרב מתריעין. ת"ר אין צ"ל חרב שאינה של שלום שודאי מתריעין אלא אפי' חרב של שלום מתריעין שאין לך חרב של שלום יותר מפרעה נכה ואעפ"כ נכשל בה

כא א מיי' פ"ב מהלכות תעניות הל' י טוש"ע א"ח סי' תקעו סעיף ט:
כב ב ג ד ה ו מיי' שם הלכה ז ח טוש"ע שם סעיף ו ז:
כג ז מיי' שם הלכה ד טוש"ע שם סעיף א:

[גי' הערוך זנדוקא]

[עי' ע"ז כח:]

[נ"ל דשתנא עי' ע"ז כח: וכן גי' הערוך]

ס"א אחי

[גי' רי"ף ורא"ש ת"ר על השדפון וכו']

[גי' רי"ף ורא"ש ברחה]

הגהות מהר"ב רנשבורג

א] רש"י ד"ה הכי קאמר וכו' והאי דקתני נראתה ביום אשדה וכו' נמחק מלת אשדה ונ"ב נ"ל אעיר:

רבינו גרשום

כרכינהו להני ביסתרקי למזבן ואמרי ליה כ"ע לישיימינהו מר. אמר להו הכי והכי שוו דבעי למיהב שווי' אילו בסתרקי להנהו זוגא דרבנן א"ל ההוא זוגא דרבנן חשדתינן דאתינן לוותך לישקלינהו מר לבסתרקי דלא בעינא להו. מסאני אוכמי' כגוים ולא רמו חוטי. ציצית: מפני שהיא מכה מהלכת. שלאחר שנראה כל שהוא אינו מפסיק: שניהם אינה משולחת דאקראי היא מחמת רעבתינתא. א"נ בשדה ביום מסיים הברייתא בשדה הסמוכה לאגם. עמדה אינה משולחת לפי שלבה גסה באגם שהוא מצויה שם. בשדה שאינה סמוכה לאגם עמדה משולחת. באגם גופיה לא הוה משולחת עד דאכלה מהן. כוכי דאגמא דציידי. צריפין דיורין קטנים שדרין בהן ציידים ועל אותו גג עלתה דס"ד לא חשיב גג קמ"ל:

הגהות הב"ח

(א) גמ' חלשא דעתיה דרבא משום דאביי איתחזי ליה בחלמא אמרו ליה מסתייך: (ב) שם האי בר עלמא דאתי הוא קרא ליה ולא אתא לגביה רהט בתריה א"ל: (ג) שם מ"ט לית לך חוטי וסיימת מסאני אוכמי כו' דיהודאה אנא דכי הוו גזרי: (ד) רש"י ד"ה מסאני אוכמי כו' שלא כמנהג היהודים. נ"ב עי' בתוס' פרק בן סורר ומורה דף ע"ד ובפ' הכונס דף נ"ט: (ה) ד"ה זנדוקנא כו' האסורין של מלך הס"ד: (ו) ד"ה עד דעבדי שלמא. דהבאת שלום בין אדם לחבירו היא אחד מן הדברים שאדם אוכל פירותיהן בעוה"ז והקרן קיימת לעוה"ב הס"ד: (ז) ד"ה שדפון כו' אי נמי מעשה שהיה כך היה הס"ד: (ח) ד"ה הכי קאמר כו' והאי דקתני נראתה ביום אעיר קאי דאם נראתה בשדה אפילו ביום אינה: (ט) ד"ה כי תניא כו' רצתה לא באגם גופא דכיון דהיינו: (י) ד"ה אין צריך לומר כו' שמתריעין עליה הס"ד ומה"ד אלא כו':

גליון הש"ס

גמ' איכא בהאי שוקא. עיין בתורת חיים סנהדרין דף פח ע"ב ד"ה שלחו מתם:

עין משפט נר מצוה

כד א מיי' פ"ב מהל' תענית הלכה יא טוש"ע א"ח סימן תקעו סעיף ח:
כה ב מיי' פ"ב מהלכות טומאת מת הל' ד:
כו ג מיי' פ"א מהל' תענית הלכה ט טוש"ע א"ח סימן תקעח סעיף א:
כז ד מיי' פ"ב מהל' תענית הלכה ה טוש"ע א"ח סימן תקעו סעיף ג:
כח ה ו מיי' שם הל' טו טוש"ע שם סעיף יא:

גמרא

"וישלח אליו מלאכים, לאמר: מה לי ולך, מלך יהודה? לא עליך אתה היום, כי אל בית מלחמתי; ואלהים אמר לבהלני: חדל לך מאלהים, אשר עמי, ואל ישחיתך". (א) מאי "אלהים, אשר עמי"? אמר רב יהודה אמר רב: זו ע"ז. אמר: הואיל וקא בטח בע"ז – יכילנא ליה. (ב) "ויורו היורים למלך יאשיהו, ויאמר המלך לעבדיו העבירוני, כי החליתי מאד". מאי "כי החליתי מאד"? *אמר רב יהודה אמר רב: מלמד שעשו כל גופו ככברה. אמר ר' שמואל בר נחמני אמר רבי *(יוחנן) מפני מה נענש יאשיהו – מפני שהיה לו לימלך בירמיהו, ולא נמלך. מאי דרש? "וחרב לא תעבור בארצכם". מאי "חרב"? אילימא: חרב שאינה של שלום, והכתיב "ונתתי שלום בארץ"! אלא, אפילו (ג) של שלום. והוא אינו יודע שאין דורו דומה יפה. כי הוה ניחא נפשיה, חזא ירמיהו שפוותיה דקא מרחשן, אמר: שמא, ח"ו, מילתא דלא מהגנא אמר אגב צעריה. גחין ושמעיה דקא מצדיק עליה דינא אנפשיה, אמר "צדיק הוא ה', כי פיהו מריתי". פתח עליה ההיא שעתא "רוח אפינו, משיח ה'". § "מעשה וירדו זקנים מירושלים לעריהם" כו'. § איבעיא להו: כמלא תנור תבואה, או דלמא כמלא תנור פת? תא שמע: [א]כמלא פי תנור. ועדיין תיבעי להו: ככיסויא דתנורא, או דלמא כי דרא דריפתא דהדר ליה לפומא דתנורא? תיקו. § "ועוד גזרו תענית על שאכלו זאבים" כו'. § אמר עולא משום ר' שמעון בן יהוצדק: *מעשה ובלעו זאבים שני תינוקות והקיאום דרך בית הרעי. ובא מעשה לפני חכמים, [ב]וטיהרו את הבשר, וטמאו את העצמות. § "על אלו מתריעין בשבת" כו'. § תנו רבנן: (ד) *עיר שהקיפוה נכרים או נהר, ואחד ספינה המיטרפת בים, ואחד יחיד שנרדף מפני נכרים או מפני לסטין, *ומפני רוח רעה – [ג]על כולן יחיד רשאי לסגף את עצמו בתענית. רבי יוסי אומר: אין היחיד רשאי לסגף את עצמו בתענית, שמא יצטרך לבריות, ואין הבריות מרחמות עליו. אמר רב יהודה אמר רב: מ"ט דרבי יוסי? דכתיב "ויהי האדם לנפש חיה" – נשמה שנתתי בך, החייה. § "שמעון התימני אומר: אף על הדבר" כו'. § איבעיא להו: לא הודו לו חכמים בשבת, [ד]אבל בחול – הודו לו? או דלמא לא הודו לו כלל? ת"ש, דתניא: מתריעין על הדבר בשבת, ואצ"ל בחול. ר' חנן בן פיטום, תלמידו של ר' עקיבא, משום רבי עקיבא אומר: אין מתריעין על הדבר כל עיקר. § "על כל צרה שלא תבא על הצבור" כו'. § ת"ר על כל צרה שלא תבא על הצבור מתריעין עליה, חוץ מרוב גשמים. מ"ט? אמר ר' (א) יוחנן: [ה]לפי שאין מתפללין על רוב הטובה. ואמר רבי יוחנן: מניין שאין מתפללין על רוב הטובה – שנאמר "הביאו את כל המעשר אל בית האוצר" וגו' *)מאי "עד בלי די"? אמר רמי בר *רב (יוד) עד שיבלו שפתותיכם מלומר "די". אמר (ב) רמי בר רב יוד: [ו]ובגולה מתריעין עליה. תניא נמי הכי: שנה שגשמיה מרובין, אנשי משמר שולחין לאנשי מעמד: תנו עיניכם באחיכם שבגולה שלא יהא בתיהם קבריהם. שאלו את ר' אליעזר: עד היכן גשמים יורדין ויתפללו שלא ירדו? אמר להם: כדי שיעמוד אדם בקרן אפל, וישכשך רגליו במים. והתניא "ידיו"! רגליו כידיו קאמינא. אמר רבה בר בר חנה: לדידי חזיא לי קרן אפל, דקם ההוא טייעא כי רכיב גמלא ונקיט רומחא בידיה מתחזי (ג) איניבא. ת"ר: "ונתתי גשמיכם בעתם". לא שכורה ולא צמאה, אלא בינונית. שכל זמן שהגשמים מרובין – מטשטשין את הארץ, ואינה מוציאה פירות. דבר אחר: בעתם

[דה"ב לה; שם; ויקרא כו; איכה א; שם ד; בראשית ב; מלאכי ג; ויקרא כו]

א) [גי' רי"ף ורא"ש אמר ר' אבא אמר שמואל לפי] ב) [גי' רי"ף ורא"ש ר"י אמר רב וכן גי' רש"א] ג) [נ"ל יניבא פי' תולעת כדאיתא בחולין פה: ר' חייא נפל ליה יניבא ערוך ערך אנבא] ○) ויקרא כו

רש"י

וישלח אליו מלאכים לאמר מה לי ולך מלך יהודה לא עליך אתה היום כי אל בית מלחמתי ואלהים אמר לבהלני חדל לך מאלהים אשר עמי וגו' לא עליך אני הולך היום. יאשיה יצא לקראתו למלחמה, ולא נתנו לעבור בארצו, ושלח לו פרעה נכה מלאכים לאמר כו': מאן אלהים. דקאמר ליה פרעה נכה "חדל לך מאלהים אשר עמי" (ה): מלמד. מדכתיב "ויורו המורים", דמשמע: יריות רבות יורו המורים: *אמר רב יהודה אמר רב מלמד שעשו כל גופו ככברה: הא כתיב ונתתי שלום בארץ. ולמאי הלכתא כתביה רחמנא לאידך קרא "וחרב לא תעבור בארצכם" – אלא אפילו חרב של שלום: שאין דורו דומה יפה. בעיני המקום: איבעיא להו כמלא תנור תבואה. דהיינו שיעור גדול יותר ממלא תנור פת, דשיעור קטן הוא, שאין דרך למלאות כל חלל התנור פת, אלא בדפנות מדביקין אותו: ת"ש. דקתני חדא כי האי לישנא כמלא פי התנור, דהיינו פת. דאילו תבואה לא מלי קיימא על פי התנור: או דלמא כי דרא דריפתא. שורה של לחם הדבוקין זה אצל זה בפי התנור. אי נמי: שמדביקין זה למעלה מזה עד פי התנור: ובלען. כשהן שלימין: וטהרו את הבשר. שאינו מטמא טומאת מת, דנתעכל ונתבטל תוך מעיו. וכגון ששהו ימי עיכול, ופירשא בעלמא הוא: וטימאו את העצמות. דלא מתעכלו: מפני רוח רעה. שנכנס בו רוח שידה, ורץ והולך, ושמא יטבע בנהר או יפול וימות: לסגף. "לענות נפש" מתרגמינן: לסגפא נפש (במדבר ל): יצטרך לבריות. כי אין בו כח להרויח ולהתפרנס מיגיעו: דכתיב לנפש חיה. החייה: (ו) חנן בן פטום אומר אין מתריעין על הדבר. אפי' בחול, דגזירה היא: רמי בר רב יוד. חכם ששמו יוד: ובגולה. בבל, שהיא במצולה: מתריעין על רוב גשמים. שלא ירדו: שלא יהו בתיהם קבריהן. שעמוקה היא, ונטבעים בתיהם במים: אנשי משמר ואנשי מעמד. מפרש בשלשה פרקים לקמן (דף כו.): תנו עיניכם. התבוננו בתפלתכם בתעניות עליהם, שלא ירדו רוב גשמים: קרן אפל. אבן סלע גבוה, וכך שמו: וישכשך רגליו במים. כלומר: לעולם אין מתפללין: והתניא ידו. עד שישכשך ידו (ז): רגלו כידו. וכיון דיכול לשכשך ברגלו, אי שוחה – יכול לשכשך בידו נמי: טייעא. סוחר ישמעאל: ומיתחזי. האי טייעא וגמליה ורומחא לרבה בר בר חנה דהוה על קרן אפל: איניבא. תולעת. ל"א: כי אננא לינדינ"א בלע"ז: לא שכורה. לא שתויה יותר מדאי, שמטשטשין את הארץ: דכתיב

תוספות

כמלא תנור תבואה או דלמא כמלא תנור פת. כמלא תנור תבואה הוי פי' כמלא חלל התנור תבואה, דהיינו יותר ממלא תנור פת. תא שמע: כמלא פי תנור פת, ואם כן איירי בפת: ועדיין תבעי לך כמלא פי תנור כמלא עגול פי תנור. דהיינו שורה של לחם סביבות פי התנור. או דלמא כי דרא דריפתא, ואהדר ליה לפומיה דתנורא שורות שורות של לחם זו למעלה מזו, עד פי התנור: וטהרו את הבשר. פירוש: לפי שנתעכלו במעי הזאבים, וטמאו את העצמות דלא מיעכלו: ועל כולן רשאי לסגף עצמו בתענית. פי': לענות נפש מתרגמינן: לסגפא נפש: ר' יוסי אומר אין היחיד רשאי לסגף. וצ"ל דהני תנאי ל"פ בהא דמיירי הני אמוראי בפרקין דלעיל (דף יא:) אם נקרא חוטא או נקרא קדוש וכו'. דהאמוראי פליגי במאי דמצי לצעורי נפשיה, והני תנאי פליגי בדלא מצי לצעורי נפשיה: לאנשי (ח) משמר. פי': דהיינו אנשי מעמד. דיש בישראל שהיו נחלקים למעמדות להתפלל, שיתפללו על אחיהם שבגולה. פי': לפי שגגותיהם שוים, ונימוקים מחמת גשמים: קרן אפל. פי': שם מקום: אינבא. פירוש לנד"א בלע"ז, מחמת גובהו של הר: *בלילי רביעיות ובלילי שבתות. פי': שלא היו בני אדם הולכין בדרכים באותן לילות, מפני אגרת בת מחלת, כדמפרש במסכת פסחים (דף קיב:): השולה

מסורת הש"ס

[עי' רש"י שבת ע' ד"ה ה"ג וכו'] מו"ק כח: [סנהדרין מח:] [נ"ל יונתן] מנחות סט: לעיל יד. ומפני רוח רעה מתריעין בשבת ועל כולן כל"ל רש"א *) לעיל ט. שבת לב: מכות כג. [לעיל ט. ובשבת ובמכות איתא חמא וכן לא אמר רב ובכרש"י כאן הגירסא רבי יוד הוא שם חכם כל"ל דשמיה שמו זה דלקמן בסמוך דאמר ובגולה מתריעין וכו']

רבינו חננאל

יאשיהו ונהרג דכתיב ויורו המורים למלך יאשיהו ואמר עשאוה ככברה ולמה נענש מפני שלא נמלך בירמיהו כד הוה ניח נפשיה שמעיה ירמיהו דהוה קאמר צדיק הוא ה' כי פיהו מריתי פתח עליה ירמיהו רוח אפינו משיח ה': ועוד גזרו תענית על שבלעו זאבים ב' תינוקות בעבר הירדן והקיאום דרך בית רעי וטיהרו הבשר וטמאו העצמות מ"ט כיון דבשר עביד להתעכולי כמעוכל הוא וכפרש הוא חשוב וכגללים שאין להם טומאה אבל העצמות דאקישי טפי לא עבידי לאיתעכלי ובחזקתייהו קימי לפיכך מטמאי. ומפורש זה כאשר אמרנו במנחות בפ' ר' ישמעאל אומר בבעיא דרמי בר חמא בפיל שבלע כפיפה מצרית והקיאה דרך בית הרעי כו' ואמרינן תפשוט ליה מהא דאמר עולא מעשה שבלעו ב' זאבים ב' תינוקות והקיאום דרך הרעי כו': על אלו מתריעין בשבת על עיר שהקיפוה נכרים כו' ואוקימנא בפרק הראשון דהתרעה זו בעננו. ר' יוסי אומר לעזרה ולא לצעקה: ת"ר עיר שהקיפוה נכרים נהר וספינה המטורפת בים. ויחיד הנרדף לפני נכרים או מפני רוח רעה או מפני לסטים מתריעין עליהן בשבת. ועל כולן יחיד רשאי לסגף עצמו בתענית ר' יוסי אומר אין היחיד רשאי לסגף עצמו בתענית שמא יצטרך לבריות ואין מרחמין עליו. ואמרי' מ"ט דר' יוסי כתיב ויהי האדם לנפש חיה. נשמה שנתתי בך החיה. שמעון התימני אומר מתריעין אף על הדבר. [משום ר"ע אמרו אין מתריעין על הדבר] כל עיקר. על כל צרה הבאה על הצבור מתריעין עליהן חוץ מרוב גשמים. מעשה שאמרו בחוני המעגל התפלל אולי ירדו גשמים. עוד אמר להם צאו וראו אם נמחית אבן הטוען פי' כדאמרן בפרק אלו מציאות ת"ר אבן הטוען היתה בירושלים כל מי שאבדה לו אבדה נפנה לשם וכל המוצא אבדה נפנה לשם המוצא היה עולה על אותה אבן והיה מכריז מי שאבדה לו אבדה יבא ויתן סימניה ויקח. ומי שאבדה לו אבדה היה נותן סימניה ונוטלה וזו ששנינו צאו וראו אם נמחית אבן הטוען. והוו רבותי מפרשין אם נמחית אבן הטוען מלשון וימחה את כל היקום כלומר אם כיסוה המים כאלו נמחית מן העולם עד שראינו בירושלמי פירוש אחרת כשם שאי אפשר לאבן הזה להמחות כך אי אפשר להתפלל על הגשמים שילכו שלח לו שמעון בן שטח צריך אתה להתנדות אלו נגזרה גזרה בימי אליהו שנשבע שלא יבא מטר אלא לפי דברו ונשבעת אתה שעתה מיד יבא מטר לא נמצאת מביא רבים לידי חטא וחלול השם וכל המביא הרבים לידי חלול השם צריך נדוי וכל המעכב את הרבים מלעשות מצוה צריך נידוי. מניין שאין מתפללין על רוב גשמים שנאמר והריקותי לכם ברכה עד בלי די ואמר רב עד שיבלו שפתותיכם מלומר די. ובגולה מתריעין על רוב גשמים. תניא נמי הכי שנה שגשמיה מרובים אנשי משמר שולחין לאנשי מעמד תנו עיניכם לאחיכם שבגולה שלא יפלו עליהן בתיהן. יניבא תולעת דגרסינן בכיסוי הדם נפל ליה לר' חייא יאניבא בכיתניה. פי' גאון גירסא כך הוא כינבא ונבא זהו מן כנים. כגון הא דגרס בפרק (ר' אליעזר אומר תולין) [שמונה שרצים קז:] הטפויין וביצי כנים. ועוד בפרק (ב"ש אומר) [שלשה מינים אסורין בנזיר (לט.)] ת"ש מאנבא חיה דמשתכחא בעיקבא ואנבא מיתה משתכחא ברישא דמזיא ובלשון ישמעאל קורין אותן ציבאן והדעת נוטה על הפירוש שפירשנו אנו. שאלו לר' אליעזר עד מתי יהו הגשמים יורדין ולא יתפללו עליהן שלא ירדו גשמים אמר להן עד כדי שישב אדם (במקום אפל) בקרן אפל וישכשך רגלו כידו במים: ת"ר ונתתי גשמיכם בעתם לא שכורה ולא צמאה אלא בינונית שבזמן שהגשמים רבים מטשטשין את הארץ ואינה עושה פירות.

רבינו גרשום

והכתיב ונתתי שלום ואין צריך לומר חרב שאינה של שלום שאינה עוברת: שאין דורו דומה יפה שאין מעשה ידי הדור יפה שלפיכך הוא בא: כמלא תנור תבואה כמו שהיה קרקע התנור מכוסה מתבואה. כמלא תנור פת היינו מעט. כמלא פי תנור משמע פת שהוא סביב הפה. כי כיסא דתנורא ככיסוי פי התנור דהיינו פת אחד: וטיהרו את הבשר שהרי נתעכל וטמאו את העצמות. שלא נתעכל: לסגף לענות כדמתרגמינן לענות לסגפא: או לא הודו לו כלל. דאין מתריעין על הדבר כלל אפי' בחול בזמן שישנו במקום אחד. מאי טעמא אין מתריעין על רוב גשמים: ובגולה מתריעין על רוב גשמים לפי שהן יושבין באגם ורוב גשמים קשה להם. תנו עיניכם שתתפללו. אופל הר גבוה: לשפשף במים. מילתא דלא אפשר רגלו כידו (למ"ה) רגלו או ידו. אינבא. לנטרא: בלילי רביעיות שאין בני אדם מצויים לחוץ מפני אגרת בת מחלת. אם נמחת נתכסה. צריך אתה להתנדות שמטיח דברים כלפי מעלה:

הגהות הב"ח

(א) גמ' ואל ישחיתך מאן אלהים אמר רב יהודה אמר רב כו' כצ"ל ותיבות אשר עמי נמחק: (ב) שם יכילנא ליה וכתיב ויורו היורים וכו' כי החליתי מאד אמר רב יהודה אמר רב עשו כל גופו וכו' כצ"ל ותיבות מאי כי החליתי מאד ותיבת מלמד נמחק: (ג) שם שלום בארץ אלא אפילו חרב של שלום כו' כי הוה קא ניחא נפשיה: (ד) שם ת"ר אחד עיר שהקיפוה נכרים: (ה) רש"י ד"ה מאן אלהים כו' אשר עמי הס"ד ואח"כ מה"ד אמר יאשיהו הואיל וקא בטח פרעה בע"ז יכילנא ליה והיינו דכתיב ולא הסיב יאשיהו לא הסיבו כלום הס"ד ואח"כ מה"ד כל גופו מדכתיב ויורו כו' המורים הס"ד ואח"כ מה"ד ה"ג אמר רב יהודה אמר רב עשו כל גופו ככברה הס"ד ותיבת מלמד נמחק: (ו) ד"ה דכתיב כו' החייה הס"ד ואח"כ מה"ד רבי חנן בן כו': (ז) ד"ה והתניא וכו' ידו במים הס"ד: (ח) תום' ד"ה לאנשי מעמד פי' היינו אנשי מעמד כו'. נ"ב עי' לקמן דף כ"ז:

בעתם — בלילי רביעיות ובלילי שבתות. שכן מצינו *בימי שמעון בן שטח, *שירדו להם גשמים בלילי רביעיות ובלילי שבתות, עד שנעשו חטים ככליות ושעורים כגרעיני זיתים ועדשים כדינרי זהב. וצררו מהם דוגמא לדורות, להודיע כמה החטא גורם, שנאמר (ירמיהו ה) °"עונותיכם הטו אלה, וחטאתיכם מנעו הטוב מכם". וכן מצינו בימי הורדוס שהיו עוסקין בבנין בהמ"ק והיו יורדין גשמים בלילה. למחר נשבה הרוח, ונתפזרו העבים, וזרחה החמה, ויצאו העם למלאכתן, וידעו שמלאכת שמים בידיהם.§ "מעשה ששלחו לחוני המעגל" וכו'.§

ת"ר: פעם אחת, יצא רוב אדר ולא ירדו גשמים. שלחו לחוני המעגל: התפלל וירדו גשמים. התפלל ולא ירדו גשמים. עג עוגה, ועמד בתוכה, כדרך שעשה חבקוק הנביא, שנאמר (חבקוק ב) °"על משמרתי אעמדה, ואתיצבה על מצור" וגו'. אמר לפניו: רבונו של עולם! בניך שמו פניהם עלי, שאני כבן בית לפניך. נשבע אני בשמך הגדול שאיני זז מכאן עד שתרחם על בניך. התחילו גשמים מנטפין. אמרו לו תלמידיו: רבי, ראינוך, ולא נמות. כמדומין אנו שאין גשמים יורדין אלא להתיר שבועתך. אמר: (א) לא כך שאלתי, אלא גשמי בורות, שיחין, ומערות. ירדו בזעף, עד שכל טפה וטפה כמלא פי חבית. ושיערו חכמים שאין טפה פחותה מלוג. אמרו לו תלמידיו: רבי, ראינוך, ולא נמות. כמדומין אנו שאין גשמים יורדין אלא לאבד העולם. אמר לפניו: לא כך שאלתי, אלא גשמי רצון, ברכה, ונדבה. ירדו כתיקנן, עד שעלו כל העם להר הבית מפני הגשמים. אמרו לו: רבי, כשם שהתפללת שירדו, כך התפלל וילכו להם. אמר להם: כך מקובלני שאין מתפללין על רוב הטובה. אעפ"כ הביאו לי פר הודאה. הביאו לו פר הודאה. סמך שתי ידיו עליו, ואמר לפניו: רבש"ע עמך ישראל שהוצאת ממצרים אינן יכולין (ב) לא ברוב טובה ולא ברוב פורענות. כעסת עליהם — אינן יכולין לעמוד. השפעת עליהם טובה — אינן יכולין לעמוד. יהי רצון מלפניך שיפסקו הגשמים ויהא ריוח בעולם. מיד נשבה הרוח, ונתפזרו העבים, וזרחה החמה, ויצאו העם לשדה והביאו להם כמהין ופטריות. (ברכות יט. לעיל יט:) *שלח לו שמעון בן שטח: אלמלא חוני אתה — גוזרני עליך נידוי. [א] שאילו שנים כשני אליהו שמפתחות גשמים בידו של אליהו, לא נמצא שם שמים מתחלל על ידך? אבל מה אעשה לך, שאתה מתחטא לפני המקום ועושה לך רצונך, כבן שמתחטא על אביו ועושה לו רצונו. ואומר לו: אבא, הוליכני לרחצני בחמין, שטפני בצונן, תן לי אגוזים, שקדים, אפרסקים, ורמונים — ונותן לו. ועליך הכתוב אומר (משלי כג) °"ישמח אביך ואמך ותגל יולדתך". תנו רבנן: מה שלחו בני לשכת הגזית לחוני המעגל? (איוב כב) °"ותגזר אומר, ויקם לך, ועל דרכיך נגה אור". "ותגזר אומר" — אתה גזרת מלמטה, והקדוש ברוך הוא מקיים מאמרך מלמעלה. "ועל דרכיך נגה אור" — דור שהיה אפל הארת בתפלתך. 'כי השפילו, ותאמר: גוה' — דור שהיה שפל, הגבהתו בתפלתך. 'ושח עינים יושיע' — דור ששח בעונו, הושעתו בתפלתך. 'ימלט אי נקי' — דור שלא היה נקי, מלטתו בתפלתך. 'ונמלט בבור כפיך' — מלטתו במעשה ידיך הברורין. אמר ר' יוחנן: כל ימיו של אותו צדיק, היה מצטער על מקרא זה (תהלים קכו) °"שיר המעלות: בשוב ה' את שיבת ציון, היינו כחולמים". אמר: מי איכא דניים שבעין שנין בחלמא? יומא חד הוה אזל באורחא, חזייה להההוא גברא דהוה נטע חרובא. אמר ליה: האי עד כמה שנין טעין? אמר ליה: עד שבעין שנין. אמר ליה: פשיטא לך דחיית שבעין שנין? אמר ליה: (ג) האי [גברא] עלמא בחרובא אשכחתיה. כי היכי דשתלי לי אבהתי, שתלי נמי לבראי. יתיב קא כריך ריפתא, אתא ליה שינתא, נים. אהדרא ליה משוניתא איכסי מעינא, ונים שבעין שנין. כי קם, חזייה לההוא גברא דהוה קא מלקט מינייהו. אמר ליה: את הוא דשתלתיה? אמר ליה: בר בריה אנא. אמר ליה: שמע מינה דניימי שבעין שנין. חזא לחמריה דאתיילידא ליה רמכי רמכי. אזל לביתיה אמר להו: בריה דחוני המעגל מי קיים? אמרו ליה: בריה ליתא, בר בריה איתא. אמר להו: אנא חוני המעגל. לא הימנוהו. אזל לבית המדרש שמעינהו לרבנן דקאמרי: נהירן שמעתתין כבשני חוני המעגל, דכי הוי עייל לבית מדרשא כל קושיא דהוו להו לרבנן הוה מפרק להו. אמר להו: אנא ניהו. לא הימנוהו, ולא עבדי ליה יקרא כדמבעי ליה. חלש דעתיה, בעי רחמי, ומית. אמר רבא, היינו דאמרי אינשי: או חברותא [ב"ב טז:] *או מיתותא. אבא חלקיה בר בריה דחוני המעגל הוה, וכי מצטריך עלמא למיטרא הוו משדרי רבנן לגביה, ובעי רחמי ואתי מיטרא. זימנא חדא איצטריך עלמא למיטרא, שדור רבנן זוגא דרבנן לגביה למבעי רחמי דניתי מיטרא. אזול לביתיה ולא אשכחוהו. אזול בדברא ואשכחוהו דהוה קא רפיק. (ד) יהבו ליה שלמא ולא

(ה) דכתיב בעתם. זהו בלילי רביעיות ובלילי שבתות, דאין טורח לבני אדם, דאינם הולכין לדרכים בלילי רביעיות מפני אגרת בת מחלת, בפסחים (דף קיב:): שכן מצינו. כלומר: ושמא תאמר אין סיפק בגשמים של ד' לילות בשבת — מצינו בימי שמעון בן שטח כו': וצררו. קשרו ואצרו: הורדוס. סתר בנין (תורה אור) דעזרה, ובנה בנין יפה ממנו, בב"ב (דף ד.): עוגה. שורה עגולה, כמו עוגה שהיא עגולה: כדרך שעשה חבקוק. כדמפרש בתרגום של תפלת חבקוק (ו) "על משמרתי אעמדה" — כמין בית האסורים עשה וישב: ראינוך ולא נמות. נראה אותך ולא נמות. בניחותא: השתדל שלא נמות ברעב מפני עצירת גשמים: פר הודאה. להתודות עליו, ועשה (ז) לו סמיכה, והביאו שלמים. חוני בזמן הבית היה: כמהין ופטריות. בולי"ן בלע"ז, שיצאו מלחלוח הגשמים וידעו כי של ברכה היו: אלמלא חוני אתה. ואדם גדול (ח): לנדות. שמנדין על כבוד הרב, שהטיח דברים ואמר: לא כך שאלתי: שאלמלא היו שנים כשני אליהו. גזירת עצירת גשמים, ומפתח של גשמים בידו של אליהו גרסינן: לא נמצא שם שמים מתחלל. בתמיה (ט). שאליהו נשבע "חי ה' אם יהיה השנים האלה טל ומטר כי אם לפי דברי" (מלכים א יז), ואתה נשבע שאין אתה זז עד שירדו גשמים: נמצא שם שמים מתחלל על ידך. דזה או זה בא לידי שבועת שוא: מתחטא. לשון חטא, כלומר (י): הוי הולך וחוטא: לשכת הגזית. סנהדרין: דור שהיה אפל. מרוב צער שלא ירדו גשמים: הושעת בתפלתך. מן המיתה, שהבאת עליהם שובע: של אותו צדיק. חוני המעגל היה מצטער על המקרא הזה: שיר המעלות. לשון עילוי: היינו כחולמים. כחלום נדמה גלות בבל שהיה שבעים שנה: שבעין שני בחלמא. בתמיה: מי איתא דניים שבעין שנין בחלמיה (כ) — ויש אדם ישן שבעים שנה בשינה אחת? עד שבעין שנין. לא טעין פירא בטעינא קמייתא: יתיב. חוני המעגל וקא כריך ריפתא: הכי גרסי': אנא עלמא בחרובא אשכחתיה, כי היכי דשתלי לי אבהתי אנא נמי אישתיל לבראי: אהדרא ליה משוניתא. עלתה סביבותיו אבן סלע: ואיכסי מעינא דאינשי. ולא אשכחוהו התם: רמכי רמכי. וולדי וולדות כאלו השנים דניים. מעוברת זכר היתה, וחזר ובא עליה, והולידו: אמר להו. שאל להון: בנו של חוני המעגל קיים הוא: נהירנא לן הנך שמעתתא. מוגהת לנו שמועה זו כאילו למדנוה בחייו של חוני המעגל, שהיה מפרקה לנו ומגיה לנו יפה יפה: או חברותא או מיתותא. ולא גרסינן הכא כחברי דאיוב, אלא בבבא בתרא (דף טז:), גבי מעשה דאיוב, אם אין חביריו של אדם נוהגין בו כבוד כבתחילה — נוח לו שימות. אי *נמי משום (ל) הנך בריוני לא כתוב בספרינו: רפיק בדברא. עודר בשדה: לא

[עי' תוספות שבת טז: ד"ה לאמר וכו']

רבינו חננאל

בעתם בלילי ד' ובלילי ז'. וכן היו בימי שמעון בן שטח עד שנעשו חטים ככליות שעורים כזיתים ועדשים כדינרין וצררו מהם דוגמא לדורות להודיע כמה החטא גורם שנאמר וחטאתיכם מנעו הטוב מכם. וכן מצינו בבנין בהמ"ק ירדו גשמים בלילות ולמחר נשבה הרוח ונתפזרו העבים וזרחה השמש והשכימו כל אחד ואחד למלאכתן להודיע שמלאכת שמים בידיהם: ת"ר פעם אחת יצא רוב אדר ולא ירדו גשמים שלחו לחוני המעגל להתפלל התפלל ולא ירדו גשמים כו'. מעשה בחוני המעגל דנים ע' שנה כו' ומעשה דאבא חלקיהו בר בריה דחוני המעגל דאצטריך עלמא למיטרא ושדרו רבנן לוותיה ואשכחוה רבנן דקא רפיק בדברא יהבו ליה שלמא כו'

רבינו גרשום

ת"ר פעם אחת וכו' היינו (פ"ע) [פ"א] עצמו דמתניתין: עג עוגה וצר צורה. ראינוך ולא נמות בתימא. בשביל שראינוך לא נמות. שאלו היו שנים כשני אליהו שאין מפתחות של מטר ביד הקב"ה לא נמצא שם שמים מתחלל. שנמצאת מחלל את שבועתו: משוניתא סלע: רמכי ולדות. אי חברא שיהא לו חבר טוב שנוהג לו כבוד:

הגהות הגר"א

א] גמרא גוזרני עליך נדוי. נ"ב ולא עוד אלא:

הגהות הב"ח

(א) גמ' אלא להתיר שבועתך אמר לפניו לא כך שאלתי כו' אלא לאבד העולם אמר להם לא תמותו אמר לפניו: (ב) שם אינן יכולין לעמוד לא: (ג) דחיית שבעין שנין א"ל אנא עלמא בחרובא אשכחתיה: (ד) שם בסה"ע דהוה קא רפיק בדברא יהבו ליה שלמא: (ה) רש"י בריש העמוד צ"ל ד"א בעתם ותיבת דכתיב נמחק. זהו כו' דאינן טורח על בני אדם דאינם: (ו) ד"ה כדרך כו' תפלת חבקוק הס"ד: (ז) ד"ה פר כו' ועשה עליו סמיכה והביאו: (ח) ד"ה אלמלא כו' ואדם גדול אתה הס"ד: (ט) ד"ה לא נמצא כו' בתמיה שאם אליהו היה נשבע חי ה' וכו' שאין אתה זז משם עד שירדו גשמים נמצא כל"ל והד"א: (י) ד"ה מתחטא כו' כלומר הולך וחוטא הס"ד ותיבת הוי נמחק ואח"כ מה"ד בני לשכת כו': (כ) ד"ה שבעין כו' שבעין שנין בחלמיה כלומר ויש אדם ישן: (ל) ד"ה או חברותא כו' אי נמי משום הנהו בריוני לא כתוב:

וְלָא אַסְבַּר לְהוּ אַפֵּיהּ. בְּפַנְיָא, כִּי הֲוָה מְנַקֵּט צִיבֵי, דָּרָא צִיבֵי וּמָרָא בְּחַד כַּתְפָּא, וּגְלִימָא בְּחַד כַּתְפָּא. כּוּלָּהּ אוֹרְחָא לָא סַיֵּים מְסָאנֵי. כִּי מָטֵי לְמַיָּא, סַיֵּים מְסָאנֵיהּ. כִּי מְטָא לְהִיזְמֵי וְהִיגֵי, דַּלְיִנְהוּ לְמָנֵיהּ. (א) כִּי מְטָא לְמָתָא, נָפְקָא דְּבֵיתְהוּ לְאַפֵּיהּ כִּי מִיקַּשְּׁטָא. כִּי מְטָא לְבֵיתֵיהּ, עֲלַת דְּבֵיתְהוּ בְּרֵישָׁא, וַהֲדַר עָיֵיל אִיהוּ, וַהֲדַר עָיְילֵי רַבָּנַן. יָתֵיב וְכָרֵיךְ רִיפְתָּא, וְלָא אֲמַר לְהוּ לְרַבָּנַן, (ב) "תּוּ כְּרוֹכוּ". פְּלַג רִיפְתָּא לִינוּקֵי; לְקַשִּׁישָׁא — חֲדָא, וּלְזוּטְרָא — תְּרֵי. אֲמַר לָהּ לִדְבֵיתְהוּ: יָדַעֲנָא דְּרַבָּנַן (ג) מִשּׁוּם מִיטְרָא קָא אָתוּ. נִיסַּק לְאִיגְּרָא, וְנִיבָּעֵי רַחֲמֵי. אֶפְשָׁר דְּמַרְצֵי הַקָּדוֹשׁ בָּרוּךְ הוּא וְיֵיתֵי מִיטְרָא, וְלָא נַחֲזִיק טִיבוּתָא לְנַפְשִׁין. סַקוּ לְאִיגְּרָא, קָם אִיהוּ בַּחֲדָא זָוִיתָא, וְאִיהִי בַּחֲדָא זָוִיתָא. קַדִּים סְלוּק עֲנָנֵי מֵהָךְ זָוִיתָא דִּדְבֵיתְהוּ. כִּי נָחֵית, אֲמַר לְהוּ: אַמַּאי אָתוּ רַבָּנַן? אֲמַרוּ לֵיהּ: שַׁדְּרִי לָן רַבָּנַן לְגַבֵּי דְּמָר לְמִיבָּעֵי רַחֲמֵי אַמִּיטְרָא. אֲמַר לְהוּ: בָּרוּךְ הַמָּקוֹם שֶׁלֹּא הִצְרִיךְ אֶתְכֶם לְאַבָּא חִלְקִיָּה. אֲמַרוּ לֵיהּ: יָדְעִינַן דְּמִיטְרָא מֵחֲמַת מָר הוּא דַּאֲתָא, אֶלָּא לֵימָא לָן מָר הָנֵי מִילֵּי דְּתַמְיְהָא לָן: מַאי טַעֲמָא כִּי יָהֵיבְנָא לְמָר שְׁלָמָא לָא אַסְבַּר לָן מָר אַפֵּיהּ? אֲמַר לְהוּ: שְׂכִיר יוֹם הֲוַאי, וְאָמִינָא לָא אִיפַּגַּר. וּמַאי טַעֲמָא דָּרָא מָר צִיבֵי אַחַד כַּתְפֵיהּ וּגְלִימָא אַחַד כַּתְפֵיהּ? אֲמַר לְהוּ: טַלִּית שְׁאוּלָה הָיְתָה. לְהָכִי שְׁאִלִי, וּלְהָכִי לָא שְׁאִלִי. מַאי טַעֲמָא כּוּלָּהּ אוֹרְחָא לָא סַיֵּים מָר מְסָאנֵיהּ, וְכִי מָטֵי לְמַיָּא סַיֵּים מְסָאנֵיהּ? אֲמַר לְהוּ: כּוּלָּהּ אוֹרְחָא חָזֵינָא, בְּמַיָּא — לָא קָא חָזֵינָא. מ"ט כִּי מְטָא מָר לְהִיזְמֵי וְהִיגֵי, דַּלְיִנְהוּ לְמָנֵיהּ? אֲמַר לְהוּ: *זֶה מַעֲלֶה אֲרוּכָה, וְזֶה אֵינָהּ מַעֲלָה אֲרוּכָה. מַאי טַעֲמָא כִּי מְטָא מָר לְמָתָא, נָפְקָא דְּבֵיתְהוּ דְּמָר כִּי מִיקַּשְּׁטָא? אֲמַר לְהוּ: כְּדֵי שֶׁלֹּא אֶתֵּן עֵינַי בְּאִשָּׁה אַחֶרֶת. מַאי טַעֲמָא עָיְילָא הִיא בְּרֵישָׁא, וַהֲדַר עָיֵיל מָר אַבַּתְרָהּ, וַהֲדַר עָיְילִינַן אֲנַן? אֲמַר לְהוּ: מִשּׁוּם דְּלָא בְּדַקִיתוּ לִי. מַאי טַעֲמָא כִּי כָּרֵיךְ מָר רִיפְתָּא, לָא אֲמַר לָן "אֵיתוּ כְּרוֹכוּ"? מִשּׁוּם דְּלָא נְפִישָׁא רִיפְתָּא, וְאָמִינָא לָא אַחֲזִיק בְּהוּ בְּרַבָּנַן טִיבוּתָא בְּחִנָּם. מַאי טַעֲמָא יָהֵיב מָר לִינוּקָא קַשִּׁישָׁא חֲדָא רִיפְתָּא וּלְזוּטְרָא תְּרֵי? אֲמַר לְהוּ: הַאי קָאֵי בְּבֵיתָא, וְהַאי יָתֵיב בְּבֵי כְּנִישְׁתָּא. וּמַאי טַעֲמָא קַדִּים סְלוּק עֲנָנֵי מֵהָךְ זָוִיתָא דַּהֲוָות קָיְימָא דְּבֵיתְהוּ דְּמָר לַעֲנָנָא דִּידֵיהּ? מִשּׁוּם דְּאִיתְּתָא שְׁכִיחָא בְּבֵיתָא, וְיָהֲבָא רִיפְתָּא לַעֲנִיֵּי, *וּמְקָרְבָא הֲנָיָיתַהּ, [וַאֲנָא יָהֵיבְנָא] זוּזָא, וְלָא מְקָרְבָא הֲנָיָיתֵיהּ. אִי נַמִּי, (ד) הָנְהוּ בִּרְיוֹנֵי דַּהֲווּ בְּשִׁיבָבוּתָן, [אֲנָא] בְּעַי רַחֲמֵי דְּלֵימוּתוּ, וְהִיא °בָּעְיָא רַחֲמֵי דְּלִיהַדְרוּ בִּתְיוּבְתָּא, [וְאַהְדָרוּ.] חָנָן הַנֶּחְבָּא בַּר בְּרַתֵּיהּ דְּחוֹנִי הַמְעַגֵּל הֲוָה. כִּי (ה) מִצְטְרִיךְ עָלְמָא לְמִיטְרָא, הֲווּ מְשַׁדְּרִי רַבָּנַן יָנוּקֵי דְּבֵי רַב לְגַבֵּיהּ, וְנָקְטִי לֵיהּ בְּשִׁיפּוּלֵי גְלִימֵיהּ, וַאֲמַרוּ לֵיהּ: אַבָּא, אַבָּא, הַב לָן מִיטְרָא! אָמַר לִפְנֵי הקב"ה: רבש"ע עֲשֵׂה בִּשְׁבִיל אֵלּוּ שֶׁאֵין מַכִּירִין בֵּין אַבָּא דְּיָהֵיב מִיטְרָא לְאַבָּא דְּלָא יָהֵיב מִיטְרָא. וְאַמַּאי קָרֵי לֵיהּ חָנָן הַנֶּחְבָּא? מִפְּנֵי שֶׁהָיָה מַחְבִּיא עַצְמוֹ בְּבֵית הַכִּסֵּא. אֲמַר לֵיהּ רַבִּי זְרִיקָא לְרַב סָפְרָא: *תָּא חֲזִי [מָה] בֵּין תַּקִּיפֵי דְּאַרְעָא דְּיִשְׂרָאֵל לַחֲסִידֵי דְּבָבֶל. חֲסִידֵי דְּבָבֶל — רַב הוּנָא וְרַב חִסְדָּא. כִּי הֲוָה מִצְטְרִיךְ עָלְמָא לְמִיטְרָא, אָמְרִי: נִיכְנִיף (ו) הֲדָדֵי וְנִיבָּעֵי רַחֲמֵי. אֶפְשָׁר דְּמִירַצֵּי הַקָּדוֹשׁ בָּרוּךְ הוּא דְּיֵיתֵי מִיטְרָא. תַּקִּיפֵי דְּאַרְעָא דְּיִשְׂרָאֵל — כְּגוֹן ר' יוֹנָה אֲבוּהּ דְּרַבִּי מָנִי, כִּי הֲוָה מִצְטְרִיךְ עָלְמָא לְמִיטְרָא, הֲוָה עָיֵיל לְבֵיתֵיהּ, וַאֲמַר לְהוּ: הָבוּ לִי גְּוָאלְקִי, וְאֵיזִיל וְאַיְיתִי לִי בְּזוּזָא עִיבּוּרָא. כִּי הֲוָה נָפֵיק לְבָרָא, אָזֵיל וְקָאֵי בְּדוּכְתָּא עֲמִיקְתָּא, דִּכְתִיב °"מִמַּעֲמַקִּים קְרָאתִיךָ ה'". וְקָאֵי בְּדוּכְתָּא צְנִיעָא, (ז) וּמְכַסֵּי בְּשַׂקָּא, וּבָעֵי רַחֲמֵי, וְאָתֵי מִיטְרָא. כִּי הֲוָה אָתֵי לְבֵיתֵיהּ, אָמְרִי לֵיהּ: אַיְיתִי (ח) מָר עִיבּוּרָא? אֲמַר לְהוּ: אָמִינָא, הוֹאִיל וַאֲתָא מִיטְרָא הַשְׁתָּא, רְוַח עָלְמָא. וְתוּ, רַבִּי מָנִי בְּרֵיהּ הֲווּ קָא מְצַעֲרִי לֵיהּ דְּבֵי נְשִׂיאָה. אִישְׁתַּטַּח עַל קִבְרָא דַּאֲבוּהּ, אֲמַר לֵיהּ: אַבָּא, אַבָּא, הָנֵי מְצַעֲרוּ לִי. יוֹמָא חַד הֲווּ קָא חָלְפִי הָתָם, אִינְקוּט כַּרְעָא דְּסוּסְוָותַיְיהוּ, עַד דְּקַבִּילוּ עֲלַיְיהוּ דְּלָא קָא מְצַעֲרוּ לֵיהּ. וְתוּ, רַבִּי מָנִי הֲוָה שְׁכִיחַ קַמֵּיהּ דְּרַבִּי יִצְחָק בֶּן אֶלְיָשִׁיב. אֲמַר לֵיהּ: עֲתִירֵי דְּבֵי חָמִי קָא מְצַעֲרוּ לִי. אֲמַר: לִיעֲנוּ, וְאִיעֲנוּ. אֲמַר: קָא דָּחֲקוּ לִי. אֲמַר: לִיעַתְרוּ, וְאִיעַתְרוּ. אֲמַר: לָא מִיקַּבְּלִי עֲלַי אֱינָשֵׁי בֵּיתִי. א"ל: מַה שְּׁמָהּ? חַנָּה. תִּתְיַיפִּי חַנָּה, וְנִתְיַיפַּת. אֲמַר לֵיהּ: קָא מְגַנְדְּרָא עֲלַי. א"ל: אִי הָכִי — תַּחֲזוֹר חַנָּה לְשַׁחֲרוּרִיתָהּ. וְחָזְרָה חַנָּה לְשַׁחֲרוּרִיתָהּ. הָנְהוּ תְּרֵי תַּלְמִידֵי דַּהֲווּ קַמֵּיהּ דְּרַבִּי יִצְחָק בֶּן אֶלְיָשִׁיב אֲמַרוּ לֵיהּ: נִיבְּעֵי מָר רַחֲמֵי עֲלַן דְּנִיחְכַּם טוּבָא! אֲמַר לְהוּ: עִמִּי הָיְתָה, וְשִׁלַּחְתִּיהָ. רַבִּי יוֹסֵי בַּר אָבִין הֲוָה שְׁכִיחַ קַמֵּיהּ דְּר' יוֹסֵי דְּמִן יוֹקֶרֶת. שַׁבְקֵיהּ וַאֲתָא לְקַמֵּיהּ דְּרַב אָשֵׁי.

יוֹמָא

לָא אַסְבַּר לְהוּ אַפֵּיהּ. לֹא הֶחֱזִיר לָהֶם פָּנָיו: בְּפַנְיָא. לִפְנוֹת עֶרֶב, כְּשֶׁהָלַךְ לְבֵיתוֹ: דַּלְיִנְהוּ לְמָנֵיהּ. הִגְבִּיהַּ בְּגָדָיו אַחַר כְּתֵיפָיו, כְּדֵי שֶׁלֹּא יִקָּרְעוּ: כִּי מִיקַּשְּׁטָא. בְּתַכְשִׁיטִין: לְאִיגְּרָא. עֲלִיָּיה: זָוִיתָא. זָוִית: מִזָּוִיתָא דִּדְבֵיתְהוּ. מֵאוֹתוֹ הָרוּחַ שֶׁאִשְׁתּוֹ שָׁם עָלוּ הֶעָבִים תְּחִלָּה, שֶׁהִיא נַעֲנֵית תְּחִילָּה: לָא אִפַּגַּר. לֹא אֶתְבַּטֵּל מִמְּלַאכְתִּי, כְּמוֹ: יוֹמָא דְּמִיפַּגְּרִי רַבָּנָן (שבת דף קכט:): מ"ט דָּרֵית. מַדּוּעַ נָשָׂאתָ הַטַּלִּית עַל כָּתֵף אַחַת, וְלֹא נָתַתָּ בְּכָתֵף תַּחַת הַמַּשּׂאוֹי: לְהָכִי שְׁאִלָּה לִי. לְהִתְעַטֵּף בָּהּ: וּלְהָכִי לָא שְׁאִלָּה לִי. לְהַטִּיל עָלֶיהָ קוֹצִין, לְקָרְעָהּ: בְּמַיָּא לָא חָזֵינַן. מַה דְּאִית בָּהּ, וְשֶׁמָּא יִשְּׁכֶנּוּ דָּג אוֹ נָחָשׁ: דְּלָא בְּדַקִיתוּ לִי. אִם כְּשֵׁרִים אִם פְּרִיצִים, דְּאָמַר מָר (במס' דרך ארץ רבה פ"ה): כָּל אָדָם יְהִי בְּעֵינֶיךָ כְּלִסְטִים: (ט) טוֹבַת הֲנָאָה חִנָּם. דְּאֵינְהוּ לָא הֲווּ קָא אָכְלִי, דְּלֵיכָּא רִיפְתָּא, וְקָא מַחֲזִיקִינַן בְּהוּ טוֹבָה חִנָּם: יָנוּקָא קָאֵי בְּבֵי כְּנִישְׁתָּא. קַמֵּי רַבֵּיהּ, וְלָא אָתֵי כּוּלֵּי יוֹמָא: דְּאִיתְּתָא שְׁכִיחָא בְּבֵיתָא. כָּל יוֹמָא, וְכִי מִילְּטְרִיךְ עַנְיָא מִידִי — חָזְיָא וְיָהֲבָה (י): וְעוֹד דִּמְקָרְבָא הֲנָיָיתַהּ. שֶׁדְּבַר אֲכִילָה הִיא נוֹתֶנֶת לֶעָנִי, וְהוּא בְּלֹא טוֹרַח, מִמַּה שֶּׁהָיְתָה נוֹתֶנֶת מָעוֹת וְיַטְרִיחַ הֶעָנִי עַד שֶׁיִּקְנֶה: אִי נַמִּי. אַהָכִי קָדֵים עֲנָנֵי דִּידָהּ: מִשּׁוּם בִּרְיוֹנֵי. בּוּרִים עַמֵּי הָאָרֶץ: יָנוּקֵי דְּבֵי רַב. לְהַמְרִיךְ לִבּוֹ, וְיִתְכַּוֵּין בִּתְפִלָּתוֹ: בְּשִׁיפּוּלֵי. בְּשׁוּלֵי בְּגָדָיו: אַבָּא אַבָּא. כָּךְ רְגִילִים לִקְרוֹתוֹ, כְּיָתוֹם שֶׁאוֹמֵר אָבִי: שֶׁאֵין מַכִּירִין. בֵּין

(כ) *חוֹנִי לְאַבָּא, כִּסְבוּרִין עָלַי שֶׁאֲנִי אֲבִיהֶן: ה"ג: שֶׁהָיָה מַחְבִּיא. וְלֹא גָּרְסִי' שֶׁהָיָה מַחְבִּיא בְּבֵית הַכִּסֵּא (ל) — כִּי הֲוָה בָּעֵי רַחֲמֵי אַמַּיָּא הָיָה מַחְבִּיא עַצְמוֹ מֵרוֹב עֲנָוָה. וּמַאן דְּגָרֵס בֵּית הַכִּסֵּא — כְּלוֹמַר: מִתְחַבֵּא בִּבְגָדָיו כְּשֶׁהוּא נִכְנָס לְהָסֵךְ אֶת רַגְלָיו, מֵרוֹב צְנִיעוּת: רַב הוּנָא וְרַב חִסְדָּא. חֲסִידֵי דְּבָבֶל מְפַרְסְמִין אֶת הַדָּבָר, וְשֶׁל אֶרֶץ יִשְׂרָאֵל צְנוּעִין וְלֹא מוֹדִיעִין שֶׁבָּא הַמָּטָר בִּשְׁבִילָם: תָּא לִיכְנִיף אַהֲדָדֵי. (מ) אַלְמָא: מִשּׁוּם חַד מִינַּיְיהוּ לָא אָתֵי מִיטְרָא: תַּקִּיפֵי דְּאֶרֶץ יִשְׂרָאֵל רַבִּי יוֹנָה. וְקָא חָזֵינַן (נ) דְּמֵחֲמָתֵיהּ אָתֵי מִיטְרָא: גְּוָאלְקָא. טסק"א בְּלַעַ"ז: וְאַיְיתֵי בְּזוּזָא עִיבּוּרָא. דָּגָן, מִשּׁוּם כַּפְנָא (ס). שֶׁאֲפִילּוּ לִבְנֵי בֵּיתוֹ לֹא הָיָה מוֹדִיעַ: אַיְיתֵי לָן מָר מֵעִיבּוּרָא. דְּבָעֵית לְמִיזְבַּן: רַוְוחָא עָלְמָא. דְּלֶיהֱוֵי שׂוֹבַע, וְאַהָכִי לָא זַבְנֵי בְּיוֹקְרָא דְּהַשְׁתָּא: הֲווּ קָא חָלְפִי. דְּבֵי נְשִׂיאָה: הָתָם. עִלָּוֵיהּ מְעַרְתָּא דְּרַבִּי יוֹנָה: אִינְקוּט. נִדְבְּקוּ בַּקַּרְקַע שֶׁעַל גַּבֵּי מְעָרָה, וְלֹא הָיוּ יְכוֹלִין לָזוּז מִמְּקוֹמָן (ע): עֲתִירֵי דְּבֵי חָמִי. עֲשִׁירִים שֶׁל בֵּית חָמִי: לִיעֲנוּ. יִהְיוּ עֲנִיִּים: קָא דָּחֲקִי לִי. לִיתֵּן לָהֶן פַּרְנָסָה: לָא מִקַּבְּלִי עֲלַי אֱינָשֵׁי בֵּיתִי. אֵין אִשְׁתִּי מְקוּבֶּלֶת עָלַי, שֶׁאֵינָהּ יָפָה: מְגַנְדְּרָא. מִתְגַּדֶּלֶת עָלַי מִתּוֹךְ גַּבְהוּת יוֹפְיָהּ. מְגַנְדְּרָא — מִלְּשׁוֹן "מָקוֹם הִנִּיחוּ לִי אֲבוֹתַי לְהִתְגַּדֵּר בּוֹ" (חולין דף ז.): עִמִּי הָיְתָה וְשִׁלַּחְתִּיהָ. (פ) דָּבָר זֶה הָיָה בְּיָדִי, שֶׁכָּל מַה שֶּׁאֲנִי מְבַקֵּשׁ הָיוּ נוֹתְנִין לִי, וְעַכְשָׁיו אֵין תְּפִלָּתִי מְקוּבֶּלֶת כָּל כָּךְ (צ): דְּמִן דְּיוֹקֶרֶת. מָקוֹם:

יוֹמָא

רבינו חננאל

מעשה בחנין הנחבא בר ברתיה דחוני המעגל (פי' קבלה בידינו הוא שהיו חכמים מתעסקין למנותו פרנס על הצבור ולא קביל והלך ונחבא לפיכך היו קורין אותו חנין הנחבא) דכי הוה אצטריך עלמא מיטרא שדרו רבנן ינוקי דבי רב ומנקטי ליה לגלימיה ואמרי ליה אבא אבא הב לן מיטרא אמר רבון העולמים עשה בשביל אלו שאין יודעין איזה אב נותן מטר. תא חזי חסידי דבבל מיכנפי ובעו רחמי אולי מירצי קב"ה אבל חסידי ארץ ישראל כגון חנין זה וכגון ר' יונה [אבוה דר' מני] כד הוה אצטריך עלמא למיטרא שקיל (אבוה דר' מני) ואלקי. פי' שקים אמר איזיל איזבין חטי אזל קאי בדוכתיה עמיקתא מיכסי שקא בצנעא בעי רחמי ואתי מיטרא כו'. ר' מני בריה הוו מצערי ליה דבי נשיאה אזל אישתטח אמערתא דאבוה הוו מחלפי התם אנקוט כרעיה דסוסוותיהו כו'. הוה שכיח קמיה דר' יצחק בן אלישיב. א"ל עתירי דבי חמוה קא מצערו לי א"ל ליענו ואיענו כו' עד חזרה חנה לשחרוריתה. תרי תלמידי הוו שכיחי קמיה אמרו ליה ליבעי עלן מר רחמי דניחכם. אמר להו עמי היתה אותה תפלה ושלחתיה. ר' יוסי ב"ר אבין

רבינו גרשום

איפגר. איבטל: להכי שאלה להתעטף ולהכי לא שיילה למידר משאוי עלה. מחביא עצמו מתפלל בחשאי: מחביא בבית הכסא צנוע: לחסידי דבבל. שהיו מתפללין בפרהסיא ותקיפי דארעא דישראל מתפללין בצינעא *) וקול התור מכאן שהמלאך דומה לתור דהיינו עגל. קואלקא. בוצלא: דבי חמיו. לא מקבלי אינשי בית עלי דהויא מכוערת טפי: עמי היתה ושלחתיה. כלומר בתחילה היה לבי לכך אבל כבר קבלתי עלי שלא להטריח את קוני:

*) מתיבות וקול התור עד דהיינו עגל לא שייך כאן ומקומו להלן כה ע"ב:

הגהות הב"ח

(א) גמ' להיזמי והיגי דלינהו למניה וסיים מסאניה כי מטא למתא: (ב) שם איתו כרוכו: (ג) שם ידענא דרבנן אמטול מיטרא קא אתו: (ד) שם אי נמי משום הנהו בריוני כו'. נ"ב עי' פרש"י בסוף עמוד א': (ה) שם הוה מצטריך: (ו) שם אמרי ניכניף לגבי הדדי וניבעי רחמי: (ז) שם וקאי בדוכתא צניעא והוה מיכסי בשקא כו': (ח) שם אמרי ליה אייתי לן מר עיבורא: (ט) רש"י ד"ה דלא כו' כלסטים מה"ד טיבותא טובת הנאה כו': (י) ד"ה דאיתתא וד"ה ועוד הד"א: (כ) ד"ה שאין מכירין בין חנן לאביהן שבשמים כסבורין עלי: (ל) ד"ה ה"ג וכו' כלומר מתחבא כו': (מ) ד"ה תא ליכניף אהדדי אלמא בפרהסיא היו עושין ולא בצינעא ל"א נכניף אהדדי אלמא משום חד מינייהו לא הוה אתי: (נ) ד"ה תקיפי כו' וקא חזינן כו' דמחמתיה בלחוד אתי מיטרא: (ס) ד"ה ואייתי כו' דגן משום כפנא כמ"ש התוס' ואח"כ מה"ד בדוכתא עמיקתא בעמק או תחת הסלע כדי שלא יראוהו בני אדם שאפילו לבני ביתו: (ע) ד"ה אינקוט כו' לזוז ממקומן שלא הניחם לילך עד שיקבלו עליהם שלא לנער עוד את רבי מני בנו הס"ד ואח"כ מה"ד הוה שכיח ר' מני לפני ר' יצחק בן אלישיב הס"ד: (פ) ד"ה עמי היתה ושלחתיה. נ"ב ס"א כלומר שקבלתי עלי שלא להתפלל על ענין זה שהתפללתי קודם: (צ) בא"ד מקובלת כל כך ומפני שלא רצה להטריח לפני המקום אמר כן הס"ד:

גליון הש"ס

גמ' בעיא רחמי דליהדרו בתיובתא. עיין ברכות ד' י ע"א:

מסורת הש"ס

[נ"ל קוני הגהת יעב"ץ]

[ב"ק נח:]

[כתובות סז:]

[חולין קכב: מגילה כח]

תהלים קל

כט א ב מיי' פ"א מהל' שבת הל' א סמג לאוין סה:

יומא חד שמעיה. רב אשי לרבי יוסי בר אבין. ל"א: יומא חד שמעיה רבי יוסי בר אבין לרב אשי דקא גריס: אמר שמואל השולה דג מן הים בשבת כיון דיבש בו כסלע, אע"פ שהוא מפרכס לאחר כן, ובעוד שהוא מפרכס השליכו בים — חייב משום נטילת נשמה, שהיא אב מלאכה, דתנן (שבת עג.) השוחטו כו'. אמר ליה רבי יוסי: ובין סנפיריו, דודאי לא חי. ובשאין מחוסר לידה עסקינן, כגון שלדו בתוך הסל והניחו במים לחיות, כדרך שעושין הדייגין: א"ל. רב אשי: ולא סבר לה מר דהאי ובין סנפיריו רבי יוסי בר אבין אמרה? כלומר, מ"ט לא אמרת ליה משמיה? שכל האומר דבר תורה אור בשם אומרו מביא גאולה לעולם: סנפיריו. שפורח בהן: לא תינקטו לי בדעתייכו. אל תחשדוני שלא הבאתי לכם מזונות עד עכשיו: דסגאי. שטרחתי ואיחרתי: דהוה כריא בהוצא. סותר גדר קוצים, כדי להסתכל דרך הנקב: אמר ליה רבי יוסי מאי האי. מה אתה מעיין כאן: אינשו. שכחו: טשו מפניו. היו מתכסים: העבודה. שבועה: ביתום ויתומה. לזווג זה לזו: אכלבא. אוצר של חטים: אוהבך. הקב"ה: אלא כאחד מעניי ישראל. משום דמעשה נסים הוא, ואסור לאדם להנות ממעשה נסים, כדאמר לעיל (דף כ:): ואם עושין לו נס — מנכין לו מזכיותיו: רבי יהודה נשיאה. היה בנו של רבן גמליאל בר רבי: לשמואל הרמתי. שמורידין גשמים בשבילו, דכתיב *"הלא קציר חטים היום". ועכשיו באין כל ישראל והפילו על ר' יהודה בן גמליאל דלוותא, ולייכא דמשגח ביה: שנתקע. תקוע: והא לא קבלינן מאתמול. בהדייהו (ה) גרירין. (גררינן) גרורין ומשוכין אנו אחריהן, וכמי שקבלנו עלינו: זעירא דמן חברייא. צעיר שבחבירים. והאי דקרי ליה הכי — משום דאושעיא אחרינא הוה קשיש: מעיני העדה. זקנים, מאירי עיני העם: בזמן שעיניה יפות אין כל גופה וכו'. כלומר, כל גופה יפה: אין עיניה יפות כו'. הואיל והנהו דבי נשיאה דהוו "עיני העדה" רשעים — דלית טעם אין צריכין לבדוק מה מעשיהם, לכך לא מעגמנו מן שמים: אתו עבדי דריש גלותא וקא מצערו ליה. לאושעיא. אמרו ליה בני מתא. לעבדי דבי נשיאה: מצער לן. מחרף ומגדף אותנו: נחית קמיה. לפני התיבה: נשב. כמו נשב: בקוסטא דחיקא. בכפר דחוק, שיש בו עניות ביותר: פירא דכוורי. מחילות של דגים: כל מאן דפשע. דלא בעי (ו) מיקרי משחדינא ליה כו': ומסדרינא ליה ומפייסינא ליה. מתקנין כסדר:

ה"ג

יומא חד שמעיה דקא גריס: אמר שמואל: *אהשולה דג מן הים בשבת, כיון שיבש בו כסלע, חייב. א"ל: ולימא מר בובין סנפיריו. אמר ליה: ולא סבר לה מר דההיא רבי יוסי בן רבי אבין אמרה? אמר ליה: אנא ניהו. א"ל: ולאו קמיה דר' יוסי דמן יוקרת הוה שכיח מר? א"ל: (*הין.) א"ל: ומ"ט שבקיה מר ואתא הכא? אמר ליה: גברא דעל בריה ועל ברתיה לא חס — עלי דידי היכי חייס? בריה מאי היא? יומא חד הוו אגרי ליה אגירי בדברא. נגה להו, ולא אייתי להו ריפתא. אמרו ליה לבריה: (א) כפינן! הוו יתבי תותי תאינתא. אמר: תאנה, תאנה! הוציאי פירותיך, ויאכלו פועלי אבא. אפיקו, ואכלו. אדהכי והכי אתא אבוה, אמר להו: לא תינקטו בדעתייכו, דהאי דנגהנא אמצוה טרחנא, ועד השתא הוא דסגאי. אמרו ליה: רחמנא לישבעך, כי היכי דאשבען ברך! אמר להו: מהיכא? אמרו: הכי והכי הוה מעשה. אמר לו: בני, אתה הטרחת את קונך להוציא תאנה פירותיה שלא בזמנה — יאסף שלא בזמנו. ברתיה מאי היא? הויא ליה ברתא בעלת יופי. יומא חד חזיא לההוא גברא דהוה כריא בהוצא וקא חזי לה. אמר לה: מאי האי? אמר ליה: רבי, אם ללוקחה לא זכיתי, לראותה לא אזכה? אמר לה: בתי, קא מצערת להו לבריתא. שובי לעפריך, ואל יכשלו ביך בני אדם. (ב) הויא ליה ההוא חמרא, כדהוו אגרי לה כל יומא, לאורתא הוו משדרי לה אגרה אגבה, ואתיא לבי מרה. ואי טפו לה או בצרי לה — לא אתיא. יומא חד אינשו זוגא דסנדלי עלה, ולא אזלה עד דשקלונהו מינה, והדר אזלה. אלעזר איש בירתא כד הוו חזו ליה גבאי צדקה, הוו טשו מיניה, דכל מאי דהוה גביה יהיב להו. יומא חד הוה סליק לשוקא למזבן נדוניא לברתיה. חזיוהו גבאי צדקה טשו מיניה. אזל ורהט בתרייהו. אמר להו: אשבעתיכו, במאי עסקיתו? אמרו ליה: ביתום ויתומה. אמר להן: העבודה! שהן קודמין לבתי. שקל כל דהוה בהדיה ויהב להו. פש ליה חד זוזא, זבן (ג) ליה חיטי, ואסיק שדייה באכלבא. אתאי דביתהו, אמרה לה לברתיה: מאי אייתי אבוך? אמרה לה: כל מה דאייתי, באכלבא שדייה. אתיא למיפתח בבא דאכלבא, חזת אכלבא דמליא חיטי, וקא נפקא בצינורא דדשא, ולא מיפתח בבא מחיטי. אזלא ברתיה לבי מדרשא, אמרה ליה: בא וראה מה עשה לך אוהבך! אמר לה: העבודה! הרי הן הקדש עליך, ואין לך בהן אלא כאחד מעניי ישראל. ר' יהודה נשיאה גזר תעניתא. בעי רחמי ולא אתא מיטרא. אמר: כמה איכא משמואל הרמתי ליהודה בן גמליאל! אוי לו לדור שכן נתקע! אוי לו למי שעלתה בימיו כך! חלש דעתיה, ואתא מיטרא. דבי נשיאה גזר תעניתא, ולא אודעינהו לרבי יוחנן ולריש לקיש. לצפרא אודעינהו. אמר ליה ריש לקיש לרבי יוחנן: הא לא קבילנא עלן מאורתא! אמר ליה: אנן בתרייהו גררינן. דבי נשיאה גזר תעניתא, ולא אתא מיטרא. תנא להו אושעיא זעירא *דמן חברייא: °"והיה, אם מעיני העדה נעשתה לשגגה". משל לכלה שהיא בבית אביה. כל זמן שעיניה יפות, אין כל גופה צריכה בדיקה. עיניה *)טרוטות, כל גופה צריכה בדיקה. אתו עבדיה ורמו ליה סודרא בצואריה, וקא מצערו ליה. אמרו (*ליה) בני מאתיה: שבקיה, דהא נמי מצער לן. כיון דחזינן דכל מיליה לשום שמים, לא אמרי ליה (ד) מידי ושבקינן ליה. אתון נמי שבקוהו. רבי גזר תעניתא, ולא אתא מיטרא. נחית קמיה אילפא, ואמרי לה רבי אילפי, *אמר: "משיב הרוח" — *ונשא זיקא, "מוריד הגשם" — ואתא מיטרא. אמר ליה: מאי עובדך? אמר ליה: דיירנא בקוסטא דחיקא דלית ביה חמרא לקידושא ואבדלתא. טרחנא ואתינא חמרא לקידושא ואבדלתא, ומפיקנא להו ידי חובתייהו. רב איקלע להההוא אתרא. גזר תעניתא, ולא אתא מיטרא. נחית קמיה שליחא דצבורא. אמר: "משיב הרוח", ונשב זיקא. אמר: "מוריד הגשם" — ואתא מיטרא. אמר ליה: מאי עובדך? אמר ליה: מיקרי דרדקי אנא, ומקרינא לבני עניי כבני עתירי. וכל דלא אפשר ליה, לא שקלינא מיניה מידי. ואית לי פירא דכוורי, וכל מאן דפשע, משחדינא ליה מינייהו, ומסדרינן ליה, ומפייסינן ליה, עד דאתי וקרי. רב נחמן גזר תעניתא. בעא רחמי, ולא אתא מיטרא. אמר: שקלוה לנחמן, חבוטו מן גודא לארעא. חלש דעתיה, ואתא מיטרא. רבה גזר תעניתא. בעי רחמי, ולא אתא מיטרא. אמרו ליה: והא רב יהודה כי הוה גזר תעניתא, אתא מיטרא! אמר להו: מאי אעביד? אי משום תנויי — אנן עדיפינן מינייהו, דבשני דרב יהודה *כל תנויי בנזיקין

*) [עי' רש"י שבת לה.]

השולה דג מן הים. שולה כמו מגביה. כיון שיבש בו כסלע(ז), שעדיין הוא מפרכס, ובשעה שמפרכס חזר והשליכו לים — חייב משום נטילת נשמה שהיא אב מלאכה, דתנן (שבת דף עג.): השוחטו והמפשיטו, גבי אבות מלאכות:

הא

רבינו חננאל

שמע לרב אשי דתני אמר שמואל השולה דג מן הים כיון שיבש בו כסלע חייב. א"ל איהו ובין סנפירין. א"ל רב אשי הני דבי ר' יוסי אינון א"ל אנא הוא א"ל רב אשי ואמאי שבקת לר' יוסי דמן יוקרת רבך א"ל גברא דלא חס אבריה ואברתיה עלי דידי חיים. בריה וברתיה מאי היא כו'. כלבא אוצר. ר' יהודה נשיאה גזר תעניתא ולא אתא מיטרא. אמר משמואל הרמתי שאמר הלא קציר חטים היום כו' וכיון שקרא בא המטר הגיע שפלות הדור ליהודה בן גמליאל שהוא פרנס הדור וצועק ואינו נענה. אוי לו לדור הנתקע לכך אוי מי שעלתה בימיו צרה ואין מי שראוי להתפלל ולהשיב חימה. חלש דעתיה [דר"י נשיאה] ואתא מיטרא. דבי נשיאה גזר תענית ולא אודועינהו לר' יוחנן ולר"ש בן לקיש לצפרא אודיעינהו אמר ר"ל לא קבלנו עלינו מאתמול. א"ר יוחנן ניתיב בתעניתא דאנו בתרייהו גרירינן. דבי נשיאה גזור תעניתא בעו רחמי ולא אתא מיטרא. תנא להו והיה אם מעיני העדה נעשתה לשגגה. משל לכלה בזמן שעיניה יפין אין הגוף צריך בדיקה כו' כלומר פרנסי הדור הוא דלא מעלי. רבי אילפי ירד לפני התיבה לפני ר' אמי אמר משיב הרוח אתא זיקא אמר מוריד הגשם אתא מטרא אמרי ליה מאי עובדך אמר להו בקיפא פי' בכפר דחוק דאירנא וטרחנא ומייתינא קדושא ואבדלתא ומפקנא להו ידי חובתיהו. וכן ההוא שליחא דצבורא דנחית קמי דרבא ושאלוהו ואמר מקרי ינוקי אנא ומקרינא לבני עניי כבני עתירי ואית לי פירא (דסורי) דכוורי דמפרנסנא מיניה כל

רבינו גרשום

שיבש בו כסלע חייב משום צידה ומשום נטילת נשמה: אמר ליה ר' יוסי בר ר' אבין ובין סנפיריו א"ל רב יוסף הא בין סנפיריו ר' יוסי היא. כלבא גורן. משמואל הרמתי שהיה מבקש ומביא מטר אפי' בימי קציר חטים דכתיב הלא קציר חטים וגו': בתרייהו דבי נשיאה אזלינן וכי קבילו אינהו הוי כמו קבילו אנו. מעיני העדה עיקר העדה היינו דבי נשיאה. קוסא אתרא. דחיקא. בני אדם דחוקים:

שבת קז: | ל"ל הן | שמואל א יב | [עי' פרש"י ותוס' חולין יב: ד"ה דמן ופרש"י שם לא. ד"ה זעירא] | במדבר טו | [ל"ל להו] | [לקמן כה: ב"מ פה:] | [ל"ל ונשב וכן לקמן בסמוך וכן לקמן כה: וב"מ פה: איתא ונשב אמנם לפני רש"י היה הגירסא ונשא הלכך פי' רש"י הכא ונשא כמו ונשב] | ברכות כ. סנהדרין קו: ע"ש

הגהות הב"ח

(א) גמ' ליה לבריה כפינן הוו יתבי: (ב) שם ואל יכשלו ביך בני אדם וכן הוה הויא ליה ההיא חמרא: (ג) שם חד זוזא זבן ביה חיטי ואסיק כו' מאי אייתי לך אבוך אמרה: (ד) שם לא אמרי ליה ולא מידי ושבקינן ליה: (ה) רש"י ד"ה והא לא כו' בהדייהו כלאמרינן לעיל מאימתי מקבל רב אמר במנחה ושמואל אמר בתפלת המנחה הס"ד: (ו) ד"ה כל מאן דפשע דלא בעי מיקרי הס"ד ואח"כ מה"ד משחדינא ליה כוורי כי היכי דגמיר הס"ד: (ז) תוס' ד"ה השולה כו' שיבש בו כסלע אע"פ שעדיין הוא מפרכס ובשעה:

[ועיין בסנהדרין קו: בפרש"י ועי' בפי' רש"י ברכות כ.]

ל א ב ג מיי' פ"ד מהל' עבודת יוה"כ הלכה א:

ה"ג בנזיקין הוה. למודם לא היה גדול אלא בסדר נזיקין: שכובשת ירק בקדירה. במסכת [*טהרות] היא, בפ' שני (מ"א*) גבי ידות מיירי. דקיי"ל (עוקצין פ"א משנה א): כל ידות האוכלין, אם נגעה טומאה בהן – נטמא גם האוכל הצריך לידות, דיד מכניס ומוציא, כדאמרינן ב"העור והרוטב" (חולין דף קיח.): "מכל האוכל" – לרבות הידות. וקתני התם: אשה שהיא כובשת ירק, דידות שלהן טהורין, דכשהיא עוצרת אותם – הידות משתברות, וא"א ליטול הירקות בידות שלהן, שנשמט ונפסק האוכל מן היד, מחמת כבישה: כובשת. סול"ן בלע"ז, עוצרת שיצא המשקה שלהן ויבשו. דרך אשה בכך כובשת ירק ממים, שישתמרו לזמן מרובה: טהורין. העלין והקלחין: ואמרי לה. כי מטא לאידך בפרק שני (דעוקצין משנה א) "זיתים שכבשן בטרפיהן". כתרגומו: עלה – טרפא (בראשית ח), עלין שלהן דהיינו ידות: טהורין. הידות להביא טומאה לאוכל, דתו לא חזי למהוי בית יד: הוויות דרב ושמואל. עומק גדול, ולא הוה נהירא ליה: תליסר מתיבתא. שלש עשרה ישיבות איכא בהך מתא דגמרי מסכת עוקצין: כי הוה שליף חד מסאנא. משום עינוי: דחזא מידי. חס ושלום בעודדי בישי: פרצי בריפתא. זורקים אותם זה לזה (ג): ניעשייה. יעשנו שיצא לחוץ: אכוספא דתמרי. על כלי מלא תמרים, או פסולת של תמרים: קאימנא אנהר פפא. ההוא יומא דעבד רב יהודה הכי: חלא. חול: דסמידא. סולת, והן עצמן מוכרין אותו: אמר להו מעשה נסים כו'. וכמה דאפשר להתרחק ממעשה נסים – יותר טוב ונכון: דפרזינא. מקום: אקריון. הקרוני, הייתי קורא בחלומי: נגדא. מלקות: איפרא הורמיז. כך שמה איפרא חן יופי שדים היה *לה: מאי היא. מאי עביד להו: אמרה ליה. דכל אימת דבעי מיטרא: זימנא דמיטרא הוא. ואפילו לא בעו – נמי אתי מיטרא: שלחה ליה לרבא. דרחמא ליה לרבא: אבותינו ספרו לנו פועל פעלת בימיהם בימי קדם. שהיית מפליא להם נסים (ד): עד דשפיך מרזבי דציפורי. שקילחו מים מן המרזיבות, עד ששוטפין בחוצות ויורדין ושופכין לדיגלת. לנהר חדקל: אשני מטתך. אל תשכב במטתך הלילה: בסכיני. שרצו שדים להורגו, וחתכו את מטתו. והיינו דאמרי' בשחיטת חולין בפרק "הזרוע" (דף קלג.), וליקריוה לרבא? רבא נזוף הוה. לא מצינו לו נזיפה בכל התלמוד אלא בזה המעשה, כשביקש הגשמים בתמוז שלא לצורך: הכי גרסינן: ר"פ גזר תעניתא חלש לביה טעים מידי בעא רחמי ולא אתא מיטרא: אי שריף מר חדא פינכא דדייסא. מלשון "שורפה חיה" (ע"ז דף כט:) (ה). פינכא – מלא כף, כמו מלחיך פינכי (פסחים דף מט.). דייסא – טריי"ס בלע"ז. ולחוכא קאמר ליה הכי, משום דטעים ברישא והדר בעא רחמי: רבי חנינא בן דוסא. תנא הוא: כל העולם כולו בצער. שמבקשין מים לשדותיהן: בנחת. שאני יושב בביתי, ואיני צריך לגשמים, לפי שאין לי שדות: מאי אהניא ליה צלותיה דכהן גדול. כשהיה מתפלל תפלה קצרה ביום הכפורים, שהיה אומר: אל יכנס לפניך תפלת עוברי דרכים, דר' חנינא מבטל ליה לצלותיה דכהן גדול, שאעפ"כ שמע הקב"ה תפלתו ופסיק מיטרא: שחונה. חמה. כמו "חמותי ראיתי אור" (ישעיהו מד), תירגם יונתן בן עוזיאל: שחינת: אם שחונה תהא גשומה. כשהיא חמה צריכה הארץ לגשמים מאד ותדיר: בת קול יוצאת ואומרת כל העולם כולו. ולא גרסי' מהר חורב: קב חרובים מערב שבת לערב שבת. כל השבת היה ניזון בכך. חסר לחם היה, ומתגלגל היה בחרובין: אקטרתא. דבר שמעלה עשן כקיטור הכבשן (ו):

משום

תורה אור

בנזיקין הוה, ואנן קא מתנינן בשיתא סדרין. וכי הוה מטי רב יהודה בעוקצין: *"האשה שכובשת ירק בקדירה", ואמרי לה: *"זיתים שכבשן בטרפיהן טהורין", אמר: הוויי' דרב ושמואל קא חזינא הכא! ואנן קא מתנינן בעוקצין תליסר מתיבתא. ואילו רב יהודה כי הוה שליף חד מסאנא – אתי מיטרא. ואנן קא צווחינן כולי יומא, וליכא דאשגח בן! אי משום עובדא, אי איכא דחזא מידי – לימא! אבל מה יעשו גדולי הדור, שאין דורן דומה יפה? רב יהודה חזא הנהו בי תרי דהוו קא פרצי בריפתא, אמר: שמע מינה איכא שבעא בעלמא. יהיב עיניה, הוה כפנא. אמרו ליה רבנן לרב כהנא בריה דרב נחוניא שמעיה: (א) מר, דשכיח קמיה, ניעשייה דליפוק בפתחא דסמוך לשוקא. עשייה ונפק לשוקא. חזא כנופיא. אמר להו: מאי האי? אמרו ליה: אכוספא דתמרי קיימי דקא מזדבן. אמר: שמע מינה כפנא בעלמא. אמר ליה לשמעיה: שלוף לי מסאניי. שלף ליה חד מסאנא, ואתא מיטרא. כי מטא למישלף אחרינא, אתא אליהו ואמר ליה: אמר הקדוש ברוך הוא: אי שלפת אחרינא, מחריבנא לעלמא. אמר רב מרי ברה דבת שמואל: אנא הוה קאימנא אגודא דנהר פפא, חזאי למלאכי דאידמו למלחי דקא מייתי חלא ומלונהו לארבי, והוה קמחא דסמידא. (ב) אתו כולי עלמא למיזבן. אמר להו: מהא לא תיזבנון, דמעשה נסים הוא. למחר אתיין ארבי דחיטי *דפרזינא. רבא איקלע להגרוניא. גזר תעניתא, ולא אתא מיטרא. אמר להו: ביתו כולי עלמא בתעניתייכו. למחר אמר להו: מי איכא דחזא חילמא, לימא. אמר להו ר' אלעזר מהגרוניא: לדידי אקריון בחלמי: "שלם טב לרב טב מריבון טב דמטוביה מטיב לעמיה". אמר: שמע מינה *עת רצון היא מבעי רחמי. בעי רחמי, ואתי מיטרא. ההוא גברא דאיחייב נגדא בבי דינא דרבא משום דבעל נכרית נגדיה רבא ומית. אשתמע מילתא בי שבור מלכא, בעא לצעורי לרבא. אמרה ליה איפרא הורמיז, אימיה דשבור מלכא, לבריה: לא ליהוי לך עסק דברים בהדי יהודאי, דכל מאן דבעיין ממרייהו – יהיב להו. אמר לה: מאי היא? בעין רחמי ואתי מיטרא. אמר לה: ההוא משום דזימנא דמיטרא הוא. אלא לבעו רחמי האידנא, בתקופת תמוז, וליתי מיטרא. שלחה ליה לרבא: כוין דעתך, ובעי רחמי דליתי מיטרא. בעי רחמי, ולא אתי מיטרא. אמר לפניו: רבונו של עולם! °"אלהים, באזנינו שמענו, אבותינו ספרו לנו, פועל פעלת בימיהם, בימי קדם", ואנו בעינינו לא ראינו. אתא מיטרא עד דשפוך מרזבי *דצפורי לדיגלת. אתא אבוה איתחזי ליה בחלמיה, ואמר ליה: מי איכא דמיטרח קמי שמיא כולי האי? אמר ליה: שני דוכתיך. שני דוכתיה. למחר אשכחיה דמרשם פורייה בסכיני. רב פפא גזר תעניתא, ולא אתא מיטרא. חלש ליביה, שרף פינכא דדייסא, ובעי רחמי, ולא אתא מיטרא. אמר ליה רב נחמן בר *אושפזתי: אי שריף מר פינכא אחריתי דדייסא, אתי מיטרא. איכסיף וחלש דעתיה, ואתא מיטרא. *)ר' חנינא בן דוסא הוה קא אזיל באורחא אתא מיטרא. אמר לפניו: רבונו של עולם! כל העולם כולו בנחת, וחנינא בצער? פסק מיטרא. כי מטא לביתיה, אמר לפניו: רבונו של עולם! כל העולם כולו בצער, וחנינא בנחת? אתא מיטרא. אמר רב יוסף: מאי אהניא ליה צלותא דכהן גדול לגבי רבי חנינא בן דוסא? דתנן: *[א]היה מתפלל תפלה קצרה בבית החיצון. *מאי מצלי? רבין בר אדא ורבא בר אדא דאמרי תרוייהו משמיה דרב יהודה: יהי רצון מלפניך, ה' אלהינו, שתהא השנה הזו גשומה ושחונה. שחונה מעלייתא היא? אדרבה, גריעותא היא! אלא: [ב]אם שחונה – תהא גשומה וטלולה. ואל יכנס לפניך תפילת עוברי דרכים. רב אחא בריה דרבא מסיים משמיה דרב יהודה: [ג]לא יעדי עביד שולטן מדבית יהודה, ואל יהו עמך ישראל צריכין להתפרנס זה מזה, ולא לעם אחר. אמר רב יהודה אמר רב: *בכל יום ויום בת קול יוצאת ואומרת: כל העולם כולו ניזון בשביל חנינא בני, וחנינא בני דיו בקב חרובים מע"ש לע"ש. הוה רגילא דביתהו למיחמא תנורא כל מעלי דשבתא ושדייא אקטרתא,

משום

*) יומא נג:

רבינו גרשום

האשה שכובשת ירק בקדירה ונגע טומאה לקלח אין מביאין טומאה לירק כיון דנכבשו בטיל ליה בתורת יד: זיתים בטרפיהן טרפא נמי הם ידות: אנא קיימנא בההיא שעתא: דפרונאי מקום: שחונה חמימה:

הגהות הב"ח

(א) גמ' שמעיה דמר דשכיח: (ב) שם ואתו כולי עלמא למיזבן מיניה ואמינא להו מהא כו' להגרוניא גזר תעניתא בעא רחמי ולא אתא כו' בתעניתייכו ביתו למחר אמר להו כו' עם הלכון היא למבעי רחמי בעי רחמי: (ג) רש"י ד"ה פרצי כו' זה לזה כמשחקין זה עם זה הס"ד: (ד) ד"ה אבותינו כו' מפליא להם נסים אבל בעינינו לא ראינו כלומר עכשיו הכלה לנו נפלאותיך הס"ד: (ה) ד"ה אי שריף כו' מל' טורפה חיה אי אכיל מר חדא פינכא מלא קף: (ו) ד"ה אקטרתא כו' כקיטור הכבשן כדי שיהיו סבורין השכנים שאופה בתנור הס"ד:

[וע"ע רש"י נדה כ: ד"ה איפרא ועי' תוס' גיטין יח. ד"ה הורמין וכו' הקשו על פרש"י]

רבינו חננאל

מאן דפשע משחרינא ליה בהו עד דקרי *) בימי רב יהודה מצלו ואתי מטרא. אמרי אי משום תורה כלהו תנויי בנזיקין הוה ואנן מתנינן טובא. וכי הוה רב יהודה מטי להאשה שכובשת ירק בקדירה ואמרי לה זיתים שכבשן בטרפיהן זו היא משנה בעוקצין פ"ב. הוה א' הויה דרב ושמואל קא חזינא הכא כלומר זו קושיא גדולה היא ואנן האידנא מתנינן י"ג מתיבתא בעוקצין אלא מה יעשו פרנסי גדולי הדור שאין דורן יפה: רב יהודה שלף מסניה למבעי רחמי אמטרא אתחזי ליה חלמא אי שלפת אחרינא מחריב עלמא. ההוא דבעל כותית נגדיה רב יהודה ומית אכלו ביה קורצי. הלשינו עליו שהמית אדם. פי' אכלו קראו עליו מלשינות כדמתרגם קרא בגרון אל תחשוך אכלי. בעא שבור מלכא לצעוריה כו'. ר' חנינא בן דוסא הוה אזיל באורחא אתא מיטרא אמר רבון העולמים כל העולם בנחת וחנינא בצער פסק מיטרא כי אתא לביתיה אמר כל העולם בצער וחנינא בנחת אתא מיטרא אמר רב יוסף מאי אהני צלותא דכ"ג דהוה מצלי ביוה"כ יר"מ שאם תהיה השנה הזאת שחונה תהיה גשומה ואל תכנס לפניך תפלת עוברי דרכים שמתפללין לפסוק המטר הנה ר' חנינא התפלל ופסק המטר. ועוד היה מתפלל ואל יעדי עביד שלטון מדבית יהודה. ואל יהו עמך בית ישראל צריכין זה לזה לפרנסה: בכל יום ויום ב"ק יוצאה ואומרת כל העולם כולו ניזון בשביל חנינא בני וחנינא בני דיו קב חרובין מע"ש לע"ש:

*) נראה דצ"ל אמרו ליה רבנן [illegible]

טהרות פ"ב מ"א

עוקצין פ"ב מ"א

גליון הש"ס

גמ' א"ל שני דוכתיך. עיין חולין דף קלג ע"א רש"י ד"ה נזוף:

[גי' הערוך ערך ארזן א' דארזנאי פי' ספינות מלחות ארז]

[ברכות ח. יומא סט. יבמות עב. סנהדרין סד.]

תהלים מד

[נ"ל דמחווז וכ"א בע"י]

[גי' הערוך אושפרתי פי' הוא שם אמו של רב פפא]

יומא נב: ע"ש

שם נג:

ברכות יז: חולין פו.

לא א מיי' פ"ה מהל' נזקי ממון הל' ב סמג עשין סח טוש"ע ח"מ סימן תט סעיף א:

מִשּׁוּם כִּיסוּפָא. שֶׁהָיוּ שְׁכֵינוֹתֶיהָ אוֹפוֹת עִיסָּה לִכְבוֹד שַׁבָּת, וְהִיא אֵינָהּ עוֹשָׂה כְּלוּם: אַגְנָא. עֲרֵיבָה: מְסָא. עֶתֶר שֶׁמּוֹלִיאִין בּוֹ הַלֶּחֶם. מַרְדֶּה – פאלי"א בְּלַעַ"ז. וּמַרְדֶּה וּמָסָא חֲדָא מִילְּתָא הִיא (ד): תָּנָא אַף הִיא לְהָבִיא מַרְדֶּה נִכְנְסָה. פל"א בְּלַעַ"ז, עַל שֵׁם שֶׁרוֹדִין בָּהּ פַּת מִן הַתַּנּוּר*. שֶׁלֹּא הָיְתָה שׁוֹאֶלֶת מִפְּנֵי שֶׁרְגִילָה בְּנִיסִּין: חַזְיָא. דְּבֵיתְהוּ בַּחֲלוֹמָהּ: מִישְׁקָל לָא שָׁקְלִי. בָּתַר דְּיָהֲבִי. כָּל הֵיכָא דְּתָנֵי בֵּי שִׁמְשֵׁי הַיְינוּ עֶרֶב שַׁבָּת, לֹא שָׁמַעְתִּי טַעַם*: בְּמָנָא דְחַלָּא. בִּכְלִי שֶׁיֵּשׁ בּוֹ הַחוֹמֶץ, וְשַׂמְתִּי הַחוֹמֶץ בַּנֵּר וְיִכְבֶּה הַנֵּר: עַד שֶׁנָּטְלוּ מִמֶּנּוּ אוֹר לְהַבְדָּלָה. הִדְלִיק מִמֶּנּוּ נֵר אַחֵר לֵיהָנוֹת בּוֹ, וְנֵר תּוֹרָה אוֹר שֶׁל מַעֲשֵׂה נִסִּים כִּיבָּה, כִּי הֵיכִי דַּעֲבַד רַב יְהוּדָה (לעיל דף כד:) בְּחַלָּה דַּהֲוָה סְמִידָא: קָא מַפְסְדֵי לָן. שָׂדוֹת: דּוּבִּים. וְזוֹאֵבִים בַּשָּׂדוֹת: וְלָא מָטוּ כְּשׁוּרֵי. אֵין הַקּוֹרוֹת מַגִּיעוֹת מִכּוֹתֶל לְכוֹתֶל: אִיכּוּ נִימְטוּ כְּשׁוּרַיִךְ. יַאֲרִיכוּ הַקּוֹרוֹת: סְנִיפִּין הָיוּ. הַקּוֹרוֹת שֶׁל חֻלְיוֹת הָיוּ, בְּמַעֲשֵׂה נֵס נִדְבְּקוּ לָהֶן חֲתִיכוֹת קְטַנּוֹת לְאׇרְכָּן: ר"א בֶּן פְּדָת. אֲמוֹרָא הָיָה, וְהוּא הַנִּקְרָא מָרָא דְאַרְעָא דְּא"י בְּמַסֶּכֶת נִדָּה (דף כ:). בַּעַל הוֹרָאוֹת הָיָה, וְהוּא שִׁימֵּשׁ רַבִּי יוֹחָנָן *)אַחֲרֵי מוֹת רֵישׁ לָקִישׁ, וְהָיָה דָּחוּק וְעָנִי: עֲבַד מִילְּתָא. הִקִּיז דָּם: בְּרָא דְתוּמָא. בֶּן הַשּׁוּם, גֶּלַע שֶׁל שׁוּם: חֲלַשׁ לִיבֵּיהּ. נִתְעַלְּפָה: צוּצִיתָא. נִיצוֹץ: מֵאַפּוּתֵיהּ. מִמִּצְחוֹ: כּוּלֵּי הַאי וְאֶפְשָׁר. בִּתְמִיָּה: כּוּלֵּי הַאי עָבַדְתְּ, וְאַכַּתִּי הַךְ סְפֵיקָא דִּלְמָא לָא מִיתְרַמֵּינָא בְּשַׁעְתָּא דִמְזוֹנֵי? דְּחַיֵּי נְפִישָׁא אוֹ דְּחָיֵינָא. יְמֵי חַיַּי שֶׁחָיִיתִי כְּבָר הֵם רַבִּים מִמַּה שֶּׁאֲנִי עָתִיד לִחְיוֹת: אֲמַר דְּחָיִית. מַה שֶּׁכְּבָר חָיִיתָ מְרוּבִּים מִמַּה שֶּׁאַתָּה עָתִיד לִחְיוֹת. וְהַיְינוּ דְּקָא בָּכֵי כִּי אֲמַר שְׁכִינָה הָכִי. וְהַאי דַּחַיְיךְ – מִשּׁוּם י"ג נַהֲרְוָותָא לִרְחוֹץ בָּהֶן, וּלְטַיֵּיל בָּהֶן מִזֶּה לָזֶה: אִי הָכִי לָא בָּעֵינָא. דְּתִיחָרְבֵיהּ לְעָלְמָא: וְתוּ לָא. וְכִי אֵין אַתָּה נוֹתֵן לִי דְּבָרִים אֲחֵרִים: א"ל וּלְחַבְרָךְ מַאי קָא יָהֵבִינָא. אֲנָא מִגַּבְרָא דְּלֵית לֵיהּ בָּעֵינָא לָא גָּרֵיס בְּסֵפֶר רַבִּי. וּבְסֵפֶר שֶׁלִּי כָּתוּב: בְּאַסְקְטוּלָא אַפּוּתַאי. הַיְינוּ נוּלִיתָא דִּנְפַק מִינֵּיהּ, שֶׁמַּדְבִּיק אֶצְבַּע גְּדוֹלָה עִם הַגּוּדָל, וּמַכֶּה בְּצִפּוֹרֶן הָאֶצְבַּע: אִיגְרוּ בָּךְ גִּירַי. כְּלוֹמַר: הִכֵּיתִי בְּחִיצַּי. לְחֶדְוָוה בְּעָלְמָא אָמַר כֵּן: הָא אֲנָא וְהָא בַּר לִיוַאי. הוּא אִישׁ אֶחָד וַאֲנִי אִישׁ אֶחָד, הוּא עָדִיף מִינַּאי: דִּתְבְרִי. שׁוֹבְרִים: שֶׁיָּבֹא מָטָר בִּשְׁבִילֵנוּ. מְקַבְּלִים אַתֶּם עֲלֵיכֶם, וּמַסְכִּימִין לָדַעַת אֶחָד: כַּמָּה עַזִּין. דְּלָא כַּסִּין מְעוּנָּנָא: לֵוִי אַחְוֵי קִידָּה. נוֹעֵץ שְׁנֵי גוּדָלָיו בָּאָרֶץ, וְשׁוֹחֶה וְנוֹשֵׁק אֶת הָרִצְפָּה: הָא וְהָא גָּרְמָא לֵיהּ. הַחֵטְא גָּרַם לוֹ שֶׁנִּצְלַע בְּקִידָּה:

וְאֵין

מִשּׁוּם כִּיסוּפָא. הֲוָה לָהּ הָהִיא שִׁיבַבְתָּא בִּישְׁתָא, אֲמָרָה: מִכְּדִי יָדַעְנָא דְּלֵית לְהוּ וְלָא מִידֵי. מַאי כּוּלֵּי הַאי? אֲזַלָא וְטַרְפָא אַבָּבָא. אִיכְסְפָא וְעַיְילָא לְאִינְדְּרוֹנָא. אִיתְעֲבִיד לָהּ נִיסָּא דְּחָזְיָא לְתַנּוּרָא מְלֵא לַחְמָא וְאַגְנָא מְלֵא לִישָׁא. אֲמָרָה לָהּ: פְּלָנִיתָא, פְּלָנִיתָא! אַיְיתִי מָסָא, דְּקָא חָרִיךְ לַחְמִיךְ. אֲמָרָה לָהּ: אַף אֲנָא לְהָכִי עָיֵילִי. תָּנָא: אַף הִיא לְהָבִיא מַרְדֶּה נִכְנְסָה, מִפְּנֵי שֶׁמְּלוּמֶּדֶת בְּנִסִּים. (א) אֲמָרָה לֵיהּ דְּבֵיתְהוּ: עַד אֵימַת נֵיזִיל וְנִצְטַעַר כּוּלֵּי הַאי? אֲמַר לָהּ: מַאי נַעֲבֵיד? בְּעֵי רַחֲמֵי דְּנֵיתְבוּ לָךְ מִידֵי.* בְּעָא רַחֲמֵי, יָצְתָה כְּמִין פִּיסַּת יָד וְיָהֲבוּ לֵיהּ חַד כַּרְעָא דְּפָתוֹרָא דְּדַהֲבָא. (*חֲזַאי) בְּחֶלְמָא עֲתִידִי צַדִּיקֵי דְּאָכְלִי אַפָּתוֹרָא דְּדַהֲבָא דְּאִית לֵיהּ תְּלָת כַּרְעֵי, (*וְאַתְּ) אוֹכֶלֶת אַפָּתוֹרָא דִּתְרֵי כַּרְעֵי. (*אֲמָרָה לֵיהּ:) נִיחָא לָךְ דְּמֵיכָל אָכְלִי כּוּלֵּי עָלְמָא אַפָּתוֹרָא דְּמִשְׁלַם, וַאֲנַן אַפָּתוֹרָא דְּמִחֲסַר? אֲמָרָה לֵיהּ: וּמַאי נַעֲבֵיד? בְּעֵי רַחֲמֵי דְּנִשְׁקְלִינְהוּ מִינָּךְ. בְּעֵי רַחֲמֵי וּשְׁקָלוּהוּ. תָּנָא: גָּדוֹל הָיָה נֵס אַחֲרוֹן יוֹתֵר מִן הָרִאשׁוֹן. דִּגְמִירִי דְּמֵיהַב יָהֲבִי, מִישְׁקַל – לָא שָׁקְלִי. חַד בֵּי שִׁמְשֵׁי חַזְיֵיהּ לִבְרַתֵּיהּ דַּהֲוָות עֲצִיבָא. אֲמַר לָהּ: בִּתִּי, *לָמַּאי עֲצִיבַתְּ? אֲמָרָה לֵיהּ: כְּלִי שֶׁל חוֹמֶץ נִתְחַלֵּף לִי בִּכְלִי שֶׁל שֶׁמֶן, וְהִדְלַקְתִּי מִמֶּנּוּ אוֹר לַשַּׁבָּת. אֲמַר לָהּ: בִּתִּי, מַאי אִיכְפַּת לָךְ? מִי שֶׁאָמַר לַשֶּׁמֶן וְיִדְלוֹק הוּא יֹאמַר לַחוֹמֶץ וְיִדְלוֹק. תָּנָא: הָיָה דּוֹלֵק וְהוֹלֵךְ כָּל הַיּוֹם כּוּלּוֹ, עַד שֶׁהֵבִיאוּ מִמֶּנּוּ אוּר לְהַבְדָּלָה. ר' חֲנִינָא בֶּן דּוֹסָא הֲווּ לֵיהּ הָנָךְ עִיזֵּי. אֲמַרוּ לֵיהּ: קָא מַפְסְדָן.(ב) אֲמַר: אִי קָא מַפְסְדָן, נִיכְלִינְהוּ דּוּבֵּי. וְאִי לָא, כָּל חֲדָא וַחֲדָא תֵּיתֵי לְאוּרְתָּא דּוּבָּא בְּקַרְנַיְיהוּ. לְאוּרְתָּא אַיְיתִי כָּל חֲדָא וַחֲדָא דּוּבָּא בְּקַרְנַיְיהוּ. הֲוָה לֵיהּ הַהִיא שִׁיבַבְתָּא דְּקָא בָּנְיָא בֵּיתָא, וְלָא מָטוּ כְּשׁוּרֵי. אָתְיָא לְקַמֵּיהּ, אֲמָרָה לֵיהּ: בָּנִיתִי בֵּיתִי וְלָא קָמָטוּ כְּשׁוּרַאי! אֲמַר לָהּ: מַה שְּׁמֵךְ? אֲמָרָה לֵיהּ: אִיכּוּ. אֲמַר: אִיכּוּ, נִימְטוּ כְּשׁוּרַיִךְ. תָּנָא: הִגִּיעוּ, עַד שֶׁיָּצְאוּ אַמָּה לְכָאן וְאַמָּה לְכָאן. וְיֵשׁ אוֹמְרִין: *סְנִיפִּין עֲשָׂאוּם. תַּנְיָא, פְּלִימוֹ אוֹמֵר: אֲנִי רָאִיתִי אוֹתוֹ הַבַּיִת, וְהָיוּ קוֹרוֹתָיו יוֹצְאוֹת אַמָּה לְכָאן וְאַמָּה לְכָאן. וְאָמְרוּ לִי: בַּיִת זֶה שֶׁקֵּירָה ר' חֲנִינָא בֶּן דּוֹסָא בִּתְפִלָּתוֹ. *וְר' חֲנִינָא בֶּן דּוֹסָא מֵהֵיכָן הֲווּ לֵיהּ עִזִּים?[א] וְהָא עָנִי הָוֵי! וְעוֹד, אָמְרוּ חֲכָמִים: *א"אֵין מְגַדְּלִין בְּהֵמָה דַּקָּה בְּא"י. אָמַר רַב פִּנְחָס: מַעֲשֶׂה וְעָבַר אָדָם אֶחָד עַל פֶּתַח בֵּיתוֹ וְהִנִּיחַ שָׁם תַּרְנְגוֹלִין, וּמְצָאָתָן אִשְׁתּוֹ שֶׁל ר' חֲנִינָא בֶּן דּוֹסָא, וְאָמַר לָהּ: אַל תֹּאכְלִי מִבֵּיצֵיהֶן. וְהִרְבּוּ בֵּיצִים וְתַרְנְגוֹלִין, וְהָיוּ מְצַעֲרִין אוֹתָם. וּמְכָרָן, וְקָנָה בִּדְמֵיהֶן עִזִּים. פַּעַם אַחַת עָבַר אוֹתוֹ אָדָם שֶׁאָבְדוּ מִמֶּנּוּ הַתַּרְנְגוֹלִין, וְאָמַר לַחֲבֵירוֹ: בְּכָאן הִנַּחְתִּי הַתַּרְנְגוֹלִין שֶׁלִּי. שָׁמַע ר' חֲנִינָא, אָמַר לוֹ: יֵשׁ לְךָ בָּהֶן סִימָן? אָמַר לוֹ: הֵן. נָתַן לוֹ סִימָן וְנָטַל אֶת הָעִזִּין. וְהֵן הֵן *עִיזֵּי דְּאַיְיתוּ דּוּבֵּי בְּקַרְנַיְיהוּ. רַבִּי אֶלְעָזָר בֶּן פְּדָת דְּחִיקָא לֵיהּ מִילְּתָא טוּבָא. עֲבַד מִילְּתָא, וְלָא הֲוָה לֵיהּ מִידֵי לְמִטְעַם. שְׁקַל בְּרָא דְתוּמָא וְשַׁדְיֵיהּ בְּפוּמֵּיהּ. חֲלַשׁ לִבֵּיהּ וְנִים. אֲזוּל רַבָּנַן לְשַׁיּוּלֵי בֵּיהּ, חַזְיוּהוּ דְּקָא בָּכֵי וְחָיֵיךְ, וּנְפַק צוּצִיתָא דְנוּרָא מֵאַפּוּתֵיהּ. כִּי אִתְּעַר, אֲמַרוּ לֵיהּ: מ"ט קָבָכֵית וְחָיְיכַתְּ? אֲמַר לְהוּ: דַּהֲוָה יָתֵיב עִמִּי הַקָּב"ה, וַאֲמַרִי לֵיהּ: עַד מָתַי אֶצְטַעַר בְּהַאי עָלְמָא? וַאֲמַר לִי: אֶלְעָזָר בְּנִי, נִיחָא לָךְ דְּאַפְכֵיהּ לְעָלְמָא מֵרֵישָׁא? אֶפְשָׁר דְּמִתְיַלְדַתְּ בְּשַׁעְתָּא דִמְזוֹנֵי. אֲמַרִי לְקַמֵּיהּ: כּוּלֵּי הַאי, "וְאֶפְשָׁר"? אֲמַרִי לֵיהּ: דְּחָיֵי טְפֵי, אוֹ דְּחָיֵינָא? א"ל: דְּחָיִית. אֲמַרִי לְקַמֵּיהּ: א"כ, לָא בָּעֵינָא. אֲמַר לִי: בְּהַאי אַגְרָא דְּאָמְרַתְּ "לָא בָּעֵינָא", יָהֵיבְנָא לָךְ לְעָלְמָא דְּאָתֵי תְּלֵיסְרֵי נַהֲרְוָותָא דְּמִשְׁחָא אֲפַרְסְמוֹן דַּכְיָין *כִּפְרָת וְדִיגְלַת, דְּמִעַנְּגַתְּ בְּהוּ. אֲמַרִי לְקַמֵּיהּ: הַאי, וְתוּ לָא? אֲמַר לִי: וּלְחַבְרָךְ מַאי יָהֵיבְנָא? אֲמַרִי לֵיהּ: וַאֲנָא מִגַּבְרָא דְּלֵית לֵיהּ בָּעֵינָא? מָחְיַין בְּאַסְקוּטְלָא *אַפּוּתַאי, וַאֲמַר לִי: אֶלְעָזָר, בְּרִי, *גִּירַי בָּךְ, גִּירַי! ר' חָמָא בַּר חֲנִינָא גְּזַר תַּעֲנִיתָא, וְלָא אֲתָא מִיטְרָא. אֲמַרוּ לֵיהּ: וְהָא רַבִּי יְהוֹשֻׁעַ בֶּן לֵוִי גְּזַר תַּעֲנִיתָא, וְאָתֵי מִיטְרָא! אֲמַר לְהוּ: הָא אֲנָא, הָא בַּר לִיוָאֵי! אֲמָרוּ לֵיהּ: דְּנֵיתֵי וְנִיכַוֵּין דַּעְתִּין. אֶפְשָׁר דְּתָבְרִי צִיבּוּרָא לִבַּיְיהוּ, דְּאָתֵי מִיטְרָא. בְּעוֹן רַחֲמֵי, וְלָא אָתֵי מִיטְרָא. אֲמַר לְהוּ: נִיחָא לְכוּ שֶׁיָּבֹא מָטָר בִּשְׁבִילֵנוּ? אָמְרוּ לֵיהּ: הֵן. אָמַר: רָקִיעַ, רָקִיעַ, כַּסִּי פָּנֶיךָ! לָא אִיכַּסִּי. אָמַר: כַּמָּה עַזִּין פְּנֵי רָקִיעַ! אִיכַּסִּי, (ג) וַאֲתָא מִיטְרָא. לֵוִי גְּזַר תַּעֲנִיתָא, וְלָא אֲתָא מִיטְרָא, אָמַר לְפָנָיו: רִבּוֹנוֹ שֶׁל עוֹלָם! עָלִיתָ וְיָשַׁבְתָּ בַּמָּרוֹם וְאֵין אַתָּה מְרַחֵם עַל בָּנֶיךָ! אֲתָא מִיטְרָא, וְאִיטְלַע. אָמַר רַבִּי אֶלְעָזָר: *לְעוֹלָם אַל יַטִּיחַ אָדָם דְּבָרִים כְּלַפֵּי מַעְלָה, שֶׁהֲרֵי אָדָם גָּדוֹל הֵטִיחַ דְּבָרִים כְּלַפֵּי מַעְלָה, וְאִיטְלַע! וּמַנּוּ? לֵוִי. וְהָא גָּרְמָא לֵיהּ? וְהָא לֵוִי אַחְוֵי קִידָּה קַמֵּיהּ דְּרַבִּי וְאִיטְלַע! הָא וְהָא גָּרְמָא לֵיהּ. רַבִּי חִיָּיא בַּר לוּלְיָינִי שְׁמָעִינְהוּ לְהָנָךְ עֲנָנֵי דְּקָאָמְרִי: נֵיתוּ וְנִיתְבֵי מַיָּא בְּעַמּוֹן וּמוֹאָב. אָמַר לְפָנָיו: רִבּוֹנוֹ שֶׁל עוֹלָם! כְּשֶׁנָּתַתָּ תּוֹרָה לְעַמְּךָ יִשְׂרָאֵל, חָזַרְתָּ עַל כָּל אוּמּוֹת הָעוֹלָם, וְלֹא קִיבְּלוּהָ. וְעַכְשָׁיו אַתָּה נוֹתֵן לָהֶם מָטָר? שְׁדוֹ הָכָא! שַׁדְיוּהּ אַדּוּכְתַּיְהוּ. *דָּרַשׁ רַבִּי חִיָּיא בַּר לוּלְיָינִי: מַאי דִּכְתִיב °"צַדִּיק כַּתָּמָר יִפְרָח כְּאֶרֶז בַּלְּבָנוֹן יִשְׂגֶּה"? אִם נֶאֱמַר תָּמָר, לָמָּה נֶאֱמַר אֶרֶז, וְאִם נֶאֱמַר אֶרֶז, לָמָּה נֶאֱמַר תָּמָר? אִילּוּ נֶאֱמַר תָּמָר, וְלֹא נֶאֱמַר אֶרֶז, הָיִיתִי אוֹמֵר: מַה תָּמָר

אֵין

הא והא גרמו ליה. פי' הרלב"ד: הא כדעבד, דאחוי הקידה קמי רבי – איטלע. והא דהטיח דברים כלפי מעלה גרמא ליה דאיטלע:

שאני

עי' שבת קיז: רש"י ד"ה מרדה [וכתובות קג. מפרש רש"י טעס ועיין רש"י שבת פו: ד"ה וליטבלו וכו']

[נ"ל חזוא עי' רש"י]

[נ"ל ואיהו אפתורא גירס' ע"י]

*) [כלאיתא ב"מ פד.]

ב"ק עט:

ב"מ קו.

[גי' הערוך אאפותא פי' מצח]

סוכה נג: מגילה כב.

ב"ב פ: תהלים צב

נ"א ממטובתא דגנזיא לצדיקי לעלמא דאתי

[נ"ל אמר לה וכן איתא בע"י]

[נ"ל אמאי וכ"ה בדפו"י]

גליון הש"ס

גמרא בעי רחמי יצתה כמין פיסת יד. עי' שמות רבה פ' נ"ב: **רש"י** ד"ה כל היכא כו' לא שמעתי טעם. עיין ברכות דף כה ע"ב ד"ה מאן שמעת ליה וש"נ: **תוספות** ד"ה והא וכו' פי' הרלב"ד. הובא עוד שמעתא דרלב"ד בתוספות יומא דף יח ע"ב ד"ה לא ע"ש:

[עי' ערוך ערך סנף]

[עי' בע"י וכת"י שם הכל זה איתו מן הגמרא מהיכן על דאיתו דובי בקרנייהו]

הגהות הב"ח

(א) גמ' מפני שמלומדת בנסים היתה אמרה ליה דביתהו כו' אמר לה מאי נעביד אמרה ליה בעי רחמי דניתבו כו' ומאי נעביד אמרה ליה בעי רחמי כו' דגמירי מן שמיא מיהב יהבי: (ב) שם אמרו ליה קא מפסדן עיזך אמר אי כו': (ג) שם כמה עזין פני רקיע ולא איכסי בעיבא ואתא מיטרא: (ד) רש"י ד"ה מרדה כו' ואח"כ מה"ד תנא אף היא להביא מרדה נכנסה שלא היתה כו' על שם שרודין בה פת מן התנור הס"ד ואח"כ מה"ד מפני שרגילה בנסים כו':

הגהות הגר"א

[א] גמ' (והא עני הוי ועוד א"ח א"מ בהמה דקה בא"י) תא"מ:

תיבות כפרת ודיגלת ליתא בע"י

ס"א אגרי [עי' פי' הערוך ערך גר]

רבינו גרשום

מרדה לרדות הפת: סניפין שמלאכים הארוכים בחתכי קורה: מגביהו מן הקרקע שלא יקוץ סמוך לקרקע שיחליף גזעו:

רבינו חננאל

חד [בי] שימשא איחלף לברתיה ורמייא חלא לשרגא דשבתא והוות עציבא א"ל אבוה אל תעצבי מי שאמר לשמן וידלוק [יאמר לחומץ וידלוק] תנא [היה דולק] כל השבת עד דשקיל מיניה אור להבדלה: ר' אלעזר בן פדת הוה דחיק ליה עלמא הקיז ולא הוה ליה מידי למיכל אשכח בר תומא שדא לפומא חלש לביה עיילו רבנן לשיוליה ביה ומצאוהו ישן חזייה דבכא ואחיך ונפיק ציציתא דנורא מאפותיה כשהקיץ משנתו אמרו ליה מאי היא. אמר להו חזאי שכינה בחלמא ואמרי קמיה עד מתי אהא בהאי דוחקא אתאמר לי מקמיה ניחא לך דליחרב עלמא ואבריה מרישא אפשר דמתיילדת בשעתא דמזוני אמרי קמיה כולי האי ואולי לא בעינא [א"ל בהאי] אגרא [דאמרת] לא בעינא יהיבנא לך לעלמא דאתי י"ג מעיינתא דמשכי אפרסמון דכייא כו' עד מחיין באסקוטלא אפותאי כלומר הכהו מלאך באצבעו על מצחו ונראת להן ההכאה כניצוצת של אש כשכופף אדם אצבעו על בוהנו ושומט אותה בכח ומכה את חבירו נקראת המכה ההיא אסקוטלא. אפותא פדחת. לוי גזר תעניתא ולא אתי מיטרא אמר רבון העולמים אינך משגיח בצער בניך ומרחם עליהם כלומר ראוים הם להתרחם ואינך מרחם ולפי

נ"ל אין

לב א מיי' פכ"ג מהל' מכירה הלכה טו סמג עשין מב טוש"ע ח"מ סימן ריו סעיף יד:
לג ב מיי' פ"ד מהלכות תענית הלכה יט טוש"ע א"ח סימן תקעה סעיף יא:

תורה אור

אין גזעו מחליף — אף צדיק ח"ו אין גזעו מחליף, לכך נאמר ארז. אילו נאמר ארז, ולא נאמר תמר, הייתי אומר: מה ארז אין עושה פירות, אף צדיק, ח"ו אין עושה פירות. לכך נאמר תמר ונאמר ארז. וארז גזעו מחליף? והתניא: *[א]הלוקח אילן מחבירו לקוץ — מגביהו מן הקרקע טפח, וקוצץ. בסדן השקמה — שני טפחים. בבתולת השקמה — שלשה טפחים. בקנים ובגפנים — מן הפקק ולמעלה. בדקלים ובארזים — חופר למטה ומשריש, לפי שאין גזעו מחליף. הכא במאי עסקינן? בשאר מיני ארזים, כדרבה בר הונא, דאמר רבה בר הונא: *עשרה מיני ארזים הן, שנאמר °"אתן במדבר ארז, שיטה, והדס" וגו'. (ישעיהו מא) ת"ר: מעשה ברבי אליעזר שגזר שלש עשרה תעניות על הצבור, ולא ירדו גשמים. באחרונה, התחילו הצבור לצאת. אמר להם: תקנתם קברים לעצמכם? געו כל העם בבכיה, וירדו גשמים. שוב מעשה בר' אליעזר שירד לפני התיבה ואמר עשרים וארבע ברכות, ולא נענה. ירד רבי עקיבא אחריו, ואמר: אבינו, מלכנו, אין לנו מלך אלא אתה. אבינו, מלכנו, למענך רחם עלינו, וירדו גשמים. הוו מרנני רבנן. יצתה בת קול ואמרה: לא מפני שזה גדול מזה, אלא שזה מעביר על מדותיו, וזה אינו מעביר על מדותיו. ת"ר: עד מתי יהו הגשמים יורדין, והצבור פוסקין מתעניתם? כמלא ברך המחרישה. דברי רבי מאיר. *וחכמים אומרים: [ב]בחרבה — טפח. בבינונית — טפחיים. בעבודה — שלשה טפחים. תניא: *רבי שמעון בן אלעזר אומר: אין לך טפח מלמעלה, שאין תהום יוצא לקראתו שלשה טפחים. והא תניא: טפחיים! לא קשיא: כאן — בעבודה, כאן — בשאינה עבודה. א"ר אלעזר: כשמנסכין את המים בחג, תהום אומר לחבירו: אבע מימיך, קול שני ריעים אני שומע, שנאמר °"תהום אל תהום קורא לקול צנוריך" וגו'. (תהלים מב) אמר רבה: לדידי חזי לי האי רידיא דמי לעיגלא (תלתא) ופירסא* שפוותיה, וקיימא בין תהומא תתאה לתהומא עילאה. לתהומא עילאה א"ל: חשור מימיך, לתהומא תתאה א"ל: אבע מימיך, שנא' °"הנצנים נראו בארץ" וגו'. (שה"ש ב) § היו מתענין, וירדו גשמים קודם הנץ החמה כו'. § ת"ר: היו מתענין, וירדו להם גשמים קודם הנץ החמה — לא ישלימו. לאחר הנץ החמה — ישלימו, דברי ר' מאיר. ר' יהודה אומר: קודם חצות — לא ישלימו. לאחר חצות — ישלימו. רבי יוסי אומר: קודם ט' שעות — לא ישלימו. לאחר ט' שעות — ישלימו, שכן מצינו באחאב מלך ישראל שהתענה מתשע שעות ולמעלה, שנאמר °"הראית כי נכנע אחאב" וגו'. (מלכים א כא) ר' יהודה נשיאה גזר תעניתא, וירדו להם גשמים לאחר הנץ החמה. סבר לאשלומינהו. א"ל רבי אמי: קודם חצות ואחר חצות שנינו. שמואל הקטן גזר תעניתא, וירדו להם גשמים קודם הנץ החמה. כסבורין העם לומר שבחו של צבור הוא, אמר להם: אמשול לכם [משל.] למה הדבר דומה? לעבד שמבקש פרס מרבו. אמר להם: תנו לו ואל אשמע קולו. שוב שמואל הקטן גזר תעניתא, וירדו להם גשמים לאחר שקיעת החמה. כסבורים העם לומר שבחו של צבור הוא. אמר להם שמואל: לא שבח של צבור הוא. אלא אמשול לכם משל. למה הדבר דומה — לעבד שמבקש פרס מרבו, ואמר להם: המתינו לו עד שיתמקמק ויצטער, ואחר כך תנו לו. ולשמואל הקטן, שבחו של צבור היכי דמי? אמר: *"משיב הרוח" — ונשב זיקא, אמר: "מוריד הגשם" — ואתא מיטרא. § "מעשה וגזרו תענית בלוד" כו'. § ונימא הלל מעיקרא? *)אביי ורבא דאמרי תרוייהו: לפי שאין אומרים הלל אלא

*) גי' רא"ש רב ושמואל

*אין גזעו מחליף. אם נפסק: אף צדיק. אין לו זכר, לצדיק אין גזעו מחליף — אינו בתחיית המתים: צדיק אינו עושה פירות. אין לו שכר לעתיד: בתולת השקמה. נטיעה שלא נקצצה מעולם: סדן. שכבר הזקין, טרונ"ק בלע"ז, שנקצץ וחוזר ומתעבה. והוא מלשון: סדנא בסדניה יתיב (פסחים דף כח.): שני טפחים. שכבר גזעו מחליף: מן הפקק. קשר התחתון: מיני ארזים. שנאמר "אתן במדבר ארז שטה והדס" וגו' — ובליר להו תלת, ובראש השנה (דף כג.) מפרש: הוסיפו עליהם אלונים אלמונים אלמוגים: מעשה ברבי אליעזר בן הורקנוס. י"ג תעניות שהתענו והלכו עד שגמרו י"ג, כדתנן (לעיל דף יב:): עברו אלו ולא נענו כו': התחילו הצבור לצאת. מבית הכנסת: קברים תקנתם. בתמיה. אין לכם, אלא לכו קברו עצמכם מפני הרעב: געו. נעקו, כמו "אם יגעה שור על בלילו" (איוב ו) "הלוך וגעו" (שמואל א ו): ויהיו הצבור פוסקין מתעניתם. דתנן (בראשית): עברו אלו ולא נענו ב"ד גוזרין עוד כו', אבל נענו — שוב אין צריכין להתענות. והני מילי — לצבור, אבל יחיד שהיה מתענה על החולה ונתרפא, או על צרה ועברה — הרי מתענה ומשלים, כדאמרן לעיל (דף י:). כך שמעתי: כמלא ברך המחרישה. אם טשטשו הגשמים בעומק הקרקע כשיעור שורת מענית המחרישה: ברך. הוא הכלי שחורשין בו, ומבריכין אותו סמוך לקרקע כשחורשין בו. כלומר (א), מילא התלם שיראו המים בתלם מחרישתו, שקורין קולטר"א: בחרבה. קרקע יבשה טפח, כיון דחריבה היא, ונכנסו בה הגשמים טפח — ודאי רוב גשמים ירדו: בעבודה. חרושה, כגון שדה ניר הנכנסים בה גשמים הרבה — ג' טפחים, דאפי' בגשמים מועטין נכנסין בה בטפח או בטפחיים: אין לך כל טפח. כשנכנסו הגשמים בעומק הקרקע טפח — תהום עולה ומתגבר ג' טפחים. ואע"ג דסומכא דארעא אלפא גרמידי בפרק "החליל" (סוכה דף נג:) — אפ"ה רטיבותא מהנייא: והתניא. תהום יוצא לקראתו ב' טפחים: הא דקתני טפחיים ותו לא בעבודה. דאע"ג דנכנסו טפח בקרקע — פורתא הוא דנחית, ואהכי לא נפיק בהו לקבליה שלשה טפחים, אלא פורתא, טפחיים: בשאינה עבודה. דכי נכנסו בה טפח טפי הוא דנחית, ונפיק תהום לקיבליה ג' טפחים: אבע. לשון נחל נובע: קול שני ריעים. ניסוך המים וניסוך היין: תהום אל תהום קורא. מים עליונים ומים תחתונים: צנוריך. אותן שני ספלים: האי רידיא. מלאך הממונה על הגשמים כך שמו: דמי לעיגלא. ול"ג תלתא: בין תהומא עילאה לתתאה. בין הרקיע לאוקיינוס, היכא דנשקי ארעא ורקיע: תהומא עלאה. מים העליונים: חשור מימיך. ברקיע: אבע מימיך. למטה בקרקע: הנצנים נראו בארץ. כלומר, כשמנסכין מים בחג שהניסוכין נראו בארץ, שאין באין אלא משנה לחבירתה כנגד זה שאינו יוצא אלא משנה לשנה. ועת הזמיר הגיע — זמירות החג, אז קול התור — מלאך דומה לשור, תרגום שור — תור, שבשעה שמנסכין מים בחג הוא אומר כן. לשון אחר: כמשמעו, הנצנים נראו והזמיר הגיע, בשעה שקול התור נשמע: *קודם הנץ החמה לא ישלימו. דאכתי לא חל עלייהו תענית כי נחתי גשמים: קודם חצות. דחצות זמן אכילה היא. מחצות ואילך חל התענית, כיון שלא סעדו בשעת סעודה: ועשו יו"ט. מתוך שמחה: הלל הגדול. "הודו לאלהי האלהים כי לעולם חסדו". ומפני שנאמר בו "נותן לחם לכל בשר", כדאמרינן בשילהי פסחים (דף קיח.): שכן מצינו כו'. כלומר, שאין לך אדם בעולם שאין תענית חל עליו מט' שעות ואילך, אפי' בני מלכים שדרכן לאכול בט' שעות, שעד ג' שעות הן ישנים במטותיהן ושוהין ששה שעות ואוכלין, וכדאמרינן בפסחים (דף קז:): אפי' אגריפס המלך, שרגיל לאכול בט' שעות ביום — לא יאכל עד שתחשך. שנאמר "הראית כי נכנע אחאב מפני", ואחאב לא חלה תעניתו עליו אלא מט' שעות ואילך, ועד ט' שעות היה יכול לאכול, שלא גמר בדעתו להתענות. אלא שבא אליהו אותו היום שנכנס בכרם נבות היזרעאלי, ואמר ליה "הרצחת וגם ירשת" וגו' (מלכים א כא), "ילקו הכלבים" וגו' (בראשית), וכתיב "ויצום" — שהתענה אותו היום: הכי גרסינן. שמואל הקטן גזר תעניתא וירדו גשמים קודם הנץ החמה: שבח צבור הוא. שעדיין לא קראו ונענו: למה הדבר דומה. וכו': אלא

רבינו חננאל

שהטיח דברים הללו איטלע ונעשה פיסח. והיינו דאמרינן בכל מקום לעולם לא יטיח אדם דברים כלפי למעלה שהרי אדם גדול הטיח דברים כלפי למעלה ואיטלע ומנו לוי. זה שדרשו [צדיק כתמר יפרח] כארז בלבנון ישגה. תמר עושה פירות ואין גזעו מחליף ארז גזעו מחליף ואין עושה פירות לפיכך נמשלו הצדיקים כתמר לעשות פירות וכארז להחליף גזעו ואקשינן וכי ארז גזעו מחליף והתני' הלוקח (לולב) אילן מחבירו לקוץ מגביהו מן הקרקע טפח בדקלין ובארזין חופר ומשרש לפי שאין גזעם מחליף ושנינן האי ארז שנמשלו בו הצדיקים כגון שטה והדס ועץ שמן וכדרבא דאמר עשרה מיני ארזים הן והללו כולן גזעם מחליף זולתי הארז לבדו. והא דר' אליעזר דירד לפני התיבה ואמר כ"ד ברכות ולא ירדו גשמים וירד אחריו ר' עקיבא ואמר אבינו מלכנו אבינו אתה ואין לנו מלך אלא אתה אבינו מלכינו רחם עלינו ומיד ירדו גשמים הוו מרננו (כ"ע) רבנן. יצתה ב"ק ואמרה לא מפני שרבי עקיבא גדול מר' אליעזר אלא ר' עקיבא מעביר על מדותיו ור' אליעזר עומד על מדותיו ואינו מעביר: ת"ר עד היכן גשמים יורדין וצבור פוסקין מתעניתן כמלוא ברך המחרישה. פי' כשיעור חפירת האת בחרישה אם ירדו הגשמים כשיעור הזה ר' יהודה אומר בחרבה טפח בבינונית טפחים בעבודה שלשה טפחים וקיי"ל כר' יהודה: תניא אין לך טפח שיורד מלמעלה שאין תהום עולה לקראתו טפחיים ואם שדה עבודה שלשה טפחים. א"ר אליעזר בשעה שמנסכין מים בחג תהום אומר לחבירו אבע מימך קול ב' רעים אני שומע פי' קול ב' צנורים ניסוך המים וניסוך היין הנמשכין מנקבי הספלים שעל המזבח כדכתיב תהום אל תהום קורא לקול צנוריך. אמר רבה בר בר חנה לדידי חזי לי הא רידיא דמיא לעגלא תלתא פי' בת ג' שנים וקיימי בין תהומא עלאה לתהומא תתאה כדכתיב הנצנים נראו בארץ עת הזמיר הגיע וקול התור נשמע בארצנו פי' קול עגלא הוא קול התור הכתוב כפסוק כי העגל הוא השור: **מתני'** היו מתענין וירדו גשמים כו'. חזינן דסוגיא (דשמעתין) דירושלמי הכי סלקן קודם חצות לא ישלימו (והא תנן) [והא אמרינן] נמי בגמרא ר' אמי ור' יהודה נשיאה בתר דאהדריה ר' אמי דאמר אחר חצות שנינו ולכ"ע אין אומרים הלל הגדול אלא על נפש שבעה ואי איכא אתרא דחיישי משום שכרות גומרין הלל הגדול ואח"כ אוכלין. הלל הגדול *)דכתיב ביה מעלה נשיאים מקצה הארץ ברקים למטר עשה דאמר ר' יוחנן הלל הגדול משעומדין בבית ה' עד סוף הלל הגדול. ואסיקנא שאין שבח לצבור אם ירדו גשמים קודם הנץ החמה אלא אם אמרו משיב הרוח אתא זיקא מוריד הגשם ואתא מטרא זהו שבח צבור והכל פשוטה היא: **ירוש%מי** ר' אחא ור' אבהו בשם ר' יוסי בר' חנינא אסור להתענות עד שש שעות בשבת. א"ר יוסי ב"ר אבין מתניתין היא קודם חצות לא ישלימו עד כדון צפרא הוא לאחר חצות ישלימו כבר עבר רובו של יום בקדושה. ריב"ז כד הוה בעי דייחות מיטרא הוה אמר לספריה אזל קום קמיה היכלא ואמרו בגין דר' בעי מספרא ולית בחיילי' מצטער ומיד מיטרא נחית. רב אדא בר אהבה כד הוה שליף מסאניה הוה מיטרא נחית וכד הוה שליף תרווייהו הוה עלמא טייף מפולת בתים הוה תמן והוה רב מייתי חד מן תלמידוי בביתא עד דהוו מפנין ביתא וכיון דהיה נפיק מביתא מיד הוה נפיל ואית דאמרי (א') רב אדא בר אהבה הות. שלחו לו חכמים מה מעשים טובים יש בידך שלח להם מימי לא קדמני אדם בבית הכנסת ולא הנחתי אדם בבית הכנסת ויצאתי ולא הלכתי ד' אמות בלא תורה ובלא תפילין ולא הזכרתי דברי תורה במקום מטונף ולא הצעתי וישנתי שינת קבע אלא שינת עראי. ולא כיניתי שם לחבירי. ולא צעדתי בין החברים ולא שמחתי בתקלת חבירי. ולא עלה קללת חבירי על מטתי. ולא עברתי בשוק אצל מי שהוא חייב לי. ולא הקפדתי בתוך ביתי לקיים מה שנאמר אתהלך בתם לבבי בקרב ביתי: **) קבלה ביד חכמים כי ביום שנהרג נבות בו ביום הגיע השמועה לאיזבל ובו ביום ירד אחאב אל כרמו לרשתי ובו ביום אמר לו אליהו הרצחת וגם ירשת ומיד נכנע שנאמר ויהי כשמוע אחאב את הדברים האלה ויקרע את בגדיו וישם שק על בשרו ויצום וישכב בשק ויהלך אט. וגמירי דההיא שעתא שעה תשיעית הואי וצם שלש שעות האחרונות מן היום ונחשב צום דכתיב הראית כי נכנע אחאב אבל ראיה ברורה שנתענה אחאב מתשע שעות ולמעלה ליכא:

הדרן עלך סדר תעניות האלו האמור

*) נראה דחסר וצ"ל הלל הגדול צריך להתחיל ממזמור הללו את שם ה' שעומדים בבית ה' וגו' דכתיב ביה מעלה נשיאים וכו'. **) קאי אמ"ש בגמרא שכן מצינו באחאב כו'.

ב"ב פ:

ר"ה כג. סוכה לז. ב"ב פ:

[מד"ה קודם עד ד"ה שכן מלינו שייך לפני המתנה לעיל יט.]

גי' רי"ף ורא"ש ר' יהודה אומר

[תוספתא פ"ב]

הגהות הב"ח

(א) רש"י ד"ה ככך כו' כלומר מלוה התלם שירחו:

[ס"א ופריטא]

[לעיל כה. ב"מ פה:]

רבינו גרשום

ארז עצמו אין גזעו מחליף שאר מיני ארזים גזען מחליף: כמלא ברך המחרישה. גומות של מחרישה: כאן בעבודה שהיא מפורדת דרכה ונכנסת בה מים טפח מהרה (אין שוה) מלמטה טפחים ובשאינה עבודה שהיא קשה עד שנכנס טפח מלמעלה עולה ג' טפחים מלמטה: שני ריעים ניסוך המים וניסוך היין קול צינוריך היינו שני ניסוכין: שנענה מט' שעות ולמעלה שהיה רגיל לאכול בט' שכן דרך אדם לאכול בשש ומלך שישן עד שלש שעות אוכל [בט'] ולפי שלא אכל בט' אלא בעשר חשיב תענית: קודם חצות שנינו דאין משלימין ואין צריך לו להשלים: דשכיחא ביה שכרות ולא מצי מכווני לאחר אכילה:

הדרן עלך סדר תעניות

אֶלָּא בְּנֶפֶשׁ שְׂבֵעָה. מִתּוֹךְ שֶׁכָּתוּב בּוֹ "נוֹתֵן לֶחֶם לְכָל בָּשָׂר" (תהלים קלו) – נָאֶה לְהֵאָמֵר עַל הַשּׂוֹבַע: דַּאֲבִי גּוֹבָר. שֵׁם אָדָם, אוֹ מָקוֹם: דִּשְׁכִיחַ בְּהוּ. יַיִן וְשִׁכְרוּת, וּפָשְׁעִי וְלֹא יֹאמְרוּ הַלֵּל:

הדרן עלך סדר תעניות אלו

בְּשְׁלֹשָׁה פְּרָקִים בְּמוּסָף. מְפָרֵשׁ בַּגְּמָרָא: נְעִילַת שְׁעָרִים. מְפוֹרָשׁ בִּבְרָכוֹת יְרוּשַׁלְמִי בְּפֶרֶק "תְּפִלַּת הַשַּׁחַר" אֵימָתַי נְעִילָה: יֵשׁ אוֹמְרִים נְעִילַת שַׁעֲרֵי מִקְדָּשׁ, וְי"א נְעִילַת שַׁעֲרֵי שָׁמַיִם, שֶׁנּוֹעֲלִים אוֹתָן לְעֵת עֶרֶב בִּגְמַר תְּפִלָּה. וְנוֹהֲגִין הָיוּ לְהִתְפַּלֵּל תְּפִלַּת נְעִילָה בְּכָל תַּעֲנִיתָם, כְּדֶרֶךְ שֶׁמִּתְפַּלְּלִין בְּיוה"כ: אֵלּוּ הֵן מַעֲמָדוֹת. הַמִּתְעַנִּין מִתְפַּלְּלִין בְּעָרֵיהֶם שֶׁיִּתְקַבֵּל בְּרָצוֹן קָרְבַּן אֲחֵיהֶם כִּדְלְקַמָּן: לְפִי שֶׁנֶּאֱמַר צַו אֶת בְּנֵי יִשְׂרָאֵל וגו'. שֶׁהַתָּמִיד בָּא מִן הַשְּׁקָלִים שֶׁל כָּל יִשְׂרָאֵל, וְאִי אֶפְשָׁר שֶׁיְּהוּ כָּל יִשְׂרָאֵל עוֹמְדִין עַל גַּבֵּי קָרְבָּנָם, וּמִינּוּ מַעֲמָדוֹת לִהְיוֹת בִּמְקוֹמָם: נְבִיאִים הָרִאשׁוֹנִים. שְׁמוּאֵל וְדָוִד, בַּגְּמָרָא מְפָרֵשׁ: עַל כָּל מִשְׁמָר. אַרְבָּעָה וְעֶשְׂרִים מִשְׁמָרוֹת שֶׁל כֹּהֲנִים הָיוּ, וּשְׁמוּאֵל וְדָוִד תִּיקְּנוּם. וְעַל כָּל מִשְׁמָר הָיָה מַעֲמָד בִּירוּשָׁלַיִם, שֶׁקְּבוּעִין וְעוֹמְדִין בָּעִיר וְעוֹמְדִין עַל קָרְבַּן אֲחֵיהֶם. וּלְבַד אֵלּוּ הַדָּרִים בִּירוּשָׁלַיִם הָיוּ מַעֲמָדוֹת בְּכָל עִיר, שֶׁיִּשְׂרָאֵל נֶחְלְקוּ לְכ"ד מַעֲמָדוֹת כְּנֶגֶד אַרְבָּעָה וְעֶשְׂרִים מִשְׁמָרוֹת, כִּדְתַנְיָא בִּבְרַיְיתָא שֶׁל מ"ט מִדּוֹת. וְהַיְינוּ דִּתְנַן: הָיָה מַעֲמָד בִּירוּשָׁלַיִם כֹּהֲנִים לְוִיִּם וְיִשְׂרְאֵלִים: כֹּהֲנִים וּלְוִיִּם. שֶׁל מִשְׁמָר הָיוּ עוֹלִים (א) בִּירוּשָׁלַיִם, כֹּהֲנִים לָעֲבוֹדָה וּלְוִיִּם לַשִּׁיר, וּמִכָּל הַמַּעֲמָדוֹת הָיוּ קְבוּעִין בִּירוּשָׁלַיִם לַעֲמוֹד עַל קָרְבַּן אֲחֵיהֶם: וְהַשְּׁאָר הָיוּ מִתְכַּנְּסִין לְעָרֵיהֶם. וּמִתְפַּלְּלִין עַל קָרְבַּן אֲחֵיהֶם שֶׁיִּתְקַבֵּל בְּרָצוֹן, וּמִתְעַנִּין וּמוֹלִיכִין סֵפֶר תּוֹרָה בְּיוֹם תַּעֲנִיתָם: וְקוֹרִין בְּמַעֲשֵׂה בְרֵאשִׁית. וּבַגְּמָרָא מְפָרֵשׁ טַעְמָא: בַּיּוֹם הָרִאשׁוֹן. שֶׁל שָׁבוּעַ: קוֹרִין בְּרֵאשִׁית כו'. פָּרָשָׁה רִאשׁוֹנָה וּפָרָשַׁת יְהִי רָקִיעַ, לְפִי שֶׁאֵין בְּפָרָשַׁת בְּרֵאשִׁית לְבַדָּהּ ט' פְּסוּקִים כְּדֵי קְרִיאַת כֹּהֵן לֵוִי יִשְׂרָאֵל, וְכֵן כּוּלָּן: בַּשִּׁשִּׁי וַתּוֹצֵא הָאָרֶץ עַד וַיְכוּלּוּ. לְפִי שֶׁבְּפָרָשַׁת תּוֹצֵא הָאָרֶץ אֵין בָּהּ אֶלָּא שְׁמוֹנָה פְּסוּקִים, לְפִיכָךְ אוֹמֵר "וַיְכוּלּוּ": פָּרָשָׁה גְּדוֹלָה. שֶׁבַּפָּרָשִׁיּוֹת הַלָּלוּ קוֹרִין אוֹתָהּ בִּשְׁנַיִם, כְּגוֹן פָּרָשָׁה רִאשׁוֹנָה שֶׁל בְּרֵאשִׁית יֵשׁ בָּהּ חֲמִשָּׁה פְּסוּקִים הָיוּ קוֹרִין אוֹתָהּ בִּשְׁנַיִם, כִּדְאָמְרִינַן בַּגְּמָרָא "יְהִי רָקִיעַ" בְּאֶחָד, וּבַיּוֹם הַשֵּׁנִי "יְהִי רָקִיעַ" בְּאֶחָד "יִקָּווּ" – בִּשְׁנַיִם, שֶׁיֵּשׁ בָּהּ ה' פְּסוּקִים. בַּיּוֹם הַשְּׁלִישִׁי "יִקָּווּ" – בְּאֶחָד, שֶׁאֵין בָּהּ אֶלָּא ה' פְּסוּקִים, וְ"יְהִי מְאוֹרוֹת" – בִּשְׁנַיִם, שֶׁיֵּשׁ בָּהּ ו' פְּסוּקִים: וְקוֹרִין אוֹתָהּ עַל פִּיהֶן. כָּל אֶחָד בִּפְנֵי עַצְמוֹ. וּבְעֵי בַּגְּמָרָא מַאי קָאָמַר, מֵעִיקָּרָא קָתָנֵי פָּרָשָׁה קְטַנָּה כו', דְּמַשְׁמַע דְּבְסֵפֶר תּוֹרָה קוֹרִין, וַהֲדַר תָּנָא עַל פִּיהֶם. פָּרָשָׁה בִּנְעִילָה לֵיכָּא: כָּל יוֹם שֶׁיֵּשׁ בּוֹ הַלֵּל אֵין בּוֹ מַעֲמָד (ד) שַׁחֲרִית. אוֹתָן שֶׁהָיוּ בִּירוּשָׁלַיִם לֹא הָיוּ מִתְפַּלְּלִין עַל קָרְבַּן אֲחֵיהֶם שֶׁיֵּשׁ בּוֹ הַלֵּל, לְפִי שֶׁאֵין לָהֶן פְּנַאי לַעֲשׂוֹת מַעֲמָדָם שֶׁקּוֹרִין אֶת הַלֵּל, וּמִפְּנֵי הַהַלֵּל הָיוּ דּוֹחִין אֶת הַמַּעֲמָד: קָרְבַּן מוּסָף. יוֹם שֶׁיֵּשׁ בּוֹ קָרְבַּן מוּסָף בִּירוּשָׁלַיִם אֵין (ה) מַעֲמָד בִּנְעִילָה בִּירוּשָׁלַיִם, וְכָל שֶׁכֵּן בַּמִּנְחָה הַסְּמוּכָה לַמּוּסָף. לְפִי שֶׁהָיוּ טְרוּדִין בַּמּוּסָף, שֶׁיֵּשׁ בּוֹ לְהַקְרִיב בְּהֵמוֹת יוֹתֵר מִתָּמִיד שֶׁהוּא אֶחָד. אֵין לְךָ מוּסָף בְּלֹא שְׁתֵּי בְהֵמוֹת, וְלֹא הָיָה לָהֶם פְּנַאי כְּלָל, שֶׁהַכֹּהֲנִים שֶׁל מַעֲמָד טְרוּדִים בַּמּוּסָף וְיִשְׂרָאֵל שֶׁבָּהֶן הָיוּ טְרוּדִים לַחְטוֹב עֵצִים וְלִשְׁאוֹב מַיִם, וְדוֹחֶה אֲפִי' מַעֲמַד דִּנְעִילָה: קָרְבַּן עֵצִים. בַּגְּמָרָא מְפָרֵשׁ: כְּגוֹן אֶחָד מִט' זְמַנִּים. וְאוֹתוֹ יוֹם שֶׁהָיָה בּוֹ קָרְבַּן עֵצִים, אֲפִילּוּ לֹא הָיָה בּוֹ מוּסָף – הָיָה נִדְחֶה מַעֲמָד שֶׁל מִנְחָה מִפְּנֵי קָרְבַּן עֵצִים, מִפְּנֵי שֶׁקָּרְבַּן עֵצִים קוֹדֵם לַמִּנְחָה וְדוֹחֶה מַעֲמָד הַסָּמוּךְ לוֹ [וְלֹא] שֶׁל נְעִילָה: כָּךְ הָיָה רַבִּי יְהוֹשֻׁעַ דּוֹרֵשׁ קָרְבַּן מוּסָף אֵין (ו) בַּמִּנְחָה. וְטַעְמָא מְפָרֵשׁ בַּגְּמָרָא: זְמַן עֲצֵי כֹהֲנִים וְהָעָם. שֶׁמִּתְנַדְּבִים עֵצִים: תִּשְׁעָה. בְּאֵלּוּ הַט' זְמַנִּים הָיוּ הַכֹּהֲנִים וְהָעָם מִתְנַדְּבִים לְהָבִיא עֵצִים, וְהָיוּ מַקְרִיבִין קָרְבָּן אוֹתוֹ הַיּוֹם. וַאֲפִילּוּ הָיוּ עֵצִים הַרְבֵּה בַּמַּעֲרָכָה – הָיוּ אֵלּוּ מִתְנַדְּבִין, וּמַקְרִיבִין בְּאֵלּוּ תִּשְׁעָה זְמַנִּים: בְּנֵי אָרַח בֶּן יְהוּדָה. שֶׁכְּשֶׁעָלוּ בְּנֵי הַגּוֹלָה הֵם הִתְנַדְּבוּ תְּחִילָּה בְּאֶחָד בְּנִיסָן (ז), וְסִפֵּק לָהֶם עֵצִים עַד כ' בְּתַמּוּז שֶׁהִתְנַדְּבוּ בְּנֵי דָוִד. אָרַח – שְׁמוּאֵל, וּמִשֵּׁבֶט יְהוּדָה הָיָה: בְּנֵי דָוִד. מִמִּשְׁפַּחַת דָּוִד הַמֶּלֶךְ: סְנָאָה בֶּן בִּנְיָמִין זַתּוּא בֶּן יְהוּדָה בְּנֵי גּוֹנְבֵי עֱלִי וּבְנֵי קוֹצְעֵי קְצִיעוֹת מִשְׁפָּחָה אַחַת הֵן. וּבַגְּמָרָא מְפָרֵשׁ אַמַּאי מִיקְּרוּ הָכִי: בְּנֵי עָדִין בְּאֶחָד בְּטֵבֵת שָׁבוּ בְּנֵי פַּרְעוֹשׁ שְׁנִיָּה. וּבַגְּמָרָא מְפָרֵשׁ אַמַּאי קָבְעוּ לָהֶן אֵלּוּ הַזְּמַנִּים: בְּאֶחָד בְּטֵבֵת. שֶׁהָיָה ר"ח [וַחֲנוּכָּה] לֹא הָיָה בּוֹ מַעֲמָד כּוּ':

נִשְׁתַּבְּרוּ

יומא פז: | במדבר כח | שם ח. ע"ש פרש"י | ירושלמי ל"ג | מגילה כב. | [יומא ז:]

תורה אור

[א] אֶלָּא עַל נֶפֶשׁ שְׂבֵעָה וְכֶרֶס מְלֵאָה. אִינִי? וְהָא רַב פָּפָּא אִיקְלַע לְבֵי כְנִישְׁתָּא דַּאֲבִי גּוֹבָר, וְגָזַר תַּעֲנִית, וְיָרְדוּ לָהֶם גְּשָׁמִים עַד חֲצוֹת, וְאָמַר הַלֵּל, וְאַחַר כָּךְ אָכְלוּ וְשָׁתוּ! שָׁאנֵי בְּנֵי מְחוֹזָא, דִּשְׁכִיחִי בְּהוּ שִׁכְרוּת.§

הדרן עלך סדר תעניות אלו

בִּשְׁלֹשָׁה *פְּרָקִים בַּשָּׁנָה כֹּהֲנִים נוֹשְׂאִין אֶת כַּפֵּיהֶן אַרְבַּע פְּעָמִים בַּיּוֹם: בְּשַׁחֲרִית, בְּמוּסָף, בְּמִנְחָה, וּבִנְעִילַת שְׁעָרִים: בְּתַעֲנִיּוֹת, וּבְמַעֲמָדוֹת, וּבְיוֹם הַכִּפּוּרִים. אֵלּוּ הֵן מַעֲמָדוֹת: לְפִי שֶׁנֶּאֱמַר °"צַו אֶת בְּנֵי יִשְׂרָאֵל. אֶת קָרְבָּנִי, לַחְמִי". [ב] וְכִי הֵיאַךְ *קָרְבָּנוֹ שֶׁל אָדָם קָרֵב וְהוּא אֵינוֹ עוֹמֵד עַל גַּבָּיו? הִתְקִינוּ נְבִיאִים הָרִאשׁוֹנִים עֶשְׂרִים וְאַרְבָּעָה מִשְׁמָרוֹת. עַל כָּל מִשְׁמָר וּמִשְׁמָר הָיָה מַעֲמָד בִּירוּשָׁלַיִם שֶׁל כֹּהֲנִים, שֶׁל לְוִיִּם, וְשֶׁל יִשְׂרְאֵלִים. [ג] הִגִּיעַ זְמַן הַמִּשְׁמָר לַעֲלוֹת, כֹּהֲנִים וּלְוִיִּם — עוֹלִים לִירוּשָׁלַיִם, וְיִשְׂרָאֵל שֶׁבְּאוֹתוֹ מִשְׁמָר — מִתְכַּנְּסִין לְעָרֵיהֶן וְקוֹרִאין בְּמַעֲשֵׂה בְרֵאשִׁית. ([ד] וְאַנְשֵׁי הַמַּעֲמָד הָיוּ מִתְעַנִּין אַרְבָּעָה יָמִים בַּשָּׁבוּעַ — מִיּוֹם ב' וְעַד יוֹם חֲמִישִׁי. וְלֹא הָיוּ מִתְעַנִּין עֶרֶב שַׁבָּת, מִפְּנֵי כְבוֹד הַשַּׁבָּת, וְלֹא בְּאֶחָד בַּשַּׁבָּת, כְּדֵי שֶׁלֹּא יֵצְאוּ מִמְּנוּחָה וָעוֹנֶג לִיגִיעָה וְתַעֲנִית וְיָמוּתוּ.) *[ה] בַּיּוֹם הָרִאשׁוֹן — "בְּרֵאשִׁית" וִ"יהִי רָקִיעַ". בַּשֵּׁנִי — "יְהִי רָקִיעַ" וְ"יִקָּווּ הַמַּיִם". בַּשְּׁלִישִׁי — "יִקָּווּ הַמַּיִם" וִ"יהִי מְאוֹרוֹת". בָּרְבִיעִי — "יְהִי מְאוֹרוֹת" וְ"יִשְׁרְצוּ הַמַּיִם". בַּחֲמִישִׁי — "יִשְׁרְצוּ הַמַּיִם" וְ"תוֹצֵא הָאָרֶץ". בַּשִּׁשִּׁי — "תּוֹצֵא הָאָרֶץ" "וַיְכֻלּוּ הַשָּׁמַיִם". [ו] פָּרָשָׁה גְּדוֹלָה קוֹרִין אוֹתָהּ בִּשְׁנַיִם, וְהַקְּטַנָּה — בְּיָחִיד, בְּשַׁחֲרִית בְּמוּסָף. וּבְמִנְחָה נִכְנָסִין וְקוֹרִין עַל פִּיהֶן כְּקוֹרִין אֶת שְׁמַע. עֶרֶב שַׁבָּת בְּמִנְחָה לֹא הָיוּ נִכְנָסִין, מִפְּנֵי כְבוֹד הַשַּׁבָּת. [ז] כָּל יוֹם שֶׁיֵּשׁ בּוֹ הַלֵּל — אֵין (א) מַעֲמָד בְּשַׁחֲרִית. קָרְבַּן מוּסָף — אֵין בִּנְעִילָה. קָרְבַּן עֵצִים — אֵין בְּמִנְחָה, דִּבְרֵי ר' עֲקִיבָא. אָמַר לוֹ בֶּן עַזַּאי: [ח] כָּךְ הָיָה רַבִּי יְהוֹשֻׁעַ שׁוֹנֶה: קָרְבַּן מוּסָף — אֵין בְּמִנְחָה. קָרְבַּן עֵצִים — אֵין בִּנְעִילָה. חָזַר רַבִּי עֲקִיבָא לִהְיוֹת שׁוֹנֶה כְּבֶן עַזַּאי. זְמַן עֲצֵי כֹהֲנִים וְהָעָם תִּשְׁעָה: בְּאֶחָד בְּנִיסָן — בְּנֵי אָרַח בֶּן יְהוּדָה. בְּעֶשְׂרִים בְּתַמּוּז — בְּנֵי דָוִד בֶּן יְהוּדָה. בַּחֲמִשָּׁה בְּאָב — בְּנֵי פַרְעוֹשׁ בֶּן יְהוּדָה. בְּשִׁבְעָה בּוֹ — בְּנֵי יוֹנָדָב בֶּן רֵכָב. בַּעֲשָׂרָה בּוֹ — בְּנֵי סְנָאָה בֶּן בִּנְיָמִן. בַּחֲמִשָּׁה עָשָׂר בּוֹ — בְּנֵי (ב) זַתּוּא בֶּן יְהוּדָה, וְעִמָּהֶם כֹּהֲנִים וּלְוִיִּם, וְכָל מִי שֶׁטָּעָה בְּשִׁבְטוֹ, וּבְנֵי גוֹנְבֵי עֱלִי וּבְנֵי קוֹצְעֵי קְצִיעוֹת. בְּעֶשְׂרִים בּוֹ — בְּנֵי פַחַת מוֹאָב בֶּן יְהוּדָה. בְּעֶשְׂרִים בֶּאֱלוּל — בְּנֵי עָדִין בֶּן יְהוּדָה. בְּאֶחָד בְּטֵבֵת — שָׁבוּ בְּנֵי פַרְעוֹשׁ שְׁנִיָּה. בְּאֶחָד בְּטֵבֵת לֹא הָיָה בּוֹ מַעֲמָד, שֶׁהָיָה בּוֹ הַלֵּל וְקָרְבַּן מוּסָף וְקָרְבַּן עֵצִים. [ט] חֲמִשָּׁה דְבָרִים אֵירְעוּ אֶת אֲבוֹתֵינוּ בְּשִׁבְעָה עָשָׂר בְּתַמּוּז, וַחֲמִשָּׁה בְּתִשְׁעָה בְּאָב. *בְּשִׁבְעָה עָשָׂר בְּתַמּוּז

נִשְׁתַּבְּרוּ

שאני בני מחוזא דשכיחי בהו שכרות. ולהכי היו אומרים הלל הגדול קודם שיאכלו וישתו. ובפסוקי דזמרה נוהגין לומר שחרית, ודווקא בפסוקי דזמרה קודם התפלה, אבל בשעת תפלה אין אומרים אותו אלא בנפש שבעה וכרס מלאה:

הדרן עלך סדר תענית אלו

בכל יום שיש בו הלל אין בו מעמד שחרית. פי': דהיינו חנוכה, דבשאר יום טוב לא משכחת לה בלא קרבן מוסף:

קרבן מוסף אין בו נעילה. פירוש: יום שקרבין בו מוסף – אין בו נעילה, לפי שטרודין הם במוסף ואין להם פנאי לומר נעילה:

קרבן עצים אין בו מנחה. משום דעד המנחה היו טרודים בקרבן העצים. אבל יש בו נעילה, דכל כך לא היו מאחרים עד שעת נעילה, דאמר בן עזאי כך היה וכו':

מנחה

עין משפט נר מצוה

לד א מיי' פ"א מהל' תענית הלכה טז [וטוש"ע א"ח סימן תקעה סעיף יא]:

א ב מיי' פ"ו מהלכות כלי מקדש הלכה א סמג עשין קעב:

ב ג מיי' שם הלכה ב:

ג ד מיי' שם הלכה ג:

ד ה מיי' שם הלכה ו:

ה ו מיי' שם הלכה ז:

ו ז ח מיי' שם הלכה ח:

ז ט מיי' פ"ה מהלכות תענית הלכה ב סמג עשין מד"ס ג טור א"ח סימן תקמט:

רבינו חננאל

בשלשה פעמים בשנה הכהנים נושאין את כפיהם כו'.

רבינו גרשום

בשלשה פרקים כו' בתעניות ובמעמדות ודאי מעמדות הן בכל יום אלא לכך חשיב פרק בפני עצמו דלא כל ישראל הן אלא של אותו משמר ובתעניות יש כל ישראל ויש מהן ד' פרקים ביום:

הגהות הב"ח

(א) מתני' כל יום שיש בו הלל אין בו מעמד בשחרית כו' אין בו בנעילה כו' אין בו במנחה כו' כצ"ל וכן בסמוך: (ב) שם בט"ו בו בני זתוא. נ"ב ס"א זתא: (ג) רש"י ד"ה כהנים כו' היו עולים לירושלים כהנים כו' על קרבן אחיהם והשאר היו כו' כצ"ל והד"א: (ד) ד"ה כל יום כו' אין בו מעמד בשחרית אותן וכו' אחיהם ביום שיש בו הלל: (ה) ד"ה קרבן כו' אין בו מעמד בנעילה כו' שהוא אחד דאין לך מוסף: (ו) ד"ה כך היה כו' אין בו במנחה: (ז) ד"ה בני ארח כו' באחד בניסן וספקו להם עצים כו' בני דוד ארח כך שמו ומשבט יהודה היה כצ"ל ותיבת שמואל נמחק:

ח א מיי' פ"ה מהלכות תענית הלכה ו סמג עשין מד"ס ג טוש"ע א"ח סי' תקנא סעיף א:

רש"א מ"ז

ט ב מיי' וסמג שם טוש"ע א"ח שם סעיף ג:

י ג מיי' שם הלכה ז סמג שם טוש"ע א"ח סימן תקנב סעיף א:

יא ד ה מיי' פי"ד מהל' תפלה הלכה א ב סמג עשין כ טוש"ע א"ח סימן קכט סעיף א:

סנהדרין ע:

יב ו מיי' שם פט"ו הלכה ד סמג שם טוש"ע א"ח סימן קכח סעיף לח:

נִשְׁתַּבְּרוּ הַלּוּחוֹת, (א) וּבָטֵל הַתָּמִיד, וְהוּבְקְעָה הָעִיר, וְשָׂרַף אַפּוֹסְטְמוֹס אֶת הַתּוֹרָה (ב) וְהֶעֱמִיד צֶלֶם בַּהֵיכָל. בְּתִשְׁעָה בְּאָב נִגְזַר עַל אֲבוֹתֵינוּ שֶׁלֹּא יִכָּנְסוּ לָאָרֶץ, *וְחָרַב הַבַּיִת בָּרִאשׁוֹנָה וּבַשְּׁנִיָּה, וְנִלְכְּדָה בֵּיתָר, וְנֶחְרְשָׁה הָעִיר. [א]מִשֶּׁנִּכְנָס אָב, מְמַעֲטִין בְּשִׂמְחָה. *[ב]שַׁבָּת שֶׁחָל תִּשְׁעָה בְּאָב לִהְיוֹת בְּתוֹכָהּ — אָסוּר מִלְּסַפֵּר וּמִלְּכַבֵּס. וּבַחֲמִישִׁי מוּתָּרִין מִפְּנֵי כְבוֹד הַשַּׁבָּת. *[ג]עֶרֶב תִּשְׁעָה בְּאָב — לֹא יֹאכַל אָדָם שְׁנֵי תַבְשִׁילִין. לֹא יֹאכַל בָּשָׂר וְלֹא יִשְׁתֶּה יַיִן. רַבָּן שִׁמְעוֹן בֶּן גַּמְלִיאֵל אוֹמֵר: יְשַׁנֶּה. רַבִּי יְהוּדָה מְחַיֵּיב בִּכְפִיַּית הַמִּטָּה, וְלֹא הוֹדוּ לוֹ חֲכָמִים. *אָמַר רַבָּן שִׁמְעוֹן בֶּן גַּמְלִיאֵל: לֹא הָיוּ יָמִים טוֹבִים לְיִשְׂרָאֵל כַּחֲמִשָּׁה עָשָׂר בְּאָב וּכְיוֹה"כ, שֶׁבָּהֶן בְּנוֹת יְרוּשָׁלַיִם יוֹצְאוֹת בִּכְלֵי לָבָן שְׁאוּלִין, *שֶׁלֹּא לְבַיֵּישׁ אֶת מִי שֶׁאֵין לוֹ. (ג) כָּל הַכֵּלִים טְעוּנִין טְבִילָה. וּבְנוֹת יְרוּשָׁלַיִם יוֹצְאוֹת וְחוֹלוֹת בַּכְּרָמִים. וּמֶה הָיוּ אוֹמְרוֹת? בָּחוּר! שָׂא נָא עֵינֶיךָ וּרְאֵה מָה אַתָּה בּוֹרֵר לָךְ. אַל תִּתֵּן עֵינֶיךָ בַּנּוֹי. תֵּן עֵינֶיךָ בַּמִּשְׁפָּחָה, °"שֶׁקֶר הַחֵן, וְהֶבֶל הַיּוֹפִי, אִשָּׁה יִרְאַת ה' הִיא תִתְהַלָּל". וְאוֹמֵר °"תְּנוּ לָהּ מִפְּרִי יָדֶיהָ, וִיהַלְלוּהָ בַשְּׁעָרִים מַעֲשֶׂיהָ". וְכֵן הוּא אוֹמֵר °"צְאֶינָה וּרְאֶינָה, בְּנוֹת צִיּוֹן, בַּמֶּלֶךְ שְׁלֹמֹה בָּעֲטָרָה שֶׁעִטְּרָה לּוֹ אִמּוֹ בְּיוֹם חֲתֻנָּתוֹ, וּבְיוֹם שִׂמְחַת לִבּוֹ". "בְּיוֹם חֲתֻנָּתוֹ" — זֶה מַתַּן תּוֹרָה. "וּבְיוֹם שִׂמְחַת לִבּוֹ" — זֶה בִּנְיַן בֵּית הַמִּקְדָּשׁ, שֶׁיִּבָּנֶה בִּמְהֵרָה בְיָמֵינוּ.

§ **גמ'** "בִּשְׁלֹשָׁה פְּרָקִים בַּשָּׁנָה כֹּהֲנִים נוֹשְׂאִין אֶת כַּפֵּיהֶם" כו'. § תַּעֲנִיּוֹת וּמַעֲמָדוֹת מִי אִיכָּא מוּסָף? חַסּוּרֵי מִיחַסְּרָא וְהָכִי קָתָנֵי: בִּשְׁלֹשָׁה פְּרָקִים כֹּהֲנִים נוֹשְׂאִין אֶת כַּפֵּיהֶן כָּל זְמַן שֶׁמִּתְפַּלְּלִין, וְיֵשׁ מֵהֶן אַרְבָּעָה פְּעָמִים בְּיוֹם, שַׁחֲרִית, וּמוּסָף, מִנְחָה, וּנְעִילַת שְׁעָרִים. וְאֵלּוּ הֵן שְׁלֹשָׁה פְּרָקִים: תַּעֲנִיּוֹת, וּמַעֲמָדוֹת, וְיוֹם הַכִּפּוּרִים. א"ר נַחְמָן אָמַר רַבָּה בַּר אֲבוּהּ: זוֹ דִּבְרֵי רַבִּי מֵאִיר, אֲבָל חֲכָמִים אוֹמְרִים: שַׁחֲרִית וּמוּסָף — יֵשׁ בָּהֶן נְשִׂיאַת כַּפַּיִם, מִנְחָה וּנְעִילָה — אֵין בָּהֶן נְשִׂיאַת כַּפַּיִם. *מַאן חֲכָמִים — ר' יְהוּדָה הִיא, דְּתַנְיָא: שַׁחֲרִית וּמוּסָף, מִנְחָה וּנְעִילָה כּוּלָּן יֵשׁ בָּהֶן נְשִׂיאַת כַּפַּיִם. דִּבְרֵי ר"מ, ר"י אוֹמֵר: שַׁחֲרִית וּמוּסָף יֵשׁ בָּהֶן נְשִׂיאַת כַּפַּיִם, מִנְחָה וּנְעִילָה — אֵין בָּהֶן נְשִׂיאַת כַּפַּיִם. רַבִּי יוֹסֵי אוֹמֵר: נְעִילָה יֵשׁ בָּהּ נְשִׂיאַת כַּפַּיִם, מִנְחָה — אֵין בָּהּ נְשִׂיאַת כַּפַּיִם. בְּמַאי קָמִיפַּלְגִי? רַבִּי מֵאִיר סָבַר: כָּל יוֹמָא טַעְמָא מַאי לָא פָּרְשִׂי כָּהֲנֵי יְדַיְיהוּ בְּמִנְחָתָא — מִשּׁוּם שִׁכְרוּת. הָאִידָּנָא לֵיכָּא שִׁכְרוּת. רַבִּי יְהוּדָה סָבַר: שַׁחֲרִית וּמוּסָף, דְּכָל יוֹמָא לָא שְׁכִיחַ שִׁכְרוּת — לָא גָּזְרוּ בְּהוּ רַבָּנַן. מִנְחָה וּנְעִילָה, דְּכָל יוֹמָא שְׁכִיחָא שִׁכְרוּת — גָּזְרוּ בְּהוּ רַבָּנַן. רַבִּי יוֹסֵי סָבַר: מִנְחָה, דְּאִיתַהּ בְּכָל יוֹמָא — גָּזְרוּ בַּהּ רַבָּנַן. נְעִילָה, דְּלֵיתַהּ בְּכָל יוֹמָא — לָא גָּזְרוּ בַּהּ רַבָּנַן. אָמַר רַב יְהוּדָה אָמַר רַב: הֲלָכָה כְּרַבִּי מֵאִיר. וְרַבִּי יוֹחָנָן אָמַר: נָהֲגוּ הָעָם כְּרַבִּי מֵאִיר. וְרָבָא אָמַר: מִנְהָג כְּרַבִּי מֵאִיר. מַאן דְּאָמַר הֲלָכָה כְּרַבִּי מֵאִיר, דָּרְשִׁינַן לַהּ בְּפִירְקָא. מַאן דְּאָמַר מִנְהָג, — מִדְרַשׁ לָא דָּרְשִׁינַן, אוֹרוּיֵי מוֹרֵינַן. וּמַאן דְּאָמַר נָהֲגוּ — אוֹרוּיֵי לָא מוֹרֵינַן, וְאִי עָבֵיד, — עָבֵיד, וְלָא מְהַדְּרִינַן לֵיהּ. וְרַב נַחְמָן אָמַר: הֲלָכָה כְּרַבִּי יוֹסֵי. [ד]וַהֲלָכָה כְּרַבִּי יוֹסֵי. (ד) וְהָאִידָּנָא מ"ט פָּרְשִׂי כָּהֲנֵי יְדַיְיהוּ בְּמִנְחָתָא דְּתַעֲנִיתָא? [ה]כֵּיוָן דְּבְסָמוּךְ לִשְׁקִיעַת הַחַמָּה קָא פָּרְשִׂי — כִּתְפִלַּת נְעִילָה דָּמְיָא. דְּכוּלֵּי עָלְמָא מִיהַת [ו]שִׁכּוֹר אָסוּר בִּנְשִׂיאַת כַּפַּיִם. מְנָהָנֵי מִילֵּי? אָמַר רַבִּי יְהוֹשֻׁעַ בֶּן לֵוִי מִשּׁוּם בַּר קַפָּרָא: לָמָּה נִסְמְכָה פָּרָשַׁת כֹּהֵן מְבָרֵךְ לְפָרָשַׁת נָזִיר? לוֹמַר: מַה נָּזִיר אָסוּר בְּיַיִן, אַף כֹּהֵן מְבָרֵךְ אָסוּר בְּיַיִן. מַתְקִיף לַהּ אֲבוּהּ דְּרַבִּי זֵירָא, וְאָמְרִי לַהּ אוֹשַׁעְיָא בַּר זַבְדָּא: אִי מַה נָּזִיר אָסוּר בְּחַרְצָן, אַף כֹּהֵן מְבָרֵךְ אָסוּר בְּחַרְצָן! א"ר יִצְחָק, אָמַר קְרָא: "לְשָׁרְתוֹ וּלְבָרֵךְ בִּשְׁמוֹ". מַה מְּשָׁרֵת מוּתָּר בְּחַרְצָן, אַף כֹּהֵן מְבָרֵךְ מוּתָּר בְּחַרְצָן. אִי

משלי לא | שם | שה"ש ג | [עירובין סה. וש"נ]

מנחה ונעילה דכל יומא שכיחי בהו שכרות גזרו רבנן. אפילו ביומא דתענית דלית בהו שכרות. וקשיא: דהכא משמע דבמנחה שייכא שכרות ובפ"ק דשבת (דף י. ושם) קאמר בהדיא דבמנחה לא שייכא שכרות! וי"ל: דהא דקאמר התם דבמנחה לא שייכא שכרות! ר"ל לגבי ערבית שכרות דמנחה לאו כלום (לגבי שבת) דיותר שכיח שכרות בערבית (יותר) מבמנחה, אבל לעולם במנחה שייך שכרות לגבי שחרית ומוסף:

ומאן דאמר נהגו אורויי נמי לא מורינן. פירשנו בפ"ק דראש השנה (דף טו: ד"ה וכי):

והאידנא נהוג עלמא דפרסי כהני ידייהו במנחה (ז) סמוך לשקיעת החמה. ולכך לא נהגו העם לומר נשיאת כפים במנחה ביום הכפורים לפי שמתפללין מנחה בעוד היום גדול, אבל במנחה בשאר תעניות יש נשיאת כפים. אבל מכל מקום בנעילה ביום הכפורים יש נשיאת כפים: אי

נִשְׁתַּבְּרוּ הַלּוּחוֹת. בַּגְּמָ' מְפָרֵשׁ: וּבָטֵל הַתָּמִיד. לְפִי שֶׁגָּזְרָה הַמַּלְכוּת גְּזֵרָה מִלְּהַקְרִיב עוֹד: וְהוּעֲמַד צֶלֶם בַּהֵיכָל. שֶׁהֶעֱמִידוֹ מְנַשֶּׁה, כִּדְמְפוֹרָשׁ בְּתַרְגּוּם יְרוּשַׁלְמִי בְּפָרָשַׁת "הַשָּׁמַיִם כִּסְאִי" וגו' (ישעיהו סו): עַל אֲבוֹתֵינוּ. דּוֹר הַמִּדְבָּר "אִם יִרְאֶה אִישׁ בָּאֲנָשִׁים הָאֵלֶּה הַדּוֹר הָרָע הַזֶּה אֶת הָאָרֶץ" וגו' (דברים א): בֵּיתָר. עִיר גְּדוֹלָה, וְהָיוּ יִשְׂרָאֵל דָּרִין בָּהּ, בְּמַסֶּכֶת גִּיטִּין, פֶּרֶק "הַנִּיזָּקִין" (דף נז.): אַשְּׁקָא דְרִיסְפַּק חֲרֵב בֵּיתָר: שַׁבָּת שֶׁחָל תִּשְׁעָה בְּאָב כו'. שָׁבוּעַ: בַּחֲמִישִׁי מוּתָּרִין. אִם חָל תִּשְׁעָה בְּאָב בְּעֶרֶב שַׁבָּת — מוּתָּרִין לְכַבֵּס בַּחֲמִישִׁי, וּכְשֶׁחָל ט' בְּאָב בְּד' בְּשַׁבָּת — לָא אִיצְטְרִיךְ לְמִיתְנֵי דְּמוּתָּרִין, כִּדְאָמְרִינַן בַּגְּמָרָא: לֹא שָׁנוּ אֶלָּא לְפָנָיו כו': שְׁנֵי תַבְשִׁילִין. *בָּשָׂר וְדָגִים, אוֹ בָּשָׂר וּבֵיצִים שֶׁעָלָיו, אוֹ דָּג וּבֵיצָה שֶׁעָלָיו, כִּדְאָמַר בְּפֶרֶק "עַרְבֵי פְסָחִים" (דף קיד:): יְשַׁנֶּה. בַּגְּמָרָא מְפָרֵשׁ: כְּפִיַּית הַמִּטָּה. עַל פָּנֶיהָ, וְלֹא יִישַׁן עָלֶיהָ: שְׁאוּלִין. שֶׁכּוּלָּן שׁוֹאֲלוֹת זוֹ מִזּוֹ, אֲפִילּוּ עֲשִׁירוֹת, כְּדֵי שֶׁלֹּא לְבַיֵּישׁ כו': טְעוּנִין טְבִילָה. קוֹדֶם שֶׁיִּלְבְּשׁוּם, לְפִי שֶׁאֵין כָּל אַחַת בְּקִיאָה בַּחֲבֶרְתָּהּ, שֶׁמָּא נִדָּה הָיְתָה: וְחוֹלוֹת. כְּמוֹ "לָחוּל בַּמְּחוֹלוֹת" (שופטים כא): בַּמֶּלֶךְ שְׁלֹמֹה. בַּמֶּלֶךְ שֶׁהַשָּׁלוֹם שֶׁלּוֹ: אִמּוֹ. כְּנֶסֶת יִשְׂרָאֵל: זֶה מַתַּן תּוֹרָה. יוֹם הַכִּפּוּרִים, שֶׁנִּיתְּנוּ בּוֹ לוּחוֹת הָאַחֲרוֹנוֹת: **גמ'** כָּל זְמַן שֶׁמִּתְפַּלְּלִין. דְּהַיְינוּ שַׁחֲרִית וּמִנְחָה וּנְעִילָה: (ה) יֵשׁ מֵהֶן אַרְבָּעָה פְּעָמִים בְּיוֹם. יוֹם הַכִּפּוּרִים, שֶׁיֵּשׁ בּוֹ מוּסָף: כָּל יוֹמָא מַאי טַעְמָא לָא פָּרְשִׂי כָּהֲנֵי יְדַיְיהוּ בְּמִנְחָה. דְּכָל יוֹמָא שְׁכִיחָא בֵּיהּ שִׁכְרוּת, שֶׁכְּבָר סָעַד, וּזְמִנִין דְּמָשְׁכָא סְעוּדָתֵיהּ וּמִשְׁתַּכֵּר, וּפָרֵישׂ יָדֵיהּ בַּהֲדֵי חַמְרֵיהּ. וְכֹהֵן שְׁתוּי יַיִן אָסוּר לִישָּׂא אֶת כַּפָּיו, שֶׁנֶּאֱמַר "יַיִן וְשֵׁכָר אַל תֵּשְׁתְּ בְּבוֹאֲכֶם" וגו' (ויקרא י), וּנְשִׂיאַת כַּפַּיִם מֵעֵין עֲבוֹדָה, כִּדְלְקַמָּן: הָאִידָּנָא. בַּתַּעֲנִיּוֹת וּבַמַּעֲמָדוֹת לָא שְׁכִיחָא שִׁכְרוּת, וּבַמַּעֲמָדוֹת נַמִי מִתְעַנִּין כִּדְלְקַמָּן (דף כז:): גָּזְרִינַן. תַּעֲנִית אַטּוּ שְׁאָר יָמִים: נְעִילָה דְּלֵיתָהּ בְּכָל יוֹמָא. אֶלָּא בְּיוֹם הַתַּעֲנִית: דְּדָרְשִׁינַן בְּפִירְקָא. הֲלָכָה כְּרַבִּי מֵאִיר, דְּבָעֵינַן דְּלֵיקוּם כְּווֹתֵיהּ עָלְמָא: אוֹרוּיֵי אוֹרֵינַן. כְּרַבִּי מֵאִיר — אִי אָתוּ לְקַמָּן, אֲבָל בְּפִירְקָא — לָא דָּרְשִׁינַן, דְּלָא פְּשִׁיטָא לֵיהּ כּוּלֵּי הַאי דְּתֶיהֱוֵי הֲלָכָה כְּר"מ. וּמ"ד נָהֲגוּ — מַשְׁמַע: הֵן נָהֲגוּ מֵאֲלֵיהֶן, אֲבָל אֵינוֹ עִיקָּר. וּמִנְהָג מַשְׁמַע — תּוֹרַת מִנְהָג יֵשׁ בַּדָּבָר, וּמִנְהָג כָּשֵׁר הוּא: וְרַב נַחְמָן אָמַר הֲלָכָה כְּרַבִּי יוֹסֵי וַהֲלָכָה כְּרַבִּי יוֹסֵי. גְּמָרָא קָא פָּסֵיק וּמְהַדַּר סְתָמָא, וּמוֹקֵי לַהּ הֲלָכָה כְּרַבִּי יוֹסֵי. וְאַהָכִי קָא פָּרֵיךְ וְאֶלָּא הָאִידָּנָא כו': כֵּיוָן דִּסְמוּךְ לִשְׁקִיעַת הַחַמָּה וכו'. שֶׁמְּאַחֲרִין (ו) עַד שְׁקִיעַת הַחַמָּה, וּמִתְפַּלְּלִין כָּל שָׁעָה, וְאֵינָן הוֹלְכִין לְבֵית הַכְּנֶסֶת מִשֵּׁשׁ שָׁעוֹת וּמֶחֱצָה וּלְמַעְלָה כְּמוֹ שֶׁהָיוּ עוֹשִׂין לְאוֹתָן הַיָּמִים: כִּתְפִלַּת נְעִילָה דָּמְיָא. דְּהַשְׁתָּא לֵיכָּא לְמֵיגְזַר מִשּׁוּם מִנְחָה דְּכָל יוֹמָא, דְּמִנְחָתָא כִּי הָא לֵיתָא בְּכָל יוֹמָא: שִׁכּוֹר מִיהָא אָסוּר בִּנְשִׂיאַת כַּפַּיִם. דַּאֲפִילּוּ ר"מ לָא קָאָמַר אֶלָּא מִשּׁוּם דְּהָאִידָּנָא לָאו שִׁכְרוּת הוּא: פָּרָשַׁת כֹּהֵן מְבָרֵךְ. "כֹּה תְבָרְכוּ אֶת בְּנֵי יִשְׂרָאֵל אָמוֹר לָהֶם" (במדבר ו): מַה מְּשָׁרֵת כו'. עוֹבֵד עֲבוֹדָה, דְּלָא מִיתְּסַר אֶלָּא שְׁתוּיֵי יַיִן מַמָּשׁ, דִּכְתִיב "יַיִן וְשֵׁכָר אַל תֵּשְׁתְּ" וגו', הָא בְּחַרְצָן — מוּתָּר: מַאי

[ר"ה יח:]

יבמות מג.

[כוונת רש"י בשר מליח דשרי כדאיתא לקמן ל. בברייתא תנא אבל אוכל הוא בשר מליח כו']

[פסחים פב. וש"נ]

תורה אור

רבינו חננאל

ואקשינן וכי תעניות אית בהו מוסף ותרצינן לה הכי בג' פרקים כהנים נושאין את כפיהם כ"ז שמתפללין ויש מהן ד' פעמים ביום בשחרית במוסף ובמנחה ובנעילה. ואלו הן ג' פרקים תעניות ומעמדות ויוה"כ. וסתם מתני' ר' מאיר היא דלא משכחת לה דנושאין כפיהם כל זמן שמתפללין אלא לרבי מאיר דתני שחרית ומוסף מנחה ונעילה יש בהן נשיאות כפים דברי ר' מאיר וטעמא דר' מאיר מפורש הוא כיון דביום הכפורים ובמעמדות ליכא שכרות במנחה נושאין כפיהם ולא גזרינן. ור' יהודה תני שחרית ומוסף בלבד יש בהן נשיאות כפים דבכל יומא לית בהו שכרות לפיכך לא גזרינן בהו. שמעינן מינה דר' יהודה אין אדם רשאי ליכול אלא אחר תפלת מוסף. אבל במנחה דבשאר יומי אית בהו שכרות גזרינן בהו ביוה"כ ובמעמדות ר' יוסי אומר מנחה אין בה נשיאות כפים משום דאיתא כל יומא ואתי לאחלופי גזרינן אבל נעילה דליתא אלא ביוה"כ ובמעמדות יש בה נשיאות כפים דכיון דליתא כל יומא לא גזרינן. ואסיקנא דהלכתא כר' יוסי דאמר שחרית ומוסף ונעילה יש בהן נשיאות כפים מנחה אין בה נשיאות כפים. והאידנא דלא מצלו מנחה דתעניתא אלא סמוך לשקיעת החמה כדאוקימנא (לעיל יב:) דרביעית היום האחרון הוא דמתפללין בו תפלת תענית כדכתיב ובמנחת הערב קמתי מתעניתי וגו' בנעילה דמיא ויש בה נשיאות כפים. ואע"ג דאמר רב הלכתא כרבי מאיר ודרשינן לה בפירקא ורב הונא אמר מנהג כר"מ אוריי מורינן הכי בפרקא לא דרשי לה (ואף ר') [ור' יוחנן אמר] נהגו כר"מ לא דרשי ולא מורינן כוותיה ואי עביד לא מהדרינן ליה: ודייקי כו' אלמא שכור אסור בנשיאת כפים מנא לן ופשיט דכתיב לשרתו ולברך בשמו אתקש (משרת ולו למברך) [מברך למשרת] ולנזיר מה משרת אסור ביין שנאמר יין ושכר אל תשת אף מברך אסור ביין ושכר דקיימא לן כל המשכר [אסור] ומותר בחרצן אי הכי למאי אתקש לנזיר להכשיר

הגהות הב"ח

(א) במשנה ובוטל התמיד: (ב) והעמידו צלם בהיכל. נ"ב גי' רש"י והועמד: (ג) שם את מי שאין לו וכל הכלים טעונין: (ד) גמ' והלכה כר' יוסי ואלא האידנא מ"ט פרסי כו' כיון דסמוך לשקיעת החמה: (ה) רש"י ד"ה ויש מהן: (ו) ד"ה כיון דסמוך כו' שמאחרים עד שקיעת החמה. נ"ב נראה שרש"י דקדק לבאר שלא יסמכו עלה דהאי להתחיל מנחה סמוך לשקיעת החמה דזה אסור אלא ר"ל שכבר התחילו בזמנו קאמר דמתפללין כל שעה ומאחרין עד שקיעת החמה: (ז) תוס' ד"ה והאידנא כו' ידייהו במנחה כיון דסמוך לשקיעת החמה כו' בשאר תעניות יש לומר נשיאת כפים כו' ביוה"כ יש לומר נשיאת כפים:

רבינו גרשום

במוסף דהיינו יוה"כ שיש בו מוסף: אמר רב נחמן זו דקתני נושאין כפיהן בשחרית במוסף במנחה בנעילה ר"מ היא. כל יומא טעמא מאי אין נושאין כפיהן *) האידנא בתענית ובמעמדות וביוה"כ (ובמעמדות) דאית בהו תענית נמי שכיחא שכרות להכי נושאין כפיהן בכל ד' תפלות שבהן: מנחה ונעילה דבשאר יומי שכיחא שכרות גזרו בהו רבנן בהני דלמא אתי למיעבד בשאר יומי נמי: אבל אורויי מורינן כרבי מאיר למאן דבעי כמאן הלכה: והואיל והלכה כרבי יוסי האידנא מאי טעמא פרסי כהני ידייהו ביום הכפורים במנחה כיון דבשקיעת החמה פרסי שהוו מאחרין לתפלת המנחה: שכור אסור בנשיאת כפים דקתני מאי טעמא לא דשכיחא ביה שכרות: **) מהו משרת מותר דכתיב יין ושכר אל תשת אבל אוכל הוא חרצן: אף כהן מברך לא יהא בעל מום והא קיימא לן דבעל מום מברך אלא אם כן יהו מומין שבגלוי. הא איתקש לנזיר מה נזיר בעל מום אף מברך בעל מום: מאי חזית דאקשית לקולא דאקשת ליה לנזיר דבעל מום מותר ואקשת ליה למשרת דבחרצן מותר אקיש לחומרא ונימא מה נזיר אסור בחרצן אף מברך אסור בחרצן ומה משרת בעל מום לא אף מברך בעל מום לא:

*) אולי צ"ל במנחה משום שכרות האידנא וכו' דאית בהו תענית ליכא שכרות ולהכי וכו'. **) צ"ל מה משרת מותר בחרצן וכו' אף כהן מברך מותר בחרצן: אף כהן וכו'.

אסמכתא

אִי מַה מְשָׁרֵת בַּעַל מוּם לֹא, אַף כֹּהֵן מְבָרֵךְ בַּעַל מוּם לֹא! הָא אִיתַּקַּשׁ לְנָזִיר! וּמַאי חָזֵית דְּמַקַּשְׁתְּ לְקוּלָּא? אַקֵּישׁ לְחוּמְרָא! אַסְמַכְתָּא נִינְהוּ מִדְּרַבָּנַן, וּלְקוּלָּא.§ "אֵלּוּ הֵן מַעֲמָדוֹת לְפִי שֶׁנֶּאֱמַר 'צַו אֶת בְּנֵי יִשְׂרָאֵל' כו'.§ מַאי קָאָמַר? ה"ק: אֵלּוּ הֵן מַעֲמָדוֹת. וּמַה טַּעַם תִּיקְּנוּ מַעֲמָדוֹת? לְפִי שֶׁנֶּאֱמַר °"צַו אֶת בְּנֵי יִשְׂרָאֵל וְאָמַרְתָּ אֲלֵיהֶם: אֶת קָרְבָּנִי, לַחְמִי לְאִשַּׁי". וְהֵיאַךְ קָרְבָּנוֹ שֶׁל אָדָם קָרֵב וְהוּא אֵינוֹ עוֹמֵד עַל גַּבָּיו? הִתְקִינוּ נְבִיאִים הָרִאשׁוֹנִים עֶשְׂרִים וְאַרְבָּעָה מִשְׁמָרוֹת. עַל כָּל מִשְׁמָר וּמִשְׁמָר הָיָה מַעֲמָד בִּירוּשָׁלַיִם שֶׁל כֹּהֲנִי' וְשֶׁל לְוִיִּם, וְשֶׁל יִשְׂרְאֵלִים. הִגִּיעַ זְמַן מִשְׁמָר לַעֲלוֹת — כֹּהֲנִים וּלְוִיִּם עוֹלִין לִירוּשָׁלַיִם. ת"ר: עֶשְׂרִים וְאַרְבָּעָה מִשְׁמָרוֹת[א] (א) בְּאֶרֶץ יִשְׂרָאֵל, וּשְׁתֵּים עֶשְׂרֵה בִּירִיחוֹ. שְׁתֵּים עֶשְׂרֵה בִּירִיחוֹ?! נְפִישָׁן לְהוּ טוּבָא! אֶלָּא: שְׁתֵּים עֶשְׂרֵה מֵהֶן בִּירִיחוֹ. הִגִּיעַ זְמַן הַמִּשְׁמָר לַעֲלוֹת, חֲצִי הַמִּשְׁמָר הָיָה עוֹלֶה מֵאֶרֶץ יִשְׂרָאֵל לִירוּשָׁלַיִם, וַחֲצִי הַמִּשְׁמָר הָיָה עוֹלֶה *מִירִיחוֹ כְּדֵי שֶׁיְּסַפְּקוּ מַיִם וּמָזוֹן לַאֲחֵיהֶם שֶׁבִּירוּשָׁלַיִם. אָמַר רַב יְהוּדָה אָמַר שְׁמוּאֵל: כֹּהֲנִים וּלְוִיִּם וְיִשְׂרְאֵלִים מְעַכְּבִין אֶת הַקָּרְבָּן. בְּמַתְנִיתָא תָּנָא ר"ש בֶּן אֶלְעָזָר: (ב) כֹּהֲנִים, וּלְוִיִּם וּכְלֵי שִׁיר מְעַכְּבִין אֶת הַקָּרְבָּן. בְּמַאי קָמִיפַּלְגִי? מָר סָבַר: *[ב]עִיקַּר שִׁירָה בַּפֶּה. וּמָר סָבַר: עִיקַּר שִׁירָה בִּכְלִי. אָמַר רַב (א) חָמָא בַּר גּוּרְיָא אָמַר רַב: [ג]מֹשֶׁה תִּיקֵּן לָהֶם לְיִשְׂרָאֵל שְׁמוֹנָה מִשְׁמָרוֹת, אַרְבָּעָה מֵאֶלְעָזָר וְד' מֵאִיתָמָר. בָּא שְׁמוּאֵל וְהֶעֱמִידָן עַל שֵׁשׁ עֶשְׂרֵה. בָּא דָּוִד וְהֶעֱמִידָן עַל עֶשְׂרִים וְאַרְבָּעָה, שֶׁנֶּאֱמַר °"בִּשְׁנַת הָאַרְבָּעִים לְמַלְכוּת דָּוִד נִדְרָשׁוּ, וַיִּמָּצֵא בָהֶם גִּבּוֹרֵי חַיִל בְּיַעְזֵיר גִּלְעָד". מֵיתִיבִי: מֹשֶׁה תִּיקֵּן לָהֶם לְיִשְׂרָאֵל שְׁמוֹנָה מִשְׁמָרוֹת, אַרְבָּעָה מֵאֶלְעָזָר וְאַרְבָּעָה מֵאִיתָמָר. [ד]בָּא דָוִד וּשְׁמוּאֵל וְהֶעֱמִידָן עַל עֶשְׂרִים וְאַרְבַּע, שֶׁנֶּאֱמַר: °"הֵמָּה יִסַּד דָּוִד וּשְׁמוּאֵל הָרוֹאֶה בֶּאֱמוּנָתָם"! הָכִי קָאָמַר: מִיסוֹדוֹ שֶׁל דָּוִד וּשְׁמוּאֵל הָרָמָתִי הֶעֱמִידוּם עַל עֶשְׂרִים וְאַרְבַּע. תַּנְיָא אִידָךְ: מֹשֶׁה תִּיקֵּן לָהֶם לְיִשְׂרָאֵל שֵׁשׁ עֶשְׂרֵה מִשְׁמָרוֹת, שְׁמוֹנָה מֵאֶלְעָזָר וּשְׁמוֹנָה מֵאִיתָמָר, וּכְשֶׁרַבּוּ בְּנֵי אֶלְעָזָר עַל בְּנֵי אִיתָמָר, חִלְּקוּם וְהֶעֱמִידוּם עַל עֶשְׂרִים וְאַרְבַּע, שֶׁנֶּאֱמַר °"וַיִּמָּצְאוּ בְנֵי אֶלְעָזָר רַבִּים לְרָאשֵׁי הַגְּבָרִים מִן בְּנֵי אִיתָמָר, וַיַּחְלְקוּם. לִבְנֵי אֶלְעָזָר רָאשִׁים לְבֵית אָבוֹת שִׁשָּׁה עָשָׂר וְלִבְנֵי אִיתָמָר לְבֵית אֲבוֹתָם שְׁמוֹנָה". וְאוֹמֵר: °"בֵּית אָב אֶחָד אָחֻז לְאֶלְעָזָר, וְאָחֻז אָחֻז לְאִיתָמָר". מַאי "וְאוֹמֵר"? וְכִי תֵּימָא כִּי הֵיכִי דִּנְפִישִׁי בְּנֵי אֶלְעָזָר, הָכָא נַמִי דִּנְפִישִׁי בְּנֵי אִיתָמָר — שְׁמוֹנָה מֵעִיקָּרָא אַרְבָּעָה הֲווֹ, ת"ש "בֵּית אָב אֶחָד אָחֻז לְאֶלְעָזָר, וְאָחֻז אָחֻז לְאִיתָמָר". תְּיוּבְתָּא דְּרַב (ב) חָמָא בַּר גּוּרְיָא! אָמַר לָךְ רַב (ג) חָמָא בַּר גּוּרְיָא: תַּנָּאֵי הִיא, וַאֲנָא דַּאֲמַרִי כִּי הַאי תַּנָּא דְּאָמַר שְׁמוֹנָה. ת"ר: (ד) אַרְבָּעָה מִשְׁמָרוֹת עָלוּ מִן הַגּוֹלָה, וְאֵלּוּ הֵן: יְדַעְיָה, [חָרִים,] פַּשְׁחוּר, וְאִימֵּר. עָמְדוּ נְבִיאִים שֶׁבֵּינֵיהֶם וְחִלְּקוּם

א) ס"א חסדא ב ג) ס"א חסדא ד) ערכין יב:

במדבר כח · דה"א כו · שם ט · שם כד · שם

רש"י

מאי קאמר. דקא בעי מאי ניהו מעמדות, ומייתי קרא "את קרבני לחמי לאשי" וגו': הכי קאמר אלו הן מעמדות. דלקמן. וטעמא מאי תקון מעמדות — לפי שנאמר "צו את בני ישראל ואמרת אליהם את קרבני לחמי לאשי" וגו': ה"ג: תנו רבנן כ"ד משמרות היו בא"י וי"ב ביריחו י"ב ביריחו בתמיה נפישי להו טובא! אלא אימא: וי"ב מהן ביריחו. ברישא משמע לבד הכ"ד שבעיירות א"י היו י"ב ביריחו, דהוו להו ל"ו. וי"ב מהן, משמע שמאותן הכ"ד היו י"ב ביריחו: ה"ג: הגיע זמן המשמר חצי המשמר עולה לירושלים וחצי המשמר עולה ליריחו כדי שיספקו מים ומזון לאחיהם שבירושלים. כלומר, כיצד היו י"ב ביריחו? כשהגיע זמן המשמר לעלות לירושלים בשבת, מתחלקים אנשי המשמר, חציין הולכין לירושלים לעבודה וחציין הולכין ליריחו הסמוכה לירושלים, ומתקנין שם מים ומזון לאחיהם. וכך עושין כל הכ"ד משמרות. נמצא י"ב ביריחו א]. לשון אחר נהירא לי: מעכבין את הקרבן. אם אין מעמד מכוון בירושלים, כדתנן (לעיל דף כו.): על כל משמר היה מעמד בירושלים, של כהנים לוים וישראלים. כיון דכולהו בעלים בעינן דליהוי (ג) כמוהו על גבי עבודה: וכלי שיר מעכבין את הקרבן. פלוגתא בשילהי מסכת סוכה (דף נ:), ובערכין (דף יא.) מפורשת: עיקר שירה בפה. וכלי לבסומי קלא בעלמא, וכיון דאיכא לוים — לא מעכב משום כלי שיר: עיקר שירה בכלי. אבוב, וכן בפרק "החליל" (ברא שית): ארבעה מאלעזר. מבניו של אלעזר, שעשה מהן ד' משמרות. וגמרא גמר לה: המה יסד דוד ושמואל הרואה באמונתם. ותיובתא דרב חמא, דאמר: שמואל העמידם על י"ו, ודוד העמידן על כ"ד. דהא שמעי' מינה דתרוייהו בהדי הדדי תקינינהו: מיסודו של שמואל הרמתי. שהעמידן על י"ו, בא דוד והעמידן על כ"ד. אית ספרים שכתוב בהן: מיסודו של שמואל ודוד העמידום על כ"ד, כלומר: שניהם הועילו בדבר, ושמואל העמידם על י"ו ודוד על כ"ד: וימצאו בני אלעזר רבים לראשי הגברים מבני איתמר ויחלקו בני אלעזר ראשים לבית אבותם ששה עשר ולבני איתמר ראשים לבית אבותם שמונה ואומר בית אב אחד אחוז לאלעזר ואחוז אחוז לאיתמר. "וימצאו בני אלעזר רבים לראשי הגברים" — כלומר, ראשי הגברים של בני אלעזר היו רבים מאיתמר. והאי "וימצאו" — משמע דקודם לכן היו קבועים, ועכשיו הוסיפו עליהן, "ויחלקום" לי"ו בית אב. "אחד אחוז" שהיה מתחילה לאלעזר דהיינו ח', אחוז אחד בגורל דהיינו נמי ח', והוו להו י"ו: ואחוז אחוז לאיתמר. מה שהיה מתחילה אחוז לאיתמר אחוזים עתה כבתחילה, שלא הרבו עליהם שום בית אב: מאי ואומר. וכי תימא מעיקרא הוו ד' לאלעזר וד' לאיתמר: וכי היכי דנפישי בני אלעזר הכי נמי נפישי בני איתמר. ומיהו, בני אלעזר נפישי טפי, דהא לאיתמר לא אוקמינהו אלא על ח', ולאלעזר על י"ו: תא שמע ואחוז אחוז לאיתמר. אלמא כדקיימי קיימי, ושמע מינה דמשה תיקן להם י"ו, ח' מזה וח' מזה, וקשיא לרב חמא דאמר ד' וד'. והא דכתב לעיל ובשנת הארבעים וגו' המה יסד — במה שהוסיפו עליהן עד כ"ד משמעי, [אבל] משה תיקן להם י"ו משמרות: תנאי היא. דהא איכא תנא דלעיל דקתני משה תיקן להן ח' משמרות משניהן, ואנא קאימנא כוותיה: עלו מן הגולה. בבית שני. והשאר לא עלו, שהרבה מישראל נשתיירו, ולא רצו לעלות: פשחור ואימר. ומבעיא לי, דפשחור (ד) לא כתיב גבי כ"ד משמרות (דה"א כד):

תוספות

אי מה משרת בעל מום לא אף מברך בעל מום לא. פי': כיון דילפינן ג"ש ממשרת — נימא כמו משרת, דמשרת בעל מום — לא, אף מברך וכו'. ומשני: הא איתקש לנזיר וכו'. מכאן נראה דבעל מום מברך ברכת כהנים, *מדקא חזינן דהתלמוד רוצה ללמוד מברך ממשרת ולבעל מום ודחינן ליה. אם כן נראה דלענין נשיאת כפים כהן בעל מום נושא כפיו. ומכאן יש להוכיח דכהן שהמיר דתו — נושא כפיו, וכשר לישא כפיו ולקרות בתורה כמו שלא המיר. וראיה *מהא דכהנים ששימשו בבית חוניו לא ישמשו במקדש, אבל נוטלים חלק עם אחיהם כמו בעלי מומין. מדקאמר שהם כבעלי מומין משמע דכל עבודה שבעל מום ראוי לעשות יעשו, וכהן בעל מום נושא כפיו*:

ומאי חזית דאקשת לקולא אקיש לחומרא. פי': מאי חזית דמקשת כהן לנזיר להקל, ולומר כמו שנזיר הוי בעל מום — כמו כן כהן בעל מום כשר. ואקשת למשרת, מה משרת מותר בחרצן — אף כהן מברך מותר בחרצן. אקשה לחומרא, פירוש: ונימא דכמו שנזיר אסור בחרצן אף כהן אסור בחרצן, וכמו כהן משרת אסור בעל מום אף כהן מברך בעל מום אסור! ומשני: אסמכתא וכו':

מר סבר עיקר שירה בפה. ולכך הכל כשרים, אפילו פסולים אפילו ממזרים, לומר שירה, דלא הוי אלא בפה. ולמאן דאמר עיקר שירה בכלי, אם כן צריך שיהו כהנים או לוים, דהא הכלי זמר היה קדוש:

רבינו חננאל

להכשיר בו בעל מום להיות כשר לברכה. ואמרינן מה ראית להקשות לקולא אקשתו למשרת להיות מותר בחרצן. ואקשתו לנזיר להיות בעל מום כשר לברכה. אדרבה הקשהו לחומרא. הקשהו למשרת להיות כהן בעל מום פסול בנשיאות כפים והקשהו לנזיר להיות אסור בחרצן. ושנינן אסמכתא בעלמא היא. פי' דרשת סמוכין מדרבנן היא הלכך לקולא דרשינן. וכתיב נמי לעמוד לשרת *) מה משרת עומד אף נשיאות כפים מעומד: **פיסקא** אלו הן המעמדות. מה טעם תקינו מעמדות לפי שנאמר צו את בני ישראל: **ירושלמי** א"ר יונה תמידין קרבנן דכל ישראל אינון וא"ת יהיו כל ישראל כל השנה כולה בירושלים עומדים על קרבנן. לא חייבתם התורה אלא ג' רגלים בשנה. ואם יש לומר יהיו יושבין בטילין בעריהם הא כתיב ואספת דגנך הנם מוזהרין לאסוף דגנם ותירושם של כל השנה כולה. התקינו הנביאים הראשונים כ"ד משמרות ועל כל משמר ומשמר היה מעמד בירושלים של כהנים ושל לוים ושל ישראל: ת"ר כ"ד משמרות היו בא"י מהן י"ב ביריחו. הגיע זמן המשמר לעלות חצי המשמר עולה מא"י וחצי משמר מיריחו כדי שיספקו מים ומזון לאחיהם. כלומר חצי המשמר הנותר מספיקין צורכי העולים. ובפעם אחרת מתחליפים. מי שלא עלה יעלה עכשיו. מי שעלה כבר ישב עתה בביתו ויספק צרכי העולים: **ירושלמי** תני ר' שמעון בן אלעזר ישראל והכהנים והלוים וכלי שיר מעכבין את הקרבן שנאמר כל הקהל משתחוים אלו ישראל. והשיר משורר אלו הלוים והחצוצרות מחצצרים אלו הכהנים הכל עד לעלות העולה. הכל מעכבין את הקרבן. אמר רב חסדא אמר רב משה תקן לישראל שמונה משמרות. ד' מאלעזר וד' מאיתמר. בא שמואל והעמידן על שש עשרה. בא דוד והעמידן עד כ"ד. שנאמר בשנת הארבעים למלכות דוד נדרשו. ואותבינן עליה מהא דתניא משה תיקן להם לישראל ט"ז משמרות. ח' מאלעזר וח' מאיתמר וכשרבו בני אלעזר על בני איתמר חלקום לכ"ד שנאמר וימצאו בני אלעזר רבים לראשי הגברים מבני איתמר ויחלקום לבני אלעזר ראשים לבית אבות ששה עשר. ולבני איתמר לבית אבותם שמונה. הוי ח' לאלעזר וח' מאיתמר כגון שהיו ח' אלפים מזה וח' אלפים [מזה] כל משמר אלף רבו בני אלעזר וכאשר דרשום נמצאו י"ו אלף ובני איתמר ח' אלפים כמו שהיו חלקו בני אלעזר לי"ו משמר אלף של כל משמר ובני איתמר נשארו ח' משמרות כמו שהוא וזהו שכתב ויחלקום לבני אלעזר ראשים לבית אבות ששה עשר ולבני איתמר לבית אבותם שמונה. וכתיב בית אב אחד אחוז לאלעזר ואחוז אחוז לאיתמר כל האחוז שהיה לאיתמר מקודם הוא האחוז עתה. אבל לבני אלעזר הוסיפו ח' אחרים. תיובתא דרב חסדא דאמר משה תיקן להם לישראל ח' משמרות כו' הנה זה הברייתא תנא י"ו משמרות תיקן להם משה לישראל. ושנינן תנאי היא ואנא דאמרי כי האי תנא דתניא משה תיקן לישראל ח' משמרות ד' מאלעזר וד' מאיתמר אכתי סיפא דקתני באו שמואל

*) דברי רבינו אין לו ביאור לכאורה ואולי לחסר איזה תיבות ונ"ל ועיקר הקושיא לפרתו ולכך בשמו לענין עמידה אתי דכתיב התם לעמוד לשרת ואמרינן מה משרת עומד וכו' כנ"ל וכ"ה בסוטה ד' לח ע"ש ועי' תוס' מנחות קט. סד"ה לא וברא"ש פ"ג דמגילה סי' יט.

עין משפט נר מצוה

יג א מיי' פט"ו מהל' תפלה הל' ב סמג עשין יט טוש"ע א"ח סימן קכח סעיף ל:
כ"ה במגילה כד: ע"ש
יד ב מיי' פ"ג מהל' כלי המקדש הל' ג סמג עשין קסט:
טו ג ד מיי' שם פ"ד הלכה ג סמג עשין קעג:
[מנחות דף קט. וע"ש בתוס' ד"ה לא]
[וע"ע תוס' סוטה לט: ד"ה כי מהדר ותוס' מנחות קט: ד"ה לא]

מסורת הש"ס

ס"א ליריחו
סוכה נא. [ערכין יא: ע"ז מז:]

הגהות מהר"ב רנשבורג

א] רש"י ד"ה ה"ג הגיע זמן וכו'. לשון אחר נהירא לי. נ"ל ולא נהירא לי:

הגהות הב"ח

(א) גמ' ת"ר כ"ד משמרות היו בא"י כו' אלא אימא ושתים עשרה מהן: (ב) שם ר"ש בן אלעזר אומר כהנים: (ג) רש"י ד"ה כהנים כו' בעינן דליהוי כולהו לגבי עבודה: (ד) ד"ה פשחור כו' לא כתיב גבי כ"ד משמרות ולא הגורל ליהויריב לידעיה השני כו' ולא קא חשיב פשחור ולפע"ד יש לתרץ דכיון דבפרשה ב' כתוב העולים מן הכהנים היו ארבע משמרות ולא קא חשיב פשחור מכ"ד משמרות היה עוד שם אחד של נמי נשתנה שמם לפי השעה כדפרק ב' כתוב בסדר פנחס אלא משפחות השבטים:

גליון הש"ס

גמ' מדרבנן ולקולא. כעין זה שבת דף פג ע"ב:

הגהות הגר"א

[א] גמ' ת"ר כ"ד משמרות. נ"ב של לוים:

רבינו גרשום

אסמכתא דרבנן הוא הא דמקשינן מברך לנזיר ולמשרת מדרבנן היא: ה"ק ואלו הן מעמדות דקתני לקמיה התקינו נביאים הראשונים כ"ד משמרות (כל) [של] כהנים על כל משמר היה מעמד בירושלים כהנים ולוים שבמשמר עולין בירושלים וישראל שבאותו משמר מתענין וכו' ומקצתן עולין לירושלים כדי שיעמדו על הקרבנות: אי הכי נפישי להו דמשמע דהוי ל"ו משמרות אלא אימא שתים עשרה כלומר מאותן עשרים וארבעה הוי מהן שתים עשרה מיריחו ושתים עשרה מכל שאר ישראל: כיצד הגיע זמן משמרות לעלות חצי משמר עולה מא"י וחצי משמר מיריחו וכן כל משמר ומשמר עולה חצי מא"י וחצי מיריחו דהיינו שתים עשרה מא"י ושתים עשרה מיריחו ולמה כל משמר חציו מיריחו לפי שהן קרובין לירושלים מספקין מזון לאחיהן שאר חצי משמר הבאין מא"י ממקום רחוק ואין יכולין להביא מזון עמהן: עיקר שירה בפה ואין צריך כלי שיר: בא דוד ושמואל והעמידום בין שניהם כ"ד קשיא לרב חסדא דאמר שמואל תיקן י"ו ודוד כ"ד תריץ הכי קאמר מיסודו של שמואל הרמתי שהוא העמידן על י"ו חזר דוד והעמידן על כ"ד. מיתיבי משה תקן י"ו משמרות וקשיא לרב חסדא דאמר ח' משמרות וכשרבו בני אלעזר חילקום לי"ו משמרות היינו כ"ד משמרות וכי תימא כי היכי דנפישי בני אלעזר כן רבו בני איתמר ולעולם בימי משה הוא ארבע מאלעזר וארבע מאיתמר כדאמר רב חסדא והתרבו בני אלעזר והעמידום על י"ו נתרבו בני איתמר והעמידום על ח' והיינו דכתיב וימצאו בני אלעזר וגו'. ת"ש בית אב אחד אחוז לאלעזר ואחוז אחוז לאיתמר כלומר כל בית אב אחד של אלעזר חילקו לשנים אבל בני איתמר כדקיימי בימי משה קיימי עכשיו ומדכתיב ולבני איתמר לבית אבותם שמונה אלמא דבימי משה הא שמונה מאלעזר ושמנה

טז א מיי' פי"ב מהל' תפלה הלכה ג סמג עשין יט טוש"ע א"ח סימן קלז סעיף ג:
יז ב מיי' פ"ג שם ה"ד סמג שם טוש"ע א"ח סי' תכג סעיף ב:

וחלקום והעמידום על עשרים וארבעה. בללום ונתנום בקלפי. בא ידעיה ונטל חלקו וחלק חבריו — שש. בא [חרים] ונטל חלקו וחלק חבריו — שש. וכן פשחור, וכן אימר. וכן התנו נביאים שביניהם, שאפי' (*יהוידיב) ראש משמרת עולה, לא ידחה ידעיה ממקומו, אלא ידעיה עיקר (*ויהוידיב) טפל לו.§ "וישראל שבאותו משמר מתכנסין בעריהן וקורין במעשה בראשית".§ מנהני מילי? א"ר יעקב בר אחא *אמר רב אסי: *אלמלא מעמדות, לא נתקיימו שמים וארץ, שנאמר °"ויאמר: ה' אלהים, במה אדע כי אירשנה?" אמר אברהם: רבש"ע! שמא ישראל חוטאין לפניך, אתה עושה להם כדור המבול וכדור הפלגה? א"ל: לאו. אמר לפניו: רבש"ע! הודיעני, במה אירשנה? א"ל: °"קחה לי עגלה משולשת ועז משולשת" וגו'. אמר לפניו: רבש"ע! תינח בזמן שבית המקדש קיים. בזמן שאין בית המקדש קיים מה תהא עליהם? אמר לו: כבר תקנתי להם סדר קרבנות. בזמן שקוראין בהן לפני — מעלה אני עליהם כאילו הקריבום לפני, ואני מוחל להם על כל עונותיהם. ת"ר: *"אנשי א) [א] משמר היו מתפללין על קרבן אחיהם שיתקבל ברצון. ואנשי מעמד מתכנסין לבית הכנסת ויושבין ד' תעניות: בשני בשבת, בשלישי, ברביעי, ובחמישי. בשני — על יורדי הים. בשלישי — על הולכי מדברות. ברביעי — על אסכרא שלא תיפול על התינוקות. בחמישי — על עוברות ומיניקות. עוברות — שלא יפילו. מיניקות — שיניקו את בניהם. ובערב שבת לא היו מתענין מפני כבוד השבת, ק"ו בשבת עצמה. באחד בשבת מ"ט לא? אמר ר' יוחנן: מפני הנוצרים. ר' שמואל בר נחמני אמר: מפני שהוא שלישי ליצירה. ריש לקיש אמר: מפני נשמה יתירה. דאמר ריש לקיש: *נשמה יתירה ניתנה בו באדם בע"ש, במוצאי שבת נוטלין אותה ממנו, שנאמר °"שבת וינפש" — כיון ששבת, וי, אבדה נפש.§ "ביום הראשון" "בראשית", "ו"יהי רקיע".§ *תנא: "בראשית" — בשנים. "יהי רקיע" — באחד. בשלמא "יהי רקיע" באחד, תלתא פסוקי הוו. אלא "בראשית" בשנים *)(מ"ט) ה' פסוקי הויין, (*ותנן:) *א הקורא בתורה אל יפחות מג' פסוקים! רב אמר: ב דולג. ושמואל אמר: פוסק. ורב, דאמר דולג, מ"ט לא אמר פוסק? קסבר: כל פסוקא *דלא פסקיה משה — אנן לא פסקינן ליה. ושמואל אמר: פוסק. ומי פסקינן? והאמר רבי חנינא קרא: צער גדול היה לי אצל ר' חנינא הגדול, ולא התיר לי לפסוק אלא לתינוקות של בית רבן, הואיל ולהתלמד עשוין. *ושמואל: התם טעמא מאי — משום דלא אפשר. הכא נמי — לא אפשר. ושמואל אמר: פוסק. מ"ט לא אמר: דולג? גזירה משום הנכנסין, וגזירה משום היוצאין. מיתיבי: *פרשה של ששה פסוקים קורין אותה בשנים, ושל חמשה (א) [ביחיד. ואם] הראשון קורא ג' השני קורא שנים מפרשה זו, ואחד מפרשה אחרת. וי"א: ג' לפי שאין מתחילין בפרשה פחות משלשה פסוקין. למ"ד דולג — לידלוג, ולמאן דאמר פוסק — ליפסוק! שאני התם

דאית

*) [ליתא במגילה]

שמות לג · שם לד

תוספות

רב אמר דולג. פי': הראשון קורא מראש הפרשה ג' פסוקים, והשני שאין לו כי אם שני פסוקים — מדלג פסוק אחד וקורא ממה שקרא הראשון. וכן נמי בראשי חדשים מדלגין. והקשה ה"ר יהודה בר נתן: ואמאי מדלגין? אמאי אינו קורא למעלה בפרשה? דהא בשבת בחוש"מ קורא הוא מ"ראה אתה אומר אלי" (שמות לג) אע"פ שעיקר הפרשה אינה מתחלת כי אם מ"פסל לך" (שם לד)! וי"ל: דמ"ה הוא קורא ראה בפרשה של מעלה לפי שכל אותה הפרשה משתעי בחד עניינא. אבל פרשה דר"ח, לעיל מינה לא משתעי כלל מחד עניינא, ולכך אינו קורא בפרשה של מעלה, אלא דולג. ומזה ראיה למנהגנו אהא דלא קרינן בכל שבת ושבת פרשה של שבת כמו שאנו עושין בי"ט, שאנו קורין פרשיות לפי המאורע — לפי שאין בפרשה של שבת שלשה פסוקים. דאין לומר שנדלג לעיל, דלא הוי מחד עניינא:

גזרה משום הנכנסין והיוצאין. פי': שהנכנסין שלא ראו (ה) הראשונים שקרא ג' פסוקים ויראו השני שקורא פסוק אחד מלמעלה יאמרו שהראשון לא קרא אלא שני פסוקים. והיוצאין, כשהראשון קורא שלשה פסוקים ואינו משייר אלא שני פסוקים, איכא גזירת יוצאין, דסברי האי שני סגיא ליה בשני פסוקים:

מה

רש"י

וחלקום. לכ"ד, וכתבו כנוי של כל אחד ואחד בחלק: בללום ונתנום בקלפי. כתבו על כ"ד חתיכות קלף ראשי משמרות שחלקו מאותן ד': בא ידעיה. משמרה של ידעיה, בא אחד מהן ונוטל חלקו וחלק ה' חתיכות קלף דהוו להו שש, ומי שהיה עולה בידו ראשון היה לשבת ראשונה שבסדר, שהיו עולין בידו זו אחר זו — כך היו עובדין בשבתותיהן זו אחר זו: וכך התנו. שאפי' יהויריב שהיה במקדש ראשון ראשון למשמרות, עולה מן הגולה: לא ידחה ידעיה. הואיל ומתחלה לא עלה יהויריב, אלא כל משמרות הנעשות מידעיה קודמות לעבודה ליהויריב, ויהויריב בא ועובד אחריהן במקום משמר אחר וששה דידעיה עושין אותן ה' שלא להרבות במשמרות: א"ר אסי לפי שאלמלא מעמדות. עיסקי קרבנות שישראל עושין, הן היו כלים בחטאתן. ומשהן כלין — שמים וארץ העומדים בזכותן אין מתקיימין כו': כאנשי דור המבול. שמאחר שהן כלין אין העולם מתקיים, והואיל שעל עיסקי קרבן העולם עומד, לכך קורין אנשי מעמד בעריהן במעשה בראשית: כבר תקנתי להם כו'. כל זמן שקורין בהן כו' מהיכא יליף לה להאי. גמגום: ת"ר אנשי משמר מתפללין על קרבן אחיהן. תמידים שבכל יום: אנשי משמר. (ג) אותן כ"ד שהיו בעריהן: בשני על יורדי הים. דכתיב בשני (בראשית א) "יהי רקיע בתוך המים", וצריך להזכיר ולרצות על הדבר: בשלישי על הולכי מדברות. דכתיב "ותראה היבשה" — תהי ראויה יבשה להולכיה, שלא יזוקו מפני חיות רעות: ברביעי על האסכרא. שבו נתלו המאורות, וכתיב ביה (בראשית) "יהי מארת" — מארת כתיב: ועל עוברות כו'. דכתיב ביה (שם) "ישרצו המים שרץ נפש חיה": מפני הנוצרים. שעושים אותו יום טוב שלהם: שלישי ליצירה. דאדם נברא ביום ששי, ובכל יום שלישי הוי חלוש, כדכתיב (בראשית לד) "ויהי ביום השלישי בהיותם כואבים": נשמה יתירה. שנוטלין אותה ממנו, והוי חלש: נשמה יתירה. שמרחיבים דעתו לאכילה ושתיה: כיון ששבת. שנח ושמר את השבת: ווי אבדה נפש. וינפש דורש בנוטריקון: ווי נפש: בראשית בשנים. כהן ולוי קורין ביום תענית בראשית: תלתא פסוקי הוי. וסגיא בהו לחד גברא: רב אמר דולג. הראשון קורא שלשה פסוקים, והשני מתחיל בפסוק שסיים בו הראשון, והשנים עמו — הרי שלשה. ומשום אין משיירין בפרשה פחות משלשה פסוקים ליכא, משום דלא אפשר: פוסק. מפסיק הפסוק לשנים, ראשון קורא שני פסוקים וחצי, ולוי משלים חצי אותו הפסוק שקרא הכהן עם שנים הנותרים: ר' חנינא קרא. שהיה בעל מקרא, ויודע בגירסא ובקי בטעמיה: צער גדול. הרבה טרחתי וחזרתי עליו שיתיר לי לפסוק הפסוק לשנים לצורך תינוקות שלומדים לפני, שאינן יכולין לקרוא פסוק כולו: הכי נמי לא אפשר. גבי ס"ת (ג). ודילוג אי אפשר, משום הנכנסין והיוצאין, אם שני דולג ומתחיל בפסוק שסיים בו הראשון, בני אדם הנכנסין שלא שמעו קריאת הראשון סבורין לומר שלא קרא הראשון אלא שני פסוקים ונפיק מיניה חורבא, וכשהראשון קורא ג' פסוקים ואינו משייר אלא שנים איכא גזרת יוצאין דסברי האי שני דסגיא ליה בשני פסוקים: מיתיבי פרשה של ששה פסוקים. אשאר ימות השנה קאי: ויש אומרים שלשה. מפרשה אחריתי: הכי גרסינן: למאן דאמר*) דולג לידלוג למ"ד פוסק ליפסוק. כלומר, פרשה של חמשה פסוקין (ד) אמאי קורא שני שלשה פסוקין בפרשה אחרת? לידלוג או ליפסוק:

דאית

*) [ע' רש"י במגיל' כב. ד"ה למאן וקל"ע]

רבינו חננאל

שמואל ודוד והעמידום על (י"ו) [כ"ד] קשיא לרב חסדא ושנינן הכי מיסוד של שמואל שהוסיף על שתיקן משה. בא דוד והוסיף על מה שתיקן שמואל [והעמידום על כ"ד] שנא' המה יסד דוד ושמואל הרואה באמונתם: ת"ר ד' משמרות עלו מן הגולה. ידעיה חרים פשחור אימר. עמדו הנביאים שביניהם וחלקום לכ"ד משמרות בללום ונתנום בקלפי בא ידעיה ונטל חלקו וחלק חבירו שש וכן חרים וכן פשחור וכן אימר וכן התנו נביאים שביניהם שאע"פ שיהויריב ראש משמרה עולה לא ידחה ידעיה ממקומו אלא ידעיה עיקר ויהויריב טפל לו עמדו ראשי א) משמרות וקבעו עצמן בתי אבות. משמר שהיה בו ה' בתי אבות ג' מקריבין ב) ג' ימים וב' מקריבין ד' ימים. ומי שהיה בו ג) ו' בית אבות כל אחד מקריב יומו וכן כולן. יש מי שקבעו עצמן לעולם. בית אב שהיה בשבת לעולם אינו מקריב אלא בשבת. ומי שהוא ביום ראשון לעולם ביום ראשון. ויש שמגדילין ד) על כל משמר. ויש שהוא מגדילין בכל שבוע ושבוע: ירושלמי ר' הוה ממני (מוציאין) [תרין מנויין] אי הוין כדי הוין מתקיימין ואין לא הוו מסתלקין מדרמך. תרגום ויישן ויחלום ודמוך וחלם. (ר') פקיד לבריה לא תעביד כן אלא מני כולהו כחדא ומני ר' חמא בר' חנינא בראש. ולמה לא מנייה ר' בגין שהשיבו ברבים. ומה השיבו ר' הוה יתיב מתני [יחזקאל ז] ופלטו פליטיהם והיו אל ההרים כיוני הגאיות כולם (הומות) [הומיות אמר] ליה רבי חנינא (כלם) הומות א"ל הן קריתיה א"ל קומי רב המנונא דבבל. א"ל כד תיחות תמן אמור ליה דמנייתך חכים וידע דלא מיתמני ביומוי. מן דמך ר' א' איני מקבל עד דתמני ר' אפס דדרומא והוה תמן חד סב ה) א"ר חנינא קדמאי אנא תניין וקביל עליה ר' חנינא מתמנן תליתאי שמואל ודבית שילה הוי עיילין שאלין בשלמא דנשיאה כל יומא והוו דבית שילה עלין ויתבין קדמאי פלגו יקר לשמואל ואותיביה קדמאי על רב לתמן פלג ליה שמואל יקר ואותיביה קדמאי אמרו דבית שילה אנן תניין וקביל שמואל עלויה מיתב תליתאי. המה יסד דוד ושמואל הרואה באמונתם אומנות גדולה היתה שאין משמר נוטל ושונה בשדה אחוזה עד שיטול חבירו. תנא בתוספתא. אלו משמרות כהנים לוים וישראלים עמדו נביאים שביניהם וקבעום כ"ד משמרות שנאמר צו את בני ישראל אי אפשר לומר כל ישראל אלא מלמד ששלוחו של אדם כמותו הגיע זמן המשמר כהנים ולוים עולין בירושלים וישראל שבאותו משמר שאין יכולין לעלות לירושלים מתקבצין בעריהם וקורין בענין קרבנות ובענין מעשה בראשית ובטלין מן המלאכה (של) [כל] אותה שבת ולמה קורין בקרבנות ובמעשה בראשית ללמדך שאלמלא המעמדות שמתקבצין וקורין לא נתקיימו מעשה בראשית שנא' אם לא בריתי יומם ולילה חקות שמים וארץ לא שמתי. וכתיב ויאמר ה' במה אדע כי אירשנה. אמר אברהם לפני הקב"ה רבש"ע מתיירא אני שמא ישראל יחטאו כו': ת"ר אנשי

א) מכאן עד ויש מהם שמגדילין הוא לשון התוספתא למכילתין פ"ב ובירושלמי כאן ה"ב. ב) בתוספתא הגי' שלשה מקריבין שני ימים [ור"ל לכל אחד מהבתי אבות מקריבין שני ימים] ושנים מקריבין יום אחד משמר שיש בו ששה חמשה מקריבין חמשה ימים ואחד מקריב שני ימים עכ"ל התוספתא אכן בירושלמי הגי' כמש"כ רבינו וכן צ"ל גם בתוספתא ודו"ק. ג) נראה דצ"ל ומי שהי' בו ז' בתי אבות וכ"ה בתוספתא ובירושלמי. ד) בירושלמי הגי' שמגרילין וע"ש במפרש. ה) אמר אי חנינא קדמאי אנא תניין אין ר' אפס דרומאה קדמאי אנא תניין כ"ה בירושלמי.

ל"ל יהויריב · ל"ל ויהויריב · [ע' תוספות מגילה כח.]

גליון הש"ס

גמ' אמר רב אסי אלמלא מעמדות. ע' תוי"ט פ"ד מ"ב דלפנות:

הגהות מהר"ב רנשבורג

א] גמ' ת"ר אנשי משמר. נ"ב גלע"ד של"ל איפכא לאנשי משמר היו מתפללין ולאנשי מעמד מתכנסין לבהכ"נ וכן מוכח בתמיד' וברמב"ם פ"ו מהלכות כלי מקדש הלכה א' ב' ג' ודו"ק:

[מס' סופרים פי"ז ה"ה ע"ש]

הגהות הגר"א

[א] גמ' ת"ר אנשי משמר (רשום עליו אות ב') היו כו' ואנשי מעמד (רשום עליו אות א') כלומר דצ"ל להיפך:

[כלה טז:] · מגילה כב: · [ל"ל ותניא] ג"ז שם · [מגילה שם ברכות יב:] · [במגילה שם ליתא] · מגילה שם ע"ש

הגהות הב"ח

(א) גמ' קורין אותה בשנים ושל חמשה ביחיד הראשון קורא: (ב) רש"י ד"ה אנשי משמר שהיו בירושלים: (ג) ד"ה ה"ג לא אפשר גבי ס"ת דבדלוג אי אפשר: (ד) ד"ה למאן כו' אמאי קורא שני כו' נ"ב עי' פ"ג דמגילה דף כב ע"א אפשר דמייתי התם מיירי בקריאה ככר ע"ש אבל ברייתא דהכא תנא קורא לכתחילה קשיא אמאי קורא לידלג או ליפסק: (ה) תום' ד"ה גזירה כו' שלא ראו את הראשון שקרא כו' ויראו את השני:

רבינו גרשום

ושמנה מאיתמר וקשיא לרב חסדא אמר לך רב חסדא תנאי הוא דאשכחן תנא דלעיל דתניא משה תיקן ד' מאלעזר וד' מאיתמר ואנא דאמרי כוותיה: בללום ונתנום בקלפי שכשחלקו כל משמר לו' משמרות היה מחלוקת ביניהם שזו אומר אני עולה תחלה וזו אומר אני עולה תחלה מה עשו כתבו שמות ראשי של אותן ה' משמרות שהוסיפו ממשמר ידעיה ובא ידעיה ונטל חלקו וחלק חבריו שהניח ידיו בקלפי ואומר שם אותה משמורה שעולה בידי תחלה היא עולה תחלה אחרי וכן בשניה וכן בשלישית וכן ברביעית וכן חמישית וכן עשה חרים וכו'. שאפי' יהויריב עולה שהוא לא רצה לעלות עם עזרא: מנה"מ דקורין במעמדות מעשה בראשית אמר רב אסי אילמלא מעמדות כלומר קרבנות לא נתקיימו שמים וארץ שנא' ויאמר ה' אלהים במה אדע וגו' קחה לי עגלה משולשת וגו' דהיינו קרבנות לפיכך קוראין במעשה בראשית כשעוסקין בקרבנות לפי שכל מעשה בראשית אינו מתקיים אלא בשביל הקרבנות: אנשי משמר היו מתפללין על קרבן אחיהם שיתקבל ברצון שבו כהנים של משמר נחלק לז' בתי אבות וכל בית אב עובד יום אחד וביום שבית אב עובד שאר כל כהנים אנשי משמר ז' בתי אבות מתפללין על קרבן שמקריבין אחיהם בית אב שביעי שיתקבל ברצון: אנשי מעמד היו יושבין ד' תעניות כלו' אותן ישראל של מעמד כדאמרנו לעיל במשנתנו שמתכנסין בעריהן יושבין ד' תעניות על יורדי הים לפי שנאמר בו והיה רקיע בתוך המים על הולכי מדברות לפי שנאמר בו ותראה היבשה על אסכרא לפי שנאמר בו יהי מאורות מארת כתיב דמשמע מארה על עוברות ומיניקות לפי שנאמר בו ישרצו המים נפש חיה דהיינו דמעוברות. מפני הנוצרים לפי שיום חג שלהם באחד בשבת ואם היו ישראל מתענין היו כועסים. שלישי דיצירה שאדם נוצר בערב שבת

יח א מיי' פ"ו מהל' כלי המקדש הל' ז:

דאית ליה רווחא. "פרשה גדולה קורין אותה בשנים בשחרית ובמוסף ובמנחה קורין על פיהן" כו'. § איבעיא להו: היכי קאמר? בשחרית ובמוסף קורין אותה בספר, ובמנחה קורין אותה על פה כקורין את שמע או דלמא הכי קתני: בשחרית קורין אותה בספר, ובמוסף ובמנחה קורין אותה על פה כקורין את שמע. תא שמע, דתניא: בשחרית ובמוסף נכנסין לבית הכנסת וקורין כדרך שקורין כל השנה ובמנחה יחיד קורא אותה על פה. אמר ר' יוסי: וכי יחיד יכול לקרות דברי תורה על פה בצבור? אלא: [א]כולן נכנסין וקורין אותה על פה כקורין את שמע. § "כל יום שיש בו הלל אין בו מעמד" כו'. § מה הפרש בין זה לזה? הללו דברי תורה, והללו דברי סופרים. § "זמן עצי כהנים והעם" כו'. § ת"ר: למה הוצרכו לומר זמן עצי כהנים והעם? אמרו: כשעלו בני הגולה, לא מצאו עצים בלשכה, ועמדו אלו והתנדבו משלהם. וכך התנו נביאים שביניהן: שאפי' לשכה מלאה עצים — יהיו אלו מתנדבין משלהן, שנאמר (נחמיה י) "והגורלות הפלנו על קרבן העצים הכהנים, הלוים, והעם, להביא לבית אלהינו, לבית אבותינו, לעתים מזומנים שנה בשנה, לבער על מזבח ה' אלהינו, ככתוב בתורה". § "ועמהם כהנים ולוים וכל מי" כו'. § תנו רבנן: מה היו בני גונבי עלי ובני קוצעי קציעות? אמרו: פעם אחת גזרה המלכות גזירה על ישראל שלא יביאו עצים למערכה ושלא יביאו בכורים לירושלים, והושיבו פרוזדאות על הדרכים כדרך שהושיב ירבעם בן נבט שלא יעלו ישראל לרגל. מה עשו כשרין *)(*שבאותו הדור ויראי חטא)? הביאו סלי בכורים וחיפום בקציעות, ונטלום ועלי על כתפיהן. וכיון שהגיעו אצל פרוזדאות, אמרו להם: להיכן אתם הולכין? אומרין להם: לעשות שני עיגולי דבילה במכתשת שלפנינו ובעלי שעל כתפינו. כיון שעברו מהן — עיטרום בסלים והביאום לירושלים. תנא: הן הן בני סלמאי הנתופתי. ת"ר: מה הן בני סלמאי הנתופתי? אמרו: פעם אחת גזרה המלכות גזירה על ישראל שלא יביאו עצים למערכה, והושיבו פרוזדאות על הדרכים כדרך שהושיב ירבעם בן נבט על הדרכים שלא יעלו ישראל לרגל. מה עשו יראי חטא שבאותו הדור? הביאו גזיריהן ועשו סולמות, והניחו על כתפיהם והלכו להם. כיון שהגיעו אצלן, אמרו להם: להיכן אתם הולכין? אמרו להם: להביא גוזלות משובך שלפנינו, ובסולמות שעל כתפינו. כיון שעברו מהן — פירקום והביאום, והעלום לירושלים. ועליהם ועל כיוצא בהם הוא אומר (משלי י) "זכר צדיק לברכה", ועל ירבעם בן נבט וחבריו נאמר: "ושם רשעים ירקב". § "בעשרים בו בני פחת מואב בן יהודה". § תנא: בני פחת מואב בן יהודה הן הן בני דוד בן יהודה. דברי ר' מאיר. רבי יוסי אומר: הן הן בני יואב בן צרויה. § "בעשרים באלול, בני עדין בן יהודה" וכו'. § תנו רבנן: בני עדין בן יהודה הן הן בני דוד בן יהודה. דברי רבי יהודה. רבי יוסי אומר: הן הן בני יואב בן צרויה. § "באחד בטבת, שבו בני פרעוש שניה" כו'. § מני מתני'? לא ר' מאיר, ולא רבי יהודה, ולא רבי יוסי. אי ר"מ — ליתני שבו בני דוד בן יהודה שניה. אי רבי יהודה — ליתני שבו בני דוד בן יהודה שניה. אי רבי יוסי — ליתני שבו בני יואב בן צרויה שניה! לעולם ר' יוסי, ותרי תנאי אליבא דר' יוסי. § "באחד בטבת לא היה בו מעמד" כו'. § אמר ליה מר קשישא בריה דרב חסדא לרב אשי: מאי

*) [נ"ל ויראי חטא שבאותו הדור]

רש"י

דאית ליה רווחא. שיכול לקרות מפרשה אחרת. אבל הכא לית ליה רווחא, דהא לא מצי למיקרי אלא "בראשית" ו"יהי רקיע": מה הפרש בין זה לזה. מאי שנא דקרבן עצים דחי מעמד דנעילה, ומעמד דמנחה לא דחי? הללו דברי תורה. מנחה, כדאמרי' בברכות (דף כו:): יצחק אבינו תיקן תפלת מנחה, שנאמר (בראשית כד) "ויצא יצחק לשוח בשדה לפנות ערב", ודנעילה מדברי סופרים. וצריכין חיזוק לא גרסינן [א] הכא: עמדו אלו. זמן דקתני במתני' – אהכי הוצרכו למנות, משום ההיא תקנה דעבוד להו הנך נביאים כי היכי דלא לידחינהו מאתרייהו: פרוזדאות. שומרים: בכורים. אדם נכנס לתוך שדהו ורואה אשכול שביכר, תאנה שביכרה – קושר עליה גמי ועושה אותה בכורים: בקציעות. תאנים יבשים, כותשין אותן ועושין מהן עגולין: ה"ג: והעלי על כתפיהן. (*בוכנא): במכתשת שלפנינו. שהוא במקום אחר (א) לפני בסמוך. וזהו גונבי עלי – על שם שמתגנבין מן הפרוזדאות על עסקי עלי: הן הן בני סלמאי הנתופתי. כעין מעשה זה עשו(ב): הן הן בני דוד בן יהודה. דוד מלך ישראל. ואהכי קרו ליה פחת מואב – שבא מרות המואביה: יואב בן צרויה. שבא מרות המואביה. כי צרויה אם יואב אחות דוד היתה, שנאמר (דה"א ב) "ואחיותיהם צרויה ואביגיל": בני עדין הן הן בני דוד. להכי קרי ליה בספר שמואל (ב כג) עדינו העצני, *שבשעה שעוסק בתורה – מעדן עצמו כתולעת, וכשיוצא למלחמה – מתקשה כעץ: הן הן בני יואב בן צרויה. פלוגתא היא (*במס' חגיגה) חד אמר עדינו העצני זה דוד, *וחד אמר זה יואב: ליתני שבו בני דוד שניה. דהא קאמר ר' מאיר פחת מואב היינו דוד: ולר' יהודה. בני עדין היינו דוד. ובמתניתין קתני ברישא בני דוד והדר קתני בני פחת מואב, דלר"מ ולר' יהודה בני עדין – היינו דוד, שבו שניה מיבעי ליה: ולר' יוסי. דאמר פחת מואב ועדין היינו יואב, שבו שניה מיבעי ליה: לעולם ר' יוסי ותרי תנאי אליבא דר' יוסי. דמאן דאמר בני עדין בן יהודה היינו בני יואב – לא סבר ליה דבני פחת מואב היינו יואב, ולהכי לא קתני שבו בני יואב שניה. ולא סבירא ליה נמי דהן הן בני דוד – דאם כן שבו בני דוד שניה מיבעי ליה למיתני, אלא משפחה אחרת הן. ומאן דאמר בני פחת מואב היינו בני יואב – לא סבירא ליה דבני עדין היינו יואב, אלא משפחה אחרת הן: מאי

תוספות

מה הפרש בין זה לזה. כלומר: מה הפרש בין קרבן מוסף לקרבן עצים, דקרבן מוסף דוחה מנחה וקרבן עצים לא דחי מנחה? הללו דברי תורה. מוסף, ולהכי קדחי מנחה דהוי מדברי תורה. אבל קרבן עצים, דהוי מדברי סופרים, והלכך לא דחיא אלא נעילה דהויא מדברי סופרים, אבל לא דחיא מנחה דהויא מדברי תורה: בני פחת מואב וכו' הן הן בני דוד. ולכך נקראו בני פחת, (ג) שבאו מרות המואביה:

הן הן בני יואב בן צרויה. פירוש: דצרויה היתה *אחות דוד, כדכתיב (דה"א ב) "ואחיותיהם צרויה", והם באים מזרע רות המואביה:

אי ר"מ. דקאמר בני פחת מואב בן יהודה הן הן בני דוד בן יהודה, ליתני במתניתין כי קאמר בעשרים כו' בני פחת מואב בן יהודה היה, ה"ל למיתני בני דוד בן יהודה שבו שניה, כמו שאומר שבו בני פרעוש שניה. אי ר' יהודה, דקאמר בני עדין בן יהודה הן הן בני דוד בן יהודה – ליתני שבו בני דוד בן יהודה שניה. אי ר' יוסי – ליתני שבו בני יואב שניה! ומשני: תרי תנאי ואליבא דר' יוסי. וקשיא: אמאי לא מוקי אליבא דר"מ ותרי תנאי אליבא דר"מ? שהרי טפי יש לן לאוקמא כר"מ דסתמא דמתני' כר' מאיר! ונראה לי: דלהכי מוקי לה כרבי יוסי, משום דרבי יוסי נימוקו עמו, ומסתברא כוותיה בכל מקום ואפילו מחביריו:

ויוס

רבינו חננאל

משמר. מתפללין על קרבן אחיהם שיתקבל ברצון. ואנשי מעמד מתענין ד' תעניות בשבוע. בשני על יורדי הים. שנאמר ויאמר אלהים יהי רקיע בתוך המים וגו'. בשלישי על הולכי מדברות שנאמר יקוו המים ותראה היבשה. בד' על האסכרה שלא תעל בתינוקות שנאמר יהי מאורות. מארת כתיב חסר ו'. בה' על עוברות שלא יפילו ועל המניקות שיגדלו בניהם שנאמר ישרצו המים שרץ [נפש חיה]. בע"ש לא היו מתענין מפני כבוד בשבת וכ"ש שבת עצמה.א) וסנהדרין לבתי אבות מתענין עמהם. באחד בשבת מ"ט לא. ר' יוחנן אומר מפני הנוצרים. פי' שיו"ט שלהם הוא. ר' שמואל ב"נ אומר מפני שהוא שלישי ליצירה. וכתיב ויהי ביום השלישי בהיותם כאבים. כלומר נברא האדם בששי הנה ששי ושבת ויום ראשון הרי שלש ליצירה והוא עדיין חלש. ר' שמעון בן לקיש אמר מפני נשמה יתירה שנתנת לאדם בשבת כדי לאכול ולשתות ולשמוח ולהתענג כגבור בשתיית היין ואם אין בו כח גדול אין בו יכולת לשתות ובמ"ש ניטלת מן האדם. ונשתייר תשוי כח לפיכך אין בו יכולת. כדכתיב שבת וינפש. כיון ששבת ווי אבדה נפש. כלומר אבדה הנפש היתירה: מתני' וישראל שבאותו משמר מתכנסין בעריהם. פי' קבלנו מרבותינו שהיו בכל יום קורין פרשת קרבנות. ואח"כ היו קורין סדר בראשית. ביום הראשון בראשית ויהי רקיע. תנא בראשית בשנים אמאי בשנים והא ה' פסוקי נינהו. ותנא הקורא בתורה לא יפחות מג' פסוקים. רב אמר דולג. פי' הראשון קורא שלשה. השני חוזר וקורא אחד מאלו השלשה שקראם הראשון והשני פסוקים הנותרים מן הפרשה. ושמואל אמר פוסק הפסוק אחד לשנים כל אחד קורא שלשה. רב אמר דולג. כל פסוקא דלא פסקיה משה אנן לא פסקינן ליה. וקיי"ל כרב וכבר פירשנוהו במגילה. פי' בשחרית במוסף כו'. תנא בשחרית ובמוסף נכנסין בכנסת וקורא בתורה בצבור. ע"ש לא היו נכנסין מפני כבוד השבת: מתני' כל יום שיש בו הלל ואין בו מוסף כגון חנוכה וכיוצא בו לא היה בו בשחרית כלומר לא היה בו מעמד בשחרית לא היו אנשי מעמד נכנסין בכנסת וקורין פרשיותיהן בשחרית וכל יום שיש בו קרבן מוסף כגון ר"ח וחש"מ אין בו לאנשי מעמד קריאה במנחה. כל יום שיש בו קרבן עצים כגון אלו ט' ימים שאנו עתידין לפרשן כדתנא זמן עצי הכהנים והעם ט' אין לאנשי המעמד תפלה בנעילה. אמר בן עזאי משום ר' יהושע כל יום שיש בו קרבן מוסף אין מעמד ב) בנעילה. קרבן עצים אין במנחה. ואמרינן מה הפרש בין זה לזה. ופרקינן הללו דברי תורה כלומר הימים שיש בהן קרבן מוסף כגון ר"ח וחולו של מועד מן התורה אסורים בתענית ואין צריכין [חיזוק] אלא דוחין המעמד שבנעילה. ואע"פ שאינה תדירה. ואינו דבר ידוע. אבל זמן הכהנים שהוא אסור בתענית מדרבנן צריך חיזוק. לפי' אין בו מעמד במנחה שהוא תדיר והוא ידוע. וכיון שרואין כי דוחה את המנחה נוהגין בו יו"ט. כדתניא [במגלת תענית] ואלו ימים זמן עצי הכהנים והעם אסורין בהספד ותענית: ת"ר למה הוזכרו זמן עצי הכהנים והעם להמנות כשעלו ישראל מן הגולה לא מצאו עצים למערכה ועמדו אלו והתנדבו משלהם. פי' גונבין עלי וקוצעי קציעות גונבין דעת יושבי פרדסאות באמרם להם כי התאנים הבכורות הללו אנו הולכים בהן לכתוש במכתש שלפנינו ובעלי שעל כתפינו לעשותן קציעה של דבילה. פי' עלי יד המכתש כדכתיב אם תכתוש את האויל במכתש בתוך הריפות בעלי. דברים פשוטים הן

א) כן הוא בירושלמי. ב) כן היתה גרסת רבינו להיפך מגרסא שלנו במתני' בדברי ר"ע וב"ע.

[נ"ל בוכנא]

[מו"ק טז:]

כמו"ק טז: כנ"ל

[לא נמצא שם דחד אמר זה יואב ובתיקוני כלי שרת תקנתי על נכון]

נ"ל בת ישי

הגהות הב"ח

(א) רש"י ד"ה במכתשת כו' במקום אחר לפנינו בסמוך: (ב) ד"ה הן הן כו' עשו בסמוך הס"ד: (ג) תוס' ד"ה בני פחת מואב שבאו מרות:

הגהות הגר"א

[א] רש"י ד"ה הללו. וצריכין חיזוק ל"ג. נ"ב אבל הגאונים גרסי וערש"ב:

רבינו גרשום

שבת והוי אחד בשבת שלישי ויש בו חולשא. במוצאי שבת ניטלת ממנו ויש בו חולשא: במוסף במנחה וכו' ופי' בגמ' רב אמר דולג שראשון קורא ג' פסוקים ושמואל אמר פוסק שאינו דולג משום גזרה משום הנכנסין ומשום היוצאין שאם קורא ראשון ג' פסוקים שלמין א' היוצא לאחר כששיים הראשון שלא נשתייר לשני לקרות אלא ב' פסוקין וכן אם מתחיל השני בפסוק הג' הנכנס לאחר שסיים הראשון כששומע ששני קורא הג' אומר לא קרא הראשון אלא ב' פסוקים: דאית ביה רווחא שיכול לקרות פסוק אחד מפרשה אחרת אבל דלא מצי למקרי מפרשה אחרת דאית לה למיקרא למחר או דולג או פוסק. ובמנחה קורין על פיהן מה שקורין שחרית בספר כדרך שקורין כל השנה בספר: ערב שבת במנחה לא היו נכנסין לקרות בפה לפי שהן עוסקין לכבוד שבת לטרוח בסעודת שבת והאי דקתני בששי ותצא וגו' היינו בשחרית בספר: אין בו מעמד שחרית כלומר אין קורין מה שקורין במעמדות לפי שעוסקין בהלל. קרבן מוסף אין בו נעילה כלומר שיש בו קרבן מוסף אין בו תפלת נעילה ואין קורין במעמדות לפי שעוסקין בקרבן וקסבר דתפלת נעילה קודם לתפלת מנחה ולפי שתפלת מוסף עד הערב עוסקין במוסף בשעת נעילה. קרבן עצים אין במנחה כלומר ביום שמביאין קרבן עצים אין קוראין במעמדות במנחה. לפי שעוסקין בקרבן עצים: קרבן מוסף אין במנחה כלומר מנחה קודם לנעילה ובשעת מנחה עוסקין במוסף ואין פנאי לקרות במעמדות: מה הפרש בין זה לזה כלומר מ"ש דמוסף דוחה מנחה ואין דוחה נעילה וקרבן עצים דוחה אפי' נעילה: הללו קרבן מוסף דברי תורה ואין צריכין חיזוק ואין צריך שיהא דוחה אלא מנחה שסמוך לו אבל קרבן עצים שהן מדברי סופרים וצריכין חיזוק לפיכך עשו בו חיזוק שדוחה אפי' נעילה שאינו סמוך לו: ועמהן עם זתוא שהוא אחרון כהנים ולוים וכל מי שטעה שבטו שאינו יודע מאיזה שבט הוא: שבו בני פרעוש שניה. הן הולכין פעם שניה להביא עצים. באחד בטבת לא היה בו מעמד כל היום שהיה בו הלל בשחרית וקרבן מוסף במנחה וקרבן עצים בנעילה: למה הוצרכו לקבוע הני זמנים להביא עצים למערכה: פרדסאות. ממונים: בקציעות. של דבילה: עיטרום בסלים כמצוה דכתיב ונתת בטנא. פרקום והביאום. עצים של סולמות לירושלים לקרבן עצים. בני פחת מואב הן בני דוד ולהכי קרי ליה מואב משום דאתי מרות המואביה הן בני יואב דאתי נמי ממואב מאמו: הן בני דוד ועל שם עדינו העצני קרי ליה בני עדין. הן בני יואב ועל שם דוד שהיה ראש משפחותם קרי להו בני עדין על שם דוד. אי ר"מ ליתני נמי שבו בני דוד שניה דר"מ קאמר הני פחת מואב הן בני דוד כיון דתרוייהו קתני להו במתניתין כדתני בני דוד איבעי להו למיתני שבו שניה דכבר קתני דבאו פעם ראשונה דקתני באו בני פחת מואב. אי ר' יהודה ליתני שבו בני דוד שניה נמי דהא תני במתניתין שתי פעמים בני דוד דר' יהודה אמר דבני עדין הן בני דוד אי ר' יוסי ליתני שבו בני יואב שניה. תרי תנאי אליבא דר' יוסי דהאי תנא דאמר אליבא דר' יוסי בני פחת מואב הני בני יואב לא אמר דר' יוסי אמר בני עדין הן בני יואב ומאן דאמר אליבא דר' יוסי בני עדין הן בני יואב לא אמר דר' יוסי אמר בני פחת מואב הן בני יואב ולא תני במתניתין בני יואב אלא פעם אחת להכי לא קתני שבו בני

מַאי שְׁנָא הַלֵּל דְּדָחֵי דִּידֵיהּ, וּמַאי שְׁנָא מוּסָף דְּלָא דָּחֵי דִּידֵיהּ? א"ל רַב אָשֵׁי: הַשְׁתָּא דְּלָאו דִּידֵיהּ דָּחֵי — דִּידֵיהּ לֹא כׇּל שֶׁכֵּן! אֲמַר לֵיהּ: הָכִי קָאָמֵינָא לָךְ: לָא לִידְחֵי אֶלָּא דִּידֵיהּ! אֲמַר לֵיהּ: אִיכָּא ר' יוֹסֵי דְּקָאֵי כְּוָותָךְ. דְּתַנְיָא, ר' יוֹסֵי אוֹמֵר: כׇּל יוֹם שֶׁיֵּשׁ בּוֹ מוּסָף — יֵשׁ בּוֹ מַעֲמָד. מַעֲמָד דְּמַאי? אִילֵּימָא מַעֲמָד דְּשַׁחֲרִית — הָא תַּנָּא קַמָּא נַמִי הָכִי קָאָמַר. אֶלָּא מַעֲמָד דְּמוּסָף — דִּידֵיהּ נַמִי לָא דָּחֵי?! אֶלָּא דְּמִנְחָה [א] — קׇרְבַּן עֵצִים דָּחֵי! אֶלָּא לָאו — דִּנְעִילָה. שְׁמַע מִינַּהּ: דִּידֵיהּ — דָּחֵי, דְּלָאו דִּידֵיהּ — לָא דָּחֵי, שְׁמַע מִינַּהּ. וְלִיתְנֵי נַמִי: בְּאֶחָד בְּנִיסָן לֹא הָיָה בּוֹ מַעֲמָד, מִפְּנֵי שֶׁיֵּשׁ בּוֹ הַלֵּל וְקׇרְבַּן מוּסָף וְקׇרְבַּן עֵצִים! אֲמַר רָבָא: זֹאת אוֹמֶרֶת הַלֵּילָא דְּבְרֵישׁ יַרְחָא לָאו דְּאוֹרָיְיתָא. דְּאָמַר רַבִּי יוֹחָנָן מִשּׁוּם רַבִּי שִׁמְעוֹן בֶּן יְהוֹצָדָק: *[א]שְׁמוֹנָה עָשָׂר יוֹם בַּשָּׁנָה יָחִיד גּוֹמֵר בָּהֶן אֶת הַלֵּל, וְאֵלּוּ הֵן: שְׁמוֹנַת יְמֵי הֶחָג, וּשְׁמוֹנַת יְמֵי חֲנוּכָּה, וְיוֹם טוֹב הָרִאשׁוֹן שֶׁל פֶּסַח, וְיוֹם טוֹב (רִאשׁוֹן) שֶׁל עֲצֶרֶת. [ב]וּבַגּוֹלָה, עֶשְׂרִים וְאֶחָד יוֹם, וְאֵלּוּ הֵן: [ג]תִּשְׁעַת יְמֵי הֶחָג, [ד]וּשְׁמוֹנַת יְמֵי חֲנוּכָּה, [ה]וּשְׁנֵי יָמִים הָרִאשׁוֹנִים שֶׁל פֶּסַח, [ו]וּב' יָמִים טוֹבִים שֶׁל עֲצֶרֶת. רַב אִיקְלַע לְבָבֶל, חֲזִינְהוּ דְּקָא קָרוּ הַלֵּילָא בְּרֵישׁ יַרְחָא. סְבַר לְאַפְסוֹקִינְהוּ. כֵּיוָן דַּחֲזָא דְּקָא מְדַלְּגֵי דַּלּוֹגֵי, אֲמַר: שְׁמַע מִינַּהּ, [ז]מִנְהַג אֲבוֹתֵיהֶם בִּידֵיהֶם. תָּנָא: יָחִיד לֹא יַתְחִיל, וְאִם הִתְחִיל, גּוֹמֵר.§ "ה' דְּבָרִים אֵירְעוּ אֶת אֲבוֹתֵינוּ בְּשִׁבְעָה עָשָׂר בְּתַמּוּז" כו'§ "נִשְׁתַּבְּרוּ הַלּוּחוֹת". מְנָלַן? דְּתַנְיָא: *בְּשִׁשָּׁה לַחֹדֶשׁ נִיתְּנוּ עֲשֶׂרֶת הַדִּבְּרוֹת לְיִשְׂרָאֵל. רַבִּי יוֹסֵי אוֹמֵר: בְּשִׁבְעָה בּוֹ. מַאן דְּאָמַר בְּשִׁשָּׁה נִיתְּנוּ — בְּשִׁשָּׁה נִיתְּנוּ, וּבְשִׁבְעָה עָלָה מֹשֶׁה. מ"ד בְּשִׁבְעָה — בְּשִׁבְעָה נִיתְּנוּ, וּבְשִׁבְעָה עָלָה מֹשֶׁה, דִּכְתִיב °"וַיִּקְרָא אֶל מֹשֶׁה בַּיּוֹם הַשְּׁבִיעִי" וּכְתִיב °"וַיָּבֹא מֹשֶׁה בְּתוֹךְ הֶעָנָן וַיַּעַל אֶל הָהָר, וַיְהִי מֹשֶׁה בָּהָר אַרְבָּעִים יוֹם וְאַרְבָּעִים לָיְלָה". עֶשְׂרִים וְאַרְבָּעָה דְּסִיוָן, וְשִׁיתְסַר דְּתַמּוּז, מְלוֹ לְהוּ אַרְבְּעִין. בְּשִׁיבְסַר בְּתַמּוּז נְחֵית, אֲתָא, וְתַבְרִינְהוּ לְלוּחוֹת. וּכְתִיב °"וַיְהִי כַּאֲשֶׁר קָרַב אֶל הַמַּחֲנֶה, וַיַּרְא אֶת הָעֵגֶל. וַיַּשְׁלֵךְ מִיָּדָיו אֶת הַלּוּחוֹת, וַיְשַׁבֵּר אוֹתָם תַּחַת הָהָר".§ "בָּטַל הַתָּמִיד" — גְּמָרָא.§ "הוּבְקְעָה הָעִיר". בְּי"ז הֲוָה? וְהָכְתִיב °"בַּחֹדֶשׁ הָרְבִיעִי, בְּתִשְׁעָה לַחֹדֶשׁ, וַיֶּחֱזַק הָרָעָב בָּעִיר". וּכְתִיב בַּתְרֵיהּ °"וַתִּבָּקַע הָעִיר" וגו'! אֲמַר רָבָא: לָא קַשְׁיָא. כָּאן — בָּרִאשׁוֹנָה, כָּאן — בַּשְּׁנִיָּה. דְּתַנְיָא: בָּרִאשׁוֹנָה, הוּבְקְעָה הָעִיר בְּתִשְׁעָה בְּתַמּוּז, בַּשְּׁנִיָּה, בְּשִׁבְעָה עָשָׂר בּוֹ.§ "שָׂרַף אַפּוֹסְטְמוֹס אֶת הַתּוֹרָה" — גְּמָרָא.§ "הֶעֱמִיד צֶלֶם בַּהֵיכָל". מְנָלַן? דִּכְתִיב °"וּמֵעֵת הוּסַר הַתָּמִיד, וְלָתֵת שִׁקּוּץ שׁוֹמֵם". וְחַד הֲוָה? וְהָכְתִיב °"וְעַל כְּנַף שִׁקּוּצִים מְשׁוֹמֵם"! אֲמַר רָבָא: תְּרֵי הֲווּ, וְנָפַל חַד עַל חַבְרֵיהּ וְתַבְרֵיהּ לֵיהּ לִידֵיהּ, וְאִשְׁתְּכַח דַּהֲוָה כְּתִיב: (א) אַנְתְּ

מקורות בשולי הגמרא: שמות כד; שם; שם לב; ירמיהו נב; שם; דניאל יב; שם ט.

תורה אור

רש"י

מַאי שְׁנָא הַלֵּל דְּדָחֵי דִּידֵיהּ. מַעֲמָד דְּשַׁחֲרִית: וּמַאי שְׁנָא מוּסָף דְּלָא דָּחֵי דִּידֵיהּ. דְּקָתָנֵי: יוֹם שֶׁיֵּשׁ בּוֹ מוּסָף אֵין בּוֹ (ב) מִנְחָה, וְלָא קָתָנֵי אֵין בּוֹ מוּסָף, דְּלָא דָּחֵי דִּידֵיהּ אֶלָּא דְּמִנְחָה: הָכִי קָאָמֵינָא. הָכִי קָא בָּעֵינָא לְמֵימַר: אֶלָּא דִּידֵיהּ. דְּמוּסָף: ה"ג: רַבִּי יוֹסֵי אוֹמֵר כׇּל יוֹם שֶׁיֵּשׁ בּוֹ מוּסָף יֵשׁ בּוֹ מַעֲמָד. וְאַתָּנָא קַמָּא פָּלֵיג, דְּאָמַר: יוֹם שֶׁיֵּשׁ בּוֹ מוּסָף אֵין בּוֹ (ג) נְעִילָה, וַאֲתָא ר' יוֹסֵי לְמֵימַר דְּיֵשׁ בּוֹ מַעֲמָד, אע"פ שֶׁיֵּשׁ בּוֹ מוּסָף: אֶלָּא לָאו דִּנְעִילָה הוּא. דְּאָמַר ר' יוֹסֵי דְּיֵשׁ בּוֹ מַעֲמָד, וְאֵין מוּסָף דּוֹחֶה אוֹתוֹ: בְּאֶחָד בְּנִיסָן. דְּאִית בֵּיהּ הַלֵּל דְּרֹאשׁ חֹדֶשׁ: (ד) קׇרְבַּן עֵצִים. (קׇרְבַּן מוּסָף) דִּבְנֵי אָרַח בֶּן יְהוּדָה: זֹאת אוֹמֶרֶת. מִדְּלָא קָתָנֵי נַמִי בְּאֶחָד בְּנִיסָן — אַלְמָא הַלֵּל דְּרֹאשׁ חֹדֶשׁ לָא דָּחֵי לֵיהּ לְמַעֲמָד, שְׁמַע מִינַּהּ דְּלָאו דְּאוֹרָיְיתָא הֲוָה א], אֶלָּא מִנְהָגָא כִּדְלְקַמָּן: מִנְהַג אֲבוֹתֵיהֶם בִּידֵיהֶן. אֲבָל הַלֵּל דַּחֲנוּכָּה, כְּגוֹן בְּאֶחָד בְּטֵבֵת — וַדַּאי דָּחֵי, דְּכֵיוָן דִּנְבִיאִים תִּיקְּנוּהוּ שֶׁיְּהוּ אוֹמְרִים אוֹתוֹ עַל כׇּל פֶּרֶק וּפֶרֶק וְעַל כׇּל צָרָה שֶׁלֹּא תָּבֹא עֲלֵיהֶן, כְּשֶׁנִּגְאָלִין יְהוּ אוֹמְרִין אוֹתוֹ עַל גְּאוּלָּתָן — כִּדְאוֹרָיְיתָא דָּמֵי: יָחִיד. כְּלוֹמַר, אֲפִי' יָחִיד גּוֹמֵר בָּהֶן אֶת הַהַלֵּל. שֶׁכׇּל אֶחָד וְאֶחָד חַיָּיב לִגְמוֹר בּוֹ אֶת הַהַלֵּל. בְּמַסֶּכֶת עֲרָכִין מְפוֹרָשׁ מַאי שְׁנָא דְּגוֹמֵר כׇּל יְמֵי הֶחָג, וּבְפֶסַח לֹא גּוֹמֵר אֶלָּא יוֹם רִאשׁוֹן — מִשּׁוּם דְּחַג הַסּוּכּוֹת חָלוּק בְּקׇרְבְּנוֹתָיו, וְכׇל אֶחָד וְאֶחָד כְּחַג בִּפְנֵי עַצְמוֹ דָּמֵי: וּבַגּוֹלָה. שֶׁעוֹשִׂין שְׁנֵי יָמִים טוֹבִים מִשּׁוּם סְפֵיקָא: דִּמְדַלְּגֵי דַּלּוֹגֵי. כְּגוֹן חֲנַן, דִּמְדַלְּגִין "לֹא לָנוּ ה' לֹא לָנוּ", וּמַתְחִיל מִן "ה' זְכָרָנוּ יְבָרֵךְ": לֹא יַתְחִיל. אֵינוֹ צָרִיךְ לְהַתְחִיל בְּרֹאשׁ חֹדֶשׁ: ר' יוֹסֵי אוֹמֵר בְּשִׁבְעָה. וְטַעֲמַיְיהוּ מִקְרָא בְּמַסֶּכֶת שַׁבָּת בְּפֶרֶק ר"ע: בְּשִׁבְעָה עָלָה מֹשֶׁה. לְקַבֵּל הַלּוּחוֹת. כְּלוֹמַר, וַדַּאי לֵיכָּא מַאן דְּפָלֵיג עֲלַהּ דְּמַתְנִי' דְּקָתָנֵי דְּבְי"ז בְּתַמּוּז נִשְׁתַּבְּרוּ הַלּוּחוֹת — מִכְּלָל דְּכוּלְּהוּ סְבִירָא לְהוּ דִּבְשִׁבְעָה עָלָה (ה), וְלָאו מִקְרָא נָפְקָא לָן דִּבְשִׁבְעָה עָלָה, דְּהַאי דִּכְתִיב "וַיִּשְׁכֹּן כְּבוֹד ה' עַל הַר סִינַי וַיְכַסֵּהוּ הֶעָנָן שֵׁשֶׁת יָמִים וַיִּקְרָא אֶל מֹשֶׁה בַּיּוֹם הַשְּׁבִיעִי" — אִיכָּא מַאן דְּדָרֵישׁ לֵיהּ בְּמַסֶּכֶת יוֹמָא כִּי אַחַר מַתַּן תּוֹרָה הֲוָה. מִשִּׁבְעָה בְּסִיוָן עַד י"ז בְּתַמּוּז אִיכָּא מ' יוֹם: כ"ד דְּסִיוָן שֶׁהוּא מָלֵא, וְי"ו דְּתַמּוּז — הֲרֵי מ' יוֹם שֶׁעָמַד מֹשֶׁה בָּהָר: גְּמָרָא. כָּךְ קִיבַּלְנוּ מֵאֲבוֹתֵינוּ: וּמֵעֵת הוּסַר הַתָּמִיד לָתֵת שִׁקּוּץ שׁוֹמֵם וגו'. דְּבְעֵת שֶׁהוּסַר וְנִתְבַּטֵּל הַתָּמִיד — בְּאוֹתוֹ הַיּוֹם נָתַן שִׁקּוּץ שׁוֹמֵם, דְּהַיְינוּ הוֹעֲמַד צֶלֶם בַּהֵיכָל: ה"ג: וְהָא כְּתִיב עַל כְּנַף שִׁקּוּצִים. כְּלוֹמַר הָא כְּתִיב קְרָא אַחֲרִינָא, דִּכְתִיב בֵּיהּ "שִׁקּוּצִים", דְּמַשְׁמַע תְּרֵי: תְּרֵי הֲווּ. שֶׁהֶעֱמִידָן מְנַשֶּׁה בַּהֵיכָל: וְנָפַל חַד עַל חַבְרֵיהּ וְקַטְעֵיהּ לִידֵיהּ. וְהַנִּקְטָע לָא קָא חָשֵׁיב, וְהַיְינוּ דִּכְתִיב שִׁקּוּץ אֶחָד: אִשְׁתְּכַח דִּכְתִיב. עַל הַהוּא צֶלֶם הָכִי: אַנְתְּ

תוספות

ויום טוב הראשון של פסח. הוא גומר הלל. אבל שמונה ימי פסח — לא, משום דלא דמי לחנוכה וסוכות. דחנוכה — דינא הוא לגמור הלל, דכל הח' ימים היה הנס מתגדל, והיה כל חד וחד יום טוב. וכן בסוכות *כל יומא ויומא הוי י"ט לעצמו, לפי שפרי החג מתמעטין והולכין. אבל פסח אינו משתנה לא מקרבנות ולא מיום טוב, לכך אין גומרים בו ההלל אלא יום הראשון, והאידנא דגומרין תרי יומי — משום דעבדינן אותו מספק הוי חד יומא לענין קריאת הלל, וכן ביום שני של עצרת, וכן יום של שמחת תורה. ומש"ה יש לנו כ"א יום לגמור הלל:

אמר שמע מינה מנהג אבותיהם בידיהם. י"מ דאמנהג לא מברכינן (ו), מהכא. וכן משמע בסוכה בפרק "לולב וערבה" (דף מד:) דקאמר, *אמר אביי: הוה קאימנא קמיה דר' יצחק, ואייתי ההיא ערבה לקמיה, שקל חביט חביט ולא בריך. קסבר: ערבה מנהג נביאים היא. אלמא: אמנהג לא מברכינן. אבל רבינו תם פסק דמברכינן, דאי איתא דלא מברכינן — אם כן מאי קאמר בגמרא כיון דשמעינהו דמדלגי ואזלי שמע מינה מנהג אבותיהם בידיהם, וכי לא היה לו להכיר אי משום מנהג — קרו ליה לא מברכי, אי איתא דאמנהג לא מברכינן. ואי מברכי — לא מנהג הוא. וכי תימא דלא בא בתחילת קריאת הלל — הא לא מצי אמרת, דהא רב איקלע לבבל קאמר, דאי איתא דבאמצע תפלה בא — הוה ליה למימר איקלע לבי כנישתא. ומדלא אמר מדלא ברכי מנהג הוא — שמע מינה דאמנהגא נמי מברכינן. וההיא דסוכה דמשמע דאמנהגא לא מברכינן, היינו דווקא אמנהג דערבה, דלא הוי אלא מנהג טלטול בעלמא, ואמנהג דטלטול לא מברכינן. אבל בשאר מנהג, כמו קריאת הלל ואחריני כמו אותו מנהג — ודאי מברכינן. וכן הלכה למעשה. ולפי זה יש ליזהר שלא לדבר באמצע ההלל, כיון שבירך, דאם כן הוי מפסיק. ונראה דאין יחיד מחויב לקרות ההלל, אכן אם רוצה לחייב עצמו — הרשות בידו*:

ואשתכח דכתיב עילויה. על אותו יד. פירוש: מצאו כתוב על היד שנחתכה מן הצלם: אנת צבי לאחרובי ביתיה, כלומר ביתו של הקב"ה (ז), אשלמת ליה כלומר: וכחך נתת לו. ויש מפרשים דהכתיבה הוה על הצלם השלם, וה"ק: אשכחי' עליה, על הצלם השלם, אנת צבי לאיחרובי ביתיה. כלומר: אתה רצית להחריב ביתו של הקדוש ברוך הוא, וידך אשלמת ליה — לכך שלמתי את ידך להקדוש ברוך הוא, שחתכתי:

רבינו חננאל

הן. תנא לפי שמסרו עצמן על המצות נזכרין לברכה. כדכתיב זכר צדיק לברכה. זמן עצי הכהנים והעם תשעה. באחד בניסן בני ארח בן יהודה כו'. מני מתני' אינה לר' מאיר דאמר בני פחת מואב הן הן בני דוד בן יהודה דאי ר' מאיר היא כיון שהקריבו בני דוד בן יהודה (כ"ג) [כ'] בתמוז ובאו בני פחת מואב להקריב בכ' באב היה לו לומר אם בני פחת מואב הן בני דוד בן יהודה שבו בני פחת מואב שניה כמו שאמר בני פרעוש שניה. אי מתני' ר' יהודה היא כיון דאמר בני עדין בן יהודה הן בני דוד בן יהודה היה לו לומר שבו בני עדין בן יהודה שניה אי ר' יוסי כיון דאמר בני פחת מואב בן יהודה בני יואב בן צרויה הן ובני עדין הן הן בני יואב בן צרויה היה לו לומר שבו בני עדין שניה. ואוקמיה לר' יוסי ותרי תנאי אליבא דר' יוסי: באחד בטבת לא היה בו מעמד מפני שיש בו הלל שהיא חנוכה והלל דוחה מעמד של שחרית ויש בו קרבן מוסף של ר"ח שדוחה מעמד של נעילה וכ"ש של מוסף דבהדיא תנינן באחד בטבת לא הוה בו מעמד כלל והוא זמן קרבן עצים. דתנן באחד בטבת שבו בני פרעוש שניה וקרבן עצים דוחה מעמד דמנחה ואוקימנא למתני' דתנא דידן סבר קרבן מוסף דוחה מעמד דנעילה ומעמד דמוסף. ור' יוסי פליג עליה. דתניא ר' יוסי אומר כל יום שיש בו מוסף יש בו מעמד ואוקימנא יש בו מעמד בנעילה. דסבר דידיה דחי דלאו דידיה לא דחי. דייק רבא מדלא קתני באחד בניסן לא היה בו מעמד והנה יש בו קרבן עצים וקרבן מוסף (כגון) [והלל כמו] אחד בטבת (שאו') [ש"מ] הלל דחנוכה הוא כמו הלל של תורה. אבל הלל דר"ח לאו דאורייתא הוא. דא"ר יוחנן משום רבי שמעון בן יהוצדק י"ח ימים בשנה יחיד גומר בהן את הלל ואלו הן ח' ימי החג וח' ימי חנוכה ויו"ט הראשון של פסח ויו"ט של עצרת. ובגולה כ"א יום ט' ימי החג וח' ימי חנוכה וב' ימים של פסח וב' ימים של עצרת. רב אקלע לבבל ושמע דקרו הלל בר"ח בעא למיפסקינהו כיון דשמע להן דפסקי שבק להו. אמר מנהג אבותיהם בידיהם. תנא יחיד לא יתחיל בברכה בזמן שקורין בהן כגון ר"ח וחוש"מ פסח ואם טעה ובירך בא"י אמ"ה אקב"ו לקרוא (והתחיל לגמור) [את הלל גומר] וזהו אם התחיל גומר וקיי"ל הכי דאין חובה: ה' דברים אירעו את אבותינו וכו' נשתברו הלוחות מנלן לפי שעלה משה למרום בז' בסיון דכתיב ויקרא אל משה ביום השביעי מתוך הענן נמצא שעמד משה במרום כ"ד ימים תשלום סיון וי"ו מתמוז הרי מ' יום. כדכתיב ויהי משה בהר ארבעים יום. למחר ירד ושבר לוחות ונמצאת שבירת הלוחות בי"ז בתמוז. בטל תמיד גמרא. *) כר' לוי דאמר אף בימי מלכות הרשעה היו משלשלין להן קופות של זהב. והן היו מעלין להן שני כבשים. ובסוף העלו להן ב' חזירים ומצאו אותה שגרמו העונות ובטל התמיד ונחרב הבית. והובקעה העיר בחרבן השני י"ז כדתנא בט' לחדש הרביעי הובקעה העיר בראשונה ובשניה בי"ז שרף אפוסטמוס בי"ז בתמוז את התורה גמרא: ירושלמי היכן שרפה **) העמיד צלם בהיכל מנלן דכתיב ומעת הוסר ובטל התמיד ניתן השקוץ בהיכל. הנה בפירוש כי מעת שהוסר ובטל התמיד ניתן השקוץ בהיכל. וכבר אמרנו בי"ז בטל התמיד

*) חסר כאן וצ"ל כבירושלמי ר' סימון בשם ר"י בן לוי בימי מלכות וכו' ואמר ר' אף בימי כו'. **) נראה שחסר כאן ועי' בירושלמי.

רבינו גרשום

בני יואב שניה: מ"ש הלל דדחי דידיה ומ"ש מוסף דלא דחה דידיה התם קאי דקתני במתניתין יש בו הלל אין בו מעמד דשחרית קרבן מוסף אין בו במנחה ופריך מר קשישא מ"ש הלל דדחי מעמד בתפלה דידיה דהיינו שחרית ומוסף לא דחי מעמד בתפלה דידיה דקתני מוסף אין במנחה דמשמע אבל במוסף עצמו איכא מעמד: א"ל ומי בעיא לך דמוסף דחי דידיה השתא מנחה דלא הוה דידיה דחי ליה דמוסף דידיה דמוסף מיבעיא אמאי *) דחי נמי במנחה הא הלל לא דחי אלא דידיה דשחרית לחודיה: ר' יוסי קאי כוותך. דמוסף לא דחי אלא מעמד דמוסף ולא דמנחה: דידיה נמי לא דחי. תמי' וכי מוסף לא דחי מעמד שבמוסף: י"ח יום גומרין את ההלל ולא קתני ר"ח. לא יתחיל הלל בר"ח: ובשבעה (עשר) [עלה] ואותו יום לא חשבינן אלא מכן ואילך חשיב מ' יום כ"ג דסיון שהוא מלא וי"ז בתמוז הרי מ' נמצא שבמ' ירד ושבר את הלוחות. מעת הוסר התמיד לתת שקוץ כלומר ביום שהוסר התמיד הקים צלם וכבר אמר בי"ז בטל התמיד (דכתיב עלה לליצנותא) בט' באב נגזרה גזרה על אבותינו שלא יכנסו לארץ ובערב ט"ב חזרו מרגלים ולמחר קבעו ט"ב: דרך שלשת ימים הרי כ"ב דיום עשרים עצמו דאייר הוא מחשבון הג' ימים וכתיב עד חדש ימים דהיינו (כ"מ) [כט] ימים וחשוב ז' דאייר לפי שהוא חסר וכ"ב דסיון הרי החדש ימים ועדין נשתיירו ח' דסיון לפי שהוא מלא וכתיב ותסגר מרים שבעת ימים הרי כ"ט דסיון ובאותו יום עצמו שלח מרגלים וכתיב וישובו מקץ ארבעים יום חשוב ב' דסיון וכ"ט דתמוז הרי ל"א וח' דאב דאמרת דבערב

*) חסר כאן וצ"ל הכי קאמינא לך לא לדחי אלא דידיה ואמאי דחי וכו'.

עין משפט נר מצוה

יט א מיי' פ"ג מהל' מגילה וחנוכה הל' ו:
[הגהות מבואר להדיא בגמרא ערכין י:]
כ ב מיי' שם הלכה ז: [רב אלפס שבת פ"ב דף יא:]
כא ג מיי' שם טוש"ע א"ח סימן תרמד סעיף א:
כב ד מיי' שם טוש"ע א"ח סימן תרפג:
כג ה מיי' שם טוש"ע א"ח סימן תפח סעיף א:
כד ו מיי' שם טוש"ע א"ח סימן תלב סעיף א:
כה ז מיי' שם טוש"ע א"ח סימן תכב סעיף ב:
[נ"ל אמר אביי כו' קמיה דרבי אלעזר בר צדוק]
[וע"ע תוס' ברכות יד: ד"ה ימים ותו' ערכין י: ד"ה י"ח ותו' סוכה מד: ד"ה כאן]

מסורת הש"ס

ערכין י: [תוספ' סוכה פ"ג] ע"ש מס' סופרים פ"כ הל' ט ע"ש]
שבת פו: יומא ד:

הגהות הב"ח

(א) גמ' כתוב ואשתכח דהוה כתיב עילויה אנת גרמת לאחרובי ביתיה וידך אשלימית ליה: (ב) רש"י ד"ה ומ"ש מוסף כו' אין בו במנחה ולא קתני אין בו במוסף נעילה: (ג) ד"ה כ"ר יוסי כו' אין בו נעילה ואתא: (ד) ד"ה באחד כו' דר"ח מה"ד וקרבן מוסף וקרבן עצים דבני ארח: (ה) ד"ה בשבעה כו' ס"ל דבשבעה עלה ולא כשבע דמקרא נפקא לן כו' מתן תורה הוה משבעה כו' והד"א: (ו) תוס' ד"ה אמר כו' לא מברכינן כדמוכח הכא וכן משמע כו' דקאמר אמר אביי הוה קאימנא קמיה דר' אלעזר בר צדוק ואייתי ההוא גברא ערבה קמיה: (ז) שם ד"ה ואשתכח כו' ביתו של הקב"ה וידך אשלמת וכו' להקב"ה שחתכתי ידך הס"ד:

הגהות הגר"א

[א] גמ' אלא דמנחה ודנעילה וה"ג מ"ש כו'. כל"ל:

הגהות מהר"ב רנשבורג

א] רש"י ד"ה זאת אומרת וכו' אלא מנהגא כדלקמן מנהג וכו'. נ"ב הכל דבור אחד ודו"ק:

רש"י

אנת צבית לאחרובי ביתיה וידך אשלימת ליה. משל אומר לחבירו: אתה רצית להחריב ביתו של מקום, שהטית ישראל אחריך – ואני עשיתי בך נקמה ושלמתי לך ידי. ל"א: אנת צבית לאחרובי ביתא וידך [אושליתא] לי. לשון שאילת [כלים], כלומר: ועלה בידי: ואמר רבי חמא בר חנינא אותו היום וכו'. מהר, לשון מהר, עכשיו. כשתטול י"ט ימים מחדש אייר קודם עליית הענן פשו להו י', והנהו י' היו בין דרך שלשת ימים וז' דהסגרת מרים, וחדש (ה) של כ"ט ימים שאכלו בשר – הוה ל"ט. והשתא אשתכח דמשה שלח מרגלים בכ"ט דסיון: הני ארבעים נכי חד. ב' מסיון וכ"ט מתמוז – הוה ל"א, וח' מאב – הוה ל"ט: וחובה על ידי חייב. היינו תשעה באב, דרגילין להיות בו רעות: ה"ג. מגלגלין זכות ע"י זכאי: מוצאי שבת. יום ראשון: מוצאי שביעית. שמינית: דוכן. מקום עשוי כעין אצטבא, ועליו לוים עומדין לשורר: וישב עליהם את אונם וברעתם יצמיתם ה' אלהינו. במזמור "אל נקמות ה'", והוא שיר של יום רביעי. והאי דאמרי ליה ביום ראשון – איליא בעלמא (ו) הוה דנפל בפומייהו, כדאמרינן בערכין (דף יב.). פי' איליא – קינה, שכן תרגום יונתן בן עוזיאל "שא קינה" (יחזקאל כח) – טול אילייא. וכמו "אלי כבתולה חגורת שק על בעל נעוריה" (יואל א), שפירושו: קונני ובכי: נחרשה העיר. כדכתיב (מיכה ג) "ציון שדה תחרש", שנחרשה כולה ונעשית כשדה חרושה: בעל החוטם. בעל קומה וצורה. ל"א: גדול הדור: מתבקש. ליהרג. ברמז אמר ליה, שלא יכירו בו אנשי המלך: טשא. נחבא. כמו "טשו במערתא" (שבת דף לג:): אזל. האדון אצל רבן גמליאל בצנעא: ומית חד מינייהו. מן היועצין, וכסבורין שאירע להן על שהרעו לגזור: גיא חזיון. ירושלים, שהכל מסתכלין שם: מקרקר. לשון יללה: קיר ושוע. מקונן וזועק, לשון "הנה קול שועת בת עמי" (ירמיהו ח). קיר – כמו קירי דבשחיטת חולין (דף *קלט:): אל ההר. בשביל הר ציון ששמם: משנכנס אדר. ימי נסים היו לישראל: פורים ופסח: ניזיל

גמרא

תורה אור

אנת צבית לחרובי ביתא, ידך אשלימת ליה. "בתשעה באב נגזר על אבותינו שלא יכנסו לארץ". מנלן? דכתיב "ויהי בחדש הראשון בשנה השנית, באחד לחדש, הוקם המשכן". ואמר מר: *שנה ראשונה עשה משה את המשכן, שניה הקים משה את המשכן ושלח מרגלים. וכתיב: "ויהי בשנה השנית, בחדש השני בעשרים בחדש, נעלה הענן מעל משכן העדות". וכתיב "ויסעו מהר ה' דרך שלשת ימים". אמר רבי חמא בר חנינא: *אותו היום סרו מאחרי ה'. וכתיב "והאספסוף אשר בקרבו התאוו תאוה, וישובו ויבכו גם בני ישראל" וגו'. וכתיב "עד חדש ימים" וגו', דהוו להו עשרין ותרתין בסיון. וכתיב "ותסגר מרים שבעת ימים" – דהוו להו עשרין ותשעה בסיון. וכתיב "שלח לך אנשים". ותניא: בעשרים ותשעה בסיון שלח משה מרגלים. וכתיב "וישובו מתור הארץ מקץ ארבעים יום". הני ארבעים יום נכי חד הוו! אמר אביי: *תמוז דההיא שתא מלויי מליוה, דכתיב "קרא עלי מועד לשבור בחורי". וכתיב "ותשא כל העדה ויתנו את קולם, ויבכו העם בלילה ההוא". *אמר רבה אמר ר' יוחנן: (א) (*אותו היום ערב) תשעה באב היה. אמר להם הקב"ה: אתם בכיתם בכיה של חנם, ואני קובע לכם בכיה לדורות. "חרב הבית בראשונה" (ב) – דכתיב "ובחדש החמישי, בשבעה לחדש, היא שנת תשע עשרה [שנה] למלך נבוכדנצר מלך בבל, בא נבוזראדן, רב טבחים, עבד מלך בבל, ירושלם. וישרוף את בית ה'" וגו'. וכתיב "ובחדש החמישי, בעשור לחדש, היא שנת תשע עשרה [שנה] למלך *נבוכדנצר מלך בבל, בא נבוזראדן, רב טבחים, עמד לפני מלך בבל בירושלם" וגו'. ותניא: אי אפשר לומר בשבעה, שהרי כבר נאמר בעשור. ואי אפשר לומר בעשור, שהרי כבר נאמר בשבעה. הא כיצד? בשבעה נכנסו נכרים להיכל, ואכלו וקלקלו בו שביעי שמיני, אותשיעי סמוך לחשכה הציתו בו את האור, והיה דולק והולך כל היום כולו, *שנאמר "אוי לנו, כי פנה היום, כי ינטו צללי ערב". והיינו דאמר רבי יוחנן: (ג) אלמלי הייתי באותו הדור – לא קבעתיו אלא בעשירי, מפני שרובו של היכל בו נשרף. ורבנן? אתחלתא דפורענותא עדיפא. "ובשניה". מנלן? דתניא: *מגלגלין זכות ליום זכאי, וחובה ליום חייב. אמרו: א] כשחרב בית המקדש בראשונה (ד) אותו היום ערב תשעה באב היה, ומוצאי שבת היה, ומוצאי שביעית היתה, ומשמרתה של יהויריב היתה, והלוים היו אומרי' שירה ועומדין על דוכנם. ומה שירה היו אומרים – "וישב עליהם את אונם, וברעתם יצמיתם". ולא הספיקו לומר "יצמיתם ה' אלהינו", עד שבאו נכרים וכבשום. *וכן בשניה. "נלכדה ביתר". גמרא. *"נחרשה העיר". תניא: *כשחרב טורנוסרופוס הרשע את ההיכל, נגזרה גזרה על רבן גמליאל להריגה. בא אותו הגמון ועמד בבית המדרש, ואמר: בעל החוטם מתבקש, בעל החוטם מתבקש. שמע רבן גמליאל. אזל טשא מינייהו. אזל לגביה בצנעא. א"ל: אי מצילנא לך, מייתית לי לעלמא דאתי? א"ל: הן. א"ל: אשתבע לי. אשתבע ליה. סליק לאיגרא, נפיל, ומית. וגמירי, דכי גזרי גזירתא ומית חד מינייהו – מבטלי לגזירתייהו. יצתה בת קול ואמרה: אותו הגמון מזומן לחיי העולם הבא. תנו רבנן: משחרב הבית בראשונה, נתקבצו כיתות כיתות של פרחי כהונה ומפתחות ההיכל בידן, ועלו לגג ההיכל ואמרו לפניו: רבונו של עולם! הואיל ולא זכינו להיות גזברין נאמנים – יהיו מפתחות מסורות לך. וזרקום כלפי מעלה, ויצתה כעין פיסת יד וקיבלתן מהם. והם קפצו ונפלו לתוך האור. ועליהן קונן ישעיהו הנביא "משא גיא חזיון. מה לך איפוא, כי עלית כולך לגגות? תשואות מלאה, עיר הומיה, קריה עליזה, חלליך לא חללי חרב, ולא מתי מלחמה". אף בהקב"ה נאמר "מקרקר קיר ושוע אל ההר". § "משנכנס אב, ממעטין בשמחה" כו' § אמר רב יהודה בריה דרב שמואל בר שילת משמיה דרב: כשם שמשנכנס אב ממעטין בשמחה – כך משנכנס אדר מרבין בשמחה,

אמר

שמות מ; במדבר ט; שם י; שם; שם יא; שם; שם יב; שם יג; שם; איכה א; במדבר יד; מלכים ב כה; ירמיהו נב; שם ו; ישעיה כב; שם

תוספות

(ז) **דכתיב** עד חדש ימים הוו להו כ"ב בסיון. פי': חשוב מעשרים ימים של ר"ח אייר עד סופו – תמצא ט' ימים, נמצא בכ' בסיון כ"ט, ועד חדש ימים – הוי שלשים ימים. אם כן לפי זה תמצא מעשרים ושנים לחדש השני דזה אייר חדש שלם עד כ"ב דסיון, וג' ימים שנסעו מהר ה' – הרי ל"ג. דל מינייהו ב' ימים דבעשרים בחדש נעלה הענן – ואייתר להו שני ימים. פשו כ"ג, דל יומא מן שלשה שהאחד מן הג' ימים היה בכלל החדש (ח), שאייר חסר – פש להו כ"ב*:

אמר אביי תמוז דההיא שתא מלויי מליוה. ועשו אותו משלשים ימים, כדי שיכלו המ' ימים בתשעה באב. שלשים יום דתמוז ואחד דסיון, דבכ"ט שלח המרגלים. ותשעה באב – הרי ארבעים ימים. וביום תשעה באב שבו המרגלים מתור הארץ: **וישב** עליהם את אונם וברעתם יצמיתם ולא הספיקו לומר יצמיתם ה' אלהינו עד שבאו האויבים וכו'. פי': באותו פסוק יש ב' פעמים "יצמיתם", ולא הספיקו לומר השני עד שבאו וכבשום. ואומר ר"י: *אע"ג דאין אותו פסוק כלל במזמור שיר של מוצ"ש – אירע להם כך שאמרו אותו פסוק. ובירושל' מפרש: איליא נקט, פירוש: איליא הוי כמו "אלי כבתולה", דהוי לשון קינה, כמו שקורין העולם ריאוני"א בלע"ז:

אמר

רבינו חננאל

וה' דברים אירעו את אבותינו בט' באב נגזר על אבותינו שלא יכנסו לארץ מנא לן. דתניא בכ"ט בסיון שלח המרגלים הנה שני ימים הנותרים מסיון ול' יום של תמוז שאותה שנה תמוז מלא היה. דכתיב קרא עלי מועד לשבור בחורי הרי ל"ב וח' ימים באב הרי מ' יום שלמים. נמצאו שהגיעו ט' באב. אמר רבה אמר ר' יוחנן אותו היום ט' באב היה והיו ישראל יושבים ובוכים. אמר הקב"ה אתם בכיתם בכיה של חנם אני אקבע לכם בכיה לדורות. חרב הבית בראשונה שנאמר בחדש החמישי בעשור לחדש בא נבוזראדן וגו' וכתיב אחרי' וישרוף את בית ה' ואת בית המלך וכתיב קרא אחרינא בחדש החמישי בשבעה לחדש היא שנת תשע עשרה בא נבוזראדן רב טבחים עבד מלך בבל וישרוף את בית ה' ואת בית המלך. אי אפשר לומר בשבעה שכבר נאמר בעשרה ואי אפשר לומר בעשרה שכבר נאמר וכו' ואכלו וקלקלו בו ז' וח' ט' בו בערב (באב) הציתו סמוך לחשכה והיה דולק והולך כל היום שנא' אוי לנו כי פנה היום כי ינטו צללי ערב. א"ר יוחנן אלמלא הייתי באותו הדור לא קבעתיו אלא בעשירי מפני שרובו של היכל בעשירי נשרף. ותנא דידן תחלת פורענותא עדיפא. ובשניה דתניא ר' יוסי אומר מגלגלין זכות ליום זכאי וחובה ליום חייב. כשחרב הבית בראשונה ט' באב היה ומ"ש ומוצאי שביעית היתה ומשמרת יהויריב היתה כו'. נלכדה ביתר ונחרשה העיר גמרא. פי' שאמר הנביא לתת

הגהות מהר"י לנדא

א] גמ' כשחרב בהמ"ק בראשונה אותו היום תשעה באב היה כל"ל:

הגהות הב"ח

(א) גמ' אותו היום ערב. תא"מ ונ"ב ס"א אותו היום תשעה באב היה: (ב) שם חרב הבית בראשונה מנלן דכתיב ובחדש: (ג) שם לאמר ר' יוחנן אלמלי. נ"ב ע' ר"פ הקורא עומד בתוס' ד"ה אלמלא: (ד) שם כשחרב בהמ"ק בראשונה (אותו היום ערב ת"ב היה) תא"מ ונ"ב ס"א אותו היום תשעה באב היה: (ה) רש"י ד"ה אמר רבי חמא כו' וחדש של כ"ט ימים. נ"ב מפרש"י מבואר דמפרש עד חדש ימים וגו' חדש של לבנה דהיינו כ"ט י"ב תשל"ג ונמצא שלשה ימים שסרו הוו כ' וכ"א וכ"ב מאייר נשארו שבעה מאייר וכ"ב מסיון שבו כלה חדש ימים שאכלו בשר דהיינו כ"ט יום עוד ס"ל לרש"י דהמרגלים באו בסוף שמיני לאב שהרי ליל ט' בכו בכיה של חנם והוקבע לדורות אבל התוס' נחלקו עליו וס"ל דעד חדש ימים וגו' הוה חדש שלם של שלשים יום שלמים ונדחקו לפרש דיום ג' שסרו דהיינו כ"ב מאייר נחשב לכאן ולכאן דיום הג' שסרו הוא עלמו היום הראשון מהחדש שאכלו בשר ועוד נחלקו וס"ל דכ"ט דסיון שבו שלח מרגלים אינו נחשב בחשבון מ' יום דמרגלים אלא הוא נחשב מז' ימים דהסגרת מרים ולא נשאו המרגלים רגליהם אלא ביום ל' דסיון ולפי זה לריך לפרש דלא שבו המרגלים אלא בט' באב בסוף היום שאז בכו בכיה של חנם ונקבע עליהם בכיה לדורות כי לעת הערב סמוך לחשיכה הליתו בו האש ולפי זה לא גרסינן אותו היום ערב תשעה באב היה כו' אלא ה"ג אותו היום ט' באב היה: (ו) ד"ה וישב כו' אילייא בעלמא הוא דנפל: (ז) תום' ד"ה וכתיב כו' מעשרים ימים של חדש אייר וכו' הוי שלשים יום א"כ: (ח) בא"ד היה בכלל החדש פש להו כ"ב כל"ל ותיבות שאייר חסר נמחק:

רבינו גרשום

דבערב ט"ב חזרו א"כ לא הוו בדרך אלא מ' נכי חדא וקרא אמר ארבעים: תמוז מליוה ואיכא ל' דתמוז נמצא בערב ט"ב מ' מלאים ולמחר קבעי לט"ב. קרא עלי מועד שקבעו תמוז של שלשים. וחובה ע"י חייב לפי שבט"ב היה כבר חייב ששרף בו בראשונה. כשהרס משמע נחרש: בעל החוטם כלומר עין שבהם חשוב שבהם. דבטלי קצרי. לכבס וללבוש מאי כבוד שבת איכא במאי דלבוש בחמישי אלא לאו להניח וללבוש בשבת דהיינו כבוד שבת טעמא דבחמישי לפי שהוא קרוב לשבת אבל שאר יומי אפילו להניח וקשיא לרב הונא:

מסורת הש"ס / עין משפט

כו א טוש"ע א"ח סימן תקנת:

רש"א

[סנהדרין סט: זבחים קיח: ערכין יג:]

[שבת קטז:]

פסחים עז: שבועות י:

סוטה לה. [סנהדרין קד:]

[ע"ש ברש"י ל"ע ולענ"ד נ"ל כמו מקרקרן דבשחיטת חולין נג:]

[ר"ה יח:]

[בשהרס כל"ל ועיין תי"ט]

עי' מהרש"א

[כל זה איתא בערכין יא: ומשני רבא ולאותיותא רב אשי אליליא בעלמא כו']

[נ"ל אותה לילה ליל וכן איתא בע"י]

[לפניו בקרא נבוזראדר]

נ"א של עשירי

ערכין יא:

תהלים צד

גי' עין יעקב נחרשה העיר נמי גמרא. תניא כשחרש כו' ובעוד ס' תקמב מעתיק נחרשה העיר שחרש טורנוסרופוס כו'

אָמַר רַב פַּפָּא: א) הִלְכָּךְ, בַּר יִשְׂרָאֵל דְּאִית לֵיהּ דִּינָא בַּהֲדֵי נָכְרִי — לִישְׁתַּמֵּיט מִינֵּיהּ בְּאָב, דְּרִיעַ מַזָּלֵיהּ, וְלִימְצִי נַפְשֵׁיהּ בַּאֲדָר, *דְּבָרִיא מַזָּלֵיהּ. °"לָתֵת לָכֶם אַחֲרִית וְתִקְוָה". (ירמיהו כט) אָמַר רַב יְהוּדָה בְּרֵיהּ דְּרַב שְׁמוּאֵל בַּר שֵׁילַת מִשְּׁמֵיהּ דְּרַב: אֵלּוּ דְּקָלִים וּכְלֵי פִשְׁתָּן. °"וַיֹּאמֶר רְאֵה, רֵיחַ (בראשית כז) בְּנִי כְּרֵיחַ שָׂדֶה אֲשֶׁר בֵּרֲכוֹ ה'". אָמַר רַב יְהוּדָה בְּרֵיהּ דְּרַב שְׁמוּאֵל בַּר שֵׁילַת מִשְּׁמֵיהּ דְּרַב: כְּרֵיחַ שָׂדֶה שֶׁל תַּפּוּחִים.§ "שַׁבָּת שֶׁחָל תִּשְׁעָה בְּאָב לִהְיוֹת בְּתוֹכָהּ, אֲסוּרִין לְסַפֵּר וּלְכַבֵּס".§ אָמַר רַב נַחְמָן: לֹא שָׁנוּ אֶלָּא לְכַבֵּס וְלִלְבּוֹשׁ, אֲבָל לְכַבֵּס וּלְהַנִּיחַ — מוּתָּר. וְרַב שֵׁשֶׁת אָמַר: אֲפִילּוּ לְכַבֵּס וּלְהַנִּיחַ אָסוּר. אָמַר רַב שֵׁשֶׁת: תֵּדַע, דְּבָטְלִי קָצְרֵי דְּבֵי רַב. מְתִיב רַב הַמְנוּנָא: (א)*"בַּחֲמִישִׁי מוּתָּרִים מִפְּנֵי כְבוֹד הַשַּׁבָּת". לְמַאי? אִילֵימָא לְכַבֵּס וְלִלְבּוֹשׁ — מַאי כְּבוֹד שַׁבָּת אִיכָּא? אֶלָּא — לְהַנִּיחַ. וּבַחֲמִישִׁי הוּא דִּשְׁרֵי, אֲבָל הַשַּׁבָּת כּוּלָּהּ — אָסוּר! לְעוֹלָם, לְכַבֵּס וְלִלְבּוֹשׁ, וּכְשֶׁאֵין לוֹ אֶלָּא חָלוּק אֶחָד. *דְּאָמַר רַב אַסִּי א"ר יוֹחָנָן: ב) מִי שֶׁאֵין לוֹ אֶלָּא חָלוּק אֶחָד — מוּתָּר לְכַבְּסוֹ בְּחוּלּוֹ שֶׁל מוֹעֵד. אִיתְּמַר נַמִי, אָמַר רַבִּי בִּנְיָמִין אָמַר ר' אֶלְעָזָר: לֹא שָׁנוּ אֶלָּא לְכַבֵּס וְלִלְבּוֹשׁ, אֲבָל לְהַנִּיחַ — מוּתָּר. מֵיתִיבֵי: ג) אָסוּר לְכַבֵּס לִפְנֵי תִּשְׁעָה בְּאָב, אֲפִילּוּ לְהַנִּיחַ לְאַחַר תִּשְׁעָה בְּאָב. וְגִיהוּץ שֶׁלָּנוּ כְּכִיבּוּס שֶׁלָּהֶן. וּכְלֵי פִשְׁתָּן אֵין בָּהֶם מִשּׁוּם גִּיהוּץ. תְּיוּבְתָּא. ד) שְׁלַח רַב יִצְחָק בַּר גִּיּוֹרֵי מִשְּׁמֵיהּ דְּרַבִּי יוֹחָנָן: אע"פ שֶׁאָמְרוּ כְּלֵי פִשְׁתָּן אֵין בָּהֶן מִשּׁוּם גִּיהוּץ — אֲבָל אָסוּר לְלוֹבְשָׁן בְּשַׁבָּת שֶׁחָל תִּשְׁעָה בְּאָב לִהְיוֹת בְּתוֹכָהּ. אָמַר רַב: לֹא שָׁנוּ אֶלָּא לְפָנָיו, ה) אֲבָל לְאַחֲרָיו — מוּתָּר. וּשְׁמוּאֵל אָמַר: אֲפִילּוּ לְאַחֲרָיו נַמִי אָסוּר. מֵיתִיבֵי: "שַׁבָּת שֶׁחָל תִּשְׁעָה בְּאָב לִהְיוֹת בְּתוֹכָהּ אָסוּר לְסַפֵּר וּלְכַבֵּס. וּבַחֲמִישִׁי מוּתָּרִין מִפְּנֵי כְבוֹד הַשַּׁבָּת. כֵּיצַד? חָל לִהְיוֹת בְּאֶחָד בְּשַׁבָּת — מוּתָּר לְכַבֵּס כָּל הַשַּׁבָּת כּוּלָּהּ. בְּשֵׁנִי, בִּשְׁלִישִׁי, בִּרְבִיעִי, וּבַחֲמִישִׁי, לְפָנָיו — אָסוּר, לְאַחֲרָיו — מוּתָּר. חָל לִהְיוֹת בְּעֶרֶב שַׁבָּת — מוּתָּר לְכַבֵּס בַּחֲמִישִׁי, מִפְּנֵי כְבוֹד הַשַּׁבָּת. וְאִם לֹא כִּבֵּס בַּחֲמִישִׁי בְּשַׁבָּת — מוּתָּר לְכַבֵּס בְּעֶרֶב שַׁבָּת מִן הַמִּנְחָה וּלְמַעְלָה". *לָיֵיט עֲלָהּ אַבַּיֵּי, וְאִיתֵּימָא רַב אַחָא בַּר יַעֲקֹב, אַהָא. *חָל לִהְיוֹת בַּשֵּׁנִי וּבַחֲמִישִׁי — קוֹרִין שְׁלֹשָׁה וּמַפְטִיר אֶחָד. בַּשְּׁלִישִׁי וּבָרְבִיעִי — קוֹרֵא אֶחָד וּמַפְטִיר אֶחָד. רַבִּי יוֹסֵי אוֹמֵר: ו) לְעוֹלָם קוֹרִין שְׁלֹשָׁה וּמַפְטִיר אֶחָד. תְּיוּבְתָּא דִּשְׁמוּאֵל! אָמַר לָךְ שְׁמוּאֵל: תַּנָּאֵי הִיא. דְּתַנְיָא: *ז)"תִּשְׁעָה בְּאָב שֶׁחָל לִהְיוֹת בְּשַׁבָּת, וְכֵן עֶרֶב תִּשְׁעָה בְּאָב שֶׁחָל לִהְיוֹת בְּשַׁבָּת — אוֹכֵל וְשׁוֹתֶה כָּל צָרְכּוֹ, וּמַעֲלֶה עַל שׁוּלְחָנוֹ אֲפִילּוּ כִּסְעוּדַת שְׁלֹמֹה בִּשְׁעָתוֹ. וְאָסוּר לְסַפֵּר וּלְכַבֵּס מֵר"ח וְעַד הַתַּעֲנִית. דִּבְרֵי רַבִּי מֵאִיר. רַבִּי יְהוּדָה אוֹמֵר: כָּל הַחֹדֶשׁ כּוּלּוֹ אָסוּר. רשב"ג אוֹמֵר: אֵינוֹ אָסוּר אֶלָּא אוֹתָהּ שַׁבָּת בִּלְבַד. וְתַנְיָא אִידָךְ: וְנוֹהֵג אֵבֶל מֵרֹאשׁ חֹדֶשׁ וְעַד הַתַּעֲנִית, דִּבְרֵי ר' מֵאִיר. רַבִּי יְהוּדָה אוֹמֵר: כָּל הַחֹדֶשׁ כּוּלּוֹ אָסוּר. רשב"ג אוֹמֵר: אֵינוֹ אָסוּר אֶלָּא אוֹתָהּ שַׁבָּת בִּלְבַד. אָמַר ר' יוֹחָנָן: וּשְׁלָשְׁתָּן מִקְרָא אֶחָד דָּרְשׁוּ, דִּכְתִיב: °"וְהִשְׁבַּתִּי כָּל מְשׂוֹשָׂהּ, חַגָּהּ, חָדְשָׁהּ, וְשַׁבַּתָּהּ". (הושע ב) מַאן דְּאָמַר מֵר"ח וְעַד הַתַּעֲנִית

מֵחַגָּהּ

נֵיזִיל בַּהֲדֵיהּ. בְּעַרְכָּאוֹת שֶׁלָּהֶן: *וְנָתַתִּי לָכֶם אַחֲרִית וְתִקְוָה. אַיְּידֵי דַּאֲיְירֵי רַב יְהוּדָה לְעֵיל, נָקֵיט וְאָזֵיל: דְּקָלִים. לְהִתְפַּרְנֵס מֵהֶן, שֶׁיֵּשׁ מֵהֶן בְּבָבֶל הַרְבֵּה, כִּדְאָמְרִינַן בְּפ"ק (דף ט:): עוּלָּא אִיקְלַע לְבָבֶל חֲזָא מְלָא צַנָּא דְּתַמְרֵי כו': כְּלֵי פִשְׁתָּן. לִלְבּוֹשׁ: לֹא שָׁנוּ. בְּמַתְנִי' שֶׁכָּל הַשָּׁבוּעַ אָסוּר לְכַבֵּס: אֲפִילּוּ לְכַבֵּס וּלְהַנִּיחַ. כְּדֵי שֶׁיִּלְבּוֹשׁ לְאַחַר זְמַן לְאַחַר ט' בְּאָב — אָסוּר, דְּנִרְאֶה כְּמַסִּיחַ דַּעְתּוֹ, שֶׁעוֹסֵק בְּכִיבּוּס בְּגָדִים: אָמַר רַב שֵׁשֶׁת תֵּדַע. דַּאֲפִי' לְכַבֵּס וּלְהַנִּיחַ אָסוּר: קָצְרֵי. כָּךְ שְׁמָם *בִּלְשׁוֹן יִשְׁמָעֵאל, וְהֵם כּוֹבְסִין. שָׁמַעְתִּי אוֹמְרִים עַל שֵׁם שֶׁמְּקַצְּרִין בִּגְדֵי צֶמֶר כְּשֶׁדּוֹרְסִין אוֹתָן בְּרַגְלֵיהֶן בְּמַיִם שֶׁקּוֹרִין פורלוי"ר, וְהַיְינוּ דְּמְתַרְגְּמִינַן "עֵין רוֹגֵל" (שמואל ב יז) — עֵינָא דְּקַצְּרָא: אִילֵימָא לְכַבֵּס וְלִלְבּוֹשׁ. מִיָּד בַּחֲמִישִׁי, מַאי כְּבוֹד שַׁבָּת אִיכָּא? אֶלָּא. לָאו לְכַבֵּס וּלְהַנִּיחַ עַד הַשַּׁבָּת: לְעוֹלָם לְכַבֵּס וְלִלְבּוֹשׁ. מִיָּד בַּחֲמִישִׁי (ב): וּבְמִי שֶׁאֵין לוֹ אֶלָּא חָלוּק אֶחָד. דְּאֵין לוֹ לְהַחֲלִיף. וּמַאי מִפְּנֵי כְבוֹד הַשַּׁבָּת, דְּאִי לָא מְכַבֵּס הַשְׁתָּא בַּחֲמִישִׁי — תּוּ לָא מָצֵי לְכַבֵּס לֵיהּ: (ג) חוּלּוֹ שֶׁל מוֹעֵד. שֶׁאֵין לוֹ אֶלָּא חָלוּק אֶחָד, דְּלָא סַגְיָא דְּלָא מְכַבֵּס מִפְּנֵי הַכְּנִימָה. וַאֲפִי' כִּיבֵּס לִפְנֵי הַמּוֹעֵד — מוּתָּר לְכַבְּסָהּ בַּמּוֹעֵד: וְגִיהוּץ שֶׁלָּנוּ. אֵינוֹ יָפֶה אֶלָּא כְּכִיבּוּס שֶׁלָּהֶן, וְאָסוּר לִנְהוֹג לִפְנֵי תִּשְׁעָה בְּאָב אֲפִילּוּ לְהַנִּיחַ לְאַחַר תִּשְׁעָה בְּאָב, אֲבָל כִּיבּוּס שֶׁלָּנוּ — מוּתָּר: כְּלֵי פִשְׁתָּן אֵין בָּהֶן. לֵיאָסֵר מִשּׁוּם גִּיהוּץ, אֶלָּא בִּכְלֵי מֵילַת, לוסקי"י בְּלַעַ"ז: לֹא שָׁנוּ. שֶׁאָסוּר לְלוֹבְשׁוֹ בַּשָּׁבוּעַ שֶׁחָל תִּשְׁעָה בְּאָב לִהְיוֹת בְּתוֹכָהּ, אֶלָּא בַּיָּמִים שֶׁלִּפְנֵי תִּשְׁעָה בְּאָב, שֶׁאִם חָל בְּיוֹם רְבִיעִי — אָסוּר לְלוֹבְשׁוֹ רִאשׁוֹן וְשֵׁנִי וּשְׁלִישִׁי: אֲבָל לְאַחֲרָיו. חֲמִישִׁי וְשִׁשִּׁי [א] א) וּשְׁבִיעִי מוּתָּר: חָל לִהְיוֹת בְּאֶחָד בְּשַׁבָּת מוּתָּר לְכַבֵּס כָּל הַשַּׁבָּת כּוּלָּהּ. דְּהַיְינוּ לְאַחֲרָיו: חָל לִהְיוֹת בַּשֵּׁנִי אוֹ בַּשְּׁלִישִׁי וּבָרְבִיעִי וּבַחֲמִישִׁי כו': לָיֵיט עֲלָהּ אַבַּיֵּי וְאִיתֵּימָא רַב אַחָא בַּר יַעֲקֹב אַהָא. הַמְכַבֵּס בְּתִשְׁעָה בְּאָב, אֲפִילּוּ מִן הַמִּנְחָה וּלְמַעְלָה. וְאַדְּקָאֵי בְּבָרַיְיתָא מַפְסִיק לָהּ לְמִילְּתָא, וְקָאָמַר: לָיֵיט עֲלָהּ אַבַּיֵּי כו': חָל לִהְיוֹת בַּשֵּׁנִי כו'. סֵיפָא דְּהַהִיא בָּרַיְיתָא גּוּפָהּ הִיא: וּמַפְטִיר. (ה) מֵאוֹתָן שְׁלֹשָׁה אַחֲרוֹן מַפְטִיר, מִתּוֹךְ שֶׁאֵין מוֹסִיפִין בְּחוֹל יוֹתֵר מִג' אֲנָשִׁים וְלֹא בְּר"ח עַל ד', שֶׁאֵין לָנוּ לְהוֹסִיף אֶלָּא בְּשַׁבָּת וּבְי"ט, כִּדְמְפָרֵשׁ בִּמְגִילָּה (דף כא.). וּלְפִיכָךְ קוֹרִין ג', דִּזְמַן סֵפֶר תּוֹרָה הוּא, וּבְלָאו הָכִי הֲווּ קָרוּ שְׁלֹשָׁה, שֶׁהוּא מְתַקֶּנֶת עֶזְרָא לִקְרוֹת בַּשֵּׁנִי וּבַחֲמִישִׁי כֹּהֵן וְלֵוִי וְיִשְׂרָאֵל: קוֹרֵא אֶחָד וּמַפְטִיר אֶחָד. אֶחָד קוֹרֵא וְהוּא עַצְמוֹ הַמַּפְטִיר. קָתָנֵי מִיהַת לְאַחֲרָיו מוּתָּר. תְּיוּבְתָּא דִּשְׁמוּאֵל: וְכֵן עֶרֶב תִּשְׁעָה בְּאָב שֶׁחָל לִהְיוֹת בְּשַׁבָּת. *אֵינוֹ מַפְסִיק סְעוּדָתוֹ, וְאֵינוֹ מְמַעֵט בְּתַבְשִׁילִין, אֶלָּא אוֹכֵל כָּל צָרְכּוֹ וּמַעֲלֶה עַל שׁוּלְחָנוֹ אֲפִי' כִּסְעוּדַּת שְׁלֹמֹה בִּשְׁעָתוֹ. דִּפְלוּגְתָּא הִיא בְּמַסֶּכֶת גִּיטִּין בְּפֶרֶק ["מִי שֶׁאֲחָזוֹ"] (דף סח:), דְּאִיכָּא לְמַאן דְּאָמַר: מֶלֶךְ וְהֶדְיוֹט וּמֶלֶךְ, וְאִיכָּא לְמַאן דְּאָמַר: מֶלֶךְ וְהֶדְיוֹט. כְּלוֹמַר, כְּשֶׁנִּטְרַד — שׁוּב לֹא חָזַר לְמַלְכוּתוֹ. לְפִיכָךְ הוּצְרַךְ לוֹמַר "בִּשְׁעָתוֹ" — בְּעֵת מַלְכוֹ וְתָקְפּוֹ, שֶׁהָיָה אוֹכֵל הוּא וְשָׂרָיו ס' כּוֹר סוֹלֶת כו': וְעַד הַתַּעֲנִית. אַלְמָא דִּסְבִירָא לֵיהּ לְרַבִּי מֵאִיר לְפָנָיו אָסוּר לְאַחֲרָיו מוּתָּר, וְרַבִּי יְהוּדָה וְרַבָּן (*גַּמְלִיאֵל) סְבִירָא לְהוּ דַּאֲפִילּוּ לְאַחֲרָיו נַמִי אָסוּר:

מֵחַגָּהּ

תורה אור

אמר רב פפא הלכך האי בר ישראל דאית ליה דינא בהדי נכרי לישתמיט וכו'. פירוש: משום דאמר לעיל מגלגלין חובה ליום חייב: **של** תפוחים. י"מ: תפוחים — *כריח אתרוגים: **קצרי** דבי רב. פירוש: כובסין הבגדים, ולכך קרי להו קצרי על שם שמקצרין הבגדים ע"י רחיצת המים: **מי** שאין לו אלא חלוק אחד מותר לכבס במועד. (*ובטבול יום) ובפ' "אלו מגלחין" (מו"ק דף יד.) דקאמר: וליטעמיך, הא דאמר רבי אסי אמר רבי יוחנן מי שאין לו אלא חלוק אחד וכו', דפריך, יאמרו: כל החלוקים אסורים לכבס בחול המועד וחלוק זה מותר? ומתרץ: זה אזורו מוכיח עליו, שאין לו אלא חלוק אחד. וא"כ דוקא להם, אבל לנו — ודאי אסור, אפי' אין לנו אלא חלוק אחד, שאין אנו אוגדין אזור על חלוקות שלנו, ולא הוי אזורו מוכיח עליו. וכן צריך ליזהר שלא לכבס המטפחת בחול המועד, אע"ג שאין לנו אלא אחת. אבל מ"מ יש לנשים לכבס בגדי התינוקות כדי לשכוב, דהוי כמי שאין לו אלא חלוק אחד, שיש רגילות להחליף בגדיהם, וכל שעה צריך לו כל בגדיו. ועל זה נהגו העולם לכבסם בחול המועד:

בשני ובחמישי קורין שלש ומפטיר אחד. מכאן מוכיח רבינו תם דמפטיר עולה למנין שבעה, מדקאמר: קורין שלש ומפטיר אחד, שמפטיר אחד מן הג', דקא מיבעיא ליה במגילה (דף כג. ושם): מפטיר עולה למנין שבעה או לא, משמע מהכא דעולה:

ותרוייהו

כז א טוש"ע א"ח סימן תקנא סעיף א:

[עי' תוס' שבת פח. ד"ה פריו קודם]

כח ב מיי' פ"ז מהל' י"ט הלכה כא סמג לאוין עה טוש"ע שם סימן תקלד סעיף א:

[צ"ל ובחולין דף קז:]

כט ג ד מיי' פ"ה מהל' תענית הלכה ו סמג עשין מד"ס ג טוש"ע שם סימן תקנא סעיף ג:

ל ה מיי' שם טוש"ע שם סעיף ד:

לא ו מיי' פי"ב מהל' תפלה הלכה טז טור א"ח סימן תקנט:

לב ז מיי' פ"ה מהל' תענית הלכה ח טוש"ע א"ח סימן תקנב סעיף י:

[לעיל כו:]

מ"ק יד. יח. חולין קז:

רבינו חננאל

לתת לכם אחרית ותקוה. אמרינן משמיה דרב אלו דקלין וכלי פשתן. ראה ריח בני כריח שדה. כריח שדה של תפוחין: בגדים מגוהצין אסור ללובשן בשבת שחל ט' באב להיות בתוכה עד יום תענית ואפילו הן בגדים של פשתן. פי' גיהוץ בלשון ישמעאל צקל והוא מעברי ליה חומרתא (כתובות י:) שבת שחל להיות ט' באב בתוכה אסור לספר ולכבס. ובחמישי מותר מפני כבוד השבת. אוקימנא בזמן שחל ט' באב בע"ש בה' שמקודם יום ט' באב התירו לו לכבס וללבוש כשאין לו אלא חלוק אחד ומותר לכבסו אפילו בחוש"מ. כבוס *) חלוקת רב נחמן ורב ששת היא וקיי"ל בהא כרב ששת דא' אפילו לכבס ולהניח אחר ט' באב אסור תדע דקא בטלי קצרי דבי רב ומותבינן מהא דתניא אסור לכבס לפני ט' באב ואפילו להניח לאחר ט' באב וגיהוץ של בני ארץ בבל כבוס של בני א"י. וכלי פשתן אין בהן משום גיהוץ. אבל אסור ללובשן בשבת שחל ט' באב להיות בתוכה: [שבת שחל ט"ב להיות בתוכה] אסורין לספר ולכבס ובחמישי מותרין מפני כבוד השבת כיצד חל להיות באחד בשבת מותרין לכבס כל השבת כולה חל להיות ט' באב בב' או בג' או בד' או בה' לפניו אסור לאחריו מותר. חל ט' באב להיות בע"ש מותרין לכבס בחמישי. פי' מי שאין לו אלא חלוק אחד ואם לא כיבס בה' יכבס בע"ש בט' באב עצמו מן המנחה ולמעלה. לייט אביי מי שהצריך ודחק עצמו לכך. ובקריאת הספר קיי"ל כר' יוסי דאמר לעולם קורין ג' בט' באב ומפטיר

*) נראה דצ"ל וכבוס להניח לאחר ת"ב.

[צ"ל נתת]

[גירסת רא"ש דתקיף מולי']

[ע' ב"ק קיט: וברש"י שם]

הגהות הב"ח

(א) גמ' ובחמישי מותרי מפני כבוד השבת מא מותרין אילימא לכבס כו הוא דשרי אבל כל השבו כולה: (ב) רש"י ד"ה לעולם כו' מיד בחמיש ובמי שאין כו' הד"א (ג) ד"ה בחולו של מועד דכיון שאין לו אלא חלוק אחד דלא סגי דלא מכבס ליה מפני הכנימה (ד) ד"ה ומפטיר אחד מאותן שלש:

הגהות מהר"ב רנשבורג

א] רש"י ד"ה אבל לאחרי וכו' ושביעי. נמחק מלת ושביעי:

[קדושין לג: וש"נ]

[מגילה כב:]

עירובין מ:

הגהות הגר"א

[א] רש"י ד"ה אבל ושביעי. רשום קו עליו למחקו:

[עי' בהג"ה בא"ח סי' תקנב ס"ק יב כוונת רש"י במ"ש אינו מפסיק סעודתו]

[צ"ל שמעון בן גמליאל]

רבינו גרשום

לעולם לכבס וללבוש בחמישי ודאמרת מאי כבוד שבת איכא דלית ליה אלא אותו חלוק ולא מצי להמתין עד שבת והיינו כבוד שבת דמכבס ליה ולהכי שאר יומי אסור אבל להניח לא הוי אסור וגיהוץ שלנו אסור. לייט עלה אביי במאן דכבים בע"ש בט' באב מן המנחה ולמעלה קורין ג' הואיל וכל חמישי ושני קורין ג'. מפטיר אסוף אסיפם. תיובתא דשמואל הא דקתני מותר לכבס כל השבוע ושמואל אמר

מֵ"חַגָּהּ". וּמ"ד כָּל הַחֹדֶשׁ כּוּלּוֹ אָסוּר מֵ"חָדְשָׁהּ". וּמ"ד כָּל הַשַּׁבָּת כּוּלָּהּ אָסוּר מִ"שַּׁבַּתָּהּ". אָמַר רָבָא: הֲלָכָה כְּרשב"ג. וְאָמַר רָבָא: הֲלָכָה כְּרַבִּי מֵאִיר. וְתַרְוַיְיהוּ לְקוּלָּא. וּצְרִיכָא, דְּאִי אַשְׁמוּעִינַן הֲלָכָה כְּר' מֵאִיר, הֲוָה אָמִינָא: אפי' מֵר"ח, קמ"ל: הֲלָכָה כְּרשב"ג. וְאִי אַשְׁמוּעִינַן הֲלָכָה כְּרשב"ג, הֲוָה אָמִינָא: אֲפִילּוּ לְאַחֲרָיו, קמ"ל הֲלָכָה כְּרַבִּי מֵאִיר.§ "עֶרֶב תִּשְׁעָה בְּאָב, לֹא יֹאכַל אָדָם ב' תַּבְשִׁילִין" כו'.§ אָמַר רַב יְהוּדָה: לֹא שָׁנוּ אֶלָּא מִשֵּׁשׁ שָׁעוֹת וּלְמַעְלָה, אֲבָל מִשֵּׁשׁ שָׁעוֹת וּלְמַטָּה — מוּתָּר. וְאָמַר רַב יְהוּדָה: לֹא שָׁנוּ אֶלָּא בִּסְעוּדָה הַמַּפְסִיק בָּהּ, אֲבָל בִּסְעוּדָה שֶׁאֵינוֹ מַפְסִיק בָּהּ — מוּתָּר. אוְתַרְוַיְיהוּ לְקוּלָּא. וּצְרִיכָא, דְּאִי אַשְׁמְעִינַן בִּסְעוּדָה הַמַּפְסִיק בָּהּ — הֲוָה אָמִינָא: אֲפִי' מִשֵּׁשׁ שָׁעוֹת וּלְמַטָּה, קמ"ל: מִשֵּׁשׁ שָׁעוֹת וּלְמַעְלָה. וְאִי אַשְׁמְעִינַן מִשֵּׁשׁ שָׁעוֹת וּלְמַעְלָה, הֲוָה אָמִינָא: אֲפִי' בִּסְעוּדָה שֶׁאֵינוֹ מַפְסִיק בָּהּ. קמ"ל בִּסְעוּדָה הַמַּפְסִיק בָּהּ. תַּנְיָא כְּלִישָּׁנָא קַמָּא, תַּנְיָא כְּלִישָּׁנָא בַּתְרָא. תַּנְיָא כְּלִישָּׁנָא בַּתְרָא: הַסּוֹעֵד עֶרֶב תִּשְׁעָה בְּאָב, אִם עָתִיד לִסְעוֹד סְעוּדָה אַחֶרֶת — מוּתָּר לֶאֱכוֹל בָּשָׂר וְלִשְׁתּוֹת יַיִן. וְאִם לָאו — אָסוּר לֶאֱכוֹל בָּשָׂר וְלִשְׁתּוֹת יַיִן. תַּנְיָא כְּלִישָּׁנָא קַמָּא: עֶרֶב תִּשְׁעָה בְּאָב, לֹא יֹאכַל אָדָם שְׁנֵי תַבְשִׁילִין. לֹא יֹאכַל בָּשָׂר וְלֹא יִשְׁתֶּה יַיִן. רַבָּן שִׁמְעוֹן בֶּן גַּמְלִיאֵל אוֹמֵר: יְשַׁנֶּה. אָמַר רַבִּי יְהוּדָה: כֵּיצַד מְשַׁנֶּה? אִם הָיָה רָגִיל לֶאֱכוֹל שְׁנֵי תַבְשִׁילִין — יֹאכַל מִין אֶחָד, וְאִם הָיָה רָגִיל לִסְעוֹד בַּעֲשָׂרָה בְּנֵי אָדָם — סוֹעֵד בַּחֲמִשָּׁה. הָיָה רָגִיל לִשְׁתּוֹת עֲשָׂרָה כּוֹסוֹת — שׁוֹתֶה חֲמִשָּׁה כּוֹסוֹת. בַּמֶּה דְּבָרִים אֲמוּרִים — מִשֵּׁשׁ שָׁעוֹת וּלְמַעְלָה, אֲבָל מִשֵּׁשׁ שָׁעוֹת וּלְמַטָּה — מוּתָּר. תַּנְיָא אִידָךְ: עֶרֶב תִּשְׁעָה בְּאָב, לֹא יֹאכַל אָדָם שְׁנֵי תַבְשִׁילִין. לֹא יֹאכַל בָּשָׂר וְלֹא יִשְׁתֶּה יַיִן. דִּבְרֵי ר"מ. וַחכ"א: יְשַׁנֶּה, וּמְמַעֵט בְּבָשָׂר וּבְיַיִן. כֵּיצַד מְמַעֵט? אִם הָיָה רָגִיל לֶאֱכוֹל לִיטְרָא בָּשָׂר — יֹאכַל חֲצִי לִיטְרָא. הָיָה רָגִיל לִשְׁתּוֹת לוֹג יַיִן — יִשְׁתֶּה חֲצִי לוֹג יַיִן. וְאִם אֵינוֹ רָגִיל כָּל עִיקָּר — אָסוּר. רשב"ג אוֹמֵר: אִם הָיָה רָגִיל לֶאֱכוֹל צְנוֹן אוֹ מָלִיחַ אַחַר סְעוּדָתוֹ — הָרְשׁוּת בְּיָדוֹ. תַּנְיָא אִידָךְ: כָּל שֶׁהוּא מִשּׁוּם תִּשְׁעָה בְּאָב — אָסוּר לֶאֱכוֹל בָּשָׂר וְאָסוּר לִשְׁתּוֹת יַיִן, וְאָסוּר לִרְחוֹץ. כָּל שֶׁאֵינוֹ מִשּׁוּם ט"ב — מוּתָּר לֶאֱכוֹל בָּשָׂר וְלִשְׁתּוֹת יַיִן, וְאָסוּר לִרְחוֹץ. ר' יִשְׁמָעֵאל בְּר' יוֹסֵי אוֹמֵר מִשּׁוּם אָבִיו: כָּל שָׁעָה שֶׁמּוּתָּר לֶאֱכוֹל [א] בָּשָׂר מוּתָּר לִרְחוֹץ. ת"ר: כָּל מִצְוֹת הַנּוֹהֲגוֹת בְּאָבֵל נוֹהֲגוֹת בְּט' בְּאָב: באָסוּר בַּאֲכִילָה וּבִשְׁתִיָּה, *וּבְסִיכָה, וּבִנְעִילַת הַסַּנְדָּל, וּבְתַשְׁמִישׁ הַמִּטָּה. וְאָסוּר לִקְרוֹת בַּתּוֹרָה, בַּנְּבִיאִים, וּבַכְּתוּבִים, וְלִשְׁנוֹת בַּמִּשְׁנָה, בַּתַּלְמוּד, וּבַמִּדְרָשׁ, וּבַהֲלָכוֹת וּבָאַגָּדוֹת. אֲבָל קוֹרֵא הוּא בְּמָקוֹם שֶׁאֵינוֹ רָגִיל לִקְרוֹת, וְשׁוֹנֶה בְּמָקוֹם שֶׁאֵינוֹ רָגִיל לִשְׁנוֹת. וְקוֹרֵא בְּקִינוֹת, בְּאִיּוֹב, וּבַדְּבָרִים הָרָעִים שֶׁבְּיִרְמְיָה. וְתִינוֹקוֹת שֶׁל בֵּית רַבָּן *)[ב] בְּטֵלִין, מִשּׁוּם שֶׁנֶּאֱמַר °"פִּקּוּדֵי ה' יְשָׁרִים, מְשַׂמְּחֵי לֵב". ר' יְהוּדָה אוֹמֵר: אַף אֵינוֹ קוֹרֵא בְּמָקוֹם שֶׁאֵינוֹ רָגִיל לִקְרוֹת, וְאֵינוֹ שׁוֹנֶה בְּמָקוֹם שֶׁאֵינוֹ רָגִיל לִשְׁנוֹת. אֲבָל קוֹרֵא הוּא בְּאִיּוֹב, וּבְקִינוֹת, וּבַדְּבָרִים הָרָעִים שֶׁבְּיִרְמְיָהוּ. וְתִינוֹקוֹת שֶׁל בֵּית רַבָּן בְּטֵלִים בּוֹ, מִשּׁוּם שֶׁנֶּאֱמַר "פִּקּוּדֵי ה' יְשָׁרִים, מְשַׂמְּחֵי לֵב".§ "לֹא יֹאכַל בָּשָׂר וְלֹא יִשְׁתֶּה יַיִן".§ תָּנָא: *ג"אֲבָל אוֹכֵל הוּא בָּשָׂר מָלִיחַ וְשׁוֹתֶה יַיִן מִגִּתּוֹ". בָּשָׂר מָלִיחַ עַד כַּמָּה? אָמַר רַב חִינְנָא בַּר כָּהֲנָא מִשְּׁמֵיהּ דִּשְׁמוּאֵל: דכָּל זְמַן (*שֶׁאֵינוֹ) כִּשְׁלָמִים. וְיַיִן מִגִּתּוֹ עַד כַּמָּה? כָּל זְמַן שֶׁהוּא תּוֹסֵס. תָּנָא: **)ה"יַיִן תּוֹסֵס אֵין בּוֹ מִשּׁוּם גִּילּוּי. ווְכַמָּה תְּסִיסָתוֹ — ג' יָמִים. אָמַר רַב יְהוּדָה אָמַר רַב: זכָּךְ הָיָה מִנְהָגוֹ שֶׁל רַבִּי יְהוּדָה בְּרַבִּי אִילְעַאי: עֶרֶב תִּשְׁעָה בְּאָב מְבִיאִין לוֹ פַּת חֲרֵיבָה בְּמֶלַח, וְיוֹשֵׁב

בֵּין

*) [גירס' הרי"ף והרא"ש אינן בטילין בו דברי ר"מ ר' יהודה אומר אף אינו קורא במקום וכו' ותינוקות של בית רבן בטלין בו משום שנאמר פקודי ה' ישרים משמחי לב וע"ע טור א"ח ר"ס תקנד] **) [סנהדרין ע. ע"ז ל. תוספתא תרומות פ"ז]

תורה אור

°תהלים יט

רש"י

מֵחַגָּהּ. כְּלוֹמַר, יָלֵיף טַעְמָא מִן "חַגָּהּ", דְּהַיְינוּ ר"ח שֶׁנִּקְרָא חַג, כִּדְאָמְרִי' לְעֵיל (דף כט.) "קָרָא עָלַי מוֹעֵד": הֲלָכָה כְּר"מ. דִּלְפָנָיו אָסוּר וּלְאַחֲרָיו מוּתָּר: הֲלָכָה כְּרַבָּן שִׁמְעוֹן בֶּן גַּמְלִיאֵל. דְּאֵין אִיסּוּר נוֹהֵג אֶלָּא בְּאוֹתָהּ שַׁבָּת: תַּרְוַיְיהוּ לְקוּלָּא. כִּדְמְפָרֵשׁ וְאָזֵיל, דִּבְלְפָנָיו מוֹקֵי הֲלָכָה כְּר"מ — דִּלְפָנָיו וְלֹא לְאַחֲרָיו, וּבְאוֹתָהּ שַׁבָּת — אֲבָל קוֹדֶם אוֹתָהּ שַׁבָּת אֲפִילּוּ לְפָנָיו מוּתָּר: מִשֵּׁשׁ שָׁעוֹת וּלְמַטָּה. כְּלַפֵּי הַשַּׁחַר: הַמַּפְסִיק בָּהּ. דְּשׁוּב אֵינוֹ אוֹכֵל עוֹד מֵאוֹתָהּ סְעוּדָה וְאֵילָךְ: ה"ג: כֵּיצַד יְשַׁנֶּה א"ר יְהוּדָה אִם הוּא רָגִיל כו': בַּעֲשָׂרָה. שֶׁהָיוּ סוֹעֲדִין עִמּוֹ לִכְבוֹדוֹ: וחכ"א יְשַׁנֶּה. אַשְּׁנֵי תַבְשִׁילִין קָיְימִי (א), בָּשָׂר וְיַיִן יְמַעֵט: מָלִיחַ. דָּג אוֹ בָּשָׂר מָלִיחַ, דְּאֵין בּוֹ טַעַם כָּל כָּךְ אַחַר שֶׁשָּׁהָה שְׁלֹשָׁה יָמִים בְּמֶלַח, כִּדְלְקַמָּן (ב). כִּשְׁלָמִים "וְהַנּוֹתָר מִבְּשַׂר זֶבַח הַשְּׁלָמִים" וגו', טְפֵי לָא אַשְׁכַּחַן דְּמִקְרֵי בָּשָׂר: כָּל שֶׁהוּא מִשּׁוּם ט' בְּאָב. כְּגוֹן סְעוּדָה הַמַּפְסִיק בָּהּ: כָּל שֶׁאֵינוֹ מִשּׁוּם ט"ב. כְּגוֹן סְעוּדָה הַמַּפְסִיק בָּהּ בְּתַעֲנִית צִבּוּר, אִי נַמִּי סְעוּדָה שֶׁאֵינוֹ מַפְסִיק בָּהּ: ה"ג: ר' יִשְׁמָעֵאל בְּר' יוֹסֵי אוֹמֵר מִשּׁוּם אָבִיו כָּל שָׁעָה שֶׁמּוּתָּר לֶאֱכוֹל מוּתָּר לִרְחוֹץ. וְלָא גָּרְסִינַן בָּשָׂר. כְּלוֹמַר, אֲפִילּוּ בִּשְׁעַת סְעוּדָה הַמַּפְסִיק מוּתָּר לִרְחוֹץ, הוֹאִיל וּמוּתָּר לֶאֱכוֹל: אָסוּר בַּאֲכִילָה וּבִשְׁתִיָּה. הָנֵי אֵין נוֹהֲגִין בְּאֵבֶל, דְּקָא חָשֵׁיב נַמִּי אִיסּוּרִים שֶׁנּוֹהֲגִין בּוֹ לְבַד מֵהָנֵי דִּנְהִיגֵי בְּאֵבֶל: רְחִיצָה סִיכָה וּנְעִילָה כו': וְאָסוּר לִקְרוֹת בַּתּוֹרָה כו'. דִּכְתִיב בְּהוּ "מְשַׂמְּחֵי לֵב" (ג): בְּמָקוֹם שֶׁאֵינוֹ רָגִיל לִקְרוֹת. דְּכֵיוָן דְּלָא יָדַע — אִית לֵיהּ צַעֲרָא: עַד כַּמָּה. הָוֵי בָּשָׂר גָּמוּר, דְּלָא הָוֵי בָּשָׂר מָלִיחַ — כָּל זְמַן שֶׁהוּא כִּשְׁלָמִים, שֶׁלֹּא שָׁהָה בְּמִלְחוֹ אֶלָּא שְׁנֵי יָמִים וְלַיְלָה אֶחָד, כִּזְמַן אֲכִילַת שְׁלָמִים. וּלְהָכִי נָקַט כִּשְׁלָמִים, דְּבִזְמַן אֲכִילַת שְׁלָמִים אַשְׁכַּחַן דְּאִקְרִי "בָּשָׂר", דִּכְתִיב (ויקרא ז) *"וְהַנּוֹתָר מִבְּשַׂר זֶבַח הַשְּׁלָמִים" וגו'. טְפֵי לָא אַשְׁכַּחַן דְּמִקְרֵי בָּשָׂר, שֶׁהַטַּעַם נִפְסָל אַחֲרֵי ב' וְג' יָמִים: יַיִן מִגִּתּוֹ. חָדָשׁ וּמָתוֹק, וְאֵינוֹ טוֹב כְּיַיִן יָשָׁן, וּמְשַׁלְשֵׁל וּמַזִּיק: תּוֹסֵס. רוֹתֵחַ: אֵין בּוֹ מִשּׁוּם גִּילּוּי. שֶׁאֵין נָחָשׁ שׁוֹתֵהוּ, כִּי יִבְרַח מֵרְתִיחָתוֹ:

תוספות

ותרוייהו לקולא. כלומר, תרוייהו כדר"מ דאמר מר"ח ועד התענית, וכרשב"ג דאמר אינו אסור אלא אותה שבת בלבד, הלכה כתרוייהו לקולא. כלומר, דאינו אסור אלא אותה שבת בלבד כרשב"ג, ודוקא [עד] התענית, אבל לאחר התענית — מותר, דהלכה כר"מ דאמר דאינו אסור אלא עד התענית. ואע"ג דשלחו משמיה דר' יוחנן דכלי פשתן מותר לכבס במועד — מ"מ החמיר לנו מורינו רש"י לתת סדינין שלנו לכובס אותה שבוע שהיה בה ט"ב קודם התענית [ג]. אבל היכא דחל ט"ב בה' בשבת — מותר לכבס ולספר מחמשי ואילך מפני כבוד השבת, דאין להמתין עד ערב שבת מפני טורח השבת*:

ערב ט"ב לא יאכל אדם ב' תבשילין. פירוש ב' תבשילין: ר"ל בשתי קדירות, כגון שקורין העולם אכלנו ב' מינים, שקורין מייסו"ן. אבל אין לאסור לאכול תבשיל שעושין מבצלים ומגבינה ומביצים, דאע"ג דאין רגילין העולם לאכול בצלים חיין, כדאמר בעירובין (ד' כט.): אכל בצל והשכים ומת וכו', שקשין לכל גופו של אדם כחרבות — אעפ"כ, מאחר שאין עושין מהם תבשיל בעצמו אם לא ישימו (ד) או שומן או שום דבר שנותן בהם טעם — אינו קרוי תבשיל כדי לאסור הבצלים שמשימין עמהם. אבל מן גבינה המבושל בקדירה אין חששא לאכול, דכל דבר שהוא נאכל כמו שהוא חי, כמו חלב, כמו גבינה, כמו תפוחים — אין בהם תורת בשול כלל וכלל: ואם היה רגיל לסעוד בעשר יסעוד בחמשה. צריך למעט בכבודו: ואע"ג דקאמר התלמוד דבשר מליח מותר כל זמן שאינו כשלמים, כלומר שעבר יותר מב' ימים משחיטתו — אפ"ה לדידן אסור לאכול בשר, אפי' מלוח, מזמן מרובה, כיון דאנו רגילים לאכול בשר מליח. וכן צריך למעט בשתייתו, שאם היה רגיל לשתות עשרה כוסות משכר או ממשקה אחר — לא ישתה כי אם חמשה. וצריך לשנות מקומו שהוא רגיל לאכול בו, כמו שהיה מנהגו של רבי יהודה בר' אילעאי, שישב ואכל ערב ט"ב בין תנור לכיריים, מקום שהיה מנוול:

כל

עין משפט נר מצוה

לג א מיי' פ"ה מהל' תענית הלכה ז סמג עשין ג טוש"ע א"ח סימן תקנב סעיף א וסעיף ט:
לד ב מיי' שם הלכה י סמג שם טוש"ע שם סי' תקנד סעיף א:
לה ג ד מיי' שם הלכה ז סמג שם (טוש"ע שם סי' תקנב סעיף ב):
לו ה ו מיי' פי"א מהל' רוצח ושמירת נפש הלכה ח סמג עשין עט וטור י"ד סימן קטז:
לז ז מיי' פ"ה מהל' תענית הלכה ט טוש"ע א"ח סימן תקנב סעיף ו:

[עי' ב"י בא"ח סי' תקנא מה שתמה על דברי תוס' אלו]

רבינו חננאל

ומפטיר אחד. ואסיקנא הלכתא (כר' יוחנן) כרשב"ג דאמר אינו נוהג אלא אותה שבת בלבד שחל ט' באב להיות בתוכה. והלכתא כר' מאיר דאמר עד התענית. אבל לאחר התענית שאר א) שבוע מותר. וזהו פי' הלכתא כתרווייהו לקולא: ערב ט' באב לא יאכל ב' תבשילין כו' ואפילו אורז ועדשים. אבל אוכל תבשיל אחד בלבד שלא יהיה אותו תבשיל בשר ואם הוא בשר בן ג' ימים מותר. דא' כל בשר שאינו כשלמים בן ב' ימים ולילה אחד כדכתיב ביום זבחכם יאכל וממחרת וגו' אינו קרוי בשר אלא מליח ויין תוסס נמי כגון שנסחט בתוך ג' ימים מותר שאינו עדיין יין. אמר רב יהודה אמר רב ל"ש לא יאכל ב' תבשילין ולא יאכל בשר ולא ישתה יין בערב ט' באב משעה שיעברו שש שעות מן היום כגון שיקבע סעודתו משעה שביעית ולמעלה. והני מילי בסעודה שהוא מפסיק בה כלומר בתענית. אבל אם בדעתו לאכול עדיין פעם אחרת או קודם שעה ששית מותר ב) (מתשתא מיבררי). הני מילי פשוטות הן. רשבג"א אם היה רגיל לאכול אחר סעודתו צנון או מלח הרשות בידו: ת"ר כל שהוא משום ט' באב אסור לאכול בשר ולשתות יין ואסור לרחוץ ג) משעה שאסור לאכול אסור לרחוץ. ואע"ג דתנינן נוהג אבל עד התענית ואמרינן הלכתא אבל אסור לרחוץ כל גופו בין בחמין בין בצונן כל ז' אבל פניו ידיו ורגליו בחמין אסור בצונן מותר. הא גרסינן בפסחים פרק מקום שנהגו (דף נד:) אין בין ט' באב ליוה"כ כו' מסייע ליה לר' אלעזר דאמר אסור לאדם שיושיט אצבעו במים בט' באב כדרך שאסור ביוה"כ. אע"ג דמותבינן עליה הא משני רב פפא חמורי לא קתני. וגרסינן בפ' יוה"כ (יומא עח.) מטפחת היה לו לריב"ל (ביוה"כ) [עיוה"כ] מקנח פניו ידיו ורגליו למחר מעבירה ע"ג עיניו ואינו חושש. ערב ט' באב שורה במים ועושה כמין כלים נגובים למחר מעביר ע"ג עיניו ואינו חושש ש"מ מהני כלהו דרחיצת פניו ידיו ורגליו בט' באב אפילו בצונן אסור אלא אם היו מטונפות: ת"ר כל מצות הנוהגות באבל נוהגות בט' באב. אסור ברחיצה ובסיכה ובנעילת הסנדל ובתשמיש המטה. שלח רב ד) הגאון בלשון הזה יהא בנדוי כל מי שעושה אחת מכל אלו בט' באב כל היום. וא' לקרות בתורה בנביאים ובכתובים ולשנות במשנה בתלמוד כו'. ר' יהודה ה) אומר אינו קורא אלא במקום שאינו רגיל לקרות מפני שצער הוא לו וקורא באיוב ובקינות פי' איכה ובדברים הרעים שבירמיה ותינוקות של בית רבן בטלים משום פקודי ה' ישרים משמחי לב. תנא יין תוסס אין בו משום גילוי. וכמה תסיסתו ג' ימים. לפיכך בערב ט' באב מותר:

א) אולי צ"ל כל שאר ימי השבוע מותר. ב) אולי צ"ל מחלוקת ר"מ וחכמים פשוטות הן. ג) אולי צ"ל ר' ישמעאל בר"י אמר משעה שמותר לאכול מותר לרחוץ. ד) אולי צ"ל רב האי גאון. ה) נראה דצ"ל ר"י אומר אף אינו קורא במקום שאינו רגיל וכו'.

מסורת הש"ס

[צ"ל ואם האכל יאכל מבשר]

[צ"ל וברחיצה ובסיכה וע' ברי"ף ובר"ש דלא גרסי באכיל' ובשתי']

[סנהדרין ע.]

[צ"ל שהוא וכ"א בסנהדרין ע. וכן בפרש"י דהכא ודהתם]

הגהות הב"ח

(א) רש"י ד"ה וחכ"א ישנה אשני תבשילין קיימי אבל בשר ויין: (ב) ד"ה מליח כו' כדלקמן הס"ד והשאר נמחק: (ג) ד"ה ואסור לקרות כו' משמחי לב במקום שהוא רגיל הס"ד: (ד) תום' ד"ה ערב כו' אם לא ישימו בו שומן או:

הגהות הגר"א

[א] גמרא כל שעה שמותר לאכול (בשר) תז"מ (וכן מחקו רש"י וכן בתוספתא ליתא): [ב] שם ותינוקות של ב"ר אינן בטלין ר' יהודה כו'. כצ"ל (וכ"ה ברי"ף ורא"ש ובא"ז וגירסתם בת"ק דברי ר"מ וכ"ד הפוסקים שפסקו כר' יהודה): [ג] תום' סד"ה ותרוייהו. (אבל היכא כו' עד טורח השבת) תא"מ (וכבר תמה הב"י ע"ז):

רבינו גרשום

אמר לאחריו נמי אסור: מחגה מה חגה ח' ימים אף מיעוט שמחה ח' ימים: ותרוייהו לקולא הלכה כר"מ דאמר אין אסור אלא עד התענית והלכה כרשב"ג דאין איסור אלא אותה שבת והוא שלפני ט' באב: בסעודה המפסיק סעודה אחרונה שמקבל עליו תענית. אבל בסעודה שאין מפסיק כגון סעודה שאוכל קודם לכן שעדיין יאכל אחריה. כל שהוא משום ת"ב היינו ט' באב עצמו כל שאינו משום ת"ב שאר תעניות. קורא הוא במקום שאינו רגיל לקרות לפי שמצטער: כל זמן שהוא כשלמים שני ימים ולילה אחד אינו אוכל בערב ת"ב אבל אחר כן אוכל שבטל מתורת בשר.

לח א מיי' פ"ה מהל' תענית הל' י סמג עשין ג טוש"ע א"ח סי' תקנד סעיף כב:
לט ב מיי' שם טוש"ע שם סעיף כד:
מ ג ד טוש"ע שם סעיף כה:
מא ה מיי' פ"ה מהל' אבל הלכה יח טור י"ד סימן שפז:

בֵּין תַּנּוּר לַכִּירַיִים, וְאוֹכֵל, וְשׁוֹתֶה עָלֶיהָ קִיתוֹן שֶׁל מַיִם, וְדוֹמֶה כְּמִי שֶׁמֵּתוֹ מוּטָּל לְפָנָיו. תְּנַן הָתָם: *[א]מָקוֹם שֶׁנָּהֲגוּ לַעֲשׂוֹת מְלָאכָה בְּט' בְּאָב, עוֹשִׂין. מָקוֹם שֶׁנָּהֲגוּ שֶׁלֹּא לַעֲשׂוֹת — אֵין עוֹשִׂין. וּבְכָל מָקוֹם ת"ח בְּטֵלִים. רשב"ג אוֹמֵר: לְעוֹלָם יַעֲשֶׂה כָּל אָדָם עַצְמוֹ כְּתַלְמִיד חָכָם. תַּנְיָא נַמִי הָכִי, רשב"ג אוֹמֵר: לְעוֹלָם יַעֲשֶׂה אָדָם עַצְמוֹ כְּתַלְמִיד חָכָם, כְּדֵי שֶׁיִּתְעַנֶּה. תַּנְיָא אִידָךְ: *"רשב"ג אוֹמֵר: כָּל הָאוֹכֵל וְשׁוֹתֶה בְּט' בְּאָב — כְּאִילּוּ אוֹכֵל וְשׁוֹתֶה בְּיוה"כ. ר"ע אוֹמֵר: [ב]כָּל הָעוֹשֶׂה מְלָאכָה בְּתִשְׁעָה בְּאָב — אֵינוֹ רוֹאֶה סִימַן בְּרָכָה לְעוֹלָם. וַחכ"א: כָּל הָעוֹשֶׂה מְלָאכָה בְּט' בְּאָב וְאֵינוֹ מִתְאַבֵּל עַל יְרוּשָׁלַיִם — אֵינוֹ רוֹאֶה בְּשִׂמְחָתָהּ, שֶׁנֶּאֱ' *°"שִׂמְחוּ אֶת יְרוּשָׁלַםִ, וְגִילוּ בָהּ, כָּל אוֹהֲבֶיהָ שִׂישׂוּ אִתָּהּ מָשׂוֹשׂ, כָּל הַמִּתְאַבְּלִים עָלֶיהָ". מִכָּאן אָמְרוּ: *[ג]כָּל הַמִּתְאַבֵּל עַל יְרוּשָׁלַיִם זוֹכֶה וְרוֹאֶה בְּשִׂמְחָתָהּ, וְשֶׁאֵינוֹ מִתְאַבֵּל עַל יְרוּשָׁלַיִם — אֵינוֹ רוֹאֶה בְּשִׂמְחָתָהּ. *תַּנְיָא נַמִי הָכִי: [ד]"כָּל הָאוֹכֵל בָּשָׂר וְשׁוֹתֶה יַיִן בְּט' בְּאָב, עָלָיו הַכָּתוּב אוֹמֵר °"וַתְּהִי עֲוֹנוֹתָם עַל עַצְמוֹתָם"". §"רַבִּי יְהוּדָה מְחַיֵּיב בִּכְפִיַּית הַמִּטָּה, וְלֹא הוֹדוּ לוֹ חֲכָמִים". § תַּנְיָא: אָמְרוּ לוֹ לְרַבִּי יְהוּדָה: לִדְבָרֶיךָ, עוּבָּרוֹת וּמֵנִיקוֹת מַה תְּהֵא עֲלֵיהֶן? אָמַר לָהֶם: אַף אֲנִי לֹא אָמַרְתִּי אֶלָּא בְּיָכוֹל. תַּנְיָא נַמִי הָכִי: "מוֹדֶה ר' יְהוּדָה לַחֲכָמִים בְּשֶׁאֵינוֹ יָכוֹל. וּמוֹדִים חֲכָמִים לְרַבִּי יְהוּדָה בְּיָכוֹל". מַאי בֵּינַיְיהוּ? אִיכָּא בֵּינַיְיהוּ שְׁאָר מִטּוֹת, כִּדְתַנְיָא: *[ה]"כְּשֶׁאָמְרוּ לִכְפּוֹת הַמִּטָּה, לֹא מִטָּתוֹ בִּלְבַד הוּא כּוֹפֶה, אֶלָּא כָּל הַמִּטּוֹת כּוּלָּן הוּא כּוֹפֶה. אָמַר רָבָא: הִלְכְתָא כְּתַנָּא דִּידָן, *וְלֹא הוֹדוּ לוֹ חֲכָמִים כָּל עִיקָּר. § "א"ר שִׁמְעוֹן ב"ג לֹא הָיוּ יָמִים טוֹבִים לְיִשְׂרָאֵל כַּחֲמִשָּׁה עָשָׂר בְּאָב וּכְיוה"כ". § *בִּשְׁלָמָא יוֹם הַכִּפּוּרִים — מִשּׁוּם דְּאִית בֵּיהּ סְלִיחָה וּמְחִילָה, יוֹם שֶׁנִּיתְּנוּ בּוֹ לוּחוֹת הָאַחֲרוֹנוֹת. אֶלָּא ט"ו בְּאָב מַאי הִיא? אָמַר רַב יְהוּדָה אָמַר שְׁמוּאֵל: יוֹם שֶׁהוּתְּרוּ שְׁבָטִים לָבוֹא זֶה בָּזֶה. מַאי דְּרוּשׁ? °"זֶה הַדָּבָר אֲשֶׁר צִוָּה ה' לִבְנוֹת צְלָפְחָד" וגו' — דָּבָר זֶה לֹא יְהֵא נוֹהֵג אֶלָּא בְּדוֹר זֶה. אָמַר רַב יוֹסֵף אָמַר רַב נַחְמָן: יוֹם שֶׁהוּתַּר שֵׁבֶט בִּנְיָמִין לָבוֹא בַּקָּהָל, שֶׁנֶּאֱמַר °"וְאִישׁ יִשְׂרָאֵל נִשְׁבַּע בַּמִּצְפָּה, לֵאמֹר אִישׁ מִמֶּנּוּ לֹא יִתֵּן בִּתּוֹ לְבִנְיָמִן לְאִשָּׁה". מַאי דְּרוּשׁ? אָמַר רַב: "מִמֶּנּוּ", וְלֹא מִבָּנֵינוּ. (*אָמַר) רַבָּה בַּר בַּר חָנָה א"ר יוֹחָנָן: יוֹם שֶׁכָּלוּ בּוֹ מֵתֵי מִדְבָּר. דְּאָמַר מָר: עַד שֶׁלֹּא כָּלוּ מֵתֵי מִדְבָּר, לֹא הָיָה דִּבּוּר עִם מֹשֶׁה, שֶׁנֶּאֱמַר °"וַיְהִי, כַּאֲשֶׁר תַּמּוּ כָּל אַנְשֵׁי הַמִּלְחָמָה לָמוּת, וַיְדַבֵּר ה' אֵלַי". אֵלַי הָיָה הַדִּבּוּר. עוּלָּא אָמַר: יוֹם שֶׁבִּיטֵּל הוֹשֵׁעַ בֶּן אֵלָה *פְּרוֹסְדִיּוֹת *שֶׁהוֹשִׁיב יָרָבְעָם בֶּן נְבָט עַל הַדְּרָכִים, שֶׁלֹּא יַעֲלוּ יִשְׂרָאֵל לָרֶגֶל, וְאָמַר: לְאֵיזֶה

ישעיהו סו | יחזקאל לב | במדבר לו | שופטים כא | דברים ב

רש"י

בֵּין תַּנּוּר לַכִּירַיִים. מָקוֹם מְנֻוָּול שֶׁבַּבַּיִת: אֵינוֹ רוֹאֶה סִימַן בְּרָכָה. מֵאוֹתָהּ מְלָאכָה: כָּל הָאוֹכֵל בָּשָׂר וְשׁוֹתֶה יַיִן בְּתִשְׁעָה בְּאָב עָלָיו הַכָּתוּב אוֹמֵר וַתְּהִי עֲוֹנוֹתָם עַל עַצְמוֹתָם. בְּתִשְׁעָה בְּאָב, כְּלוֹמַר בַּסְּעוּדָה הַמַּפְסִיק בָּהּ: עוּבָּרוֹת וּמֵנִיקוֹת. שֶׁאֵינָן יְכוֹלוֹת לִישֹׁן עַל גַּבֵּי קַרְקַע: בְּיָכוֹל. שֶׁאֶפְשָׁר לוֹ: מַאי בֵּינַיְיהוּ. כֵּיוָן דְּזֶה מוֹדֶה לוֹ בְּיָכוֹל, וְזֶה מוֹדֶה לוֹ בְּשֶׁאֵינוֹ יָכוֹל: שְׁאָר מִטּוֹת. שֶׁבַּבַּיִת, שֶׁאֵינוֹ שׁוֹכֵב בָּהֶן. ר' יְהוּדָה דִּמְחַיֵּיב בְּמַתְנִי' בִּכְפִיַּית הַמִּטָּה — קָמְחַיֵּיב נַמִי בְּיָכוֹל בִּשְׁאָר מִטּוֹת. וְרַבָּנַן סָבְרִי: מִטָּתוֹ כּוֹפֶה וְלֹא שְׁאָר מִטּוֹת, וְכִדְתַנְיָא גַּבֵּי אָבֵל: שֶׁנִּיתְּנוּ בּוֹ לוּחוֹת אַחֲרוֹנוֹת. שֶׁבְּי"ז בְּתַמּוּז יָרַד מֹשֶׁה מִן הָהָר תְּחִלָּה וְשִׁיבֵּר אֶת הַלּוּחוֹת, וּבִי"ח טָחַן אֶת הָעֵגֶל, וְדָן אֶת הַפּוֹשְׁעִים, וְעָלָה לַמָּרוֹם. נִשְׁתַּהָה שָׁם שְׁמוֹנִים יוֹם, אַרְבָּעִים יוֹם עָמַד בִּתְפִלָּה, דִּכְתִיב (דברים ט) "וָאֶתְנַפַּל לִפְנֵי ה' אַרְבָּעִים יוֹם וְאַרְבָּעִים לַיְלָה", וְאַרְבָּעִים יוֹם עָמַד כְּבָרִאשׁוֹנָה. חֲשׁוֹב מִי"ז בְּתַמּוּז עַד יוֹם הַכִּפּוּרִים — וְהָווּ לְהוּ שְׁמוֹנִים יוֹם: שְׁנֵים עָשָׂר שֶׁנִּשְׁתַּיְּירוּ מִתַּמּוּז דְּהוּא חָסֵר, וּשְׁלֹשִׁים דְּאָב, וְתִשְׁעָה וְעֶשְׂרִים דֶּאֱלוּל — הֲרֵי אֶחָד וְשִׁבְעִים, וְתִשְׁעָה דְּתִשְׁרֵי — הֲרֵי שְׁמוֹנִים יוֹם. וְלֵיל יוֹם (א) הַשְּׁלִישִׁים כְּנֶגֶד לֵילוֹ שֶׁל י"ז תַּמּוּז דְּלָא הֲוָה בְּחוּשְׁבָּנֵיהּ, דְּהָא נְפַק לֵיהּ כְּבָר בְּשָׁעָה שֶׁעָלָה — הָשְׁתָּא הָוֵי לְהוּ פ' שְׁלֵמִין, לַיְלָה וָיוֹם. וּבוֹקֶר יוֹם כִּפּוּר יָרַד, שֶׁהוּא עֲשָׂרָה בְּתִשְׁרֵי. וְאוֹתוֹ הַיּוֹם נִקְבַּע לְיוֹם כִּפּוּר — לְהוֹדִיעַ שֶׁמָּחַל וְנִיחַם עַל הָרָעָה אֲשֶׁר דִּבֵּר לַעֲשׂוֹת לְעַמּוֹ, וְעַל כֵּן נִקְבַּע יוֹם כִּפּוּר בַּעֲשָׂרָה בְּתִשְׁרֵי, כָּךְ שָׁמַעְתִּי: שֶׁהוּתְּרוּ שְׁבָטִים לָבֹא זֶה בָּזֶה. דְּרַחֲמָנָא אֲמַר "וְכָל בַּת יוֹרֶשֶׁת נַחֲלָה" וגו' (במדבר לו), וּכְתִיב (בראשית) "וְלֹא תִסּוֹב נַחֲלָה מִמַּטֶּה לְמַטֶּה אַחֵר, כִּי אִישׁ בְּנַחֲלָתוֹ יִדְבְּקוּ בְּנֵי יִשְׂרָאֵל", וְעָמְדוּ וְהִתִּירוּ דָּבָר זֶה בַּחֲמִשָּׁה עָשָׂר בְּאָב: זֶה הַדָּבָר אֲשֶׁר צִוָּה ה' לִבְנוֹת צְלָפְחָד וגו'. "זֶה" מִיעוּט הוּא. כְּלוֹמַר, לֹא יִהְיֶה דָּבָר זֶה נוֹהֵג אֶלָּא בְּדוֹר זֶה, בַּדּוֹר שֶׁל בְּנוֹת צְלָפְחָד: לָבֹא בַּקָּהָל. לִישָּׂא נָשִׁים, לְפִי שֶׁנִּשְׁבְּעוּ יִשְׂרָאֵל מִלְּהִינָּשֵׂא לָהֶם, כִּדְכְתִיב בְּשׁוֹפְטִים (כא): מִמֶּנּוּ. מִיעוּט הוּא, דִּכְתִיב "אִישׁ מִמֶּנּוּ לֹא יִתֵּן בִּתּוֹ לְבִנְיָמִין" — לֹא גָּזְרוּ אֶלָּא מֵהֶם (מִמֶּנּוּ), אֲבָל מִבְּנֵיהֶם לֹא גָּזְרוּ: שֶׁכָּלוּ מֵתֵי מִדְבָּר. דְּתַנְיָא: כָּל אַרְבָּעִים שָׁנָה שֶׁהָיוּ בַּמִּדְבָּר, בְּכָל עֶרֶב תִּשְׁעָה בְּאָב הָיָה הַכָּרוֹז יוֹצֵא וְאוֹמֵר: צְאוּ לַחֲפוֹר. וְהָיָה כָּל אֶחָד וְאֶחָד יוֹצֵא וְחוֹפֵר לוֹ קֶבֶר, וְיָשֵׁן בּוֹ, שֶׁמָּא יָמוּת קוֹדֶם שֶׁיַּחְפּוֹר. וּלְמָחָר הַכָּרוֹז יוֹצֵא וְקוֹרֵא: יִבָּדְלוּ חַיִּים מִן הַמֵּתִים! וְכָל שֶׁהָיָה בּוֹ נֶפֶשׁ חַיִּים — הָיָה עוֹמֵד וְיוֹצֵא. וְכָל שָׁנָה הָיוּ עוֹשִׂין כֵּן, וּבִשְׁנַת אַרְבָּעִים שָׁנָה עָשׂוּ, וּלְמָחָר עָמְדוּ כּוּלָּן חַיִּים. וְכֵיוָן שֶׁרָאוּ כָּךְ, תָּמְהוּ וְאָמְרוּ: שֶׁמָּא טָעִינוּ בַּחֶשְׁבּוֹן הַחֹדֶשׁ? חָזְרוּ וְשָׁכְבוּ בְּקִבְרֵיהֶן בַּלֵּילוֹת עַד לֵיל חֲמִשָּׁה עָשָׂר, וְכֵיוָן שֶׁרָאוּ שֶׁנִּתְמַלְּאָה הַלְּבָנָה בְּט"ו, וְלֹא מֵת אֶחָד מֵהֶם — יָדְעוּ שֶׁחֶשְׁבּוֹן חֹדֶשׁ מְכוּוָּן, וּכְבָר מ' שָׁנָה שֶׁל גְּזֵרָה נִשְׁלְמוּ, קָבְעוּ אוֹתוֹ הַדּוֹר לְאוֹתוֹ הַיּוֹם יו"ט: דְּאָמַר מָר כו'. לְפִיכָךְ יו"ט הוּא: לֹא הָיָה הַדִּבּוּר עִם מֹשֶׁה. בְּיִחוּד וְחִיבָּה, דִּכְתִיב "וַיְדַבֵּר ה' אֵלַי לֵאמֹר" — אֵלַי נִתְיַיחֵד הַדִּיבּוּר. וְאַע"ג דְּמִקַּמֵּי הָכִי כְּתִיבִי קְרָאֵי בְּהוּ "וַיְדַבֵּר", אִיכָּא דְּאָמְרִי: לֹא הָיָה פֶּה אֶל פֶּה, אֶלָּא בְּחֶזְיוֹן לַיְלָה. גִּמְגּוּם: לְאֵיזֶה

תוספות

כל העושה מלאכה בתשעה באב אינו רואה סימן ברכה לעולם. כלומר באותה מלאכה שרגיל לעשות בתשעה באב אינו רואה סימן ברכה לעולם. וחייב אדם לצער ולמעט בכבודו ובהנאותיו, שאם היה רגיל לשכב על שני כרים — לא ישכב כי אם על אחד. אבל עוברות ומניקות אינן חייבות כולי האי, שאינם יכולות להצטער בעצמן. ואוכלין סעודה המפסקת מבעוד יום, וכן (נמי) ביום הכפורים (נמי) צריך לסעוד מבע"י, דתוספת יום הכפורים מן התורה כדכתיב (ויקרא כג) "מערב ועד ערב" וכתיב "בעצם היום הזה" (שם). אבל מכל מקום אין לאסור לשתות משאכל סעודה מפסקת ועדיין הוי היום גדול, ●כדמשמע בירושלמי דר' יוסי איקלע לבצרה, אכל סעודה מפסקת אתא לגבי דריש כנישתא והוה סעיד. אמר ליה ההוא ריש כנישתא: סעוד אצלי, אמר ליה: אכלית ואפסקית. אמר לו: אשגח עלי, דלא לימרון הדין גברא לא אשגח עליה — אכל מכל עיגול פתית, ואכל מכל תבשיל ותבשיל חד פת, ושתה מכל חבית חד כסא. והכי הלכתא: אם עדיין היום גדול לאחר שאכל סעודה המפסקת מותר לשתות אפילו ערב יוה"כ, וכל שכן ערב תשעה באב:

אמר רבא הלכה כתנא דידן ולא הודו לו חכמים. פירוש: שאין צריך לכפות המטה. והאידנא דחיישינן לכשפים — לא עבדינן כפיית המטה, ואפילו באבל:

יום שהותרו השבטים לבא זה בזה. פירוש: דהיינו י"ט:

יום שבו כלו מתי מדבר. כדאמרי' (במדרש איכה): כל ט' באב היו עושין קבריהן ושוכבין בתוכן, ולמחר הכרוז יוצא: הבדלו החיים. ואותה השנה שכלתה הגזרה — קמו כולם, והיו סבורים שמא טעו בחודש, עד שראו הלבנה מלאה — ואז ידעו שכלתה הגזרה, ועשו יו"ט. ופרשב"ם (בב"ב דף קכא.*): כל המ' שנים לא היו מתים אלא בט' באב, ●ובכל ט' באב היו מתים *כ"א אלף ופרוטרוט, ומפרש התם דאותו פרוטרוט עולה למ' שנים ט"ו אלף. וי"מ: שהיו מתים בכל יום, אך רוב המתים היו לעולם בתשעה באב. ובחמשה עשר באב פסקה הגזרה ולא מתו כלל, ועשו י"ט:

תיקנו

שולי הגליון

[ברכות יז:] פסחים נה:

[ברי"ף וברא"ש מהופכים דברי ר"ע לרשב"ג ודברי רשב"ג לר"ע]

[ב"ב ס:]

הגהות הב"ח

(א) רש"י ד"ה שניתנו כו' הרי שמונים יום וליל יום כפור השלים כנגד:

מו"ק כז. נדרים נו. סנהדרין כ.

בס"י אי' דקאמר ולא הודו

ב"ב קכא. ע"ש

גליון הש"ס

תום' ד"ה כל העושה וכו' כדמשמע בירושלמי בעירובין דף מא ע"א בתוס' ד"ה אי אתם כתבו כן בשם מדרש איכה רבתי: שם ד"ה יום שבו וכו' ובכל ט"ב היו מתים. עיין תשובת חות יאיר בסוף הספר תשוב' של הגאון מוהר"ר זצ"ל בסופו:

[בב"ב קכא. איתא רב דימי בר יוסף אמר רב נחמן יום וכו']

[גיר' הערוך פרוזדאות פי' שומרים וע' לעיל כח. והושיבו פרוזלאות כו']

גיטין נז.

ברי"ף וברא"ש ליתא תנ"ה

[ע"ש ברשב"ם וע' מהרש"א]

מתים מת"ר אלף בפרוטרוט כצ"ל

[גיטין פח.] [ושם הגי' פרדסיות וכן הגי' בב"ב קכא:]

רבינו חננאל

ר' אומר כל האוכל ושותה בט' באב כאלו אוכל ושותה ביוה"כ. ר' עקיבא אומר העושה מלאכה בט' באב אינו רואה סימן ברכה לעולם. והכ"א העושה מלאכה בט' באב אינו רואה בשמחת ירושלים שנאמר שמחו את וגו' שישו אתה משוש כל המתאבלים עליה. כל שאינו מתאבל על ירושלים אינו רואה בשמחתה. וכל האוכל בט' באב עליו הכתוב אומר ותהי עונותם על עצמותם. עונותיו חקוקים על עצמותיו. ר' יהודה מחייב בכפיית המטה ולא הודו לו חכמים. תנא מודה ר' יהודה לחכמים בשאינו יכול כגון עוברות ומיניקות וכיוצא בהן שאין כופין מטותיהן. ומודים חכמים לר' יהודה שכופה כל אדם מטתו מי שהוא יכול לישן על הקרקע ואמר רבא הלכתא כתנא דידן דקתני לא הודו לו חכמים. מנהגו של ר' יהודה ברבי אלעאי בערב ט' באב היה יושב בין תנור לכיריים ואוכל פת חריבה במלח. ושותה קיתון של מים ודומה כמי שמתו מוטל לפניו: ארשב"ג לא היו ימים טובים לישראל כט"ו באב וכיוה"כ. בשלמא יוה"כ משום שהוא יום שנתנו לוחות האחרונות לפי שכשתחשב מז' בסיון שעלה משה לקבל לוחות הראשונות מ' יום עד י"ז בתמוז שנא' ואתנפל לפני ה' וגו' עד כ"ט באב ומיד א"ל הקב"ה למשה עלה אלי ההרה. ועלה ביום ל' של אב (עשה ג') [עמד מ'] יום וירד בלוחות האחרונות והוא יוה"כ לפיכך ראוי להיות יו"ט. אלא ט"ו באב מפני מה הוא יו"ט ואמרי' יום שהותרו שבטים לבוא זה בזה. דדרוש זה הדבר שכתוב בענין ולא תסוב נחלה ממטה למטה אחד. לא יהא נוהג אלא באותו דור שנכנסו לארץ. ולהם נחלקה הארץ בלבד. ור' יוחנן אמר שהותר שבט בנימין דדרוש איש ממנו לא יתן בתו לבנימין ממנו ולא מבנינו. רב נחמן אמר יום שכלו בו מתי מדבר. ומצינו בפירוש בירושלמי ר' אבון אמר שבטל בו החפירה דא"ר לו בכל ערב ט' באב היה משה רבינו מוציא כרוז במחנה ישראל צאו לחפור היו יוצאין (עצמן) וחופרין קברות וכל אחד ישן בקברו. ובשחר מי שנמצא חי חזר למחנה והמתים נשארו בקבריהן ומוצאין עצמן בכל שנה חסרים ט"ו אלף ופרוטרוט בשנת ל"ח שנה עשו כמנהג כל השנים עמדו כולן לא מת אחד מהן. אמרו טעינו בחשבון אינו היום ט' באב וכן אמרו בי"א בי"ב ובי"ג ובי"ד כיון שהגיע ט"ו באב וראו הלבנה מלאה

רבינו גרשום

מחייב בכפיית המטה לכוף מטתו כאבל: עוברות ומיניקות שאי אפשר להם בלא מטות מה תהא עליהם: שאר מטות שאינו שוכב עליה דר' יהודה מחייב לכוף כל המטות שבבית וחכ"א אינו חייב לכוף אלא מטתו בלבד: כל הכלים המשאילות זו לזו טעונות טבילה שמא דנדה היו. יום שכלו מתי מדבר וקבעו יום טוב לפי שחזר הדיבור למשה. יום שפוסקין מלכרות עצים למערכה ומיכן ואילך מוסיפין לעסוק בתורה:

רש"י

לְאֵיזֶה שֶׁיִּרְצֶה יַעֲלוּ. הוֹשֵׁעַ בֶּן אֵלָה רָשָׁע הָיָה, דִּכְתִיב (מלכים ב יז) "וַיַּעַשׂ הָרַע בְּעֵינֵי ה' רַק לֹא כְּמַלְכֵי יִשְׂרָאֵל", וְהַיְינוּ דְּקָאָמַר "רַק" – שֶׁבִּטֵּל אֶת הַפְּרוֹסְדָאוֹת, וְאָמַר: לְאֵיזֶה שֶׁיִּרְצוּ יַעֲלוּ: הֲרוּגֵי בֵיתָר. בְּפֶרֶק "הַנִּיזָּקִין" (גיטין דף נז.): מִלִּכְרוֹת. לְפִי שֶׁהֵן לַחִין, וּמֵאוֹתוֹ הַזְּמַן אֵין כֹּחַ בַּחַמָּה לְיַבְּשָׁן. וְחָיְישִׁינַן מִפְּנֵי הַתּוֹלַעַת, לְפִי שֶׁעֵץ שֶׁיֵּשׁ בּוֹ תּוֹלַעַת פָּסוּל לַמַּעֲרָכָה, כִּדְאָמְרִינַן (מדות פ"ב מ"ה): יוֹם תְּבַר מַגָּל. שְׁבִירַת הַגַּרְזֶן, שֶׁפָּסַק הַחוֹטֵב מִלַּחְטוֹב עֵצִים: מִכָּאן וְאֵילָךְ. מֵחֲמִשָּׁה עָשָׂר בְּאָב וְאֵילָךְ, דְּמוֹסִיף לֵילוֹת עַל הַיָּמִים לַעֲסוֹק בַּתּוֹרָה – יוֹסִיף חַיִּים עַל חַיָּיו: דְּלָא יוֹסִיף. לַעֲסוֹק בַּתּוֹרָה בַּלֵּילוֹת: תִּקְבְּרֵיהּ אִימֵּיהּ. כְּלוֹמַר: יָמוּת בְּלֹא עִתּוֹ: בַּת מֶלֶךְ. אַף עַל פִּי שֶׁהָיָה לָהּ – שׁוֹאֶלֶת מִבַּת כֹּהֵן גָּדוֹל כו', שֶׁלֹּא לְבַיֵּישׁ אֶת הַשּׁוֹאֶלֶת מִתּוֹךְ שֶׁאֵין לָהּ: מִבַּת כֹּהֵן גָּדוֹל. שֶׁהוּא קָרוֹב וְסָמוּךְ לַמַּלְכוּת: סְגָן. כֹּהֵן חָשׁוּב, מְמוּנֶּה תַּחַת כֹּהֵן גָּדוֹל לִהְיוֹת תַּחְתָּיו בְּיוֹם הַכִּפּוּרִים. אִם יֶאֱרַע פְּסוּל בְּכֹהֵן גָּדוֹל בְּיוֹם הַכִּפּוּרִים – יְשַׁמֵּשׁ זֶה הַסְּגָן תַּחְתָּיו: מְשׁוּחַ מִלְחָמָה. הוּא הַכֹּהֵן הַמַּכְרִיז בַּמִּלְחָמָה *"מִי הָאִישׁ הַיָּרֵא וְרַךְ הַלֵּבָב" וגו' (דברים כ): אֲפִילּוּ מְקוּפָּלִין וּמוּנָּחִין בְּקוּפְסָא'. אִיסְקוּרְיי"ן: צְרִיכִין טְבִילָה. כּוּלָּן, שֶׁלֹּא לְבַיֵּישׁ אֶת שֶׁצְּרִיכָה טְבִילָה: שֶׁאֵין אִשָּׁה אֶלָּא לְבָנִים. אִם בָּנֶיךָ יִהְיוּ מְיוּחָסִין הַכֹּל קוֹפְצִין עֲלֵיהֶם, בֵּין זְכָרִים בֵּין נְקֵבוֹת: עַל מְנָת שֶׁתְּעַטְּרוּנוּ בִּזְהוּבִים. שֶׁאַחֲרֵי הַנִּשּׂוּאִין תִּתְּנוּ לָנוּ תַּכְשִׁיטִין. וּמִילְּתָא בְּעָלְמָא הוּא דְּאָמְרִי, כְּלוֹמַר: וּבִלְבַד שֶׁתִּתְּנוּ לָנוּ מַלְבּוּשִׁים נָאִים: מָחוֹל. סָבִיב, לְשׁוֹן "מְחוֹל הַכֶּרֶם" (כלאים פ"ד מ"א): מַרְאֶה בְּאֶצְבָּעוֹ. וְאוֹמֵר: זֶה ה' קִוִּינוּ לוֹ וְיוֹשִׁיעֵנוּ, זֶה ה' קִוִּינוּ לוֹ נָגִילָה וְנִשְׂמְחָה בִּישׁוּעָתוֹ:

גמרא

תורה אור

לְאֵיזֶה שֶׁיִּרְצוּ יַעֲלוּ. *רַב מַתָּנָה אָמַר: יוֹם שֶׁנִּתְּנוּ הֲרוּגֵי בֵיתָר לִקְבוּרָה. וְאָמַר רַב מַתָּנָה: *אוֹתוֹ יוֹם שֶׁנִּתְּנוּ הֲרוּגֵי בֵיתָר לִקְבוּרָה [א]תִּקְּנוּ בְּיַבְנֶה 'הַטּוֹב וְהַמֵּטִיב'. 'הַטּוֹב' – שֶׁלֹּא הִסְרִיחוּ. 'וְהַמֵּטִיב' – שֶׁנִּתְּנוּ לִקְבוּרָה. רַבָּה וְרַב יוֹסֵף דְּאָמְרִי תַּרְוַיְיהוּ: יוֹם שֶׁפָּסְקוּ מִלִּכְרוֹת עֵצִים לַמַּעֲרָכָה, (*תַּנְיָא) רַבִּי אֱלִיעֶזֶר הַגָּדוֹל אוֹמֵר: מֵחֲמִשָּׁה עָשָׂר בְּאָב וְאֵילָךְ תָּשַׁשׁ כֹּחָהּ שֶׁל חַמָּה, וְלֹא הָיוּ כּוֹרְתִין עֵצִים לַמַּעֲרָכָה, לְפִי שֶׁאֵינָן יְבֵשִׁין. אָמַר רַב מְנַשְּׁיָא: וְקָרוּ לֵיהּ יוֹם תְּבַר מַגָּל. מִכָּאן וְאֵילָךְ דְּמוֹסִיף – יוֹסִיף, וּדְלָא מוֹסִיף – (*יֶאֱסֵף.) (*תָּנֵי רַב יוֹסֵף:) מַאי "יֶאֱסֵף"? אָמַר רַב יוֹסֵף תִּקְבְּרֵיהּ אִימֵּיהּ. § "שֶׁבָּהֶן בְּנוֹת יְרוּשָׁלַיִם" כו'. § ת"ר: בַּת מֶלֶךְ שׁוֹאֶלֶת מִבַּת כֹּהֵן גָּדוֹל, בַּת כֹּהֵן גָּדוֹל מִבַּת סְגָן, וּבַת סְגָן מִבַּת מְשׁוּחַ מִלְחָמָה, וּבַת מְשׁוּחַ מִלְחָמָה מִבַּת כֹּהֵן הֶדְיוֹט, וְכָל יִשְׂרָאֵל שׁוֹאֲלִין זֶה מִזֶּה, כְּדֵי *שֶׁלֹּא יִתְבַּיֵּישׁ אֶת מִי שֶׁאֵין לוֹ. § "כָּל הַכֵּלִים טְעוּנִין טְבִילָה". § אָמַר רַבִּי אֶלְעָזָר: אֲפִילּוּ מְקוּפָּלִין וּמוּנָּחִין בְּקוּפְסָא. § "בְּנוֹת יִשְׂרָאֵל יוֹצְאוֹת וְחוֹלוֹת בַּכְּרָמִים". § תָּנָא: "מִי שֶׁאֵין לוֹ אִשָּׁה נִפְנֶה לְשָׁם". § *"מְיוּחָסוֹת שֶׁבָּהֶן הָיוּ אוֹמְרוֹת בָּחוּר" וכו'. § תָּנוּ רַבָּנַן: יְפֵיפִיּוֹת שֶׁבָּהֶן מָה הָיוּ אוֹמְרוֹת – תְּנוּ עֵינֵיכֶם לְיוֹפִי, שֶׁאֵין הָאִשָּׁה אֶלָּא לְיוֹפִי. מְיוּחָסוֹת שֶׁבָּהֶן מָה הָיוּ אוֹמְרוֹת – תְּנוּ עֵינֵיכֶם לַמִּשְׁפָּחָה, לְפִי *שֶׁאֵין הָאִשָּׁה אֶלָּא לְבָנִים. מְכוֹעָרוֹת שֶׁבָּהֶם מָה הָיוּ אוֹמְרוֹת – קְחוּ מִקַּחֲכֶם לְשׁוּם שָׁמַיִם, וּבִלְבַד שֶׁתְּעַטְּרוּנוּ בִּזְהוּבִים. אָמַר עוּלָּא בִּירָאָה אָמַר רַבִּי אֶלְעָזָר: עָתִיד הַקָּדוֹשׁ בָּרוּךְ הוּא לַעֲשׂוֹת מָחוֹל לַצַּדִּיקִים, וְהוּא יוֹשֵׁב בֵּינֵיהֶם בְּגַן עֵדֶן, וְכָל אֶחָד וְאֶחָד מַרְאֶה בְּאֶצְבָּעוֹ, שֶׁנֶּאֱמַ' (ישעיהו כה) °"וְאָמַר בַּיּוֹם הַהוּא הִנֵּה, אֱלֹהֵינוּ זֶה קִוִּינוּ לוֹ וְיוֹשִׁיעֵנוּ. זֶה ה' קִוִּינוּ לוֹ. נָגִילָה וְנִשְׂמְחָה בִּישׁוּעָתוֹ". §

הדרן עלך בשלשה פרקים וסליקא לה מסכת תענית

תוספות

תיקנו ביבנה הטוב והמטיב. פירוש: בברכת המזון. ומש"ה תקנו יותר על היין "הטוב והמטיב" טפי מבשאר דברים, לפי שהיו [כמו] גדר בכרם, ולא נסרחו: **יום** תבר מגל. פירוש: שמונעין מלכרות עצים למערכה. פירוש: משום שחלש כחה של חמה, ומגדלין התולעים באילנות, ועצים מתולעים פסולים למערכה. כדאמר [במדות] (פ"ב מ"ה) שהכהנים בעלי מומין הם מנקרים העצים ומסירין העצים מתולעים, שפסולות למערכה:

דלא מוסיף יאסף. פי': אותו שאינו מוסיף מן הלילות על הימים – יאסף: **מאי** יאסף תקבריה אימיה. תימה: וכי היה מסופק מאי יאסף? אלא נראה לומר דלא מוסיף יסיף (א) ומיהא קבעי גמרא מאי יסיף, אבל לעולם הוה ידע דיאסף הוא לשון מיתה, כדכתיב (בראשית מט) "ויגוע ויאסף אל עמיו": **כל** אחד ואחד מראה הקדוש ברוך הוא באצבעו, שנאמר "הנה אלהינו זה קוינו לו וגו' נגילה ונשמחה בישועתו":

הדרן עלך בשלשה פרקים וסליקא לה מסכת תענית

רבינו חננאל

מלאה אמרו ודאי בטל הקב"ה אותה גזרה לפיכך עשאוהו יו"ט. רב מתנה אמר יום שנתנו הרוגי ביתר לקבורה בו ביום תקנו הטוב והמטיב הטוב שלא הסריחו והמטיב שנתנו לקבורה. יום שפוסקין בו לכרות עצים למערכה כדתניא ר"א הגדול אומר מט"ו באב תשש כחה של חמה ולא היו כורתים עצים למערכה מפני שאין יבשים וכיון שאין יבשים מתליעין וקרו ליה יום תבר מגל. כלומר מעתה אין אנו צריכין מגל לחתוך בו עצים. [מכאן ואילך] פי' מט"ו באב מי שמוסיף מן הלילה ליום כלומר עומד בלילה ושונה שכבר האריך הלילה. ומי שלא יוסיף תקבריה אימיה שאינו מן החכמים שמנדדין שינה מעיניהם בעולם הזה וחיים לעוה"ב: הדרן עלך בשלשה פרקים

רבינו גרשום

שש כחה של חמה. ואינה מייבשת העצים. יום תבר מגל כלומר מיכן ואילך אין צריכין המגל לכרות עצים: ודלא מוסיף מלילות על הימים לעסוק בתורה [יוסף] לפי שכבר גדולין הלילות: אפי' מקופלין חיישינן שמה ישבה עליהן נדה. לעשות מחול להצדיקים שהצדיקים עושין מחול והקב"ה יושב באמצע ומראין זה לזה ואומרים הנה אלהינו זה קוינו לו ויושיענו זה ה' קוינו לו נגילה ונשמחה בישועתו:

הדרן עלך בשלשה פרקים וכולה מסכתא ופרקיהון ארבעה וסימניהן הזכרת סדר תעניות שלשה:

מסורת הש"ס: ב"ב קכא: | ברכות מח: | [גיר' ע"י דתניא] | [ב"ב ליתא אלא כך איתא אי יסיף תני רב יוסף תקבריה אימיה] | [אם שנ"ל אל ירך לבבכם י' עי' פרק בתורה מכות יא. וכסוטה מג.] | כתובות נט:

הגהות הב"ח: (א) תוס' ד"ה מאי כו' דלא סיף יסיף ומשום הכי קבעי גמרא מאי:

עין משפט נר מצוה: מב א מיי' פ"ב מהל' ברכות הל' א: | [נ"ל יסיף כך אי' בב"ב וע"ש ברשב"ם] | [פסחים פב. וש"נ] | [עי' הגיר' בע"י]

The following paragraph is recited three times:

הַדְרָן עֲלָךְ מַסֶּכֶת תַּעֲנִית וְהַדְרָךְ עֲלָן, דַּעְתָּן עֲלָךְ מַסֶּכֶת
תַּעֲנִית וְדַעְתָּךְ עֲלָן, לָא נִתְנְשֵׁי מִנָּךְ מַסֶּכֶת תַּעֲנִית וְלָא
תִתְנְשֵׁי מִנָּן, לָא בְּעָלְמָא הָדֵין וְלָא בְּעָלְמָא דְאָתֵי.

יְהִי רָצוֹן מִלְּפָנֶיךָ יהוה אֱלֹהֵינוּ וֵאלֹהֵי אֲבוֹתֵינוּ,
שֶׁתְּהֵא תוֹרָתְךָ אֻמָּנוּתֵנוּ בָּעוֹלָם הַזֶּה, וּתְהֵא עִמָּנוּ
לָעוֹלָם הַבָּא. חֲנִינָא בַּר פַּפָּא, רָמֵי בַּר פַּפָּא, נַחְמָן
בַּר פַּפָּא, אֲחַאי בַּר פַּפָּא, אַבָּא מָרִי בַּר פַּפָּא, רַפְרָם
בַּר פַּפָּא, רָכִישׁ בַּר פַּפָּא, סוּרְחַב בַּר פַּפָּא, אַדָּא בַּר
פַּפָּא, דָּרוּ בַּר פַּפָּא.

הַעֲרֶב נָא יהוה אֱלֹהֵינוּ אֶת דִּבְרֵי תוֹרָתְךָ בְּפִינוּ וּבְפִי
עַמְּךָ בֵּית יִשְׂרָאֵל, וְנִהְיֶה אֲנַחְנוּ וְצֶאֱצָאֵינוּ (וְצֶאֱצָאֵי
צֶאֱצָאֵינוּ) וְצֶאֱצָאֵי עַמְּךָ בֵּית יִשְׂרָאֵל, כֻּלָּנוּ יוֹדְעֵי
שְׁמֶךָ וְלוֹמְדֵי תוֹרָתְךָ לִשְׁמָהּ. מֵאֹיְבַי תְּחַכְּמֵנִי מִצְוֹתֶךָ תהלים קיט
כִּי לְעוֹלָם הִיא־לִי: יְהִי־לִבִּי תָמִים בְּחֻקֶּיךָ לְמַעַן לֹא
אֵבוֹשׁ: לְעוֹלָם לֹא־אֶשְׁכַּח פִּקּוּדֶיךָ כִּי־בָם חִיִּיתָנִי:
בָּרוּךְ אַתָּה יהוה לַמְּדֵנִי חֻקֶּיךָ: אָמֵן אָמֵן אָמֵן סֶלָה
וָעֶד.

מוֹדִים אֲנַחְנוּ לְפָנֶיךָ יהוה אֱלֹהֵינוּ וֵאלֹהֵי אֲבוֹתֵינוּ
שֶׁשַּׂמְתָּ חֶלְקֵנוּ מִיּוֹשְׁבֵי בֵּית הַמִּדְרָשׁ, וְלֹא שַׂמְתָּ חֶלְקֵנוּ
מִיּוֹשְׁבֵי קְרָנוֹת. שֶׁאָנוּ מַשְׁכִּימִים וְהֵם מַשְׁכִּימִים,
אָנוּ מַשְׁכִּימִים לְדִבְרֵי תוֹרָה, וְהֵם מַשְׁכִּימִים לִדְבָרִים
בְּטֵלִים. אָנוּ עֲמֵלִים וְהֵם עֲמֵלִים, אָנוּ עֲמֵלִים וּמְקַבְּלִים
שָׂכָר, וְהֵם עֲמֵלִים וְאֵינָם מְקַבְּלִים שָׂכָר. אָנוּ רָצִים וְהֵם
רָצִים, אָנוּ רָצִים לְחַיֵּי הָעוֹלָם הַבָּא, וְהֵם רָצִים לִבְאֵר
שַׁחַת, שֶׁנֶּאֱמַר: וְאַתָּה אֱלֹהִים תּוֹרִדֵם לִבְאֵר שַׁחַת תהלים נה
אַנְשֵׁי דָמִים וּמִרְמָה לֹא־יֶחֱצוּ יְמֵיהֶם וַאֲנִי אֶבְטַח־בָּךְ:

יְהִי רָצוֹן מִלְּפָנֶיךָ יהוה אֱלֹהַי, כְּשֵׁם שֶׁעֲזַרְתַּנִי לְסַיֵּם
מַסֶּכֶת תַּעֲנִית כֵּן תְּעַזְּרֵנִי לְהַתְחִיל מַסֶּכְתּוֹת וּסְפָרִים
אֲחֵרִים וּלְסַיְּמָם, לִלְמֹד וּלְלַמֵּד לִשְׁמֹר וְלַעֲשׂוֹת
וּלְקַיֵּם אֶת כָּל דִּבְרֵי תַלְמוּד תּוֹרָתְךָ בְּאַהֲבָה, וּזְכוּת
כָּל הַתַּנָּאִים וְאָמוֹרָאִים וְתַלְמִידֵי חֲכָמִים יַעֲמֹד לִי
וּלְזַרְעִי שֶׁלֹּא תָמוּשׁ הַתּוֹרָה מִפִּי וּמִפִּי זַרְעִי וְזֶרַע זַרְעִי
עַד עוֹלָם, וְיִתְקַיֵּם בִּי: בְּהִתְהַלֶּכְךָ תַּנְחֶה אֹתָךְ בְּשָׁכְבְּךָ משלי ו
תִּשְׁמֹר עָלֶיךָ וַהֲקִיצוֹתָ הִיא תְשִׂיחֶךָ: כִּי־בִי יִרְבּוּ יָמֶיךָ משלי ט
וְיוֹסִיפוּ לְךָ שְׁנוֹת חַיִּים: אֹרֶךְ יָמִים בִּימִינָהּ בִּשְׂמֹאולָהּ משלי ג
עֹשֶׁר וְכָבוֹד: יהוה עֹז לְעַמּוֹ יִתֵּן יהוה יְבָרֵךְ אֶת־עַמּוֹ תהלים כט
בַשָּׁלוֹם:

The following paragraph is recited three times:

הַדְרָן We shall return to you, tractate *Ta'anit,* and your glory is upon us. Our thoughts are upon you, tractate *Ta'anit,* and your thoughts are upon us. We will not be forgotten from you, tractate *Ta'anit,* and you will not be forgotten from us; neither in this world nor in the World-to-Come.

יְהִי רָצוֹן May it be Your will, Lord our God and God of our ancestors, that Your Torah will be our avocation in this world and will accompany us to the World-to-Come. Ḥanina bar Pappa, Ramei bar Pappa, Naḥman bar Pappa, Aḥai bar Pappa, Abba Mari bar Pappa, Rafram bar Pappa, Rakhish bar Pappa, Surḥav bar Pappa, Adda bar Pappa, Daru bar Pappa.

הַעֲרֶב נָא Please, Lord our God, make the words of Your
Torah sweet in our mouths and in the mouths of Your
people, the house of Israel, so that we, our descendants
(and their descendants), and the descendants of Your
people, the house of Israel, may all know Your name and
study Your Torah for its own sake. Your commandments *Psalms 119*
make me wiser than my enemies, for they are ever with
me. Let my heart be undivided in Your statutes, in order
that I may not be put to shame. I will never forget Your
precepts, for with them You have quickened me. Blessed
are You, O Lord; teach me Your statutes. Amen, Amen,
Amen, Selah, Forever.

מוֹדִים We give thanks before You, Lord Our God and
God of our ancestors, that You have placed our lot
among those who sit in the study hall and that you have
not given us our portion among those who sit idly on
street corners. We rise early and they rise early. We rise
early to pursue matters of Torah and they rise early to
pursue frivolous matters. We toil and they toil. We toil
and receive a reward and they toil and do not receive a
reward. We run and they run. We run to the life of the
World-to-Come and they run to the pit of destruction,
as it is stated: But You, God, will bring them down into *Psalms 55*
the pit of destruction; men of blood and deceit shall not
live out half their days; but as for me, I will trust in You.

יְהִי רָצוֹן May it be Your will, Lord my God, just as you
have assisted me in completing tractate *Ta'anit* so assist
me to begin other tractates and books and conclude
them to learn and to teach, to observe and to perform,
and to fulfill all the teachings of Your Torah with love.
And may the merit of all the *tanna'im* and *amora'im* and
Torah scholars stand for me and my descendants so that
the Torah will not move from my mouth and from the
mouths of my descendants and the descendants of my
descendants forever. And may the verse: When you *Proverbs 6*
walk, it shall lead you, when you lie down, it shall watch
over you; and when you awaken, it shall talk with you
be fulfilled in me. For in the Torah your days shall be *Proverbs 9*
multiplied, and the years of your life shall be increased.
Length of days is in her right hand; in her left hand are *Proverbs 3*
riches and honor. May the Lord give strength to His *Psalms 29*
people; the Lord will bless His people with peace.

The following קדיש *requires the presence of a* מנין*.*

יִתְגַּדַּל וְיִתְקַדַּשׁ שְׁמֵהּ רַבָּא
בְּעָלְמָא דְּהוּא עָתִיד לְאִתְחַדָּתָא
וּלְאַחֲיָאָה מֵתַיָּא, וּלְאַסָּקָא יָתְהוֹן לְחַיֵּי עָלְמָא
וּלְמִבְנֵא קַרְתָּא דִירוּשְׁלֵם, וּלְשַׁכְלָלָא הֵיכְלֵהּ בְּגַוַּהּ
וּלְמֶעְקַר פָּלְחָנָא נֻכְרָאָה מֵאַרְעָא
וְלַאֲתָבָא פָּלְחָנָא דִשְׁמַיָּא לְאַתְרֵהּ
וְיַמְלִיךְ קֻדְשָׁא בְּרִיךְ הוּא בְּמַלְכוּתֵהּ וִיקָרֵהּ
(נוסח ספרד: וְיַצְמַח פּוּרְקָנֵהּ וִיקָרֵב מְשִׁיחֵהּ)
בְּחַיֵּיכוֹן וּבְיוֹמֵיכוֹן וּבְחַיֵּי דְכָל בֵּית יִשְׂרָאֵל
בַּעֲגָלָא וּבִזְמַן קָרִיב, וְאִמְרוּ אָמֵן.

יְהֵא שְׁמֵהּ רַבָּא מְבָרַךְ לְעָלַם וּלְעָלְמֵי עָלְמַיָּא.

יִתְבָּרַךְ וְיִשְׁתַּבַּח וְיִתְפָּאַר וְיִתְרוֹמַם וְיִתְנַשֵּׂא
וְיִתְהַדָּר וְיִתְעַלֶּה וְיִתְהַלָּל
שְׁמֵהּ דְּקֻדְשָׁא בְּרִיךְ הוּא
לְעֵלָּא מִן כָּל בִּרְכָתָא
/בעשרת ימי תשובה: לְעֵלָּא לְעֵלָּא מִכָּל בִּרְכָתָא/
וְשִׁירָתָא, תֻּשְׁבְּחָתָא וְנֶחֱמָתָא, דַּאֲמִירָן בְּעָלְמָא
וְאִמְרוּ אָמֵן. (קהל: אָמֵן)

עַל יִשְׂרָאֵל וְעַל רַבָּנָן
וְעַל תַּלְמִידֵיהוֹן וְעַל כָּל תַּלְמִידֵי תַלְמִידֵיהוֹן
וְעַל כָּל מָאן דְּעָסְקִין בְּאוֹרַיְתָא
דִּי בְּאַתְרָא (בארץ ישראל: קַדִּישָׁא) הָדֵין, וְדִי בְּכָל אֲתַר וַאֲתַר
יְהֵא לְהוֹן וּלְכוֹן שְׁלָמָא רַבָּא
חִנָּא וְחִסְדָּא, וְרַחֲמֵי, וְחַיֵּי אֲרִיכֵי, וּמְזוֹנֵי רְוִיחֵי
וּפֻרְקָנָא מִן קֳדָם אֲבוּהוֹן דִּי בִשְׁמַיָּא
וְאִמְרוּ אָמֵן.

יְהֵא שְׁלָמָא רַבָּא מִן שְׁמַיָּא
וְחַיִּים (טוֹבִים) עָלֵינוּ וְעַל כָּל יִשְׂרָאֵל
וְאִמְרוּ אָמֵן.

Bow, take three steps back, as if taking leave of the Divine Presence, then bow, first left, then right, then center, while saying:

עֹשֶׂה שָׁלוֹם/ בעשרת ימי תשובה: הַשָּׁלוֹם/ בִּמְרוֹמָיו
הוּא יַעֲשֶׂה בְרַחֲמָיו שָׁלוֹם, עָלֵינוּ וְעַל כָּל יִשְׂרָאֵל
וְאִמְרוּ אָמֵן.

The following Kaddish requires the presence of a minyan.

Magnified and sanctified may His great name be,
in the world that will in future be renewed,
reviving the dead and raising them up to eternal life.
He will rebuild the city of Jerusalem
and in it re-establish His Temple.
He will remove alien worship from the earth
and restore to its place the worship of Heaven.
Then the Holy One, blessed be He,
will reign in His sovereignty and splendor.
May it be in your lifetime and in your days,
(*Nusaḥ Sepharad:* make His salvation flourish,
and hasten His messiah,)
and in the lifetime of all the House of Israel,
swiftly and soon – and say: Amen.

May His great name be blessed for ever and all time.

Blessed and praised,
glorified and exalted,
raised and honored,
uplifted and lauded
be the name of the Holy One,
blessed be He,
beyond any blessing,
song, praise and consolation uttered in the world –
and say: Amen.

To Israel, to the teachers,
their disciples and their disciples' disciples,
and to all who engage in the study of Torah,
in this (*in Israel add:* holy) place or elsewhere,
may there come to them and you great peace,
grace, kindness and compassion,
long life, ample sustenance and deliverance,
from their Father in Heaven –
and say: Amen.

May there be great peace from heaven,
and (good) life for us and all Israel –
and say: Amen.

Bow, take three steps back, as if taking leave of the Divine Presence, then bow, first left, then right, then center, while saying:

May He who makes peace in His high places,
in His compassion make peace for us and all Israel –
and say: Amen.

לוח ספרים ופירושים

רשימת הספרים והפירושים אשר הובאו במסכת תענית

אגדות התלמוד — למחבר שלא נודע שמו, קובץ עתיק של אגדות סהתלמוד עם ביאור.

אהבת איתן — לר' אברהם בעל "משכיל לאיתן", על אגדות הש"ס.

אוצר הכבוד — לר' טודרוס אבולעפיא, פירוש לאגדות הש"ס.

אליה רבה — לר' אליהו שפירא, ביאור על שולחן ערוך אורח חיים.

אלשיך — לר' משה אלשיך, פירוש לתורה.

אשכול — לר' אברהם בר יצחק מנרבונה, ספר חידושי הלכה.

אשל אברהם — לר' אברהם דוד מבוטשאטש, ביאורים לשולחן ערוך.

באור הלכה — לר' ישראל מאיר הכהן, חלק מ"משנה ברורה".

באר הגולה — לר' משה רבקה"ש, הערות ומקורות לשולחן ערוך.

באר היטב — לר' יהודה אשכנזי, קיצור פסקי דינים וביאור שולחן ערוך.

בית חדש — לר' יואל סירקיש הלוי, פירושו על ה"טורים" ומהגהותיו על הש"ס.

בית יוסף — לר' יוסף קארו פירושו על ספר ה"טורים".

גאונים — הכוונה בעיקר לדבריהם המובאים ב"אוצר הגאונים" לר' בנימין מנשה לוין.

גבורות ארי — לר' אריה ליב, בעל ה"שאגת אריה", חידושים למסכתות אחדות.

גר"א — בעיקר ביאורו של הגר"א לשולחן ערוך. לעתים גם מהגהותיו לש"ס.

דקדוקי סופרים — לר' נתן נטע רבינוביץ, חילופי נוסחאות בש"ס.

דרוש וחידוש — לר' עקיבא איגר, חידושים על מסכתות הש"ס.

דרכי משה — לר' משה איסרליש, פירושו על ה"טורים".

דרש משה — לר' משה ב"ר יצחק מפיזענק, חידושים.

דברי שלמה — לר' שלמה כהן, הגהותיו לש"ס.

הכותב — לר' יעקב בן חביב מלקט "עין יעקב", פירוש על אגדות הש"ס.

הגהות מיימוניות — לר' מאיר הכהן, הערות ומקורות ל"יד החזקה".

השגות הראב"ד — לר' אברהם בן דוד, השגות והערות ל"יד החזקה".

השלמה — לרבינו משולם ב"ר משה מבדרש, השלמה להלכות הרי"ף.

חיי אדם — לר' אברהם דנציג, פסקי דינים בקיצור.

חכמת מנוח — לר' מנוח הענדיל ב"ר שמריה, הגהות והערות על הש"ס.

טור, טורים — ספר הטורים לר' יעקב בן הרא"ש, פסקי הלכות.

טורי זהב — לר' דוד ב"ר שמואל הלוי חריף, פירוש לשולחן ערוך.

יוחסין — לר' אברהם זכות. על תולדות ישראל.

יערות דבש — לר' יהונתן אייבשיץ, ספר דרשות.

כל בו — ספר הלכות למחבר קדמון אשר לא נודע שמו.

כלי יקר — לר' שלמה אפרים מלונציץ, פירושו על התורה.

כסף משנה — לר' יוסף קארו, פירוש על ה"יד החזקה".

כפתור ופרח — לר' אישתורי הפרחי, הלכות הנוגעות לארץ ישראל.

כפתור ופרח — לר' יעקב לוצאטו, ביאור אגדות.

לחם משנה — לר' אברהם די בוטון, פירוש על ה"יד החזקה".

מאירי — ספר "בית הבחירה" לרבינו מנחם בן שלמה לבית מאיר, בעיקר על ההלכה שבתלמוד.

מגיד משנה — לר' וידאל די טולושא. ראשון המפרשים ל"יד החזקה".

מגן אברהם — לר' אברהם גומבין, פירוש על שולחן ערוך אורח חיים.

מהר"ל — מורנו הרב ר' יהודה ליוואי מפראג, בעיקר ביאוריו לאגדות התלמוד (וכן מספרו "בא הגולה").

מהרש"א — מורנו הרב ר' שמואל אליעזר איידליש, חידושי הלכות ואגדות לתלמוד.

מוהריק"ש — מורנו הרב ר' יוסף קאשטרו, שאלות ותשובות.

מחזור ויטרי — לר' שמחה מויטרי, ספר דינים ומנהגים.

מחצית השקל — לר' שמואל הלוי מקעלין, ביאור על פירוש "מגן אברהם" לשולחן ערוך אורח חיים.

מכתם — לרבינו דוד ב"ר לוי, חידושי הלכה.

מלאכת שלמה — לר' שלמה עדני, ביאור על המשנה.

מנחת בכורים — לר' שמואל אביגדור מקרלין, פירוש לתוספתא.

מרדכי — רבינו מרדכי ב"ר הלל אשכנזי, קיצור דינים מן הש"ס.

משנה ברורה — לר' ישראל מאיר הכהן, פירוש לשולחן ערוך.

נזר הקדש — לר' יחיאל מיכל ב"ר עוזיאל, פירוש למדרש רבה.

נמוקי יוסף — לרבינו יוסף חביבא, פירוש להלכות הרי"ף.

נפש החיים — לר' חיים מוואלוזין, דרשות והגות.

סידור הרב — הכוונה לסידור שנערך על ידי ר' שניאור זלמן מלאדי, עם ביאור ופסקי דינים.

ספר הבתים — ספר דינים קדום, המובא בספרי הראשונים.

ספר המאורות — לרבינו מאיר ב"ר שמעון המעילי מנרבונה, פירוש למסכת תענית.

ספר חסידים — לר' יהודה החסיד. הוראות והדרכות במוסר.

ספר מצוות גדול (סמ"ג) — לר' משה מקוצי, על תרי"ג מצוות.

עיון יעקב — לר' יעקב ב"ר יוסף ריישר, פירוש ל"עין יעקב".

עטרת זקנים — לר' מנחם מענדל אוירבך, פירוש לשולחן ערוך.

עץ יוסף — לר' חנוך זונדל ב"ר יוסף, ביאור ל"עין יעקב".

ערוך — לר' נתן יחיאל מרומי, המילון התלמודי הראשון.

ערוך השולחן — לר' יחיאל מיכל אפשטיין, קובץ פסקי הלכה.

עשרה מאמרות — לר' מנחם עזריה מפאנו, קובץ ספריו הקטנים בהלכה ובקבלה.

פירוש המשניות לרמב"ם — פירוש הרמב"ם למשנה, הקרוי "ספר המאור".

פרי חדש — לר' חזקיה די סילוא, חידושי הלכות.

פרי מגדים — לר' יוסף תאומים, פירוש למפרשי השולחן ערוך.

פרישה — לר' יהושע פלק הכהן, על ה"טור", מן הספר "דרישה ופרישה".

פתח עינים — לר' חיים יוסף דוד אזולאי, ביאור למסכתות הש"ס (בעיקר האגדה).

קרבן העדה — לר' דוד פרנקל, פירוש לתלמוד הירושלמי.

קרבן נתנאל — לר' נתנאל וייל, ביאור על הלכות הרא"ש.

קרן אורה — לר' יצחק ב"ר אהרן קארלין, חידושים למסכתות הש"ס.

ר"א — מפרש קדום, שאולי הוא ר' אלייקים, בן זמנו של רש"י. מתוך קובץ על מסכת תענית.

ראב"ד — רבינו אברהם בן דוד. מתוך הגהותיו על ה"יד החזקה" ומפירושיו לתלמוד המובאים בדברי הראשונים.

רא"ה — רבינו אהרן הלוי, בן דורו של הרשב"א, מחידושיו.

רא"ש — רבינו אשר, הכוונה בעיקר מפסקי ההלכה שלו לתלמוד.

ראש יוסף — לר' יוסף ב"ר יעקב מפינטשוב, חידושים על אגדות הש"ס.

ראשון לציון — לר' חיים בן עטר לר' חיים בן עטר, חידושים לכמה מסכתות.

רבינו בחיי — רבינו בחיי בן אשר, פירוש לתורה ("כד הקמח").

ר"ג, רגמ"ה — רבינו גרשום מאור הגולה, פירושו לתלמוד.

רד"ק — ר' דוד קמחי, הכוונה בעיקר לספרו "מכלול" וגם לפירושו למקרא.

רה"ג — רב האי גאון, בעיקר דברים המובאים בשאלות ותשובות וקבצי תורת הגאונים.

רז"ה — ר' זרחיה הלוי, מחבר ספר "המאור".

ר"ח — רבינו חננאל מקירואן, פירושו לתלמוד.

רבינו יהונתן — רבינו יהונתן מלוניל, פירושו על הרי"ף.

ריא"ז — לר' ישעיה אור זרוע, פסקי הלכות.

ריב"ש — רבינו יצחק בר ששת, חידושים.

ריא"ף — ר' יאשיה פינטו, הכוונה לפירושו על "עין יעקב".

ריבב"ן — ר' יהודה ב"ר בנימין הרופא מן הענוים, פירוש לרי"ף.

רי"ד — רבינו ישעיה דיטראני, פירושיו למסכתות שונות בתלמוד של, וכן "פסקי הרי"ד" — פסקיו לפי סדר התלמוד.

ריטב"א — ר' יום טוב אלאשבילי הכוונה לביאורו לש"ס.

ריעב"ץ — ר' יעקב עמדין ב"ר צבי, הגהות על הש"ס.

רי"ף — רבינו יצחק אלפסי ספר הלכותיו.

רמ"א — ר' משה איסרליש, בעיקר חידושים והגהות (ספר ה"מפה") לשולחן ערוך.

רמב"ם — רבינו משה בן מימון, הכוונה לספר "יד החזקה", לעתים גם לדבריו ב"פירוש המשניות".

רמב"ן — רבינו משה בן נחמן, מחידושיו לש"ס.

רמת שמואל — לר' שמואל הלוי, חידושים לכמה מסכתות.

ר"ן — רבינו נסים, הכוונה בעיקר לפירושו על הרי"ף.

ר"נ גאון — רבינו נסים גאון, מחבר "המפתח למנעול התלמוד" ועוד, מדבריו.

רב עמרם גאון — הכוונה לסידור קדמון שנערך על ידי רב עמרם גאון.

רע"ב — ר' עובדיה מברטנורא, פירוש למשנה.

ר"צ חיות — ר' צבי חיות, הגהות וחידושים לש"ס.

רב צמח גאון — מדבריו ב"אוצר הגאונים" ושאר מקורות.

רשב"א — רבינו שלמה בן אברהם בן אדרת, הכוונה בעיקר לחידושיו לש"ס.

רש"ש — ר' שמואל שטראשון, הגהותיו על הש"ס.

שאילתות — לר' אחאי גאון, פסקי הלכה מסודרים לפי פרשיות השבוע.

שולחן ערוך הרב — לר' שניאור זלמן מלאדי, ספר הלכות.

שו"ע — שולחן ערוך (וחלקיו: אורח חיים, יורה דעה, חושן משפט, אבן העזר) לר' יוסף קארו.

שושנת יעקב — לר' יעקב ב"ר שמואל קמחי, חידושים למסכת תענית.

שיטה — פירוש למסכת תענית לאחד הראשונים, אולי רבינו חיים ב"ר שמואל בן דוד מטודילו, כנראה בן זמנו של הרשב"א.

שיטה מקובצת — פירוש על כמה מסכתות, המיוחס לר' בצלאל אשכנזי.

ש"ך — שפתי כהן, פירוש ר' שבתי כהן לשולחן ערוך "אורח חיים" "יורה דעה".

שני לוחות הברית — לר' ישעיהו הלוי הורביץ, ספר מוסר והלכה.

שפת אמת — לר' יהודה לייב אלתר, חידושים למסכתות התלמוד.

שערי תשובה — לר' חיים מרדכי מרגליות, קובץ תשובות לפי סדר שולחן ערוך.

תוספות הרא"ש — פירוש רבינו אשר לכמה מסכתות.

תוספות יום טוב — לר' יום טוב ליפמן הלר, פירוש למשנה.

תוספות רי"ד — לרבינו ישעיה די טראני (הראשון), פירושים לכמה ממסכתות הש"ס.

תורת חיים — לר' אברהם חיים שור, חידושים לכמה מסכתות.

תלמיד הרמב"ן — פירוש להלכות הרי"ף למס' תענית שכתב אחד מתלמידי הרמב"ן.

פירוש רש"י לתענית — כבר העירו חכמים רבים שכנראה אין הפירוש הנדפס בגמרות על מסכת תענית פירושו של רש"י, אלא אולי של אחד מתלמידיו.

לוח ראשי תיבות

שהובאו בצורה זו בתסכת תענית

אדר״נ — אבות דר׳ נתן.
אג״ב — אגדת בראשית.
אה״ע — אבן העזר.
או״ח — אורח חיים.
א״י — ארץ ישראל.
איכ״ר — איכה רבה.
אסת״ר — אסתר רבה.
א״ר — אליה רבה.
ב״ב — בבא בתרא.
באה״ג — באר הגולה.
בה״ט — באר היטב.
בה״ל — ביאור הלכה.
ב״ח — בית חדש.
ב״י — בית יוסף.
ב״מ — בבא מציעא.
במדב״ר — במדבר רבה.
ב״ק — בבא קמא.
ב״ר — בראשית רבה.
גר״א — גאון ר׳ אליהו (מוילנא).
גבו״א — גבורות ארי.
דב״ר — דברים רבה.
ד״ה — דיבור המתחיל.
דה״י — דברי הימים.
ד״מ — דרכי משה.
דפו״י — דפוס ישן, דפוסים ישנים.
דק״ס — דקדוקי סופרים.
ה״... — הלכה, כגון: ה״א — הלכה א׳, ה״ב — הלכה ב׳ וכו׳..
הג״מ — הגהות מיימוניות.
הקב״ה — הקדוש ברוך הוא.
ויק״ר — ויקרא רבה.
וכיו״ב — וכיוצא בזה.
וכ״נ — וכן נראה.
ז״ח — זוהר חלק..., כגון: זח״א — זוהר חלק א׳, זח״ב — זוהר חלק ב׳..

חו״ל — חוץ לארץ.
חו״מ — חושן משפט.
חז״ל — חכמינו זכרונם לברכה.
ט״ז — טורי זהב.
יו״ד — יורה דעה.
כ״מ — כסף משנה.
כ״נ — כן נראה.
כצ״ל — כך צריך להיות.
כת״י — כתב יד, כתבי יד.
כתי״מ — כתב יד מינכן.
לח״מ — לחם משנה.
מ״... — משנה. כגון: מ״א — משנה א׳, מ״ב — משנה ב׳ וכו׳..
מ״א — מגן אברהם.
מ״ב — משנה ברורה.
מג״א — מגן אברהם.
מהר״ל — מורנו הרב רבי (יהודה) ליוואי (מפראג).
מהרש״א — מורנו הרב שמואל אלעזר איידליש.
מוהריק״ש — מורנו הרב יוסף קאשטרו.
מו״ק — מועד קטן.
מחצה״ש — מחצית השקל.
מלא״ש — מלאכת שלמה.
מ״מ — מגיד משנה.
מנ״ב — מנחת בכורים.
מס׳ .
נ״ך — נביאים כתובים.
נמו״י — נמוקי יוסף.
סמ״ג — ספר מצוות גדול.
עה״ש — ערוך השולחן.
עה״ת — על התורה.
ע״ז — עבודה זרה.

עט״ז — עטרת זקנים.
ע״י — עין יעקב, על ידי.
עפ״י — על פי.
עי״ש, עיי״ש — עיין שם.
פ״... — פרק, פרשה. כגון: פ״א — פרק א׳. פ״א — פרשה א׳ וכו׳..
פ״ח — פרי חדש.
פיה״מ — פירוש המשניות (לרמב״ם).
פמ״ג — פרי מגדים.
פסדר״כ — פסיקתא דרב כהנא.
פסידר״כ — פסיקתא דרב כהנא.
פסי״ר — פסיקא רבתי.
פרדר״א — פרקי דר׳ אליעזר.
פר״ח — פרי חדש.
צ״ל — צריך להיות, צריך לומר.
קה״ר — קהלת רבה.
ר׳ — ראה, רב, רבי, רבינו..
ר״א — ר׳ אליקים.
ראב״ד — רבינו אברהם בן דוד.
רא״ה — ר׳ אהרן הלוי.
רא״ש — רבינו אשר.
ר״ג — רבינו גרשום.
רגמ״ה — רבינו גרשום מאור הגולה.
רד״ק — ר׳ דוד קמחי.
ר״ה — ראש השנה.
רה״ג — רב האי גאון.
רו״ר — רות רבה.
רז״ה — רבינו זרחיה הלוי.
ר״ח — רבינו חננאל.
ריא״ז — רבינו ישעיה אור זרוע.
ריא״ף — ר׳ יאשיה פינטו.
ריבב״ן — ר׳ יהודה בן בנימין.
ריב״ש — רבינו יצחק בר ששת.
רי״ד — ר׳ ישעיה דיטראני.

ריטב״א — רבינו יום טוב בן אברהם (אלאשבילי).
ריעב״ץ — ר׳ יעקב עמדין ב״ר צבי.
רי״ף — ר׳ יצחק אלפסי.
רמ״א — ר׳ משה איסרליש.
רמב״ם — רבינו משה בן מיימון.
רמב״ן — רבינו משה בן נחמן.
ר״נ — רבינו נסים (בן ראובן).
ר״נ גאון — רבינו נסים גאון.
רע״ב — ר׳ עובדיה מברטנורא.
רע״ג — רב עמרם גאון.
רעק״א — ר׳ עקיבא איגר.
ר״צ חיות — ר׳ צבי חיות.
רשב״א — רבינו שלמה בן אברהם בן אדרת.
רשב״י — רבי שמעון בן יוחאי.
רש״י — רבינו שלמה יצחקי.
רש״ש — ר׳ שמואל שטראשון..
שה״ר — שיר השירים רבה.
שוח״ט — שוחר טוב.
שו״ע — שולחן ערוך.
שועה״ר — שולחן ערוך הרב.
שטמ״ק — שיטה מקובצת.
ש״ך — שפתי כהן.
של״ה — שני לוחות הברית.
שמו״ר — שמות רבה.
שע״ת — שערי תשובה.
שפ״א — שפת אמת.
תו״כ — תורת כהנים.
תוס׳ — תוספות.
תוי״ט — תוספות יום טוב.
תורי״ד — תוספות רי״ד.
תנדב״א — תנא דבי אליהו.
תנדבא״ז — תנא דבי אליהו זוטא.
תנדבא״ר — תנא דבי אליהו רבה

מְגִילָּה

נִקְרֵאת *בְּי"א, בְּי"ב, בְּי"ג, בְּי"ד, בְּט"ו, לֹא פָּחוֹת וְלֹא יוֹתֵר. ^א^כְּרַכִּין הַמּוּקָּפִין חוֹמָה מִימוֹת יְהוֹשֻׁעַ בִּן נוּן קוֹרִין בְּט"ו, ^ב^כְּפָרִים וַעֲיָירוֹת גְּדוֹלוֹת קוֹרִין בְּי"ד, ^ג^אֶלָּא שֶׁהַכְּפָרִים מַקְדִּימִין לְיוֹם הַכְּנִיסָה. כֵּיצַד? חָל לִהְיוֹת י"ד בַּשֵּׁנִי — כְּפָרִים וַעֲיָירוֹת גְּדוֹלוֹת קוֹרִין בּוֹ בַּיּוֹם, וּמוּקָּפוֹת חוֹמָה לְמָחָר. חָל לִהְיוֹת בַּשְּׁלִישִׁי אוֹ בָּרְבִיעִי — כְּפָרִים מַקְדִּימִין לְיוֹם הַכְּנִיסָה, וַעֲיָירוֹת גְּדוֹלוֹת קוֹרִין בּוֹ בַּיּוֹם, וּמוּקָּפוֹת חוֹמָה לְמָחָר. חָל לִהְיוֹת בַּחֲמִישִׁי — כְּפָרִים וַעֲיָירוֹת גְּדוֹלוֹת קוֹרִין בּוֹ בַּיּוֹם, וּמוּקָּפוֹת חוֹמָה לְמָחָר. חָל לִהְיוֹת ע"ש — כְּפָרִים מַקְדִּימִין לְיוֹם הַכְּנִיסָה, וַעֲיָירוֹת גְּדוֹלוֹת וּמוּקָּפוֹת חוֹמָה קוֹרִין בּוֹ בַּיּוֹם. חָל לִהְיוֹת בַּשַּׁבָּת — כְּפָרִים וַעֲיָירוֹת גְּדוֹלוֹת מַקְדִּימִין וְקוֹרִין לְיוֹם הַכְּנִיסָה, וּמוּקָּפוֹת חוֹמָה לְמָחָר. חָל לִהְיוֹת אַחַר הַשַּׁבָּת — כְּפָרִים מַקְדִּימִין לְיוֹם הַכְּנִיסָה, וַעֲיָירוֹת גְּדוֹלוֹת קוֹרִין בּוֹ בַּיּוֹם, וּמוּקָּפוֹת חוֹמָה לְמָחָר.§ **גמ'** "מְגִילָּה נִקְרֵאת בְּי"א" מְנָלַן? *מְנָלַן?! כִּדְבָעֵינַן לְמֵימַר לְקַמָּן: *חֲכָמִים הֵקִילוּ עַל הַכְּפָרִים לִהְיוֹת מַקְדִּימִין לְיוֹם הַכְּנִיסָה כְּדֵי שֶׁיְּסַפְּקוּ מַיִם וּמָזוֹן לַאֲחֵיהֶם שֶׁבַּכְּרַכִּים! [לקמן ד. יט:] אֲנַן הָכִי קָאָמְרִינַן: מִכְּדִי, כּוּלְּהוּ אַנְשֵׁי כנה"ג תַּקְנִינְהוּ, דְּאִי ס"ד אַנְשֵׁי כנה"ג י"ד וְט"ו תַּקּוּן — אָתוּ רַבָּנַן וְעָקְרִי תַּקַּנְתָּא דְּתַקִּינוּ אַנְשֵׁי כנה"ג? וְהָתְנַן: *^ד^אֵין ב"ד יָכוֹל לְבַטֵּל דִּבְרֵי ב"ד חֲבֵירוֹ אא"כ גָּדוֹל מִמֶּנּוּ בְּחָכְמָה וּבְמִנְיָן! אֶלָּא פְּשִׁיטָא — כּוּלְּהוּ אַנְשֵׁי כנה"ג תַּקִּינוּ. הֵיכָא רְמִיזָא? *אָמַר רַב שֶׁמֶן בַּר אַבָּא א"ר יוֹחָנָן: אָמַר קְרָא: °"לְקַיֵּים אֶת יְמֵי הַפּוּרִים הָאֵלֶּה בִּזְמַנֵּיהֶם" (אסתר ט) — זְמַנִּים הַרְבֵּה תִּקְּנוּ לָהֶם. הַאי מִיבְּעֵיא לֵיהּ לְגוּפֵיהּ! א"כ לֵימָא קְרָא "זְמַן". מַאי "זְמַנֵּיהֶם"? זְמַנִּים טוּבָא. וְאַכַּתִּי מִיבְּעֵי לֵיהּ: *זְמַנּוֹ שֶׁל זֶה לֹא כִּזְמַנּוֹ שֶׁל זֶה! א"כ לֵימָא קְרָא "זְמַנָּם". מַאי "זְמַנֵּיהֶם"? שָׁמְעַתְּ מִינָּהּ כּוּלְּהוּ. אֵימָא: זְמַנִּים טוּבָא! "זְמַנֵּיהֶם" דּוּמְיָא דִּ"זְמַנָּם", מָה "זְמַנָּם" תְּרֵי — אַף "זְמַנֵּיהֶם" תְּרֵי. וְאֵימָא תְּרֵיסַר וּתְלֵיסַר! *כִּדְאָמַר רַב שְׁמוּאֵל בַּר יִצְחָק: י"ג זְמַן קְהִילָּה לַכֹּל הִיא, וְלָא צָרִיךְ לְרַבּוּיֵי. הָכָא נַמִי י"ג זְמַן קְהִילָּה לַכֹּל הִיא וְלָא צָרִיךְ לְרַבּוּיֵי. וְאֵימָא שִׁיתְּסַר וְשִׁיבְסַר! °"וְלֹא יַעֲבוֹר" (שם) כְּתִיב. וְר' שְׁמוּאֵל בַּר נַחְמָנִי אָמַר: אָמַר קְרָא: °"כַּיָּמִים אֲשֶׁר נָחוּ בָהֶם הַיְּהוּדִים" (שם). "יָמִים" "כַּיָּמִים" — לְרַבּוֹת י"א וְי"ב. וְאֵימָא תְּרֵיסַר וּתְלֵיסַר! אר"ש בַּר יִצְחָק: י"ג זְמַן קְהִילָּה לַכֹּל הִיא, וְלָא צְרִיךְ לְרַבּוּיֵי. וְאֵימָא שִׁיתְּסַר וְשִׁיבְסַר! "וְלֹא יַעֲבוֹר" כְּתִיב. ר"ש בַּר נַחְמָנִי מ"ט לָא אָמַר מִ"בִּזְמַנֵּיהֶם"? זְמַן זְמַנָּם זְמַנֵּיהֶם לָא מַשְׁמַע לֵיהּ. וְרַב שֶׁמֶן בַּר אַבָּא, מ"ט לָא אָמַר מִ"כַּיָּמִים"? אָמַר לָךְ: הַהוּא לְדוֹרוֹת הוּא דִּכְתִיב. אָמַר רַבָּה בַּר בַּר חָנָה א"ר יוֹחָנָן: זוֹ דִּבְרֵי ר"ע סְתִימְתָּאָה דְּדָרֵישׁ זְמַן זְמַנָּם זְמַנֵּיהֶם. אֲבָל חכ"א: אֵין קוֹרִין אוֹתָהּ אֶלָּא בִּזְמַנָּהּ. מֵיתִיבִי: א"ר יְהוּדָה *^ה^אֵימָתַי — בִּזְמַן שֶׁהַשָּׁנִים כְּתִיקְנָן, וְיִשְׂרָאֵל שְׁרוּיִין עַל אַדְמָתָן. אֲבָל בַּזְּמַן הַזֶּה, הוֹאִיל וּמִסְתַּכְּלִין בָּהּ — אֵין קוֹרִין אוֹתָהּ אֶלָּא בִּזְמַנָּהּ. רַבִּי יְהוּדָה אַלִּיבָּא דְּמַאן? אִילֵימָא אַלִּיבָּא דְּר"ע — אֲפִילּוּ בַּזְּמַן הַזֶּה אִיתָא לְהַאי תַּקַּנְתָּא. אֶלָּא לָאו — אַלִּיבָּא דְּרַבָּנַן, וּבִזְמַן שֶׁהַשָּׁנִים כְּתִיקְנָן וְיִשְׂרָאֵל שְׁרוּיִין עַל אַדְמָתָן מִיהָא קָרֵינַן! תְּיוּבְתָּא דְּרַבִּי יוֹחָנָן! תְּיוּבְתָּא. א"ד: אָמַר רַבָּה בַּר בַּר חָנָה אָמַר ר' יוֹחָנָן: זוֹ דִּבְרֵי ר"ע סְתִימְתָּאָה. אֲבָל חֲכָמִים אָמְרוּ: בַּזְּמַן הַזֶּה, הוֹאִיל וּמִסְתַּכְּלִין בָּהּ אֵין קוֹרִין אוֹתָהּ אֶלָּא בִּזְמַנָּהּ. תַּנְיָא נַמִי הָכִי: אָמַר רַבִּי יְהוּדָה: אֵימָתַי — בִּזְמַן שֶׁהַשָּׁנִים כְּתִיקְנָן וְיִשְׂרָאֵל שְׁרוּיִין עַל אַדְמָתָן, אֲבָל בַּזְּמַן הַזֶּה, הוֹאִיל וּמִסְתַּכְּלִין בָּהּ — אֵין קוֹרִין אוֹתָהּ אֶלָּא בִּזְמַנָּהּ. רַב אַשִׁי קַשְׁיָא לֵיהּ דְּר' יְהוּדָה אַדְּר' יְהוּדָה, וּמוֹקִים

רש"י

מְגִילָּה נִקְרֵאת בִּי"א וכו'. פְּעָמִים בָּזֶה וּפְעָמִים בָּזֶה. וּלְקַמָּן מְפָרֵשׁ וְאָזֵיל: לֹא פָּחוֹת וְלֹא יוֹתֵר. לֹא פָּחוֹת מִי"א וְלֹא יוֹתֵר מִט"ו: מִימוֹת יְהוֹשֻׁעַ. בַּגְּמָ' מְפָרֵשׁ לָהּ: אֶלָּא שֶׁהַכְּפָרִים מַקְדִּימִין לְיוֹם הַכְּנִיסָה. כְּלוֹמַר, מֵאַחַר שֶׁהַמּוּקָּפִין קוֹרִין בְּט"ו וְשֶׁאֵין מוּקָּפִין קוֹרִין בְּי"ד, הֲרֵי הַכֹּל בִּכְלָל, אוֹ הֵיכִי מַשְׁכַּחַת י"א, י"ב, י"ג? אֶלָּא שֶׁהַכְּפָרִים נָתְנוּ לָהֶן חֲכָמִים רְשׁוּת לְהַקְדִּים קְרִיאָתָהּ לְיוֹם הַכְּנִיסָה, יוֹם שֵׁנִי בְּשַׁבָּת שֶׁלִּפְנֵי י"ד, אוֹ חֲמִישִׁי בְּשַׁבָּת, שֶׁהוּא יוֹם כְּנִיסָה, שֶׁהַכְּפָרִים מִתְכַּנְּסִין לָעֲיָירוֹת לְמִשְׁפָּט, לְפִי שֶׁבָּתֵּי דִּינִין יוֹשְׁבִין בָּעֲיָירוֹת בַּשֵּׁנִי וּבַחֲמִישִׁי כְּתַקָּנַת עֶזְרָא (ב"ק דף פב.). וְהַכְּפָרִים אֵינָן בְּקִיאִין לִקְרוֹת, וּצְרִיכִין שֶׁיִּקְרָאֶנָּה לָהֶם אֶחָד מִבְּנֵי הָעִיר, וְלֹא הִטְרִיחוּם חֲכָמִים לְהִתְאַחֵר וְלָבֹא בְּיוֹם י"ד, וּפְעָמִים שֶׁיּוֹם הַכְּנִיסָה בְּי"ג וּפְעָמִים שֶׁהוּא בְּי"א: חָל אַרְבָּעָה עָשָׂר לִהְיוֹת בְּעֶרֶב שַׁבָּת עֲיָירוֹת וּמוּקָּפִין חוֹמָה קוֹרִין בּוֹ בַּיּוֹם. שֶׁאֵין קְרִיאַת הַמְּגִילָּה בְּשַׁבָּת, גְּזֵירָה שֶׁמָּא יִטְלֶנָּה בְּיָדוֹ. וְאִם תֹּאמַר: יְאַחֲרוּ הַמּוּקָּפִין עַד אַחַר שַׁבָּת? הֲוָה לֵיהּ ט"ז, וְאָמַר קְרָא "וְלֹא יַעֲבוֹר": חָל לִהְיוֹת אַחַר שַׁבָּת כְּפָרִים מַקְדִּימִין לְיוֹם הַכְּנִיסָה. דַּהֲוָה לֵיהּ י"א, וְטָפֵי לֹא מַשְׁכַּחַת לָהּ יוֹם הַכְּנִיסָה שֶׁלִּפְנֵי פּוּרִים מוּקְדָּם לוֹ, דְּמִיּוֹם הַכְּנִיסָה לְיוֹם הַכְּנִיסָה לֹא מַקְדְּמִינַן: **גמ'** ה"ג: מְנָלַן מְנָלַן כִּדְבָעֵינַן לְמֵימַר לְקַמָּן וכו'. וְהָכִי פֵּירוּשָׁא: מְנָלַן דְּי"א וְי"ב וְי"ג חֲזוּ לְקִרְיָיה? דְּי"ד וְט"ו הוּא דִּכְתִיב בִּקְרָא! וְקָא מְהַדַּר גְּמָרָא: מְנָלַן?! בִּתְמִיָּה, הַאי לָאו חוֹבָה, הִיא אֶלָּא חֲכָמִים הֵקִילוּ עֲלֵיהֶן, כִּדְבָעֵינַן לְמֵימַר לְקַמָּן: כְּדֵי שֶׁיְּסַפְּקוּ. שֶׁיְּהוּ פְּנוּיִין בְּיוֹם פּוּרִים לְהַסְפִּיק צָרְכֵי סְעוּדַת פּוּרִים לִבְנֵי הָעֲיָירוֹת: אֲנַן הָכִי קָאָמְרִינַן. אֲנַן דְּמִיבַּעְיָא לַן מְנָלַן, הָכִי קָאָמְרִינַן: מִכְּדִי. מִדְּהֵקִילוּ חֲכָמִים עַל הַכְּפָרִים לְהַקְדִּים — עַל כָּרְחָךְ אַנְשֵׁי כְּנֶסֶת הַגְּדוֹלָה שֶׁתִּיקְּנוּ בִּימֵי מָרְדְּכַי וְאֶסְתֵּר אֶת שִׂמְחַת הַפּוּרִים וּקְרִיאַת הַמְּגִילָּה — כּוּלְּהוּ הָנֵי זִימְנֵי תִּיקּוּן, וְנָתְנוּ רְשׁוּת לִקְרוֹת: דְּאִי סָלְקָא דַּעְתָּךְ. י"ד וְט"ו תַּקּוּן הַכְּתוּבִין בַּמְּגִילָּה, וְתוּ לָא: הֵיכִי אָתוּ רַבָּנַן. דְּבַתְרַיְיהוּ וְעָקְרוּ תַּקַּנְתָּא, וְהִתִּירוּ לְהַקְדִּים? בִּתְמִיָּה: אֶלָּא פְּשִׁיטָא אִינְהוּ תַּקּוּן. וְכֵיוָן דְּאִינְהוּ תַּקּוּן, וַדַּאי רַמְזִינְהוּ בִּמְגִילַּת אֶסְתֵּר, הַיְינוּ דְּמִיבַּעְיָא לַן הֵיכָא רְמִיזָא, וּמְנָלַן: לְגוּפֵיהּ. לְי"ד וְט"ו הַמְפוֹרָשִׁין בַּסֵּפֶר: לֵימָא קְרָא. "אֶת יְמֵי הַפּוּרִים הָאֵלֶּה בַּזְּמַן" — דְּמַשְׁמַע: בַּזְּמַן הַמְפוֹרָשׁ לָהֶם: וְאַכַּתִּי מִיבְּעֵי לֵיהּ. הַאי דְּנָקַט זְמַנִּים לְשׁוֹן רַבִּים: זְמַנּוֹ. שֶׁל מוּקָּפִין לָאו כִּזְמַנּוֹ שֶׁל פְּרָזִים. דְּאִי כָּתוּב "בַּזְּמַן", הֲוָה מַשְׁמַע זְמַן אֶחָד לִשְׁנֵיהֶן, אִי בָּעוּ — לִיקְרוּ בְּאַרְבֵּיסַר, וְאִי בָּעוּ — לִיקְרוּ בַּחֲמֵיסַר: זְמַנֵּיהֶם דּוּמְיָא דִּזְמַנָּם. רִבּוּיָא דְּדָרְשִׁינַן לִקְרָא לְיִיתּוּרָא דְּיוּ"ד וְהֵ"א, דּוּמְיָא דְּעִיקַּר הַזְּמַן דְּנָפְקָא לַן מִזְּמַנָּם הוּא דְּקָא מְרַבֶּה, דּוּמְיָא דִּידְהוּ: זְמַן קְהִלָּה לַכֹּל הִיא. הַכֹּל נִקְהֲלוּ לְהִנָּקֵם מֵאוֹיְבֵיהֶם בֵּין בְּשׁוּשַׁן בֵּין בִּשְׁאָר מְקוֹמוֹת, כְּמוֹ שֶׁכָּתוּב בַּסֵּפֶר. הִלְכָּךְ לֹא צָרִיךְ קְרָא לְרַבּוּיֵי שֶׁיְּהֵא רָאוּי לְקִרְיָיה, דְּעִיקַּר הַנֵּס בּוֹ הָיָה: יָמִים כַּיָּמִים. לְעֵיל מִינֵּיהּ כְּתִיב י"ד וְט"ו יִשְׂמְחוּ, וּכְתִיב "כַּיָּמִים אֲשֶׁר נָחוּ בָהֶם הַיְּהוּדִים" וגו', וַהֲוָה לֵיהּ לְמִיכְתַּב: יָמִים אֲשֶׁר נָחוּ, דְּמַשְׁמַע הֵם הֵם יָמִים אֲשֶׁר נָחוּ, מַאי "כַּיָּמִים" — לְרַבּוֹת שָׁנִים אֲחֵרוֹת כִּדוּגְמָתָן: לְדוֹרוֹת הוּא דִּכְתִיב. לְהָכִי שַׁיָּיךְ לִישָּׁנָא דִּקְרָא "כַּיָּמִים", כְּלוֹמַר: יַעֲשׂוּ לְדוֹרוֹת י"ד וְט"ו כַּאֲשֶׁר הָיָה בִּימֵי הַנֵּס יָמִים אֲשֶׁר נָחוּ בָהֶם, הִלְכָּךְ לָא אִיכָּא לְרַבּוּיֵי מֵהָכָא שָׁנִים אֲחֵרִים: זוֹ דִּבְרֵי ר' עֲקִיבָא. הָכִי גְּמִיר רַבִּי יוֹחָנָן מֵרַבֵּיהּ דְּמַתְנִי' ר"ע אֲמָרָהּ: סְתִימְתָּאָה. הַרְבֵּה סְתָם מִשְׁנָה סְתָמָם ר' שֶׁהֵן דִּבְרֵי ר' עֲקִיבָא. וי"מ — סְתִימְתָּאָה — כָּל הַסְּתוּמִין תַּלְמִידָיו הָיוּ, כִּדְאָמַר בְּסַנְהֶדְרִין (דף פו.): סְתָם מִשְׁנָה ר"מ, סְתָם תּוֹסֶפְתָּא ר' נְחֶמְיָה, סְתָם סִפְרָא רַבִּי יְהוּדָה, וְכוּלְּהוּ סְתִימְתָּאֵי אַלִּיבָּא דְּר' עֲקִיבָא. אַךְ קָשֶׁה בְּעֵינַי לְפָרֵשׁ כֵּן, שֶׁמָּצִינוּ בְּכַמָּה מְקוֹמוֹת בְּשֵׁם ר"א בְּר' יוֹסֵי סְתִימְתָּאֵי, רַבִּי מְנַחֵם בַּר רַבִּי יוֹסֵי סְתִימְתָּאֵי לְקַמָּן בְּפֶרֶק "בְּנֵי הָעִיר" (דף כו.*) [ועי' רש"י בכורות ל. ד"ה תיתי]: אֵימָתַי. הֵקִילוּ חֲכָמִים עַל הַכְּפָרִים: בִּזְמַן שֶׁהַשָּׁנִים כְּתִיקְנָן. שֶׁהַשָּׁנִים מִתְעַבְּרוֹת עַל פִּי בֵּית דִּין, וְהֶחֳדָשִׁים הַמְקַדְּשִׁין בְּבֵית דִּין שׁוֹלְחִין שְׁלוּחֵיהֶן לְהוֹדִיעַ אֵימָתַי הוּקְדַּשׁ נִיסָן, וְעוֹשִׂין מוֹעֲדִים ע"פ שְׁלוּחִין: כְּשֶׁשְּׁרוּיִין עַל אַדְמָתָם. וְהַשְּׁלוּחִין מַגִּיעִין עַד הַפֶּסַח לִקְצֵה אֶרֶץ יִשְׂרָאֵל: אֲבָל בַּזְּמַן הַזֶּה. שֶׁפָּסְקוּ כָּל אֵלֶּה וְיִשְׂרָאֵל נִפְרְדוּ, וְלֹא יַגִּיעוּ שְׁלוּחֵי ב"ד אֶצְלָם — הַכֹּל צוֹפִין לְמִקְרָא מְגִילָּה וְאוֹמְרִים יוֹם י"ד בַּאֲדָר קָרֵינַן הַמְּגִילָּה, נִשְׁאֲרוּ לַאֲדָר ט"ו יוֹם וְט"ו שֶׁל נִיסָן עוֹשִׂין פֶּסַח וְאִם תַּקְדִּים קְרִיאָתָהּ יַעֲשׂוּ פֶּסַח לְסוֹף שְׁלֹשִׁים יוֹם שֶׁל קְרִיאָה, וְנִמְצְאוּ אוֹכְלִין חָמֵץ בַּיָּמִים אַחֲרוֹנִים (בַּיּוֹם) שֶׁל פֶּסַח: בַּזְּמַן הַזֶּה נַמִי אִיתָא לְהָא תַּקַּנְתָּא. דְּהָא רַבִּי עֲקִיבָא בַּזְּמַן הַזֶּה [הֲוָה], וְאָמַר בְּמַתְנִי' דְּמַקְדִּימִין: אֶלָּא לָאו אַלִּיבָּא דְּרַבָּנַן. דַּהֲווּ מִקַּמֵּי ר"ע, אֲמָרָהּ: מִיהָא קָרֵינַן. אַלְמָא, רַבָּנַן נַמִי דָּרְשֵׁי זְמַן זְמַנָּם זְמַנֵּיהֶם: אִיכָּא דְּאָמְרִי אָמַר רַבָּה זוֹ דִּבְרֵי ר' עֲקִיבָא סְתִימְתָּאָה. וְלָא גָּרְסִינַן לְהַאי לִישָּׁנָא דְּדָרֵישׁ זְמַן זְמַנָּם זְמַנֵּיהֶם, דְּהָא רַבָּנַן דִּפְלִיגִי עֲלֵיהּ נַמִי דָּרְשֵׁי לֵיהּ, אֶלָּא שֶׁהֶחְמִירוּ לְאַחַר חוּרְבָּן מִשּׁוּם דְּמִסְתַּכְּלִין בָּהּ: קַשְׁיָא דר"י. דְּהָא בָּרַיְיתָא דִּלְעֵיל אַדְּר' יְהוּדָה דְּמַתְנִי', כִּדְמְפָרֵשׁ וְאָזֵיל: וְאוֹקֵי

רבינו חננאל

מגילה נקראת בי"א בי"ב בי"ג בי"ד בט"ו לא פחות ולא יותר. והא לא כתב קרא אלא בי"ד ובט"ו והני כולהו מנא לן. ואמרינן כדבעינן למימר לקמן חכמים הקילו על הכפרים שיהיו מקדימין ליום הכניסה וקורין בי"א ובי"ב ובי"ג פי' יום הכניסה יום ב' ויום ה' נקרא יום הכניסה. מפני שנכנסין בני הכפרים בכרכים כדי שיתפללו בצבור ויקראו בס"ת. וביום שנכנסין מספקים מים ומזון לאחיהם שבכרכים ואם חל יום י"ד ביום ג' התירו לכפרים לקרוא המגילה ביום ב' שהוא י"ג לחדש. ואם חל להיות י"ד ברביעי קורין הכפרים ביום ב' שהוא י"ב לחדש. ואם חל י"ד להיות באחד בשבת מקדימין וקורין ביום ה' שהוא י"א לחדש. הקילו עליהן מפני שמספיקים מים ומזון לאחיהם שבכרכים. ואם יכנסו ביום ג' או ביום ד' מפני קריאת המגילה אינן יכולין לבוא ביום ה' שהוא יום הכניסה וכן דרך זו השמועה. ואקשינן ואיך הקילו חכמים ועקרו י"ד ויום ט"ו שהן תקנת אנשי כנסת הגדולה ותקנו הם י"א וי"ב וי"ג לבני הכפרים. והא אין ב"ד יכול לבטל דברי ב"ד חבירו וכו'. ופרקינן הני נמי מסורת היה בידם על פה כי אנשי כנסת [הגדולה] תקנום. מדכתיב לקיים את (דברי) [ימי] הפורים האלה בזמניהם. ולא כתיב זמן או זמנם. דמשמע זמנם של פרזים לא הוא זמן של בן כרך. אלא כתיב זמניהם. דייקינן מינה כי זמנים הרבה תיקנו להן חכמים. והן י"א וי"ב בי' ימים כנגד י"ד וט"ו. אבל י"ג לא צריך קרא לרבויי דהוא זמן קהלה לכל. ולא יתכן לומר ט"ז וי"ז דכתיב ולא יעבור. כלומר ולעבור ולעשות ימי הפורים אחר יום ט"ו. ור"ש בר נחמני מכימים דכתיב לרבות י"א וי"ב כו'. ואידך כימים כלומר כמו הימים אשר נחו בהם עשו אותם גם פורים. א"ר יוחנן משנה זו מגילה נקראת. בי"א בי"ב כו'. שנעשית סתומה דברי ר' עקיבא הן. אבל חכמים אומרים אין קורין אותה אלא בזמנה והן י"ד וט"ו בלבד. ואותבינן עלה מהא דתניא א"ר יהודה אימתי קורין בי"א בי"ב ובי"ג בזמן שהשנים כתקנן. וישראל שרוין על אדמתם. אבל עתה אע"פ שבזמן הזה השנים כתיקנן. הואיל ומסתכלין בה אין קורין

עין משפט נר מצוה

א א מיי' פ"א מהלכות מגילה הלכה ד סמג עשין ד טור ש"ע א"ח סי' תרפח סעיף ו:
ב ב מיי' שם הלכה ט טוש"ע שם סעיף ג:
ג ג מיי' שם הלכה ו ז סמג שם:
ד ד מיי' פ"ב מהלכות ממרים הלכה ב:
ה ה מיי' פ"א מהל' מגיל' הלכה ט:

מסורת הש"ס

יבמות יג:
[עי' תוס' זבחים פט. ד"ה מנלן וכו' מה שהקשו בסוגיא דהכא והניחו בקושיא]
מו"ק ג: גיטין לו. עדיות פ"א מ"ה ע"ש לו.
[יבמות יג:]
[לקמן ד:]
[גי' רי"ף ואימא תריסר ותליסר י"ג זמן כו' וגי' רא"ש א"ר שמואל בר יצחק י"ג זמן כו']
תענית יח: ע"ש

גליון הש"ס

גמ' מתני' אלא שהכפרים כו'. עיין מדרש תנחומא פרשת בראשית פי' חלש בההיא דיני הכניסה: **שם** ולא יעבור כתיב. לקמן דף ה ע"א:

ו א מיי' פ"א מהלכות מגילה הלכה ו:
ז ב ג ד ה מיי' שם הלכה ד ה ו סמג עשין ד טוש"ע א"ח סי' תרפח סעיף ב:

ועוד האמר רב חסדא מ"ם וסמ"ך כו'. השתא סלקא דעתך דמנצפ"ך מיירי בסתומות. ותימה: דבמסכת שבת פרק "הבונה" (דף קד. ושם) משמע איפכא, מדקאמר התם: בשלמא פתוח ועשאו סתום – עילויי עליה, דאמר רב חסדא כו'. אלא סתום ועשאו פתוח גרועי גרעיה, דא"ר ירמיה מנצפ"ך [צופים אמרום]. אלמא מנצפ"ך איירי בפתוחות! ואור"י: דגמ' [דשבת] מסיק ליה וקתני, דידע מתחילה מילתיה דרב חסדא, וגם איירי ליה מעיקרא בפתוחות, הוצרך להעמיד מנצפ"ך בפתוחות ולא תקשה דרב חסדא. והכא ה"ק: ותסברא והכתיב "אלה המצות"? והך קושיא איתותב בין בפתוחות בין בסתומות. ועוד: את"ל דבסתומות איירי – *אכתי תקשה והאמר רב חסדא מ"ס וסמ"ך וכו'. וכן פירש"ת, וז"ל שהגיה בספר הישר: מנצפ"ך צופים אמרום כמו "קול צופיך" (ישעיה נב) = נביאים. "צופים מהר אפרים" (שמואל א א) *ממאתים נביאים (*מצופים) שעמדו להם לישראל, והיו צופים הללו לאחר שטרף אמון את התורה. ומשום לשון נופל על הלשון נקרא מנצפ"ך, בלשון צופיך. ותסברא והכתיב "אלה המצות", ועוד: והאמר רב חסדא מ"ס וסמ"ך שבלוחות וכו'. ומשני: אין, מהוי הוי, ולא קשיא מידי, דרבי ירמיה מוקי לה בסתומות. וכי מטי במגילה פריך מהא דרב חסדא, דהכי אורחיה, זיל הכא קא מדחי ליה "מאלה המצות" נמי פריך, ומשני שפיר. ומתוך הסוגיא דמגילה ושבת מוכח תרוייהו. ורבי ירמיה קאמר מנצפ"ך צופים אמרום – אפתוחות ואסתומות, וכדמסיק התלמוד*: מבטלין

[ס"א נמי] [לקמן יד.] [נ"ל צופים] [גי' רי"ף רבן] [ועי' תוספת שבת קד. ד"ה גרועי]

תורה אור

ומוקים לה לברייתא כר' יוסי בר יהודה: ומי אמר ר"י בזמן הזה הואיל ומסתכלין בה אין קורין אותה אלא בזמנה? ורמינהי, *א"ר יהודה: [א]אימתי – מקום שנכנסין בשני ובחמישי, אבל מקום שאין נכנסין בשני ובחמישי – אין קורין אותה אלא בזמנה. מקום שנכנסין בשני ובחמישי מיהא קרינן, ואפילו בזמן הזה! ומוקים לה לברייתא כרבי יוסי בר יהודה. ומשום דקשיא ליה דרבי יהודה אדר' יהודה מוקים לה לברייתא כרבי יוסי בר יהודה?! רב אשי שמיע ליה דאיכא דתני לה כרבי יהודה, ואיכא דתני לה כרבי יוסי בר יהודה, ומדקשיא ליה דרבי יהודה אדרבי יהודה אמר: מאן דתני לה כרבי יהודה – לאו דווקא, מאן דתני לה כרבי יוסי בר יהודה – דווקא.§ "כרכים המוקפים חומה מימות יהושע בן נון קורין בחמשה עשר" וכו'.§ מנהני מילי? אמר *רבא: דאמר קרא: °"על כן היהודים הפרזים (אסתר ט) היושבים בערי הפרזות" וגו' מדפרזים בארבעה עשר – מוקפין בחמשה עשר. ואימא: פרזים בארבעה עשר – מוקפין כלל כלל לא! ולאו ישראל נינהו? ועוד, "מהודו ועד כוש" כתיב. ואימא: פרזים בארביסר, מוקפין בארביסר ובחמיסר, כדכתיב: °"להיות עושים את יום (שם) ארבעה עשר לחדש אדר ואת יום חמשה עשר [בו] בכל שנה"! אי הוה כתב: "את יום ארבעה עשר וחמשה עשר" – כדקאמרת, השתא דכתיב: "את יום ארבעה עשר ואת יום חמשה עשר" – אתא *"את" ופסיק: הני בארבעה עשר, והני בחמשה עשר. ואימא: פרזים בארביסר, מוקפין – אי בעו בארביסר, אי בעו בחמיסר! אמר קרא: "בזמניהם" – זמנו של זה לא זמנו של זה. ואימא בתליסר! כשושן. אשכחן עשייה; זכירה מנלן? אמר קרא: °"והימים האלה נזכרים ונעשים", (שם) איתקש זכירה לעשייה. מתני' דלא כי האי תנא, דתניא, *רבי יהושע בן קרחה אומר: כרכין המוקפין חומה מימות אחשורוש קורין בחמשה עשר. מ"ט דרבי יהושע בן קרחה? כי שושן, [ג]מה שושן מוקפת חומה מימות אחשורוש וקורין בחמשה עשר – אף כל שמוקפת חומה מימות אחשורוש קורין בחמשה עשר. ותנא דידן מ"ט? יליף "פרזי" "פרזי", כתיב הכא: °"על כן היהודים הפרזים" וכתיב התם: °"לבד מערי הפרזי הרבה (שם, דברים ג) מאד". מה להלן [א*]מוקפת חומה מימות יהושע בן נון – אף כאן [ב*]מוקפת חומה מימות יהושע בן נון. בשלמא רבי יהושע בן קרחה לא אמר כתנא דידן – דלית ליה "פרזי" "פרזי". אלא תנא דידן מ"ט לא אמר כר' יהושע בן קרחה? מ"ט? דהא אית ליה "פרזי" "פרזי"! הכי קאמר: אלא שושן [ג]דעבד' כמאן? לא כפרזים ולא כמוקפין! אמר רבא, ואמרי לה כדי: [ג]שאני שושן הואיל ונעשה בה נס. בשלמא לתנא דידן – היינו דכתיב: °"מדינה ומדינה ועיר ועיר". "מדינה ומדינה" – לחלק בין (אסתר ט) מוקפין חומה מימות יהושע בן נון למוקפת חומה מימות אחשורוש. "עיר ועיר" נמי – לחלק בין שושן לשאר עיירות. אלא לרבי יהושע בן קרחה, בשלמא "מדינה ומדינה" – לחלק בין שושן לשאר עיירות, אלא "עיר ועיר" למאי אתא? אמר לך רבי יהושע בן קרחה: ולתנא דידן מי ניחא? כיון דאית ליה "פרזי" "פרזי", "מדינה ומדינה" למה לי? אלא, קרא לדרשה הוא דאתא, וכדרבי יהושע בן לוי הוא דאתא. דאמר רבי יהושע בן לוי: *[ד]כרך וכל הסמוך לו וכל הנראה עמו נידון ככרך. עד כמה? אמר רבי ירמיה ואיתימא רבי חייא בר אבא: [ה]כמחמתן לטבריא, מיל. *ולימא מיל! הא קא משמע לן: דשיעורא דמיל כמה הוי? כמחמתן לטבריא. *ואמר רבי ירמיה ואיתימא רבי חייא בר אבא: מנצפ"ך צופים אמרום. ותסברא?! והכתיב: °"אלה המצות" *שאין (ויקרא כז) נביא רשאי לחדש דבר מעתה! ועוד, האמר רב חסדא: מ"ם וסמ"ך שבלוחות
בנס

ואוקי לה להך ברייתא. דלעיל כרבי יוסי בר יהודה: אימתי. מקדימים: מקום שנכנסים כו'. במקום שבית דין קבוע והכפרים נכנסים שם ליום הדין כשיש להם הריב: אבל מקום שאין נכנסין. דהך הקדמה לאו קולא היא לכפרים – אין קורין אותה אלא בזמנה: משום דקשיא ליה כו'. בתמיה: הפרזים. עיר שאין לה חומה, ומתוך כך ישיבתה נפוץ ופרוז, ומרוחקין משכונה לשכונה: מוקפין בט"ו. שהרי שני ימים כתובין שם, ומדקבע י"ד לפרזים – שדייה ט"ו למוקפין: כלל כלל לא. וחמשה עשר דכתיב במגילה שדייה לשושן, כדרך שנחו בו בשעת הנס: מהודו ועד כוש כתיב. שקיבלו עליהם פורים, דכתיב "וישלח ספרים בכל מדינות המלך אחשורוש וגו' לקיים עליהם", ואע"ג דלא כתב הודו וכוש בהאי קרא, כיון דכתיב בכל מדינות המלך אחשורוש – הרי מהודו ועד כוש: כדכתיב להיות עושים. מסקנא דקושיא היא, ולא פירוקא הוא: ואימא פרזים בי"ד. דהא קבעינהו קרא, אבל מוקפין דלא קבעינהו קרא, אי בעו בארביסר – ליקרו, אי בעו בחמיסר – ליקרו: ואימא מוקפין בי"ג. וקרא דכתיב בחמשה עשר – לשושן הוא דקבע, כדרך שעשו בט"ו בשנה ראשונה: ומשני כשושן. כיון דלא רמז לך הכתוב זמן המוקפין אימת הוא, ואשכחן שושן שעשו בט"ו – מסתברא שאותו היום שייר למוקפין: אשכחן עשייה. דמשתה ויום טוב שתהא לפרזים בי"ד, ומוקפין בט"ו: זכירה. קריאת המגילה: מנלן. שנקבע להם זמן לפרזים בארבעה עשר? הא בהאי קרא ד"על כן היהודים הפרזים היושבים בערי הפרזות עושים את יום ארבעה עשר" וגו' עשייה הוא דכתיבא: איתקש זכירה לעשייה. הלכך זמן אחד להם: וכתיב התם. בביאת הארץ בימי משה ויהושע "לבד מערי הפרזי הרבה מאד": מה להלן מימות יהושע. ולא גרסינן מה להלן מוקפין חומה מימות יהושע, דהא פרזים לאו מוקפין חומה נינהו: אף כאן מימות יהושע. אף פרזים האמור כאן במעשה המן – בפרזי דיהושע קאמר, ואע"ג דלאחר כן נעשה מוקף – הוי פרזים לענין מגילה: פרזי פרזי. לא גמיר גזירה שוה מרביה, ואין אדם דן גזירה שוה מעצמו, אלא אם כן קיבלה מרבו: הכי קאמר אלא שושן דעבדה כמאן. אי ילפינן הך גזירה שוה, היאך עשו אותן שבשושן בט"ו? הא פרזי הוא, ולא ידעינן בה שהוקפה מימות יהושע: הואיל ונעשה בה נס. שניתן להם גם מחר לעשות כדת היום להרוג בשונאיהם שני ימים – על כרחן לא נחו עד ט"ו, וכן קבעוה לדורות: מדינה ומדינה עיר ועיר. גבי זכירה ועשייה כתיב "והימים האלה נזכרים ונעשים" וגו'. משמע מדינה ומדינה כמנהגה ועיר ועיר כמנהגה, למדנו שיש מנהג חלוק במדינות, ומנהג חלוק בעיירות, לחלק בין שושן לשאר עיירות, ואע"פ שאף היא בכלל פרזים – הוקבעה בט"ו: הכי גרסינן. אלא לר' יהושע בן קרחה בשלמא מדינה ומדינה לחלק בין מוקפין חומה מימות אחשורוש לשאין מוקפין מימות אחשורוש: עיר ועיר למאי. הרי כל הפרזים שוין וכל המוקפין שוים, ואין חילוק בין עיר ועיר: וכר' יהושע בן לוי. ובחלוק לא איירי כלל, אלא ה"ק: כל עיר ועיר הסמוך למדינה שתהא כמותה: נידון ככרך. וקורין בט"ו הסמוך, אע"ג שאינו נראה, נראה אע"פ שאינו סמוך, הכי מפרש לקמן: עד כמה. חשיב לה סמוך: מנצפ"ך. כפל אותיות: צופים אמרום. נביאי הדורות:
בנס

[לקמן ז: ה.] [ב"ק סה: ע"ז נב:] [תוספתא פ"א ושם א"ר רבי יהודה ב"ק] [לקמן ג:] [פסחים מו.] [שבת קט.] [יומא פ. תמורה טז.]

רבינו חננאל

קורין אותה אלא בזמנה. ר' יהודה אליבא דמאן אי נימא אליבא דר' עקיבא אפי' בזמן הזה קורין אותה בי"א ובי"ב ובי"ג. והא תקנת אנשי כנה"ג הן. אלא ודאי ר' יהודה אליבא דרבנן ובזמן שהשנים כתיקנן וישראל שרויין על אדמתם מיהא קורין בי"א ובי"ב. תיובתא דר' יוחנן. איכא דאמרי א"ר [יוחנן] זו המשנה דברי ר' עקיבא הן. אבל חכ"א בזמן הזה הואיל ומסתכלין א) בה. האביונים מסתכלין בקריאת המגילה כי בעת קריאת המגילה מחלקין מעות פורים לעניים ומשלחין להן מתנות אין קורין אותה אלא בזמנה בי"ד תניא נמי הכי רב אשי קשיא ליה ומי א"ר יהודה הכי אבל בזמן הזה הואיל ומסתכלין בה אין קורין אותה אלא בזמנה. והאי ב) שאמר גאון ז"ל כך אנו שונין ומסתכנין. ופירש אם השנים כתיקנם שיכולין ישראל להעמיד דתותיהן ואין עליהן סכנה *) אין קורין אותה אלא בזמנה. אבל אנו כך שנינו. א"ר יהודה אימתי מקום שנכנסים בב' ובה' אבל מקום שאין נכנסים אין קורין אותה אלא בזמנה. מקום שנכנסים בב' ובה' מיהא קרינן בי"א ובי"ב ואפי' בזמן הזה. ושמיע ליה לרב אשי דאיכא מאן דתני לה לברייתא כר' יוסי ב"ר יהודה **) דוקא הוא דלא תקשי לך דר' יהודה אדר' יהודה: **כרכין** המוקפין חומה מימות יהושע בן נון קורין בט"ו. ואקימנא בגמ' פרזים. כתיב הכא הפרזים היושבים בערי הפרזות עושים את יום ארבעה עשר. וכתיב התם לבד מערי הפרזי. מה להלן דכתיב הפרזי וקרי להני פרזי ומוקפות חומות דבהדיהן מימות יהושע בן נון כמו הנך קורין בט"ו ואימא מוקפין חומה קורין בי"ד וט"ו. ופרקינן אי הוה כתיב את יום י"ד וט"ו כדקא אמרת. השתא כתיב את יום ארבעה עשר ואת יום חמשה עשר. שמעינן הני בי"ד והני בט"ו לית מאן דעביד ב' ימים לכל מקום ומקום יומו יום אחד. תוב ליכא למימר דמוקפין אי בעו בי"ד אי בעו בט"ו דהא פרשינן לעיל מדכתיב זמניהן דייקינן דכל חד בזמנו. וזמנו של זה לא זמנו של זה. כלומר אין הפרזים קורין בט"ו ולא המוקפין בי"ד. ואומר בי"ג כלומר מוקפין אי בעו בט"ו. אי בעו בי"ג. ופרקינן כשושן מה שושן אע"ג דלא מוקפת חומה מימות יהושע בן נון היא. מיהא כיון דהיא מוקפת חומה קרו בט"ו. אף כל שהיא מוקפת חומה קרו בט"ו. ואיתקש זכירה לעשייה דכתיב והימים האלה נזכרים ונעשים. מתני' דלא כר' יהושע בן קרחה דתני מוקפין חומה מימות אחשורוש קורין בט"ו ותנא דידן אמר שאני שושן דאע"ג דלאו מוקפת חומה מימות יהושע בן נון היא הואיל ונעשה בה נס לפיכך קראו בט"ו. ואקשינן בשלמא לתנא דידן כתיב מדינה ומדינה עיר ועיר. מדינה ומדינה לחלק בין דתרווייהו מוקפות חומה אינון. המוקפות חומה מימות יהושע בן נון קרו בט"ו. והמוקפות אחרי כן קרו בי"ד. עיר ועיר נמי לחלק בין שושן לשאר עיירות. בשושן בט"ו בשאר עיירות בי"ד. אלא לר' יהושע בן קרחה עיר ועיר למה לי. ואמרינן ולתנא דידן כיון דגמר פרזים פרזים כדאמרינן מדינה ומדינה למה לו. אלא לכר"ע קרא יתירא הוא שנא' מדינה ***) וכל הסמוך למדינה כמדינה היא. וכן עיר ועיר דאמר ריב"ל כרך וכל הסמוך לו וכל הנראה עמו נידון ככרך. וכמה יהיה מחוץ לכרך הסמוך לו שיחשב כמו כרך. ואוקימנא מיל כמחמתן לטבריא וזה שיעור המיל: **א"ר** ירמיה ואיתימא ר' חייא בר אבא מנצפ"ך צופים אמרום

הגהות הגר"א
[א] [ב] גמ' (מוקפת חומה) תא"מ (וכן מחקו רש"י): [ג] שם דעבדה. רשום קו עליו למחקו:

א) עיין בערוך ערך סכל א'. ב) הרמב"ן במלחמות כתב בזה הלשון וזו היא גירסתו של רבינו האי גאון ז"ל. *) חסר אבל בזמן שהיו מסתכנין ישראל בדתיהן אין קורין כו'. וכ"ה ברי"ף ז"ל. **) נראה דחסר וצ"ל ומדקשיא ליה דר"י אדר"י אמר מאן דתני לה כר"י ב"ר יוסי דוקא וכו'. ***) נראה דצ"ל אלא נאמר מדינה ומדינה ואשמעינן דכל הסמוך וכו'.

בְּנֵם הָיוּ עוֹמְדִין! אִין, מַהֲוָה הֲווּ, וְלָא הֲווּ יָדְעִי הֵי בְּאֶמְצַע תֵּיבָה וְהֵי בְּסוֹף תֵּיבָה, וְאָתוּ צוֹפִים וְתַקִּינוּ: פְּתוּחִין בְּאֶמְצַע תֵּיבָה וּסְתוּמִין בְּסוֹף תֵּיבָה. סוֹף סוֹף "אֵלֶּה הַמִּצְוֹת" — שֶׁאֵין נָבִיא עָתִיד לְחַדֵּשׁ דָּבָר מֵעַתָּה! אֶלָּא שְׁכָחוּם וְחָזְרוּ וִיסָדוּם. וא"ר יִרְמְיָה וְאִיתֵּימָא רַבִּי חִיָּיא בַּר אַבָּא: תַּרְגּוּם שֶׁל תּוֹרָה — אוּנְקְלוֹס הַגֵּר אֲמָרוֹ מִפִּי ר' אֱלִיעֶזֶר וְר' יְהוֹשֻׁעַ. תַּרְגּוּם שֶׁל נְבִיאִים — יוֹנָתָן בֶּן עוּזִּיאֵל אֲמָרוֹ מִפִּי חַגַּי זְכַרְיָה וּמַלְאָכִי, וְנִזְדַּעְזְעָה אֶרֶץ יִשְׂרָאֵל אַרְבַּע מֵאוֹת פַּרְסָה עַל אַרְבַּע מֵאוֹת פַּרְסָה. יָצְתָה בַּת קוֹל וְאָמְרָה: מִי הוּא זֶה שֶׁגִּילָּה סְתָרַיי לִבְנֵי אָדָם? עָמַד יוֹנָתָן בֶּן עוּזִּיאֵל עַל רַגְלָיו וְאָמַר: אֲנִי הוּא שֶׁגִּלִּיתִי סְתָרֶיךָ לִבְנֵי אָדָם; גָּלוּי וְיָדוּעַ לְפָנֶיךָ שֶׁלֹּא לִכְבוֹדִי עָשִׂיתִי, וְלֹא לִכְבוֹד בֵּית אַבָּא, אֶלָּא לִכְבוֹדְךָ עָשִׂיתִי, שֶׁלֹּא יִרְבּוּ מַחֲלוֹקֶת בְּיִשְׂרָאֵל. וְעוֹד בִּיקֵּשׁ לְגַלּוֹת תַּרְגּוּם שֶׁל כְּתוּבִים, יָצְתָה בַּת קוֹל וְאָמְרָה לוֹ: דַּיֶּיךָּ! מ"ט — מִשּׁוּם דְּאִית בֵּיהּ קֵץ מָשִׁיחַ. וְתַרְגּוּם שֶׁל תּוֹרָה, אוּנְקְלוֹס הַגֵּר אֲמָרוֹ? וְהָא *אָמַר רַב אִיקָא בַּר אָבִין אָמַר רַב חֲנַנְאֵל אָמַר רַב: מַאי דִּכְתִיב °"וַיִּקְרְאוּ בַסֵּפֶר תּוֹרַת הָאֱלֹהִים מְפוֹרָשׁ וְשׂוֹם שֶׂכֶל וַיָּבִינוּ בַּמִּקְרָא"? "וַיִּקְרְאוּ בַסֵּפֶר תּוֹרַת הָאֱלֹהִים" — זֶה מִקְרָא; "מְפוֹרָשׁ" — זֶה תַּרְגּוּם; "וְשׂוֹם שֶׂכֶל" — אֵלּוּ הַפְּסוּקִין; "וַיָּבִינוּ בַּמִּקְרָא" — אֵלּוּ פִּיסְקֵי טְעָמִים, וְאָמְרִי לַהּ: אֵלּוּ הַמָּסוֹרֶת. שְׁכָחוּם וְחָזְרוּ וִיסָדוּם. מַאי שְׁנָא דְּאוֹרַיְיתָא דְּלָא אִזְדַּעְזְעָה, וְאַדִּנְבִיאֵי אִזְדַּעְזְעָה? דְּאוֹרַיְיתָא מִיפָּרְשָׁא מִלְּתָא; דִּנְבִיאֵי אִיכָּא מִילֵּי דְּמִיפָּרְשָׁן, וְאִיכָּא מִילֵּי דְּמִסַּתְּמָן. דִּכְתִיב: °"בַּיּוֹם הַהוּא יִגְדַּל הַמִּסְפֵּד בִּירוּשָׁלַםִ כְּמִסְפַּד הֲדַדְרִמּוֹן בְּבִקְעַת מְגִידּוֹן", *וְאָמַר רַב יוֹסֵף: *אִלְמָלֵא תַּרְגּוּמָא דְּהַאי קְרָא לָא יָדַעְנָא מַאי קָאָמַר: בְּיוֹמָא הַהוּא יִסְגֵּי מִסְפְּדָא בִּירוּשְׁלֵים כְּמִסְפְּדָא דְּאַחְאָב בַּר עָמְרִי דִּקְטַל יָתֵיהּ הֲדַדְרִימּוֹן בֶּן טַבְרִימּוֹן בְּרָמוֹת גִּלְעָד, וּכְמִסְפְּדָא דְּיֹאשִׁיָּה בַּר אָמוֹן דִּקְטַל יָתֵיהּ פַּרְעֹה חֲגִירָא בְּבִקְעַת מְגִידּוֹ. *°"וְרָאִיתִי אֲנִי דָנִיֵּאל לְבַדִּי אֶת הַמַּרְאָה וְהָאֲנָשִׁים אֲשֶׁר הָיוּ עִמִּי לֹא רָאוּ אֶת הַמַּרְאָה אֲבָל חֲרָדָה גְדֹלָה נָפְלָה עֲלֵיהֶם וַיִּבְרְחוּ בְּהֵחָבֵא". א*) מַאן נִינְהוּ אֲנָשִׁים? אָמַר ר' יִרְמְיָה וְאִיתֵּימָא רַבִּי חִיָּיא בַּר אַבָּא: זֶה חַגַּי זְכַרְיָה וּמַלְאָכִי. *אִינְהוּ עֲדִיפֵי מִינֵּיהּ, וְאִיהוּ עָדִיף מִינַּיְיהוּ. אִינְהוּ עֲדִיפֵי מִינֵּיהּ — דְּאִינְהוּ נְבִיאֵי, וְאִיהוּ לָאו נָבִיא. אִיהוּ עָדִיף מִינַּיְיהוּ — דְּאִיהוּ חֲזָא וְאִינְהוּ לָא חֲזוֹ. וְכִי מֵאַחַר דְּלָא חֲזוֹ מ"ט אִיבְעִיתוּ? אע"ג דְּאִינְהוּ לָא חֲזוֹ — מַזָּלַיְיהוּ חֲזוֹ. אָמַר רָבִינָא: שְׁמַע מִינַּהּ, הַאי מַאן דְּמִיבְעִית — אע"ג דְּאִיהוּ לָא חָזֵי, מַזָּלֵיהּ חָזֵי. מַאי תַּקַּנְתֵּיהּ? *לִיקְרֵי ק"ש. וְאִי קָאֵים בִּמְקוֹם הַטִּנּוֹפֶת — לִינְשׁוֹף מִדּוּכְתֵּיהּ אַרְבַּע גַּרְמִידֵי. וְאִי לָא — לֵימָא הָכִי: "עִיזָּא דְּבֵי טַבָּחֵי שַׁמִּינָא מִינַּאי". § וְהַשְׁתָּא דְּאָמְרַתְּ "מְדִינָה וּמְדִינָה" "וְעִיר וָעִיר" לִדְרָשָׁה, "מִשְׁפָּחָה וּמִשְׁפָּחָה" לְמַאי אֲתָא? אָמַר רַבִּי יוֹסֵי בַּר חֲנִינָא: לְהָבִיא מִשְׁפְּחוֹת כְּהוּנָּה וּלְוִיָּה שֶׁמְּבַטְּלִין עֲבוֹדָתָן וּבָאִין לִשְׁמוֹעַ מִקְרָא מְגִילָּה. דְּאָמַר רַב יְהוּדָה אָמַר רַב: *אכֹּהֲנִים בַּעֲבוֹדָתָן, וּלְוִיִּם בְּדוּכָנָן, וְיִשְׂרָאֵל בְּמַעֲמָדָן — כּוּלָּן מְבַטְּלִין עֲבוֹדָתָן וּבָאִין לִשְׁמוֹעַ מִקְרָא מְגִילָּה. תַּנְיָא נַמִּי הָכִי: כֹּהֲנִים בַּעֲבוֹדָתָן, וּלְוִיִּם בְּדוּכָנָן, וְיִשְׂרָאֵל בְּמַעֲמָדָן — כּוּלָּן מְבַטְּלִין עֲבוֹדָתָן וּבָאִין לִשְׁמוֹעַ מִקְרָא מְגִילָּה. מִכָּאן סָמְכוּ שֶׁל בֵּית רַבִּי שֶׁמְּבַטְּלִין תַּלְמוּד תּוֹרָה וּבָאִין לִשְׁמוֹעַ מִקְרָא מְגִילָּה, קַל וָחוֹמֶר מֵעֲבוֹדָה. וּמָה עֲבוֹדָה שֶׁהִיא חֲמוּרָה — מְבַטְּלִינַן, תַּלְמוּד תּוֹרָה — לֹא כָּל שֶׁכֵּן?! וַעֲבוֹדָה חֲמוּרָה מִתַּלְמוּד תּוֹרָה? וְהָכְתִיב: °"וַיְהִי בִּהְיוֹת יְהוֹשֻׁעַ בִּירִיחוֹ וַיִּשָּׂא עֵינָיו וַיַּרְא וְהִנֵּה אִישׁ עוֹמֵד לְנֶגְדּוֹ [וגו'] וַיִּשְׁתָּחוּ (לְאַפָּיו)". *וְהֵיכִי עָבֵיד הָכִי? וְהָאָמַר רַבִּי יְהוֹשֻׁעַ בֶּן לֵוִי: אָסוּר לְאָדָם שֶׁיִּתֵּן שָׁלוֹם לַחֲבֵירוֹ בַּלַּיְלָה, חָיְישִׁינַן שֶׁמָּא שֵׁד הוּא! שָׁאנֵי הָתָם דַּאֲמַר לֵיהּ: "כִּי אֲנִי שַׂר צְבָא ה'". וְדִלְמָא מְשַׁקְּרִי? גְּמִירִי דְּלָא מַפְּקִי שֵׁם שָׁמַיִם לְבַטָּלָה. *אֲמַר לוֹ: אֶמֶשׁ בִּטַּלְתֶּם תָּמִיד שֶׁל בֵּין הָעַרְבַּיִם, וְעַכְשָׁיו בִּטַּלְתֶּם תַּלְמוּד תּוֹרָה! אֲמַר לוֹ: עַל אֵיזֶה מֵהֶן בָּאתָ? אֲמַר לוֹ: "עַתָּה בָאתִי". מִיָּד ב)°"וַיָּלֶן יְהוֹשֻׁעַ בַּלַּיְלָה הַהוּא בְּתוֹךְ הָעֵמֶק". אָמַר רַבִּי יוֹחָנָן: מְלַמֵּד

א) שהיה דניאל מתמה עליהם שהוא ראה והמה לא ראו ומשני שהיו חזו"מ שהיו להם מעלה גדולה ממנו שהיו נביאים והם לא ראו זה היתה התמיה שלו

ב) [וכן איתא בסנהדרין מד: ועי' בתוס' דהכא ד"ה וילן וכו' אבל בעירובין סג: איתא וילך וכו' אמר רבי יוחנן מלמד שהלך בעומקה וכו' וע"ש בתוס' ד"ה מיד ילך וכו']

רש"י

בְּנֵם הָיוּ עוֹמְדִין. שֶׁהָיְתָה חֲקִיקָתָן מִשְּׁנֵי עֶבְרֵיהֶן. הִלְכָּךְ, שְׁאָר אוֹתִיּוֹת יֵשׁ לָהֶן מְקוֹם דָּבֵק, אֶלָּא מֵ"ם וְסָמֶ"ךְ הָיְתָה בָּאֲוִיר (וְדַוְקָא בִּסְתוּמִים). וְאֶפְשָׁר הָיָה לוֹ לְתָרֵץ הָךְ (בָּרַיְיתָא) דְּרַב חִסְדָּא בִּסְתוּמִין, וְכִי אִתְּמַר הָךְ דְּרַבִּי יִרְמְיָה — בִּפְתוּחִין, וְהָכִי מוּכָח בְּפֶרֶק "הַבּוֹנֶה" בְּמַסֶּכֶת שַׁבָּת, אֶלָּא הָא *פָּרֵיךְ לָהּ מִילְּתָא דְּשַׁוְיָא לְתַרְוַיְיהוּ: *מַהֲוָה הֲווּ כו'. וְאוֹרְחָא דְּסוּגְיָא דִּגְמָרָא *(לְהַקְשׁוֹת) דָּבָר שֶׁאֵינוֹ, עַד דְּטָרַח וּמַעֲמִידָהּ עַל בּוּרְיָהּ. מִפִּי רַבִּי ע"כ: שֶׁלֹּא יִרְבּוּ מַחֲלוֹקֶת. לְפָרֵשׁ מִקְרָאוֹת הַסְּתוּמִים: קֵץ מָשִׁיחַ. בְּסֵפֶר דָּנִיֵּאל: וַיִּקְרְאוּ בַסֵּפֶר תּוֹרַת הָאֱלֹהִים וגו'. בְּסֵפֶר עֶזְרָא כְּתִיב: זֶה מִקְרָא. לָשׁוֹן עִבְרִי שֶׁל חוּמָשׁ: הַפְּסוּקִים. הֵיאָךְ נִפְסָקִין: פִּיסְקֵי הַטְּעָמִים. הַנְּגִינוֹת קְרוּיִין טְעָמִים: אִלְמָלֵא תַּרְגּוּמָא דְּהַאי קְרָא וכו'. שֶׁלֹּא מָצִינוּ בְּכָל הַמִּקְרָא הֶסְפֵּד לַהֲדַדְרִימּוֹן בְּבִקְעַת מְגִידּוֹ. וְיוֹנָתָן תִּרְגְּמוֹ לִשְׁנֵי הֶסְפֵּידוֹת: הֲדַדְרִימּוֹן בְּרָמוֹת גִּלְעָד (מלכים א כב), וְיֹאשִׁיָּהוּ בְּבִקְעַת מְגִידּוֹ, כִּדְמְפָרֵשׁ בְּסֵפֶר מְלָכִים (ב כג): דְּאִינְהוּ נְבִיאֵי. שֶׁנִּתְנַבְּאוּ לְיִשְׂרָאֵל בִּשְׁלִיחוּתוֹ שֶׁל מָקוֹם, וְהוּא לֹא נִשְׁתַּלַּח לְיִשְׂרָאֵל בְּשׁוּם נְבוּאָה: מַאי טַעְמָא אִיבְעִיתוּ. דִּכְתִיב בִּקְרָא "אֲבָל חֲרָדָה גְדוֹלָה נָפְלָה עֲלֵיהֶם וַיִּבְרְחוּ בְּהֵחָבֵא": מַזָּלַיְיהוּ. שַׂר שֶׁל כָּל אָדָם לְמַעְלָה: לִינְשׁוֹף. יְדַלֵּג: וְיִשְׂרָאֵל בְּמַעֲמָדָן. עוֹמְדִין עַל תְּמִידֵי צִבּוּר בִּשְׁעַת הַקָּרְבָּן, כִּדְתְנַן בְּמַסֶּכֶת תַּעֲנִית (דף כו.): "תִּשְׁמְרוּ לְהַקְרִיב לִי בְּמוֹעֲדוֹ", הֵיאָךְ שׁוֹמֵר אִם אֵינוֹ עוֹמֵד עַל גַּבָּיו? תִּיקְּנוּ נְבִיאִים הָרִאשׁוֹנִים כ"ד מִשְׁמָרוֹת, עַל כָּל מִשְׁמָר וּמִשְׁמָר הָיָה מַעֲמָד כו': וְהֵיכִי עָבֵיד הָכִי. שֶׁהִשְׁתַּחֲוָה לוֹ, דִּכְתִיב "וַיִּפּוֹל עַל פָּנָיו וַיִּשְׁתָּחוּ": אֶמֶשׁ בִּיטַּלְתֶּם כו'. בִּתְשׁוּבָה שֶׁהֱשִׁיבוֹ "עַתָּה בָאתִי" אָנוּ לְמֵדִין תְּחִלַּת דִּבְרֵי הַמַּלְאָךְ. הֶאֱשִׁימָן בִּשְׁנֵי דְבָרִים: אֶמֶשׁ, כְּלוֹמַר כְּשֶׁהֶעֱרִיב הַיּוֹם, הָיָה לָכֶם לְהַקְרִיב תָּמִיד הָעֶרֶב וּבִטַּלְתֶּם אוֹתוֹ, וְנִשְׁתַּהִיתֶם בְּמַחֲרַב הָעִיר חִנָּם, שֶׁאֵין זְמַן מִלְחָמָה בַּלַּיְלָה [מִשֶּׁחֲשַׁךְ]: וְעַכְשָׁיו. שֶׁהוּא לַיְלָה, הָיָה לָכֶם לַעֲסוֹק בַּתּוֹרָה, שֶׁהֲרֵי אֵינְכֶם נִלְחָמִים בַּלַּיְלָה: עַתָּה בָאתִי. עַל שֶׁל עַכְשָׁיו: מִיָּד וַיָּלֶן יְהוֹשֻׁעַ בַּלַּיְלָה הַהוּא בְּתוֹךְ הָעֵמֶק. לֹא בְּאוֹתוֹ הַלַּיְלָה כְּתִיב, אֶלָּא בַּלַּיְלָה שֶׁצָּר עַל הָעַי, וְהָכִי קָאָמַר: מִיָּד חָזַר יְהוֹשֻׁעַ מִדְּבָרָיו, וּכְשֶׁבָּא לַיְלָה אַחֵר בְּמָצוֹר — עָסַק בַּתּוֹרָה: הָא

תוספות

מבטלין כהנים מעבודתן לשמוע מקרא מגילה. וקשה: אמאי מבטלין? והלא אחר הקריאה יש הרבה שהות לעבודה! ויש לומר: דכיון דמשהאיר היום הוי זמן עבודה, והם מניחין אותה בשביל הקריאה – משום הכי קרי ליה ביטול. וא"ת: ויעשו עבודתן מיד, ואחר כך יקראו המגילה לבדם! וי"ל: דטוב לקרות עם הצבור, משום דהוי טפי פרסומי ניסא:

חיישינן שמא שד הוא. פירש ריב"א: דדוקא חוץ לעיר, [היכא דשכיחי מזיקין], כגון בשדה ובלילה. וכן היה יהושע צר על יריחו בשדה רחוק ממחנה ישראל. אבל במקום שבני אדם מצויין – אין לחוש, דאל"כ אדם שאמר לנו [בלילה בעיר] "כתבו גט לאשתי" היכי כתבינן? ניחוש שמא שד הוא [ולא נכתוב] עד דנחזי ליה בבואה דבבואה. ולא אשכחן דפריך ליה גמרא אלא גבי מי שהושלך בבור, פרק "התקבל" (גיטין דף סו. ושם):

אמש בטלתם תמיד של בין הערבים. קשה: אמאי בטלוהו? בשלמא תלמוד תורה בטלו – לפי שהיו צריס על העיר כל ישראל, אבל הכהנים אמאי לא היו מקריבים התמיד? וי"ל: לפי שהארון לא היה במקומו, כדאמר פרק "הדר" (עירובין דף סג:), והכהנים נושאין את הארון. וא"ת: והיכי משמע לישנא דקרא דבטלו התמיד ותלמוד תורה? ויש לומר: דה"פ: מדקאמר "הלנו אתה" הכי קאמר: בשביל תלמוד תורה באת, דכתיב "תורה צוה לנו" – אם לצרינו, או בשביל הקרבנות שמגינים עלינו מצרינו:

עתה באתי. פי' ריב"ן: על תלמוד תורה באתי, דכתיב ביה "ועתה כתבו לכם [את] השירה הזאת" (דברים לא): *וילן יהושע בלילה ההוא בתוך העמק. לא כתיב בהאי קרא כן, אלא כשצר על יריחו כתיב "וילן בלילה ההוא בתוך העם" וכשצר על העי כתיב "וילך *בלילה ההוא בתוך העמק". ודרך התלמוד הוא לקצר הפסוקים ולערבם יחד, כמו "ונתן הכסף וקם לו" (ערכין דף לג.)*:

רבינו חננאל

אמרום. כלומר האותיות הללו חכמים תקנום. ואקשינן ואלה המצות שאין נביא רשאי לחדש דבר מעתה ופרקינן לעולם מתוקנים היו. וכן היה. מסורת בידם מהנביאים להיות הפתוחים באמצע תיבה. והסתומים בסוף תיבה ושכחום וחזרו הצופים ויסדום. והוא עוד אמר תרגום של תורה אונקלוס הגר אמרו מפי ר' אליעזר ור' יהושע כאשר למדו אותו כך לימדוהו לאחרים. ושל נביאים יונתן בן עוזיאל אמרו כמו שהיה מסורת בידם של חכמים מפי חגי זכריה ומלאכי. ותרגום של כתובים נמנע מן השמים לגלותו משום דאית ביה קץ משיח. ואקשינן והא תרגום של תורה בימי עזרא הוה דכתיב (ויכתבו) [ויקראו] בספר תורת האלהים מפורש. ואמרינן מפורש זה תרגום ושום שכל אלו פסוקים. ויבינו במקרא זה פיסוק טעמים ואמרי לה אלו המסורת. ופרקינן אין תרגום מיהוה הוה בידייהו מקמי עזרא ושכחוהו רובא דאינשי ואתא אונקלוס ויסדיה למיקרי ביה בצבור. מיהו מילי דאורייתא מיגליין. כלומר רובן מפורשין הן. אבל של נביאים מסותמין הן. דהא לולי התרגום של זה הפסוק ביום ההוא יגדל המספד בירושלם כמספד הדרימון וגו'. לא הוינן ידעינן פירושא דהאי פסוקא ולפיכך נזדעזע העולם שגילה הטעמים שהיו נעלמים. וראיתי אני דניאל לבדי המראה וגו'. מאן נינהו אנשים שהיו עמו זה חגי זכריה ומלאכי. ולמה נפלה חרדה גדולה עליהם. דאע"ג דאינהו לא חזו מזלייהו חזו: וכיון דמדינה ומדינה (הוא) לדרשה הוא דאתיין כדאמרן משפחה [ומשפחה] מאי דרשת בה ואסיקנא משפחות כהנים ולוים. וכדתניא כהנים המתעסקין בעבודתן ולוים בדוכנם וישראל במעמדן כולן מבטלין עבודתן ובאין לשמוע מקרא מגילה מיכן סמכו של בית ר' שמבטלין תלמוד תורה ובאין לשמוע מקרא מגילה. אם הכהנים מבטלין עבודתן ת"ת לא כל שכן. ואקשינן וכי עבודה חמורה מדברי תורה והכתיב ויהי בהיות יהושע ביריחו וישא עיניו וירא והנה וגו' ויאמר לא כי אני שר צבא ה' עתה באתי. א"ל אמש בטלתם תמיד של

עין משפט נר מצוה

ח א מיי' פ"א מהלכות מגילה הלכה א סמג עשין ד טור ש"ע א"ח סי' תרפז סעיף ב:

נדרים לז:

[ועי' תוס' עירובין סג: דגרסי וילך ע"ש]

[יהושע]

[ועי' תוס' שבת קכח. ועירובין טו: ד"ה בכתיבה ובמו"ק ח. ד"ה נפקא ולקמן כ. ד"ה דכתיב ומנחות מד: ד"ה מנחתם]

מסורת הש"ס

איתו בפי' אחרים

נ"א פריך

נ"א ומשני מהוה

[נ"ל לתרץ]

נחמיה ח

זכריה יב

דניאל י

מו"ק כח:

[ועי' תוס' ב"ק ג: ד"ה כלמתרגם]

[סנהדרין נג:]

[שם לג.]

[שם ע"ש]

[ערכין ד. ושם איתא ר"י אמר שמואל]

יהושע ה

סנהדרין מד.

עירובין סג: [סנהדרין שם]

יהושע ח

גליון הש"ס

גמ' שכחום וחזרו ויסדום. לקמן יח ע"א סוכה מד ע"א: שם אונקלוס הגר אמרו. עי' ירושלמי דמסכתין פ"א הלכה ט: שם כמספדא דאחאב. עי' ב"ק יז ע"א תוד"ה והלא: רש"י ד"ה ויקראו כו' בספר עזרא כתיב. עי' סוכה יב ע"א ברש"י ד"ה לאו הכי ומ"ש שם: תום' ד"ה מבטלין כו' והלא אחר כו'. עי' פסקי תוס' ערכין אות כ:

מְלַמֵּד שֶׁלָּן בְּעוֹמְקָהּ שֶׁל הֲלָכָה. *וְאָמַר רַב שְׁמוּאֵל בַּר אוּנְיָא: גָּדוֹל תַּלְמוּד תּוֹרָה יוֹתֵר מֵהַקְרָבַת תְּמִידִין, שֶׁנֶּאֱמַר: "עַתָּה בָאתִי"! לָא קַשְׁיָא: הָא — דְּרַבִּים, וְהָא — דְּיָחִיד. וּדְיָחִיד קַל? וְהָתְנַן: *[א]נָשִׁים בַּמּוֹעֵד מְעַנּוֹת, אֲבָל לֹא מְטַפְּחוֹת. ר' יִשְׁמָעֵאל אוֹמֵר: אִם הָיוּ סְמוּכוֹת לַמִּטָּה — מְטַפְּחוֹת. בְּרָאשֵׁי חֳדָשִׁים בַּחֲנוּכָּה וּבְפוּרִים — מְעַנּוֹת וּמְטַפְּחוֹת בָּזֶה וּבָזֶה,(א) אֲבָל לֹא מְקוֹנְנוֹת. וְאָמַר רַבָּה בַּר הוּנָא: *[ב]אֵין מוֹעֵד בִּפְנֵי תַלְמִיד חָכָם, כׇּל שֶׁכֵּן חֲנוּכָּה וּפוּרִים! [מו"ק כח:] כְּבוֹד תּוֹרָה קָאָמְרַתְּ. כְּבוֹד תּוֹרָה דְּיָחִיד — חָמוּר; תַּלְמוּד תּוֹרָה דְּיָחִיד — קַל. אָמַר רָבָא: פְּשִׁיטָא לִי: עֲבוֹדָה וּמִקְרָא מְגִילָּה — מִקְרָא מְגִילָּה עָדִיף, מִדְּר' יוֹסֵי בַּר חֲנִינָא. תַּלְמוּד תּוֹרָה וּמִקְרָא מְגִילָּה — מִקְרָא מְגִילָּה עָדִיף, מִדְּסָמְכוּ שֶׁל בֵּית רַבִּי. תַּלְמוּד תּוֹרָה וּמֵת מִצְוָה — מֵת מִצְוָה עָדִיף, מִדְּתַנְיָא: *[ג]מְבַטְּלִין תַּלְמוּד תּוֹרָה לְהוֹצָאַת מֵת וּלְהַכְנָסַת כַּלָּה. עֲבוֹדָה וּמֵת מִצְוָה — מֵת מִצְוָה עָדִיף, מִ"וּלְאַחֹתוֹ" דְּתַנְיָא: [במדבר ו] *"וּלְאַחוֹתוֹ" מַה תַּ"ל? הֲרֵי שֶׁהָיָה הוֹלֵךְ לִשְׁחוֹט אֶת פִּסְחוֹ וְלָמוּל אֶת בְּנוֹ, וְשָׁמַע שֶׁמֵּת לוֹ מֵת, יָכוֹל יִטַּמֵּא — אָמַרְתָּ: לֹא יִטַּמָּא. יָכוֹל כְּשֵׁם שֶׁאֵינוֹ מִיטַּמֵּא לַאֲחוֹתוֹ כָּךְ אֵינוֹ מִיטַּמֵּא לְמֵת מִצְוָה — תַּ"ל "וּלְאַחוֹתוֹ": לַאֲחוֹתוֹ הוּא דְּאֵינוֹ מִיטַּמֵּא, [ד]אֲבָל מִיטַּמֵּא לְמֵת מִצְוָה. בָּעֵי רָבָא: מִקְרָא מְגִילָּה וּמֵת מִצְוָה הֵי מִינַּיְיהוּ עָדִיף? מִקְרָא מְגִילָּה עָדִיף מִשּׁוּם פִּרְסוּמֵי נִיסָּא, אוֹ דִּלְמָא מֵת מִצְוָה עָדִיף — מִשּׁוּם כְּבוֹד הַבְּרִיּוֹת? בָּתַר דְּבַעְיָא הֲדַר פַּשְׁטַהּ: [ה]מֵת מִצְוָה עָדִיף. *דְּאָמַר מַר: גָּדוֹל כְּבוֹד הַבְּרִיּוֹת שֶׁדּוֹחֶה אֶת לֹא תַעֲשֶׂה שֶׁבַּתּוֹרָה. גּוּפָא, *א"ר יְהוֹשֻׁעַ בֶּן לֵוִי: [ו]כְּרַךְ וְכׇל הַסָּמוּךְ לוֹ וְכׇל הַנִּרְאֶה עִמּוֹ נִדּוֹן כִּכְרַךְ. [לעיל ב:] תָּנָא: [ז]סָמוּךְ — אע"פ שֶׁאֵינוֹ נִרְאֶה, נִרְאֶה — אע"פ שֶׁאֵינוֹ סָמוּךְ. בִּשְׁלָמָא נִרְאֶה אע"פ שֶׁאֵינוֹ סָמוּךְ — מַשְׁכַּחַתְּ לָהּ כְּגוֹן דְּיָתְבָה בְּרֹאשׁ הָהָר. אֶלָּא סָמוּךְ אע"פ שֶׁאֵינוֹ נִרְאֶה, הֵיכִי מַשְׁכַּחַתְּ לָהּ? א"ר יִרְמְיָה: שֶׁיּוֹשֶׁבֶת בְּנַחַל. וְא"ר יְהוֹשֻׁעַ בֶּן לֵוִי: [ח]כְּרַךְ שֶׁיָּשַׁב וּלְבַסּוֹף הוּקַּף — נִדּוֹן כִּכְפָר. מ"ט — דִּכְתִיב: [ויקרא כה] "וְאִישׁ כִּי יִמְכּוֹר בֵּית מוֹשַׁב עִיר חוֹמָה" — *[ט]שֶׁהוּקַּף וּלְבַסּוֹף יָשַׁב, וְלֹא שֶׁיָּשַׁב וּלְבַסּוֹף הוּקַּף. [לקמן ה.] וְאָמַר ריב"ל: [י]כְּרַךְ שֶׁאֵין בּוֹ עֲשָׂרָה בַּטְלָנִין — נִדּוֹן כִּכְפָר. מַאי קמ"ל? תְּנֵינָא: *אֵיזוֹ הִיא עִיר גְּדוֹלָה — כׇּל שֶׁיֵּשׁ בָּהּ עֲשָׂרָה בַּטְלָנִין; פָּחוֹת מִכָּאן — הֲרֵי זֶה כְּפָר. כְּרַךְ אִיצְטְרִיךְ לֵיהּ, אע"ג דְּמִיקַּלְעֵי לֵיהּ מֵעָלְמָא. וְאָמַר ריב"ל: כְּרַךְ שֶׁחָרַב וּלְבַסּוֹף יָשַׁב — נִדּוֹן כִּכְרַךְ. מַאי חָרַב? אִילֵימָא חָרְבוּ חוֹמוֹתָיו, יָשַׁב — אִין, לֹא יָשַׁב — לָא? וְהָא תַּנְיָא, *רַבִּי אֱלִיעֶזֶר בַּר יוֹסֵי אוֹמֵר: [ויקרא כה] "אֲשֶׁר לוֹא חוֹמָה" — [כ]אַף עַל פִּי שֶׁאֵין לוֹ עַכְשָׁיו, וְהָיָה לוֹ קוֹדֶם לָכֵן. אֶלָּא: מַאי חָרַב — שֶׁחָרַב מֵעֲשָׂרָה בַּטְלָנִין. וְאָמַר ריב"ל:

לוד

מלמד שהלך ולן בעומקה של הלכה. כל זמן ששכינה וארון שרויין שלא במקומן אסורים בתשמיש המטה לא גרס ליה הכא, דמה שייך כאן? ובפרק "הדר" (עירובין סג:) גרס ליה, דקאמר שנענש יהושע על שבטל ישראל מפריה ורביה*. י"ל דמה שנענש שלא היה לו בן זכר היה על שבטל ישראל מתשמיש, מדה כנגד מדה. אבל שאר עונש בא לו על בטול תורה:

מענות. כולן עונות כאחת. מקוננות – אחת אומרת והשאר עונות. מטפחות – יד על יד, או על ירך, או על פניס: **אין** מועד בפני תלמיד חכם. ויום שמועה כבפניו דמי: **כל** שכן חנוכה ופורים. שמותר להספידס, אע"ג דמבטל ממקרא מגילה. אלמא: ת"ת חמור ממקרא מגילה: **מת** מצוה עדיף. לאו דווקא מת מצוה, והוא הדין לכל מתים שבעולם מבטלים תלמוד תורה להוציאם. אלא איידי דנקט בסמוך גבי "ולאחותו" מת מצוה, ה"נ נקט תלמוד תורה ומת מצוה*:

מת מצוה עדיף. הקשה הר"ר אלחנן: למה לי קרא? תיפוק ליה מק"ו: ומה ת"ת דחמירא – מבטלין משום כבוד המת, עבודה דקילא – לא כל שכן, דהא אפילו תלמוד תורה דרבים מבטלין משום כבוד המת, כדאמר פ"ב דכתובות (דף יז. ושם)! וי"ל: דה"מ למאן דקרי ותני ומתני, דצריך כולי האי. אבל למאן דלא קרי ותני – לא צריך כולי האי. והכא מיירי במת מצוה דלא קרי ותני, ומשום הכי צריך קרא ד"ולאחותו": **כרך** שאין בו י' בטלנים נדון בכפר. וצ"ל דמיירי בסתם כרכים האמורים בתלמוד. *אבל המוקף חומה מימות יהושע בן נון, אפילו אין בו י' בטלנים קורין בט"ו. וה"נ משמע, דפריך בסמוך מאי קמ"ל תנינא איזו היא עיר גדולה כו'. ומשני: כרך איצטריך ליה, אע"ג דמקלעי ליה מעלמא. ואי איתא דאפילו במוקף חומה מימות יהושע בן נון צריך י' בטלנין – הוה ליה למימר מוקף מימות יהושע אצטריכא ליה, אע"ג דחשיב חומה דידהו שהגינו מן האויבים, וגם מקלעי ליה מעלמא דהוי רבותא טפי. אלא ש"מ דבמוקף מימות יהושע לא צריך י':

כרך שישב ולבסוף הוקף נדון ככפר. פירש הקונטרס דלענין בתי ערי חומה איירי, וה"נ משמע, מדאייתי קרא ד"כי ימכור". וקשה: דאם כן, בערכין (דף לג.) הו"ל להש"ס למתני, גבי הא דתני שאר דיני דבתי ערי חומה! ועוד קשה: דאם כן הל"ל נדון כערי החצרים, דשייך גבייהו! לכ"נ דלענין מגילה מיירי. מכל מקום מייתי קרא ד"כי ימכור" לאשמועינן דחומה דמתנינן גבי מגילה בכה"ג דמהני גבי ערי חומה דהיינו הוקף ולבסוף ישב כדכתיב "בית מושב עיר חומה" דמשמע שנתיישב בתוך החומה. ואם תאמר: לקמן (דף ה:) אמרינן דטבריא שימה חומתה, אע"ג דאין לה דין ערי חומה, מ"מ קורין את המגילה בט"ו [ג]דהשם מוקפין חומה כיון דמגיא מאוידים! וה"נ היה לנו לומר כשישב ולבסוף, הוקף כיון דמכסיא ומגניא! וי"ל: דשאני טבריא, דכיון דחזינן דהיקף יש מהני כהיקף חומה לגבי מגילה – גם כן דין הוא שיקראו המגילה בט"ו, שהרי היקף שלה קודם לישובה, והוי כשאר היקף דמהני בבתי ערי חומה. אבל ישב ולבסוף הוקף – לא מצינו בשום מקום דחשיב חומה שלה. וא"ת: לקמן בפרקין (שם) דקאמר "אשר לו חומה" פרט לשור אגר, פי': שאגרות חומות שלה, כגון שהבתים מדובקים יחד בעגול והוי כמו חומה סביב לעיר. ולמה לי קרא? תיפוק ליה דה"ל "ישב ולבסוף הוקף" שהרי לא נגמרה חומת העיר עד שנגמרו כל הבתים! ויש לומר: דקרא אתא לאשמועינן דאפילו היכא דקים לן שלא דר אדם שם עד שנגמרו כל הבתים – אפילו הכי לא חשיב היקף. וצריך לומר דהא דקאמר נדון ככפר – מיירי דליכא י' בטלנים, דאי יש שם עשרה בטלנין – אמאי גרע מעיירות גדולות דהוו בי"ד?: **והתניא** רבי אליעזר ברבי יוסי אומר וכו' וא"ת: אדמותבת ליה מרבי אליעזר, לסייעיה מרבנן דפליגי עליה, וסברי דקדושה ראשונה קדשה לשעתה ולא לעתיד לבא! ויש לומר: דע"כ לא סבר רבי יהושע כרבנן, דאי סבר כוותייהו – מאי מהני (*ישב ולבסוף הוקף) אם לא קדשה קדושה שנייה?: **אלא** שחרב מעשרה בטלנים. וכשלא הוקף מימות יהושע איירי, דביה לא צריך עשרה. ואם תאמר: מאי מהני מה שהיה כרך מתחילה, הוה ליה כפר שנעשה כרך שנתישבו שם עשרה! ויש לומר: דלרבותא נקט הכי, ולא מבעיא כפר שנעשה כרך, דבסתמא ליכא למיחש שמא יחסרו דיורים. אלא אפילו זה, שפסקו דיורים כבר פעם אחת, וסלקא דעתך אמינא דאיכא למיחש שמא יפסקו עוד פעם אחרת – אפילו הכי קא משמע לן דלא חיישינן:

לוד

הא דרבים. דהתם כל ישראל הוו: מענות. הספד על המת: ולא מטפחות. על לבן: אבל לא מקוננות. והתם מפרש איזהו עינוי ואיזהו קינה: עינוי – שכולן עונות כאחת, קינה – אחת אומרת וכולן עונות אחריה: ת"ת דיחיד. ביטול מלמודו קל מעבודה ופורים: מדרבי

תורה אור

יוסי בר חנינא. דדריש משפחה כו': ולאחותו מה ת"ל. גבי נזיר כתיב "על נפש מת לא יבא" (במדבר ו), הרי הכל במשמע. הדר כתיב בתריה קרא יתירא "לאביו ולאמו לאחיו ולאחותו" כו', דריש לה בספרי: לאביו לא יטמא – אבל מיטמא הוא למת מצוה. לאמו מה ת"ל – שאם היה כהן ונזיר, אע"פ שקדוש ב' קדושות – לאמו לא יטמא, אבל מיטמא הוא למת מצוה. לאחיו, שאם היה כהן גדול ונזיר – לאחיו לא יטמא, אבל מיטמא הוא למת מצוה. דעל כרחך כולהו למעוטי מת מצוה אתו. הלכך, אם אינו ענין לו – תנהו ענין לחבירו. ולאחותו מה ת"ל כו' ואם אינו ענין לאלו – תנהו ענין לענין ביטול עבודה ומילה מפני מת מצוה: שמת לו מת. אח או אחות: אמרת לא יטמא. כשם שאין נזיר מבטל נזירותו ליטמא לקרוביו, כך הוא זה לא יבטל מפסחו: את לא תעשה. דכתיב "לא תוכל להתעלם" (דברים כב) וכתיב "והתעלמת" – פעמים שאתה מתעלם, כגון זקן ואינו לפי כבודו: בנחל. מקום נמוך: שישב ולבסוף הוקף. שנתיישב תחלה בבתים ולבסוף הוקף חומה, נידון ככפר לענין בתי ערי חומה: בית מושב עיר חומה. בית מושב של עיר חומה: עשרה בטלנין. שבטלין ממלאכתן, שיהו מלויין תמיד בבית הכנסת שחרית וערבית, כדאמרינן במסכת ברכות (דף ו:): כיון שבא הקב"ה בבית הכנסת ולא מצא שם עשרה וכו': תנינא. בפירקין במתני' (ד' ה.): כרך איצטריכא ליה. דכל כרך אינו אלא מקום שווקין שנכנסים שם מכל צד, וגדול הוא יותר מעיר גדולה: דמיקלעי ליה מעלמא. אנשים הרבה, ויש הרבה מהן בטלין ממלאכה, שאין עושין מלאכה אלא במקומן. אפילו הכי בעינן קבועין, דזמנין דלא משתכחין: ישב אין. שחזר והוקף:

לוד

רבינו חננאל
של בין הערבים ועכשיו בטלתם ת"ת. ועל איזה מהן באת. א"ל עתה באתי. כלומר על ת"ת שבטלתם אותו עתה. הנה ת"ת חמור מעבודה ופרקינן התם גבי יהושע ת"ת דכל ישראל ולפיכך חמור מעבודה. אבל דיחידים כגון ת"ת דרבי עבודה חמורה ממנו. וכן פורים: אריב"ל אסור לאדם לתת שלום בלילה חיישינן שמא שד הוא ואי מזכיר לו שם שמים שרי. ות"ת דיחיד קיל והתנן נשים במועד מענות אבל לא מטפחות כו'. ואמר רבה בר רב הונא אין מועד בפני ת"ח. כ"ש חנוכה ופורים. ופרקינן כבוד תורה כגון הספד ת"ח וכיוצא בו. אפי' דיחיד חמור מפורים. אבל ת"ת דיחיד קל מעבודה ופורים. אמר רבא פשיטא לי עבודה ומקרא מגילה. מקרא מגילה עדיף. כדר' יוסי ב"ר חנינא. וכן מקרא מגילה עדיף מת"ת מדמבטלין דבי ר' ת"ת ובאין לשמוע מקרא מגילה. וכן קבורת מת מצוה עדיף. דתנן מבטלין להוצאת המת ולהכנסת כלה. *) ומסיקנא
דקבורת מת מצוה עדיף ממקרא מגילה. הגדול כבוד הבריות שדוחה את לא תעשה שבתורה. פי' כגון זקן שראה בהמת חבירו והיא נדחה. ואין כבודו להנהיג בהמה אינו חייב להשיבה. שנאמר והתעלמת ואמרינן פעמים שאתה מתעלם. באיזה צד כגון זקן שאין כבודו להנהיג לפניו בהמות שהוא פטור מלהשיב. נמצא כבוד הזקן דוחה את הכתוב לא תוכל להתעלם. וכן אם יש לפניו ב' מצות עבודה ומת מצוה. מת מצוה עדיף ויבטל עבודה. מדתניא ולאחותו דכתיבה בנזיר מה ת"ל כלומר לאחיו אינו מטמא לאחותו לא כ"ש. א"כ מה ת"ל ולאחותו. הרי שהיה הולך לשחוט את פסחו ולמול את בנו ששחיטתן אע"פ שהן מצות עשה שהוא חייב כרת. כדתנן בכריתות פרק ראשון. הפסח והמילה מצות עשה כדכתיב והאיש אשר הוא טהור ובדרך לא היה וחדל לעשות הפסח. וכתיב וערל זכר אשר לא ימול וגו'. ושמע שמת לו מת יכול יטמא **). דייקינן מדכתיב והאיש אשר הוא טהור וחדל לעשות הפסח ונכרתה. וכן ערל זכר אשר לא ימול וגו'. כלומר אינו רשאי להיטמא למתו ולבטל המצוה. ת"ל ולאחותו. הנה הנזיר מצוה שלא להיטמאות וכתיב ולאחותו מופנה ללמד ממנה לאחותו אינו מטמא אבל מטמא למת מצוה יכול לא יטמא שאם יטמא נמצא בטל מן המצוה. אע"פ שמבטל העבודה: אריב"ל כרך וכל הסמוך לו. מיל. כדאמרן [לעיל ג:] תנא סמוך בזה השיעור אע"פ שלא נראה עמו כגון שיושבת בנחל. או נראה עמו כגון שיושבת בראש ההר. אע"פ שאינו סמוך כשיעור מיל אלא יותר מזה נדון ככרך. [illegible]
[illegible]
לוד

*) מגילה דחסר כאן וג"ל מקרא מגילה ומת מצוה מאי עדיף ומסיקנא וכו'. **) נ"ל יכול יטמא תלמוד לומר לא יטמא ודייקינן לה מדכתיב וכו'.

מסורת הש"ס: [עירובין סג: ע"ש סנהדרין מד. ע"ש] · מו"ק כח: · [לקמן כט. (ע"ש בתוס') כתובות יז. (ע"ש בתוס')] · ברכות יט: נזיר מח: סנהדרין לה. זבחים ק. · שבת פא: לג: עירובין נה: מנחות לז: · [ערכין לג: ע"ש דהוא ברייתא] · [לקמן י: שבועות טז: ערכין לב. (ועי' רש"י ותוס') ערכין לב. ושם ועי' פי' תוס' על זה בחולין סה. ד"ה אע"פ] · נ"א אם לבסוף ישב

הגהות הב"ח
(א) גמ' ומטפחות בזה ובזה אין מקוננות: (ב) תוס' ד"ה כרך שישב וכו' בט"ו דהוא מוקפת חומה:

גליון הש"ס
גמ' ולהכנסת כלה. בהגהות ע"ש אה"ע סי' סה סעיף א:

עין משפט נר מצוה
ולא סתרי אהדדי דהתם קאמר שנענש על שביטל ישראל מפ"ו והכא אמר שנענש על שביטל מעבודה די"ל דמה שנענש כו'
ט א ב מיי' פ"ו מהלכות י"ט הלכה כב ופי"א מהל' אבל הלכה ד סמג עשין ב טוש"ע א"ח סימן תקמז סעיף ב וטוש"ע י"ד סימן תא סעיף ה:
י ג מיי' שם פי"ד הלכה ט טוש"ע י"ד סימן שסא סעיף א:
יא ד מיי' שם פ"ג הלכה ח טוש"ע י"ד סי' שעד סעיף א:
יב ה מיי' פ"א מהלכות מגילה הלכה א טור ש"ע א"ח סי' תרפז סעיף ב:
[ועי' תוס' כתובות יז. ד"ה להוצאת]
יג ו ז מיי' שם הלכה י טור ש"ע א"ח סי' תרפח סעיף ב:
יד ח שם סעיף א:
טו ט מיי' פי"ב מהל' שמטה ויובל הלכה יד סמג עשין קנב:
טז י מיי' פ"א מהלכות מגילה הלכה ח:
יז כ מיי' פי"ב מהלכות שמטה ויובל הלכה טו [ופ"א מהלכות מגילה ה"ד טוש"ע א"ח סי' תרפח סעיף א]:
דהיינו עיירות גדולות אבל כרך הנזכר במקרא מגילה היינו המוקף חומה

לוד ואונו וגיא החרשים מוקפות חומה מימות יהושע בן נון הוו. והני יהושע בנינהי? והא אלפעל בננהי, דכתיב: "[ו]בני אלפעל עבר ומשעם ושמר הוא בנה את אונו ואת לוד ובנותיה". ולטעמיך, (א) אסא בננהי, דכתיב: "ויבן (*אסא את ערי הבצורות אשר ליהודה)"! אמר ר' אלעזר: הני מוקפות חומה מימות יהושע בן נון הוו. חרוב בימי פילגש בגבעה, ואתא אלפעל בננהי. הדור אינפול – אתא אסא שפצינהו. דיקא נמי, דכתיב: "ויאמר ליהודה נבנה את הערים האלה" – מכלל דערים הוו מעיקרא, ש"מ. *ואריב"ל: נשים חייבות במקרא מגילה, *שאף הן היו באותו הנס. ואמר רבי יהושע בן לוי: פורים שחל להיות בשבת – שואלין ודורשין בענינו של יום. מאי אריא פורים? אפילו י"ט נמי. דתניא: *משה תיקן להם לישראל שיהו שואלין ודורשין בענינו של יום: הלכות פסח בפסח, הלכות עצרת בעצרת והלכות חג בחג. פורים איצטריכא ליה. מהו דתימא: נגזור משום דרבה, קמ"ל. *ואריב"ל: חייב אדם לקרות את המגילה בלילה ולשנותה ביום, שנאמר "אלהי אקרא יומם ולא תענה ולילה ולא דומיה לי". סבור מינה: למקרייה בליליא, ולמיתנא מתניתין דידה ביממא. אמר להו רבי ירמיה: לדידי מיפרשא לי מיניה דרבי חייא בר אבא: כגון דאמרי אינשי: אעבור פרשתא דא ואתנייה. איתמר נמי, אמר רבי חלבו אמר עולא ביראה: *חייב אדם לקרות את המגילה בלילה ולשנותה ביום, שנאמר "למען יזמרך כבוד ולא ידום ה' אלהי לעולם אודך". § "אלא שהכפרים מקדימין ליום הכניסה". § א"ר חנינא: חכמים הקילו על הכפרים להיות מקדימין ליום הכניסה *כדי שיספקו מים ומזון לאחיהם שבכרכין.
למימרא

דה"א ח | סס ב יד | סס | תהלים כב | סס ל

רש"י

לוד ואונו וגיא החרשים. מערי בנימין היו, כדכתיב "ובני אלפעל עבר ומשעם ושמר הוא בנה את לוד ואת אונו" וגו'. ובספר דברי הימים מיחסו על שבט בנימין. וגמרא גמיר לה רבי יהושע בן לוי מרבותיו דמוקפות חומה מימות יהושע בן נון הן. ובמתני' דערכין תנן תרתי מינייהו דקא מני לוד ואונו אצל ערי חומה, שאינן נוהגות אלא מימות יהושע בן נון. ולפי שחומותיהן נראות חדשות, כדאמרינן לקמן שנפלו והחזיקן, הוזקק ר' יהושע בן לוי להעיד שבכלל מוקפות חומה הן, לקרות מגילה בט"ו: ויחזק **אסא.** אינו בכל המקרא, אבל מקרא אחר כתיב "ויבן ערים ביהודה", ואע"ג דהני לאו מיהודה נינהו, ומבנימין היו – מלכי יהודה מושלים על בנימין. ומלינו באסא שאף ערי בנימין חיזק, דכתיב (ד"ה ב טז) "וישאו את אבני הרמה ואת עציה אשר בנה בעשא ויבן בה את גבע ואת המצפה", והן ערי בנימין, כדכתיב בספר יהושע: **בימי פילגש בגבעה.** שהחריבו ישראל את בנימין ואת עריו, כדכתיב "גם כל הערים הנמצאות שלחו באש" (שופטים כ): **שפצינהו.** החזיק את בדקיהן. ודומה לו ביבמות (דף סג.): טוס ולא תשפך, שפיץ ולא תבנה: **דיקא נמי.** גרס: **שאף הן היו באותו הנס.** שאף על הנשים גזר המן "להשמיד להרוג ולאבד מנער ועד זקן טף ונשים" וגו': **שואלין ודורשין.** מעמידין תורגמן לפני החכם, לדרוש אגרת פורים ברבים: **משום דרבה.** דגזר לקמן בקריאת מגילה שמא יעבירנה ארבע אמות ברשות הרבים, אף כאן גזרו דרשה אטו קרייה: **ולשנותה ביום.** זכר לנס, שהיו זועקין בימי צרתן יום ולילה: **אקרא.** במזמור "למנצח על אילת השחר" הוא, שנאמר על אסתר, כדאמרינן במסכת יומא (דף כט.): למה נמשלה אסתר כאילת כו': **סבור מינה.** בני הישיבה, ששמעו שמועה זו בלה"ק "ולשנותה ביום", היו סבורין דהאי "ולשנותה" – לשון שונה משנה הוא: **למיתני מתני' דידה.** משניות של מסכת מגילה: **אעבור פרשתא דא ואתנייה.** אסיים פרשה זו ואשנה אותה פעם שניה: **ביראה.** דמן בירי: **יזמרך כבוד.** ביום, ולא ידום בלילה. והאי קרא במזמור "ארוממך ה' כי דליתני" דרשינן בפסיקתא *) במרדכי ואסתר והמן ואחשורוש. וקריאת מגילה שבח הוא, שמפרסמין את הנס, והכל מקלסין להקדוש ברוך הוא: **למימרא**

*) [דר"כ סוף פיסקא דהעומר]

תורה אור

תוספות

לוד ואונו וגיא החרשים. הקשה ה"ר אלחנן: אמאי אצטריך ליה לרבי יהושע לאשמועינן דאונו מוקפת מימות יהושע? והא משנה שלימה היא בפרק בתרא דערכין (דף לב.): ויש לומר דאגב דאצטריך לאשמועינן לוד וגיא החרשים תנא נמי אונו בהדייהו:

הא אלפעל בננהו. קשה: אמאי לא פריך בפרק בתרא דערכין כי האי גוונא? וי"ל: דהתם לא תנן אלא אונו, והיה יודע דמצי לשנויי תרי אונו הוו. אבל הכא דהוו ג' – בשלשתן לא שייך למימר שהן כפולות:

נשים חייבות במקרא מגילה. מכאן משמע שהנשים מוציאות את אחרים ידי חובתן, מדלא קאמר "לשמוע מקרא מגילה". והכי נמי משמע בערכין (דף ג: ושם), דקאמר: הכל כשרים לקרא את המגילה, ומסיק: הכל כשרים לאתויי מאי? ומשני: לאתויי נשים – משמע להוציא אפילו אנשים. וקשה: דהא בתוספתא *תני בהדיא דטומטום אין מוציא לא את מינו ולא שאין מינו, ואנדרוגינוס מוציא את מינו ואין מוציא את שאין מינו, ופשיטא דלא עדיפא אשה מאנדרוגינוס! וכן פסקו הה"ג דאשה מוציאה מינה אבל לא אנשים! וי"ל: דסלקא דעתך דלא יועיל קריאתן אפילו להוציא הנשים, קמ"ל דחייבין. *דהכל חייבין בשמיעה עבדים נשים וקטנים:

שאף הן היו באותו הנס. פירש רשב"ם: שעיקר הנס היה על ידן; בפורים – על ידי אסתר, בחנוכה – על ידי יהודית, בפסח – שבזכות צדקניות שבאותו הדור נגאלו. *וקשה: דלשון ש"אף הן" משמע שהן טפלות, ולפירושו היה לו לומר שהן לכך נראה לי ש"אף הן" היו בספק דלהשמיד ולהרוג, וכן בפסח שהיו משועבדות לפרעה במצרים, וכן בחנוכה הגזירה היתה מאד עליהן. גבי מצה יש מקשה: למה לי היקשא *דכל שישנו ב"בל תאכל חמץ" ישנו ב"קום אכול מצה"? תיפוק ליה מטעם שהן היו באותו הנס! וי"ל: דמשום האי טעמא לא מחייבא אלא מדרבנן, אי לאו מהיקשא. ורבינו יוסף איש ירושלים תירץ: דסלקא דעתך למיפטרה מגזירה שוה דט"ו ט"ו דחג הסוכות, כדפי' פרק "אלו עוברין" (פסחים מג: ד"ה סלקא*): **פסק:** ואומר על הנסים בתפלה ובהודאה. ויש שאין אומרים "כשם", לפי שאמרו חכמים (ברכות לד.) לעולם לא ישאל אדם צרכיו לא בג' ראשונות ולא בג' ברכות אחרונות. ושטות הוא, שהרי האי טעמא לא הוי אלא למתפלל בלשון יחיד, אבל בשביל הציבור שרי. אבל נראה שאין לאומרו מטעם אחר, משום דאמרו חכמים (פסחים קיז:) דכל דבר דהוי בלהבא תקנו בלהבא, ודבדבר דהודאה הוי לשעבר, ומשום הכי תקנו בה "על הנסים" דהוי לשעבר. ובליל י"ד לאחר תפלת מעריב אומר קדיש שלם, ואחר כך קורא את המגילה, ומברך לפניה ג' ברכות ואחריה ברכה אחת עד "האל המושיע". השלים, עומד לפני התיבה ואומר ,ואתה קדוש", ואין תחילין "ובא לציון" לפי שאין גאולה בלילה. ואם מוצאי שבת הוא יאמר "ויהי נועם" קודם. וכשרוצה לקרות פושט את כולה קודם כאגרת, אבל לא גולל וקורא כמו ס"ת. ובשחר מתפלל שמונה עשרה ברכות, ואומר "על הנסים" בהודאה, ואין אומר "כשם" לפי שכל הברכה אינה אלא לשעבר, וא"כ אין לומר בה דבר שלהבא, ואחר כך אומר קדיש עד "דאמירן", ואוחז ס"ת וקורא שלשה גברי פרשת "ויבא עמלק", אע"פ שאין בה אלא ט' פסוקים, ואין מחזיר הספר תורה למקומו, אלא יושב ואוחז בידיו עד שקראו את המגילה, ומברך עליה כאשר עשה בלילה, כדפירש בפנים. ואחר כך אומר תהלה "ובא לציון" ואין אומרים "למנצח" משום דכתיב ביה צרה, וצרה בפורים לא מזכרינן. וכן אין נופלים על פניהם בי"ד ובט"ו, משום דכתיב "ימי משתה ושמחה" ואומר [(תהלים כב) "למנצח על אילת השחר"] *משום דכתיב ביה מפלה לעובדי כוכבים, וכן בליל ארבעה עשר. ואומר "פטום הקטורת", וכל הסדר כמו בחול: **פורים** שחל להיות בשבת. דווקא בשבת, לפי שאין קורין המגילה משום גזירה דרבה. אבל בחול א"צ שהרי קורין המגילה, וטפי איכא פרסומי ניסא: **מאי** איריא פורים אפילו י"ט נמי. נראה לי דה"פ: מאי איריא פורים דאין דורשין בו מקודם לכן שלשים יום, דמשום הכי לידרוש בו ביום, אפילו בי"ט, דדרשינן שלשים יום לפניו ואפילו הכי דורשין בו ביום, כדתניא (לקמן לב.) "וידבר משה את מועדי ה'" וכו'": **חייב** אדם לקרות את המגילה בלילה ולשנותה ביום. אומר ר"י: דאף על גב דמברך זמן בלילה חוזר ומברך אותו ביום, דעיקר פרסומי ניסא הוי בקריאה דיממא. וקרא נמי משמע כן, דכתיב "ולילה ולא דומיה לי" כלומר: אף על גב שקורא ביום – חייב לקרות בלילה, והעיקר הוי ביממא, כיון שהזכירו הכתוב תחילה. וגם עיקר הסעודה בימנא הוא, כדאמר לקמן (דף ז:) דאם אכלה בלילה לא יצא י"ח. והכי נמי משמע, מדכתיב "נזכרים ונעשים" ואיתקש זכירה לעשייה, מה עיקר עשייה בימאא – אף זכירה כן:
ויעבירנה

עין משפט נר מצוה

יח א מיי' פ"א מהלכות מגילה הלכה א סמג עשין ד טוש"ע א"ח סי' תרפט סעיף א:
יט ב מיי' שם הלכה יג:
כ ג מיי' פ"ג מהלכות תפלה הלכה ח:
כא ד מיי' פ"א מהלכות מגילה הלכה ג' סמג שם טוש"ע א"ח סי' תרפז סעיף א:

מסורת הש"ס

[כל ערי מצורה ביהודה]
[ערכין ג.]
[שבת כג. פסחים קח:]
לקמן לב.
[לקמן כ.]
לקמן כ.
[לעיל ב. לקמן יט.]
[דמגילה פ"ב]
דומיא דהכל כצ"ל
[סוטה יא:]
[פסחים מג:]
[ועי' תוס' פסחים קח: ד"ה היו]

הגהות הב"ח

(א) גמ' ולטעמיך הא אסא אשר ליהודה אלא אמר ר' אלעזר:

גליון הש"ס

[תוס'] ד"ה נשים וכו'. וכן [פס]קו הה"ג. עי' סוכה דף [לח] ע"א תוס' ד"ה באמת: [ש]ם ד"ה פסק כו' משום [דכ]תי' בי' מפלה לעובדי [כו]כבי' עי' לקמן דף טו [ע"]ב וביומא דף כט ע"א ול"ע:

אותו מזמור לא נמצא ...לה לשום אומה אבל ...ליהו רבה סי' תרלג ...ק ט כתב בזה"ל ובתוס' ...לה דף ד כתוב לומ' שיר ...מר לאסוף משום דיש ...פלת עמלק עכ"ל ...כ שכך היה לפניו הנוסחא בתוס'

רבינו חננאל

לוד ואונו גיא החרשים מוקפת חומה וכו'. כלומר דייקינן מדכתיב ויבן אסא את (כל הערים הבצורות אשר) [ערי מצורה] ביהודה וכי כל הערים אסא בנאם והלא [בנויים] היו. אלא שפצינהו. כך יש לומר אלפעל שפצינהו. כרכין המוקפין חומה מימות יהושע בן נון מקודשות ומשלחין מצורעין מתוכן וא"ר יהושע נשים חייבות לשמוע מקרא מגילה שאף הן היו באותו הנס. כלומר שגם הן היו בכלל להשמיד להרוג ולאבד. פורים שחל להיות בשבת. פי' אם חל ט"ו להיות בשבת שהוא פורים לבני כרכין שואלין ודורשין בענינו של יום: מהו דתימא נגזור משום דרבה. דאמר הכל חייבין במקרא מגילה ואין הכל בקיאין בה גזירה שמא יטלנה מי שאינו בקי וילך אצל מי שבקי ויעבירנה ד' אמות ברה"ר קמ"ל. וחייב אדם לקרות את המגילה

למימרא דתקנתא דכרכין הוי? והתנן: חל להיות בשני – כפרים ועיירות גדולות קורין בו ביום. ואם איתא – ליקדמו ליום הכניסה! הוו להו עשרה, ועשרה לא תקינו רבנן. ת"ש: חל להיות בחמישי – כפרים ועיירות גדולות קורין בו ביום. ואם איתא – ליקדמו ליום הכניסה, דאחד עשר הוא! מיום הכניסה ליום הכניסה לא דחינן. תא שמע, א"ר יהודה: *אימתי – במקום שנכנסים בשני ובחמישי, אבל מקום שאין נכנסים בשני ובחמישי – אין קורין אותה אלא בזמנה. ואי סלקא דעתך תקנתא דכרכין היא – משום דאין נכנסים בשני ובחמישי מפסדי להו לכרכין? לא תימא "כדי שיספקו מים ומזון", אלא אימא: מפני *שמספקים מים ומזון לאחיהם שבכרכין. § "כיצד חל להיות בשני בשבת כפרים ועיירות גדולות קורין בו ביום" וכו'. § מאי שנא רישא דנקט סידורא דירחא, ומאי שנא סיפא דנקט סידורא דיומי? איידי דמיתהפכי ליה נקט סידורא דיומי. § "חל להיות בע"ש" וכו'. § מתני' מני? אי רבי, אי רבי יוסי. מאי רבי? דתניא: חל להיות בע"ש – כפרים ועיירות גדולות, מקדימין ליום הכניסה, ומוקפין חומה קורין בו ביום. ר' אומר: אומר אני, לא ידחו עיירות ממקומן, [א]אלא אלו ואלו קורין בו ביום. מאי טעמא דת"ק? דכתיב: "בכל שנה ושנה". מה כל שנה ושנה עיירות קודמות למוקפין – אף כאן עיירות קודמות למוקפין. ואימא: "בכל שנה ושנה" מה כל שנה ושנה אין נדחין עיירות ממקומן – אף כאן לא ידחו עיירות ממקומן! שאני הכא דלא אפשר. ורבי, מ"ט? "בכל שנה ושנה", מה כל שנה ושנה אין עיירות נדחין ממקומן – אף כאן לא ידחו עיירות ממקומן. ואימא: "בכל שנה ושנה" מה כל שנה ושנה עיירות קודמות למוקפין – אף כאן נמי עיירות קודמות למוקפין! שאני הכא דלא אפשר. מאי ר' יוסי? דתניא: *חל להיות בערב שבת – מוקפין וכפרים מקדימין ליום הכניסה, ועיירות גדולות קורין בו ביום. רבי יוסי אומר: אין מוקפין קודמין לעיירות, אלא אלו ואלו קורין בו ביום. מ"ט דתנא קמא? דכתיב: "בכל שנה ושנה" – מה כל שנה ושנה עיירות בארבעה עשר, וזמנו של זה לא זמנו של זה – אף כאן עיירות בארבעה עשר, וזמנו של זה לא זמנו של זה. ואימא: "בכל שנה ושנה" – מה כל שנה ושנה אין מוקפין קודמין לעיירות – אף כאן אין מוקפין קודמין לעיירות! שאני הכא דלא אפשר. מ"ט דר' יוסי? "בכל שנה ושנה" – מה כל שנה ושנה אין מוקפין קודמין לעיירות – אף כאן אין מוקפין קודמין לעיירות. ואימא: "בכל שנה ושנה" – מה כל שנה ושנה *זמנו של זה לא זמנו של זה – אף כאן זמנו של זה לא זמנו של זה! שאני הכא דלא אפשר. וסבר רבי עיירות לא דחינן ליום הכניסה? והתניא: *חל להיות בשבת – כפרים מקדימין ליום הכניסה, [ב]ועיירות גדולות קורין בע"ש ומוקפות חומה למחר. *ר' אומר: אומר אני, הואיל ונדחו עיירות ממקומן – ידחו ליום הכניסה! הכי השתא?! התם – זמנם שבת היא, והואיל דנדחו – ידחו. והכא, זמנם ערב שבת. כמאן אזלא הא דאמר רבי חלבו א"ר הונא: פורים שחל להיות בשבת הכל נדחין ליום הכניסה. הכל נדחין סלקא דעתך?! והא איכא מוקפין דעבדי למחר! אלא כל הנדחה – ידחה ליום הכניסה. כמאן? כרבי. דכולי עלמא מיהא [ג]מגילה בשבת לא קרינן. מאי טעמא? *אמר רבה: הכל חייבין בקריאת מגילה *)(ובתקיעת שופר), ואין הכל בקיאין במקרא מגילה. גזירה שמא יטלנה בידו וילך אצל בקי ללמוד, ויעבירנה ארבע אמות ברשות הרבים. והיינו טעמא דשופר, והיינו טעמא דלולב. רב יוסף אמר: מפני שעיניהן של עניים נשואות במקרא מגילה. תניא נמי הכי: אע"פ שאמרו כפרים מקדימין ליום הכניסה – [ד]גובין בו ביום, ומחלקין בו ביום. אע"פ שאמרו? אדרבה, משום דאמרו הוא! אלא: הואיל ואמרו שכפרים מקדימין ליום הכניסה – גובין בו ביום ומחלקין בו ביום, מפני שעיניהם של עניים נשואות במקרא מגילה. [ה]אבל

שמחה

*) [ליתא בשאילתות וברי"ף ורא"ש גם מהרש"א מוחק זה]

למימרא דתקנתא דכרכין היא. כדי שיספקו, משמע: כדי שיהו פנויין ליום השמחה: אלא אימא מפני שמספקין. שכר הוא להם בשביל שהן מספקין. הלכך, היכא דאין נכנסין – לא קולא הוא לגבייהו, ואין כאן שכר: סידרא דירחא. דקתני בי"א, בי"ב, בי"ג, בי"ד, בט"ו, כסדר מנין החודש, וכשבא לפרשה נקט סדר ימי השבת ושמעינן ימי החודש לאחריה: חל להיות ערב שבת כפרים מקדימין ליום הכניסה – הרי י"ג, חל להיות בשבת(א) – הרי י"ב, חל להיות אחר השבת כפרים מקדימין ליום הכניסה – הרי י"א. ומשני: איידי דמיתהפכי ליה נקט סידורא דיומי. כלומר, ע"י שאם היה אוחז ימי השבת לפי סדר ימי החדש יהו נהפכין לו, וטועה בגירסתו השונה את המשנה, לפי שהיה צריך להזכירן לאחוריו אחר השבת – דהיינו י"א, בשבת – י"ב, ערב שבת – י"ג, מתוך כך הוא בא לדלג ולטעות, להכי נקט סידורא דיומא. וסדר החודש הבא לו לאחוריים אינו מזכירו בפיו, דהרי מאליו הוא נשמע, ואין כאן עוד טעות: מני מתני'. דקתני: חל להיות ע"ש עיירות ומוקפות חומה קורין בו ביום, אי רבי אי רבי יוסי: בכל שנה ושנה. "להיות עושים את שני הימים האלה ככתבם וכזמנם בכל שנה ושנה" – כל השנים יהו שוות: דלא אפשר. דאם כן לא יקדמו עיירות למוקפין, שאינן יכולין לקרות בשבת: מה כל שנה ושנה עיירות בי"ד. לכך אין נדחות ממקומן, ודלא כתנא קמא דרבי: זמנו של זה לא הוא זמנו של זה. הלכך לא עבד כתנא דמתני' כו': דלא אפשר. דאי לא מקדמת להו למוקפין צריך אתה לעקור עיירות מפני מוקפין, או יקראו ביום אחד: הכא ערב שבת זמנם. ואין לך צורך לדחותן: הכל חייבין. ומתוך שהוא מחוייב בדבר הוא בהול לצאת ידי חובה: ויעבירנה ארבע אמות. ואפילו לן בשדה ומגילה בידו – יש לגזור על הדבר: נשואות למקרא מגילה. לקבל מתנות האביונים, ואי אפשר בשבת: גובין בו ביום. שמקדימין בו לקרות גובין הגבאים מתנות האביונים, ומחלקין לעניים: אדרבה. משום דאמרו להקדים את הקריאה הוא דאמרו להקדים את המתנות, כדמפרש תנא טעמא ואזיל, מפני שעיניהן של עניים כו':

שמחה

ויעבירנה ארבע אמות ברשות הרבים. קשה: אמאי לא קאמר ויוציאנה מרשות היחיד לרשות הרבים, דאורחא דמילתא הוי טפי! ויש לומר: דמרה"י לרה"ר לא טעו אינשי, אבל זימנין שהמגילה קיימא כבר ברשות הרבים, ויעבירנה ארבע אמות בגווה. ועי"ל: *דלהכי לא נקט מרשות היחיד לרשות הרבים לפי [שלפעמים] שאין שם חיוב חטאת, (*כיון) שלא היתה עקירה ראשונה לשם כך, כגון המפנה חפצים מזוית לזוית ונמלך עליהן להוציאן, דפטור מהאי טעמא (שבת דף ה:): **ויעבירנה** ארבע אמות ברשות הרבים. אבל מילה בשבת אין לדחות, דהא אמירא, *שכן נכרתו עליה י"ג בריתות. וגם אין אדם מל אלא אם כן הוי בקי, דסכנה יש בדבר. אך נשאל לר"י הלוי: איך תוקעין במוצאי יום הכפורים? והלא אסור לעשות מלאכה °עד שיבדיל, ותו: שמא ילך אצל בקי, כדחיישינן בר"ה שחל בשבת. ואם כן היה לנו למיחש להאי גזירה! ותירץ: דמשום דתקיעת שופר חכמה ואין מלאכה, וגם לא חיישינן שמא ילך אצל בקי – דמשום תקיעה אחת °שאינה אלא משום זכר ליובל לא אצטריך כולי האי כראש השנה, דאורייתא היא, וצריך שלשים קולות. ורבינו שמואל אומר דדוקא בשבת ובר"ה דאם מעבירו ארבע אמות ברשות הרבים איכא איסורא דאורייתא, בהא ודאי יש לחוש. אבל במוצאי יוה"כ, דאפילו אם מעבירו ד' אמות ברשות הרבים לא הוי אלא איסור דרבנן – בהא ודאי לא גזר, דהוי גזירה לגזירה:

ורב יוסף אמר מפני שעיניהם של עניים נשואות למקרא מגילה. ע"כ צ"ל דרב יוסף לא פליג אטעמיה דרבה, דהא גבי שופר ולולב ליכא טעמא אחרינא. מכל מקום קאמר הכא טעמא אחרינא משום דאיכא נפקותא מיהא במקדש דליכא שבות ואפ"ה אסור משום האי סברא דקאמר רב יוסף:

הוה

כב א ב מיי' פ"א מהלכות מגילה הלכה יד:

[עי' תוס' ר"ה כט: ד"ה שמא ותוס' סוכה מג. ד"ה ויעבירנו ותוס' ביצה יז.]

כג ג מיי' שם הלכה יג טוש"ע א"ח סימן תרפח סעיף ו:

כד ד ה מיי' פ"ב שם הלכה יד טוש"ע שם:

[יבמות ה:]

רבינו חננאל

[המגילה] כו'. הכפרים מקדימין ליום הכניסה מפני שמספיקין מים ומזון לאחיהם שבכרכים. וכן תנא דבי שמואל ואקשינן הלא עזרא אחר שבאו לא"י ובנו הבית תיקן קריאת התורה בב' ובה' ובמנחה בשבת. ובימי מרדכי ואסתר שהיו בימי כנסת הגדולה לא היתה תקנה זו ואין שם עדיין יום הכניסה. ואיך אמר משנתינו אלא שהכפרים מקדימין ליום הכניסה ומצאנו בתלמוד א"י כך. וכי מרדכי ואסתר מתקנין סמניהן כדאמרן להיותם מקדימין ליום הכניסה על מה שעזרא עתיד לתקן יום הכניסה להיות קורין בס"ת בב' ובה'. וא"ר מנא נמי מי שסידר את המשנה סמכה למקרא משפחה ומשפחה מדינה ומדינה ועיר ועיר. כיצד חל להיות בשני כפרים ועיירות. גדולות קורין בו ביום. ומוקפין חומה למחר: **ירושלמי** כל הני דתנינן חל להיות בארביסר אנן קיימין. א"ר יוסי מתניתא אומרת כן. ומוקפת חומה למחר. א"ר יוסי לית כאן חל להיות בשני דאם מקלע צומא רבה (ע"ש) חד בשבא ואף על גב דאם חל י"ד באדר להיות בשני או בשבת יבא פסח בב' או בד' לא הביאה המשנה להוסיף שחלו ממש אלא סדור דיומי נקט. והכי קאמר אילו חל להיות בב' אין מקדימין וקורין בה'. (קורין בה') דמיום הכנים' ליום הכניסה לא דחינן חל להיות בע"ש כפרים קורין בי"ג. חל להיות בשבת כפרים ועיירות גדולות קורין בי"ב. חל להיות באחד בשבת כפרים קורין בי"א. ואקשינן ומ"ש מעיקרא נקיט סידורא דירחא כו' כדתנן מגילה נקראת בי"א כו'. פי' נקיט תנא בי"א לחדש בי"ב לחדש בי"ג לחדש. כסדר החודש. ואח"כ שנה חל להיות בשני בג' בד' ובה' בשבת באחד בשבת. ופרקינן איידי דמיתכפין ליה נקיט סידורא דיומי. פי' אלו שנה התנא סדר ימי החדש ושנה חל להיות י"ד באדר באחד בשבת כפרים מקדימין בה' ליום הכניסה שהוא י"א לחדש. חל להיות יום י"ד בד' קורין בב' בי"ב. ואם חל להיות בג' קורין הכפרים ליום הכניסה שהוא י"ג לחדש. הנה נמצאו הימים מתהפכים מאחר בשבת ליום רביעי. ומיום ד' יחזור ליום ה'. וכן בשבת ובע"ש כסדר הזה לפיכך אחז סדר הימים של שבוע. מני מתני' דקתני שאם חל י"ד להיות בע"ש כפרים מקדימין ליום הכניסה ועיירות גדולות ומוקפות חומה קורין בע"ש או ר' או ר' יוסי. ר' דתניא ר' אומר אומר אני לא שידחו עיירות ממקומן אלא אלו ואלו עיירות גדולות ומוקפות חומה קורין בע"ש. ר' יוסי מאי היא דתניא חל להיות בע"ש כו'. ר' יוסי אומר אומר אני לא שיקדמו מוקפות לעיירות אלא מוקפות ועיירות קורין בו ביום ודבריהן פשוטין הן. ואקשינן וסבר ר' לא ידחו עיירות ממקומן. והתניא חל להיות בשבת כפרים מקדימין ליום הכניסה ועיירות גדולות קורין בע"ש ומוקפות חומה למחר ביום ראשון. ר' אומר אומר אני הואיל ונדחו עיירות מיום י"ד ידחו ליום הכניסה. ופרקינן הכי השתא התם שבת זמנם ולהדחות עומדים ידחו ליום הכניסה הכא ע"ש זמנם לאו לדחויי עומדים. הלכך יקראו בזמנם. *) ור' היא דאמר כל הני דחיין ידחו ליום הכניסה כו'. דכ"ע מיהת בין ר' בין ר' יוסי בין רבנן דפליגי עלייהו. מגילה בשבת לא קרינן לה. מ"ט אמר רבה הכל חייבין במקרא מגילה ואין הכל בקיאין בה כו'. כדאמרן היינו טעמא דשופר והיינו טעמא דמגילה. כולהו חדא גזירה היא שמא יעבירנה ד' אמות ברה"ר. ואסיקנא במס' סוכה מפני מה אין לולב דוחה שבת ביום טוב ראשון והלא מצותו מן התורה אפי' בגבולין. ואוקימנא משום דלא ידעינן בקביעא דירחא ומספק לא דחינן והיינו טעמא דמגילה והיינו טעמא דשופר. רב יוסף אומר מפני שעיניהן של עניים נשואות למקרא מגילה. וכיון שקורין ליום הכניסה כך גובין ומחלקין מעות של פורים ביום הכניסה. אבל

שמחה

*) נראה דחסר וצ"ל א"ר חלבו א"ר הונא פורים שחל בשבת כל הנדחה ידחה ליום הכניסה ור' היא וכו'.

[לעיל ב: לקמן ה.]

[לקמן יט.]

הגהות הב"ח

(א) רש"י ד"ה סידרא וכו' חל להיות בשבת כפרים מקדימין ליום הכניסה הרי י"ב:

גליון הש"ס

תוס' ד"ה ויעבירנה כו' עד שיבדיל. עי' שבת דף קנ ע"ב: **בא"ד** שאינה אלא כו' עי' שבת דף קיד ע"ב תוס' ד"ה ואמאי ליתקע:

[תוספתא פ"א]

[לעיל ב.]

[תוספתא פ"א]

[לקמן ה.]

פסחים סט. סוכה מב: ר"ה כט: [ביצה יז:]

שִׂמְחָה. שֶׁל מַאֲכָל וּמִשְׁתֶּה: בִּזְמַנָּהּ. בְּי"ד, מִתּוֹךְ שֶׁהִיא חוֹבָה בּוֹ בַּיּוֹם עַל כָּל יָחִיד וְיָחִיד – קוֹרִין אוֹתָהּ אֲפִילּוּ בְּיָחִיד, דְּהַכֹּל קוֹרִין בּוֹ, וְאִיכָּא פִּרְסוּם נֵס: שֶׁלֹּא בִּזְמַנָּהּ. כְּגוֹן כְּפָרִים הַמַּקְדִּימִין לְיוֹם הַכְּנִיסָה – אֵין קוֹרִין אוֹתָהּ אֶלָּא בַּעֲשָׂרָה, דְּבָעֵינַן פִּרְסוּם נִיסָּא: וְרַב אַסִּי אָמַר בֵּין בִּזְמַנָּהּ בֵּין שֶׁלֹּא בִּזְמַנָּהּ. מִצְוָה לְחַזֵּר אַחַר עֲשָׂרָה, מִשּׁוּם פִּרְסוּמֵי נִיסָּא. אֲבָל אִי לָא אַשְׁכַּח עֲשָׂרָה – לָא אָמַר רַב אַסִּי דְּלָא לִיקְרֵי, שֶׁאֵין אִיסּוּר קְרִיאָתָהּ בְּיָחִיד, אֶלָּא מִצְוָה לְקָרוֹתָהּ בַּעֲשָׂרָה: וְחָשׁ לֵיהּ רַב לְהָא דְּרַב אַסִּי. וְחָזַר עַל עֲשָׂרָה וְקִיבְּלָן: עֶרֶב שַׁבָּת זְמַנָּם הוּא. מַשְׁמַע שֶׁהוּא זְמַן הַקָּבוּעַ לְהוּ מִימֵי אַנְשֵׁי כְּנֶסֶת הַגְּדוֹלָה, מִדְּלָא קָאָמַר מַקְדִּימִין לְעֶרֶב שַׁבָּת. לְהָכִי קָשֶׁה לֵיהּ: וְהָא שַׁבָּת זְמַנָּם הוּא, שֶׁהֲרֵי י"ד הוּקְבַּע לַפְּרָזִים. אֶלָּא לְהָכִי נְקַט הַאי לִישָּׁנָא, דְּתִשְׁמַע מִינָּהּ: הוֹאִיל וְתִיקְּנוּ לָהֶן חַכְמֵי יִשְׂרָאֵל שֶׁאַחַר כְּנֶסֶת הַגְּדוֹלָה לְהַקְדִּים מִשּׁוּם דַּרְבָּה – הֲרֵי הוּא לָנוּ כַּיּוֹם וּזְמַן הַקָּבוּעַ מִתְּחִלָּה לְכָל דְּבָרָיו, וְאַף עַל פִּי שֶׁהוּא שֶׁלֹּא בִּזְמַנָּן – הָוֵי כִּזְמַנָּן: מתני' בְּאֵלּוּ אָמְרוּ. בִּזְמַנִּים שֶׁל מְגִילָּה אָמְרוּ מַקְדִּימִין אִם חָל י"ד בְּשַׁבָּת: אֲבָל זְמַן עֲצֵי כֹהֲנִים וְהָעָם. הָאָמוּר בְּמַסֶּ' תַּעֲנִית (דף כח.), שֶׁהָיוּ מִשְׁפָּחוֹת שֶׁל יִשְׂרָאֵל שֶׁקָּבוּעַ לָהֶם יָמִים בְּכָל שָׁנָה לְהָבִיא עֵצִים לַמִּקְדָּשׁ לְצוֹרֶךְ הַמַּעֲרָכָה, וּמְבִיאִין קָרְבָּן עֵצִים עִמָּהֶן. אִם חָל לִהְיוֹת בְּשַׁבָּת – מְאַחֲרִין לְיוֹם מָחָר. וְכֵן תִּשְׁעָה בְּאָב שֶׁחָל לִהְיוֹת בְּשַׁבָּת, וְהוּא הַדִּין לְי"ז בְּתַמּוּז וְלַעֲשָׂרָה בְּטֵבֵת. וְהַאי דְּנָקַט תִּשְׁעָה בְּאָב – מִשּׁוּם דְּהוּכְפְּלוּ בּוֹ צָרוֹת וְהַכֹּל מִתְעַנִּין בּוֹ. אֲבָל שְׁאָר צוֹמוֹת, אָמְרִינַן בְּמַסֶּכֶת רֹאשׁ הַשָּׁנָה (דף יח:): רָצוּ – מִתְעַנִּין, רָצוּ – אֵין מִתְעַנִּין: וַחֲגִיגָה. אִם חָל יוֹם טוֹב בְּשַׁבָּת – דּוֹחִין שַׁלְמֵי חֲגִיגָה לְמָחָר, שֶׁהֲרֵי יֵשׁ לָהּ תַּשְׁלוּמִין כָּל שִׁבְעָה. וְכֵן "הַקְהֵל אֶת הָעָם" שֶׁהָיָה בְּשָׁנָה רִאשׁוֹנָה שֶׁל שְׁמִטָּה בְּמוֹצָאֵי יוֹם טוֹב *הָאַחֲרוֹן שֶׁל חָג, כִּדְכְתִיב "מִקֵּץ שֶׁבַע שָׁנִים בְּמוֹעֵד שְׁנַת הַשְּׁמִטָּה" (דברים לא) כִּדְאָמְרִינַן בְּמַסֶּכֶת סוֹטָה (דף מא.), שֶׁהָיָה הַמֶּלֶךְ קוֹרֵא בַּתּוֹרָה סֵפֶר מִשְׁנֵה תוֹרָה, וְכָל הָעָם חַיָּיבִין לָבוֹא וּלְהָבִיא אֶת טַפָּם, כִּדְכְתִיב "הַקְהֵל אֶת הָעָם הָאֲנָשִׁים וְהַנָּשִׁים וְהַטַּף". וּבְשַׁבָּת אִי אֶפְשָׁר, וּמַעֲבִירִין אוֹתוֹ לְמָחָר. וּבַגְּמָרָא יְרוּשַׁלְמִי מְפָרֵשׁ דְּהָא דְּלָא עָבְדִינַן לֵיהּ בְּשַׁבָּת – מִפְּנֵי הַבִּימָה, כִּדְתְנַן: בִּימָה שֶׁל עֵץ הָיוּ עוֹשִׂין לַמֶּלֶךְ בָּעֲזָרָה וְיוֹשֵׁב עָלֶיהָ. וּפָרְכִינַן הָתָם: וְלִיעַבְדָהּ מֵאֶתְמוֹל! וּמְשַׁנֵּי: דְּחִיקָא לֵיהּ עֲזָרָה: וְלֹא מַקְדִּימִין. טַעְמָא מְפָרֵשׁ בַּגְּמָרָא: גמ' עֲשָׂרָה בַּטְלָנִין. שֶׁבְּבֵית הַכְּנֶסֶת, שֶׁהֵן בְּטֵלִים מִמְּלַאכְתָּן וְנִיזּוֹנִים מִשֶּׁל צִבּוּר כְּדֵי לִהְיוֹת מְצוּיִין בַּתְּפִלָּה בְּבֵית הַכְּנֶסֶת. דְּאָמַר מַר בְּמַסֶּכֶת בְּרָכוֹת (דף ו:): כֵּיוָן שֶׁבָּא הקב"ה בְּבֵית הַכְּנֶסֶת וְאֵינוֹ מוֹצֵא שָׁם עֲשָׂרָה וכו': מִנַּיִן שֶׁאֵין מוֹנִין יָמִים לְשָׁנִים. כְּגוֹן דְּאָמַר: קוֹנָם יַיִן שֶׁאֲנִי טוֹעֵם לְשָׁנָה – מוֹנֶה י"ב חֹדֶשׁ מִיּוֹם לְיוֹם. וְאִם נָדַר בְּאֶחָד בְּנִיסָן – אָסוּר עַד אֶחָד בְּנִיסָן הַבָּא, אַע"פ שֶׁעֲדַיִין יֵשׁ י"א יוֹם שֶׁיְּמוֹת הַחַמָּה יְתֵירִין עַל יְמוֹת הַלְּבָנָה, אוֹ פְּעָמִים שֶׁהָיוּ עוֹשִׂין חֳדָשִׁים חֲסֵרִין: שָׁעוֹת לַחֳדָשִׁים. כְּגוֹן הָאוֹמֵר: זֶה גִּיטֵּךְ אִם לֹא בָּאתִי מִכָּאן עַד חֹדֶשׁ זֶה, וְהָיָה חֹדֶשׁ חָסֵר, וּבָא מִשֶּׁחֲשֵׁיכָה לְיוֹם כ"ט – אֵין אוֹמְרִים עֲדַיִין הוּא בְּתוֹךְ הַחֹדֶשׁ, שֶׁהֲרֵי חֶדְשָׁהּ שֶׁל לְבָנָה כ"ט יוֹם וּמֶחֱצָה: אַכַּתִּי לָא מְטָא זְמַן חִיּוּבַיְיהוּ. וְאִם יַקְדִּימוּהָ לֹא יֵצְאוּ יְדֵי חוֹבָתָן. וְכֵן עֲצֵי כֹהֲנִים שֶׁקָּבוּעַ לָהֶן זְמַן קָבוּעַ בִּנְדָרִים: בִּשְׁלָמָא חֲגִיגָה. דְּקָתָנֵי מְאַחֲרִים אִי אִיקְלַע בְּשַׁבָּת: אֲפִילּוּ בְּיוֹם טוֹב דִּזְמַן חֲגִיגָה הוּא. שֶׁמּוּתָּר לְהַקְרִיב שַׁלְמֵי חֲגִיגָה, וַאֲפִילּוּ הָכִי מְאַחֲרִין עוֹלַת רְאִיָּיה עַד חוּלּוֹ שֶׁל מוֹעֵד. וְהָכִי מַשְׁמַע לִישָּׁנָא דִּבְרַיְיתָא: חֲגִיגָה מְאַחֲרִין, וְעוֹד יֵשׁ דָּבָר אַחֵר שֶׁהִגִּיעַ זְמַנּוֹ מְאַחֲרִין אוֹתוֹ יוֹם אַף שֶׁהוּא זְמַן חֲגִיגָה, וְאֵיזוֹ זוֹ – עוֹלַת רְאִיָּיה, שֶׁהִיא חוֹבַת רֶגֶל, כִּדְכְתִיב "לֹא יֵרָאוּ פָנַי רֵיקָם" (שמות כג), וְאָמְרִינַן בְּמַסֶּכֶת חֲגִיגָה (דף ז.): "לֹא יֵרָאוּ פָנַי רֵיקָם" – בְּעוֹלוֹת וּזְבָחִים. וְאַף"ה בְּיוֹ"ט לֹא קְרֵבָה. וּב"ש הִיא, דְּאָמְרִי: אֵין מַקְרִיבִין בְּיוֹ"ט עוֹלָה הַיְכוֹלָה לָבֹא לְמָחָר, וַאֲפִילּוּ הִיא חוֹבַת הָרֶגֶל: מְבִיאִין שְׁלָמִים בְּיוֹ"ט. שֶׁהֵן מַאֲכַל אָדָם בְּיוֹ"ט, וּכְתִיב "אַךְ אֲשֶׁר יֵאָכֵל לְכָל נֶפֶשׁ" (שמות יב): וְאֵין סוֹמְכִין עֲלֵיהֶן. שֶׁהַסְּמִיכָה שְׁבוּת הִיא, דִּתְנַן (ביצה דף לו:), אֵלּוּ הֵן מִשּׁוּם שְׁבוּת: לֹא רוֹכְבִין עַל גַּבֵּי בְהֵמָה. וְעַל אֵלּוּ שֶׁיַּקְרִיבוּ בְּיוֹ"ט יִסְמְכוּ מֵאֶתְמוֹל, דְּלֵית לְהוּ לְבֵית שַׁמַּאי תֵּכֶף לִסְמִיכָה שְׁחִיטָה: אֲבָל לֹא עוֹלוֹת. אֵין מְבִיאִין, דִּסְבָרֵי "לָכֶם" – וְלֹא לַגָּבוֹהַּ: וּבֵית הִלֵּל אוֹמְרִים מְבִיאִין שְׁלָמִים וְעוֹלוֹת. וּמָה אֲנִי מְקַיֵּים "לָכֶם" – לָכֶם וְלֹא לְנָכְרִים: כָּל זְמַן חֲגִיגָה. כָּל הָרֶגֶל, עַד יוֹ"ט הָאַחֲרוֹן רַשַּׁאי לְשַׁהוֹתָהּ: רַב אַשִׁי אָמַר חֲגִיגָה כָּל זְמַן שֶׁנֶּאֶמְרָה בּוֹ חֲגִיגָה מְאַחֲרִין. אִם בָּאָה בְּשַׁבָּת. וַאֲפִילּוּ עֲצֶרֶת שֶׁאֵינָהּ אֶלָּא יוֹם אֶחָד – תַּשְׁלוּמִין יֵשׁ לָהּ כָּל שִׁבְעָה, וַעֲדַיִין יֵשׁ לָהּ זְמַן לִיקָּרֵב: וּמוֹדִין בַּעֲצֶרֶת שֶׁחָל לִהְיוֹת בְּשַׁבָּת. בְּמַסֶּכֶת חֲגִיגָה (דף יז.) נֶחְלְקוּ בַּעֲצֶרֶת שֶׁחָל לִהְיוֹת בְּעֶרֶב שַׁבָּת, בֵּית שַׁמַּאי אוֹמְרִים: יוֹם טְבוֹחַ שֶׁל עֲצֶרֶת אַחַר הַשַּׁבָּת. וּבֵית שַׁמַּאי לְטַעְמַיְיהוּ, דְּאָמְרִי: עוֹלוֹת אֵין מַקְרִיבִין בְּיוֹם טוֹב, הִלְכָּךְ לֹא יַקְרִיבוּ עַד לְאַחַר שַׁבָּת. וּבֵית הִלֵּל אוֹמְרִים: אֵין לָהּ יוֹם טְבוֹחַ, אֵין צָרִיךְ לְהַמְתִּין לְיוֹם טְבוֹחַ, שֶׁהַשְּׁלָמִים [וְעוֹלוֹת] קְרֵבִין בְּיוֹ"ט. וּמוֹדִין בַּעֲצֶרֶת שֶׁחָל לִהְיוֹת בְּשַׁבָּת שֶׁאֵין עוֹלַת רְאִיָּיה וְשַׁלְמֵי חֲגִיגָה קְרֵבִין בְּשַׁבָּת, וּמַמְתִּין לְיוֹם טְבוֹחַ שֶׁל קָרְבָּנוֹת הַיּוֹם לְאַחַר הַשַּׁבָּת, אַלְמָא: יֵשׁ תַּשְׁלוּמִין לַעֲצֶרֶת: בִּקְרוֹנָהּ

תורה אור

שִׂמְחָה אֵינָהּ נוֹהֶגֶת אֶלָּא בִּזְמַנָּהּ. אָמַר רַב: [א]מְגִילָּה, בִּזְמַנָּהּ — קוֹרִין אוֹתָהּ אפי' בְּיָחִיד, שֶׁלֹּא בִּזְמַנָּהּ — בַּעֲשָׂרָה. רַב אַסִּי אָמַר: בֵּין בִּזְמַנָּהּ בֵּין שֶׁלֹּא בִּזְמַנָּהּ בַּעֲשָׂרָה. *הֲוָה עוֹבָדָא וְחָשׁ לֵיהּ רַב לְהָא דְּרַב אַסִּי. וּמִי אָמַר רַב הָכִי? וְהָאָמַר רַב יְהוּדָה בְּרֵיהּ דְּרַב שְׁמוּאֵל בַּר שֵׁילַת מִשְּׁמֵיהּ דְּרַב: פּוּרִים שֶׁחָל לִהְיוֹת בַּשַּׁבָּת — עֶרֶב שַׁבָּת זְמַנָּם. עֶרֶב שַׁבָּת זְמַנָּם?! וְהָא שַׁבָּת זְמַנָּם הוּא! אֶלָּא לָאו הָכִי קָאָמַר: שֶׁלֹּא בִּזְמַנָּם — כִּזְמַנָּם, מַה זְמַנָּם אֲפִילּוּ בְּיָחִיד, אַף שֶׁלֹּא בִּזְמַנָּם — אֲפִילּוּ בְּיָחִיד! לֹא, לְעִנְיַן מִקְרָא מְגִילָּה בַּעֲשָׂרָה. אֶלָּא, מַאי עֶרֶב שַׁבָּת זְמַנָּם? לְאַפּוֹקֵי מִדְּרַבִּי, דְּאָמַר *הוֹאִיל וְנִדְחוּ עֲיָירוֹת מִמְּקוֹמָן יִדָּחוּ לְיוֹם הַכְּנִיסָה.(א) הָא קמ"ל דְּעֶרֶב שַׁבָּת זְמַנָּם הוּא.§

מתני' *[ב]אֵי זוֹ הִיא עִיר גְּדוֹלָה? כָּל שֶׁיֵּשׁ בָּהּ עֲשָׂרָה בַּטְלָנִין. פָּחוֹת מִכָּאן — הֲרֵי זֶה כְּפָר. בְּאֵלּוּ אָמְרוּ מַקְדִּימִין וְלֹא מְאַחֲרִין. אֲבָל זְמַן עֲצֵי כֹהֲנִים,(ב) וְתִשְׁעָה בְּאָב, חֲגִיגָה, וְהַקְהֵל — מְאַחֲרִין וְלֹא מַקְדִּימִין. [ג]אע"פ[א] שֶׁאָמְרוּ מַקְדִּימִין[א] וְלֹא מְאַחֲרִין — מוּתָּרִין בְּהֶסְפֵּד וּבְתַעֲנִית, וּמַתָּנוֹת לָאֶבְיוֹנִים.[ב] א"ר יְהוּדָה: [ד]אֵימָתַי — מָקוֹם שֶׁנִּכְנָסִין בַּשֵּׁנִי וּבַחֲמִישִׁי, אֲבָל מָקוֹם שֶׁאֵין נִכְנָסִין לֹא בַּשֵּׁנִי וְלֹא בַּחֲמִישִׁי — אֵין קוֹרִין אוֹתָהּ אֶלָּא בִּזְמַנָּהּ.§

גמ' תָּנָא: עֲשָׂרָה בַּטְלָנִין שֶׁבְּבֵית הַכְּנֶסֶת.§ "בְּאֵלּוּ אָמְרוּ מַקְדִּימִין וְלֹא מְאַחֲרִין".§ מ"ט? אָמַר רַבִּי אַבָּא אָמַר שְׁמוּאֵל: אָמַר קְרָא: "וְלֹא יַעֲבוֹר". וְאָמַר רַבִּי אַבָּא אָמַר שְׁמוּאֵל:[ג] [ה]מִנַּיִן שֶׁאֵין מוֹנִין יָמִים לְשָׁנִים? שנא' °"לְחָדְשֵׁי הַשָּׁנָה" (שמות יב) — חֳדָשִׁים אַתָּה מוֹנֶה לְשָׁנִים, וְאִי אַתָּה מוֹנֶה יָמִים לְשָׁנִים. וְרַבָּנַן[ד] דְּקֵיסָרִי מִשּׁוּם ר' אַבָּא אָמְרוּ: מִנַּיִן שֶׁאֵין מְחַשְּׁבִין שָׁעוֹת לַחֳדָשִׁים? שֶׁנֶּא' °"עַד חֹדֶשׁ יָמִים" (במדבר יא) — יָמִים אַתָּה מְחַשֵּׁב לַחֳדָשִׁים, וְאִי אַתָּה מְחַשֵּׁב שָׁעוֹת לַחֳדָשִׁים.§ "אֲבָל זְמַן עֲצֵי כֹהֲנִים וְתִשְׁעָה בְּאָב וַחֲגִיגָה וְהַקְהֵל מְאַחֲרִין וְלֹא מַקְדִּימִין".§ [ו]תִּשְׁעָה בְּאָב — אַקְדּוּמֵי פּוּרְעָנוּת לָא מַקְדְּמִי. [ז]חֲגִיגָה [ח]וְהַקְהֵל — מִשּׁוּם דְּאַכַּתִּי לָא מְטָא זְמַן חִיּוּבַיְיהוּ. תָּנָא: חֲגִיגָה וְכָל זְמַן חֲגִיגָה מְאַחֲרִין. בִּשְׁלָמָא חֲגִיגָה, דְּאִי מִיקְלַע בְּשַׁבְּתָא — מְאַחֲרִינַן לָהּ לְבָתַר שַׁבְּתָא. אֶלָּא זְמַן חֲגִיגָה מַאי הִיא? אָמַר רַב אוֹשַׁעְיָא, הָכִי קָאָמַר: חֲגִיגָה בַּשַּׁבָּת, וְעוֹלַת רְאִיָּיה אֲפִילּוּ בְּיוֹ"ט דִּזְמַן חֲגִיגָה — מְאַחֲרִין. מַנִּי? ב"ש הִיא, דִּתְנַן: [*ב"ש אוֹמְרִים:] מְבִיאִין שְׁלָמִים בְּיוֹ"ט וְאֵין סוֹמְכִין עֲלֵיהֶן, אֲבָל לֹא עוֹלוֹת. וּב"ה אוֹמְרִים: [ט]מְבִיאִין שְׁלָמִים וְעוֹלוֹת, וְסוֹמְכִין עֲלֵיהֶן. רָבָא אָמַר: חֲגִיגָה, כָּל זְמַן חֲגִיגָה מְאַחֲרִין, טְפֵי — לָא. דִּתְנַן: *מִי [י]שֶׁלֹּא חָג בְּיוֹ"ט הָרִאשׁוֹן שֶׁל חָג — חוֹגֵג וְהוֹלֵךְ אֶת כָּל הָרֶגֶל כּוּלּוֹ וְיוֹם טוֹב הָאַחֲרוֹן שֶׁל חָג. [כ]עָבַר הָרֶגֶל וְלֹא חָג — אֵינוֹ חַיָּיב בְּאַחֲרָיוּתוֹ. רַב אַשִׁי אָמַר: חֲגִיגָה וְכָל זְמַן חֲגִיגָה מְאַחֲרִין — [ל]וַאֲפִי' עֲצֶרֶת דְּחַד יוֹמָא מְאַחֲרִין. דִּתְנַן: מוֹדִים, שֶׁאִם חָל *עֲצֶרֶת לִהְיוֹת בְּשַׁבָּת שֶׁיּוֹם טְבוֹחַ אַחַר הַשַּׁבָּת. אָמַר רַבִּי אֶלְעָזָר אָמַר רַבִּי חֲנִינָא: רַבִּי נָטַע נְטִיעָה בְּפוּרִים, וְרָחַץ

א) תענית יח. ב) [לעיל ב: ז:] ג) [נזיר ז. ע"ש] ד) [שם]

הוה עובדא ליה רב להא דרב אסי. מכל מקום הלכתא כוותיה דרב, דהא ר' יוחנן(ג) איתא כוותיה פרק שני (דף יט:), דקאמר: הקורא במגילה הכתובה בין הכתובים (*יצא). ומסיק: הא ביחיד הא בצבור. אלמא שקורין אותה ביחיד, וכן הלכה, דרב ור' יוחנן הלכה כרבי יוחנן, וכ"ש הכא דקיימו בחד שיטתא. ועוד, דרב אסי תלמיד דרב הוה, *ורבינו יוסף איש ירושלים פסק דאף ביחיד צריך לברך, וכן נמצא בתשובת רש"י, שהשיב: נראה בעיני דלא שנא יחיד ולא שנא צבור, אחד מברך ואחרים שומעין, וכן נראה לומר מאחר שהוכחנו קריאתה ביחיד. *אי איתא שאין בה ברכה [ביחיד] – הוה ליה לפרושי (לקמן כא:) ומאי(ד) מברך דאמר בצבור:

עולת ראייה אפי' בי"ט מאחרין. הקשה הר"ר אלחנן, מהא דאמרינן פרק קמא דביצה (דף יב. ושם): השוחט עולת נדבה בי"ט לוקה. ומסיק: דאמר לך מני בית שמאי היא וכו'. וקשה: אמאי לא תני עולת ראייה, דהוי רבותא טפי, דאף על גב דהוי צורך י"ט – לוקה אליבא דב"ש? ואין לומר דלהכי נקט עולת נדבה לאשמועינן דאפילו הכי שרו בית הלל – זה אינו, דהא בפרק שני דהתם (דף יט. ושם) מוכח בהדיא דלא נחלקו ב"ה על(ה) עולה [שאינה] של י"ט, דודאי אינה קריבה בי"ט. ואם כן קשה, אמאי נקט עולת נדבה? וי"ל: דלהכי נקט עולת נדבה, למידק: הא שלמי נדבה – אינו לוקה, כיון דאיכא בהו צורך אוכל נפש, אבל איסורא מיהא איכא משום דכתיב "לכם":

כה א מיי' פ"א מהל' מגילה הלכה ז סמג עשין ד טוש"ע א"ח סי' תרצ סעיף יח:
כו ב מיי' שם הלכה ח סמג עשין ד:
כז ג מיי' שם פ"ב הלכה יג:
[ועי' בתוס' קדושין מה: ד"ה הוה]
כח ד מיי' שם פ"א הלכה ח:
כט ה מיי' פ"א מהל' קידוש החודש הל' ב (ופ"י מהלכות נדרים טוש"ע י"ד סי' רכ סעיף ד ה ו ז):
ל ו מיי' פ"ה מהלכות תענית הלכה ה סמג עשין ג טוש"ע א"ח סי' תקנ סעיף ג וסי' תקנב סעיף י:
לא ז מיי' פ"א מהלכות חגיגה הלכה ח:
לב ח [מיי'] שם פ"ג הל' ז:
לג ט מיי' שם פ"א הלכה ח ט:
לד י מיי' שם הלכה ד:
לה כ מיי' שם הל' ו:
לו ל מיי' שם הל' ז:

רבינו חננאל

שמחה שהיא סעודת פורים לא תהא אלא בזמנה שהוא יום י"ד באדר: אמר רב מגילה בזמנה כלומר בי"ד קורין אותה אפי' ביחיד שלא בזמנה כגון י"א י"ב י"ג שמקדימין ליום הכניסה אין קורין אותה אלא בעשרה וקי"ל כרב. דהא ר' יוחנן אמר בפירוש בפירקין דלקמן (דף יט.) הקורא במגילה הכתובה בין הכתובים לא יצא. ולא אמרו אלא בצבור. לאו מכלל דסבירא ליה שקורין אותה ביחיד. רב אסי אמר אפילו בזמנה בעשרה. הוה עובדא וחש לה רב ולא קראה בזמנה אלא בעשרה כרב אסי. ואקשינן ומי אמר רב שלא בזמנה קורין אותה בעשרה כלומר הקורין אותה ביום הכניסה כגון הכפרים וכיוצא בהן אין קורין אותה אלא בעשרה והאמר [רב יהודה בריה דרב שמואל בר שילת] משמיה דרב פורים שחל להיות בשבת ע"ש זמנם. ע"ש זמנם והא שבת זמנם. ופרקינן הכי קאמר ע"ש שהוא שלא בזמנו של קריאת המגילה קורין אותה כבזמנו מה זמנו אפי' ביחיד כך שלא בזמנו אפי' ביחיד. ודחינן לא לענין מקרא מגילה בעשרה. ושלא בזמנה היא ואלא מאי ע"ש זמנם. כלומר שקורין בע"ש המגילה כאילו זמנם הוא. ולאפוקי מדרבי דאמר כל הנדחין ידחו ליום הכניסה קאמר דע"ש זמנם ואע"ג דחש לה רב להא דרב אסי קי"ל כרב דאמר אפי' ביחיד: מתני' איזוהי עיר גדולה כו'. תנא עשרה בטלנים בכנסת. פחות מיכן הרי זה כפר: ירושלמי י' בטלנים בכנסת ממלאכתן *) א"ר כגון אנו שאנו צריכין תלמוד א"י רבי בא בש"ר יהודה כל שאמרו חכמים ידחה ממקומו ויקרא ובלבד בעשרה. ואנן חמין רבנן קורין אפי' ביחיד. הלכך קורין השתא אפי' ביחידי. ועוד הא"ר בא אנן חמון רבנן קורין אפי' ביחיד וקי"ל מעשה רב. מר רב צמח זצ"ל כתב בש"צ הקורא את המגילה שקורא וכורך כס"ת ורבינו האי זצו"ל אמר מנהגא דחזנן קורא ופושט כאגרת אבל קורא וכורך כס"ת לא חזו לנא לתלמודינו הכי. כפר שאין בו י' תקנתו קלקלתו ונעשה כעיר. באלו אמרו מקדימין קריאת מגילה ותרומת שקלים דכתיב ולא יעבור אבל סעודת פורים וסעודת ר"ח וספק מילה חמן עצי כהנים חגיגה וט' באב והקהל מאחרין ולא מקדימין. מנין שאין מונין ימים לשנים שנאמר לחדשי השנה חדשים אתה מונה לשנה ולא ימים וכן אין מונין שעות לחדש אלא ימים שנאמר עד חדש ימים. אבל זמן עצי הכהנים ט' באב חגיגה והקהל [מאחרין] אותם אחר שבת מ"ט ט' באב לא מקדימין פורענותא הוא חגיגה והקהל אכתי לא מטא זמן חיוביהו. תנא חגיגה כל זמן חגיגה מאחרין ואוקמה רב הושעי' הכי אי איקלע יו"ט בשבת דוחין את החגיגה שהיא שלמים באחד בשבת אבל אי איקלע בחול אע"ג דמביאין חגיגה שהוא זמן חגיגה כלומר לשחוט ולאכול חגיגה בלבד וכל כיוצא בה שנאכלים הוא מותר אבל עולת ראיה דוחין אותה למחר וזו ששנינו בתוספתא ב"ש היא דתנן ב"ש אומרים מביאין שלמים וסומכין עליהן אבל לא עולות כו'. רבא אמר כך פירושה

*) בירושלמי לפנינו איתא כגון אנו שאין אנו צריכין לתלמודינו וע"ש במפרש ואולי דגי' רבינו שאנו צריכין עוסק ודו"ק.

קדושין מה: סנהדרין כט:
[לעיל ד:]
[לעיל ג:]
ס"א הראשון ועיין ברי"ף
ביצה יט. חגיגה ז: יז: ר"ה ד:
חגיגה ט. יז. ביצה כ. ר"ה ד: [יומא ג.]
חגיגה יז.

הגהות הב"ח

(א) גמ' ידחו ליום הכניסה קמ"ל כצ"ל ותיבת הא נמחק: (ב) שם במשנה זמן עצי כהנים והעם ותשעה באב: (ג) תוס' ד"ה הוה וכו' רבי יוחנן אית ליה כוותיה בפרק שני: (ד) בא"ד הוה ליה לפרושי שאין מברך אלא בצבור: (ה) ד"ה עולות וכו' דלא נחלקו ב"ה על עולת נדבה של י"ט:

הגהות הגר"א

[א] במשנה (ולא מאחרין) תא"מ:

גליון הש"ס

גמ' הוה עובדא וחש ליה רב. עי' ר"ה דף כז ע"ב תוס' ד"ה ושמע:

ורחץ בקרונה של צפורי. לאו דוקא בקרונה, אלא כלומר בפרהסיא. ואם תאמר: מאי איריא לרחוץ? אפי׳ לאכול נמי מותר, כדתניא בר"ה (דף יח:): אין צרה ואין שלום, רצו — מתענין, לא רצו — אין מתענין וי"ל: דכיון דקבלוהו כבר אבותינו על עצמם, מסתמא גם הם קבלוהו:

בקרונה של צפורי. ביום השוק, בפרהסיא, בשעת הילוך קרונות: ולא הודו לו. מתשעה באב: אמר לפניו. [לפני] רבי אלעזר: לא כך היה. לא ביקש לעקור לגמרי, אלא אותה שנה בלבד: טובים השנים. אילו לא שמעתי(ב) הייתי טועה בדבר, עכשיו טוב לי שלימדתני האמת: בר ארביסר הוה. לא היתה (ג)מן המוקפין: וטבריא מוקפת חומה מימות יהושע. לקמן ילפינן מקרא: וכי פשיטא ליה. שהיה מבני חמיסר, מי שרי בארביסר במלאכה: לא נצרכא. במגילת תענית, שהרי כבר כתובין במגילת אסתר שאסור בהספד ותענית, אלא לאסור כו׳: שדי כיתנא. זורע פשתן: בר יומיה הוה. שקראו בו בני עירו: אפילו תימא בר יומיה הוה גרסי׳. רבי שנטע נטיעה — ביום שקראו בו נטע, ודקא קשיא לך יום טוב שאסור בעשיית מלאכה — ההוא קרא דכתיב "שמחה ומשתה ויום טוב" כתיב מעיקרא, קודם קבלה. אבל בשעת קבלה — לא קיבלו עליהן אלא שמחה ומשתה, לאוסרן בהספד ותענית, אבל י"ט לא קיבלו עליהן: ובאתריה דרבי לא נהוג גרסינן. במקומו של רבי לא נהגו איסור בדבר: נטיעה של שמחה. דכיון דפורים יום שמחה הוא — מותר לנטוע נטיעה של שמחה: כדתנן עברו אלו. י"ג תעניות שב"ד מתענין על הגשמים: ולא נענו. מן השמים: ממעטין. בנטיעה ובבנין: ותנא(ד) נטיעה נטיעה של שמחה. בנין האמור כאן שאסורין בבנין של שמחה, שנוהגין עצמן כנזופין וכאבלים: ונטיעה. האמורה כאן — נטיעה של שמחה, כגון אבורנקי — אילן שצילו נאה, כגון אילן שכופפין אותו על גבי כלונסות ויתידות, והמלכים אוכלין תחתיו בימות החמה ומתעדנין בה במיני שמחות. ובנין בית חתנות לבנו — כשמשיא אשה לבנו הראשון היה בונה לו בית, ועושה לו חופה בתוכו, אלמא: איכא נטיעה של שמחה: וערי מבצר הצדים וגו׳. בספר יהושע (יט) בנחלת נפתלי, וקיימא לן לקמן דרקת זו טבריא, וקרי ליה "ערי מבצר", אלמא: מוקפת חומה הואי: דחד גיסא שורא דימא הויא. אין לה חומה מצד אחד, אלא הים חומתה, ומספקא ליה אי חשיב היקף אי לא: חומה ולא שור איגר. בבתי ערי חומה כתיב "עיר חומה" ולא עיר שאין לה חומה בפני עצמה, אלא מוקפת בתים סמוכות זו לזו, וחומות חיצונות של בתים נעשות חומה לעיר. והיינו שור איגר — שגגותיה חומותיה. גג מתרגמינן איגר: סביב. לגבי בתי החצרים כתיב "אשר אין להם חומה סביב", מכלל דבתי ערי חומה מסובבת(ה) סביב קאמר׳: פרט לטבריא שימה חומתה. שהים שלה היא חומתה מצד האחד: כי מספקא ליה לענין מקרא מגילה. דלא מפורש בה חומה, אלא לשון פרזים ושאינן פרזים כתיב בה. ומספקא ליה האי לשון פרזים אי לשון גלוי הוא, או לשון עיר הנוחה ליכבש: כד הוינא טליא. כשהייתי נער: ואישתכח

תורה אור

וְרָחַץ *בְּקְרוֹנָהּ שֶׁל צִפּוֹרִי בְּשִׁבְעָה עָשָׂר בְּתַמּוּז, וּבִקֵּשׁ לַעֲקוֹר תִּשְׁעָה בְּאָב, וְלֹא הוֹדוּ לוֹ. אָמַר לְפָנָיו רַבִּי אַבָּא בַּר זַבְדָּא: רַבִּי, לֹא כָּךְ הָיָה מַעֲשֶׂה. אֶלָּא: תִּשְׁעָה בְּאָב שֶׁחָל לִהְיוֹת בְּשַׁבָּת הֲוָה, וּדְחִינוּהוּ לְאַחַר הַשַּׁבָּת, וְאָמַר רַבִּי: הוֹאִיל וְנִדְחָה — יִדָּחֶה, וְלֹא הוֹדוּ חֲכָמִים. קָרֵי עֲלֵיהּ °"טוֹבִים הַשְּׁנַיִם מִן הָאֶחָד" [קהלת ד]. וְרַבִּי, הֵיכִי נָטַע נְטִיעָה בְּפוּרִים? וְהָתָנֵי רַב יוֹסֵף: "שִׂמְחָה וּמִשְׁתֶּה וְיוֹ"ט", "שִׂמְחָה" — *מְלַמֵּד שֶׁאֲסוּרִים בְּהֶסְפֵּד; "מִשְׁתֶּה" — מְלַמֵּד שֶׁאָסוּר בְּתַעֲנִית; "יוֹם טוֹב" — מְלַמֵּד שֶׁאָסוּר בַּעֲשִׂיַּית מְלָאכָה! אֶלָּא: רַבִּי בַּר אַרְבֵּיסַר הֲוָה, וְכִי נָטַע — בַּחֲמֵיסַר נָטַע. אִינִי? וְהָא רַבִּי בִּטְבֶרְיָא הֲוָה, וּטְבֶרְיָא מוּקֶּפֶת חוֹמָה מִימוֹת יְהוֹשֻׁעַ בִּן נוּן הֲוַאי! אֶלָּא: רַבִּי בַּר חֲמֵיסַר הֲוָה, וְכִי נָטַע — בְּאַרְבֵּיסַר הֲוָה. וּמִי פְּשִׁיטָא לֵיהּ דִּטְבֶרְיָא מוּקֶּפֶת חוֹמָה מִימוֹת יְהוֹשֻׁעַ בִּן נוּן? וְהָא חִזְקִיָּה קָרֵי בִּטְבֶרְיָא בְּאַרְבֵּיסַר וּבַחֲמֵיסַר, מְסַפְּקָא לֵיהּ אִי מוּקֶּפֶת חוֹמָה מִימוֹת יְהוֹשֻׁעַ בִּן נוּן הִיא אִי לָא! לְחִזְקִיָּה — מְסַפְּקָא לֵיהּ, לְרַבִּי — פְּשִׁיטָא לֵיהּ. וְכִי פְּשִׁיטָא לֵיהּ מִי שָׁרֵי? וְהָכְתִיב בִּמְגִילַּת תַּעֲנִית: "אֶת יוֹם אַרְבָּעָה עָשָׂר וְאֶת יוֹם חֲמִשָּׁה עָשָׂר יוֹמֵי פוּרַיָּא אִינּוּן, דְּלָא לְמִסְפַּד בְּהוֹן". וְאָמַר רָבָא: לֹא נִצְרְכָא אֶלָּא לֶאֱסוֹר אֶת שֶׁל זֶה בָּזֶה וְאֶת שֶׁל זֶה בָּזֶה! הָנֵי מִילֵּי — בְּהֶסְפֵּד וּבְתַעֲנִית, אֲבָל מְלָאכָה — יוֹם אֶחָד וְתוּ לָא. אִינִי? וְהָא רַב חַזְיֵיהּ לְהַהוּא גַּבְרָא דַּהֲוָה קָא שָׁדֵי כִּיתָּנָא בְּפוּרַיָּא, וְלַטְיֵיהּ וְלָא צְמַח כִּיתָּנֵיהּ! הָתָם בַּר יוֹמָא הֲוָה. רַבָּה בְּרֵיהּ דְּרָבָא אָמַר: אֲפִי׳ תֵּימָא (א) בְּיוֹמֵיהּ. הֶסְפֵּד וְתַעֲנִית — קַבִּילוּ עֲלַיְיהוּ, מְלָאכָה לָא קַבִּילוּ עֲלַיְיהוּ. דְּמֵעִיקָּרָא כְּתִיב: "שִׂמְחָה וּמִשְׁתֶּה וְיוֹם טוֹב", וּלְבַסּוֹף כְּתִיב: "לַעֲשׂוֹת אוֹתָם יְמֵי מִשְׁתֶּה וְשִׂמְחָה", וְאִילּוּ "יוֹם טוֹב" לָא כְּתִיב. וְאֶלָּא רַב, מ"ט לַטְיֵיהּ לְהַהוּא גַּבְרָא? *דְּבָרִים הַמּוּתָּרִין וַאֲחֵרִים נָהֲגוּ בָּהֶן אִיסּוּר הֲוָה, וּבְאַתְרֵיהּ דְּרַבִּי לָא נְהוּג. וְאִיבָּעֵית אֵימָא: לְעוֹלָם נְהוּג, וְרַבִּי נְטִיעָה שֶׁל שִׂמְחָה נָטַע. כִּדְתְנַן: "עָבְרוּ אֵלּוּ וְלֹא נַעֲנוּ — מְמַעֲטִין בְּמַשָּׂא וּמַתָּן, בְּבִנְיָן וּבִנְטִיעָה, בְּאֵירוּסִין וּבְנִישּׂוּאִין. וְתָנָא עֲלָהּ: *בִּנְיָן — בִּנְיָן שֶׁל שִׂמְחָה; נְטִיעָה — נְטִיעָה שֶׁל שִׂמְחָה. אֵיזֶהוּ בִּנְיָן שֶׁל שִׂמְחָה — זֶה הַבּוֹנֶה בֵּית חֲתָנוּת לִבְנוֹ. אֵיזוֹ הִיא נְטִיעָה שֶׁל שִׂמְחָה — זֶה הַנּוֹטֵעַ אַבּוּרְנְקֵי שֶׁל מְלָכִים. גּוּפָא, חִזְקִיָּה קָרֵי בִּטְבֶרְיָא בְּאַרְבֵּיסַר וּבַחֲמֵיסַר, מְסַפְּקָא לֵיהּ אִי מוּקֶּפֶת חוֹמָה מִימוֹת יְהוֹשֻׁעַ בִּן נוּן הִיא אִי לָא. וּמִי מְסַפְּקָא לֵיהּ מִלְּתָא דִּטְבֶרְיָא? וְהָכְתִיב: °"וְעָרֵי מִבְצָר הַצִּדִּים צֵר וְחַמַּת רַקַּת וְכִנָּרֶת" [יהושע יט], וְקַיְימָא לַן *רַקַּת זוֹ טְבֶרְיָא! מִשּׁוּם דִּמְסַפְּקָא לֵיהּ: מִשּׁוּם דְּחַד גִּיסָא שׁוּרָא דְּיַמָּא הֲוַאת. אִי הָכִי, אַמַּאי מְסַפְּקָא לֵיהּ? וַדַּאי לָאו חוֹמָה הִיא! דְּתַנְיָא: *°"אֲשֶׁר לוֹ חוֹמָה" [ויקרא כה] — וְלֹא שׁוּר אִיגַּר; "סָבִיב" — פְּרָט לִטְבֶרְיָא שֶׁיָּמָּהּ חוֹמָתָהּ! לְעִנְיַן בָּתֵּי עָרֵי חוֹמָה לָא מְסַפְּקָא לֵיהּ; כִּי קָא מְסַפְּקָא לֵיהּ — לְעִנְיַן מִקְרָא מְגִילָּה: מַאי פְּרָזִים וּמַאי מוּקָּפִין דִּכְתִיבִי גַּבֵּי מִקְרָא מְגִילָּה? מִשּׁוּם דְּהָנֵי מִיגַּלּוּ, וְהָנֵי לָא מִיגַּלּוּ, וְהָא נַמִי מִיגַּלְיָא? אוֹ דִּלְמָא: מִשּׁוּם דְּהָנֵי מִיגְּנוּ וְהָנֵי לָא מִיגְּנוּ, וְהָא נַמִי מִיגְּנְיָא? מִשּׁוּם הָכִי מְסַפְּקָא לֵיהּ. רַב אַסִּי קָרֵי מְגִילָּה בְּהוּצָל בְּאַרְבֵּיסַר וּבַחֲמֵיסַר. מְסַפְּקָא לֵיהּ אִי מוּקֶּפֶת חוֹמָה מִימוֹת יְהוֹשֻׁעַ בִּן נוּן הִיא אִי לָא. אִיכָּא דְּאָמַר, אָמַר רַב אַסִּי: הַאי הוּצָל דְּבֵית בִּנְיָמִין מוּקֶּפֶת חוֹמָה מִימוֹת יְהוֹשֻׁעַ הִיא. אָמַר רַבִּי יוֹחָנָן: כִּי הֲוֵינָא טַלְיָא אָמֵינָא מִלְּתָא דְּשָׁאֵילְנָא לְסָבַיָּא, וְאִישְׁתַּכַּח

*) [ועי׳ תוס׳ יבמות מג. ד"ה מליסא]

ובקש לעקור תשעה באב ולא הודו לו. קשה: היכי סלקא דעתך דהאי תנא [דרבי] היה רוצה לעקור ט׳ באב לגמרי? והא אמרינן (תענית דף ל:): כל האוכל ושותה בתשעה באב אינו רואה בנחמה של ירושלים! ועוד: דהא אין בית דין יכול לבטל דברי בית דין חבירו אא"כ גדול הימנו בחכמה ובמנין! ויש לומר: דלא רצה לעוקרו *אלא מחומרא שיש בו יותר משאר תעניות. אי נמי: יש לומר דרצה לעקרו מתשיעי ולקבעו בעשירי, כדאמר ר׳ יוחנן (שם כט.): *אילו הואי התם קבעתיה בעשירי:

שאסורים בהספד. השיב רש"י וכי מי נתן כח לימי מגילת אסתר לדחות אבילות? *אי איתא דבהספד נאסר משום דכתיב "ימי משתה ושמחה": והא חזינן דכולי עלמא נהגו בו היתר. אלא ודאי לא הוי אלא לענין שאין נופלין על פניהם, דלא הוי יום צרה אלא יום שמחה: [נ"א ועוד אי]

והא רבי בטבריא הוה. נראה שהיה(ו) בימי אנטונינוס כשהיו יחד, כדאמר במס׳ ע"ז (דף י.) שרצה לשחרר בני טבריא ממס, לפי שהיו תלמידי חכמים, דקאמר: ליעביד טבריא קלניא:

דברים המותרים ואחרים נהגו בהן איסור. קשה: דהא רבי התיר בית שאן ע"י ר׳ מאיר שאכל שם עלה של ירק, בחולין (דף ו:)! וי"ל: דהתם לא נהגו איסור אלא בטעות, והכא איירי בדבר שנהגו בו איסורא במתכוין*:

ממעטין במשא ומתן. פי׳ של שמחה. דומיא דבנין ונטיעה דבסמוך(ז), אבל שאר בניינים — שרו, ואין לך משא ומתן גדול מזה*):

ממעטין. רוצה לומר שלא יהו ששים כלל — °ומיירי מתשעה באב שמארסין בו. אבל אין לפרש ממעטין אבל ששים קצת, דאם כן היה לו לפרש השיעור, מה הוא קורא ממעט:

שטובה

[ועי׳ תוס׳ פסחים נה. ד"ה הא]

לז א ב מיי׳ פ"ב מהל׳ מגילה הלכה יג סמג עשין ד טוש"ע א"ח סי׳ תרצו סעיף ג:
לח ג שם סעיף ב:
לט ד ה ו שם סעיף א:
מ ז ח מיי׳ פ"ג מהל׳ תענית הל׳ ח טוש"ע א"ח סי׳ תקעה סעיף ז:
מא ט מיי׳ פ"א מהל׳ מגילה הלכה יא סמג עשין ד טוש"ע א"ח סי׳ תרפח סעיף ד:
מב י מיי׳ פי"ב מהל׳ שמטה ויובל הל׳ יג:

אלא מחומרא שיש בו יותר משאר תענית ודורות ראשונים לא גזרו אלא רק שיהא יום תענית ולא יותר

אלו הואי התם קבעתיה בעשירי ודאי ר"י לא היה יכול להכריע כל החכמים לדעתו אלא שהרבה חכמים הסכימו לקובעו בעשירי רק הרוב הסכימו לקובעו בתשיעי וכה"ג אינו בכלל אין ב"ד רשאי וכו׳ דיש רשות ביד ב"ד אחר לקבוע הלכה כדברי יחיד כדאיתא בעדיות פ"א משנה ה

[פירוש מים נובעין וקרים. ערוך ערך קרונה]

תענית יח:

[פסחים נ: נדרים טו. פא:]

תענית יב.

שם יז:

[גי׳ הערוך אבורנקי]

[לקמן ו.]

ערכין לב:

גליון הש"ס

תוס׳ ד"ה ממעטין ר"ל וכו׳ ומיירי מט"ב. עיין פסחים דף נה ע"א ול"ע:

רבינו חננאל

פירושה חגיגה כ"ז חגיגה מאחרין כלומר כל ימי החג מאחרין מיום לחבירו אבל אם שלמו ימי החג לא דתנן מי שלא חגג (גרסינן) ביו"ט הראשון של חג חוגג והולך כל הרגל כולו עד יו"ט אחרון של חג עבר הרגל כו׳. רב אשי אמר הכי קאמר אפי׳ עצרת דחגיגתה חד יומא הוא אי איקלעי בשבת מאחרין חגיגה למחר כדתנן ומודין שאם חל להיות בשבת שיום טבוח לאחר השבת וזו המשנה אחרים היא שאומרים אין בין עצרת לעצרת אלא ד׳ ימים ואין הלכה כמותם: רבי נטע נטיעה בפורים אוקימנא דר׳ יהודה פשיטא ליה דטבריא מוקפת חומה מימות יהושע היא ורבי בר חמיסר הוא וכי נטע בארביסר נטע כו׳. ואסיקנא אפי׳ תימא ביומיה הספד ותענית קבילו עילויהו וכי אסירי הספד ותעניות כולי עלמא כדכתיב במגילת תענית ארביסר וחמיסר פוריא אינון דלא למיספד ואמר רבא לא נצרכא אלא לאסור את של זה בזה פי׳ לאסור לבן כרך בי"ד בהספד ותענית ולבן כפר בט"ו אלו ואלו אסורין בהספד ותענית בב׳ ימים הללו. אבל מלאכה אינו אסור אלא מי שנהגו בני אותו מקום איסור על עצמם כדתניא דברים המותרים ואחרים נהגו בהן איסור למלאכה [אי אתה רשאי להתירן בפניהם] ורב דלטייה לההוא גברא ולא צמח כיתניה מקום שלא נהגו לעשות מלאכה בפורים הוה. איבעית אימא רבי נטיעה של שמחה נטע דתנן עברו אלו ולא נענו ממעטין במשא ובמתן כו׳ ותנא בנין של שמחה נטיעה של שמחה מכלל שאע"פ שאסור לעשות מלאכה נטיעה של שמחה מותרת לו *) דהא מן התעניות הראשונות שנינו עברו אלו ולא נענו ב"ד גוזרין ג׳ תעניות אוכלין ושותין מבע"י ואסורין במלאכה כו׳ ללמדך שאע"פ שאסורים במלאכה מן התעניות הראשונות בנין של שמחה ונטיעה של שמחה מותרין היו **) לפיכך בא עתה לאסור אפי׳ אלו שהיו בהן מותרין עד עתה ומפני שהן של שמחה וכן בפורים אע"פ שאסורים במלאכה בנטיעה של שמחה מותרין הן לפיכך אמרנו דר׳ נטיעה של שמחה שהוא אבורנקי של מלכים נטע. רבי רחץ בקרונה של ציפורי בי"ז בתמוז וביקש לעקור ט׳ באב שחל להיות בשבת ודחוהו לאחר שבת אמר הואיל ונדחה ידחה ולא הודו לו חכמים: גופא חזקיה קרא מגילה בטבריא בי"ד

*) נראה דצ"ל דהגה בתעניות הראשונות וכו׳. **) דברי רבינו אלו צריכין באור לכאורה דהיאך אפשר דבתענית צבור שאסור במלאכה יהי׳ מותר בנין של שמחה וצ"ע ועי׳ בחדושי הרמב"ן.

הגהות הב"ח

(א) גמ׳ אפילו תימא ביומיה הוה הספד: (ב) רש"י ד"ה טובים וכו׳ שמעתי ממך הייתי: (ג) ד"ה בר ארביסר הוה לא היתה עיר מן: (ד) ד"ה ותנא עלה בנין בנין של שמחה נטיעה נטיעה וכו׳ והד"א עם ד"ה ונטיעה כו׳ של שמחה הס"ד: (ה) ד"ה סביב וכו׳ מסובבת חומה סביב: (ו) תום׳ ד"ה והא רבי וכו׳ שהיה בטבריא בימי: (ז) ד"ה ממעטין וכו׳ ונטיעה דבסמוך דבשל שמחה דוקא אסור אבל שאר בניינים:

ואישתכח כוותי: חמת זו טבריא. ולמה נקרא שמה "חמת"? על שום חמי טבריא. רקת — זו ציפורי. ולמה נקרא שמה "רקת"? משום דמידלייא כרקתא דנהרא. כינרת — זו גינוסר. ולמה נקרא שמה כינרת? דמתיקי פירא כקלא דכינרי. אמר רבא: מי איכא למאן דאמר רקת לאו טבריא היא? והא כי שכיב איניש הכא, התם ספדי ליה הכי: גדול הוא בששך, ושם לו ברקת. וכי מסקי ארונא להתם ספדי ליה הכי: אוהבי *שרידים יושבי רקת, צאו וקבלו הרוגי עומק. *כי נח נפשיה דרבי זירא פתח עליה ההוא ספדנא: ארץ שנער הרה וילדה, ארץ צבי גידלה שעשועיה. אוי נא לה, אמרה רקת, כי אבדה כלי חמדתה! אלא אמר (*רבה): חמת — זו חמי גרר; רקת זו טבריא; כינרת — זו גינוסר. ולמה נקרא שמה "רקת"? *שאפילו ריקנין שבה מלאין מצות כרמון. רבי ירמיה אמר: רקת שמה. ולמה נקרא שמה טבריא? שיושבת בטבורה של ארץ ישראל. (*רבא) אמר: "רקת" שמה. ולמה נקרא שמה טבריא? שטובה ראייתה. אמר זעירא: קטרון זו ציפורי. ולמה נקרא שמה ציפורי — שיושבת בראש ההר כצפור. וקטרון ציפורי היא? והא קטרון בחלקו של זבולון הואי, דכתיב: °"זבולון לא הוריש את יושבי קטרון ואת יושבי נהלול". וזבולון מתרעם על מדותיו הוה, שנאמר: °"זבולון עם חרף נפשו למות". מה טעם? משום ד"נפתלי על מרומי שדה". אמר זבולון לפני הקב"ה: רבונו של עולם! לאחיי נתת להם שדות וכרמים ולי נתת הרים וגבעות. לאחיי נתת להם ארצות ולי נתת ימים ונהרות. אמר לו: כולן צריכין לך ע"י חלזון, שנאמר: [°"עמים הר יקראו] ושפוני טמוני חול". תני רב יוסף: "שפוני" — זה חלזון; "טמוני" — זו טרית; "חול" — זו זכוכית לבנה. אמר לפניו: רבונו של עולם מי מודיעני?(א) אמר לו: °"שם יזבחו זבחי צדק". סימן זה יהא לך: כל הנוטל ממך בלא דמים — אינו מועיל בפרקמטיא שלו כלום. ואי סלקא דעתך קטרון זו ציפורי, אמאי מתרעם על מדותיו? והא הויא ציפורי, מילתא דעדיפא טובא! וכי תימא דלית בה זבת חלב ודבש — והאמר ריש לקיש: לדידי *חזי לי זבת חלב ודבש דציפורי, והויא ששה עשר מיל על ששה עשר מיל! וכ"ת: דלא נפישא דידיה כדאחוה — *והאמר רבה בר בר חנה אמר רבי יוחנן: לדידי חזי לי זבת חלב ודבש דכל ארעא דישראל והויא כמבי כובי עד אקרא דתולבקני — עשרין ותרתין פרסי אורכא, ופותיא שיתא פרסי! אפ"ה שדות וכרמים עדיפא ליה. דיקא נמי, דכתיב: °"ונפתלי על מרומי שדה". ש"מ. אמר רבי אבהו: °"ועקרון תעקר" — זו קסרי בת אדום, שהיא יושבת בין החולות, והיא היתה יתד תקועה לישראל בימי יוונים. וכשגברה מלכות בית חשמונאי ונצחום, היו קורין אותה אחידת מגדל *שיר. אמר רבי יוסי בר חנינא: מאי דכתיב: °"והסירותי דמיו מפיו ושקוציו מבין שיניו ונשאר גם הוא לאלהינו"? "והסירותי דמיו מפיו" — זה בית(ב) במיא שלהן; "ושקוציו מבין שיניו" — זה בית גליא שלהן; "ונשאר גם הוא לאלהינו" — אלו בתי כנסיות ובתי מדרשות שבאדום. °"והיה כאלוף ביהודה ועקרון כיבוסי" — אלו *תראטריות וקרקסיות שבאדום שעתידין שרי יהודה ללמד בהן תורה ברבים. *אמר רבי יצחק: לשם — זו פמיים; עקרון תעקר — זו קסרי בת אדום, שהיא היתה מטרופולין של מלכים. איכא דאמרי: דמרבי בה מלכי, ואיכא דאמרי: דמוקמי מינה מלכי. קסרי וירושלים, אם יאמר לך אדם: חרבו שתיהן — אל תאמן; ישבו שתיהן — אל תאמן; חרבה קסרי וישבה ירושלים, חרבה ירושלים וישבה קסרי — תאמן, שנאמר: °"אמלאה החרבה": *אם מליאה זו — חרבה זו. אם מליאה זו — חרבה זו. רב נחמן בר יצחק אמר מהכא: °"ולאום מלאום יאמץ". ואמר רבי יצחק: מאי דכתיב: °"יוחן רשע בל למד צדק"? אמר יצחק לפני הקב"ה: רבש"ע יוחן עשו! אמר לו: רשע הוא. אמר לו: "בל למד צדק"? אמר לו: °"בארץ נכוחות יעול". אמר לו: אם כן — "בל יראה גאות ה'". ואמר רבי יצחק: מאי דכתיב: °"אל תתן ה' מאויי רשע זממו אל תפק ירומו סלה"? אמר יעקב לפני הקב"ה רבונו של עולם, אל תתן לעשו הרשע תאות לבו. "זממו אל תפק" — זו גרממיא

רש"י

ואישתכח כוותי. גרסינן: רקתא דנהרא. שפת הנהר, גבוה מן הנהר, אף ציפורי יושבת בראש ההר: כי שכיב איניש הכא. כשמת אדם גדול בבבל: ספדי ליה התם. בטבריא: ששך. בבל, בחילוף א"ת ב"ש: ושם לו ברקת. יצא לו שם בטבריא: וכי מסקי ארון. של מת מבבל לקוברו בטבריא: אמרו הכי. הספדנין קורין בשווקים בלשון הזה, שיצאו לקראת המת: אוהבי שרידים. אוהבי ישראל: יושבי רקת צאו וקבלו הרוגי עמק. מתי בבל העמוקה: ר' זירא עלה מבבל לארץ ישראל ומת שם בטבריא: [ארץ צבי. ארץ] ישראל: גידלה שעשועיה. של שנער: בטיבורה. באמצעיתה: לא הוריש את יושבי קטרון. שבאה לחלקו, ועבר על מה שאמר הקב"ה "לא תחיה כל נשמה" (דברים כ) והניחן לגור שם ביניהם ולהעלות להם מס: על מדותיו. על מזלו שנמדד לו מן השמים, מדה שאינו חפץ בה: כולן צריכין לך. כל אחיך יהו צריכין לך: על ידי חלזון. חלזון עולה מן הים להרים, וצובעין בדמו תכלת, ונמכר בדמים יקרים: עמים הר יקראו. מכל השבטים יתקבצו להריך לקנות שפוני טמוני חול: שפוני זה חלזון. שהוא דבר חשוב. ספון = חשוב בלשון בברייתא: טרית. דג שקורין טונינ"א: זכוכית לבנה. היוצא מן החול. כדאמר ב"יציאות השבת" (שבת טו:). וחול של זבולון חשוב משאר חולות, וראוי לזכוכית לבנה: מי מודיעני. על זאת לתת לי דמים: כל המוצא חלזון ונוטלו בלא דמים אינו מצליח: שם יזבחו זבחי צדק. כאשר אסור גזל בעולה — כך לא יגזלו ממך כלום. שאם יטול שוה פרוטה בלא דמים — תתקלקל הצביעה והחול, ולא יועיל כלום: זבת חלב ודבש. העזים אוכלין תאנים, והדבש נוטף מהן, והחלב זב מן העזים, ונעשים כמין נחל: ששה עשר מיל. ד' פרסאות: לדידי חזי לי זבת חלב ודבש דכל ארץ ישראל. בכל מקום שהוא שם, ואם באת לצרפו יחד — הוי כמבי כובי עד אקרא דתולבקני, שם מקום: אקרא. מקום מעבר הנהר, ובלע"ז פורט"ו: עדיפא ליה. חביבי ליה: יתד תקועה. לרעה: אחידת מגדל שיר. כבושת מגדל שיר: והסירותי דמיו מפיו וגו'. גבי צור כתיב, שהוא ראש לאדום: גלייא(ג) במיא. ראשי ע"ז הם לאדום: כיבוסי. היא ירושלים: והיה אדום לאלופי יהודה. ועקרון תהיה בית תלמוד בירושלים: לשם. עיר שכיבשו בני דן: זו פמיים. שמשם ירדן יוצא, כדאמר מר: ירדן יוצא ממערת פמיים (בכורות דף נה.): מטרופולין. לשון יון: אימא של מלכות. מטר"א = אם. פולין = לשון שררה. כדאמר מר: עד שבאו דיופלי מהעיר — שני שרים (תענית דף יח:): דמרבי. שמגדלין שם בני מלכים: אמלאה החרבה. רישא דקרא "יען אמרה צור על ירושלים אמלאה החרבה": עכשיו אתמלא מחורבתה:(ד) רשע. זה עשו: בארץ נכוחות יעול. את ירושלים יחריב: אמר יצחק להקב"ה יוחן רשע זה, עשו אמר לו הקדוש ברוך הוא: רשע הוא: אמר. יצחק: בל למד צדק. כלומר, אין אדם יכול ללמד עליו צדק? אמר לו. הקב"ה: בארץ נכוחות יעול. כלומר: עתיד להחריב את ארץ ישראל: אמר יצחק. אם כן "בל יראה גאות ה'": זממו אל תפק. אל תוציאנו מנחיריו. זמם = כמין טבעת ברזל *שנותנין בחוטמה של אנקה ומשכת בו, ומתוך חוזקה אינה משתמרת כי אם בו: גרממיא

תוספות

שטובה ראייתה. שהיו שם גנות ופרדסים:

דכל הנוטל (פרוטה) ממך בלא דמים אין מועיל. דכתיב "שם יזבחו זבחי צדק", וגזל לא מהני בזבח:

טראטריות (ה) וקרקסיאות. י"מ: בתי עבודת כוכבים, ומכנה אותן טרטאכ' — לשון חרפה, וקרקסיאות — רוצה לומר בית הכסא בלשון ערב. וקשה לומר שאותן מקומות מטונפות יכול ללמוד שם תורה! אלא ודאי לשממה יהא במהרה בימינו, ורוצה לומר: בתים שמתאספים שם לוועד של עובדי עבודת כוכבים:

רבינו חננאל

בי"ד ובט"ו משום דמספקא ליה ומקשינן והא טבריא ודאי מערי מבצר הוא דכתיב ועדי מבצר הצדים צר וחמת רקת וכנרת וקי"ל דרקת זו טבריא אלא משום שימה חומתה כו'. טליא פי' נערים. דמדליא כרקתא דנהרא פי' גבוהה כשפת הנהר:

[עיין פרש"י ובערוך ערך שרד פי' אוהבי תלמידי חכמים יושבי בבית המדרש של טבריא ופי' הערוך מבואר על פי מה דאמר הש"ס בחולין קלג. אין שריד אלא ת"ח שנאמר ובשרידים אשר ה' קורא]

הגהות הב"ח

(א) גמ' מי מודיעני על זאת אמר לו וכו' שכל הנוטל: (ב) שם דמיו מפיו זה בית כריא שלהן: (ג) רש"י ד"ה גלייא וכריא ראשי: (ד) ד"ה אמלאה וכו' מחורבתה הס"ד ואח"כ מ"ה יוחן רשע: (ה) תוד"ה טראטריאות י"מ בתי כצ"ל ותי' וקרקסיאות נמחק וכו' מקומות מטונפות יטלום ללמוד וכו' וטראטריות וקרקסיאות דהכא רוצה לומר בתים כ"ב עיין בשבת דף קנ. ופ"ק דע"ז דף יח ע"ב:

כתובות קיא:

גליון הש"ס

רש"י ד"ה זממו כו'. שנותנים בחוטמה של אנקה. שבת דף נא ע"ב:

[נ"ל צור כך הגי' בע"י ובערוך ערך אחד גרים שד פי' מגדל שסורים בו לפנים שדים פ"א מגדל שהוא מוחזק בשד]

[בכורות נה.]

מו"ק כה: | [נ"ל רבא] | ברכות מ. עירובין יט. חגיגה כז. סנהדרין לז.] | [נ"ל רבה] | [כתובות קיא: ע"ש] | בערוך ערך תאטר האריך בפירושו דהגהו שתי תיבות] | פסחים מב:

תורה אור: שופטים א | שם ה | דברים לג | שם | שופטים ה | צפניה ב | זכריה ט | שם | יחזקאל כו | בראשית כה | ישעיה כו | שם | תהלים קמ

גרממיא של אדום, שאלמלי הן יוצאין מחריבין כל העולם כולו. ואמר רבי חמא בר חנינא: תלת מאה קטירי תגא איכא בגרממיא של אדום, ותלת מאה ושיתין וחמשה מרזבני איכא ברומי. ובכל יומא נפקי הני לאפי הני ומקטיל חד מינייהו, ומיטרדי לאוקמי מלכא. ואמר ר' יצחק: אם יאמר לך אדם: יגעתי ולא מצאתי — אל תאמן; לא יגעתי ומצאתי — אל תאמן; יגעתי ומצאתי — תאמן. הני מילי — בדברי תורה, אבל במשא ומתן — סייעתא הוא מן שמיא. ולדברי תורה לא אמרן אלא לחדודי, אבל לאוקמי גירסא — סייעתא מן שמיא היא. ואמר רבי יצחק: *אם ראית רשע שהשעה משחקת לו — אל תתגרה בו, שנא' °"אל תתחר במרעים" (תהלים לז). ולא עוד אלא שדרכיו מצליחין, שנא' °"יחילו דרכיו בכל עת" (שם י). ולא עוד אלא שזוכה בדין, שנאמר: "מרום משפטיך מנגדו". ולא עוד אלא שרואה בשונאיו, שנאמר: "כל צורריו יפיח בהם". איני? והאמר ר' יוחנן משום ר"ש בן יוחי: מותר להתגרות ברשעים בעולם הזה, שנא' °"עוזבי תורה יהללו רשע ושומרי תורה יתגרו בם" (משלי כח). ותניא *ר' דוסתאי בר מתון אמר: מותר להתגרות ברשעים בעולם הזה.(א) ואם לחשך אדם לומר: "אל תתחר במרעים ואל תקנא בעושי עולה" — מי שלבו נוקפו אומר כן. אלא: "אל תתחר במרעים" — להיות כמרעים, "ואל תקנא בעושי עולה" — להיות כעושי עולה. ואומר: °"אל יקנא לבך בחטאים" וגו' (שם כג). לא קשיא: הא — במילי דידיה; הא — במילי דשמיא. ואיבעית אימא: הא והא במילי דידיה. ולא קשיא: הא — בצדיק גמור; הא — בצדיק שאינו גמור. דאמר רב הונא: *מאי דכתיב: °"למה תביט בוגדים תחריש בבלע רשע צדיק ממנו" (חבקוק א)? צדיק ממנו — בולע; צדיק גמור — אינו בולע. ואי בעית אימא: שעה משחקת לו שאני.§ אמר עולא: איטליא של יון, זה כרך גדול של רומי. והויא תלת מאה פרסה, על תלת מאה פרסה. ויש בה שס"ה שווקים כמנין ימות החמה, וקטן שבכולם של מוכרי עופות, והויא ששה עשר מיל על ששה עשר מיל. ומלך סועד בכל יום באחד מהן. והדר בה אע"פ שאינו נולד בה — נוטל פרס מבית המלך; והנולד בה אע"פ שאינו דר בה — נוטל פרס מבית המלך. ושלשת אלפים בי בני יש בו, *)וחמש מאות חלונות מעלין עשן חוץ לחומה. צדו אחד ים וצדו אחד הרים וגבעות; צדו אחד מחיצה של ברזל, וצדו אחד חולסית ומצולה.§ **מתני'** [א]קראו את המגילה באדר הראשון ונתעברה השנה — קורין אותה באדר שני. *אין בין אדר הראשון לאדר השני אלא קריאת המגילה, ומתנות לאביונים.§ **גמ'** הא לענין סדר פרשיות — זה וזה שוין. מני מתני'? לא תנא קמא, ולא ר' אליעזר ברבי יוסי, ולא רשב"ג. דתניא: *קראו את המגילה באדר הראשון ונתעברה השנה — קורין אותה באדר השני, *שכל מצות שנוהגות בשני נוהגות בראשון, חוץ ממקרא מגילה. ר"א ברבי יוסי אומר: אין קורין אותה באדר השני, שכל מצות שנוהגות בשני נוהגות בראשון. רשב"ג אומר משום רבי יוסי: אף קורין אותה באדר השני, [ב]שכל מצות שנוהגות בשני אין נוהגות בראשון. ושוין בהספד ובתענית שאסורין בזה ובזה. ר"ש בן גמליאל היינו תנא קמא! אמר רב פפא: סדר פרשיות איכא בינייהו. דתנא קמא סבר: לכתחילה בשני, ואי עבוד בראשון — עבוד, בר ממקרא מגילה, דאף על גב דקרו בראשון קרו בשני. ורבי אליעזר ברבי יוסי סבר: אפילו מקרא מגילה לכתחילה בראשון. ורבן שמעון בן גמליאל סבר: אפילו סדר פרשיות, אי קרו בראשון — קרו בשני. מני? אי תנא קמא — קשיא מתנות; אי רבי אליעזר ברבי יוסי — קשיא נמי מקרא מגילה. אי רשב"ג — קשיא סדר פרשיות! לעולם ת"ק, ותנא מקרא מגילה והוא הדין מתנות לאביונים, *דהא בהא תליא. ואב"א לעולם רשב"ג היא, ומתני' חסורי מיחסרא, והכי קתני: [ג]אין בין ארבעה עשר שבאדר הראשון לי"ד שבאדר השני אלא מקרא מגילה ומתנות. הא לענין הספד ותענית — זה וזה שוין. ואילו סדר פרשיות לא מיירי. אמר רבי חייא בר אבין אמר רבי יוחנן: הלכתא כרבן שמעון בן גמליאל שאמר משום רבי יוסי. אמר רבי יוחנן: ושניהם מקרא אחד דרשו: "בכל שנה ושנה". רבי אליעזר ברבי יוסי סבר: "בכל שנה ושנה" מה כל שנה ושנה אדר הסמוך לשבט — אף כאן אדר הסמוך לשבט. ורשב"ג סבר: "בכל שנה ושנה", מה כל שנה ושנה אדר הסמוך לניסן — אף כאן אדר הסמוך לניסן. בשלמא רבי אליעזר ברבי יוסי — מסתבר טעמא, *דאין מעבירין על המצות. אלא רשב"ג מ"ט? אמר רבי טבי: טעמא דרבי שמעון בן גמליאל מסמך גאולה לגאולה עדיף. רבי אלעזר אמר: טעמא דר' שמעון ב"ג מהכא, דכתיב: "לקיים את אגרת הפורים הזאת השנית". ואיצטריך למיכתב השנית

*) [ועי' תוס' מנחות סד: ד"ה אב"א ותוס' יומא לג. ד"ה אין ותוס' זבחים נא. ד"ה אשר]

רש"י

גרממיא. שם מלכות, והיא מאדום: מרזבני. דוכסים: יגעתי. בתורה: לאוקמי גירסא. שלא תשתכח ממנו: סייעתא דשמיא. ויש יגע ואינו מוצא: יחילו. יצליחו. ודומה לו "על כן לא יחיל טובו" (איוב כ): מרום משפטיך מנגדו. מסולקין הם ממנו: יפיח בהם. בנפיחה בעלמא הן נופלים: מי שלבו נוקפו. הירא מן העבירות שבידו אומר כן: אל תתחר. אינו לשון גירוי, אלא שלא תתחוז במעשיו. כמו "ואיך תתחרה את הסוסים" (ירמיה יב) — כלומר: שאינו רץ כמותו: ואומר אל יקנא לבך בחטאים כי אם ביראת ה' כל היום. על כרחך אין קנאה זו לשון גירוי מלחמה, אלא אחיזת מעשיו, מדכתיב בסיפא "כי אם ביראת ה' כל היום": איטליא של יון. כרך גדול שנגדל בשביל עון מנשה. שבשעה שהכניס צלם בהיכל ירד גבריאל ונעץ קנה בים, *ונגדל עליו חלקה גדולה ונבנה לשם איטליא של יון. "מאיי אלישה" (יחזקאל כז) מתרגמינן "מנגוות איטליא": שווקים. חוצות: פרס. מזון: חלונות שמעלים מהן עשן חוץ לחומה. שהן גבוהים מן החומה, ואין מעשנין את החומה, וזהו חשיבות: חולסית. מקום אבנים דקות: **מתני'** אלא מקרא מגילה. כלומר: שאם עשאו בראשון לא יצא: **גמ'** סדר פרשיות. פרשת שקלים וזכור ופרה והחודש. דתנן במתניתין ד"בני העיר" *דנוהגין באדר: זה וזה שוין. שאם קראם בראשון אין צריך לחזור ולקרות בשני: שאסורין בזה ובזה. ביום ארבעה עשר וחמשה עשר שבשניהן: ואמר רב פפא. גרסינן: ורבן שמעון בן גמליאל כו'. דהא כל מצות קאמר: מתניתין הכי קתני. ולא איירי בסדר פרשיות כלל: אין מעבירין כו'. משבא לידי אקדים לעשות. דהכי תניא במכילתא "ושמרתם את המצות" — אם באת מצוה לידך אל תחמיצנה: גאולה לגאולה. פורים לפסח: השנית. בחודש השני: לבסוף

תוספות

הא לענין סדר פרשיות זה וזה שוין. שאם קראו הארבע פרשיות באדר הראשון, שעדיין לא היו יודעין שצריכין לעבר, ובתר הכי עברו השנה — אין צריך לקרותם באדר השני: **ורבי אליעזר** ברבי יוסי סבר אף מקרא מגילה [לכתחלה בראשון. ונראה דדייק מדקתני משנה יתירא: שכל מצות שנוהגות בשני נוהגות בראשון, [דמשמע] לכתחילה. ויש שנוהגין לעשות ימי משתה ושמחה בארבעה עשר ובחמשה עשר של אדר הראשון, וריהטא דמתניתין נמי משמע כן, מדקאמר אלא מקרא מגילה(ג) בלבד ומתנות עניים. מכלל דלענין משתה ושמחה זה וזה שוין. ולא נהירא, דהא אמרינן בגמרא: הא לענין הספד ותענית זה וזה שוין, מכלל דשמחה ומשתה ליכא. דע"כ לא תליא הא בהא, דאי תליא הא בהא — לאשמעינן דמשתה ושמחה נהגו בהו וממילא נאסר בהספד. דהא הימים האמורים במגילת תענית האסורים בהספד אין בהן משתה ושמחה. וכן הלכה, שאין צריך להחמיר לעשות משתה ושמחה באדר הראשון:

מסתבר טעמיה דאין מעבירין על המצות. מכאן קשה להא דאמרינן בפרק "איזהו מקומן" (זבחים דף נא. ושם) בגמרא, דקאמר: שירי הדם היה שופך על יסוד מערבי של המזבח. ודייק טעמא דאמר קרא "אל יסוד מזבח העולה". וקשה: התם למה לי קרא? תיפוק ליה דאין מעבירין על המצות, וכשהוא יוצא מפתח ההיכל שהוא מערב, ביסוד מערבי הוא דפגע ברישא! ויש מפרשים דלא שייך למימר אין מעבירין על המצות אלא היכא שיש לפניו שתי מצות, שיש לו לעשות קודם אותה דפגע ברישא. וזה אינו, דהכא ליכא אלא מצוה אחת, ואפילו הכי מפרש הטעם משום דאין מעבירין! ורבינו יהודה תירץ: דאי לאו קרא הוה אמינא דאין מעבירין לכתחילה, הא דיעבד — שרי, משום הכי איצטריך לאסור בדיעבד. אי נמי, נראה התם דמטעם דאין מעבירין לא חזינן אלא דכל מערבי של מזבח כשר, אבל יסוד — לא חזינן דצריך, משום הכי איצטריך קרא, לאשמועינן יסוד*):
נאמרה

עין משפט נר מצוה

מג א מיי' פ"א מהל' מגילה הל' יב סמג עשין מד"ס ד טור א"ח סימן תרפח:
מד ב ג מיי' פ"ב מהל' מגילה הל' יג סמג שם טור שו"ע א"ח סי' תרלז:

רבינו חננאל

מתני' קרא את המגילה באדר הראשון ונתעברה השנה כו' הא לענין פרשיות זה וזה שוין פי' פרשיות כדתנן בר"ח אדר קורין בפרשת שקלים. בשניה זכור. בשלישית פרה אדומה. ברביעית החדש הזה. בחמישי חוזרין לכסדרן ואוקימנא דבסדר פרשיות זה וזה שוין. אם קראו אותם באדר הראשון יצאו ואין צריכין לחזור ולקרות אותם באדר השני. מני מתניתין לא ת"ק ולא ר' אליעזר בר' יוסי ולא ר' אליעזר בר' יוסי ולא רשב"ג דתניא קראו את המגילה באדר הראשון ונתעברה כו'. ואמר רב פפא סדר פרשיות איכא בינייהו תנא קמא סבר פרשיות לכתחלה בשני ואי עביד בראשון תוב לא עבדי בשני לבד ממקרא מגילה דאע"ג [דקרו] בראשון קרו נמי בשני. ר' אליעזר בר' יוסי סבר אפי' מקרא מגילה לכתחלה בראשון ור"ש ב"ג סבר סדר פרשיות לכתחלה נמי בשני. ואע"ג דקרו בראשון קרו נמי בשני. מני מתני' אי ת"ק הא קתני חוץ ממקרא מגילה בלבד ומשנתנו שנינו אלא מקרא מגילה ומתנות לאביונים. הלכך קשיא ומתנות לאביונים אי ר' אליעזר בר' יוסי קשיא נמי מקרא מגילה. דהא בהדיא תני דלא מקרא מגילה ולא מתנות לאביונים אין נוהגין בשני ומתני' קתני דזה וזה נוהגים בשני. אי רשב"ג קשיא סדר פרשיות דדייקינן ממתני' הא לענין פרשיות אדר הראשון והשני שוין ורשב"ג סבר אין נוהגין אלא בשני ופרקינן לעולם מתניתין ת"ק היא ותנא בברייתא מקרא מגילה והוא הדין למתנות לאביונים דמתנות אביונים בקריאת המגילה הם תלויים. עת שקורין המגילה נותנין לעניים המתנות מפני שעיני העניים נשואות למקרא מגילה איבעית אימא לעולם מתני' רשב"ג והכי קתני אין בין י"ד דאדר הראשון ויום י"ד דאדר השני אלא מקרא מגילה ומתנות לאביונים: הא לענין הספד ותענית יום י"ד של אדר הראשון ויום י"ד דאדר השני זה וזה שוין. ואילו בסדר פרשיות תנא דידן לא קתני מידי ואסיקנא משום דרבי יוחנן הלכה כרשב"ג דאמר כל מצות הנוהגות בשני אין נוהגות בראשון ובין סדר הפרשיות ובין מקרא מגילה אין נוהגין אלא באדר השני בלבד. וא"ר יוחנן דייק רשב"ג מדכתיב כל שנה ושנה מה כל שנה ושנה אדר הסמוך לניסן כן אפילו במעוברת אדר הסמוך לניסן ואקשינן והא אין מעבירין על המצות ופרקינן מסמך גאולת אסתר לגאולת מצרים עדיפא ר' אלעזר (בר' יוסי) אומר טעמא דרשב"ג לקיים את אגרת הפורים הזאת השנית מדכתיב השנית

מסורת הש"ס

[ס"א ועלה עליו שרטון גדול]
ברכות ז: ע"ש
[דף כט.]
[ברכות ז: ע"ש מסכת ד"א רבה פ"ב ע"ש]
ברכות ז: ע"ש ב"מ עא.
*) [נ"א וכל אחד ואחד חמש מאות חלונות וכו']
שקלים ב:
[תוספ' פ"א]
[ר"ה יט:]
[שבת קלה: וש"נ]
[יומא לג. וש"נ]

הגהות הב"ח

(א) גמ' מותר להתגרות ברשעים בעולם הזה שנאמר עוזבי תורה יהללו רשע וגו' ואם לחשך אדם לומר והכתיב אל תתחר וגו' בעושי עולה אמור לו מי שלבו: (ב) תוס' ד"ה ור' אליעזר וכו' אלא מקרא מגילה ומתנות עניים כצ"ל ותיבת בלבד נמחק:

"השנית", ואיצטריך למיכתב "בכל שנה ושנה". דאי מ"בכל שנה ושנה", הוה אמינא כי קושין. קא משמע לן: "השנית". ואי אשמועינן "השנית", הוה אמינא בתחילה בראשון ובשני. קמ"ל: "בכל שנה ושנה". ורבי אליעזר בר' יוסי, האי "השנית" מאי עביד ליה? מיבעי ליה לכדרב שמואל בר יהודה, דאמר רב שמואל בר יהודה: בתחילה קבעוה בשושן, ולבסוף בכל העולם כולו. אמר רב שמואל בר יהודה: שלחה להם אסתר לחכמים: קבעוני לדורות! שלחו לה: קנאה את מעוררת עלינו לבין האומות. שלחה להם: כבר כתובה אני על דברי הימים למלכי מדי ופרס. *רב ורב חנינא ורבי יוחנן ורב חביבא מתנו. בכוליה סדר מועד כל כי האי זוגא חלופי רבי יוחנן ומעייל רבי יונתן: שלחה להם אסתר לחכמים: כתבוני לדורות. שלחו לה: °"הלא כתבתי לך שלישים", שלישים ולא רבעים. עד שמצאו לו מקרא כתוב בתורה: °"כתב זאת זכרון בספר". "כתב זאת" — מה שכתוב כאן ובמשנה תורה; "זכרון" — מה שכתוב בנביאים, "בספר" — מה שכתוב במגלה. כתנאי: "כתב זאת" — מה שכתוב כאן; "זכרון" — מה שכתוב במשנה תורה; "בספר" — מה שכתוב בנביאים, דברי רבי יהושע. ר' אלעזר המודעי אומר: "כתב זאת" — מה שכתוב כאן ובמשנה תורה; "זכרון" — מה שכתוב בנביאים; "בספר" — מה שכתוב במגילה. אמר רב יהודה אמר שמואל: אסתר אינה מטמאה את הידים. למימרא דסבר שמואל אסתר לאו ברוח הקודש נאמרה? והאמר שמואל: אסתר ברוח הקודש נאמרה! נאמרה לקרות *ולא נאמרה ליכתוב. מיתיבי: *רבי מאיר אומר: קהלת אינו מטמא את הידים, ומחלוקת בשיר השירים. ר' יוסי אומר: שיר השירים מטמא את הידים, ומחלוקת בקהלת. ר' שמעון אומר: קהלת מקולי ב"ש ומחומרי ב"ה, אבל [א]רות ושיר השירים ואסתר — מטמאין את הידים! הוא דאמר כר' יהושע. תניא, ר' שמעון בן מנסיא אומר: [ב]קהלת אינו מטמא את הידים, מפני שחכמתו של שלמה היא. אמרו לו: וכי זו בלבד אמר? והלא כבר נאמר: °"וידבר שלשת אלפים משל", ואומר: °"אל תוסף על דבריו". מאי ואומר? וכי תימא: מימר — טובא אמר, דאי בעי — איכתיב, ודאי בעי לא איכתיב, תא שמע: "אל תוסף על דבריו". תניא, ר' אליעזר אומר: אסתר ברוח הקודש נאמרה, שנאמר: °"ויאמר המן בלבו". ר' עקיבא אומר: אסתר ברוח הקודש נאמרה, שנאמר: °"ותהי אסתר נשאת חן בעיני כל רואיה". ר"מ אומר: אסתר ברוח הקודש נאמרה, שנאמר: °"ויודע הדבר למרדכי". רבי יוסי בן דורמסקית אומר: אסתר ברוח הקודש נאמרה, שנאמר: °"ובבזה לא שלחו את ידם". אמר שמואל: אי הואי התם הוה אמינא מלתא דעדיפא מכולהו, שנאמר: "קימו וקבלו" — *קימו למעלה מה שקיבלו למטה. אמר רבא: *לכולהו אית להו פירכא, לבר מדשמואל דלית ליה פירכא. דרבי אליעזר — סברא הוא, דלא הוה איניש דחשיב למלכא כוותיה, והאי כי קא מפיש טובא ואמר — אדעתיה דנפשיה קאמר. דר"ע — דלמא *כר' אלעזר, דאמר: מלמד שכל אחד ואחד נדמתה לו כאומתו. והא דרבי מאיר — דלמא כרבי חייא בר אבא, דאמר: *בגתן ותרש שני טרשיים היו. והא דרבי יוסי בן דורמסקית — דלמא פריסתקי שדור. דשמואל ודאי לית ליה פירכא. אמר (א)רבינא: *היינו דאמרי אינשי: טבא חדא פלפלתא חריפתא ממלי צני קרי. רב יוסף אמר, מהכא: °"וימי הפורים האלה לא יעברו מתוך היהודים". רב נחמן בר יצחק אומר, מהכא: "וזכרם לא יסוף מזרעם". § "ומתנות לאביונים". תני רב יוסף: "ומשלוח מנות איש לרעהו" — [ג]שתי מנות לאיש אחד; "ומתנות לאביונים" — [ד]שתי מתנות לשני בני אדם. רבי יהודה נשיאה שדר ליה לרבי אושעיא אטמא דעיגלא תלתא וגרבא דחמרא. שלח ליה: קיימת

(משלי כב; שמות יז; מלכים א ד; משלי ל; אסתר ו; שם ב; שם; שם ט)

רש"י

לבסוף קבעוה כו'. וזהו השנית: שלחה להם. בשנה שנייה לקובעה עליהם חובה: קבעוני. ליום טוב ולקרייה, להיות לי לשם: קנאה את מעוררת עלינו. שיאמרו האומות שאנו שמחים להזכיר מפלתן: כבר אני כתובה. ושם יהו רואין מה שאירע להם על ידי ישראל: רב ורב חנינא ורבי יוחנן ורב חביבא מתנו. הא דאמרינן לקמן: בכוליה סדר מועד. שהוזכרה שם זוג זה של ארבע חכמים הללו, חלופי רבי יוחנן ומכניסין רבי יונתן: שלישים. בשלשה מקומות יש לנו להזכיר מלחמת עמלק: בספר "ואלה שמות" (יז) ובמשנה תורה (כה), ובספר שמואל (א טו). וזהו שאמר שלמה: בדבר שבשלשתו אי אתה רשאי לרבעו: זאת מה שכתוב כאן ובמשנה תורה. דכל מה שכתוב בתורה קורא כתב אחד: אינה מטמאה את הידים. כשאר ספרים. דאמר ב"יציאות השבת" (דף יד.) שגזרו עליהן לטמא את הידים לתרומה, *ומחלוקת בית שמאי וב"ה היא: הוא דאמר כרבי יהושע. דאמר לעיל: 'זאת' — מה שכתוב בתורה, 'זכרון' — מה שכתוב במשנה תורה, 'בספר' — מה שכתוב בנביאים. אבל במגילה לא ניתנה ליכתב, אלא לגורסה על פה ולקרותה: והלא כבר נאמר וידבר כו'. וקהלת כבר נאמרה, וכיון דלא כתב את כולן — למדת שמה שכתב רוח הקודש היה: אל תוסף על דבריו. מקרא הוא בספר משלי: דאי בעי כתב ואי בעי לא כתב. ולעולם מה שכתב משלות בעלמא נינהו, ולא מפי הקב"ה: תא שמע אל תוסף על דבריו. מדקאסר להוסיף עליהן, שמע מינה ברוח הקודש נאמרו: ויאמר המן בלבו. מנא ידעו כותבי המגילה שכך אמר בלבו? אלא רוח הקודש גלה עליהם: ויודע הדבר למרדכי. מי גלה לו? רוח הקדש שרה עליו: ובבזה לא שלחו את ידם. היאך ידעו מה עשו הרחוקים: מפיש ואמר טובא. "יביאו לבוש מלכות", אדעתא דנפשיה קאמר, שמע מינה: זאת היתה בלבו: נדמתה לו כאומתו. והיו אומרים בפיהם: זו משלנו היא: דרבי חייא בר אבא. לקמן בפירקין: פריסתקי שדור. שלוחים שלחו להם למרדכי ואסתר שלא נגעו בביזה, שלא ירע למלך: לא יעברו. מנא ידע את העתיד? מנות. מיני מעדנים: שתי מנות לאדם אחד. דכתיב "ומשלוח מנות איש לרעהו" — שתי מנות לאדם אחד. "ומתנות לאביונים" — שתי מתנות לשני בני אדם, די לכל אחד ואחד מתנה אחת. דהא אביונים נמי תרתי משמע: עגלא תלתא. שלישי לבטן:

ה"ג

תוספות

נאמרה לקרות ולא לכתוב. משמע דסבר דמותר לקרותה ע"פ. וקשה: דהיכי פליג על סתם משנה דלקמן דפ"ב (דף יז.), (ב)דתני: קראה על פה לא יצא! ורב נמי הוא דאמר לקמן (דף יט.) שצריך לכותבה ולתופר' בגידין, ור' יוחנן נמי [אמר] (שם:) דאם קראה (ג) בין הכתובים לא יצא! לכך נר' לפר', דהא דקאמר לא ניתנה ליכתב ברוח הקודש, אבל מדרבנן ניתנה ליכתב ולקרות. ואכתי קשיא: דהא אמרינן בפ' (ד) "הממונה" במסכת יומא (דף כט.): נמשלה אסתר לאילת השחר, מה שחר סוף הלילה — אף אסתר סוף הנסים. ופריך: והא איכא חנוכה! ומשני: ניתן ליכתב קאמר. ופריך: הניחא למאן דאמר ניתן ליכתב, אלא למאן דאמר לא ניתן ליכתב — מאי איכא למימר? (ה) ואין לומר דהא דניתן ליכתב מדרבנן קרי כתיבה, דאם כן הדרא קושיין לדוכתא — דהא איכא חנוכה שניתנה לכתוב מדרבנן במגילת תענית! ותירץ הר"ר אלחנן: דכתיבה דמגילה מהניא טפי, דהא צריכה גידין ושרטוט, וכמה דברים דלא צריכי במגילת תענית:

לכולהו (ו) איכא פירכא בר מדשמואל. וקשה: דלשמואל מי ליכא פירכא? דהא רבא גופיה הוא דאמר פרק "רבי עקיבא" (שבת דף פח. ושם) (מכאן מודעא רבה לאורייתא) שקבלו שנית בימי אחשורוש, אלמא דאיצטריך קרא לדרשא אחרינא! ויש לומר: דלא חשיב האי פירכא, דהא שפיר שמעינן מינה תרתי. ולא דמי האי פירכא לשאר פירכות, דאינך, דסתר סברתם לגמרי*:

ורב נחמן אמר מהכא וזכרם לא יסוף מזרעם. דבריש דקרא לא חזינן אלא היהודים שבאותו הדור:

עין משפט נר מצוה

מה א ב מיי' פ"ט מהל' שאר אבות הטומאות הלכה ו:

מו ג מיי' פ"ב מהלכות מגילה הלכה טו סמג עשין ד טוש"ע א"ח סימן תרצה סעיף ד:

מז ד מיי' שם הלכה טז סמג שם טוש"ע א"ח סי' תרצד סעיף א:

רבינו חננאל

השנית ש"מ דבאדר השני: **קנאה** את מעוררת עלינו כלומר כיון שתיכתב ותיקבע לדורות יהיו האומות שומעין הדבר הזה ומתקנאין ואומרים נשלם גמולכם. שלישים ולא רבעים פי' לא נתן להיכתב *) זכרון עמלק פעמים אמור בתורה ויבא עמלק. וקי"ל כר' אלעזר המודעי דאמר כתוב זאת מה שכתוב כאן ובמשנה תורה. זכרון מה שכתוב בנביאים. בספר [מה] שכתוב במגילה: אסתר מטמא את הידים דברי רשב"י פי' כל כתבי הקדש מטמאין את הנוגע בהן כדתנן בסוף מסכת ידים תרגום שבעזרא ושבדניאל מטמאין את הידים תרגום שכתבו עברית ועברית שכתבו תרגום [וכתב עברי] אין מטמאין את הידים (וכתב עברי) לעולם אין מטמא עד שיכתבנו אשורית על העור בדיו אומרים צדוקים קובלים אנחנו עליכם פרושים שאתם אומרים כתבי הקדש מטמאין את הידים וכתבי המירם אינן מטמאין את הידים אמר להם ריב"ז וכי אין לנו על הפרושים אלא זו בלבד הרי הן אומרים עצמות חמור טהורין ועצמות יוחנן כה"ג טמאין. א"ל לפי חיבתן הן טומאתן שלא יעשה אדם עצמות אביו ואמו תרוודות. אמר להן אף כתבי הקדש לפי חיבתן הן טומאתן כו' כלומר גזרו עליהן טומאה שלא יהיו מצויין לנגיעתן בכל עת ומפורש במס' שבת פ"א [ד' י"ד] ובספר מ"ט גזרו ביה [טומאה] דאמר רב משרשיא בתחלה היו מצניעין אוכלין דתרומה אצל ס"ת אמרי האי קדש והאי קדש כיון דחזו דאתו לידי פסידא שהיו העכברים אוכלים הספרים גזרו ביה רבנן [טומאה] ואף אסתר מטמאה את הידים: ברוה"ק נאמרה שנא' קיימו וקבלו היהודים (מכלל שיש בה קדושה) קיימו למעלה מה שקבלו עליהם למטה וכל אלו הפסוקים כגון ויאמר המן בלבו וכיוצא בו מי מודע מה היה בלבו אלא הקב"ה: תני רב יוסף ומשלוח מנות איש לרעהו. ב' מנות לאדם אחד דכתיב מנות איש לרעהו ומתנות לאביונים. ב' מנות לב' בני אדם. ר' יהודה נשיאה שלח לר' הושעיא ירך של עגל שלישי לבטן וקנקן יין

מסורת הש"ס

סוכה ז: שבת כג:

[עדיות פ"ה מ"ג, ידים פ"ג מ"ה] [ע"ש שינוי נוסחאות ועיין בתוי"ט]

מכות כג:

[חגיגה י. וש"נ]

לקמן יג.

[ס: וכס איתא רבי יוחנן]

יומא פה. חגיגה י. אסתר ט

הגהות הב"ח

(א) גמ' אמר רבא היינו דאמרי אינשי: (ב) תוס' ד"ה נאמרה וכו' דפ"ב [דלקמן] קראה וכו': (ג) בא"ד [דאם] קראה במגילה [ה]כתובה בין הכתובים [לא יצא]: (ד) שם פרק א"ל הממונה: (ה) שם מאי [אי]כא למימר מוקים לה [כר]בי בנימין בר יפת ואין [לו]מר: (ו) ד"ה לכולהו כ"ב [עיי]ן פ"ק דחגיגה בתוס' [ד"]ה דלמא כר' יהודה בדף י' ע"א:

נראה דחסר כאן וצ"ל זכרון עמלק פעם רביעי כי פעמים אמור בתורה ויבא עמלק וזכור את וגו ופעם שלישי בנביאים זכרתי את אשר וגו' וקיי"ל וכו'.

עין משפט נר מצוה

מח א מיי' פ"ב מהל' מגילה הלכה טו סמג עשין ד טוש"ע א"ח סימן תרצה סעיף ד:

מט ב מיי' שם טוש"ע שם סעיף ב:

נ ג מיי' שם הלכה יד טוש"ע שם סעיף א:

נא ד ה ו מיי' פ"א מהלכות יו"ט הלכה ז ח סמג לאוין ע"ה טוש"ע א"ח סימן תצה סעיף א:

נב ז מיי' פ"א מהלכות שביתת עשור הלכה ב סמג לאוין סח טוש"ע א"ח סי' תריא סעיף ב:

נג ח מיי' פי"ט מהלכות סנהדרין הלכה ז סמג לאוין קנט:

גמרא

קיימת בנו רבינו "ומשלוח מנות איש לרעהו" (א)[א] "ומתנות לאביונים". רבה שדר ליה למרי בר מר ביד אביי מלא *טסקא דקשבא, ומלי כסא קמחא דאבשונא. אמר ליה אביי: השתא אמר מרי: אי חקלאה מלכא ליהוי – דיקולא מצואריה לא נחית. הדר שדר ליה איהו מלא טסקא דזנגבילא, ומלא כסא דפלפלתא אריכא. אמר אביי: השתא אמר מר: אנא שדרי ליה חוליא, ואיהו שדר לי חורפא! אמר אביי: כי נפקי מבי מר, הוה שבענא. כי מטאי להתם קריבו לי שיתין צעי דשיתין מיני קדירה, ואכלי בהו שיתין פלוגי. ובישולא בתרייתא הוו קרו ליה צלי קדר, ובעאי למיכס צעא אבתרה. אמר אביי: היינו דאמרי אינשי: כפין עניא ולא ידע. אי נמי: *רווחא לבסימא שכיח. אביי בר אבין ור' חנינא בר אבין [א]מחלפי סעודתייהו להדדי. אמר רבא: [ב]מיחייב איניש לבסומי בפוריא עד דלא ידע בין ארור המן לברוך מרדכי. רבה ורבי זירא עבדו סעודת פורים בהדי הדדי. איבסום. קם רבה שחטיה לרבי זירא. למחר בעי רחמי ואחייה. לשנה אמר ליה: ניתי מר ונעביד סעודת פורים בהדי הדדי! אמר ליה: *לא בכל שעתא ושעתא מתרחיש ניסא. אמר רבא: [ג]סעודת פורים שאכלה בלילה לא יצא ידי חובתו. מאי טעמא? "ימי משתה ושמחה" כתיב. רב אשי הוה יתיב קמיה (*דרב כהנא). נגה ולא אתו רבנן. אמר ליה: מאי טעמא לא אתו רבנן? (ג) דלמא טרידי בסעודת פורים. אמר ליה: ולא הוה אפשר למיכלה באורתא. אמר ליה: לא שמיע ליה למר הא דאמר רבא: סעודת פורים שאכלה בלילה לא יצא ידי חובתו? אמר ליה: *(אמר רבא הכי?) [אמר ליה: אין.] (א) תנא מיניה ארבעין זימנין ודמי ליה כמאן דמנח בכיסיה.§

מתני' [ד] ג) אין בין יום טוב לשבת אלא אוכל נפש בלבד.§ **גמ'** הא לענין מכשירי אוכל נפש – זה וזה שוין. מתניתין דלא כרבי יהודה. דתניא: ג) אין בין יום טוב לשבת אלא אוכל נפש. רבי יהודה מתיר אף מכשירי אוכל נפש. *מ"ט דת"ק – אמר קרא: °"הוא" – ולא מכשיריו. ור' יהודה (*אמר:) "לכם" – [ה]"לכם ד) לכל צורכיכם. ואידך נמי, הכתיב: "לכם"! לכם *ולא לגוים, לכם ולא לכלבים. ואידך נמי הא כתיב: "הוא"! כתיב "הוא" וכתיב "לכם". [ו]כאן – במכשירין שאפשר לעשותן מערב יום טוב; כאן – במכשירין שאי אפשר לעשותן מערב יום טוב.§

מתני' [ז]*אין בין שבת ליום הכפורים אלא שזה, זדונו בידי אדם וזה, זדונו בכרת.§ **גמ'** הא לענין תשלומין – זה וזה שוין. מני מתניתין? רבי נחוניא בן הקנה היא, דתניא ר' נחוניא בן הקנה היה עושה *את יום הכפורים כשבת לתשלומין. מה שבת מתחייב בנפשו ופטור מן התשלומין – אף יום הכפורים מתחייב בנפשו ופטור מן התשלומין. *תנן התם: כל חייבי כריתות שלקו נפטרו מידי כריתתן, שנאמר: °"ונקלה אחיך לעיניך" – כיון שלקה הרי הוא כאחיך, דברי רבי חנניה בן גמליאל. *אמר ר' יוחנן: חלוקין עליו חביריו על ר' חנניה בן גמליאל. אמר רבא: אמרי בי רב, תנינא: אין בין יוה"כ לשבת אלא שזה, זדונו בידי אדם וזה, זדונו בהיכרת. ואם איתא – אידי ואידי בידי אדם היא! אמר רב *נחמן: הא מני? רבי יצחק היא דאמר: מלקות בחייבי כריתות ליכא. דתניא *רבי יצחק אומר: חייבי כריתות בכלל היו. ולמה יצאת כרת באחותו? לדונה בכרת ולא במלקות. רב אשי אמר: אפי' תימא רבנן. זה – עיקר זדונו בידי אדם; וזה – עיקר זדונו בהיכרת.§

מתני'

תורה אור | שמות יב | דברים כה | ס"א

א) [ברכות כח. וש"נ] ב) [ביצה לו:] ג) שבת ס: קכל. קלז: ביצה כח. לו: [תוספתא פ"א] ד) [ביצה כח: וש"נ]

תוספות

דלא ידע בין ארור המן לברוך מרדכי. [בירושלמי]: ארורה זרש ברוכה אסתר, ארורים כל הרשעים ברוכים כל היהודים:

אין בין יו"ט לשבת. צריך לומר דה"פ: אין שום מלאכה אסורה לשבת שלא תהא אסורה ליום טוב אלא אוכל נפש בלבד, אבל שאר חלוקים יש ביניהן, שזה בסקילה וזה בלאו:

כאן במכשירין שאי אפשר לעשות מערב יו"ט. משמע מדלא (ד)פליגי אלא במכשירין מכלל דגוף המאכל שרי לעשות ביום טוב, אע"ג דאפשר לעשות מערב יו"ט. ומדרב יהודה נשמע לרבנן, דהא לא פליגי עליה אלא במכשירין. וא"כ קשיא, דאמר בפרק "המצניע" (שבת דף צה. ושם): החולב והמגבן והמרבן והרודה חלות דבש, בשבת – חייב חטאת, הזיד ביו"ט – לוקה את הארבעים. אע"ג דהוי אוכל נפש. ואפי' לרבנן דאמרי התם אחד זה ואחד זה אין בו אלא משום שבות, מ"מ מודו היכא דאיכא אב מלאכה דלוקה! ויש לומר: דודאי אוכל נפש המתקלקל אם עושהו מאתמול – מותר לעשות ביו"ט, אבל אוכל נפש דעדיף טפי כשהוא עשוי מאתמול, כגון ההוא ד"המצניע" – אסור לעשותו ביו"ט. אבל מכשירין, דלא מתקלקל כשנעשו מאתמול – בהא ודאי יש לחלק [בין] היכא דאפשר ללא אפשר:

חייבי כריתות בכלל היו. פ"ה: בכלל "ונכרתו הנפשות העושות". וקשה: דאם כן הוי ליה למימר אחותו בכלל היתה, כלומר בכלל ונכרתו הנפשות, ולא היה לו לכתוב כרת! בה ויש לומר דה"פ: חייבי כריתות בכלל היו, פי': בכלל המלקיות, דבכל אחת ואחת יש לאו. ולמה יצאת כרת באחותו בלא לאו, שהרי הכרת לא איצטריך, שהרי היתה בכלל ונכרתו, אלא ודאי יצאתה לדונה בכרת (ה). ומינה נגמר לכל האחרים, כדין דבר שהיה בכלל:

אלא

רש"י

ה"ג: קיימת בנו רבינו ומשלוח מנות. דהא תרי מנות איכא: הדר שלח ליה איהו לא גרסינן ליה הכא: טסקא דקשבא. שק מלא תמרים: דאבשונא. שנתייבשו החטים בתנור בעודן כרמל, וקמח שלהן מתוק לעולם: א"ל אביי. לרבה: השתא אמר מרי. עכשיו יאמר מרי עליך: אי חקלאה מלכא ליהוי דיקולא מצואריה לא נחית. הסל שהיה רגיל להוליך בעודנו בן כפר ומאכיל לבהמתו, לא יוריד עתה מראשו. כך אתה, נעשית מלך וראש בפומבדיתא, ואינך שולח לו אלא דברים המצויין לכל: חוליא. מתיקא: כי נפקי מבי מר. כששלחתי מבית אדוני, רבה, לילך לבית (ג) אבא מרי בר מר הייתי שבע: צעי. קערות של מיני מאכל: דאיכסייא לצעא בתראי. הייתי חפץ לכוס הקערה אחריו. כל אכילה שלא כדרכה נקרא כוסס: רווחא לבסימא שכיח. ריוח מצוי לדבר המתוק בתוך המעיים: מחלפי סעודתייהו. זה אוכל עם זה בפורים של שנה זו, ובשניה סועד חברו עמו: לאבסומי. להשתכר ביין: ואיבסום. נשתכרו: נגה ולא אתו רבנן. איחר היום, ולא באו התלמידים לבית המדרש: **מתני'** אין בין יום טוב לשבת. להיות מותר לכתחלה ביום טוב מה שאסור בשבת. אבל לענין עונשין – יש הרבה, שזה בסקילה ובכרת, וזה בלאו גרידא: **גמ'** זה וזה שוין. אסורין ביום טוב כשבת: שאפשר. כגון סכין שנפגם מערב יום טוב: שאי אפשר. כגון סכין שנפגמה ביום טוב: **מתני'** בידי אדם. יש בה מיתת ב"ד: **גמ'** אף יום הכפורים מתחייב בנפשו. דאיסור כרת כמיתת בית דין דמי: ופטורים מלשלם. אם הדליק גדישו של חבירו ביום הכפורים, שאין תשלומין אלא חיוב מיתה, שנאמר "ולא יהיה אסון ענש יענש" (שמות כא), הא אם יהיה אסון – לא יענש: כל חייבי כריתות שלקו. שהתרו בהן עדים על לאו שעמו כרת, ולקו בבית דין: נפטרו מידי כריתתן. שוב אין בית דין של מעלה נפרעין: תנינא. דחלוקין: ואם איתא. דנפטרו, אידי ואידי בידי אדם הוא, אף ביום הכפורים יש מלקות על לאו שבו, ובית דין פוטרין אותו מכרת: אמר רב נחמן. לעולם אינן חלוקין עליו חביריו, והא דקתני דאין זדונו בידי אדם: הא מני ר' יצחק היא. דאמר במסכת מכות דאין מלקין בלאו הניתן לאזהרת כרת, אפילו התרו בו למלקות. ויליף טעמיה מהאי קרא: כל חייבי כריתות. של עריות היו בכלל "ונכרתו הנפשות העושות" וגו' שכתוב בפרשת עריות (ויקרא יח): למה יצאת כרת באחותו. דכתיב ב"קדושים תהיו": "ואיש כי יקח את אחותו" וגו': לדונה בכרת ולא במלקות. אם התרו בהן. ואף על גב דנדה נמי נשנית באותה פרשה – לדבר שנתחדש בה נשנית, להערלה: אפילו תימא רבנן היא. דאמרי מלקות אבל כרת. ואפילו *הכא ליכא למילף מינה, שחלוקין על רבי חנניה, והכי קאמר מתניתין: שבת עיקר חומר זדונו בידי אדם, וזה – עיקר חומר זדונו בהכרת. ומיהו, אם התרו בו ולקה – מיפטר:

מתני'

מסורת הש"ס

[עי' תוספות ע"ז יז: ד"ה חלב פירושו של מלה תמרים]

[עירובין סב.]

[פסחים נ:]

[בשאלתות לפורים איתא דאמימר]

[בשאלתות איתא לא שמיע לי תנא מיניה וכו']

[ביצה כח. ע"ש]

[נ"ל אמר קרא]

[עי' תוספות מנחות לב: ד"ה תפילין]

שבועות לג. פסחים כט: לב. כתובות ל. [תוס' פ"א ותוס' ב"ק פ"ו]

[מכות ג. ע"ש]

[במכות איתא ר"נ בר יצחק]

[מכות יג: כג: כריתות ב:]

[נ"ל הכי]

רבינו חננאל

שלח ליה קיימת בנו רבינו *) ומתנות לאביונים כלומר נתינת אביונים נתת לי מנה אחת והיא הירך חזר שלח לו עגל וג' קנקני יין כו'. בסימא פי' שיכור: **אמר** רבא סעודת פורים שאכלה בלילה לא יצא מ"ט ימי משתה ושמחה כתיב. שיתין צעי פי' קערות במיני מטעמים: **מתני'** אין בין יו"ט לשבת אלא אוכל נפש בלבד פי' בשבת אסור ביום טוב מותר. שנאמר אך אשר יאכל לכל נפש הוא לבדו יעשה לכם כגון אפייה ובישול וכיוצא בהן אבל מכשירי אוכל נפש כגון להוציא אש מן האבנים לבשל וכגון תקון סכין לשחוט בה וכיוצא בהן זה וזה שוין. כשם שאסור בשבת כך אסור ביו"ט: **גמ'** מתניתין דלא כר' יהודה. דתניא אין בין יו"ט לשבת אלא אוכל נפש בלבד שנא' אך אשר יאכל לכל נפש כו' והאי דכתיב לכם. לכם ולא לכלבים לכם ולא לעובדי כוכבים ר' יהודה מתיר אף במכשירי אוכל נפש שאי אפשר לעשותן מעיו"ט שנא' לכם לכל צרכיכם. וגרסי' בפרק משילין פירות דאוקמה רב פפא להא דתנן אין בין יו"ט לשבת אלא אוכל נפש בלבד ב"ש היא: **ירושלמי** אין בין יו"ט לשבת אלא אוכל נפש והא איכא חייבין סקילה וכרת בשבת ואין סקילה ולא כרת ביו"ט. מכות ביום טוב ואין מכות בשבת. ואין תימא באוכל נפש מתני' היא. והא תנינן משילין פירות דרך ארובה ביו"ט אבל לא בשבת. **) א"ר יוסי והוא שמל להדליק נר של בטלה ביו"ט אמר משמיה דר' יוחנן לא תתיר ולא תאסור: [מתני'] **אין** בין יוה"כ לשבת אלא ששבת זדונו סקילה בידי אדם. ויוה"כ המחללו בזדון חייב כרת בידי שמים: [גמ'] הא לענין תשלומין זה וזה שוין שאין חייב בתשלומין דקם ליה בדרבה מיניה. מני מתני' רבי נחוניא בן הקנה שפוטר מן התשלומין בזה ובזה. דתניא ר' (יהודה) [נחוניא] בן הקנה היה עושה את יוה"כ כשבת לתשלומין כו'. תנן התם כל חייבי כריתות שלקו נפטרו מידי כריתתן. דברי רבי חנניא בן גמליאל. א"ר יוחנן חלוקין עליו חביריו על רבי חנניא בן גמליאל ואומרים אע"פ שלקו לא נפטרו אמרי בי רב תנינא שחולקין עליו חביריו דתנן אין בין שבת ליוה"כ אלא ששבת זדונו בידי אדם ויוה"כ זדונו בכרת ואם המלקות פוטרתו נמצא גם זה זדונו בידי אדם. ואוקמה רב נחמן בר יצחק כרבי יצחק דתני חייבי כריתות היו ולמה יצאת כרת באחותו לדונה בכרת ולא במלקות: וגו' גם אחותו בכלל כל חייבי כריתות היא ולמה יצאת כרת באחותו לדונה בכרת ולא במלקות:

מתני'

*) גי' רבינו כאן היה כמו דאיתא בירושלמי בפירקין בסוף הלכה ד' ובשאלתות פ' ויקהל וכן הו' גירסת בעל מנורת המאור כאן בגמ' בנר ג' כלל ד' ח"ג פ"ג. **) חסר כאן וכ"ה הלשון בירושלמי עוד מן הדא שוחקין עצי בשמים למילה ביו"ט אבל לא בשבת א"ר יוסי והוא שמל וכו'.

הגהות הב"ח

(א) גמ' ומשלוח מנות איש לרעהו רבה שדר כצ"ל ותיבות ומתנות לאביונים נמחק: (ב) שם מ"ט לא אתו רבנן א"ל דלמא: (ג) רש"י ד"ה כי נפקי וכו' לבית מרי כצ"ל ותיבת אבא נמחק: (ד) תוספות ד"ה כאן וכו' מדלא מפליג אלא במכשירין: (ה) ד"ה חייבי וכו' לדונה בכרת ולא במלקות ומינה:

הגהות הגר"א

[א] גמ' (ומתנות לאביונים) תא"מ (וכ"מ מרש"י דל"ג לה):

מתני' *אאֵין בֵּין הַמּוּדָּר הֲנָאָה מֵחֲבֵירוֹ לַמּוּדָּר מִמֶּנּוּ מַאֲכָל אֶלָּא דְּרִיסַת הָרֶגֶל, וְכֵלִים שֶׁאֵין עוֹשִׂין בָּהֶן אוֹכֶל נֶפֶשׁ.§ גמ' הָא לְעִנְיַן כֵּלִים שֶׁעוֹשִׂין בָּהֶן אוֹכֶל נֶפֶשׁ — זֶה וָזֶה שָׁוִין.§ "דְּרִיסַת הָרֶגֶל".§ הָא לָא קָפְדִי אֱינָשֵׁי! אָמַר רָבָא: הָא מַנִּי? רַבִּי אֱלִיעֶזֶר, דְּאָמַר: *וִיתּוּר אָסוּר בְּמוּדַּר הֲנָאָה.§ מתני' באֵין בֵּין נְדָרִים לִנְדָבוֹת אֶלָּא שֶׁהַנְּדָרִים חַיָּיב בְּאַחֲרָיוּתָן, וּנְדָבוֹת אֵינוֹ חַיָּיב בְּאַחֲרָיוּתָן.§ גמ' הָא לְעִנְיַן "בַּל תְּאַחֵר" — זֶה וָזֶה שָׁוִין. תְּנַן הָתָם: *גאֵי זֶהוּ נֶדֶר? הָאוֹמֵר: "הֲרֵי עָלַי עוֹלָה". אֵיזוֹ הִיא נְדָבָה? הָאוֹמֵר: "הֲרֵי זוֹ עוֹלָה". וּמַה בֵּין נְדָרִים לִנְדָבוֹת? נְדָרִים, מֵתוּ אוֹ נִגְנְבוּ אוֹ אָבְדוּ — חַיָּיב בְּאַחֲרָיוּתָן; נְדָבוֹת, מֵתוּ אוֹ נִגְנְבוּ אוֹ אָבְדוּ — אֵינוֹ חַיָּיב בְּאַחֲרָיוּתָן. מְנָהָנֵי מִילֵּי? דְּתָנוּ רַבָּנַן: *°"וְנִרְצָה לוֹ לְכַפֵּר עָלָיו". ר' שִׁמְעוֹן אוֹמֵר: אֶת שֶׁעָלָיו, חַיָּיב בְּאַחֲרָיוּתוֹ; וְאֶת שֶׁאֵינוֹ עָלָיו, אֵינוֹ חַיָּיב בְּאַחֲרָיוּתוֹ. מַאי מַשְׁמַע? א"ר יִצְחָק בַּר אַבְדִּימִי: כֵּיוָן דְּאָמַר "עָלַי" — כְּמַאן דְּטָעִין אַכַּתְפֵיהּ דָּמֵי.§ מתני' דאֵין בֵּין זָב הָרוֹאֶה שְׁתֵּי רְאִיּוֹת, לְרוֹאֶה שָׁלֹשׁ, אֶלָּא קָרְבָּן.§ גמ' הָא לְעִנְיַן מִשְׁכָּב וּמוֹשָׁב, וּסְפִירַת שִׁבְעָה — זֶה וָזֶה שָׁוִין. מְנָהָנֵי מִילֵּי? דְּתָנוּ רַבָּנַן: רַבִּי סִימַאי אוֹמֵר: *מָנָה הַכָּתוּב שְׁתַּיִם וּקְרָאוֹ "טָמֵא", שָׁלֹשׁ וּקְרָאוֹ טָמֵא. הָא כֵּיצַד? שְׁתַּיִם לְטוּמְאָה וְשָׁלֹשׁ לְקָרְבָּן. וְאֵימַר: שְׁתַּיִם לְטוּמְאָה וְלֹא לְקָרְבָּן, שָׁלֹשׁ לְקָרְבָּן וְלֹא לְטוּמְאָה! אָמַרְתָּ: עַד שֶׁלֹּא רָאָה שָׁלֹשׁ רָאָה שְׁתַּיִם. וְאֵימַר: שְׁתַּיִם לְקָרְבָּן וְלֹא לְטוּמְאָה, שָׁלֹשׁ אַף לְטוּמְאָה! לֹא ס"ד דְּתַנְיָא: °"וְכִפֶּר עָלָיו הַכֹּהֵן לִפְנֵי ה' מִזּוֹבוֹ" — מִקְצָת זָבִין מְבִיאִין קָרְבָּן וּמִקְצָת זָבִין אֵין מְבִיאִין קָרְבָּן. הָא כֵּיצַד? רָאָה שָׁלֹשׁ — מֵבִיא, שְׁתַּיִם — אֵינוֹ מֵבִיא. אוֹ אֵינוֹ אֶלָּא רָאָה ב' — מֵבִיא, רָאָה שָׁלֹשׁ — אֵינוֹ מֵבִיא? אָמַרְתָּ: עַד שֶׁלֹּא רָאָה שָׁלֹשׁ רָאָה שְׁתַּיִם. וְאִיצְטְרִיךְ דְּרַבִּי סִימַאי, וְאִיצְטְרִיךְ "מִזּוֹבוֹ". דְּאִי מִדְּרַבִּי סִימַאי — הֲוָה אָמִינָא כִּי קוּשְׁיָין. קָמַשְׁמַע לָן "מִזּוֹבוֹ". וְאִי "מִזּוֹבוֹ" — לֹא יָדַעְנָא כַּמָּה רְאִיּוֹת. קָמַשְׁמַע לָן דְּרַבִּי סִימַאי. וְהַשְׁתָּא דְּאָמַרְתְּ "מִזּוֹבוֹ" לִדְרָשָׁא, °"וְכִי יִטְהַר הַזָּב מִזּוֹבוֹ" מַאי דָּרְשַׁתְּ בֵּיהּ? הַהוּא מִיבְּעֵי לֵיהּ לִכְדְתַנְיָא: "וְכִי יִטְהַר הַזָּב" — לִכְשֶׁיִּפְסוֹק מִזּוֹבוֹ, ["מִזּוֹבוֹ"] וְלֹא *מִזּוֹבוֹ וְנִגְעוֹ; "מִזּוֹבוֹ וְסָפַר" — הלִימֵּד עַל זָב בַּעַל שְׁתֵּי רְאִיּוֹת שֶׁטָּעוּן סְפִירַת שִׁבְעָה. וַהֲלֹא דִּין הוּא: אִם מְטַמֵּא מִשְׁכָּב וּמוֹשָׁב — לֹא יְהֵא טָעוּן סְפִירַת שִׁבְעָה?! שׁוֹמֶרֶת

רש"י

מתני' אֵין בֵּין הַמּוּדָּר הֲנָאָה. מוּדַּר הֲנָאָה חָמוּר מִמּוּדַּר מַאֲכָל: דְּרִיסַת הָרֶגֶל. שֶׁהַמּוּדָּר הֲנָאָה אָסוּר לִיכָּנֵס לְבֵיתוֹ, וְהַמּוּדָּר מַאֲכָל מוּתָּר: וְכֵלִים שֶׁאֵין עוֹשִׂין בָּהֶן אוֹכֶל נֶפֶשׁ. מוּתָּר לְהַשְׁאִיל לְמוּדַּר מַאֲכָל. וְדַוְקָא בְּמָקוֹם שֶׁאֵין מַשְׂכִּירִין כַּיּוֹצֵא בָּהֶן, אֲבָל בְּמָקוֹם שֶׁמַּשְׂכִּירִין כַּיּוֹצֵא בָּהֶן – תְּנַן בְּהֶדְיָא* דְּאָסוּר, דְּכָל הֲנָאָה שֶׁאִם לֹא הֶהֱנָהוּ זֶה הָיָה מְחַסֵּר בָּהּ פְּרוּטָה – הֲנָאַת מַאֲכָל הִיא, שֶׁהֲרֵי רְאוּיָה אוֹתָהּ פְּרוּטָה לִקְנוֹת בָּהּ מַאֲכָל: גמ' הָא לְעִנְיַן כֵּלִים שֶׁעוֹשִׂין בָּהֶן אוֹכֶל נֶפֶשׁ. אָסוּר אַף בְּמוּדַּר מַאֲכָל, וַאֲפִי' בְּמָקוֹם שֶׁאֵין מַשְׂכִּירִים: הָא לָא קָפְדִי אֱינָשֵׁי. וְאַמַּאי אָסוּר בְּמוּדַּר הֲנָאָה? וִיתּוּר. דָּבָר שֶׁהָיָה מְוַותֵּר לְכָל אָדָם, וְאֵינוֹ מַקְפִּיד עָלָיו: מתני' נֶדֶר וּנְדָבָה. מְפָרֵשׁ בַּגְּמָרָא: נֶדֶר – הָאוֹמֵר "הֲרֵי עָלַי עוֹלָה", וּלְאַחַר זְמַן הִפְרִישָׁהּ – חַיָּיב בְּאַחֲרָיוּתָהּ. נְדָבָה – הָאוֹמֵר "הֲרֵי זוֹ", וְלֹא קִבְּלָהּ עָלָיו: גמ' הָא לְעִנְיַן בַּל תְּאַחֵר. וְאַף עַל גַּב דִּנְדָבָה בִּקְרָא דְּ"בַל תְּאַחֵר" לָא כְּתִיבָא, הָא מְרַבִּינַן לֵיהּ בְּמַסֶּכֶת רֹאשׁ הַשָּׁנָה מִגְּזֵרָה שָׁוָה: אֶת שֶׁעָלָיו חַיָּיב בְּאַחֲרָיוּתוֹ. הָכִי דָּרֵשׁ לֵיהּ לִקְרָא: "וְנִרְצָה לוֹ" נִדְרוֹ – לִכְשֶׁיִּתְכַּפֵּר בָּהֶן הַוְיָא נִרְצֶה, אֲבָל מִקַּמֵּי כַּפָּרָה לֹא נִרְצָה. וּבְאֵיזֶה קָרְבָּן אָמַרְתִּי לְךָ? – בְּאוֹתוֹ שֶׁעָלָיו, וְהַיְינוּ "עָלָיו" דִּקְרָא: מַאי מַשְׁמַע. דְּעָלָיו קִבֵּל אַחֲרָיוּת עָלָיו: מתני' שְׁתֵּי רְאִיּוֹת. בְּיוֹם אֶחָד, אוֹ בִּשְׁנֵי יָמִים רְצוּפִים. וְכֵן שָׁלֹשׁ, בְּיוֹם אֶחָד אוֹ בִּשְׁלֹשָׁה יָמִים רְצוּפִין, אוֹ שְׁתַּיִם בְּיוֹם אֶחָד וְאַחַת לְמָחָר: גמ' מִשְׁכָּב וּמוֹשָׁב. שָׁכַב אוֹ יָשַׁב עַל גַּבֵּי עֲשָׂרָה בְּגָדִים זֶה עַל זֶה – כּוּלָּן אֲבוֹת הַטּוּמְאָה, וַאֲפִילּוּ לֹא נָגַע בָּהֶן. וְאִילּוּ נָגַע בְּדָבָר שֶׁאֵינוֹ מִשְׁכָּב וּמוֹשָׁב – אֵינוֹ [אֶלָּא] רִאשׁוֹן לְטוּמְאָה, וְאֵינוֹ מְטַמֵּא אָדָם וְכֵלִים אֶלָּא אוֹכָלִין וּמַשְׁקִין: וּסְפִירַת שִׁבְעָה. מִשֶּׁיִּפְסוֹק צָרִיךְ לִמְנוֹת ז' נְקִיִּים קוֹדֶם שֶׁיִּטְבּוֹל, וְאִם רָאָה זוֹב בְּאַחַד מֵהֶן – סָתַר כָּל הַמְּנוּיִין: מְנָא הָנֵי מִילֵּי. דְּשָׁוִין לְטוּמְאָה וְאֵין שָׁוִין לְקָרְבָּן: מָנָה הַכָּתוּב שְׁתַּיִם. "וְאִישׁ כִּי יִהְיֶה זָב מִבְּשָׂרוֹ זוֹבוֹ טָמֵא הוּא" (ויקרא טו), הֲרֵי שְׁתֵּי זִיבוֹת מְנוּיוֹת כָּאן, וּקְרָאוֹ טָמֵא: שָׁלֹשׁ וּקְרָאוֹ טָמֵא. דִּכְתִיב "וְזֹאת תִּהְיֶה טוּמְאָתוֹ בְּזוֹבוֹ רָר בְּשָׂרוֹ אֶת זוֹבוֹ אוֹ הֶחְתִּים בְּשָׂרוֹ מִזּוֹבוֹ" (שם) – הֲרֵי לְךָ שָׁלֹשׁ, וּקְרָאוֹ טָמֵא – "טוּמְאָתוֹ הִיא": הָא כֵּיצַד. אִם מִשְּׁתַּיִם טָמֵא, לָמָּה פֵּרֵט לְךָ הַכָּתוּב שָׁלֹשׁ? שְׁתַּיִם לְטוּמְאָה. לְכָל חוֹמֶר טוּמְאַת זָב: וְלֹא לְטוּמְאָה. חֲמוּרָה, אֶלָּא כְּבַעַל קֶרִי בְּעָלְמָא: רָאָה שְׁתַּיִם. וַהֲרֵי כְּבָר יָרַד לְכָל חוֹמֶר טוּמְאָה, וּמִי הוֹצִיאוֹ? מִזּוֹבוֹ. מַשְׁמַע: מִקְצָת זוֹבוֹ: לָא יָדַעְנָא כַּמָּה רְאִיּוֹת. הַאי מִקְצָת דְּמַשְׁמַע מֵהַאי קְרָא, לָא יָדְעִינַן מַאי הִיא. שָׁלֹשׁ וְאַרְבַּע, אוֹ שְׁתַּיִם וְשָׁלֹשׁ: לִכְשֶׁיִּפְסוֹק מִזּוֹבוֹ. אֵין צָרִיךְ לִיטְבּוֹל קוֹדֶם סְפִירָה, אֶלָּא מִשֶּׁיִּפְסוֹק יִמְנֶה. הָכִי גָּרְסִינַן בְּתוֹרַת כֹּהֲנִים: "מִזּוֹבוֹ" – וְלֹא מִזּוֹבוֹ וּמִנִּגְעוֹ. שֶׁאִם הָיָה זָב וּמְצוֹרָע, וּפָסַק מִזּוֹבוֹ וְלֹא נִתְרַפֵּא עֲדַיִין מִנִּגְעוֹ – "וְסָפַר", אֵין אוֹמְרִים לוֹ אֵין סְפִירָה זוֹ נְקִיּוּת עַד שֶׁיִּטְהַר אַף מִנִּגְעוֹ, אֶלָּא מוֹנֶה וְהוֹלֵךְ מִיָּד וְעוֹלָה לוֹ לִסְפִירַת זוֹב. וְלִכְשֶׁיִּתְרַפֵּא מִצָּרַעְתּוֹ יִטְבּוֹל מִיָּד טְבִילָה רִאשׁוֹנָה שֶׁל מְצוֹרָע, וְהִיא עוֹלָה לוֹ לִטְבִילַת נִגְעוֹ וְזוֹבוֹ, וְנִטְהָר מִלְּטַמֵּא מִשְׁכָּב וּמוֹשָׁב וּלְטַמֵּא כְּלִי חֶרֶס בְּהֶיסֵּט כְּדִין זָב. וְאַף עַל פִּי שֶׁצָּרִיךְ לִסְפִירַת שִׁבְעָה לְצָרַעְתּוֹ לְעִנְיַן אֲכִילַת קֳדָשִׁים, וּטְבִילָה שְׁנִיָּה כִּדְכְתִיב בִּמְצוֹרָע (ויקרא יד) "וְרָחַץ בַּמַּיִם וְטָהֵר וְאַחַר יָבֹא אֶל הַמַּחֲנֶה וְיָשַׁב מִחוּץ לְאָהֳלוֹ שִׁבְעַת יָמִים, וְהָיָה בַּיּוֹם הַשְּׁבִיעִי יְגַלַּח אֶת כָּל שְׂעָרוֹ וגו' וְרָחַץ [אֶת] בְּשָׂרוֹ בַּמַּיִם" וגו' – אַלְמָא טְבִילָה קַמַּיְיתָא לְטַהֲרוֹ מִלְּטַמֵּא מִשְׁכָּב וּמוֹשָׁב וּכְלִי חֶרֶס בְּהֶיסֵּט: מִזּוֹבוֹ וְסָפַר. לְהָכִי סָמַךְ סְפִירָה אֵצֶל זוֹבוֹ, לְלַמֶּדְךָ שֶׁאַף בִּשְׁבִיל מִקְצַת זָב טָעוּן סְפִירָה, לִימֵּד עַל זָב בַּעַל שְׁתֵּי רְאִיּוֹת: לֹא יְהֵא טָעוּן סְפִירַת שִׁבְעָה. בִּתְמִיָּה: אַחַר שֶׁאָמַרְתָּ שְׁתַּיִם כו'. וְה"ג: הֲלֹא דִּין הוּא! אִם מְטַמֵּא מִשְׁכָּב וּמוֹשָׁב בִּשְׁתֵּי רְאִיּוֹת לְכָל חוֹמֶר טוּמְאַת זָב, מֵהֵיכָן יִתְמַעֵט מִסְּפִירָה: שׁוֹמֶרֶת

תוספות

אלא דריסת הרגל וכלים שאין עושין בהן אוכל נפש. דמודר הנאה אסור בהן, ומודר מאכל מותר במקום שאין משכירין. אבל במקום שמשכירין בפרוטה – אסור אפי' במודר מאכל, דאותה פרוטה ראויה לקנות ממנה מאכל. אבל כלים שעושין בהן אוכל נפש אסור אפילו בפחות משוה פרוטה, כיון דהוי אוכל נפש:

דריסת הרגל הא לא קפדי אינשי. קשה: דהא "בחזקת הבתים" (ב"ב דף נז:) קאמר בגמרא: אלו דברים שאין להם חזקה, ואלו דברים שיש להם חזקה, וכו' מעמיד בהמה בחצר אין להם חזקה. ומוקי לה התם בשותפין, דבהעמדה כדי לא קפדין ופריך, והתנן: השותפין שנדרו הנאה זה מזה אסורין ליכנס בחצר, ומשני לה התם. מיהו, שמעינן לה מינה דאדריסת הרגל קפדי! ולא קשה *מההיא דהתם פרק בתרא דבילה (דף לט:) דמשני התם דלעולם לא קפדי, ומני ר' אליעזר היא. דלמא התם מיירי בשותפין, אבל שאר אינשי ודאי קפדי. אבל הכא קשיא, דמיירי בסתם בני אדם, ואפי' הכי קאמר דלא קפדי! ותירץ ר"ת: דהכא מיירי בבקעה, דלא קפדי בה שום אדם. וסברא הוא לומר כן(א) דומיא (*דריסא) דכלים שאין עושין בהן אוכל נפש, דמיירי שאין משכירין כיוצא בהן, דמוקמינן לה בנדרים (דף לג:) כרבי אליעזר*:

אין בין נדר לנדבה. קשיא: אמאי לא תני שנדבה באה מן המעשר, דכתיב (דברים כז) "וזבחת שלמים" בי מעשר, ונדר אינו בא אלא מן החולין, וכיון דאמר "הרי עלי" הוי(ב) נדר! *וי"ל: דמן הדין לא תנא ליה, משום דאיירי בקרבן שהופרש כבר, ואשמעינן דאין חילוק בעבודתן. אבל בקרבן שלא הופרש – פשיטא ליה שיש הרבה חילוקים. אי נמי, דתנא ושייר. ונהי דאין בין קאמר, דמשמע דהוי דוקא, כדאמר ב"מרובה" (ב"ק דף סב: ושם) מ"מ לא קשיא, דבמסכת תענית (דף יג: ושם) אשכחן "אין בין" דשייר, דקאמרף אין בין שלש אמצעיות. וכי תימא תנא ושייר – והא "אין בין" קתני! ופריך: ותסברא "אין בין" דווקא? והא שייר תיבה! ומשני: אי משום תיבה לאו שיורא הוא. מכל מקום משמע דאי הוה משייר ליה לא הוה קשיא ליה כלל, אף על גב דקתני "אין בין"*: יש ספרים דגרסי:

ומה מצורע שאין מטמא משכב ומושב. ובתורת כהנים תני שמטמא משכב ומושב! ותירץ רש"י בפסחים (דף סז: ד"ה זב) דהיינו לטמא אוכלין ומשקין, אבל לא לטמא אדם וכלים *כגון זב: עד

מסורת הש"ס: (נדרים לג.) | שם לג: | ב"ב נז: נדרים לג: מח: | ר"ה ו. קינין פ"א מ"א [חולין קלט. ערכין כא.] | [זבחים ז:] | ויקרא ח | שם טו | שם | [נדה לז. ושם איתא ולא מנגעו אבל בת"כ איתא ולא מזובו ונגעו ועיין בקרבן אהרן] | גי' רש"א מההיא דהתם מפרק כו' ע"ש | [נ"ל דריסה] | [ועי' תוספות ב"ק נה: ד"ה זה ותוספות ב"ב נז: ד"ה רבינא] | [ועי' תוספות חגיגה ח. ד"ה אמאי ותוספות ב"ק סב: ד"ה מי קתני] | [וכב"ק ובתענית כתבו תוספות תירוץ אחר ועי' תוס' שבת ס: ד"ה אין] | ס"א כמו

הגהות הב"ח

(א) תוס' ד"ה דריסת וכו' וסברא הוא לומר כן. נ"ב לכאורה צריך לומר לפי זה הס"מ למיפרך אכלים שאין עושין בהם אוכל נפש הא לא קפדי וכ"ב התוס' בפרק חזקת הבתים: (ב) ד"ה אין בין וכו' וכיון דאמר הרי עלי הוי חובה וכו' וי"ל:

רבינו חננאל

[מתני'] אין בין המודר הנאה מחבירו למודר הימנו מאכל אלא דריסת הרגל וכלים שאין עושין בהן אוכל נפש כגון בגדים וכיוצא בהן דלמודר הנאה אסור. ואוקימנא לר' אליעזר דתני אפילו ויתור אסור במודר הנאה. פי' אפילו דברים שדרך בנ"א לוותר עליהן כגון דריסת הרגלים (וכלים שאין עושין) בחצרם שאם יכנס אדם ויהלך בה אין מקפידין עליו וכיוצא בזה אפי' כגון זה אסור. אבל למודר ממנו מאכל דריסת הרגל וכלים שאין עושין בהן אוכל נפש כגון קערה ותמחוי וכן כיוצא בהן מותר הא כלים שעושין בהן אוכל נפש כגון נפה וכברה ריחים ותנור וכיוצא בהן זה וזה שוין שניהם אסורין: מתני' אין בין נדרים לנדבות כו'. הא לבל תאחר כדכתיב כי תדור נדר לה' וגו' זה וזה שוין כלומר אם יאחר בין הנדר ובין הנדבה עובר משום בל תאחר: תנן התם איזהו נדר האומר עלי עולה איזו היא נדבה האומר הרי זו נדבה ומה ביניהם נדרים מתו או נגנבו חייבין באחריותן שנאמר ונרצה לו לכפר עליו דייקינן מעליו את שעליו. כלומר אם אמר עלי חייב באחריותו דכיון דאמר עלי כמאן דרמי אכתפיה דמי שחייב למוסרו למי שחייב לו אבל הנדבה אין חייב באחריותה: מתני' אין בין זב הרואה ב' ראיות לרואה ג' וכו'. הא לענין משכב ומושב וספירת ז' טהורין זה וזה שוין דתניא או החתים בשרו מזובו דייקינן מדכתיב מזובו שמעינן מינה אף מקצת זובו מטמא משכב ומושב להביא את שראה ב' ראיות שיטמא משכב ומושב כל הטעון משכב ומושב טעון ספירת ז'. כדתניא מזובו וספר מקצת זובו נמי טעון ספירת ז' להביא את שראה ב' ראיות שטעון ספירת ז'. מתני' מני ר' סימאי היא. דתני ר' סימאי מנה הכתוב שתים וקרא טמא שלש וקרא טמא. הא כיצד ב' לטומאה ג' אף לקרבן פי' מנה הכתוב ב' פעמים זיבות זוב וזובו וקרא טמא. שנאמר איש איש כי יהיה זב מבשרו זובו טמא הוא. עוד חזר הכתוב אחר ומנה שלש בזובו אחת זובו שתים מזובו הרי ג' שנאמר וזאת תהיה טומאתו בזובו וגו' אמר אם בשתים טמא בשלש לא כ"ש למה כתב עוד שלש ללמד כי בב' ראיות טמא הוא ופטור מן הקרבן בג' ראיות חייב אף בקרבן. ואקשינן ואימא שתים לקרבן ולא לטומאה. כלומר בב' ראיות חייב קרבן אע"פ שאינו טמא ראה שלישית חייב בטומאה ובקרבן. ופרקינן לא דתניא וכפר עליו הכהן לפני ה' מזובו. מקצת זבים מביאין קרבן ומקצת אין מביאין קרבן. וא"ת כי בעל ב' ראיות מביא קרבן. אין לך זב שאינו מביא קרבן שאינו רואה אלא ג'. אלא שכבר הקדים וראה ב' וכבר נתחייב בב'. ומכאן ולהבא אפילו ראה כמה אין חייב אלא קרבן אחד כו' ואיצטריך לדרבי סימאי לברר כי בשתי ראיות נקרא טמא. ואיצטריך מזובו לדחות הקושיא שהקשו על רבי סימאי דאי לאו מזובו הוה אמינא שתים לקרבן שלש לקרבן ולטומאה כו'. ופשוטה היא: אמר

נח א מיי' פ"א מהלכות מטמאי משכב ומושב הלכה א ב:
נט ב מיי' פ"י מהלכות טומאת צרעת הל' י:
ס ג מיי' פ"ה מהלכות מטמאי משכב ומושב הלכה ט:
סא ד מיי' פ"י מהל' טומאת צרעת הל' ח:
סב ה ו מיי' פ"א מהל' תפלין הלכה יט:
סג ז מיי' פ"ט מהל' שאר אבות הטומאות הלכה ז:

"שׁוֹמֶרֶת יוֹם כְּנֶגֶד יוֹם" תּוֹכִיחַ, אשֶׁמְּטַמְּאָה מִשְׁכָּב וּמוֹשָׁב וְאֵינָהּ טְעוּנָה סְפִירַת שִׁבְעָה. וְאַף אַתָּה אַל תִּתְמַהּ עַל זֶה, שֶׁאע"פ שֶׁמְּטַמֵּא מִשְׁכָּב וּמוֹשָׁב לֹא יְהֵא טָעוּן סְפִירַת שִׁבְעָה. תַּלְמוּד לוֹמַר: "מִזּוֹבוֹ וְסָפַר" — מִקְצָת זוֹבוֹ וְסָפַר, לִימֵּד עַל זָב בַּעַל שְׁתֵּי רְאִיּוֹת שֶׁטָּעוּן סְפִירַת שִׁבְעָה.

אָמַר לֵיהּ רַב פַּפָּא לְאַבַּיֵי: מַאי שְׁנָא הַאי "מִזּוֹבוֹ" דִּמְרַבֵּי בֵּיהּ זָב בַּעַל שְׁתֵּי רְאִיּוֹת, וּמַאי שְׁנָא הַאי "מִזּוֹבוֹ" דִּמְמַעֵט בֵּיהּ זָב בַּעַל שְׁתֵּי רְאִיּוֹת? אָמַר לֵיהּ: אִי סָלְקָא דַּעְתָּךְ הַאי לְמַעוּטֵי הוּא דַּאֲתָא — לִישְׁתּוֹק קְרָא מִינֵּיהּ. וְכִי תֵּימָא: אָתְיָא מִדִּינָא — שׁוֹמֶרֶת יוֹם כְּנֶגֶד יוֹם תּוֹכִיחַ. וְכִי תֵּימָא: הַאי מִיבְּעֵי לֵיהּ "מִזּוֹבוֹ" וְלֹא(א) מִנִּגְעוֹ — א"כ לִיכְתּוֹב קְרָא: "וְכִי יִטְהַר הַזָּב" וְלִישְׁתּוֹק. "מִזּוֹבוֹ" לָמָּה לִי? לִימֵּד עַל זָב בַּעַל שְׁתֵּי רְאִיּוֹת שֶׁטָּעוּן סְפִירַת שִׁבְעָה.§

מתני' *באֵין בֵּין מְצוֹרָע מוּסְגָּר לִמְצוֹרָע מוּחְלָט, אֶלָּא פְּרִיעָה וּפְרִימָה. אֵין בֵּין טָהוֹר מִתּוֹךְ הֶסְגֵּר לְטָהוֹר מִתּוֹךְ הֶחְלֵט אֶלָּא תִּגְלַחַת וְצִפֳּרִים.§ **גמ'** הָא לְעִנְיַן שִׁילּוּחַ [וְטוּמְאָה] — זֶה וָזֶה שָׁוִין. מְנָהָנֵי מִילֵּי? דְּתָנֵי רַב שְׁמוּאֵל בַּר יִצְחָק קַמֵּיהּ דְּרַב הוּנָא: °"וְטִהֲרוֹ הַכֹּהֵן מִסְפַּחַת הִיא וְכִבֶּס בְּגָדָיו וְטָהֵר" — טָהוֹר מִפְּרִיעָה וּפְרִימָה דְּמֵעִיקָּרָא. א"ל רָבָא: אֶלָּא מֵעַתָּה, גַּבֵּי זָב דִּכְתִיב: °"וְכִבֶּס בְּגָדָיו וְטָהֵר", הָתָם מַאי "וְטָהֵר" מֵעִיקָּרָא אִיכָּא? אֶלָּא: גטָהוֹר הַשְׁתָּא מִלְּטַמֵּא כְּלִי חֶרֶס בְּהֶיסֵּט. אע"ג דְּהָדַר חָזֵי לֹא מְטַמֵּא לְמַפְרֵעַ — ה"נ דטָהוֹר [*הַשְׁתָּא מִלְּטַמֵּא בְּבִיאָה לְמַפְרֵעַ!] אֶלָּא אָמַר רָבָא: מֵהָכָא: °"וְהַצָּרוּעַ אֲשֶׁר בּוֹ הַנֶּגַע" — מִי שֶׁצָּרַעְתּוֹ תְּלוּיָה בְּגוּפוֹ, יָצָא זֶה שֶׁאֵין צָרַעְתּוֹ תְּלוּיָה בְּגוּפוֹ אֶלָּא בְּיָמִים. אָמַר לֵיהּ אַבַּיֵי: אֶלָּא מֵעַתָּה °"כָּל יְמֵי אֲשֶׁר הַנֶּגַע בּוֹ יִטְמָא" מִי שֶׁצָּרַעְתּוֹ תְּלוּיָה בְּגוּפוֹ הוּא דְּטָעוּן שִׁילּוּחַ, וְשֶׁאֵין צָרַעְתּוֹ תְּלוּיָה בְּגוּפוֹ — אֵין טָעוּן שִׁילּוּחַ? וְכִי תֵּימָא הָכִי נַמִי — וְהָא קָתָנֵי: אֵין בֵּין מְצוֹרָע מוּסְגָּר לִמְצוֹרָע מוּחְלָט אֶלָּא פְּרִיעָה וּפְרִימָה. הָא לְעִנְיַן שִׁילּוּחַ וּלְטַמּוֹיֵי בְּבִיאָה — זֶה וָזֶה שָׁוִין! א"ל: "יְמֵי", "כָּל יְמֵי" — לְרַבּוֹת מְצוֹרָע מוּסְגָּר לְשִׁילּוּחַ. (ב)אִי הָכִי תִּגְלַחַת וְצִפֳּרִים מ"ט לֹא? דְּקָתָנֵי: אֵין בֵּין טָהוֹר מִתּוֹךְ הֶסְגֵּר לְטָהוֹר מִתּוֹךְ הֶחְלֵט אֶלָּא תִּגְלַחַת וְצִפֳּרִים! אָמַר אַבַּיֵי: אָמַר קְרָא: °"וְיָצָא הַכֹּהֵן אֶל מִחוּץ לַמַּחֲנֶה... *וְהִנֵּה נִרְפָּא נֶגַע הַצָּרַעַת" מִי שֶׁצָּרַעְתּוֹ תְּלוּיָה בִּרְפוּאוֹת, יָצָא זֶה שֶׁאֵין צָרַעְתּוֹ תְּלוּיָה בִּרְפוּאוֹת אֶלָּא בְּיָמִים.§

מתני' [א*]*האֵין בֵּין סְפָרִים לִתְפִלִּין וּמְזוּזוֹת *אֶלָּא שֶׁהַסְּפָרִים נִכְתָּבִין בְּכָל לָשׁוֹן, הוּתְפִלִּין וּמְזוּזוֹת אֵינָן נִכְתָּבוֹת אֶלָּא אַשּׁוּרִית. רשב"ג אוֹמֵר: ואַף בַּסְּפָרִים לֹא הִתִּירוּ שֶׁיִּכָּתְבוּ אֶלָּא יְוָונִית.§ **גמ'** הָא לְתוֹפְרָן בְּגִידִין, וּלְטַמֵּא אֶת הַיָּדַיִם — זֶה וָזֶה שָׁוִין.§ "וּסְפָרִים נִכְתָּבִין בְּכָל לָשׁוֹן" וכו'.§ וּרְמִינְהוּ: *זמִקְרָא שֶׁכְּתָבוֹ תַּרְגּוּם, וְתַרְגּוּם שֶׁכְּתָבוֹ מִקְרָא, וּכְתָב עִבְרִי — אֵינוֹ מְטַמֵּא אֶת הַיָּדַיִם, עַד שֶׁיִּכְתְּבֶנּוּ בִּכְתָב אַשּׁוּרִית, עַל הַסֵּפֶר, וּבִדְיוֹ. אָמַר רָבָא: לָא קַשְׁיָא: כָּאן

תורה אור: ויקרא יג; שם טו; שם יג; שם; שם יד

שבת קטו:

רש"י

שׁוֹמֶרֶת יוֹם כְּנֶגֶד יוֹם. הָרוֹאָה יוֹם אֶחָד אוֹ שְׁנַיִם בְּתוֹךְ אַחַד עָשָׂר יוֹם שֶׁבֵּין נִדָּה לְנִדָּה – מוֹנָה יוֹם אֶחָד, וְטוֹבֶלֶת בּוֹ בַּיּוֹם, תּוֹכִיחַ: שֶׁמְּטַמְּאָה מִשְׁכָּב וּמוֹשָׁב. בִּשְׁמַעְתָּא בַּתְרַיְיתָא דְּמַסֶּכֶת נִדָּה (דף עג:) מְרַבִּינַן לָהּ: מַאי שְׁנָא הַאי מִזּוֹבוֹ. מִ"זּוֹבוֹ וְסָפַר (לָהּ) [לוֹ]" דָּרַשְׁתְּ לֵיהּ (ג) דְּמִקְצָת זוֹב, וּלְאַשְׁמוּעִינַן דְּמִקְצָת זָבִין טְעוּנִין סְפִירַת שִׁבְעָה. וּבְהָא עִנְיָינָא שָׁמְעִינַן מִינֵּיהּ זָב בַּעַל שְׁתֵּי רְאִיּוֹת לִסְפִירָה, וּמַאי שְׁנָא הַאי "מִזּוֹבוֹ" דִּלְעֵיל דִּכְתִיב לְגַבֵּי קָרְבָּן וְלָא דָּרַשְׁתְּ לֵיהּ מִקְצָת זוֹב לְאֵתוּיֵי זָב בַּעַל שְׁתֵּי רְאִיּוֹת לְקָרְבָּן, אֶלָּא מִקְצָת זָבִין דָּרַשְׁתְּ לֵיהּ, וּמוֹקְמַתְּ לֵיהּ אַבַּעַל שָׁלֹשׁ רְאִיּוֹת, וּמְמַעֲטַתְּ מִינֵּיהּ בַּעַל שְׁתֵּי רְאִיּוֹת! לִישְׁתּוֹק קְרָא מִינֵּיהּ. וּמֵהֵיכָא תֵּיתֵי לָן סְפִירָה: וְכִי תֵּימָא אָתְיָא מִדִּינָא. דִּלְעֵיל, כִּדְאָמְרַתְּ אִם מְטַמֵּא מִשְׁכָּב וּמוֹשָׁב לֹא יְהֵא טָעוּן סְפִירַת שִׁבְעָה – לָא אָתְיָא, דְּהָא אָמְרַתְּ שׁוֹמֶרֶת יוֹם כְּנֶגֶד יוֹם תּוֹכִיחַ: אִם כֵּן לִיכְתּוֹב קְרָא וְכִי יִטְהַר הַזָּב. וְלָא בָּעֵי "מִזּוֹבוֹ", וּמִדִּכְתִיב "וְכִי יִטְהַר הַזָּב" וְלָא כְּתִיב "וְכִי יִטְהַר" סְתָמָא הֲוָה דָּרְשִׁינַן לֵיהּ, וְכִי יִטְהַר מִן הַזָּב. מַאי מִזּוֹבוֹ – שְׁמַע מִינָּהּ לְמִדְרַשׁ: מִקְצָת זָבִין טָעוּן סְפִירָה: **מתני'** פְּרִיעָה וּפְרִימָה. "בְּגָדָיו יִהְיוּ פְרוּמִים וְרֹאשׁוֹ יִהְיֶה פָרוּעַ": מוּחְלָט. לְאַחַר שֶׁכָּלוּ יְמֵי הַהֶסְגֵּר, וְנִרְאָה בּוֹ סִימָנֵי טוּמְאָה הָאֲמוּרִין בּוֹ: **גמ'** שִׁילּוּחַ. חוּץ לְחוֹמַת הָעִיר: וְטוּמְאָה. כָּל חוֹמֶר טוּמְאָה הָאֲמוּרָה בִּמְצוֹרָע: מְנָא הָנֵי מִילֵּי. דְּאֵין פְּרִיעָה וּפְרִימָה בְּמוּסְגָּר? דִּלְמָא גַּלֵּי לָן רַחֲמָנָא בְּמוּחְלָט, וְהוּא הַדִּין לְמוּסְגָּר, כִּדְאָמְרַתְּ לְעִנְיַן טוּמְאָה: וְטִהֲרוֹ הַכֹּהֵן מִסְפַּחַת הִיא. בִּמְצוֹרָע שֶׁבָּא לִכְלַל טָהֳרָה מִתּוֹךְ הֶסְגֵּירוֹ וְלֹא נֶחְלַט כְּתִיב, וְסֵיפֵיהּ דִּקְרָא כְּתִיב "וְכִבֶּס בְּגָדָיו וְטָהֵר", מִדְּלָא כָּתַב וְיִטְהַר לִישָּׁנָא דְּמֵעִיקָּרָא הוּא, וְהָכִי קָאָמַר: וּכְבָר קוֹדֶם טְבִילָה הָיָה טָהוֹר מִמִּקְצָת טוּמְאָה שֶׁל חוֹמֶר מְצוֹרָע: גַּבֵּי זָב דִּכְתִיב. בְּסוֹף טָהֳרָתוֹ "וְטָהֵר", מַה טָּהוֹר מֵעִיקָּרָא אָמְרַתְּ בֵּיהּ? אֶלָּא. עַל כָּרְחָךְ טָהוֹר יִהְיֶה מִכָּאן וּלְהַבָּא מִלְּטַמֵּא כְּלֵי חֶרֶס בְּהֶיסֵּט, וְאע"ג שֶׁטְּבִילָתוֹ בַּיּוֹם, וְאִם רָאָה אַחַר טְבִילָה בּוֹ בַּיּוֹם סָתַר אֶת הַכֹּל וּמְטַמֵּא לְמַפְרֵעַ מִשְׁכָּב וּמוֹשָׁב, כִּדְאָמְרִינַן בְּ"כֵּיצַד צוֹלִין" (פסחים דף פא.), וְכָל שֶׁכֵּן אָדָם, וַאֲפִילוּ הָכִי מְהַנְּיָא לֵיהּ טְבִילָה מִלְּטַמֵּא כְּלֵי חֶרֶס שֶׁהֶסִּיט בֵּין טְבִילָה לִרְאִיָּיה. וְהָכִי דָּרֵישׁ לָהּ בְּתוֹרַת כֹּהֲנִים. וְנִרְאֶה בְּעֵינַי דְּהָא דְּדָרְשִׁינַן לֵיהּ וְטָהֵר מִלְּטַמֵּא כְּלֵי חֶרֶס, מִדְּכָתְבִינְהוּ לְהַאי קְרָא בָּתַר קְרָא "אֲשֶׁר יִגַּע בּוֹ הַזָּב", דְּנָפְקָא לָן מִינֵּיהּ הֶיסֵּט כְּלֵי חֶרֶס לְזָב, וְאֵין לְךָ עוֹד טָמֵא שֶׁמְּטַמֵּא כְּלֵי חֶרֶס בְּהֶיסֵּט אֶלָּא הוּא: הָכָא נַמִי וְטָהֵר. דִּמְצוֹרָע טָהוֹר הַשְׁתָּא מִלְּטַמֵּא בְּבִיאָה(ד) מֵחוּמְרֵי מְצוֹרָע, שֶׁמְּטַמֵּא אָדָם וְכֵלִים הַנִּכְנָסִין עִמּוֹ לַבַּיִת, שֶׁאֲפִילּוּ חָזְרָה הַמִּסְפַּחַת וּפָשְׂתָה וְנִטְמָא – טָהוֹר, כִּדְכְתִיב "וְאִם פָּשֹׂה תִפְשֶׂה הַמִּסְפַּחַת בָּעוֹר" וגו', אַהֲנֵי לֵיהּ טְבִילָה לְטַהֵר אֶת הַכֵּלִים הַבָּאִין עִמּוֹ לַבַּיִת. לְפִי שֶׁמְּצוֹרָע מְטַמֵּא בְּבִיאָה, דְּתַנְיָא בְּתוֹרַת כֹּהֲנִים: "זֹאת הַתּוֹרָה לְכָל נֶגַע הַצָּרַעַת וְלַנָּתֶק וּלְצָרַעַת הַבֶּגֶד וְלַבָּיִת", מַה בַּיִת מְטַמֵּא בְּבִיאָה – אַף כּוּלָּן מְטַמְּאִין בְּבִיאָה: אֲשֶׁר בּוֹ. מַשְׁמַע(ה) מִי שֶׁצָּרַעְתּוֹ תְּלוּיָה טוּמְאָתוֹ בְּגוּפוֹ, שֶׁכָּל זְמַן שֶׁלֹּא נִתְרַפָּא מִמֶּנּוּ טָמֵא. וְהַיְינוּ מוּחְלָט, דְּגַבֵּי טָהֳרָה דִּילֵיהּ כְּתִיב "וְהִנֵּה נִרְפָּא נֶגַע הַצָּרַעַת מִן הַצָּרוּעַ": יָצָא. מוּסְגָּר שֶׁטּוּמְאָתוֹ תְּלוּיָה בִּימֵי הֶסְגֵּר, שֶׁאִם לֹא יִמְלָא בַּיּוֹם (ו) שְׁבִיעִי סִימָנֵי טוּמְאָה, שֵׂעָר לָבָן אוֹ פִּסְיוֹן, יְטַהֲרֶנּוּ. וְאע"פ שֶׁנִּגְעוֹ עוֹמֵד עָלָיו: כָּל יְמֵי אֲשֶׁר הַנֶּגַע בּוֹ וגו'. שִׁילּוּחַ כְּתִיב בְּהַאי קְרָא "מִחוּץ לַמַּחֲנֶה מוֹשָׁבוֹ": יְמֵי כָּל יְמֵי. מַלְּהָוֵה לֵיהּ לְמִיכְתַּב "יְמֵי" וּכְתִיב "כָּל יְמֵי": בִּימֵי רְפוּאָתוֹ: לְטָהוֹר מִתּוֹךְ הֶסְגֵּר. אֵין בֵּין טָהוֹר מִתּוֹךְ הֶחְלֵט אֶלָּא תִּגְלַחַת וְצִפֳּרִים. דְּאַף עַל גַּב דְּאִיכָּא קָרְבְּנוֹת אָשָׁם וְלוֹג שֶׁמֶן, מִיהוּ הָכָא בְּיוֹם טָהֳרָתוֹ וּרְפוּאָתוֹ הוּא דְּקָתָנֵי, וְלָא אַיְירֵי בְּקָרְבָּנוֹת שֶׁהֵן בַּשְּׁמִינִי: וְהִנֵּה נִרְפָּא וגו'. וּכְתִיב בָּתְרֵיהּ "שְׁתֵּי צִפֳּרִים חַיּוֹת טְהוֹרוֹת וְגִלַּח אֶת כָּל שְׂעָרוֹ": **מתני'** סְפָרִים. תּוֹרָה נְבִיאִים וּכְתוּבִים: אַשּׁוּרִית. לְשׁוֹן הַקּוֹדֶשׁ: אַף בַּסְּפָרִים לֹא הִתִּירוּ. לְהֵם לָשׁוֹן אַחֵר חוּץ מִלְּשׁוֹן הַקּוֹדֶשׁ: אֶלָּא יְוָונִית. וּבַגְּמָרָא מְפָרֵשׁ טַעְמָא: **גמ'** לְתוֹפְרָן בְּגִידִין. כָּל סִפְרֵיהֶן עֲשׂוּיִין בִּגְלָיוֹן. וַהֲלָכָה לְמֹשֶׁה מִסִּינַי הוּא ◐בִּתְפִלִּין וּמְזוּזוֹת שֶׁיְּהוּ תְּפוּרִין בְּגִידִין. וּבְסֵפֶר תּוֹרָה נֶחְלְקוּ בְּמַסֶּכֶת מַכּוֹת (דף יא.) בְּסֵפֶר תּוֹרָה שֶׁתְּפָרָהּ בְּפִשְׁתָּן, הַשְׁתָּא אַשְׁמְעִינַן מַתְנִיתִין כְּמַאן דְּפָסַל: מִקְרָא שֶׁכְּתָבוֹ תַּרְגּוּם. סֵפֶר שֶׁכָּתוּב בִּלְשׁוֹן הַקּוֹדֶשׁ, הָרָאוּי לִכְתּוֹב בּוֹ מִקְרָא כְּתָבוֹ לְשׁוֹן אֲרַמִּי: וְתַרְגּוּם. שֶׁהָיָה רָאוּי לִיכְתּוֹב בּוֹ תַּרְגּוּם כְּגוֹן "יְגַר שָׂהֲדוּתָא" (בראשית לא) כְּתָבוֹ מִקְרָא. "גַּלְעֵד", וּכְגוֹן תַּרְגּוּם (ז) כְּתָב שֶׁל דָּנִיֵּאל וְעֶזְרָא: וּכְתָב עִבְרִי. אוֹ שֶׁלֹּא שִׁינָּה אֶת הַלָּשׁוֹן, אֲבָל שִׁינָּה אֶת הַכְּתָב, שֶׁכְּתָבוֹ בִּכְתָב שֶׁל עֵבֶר הַנָּהָר. וּבְמַסֶּכֶת סַנְהֶדְרִין (דף כא:) קָרֵי לֵיהּ כְּתָבָא לִיבּוֹנָאָה: עַד שֶׁיִּכְתְּבֶנּוּ אַשּׁוּרִית. כְּתָב אַשּׁוּרִית הוּא כְּתָב שֶׁלָּנוּ: גוּפָן

תוספות

עד שיכתוב אשורית ועל הספר ובדיו. לקמן מוקי לה במגילה, וקשיא: דהא אמרינן בפרק שני (דף יח.): גיפטית לגיפטים עילמית לעילמים – יצא. ומיירי ודאי שכתוב באותו לשון שקורא, דאם לא כן – הוי קורא על פה, ולא יצא. ואם כן קשיא: אמאי לא מטמאה את הידים כיון שנתנה לקרות וליכתב בכל לשון שמכירין בה? ויש לומר: דכיון שאינה כשרה לקרות אלא למכירים בה – דין הוא שלא תטמא את הידים. אבל היכא דכתיבה אשורית (ח) כשירה אף לשאינן מכירין, ומשום הכי דין הוא שתטמאה את הידים:

בשלמא

רבינו חננאל

אמר ליה רב פפא לאביי מ"ש האי מזובו דממעיט ליה לזב בעל ב' ראיות מקרבן כדאמרן והאי מזובו מרבי ליה לזב בעל ב' ראיות לספירת ז' א"ל אביי אי לאו לרבויי אתא לשתוק קרא מיניה ולא יכתוב מזובו כלל. וכי תימא הוה אתי מן הדין כדאמרינן והלא דין הוא כו' פרכינן עלה שומרת יום כנגד יום תוכיח ונדחה הדין וא"ת האי מזובו לגופו בא. ללמד מזובו ולא מנגעו א"כ היה לו לכתוב וכי יטהר הזב וספר לו מזובו למה לי אלא לא בא מופנה אלא לרבות זב בעל ב' ראיות שטעון ספירת ז'. תנא בתוספתא אין בין זב לזבה אלא [שהזב] טעון מים חיים וזבה אינה טעונה ביאת מים חיים אין בין זבה לנדה אלא *) קרבן אין בין נדה ליולדת אלא הבאת קרבן אין בין נדה לשומרת יום כנגד יום אלא ספירת ז': [מתני'] אין בין מצורע מוסגר למצורע מוחלט אלא פריעה ופרימה**) ותגלחת וצפורין. פי' מצורע הנטהר מתוך הסגר כגון שנראתה בהרת באדם והסגירה הכהן פעם ראשונה ושניה וראה והנה כהה הנגע ולא פשה הנגע וטהר ונקרא מצורע מוסגר אין עליו אלא טבילה והערב שמש אבל אם פשתה וטמאו הכהן נעשה מצורע צמות והוא הנקרא מצורע מוחלט כדמתרגמינן לצמיתות לחלוטין ועליו כתיב והצרוע אשר בו הנגע בגדיו יהיו פרומים וראשו יהיה פרוע. וזו היא פריעה ופרימה פריעה לגדל פרע שער ראשו ולכשיטהר טעון גלוח כל שערו פי' פרימה קריעת הבגדים ושלוח צפור ושחיטת האחרת הא לענין שלוח מן המחנה כדכתיב וישלחו מן המחנה כל צרוע זה וזה שוין וכן לטמויי בביאה כדתנן בנגעים פרק ז' הטהור מתוך הסגר פטור מן הפריעה ומן הפרימה ומן התגלחת ומן הצפרים מתוך החלט חייב בכולם וזה וזה מטמאין בביאה ותנן נמי בפרק י"ג (משנה י"ב) מצורע שנכנס לבית הכלים שיש שם טמאין [אפי'] עד הקורות: מנא לן ופשיט לה רבה מהכא. והצרוע אשר בו הנגע דייקינן קרא דכתיב בו. מי שצרעתו תלויה בגופו טעון פריעה ופרימה יצא מצורע מוסגר שאין צרעתו תלויה בגופו אלא בימים כלומר במלאות ז' ימים ולא פשה הנגע נטהר. אי הכי לענין שלוח נמי דהא כתיב כל ימי אשר הנגע בו יטמא וגו'. נידוק נמי בו דכתיב בהאי קרא. ונימא מי שצרעתו תלויה בגופו טעון שילוח מחוץ למחנה יצא מצורע מוסגר שאין טעון שילוח. וא"ת אין הכי נמי והא דייקינן ממתני' דקתני אין בין מצורע מוסגר כו'. הא לענין שילוח זה וזה שוין. ופרקינן אי הוה כתיב ימי אשר הנגע בו כדקאמרת השתא דכתיב כל לרבויי מצורע [מוסגר] לשילוח אי הכי דהאי כל לרבויי אתא אפי' תגלחת וצפרין ניבעי. ופרקינן כתיב והנה נרפא נגע הצרעת מן הצרוע וצוה הכהן ולקח למטהר שתי צפרים חיות וגו'. הצרוע שצרעתו בגופו ונתרפא טעון צפרים ותגלחת יצא מצורע מוסגר שאין צרעתו תלויה ברפואות אלא בימים: [מתני'] אין [בין] ספרים לתפילין ומזוזות אלא שהספרים כו'. דייקינן מינה הא לתופרן בגידין ולטמויי את הידים ככתבי הקדש אלו ואלו שוין. ואקשינן וספרים הנכתבין בכל לשון מטמאין את הידים. והתנן בסוף מסכת ידים תרגום שבעזרא ושבדניאל מטמא את הידים תרגום שכתבו עברית

*) כ"ה גם בתוספתא דמכילתין אבל נראה דל"ל ספירת ז' וקרבן וכן לקמן אין בין נדה לשומרת יום וכו' אלא ספירת ז' נמי צריך להגיה בזה ול"ע. **) חסר כאן ול"ל אין בין טהור מתוך הסגר לטהור מתוך החלט אלא תגלחת וכו'.

הגהות מהר"ב רנשבורג

[א] מתני' אין בין ספרים כו'. נ"ב עיין מנחות דף ל"ב ע"א תוס' ד"ה תפילין וכו' ודו"ק:

רש"א

סנהדרין קו: ערכין טו.

גליון הש"ס

מתני' אין בין מצורע. עי' מ"ק ז. תד"ה אמר רבי: **עין** משפט אות ד' מיי' פ"י. לא נזכר כלל ברמב"ם מזה ופשטות דברי רמב"ם מיירי דליכא טומאה כלל למפרע אף לא טומאה קלה. ועיין בספר ראשון לציון לבעל פרי תואר: **רש"י** ד"ה לתופרן בגידין וכו' בתפילין ומזוזות. עיין תשובת חות יאיר סימן קנ"ב אות יג:

נ"ל וראה הכהן והנה כו'

[עי' תוספות שבת עט: ד"ה תפלין וכו' מה שהניחו בקושי']

לקמן יח. ידים פ"ד מ"ה ע"ש

הגהות הב"ח

(א) גמ' האי מיבעי ליה מזובו ולא מזובו ומנגעו א"כ: (ב) שם כל ימי לרבות מצורע מוסגר לשילוח (אי הכי תגלחת וצפרים וכו' ברפואות אלא בימים) תא"מ ונ"ב ס"א אין בין טהור מתוך הסגר וכו' מאי טעמא אמר אביי אמר קרא ויצא: (ג) רש"י ד"ה מאי שנא וכו' דרשת ליה למקצת וכו' לגבי קרבן דלא דרשת: (ד) ד"ה הכא נמי וכו' בביאה למפרע מחומרי: (ה) ד"ה אשר בו משמע בגופו הס"ד: ומה"ד מי שצרעתו תלויה בגופו טומאתו: (ו) ד"ה יצא מוסגר וכו' ביום שביעי סימני: (ז) ד"ה כתבו מקרא וכו' תרגום של דניאל כצ"ל ותיבת כתב נמחק: (ח) תוספות ד"ה עד וכו' דכתיבה אשורית דכשרה אף לשאינן מכירין משום הכי:

גמרא

כָּאן *בְּגוּפָן שֶׁלָּנוּ, כָּאן בְּגוּפָן שֶׁלָּהֶן. אָמַר לֵיהּ אַבַּיֵי: בְּמַאי אוֹקִימְתָּא לְהַהִיא? בְּגוּפָן שֶׁלָּהֶן? מַאי אִירְיָא מִקְרָא שֶׁכְּתָבוֹ תַּרְגּוּם וְתַרְגּוּם שֶׁכְּתָבוֹ מִקְרָא? אֲפִילּוּ מִקְרָא שֶׁכְּתָבוֹ מִקְרָא וְתַרְגּוּם שֶׁכְּתָבוֹ תַּרְגּוּם נַמִי, דְּהָא קָתָנֵי: "עַד שֶׁיִּכְתְּבֶנּוּ אַשּׁוּרִית עַל הַסֵּפֶר בִּדְיוֹ"! אֶלָּא, לָא קַשְׁיָא: הָא — רַבָּנַן, הָא — רשב"ג. אִי רשב"ג הָא אִיכָּא יְוָנִית! אֶלָּא, לָא קַשְׁיָא: כָּאן — בִּסְפָרִים, כָּאן — בִּתְפִלִּין וּמְזוּזוֹת. תְּפִלִּין וּמְזוּזוֹת מ"ט — מִשּׁוּם דִּכְתִיב בְּהוּ °"וְהָיוּ" בַּהֲוָיָיתָן יְהוּ. מַאי תַּרְגּוּם שֶׁכְּתָבוֹ מִקְרָא אִיכָּא? בִּשְׁלָמָא תּוֹרָה — אִיכָּא °"יְגַר שָׂהֲדוּתָא". אֶלָּא הָכָא, מַאי תַּרְגּוּם אִיכָּא? אֶלָּא לָא קַשְׁיָא: כָּאן — בִּמְגִילָּה, כָּאן — בִּסְפָרִים. מְגִילָּה [א]מ"ט — דִּכְתִיב בָּהּ: "כִּכְתָבָם וְכִלְשׁוֹנָם". מַאי תַּרְגּוּם שֶׁכְּתָבוֹ מִקְרָא אִיכָּא? אָמַר רַב פַּפָּא: °"וְנִשְׁמַע פִּתְגָם הַמֶּלֶךְ". רַב נַחְמָן בַּר יִצְחָק אָמַר: °"וְכָל הַנָּשִׁים יִתְּנוּ יְקָר לְבַעְלֵיהֶן". רַב אַשִׁי אָמַר: כִּי תַּנְיָא הַהִיא, בִּשְׁאָר סְפָרִים, וְרַבִּי יְהוּדָה הִיא. דְּתַנְיָא: תְּפִלִּין וּמְזוּזוֹת אֵין נִכְתָּבִין אֶלָּא אַשּׁוּרִית. וְרַבּוֹתֵינוּ הִתִּירוּ יְוָנִית. וְהָכְתִיב: "וְהָיוּ"! אֶלָּא אֵימָא: סְפָרִים נִכְתָּבִים בְּכָל לָשׁוֹן, וְרַבּוֹתֵינוּ הִתִּירוּ יְוָנִית. הִתִּירוּ?! מִכְּלָל דְּתַנָּא קַמָּא אָסַר! אֶלָּא אֵימָא: רַבּוֹתֵינוּ לֹא הִתִּירוּ שֶׁיִּכָּתְבוּ אֶלָּא יְוָנִית. וְתַנְיָא, א"ר יְהוּדָה: אַף כְּשֶׁהִתִּירוּ רַבּוֹתֵינוּ יְוָנִית — לֹא הִתִּירוּ אֶלָּא בְּסֵפֶר תּוֹרָה, וּמִשּׁוּם מַעֲשֶׂה דְּתַלְמַי הַמֶּלֶךְ.(א) דְּתַנְיָא: *מַעֲשֶׂה בְּתַלְמַי הַמֶּלֶךְ שֶׁכִּינֵּס שִׁבְעִים וּשְׁנַיִם זְקֵנִים וְהִכְנִיסָן בְּשִׁבְעִים וּשְׁנַיִם בָּתִּים וְלֹא גִּילָּה לָהֶם עַל מָה כִּינְּסָן. וְנִכְנַס אֵצֶל כָּל אֶחָד וְאֶחָד וְאָמַר לָהֶם: כִּתְבוּ לִי, תּוֹרַת מֹשֶׁה רַבְּכֶם. נָתַן הקב"ה בְּלֵב כָּל אֶחָד וְאֶחָד עֵצָה, וְהִסְכִּימוּ כּוּלָּן לְדַעַת אַחַת. • *וְכָתְבוּ לוֹ °"אֱלֹהִים בָּרָא בְּרֵאשִׁית"; °"אֶעֱשֶׂה אָדָם בְּצֶלֶם וּבִדְמוּת"; °"וַיְכַל בַּיּוֹם הַשִּׁשִּׁי וַיִּשְׁבֹּת בַּיּוֹם הַשְּׁבִיעִי"; °"זָכָר וּנְקֵבָה בְּרָאוֹ", וְלֹא כָּתְבוּ "בְּרָאָם"; °"הָבָה אֵרְדָה וְאָבְלָה שָׁם שְׂפָתָם"; °"וַתִּצְחַק שָׂרָה בִּקְרוֹבֶיהָ"; °"כִּי בְאַפָּם הָרְגוּ שׁוֹר וּבִרְצוֹנָם עִקְּרוּ אֵבוּס"; °"וַיִּקַּח מֹשֶׁה אֶת אִשְׁתּוֹ וְאֶת בָּנָיו וַיַּרְכִּיבֵם עַל נוֹשֵׂא בְּנֵי אָדָם"; °"וּמוֹשַׁב בְּנֵי יִשְׂרָאֵל אֲשֶׁר יָשְׁבוּ בְּמִצְרַיִם *וּבִשְׁאָר אֲרָצוֹת אַרְבַּע מֵאוֹת שָׁנָה"; °"וַיִּשְׁלַח אֶת זַאֲטוּטֵי בְּנֵי יִשְׂרָאֵל"; °"וְאֶל זַאֲטוּטֵי בְּנֵי יִשְׂרָאֵל לֹא שָׁלַח יָדוֹ".

לא

רש"י

גּוּפָן. כְּתִיבָה: כָּאן בְּגוּפָן שֶׁלָּנוּ. מַתְנִיתִין דְּקָתָנֵי בְּכָל לָשׁוֹן — שֶׁלֹּא שִׁינָּה אֶת הַכְּתָב, אֶלָּא שֶׁשִּׁינָּה אֶת הַלָּשׁוֹן. וּבָרַיְיתָא בְּגוּפָן שֶׁלָּהֶן: הָא. דְּקָאמַר עַד שֶׁיִּכְתְּבֶנּוּ בִּכְתָב אַשּׁוּרִית: רַבָּן שִׁמְעוֹן בֶּן גַּמְלִיאֵל הִיא. דְּפָלֵיג אַדְּרַבָּנָן בְּמַתְנִיתִין: אִי רַבָּן שִׁמְעוֹן בֶּן גַּמְלִיאֵל. אַמַּאי קָתָנֵי בְּבָרַיְיתָא עַד שֶׁיִּכְתְּבֶנּוּ אַשּׁוּרִית: אֶלָּא לָא קַשְׁיָא.

גָּרְסִינַן: וְהָיוּ הַדְּבָרִים הָאֵלֶּה. כְּתִיב בִּתְפִלִּין וּמְזוּזוֹת, שֶׁכְּתוּבִין בָּהֶן פָּרָשִׁיּוֹת שֶׁל שְׁמַע: בִּשְׁאָר סְפָרִים. נְבִיאִים וּכְתוּבִים: מִכְּלָל דְּתַנָּא קַמָּא. בִּתְמִיהָ: וְהָא תַּנָּא קַמָּא שָׁרֵי בְּכָל לָשׁוֹן! רַבּוֹתֵינוּ. אָמְרוּ רַבָּן שִׁמְעוֹן בֶּן גַּמְלִיאֵל: תַּלְמַי. מֶלֶךְ מִצְרַיִם הָיָה: אֱלֹהִים בָּרָא בְּרֵאשִׁית. אֶת הַשָּׁמַיִם. שֶׁלֹּא יֹאמַר בְּרֵאשִׁית שֵׁם הוּא, וּשְׁתֵּי רְשׁוּיוֹת הֵן, וְרִאשׁוֹן בָּרָא אֶת הַשֵּׁנִי: אֶעֱשֶׂה אָדָם. שֶׁמִּכָּאן פָּקְרוּ הָאוֹמְרִים שְׁתֵּי רְשׁוּיוֹת הֵן, דִּכְתִיב "נַעֲשֶׂה אָדָם" (בראשית א): וַיְכַל בַּיּוֹם הַשִּׁשִּׁי. שֶׁלֹּא יֹאמַר אִם כֵּן עָשָׂה מְלָאכָה בְּשַׁבָּת, דְּהָא כְּתִיב "וַיְכַל בַּיּוֹם הַשְּׁבִיעִי", וְהוּא לֹא יְקַבֵּל עָלָיו מִדְרַשׁ חֲכָמִים שֶׁדָּרְשׁוּ בּוֹ: מֶה הָיָה הָעוֹלָם חָסֵר — מְנוּחָה, בָּאתָה שַׁבָּת — בָּאתָה מְנוּחָה, וְזֶהוּ גְּמָרוֹ: זָכָר וּנְקֵבָה בְּרָאוֹ וְלֹא כָּתְבוּ בְּרָאָם. דְּמַשְׁמַע שְׁנֵי גוּפִין בָּרָא, כָּל אֶחָד זָכָר וּנְקֵבָה שְׁנֵי פַרְצוּפִין. לָכֵן כָּתְבוּ בְּרָאוֹ, שֶׁכָּךְ נִבְרָא אָדָם בִּשְׁנֵי פַרְצוּפִים: בִּקְרוֹבֶיהָ. שֶׁלֹּא יֹאמַר עַל אַבְרָהָם לֹא הִקְפִּיד דִּכְתִיב "וַיִּצְחַק", וְעַל שָׂרָה הִקְפִּיד. לְפִיכָךְ כָּתְבוּ בִּקְרוֹבֶיהָ, לוֹמַר: אַבְרָהָם בְּלִבּוֹ, וְהִיא אָמְרָה בִּקְרוֹבֶיהָ: נוֹשֵׂא בְּנֵי אָדָם. דְּמַשְׁמַע גָּמָל. שֶׁלֹּא יֹאמַר מֹשֶׁה רַבְּכֶם לֹא הָיָה לוֹ סוּס אוֹ גָּמָל: הָרְגוּ שׁוֹר. שֶׁלֹּא יֹאמַר רַצְחָנִים הָיוּ אֲבוֹתֵיכֶם, שֶׁהֲרֵי אֲבִיהֶם מֵעִיד עֲלֵיהֶם שֶׁהֵם הָרְגוּ אִישׁ. לְכָךְ כָּתְבוּ שׁוֹר, שֶׁלֹּא הָיוּ חֲשׁוּבִין בְּעֵינָיו אֶלָּא כִּבְהֵמוֹת, וְלֹא הִקְפִּיד(ב) עַל הַבְּהֵמוֹת: וּבִשְׁאָר אֲרָצוֹת. שֶׁלֹּא יֹאמַר שֶׁקֶר כָּתוּב בַּתּוֹרָה, שֶׁהֲרֵי קְהָת מִיּוֹרְדֵי מִצְרַיִם הָיָה, וּכְשֶׁאַתָּה מוֹנֶה שְׁנוֹתָיו שֶׁל קְהָת וּשְׁנוֹתָיו שֶׁל עַמְרָם וּשְׁנוֹתָיו שֶׁל מֹשֶׁה כּוּלָּן אֵין מַגִּיעוֹת לְד' מֵאוֹת שָׁנָה, כָּל שֶׁכֵּן שֶׁהַרְבֵּה מִשְּׁנוֹת הַבָּנִים נִבְלָעִין בְּתוֹךְ שְׁנוֹת הָאָבוֹת. אֶלָּא שֶׁמָּנָה הַכָּתוּב מִיּוֹם שֶׁנִּגְזְרָה גְּזֵירַת גָּלוּת מִצְרַיִם בֵּין הַבְּתָרִים, וּמִשָּׁם עַד שֶׁנּוֹלַד יִצְחָק שְׁלֹשִׁים שָׁנָה, וּמִשֶּׁנּוֹלַד יִצְחָק עַד שֶׁיָּצְאוּ יִשְׂרָאֵל מִמִּצְרַיִם אַרְבַּע מֵאוֹת שָׁנָה, צֵא מֵהֶם שִׁשִּׁים שֶׁל יִצְחָק וּמֵאָה וְל' שֶׁחַיָּה יַעֲקֹב כְּשֶׁבָּא לְמִצְרַיִם — נִשְׁאֲרוּ מָאתַיִם וָעֶשֶׂר. וְכֵן הָיְתָה הַגְּזֵרָה "כִּי גֵר יִהְיֶה זַרְעֲךָ בְּאֶרֶץ לֹא לָהֶם" (בראשית טו), וְלֹא נֶאֱמַר בְּמִצְרַיִם, אֶלָּא בְּאֶרֶץ לֹא לָהֶם. וּכְשֶׁנּוֹלַד יִצְחָק הָיָה אַבְרָהָם גֵּר בְּאֶרֶץ פְּלִשְׁתִּים, וּמֵאָז עַד שֶׁיָּצְאוּ מִמִּצְרַיִם נִמְצָא יִצְחָק וְזַרְעוֹ, שֶׁהֵן זַרְעוֹ שֶׁל אַבְרָהָם, גֵּרִים. וּשְׁלֹשִׁים שֶׁל קוֹדֶם לָכֵן לֹא נִמְנוּ בַּגְּזֵרָה, דְּהָא "זַרְעֲךָ" כְּתִיב: זַאֲטוּטֵי. לְשׁוֹן חֲשִׁיבוּת. אֲבָל נַעֲרֵי לְשׁוֹן קְטַנּוּת, וְיֹאמַר: גְּרוּעִים שֶׁלָּכֶם שְׁלַחְתֶּם לְקַבֵּל פְּנֵי שְׁכִינָה: וְאֶל זַאֲטוּטֵי בְּנֵי יִשְׂרָאֵל. בְּאוֹתָהּ פָּרָשָׁה עַצְמָהּ. וּלְפִי שֶׁכָּתְבוּ זַאֲטוּטֵי תְּחִילָּה חָזְרוּ וּכְתָבוּם כִּשְׁמָם הָרִאשׁוֹן, וְלֹא כָּתְבוּ "וְאֶל אֲצִילֵי בְּנֵי יִשְׂרָאֵל": לא

תוספות

בשלמא תורה איכא יגר שהדותא. וקשה: אמאי מפסלא בהכי? והלא אילו היה חסר כל אלו *השלש תיבות לא מפסיל בהכי, כדאמרינן בגיטין (דף ס.): ספר תורה שחסר יריעה אחת אין קורין בו. משמע: דווקא יריעה אחת, אבל פסוק אחד — לא! ודחק הקונטרס לומר דגרע טפי כשהוא כתוב תרגום מכשהוא לא נכתב כלל. ויש לומר דהכא לא בא אלא להשמיענו דהוי טעות, וצריך להגיהו:

כאן במגילה כאן בשאר ספרים — וקשה: דהך ברייתא כמאן מתוקמא? לא כרבן שמעון בן גמליאל ולא כרבנן! דאי רבנן — א"כ הוה ליה למיתני במתני' מגילה גבי תפילין ומזוזות, שאין נכתבין אלא אשורית. וכרבן שמעון בן גמליאל לא מתוקמא, שהרי הוא מתיר אף יונית. ואין לומר דהני מילי בשאר ספרים [מתיר רשב"ג יונית], אבל במגילה מודה שצריך אשורית — זה אינו, דהא בפרק שני (דף יח.) אמרי רב ושמואל דלעז יונית לכל כשר. ומסיק דאינהו אמור כרשב"ג, ומסיק נמי התם קא משמע לן דאף במגילה נמי אמרי מלתייהו! ועל כרחך צריך לומר שזה המתרץ אין סובר דרבן שמעון בן גמליאל קאי כוותיה דרב ושמואל דלקמן, אלא סובר ליה דרבן שמעון בן גמליאל לא התיר במגילה אלא אשורית, ומשום דכתיב בהו "ככתבם וכלשונם" ורב ושמואל דלקמן סבירא להו [כשינויא] דרב אשי דבסמוך: **ורב אשי אמר ההוא בשאר ספרים** ב] **ור' יהודה היא.** וקשה: דהא בפרק "כל כתבי" (שבת דף קטו: ושם) אמר רב אשי(ג): אין בין ספרים למגילה אלא שהספרים נכתבין בכל לשון, ומגילה צריך אשורית בספר ובדיו. אלמא דבשאר ספרים לא צריך אשורית וספר ודיו. ואם כן מנא ליה לרב אשי לומר דר' יהודה מחמיר ומצריך כולי האי? והא לא אשכח התם שום תנא דפליג עליה! וי"ל: דההיא ד"כל כתבי" (ג"ז שם) מיירי לענין הצלה מפני הדליקה דווקא, והכי קאמר: בשאר ספרים יש להצילם אע"ג דנכתבין בכל לשון, שהרי יש בהן כמה שמות קדושים. אבל במגילה שאין בה שום אזכרה — אין להצילה אלא אם כן כתובה כהלכתה. והכא מיירי להכשיר לקרות בהן:

אלהים ברא בראשית. פ"ה: שאם כתבו "בראשית ברא" היו אומרים בראשית שם הוא, ושתי רשויות הן. וקשה: שהרי בראשית אין שם כלל, אלא בתחלה. ועוד שכתבו לו בלשון יונית בתחלה! וי"ל: שהיונים היו יודעים שלעולם יש להזכיר הבורא בתחילה, ואם כן אלו כתבו בראשית קודם היה אומר דשתי רשויות הן, והתיבה הראשונה הוי בורא אחד, ואלהים הוי השני, משום הכי הפכו לו: **על** נושא אדם. פן יאמר להם: וכי לא היה לו למשה רבכם סוס או גמל?: (*ואל) זאטוטי בני ישראל. וקשה: אמאי לא כתבו לו "וישלח את אצילי בני ישראל" כדכתיב בסמוך, והוי לשון גדולה! ויש לומר: לפי שלא רצו לשקר, ולכך כתבו לו זאטוטי במקום נערי ובמקום אצילי, דמשמע לשון גדולה, כמו זוטו של ים (ב"מ דף כא:), ומשמע נמי לשון השפלה כדאמרינן התם*: האומר "לצולה חרבי" (ישעיה מד) — זו בבל, שהוא זוטו של עולם. פי': עומקו ותחתיתו, ושפלה מכל ארצות. כדאמרינן נמי התם (שבת דף קיג:): הלכך נקרא שמה בבל, שכל מתי מבול ננערו שם (זבחים דף קיג:):

אין

רבינו חננאל

עברית. ועברית שכתבו תרגום וכתב עברי אינו מטמא את הידים עד שיכתבנו אשורית. על עור ובדיו ופריק רבה ממתני' דקתני דכתבינן בכל לשון בגיפן שלנו*). כלומר בצורות האותיות שלנו ובלשון אחר זולתי לשה"ק. לפיכך מטמאין את הידים. שהאותיות בכתב אשורי הן. ומתני' השנויה במסכת ידים בגיפן של שאר לשונות שבאומות לפיכך אין מטמאין [את הידים]. והאי פירוקא דרבה איפריכא וסוגיא דשמעתא בפירוקא דרב אשי סלקא: (את הידים) ואקשינן אי הכי מאי איריא עברית שכתבו תרגום אפי' עברית שכתבו עברית בגיפן של שאר לשונות לא. דקתני עד שיכתבנו אשורית על העור בדיו ופרקינן לעולם ב' המשניות בגיפן שלנו. ומשנה השנויה במס' ידים לרשב"ג היא דמצריך בכל הספרים אשורית. ודחינן והא איכא יוונית לרשב"ג שהוא מתיר למה שנה עד שיכתבנו אשורית בלבד. אלא לא קשיא מתניתין בספרים ומשנה השנויה בידים בתפילין ובמזוזות. ומשנינן ודחינן ואוקמה למתני' דהתם רב אשי בשאר ספרים זולתי ס"ת. ור' יהודה היא דתניא ספרים נכתבים בכל לשון. ורבותינו [התירו] שיכתבו יוונית כו' אבל תפילין ומזוזות דברי הכל אשורית דכתי' בהו והיו בהווייתן יהו. ותניא א"ר יהודה אף כשהתירו רבותינו יוונית לא התירו אלא בס"ת. משום מעשה דתלמי המלך שכינס ע"ב זקנים בע"ב בתים אמר להם כתבו לי תורתכם. נתן הקב"ה עצה טובה בלבם והסכימה דעתם לדעת אחת. וכתבו לו אלהים ברא בראשית. אעשה אדם בצלם ובדמות כו'

*) עי' ערוך ערך גפן.

מסורת הש"ס

[גי' הערוך גיפן]

[עי' מהרש"א]

[ג"ל ואשלח את]

[במדרש]

מס' סופרים פ"א הלכה ח]

מכילתא פרשת בא

...ל ובשאר ארצות שלשי' ...נה וד' מאות שנה כך ...גי' בע"י ובילקוט פ' ...ראשית וכן בירושלמי ועי' ...א וכן איתא במס' סופרים פ"א]

הגהות הב"ח

(א) גמ' דתלמי המלך מאי היא דתניא מעשה: (ב) רש"י ד"ה הרגו וכו' לא הקפיד אלא על הבהמות: (ג) תוס' ד"ה ורב אשי אמר כי תניא ההיא וכו' אמר רב אשי דתניא אין בין וכו' מגילה עד שתהא כתובה אשורית על הספר ובדיו:

גליון הש"ס

גמ' וכתבו לו. עי' יש"ש ב"ק פ"ד סי' מ:

הגהות מהר"ב רנשבורג

[א] גמ' מ"ט דכתיב בה ככתבם וכלשונם. נ"ב נ"ל ככתבם וכזמנם וכ"כ ...פר"ח סימן תר"ל ובספר ...ורי אבן יעוש"ה: [ב] תוס' ד"ה ורב אשי וכו' ...ר' יהודה היא. נ"ב עי' ...מנחות דף לא ע"ב תוס' ד"ה עשאה כו' ודו"ק:

סד א מיי' פ"ד מהל' כלי המקדש הלכה יד:
סה ב מיי' פט"ו מהל' שגגות הלכה ז:
סו ג מיי' פ"א מהלכות עבודת יוה"כ הלכה ג:
סז ד מיי' פ"ו מהלכות בית הבחירה הלכה טו ופ"ז שם הלכה יד ופ"י מהלכות מעשה הקרבנות הלכה ה:
סח ה מיי' פ"ו מהלכות בית הבחירה הלכה טו ופ"י מהלכות מעשה הקרבנות הלכה ג ופי"א שם הלכה ה:

°"לא חמד אחד מהם נשאתי"; °"אשר חלק ה' אלהיך אתם להאיר לכל העמים"; °"וילך ויעבוד אלהים אחרים" "אשר לא צויתי לעובדם". וכתבו לו: (א) "את צעירת הרגלים", ולא כתבו לו °"את הארנבת", מפני °שאשתו של תלמי ארנבת שמה, שלא יאמר: שחקו בי היהודים והטילו שם אשתי בתורה.§ "רשב"ג אומר אף בספרים לא התירו שיכתבו אלא יונית".§ א"ר אבהו א"ר יוחנן: הלכה כרשב"ג. וא"ר(ב) יוחנן: מ"ט דרשב"ג — אמר קרא *°"יפת אלהים ליפת וישכן באהלי שם" — דבריו של יפת יהיו באהלי שם. ואימא גומר ומגוג! *א"ר חייא בר אבא: היינו טעמא דכתיב: "יפת אלהים ליפת" — יפיותו של יפת יהא באהלי שם.§ **מתני'** *[א]אין בין כהן משוח בשמן המשחה למרובה בגדים אלא פר הבא על כל המצות. [ב]אין בין כהן משמש לכהן שעבר אלא פר יום הכפורים, ועשירית האיפה.§ **גמ'** הא לענין פר יום כפורים ועשירית האיפה — זה וזה שוין. מתניתין דלא כר"מ, דאי ר"מ, [הא תניא:] *מרובה בגדים מביא פר הבא על כל המצות, דברי ר"מ. וחכ"א: אינו מביא. מ"ט דר"מ — דתניא: °"משיח". אין לי אלא משוח בשמן המשחה. מרובה בגדים מנין? ת"ל "המשיח". במאי אוקימנא? דלא כר"מ. אימא סיפא: אין בין כהן משמש לכהן שעבר אלא פר יוה"כ ועשירית האיפה. הא לכל דבריהן — זה וזה שוין. אתאן לר"מ, דתניא: *אירע בו פסול ומינו כהן אחר תחתיו — ראשון חוזר לעבודתו, שני — כל מצות כהונה גדולה עליו, דברי ר"מ. רבי יוסי אומר: [ג]ראשון חוזר לעבודתו, שני אינו ראוי לא לכהן גדול ולא לכהן הדיוט. וא"ר יוסי: °מעשה ברבי יוסף בן אולם מציפורי, שאירע בו פסול בכהן גדול ומינוהו תחתיו. ובא מעשה לפני חכמים ואמרו: ראשון חוזר לעבודתו, שני אינו ראוי לא לכהן גדול ולא לכהן הדיוט. כהן גדול — משום איבה; כהן הדיוט — משום *מעלין בקודש ולא מורידין. רישא רבנן, וסיפא ר"מ?! אמר רב חסדא: אין. רישא רבנן וסיפא ר"מ. רב יוסף °אמר: *רבי היא, ונסיב לה אליבא דתנאי.§ **מתני'** *אין בין במה גדולה לבמה קטנה אלא פסחים. זה הכלל: כל שהוא נידר ונידב, קרב בבמה; וכל שאינו לא נידר ולא נידב — אינו קרב בבמה.§ **גמ'** פסחים ותו לא? אימא: כעין פסחים. מני? ר"ש היא. דתניא, *ר"ש אומר: אף צבור לא הקריבו אלא פסחים וחובות שקבוע להם זמן, אבל חובות שאין קבוע להם זמן — הכא והכא לא קרב.§ **מתני'** *אין בין שילה לירושלים אלא שבשילה אוכלין קדשים קלים ומעשר שני בכל הרואה, [ד]ובירושלים לפנים מן החומה. וכאן וכאן, [ה]קדשי קדשים נאכלין לפנים מן הקלעים. קדושת שילה
יש

לא חמד אחד מהם נשאתי. שלא יאמר חמור לא לקח, אבל חפץ אחר לקח: להאיר לכל העמים. שאם לא כן, יאמר: הן נח מותר בע"ז ומדרשו (ע"ז נ"ה.): להחליקן בדברים כדי לטורדן מן העולם: אשר לא צויתי לעובדם. שאם לא כתבו לעובדם משמע אשר לא צויתי שיהיו, ויאמר: א"כ אלהות הן, שעל כורחו נבראו: וכתבו. במקום "ואת הארנבת" ואת צעירת הרגלים, לפי שידיה קצרות וקטנות מרגליה: יפיותו של יפת. הוא לשון יון, לשונו יפה משל כל בני יפת: **מתני'** מרובה בגדים. כהנים ששימשו בבית שני, ואף בבית ראשון מימות יאשיהו ואילך, שנגנז צלוחית של שמן המשחה: פר הבא על כל המצות. כהן משיח שהורה היתר בדבר שזדונו כרת, ועשה כהוראתו, מביא פר. שנאמר "אם הכהן המשיח יחטא לאשמת העם" וגו' (ויקרא ד): כהן המשמש. כגון שאירע בו פסול, ומינו אחר תחתיו, ועבר פסולו וחזר לעבודתו, והעבירו הבא תחתיו. הראשון קרוי משמש, והשני עבר: אלא פר יוה"כ. שאי אפשר להביא שנים. וכן עשירית האיפה חביתי כהן [גדול] שבכל יום, שאי אפשר להביא שנים: **גמ'** הא לכל דבריהן זה וזה שוין. ואם בא להקטיר או לעבוד שום עבודה — משמש בשמונה בגדים כהן שעבר ככהן המשמש: כל מצות כהונה גדולה עליו. משמש בח' בגדים, לא פורע ולא פורם, ומצווה על הבתולה, ומוזהר על האלמנה, ומקריב אונן: ואינו ראוי. לשמש לא בשמונה בגדים ככהן גדול, ולא בארבעה ככהן הדיוט: רבי היא. וסתמה אליבא דנפשיה: ונסיב ליה אליבא דתנאי. במרובה בגדים סבר לה כרבנן, ובכהן שעבר סבר לה כר' מאיר: **מתני'** אין בין במה. אין הפרש בשעת היתר הבמות בין במה גדולה, זה מזבח של משה בעודו בנוב וגבעון: לבמה קטנה. מזבח של יחיד, שכל יחיד ויחיד עושה במה לעצמו: קרב בבמה. קטנה: כל שאינו נידר ונידב כו'. בזבחים יליף לה בפרק בתרא: **גמ'** פסחים ותו לא. והא קתני סיפא: כל שאינו נידר ונידב — אינו קרב בבמה קטנה. ואילו בגדולה היו מקריבין קרבנות צבור, תמידין ומוספין. וקא ס"ד דאף חובות צבור שאין קבוע להן זמן היו קריבין בה, כגון פר העלם דבר של צבור ושעירי ע"ז: כעין פסחים. וכל חובות הקבוע להם זמן כפסחים: מני. מתניתין, דקתני דבמה קטנה אין קרב בה שום חובה, ואמר דבמה גדולה לא עדיפא מינה אלא בחובות הקבוע להן זמן: ר' שמעון היא. דאמר בפרק בתרא דזבחים: אף צבור לא הקריבו בבמה גדולה שום חובה, אלא פסחים וחובות הקבוע להן זמן. אבל חובות שאין קבוע להן זמן, כגון פר העלם דבר ושעירי ע"ז — הכא והכא לא קרב. אבל כדרבנן דהתם לא מתוקמא מתניתין, דהא אמרי: כל שהצבור מקריבין באהל מועד שבמדבר, מקריבין באהל מועד שבגלגל, דהיא במה גדולה, ואפילו פר העלם דבר. ומתניתין קתני פסח וכיוצא בהן: **מתני'** בכל הרואה. בכל מקום שיוכל לראות משם את שילה. ובפרק בתרא דזבחים יליף טעמא:
יש

אין בין כהן משוח למרובה בגדים אלא פר הבא על כל המצות. *פירוש: פר כהן משיח — שחטא בשוגג, דעשה אחת מכל מצות ה' אשר לא תעשינה ואשם בדבר שזדונו כרת. אבל לא איירי בפר העלם דבר של צבור, דכתיב ביה הכהן המשיח (יחטא), דהא מרבינן בת"כ (ג) ואפילו כהן הדיוט יכול להביאו, וכל שכן מרובה בגדים: **אין** בין כהן המשמש לכהן שעבר אלא פר יום הכפורים. קשה: אמאי נקט לכהן שעבר? דהא אפילו ביום שאירע בו פסול לכהן המשמש, ושמש זה תחתיו, הוי חילוק זה, שהפר בא מן המשמש אע"פ שאין משמש. כדאי' בירושלמי. ואם כן הוה ליה למימר בין הכהן המשמש לכהן שיעבור! וי"ל: דאי נקט לאותו שיעבור הוה משמע הא לאותו שעבר כבר, דהוי בכל שנה — יש הרבה חילוקים ביניהם. משום הכי נקט לאותו שעבר, לאשמועינן דאף בדידיה ליכא אלא חילוק זה. וא"ת: למאי דפרישית שהפר הוי מאותו שאירע בו הפסול, אע"ג שאין משמש, א"כ קשיא מהא דאמר סוף פ"ק דשבועות (דף יד:): "אשר לו" — ולא משל אחיו הכהנים. ואדרבה, היה לו לומר ולא מאותו המשמש תחתיו, דהוי רבותא טפי! ושמא משום דהוי מלתא דלא שכיחא שבקיה, ונקט מידי דשכיח כל שנה. והיא נמי ד"הקומץ רבה" (מנחות דף יט.) דקאמר דגלי רחמנא שחיטה בבעלים לא קשה לפירושינו(ד), דשרי, דכיון דזכי ליה רחמנא — הוי כאילו מקדיש משלו: **ולא** לכהן הדיוט משום מעלין בקדש וכו'. קשיא: למה ליה האי טעמא? תיפוק ליה דכיון דראוי לכהן גדול, אי לאו משום איבה א"כ אינו יכול לשמש בארבעה בגדים משום דהוה ליה מחוסר בגדים! ויש לומר: דמשום האי טעמא לא היינו מקפידין, כיון דעל פי בית דין *הוא, אי לאו טעמא דמעלין:
מני רבי שמעון היא דאמר אף צבור לא הקריבו. נראה דכיון דמוקמינן למתני' כרבי שמעון א"כ סיפא נמי אתיא כוותיה, דקתני: זה הכלל כל הנידר ונידב קרב בבמה. וקשה: דהא נזירות דהוי דבר הנידר ונידב, כדאמרינן בפרק שני דתמורה (דף יד: ושם), ואפילו הכי אית ליה לר' שמעון פ' בתרא דזבחים (דף קיז. ושם) דמנחות ונזירות אין קרב אפילו בבמה גדולה! וי"ל: דהכי מיפרשא מתניתין: זה הכלל כל הנידר ונידב, שקרב בבמה גדולה, כגון עולה ושלמים — ליחיד קרב בבמה קטנה. וכל שאינו נידר ונידב, ואע"פ שקרב בבמה גדולה — אין קרב בבמה קטנה. אבל מודה הוא דיש נידר ונידב שאין קרב לא בבמה גדולה ולא בבמה קטנה*:
שמעתי

הוריות יב.
ג"ז שם: יומא יב: [תוספתא יומא פ"א]
[עי' תוס' יומא פירושם]
[וע"ע תוס' פסחים לח: ד"ה זאת אומרת]

במדבר טז · דברים ד · שם יז · ויקרא יא · בראשית ט · ויקרא ד

[יומא ט: ע"ש]
[נ"ל אלא א"ר וכן גי' ע"י]
הוריות יח:
[לקמן כא: יומא יב: וש"נ]
[ר"ה ז: וש"נ]
זבחים קיז. קיח. ע"ש
[זבחים קיז.]
[תמורה כח:]

הגהות הב"ח

(א) גמ' וכתבו לו במקום את הארנבת את צעירת: (ב) שם הלכה כרשב"ג ואמר ר' אבהו אמר ר' יוחנן מ"ט: (ג) תום' ד"ה אין בין כהן משוח וכו' דאפילו כהן הדיוט: (ד) ד"ה אין בין כהן המשמש וכו' קשה לפירושינו היכי שחיט דכיון דזכי:

רבינו חננאל

עד שלא יאמר שחקו בי יהודים והטילו שם אשתי בתורתם. רשבג"א אף בספרים לא התירו שיכתבו אלא יוונית. מנא הני מילי א"ר יוחנן דכתיב יפת אלהים ליפת וישכון באהלי שם מיפיפותו של יפת. כלומר ממבחר בניו של יפת והיא כתיבת יון יהיו באהלי שם שהם בני ישראל. א"ר אבהו א"ר יוחנן הלכה כרשב"ג: [מתני'] אין בין כהן משוח בשמן המשחה למרובה בגדים כו'. מנא לן דכתיב אם הכהן המשיח יחטא לאשמת העם וגו'. פי' מרובה בגדים בבית שני שלא היה להם שמן המשחה היה מתמגד כ"ג בלבישת ח' בגדים. לפי שכל זמן שהיה הדיוט. היה משמש בד' בגדים לבש עוד ד' ונתרבה בד' אחרים נעשה כ"ג לפיכך נקרא מרובה בגדים. וזה מפורש בתלמוד בהוריות פ' ב' משוח בשמן המשחה בבית הראשון. מרובה בגדים בבית האחרון. ואמר ה' דברים היו. בית הראשון גדול מן האחרון. ואלו הן. אש וארון. ואורים ותומים ושמן המשחה. ורוה"ק ושאר כל הענין. הא לענין פר יוה"כ כדכתיב בזאת יבא אהרן אל הקדש בפר בן בקר וגו'. ועשירית האיפה כדכתיב זה קרבן אהרן ובניו אשר יקריבו לה' ביום המשח אותו וגו'. ומפורש בתורת כהנים שכל כהן מביא עשירית האיפה מדכתיב ובניו מרבינן אפי' הדיוטות וכ"ש מרובה בגדים. מתני' דלא כר"מ דתני מרובה בגדים מביא פר הבא על כל המצות ואקשינן אימא סיפא אין בין כהן משמש לכהן שעבר. כלומר שנפסל במום או בזולתו אלא פר יוה"כ ועשירית האיפה שהכהן המשמש הוא המביא משלו. וזה שעבר לא. הא לכל דבריהם זה וזה שוין. אתאן לר' מאיר דתני אירע בו פסול לכהן גדול ומינו אחר תחתיו כו' ופריק רב יוסף מתני' רבי היא. רישא סבר לה כרבנן. סיפא סבר לה כרבי מאיר: [מתני'] אין בין במה גדולה לבמה קטנה וכו'. ואוקימנא כעין פסחים. והן חובות הקבוע להן זמן. ומפורש בסוף פרק פרת חטאת ובסוף שחיטת קדשים בתוספתא אלו דברים שבין במה גדולה לקטנה קרן וכבש ויסוד. וריבוע וכיור וכנו בבמה גדולה ולא קטנה. *) חזה ושוק ועור העולה לבעלים בבמה קטנה. אבל נותר זמן וטמא זה וזה שוין. איזו היא במה גדולה **) בשעת איסור במה [שהי'] אהל מועד נטוי כדרכו. (אין) הארון נתון שם. איזו היא במה קטנה היתר הבמה עושה אדם במה על פתח ביתו ועל פתח חצירו ועל פתח גינתו ומקריב עליה הוא ובנו ובתו כו': [מתני'] אין בין שילה לירושלים אלא שבשילה אוכלים קדשים קלים ומעשר שני בכל הרואה. ובירושלים לפנים מן החומה כו'. פי' הרואה העומד בשילה כל מקום שרואה מלא עיניו מותר לו לאכול קדשים קלים ומע"ש ומפורש בפ' פרת חטאת. (דף קיח ע"ב) הכי א"ר אבהו כתיב בן פורת עלי עין וגו'. עין שלא רצתה להנות מדבר שאינו שלה תזכה ותאכל בקדשים כמלא עיניה. תנא רואה שאמר כולו שלא יהא דבר מפסיק וכן היה עומד בשדה ומביט משם משכן שילה מותר לו לאכול באותו מקום קדשים קלים ומע"ש. ותנן באו לשילה נאסרו הבמות. ולא היה שם תקרה אלא בית של אבנים מלמטה ויריעות מלמעלה והיא היתה מנוחה כו'. ותניא ימי אהל מועד שבשילה

*) חסר כאן מלשון התוספתא וצ"ל חזה ושוק ועור העולה לכהנים בבמה גדולה חזה ושוק ועור העולה לבעלים בבמה קטנה כ"ה שם בתוספתא ע"ש. **) לשון התוספתא שם איזו היא במה גדולה בשעת היתר במה אהל מועד נטוי כדרכו אין הארון נתון שם וכו'.

גליון הש"ס

גמ' מפני שאשתו. בירושלמי וכן במ"ר פ' שמיני איתא דאמו של תלמי ארנבתא שמה: שם מעשה בר' יוסף בן אולם. עי' תוס' ישנים יומא דף כא ע"א ד"ה ולא אירע קרי: שם אמר רבי היא ונסיב לה אליבא דתנאי. ר"ה דף ז ע"ב שבועות דף ד ע"א חולין דף פד ע"א ודף קד ע"א הוריות דף יב ע"ב: תוס' ד"ה אין בין כהן משוח וכו' פי' פר כהן משיח. עי' יומא דף נז ע"א תד"ה אני ראיתיה וקדושין דף לו ע"ב בפרש"י ד"ה אי דפנים ובתוס' ד"ה אי דפנים:

סט א מיי' פ"ו מהלכות בית הבחירה הלכה ג:
ע ב ג מיי' שם פ"ו הלכה טו סמג עשין קסג:

להקריב עכשיו וכ"ש בבמה כצ"ל

יש אחריה היתר, וקדושת ירושלים אין אחריה היתר.§ **גמ'** א"ר יצחק: שמעתי שמקריבין בבית חוניו בזמן הזה. קסבר: *בית חוניו לאו בית ע"ז היא, וקא סבר: קדושה ראשונה — קידשה לשעתה ולא קידשה לעתיד לבוא, דכתיב: °"כי לא באתם עד עתה אל המנוחה ואל הנחלה". *"מנוחה" — זו שילה, "נחלה" — זו ירושלים. מקיש נחלה למנוחה: מה מנוחה יש אחריה היתר — אף נחלה יש אחריה היתר. אמרו ליה: אמרת? אמר להו: לא. אמר רבא: האלהים! אמרה וגמירנא לה מיניה. ומ"ט קא הדר ביה? משום קושיא דרב מרי. דמותיב רב מרי: קדושת שילה יש אחריה היתר, קדושת ירושלים אין אחריה היתר. ועוד תנן: *[א]משבאו לירושלים נאסרו הבמות, ולא היה להם עוד היתר, והיא היתה לנחלה. תנאי היא, (*דתניא,) א"ר אליעזר: *שמעתי כשהיו בונין בהיכל (א)עושין קלעים להיכל, וקלעים לעזרה. אלא שבהיכל בונין מבחוץ, ובעזרה בונין מבפנים. וא"ר יהושע: [ב]שמעתי *שמקריבין אע"פ שאין בית, אוכלין קדשי קדשים אע"פ שאין קלעים, קדשים קלים ומעשר שני אע"פ שאין חומה. [ג]מפני שקדושה ראשונה — קידשה *לשעתה, °וקידשה לעתיד לבוא. (ב) מכלל דר"א סבר: לא קידשה לעתיד לבוא. א"ל רבינא לרב אשי: ממאי? דלמא דכולי עלמא קדושה ראשונה — קידשה לשעתה, וקידשה לעתיד לבוא. ומר מאי דשמיע ליה קאמר, ומר מאי דשמיע ליה קאמר. וכי תימא: קלעים לר"א למה לי? לצניעותא בעלמא. אלא, כי הני תנאי. דתניא, אמר רבי ישמעאל ברבי יוסי: למה מנו *חכמים את אלו? שכשעלו בני הגולה מצאו את אלו וקידשום, אבל הראשונות — בטלו משבטלה הארץ. אלמא קסבר: קדושה ראשונה קידשה לשעתה ולא קידשה לעתיד לבוא. ורמינהו: *אמר רבי ישמעאל ברבי יוסי: וכי אלו בלבד היו? והלא כבר נאמר: °"ששים עיר כל חבל ארגוב", וכתיב: °"כל אלה ערים בצורות חומה גבוהה"! אלא למה מנו חכמים את אלו? שכשעלו בני הגולה מצאו אלו וקידשום. קידשום?! השתא

דברים יב | דברים ג | שם

רש"י

יש אחריה היתר. כשחרבה שילה הותרו הבמות כדאמרינן במס' זבחים (דף קיט.) "כי לא באתם עד עתה אל המנוחה" – זו שילה, שנחו מלכבוש. "ואל הנחלה" – זו ירושלים. למה חלקן הכתוב, כדי ליתן היתר בין זו לזו: **גמ'** בית חוניו. מזבח חוניו. בנו של שמעון הצדיק בנה במה במצרים לשם שמים, כדאמרינן במס' מנחות (דף קט:): קסבר כו'. דאיכא למאן דאמר התם שבנאה לשם ע"ז: וקסבר קדושה. שנתקדשה ירושלים אינה קדושה לעולם, ומשחרבה הותרו הבמות: לעתיד לבא. כלומר, משתחרב: והיא היתה נחלה. האמור בפסוק "אל המנוחה ואל הנחלה": קלעים להיכל. קא סלקא דעתך במקום חומות היכל, שיהא מזבח הבנוי בעזרה קרוי "אשר פתח אהל מועד". שאלמלא כן לא היו מקריבין עד שיגמר הבנין. והם התחילו להקריב קרבנות משבאו שם בימי כורש, כמו שכתוב בספר עזרא (ג), ועד עשרים ושנים שנה אחרי כן לא נגמר הבית, בשנת שלש לדריוש האחרון: בונין מבחוץ. שהיו הקלעים פרושים לפנים מעובי החומה, שלא יכנסו הבונין לתוך ההיכל: לאו מכלל דר' אליעזר. דבעי קלעים, סבר: לא קידשה לאחר חורבן, לפיכך פירסו קלעים במקום בנין, וחזרו וקידשו בתודות ובשיר, כדאמר במס' שבועות (דף טז.): ומר מאי דשמיע ליה קאמר. ולא משום נורך קדושה: וכי תימא. כו': את אלו. עיירות נמנו בפ' בתרא דערכין לענין בתי ערי חומה, לומר שהיו מוקפות חומה מימות יהושע בן נון, ואין שם יותר מתשעה: ולמה מנאום. והלא הרבה היו שם, והתם נמי תנן: וכל כיוצא בהן: ורמינהו. מסקנא דמילתיה הוא, דאמר לעיל הני תנאי פליגי בקידשה ולא קידשה: הא

[מנחות קט:] | [זבחים קיט.] | שם קיב: | [נ"ל דתנן] | שבועות טז. זבחים קז: עדיות פ"ח מ"ו | [זבחים סב.] | חגיגה ג: [זבחים ס: קז: חולין ז. תמורה כא. ערכין לב: מכות יט. שבועות טז.] | ערכין לב:

תוספות

שמעתי שמקריבין בבית חוניו. קשיא: היאך מקריבין שם בטומאה? דהא גזרו טומאה על ארץ העמים! ויש לומר: דשמא לגבי הא לא גזרו חכמים טומאה, כיון שמן התורה יכול להקריב: **ומאי** טעמא הדר ביה משום קושיא דרב מרי. הקשה הר"ר חיים: ומתחילה היכי אמר למילתיה? וכי לא היה יודע המשנה? והלא הן שגורות בפי כל! ועוד קשיא: כיון דתנאי היא, אמאי הדר ביה? לימא אנא דאמרי כמאן דאמר לא קדשה! לכך נראה להר"ר חיים: דכ"ע מודו דמשבאו לירושלים נאסרו הבמות ושוב לא היה להן היתר: והני תנאי בהא פליגי, דמאן דאמר לא קדשה — סבר דאף במקומו של מזבח אין יכולין להקריב עכשיו*, ומאן דאמר קדשה סבר דבמקום מזבח מותר להקריב, אבל לא בבמה:

דכולי עלמא קדושה ראשונה קדשה לשעתה וקדשה לעתיד לבוא. הקשה רבינו תם: אמאי לא מייתי ראיה דרבי אליעזר אית ליה בפ' קמא דחגיגה (דף ג: ושם) דלא קדשה לעתיד לבוא, דקאמר התם: מעשה ברבי יוסי בן דורמסקית, ומסיק, אמר ר' אליעזר: כך מקובלני מרבן יוחנן בן זכאי עמון ומואב מעשרין מעשר עני בשביעית, מה טעם — משום דהרבה כרכים כבשו עולי מצרים ולא כבשום עולי בבל, וקדושה ראשונה קדשה לשעתה ולא קדשה לעתיד לבא! ותירץ רבינו תם: דמה טעם דהתם גמרא הוא דקאמר לה, ולאו מילתא דרבי אליעזר היא. ותדע, דהא במשנה דמסכת ידים (פ"ד משנה ג) דתניא מילתיה דרבי אליעזר לא תנא לה והכי פירושה: מה טעם מעשרין — משום דכי האי גוונא אשכחן בערי ישראל שהניחום עולי בבל מלקדש, למאן דאמר לא קדשה, כדי שיסמכו עליהן עניי ישראל בשביעית. וכל שכן עמון ומואב שהן חוצה לארץ, שהניחום עולי בבל מלקדש למאן דאמר לא קדש', והניחום לעניים. דהא לא איירי בעמון ומואב שטהרו בסיחון. אלא איירי באותן שהניחו ישראל בבואם ממצרים ולא כבשום, והכי נמי משמע במסכת ידים (ג"ז שם) דחשיב להו עם בבל ומצרים שהן חו"ל. והיא (ג)ד"חזקת הבתים" (ב"ב דף לח.) דקאמר: שלש ארצות לחזקה: יהודה, ועבר הירדן, והגליל. דמשמע דעמון ומואב שהיו בעבר הירדן היו א"י – מיירי בעמון ומואב שטהרו בסיחון. ועוד הקשה ר"ת מהא דאמר במס' ביצה (דף ה: ושם): וכר"ה (דף לא:): כרם רבעי היה לו לרבי אליעזר, ובקש להפקירו לעניים. וא"כ משמע דאית ליה קדשה לעתיד לבוא, ומשום שלא היה רוצה לטרוח להוליכו לירושלים? היה מפקירו לעניים, שיוליכו אותו ויאכלוהו שמה. דאי סבר לא קדשה, והיה צריך לפדותו, כאותו שבחוצה לארץ שצריך לפדותו – אמאי היה צריך להוליך לירושלים וגם מה היו העניים מרויחים אחרי שצריך לפדותו? וי"ל: משום דבראשונה כרם רבעי שבארץ ישראל היה צריך להוליכו (ד)לירושלים, גם בקש ר' אליעזר להוליכו משום דכל דבר שנאסר במנין צריך מנין אחר להתירו. והאי מייתי לה בביצה (ג"ז שם). ומכל מקום העניים היו מרויחים במה שהיו יכולים לחללו בשוה פרוטה, כדשמואל. והי דשמואל לא אמר למלתיה אלא בדיעבד, כדמשמע לישנא שחללו – היינו דווקא בזמן שבית המקדש קיים, אבל בזמן הזה – לא, *ואפילו לכתחילה. והכי נמי איתא בשאלתות דרב אחאי בפרשת "קדושים תהיו" (סוף סימן ק'): ומברך על פדיון עובר לעשייתן. וקלי ליה לדמי פדיוניה או ישליכם לנהר: [וע"ע תוס' ר"ה לא: ד"ה בקש]:

למה מנו חכמים את אלו. קשה: אמאי מייתי הך ברייתא, דלא מוכחא אלא דקדושה ראשונה לא בטלה? והאיכא תנא דאית ליה בפ' הערל (יבמות דף פב:) דקדושה ראשונה ושניה יש להן, הא שלישית אין להן, דקדושה אחרונה לא בטלה. וקדושת חוניו היתה לאחר קדושה שלישית? (ה)ויש לומר: דאפילו למאן דאמר קדושה אחרונה לא בטלה – היינו דוקא לענין תרומה בזמן הזה, אבל לכל מילי אחריני – ודאי בטלה: שאר

[ס"א שניה]

רבינו חננאל

שבשילה ש"ע חסר אחת. ותניא כשמת עלי הכהן חרבה שילה ובאו לנוב וכשמת שמואל חרבה נוב ובאו לגבעון קדושת שילה יש אחריה היתר כלומר שרתה השכינה אחר חרבנה בנוב וגבעון ובירושלים. אבל משנבנה בית עולמים אין אחריו היתר במקום אחר לעולם. א"ר יצחק שמעתי שמקריבין בבית חוניו ולאו בית ע"ז היא. וקדושת ירושלים יש אחריה היתר כו' ונדחו דבריו. ומעשה דחוניו מפורש בסוף מנחות. דבן שמעון הצדיק הוא וחלק על שמעי' אחיו כשעלה לכהונה גדולה נתקנא בו כו'. וברח והלך ובנה מזבח באלכסנדריא של מצרים. והקריב עליו קרבן כו'. ואמרינן תנאי היא. כלומר יש תנא שאומר יש אחריה היתר. דתניא א"ר אליעזר כשהיו בונין בהיכל היו עושין קלעים להיכל וקלעים לעזרה כו'. א"ר יהושע שמעתי שמקריבי' אע"פ שאין בית כו' עד מפני שקדושה ראשונה קדשה לעתיד לבוא לעולם. ודייקינן לאו מכלל דר' אליעזר בר פלוגתי' דר' יהושע סבר דקדושה ראשונה קדשה לשעתה היא ולא לעתיד. ודחי רבינא ואמר כ"ע קידשה לשעתה וקידשה לעתיד. ור' אליעזר אמר מה ששמע. ור' יהושע מה ששמע ואין ביניהם חלוקה. ואמרינן אלא ר' ישמעאל ב"ר יוסי הוא דאמר קדושה ראשונה אינה לעתיד לבוא. והוא חולק על ר' אליעזר ועל ר' יהושע דתניא בתורת כהנים (פרשת בהר פ"ד) ערי חומה המוקפות מימות יהושע בן נון. כגון קצרה הישנה של ורין. וחקרה של גוש חלב ויורפת הישנה וגמלה הרי בגליל. וגדוד הרי בעבר הירדן וחדיד ואונו וירושלים הרי ביהודה. א"ר ישמעאל ברבי יוסי לא מנו את אלו אלא שקידשום כשעלו מן הגולה. אבל הראשונות

הגהות הב"ח

(א) גמ' כשהיו בונין בהיכל עשו קלעים: (ב) שם לעתיד לבוא לאו מכלל דר' אליעזר: (ג) תוס' ד"ה דכולי עלמא וכו' ומצרים שהן חו"ל והיא דפ"ע דשביעית ומייתי לה בפ' מקום שנהגו דקאמר שלש ארצות לבעור יהודה: (ד) בא"ד צריך להוליכו לירושלים גם בקש ר' אליעזר ג"כ להוליכו כצ"ל: (ה) ד"ה למה וכו' ויש לומר. נ"ב משמע מסברת תוס' דמפרשי ראשונה אברהם ויצחק ויעקב שניה ירושת יהושע ואלו שניהם יש להם ביטול אבל שלישית ירושת עזרא אין לה ביטול וזה שלא כדברי התוס' ש... להם היינו לומר דצריך לחזור לירושה כדי לקדשם ואין להם היינו לומר דא"צ דירושה עומדת היא דלא בטלה קדושתה וכמו שפרש"י לשם אלא דלרבינו חננאל ראשונה היא ירושת אברהם ויצחק ויעקב שניה ירושת יהושע ומשם ואילך קדש... ראשונה היא ירושת יהושע שניה היא ירושת עזרא ומשם ואילך קדשה לעולם ע"ש:

גליון הש"ס

גמ' וקידשה לעתיד לבוא. עי' ברכות דף סא ע"ב:

הא אמרי. לקמן בסיפא דהא מתני' גופה דלא צריכי לקדושי, דקא מסיים ואזיל בה: וכל שתעלה בידך מסורת מאבותיך: כל המצות הללו. הנוהגות בערי חומה: שילוח מצורע, וקריאת מגילה בחמשה עשר, והבית חלוט בה לסוף שנה: אע"פ שאין כו'. אלמא סבירא ליה קדושה קמייתא לא בטלה מחמת חורבן, והיינו תנאי: וחרבו שלופה וגו'. וליערו, שהוכיחו על ביטול תורה ותמיד של בין הערבים, כדאמר לעיל בפירקין (דף ג.): ויהי דוד לכל דרכיו משכיל וה' עמו. וכתיב התם "ויהי שאול עוין את דוד" בשביל הצלחתו: אמוץ ואמציה. אמוץ אביו של ישעיה, ואמציה מלך יהודה: מלמד שכיסתה פניה בבית חמיה. לפיכך לא הכירה עכשיו, שאף בביתו לא ראה פניה שיהא מכירה: אינו מן המדה. אינו אוחז למעט מדת קרקע לכל צדדיו כלום, כדקתני: יש לו עשר אמות לכל רוח. באמצע בית קדש הקדשים היה יושב, ויש ריוח בינו לבין הכתלים עשר אמות לכל צד. וכל הבית אינו אלא כ' על כ', נמצא שאינו ממעט כלום: לפני הדביר. חלל בית קדש הקדשים שהוא לפנים מן הדביר, היא המחיצה המבדלת בין הקדש ובין קדש הקדשים: פתח לה פיתחא להאי פרשתא מהכא. כשהיה

תורה אור

רוצה לדרוש בענין איגרת פורים היה מתחיל לדרוש מקרא זה: וקמתי עליהם. בפורענות בבל כתיב: זה הכתב. אין להן כתב, אלא מאומה אחרת: נין. לשון ממשלה, וכן "ינון שמו" (תהלים עב) — ימשול ויגדל: בצאת לפני החלוץ. ביהושפט כתיב, בדברי הימים, כשילא להלחם על העמונים והגבעונים שבאו עליו: הודו לה' כי טוב. משמע: טוב שיקלסו לפניו על זאת: אחרים משיש. וכשנתחייבו כלייה בימי המן היו אויביהן שמחין להן: ושמתי כסאי בעילם. שושן הבירה היתה בעילם, דכתיב בספר דניאל (ח) "בשושן הבירה אשר בעילם המדינה": כי

(א) השתא [הא] אמרי לא צריכא לקדושי! אלא: מצאו את אלו ומנאום. ולא אלו בלבד, אלא כל שתעלה לך מסורת בידך מאבותיך שמוקפת חומה מימות יהושע בן נון — כל המצות הללו נוהגין בה, מפני שקדושה ראשונה קידשה לשעתה וקידשה לעתיד לבא. קשיא דר' ישמעאל אדר' ישמעאל! תרי תנאי אליבא דר' ישמעאל בר' יוסי. ואיבעית אימא: הא — ר' אלעזר בר יוסי אמרה, דתניא: *ר' אלעזר בר' יוסי אמר: °"אשר לוא חומה" — אע"פ שאין לו עכשיו והיה לו קודם לכן.§ "ויהי בימי אחשורוש". אמר רבי לוי ואיתימא רבי יונתן: דבר זה מסורת בידינו מאנשי כנסת הגדולה, כל מקום שנאמר "ויהי" אינו אלא לשון צער. °"ויהי בימי אחשורוש" — הוה המן. °"ויהי בימי שפוט השופטים" — הוה רעב. °"ויהי כי החל האדם לרוב" — "וירא ה' כי רבה רעת האדם". °"ויהי בנסעם מקדם" — "הבה נבנה לנו עיר". °"ויהי בימי אמרפל" — "עשו מלחמה". °"ויהי בהיות יהושע ביריחו" — "וחרבו שלופה בידו". °"ויהי ה' את יהושע" — "וימעלו בני ישראל". °"ויהי איש אחד מן הרמתים" — "כי את חנה אהב וה' סגר רחמה". °"ויהי (*כי) זקן שמואל" — "ולא הלכו בניו בדרכיו". °"ויהי דוד לכל דרכיו משכיל [וה' עמו]" — "ויהי שאול עוין את דוד". °"ויהי כי ישב המלך בביתו" — *"רק אתה לא תבנה הבית". והכתיב: °"ויהי ביום השמיני", ותניא: אותו היום היתה שמחה לפני הקדוש ברוך הוא כיום שנבראו בו שמים וארץ. כתיב הכא: "ויהי ביום השמיני", וכתיב התם: °"ויהי (*בקר) יום אחד"! הא שכיב נדב ואביהוא. והכתיב: °"ויהי בשמונים שנה וארבע מאות שנה"! והכתיב: °"ויהי כאשר ראה יעקב את רחל"! והכתיב "ויהי ערב ויהי בקר יום אחד"! והאיכא שני! והאיכא שלישי! והאיכא טובא! *אמר רב אשי: כל "ויהי" — איכא הכי, ואיכא הכי. "ויהי בימי" אינו אלא לשון צער. חמשה "ויהי בימי" הוו: "ויהי בימי אחשורוש", "ויהי בימי שפוט השופטים", "ויהי בימי אמרפל", °"ויהי בימי אחז", °"ויהי בימי יהויקים". (*א"ר) לוי: דבר זה מסורת בידינו מאבותינו: אמוץ ואמציה אחים הוו. מאי קמ"ל? כי הא *דא"ר שמואל בר נחמני אמר רבי יונתן: כל כלה שהיא צנועה בבית חמיה, זוכה ויוצאין ממנה מלכים ונביאים. מנלן? מתמר, דכתיב: °"ויראה יהודה ויחשבה לזונה כי כסתה פניה". משום דכסתה פניה ויחשבה לזונה?! אלא משום דכסתה פניה בבית חמיה, ולא הוה ידע לה, זכתה ויצאו ממנה מלכים ונביאים. מלכים — מדוד, נביאים — דא"ר לוי: מסורת בידינו מאבותינו: אמוץ ואמציה אחים היו. וכתיב: °"חזון ישעיהו בן אמוץ". וא"ר לוי: דבר זה *מסורת בידינו מאבותינו: מקום ארון אינו מן המדה. תניא נמי הכי: ארון שעשה משה יש לו עשר אמות לכל רוח. וכתיב: °"ולפני הדביר עשרים אמה אורך", *וכתיב: "כנף הכרוב האחד עשר אמות, וכנף הכרוב האחד עשר אמות". ארון גופיה היכא הוה קאי? אלא לאו שמע מינה בנס היה עומד? ר' יונתן פתח לה פיתחא להאי פרשתא מהכא: °"וקמתי עליהם וגו' והכרתי לבבל שם ושאר ונין ונכד נאם ה'". "שם" — זה הכתב; "שאר" — זה לשון; "נין" — זה מלכות; "ונכד" — זו ושתי. רבי שמואל בר נחמני פתח לה פיתחא להאי פרשתא מהכא: °"תחת הנעצוץ יעלה ברוש ותחת הסרפד יעלה הדס". "תחת הנעצוץ" — תחת המן הרשע. *שעשה עצמו ע"ז, דכתיב: °"ובכל הנעצוצים ובכל הנהלולים". "יעלה ברוש" — זה מרדכי, שנקרא ראש לכל הבשמים, שנאמר: °"ואתה קח לך בשמים ראש מר דרור" ומתרגמינן: *מרי דכי. "תחת הסרפד" — תחת ושתי הרשעה, בת בנו של נבוכדנצר הרשע, ששרף רפידת בית ה', דכתיב: °"רפידתו זהב". "יעלה הדס" — זו אסתר הצדקת שנקראת הדסה, שנאמר: °"ויהי אומן את הדסה". "והיה לה' לשם" — זו מקרא מגילה. "לאות עולם לא יכרת" — אלו ימי פורים. ר' יהושע בן לוי פתח לה פיתחא להאי פרשתא מהכא: °"והיה כאשר שש ה' עליכם להיטיב אתכם... כן ישיש... להרע אתכם". *ומי חדי הקב"ה במפלתן של רשעים? והא כתיב: °"בצאת לפני החלוץ ואומרים הודו לה' כי לעולם חסדו", וא"ר יוחנן: מפני מה לא נאמר "כי טוב" בהודאה זו? לפי שאין הקב"ה שמח במפלתן של רשעים. ואמר רבי יוחנן: מאי דכתיב: °"ולא קרב זה אל זה כל הלילה"? בקשו מלאכי השרת לומר שירה. אמר הקב"ה: מעשה ידי טובעין בים, ואתם אומרים שירה?! אמר רבי אלעזר: הוא אינו שש, אבל אחרים משיש. ודיקא נמי דכתיב: "כן ישיש", ולא כתיב "ישוש". ש"מ. רבי אבא בר כהנא פתח לה פיתחא להאי פרשתא מהכא: °"לאדם שטוב לפניו נתן חכמה ודעת ושמחה" — זה מרדכי הצדיק; "ולחוטא נתן ענין לאסוף ולכנוס" — זה המן. "לתת לטוב לפני האלהים" — זה מרדכי ואסתר, דכתיב: "ותשם אסתר את מרדכי על בית המן". רבה בר עופרן פתח לה פיתחא להאי פרשתא מהכא: °"ושמתי כסאי בעילם והאבדתי משם מלך ושרים". "מלך" — זו ושתי; "ושרים" — זה המן ועשרת בניו. רב דימי בר יצחק פתח לה פיתחא להאי פרשתא מהכא: כי

שאר זה לשון. קשה: שעדיין הם מספרין [בבבל] — בלשון ארמית! ונראה דרוצה לומר [לשון מלכות] — שהמלכים משתמשין בו, שאין שאר [העם] מכירין בו*: **רבה** בר עופרן. גרסינן. ולא גרסינן עפרון, דשם רשעים ירקב, ולא מסקו בשמייהו*: שלשה

ויקרא כה
[לעיל ג: וש"נ]
אסתר א רות א
בראשית ו
בראשית יא שם יד
יהושע ה
יהושע ו
שמואל א א
ש"א ח [נ"ל כאשר]
שם יח
[בקרא דשמואל ב ז בענין ויהי כי ישב המלך בביתו וגו' כתיב האתה תבנה לי בית לשבת]
שמואל ב ז
ויקרא ט
בראשית א
מלכים א ו
[נ"ל ערב ויהי בקר]
בראשית כט
[נ"ל אלא אמר]
ישעיה ז
ירמיה א
[נ"ל וא"ר]
סוטה י:
בראשית לח
ישעיה א
ב"ב לט. יומא כא.
מלכים א ו
[נ"ל ועשרים אמה רוחב וכן גרס בע"י במס' ב"ב עי' ב"ב לט. ותבין]
ישעיה יד
ישעיה נה
[לקמן יט.]
שם ז
שמות ל
[חולין קלט:]
שיר ג
[אסתר ב]
[ועי' תוס' ע"ז י. ד"ה שאין להם]
דברים כח
סנהדרין לט: ע"ש
ד"ה ב כ
[כדאיתא ביומא לח:]
שמות יד
קהלת ב
ירמיה מט

הגהות הב"ח

(א) גמ' השתא הא אמרי לקמן דלא צריכי לקדושי:

רבינו חננאל

הראשונות בטלו משבטלה הארץ. איני והתניא בסוף ערכין א"ר ישמעאל ב"ר יוסי וכי אלו בלבד הי' והלא כתיב ששים עיר כל חבל ארגוב. וכתיב כל אלו ערים בצורות וגו'. אלא מצאו את אלו ומנאום. ולא אלו בלבד אלא כל שתעלה מסורת מאבותיך שמוקפות חומה מימות יהושע בן נון. כל המצות האלו נוהגות בה. מפני שקדושה ראשונה קידשה לשעתה היא וקדוש לעתיד לבוא. קשיא דר' ישמעאל אדר' ישמעאל. ופרקינן תרי תנאי אליבא דר' ישמעאל. איבעי תימא הא בתרייתא ר' אלעזר בר' יוסי אמרה. דתניא ר' אלעזר בר' יוסי אומר אשר לו חומה לצמית כו'. אע"פ שאין לו עכשיו והיה לו קודם לכן. כלומר אע"פ שחרבה חומתה בקדושתה קיימא: **מסורת** בידינו מאנשי כנסת הגדולה כל ויהי לשון צעק הוא. ה' ויהי בימי הוו. ועוד מסורת ביד מאנשי כנסת הגדולה אמוץ ואמציה אחים הוו ואסיקנא כל כלה שצנועה בבית חמיה זוכה לצאת ממנה מלכים ונביאים מנא לן מתמר. ועוד מסורת בידינו מקום ארון [אינו] מן המדה. דתניא או שעשה

כִּי עֲבָדִים אֲנַחְנוּ. פָּסוּק הוּא בְּסֵפֶר עֶזְרָא, וְסֵיפָא "וַיַּט עָלֵינוּ חֶסֶד לִפְנֵי (ב) שָׂרֵי פָרַס לָתֶת *עָלֵינוּ מִחְיָה": בָּאֵשׁ בִּימֵי נְבוּכַדְנֶצַּר. שֶׁהִפִּילָנוּ לְתוֹךְ הַכִּבְשָׁן: אֵימָתַי רָאוּ כָל אַפְסֵי אֶרֶץ אֵת יְשׁוּעַת אֱלֹהֵינוּ בִּימֵי מָרְדְּכַי. שֶׁהַדָּבָר נִגְלָה לְכָל הָאוּמּוֹת, שֶׁהָלְכוּ אִגְּרוֹת בְּכָל הָעוֹלָם: ⊕מְסוֹרְבָּלִין. מְלוּבָּשִׁין בְּבָשָׂר: נַעֲשָׂה תּוֹרָה אוֹר שׂוֹנְאוֹ שֶׁל הַקָּדוֹשׁ בָּרוּךְ הוּא מַךְ. כְּמִי שֶׁלֹּא הָיָה יָכוֹל לְהוֹשִׁיעַ: אָדָם וְלֹא מֶלֶךְ. זֶה הָמָן: רַב מַתָּנָה [אָמַר] מֵהָכָא. פָּתַח פִּתְחָא: [הָדָא דִּכְתִיב כו']. מַה שֶּׁכָּתַב בַּתּוֹרָה "וְאֵין קוֹנֶה" גָּזַר הָמָן שֶׁלֹּא יְהֵא אָדָם רַשַּׁאי לִקְנוֹת מֵהֶן לְעֶבֶד: וּשְׁמוּאֵל אָמַר (ג) מֵהָכָא. פִּתְחָא לֹא מְאַסְתִּים וגו'": וְאִם לֹא תוֹרִישׁוּ וגו'. אַף אֵלּוּ נֶעֶנְשׁוּ עַל שֶׁחָמַל שָׁאוּל עַל עֲמָלֵק: אֶעֱשֶׂה לָכֶם. אַף אֵלּוּ כִּמְעַט כָּלוּ: אָחִיו שֶׁל רֹאשׁ. כְּלוֹמַר: דּוֹמֶה לוֹ: בֶּן גִּילוֹ. בֶּן מַזָּלוֹ, שֶׁשְּׁנֵיהֶן דַּעַת אַחַת הָיָה לָהֶן: בִּקֵּשׁ לְהַחֲרִיב. יְסוֹד שֶׁיִּסֵּד זְרוּבָּבֶל בְּבֵית הַמִּקְדָּשׁ בִּימֵי כּוֹרֶשׁ לִפְנֵי אֲחַשְׁוֵרוֹשׁ, כְּמוֹ שֶׁאָמוּר בְּסֵפֶר עֶזְרָא (סימן ד): שִׂטְנָה. שֶׁנִּמְנָה לְשָׂטָן לָהֶם, שֶׁלֹּא יִבְנוּהוּ: ⊕אָח. אוֹי: אַבְרָם הוּא אַבְרָהָם. פָּסוּק הוּא בְּדִבְרֵי הַיָּמִים: שֶׁמָּלַךְ מֵעַצְמוֹ. שֶׁלֹּא הָיָה מִזֶּרַע הַמְּלוּכָה: כִּי הוּא רוֹדֶה. כְּתִיב בִּשְׁלֹמֹה: כְּשֵׁם שֶׁמָּלַךְ עַל תִּפְסַח (ד) וְעַל עַזָּה וכו'. וְהָכִי קָאָמַר: כִּי הוּא רוֹדֶה בְּכָל עֵבֶר הַנָּהָר כְּמוֹ מִתִּפְסַח וְעַד עַזָּה: מָלְכוּ בְּכִיפָּה. תַּחַת כָּל כִּיפַּת הָרָקִיעַ: הָא דַּאֲמַרַן. "מֵהוֹדּוּ וְעַד כּוּשׁ": סִימָן

עזרא ט °"כִּי עֲבָדִים אֲנַחְנוּ וּבְעַבְדוּתֵנוּ לֹא עֲזָבָנוּ אֱלֹהֵינוּ וַיַּט עָלֵינוּ חֶסֶד לִפְנֵי מַלְכֵי פָרַס". אֵימָתַי? בִּזְמַן *הָמָן. רַבִּי חֲנִינָא בַּר פָּפָּא פָּתַח לָהּ פִּתְחָא לְהָא פָּרָשָׁתָא מֵהָכָא: (תהלים סו) °"הִרְכַּבְתָּ אֱנוֹשׁ לְרֹאשֵׁנוּ בָּאנוּ בָאֵשׁ וּבַמַּיִם". "בָּאֵשׁ" — בִּימֵי נְבוּכַדְנֶצַּר הָרָשָׁע; "וּבַמַּיִם" — בִּימֵי פַרְעֹה. "וַתּוֹצִיאֵנוּ לָרְוָיָה" — בִּימֵי הָמָן. רַבִּי יוֹחָנָן פָּתַח לָהּ פִּתְחָא לְהָא פָּרָשָׁתָא מֵהָכָא: (שם צח) °"זָכַר חַסְדּוֹ וֶאֱמוּנָתוֹ לְבֵית יִשְׂרָאֵל רָאוּ כָל אַפְסֵי אָרֶץ אֵת יְשׁוּעַת אֱלֹהֵינוּ". אֵימָתַי רָאוּ כָּל אַפְסֵי אָרֶץ אֵת יְשׁוּעַת אֱלֹהֵינוּ? בִּימֵי מָרְדְּכַי וְאֶסְתֵּר. רֵישׁ לָקִישׁ פָּתַח לָהּ פִּתְחָא לְהָא פָּרָשָׁתָא מֵהָכָא: °"אֲרִי נוֹהֵם וְדוֹב שׁוֹקֵק מוֹשֵׁל רָשָׁע עַל עַם דָּל". "אֲרִי נוֹהֵם" — זֶה נְבוּכַדְנֶצַּר הָרָשָׁע, דִּכְתִיב בֵּיהּ: °"עָלָה אַרְיֵה מִסֻּבְּכוֹ". "דּוֹב שׁוֹקֵק" — זֶה אֲחַשְׁוֵרוֹשׁ, דִּכְתִיב בֵּיהּ: °"וַאֲרוּ חֵיוָה אָחֳרִי תִנְיָנָה דָּמְיָה לְדֹב". *וְתָנֵי רַב יוֹסֵף: אֵלּוּ פַּרְסִיִּים, שֶׁאוֹכְלִין וְשׁוֹתִין כְּדוֹב, וּמְסוֹרְבָּלִין בָּשָׂר כְּדוֹב, וּמְגַדְּלִין שֵׂעָר כְּדוֹב, וְאֵין לָהֶם מְנוּחָה כְּדוֹב. "מוֹשֵׁל רָשָׁע" — זֶה הָמָן. "עַל עַם דָּל" — אֵלּוּ יִשְׂרָאֵל, שֶׁהֵם דַּלִּים מִן הַמִּצְוֹת. ר' אֶלְעָזָר פָּתַח לָהּ פִּתְחָא לְהָא פָּרָשָׁתָא מֵהָכָא: °"בַּעֲצַלְתַּיִם יִמַּךְ הַמְּקָרֶה וּבְשִׁפְלוּת יָדַיִם יִדְלֹף הַבָּיִת" *בִּשְׁבִיל עַצְלוּת שֶׁהָיָה לָהֶם לְיִשְׂרָאֵל, שֶׁלֹּא עָסְקוּ בַּתּוֹרָה, נַעֲשָׂה שׂוֹנְאוֹ שֶׁל הקב"ה מָךְ. וְאֵין "מָךְ" אֶלָּא עָנִי, שֶׁנֶּאֱמַר: °"וְאִם מָךְ הוּא מֵעֶרְכֶּךָ". וְאֵין "מְקָרֶה" אֶלָּא הקב"ה, שֶׁנֶּאֱמַר: °"הַמְקָרֶה בַמַּיִם עֲלִיּוֹתָיו". רַב נַחְמָן בַּר יִצְחָק פָּתַח לָהּ פִּתְחָא לְהָא פָּרָשָׁתָא מֵהָכָא: °"שִׁיר הַמַּעֲלוֹת לוּלֵי ה' שֶׁהָיָה לָנוּ יֹאמַר נָא יִשְׂרָאֵל. לוּלֵי ה' שֶׁהָיָה לָנוּ בְּקוּם עָלֵינוּ אָדָם" — ⊕"אָדָם", וְלֹא מֶלֶךְ. רָבָא פָּתַח לָהּ פִּתְחָא לְהָא פָּרָשָׁתָא מֵהָכָא: °"בִּרְבוֹת צַדִּיקִים יִשְׂמַח הָעָם וּבִמְשֹׁל רָשָׁע יֵאָנַח עָם". "בִּרְבוֹת צַדִּיקִים יִשְׂמַח הָעָם" — זֶה מָרְדְּכַי וְאֶסְתֵּר, דִּכְתִיב: "וְהָעִיר שׁוּשָׁן צָהֲלָה וְשָׂמֵחָה"; "וּבִמְשֹׁל רָשָׁע יֵאָנַח עָם" — זֶה הָמָן, דִּכְתִיב: "וְהָעִיר שׁוּשָׁן נָבוֹכָה". רַב מַתָּנָה אָמַר מֵהָכָא: °"כִּי מִי גוֹי גָּדוֹל אֲשֶׁר לוֹ אֱלֹהִים קְרוֹבִים אֵלָיו". רַב אַשִׁי אָמַר מֵהָכָא: °"אוֹ הֲנִסָּה אֱלֹהִים" וגו'.[א] "וַיְהִי בִּימֵי אֲחַשְׁוֵרוֹשׁ". אָמַר רַב: וַיי וְהִי. (א) הָדָא דִּכְתִיב: °"וְהִתְמַכַּרְתֶּם שָׁם לְאֹיְבֶיךָ לַעֲבָדִים וְלִשְׁפָחוֹת" וגו'. וּשְׁמוּאֵל אָמַר: °"לֹא מְאַסְתִּים וְלֹא גְעַלְתִּים לְכַלֹּתָם". "לֹא מְאַסְתִּים" — בִּימֵי יְוָונִים; "וְלֹא גְעַלְתִּים" — בִּימֵי נְבוּכַדְנֶצַּר, "לְכַלּוֹתָם" — בִּימֵי הָמָן; "לְהָפֵר בְּרִיתִי אִתָּם" — בִּימֵי פַרְסִיִּים, "כִּי אֲנִי ה' אֱלֹהֵיהֶם" — בִּימֵי גּוֹג וּמָגוֹג. בְּמַתְנִיתָא תָּנָא: "לֹא מְאַסְתִּים" — בִּימֵי כַּשְׂדִּים, שֶׁהֶעֱמַדְתִּי לָהֶם דָּנִיֵּאל חֲנַנְיָה מִישָׁאֵל וַעֲזַרְיָה; "וְלֹא גְעַלְתִּים" — בִּימֵי יְוָונִים, שֶׁהֶעֱמַדְתִּי לָהֶם שִׁמְעוֹן הַצַּדִּיק, וְחַשְׁמוֹנַאי וּבָנָיו, וּמַתִּתְיָה כֹּהֵן גָּדוֹל, "לְכַלּוֹתָם" — בִּימֵי הָמָן, שֶׁהֶעֱמַדְתִּי לָהֶם מָרְדְּכַי וְאֶסְתֵּר; "לְהָפֵר בְּרִיתִי אִתָּם" — בִּימֵי פַרְסִיִּים שֶׁהֶעֱמַדְתִּי לָהֶם שֶׁל בֵּית רַבִּי וְחַכְמֵי דוֹרוֹת; "כִּי אֲנִי ה' אֱלֹהֵיהֶם" — לֶעָתִיד לָבוֹא, שֶׁאֵין כָּל אוּמָּה וְלָשׁוֹן יְכוֹלָה לִשְׁלוֹט בָּהֶם. רַבִּי לֵוִי אָמַר מֵהָכָא: °"וְאִם לֹא תוֹרִישׁוּ אֶת יֹשְׁבֵי הָאָרֶץ". רַבִּי חִיָּיא אָמַר מֵהָכָא: °"וְהָיָה כַּאֲשֶׁר דִּמִּיתִי לַעֲשׂוֹת לָהֶם אֶעֱשֶׂה לָכֶם".[ב*] "אֲחַשְׁוֵרוֹשׁ", אָמַר רַב: אָחִיו שֶׁל רֹאשׁ וּבֶן גִּילוֹ שֶׁל רֹאשׁ. אָחִיו שֶׁל רֹאשׁ — אָחִיו שֶׁל נְבוּכַדְנֶצַּר הָרָשָׁע שֶׁנִּקְרָא "רֹאשׁ", שֶׁנֶּאֱמַר: °"אַנְתְּ הוּא רֵאשָׁה דִּי דַהֲבָא". בֶּן גִּילוֹ שֶׁל רֹאשׁ, הוּא הָרַג — הוּא בִּיקֵּשׁ לַהֲרוֹג, הוּא הֶחֱרִיב — הוּא בִּיקֵּשׁ לְהַחֲרִיב, שֶׁנֶּאֱמַר: °"וּבְמַלְכוּת אֲחַשְׁוֵרוֹשׁ בִּתְחִלַּת מַלְכוּתוֹ כָּתְבוּ שִׂטְנָה עַל יֹשְׁבֵי יְהוּדָה וִירוּשָׁלִָם". וּשְׁמוּאֵל אָמַר: שֶׁהוּשְׁחֲרוּ פְּנֵיהֶם שֶׁל יִשְׂרָאֵל בְּיָמָיו כְּשׁוּלֵי קְדֵרָה. וְרַבִּי יוֹחָנָן אָמַר: כָּל שֶׁזּוֹכְרוֹ אוֹמֵר "אָח לְרֹאשׁוֹ". וְרַבִּי חֲנִינָא אָמַר: שֶׁהַכֹּל נַעֲשׂוּ רָשִׁין בְּיָמָיו, שֶׁנֶּאֱמַר: °"וַיָּשֶׂם הַמֶּלֶךְ אֲחַשְׁוֵרוֹשׁ מַס". "הוּא אֲחַשְׁוֵרוֹשׁ" — הוּא בְּרִשְׁעוֹ מִתְּחִילָּתוֹ וְעַד סוֹפוֹ. °"הוּא עֵשָׂו" — הוּא בְּרִשְׁעוֹ מִתְּחִילָּתוֹ וְעַד סוֹפוֹ. °"הוּא דָתָן וַאֲבִירָם" — הֵן בְּרִשְׁעָן מִתְּחִילָּתָן וְעַד סוֹפָן. °"הוּא הַמֶּלֶךְ אָחָז" — הוּא בְּרִשְׁעוֹ מִתְּחִילָּתוֹ וְעַד סוֹפוֹ. °"אַבְרָם הוּא אַבְרָהָם" — הוּא בְּצִדְקוֹ מִתְּחִילָּתוֹ וְעַד סוֹפוֹ. °"הוּא אַהֲרֹן וּמֹשֶׁה" — הֵן בְּצִדְקָן מִתְּחִילָּתָן וְעַד סוֹפָן. °"וְדָוִד הוּא הַקָּטָן" — הוּא בְּקַטְנוּתוֹ מִתְּחִילָּתוֹ עַד סוֹפוֹ: כְּשֵׁם שֶׁבְּקַטְנוּתוֹ הִקְטִין עַצְמוֹ אֵצֶל מִי שֶׁגָּדוֹל מִמֶּנּוּ בַּתּוֹרָה — כָּךְ בְּמַלְכוּתוֹ הִקְטִין עַצְמוֹ אֵצֶל מִי שֶׁגָּדוֹל מִמֶּנּוּ בְּחָכְמָה. "הַמּוֹלֵךְ" אָמַר רַב: שֶׁמָּלַךְ מֵעַצְמוֹ. אָמְרִי לָהּ לְשֶׁבַח וְאָמְרִי לָהּ לִגְנַאי. אָמְרִי לָהּ לְשֶׁבַח: דְּלָא הֲוָה אִינִישׁ דַּחֲשִׁיב לְמַלְכָּא כְּוָותֵיהּ. וְאָמְרִי לָהּ לִגְנַאי: דְּלָא הֲוָה חָזֵי לְמַלְכוּתָא וּמָמוֹנָא יְתֵירָא הוּא דִּיהַב וְקָם. "מֵהֹדּוּ וְעַד כּוּשׁ" רַב וּשְׁמוּאֵל; חַד אָמַר: הוֹדּוּ בְּסוֹף הָעוֹלָם וְכוּשׁ בְּסוֹף הָעוֹלָם. וְחַד אָמַר: הוֹדּוּ וְכוּשׁ גַּבֵּי הֲדָדֵי הֲווּ קָיְימִי. כְּשֵׁם שֶׁמָּלַךְ עַל הוֹדּוּ וְכוּשׁ — כָּךְ מָלַךְ מִסּוֹף הָעוֹלָם וְעַד סוֹפוֹ. כַּיּוֹצֵא בַּדָּבָר אַתָּה אוֹמֵר: °"כִּי הוּא רֹדֶה בְּכָל עֵבֶר הַנָּהָר מִתִּפְסַח וְעַד עַזָּה". *רַב וּשְׁמוּאֵל; חַד אָמַר: תִּפְסַח בְּסוֹף הָעוֹלָם וְעַזָּה בְּסוֹף הָעוֹלָם. וְחַד אָמַר: תִּפְסַח וְעַזָּה בַּהֲדֵי הֲדָדֵי הֲווּ קָיְימִי. כְּשֵׁם שֶׁמָּלַךְ עַל תִּפְסַח וְעַל עַזָּה — כָּךְ מָלַךְ עַל כָּל הָעוֹלָם כּוּלּוֹ. "שֶׁבַע וְעֶשְׂרִים וּמֵאָה מְדִינָה" אָמַר רַב חִסְדָּא: בַּתְּחִילָּה מָלַךְ עַל שֶׁבַע, וּלְבַסּוֹף מָלַךְ עַל עֶשְׂרִים, וּלְבַסּוֹף מָלַךְ עַל מֵאָה. אֶלָּא מֵעַתָּה, °"וּשְׁנֵי חַיֵּי עַמְרָם שֶׁבַע וּשְׁלֹשִׁים וּמְאַת שָׁנָה" מַאי דָּרְשַׁתְּ בֵּיהּ? שָׁאנֵי הָכָא דִּקְרָא יְתֵירָא הוּא, מִכְּדֵי כְּתִיב: "מֵהֹדּוּ וְעַד כּוּשׁ", "שֶׁבַע וְעֶשְׂרִים וּמֵאָה מְדִינָה" לָמָּה לִי? ש"מ לִדְרָשָׁה.§ תָּנוּ רַבָּנַן: שְׁלֹשָׁה מָלְכוּ בְּכִיפָּה, וְאֵלּוּ הֵן: אַחְאָב *וַאֲחַשְׁוֵרוֹשׁ וּנְבוּכַדְנֶצַּר. אַחְאָב, דִּכְתִיב: (מ"א יח) °"חַי ה' אֱלֹהֶיךָ אִם יֶשׁ גּוֹי וּמַמְלָכָה אֲשֶׁר לֹא שָׁלַח אֲדֹנִי שָׁם לְבַקֶּשְׁךָ" *וגו' וְאִי לָא דַּהֲוָה מָלֵיךְ עֲלַיְיהוּ — הֵיכִי מָצֵי מַשְׁבַּע לְהוּ? נְבוּכַדְנֶצַּר — דִּכְתִיב: (ירמיה כז) °"וְהָיָה הַגּוֹי וְהַמַּמְלָכָה... אֲשֶׁר לֹא *יִתֵּן אֶת צַוָּארוֹ בְּעֹל מֶלֶךְ בָּבֶל". אֲחַשְׁוֵרוֹשׁ — הָא דַּאֲמַרַן

שְׁלֹשָׁה מָלְכוּ בְּכָל הָעוֹלָם כּוּלּוֹ. וְהָא דְּלָא חָשֵׁיב אֲלֶכְּסַנְדֵּר מוּקְדוֹן — מִשּׁוּם דְּלָא אַיְירֵי הָכָא אֶלָּא בְּאוֹתָם הַכְּתוּבִים לְהֶדְיָא:

אתה
סימן

רבינו חננאל

שעשה משה יש לו י' אמות ריוח לכל רוח. וכתיב ולפני הדביר עשרים וגו': *) ליהודים היתה אורה ושמחה וגו'. א"ר יהודה אורה זו תורה שנאמר כי נר מצוה ותורה אור. שמחה זה יו"ט שנאמר ושמחת בחגך. וששון זו מילה שנאמר שש אנכי על אמרתך. ויקר אלו תפלין שבראש: אחשורוש אחיו של ראש ובן גילו של ראש. פי' אחשורוש אח שוה לראש. אחיו של נ"נ כו' הוא אחשורוש הוא ברשעת מתחלתו ועד סופו ת"ר ג' מלכו בכיפה. אחאב ונ"נ ואחשורוש

*) לכאורה מאמר זה עד ויקר אלו תפלין שבראש אין כאן מקומו רק להלן דף ט"ז ע"ב ואולי דלפני רבינו הי' כתוב כאן.

הגהות הב"ח

(א) גמ' אמר רב ויי והי נתקיים מה שכתוב בתורה והתמכרתם שם: (ב) רש"י ד"ה כי עבדים וכו' לפני מלכי פרס: (ג) ד"ה ושמואל אמר פתח פתחא מהכא לא מאסתים: (ד) ד"ה כשם שמלך על תפסח. נ"ב הא דלא פרש"י כלום על כשם שמלך מהודו ועד כוש משום דלשם הוזכר מהודו עד כוש תחילה ולא זו אף זו קאמר אבל הכא הזכיר תפסח ועזה בסופיה דקרא קשיא וצריך לפרש דה"ק כי הוא רודה כו':

הגהות הגר"א

[א] גמ' הנסה אלהים וגו' רב אמר מהכא והתמכרתם כו' כצ"ל: [ב] שם אעשה לכם ויהי בימי אחשורוש אמר רב ויי והי אחשורוש אמר רב כו' כצ"ל:

גליון הש"ס

גמ' אדם ולא מלך. עי' ע"ז דף ג ע"א תד"ה כהנים: **רש"י** ד"ה מסורבלין מלובשין. עי' רש"י שבת דף קלא ע"ב ד"ה קטן המסורבל: **ד"ה** אח אוי. עי' סנהדרין דף קב ע"ב וברש"י שם ד"ה אח לשמים. וברש"י הושע יג טו:

[נ"ל יעבדו אתו את נבוכדנצר מלך בבל ואת אשר לא יתן וגו']

מסורת הש"ס

[נ"ל לנו]; ס"א מרדכי; עזרא ט; תהלים סו; שם צח; משלי כח; ירמיה ד; דניאל ז; ע"ז ב: קדושין עב.; קהלת י; [תענית ז:]; ויקרא כז; תהלים קד; שם קכד; משלי כט; דברים ד; שם; שם כח; ויקרא כו; במדבר לג; שם; דניאל ב; עזרא ד; אסתר י; בראשית לו; במדבר כו; דה"ב כח; דה"א א; שמות ו; שמואל א יז; מלכים א ד; סנהדרין כ:; שמות ו; מ"א יח; ירמיה כז; [נ"ל נבוכדנצר ואחשורוש]; [נ"ל ואמרו אין והשביע את הגוי ואת הממלכה וגו']

(סימן שסד"ך) וְתוּ לֵיכָּא? וְהָא אִיכָּא שְׁלֹמֹה! לֹא סְלִיק מַלְכוּתֵיהּ. הָנִיחָא לְמ"ד *מֶלֶךְ וְהֶדְיוֹט. אֶלָּא לְמ"ד מֶלֶךְ וְהֶדְיוֹט וּמֶלֶךְ, מַאי אִיכָּא לְמֵימַר? שְׁלֹמֹה מִילְּתָא אַחֲרִיתִי הֲוָה בֵּיהּ, שֶׁמָּלַךְ עַל הָעֶלְיוֹנִים וְעַל הַתַּחְתּוֹנִים, שֶׁנֶּאֱמַר: °"וַיֵּשֶׁב שְׁלֹמֹה עַל כִּסֵּא ה'". וְהָא הֲוָה סַנְחֵרִיב, דִּכְתִיב: °"מִי בְּכָל אֱלֹהֵי הָאֲרָצוֹת הָאֵלֶּה אֲשֶׁר הִצִּילוּ אֶת אַרְצָם מִיָּדִי"! הָא (א)אִיכָּא יְרוּשָׁלַיִם דְּלָא כְּבָשָׁהּ. וְהָא אִיכָּא דָּרְיָוֶשׁ, דִּכְתִיב: °"דָּרְיָוֶשׁ מַלְכָּא כְּתַב לְכָל עַמְמַיָּא אוּמַיָּא וְלִישָּׁנַיָּא דִּי דָיְרִין בְּכָל אַרְעָא שְׁלָמְכוֹן יִסְגֵּא"! הָא (ב)אִיכָּא שֶׁבַע דְּלָא מָלַךְ עֲלַיְיהוּ, דִּכְתִיב: °"שְׁפַר קֳדָם דָּרְיָוֶשׁ וַהֲקִים עַל מַלְכוּתָא לַאֲחַשְׁדַּרְפְּנַיָּא מְאָה וְעֶשְׂרִין". וְהָא אִיכָּא כּוֹרֶשׁ, דִּכְתִיב °"כֹּה אָמַר כּוֹרֶשׁ מֶלֶךְ פָּרַס כֹּל מַמְלְכוֹת הָאָרֶץ נָתַן לִי ה'"! הָתָם אִשְׁתַּבּוּחֵי הוּא דְּקָא מִשְׁתַּבַּח בְּנַפְשֵׁיהּ.§ °"בַּיָּמִים הָהֵם כְּשֶׁבֶת הַמֶּלֶךְ", וּכְתִיב בַּתְרֵיהּ: "בִּשְׁנַת שָׁלוֹשׁ לְמָלְכוֹ". אָמַר רָבָא: מַאי "כְּשֶׁבֶת"? לְאַחַר שֶׁנִּתְיַישְּׁבָה דַּעְתּוֹ. אָמַר: בֵּלְשַׁצַּר חָשֵׁב וְטָעָה, אֲנָא חָשֵׁיבְנָא וְלָא טָעֵינָא. מַאי הִיא? דִּכְתִיב: °"כִּי לְפִי מְלֹאת לְבָבֶל שִׁבְעִים שָׁנָה אֶפְקוֹד אֶתְכֶם", וּכְתִיב: °"לְמַלֹּאות לְחָרְבוֹת יְרוּשָׁלַםִ שִׁבְעִים שָׁנָה". חֲשׁוֹב אַרְבְּעִין וְחָמֵשׁ דִּנְבוּכַדְנֶצַּר, וְעֶשְׂרִים וּתְלָת דֶּאֱוִיל מְרוֹדַךְ, וְתַרְתֵּי דִּידֵיהּ – הָא *שִׁבְעִים. אַפֵּיק מָאנֵי דְּבֵי מַקְדְּשָׁא וְאִשְׁתַּמֵּשׁ בְּהוּ. וּנְבוּכַדְנֶצַּר, מְנָלַן דְּאַרְבְּעִין וְחָמֵשׁ שְׁנִין מָלַךְ? דְּאָמַר מָר: *גָּלוּ בְּשֶׁבַע, גָּלוּ בִּשְׁמוֹנֶה, גָּלוּ בִּשְׁמוֹנֶה עֶשְׂרֵה, גָּלוּ בְּתְשַׁע עֶשְׂרֵה. גָּלוּ בְּשֶׁבַע לְכִיבּוּשׁ יְהוֹיָקִים – גָּלוּת יְהוֹיָכִין, שֶׁהִיא שְׁמוֹנֶה לִנְבוּכַדְנֶצַּר. גָּלוּ בִּשְׁמוֹנֶה עֶשְׂרֵה לְכִיבּוּשׁ יְהוֹיָקִים גָּלוּת צִדְקִיָּהוּ שֶׁהִיא תְּשַׁע עֶשְׂרֵה לִנְבוּכַדְנֶצַּר. דְּאָמַר מָר: *שָׁנָה רִאשׁוֹנָה כִּיבֵּשׁ נִינְוֵה, שְׁנִיָּה כִּיבֵּשׁ יְהוֹיָקִים. וּכְתִיב: °"וַיְהִי בִשְׁלֹשִׁים וָשֶׁבַע שָׁנָה לְגָלוּת יְהוֹיָכִין מֶלֶךְ יְהוּדָה בִּשְׁנֵים עָשָׂר חֹדֶשׁ בְּעֶשְׂרִים וַחֲמִשָּׁה לַחֹדֶשׁ נָשָׂא אֱוִיל מְרוֹדַךְ מֶלֶךְ בָּבֶל [בִּשְׁנַת מַלְכוּתוֹ] אֶת רֹאשׁ יְהוֹיָכִין מֶלֶךְ יְהוּדָה וַיּוֹצֵא אוֹתוֹ מִבֵּית הַכֶּלֶא". תְּמָנֵי וּתְלָתִין וְשֶׁבַע – הֲרֵי אַרְבְּעִין וְחָמֵשׁ דִּנְבוּכַדְנֶצַּר; וְעֶשְׂרִין וּתְלָת דֶּאֱוִיל מְרוֹדַךְ – גְּמָרָא; וְתַרְתֵּי דִּידֵיהּ – הָא שִׁבְעִין. אָמַר: הַשְׁתָּא וַדַּאי תּוּ לָא מִיפַּרְקִי. אַפֵּיק מָאנֵי דְּבֵי מַקְדְּשָׁא וְאִשְׁתַּמֵּשׁ בְּהוּ. הַיְינוּ דְּקָאָמַר לֵיהּ דָּנִיֵּאל: °"וְעַל מָרֵי שְׁמַיָּא הִתְרוֹמַמְתָּ וּלְמָאנַיָּא דִּי בַיְתֵיהּ הַיְתִיו קָדָמָךְ", וּכְתִיב: °"בֵּיהּ בְּלֵילְיָא קְטִיל בֵּלְשַׁאצַּר מַלְכָּא [כַּשְׂדָּאי"], וּכְתִיב: °"וְדָרְיָוֶשׁ מָדָאָה קַבֵּל מַלְכוּתָא כְּבַר שְׁנִין שִׁתִּין וְתַרְתֵּין". אָמַר: אִיהוּ מִיטְעָא טָעֵי. אֲנָא חָשֵׁיבְנָא וְלָא טָעֵינָא. מִי כְּתִיב: "לְמַלְכוּת בָּבֶל"? "לְבָבֶל" כְּתִיב. מַאי "לְבָבֶל"? לְגָלוּת בָּבֶל. כַּמָּה בְּצִירַן? תְּמָנֵי. חָשֵׁיב וְעָיֵיל חִילּוּפַיְיהוּ. חֲדָא דְּבֵלְשַׁצַּר, וְחָמֵשׁ דְּדָרְיָוֶשׁ וְכוֹרֶשׁ, וְתַרְתֵּי דִּידֵיהּ הָא שִׁבְעִין. כֵּיוָן דַּחֲזֵי דִּמְלוּ שִׁבְעִין וְלָא אִיפְּרוּק אָמַר: הַשְׁתָּא וַדַּאי תּוּ לָא מִיפַּרְקִי. אַפֵּיק מָאנֵי דְּבֵי מַקְדְּשָׁא וְאִשְׁתַּמֵּשׁ בְּהוּ. בָּא שָׂטָן וְרִיקֵּד בֵּינֵיהֶן וְהָרַג אֶת וַשְׁתִּי. וְהָא שַׁפִּיר חָשֵׁיב! אִיהוּ נַמִי מִיטְעָא טָעֵי, דְּאִיבָּעֵי לֵיהּ לְמִימְנֵי מֵחָרְבוֹת יְרוּשָׁלַיִם. סוֹף סוֹף כַּמָּה בְּצִירַן? (*חֲדֵיסַר.) אִיהוּ כַּמָּה מָלַךְ? אַרְבֵּיסַר. בְּאַרְבֵּיסַר דִּידֵיהּ אִיבָּעֵי לֵיהּ לְמִיבְנֵי בֵּית הַמִּקְדָּשׁ. אַלְּמָה כְּתִיב: °"בֵּאדַיִן בְּטֵילַת עֲבִידַת בֵּית אֱלָהָא דִּי בִּירוּשְׁלֶם"! אָמַר רָבָא: שָׁנִים מְקוּטָּעוֹת הָווּ.
תַּנְיָא

תורה אור: דה"א כט; ישעיה לו; דניאל ו; שם; עזרא א; אסתר א; ירמיה כט; דניאל ט; ירמיה נב; דניאל ה; שם; שם ו; עזרא ד

[סנהדרין כ: גיטין סח:] [נ"ל חד סרי] [לקמן יט.] [ערכין יב.] [שם] [נ"ל חד סרי]

רש"י

סִימָן. שְׁלֹמֹה סַנְחֵרִיב דָּרְיָוֶשׁ כּוֹרֶשׁ: לָא סְלִיק מַלְכוּתֵיהּ. לֹא הִשְׁלִים מַלְכוּתוֹ, שֶׁהֲרֵי נִטְרַד, כִּדְאָמְרִינַן בְּמַסֶּכֶת גִּיטִּין (דף סח:) הָנִיחָא לְמַאן דְּאָמַר וכו'. בְּמַסֶּ' גִּיטִּין פֶּ' "מִי שֶׁאֲחָזוֹ": עַל הָעֶלְיוֹנִים. עַל הַשֵּׁדִים: כְּשֶׁבֶת הַמֶּלֶךְ. מַשְׁמַע: בִּתְחִילַּת מַלְכוּתוֹ, וַהֲדַר כְּתִיב "בִּשְׁנַת שָׁלֹשׁ": כְּשֶׁנִּתְיַישְּׁבָה דַּעְתּוֹ. שֶׁמִּתְּחִלָּה הָיָה דּוֹאֵג שֶׁיִּגָּאֲלוּ יִשְׂרָאֵל מִתַּחַת יָדוֹ, כְּשֶׁיִּגָּמְרוּ שִׁבְעִים שָׁנָה לְגָלוּת בָּבֶל, וְעַכְשָׁיו נִתְיַישְּׁבָה(ג): מַאי הִיא. חוּשְׁבְּנֵיהּ דְּבֵלְשַׁצַּר וְטָעוּתֵיהּ: לְפִי מְלֹאות לְבָבֶל. כְּסָבוּר הוּא לְמַלְכוּת בָּבֶל, מִיּוֹם שֶׁנָּטְלָה בָּבֶל מַלְכוּת, וְזֶה נְבוּכַדְנֶצַּר, נָטַל מַלְכוּת מֵאֵסַר חַדּוֹן מֶלֶךְ אַשּׁוּר: חָשֵׁב. בֵּלְשַׁצַּר: מ"ה דִּנְבוּכַדְנֶצַּר, וְכ"ג דֶּאֱוִיל מְרוֹדַךְ: וְתַרְתֵּי דִּידֵיהּ. דְּאַשְׁכְּחַן דְּבֵלְשַׁצַּר מָלַךְ תְּלָת שְׁנִין, דִּכְתִיב בְּסֵפֶר דָּנִיֵּאל, (ח) "בִּשְׁנַת שָׁלֹשׁ לְמַלְכוּת בֵּלְשַׁצַּר הַמֶּלֶךְ חָזוֹן נִרְאָה אֵלַי אֲנִי דָנִיֵּאל" וגו': גָּלוּ בְּשֶׁבַע גָּלוּ בִּשְׁמוֹנֶה. חַד גָּלוּת הוּא, וּקְרָאֵי קָא דָרֵישׁ. כְּתִיב בְּגָלוּת יְהוֹיָכִין "בִּשְׁנַת שְׁמוֹנֶה" (ד) לְמַלְכוּת נְבוּכַדְנֶצַּר בְּסוֹף סֵפֶר מְלָכִים, וּבְסֵפֶר יִרְמְיָה בְּסוֹפוֹ "אֲשֶׁר הֶגְלָה נְבוּזַרְאֲדָן בִּשְׁנַת שֶׁבַע". אֶלָּא: שְׁמוֹנֶה לְמַלְכוּת נְבוּכַדְנֶצַּר, וְשֶׁבַע לְכִיבּוּשׁ יְהוֹיָקִים, שֶׁכְּבָשׁוֹ תַּחְתָּיו בְּשָׁנָה שְׁנִיָּה לְמַלְכוּתוֹ (ה) וְלֹא הֶגְלָהוּ, וַיְהִי לוֹ עֶבֶד שָׁלֹשׁ שָׁנִים. וְי"ח וְי"ט כְּתִיב בְּגָלוּת צִדְקִיָּהוּ בְּסוֹף סֵפֶר יִרְמְיָה, וְהַיְינוּ חוּרְבוֹת יְרוּשָׁלַיִם שֶׁהִיא י"א שָׁנָה אַחַר גָּלוּת יְהוֹיָכִין, דִּכְתִיב "וַיְהִי בְּעַשְׁתֵּי עֶשְׂרֵה שָׁנָה לַמֶּלֶךְ צִדְקִיָּהוּ" וגו'. וּמַאי י"ח וְי"ט? י"ח לְכִיבּוּשׁ יְהוֹיָקִים, וְי"ט לְמַלְכוּת נְבוּכַדְנֶצַּר: דְּאָמַר מָר שָׁנָה רִאשׁוֹנָה כִּיבֵּשׁ נִינְוֵה. שֶׁהָיְתָה רֹאשׁ מַלְכוּת אַשּׁוּר, שֶׁהָיָה מֶלֶךְ בְּנִינְוֵה: שְׁנִיָּה כִּיבֵּשׁ יְהוֹיָקִים. קְרָאֵי קָא דָרֵישׁ, בְּסֵדֶר עוֹלָם, כְּתִיב בְּרֹאשׁ סֵפֶר דָּנִיֵּאל "בִּשְׁנַת שָׁלֹשׁ לְמַלְכוּת יְהוֹיָקִים בָּא נְבוּכַדְנֶצַּר בִּירוּשָׁלַיִם וַיִּתֵּן ה' אֶת יְהוֹיָקִים בְּיָדוֹ", אֶפְשָׁר לוֹמַר כֵּן? וַהֲלֹא לֹא מָלַךְ אֶלָּא בִּשְׁנַת אַרְבַּע לִיהוֹיָקִים, שֶׁנֶּאֱמַר בְּסֵפֶר יִרְמְיָה (מה) "הַדָּבָר אֲשֶׁר הָיָה בִּשְׁנַת הָרְבִיעִית לִיהוֹיָקִים הִיא שָׁנָה הָרִאשׁוֹנָה לִנְבוּכַדְנֶצַּר". אֶלָּא מַה תַּלְמוּד לוֹמַר בִּשְׁנַת שָׁלֹשׁ לְמַלְכוּת יְהוֹיָקִים – בִּשְׁנַת שְׁלֹשָׁה לְמִרְדוֹ, לְאַחַר שֶׁכִּיבְּשׁוֹ עֲבָדוֹ שְׁלֹשָׁה שָׁנִים וּמָרַד בּוֹ, שֶׁנֶּאֱמַר "וַיְהִי לוֹ [יְהוֹיָקִים] עֶבֶד שָׁלֹשׁ שָׁנִים וַיָּשָׁב וַיִּמְרָד בּוֹ" (מלכים ב כד). וְלִמֶּדְךָ כָּאן שֶׁעָמַד בְּמִרְדוֹ שָׁלֹשׁ שָׁנִים. הֲרֵי שִׁשָּׁה שָׁנִים לְכִיבּוּשׁוֹ, וּבַפַּעַם הַזֹּאת נִמְסַר בְּיָדוֹ וַהֲרָגוֹ, וְנִתְקַיֵּים בּוֹ "קְבוּרַת חֲמוֹר יִקָּבֵר" (ירמיה כב). וְהִמְלִיךְ אֶת יְהוֹיָכִין בְּנוֹ תַּחְתָּיו, וּבָא לוֹ לְבָבֶל (מדרש רבה מצורע פי"ט). אָמְרוּ לוֹ יוֹעֲצָיו: הָאָב מָרַד בְּךָ וְהִמְלַכְתָּ בְּנוֹ? מַתְלָא אָמְרַן: מִכַּלְבָּא בִּישָׁא גּוּרְיָא טָבָא לָא נָפֵיק. חָזַר עָלָיו לִתְשׁוּבַת הַשָּׁנָה וְהֶגְלָהוּ, וְהִמְלִיךְ לְצִדְקִיָּהוּ. וְכֵן כְּתִיב בְּסֵפֶר מְלָכִים בְּסוֹפוֹ. נִמְצֵאת גָּלוּת יְהוֹיָכִין בִּשְׁנַת שֶׁבַע לְכִיבּוּשׁ יְהוֹיָקִים, וַהֲרֵי הַכָּתוּב קוֹרֵא אוֹתָהּ "בִּשְׁנַת שְׁמוֹנֶה לְמַלְכוּת נְבוּכַדְנֶצַּר". בְּסֵפֶר מְלָכִים בְּסוֹפוֹ, לָמַדְנוּ שֶׁבְּשָׁנָה שְׁנִיָּה לְמַלְכוּתוֹ כִּיבְּשׁוֹ: נָשָׂא אֱוִיל מְרוֹדַךְ מֶלֶךְ בָּבֶל וגו'(ו). לָמַדְנוּ שֶׁמָּלַךְ אֱוִיל מְרוֹדַךְ בִּשְׁנַת ל"ז לְגָלוּת יְהוֹיָכִין, וּכְבָר מָלַךְ נְבוּכַדְנֶצַּר שְׁמוֹנֶה שָׁנִים קוֹדֶם גָּלוּת יְהוֹיָכִין, שְׁמוֹנֶה וְל"ז הֲרֵי מ"ה, וְכ"ג דֶּאֱוִיל מְרוֹדַךְ וְג' דְּבֵלְשַׁצַּר: אַפֵּיק מָאנֵי דְּבֵית הַמִּקְדָּשׁ. בִּשְׁנַת שְׁלִישִׁית לְמַלְכוּתוֹ: אָמַר. אֲחַשְׁוֵרוֹשׁ, אִיהוּ וַדַּאי מִיטְעָא טָעֵי: אֲנָא חָשֵׁיבְנָא כו' לְגָלוּת בָּבֶל. תְּחִילַּת גּוֹלָה שֶׁהֶגְלָה אֶת יְכָנְיָה: כַּמָּה בְּצִירַן. מִשִּׁבְעִים מִשְּׁנַת שְׁתַּיִם לְבֵלְשַׁצַּר תְּמָנֵי, אוֹתָן שְׁמוֹנָה שָׁנִים שֶׁמָּלַךְ נְבוּכַדְנֶצַּר לִפְנֵי הַגְלוֹתוֹ אֶת יְכָנְיָה, שֶׁלֹּא הָיָה לוֹ לְבֵלְשַׁצַּר לִמְנוֹתָן וּמְנָאָן: חָשֵׁב. אֲחַשְׁוֵרוֹשׁ מִב' לְבֵלְשַׁצַּר עַד שָׁלֹשׁ שֶׁלּוֹ: וְעָיֵיל. הָנָךְ תְּמָנֵי תְּחוּתַיְיהוּ: חֲדָא דְּבֵלְשַׁצַּר. דַּהֲרֵי (ז) מִשְּׁנַת שְׁתַּיִם שָׁלְמוּ שִׁבְעִים שָׁנָה לְפִי מִנְיָינוֹ, וְשׁוּב מָנָה שְׁלִישִׁית: וַחֲמִשָּׁה דְּדָרְיָוֶשׁ הַמָּדִי וְכוֹרֶשׁ הַפָּרְסִי. דִּכְתִיב "וְדָרְיָוֶשׁ מָדָאָה קַבֵּיל מַלְכוּתָא" (דניאל ו), וְאַחֲרָיו מָלַךְ כּוֹרֶשׁ הָרִאשׁוֹן שֶׁנָּתַן רְשׁוּת לִבְנֵי הַגּוֹלָה לַעֲלוֹת, שֶׁנֶּאֱמַר: "כֹּה אָמַר כּוֹרֶשׁ" וגו' (עזרא א). וְקָסָלְקָא דַּעְתָּךְ הַשְׁתָּא שֶׁמָּלְכוּ בֵּין שְׁנֵיהֶן ה' שָׁנִים, אַע"ג דְּלָא כְּתִיב בִּקְרָא: וְתַרְתֵּי דַּאֲחַשְׁוֵרוֹשׁ. כְּבָר עָבְרוּ לוֹ שְׁתֵּי שָׁנִים: מֵחָרְבוֹת יְרוּשָׁלַיִם. גָּלוּת צִדְקִיָּהוּ, שֶׁנִּשְׂרְפָה הָעִיר, וּבוֹ בְּהֶדְיָא כְּתִיב דִּלְחָרְבוֹת יְרוּשָׁלַיִם בָּעֵי לְמִימְנְיָא, דִּכְתִיב בְּסֵפֶר דָּנִיֵּאל (ט) "לְמַלֹּאות לְחָרְבוֹת יְרוּשָׁלַם שִׁבְעִים שָׁנָה": *חֲדֵיסָר. שֶׁכָּךְ עָמַד הַבַּיִת אַחַר גָּלוּת יְכָנְיָה: אִיהוּ כַּמָּה מָלַךְ אַרְבֵּיסָר. דִּכְתִיב בִּשְׁנַת שְׁתֵּים עֶשְׂרֵה הִפִּיל פּוּר הוּא הַגּוֹרָל, וְלַשָּׁנָה אַחֶרֶת נַעֲשָׂה הַנֵּס – הֲרֵי י"ג(ח). דְּמַלְכֵי אוּמּוֹת הָעוֹלָם מִתִּשְׁרֵי מָנֵינַן, וְנִתְחַדְּשָׁה הַשָּׁנָה בְּתִשְׁרֵי. וּכְתִיב לַשָּׁנָה אַחֶרֶת "לְקַיֵּים אֶת אִגֶּרֶת הַפּוּרִים הַזֹּאת הַשֵּׁנִית" – הֲרֵי י"ד: בֵּאדַיִן. בִּימֵי כּוֹרֶשׁ בְּטֵילַת עֲבִידַת בֵּית אֱלָהָא, שֶׁצִּוָּה כּוֹרֶשׁ לִבְנוֹת וְחָזַר בּוֹ עַל יְדֵי צָרֵי יְהוּדָה וּבִנְיָמִין, כְּמוֹ שֶׁכָּתוּב בְּסֵפֶר עֶזְרָא, עַד שְׁנַת תַּרְתֵּין לְמַלְכוּת דָּרְיָוֶשׁ הַשֵּׁנִי שֶׁמָּלַךְ אַחַר אֲחַשְׁוֵרוֹשׁ, וְנִקְרָא שְׁלֹשָׁה שֵׁמוֹת: דָּרְיָוֶשׁ כּוֹרֶשׁ אַרְתַּחְשַׁסְתָּא: שָׁנִים מְקוּטָּעוֹת הָיוּ. אוֹתָן שָׁנִים שֶׁמָּנִינַן לְמַעְלָה יֵשׁ בָּהֶן שֶׁנִּבְלְעוּ מִשֶּׁל אַחֲרוֹן (ט) בָּרִאשׁוֹן, כְּגוֹן לְדָרְיָוֶשׁ הַמָּדִי וְכוֹרֶשׁ שֶׁמָּנִינַן לָהֶן ה' שָׁנִים לֹא תִּמְנָא אֶלָּא ד', דִּכְתִיב "בִּשְׁנַת אַחַת לְדָרְיָוֶשׁ בֶּן אֲחַשְׁוֵרוֹשׁ" בְּסֵפֶר דָּנִיֵּאל (ט) "בִּשְׁנַת שָׁלֹשׁ לְמַלְכוּת כּוֹרֶשׁ" וגו'. וְתַנְיָא בְּסֵדֶר עוֹלָם: לֹא מָצִינוּ לְמָדַי שָׁנָה בַּכְּתוּבִים אֶלָּא זוֹ בִּלְבַד, וּלְכוֹרֶשׁ מָצִינוּ שְׁלֹשָׁה שָׁנִים בְּסֵפֶר דָּנִיֵּאל "בִּשְׁנַת שָׁלֹשׁ לְמַלְכוּת כּוֹרֶשׁ" וגו'. וְתַנְיָא נַמִי בְּסֵדֶר עוֹלָם: כּוֹרֶשׁ מָלַךְ ג' שָׁנִים מְקוּטָּעוֹת – הֲרֵי שְׁמִינִית שָׁנָה יְתֵרָה, וְגַם (י) דְּבִשְׁנוֹת נְבוּכַדְנֶצַּר וֶאֱוִיל מְרוֹדַךְ נִבְלְעָה שָׁנָה, וּכְנֶגְדּוֹ נִשְׁתָּהָה הַבִּנְיָן שְׁתַּיִם שָׁנִים לְדָרְיָוֶשׁ:
תַּנְיָא

רבינו חננאל

כו'. כשבת כשנתיישבה דעתו. אמר בלשצר מנה וטעה. אנא מנינא ולא טעינא. כתיב כי לפי מלאות [לבבל] ע' שנה אפקוד אתכם. אמר בלשצר *) מאי למלכות בבל. חשב מ"ה דנ"נ. מ"ה מנא לן. דאמר מר גלו בשבע לכיבוש יהויקים בן יאשיהו מלך יהודה היא השנה השניה לנ"נ מלך בבל. וכיבש יהויקים בשנה החמישית למלכו. נמצא משכיבש ועד שמת ז' שנים. שכל מלכות יהויקים היתה י"א שנה שנאמר אחת עשרה שנה מלך בירושלים. ואמר בנ"נ שנה ראשונה כיבש נינוה. שניה כיבש יהויקים. וכיון שמת יהויקים מלך יכניה ג' חדשים ובא נ"נ והגלהו שנאמר ויקח אותו מלך בבל בשנת שמונה למלכו. נמצא משכיבש יהויקים עד שמת יהויקים ז' שנים ויכניה ג' חדשים והגלהו. וזהו פירושו. גלו בשבע לכיבוש יהויקים שהיא שנת ח' לנ"נ. וזה שכתוב בשנת שלש למלכות יהויקים מלך יהודה בא נ"נ מלך בבל ירושלים ויצר עליה כבר פירשוהו רבותינו. בשנת שלש למרדו דהא בשנה הרביעית ליהויקי' מלך נ"נ. גלו בי"ח לכיבוש יהויקים שהיא שנת י"ט לנ"נ. שנאמר ובעשור לחדש החמישי היא תשע עשרה למלך נ"נ מלך בבל בא נבוזראדן רב טבחים וגו'. נמצא שהגלה יהויכין בשנת שמונה למלכו. ונשאר יהויכין ל"ז שנה חבוש בבית האסורים בגלות עד שמת נ"נ. שנאמר ויהי בשלשים ושבע לגלות יהויכין מלך יהודה וגו'. הנה **) מקום גלות יהויכין ח' שנים ול"ז שנה. הרי מ"ה שנה לנ"נ. הנה נמצאו שנות נ"נ מן הפסוקים. אבל כ"ג שנה למרודך גמרא ותלתא דבלשצר הרי ע' מדלא איפרוק כו'. אמר אחשורוש בלשצר טעה דאיבעי למימנא ע' לגלות. כמה בצרו ח' שנה שמלך נ"נ קודם גלות יכניה עייל תמני שני חילופייהו חדא דבלשצר. וה' שנה דכורש ודריוש וב' שנים דידיה הא שבעים כו'. היינו דכתיב בשנת שלש למלכו. כשבת כשנתיישבה דעתו דאמר תוב לא מפרקי כולה שמעתא ופשוטה היא.

*) נ"ל אמר בלשצר חשב וטעה וכו' מאי היא דכתיב כי לפי מלאת לבבל וחשב דמאי לבבל למלכות בבל חשב וכו'.

**) נראה דל"ל הנה מלך מקודם גלות יהויכין וכו'.

הגהות הב"ח

(א) גמ' הא הוה ירושלים: (ב) שם הא הויא שבע דלא מלך: (ג) רש"י ד"ה כשנתיישבה וכו' ועכשיו נתיישבה דעתו הס"ד: (ד) ד"ה גלו בשבע וכו' בשנת שמנה למלכו בסוף ספר כצ"ל ותיבת נבוכדנצר נמחק: (ה) בא"ד בשנה שניה למלכותו כדאמרינן לקמן ולא הגלהו כו' חורבות ירושלים דהויא י"א שנה וכו' כדכתיב ויהי: (ו) ד"ה נשא אויל מרודך מלך בבל וגו' בשנת מלכותו למדנו: (ז) ד"ה חדא וכו' בשנת שתים וכו' ושוב מלך שנה שלישית: (ח) ד"ה איהו כמה וכו' הרי י"ג דהא למלכי אומות: (ט) ד"ה שנים מקוטעות וכו' מאל אחרון בשל ראשון וכו' וכורש הפרסי שמנינן להם ה' שנים ולא וכו' לדריוש בן אחשורוש מזרע מדי ולא זהו אחשורוש המלך שזה קדמו שנים הרבה ותניא בסדר עולם כצ"ל ותיבות בספר דניאל בשנת שלש למלכות כורש וגו' נמחק: (י) בא"ד וגם בשנות נבוכדנצר וכו' שתים לדריוש האחרון הס"ד:

תניא נמי הכי. דבשנות נבוכדנצר ואויל מרודך נבלעה שנה: עוד שנה אחת לבבל.(י) הכי איתא בסדר עולם: "ביה בליליא קטיל בלשצר מלכא ודריוש מדאה קביל מלכותא", הרי שבעים שנה מיום שמלך נבוכדנצר, שבעים חסר אחת מיום שכיבש יהויקים, ועוד שנה אחת לבבל למלאות שבעים שנה משמשלט על ישראל, ועמד דריוש והשלימה. ואחריו בשנה אחרת מלך כורש בבבל, ונפקדו פקידה במקצת, שאמר "מי בכם מכל עמו יהי אלהיו עמו ויעל" וגו'. למדנו מברייתא זו כשמת בלשצר לא היו לכיבוש יהויקים אלא שבעים חסר אחת, ואנחנו מנינו למעלה שבעים שנה: מ"ה דנבוכדנצר, וכ"ג דאויל מרודך, ושלשה דבלשצר – הרי שנים מקוטעות היו: בינותי בספרים. לשון ספירה וחשבון: כתיב לפי מלאות לבבל. "שבעים שנה אפקוד אתכם" בספר ירמיה: וכתיב. בספר דניאל "למלאות לחרבות ירושלם שבעים שנה מספר השנים אשר היה דבר ה' אל ירמיה הנביא": לפקידה בעלמא. (כ) ואמר "לפי מלאות לבבל שבעים שנה אפקוד אתכם", וכך היתה שנפקדו בשנה אחת לכורש מלך פרס, שהיא שנת ע"א לכיבוש יהויקים שפשטה בבל על ישראל: משיח. (ל) נמשח, כמו שמן המשחה: קובל אני לך כו'. והכי קאמר: "כה אמר ה' למשיחו (מ) לכורש אשר החזקתי בימינו" וגו' "הוא יבנה את ביתי". תרי קראי כתיבי דסמיכי אהדדי. וניקוד טעם מקרא זה מוכיח על דרש זה, שאין לך טעם זרקא במקרא שאין סגול בא אחריו, וכאן נקוד למשיחו בזרקא, ולכורש נקוד במאריך – להפרישו ולנתקו מעם "למשיחו": מי בכם מכל עמו וגו'. והוא עצמו לא נשתדל בדבר: כתיב פרס ומדי הפרתמים. סמך הפרתמים אצל מדי, וכתיב "למלכי מדי ופרס" – סמך מלכי אצל מדי: בגדי כהונה. שהיו בידו שם בגדי כהן גדול (נ) שהביאן מירושלים: פיקח היה. שהקדים משתה הרחוקים יותר ממשתה בני עירו: שהשתחוו לצלם. בימי נבוכדנצר: וכי משוא פנים יש בדבר. איך זכו לנס? הם עשו לפנים. מיראה: חרי חרי. מעשה מחט, מלאכת המפתות היתה עשויה נקבים נקבים: מילת לבנה. חור לשון חיור: הראוי לכסף כו'. מטות זהב וכסף קדריש, של הראוי לזהב – לזהב, וגרוע – לכסף: מתחוטטות על בעליהן. דלפה עשה להם באבנים חטובות, כלומר: שלא באו לידי אדם אלא בטורח, שמחטטים ומחזירים בעליהן אחריהן עד שמוצאין אותן בדמים יקרים: וכן הוא אומר. שהמקרא משבח אבני יקרות, ואומר (ס) על נסיונות הרבה הן באין "כי אבני נזר מתנוססות על אדמתו". והכתוב מדבר לישראל לעתיד לבוא, שיהיו חשובין ויקרים בין האומות כאבני נזר המתנוססות: דרי דרי. שורות שורות סביב. *וסוחרת לשון "סחור סחור"*: בצהרים. והאי וסוחרת *לשון סהרא הוא: שקרא דרור לכל בעלי סחורה. עשה נחת רוח לבני מלכותו, להעביר מהן מכס של סוחרין: הראשונים. כלומר: בלשצר וחבורתו: כדת של תורה. אכילת מזבח מרובה משתיה, פר ושלשה עשרונים סולת לאכילה, ונסך חצי ההין: מיין מדינתו. יין הרגיל בו ולא ישכרהו, [ולא ישתהו] אלא לפי רצונו: כרצון מרדכי והמן. הם היו שרי המשקים במשתה: איהו בקרי. דלועין גדולות: בוציני

תניא נמי הכי: ועוד שנה(א) אחרת לבבל, ועמד דריוש והשלימה. אמר רבא: אף דניאל טעה בהאי חושבנא, דכתיב °"בשנת אחת למלכו אני דניאל בינותי בספרים". מדקאמר "בינותי" – מכלל דטעה. מ"מ קשו קראי אהדדי. כתיב: °"מלאות לבבל", וכתיב: °"לחרבות ירושלם"! אמר רבא: לפקידה בעלמא. והיינו דכתיב: °"כה אמר כורש מלך פרס: כל ממלכות הארץ נתן לי ה' אלהי השמים והוא פקד עלי לבנות לו בית בירושלם".(ב) דרש רב נחמן בר רב חסדא: מאי דכתיב: °"כה אמר ה' למשיחו לכורש אשר החזקתי בימינו", וכי כורש משיח היה? אלא א"ל הקב"ה למשיח: קובל אני לך על כורש. אני אמרתי: "הוא יבנה (ג)ביתי ויקבץ גליותי", והוא אמר: °"מי בכם מכל עמו... ויעל".§ *"חיל פרס ומדי הפרתמים", וכתיב: "למלכי מדי ופרס". אמר רבא: אתנויי אתנו בהדדי. אי מינן מלכי – מינייכו איפרכי, ואי מינייכו מלכי – מינן איפרכי. "בהראותו את עושר כבוד מלכותו"(ד) א"ר יוסי בר חנינא: מלמד שלבש בגדי כהונה. כתיב הכא: °"יקר תפארת גדולתו", וכתיב התם: °"לכבוד ולתפארת". "ובמלאות הימים האלה" וגו' רב ושמואל. חד אמר: מלך פיקח היה. וחד אמר: מלך טיפש היה. מאן דאמר מלך פיקח היה – שפיר עבד דקריב רחיקא ברישא, דבני מאתיה (ה)כל אימת דבעי מפייס להו. ומאן דאמר טיפש היה – דאיבעי ליה לקרובי בני מאתיה ברישא, דאי מרדו ביה הנך(ו) – הני הוו קיימי בהדיה. *שאלו תלמידיו את רשב"י: מפני מה נתחייבו שונאיהן של ישראל שבאותו הדור כליה? אמר להם: אמרו אתם. אמרו לו: מפני שנהנו מסעודתו של אותו רשע. (ז)אם כן שבשושן יהרגו, שבכל העולם כולו אל יהרגו! אמרו לו: אמור אתה! אמר להם: מפני שהשתחוו לצלם. אמרו לו: וכי משוא פנים יש בדבר? אמר להם: *הם לא עשו אלא לפנים – אף הקב"ה לא עשה עמהן אלא לפנים, והיינו דכתיב: °"כי לא ענה מלבו".§ "בחצר גנת ביתן המלך" רב ושמואל. חד אמר: הראוי לחצר – לחצר, הראוי לגינה – לגינה, הראוי לביתן – לביתן. וחד אמר: הושיבן בחצר – ולא החזיקתן, בגינה – ולא החזיקתן, עד שהכניסן לביתן והחזיקתן. במתניתא תנא: הושיבן בחצר ופתח להם שני פתחים, אחד לגינה ואחד לביתן. "חור כרפס ותכלת". מאי "חור"? רב אמר: חרי חרי. ושמואל אמר: מילת לבנה הציע להם. "כרפס" אמר ר' יוסי בר חנינא: כרים של פסים. "על גלילי כסף ועמודי שש מטות זהב וכסף". תניא, ר' יהודה אומר: הראוי לכסף – לכסף, הראוי לזהב – לזהב. אמר לו ר' נחמיה: א"כ אתה מטיל קנאה בסעודה! אלא, הם של כסף, ורגליהן של זהב. "בהט ושש" א"ר אסי: אבנים *שמתחוטטות על בעליהן. וכן הוא אומר: (ח)°"אבני נזר מתנוססות על אדמתו". "ודר וסוחרת" רבי אמר: דרי דרי. ושמואל אמר: אבן טובה יש בכרכי הים ודרה שמה. הושיבה באמצע סעודה ומאירה להם כצהרים. דבי רבי ישמעאל תנא: שקרא דרור לכל בעלי סחורה. "והשקות בכלי זהב וכלים מכלים שונים" – "משונים" מיבעי ליה? אמר רבא: יצתה בת קול ואמרה להם: ראשונים, כלו מפני כלים ואתם שונים(ט) בהם?! "ויין מלכות רב" אמר רב: מלמד שכל אחד ואחד השקהו יין שגדול הימנו בשנים. "והשתיה כדת (*אין אונס".) מאי "כדת"? א"ר חנן משום ר"מ: כדת של תורה. מה דת של תורה – אכילה מרובה משתיה; אף סעודתו של אותו רשע – אכילה מרובה משתיה. "אין אונס", אמר רבי אלעזר: מלמד שכל אחד ואחד השקהו מיין מדינתו. "לעשות כרצון איש ואיש" אמר רבא: לעשות כרצון מרדכי והמן. מרדכי – דכתיב: "איש יהודי". המן – "איש צר ואויב". "גם ושתי המלכה עשתה משתה נשים בית המלכות". "בית הנשים" מיבעי ליה? אמר רבא: שניהן לדבר עבירה נתכוונו. היינו דאמרי אינשי: *איהו *בקרי ואתתיה בבוציני

תורה אור: דניאל ט; ירמיה כט; דניאל ט; עזרא א; ישעיה מה; עזרא א; אסתר א; שמות כח; איכה ג; זכריה ט

אתה מטיל קנאה. וא"ת: למ"ד לעיל הראוי לגינה לגינה, הראוי לחצר לחצר, א"כ אתה מטיל קנאה בסעודה! י"ל: דסבירא ליה דכיון שלא היו רואין זה את זה ליכא קנאה: **כדת** של תורה אכילה מרובה משתיה. והא דאמרינן בנדה (דף כד: וסס): כל שאכילתו מרובה משתייתו עלמותיו סכויין – היינו באוכל יותר מדאי:

ספרחה

רבינו חננאל

והא קשו קראי אהדדי ופריק רבא לפי מלאת לבבל לפקידה בעלמא ולחורבות ירושלים לגאולה. אבנים מתחוטטות על בעליהן. מחטיאות בעליהן. כלומר כל מי שנמצאת בידו מתחייב למלכות *) שאינן ראויות להדיוט אלא למלכות בלבד. וכן בעליהן כיון שנמצאות בידיהם נסים ובורחין שמתיראין מן המלכות. מה דת של תורה אכילה מרובה משתיה. פי' התמיד כבש. שיש בו כמה רביעיות. ונסכו רביעית ההין יין בלבד. איהו

*) וכן העתיק הערוך בערך חט א' בשם רבינו ע"ש.

הגהות הב"ח

(א) גמ' ועוד שנה אחת יש לבבל ועמד וכו' ואף דניאל וכו' בינותי בספרים מספר השנים אשר היה דבר ה' אל ירמיה הנביא למלאות לחרבות ירושלים שבעים שנה מדקאמר אני בינותי בספרים מכלל דאיהו נמי טעה מ"מ קשו: (ב) שם לבנות לו בית בירושלים וכתיב מי בכם מכל עמו יהי אלהיו עמו ויעל דרש רב נחמן: (ג) שם הוא יבנה עירי ויקבץ גלותי: (ד) שם כבוד מלכותו ואת יקר וגו' אמר רבי יוסי וכו' בגדי כהונה ונתעטף ועמד כתיב הכא: (ה) שם דבני מאתיה מיקף כייפי ליה כל אימת דבעי בהו מקרב להו ומאן דאמר טיפש: (ו) שם מרדו ביה הנך קיימי הני והוו בהדיה: (ז) שם של אותו רשע אמר להם אם כן: (ח) שם וכן הוא אומר כי אבני: (ט) שם ואתם שונים בהן: (י) רש"י ד"ה ועוד שנה אחת לבבל. רישא דברייתא הכי איתא: (כ) ד"ה לפקידה בעלמא נאמר האי לפי מלאות לבבל שבעים שנה דהא אפקוד אתכם כתיב וכך היה שנפקדו וכו' שפשטה יד בבל: (ל) ד"ה משיח הוא כמו נמשח בשמן כצ"ל ותיבת כמו נמחק: (מ) ד"ה קובל וכו' למשיחו על כורש אני קובל אשר החזקתי וכו' יבנה את עירי תרי קראי: (נ) ד"ה בגדי כהונה וכו' כהן גדול שהביא נבוכדנצר מירושלים: (ס) ד"ה וכן הוא וכו' ואומר שעל ידי נסיונות:

גליון הש"ס

גמ' שאלו תלמידיו. עי' מדרש שיר השירים בפסוק זאת קומתך דמתה לתמר: **שם** הם לא עשו אלא לפנים. עי' סנהדרין דף סא ע"ב. ועי' ע"ז דף ג ע"א תוס' ד"ה שלא השתחוו: **רש"י** ד"ה דרי דרי וכו' וסוחרת לשון סחור. כי סביב תרגומו סחור סחור (ויקרא א ה): **שם** ד"ה כצהרים וכו' לשון סהרא הוא. עי' לקמן דף יג ע"א רש"י ד"ה אסתהר:

מסורת הש"ס: כתיב חיל כו' כצ"ל | [ע' תוס' ע"ז ג. ד"ה שלא וכו'] | ערוך ערך חט א' כתב זה פירוש ע"ז בשם ר"ג ור"ח ע"ש] | [בע"י ליתא] | [שבת יג.] | סוטה י. [עי' בערוך ערך קר ד]

תורה אור

בבוציני. "ביום השביעי כטוב לב המלך ביין". אטו עד השתא לא טב לביה בחמרא? אמר רבא: יום השביעי שבת היה. שישראל אוכלין ושותין, מתחילין בד"ת ובדברי תשבחות. אבל אומות העולם שאוכלין ושותין — אין מתחילין אלא בדברי תיפלות. וכן בסעודתו של אותו רשע הללו אומרים: מדיות נאות; והללו אומרים: פרסיות נאות, אמר להם אחשורוש: כלי שאני משתמש בו אינו לא מדיי ולא פרסי אלא כשדיי. רצונכם לראותה? אמרו לו: אין, ובלבד שתהא ערומה. *שבמדה שאדם מודד בה מודדין לו, מלמד שהיתה ושתי הרשעה מביאה בנות ישראל ומפשיטן ערומות ועושה בהן מלאכה בשבת.(א) היינו דכתיב: "אחר הדברים האלה כשוך חמת המלך אחשורוש זכר את ושתי ואת אשר עשתה ואת אשר נגזר עליה" כשם שעשתה — כך נגזר עליה. "ותמאן המלכה ושתי". מכדי פריצתא הואי, דאמר מר: שניהן לדבר עבירה נתכוונו. מ"ט לא אתאי? א"ר יוסי בר חנינא: מלמד שפרחה בה צרעת. במתניתא תנא: [בא גבריאל ועשה לה זנב.] "ויקצף המלך מאד".(ב) אמאי דלקה ביה כולי האי? אמר רבא: שלחה ליה: *בר אהורייריה דאבא! אבא לקבל אלפא חמרא שתי, ולא רוי, וההוא גברא אשתטי בחמריה! מיד "וחמתו בערה בו". "ויאמר המלך לחכמים". מאן חכמים? רבנן. "יודעי העתים" — שיודעין לעבר שנים ולקבוע חדשים. אמר להו: דיינוה לי! אמרו: היכי נעביד? נימא ליה: קטלה — למחר פסיק ליה חמריה(ג) ובעי לה מינן. נימא ליה: שבקה — קא מזלזלה במלכותא. אמרו לו: מיום שחרב בית המקדש וגלינו מארצנו, ניטלה עצה ממנו, ואין אנו יודעין לדון דיני נפשות. זיל לגבי עמון ומואב, דיתבי בדוכתייהו כחמרא דיתיב על דורדייה. וטעמא אמרו ליה, דכתיב: °"שאנן מואב מנעוריו ושוקט הוא אל שמריו ולא הורק מכלי אל כלי ובגולה לא הלך על כן עמד טעמו בו וריחו לא נמר". מיד — "והקרוב אליו כרשנא שתר אדמתא תרשיש". א"ר לוי: כל פסוק זה על שום קרבנות נאמר. "כרשנא" אמרו מלאכי השרת לפני הקב"ה: רבש"ע, כלום הקריבו לפניך כרים בני שנה כדרך שהקריבו ישראל לפניך? "שתר" כלום הקריבו לפניך שתי תורין? "אדמתא" כלום בנו לפניך מזבח אדמה? "תרשיש" כלום שימשו לפניך בבגדי כהונה דכתיב בהו: °"תרשיש ושהם וישפה". "מרס" כלום מירסו בדם לפניך? "מרסנא" כלום מירסו במנחות לפניך? "ממוכן" כלום הכינו שלחן לפניך? "ויאמר ממוכן". תנא: ממוכן זה המן. ולמה נקרא שמו ממוכן? שמוכן לפורענות. אמר רב כהנא: •מכאן שההדיוט קופץ בראש. "להיות כל איש שורר בביתו" אמר רבא: •אלמלא אגרות הראשונות לא נשתייר משונאיהן של ישראל שריד ופליט; אמרי מאי האי דשדיר לן "להיות כל איש שורר בביתו"? פשיטא! אפילו קרחה בביתיה פרדשכא ליהוי! "ויפקד המלך פקידים". א"ר: מאי דכתיב °"כל ערום יעשה בדעת וכסיל יפרוש אולת"? "כל ערום יעשה בדעת" — זה דוד, דכתיב: °"ויאמרו לו עבדיו יבקשו לאדני המלך נערה בתולה". כל מאן דהוה ליה ברתא — אייתה ניהליה. "וכסיל יפרוש אולת" — זה אחשורוש, דכתיב: "ויפקד המלך פקידים". כל מאן דהוה ליה ברתא — איטמרה מיניה. "איש יהודי היה בשושן הבירה" וגו'. "איש ימיני". מאי קאמר? אי ליחוסא קאתי — ליחסיה (ד)ואזיל עד בנימין! אלא מאי שנא הני? תנא: כולן על שמו נקראו. "בן יאיר" — בן שהאיר עיניהם של ישראל בתפלתו; "בן שמעי" — בן ששמע אל תפלתו; "בן קיש" — שהקיש על שערי רחמים ונפתחו לו. קרי ליה "יהודי" — אלמא מיהודה קאתי, וקרי ליה "ימיני" — אלמא מבנימין קאתי! *אמר רב נחמן: מרדכי מוכתר בנימוסו היה. *אמר רבה בר בר חנה אמר ר' יהושע בן לוי: אביו מבנימין ואמו מיהודה. ורבנן אמרי: משפחות מתגרות זו בזו. משפחת יהודה אומרת: אנא גרים דמתיליד מרדכי, דלא קטליה דוד לשמעי בן גרא. ומשפחת בנימין אמרה: מינאי קאתי. רבא אמר: כנסת ישראל אמרה לאידך גיסא: ראו מה עשה לי יהודי ומה שילם לי ימיני. מה עשה לי יהודי — דלא

ירמיה מח

שמות כח

משלי יג

מלכים א א

רש"י

בוציני. דלועין קטנות. כלומר, דבאותו מין עצמו, זה נואף וזו נואפת. הוא אומר להראות את יופיה, והיא לכך נתכוונה שיסתכלו ביופיה: פריצתא הואי. פרוצה היתה: מלמד שפרחה בה צרעת. וילף בירושלמי מ"אשר נגזר עליה", וכתיב "וישב בית החפשית מצורע כי נגזר מבית ה'" (דה"ב כו), מה להלן צרעת – אף כאן צרעת: אהורייריה. שומרי הסוסים: לקבל אלפא חמרא שתי. כן העיד הכתוב עליו (דניאל ה): פסיק ליה. יפיג יינו מעט מעליו: על דורדייה. על שמריו: וטעמא אמרו ליה. ויפה אמרו לו, דודאי כן הוא, שמתוך שהאדם שקט דעתו מיושבת עליו, שנאמר "שאנן מואב מנעוריו ושוקט הוא אל שמריו", וסיפיה דקרא "על כן עמד טעמו בו וריחו לא נמר": פסוק זה על קרבנות נאמר. "והקרוב אליו" – לשון הקרבת קרבן. מלאכי השרת הזכירו לפני הקב"ה את הקרבנות שהקריבו ישראל לפניו לעשות להם נקמה בושתי, ותבא אסתר ותמלוך תחתיה: כרשנא. כלום הקריבו לפניך כרים בני שנה: שתר. שתי תורים: מרס. שמירסו את הדם, שלא יקרש ושוב לא יהא ראוי לזריקה: מרסנא. מירסו במנחות לבוללן. ממרס לשון מגיס: מוכן לפורענות. עומד להיות תלוי: מכאן שההדיוט קופץ בראש. שהרי מנה אותו הכתוב לבסוף, אלמא גרוע הוא מכולן, והוא קפץ בראש: אלמלא אגרות ראשונות. שהוחזק כהן שוטה בעיני האומות: לא נשתייר משונאי ישראל שריד ופליט. שהיו ממהרין להורגן במצות המלך באגרות האחרונות, ולא היו ממתינים ליום המועד: אמרי מאי האי דשדר לן. אומרים האומות: מה זה ששלח לומר לנו להיות כל איש שורר בביתו? (ה) שאף הגרדן שורר בביתו: פרדשכא. פקיד ונגיד: נערה. דוד לא ביקש אלא נערה אחת(ו), כל אדם הראה לשלוחיו את בתו אולי תיטב בעיניו. ואחשורוש כסיל, נויה לקבץ את כולן — הכל יודעין שלא יקח אלא אחת, ואת כולן יבעל. מאן דהוה ליה ברתא — מטמרה: מוכתר בנימוסו היה. בשמות נאין. נימוס — שם בלשון יון: א] •(*נערי) לא גרסינן, אלא הכי גרסינן: אמר רבה בר בר חנה אמר רבי יהושע בן לוי כו': דלא

תוספות

שפרחה בה צרעת. בירושלמי מפרש דילפינן "נגזר" דכתיב גבי ושתי מ"נגזר" דכתיב גבי עוזיה כשנצטרע, דכתיב ביה "נגזר מבית ה'" (דה"ב כו): זיל לגבי עמון ומואב דיתבי בדוכתייהו כחמרא. וקשה: דהא פרק "תפלת השחר" (ברכות דף כח.) פריך: וכי עמון במקומו יושב? והלא בא סנחריב ובלבלו! לכך פר"ת דגרסינן הכא מואב לחוד, דקרא נמי לא הזכיר אלא מואב, דכתיב "שאנן מואב". ובברכות נמי לא גרסינן אלא עמון, ומזה הטעם התירו ליהודה גר העמוני לבא בקהל. אבל משמע דגרי אינך לא רצו להתיר לבא בקהל לפי שלא בלבל סנחריב מצרים ולא בלבל מואב ומיהו, קשה: דבברכות משמע, באותה שהבאתי, שסנחריב בלבל עמון, ובירמיה חשיב להו באותן שהגלה נבוכדנצר! וי"ל: לפי שסנחריב היה ראשון שבלבל – נקרא הכל על שמו, ועליו כתיב "ואסיר גבולות עמים ועתידותיהם שוסתי", אבל ודאי עיקר החורבן היה ע"י נבוכדנצר*:

ממוכן *יש מדרש שהיה דניאל, ולפי שהיה נשוי לשרית שהיתה גדולה ממנו שלא היה יכול לכופה לדבר כלשונו, יעץ לעשות כן: כל

רבינו חננאל

בקרי ואיתתי' בבוציני. פי' שניהם לזנות. מוכתר בנימוסו. [הי' כעדי] פי' מצויין בדתי כל התורה היה (בצדי) *) שהיה בחורו יודע וזהיר במצות. ורבה בר רב הונא עדיף מיניה בענותנות דהא אמר רבא תלת מילי בעאי משמיא. חכמתיה דרב הונא. ועיתריה דרב חסדא יהבו לי. ענותנותיה דרבה בר רב הונא לא יהבו לי.

*) נ"ל מצויין בדתי כל התורה היה כעדי שהי' ידוע בדורו וזהיר במצות וכ"ה בערוך ערך נמס ב'.

[וע"ע תוס' יבמות עו: ד"ה מנימין ותוס' סוטה ט.]

[עי' פרקי דר"א פמ"ט]

[סוטה ח:]

ס"א לא גרים בר

[נ"ל כעדי עי' בע בפרש"י שם עי' בער ערך נמס וערך עדי]

[בע"י גריס רבה בר ר הונא ורבה בר בר חנ משמיה דרבי יהושע ב לוי אמרו אביו מבנימ וכו' וע"ש בפרש"י ובערו ערך נמס ב כתב בזה מרדכי מוכתר בנמוסו הי כעדי פירוש מצוין בדי התורה כעדי שהיה ידו בדורו וזהיר במצות וכ ע"

הגהות הב"ח

(א) גמ' מלאכה בשבת לפיכך נגזר עליה בשבת היינו דכתיב: (ב) שם ויקצף המלך מאד וחמתו בערה בו אמאי דלקה: (ג) שם פסיק ליה חמריה ודכיר לה ובעי לה מינן: (ד) שם ליחסיה וליזיל עד בנימין מאי שנא הני תלתא תנא כולן כצ"ל ותיבת אלא נמחק: (ה) רש"י ד"ה אמרי מאי וכו' להיות כל איש שורר בביתו פשיטא שאף הגרדן: (ו) ד"ה נערה וכו' נערה אחת לפיכך כל אדם וכו' ואחשורוש היה כסיל וכו' מטמרה מיניה הס"ד:

גליון הש"ס

גמ' אמר ר"כ מכאן שההדיוט כו'. עי' ירושל' פרק ד דסנהדרין ה"ז: שם אמר רבא אלמלא. ע"ל כא ע"א תד"ה אלמלא: רש"י ד"ה נערי לא גרסי'. עי' דבר נחמד בספר מקום שמואל:

הגהות מהר"ב רנשבורג

א] רש"י ד"ה נערי לא גרסינן. כ"ב עיין בזה בספר מקום שמואל בשער התירוצים:

[בע"י איתא תוספת יש ספרים דגרסי איש יהודי היה בשושן הבירה וגו' אמר רב נחמן מוכתר בנימוסו היה פי' שמות נאים והגונים כדדריש שכולם על שמו נקראים וי"ס דגרסי קרי ליה יהודי וקרי ליה ימיני יהודי אלמא מיהודה קאתי ימיני אלמא מבנימין קאתי אמר רב נחמן מרדכי מוכתר מוכתר בנימוסו היה ולא נהירא דמה ענין זה לזה ומיהו יש ליישבו מוכתר בנימוסו מוכתר בשמות נאים ובמעשים נאים ובטכסיסי מלכות ולכך קוריו של שם יהודה שהיה חשוב מכל השבטים ויצאו ממנו מלכים]

דלא קטליה דוד לשמעי, דאתיליד מיניה מרדכי, דמיקני ביה המן. ומה שילם לי ימיני — דלא קטליה שאול לאגג, דאתיליד מיניה המן, דמצער לישראל. רבי יוחנן אמר: לעולם מבנימן קאתי. ואמאי קרי ליה "יהודי"? על שום שכפר בע"ז. שכל הכופר בע"ז נקרא "יהודי", כדכתיב: °"איתי גוברין יהודאין" וגו'. (דניאל ג) רבי שמעון בן פזי, כי הוה פתח בדברי הימים, אמר הכי: כל דבריך, אחד הם, ואנו יודעין לדורשן. °"ואשתו היהודיה ילדה את ירד אבי גדור ואת חבר אבי שוכו ואת יקותיאל אבי זנוח ואלה בני בתיה בת פרעה אשר לקח מרד". (דה"א ד) אמאי קרי לה "יהודיה" — על שום שכפרה בע"ז, דכתיב: °"ותרד בת פרעה לרחוץ על היאור", (שמות ב) *ואמר רבי יוחנן: שירדה לרחוץ מגילולי בית אביה. ילדה? והא רבויי רביתיה! לומר לך: *שכל המגדל יתום ויתומה בתוך ביתו מעלה עליו הכתוב כאילו ילדו. "ירד" — זה משה. ולמה נקרא שמו "ירד"?[א] שירד להם לישראל מן בימיו. *"גדור" — שגדר פרצותיהן של ישראל. "חבר" — שחיבר את ישראל לאביהן שבשמים. "סוכו" — שנעשה להם לישראל כסוכה. "יקותיאל" — שקוו ישראל לאל בימיו. "זנוח" — שהזניח עונותיהן של ישראל. "אבי" "אבי" "אבי" — אב בתורה, אב בחכמה, אב בנביאות. "ואלה בני בתיה... אשר לקח מרד". וכי מרד שמו? והלא כלב שמו! אמר הקב"ה יבא כלב שמרד בעצת מרגלים וישא את(א) בת פרעה שמרדה בגלולי בית אביה. "אשר הגלה מירושלים". אמר רבא: שגלה מעצמו. "ויהי אומן את הדסה". קרי לה "הדסה" וקרי לה "אסתר". תניא ר"מ אומר: אסתר שמה. ולמה נקראת שמה הדסה? על שם הצדיקים *שנקראו "הדסים". וכן הוא אומר: °"והוא עומד בין ההדסים". (זכריה א) רבי יהודה אומר: הדסה שמה. ולמה נקראת שמה אסתר? על שם שהיתה מסתרת דבריה, שנאמר: "אין אסתר מגדת את עמה" וגו'. ר' נחמיה אומר: הדסה שמה. ולמה נקראת אסתר? שהיו אומות העולם קורין אותה על שום אסתהר. בן עזאי אומר: אסתר, לא ארוכה ולא קצרה היתה, אלא בינונית כהדסה. ר' יהושע בן קרחה אמר: *אסתר ירקרוקת היתה וחוט של חסד משוך עליה. "כי אין לה אב ואם" — "ובמות אביה ואמה" למה לי? אמר רב אחא: עיברתה — מת אביה; ילדתה — מתה אמה. "ובמות אביה ואמה לקחה מרדכי לו לבת". תנא משום ר"מ: אל תקרי "לבת" אלא לבית. וכן הוא אומר: °"ולרש אין כל כי אם כבשה אחת קטנה אשר קנה ויחיה ותגדל עמו ועם בניו יחדו מפתו תאכל ומכוסו תשתה ובחיקו תשכב ותהי לו כבת". (שמואל ב יב) משום דבחיקו תשכב, הוות ליה (*לבת)? אלא (*לבית) — הכי נמי לבית. "ואת שבע הנערות" וגו' — אמר רבא: שהיתה מונה בהן ימי שבת. "וישנה ואת נערותיה" וגו' אמר רב: שהאכילה מאכל יהודי. ושמואל אמר: שהאכילה *קדלי דחזירי. ור' יוחנן אמר: זרעונים. וכן הוא אומר: °"ויהי המלצר נושא את פת בגם... ונותן להם זרעונים". (דניאל א) "ששה חדשים בשמן המור". *מאי "שמן המור"? ר' חייא בר אבא אמר: סטכת. רב הונא אמר: שמן זית שלא הביא שליש. תניא רבי יהודה אומר: אנפקינון — שמן זית שלא הביא שליש. ולמה סכין אותו? שמשיר את השיער ומעדן את הבשר. "בערב היא באה ובבקר היא שבה". אמר רבי יוחנן: מגנותו של אותו רשע למדנו שבחו, שלא היה משמש מטתו ביום. "ותהי אסתר נשאת חן". אר"א: *מלמד שלכל אחד ואחד נדמתה לו כאומתו. "ותלקח אסתר אל המלך אחשורוש אל בית מלכותו בחדש העשירי הוא חדש טבת" — ירח שהגוף נהנה מן הגוף. "ויאהב המלך את אסתר מכל הנשים ותשא חן וחסד לפניו מכל הבתולות". אמר רב: ביקש לטעום טעם בתולה — טעם, טעם בעולה — טעם. "ויעש המלך משתה גדול". עבד משתיא — ולא גליא ליה; דלי כרגא — ולא גליא ליה; שדר פרדישני — ולא גליא ליה. "ובהקבץ בתולות שנית" וגו' אזיל שקל עצה ממרדכי. אמר: אין אשה מתקנאה אלא בירך חבירתה — ואפי' הכי לא גליא ליה, דכתיב: "אין אסתר מגדת מולדתה" וגו'. אמר רבי אלעזר: מאי דכתיב:

לא

רש"י

*דלא קטליה דוד לשמעי. שהיה חייב מיתה: לאידך גיסא. לצערה ולא לשבח: איש יהודי ואיש ימיני גרמו לי הצער הזה: איתי גוברין יהודאין כו'. וסיפיה דקרא "לאלהך לא פלחין": כל דבריך אחד הן. כנגד הספר היה אומר: כל דבריך, דברי הימים, אחת הן. הרבה שמות אתה מזכיר, פלוני ופלוני, וכולן אדם אחד הן: ואנו יודעין לדורשן. ואע"פ שסתמת אותן, אנו נותנין את לבינו עד שאנו יודעין לדורשן. משום דאמרינן לעיל כל הכופר בע"ז נקרא יהודי נקט לה הכא: ואשתו היהודיה וגו'. והלא בתיה שמה, דהא כתיב בסופיה "ואלה בני בתיה": לרחוץ. לטבול (*לשון) גירות: והלא כלב שמו. שבכלב משתעי קרא: הכי גרסינן: וישא בתיה שמרדה בגילולי בית אביה. ולכך נשתנה שמה בליקוחין הללו: שגלה מעצמו. מדלא כתיב "אשר היה מן הגולה אשר הגלתה", וכתיב "אשר הגלה עם הגולה", משמע שלא היה כשאר ישראל שגלו על כרחן, והוא גלה מעצמו, כמו שעשה ירמיה שגלה מעצמו, עד שאמר לו הקב"ה לחזור: בין ההדסים אשר במצולה. בין הצדיקים שגלו לבבל, ובשכינה משתעי קרא: אסתהר. ירח, יפה כלבנה: ירקרוקת היתה. כהדסה זו: אלא חוט של חסד משוך עליה. מאת הקב"ה, לכך נראית יפה לאומות ולאחשורוש: ובמות אביה ואמה תרי ל"ל. מאחר דכתיב "כי אין לה אב ואם", אלא ללמדנו שאפי' יום אחד לא היה לה אב ואם: בשעה שנתעברה אמה מת אביה. נמצא שלא היה לה אב משעה שנראה להקרות אב: וכשילדתה אמה מתה. ולא נראית לקרות אם: ולרש אין כל. באוריה משתעי קרא: כבשה אחת. (ב) בת שבע: שהיתה מונה בהן ימי שבת. שהיתה משרתת לה אחת באחד בשבת, ואחת בשני בשבת, ואחת בשלישי בשבת, וכן כולן. וכשהגיע יום שפחה של שבת יודעת שהיום שבת: *כתלי דחזירי. בקונ"ם שמינית. ומתוך אונסה לא נענשה: וכן הוא אומר. שהזרעונים טובים לצדיקים להבדילן ממאכל טמא: ויהי המלצר נושא את פת בגם ויין משתיהם וגו'. וכתיב בההוא ענינא "ולמקצת ימים עשרה נראה מראיהם טוב ובריאי בשר" וגו': אנפקינון שמן זית שלא הביא שליש. גבי מנחות תנן: *אין מביאין אנפקינון, ואם הביא – פסול. ועלה קאי ר' יהודה ואמר מהו אנפקינון: מעדן. (ג) מצהיב: מגנותו של אותו רשע. גנותו הוא זה, שהוא בועל נשים ומשלחן: שהגוף נהנה מן הגוף. מפני הצינה. והעיד לך הכתוב שהיו מתכוונין מן השמים לחבבה על בעלה: ביקש לטעום כו'. לכך נאמר "מכל הנשים ומכל הבתולות": עבד משתיא כו'. חוזר לכמה עניינים לפייסה שתגלה לו מולדתה, ולא הועיל. וסמוך לה להאי קרא "ובהקבץ בתולות שנית וגו' אין אסתר מגדת מולדתה ואת עמה" וגו' עבד משתיא סעודה לכבודה, מה שלא עשה בשאר נשים: דלי כרגא. אמר: בשביל אסתר אני מניח לכם מכסי גולגלתכם, היינו "והנחה למדינות עשה": שדר פרדישני. דורונות לשרים בשמה, והיינו דכתיב "ויתן משאת כיד המלך":

לא

תוספות

כל הכופר בע"ז נקרא יהודי שנאמר "איתי גוברין יהודאין".* על שם יהודי, שהרי אמר ב"חלק" (סנהדרין דף נג:) דלא הוו משבט יהודה: אשר הגלה שגלה מעצמו. ודריש ליה מדלא כתיב "הוגלה": קדלי דחזירי. וס"ו, היא לא היתה אוכלת:

וטובלת

רבינו חננאל

כל המגדל יתום בתוך ביתו מעלה עליו הכתוב כאילו הוא ילדו: נקראת הדסה מפני דהיתה צדקת. שהצדיקים נקראים הדסים: לקחה מרדכי לו לבת: תנא משום רבי מאיר לבית:

[בע"י איתא בזה"ל תימה איך שקראם יהודאין לפי שהיו משבט יהודה כדכתיב (דניאל א) ויהי בהם מבני יהודה דניאל חנניה מישאל ועזריה וי"ל דאתיא כר"ש בר נחמני דאמר בפרק חלק נג: דניאל מבני יהודה חנניה מישאל ועזריה משאר שבטים]

הגהות הב"ח

(א) גמ' וישא את בתיה בת פרעה: (ב) רש"י ד"ה כבשה אחת זו בת שבע: (ג) ד"ה מעדן מצהיב ומצהיל הס"ד:

הגהות הגר"א

[א] גמ' (שירד להם לישראל מן בימיו) תא"מ ונ"ב שהוריד תורה לישראל:

[נ"ל כבית וכן איתא בע"י]

[פירוש עורף של חזרת כלומר ראש של חסא ערוך ערך קתל ועיין תוספות ד"ה קדלי]

גליון הש"ס

גמ' ואשתו היהודיה. עי' מ"ר ריש ויקרא: **שם** על שם הצדיקים. עי' ברכות דף כו ע"ב תוד"ה ואין שיחה: **רש"י** ד"ה אסתהר ירח. כי ירח תרגומו סהרא (בראשית לז ט):

מסורת הש"ס

תיבת דלא עד תיבת עד הזה שייך לעמוד הקודם

[נ"ל לשום]

[סוטה יב:]

סנהדרין יט:

גי' ע"י ובשבילו

[סנהדרין נג. ע"ש ועי' תוס' ברכות כו: ד"ה ואין שיחה]

בערוך הגי' קתלי

[לקמן טו.]

[מנחות פה:]

[נ"ל כבת]

חים מג. ע"ש מ"ק ט: ...ש שבת פ. ע"ש מנחות פו. ע"ש

[לעיל ז.]

°"לֹא יִגְרַע מִצַּדִּיק עֵינָיו"? בִּשְׂכַר צְנִיעוּת שֶׁהָיְתָה בָּהּ בְּרָחֵל — זָכְתָה וְיָצָא מִמֶּנָּה שָׁאוּל. וּבִשְׂכַר צְנִיעוּת שֶׁהָיָה בּוֹ בְּשָׁאוּל — זָכָה וְיָצְאת מִמֶּנּוּ אֶסְתֵּר. *וּמַאי צְנִיעוּת הָיְתָה בָּהּ בְּרָחֵל? דִּכְתִיב: °"וַיַּגֵּד יַעֲקֹב לְרָחֵל כִּי אֲחִי אָבִיהָ הוּא". וְכִי אֲחִי אָבִיהָ הוּא? וַהֲלֹא בֶּן אֲחוֹת אָבִיהָ הוּא? אֶלָּא אָמַר לָהּ: מִנְּסְבָא לִי? אָמְרָה לֵיהּ: אִין. מִיהוּ אַבָּא רַמָּאָה הוּא וְלָא יָכְלַתְּ לֵיהּ. אָמַר לָהּ:(א) אָחִיו אֲנָא בְּרַמָּאוּת. אָמְרָה לֵיהּ: וּמִי שָׁרֵי לְצַדִּיקֵי לְסַגּוּיֵי בְּרַמְיוּתָא? אָמַר לָהּ: אִין. °"עִם נָבָר תִּתָּבָר וְעִם עִקֵּשׁ תִּתַּפָּל". אָמַר לָהּ: וּמַאי רַמְיוּתָא? אָמְרָה לֵיהּ: אִית לִי אַחְתָּא דְּקַשִּׁישָׁא מִינַּאי, וְלָא מַנְסֵיב לִי מִקַּמַּהּ. *מָסַר לָהּ סִימָנִים. כִּי מְטָא לֵילְיָא, אָמְרָה: הָשְׁתָּא מִיכַּסְפָא אַחְתַּאי. מְסַרְתִּינְהוּ נִיהֲלָהּ. וְהַיְינוּ דִּכְתִיב: °"וַיְהִי בַבֹּקֶר וְהִנֵּה הִיא לֵאָה", מִכְּלָל דְּעַד הָשְׁתָּא לָאו לֵאָה הִיא?! אֶלָּא: מִתּוֹךְ סִימָנִין שֶׁמָּסְרָה רָחֵל לְלֵאָה לָא הֲוָה יָדַע עַד הָשְׁתָּא. לְפִיכָךְ זָכְתָה וְיָצָא מִמֶּנָּה שָׁאוּל. וּמָה צְנִיעוּת הָיְתָה בְּשָׁאוּל? דִּכְתִיב: °"וְאֶת דְּבַר הַמְּלוּכָה לֹא הִגִּיד לוֹ אֲשֶׁר אָמַר שְׁמוּאֵל"(ב) — זָכָה וְיָצְאת מִמֶּנּוּ אֶסְתֵּר. *וְאָמַר רַבִּי אֶלְעָזָר: כְּשֶׁהקב"ה פּוֹסֵק גְּדוּלָּה לְאָדָם פּוֹסֵק לְבָנָיו וְלִבְנֵי בָנָיו עַד סוֹף כָּל הַדּוֹרוֹת, שֶׁנֶּאֱמַר: °"וַיּוֹשִׁיבֵם לָנֶצַח וַיִּגְבָּהוּ" (וגו'), וְאִם הִגִּיס דַּעְתּוֹ — הקב"ה מַשְׁפִּילוֹ, שֶׁנֶּאֱמַר: °"וְאִם אֲסוּרִים בַּזִּקִּים" וגו'. "וְאֶת מַאֲמַר מָרְדֳּכַי אֶסְתֵּר עוֹשָׂה" אָמַר רַבִּי שֶׁהָיְתָה מַרְאָה דַּם נִדָּה לַחֲכָמִים. "כַּאֲשֶׁר הָיְתָה בְאָמְנָה אִתּוֹ" — אָמַר רַבָּה בַּר לִימָא *(מִשְּׁמֵיהּ דְּרַב:) שֶׁהָיְתָה עוֹמֶדֶת מֵחֵיקוֹ שֶׁל אֲחַשְׁוֵרוֹשׁ וְטוֹבֶלֶת וְיוֹשֶׁבֶת בְּחֵיקוֹ שֶׁל מָרְדֳּכַי. "בַּיָּמִים הָהֵם וּמָרְדֳּכַי יוֹשֵׁב בְּשַׁעַר הַמֶּלֶךְ קָצַף בִּגְתָן וָתֶרֶשׁ". אָמַר ר' חִיָּיא בַּר אַבָּא אָמַר רַבִּי יוֹחָנָן: הִקְצִיף הקב"ה אָדוֹן עַל עֲבָדָיו לַעֲשׂוֹת רְצוֹן צַדִּיק. וּמַנּוּ — יוֹסֵף, שֶׁנֶּאֱמַר: °"וְשָׁם אִתָּנוּ נַעַר עִבְרִי" וגו'. עֲבָדִים עַל אֲדוֹנֵיהֶן לַעֲשׂוֹת נֵס לְצַדִּיק, וּמַנּוּ — מָרְדֳּכַי, [א*]דִּכְתִיב: "וַיִּוָּדַע הַדָּבָר לְמָרְדֳּכַי" וגו'. *אָמַר רַבִּי יוֹחָנָן: בִּגְתָן וָתֶרֶשׁ °שְׁנֵי טַרְסִיִּים הֲווּ, וְהָיוּ מְסַפְּרִין בִּלְשׁוֹן טוּרְסִי, וְאוֹמְרִים: מִיּוֹם שֶׁבָּאת זוֹ לֹא רָאִינוּ שֵׁינָה בְּעֵינֵינוּ. בֹּא וְנַטִּיל אֶרֶס בַּסֵּפֶל כְּדֵי שֶׁיָּמוּת. וְהֵן לֹא הָיוּ יוֹדְעִין כִּי מָרְדֳּכַי מִיּוֹשְׁבֵי לִשְׁכַּת הַגָּזִית הָיָה, וְהָיָה יוֹדֵעַ בְּשִׁבְעִים לָשׁוֹן. אָמַר לוֹ: וַהֲלֹא אֵין מִשְׁמַרְתִּי וּמִשְׁמַרְתְּךָ שָׁוָה! אָמַר לוֹ: אֲנִי אֶשְׁמוֹר מִשְׁמַרְתִּי וּמִשְׁמַרְתְּךָ. וְהַיְינוּ דִּכְתִיב: "וַיְבֻקַּשׁ הַדָּבָר וַיִּמָּצֵא" — שֶׁלֹּא נִמְצְאוּ בְּמִשְׁמַרְתָּן. "אַחַר הַדְּבָרִים הָאֵלֶּה", *(אַחַר מַאי?) אָמַר רָבָא: אַחַר שֶׁבָּרָא הקב"ה רְפוּאָה לַמַּכָּה, דְּאָמַר ר"ל: אֵין הקב"ה מַכֶּה אֶת יִשְׂרָאֵל אא"כ בּוֹרֵא לָהֶם רְפוּאָה תְּחִילָּה, שֶׁנֶּאֱמַר: °"כְּרָפְאִי לְיִשְׂרָאֵל וְנִגְלָה עֲוֹן אֶפְרַיִם" — אֲבָל אוּמּוֹת הָעוֹלָם אֵינוֹ כֵּן, מַכֶּה אוֹתָן וְאח"כ בּוֹרֵא לָהֶם רְפוּאָה, שֶׁנֶּאֱמַר: °"וְנָגַף ה' אֶת מִצְרַיִם נָגוֹף וְרָפוֹא". "וַיִּבֶז בְּעֵינָיו לִשְׁלוֹחַ יָד בְּמָרְדֳּכַי לְבַדּוֹ" אָמַר רָבָא: בַּתְּחִילָּה בְּמָרְדֳּכַי לְבַדּוֹ, וּלְבַסּוֹף בְּעַם מָרְדֳּכַי, וּמַנּוּ — רַבָּנַן; וּלְבַסּוֹף בְּכָל הַיְּהוּדִים. "הִפִּיל פּוּר הוּא הַגּוֹרָל". תָּנָא: כֵּיוָן שֶׁנָּפַל פּוּר בְּחוֹדֶשׁ אֲדָר שָׂמַח שִׂמְחָה גְּדוֹלָה. אָמַר: נָפַל לִי פּוּר בְּיֶרַח שֶׁמֵּת בּוֹ מֹשֶׁה. וְלֹא הָיָה יוֹדֵעַ *שֶׁבְּשִׁבְעָה בַּאֲדָר מֵת וּבְשִׁבְעָה בַּאֲדָר נוֹלַד. "יֶשְׁנוֹ עַם אֶחָד". אָמַר רָבָא: לֵיכָּא דְּיָדַע לִישָּׁנָא בִּישָׁא כְּהָמָן. אָמַר לֵיהּ: תָּא נֵיכְלִינְהוּ. אָמַר לֵיהּ מִסְתְּפִינָא מֵאֱלָהֵיו דְּלָא לֶיעְבֵּיד בִּי כִּדְעָבַד בְּקַמָּאֵי. אָמַר לֵיהּ: יָשְׁנוּ מִן הַמִּצְוֹת. אָמַר לֵיהּ: אִית בְּהוּ רַבָּנַן. אָמַר לֵיהּ: עַם אֶחָד הֵן. שֶׁמָּא תֹּאמַר קָרְחָה אֲנִי עוֹשֶׂה בְּמַלְכוּתְךָ — מְפוּזָּרִין הֵם בֵּין הָעַמִּים. שֶׁמָּא תֹּאמַר: אִית הֲנָאָה מִינַּיְיהוּ — "מְפוֹרָד", כְּפְרֵידָה זוֹ שֶׁאֵינָהּ עוֹשָׂה פֵּירוֹת. וְשֶׁמָּא תֹּאמַר: אִיכָּא מְדִינְתָּא מִינַּיְיהוּ — ת"ל "בְּכֹל מְדִינוֹת מַלְכוּתֶךָ". "וְדָתֵיהֶם שׁוֹנוֹת מִכָּל עָם" — דְּלָא אָכְלִי מִינַּן, וְלָא נָסְבִי מִינַּן, וְלָא מַנְסְבִי לַן. "וְאֶת דָּתֵי הַמֶּלֶךְ אֵינָם עוֹשִׂים" — דְּמַפְּקִי לְכוּלָּא שַׁתָּא בְּשה"י פה"י. "וְלַמֶּלֶךְ אֵין שֹׁוֶה לְהַנִּיחָם" — דְּאָכְלוּ וְשָׁתוּ וּמְבַזּוּ לֵיהּ לְמַלְכוּת. וַאֲפִילּוּ נוֹפֵל זְבוּב בְּכוֹסוֹ שֶׁל אֶחָד מֵהֶן — זוֹרְקוֹ וְשׁוֹתֵהוּ; וְאִם אֲדוֹנִי הַמֶּלֶךְ נוֹגֵעַ בְּכוֹסוֹ שֶׁל אֶחָד מֵהֶן — חוֹבְטוֹ בְּקַרְקַע וְאֵינוֹ שׁוֹתֵהוּ. "אִם עַל הַמֶּלֶךְ טוֹב יִכָּתֵב לְאַבְּדָם וַעֲשֶׂרֶת אֲלָפִים כִּכַּר כֶּסֶף" וגו'. אָמַר רֵישׁ לָקִישׁ: גָּלוּי וְיָדוּעַ לִפְנֵי מִי שֶׁאָמַר וְהָיָה הָעוֹלָם שֶׁעָתִיד הָמָן לִשְׁקוֹל שְׁקָלִים עַל יִשְׂרָאֵל, לְפִיכָךְ הִקְדִּים שִׁקְלֵיהֶן לִשְׁקָלָיו. וְהַיְינוּ דִּתְנַן: *בְּאֶחָד בַּאֲדָר מַשְׁמִיעִין עַל הַשְּׁקָלִים וְעַל הַכִּלְאַיִם. "וַיֹּאמֶר הַמֶּלֶךְ לְהָמָן הַכֶּסֶף נָתוּן לָךְ וְהָעָם לַעֲשׂוֹת בּוֹ כַּטּוֹב בְּעֵינֶיךָ". אָמַר רַבִּי אַבָּא: מָשָׁל

(איוב לו; בראשית כט; שמואל ב כב; בראשית כט; שמואל א י; איוב לו; שם; בראשית מא; הושע ז; ישעיה יט)

רש"י

לֹא יִגְרַע מִצַּדִּיק עֵינָיו. נוֹתֵן עֵינָיו בְּמַעֲשֵׂה הַצַּדִּיקִים לְשַׁלֵּם לָהֶם(ג) אַף לְיָמִים רַבִּים מִדָּה כְּמִדָּה: זָכְתָה וְיָצָא מִמֶּנָּה שָׁאוּל. שֶׁהָיָה צָנוּעַ: זָכָה וְיָצָאת מִמֶּנּוּ אֶסְתֵּר. בְּתַרְגּוּם שֶׁל מְגִילָּה מְיַיחֵס מָרְדֳּכַי וְעוֹשֵׂהוּ עֲשִׂירִי לְשָׁאוּל, וּמִשָּׁאוּל עַד בִּנְיָמִין. וּכְתִיב "הִיא אֶסְתֵּר בַּת דּוֹדוֹ", וְאֵין לוֹ רְאָיָה אַחֶרֶת בַּכְּתוּבִים שֶׁיָּצְאָה מִשָּׁאוּל: מְסַרְתָּן. לְלֵאָה, וְהוּא צְנִיעוּת, שֶׁלֹּא יִתְפַּרְסֵם הַדָּבָר שֶׁמָּסַר לָהּ סִימָנִין: שֶׁנֶּאֱמַר לֹא יִגְרַע מִצַּדִּיק עֵינָיו. וְסֵיפֵיהּ דִּקְרָא "וַיּוֹשִׁיבֵם לָנֶצַח וַיִּגְבָּהוּ" — וְהַיְינוּ גְּדוּלָּה לְדוֹרוֹת: וְאִם הֵגִיס דַּעְתּוֹ כו'. הָכִי סָמְכִי קְרָאֵי: "וַיּוֹשִׁיבֵם לָנֶצַח וַיִּגְבָּהוּ וְאִם אֲסוּרִים בַּזִּקִּים" — עַל יְדֵי שֶׁמַּגְבִּיהִין עַצְמָן בָּאִין לִידֵי עֲנִיּוּת וְיִסּוּרִים: וְטוֹבֶלֶת. מֵחֲמַת נְקִיּוּת, שֶׁלֹּא תְּהֵא מְאוּסָה לַצַּדִּיק מִשְּׁכִיבָתוֹ שֶׁל אֲחַשְׁוֵרוֹשׁ: אָדוֹן עַל עֲבָדָיו. "וַיִּקְצוֹף פַּרְעֹה עַל שְׁנֵי סָרִיסָיו": לְשׁוֹן טוּרְסִי. שֵׁם מָקוֹם: לֹא רָאִינוּ שֵׁינָה. מִתּוֹךְ שֶׁהָיְתָה חֲבִיבָה עָלָיו הָיָה מַרְבֶּה בְּתַשְׁמִישׁ, וְצָמֵא לִשְׁתּוֹת: מִשְׁמַרְתִּי וּמִשְׁמַרְתְּךָ. אַתָּה מְמוּנֶּה עַל עֲבוֹדָה אַחַת, וַאֲנִי מְמוּנֶּה עַל עֲבוֹדָה אַחֶרֶת: ה"ג: אַחַר הַדְּבָרִים הָאֵלֶּה גִּדַּל הַמֶּלֶךְ* אֶת הָמָן וגו'. בָּתַר בִּגְתָן וָתֶרֶשׁ כְּתִיב: וְקָא בָּעֵי תַּלְמוּדָא: אַחַר מַאי. מַה הֵעִיד עָלָיו הַכָּתוּב שֶׁלֹּא גִּידְּלוֹ עַד שֶׁבָּא מַעֲשֶׂה הַזֶּה: אַחַר שֶׁבָּרָא הַקָּדוֹשׁ ב"ה רְפוּאָה לַמַּכָּה. [מהרש"ל]

הָעֲתִידָה לָבֹא לְאַחַר זְמַן: כְּרָפְאִי לְיִשְׂרָאֵל. וְאַחַר כָּךְ נִגְלָה עֲוֹן אֶפְרַיִם, ע"י מַכָּה שֶׁאֲנִי מֵבִיא עֲלֵיהֶן: הִפִּיל פּוּר. וּמַהוּ פּוּר, הוּא הַגּוֹרָל. מִיּוֹם לְיוֹם, בְּאֵיזוֹ יוֹם יִפּוֹל הַגּוֹרָל. וְכֵן מֵחוֹדֶשׁ לְחוֹדֶשׁ. וְהַגּוֹרָל שֶׁל כּוּלָּן הֵטִיל בְּיוֹם אֶחָד, וְנָפַל לוֹ הַגּוֹרָל עַל(ד) אֶחָד: בְּשִׁבְעָה בַּאֲדָר מֵת מֹשֶׁה. שֶׁנֶּאֱמַר (תורה אור) "וְהָעָם עָלוּ מִן הַיַּרְדֵּן בֶּעָשׂוֹר לַחוֹדֶשׁ הָרִאשׁוֹן" (יהושע ד). צֵא מֵהֶם לְמַפְרֵעַ שְׁלֹשִׁים יוֹם שֶׁאֶבְלוּ שֶׁל מֹשֶׁה, וּשְׁלֹשָׁה יָמִים שֶׁהֵכִינוּ לָהֶם צֵידָה, שֶׁנֶּאֱמַר "הָכִינוּ לָכֶם צֵידָה כִּי בְּעוֹד שְׁלֹשֶׁת יָמִים אַתֶּם עוֹבְרִים" וגו' (שם א), הֲרֵי בְּשִׁבְעָה בַּאֲדָר מֵת מֹשֶׁה: וּבְשִׁבְעָה בַּאֲדָר נוֹלַד. דִּכְתִיב "בֶּן מֵאָה וְעֶשְׂרִים שָׁנָה אָנֹכִי הַיּוֹם" (דברים לא): הַיּוֹם מָלְאוּ יָמַי וּשְׁנוֹתַי, כְּדַאי הַלֵּידָה שֶׁתְּכַפֵּר עַל הַמִּיתָה: אִית בְּהוּ רַבָּנַן. מִתְּשׁוּבָתוֹ שֶׁל הָמָן לָמֵדִין שֶׁכָּךְ הָיָה אֲחַשְׁוֵרוֹשׁ מְשִׁיבוֹ: קָרְחָה אֲנִי עוֹשֶׂה בְּמַלְכוּתְךָ. שֶׁמַּלְכוּת אַחַת מְלֵיאָה מֵהֶם: מְדִינְתָּא. מְדִינָה קְטַנָּה: וְלָא נָסְבִי מִינַּן. נָשִׁים: וְאֶת דָּתֵי הַמֶּלֶךְ אֵינָם עוֹשִׂים. אוֹנְגָּרִיּוֹת וּמִסִּים וְגוּלְגָּלִיּוֹת וְאַרְנוֹנוֹת אֵינָן נוֹתְנִין: דְּמַפְּקֵי לֵיהּ לְשַׁתָּא בְּשה"י פה"י. שַׁבָּת הַיּוֹם, פֶּסַח הַיּוֹם, וְאָנוּ אֲסוּרִים בִּמְלָאכָה: אֵין שֹׁוֶה. אֵין נָאֶה, וְאֵין חֲשַׁשׁ לְהַנִּיחָן: מַשְׁמִיעִין. בֵּית דִּין מַכְרִיזִין שֶׁיָּבִיאוּ שְׁקָלִים לַמִּקְדָּשׁ: וְעַל הַכִּלְאַיִם. שֶׁגָּדְלוּ הַזְּרָעִים קְצָת, וְנִיכָּר נִיכָּר, וְעוֹקְרִין אוֹתָן מִשְּׂדוֹתֵיהֶן בְּהַכְרָזַת בֵּית דִּין: מָשָׁל

תוספות

וטובלת ויושבת בחיקו של מרדכי. ואם תאמר: והא לא הוי שם הבחנת שלש' חדשים, שהרי בכל יום היה אותו רשע מלוי אצלה! וי"ל: שהיתה משמשת במוך: [מהרש"ם]

הכסף נתון לך. גימטריא ד"הכסף" עולה "העץ", רמז לו שיתלה עליו*:

רבינו חננאל

אמר לו והלא אין משמרתי ומשמרתך שוה. א"ל אני אשמור משמרתי ומשמרתך. פי' א"ל אני אשמור משמרתי בתחלת הלילה עד החק שאנו קבועים. ואשמור עוד ממך בחצי הלילה במשמרתך ועשו כך ונתבקש במשמרתו שבתחלת הלילה. שכל השומר בתחלת הלילה כשיעמוד אחר לשמור ישן מי שכבר שמר. ונמצא זה שומר שלא במשמרתו לפיכך נתבררה עליו העצה: אין הקב"ה מכה את ישראל עד שבורא להם רפואה שנאמר כרפאי לישראל וגו':

הגהות הב"ח

(א) גמ' אמר לה אי רמאי הוא אחיו אנא ברמאות: (ב) שם אמר שמואל לפיכך זכה ויצאת ממנו אסתר אסתר מאי היא דכתיב אין אסתר מגדת ואמר רבי אלעזר וכו' שנאמר לא יגרע מצדיק עיניו ויושיבם לנצח: (ג) רש"י ד"ה לא יגרע וכו' לשלם להן גמולן אף לימים: (ד) ד"ה הפיל פור וכו' הגורל על אחד הס"ד:

גליון הש"ס

גמ' שני טרסיים. עי' חולין דף נז ע"ב תד"ה מטלית:

עיין תוספות לקמן טז. ד"ה ודתי (וכו')

הגהות הגר"א

[א] גמ' (דכתיב) תז"

מסורת הש"ס

ב"ב קכג. ע"ש

ס"א וכי מטא הה יומא מעייל לה לגבך כ עשה יעקב מסר

[זבחים קב. ע"ש]

שם

[ילקוט וכע"י ליתא]

ברכות מח

[לעיל ז. ע"ש]

[ילקוט ליתא מאי אח

[קדושין לח. סוטה יב:]

שקלים ב. לקמן כט. מ"ו.

מָשָׁל דַּאֲחַשְׁוֵרוֹשׁ וְהָמָן כו'. כְּלוֹמַר יֵשׁ לִלְמוֹד מֵאֲחַשְׁוֵרוֹשׁ שֶׁאַף בְּדַעְתּוֹ הָיָה לְהַשְׁמִידָן: (*לְהַחֲזִירָן) לְמוּטָב. שֶׁגָּזְרוּ עֲלֵיהֶן תַּעֲנִיּוֹת לִתְשׁוּבָה, כִּדְכְתִיב "צוֹם וּבְכִי וּמִסְפֵּד שַׂק וָאֵפֶר יוּצַּע לָרַבִּים": חוּץ מִמִּקְרָא מְגִילָּה. וְאִם תֹּאמַר: נֵר חֲנוּכָּה? כְּבָר פָּסְקוּ הַנְּבִיאִים, אֲבָל בִּימֵי מָרְדְּכַי הָיוּ חַגַּי זְכַרְיָה וּמַלְאָכִי: מֵעַבְדוּת לְחֵירוּת. תורה אור בִּיצִיאַת מִצְרַיִם אָמְרוּ שִׁירָה עַל הַיָּם: הַלֵּל נַמִּי נֵימָא. שֶׁהִיא שִׁירָה: הָכִי גָּרְסִי': אָמַר רָבָא בִּשְׁלָמָא הָתָם כו' וְלֹא עַבְדֵי פַּרְעֹה. שֶׁהֲרֵי לְחֵירוּת יָצְאוּ: אַכַּתִּי עַבְדֵי אֲחַשְׁוֵרוֹשׁ אֲנַן. דְּלֹא נִגְאֲלוּ אֶלָּא מִן הַמִּיתָה: בֵּין לְרָבָא. דְּאָמַר לְהָכִי לֹא אָמְרֵי הַלֵּל דְּאַכַּתִּי עַבְדֵי אֲחַשְׁוֵרוֹשׁ הֲווּ, הָא לָאו הָכִי – אָמְרִינַן: בֵּין לְרַב נַחְמָן. דְּאָמַר קְרִיאַת מְגִילָּה בִּמְקוֹם הַלֵּל:(ד) הוּכְשְׁרוּ שְׁאָר אֲרָצוֹת לוֹמַר שִׁירָה. עַל נֵס הַמְאוֹרָע לָהֶם: וְתוּ לֵיכָּא. נְבִיאִים: נְבוּאָה שֶׁהוּצְרְכָה לְדוֹרוֹת. לִלְמוֹד תְּשׁוּבָה אוֹ הוֹרָאָה, וְכָל הָנָךְ מ"ח הוּצְרְכוּ. וּבַהֲלָכוֹת גְּדוֹלוֹת(ה) מְנוּיִין מִסֵּדֶר עוֹלָם[א]: אַבְרָהָם, יִצְחָק, יַעֲקֹב, מֹשֶׁה וְאַהֲרֹן, יְהוֹשֻׁעַ, פִּנְחָס – "וַיַּעַל מַלְאַךְ ה' מִן הַגִּלְגָּל אֶל הַבֹּכִים" (שופטים ב), זֶה פִּנְחָס. "וַיָּבֹא אִישׁ הָאֱלֹהִים אֶל עֵלִי" (שמואל א ב) – זֶה אֶלְקָנָה. עֵלִי, שְׁמוּאֵל, גָּד, נָתָן, דָּוִד, שְׁלֹמֹה, עִדּוֹ – קָרָא *אֶל הַמִּזְבֵּחַ בְּבֵית אֵל, מִיכָיְהוּ בֶּן יִמְלָה בִּימֵי אַחְאָב, עוֹבַדְיָה, אֲחִיָּה הַשִּׁילוֹנִי, יֵהוּא בֶּן חֲנָנִי בִּימֵי אָסָא, עֲזַרְיָה בֶּן עוֹדֵד, חֲזִיאֵל [הַלֵּוִי] מִבְּנֵי מַתַּנְיָה, אֱלִיעֶזֶר בֶּן דּוֹדוֹ מִמָּרֵשָׁה – כּוּלָּן בִּימֵי יְהוֹשָׁפָט, בְּדִבְרֵי הַיָּמִים (ב יט). וּבִימֵי יָרָבְעָם בֶּן יוֹאָשׁ – הוֹשֵׁעַ עָמוֹס, וּבִימֵי יוֹתָם – מִיכָה הַמּוֹרַשְׁתִּי, וּבִימֵי אֲמַצְיָה – אָמוֹץ, אָמוֹץ אָמַר לַאֲמַצְיָה "מַדּוּעַ דָּרַשְׁתָּ אֱלֹהֵי אֱדוֹם". וְאֵלִיָּהוּ, וֶאֱלִישָׁע, וְיוֹנָה בֶּן אֲמִתַּי, יְשַׁעְיָה. בִּימֵי מְנַשֶּׁה – יוֹאֵל, נַחוּם, חֲבַקּוּק. בִּימֵי יֹאשִׁיָּה – צְפַנְיָה, אוּרִיָּה מִקִּרְיַת יְעָרִים, יִרְמְיָה. בַּגּוֹלָה – יְחֶזְקֵאל, דָּנִיֵּאל. בִּשְׁנַת ב' לְדָרְיָוֶשׁ – בָּרוּךְ, נֵרִיָּה, שְׂרָיָה, מַחְסֵיָה, חַגַּי, זְכַרְיָה, מַלְאָכִי, וּמָרְדְּכַי בִּלְשָׁן. בְּסֵדֶר עוֹלָם. וְעַל דָּנִיֵּאל אָמְרִינַן לְעֵיל (דף ג.) אִינְהוּ נְבִיאֵי וְאִיהוּ לָאו נָבִיא, אֶלָּא אַפֵּיק דָּנִיֵּאל וְעַיֵּיל שְׁמַעְיָה שֶׁאָמַר לִרְחַבְעָם אַל תַּעֲלוּ וְאַל תִּלָּחֲמוּ עִם אֲחֵיכֶם בְּנֵי יִשְׂרָאֵל. *שְׁנַיִם לֹא יָדַעְתִּי[ב]: נִתְבַּצֵּר לָהֶם. לְשׁוֹן גָּבוֹהַּ, כְּמוֹ "וּבְצוּרוֹת בַּשָּׁמַיִם" (דברים ט): כְּשֶׁהִיא אֲחוֹת אַהֲרֹן. וַעֲדַיִין לֹא נוֹלַד מֹשֶׁה: פְּתִילוֹת לַמִּקְדָּשׁ. (ו) מִשְׁכַּן שִׁילֹה: מִשּׁוּם יִחוּד. שֶׁהוּא גָּבוֹהַּ, וְאֵין לוֹ צֵל, וְאֵין אָדָם יָכוֹל לְהִתְיַיחֵד שָׁם עִמָּהּ כְּמוֹ בַּבַּיִת: לֵב אֶחָד. שָׂרָף יֵשׁ לוֹ כְּמוֹ אִילָן, אֲבָל אֵין לוֹ בַּעֲנָפָיו אֶלָּא בְּגִזְעוֹ עַל פְּנֵי כָּל גּוֹבְהוֹ: רָמָה קַרְנִי וְלֹא רָמָה פַּכִּי. זוֹ הִיא נְבוּאָתָהּ, שֶׁנִּתְנַבְּאִית עַל שָׁאוּל וְיֵהוּא שֶׁלֹּא תִּימָּשֵׁךְ מַלְכוּתָן. בִּמְשִׁיחַת דָּוִד וּשְׁלֹמֹה כְּתִיב קֶרֶן הַשֶּׁמֶן, וּבִמְשִׁיחַת שָׁאוּל וְיֵהוּא כְּתִיב פַּךְ: וְכִי רוֹאִין דָּם בַּלַּיְלָה. שֶׁנֶּאֱמַר (שמואל א כה) "אִם אַשְׁאִיר לְנָבָל עַד אוֹר הַבֹּקֶר מַשְׁתִּין בְּקִיר", שְׁמַע מִינָּהּ דַּהֲוָה בַּלַּיְלָה, וְכִי מַרְאִין דָּם בַּלַּיְלָה אִם טָמֵא אוֹ טָהוֹר? הֲלֹא צָרִיךְ לְהַבְחִין מַרְאִיתוֹ, אִם מֵה' דָּמִים הַטְּמֵאִים בָּאִשָּׁה הוּא: וְכִי דָּנִין דִּינֵי נְפָשׁוֹת בַּלַּיְלָה. וְהָא כְּתִיב (ירמיה כא) "דִּינוּ לַבֹּקֶר מִשְׁפָּט", וּכְתִיב "וְהוֹקַע אוֹתָם לַה' ב)נֶגֶד הַשָּׁמֶשׁ" (במדבר כה): כְּלִיתַנִי

מָשָׁל דַּאֲחַשְׁוֵרוֹשׁ וְהָמָן לְמָה הַדָּבָר דּוֹמֶה? לִשְׁנֵי בְנֵי אָדָם, לְאֶחָד הָיָה לוֹ תֵּל בְּתוֹךְ שָׂדֵהוּ וּלְאֶחָד הָיָה לוֹ חָרִיץ בְּתוֹךְ שָׂדֵהוּ. בַּעַל חָרִיץ אָמַר: מִי יִתֵּן לִי תֵּל זֶה בְּדָמִים! בַּעַל הַתֵּל אָמַר: מִי יִתֵּן לִי חָרִיץ זֶה בְּדָמִים! לְיָמִים נִזְדַּוְּוגוּ זֶה אֵצֶל זֶה. אָמַר לוֹ בַּעַל חָרִיץ לְבַעַל הַתֵּל: מְכוֹר לִי תִּילְּךָ! אָמַר לוֹ: טוֹל אוֹתָהּ בְּחִנָּם, וְהַלְוַאי! "וַיָּסַר הַמֶּלֶךְ אֶת טַבַּעְתּוֹ". אָמַר רַבִּי אַבָּא בַּר כָּהֲנָא: גְּדוֹלָה הֲסָרַת טַבַּעַת יוֹתֵר מֵאַרְבָּעִים וּשְׁמוֹנָה נְבִיאִים וְשֶׁבַע נְבִיאוֹת שֶׁנִּתְנַבְּאוּ לָהֶן לְיִשְׂרָאֵל, שֶׁכּוּלָּן לֹא הֶחֱזִירוּם לְמוּטָב, וְאִילּוּ הֲסָרַת טַבַּעַת הֶחֱזִירָתָן לְמוּטָב. ת"ר: אַרְבָּעִים וּשְׁמוֹנָה נְבִיאִים וְשֶׁבַע נְבִיאוֹת נִתְנַבְּאוּ לָהֶם לְיִשְׂרָאֵל, וְלֹא פָּחֲתוּ וְלֹא הוֹתִירוּ עַל מַה שֶּׁכָּתוּב בַּתּוֹרָה חוּץ מִמִּקְרָא מְגִילָּה. מַאי דְּרוּשׁ? אָמַר רַבִּי חִיָּיא בַּר אָבִין אָמַר רַבִּי יְהוֹשֻׁעַ בֶּן קָרְחָה:(א) וּמָה מֵעַבְדוּת לְחֵירוּת אָמְרִי' שִׁירָה – מִמִּיתָה לְחַיִּים לֹא כׇּל שֶׁכֵּן?! אִי הָכִי הַלֵּל נַמִּי נֵימָא!(ב) *לְפִי *שֶׁאֵין אוֹמְרִים הַלֵּל עַל נֵס שֶׁבְּחוּצָה לָאָרֶץ. יְצִיאַת מִצְרַיִם דְּנֵס שֶׁבְּחוּצָה לָאָרֶץ, הֵיכִי אָמְרִינַן שִׁירָה? כִּדְתַנְיָא: עַד שֶׁלֹּא נִכְנְסוּ יִשְׂרָאֵל לָאָרֶץ הוּכְשְׁרוּ כׇּל אֲרָצוֹת לוֹמַר שִׁירָה. מִשֶּׁנִּכְנְסוּ יִשְׂרָאֵל לָאָרֶץ, לֹא הוּכְשְׁרוּ כׇּל הָאֲרָצוֹת לוֹמַר שִׁירָה. רַב נַחְמָן אָמַר: *קְרִיָּיתָא זוֹ הַלֵּילָא. א)(ג) רָבָא אָמַר: בִּשְׁלָמָא הָתָם °"הַלְלוּ עַבְדֵי ה'" – וְלֹא עַבְדֵי פַרְעֹה, אֶלָּא הָכָא – "הַלְלוּ עַבְדֵי ה'" וְלֹא עַבְדֵי אֲחַשְׁוֵרוֹשׁ? אַכַּתִּי עַבְדֵי אֲחַשְׁוֵרוֹשׁ אֲנַן. *בֵּין לְרָבָא בֵּין לְר"נ קַשְׁיָא: וְהָא תַּנְיָא: מִשֶּׁנִּכְנְסוּ לָאָרֶץ לֹא הוּכְשְׁרוּ כׇּל הָאֲרָצוֹת לוֹמַר שִׁירָה! כֵּיוָן שֶׁגָּלוּ – חָזְרוּ לְהֶכְשֵׁירָן הָרִאשׁוֹן. וְתוּ לֵיכָּא? וְהָכְתִיב: °"וַיְהִי אִישׁ אֶחָד מִן הָרָמָתַיִם צוֹפִים" – אֶחָד מִמָּאתַיִם צוֹפִים שֶׁנִּתְנַבְּאוּ לָהֶם לְיִשְׂרָאֵל! מִיהְוָה טוּבָא הֲווּ, כִּדְתַנְיָא: הַרְבֵּה נְבִיאִים עָמְדוּ לָהֶם לְיִשְׂרָאֵל, כִּפְלַיִם כְּיוֹצְאֵי מִצְרַיִם. אֶלָּא נְבוּאָה שֶׁהוּצְרְכָה לְדוֹרוֹת – נִכְתְּבָה, וְשֶׁלֹּא הוּצְרְכָה – לֹא נִכְתְּבָה. רַבִּי שְׁמוּאֵל בַּר נַחְמָנִי אָמַר: אָדָם הַבָּא מִשְּׁתֵּי רָמוֹת שֶׁצּוֹפוֹת זוֹ אֶת זוֹ. רַבִּי חָנִין אָמַר: אָדָם הַבָּא מִבְּנֵי אָדָם שֶׁעוֹמְדִין בְּרוּמוֹ שֶׁל עוֹלָם. וּמַאן נִינְהוּ? בְּנֵי קֹרַח, דִּכְתִיב: °"וּבְנֵי קֹרַח לֹא מֵתוּ". *תָּנָא מִשּׁוּם רַבֵּינוּ: מָקוֹם נִתְבַּצֵּר לָהֶם בְּגֵיהִנָּם, וְעָמְדוּ עָלָיו. שֶׁבַע נְבִיאוֹת מַאן נִינְהוּ? שָׂרָה, מִרְיָם, דְּבוֹרָה, חַנָּה, אֲבִיגַיִל, חוּלְדָּה וְאֶסְתֵּר. שָׂרָה – דִּכְתִיב: °"אֲבִי מִלְכָּה וַאֲבִי יִסְכָּה", *וְאָמַר ר' יִצְחָק: "יִסְכָּה" זוֹ שָׂרָה. וְלָמָּה נִקְרָא שְׁמָהּ "יִסְכָּה"? שֶׁסָּכְתָה בְּרוּחַ הַקֹּדֶשׁ, שֶׁנֶּאֱמַר: °"כֹּל אֲשֶׁר תֹּאמַר אֵלֶיךָ שָׂרָה שְׁמַע בְּקֹלָהּ". ד"א: "יִסְכָּה" שֶׁהַכֹּל סוֹכִין בְּיוֹפְיָהּ. מִרְיָם – דִּכְתִיב: °"וַתִּקַּח מִרְיָם הַנְּבִיאָה אֲחוֹת *)אַהֲרֹן", **)וְלֹא אֲחוֹת מֹשֶׁה? אָמַר ר"נ אָמַר רַב: שֶׁהָיְתָה מִתְנַבְּאָה כְּשֶׁהִיא אֲחוֹת אַהֲרֹן, וְאוֹמֶרֶת: עֲתִידָה אִמִּי שֶׁתֵּלֵד בֵּן שֶׁיּוֹשִׁיעַ אֶת יִשְׂרָאֵל. וּבְשָׁעָה שֶׁנּוֹלַד נִתְמַלֵּא כׇּל הַבַּיִת כּוּלּוֹ אוֹרָה. עָמַד אָבִיהָ וּנְשָׁקָהּ עַל רֹאשָׁהּ, אָמַר לָהּ: בִּתִּי, נִתְקַיְּימָה נְבוּאָתֵיךְ! וְכֵיוָן שֶׁהִשְׁלִיכוּהוּ לַיְאוֹר – עָמַד אָבִיהָ וּטְפָחָהּ עַל רֹאשָׁהּ וְאָמַר לָהּ: בִּתִּי, הֵיכָן נְבוּאָתֵיךְ? הַיְינוּ דִּכְתִיב: °"וַתֵּתַצַּב אֲחֹתוֹ מֵרָחוֹק לְדֵעָה" – לָדַעַת מַה יְּהֵא בְּסוֹף נְבוּאָתָהּ. דְּבוֹרָה – דִּכְתִיב: °"וּדְבוֹרָה אִשָּׁה נְבִיאָה אֵשֶׁת לַפִּידוֹת". מַאי "אֵשֶׁת לַפִּידוֹת"? שֶׁהָיְתָה עוֹשָׂה פְּתִילוֹת *לַמִּקְדָּשׁ. °"וְהִיא יוֹשֶׁבֶת תַּחַת תּוֹמֶר". מַאי שְׁנָא "תַּחַת תּוֹמֶר"? אָמַר ר' שִׁמְעוֹן בֶּן *אַבְשָׁלוֹם: מִשּׁוּם יִחוּד. דָּבָר אַחֵר: *מַה תָּמָר זֶה אֵין לוֹ אֶלָּא לֵב אֶחָד – אַף יִשְׂרָאֵל שֶׁבְּאוֹתוֹ הַדּוֹר לֹא הָיָה לָהֶם אֶלָּא לֵב אֶחָד לַאֲבִיהֶן שֶׁבַּשָּׁמַיִם. חַנָּה – דִּכְתִיב: °"וַתִּתְפַּלֵּל חַנָּה וַתֹּאמַר עָלַץ לִבִּי בַּה' רָמָה קַרְנִי בַּה'". *"רָמָה קַרְנִי" וְלֹא רָמָה פַּכִּי. דָּוִד וּשְׁלֹמֹה שֶׁנִּמְשְׁחוּ בְּקֶרֶן – נִמְשְׁכָה מַלְכוּתָן; שָׁאוּל וְיֵהוּא שֶׁנִּמְשְׁחוּ בְּפַךְ – לֹא נִמְשְׁכָה מַלְכוּתָן. °"אֵין קָדוֹשׁ כַּה' כִּי אֵין בִּלְתֶּךָ". *אָמַר רַב יְהוּדָה בַּר מְנַשְּׁיָא: אַל תִּקְרֵי "בִּלְתֶּךָ" אֶלָּא "לְבַלּוֹתֶךָ". שֶׁלֹּא כְּמִדַּת הקב"ה מִדַּת בָּשָׂר וָדָם. מִדַּת בָּשָׂר וָדָם – מַעֲשֵׂה יָדָיו מְבַלִּין אוֹתוֹ. אֲבָל הַקָּדוֹשׁ בָּרוּךְ הוּא – מְבַלֶּה מַעֲשֵׂה יָדָיו. °"וְאֵין צוּר כֵּאלֹהֵינוּ" – *אֵין צַיָּיר כֵּאלֹהֵינוּ. אָדָם צָר צוּרָה עַל גַּבֵּי הַכּוֹתֶל וְאֵינוֹ יָכוֹל לְהַטִּיל בָּהּ רוּחַ וּנְשָׁמָה, קְרָבִים וּבְנֵי מֵעַיִם. אֲבָל הקב"ה צָר צוּרָה בְּתוֹךְ צוּרָה וּמַטִּיל בָּהּ רוּחַ וּנְשָׁמָה, קְרָבַיִם וּבְנֵי מֵעַיִם. אֲבִיגַיִל – דִּכְתִיב: °"וְהָיָה הִיא רוֹכֶבֶת עַל הַחֲמוֹר וְיוֹרֶדֶת בְּסֵתֶר הָהָר". "בְּסֵתֶר הָהָר"? "מִן הָהָר" מִיבְּעֵי לֵיהּ! אָמַר רַבָּה בַּר שְׁמוּאֵל: עַל עִסְקֵי דָּם הַבָּא מִן הַסְּתָרִים. נָטְלָה דָּם וְהֶרְאֲתָה לוֹ. אָמַר לָהּ: וְכִי מַרְאִין דָּם בַּלַּיְלָה? אָמְרָה לוֹ: וְכִי דָּנִין דִּינֵי נְפָשׁוֹת בַּלַּיְלָה? אָמַר לָהּ:

א) גי' רי"ף ורא"ש מתקיף לה רבא מי דמי בשלמא. ב) נגד השמש ודוד אמר אם אשאיר לנבל מכל אשר לו עד אור הבקר.

רבינו חננאל

ת"ר מ"ח נביאים וז' נביאות לא פחתו ולא הותירו על מה שכתוב בתורה אפי' אות אחת חוץ ממקרא מגילה. ואלו הן מ"ח נביאים. משה. ואהרן. ואסיר. ואלקנה. ואביאסף בני קרח נתנבאו במדבר. יהושע פינחס. אלקנה. גד החוזה. נתן הנביא. אסף.

וחנניה לא ידעתי א' עודד הנביא ד"ה ב ט"ו לפי פי' רד"ק ואחד חנני הרואה ד"ה ב ט"ז שהתנבא על אסא ולפי פשוטו כשמזכיר הנביא בשמו ושם אביו בנבואה בידוע שהוא נביא בן נביא וא"כ עזריה בן עודד ויהוא בן חנני נחשבים לנביאים המה ואביהם גם יש לחשוב זכריה בן יהוידע הכהן ד"ה ב כ"ד גם עודד הנביא שהתנבא בימי פקח בן רמליהו דה"ב כ"ח

משום יחוד. כשבאין אליה בני ישראל למשפט: **דכתיב** ותתפלל חנה ותאמר עלץ לבי בה'. וה"נ הוה מצי לאתויי כל הפרשה, שכל הנבואה על סנחריב נבוכדנצר והמן, כמו שתרגם יונתן. אלא קרא דריש פרשתא נקט: מורד

מורד

הגהות הב"ח

(א) גמ' אמר ר' יהושע בן קרחה קל וחומר ומה מעבדות לחירות: (ב) שם הלל נמי נימא אמר ר' יצחק לפי שאין וכו' שבחוצה לארץ והרי יציאת מצרים דנס שבחוצה לארץ ואמרי' הלילא התם כדתניא עד כו"ל: (ג) שם קרייתא זו הלילא מתקיף לה רבא מי דמי בשלמא התם: (ד) רש"י ד"ה בין לר' נחמן וכו' הלל הס"ד ואח"כ מ"ה לא הוכשרו: (ה) ד"ה נבואה וכו' ובהלכות גדולות הן מנויין ורובן יש ללמוד מסדר עולם וכו' קרא על המזבח וכו' בימי יאשיה צפניה וירמיה ואוריה מקרית יערים ליהויקים בגולה יחזקאל דניאל: (ו) ד"ה פתילות למקדש. למשכן שילה בשעה שבני אדם באין ליטול עצה ממנה יושבת תחת תומר שלא תשב עמהם בסתר משום יחוד שהוא גבוה ואין לו צל ואין אדם יכול להתייחד שם עמה כמו בבית ותחת שאר אילנות יש צל שיש להם ענפים סמוך לעיקרן הס"ד:

הגהות הגר"א

[א] רש"י ד"ה נבואה כו' אברהם כו'. נ"ב אבל בסדר עולם לא חשיב אברהם יצחק ויעקב משה ואהרן עלי שלמה נריה מחסיה וחשיב במקומם ג' בני קרח אסף והימן ואיתן וידותן וזכריהו הכהן אל כי לא חשיב במ"ח נביאים רק אחר מות משה אף שבנביאות חשיב כי לא היו רק ז' וכן נריה ומחסיה לא נכתבו נבואתן ולא נקראו נביאים וכן עלי ושלמה וע"ל ט"ו ברוך בן נריה כו': [ב] שם בסה"ד שנים לא ידעתי. נ"ב והם חנני ועודד:

מסורת הש"ס

[נ"ל להחזירתן]

הנבואת יעדי החוזה ד"ה ב ט ולאפשר עידו זה הנזכר בד"ה ב יב היינו יעדי

ערכין י: ע"ש

תהלים קיג

[ערכין י: ע"ש היטב]

שמואל א א

במדבר כו

סנהדרין קי.

בראשית יא

סנהדרין סט:

בראשית כא

שמות טו

*) [סוטה יב: ע"ש]

**) [נ"ל וגו' אחות אהרון ולא וכו']

שמות ב

שופטים ד

שם

[למשכן וכן איתא בילקוט]

[סוכה מה:]

אבי שלום ועי' תוס' ב"ח: ד"ה דלא ותוס' כתובות קד: ד"ה שני

שמואל א ב

כריתות ו. הוריות יב.

ברכות י.

שם

ברכות י. ע"ש

שמואל א כה

עין משפט נר מצוה

עא א מיי' פ"ג מהל' מלכים הלכה ח סמג עשין נו:

רבינו חננאל

הימן. ידותון. שמואל. דוד. *) אחיה. שמעיה. עידו. עזריה בן עודד. חנני הרואה. יהוא בן חנני. אליהו. מיכיהו. עובדיהו. אלישע. (יחזקאל). אליעזר בן דודיהו. יונה בן [אמתי] זכריה בן יהודע. אמוץ. חבקוק. צפניהו בן כושי. ירמיה. ישעיה. יחזקאל. דניאל. ברוך בן נריה. עזריה בן מחסיה. מרדכי בלשן. הושע בן בארי. עמוס. מיכה המורשתי. יואל בן פתואל. נחום. חגי. זכריה. ומלאכי. ז' נביאות שרה. מרים. דבורה. חולדה. חנה. אביגיל. ואסתר:

*) אולי צ"ל כאן שלמה.

תוספות

מורד במלכות הוא ולא צריך למידייניה. קשה: א"כ היאך גרס פרק "אחד דיני ממונות" (סנהדרין דף לו. ושם) דדיני נפשות מתחילין מן הצד, מדכתיב גבי נבל "ויחגרו איש חרבו ויחגור גם דוד חרבו" (ש"א כה), והא מורד במלכות הוה ולא בעי למידייניה! ועוד קשה: היאך ישב דוד בדין, והא אין מושיבין מלך בסנהדרין, כדאמרינן במסכת סנהדרין פרק "כ"ג"! (דף יח:) וע"ק מפ' "במה בהמה יוצאה" (שבת דף נו.) גבי אוריה, דקאמר: שהיה לו לדונו בסנהדרין, ואמאי? והא מורד במלכות היה! וי"ל: דהכא ה"פ: מורד במלכות הוא ולא צריך למידייניה כשאר דיני נפשות, שדנין בו ביום לזכות וביום שלאחריו לחובה, אלא אפילו בו ביום גומרין לחובה. והיינו הא דקאמרה ליה אביגיל: וכי דנין דיני נפשות בלילה, היה לך להמתין לגמור עד למחרת. והוא השיב לה: מורד במלכות הוה ואין צריך להמתין עד למחר. אבל לדונו ודאי צריך. וגם לא קשה מהא שישב דוד בסנהדרין, דהא דאין מושיבין מלך בסנהדרין, היינו משום דלא הוי כבודו להיות יושב ושותק, אבל גבי מורד כבודו הוא להיות יושב ושותק, לפי שהוא נוגע בדבר:

ה"ג: מאי מבוא בדמים תרי דמים דם נדה ושפיכות דמים מלמד שגלתה שוקה. ולא גרסינן: איכא דאמרי מלמד שגלתה שוקה. דהא השתא מפרש מאי תרי דמים, ועד השתא לא פריש להו:

שגלתה שוקה והלך דוד לאורה ג' פרסאות. קשה: היאך אותה לדיקת גלתה שוקה לפני דוד? ועוד קשה: דמחזי כגוזמא לומר שהלך לאור שוקה ג' פרסאות! וי"ל: דנמצא בספרים מדויקים שנקוד בהן לאורה, כלומר לאור שלה, פירוש: נתאוה לה דוד והלך באור חמימות שלש פרסאות:

דאיגיירה ונסבה יהושע. קשיא: היאך נסבה? הא אמרי' פ' "הערל" (יבמות דף עו. ושם) דאפילו בגירותן *לית להו חתנות! וצריך לומר שלא היתה משבעה עממין, אלא משאר עממין ובאת לגור שם. *ויש מפרשים: שרצו לומר שלא הוזהרו על לאו ד"לא תתחתן" עד לאחר שנכנסו לארץ. וזה אינו: דאמרי' במדרש דנתינים באו להתגייר בימי משה כמו בימי יהושע, ואף על פי כן לא הותרו לבא בקהל, אלא היו חוטבי עצים ושואבי מים. אלמא דקודם שעברו את הירדן ונכנסו לארץ הוזהרו עליהם*:

ארבע

גמרא

אמורד במלכות הוא, ולא צריך למידייניה. אמרה לו: עדיין שאול קיים, ולא יצא טבעך בעולם. אמר לה: °"ברוך טעמך וברוכה את אשר כליתני [היום הזה] מבא בדמים". "דמים" תרתי משמע! [א]אלא מלמד שגילתה את שוקה, והלך לאורה ג' פרסאות. אמר לה: השמיעי לי! אמרה לו: °"לא תהיה זאת לך לפוקה", "זאת" — מכלל דאיכא אחריתי. ומאי ניהו? מעשה דבת שבע. ומסקנא הכי הואי. °"והיתה נפש אדוני צרורה בצרור החיים". כי הוות מיפטרא מיניה אמרה ליה: °"והטיב ה' לאדוני וזכרת את אמתך". אמר רב נחמן: היינו דאמרי אינשי: איתתא בהדי שותא פילכא. איכא דאמרי: *שפיל ואזיל בר אווזא ועינוהי מיטייפי. חולדה — דכתיב: °"וילך חלקיהו הכהן ואחיקם ועכבור" וגו'. ובמקום דקאי ירמיה היכי מתנביא איהי? אמרי בי רב משמיה דרב: חולדה קרובת ירמיה היתה, ולא הוה מקפיד עליה. ויאשיה גופיה היכי שביק ירמיה ומשדר לגבה? אמרי דבי רבי שילא: מפני שהנשים רחמניות הן. ר' יוחנן אמר: ירמיה לא הוה התם, *שהלך להחזיר עשרת השבטים. *ומנלן דאהדור? דכתיב: °"כי המוכר אל הממכר לא ישוב". אפשר יובל בטל, ונביא מתנבא עליו שיבטל? אלא מלמד שירמיה החזירן, ויאשיהו בן אמון מלך עליהן, דכתיב: °"ויאמר מה הציון הלז אשר אני רואה? ויאמרו אליו אנשי העיר: הקבר איש האלהים אשר בא מיהודה ויקרא את הדברים האלה אשר עשית על המזבח בבית אל". וכי מה טיבו של יאשיהו על המזבח בבית אל? אלא מלמד שיאשיהו מלך עליהן. רב נחמן אמר: מהכא: °"גם יהודה שת קציר לך בשובי שבות עמי". אסתר — דכתיב: °"ויהי ביום השלישי ותלבש אסתר מלכות". *"בגדי מלכות" מיבעי ליה! אלא: שלבשתה רוח הקדש. כתיב הכא: "ותלבש", וכתיב התם: °"ורוח לבשה את עמשי" וגו'. אמר רב נחמן: לא יאה יהירותא לנשי. תרתי נשי(א) יהירן הויין, וסניין שמייהו. חדא שמה זיבורתא, וחדא שמה כרכושתא. זיבורתא — כתיב בה: °"ותשלח ותקרא לברק", ואילו איהי לא אזלה לגביה. כרכושתא כתיב בה: °"אמרו לאיש", ולא אמרה "אמרו למלך". אמר רב נחמן: חולדה(ב) מבני בניו של יהושע היתה. כתיב הכא: °"בן חרחס", וכתיב התם: *°"בתמנת חרס". איתיביה רב עינא סבא לרב נחמן: שמונה נביאים והם כהנים יצאו מרחב הזונה. ואלו הן: נריה ברוך, ושריה, מחסיה ירמיה חלקיה, חנמאל ושלום. רבי יהודה אומר: אף חולדה הנביאה מבני בניה של רחב הזונה היתה. כתיב הכא: "בן תקוה", וכתיב התם: °"את תקות חוט השני". אמר ליה: *עינא סבא! ואמרי לה *פתיא אוכמא! מיני ומינך תסתיים שמעתא. דאיגיירא ונסבה יהושע. ומי הוו ליה זרעא ליהושע? והכתיב: °"נון בנו יהושע בנו"! בני — לא הוו ליה; בנתן — הוו ליה. בשלמא

תורה אור: שמואל א כה · שם · שם · שם · מלכים ב כב · יחזקאל ז · מ"ב כג · הושע ו · אסתר ה · דה"א יב · שופטים ד · מלכים ב כב · מלכים ב כב · יהושע כד · יהושע ב · דה"א ז

רש"י

כליתני. מנעת אותי: בדמים. דם נדה ושפיכות דמים: שגילתה שוקה. ונתאוה לה, ותבעה ולא שמעה לו, כדמסיים ואזיל: לפוקה. (ג) כמו "פיק ברכים" (נחום ב): הכי גרסי': זאת מכלל דאיכא אחריתי ומאי ניהו מעשה דבת שבע ומסקנא הכי הוה. והכי פירושה: מדקאמרה ליה "ולא תהיה זאת לך לפוקה", מכלל שהתנבאתה לו שסופו להכשל בביאה אחרת, ומאי ניהו — בת שבע. ומסקנא הכי הוה — סוף שעלתה לו כך. אלמא נביאה הוות, שנתקיימה נבואתה: בהדי שותא פילכא. עם שהאשה מדברת היא טווה. כלומר, עם שהיא מדברת עמו על בעלה — הזכירה לו את עצמה, שאם ימות(ד) ישאנה: מיטייפי. צופין למרחוק. ודוגמתו במס' כתובות (דף ס.): נטוף עיניך: ובמקום ירמיה היכי מיתנביא היא. הרי ירמיה עמד משנת י"ג ליאשיה, שנאמר "אשר היה דבר ה' אל ירמיה" וגו' (ירמיה א), והספר נמצא בשנת י"ח ליאשיה, ועליו שלח אל חולדה: כי המוכר אל הממכר לא ישוב. יחזקאל אמרו, והוא נתנבא בתוך (*י"ד) שנה שבין גלות יכניה לחרבות ירושלים, ומתנבא שיהא בטל היובל והמוכר שדהו לא ישוב לו: אפשר יובל בטל. משגלו עשרת השבטים בימי חזקיה, שנאמר "לכל יושביה" (ויקרא כה) — בזמן שכל יושביה עליה, ולא בזמן שגלו מקצתן. נמצא משגלו שבט ראובן וגד וחצי שבט מנשה [כבר] בטלו היובלות, ויחזקאל היה מתנבא לאחר זמן שיבטל? אלא מלמד שירמיה החזירן. בשנה שנמצא הספר, והיא שנת שמונה עשרה ליאשיהו. וכששלח על דברי הספר אל חולדה לא היה שם ירמיה(ה), וחזרו למנות את היובל, ולא הספיקו למנות אלא שמיטות עד שחרב הבית: ויאמר מה הציון הלז. ביאשיהו כתיב, בהיותו בבית אל, ושרף עצמות הכומרים בבית אל על המזבח שעשה ירבעם: מה טיבו בבית אל. והלא (*משל) מלכי ישראל *היה, שהרי שם העמיד ירבעם את העגל: שת קציר. עשה חיל וגדולה, כמו(ו) *"ועשה קציר כמו נטע" (איוב יד): לא נאה יוהרא לנשי. לא נאה חשיבות לנשים: וסניין שמייהו. שמותיהן מאוסות: זיבורתא. דבורה: כרכושתא. חולדה: בן חרחס. ואע"ג דקרא על בעלה קא מסהיד, מיהו במעשיה כתיב: אמר ליה עינא סבא מיני ומינך תסתיים שמעתא. כלומר, על ידי ועל ידך תתפרש אמיתו של דבר, הא והא הואי: נון בנו יהושע בנו. את שבט אפרים מייחס הכתוב עד יהושע, ומיהושע ולמטה לא ייחס איש:

מסורת הש"ס

ב"ק נב:

[צ"ל י"א]

[עי' רש"י במשנה סנהד קי. ד"ה עשרת וכו']

[צ"ל של]

צ"ל היתה

[לקמן טו. ע"ש]

[עי' פרש"י בערכין]

[עי' ב"ב קכב:]

[ברכות נ. ע"ש פר פסחים פח. ע"ש טז: פרש"י]

[פי' דאסורין בלאו דלא תתחתן אף לאחר שנתגיירו]

[ועי' תוס' סוטה לה: ד"ה לרבות]

[ועי' תוס' גיטין מו. ד"ה כיון]

מלכים ב כב

[פסחים פח.]

דה"א ז

הגהות הגר"א

[א] גמ' (אלא מ' שגילתה א"ש וה"ל ג"פ השמיעי לי אמרה תא"מ:

הגהות הב"ח

(א) גמ' תרתי נשי נביאתא יהירין הווין: (ב) שם אמר רב נחמן חולדה הנביאה מבני: (ג) רש"י ד"ה לפוקה לשון כשלון ברכים כמו ופיק ברכים: (ד) ד"ה בהדי שותא וכו' שאם ימות נבל ישאנה: (ה) ד"ה אלא מלמד וכו' לא היה שם ירמיה ויאשיהו המלך מלך עליהם וחזרו למנות וכו' אלא חמש שמיטות: (ו) ד"ה שת קציר וכו' וגדולה כמו תשלח ועשה קציר:

גליון הש"ס

רש"י ד"ה בהדי כו' שהאשה מדברת. עיין סוכה דף נו ע"ב רש"י ד"ה שותא:

בִּשְׁלָמָא אִינְהוּ — מִיפְּרְשִׁי. אֶלָּא אֲבְהָתַיְיהוּ
מְנָלַן? כִּדְעוּלָּא. דְּאָמַר עוּלָּא: כָּל מָקוֹם ששְּׁמוֹ
וְשֵׁם אָבִיו בִּנְבִיאוּת — בְּיָדוּעַ שֶׁהוּא נָבִיא בֶּן
נָבִיא; שְׁמוֹ וְלֹא שֵׁם אָבִיו — בְּיָדוּעַ שֶׁהוּא נָבִיא
וְלֹא בֶּן נָבִיא; שְׁמוֹ וְשֵׁם עִירוֹ מְפוֹרָשׁ — בְּיָדוּעַ
שֶׁהוּא (א) מֵאוֹתָהּ הָעִיר, שְׁמוֹ וְלֹא שֵׁם עִירוֹ
— בְּיָדוּעַ שֶׁהוּא מִירוּשָׁלַיִם. בְּמַתְנִיתָא תָּנָא: כָּל שֶׁמַּעֲשָׂיו (ב) וּמַעֲשֵׂה אֲבוֹתָיו
צפניה א סְתוּמִין, וּפֵרֵט לְךָ הַכָּתוּב בְּאֶחָד מֵהֶן לְשֶׁבַח, כְּגוֹן °"דְּבַר ה' אֲשֶׁר הָיָה אֶל
צְפַנְיָה בֶּן כּוּשִׁי בֶּן גְּדַלְיָה" — בְּיָדוּעַ שֶׁהוּא צַדִּיק בֶּן צַדִּיק. וְכָל שֶׁפֵּרֵט לְךָ
ירמיה מא הַכָּתוּב בְּאֶחָד מֵהֶן לִגְנַאי, כְּגוֹן: °"וַיְהִי בַּחֹדֶשׁ הַשְּׁבִיעִי בָּא יִשְׁמָעֵאל בֶּן נְתַנְיָה
בֶּן אֱלִישָׁמָע" — בְּיָדוּעַ שֶׁהוּא רָשָׁע בֶּן רָשָׁע. *אָמַר רַב נַחְמָן: מַלְאָכִי זֶה מָרְדֳּכַי.
וְלָמָּה נִקְרָא שְׁמוֹ מַלְאָכִי? שֶׁהָיָה מִשְׁנֶה לַמֶּלֶךְ. מֵיתִיבִי: בָּרוּךְ בֶּן נֵרִיָּה
וּשְׂרָיָה בֶּן[א] מַעֲשֵׂיָה, וְדָנִיֵּאל, וּמָרְדֳּכַי בִּלְשָׁן, וְחַגַּי, זְכַרְיָה וּמַלְאָכִי — כּוּלָּן
נִתְנַבְּאוּ בִּשְׁנַת שְׁתַּיִם לְדָרְיָוֶשׁ! תְּיוּבְתָּא. תַּנְיָא, אָמַר רַבִּי יְהוֹשֻׁעַ בֶּן קָרְחָה:
מַלְאָכִי זֶה עֶזְרָא. וְחכ"א: מַלְאָכִי שְׁמוֹ. אָמַר רַב *נַחְמָן: מִסְתַּבְּרָא כְּמַאן
מלאכי ב דְּאָמַר: מַלְאָכִי זֶה עֶזְרָא, דִּכְתִיב בִּנְבִיאוּת מַלְאָכִי: °"בָּגְדָה יְהוּדָה וְתוֹעֵבָה
נֶעֶשְׂתָה בְיִשְׂרָאֵל וּבִירוּשָׁלָםִ כִּי חִלֵּל יְהוּדָה קֹדֶשׁ ה' אֲשֶׁר אָהֵב וּבָעַל בַּת אֵל
עזרא י נֵכָר". וּמַאן אַפְרֵישׁ נָשִׁים גּוֹיוֹת? עֶזְרָא, דִּכְתִיב: °"וַיַּעַן שְׁכַנְיָה בֶן יְחִיאֵל מִבְּנֵי
עֵילָם וַיֹּאמֶר לְעֶזְרָא: אֲנַחְנוּ מָעַלְנוּ בֵאלֹהֵינוּ וַנֹּשֶׁב נָשִׁים נָכְרִיּוֹת". תָּנוּ רַבָּנַן:
אַרְבַּע נָשִׁים יְפֵיפִיּוֹת הָיוּ בָּעוֹלָם: שָׂרָה (*וַאֲבִיגַיִל, רָחָב) וְאֶסְתֵּר. וּלְמַאן דְּאָמַר
*אֶסְתֵּר יְרַקְרוֹקֶת הָיְתָה, מַפֵּיק אֶסְתֵּר וּמְעַיֵּיל וַשְׁתִּי. תָּנוּ רַבָּנַן: רָחָב בִּשְׁמָהּ זִינְּתָה;
יָעֵל בְּקוֹלָהּ, אֲבִיגַיִל בִּזְכִירָתָהּ, מִיכַל בַּת שָׁאוּל בִּרְאִיָּיתָהּ. *אָמַר רַבִּי יִצְחָק: כָּל
הָאוֹמֵר "רָחָב" "רָחָב" — מִיָּד נִיקְרִי. א"ל רַב נַחְמָן: אֲנָא אָמֵינָא "רָחָב, רָחָב" וְלָא אִיכְפַּת
לִי. אָמַר לֵיהּ: כִּי קָאָמֵינָא — בְּיוֹדְעָהּ וּבְמַכִּירָהּ. "וּמָרְדֳּכַי יָדַע אֶת כָּל אֲשֶׁר נַעֲשָׂה".
מַאי אָמַר? רַב אָמַר: גָּבַהּ (ג) הָמָן מֵאֲחַשְׁוֵרוֹשׁ. וּשְׁמוּאֵל אָמַר: גָּבַר מַלְכָּא עִילָּאָה
מִמַּלְכָּא תַּתָּאָה. "וַתִּתְחַלְחַל הַמַּלְכָּה". מַאי *"וַתִּתְחַלְחַל"? אָמַר רַב: שֶׁפֵּירְסָה נִדָּה.
וְר' יִרְמְיָה אָמַר: שֶׁהוּצְרְכָה לִנְקָבֶיהָ. "וַתִּקְרָא אֶסְתֵּר לַהֲתָךְ". *אָמַר רַב: הֲתָךְ זֶה
דָּנִיֵּאל. וְלָמָּה נִקְרָא שְׁמוֹ הֲתָךְ? שֶׁחֲתָכוּהוּ מִגְּדוּלָּתוֹ. וּשְׁמוּאֵל אָמַר: שֶׁכָּל
דִּבְרֵי מַלְכוּת נֶחְתָּכִין עַל פִּיו. "לָדַעַת מַה זֶּה וְעַל מַה זֶּה". אָמַר רַבִּי
יִצְחָק: שָׁלְחָה לוֹ: שֶׁמָּא עָבְרוּ יִשְׂרָאֵל עַל חֲמִשָּׁה חוּמְשֵׁי תוֹרָה, דִּכְתִיב
שמות לב בָּהֶן: °"מִזֶּה וּמִזֶּה הֵם כְּתוּבִים". "וַיַּגִּידוּ לְמָרְדֳּכַי אֵת דִּבְרֵי אֶסְתֵּר", וְאִילּוּ אִיהוּ
לָא אֲזַל לְגַבַּהּ. מִכָּאן *שֶׁאֵין מְשִׁיבִין עַל הַקַּלְקָלָה. "לֵךְ כְּנוֹס אֶת כָּל
הַיְּהוּדִים" וגו' עַד "אֲשֶׁר לֹא כַדָּת". אָמַר רַבִּי אַבָּא: שֶׁלֹּא כַּדָּת (ד) הָיָה,
שֶׁבְּכָל יוֹם וְיוֹם עַד עַכְשָׁיו — בְּאוֹנֶס, וְעַכְשָׁיו — בְּרָצוֹן. "וְכַאֲשֶׁר אָבַדְתִּי אָבָדְתִּי" — כְּשֵׁם
שֶׁאָבַדְתִּי מִבֵּית אַבָּא כָּךְ אוֹבַד מִמְּךָ. "וַיַּעֲבוֹר מָרְדֳּכַי". אָמַר רַב: שֶׁהֶעֱבִיר יוֹם
רִאשׁוֹן שֶׁל פֶּסַח בְּתַעֲנִית. וּשְׁמוּאֵל אָמַר: דַּעֲבַר *עַרְקוּמָא דְּמַיָּא. "וַיְהִי בַּיּוֹם
[אסתר ד] הַשְּׁלִישִׁי וַתִּלְבַּשׁ אֶסְתֵּר מַלְכוּת". "בִּגְדֵי מַלְכוּת" מִיבְּעֵי לֵיהּ! אָמַר רַבִּי אֶלְעָזָר אָמַר
רַבִּי חֲנִינָא: *מְלַמֵּד שֶׁלְּבָשַׁתָּה רוּחַ הַקֹּדֶשׁ. כְּתִיב הָכָא: "וַתִּלְבַּשׁ", וּכְתִיב הָתָם:
דה"א יב °"וְרוּחַ לָבְשָׁה אֶת עֲמָשַׂי". וְאָמַר רַבִּי אֶלְעָזָר אָמַר ר' חֲנִינָא: לְעוֹלָם)אַל תְּהִי
בִּרְכַּת הֶדְיוֹט קַלָּה בְּעֵינֶיךָ, שֶׁהֲרֵי שְׁנֵי גְדוֹלֵי הַדּוֹר בֵּרְכוּם שְׁנֵי הֶדְיוֹטוֹת וְנִתְקַיְּימָה
שמואל ב כד בָּהֶן, וְאֵלּוּ הֵן: דָּוִד וְדָנִיֵּאל; דָּוִד — דְּבָרְכֵיהּ אֲרַוְנָה, דִּכְתִיב: °"וַיֹּאמֶר אֲרַוְנָה אֶל הַמֶּלֶךְ"
דניאל ו (ה) וגו'. דָּנִיֵּאל — דְּבָרְכֵיהּ דָּרְיָוֶשׁ, דִּכְתִיב: °"אֱלָהָךְ דִּי אַנְתְּ פָּלַח לֵיהּ בִּתְדִירָא הוּא
יְשֵׁיזְבִנָּךְ". וְאָמַר רַבִּי אֶלְעָזָר אָמַר ר' חֲנִינָא: *אַל תְּהִי קִלְלַת הֶדְיוֹט קַלָּה בְּעֵינֶיךָ,
בראשית כ שֶׁהֲרֵי אֲבִימֶלֶךְ קִלֵּל אֶת שָׂרָה, °"הִנֵּה הוּא לָךְ כְּסוּת עֵינַיִם" וְנִתְקַיֵּים בְּזַרְעָהּ — °"וַיְהִי
שם כז כִּי זָקֵן יִצְחָק וַתִּכְהֶיןָ עֵינָיו". וְאָמַר רַבִּי אֶלְעָזָר אָמַר ר' חֲנִינָא: בֹּא וּרְאֵה שֶׁלֹּא
כְּמִדַּת הקב"ה מִדַּת בָּשָׂר וָדָם; מִדַּת בָּשָׂר וָדָם — אָדָם שׁוֹפֵת קְדֵרָה וְאח"כ נוֹתֵן
לְתוֹכָהּ מַיִם, אֲבָל הקב"ה — נוֹתֵן מַיִם וְאַחַר כָּךְ שׁוֹפֵת הַקְּדֵרָה, לְקַיֵּים מַה שֶּׁנֶּאֱמַר:
ירמיה י °"לְקוֹל תִּתּוֹ הֲמוֹן מַיִם בַּשָּׁמַיִם". וְאָמַר ר"א אָמַר רַבִּי חֲנִינָא: *כָּל הָאוֹמֵר דָּבָר בְּשֵׁם
אוֹמְרוֹ מֵבִיא גְאוּלָּה לָעוֹלָם, שֶׁנֶּאֱמַר: "וַתֹּאמֶר אֶסְתֵּר לַמֶּלֶךְ בְּשֵׁם מָרְדֳּכָי". וְאָמַר ר"א אָמַר רַבִּי חֲנִינָא: צַדִּיק
אָבַד — לְדוֹרוֹ אָבַד. מָשָׁל לְאָדָם שֶׁאָבְדָה לוֹ מַרְגָּלִית, כָּל מָקוֹם שֶׁהִיא — מַרְגָּלִית שְׁמָהּ, לֹא אָבְדָה אֶלָּא
לְבַעְלָהּ. "וְכָל זֶה אֵינֶנּוּ שׁוֶֹה לִי". אָמַר רַבִּי אֶלְעָזָר אָמַר רַבִּי חֲנִינָא: בְּשָׁעָה שֶׁרָאָה הָמָן אֶת מָרְדֳּכַי יוֹשֵׁב
בְּשַׁעַר הַמֶּלֶךְ, אָמַר: "כָּל זֶה אֵינֶנּוּ שׁוֶֹה לִי".(ו) כִּדְרַב חִסְדָּא, דְּאָמַר רַב חִסְדָּא: זֶה בָּא בִּפְרוֹזְבּוּלִי וְזֶה בָּא
בִּפְרוֹזְבּוּטִי

*) ברכות ז.

רש"י

בִּשְׁלָמָא.(ז) יִרְמְיָה וַחֲנַמְאֵל דִּכְתִיב "וַיָּבֹא אֵלַי חֲנַמְאֵל בֶּן דֹּדִי כִּדְבַר ה'" (ירמיה לב). בָּרוּךְ וּשְׂרָיָה מָצִינוּ שֶׁהָיוּ תַּלְמִידֵי יִרְמְיָה, בָּרוּךְ — דִּכְתִיב "מִפִּיו יִקְרָא אֵלַי אֵת הַדְּבָרִים הָאֵלֶּה וַאֲנִי כּוֹתֵב עַל הַסֵּפֶר בַּדְּיוֹ" (ירמיה לו), וּשְׂרָיָה בְּתוֹךְ סֵפֶר יִרְמְיָה (נא): "הַדָּבָר אֲשֶׁר צִוָּה יִרְמְיָה אֶת שְׂרָיָה בֶּן מַחְסֵיָה" וגו'. וּמָצִינוּ בְּתַלְמִידֵי נְבִיאִים שֶׁהָיוּ נְבִיאִים: נָחָה רוּחַ אֵלִיָּהוּ עַל אֱלִישָׁע, וִיהוֹשֻׁעַ תַּלְמִיד מֹשֶׁה. וּלְקַמָּן תַּנְיָא בְּבָרַיְיתָא: בָּרוּךְ בֶּן נֵרִיָּה, וּשְׂרָיָה בֶּן מַחְסֵיָה, וְדָנִיֵּאל, וּמָרְדֳּכַי, וְחַגַּי, זְכַרְיָה וּמַלְאָכִי, כּוּלָּן נִתְנַבְּאוּ בִּשְׁנַת שְׁתַּיִם לְדָרְיָוֶשׁ: יִשְׁמָעֵאל בֶּן נְתַנְיָה. הוּא שֶׁהָרַג אֶת גְּדַלְיָהוּ בֶּן אֲחִיקָם הַצַּדִּיק: בִּשְׁנַת שְׁתַּיִם לְדָרְיָוֶשׁ. הָאַחֲרוֹן, נִתְנַבְּאוּ לִבְנֵי הַגּוֹלָה שֶׁיַּחְזְרוּ לְבֵית הַמִּקְדָּשׁ. שֶׁנִּתְבַּטְּלָה הַמְּלָאכָה זֶה שְׁמוֹנֶה עֶשְׂרֵה שָׁנָה עַל יְדֵי שֹׁמְרוֹנִים מִשֶּׁהִתְחִילוּ בָּהּ בִּימֵי כּוֹרֶשׁ: בָּגְדָה יְהוּדָה. סֵיפֵיהּ דִּקְרָא "וּבָעַל בַּת אֵל נֵכָר": בִּשְׁמָהּ זִינְּתָה. הַמַּזְכִּיר אֶת שְׁמָהּ נִגְרָר אַחַר תַּאֲוַת זְנוּת: נִקְרִי. רוֹאֶה קֶרִי: ה"ג: מַאי אָמַר. כְּשֶׁצָּעַק זְעָקָה גְּדוֹלָה וּמָרָה, מֶה הָיָה אוֹמֵר בְּצַעֲקָתוֹ? רַב אָמַר. כָּךְ הָיָה צוֹעֵק: גָּבַהּ הָמָן מֵאֲחַשְׁוֵרוֹשׁ. שֶׁמְּלָאוֹ לִבּוֹ לְדַבֵּר מַה שֶּׁלֹּא עָלָה עַל לֵב אֲחַשְׁוֵרוֹשׁ: גָּבַר מַלְכָּא עִילָּאָה. כִּינּוּי הוּא לְהֵיפּוּךְ, בְּלָשׁוֹן נְקִיָּה: וַתִּתְחַלְחַל. נִתְמַסְמֵס חֲלַל גּוּפָהּ: שֶׁחֲתָכוּהוּ מִגְּדוּלָּתוֹ. בִּימֵי אֲחַשְׁוֵרוֹשׁ. שֶׁהֲרֵי בֵּלְשַׁאצַּר הִשְׁלִיטוֹ תְּלָתָא בְּמַלְכוּתוֹ, וְכֵן דָּרְיָוֶשׁ הַמָּדִי, שֶׁנֶּאֱמַר "וְעֵלָּא מִנְּהוֹן סָרְכִין תְּלָתָא דִּי דָנִיֵּאל חַד מִנְּהוֹן" (דניאל ו), וְכֵן כּוֹרֶשׁ שֶׁנֶּאֱמַר "וְדָנִיֵּאל הַצְלַח בְּמַלְכוּת דָּרְיָוֶשׁ וּבְמַלְכוּת כּוֹרֶשׁ פָּרְסָאָה" (שם). וּכְשֶׁמָּלַךְ אֲחַשְׁוֵרוֹשׁ חֲתָכוֹ מִגְּדוּלָּתוֹ: וְאִילּוּ אִיהוּ. דָּנִיֵּאל לָא אָזֵיל לְהָשִׁיב שְׁלִיחוּתוֹ: עַל הַקַּלְקָלָה. שֶׁהָיְתָה אֶסְתֵּר מוּנַעַת לָבֹא אֶל הַמֶּלֶךְ, לְפִיכָךְ לֹא הֵשִׁיב הֲתָךְ אֶת שְׁלִיחוּתוֹ, וְאֶסְתֵּר שָׁלְחָה דְּבָרֶיהָ ע"י אֲחֵרִים: עַד עַכְשָׁיו. נִבְעַלְתִּי בְּאוֹנֶס: וְעַכְשָׁיו. מִכָּאן וְאֵילָךְ מִדַּעְתִּי: אָבַדְתִּי מִמְּךָ. וַאֲסוּרָה אֲנִי לְךָ, דְּאֵשֶׁת יִשְׂרָאֵל שֶׁנֶּאֶנְסָה מוּתֶּרֶת לְבַעְלָהּ, וּבְרָצוֹן — אֲסוּרָה לְבַעְלָהּ: יו"ט רִאשׁוֹן שֶׁל פֶּסַח. שֶׁהֲרֵי בְּי"ג בְּנִיסָן נִכְתְּבוּ הָאִגְּרוֹת וְנִיתַּן הַדָּת בְּשׁוּשָׁן, וְי"ד וַחֲמִשָּׁה עָשָׂר וְשִׁשָּׁה עָשָׂר הִתְעַנּוּ, וּבְשִׁשָּׁה עָשָׂר *נִתְלָה הָמָן בָּעֶרֶב: דַּעֲבַר עַרְקוּמָא דְּמַיָּא. לֶאֱסוֹף הַיְּהוּדִים שֶׁבְּעֵבֶר הַשֵּׁנִי: שׁוֹפֵת אֶת הַקְּדֵרָה. מוֹשִׁיבָהּ עַל הַכִּירָה, הִיא קְרוּיָה שְׁפִיתָה: וְזֶה בָּא בִּפְרוֹזְבּוּלִי. מָרְדֳּכַי בָּא אֵלָיו בְּטַעֲנַת עוֹשֶׁר, הָמָן בָּא בְּטַעֲנַת עוֹנִי. שֶׁמָּכַר הָמָן אֶת עַצְמוֹ לְמָרְדֳּכַי קוֹדֶם לָכֵן יָמִים רַבִּים בְּכִכְּרֵי לֶחֶם: בּוּלִי. לְשׁוֹן עוֹשֶׁר, כִּדְאָמְרִינַן (גיטין דף לז.) "וְשָׁבַרְתִּי אֶת גְּאוֹן עוּזְּכֶם" — אֵלּוּ בּוּלָאוֹת שֶׁבִּיהוּדָה:

בּוּטֵי

תוספות

ארבע נשים יפיפיות היו בעולם. קשה: אמאי לא חשיב חוה? דהא אמרינן בפ' "חזקת הבתים" (ב"ב דף נח.) שרה לפני חוה כקוף בפני אדם! ויש לומר: דלא חשיב אלא אותן הנולדות מאשה: **כשם** שאבדתי מבית אבא כך אבדתי ממך. וא"ת: אמאי לא היה מגרשה ותהא מותרת להחזירנה? י"ל: לפי שכל מעשה הגט הוא ע"פ עדים, והיה ירא פן יתפרסם הדבר למלכות*: **ביום** השלישי. בזכות תורה נביאים וכתובים. א"נ: כהנים לוים וישראלים. אי נמי: משה ואהרן ומרים. אי נמי: שלישי דמתן תורה:

זה

[ועי' תוס' סנהדרין עד: סד"ה והא]

רבינו חננאל

כל ששמו ושם אביו בנבואה בידוע שהוא נביא בן נביא. וכן כל ששמו ושם עירו (ו) מפורש בידוע שהוא *) מירושלים וכן כל שמעשיו ומעשה אבותיו סתומין ופרט הכתוב באחד מהן אם לשבח כולן צדיקים. ואם לגנאי כולן רשעים: **אמר** רב מלאכי זה מרדכי. ר' יהושע בן קרחה אומר מלאכי זה עזרא. ומסתברא כמ"ד מלאכי זה עזרא: **ויגידו** למרדכי ואילו איהו לא אזל. מיכן שאין משיבין על הקלקלה. [ויעבור מרדכי וכו'] ושמואל אמר דעבר עורקמא דמיא. כל האומר דבר בשם אומרו מביא גאולה לעולם שנאמר ותאמר אסתר למלך בשם מרדכי. צדיק אבד לדורו אבד משל כו'.

*) נ"ל שהוא מאותה העיר שמו ולא שם עירו בידוע שהוא מירושלים.

הגהות הב"ח

(א) גמ' בידוע שהוא נביא מאותה העיר: (ב) שם כל שמעשיו סתומין ומעשה אבותיו וכו' בן צדיק וכל שמעשיו ומעשה אבותיו סתומין ופרט לך הכתוב: (ג) שם גבה לבו של המן מאחשורוש: (ד) שם אמר ר' אבא שלא כדת כל יום ויום שבכל יום ויום באונס ועכשיו ברצון כצ"ל: (ה) שם ויאמר ארונה אל המלך ה' אלהיך ירצך וגו': (ו) שם כל זה איננו שוה לי וכי משום דרואה מרדכי יושב בשער המלך אמר כל זה איננו שוה לי אלא כדרב חסדא דאמר: (ז) רש"י ד"ה בשלמא אינהו ירמיה וחנמאל ברוך ושריה מיפרשי בנבואה חנמאל דכתיב ויבא אלי:

הגהות הגר"א

[א] גמ' מעשיה. נ"ל מחסיה:

גליון הש"ס

גמ' ששמו ושם אביו עי' ב"ב דף טו ע"ב תוס' ד"ה בלעם ובמהר"ש אליילס בח"א שם: **שם** כל האומר רחב. עיין סנהדרין מה ע"א תד"ה אלא: **שם** ואילו איהו לא אזיל לגביה. עי' ב"ב דף ד ע"א תוס' ד"ה שכל:

מסורת הש"ס

[ע"י ... אמר רב מלאכי וכו']

ע"י אמר רב נחמן בר יצחק

[נ"ל רחב ואביגיל]

[לעיל יג.]

תענית ה:

נדה עא. סוטה כ:

ב"ב ז.

ע"ז י:

[...פרש"י לקמן כח: ד"ה עורקמא]

...לה המן בערב ר"ל ...ערב אחר יום ששה עשר ..."ל טז. ברש"י ד"ה ...כות קמילה וד"ה לתעניתו

לקמן כח. ב"ק נג. ע"ש

...ות פ"ו מ"ו [נדה יט: חולין קד:]

בפרוזבוטי. אמר רב פפא: וקרו ליה עבדא דמזדבן(א) בטלמי. "וכל זה איננו שוה לי" — מלמד שכל גנזיו של אותו רשע חקוקין על לבו. ובשעה שרואה את מרדכי יושב בשער המלך, אמר: "כל זה איננו שוה לי". ואמר *ר' אלעזר אמר רבי חנינא: עתיד הקב"ה להיות עטרה בראש כל צדיק וצדיק, שנאמר: °"ביום ההוא יהיה ה' צבאות לעטרת צבי" [וגו']. מאי "לעטרת צבי ולצפירת תפארה"? לעושין צביונו ולמצפין תפארתו. יכול לכל? ת"ל: "לשאר עמו" — *למי שמשים עצמו כשירים. "ולרוח משפט" — זה הדן את יצרו. ו"ליושב על המשפט" — זה הדן דין אמת לאמתו. "ולגבורה" — זה המתגבר על יצרו. "משיבי מלחמה"(ב) — שנושאין ונותנין במלחמתה של תורה. "שערה" — [אלו ת"ח] שמשכימין ומעריבין בבתי כנסיות ובבתי מדרשות. אמרה מדת הדין לפני הקב"ה: רבונו של עולם! מה נשתנו אלו מאלו? אמר לה הקדוש ברוך הוא: ישראל עסקו בתורה, אומות העולם לא עסקו בתורה. אמר ליה: "גם אלה ביין שגו ובשכר תעו... פקו פליליה". אין "פקו" אלא גיהנם, שנאמר: °"ולא תהיה זאת לך לפוקה". ואין "פליליה" אלא דיינין, שנאמר: °"ונתן בפלילים". "ותעמד בחצר בית המלך הפנימית". א"ר לוי: כיון שהגיעה לבית הצלמים — נסתלקה הימנה שכינה. אמרה: °"אלי אלי למה עזבתני". שמא אתה דן על שוגג כמזיד ועל אונס כרצון? או שמא על שקראתיו "כלב", שנאמר: °"הצילה מחרב נפשי מיד כלב יחידתי"? חזרה וקראתו "אריה", שנאמר: °"הושיעני מפי אריה". "ויהי כראות המלך את אסתר המלכה". אמר רבי יוחנן: ג' מלאכי השרת נזדמנו לה באותה שעה. אחד שהגביה את צוארה, ואחד שמשך חוט של חסד עליה, ואחד שמתח את השרביט. וכמה? אמר רבי ירמיה: שתי אמות היה והעמידו על שתים עשרה; ואמרי לה: על שש עשרה; ואמרי לה: על עשרים וארבע. במתניתא תנא: על ששים. וכן אתה מוצא באמתה של בת פרעה, וכן אתה מוצא בשיני רשעים, דכתיב: °"שיני רשעים שברת". ואמר ריש לקיש: *אל תקרי "שברת" אלא "שריבבת". •רבה בר עופרן אמר משום ר"א, ששמע מרבו, ורבו מרבו: מאתים. "ויאמר לה המלך *לאסתר המלכה מה בקשתך... עד חצי המלכות... ותעש". "חצי המלכות" ולא כל המלכות, ולא דבר שחוצץ למלכות, ומאי ניהו? בנין בית המקדש. "יבא המלך והמן אל המשתה". ת"ר: מה ראתה אסתר שזימנה את המן? ר"א אומר: פחים טמנה לו, שנאמר: °"יהי שלחנם לפניהם לפח". ר' יהושע אומר: מבית אביה למדה, שנאמר: °"אם רעב שונאך האכילהו לחם" וגו'. ר"מ אומר: כדי שלא יטול עצה וימרוד. ר' יהודה אומר: כדי שלא יכירו בה שהיא יהודית. ר' נחמיה אומר: כדי שלא יאמרו ישראל: אחות יש לנו בבית המלך, ויסיחו דעתן מן הרחמים. ר' יוסי אומר: כדי שיהא מצוי לה בכל עת. ר"ש בן מנסיא אומר: אולי ירגיש המקום ויעשה לנו נס. רבי יהושע בן קרחה אומר: אסביר לו פנים, כדי שיהרג הוא והיא. רבן גמליאל אומר: מלך הפכפכן היה. אמר רבי גמליאל: עדיין צריכין אנו למודעי. דתניא, ר' אליעזר המודעי אומר: קנאתו במלך קנאתו בשרים. רבה אמר: °"לפני שבר גאון". אביי ורבא דאמרי תרוייהו: °"בחומם אשית את משתיהם" וגו'. אשכחיה רבה בר אבוה לאליהו. א"ל: כמאן חזיא אסתר ועבדא הכי? א"ל: ככולהו תנאי וככולהו אמוראי. "ויספר להם המן את כבוד עשרו ורוב בניו". וכמה רוב בניו? אמר רב: ל' עשרה מתו, ועשרה נתלו ועשרה מחזרין על הפתחים. ורבנן אמרי: אותן שמחזרין על הפתחים שבעים הויא, דכתיב: °"שבעים בלחם נשכרו". אל תקרי "שבעים" אלא "שבעים". ורמי בר אבא אמר: כולן מאתים ושמונה הוו, שנאמר: "ורוב בניו". "ורוב" בגימטריא מאתן וארביסר הוו! •אמר רב נחמן בר יצחק: "ורב" כתיב. "בלילה ההוא נדדה שנת המלך". אמר רבי תנחום: נדדה שנת מלכו של עולם. ורבנן אמרי: נדדו עליונים, נדדו תחתונים. רבא אמר: שנת המלך אחשורוש ממש. נפלה ליה מילתא בדעתיה, אמר: מאי דקמן דזמינתיה אסתר להמן? דלמא עצה קא שקלי עילויה דההוא גברא למקטליה. הדר אמר: אי הכי, לא הוה גברא דרחים לי דהוה מודע לי? הדר אמר: דלמא איכא איניש דעבד בי טיבותא ולא פרעתיה, משום הכי מימנעי אינשי ולא מגלו לי. מיד — "ויאמר להביא את ספר הזכרונות דברי הימים". "ויהיו נקראים" — מלמד שנקראים מאיליהן. "וימצא כתוב". "כתב" מבעי ליה! מלמד ששמשי

בוטי. לשון עניות, כמו "והעבט תעביטנו" (דברים טו), במסכת גיטין (דף לז.): בטולמי. נהמא. "בככרות לחם עשרים לחם שעורים" (מלכים ב ד) מתרגמינן: עשרין טולמין דלחמא: לרוח משפט. לשופטים את רוחן יהיה לעטרה: דן את יצרו. כופהו לשוב בתשובה: ומתגבר על יצרו. אינו הולך אחריו לעבור עבירה: שמשכימין כו'. והיינו שערה — שעושין [שנעשים שוערים] לפתוח דלתות בהשכמה, ולאחר [שם עד] זמן נעילתו: גם אלה. אלו הרשעים הנידונין בגיהנם: ביין שגו. כלומר: אף הם עשו כהם, לפיכך דנם: פקו פליליה. לגיהנם נשפטו: אלי אלי למה עזבתני. במזמור "אילת השחר" הוא: על אונס. [אע"פ] שאני באה אליו מאליי — אונס הוא: הצילה מחרב נפשי. באותו מזמור הוא: אמתה של בת פרעה. "ותשלח את אמתה ותקחה" (שמות ב): בשיני רשעים. עוג מלך הבשן, במס' ברכות פרק "הרואה" (דף נד:) *[שעקר הר בת ג' פרסי להשליכו על ישראל, ונתנו על ראשו, ושלח הקב"ה נמלים ונקבוהו, ונכנס בצוארו. בקש לשומטו — ונשתרבבו שיניו לכאן ולכאן]: אל תקרי שברת אלא שרבבת. גרסינן. ומ"שיני רשעים" נפיק להאי דרשה, דליכתוב קרא "ושן רשע", אלא י' דשיני וי"ם דרשעים הרי ששים: ולא דבר שחוצץ במלכות. בנין הבית, שהוא באמצע של עולם, כדאמרי' בסדר יומא (דף נד:): אבן שתיה שממנה נשתת העולם: מבית אביה למדה. שמעה התינוקות אומרים כן: וימרוד. במלך, שהיתה שעתו מגלחת: שיהא מצוי לה. אולי תוכל להכשילו בשום דבר לפני המלך: ירגיש הקב"ה. שאף אני מקרבת שונאיהן של ישראל. אי נמי ירגיש שאני צריכה להחניף רשע זה ולזלזל בכבודי: שיהרג הוא והיא. שישחדני המלך ממנו, ויהרוג את שניהם. [נ"א: וכי גזרי גזירה ומית חד מינייהו בטלי הגזירה]*: מלך הפכפך היה. וחוזר בדיבורו, אמרה: שמא אוכל לפתותו ולהורגו, ואם לא יהא מזומן — תעבור השעה ויחזור בו: בחומם אשית את משתיהם. על בלשצר וסיעתו נאמר, בשובם מן המלחמה. שדריוש וכורש היו צרין על בבל ונצחן בלשצר אותו היום, והיו עייפים וחמים, וישבו לשתות ונשתכרו, ובאותו היום נהרג. ואף אסתר אמרה: מתוך משתיהן של רשעים באה להם פורענות: שבעים בלחם נשכרו. יונתן תרגם על בניו של המן: שנת מלכו של עולם. דוגמא, "ויקץ כישן ה'" (תהלים עח) — לנקום נקמתו: נדדו עליונים. שהיו מלאכים מבהילים אותו כל הלילה, ואמרו לו: כפוי טובה, שלם טובה למי שעשאך, לשון מורי. ויש אומרים: [נדדו עליונים] כדי שירבו בתחנונים לבקש על הדבר: מאי דקמן דזמינתיה. כלומר: מה זאת הבאה לפני עכשיו דבר חדש כזה: כתוב. משמע שהיה כתוב מחדש. כתב משמע מעיקרא, וימצא כתוב בספר זכרון לפניו אשר הגיד מרדכי: שמשי

זה הדן דין אמת לאמתו. נראה דמשום הכי נקט אמת, לאשמועינן דדיין מרומה צריך לחקור העדים בטוב עד שיתברר האמת. ואז ידונו אותו לאמתו*: [ה"ג: אל תקרי שברת אלא שרבבת. ל' אשתרבובי (סוכה ה.) ול"ג שריבבת]:

רבינו חננאל

בולי ובוטי. פי' עשירים ודלים: **עתיד** הקב"ה להיות עטרה בראש כל צדיק וצדיק שנאמר ביום ההוא יהיה ה' צבאות לעטרת צבי וגו': **שערה** שמשכימין ומעריבין בבתי כנסיות ובבתי מדרשות. אמרה מדת הדין לפני הקב"ה כו' א"ל רבה בר אבוה לאליהו כמאן חזא אסתר דעבדא הכי. א"ל ככולהו תנאי וככולהו אמוראי.

הגהות הב"ח

(א) גמ' עבדא דמזדבן בטולמי דנהמא ואמר ר' אלעזר אמר ר' חנינא כצ"ל ותיבות וכל זה איננו שוה לי מלמד וכו' אמר כל זה איננו שוה לי נמחק: (ב) שם משיבי מלחמה אלו שנושאין:

ס"א

גליון הש"ס

גמ' רבה בר עופרן. ע"ל י ע"ב תד"ה רבה: **שם** אמר רנב"י ורב כתיב. כעין זה יומא לח ע"ב ודף עה ע"ב:

תורה אור

ישעיה כח

שמואל א כה

שמות כא

תהלים כב

שם

שם

שם ג

ברכות נד: סוטה יב:

[נ"ל מה לך אסתר המלכה ומה]

תהלים סט

משלי כה

משלי טז

ירמיה נא

שמואל א ב

[סוף תענית כט ע"א]

[סנהדרין קיח: ע"ש ס' שינויים ובפרש"י שם]

[ר"ה יז:]

[ועי' תוס' ב"ב ח: דין]

שמשי. סופר המלך, שונא ישראל היה, ומימות כורש היה, כמו שנאמר בספר עזרא (סימן ד) שכתב שטנה על בנין הבית, עד (ג) שבא כורש וביטלו. ואף בימי אחשורוש עשה כן, שנאמר (שם) "ובמלכות אחשורוש בתחלת מלכותו כתב שטנה": לו הכין. לצורך עצמו: דיסקרתא. כפר: נהרא. ליטול מכם: לרבנן. תלמידיו: הלכות קמיצה. דורש בענינו של יום, וששה עשר בניסן היה, הוא יום תנופת העומר: ואשקול למזייא. ואטול שערי: אסרתינהו. נותה עליהן להחביאן: אומני. ספרים: זוזא. זוג של ספרים, כעין מספרים: עציץ. כלי חרס: ולתעניתו. יום שלישי לתענית היה, שהתחילו להתענות בי"ד בניסן. ומה שאמר המקרא ליום אתמול שלישי, "ויהי ביום השלישי ותלבש אסתר מלכות" — יום שלישי לשילוח הרגלים היה: אם מזרע היהודים. יש זרע ביהודים, שאם הוא בא מהם – לא תוכל לו: מלמד שהביאוהו בבהלה. ולא רחץ יפה מטינופו: שוה. חושש: מלמד שהיתה מחווה כנגד אחשורוש. מרבוי (ד) אתה לומד "איש צר ואויב המן הרע הזה": נופל. לשון עושה והולך. נופל ורוצה לזקוף, והמלאך מפילו: וישלך עליו. הקב"ה משליך פורענות על הרשע בלי חמלה: מידו ברוח יברח. בני סייעתו וחבריו בורחים מידו: אחת של אסתר. שהיה כעוס אחשורוש על מה שעשה המן לאסתר: דבר שנצטער בו אותו צדיק. "לעבד נמכר יוסף" על ידי קנאת אחיו: יכשל

תורה אור [אסתר ו] [שם] [שם] [שם] [סנהדרין לח. קה.]

ששמשי מוחק וגבריאל כותב. אמר רבי אסי, דרש ר' שילא איש כפר תמרתא: ומה כתב שלמטה שלזכותן של ישראל אינו נמחק — כתב שלמעלה לא כל שכן? °"לא נעשה עמו דבר". אמר רבא: לא מפני שאוהבין את מרדכי אלא מפני ששונאים את המן. °"הכין לו", תנא: לו הכין. "ועשה כן למרדכי", אמר ליה: מנו מרדכי? אמר ליה: °"היהודי". אמר ליה: טובא מרדכי איכא ביהודאי! אמר ליה: °"היושב בשער המלך". אמר ליה:(א) סגי ליה בחד דיסקרתא, אי נמי בחד נהרא! אמר ליה: הא נמי הב ליה, "אל תפל דבר מכל אשר דברת". "ויקח המן את הלבוש ואת הסוס", אזל אשכחיה דיתבי רבנן קמיה ומחוי להו הלכות קמיצה לרבנן. כיון דחזייה מרדכי דאפיק לקבליה וסוסיה מיחד בידיה, מירתת. אמר להו לרבנן: האי רשיעא למיקטל נפשי קא אתי, זילו מקמיה די לא תכוו בגחלתו! בההיא שעתא נתעטף מרדכי וקם ליה לצלותא. אתא המן ויתיב ליה קמייהו ואוריך עד דסליק מרדכי לצלותיה. אמר להו: במאי עסקיתו? אמרו ליה: בזמן שבית המקדש קיים, מאן דמנדב מנחה, מייתי מלי קומציה דסולתא ומתכפר ליה. אמר להו: אתא מלי קומצי קמחא דידכו, ודחי עשרה אלפי ככרי כספא דידי. אמר ליה: רשע! *עבד שקנה נכסים — עבד למי, ונכסים למי? אמר ליה: קום לבוש הני מאני, ורכוב האי סוסיא, דבעי לך מלכא. אמר ליה: לא יכילנא עד דעיילנא לבי בני ואשקול למזייא, דלאו אורח ארעא לאשתמושי במאני דמלכא הכי. שדרה אסתר ואסרתינהו לכולהו בי בני, ולכולהו אומני. עייליה איהו לבי בני, ואסחיה, ואזיל ואייתי זוזא מביתיה, וקא שקיל ביה מזייה. בהדי דקא שקיל ליה אינגד ואיתנח. אמר ליה: אמאי קא מיתנחת? אמר ליה: גברא דהוה חשיב ליה למלכא מכולהו רברבנוהי, השתא לישוייה בלאני וספר? אמר ליה: רשע, ולאו ספר של כפר קרצום היית? תנא: המן, ספר של כפר קרצום היה, עשרים ושתים שנה. בתר דשקלינהו למזייה, לבשינהו למאניה. אמר ליה: סק ורכב. אמר ליה: לא יכילנא, דכחישא חילאי מימי תעניתא. גחין וסליק. כי סליק בעט ביה. אמר ליה: לא כתיב לכו °"בנפל אויבך אל תשמח"? [משלי כד] אמר ליה: הני מילי — בישראל, אבל בדידכו כתיב: °"ואתה על במותימו תדרוך". [דברים לג] °"ויקרא לפניו: ככה יעשה לאיש אשר המלך חפץ ביקרו". [אסתר ו] כי הוה נקיט ואזיל בשבילא דבי המן, חזיתיה ברתיה דקיימא אאיגרא. סברה: האי דרכיב — אבוה, והאי דמסגי קמיה — מרדכי. שקלה עציצא דבית הכסא ושדיתיה ארישא דאבוה. דלי עיניה וחזת דאבוה הוא, נפלה מאיגרא לארעא ומתה. והיינו דכתיב: "וישב מרדכי אל שער המלך". אמר רב ששת: ששב לשקו ולתעניתו. "והמן נדחף אל ביתו אבל וחפוי ראש". "אבל" — על בתו, "וחפוי ראש" — על שאירע לו. "ויספר המן לזרש אשתו ולכל אוהביו" וגו', קרי להו "אוהביו" וקרי להו "חכמיו". אמר רבי יוחנן: כל האומר דבר חכמה, אפילו באומות העולם — נקרא חכם. "אם מזרע היהודים מרדכי" וגו', אמרו ליה: אי משאר שבטים קאתי — יכלת ליה; ואי משבט יהודה ובנימין ואפרים ומנשה — לא יכלת ליה. יהודה — דכתיב: °"ידך בערף אויביך". [בראשית מט] אינך — דכתיב בהו: °"לפני אפרים ובנימין ומנשה עוררה את גבורתך". [תהלים פ] °"כי נפל תפול לפניו". [אסתר ו] דרש ר' יהודה בר אלעאי: שתי נפילות הללו, למה? אמרו לו: אומה זו, משולה לעפר ומשולה לכוכבים. כשהן יורדין — יורדין עד עפר, וכשהן עולין — עולין עד לכוכבים. °"וסריסי המלך הגיעו ויבהילו" — מלמד [שם ו] שהביאוהו בבהלה. "כי נמכרנו אני ועמי וגו' כי אין הצר שוה בנזק המלך". אמרה לו: צר זה אינו שוה בנזק של מלך, איקני בה בושתי — וקטלה; השתא איקני בדידי — ומבעי למקטלי. "ויאמר המלך אחשורוש ויאמר לאסתר המלכה". "ויאמר" "ויאמר" למה לי? אמר רבי אבהו: בתחלה על ידי תורגמן. כיון דאמרה ליה: (ג) מדבית שאול קאתינא — מיד: "ויאמר לאסתר המלכה". § "ותאמר אסתר איש צר ואויב המן הרע הזה". אמר ר' אלעזר: מלמד שהיתה מחווה כלפי אחשורוש, ובא מלאך וסטר ידה כלפי המן. § "והמלך קם בחמתו" וגו' "והמלך שב מגנת הביתן". מקיש שיבה לקימה. מה קימה בחימה — אף שיבה בחימה. דאזל ואשכח למלאכי השרת דאידמו ליה כגברי, וקא עקרי לאילני דבוסתני. ואמר להו: מאי עובדייכו? אמרו ליה: דפקדינן המן. אתא לביתיה — "והמן נופל על המטה". "נופל"? "נפל" מיבעי ליה! אמר רבי אלעזר: מלמד שבא מלאך והפילו עליה. אמר: ויי מביתא ויי מברא! "ויאמר המלך: הגם לכבוש את המלכה עמי בבית". "ויאמר חרבונה" וגו' אמר רבי אלעזר: אף חרבונה רשע באותה עצה היה. כיון שראה שלא נתקיימה עצתו — מיד ברח. והיינו דכתיב: °"וישלך עליו ולא יחמול מידו ברוח יברח". [איוב כז] "וחמת המלך שככה". שתי שכיכות הללו למה? אחת של מלכו של עולם, ואחת של אחשורוש, ואמרי לה: אחת של אסתר ואחת של ושתי. °"לכלם נתן לאיש חליפות שמלות ולבנימן נתן... חמש חליפות". [בראשית מה] אפשר דבר שנצטער בו אותו צדיק יכשל

ודחי עשרה אלפי ככרי כספא. שמעתי שעשרה אלפי ככר כסף עולין חצי שקל לכל אחד מישראל, שהיו שש מאות אלף כשיצאו ממצרים, ואמר שיתן לאחשורוש כל פדיונם(ה). ודוק ותשכח: צריך

(א) גמ' אמר ליה ההוא סגי ליה: (ב) שם כיון דאמרה ליה בת מלכים אנא מדבית שאול: (ג) רש"י ד"ה שמשי סופר וכו' עד שלא כורש וכו' כתבו שטנה והוא בסדר עולם שבני המן כתבו שטנה הס"ד: (ד) ד"ה מלמד שהיתה וכו' מריבוי דבר זה אתה לומד שהיה לה לומר המן הרע הזה אלא שהיתה רוצה לומר על אחשורוש איש צר ואויב ועל המן הרע הזה: (ה) תוס' ד"ה ודחי וכו' כל פדיונם. נ"ב פי' הככר הוא ס' מנה [ושל קדש ק"כ מנה] והמנה כ"ה סלעים [והמן נתן עשרת אלפים ככרות של חול שהם ה' אלפים של קדש והמחצית השקל בעד ת"ר אלף משנה אחת עולה מאת ככר של קדש] וימי שנותינו שבעים שנה ומבן כ' ומעלה נתנו כופר נפש והמן נתן בעד חמשים שנה בעד ת"ר אלף:

גליון הש"ס

גמ' עבד שקנה נכסים. ע"ל טו ע"א רש"י ד"ה וזה בא:

עין משפט
נר מצוה

עב א טור א"ח סי' כה:
עג ב מיי' פ"ב מהל' מגילה הלכה יב סמג עשין ד טוש"ע א"ח סי' תרל סעיף טו:
עד ג טוש"ע שם סימן תרצא סעיף ד:
עה ד מיי' פ"ז מהל' ס"ת הל' י ופ"ח שם הלכה ד סמג עשין כה טוש"ע י"ד סי' ערה סעיף ג ד:
עו ה ו טוש"ע א"ח סי' תרצא סעיף ג:

יִכָּשֵׁל בּוֹ?! דְּאָמַר רָבָא בַּר מַחְסְיָא אָמַר רַב חָמָא בַּר גּוּרְיָא, אָמַר רַב: *בִּשְׁבִיל מִשְׁקַל שְׁנֵי סְלָעִים מֵילָת שֶׁהוֹסִיף יַעֲקֹב לְיוֹסֵף מִשְּׁאָר אֶחָיו — נִתְגַּלְגֵּל הַדָּבָר וְיָרְדוּ אֲבוֹתֵינוּ לְמִצְרַיִם. אָמַר רַבִּי בִּנְיָמִין בַּר יֶפֶת: רֶמֶז רָמַז לוֹ שֶׁעָתִיד בֵּן לָצֵאת מִמֶּנּוּ, שֶׁיֵּצֵא מִלִּפְנֵי הַמֶּלֶךְ בַּחֲמִשָּׁה לְבוּשֵׁי מַלְכוּת, שֶׁנֶּאֱמַר: "וּמָרְדֳּכַי יָצָא... בִּלְבוּשׁ מַלְכוּת, תְּכֵלֶת" וגו'. °"וַיִּפּוֹל עַל צַוְּארֵי בִנְיָמִין אָחִיו" — כַּמָּה צַוָּארִין הָווּ לֵיהּ לְבִנְיָמִין? אָמַר רַבִּי אֶלְעָזָר: בָּכָה עַל שְׁנֵי מִקְדָּשִׁים שֶׁעֲתִידִין לִהְיוֹת בְּחֶלְקוֹ שֶׁל בִּנְיָמִין וַעֲתִידִין לֵיחָרֵב. "וּבִנְיָמִן בָּכָה עַל צַוָּארָיו" — בָּכָה עַל מִשְׁכַּן שִׁילֹה, שֶׁעָתִיד לִהְיוֹת בְּחֶלְקוֹ שֶׁל יוֹסֵף וְעָתִיד לֵיחָרֵב. °"וְהִנֵּה עֵינֵיכֶם רוֹאוֹת וְעֵינֵי אָחִי בִנְיָמִין". אָמַר רַבִּי אֶלְעָזָר: אָמַר לָהֶם: כְּשֵׁם שֶׁאֵין בְּלִבִּי עַל בִּנְיָמִין אָחִי, שֶׁלֹּא הָיָה בִּמְכִירָתִי — כָּךְ אֵין בְּלִבִּי עֲלֵיכֶם. "כִּי פִי הַמְדַבֵּר אֲלֵיכֶם", כְּפִי — כֵּן לִבִּי. °"וּלְאָבִיו שָׁלַח כְּזֹאת עֲשָׂרָה חֲמוֹרִים נוֹשְׂאִים מִטּוּב מִצְרָיִם". מַאי "מִטּוּב מִצְרָיִם"? אָמַר ר' בִּנְיָמִין בַּר יֶפֶת אָמַר רַבִּי אֶלְעָזָר: שָׁלַח לוֹ יַיִן [יָשָׁן,] שֶׁדַּעַת זְקֵנִים נוֹחָה הֵימֶנּוּ. °"וַיֵּלְכוּ גַּם אֶחָיו וַיִּפְּלוּ לְפָנָיו". אָמַר רַבִּי בִּנְיָמִין בַּר יֶפֶת אָמַר רַבִּי אֶלְעָזָר: הַיְינוּ דְּאָמְרִי אֱינָשֵׁי: תַּעֲלָא בְּעִידָּנֵיהּ סְגִיד לֵיהּ. תַּעֲלָא? מַאי בְּצִירוּתֵיהּ מֵאַחֲווּהּ? אֶלָּא, אִי אִיתְּמַר הָכִי אִיתְּמַר: °"וַיִּשְׁתַּחוּ יִשְׂרָאֵל עַל רֹאשׁ הַמִּטָּה". אָמַר רַבִּי בִּנְיָמִין בַּר יֶפֶת אָמַר רַבִּי אֶלְעָזָר: תַּעֲלָא בְּעִידָּנֵיהּ סְגִיד לֵיהּ. °"וַיְנַחֵם אוֹתָם וַיְדַבֵּר עַל לִבָּם". אָמַר רַבִּי בִּנְיָמִין בַּר יֶפֶת אָמַר רַבִּי אֶלְעָזָר: מְלַמֵּד שֶׁאָמַר לָהֶם דְּבָרִים שֶׁמִּתְקַבְּלִין עַל הַלֵּב. וּמָה עֲשָׂרָה נֵרוֹת לֹא יָכְלוּ לְכַבּוֹת נֵר אֶחָד — נֵר אֶחָד הֵיאַךְ יָכוֹל לְכַבּוֹת עֲשָׂרָה נֵרוֹת? °"לַיְּהוּדִים הָיְתָה אוֹרָה וְשִׂמְחָה וְשָׂשׂוֹן וִיקָר". אָמַר רַב יְהוּדָה: "אוֹרָה" — זוֹ תּוֹרָה. וְכֵן הוּא אוֹמֵר: °"כִּי נֵר מִצְוָה וְתוֹרָה אוֹר". "שִׂמְחָה" — זֶה יוֹם טוֹב. וְכֵן הוּא אוֹמֵר: °"וְשָׂמַחְתָּ בְּחַגֶּךָ". "שָׂשׂוֹן" — זוֹ מִילָה. וְכֵן הוּא אוֹמֵר: °"שָׂשׂ אָנֹכִי עַל אִמְרָתֶךָ". "וִיקָר" — אֵלּוּ תְּפִלִּין. וְכֵן הוּא אוֹמֵר: °"וְרָאוּ כָּל עַמֵּי הָאָרֶץ כִּי שֵׁם ה' נִקְרָא עָלֶיךָ וְיָרְאוּ מִמֶּךָּ", *וְתַנְיָא, רַבִּי אֱלִיעֶזֶר הַגָּדוֹל אוֹמֵר: [א]אֵלּוּ תְּפִלִּין שֶׁבָּרֹאשׁ. "וְאֵת פַּרְשַׁנְדָּתָא... וגו' עֲשֶׂרֶת בְּנֵי הָמָן". אָמַר רַב אַדָּא דְּמִן יָפוֹ: [ב]עֲשֶׂרֶת בְּנֵי הָמָן, וַ"עֲשֶׂרֶת" — צָרִיךְ לְמֵימְרִינְהוּ בִּנְשִׁימָה אַחַת. מַאי טַעְמָא? כּוּלְּהוּ בַּהֲדֵי הֲדָדֵי נְפַקוּ נִשְׁמָתַיְיהוּ. אָמַר רַבִּי יוֹחָנָן: [ג]וָיו דְּ"וַיְזָתָא" צָרִיךְ לְמִימְתְּחָהּ בִּזְקִיפָא *)כִּמְוּרְדִּיָּא דְּלִבְרוּת. מַאי טַעְמָא? כּוּלְּהוּ בְּחַד זְקִיפָא אִזְדְּקִיפוּ. אָמַר רַבִּי חֲנִינָא בַּר פָּפָּא, דָּרַשׁ ר' שֵׁילָא אִישׁ כְּפַר תְּמַרְתָּא: [ד]כָּל הַשִּׁירוֹת כּוּלָּן נִכְתָּבוֹת אָרִיחַ עַל גַּבֵּי לְבֵנָה וּלְבֵנָה עַל גַּבֵּי אָרִיחַ, [ה]חוּץ מִשִּׁירָה זוֹ וּמַלְכֵי כְנַעַן, שֶׁאָרִיחַ עַל גַּבֵּי אָרִיחַ, וּלְבֵנָה עַל גַּבֵּי לְבֵנָה. מ"ט? שֶׁלֹּא תְּהֵא תְּקוּמָה לְמַפַּלְתָּן. "וַיֹּאמֶר הַמֶּלֶךְ לְאֶסְתֵּר הַמַּלְכָּה בְּשׁוּשַׁן הַבִּירָה הָרְגוּ הַיְּהוּדִים". אָמַר רַבִּי אַבָּהוּ: מְלַמֵּד שֶׁבָּא מַלְאָךְ וּסְטָרוֹ עַל פִּיו. "וּבְבֹאָהּ לִפְנֵי הַמֶּלֶךְ אָמַר עִם הַסֵּפֶר". "אָמַר"? "אָמְרָה" מִיבְּעֵי לֵיהּ? אָמַר רַבִּי יוֹחָנָן: אָמְרָה לוֹ: יֵאָמֵר בַּפֶּה מַה שֶּׁכָּתוּב בַּסֵּפֶר. "דִּבְרֵי שָׁלוֹם וֶאֱמֶת". אָמַר רַבִּי תַּנְחוּם, וְאָמְרִי לָהּ אָמַר רַבִּי אַסִּי: מְלַמֵּד *[ו]שֶׁצְּרִיכָה שִׂרְטוּט כַּאֲמִיתָהּ שֶׁל תּוֹרָה. "וּמַאֲמַר אֶסְתֵּר קִיַּם". "מַאֲמַר אֶסְתֵּר" — אִין, "דִּבְרֵי הַצּוֹמוֹת" — לָא?! אָמַר רַבִּי יוֹחָנָן: (א) "דִּבְרֵי הַצּוֹמוֹת..." "וּמַאֲמַר אֶסְתֵּר קִיַּם (*אֶת יְמֵי) הַפּוּרִים הָאֵלֶּה". "כִּי מָרְדֳּכַי הַיְּהוּדִי מִשְׁנֶה לַמֶּלֶךְ אֲחַשְׁוֵרוֹשׁ וְגָדוֹל לַיְּהוּדִים וְרָצוּי לְרוֹב אֶחָיו". "לְרוֹב אֶחָיו" — וְלֹא לְכָל אֶחָיו, מְלַמֵּד: שֶׁפֵּירְשׁוּ מִמֶּנּוּ מִקְצָת סַנְהֶדְרִין. אָמַר רַב יוֹסֵף: גָּדוֹל ת"ת יוֹתֵר מֵהַצָּלַת נְפָשׁוֹת, דְּמֵעִיקָּרָא חָשֵׁיב לֵיהּ לְמָרְדֳּכַי בָּתַר ד' וּלְבַסּוֹף בָּתַר חֲמִשָּׁה. מֵעִיקָּרָא כְּתִיב: °"אֲשֶׁר בָּאוּ עִם זְרוּבָּבֶל, יֵשׁוּעַ, נְחֶמְיָה, שְׂרָיָה, רְעֵלָיָה, מָרְדֳּכַי בִּלְשָׁן", וּלְבַסּוֹף כְּתִיב: °"הַבָּאִים עִם זְרוּבָּבֶל, יֵשׁוּעַ, נְחֶמְיָה, עֲזַרְיָה, רַעַמְיָה, נַחֲמָנִי, מָרְדֳּכַי, בִּלְשָׁן". אָמַר רַב וְאִיתֵּימָא רַב שְׁמוּאֵל בַּר מַרְתָּא: גָּדוֹל תַּלְמוּד תּוֹרָה יוֹתֵר מִבִּנְיַן בֵּית הַמִּקְדָּשׁ, שֶׁכָּל זְמַן שֶׁבָּרוּךְ בֶּן נֵרִיָּה קַיָּים — לֹא הִנִּיחוֹ עֶזְרָא וְעָלָה. אָמַר רַבָּה אָמַר רַב יִצְחָק בַּר שְׁמוּאֵל בַּר מַרְתָּא: גָּדוֹל תַּלְמוּד תּוֹרָה יוֹתֵר מִכִּבּוּד אָב וָאֵם, שֶׁכָּל אוֹתָן שָׁנִים שֶׁהָיָה יַעֲקֹב אָבִינוּ בְּבֵית עֵבֶר לֹא נֶעֱנַשׁ. דְּאָמַר מָר: לָמָּה

צריך לאומרן בנשימה אחת. נראה דהיינו לכתחילה, אבל בדיעבד יצא:

אמרה מיבעי ליה. דמשמע דהכי קאמר: ובבואה לפני המלך. אמרה לו מלבד הספר (ג) שעמו לעשות ולשלוח בכל המדינות, אמרה לו עוד ישוב *)מחשבתו הרעה. דכיון דקאמר בבואה אמר — משמע שיש לנו לומר מה שאמרה:

הדרן עלך מגילה נקראת

*) [ישוב מחשבתו הרעה ומשני יאמר בפה דכיון דקאמר כו' כצ"ל וכן הגיה הרמ"א בגמ' שלו]

רש"י

יִכָּשֵׁל בּוֹ. גָּרְסִי', וְלָא גָּרְסִי' זַרְעוֹ: כַּמָּה צַוָּארִין הָיוּ לוֹ לְבִנְיָמִין. לָא גָּרְסִינַן, שֶׁכֵּן דֶּרֶךְ הַמִּקְרָא לִכְתּוֹב "צַוָּארֵי" לְשׁוֹן רַבִּים: "עַל חֶלְקַת צַוָּארָיו" (בראשית כז), "בָּכָה עַל צַוָּארָיו": שִׁיגֵּר לוֹ יַיִן. לְפִי שֶׁדַּעַת זְקֵנִים נוֹחָה הֵימֶנּוּ, זֶה הַדָּבָר הַטּוֹב לוֹ מִן הַכֹּל: תַּעֲלָא. שׁוּעָל: בְּעִידָּנֵיהּ. אִם תִּרְאֶה שַׁעְתּוֹ מַצְלַחַת: תַּעֲלָא. קָרֵי לֵיהּ יוֹסֵף לִפְנֵי אֶחָיו, מַאי בְּצִירוּתֵיהּ מֵאַחֲווּהּ: אוֹרָה זוֹ תּוֹרָה. שֶׁגָּזַר עֲלֵיהֶן הָמָן שֶׁלֹּא יַעַסְקוּ בַּתּוֹרָה: זֶהוּ יוֹם טוֹב. קִיְּימוּ עֲלֵיהֶם יָמִים טוֹבִים: זוֹ מִילָה. וְעַל כָּל אֵלֶּה גָּזַר: אִמְרָתֶךָ. זוֹ מִילָה, שֶׁנִּיתְּנָה בְּמַאֲמָר וְלֹא בְּדִיבּוּר, "וַיֹּאמֶר ה' אֶל אַבְרָהָם וְאַתָּה אֶת בְּרִיתִי תִשְׁמוֹר" (בראשית יז). וּמָצִינוּ *שֶׁדָּוִד שָׂמַח עָלֶיהָ, שֶׁנֶּאֱמַר "לַמְנַצֵּחַ עַל הַשְּׁמִינִית" (תהלים ו), כְּשֶׁהָיָה בְּבֵית הַמֶּרְחָץ וְרָאָה עַצְמוֹ בְּלֹא תוֹרָה וּבְלֹא מִצְוֹת, כֵּיוָן (*שֶׁנִּסְתַּכֵּל) בַּמִּילָה — שָׂמַח*: עֲשֶׂרֶת בְּנֵי הָמָן וַעֲשֶׂרֶת. הַזְכָּרַת שְׁמוֹתָן וְתֵיבָה הַסְּמוּכָה אַחֲרֵיהֶן, כְּלוֹמַר (ב) נִשְׁמָתָן נָפְלוּ כְּאֶחָד: זְקִיפָא. פורק"א בְּלַעַז, *בַּד אֶחָד, זֶה לְמַטָּה מִזֶּה: אָרִיחַ. הוּא הַכְּתָב: לְבֵנָה. הוּא חָלָק, שֶׁהוּא כִּפְלַיִים מִן הַכְּתָב. וְהֶאֱרִיחַ חֲלִי לְבֵנָה: שֶׁלֹּא תְּהֵא לָהֶם תְּקוּמָה. שֶׁלֹּא יְהֵא לָהֶם מָקוֹם לְהַרְחִיב צְעָדָיו תַּחְתָּיו: מְלַמֵּד שֶׁבָּא מַלְאָךְ כו'. שֶׁהֲרֵי הִתְחִיל לְדַבֵּר בִּלְשׁוֹן כַּעַס, וְסוֹפוֹ אָמַר "מַה שְּׁאֵלָתֵךְ": הָכִי גָּרְסִינַן: אָמַר רַב נַחְמָן יֵאָמֵר בַּפֶּה מַה שֶּׁנִּכְתַּב בִּסְפָרִים. וְלָא גָּרְסִינַן אָמְרָה לוֹ. וְהָכִי פֵּירוּשָׁהּ, סֵדֶר הַמִּקְרָאוֹת כָּךְ הוּא: "וְקִבֵּל הַיְּהוּדִים אֵת אֲשֶׁר הֵחֵלּוּ לַעֲשׂוֹת כִּי הָמָן בֶּן הַמְּדָתָא הָאֲגָגִי וגו' וּבְבֹאָהּ לִפְנֵי הַמֶּלֶךְ אָמַר עִם הַסֵּפֶר" וגו'. וּמָרְדֳּכַי כָּתַב אֲלֵיהֶם שֶׁיַּעֲשׂוּ פוּרִים כִּי הָמָן בִּיקֵּשׁ לְאַבְּדָם, וּמַה שֶּׁבָּאת אֶסְתֵּר לִפְנֵי הַמֶּלֶךְ [לְהִתְחַנֵּן לוֹ], כָּל זֶה יֵאָמֵר שָׁנָה בְּשָׁנָה: עִם הַסֵּפֶר. שֶׁתְּהֵא מְגִילָּה כְּתוּבָה לִפְנֵיהֶם בִּשְׁעַת קְרִיאָה: כַּאֲמִיתָהּ שֶׁל תּוֹרָה. °כְּסֵפֶר תּוֹרָה עַצְמוֹ. שִׂרְטוּט הֲלָכָה לְמֹשֶׁה מִסִּינַי: דִּבְרֵי הַצּוֹמוֹת וְזַעֲקָתָם וּמַאֲמַר אֶסְתֵּר. כָּךְ סְמוּכִים הַמִּקְרָאוֹת: שֶׁפֵּירְשׁוּ מִמֶּנּוּ. לְפִי שֶׁבָּטֵל מִדִּבְרֵי תוֹרָה וְנִכְנַס לִשְׂרָרָה: מֵעִיקָּרָא. בִּימֵי כּוֹרֶשׁ, כְּשֶׁעָלָה (עִם) זְרוּבָּבֶל מִן הַגּוֹלָה וּמָרְדֳּכַי עִמּוֹ, *וְנִמְנוּ בְּסֵפֶר עֶזְרָא. כ"ד שָׁנָה הָיָה בֵּין מִנְיָן לְמִנְיָן בִּימֵי כּוֹרֶשׁ לְדָרְיָוֶשׁ הָאַחֲרוֹן, וּלְפִי שֶׁנַּעֲשָׂה מָרְדֳּכַי שַׂר בֵּינְתַיִים יָרַד מֵחֲשִׁיבוּתוֹ אֵצֶל חֲכָמִים: שֶׁכָּל זְמַן שֶׁבָּרוּךְ בֶּן נֵרִיָּה קַיָּים לֹא הִנִּיחוֹ עֶזְרָא וְעָלָה. שֶׁיֵּשׁ לְךָ לִתְמוֹהַּ לָמָּה לֹא עָלָה עֶזְרָא עִם זְרוּבָּבֶל בִּימֵי כּוֹרֶשׁ, עַד הַשָּׁנָה הַשְּׁבִיעִית לְדָרְיָוֶשׁ הָאַחֲרוֹן לְאַחַר שֶׁנִּבְנָה הַבַּיִת, כְּמוֹ שֶׁכָּתוּב בְּעֶזְרָא "וַיָּבֹא יְרוּשָׁלַםִ בַּחֹדֶשׁ הַחֲמִישִׁי הִיא שְׁנַת הַשְּׁבִיעִית לַמֶּלֶךְ" וגו' (עזרא ז). וּבַמִּדְרָשׁ, שֶׁהָיָה לוֹמֵד תּוֹרָה מִפִּי בָּרוּךְ בֶּן נֵרִיָּה בְּבָבֶל, וּבָרוּךְ לֹא עָלָה מִבָּבֶל, וּמֵת שָׁם בְּתוֹךְ הַשָּׁנִים הַלָּלוּ. וְדַאֲמַרַן לְעֵיל בָּרוּךְ נִתְנַבֵּא בִּשְׁנַת שְׁתַּיִם לְדָרְיָוֶשׁ — בְּבָבֶל הָיָה מִתְנַבֵּא, וְשׁוֹלֵחַ סְפָרִים לִירוּשָׁלַיִם: יַעֲקֹב לָמַד תּוֹרָה י"ד שָׁנָה בְּבֵית עֵבֶר. כְּשֶׁפֵּירֵשׁ מֵאָבִיו לָלֶכֶת לְחָרָן, וְלֹא נֶעֱנַשׁ עֲלֵיהֶן עַל כִּיבּוּד אָבִיו, וּבִשְׁאָר כָּל הַשָּׁנִים שֶׁנִּשְׁתַּהָה בְּבֵית לָבָן וּבַדֶּרֶךְ — נֶעֱנַשׁ, כִּדְמְפָרֵשׁ וְאָזֵיל: לָמָּה

רבינו חננאל

וילכו גם אחיו וגו'. היינו דאמרי אינשי תעלא בזמנא סגיד ליה אלו כולן פשוטות הן: **עשרת** בני המן צריך למימרינהו בנשימה אחת הקורא את המגילה מ"ט כולהו כי הדדי נפקי נשמתייהו. ו' דויזתא צריך למימתחיה דכולהו בחד זקיפא איזדקיפו: כל השירות נכתבות אריח על גבי לבינה ולבינה ע"ג אריח אבל עשרת בני המן ומלכי כנען נכתבין אריח ע"ג אריח ולבנה ע"ג לבנה. מ"ט אמר ר' אבהו כדי שלא תהא תקומה במפלתן של רשעים: **דברי** הצומות וזעקתם. ומאמר אסתר קיים דברי הפורים. אמר רב יוסף גדול ת"ת יותר מהצלת נפשות ממרדכי דמעיקרא קא חשיב ליה בתר ארבעה ובסוף חשיב ליה בתר חמשה שנאמר אשר באו עם זרובבל ישוע נחמיה וגו'. ובסוף כתיב הבאים עם זרובבל ישוע נחמיה עזריה רעמיה נחמני מרדכי בלשן. למה נקרא שמו בלשן שיודע ע' לשונות. רצוי לרוב אחיו מלמד שפירשו ממנו מקצת סנהדרין: **דברי** שלום ואמת מלמד שצריכה שרטוט כאמיתה של תורה. *) אמר משמיה דרב גדול ת"ת מבנין בהמ"ק. שכ"ז שהי' ברוך בן נריה קיים לא הניחו עזרא ועלה. ועוד אמר משמו גדול ת"ת מכבוד אב ואם. שכל השנים שהיה יעקב בבית עבר ולמד תורה לא נענש עליהן. מנא הני מילי אמר ר' יוחנן

*) אולי צ"ל אמר רב שמואל בר מרתא משמיה דרב.

הגהות הב"ח

(א) גמ' אמר ר' יוחנן הכי קאמר דברי הצומות: (ב) רש"י ד"ה עשרת וכו' כלומר שנשמתן נפלו כאחד: (ג) תוס' ד"ה אמרה וכו' מלבד הספר שאמר לעשות:

מסורת הש"ס

[מנחות דף מג:] [נ"ל שנזכר] [כדאי' במנחות מג:] [נ"ל בנמן]

שבת י: ע"ש

ונמנו בספר עזרא ומ... לאחר ד' אנשים ולב שכנמנו מנין שני לבנינה הבית כספר ע כ"ד שנה בין מנין כל למנין שני ימי כ אחשורוש וז' שנים לדריוש האחרון

בראשית מה; שם מה; שם מה; שם נ; אסתר ח; משלי ו; דברים טז; תהלים קיט; דברים כח

ברכות ו. גז. (סוטה חולין פט.) מנחות לה:

*) [עי' ב"מ פז. כפי' ר"ס] שם

[עי' תוס' גיטין ו: ד"ה ותוס' סוטה ח: מנחות ל"ב ד"ה]

עזרא ב; נחמיה ז

גליון הש"ס

גמ' ששון זו מילה. שבת דף קל ע"א בר"ה שש: רש"י ד"ה כאמיתה. כס"ת עצמו. מנחות דף לב ע"ב ת"ה הא מורין:

*לָמָּה נִמְנוּ שְׁנוֹתָיו שֶׁל יִשְׁמָעֵאל? כְּדֵי לְיַחֵס בָּהֶן שְׁנוֹתָיו שֶׁל יַעֲקֹב. דִּכְתִיב: °"וְאֵלֶּה שְׁנֵי חַיֵּי יִשְׁמָעֵאל מְאַת שָׁנָה וּשְׁלֹשִׁים שָׁנָה וְשֶׁבַע שָׁנִים". כַּמָּה קָשִׁישׁ יִשְׁמָעֵאל מִיִּצְחָק? אַרְבֵּיסַר שְׁנִין דִּכְתִיב: °"וְאַבְרָם בֶּן שְׁמֹנִים שָׁנָה וְשֵׁשׁ שָׁנִים בְּלֶדֶת הָגָר אֶת יִשְׁמָעֵאל לְאַבְרָם". וּכְתִיב: °"וְאַבְרָהָם בֶּן מְאַת שָׁנָה בְּהִוָּלֶד לוֹ אֵת יִצְחָק בְּנוֹ". וּכְתִיב: °"וְיִצְחָק בֶּן שִׁשִּׁים שָׁנָה בְּלֶדֶת אוֹתָם". בַּר כַּמָּה הֲוָה יִשְׁמָעֵאל כִּדְאוֹלִיד יַעֲקֹב? בַּר שִׁבְעִים וְאַרְבָּעָה. כַּמָּה פַּיְישָׁן מִשְּׁנֵיהּ? שִׁתִּין וּתְלָת. וְתַנְיָא: הָיָה יַעֲקֹב אָבִינוּ בְּשָׁעָה שֶׁנִּתְבָּרֵךְ מֵאָבִיו בֶּן שִׁשִּׁים וְשָׁלֹשׁ שָׁנָה, וּבוֹ בַּפֶּרֶק מֵת יִשְׁמָעֵאל, דִּכְתִיב: °"וַיַּרְא עֵשָׂו כִּי בֵרַךְ וגו' וַיֵּלֶךְ עֵשָׂו אֶל יִשְׁמָעֵאל וַיִּקַּח אֶת מַחֲלַת בַּת יִשְׁמָעֵאל אֲחוֹת נְבָיוֹת". מִמַּשְׁמַע שֶׁנֶּאֱמַר "בַּת יִשְׁמָעֵאל", אֵינִי יוֹדֵעַ שֶׁהִיא אֲחוֹת נְבָיוֹת? מְלַמֵּד שֶׁקִּידְּשָׁהּ יִשְׁמָעֵאל וּמֵת, וְהִשִּׂיאָהּ נְבָיוֹת אָחִיהָ. שִׁתִּין וּתְלָת וְאַרְבֵּיסַר עַד דְּמוֹלִיד יוֹסֵף — הָא שִׁבְעִין וְשִׁבְעָה. וּכְתִיב: °"וְיוֹסֵף בֶּן שְׁלֹשִׁים שָׁנָה בְּעָמְדוֹ לִפְנֵי פַּרְעֹה" — הָא מְאָה וְשִׁבַע, שַׁב דְּשָׂבְעָא וְתַרְתֵּי דְּכַפְנָא — הָא מְאָה וְשִׁיתְּסַר. וּכְתִיב: °"וַיֹּאמֶר פַּרְעֹה אֶל יַעֲקֹב כַּמָּה יְמֵי שְׁנֵי חַיֶּיךָ. וַיֹּאמֶר יַעֲקֹב אֶל פַּרְעֹה יְמֵי שְׁנֵי מְגוּרַי שְׁלֹשִׁים וּמְאַת שָׁנָה". מְאָה וְשִׁיתְּסַר הָוְיָין! אֶלָּא ש"מ אַרְבַּע עֶשְׂרֵה שְׁנִין דַּהֲוָה בְּבֵית עֵבֶר — לָא חֲשֵׁיב לְהוּ. דְּתַנְיָא:(א) הָיָה יַעֲקֹב בְּבֵית עֵבֶר מוּטְמָן אַרְבַּע עֶשְׂרֵה שָׁנָה. עֵבֶר מֵת לְאַחַר שֶׁיָּרַד יַעֲקֹב אָבִינוּ לַאֲרַם נַהֲרַיִם שְׁתֵּי שָׁנִים.(ב) יָצָא מִשָּׁם וּבָא לוֹ לַאֲרַם נַהֲרַיִם. נִמְצָא, כְּשֶׁעָמַד עַל הַבְּאֵר בֶּן שִׁבְעִים וְשֶׁבַע שָׁנָה. וּמְנָלַן דְּלָא מִיעֲנַשׁ? דְּתַנְיָא: נִמְצָא, יוֹסֵף שֶׁפֵּירַשׁ מֵאָבִיו, עֶשְׂרִים וּשְׁתַּיִם שָׁנָה, כְּשֵׁם שֶׁפֵּירַשׁ יַעֲקֹב אָבִינוּ מֵאָבִיו. דְּיַעֲקֹב תְּלָתִין וְשִׁיתָּא הָוְיָין! אֶלָּא:(ג) אַרְבֵּיסַר דַּהֲוָה בְּבֵית עֵבֶר לָא חֲשֵׁיב לְהוּ. סוֹף סוֹף דְּבֵית לָבָן עֶשְׂרִין שְׁנִין הָוְיָין! אֶלָּא, מִשּׁוּם דְּאִשְׁתַּהִי בְּאוֹרְחָא תַּרְתֵּין שְׁנִין. דְּתַנְיָא: יָצָא מֵאֲרַם נַהֲרַיִם וּבָא לוֹ לְסֻכּוֹת, וְעָשָׂה שָׁם שְׁמוֹנָה עָשָׂר חוֹדֶשׁ, שֶׁנֶּאֱמַר: °"וְיַעֲקֹב נָסַע סֻכֹּתָה וַיִּבֶן לוֹ בָּיִת וּלְמִקְנֵהוּ עָשָׂה סֻכֹּת". וּבְבֵית אֵל עָשָׂה שִׁשָּׁה חֳדָשִׁים, וְהִקְרִיב זְבָחִים.§

הדרן עלך מגילה נקראת

הַקּוֹרֵא [א]אֶת הַמְּגִילָּה לְמַפְרֵעַ — לֹא יָצָא. [ב]קְרָאָהּ עַל פֶּה, [ג]קְרָאָהּ *תַּרְגּוּם בְּכָל לָשׁוֹן — לֹא יָצָא. אֲבָל קוֹרִין אוֹתָהּ לַלּוֹעֲזוֹת בְּלַעַז; [ד]וְהַלּוֹעֵז שֶׁשָּׁמַע אַשּׁוּרִית — יָצָא. [ה]קְרָאָהּ סֵירוּגִין, [ו]וּמִתְנַמְנֵם — יָצָא. [ז]הָיָה כּוֹתְבָהּ, דּוֹרְשָׁהּ, וּמַגִּיהָהּ, אִם כִּוֵּן לִבּוֹ — יָצָא, וְאִם לָאו — לֹא יָצָא. [ח]הָיְתָה כְּתוּבָה בְּסַם וּבְסִיקְרָא וּבְקוֹמוֹס וּבְקַנְקַנְתּוֹם, עַל הַנְּיָיר וְעַל הַדִּפְתְּרָא — לֹא יָצָא, עַד שֶׁתְּהֵא כְּתוּבָה אַשּׁוּרִית, *עַל הַסֵּפֶר, וּבִדְיוֹ.§ **גמ'** מה"מ? אֲמַר רָבָא: דַּאֲמַר קְרָא "כִּכְתָבָם וְכִזְמַנָּם", מַה זְּמַנָּם לְמַפְרֵעַ לָא — אַף כְּתָבָם לְמַפְרֵעַ לָא. מִידֵי קְרִיאָה כְּתִיבָה הָכָא? עֲשִׂיָּיה כְּתִיבָה, דִּכְתִיב "לִהְיוֹת עוֹשִׂים אֶת שְׁנֵי הַיָּמִים"! אֶלָּא מֵהָכָא: דִּכְתִיב "וְהַיָּמִים הָאֵלֶּה נִזְכָּרִים וְנַעֲשִׂים", אִיתְקַשׁ זְכִירָה לַעֲשִׂיָּיה, מַה עֲשִׂיָּיה לְמַפְרֵעַ לָא — אַף זְכִירָה לְמַפְרֵעַ לָא. תָּנָא: [ט]וְכֵן בְּהַלֵּל, [י]וְכֵן בִּקְרִיאַת שְׁמַע, וּבִתְפִלָּה. הַלֵּל מְנָלַן? רַבָּה אָמַר: דִּכְתִיב °"מִמִּזְרַח שֶׁמֶשׁ עַד מְבוֹאוֹ". רַב יוֹסֵף אָמַר: °"זֶה הַיּוֹם עָשָׂה ה'", רַב אַוְיָא אָמַר: °"יְהִי שֵׁם ה' מְבוֹרָךְ", וְרַב נַחְמָן בַּר יִצְחָק, וְאִיתֵּימָא ר' אַחָא בַּר יַעֲקֹב, אָמַר מֵהָכָא: °"מֵעַתָּה וְעַד עוֹלָם". ק"ש — דְּתַנְיָא: *ק"ש כִּכְתָבָהּ דִּבְרֵי רַבִּי, וַחֲכ"א: [כ]בְּכָל לָשׁוֹן. מ"ט דְּרַבִּי? אָמַר קְרָא: וְהָיוּ

לָמָּה נִמְנוּ שְׁנוֹתָיו שֶׁל יִשְׁמָעֵאל. מַה לָּנוּ לִמְנוֹת שְׁנוֹת הָרְשָׁעִים: לְהִתְיַיחֵס בָּהֶן שְׁנוֹתָיו שֶׁל יַעֲקֹב. עַל יְדֵי מִנְיַן שְׁנוֹת יִשְׁמָעֵאל אָנוּ לְמֵדִין [בְּאֵיזֶה פֶּרֶק מִשְּׁנוֹת יַעֲקֹב עָבְרוּ עָלָיו כָּל הַקּוֹרוֹת וְהַמּוֹצְאוֹת אוֹתוֹ: מֵהֶן אָנוּ לְמֵדִין] שֶׁשִּׁימֵּשׁ בְּבֵית עֵבֶר י"ד שָׁנָה. כֵּיצַד? אַבְרָהָם בֶּן פ"ו שָׁנָה כְּשֶׁנּוֹלַד יִשְׁמָעֵאל, וּכְשֶׁנּוֹלַד יִצְחָק הָיָה בֶּן מֵאָה שָׁנָה — הֲרֵי הָיוּ לְיִשְׁמָעֵאל י"ד שָׁנָה. וְיִצְחָק קָדַם לְיַעֲקֹב שִׁשִּׁים שָׁנָה — הֲרֵי לְיִשְׁמָעֵאל ע"ד. כַּמָּה פָּיְישָׁן מִשְּׁנוֹתָיו שֶׁל יִשְׁמָעֵאל — ס"ג, נִמְצָא שֶׁהָיָה יַעֲקֹב כְּשֶׁמֵּת יִשְׁמָעֵאל בֶּן ס"ג שָׁנָה: וְתַנְיָא הָיָה יַעֲקֹב כו'. וְתַנְיָא נַמִּי הָכִי שֶׁהָיָה יַעֲקֹב כְּשֶׁנִּתְבָּרֵךְ מֵאָבִיו בֶּן ס"ג, וּבוֹ בַּפֶּרֶק מֵת יִשְׁמָעֵאל, שֶׁנֶּאֱמַר "וַיֵּלֶךְ עֵשָׂו אֶל יִשְׁמָעֵאל" וגו': מְלַמֵּד שֶׁקִּידְּשָׁהּ יִשְׁמָעֵאל. אָבִיהָ, וּמֵת. וְהִשִּׂיאָהּ נְבָיוֹת אָחִיהָ: וְאַרְבַּע עֶשְׂרֵה שָׁנָה. הָיָה יַעֲקֹב בְּבֵית לָבָן עַד דְּאוֹלִיד יוֹסֵף, דִּכְתִיב "עֲבַדְתִּיךָ אַרְבַּע עֶשְׂרֵה שָׁנָה בִּשְׁתֵּי בְנוֹתֶיךָ" וגו' (בראשית לא), וּכְשֶׁנּוֹלַד יוֹסֵף שָׁלְמוּ שְׁנֵי עַבְדוּת הַבָּנוֹת, שֶׁנֶּאֱמַר "וַיְהִי כַּאֲשֶׁר יָלְדָה רָחֵל אֶת יוֹסֵף" וגו' (שם ל). וּמִשָּׁם וָהָלְאָה עָבַד אוֹתוֹ בִּשְׂכַר הַצֹּאן — הֲרֵי בֶּן ע"ז הָיָה יַעֲקֹב כְּשֶׁנּוֹלַד יוֹסֵף, וּכְתִיב "וְיוֹסֵף בֶּן שְׁלֹשִׁים שָׁנָה בְּעָמְדוֹ לִפְנֵי פַרְעֹה", — נִמְצָא יַעֲקֹב בֶּן מֵאָה וָשֶׁבַע [שָׁנִים כְּשֶׁהָיָה יוֹסֵף בֶּן שְׁלֹשִׁים שָׁנָה]. וְנִשְׁתַּהָה יַעֲקֹב לֵישֵׁב בְּאֶרֶץ כְּנַעַן שֶׁלֹּא יָרַד לְמִצְרַיִם: שִׁבְעָה דְּשָׂבְעָא וּתְרֵין דְּכַפְנָא. דִּכְתִיב "כִּי זֶה שְׁנָתַיִם הָרָעָב בְּקֶרֶב הָאָרֶץ" וגו' (בראשית מה), הֲרֵי בֶּן קי"ו הָיָה יַעֲקֹב כְּשֶׁיָּרַד לְמִצְרַיִם, וּקְרָא כְּתִיב "שְׁלֹשִׁים וּמְאַת שָׁנָה". נִמְצָא, מִשֶּׁנָּסַע מִבֵּית אָבִיו עַד שֶׁבָּא לְבֵית לָבָן אַרְבַּע עָשָׂר, וְאוֹתָן הַשָּׁנִים הָיָה בְּבֵית עֵבֶר. וְלָא חֲשֵׁיב לְהוּ לָא גָּרְסִינַן הָכָא, עַד לְקַמָּן: עֵבֶר מֵת לְאַחַר יְרִידָתוֹ שֶׁל יַעֲקֹב לַאֲרַם נַהֲרַיִם. וּבָא לְבֵית לָבָן, וְעָמַד שָׁם שְׁתֵּי שָׁנִים. לֵא וַחֲשׁוֹב שְׁנוֹתָיו שֶׁל עֵבֶר, וְנִמְצָא שֶׁמֵּת כְּשֶׁהָיָה יַעֲקֹב בֶּן שִׁבְעִים וָתֵשַׁע שָׁנָה, וְהַיְינוּ שְׁתֵּי שָׁנִים מִשֶּׁבָּא לְבֵית לָבָן, כְּשֶׁתַּחֲשׁוֹב י"ד שָׁנָה שֶׁשִּׁימֵּשׁ בְּבֵית עֵבֶר: יָצָא. יַעֲקֹב מִבֵּית עֵבֶר שְׁתֵּי שָׁנִים לִפְנֵי מִיתָתוֹ שֶׁל עֵבֶר: נִמְצָא כְּשֶׁעָמַד כו'. הָכִי גָּרְסִינַן: מְנָלַן דְּלָא אִיעֲנַשׁ עֲלַיְיהוּ — דְּתַנְיָא: נִמְצָא יוֹסֵף כְּשֶׁפֵּירֵשׁ מֵאָבִיו שֶׁלֹּא רָאָהוּ עֶשְׂרִים וּשְׁתַּיִם שָׁנָה, כְּדֶרֶךְ שֶׁפֵּירֵשׁ יַעֲקֹב מִבֵּית אָבִיו שֶׁלֹּא כִּיבְּדוֹ, נִתְאַבֵּל עַל יוֹסֵף כ"ב שָׁנָה. כֵּיצַד? יוֹסֵף בֶּן שְׁבַע עֶשְׂרֵה שָׁנָה הָיָה כְּשֶׁפֵּירֵשׁ מֵאָבִיו. וּכְשֶׁמָּלַךְ עַל מִצְרַיִם הָיָה בֶּן שְׁלֹשִׁים שָׁנָה, שֶׁנֶּאֱמַר "וְיוֹסֵף בֶּן שְׁלֹשִׁים שָׁנָה בְּעָמְדוֹ לִפְנֵי פַרְעֹה" — הֲרֵי י"ג, וְשִׁבְעָה דְּשָׂבְעָא, וּתְרֵין דְּכַפְנָא — הֲרֵי עֶשְׂרִים וּשְׁתַּיִם שָׁנָה שֶׁנִּתְכַּסָּה יוֹסֵף מֵאָבִיו. וְיַעֲקֹב עָמַד עֶשְׂרִים שָׁנָה בְּבֵית לָבָן, וְי"ד שָׁנָה בְּבֵית עֵבֶר: אֶלָּא שְׁמַע מִינָּהּ. י"ד דְּבֵית עֵבֶר לָא חֲשֵׁיב לְהוּ, דְּלָא אִיעֲנַשׁ עֲלַיְיהוּ: אִי הָכִי בְּצִירָא לְהוּ. וְאֵין כָּאן אֶלָּא עֶשְׂרִים דְּבֵית לָבָן: אִישְׁתַּהִי ב' שָׁנִים בְּאוֹרְחָא. דִּבְשׁוּבוֹ מֵאֲרַם נַהֲרַיִם לָבֹא לְיִצְחָק אָבִיו וַיִּבֶן לוֹ בַּיִת לִימוֹת הַחוֹרֶף, עָשָׂה סוּכּוֹת ב' פְּעָמִים שְׁנֵי יְמוֹת הַקַּיִץ — הֲרֵי י"ח, וּבְבֵית אֵל עָשָׂה שִׁשָּׁה חֳדָשִׁים כְּשֶׁיָּצָא מִשְּׁכֶם, שֶׁנֶּאֱמַר "קוּם עֲלֵה בֵית אֵל" וגו' (בראשית לה):

הדרן עלך מגילה נקראת

הַקּוֹרֵא. לַלּוֹעֲזוֹת. כָּל שֶׁאֵינוֹ לְשׁוֹן הַקּוֹדֶשׁ נִקְרָא לַעַז. וּלְקַמָּן פָּרֵיךְ: וְהָא אָמַרְתְּ קְרָאָהּ בְּכָל לָשׁוֹן לֹא יָצָא: סֵירוּגִין. בַּגְּמָרָא מְפָרֵשׁ קוֹרֵא מְעַט וּפוֹסֵק, (*וְשׁוֹהֶה) וְחוֹזֵר וּפוֹסֵק: הָיָה כּוֹתְבָהּ אוֹ דּוֹרְשָׁהּ. וּמִתּוֹךְ כָּךְ קוֹרְאָהּ, אִם כִּוֵּן לִבּוֹ — יָצָא: דִּיפְתְּרָא וּנְיָיר. מְפָרֵשׁ בַּגְּמָ': עַל הַסֵּפֶר. קְלָף: **גמ'** מְנָהָנֵי מִילֵּי. דִּלְמַפְרֵעַ לֹא יָצָא: מַה זְּמַנָּם לְמַפְרֵעַ לֹא. דְּאִי אֶפְשָׁר שֶׁיְּהֵא ט"ו קוֹדֶם לְי"ד: מִמִּזְרַח שֶׁמֶשׁ עַד מְבוֹאוֹ. כְּשֵׁם שֶׁשְּׁקִיעַת וּזְרִיחַת הַחַמָּה לֹא יֵהָפְכוּ, כָּךְ מְהוּלָּל שֵׁם ה', וְלֹא לְמַפְרֵעַ: זֶה הַיּוֹם. כְּסֵדֶר הַיּוֹם, שֶׁאֵינוֹ מִשְׁתַּנֶּה בִּשְׁעוֹתָיו לְהֵיפֵךְ, כָּךְ לְמַפְרֵעַ לֹא: יְהִי שֵׁם ה' מְבוֹרָךְ. כַּהֲוָיָיתוֹ יְהֵא הִלּוּל הַשֵּׁם וּבִרְכָתוֹ כְּסִדְרוֹ: כִּכְתָבָהּ. בִּלְשׁוֹן הַקּוֹדֶשׁ, וְלֹא בְּלָשׁוֹן אַחֵר: וְהָיוּ

רבינו חננאל

לא נמנו שנותיו של ישמעאל אלא כדי ליחס שנותיו של יעקב אבינו. מצינו שהיה ישמעאל גדול מיצחק י"ד שנה. ויצחק גדול מיעקב ס' שנה נמצא ישמעאל גדול מיעקב ע"ד שנה ובו בפרק שנתברך יעקב אבינו מת ישמעאל וכל שנותיו היו קל"ז הסר מהן ע"ד שנה נשארו ס"ג שנה נמצא בעת שיצא לארם נהרים בן ס"ג שנה. וי"ד בבית עבר. וכ' שנה בבית לבן שנאמר זה לי עשרים שנה בביתך וגו' הרי צ"ז שנה והיה יוסף בעת צאת יעקב מאצל לבן בן [שש] שנים כי אחר י"ד שנה נולד ונשתהה שנתים בדרך נמצא יעקב כשבא אל יצחק אביו בן צ"ט שנה נתכסה יעקב מיצחק אביו ל"ו שנה כשנגנב [יוסף] היה בן י"ז שנה. וי"ג שנה עשה בבית אדוניו ובבית הסהר [וז' דשובע] ושנתים הרעב הרי י"ג שנה וז' שנה ושתי שנים הרי כ"ב נתכסה יוסף מיעקב אבינו כשיעור השנים שנתכסה יעקב מיצחק אביו זולתי י"ד שנים שהיה יעקב למד תורה בבית עבר. ולא נמנו עליהם. וכל זה החשבון מפורש מן הפסוקים הנזכרים בגמ' ולפי זו השמועה היה יוסף בשעה שהגיע אל יצחק אבי אביו בן ח' שנים ויעקב היה בן צ"ט שנתאחרו שנתים בדרך נמצא יעקב בעת שנגנב יוסף בן ק"ח שנה. וכ"ב נתכסה ממנו הרי שלשים ומאת שנה כדכתיב שלשים ומאת שנה וגו':

הדרן עלך מגילה נקראת

*) **הקורא** את המגילה לא יצא מנא לן אמר רבא דאמרינן ככתבם וכזמנם מה י"ד שהוא זמנם אם יעבור לא יתכן להחזירו למפרע ולקרותה ביום י"ד שכבר עבר כך קריאתה למפרע לא אע"ג דהאי קרא ככתבם וכזמנם בעשיה כתיב איתקש זכירה לעשיה שנא' והימים האלה נזכרים ונעשים. תנא וכן בהלל וכן בק"ש וכן בתפלה למפרע לא יצא הלל דכתיב ביה ממזרח שמש עד מבאו מהלל שם ה' כשם שאי אפשר

*) לפני רבינו חננאל היה פרק הקורא את המגילה למפרע פרק שלישי ואנחנו הגהנו דברי רבינו לפי הסדר אשר לפנינו.

הגהות הב"ח

(א) גמ' ותניא היה יעקב אבינו בבית עבר מוטמן ומשמש ארבע עשרה שנה לאחר שירד כצ"ל ותבת עבר מת נמחק: (ב) שם שתי שנים מת עבר יצא משם ובא לו לארם וכו' בן ע"ה שנה היה ומנלן דלא איענש יעקב אבינו עליה דתניא: (ג) שם אלא שמע מינה ארביסר:

עין משפט נר מצוה

א א מיי' פ"ב מהלכות מגלה הלכה א סמג עשין מד"ס ד טוש"ע א"ח סימן תרל סעיף ו:
ב ב מיי' שם הלכה ג טוש"ע שם סעיף ג וסעיף ז:
ג ג מיי' שם הלכה ד טוש"ע שם סעיף ט:
ד ד מיי' שם הלכה ג טוש"ע שם סעיף ח:
ה ה מיי' שם הלכה א טוש"ע שם סעיף ה:
ו ו מיי' שם הלכה ה טוש"ע שם סעיף יב:
ז ז מיי' שם טוש"ע שם סעיף יג:
ח ח מיי' שם הלכה ט טור וש"ע א"ח סימן תרלא סעיף א ב וע"ש:
ט ט מיי' פ"ג מהלכות חנוכה הלכה ט סמג עשין ה טוש"ע א"ח סי' תכב סעיף ו:
י י מיי' פ"ב מהלכות ק"ש הלכה יא סמג עשין יח טוש"ע א"ח סימן סב סעיף א:
יא כ מיי' שם הלכה י וסמג שם טוש"ע א"ח סימן סב סעיף ב:

מסורת הש"ס

[יבמות סז.] · [עיין ברש"י לקמן יח. ד"ה קראה] · [עיין תוספות לקמן יט. ד"ה על] · [תוספתא' פ"ב] · ברכות יג. סוטה לב: · [נ"ל וקורא מעט]

תורה אור: בראשית כה · שם טז · שם כא · שם כה · שם כח · שם מא · שם מז · שם לג · תהלים קיג · שם קיח · שם קיג · שם

כל התורה בכל לשון נאמרה. פירש הקונטרס: שנתנה לקרות בכל לשון שרוצה לקרות בספר תורה. וקשה: שהרי קריאת התורה אינה מן התורה אלא מדרבנן, לבד מפרשת זכור דהוי דאורייתא! ונראה דהכי פירושא: כל קריאה שבתורה, כגון מצות חליצה, ופרשת עגלה ערופה, ווידוי מעשר ובכורים, וכל אלו השנויין פרק "אלו נאמרין" בסוטה (דף לב. ושם)*:

דאי בלשון הקודש נאמרה למה לי למיכתב וכו'. קשיא: *דהא בפרק "אלו נאמרים" בסוטה (דף לג. ושם) מצריך קרא בין למאן דאמר בכל לשון נאמרה, בין למאן דאמר בלשון הקודש נאמרה! ויש לומר: דהתם בעי לאוקמי רבוי אליבא דכולי עלמא, למאן דאמר בכל לשון נאמרה – צריך קרא לרבויי לשון הקדש, ולמאן דאמר בלשון הקודש נאמרה – צריך לרבויי בכל לשון:

הסדיר שמונה עשרה ברכות על הסדר. מכאן קשיא למה שפרש"י בברכות (דף לד. ושם) גבי אמצעיות אין להן סדר, דפירש דאם טעה באחת מן הברכות ושכח אחת מהן – שצריך לחזור, שאומר אותה ברכה ששכח במקום שנזכר, וגומר תפלתו, וקשיא: דאם כן הוא אומר השמונה עשרה ברכות למפרע, והכא חזינא דשמעון הפקולי התקין אותן על הסדר! אלא נראה לפרש התם: אין להן סדר – דלא הוו כשלש ראשונות ושלש אחרונות דחוזר לראש השלשה כשטעה באחת מהן, אלא חוזר לאותה ששכח, וגומר ממנה ולמטה הכל כסדר. אבל ב"עננו" אין חוזר, כיון שעבר מקומו. והכי נמי אמרינן לקמן (דף יח:) גבי מגילה, שאם השמיט פסוק אחד – שמתחיל וקורא מאותו פסוק ולמטה*:

ודוד כי אמרה בפרשת תשיעית אמרה. פירש הקונטרס: ואף על גב דליכא אלא ח' מזמורים עד התם, "אשרי האיש" ו"למה רגשו גוים" תרתי ניהו. וקשיא, דהא פרק קמא דברכות (דף י.) אמר דחדא פרשה היא, ומסיק התם דכל פרשה שהיתה חביבה לדוד התחיל בה באשרי וסיים בה באשרי, כגון זו שמתחלת ב"אשרי האיש" ומסיימת ב"אשרי כל חוסי בו" והיינו סוף ד"למה רגשו". אלמא דחדא פרשה היא! וצריך לומר ד"למנצח על מות" ו"למה ה' תעמוד ברחוק" – תרתי ניהו. דאי

[ועי' תוס' ברכות לד. ד"ה אמצעיות]

תורה אור

°"והיו" – בהויתן יהו. ורבנן מ"ט? אמר קרא: °"שמע" – בכל לשון שאתה שומע. ורבי נמי, הא כתיב: "שמע"! ההוא מיבעי ליה: השמע לאזניך מה שאתה מוציא מפיך. ורבנן סברי כמאן דאמר: *[א]הקורא את שמע ולא השמיע לאזנו – יצא. ורבנן נמי, הכתיב: "והיו"! ההוא מיבעי ליה שלא יקרא למפרע. ורבי, שלא יקרא למפרע מנא ליה? מ"דברים" "הדברים". ורבנן – "דברים" "הדברים" לא משמע להו. לימא קסבר רבי כל התורה כולה בכל לשון נאמרה, דאי סלקא דעתך בלשון הקודש נאמרה – למה לי למכתב "והיו"? איצטריך, סלקא דעתך "שמע" כרבנן – כתב רחמנא "והיו". לימא קסברי רבנן כל התורה בלשון הקודש נאמרה, דאי סלקא דעתך בכל לשון נאמרה – למה לי למכתב "שמע"? איצטריך, סלקא דעתך אמינא "והיו" כרבי – כתב רחמנא "שמע". תפלה מנא לן? דתניא: *שמעון הפקולי הסדיר שמונה עשרה ברכות לפני רבן גמליאל על הסדר ביבנה. אמר רבי (א) יוחנן, ואמרי לה במתניתא תנא: *[ב]מאה ועשרים זקנים ובהם כמה נביאים תיקנו שמונה עשרה ברכות על הסדר. *ת"ר: [ג]מנין שאומרים אבות? שנאמר: °"הבו לה' בני אלים". ומנין שאומרים גבורות? שנאמר: °"הבו לה' כבוד ועוז". ומנין שאומרים קדושות? שנאמר: °"הבו לה' כבוד שמו השתחוו לה' בהדרת קדש". ומה ראו לומר בינה אחר קדושה? שנאמר: °"והקדישו את קדוש יעקב ואת אלהי ישראל יעריצו" וסמיך ליה: "וידעו תועי רוח בינה". ומה ראו לומר תשובה אחר בינה? דכתיב: °"ולבבו יבין ושב ורפא לו". אי הכי לימא רפואה בתרה דתשובה! לא ס"ד דכתיב: °"וישוב אל ה' וירחמהו ואל אלהינו כי ירבה לסלוח..." ומאי חזית דסמכת אהא, סמוך אהא! כתב קרא אחרינא: °"הסולח לכל עוניכי הרופא לכל תחלואיכי, הגואל משחת חייכי" למימרא דגאולה ורפואה בתר סליחה היא. והכתיב: "ושב ורפא לו"! ההוא – לאו רפואה דתחלואים היא, אלא רפואה דסליחה היא. ומה ראו לומר גאולה בשביעית? אמר רבא: מתוך שעתידין ליגאל בשביעית, לפיכך קבעוה בשביעית. והאמר מר: *בששית – קולות, בשביעית – מלחמות, במוצאי שביעית בן דוד בא! מלחמה נמי אתחלתא דגאולה היא. ומה ראו לומר רפואה בשמינית? אמר רבי אחא: מתוך שנתנה מילה בשמינית, שצריכה רפואה, לפיכך קבעוה בשמינית. ומה ראו לומר ברכת השנים בתשיעית? אמר רבי אלכסנדרי: כנגד מפקיעי שערים, דכתיב: °"שבור זרוע רשע", ודוד כי אמרה – בתשיעית אמרה. ומה ראו לומר קיבוץ גליות לאחר ברכת השנים? דכתיב: °"ואתם הרי ישראל ענפכם תתנו ופריכם תשאו לעמי ישראל כי קרבו לבוא". וכיון שנתקבצו גליות – נעשה דין ברשעים, שנאמר: °"ואשיבה ידי עליך ואצרוף כבור סיגיך" וכתיב: °"ואשיבה שופטיך כבראשונה". וכיון שנעשה דין מן הרשעים – כלו הפושעים, וכולל זדים עמהם, שנאמר: °"ושבר פושעים וחטאים יחדיו...(א) (יכלו".) וכיון שכלו הפושעים – מתרוממת קרן צדיקים, דכתיב: °"וכל קרני רשעים אגדע תרוממנה קרנות צדיק", וכולל גירי הצדק עם הצדיקים, שנאמר: °"מפני שיבה תקום והדרת פני זקן", וסמיך ליה: "וכי יגור אתכם גר". והיכן מתרוממת קרנם? בירושלים, שנאמר: °"שאלו שלום ירושלים ישליו אוהביך". וכיון שנבנית ירושלים – בא דוד, שנאמר:

אחר

(דברים ו; שם; תהלים כט; שם; שם; ישעיה כט; ישעיה ו; הושע יד; תהלים קג; תהלים י; יחזקאל לו; ישעיה א; שם; תהלים עה; ויקרא יט; תהלים קכב)

א) גירסת הרי"ף א"ר יצחק ואיתימא ר' חייא בר אבא ואמרי לה וכו' וגירסת הרא"ש א"ר ירמיה ואיתימא רחב"א ואמרי לה וכו'.

והיו הדברים האלה בהויתן. בלשון הקודש: שלא יקרא למפרע. אלמא: קריאת שמע למפרע לא. ומהכא יליף תנא דלעיל טעמא: בכל לשון נאמרה. לקרותה בכל לשון, ולכן איצטריך בקריאת שמע "והיו": איצטריך. "והיו", דלא תימא: "שמע", בכל לשון שאתה שומע, כרבנן: על הסדר. כמשפט המקראות, וכדיליף לקמן: הפקולי. יש אומרים שמשתכר בצמר גפן, שנקרא פקולא: הבו לה'. הזכירו לפניו את אילי הארץ: הבו לה' כבוד שמו. סיפיה דקרא "בהדרת קודש": ומה ראו לומר גאולה בשביעית. ולא רפואה אחר סליחה, כדכתיב קרא "הסולח לכל עוניכי הרופא לכל תחלואיכי": מתוך שעתידין ליגאל בשביעית. שבוע שבן דוד בא בו חלוק משאר שנים, כדאמרינן בפרק "חלק" (דף צז.): שנה ראשונה רעב ולא רעב כו', עד ובשביעית מלחמות, ובמוצאי שביעית בן דוד בא: אתחלתא דגאולה היא. ואע"ג דהאי גאולה לאו גאולה דגלות היא, אלא שיגאלנו מן הצרות הבאות עלינו תמיד, דהא ברכת קיבוץ ובנין ירושלים וצמח דוד יש לכל אחת ואחת ברכה לעצמה לבד מגאולה זו, אפילו הכי, כיון דשם גאולה עלה – קבעוה בשביעית: שבור זרוע רשע. אלו המייקרין את התבואה ומפקיעין את השער. ומאי דבמפקיעי שערים כתיב – דכתיב בההיא פרשתא "יארב במסתר כאריה" בסופו "יארוב לחטוף עני", וכי הליסטים אורב את העני? והלא את העשיר הוא אורב! אלא במפקיעי שערים הכתוב מדבר, שרוב דעתם לעניים הוא. וקא בעי דוד רחמי עלה דמילתא: "שבור זרוע רשע" ותן שובע בעולם, ובכך זרועו שבור. "ורע תדרוש רשעו בל תמצא", וזה שהיה בדעתו להיות רשע, כשתדרוש רשעו לא תמצא עולה, שלא הספיק לעשותה: בפרשה תשיעית אמרה. *ואם תאמר שמינית היא? – "אשרי" ו"למה רגשו גויים" תרתי פרשתא היא: ופריכם תשאו לעמי ישראל כי קרבו לבא. אלמא: קיבוץ גליות בעת ברכת השנים היא: וכיון שנתקבצו גליות נעשה דין ברשעים. קודם שנתיישבו בירושלים, שנאמר "ואסירה כל בדיליך", ועל ידי כן "ואשיבה שופטיך כבראשונה ויועציך כבתחלה" כמו לשעבר. "ציון במשפט תפדה ושביה בצדקה" – לכן סמכם לקבוץ גליות, והשיבה שופטינו ויועצינו במשפט: כלו המינים. תלמידי ישו הנוצרי, לכך סמכו לה ברכת המינים, שנאמר "עוזבי ה'" – אלו המינים, "ושבר פושעים" – היינו זדים, כדאמר: "פשעים" – אלו המרדין (יומא דף לו:):

אחר

(דברים ו; שם; תהלים כט; שם; ישעיה כט; שם; שם ו; תהלים קג)

רבינו חננאל

אפשר לזרוח השמש מן המערב כך הלל למפרע לא ק"ש לרבנן מוהיו שלא יקרא למפרע כלומר יהיו כמות שהן לר' מהדברים כלומר הדברים כסדרן תפלה דתני שמעון הפקולי [הסדיר] י"ח ברכות לפני ר"ג על הסדר. במתניתין תנא ק"כ זקנים ובהם כמה נביאים תקנו י"ח ברכות על הסדר. מנין שאומרים אבות שנאמר הבו לה' בני אלים והן האבות גבורי התורה והמצות כדכתיב ואת אילי הארץ לקח. גבורת גשמים שנאמר הבו לה' כבוד ועז ונקראו גבורות שיורדין בגבורה כמפורש בתחלת תעניות ועז היא גבורה ואומר מטרות עז ומנין שאומרים קדושה שנא' הבו לה' כבוד שמו השתחוו לה' בהדרת קדש בינה אחר קדושה שנאמר והקדישו את קדוש יעקב וכתיב בתריה וידעו תועי רוח בינה תשובה אחר בינה שנאמר ולבבו יבין ושב סליחה אחר תשובה שנאמר וישוב אל ה' וירחמהו וגו' תקנו גאולה בשביעית שעתידין ישראל להיגאל בשביעית ורפואה בשמינית כנגד מילה שהיא בשמיני וצריכה רפואה וברכת השנים בתשיעית כנגד מפקיעי שערים שנאמר שבור זרוע רשע ורע ודוד כי אמרה בפרשת תשיעית אמרה קבוץ גליות אחר ברכת השנים שנאמר ואתם הרי ישראל ענפיכם תתנו ופריכם תשאו לעמי ישראל כי קרבו לבוא. אחר קבוץ גליות ברכת משפט שנאמר ואשיבה ידי עליך ואשיבה שופטיך ואחריה כלות הזדים שנאמר ושבר רשעים וחטאים ואחריה ברכת צדיקים ואחריה ברכת

יב א מיי' פ"ב מהלכות ק"ש הלכה ח סמג עשין יח טור וש"ע א"ח סימן סב סעיף ג:
יג ב מיי' פ"א מהלכות תפלה הלכה ד סמג עשין יט טור א"ח סימן קיב:
[וע"ע תוספות ברכות יג. ד"ה בלה"ק]
[עיין רש"א]
יד ג טור א"ח סי' קיג:

ברכות טו. לקמן יט:
[ברכות כח:]
[לקמן יח.]
ר"ה לב.
סנהדרין לז.

הגהות הב"ח

(א) גמ' ד"ה והחטאים יחד ועוזבי ה' יכלו וכיון שכ...

ס"א וא"ת עשירית ה אשרי ולמה רגשו חדא ה ולפי גירסא זו נ"ל דס אשרי ולמה רגשו חדא ה ולמנצח על מות ולמה תעמוד גם כן חדא ואם ה"ל שמינית

אחר ישובו בני ישראל. אחר ישובו לבית המקדש, ובקשו הקב"ה ואת דוד מלכם: זובח תודה. אחר זביחה תן הודאה: וירד. מעשות החטאת והעולה וגו': חדא מילתא היא. אף הודאה עבודה של מקום הוא: אסור לספר. בקביעות ברכה: למי שיכול. ואין מי שיכול לספר את כולו, לפיכך אין נראה לספר מדעתו אלא את מה שתקנו חכמים: היסופר לו כי אדבר. הכי דריש ליה: היסופר שבחו כולו כי ארבה לו דברי שבח, אם אמר לעשות כן – כי יבולע: סמא דכולה משתוקא. מובחר כל הסממנין היא השתיקה, שלא להרבות דברים. והיינו "לך דומיה תהלה": מלה בסלע משתוקא בתרין. אם תרצה לקנות הדבור בסלע, תקנה השתיקה בשתים: *קראה תרגום בכל לשון. זו ואין צ"ל זו קתני: מיתיבי. לרב ושמואל, דקתני הכא: יוונית לא יצא: הא לא דמיא. תירוצא הוא: גיפטית לגיפטים יצא. והכי נמי תנן במתני': ללועזות בלעז: עברית. לשון עבר הנהר: עילמית. לשון עילם: (א) מתני' כברייתא. זו מיתוקמא. קראה בכל לשון, דקתני מתני' לא יצא – כגון גיפטית למדיים, ומדית לגיפטים. אבל קורין אותו ללועזות בלעז איש כלשונו: ופרסומי ניסא. אע"פ שאין יודעין מה ששומעין, שואלין את השומעין ואומרין מה היא הקרייה הזו, ואיך היה הנס, ומודיעין להן: לא הוו ידעי רבנן. תלמידי רבינו הקדוש: חלוגלוגות. מין ירק הוא, ושנוי בכמה מקומות במשנה ובברייתא: פרפחיני. פיקל"י בלעז: מסלסל בשערך. למדנו שהסלסול לשון חיפוש והיפוך: טאטיתא. אישקופ"א בלעז:

סירוסין

תורה אור

הושע ג °"אחר ישובו בני ישראל ובקשו את ה' אלהיהם ואת דוד מלכם". וכיון שבא דוד – באתה תפלה, שנאמר: ישעיה נו °"והביאותים אל הר קדשי ושמחתים בבית תפלתי". וכיון שבאת תפלה באת עבודה, שנאמר: "עולותיהם וזבחיהם לרצון על מזבחי". וכיון שבאת "עבודה" – באתה תודה, שנאמר: תהלים נ °"זובח תודה יכבדנני". ומה ראו לומר ברכת כהנים אחר "הודאה"? – דכתיב: ויקרא ט °"וישא אהרן את ידיו אל העם ויברכם וירד מעשות החטאת והעולה והשלמים". אימא קודם עבודה? לא ס"ד, דכתיב: "וירד מעשות החטאת" וגו' מי כתיב "לעשות"? "מעשות" כתיב. ולימרה אחר העבודה! לא ס"ד, דכתיב "זובח תודה". מאי חזית דסמכת אהאי? סמוך אהאי! מסתברא עבודה והודאה חדא מילתא היא. ומה ראו לומר "שים שלום" אחר ברכת כהנים? דכתיב: במדבר ו °"ושמו את שמי על בני ישראל ואני אברכם". ברכה דהקב"ה – שלום, שנאמר: תהלים כט °"ה' יברך את עמו בשלום". וכי מאחר *דמאה ועשרים זקנים ומהם כמה נביאים תקנו תפלה על הסדר, שמעון הפקולי מאי הסדיר? •שכחום, וחזר וסדרום. •מכאן ואילך, אסור לספר בשבחו של הקב"ה. *דא"ר אלעזר: מאי דכתיב: שם קו °"מי ימלל גבורות ה' ישמיע כל תהלתו"? למי נאה למלל גבורות ה' – למי שיכול להשמיע כל תהלתו. אמר רבה בר בר חנה א"ר יוחנן: המספר בשבחו של הקב"ה יותר מדאי – נעקר מן העולם, שנאמר: איוב לז °"היסופר לו כי אדבר, אם אמר איש כי יבלע". דרש ר' יהודה איש כפר גבוריא, ואמרי לה איש כפר גבור חיל: מאי דכתיב תהלים סה °"לך דומיה תהלה"? סמא דכולה משתוקא. כי אתא רב דימי אמר: אמרי במערבא: *)מלה – בסלע, משתוקא – בתרין.§ "קראה על פה לא יצא" וכו'.§ מנלן? אמר רבא: אתיא 'זכירה' 'זכירה'. כתיב הכא: "והימים האלה נזכרים", וכתיב התם: שמות יז °"כתב זאת זכרון בספר". מה להלן בספר – אף כאן בספר. וממאי דהאי זכירה קריאה היא? דלמא עיון בעלמא! לא סלקא דעתך, (*דכתיב) °"זכור". יכול בלב? כשהוא אומר "לא תשכח" [נ"ל דתניא] [דברים כה] הרי שכחת הלב אמור. הא מה אני מקיים "זכור" – בפה.§ "קראה תרגום לא יצא" וכו'.§ היכי דמי? אילימא דכתיבה מקרא, וקרי לה תרגום – היינו על פה! לא צריכא, דכתיבה תרגום וקרי לה תרגום.§ "אבל קורין אותה ללועזות בלעז" וכו'.§ והא אמרת קראה בכל לשון לא יצא! רב ושמואל דאמרי תרוייהו: בלעז יווני. היכי דמי? אילימא דכתיבה אשורית וקרי לה יוונית – היינו על פה! א"ר אחא א"ר אלעזר: שכתובה בלעז יוונית. וא"ר אחא א"ר אלעזר: מנין שקראו הקב"ה ליעקב "אל"? שנאמר: בראשית לג °"ויקרא לו אל אלהי ישראל". דאי סלקא דעתך למזבח קרא ליה יעקב "אל" – "ויקרא לו יעקב" מיבעי ליה! אלא ויקרא לו ליעקב "אל". ומי קראו "אל"? אלהי ישראל. מיתיבי: קראה גיפטית עברית, עילמית, מדית, יוונית – לא יצא! הא לא דמיא אלא להא [א]גיפטית לגיפטים, עברית לעברים, עילמית לעילמים, יוונית ליוונים – יצא. אי הכי, רב ושמואל אמאי מוקמי לה למתני' בלעז יוונית? לוקמה בכל לעז! [אלא, מתניתין כברייתא.] וכי איתמר דרב ושמואל – בעלמא איתמר: *רב ושמואל דאמרי [תוספות לעיל ט. ד"ה כאן במגילה] תרוייהו: לעז יווני לכל כשר. והא קתני יוונית ליוונים – אין, לכולי עלמא – לא! אינהו דאמור כרשב"ג – דתנן, לעיל ח: *רשב"ג אומר: אף ספרים לא התירו שיכתבו אלא יוונית. ולימרו הלכה כרשב"ג! אי אמרי הלכה כרשב"ג הוה אמינא: הני מילי – שאר ספרים, אבל מגילה דכתיב בה "ככתבם" אימא לא – קמ"ל.§ "והלועז ששמע אשורית יצא" וכו'.§ והא לא ידע מאי קאמרי! מידי דהוה אנשים ועמי הארץ. מתקיף לה רבינא, אטו אנן "האחשתרנים בני הרמכים" מי ידעינן? אלא מצות קריאה ופרסומי ניסא – הכא נמי מצות קריאה ופרסומי ניסא.§ "קראה סירוגין יצא" וכו'.§ ר"ה כו: לא הוו ידעי רבנן *מאי "סירוגין". שמעוה לאמתא דבי רבי, דקאמרה להו לרבנן דהוי עיילי פסקי פסקי לבי רבי: עד מתי אתם נכנסין סירוגין סירוגין? לא הוו ידעי רבנן מאי "חלוגלוגות". שמעוה לאמתא דבי רבי דאמרה ליה להוא גברא דהוה קא מבדר פרפחיני: עד מתי משלי ד אתה מפזר חלוגלוגך? לא הוו ידעי רבנן מאי °"סלסלה ותרוממך". שמעוה *לאמתא דבי רבי דהוות אמרה [ר"ה שם ע"ש נזיר ג.] להההוא גברא דהוה מהפך במזייה אמרה ליה: עד מתי אתה מסלסל בשערך. לא הוו ידעי רבנן מאי תהלים נה °"השלך על ה' יהבך". אמר רבה בר בר חנה: זימנא חדא הוה אזילנא בהדי ההוא טייעא וקא דרינא ישעיה יד טונא ואמר לי: שקול יהביך ושדי אגמלאי. לא הוו ידעי רבנן מאי °"וטאטאתיה במטאטא השמד". שמעוה לאמתא דבי רבי דהוות אמרה לחברתה: שקולי טאטיתא וטאטי ביתא. ת"ר: קראה סירוגין – יצא,

סירוסין

*) בערוך [ערך מלת] גרס מילא בסלע משתוקא כאבן טבא

דאי סלקא דעתך למזבח קרי ליה יעקב אל. (ב) נראה דהכי נמי כתיב (שמות יז) "ויקרא שמו ה' נסי" "ויקרא לו ה' שלום" (שופטים ו) ומתרגמי': ופלח וכו'. מ"מ, יש לומר דהתם על שם הנס ועל שם השלום שאירע להן היו קוראין למזבח כן, אבל הכא ליכא שום מעשה שנוכל לומר שע"י כן קראו יעקב אל. ואם איתא שיעקב קראו אל – הוי ליה לפרושי להדיא:

נקוט

רבינו חננאל

דוד שנאמר אחר ישובו בני ישראל ובקשו את ה' ואת דוד מלכם. ואחר תפלה עבודה שנא' ושמחתים בבית תפלתי עולותיהם וזבחיהם לרצון ואחר עבודה הודאה שנאמר זובח תודה יכבדנני. אחריהן ברכת כהנים שנאמר וישא אהרן את ידיו אל העם ויברכם מלמד שעשה החטאת ואח"כ ברך את העם. אחר ברכת [כהנים] שלום שנא' ואני אברכם. וברכת הקב"ה היא שלום שנא' ה' עוז לעמו יתן ה' יברך את עמו בשלום מיכן ואילך אסור לספר בשבחו של הקב"ה שנאמר מי ימלל גבורות ה' וגו'. מי נאה למלל גבורות ה' למי שיכול להשמיע כל תהלתו. א"ר אלעזר כל המספר בשבחו של הקב"ה יותר מדי נעקר מן העולם. שנאמר אם אמר איש כי יבולע וכתיב לך דומיה תהלה אלהים בציון כלומר הדומיה היא תהלתך. סמא דכולא משתוקא מלה בסלע ומשתוקא בתרתי: קראה על פה לא יצא דאתיא זכירה זכירה כתיב הכא נזכרים ונעשים וכתיב התם כתוב זאת זכרון בספר ופרישנא זכור בפה מה שכתוב בספר. קראה תרגום אוקימנה בשכתובה תרגום וקראה תרגום לא יצא וכ"ש אם כתובה אשורית וקראה תרגום דהיינו על פה. בכל לשון לא יצא אבל קורין אותה ללועזות בלעז. ואוקמוה רב ושמואל בשכתובה בלעז יווני וקורין אותה ללועז יווני. ואותבינן עלייהו קראה גיפטית עיברית עילמית מדית יונית בכל לשון לא יצא. ופרקינן לא דמיא מתניתין אלא לסיפא גיפטית לגיפטים עברית לעברים יונית ליונים יצא אי הכי רב ושמואל לוקמה מתניתין בכל לעז אין מתניתין כברייתא ודרב ושמואל בעלמא אתמר ואליבא דרבן שמעון בן גמליאל דאמר אף בספרים לא התירו שיכתבו אלא יונית אמרו בלעז יונית לכל כשר דיונית לרשב"ג כאשורית לת"ק היא וקי"ל כמתניתין וכפירושא דברייתא. והלועז ששמע אשורית אע"ג דלא ידע מאי קאמר יצא מ"ט דהא איכא מצות קריאה ופרסומי ניסא וכגון [נשים] ועמי הארץ דלא ידעין פירוש האחשתרנים בני

עין משפט נר מצוה

טו א מיי' פ"ב מהל' מגילה הלכה ד סמג עשין ד טוש"ע א"ח סימן תרצ סעיף ט:

*) אפילו הכי נפקין י"ח: קראה סירוגין יצא פי' פיסקי פיסקי כגון שקורא ומפסיק ביני ביני וחוזר ומתחיל ממקום שפסק. סלסלה פירוש הפוך בה והפוך בה כלומר התעסק בתורתך תמיד. מטאטא שמכבדין

נראה מזה קצת דגי' אחרת היה לרבינו בגמ' דדוקא ע"ה הוא דלא ידעי הפירוש של האחשתרנים וצ"ע.

מסורת הש"ס: [שייך במשנה דלעיל יז.] · [לעיל יז:] · מכות י. הוריות יג: · איוב לז · תהלים סה · שמות יז · [נ"ל דתניא] דברים כה · בראשית לג · [תוספות לעיל ט. ד"ה כאן במגילה] · לעיל ח: · ר"ה כו: · משלי ד · [ר"ה שם ע"ש נזיר ג.] · תהלים נה · ישעיה יד

הגהות הב"ח

(א) רש"י ד"ה עילמית לשון עילם הס"ד ואח"כ מה"ד לוקמה בכל לע"ז ומתניתין וכו' וקראה: (ב) תוספות ד"ה דאי ס"ד וכו' יעקב אל ואף על גב דהכי נמי כתיב ויקרא שמו ה' נסי:

גליון הש"ס

גמרא שכחום וחזר וסדרום. לעיל דף ג ע"א סוכה דף מד ע"א: שם מכאן ואילך אסור לספר. עיין לקמן דף כה ע"א:

טז א מיי' פ"ב מהלכות מגילה הלכה א טוש"ע א"ח סימן תרצ סעיף ה:
יז ב מיי' פ"ז מהל' יבום וחליצה הלכה ח סמג עשין נא טוש"ע אה"ע סימן קנט סעיף ה:
יח ג ד ה מיי' פ"ב מהל' מגילה הלכה י סמג עשין מד"ס ד טוש"ע א"ח סימן תרצ סעיף ג:
יט ו מיי' שם הלכה א טוש"ע שם סעיף ו:
כ ז מיי' פ"ב שם הלכה ב:
כא ח מיי' שם פ"ב הלכה ו טוש"ע שם סעיף יג:
כב ט מיי' פ"א מהל' תפילין הלכה יב טוש"ע י"ד סימן רעד סעיף ב:
כג י מיי' שם טוש"ע א"ח סי' לב סעי' ו
כד כ מיי' שם טוש"ע י"ד סימן רפח סעיף ח:
כה ל מיי' שם טוש"ע א"ח סימן לב סעיף כט וסעיף לא:

סירוסין – לא יצא. ר' מונא אומר משום רבי יהודה: אף בסירוגין, אם שהה כדי לגמור את כולה – חוזר לראש. אמר רב יוסף: הלכה כר' מונא שאמר משום ר' יהודה. א"ל אביי לרב יוסף: כדי לגמור את כולה, מהיכא דקאי לסיפא, או דלמא מרישא לסיפא? א"ל: מרישא לסיפא. דא"כ *נתת דבריך לשיעורין. אמר ר' אבא א"ר ירמיה בר אבא אמר רב: הלכה כרבי מונא. ושמואל אמר: [א]אין הלכה כרבי מונא. בסורא מתנו הכי. בפומבדיתא מתנו הכי: אמר רב כהנא אמר רב: הלכה כרבי מונא. ושמואל אמר: אין הלכה כר' מונא. רב ביבי מתני איפכא, רב אמר: אין הלכה כר' מונא, ושמואל אמר: הלכה כר' מונא. אמר רב יוסף: נקוט דרב ביבי בידך, *דשמואל הוא דחייש ליחידאה. דתנן: *שומרת יבם, שקידש אחיו את אחותה, משום ר' יהודה בן בתירה. אמרו: אומרים לו: המתן עד שיעשה אחיך הגדול מעשה. אמר שמואל: [ב]הלכה כר' יהודה בן בתירה. ת"ר: [ג]השמיט בה סופר אותיות או פסוקין, וקראן הקורא [א] כמתורגמן המתרגם – יצא. מיתיבי: [ד]היו בה אותיות מטושטשות או מקורעות, אם רשומן ניכר – כשרה; ואם לאו – פסולה. [ה]לא קשיא: הא – בכולה, הא – במקצתה. ת"ר: *[ו]השמיט בה הקורא פסוק אחד, לא יאמר: "אקרא את כולה ואח"כ אקרא אותו פסוק", אלא קורא מאותו פסוק ואילך. [ז]נכנס לבית הכנסת ומצא צבור שקראו חציה, לא יאמר: "אקרא חציה עם הצבור ואח"כ אקרא חציה" אלא קורא אותה מתחילתה ועד סופה.§ "מתנמנם יצא" וכו'.§ היכי דמי *מתנמנם? אמר רב אשי: נים ולא נים *)תיר ולא תיר, דקרו ליה ועני, ולא ידע לאהדורי סברא, וכי מדכרו ליה – מידכר.§ "היה כותבה, דורשה, ומגיהה, אם כוון לבו יצא" וכו'.§ היכי דמי? אי דקא מסדר פסוקא פסוקא וכתב לה – כי כוון לבו מאי הוי? על פה הוא! אלא דכתב פסוקא פסוקא וקרי ליה. ומי יצא? והאמר *רבי חלבו אמר רב חמא בר גוריא אמר רב: הלכה כדברי האומר כולה. ואפי' למ"ד מ"איש יהודי" צריכה שתהא כתובה כולה! [ח]אלא, דמנחה מגילה קמיה, וקרי לה מינה פסוקא פסוקא, וכתב לה. לימא מסייע ליה לרבה בר בר חנה, דאמר רבה בר בר חנה א"ר יוחנן: [ט]אסור לכתוב אות אחת *שלא מן הכתב? דלמא דאתרמויי ליה אתרמויי. גופא, אמר רבה בר בר חנה א"ר יוחנן: אסור לכתוב אות אחת שלא מן הכתב. מיתיבי, *אמר רשב"א: מעשה בר' מאיר שהלך לעבר שנה **)בעסיא ולא היה שם מגילה וכתבה מלבו וקראה! א"ר אבהו: שאני רבי מאיר דמיקיים ביה °"ועפעפיך יישירו נגדך". אמר ליה רמי בר חמא לרבי ירמיה מדפתי: מאי "ועפעפיך יישירו נגדך"? אמר לו: אלו דברי תורה דכתיב בהו °"התעיף עיניך בו ואיננו", ואפילו הכי – מיושרין הן אצל ר' מאיר. רב חסדא אשכחיה לרב חננאל דהוה כתב ספרים שלא מן הכתב. אמר ליה: ראויה כל התורה כולה ליכתב על פיך, אלא כך אמרו חכמים: אסור לכתוב אות אחת שלא מן הכתב. מדקאמר כל התורה כולה ראויה שתיכתב על פיך – מכלל דמיושרין הן אצלו, והא רבי מאיר כתב! שעת הדחק שאני. אביי שרא לדבי בר *חבו למיכתב תפלין ומזוזות שלא מן הכתב. כמאן? כי האי תנא. דתניא ר' ירמיה אומר משום רבינו: *תפלין ומזוזות נכתבות שלא מן הכתב, ואין צריכות שרטוט. והלכתא: [י]תפלין – אין צריכין שרטוט, [כ]מזוזות – צריכין שרטוט. [ל]אידי ואידי נכתבות שלא מן הכתב. מ"ט – מיגרם גריסין.§ "היתה כתובה בסם" כו'.§ *סם – סמא, סקרא – אמר רבה בר בר חנה: סקרתא שמה. קומוס – קומא.

קנקנתום

*) [עי' תוספות תענית יב: וע"ע היטב תוספות נדה סג.] **) [עי' תוספות יבמות קטו. ד"ה א"ר עקיבא]

רש"י

סירוסין. למפרע. כמו "הרס את המקרא ודרשהו", וכן "יצא מחותך או מסורס" (נדה דף כח.): דחייש ליחידאה. במקום שהיחיד מחמיר ורבים מקילין: שומרת יבם. מלפה ליבמה. ומלוה בגדול ליבם. בא אחד מן האחין וקידש את אחותה של יבמה אחר שנפלה היבמה לפניהן: אומרים לו המתן. מלכונסה: עד שיעשה אחיך הגדול מעשה. ביבמתו, או לחלוץ או ליבם. אבל בעוד היבמה לפני כולן לחלוץ או לייבם – הרי היא לכל אחד כאשתו על ידי זיקת יבום, ואסור באחותה משום אחות אשה. דקסבר: יש זיקה אפי' בתרי, וכל שכן בחד. ופליגי רבנן עליה, ואמרי: הואיל ושני אחים הן – אין זיקתו מיוחדת להיות מוטלת על אחד מהן להיות כאשתו, ומותר באחותה: השמיט. דילג בה הסופר פסוק אחד, וקראן הקורא: כמתורגמן המתרגם. על פה: תיר. ער: אהדורי סברא. דבר הבא מבינת הלב: דקא מסדר פסוקא. על פה וכתב ליה. וקתני: יצא, ע"י קריאת אותו סידור: הלכה כדברי האומר כולה. צריך לקרות. ופליגי בה תנאי במתני' מהיכן קורא אדם את המגילה ויוצא בה ידי חובתו, רבי מאיר אומר: כולה, ר' יהודה אומר: מ"איש יהודי": דמנחא מגילה קמיה. ומעתיק ממנה: מסייע ליה לרבה. מתני' דקתני יצא. וליכא לאוקמה אלא במעתיק מן הכתב, מסייע ליה לרבה: דלמא דאיתרמי ליה. לעולם מותר לכתוב בלא העתק, ומתני' – דאתרמי ליה מגילה ומעתיק ממנה. ואיצטריך לאשמעינן דהיכא דמעתיק ממנה, אם כוון לבו – יצא: התעיף עיניך בו ואיננו. אם תכפול עיניך ממנה הרי היא משתכחת ממך כהרף עין: דבי בר חבו. מוכר תפילין הוה, כדאמרינן בבבא מציעא (דף כט:): תפילין דבי בר חבו שכיחי: והלכתא כו'. כך הלכה למשה מסיני: מיגרם גריסין. שגורות בפי הכל: סמא. *זרניך בלשון קודש, אורפמניט"ו בלעז: סקרתא. צבע אדום שצובעין בו תריסין: קומא. שרף אילן:

חרפא

תוספות

נקוט דרב ביבי בידך. דאמר רב אין הלכה כרבי מונא שאמר שחוזר לראש. וכן הלכה דאין צריך לחזור לראש, דהלכה כרב באיסורי דאמר כן, ורבי יוחנן קאי כוותיה בפרק בתרא דר"ה (דף לד: ושם) דאמר: שאם שמע תשע תקיעות בתשע שעות ביום יצא, ומסיים התם: תניא נמי הכי, ומייתי הא, ופריך: והא אמר רבי יוחנן משום ר"ש בן יהוצדק שאם שהה כדי לגמור את כולה חוזר לראש! ומשני: הא דידיה הא דרביה. ומדתניא כוותיה – שמע מינה הלכתא כוותיה. ומכאן סומך ר"י כשעומד "באמת ויציב" שממתין עד שיאמר עם הצבור "קדושה" ו"ברכו" ו"אמן יהא שמיה רבא":

שקידש אחיו את אחותה. דווקא קידש אומרים לו המתן מלישא, דכיון דאינה עדיין אלא ארוסה נראה שנושא אחות זקוקתו. אבל אם נשאה – אשתו גמורה היא, ואין צריך להמתין, דהא פקע זיקה לגמרי. ודוקא קידש אחר נפילה, אבל קודם נפילה, שלא היתה אחות זקוקתו בשעת הקדושין אין אומרים לו "המתן", שהרי לא היתה שום זיקה מעולם. וטעמא דר' יהודה משום דסבר יש זיקה:

תפלין אינן צריכין שרטוט. פירש ר"ת: דכן הלכה:

__קנקנתום__ תרתא דאושכפי. פירש הקונטרס: ארמינט"א. וקשיא: דא"כ, יהא אסור להטיל ארמינ"ט לתוך הדיו! אלא ש"מ: דקנקנתום לא הוי ארמינ"ט. דהכי נמי משמע התם, דמפרש טעמא דקנקנתום אסור משום דכתיב (במדבר ה) וכתב ומחה גבי סוטה כתב שיכול למחות, ודיו שיש בו קנקנתום אינו יכול למחות. וא"כ ש"מ דקנקנתום לאו היינו ארמינ"ט, שהרי בכל יום אנו מטילין ארמינ"ט לתוך הדיו שלנו, ואפ"ה מחקינן ליה שפיר. ונראה כדפי' רשב"ם בעירובין (דף יג. ושם) דקנקנתום היינו ויטריול"ו. ונהי דאמרינן התם שהיא ירוקה, מ"מ י"ל שמשחרת כששוחקים אותה הדק הדק:

דיפתרא

[שבת לה: גטין יז. ב"ב כט. חולין ט. לב.] [יבמות פג.] שם יח: מא. שייך לדף יט. [עירובין יג.] [תוספתא פ"ב] תענית יב. פסחים קב: יבמות נב. נדה סג. [לקמן יט.] [שם] מנחות לב. [תוספתא פ"ב] משלי ד שם כג [גי' הערוך חבו] מנחות לב: גיטין יט. שבת קד:

רבינו חננאל

שמכבדין בו הבית. יהבך המשאוי שלך. ת"ר קראה סירוגין יצא כדאמרי'. סירוסין *) חדא חדא אחד זולתי אחד. כגון שקורא פסוק ומניח פסוק וקורא פסוק שלישי וחוזר וקורא הפסוק השני שהניח כי האי גוונא לא יצא ר' מונא אמר משום ר' יהודה אף בסירוגין אם שהה כדי לגמור את כולה אע"ג שחזר וקרא הנשאר והשלימה לא יצא. ואוקימנא בששהה לגמור את כולה מרישא לסיפא מויהי בימי אחשורוש עד כי מרדכי היהודי. ואסיקנא אמר רב יוסף נקוט דרב ביבי בידך דאמר רב אין הלכה כר' מונא ושמואל אמר הלכה כר' מונא דשמעינן לשמואל דחייש ליחידאה דתנן שומרת יבם שקידש אחיו את אחותה כו'. ופשוטה היא וקי"ל כרב דאיסורא היא ולא חיישינן לשמואל אלא אם קראה סירוגין אפילו שהה כמה יצא ואע"ג דא"ר יוחנן משום רבי שמעון בן יהוצדק באחרית ראש השנה בהלל ובמגילה אם שהה כדי לגמור את כולה חוזר לראש הא אמר ר' יוחנן לר' אבהו לדידי לא סבירא לי. ואמר שמע ט' תקיעות בט' שעות ביום יצא ותניא כוותיה ובתלמוד ארץ ישראל אמרו משמיה דרב הלכתא כר' מונא שאמר משום ר' יהודה שאמר משום ר' יוסי הגלילי. ת"ר השמיט בה סופר פסוק ואותיות וקראן הקורא כמתורגמן המתרגם כלומר דרך המתרגם שמוסיף דברים מלבו לברר הטעם ונמצא קורא אותן הדברים על פה כן גם הקורא את פסוק ואותיות על פה אעפ"כ יצא דרמינן עלה מהא דתניא היו בה אותיות מטושטשות או מקורעות אם רשומן ניכר יצא ואם לאו לא יצא וממתניתין נמי דקתני קראה על פה לא יצא ופרקינן הני מילי בכולה אבל פסוק או אותיות על פה אם **) עשה וקראן על פה יצא: ת"ר השמיט בה הקורא פסוק לא יאמר הקורא אקרא את כולה עם הצבור ואחזור ואקרא אותו פסוק אלא קורא אותה מאותו פסוק וכן מי שנכנס לבית הכנסת ומצא צבור שקראו חציה לא יאמר אקרא מיכן ואח"כ אחזור ואקרא חציה הראשון אלא קורא אותה מתחלתה ועד סוף. קראה מתנמנם יצא אוקמה רב אשי כגון דנים ולא נים תיר ולא תיר ואי קרו ליה עני ולא ידע לאהדורי סברא וכי מדכרו ליה מדכר אם הוא מתנמנם כי האי גוונא יצא ואם לאו לא יצא. היה כותבה דורשה ומגיהה אם כוון לבו לצאת יצא דהא כתבה כולה ומנחא קמיה אלא כותבה היכי דמי כותבה מיכן שארבעה עשר מותר בעשיית מלאכה מיהו בעינן לקרותה ממגילה שהיא כתובה כולה. ואוקימנא בדמנחא מגילה שלמה כתובה כולה קמיה וקרי בהא פסוקא פסוקא וכתיב ליה וכרבי יוחנן דאמר אסור לכתוב אפילו אות אחת שלא מן הכתב ואע"פ דאמר דכתב ר"מ באסיא מלבו מגלה וקראה והיה בקי בתורה כולה שהיה יודע ע"פ האי אמרינן שעת הדחק היתה שלא היתה שם אחרת ומפני שעת הדחק התירו לו אבל זולתי שעת הדחק לא ואפילו למי שהוא [בקי] כר"מ וקי"ל שכתב אחת מלבו והניחה לפניו וכתב אחרת ממנה כותב מן הכתובה דמנחא קמיה. אביי שרא לרבי בר הבו למכתב תפלין ומזוזות שלא מן הכתב כי האי תנא ואסיקנא והלכתא מזוזה צריכה שרטוט תפלין אין צריכין שרטוט ואלו ואלו נכתבים שלא מן הכתב מ"ט

מגרם

*) אולי צ"ל סירוסין בירושלמי אלא פרא אלא אחד זולתו אחד כגון וכו' וכ"ה בירושלמי שם כסך לשנא ורבינו מפרש דפרא אלא היינו זולתי אחד. **) אולי צ"ל אם השמיט וקרא וכו'.

גליון הש"ס

גמרא עד שיעשה אחיך הגדול. במתניתין יבמות דף מא אינו ואולם במתניתין במשניות איתא כן ועיין בתוי"ט שם: **שם** שהלך לעבר שנה. עיין יבמות קטו ע"א תוד"ה אמר ר"ע: **שם** שאני ר"מ. עיין מ"ר בראשית ס"פ ל"ו שתירץ ששתי מגילות כתב גנז הראשונה וקיים השניה:

הגהות הגר"א

[א] גמ' כמתורגמן המתרגם. נ"ב לפרש"י כל זה שפת יתר הוא אבל הפירוש הוא שקראן בלשון תרגום לפי שהיו רגילין בתרגום בעל פה וקמ"ל דאף למכיר אשורית יוצא בלעז וקמ"ל אף שקרא בב' לשונות יוצא דהא צריך לקרות כולה ואף המיעוט מעכב מדקאמר (לעיל ע"א) אטו אנן כו' וכ"ה להדיא הפירוש הנ"ל בירושלמי ומ"ש בירושלמי מי שיודע גם אשורית אין יוצא בלעז היינו אשורית דלא כגמ' דילן וקי"ל כגמ' דילן דבזה אף לועז לא יצא מ"מ פשטא דמתני' דקאמר והלועז כו' וגמ' כו' ופשטא דירושלמי משמע כדברי הרמב"ן דלא יצא אלא הלועז דוקא וכאן דוקא במקצתה כי היכי דיצא בעל פה אלא שי"ל דגמ' דילן ס"ל כשמואל בירושלמי דלא כר' אבהו מדפריך גמ' מעל פה ולא פריך מתרגום (ועמ"ש רבינו בא"ח סימן תר"ץ)

חרתא דאושכפי. סם שצובעין בו מנעלים שחורין: **קמיח.** כמיס: **ולא עפיץ.** מעובד בעפצים שקורין גל"ש: **מחקא.** מין עשבים עשוי על ידי דבק: **מתני' בן עיר.** שזמנו בארבעה עשר: **שהלך לכרך.** שזמנו בחמשה עשר: **אם עתיד לחזור.** מפרש בגמ': **קורא כמקומו.** כחובת מקומו, בן עיר בארבעה עשר, בן כרך בחמשה עשר: **גמ' לא שנו.** דבן כרך שהלך לעיר ועתיד לחזור למקומו קורא בחמשה עשר ולא בארבעה עשר: **אלא שעתיד לחזור בליל ארבעה עשר.** אם קודם עמוד השחר יצא מן העיר, הוא דקתני שאינו צריך לקרות עמהן בלילי י"ד, אע"פ שעודנו שם, הואיל וביום לא יהיה שם – אין זה אפילו פרוז בן יומו: **אבל אין עתיד.** לצאת משם בלילה, דהשתא הוי פרוז לאותו יום אע"פ שעתיד לחזור, למחר ליום (*אחר) – נקרא פרוז, וקורא עמהן בין בלילי י"ד בין בי"ד. וה"ה לבן עיר שהלך לכרך, אם עתיד לחזור בלילי ט"ו, שלא יהא שם ביום ט"ו – לא הוי מוקף ליומו, וקורא בי"ד כחובת מקומו ואעפ"י שהוא בכרך. אבל אין עתיד לחזור בלילי ט"ו – אין צריך לקרותה בי"ד, וממתין וקורא עמהן, אע"פ שסופו לחזור לאחר זמן: **מנא (א) ליה.** דמשום ההוא יומא חשיב כוותייהו: **בן כפר.** שהקדים וקרא ליום הכניסה, ואח"כ הלך לעיר והיה שם לילי י"ד: **בין כך ובין כך.** אפילו עתיד לחזור ולצאת משם קודם היום – קורא עמהן בלילה: **כבני העיר בעי מקרי.** כל הפרזים זמנם בארבעה עשר, בין כפרים בין עיירות, ורבנן הוא דאקילו עלייהו להקדים ליום הכניסה: **והני מילי.** דאקילו עלייהו דאין צריך לחזור ולקרות בארבעה עשר – כי איתיה בכפר: *__מאחר הדברים האלה.__ גידל המלך וכו': **כל תוקף.** לקיים אגרת הפורים על תוקף הקפיד להזכיר: **תוקפו של אחשורוש.** ומתחלתה היא מדברת בתוקפו, עד סופה: **ומה ראו על ככה.** המגילה נכתבת ונקראת להודיע לדורות מה ראו באותו הזמן שעשו מה שעשו, ומפרש "על ככה" עשו, ולפרש מה הגיע על העושים: **נקראת ספר.** "ונכתב בספר": **שאם תפרה בחוטי פשתן פסולה.** דאיכא למאן דאמר במסכת מכות (דף יא.) ספר תורה שתפרו בפשתן פסולה: **ונקראת אגרת.** לומר שאינה חמורה כספר: **שיהו משולשין.** שיהא מראש התפר] עד מקום תפירת הגיד כמתמנו ועד הגיד השני, ומן השני לשלישי כמשלישי לסוף התפר: **הכתובה בין הכתובים.** ספרים שהיו בימי החכמים כולן בגליון, כספר תורה שלנו: **לא יצא.** דבעינן אגרת לעצמה, דמיפרסם ניסא טפי. דכי קורהא בין הכתובים נראה כקורא במקרא: **אי מחסרא או מייתרא.** ארוכה מששאר הקלפים למעלה או למטה, או קצרה מהן, ויש לה היכר לעצמה:

דיפתרא דמליח וקמיח ולא עפיץ. קשיא: א"כ היאך כותבין על קלפים שלנו, דלא עפילי, ספר תורה ותפלין ומגילה? ותירץ רבינו תם: שהסיד שאנו נותנין בקלפים שלנו מהני כעפצים. ותדע: דבפרק שני דגיטין (דף יט.) אמר דבלא עפיץ יכול להזדייף, ושלנו אין יכול להזדייף על הלבן*:

*__על__ הספר ובדיו. פירש ר"ת: שהדיו שלנו הוא דיו גמור, אבל של עפצים לא הוי דיו. והכי משמע פ"ב דגיטין (גז"ש) (ב), דתניא: בכל כותבין בדיו ובסם, ומסיק: בכל דבר של קיימא. ומסיק: לאתויי מאי? ומשני: לאתויי הא דתנא רבי חייא כתבו במי טריא ועפצא כשר. ומדאצטריך לאתויי עפצא מרבוייא בתר דתני דיו, שמע מינה דעיקר דיו לא הוי מעפצא. ומטעם זה רצה לפסול ספר תורה הכתובה מדיו של עפצים. והאשכנזים השיבו לו דהתם מיירי במים ששרו בהן עפצים, אבל אותו שעשו מגוף העפצים – ודאי הוא טוב. ומ"מ נראה דאותו שלנו הוי עיקר דיו, כדמשמע פרק "כל היד" (נדה דף כ.) דרבי אמי פלי קורטא דדיותא ובדיק, פירוש: ומשבר חתיכה של דיו ובדיק ביה דם שחור. ובאותו שלנו שייך שבירה ולא באותו של עפצים: **בן** כפר שהלך לעיר בין כך ובין כך קורא עמהם. פירש רש"י: ואע"פ שקרא כבר ליום הכניסה. וקשיא: למה יחזור ויקרא שני פעמים? ומ"מ נראה דשפיר פי' רש"י, דכיון שהיה בעיר בלילה – נעשה כבני העיר, ואע"פ שעתיד לחזור (ג) (בו) בי"ד, ואע"פ שקרא ביום הכניסה. דהא דאמרי' כפרים מקדימים ליום הכניסה כדי שיספיקו מים ומזון לאחיהם שבכרכים ופטורים ממגילה – היינו דווקא כשאינם שוהים שם בליל י"ד, אלא ביום י"ד באים שם. אבל כששוהים שם בליל ארבעה עשר – ודאי דינם כבני העיר, אע"פ שקראו כבר: **ובלבד** שיהו משולשין. נראה כמו שפרש"י: שיהיה מראש התפר עד הגיד כמגיד לגיד חבירו, בין מלמעלה בין מלמטה. והכי נמי משמע במכות (דף ט: ושם) גבי ערי מקלט, דקאמר "ושלשת" שיהו משולשין: מדרום לחברון כמחברון לשכם, ומשכם לקדש כמקדש לצפון. שמע מינה דמשולשין משמע הכי. ולא כמו שמפרשים שיהיה הגיד בראש הדף ובאמצעיתו ובסופו*: שיור

עיר תורה אור

קנקנתום – חרתא דאושכפי. "דיפתרא" – דמליח וקמיח ולא עפיץ. "נייר" – מחקא. § "עד שתהא כתובה אשורית"; § דכתיב: "ככתבם וכזמנם". § "על הספר ובדיו" וכו'. § מנלן? אתיא "כתיבה" "כתיבה". כתיב הכא: °"ותכתב אסתר המלכה", וכתיב התם: °"ויאמר להם ברוך מפיו יקרא אלי את כל הדברים האלה ואני כותב על הספר בדיו". § **מתני'** [א]בן עיר שהלך לכרך ובן כרך שהלך לעיר, אם עתיד לחזור למקומו – קורא כמקומו; ואם לאו – קורא עמהן. ומהיכן קורא אדם את המגילה ויוצא בה י"ח? ר"מ אומר: [ב]כולה. ר' יהודה אומר: מ"איש יהודי". רבי יוסי אומר: מ"אחר הדברים האלה". § **גמ'** אמר רבא: [ג]לא שנו אלא שעתיד לחזור בלילי י"ד, אבל אין עתיד לחזור בלילי ארבעה עשר – קורא עמהן. אמר רבא: מנא אמינא לה? דכתיב: °"על כן היהודים הפרזים היושבים בערי הפרזות". מכדי כתיב: "היהודים הפרזים", למה לי למיכתב "היושבים בערי הפרזות"? הא קמ"ל: דפרוז בן יומו, נקרא פרוז. אשכחן פרוז. מוקף מנא לן? סברא הוא. מדפרוז בן יומו קרוי פרוז – מוקף בן יומו קרוי מוקף. ואמר רבא: בן כפר, שהלך לעיר – בין כך ובין כך, קורא עמהן. מאי טעמא? האי כבני העיר בעי למקרי, *ורבנן הוא דאקילו על הכפרים *כדי שיספקו מים ומזון לאחיהם שבכרכין. הני מילי – כי איתיה בדוכתיה, אבל כי איתיה בעיר – כבני עיר בעי למקרי. איתיביה אביי: בן כרך שהלך לעיר – בין כך ובין כך קורא כמקומו. בן כרך ס"ד באם עתיד לחזור תליא מילתא! אלא לאו – בן כפר! ולאו תרוצי מתרצת? תני: קורא עמהן. § "מהיכן קורא אדם את המגילה" וכו'. § תניא, *רשב"י אומר: מ"בלילה ההוא". א"ר יוחנן: וכולן, מקרא אחד דרשו: "ותכתב אסתר המלכה... ומרדכי היהודי את כל תוקף". מאן דאמר כולה – תוקפו של אחשורוש. ומאן דאמר מ"איש יהודי" – תוקפו של מרדכי. ומ"ד מ"אחר הדברים האלה" – תוקפו של המן. ומ"ד מ"בלילה ההוא" – תוקפו של נס. רב הונא אמר: מהכא: "ומה ראו על ככה ומה הגיע אליהם". מ"ד כולה – מה ראה אחשורוש שנשתמש בכלים של בית המקדש. "על ככה" – משום דחשיב *שבעים שנין ולא איפרוק. "ומה הגיע אליהם"? דקטל ושתי. ומ"ד מ"איש יהודי", מה ראה מרדכי דאיקני בהמן? "על ככה" – *דשוי *נפשיה ע"ז "ומה הגיע אליהם" – דאתרחיש ניסא. ומ"ד מ"אחר הדברים האלה" מה ראה המן שנתקנא בכל היהודים? "על ככה" משום ד"מרדכי לא יכרע ולא ישתחוה". "ומה הגיע אליהם"? "ותלו אותו ואת בניו על העץ". ומ"ד מ"בלילה ההוא" מה ראה אחשורוש להביא את ספר הזכרונות? "על ככה" – דזמינתיה אסתר להמן בהדיה. "ומה הגיע אליהם"? דאתרחיש ניסא. *א"ר חלבו אמר רב חמא בר גוריא אמר רב: הלכה כדברי האומר כולה. ואפי' למאן דאמר *מ"איש יהודי" – [ד]צריכה שתהא כתובה כולה. וא"ר חלבו אמר רב חמא בר גוריא אמר רב: מגילה נקראת "ספר" ונקראת "אגרת". נקראת "ספר" – [ה]שאם תפרה בחוטי פשתן פסולה. ונקראת "אגרת" – [ו]שאם הטיל בה שלשה חוטי גידין כשרה. אמר רב נחמן: ובלבד שיהו משולשין. אמר רב יהודה אמר שמואל: [ז]הקורא במגילה הכתובה בין הכתובים – לא יצא. אמר רבא: [ח]לא אמרן אלא דלא מחסרא ומייתרא פורתא, אבל מחסרא ומייתרא פורתא – לית לן בה. לוי בר שמואל הוה קא קרי קמיה דרב יהודה במגילה הכתובה

ומחו

מסורת הש"ס: אסתר ט | ירמיה לו | אסתר ט

הגהות הב"ח
(א) רש"י ד"ה מנא אמינא לה דמשום ההוא: (ב) תוס' ד"ה על הספר וכו' דתנן בכל כותבין בדיו ובסם ובסיקרא ובכל דבר: (ג) ד"ה בן כפר וכו' שעתיד לחזור בליל י"ד ואע"פ:

[נ"ל אחד]

הגהות מהר"ב רנשבורג
א] רש"י ד"ה שיהו משולשין שיהא מראש התפר וכו'. נ"ב עיין מהר"מ שי"ף שהאריך והגיה בלשון רש"י פעמים הספר תחת התפר. ועיין בכורות דף לט ע"א תוספות ד"ה שיהיו וכו' משמע כדבריו ודבריהם סותרים להדדי ישוע"ה וצ"ע:

[לעיל ב. ז.]

[לעיל ז: מסיק הגמרא מפני שמספקין]

[שייך לעיל במשנה]

[תוס' פ"ב ושם איתא רשב"א]

גליון הש"ס
תוספות ד"ה ובלבד שיהו כו' מראש התפר. עיין בכורות דף לט ע"א תוספות ד"ה שיהיו משולשים ושם איתא מראש הדף וכו' וכן נכון:

[לעיל יח:]

[לעיל י:]

[ועיין תוספות שבת עב: ותוס' סנהדרין סח: ד"ה רבה אמר]

[לעיל יח:]

[שם]

[ג"ל בפנים בגמרא עמוד שני]

עין משפט נר מצוה

כו א מיי' פ"א מהלכות מגילה הלכה י טוש"ע א"ח סי' תרפח סעי' ה:

[וע"ע תוספות שבת עט: ד"ה קלף ותוס' מנחות לא: ד"ה הא]

כז ב מיי' שם הלכה ג טור ש"ע א"ח סי' תרל סעיף ג:

כח ג מיי' שם הלכה י טור וש"ע א"ח סי' תרפח סעיף ה:

כט ד מיי' פ"ב שם הל' ו טוש"ע א"ח סי' תרל סעיף ג:

ל ה ו מיי' פ"ב מהלכות מגילה הלכה יא סמג עשין ד טוש"ע א"ח סי' תרלא סעיף ה ו:

לא ז ח מיי' שם הלכה ח טוש"ע שם סעיף ח:

רבינו חננאל

מגרם גרסי להו. היתה כתובה בסם בסיקרא בקומוס כו'. סם. סמא. סקרא. סיקרתא שמה. קומוס. קומא. קנקנתום חרתא דאושכפי דיפתרא דמליח וקמיח ולא עפיץ נייר מחקא באלו כולו [לא] יצא עד שתהא כתובה על העור ובדיו דגמר כתיבה כתיבה *) ויאמר להם ברוך מפיו יקרא אלי את כל הדברים האלה ואני כותב על הספר בדיו: **מתני'** בן עיר שהלך לכרך ובן כרך שהלך לעיר אם עתיד לחזור קורא כמקומו אמר רבא ל"ש בן כרך שהלך לעיר קורא כמקומו אלא שעתיד לחזור בליל י"ד ונזדמן לו ונתעכב לו ולא חזר קורא בט"ו כבני מקומו. אבל אינו עתיד לחזור בלילי י"ד קורא עמהם דכתיב על כן היהודים הפרזים למה לי עוד היושבים בערי הפרזות לא בא אלא ללמד דפרוז בן יומו קרוי פרוז. וכן מוקף בן יומו קרוי מוקף: **ירושלמי** ניחא בן כרך שהלך לעיר שזמנו מאוחר בן עיר שהלך לכרך ואין זמנו מוקדם **) לפיכך שנינו אם עתיד לחזור יום חזר הרי חוזר ואם לא נעשה מוקף. א"ר יודן לית כן בן עיר שהלך לכרך א"ר יוסי אית כאן בעתיד להשתקע כו' נתברר הפירוש שפירשנו. אמר רבה בן כפר שהלך לעיר בין עתיד לחזור בכפר בין אינו עתיד לחזור קורא עמהם בי"ד דלא תקינו ליה רבנן לאקדומי ליום הכניסה אלא כי איתיה בכפר אבל כי איתיה בעיר כבני העיר בעי למיקרא. ומותיב אביי עליה ומתרץ הכי בן כפר שהלך לעיר בין כך ובין כך קורא עמהם: **מהיכן** קורא את המגילה ויוצא בה רבי מאיר אומר כו'. ואסיקנא כדברי האומר את כולה אמר [רבי חלבו אמר רב חמא בר גוריא] משמיה דרב מגילה נקראת ספר ללמד שאם תפרה בפשתן פסולה כספר תורה נקראת אגרת שאם הטיל בה ג' חוטי גידין כשרה. ובלבד שיהו משולשין כלומר החוט כרוך זה אחר זה ג' פעמים ג' בב' קצוות וג' באמצע. הקורא במגילה הכתובה בין הכתובים פירוש אם הן כולן כתובים שנכתבו מגילה ומגילת אסתר בכללן. והיו רוחב היריעות הכתובות כולן מדה אחת פסולה ואם מיחסרא או מייתרא כגון שכל יריעה רחבה ג' זרתות והיריעות שכתובה בהן מגילת אסתר רחבן ג'

*) כתיב הכא ותכתוב אסתר המלכה וכתיב התם ויאמר כו'. **) נראה דצ"ל כלומר ואיך שנינו אם עתיד לחזור אם חזר הרי חזר ואם לא כו'.

תורה אור

הַכְּתוּבָה בֵּין הַכְּתוּבִים. אֲמַר לֵיהּ: הֲרֵי אָמְרוּ הַקּוֹרֵא בִּמְגִילָּה הַכְּתוּבָה בֵּין הַכְּתוּבִים לֹא יָצָא. א"ר חִיָּיא בַּר אַבָּא א"ר יוֹחָנָן: הַקּוֹרֵא בִּמְגִילָּה הַכְּתוּבָה בֵּין הַכְּתוּבִים — לֹא יָצָא. וּמָחוּ לָהּ אַמּוֹחָא: א בְּצִבּוּר שָׁנוּ. וְאָמַר רַבִּי חִיָּיא בַּר אַבָּא א"ר יוֹחָנָן: שִׁיּוּר הַתֶּפֶר — הֲלָכָה לְמֹשֶׁה מִסִּינַי. וּמָחוּ לָהּ אַמּוֹחָא: וְלֹא אָמְרוּ ב אֶלָּא כְּדֵי שֶׁלֹּא יִקָּרַע. וְאָמַר רַבִּי חִיָּיא בַּר אַבָּא א"ר יוֹחָנָן: אִלְמָלֵי נִשְׁתַּיֵּיר בִּמְעָרָה שֶׁעָמַד בָּהּ מֹשֶׁה וְאֵלִיָּהוּ כִּמְלֹא נֶקֶב מַחַט סִדְקִית — לֹא הָיוּ יְכוֹלִין לַעֲמוֹד מִפְּנֵי הָאוֹרָה, שֶׁנֶּאֱמַר: "כִּי לֹא יִרְאַנִי הָאָדָם וָחָי". (שמות לג) וְאָמַר ר' חִיָּיא בַּר אַבָּא א"ר יוֹחָנָן: מַאי דִּכְתִיב "וַעֲלֵיהֶם כְּכָל הַדְּבָרִים אֲשֶׁר דִּבֶּר ה' עִמָּכֶם בָּהָר"? (דברים ט) *מְלַמֵּד שֶׁהֶרְאָהוּ הקב"ה לְמֹשֶׁה דִּקְדּוּקֵי תוֹרָה וְדִקְדּוּקֵי סוֹפְרִים וּמַה שֶּׁהַסּוֹפְרִים עֲתִידִין לְחַדֵּשׁ. וּמַאי נִיהוּ? מִקְרָא מְגִילָּה.§

מתני' *ג הַכֹּל כְּשֵׁרִין לִקְרוֹת אֶת הַמְּגִילָּה חוּץ מֵחֵרֵשׁ שׁוֹטֶה וְקָטָן. ר' יְהוּדָה מַכְשִׁיר בְּקָטָן.§

גמ' מַאן תַּנָּא חֵרֵשׁ דִּיעֲבַד נַמִי לֹא? אָמַר רַב מַתָּנָה: ר' יוֹסֵי הִיא, דִּתְנַן: *הַקּוֹרֵא אֶת שְׁמַע וְלֹא הִשְׁמִיעַ לְאָזְנוֹ — יָצָא. רַבִּי יוֹסֵי אוֹמֵר: לֹא יָצָא. וּמִמַּאי דְּרַבִּי יוֹסֵי הִיא, וְדִיעֲבַד נַמִי לָא? דִּלְמָא רַבִּי יְהוּדָה הִיא, וּלְכַתְּחִלָּה הוּא דְּלָא, הָא דִּיעֲבַד — שַׁפִּיר דָּמֵי! לָא סָלְקָא דַּעְתָּךְ, דְּקָתָנֵי חֵרֵשׁ דּוּמְיָא דְּשׁוֹטֶה וְקָטָן. מַה שׁוֹטֶה וְקָטָן דִּיעֲבַד נַמִי לָא, אַף חֵרֵשׁ — דִּיעֲבַד נַמִי לָא. וְדִלְמָא הָא כִּדְאִיתָא וְהָא כִּדְאִיתָא! מִדְּקָתָנֵי סֵיפָא: רַבִּי יְהוּדָה מַכְשִׁיר בְּקָטָן — מִכְּלָל דְּרֵישָׁא לָאו ר' יְהוּדָה הִיא. (א*) וְדִלְמָא כּוּלָּהּ ר' יְהוּדָה הִיא? מִי דָּמֵי? רֵישָׁא לִפְסוּלָה, וְסֵיפָא לִכְשֵׁירָה. וְדִלְמָא כּוּלָּהּ ר' יְהוּדָה הִיא, וּתְרֵי גַּוְונֵי קָטָן קָתָנֵי לַהּ. וְחַסּוּרֵי מִיחַסְּרָא וְהָכִי קָתָנֵי: הַכֹּל כְּשֵׁרִין לִקְרוֹת אֶת הַמְּגִילָּה חוּץ מֵחֵרֵשׁ שׁוֹטֶה וְקָטָן. בד"א — בְּקָטָן שֶׁלֹּא הִגִּיעַ לְחִינּוּךְ, אֲבָל בְּקָטָן שֶׁהִגִּיעַ לְחִינּוּךְ — אֲפִילּוּ לְכַתְּחִלָּה, שֶׁר' יְהוּדָה מַכְשִׁיר בְּקָטָן. בְּמַאי אוֹקִימְתָּא? כְּר' יְהוּדָה, וְדִיעֲבַד. אֶלָּא הָא דְּתָנֵי: (ר') יְהוּדָה בְּרֵיהּ דְּרַבִּי שִׁמְעוֹן בֶּן פָּזִי: חֵרֵשׁ הַמְדַבֵּר וְאֵינוֹ שׁוֹמֵעַ — תּוֹרֵם לְכַתְּחִלָּה, מַנִּי? אִי רַבִּי יְהוּדָה — דִּיעֲבַד אִין, לְכַתְּחִלָּה לָא. אִי רַבִּי יוֹסֵי — דִּיעֲבַד נַמִי לָא! וְאֶלָּא מַאי? ר' יְהוּדָה וַאֲפִי' לְכַתְּחִלָּה? אֶלָּא הָא *דְּתַנְיָא: ד לֹא יְבָרֵךְ אָדָם בִּרְכַּת הַמָּזוֹן בְּלִבּוֹ, וְאִם בֵּירַךְ — יָצָא, מַנִּי? לָא רַבִּי יְהוּדָה וְלָא רַבִּי יוֹסֵי. אִי ר' יְהוּדָה — אֲפִי' לְכַתְּחִלָּה. אִי ר' יוֹסֵי — אֲפִי' דִּיעֲבַד נַמִי לָא! לְעוֹלָם

רש"י

וּמָחוּ לָהּ אַמּוֹחָא. לְאַחַר שֶׁאָמַר שְׁמוּעָה זוֹ הִכָּה עַל קָדְקֳדָהּ. כְּלוֹמַר, סָתַר מִקְלָתָהּ, וְאָמַר: לֹא אָמְרוּ אֶלָּא בְּצִבּוּר: שִׁיּוּר הַתֶּפֶר. כְּשֶׁתּוֹפְרִין יְרִיעוֹת שֶׁל סֵפֶר תּוֹרָה לְחַבְּרָן יַחַד, מְשַׁיְּירִין בַּתֶּפֶר לְמַעְלָה וּלְמַטָּה: וּמָחוּ לָהּ אַמּוֹחָא. לְאַחַר שֶׁאֲמָרָהּ הִכָּה עַל מוֹחָהּ, כְּלוֹמַר חָזַר וְסָתַר, וְאָמַר: לָאו הֲלָכָה לְמֹשֶׁה מִסִּינַי הוּא, אֶלָּא חֲכָמִים אָמְרוּ: כְּדֵי שֶׁלֹּא יִקָּרַע. שֶׁאִם אֵינוֹ מְשַׁיֵּיר, מְהַדֵּק בְּחָזְקָה כְּשֶׁהוּא מְהַדְּקוֹ לְסֵפֶר תּוֹרָה, וְהוּא נִקְרָע. אֲבָל עַכְשָׁיו, כְּשֶׁהוּא מְהַדְּקוֹ בְּכֹחַ וּמַתְחִיל לְהַרְחִיב וְרוֹצֶה לְהִיקָּרַע — מוֹנֵעַ מִלְּהַדְּקוֹ יוֹתֵר: מְעָרָה שֶׁעָמַד בָּהּ מֹשֶׁה. כְּשֶׁעָבַר הקב"ה לְפָנָיו, שֶׁנֶּאֱמַר "וְשַׂמְתִּיךָ בְּנִקְרַת הַצּוּר" (שמות לג). וְאֵלִיָּהוּ אַף הוּא עָמַד בְּאוֹתָהּ מְעָרָה וְעָבַר הקב"ה לְפָנָיו, שֶׁנֶּאֱמַר "וַיָּבֹא שָׁם אֶל הַמְּעָרָה וגו' וַיֹּאמֶר צֵא וְעָמַדְתָּ בָהָר וגו' וְהִנֵּה ה' עוֹבֵר" וגו' (מלכים א יט): מַחַט סִידְקִית. שֶׁלָּנוּ, שֶׁהִיא דַּקָּה וְתוֹפְרִין בָּהּ סִדְקֵי בְגָדִים. וְיֵשׁ מַחַט אַחֶרֶת גַּסָּה, שֶׁנִּקְרֵאת מַחַט שֶׁל שַׂקָּאִין: אִלְמָלֵי נִשְׁתַּיֵּיר בָּהּ נֶקֶב. כְּפִי מַחַט, כְּשֶׁעָבַר עֲלֵיהֶן הקב"ה, כְּמוֹ שֶׁנֶּאֱמַר "וְשַׂכּוֹתִי כַפִּי עָלֶיךָ עַד עָבְרִי" (שמות לג): דִּקְדּוּקֵי תוֹרָה. רִיבּוּיִין אֶתִין וְגַמִּין, מִיעוּטִין אַכִין וְרַקִּין: דִּקְדּוּקֵי סוֹפְרִים. שֶׁדִּקְדְּקוּ הָאַחֲרוֹנִים מִלְּשׁוֹן מִשְׁנַת הָרִאשׁוֹנִים: לֹא יָצָא. דִּיעֲבַד הוּא: וּמִמַּאי. דְּחוּץ מֵחֵרֵשׁ דְּקָאָמַר מַתְנִי' אֲפִי' בְּדִיעֲבַד קָאָמַר, וְר' יוֹסֵי הִיא דְּפָסַל בְּדִיעֲבַד: וּלְכַתְּחִלָּה הוּא דְּלָא. וּבְהָא אִיכָּא לְמֵימַר דַּאֲפִי' ר' יְהוּדָה מוֹדֶה, דְּהָא לָא שָׁמְעִינַן לֵיהּ דְּפָלֵיג אֶלָּא בְּדִיעֲבַד: מִדְּסֵיפָא רַבִּי יְהוּדָה. דְּקָתָנֵי: וְר' יְהוּדָה מַכְשִׁיר בְּקָטָן: לָא דָּמֵי רֵישָׁא לִפְסוּלָהּ וְסֵיפָא לְהֶכְשֵׁירָהּ לָא גָּרְסִינַן לֵיהּ, דְּלִישָּׁנָא יְתֵירָא הוּא. אֶלָּא הָכִי גָּרְסִינַן: וְדִלְמָא רַבִּי יְהוּדָה הִיא וּתְרֵי גַּוְונֵי קָטָן, וְחַסּוּרֵי מִיחַסְּרָא כו' הַכֹּל כְּשֵׁרִין לִקְרוֹת אֶת הַמְּגִילָּה חוּץ מֵחֵרֵשׁ שׁוֹטֶה וְקָטָן. הָא כִּדְאִיתָא וְהָא כִּדְאִיתָא, חֵרֵשׁ לְכַתְּחִילָּה וְשׁוֹטֶה אֲפִילּוּ בְּדִיעֲבַד: בד"א בְּקָטָן שֶׁלֹּא הִגִּיעַ לְחִינּוּךְ. לְחִינּוּךְ מִצְוֹת, כְּגוֹן בֶּן תֵּשַׁע וּבֶן עֶשֶׂר, כִּדְאָמְרִינַן בְּיוֹמָא בְּפֶרֶק בַּתְרָא (דף פב.): בְּמַאי אוֹקִימְתָּא כְּר' יְהוּדָה. וְאַשְׁמְעַתְּ לָן דְּכִי אָמַר רַבִּי יְהוּדָה בְּלֹא הִשְׁמִיעַ לְאָזְנוֹ יָצָא — בְּדִיעֲבַד קָאָמַר, וְלֹא לְכַתְּחִילָּה: אֶלָּא הָא דְּתַנְיָא כו' תּוֹרֵם. וְאע"פ שֶׁהוּא צָרִיךְ לְבָרֵךְ, וְאֵין אָזְנָיו שׁוֹמְעוֹת הַבְּרָכָה שֶׁהוּא מוֹצִיא מִפִּיו: אֶלָּא מַאי. בָּעֵית לְמֵימַר דְּרַבִּי יְהוּדָה דְּאָמַר בְּלֹא הִשְׁמִיעַ לְאָזְנוֹ יָצָא אֲפִילּוּ לְכַתְּחִילָּה, כִּי הֵיכִי דְּתֵיקוּם הָא דְּר"י בְּרֵיהּ דְּר"ש בֶּן פָּזִי אַלִּיבֵּיהּ, וְהַאי דְּקָא מִיפַּלְגֵי בְּדִיעֲבַד — לְהוֹדִיעֲךָ כֹּחוֹ דְּר' יוֹסֵי: אֶלָּא הָא דְּתַנְיָא כו' מַנִּי: לְעוֹלָם

תוספות

שיור התפר הלכה למשה מסיני. נראה דאף במגילה ובשאר ספרים בעינן שיור התפר, כיון דטעמא הוי כדי שלא יקרע:

חוץ מחרש. סתם חרש *הוי אינו שומע ואינו מדבר, אבל חרש דהכא מדבר הוא, מדקרי המגילה, ופקח הוא לכל דבריו חוץ מדבר זה שצריך שישמיע לאזנו:

ורבי יהודה מכשיר. קשה: באיזה קטן מיירי? אי בלא הגיע לחינוך — מאי טעמא דרבי יהודה דמכשיר? והא אמרינן בסוף פ' בתרא דראש השנה (דף כט.) כל שאינו מחויב בדבר אין מוציא אחרים ידי חובתן. ואי הגיע לחינוך — מאי טעמא דרבנן דפסלי? והלא כל האחרים נמי אין חייבין אלא מדרבנן! וא"כ קשיא: אמאי לא אמרינן דאתי דרבנן ומפיק דרבנן? דהכי נמי אמרינן פ' "מי שמתו" (ברכות דף כ: ושם) דבן מברך לאביו אע"פ שהוא קטן, ויוצא בברכתו, ומוקי לה התם כגון שאכל האב כזית או כביצה דהוי שיעורא דרבנן, ואתי קטן שחיובו דרבנן, ומפיק האב שלא אכל אלא שיעורא דרבנן. ואמאי לא אמרינן כן במגילה, וכן בפ' "לולב הגזול" (סוכה דף לח: ושם) דאמר: אין קטן מוציא [בקריאת הלל] ועונין אחריו מה (ב) שהן אומרים מאי שנא מברכת המזון? וי"ל: דלעולם מיירי בקטן שהגיע לחינוך, ואפ"ה פסלו רבנן. משום דמגילה ליכא חיובא אפילו בגדולים אלא מדרבנן, וקטן אין מחויב אלא מדרבנן אפילו בשאר מצות, ובגדול ליכא אלא חד דרבנן במגילה, שהרי בשאר מצות הוא חייב דאורייי', ולא אתי תרי דרבנן ומפיק חד דרבנן. אבל ההיא דבהמ"ז מיירי שהקטן אכל כדי שביעה דהוי חיובא דאורייתא, וליכא אלא חד דרבנן, ומפיק האב שלא אכל אלא שיעורא דרבנן. ומ"מ קשיא, דקאמרינן *דרב ששת ורב יוסף אמרי אגדתא בלילי פסחים ומוציאין האחרים, משום דסברי מצה בזמן הזה דרבנן. [פסחים קטז:] ולפי מה שפירש' קשה: היכי אתו אינהו דהוו תרי דרבנן, דהא סומא פטור מלומר האגדה, ומפקי האחרים דחייבים מיהא דרבנן, וליכא בהו אלא חד דרבנן! וי"ל: דסומא עדיף מקטן, שהרי נתחייב כבר מדאורייתא, משא"כ בקטן*):

ודלמא ר' יהודה היא. משום דפסיק התם כרבי יהודה, דחיק לאוקומי מתני' כוותיה:

אלא הא דתניא לא יברך אדם ברכת המזון בלבו. קשיא: היכי מדמינן ברכת המזון לקריאת שמע? בשלמא מגילה איכא למימר דסבר כמאן דאמר דצריך בקריאת שמע השמעת אוזן, וסבר דתקינו רבנן מגילה כעין דאורייתא. אבל ברכת המזון דהוי דאורייתא ולא כתיב ביה 'שמע', מנלן לתקן ביה דצריך שישמיע לאזנו? ויש לומר: דקים ליה דגמרינן ברכת המזון מקריאת שמע:

*) [וע"ע תוס' לקמן כד. ד"ה אבל וד"ה מי ותוס' עירובין נו. ד"ה דלמא]

עין משפט נר מצוה

[תרומות פ"א מ"ב]

לב א מיי' פ"ב מהל' מגילה הלכה ח סמג עשין ד טוש"ע או"ח סי' תרצ סעיף ח:

לג ב מיי' פ"ט מהל' ס"ת הלכה יד סמג עשין כה טוש"ע יו"ד סי' רעח סעיף א [וטוש"ע או"ח סי' תרצא סעיף ז]:

לד ג מיי' פ"א מהלכות מגילה הלכה ב סמג עשין ד טוש"ע או"ח סי' תרפט סעיף ב:

לה ד מיי' פ"א מהלכות ברכות הלכה ז:

רבינו חננאל

ג' זרתות וחצי זרת או ב' זרתות וחצי שנראית מגילה בפני עצמה כשרה. אמר ר' יוחנן הקורא במגילה הכתובה בין הכתובים לא יצא ומחו לה אמוחא לא אמרן לא יצא אלא בצבור ש"מ קורין אותה ביחיד כרב. ושיור התפר פי' שיניח כמו אצבע ועוד בתחלה ואחר כך יתפור בגידין הל"מ היא ואוקימנא כדי שלא יקרע. וא"ר יוחנן אלמלא נשתייר במערה שעמד בה משה ואליהו כמלוא מחט נקב סידקית לא יכלו לעמוד מפני האורה דכתיב כי לא יראני האדם וחי. ומאי דכתיב ועליהם ככל הדברים דייקינן מן עליהם מלמד שהראהו הקב"ה למשה בסיני דקדוקי תורה ודקדוקי סופרים ומה שעתידין לחדש ומאי ניהו מקרא מגילה: **ירושלמי** וזכרם לא יסוף מזרעם מיכן שקבעו להם חכמים מסכת': **מתני'** הכל כשרים לקרוא את המגילה חוץ מחרש שוטה וקטן רבי יהודה מכשיר בקטן מאן תנא חרש אפילו דיעבד לא ואוקמה רב מתנה לר' יוסי דתנן הקורא את שמע ולא השמיע לאזנו יצא ר' יוסי אומר לא יצא פירוש כיון שלא שמע הרי הוא כחרש לפיכך [לא יצא] ואמרי' ודילמא מתניתין ר"י היא ולכתחלה הוא דלא הא דיעבד שפיר דמי ודחינן מדקתני חרש בהדי שוטה דשמעינן מיכן חרש דומיא דשוטה מה שוטה דיעבד פסול אף חרש נמי כן. ואמרינן ודילמא הא כדאיתיה והא כדאיתיה כלומר אע"פ ששנאה כאחד כל אחד יש לו דרך [אחר] ודחינן מדסיפא רבי יהודה מכשיר בקטן רישא דפסיל בקטן לאו ר' יהודה היא דאם כן קשיא דר' יהודה אדר' יהודה ופריק כולה ר' יהודה היא ותרי גווני קטן רישא בקטן שלא הגיע לחינוך והוא כדתנן בפרק יוה"כ תינוקות אין מענין אותן (לשעות) ביוה"כ אבל מחנכין אותן קודם שנה או שנתים כדי להרגילן למצו' וא"ר יוחנן בן עשר בן י"א מחנכין אותן לשעות כו' ולפיכך פסול אבל סיפא דקתני ר' יהודה מכשיר בקטן הוא קטן שהגיע לחינוך מבן י"א שנה ולמעלה ולפיכך אמר כשר ואפילו לכתחלה כשר ודר' במאי אוקימתא למתניתין כר' יהודה ורישא כולה דיעבד אין לכתחלה לא (ר' אומר) הא דתני חרש המדבר ואינו שומע תורם לכתחלה מני אי רבי יהודה דאי עבד מכשיר אבל לכתחלה לא ורבי יוסי לכתחלה ולא דיעבד מכשיר הא דקתני תורם לכתחלה מני היא. ומתמהינן ולאו מאי הא דתני חרש תורם לכתחלה ר' יהודה היא וקשיא לן אי הכי היה לו להקשות אי ר' יהודה מכש... בקטן

הגהות הב"ח

(א) גמ' לאו ר' יהודה ... (ודלמא כולה וכו' לכשי... תא"מ ונ"ב רש"י לא ג... ליה: (ב) תוס' ד"ה ... יהודה וכו' אחריו שהוא אומר:

גליון הש"ס

גמרא בצבור שנו. לעיל דף ד ע"א תו' ... הוה עובדא: **רש"י** ... מחט סדקית וכו' ויש מ... אחרת. במתני' דשבת קכב ע"ב: **תוס'** ... ור"י מכשיר וכו' ולא ... תרי דרבנן. עיין לקמן כד ע"א תוס' ד"ה א... **בא"ד** וי"ל דסו... עדיף. עיין לקמן דף ... ע"א תוס' ד"ה מי ... רהא: **תוס'** ד"ה ודל... ר"י היא משום דפס... כעין זה שבת קג ... תוס' ד"ה לעולם:

מסורת הש"ס

[עי' ברכות ה. ועי' פי' על זה בהקדמת התוי"ט]

ברכות טו. [ערכין ב:]

ג"ז שם לעיל יז:

ברכות טו.

לְעוֹלָם ר' יְהוּדָה, וַאֲפִי' לְכַתְּחִילָּה. וְלָא קַשְׁיָא: הָא — דִּידֵיהּ, הָא — דְּרַבֵּיהּ. דְּתַנְיָא, ר' יְהוּדָה אוֹמֵר מִשּׁוּם ר"א בֶּן עֲזַרְיָה: הַקּוֹרֵא אֶת שְׁמַע צָרִיךְ שֶׁיַּשְׁמִיעַ לְאׇזְנוֹ, שֶׁנֶּאֱמַר: °"שְׁמַע יִשְׂרָאֵל ה' אֱלֹהֵינוּ ה' אֶחָד" — הַשְׁמַע לְאׇזְנֶיךָ מַה שֶּׁאַתָּה מוֹצִיא מִפִּיךָ. ר"מ אוֹמֵר: °"אֲשֶׁר אָנֹכִי מְצַוְּךָ הַיּוֹם עַל לְבָבֶךָ" — אַחַר כַּוָּונַת הַלֵּב הֵן הֵן הַדְּבָרִים. הַשְׁתָּא דְּאָתֵית לְהָכִי, אֲפִילּוּ תֵּימָא רַבִּי יְהוּדָה כְּרַבֵּיהּ סְבִירָא לֵיהּ. וְהָא דְּתָנֵי יְהוּדָה בְּרֵיהּ דְּר' שִׁמְעוֹן בֶּן פָּזִי — ר"מ הִיא. § "רַבִּי יְהוּדָה מַכְשִׁיר בְּקָטָן". § (*דְּתַנְיָא) *א"ר יְהוּדָה: קָטָן הָיִיתִי וּקְרִיתִיהָ לְמַעְלָה מֵרַבִּי טַרְפוֹן וּזְקֵנִים בְּלוֹד. אָמְרוּ לוֹ: *אֵין מְבִיאִין רְאָיָה מִן הַקָּטָן. תַּנְיָא, אָמַר רַבִּי: *קָטָן הָיִיתִי וּקְרִיתִיהָ לְמַעְלָה מֵרַבִּי יְהוּדָה. אָמְרוּ לוֹ: אֵין מְבִיאִין רְאָיָה מִן הַמַּתִּיר. וְלֵימְרוּ לֵיהּ: אֵין מְבִיאִין רְאָיָה מִן הַקָּטָן! חֲדָא וְעוֹד קָאָמְרוּ לֵיהּ. חֲדָא — דְּקָטָן הָיִיתָ. וְעוֹד: אֲפִילּוּ גָּדוֹל הָיִיתָ — אֵין מְבִיאִין רְאָיָה מִן הַמַּתִּיר. §

מתני' [א]אֵין קוֹרִין אֶת הַמְּגִילָּה, [ב]וְלֹא מָלִין, [ג]וְלֹא טוֹבְלִין, [ד]וְלֹא מַזִּין, [ה]וְכֵן שׁוֹמֶרֶת יוֹם כְּנֶגֶד יוֹם — לֹא תִּטְבּוֹל עַד שֶׁתָּנֵץ הַחַמָּה. *וְכוּלָּן שֶׁעָשׂוּ מִשֶּׁעָלָה עַמּוּד הַשַּׁחַר — כָּשֵׁר. §

גמ' מְנָלַן? דְּאָמַר קְרָא: °"וְהַיָּמִים הָאֵלֶּה נִזְכָּרִים וְנַעֲשִׂים" בַּיּוֹם — אִין, בַּלַּיְלָה — לָא. לֵימָא תֶּיהְוֵי תְּיוּבְתָּא דְּר' יְהוֹשֻׁעַ בֶּן לֵוִי, *דְּאָמַר ריב"ל: חַיָּיב אָדָם לִקְרוֹת אֶת הַמְּגִילָּה בַּלַּיְלָה וְלִשְׁנוֹתָהּ בַּיּוֹם? כִּי קָתָנֵי אַדְּיוֹם. § "וְלֹא מָלִין" וְכוּ'. § דִּכְתִיב: °"וּבַיּוֹם הַשְּׁמִינִי יִמּוֹל". § "וְלֹא טוֹבְלִין וְלֹא מַזִּין" וְכוּ'. § דִּכְתִיב: °"וְהִזָּה הַטָּהֹר עַל הַטָּמֵא [וגו'] בַּיּוֹם הַשְּׁבִיעִי", וְאִתְקַשׁ טְבִילָה לְהַזָּאָה. § "וְכֵן שׁוֹמֶרֶת יוֹם כְּנֶגֶד יוֹם לֹא תִּטְבּוֹל עַד שֶׁתָּנֵץ הַחַמָּה" וְכוּ'. § פְּשִׁיטָא! מ"ש שׁוֹמֶרֶת יוֹם כְּנֶגֶד יוֹם מִכׇּל חַיָּיבֵי טְבִילוֹת? אִיצְטְרִיךְ. סָלְקָא דַּעְתָּךְ אָמֵינָא תֶּיהְוֵי כִּרְאִיָּה רִאשׁוֹנָה שֶׁל זָב, וּרְאִיָּה רִאשׁוֹנָה שֶׁל זָב אִיתְקַשׁ לְבַעַל קֶרִי, דִּכְתִיב: °"זֹאת תּוֹרַת הַזָּב וַאֲשֶׁר תֵּצֵא מִמֶּנּוּ שִׁכְבַת זָרַע". מַה בַּעַל קֶרִי טוֹבֵל בַּיּוֹם — הַאי נָמֵי לִיטְבּוֹל בְּיוֹמֵיהּ. וְהָא בִּימָמָא לָא מָצֵי טָבְלָה,(א) דִּכְתִיב: °"כׇּל יְמֵי זוֹבָהּ כְּמִשְׁכַּב נִדָּתָהּ יִהְיֶה לָּהּ" — בְּלֵילְיָא מִיהַת לִיעֲבִיד מִקְצָת שִׁימּוּר וְתִיטְבּוֹל, קמ"ל: כֵּיוָן דְּבָעֲיָא סְפִירָה —

סְפִירָה

תורה אור: דברים ו | שם | אסתר ט | ויקרא יב | במדבר יט | ויקרא טו | שם

[תוספתא פ"ב]

רש"י

לְעוֹלָם רַבִּי יְהוּדָה. וַאֲפִי' לְכַתְּחִילָּה מַכְשִׁיר. וּמַתְנִי' רַבִּי יוֹסֵי הִיא, וַאֲפִי' דִּיעֲבַד לָא: וְהַאי. דְּתוֹרֵם לְכַתְּחִילָּה ר' יְהוּדָה: וְהַאי. דְּבִרְהמ"ז: דְּרַבֵּיהּ. מִשְּׁמוֹ שֶׁל ר' אֶלְעָזָר בֶּן עֲזַרְיָה אֲמָרָהּ, שֶׁצָּרִיךְ לְהַשְׁמִיעַ. וְהַאי לִישָּׁנָא מַשְׁמַע לְכַתְּחִילָּה, אֲבָל דִּיעֲבַד יָצָא: וְהַשְׁתָּא דְּאָתֵית לְהָכִי. לְאַשְׁמוּעִינַן הָא פְּלוּגְתָּא דְּר' יְהוּדָה וְר"מ: אֲפִי' תֵּימָא ר' יְהוּדָה. דְּאָמַר בְּק"ש יָצָא, דִּיעֲבַד — אִין, לְכַתְּחִילָּה — לָא. וּמַתְנִי' נָמֵי לְכַתְּחִילָּה הוּא דְּפָסְלָה לְחֵרֵשׁ, וְר' יְהוּדָה הִיא. וְכֵן דְּבִרְכַּת הַמָּזוֹן נָמֵי ר' יְהוּדָה הִיא. וּדְקַשְׁיָא לָךְ הָא דִּיהוּדָה בְּרֵיהּ דְּר' שִׁמְעוֹן בֶּן פָּזִי מַנִּי, לָא ר' יְהוּדָה וְלָא ר' יוֹסֵי — ר"מ הִיא, דְּמַכְשַׁר לְכַתְּחִילָּה: מִן הַמַּתִּיר. ר' יְהוּדָה שֶׁקָּרִיתָ לְפָנָיו הוּא הַמַּתִּיר אֶת הַקָּטָן, וְאֵין לְךָ לְהָבִיא רְאָיָה מִמֶּנּוּ, שֶׁהֲרֵי רַבִּים חוֹלְקִין עָלָיו:

מתני' וְלֹא טוֹבְלִין. מִשֶּׁיַּגִּיעַ שְׁבִיעִי לְזָב וְלִטְמֵא מֵת אֵין אוֹמְרִים מִשֶּׁחֲשֵׁיכָה בִּכְנִיסַת שְׁבִיעִי רָאוּי לִטְבּוֹל, אע"ג דְּלַיְלָה תְּחִילַּת יוֹם הִיא — הָכָא יוֹם בָּעֵינַן. אֲבָל מִשֶּׁעָבַר הַיּוֹם מוּתָּר לִטְבּוֹל בַּלַּיְלָה. וּבַגְּמָרָא יָלֵיף לָהּ לְכוּלְּהוּ: וְכֵן שׁוֹמֶרֶת יוֹם כְּנֶגֶד יוֹם. בַּגְּמָרָא מְפָרֵשׁ מַאי שְׁנָא דְּנָקַט לְהָא תּוּ בְּאַנְפֵּי נַפְשָׁהּ, הָא תְּנָא לֵיהּ "אֵין טוֹבְלִין": עַד הָנֵץ הַחַמָּה. שֶׁלֹּא מְסַפֵּק לַיְלָה: וְכוּלָּן שֶׁעָשׂוּ כו'. דְּמֵעֲלוֹת הַשַּׁחַר יְמָמָא הוּא, אֲבָל לְפִי שֶׁאֵין הַכֹּל בְּקִיאִין בּוֹ צְרִיכִין לְהַמְתִּין עַד הָנֵץ הַחַמָּה: **גמ'** כִּי קָתָנֵי. עַד שֶׁתְּהֵא הָנֵץ הַחַמָּה אַדְּיוֹם אַקְּרִיָּיה שְׁנִיָּה, וְקָאָמַר שֶׁיְּהֵא שֶׁל יוֹם בַּיּוֹם: וְאִיתְקַשׁ טְבִילָה. דִּכְתִיב בְּסֵיפֵיהּ "וְרָחַץ בַּמַּיִם", וְה"ה לְזָב וְזָבָה: ה"ג. פְּשִׁיטָא מַאי שְׁנָא שׁוֹמֶרֶת יוֹם כְּנֶגֶד יוֹם כו': שׁוֹמֶרֶת יוֹם כְּנֶגֶד יוֹם. לְאַחַר שֶׁכָּלָה שִׁבְעָה יְמֵי נִדָּה נִכְנָסִין י"א יוֹם הַקְּרוּיִין יְמֵי זִיבָה, שֶׁאִם תִּרְאֶה בָּהֶן ג' יָמִים רְצוּפִין — הֲרֵי הִיא זָבָה, וּטְעוּנָה סְפִירַת שִׁבְעָה וְקׇרְבָּן. וְאִם תִּרְאֶה יוֹם אֶחָד — שׁוֹמֶרֶת יוֹם לַמָּחֳרָת וְטוֹבֶלֶת. וּמִקְּרָאֵי יָלֵיף לָהּ בְּתוֹרַת כֹּהֲנִים, וּמַיְיתִי לָהּ בִּשְׁמַעְתָּא בַּתְרַיְיתָא דְּמַסֶּכֶת נִדָּה: תֶּיהְוֵי. הָךְ רְאִיָּה שֶׁל זָבָה כִּרְאִיָּה רִאשׁוֹנָה שֶׁל זָב, דְּאִיתְקַשׁ לְבַעַל קֶרִי, דִּכְתִיב "זֹאת תּוֹרַת הַזָּב וַאֲשֶׁר תֵּצֵא מִמֶּנּוּ שִׁכְבַת זָרַע". חֲדָא זִיבָה כְּתִיב הָכָא, וְהַיְינוּ רְאִיָּה רִאשׁוֹנָה, וַ"אֲשֶׁר תֵּצֵא מִמֶּנּוּ שִׁכְבַת זָרַע" — הַיְינוּ בַּעַל קֶרִי: מִשּׁוּם דִּכְתִיב יִהְיֶה גָּרְסִינַן. "כׇּל יְמֵי זוֹב טוּמְאָתָהּ כְּמִשְׁכַּב נִדָּתָהּ יִהְיֶה לָּהּ". וְהָךְ קְרָא בְּרָאִיַּית שׁוֹמֶרֶת יוֹם כְּנֶגֶד יוֹם קָאֵי, מֵרִבּוּיֵי "כׇּל יְמֵי" דָּרְשִׁינַן לָהּ בְּמַסֶּכֶת נִדָּה (דף עג.). וְאָמְרִינַן הָתָם: "יִהְיֶה לָּהּ" — מְלַמֵּד שֶׁסּוֹפֶרֶת אֶחָד לְאֶחָד, קְצָת מִיּוֹם הַמָּחֳרָת. הִלְכָּךְ, בַּלַּיְלָה מִיהַת תִּטְבּוֹל, דַּעֲבָדָה קְצָת שִׁימּוּר:

[נ"ל תניא] [סנהדרין נב:] [תוספתא שם] [פרה סוף פי"ב] לעיל ד.

תוספות

ולא טובלין ולא מזין אלא ביום. קשיא: דהתנן במסכת פרה (פי"ב משנה י"א): אין טובלין האזוב בלילה ומזין ביום, אבל הוא עצמו טובל בלילה ומזין עליו ביום. והכא אמרינן דצריך לטבול ביום! ופר"ת: דשתי טבילות הן, אחת לפני ההזאה כדי לקבל ההזאה, ואותה הויא בלילה, כדתנן במסכת יבמות (דף מו:). ואחת לאחר ההזאה, והיינו ההיא דכתיבא בקרא, וההיא הויא ביממא. והכי נמי משמע פ"ב דכריתות (דף ט.) דאיכא טבילה לפני ההזאה, דקאמרינן: מה אבותיכם לא נכנסו לברית אלא במילה וטבילה והרצאת דמים, והרצאת דמים נפקא לן מ"ויזרוק את הדם" וטבילה נפקא לן משום דגמירי דאין הזאה בלא טבילה לפניה כדי לקבל ההזאה. והזאת פרה במקום אותה הזאה עומדת, ואם כן צריך טבילה לפניה, *וגם צריך טבילה לאחריה, דהא בספרי קתני: שאם הקדים טבילה להזאה — לא עשה ולא כלום. אלמא: שיש טבילה לאחר הזאה, כדמשמע התם, ואחת קודם ההזאה כדמשמע בכריתות ובכמה מקומות בגמרתנו, שמזכיר טבילה לפני ההזאה. ומ"מ קשה: הכא באיזה טבילה מיירי? אי בטבילה דלפני ההזאה, כדמשמע לישנא דנקט טובלין — ברישא אם כן הויא אפילו בלילה, כדפרישית! ואי מיירי באותה שלאחר הזאה — מאי איריא משום דאיתקש להזאה? תיפוק ליה משום דהויא לאחר ההזאה, ואינה אלא ביום! ולמעוטי לילה שלאחר ההזאה דהיינו ליל שמיני לא איצטריך, דכיון דעבר שביעי — פשיטא דמותר לטבול בכל עת שירצה. וגם רש"י פירש כן, דמשעבר היום מותר לטבול בלילה. לכך נראה כפירוש ריב"א: דהכא מיירי בטבילת אזוב, דהויא ביממא, כדתנן במסכת (פרה שם) ולהכי נקט טובלין ואח"כ מזין. וה"נ משמע בירושלמי, דמייתי קרא ד"וטבל והזה" למדרשא דאתקש טבילה להזאה, והיינו טבילת אזוב. *ומיהו קשה לר"י: דהא אמר בשלהי מסכת יומא (דף פח.) הזב והזבה וטמא מת (ג) טבילתן ביום, ר' יוסי אומר: מן המנחה ולמעלה לא יטבול. פירוש: אחר שהתפלל תפלת המנחה, דתפילת נעילה יכול הוא לאומרה בלילה. ופשיטא דהיינו ביום שלאחר ההזאה, *דאי לפני ההזאה היאך מותר לטבול ביום הכפורים? אי משום דטבילה בזמנה מצוה — מכל מקום ההזאה הויא שבות, כדאמר פרק אלו דברים (פסחים דף סה:), והיאך יכול לעשות? ואם תפרש שהזה מאתמול ועכשיו הוא טובל בשמיני — אין זו טבילה בזמנה, ולא דחיא יום הכפורים! וי"ל: שקיבל ההזאה מקטן, או בשוגג, או שעבר והזה:

דכתיב וביום השמיני ימול. קשיא: דבפרק "ר' אליעזר אומר אם לא הביא" (שבת דף קלג. ושם) דריש האי קרא, לומר אפילו בשבת, ולא בלילה, ותניא התם כוותיה דרבי יוחנן! וי"ל: דהכא מייתי הדרשה הפשוטה יותר, כראיית נגעים*. והקשה ה"ר אפרים: כיון דמילה אינה בלילה, אם כן הויא מצות עשה שהזמן גרמא שהנשים פטורות ממנה, וא"כ קשיא למה לי בפ"ק דקדושין (דף כט. ושם) קרא ד"אותו" לומר דאשה אינה חייבת למול? תיפוק ליה דמצות עשה שהזמן גרמא היא! וי"ל: דאי לאו "אותו" הוה אמינא דהאי דנשים פטורות ממצות עשה שהזמן גרמא — היינו היכא דליכא כרת, דומיא דמצה ושמחה והקהל דלית בהו כרת, ומנייהו ממעטינן נשים. אבל מילה שיש בה כרת, ונכרתו עליה שלש עשרה בריתות — הוה אמינא דמחייב בהו נשים למול את בנייהו, קמ"ל "אותו" דלא. אי נמי למילה שלא בזמנה, וכמאן דאמר *) דנוהגין בין ביום בין בלילה**):

מאי שנא שומרת יום כנגד יום וכו'. אי "ולא טובלין" דלעיל מיירי בטבילת אדם — אתי שפיר, דבעי מאי שנא שהזכיר בפני עצמה. אבל אי איירי בטבילת אזוב צריך לפרש הכי: מאי שנא שהזכיר שומרת יום, לומר שהיא ביום, מכל שאר חייבי טבילות:

ספירה

*) [יבמות עב:] **) [ועי' תוס' יבמות עב: ד"ה אין ותוס' קדושין כט. ד"ה אותו]

[בסנהדרין לד: ועי' תוספ' שם ד"ה כתיב ובתו' מו"ק ח: ד"ה נפקא ותוס' זבחים קיז. ד"ה והתורה]

עין משפט נר מצוה

לו א טוש"ע א"ח סימן תרפז סעיף א:

לז ב מיי' פ"א מהלכות מילה הלכה ח סמג עשין כח טוש"ע י"ד סי' רסב סעיף א:

לח ג מיי' פ"א מהלכות מקואות הלכה ו סמג עשין רמח:

לט ד מיי' פי"א מהל' פרה אדומה הלכה א סמג עשין רלג:

מ ה מיי' פ"ו מהלכות אסורי ביאה הלכה ט סמג לאוין קיא ועשין רמג טור יד סימן קפג:

רבינו חננאל

בקטן ובחרש ופרקינן חדא מתרתי אותיב ליה אלא הא דתניא לא יברך אדם לכתחלה ברכת המזון בלבו ואם בירך יצא כו' ופרקינן לעולם תרווייהו רבי יהודה והא דתני חרש תורם לכתחלה דידיה ומתניתין דאוקימנא דאיעבד והא דתני ואם ברך יצא תני לה רבי יהודה משמיה דרביה דתניא ר' יהודה אומר משום רבי אלעזר בן עזריה הקורא את שמע צריך להשמיע לאזנו שנאמר שמע ישראל השמע לאזניך לכתחלה מה שאתה מוצא מפיך ר' מאיר אומר כשהוא אומר אשר אנכי מצוך היום על לבבך אחר כוונת הלב הן הן הדברים כלומר אין צריך להשמיע ואפילו לא הוציא את הדברים מפיו אלא בירך בלבו יצא והדר אוקימנה למתניתין רבי יהודה לכתחלה לא יקרא החרש ודאיעבד יצא וכן אם בירך בלבו לכתחלה לא אבל בדיעבד יצא. והא דתניא חרש תורם לכתחלה ר' מאיר היא: תניא א"ר קטן הייתי וקראתיה למעלה מרבי יהודה כו' אמרו חדא דקטן היית ואין עדות מקטן. ועוד ר' יהודה שקראת למעלה ממנו (מכשיר) [מתיר] הוא ואין מביאין ראיה מן המתיר וקי"ל כלישנא בתרא דרב יוסף דאמר [בברכות טו] מחלוקת בק"ש אבל בשאר מצות דברי הכל יצא. ואמר רב חסדא א"ר שילא הלכתא כר' יהודה ועוד אמר הלכתא כר' יהודה שאמר משום ר' אליעזר בן עזריה הלכך לכתחלה לא מוקמינן חרש מדבר ואינו שומע למפרס על שמע ולברך ברכת המזון ואי עבד שפיר דמי: **ירושלמי** ר' יוסי אומר כתיב והאזנת למצותיו השמע לאזנך מה שאתה מוצא מפיך בר קפרא אמר צריך לקרותה בפני הנשים והקטנים שאף הם היו בספק נפשות. אין קורין את המגלה אלא ביום שנאמר והימים האלה נזכרים ונעשים וגו' ביום ולא בלילה והני מילי בקריאה של יום כדקתני ולשנותה ביום

ולא מוהלין דכתיב וביום השמיני ימול ולא טובלין ולא מזין דכתיב והזה הטהור על הטמא ביום השלישי ואתקש טבילה להזאה שנאמר והזה ורחץ אלו כולן וכן שומרת יום כנגד יום כגון שראתה בי"א יום שבין נדה לנדה שהן ימי זיבה [יום א'] הדין לישב שלא תגע בדבר ולא תטהר למחר יום ב' ואם לא ראתה בו דם טובלת ביום ג' *) לראייתה משתנץ החמה וטהורה אבל קודם שתנץ החמה לא: **ירושלמי** כל חייבי טבילות טבילתן ביום נדה ויולדת טבילתן בלילה נדה שעבר זמנה פירוש אחר ז' ימים לנדה דאורייתא או אחרי ז' נקיים (וספק זובה) [לזבה] טובלת בין ביום בין בלילה. דרש ר' חייא בר בא לצודיא נדה שעבר זמנה טובלת אפילו ביום תמן אמרו אפילו עובר זמנה לא מפני חמותה ומפני כלתה אשה משל בית רבותינו ראוה טובלת כדרכה ביום ואמרו עוברת זמן היתה. נדה שנאנסה

*) עי' נדה ע"ב. ובמשנה טבלה ביום שלאחריו כו' וצ"ע.

הגהות הב"ח

(א) גמ' לא מצי טבלה משום דכתיב כל: (ב) תום' ד"ה ולא טובלין וכו' הזאה וטמא מת טובלין כדרכן ביום הכפורים ר' יוסי אומר:

גליון הש"ס

תוס' ד"ה ולא טובלין וכו' וגם לריך טבילה לאחריה. עי' תוס' חגיגה דף כג ע"א תוס' ד"ה טעמו: בא"ד דאי לפני ההזאה היאך מותר לטבול ביוה"כ. עי' שבת דף קיא ע"א תוס' ד"ה לא תוס'.

ספירה – בימָמא היא.§ "וכולן שעשו משעלה עמוד השחר כשר".§ מנהני מילי? אמר רבא: דאמר קרא: "ויקרא אלהים לאור יום" – *למאיר ובא קראו יום. אלא מעתה "ולחשך קרא לילה", [למחשיך ובא קרא לילה?] הא קיי"ל דעד צאת הכוכבים לאו לילה הוא! אלא אמר רבי זירא, מהכא: *"ואנחנו עושים במלאכה וחצים מחזיקים ברמחים מעלות השחר עד צאת הכוכבים", ואומר: "(*והיה) לנו הלילה (*למשמר)" מאי "ואומר"? וכ"ת משעלה עמוד השחר לאו יממא, ומכי ערבא שמשא ליליא, ואינהו מקדמי ומחשכי – ת"ש "(*והיה) לנו הלילה משמר והיום מלאכה".§ **מתני'** א כל היום כשר לקריאת המגילה, ב ולקריאת ההלל, ג ולתקיעת שופר, *ד ולנטילת לולב, ה ולתפלת המוספין, ו ולמוספין, ז ולוידוי הפרים, ח ולוידוי מעשר, ט ולוידוי יוהכ"פ, י לסמיכה, לשחיטה, לתנופה, להגשה, לקמיצה, ולהקטרה, למליקה, ולקבלה, ולהזיה, כ ולהשקיית סוטה, ל ולעריפת העגלה, מ ולטהרת המצורע. *כל הלילה כשר נ לקצירת העומר, ס ולהקטר חלבים ואברים. *ע זה הכלל: דבר שמצותו ביום – כשר כל היום, דבר שמצותו בלילה – כשר כל הלילה.§ **גמ'** מנלן? דאמר קרא: "והימים האלה נזכרים ונעשים". לקריאת ההלל – דכתיב: "ממזרח שמש עד מבואו". (*רבי יוסי) אומר: "זה היום עשה ה'". "ולנטילת לולב" – דכתיב: "ולקחתם לכם ביום הראשון". "ולתקיעת שופר" – דכתיב: "יום תרועה יהיה לכם". ולמוספין – דכתיב: "דבר יום ביומו". "ולתפלת המוספין" – כמוספין שוויה רבנן. "ולוידוי פרים" – דיליף 'כפרה' 'כפרה' מיום הכפורים. דתניא *גבי יוה"כ: "וכפר בעדו ובעד ביתו" פ בכפרת דברים הכתוב מדבר, וכפרה ביממא הוא, דכתיב: "ביום הזה יכפר עליכם".§ "ולוידוי מעשר" וכו'.§ דכתיב: "ואמרת לפני ה' אלהיך בערתי הקדש מן הבית" וסמיך ליה: "היום הזה ה' אלהיך מצוך".§ "לסמיכה ולשחיטה".§ דכתיב: "וסמך ושחט" וכתיב בה בשחיטה: "ביום זבחכם". "ולתנופה" – דכתיב: "ביום הניפכם את העומר". "ולהגשה" – דאיתקש לתנופה, דכתיב: "ולקח הכהן מיד האשה את מנחת הקנאות והניף... והקריב". "ולמליקה ולקמיצה ולהקטרה ולהזיה" – דכתיב: "ביום צוותו את בני ישראל". "ולהשקיית סוטה" – *אתיא 'תורה' 'תורה'. כתיב הכא: "ועשה לה הכהן את כל התורה הזאת", וכתיב התם: "על פי התורה אשר יורוך ועל המשפט". מה

(בראשית א; נחמיה ד; שם; תהלים קיג; שם קיח; ויקרא כג; במדבר כט; ויקרא כג; שם טז; שם; דברים כו; ויקרא ג; שם יט; שם כג; במדבר ה; ויקרא ז; במדבר ה; דברים יז)

רש"י

קמ"ל. כיון דהאי אחד לאחד משום ספירה היא, מדוגמת ספירת ז', כל ספירה דימָמא היא, דכתיב "וספרה לה שבעת ימים" (ויקרא טו): מקדמי. מקדימין: מחשכי. מעריבין: ת"ש (*והיה) לנו הלילה למשמר והיום למלאכה. ש"מ: כל זמן שעסוקים במלאכה קרי יום, ולא קדמותא וחשכותא: **מתני'** כל היום כשר. ואע"ג דקיימא לן* זריזין מקדימין למצות, דכתיב "וישכם אברהם בבקר" (בראשית כב), אפילו הכי כשר כל היום: לוידוי פרים. פר העלם דבר של צבור, ופר כהן משיח, שמתודין עליו חטא שהביאוהו עליו, כדאמרינן במסכת יומא (דף לו:): "והתודה" על חטאת עון חטאת. כתיב הכא "וכפר עליו הכהן" (ויקרא ד) וכתיב התם ביום הכפורים "יעמד חי לפני ה' לכפר עליו" וגו' (ויקרא טז), מה להלן כפרת דברים וביום, כדיליף לקמן – אף כאן כפרת דברים וביום: למליקה. של עוף: לקבלה. לקבלת הדם: להזיה. לזריקת הדם, והזיית פרים הנשרפין וחטאות הפנימיות שהיא זריקה שלהן: **גמ'** בכפרת דברים. וידוי. במס' יומא (דף לו:) מסיים לה: אתה אומר בכפרת דברים, או אינו אלא בכפרת דמים? הרי הוא אומר "ושחט את פר החטאת אשר לו", למדנו שעדיין לא נשחט הפר: כי ביום הזה יכפר עליכם. אלמא כפרתו ביום: והניף והקריב. והקרבה היא הגשה, דאי אפשר לומר הך הקרבה היא הקטרת הקומץ – דהא כתיב בתריה "וקמץ והקטיר". ומה היא הגשה? – מגיש את המנחה ומגיעה בקרן מערבית דרומית של מזבח כנגד חודה של קרן, ואח"כ קומץ. ומקראי יליף לה במסכת סוטה (דף יד:) ובמנחות (דף יט:): לקמיצה ולהקטרה. בהקטרת קומץ קאמר, שהיא במנחה כנגד זריקת דם בזבחים, ואינה כשרה אלא ביום. אבל הקטר חלבים ואברים – תנן במתני' דכשרים כל הלילה: ביום צוותו. להקריב את קרבניהם. וכל הני הקרבת הקרבן נינהו, דאילו הקטרת קומץ הקרבה (א) היא, וקמיצה איתקש להקטרה, דכתיב "וקמץ והקטיר". מליקת עוף, מליקתו והזייתו כאחת, והזייתו היא הקרבתו. קבלת דם – הקרבה קרי לה, דאמר מר (חגיגה דף יא.): "והקריבו", זו קבלת הדם. א"נ: להקריב, כל צורכי הקרבה; קמיצה ומליקה וקבלה כולן צרכי הקרבה הן, ואי אפשר בלא הן. אבל הגשה ותנופה אינן מעכבין:

משפט

תוספות

ספירה ביממא היא. מכאן קשיא לפירוש רש"י ד"כילד צולין" (פסחים דף פא. ושם) דפריך: ולר' יוסי דאמר מקצת היום ככולו, וזבה שראתה בשבעה לספירתה אינה סותרת, אם כן, זבה גדולה לדידיה היכי משכחת לה? ומשני: [בראתה כל שני] בין השמשות, דאז הוי סוף היום ותחלת האחר בטומאה. וקשיא: אמאי לא אמר ברואה בלילות? דהא ספירת לילה לאו ספירה היא, ונמצא שכל היום טמא, כיון שתחילתו הוי טמא! וי"ל: דסבר ר' יוסי דסוף היום מהני לשמור כמו תחלת היום. וה"נ משמע פרק שני דנזיר (דף טז.) בסופו, דקאמר: [לר"י זבה גמורה] היכי משכח לה? אי דחזי בפלגא דיומא – אידך פלגא ליהוי לה שימור, ואם תאמר: אם כן רבי יוסי דסבר מקצת היום ככולו, א"כ היה לו להקשות ר' יוסי ככותאי אמרה לשמעתיה, כדקפריך לרב בנדה (דף סט.) וי"ל: דכותאי אמרי אפי' מיום ראשון שפסקה בו, דסופרתו ליום ראשון, ור' יוסי לא אמר אלא מיום שבעה*: והא קי"ל **דעם צאת הכוכבים ליליא הוא.** ואם תאמר: כיון דקיי"ל דבצאת הכוכבים הוי ליליא, א"כ אמאי פליגי ר' יוסי ור' יהודה בבין השמשות?* לימרו בצאת הכוכבים! וי"ל: דאף בשיעור צאת הכוכבים יש חילוק, שיש כוכבים נראין ביום*:

והיה לנו הלילה למשמר. קשיא: דהא אמרינן בברכות (דף ב: ושם) גבי צאת הכוכבים לילה הוא, ואע"פ שאין ראיה לדבר זכר לדבר – דכתיב "והיה לנו הלילה למשמר", ואמאי לא הוי ראייה גמורה כדמפקינן הכא מקרא? ויש לומר: דהתם בעי לאסוקי דזמן שכיבה דגבי ק"ש הוי צאת הכוכבים, ומש"ה קאמרינן התם דאין זו ראייה גמורה. דנהי דהוי לילה באותה שעה, מ"מ לא הוי זמן שכיבה לכל אדם: **ולוידוי** יוה"כ דתניא. קשיא: אמאי איצטריך למימר האי? כיון דתנא כל היום כשר לסמיכה, והלא הוידוי אינו אלא בשעת סמיכה! וי"ל: דאי לאו האי הוה אמינא דוידוי זה (*כוידוי) דשאר סמיכות, דאינו כשר כל היום. ויגרוס נמי לסמיכה שלא תהא כשרה כל היום כשאר סמיכות, משו"ה איצטריך למתני הוידוי:

לקמיצה ולהקטרה דכתיב ביום צוותו. אבל שחיטה לא מפקינן מהאי קרא, דלאו עבודה היא, שהרי כשרה בזר. וקרא משתעי בעבודה, דכתיב "להקריב את קרבניהם", וכן תנופה והגשה *אין צריך בהו כהן במנחה לפני הקמיצה:

*כל הלילה כשר לקצירת העומר – אומר ר"ת: שאם שכח לברך בלילה לא יברך ביום, כדמשמע בהאי סתמא דמתני'. דנהי דאיכא סתמא במנחות (דף עא.) דתני נקצר ביום כשר בדיעבד, מ"מ סתמא דהכא עדיפא, דהא קתני לה גבי הלכתא פסיקתא דדינא. ועוד נראה: דאפי' למאן דמכשר קצירת העומר ביום דיעבד, מודה הוא גבי ספירה דאין לברך ביום, משום דשנה עליה הכתוב לעכב, דכתיב (ויקרא כג) "תמימות" ואי אתה מוצא תמימות אלא כשאתה מונה בלילה. וכן כתוב ב"הלכות עצרת". ובה"ג כתב: דהיכא דאינשי לברך בלילה ימנה למחר בלא ברכה וכן הלכה. אבל אם שכח לילה ויום – לא ימנה עוד בברכה, דבעינן "תמימות" וליכא. *)ואחר שבירך על הספירה אומר "יה"ר שיבנה וכו'" מה שאין כן בתקיעת שופר ולולב, והיינו טעמא לפי שאין (ב) אלא הזכרה עתה לבנין ביהמ"ק, אבל לשופר ולולב יש עשיה:

*) [עי' תוספות מנחות סו. סד"ה זכר למקדש]

ולהקטיר

מסורת הש"ס

[נ"ל והיה כו' משמר והיום מלאכה]
[בפסחים ד.]
ברכות ב: פסחים ב.
[ברכות שם]
[נ"ל והיה]
[נ"ל משמר והיום מלאכה]
[נ"ל והיה]
[סוכה לח.]
מנחות עב.
[הא דלא תנא נמי להרחה עי' תוס' יומא כו: תוס' ד"ה אלא ותוספות זבחים פו: ד"ה אלא]
[נ"ל רב יוסף]
יומא ל.
[סוטה יז: ע"ש בתוספות ד"ה מה משפט וכו' ועי' פרש"י ומפרשים באופן אחר]

הגהות הב"ח

(א) רש"י ד"ה ביום צוותו וכו' הקטרת קומץ הקרבה היא וקמילה: (ב) תום' ד"ה כל הלילה וכו' לפי שאין עה אלא הזכרה לבנין:

עין משפט נר מצוה

מא א מיי' פ"א מהל' מגילה הל' ג סמג עשין מד"ס ד טוש"ע א"ח סימן תרפז סעיף א:
מב ב מיי' פ"ג מהל' חנוכה הלכה ה:
מג ג טוש"ע א"ח סימן תקפח סעיף א:
מד ד מיי' פ"ז מהלכות לולב הלכה י סמג עשין מד טוש"ע א"ח סימן תרנב סעיף א:
מה ה מיי' פ"ג מהל' תפלה הלכה ה סמג עשין יט טוש"ע א"ח סימן רפו סעיף א:
מו ו מיי' פ"ד מהלכות מעשה הקרבנות הל' ו סמג עשין קפב:
מז ז מיי' פ"ב מהלכות עבודת יוה"כ הל' ז:
מח ח מיי' פ"א מהל' מעשר שני הל' ד:
מט ט מיי' פ"ג מהל' עבודת יוה"כ הלכה ה:
נ י מיי' פ"ד מהלכות מעשה הקרבנות הלכה יג סמג עשין קפב:
[וע"ע תוספות פסחים פא. ד"ה אי נמי וכו']
נא כ מיי' פ"ג מהל' סוטה הלכה ה סמג עשין נו:
[שבת לד:]
[וע"ע תוספות פסחים ב. ד"ה והא]
נב ל מיי' פ"י מהלכות רוצח הלכה ה סמג עשין עח:
נג מ מיי' פ"ו מהל' טומאת צרעת הלכה ג סמג עשין רלו ורלז:
נד נ מיי' פ"ז מהלכות תמידין ומוספין הל' ז סמג עשין קנב:
נה ס מיי' פ"ד מהל' מעשה הקרבנות הל' ו סמג עשין קפו:
נו ע מיי' פ"ב מהלכות עבודת יוה"כ הל' ו:
[נ"ל אינו כוידוי]

גליון הש"ס

גמרא דכתיב וסמך ושחט. עיין מנחות דף צג ע"ב ד"ה ידו: תוספות ד"ה לקמיצה וכו' וכן תנופה והגשה. עיין קדושין דף לו ע"ב תוס' ד"ה הסמיכות ונע"ג:
[עיין תוספות מנחות ע. ד"ה מקמילה]
שייך למתני'

רבינו חננאל

שנאנסה וטבלה ר' שמי בשם רב טהורה לביתה וטמאה לטהרות רבי אלעזר משום ר' חנינא טמאה בין לביתה בין לטהרות שנאמר וכבס שנית וטהר מה הראשונה לדעת שנאמר וצוה הכהן וכבסו אף שניה לדעת: וכולן שעשו משעלה עמוד השחר כשר שנאמר ואנחנו עושים במלאכה חצים מחזיקים ברמחים מעלות השחר ועד צאת הכוכבים ש"מ מעלות השחר ועד צאת הכוכבים יום הוא שנאמר והיום למלאכה כלומר לא היו עושי מלאכה אלא ביום: [מתני'] כל היום כשר לקריאת המגילה כו': **ירושלמי** לקריאת המגילה [שנאמר] ביום אשר שברו אויבי היהודים וגו' לקריאת ההלל שנאמר זה היום עשה ה' לתקיעת שופר שנאמר יו תרועה יהיה לכם למוספין שנא' ביום צוותו את בני ישראל ואיתקש תפלת המוספין למוספין לנטילת לולב שנאמר ולקחתם לכם ביום הראשון וגו' (פירוש) לודוי הפרים ולודוי המעשר ולודוי יוה"כ לסמיכה לשחיט ולתנופה ולכפרה ולהגשה לקמיצה ולהקטרה למליקה ולקבלה להזאה להשקאת סוטה לעריפת העגלה לטהר את המצורע אלו כולן כשרים כל היום. כל הלילה כשר לקצירת העומר ולהקטיר חלבים ואימור זה

משְׁפָּט בַּיּוֹם. דִּכְתִיב "וְהָיָה בְּיוֹם הַנְחִילוֹ אֶת בָּנָיו" (דברים כא), אוּרְעָה כָּל הַפָּרָשָׁה כּוּלָּהּ לִהְיוֹת דִּין, בְּמַסֶּ' סַנְהֶדְרִין בְּפֶ' "אֶחָד דִּינֵי מָמוֹנוֹת" (דף לד:): לְטָהֳרַת מְצוֹרָע. בִּצְפָּרִים וְעֵץ אֶרֶז וְאֵזוֹב וּשְׁנִי תוֹלַעַת: דְּאָמַר מָר קְצִירָה וּסְפִירָה בַּלַּיְלָה. וְיָלֵיף לָהּ בְּמַסֶּ' מְנָחוֹת מִקְּרָאֵי: כָּל הַלַּיְלָה עַד הַבּוֹקֶר. "עַל מוֹקְדָהּ עַל הַמִּזְבֵּחַ כָּל הַלַּיְלָה עַד הַבּוֹקֶר": וּכְר' יוֹסֵי. דְּאָמַר בְּמַסֶּכֶת מְנָחוֹת: אֲפִילּוּ סִילֵּק אֶת הַיְשָׁנָה שַׁחֲרִית וְסִידֵּר אֶת הַחֲדָשָׁה עַרְבִית – אַף זוֹ הָיְתָה תָּמִיד. וּמַהוּ תָּמִיד – שֶׁלֹּא יָלִין שׁוּלְחָן בְּלֹא לֶחֶם. אֲבָל לְרַבָּנָן – טִפְחוֹ שֶׁל זֶה מְסַדֵּר בְּצַד טִפְחוֹ שֶׁל מְסַלֵּק:

הדרן עלך הקורא למפרע

הַקּוֹרֵא עוֹמֵד וְיוֹשֵׁב. אִם רָצָה עוֹמֵד, אִם רָצָה יוֹשֵׁב: קְרָאוּהָ שְׁנַיִם. יַחַד – יָצְאוּ, וְלָא אָמְרִינַן: אֵין שְׁנֵי קוֹלוֹת נִשְׁמָעִין כְּאֶחָד: לֹא יְבָרֵךְ. אֵין צָרִיךְ לְבָרֵךְ: בְּשֵׁנִי וּבַחֲמִישִׁי בְּשַׁבָּת וּבְשַׁבָּת בְּמִנְחָה. עֶזְרָא תִּיקֵּן שֶׁיְּהוּ קוֹרִין בְּשֵׁנִי וּבַחֲמִישִׁי, בְּבָבָא קַמָּא בְּפֶרֶק "מְרוּבֶּה" (דף פב.). וְהָכָא אַשְׁמְעִינַן דִּשְׁלֹשָׁה הֵן: כֹּהֵן וְלֵוִי וְיִשְׂרָאֵל: וְאֵין מוֹסִיפִין עֲלֵיהֶן. שֶׁלֹּא יִקְשֶׁה לַצִּבּוּר, מִפְּנֵי שֶׁהֵן יְמֵי מְלָאכָה. וְשַׁבָּת בְּמִנְחָה סָמוּךְ לַחֲשֵׁיכָה הוּא, שֶׁהֲרֵי כָּל הַיּוֹם הָיוּ רְגִילִין לִדְרוֹשׁ: וְאֵין מַפְטִירִין. מִשּׁוּם הַאי טַעְמָא גּוּפֵיהּ: הַפּוֹתֵחַ וְהַחוֹתֵם. בַּגְּמָ' מְפָרֵשׁ: וְאֵין מוֹסִיפִין עֲלֵיהֶן. בְּרָאשֵׁי חֳדָשִׁים וְחוֹל הַמּוֹעֵד נַמִי אִיכָּא בִּיטּוּל מְלָאכָה, דִּמְלֶאכֶת דָּבָר הָאָבֵד מוּתֶּרֶת: **גְּמָ'** מַה שֶּׁאֵין כֵּן בַּתּוֹרָה. שֶׁאֵין קוֹרִין בַּתּוֹרָה בְּצִבּוּר מְיוּשָּׁב: כִּבְיָכוֹל. נֶאֱמַר בְּהַקָּבָּ"ה כְּבְאָדָם, שֶׁיָּכוֹל לְהֵאָמֵר בּוֹ כֵּן: שֶׁלֹּא יֵשֵׁב עַל גַּבֵּי הַמִּטָּה. אֶלָּא אוֹ שְׁנֵיהֶם עַל גַּבֵּי הַמִּטָּה אוֹ שְׁנֵיהֶם עַל גַּבֵּי קַרְקַע: וְלוֹמֵד. מִפִּי הַגְּבוּרָה: יוֹשֵׁב וְשׁוֹנֶה. שׁוֹנֶה לְבַדּוֹ מַה שֶּׁלָּמַד: רַכּוֹת. דְּבָרִים רַכִּים וְנוֹחִים, שֶׁאָדָם מָהִיר לְשָׁמְעָן: וּבִלְבַד

תורה אור

*מַה מִּשְׁפָּט בַּיּוֹם — אַף כָּאן בַּיּוֹם.§ "וְלַעֲרִיפַת הָעֶגְלָה".§ אָמְרִי דְּבֵי רַבִּי יַנַּאי: *"כַּפָּרָה" כְּתִיב בָּהּ כְּקֳדָשִׁים.§ "וּלְטָהֳרַת מְצוֹרָע".§ דִּכְתִיב: °"זֹאת תִּהְיֶה תּוֹרַת הַמְּצוֹרָע בְּיוֹם טָהֳרָתוֹ".§ "כָּל הַלַּיְלָה כָּשֵׁר לִקְצִירַת הָעוֹמֶר" וכו'.§ דְּאָמַר מָר: *קְצִירָה [א]וּסְפִירָה בַּלַּיְלָה, וַהֲבָאָה בַּיּוֹם.§ "וּלְהֶקְטֵר חֲלָבִים וְאֵבָרִים".§ דִּכְתִיב: °"כָּל הַלַּיְלָה עַד הַבּוֹקֶר".§ "זֶה הַכְּלָל: דָּבָר שֶׁמִּצְוָתוֹ בַּיּוֹם כָּשֵׁר כָּל הַיּוֹם".§ זֶה הַכְּלָל לְאַתּוּיֵי מַאי? לְאַתּוּיֵי סִידּוּר בָּזִיכִין וְסִלּוּק בָּזִיכִין, וּכְר' יוֹסֵי. דְּתַנְיָא, *רַבִּי יוֹסֵי אוֹמֵר: סִילֵּק אֶת הַיְשָׁנָה שַׁחֲרִית וְסִידֵּר אֶת הַחֲדָשָׁה עַרְבִית — אֵין בְּכָךְ כְּלוּם. וּמָה אֲנִי מְקַיֵּים (°*"לִפְנֵי ה' תָּמִיד"?) שֶׁלֹּא *יְהֵא שׁוּלְחָן בְּלֹא לֶחֶם.§ "דָּבָר שֶׁמִּצְוָתוֹ בַּלַּיְלָה כָּשֵׁר כָּל הַלַּיְלָה".§ לְאַתּוּיֵי מַאי? [ב]לְאַתּוּיֵי אֲכִילַת פְּסָחִים, וּדְלָא כְּר' אֶלְעָזָר בֶּן עֲזַרְיָה. דְּתַנְיָא, *"וְאָכְלוּ אֶת הַבָּשָׂר בַּלַּיְלָה הַזֶּה" א"ר אֶלְעָזָר בֶּן עֲזַרְיָה: נֶאֱמַר כָּאן "בַּלַּיְלָה הַזֶּה", וְנֶאֱמַר לְהַלָּן °"וְעָבַרְתִּי בְאֶרֶץ מִצְרַיִם בַּלַּיְלָה הַזֶּה". מַה לְּהַלָּן עַד חֲצוֹת — אַף כָּאן עַד חֲצוֹת.§

הדרן עלך הקורא למפרע

הַקּוֹרֵא [ג]אֶת הַמְּגִילָּה — עוֹמֵד וְיוֹשֵׁב. קְרָאָהּ אֶחָד, קְרָאוּהָ שְׁנַיִם — יָצְאוּ. מְקוֹם שֶׁנָּהֲגוּ לְבָרֵךְ — יְבָרֵךְ. וְשֶׁלֹּא לְבָרֵךְ — לֹא יְבָרֵךְ. [ד]בְּשֵׁנִי וַחֲמִישִׁי, בְּשַׁבָּת בְּמִנְחָה — קוֹרִין שְׁלֹשָׁה, אֵין פּוֹחֲתִין מֵהֶן וְאֵין מוֹסִיפִין עֲלֵיהֶן, וְאֵין מַפְטִירִין בְּנָבִיא. הַפּוֹתֵחַ וְהַחוֹתֵם בַּתּוֹרָה — מְבָרֵךְ לְפָנֶיהָ וּלְאַחֲרֶיהָ. [ה]בְּרָאשֵׁי חֳדָשִׁים [ו]וּבְחוּלּוֹ שֶׁל מוֹעֵד — קוֹרִין אַרְבָּעָה, אֵין פּוֹחֲתִין מֵהֶן וְאֵין מוֹסִיפִין עֲלֵיהֶן, וְאֵין מַפְטִירִין בְּנָבִיא. הַפּוֹתֵחַ וְהַחוֹתֵם בַּתּוֹרָה — מְבָרֵךְ לְפָנֶיהָ וּלְאַחֲרֶיהָ. זֶה הַכְּלָל: כָּל שֶׁיֵּשׁ בּוֹ מוּסָף וְאֵינוֹ יוֹם טוֹב — קוֹרִין אַרְבָּעָה. [ז]בְּיוֹם טוֹב — חֲמִשָּׁה. [ח]בְּיוה"כ — שִׁשָּׁה, [ט]בְּשַׁבָּת — שִׁבְעָה. אֵין פּוֹחֲתִין מֵהֶן, [י]אֲבָל מוֹסִיפִין עֲלֵיהֶן, [כ]וּמַפְטִירִין בְּנָבִיא. הַפּוֹתֵחַ וְהַחוֹתֵם בַּתּוֹרָה — מְבָרֵךְ לְפָנֶיהָ וּלְאַחֲרֶיהָ.§ **גְּמָ'** תָּנָא: [ל]מַה שֶּׁאֵין כֵּן בַּתּוֹרָה. מְנָהָנֵי מִילֵּי? אָמַר רַבִּי אַבָּהוּ: דְּאָמַר קְרָא: °"וְאַתָּה פֹּה עֲמֹד עִמָּדִי". וְאָמַר רַבִּי אַבָּהוּ: *אִלְמָלֵא מִקְרָא כָּתוּב אִי אֶפְשָׁר לְאוֹמְרוֹ, כִּבְיָכוֹל אַף הקב"ה בַּעֲמִידָה. וא"ר אַבָּהוּ: [מ]מִנַּיִן לָרַב שֶׁלֹּא יֵשֵׁב עַל גַּבֵּי מִטָּה וְיִשְׁנֶה לְתַלְמִידוֹ עַל גַּבֵּי קַרְקַע? שֶׁנֶּאֱמַר: "וְאַתָּה פֹּה עֲמֹד עִמָּדִי". ת"ר: [נ]מִימוֹת מֹשֶׁה וְעַד רַבָּן גַּמְלִיאֵל לֹא הָיוּ לְמֵדִין תּוֹרָה אֶלָּא מְעוּמָּד. מִשֶּׁמֵּת רַבָּן גַּמְלִיאֵל יָרַד חוֹלִי לָעוֹלָם וְהָיוּ לְמֵדִין תּוֹרָה מְיוּשָּׁב. וְהַיְינוּ דִּתְנַן: *מִשֶּׁמֵּת רַבָּן גַּמְלִיאֵל(א) בָּטֵל כְּבוֹד תּוֹרָה. כָּתוּב אֶחָד אוֹמֵר: °"וָאֵשֵׁב בָּהָר", וְכָתוּב אֶחָד אוֹמֵר: °"וְאָנֹכִי עָמַדְתִּי בָהָר"! אָמַר רַב: עוֹמֵד וְלוֹמֵד, יוֹשֵׁב וְשׁוֹנֶה. ר' חֲנִינָא אָמַר: לֹא עוֹמֵד וְלֹא יוֹשֵׁב אֶלָּא שׁוֹחֶה. רַבִּי יוֹחָנָן אָמַר: אֵין יְשִׁיבָה אֶלָּא לְשׁוֹן עַכָּבָה, שֶׁנֶּאֱמַר: °"וַתֵּשְׁבוּ בְקָדֵשׁ יָמִים רַבִּים". רָבָא אָמַר: רַכּוֹת מְעוּמָּד, וְקָשׁוֹת מְיוּשָּׁב.§ "קְרָאָהּ אֶחָד קְרָאוּהָ שְׁנַיִם יָצְאוּ" וכו'.§ תָּנָא:

ולהקטיר חלבים(ב) כל הלילה עד הבוקר. והיינו דוקא שנתעכלו האברים קודם חצות, שנשלטה בהן האור. אבל אם לא שלטה בהן אין *נמשכין אחר חצות, כדאמר ר' יוחנן סוף פ"ק דיומא (דף כ:): **לאתויי** אכילת פסחים ודלא כרבי אלעזר ב"ע. מ"מ נראה דהלכה כר' אלעזר, דהא איכא סתמא ב"ערבי פסחים" (פסחים קכ: ושם) דקאי כוותיה, דתנן: הפסח אחר חצות מטמא את הידים, וכן משנה ב"איזהו מקומן" (זבחים דף נו:) וסתמא בסוף פ"ק דברכות (דף ט.) גבי מעשה ובאו בניו של רבן גמליאל מבית המשתה וכו', אמר להם: כל מה שאמרו חכמים עד חצות מצותן עד שיעלה עמוד השחר ואילו אכילת פסחים לא קתני! ומוקי לה כראב"ע, דאמר עד חצות. וא"כ צריך ליזהר לאכול מצה בלילי פסחים קודם חצות, ואפילו מצה של אפיקומן, שהרי חיוב מצה בזמן הזה הוה דאורייתא. *אבל בהלל של אחר אפיקומן אין להחמיר כל כך, שהרי מדרבנן הוא:

הדרן עלך הקורא למפרע

הקורא. ואין מפטירין בנביא. קשיא לר"ת: דהא בפרק "במה מדליקין" (שבת דף כד. ושם) אמר רב אחדבוי(ג) שאלמלא שבת אין נביא במנחה ביום טוב שחל להיות בשבת! וצריך לומר: דהאי דקאמר התם דמפטיר בנביא במנחה בשבת כשחל ביו"ט – לאו דוקא נביא, אלא רוצה לומר בכתובים, כדאמרינן פרק "כל כתבי" (שם קטז:): בנהרדעא פסקי סדרא בכתובים במנחה בשבתא, ופסקי – היינו הפטרה. ומקומות יש שנוהגין לעשות כן. והטעם שמפטיר במנחה בתענית ולא בשחרית – משום דכתיב בה "שמרו משפט ועשו צדקה" (ישעיה נו) ואגרא דתעניתא צדקתא* לעת ערב, ומש"ה נכון לאומרו בערב אחר שעשו צדקה:

הפותח והחותם בתורה מברך לפניה ולאחריה. קשיא: אמאי תנא הך מילתא הכא ג' פעמים? דהא בחד זימנא סגיא! וי"ל: דהוה סלקא דעתך דכל דטפי מילתא מחבריה מברך לפניה ולאחריה, מש"ה אצטריך למתני בכולהו:

אלמלא מקרא כתוב. קשיא, שיש "אלמלא" שרוצה לומר אילו לא, כגון הכא, וכגון: אלמלא אגרות הראשונות (לעיל דף יט:), וכן הרבה ויש "אלמלא" שרוצה לומר אילו היה: אלמלא נגדוה לחנניה מישאל ועזריה (כתובות דף לג:), וכן אלמלא לוי אתה וכו' (לקמן דף כד:). ומאי שנא? ואומר ר"ת: דהיכא שיש אל"ף בסוף אלמלא רוצה לומר: אילו לא, והיכא דכתי' אלמלי ביו"ד – רוצה לומר: אילו היה:

תנא

רבינו חננאל

זה הכלל דבר שמצותו ביום כשר כל היום לאתויי סידור בזיכין וכר' יוסי דתניא ר' יוסי אומר אפילו סילק לחם הפנים הישנה שחרית וסידר החדשה ערבית אין בכך כלום. ומה אני מקיים לחם הפנים לפני תמיד שלא ילין שלחן בלא לחם: כל דבר שמצותו בלילה כשר כל הלילה לאתויי אכילת פסחים ודלא כר' אלעזר בן עזריה דתני עד חצות: **ירושלמי** דבר שדוחה את השבת ביום מהו ידחו מכשיריו בלילה והתנינן העמידו עושה חביתין לעשות חביתין תיפתר בחול. תני ר' אחא זה סדר התמיד לעבודת בית אלהינו בין בחול בין בשבת: **הדרן עלך הקורא את המגילה**

קורא את המגילה עומד ויושב יצא. תנא מה שאין כן בתורה שנאמר ואתה פה עמוד עמדי. אמר רב מנין לרב שלא ישב ע"ג מטה ותלמיד ע"ג קרקע וישנה שנאמר ואתה פה עמוד כלומר התלמיד כמו הרב: **ת"ר** מימות [משה] ועד ר"ג היו למדין תורה מעומד. משמת ר"ג ירד חולי לעולם והתחילו לישב ולשנות והיינו דתנן במס' סוטה משמת ר"ג בטל כבוד התורה: **כתוב** אחד אומר ואשב בהר ארבעים יום וכתוב אחד אומר ואנכי עמדתי בהר. ואסיקנא רכות מעומד וקשות מיושב: **מתני'** קראה אחד את המגילה או קראוה שנים ביחד יצאו.

תנא

עין משפט נר מצוה

נז א מיי' פ"ז מהלכות תמידין הלכה ו סמג עשין ר טוש"ע א"ח סימן תפט סעיף א:

נח ב מיי' פ"ח מהל' קרבן פסח הלכה יד סמג עשין רכו:

א ג מיי' פ"ב מהלכות מגילה הלכה ז סמג עשין מד"ס ד טוש"ע א"ח סי' תרצ סעיף א:

ב ד מיי' פי"ב מהלכות תפלה הלכה טז טור ש"ע א"ח סי' קלה סעיף א:

ג ה מיי' שם טוש"ע א"ח סימן תכג סעיף א:

ד ו מיי' שם טוש"ע א"ח סי' תרסג סעיף א:

[עי' תוספות זבחים נז: ד"ה ואיבעי' אימא]

[נ"ל לפני תמיד (שמות כה) וכן איתא במנחות במשנה ובברייתא צט: וכן איתא בתוספתא]

ה ז מיי' שם טוש"ע א"ח סי' תפח סעיף ג וסי' תלד סעיף א:

ו ח מיי' שם טוש"ע א"ח סימן תרכא סעיף א:

ז ט י מיי' שם טוש"ע א"ח סי' רפב סעיף א:

ח כ מיי' שם הלכה ב טוש"ע שם סעיף ד וסי' תפח סעיף ג וסימן תלד סעיף א וסי' תרכא סעיף א:

ט ל מיי' שם הלכה יא טוש"ע א"ח סי' קמא סעיף א:

י מ מיי' פ"ד מהלכות ת"ת הלכה ב טוש"ע י"ד סי' רמו סעיף ט:

יא נ מיי' שם:

[ברכות ו: וע"ע סנהדרין לה.]

מסורת הש"ס

[ר"ה כה: סנהדרין יח:]

[קדושין נז. ע"ז כט: זבחים ע: חולין יח.]

מנחות צו.

[לט: [תוספ' מנחות פי"א]

[ג' במנחות לט: שלא ילין]

[ברכות ט. פסחים קכ: זבחים נז: מכילתא דר"י פרשת בא]

ויקרא יד | שם ו | שם כד | שמות יב | דברים ה | סוטה מט. | דברים ט | שם א

הגהות הב"ח

(א) גמ' משמת רבן גמליאל בטל: (ב) תוס' ד"ה ולהקטיר חלבים דכתיב כל וכו' אבל אם לא שלטה בהן האור אין נמשכין: (ג) שם ד"ה הקורא וכו' אמר רב אחדבוי ביו"ט שחל להיות בשבת שאלמלא שבת אין נביא במנחה וצריך לומר במנחה בשבת לאו דוקא נביא כו"ל ותיבות כשחל ביו"ט נמחק:

גליון הש"ס

גמ' אלמלא מקרא כתוב. עיין לעיל דף יז ע"ב סוטה דף יג ע"ב:

תנא: [א]מה שאין כן בתורה. *תנו רבנן: [ב]בתורה אחד קורא ואחד מתרגם, ובלבד שלא יהא אחד קורא ושנים מתרגמין. [ג]ובנביא אחד קורא ושנים מתרגמין, ובלבד שלא יהו שנים קורין ושנים מתרגמין. [ד]ובהלל [ה]ובמגילה – אפילו עשרה קורין (א)ועשרה מתרגמין. מאי טעמא? כיון דחביבה – יהבי דעתייהו, ושמעי.§ [ו]"מקום שנהגו לברך יברך".§ אמר אביי: [ז]לא שנו אלא לאחריה, אבל לפניה – מצוה לברך. דאמר רב יהודה אמר שמואל: *[ח]כל המצות כולן מברך עליהן עובר לעשייתן. מאי משמע דהאי "עובר" לישנא דאקדומי הוא? אמר רב נחמן בר יצחק: אמר קרא: °"וירץ אחימעץ דרך הככר ויעבר את הכושי". (ש"ב יח) אביי אמר מהכא: °"והוא עבר לפניהם". (בראשית לג) ואיבעית אימא מהכא: °"ויעבר מלכם לפניהם וה' בראשם". (מיכה ב) [ט]לפניה מאי מברך? רב ששת מקטרזיא איקלע לקמיה דרב אשי. ובריך מנ"ח. לאחריה מאי מברך? *"ברוך אתה ה' אלהינו מלך העולם (*האל) הרב את ריבנו והדן את דיננו והנוקם את נקמתנו והנפרע לנו מצרינו והמשלם גמול לכל אויבי נפשנו. ברוך אתה ה' הנפרע לישראל מכל צריהם". רבא אמר: "האל המושיע". אמר רב פפא: *[י]הלכך נימרינהו לתרוייהו: "ברוך אתה ה' הנפרע לישראל מכל צריהם האל המושיע".§ "בשני ובחמישי, בשבת במנחה קורין שלשה" וכו'.§ הני שלשה כנגד מי? *אמר רב אסי: כנגד תורה נביאים וכתובים. רבא אמר: כנגד כהנים לוים וישראלים. אלא הא דתני רב שימי: [כ]אין פוחתין מי' פסוקין בבית הכנסת, "וידבר" עולה מן המנין, הני עשרה כנגד מי? א"ר יהושע בן לוי: *כנגד עשרה בטלנין שבבית הכנסת. רב יוסף אמר: *כנגד עשרת הדברות שנאמרו למשה בסיני. (*רבי לוי אמר: כנגד עשרה הילולין שאמר דוד בספר תהלים.) *ורבי יוחנן אמר: כנגד עשרה מאמרות שבהן נברא העולם. הי נינהו? "ויאמר" דבראשית? הני תשעה הוו! "בראשית" נמי מאמר הוא, דכתיב: °"בדבר ה' שמים נעשו וברוח פיו כל צבאם". (תהלים לג) אמר רבא: [ל]ראשון שקרא ד' – משובח; שני שקרא ד' – משובח; שלישי שקרא ד' – משובח. ראשון שקרא ד' משובח – דתנן: *[מ]בשלש קופות של שלש(ב) סאין שבהן תורמין את הלשכה, והיה כתוב עליהן אב"ג, *לידע איזו מהן נתרמה ראשון להקריב ממנה ראשון, שמצוה בראשון. אמצעי שקרא ארבעה משובח – דתניא:* °"אל מול פני המנורה יאירו" (במדבר ח) [נ]מלמד שמצדד פניהם כלפי נר מערבי, ונר מערבי כלפי שכינה. ואמר *רבי יוחנן: מכאן שאמצעי משובח. ואחרון שקרא ארבעה משובח – משום *[ס]מעלין בקדש ולא מורידין. רב פפא איקלע לבי כנישתא דאבי גובר וקרא ראשון ארבעה, ושבחיה רב פפא.§ "אין פוחתין מהן ואין מוסיפין".§ תנא: הפותח מברך לפניה, והחותם מברך לאחריה, [ע]והאידנא דכולהו מברכי לפניה ולאחריה – היינו טעמא דתקינו רבנן: גזירה משום הנכנסין ומשום היוצאין.§ "בראשי חדשים ובחולו של מועד קורין ארבעה" וכו'.§ בעא מיניה עולא בר רב מרבא: פרשת ראש חודש כיצד קורין אותה? °"צו את בני ישראל ואמרת אליהם את קרבני לחמי" (במדבר כח) דהויין תמניא פסוקי, היכי נעביד? ניקרי תרי תלתא תלתא פסוקין – פשו להו תרי, [פ]ואין משיירין בפרשה פחות משלשה פסוקין. ניקרי ארבעה ארבעה – פשו להו שבעה: "וביום השבת" הויין תרי, "ובראשי חדשיכם" הויין חמשה. היכי נעביד? ניקרי תרי מהא וחד מהנך,
אין

רש"י

תורה אור

ובלבד שלא יהא אחד קורא ושנים מתרגמין. וכל שכן שאין שנים קורין, וטעמא משום דתרי קלי לא מישתמעי: ובנביא אפילו אחד קורא ושנים מתרגמין. שהתרגום אינו אלא להשמיע לנשים ועמי הארץ שאינן מכירין בלשון הקודש, והתרגום הוא לעז הבבליים, ובתרגום של תורה צריכין אנו לחזור שיהו מבינין את המצות, אבל בשל נביאים לא קפדי עלייהו כולי האי: ועשרה מתרגמין. (ג) לא גרסינן, שאין תרגום בכתובים: ויעבר את הכושי. ויקדם את הכושי: מקטרזיא. מקום: מנ"ח. על מקרא מגילה, ושעשה נסים, ושהחיינו: וידבר עולה מן המנין. "וידבר ה' אל משה לאמר", אע"פ שאין ללמוד ממנו כלום: בראשית נמי. דמשתעי בשמים ובארץ (ד), דכתיב "בדבר ה' שמים נעשו וברוח פיו כל צבאם": מאמר הוא. אף הן במאמר נבראו: נר מערבי. הוא נר אמצעי. למאן דאמר נרות צפון ודרום מונחין – הוי אמצעי משוך קימעא כלפי מערב חוץ מאחר נרות. דלמאן דאמר מערב ומזרח מונחין – לא, משום דהוי מערבי השני כלפי מזרח, הכי איתא במנחות: תורמין. כהנים את הלשכה, נותנין משקלי שנה זו לתוכה לקנות מהן קרבנות צבור לכל השנה: אל מול פני המנורה יאירו שבעת הנרות. למול פני נר שבגוף המנורה, שהוא אמצעי, היה מצדד פני ששה הנרות: ראשון. מן שלשה שקרא ארבעה פסוקים משובח, וכן שני, וכן שלישי. אם לא עשה הראשון ועשה השני, או אם לא קראו לא הראשון ולא השני ארבעה פסוקים וקרא אותן השלישי – משובח. ואם יש להן ריוח בפרשה וקראו כל אחד ארבעה פסוקים – כולן משובחין: משום הנכנסין. שאם יכנס אדם לבית הכנסת אחר שבירך ראשון, ואם לא ישמע את האחרים מברכין, יאמר: אין ברכה בתורה לפניה: ומשום היוצאין. ולא שמעו את החותם מברך לאחריה, והראשונים לא ברכו, יאמרו היוצאים: אין ברכה בתורה לאחריה: כיצד קורין. בד' בני אדם: אין משיירין בפרשה כו'. לקמן מפרש טעמא. ואין מתחילין נמי לקמן אמרינן לה, ומפרש טעמא:
ליקרי

תוספות

תנא מה שאין כן בתורה. פירוש: שאין קורא אלא אחד. מכאן קשיא למה שפירש רבינו משולם בפרק קמא דבבא בתרא (דף טו. ושם) ו"בהקומץ רבה" (מנחות דף ל: ושם) דשמונה פסוקים שבתורה יחיד קורא אותן, פירוש "יחיד קורא אותן" – שלא יקרא שליח צבור עמו בפרשת "ויעל משה" כשמסיימין את התורה. וקשיא: שהרי בימיהם לא היה שליח צבור קורא עמהם, כדאמר הכא. ועכשיו נמי לא התקינו אלא שלא לבייש מי שאין יודע לקרות! לכך נראה כמו שפירש רש"י ב"הקומץ": יחיד קורא אותן לבדו, ולא יהיו שנים מפסיקין וקוראין באותן שמונה פסוקים, שמתחילין מ"ויעל" לפי שסוף תחילת הפרשה*:

ובמגילה אפילו עשרה קורין (ה) ועשרה מתרגמין. רש"י מוחק מתרגמין, לפי שאין מתרגמין תרגום בכתובים. ובתוס' מתקו, דודאי יש תרגום, אבל לא עשאו יהונתן, אלא מימי התנאים נעשה*:

כנגד תורה נביאים – וכתובים. קשה: דהא לקמן (דף כג.) אמר כנגד (ו) שומרי הסף! וי"ל: דהתם לא הוי עיקר התקנה, דהא לא תקנו ארבעה כנגד הא, שלשה שומרי הסף וסריס אחד. ואיתא בירושלמי: איכא סריס אחד שיושב *ומתרך ההלכות ומעמידן על עקרן, ואפ"ה לא תקנו כנגדו – ש"מ דעיקר התקנה לא היתה אלא כנגד תורה ונביאים וכתובים:

אין פוחתין מעשרה פסוקים בבהכ"נ. וא"ת: והרי פרשת עמלק, דליכא אלא תשעה פסוקים! י"ל: דשאני פרשת עמלק דסידרא דיומא הוא, ומפסיק ענינא ביה, ומש"ה אין לחוש. דהכי נמי אמרינן לקמן (דף כג.) דאין מפטירין פחות מכ"א פסוקים, והיכא דסליק ענינא – קורין שפיר בפחות:

מסורת הש"ס

[ר"ה כז. תוספתא פ"ג] פסחים ז: קיט: סוכה לט. מנחות לה: נדה סג. [גירסת רב אלפס א"ר יוחנן ברוך וכו' ועי' ג"כ בהרא"ש] [ברכות נט. סו.] תענית ז. [לקמן כד.] [ר"ה לב.] [שם] [עי' יומא סב. סד.] במדבר ח [במנחות לח. איתא רבי נתן] [לעיל ט: וש"נ] במדבר כח

עין משפט נר מצוה

יב א מיי' פי"ב מהל' תפלה הלכה י טוש"ע א"ח סי' קמא סעיף ב:
יג ב מיי' שם הלכה יג:
יד ג מיי' שם הלכה יב:
טו ד טוש"ע א"ח סי' תפח סעיף ב:
טז ה מיי' פ"א מהלכות מגילה הלכה ז טור ש"ע א"ח סי' תרצ סעיף ב:
יז ו ז מיי' פ"א שם הלכה ג טוש"ע א"ח סי' תרצב סעיף א:
יח ח מיי' פי"א מהלכות ברכות הלכה ב טור ש"ע א"ח סימן כה סעיף ח:
[עי' תוספות ב"ב טו. ד"ה שמונה כו' ביארו יותר]
יט ט י מיי' פ"א מהל' מגילה הלכה ג טור ש"ע א"ח סימן תרצב סעיף א:
[ועי' תוספת שבת קטו. ד"ה ונידו וכו' ולכאורה מסוגיא דהכא תיובתא כלפי שטותאתה דרס"ג הכא למוחק ותגלה ומלישב]
כ כ מיי' פי"ב מהלכות תפלה הלכה ג סמג עשין יט טוש"ע א"ח סי' קלז סעיף א:
[ברב אלפס והרא"ש ליתא ועמ"ש הטור סימן תרלב בשם רב עמרם]
כא ל מיי' שם הלכה ב טוש"ע א"ח שם
כב מ מיי' פ"ב מהלכות שקלים הלכה ז:
כג נ מיי' פ"ג מהלכות בית הבחירה הלכה ח:
כד ס מיי' פ"ד מהלכות כלי המקדש הלכה ...
כה ע מיי' פי"ב מהל' תפלה הלכה ה טור ש"ע א"ח סי' קלט סעיף ד:
[ב"ק פב.]
[מלתא דרבי לוי ליתא בכת"י אלפס וברא"ש וכן מוכרח דלא גרסינן לה ...]
כו פ מיי' שם ה"ג טוש"ע א"ח סי' קלח סעיף א:
יומא סב. סד. שקלים ה.
מנחות לח.

רבינו חננאל

תנא מה שאין כן בתורה: ת"ר [בתורה] אחד קורא ואחד מתרגם ובלבד שלא יהו שנים קורין או שנים מתרגמין. ובנביא אחד קורא ושנים מתרגמין ובלבד שלא יהו שנים קורין. ובהלל ובמגילה אפי' עשרה קורין ועשרה מתרגמין יצאו. מ"ט כאן דחביבא להו מכווני דעתייהו: מקום שנהגו לברך יברך הני מילי לאחריה אבל לפניה מצוה לברך. דקי"ל כל המצות מברך עליהן עובר לעשייתן. ופרשן דהאי עובר לישנא דאקדומי הוא כדכתיב וילך ויעבר את הכושי. ומברך לפניה מנ"ח סימן. ולאחריה מברך האל הרב את ריבנו והדן את דיננו וגו' וחותם ברוך הנפרע לישראל מכל צריהם האל המושיע: **מתני'** בשני ובחמישי ובמנחה בשבת קורין ג' אין פוחתין ואין מוסיפין עליהן ואין מפטירין בנביא. והני ג' כנגד כהנים לוים וישראלים. אין פוחתין מעשרה פסוקים בבהכ"נ וידבר עולה מן המנין והני עשרה כנגד י' הדברות שנאמר למשה בסיני. ר' יוחנן אומר כנגד עשרה מאמרות שבהן נברא העולם. ובראשית נמי מאמר הוא שנאמר בדבר ה' שמים נעשו. אמר רבא ראשון שקרא ארבעה משובח. דתניא אמר ר' יוסי למה היה כתוב בקופות שתורמין בהן את הלשכה א' ב' ג' לידע איזה מהן נתרמה ראשון שמצוה בראשון פי' הקופה שהיה כתוב בה אלף היא היתה ראשונה ומן השקלים שבתוכה קונין הקרבנות ומקריבין עד שישלמו ועוד מן השניה ואחריה עד השלישית. אמצעי משובח מן המנורה: אחרון משובח מעלין בקודש ולא מורידין. שיבח רב פפא לראשון שקרא ד'. הפותח והחותם בתורה מברך לפניה ולאחריה. אוקימנא גזירה משום הנכנסים ומשום היוצאים דאי לא גזירה הפותח מברך לפניה וחותם לאחריה בלבד בר"ח ובחוש"מ קורא ד' ומיבעיא לן פרשת צו שהיא ח' פסוקים
האיך

הגהות הב"ח

(א) גמ' עשרה קורין (ועשרה מתרגמין) תא"מ ונ"ב ס"א אין זה: (ב) שם בשלש קופות של שלש שלש סאין תורמין כצ"ל ותיבת שבהן נמחק: (ג) רש"י ד"ה ועשרה מתרגמין. נ"ב עיין לעיל דף ג ע"א: (ד) ד"ה בראשית וכו' ובארץ מאמר הוא אף הן במאמר נבראו דכתיב בדבר וכו' כל צבאם הס"ד ואח"כ מה"ד ראשון מן שלשה וכו' משובחין הס"ד ואח"כ מה"ד תורמין את הלשכה הכהנים נותנין וכו' לכל השנה הס"ד ואח"כ מה"ד אל מול וכו' ששה הנרות הס"ד ואח"כ מה"ד נר מערבי וכו' במנחות הס"ד ואח"כ מה"ד משום הנכנסין: (ה) תום' ד"ה ובמגילה וכו' רש"י מוחק ועשרה מתרגמין: (ו) ד"ה כנגד וכו' כנגד שלשה שומרי הסף וכו' דהא לא תקנו ארבעה כנגד שלשה שומרי הסף ואחד כנגד סריס אחד שאין בירושלים שיושב ומתרך ההלכות ומעמידן על עקרן אלא סריס אחד ואפילו הכי:

אין מתחילין בפרשה פחות משלשה פסוקים. ליקרי תרי מהא ותלתא מהך — פשו להו תרי! אמר לו: זו לא שמעתי, כיוצא בה שמעתי, דתנן: *ביום הראשון "בראשית" ו"יהי רקיע". ותני עלה: "בראשית" — בשנים, "יהי רקיע" — באחד. והוינן בה: בשלמא "יהי רקיע" באחד — דתלתא פסוקי הוו. אלא "בראשית" בשנים? חמשה פסוקי הוו, ותניא:* הקורא בתורה לא יפחות משלשה פסוקים! ואיתמר עלה: רב אמר: דולג, ושמואל אמר: פוסק. רב אמר דולג. מאי טעמא לא אמר פוסק? קסבר *כל פסוקא דלא פסקיה משה אנן לא פסקינן ליה. ושמואל אמר פסקינן ליה? והא אמר רבי חנניא קרא: צער גדול היה לי אצל רבי חנינא הגדול, ולא התיר לי לפסוק אלא לתינוקות של בית רבן, הואיל ולהתלמד עשויין! התם טעמא מאי? משום דלא אפשר; הכא נמי — לא אפשר. ושמואל אמר פוסק. מאי טעמא לא אמר דולג? גזירה משום הנכנסין ומשום היוצאין. מיתיבי: *פרשה של ששה פסוקים קורין אותה בשנים, ושל חמשה פסוקים — ביחיד. קרא ראשון שלשה — השני קורא שנים מפרשה זו ואחד מפרשה אחרת. ויש אומרים שלשה, לפי שאין מתחילין בפרשה פחות משלשה פסוקים. ואם איתא, למאן דאמר דולג — נדלוג, ולמאן דאמר *פוסק — נפסוק! שאני התם דאפשר בהכי. אמר רבי תנחום אמר ריב"ל: הלכה כיש אומרים. ואמר רבי תנחום אמר ריב"ל: כשם שאין מתחילין בפרשה פחות מג' פסוקים — כך אין משיירין בפרשה פחות משלשה פסוקים. פשיטא! השתא ומה אתחלתא דקא מקיל תנא קמא — מחמירי יש אומרים, שיור דמחמיר ת"ק לא כ"ש דמחמירי יש אומרים?! מהו דתימא: נכנסין — שכיחי; יוצאין — לא שכיחי דמנחי ספר תורה ונפקי, קמ"ל. ות"ק מ"ש שיורי דלא — משום יוצאין, אתחולי נמי — גזירה משום הנכנסין! אמרי: מאן דעייל — שיולי שייל. שלח ליה רבה בריה דרבא לרב יוסף: הלכתא מאי? שלח ליה: הלכתא דולג, ואמצעי דולגין (ושאין)! § "זה הכלל, כל שיש בו מוסף" וכו'. § איבעיא להו: תענית צבור, בכמה? ראש חדש ומועד דאיכא קרבן מוסף — ארבעה, אבל הכא דליכא קרבן מוסף — לא, או דלמא: הכא נמי איכא מוסף תפלה? ת"ש: בראשי חדשים ובחולו של מועד קורין ארבעה. הא בתענית צבור — ג'! אימא רישא: בשני ובחמישי, ובשבת במנחה קורין ג', הא תענית צבור — ארבעה! *אלא, מהא ליכא למישמע מינה. ת"ש דרב איקלע לבבל בתענית צבור. קם קרא בסיפרא, פתח בריך, חתים ולא בריך. נפול כולי עלמא אאנפייהו, ורב לא נפל על אפיה. מכדי רב בישראל קרא, מאי טעמא חתם ולא בריך? לאו משום דבעי למיקרי אחרינא בתריה? לא, רב בכהני קרא, דהא *רב הונא קרי בכהני. בשלמא רב הונא קרי בכהני — דהא אפילו רב אמי ורב אסי *דכהני חשיבי דארעא ישראל, מיכף כייפו ליה לרב הונא. אלא רב, הא איכא שמואל דכהנא הוה ודבר עליה! שמואל נמי מיכף הוה כייף ליה לרב, ורב הוא דעבד ליה כבוד. וכי עביד ליה — בפניו, שלא בפניו — לא עביד ליה. הכי נמי מסתברא דרב בכהני קרא, דאי סלקא דעתך בישראל קרא — לפניה מאי טעמא בריך? לאחריה נמי לבריך? לאחר תקנה. אי הכי, לאחריה נמי לבריך? שאני היכא דיתיב רב דמיעל עיילי, מיפק

מיפק

ליקרי. שלישי תרי מהא שני מקראות דפרשת "וביום השבת", ותלתא קראי מ"בראשי חדשיכם", פשו להו תרי וכו': ביום הראשון. גבי מעמדות תנן ליה במסכת תענית, ביום הראשון באחד בשבת: דולג. השני חוזר ומתחיל פסוק שגמר בו שלפניו: פוסק. הראשון קורא חצי הפסוק השלישי, ופוסקו: גזירה משום הנכנסין. שישמעו השני מתחיל פסוק זה, ויאמרו: לא קרא ראשון אלא שנים. וכן היוצאין שישמעו את הראשון קורא שלשה, ויצאו מבית הכנסת ויאמרו: לא יקרא השני אלא שנים: הכי גרסינן. קרא ראשון שלשה השני קורא שנים מפרשה זו כו': למ"ד דולג נדלוג. למאן דאמר *פוסק ליכא למיפרך, דהא קרא ראשון שלשה קתני, דאי אפשר עוד לחזור: שאני התם דאפשר בהכי. לקרות מפרשה זו לאחריה. דהך מתניתא קיימא בשני ובחמישי, שהוא יכול לקרות מה שירצה, שהכל מעניינו של יום: כשם שאין מתחילין בפרשה בפחות משלשה פסוקים. גזירה משום הנכנסין, שיהו סבורים לא קרא זה אלא שני פסוקים של התחלת פרשה זו, שהרי לא היו בבית הכנסת ולא שמעו שקרא מפרשה העליונה: כך אין משיירין כו'. גזירה משום היוצאין, שסבורין שהקורא אחריו של זה לא יקרא אלא שני פסוקים הנותרים: שיור דקא מחמיר תנא קמא. דקתני ושל חמשה ביחיד, ולא אמרינן יקרא הראשון שלשה ויפסוק אם ירצה: נכנסין שכיחי. לפיכך החמירו יש אומרים בהתחלה: שיולי משאיל. כשישמע שקורא השני שלשה מקראות, והראשון לא קרא מפרשה זו אלא שנים, ישאל היאך קרא הראשון שני פסוקים ולא יותר? ויאמרו לו שקרא מפרשה העליונה: הלכתא מאי. בשל מעמדות: ואמצעי דולג. שאם לא ידלג הוא יהא צריך (א) להתחיל בפרשה פחות משלשה פסוקים, ואם יקרא שלשה מן השניה — נמצא קורא כולה: מוסף. (ב) פסקא תפלת "עננו" ברכה יתירה: מכדי רב בישראל קרא. שהרי רב לא היה לא כהן ולא לוי: דהא רב הונא קרא בכהני. במסכת גיטין, ב"הניזקין" (דף נט:): הא איכא שמואל. בנהרדעא, שהוא ממדינת בבל, דכהנא הוא: ודבר עילויה. נהוג היה להיות למעלה מרב, כדאמרינן בפרק "מרובה" (ב"ק פ.): רב לא עייל לקמיה דשמואל: ורב הוא דעביד. להאי דאדבריה עליה — כבוד הוה עביד ליה, משום דלייטיה רב לשמואל דלא לוקמי בני, במס' שבת פ' "שמונה שרצים" (דף קח.): שלא בפניו לא עביד ליה. ושמואל לא היה בבבל, אלא בנהרדעא:

תורה אור

אין מתחילין בפרשה פחות מג' פסוקים. גזירה משום הנכנסין, שלא יטעו לומר שאותו שקרא לפניו לא קרא אלא שני פסוקים. וקשה על מנהג שלנו, שאנו קורין בפרשת "ויחל" בתעניות, והראשון מתחיל שם, והוא לסוף *שני פסוקים מפרשה שלמעלה. וכן המפטיר ביו"ט בחול המועד דפסח שמתחיל מ"והקרבתם" שהוא לסוף שני פסוקים מראש הפרשה! ויש לומר: דשאני אלו הפרשיות, שהרי ידועות הן לעולם, וליכא למטעי. וכן פרשה של ראש חדש שהשלישי קורא "וביום השבת"(ג) אין לחוש שמא יאמרו הנכנסים שהשלישי לא קרא אלא שני פסוקים מ"וביום השבת" — שהרי הדבר ידוע לעולם. וגם יש להם לחשוב שא"כ לא היה לו להניח כשהגיע לפרשה, שהרי גם זו מעין פרשה שהניח בה: **ואם** איתא למאן דאמר דולג לדלוג. פירש הקונטרס: דלמאן דאמר פוסק לא קשיא מידי, דכיון שקרא הראשון שלשה פסוקים — אין לפסוק עוד. וקשה: דהא מאן דאמר פוסק אית ליה שפיר נמי דולג, אי לאו גזירה משום הנכנסין והיוצאין. והכא, נהי שאין אנו יכולין לתקן מה (ד) שעשו הראשונים שהטעו את היוצאים, שיסברו שהבא אחריו לא יקרא אלא שני פסוקים, מכל מקום היה להם לתקן שלא יטעו הנכנסין, לפי שמתחיל זה בשני פסוקים סמוך לפרשה! לכך נראה לפרש דלמאן דאמר פוסק לא קשיא מידי, דלדידיה תרלי שפיר: שאני הכא (ה) היכא דלא אפשר, אבל היכא דאפשר שלא לפסוק — פשיטא שאין להפסיק. אבל למ"ד דולג תקשה: **שאני** התם דאפשר. קשיא: היאך נהגו העולם בחולו של מועד של חג שקורא הרביעי כל מה שקראו השנים? והא הכא דלא שרינן לא דולג ולא פוסק אלא היכא דלא אפשר, ואפילו היכא (ו) דקאמר משום הנכנסין והיוצאין. מיהו, הא פשיטא לן שאם קרא אותו שלפני האחרון עד שני פסוקים מסוף הפרשה שבפסח או בעצרת, שהאחרון דולג למעלה, ולא יקרא שני פסוקים שהניח האחר, וגם מפרשה של אחריה, כגון דלא הוי מעניינו של יום:

כז א מיי' פי"ב מהלכות תפלה הלכה ג טוש"ע א"ח סי' קלח סעיף א:

[עי' רש"א ותשובת מהרי"ל סי' קם ובמגן אברהם סי' קלח ס"ק ב]

כח ב מיי' פ"ו מהלכות כלי המקדש הלכה ו:

כט ג מיי' פי"ב מהל' תפלה הלכה ג טור ש"ע א"ח סי' קלז סעיף ב:

ל ד מיי' פי"ג שם הלכה ז טוש"ע א"ח סי' תכג סעיף ב:

תענית כז:

רבינו חננאל

האיך יקראו אותה ג' בני אדם כו'. רב אמר דולג כלומר כהן קורא ג' ולוי חוזר וקורא פסוק אחד מן הפסוקים שלשה שקרא כהן וב' אחרים נשארו ג' ישראל קורא אותן. ושמואל א' פוסק כלומר פוסק פסוק אחד לשנים. ועושה השמונה תשעה וקורין השלשה משלשה שלשה משום דלא אפשר אלא בהכי. ואותבינן עליה דרב מהא דתניא פרשה של ששה פסוקים קורין אותה שנים של חמשה יחיד קורא אותה קרא אחד ג' והניח ב' השני קורא אותם שנים ופסוק אחד מן הפרשה של אחריה. וי"א ג' קורין מן הפרשה של אחריה שאין מתחילין מן הפרשה פחות מג' פסוקים. ופריק רב שאני התם דאפשר בהכי כלומר אפשר לו לקרות מן הפרשה שאחריה אבל בענין בראשית שהשלישי רוצה לקרות ויהי רקיע. ובענין צו את בני ישראל דסליק עניינא שאי אפשר לשלישי לקרות מן ובראשי חדשיכם דהא רביעי קורא ובראשי חדשיכם. וכיון דלא אפשר להו לקרות מן הפרשה של אחריה שאחר רוצה לקרותה הלכך דולגין. אריב"ל הלכה כיש אומרים. ועוד א' כשם שאין מתחילין בפרשה פחות מג' פסוקים כך אין משיירין פחות מג' פסוקים. ומתמהינן השתא ומה התחלה דמקיל ת"ק ואמר אחד מפרשה אחרת מחמיר י"א ואומר שלשה. שאין מתחילין בפרשה פחות מג' פסוקים *) שיורי דחמיר במשייר ת"ק ואמר פרשה של חמשה יחיד קורא אותה כולה ואם קרא ג' והניח ב' דאיעבד אבל לכתחלה (ג') שלשה צריך להניח לא כ"ש דמחמרי י"א וכיון שאמר הלכה כי"א למה הוצרך לומר כשם שאין מתחילין כך אין משיירין. ופרקינן מהו דתימא נכנסין שכיחי והנכנס ששמע שלא קרא הפרשה שהתחיל בה אלא פסוק אחד ולא ידע שכבר קרא מן הפרשה שלפניה ב' פסוקים ילך ויאמר הקורא פסוק אחד יצא לפיכך גזרי שצריך לקרות המתחיל בפרשה ג' פסוקים אבל להניח ב' פסוקים בפרשה הוה גזר דהא שומע דהעולה אחריו קורא אותן שני פסוקים ושלשה מפרשה אחרת ולא אתי למיטעא ולמימר דתרי סגיא וא"ת שמא יצא אחר מן הכנסת **) ולא ישמע מה שקרא מן הפרשה האחרת קמ"ל. ואסיקנא

נראה דצ"ל שיורי דמחמיר ת"ק לשייר ואמר כו'. **) נראה דחסר כאן וצ"ל ולא ישמע מה שיקרא מן הפרשה שלאחריה זה לא שכיח דמנחי ס"ת ונפקי קמ"ל.

תענית כו.

ברש"י תענית כז: ד"ה הכי גרסינן וכו' וע"ע

[עי' ברכות יב:]

תענית כז: ע"ש

ק נפסוק לדעת רש"י ליה וכ"ל הקושיא קאי אל דתני ושל חמשה ביחיד

נדרים עב. ברכות כה. וש"נ

[גיטין נט:]

שם

הגהות הב"ח

[illegible] (א) רש"י ד"ה ואמצעי וכו' יהא צריך לשייר שלשה: (ב) ד"ה מוסף. נ"ב כצ"ל ותיבת פסקא נמחק: (ג) תוס' ד"ה אין מתחילין וכו' וביום השבת רביעי ובראשי חדשיכם לחוש: (ד) ד"ה ואם לא כו' לתקן מה שעשה הראשון שהטעה את היוצאים: (ה) בא"ד שאני [illegible] דלא כצ"ל ותיבת [illegible] נמחק: (ו) ד"ה שאני ואפילו היכא דאיכא משום:

גליון הש"ס

רש"י ד"ה בשלמא רב הונא קרי בכהני. עי' לקמן דף כח ע"א תוד"ה כי קאמר:

תורה אור

מֵיפַּק לָא נָפְקִי. ת"ש: זֶה הַכְּלָל: כָּל שֶׁיֵּשׁ בּוֹ בִּיטּוּל מְלָאכָה לָעָם, כְּגוֹן תַּעֲנִית צִבּוּר וְתִשְׁעָה בְּאָב — [א]קוֹרִין ג', וְשֶׁאֵין בּוֹ בִּיטּוּל מְלָאכָה לָעָם, כְּגוֹן רָאשֵׁי חֳדָשִׁים וְחוּלּוֹ שֶׁל מוֹעֵד — קוֹרִין ד', שְׁמַע מִינַּהּ. אָמַר רַב אַשִׁי: וְהָא אֲנַן לָא תְּנַן הָכִי: "זֶה הַכְּלָל: כָּל יוֹם שֶׁיֵּשׁ בּוֹ מוּסָף וְאֵינוֹ יוֹם טוֹב — קוֹרִין אַרְבָּעָה", לְאַתּוּיֵי מַאי? לָאו לְאַתּוּיֵי תַּעֲנִית צִיבּוּר וְתִשְׁעָה בְּאָב? וּלְרַב אַשִׁי מַתְנִיתִין מַנִּי? לָא תַּנָּא קַמָּא וְלָא רַבִּי יוֹסֵי, דְּתַנְיָא: *חָל לִהְיוֹת בְּשֵׁנִי וּבַחֲמִישִׁי — קוֹרִין ג' וּמַפְטִיר אֶחָד. בַּשְּׁלִישִׁי וּבָרְבִיעִי קוֹרֵא אֶחָד וּמַפְטִיר אֶחָד. רַבִּי יוֹסֵי אוֹמֵר: לְעוֹלָם קוֹרִין ג' וּמַפְטִיר אֶחָד. וְאֶלָּא קַשְׁיָא "זֶה הַכְּלָל"? לָא, לְאַתּוּיֵי רֹאשׁ חוֹדֶשׁ וּמוֹעֵד. הָא בְּהֶדְיָא קָתָנֵי לָהּ: בְּרָאשֵׁי חֳדָשִׁים וּמוֹעֵד קוֹרִין אַרְבָּעָה! סִימָנָא בְּעָלְמָא יָהֵיב, דְּלָא תֵּימָא יו"ט וְחוּלּוֹ שֶׁל מוֹעֵד כִּי הֲדָדֵי נִינְהוּ. אֶלָּא *נְקוֹט הַאי כְּלָלָא בְּיָדָךְ: כָּל דְּטָפֵי לֵיהּ מִילְּתָא מֵחַבְרֵיהּ, טָפֵי לֵיהּ גַּבְרָא יְתֵירָא. הִלְכָּךְ [ב]בְּר"ח וּמוֹעֵד, דְּאִיכָּא קָרְבַּן מוּסָף — קוֹרִין אַרְבָּעָה; בְּיו"ט דְּאָסוּר בַּעֲשִׂיַּית מְלָאכָה — חֲמִשָּׁה; בְּיוה"כ דַּעֲנוּשׁ כָּרֵת — שִׁשָּׁה; שַׁבָּת דְּאִיכָּא אִיסּוּר סְקִילָה — שִׁבְעָה.

גּוּפָא, רַב אִיקְּלַע לְבָבֶל בְּתַעֲנִית צִבּוּר, קָם קְרָא בְּסִפְרָא, פְּתַח — בְּרִיךְ, חָתַם — וְלָא בְּרִיךְ. נְפוּל כּוּלֵּי עָלְמָא אַאַנְפַּיְיהוּ — וְרַב לָא נְפַל עַל אַנְפֵּיהּ. מ"ט רַב לָא נְפֵיל עַל אַפֵּיהּ? [ג]רִצְפָּה שֶׁל אֲבָנִים הָיְתָה, וְתַנְיָא: °"וְאֶבֶן מַשְׂכִּית לֹא תִתְּנוּ בְּאַרְצְכֶם לְהִשְׁתַּחֲוֹת עָלֶיהָ", "עָלֶיהָ" אִי אַתָּה מִשְׁתַּחֲוֶה בְּאַרְצְכֶם, [ד]אֲבָל אַתָּה מִשְׁתַּחֲוֶה עַל אֲבָנִים שֶׁל בֵּית הַמִּקְדָּשׁ. כִּדְעוּלָּא, דְּאָמַר עוּלָּא: לֹא אָסְרָה תּוֹרָה אֶלָּא רִצְפָּה שֶׁל אֲבָנִים בִּלְבַד. אִי הָכִי מַאי אִירְיָא רַב? אֲפִילּוּ כּוּלְּהוּ נַמִי! קַמֵּיהּ דְּרַב הֲוַאי. וְלֵיזִיל לְגַבֵּי צִיבּוּרָא, וְלִינְפּוֹל עַל אַפֵּיהּ! לָא בָּעֵי לְמִיטְרַח צִיבּוּרָא. וְאִיבָּעֵית אֵימָא: רַב פִּישּׁוּט יָדַיִם וְרַגְלַיִם הֲוָה עָבֵיד, וְכִדְעוּלָּא, דְּאָמַר עוּלָּא: [ה]לֹא אָסְרָה תּוֹרָה אֶלָּא פִּישּׁוּט יָדַיִם וְרַגְלַיִם בִּלְבַד. וְלִיפּוֹל עַל אַפֵּיהּ וְלָא לֶיעְבִיד פִּישּׁוּט יָדַיִם וְרַגְלַיִם! לָא מְשַׁנֵּי מִמִּנְהֲגֵיהּ. וְאִיבָּעֵית אֵימָא: *אָדָם חָשׁוּב שָׁאנֵי, *כִּדְרַבִּי אֶלְעָזָר. דְּאָמַר רַבִּי אֶלְעָזָר: [ו]אֵין אָדָם חָשׁוּב רַשַּׁאי לִיפּוֹל עַל פָּנָיו אֶלָּא אִם כֵּן נַעֲנֶה כִּיהוֹשֻׁעַ בִּן נוּן, דִּכְתִיב: °"וַיֹּאמֶר ה' אֶל יְהוֹשֻׁעַ קוּם לָךְ" [וגו'.] תָּנוּ רַבָּנַן: *"קִידָּה" — עַל אַפַּיִם, שֶׁנֶּאֱמַר: °"וַתִּקֹּד בַּת שֶׁבַע אַפַּיִם אֶרֶץ". "כְּרִיעָה" — עַל בִּרְכַּיִם, וְכֵן הוּא אוֹמֵר: °"מִכְּרוֹעַ עַל בִּרְכָּיו". "הִשְׁתַּחֲוָאָה" — זוֹ פִּישּׁוּט יָדַיִם וְרַגְלַיִם, שֶׁנֶּאֱמַר: °"הֲבוֹא נָבוֹא אֲנִי וְאִמְּךָ וְאַחֶיךָ לְהִשְׁתַּחֲוֹת לְךָ אָרְצָה". *לֵוִי אַחְוֵי קִידָּה קַמֵּיהּ דְּרַבִּי, וְאִיטְלַע. וְהָא קָא גָּרְמָא לֵיהּ? וְהָאָמַר רַבִּי אֶלְעָזָר: לְעוֹלָם אַל יַטִּיחַ אָדָם דְּבָרִים כְּלַפֵּי מַעְלָה, שֶׁהֲרֵי אָדָם גָּדוֹל הֵטִיחַ דְּבָרִים כְּלַפֵּי מַעְלָה וְאִיטְלַע. וּמַנּוּ — לֵוִי! הָא וְהָא גָּרְמָא לֵיהּ. *אָמַר רַב חִיָּיא בַּר אָבִין: חָזֵינָא לְהוּ לְאַבַּיֵי וְרָבָא

ויקרא כו | יהושע ז | מ"א א | שם ח | בראשית לז

רש"י

מֵיפַּק לָא נָפְקִי. הִלְכָּךְ, לְפָנֶיהָ בְּרִיךְ – גְּזֵירָה מִשּׁוּם הַנִּכְנָסִין כְּדְאָמְרִינַן לְעֵיל, לְאַחֲרֶיהָ לָא בְּרִיךְ – דְּלָא חָיֵישׁ לַיּוֹצְאִין: זֶה הַכְּלָל כָּל שֶׁיֵּשׁ בּוֹ בִּיטּוּל מְלָאכָה לָעָם. כַּמָּה שֶׁהֵן מְאַחֲרִין בְּבֵית הַכְּנֶסֶת: כְּגוֹן תַּעֲנִית צִבּוּר. שֶׁמּוּתָּר בִּמְלָאכָה. רוֹב תַּעֲנִית לְצִבּוּר מוּתָּרִין בִּמְלָאכָה, חוּץ מִשֶּׁל גְּשָׁמִים הָאֶמְצָעִיִּים וְהָאַחֲרוֹנִים: וְתִשְׁעָה בְּאָב. נַמִי מוּתָּר בִּמְלָאכָה, אֶלָּא בְּמָקוֹם שֶׁנָּהֲגוּ: רָאשֵׁי חֳדָשִׁים. אֵין בּוֹ בִּיטּוּל מְלָאכָה כָּל כָּךְ, שֶׁאֵין הַנָּשִׁים עוֹשׂוֹת מְלָאכָה בָּהֶן. וְהָכִי נַמִי אָמְרִינַן בְּמַסֶּ' רֹאשׁ הַשָּׁנָה (דף כג.) גַּבֵּי מַשּׂוּאוֹת: מִשּׁוּם בִּיטּוּל מְלָאכָה לָעָם שְׁנֵי יָמִים. וְשָׁמַעְתִּי מִפִּי מוֹרִי הַזָּקֵן ז"ל, שֶׁנִּיתְּנָה לָהֶם מִצְוָה זוֹ בִּשְׁבִיל שֶׁלֹּא פֵּירְקוּ נִזְמֵיהֶן בָּעֵגֶל (תּוֹסֶפְתָּא. וַאֲנִי מְצָאתִי בְּפֶרֶק מ"ה דִּבְרַיְיתָא דְּרַבִּי אֱלִיעֶזֶר: שָׁמְעוּ הַנָּשִׁים וְלֹא רָצוּ לִיתֵּן נִזְמֵיהֶן לְבַעֲלֵיהֶן, אֶלָּא אָמְרוּ לָהֶן: אַתֶּם רוֹצִים לַעֲשׂוֹת פֶּסֶל וּמַסֵּכָה שֶׁאֵין בּוֹ כֹּחַ לְהַצִּיל. וְנָתַן הקב"ה שְׂכָרָן שֶׁל נָשִׁים בָּעוֹלָם הַזֶּה, שֶׁיְּהוּ מְשַׁמְּרוֹת רָאשֵׁי חֳדָשִׁים יוֹתֵר מִן הָאֲנָשִׁים. וְלָעוֹה"ב הֵן עֲתִידוֹת לְהִתְחַדֵּשׁ כְּמוֹ רָאשֵׁי חֳדָשִׁים, שֶׁנֶּאֱמַר "תִּתְחַדֵּשׁ כַּנֶּשֶׁר נְעוּרָיְיכִי" ע"כ). וּמִקְרָא מְסַיְּיעוֹ, דִּכְתִיב "אֲשֶׁר נִסְתַּרְתָּ שָׁם בְּיוֹם הַמַּעֲשֶׂה" (שמואל א כ), וְתִרְגֵּם יוֹנָתָן: בְּיוֹמָא דְחוֹלָא. וְהָתָם נַמִי גַּבֵּי ר"ח קָאֵי, דְּקָאָמַר לֵיהּ "מָחָר חוֹדֶשׁ" וְקָרֵי לֵיהּ לְעֶרֶב ר"ח "יוֹם הַמַּעֲשֶׂה", אַלְמָא: רֹאשׁ חֹדֶשׁ לָאו יוֹם הַמַּעֲשֶׂה הוּא. וּמוֹעֵד נַמִי לָאו בִּיטּוּל מְלָאכָה לָעָם, שֶׁהֲרֵי בָּאִין לְבֵית הַכְּנֶסֶת יוֹתֵר מִימוֹת הַחוֹל, לְפִי שֶׁאֵין עוֹשִׂין בּוֹ מְלָאכָה אֶלָּא בְּדָבָר הָאָבֵד: וּלְרַב אַשִׁי. דְּאָמַר: זֶה הַכְּלָל דְּמַתְנִי' לְאַתּוּיֵי נַמִי תִּשְׁעָה בְּאָב, דְּאִית בֵּיהּ מוּסָף תְּפִלַּת "עֲנֵנוּ": מַתְנִי' מַנִּי כו' חָל לִהְיוֹת כו'. גַּבֵּי תִּשְׁעָה בְּאָב תַּנְיָא לָהּ, בְּשְׁמַעְתָּא בַּתְרַיְיתָא דְּמַסֶּ' תַּעֲנִית: קוֹרֵא אֶחָד וּמַפְטִיר אֶחָד. הַקּוֹרֵא הוּא הָוֵי הַמַּפְטִיר: סִימָנָא בְּעָלְמָא. הָא דַּהֲדַר נָקֵיט לֵיהּ בְּזֶה הַכְּלָל, סִימָנָא יָהֵיב לָן כו': כָּל דְּטָפֵי מִילְּתָא מֵחַבְרֵיהּ. כָּל יוֹם הָעוֹדֵף דָּבָר מֵחֲבֵירוֹ: לֹא אָסְרָה תּוֹרָה. בְּפָסוּק זֶה אֶלָּא שֶׁלֹּא יַעֲשׂוּ רִצְפַּת אֲבָנִים בְּבהכ"נ, דּוּגְמַת שֶׁל מִקְדָּשׁ: לָא בָּעֵי מַטְרַח צִבּוּרָא. שֶׁאִם יֵלֵךְ יַעַמְדוּ מִפָּנָיו: פִּישּׁוּט יָדַיִם וְרַגְלַיִם. כְּשֶׁהָיָה נוֹפֵל עַל פָּנָיו, וּשְׁאָר הַצִּבּוּר לֹא הָיוּ עוֹשִׂין כֵּן: לָא מְשַׁנֵּי. לֹא הָיָה רוֹצֶה לְשַׁנּוֹת מִמִּנְהָגוֹ: וְאִיבָּעֵית אֵימָא. לֹא הָיָה רָגִיל לִיפּוֹל עַל פָּנָיו. (א) כְּלוֹמַר שֶׁהָיָה אָדָם חָשׁוּב, וְאֵינוֹ נוֹפֵל עַל פָּנָיו: אא"כ נַעֲנֶה. כְּלוֹמַר: אא"כ בָּטוּחַ בְּמַעֲשָׂיו שֶׁהוּא נַעֲנֶה בִּתְפִלָּתוֹ: לָמָּה זֶה אַתָּה נוֹפֵל עַל פָּנֶיךָ. אַלְמָא, אֵין לוֹ לַעֲשׂוֹת: קִידָּה. הָאֲמוּרָה בְּכָל מָקוֹם – אֵינָהּ אֶלָּא עַל אַפַּיִם: אַרְצָה. מַשְׁמַע: כּוּלּוֹ שָׁטוּחַ אַרְצָה: אַחְוֵי קִידָּה. נוֹעֵץ גּוּדָלָיו וְנִשְׁעָן עֲלֵיהֶם, וְשׁוֹחֶה עַד שֶׁנּוֹשֵׁק אֶת הָרִצְפָּה וְזוֹקֵף. וּמִתּוֹךְ שֶׁאֵינוֹ יָכוֹל לְהִשָּׁעֵן עַל גּוּדָלָיו, וְאֵין יָדָיו מְסַיְּיעוֹת אוֹתוֹ בִּזְקִיפָתוֹ וְצָרִיךְ לְהִתְאַמֵּץ בְּמָתְנָיו – וּמִתּוֹךְ כָּךְ נִצְלָע בְּבוּקְא דְּאַטְמָא: הֵטִיחַ דְּבָרִים כְּלַפֵּי מַעְלָה. בְּמַסֶּכֶת תַּעֲנִית: עָלִיתָ לַמָּרוֹם וְאֵין אַתָּה מַשְׁגִּיחַ עַל בָּנֶיךָ: הָא וְהָא גָּרְמָא לֵיהּ. לְפִי שֶׁהֵטִיחַ – נִתְקַלְקֵל בִּשְׁעַת הַסַּכָּנָה: דַּמַלְּיֵי

תוספות

ושאין בהן ביטול מלאכה כגון ראש חדש קורין ארבעה. וקשיא: דהא בפרק "אין דורשין" בחגיגה (דף יח. ושם) אמרינן: ראש חדש יוכיח, שיש בו קרבן מוסף ומותר בעשיית מלאכה! וי"ל: דודאי מותר הוא בעשיית מלאכה לאנשים, אבל נשים אסורות במלאכה, לפי שלא פרקו נזמיהן במעשה העגל*:

ולרב אשי מתני' מני לא תנא קמא ולא רבי יוסי דתניא כו' רבי יוסי אומר לעולם קורין שלשה ומפטיר אחד. וא"ת: דלמא ר' יוסי היא, והכי קאמר: לעולם קורין שלשה, והרביעי דהוי מפטיר אחד. ולא בעי למימר אחד מן השלשה! וי"ל: דכי היכי דלת"ק ליכא למימר מפטיר אחד דהיינו רביעי, דהא (ב) הוא ממעט בט' באב שהוא בשלישי וברביעי יותר מבשני וה' דעלמא, וא"כ מסתמא לא יחמיר בט' באב שהוא בב' וה' לקרות רביעי, ואינו מחמיר לקרות אלא להפטיר. הכי נמי לר' יוסי, הוי המפטיר אחד מן השלשה שקראו:

ואיבעית אימא רב פישוט ידים ורגלים הוא דעבד כדעולא. וקשה: וכי לא היה יודע (ג) דמלי לשנויי הכי? וכי ס"ד מעיקרא שיהא אסור בלא פישוט ידים ורגלים? וי"ל: דמעיקרא אסר ליה מדרבנן בלא פישוט ידים ורגלים, ובסוף קאמר ואיבעית אימא אין אסור מדרבנן, ורב פישוט ידים ורגלים הוא דעביד דאסור מן התורה. ומיהו, קשה ללישנא קמא דאסור מדרבנן בלא פישוט ידים ורגלים. יש לתמוה על בתי כנסיות שלנו שיש בהן רצפה, היאך נופל שליח צבור על פניו? ונראה לי דמצלי אצלויי, ובהכי שרי. והכי נמי משמע בסמוך, דמייתי ההיא דפרק "אין עומדין" דברכות (דף לד: ושם) דחזינן להו לאביי ורבא דמצלי אצלויי. כן פירש רב האי גאון:

אין אדם חשוב רשאי ליפול על פניו. בירושלמי מפרש: היכא שמתפלל בשביל הצבור, אבל בינו לבין עצמו – שפיר דמי:

קידה על אפים. לא מכח הקרא הוא מפיק לה, דהא כתיב נמי (ישעיה מט) "אפים ארץ ישתחוו לך" אלא הכי גמיר ליה מרביה (ד) דגבי לשון קידה שייך אפים:

עין משפט נר מצוה

לא א מיי' פי"ב מהלכות תפלה הלכה טז טור א"ח סי' תקנט וסי' תקעט:

[וע"ע תוס' חגיגה יח. ד"ה ר"ח ותוס' ר"ה כג. ד"ה משום ותוס' שבת כד. ד"ה או דלמא]

לב ב מיי' שם טור א"ח סימן תקנט:

לג ג מיי' פ"ו מהלכות ע"ז הלכה ו ופ"ה מהל' תפלה הלכה יד טוש"ע א"ח סי' קלא סעיף ח בהג"ה:

לד ד ה מיי' פ"ה מהל' תפלה הלכה יד ופ"ו מהלכות ע"ז הלכה ז:

לה ו מיי' פ"ה מהלכות תפלה הל' יד טוש"ע א"ח סימן קלא סעיף ח:

רבינו חננאל

ואסיקנא הלכתא דולג והלכתא אמצעי דולג: **מתני'** ביו"ט חמשה וביוה"כ ששה וכו' ואסיקנא נקוט האי כללא בידך כל דטפי מלתא מחבריה טפי בה גברא יתירא בר"ח ובמועד דאיכא קרבן מוסף קורין ד' ביו"ט דאסור בעשיית מלאכה ה' ביוה"כ דענוש כרת ו' בשבת דאיסורו בסקילה ז': גופא רב איקלע לתענית צבור קם קרא בספרא במקום כהן ואפילו רב אמי ורב אסי כהני חשיבי מיכף הוו כייפי ליה ושמואל דהוא כהן לא הוה התם פתח בריך חתים לא בריך. נפל כ"ע אאפייהו ורב לא נפל משום דרצפה של אבנים הוות קמיה דתניא ואבן משכית לא תתנו בארצכם. פי' רצפה כדכתיב על רצפת בהט ושש ודר וסוחרת וכדתנינן עמוד והפג על הרצפה וברצפה של אבני בית המקדש אתה משתחוה ולא ברצפה זולתי המקדש ואקשינן אי הכי לכ"ע אסיר ופרקינן קמיה דרב הואי איבעית אימא פישוט ידים ורגלים הוה עביד רב וכדעולא דאמר לא אסרה תורה אלא פישוט ידים ורגלים. איבעית אימא אמאי לא נפיל רב אאפיה משום דר' אלעזר דאמר אין אדם חשוב רשאי ליפול על פניו בצבור אא"כ נענה כיהושע בן נון שנאמר ויאמר ה' אל יהושע קום לך וגו': **ת"ר** קידה על אפים כריעה על ברכים השתחויה פישוט ידים ורגלים. וכולהו מקראי. לוי אחוי קידה קמיה דר' ונפל ואיטלע והאי גרמא ליה והא"ר אלעזר לעולם אל יטיח אדם דברים כלפי מעלה כו' ואסיקנא בתחלת ר' *) ישמעאל רבי אמי בשם רבנן דתמן לא התירו השתחויה אלא לתענית צבור ובלבד על הצד. ר' ינוי זעירא בשם אבהתיה כל מי שיפול על פניו ואינו כשר כיהושע [שאם יפול על פניו] יאמר לו מן השמים קום לך אל יפול ובלבד יחיד על הצבור. רב מפ בבי' רב אחא. ורב [אמי] מפקד לאינש בייתיה כד דהוון נפקין לתעניתא לא תהוון רבעין כאורחכון. ר' יונה ורב אחא רבעין על סטרהון. אמר ר' שמואל חמית ר' אבהו רבע כי אורח בי"ט

*) נ"ל ואסיקנא בירושלמי בפ' ר' ישמעאל הלכה א' רב אמי וכו'.

מסורת הש"ס

תענית כט:

[שבת קמז. וש"נ]

[שבת נח. וש"נ] תענית יד.

ברכות לד: שבועות טז

תענית כה. סוכה נג.

[ברכות לד: ע"ש]

הגהות הב"ח

(א) רש"י ד"ה ואיבעית אימא וכו' על פניו שהיה אדם: (ב) תום' ד"ה ולרב אשי וכו' דהא ממעט בט' באב כשחל בשלישי וברביעי: (ג) ד"ה ואיבעית אימא וכו' לא היה יודע דמצי לשנויי: (ד) ד"ה קידה וכו' גמיר ליה מרביה מייתי קרא אלא דגבי לשון קידה:

וְרָבָא דִּמְצַלֵּי אַצְלוּיֵי.§ בְּיו"ט חֲמִשָּׁה, בְּיוה"כ שִׁשָּׁה כו'.§ מַתְנִי' מַנִּי? לֹא ר' יִשְׁמָעֵאל וְלֹא רַבִּי עֲקִיבָא. דְּתַנְיָא: *בְּיו"ט — חֲמִשָּׁה, וּבְיוה"כ — שִׁשָּׁה, וּבְשַׁבָּת — שִׁבְעָה, אֵין פּוֹחֲתִין מֵהֶן וְאֵין מוֹסִיפִין עֲלֵיהֶן, דִּבְרֵי ר' יִשְׁמָעֵאל. ר"ע אוֹמֵר: בְּיו"ט — חֲמִשָּׁה, וּבְיוֹם הַכִּפּוּרִים — שִׁבְעָה, וּבְשַׁבָּת — שִׁשָּׁה, אֵין פּוֹחֲתִין מֵהֶן אֲבָל מוֹסִיפִין עֲלֵיהֶן. מַנִּי? אִי ר' יִשְׁמָעֵאל — קַשְׁיָא תּוֹסֶפֶת. אִי ר"ע — קַשְׁיָא שִׁשָּׁה וְשִׁבְעָה! אָמַר רָבָא: תַּנָּא דְּבֵי רַבִּי יִשְׁמָעֵאל הִיא. דְּתָנָא דְּבֵי ר' יִשְׁמָעֵאל: בְּיוֹם טוֹב — חֲמִשָּׁה, בְּיוה"כ — שִׁשָּׁה, בְּשַׁבָּת — שִׁבְעָה, אֵין פּוֹחֲתִין מֵהֶן אֲבָל מוֹסִיפִין עֲלֵיהֶן, דִּבְרֵי ר' יִשְׁמָעֵאל. קַשְׁיָא דְּר' יִשְׁמָעֵאל אַדְּר' יִשְׁמָעֵאל! תְּרֵי תַּנָּאֵי אַלִּיבָּא דְּרַבִּי יִשְׁמָעֵאל. מַאן תְּנָא לְהָא דְּתַנְיָא: *[א]בְּיו"ט מְאַחֲרִין לָבוֹא וּמְמַהֲרִין לָצֵאת; בְּיוֹם הַכִּפּוּרִים מְמַהֲרִין לָבוֹא, וּמְאַחֲרִין לָצֵאת; [ב]וּבְשַׁבָּת מְמַהֲרִין לָבוֹא, [ג]וּמְמַהֲרִין לָצֵאת? לֵימָא ר"ע, דְּאִית לֵיהּ גַּבְרָא יְתֵירָא? אֲפִילּוּ תֵּימָא רַבִּי יִשְׁמָעֵאל, דְּנָפֵישׁ סִידּוּרָא דְּיוֹמָא. הָנֵי שְׁלֹשָׁה *חֲמִשָּׁה [א] וְשִׁבְעָה כְּנֶגֶד מִי? פְּלִיגִי בָּהּ רַבִּי יִצְחָק בַּר נַחְמָנִי וְחַד דְּעִמֵּיהּ, וּמַנּוּ? רַבִּי שִׁמְעוֹן בֶּן פַּזִּי. וְאָמְרִי לָהּ: ר' שִׁמְעוֹן בֶּן פַּזִּי וְחַד דְּעִמֵּיהּ, וּמַנּוּ? רַבִּי יִצְחָק בַּר נַחְמָנִי, וְאָמְרִי לָהּ ר' שְׁמוּאֵל בַּר נַחְמָנִי. חַד אָמַר: כְּנֶגֶד בִּרְכַּת כֹּהֲנִים. וְחַד אָמַר: כְּנֶגֶד שְׁלֹשָׁה שׁוֹמְרֵי הַסַּף, חֲמִשָּׁה מֵרוֹאֵי פְּנֵי הַמֶּלֶךְ, שִׁבְעָה רוֹאֵי פְּנֵי הַמֶּלֶךְ. תָּנֵי רַב יוֹסֵף: ג' חֲמִשָּׁה וְשִׁבְעָה: שְׁלֹשָׁה שׁוֹמְרֵי הַסַּף, חֲמִשָּׁה מֵרוֹאֵי פְּנֵי הַמֶּלֶךְ, שִׁבְעָה רוֹאֵי פְּנֵי הַמֶּלֶךְ. אָמַר לֵיהּ אַבָּיֵי: עַד הָאִידָּנָא מַאי טַעְמָא לָא פָּרֵישׁ לָן מָר? אָמַר לֵיהּ: לָא הֲוָה יָדַעְנָא דִּצְרִיכְתּוּ לֵיהּ. *וּמִי בָּעִיתוּ מִינַּאי מִילְּתָא וְלָא אֲמַרִי לְכוּ. אָמַר לֵיהּ יַעֲקֹב מִינָאָה לְרַב יְהוּדָה: הָנֵי שִׁשָּׁה דְּיוה"כ כְּנֶגֶד מִי? אָמַר לֵיהּ: כְּנֶגֶד שִׁשָּׁה שֶׁעָמְדוּ מִימִינוֹ שֶׁל עֶזְרָא וְשִׁשָּׁה מִשְּׂמֹאלוֹ, שֶׁנֶּאֱמַר: °"וַיַּעֲמֹד עֶזְרָא הַסּוֹפֵר עַל מִגְדַּל עֵץ אֲשֶׁר עָשׂוּ לַדָּבָר וַיַּעֲמֹד אֶצְלוֹ מַתִּתְיָה וְשֶׁמַע וַעֲנָיָה וְאוּרִיָּה וְחִלְקִיָּה וּמַעֲשֵׂיָה עַל יְמִינוֹ וּמִשְּׂמֹאלוֹ פְּדָיָה וּמִישָׁאֵל וּמַלְכִּיָּה וְחָשֻׁם וְחַשְׁבַּדָּנָה זְכַרְיָה מְשֻׁלָּם". הָנֵי שִׁבְעָה הָווּ! הַיְינוּ זְכַרְיָה הַיְינוּ מְשֻׁלָּם. וְאַמַּאי קָרְאוֹ מְשֻׁלָּם? *דִּמְשַׁלַּם בְּעוֹבָדֵיהּ. ת"ר: *[ד]הַכֹּל עוֹלִין לְמִנְיַן שִׁבְעָה, וַאֲפִילּוּ קָטָן, °וַאֲפִילּוּ אִשָּׁה. אֲבָל אָמְרוּ חֲכָמִים: אִשָּׁה לֹא תִּקְרָא בַּתּוֹרָה, °מִפְּנֵי כְּבוֹד צִבּוּר. אִיבַּעְיָא לְהוּ: °מַפְטִיר, מַהוּ שֶׁיַּעֲלֶה לְמִנְיַן שִׁבְעָה? רַב הוּנָא וְר' יִרְמְיָה בַּר אַבָּא. חַד אָמַר: עוֹלֶה, [ה]וְחַד אָמַר: אֵינוֹ עוֹלֶה. מ"ד עוֹלֶה — דְּהָא קָרֵי. וּמ"ד אֵינוֹ עוֹלֶה — כִּדְעוּלָּא, דְּאָמַר עוּלָּא: מִפְּנֵי מָה [ו]הַמַּפְטִיר בַּנָּבִיא צָרִיךְ שֶׁיִּקְרָא בַּתּוֹרָה תְּחִלָּה? מִפְּנֵי כְבוֹד תּוֹרָה. וְכֵיוָן דְּמִשּׁוּם כְּבוֹד תּוֹרָה הוּא — לְמִנְיָנָא לָא סָלֵיק. מֵיתִיבִי: [ז]הַמַּפְטִיר בַּנָּבִיא לֹא יִפְחוֹת מֵעֶשְׂרִים וְאֶחָד פְּסוּקִין כְּנֶגֶד שִׁבְעָה שֶׁקָּרְאוּ בַּתּוֹרָה. וְאִם אִיתָא, עֶשְׂרִים וְאַרְבָּעָה הָוְיָין! כֵּיוָן דְּמִשּׁוּם כְּבוֹד תּוֹרָה הוּא,

כְּנֶגְדוֹ

רש"י

דִּמְצַלֵּי אַצְלוּיֵי. עַל צִדֵּיהֶן, וְלֹא נוֹפְלִין עַל פְּנֵיהֶן מַמָּשׁ, לְפִי שֶׁאֵין אָדָם חָשׁוּב רַשַּׁאי לִיפּוֹל עַל פָּנָיו: הָכִי גָּרְסִינַן. תַּנָּא דְּבֵי ר' יִשְׁמָעֵאל הִיא: בְּיו"ט מְאַחֲרִין לָבֹא. לְבֵית הַכְּנֶסֶת, שֶׁצָּרִיךְ לִטְרוֹחַ בִּסְעוּדַת יו"ט, כָּךְ מְפוֹרָשׁ בְּמַסֶּכֶת סוֹפְרִים*: וּמְמַהֲרִין לָצֵאת. מִשּׁוּם שִׂמְחַת יוֹם טוֹב: וּבְשַׁבָּת מְמַהֲרִין לָבֹא. שֶׁכְּבָר תִּיקְּנוּ תּוֹרָה אוֹר הַכֹּל מֵעֶרֶב שַׁבָּת, וְיָפֶה לְמַהֵר בִּיאָתָן לִקְרוֹת שְׁמַע כְּוָתִיקִין: וּמְמַהֲרִין לָצֵאת. מִשּׁוּם עוֹנֶג שַׁבָּת: בִּרְכַּת כֹּהֲנִים. שָׁלֹשׁ תֵּיבוֹת בְּפָסוּק רִאשׁוֹן, וַחֲמִשָּׁה בְּפָסוּק שֵׁנִי, וְשִׁבְעָה בְּפָסוּק שְׁלִישִׁי: חֲמִשָּׁה מֵרוֹאֵי פְּנֵי הַמֶּלֶךְ וְשִׁבְעָה רוֹאֵי פְּנֵי הַמֶּלֶךְ. שִׁבְעָה הֵם, כְּדִכְתִיב "שִׁבְעַת שָׂרֵי פָּרַס וּמָדַי". וּמֵהֶם יֵשׁ חֲמִשָּׁה חֲשׁוּבִים, כְּדִכְתִיב בְּסוֹף מְלָכִים. "שְׁלֹשָׁה שׁוֹמְרֵי הַסַּף" בְּסוֹף סֵפֶר מְלָכִים, וּכְנֶגְדָּן תִּיקְּנוּ אֵלּוּ מֵעֵין דְּבַר מַלְכוּת: דִּמְשַׁלַּם בְּעוֹבָדֵיהּ. תָּמִים בְּמַעֲשָׂיו: מִפְּנֵי כְּבוֹד תּוֹרָה. שֶׁלֹּא יְהֵא כְּבוֹד תּוֹרָה וּכְבוֹד נָבִיא שָׁוֶה, וְכֵיוָן דְּמִשּׁוּם כְּבוֹד תּוֹרָה הוּא וְלֹא מִשּׁוּם חוֹבָה — לָאו מִמִּנְיָנָא הוּא: כְּנֶגֶד ז' שֶׁקָּרְאוּ בַּתּוֹרָה. לֹא פִּיחֵת כָּל אֶחָד מִג' פְּסוּקִים: וְאִם אִיתָא. דְּהָיְינוּ עוֹלֶה מִן הַמִּנְיָן — הָווּ לְהוּ שְׁמוֹנָה שֶׁקָּרְאוּ בַּתּוֹרָה, וְכ"ד בָּעֵינַן בַּנָּבִיא:

תוספות

הני שלשה וחמשה כנגד מי. אבל מששה של יום הכפורים לא בעי עד לקמן. קשיא: אמאי לא בעי מד' של ראש חדש כנגד מי, וכן של חולו של מועד? וי"ל: דקים ליה דטעמא דמוסף חשיב לטפויי חד גברא, אבל לטפויי כל כך(א) ביו"ט וביוה"כ ובשבת – לא ס"ל משום *כרת וסקילה, אי לא משכחינן כנגד מי: **שבעה** רואי פני המלך. פירש הקונטרס דאחשורוש. וקשיא לומר שתקנו חכמים כנגד ענינו של אותו רשע! לכך פירש ר"ת: אותן הכתובים בספר ירמיה (נב), ובמלכים (ב כה) כתיב ה'. ובירושלמי מפרש שהשנים שלא הוזכרו במלכים הם סופרי הדיינין: **אמר** יעקב. מלעה גרסינן שאם הוה מין *לא היה מזכירו יעקב, דהא כתיב "שם רשעים ירקב" (משלי י): **חד אמר** עולה וחד אמר אין עולה. פסק ר"ת: דקיימא לן *כמ"ד עולה. ולכך אנו נוהגין בתעניות במנחה ובט"ב שהשלישי מפטיר. וכן ביום הכפורים במנחה, אבל בשבתות ובימים טובים וביוה"כ שחרית – המפטיר לא הוי מן המנין, דכיון שמותר להוסיף עליהם יכולין אנו לעשות מנהגינו אליבא דכולי עלמא. דאי הוי הלכה כמ"ד אין עולה – עבדינן שפיר, ואפילו הוי נמי הלכה כמאן דאמר עולה – מ"מ אין לחוש, שהרי מותר להוסיף. ואע"ג דאמרינן לקמן (דף כט:) של להיות בואתה תצוה קורין שיתא ב"ואתה תצוה" וחד ב"כי תשא" – מכל מקום נהגו עכשיו לקרות המפטיר שהוא שמיני, כל זה כדי לנהוג מנהגינו. וחזן שטעה וגמר כל הסדר של שבת – יחזור ויקרא(ב) השביעי, וכן אם הוא יו"ט וקרא כל המנין שהוא צריך, ושכח לקרות בחובת היום – יחזור ספר תורה ויקרא אחר בחובת היום. ואחרון שקרא קודם הוי כמאן דליתיה. אבל בשבת של חנוכה או בר"ח של חנוכה – (ג) אין צריך, כדאיתא ב"ילמדנו" דחנוכה* דהלכתא אין משגיחין בחנוכה כל עיקר. וימים שיש בהן קרבן מוסף גומר קדיש קודם. שיוציא ספר תורה ובימים שאין בהן קרבן מוסף אין גומר קדיש קודם ובשבת לא יקרא פחות מאחד ועשרים פסוקים לשבעה בני אדם, כל חד וחד שלשה פסוקים ובמנחה ובשני ובחמישי עשרה פסוקים. ואם שכח ולא קרא כל כך – יחזור ויקרא: **כיון** דמשום כבוד תורה הוא כנגדו נמי לא בעי. וקשיא: לפי מנהגינו שאנו נוהגין בכל שבתות השנה שהמפטיר חוזר וקורא מה שקראו הראשונים, ואין קורא כלל אחר כך, אם כן מאי קא משני כיון דמשום כבוד התורה הוא כנגדו נמי לא בעינן? אדרבה, היה לו לומר דאין קורא אלא מה שקראו הראשונים – כנגדו לא בעינן. אלא שמע מינה דבימי התנאים היה המפטיר קורא מה שלא קראו הראשונים. והכי נמי משמע מדתקינו ג' פסוקים כנגדו למפטיר בנביא כנגד מה שקרא בתורה למאן דאמר עולה, כדאמרינן בסמוך. א"כ שמע מינה שהוא קורא מה שלא קראו הראשונים. וא"כ קשה: למה אין אנו נוהגין לעשות כן? ונראה לפי שבימי החכמים לא היו אומרים קדיש בין אותן שקראו קודם המפטיר והמפטיר, ולכך היה המפטיר מסיים. אבל אחר שנסדר הש"ס ותקנו לומר קדיש בין אותם שקראו ראשונה והמפטיר, כמו שתקנו לומר "ברוך ה' לעולם אמן ואמן" ו"יראו עינינו" אחר השכיבנו שלא היו אומרים בימי התנאים, °והם תקנוהו להודיע שתפלת ערבית רשות, והכי נמי תקנו לומר קדיש בין השבעה למפטיר להודיע שאינו ממנין השבעה. והר"ר אליהו הנהיג את בני עירו שאפילו כשמוציאין שני ספרי תורות או שלשה – נוהג מנהג זה שיקראו הראשונים הכל, והמפטיר חוזר וקורא ממה שקראו הראשונים. וכן הנהיג רבינו משלם. וכן נוהגין עכשיו בכל צרפת. ושינו את מנהג רש"י ורבותיו ור"ת. והא שאין מוציאין ב' ספרי תורות בכל השבתות לקרות בשניה "וביום השבת" כמו שעושין ביו"ט – נראה לפי שאין בפרשה אלא שני פסוקים, ואין קורין בתורה פחות מג' פסוקים, ואין להתחיל בפרשה שלמעלה או לסיים בפרשה שלמטה משום דלא הוי מענינו של יום. ועוד י"ל: לפי שצריך להפטיר בכל שבת מענינו של יום. ואי קרינן בשל שבת – א"כ יהא צריך להפטיר בדסליק מיניה, והיינו בשבת, וא"כ יהו כל ההפטרות מענין אחד. ועוד י"ל: לפי שלעולם אין קורין בספר תורה שני בקרבנות אלא באותן שבאין לכפרה, כדפירש לקמן פרק "בני העיר" (דף לא.) שקורין בהן ביו"ט, ומהני לישראל כאילו הקריבום. אבל קרבנות שבת – אינן באין לכפרה, ומש"ה אין קורין בהן:

לא

ירושלמי משה התקין לישראל שיהיו קורין בתורה בשבתות ובי"ט ובר"ח ובחוש"מ שנאמר וידבר משה את מועדי ה' אל בני ישראל עזרא תיקן שיהיו קורין ג' בתורה בשני ובחמישי ובשבת במנחה אבל הקריאה בתורה מימות משה רבינו היתה שלא ישארו ג' ימים בלא קריאה בתורה והוא תיקן טבילה לבעלי קריין ושיהו בתי דינין יושבין בעיירות בב' ובה' ושיהו רוכלין כו'. הלעוזות לא נהגו להיות קורין גהו"ז אלא אחד קורא כל הפרשה היה אחד יודע כל הפרשה קורין אותה כולה. ז' יודעין ג' פסוקים כולן קורין אותן אחד יודע ג' פסוקים קורא חוזר וקורא. ר' זעירא בשם ר' ירמיה העבד עולה למנין ז'. והא אסור לאדם ללמד עבדו תורה תיפתר בשלמד מעצמו או שלמדו רבו כטבי. וידבר עולה מג' פסוקים [רבי חלבו רבי מתנה שמואל בר שילת] משמיה דרב ז' חוץ המפטיר התיב ר' חנינא כו': **ת"ר** הכל עולין למנין ז' אפילו אשה אפילו קטן אבל אמרו חכמים אשה לא תקרא בתורה מפני כבוד הצבור המפטיר שקורא בתורה חד אמר עולה למנין ז' וחד אמר אינו עולה ואותבינן על מאן דאמר אינו עולה למנין שבעה אלא צריך ז' והוא. מהא דתניא המפטיר בנביא לא יפחות מכ"א פסוקים ג' פסוקים לכל אחד כנגד ז' שקראו בתורה ואם איתא דתמני בעינן בהדי המפטיר כ"ד פסוקי בעינן. ופרקינן המפטיר כיון דמשום

כבוד

מסורת הש"ס

[פי"ח ה"ד]

[תוספתא פ"ג]

[מס' סופרים פי"ח ה"ד ע"ש ונ"ע]

סנהדרין י: [עי' תוספות לעיל כא: ד"ה כנגד]

[סוכה יד: נזיר יט. סנהדרין י:]

נחמיה ח

[הוריות יא: כריתות ה:]

[תוספת' פ"ג]

הגהות הב"ח

(א) תוס' ד"ה הני וכו' אבל לטפויי כל כך בשבת וביום טוב משום מלאכה וכרת וסקילה לא ס"ל אי לא אשכחינן: (ב) ד"ה חד אמר וכו' יחזור ויקרא מה שקרא השביעי וכן: (ג) בא"ד או בר"ח של חנוכה ושבת אין צורך לקרות לחנוכה כדאי' לקמן דף כט דהלכתא כל"ל ותיבות בילמדנו לחנוכה נמחק:

הגהות הגר"א

[א] גמרא הני שלשה חמשה שבעה כנגד מי כו' כצ"ל:

עין משפט נר מצוה

לו א טוש"ע א"ח סי' תקכט סעיף א בהגה"ה:

לז ב טוש"ע א"ח סי' קסז סעיף ב:

נ"ל מלאכה כרת. מהרש"א

לח ג טוש"ע א"ח סי' רפא בהג"ה:

לט ד מיי' פי"ב מהל' תפלה הלכה יז סמג עשין יט טוש"ע א"ח סי' רפב סעיף ג:

מ ה ו מיי' שם הלכה יז טוש"ע שם סעיף ד בהגה"ה:

[ועי' תוספות ע"ז יז. ד"ה ויעקב כו' אבל יעקב מינאה דר' אבהו וכו' ומלוה לייסב]

[עי' תוספת תענית כט: ד"ה בשני]

מא ז מיי' שם הלכה יג טוש"ע א"ח סי' רפב סעיף א:

גליון הש"ס

גמ' ואפי' אשה. עי' ר"ה דף לג ע"א תוס' ד"ה הא ר' יהודה: **שם** מפני כבוד צבור. לקמן דף כד ע"ב וש"נ: **שם** מפטיר מהו שיעלה. עי' תענית ד' כט ע"ב תד"ה בשני ובחמישי: **תוס'** ד"ה כיון וכו' והם תקנוהו להודיע שת"ע רשות. עי' ברכות דף ב ע"א תד"ה מברך ודף ד ע"ב תד"ה אמר ר' יוחנן ודף כז ע"ב תוס' ד"ה והלכתא:

[וכן לקמן בסוגין כט:]

רבינו חננאל

בי"ט ה'. וביוה"כ ו' בשבת ז' אין פוחתין מהן אבל מוסיפין עליהן. וכשמוסיפין ב' קורין בס"ת מאחרין לצאת וכשפוחתין ממהרין לצאת. הני ג' שקורין בשני ובחמישי ובשבת במנחה ובתעניות ובט' באב וכיוצא בהן. וה' שקורין ביו"ט וז' שקורין בשבת כנגד [ברכת] כהנים הפסוק הראשון ג' תיבות והשני ה' והשלישי ז' תני רב יוסף ג' כנגד שומרי הסף ה' מרואי פני המלך שנא' וחמשה אנשים מרואי פני המלך. שבעה מרואי פני המלך דכתיב ושבעה אנשים מרואי פני המלך ו' דיוה"כ כנגד ששה שעמדו מימינו של עזרא ומשמאלו שנאמר ויעמד אצלו מתתיה ושמע ועניה ואוריה וחלקיה ומעשיה על ימינו ומשמאלו פדיה וגו':

תורה אור

כְּנֶגְדּוֹ נַמִּי לָא בָּעֵי. מַתְקִיף לָהּ רָבָא: וַהֲרֵי °"עוֹלוֹתֵיכֶם סְפוּ" דְּלָא הָוְיָין עֶשְׂרִין וְחַד, וְקָרֵינַן! (ירמיה ז) אשָׁאנֵי הָתָם דִּסְלִיק עִנְיָנָא. וְהֵיכָא דְּלָא סְלִיק עִנְיָינָא לָא? וְהָאָמַר רַב שְׁמוּאֵל בַּר אַבָּא: זִמְנִין סַגִּיאִין הֲוָה קָאֵימְנָא קַמֵּיהּ דְּר' יוֹחָנָן, וְכִי הֲוָה קָרֵינַן עֲשָׂרָה פְּסוּקֵי, אָמַר לָן: אַפְסִיקוּ! מָקוֹם שֶׁיֵּשׁ תּוּרְגְּמָן שָׁאנֵי, דְּתָנֵי רַב תַּחְלִיפָא בַּר שְׁמוּאֵל: לֹא שָׁנוּ אֶלָּא בְּמָקוֹם שֶׁאֵין תּוּרְגְּמָן, באֲבָל מָקוֹם שֶׁיֵּשׁ תּוּרְגְּמָן — פּוֹסֵק.§ **מתני'** גאֵין פּוֹרְסִין עַל שְׁמַע, דוְאֵין עוֹבְרִין לִפְנֵי הַתֵּיבָה, הוְאֵין נוֹשְׂאִין אֶת כַּפֵּיהֶם, ווְאֵין קוֹרִין בַּתּוֹרָה, זוְאֵין מַפְטִירִין בַּנָּבִיא, חוְאֵין עוֹשִׂין מַעֲמָד וּמוֹשָׁב, וְאֵין אוֹמְרִים בִּרְכַּת אֲבֵלִים טוְתַנְחוּמֵי אֲבֵלִים, יוּבִרְכַּת חֲתָנִים, כוְאֵין מְזַמְּנִין (א) בְּשֵׁם פָּחוֹת מֵעֲשָׂרָה. לוּבְקַרְקָעוֹת — תִּשְׁעָה וְכֹהֵן, מוְאָדָם כַּיּוֹצֵא בָּהֶן.§ **גמ'** *מה"מ? אָמַר ר' חִיָּיא בַּר אַבָּא א"ר יוֹחָנָן: דְּאָמַר קְרָא °"וְנִקְדַּשְׁתִּי בְּתוֹךְ בְּנֵי יִשְׂרָאֵל" — נכָּל דָּבָר שֶׁבִּקְדוּשָּׁה לֹא יְהֵא פָּחוֹת מֵעֲשָׂרָה. מַאי מַשְׁמַע? דְּתָנֵי ר' חִיָּיא: *אָתְיָא "תּוֹךְ" "תּוֹךְ", כְּתִיב הָכָא "וְנִקְדַּשְׁתִּי בְּתוֹךְ בְּנֵי יִשְׂרָאֵל" (ויקרא כב) וּכְתִיב הָתָם °"הִבָּדְלוּ מִתּוֹךְ הָעֵדָה", (במדבר טז) וְאָתְיָא "עֵדָה" "עֵדָה", דִּכְתִיב הָתָם °"עַד מָתַי לָעֵדָה הָרָעָה הַזֹּאת" (שם יד) מַה לְּהַלָּן עֲשָׂרָה — אַף כָּאן עֲשָׂרָה.§ "וְאֵין עוֹשִׂין מַעֲמָד וּמוֹשָׁב פָּחוֹת מֵעֲשָׂרָה".§ כֵּיוָן דְּבָעֵי לְמֵימַר *"עִמְדוּ יְקָרִים, עֲמוֹדוּ! שְׁבוּ יְקָרִים, שְׁבוּ!" – בְּצִיר מֵעֲשָׂרָה לָאו אוֹרַח אַרְעָא.§ "וְאֵין אוֹמְרִים בִּרְכַּת אֲבֵלִים וּבִרְכַּת חֲתָנִים" (וכו').§ מַאי בִּרְכַּת אֲבֵלִים? בִּרְכַּת רְחָבָה. דְּא"ר יִצְחָק א"ר יוֹחָנָן: *בִּרְכַּת אֲבֵלִים בַּעֲשָׂרָה, סוְאֵין אֲבֵלִים מִן הַמִּנְיָן. בִּרְכַּת חֲתָנִים בַּעֲשָׂרָה — עוַחֲתָנִים מִן הַמִּנְיָן.§ "וְאֵין מְזַמְּנִין עַל הַמָּזוֹן בְּשֵׁם פָּחוֹת מֵעֲשָׂרָה" (וכו').§ *◦כֵּיוָן דְּבָעֵי לְמֵימַר "נְבָרֵךְ לֵאלֹהֵינוּ" — בְּצִיר מֵעֲשָׂרָה לָאו אוֹרַח אַרְעָא.§ "וְהַקַּרְקָעוֹת תִּשְׁעָה וְכֹהֵן וְאָדָם כַּיּוֹצֵא בָּהֶן" (וכו').§ מנה"מ אָמַר שְׁמוּאֵל: עֲשָׂרָה *כֹּהֲנִים כְּתוּבִים בַּפָּרָשָׁה, חַד לְגוּפֵיהּ, (*וְחַד לְמַעוּטֵי), וְאִידָךְ הָוֵי מִיעוּט אַחַר מִיעוּט *וְאֵין מִיעוּט אַחַר מִיעוּט אֶלָּא לְרַבּוֹת: תִּשְׁעָה יִשְׂרְאֵלִים וְחַד כֹּהֵן. וְאֵימָא חֲמִשָּׁה כֹּהֲנִים וַחֲמִשָּׁה יִשְׂרְאֵלִים! קַשְׁיָא.§ "וְאָדָם כַּיּוֹצֵא בָּהֶן".§ אָדָם מִי קָדוֹשׁ? אָמַר רַבִּי אַבָּהוּ: בְּאוֹמֵר "דָּמַי עָלַי". דְּתַנְיָא: פהָאוֹמֵר "דָּמַי עָלַי" — שָׁמִין אוֹתוֹ כְּעֶבֶד. וְעֶבֶד אִיתַּקַּשׁ לְקַרְקָעוֹת, דִּכְתִיב °"וְהִתְנַחַלְתֶּם אוֹתָם לִבְנֵיכֶם אַחֲרֵיכֶם לָרֶשֶׁת אֲחֻזָּה".§ **מתני'** צהַקּוֹרֵא בַּתּוֹרָה לֹא יִפְחוֹת מִשְּׁלֹשָׁה פְּסוּקִים, קוְלֹא יִקְרָא לַמְּתוּרְגְּמָן יוֹתֵר מִפָּסוּק אֶחָד. וּבַנָּבִיא

(ויקרא כה)

רש"י

כְּנֶגְדּוֹ נַמִּי לָא בָּעֵינַן. לִקְבּוֹעַ ג' פְּסוּקִים בַּנָּבִיא כְּנֶגֶד אוֹתָן שֶׁקּוֹרֵא הַמַּפְטִיר בַּתּוֹרָה: מָקוֹם שֶׁיֵּשׁ תּוּרְגְּמָן שָׁאנֵי. שֶׁיֵּשׁ טוֹרַח לַצִּבּוּר: **מתני'** אֵין פּוֹרְסִין עַל שְׁמַע. מִנְיָן הַבָּא לְבֵית הַכְּנֶסֶת לְאַחַר שֶׁקָּרְאוּ הַצִּבּוּר אֶת שְׁמַע, עוֹמֵד אֶחָד וְאוֹמֵר קַדִּישׁ וּבָרְכוּ וּבְרָכָה רִאשׁוֹנָה שֶׁבִּקְרִיאַת שְׁמַע. פּוֹרְסִין לְשׁוֹן חֲצִי הַדָּבָר: וְאֵין עוֹבְרִין לִפְנֵי הַתֵּיבָה. שְׁלִיחַ לַצִּבּוּר: וְאֵין נוֹשְׂאִין כַּפֵּיהֶן. הַכֹּהֲנִים: אֵין קוֹרִין בַּתּוֹרָה. בְּלַצִּבּוּר: אֵין עוֹשִׂין מַעֲמָד וּמוֹשָׁב. לְמֵת, כְּשֶׁנּוֹשְׂאִין אֶת הַמֵּת לְקוֹבְרוֹ הָיוּ יוֹשְׁבִין ז' פְּעָמִים לִבְכּוֹת אֶת הַמֵּת, וְהָרוֹצֶה לְסוֹפְדוֹ — יִסְפּוֹד. וְהָכִי תַּנְיָא (ב"ב דף ק:): אֵין פּוֹחֲתִין מִשִּׁבְעָה מַעֲמָדוֹת וּמוֹשָׁבוֹת לְמֵת, כְּגוֹן: עִמְדוּ יְקָרִים עֲמוֹדוּ, שְׁבוּ יְקָרִים שְׁבוּ: בִּרְכַּת אֲבֵלִים. מְפָרֵשׁ בַּגְּמָ': וְתַנְחוּמֵי אֲבֵלִים. כְּשֶׁחוֹזְרִין מִן הַקְּבָרוֹת עוֹמְדִין וּמְנַחֲמִין אֶת הָאָבֵל. וְאֵין שׁוּרָה פְּחוּתָה מֵעֲשָׂרָה, בְּמַסֶּכֶת סַנְהֶדְרִין (דף יט.): וְאֵין מְזַמְּנִין עַל הַמָּזוֹן בַּשֵּׁם. "נְבָרֵךְ אֱלֹהֵינוּ": וְהַקַּרְקָעוֹת. שֶׁל הֶקְדֵּשׁ, הַבָּא לְפוֹדוֹתָן צָרִיךְ עֲשָׂרָה, וְאֶחָד מֵהֶן כֹּהֵן: וְאָדָם כַּיּוֹצֵא בָּהֶן. אִם בָּא (ב) לִפְדּוֹת מִיַּד הֶקְדֵּשׁ. וּבַגְּמָ' מְפָרֵשׁ לָהּ: **גמ'** עֵדָה. אֵין פְּחוּתָה מֵעֲשָׂרָה, שֶׁנֶּאֱמַר "עַד מָתַי לָעֵדָה הָרָעָה הַזֹּאת", יָצְאוּ יְהוֹשֻׁעַ וְכָלֵב: לָאו אוֹרַח אַרְעָא. לְהַטְרִיחַ שָׁלִיחַ לְכָךְ וְלִקְרוֹתָן יְקָרִים, דְּא"כ מַה הִנַּחְתָּ לַמְרוּבִּין? אֵין אֲבֵלִים מִן הַמִּנְיָן. שֶׁהֲרֵי הוּא אוֹמֵר בְּרָכָה לַמְנַחֲמִים בִּפְנֵי עַצְמָן: אַחֵינוּ, בַּעַל הַגְּמוּל יְשַׁלֵּם לָכֶם גְּמוּלְכֶם הַטּוֹב, בא"י מְשַׁלֵּם הַגְּמוּל. וְלָאֲבֵלִים בִּפְנֵי עַצְמָן: אַחֵינוּ, בַּעַל נֶחָמוֹת יְנַחֵם אֶתְכֶם, בא"י מְנַחֵם אֲבֵלִים. וְאֵינוֹ כּוּלָּן יַחַד: י' כֹּהֲנִים כְּתוּבִים. בְּפָרָשַׁת הֶקְדֵּשׁוֹת, שְׁלֹשָׁה בָּעֲרָכִין וּשְׁלֹשָׁה בִּבְהֵמָה וְאַרְבָּעָה בַּקַּרְקָעוֹת, וְכֵיוָן דְּמַשְׁלְמִי בְּהוּ עֲשָׂרָה — בָּעֵינַן עֲשָׂרָה גַּבְרֵי: חַד לְגוּפֵיהּ. דְּכֹהֵן בָּעֵינַן: וְאֵימָא חֲמִשָּׁה כֹּהֲנִים וַחֲמִשָּׁה יִשְׂרְאֵלִים. כֵּיוָן דְּטַעְמָא מִשּׁוּם מִיעוּט אַחַר מִיעוּט הוּא, הַשְּׁלִישִׁי אֵינוֹ מִיעוּט אַחַר מִיעוּט. וְכֵיוָן דְּדָרַשְׁתְּ לֵיהּ (ג) שְׁנֵי מִיעוּט אַחַר מִיעוּט — אִיתְרַבֵּי לְיִשְׂרָאֵל, כִּי הָדַר אָתָא כֹּהֵן שְׁלִישִׁי — אַשְׁמוּעִינַן דְּלֶיהֱוֵי כֹּהֵן וְלֹא יִשְׂרָאֵל, וְכֵן ה' וְכֵן ז' וְכֵן ט': עֶבֶד אִיתַּקַּשׁ לְקַרְקָעוֹת. שֶׁנֶּאֱמַר "וְהִתְנַחַלְתֶּם אוֹתָם לִבְנֵיכֶם אַחֲרֵיכֶם לָרֶשֶׁת אֲחוּזָּה, לְעוֹלָם בָּהֶם תַּעֲבוֹדוּ": **מתני'** וְלֹא יִקְרָא לַמְּתוּרְגְּמָן יוֹתֵר מִפָּסוּק אֶחָד. שֶׁלֹּא יִטְעֶה מְתוּרְגְּמָן (מִן) הַמְּתַרְגֵּם עַל פֶּה:

וּבַנָּבִיא

תוספות

לא שנו אלא במקום שאין מתרגמין. ועל זה אנו סומכין שאין אנו מתרגמין הפטרות ◦שבכל ימות השנה, וכן הפרשיות:

אין פורסין על שמע פחות מעשרה. בירושלמי מפרש שאם התחילו בעשרה ויצאו מקצתן – אפ"ה גומרין, ועל היוצאים הוא אומר "ועוזבי ה' יכלו" (ישעיה א), וכן הלכה:

ואין פורסין על שמע. הקונטרס פירש: בני אדם שבאו בבית הכנסת אחר שהתפללו הצבור, ורוצים לומר קדיש וברכו – צריך עשרה. ור"ת פירש: דבשבעה שלא שמעו עם שלש אחרים סגי. וה"נ איתא במס' סופרים*: רבותינו שבמערב אומרים בשבעה, ונותנים טעם לדבריהם, דכתיב "בפרוע פרעות בישראל בהתנדב עם ברכו ה'" (שופטים ה) דאיכא שבע תיבות. וי"א אפילו בששה, משום ד"ברכו" הוי הששי. ור"ת כתב בספר הישר: בחמשה, משום דליכא אלא חמש תיבות עד "ברכו". ונ"ל אפילו בשלשה שלא שמעו. והכי פירושו דקרא: בפרוע פרעות בישראל, שלא עשו מה שמוטל עליהם לעשות – אז יתנדב העם לברך ה', וליכא אלא שלש תיבות עד בהתנדב. ותלמידי רש"י פירשו משמו דאפילו בשביל אחד שלא שמע יכולים הם לפרוס על שמע, ואפילו אותו ששמע כבר יכול להוציא אותן שלא שמעו. כמו שאנו רואים שליח צבור, שאף על פי שהתפלל כבר השמונה עשרה ברכות בלחש – חוזר ומתפלל בקול רם, ואע"פ שכולנו בקיאין עכשיו, מ"מ י"ל דאין זה ראייה כל כך, דשאני השמונה עשרה ברכות שהרי אם היה מתפלל מתחילה בקול רם – שמא לא יכוונו לבם להגיע עם שליח צבור במקום קדושה ומודים. ור"ת לא היה רוצה לעשות אפילו לעצמו:

ואמר ר' יצחק א"ר יוחנן ברכת אבלים בעשרה. פירש ר"י דלא איירי בברכת המזון, שהרי לא היתה ברחוב העיר, כדפי' פרק קמא דכתובות (דף ח: ושם). אלא איירי בברכות שהיו אומרים ברחוב העיר במעמדות. שהיו עושין לנחם אבלים, אבל בשל ברכת המזון סגי בשלשה והוא עצמו מצטרף, כדפירש הטעם שם: **עשרה** כהנים כו'. קשיא לי אמאי לא בעי אחד עשר, דאין ב"ד שקול בכל דבר שהוא תלוי שעומד בשקול הדעת*: **ואדם** מי קדוש. פירש הקונטרס פ"ק דסנהדרין (דף טו.): והא אין נמכר בשוק כעבד לכן אין קדוש. וקשיא: אמאי לא קאמר דמיירי בעבד כנעני, שיכול אדם להקדישו. דהא עבד כנעני שפיר קרוי אדם, כדאמרינן פ' "השולח" (גיטין לח: ושם*): "כל חרם אשר יחרם מן האדם לא יפדה" – לרבות עבדו ושפחתו הכנעניים! וי"ל: דאי איתא דמיירי בעבד כנעני סגי בשלשה, אבל בעשרה לא. כדאיתא בירושלמי גזרה שמא ישמעו ויברחו. וא"ת: אימא דההיא ירושלמי איירי בדינא דרבנן, אבל בדינא דאורייתא צריך עשרה, וא"כ הדר קושיין לדוכתיה, דכי פריך אדם מי קדיש – לישני דמיירי בעבד כנעני! וי"ל: דפשיטא ליה דמתניתין חשיב ותני הדינין שצריך לעשות, וא"כ אי איתא דאיירי בעבד הא הוה בשלשה. ועוד: נראה דסבר ליה למקשן דאי איתא דמיירי בעבד – הוה ליה לפרושי בהדיא הקרקעות והעבדים תשעה וכהן, כדקתני בכל מקום הקרקעות והעבדים. [וע"ע תוספות סנהדרין טו. ד"ה אדם]: **שמין** אותו כעבד ועבד איתקש לקרקעות דכתיב "והתנחלתם אותם" וגו'. משמע דעבד עברי איתקש לקרקעות, והכי נמי משמע פלק קמא דקדושין (דף ז. ושם) דאשה הוה לה נכסים שיש להן אחריות מטעם דעבד איתקש לקרקע. וקשיא: דהיינו דווקא עבד כנעני דעליה כתיב קרא ד"והתנחלתם", אבל עבד עברי לא מצינו כלל דאיתקש לקרקע! ודאי ההיא דקדושין יש לדחות כדפירש' שם, אבל הכא קשיא:

וכנביא

רבינו חננאל

כבוד תורה קרי פי' *) שלא בנביאים עד שיקרא בתורה. כנגדו לא צריך והדעת נוטה שאינו עולה ואי סליק ענין ההפטרה לא חיישינן לכ"א פסוקים וכן אי איכא תורגמן אפי' לא קרא מזה ההפטרה אלא ב' פסוקים פוסק כר' יוחנן ודיו: [מתני'] אין פורסין על שמע ואין עוברין לפני התיבה. ואין נושאין כפיהן ואין קורין בתורה ואין מפטירין בנביא ואין עושין מעמד ומושב. ואין אומרים ברכת אבלים שהיא ברכת רחבה וא"ר יוחנן ברכת אבלים בעשרה ואין אבלים מן המנין ותנחומי אבלים וברכת חתנים. ואין מזמנין על המזון בשם פחות מי' מנא לן. וא' משום ר' יוחנן דכתיב ונקדשתי בתוך בני ישראל וכתיב התם הבדלו מתוך העדה וכתיב עד מתי לעדה הרעה הזאת וכלב נשארו המרגלים י' והן שנקראו העדה ומפורש בתלמוד א"י מהאי קרא בבני יעקב לשבור בר בתוך הבאים וכתיב ויבואו אחי יוסף עשרה. ואקשי' בירושלמי מכיון דתנינן אין פורסין את שמע לריזא מילה תנינן אין עוברין לפני התיבה פחות מי' ופרקינן לכן צריכה בהדה דתני אין פורסין את שמע פחות מי' התחילו בי' והלכו מקצתן גומרים וכן כולן השנוין במשנתינו כיוצא בהן ועל כולן הוא אומר ועוזבי ה' יכלו. וכן אדם שאמר דמי עלי שמין אותו כעבד ולא יהיה פחות מעשרה.

הקורא

*) נראה דצ"ל שלא יתחיל לקרות בנביאים עד שיקרא וכו'.

עין משפט נר מצוה

מב א מיי' פי"ב מהל' תפלה הלכה יג טוש"ע א"ח סי' רפד סעיף א:

מג ב מיי' שם הלכה יג טוא"ח שם סמג עשין יט:

מד ג מיי' פ"ח מהלכות תפלה הלכה ה סמג שם טוש"ע א"ח סי' נה סעיף א וסי' סט סעיף א:

מה ד מיי' שם טוש"ע א"ח סי' סט סעיף א:

[פי' הל"ז]

מו ה מיי' שם טוש"ע א"ח סי' קכח סעיף א:

מז ו מיי' שם הלכה ד ופי"ב הלכה ג טוש"ע א"ח סי' קמג סעיף א:

מח ז מיי' פ"ח שם הל"ד:

מט ח מיי' פי"ב מהל' אבל הלכה ד טוש"ע י"ד סי' שעו:

נ ט מיי' פי"ג מהלכות אבל הלכה א סמג עשין מד"ס ב טור שם:

נא י מיי' פ"ב מהלכות ברכות הלכה י ופ"י מהלכות אישות הלכה ה טוש"ע אה"ע סי' סא סעיף ד:

נב כ מיי' פ"ה מהלכות ברכות הלכה ד סמג עשין כז טוש"ע א"ח סימן קצב סעיף א:

נג ל מ מיי' פ"ח מהל' ערכין הלכה ב:

נד נ מיי' פ"ח מהלכות תפלה הלכה ד טור ש"ע א"ח סי' סט סעיף א:

נה ס מיי' פי"ג מהל' אבל הלכה א סמג עשין מד"ס ב טור י"ד סי' שעו:

נו ע מיי' פ"ב מהלכות ברכות הלכה י ופ"י מהל' אישות הל"ה טוש"ע אה"ע סי' סב סעיף ד:

נז פ מיי' פ"ח מהלכות ערכין הלכה ב:

נח צ מיי' פי"ב מהלכות תפלה הלכה ג טור ש"ע א"ח סי' קלז סעיף א:

נט ק מיי' שם הלכה י טוש"ע א"ח סי' קמה סעיף א:

[עי' תוס' ערכין יט: ד"ה או דלמא]

[ע"ש דמייתי קרא אחרינא]

גליון הש"ס

גמ' כיון דבעי למימר נברך לאלהינו. עי' ברכות דף מט ע"ב תוס' ד"ה נברך: תום' ד"ה לא שנו וכו' שבכל ימות השנה. עי' לקמן דף כד ע"א תוס' ד"ה ואם היו:

[סנהדרין ב.]

ברכות כא: ע"ש

[ברכות כא: ע"ש סנהדרין עד: ע"ש]

ב"ב ק:

כתובות ח.

[ברכות מה:]

סנהדרין טו.

[בסנהדרין ליתא]

[יומא מג. וש"נ]

[סנהדרין טו.]

הגהות הב"ח

(א) במשנה ואין מזמנין על המזון בשם: (ב) רש"י ד"ה ואדם וכו' אם בא לפטור עצמו מיד: (ג) ד"ה ואימא חמשה וכו' דכיון דדרשת ליה כהן שני מיעוט:

גמרא

תורה אור

א ובנביא שלשה. היו שלשתן שלש פרשיות – קורין אחד אחד. ב מדלגין בנביא, ואין מדלגין בתורה. ועד כמה הוא מדלג? עד כדי שלא יפסוק המתורגמן.§ גמ' הני ג' פסוקין כנגד מי? ●אמר רב אסי: כנגד תורה נביאים וכתובים. ולא יקרא למתורגמן יותר מפסוק אחד ובנביא ג' פסוקים, ואם היו שלשתן שלש פרשיות – קורא אחד אחד, כגון °"כי כה אמר ה' חנם נמכרתם" °"כי כה אמר ה' אלהים מצרים ירד עמי בראשונה" °"ועתה מה לי פה נאם ה'".§ "מדלגין בנביא ואין מדלגין בתורה".§ ורמינהי: *קורא °"אחרי מות" °ו"אך בעשור". והא קא מדלג! אמר אביי: לא קשיא: כאן בכדי שיפסוק התורגמן, וכאן – בכדי שלא יפסוק התורגמן. והא עלה קתני: מדלגין בנביא ואין מדלגין בתורה, ועד כמה הוא מדלג – עד כדי שלא יפסוק התורגמן, מכלל דבתורה כלל כלל לא! אלא אמר אביי: לא קשיא: כאן – בענין אחד, כאן – בשתי ענינות. והתניא: מדלגין בתורה בענין אחד, ובנביא בשני ענינין. כאן וכאן בכדי שלא יפסוק התורגמן. תניא אידך: *ג אין מדלגין מנביא לנביא, ובנביא של שנים עשר – מדלג, ובלבד שלא ידלג מסוף הספר לתחילתו.§ מתני' המפטיר בנביא הוא פורס על שמע, והוא עובר לפני התיבה, והוא נושא את כפיו. ואם היה קטן – אביו או רבו עוברין על ידו. קטן קורא בתורה ומתרגם, ד אבל אינו פורס על שמע ואינו עובר לפני התיבה, ה ואינו נושא את כפיו. ו פוחח פורס את שמע ומתרגם, אבל אינו קורא בתורה, ז ואינו עובר לפני התיבה, ואינו נושא את כפיו. ח סומא פורס את שמע ומתרגם, רבי יהודה אומר: כל שלא ראה מאורות מימיו – אינו פורס על שמע.§ גמ' מ"ט? רב פפא אמר: משום כבוד, רבה בר שימי אמר: משום דאתי לאינצויי. מאי בינייהו? איכא בינייהו דעביד בחנם. תנן: ואם היה קטן – אביו או רבו עוברין על ידו. אי אמרת משום (א) נצויי – קטן בר נצויי הוא? אלא מאי משום כבוד – קטן בר כבוד הוא?! אלא: איכא כבוד אביו וכבוד רבו,

הכא

(ישעיה נב; שם; שם; ויקרא טז; ויקרא כג)

רש"י

ובנביא שלשה. אם ירצה, ולא איכפת לן אם יטעה, דלא נפקא מיניה הוראה: ואם היו שלשתן כו'. בגמ' מפרש היכא משכחת לה רצופין: מדלגין בנביא. מפרשה לפרשה: ואין מדלגין בתורה. שהשומע את הקופץ ממקום למקום אין לבו מיושב לשמוע: ועד כמה הוא מדלג. בנביא: שלא יפסוק התורגמן. שלא ידלג ממקום שהוא קורא אלא כדי שיוכל לגול את הספר ולקרות במקום הדילוג קודם שיגמור התורגמן תרגום המקרא שידלג זה, משום שאין כבוד לצבור לעמוד שם בשתיקה: גמ' קורא. כהן גדול "אחרי מות" ביום הכפורים – משנה היא במסכת יומא – ו"אך בעשור לחודש". ויש כאן דילוג, דפרשת "אך בעשור לחדש השביעי" בפרשת "אמור אל הכהנים": כאן בכדי שלא יפסוק המתורגמן. והאי בכדי שלא יפסוק הוא, שהרי סמוכין הן: והא קתני. גרסינן, ולא גרסינן עלה: בענין אחד. ששניהן מדברין בדבר אחד, ואין כאן טירוף הדעת. הלכך, כי לא מפסיק תורגמן – מדלג, שהרי שניהן בענין יוה"כ מדברים. ומתני' דקתני כלל לא – בשני ענינים, כגון מפרשת נגעים לפרשת זבין: והתניא. בניחותא: אין מדלגין מנביא לנביא. שיש כאן טירוף יותר מדאי: מסוף הספר לתחילתו. למפרע: מתני' המפטיר בנביא. מי שרגיל להפטיר בנביא, תקנו חכמים שיהא פורס את שמע: הוא עובר לפני התיבה. להוציא את הצבור בקדושה שבתפלה: על ידו. בשבילו: קטן אינו פורס על שמע. לפי שהוא בא להוציא רבים ידי חובתן. וכיון שאינו מחוייב בדבר – אינו מוציא אחרים ידי חובתן: ואינו נושא את כפיו. אם כהן הוא, שאין כבוד של צבור להיות כפופין לברכתו: פוחח. (ב) במס' סופרים *מפרש: כל שכרעיו נראין. "ערום ויחף" מתרגם: ערטילאי ופחח (ישעיה כ): פורס את שמע. דהא מחוייב בברכה: אבל אינו קורא בתורה. משום כבוד תורה. וכן לפני התיבה, וכן בנשיאות כפים – גנאי הוא לצבור: גמ' משום כבוד. להעביר לפני התיבה, הואיל וממליא עצמו לדבר שאינו כבודו, תיקנו לו זו לכבוד: משום אינצויי. הדבר בא לידי מחלוקת: אני מפטיר ואתה תעבור לפני התיבה: דקא עביד בחנם. הבא לעבור לפני התיבה אינו נוטל שכר,

דהכא

תוספות

ובנביא שלשה. ועכשיו אין אנו מקרין למתורגמן אפילו בנביא אלא פסוק אחד, שלא יבא לטעות. רק בתחילת ההפטרה אנו מקרין ג' למתורגמן, להודיע כי כן הדין, אי לא דחיישינן שיטעה: ואם היו שלשתן של שלש פרשיות קורין אחד אחד. קשיא על מה שאנו מתרגמין "ויאמר יהושע אל העם התקדשו" (יהושע ג) ויש שם ג' פסוקים עד בעת ההיא, ומקרין אותן למתרגם שלשתן ביחד, ואע"פ שיש פרשה בסוף שני פסוקים. והא שאנו מתרגמין הפטרות של פסח ועצרת טפי משאר י"ט – לפי שהן מדברות בנס היום, כדי לפרסם הנס, וכן במתן תורה כדי לפרסם הנס: אבל אינו פורס על שמע. ואפילו לרבי יהודה דמכשיר ליה במגילה לעיל (דף יט:)(ג) – הכא מודה שלא יוציא אחרים ידי חובתן בדבר שבקדושה. משום דבקטן איכא ב' דרבנן, כדפרישית לעיל לרבנן דרבי יהודה. אבל במגילה יש להקל, לפי שטף ונשים היו בספק ד"להרוג ולהשמיד" לפיכך עשאו רבי יהודה כגדול: פוחח. (ד) ערום ויחף פ"ה מתרגמינן ערטילאי ופחי. וליתא, *דפחי הוא תרגום של ערום. וכן פירש רב אלפס דפחי זהו אותו שלבוש בגדים קרועין, והכי נמי משמע פרק קמא דמס' קידושין*: ואינו עובר לפני התיבה. קשה: מאי איריא קטן! אפילו גדול נמי אינו עובר לפני התיבה אא"כ נתמלא זקנו, כדתניא סוף פ"ק דחולין (דף כד: ושם): נתמלא זקנו – ראוי לעשות שליח צבור, ולירד לפני התיבה, אבל בענין אחר לא! וי"ל: דהתם מיירי בתענית צבור, כדתנן בתענית (דף טז.) דאין מורידין לפני התיבה אלא זקן ורגיל (*ומי שנתמלא זקנו) ומי שטפולו מרובה. והא דקתני התם גבי נתמלא זקנו ראוי לעשות ש"ץ – היינו להיות ש"ץ בקביעות, אבל באקראי בעלמא – יכול להיות משהביא ב' שערות. ולא כמו שפירש רש"י שם, דפירש דמיירי לתקיעת שופר ולהמנות פרנס על הצבור ולהלקות ולנדות: ואין נושא כפיו. משמע: הא אם הביא ב' שערות – ישא כפיו. וקשה: דהא סוף פ"ק דחולין (דף כד: ושם) אמר דאין נושא את כפיו עד שיתמלא זקנו! ועוד קשה: דמשמע סוף פרק "לולב הגזול" (סוכה דף מב.) קטן היודע לישא את כפיו חולקין לו תרומה בגורן, ואפיו קטן ממש! וי"ל: דההיא ד"לולב הגזול" מיירי עם כהנים גדולים, ללמוד ולהתחנך. והא דפסלינן הכא קטן – מיירי בשאין גדולין עמו. וההיא דחולין דבעי מלוי זקן – מיירי לישא כפיו תדיר בקביעות, אבל באקראי בעלמא – יכול הוא לישא כפיו אע"פ שלא נתמלא זקנו כדי לאחזוקי נפשיה בכהני: (וע"ע תוס' יבמות לט: ד"ה ואלו) מי שלא ראה מאורות לא יפרוס על שמע. קשה: דהא רבי יהודה הוא דאמר פרק "החובל" (ב"ק דף פז. ושם): סומא פטור מכל המצות. וא"כ, אי איירי הכא בסומא – אפילו ראה מאורות ונסתם נמי! ומפרש בירושלמי, דלא מיירי בסומא ממש, אלא מיירי שהוא בבית אפל. ועוד י"ל: דמיירי שפיר בסומא, והא דפטרינן התם סומא – היינו מן התורה, ●אבל מדרבנן מיהא חייב. ואפילו נסתמא משנולד – מ"מ חייב הוא מדרבנן, שלא יהא כנכרי, ולא יהא נוהג בו דת יהודי כלל. דלא דמי לנשים דפטורים ממצות עשה שהזמן גרמא, אפילו מאותן שאינן אלא מדרבנן, שהרי בנר חנוכה ובארבע כוסות ובמקרא מגילה דלא הוו אלא מדרבנן לא מחייבי אלא לפי שהן היו באותו הנס – התם היינו טעמא שאפילו נפטור אותן מכל מצות עשה שהזמן גרמא – מ"מ עדיין יש להן מצות רבות. אבל סומא אם נפטור אותו מכל מצות, אפי' מאותן שאינן אלא מדרבנן – א"כ יהא חשוב כנכרי. ואע"ג דפירש' לעיל דקטן דאית(ה) תרי מדרבנן שהוא קטן ופריסת שמע דלא הוי אלא מדרבנן אין יכול להוציא אחרים גדולים, דליכא אלא חד דרבנן – פריסת שמע, ●אפ"ה, סומא שיש בו תרי מדרבנן יוציא שפיר האחרים, דכיון שהוא גדול ובר דעת – עדיף טפי מקטן: [וע"ע תוס' עירובין לו. ד"ה דילמא וכו' ותוס' לעיל יט: ד"ה ור"י מכשיר]

כשאתה

מסורת הש"ס

[לעיל כא:]

יומא סח: סוטה מא.

[תוספ' פ"ג]

[פי"ד הט"ו]

עין משפט נר מצוה

ם א מיי' פי"ב מהל' תפלה הלכה יד:

סא ב ג מיי' שם הלכה יג סמג עשין יט טוש"ע א"ח סי' קמד סעיף א:

סב ד מיי' פ"ח מהל' תפלה הלכה יא טוש"ע א"ח סי' נג סעיף ו:

סג ה מיי' פט"ו שם הלכה ד טוש"ע א"ח סי' קכח סעיף לד:

סד ו מיי' פ"ח שם הלכה יב:

סה ז מיי' שם טוש"ע א"ח סי' נג סעיף יג:

סו ח מיי' שם טוש"ע א"ח סי' סט סעיף ב:

[כוונת תוספות דליתא כן בתרגום אלא דמתרגם על ערום ויחף פחח ויחף וכן האמת בתרגום שלפנינו וכן איתא ברש"י ישעיה על פסוק ערום ת"י פחח]

גליון הש"ס

גמ' א"ר אסי כנגד תורה. עי' מ"ר פ' תבא: תוס' ד"ה מי שלא וכו' אבל מדרבנן מיהא חייב. עי' ר"ה דף לג ע"א תד"ה הא ר' יהודה: בא"ד אפ"ה סומא שיש בו תרי מדרבנן. עי' לעיל דף יט ע"ב תוס' ד"ה ור' יהודה:

רבינו חננאל

הקורא בתורה לא יפחות לו מג' פסוקים כנגד תורה נביאים וכתובים ולא יקרא לתורגמן בתורה יותר מפסוק אחד ובנביא ג' ואם היו שלשתן ג' פרשיות כגון כי כה אמר ה' חנם נמכרתם כי כה אמר ה' מצרים ירד עמי בראשונה ועתה מה לי פה כגון אלו קורין א' א'. מדלגין בתורה בענין אחד כגון אחרי מות ואך בעשור אע"פ שהן מרוחקין זה מזה כיון שהן ענין אחד מדלגין ובנביא מדלגין אפילו בב' ענינות. וכאן וכאן כדי שלא יפסיק המתורגמן. פי' משעה שיפסיק עד שיכרוך הספר ויגיע למקום שרוצה לקרות שיעור שישלים המתרגם הפסוק שמתרגם לא יותר. ואין מדלגין מנביא לנביא כגון מישעיה לירמיה וכיוצא בו ובנביא של י"ב והוא ספר תרי עשר מדלגין מנביא לנביא ובלבד שלא ידלג מסוף הספר לתחלתו שהוא למפרע. המפטיר בנביא הוא פורס את שמע והוא עובר לפני התיבה ואם הוא כהן הוא נושא את כפיו. מ"ט. רב פפא אמר משום כבוד. רבא בר שימי א' משום אינצויי כלומר חיישינן דלמא אתו למימר אני מפטיר וזה פורס על שמע. וכי זה גדול ממני ליקח שכר. הלכך התקינו להיות המפטיר פורס על שמע עובר לפני התיבה כו'. *) ואין עושין בחנם אלא משום כבוד. אבל לא מינצו אלא במקום שהפורס על שמע העובר לפני התיבה נוטל שכר ואם היה המפטיר קטן שאינו ראוי לעבור לפני התיבה ולא לפרוס על שמע אביו או רבו עוברין על ידו דאי לאו הכי אתי רבו לאינצויי.

קטן

*) נראה דחסר כאן ואם עושין בחנם אינו אלא משום כבוד כו'.

הגהות הב"ח

(א) גמ' אי אמרת משום [אי]נצויי קטן: (ב) רש"י [ד"ה] פוחח ערום ויחף [מת]רגמינן ערטילאי ופחח [ובמ]ס' סופרים מפרש כל [שכר]עיו נראין הס"ד. ונ"ב ...ה דרש"י בא ליישב מה ...קה דאי פוחח דהכא ...ף ברגליו לחוד קאמר ...אי אינו נושא כפיו הא ... לחלוץ מנעליו בשעה ...שא כפיו דמהאי טעמא ...מין ברגליו אינו נושא ... כיון שהוא יחף ...תכלים בו כדפי' ...יא בדף זה בע"ב על ...הביא מסכת סופרים ...חח דהכא כל שכרעיו ...ין דהיינו דאין לו בתי ...יס דזה נמי נקרא פוחח שהולך יחף לגמרי שאין לו אף בתי שוקים ומש"ה פי' רש"י בסמוך דאית ביה משום ולא יראה בך ...ת דבר דכיון דאין לו כלל בתי שוקים אית ביה איסור ראיית ערוה אבל בחולץ מנעליו ואית ליה בתי שוקים אע"ג דיחף הוא ... ביה איסור דראיית ערוה ולא הוה קמיבעי ליה מידי בקטן: (ג) תוס' ד"ה אבל וכו' במגילה לעיל דף יט. נ"ב ע"ש בתוס' ...ה ור' יהודה: (ד) ד"ה פוחח. פ"ה ערום ויחף מתרגמינן ערטילאי ופחח וליתא דפחח הוא תרגום וכו' רב אלפס דפוחח זהו ...ו וכו' פרק י"ד דמסכת סופרים הס"ד. ונ"ב וז"ל שם הלכה טו פוחח הנראים כרעיו או בגדיו פרומים או מי שראשו מגולה ...ס את שמע ע"כ וכבר כתבתי ברש"י דפוחח כשאין לו בתי שוקים ולא יחף: (ה) ד"ה מי שלא וכו' לעיל דקטן דאית ביה תרתי מדרבנן שהוא קטן ופריסת שמע נמי דלא הוי וכו' סומא שיש בו תרתי מדרבנן מוציא שפיר:

תוספות

כשאתה מגיע אצל וחכיתי לה'. קשה: כיון שלא היה יכול לומר חי"ת א"כ היאך הורידו רבי לפני התיבה כשגזר תענית, כדאי' ב"השוכר את הפועלים" (ב"מ דף פה:), והא אין מורידין לא מאנשי חיפה ולא מאנשי בית שאן לפי שקוראין לאלפין עיינין ולעיינין אלפין! וי"ל: דכשהיה מתכוין לקרות החי"ת קורא אותה שפיר ע"י טורח, אבל לא היה בקל. ולפי שאמר ליה אליהו שעל ידו תמהר הגאולה – לפיכך הורידו*:

אם היה דש בעירו מותר. ואפילו במומין שבידו, כדאמר בירושלמי בההוא כהן דהוו ידיה עקישי, אתא לקמיה דרבי נפתלי אמר ליה: כיון שאתה דש בעירך – מותר:

סכנה ואין בה מצוה. פר"ת: בשעת הסכנה יכול להסתכן בהן, ולא תגין עליו המצוה, ולא יעשה לו נס כמו לאלישע בעל הכנפים (שבת דף מט.):

בתפרן. כשהוא תופר בית מושבם צריך ליזהר שלא ימשוך חוט התפירה יותר מדאי ויתקלקל הריבוע. ור"ת פירש: דצריך שיהא התפר עצמו מרובע:

יברכוך

גמרא

הָכָא נַמִי אִיכָּא נְצוּיֵי אָבִיו וּנְצוּיֵי רַבּוֹ.§ "פּוֹחֵחַ פּוֹרֵס עַל שְׁמַע" וכו'.§ בְּעָא מִינֵּיהּ עוּלָּא בַּר רַב מֵאַבַּיֵי: קָטָן פּוֹחֵחַ מַהוּ שֶׁיִּקְרָא בַּתּוֹרָה? אֲמַר לֵיהּ: וְתִיבְּעֵי לָךְ עָרוֹם? עָרוֹם מַאי טַעְמָא לָא – °מִשּׁוּם כְּבוֹד צִבּוּר, הָכָא נַמִי – מִשּׁוּם כְּבוֹד צִבּוּר.§ "סוּמָא פּוֹרֵס עַל שְׁמַע" וכו'.§ תַּנְיָא, *אָמְרוּ לוֹ לְרַבִּי יְהוּדָה: הַרְבֵּה צָפוּ לִדְרוֹשׁ בַּמֶּרְכָּבָה וְלֹא רָאוּ אוֹתָהּ מִימֵיהֶם. וְר' יְהוּדָה: הָתָם *בְּאַבַנְתָּא דְּלִיבָּא תַּלְיָא מִילְּתָא, וְהָא קָא מִיכַּוֵּין וְיָדַע. הָכָא – מִשּׁוּם הֲנָאָה הוּא, וְהָא לֵית לֵיהּ הֲנָאָה. וְרַבָּנַן: אִית לֵיהּ הֲנָאָה, כְּרַבִּי יוֹסֵי. דְּתַנְיָא, א"ר יוֹסֵי: כָּל יָמַי הָיִיתִי מִצְטַעֵר עַל מִקְרָא זֶה °"וְהָיִיתָ מְמַשֵּׁשׁ בַּצָּהֳרַיִם כַּאֲשֶׁר יְמַשֵּׁשׁ הָעִוֵּר בָּאֲפֵלָה", וְכִי מָה אִכְפַּת לֵיהּ לְעִוֵּר בֵּין אֲפֵילָה לְאוֹרָה? עַד שֶׁבָּא מַעֲשֶׂה לְיָדִי. פַּעַם אַחַת הָיִיתִי מְהַלֵּךְ בְּאִישׁוֹן לַיְלָה וַאֲפֵלָה, וְרָאִיתִי סוּמָא שֶׁהָיָה מְהַלֵּךְ בַּדֶּרֶךְ וַאֲבוּקָה בְּיָדוֹ. אָמַרְתִּי לוֹ: בְּנִי, אֲבוּקָה זוֹ לָמָּה לָךְ? אָמַר לִי: כָּל זְמַן שֶׁאֲבוּקָה בְּיָדִי – בְּנֵי אָדָם רוֹאִין אוֹתִי, וּמַצִּילִין אוֹתִי מִן הַפְּחָתִין וּמִן הַקּוֹצִין וּמִן הַבַּרְקָנִין.§ **מתני'** [א]כֹּהֵן שֶׁיֵּשׁ בְּיָדָיו מוּמִין לֹא יִשָּׂא אֶת כַּפָּיו. ר' יְהוּדָה אוֹמֵר: [ב]אַף מִי שֶׁהָיוּ יָדָיו צְבוּעוֹת *סָטִים לֹא יִשָּׂא אֶת כַּפָּיו מִפְּנֵי שֶׁהָעָם מִסְתַּכְּלִין בּוֹ.§ **גמ'** (א) [ג]תָּנָא: מוּמִין שֶׁאָמְרוּ – בְּפָנָיו, יָדָיו וְרַגְלָיו. אָמַר ר' יְהוֹשֻׁעַ בֶּן לֵוִי: יָדָיו בּוֹהַקְנִיּוֹת – לֹא יִשָּׂא אֶת כַּפָּיו. תַּנְיָא נַמִי הָכִי: [ד]יָדָיו בּוֹהַקְנִיּוֹת – לֹא יִשָּׂא אֶת כַּפָּיו. עֲקוּמוֹת, עֲקוּשׁוֹת – לֹא יִשָּׂא אֶת כַּפָּיו. אָמַר רַב אַסִּי: [ה]חֵיפָנִי (*וּבֵשָׁנִי) לֹא יִשָּׂא אֶת כַּפָּיו. תַּנְיָא נַמִי הָכִי: [ו]אֵין מוֹרִידִין לִפְנֵי הַתֵּיבָה לֹא אַנְשֵׁי בֵּית שְׁאָן, וְלֹא אַנְשֵׁי בֵּית חֵיפָה, וְלֹא אַנְשֵׁי טִבְעוֹנִין, מִפְּנֵי *שֶׁקּוֹרִין לְאָלְפִין עַיְינִין וּלְעַיְינִין אָלְפִין. אֲמַר לֵיהּ רַבִּי חִיָּיא לְר' שִׁמְעוֹן בַּר רַבִּי: °אִלְמָלֵי אַתָּה לֵוִי פָּסוּל אַתָּה מִן הַדּוּכָן, מִשּׁוּם דַּעֲבֵי קָלָךְ. אֲתָא אֲמַר לֵיהּ לַאֲבוּהּ. אֲמַר לֵיהּ: זִיל אֵימָא לֵיהּ: כְּשֶׁאַתָּה מַגִּיעַ אֵצֶל °"וְחִכִּיתִי לַה'" לֹא נִמְצֵאתָ מְחָרֵף וּמְגַדֵּף? אָמַר רַב הוּנָא: זַבְלְגָן לֹא יִשָּׂא אֶת כַּפָּיו. וְהָא הַהוּא דַּהֲוָה בְּשִׁיבָבוּתֵיהּ דְּרַב הוּנָא, וַהֲוָה פָּרֵיס יְדֵיהּ! הַהוּא דָּשׁ בְּעִירוֹ הֲוָה. תַּנְיָא נַמִי הָכִי: [ז]זַבְלְגָן לֹא יִשָּׂא אֶת כַּפָּיו, וְאִם הָיָה דָּשׁ בְּעִירוֹ – מוּתָּר. א"ר יוֹחָנָן: [ח]סוּמָא בְּאַחַת מֵעֵינָיו לֹא יִשָּׂא אֶת כַּפָּיו. וְהָא הַהוּא דַּהֲוָה בְּשִׁיבָבוּתֵיהּ דְּרַבִּי יוֹחָנָן, דַּהֲוָה פָּרֵיס יְדֵיהּ! הַהוּא דָּשׁ בְּעִירוֹ הֲוָה. תַּנְיָא נַמִי הָכִי: סוּמָא בְּאַחַת מֵעֵינָיו לֹא יִשָּׂא אֶת כַּפָּיו, וְאִם הָיָה דָּשׁ בְּעִירוֹ – מוּתָּר: "ר"י אוֹמֵר מִי שֶׁהָיוּ יָדָיו צְבוּעוֹת לֹא יִשָּׂא אֶת כַּפָּיו".§ תָּנָא: [ט]אִם רוֹב אַנְשֵׁי הָעִיר מְלַאכְתָּן בְּכָךְ – מוּתָּר.§ **מתני'** [י]הָאוֹמֵר "אֵינִי עוֹבֵר לִפְנֵי הַתֵּיבָה בִּצְבוּעִין" – אַף בִּלְבָנִים לֹא יַעֲבוֹר. "בְּסַנְדָּל אֵינִי עוֹבֵר" – אַף יָחֵף לֹא יַעֲבוֹר. [כ]הָעוֹשֶׂה תְּפִלָּתוֹ עֲגוּלָּה – סַכָּנָה וְאֵין בָּהּ מִצְוָה. נְתָנָהּ עַל מִצְחוֹ אוֹ עַל פַּס יָדוֹ – הֲרֵי זוֹ דֶּרֶךְ הַמִּינוּת. °[ל]*צִיפָּן זָהָב וּנְתָנָהּ עַל בֵּית אוּנְקְלִי שֶׁלּוֹ – ה"ז דֶּרֶךְ הַחִיצוֹנִים.§ **גמ'** מ"ט? חָיְישִׁינַן שֶׁמָּא מִינוּת נִזְרְקָה בּוֹ.§ "הָעוֹשֶׂה תְּפִלָּתוֹ עֲגוּלָּה סַכָּנָה וְאֵין בָּהּ מִצְוָה".§ לֵימָא תְּנֵינָא לְהָא דְּתָנוּ רַבָּנַן: *) [מ]תְּפִלִּין מְרוּבָּעוֹת הֲלָכָה לְמֹשֶׁה מִסִּינַי! וְאָמַר רָבָא: בְּתִפְרָן וּבַאֲלַכְסוֹנָן – אָמַר רַב פָּפָּא: מַתְנִיתִין דַּעֲבִידָא כִּי אַמְגּוּזָא.§ **מתני'** הָאוֹמֵר

יְבָרֶכְךָ

*) מנחות לה. [ע"ש שבת כח:]

[נ"ל צִיפָּה [מעי"ן]]

רש"י

דְּהָכָא אִיכְּלוּיֵי לֵיכָּא, מִשּׁוּם כָּבוֹד אִיכָּא: קָטָן פּוֹחֵחַ מַהוּ שֶׁיִּקְרָא בַּתּוֹרָה. גָּדוֹל פּוֹחֵחַ הוּא דְּאָסוּר מִשּׁוּם "וְלֹא יִרְאֶה בְךָ עֶרְוַת דָּבָר" (דברים כג), אֲבָל קָטָן אֵינוֹ מוּזְהָר, אוֹ דִּלְמָא לָא פָּלֵיג מַתְנִי' בֵּין קָטָן לְגָדוֹל: לִדְרוֹשׁ בַּמֶּרְכָּבָה. דִּיחֶזְקֵאל: פְּחָתִים. גּוּמוֹת:

תורה אור

מתני' כֹּהֵן שֶׁיֵּשׁ בְּיָדָיו מוּמִין. לְפִי שֶׁהָעָם מִסְתַּכְּלִין בּוֹ, וְאָמְרִינַן בְּמַסֶּכֶת חֲגִיגָה (דף טז.): הַמִּסְתַּכֵּל בַּכֹּהֲנִים בְּשָׁעָה שֶׁנּוֹשְׂאִין אֶת כַּפֵּיהֶן עֵינָיו כֵּהוֹת, לְפִי שֶׁהַשְּׁכִינָה שׁוֹרָה עַל יְדֵיהֶן*: **גמ'** בּוֹהַקְנִיּוֹת. לונטיי"ש בְּלַעַ"ז: עֲקוּמוֹת. כְּפוּפוֹת: עֲקוּשׁוֹת. לְגַבֵּיהֶן: חֵיפָנִי וּבֵישָׁנִי. כֹּהֵן שֶׁהוּא מֵאַנְשֵׁי חֵיפָה וּמֵאַנְשֵׁי בֵּית שְׁאָן מְגַמְגְּמִין בִּלְשׁוֹנָן הֵן: מִפְּנֵי שֶׁקּוֹרִין לְאָלְפִין עַיְינִין וּלְעַיְינִין אָלְפִין. וְאִם הָיוּ עוֹשִׂין בִּרְכַּת כֹּהֲנִים הָיוּ אוֹמְרִים יָאֵר – יָעֵר ה' פָּנָיו, וּלְשׁוֹן קְלָלָה הוּא. כִּי יֵשׁ פָּנִים שֶׁיִּתְפָּרְשׁוּ לְשׁוֹן כַּעַס, כְּמוֹ "פָּנַי יֵלֵכוּ" (שמות לג), "אֶת פָּנַי" (ויקרא כ), וּמְתַרְגְּמִינַן יָת רוּגְזִי וּמֵעַי"ן עוֹשִׂין אָלְפִי"ן, וּפוֹגְמִין תְּפִלָּתָן. וּדְאָמְרִינַן (ברכות לב.) דְּבֵי ר"א קוֹרִין לְאָלְפִין עַיְינִין וּלְעַיְינִין אָלְפִין – הַהוּא בִּדְרָשָׁה: *פָּנָיו יָדָיו וְרַגְלָיו. הַנּוֹשֵׂא אֶת כַּפָּיו חוֹלֵץ מִנְעָלָיו, כִּדְתַנְיָא (סוטה דף מ.). וְאִם יֵשׁ בּוֹ מוּם יִסְתַּכְּלוּ בּוֹ, וּמִתּוֹךְ כָּךְ רוֹאִין אֶת יָדָיו: דַּעֲבֵי קָלָךְ. וְתַנְיָא בְּ"הַכֹּל שׁוֹחֲטִין" (חולין דף כד.): בְּשִׁילֹה וּבְבֵית עוֹלָמִים הַלְוִיִּם נִפְסָלִין בְּקוֹל: אֵצֶל וְחִכֵּיתִי לַה'. מִקְרָא זֶה בְּסֵפֶר יְשַׁעְיָה: לֹא נִמְצֵאתָ מְחָרֵף וּמְגַדֵּף. שֶׁהָיָה קוֹרֵא לְחֵיתִי"ן הֵיהִי"ן, נִרְאֶה כְּאוֹמֵר וְהִכֵּיתִי: זַבְלְגָן. עֵינָיו זוֹלְפוֹת דִּמְעָה: לֹא יִשָּׂא אֶת כַּפָּיו. לְפִי שֶׁמִּסְתַּכְּלִין בּוֹ: דָּשׁ בְּעִירוֹ הֲוָה. כְּבָר הָיוּ רְגִילִין אַנְשֵׁי עִירוֹ וְלֹא הָיוּ מִסְתַּכְּלִין בּוֹ עוֹד. דָּשׁ לְשׁוֹן (ב) מַרְגִּיל, כְּמוֹ כֵּיוָן דְּדָשׁ דָּשׁ (בגיטין דף נו:): *סְטִים. קרו"ג: **מתני'** אַף בִּלְבָנִים לֹא יַעֲבוֹר. טַעְמָא מְפָרֵשׁ בַּגְּמָ': הָעוֹשֶׂה תְּפִלָּתוֹ עֲגוּלָּה. תְּפִילִּין שֶׁבְּרֹאשׁוֹ, עֲגוּלָּה כְּבֵיצָה וּכְאֱגוֹז: סַכָּנָה. שֶׁלֹּא תִּכָּנֵס בְּרֹאשׁוֹ: וְאֵין בָּהּ מִצְוָה. דִּמְרוּבָּעוֹת בָּעֵינַן: נְתָנָהּ עַל מִצְחוֹ. שֶׁל רֹאשׁ, וְשֶׁל יָד עַל פַּס יָדוֹ: הֲרֵי זוֹ דֶּרֶךְ הַמִּינוּת. שֶׁמְּבַזִּין מִדְרַשׁ חֲכָמִים וְהוֹלְכִין אַחַר הַמַּשְׁמָע, כְּמַשְׁמָעָן בֵּין עֵינֶיךָ מַמָּשׁ, וְעַל יָדְךָ מַמָּשׁ, וְרַבּוֹתֵינוּ דָּרְשׁוּ בִּמְנָחוֹת (דף לז:) בִּגְזֵירָה שָׁוָה "בֵּין עֵינֶיךָ" – זֶה קָדְקֹד, מָקוֹם שֶׁמּוֹחוֹ שֶׁל תִּינוֹק רוֹפֵס. וְ"עַל יָדְךָ" – גּוֹבַהּ הַיָּד, קִיבּוֹרֶת בְּרֹאשׁ הַזְּרוֹעַ, שֶׁתְּהֵא שִׂימָה כְּנֶגֶד הַלֵּב: עַל בֵּית אוּנְקְלִי. עַל בֵּית יָד לְבוּשׁוֹ מִבַּחוּץ: הֲרֵי זֶה דֶּרֶךְ חִיצוֹנִים. בְּנֵי אָדָם הַהוֹלְכִים אַחֲרֵי דַּעְתָּם חוּץ מִדַּעַת חֲכָמִים, דְּבָעֵינַן "לְךָ לְאוֹת" וְלֹא לַאֲחֵרִים לְאוֹת (שם): צִיפָּן זָהָב. נַמִי כְּתִיב "לְמַעַן תִּהְיֶה תּוֹרַת ה' בְּפִיךָ" (שמות יג), שֶׁיְּהֵא הַכֹּל מִבְּהֵמָה טְהוֹרָה: **גמ'** שֶׁמָּא מִינוּת נִזְרְקָה בּוֹ. כּוֹמְרִין תַּלְמִידֵי יֵשׁוּ הַנּוֹצְרִי מַקְפִּידִין בְּכָךְ: בְּתִפְרָן וּבַאֲלַכְסוֹנָן. כְּשֶׁהוּא תּוֹפֵר בֵּית מוֹשָׁבָן צָרִיךְ לִיזָּהֵר שֶׁלֹּא יְקַלְקֵל רִיבּוּעָן בִּמְשִׁיכַת חוּט הַתְּפִירָה, וְצָרִיךְ שֶׁיְּהֵא לָהֶן אֲלַכְסוֹן כְּהִלְכָתוֹ (ג) בִּמְרוּבָּע, שֶׁתְּהֵא אֶצְבַּע בְּרוֹחַב וּבְאוֹרֶךְ, שֶׁיְּהֵא אֶצְבַּע וּשְׁנֵי חוּמְשִׁין בַּאֲלַכְסוֹן: כִּי אַמְגּוּזָא. עֲגוּלּוֹת כֶּאֱגוֹז. אֲבָל עֲגוּלָּה כְּבֵיצָה וְכַעֲדָשָׁה – שַׁפִּיר דָּמֵי, וְלָא תְּסַיְּיעָא לְבָרַיְיתָא מִמַּתְנִיתִין:

מתני'

עין משפט נר מצוה

סז א מיי' פט"ו מהל' תפלה הלכה ב סמג עשין ב טוש"ע א"ח סי' קכח סעיף ל:

סח ב מיי' שם טוש"ע שם סעיף לב:

סט ג ד מיי' שם טוש"ע שם סעיף ל:

[עי' תוס' ב"מ שתירצו באופן אחר]

ע ה מיי' שם הלכה א טוש"ע שם סעיף לג:

[תוספ' פ"ג]

עא ו מיי' פ"ח שם הלכה יב טוש"ע א"ח סי' נג סעיף יב:

עב ז ח מיי' פט"ו שם הלכה ב טוש"ע א"ח סי' קכח סעיף ל:

עג ט מיי' שם טוש"ע שם סעיף לב:

עד י מיי' פ"י שם הלכה ה טוש"ע א"ח סי' נג סעיף יח:

עה כ מיי' פ"ד מהל' תפילין הלכה ג:

עו ל מיי' פ"ג שם הלכה טו טוש"ע א"ח סי' לב סעיף מח:

עז מ מיי' שם הלכה א טוש"ע שם סעיף לט:

רבינו חננאל

קטן קורא בתורה ומתרגם. פוחח פורס על שמע שיקרא יוצר אור שתים לפני א) התיבה להתפלל י"ח ברכות בצבור ואינו נושא את כפיו משום כבוד צבור פי' פוחח לבוש בגד קרוע ואין בבגדיו בתי ידים אלא ידיו כמו ערומות כמה דמתרגמינן (ישעי' כ') כמה דמהלך עבדי ישעיהו פחח ויחף תלת שנין: ירושלמי סוף משקין מת לו מת קורע. מת לו מת אחר מרחיק ג' אצבעות וקורע שלמו מלפניו מתחיל מלאחריו שלמו מלמעלה מתחיל מלמטה שלמו אלו ואלו ר' חייא בר אדא דמן יפו אמר נעשה כפוחח. סומא פורס על שמע ומתרגם ר' יהודה אומר כל שלא ראה מימיו לא יפרוס את שמע כלומר לא יברך בא"י יוצר המאורות שלא נהנה ונמצא מוציא שם שמים לבטלה. ר' שמעון בר ר' הוה קליה עב ואמר לו ר' חייא שלא היה יכול לקרות חי"ת אלא היה קורא לחיתי"ן ב) היהי"ן לפיכך א"ל כשאתה מגיע לקרוא וחכיתי לה' נמצא שונא ישראל מוציאן בלשון הכאה ונמצא מחרף ומגדף. תניא זבלגן לא ישא את כפיו. ואם היה דש בעירו מותר. פי' דש בעירו ידוע ומפורסם. העו[שה] תפלתו עגולה פי' העושה תפילין עגולין כאגוז אלא תנינן תפילין מרובעות הל"מ. ואמר רבא בתופרן ובאלכסונן. ג) פי' פעמים שנופל על פניו ברחום וחנון ואם הן תפילין על ראשו עגולין יר[ד] מוחו. וזו היא סכנה. ואין מצותן אלא מרובעות נתנה על מצחו או על פס ידו הרי זו דרך המינות. ציפה זהב ונתנה על בית יד של אונקלו פי' אצילי ידיו הרי זה דרך החיצו[נים] א"ר

א) נ"ל ואינו עובר לפני התיבה וכו'. ב) מלשון רבינו משמע דר"ח אמר כן לר"ש בר ר' דלא כמו דאיתא בגמ' לפנינו ואולי דגי' אחרת היה לו וצ"ע. ג) נראה דצ"ל סכנה ואין בה מצוה פי' וכו'.

שוליים

[ועמ"ש תוס' בחגיגה ד"ה בכהנים וכו' לד פרש"י דהכא והתו[ם] הטעם ע"פ הירוש[למי] משום היסח הדעת ע'[...]]

[פירוש בהבנת הלב תוס' ע"ז כח: ד"ה שור דעינא ולדעת רש"י אב דליבא הן טרפשי הלב]

[דיבור זה שייך קודם בוהקניות]

[גי' סה"מ ורמב"ם ור[...] אסטים ופואה ו[...] אסטים וקוצה]

[נ"ל ובישני]

[ברכות לב.]

[שייך לעיל במשנה]

הגהות הב"ח

(א) גמ' (תנא מ[ומין] שאמרו בפניו ידיו ור[גליו] תא"מ ונ"ב הרא"ש ו[...] לא גרסי הך ברייתא אלפס גרס לה ועי' ב[...] א"ח סי' קכח: (ב) ר[ש"י] ד"ה דש בעירו וכו' רגיל כמו: (ג) ד"ה ב[תפרן] וכו' אלכסון כהלכתו ש[...] מרובע אצבע:

גליון הש"ס

גמ' משום כבוד [צבור] לעיל דף כג ע"א יומא [...] ע ע"א גיטין דף ס [...] סוטה דף לט ע"ב: [...] אלמלי. עי' לעיל דף [...] ע"א תוס' ד"ה אל[...] מתני' ציפן [...] סנהדרין דף מח ע"[ב]

*"יברכוך טובים" — הרי זו דרך *המינות, א"על קן צפור יגיעו רחמיך" ו"על טוב יזכר שמך", ב"מודים מודים" — משתקין אותו. המכנה בעריות — משתקין אותו, האומר: °"ומזרעך לא תתן להעביר למולך" "לא תתן לאעברא בארמיותא" — משתקין אותו בנזיפה.§ **גמ'** *בשלמא "מודים מודים" — דמיחזי כשתי רשויות, ו"על טוב יזכר שמך" נמי, דמשמע: על טוב — אין, ועל רע — לא, ותנן: *גחייב אדם לברך על הרעה כשם שהוא מברך על הטובה. אלא, "על קן צפור יגיעו רחמיך" מ"ט?(א) פליגי בה תרי אמוראי במערבא: ר' יוסי בר אבין ור' יוסי בר זבידא, חד אמר: מפני שמטיל קנאה במעשה בראשית, וחד אמר: מפני שעושה מדותיו של הקב"ה רחמים, ואינן אלא גזירות. ההוא דנחית קמיה דרבה, אמר: אתה חסת על קן צפור אתה חוס ורחם עלינו, (*אתה חסת על אותו ואת בנו אתה חוס ורחם עלינו) אמר רבה: כמה ידע האי מרבנן לרצויי למריה! א"ל אביי: והא "משתקין אותו" תנן! *ורבה? לחדודי לאביי הוא דבעא. ההוא דנחית קמיה דרבי חנינא, דאמר: האל הגדול הגבור והנורא האדיר והחזק והאמיץ. אמר ליה: סיימתינהו לשבחיה דמרך?! השתא הני תלתא, אי לאו דכתבינהו משה באורייתא ואתו(ב) כנסת הגדולה ותקנינהו, אנן לא אמרינן להו, ואת אמרת כולי האי? משל לאדם שהיו לו אלף אלפי אלפים דינרי זהב, והיו מקלסין אותו (באלף) דינרי כסף. לא *גנאי הוא לו? אמר רבי חנינא: ההכל בידי שמים, חוץ מיראת שמים, שנאמר °"ועתה ישראל מה ה' אלהיך שואל מעמך כי אם ליראה". מכלל דיראה מילתא זוטרתי היא? אין, לגבי משה רבינו מילתא זוטרתי היא, משל לאדם שמבקשין הימנו כלי גדול ויש לו — דומה עליו ככלי קטן, קטן ואין לו — דומה עליו ככלי גדול. *אמר רבי זירא: והאומר "שמע שמע" כאומר "מודים מודים" דמי. מיתיבי: הקורא את שמע וכופלה — הרי זה מגונה. מגונה הוא דהוי, שתוקי לא משתקינן ליה! לא קשיא: הא — דאמר מילתא מילתא ותני לה, הא — דאמר פסוקא פסוקא ותני לה. א"ל רב פפא לרבא — ודלמא מעיקרא לא כיון דעתיה והשתא כיון דעתיה? אמר ליה: חברותא כלפי שמיא?! אי לא מכוין דעתיה — מחינא ליה בארזפתא דנפחא עד דמכוין דעתיה.§ "המכנה בעריות משתקין אותו".§ תנא רב יוסף: קלון אביו וקלון אמו.§ "האומר ומזרעך לא תתן להעביר" וכו'.§ תנא דבי רבי ישמעאל: בישראל הבא על הנכרית והוליד ממנה בן לע"ז הכתוב מדבר.§ **מתני'** זמעשה ראובן נקרא ולא מתרגם, מעשה תמר נקרא ומתרגם, מעשה עגל הראשון נקרא ומתרגם והשני נקרא ולא מתרגם. ברכת כהנים, מעשה דוד ואמנון(ג) — *נקראין ולא מתרגמין. אין מפטירין במרכבה, ורבי יהודה מתיר. ר' אליעזר אומר: אין מפטירין °ב"הודע את ירושלם".§ **גמ'** תנו רבנן: *יש נקרין ומתרגמין, ויש נקרין ולא מתרגמין,[א] ויש לא נקרין ולא מתרגמין. אלו נקרין ומתרגמין.§ בל"ת עק"ן נשפ"ה סימן.§ מעשה בראשית נקרא ומתרגם. פשיטא! מהו דתימא: אתו לשיולי מה למעלה מה למטה, ומה

(ויקרא יח) (דברים י) (יחזקאל טז) — תורה אור

רש"י

מתני' יברכוך טובים ה"ז דרך מינות. שאינו כולל רשעים בשבחו של מקום, וחכמים למדו (כריתות דף ו:) מחלבנה שריחה רע ומנאה הכתוב בין סממני הקטורת, שמצריכן הכתוב בהרצאתן להיותן באגודה אחת: על קן צפור יגיעו רחמיך. (ד) כלשון הזה: רחמיך מגיעין על קן צפור, כך חוס ורחם עלינו: ועל טוב יזכר שמך. על טובותיך נודה לך. או שאמר שני פעמים 'מודים' כשהוא כורע — משתקין אותו. ובגמרא מפרש לה: המכנה בעריות. בגמרא מפרש שדורש פרשת עריות בכינוי, ואומר: לא ערוה ממש דיבר הכתוב, אלא כינה הכתוב בלשונו וקרא אותה ערוה, המגלה קלון אביו וקלון אמו ברבים. כינוי הוא לשון היפך, שמהפך דיבורו לשבח או לגנאי, והרבה יש בלשון חכמים. בספרי: "אספה לי שבעים איש" (במדבר יא) "ואל אראה ברעתי" (שם) — ברעתם היה לו לומר, אלא שכינה הכתוב. כיוצא בדבר "וימירו את כבודם בתבנית שור אוכל עשב" (תהלים קו) — כבודי היה לו לומר, אלא שכינה הכתוב: האומר ומזרעך לא תתן להעביר למולך. לא תבא על הנכרית ותוליד בן לע"ז: משתקין אותו בנזיפה. שעוקר הכתוב ממשמעו שהוא עבודת חוק לאמוריים להעביר בניהן לאש, ונותן כרת לבא על הנכרית, ומחייב חטאת על השוגג ומיתת ב"ד על המזיד בהתראה: **גמ'** כשתי רשויות. ומקבל ומודה אלוה אחר אלוה: על הרעה. "ברוך דיין האמת": על הטובה. "ברוך הטוב והמטיב": מטיל קנאה. לומר: על העופות חס, ועל הבהמות וחיות אינו חס: ואינן אלא גזירת מלך. להטיל עלינו עולו, להודיע שאנחנו עבדיו ושומרי מצותיו: דכתבינהו משה בתורה. "האל הגדול הגבור והנורא אשר לא ישא פנים" (דברים י): אנשי כנסת הגדולה. בספר עזרא (נחמיה ט) "ועתה אלהינו האל הגדול הגבור והנורא שומר הברית והחסד": חוץ מיראת שמים. אותה מסורה בידי אדם, שיהא הוא עצמו מכין לבו לכך. אע"ג שהיכולת בידו להכין לבבו אליו, דכתיב "הנה כחומר ביד היוצר כן אתם בידי בית ישראל" (ירמיה יח), ואומר "והסירותי את לב האבן מבשרכם" (יחזקאל לו): אמר מילתא מילתא ותני לה. כל תיבה אומר ושונה — אין כאן משמעות שתי רשויות, אלא מגונה וסכל הוא: חברותא כלפי שמיא. וכי כמנהג חבירו נוהג בהקב"ה לדבר לפניו שלא במתכוין, וחוזר ומרצה לו בכופלו שלא כיון בראשונה? מרזפתא. מרטי"ל בלע"ז. "ותשם את המקבת" מתרגמינן: מרזפתא (שופטים ד): תני רב יוסף. לפרושי מכנה דמתני', כדמתרגם "ערות אביך וערות אמך" — קלנא דאבוך וקלנא דאמך, ולא תגלה שום דבר קלון שבהן: תנא דבי רבי ישמעאל. לפרש מתני' בישראל הבא על הכותית הכתוב מדבר: **מתני'** מעשה ראובן. "וישכב את בלהה פילגש אביו" (בראשית לה): נקרא. בבית הכנסת: ולא מתרגם. חיישינן לגנותו: מעשה תמר. ויהודה: ומעשה עגל הראשון. כל פרשת העגל עד א]"ואשליכהו באש" (שמות לב). ומה שחזר אהרן וספר המעשה הוא קרוי "מעשה עגל השני", הוא שכתוב בו "ויצא העגל הזה"(ה). ולא יתרגם, פן יטעו עמי הארץ ויאמרו ממש היה בו, שיצא מאליו. אבל המקרא אין מבינין: "הודע את ירושלם. את תועבותיה", פרשה היא ביחזקאל: **גמ'** ויש לא נקרין ולא מתרגמין. מפרש בסיפא: מעשה דוד ואמנון לא נקרין בהפטרה: מעשה בראשית כו'. ואמרינן במסכת חגיגה (דף יא:), המסתכל בארבעה דברים ראוי לו כאילו לא בא לעולם, והתם *מפרש טעמא: אין רצונו של מלך שיזכירו שמו על אשפה כו':

קמ"ל

תוספות

יברכוך טובים. פי': שמוציא את הפושעים מן הכלל. אי נמי: משום דמחזי כשתי רשויות, כלומר: אלהים טובים:

מפני שעושה מדותיו של הקב"ה רחמים והן אינם אלא גזירות. *ק' להר"ר אלחנן על מה *שיסד הקליר בקדושת' שאנו אומרים ביום ב' של פסח: לדקו אותו ואת בנו(ו) לא תשחטו ביום אחד. דמשמע שר"ל שהקב"ה חס על אותו ואת בנו, והוא אינו אלא גזירה:

הכל בידי שמים חוץ מיראת שמים. קשה: דהא בפרק "אלו נערות" (כתובות דף ל. ושם) אמרינן: הכל בידי שמים חוץ מצנים ופחים! ונראה דהכא מיירי בתולדות האדם, אם יהיה חכם או טפש עני או עשיר גבור או חלש, *דהכל נגזר עליו חוץ מן היראה, כדכתיב "אל יתהלל (ז)עשיר בעשרו והגבור בגבורתו כי אם בזאת יתהלל המתהלל השכל וידוע אותי" (ירמיה ט). והתם מיירי במאורעות האדם העתידות לבא אליו אחר שנולד, שגם הם בידי שמים חוץ מצנים ופחים. פירוש: הקור והחום. ולא קשה מהא דכתיב "לפני קרתו מי יעמוד" (תהלים קמז), דה"פ: אם ישלחנה בפעם אחת. כדכתיב בראש הפסוק "משליך קרחו כפתים". וגם לא קשה מהא דכתיב "ואין נסתר מחמתו" (שם יט) — דההיא בעוברי דרכים הוא דקאמר, אבל כל זמן שהוא בביתו — ודאי יכול הוא לינצל ממנו:

אין מפטירין במרכבה ורבי יהודה מתיר. וקיימא לן כר' יהודה:

מה

עין משפט נר מצוה

עח א מיי' פ"ט מהל' תפלה הלכה ז:

[עי' תוי"ט פ"ה דברכות מ"ג]

[גי' רמב"ם דרך הצדוקים]

עט ב מיי' שם הלכה ד טוש"ע א"ח סימן קכא סעיף ב:

פ ג מיי' פ"י מהלכות ברכות הל' ג סמג עשין כז טוש"ע שם סימן רכב סעיף ג:

פא ד מיי' פ"ט מהל' תפלה הלכה ז:

פב ה מיי' פ"ה מהל' תשובה הלכה ב:

[נדה טז: ע"ש בתוס']

פג ו מיי' פ"ב מהלכות ק"ש הלכה יא סמג עשין יח טוש"ע א"ח סימן סא סעיף ט:

פד ז מיי' פי"ב מהל' תפלה הלכה יב סמג עשין יט:

רבינו חננאל

א"ר חנינא הכל בידי שמים חוץ מיראת שמים שנאמר מה ה' אלהיך שואל מעמך וגו'. וכי שואל אדם דבר שאינו ברשותו אלא מיכן ראיה שיראת שמים בידו של אדם היא. פי' ארזפתא דנפחי קורנס של נפחים. המכנה בעריות. כלומר הקורא *) הפסיק ערות אביו ואמו לא יגלה ערות אביך וערות אמך כדכתב קרא וכן כל עריות משתקין אותו ואומר לו קרוא הפסוק כמו שכתב וכי אתה מברר מילין מה שלא בירר משה רבינו ברוה"ק. מעשה ראובן נקרא ולא מיתרגם עד קללות וברכות ניקרין ומתרגמין. ולא יהא אחד מתחיל ואחד

*) כלומר שקורא הפסוק ערות אביך וערות אמך ערות אביו וערות אמו לא יגלה וכן כל עריות וכו' ומפרש כפי' הרמב"ם בפירוש המשניות וכן משמע קצת גם בערוך ערך כן.

הגהות הב"ח

(א) גמ' מאי טעמא לא פליגו בה: (ב) שם ואתו אנשי כנסת הגדולה ותקניינהו אנן לא הוה אמרינן: (ג) במשנה מעשה דוד ואמנון לא נקראין: (ד) רש"י ד"ה על קן צפור יגיעו רחמיך לשון הווה רחמיך: (ה) ד"ה מעשה עגל וכו' העגל הזה נקרא ולא מתרגם: (ו) תוס' ד"ה מפני וכו' אותו ואת בנו ביום אחד בל תשחטו דמשמע כצ"ל: (ז) ד"ה הכל וכו' כדכתיב אל יתהלל חכם בחכמתו אל יתהלל עשיר בעשרו:

גליון הש"ס

גמ' גנאי הוא לו. עיין לעיל דף יח ע"א: **תוס'** ד"ה מפני. שיסד הקליר עיין חגיגה דף יג ע"א תוס' ד"ה ורגלי החיות:

מסורת הש"ס

ברכות לג. ע"ש

שם לג:

שם נד.

[בברכות ובע"י ליתא]

[ברכות לג: וש"נ]

ברכות לג: ע"ש נדה טז:

ברכות לג: [סוכה נג:]

[ברכות לד.]

[עי' תוי"ט]

[תוספתא פ"ג]

[דף טז.]

הגהות הגר"א

[א] גמ' ויש לא נקרין ולא מתרגמין תא"מ:

הגהות מהר"ב רנשבורג

א] רש"י ד"ה מעשה תמר ו' עד ואשליכהו. מלת ואשליכהו נמחק וצ"ב ויש"ף:

ומה לפנים ומה לאחור, קמ"ל. "מעשה לוט ושתי בנותיו נקרא ומתרגם". פשיטא! מהו דתימא: ניחוש לכבודו דאברהם, קמ"ל. "מעשה תמר ויהודה נקרא ומתרגם", פשיטא! מהו דתימא: ליחוש לכבודו דיהודה, קמ"ל: שבחיה הוא דאודי. "מעשה עגל הראשון נקרא ומתרגם" פשיטא! מהו דתימא: ליחוש לכבודן של ישראל, קמ"ל: כל שכן דניחא להו דהויא להו כפרה. "קללות וברכות נקרין ומתרגמין", פשיטא! מהו דתימא: ניחוש דלמא (א)*פייגא דעתייהו דצבורא, קמ"ל. "אזהרות ועונשין נקרין ומתרגמין", פשיטא! מהו דתימא: ניחוש דלמא אתו למעבד מיראה, קמ"ל. "מעשה אמנון ותמר נקרא ומתרגם", ["מעשה אבשלום נקרא ומתרגם"] פשיטא! מהו דתימא: ליחוש ליקריה דדוד, קמ"ל. "מעשה פילגש בגבעה נקרא ומתרגם", פשיטא! מהו דתימא: ליחוש לכבודו דבנימין, קמ"ל. (יחזקאל טז) °"הודע את ירושלם את תועבותיה נקרא ומתרגם", פשיטא! לאפוקי מדרבי אליעזר. דתניא: *מעשה באדם אחד שהיה קורא למעלה מרבי אליעזר "הודע את ירושלם את תועבותיה", אמר לו: עד שאתה בודק בתועבות ירושלים — צא ובדוק בתועבות אמך. בדקו אחריו ומצאו בו שמץ פסול.§ "ואלו נקרין ולא מתרגמין" (רעבד"ן סימן) "מעשה ראובן נקרא ולא מתרגם". ומעשה ברבי חנינא בן גמליאל שהלך לכבול, והיה קורא חזן הכנסת (בראשית לה) °"ויהי בשכון ישראל" ואמר לו למתורגמן: (*הפסק), אל תתרגם אלא אחרון, ושיבחוהו חכמים. "מעשה עגל השני נקרא ולא מתרגם". איזה מעשה עגל השני? (שמות לב) מן °"ויאמר משה" עד "וירא משה" תניא, ר"ש בן אלעזר אומר: לעולם יהא אדם זהיר בתשובותיו, שמתוך תשובה שהשיבו אהרן למשה פקרו המערערים, (שם) שנאמר °"ואשליכהו באש ויצא העגל הזה".§ "ברכת כהנים נקרין ולא מתרגמין". מ"ט? משום דכתיב (במדבר ו) °"ישא".§ [א]"מעשה דוד ואמנון [א]לא נקרין ולא מתרגמין". והא אמרת מעשה אמנון ותמר נקרא ומתרגם! לא קשיא: [א]הא — דכתיב אמנון בן דוד, הא — דכתיב אמנון סתמא. ת"ר: *כל המקראות הכתובין בתורה לגנאי קורין אותן לשבח, כגון (דברים כח) °"ישגלנה" — "ישכבנה", (שם) °"בעפולים" — "בטחורים", (מ"ב ו) °"חריונים" — "דביונים", (שם יח) °"לאכול את חוריהם ולשתות את מימי שיניהם" — "לאכול את צואתם ולשתות את מימי רגליהם", (שם י) °"למחראות" — "למוצאות". ר' יהושע בן קרחה אומר: למחראות — כשמן, מפני שהוא גנאי לעבודה זרה. *אמר רב נחמן: כל ליצנותא אסירא [ב]בר מליצנותא דעבודה זרה דשריא, דכתיב (ישעיה מו) °"כרע בל קרס נבו" וכתיב (שם) °"קרסו כרעו יחדיו לא יכלו מלט משא" וגו'. ר' ינאי אמר מהכא: (הושע י) °"לעגלות בית און יגורו שכן שומרון כי אבל עליו עמו וכמריו עליו יגילו על כבודו כי גלה ממנו", אל תקרי "כבודו" אלא כבידו. אמר רב הונא בר מנוח משמיה דרב אחא בריה דרב איקא: שרי ליה לבר ישראל למימר ליה לנכרי שקליה לעבודה זרה ואנחיה בשין תיו שלו. אמר רב אשי: האי מאן דסנאי שומעניה שרי ליה לבזוייה בגימ"ל ושי"ן. האי מאן דשפיר שומעניה — שרי לשבוחיה, ומאן דשבחיה — *ינוחו לו ברכות על ראשו.§

הדרן עלך הקורא את המגילה עומד

בני העיר שמכרו רחובה של עיר — לוקחין בדמיו בית הכנסת, [ג]בית הכנסת — לוקחין תיבה, תיבה — לוקחין מטפחות, מטפחות — יקחו

רש"י

קמ"ל שבחו הוא. שבח הוא ליהודה המקרייה: דאודי. שהודה (ב)מחטאו: מאהבה. של ברכות: ומיראה. של קללות, ואין לבן לשמים: פייגי דעתייהו. יחלוש דעתן כששמעו שיהו נענשין, ויאמרו: טוב ליהנות מן העולם הזה בכל רצוננו, הואיל וסופנו ליענש: אל תתרגם אלא אחרון. "ויהיו בני יעקב שנים עשר". והפסוק הזה נפסק בהפסק פרשה, לכך קורהו אחרון, כאילו הוא פסוק לעצמו: מן "ויאמר משה אל אהרן. מה עשה לך העם הזה"(ג): פקרו המינין. העיזו פניהם, לומר יש ממש בע"ז: משום ישא. שלא יאמרו: הקב"ה נושא להן פנים. ואינן יודעין שכדאי הן ישראל לשאת להן פנים, כדאמרינן בברכות (דף כ:): לא כדאי הם ישראל לשאת להן פנים? אני אמרתי "ואכלת ושבעת וברכת" (דברים ח), והן מחמירין על עצמן עד כזית עד כביצה: ישגלנה. לשון משכב, כדכתיב "והשגל יושבת אצלו" (נחמיה ב). וי"מ: *כלבתא: בעפולים. לשון מפורש הוא לגנאי יותר מטחורים, ושניהן בנקב בית הריעי: חריונים. חרי לשון ריעי: דביונים. הזב מן היונים, שלא לפרש שהיו ישראל אוכלין גלליהן בשומרון: את חוריהם. ריעי היוצא דרך הנקב: מימי שיניהם. שינים יש לברכשתא, ויוצא לחה ורכה קרויה מימי שיניהן: למחראות. גבי עבודה זרה כתיב בספר מלכים, כי חור לשון מוצא ריעי הוא: לעגלות בית און. לקול השמועה הבאה על עגלי בית און יגורו שכיניהם שבשומרון, כי אבל עליו על העגל: וכמריו (ד)(אשר) עליו יגילו. אשר היו רגילין לשמוח עליו, עתה יתאבלו על כבודו כי גלה ממנו: אלא כבידו. כובד משאו של ריעי *תהיה בו, וכובד עגבותיו. ודומה לו בספר ישעיה (*"כרעו קרסו) יחדיו לא יכלו מלט משא" וגו' — הוא משא של ריעי. ורבותי מפרשין: וכמריו עליו יגילו — ממש, לשון שמחה, שהיכל משאוי שלהן. אבל אין לפרש כן, שהעגל כולו גלה כאחד, שנטלו סנחריב: שי"ן ותי"ו. לשון "וחשופי שת ערות מצרים" (ישעיה כ): דסני שומעניה. שיוצאות עליו שמועות רעות ושנואות, שהוא נואף: בג' ושי"ן. (ה)בר גירתא — זונה, שמה סריי = שם מוסרת. כך הוא בתשובות הגאונים. מותר לבזות גם את אמו שילדתו. ורבותי מפרשים: גיופא שייטא שטייא:

הדרן עלך הקורא את המגילה עומד

בני העיר שמכרו רחובה של עיר. יש בו קדושה, כדמפרש בגמ' הואיל ומתפללין בו בתעניות ובמעמדות: לוקחין

תוספות

מה לפנים מה לאחור. פי': *מה בסוף גבולי העולם למזרח ולמערב. א"נ: מה היה קודם ששת ימי בראשית, ומה יהיה אחר שיכלה העולם: *מעשה של עגל השני נקרא ולא מתרגם. פירש רש"י: שלא יאמרו ממשות היה בו, מדקאמר אהרן "ויצא העגל הזה". וקשה: דהא בירושלמי פליגי אמוראי, ואיכא מאן דאמר מן ויאמר "עד לשמצה בקמיהם" (*היה) מעשה עגל השני, והיינו סיפיה דקרא ד"וירא משה", ולפרש"י לא היה לו לומר אלא עד תחלת הפסוק! לכן נראה כדמפרש בירושלמי, דהטעם הוי לפי שאין דומה גנאי של יחיד ביחיד, או של צבור בצבור, לגנאי של יחיד בצבור, ומשום כבודו של אהרן לא רצו לתרגם:

הדרן עלך הקורא את המגילה עומד

בני העיר *הואיל והעם מתפללין בו בתעניות ובמעמדות. לא גרס ובמעמדות, שהרי גבי מעמדות לא מצינו רחוב, אלא לבית הכנסת היו הולכין, כדתניא בפ' בתרא דתענית (דף כו.): כיון

עין משפט נר מצוה

[עיין תוס' חגיגה יא: ד"ה יכול]

[שייך לעיל במשנה]

פה א מיי' פי"ב מהל' תפלה הל' יב סמג עשין יט:

[נ"ל היא]

פו ב טוש"ע י"ד סימן קמז סעיף ה:
א ג מיי' פי"א מהל' תפלה הל' יד טור ש"ע א"ח סימן קנג סעיף ב:

[מפרש"י נראה דגריס דלמא אתו למעבד מאהבה ומיראה ולקמן גבי אזהרות ועונשין גרס דלמא פייגי דעתייהו וכ"כ מהרש"א וע"ע בע"י]

רבינו חננאל

גומר אלא המתחיל הוא גומר את כולם תניא לעולם יהא אדם זהיר בתשובותיו שמתוך תשובה שמשיב אהרן אל משה פקרו המינין שנאמר ואשליכהו באש ויצא העגל הזה. ברכת כהנים נקרא ולא מיתרגם. מ"ט משום ישא ה' פניו אליך: ירושלמי לא נקראין. ר' בא בעא מר' יוסי מ"ט א"ל כה תברכו לברכה ניתנה ולא לקריאה תוספתא מעשה דוד בבת שבע לא נקראין ולא מתרגמין והסופר מלמד כדרכו תנו רבנן כל המקראות שכתובים לגניי כגון ישגלנה קורין אותה ישכבנה וכגון בעפולים קורין אותם בטחורים חריונים קורין אותן דביונים וחוריהן קורין אותם צואתם ולמחראות קורין אותן למוצאות אלו בלשון הקודש הן גניי גדול בלשון הזה לפיכך משנים אותם שלא להוציא דבר מגונה מפיו אמר רב נחמן כל ליצנותא אסורה בר ליצנותא דעבודה זרה דכתיב כרע בל קרס נבו וכתיב קרסו כרעו יחדו וגו'. ר' ינאי אומר מהכא על כבודו כי גלה ממנו כלומר עמו של עגל מתאבלין והכומרים שהיו עליו מגילין עכשיו מתעצבין על כבודו כי גלה כלומר לקה בכבידו וחלה וגלה הכבד שלו ניטל כולו בדרך ליצנות כיון שאינו יכול להועיל ניטל כבידו. שרי לעובד כוכבים למימר שקליה לעבודה זרה ואנחיה בשת שלך דכתיב וחשופי שת ערות מצרים ופירושו מקום השתנת מי רגלים ובתחת מקום הצואה. ואמר רב אשי מאן דסני שומעניה כגון השותה בד' מיני זמר וכיוצא בו כ
שמצינו באלישע אחר שהוציאוהו אלו הדברים לתרבות רעה ומפורש בחגיגה וכ"ש בדבר שהוא יותר מזה שרי לבזוייה בשי"ן וגימ"ל כלומר כל מי ששמעו רע מותר לבזותו בן זונה דגיירא וגיירתי ונגלו שוליך ונחמ
עקביך ופי' בן גויה בן עכו"ם. כדגרסינן כמאן קרינא לרשיעא בר צדיקא רשיעא בר רשיעא כי האי תנא כו' א) ר' יהודה בן קרחה אומר וישימם למחוראות קורין אותן ככתבו מפני שגנייי לע"ז הוא. הכת
ליחיד אין מכנין אותו לרבים כתוב לרבים אין מכנים אותו ליחיד ר"י אומר המתרגם פסוק בצורתו הרי זה בדאי והמוסיף הרי זה מגדף פירוש המתרגם ב) השם בצורתו בדאי והמוסיף עליו זולתי התרגום שלנו ה
זה מגדף. תורגמן העומד לפני חכם אינו ג) אביו או רבו: ירושלמי תפילין ומזוזה מי קודם שמואל אמר מזוזה קודמת שכן נוהגת בשבתות ובי"ט משא"כ בתפילין רב הונא אמר תפילין קודמין שנוהגין במפר
ימים והולכי מדברות משא"כ במזוזה. מתניתין מסייעא לשמואל תפלה שבלו עושין אותה מזוזה מזוזה שבלה אין עושין אותה תפלה למה שמעלין בקדש ולא מורידין: הדרן עלך הקורא את המגילה עומ

א) נ"ל תוספתא ר' יהושע בן קרחה אומר וכו'. ב) עי' תוס' קדושין דף מ"ט ד"ה המתרגם מש"כ בשם רבינו ז"ל וע"ע בערוך ערך תרגם. ג) חסר כאן וכן איתא בתוספתא שם אינו רשאי לא לפחות ולא להוסיף ולא לשנות אא"כ יהיה אביו או רבו.

הגהות הב"ח

(א) גמ' וברכות נק ומתרגמין פשיטא מ דתימא ניחוש דלמא ל למיעבד מאהבה ומיר קמ"ל אזהרות ועונ נקרין ומתרגמין פשי מהו דתימא ניחוש דלו פייגא דעתייהו דצבו קמ"ל מעשה אמנון כו' (ב) רש"י ד"ה דאו שהודה על חטאו: (ג) ד מן ויאמר וכו' העם ה שחזר אהרן וספר המע נקרא מעשה העגל ה הס"ד: (ד) ד"ה וכמ עליו כצ"ל ותיבת א נמחק: (ה) ד"ה בגימ ושי"ן. נ"ב בר גיור תרגום ירושלמי הנו והטולפת גיורא וגיורת

[עי' ר"ה ז.]

גליון הש"ס

גמ' דלמא פייגא. ע ברא"ש ויגש פ' מ"ו פס י':

[מס' סופרים פ"ט הי"

[בע"י ליתא]

[נ"ל שהיה]

[נ"ל קרסו כרעו]

[תוספתא פ"ג]

סנהדרין סג: ע"ש

הגהות מהר"ב רנשבורג

א] גמ' מעשה דוד ואמ נקרין ולא מתרגמין כצ"

[ברכות לג. שבת לא. ע ס:]

הגהות הגר"א

[א] גמ' מעשה דוד ואמ (לא) תז"מ (וכגירסא ש במתני' וע' תוי"ט):

(א) יִקְחוּ סְפָרִים, סְפָרִים — לוֹקְחִין תּוֹרָה. אֲבָל אִם מָכְרוּ תּוֹרָה — לֹא יִקְחוּ סְפָרִים, סְפָרִים — לֹא יִקְחוּ מִטְפָּחוֹת, מִטְפָּחוֹת — לֹא יִקְחוּ תֵּיבָה, תֵּיבָה — לֹא יִקְחוּ בֵּית הַכְּנֶסֶת, בֵּית הַכְּנֶסֶת — לֹא יִקְחוּ אֶת הָרְחוֹב, וְכֵן בְּמוֹתְרֵיהֶן.§ **גמ'** בְּנֵי הָעִיר שֶׁמָּכְרוּ רְחוֹבָהּ שֶׁל עִיר. אָמַר רַבָּה בַּר בַּר חָנָה אָמַר רַבִּי יוֹחָנָן: זוֹ דִּבְרֵי ר' מְנַחֵם בַּר יוֹסֵי סְתוּמְתָּאָה, אֲבָל חכ"א: אהָרְחוֹב אֵין בּוֹ מִשּׁוּם קְדוּשָּׁה. וְר' מְנַחֵם בַּר יוֹסֵי מַאי טַעְמֵיהּ? — הוֹאִיל וְהָעָם מִתְפַּלְּלִין בּוֹ בְּתַעֲנִיּוֹת וּבְמַעֲמָדוֹת. — וְרַבָּנַן: הַהוּא אַקְרַאי בְּעָלְמָא.§ "בֵּית הַכְּנֶסֶת לוֹקְחִין תֵּיבָה".§ אָמַר רַבִּי שְׁמוּאֵל בַּר נַחְמָנִי א"ר יוֹנָתָן: בלֹא שָׁנוּ אֶלָּא בֵּית הַכְּנֶסֶת שֶׁל כְּפָרִים, אֲבָל בֵּית הַכְּנֶסֶת שֶׁל כְּרַכִּין, כֵּיוָן דְּמֵעָלְמָא אָתוּ לֵיהּ — לָא מָצוּ מְזַבְּנֵי לֵיהּ, דַּהֲוָה לֵיהּ דְּרַבִּים. אָמַר רַב אַשִׁי: הַאי בֵּי כְנִישְׁתָּא דְּמָתָא מְחַסְיָא, אַף עַל גַּב דְּמֵעָלְמָא אָתוּ לָהּ, כֵּיוָן דְּאַדַּעְתָּא דִּידִי קָאָתוּ אִי בָּעֵינָא מְזַבְּנִינָא לָהּ. מֵיתִיבִי, *א"ר יְהוּדָה: מַעֲשֶׂה בְּבֵית הַכְּנֶסֶת שֶׁל טוּרְסִיִּים שֶׁהָיָה בִּירוּשָׁלַיִם שֶׁמְּכָרוּהָ לְרַבִּי אֱלִיעֶזֶר, וְעָשָׂה בָּהּ כָּל צְרָכָיו. וְהָא הָתָם דִּכְרַכִּים הֲוָה! הַהִיא בֵּי כְנִישְׁתָּא זוּטֵי הֲוָה, וְאִינְהוּ עֲבָדוּהָ. מֵיתִיבִי: °"בְּבֵית אֶרֶץ אֲחוּזַּתְכֶם" (ויקרא יד) — *גאֲחוּזַּתְכֶם מִיטַּמֵּא בִּנְגָעִים, וְאֵין יְרוּשָׁלַיִם מִיטַּמֵּא בִּנְגָעִים. אָמַר רַבִּי יְהוּדָה: אֲנִי לֹא שָׁמַעְתִּי אֶלָּא מְקוֹם מִקְדָּשׁ בִּלְבָד. הָא בָּתֵּי כְנֵסִיּוֹת וּבָתֵּי מִדְרָשׁוֹת מִיטַּמְּאִין, אַמַּאי? הָא דִּכְרַכִּין הָווּ! אֵימָא: א"ר יְהוּדָה: אֲנִי לֹא שָׁמַעְתִּי אֶלָּא מָקוֹם מְקוּדָּשׁ בִּלְבָד. בְּמַאי קָמִיפַּלְגִי? ת"ק סָבַר: *דלֹא נִתְחַלְּקָה יְרוּשָׁלַיִם לִשְׁבָטִים, וְרַבִּי יְהוּדָה סָבַר: נִתְחַלְּקָה יְרוּשָׁלַיִם לִשְׁבָטִים, וּבִפְלוּגְתָּא דְּהָנֵי תַּנָּאֵי, דְּתַנְיָא: מֶה הָיָה בְּחֶלְקוֹ שֶׁל יְהוּדָה — הַר הַבַּיִת, הַלְּשָׁכוֹת וְהָעֲזָרוֹת. וּמֶה הָיָה בְּחֶלְקוֹ שֶׁל בִּנְיָמִין — אוּלָם וְהֵיכָל וּבֵית קָדְשֵׁי הַקֳּדָשִׁים. וּרְצוּעָה הָיְתָה יוֹצֵאת מֵחֶלְקוֹ שֶׁל יְהוּדָה וְנִכְנֶסֶת בְּחֶלְקוֹ שֶׁל בִּנְיָמִין, וּבָהּ מִזְבֵּחַ בָּנוּי, וְהָיָה בִּנְיָמִין הַצַּדִּיק מִצְטַעֵר עָלֶיהָ בְּכָל יוֹם לְבוֹלְעָהּ, שֶׁנֶּאֱמַר °"חוֹפֵף עָלָיו כָּל הַיּוֹם" (דברים לג), *לְפִיכָךְ זָכָה בִּנְיָמִין וְנַעֲשָׂה אוּשְׁפִּיזְכָן לַשְּׁכִינָה. *וְהַאי תַּנָּא סָבַר: לֹא נִתְחַלְּקָה יְרוּשָׁלַיִם לִשְׁבָטִים. דְּתַנְיָא: *) האֵין מַשְׂכִּירִים בָּתִּים בִּירוּשָׁלַיִם, מִפְּנֵי שֶׁאֵינָן שֶׁלָּהֶן. ר"א **)(בַּר צָדוֹק) אוֹמֵר: אַף לֹא מִטּוֹת. לְפִיכָךְ עוֹרוֹת קָדָשִׁים — בַּעֲלֵי אוּשְׁפִּיזִין נוֹטְלִין אוֹתָן בִּזְרוֹעַ. אָמַר אַבַּיֵי: ש"מ אוֹרַח אַרְעָא לְמִישְׁבַּק אֱינָשׁ גּוּלְפָּא וּמַשְׁכָּא בְּאוּשְׁפִּיזֵיהּ. אָמַר רָבָא ולֹא שָׁנוּ אֶלָּא שֶׁלֹּא מָכְרוּ שִׁבְעָה טוֹבֵי הָעִיר בְּמַעֲמַד אַנְשֵׁי הָעִיר אֲבָל מָכְרוּ שִׁבְעָה טוֹבֵי הָעִיר בְּמַעֲמַד אַנְשֵׁי הָעִיר — אֲפִילּוּ

לְמִישְׁתְּיָא

*) [תוס' מ"ש פט"ז] **) [בתוספתא איתא בר' שמעון]

רש"י

לוקחין ספרים. נביאים וכתובים: אבל מכרו תורה כו'. שמעלין בקדש ולא מורידין – תוספתא: "מעלין בקדש" דכתיב "ויקם משה את המשכן" (שמות מ). בצלאל עשה, ומשה שהיה גדול ממנו הקימו. ולא מורידים – דכתיב "את מחתות החטאים האלה בנפשותם ועשו אותם רקועי פחים צפוי למזבח כי הקריבום לפני ה' ויקדשו" וגו' (במדבר יז), כיון שהוקדשו – הוקדשו. *עד כאן: וכן במותריהן. מכרו ספרים ולקחו מתקנת הדמים תורה – לא יקחו מן המותר דבר שקדושתו פחותה: **גמ'** זו דברי ר' מנחם כו'. בהדיא אמרינן בתוספתא דמגילה (פ"ב) דהוא אמרה: הואיל והעם מתפללים בו בתעניות ובמעמדות. כדתנן במסכת תעניות (דף טו.): עברו אלו ולא נענו – מוציאין את התיבה לרחובה של עיר. – תוספתא. ובמעמדות (ב) תנן: מתכנסין בעריהן וקורין במעשה בראשית. ותניא בגמרא: אנשי מעמד נכנסין לבית הכנסת ויושבין ארבע תעניות בשבת. אפשר בית הכנסת היה להם קבוע ברחובה של עיר ומתכנסין שם המעמד כולו, כדרך ששנינו בביכורים (פ"ג משנה ב): כל העיירות שבמעמד מתכנסין *לעיירות של מעמד, ולנין ברחובה של עיר ולא היו נכנסין לבתים ולנין שם, והיה הממונה אומר "קומו ונעלה ציון אל ה' אלהינו". הא למדת: כינוס עיירות ברחוב היתה, ואקראי הוי, שמעמד (ג) הזה אינו חוזר חלילה עד חצי שנה. ובתלמידי רבינו יצחק הלוי מצאתי: °ובמעמדות לא גרסינן. ומפרש שלא היתה תפלתן ברחוב. עד כאן: אקראי בעלמא. אינו תדיר: לא שנו. דיכולין למכור בית הכנסת אלא של כפרין: אבל של כרכין. הוה להו בתי כנסיות דרבים, והכל בעליהן, ואין בני העיר לבדם בעלים להם: טורסיים. °צורפי נחושת: ואין ירושלים מטמאה בנגעים. דלאו אחוזה היא, כדאמרי' לקמן, דסבירא ליה להאי תנא לא נתחלקה ירושלים לשבטים, ולא נפלה בגורל לא ליהודה ולא לבנימין: אני לא שמעתי. שלא יהא מיטמא אלא מקום מקדש בלבד, משום דבית של קודש הוא, וגבי נגעים "ובא אשר לו הבית" (ויקרא יד) בעינן. אבל ירושלים מיטמא בנגעים, דסבר נתחלקה לשבטים, ו"אחוזתכם" קרינא ליה. קתני מיהת לרבי יהודה דאית ליה נתחלקה, לא שנו אלא מקום מקדש, אבל בתי כנסיות ובתי מדרשות שבה (ד) – כשאר בתי העיר, ואע"ג דשל כרך הוא: מקודש. אף בתי כנסיות משמע: הר הבית. בכניסתו מצד המזרח, כל מה שיש שם פנוי קרוי הר הבית, שאין לה שם אחר: והלשכות. שבתוך החיל: והעזרות. שלשתן, עזרת נשים ועזרת ישראל הן אחת עשרה אמה שישראל רשאין ליכנס לפנים מן השער, ואחריהם לצד מערב לעזרת כהנים י"א אמה שבין דריסת רגלי ישראל למזבח החילון: ומה היה בחלקו של בנימין אולם והיכל. (ה) מצד מערב. עכשיו יותר בנתיים מקום המזבח ל"ב אמה, ובין האולם והמזבח כ"ב אמה שלא פירש של מי הוא. חזר ופירש רצועה יוצאה כו', לימדך כאן: רצועה זו לבדה ליהודה, אבל צפונו של מזבח ודרומו ומערבו – של בנימין. ובמסכת זבחים אמרינן שאין ליהודה באותה הרצועה אלא המזרחית מקום היסוד, ולכך לא היה יסוד למזרחו של מזבח: והיה בנימין הצדיק. צופה ברוח הקדש שכן עתיד להיות, ומצטער עליה: חופף עליו. אדם המצטער חופף ומתחכך בבגדיו. לשון שפשוף, כמו: נזיר חופף ומפספס (נזיר דף מב.): אושפיזכן. שהיה ארון בחלקו: והאי תנא סבר כו'. והיינו תנאי דאמרן לעיל: אין משכירין. בעלי בתים את בתיהם לעולי רגלים, אלא בחנם נותנין להן, ונכנסין לתוכן: עורות קדשים. תודה ושלמים, שהעורות לבעלים: גולפא. קנקן של חרס שנשתמש בו: ומשכא. אם שחט בהמה: לא שנו. דאין מורידין דמים מקדושתן °ובית הכנסת (ו) בחשיבותו עומד אף ביד לוקח, דומיא דספרים לוקח בהן ס"ת, והלה מנהיג ספרים בהווייתן: אלא שלא מכרו. הטובים ברשות העם. [אבל אם מכרו וכו']. פקעה קדושה מן החפץ ומן הדמים, ומותר לעשות מהן כל רצונם. והיינו דבעא מיניה רבינא מרב אשי על תילא דבי כנישתא מהו למיזרעה. אלמא, במכר כל דהו הבית והמעות בקדושתייהו קיימי:

לְמִישְׁתָּא

תוספות

כיון דמעלמא קאתו לה. נראה לפרש הכי: כיון שרוב בני אדם רגילים ללכת שם להתפלל, אף על פי שאין נותנים כלום בבנינו – מכל מקום כיון דלדעת אותן רבים נעשה – חמורה קדושתו ואינן יכולין למוכרו. ועוד יש לפרש: כיון שרבים נותנים בבנינו ובשאר צרכיו. ובסמוך נמי, דקאמר רב אשי דאדעתא דידי קאתו – היינו ממה שנותנים בו לעשות רצונו:

ואמאי והא דכרכים נינהו. משמע דסבירא ליה למקשן דכיון דלא מיזדבני דאין להן ליטמא בנגעים, משום דלא מיקרי "אחוזתכם" וגם לא קרינן ביה "אשר לו הבית". וקשה: דהא בפ"ק דיומא (דף יא.) מחייב ר"מ בית הכנסת של כרכים במזוזה, וגם מוקי ברייתא דהתם דקאמר דבית הכנסת מיטמא בנגעים כוותיה! ועוד קשה: אמאי נקט של כרכים? דהא (ר"מ) *לא מפליג התם בין של כרכים לשל כפרים לענין נגעים ומזוזה! ויש לומר: דודאי המקשן טעה בתרתי: חדא דאין חילוק בין כרכים לשל כפרים כדמסיק התם לרבנן דר"מ, דהיינו ר' יהודה. וגם טעה בהא, דאע"ג דלא מיזדבני – יש להן ליטמא בנגעים לרבי מאיר:

ורצועה יוצאה מחלק יהודה לחלק בנימין ובה היה מזבח בנוי. קשה: דהא בפרק "איזהו מקומן" (זבחים דף נג:) אמר דקרן דרומית מזרחית לא היה יסוד, לפי שלא היה יסוד אלא בחלקו של טורף – (ז) בנימין, דכתיב "בנימין זאב יטרף" (בראשית מט), אלמא שכל המזבח בנוי בחלקו של בנימין! וי"ל: אותו קרן דרומית מזרחית שלא היה בו יסוד שהיה בחלק יהודה על זה היה מצטער בנימין לבולעה, כדי שיהא כל המזבח בחלקו: אף לא המטות. פירש הר"ר יוסף: דסבירא ליה דכיון שהקרקע מקום המטות לא היה מיוחד לבעלים, לא היה כח בידם להשכירם שכירות שלם. ומכל מקום, מחמת מטלטליהם היו נוטלין עורות הקדשים:

אוגורה

עין משפט נר מצוה

ב א מיי' פי"א מהל' תפלה הלכה כא טוש"ע א"ח סי' קנד סעיף א:
ג ב מיי' שם הל' טז טוש"ע שם סי' קנג סעיף ז:
ד ג מיי' פי"ד מהל' טומאת צרעת הלכה יא ופ"ז מהלכות בית הבחירה הלכה יד:
ה ד מיי' שם ופ"ט מהל' רוצח הלכה ד:
ו ה מיי' פ"ז מהלכות בית הבחירה הל' יד:
ז ו מיי' פי"א מהלכות תפלה הלכה יז טוש"ע א"ח סי' קנג סעיף ז:

לא מפליג התם ור"ל למסקנא דהתם החילוק הוא בין אית ביה בית דירה או לא ודכפרים ודכרכים שוה לכ"ע ועי' במהרש"א

מסורת הש"ס

[וכן איתא בהדיא במנחות לט. ויליף דמעלין מאת מחתות החטאים וכו' ודלא מורידין יליף מויקם משה את המשכן וכו' וע"ש בפרש"י ונ"ע וכן בשבת כא: כתב רש"י ד"ה מעלין בקדש ואין מורידין מקראי ילפינן לה במנחות פרק שתי הלחם]

[לעיר של ראש המעמד]

[תוספתא פ"ב]

יומא יב. ב"ק פב:

[סוטה מה.]

יומא יב. זבחים נג: קיח:

[עי' סוטה לז.]

[שנאמר ובין כתפיו שכן כל"ל וכן הוא להדיא הגי' ביומא ובזבחים]

רבינו חננאל

בני העיר שמכרו רחובה של עיר לוקחין בדמיה בית הכנסת כו' אוקימנא א) פיד"ר מל' סתימתאה זו חמשנה אע"פ שהיא סתם משנה אינה לר' מאיר כדקי"ל סתם משנה ר"מ היא ב) אלא ר"ע היא או לר' מנחם ב"ר יוסי זו המשנה והיא שנויה סתם ולא כל דבריהם של חכמים הללו בכל המשנה סתומין הן אלא המשניות שהזכירום בלבד ג) לר' מנחם בר' יוסי סתימתאה דסבר הואיל והעם מתפללין בה בתעניות ובמעמדות יש בה קדושה אבל חכמים אומרים אקראי בעלמא היא. הלכך הרחוב אין בו משום קדושה. בית הכנסת לוקחין תיבה אוקימנא בבית הכנסת של כפרים אבל כנסת של כרכים לא מזדבנא משום שהיא של רבים. אמר רב אשי כנשתא דמתא מחסיא אע"ג דמעלמא קא אתו לה ושל רבים היא כיון דאדעתא דידי אתו אי בעינא מצינא מזביננא לה ובית הכנסת של טרסיים בירושל' שקנאה ר' אלעזר בן עזריה הם עשאוה לעצמן ולא מסרוה לרבים לפיכך מכרוה. ובית הכנסת של כרכין אין מוכרין לפי שאינה שלהן והתניא [אחוזתכם] מטמא בנגעים ואין ירושלים מטמאה בנגעים א"ר יהודה אני לא שמעתי שאין מטמא בנגעים אלא בית המקדש הא בתי כנסיות וירושלים מטמאין אמאי והא דכרכים נינהו ופרקינן אימא לא שמעתי אלא מקום מקודש ואפי' בתי כנסיות במשמע. במאי פליגי ת"ק סבר לא נתחלקה ירושלים לשבטים ואינה אחוזה לפיכך אינה מטמאה ור' יהודה סבר נתחלקה ואחוזתם היא זולתי מקום מקודש וכי הני תנאי מה היה בחלקו של יהודה הר הבית לשכות ועזרות מה היה בחלקו של בנימין כו' האי תנא סבר נתחלקה וחלק יהודה ובנימין היא. והאי תנא סבר לא נתחלקה דתניא אין משכירין בתים בירושלים לפי שאינן שלהן כו' אמר אביי שמע מינה דרך ארץ להניח אכסניא לבעל הבית הקנקן שקנה בו היין ושתאו והעור של כבש שנשחט ואכלו. אמר רבא לא שנו מכרו רחוב לוקחין בדמיו בית הכנסת כך וכך כו' אלא אם לא מכרו ז' טובי העיר במעמד אנשי

א) נ"ל זו דברי ר' מנחם בר"י סתימתאה פי' זו המשנה אע"פ וכו'. ב) נראה דל"ל ולא ר"ע היא אלא לר' מנחם בר"י היא וכו'. ג) אולי נ"ל וטעמיה דר' מנחם בר"י וכו'.

הגהות הב"ח

(א) במשנה לוקחין ספרים: (ב) רש"י ד"ה תוספתא ובמעמדות והא דתנן וכו' אפשר דבית הכנסת וכו' נכנסין לבתים ולמשכים היה הממונה כו' כל"ל ותיבות ולנין שם נמחק ונ"ב פי' כל אנשי העיירות של אנשי מעמד מתכנסין לעיר של ראש המעמד: (ג) בא"ד ואקראי הוה שמעמד הזה. נ"ב [חסר ההתחלה ונשאר זה הלשון] הכא בביכורים דמתכנסין לעיר של מעמד ולנין ברחובה של עיר קמיירי הכא דהיו מתפללין בצבור ברחובה של עיר באותן הימים שהיו לנין שם ואקראי בעלמא הוה פעם אחת בשנה ואפ"ה לר' מנחם יש בהן משום קדושה ולא דמי להא דקאמר לקמן בסוף דף כ"ז אי הכי קדשתינהו לכולהו שבילי דנהרדעא דהתם בהתפלל ביחיד בלין כ"ע מודו דאין בו משום קדושה: (ד) ד"ה אני לא וכו' ובתי מדרשות שבה מטמאין כשאר בתי: (ה) ד"ה ומה היה וכו' אולם והיכל ובית קדשי הקדשים שהוא לצד מערב עכשיו נשאר בנתיים מקום המזבח וכו' באותה הרצועה אלא קרן מזרחית דרומית מקום היסוד: (ו) ד"ה לא שנו וכו' ובית הכנסת בקדושתו עומד וכו' מנהיג ספרים בקדושתן אלא שלא מכרו שבעה הטובים: (ז) תוס' ד"ה ורצועה וכו' של טורף שהוא בנימין:

גליון הש"ס

רש"י ד"ה תוספתא ובמעמדות וכו'. ובמעמדות לא גרסינן בחי' הרמב"ן ב"ב דף עז ד"ה אין אותיות כתב דאשגירות לישנא הוא ולאו דוקא מעמדות: **שם** ד"ה טורסיים צורפי נחושת. עי' חולין דף נז ע"ב תד"ה מטלית. ע"ז דף יז ע"ב תד"ה רבן: **שם** ד"ה לא שנו כו' ובכה"נ בחשיבותו. מבואר דס"ל לרש"י דבלאו מעמד אנשי העיר אין מורידין דמים מקדושתן וגם הבהכ"נ בחשיבותו ובמעמד אנשי העיר בהכ"נ והדמים יוצאים לחולין ותמוה לי מזה דברי רש"י לקמן כז ע"ב ד"ה ורבנן וכו' דכיון דשקיל דמי ומעלה להו בקדושה וכו' וממ"נ אם במכרו במעמד אנשי העיר לא צריך להעלות הדמים בקדושה ואעפ"כ הלוקח מה דבעי עביד דהא בהכ"נ יוצא לחולין והמעות מותר אפי' למישתי בי' שכרא ובלא מעמד אנשי העיר אף אם מעלין הדמים בקדושה מ"מ הבהכ"נ בקדושתה קאי ונע"ג:

לְמִישְׁתָּא בֵּיהּ שִׁיכְרָא(א) שַׁפִּיר דָּמֵי. רָבִינָא הֲוָה לֵיהּ הַהוּא תִּילָא(ב) דְּבֵי כְנִישְׁתָּא אֲתָא לְקַמֵּיהּ דְּרַב אַשִׁי, אֲמַר לֵיהּ: מַהוּ לְמִיזְרְעָהּ? אֲמַר לֵיהּ: זִיל זְבָנֵיהּ מִשִּׁבְעָה טוּבֵי הָעִיר בְּמַעֲמַד אַנְשֵׁי הָעִיר, וּזְרָעָהּ. רָמִי בַּר אַבָּא הֲוָה קָא בָּנֵי בֵּי כְנִישְׁתָּא, הֲוָה הַהִיא כְּנִישְׁתָּא עַתִּיקָא הֲוָה בָּעֵי לְמִיסְתְּרֵיהּ וּלְאַתּוּיֵי לִיבְנֵי וְכַשּׁוּרֵי מִינָּהּ, וְעַיּוּלֵי לְהָתָם. יָתֵיב וְקָא מִיבַּעְיָא לֵיהּ הָא דְּרַב חִסְדָּא. דַּאֲמַר רַב חִסְדָּא: *לָא לִיסְתּוֹר בֵּי כְנִישְׁתָּא עַד דְּבָנֵי בֵּי כְנִישְׁתָּא אַחֲרִיתִי, הָתָם — מִשּׁוּם פְּשִׁיעוּתָא, כִּי הַאי גַּוְונָא מַאי? אֲתָא לְקַמֵּיהּ דְּרַב פַּפָּא — וְאָסַר לֵיהּ, לְקַמֵּיהּ דְּרַב הוּנָא — וְאָסַר לֵיהּ. אֲמַר רָבָא: הַאי בֵּי כְנִישְׁתָּא, חִלּוּפָהּ וְזַבּוּנָהּ — שָׁרֵי, אוֹגוּרָהּ וּמַשְׁכּוּנָהּ — אָסוּר. מַאי טַעְמָא — בִּקְדוּשָּׁתָהּ קָאֵי. לִיבְנֵי נַמִי, חַלּוּפִינְהוּ וְזַבּוּנִינְהוּ — שָׁרֵי, אוֹזוֹפִינְהוּ — אָסוּר. הָנֵי מִילֵּי — בְּעַתִּיקָתָא, אֲבָל בַּחֲדַתָּא — לֵית לָן בָּהּ. וַאֲפִילּוּ לְמַאן דְּאָמַר *הַזְמָנָה מִילְּתָא הִיא — ה"מ כְּגוֹן הָאוֹרֵג בֶּגֶד לְמֵת, אֲבָל הָכָא — *כְּטָווּי לְאָרִיג דָּמֵי, וְלֵיכָּא לְמַאן דְּאָמַר. *מַתָּנָה, פְּלִיגֵי בָּהּ רַב אַחָא וְרָבִינָא, חַד אָסַר וְחַד שָׁרֵי. מַאן דְּאָסַר — *בְּהַאי תִּפְקַע קְדוּשָּׁתָהּ? וּמַאן דְּשָׁרֵי: אִי לָאו דַּהֲוָה לֵיהּ הֲנָאָה מִינֵּיהּ — לָא הֲוָה יָהֵיב לֵיהּ, הֲדַר הֲוָה לֵיהּ מַתָּנָה כִּזְבִינֵי. ת"ר: תַּשְׁמִישֵׁי מִצְוָה — נִזְרָקִין, תַּשְׁמִישֵׁי קְדוּשָּׁה — נִגְנָזִין. וְאֵלּוּ הֵן תַּשְׁמִישֵׁי מִצְוָה: סוּכָּה, לוּלָב, שׁוֹפָר, צִיצִית. וְאֵלּוּ הֵן תַּשְׁמִישֵׁי קְדוּשָּׁה: דְּלוּסְקְמֵי סְפָרִים, תְּפִילִּין וּמְזוּזוֹת, וְתִיק שֶׁל ס"ת, וְנַרְתִּיק שֶׁל תְּפִילִּין וּרְצוּעוֹתֵיהֶן. אֲמַר רָבָא: מֵרֵישׁ הֲוָה אָמֵינָא הַאי כּוּרְסְיָא תַּשְׁמִישׁ דְּתַשְׁמִישׁ הוּא, וְשָׁרֵי. כֵּיוָן דַּחֲזֵינָא דְּמוֹתְבִי עֲלָוֵיהּ ס"ת, אָמֵינָא: תַּשְׁמִישׁ קְדוּשָּׁה הוּא, וְאָסוּר. וַאֲמַר רָבָא: מֵרֵישׁ הֲוָה אָמֵינָא הַאי פְּרִיסָא תַּשְׁמִישׁ דְּתַשְׁמִישׁ הוּא, כֵּיוָן דַּחֲזֵינָא דְּעָיְיפִי לֵיהּ וּמַנְחִי סִיפְרָא עֲלָוֵיהּ אָמֵינָא: תַּשְׁמִישׁ קְדוּשָּׁה הוּא, וְאָסוּר. וַאֲמַר רָבָא: הַאי תֵּיבוּתָא דְּאִירְפַּט, מֵיעְבְּדָהּ תֵּיבָה זוּטַרְתִּי — שָׁרֵי, כּוּרְסַיָּיא — אֲסִיר. וַאֲמַר רָבָא: הַאי *פְּרִיסָא דְּבָלָה, לְמֵיעְבְּדֵיהּ פְּרִיסָא לְסִפְרֵי — שָׁרֵי, לְחוּמָּשִׁין — אֲסִיר. וַאֲמַר רָבָא: הָנֵי *)זְבִילֵי דְּחוּמָּשֵׁי, וְקַמְטְרֵי דְּסִפְרֵי — תַּשְׁמִישׁ קְדוּשָּׁה נִינְהוּ, וְנִגְנָזִין. פְּשִׁיטָא! מַהוּ דְּתֵימָא: הָנֵי לָאו לְכָבוֹד עֲבִידָן, לְנַטּוּרֵי בְּעָלְמָא עֲבִידִי, קמ"ל. הַהוּא בֵּי כְנִישְׁתָּא דִּיהוּדָאֵי רוֹמָאֵי דַּהֲוָה פְּתִיחַ לְהַהוּא *אִידְרוֹנָא, דַּהֲוָה מַחֵית בֵּיהּ מֵת, וַהֲווּ בָּעוּ כָּהֲנֵי לְמֵיעַל לְצַלּוֹיֵי הָתָם. אֲתוּ אֲמַרוּ לֵיהּ לְרָבָא, אֲמַר לְהוּ: דְּלוּ תֵּיבוּתָא, אוֹתְבוּהָ, דַּהֲוָה לֵיהּ כְּלִי עֵץ הֶעָשׂוּי לְנַחַת, *וּכְלִי עֵץ הֶעָשׂוּי לְנַחַת — אֵינוֹ מְקַבֵּל טוּמְאָה, וְחוֹצֵץ בִּפְנֵי הַטּוּמְאָה. אֲמַרוּ לֵיהּ רַבָּנַן לְרָבָא: וְהָא זִמְנִין דִּמְטַלְטְלִי לֵיהּ כִּי מַנַּח סֵפֶר תּוֹרָה עֲלָוֵיהּ, וַהֲוָה לֵיהּ מִיטַּלְטֵל מָלֵא וְרֵיקָם! אִי הָכִי לָא אֶפְשָׁר. אָמַר מָר זוּטְרָא: מִטְפָּחוֹת סְפָרִים שֶׁבָּלוּ עוֹשִׂין אוֹתָן תַּכְרִיכִין לְמֵת מִצְוָה, וְזוֹ הִיא גְּנִיזָתָן. וְאָמַר רָבָא: סֵפֶר תּוֹרָה שֶׁבָּלָה גּוֹנְזִין אוֹתוֹ אֵצֶל תַּלְמִיד חָכָם, וַאֲפִילּוּ שׁוֹנֶה הֲלָכוֹת. אָמַר רַב אַחָא בַּר יַעֲקֹב: וּבִכְלִי חֶרֶס, שֶׁנֶּאֱמַר "וּנְתַתָּם בִּכְלִי חָרֶשׂ לְמַעַן יַעַמְדוּ יָמִים רַבִּים" (ירמיה לב). (*וַאֲמַר) רַב פַּפִּי מִשְּׁמֵיהּ *דְּרָ': מִבֵּי כְנִישְׁתָּא לְבֵי רַבָּנַן — שָׁרֵי, מִבֵּי רַבָּנַן לְבֵי כְנִישְׁתָּא — אֲסִיר. וְרַב פַּפָּא מִשְּׁמֵיהּ דְּרָבָא מַתְנֵי אִיפְּכָא, אָמַר רַב אַחָא: כְּוָותֵיהּ

*) [פי' עושין סביב הספר מסגרת של עור לשמור הספר וענין מדור הוא כמו יזבלני אישי. ערוך]

רש"י

לְמִישְׁתָּא בֵּיהּ שִׁיכְרָא. לִקְנוֹת בְּדָמִים וְלַעֲשׂוֹת שֵׁכָר לִשְׁתּוֹת: תִּילָא. כָּל בַּיִת הָרוּס קָרוּי תֵּל, כְּמוֹ "וְהָיְתָה תֵּל עוֹלָם" (דברים יג): בְּשׁוּרֵי. קוֹרוֹת שֶׁל בֵּית הַכְּנֶסֶת יָשָׁן הָיוּ צְרִיכִין לִתְּתָן בֶּחָדָשׁ: הָא דְּאָמַר רַב חִסְדָּא. בְּבָבָא בַּתְרָא, בְּ"הַשּׁוּתָּפִין": מִשּׁוּם פְּשִׁיעוּתָא. שֶׁמָּא יִפְשַׁע (אֶלָּא) וְיִתְיָיאֵשׁ, וְלֹא יִבְנֶה אַחֵר: כִּי הַאי גַּוְונָא מַאי. שֶׁאֵין סְתִירָתוֹ אֶלָּא לְבִנְיָנוֹ שֶׁל זֶה: חִלּוּפֵי וְזַבּוּנֵי. חָלָה קְדוּשָּׁתוֹ עַל הַחִילּוּף אוֹ עַל הַדָּמִים, וְהוּא יָצָא מִן הַקְּדוּשָּׁה לְהִשְׁתַּמֵּשׁ בּוֹ: לִיבְנֵי. לְבֵינִים שֶׁל בֵּית הַכְּנֶסֶת: בְּעַתִּיקֵי. שֶׁנִּבְנוּ כְּבָר בַּכּוֹתֶל בֵּית הַכְּנֶסֶת (ג) שֶׁנָּפַל: אֲבָל בַּחֲדַתָּא. שֶׁנַּעֲשָׂה לְשֵׁם בֵּית הַכְּנֶסֶת — לֵית לָן בָּהּ: וַאֲפִי' לְמ"ד. בְּמַסֶּכֶת סַנְהֶדְרִין, בְּפֶרֶק "נִגְמַר הַדִּין" (דף מז:) גַּבֵּי אוֹרֵג בֶּגֶד לְמֵת דְּאָסוּר בְּהַזְמָנָה, *בְּתַכְרִיכֵי הַמֵּת דַּאֲסִירֵי בַּהֲנָאָה, דְּגָמְרִינַן "שָׁם" "שָׁם" מֵעֶגְלָה עֲרוּפָה, כִּדְמְפָרֵשׁ הָתָם: הָנֵי מִילֵּי בְּאוֹרֵג בֶּגֶד לְמֵת. שֶׁאֵינוֹ חָסֵר אֶלָּא אֲרִיגָה, וְכֵיוָן שֶׁנֶּאֱרַג — מִיָּד הַוְיָא רָאוּי לְפוֹרְשׂוֹ עַל הַמֵּת(ד). אֲבָל לְבֵנִים מְחוּסָּרִים עֲשִׂיָּיה, לִבְנוֹתָן בַּכּוֹתֶל. וְהִלְכָּךְ דְּשֶׁל לְבֵנִים דְּבֵית הַכְּנֶסֶת הָוֵה לֵיהּ כְּטָווּי לְאָרִיג, וְלֵיכָּא לְמ"ד דְּבִכִי הַאי גַּוְונָא דְּהַזְמָנָה מִילְּתָא הִיא: מַתָּנָה. נָתְנוּ בְּנֵי הָעִיר בֵּית כְּנֶסֶת לְתַשְׁמִישֵׁי חוֹל: וְתַשְׁמִישֵׁי מִצְוָה. דְּבָרִים שֶׁשִּׁמְּשׁוּ בָּהֶן מִצְוָה: דְּלוּסְקְמֵי. כְּמוֹ אַמְתַּחַת וְשַׂק לָשׂוּם בּוֹ [סֵפֶר]: תִּיק וְנַרְתִּיק. חֲדָא הִיא, אֶלָּא שֶׁלְּשׁוֹן תִּיק נוֹפֵל עַל דָּבָר אָרוֹךְ, וּלְשׁוֹן נַרְתִּיק נוֹפֵל עַל דָּבָר קָצָר: כּוּרְסַיָּא. בִּימָה שֶׁל עֵץ: תַּשְׁמִישׁ דְּתַשְׁמִישׁ. שֶׁפּוֹרֵס מַפָּה עָלָיו, וְאַחַר כָּךְ נוֹתֵן סֵפֶר תּוֹרָה עָלָיו: דְּמוֹתְבִי סֵפֶר תּוֹרָה עֲלֵיהּ. בְּלֹא מַפָּה: פְּרִיסָא. יְרִיעָה שֶׁפּוֹרְסִין סְבִיבוֹת הָאָרוֹן מִבִּפְנִים: תַּשְׁמִישׁ דְּתַשְׁמִישׁ הוּא. תַּשְׁמִישׁ שֶׁל אָרוֹן: דְּעָיְיפִי לֵיהּ. פְּעָמִים שֶׁכּוֹפְלִין אוֹתוֹ תַּחַת ס"ת: דְּאִירְפַּט. אָרוֹן שֶׁנִּתְקַלְקֵל וְנִפְרַד מֵחִבּוּרוֹ. וְיֵשׁ דּוּגְמָתוֹ בְּבָרַיְיתָא בִּיבָמוֹת (דף קב.): מִנְעָל הַמְרוּפָּט: תֵּיבוּתָא זוּטַרְתִּי. לַעֲשׂוֹת תֵּיבָה קְטַנָּה, מִן הַגְּדוֹלָה הָרִאשׁוֹנָה: מֵיעְבְּדָא כּוּרְסַיָּא. בִּימָה: אָסוּר. שֶׁיָּרְדָה מִקְּדוּשָּׁתָהּ: פְּרִיסָה דְּבָלָה. יְרִיעוֹת הָאָרוֹן שֶׁבָּלוּ: לְחוּמָּשִׁין. יֵשׁ סְפָרִים שֶׁהֵן עֲשׂוּיִין כָּל חוּמָּשׁ לְבַדּוֹ, וְכוּלָּן בְּגִלָּיוֹן: זְבִילֵי. כְּמִין דְּלוּסְקְמֵי: קַמְטְרָא. אַרְגָּז, שֶׁקּוֹרִין אשקרינ"יו. וְהַרְבֵּה יֵשׁ בְּתַרְגּוּם שֶׁל יוֹנָתָן בֶּן עוּזִּיאֵל: (ה) "חֲבָלִים חֲבוּשִׁים" (יחזקאל כז), אַרְגָּזִים אַמְלִין דְּזָהוֹרִיתָא בְּקַמְטְרִין. וְכֵן "לַאֲשֶׁר עַל הַמֶּלְתָּחָה" — לִדְעַל קַמְטְרַיָּ' (מלכים ב י): בֵּי כְנִישְׁתָּא דְּרוֹמָאֵי. אַנְשֵׁי יִשְׂרָאֵל בָּאוּ מֵרוֹמִי לִמְחוֹזָא, וְנִתְיַישְּׁבוּ שָׁם, וְעָשׂוּ לָהֶם בֵּית הַכְּנֶסֶת: אִידְרוֹנָא. חֶדֶר שֶׁמַּשִּׂימִין בּוֹ מֵת, וְהָיָה מוּנָּח בּוֹ מֵת עַד שֶׁלֹּא נִקְבַּר: מָחֵית. כְּמוֹ מוּנָּח, כִּדְמְתַרְגְּמִינַן: "וַתַּנַּח בִּגְדוֹ אֶצְלָהּ" — וְאַחִיתְתֵיהּ (בראשית לט): בָּעוּ כָּהֲנֵי לְמֵיעַל וּלְצַלּוֹיֵי. בְּהַהוּא כְּנִישְׁתָּא אֵין יְכוֹלִין לִיכָּנֵס מִפְּנֵי הַטּוּמְאָה הַנִּכְנֶסֶת בְּבֵית הַכְּנֶסֶת דֶּרֶךְ הַפֶּתַח מִבַּיִת לְבַיִת, דְּהָכִי תְּנַן בְּמַסֶּכֶת אֳהָלוֹת (פ"ג משנה ז): דְּלוּ תֵּיבוּתָא. הַגְבִּיהוּ הָאָרוֹן מִמְּקוֹמוֹ: כְּלִי עֵץ הֶעָשׂוּי לְנַחַת. בְּמָקוֹם אֶחָד אֵינוֹ מְקַבֵּל טוּמְאָה, דְּאִיתְקַשׁ כְּלֵי עֵץ לְשַׂק לְעִנְיַן טוּמְאָה, דִּכְתִיב "וְכָל כְּלִי עֵץ אוֹ בֶגֶד אוֹ עוֹר אוֹ שָׂק" (ויקרא יא), מַה שַּׂק הַמִּיטַּלְטֵל אַף כְּלִי עֵץ הַמִּיטַּלְטֵל — כָּל דָּבָר הַמְקַבֵּל טוּמְאָה אֵינוֹ חוֹצֵץ בִּפְנֵי הַטּוּמְאָה: מִטְפְּחוֹת סְפָרִים. אַף שֶׁל ס"ת: וַאֲפִילּוּ שׁוֹנֶה הֲלָכוֹת. כְּלוֹמַר אֲפִילּוּ לֹא שִׁימֵּשׁ תַּלְמִידֵי חֲכָמִים בְּהַתַּלְמוּד וּבַגְּמָרָא אֶלָּא בְּמִשְׁנָיוֹת וּבְבָרַיְיתוֹת: מִבֵּי כְנִישְׁתָּא לְבֵי רַבָּנַן. לַעֲשׂוֹת

תוספות

אוגורה ומשכונה אסור. קשה: דהא רבי מאיר לא אסר במתניתין אלא ממכר עולם, אבל על תנאי — שרי ומאי שנא? ונראה לי: דהאי דר"מ שרי למכור על תנאי — היינו של רבים לרבים להתפלל שם, דאין במכר זה זלזול. והא דאסרי' הכא משכנתא — הוי דיחיד, משום זלזול:

תשמישי קדושה וכו' נרתק של תפילין ורצועותיהן. מכאן משמע שהדל"ת והיו"ד שבקשר הרצועה אינן אותיות גמורות, ולא הוי הלכה למשה מסיני כי אם השי"ן שבבתים, מדלא קרי הכא לרצועות אלא תשמישי קדושה. והכי נמי משמע ב"הקומץ רבה" (מנחות דף לה: ושם) דלא קרי להו אלא תשמישי קדושה. והכי נמי משמע בפרק שני דשבת (דף כח:), דפריך: והאמר אביי שי"ן של תפילין הלכה למשה מסיני. ולא פריך כך מן הדל"ת והיו"ד. ולא קשה מההיא דמנחות (דף לה:) גבי "וראו כל עמי הארץ כי שם ה' נקרא עליך ויראו ממך", ואמרו: אלו תפילין שבראש, שיש לפרש הטעם לפי שהן לעולם בגובה של ראש, ונראים לעולם שפיר אות. אבל אותן של יד — אינן נראין ואין בהן אות, כדכתיב "והיו לך לאות" ודרשינן (מנחות דף לז:): ולא לאחרים לאות. אבל למה שפרש"י התם דהטעם הוי משום שיש בהן השי"ן והדל"ת דהוי רוב אותיות של שדי, לפירוש זה קשה, (ו)כדמשמע בכל הני שהבאתי דהיו"ד והדל"ת לא חשיבי אותיות*:

מריש הוה אמינא האי פריסא תשמיש דתשמיש הוא. פי' הקונטרס: יריעה שפורסין סביב הארון בתוכו. וקשה: שהרי הארון עצמו הוי תשמיש קדושה(ז), ואמר (*התם) שאסור לעשות ממנו כורסיא, אלמא שהתיבה קדושה יותר מן הפורסין! לכך נראה לי: שפורסין אותה סביב הארון מבחוץ: [נ"ל הכא]

עין משפט נר מצוה

ח א מיי' פי"א מהל' תפלה הל' יב טוש"ע א"ח סי' קנב סעיף א:
ט ב מיי' שם טוש"ע שם בהגה"ה:
י ג ד מיי' שם הלכה כ טוש"ע שם סי' קנג סעיף יא:
יא ה מיי' פ"י מהלכות ס"ת הלכה ד ופ"ג מהל' ציצית הל' ט סמג עשין כה טור ש"ע א"ח סי' כא סעיף א:
יב ו ז ח מיי' פ"י מהל' ס"ת הל' ד טוש"ע א"ח סימן קנד סעיף ג וטור ש"ע י"ד סימן רפב סעיף יב:
יג ט י (מיי' שם) טוש"ע א"ח שם סעיף ו וטוש"ע י"ד שם סעיף יג:
יד כ מיי' שם הלכה ד טוש"ע א"ח שם ס"ג וטוש"ע י"ד שם סעיף יב:
טו ל מיי' פ"ג מהלכות כלים הלכה א ופ"ו מהל' טומאת מת הלכה ב:
טז מ מיי' פי"ב מהל' טומאת מת הלכה ב ופי"ג הלכה ג:
יז נ מיי' פ"י מהלכות ס"ת הלכה ג סמג עשין כה טוש"ע א"ח סי' קנד סעיף ד טוש"ע י"ד סי' רפב סעיף יא:
יח ס ע מיי' שם סמג שם טוש"ע א"ח שם סעיף ה וטוש"ע י"ד שם סעיף י:
יט פ מיי' פי"א מהלכות תפלה הל' יד טוש"ע א"ח סימן קנג סעיף א:

[ועי' תוס' ברכות ו. ד"ה אלו כו']

רבינו חננאל

העיר אבל אם מכרו ז' טובי העיר במעמד אנשי העיר אפילו למישתא בה שיכרא כלומר להוציא הדמין לחולין שפיר דמי הרשות בידו. רב אשי א"ל לרבינא זיל זבין ההוא תילא דכנשתא מז' טובי העיר במעמד אנשי העיר וזרעיה. ר' אמי הוה בי כנשתא ובעא למיסתר כנישתא עתיקתא ולאיתויי כשורי מינה ולעיולינהו בחדתא דבני ואסרו ליה רב פפי ורב הונא בר תחליפא. אמר רבא בי כנשתא חלופה וזבונה כדאמרן כזביני דמי ושרי אבל להשכירה ולמשכנה אסיר. מ"ט בקדושתא קיימא וקא משתמשי בקדש. לבינים נמי חלופינהו וזבנינהו שרי אוזופינהו אסיר והני מילי בעתיקתא שהרסו בית הכנסת והוציאו אותם מן הכתלים אבל לבינים חדשים שעדיין לא בנאום בבית הכנסת שרי ואפילו למ"ד הזמנה מילתא היא הני מילי כגון אורג בגד למת דחזי לאישתמושי ביה ואסיר אבל הני ליבני א) מפריש במטוה וארוג בו דמי דליכא מ"ד דילמא אתנן עלייהו מעיקרא. ת"ר תשמישי מצוה נזרקין. פירוש כיון שנתקיימה המצוה ושלמה נורקים כגון עצי סוכה וד' מינים שבלולב ושופר וציצית אלו וכיוצא בה אין בהו קדושה אבלן כגון דלוסקומי ספרים ותפילין ורצועותיהן ונרתיקן ומזוזות ותיק של ספר וכיוצא בהן תשמישי קדושה הן ונגנזין וכן כסא אע"פ שמניחין בו ס"ת לפרקים וכן פריסא שכופלין אותה ופורשין עליה ספר תורה או פורסין אותה על ס"ת וזבילי דחומשי וקמטרי דסיפרי כל אלו תשמישי קדושה הן ונגנזין. תיבה דאירפט פירוש שנתחלחלה כדגרסינן מנעל מרופט (שבת קמא) וזקנים מרפטו שפתייהו (שם דף קנב) מותר לעשות ממנה תיבה קטנה אבל כסא אסור דלא מיחדא תשמישיה לס"ת ב) כורסיא נמי שנשברה מותר לעשותו מותר לחתוך הבלוי ולעשותו קטן אבל פריסא לחומשין לא. אמר רבא ספר תורה שבלה גונזין אותו בכלי חרש אצל תלמיד חכם ואפילו שונה הלכות. מטפחות ספרים שבלו עושין אותן תכריכין למת מצוה. וזו היא גניזתן. ההיא כנישתא דהוה פתוחה לאידרונא דהוה מחית בה מת בעו כהנים מיעל צלויי בכנשתא התם. אמר להו רבא דלו תיבה אותבוה אבבא דליהוי כלי עץ העשוי לנחת כלומר מה שאינו מטלטל וכל כלי עץ העשוי לנחת אינו מקבל טומאה וחוצץ בפני הטומאה אמרו ליה רבנן והא זימנא דמטלטלין לה כי מנח סיפרא עילויה והוה ליה מיטלטל מלא וריקן אמר להו המטלטל מלא וריקן אינו עשוי לנחת לעולם וכל דבר שמקבל טומאה אינו חוצץ בפני הטומאה

א) אולי צ"ל כמפריש מטווה לארוג בו דמי דליכא למ"ד דלימא דבעי דאתני עלייהו מעיקרא כצ"ל ועי' היטב במנחות דף לד ע"ב. ב) לכאורה נראה דצ"ל פריסא שבלה מותר לחתוך הבלוי וכו' כצ"ל ואולי דגי' אחרת היה לרבינו בכאן וצ"ע.

מסורת הש"ס

בבא בתרא ג:
[נ"ל כתכריכי יעב"ץ]
בריה דרב יהושע
[ברכות כג: סנהדרין מז: מח. מנחות לד:]
[סנהדרין מח.]
[ב"מ עז. ע"ש]
[רב אלפס גרס במאי והרא"ש גרס אמאי]
[וילון שפורסין לפני התיבה פ"א מטפחת שמכסין בו ס"ת. ערוך]
[עי' בפ' מקץ מג פ"ל תרגום של ויבא החדרה ועאל לאדרון]
[חגיגה כו: יומא כא: מנחות לו:]
[נ"ל אמר]
[נ"ל דרבא]

הגהות הב"ח

(א) גמ' למשתא ביה שיכרא ולמשתא ביה פרי שפיר דמי. נ"ב ס"א ועיין בר"ן: (ב) שם ההוא תילא. נ"ב ע"ל בתוס' דף כח ע"ב בד"ה בתי: (ג) רש"י ד"ה בעתיקי וכו' ונפל: (ד) ד"ה הני מילי וכו' על המת הס"ד ואח"כ מה"ד אבל וכו' והלכך בשלבנו לבית הכנסת כצ"ל ותיבת לבינים נמחק: (ה) ד"ה קמטרא וכו' בן עוזיאל בחבלים חבושים וארוזים באמלין דזהוריתא למתתין בקמטרין: (ו) תוס' ד"ה תשמישי וכו' קשה מדמשמע בכל הני: (ז) ד"ה מריש וכו' תשמיש קדושה מדאמר רבא תיבותא שאסור עשות וכו' יותר מן הפריסא לכך נראה:

גליון הש"ס

גמ' א"ל מהו למזרעיה. עי' לקמן דף כח ע"ב תד"ה בתי כנסיות ובכרי"ף ליתא להנך תיבות מהו למזרעיה: **שם** פליגי בה רב אחא ורבינא. עיין ב"מ דף עז ע"א ועיין בר"ש רפ"ב דמעשרות: **שם** לנטורי בעלמא עבידן ובאדרונא דמיא גירסת הרי"ף: **שם** וחוצץ בפני הטומאה. עיין ב"ב דף כ ע"א תד"ה הוא גופה:

כוותיה דרב פפי מסתברא, דא"ר יהושע בן לוי: בהכ"נ מותר לעשותו בית המדרש, ש"מ. דרש בר קפרא: מאי דכתיב "וישרף את בית ה' ואת בית המלך ואת כל בתי ירושלם ואת כל בית גדול שרף באש". "בית ה'" – זה בהמ"ק, "בית המלך" – אלו פלטרין של מלך, "ואת כל בתי ירושלם" – כמשמען, "ואת כל בית גדול שרף באש" ר' יוחנן ור' יהושע בן לוי חד אמר: מקום שמגדלין בו תורה, וחד אמר: מקום שמגדלין בו תפלה. מ"ד תורה, דכתיב "ה' חפץ למען צדקו יגדיל תורה ויאדיר". ומ"ד תפלה דכתיב "ספרה נא... הגדולות אשר עשה אלישע". ואלישע דעבד – ברחמי הוא דעבד. תסתיים דר' יהושע בן לוי הוא דאמר מקום שמגדלין בו תורה, דאמר ר' יהושע בן לוי: בית הכנסת מותר לעשותו בית המדרש, ש"מ. § "אבל מכרו תורה לא יקחו ספרים" וכו'. § איבעיא להו: מהו למכור ס"ת ישן ליקח בו חדש? כיון דלא מעלי ליה – אסור, או דלמא כיון דליכא לעלויי עילוייא אחרינא – שפיר דמי? תא שמע: אבל מכרו תורה – לא יקחו ספרים. ספרים הוא דלא, הא תורה בתורה – שפיר דמי! מתני' דיעבד, כי קא מיבעיא לן – לכתחלה. ת"ש: גוללין ס"ת במטפחות חומשין וחומשין במטפחות נביאים וכתובים. אבל לא נביאים וכתובים במטפחות חומשין, ולא חומשין במטפחות ס"ת. קתני מיהת: גוללים ס"ת במטפחות חומשין, מטפחות חומשין – אין, מטפחות ס"ת – לא. אימא סיפא: ולא חומשין במטפחות ס"ת. הא תורה בתורה – ש"ד! *אלא, מהא ליכא למשמע מינה. תא שמע: *מניחין ס"ת על גבי תורה, ותורה ע"ג חומשין וחומשין ע"ג נביאים וכתובים. אבל לא נביאים וכתובים ע"ג חומשין, ולא חומשין על גבי תורה. הנחה קאמרת? שאני הנחה דלא אפשר. דאי לא תימא הכי – מיכרך היכי כרכינן? והא קא יתיב דפא אחבריה! אלא, כיון דלא אפשר – שרי, הכא נמי כיון דלא אפשר – שרי. ת"ש: דאמר רבה בר בר חנה א"ר יוחנן משום רשב"ג: לא ימכור אדם ס"ת ישן ליקח בו חדש. התם משום פשיעותא, כי קאמרינן – כגון דכתיב ומנח לאיפרוקי, מאי? ת"ש, דא"ר יוחנן משום ר"מ: *אין מוכרין ס"ת אלא *ללמוד תורה, ולישא אשה, ש"מ: תורה בתורה שפיר דמי. דלמא שאני למוד, *שהלמוד מביא לידי מעשה. אשה נמי – "לא תהו בראה לשבת יצרה", אבל תורה בתורה – לא. ת"ר: לא ימכור אדם ס"ת אע"פ שאינו צריך לו, יתר על כן ארשב"ג: *אפי' אין לו מה יאכל *ומכר ס"ת או בתו – אינו רואה סימן ברכה לעולם. § "וכן במותריהן". § אמר רבא: ל"ש אלא שמכרו והותירו, אבל גבו והותירו מותר. איתיביה אביי: בד"א שלא התנו אבל התנו – אפילו לדוכסוסיא מותר. ה"ד? אילימא שמכרו והותירו – כי התנו מאי הוי? אלא שגבו והותירו, טעמא – דהתנו, הא לא התנו – לא! לעולם שמכרו והותירו, וה"ק: בד"א – שלא התנו שבעה טובי העיר במעמד אנשי העיר, אבל התנו שבעה טובי העיר במעמד אנשי העיר – אפילו לדוכסוסיא נמי מותר.

א"ל אביי להההוא מרבנן דהוה מסדר מתניתא קמיה דרב ששת: מי שמיע לך מרב ששת מאי דוכסוסיא? אמר ליה: הכי אמר רב ששת: פרשא דמתא. אמר אביי: הלכך, האי צורבא מרבנן דשמע ליה מילתא ולא ידע פירושא – לישיילה קמיה דשכיח קמיה רבנן, דלא אפשר דלא שמיע ליה מן גברא. רבה אמר רבי יוחנן: משום ר"מ: בני העיר שהלכו לעיר אחרת ופסקו עליהן צדקה – נותנין, וכשהן באין מביאין אותה עמהן, ומפרנסין בה עניי עירן, תניא נמי הכי: בני העיר שהלכו לעיר אחרת ופסקו עליהן צדקה – נותנין, וכשהן באין מביאין אותה עמהן. ויחיד שהלך לעיר אחרת ופסקו עליו צדקה – תנתן לעניי אותה העיר. ר"ה גזר תעניתא, על לגביה רב חנה בר חנילאי וכל בני מתיה, רמו עלייהו צדקה ויהבו. כי בעו למיתי, אמרו ליה: נותבה לן מר, וניזול ונפרנס בה עניי מאתין! אמר להו: תנינא, בד"א – בשאין שם חבר

רש"י

לעשות מבית הכנסת בית המדרש: ויישרף את בית ה' ואת כל בית גדול. בנבוזראדן כתיב: תסתיים. יש סימן: מותר לעשות בית המדרש. אלמא: בית המדרש הוי בית גדול: דיעבד. שמכרוהו כבר, כדקתני: מכרו תורה. ומשום הכי מותר ליקח בדמיו ספר תורה, שאם לאו – מה יקחו מהם? כי קא מיבעיא לן – למכור לכתחילה לכך: חומשין. ספר תורה שאין בו אלא חומש אחד: אבל לא נביאים וכתובים במטפחות ספר תורה. שמוריד המטפחות מקדושתן: במטפחות של חומשין. דקא מעלי להו למטפחות: אבל במטפחות ספר תורה לא. אלמא: אין משנין לגריעותא בה, אלא למעלה הימנה: אימא סיפא ולא חומשין במטפחות של ספר תורה. דהא ירידה היא: וקא מותיב דפא אחבריה. דף נגלל על חבירו: משום פשיעותא. שמא משימכור שוב לא יקנה, ומתוך כך יפסדו הדמים: כי קאמרינן דמנח לאיפרוקי. שכתוב כבר החדש בבית הסופר, ואינו מעוכב אלא לתת לו דמים: אלא ללמוד תורה. להתפרנס בו כשלומד תורה. וקס"ד דה"ה לקנות ספר תורה: שאינו צריך לו. שיש לו אחר: אינו רואה סימן ברכה לעולם. באותן הדמים: שמכרו והותירו. מכרו אחד מן הקדושות הללו, ולקחו ממקצת הדמים קדושה מעולה, והותירו מהן: אבל גבו. מעות מן הצבור לצורך ספר תורה, וקנאוהו, ונותר בידן מן הדמים – מותר להורידן, שהרי עדיין לא באו לשימוש קדושה חמורה: שלא התנו. על מנת לעשות רצונו מן הדמים: לדוכסוסיא. מפרש לקמן: כי התנו מאי הוי. הא דמי קדושה הן: וטעמא דהתנו. כשגבו לעשות רצונו וחפצו ממותר הדמים: פרשא דמתא. בני העיר שוכרין אדם רוכב סוס, שיהא להן מזומן לשולחו בשליחות למושל העיר כשיצטרכו: נותנין. אותה לגבאי אותה העיר, כדי שלא יחשדום בפוסקים ואינן נותנין: וכשהן באים. וחוזרים למקומן, תובעים אותן מן הגבאים, ומפרנסין בה עניי עירן:

תוספות

כוותיה דרב פפי מסתברא. מהכא משמע דהלכה כר' יהושע בן לוי לגבי דר' יוחנן, מדמייתי ראיה דהלכה כרב פפי, משום דרבי יהושע בן לוי קאי כוותיה, אע"ג דרבי יוחנן פליג עליה*: אבל התנו ז' טובי העיר במעמד כו'. קשה: דכיון שהתנו ז' טובי העיר במעמד אנשי העיר למה לי להותירו? ואמאי נקטיה, והא אפי' בכל הדמים יכולין הן לעשות מה שירצו, כדאמר לעיל: אפילו למישתי ביה שיכרא, ופרש"י לקנות מן הדמים שכר לשתות! ויש לומר: דנקט והותירו, לאשמועינן דאף במותר בעי תנאי. דסלקא דעתך דאם קנו מן הדמים דבר קדושה והותירו, דמותר לעשות מן המותר כל מה שירצו, אפילו בלא תנאי – קמ"ל דלא:

עין משפט נר מצוה

כ א מיי' פ"י מהל' ס"ת הל' ה טוש"ע י"ד סי' רפב סעיף יט:
[וע"ע תוס' חולין לז ד"ה אמר רבא וכו' שר"ת עצמו שכתב זה לראייה חזר מזה ע"ש פירושו בסוגיא דהכא וע' תוס' עירובין סה: ד"ה איקלעו]
כא ב ג ד מיי' שם הלכה ב טוש"ע יו"ד סימן ער סעיף א טוש"ע א"ה סימן א סעיף ב:
כב ה ו מיי' פי"א מהל' תפלה הלכ' טו יח טור ש"ע א"ח סימן קנג סעיף ה:
כג ז ח ט מיי' פ"ז מהל' מתנות עניים הלכה יד טוש"ע י"ד סימן רנו סעיף ו:

מסורת הש"ס

כות כה. וש"נ וע' נדרים עב.
[תוספ' פ"ג]
[ב"ב קנא.]
תוס' ב"ב ח: ד"ה פליון]
קדושין ד' מ: [ב"ק יז.]
מס' ד"א פ' יח
נ"א והמוכר [נ"ל ומוכר וכ"א בשאלתות פרשה נח סי' ה]

גליון הש"ס

גמ' אלא ללמוד תורה. ע' ... דף ח ע"ב תד"ה ... ע"ז דף יג ... תד"ה ללמוד תורה: שם אשה נמי. ע' ב"ב ד' ... ע"א תד"ה שנא'. ... גיגה ד' ב ע"ב תד"ה תהו ובגיטין ד' מא ע"ב תד"ה לא תהו:

רבינו חננאל

בית הכנסת מותר לעשותו בית המדרש. כתיב ואת בית גדול שרף באש. ריב"ל אמר בית המדרש הוא מקום שמגדלין בו תורה כדכתיב יגדיל תורה ויאדיר. ור' יוחנן אמר בית הכנסת מקום שמגדלין בו תפלה: פיסקא אבל (מקום) אם מכרו תורה לא יקחו ספרים איבעיא להו מהו למכור ס"ת ישן וליקח בדמיו חדש. ודייקינן ממתניתין דקתני אם מכרו תורה לא יקחו ספרים הא תורה*) דיעבד שרי. ומיבעיא לן לכתחילה מאי ואתינן למיפשטה מהא דתניא גוללין ס"ת במטפחות חומשין. וחומשין במטפחות נביאים וכתובים כו' ואסיקנא ליכא למשמע מינה. ת"ש מניחין תורה ע"ג תורה. ותורה ע"ג חומשין כו' ודחינן שאני הנחה דלא אפשר כמה דלא אפשר למכרכיה ולא ליתב דפא אחבריה אלא כשם שכורכין כך מניחין תורה ע"ג תורה. ת"ש מהא אין מוכרין ס"ת אפילו ישן ליקח בו חדש. ודחינן התם משום פשיעה שמא ימכר הישן ולא יזדמן לו לקנות חדש. כי קא מיבעיא לן דמנח ס"ת לימכר מהו למכור ישן ולקנות מיד זה החדש. ת"ש אין מוכרין ס"ת אלא ללמוד תורה ולישא אשה ש"מ תורה בתורה שרי. ודחינן שאני תלמוד תורה דאמר מר גדול תלמוד שהתלמוד מביא לידי מעשה ולא איפשיט בהדיא הלכך אין מוכרין ס"ת לכתחלה. ת"ר לא ימכור אדם ס"ת אע"פ שאין צריך לו יתר על כן ארשב"ג אפילו אין לו מה יאכל ומכר ס"ת או בתו אינו רואה סימן ברכה לעולם: פיסקא מכרו בית הכנסת לא יקחו רחוב וכן במותריהן. אמר רבא לא שנו שאם מכרו רחוב יקחו בדמים בית הכנסת וכן במותריהן. כלומר אם מכרו רחוב וקנו כנסת ונשארו מן הדמים לא יקנו אלא כנסת. וכן כל השנוים במשנתנו לא שנו אלא אם מכרו והותירו אבל אם גבו מעות לקנות בית הכנסת וקנו בית הכנסת והותירו מן המעות מותר להן לקנות מה שרוצה. קתני מיהא אם מכרו רחוב לא יקחו אלא בית הכנסת כו' ומותבינן עליה מהא בד"א שלא התנו. ואוקימנה הכי בד"א שלא התנו בשעה שמכרו אבל אם התנו מעיקרא. ואמר בשעה שמכרו ז' טובי העיר במעמד אנשי העיר אפילו לדוכססיא שהוא פרשא דמתא שרי. א"ר יוחנן בני העיר שהלכו לעיר אחרת ופסקו עליהן צדקה נותנין וכשבאין מביאין אותה עמהן ומפרנסין בה עניי עירם. אבל יחיד שהלך לעיר אחרת ופסקו עליו צדקה תנתן לעניי אותה העיר. רב הונא גזר תעניתא עול לגביה רב הונא בר חנילאי וכל בני מאתיה רמו עליה צדקה ויהבו כדבעו למיהדר אמרו ליה ליהב לן

*) נ"ל בתורה ש"ד מתני' דיעבד וכו'.

כד א מיי' פי"א מהל' תפלה הל' יז סמג עשין יט טוש"ע א"ח סי' קנג ס"ט:
כה ב מיי' פ"ג מהל' ק"ש הל' ב טוש"ע א"ח סי' עח:
כו ג מיי' פ"ד מהל' תפלה הלכה יד סמג עשין יח טוש"ע א"ח סימן צב סעיף ח:

חבר עיר אבל יש שם חבר עיר — תינתן לחבר עיר. וכ"ש דעניי דידי ודידכו עלי סמיכי.§ **מתני'** אין מוכרין את של רבים ליחיד מפני שמורידין אותו מקדושתו, דברי רבי מאיר. אמרו לו: א"כ אף לא מעיר גדולה לעיר קטנה.§ **גמ'** שפיר קאמרי ליה רבנן לר"מ! ור"מ: מעיר גדולה לעיר קטנה — מעיקרא קדישא, השתא נמי קדישא, מרבים ליחיד — ליכא קדושה. ורבנן: אי איכא למיחש — כי האי גוונא נמי איכא למיחש, משום "ברוב עם הדרת מלך".§ **מתני'** אין מוכרין בית הכנסת אלא על תנאי שאם ירצו יחזירוהו, דברי ר"מ. וחכ"א: מוכרין אותו ממכר עולם, חוץ מארבעה דברים: למרחץ, ולבורסקי, לטבילה, ולבית המים. ר' יהודה אומר: מוכרין אותה לשם חצר, והלוקח מה שירצה יעשה.§ **גמ'** ולר"מ היכי דיירי בה? הא הויא לה רבית! א"ר יוחנן: ר"מ בשיטת ר"י אמרה, דאמר: צד אחד ברבית — מותר. דתניא: הרי שהיה נושה בחבירו מנה ועשה לו שדהו מכר, בזמן שמוכר אוכל פירות — מותר, לוקח אוכל פירות — אסור. ר' יהודה אומר אפילו לוקח אוכל פירות מותר. וא"ר יהודה: מעשה בביתוס בן זונן שעשה שדהו מכר על פי ראב"ע, ולוקח אוכל פירות היה. אמרו לו: משם ראיה?! מוכר אוכל פירות היה, ולא לוקח. מאי בינייהו? צד אחד ברבית איכא בינייהו. מר סבר: צד אחד ברבית — מותר, ומר סבר: צד אחד ברבית — אסור. רבא אמר: דכ"ע צד אחד ברבית אסור, והכא רבית ע"מ להחזיר איכא בינייהו. מר סבר: רבית ע"מ להחזיר — מותר, ומר סבר: אסור.§ וחכ"א מוכרין אותו ממכר עולם" וכו'.§ אר"י אמר שמואל: מותר לאדם להשתין מים בתוך ד' אמות של תפלה. אמר רב יוסף: מאי קמ"ל? תנינא, ר' יהודה אומר: מוכרין אותה לשום חצר, ולוקח מה שירצה יעשה. ואפילו רבנן לא קאמרי אלא בית הכנסת דקביע קדושתיה, אבל ד"א דלא קביע קדושתייהו — לא. תני תנא קמיה דרב נחמן: המתפלל מרחיק ד"א ומשתין, והמשתין מרחיק ד"א ומתפלל. א"ל: בשלמא המשתין מרחיק ד"א ומתפלל תנינא: כמה ירחיק מהן ומן הצואה — ד"א, אלא המתפלל מרחיק ד"א ומשתין למה לי? אי הכי, קדשתינהו לכולהו שבילי דנהרדעא! תני: ישהה. בשלמא משתין ישהה כדי הילוך ד"א — משום ניצוצות, אלא מתפלל ישהה כדי הילוך ד"א ל"ל? אמר רב אשי: שכל ד"א תפלתו סדורה בפיו ורחושי מרחשן שפוותיה.§ זלפ"ן סימן.§ שאלו תלמידיו את רבי זכאי: במה הארכת ימים? אמר להם: מימי לא השתנתי מים בתוך ד"א של תפלה, ולא כניתי שם לחבירי, ולא ביטלתי קידוש היום. אמא זקינה היתה לי, פעם אחת מכרה כפה שבראשה והביאה לי קידוש היום. תנא: כשמתה הניחה לו ג' מאות גרבי יין, כשמת הוא הניח לבניו שלשת אלפים גרבי יין. רב הונא הוה אסר ריתא וקאי קמיה דרב, אמר ליה: מאי האי? א"ל: לא הוה לי(א) קידושא, ומשכנתיה להמייניא, ואתאי ביה קידושא. א"ל: יהא רעוא דתיטום בשיראי. כי איכלל רבה בריה, רב הונא איניש גוצא הוה, גנא אפוריא, אתיין בנתיה וכלתיה שלחן ושדיין מנייהו עליה, עד דאיטום בשיראי. שמע רב ואיקפד, אמר: מאי טעמא לא אמרת לי כי (ב)ברכתיך "וכן למר"? שאלו תלמידיו את ר"א בן שמוע: במה הארכת ימים? אמר להם: מימי לא עשיתי קפנדריא לב"ה, ולא פסעתי על ראשי עם קדוש, ולא נשאתי כפי בלא ברכה. שאלו תלמידיו את ר' פרידא: במה הארכת ימים? אמר להם: מימי לא קדמני אדם לבית המדרש ולא

חבר עיר. תלמיד חכם המתעסק בצרכי צבור: ליכא קדושה. שאין אומרים דבר שבקדושה פחות מעשרה: ורבנן. אמרי: אי איכא למיחש בין רב למעט — הכא נמי איכא למיחש משום "ברוב עם הדרת מלך", ולא משכחת מכירה בבית הכנסת. אלא לא חיישינן, דכיון דשקיל דמי ומעלי להו בקדושה מעולה — כל דבעי לוקח עביד, חוץ מד' דברים כדקתני סיפא: **מתני'** אלא על תנאי. ואפילו מרבים לרבים אסר ר' מאיר מכירת חלוטין, דדרך בזיון הוא, [כלומר: אינן בעיניו לכלום]: וחכמים אומרים וכו' ממכר עולם. (ג)ליחיד, ולכל תשמיש, חוץ מד' דברים: לבית המים. [א]לכביסה. אי נמי: לבית מי רגלים: **גמ'** בד' אמות של תפלה. לאחר זמן: קדשתינהו לכולהו שבילי דנהרדעא. שאין לך ד"א בהן שלא התפללו בהן עוברי דרכים: תני ישהה. כדי הילוך ארבע אמות: משום ניצוצות. שלא יטנפו בגדיו בניצוצות שבאמתו: במה הארכת ימים. באיזה זכות: כפה. לעיף: אסר ריתא.(ד) מין גמי: דתיטום בשיראי. סתום ומכוסה במעילין. "סתמום פלשתים" תרגומו טמונין פלשתאי (בראשית כו): איכלל. כשנכנס לחופה: [שלחן]. היו פושטות בגדיהן: וכן למר. אף אתה תהא מבורך לכך, שמא היה עת רצון, ותתקיים אף בי: קפנדריא. מקצר הילוכו דרך בית הכנסת: ולא פסעתי על ראשי עם קודש. כשהיו התלמידין בבית המדרש על גבי קרקע, ההולך על גבי מסיבתן לישב למקומן נראה כפוסע על ראשי העם: ולא נשאתי(ה) כפי. לדוכן לברכת כהנים. לפי שהכהנים צריכין לברך "ברוך אתה ה' אלהינו מלך העולם אשר קדשנו (במצותיו וצונו) בקדושתו של אהרן", במסכת סוטה (דף לט.):

רבי יהודה סבר צד אחד ברבית מותר. קשה: מאי שנא מלוה סאה בסאה דאמר ב"איזהו נשך" (ב"מ דף סג. ושם) דאסור משום דאיכא צד אחד ברבית, דשמא תייקר התבואה! ויש לומר: דשאני הכא דלא הוי דרך הלואה, אלא בתורת מכר אתא לידיה. והכי קשה: מאי שנא ממשכן לו בית משכן לו שדה, דאמר התם (דף סה:) דאפי' אמר ליה לכשתרצה למוכרם לא תמכרם אלא לי בדמים הללו, ואכל פירות (יותר ממה שהלוה) — אסור. ואמר רב הונא בריה דר' יהושע דלא כר' יהודה, דאי כר' יהודה — האמר צד אחד ברבית מותר. והכא ליכא כי אם צד אחד ברבית, דשמא לא ימכרם, וגם הוי הלואה מדקאמר "משכן" — ואפילו הכי שרי רבי יהודה! וי"ל: דהכתי לא דמי כלל להלואת סאה בסאה, דהתם ליכא צד מכר כלל, אבל הכא וגבי משכן — איכא צד אחד מכר:

רבא אמר רבית על מנת להחזיר איכא בינייהו. ולרבי מאיר דמתני', סבירא ליה שהיו מתנין להחזיר שכירות בית הכנסת כשחזרו, ובהכי שרו כר' יהודה*:

לא השתנתי בתוך ד' אמות של תפלה. ואפילו היכא שיש היתר גמור, כגון ששהה כדי הילוך ד' אמות:

ולא כניתי שם לחבירי. אפילו כינוי דלא הוי גנאי, והא דאמרינן (ב"מ דף נח:) דהמכנה שם לחבירו אין לו חלק לעולם הבא — היינו בכינוי של פגם משפחה:

הניחה לו ג' (*אלפים) גרבי יין. דאמרינן: הזהיר בקידוש היום זוכה וממלאים לו גרבי יין (שבת דף כג:):

שאלו תלמידיו את ר' פרידא במה הארכת ימים כו'. קשה: *דאדרבה, היה בזכות שהיה שונה לתלמיד אחד ארבע מאות זימני, ונפק בת קול (ו)ואמר: ניחא ליך דליזכי כולי דריה לעלמא דאתי או דליחיי ד' מאה שנין? אמר הקב"ה: יהבו ליה הא והא (עירובין דף נד:). וי"ל: דמעיקרא לא ידע כן, עד לבסוף שראה שחיה כל כך*:

[ועי' תוס' עירובין נד: תרצו עוד באופן אחר]

רבינו חננאל

לן מר כו' עד בד"א שאין שם חבר עיר אבל יש חבר עיר תנתן לחבר עיר. כ"ש דעניי דידכו נמי עלי סמיכי: **מתני'** אין מוכרין של רבים ליחיד כו' אין מוכרין בית הכנסת אלא על תנאי. פירוש בית הכנסת דיחיד אימתי [שירצה] יחזירוהו דברי ר"מ. ואקשינן עלה ולר"מ היכי דיירי בה והלא רבית הוא. ואוקמה ר' יוחנן ר"מ בשיטת רבי יהודה אמרה דתניא הרי שהיה נושה בחברו מנה ועשה לו שדהו מכר כו' צד אחד ברבית. פירוש אם תהיה הלואה שתים בשלש וכיוצא בה הרי זו רבית גמורה משני צדדין גבי מלוה וגבי לוה ושניהן עוברין אבל העושה שדהו מכר על תנאי גבי לוקח הוי רבית דאי מייתי זוזיה מהדר ליה בעל כורחיה אבל גבי מוכר לא הוי דאי בעי לא מהדר ליה לעולם ולא אתי לידי איסור רבית. ואפילו מהדר ליה לא הוי רבית אלא כשיחזיר ומן מוכח מהשתא שיחזיר ושמא לא יחזיר לעולם וסבר לה ר' מאיר כר' יהודה דתניא צד אחד ברבית מותר. רבא אמר כולי עלמא צד אחד ברבית אסור והכא ברבית ע"מ להחזיר איכא בינייהו. ת"ק סבר רבית אפילו על מנת להחזירו כשיביא לו מעותיו אסור. ור' יהודה סבר כיון דבעידנא דמייתי ליה מעותיו מהדר ליה מאי דאכל מן הפירות שרי דלאו רבית דאסרה תורה הוא: **פיסקא** וחכ"א מוכרין איתו ממכר עולם חוץ מד' דברים למרחץ לבורסקי לבית הטבילה לבית המים. אמר שמואל מותר להשתין בתוך ד' אמות של תפלה והני מילי כגון בית או דרך וכיוצא בהן דלא קביעא קדושתייהו *) כגון בית הכנסת לא. ואסיקנא המתפלל מרחיק ד' אמות מהן דתנן כמה ירחיק מהן ומן הצואה ד' אמות. וכן המשתין צריך לשהות כדי הילוך ד' אמות ואח"כ יתפלל משום ניצוצות. וכן המתפלל צריך לשהות כדי הילוך ד' אמות וישתין. שכל הילוך ד' אמות תפלה סדורה בפיו ורחושי מרחשי שפוותיה. שאלו אלו כולן במה שהאריכו ימים כו' עד מתניתין ופשוטות הן. מתניתין

*) נראה דצ"ל אבל בהכנ"ס דקביע קדושתי' לא וכו':

הגהות הב"ח

(א) גמ' א"ל לא הוה לי חמרא לקידושא וכו' ואתאי ביה יין קידושא: (ב) שם כי ברכתיו וכן למר. נ"ב אע"פ דלא היה שום ריוח לרב הונא בהא דהוו שדיין מנייהו עליה אפ"ה איקפד רב דשמא היה עת רצון ובדידיה הוה הדבר תלה ומתקיים דהיה מגיע לעושר גדול: (ג) רש"י ד"ה וחכ"א וכו' ממכר עולם ואפילו ליחיד: (ד) ד"ה אסר ריתא חגור עשב מין גמי: (ה) ד"ה ולא נשאתי את כפי לדוכן לברך ברכת כהנים בלא ברכה לפי שהכהנים: (ו) תוס' ד"ה שאלו וכו' בת קול ואמרה ליה ניחא לך דליזכו אנא ודראי לעלמא דאתי או דליסופי לך חיי ד' מאה שנין אמר דניזכו אנא ודראי לעלמא דאתי אמר הקב"ה יהבו:

הגהות הגר"א

[א] רש"י ד"ה לבית המים (לכביסה אי נמי) תא"מ:

(א) וְלֹא בֵּרַכְתִּי לִפְנֵי כֹהֵן, *וְלֹא אָכַלְתִּי מִבְּהֵמָה שֶׁלֹּא הוּרְמוּ מַתְּנוֹתֶיהָ. *דְּא"ר יִצְחָק א"ר יוֹחָנָן: אָסוּר לֶאֱכוֹל מִבְּהֵמָה שֶׁלֹּא הוּרְמוּ מַתְּנוֹתֶיהָ. וְאָמַר ר' יִצְחָק: *כָּל הָאוֹכֵל מִבְּהֵמָה שֶׁלֹּא הוּרְמוּ מַתְּנוֹתֶיהָ — כְּאִילּוּ אוֹכֵל טְבָלִים. [א]וְלֵית הִלְכְתָא כְּוָותֵיהּ. "וְלֹא בֵּרַכְתִּי לִפְנֵי כֹהֵן", לְמֵימְרָא דְּמַעַלְיוּתָא הִיא? וְהָא א"ר יוֹחָנָן: כָּל תַּלְמִיד חָכָם שֶׁמְּבָרֵךְ לְפָנָיו, אֲפִילּוּ כ"ג עַם הָאָרֶץ — אוֹתוֹ ת"ח חַיָּיב מִיתָה, שֶׁנֶּאֱמַר °"כָּל מְשַׂנְאַי אָהֲבוּ מָוֶת". *אַל תִּקְרֵי "מְשַׂנְאַי" אֶלָּא "מַשְׂנִיאַי"! כִּי קָאָמַר אִיהוּ — בְּשָׁוִין. שָׁאֲלוּ תַּלְמִידָיו אֶת רַבִּי נְחוּנְיָא בֶּן הַקָּנָה: בַּמֶּה הֶאֱרַכְתָּ יָמִים? אָמַר לָהֶם: מִיָּמַי לֹא נִתְכַּבַּדְתִּי בִּקְלוֹן חֲבֵרִי, וְלֹא עָלְתָה עַל מִטָּתִי קִלְלַת חֲבֵרִי, וְוַתְּרָן בְּמָמוֹנִי הָיִיתִי. "לֹא נִתְכַּבַּדְתִּי בִּקְלוֹן חֲבֵרִי" — כִּי הָא דְּרַב הוּנָא דְּרֵי מָרָא אַכַּתְפֵּיהּ, אֲתָא רַב חָנָא בַּר חֲנִילַאי וְקָא *דָּרֵי מִינֵּיהּ. א"ל: אִי רְגִילַתְּ דְּדָרֵית בְּמָאתִיךְ — דְּרֵי, וְאִי לָא — אִתְיַיקּוּרֵי אֲנָא בְּזִילוּתָא דִּידָךְ, לָא נִיחָא לִי. "וְלֹא עָלְתָה עַל מִטָּתִי קִלְלַת חֲבֵרִי" — כִּי הָא דְּמָר זוּטְרָא, כִּי הֲוָה סָלֵיק לְפוּרְיֵיהּ אָמַר: שָׁרֵי לֵיהּ (ב) לְכָל מַאן דְּצַעֲרָן. "וַתְּרָן בְּמָמוֹנִי הָיִיתִי" — *דַּאֲמַר מָר: אִיּוֹב וַתְּרָן בְּמָמוֹנֵיהּ הֲוָה, שֶׁהָיָה מַנִּיחַ פְּרוּטָה לַחֶנְוָנִי מִמָּמוֹנֵיהּ. שָׁאַל ר"ע אֶת רַבִּי נְחוּנְיָא הַגָּדוֹל, (אָמַר לוֹ): בַּמֶּה הֶאֱרַכְתָּ יָמִים? אָתוּ *גַּוְוזֵי וְקָא מָחוּ לֵיהּ. סְלֵיק יָתֵיב אַרֵישָׁא דְּדִיקְלָא, א"ל: רַבִּי, אִם נֶאֱמַר °"כֶּבֶשׂ" לָמָּה נֶאֱמַר "אֶחָד"? אֲמַר לְהוּ: צוּרְבָא מִדְּרַבָּנַן הוּא, שַׁבְקוּהוּ. א"ל: "אֶחָד" — *מְיוּחָד שֶׁבְּעֶדְרוֹ. א"ל: מִיָּמַי לֹא קִבַּלְתִּי מַתָּנוֹת, וְלֹא עָמַדְתִּי עַל מִדּוֹתַי, וְוַתְּרָן בְּמָמוֹנִי הָיִיתִי. "לֹא קִבַּלְתִּי מַתָּנוֹת", כִּי הָא *דְּר' אֶלְעָזָר, כִּי הֲווּ מְשַׁדְּרִי לֵיהּ מַתָּנוֹת מִבֵּי נְשִׂיאָה לָא הֲוָה שָׁקֵיל, כִּי הֲוָה מְזַמְּנִי לֵיהּ — לָא הֲוָה אָזֵיל, אֲמַר לְהוּ: לָא נִיחָא לְכוּ דְּאֶחְיֶה? דִּכְתִיב °"שׂוֹנֵא מַתָּנוֹת יִחְיֶה". ר' זֵירָא, כִּי הֲווּ מְשַׁדְּרִי לֵיהּ מִבֵּי נְשִׂיאָה — לָא הֲוָה שָׁקֵיל, כִּי הֲוָה מְזַמְּנִי לֵיהּ — אָזֵיל, אֲמַר: אִתְיַיקּוּרֵי דְּמִתְיַיקְּרִי בִּי. "וְלֹא עָמַדְתִּי עַל מִדּוֹתַי" — *דַּאֲמַר רָבָא: [ב]כָּל הַמַּעֲבִיר עַל מִדּוֹתָיו מַעֲבִירִין מִמֶּנּוּ כָּל פְּשָׁעָיו, שֶׁנֶּאֱמַר[א] °)"נוֹשֵׂא עָוֹן וְעוֹבֵר עַל פֶּשַׁע" לְמִי נוֹשֵׂא עָוֹן — לְמִי שֶׁעוֹבֵר עַל פֶּשַׁע. *שָׁאַל רַבִּי אֶת ר' יְהוֹשֻׁעַ בֶּן קָרְחָה: בַּמֶּה הֶאֱרַכְתָּ יָמִים? א"ל: קַצְתָּ בְּחַיַּי? אָמַר לוֹ: רַבִּי, *תּוֹרָה הִיא וְלִלְמוֹד אֲנִי צָרִיךְ, א"ל: מִיָּמַי לֹא נִסְתַּכַּלְתִּי בִּדְמוּת אָדָם רָשָׁע. דְּאָמַר ר' יוֹחָנָן: אָסוּר לְאָדָם לְהִסְתַּכֵּל בְּצֶלֶם דְּמוּת אָדָם רָשָׁע, שֶׁנֶּאֱמַר °"לוּלֵא פְּנֵי יְהוֹשָׁפָט מֶלֶךְ יְהוּדָה אֲנִי נוֹשֵׂא אִם אַבִּיט אֵלֶיךָ וְאִם אֶרְאֶךָּ", ר"א אָמַר: עֵינָיו כֵּהוֹת, שֶׁנֶּאֱמַר °"וַיְהִי כִּי זָקֵן יִצְחָק וַתִּכְהֶיןָ עֵינָיו מֵרְאֹת", מִשּׁוּם דְּאִסְתַּכֵּל בְּעֵשָׂו הָרָשָׁע. וְהָא גְּרָמָא לֵיהּ? *וְהָאָמַר ר' יִצְחָק: לְעוֹלָם אַל תְּהִי קִלְלַת הֶדְיוֹט קַלָּה בְּעֵינֶיךָ, שֶׁהֲרֵי אֲבִימֶלֶךְ קִלֵּל אֶת שָׂרָה וְנִתְקַיֵּים בְּזַרְעָהּ, שֶׁנֶּאֱמַר °"הִנֵּה הוּא לָךְ כְּסוּת עֵינַיִם", אַל תִּקְרֵי כְּסוּת אֶלָּא כְּסִיַּית עֵינַיִם! הָא וְהָא גָּרְמָא לֵיהּ. רָבָא אֲמַר מֵהָכָא: °°)"שְׂאֵת פְּנֵי רָשָׁע לֹא טוֹב". בִּשְׁעַת פְּטִירָתוֹ א"ל: [רַבִּי], בָּרְכֵנִי! א"ל: יְהִי רָצוֹן שֶׁתַּגִּיעַ לַחֲצִי יָמַי. וּלְכוּלְּהוּ לָא? אָמַר לוֹ: הַבָּאִים אַחֲרֶיךָ בְּהֵמָה יִרְעוּ? אֲבוּהּ בַּר אִיהִי וּמִנְיָמִן בַּר אִיהִי, חַד אֲמַר: תֵּיתֵי לִי דְּלָא אִסְתַּכַּלִי בְּכוּתִי, וְחַד אֲמַר: תֵּיתֵי לִי דְּלָא עֲבַדִי שׁוּתָּפוּת בַּהֲדֵי כּוּתִי. *שָׁאֲלוּ תַּלְמִידָיו אֶת ר' זֵירָא: בַּמֶּה הֶאֱרַכְתָּ יָמִים? אָמַר לָהֶם: מִיָּמַי לֹא הִקְפַּדְתִּי בְּתוֹךְ בֵּיתִי, וְלֹא צָעַדְתִּי בִּפְנֵי מִי שֶׁגָּדוֹל מִמֶּנִּי, [ג]וְלֹא הִרְהַרְתִּי בַּמְּבוֹאוֹת הַמְטוּנָּפוֹת, וְלֹא הָלַכְתִּי ד"א בְּלֹא תּוֹרָה וּבְלֹא תְּפִילִּין, [ד]וְלֹא יָשַׁנְתִּי בְּבֵית הַמִּדְרָשׁ לֹא שֵׁינַת קֶבַע וְלֹא שֵׁינַת עֲרַאי, וְלֹא שַׂשְׂתִּי בְּתַקָּלַת חֲבֵירַי, וְלֹא קָרָאתִי לַחֲבֵירִי (*בַּחֲנִיכָתוֹ) וְאָמְרִי לַהּ *)(בַּחֲכִינָתוֹ).§ **מתני'** וְעוֹד א"ר יְהוּדָה: בֵּית הַכְּנֶסֶת שֶׁחָרַב אֵין מַסְפִּידִין בְּתוֹכוֹ, וְאֵין מַפְשִׁילִין בְּתוֹכוֹ חֲבָלִים, וְאֵין פּוֹרְשִׂין לְתוֹכוֹ מְצוּדוֹת, וְאֵין שׁוֹטְחִין עַל גַּגּוֹ פֵּירוֹת, וְאֵין עוֹשִׂין אוֹתוֹ קַפֶּנְדַּרְיָא, שֶׁנֶּאֱמַר °"וַהֲשִׁמּוֹתִי אֶת מִקְדְּשֵׁיכֶם" — [ה]קְדוּשָּׁתָן אַף כְּשֶׁהֵן שׁוֹמְמִין. עָלוּ בּוֹ עֲשָׂבִים — לֹא יִתְלוֹשׁ, מִפְּנֵי עָגְמַת נֶפֶשׁ.§ **גמ'** ת"ר: *[ו]בָּתֵּי כְנֵסִיּוֹת אֵין נוֹהֲגִין בָּהֶן קַלּוּת רֹאשׁ: אֵין אוֹכְלִין בָּהֶן, וְאֵין שׁוֹתִין בָּהֶן, וְאֵין

°) מיכה ז °°) משלי יח *) [נ"ל בחניכתו כך הגי' בע"י ומעתה מובן פרש"י על נכון דמייתי ראייה ממשנה גיטין פז:]

רש"י

מַתְּנוֹתֶיהָ. הַזְּרוֹעַ וְהַלְּחָיַיִם וְהַקֵּיבָה: וְלֹא בֵּרַכְתִּי. בִּסְעוּדָה לִפְנֵי כֹהֵן, דְּאָמַר מַר (גיטין דף נט:): "וְקִדַּשְׁתּוֹ" (ויקרא כא) — לְכָל דָּבָר שֶׁבִּקְדוּשָּׁה, לִפְתּוֹחַ רִאשׁוֹן וּלְבָרֵךְ רִאשׁוֹן: מַשְׂנִיאַי. שֶׁגּוֹרְמִין לִבְנֵי אָדָם לִשְׂנוֹאתוֹ, שֶׁהָרוֹאֶה תַּלְמִיד חָכָם שָׁפָל לִפְנֵי עַם הָאָרֶץ אוֹמֵר: אֵין נַחַת רוּחַ בַּתּוֹרָה: לֹא נִתְכַּבַּדְתִּי כו'. מְפָרֵשׁ לַהּ וְאָזֵיל: מָרָא. פורי"ש בְּלַעַז: וְקָא שָׁקֵיל מִינֵּיהּ. לְכַבְּדוֹ, וְיִשָּׂאֶנָּה הוּא: דָּרֵית בְּמָאתִיךְ. שֶׁאַתָּה נוֹשֵׂא כְּלִי כָּזֶה בְּעִירְךָ: גַּוְוזֵי. סָרִיסִין. הָיוּ עֲבָדִים מְשָׁרְתִים אוֹתוֹ, וְקָא מָחוּ לֵיהּ לְר"ע, סְבוּרִין הָיוּ שֶׁהָיָה קָץ בְּחַיָּיו: אִם נֶאֱמַר כֶּבֶשׂ. "אֶת הַכֶּבֶשׂ אֶחָד תַּעֲשֶׂה בַבֹּקֶר": וְלֹא עָמַדְתִּי עַל מִדּוֹתַי. לְשַׁלֵּם גְּמוּל רַע לְמִי שֶׁצִּיעֲרַנִי: לִלְמוֹד אֲנִי צָרִיךְ. אוּלַי אוּכַל לְקַיֵּים: לוּלֵא פְּנֵי יְהוֹשָׁפָט מֶלֶךְ יְהוּדָה אֲנִי נוֹשֵׂא אִם אַבִּיט אֵלֶיךָ וְאִם אֶרְאֶךָּ. אֱלִישָׁע אָמַר כֵּן לִיהוֹרָם: הַבָּאִים אַחֲרֶיךָ בְּהֵמָה יִרְעוּ. בִּתְמִיָּה: (ג) אֵין טוֹב לְךָ לִחְיוֹת יָמִים רַבִּים כָּמוֹנִי, שֶׁא"כ לֹא יִטְּלוּ בָּנֶיךָ בִּגְדוּלָּתְךָ. וְאַתָּה נָשִׂיא, וְהֵם כָּל יְמֵיהֶם יִהְיוּ הֶדְיוֹטוֹת: הִרְהַרְתִּי. דִּבְרֵי תוֹרָה: בְּלֹא תּוֹרָה. גִּרְסָתִי שְׁגוּרָה בְּפִי תָּמִיד: *(בַּחֲנִיכָתוֹ). אִם כִּינּוּ שֵׁם לַחֲבֵירוֹ לִגְנַאי: וְאָמְרִי לַהּ (*בַּחֲכִינָתוֹ). אֲפִילּוּ אוֹתוֹ כִּינּוּי שֶׁמְּסוּדָּר וּבָא לוֹ מִמִּשְׁפַּחְתּוֹ שֵׁם דּוֹפִי. כְּמוֹ "כָּתַב חֲנִיכָתוֹ וַחֲנִיכָתָהּ" דְּמַסֶּכֶת גִּיטִּין (דף פז:): **מתני'** מַפְשִׁילִין חֲבָלִים. וְהוּא הַדִּין לְכָל מְלָאכוֹת, אֶלָּא לְפִי שֶׁהַפְשָׁלַת חֲבָלִים צָרִיךְ מָקוֹם מְרוּוָח פָּנוּי, וּבֵית הַכְּנֶסֶת גָּדוֹל הוּא וְרָאוּי וּמַסְפִּיק לְכָךְ: מִפְּנֵי עָגְמַת נֶפֶשׁ. מַנִּיחִין בּוֹ עֲשָׂבִים, כְּדֵי שֶׁתְּהֵא עָגְמַת נֶפֶשׁ לְרוֹאֵיהֶן וְשֶׁיַּזְכִּירוּ אֶת יְמֵי בִּנְיָינוֹ, וְאֶת שֶׁהָיוּ רְגִילִין לְהִתְאַסֵּף שָׁם — יְבַקְּשׁוּ רַחֲמִים שֶׁיַּחְזְרוּ לְקַדְמוּתוֹ: **גמ'** אֵין אוֹכְלִין בָּהֶן כו'. וְלֹא גָּרְסִינַן "וְאֵין אוֹכְלִין בָּהֶן", דְּכוּלְּהוּ פֵּירוּשָׁא דְּקַלּוּת רֹאשׁ הֵן. לְשׁוֹן קַלּוּת — שֶׁמְּקִילִין אוֹתָהּ: וְאֵין

תוספות

כי קאמר איהו בשוין. וקשה מאי רבותא והא כתיב וקדשתו לכל דבר שבקדושה *לברך ראשון וי"ל דשוין לאו דוקא אלא כלומר שהכהן נמי תלמיד חכם אמנם אינו חשוב כמותו ואפי' הכי לא היה רבי פרידא רוצה לקרות לפניו וגם צריך לומר דשאר כהנים היו כפופים לרבי פרידא דאל"כ לא הוי רבותא כדחזינן פרק הניזקין (גיטין דף נט. ושם) דרב הונא לא הוי קרי בכהני אי לאו דרבי אמי ורבי אסי כהני חשיבי דארעא דישראל הוו כייפי ליה ועי"ל דהא דאמר התם דרב הונא לא הוה קרי בכהני אלא משום דשאר כהני כייפו ליה היינו דווקא בשבתות וי"ט דאיכא כינופיא אבל בב' ובה' קורא שפיר בפני כהן אע"ג דלא הוי גדול כ"כ ולדיוקא זה יש בהדיא פרק הניזקין ורבי פרידא לא רצה לקרות בפני כהן אפילו בב' ובה' ורש"י פירש דהכא מיירי בברכת המזון וה"נ משמע לישנא דלא ברכתי מדלא קאמר ולא קריתי וברכת המזון לא נתקן להן משום דרכי שלום ואפי' הכי לא היה רוצה רבי פרידא לברך בפני הכהן: **תיתי** לי דלא עבדי שותפות עם הכותי. אפי' בענין שאינו יכול לבא לידי שבועה ואפילו יחול עליו שבועה יפטרנו דסרי בשאר בני אדם אפ"ה לא היה רוצה לעשות*:

ועוד א"ר יהודה בית הכנסת שחרב. קשה מאי ועוד דהא לעיל הוה מקיל טפי מחכמים והכא הוא מחמיר ואם כן מאי ועוד וי"ל דקאי אהא דאמר ר' יהודה ברישא מוכרין אותו לשם חצר ודוקא לשם חצר קאמר אבל סתם אינה יורדת מקדושתה והיינו ועוד דאמר ר' יהודה כלומר ועוד חומרא אחרת מלבד הראשונה*:

אין אוכלין ואין שותין בהן. והא דאמר בריש ערבי פסחים (פסחים דף קא. ושם) דאורחין אכלו ושתו (ד) בבי כנישתא רוצה לומר בחדר הסמוכה לבית הכנסת:

בתי

עין משפט נר מצוה

[מו"ק כח:]

כז א מיי' פ"ט מהל' בכורים הל' יד:

כח ב מיי' פ"ב מהל' תשובה הלכה י טוש"ע א"ח סי' תרו סעיף א בהג"ה:

כט ג מיי' פ"ג מהל' ק"ש הלכה ד טוש"ע א"ח סי' פה סב:

ל ד מיי' פ"ד מהל' ת"ת הל' ט טוש"ע י"ד סי' רמו סעיף טז:

לא ה מיי' פי"א מהל' תפלה הלכה יא סמג עשין יט טוש"ע א"ח סי' קנא סעיף י:

לב ו מיי' שם הלכה ו טוש"ע שם סעיף א:

הגהות הגר"א

[א] גמרא נושא עון ועובר על פשע למי עובר על פשע למי שנושא עון (כך שמע הכותב מפיו):

[עי' תוס' בכורות ב: ד"ה שמא ותוס' סנהדרין סג: ד"ה אסור]

גליון הש"ס

גמ' שאל רבי את ר' יהושע ב"ק. עי' ב"ב דף קיג ע"א תוד"ה ומטו בה: **שם** להסתכל בצלם. דוקא להסתכל בו ביותר ולהתבונן בו בצלמו ובדמותו אבל ראיה בעלמא שרי מ"א סס"י רכו:

[עי' תוס' עירובין כג. ד"ה אי לימא]

רבינו חננאל

[מתני'] ועוד א"ר יהודה בית הכנסת שחרב אין מספידין בו ואין מפשילין לתוכו חבלים ואין פורשין בתוכו מצודות ואין שוטחין על גגו פירות ואין עושין אותו קפנדריא שנאמר והשמותי את מקדשיכם קדושתן בהן אף כשהן שוממין. עלו בו עשבים לא יתלוש מפני עגמת נפש: ת"ר בתי כנסיות אין נוהגין בהן קלות ראש אין אוכלין ואין שותין

הגהות הב"ח

(א) גמ' ולא אכלתי מבהמה שלא הורמו מתנותיה ולא ברכתי לפני כהן דאמר רבי יצחק: (ב) שם שרי ליה מריה לכל מאן: (ג) רש"י ד"ה הבאים וכו' בתמיה כלומר אין טוב: (ד) תוס' ד"ה אין אוכלין וכו' ושתו וגנו בבי כנישתא:

מסורת הש"ס

[חולין לז: מז.]

[חולין קלב: ע"ש]

וע"ש שהוא רבה בר בר חנה

[מלכים ב ג] שבת קיז. עירובין לט.]

[נ"ל בחכינתו]

[נ"ל בחניכתו]

ב"ב דף טו:

[גיר' הערוך גואזי]

[יומא לד: ע:]

[חולין מד:]

משלי ח

ס"א שקיל

במדבר כח

משלי טו

ר"ה דף יז. יומא דף כג. ודף פז:

ברכות סב.

מלכים ב ג

בראשית כז

לעיל טו. ע"ש ב"ק צג.

בראשית כ

תענית כ: ע"ש

ויקרא כו

[תוספ' פ"ב]

וְאֵין נֵיאוֹתִין בָּהֶם, וְאֵין מְטַיְּילִין בָּהֶם, וְאֵין נִכְנָסִין בָּהֶן בַּחַמָּה מִפְּנֵי הַחַמָּה וּבַגְּשָׁמִים מִפְּנֵי הַגְּשָׁמִים, וְאֵין מַסְפִּידִין בָּהֶן הֶסְפֵּד שֶׁל יָחִיד. אֲבָל קוֹרִין בָּהֶן, וְשׁוֹנִין בָּהֶן, וּמַסְפִּידִין בָּהֶן הֶסְפֵּד שֶׁל רַבִּים. א"ר יְהוּדָה: אֵימָתַי — בְּיִשּׁוּבָן, אֲבָל בְּחוּרְבָּנָן — מַנִּיחִין אוֹתָן וְעוֹלִין בָּהֶן עֲשָׂבִים, וְלֹא יִתְלוֹשׁ מִפְּנֵי עָגְמַת נֶפֶשׁ. עֲשָׂבִים — מַאן דְּכַר שְׁמַיְיהוּ? חַסּוּרֵי מִיחַסְּרָא וְהָכִי קָתָנֵי: וּמְכַבְּדִין אוֹתָן, וּמַרְבִּיצִין אוֹתָן כְּדֵי שֶׁלֹּא יַעֲלוּ בָּהֶן עֲשָׂבִים. א"ר יְהוּדָה: אֵימָתַי — בְּיִשּׁוּבָן, אֲבָל בְּחוּרְבָּנָן — מַנִּיחִין אוֹתָן לַעֲלוֹת. עָלוּ בָּהֶן עֲשָׂבִים — לֹא יִתְלוֹשׁ, מִפְּנֵי עָגְמַת נֶפֶשׁ. א"ר אַסִּי: בָּתֵּי כְנֵסִיּוֹת שֶׁבְּבָבֶל עַל תְּנַאי הֵן עֲשׂוּיִין, וְאעפ"כ אֵין נוֹהֲגִין בָּהֶן קַלּוּת רֹאשׁ. וּמַאי נִיהוּ — [א]חֶשְׁבּוֹנוֹת. אָמַר רַב אַסִּי: בהכ"נ שֶׁמְּחַשְּׁבִין בּוֹ חֶשְׁבּוֹנוֹת — מַלִּינִין בּוֹ אֶת הַמֵּת. מַלִּינִין סָלְקָא דַּעְתָּךְ? לָא סַגִּי דְּלָאו הָכִי! אֶלָּא: לַסּוֹף שֶׁיָּלִינוּ בּוֹ מֵת מִצְוָה. § "וְאֵין נֵיאוֹתִין בָּהֶן". § אָמַר רָבָא: [ב]חֲכָמִים וְתַלְמִידֵיהֶם מוּתָּרִין. דְּאָמַר ריב"ל: מַאי בֵּי רַבָּנַן — בֵּיתָא דְּרַבָּנַן. § "וְאֵין נִכְנָסִין בָּהֶן בַּחַמָּה מִפְּנֵי הַחַמָּה וּבַגְּשָׁמִים מִפְּנֵי הַגְּשָׁמִים". § כִּי הָא דְּרָבִינָא וְרַב אַדָּא בַּר מַתָּנָה הֲווּ קָיְימִי וְשָׁאֲלִי שְׁאֵילְתָא מֵרָבָא, אֲתָא זִילְחָא דְּמִיטְרָא. עָיְילִי לְבֵי כְנִישְׁתָּא. אָמְרִי: הַאי דְּעָיְילִינַן לְבֵי כְנִישְׁתָּא — לָאו מִשּׁוּם מִיטְרָא, אֶלָּא מִשּׁוּם *דִּשְׁמַעְתָּא בְּעָא צִילּוּתָא כְּיוֹמָא *דְּאִסְתְּנָא. א"ל רַב אַחָא בְּרֵיהּ דְּרָבָא לְרַב אַשִׁי: אִי אִצְטְרִיךְ לֵיהּ לְאִינִישׁ לְמִיקְרֵי גַּבְרָא מִבֵּי כְנִישְׁתָּא, מַאי? א"ל: [ג]אִי צוּרְבָא מֵרַבָּנַן הוּא — לֵימָא הִלְכְתָא, וְאִי תַּנָּא הוּא — לֵימָא מתני', וְאִי קָרָא הוּא, לֵימָא פְּסוּקָא. וְאִי לָא — לֵימָא לֵיהּ לְיָנוּקָא: אֵימָא לִי פְּסוּקָךְ. א"נ, נִישְׁהֵי פּוּרְתָּא וְנֵיקוּם. § "וּמַסְפִּידִין בָּהֶן הֶסְפֵּד שֶׁל רַבִּים". § ה"ד הֶסְפֵּידָא דְּרַבִּים? [ד]מַחְוֵי רַב חִסְדָּא: כְּגוֹן הֶסְפֵּידָא דְּקָאֵי בֵּיהּ רַב שֵׁשֶׁת, מַחְוֵי רַב שֵׁשֶׁת: כְּגוֹן הֶסְפֵּידָא דְּקָאֵי בֵּיהּ רַב חִסְדָּא. רַפְרָם אַסְפְּדַהּ לְכַלָּתֵיהּ בְּבֵי כְנִישְׁתָּא, אֲמַר: מִשּׁוּם יְקָרָא דִּידִי וּדְמִיתָא אֲתוּ כּוּלֵּיהּ עָלְמָא. ר' זֵירָא סַפְדֵיהּ לְהַהוּא מֵרַבָּנַן בְּבֵי כְנִישְׁתָּא, אֲמַר: אִי מִשּׁוּם יְקָרָא דִּידִי, אִי מִשּׁוּם יְקָרָא (א)דִּידֵיהּ, דְּמִיתָא, אֲתוּ כּוּלֵּי עָלְמָא. רֵישׁ לָקִישׁ סַפְדֵיהּ לְהַהוּא צוּרְבָא מֵרַבָּנַן דִּשְׁכִיחַ בְּאַרְעָא דְּיִשְׂרָאֵל, דַּהֲוֵי תָּנֵי הִלְכְתָא בכ"ד שׁוּרָתָא, אֲמַר: וַוי, חָסְרָא אַרְעָא דְּיִשְׂרָאֵל גַּבְרָא רַבָּה. הַהוּא דַּהֲוֵי תָּנֵי הִלְכְתָא סִיפְרָא וְסִיפְרֵי וְתוֹסֶפְתָּא, וּשְׁכִיב. אֲתוּ וַאֲמַרוּ לֵיהּ לְרַב נַחְמָן:(ב) לִיסְפְּדֵיהּ מָר! אֲמַר: הֵיכִי נִסְפְּדֵיהּ? הֵי צַנָּא דִּמְלֵי סִיפְרֵי דְּחָסַר! *תָּא חֲזִי מַה בֵּין תַּקִּיפֵי דְּאַרְעָא דְּיִשְׂרָאֵל לַחֲסִידֵי דְּבָבֶל. תְּנַן הָתָם: *[ה]וּדְאִשְׁתַּמֵּשׁ בְּתָגָא חֲלָף, *תָּנֵי רֵישׁ לָקִישׁ: זֶה הַמִּשְׁתַּמֵּשׁ בְּמִי שֶׁשּׁוֹנֶה הֲלָכוֹת, (ג)כִּתְרָהּ שֶׁל תּוֹרָה, וַאֲמַר עוּלָּא: לִשְׁתַּמֵּשׁ אִינִישׁ בְּמַאן דְּתָנֵי אַרְבָּעָה וְלָא לִשְׁתַּמֵּשׁ בְּמַאן דְּמַתְנֵי אַרְבָּעָה. כִּי הָא דְּרֵישׁ לָקִישׁ הֲוָה אָזֵיל בְּאוֹרְחָא, מְטָא עוּרְקְמָא דְּמַיָּא, אֲתָא הַהוּא גַּבְרָא אַרְכְּבֵיהּ אַכַּתְפֵּיהּ, וְקָא מְעַבַּר לֵיהּ. א"ל: קְרֵית? אֲמַר לֵיהּ: קְרֵינָא. תְּנֵית? תְּנֵינָא אַרְבָּעָה סִידְרֵי מִשְׁנָה. א"ל: פְּסַלְתְּ לָךְ אַרְבָּעָה טוּרֵי, וְטָעַנַתְּ בַּר לָקִישׁ אַכַּתְפָךְ?! שְׁדֵי בַּר לָקִישׁ בְּמַיָּא! אֲמַר לֵיהּ: נִיחָא לִי דְּאַשְׁמְעִינַן לְמָר. אִי הָכִי גְּמוֹר מִינִּי הָא מִלְּתָא דַּאֲמַר ר' זֵירָא: [ו]בְּנוֹת יִשְׂרָאֵל הֵן *הֶחְמִירוּ עַל עַצְמָן, שֶׁאֲפִילּוּ רוֹאוֹת טִיפַּת דָּם כְּחַרְדָּל יוֹשְׁבוֹת עָלָיו שִׁבְעָה נְקִיִּים. תָּנָא דְּבֵי אֵלִיָּהוּ: כָּל *הַשּׁוֹנֶה הֲלָכוֹת מוּבְטָח לוֹ שֶׁהוּא בֶּן עוֹלָם הַבָּא, שֶׁנֶּאֱמַר °"הֲלִיכוֹת עוֹלָם לוֹ", אַל תִּקְרֵי הֲלִיכוֹת — אֶלָּא הֲלָכוֹת. ת"ר: מְבַטְּלִין

רש"י

וְאֵין נֵיאוֹתִין. וְאֵין מִתְקַשְּׁטִין לְתוֹכוֹ, וְאֵין מְטַיְּילִין שָׁם: הֶסְפֵּד שֶׁל רַבִּים. שֶׁל תַּלְמִיד חָכָם שֶׁמֵּת, שֶׁצְּרִיכִין לְהִתְאַסֵּף וּלְהַסְפִּידוֹ. וּבֵית הַכְּנֶסֶת רָאוּי לְכָךְ, לְפִי שֶׁהוּא בַּיִת גָּדוֹל: מַאן דְּכַר שְׁמַיְיהוּ. הֵיכָא שָׁמְעִינַן לְתַנָּא קַמָּא לַעֲשׂוֹת בָּהֶן דָּבָר שֶׁמּוֹנְעִים מִלַּעֲלוֹת עֲשָׂבִים: אֵימָתַי. מְכַבְּדִין וּמַרְבִּיצִין אוֹתָן בְּיִשּׁוּבָן. לְאַחַר שֶׁמְּכַבְּדִין מְזַלְּפִין אֶת הַמַּיִם לְהַרְבִּיץ אֶת הָאָבָק: עַל תְּנַאי. עַל מְנָת שֶׁיִּשְׁתַּמְּשׁוּ בָּהֶן: מַלִּינִין בּוֹ. מַשְׁמַע: דְּחוֹבָה הִיא לְהָלִין בּוֹ אֶת הַמֵּת: לַסּוֹף שֶׁיָּלִינוּ בּוֹ מֵתֵי מִצְוָה. שֶׁיָּמוּתוּ בָּעִיר מֵתִים שֶׁאֵין לָהֶן קוֹבְרִין: מַאי בֵּי רַבָּנָן. לָמָּה קוֹרִין בָּתֵּי מִדְרָשׁוֹת "בֵּי רַבָּנָן" — לְפִי שֶׁבֵּיתָם הוּא לְכָל דָּבָר: זִילְחָא דְּמִטְרָא. זֶרֶם מַיִם שֶׁבָּאִין בְּכֹחַ: לָאו מִשּׁוּם מִיטְרָא. שֶׁיָּגֵן עָלֵינוּ מִפְּנֵי הַגְּשָׁמִים, שֶׁאִם לֹא הָיִינוּ עוֹסְקִין בִּשְׁמַעְתָּא — לֹא הָיִינוּ נִכְנָסִין: צִילּוּתָא. דַּעַת צְלוּלָה וּמְיוּשֶּׁבֶת, שֶׁאֵינוֹ טָרוּד בִּכְלוּם מַחֲשָׁבָה: אִי צְרִיכָא לֵיהּ אִינִישׁ לְמִקְרֵי גַּבְרָא מִבֵּי כְנִישְׁתָּא מַאי נִיעֲבִיד. מֵאַחַר שֶׁאֵין נִכְנָסִין בָּהֶן שֶׁלֹּא לְצוֹרֶךְ: לֵימָא לִינוּקָא. שֶׁהַתִּינוֹקוֹת הָיוּ רְגִילִין לִקְרוֹת בְּבֵית הַכְּנֶסֶת: כְּגוֹן הֶסְפֵּידָא דְּקָאֵי בֵּי רַב שֵׁשֶׁת. אִם יָמוּת אָדָם אֶחָד בֵּי רַב שֵׁשֶׁת: אֲמַר אִי מִשּׁוּם יְקָרָא דִּידִי אִי מִשּׁוּם יְקָרָא דְּמִיתָא. הָוֵה לֵיהּ הֶסְפֵּד שֶׁל רַבִּים: אֲתוּ כּוּלֵּי עָלְמָא. לִסְפּוֹד: דַּהֲוָה תָּנֵי הִלְכְתָא. שֶׁהָיָה שׁוֹנֶה מִשְׁנָיוֹת לַתַּלְמִידִים: בְּכ"ד שׁוּרוֹת. שֶׁל תַּלְמִידִים: הָכִי גָּרְסִינַן. חָסְרָא לֵיהּ אַרְעָא דְּיִשְׂרָאֵל גַּבְרָא רַבָּה: הֵיכִי אַסְפִּיד. בְּמַאי אֶסְפְּדֶנּוּ: הֵי צַנָּא מְלֵא סִיפְרֵי. אֵינוֹ אֶלָּא כְּסַל שֶׁמִּילְּאוּהוּ סְפָרִים, וְאֵין מֵבִין מַה בְּתוֹכָהּ. אַף שׁוֹנֶה הֲלָכוֹת וְלֹא שִׁימֵּשׁ ת"ח לִלְמוֹד, שֶׁיְּבִינוּהוּ טַעֲמֵי מִשְׁנָה. וּפְעָמִים שֶׁדִּבְרֵי מִשְׁנָה סוֹתְרִין זֶה אֶת זֶה, וְצָרִיךְ לְתָרְצָהּ, כְּגוֹן: הָכָא בְּמַאי עָסְקִינַן, וּכְגוֹן: הָא מַנִּי — רַבִּי פְּלוֹנִי הִיא, וּכְגוֹן: חַסּוּרֵי מִיחַסְּרָא, אֵינוֹ יוֹדֵעַ מַה שּׁוֹנֶה: תַּקִּיפֵי אַרְעָא דְּיִשְׂרָאֵל. רֵישׁ לָקִישׁ, דְּאָמְרִינַן בְּמַסֶּכֶת יוֹמָא (דף ט:), דַּאֲפִילּוּ בַּהֲדֵי רַבָּה בַּר בַּר חָנָה לָא מִשְׁתָּעֵי, דְּמַאן דְּמִשְׁתָּעֵי בַּהֲדֵי רֵישׁ לָקִישׁ בְּשׁוּקָא יָהֲבִין לֵיהּ עִיסְקָא בְּלָא סָהֲדֵי. רַב נַחְמָן בַּר יִצְחָק מֵחֲסִידֵי בָּבֶל, בְּשִׁילְהֵי מַסֶּכֶת סוֹטָה (דף מט:), דְּקָאָמַר לֵיהּ: לָא תִּיתְנֵי יִרְאַת חֵטְא — דְּאִיכָּא אֲנָא: בְּתָגָא. כֶּתֶר תּוֹרָה: חֲלַף. עָבַר מִן הָעוֹלָם: עוּרְקְמָא דְּמַיָּא. שְׁלוּלִית שֶׁל מַיִם מְכוּנָּסִין: דְּאַשְׁמָעִי'. שֶׁאֲשַׁמֵּשׁ לַאֲדוֹנִי: שֶׁהֶחְמִירוּ עַל עַצְמָן. דְּמִדְּאוֹרַיְיתָא אֵין צְרִיכָה שִׁבְעָה נְקִיִּים אֶלָּא הָרוֹאָה שְׁלוֹשָׁה יָמִים רְצוּפִים בְּתוֹךְ י"א יוֹם שֶׁבֵּין נִדָּה לְנִדָּה, אֲבָל בִּתְחִלַּת נִדָּתָהּ — אֲפִילּוּ רָאֲתָה כָּל שִׁבְעָה וּפָסְקָה לָעֶרֶב — טוֹבֶלֶת בַּלַּיְלָה. וְהֵן הֶחְמִירוּ עַל עַצְמָן, לְפִי שֶׁאֵין הַכֹּל בְּקִיאִים בְּפֶתַח נִדָּתָהּ אֵימָתַי הֵן עוֹמְדוֹת בְּי"א יָמִים שֶׁבֵּין נִדָּה לְנִדָּה. וְאִם תֹּאמַר: לֹא יַחְמִירוּ אֶלָּא בְּג' רְצוּפִין, כְּדִכְתִיב "יָמִים רַבִּים בְּלֹא עֵת נִדָּתָהּ" (ויקרא טו) — פְּעָמִים שֶׁרְאִיַּית דַּם נִדָּה(ד) מַזְקִיקָתָהּ לְשִׁבְעָה נְקִיִּים מִן הַתּוֹרָה. כֵּיצַד? הִתְחִילָה לִסְפּוֹר שִׁבְעָה נְקִיִּים לְאַחַר שֶׁהָיְתָה זָבָה גְּמוּרָה, וְסָפְרָה שִׁבְעָה נְקִיִּים, וּבַשְּׁבִיעִי רָאֲתָה אֲפִי' כְּחַרְדָּל — סָתְרָה הַכֹּל, וּצְרִיכָה לַחֲזוֹר וְלִסְפּוֹר שִׁבְעָה נְקִיִּים. אִי נַמִי: שֶׁמָּא רָאֲתָה שְׁנֵי יָמִים וְלֹא יָדְעָה, וְהַיּוֹם רָאֲתָה וְיָדְעָה, דְּהָווּ לְהוּ שְׁלֹשָׁה יָמִים רְצוּפִין, וּצְרִיכָה שִׁבְעָה נְקִיִּים, וְעַל כֵּן הֶחְמִירוּ: לְהַכְנָסַת

תוספות

בתי כנסיות של בבל על תנאי הן עשויין. רוצה לומר: כל זמן שהן בטלין. דהא חזינן בברייתא דלעיל וגם(ה) שהאמוראים לא היו רוצים ליכנס בהן בגשמים מפני גשמים, אלא משום דשמעתא בעי צילותא. והכא איירי כשחרב, דאז מהני התנאי. ודווקא לאותן שבבבל מהני התנאי, שהרי לעת בא גואל במהרה בימינו תפקע קדושתן, אבל לאותן שבארץ ישראל — לא מהני תנאי, שהרי קדושתן לעולם קיימת. וא"ת: כיון דמהני תנאי לאותן שבבבל, א"כ קשה מההיא דלעיל (דף כו:) דרבינא דהוה ליה(ו) בי כנישתא בארעיה, ואמר ליה רב אשי: זיל זבנה משבעה טובי העיר. ואמאי איצטריך לעשות כן אחר שנחרב? וי"ל: משום דזריעה דזריעה הוי קלות ראש ביותר ועגמת נפש, ומשום הכי אסור אפי' בחורבנה*:

ואעפ"כ אין נוהגין בהן קלות ראש. פירוש: בבנינה. שהרי בחורבנה שרי בכל הני. ואצטריך לאשמועינן, משום דסלקא דעתך אמינא דדווקא אכילה ושתיה דהוי קלות ראש ביותר הוא דאסור, אבל חשבונות דלא הוי קלות ראש כל כך — סלקא דעתך אמינא דשריא, קמ"ל דלא: שאפילו רואות טפת דם כחרדל יושבות עליה שבעה נקיים. ולא קשיא מהא דאמר בנדה (דף סו.) ובפרק "יוצא דופן" (שם ד' מג.) שאפילו כעין חרדל טמא. דשמא התם לא איירי להצריכה שבעה נקיים, אלא להיות נדה דאורייתא. וקשיא: היאך מלינו טפה כחרדל הגורמת שבעה נקיים בדאורייתא? דודאי לא תקנו חכמים דבר דלית דכוותה דאורייתא! ויש לומר: דאשכחנא בה שפיר בז' לספירתה, שסותרת הכל:

רבינו חננאל

ואין ניאותין ואין מטיילין בהן ואין נכנסין בהן מפני החמה ומפני הגשמים ואם צריכי לעיוני בשמעתא דשמעתא צריכא צילותא אע"ג דמיחזי דמפני החמה או מפני הגשמים קא עיילי שרי. וקורין בהן ושונין בהן ומספידין בהן הספד של רבים כגון הספידא דקאי בי רב חסדא או רב ששת וכיוצא בהן. רפרם ספדא לכלתיה בכנישתא כו' ור' זירא ספדיה לההוא מרבנן בכנישתא כו': ומכבדין ומרבצין אותן. א"ר יהודה אימתי בישובן אבל בחרבנן מניחין אותן ועולין בהן עשבים מפני עגמת נפש שנראין כשדה זרע. א"ר אסי בתי כנסיות שבבבל על תנאי הן עשוין. כל שעה שירצה יחזיר לקדמותיה ואף על פי כן אין נוהגין בהן קלות ראש. ומה נינהו חשבונות דאמר רב ששת בתי כנסיות שמחשבין בהן חשבונות של רבים לסוף מלינין בהן מת מצוה. ואין ניאותין בהן אמר רבא חכמים ותלמידיהן מותרין בהן. מאי בי רבנן. ביתא דרבנן. מאן דאיצטריך למיעל

עין משפט נר מצוה

לג א ב ג מיי' פי"א מהל' תפלה הלכה ו ז ט סמג עשין יט טוש"ע א"ח סי' קנא ס"א:
לד ד מיי' שם הלכה ז טוש"ע א"ח שם וטוש"ע י"ד סי' שדמ סעיף יט:
לה ה סמג עשין יב טוש"ע י"ד סי' רמו סעיף כא בהגה"ה:
לו ו מיי' פי"א מהל' אסורי ביאה הל' ד סמג לאוין קיא טוש"ע י"ד סימן קפג:

[ועי' תוס' ב"ב ג: ד"ה ועיילי]

[כשמנשבת רוח לפונית שנקרא' אסתנא יום אורה היא ונוחה לכל עי' רש"י בעירובין וכן תוס' בקדושין יב: ד"ה הא דרוח לפוני' מונעת הגשמים]

[תענית כג: חולין קכב.]

אבות פ"א מי"ג
[גי' הערוך ערך תג אמר ריש לקיש כו']

תורה אור
חבקוק ג

מסורת הש"ס

עירובין סה. ע"ש
ברכות לא. נדה דף סו.
שם דף עג.

הגהות הב"ח

(א) גמ' אי משום יקרא דמיתא כצ"ל ותיבת דידיה נמחק: (ב) שם ואמרו ליה לרב נחמן בר יצחק ליספדיה מר: (ג) שם המשתמש במי ששונה ההלכות ואמר עולא כצ"ל ותיבות כתרה של תורה נמחק: (ד) רש"י ד"ה שהחמירו וכו' פעמים שראיית דם נדה פעם אחת מזקיקתה: (ה) תוס' ד"ה בתי וכו' וגם האמוראים שלא היו: (ו) בא"ד דהוה ליה תילא בי כנישתא:

מְבַטְּלִין תַּלְמוּד תּוֹרָה לְהוֹצָאַת הַמֵּת וּלְהַכְנָסַת הַכַּלָּה. *אָמְרוּ עָלָיו עַל ר' יְהוּדָה בְּר' אֶלְעַאי שֶׁהָיָה מְבַטֵּל ת"ת לְהוֹצָאַת הַמֵּת וּלְהַכְנָסַת הַכַּלָּה. בד"א — בְּשֶׁאֵין שָׁם כָּל צוֹרְכּוֹ, אֲבָל יֵשׁ שָׁם כָּל צוֹרְכּוֹ — אֵין מְבַטְּלִין. וְכַמָּה כָּל צוֹרְכּוֹ? אֲמַר רַב שְׁמוּאֵל בַּר אִינְיָא מִשְּׁמֵיהּ דְּרַב: תְּרֵיסַר אַלְפֵי גַּבְרֵי וְשִׁיתָּא אַלְפֵי שִׁיפּוּרֵי. וְאָמְרִי לָהּ: תְּרֵיסַר אַלְפֵי גַּבְרֵי, וּמִינַּיְיהוּ שִׁיתָּא אַלְפֵי שִׁיפּוּרֵי. עוּלָּא אֲמַר: כְּגוֹן דְּחָיְיצֵי גַּבְרֵי מֵאַבּוּלָא עַד סִיכְרָא. רַב שֵׁשֶׁת אָמַר: כִּנְתִינָתָהּ כָּךְ נְטִילָתָהּ. מַה נְּתִינָתָהּ בְּשִׁשִּׁים רִיבּוֹא — אַף נְטִילָתָהּ בְּס' רִיבּוֹא. ה"מ — לְמַאן דְּקָרֵי וְתָנֵי, אֲבָל לְמַאן דְּמַתְנֵי — לֵית לֵיהּ שִׁיעוּרָא. תַּנְיָא, ר"ש בֶּן יוֹחַי אוֹמֵר: בּוֹא וּרְאֵה כַּמָּה חֲבִיבִין יִשְׂרָאֵל לִפְנֵי הקב"ה. שֶׁבְּכָל מָקוֹם שֶׁגָּלוּ — שְׁכִינָה עִמָּהֶן. גָּלוּ לְמִצְרַיִם — שְׁכִינָה עִמָּהֶן, שֶׁנֶּאֱמַר: "הֲנִגְלֹה נִגְלֵיתִי לְבֵית אָבִיךָ בִּהְיוֹתָם בְּמִצְרַיִם" וגו', גָּלוּ לְבָבֶל — שְׁכִינָה עִמָּהֶן, שֶׁנֶּאֱמַר: "לְמַעַנְכֶם שֻׁלַּחְתִּי בָבֶלָה". וְאַף כְּשֶׁהֵן עֲתִידִין לִיגָּאֵל שְׁכִינָה עִמָּהֶן, שֶׁנֶּאֱמַר: "וְשָׁב ה' אֱלֹהֶיךָ אֶת שְׁבוּתְךָ", "וְהֵשִׁיב" לֹא נֶאֱמַר אֶלָּא "וְשָׁב", מְלַמֵּד שֶׁהקב"ה שָׁב עִמָּהֶן מִבֵּין הַגָּלֻיּוֹת.(א) בְּבָבֶל הֵיכָא? אֲמַר אַבַּיֵי: בְּבֵי כְנִישְׁתָּא דְּהוּצָל, וּבְבֵי כְנִישְׁתָּא דְּשָׁף וְיָתֵיב בִּנְהַרְדְּעָא. וְלָא תֵּימָא הָכָא וְהָכָא, אֶלָּא: זִמְנִין הָכָא, וְזִמְנִין הָכָא. אֲמַר אַבַּיֵי: תֵּיתֵי לִי, דְּכִי מַרְחֵיקְנָא פַּרְסָה — עָיְילְנָא וּמְצַלֵּינָא הָתָם. אֲבוּהּ דִּשְׁמוּאֵל [וְלֵוִי] הֲווּ יָתְבִי בִּכְנִישְׁתָּא דְּשָׁף וְיָתֵיב בִּנְהַרְדְּעָא, אָתְיָא שְׁכִינָה, שְׁמַעוּ קוֹל רִיגְשָׁא. [קָמוּ וּנְפַקוּ רַב שֵׁשֶׁת הֲוָה יָתֵיב בְּבֵי כְנִישְׁתָּא דְּשָׁף וְיָתֵיב בִּנְהַרְדְּעָא אָתְיָא שְׁכִינָה] וְלָא נְפַק. אָתוּ מַלְאֲכֵי הַשָּׁרֵת וְקָא מְבַעֲתוּ לֵיהּ, אֲמַר לְפָנָיו: *רבש"ע! עָלוּב וְשֶׁאֵינוֹ עָלוּב(ב) מִי נִדְחֶה מִפְּנֵי מִי? אֲמַר לְהוּ: שַׁבְקוּהוּ. "וָאֱהִי לָהֶם לְמִקְדָּשׁ מְעַט", אָמַר רַבִּי יִצְחָק: אֵלּוּ בָּתֵּי כְנֵסִיּוֹת וּבָתֵּי מִדְרָשׁוֹת שֶׁבְּבָבֶל. וְר"א אָמַר: זֶה בֵּית רַבֵּינוּ שֶׁבְּבָבֶל. דָּרַשׁ רָבָא: מַאי דִּכְתִיב "ה' מָעוֹן אַתָּה הָיִיתָ לָּנוּ" — אֵלּוּ בָּתֵּי כְנֵסִיּוֹת וּבָתֵּי מִדְרָשׁוֹת. אֲמַר *אַבַּיֵי: מֵרֵישׁ הֲוַאי גָּרֵיסְנָא בְּבֵיתָא וּמְצַלֵּינָא בְּבֵי כְנִשְׁתָּא, כֵּיוָן דִּשְׁמָעִית לְהָא דְּקָאָמַר דָּוִד "ה' אָהַבְתִּי מְעוֹן בֵּיתֶךָ"(ג) — הֲוַאי גָּרֵיסְנָא בְּבֵי כְנִישְׁתָּא. תַּנְיָא, וְר"א הַקַּפָּר אוֹמֵר: עֲתִידִין בָּתֵּי כְנֵסִיּוֹת וּבָתֵּי מִדְרָשׁוֹת שֶׁבְּבָבֶל שֶׁיִּקָּבְעוּ בא"י, שֶׁנֶּאֱמַר "כִּי כְּתָבוֹר בֶּהָרִים וּכְכַרְמֶל בַּיָּם יָבֹא", וַהֲלֹא דְּבָרִים ק"ו: וּמָה תָּבוֹר וְכַרְמֶל שֶׁלֹּא בָּאוּ אֶלָּא לְפִי שָׁעָה לִלְמוֹד תּוֹרָה — נִקְבָּעִים בְּאֶרֶץ יִשְׂרָאֵל, בָּתֵּי כְנֵסִיּוֹת וּבָתֵּי מִדְרָשׁוֹת שֶׁקּוֹרִין וּמַרְבִּיצִין בָּהֶן תּוֹרָה — עאכ"ו. דָּרַשׁ בַּר קַפָּרָא: מַאי דִּכְתִיב "לָמָּה תְּרַצְּדוּן הָרִים גַּבְנוּנִּים", יָצְתָה בַּת קוֹל וְאָמְרָה לָהֶם: לָמָּה תִּרְצוּ דִּין עִם סִינַי? כּוּלְּכֶם בַּעֲלֵי מוּמִים אַתֶּם אֵצֶל סִינַי. כְּתִיב הָכָא "גַּבְנוּנִּים" וּכְתִיב הָתָם "אוֹ גִבֵּן אוֹ דַק", אָמַר רַב אַשִׁי: ש"מ הַאי מַאן דְּיָהִיר — בַּעַל מוּם הוּא. § "אֵין עוֹשִׂין אוֹתוֹ קַפֶּנְדַּרְיָא". § מַאי *קַפֶּנְדַּרְיָא? אָמַר רָבָא: קַפֶּנְדַּרְיָא כִּשְׁמָהּ — מַאי כִּשְׁמָהּ? כְּמַאן דְּאָמַר: אַדְּמַקִּיפְנָא אַדָּרֵי אֵיעוֹל בְּהָא. א"ר אַבָּהוּ: אִם הָיָה שְׁבִיל מֵעִיקָּרָא — מוּתָּר. אר"נ בַּר יִצְחָק: הַנִּכְנָס ע"מ שֶׁלֹּא לַעֲשׂוֹת קַפֶּנְדַּרְיָא — מוּתָּר לַעֲשׂוֹתוֹ קַפֶּנְדַּרְיָא. וא"ר חֶלְבּוֹ אָמַר ר"ה: הַנִּכְנָס לְבהכ"נ לְהִתְפַּלֵּל[א] מוּתָּר לַעֲשׂוֹתוֹ קַפֶּנְדַּרְיָא, שֶׁנֶּא' "וּבְבֹא עַם הָאָרֶץ לִפְנֵי ה' בַּמּוֹעֲדִים הַבָּא דֶּרֶךְ שַׁעַר צָפוֹן לְהִשְׁתַּחֲוֹת יֵצֵא דֶּרֶךְ שַׁעַר נֶגֶב". § "עָלוּ בּוֹ עֲשָׂבִים לֹא יִתְלוֹשׁ מִפְּנֵי עָגְמַת נֶפֶשׁ". § וְהָתַנְיָא: אֵינוֹ תּוֹלֵשׁ וּמַאֲכִיל, אֲבָל תּוֹלֵשׁ וּמַנִּיחַ! כִּי תְּנַן נַמִּי מַתְנִי' — תּוֹלֵשׁ וּמַאֲכִיל תְּנַן. ת"ר: *בֵּית הַקְּבָרוֹת אֵין נוֹהֲגִין בָּהֶן קַלּוּת רֹאשׁ: אֵין מַרְעִין בָּהֶן בְּהֵמָה, וְאֵין מוֹלִיכִין בָּהֶן אַמַּת הַמַּיִם, וְאֵין מְלַקְּטִין בָּהֶן עֲשָׂבִים, וְאִם לִיקֵּט — שׂוֹרְפָן בִּמְקוֹמָן מִפְּנֵי כְבוֹד מֵתִים. אַהַיָּיא? אִילֵימָא אַסֵּיפָא — כֵּיוָן שֶׁשּׂוֹרְפָן בִּמְקוֹמָן מַאי כְּבוֹד מֵתִים אִיכָּא? אֶלָּא אַרֵישָׁא. §

מתני' ר"ח אֲדָר שֶׁחָל לִהְיוֹת בְּשַׁבָּת — קוֹרִין בְּפָרָשַׁת שְׁקָלִים. חָל לִהְיוֹת בְּתוֹךְ הַשַּׁבָּת — מַקְדִּימִין לְשֶׁעָבַר, וּמַפְסִיקִין לְשַׁבָּת אַחֶרֶת, בַּשְּׁנִיָּה "זָכוֹר", בַּשְּׁלִישִׁית "פָּרָה אֲדוּמָּה", בָּרְבִיעִית "הַחוֹדֶשׁ הַזֶּה לָכֶם", בַּחֲמִישִׁית חוֹזְרִין לְכִסְדְּרָן. לַכֹּל מַפְסִיקִין, בְּרָאשֵׁי חֳדָשִׁים, בַּחֲנוּכָּה, וּבְפוּרִים, בְּתַעֲנִיּוֹת, וּבְמַעֲמָדוֹת, וּבְיוה"כ. §

גמ' תְּנַן הָתָם: בְּאֶחָד בַּאֲדָר מַשְׁמִיעִין עַל הַשְּׁקָלִים וְעַל

לְהַכְנָסַת כַּלָּה. לְלַוּוֹתָהּ מִבֵּית אָבִיהָ לְבֵית חוּפָּתָהּ: כְּגוֹן דְּחָיְיצֵי גַּבְרֵי מֵאַבּוּלָא לְסִיכְרָא. מְחִיצַּת אֲנָשִׁים מִשַּׁעַר הָעִיר עַד בֵּית הַקְּבָרוֹת, מָקוֹם שֶׁסּוֹפְדִין אוֹתוֹ שָׁם: כִּנְתִינָתָהּ. שֶׁל תּוֹרָה: דְּשָׁף וְיָתֵיב. וּבְנָאָהּ יְכָנְיָה וְסִיעָתוֹ מֵאֲבָנִים וְעָפָר שֶׁהֵבִיאוּ עִמָּהֶן בְּגָלוּתָן, לְקַיֵּים מַה שֶּׁנֶּאֱמַר "כִּי רָצוּ עֲבָדֶיךָ אֶת אֲבָנֶיהָ וְאֶת עֲפָרָהּ יְחוֹנֵנוּ" (תהלים קב): דְּכִי מַרְחֵיקְנָא פַּרְסָה. (ד) אֲנִי נִכְנָס לְהִתְפַּלֵּל בְּתוֹכוֹ: רַב שֵׁשֶׁת. סַגִּי נְהוֹר הֲוָה: בֵּית רַבֵּינוּ. רַב: וּכְכַרְמֶל בַּיָּם יָבוֹא. לָמַדְנוּ שֶׁעָבַר כַּרְמֶל אֶת הַיָּם, וְאֵימָתַי הָיָה — בִּשְׁעַת מַתַּן תּוֹרָה: כִּשְׁמָהּ. כְּמַשְׁמָעָהּ: אַדְּמַקִּיפְנָא אַדָּרֵי אֵיעוֹל בְּהָא. בְּעוֹד שֶׁאַקִּיף שׁוּרוֹת שֶׁל בָּתִּים הַלָּלוּ אֶכָּנֵס דֶּרֶךְ הַבַּיִת הַזֶּה, וַאֲקַצֵּר אֶת הַדֶּרֶךְ מִמָּבוֹי לְמָבוֹי, וּבֵית הַכְּנֶסֶת בֵּין שְׁנֵיהֶן: מֵעִיקָּרָא. קוֹדֶם שֶׁנִּבְנָה בֵּית הַכְּנֶסֶת שָׁם: אַרֵישָׁא. מִשּׁוּם כְּבוֹדָן שֶׁל מֵתִים. אַ"אֵין נוֹהֲגִין בָּהֶן קַלּוּת רֹאשׁ" קָאֵי:

מתני' קוֹרִין בְּפָרָשַׁת שְׁקָלִים. לְהוֹדִיעַ שֶׁיָּבִיאוּ שִׁקְלֵיהֶן בַּאֲדָר, כְּדֵי שֶׁיַּקְרִיבוּ בְּאֶחָד בְּנִיסָן מִתְּרוּמָה חֲדָשָׁה, כִּדְאָמְרִינַן בַּגְּמָרָא: וּמַפְסִיקִין לְשַׁבָּת הַבָּאָה. מִלּוֹמַר פָּרָשָׁה שְׁנִיָּה, כְּדֵי שֶׁתִּקָּרֵא פָּרָשַׁת זָכוֹר בַּשַּׁבָּת הַסְּמוּכָה לְפוּרִים, לִסְמוֹךְ מְחִיַּית עֲמָלֵק לִמְחִיַּית הָמָן: פָּרָה אֲדוּמָּה. לְהַזְהִיר אֶת יִשְׂרָאֵל לִטַּהֵר, שֶׁיַּעֲשׂוּ פִּסְחֵיהֶן בְּטָהֳרָה: בָּרְבִיעִית הַחוֹדֶשׁ הַזֶּה לָכֶם. שֶׁשָּׁם פָּרָשַׁת הַפֶּסַח. וּבְתַלְמוּד יְרוּשַׁלְמִי גָּרְסִינַן: אָמַר ר' חָמָא, בְּדִין הוּא שֶׁיִּקְדּוֹם הַחוֹדֶשׁ לְפָרָשַׁת פָּרָה, שֶׁהֲרֵי בְּאֶחָד בְּנִיסָן הוּקַם הַמִּשְׁכָּן וּבַשֵּׁנִי לוֹ נִשְׂרְפָה הַפָּרָה, וּמִפְּנֵי מָה הִקְדִּימוּהָ — שֶׁהִיא טָהֳרָתָן שֶׁל יִשְׂרָאֵל: לַכֹּל מַפְסִיקִין. מִלִּקְרוֹת בְּעִנְיַן הַיּוֹם, וְקוֹרִין בְּעִנְיַן מוֹעֵד מֵעֵין הַמְּאוֹרָע: לְמַעֲמָדוֹת. וְקוֹרִין בְּמַעֲשֵׂה בְרֵאשִׁית, כִּדְקָתָנֵי לְקַמָּן בְּמַתְנִי': **גמ'** מַשְׁמִיעִין עַל הַשְּׁקָלִים. בְּהַכְרָזַת בֵּית דִּין:

מבטלין תלמוד תורה להוצאת המת. ולא קשיא מההיא דמס' דרך ארץ (זוטא פ"ח) דאמרי': מעשה ברבי עקיבא שמצא מת מצוה בדרך ונשאו ארבעה מילין עד שהביאו לבית הקברות, וכשבא אצל ר' יהושע ור' אליעזר וספר להם, אמרו לו: על כל פסיעה ופסיעה שפסעת כאילו שפכת דם נקי! — לא היה מפני שבטל למודו, אלא משום שהזיזו ממקומו, ומת מצוה קונה מקומו*:

הני מילי למאן דקרי ותני אבל למאן דמתני לית ליה שיעורא — ממילא שמעינן דלמאן דלא קרי ותני אית ליה שיעורא ואין מבטלין תלמוד תורה בשבילו אלא כדי צורכו, להתעסק בו. ודוקא לענין ביטול תורה, אבל לענין ביטול מלאכה — אסור לכל בני העיר, שהרי בפרק "אלו מגלחין" (מו"ק דף כז: ושם) לא מחלק בענין איסור מלאכה בין מאן דקרי ותני למאן דלא קרי ותני*:

אין מרעין בהן בהמות. משום כבודן של מתים. אבל האילנות שנוטעין בהן — מותרין, ואין בהם משום כבודן של מתים, אחרי שאינן על הקברים עצמן:

לכל מפסיקין וכו' וליום הכפורים. צריך לומר דמיירי במנחת יום הכפורים שחל להיות בשבת, והא קאמר שמפסיקין מן הסדר שחל באותו שבת, וקורין בפרשת עריות. וכן בכל הני שאין קורין אלא ג' כגון תעניות ומעמדות וחנוכה ופורים. דליכא למימר דמיירי ביום הכפורים שחרית שקורין בפרשת אחרי מות בחול שהיה ובשבת שבעה — דא"כ אמאי נקט יום הכפורים? אפילו שאר מועדות נמי! ועל

רבינו חננאל

למיעל בי כנישתא אי צורבא מרבנן הוא לימא שמעתא. אי תנא הוא לימא הלכתא. אי קרא הוא לימא פסוקא. ואי לא לימא ליה לינוקא מאי פסוקיך. ומשתמש בתגא חלף. פירוש המשתמש במאן דמתני שמעתא ראוי להריגה. כל השונה הלכות מובטח לו שהוא בן עוה"ב שנאמר הליכות עולם לו: ת"ר מבטלין תלמוד תורה להוצאת המת ולהכנסת כלה. בד"א כשאין שם כל צרכו. וכמה כל צרכו י"ב אלפי גברי ושיתא אלפי שיפורי כו'. והני מילי למאן דתני וקרי פירוש קרא או תנא אבל דמתני שמעתא לית ליה שיעורא. תניא רשב"י ביבין ישראל שבכ"מ שגלו גלה שכינה עמהם כו' ופשוטה היא. עד דרש רבא ה' מעון אתה היית לנו אלו בתי כנסיות ומדרשות. אמר רבא כיון דשמעית להא לא יתיבנא וגריסנא אלא בבי כנישתא שנאמר ה' אהבתי מעון ביתך וגו'. אין עושין בית הכנסת קפנדריא ואם היה שביל מעיקרא מותר. פירוש קפנדריא לשון יון כשתהיה חצר שיש לה ב' פתחים אחד במזרח ואחד במערב הנכנס בזה ויוצא כנגדו מפסיק חצר נקרא קפנדריא. אמר רב נחמן הנכנס בבית הכנסת על מנת כו'. אמר רב הונא הנכנס לבית הכנסת להתפלל מותר לעשותו קפנדריא שנאמר ובבוא עם הארץ לפני ה' במועדים וגו' אוקימנא למתניתין הכי. עלו בו עשבים לא יתלוש להאכיל אבל תולש ומניח מפני עגמת נפש: ת"ר בבית הקברות אין נוהגין בהן קלות ראש וכו' עד אם ליקט שורפן במקומן: **מתני'** ר"ח שחל להיות בשבת קורין בפרשת שקלים

עין משפט נר מצוה

לז א מיי' פי"ד מהל' אבל הל' ט סמג עשין ג טוש"ע י"ד סימן שסא סעיף א:

לח ג ד ה ו מיי' פי"א מהל' תפלה הל' ח סמג עשין יח טוש"ע א"ח סימן קנא סעי' ה:

[עי' תוס' כתובות יז. ד"ה מבטלין]

לט ז מיי' שם הלכה יא טור ש"ע שם סעיף י:

מ ח מיי' פי"ד מהל' אבל הל' יג סמג עשין מד"ס ג טוש"ע י"ד סימן שסח סעיף א:

מא ט מיי' פי"ג מהל' תפלה הלכה כ סמג עשין יט טוש"ע א"ח סימן תרפה סעיף א:

[וע"ע תוס' כתובות יז: ד"ה אבל]

מב י מיי' שם טוש"ע שם סעיף ח:

מג כ מיי' שם טוש"ע שם סעיף ב:

מד ל מיי' שם טוש"ע שם ס"ג:

מה מ מיי' שם טוש"ע שם סעיף ד:

מו נ מיי' פ"א מהל' שקלים הלכה ט סמג עשין מח:

[גי' הילקוט בתהלים רמז תש"ד רבא וכן גרס עין יעקב]

מסורת הש"ס

כתובות דף יז. לעיל ד' ג: | [אבות דר"נ פ"ד] | [תענית טז.] | [ברכות ח. ע"ש] | [ברכות סב: ע"ש] | [שמחות פי"ד ע"ש] | ...יל דף יג: | ...ק דף ו. | שקלים דף ב.

תורה אור: תהלים קב | ש"א ב | ישעיה מג | דברים ל | יחזקאל יא | תהלים צ | תהלים כו | ירמיה מו | תהלים סח | ויקרא כא | יחזקאל מו

הגהות הב"ח

(א) גמ' מבין הגלויות ...ינה בבבל היכא צריך ...ר אביי: (ב) שם ושאינו ...ב יכול ושאינו יכול מי ...זה: (ג) שם מעון ביתך ...הואי גריסנא אלא בבי ...שתא היכא דמצלינא ...יא: (ד) רש"י ד"ה דכי ...חיקנא פרסה (אני וכו' ...וכו) תא"מ ונ"ב ס"א ...אני מהלך בדרך באותו ...ום אפילו אני מרבה עלי ...הדרך אני נכנס שם ומתפלל בתוכו:

גליון הש"ס

...' בבי כנישתא דשף. ...ין ברמב"ן במלחמות ...ר"ד לכתובות: **שם** ...יש הואי גריסנא. עיין ברכות ד' ח ע"א:

הגהות הגר"א

[א] גמ' מותר. נ"ב מלוה ... גירסת הרא"ש (וכאן ...ל ברא"ש דברכות איתא ...ותר). והרי"ף בברכות:

אוְעַל הַכִּלְאַיִם. בִּשְׁלָמָא עַל הַכִּלְאַיִם – דִּזְמַן זְרִיעָה הִיא, אֶלָּא עַל הַשְּׁקָלִים מְנָלַן? אָמַר ר' טָבִי אָמַר רַבִּי יֹאשִׁיָּה: דְּאָמַר קְרָא °"זֹאת עֹלַת חֹדֶשׁ בְּחָדְשׁוֹ", *אָמְרָה תּוֹרָה: בחַדֵּשׁ וְהָבֵא קָרְבָּן מִתְּרוּמָה חֲדָשָׁה. וְכֵיוָן דִּבְנִיסָן בָּעֵי אַקְרוּבֵי מִתְּרוּמָה חֲדָשָׁה, °קָדְמִינַן וְקָרֵינַן בְּאֶחָד בַּאֲדָר, כִּי הֵיכִי דְּלֵיתוּ שְׁקָלִים לַמִּקְדָּשׁ. כְּמַאן – דְּלָא כְּרַבָּן שִׁמְעוֹן בֶּן גַּמְלִיאֵל. דְּאִי רַבָּן שִׁמְעוֹן בֶּן גַּמְלִיאֵל – הָאָמַר שְׁתֵּי שַׁבָּתוֹת, דְּתַנְיָא: *גשׁוֹאֲלִין בְּהִלְכוֹת הַפֶּסַח קוֹדֶם לַפֶּסַח שְׁלֹשִׁים יוֹם, רַבָּן שִׁמְעוֹן בֶּן גַּמְלִיאֵל אוֹמֵר: שְׁתֵּי שַׁבָּתוֹת! אֲפִילּוּ תֵּימָא רַבָּן שִׁמְעוֹן בֶּן גַּמְלִיאֵל, כֵּיוָן דְּאָמַר מָר: *דבַּחֲמִשָּׁה עָשָׂר בּוֹ שׁוּלְחָנוֹת יוֹשְׁבִין בַּמְּדִינָה, וּבְכ"ה יוֹשְׁבִין בַּמִּקְדָּשׁ – מִשּׁוּם שׁוּלְחָנוֹת *)קָדְמִינַן וְקָרֵינַן. מַאי פָּרָשַׁת שְׁקָלִים? רַב אָמַר: °"צַו אֶת בְּנֵי יִשְׂרָאֵל וְאָמַרְתָּ אֲלֵיהֶם אֶת קָרְבָּנִי לַחְמִי" וּשְׁמוּאֵל אָמַר: ה°"כִּי תִשָּׂא". בִּשְׁלָמָא לְמַאן דְּאָמַר "כִּי תִשָּׂא" – הַיְינוּ דְּקָרֵי לַהּ פָּרָשַׁת שְׁקָלִים, דִּכְתִיב בַּהּ שְׁקָלִים. אֶלָּא לְמַאן דְּאָמַר "אֶת קָרְבָּנִי לַחְמִי", (א)הָכָא מִידֵּי שְׁקָלִים כְּתִיבֵי הָתָם? אִין, טַעְמָא מַאי – כִּדְר' טָבִי. בִּשְׁלָמָא לְמ"ד "צַו אֶת בְּנֵי יִשְׂרָאֵל" – מִשּׁוּם דִּכְתִיבֵי קָרְבָּנוֹת הָתָם, כִּדְר' טָבִי. אֶלָּא לְמ"ד "כִּי תִשָּׂא", קָרְבָּנוֹת מִי כְּתִיבֵי? שְׁקָלִים לָאֲדָנִים כְּתִיבֵי! כִּדְתָנֵי רַב יוֹסֵף: שָׁלֹשׁ תְּרוּמוֹת הֵן, שֶׁל מִזְבֵּחַ לַמִּזְבֵּחַ, וְשֶׁל אֲדָנִים לָאֲדָנִים, וְשֶׁל בֶּדֶק הַבַּיִת לְבֶדֶק הַבַּיִת. בִּשְׁלָמָא לְמַאן דְּאָמַר "כִּי תִשָּׂא" הַיְינוּ דְּשָׁנֵי הַאי רֹאשׁ חֹדֶשׁ מִשְּׁאָר רָאשֵׁי חֳדָשִׁים, אֶלָּא לְמ"ד "צַו... אֶת קָרְבָּנִי" מַאי שָׁנֵי? שָׁנֵי, דְּאִילּוּ רָאשֵׁי חֳדָשִׁים – קָרוּ שִׁיתָּא בְּעִנְיָינָא דְּיוֹמָא, וְחַד בְּדְרֹאשׁ חוֹדֶשׁ. וְאִילּוּ הָאִידָּנָא כּוּלְּהוּ בְּדְרֹאשׁ חוֹדֶשׁ. הָנִיחָא לְמַאן דַּאֲמַר *לְסֵדֶר פָּרָשִׁיּוֹת הוּא חוֹזֵר, אֶלָּא לְמַאן דַּאֲמַר לְסֵדֶר הַפְטָרוֹת הוּא חוֹזֵר, וּפָרָשְׁתָּא דְּיוֹמָא קָרֵינַן, מַאי שָׁנֵי? שָׁנֵי, דְּאִילּוּ רָאשֵׁי חֳדָשִׁים קָרוּ שִׁיתָּא בְּעִנְיָינָא דְּיוֹמָא, וְחַד קָרֵי בְּדְרֹאשׁ חוֹדֶשׁ, וְאִילּוּ הָאִידָּנָא קָרוּ תְּלָתָא בְּעִנְיָינָא דְּיוֹמָא וְאַרְבָּעָה קָרוּ בְּדְרֹאשׁ חוֹדֶשׁ. מֵיתִיבִי: *ור"ח אֲדָר שֶׁחָל לִהְיוֹת בְּשַׁבָּת קוֹרִין בְּפָרָשַׁת שְׁקָלִים, וּמַפְטִירִין בִּ"יהוֹיָדָע הַכֹּהֵן". בִּשְׁלָמָא לְמ"ד "כִּי תִשָּׂא" – הַיְינוּ דְּמַפְטִירִין בִּ"יהוֹיָדָע הַכֹּהֵן", דְּדָמֵי לֵיהּ, דִּכְתִיב *°"כֶּסֶף נַפְשׁוֹת עֶרְכּוֹ", אֶלָּא לְמ"ד "אֶת קָרְבָּנִי לַחְמִי" מִי דָּמֵי? דָּמֵי, כִּדְר' טָבִי. מֵיתִיבִי: *חָל לִהְיוֹת בְּפָרָשָׁה הַסְּמוּכָה לָהּ, בֵּין מִלְּפָנֶיהָ וּבֵין מִלְּאַחֲרֶיהָ – קוֹרִין אוֹתָהּ, וְכוֹפְלִין אוֹתָהּ. בִּשְׁלָמָא לְמ"ד "כִּי תִשָּׂא" – הַיְינוּ דְּמִתְרַמֵּי בְּהַהוּא זִימְנָא, אֶלָּא לְמ"ד "צַו אֶת קָרְבָּנִי", מִי מִתְרַמֵּי בְּהַהוּא זִימְנָא? אִין, לִבְנֵי מַעַרְבָא זדְּמַסְקֵי לִדְאוֹרַיְיתָא בִּתְלָת שְׁנִין. תַּנְיָא כְּוָותֵיהּ דִּשְׁמוּאֵל: ר"ח אֲדָר שֶׁחָל לִהְיוֹת בְּשַׁבָּת קוֹרִין "כִּי תִשָּׂא" וּמַפְטִירִין בִּ"יהוֹיָדָע הַכֹּהֵן". א"ר יִצְחָק נַפָּחָא: חר"ח אֲדָר שֶׁחָל לִהְיוֹת בְּשַׁבָּת מוֹצִיאִין שָׁלֹשׁ תּוֹרוֹת וְקוֹרִין בָּהֶן, אֶחָד בְּעִנְיָינוֹ שֶׁל יוֹם, וְאֶחָד בְּשֶׁל ר"ח, וְאֶחָד בְּ"כִי תִשָּׂא". וְא"ר יִצְחָק נַפָּחָא: *טר"ח טֵבֵת שֶׁחָל לִהְיוֹת בְּשַׁבָּת מְבִיאִין שָׁלֹשׁ תּוֹרוֹת וְקוֹרִין בָּהֶן: אֶחָד בְּעִנְיָינוֹ שֶׁל יוֹם, וְאֶחָד בְּדְרֹאשׁ חוֹדֶשׁ, וְאֶחָד בַּחֲנוּכָּה. וּצְרִיכָא: דְּאִי אִיתְּמַר בְּהָא – בְּהָא קָאָמַר ר' יִצְחָק, אֲבָל בְּהַךְ – כְּרַב ס"ל, דְּאָמַר פָּרָשַׁת שְׁקָלִים "אֶת קָרְבָּנִי לַחְמִי", וּבִשְׁתֵּי תוֹרוֹת סַגִּי, קמ"ל. וְלֵימָא הָא וְלָא בָּעֲיָא הַךְ! *חֲדָא מִכְּלַל חֲבֵירְתָּהּ אִיתְּמַר. אִיתְּמַר, ר"ח טֵבֵת שֶׁחָל לִהְיוֹת בְּחוֹל, א"ר *)יִצְחָק: יקָרוּ תְּלָתָא בְּר"ח. וְחַד בַּחֲנוּכָּה. וְרַב דִּימִי דְּמִן חֵיפָא אֲמַר: קָרוּ תְּלָתָא בַּחֲנוּכָּה וְחַד בְּר"ח. אֲמַר ר' מָנִי: כְּוָותֵיהּ דְּרַבִּי יִצְחָק נַפָּחָא מִסְתַּבְּרָא, דְּתָדִיר וְשֶׁאֵינוֹ תָּדִיר – תָּדִיר קוֹדֶם. א"ר אָבִין: כְּוָותֵיהּ דְּרַב דִּימִי מִסְתַּבְּרָא, מִי גָּרַם לָרְבִיעִי שֶׁיָּבֹא – ר"ח, הִלְכָּךְ רְבִיעִי בְּר"ח בָּעֵי מִיקְרֵי. מַאי הָוֵי עֲלַהּ? רַב יוֹסֵף אָמַר: אֵין מַשְׁגִּיחִין בְּרֹאשׁ חוֹדֶשׁ. וְרַבָּה אָמַר: אֵין מַשְׁגִּיחִין בַּחֲנוּכָּה. וְהִלְכְתָא: אֵין מַשְׁגִּיחִין בַּחֲנוּכָּה, (ב)וְר"ח עִיקָּר. אִיתְּמַר, חָל לִהְיוֹת בְּ"וְאַתָּה תְּצַוֶּה", אָמַר רַבִּי יִצְחָק נַפָּחָא: קָרוּ שִׁיתָּא מִ"וְאַתָּה תְּצַוֶּה" עַד "כִּי תִשָּׂא", וְחַד מִ"כִּי תִשָּׂא" עַד "וְעָשִׂיתָ" אָמַר אַבַּיֵי: אָמְרִי

*) [נ"ל ר' יצחק נפחא]

וְעַל הַכִּלְאַיִם. לַעֲקוֹר כִּלְאֵי הַזְּרָעִים הַנִּיכָּרִין בֵּין הַתְּבוּאָה: (ג) חוֹדֶשׁ בְּחָדְשׁוֹ לְחָדְשֵׁי הַשָּׁנָה. כָּל הָנֵי חֳדָשִׁים לָמָּה לִי? אֶלָּא אָמְרָה תּוֹרָה. יֵשׁ לְךָ חוֹדֶשׁ שֶׁאַתָּה צָרִיךְ לְחַדְּשׁוֹ בַּהֲבָאַת עוֹלוֹת תְּמִידִין וּמוּסָפִין מִתְּרוּמָה חֲדָשָׁה – וְזֶהוּ נִיסָן, כִּדְאָמְרִינַן בְּרֹאשׁ הַשָּׁנָה דְּגָמְרִינַן שָׁנָה שָׁנָה מִנִּיסָן, דִּכְתִיב "רִאשׁוֹן הוּא לָכֶם לְחָדְשֵׁי הַשָּׁנָה" (שמות יב): כְּמַאן. מַקְדְּמִינַן כּוּלֵּי הַאי, דְּלָא כְּרַבָּן שִׁמְעוֹן בֶּן גַּמְלִיאֵל: בְּט"ו בַּאֲדָר שׁוּלְחָנוֹת. בַּעֲלֵי מַטְבְּעוֹת, הַמְחַלְּפִין שִׁקְלֵי כֶסֶף בִּפְרוּטוֹת: יוֹשְׁבִין בַּמִּקְדָּשׁ. הוּא סִימָן שֶׁכְּבָר קָרֵב זְמַן לִתְרוֹם אֶת הַלִּשְׁכָּה בְּשָׁלֹשׁ קוּפּוֹת, וִימַהֲרוּ וְיָבִיאוּ. דְּמֵאוֹתוֹ הַיּוֹם מַתְחִילִין לְמַשְׁכֵּן אֶת הַמְעַכְּבִים: מִשּׁוּם שׁוּלְחָנוֹת קָדְמִינַן. לְאֶחָד בַּאֲדָר, דְּהַיְינוּ שְׁתֵּי שַׁבָּתוֹת. וְטַעְמָא דְּרַבָּן שִׁמְעוֹן בֶּן גַּמְלִיאֵל וְרַבָּנָן בְּפ"ק דִּפְסָחִים (דף ו.): טַעְמָא כִּדְרַבִּי טָבִי. טַעְמָא מַאי מַיְיתִינַן שְׁקָלִים בַּאֲדָר – כִּדְרַבִּי טָבִי, שֶׁיַּקְרִיבוּ קָרְבָּנוֹת בְּאֶחָד בְּנִיסָן מִתְּרוּמָה חֲדָשָׁה. וְהָךְ מִנְוֵיהּ הָתָם כְּתִיבָא: שְׁקָלִים לַאֲדָנִים כְּתִיבֵי. הָתָם, כְּדִכְתִיב "וְלָקַחְתָּ אֶת כֶּסֶף הַכִּפּוּרִים וְנָתַתָּ אוֹתוֹ עַל עֲבוֹדַת אֹהֶל מוֹעֵד", וְהֵן הַשְּׁקָלִים שֶׁנַּעֲשׂוּ מֵהֶן אַדְנֵי הַמִּשְׁכָּן, כְּדִכְתִיב "וְכֶסֶף פְּקוּדֵי הָעֵדָה וגו' וַיְהִי מְאַת כִּכַּר הַכֶּסֶף לָצֶקֶת אֵת אַדְנֵי הַקֹּדֶשׁ" וגו': שָׁלֹשׁ תְּרוּמוֹת. נֶאֶמְרוּ שָׁם: "מַחֲצִית הַשֶּׁקֶל תְּרוּמָה לַה'", "יִתֵּן תְּרוּמַת ה'", לָתֵת אֶת תְּרוּמַת ה'". תְּרוּמַת אֲדָנִים הָיְתָה לָאֲדָנִים, וּתְרוּמַת מִזְבֵּחַ לַמִּזְבֵּחַ, לִקְנוֹת מֵהֶן קָרְבָּנוֹת צִבּוּר לְכָל הַשָּׁנָה, דִּכְתִיב בַּהּ "לְכַפֵּר עַל נַפְשֹׁתֵיכֶם": לְבֶדֶק הַבַּיִת. הִיא לֹא הָיְתָה שָׁוָה בְּכוּלָּן, אֶלָּא אִישׁ כְּפִי נִדְבָתוֹ, שֶׁנֶּאֱמַר "וַיָּבֹאוּ הָאֲנָשִׁים עַל הַנָּשִׁים כֹּל נְדִיב לֵב" וגו' (שמות לה): הָנִיחָא לְמַאן דְּאָמַר. בְּפִרְקִין, הַאי דְּקָתָנֵי מַתְנִי' בַּחֲמִישִׁית חוֹזְרִין לְכִסְדְרָן: לְסֵדֶר פָּרָשִׁיּוֹת הוּא חוֹזֵר. שֶׁקְּרָאוּ אֶת אֵלּוּ, וְהִפְסִיקוּ מִלִּקְרוֹת אֶת פָּרָשַׁת הַשַּׁבָּת, אִיכָּא לְמֵימַר כִּדְאָמַר הָאִידָּנָא קָרוּ כּוּלְּהוּ בִּדְרֹאשׁ חוֹדֶשׁ. אֶלָּא לְמַאן דְּאָמַר כו' דִּמְפָרֵשׁ חוֹזְרִין לְכִסְדְרָן לְסֵדֶר הַהַפְטָרוֹת – אַלְמָא הַהַפְטָרוֹת הוּפְסְקוּ עַד הֵנָּה אֲבָל לֹא הַפָּרָשִׁיּוֹת, דְּעַד הָשְׁתָּא הֲווּ קָרוּ נַמִי מֵעִנְיָנָא דְּיוֹמָא, מַאי שָׁנֵי? כִּדְרַבִּי טָבִי. "זֹאת עוֹלַת חוֹדֶשׁ" בִּשְׁקָלִים אָמַר: חָל לִהְיוֹת. ר"ח אֲדָר בַּפָּרָשָׁה הַסְּמוּכָה לְפָרָשַׁת שְׁקָלִים: וְכוֹפְלִין אוֹתָהּ. בְּשַׁבָּת שְׁנִיָּה, אַע"פ שֶׁקְּרָאוּהָ בָּרִאשׁוֹנָה: בְּהַהוּא זִימְנָא. בְּאוֹתוֹ פֶּרֶק שֶׁל אֲדָר: מִי מִתְרַמֵּי. וַהֲלֹא בְּפָרָשַׁת פִּינְחָס הִיא, שֶׁהִיא סְמוּכָה לְחוֹדֶשׁ אָב: דְּמַסְקִי אוֹרַיְיתָא. מְסַיְּימִין חֲמִשָּׁה חוּמָּשִׁין פַּעַם אַחַת לְשָׁלֹשׁ שָׁנִים, וְלֹא בְּכָל שָׁנָה כְּמוֹ שֶׁאָנוּ עוֹשִׂין: אֵין מַשְׁגִּיחִין. (ד) לַעֲשׂוֹת עִיקָּר: אָמְרִי

על הכלאים דזמן זריעה היא. לאו דוקא זמן זריעה, שהרי לא הוי הזמן שמפרש ב"המקבל" (ב"מ דף קו:). אלא רוצה לומר: סוף זריעה, וכבר גדלו התבואות והזרעים, ואז הכלאים ניכרין. אבל קודם לכן אינן ניכרין: חדא מכלל חבירתה איתמר. וא"ת: ומאן דאמר מכללא, אמאי אמרה? והא כיון דידעינן אידך – כל שכן הא! ויש לומר: דמאן דאמרה באתריה דרב הוה, דסבר דראש חודש אדר שחל להיות בשבת שאין מוציאין כי אם שתי תורות, ולא הוו ידעי כלל אידך דרבי יצחק. ומזה הטעם איצטריך לאשמועינן ההיא דראש חודש טבת שחל להיות בשבת דמוציאין שלשה ספרי תורה:

והלכתא אין משגיחין בחנוכה. פירוש: לעשותו עיקר, ואע"ג דהלכתא כרבה לגבי רב יוסף*, מ"מ הוצרך לפסוק הלכה כוותיה, משום דפליגי עליה שאר אמוראי*): עדיין

*) [דומה לזה כתבו תוס' יבמות לט. סד"ה אע"ג]

רבינו חננאל

שקלים. תנן התם במסכת שקלים באחד באדר משמיעין על השקלים כו' מכריזין שיכין כל אדם שקלו ויביאהו למקדש. ולמה באחד באדר דקי"ל כר' טבי דמצריך לאיתויי הקרבנות שמקריבין בר"ח ניסן מן השקלים של שנה זו מן התרומה שנתרמה כדתנן בשלש קופות של שלש סאין כו'. והא שמועה דר' טבי בר"ה פרק א' וכיון דבעינן לאקרובי מן השקלים החדשים באחד בניסן מקדמינן להשמיע באחד באדר כדתניא שואלין בהלכות הפסח קודם לפסח ל' יום. אמרינן מתניתין נמי כרשב"ג דאמר שואלין בהלכות הפסח קודם לפסח ב' שבתות. כיון ששנינו בט"ו באדר שולחנות ישבו במדינה כדי לקבל השקלים מכל אדם. מקדמינן ומכרזינן קודם ט"ו. מ פרשת שקלים. רב אמר צו את בני ישראל את קרבני לחמי וגו' ושמואל אמר כי תשא. בשלמא לשמואל היינו דקרינן מכי תשא תרומה לה'. יתן תרומת ה'. לתת את תרומת ה' לכפר חדא לאדנים וחדא למזבח וחד לבדק הבית אלא לרב בצו את קרבני מי כתיב שקלים התם. איכא דאמרי בשלמא לשמואל דאמר בכי תשא היינו דשאני ר"ח [אדר] דבכל ראשי חדשים קורין בצו. ובר"ח אדר בכי תשא אלא ל מאי שאני. ואמרינן דבכל ר"ח שחל להיות בשבת קרו שיתא בעניינא דיומא בפרשה של אותה שבת וחד קרי בדר"ח. ובר"ח אדר מניחין פרשת היום וקורין כולן בצו את בני ישראל. הניחא לר' אמי דאמר דתנינן בחמישית חוזרין לסידרן לסדר פרשיות חוזרין מכלל שאלו ד' שבתות לא קרינן ענין היום והאידנא חוזרין לענין היום אלא לר' ירמיה דאמר לסדר הפטרות הן חוזרין אבל סדר פרשיות לעולם קו אותן כל פרשה בזמנה מאי איכא למימר. ומותבינן לרב מאי דמי הפטרה דיהוידע לצו את בני ישראל ופרקינן כר' טבי דמצריך קרבן ראש חודש ניסן מתרומה חדשה. ותוב מותבינן לרב מחל להיות רא חודש אדר בפרשה הסמוכה לה כו' איך יתכן לחול פרשת פינחס באחד באדר ופרקינן תמצא בענין הזה לבני מערבא שמסיימין התורה לשלש שנים ופוסקין כל פרשה ג' פרשיות אפשר דמיתרמי להו כי ה גוונא ועליהן תניא זו הברייתא. תניא כשמואל ראש חודש אדר שחל להיות בשבת קורין בכי תשא ומפטירין ביהוידע הכהן. ר' יצחק נפחא אמר ר"ח אדר שחל להיות בשבת מוציאין ג' תורות וקוו א' בענין היום ואחד בר"ח וא' בחנוכה. ר"ח טבת שחל להיות בחול. אמר ר' יצחק נפחא ג' קורין בר"ח ואסיקנא כוותיה. אין משגיחין בחנוכה ור"ח עיקר. אתמר חל ר"ח אדר להיות בואתה תצו

עין משפט נר מצוה

מז א מיי' פ"ב מהל' כלאים הלכה טו:
מח ב מיי' פ"ב מהל' שקלים הלכה ה ופ"ד הל' יא סמג עשין מה:
מט ג טוש"ע א"ח סי' תכט סעיף א:
נ ד מיי' פ"א מהל' שקלים הלכה ט:
נא ה ו מיי' פי"ג מהל' תפלה הלכה כ כב סמג עשין יט טוש"ע א"ח סימן תרפה סעיף א:
נב ז מיי' שם הלכה א:
נג ח מיי' שם הלכה כג סמג שם טוש"ע שם:
נד ט י מיי' שם הל' כד סמג שם טוש"ע א"ח סי' תרפד סעיף ג:

[ע' תוס' ב"ב קיד: ד"ה והילכתא ותוס' גיטין עד: ד"ה הא ותוס' מנחות לב. ד"ה מנעל ותוס' ב"ק נו: ד"ה בההיא ותוס' ב"מ כט. ד"ה והוי שואל]

הגהות הב"ח

(א) גמ' את קרבני לחמי מידי שקלים כתיבי התם אין טעמא כדר' טבי כצ"ל ותיבת הכא ותיבת מאי נמחק: (ב) שם והלכתא אין משגיחין בחנוכה כל עיקר כצ"ל ותיבות וראש חודש נמחק: (ג) רש"י ד"ה חודש הד"א עם ד"ה אלא: (ד) ד"ה אין משגיחין. בחנוכה לעשותו עיקר:

[תוספ' פ"ג לקמן ל.]

מסורת הש"ס

במדבר כח

ר"ה דף ז. יומא דף ס

פסחים ד' ו. סנהדרין ע"ז ד' ה: [תוספתא ר"ה ז. בכורות נח.]

שקלים פ"ק דף ב. מ"ג

*) [ע' תוס' בכורות ד"ה בפרוס]

סם

שמות ל

גליון הש"ס

גמ' קדמינן וקרינן. בכורות דף נז ע"ב תד"ה בפרוס:

[לקמן ל:]

[תוספ' פ"ג]

מלכים ב יב

[נ"ל כסף עובר איש כו' וכן איתא בהרא"ש]

יומא ד' ע. [סוטה מא.]

[עירובין כ. יבמות פח: מנחות מח. בכורות נדה יח:]

אָמְרִי אוּקוּמֵי הוּא דְּמוּקְמִי הָתָם. כְּלוֹמַר: אֵין הַדָּבָר נִיכָּר לְשֵׁם פָּרָשַׁת שְׁקָלִים, אֶלָּא סָבְרֵי שֶׁלֹּא נִסְתַּיְּימָה פָּרָשַׁת "וְאַתָּה תְּצַוֶּה" עַד כָּאן: וְחַד תָּאנֵי וְקָרֵי. חוֹזֵר וְשׁוֹנֶה לִקְרוֹת מִ"כִּי תִשָּׂא" עַד "וְעָשִׂיתָ כִּיּוֹר נְחֹשֶׁת" וגו': כּוֹפְלָהּ בְּשַׁבָּתוֹת. שֶׁקּוֹרִין אוֹתָהּ שְׁנֵי שַׁבָּתוֹת זוֹ אַחַר זוֹ: רַב אָמַר מַקְדִּימִין. וְקוֹרִין בְּ"כִי תִשָּׂא" לְשַׁבָּת שֶׁעָבַר, כִּדְתְנַן בְּמַתְנִי': דְּאִם כֵּן. דִּמְאַחֲרִין – בָּצְרֵי לְהוּ לְשׁוּלְחָנוֹת מִשְּׁנֵי שַׁבָּתוֹת, דְּאָמְרִינַן לְעֵיל מִשּׁוּם שֶׁשּׁוּלְחָנוֹת הוּצְרְכוּ לֵישֵׁב בַּמְּדִינָה בְּט"ו מַקְדִּימִין וְקוֹרִין מֵרֹאשׁ חוֹדֶשׁ, שֶׁיְּהוּ דּוֹרְשִׁין שְׁתֵּי שַׁבָּתוֹת לִפְנֵיהֶן, כְּרַבָּן שִׁמְעוֹן בֶּן גַּמְלִיאֵל. וְאִם תְּאַחֵר עַד לְמָחֳרַת רֹאשׁ חֹדֶשׁ – אֵין כָּאן הַקְדָּמָה שְׁתֵּי שַׁבָּתוֹת: תורה אור

אָמְרִי: אוּקוּמֵי הוּא דְּקָא מוֹקְמִי הָתָם. אֶלָּא אֲמַר אַבָּיֵי: [א]קָרוּ שִׁיתָּא מִ"וְאַתָּה תְּצַוֶּה" עַד "וְעָשִׂיתָ", וְחַד תָּנֵי וְקָרֵי מִ"כִּי תִשָּׂא" עַד "וְעָשִׂיתָ", מֵיתִיבִי: *חָל לִהְיוֹת בַּפָּרָשָׁה הַסְּמוּכָה לָהּ, בֵּין מִלְּפָנֶיהָ בֵּין מִלְּאַחֲרֶיהָ — קוֹרִין אוֹתָהּ וְכוֹפְלִין אוֹתָהּ. בִּשְׁלָמָא לְאַבָּיֵי — נִיחָא, אֶלָּא לְר' יִצְחָק נַפָּחָא קַשְׁיָא! אָמַר לָךְ ר' יִצְחָק נַפָּחָא: וּלְאַבָּיֵי מִי נִיחָא? תֵּינַח לְפָנֶיהָ, לְאַחֲרֶיהָ הַפּוֹתַחַת הֵיכִי מַשְׁכַּחַתְּ לָהּ? אֶלָּא מַאי אִית לָךְ לְמֵימַר — כּוֹפְלָהּ בְּשַׁבָּתוֹת, הָכָא נַמִי — כּוֹפְלָהּ בְּשַׁבָּתוֹת. חָל לִהְיוֹת בְּ"כִי תִשָּׂא" עַצְמָהּ, א"ר יִצְחָק נַפָּחָא: קָרוּ שִׁיתָּא מִן "וְעָשִׂיתָ" עַד "וַיַּקְהֵל" וְחַד קָרֵי מִ"כִּי תִשָּׂא" עַד "וְעָשִׂיתָ". מַתְקִיף לָהּ אַבָּיֵי: הַשְׁתָּא אָמְרִי: לְמַפְרֵעַ הוּא דְּקָרֵי! אֶלָּא אֲמַר אַבָּיֵי: קָרוּ שִׁיתָּא עַד "וַיַּקְהֵל" וְחַד תָּנֵי וְקָרֵי מִ"כִּי תִשָּׂא" עַד "וְעָשִׂיתָ". תַּנְיָא כְּוָותֵיהּ דְּאַבָּיֵי: חָל לִהְיוֹת בְּ"כִי תִשָּׂא" עַצְמָהּ — קוֹרִין אוֹתָהּ וְכוֹפְלִין אוֹתָהּ. § "חָל לִהְיוֹת בְּתוֹךְ הַשַּׁבָּת מַקְדִּימִין לְשַׁבָּת שֶׁעָבְרָה". § אִיתְּמַר, ר"ח אֲדָר שֶׁחָל לִהְיוֹת בְּעֶרֶב שַׁבָּת, רַב אָמַר: מַקְדִּימִין, וּשְׁמוּאֵל אָמַר: מְאַחֲרִין. רַב אָמַר: [ב]מַקְדִּימִין, דְּאִם כֵּן — בָּצְרֵי לְהוּ יוֹמֵי שׁוּלְחָנוֹת, וּשְׁמוּאֵל אָמַר: מְאַחֲרִין, אָמַר לָךְ: סוֹף סוֹף חֲמֵיסַר בְּמַעֲלֵי שַׁבְּתָא מִיקְלַע, וְשׁוּלְחָנוֹת לָא נָפְקֵי עַד חַד בְּשַׁבָּא, הִלְכָּךְ מְאַחֲרִין. תְּנַן: חָל לִהְיוֹת בְּתוֹךְ הַשַּׁבָּת מַקְדִּימִין לְשֶׁעָבַר, וּמַפְסִיקִין לְשַׁבָּת אַחֶרֶת. מַאי לָאו — אֲפִילּוּ בְּע"ש! לָא, בְּתוֹךְ הַשַּׁבָּת דַּוְקָא. ת"ש: אֵיזוֹ הִיא שַׁבָּת רִאשׁוֹנָה — כָּל שֶׁחָל ר"ח אֲדָר לִהְיוֹת בְּתוֹכָהּ, וַאֲפִילּוּ בְּעֶרֶב שַׁבָּת. מַאי לָאו — אֲפִילּוּ בְּע"ש דּוּמְיָא דְּתוֹכָהּ, מַה תּוֹכָהּ — מַקְדִּימִין, אַף ע"ש — מַקְדִּימִין! אָמַר שְׁמוּאֵל: בָּהּ, וְכֵן תָּנָא דְּבֵי שְׁמוּאֵל: בָּהּ. כְּתַנָּאֵי: מַסְרְגִין לְשַׁבָּתוֹת, דִּבְרֵי ר' יְהוּדָה הַנָּשִׂיא. ר"ש בֶּן אֶלְעָזָר אוֹמֵר: אֵין מַסְרְגִין. אָמַר ר"ש בֶּן אֶלְעָזָר: אֵימָתַי אֲנִי אוֹמֵר אֵין מַסְרְגִין — בִּזְמַן שֶׁחָל לִהְיוֹת בְּע"ש, אֲבָל בִּזְמַן שֶׁחָל לִהְיוֹת בְּתוֹךְ הַשַּׁבָּת — מַקְדִּים וְקוֹרֵא מִשַּׁבָּת שֶׁעָבְרָה, אע"פ שֶׁהוּא שְׁבָט. § "בַּשְּׁנִיָּה זָכוֹר" וכו'. § אִיתְּמַר, פּוּרִים שֶׁחָל לִהְיוֹת בְּע"ש, רַב אָמַר: [ג]מַקְדִּימִין פָּרָשַׁת זָכוֹר, וּשְׁמוּאֵל אָמַר: מְאַחֲרִין. רַב אָמַר: מַקְדִּימִין, כִּי הֵיכִי דְּלָא תִּיקְדּוֹם עֲשִׂיָּה לִזְכִירָה. וּשְׁמוּאֵל אָמַר: מְאַחֲרִין, אָמַר לָךְ: כֵּיוָן דְּאִיכָּא מוּקָּפִין דְּעָבְדִי בַּחֲמֵיסַר — עֲשִׂיָּה וּזְכִירָה בַּהֲדֵי הֲדָדֵי קָא אָתְיָין. תְּנַן: בַּשְּׁנִיָּה זָכוֹר. וְהָא כִּי מִיקְלַע רֵישׁ יַרְחָא בְּשַׁבָּת מִיקְלַע פּוּרִים בְּעֶרֶב שַׁבָּת, וְקָתָנֵי: בַּשְּׁנִיָּה זָכוֹר! אָמַר רַב פַּפָּא: מַאי שְׁנִיָּה — שְׁנִיָּה לְהַפְסָקָה. תָּא שְׁמַע: [ד]אֵיזוֹ שַׁבָּת שְׁנִיָּה — כָּל שֶׁחָל פּוּרִים לִהְיוֹת בְּתוֹכָהּ, וַאֲפִילּוּ בְּעֶרֶב שַׁבָּת. מַאי לָאו עֶרֶב שַׁבָּת דּוּמְיָא דְּתוֹכָהּ, מַה תּוֹכָהּ — מַקְדִּימִין, אַף עֶרֶב שַׁבָּת מַקְדִּימִין! אָמַר שְׁמוּאֵל: בָּהּ, וְכֵן תָּנָא דְּבֵי שְׁמוּאֵל: בָּהּ. חָל לִהְיוֹת בַּשַּׁבָּת עַצְמָהּ, אָמַר ר"ה: לְדִבְרֵי הַכֹּל אֵין מַקְדִּימִין. וְרַב נַחְמָן אָמַר: עֲדַיִין הִיא מַחֲלוֹקֶת. אִיתְּמַר נַמִי, א"ר חִיָּיא בַּר אַבָּא אָמַר רַבִּי אַבָּא אֲמַר רַב: פּוּרִים שֶׁחָל לִהְיוֹת בַּשַּׁבָּת — מַקְדִּים וְקוֹרֵא בַּשַּׁבָּת שֶׁעָבְרָה "זָכוֹר". § "בַּשְּׁלִישִׁית פָּרָה אֲדוּמָּה" וכו'. § תָּנוּ רַבָּנַן: [ה]אֵיזוֹ הִיא שַׁבָּת שְׁלִישִׁית — כָּל שֶׁסְּמוּכָה לְפוּרִים מֵאַחֲרֶיהָ. אִיתְּמַר: ר' חָמָא בְּר' חֲנִינָא אֲמַר: שַׁבָּת הַסְּמוּכָה לְר"ח נִיסָן. וְלָא פְּלִיגִי; הָא — דְּאִיקְלַע ר"ח נִיסָן בְּשַׁבָּת, הָא דְּאִיקְלַע בְּאֶמְצַע שַׁבָּת. § "בָּרְבִיעִית °הַחֹדֶשׁ הַזֶּה לָכֶם" (שמות יב). § תָּנוּ רַבָּנַן: [ו]ר"ח אֲדָר שֶׁחָל לִהְיוֹת בְּשַׁבָּת — קוֹרִין "כִּי תִשָּׂא" וּמַפְטִירִין בִּ"יהוֹיָדָע", וְאֵי זוֹ הִיא שַׁבָּת רִאשׁוֹנָה — כָּל שֶׁחָל ר"ח אֲדָר לִהְיוֹת בְּתוֹכָהּ, וַאֲפִילּוּ בְּעֶרֶב שַׁבָּת. [ז]בַּשְּׁנִיָּה — "זָכוֹר" וּמַפְטִירִין °"פָּקַדְתִּי" (שמואל א טו), וְאֵי זוֹ הִיא שַׁבָּת שְׁנִיָּה — כָּל שֶׁחָל פּוּרִים לִהְיוֹת בְּתוֹכָהּ, וַאֲפִילּוּ בְּעֶרֶב שַׁבָּת. [ח]בַּשְּׁלִישִׁית — פָּרָה אֲדוּמָּה, וּמַפְטִירִין °"וְזָרַקְתִּי עֲלֵיכֶם" (יחזקאל לו), וְאֵי זוֹ הִיא שַׁבָּת שְׁלִישִׁית — כָּל שֶׁסְּמוּכָה לְפוּרִים מֵאַחֲרֶיהָ. [ט]בָּרְבִיעִית "הַחֹדֶשׁ הַזֶּה" וּמַפְטִירִין °"כֹּה אָמַר ה' [אֱלֹהִים] בָּרִאשׁוֹן בְּאֶחָד לַחֹדֶשׁ" (שם מה) וְאֵיזוֹ

חֲמֵיסַר בְּמַעֲלֵי שַׁבְּתָא מִיקְלַע. וְאוֹתוֹ הַיּוֹם לֹא יַתְחִילוּ לָצֵאת וְלֵישֵׁב בַּמְּדִינָה, מִפְּנֵי כְּבוֹד הַשַּׁבָּת: לָא נָפְקֵי עַד חַד בְּשַׁבָּת. וְכִי מְאַחֲרַתְּ נַמִי אִיכָּא שְׁתֵּי שַׁבָּתוֹת, הִלְכָּךְ מְאַחֲרִין, כְּדֵי שֶׁלֹּא תִּצְטָרֵךְ לְהַפְסִיק בֵּין ב' פָּרָשִׁיּוֹת: בְּתוֹךְ שַׁבָּת דַּוְקָא. דְּאִי מְאַחֲרַתְּ וַדַּאי בָּצְרֵי לְהוּ יוֹמֵי לְשׁוּלְחָנוֹת: אָמַר שְׁמוּאֵל. הַאי בְּתוֹכָהּ דְּקָתָנֵי – לָאו תּוֹךְ שָׁבוּעַ, אֶלָּא תּוֹךְ שַׁבָּת עַצְמוֹ: וְכֵן תָּנָא דְּבֵי שְׁמוּאֵל. בְּתוֹסֶפְתָּא(א) דִּיהָךְ בָּרַיְיתָא: אֵי זוֹ הִיא שַׁבָּת רִאשׁוֹנָה – כָּל שֶׁחָל ר"ח אֲדָר לִהְיוֹת בָּהּ בְּיוֹם שַׁבָּת עַצְמוֹ, וַאֲפִילּוּ חָל בְּעֶרֶב שַׁבָּת שֶׁל אֶתְמוֹל – כְּאִילּוּ חָל בָּהּ. אַלְמָא: מְאַחֲרִין אַשְׁמוּעִינַן: מַסְרְגִין. לְשׁוֹן סֵירוּגִין. כְּלוֹמַר: מַפְסִיקִין לְשַׁבָּתוֹת בֵּין פָּרָשָׁה רִאשׁוֹנָה לִשְׁנִיָּה, כְּשֶׁחָל ר"ח בְּחוֹל שֶׁמַּקְדִּימִין לְשֶׁעָבַר, דְּאִ"כ בָּצְרֵי לְהוּ יוֹמֵי לְשׁוּלְחָנוֹת. וּמַפְסִיקִין לְשַׁבָּת הַבָּאָה, וּלְשַׁבָּת שְׁלִישִׁית קוֹרִין "זָכוֹר" כְּדֵי שֶׁתְּהֵא סְמוּכָה זָכוֹר לְפוּרִים: אֵין מַסְרְגִין. כִּדְמְפָרֵשׁ וְאָזֵיל: אֵימָתַי אֲנִי אוֹמֵר אֵין מַסְרְגִין בִּזְמַן שֶׁחָל לִהְיוֹת בְּעֶרֶב שַׁבָּת. דְּכִי נַמִי מְאַחֲרִין לָא בָּצְרֵי יוֹמֵי לְשׁוּלְחָנוֹת, כִּדְאָמַר שְׁמוּאֵל לְעֵיל: סוֹף סוֹף שׁוּלְחָנוֹת לָא יָתְבֵי עַד חַד בְּשַׁבָּת, הִלְכָּךְ מְאַחֲרִין, וְאֵין כָּאן סֵירוּג: אֲבָל בִּזְמַן שֶׁחָל לִהְיוֹת בְּתוֹךְ הַשַּׁבָּת. דְּאִי מְאַחֲרַתְּ לָהּ בָּצְרֵי לְהוּ יוֹמָא לְשׁוּלְחָנוֹת – עַל כָּרְחָךְ נַקְדִּים, וְיֵשׁ כָּאן סֵירוּג: הָכִי גָּרְסִינַן. כִּי הֵיכִי דְּלָא לִיקְדּוֹם עֲשִׂיָּיה לִזְכִירָה: תְּנַן בַּשְּׁנִיָּה זָכוֹר. קָא סָלְקָא דַּעְתָּךְ אַרֹאשׁ חוֹדֶשׁ אֲדָר שֶׁחָל לִהְיוֹת בַּשַּׁבָּת קָאֵי, דְּמַיְירֵי בֵּיהּ רֵישָׁא דְּמַתְנִיתִין: שְׁנִיָּה לַהַפְסָקָה. כְּלוֹמַר: לָאו אַרֵישָׁא קָאֵי, אֶלָּא אַסֵּיפָא קָאֵי, דְּקָתָנֵי: חָל לִהְיוֹת בְּתוֹךְ הַשַּׁבָּת – מַקְדִּימִין לְשֶׁעָבַר וּמַפְסִיקִין לַשַּׁבָּת הַבָּאָה. וַעֲלָהּ קָאֵי וְאָמַר: בַּשַּׁבָּת שֶׁל אַחַר הַפְסָקָה קוֹרִין "זָכוֹר", וּבְתוֹךְ שָׁבוּעַ שֶׁלְּאַחֲרֶיהָ יְהֵא פּוּרִים: אֵיזוֹ הִיא שַׁבָּת שְׁנִיָּה. כְּלוֹמַר: שַׁבָּת שֶׁל פָּרָשָׁה שְׁנִיָּה, פָּרָשַׁת "זָכוֹר": בְּתוֹכָהּ. לְאַחֲרֶיהָ, וַאֲפִילּוּ חָל פּוּרִים בְּעֶרֶב שַׁבָּת: בָּהּ. בְּיוֹם שַׁבָּת עַצְמוֹ קוֹרִין הַפָּרָשָׁה בּוֹ בַּיּוֹם, וַאֲפִילּוּ חָל בְּעֶרֶב שַׁבָּת אֶתְמוֹל – כְּאִילּוּ חָל לַשַּׁבָּת שֶׁלְּמָחָר, וְהַיְינוּ כִּשְׁמוּאֵל: חָל לִהְיוֹת פּוּרִים בְּשַׁבָּת. דִּבְרֵי הַכֹּל אֵין קוֹרִין "זָכוֹר" לְשֶׁעָבַר, דְּהָא הַשְׁתָּא לֹא קָדְמָה עֲשִׂיָּיה לִזְכִירָה, וְגַבֵּי מוּקָּפִין קָדְמָה זְכִירָה לַעֲשִׂיָּיה: עֲדַיִין הִיא מַחֲלוֹקֶת. אַף בְּזוֹ אָמַר רַב מַקְדִּימִין, כְּדֵי שֶׁתִּתְקַדֵּם זְכִירָה לַעֲשִׂיָּיה דְּעֲיָירוֹת: אֵיזוֹ הִיא שַׁבָּת שְׁלִישִׁית. שֶׁקּוֹרִין בּוֹ פָּרָשָׁה שְׁלִישִׁית: הָא דְּאִיקְלַע רֹאשׁ חוֹדֶשׁ נִיסָן בְּיוֹם הַשַּׁבָּת. שֶׁלֹּא הוּלְכַךְ לְהַקְדִּים פָּרָשַׁת הַחוֹדֶשׁ לַשַּׁבָּת שֶׁעָבְרָה, קָרֵינַן לַשַּׁבָּת שֶׁעָבְרָה פָּרָה אֲדוּמָּה כְּרַבִּי(ב) חָמָא בַּר' חֲנִינָא. וְלֹא בַּסְּמוּכָה לְפוּרִים, לִסְמוֹךְ אַזְהָרַת טְמֵאִים לְפֶסַח. וְהֵיכָא דְּחָל רֹאשׁ חוֹדֶשׁ נִיסָן בְּאֶמְצַע שַׁבָּת, שֶׁהוּצְרְכוּ לִקְרוֹת פָּרָשַׁת הַחוֹדֶשׁ בַּשַּׁבָּת שֶׁלְּפָנֶיהָ – הוּזְקְקוּ לְהַקְדִּים פָּרָשַׁת פָּרָה לַשַּׁבָּת שֶׁלִּפְנֵי שַׁבָּת [זוֹ], שֶׁהִיא סְמוּכָה לְפוּרִים מֵאַחֲרֶיהָ: תָּנוּ רַבָּנַן כו'. בָּרַיְיתָא זוֹ מְפוֹרֶשֶׁת לְמַעְלָה בְּסֵירוּגִין, לְרַב כִּדְאִית לֵיהּ, וְלִשְׁמוּאֵל כִּדְאִית לֵיהּ: וְאִי

[לעיל כט:]

עדיין היא מחלוקת איתמר נמי וכו'. קשיא: אמאי לא פריך מברייתא, דקתני: איזוהי שבת שניה – כל שחל פורים להיות בתוכה ואפילו בערב שבת. ולרב הוי מצי למימר ואפי' בשבת שלאחר כך, וכל שכן בערב שבת שלפניה שמקדימין לשבת שעברה! וי"ל: דהך ברייתא היינו ברייתא דבסמוך, אחר מתני' דברביעית החדש הזה, ואגב דתני ואפילו בערב שבת גבי שבת ראשונה וגבי שבת רביעית, דהוי דוקא – תנא נמי בהא בערב שבת ולא בשבת, אף על גב דלא הוי דוקא: ושאר

הגהות הב"ח

רש"י ד"ה וכן תנא שמואל בתוספתא שלהן נ"א זו היא: (ב) ד"ה דאיקלע וכו' כרבי חמא בר' חנינא:

עין משפט נר מצוה

נה א מיי' פי"ג מהל' תפלה הלכה כב:
נו ב ג מיי' שם הלכה כ טוש"ע א"ח סימן תרפה סעיף ה:
נז ד ה מיי' שם הלכה כ:
נח ו מיי' שם טוש"ע שם סעיף א:
נט ז מיי' שם טוש"ע שם סעיף ב:
ס ח מיי' שם טוש"ע שם סעיף ג:
סא ט מיי' שם טוש"ע שם סעיף ד:

רבינו חננאל

אמר אביי קרו שיתא מואתה תצוה עד ועשית כיור נחשת וחד חוזר וקורא מכי תשא עד ועשית כיור נחשת. וקי"ל כוותיה. חל להיות ר"ח אדר בכי תשא עצמה. אמר אביי קרו ו' מכי תשא עד ויקהל. וחד חוזר וקורא מכי תשא ועד ועשית כיור נחשת וקי"ל כוותיה דתניא כוותיה: אתמר ר"ח אדר שחל להיות בע"ש רב אמר מקדימין וקורין פרשת שקלים בשבת שהיא כ"ו יום בשבט. שאם לא תקרא כך אלא בשבת שהיא ב' ימים באדר בצרי יומי דשלחנות דבעינן משעה שמשמיעין בשקלים עד ט"ו ואח"כ יוצאין השלחנות והנה אם תשמע בב' ימים לאדר נמצאו השלחנות יוצאין בי"ד יום. ופריק שמואל דאמר מאחרין וקורין בשבת שהיא שני ימים באדר כיון דשלחנות כל אימת דחל ר"ח אדר בע"ש לא נפקי עד חד בשבת לא בצרי ואקשינן לשמואל דתניא איזו היא שבת ראשונה כל שחל ר"ח אדר להיות בתוכה ודייקינן מאי לאו ע"ש דומיא דתוכה מה כשחל להיות בתוכה מקדמינן וקרינן פרשת שקלים אף כשחל ר"ח אדר בע"ש מקדמינן וקרינן משבת שעברה. ופריק שמואל לא תימא בתוכה אלא בה. וכך היא סוגיא דמתניתין. איזו היא שבת ראשונה כל שחל ר"ח אדר להיות בתוכה. ואפי' בע"ש פירוש בה בשב' עצמה. כשם כשחל ר"ח אדר בשבת עצמה קורין בה פרשת שקלים כך אפילו אם חל להיות בע"ש קורין בשבת עצמה. והא פלוגתא דרב ושמואל כתנאי היא דתניא מסרגין לשבתות דברי ר' יהודה כו'. פירוש מסרגין מפסיקין כדתנן קראה סירוגין ומפרשינן פיסקי פיסקי. ואמר ר' שמעון אימתי אני אומר אין מסרגין. כלומר שאין מפסיקין אלא שקורין שבת אחר שבת בזמן שחל ר"ח

להיות ע"ש מכלל דסבר שקורין פרשת שקלים למחר כשמואל ולפיכך אין מפסיקין. ות"ק סבר מקדימין וקורין משעה שעברה אע"פ שהיא שבט כרב ומפסיקין בשבת שהיא שני ימים באדר. וקי"ל כרב.
...ג דפריק שמואל לטעמיה לית הלכתא כוותיה: ת"ר ר"ח אדר שחל להיות בשבת קורין בכי תשא ומפטירין ביהוידע. ואיזו היא שבת ראשונה כל שחל ר"ח אדר להיות בתוכה ואפילו בע"ש.
...יה זכור ומפטירין כה אמר ה' צבאות פקדתי. איזו היא שבת שניה כל שחל פורים להיות בתוכה ואפי' בע"ש. בשלישית פרה אדומה ומפטירין וזרקתי עליכם. ואיזו היא שבת שלישית כל שסמוכה לפורים
...ריה. וזה כשחל ר"ח ניסן באמצע שבת אבל אם חל ר"ח ניסן להיות בשבת נמצאת שבת שלישית הסמוכה לר"ח ניסן. ברביעית החדש הזה. ומפטירין כה אמר ה' בראשון באחד לחדש כו'

סב א מיי' פי"ג מהל' תפלה הלכה כ:
סג ב מיי' שם טוש"ע א"ח סימן תרפה:
סד ג מיי' פ"א מהל' תעניות הלכה יז טוש"ע א"ח סימן תקעו סעיף יט:
סה ד מיי' פי"ג מהל' תפלה הל' ח טוש"ע א"ח סימן תצ סעיף א:

תורה אור

[א]וְאֵיזוֹ הִיא שַׁבָּת רְבִיעִית – כָּל שֶׁחָל ר"ח נִיסָן לִהְיוֹת בְּתוֹכָהּ, וַאֲפִילּוּ בְּע"ש. § "בַּחֲמִישִׁית חוֹזְרִין לִכְסִדְרָן" וכו'. § לְסֵדֶר מַאי? ר' אַמִּי אָמַר: לְסֵדֶר פָּרָשִׁיּוֹת הוּא חוֹזֵר, ר' יִרְמְיָה אָמַר: *[ב]לְסֵדֶר הַפְטָרוֹת הוּא חוֹזֵר. אָמַר אַבַּיֵי: כְּוָותֵי' דְּר' אַמִּי מִסְתַּבְּרָא. דִּתְנַן: לַכֹּל מַפְסִיקִין: לְרָאשֵׁי חֳדָשִׁים, לַחֲנוּכָּה וּלְפוּרִים, לְתַעֲנִיּוֹת וּלְמַעֲמָדוֹת, וּלְיוה"כ. בִּשְׁלָמָא לְמ"ד לְסֵדֶר פָּרָשִׁיּוֹת הוּא חוֹזֵר – הַיְינוּ דְּאִיכָּא פָּרָשָׁה בַּחוֹל, אֶלָּא לְמ"ד לְסֵדֶר הַפְטָרוֹת הוּא חוֹזֵר – הַפְטָרָה בַּחוֹל מִי אִיכָּא? וְאִידָךְ: הָא כִּדְאִיתָא, וְהָא כִּדְאִיתָא. וּבְתַעֲנִיּוֹת לָמָּה לִי הַפְסָקָה? לִיקְרֵי מִצַּפְרָא בְּעִנְיָנָא דְיוֹמָא, וּבְמִנְחָה בְּתַעֲנִיתָא! מְסַיֵּיעַ לֵיהּ לְר"ה, דַּאֲמַר ר"ה: *מִצַּפְרָא כִּינּוּפְיָא. [ג]הֵיכִי עָבְדִינַן? אֲמַר אַבַּיֵי: מִצַּפְרָא לְפַלְגֵיהּ דְּיוֹמָא מְעַיְּינִינַן בְּמִילֵּי דְמָתָא, מִפַּלְגֵיהּ דְּיוֹמָא לְפַנְיָא – רִיבְעָא דְיוֹמָא(א) קָרוּ וּמַפְטְרִי, וְרִיבְעָא דְיוֹמָא בָּעוּ רַחֲמֵי, שֶׁנֶּאֱמַר °"וַיִּקְרְאוּ בְּסֵפֶר (נחמיה ט) תּוֹרַת ה' אֱלֹהֵיהֶם רְבִיעִית הַיּוֹם וּרְבִיעִית (הַיּוֹם) מִתְוַדִּים וּמִשְׁתַּחֲוִים". וְאֵיפוֹךְ אֲנָא! לָא ס"ד דִּכְתִיב °"וְאֵלַי יֵאָסְפוּ כֹּל חָרֵד בְּדִבְרֵי אֱלֹהֵי יִשְׂרָאֵל עַל מַעַל (עזרא ט) הַגּוֹלָה וַאֲנִי יוֹשֵׁב מְשׁוֹמֵם עַד לְמִנְחַת הָעֶרֶב" וּכְתִיב "וּבְמִנְחַת הָעֶרֶב קַמְתִּי מִתַּעֲנִיתִי". § **מתני'** [ד]בַּפֶּסַח קוֹרִין בְּפָרָשַׁת מוֹעֲדוֹת שֶׁל תּוֹרַת כֹּהֲנִים, בָּעֲצֶרֶת (דברים טז) °"שִׁבְעָה שָׁבוּעוֹת", בְּרֹאשׁ הַשָּׁנָה °"בַּחֹדֶשׁ הַשְּׁבִיעִי בְּאֶחָד לַחֹדֶשׁ", בְּיוה"כ (ויקרא כג) °"אַחֲרֵי מוֹת". בְּיו"ט הָרִאשׁוֹן שֶׁל חַג קוֹרִין בְּפָרָשַׁת מוֹעֲדוֹת שֶׁבְּתוֹרַת כֹּהֲנִים, (שם טז) וּבִשְׁאָר כָּל יְמוֹת הֶחָג בְּקָרְבְּנוֹת הֶחָג. בַּחֲנוּכָּה °בַּנְּשִׂיאִים, (במדבר ז) בַּפּוּרִים – °"וַיָּבֹא עֲמָלֵק", (שמות יז) בְּרָאשֵׁי חֳדָשִׁים – °"וּבְרָאשֵׁי חָדְשֵׁיכֶם". (במדבר כח) בַּמַּעֲמָדוֹת בְּמַעֲשֵׂה בְרֵאשִׁית, בַּתַּעֲנִיּוֹת

בְּרָכוֹת

ושאר ימות החג קורין בקרבנות החג – והא שאנו מעמידין ספר תורה שניה במועדות, וקורין בקרבנות היום – לא מצינו סמך בתלמוד, אלא בסדר רב עמרם ישנו. וקצת יש סמך לדבר מהא דאמר לקמן (דף לא:): אמר אברהם לפני הקב"ה רבש"ע וכו', אמר לו הקב"ה: כבר תקנתי להם סדר קרבנות, כל זמן שקורין בהן:

והאידנא

ואי זו היא שבת רביעית כו' ואפילו בערב שבת. בְּהָא מוֹדֶה שְׁמוּאֵל דְּעֶרֶב שַׁבָּת דּוּמְיָא דְּתוֹכָהּ, וּמַקְדִּימִין. דְּא"א מְאַחֲרִין – קָדְמָה עֲשִׂיָּיה לִשְׁמִיעָה. וַאֲנַן נוֹהֲגִין בְּכוּלְּהוּ כְּרַב, חוּץ מִפּוּרִים שֶׁחָל לִהְיוֹת בְּשַׁבָּת עַצְמָהּ, דְּהַהִיא לָא אִיקְלַע כְּלָל. דְּא"כ הָוֵי ר"ח אֲדָר בְּאֶחָד בְּשַׁבָּת, וְרֹאשׁ חוֹדֶשׁ נִיסָן בִּשְׁנֵי בְּשַׁבָּת, שֶׁהֲרֵי אֲדָר לְעוֹלָם חָסֵר – וְא"כ הָוֵה לֵיהּ פֶּסַח בִּשְׁנֵי בְּשַׁבָּת, וְקַיְימָא לָן דְּלָא בד"ו פֶּסַח לְעוֹלָם. וְיָמִים הָרְאוּיִין לִקְבִיעַת רֹאשׁ חוֹדֶשׁ אֲדָר זבד"ו. וְסִימָן מָסוֹרֶת הַפְסָקַת פָּרָשִׁיּוֹת כָּךְ: זט"ו ב"ו ד"ד וי"ו. זֶהוּ פֵּירוּשׁ זט"ו: אִם בָּא רֹאשׁ חוֹדֶשׁ אֲדָר בְּשַׁבָּת – יְהֵא לְךָ הַפְסָקַת פָּרָשָׁה בְּיוֹם חֲמִשָּׁה עָשָׂר וְלֹא יוֹתֵר; שֶׁהֲרֵי בְּיוֹם רֹאשׁ חוֹדֶשׁ קוֹרִין פָּרָשַׁת שְׁקָלִים, וּלְשַׁבָּת הַבָּאָה פָּרָשַׁת "זָכוֹר", כִּדְתַנְיָא בְּבָרַיְיתָא: אֵי זוֹ הִיא שַׁבָּת שְׁנִיָּה – כָּל שֶׁחָל פּוּרִים לִהְיוֹת בְּתוֹכָהּ, וַאֲפִילּוּ בְּעֶרֶב שַׁבָּת. וּמַתְנִי' נַמִי תְּנַן בַּשְּׁנִיָּה זָכוֹר. וְהַיְינוּ כְּרַב, דְּאָמַר פּוּרִים שֶׁחָל לִהְיוֹת בְּע"ש מַקְדִּימִין. וְעַכְשָׁיו יָחוּל פּוּרִים בְּעֶרֶב שַׁבָּת, וְאָנוּ מַקְדִּימִין כְּרַב. אֲבָל לְשַׁבָּת שְׁלִישִׁית שֶׁל אֲדָר שֶׁהוּא יוֹם ט"ו לַחוֹדֶשׁ – מַפְסִיקִין, וּבְשַׁבָּת רְבִיעִית(ב) (לַחוֹדֶשׁ) שֶׁהִיא סְמוּכָה לְפוּרִים שֶׁל מוּקָּפִין מֵאַחֲרֵיהֶן קוֹרִין פָּרָה אֲדוּמָּה, דְּתַנְיָא בְּבָרַיְיתָא: אֵי זוֹ הִיא שַׁבָּת שֶׁל פָּרָשַׁת פָּרָה – כָּל שֶׁסְּמוּכָה לְפוּרִים מֵאַחֲרֶיהָ. וְאוֹקִימְנָא הֵיכָא דְּחָל ר"ח נִיסָן בְּחוֹל, וְזֶה יָחוּל בְּאֶחָד בְּשַׁבָּת שֶׁהוּא חוֹל. וּפָרָשַׁת הַחוֹדֶשׁ קוֹרִין בְּשַׁבָּת שֶׁלְּאַחֲרֶי', שֶׁהֲרֵי הִיא סְמוּכָה לְר"ח נִיסָן, הֲרֵי לְךָ פֵּי' זט"ו. פֵּירוּשׁ ב"ו: אִם בָּא ר"ח אֲדָר בִּשְׁנֵי בְּשַׁבָּת – תְּהֵא הַפְסָקָה בְּשַׁבָּת שֶׁלְּאַחַר ר"ח, שֶׁהוּא יוֹם שִׁשָּׁה לַאֲדָר. שֶׁהֲרֵי הִקְדַּמְתָּ פָּרָשַׁת שְׁקָלִים בְּשַׁבָּת שֶׁעָבְרָה, כִּדְתַנַן: חָל לִהְיוֹת בְּתוֹךְ הַשַּׁבָּת – מַקְדִּימִין לְשֶׁעָבַר וּמַפְסִיקִין לְשַׁבָּת הַבָּאָה. וְשׁוּב אֵין לְךָ הַפְסָקָה בָּהֶן, שֶׁהֲרֵי שַׁבָּת שֶׁלְּאַחֲרֶיהָ נִקְרֵאת פָּרָשַׁת זָכוֹר וְהוּא יוֹם י"ג לַחוֹדֶשׁ, וּפוּרִים לְיוֹם מָחָר, וְשַׁבָּת שֶׁל אַחֲרֶיהָ פָּרָשַׁת פָּרָה אֲדוּמָּה שֶׁהִיא סְמוּכָה מֵאַחֲרֶיהָ, וְשַׁבָּת שֶׁל אַחֲרֶיהָ יוֹם כ"ז לַחוֹדֶשׁ קוֹרִין פָּרָשַׁת הַחוֹדֶשׁ שֶׁהִיא סְמוּכָה לְר"ח נִיסָן, וַהֲרֵי לְךָ פֵּירוּשׁ ב"ו. פֵּי' ד"ד: אִם בָּא ר"ח אֲדָר בְּד' בְּשַׁבָּת – תְּהֵא לְךָ הַפְסָקָה בְּד' לַחוֹדֶשׁ, שַׁבָּת שֶׁל אַחַר ר"ח. שֶׁהֲרֵי הִקְדַּמְתָּ פָּרָשַׁת שְׁקָלִים בְּשַׁבָּת שֶׁלִּפְנֵי ר"ח, כָּל הַטַּעַם כְּטַעַם פֵּירוּשׁוֹ שֶׁל ב"ו, וְאֵין לְךָ עוֹד הַפְסָקָה בָּהֶן, וַהֲרֵי לְךָ פֵּירוּשׁ ד"ד. פֵּירוּשׁ וי"ו: אִם בָּא ר"ח בְּשִׁשִּׁי בְּשַׁבָּת – יְהֵא לְךָ הַפְסָקָה אַחַת לְיוֹם מָחָר, שֶׁהוּא שֵׁנִי לַחוֹדֶשׁ, וְהַשְּׁנִיָּה בְּיוֹם שִׁשָּׁה עָשָׂר. הָרִאשׁוֹנָה בְּיוֹם מָחָר – כִּדְתַנְיָא: חָל לִהְיוֹת בְּתוֹךְ הַשַּׁבָּת – מַקְדִּימִין לְשֶׁעָבַר וּמַפְסִיקִין לְשַׁבָּת שְׁנִיָּה, דִּסְבִירָא לָן כְּרַב דְּאָמַר: ע"ש כְּאֶמְצַע שַׁבָּת, וּמַקְדִּימִין לְשֶׁעָבַר וּמַפְסִיקִין לְשַׁבָּת הַבָּאָה. וּפָרָשַׁת זָכוֹר בְּשַׁבָּת שֶׁל אַחֲרֶיהָ, שֶׁהוּא יוֹם תִּשְׁעָה לַחוֹדֶשׁ וְהִיא סְמוּכָה לְפוּרִים. וּבְשַׁבָּת שֶׁלְּאַחַר פּוּרִים שֶׁהוּא שִׁשָּׁה עָשָׂר לַחוֹדֶשׁ – יַפְסִיק פַּעַם שְׁנִיָּה. וְאַף עַל פִּי שֶׁסְּמוּכָה מֵאַחֲרֶיהָ לֹא תִּקָּרֵא פָּרָה אֲדוּמָּה, כִּדְאָמַר רַב חָמָא בַּר חֲנִינָא לְעֵיל, דְּהֵיכָא דְּחָל רֹאשׁ חֹדֶשׁ נִיסָן בְּשַׁבָּת קוֹרִין פָּרָשָׁה שְׁלִישִׁית בְּשַׁבָּת הַסְּמוּכָה לְר"ח נִיסָן, כְּדֵי שֶׁתִּקָּרֵא פָּרָשַׁת הַחוֹדֶשׁ בְּשַׁבָּת שֶׁל רֹאשׁ חוֹדֶשׁ, וּפָרָשַׁת פָּרָה בְּשַׁבָּת שֶׁלְּפָנֶיהָ וְהוּא יוֹם כ"ג לַחֹדֶשׁ. דֶּרֶךְ קְצָרָה: סִימַן יְמֵי קְבִיעַת ר"ח אֲדָר – זבד"ו, וְסִימַן הַהַפְסָקוֹת – זט"ו ב"ו ד"ד וי"ו. חָל ר"ח אֲדָר בְּשַׁבָּת בְּיוֹם ז' – הַהַפְסָקָה בְּט"ו לַחוֹדֶשׁ וְלֹא יוֹתֵר. חָל ר"ח אֲדָר בְּיוֹם ב' – הַפְסָקָה בְּו' לַחוֹדֶשׁ וְלֹא יוֹתֵר. חָל רֹאשׁ חֹדֶשׁ אֲדָר בְּיוֹם ד' – הַפְסָקָה בְּיוֹם ד' וְלֹא יוֹתֵר. חָל רֹאשׁ חוֹדֶשׁ אֲדָר בְּיוֹם שִׁשִּׁי – הַפְסָקָה בְּיוֹם ב' לַחֹדֶשׁ וּבְיוֹם י"ו לַחֹדֶשׁ: **לְסֵדֶר פָּרָשִׁיּוֹת.** שֶׁבְּשַׁבָּתוֹת הַלָּלוּ הִפְסִיקוּ סֵדֶר פָּרָשִׁיּוֹת, דְּלֹא קָרְאוּ אֶלָּא אַרְבַּע פָּרָשִׁיּוֹת הַלָּלוּ: **לְסֵדֶר הַפְטָרוֹת הוּא חוֹזֵר.** שֶׁעַד הֵנָּה מַפְטִירִין מֵעֵין אַרְבַּע פָּרָשִׁיּוֹת הַלָּלוּ הַשְּׁנוּיוֹת לְעֵיל בְּבָרַיְיתָא: **לְתַעֲנִיּוֹת וּלְמַעֲמָדוֹת.** עַל כָּרְחָךְ הָנֵי בְּשַׁבָּת לָא הָווּ, וְקָתָנֵי מַפְסִיקִין, וּבְחוֹל לֵיכָּא הַפְטָרָה: **הָא כִּדְאִיתָא כו'.** וַדַּאי מַפְסִיקִין בְּחוֹל פָּרָשַׁת הַיּוֹם. אֲבָל בְּשַׁבָּת שֶׁיֵּשׁ הַפְטָרָה – מַפְסִיקִין בְּהַפְטָרוֹת, וְקוֹרִין בְּהַפְטָרָה מֵעֵין הַמְּאוֹרָע: **וּבְתַעֲנִיּוֹת לָמָּה לִי הַפְסָקַת.** פָּרָשִׁיּוֹת? לְרַבִּי יִרְמְיָה פָּרֵיךְ, דְּאָמַר הֵיכָא דְּאֶפְשָׁר לָא מַפְסְקִינַן. תַּעֲנִיּוֹת, כֵּיוָן דְּאִיכָּא קְרִיאָה בְּמִנְחָה, לָמָּה יַפְסִקוּ שַׁחֲרִית? **מִצַּפְרָא כִּינּוּפְיָא.** מְאַסְּפִין בְּנֵי אָדָם, וּבוֹדְקִין וּמַזְהִירִין אִם יֵשׁ בְּיָדָם עֲבֵירָה וְיִבָּדְלוּ, כְּדֵי שֶׁיִּתְקַבֵּל הַתַּעֲנִית. לְפִיכָךְ אֵין פְּנַאי בְּשַׁחֲרִית לִקְרוֹת בַּתּוֹרָה: **בְּמִילֵּי דְמָתָא.** בּוֹדְקִים אִם תִּהְיֶה עֲבֵירָה בְּיָדָם: **וְאֵיפוֹךְ אֲנָא.** לוֹמַר דְּהָנֵי ב' רְבִיעִיּוֹת דִּקְרָא(ג) שַׁחֲרִית פַּלְגִינְהוּ: **וּבְמִנְחַת הָעֶרֶב וגו'.** וְסֵיפָא דִּקְרָא "וָאֶפְרְשָׂה כַפַּי אֶל ה'", אַלְמָא: לְפַנְיָא בָּעוּ רַחֲמֵי. וְהָנֵי קְרָאֵי תַּרְוַיְיהוּ בְּסֵפֶר עֶזְרָא: **מתני'** פָּרָשַׁת מוֹעֲדוֹת שֶׁבְּתוֹרַת כֹּהֲנִים. "שׁוֹר אוֹ כֶשֶׂב" (וַיִּקְרָא כב). וּבְיוֹמָא קַמָּא מַיְירֵי. וּבְבָרַיְיתָא אָמְרִינַן בָּהּ: וּשְׁאָר כָּל יְמוֹת הַפֶּסַח מְלַקֵּט וְקוֹרֵא מֵעִנְיָנוֹ שֶׁל פֶּסַח, וּמַאי דְּשַׁיֵּיר בְּמַתְנִי' תָּנָא בְּבָרַיְיתָא: **שִׁבְעָה שָׁבוּעוֹת.** ד"כָּל הַבְּכוֹר": **בַּחֹדֶשׁ הַשְּׁבִיעִי.** ד"שׁוֹר אוֹ כֶשֶׂב": **קוֹרִין בְּקָרְבְּנוֹת הֶחָג.** בְּפָרָשַׁת פִּינְחָס. כֵּיצַד? יוֹם רִאשׁוֹן וְיוֹם שֵׁנִי קוֹרֵא הַמַּפְטִיר בַּחֲמִשָּׁה עָשָׂר. וְאע"פ שֶׁיּוֹם שֵׁנִי הוּא, אֵין קוֹרִין בּוֹ "וּבַיּוֹם הַשֵּׁנִי" לְהַרְאוֹת שֶׁהוּא סְפֵק יוֹם שֵׁנִי – דִּגְנַאי הוּא לִקְרוֹת יו"ט בִּסְפֵק חוֹל. יוֹם רִאשׁוֹן שֶׁל חוֹל הַמּוֹעֵד שֶׁהוּא סְפֵק שֵׁנִי סְפֵק שְׁלִישִׁי – קוֹרֵא רִאשׁוֹן בַּיּוֹם הַשֵּׁנִי, וְתִנְיָינָא בַּיּוֹם הַשְּׁלִישִׁי, תְּלִיתָאָה בַּיּוֹם הָרְבִיעִי, הָרְבִיעִי שֶׁהוּא נוֹסָף בִּשְׁבִיל חש"מ הוּא קוֹרֵא אֶת סְפֵיקֵי הַיּוֹם – בַּיּוֹם הַשֵּׁנִי וּבַיּוֹם הַשְּׁלִישִׁי. וְכֵן לְמָחָר קוֹרֵא רִאשׁוֹן בַּיּוֹם הַשְּׁלִישִׁי, שֵׁנִי קוֹרֵא בַּיּוֹם הָרְבִיעִי, שְׁלִישִׁי קוֹרֵא בַּיּוֹם הַחֲמִישִׁי, וְהָרְבִיעִי בַּיּוֹם הַשְּׁלִישִׁי וּבַיּוֹם הָרְבִיעִי שֶׁהֵן סְפֵיקֵי הַיּוֹם. וְכֵן תָּמִיד, הָרְבִיעִי קוֹרֵא מַה שֶּׁקָּרָא רִאשׁוֹן וְשֵׁנִי. חוּץ מִיּוֹם אַחֲרוֹן שֶׁל חש"מ, שֶׁא"א לִקְרוֹת "בַּיּוֹם הַשְּׁמִינִי" – לְפִי שֶׁאֵינוֹ מִימֵי הֶחָג אֶלָּא רֶגֶל לְעַצְמוֹ. לְפִיכָךְ יוֹם ז' שֶׁל חש"מ רִאשׁוֹן קוֹרִין בַּיּוֹם הַחֲמִישִׁי, שֵׁנִי קוֹרֵא בַּיּוֹם הַשִּׁשִּׁי, שְׁלִישִׁי קוֹרֵא בַּיּוֹם הַשְּׁבִיעִי, וְהָרְבִיעִי קוֹרֵא בַּיּוֹם הַשִּׁשִּׁי וּבַיּוֹם הַז', שֶׁהֵן סְפֵיקֵי הַיּוֹם: **בַּחֲנוּכָּה בַּנְּשִׂיאִים.** דְּהָוֵי נַמִי חֲנוּכַּת הַמִּזְבֵּחַ: **בְּמַעֲשֵׂה בְרֵאשִׁית.** בְּמַסֶּכֶת תַּעֲנִית בְּפֶרֶק בַּתְרָא (דף כו.) שְׁנוּיָה סֵדֶר קְרִיאָתָן: בַּיּוֹם הָרִאשׁוֹן – "בְּרֵאשִׁית" וִ"יהִי רָקִיעַ", בַּשֵּׁנִי – "יְהִי רָקִיעַ" וְ"יִקָּווּ הַמַּיִם", בַּג' – "יִקָּווּ הַמַּיִם" וִ"יהִי מְאוֹרוֹת", בָּרְבִיעִי – "יְהִי מְאוֹרוֹת" וְ"יִשְׁרְצוּ הַמַּיִם", בַּחֲמִישִׁי – "יִשְׁרְצוּ הַמַּיִם" וְ"תוֹצֵא הָאָרֶץ", בַּשִּׁשִּׁי – "תּוֹצֵא הָאָרֶץ" "וַיְכֻלּוּ הַשָּׁמַיִם". וְהָתָם (דף כז:) *מְפָרֵשׁ טַעְמָא מַאי קוֹרִין בְּמַעֲשֵׂה בְרֵאשִׁית בַּמַּעֲמָדוֹת, שֶׁבִּשְׁבִיל הַקָּרְבָּנוֹת מִתְקַיְּימִים שָׁמַיִם וָאָרֶץ:

בְּרָכוֹת

[לעיל כט:]
תענית יב: ע"ש
[וכן לקמן לא:]

רבינו חננאל

בחמישי' חוזרין לכסדרן. לסדרן מאי ר' ירמיה אמר לסדר הפטרות וקי"ל כוותיה. ואקשינן לר' ירמיה ממשנתנו דתני לכל מפסיקין לתעניות ולמעמדות כלומר מניחין ענינו של יום וקורין [בענין] תעניות ובענין המעמדו' ענין מעמדות כדתנן במעמדו' במעשה בראשית. ומפורש בפ' בשלשה פרקים הכהנים כו' תעניות כדתנן ברכות וקללות ואי אמרת לסדר ההפטרות הפטרה בחול מי איכא דפסיק לה ואמר הפטרה דתעניות והפטרה דמעמדות. ופריק במקום שיש הפטרה כגון אלו השבתות שפירשנו מפסיקין להפטרה וקורין בהפטרה של זה הענין ובמקום שאין הפטרה בחול כגון שני וחמישי מפסיקין לסדר פרשיות ולא קשיא הא כדאיתא והא כדאיתא:

ירושלמי ר' בא בשם ר' חייא בר אשי אין מפסיקין בין פורים לפרה. ר' לוי אמר אין מפסיקין בין פרה להחודש. וסימניהן של פרשיות הללו בין הכוסות הללו אם רצה לשתות ישתה בין שלישי לרביעי לא ישתה. ובדין הוא שיקדום החדש לפרה שבאחד בניסן הוקם המשכן ובשני ימים בניסן נשרפה הפרה. ולמה הקדימוה. מפני שהיא טהרתו של כל ישראל. ואקשינן בתעניות למה לי הפסקה ליקרו בצפרא בענינא דיומא כו'. ואוקימנא מצפרא כנופיא ועד פלגיה דיומא מעייני במילי דמתא. ומפלגיה דיומא רבעא דיומ' קרו ומפטרי ורבעא דיומא בעו רחמי שנאמר ויקראו בספר תורת האלהים רביעית היום [ורביעית] מתודים ומשתחוים לה' אלהיהם. וכתיב ובמנחת הערב קמתי מתעניתי. ש"מ דתפלה דתענית' במנחת הערב: בפסח קורין בפרשת מועדו' שבתורת כהנים:

הגהות הב"ח

(א) גמ' ריבעא די' קרינן בספרא ומפ' (ב) רש"י ד"ה ואיזו וכו' ובשבת רביעית יום כ"ב לחודש סמוכה: (ג) ד"ה ואנא וכו' בשחרית פלג'

ברכות וקללות. אין מפסיקין בקללות, אלא אחד קורא את כולן. בשני ובחמישי, בשבת במנחה — קורין כסדרן, ואין עולים להם מן החשבון, שנאמר: °"וידבר משה את מועדי ה' אל בני ישראל" — מצותן שיהו קורין כל אחד ואחד בזמנו. § **גמ'** ת"ר: בפסח קורין בפרשת מועדות, ומפטירין בפסח °גלגל. והאידנא דאיכא תרי יומי, [א]יומא קמא בפסח גלגל, [ב]ולמחר — בפסח °יאשיהו. ושאר ימות הפסח מלקט וקורא מעניינו של פסח. מאי היא? אמר רב פפא: מאפ"ו סימן. יום טוב האחרון של פסח קורין °"ויהי בשלח" ומפטירין °"וידבר דוד" ולמחר °"כל הבכור", ומפטירין °"עוד היום". אמר אביי: והאידנא [ג]נהוג עלמא למיקרי: משך תורא קדש בכספא פסל במדברא שלח בוכרא. בעצרת °"שבעה שבועות" ומפטירין °בחבקוק, אחרים אומרים: °"בחדש השלישי" ומפטירין °במרכבה. והאידנא [ד]דאיכא תרי יומי — עבדינן כתרוייהו, ואיפכא. בראש השנה °"בחדש השביעי" ומפטירין °"הבן יקיר לי אפרים", ויש אומרים °"וה' פקד את שרה" ומפטירין °בחנה. [ה]והאידנא דאיכא תרי יומי, יומא קמא — כיש אומרים, למחר °"והאלהים נסה את אברהם" ומפטירין "הבן יקיר". [ו]ביוה"כ קורין °"אחרי מות" ומפטירין °"כי כה אמר רם ונשא", [ז]ובמנחה קורין בעריות ומפטירין ביונה. אמר ר' יוחנן: כל מקום שאתה מוצא גבורתו של הקב"ה אתה מוצא ענוותנותו; דבר זה כתוב בתורה *ושנוי בנביאים ומשולש בכתובים. כתוב בתורה — °"כי ה' אלהיכם הוא אלהי האלהים ואדוני האדונים" וכתיב בתריה "עושה משפט יתום ואלמנה". שנוי בנביאים — °"כה אמר רם ונשא שוכן עד וקדוש" וגו' וכתיב בתריה "ואת דכא ושפל רוח". משולש בכתובים — דכתיב °"סולו לרוכב בערבות ביה שמו" וכתיב בתריה "אבי יתומים ודיין אלמנות". [ח]יו"ט הראשון של חג קורין בפרשת מועדות שבתורת כהנים, ומפטירין °"הנה יום בא לה'", והאידנא דאיכא תרי יומי, [ט]למחר מיקרא ה"נ קרינן, אפטורי מאי מפטירין? °[י]"ויקהלו אל המלך שלמה", [כ]ושאר כל ימות החג. קורין בקרבנות החג [ל]יו"ט האחרון *קורין "כל הבכור" מצות וחוקים ובכור, ומפטירין °"ויהי ככלות שלמה", [מ]למחר קורין "וזאת הברכה" ומפטירין °"ויעמד שלמה". אמר רב הונא אמר רב: [נ]שבת שחל להיות בחולו של מועד, בין בפסח בין בסוכות, מקרא קרינן °"ראה אתה", אפטורי, בפסח — °"העצמות היבשות", ובסוכות — °"ביום בא גוג". [ס]בחנוכה — בנשיאים, ומפטירין °בנרות דזכריה. [ע]ואי מיקלעי שתי שבתות, קמייתא — בנרות דזכריה, בתרייתא — °בנרות שלמה. [פ]בפורים — °"ויבא עמלק". [צ]בראשי חדשים — °"ובראשי חדשיכם". [ק]ראש חדש שחל להיות בשבת מפטירין °"והיה מדי חדש בחדשו". [ר]חל להיות באחד בשבת, מאתמול מפטירין °"ויאמר לו יהונתן מחר חדש". אמר רב הונא(א) ראש

רש"י

ברכות וקללות. ד"אם בחקותי", להודיע שעל עסקי תורה באה פורענות לעולם, ויחזרו בתשובה ויגלו מגלה שהן מתענין עליה: אין מפסיקין בקללות. כדמפרש מילתא: שאין שנים קורין בהן, אלא אחד קורא את כולן, ושנים הראשונים קורין כסדרן. בענין סדר הפרשיות.(ב) ותנאי פליגי בה בברייתא בגמרא היכן מתחיל בשני ובחמישי: ואין עולה להן מן החשבון. כשיגיע יום שבת יחזרו מה שקראו בשבת במנחה ובשני ובחמישי: שנאמר וידבר משה את מועדי ה' אל בני ישראל. אכולה מתני' קאי, ללמוד מכאן שמצוה לקרות ביום המועד מענייני המועדות: **גמ'** הכי גרסינן: ת"ר בפסח קורין בפרשת מועדות כו'. ברייתא שלימה היא עד "ושאר כל ימות החג קורין בקרבנות החג". אלא שבעלי הגמרא אפסיקוה לפרש בכל מועד יום ביום מה תיקנו האחרונים שנהגו לעשות ב' ימים לקרות ביום שני, לפי שהברייתא נשנית בארץ ישראל שאין עושין י"ט אלא יום אחד: בפסח גלגל. ביהושע(ג): ושאר כל ימות הפסח סימן **מאפ**"ו. "משכו וקחו לכם צאן", "אם כסף תלוה את עמי", "פסל לך", "וידבר" שבבהעלותך. (ד)ויום טוב שני קורין ביום ראשון "שור או כשב": ויהי בשלח פרעה. לפי שביום ז' של פסח אמרו שירה על הים: ומפטירין וידבר דוד. שהיא שירה כמותה, ומדבר בה מיציאת מצרים "עלה עשן באפו" וגו' "וישלח חציו ויפיצם" וגו': עוד היום. לפי שמפלתו של סנחריב בליל פסח היה: ומפטירין בחבקוק. שמדבר במתן תורה "אלוה מתימן יבוא" במתן תורה(ה): במרכבה. דיחזקאל, על שם שנגלה בסיני (ו)ברבוא רבבות אלפי שנאן: והאידנא דאיכא תרי יומי עבדינן כתרוייהו **ואיפכא**. דקאמרי אחרים דאינהו בתראי לתנא קמא, בחדש השלישי ומפטיר במרכבה — ביום הראשון קרינן להו, ודקאמר תנא קמא בעצרת שבעה שבועות ומפטירין בחבקוק — קרינן ביום השני ואיפכא, דמתן תורה בששי בסיון: הבן יקיר לי **אפרים**. משום(ז) "זכור אזכרנו" "רחם ארחמנו": מפטירין בחנה. לפי שפקידתה היתה בראש השנה. ועקידת יצחק מזכירין כדי שתזכר לנו היום במשפט: כי כה **אמר** רם ונשא. ואמר "סולו סולו" שמדבר במדת התשובה: "הלא זה צום אבחרהו" (ישעיה נח): קורין בעריות. שמי שיש עבירות בידו יפרוש מהן, לפי שהעריות עבירה מצויה, שנפשו של אדם מחמדתן ויצרו תוקפו: הנה יום **בא** לה'. דכתיב ביה "לחוג את חג הסוכות": ויקהלו. על שם שחנוכת הבית היתה באותה אסיפה, ובחג הסוכות: קורין כל הבכור. אלא שמתחילין "עשר תעשר", לפי שיש באותה פרשה מצות וחוקים הרבה הנהוגות בחג באותו זמן, שהוא זמן אסיף, ועת שהעניים צריכין לאסוף מאכל לביתם. ועוד יש באותה פרשה: מצות מעשר עני, ומצות "נתון תתן" ו"פתוח תפתח" ו"העניק תעניק" לעבד עברי, ושילוח חפשי, ו"העבט תעביטנו": ויהי ככלות שלמה. על שם "ביום השמיני שלח את העם": מקרא קרינן ראה **אתה**. שיש שם מצות שבת ורגלים וחולו של מועד, דכתיב "את חג המצות תשמור", ומכאן למדנו איסור מלאכת חולו של מועד במסכת חגיגה (דף יח.): בעצמות היבשות. שיצאו ממצרים לפני הקץ: ביום **בא** גוג. והיא המלחמה האמורה בזכריה ב"הנה יום בא לה'": נרות דזכריה. "רני ושמחי" על שם "ראיתי והנה מנורת זהב כולה" וגו': נרות דשלמה. "ויעש חירום [וגו'] ואת המנורות חמש מימין" וגו':

עד

תוספות

והאידנא נהוג עלמא למקרי משך תורא וכו'. אומר ר"י: דזה הסדר לא ישתנה רק כשחל פסח ביום חמישי. שא' ב' קורין משך תורא וביום שלישי שהוא שבת של חול המועד קורין "ראה אתה אומר אלי" ובכללה הוי "פסל לך", כדאמרינן לקמן דשבת של חול המועד בין בניסן בין בתשרי קורין "ראה אתה אומר אלי" וביום ד' וחמישי וששי של פסח שהוא אב"ג דשבת לא יקראו "פסל לך" בחמישי של פסח כמו שרגילין בשאר שנים, אלא ביום(ח) ארבע וחמישי וששי יקראו: קדש, בכספא, במדברא:

במנחה קורין בעריות. לפי שהנשים מקושטות בשביל כבוד היום, לפיכך צריך להזכירם שלא יכשלו בהן. ובמדרש יש שלכך קורין בעריות לפי שישראל עושין רמז להקב"ה, שכשם שהזהיר אותם שלא לגלות ערוה — כך לא תגלה ערותם בעונותם:

למחר קרינן וזאת הברכה ומפטירין ויעמוד שלמה. ויש מקומות שנהגו להפטיר ב"ויהי אחרי מות משה", ושיבוש הוא שהרי הש"ס אין אומר כן. ויש אומרים שרב האי גאון תקן לומר "ויהי אחרי מות משה", אבל אינן יודעין הסברא אמאי שנה סדר הש"ס:

מפטיר "ויאמר לו יהונתן מחר חדש". קשיא: אמאי אין עושין כן כשחל ר"ח אדר וראש חדש ניסן באחד בשבת? ואמאי מפטירין ביהוידע, "ובראשון באחד לחדש"! וי"ל: משום דהפטרה דיהוידע מדברת בשקלים, ומזכרת שראש חדש אדר יהיה באותו שבוע*: [ע' רש"א]

ראש

עין משפט נר מצוה

סו א מיי' פי"ג מהל' תפלה הלכה ח טוש"ע א"ח סי' תפח ס"ג:
סז ב מיי' שם טוש"ע א"ח סי' תל סעיף א:
סח ג מיי' שם טוש"ע שם סעיף ה:
סט ד מיי' שם הל' ט טוש"ע א"ח סי' תלד סעיף א ב:
ע ה מיי' שם הלכ' י טוש"ע א"ח סי' תקפד סעי' ב וסי' תרא סעי' א:
עא ו מיי' שם הל' יא טוש"ע א"ח סי' תרכא סעיף א:
עב ז מיי' שם טוש"ע א"ח סי' תרכב סעיף ב:
עג ח מיי' שם הלכה יב טוש"ע א"ח סי' תרנט:
עד ט י מיי' שם טוש"ע א"ח סי' תרסב סעיף ג:
עה כ מיי' שם טוש"ע א"ח סי' תרסג סעיף א:
עו ל מיי' שם טוש"ע א"ח סי' תרסח סעיף ב:
עז מ מיי' שם טוש"ע א"ח סי' תרסט סעיף א:
עח נ מיי' שם הלכה טז טוש"ע א"ח סי' תל סעי' ה וסי' תרסג סעיף ג:
עט ס ע מיי' שם הל' יז טוש"ע א"ח סי' תרפד:
פ פ מיי' שם טוש"ע א"ח סי' תרצג סעי' ד:
פא צ מיי' שם הל' ד טוש"ע א"ח סי' תכג סעי' ב:
פב ק מיי' שם טוש"ע א"ח סי' תכה סעיף א:
פג ר מיי' שם טוש"ע שם סעיף ג:

רבינו חננאל

אסיקנא והאידנא נהוג עלמא משך. תורא. קדש. בכספא. פסל. מדברא. שלח. בוכרא. וקורין ומפטירין כאשר כתוב בגמרא. ופשוטה

מסורת הש"ס

תוס' ר"ה לב. ד"ה [מתחיל]

[בתרגום דף רסח. עתיק קורין מצות וחוקים וכל הבכור ומפטירין וכו' והיא גרסא נכונה]

הגהות הב"ח

(א) גמ' אמר רב הונא אמר רב ראש חדש: (ב) רש"י ד"ה קורין כסדרן. בענין סדר הפרשיות ואין עולה להן מן החשבון וכו' ובשני ובחמישי ותנאי פליגי בה בשני ובחמישי הס"ד ואח"כ מ"ד שנאמר: (ג) ד"ה בפסח גלגל ביהושע בעת ההיא הס"ד: (ד) ד"ה ושאר כל ימות הפסח וכו' שבבהעלותך וביום שני קורין משכו וביום ראשון שור כצ"ל ותיבת טוב נמחק: (ה) ד"ה ומפטירין בחבקוק וכו' במתן תורה משתעי הס"ד: (ו) ד"ה במרכבה וכו' שנגלה בסיני על פי שנאן: (ז) ד"ה הבן יקיר לי אפרים משום דכתיב ביה זכור וכו' ארחמנו דקמיירי בזכרונות הס"ד ואח"כ מה"ד ומפטירין וכו' בראש השנה הס"ד ואח"כ מה"ד והאלהים נסה את אברהם ועקידת יצחק מזכירין כדי שיזכור לנו עקידתו היום במשפט: (ח) תוס' ד"ה והאידנא וכו' אלא ביום רביעי חמישי וששי יקראו קדש:

אראש חֹדֶשׁ אָב שֶׁחָל לִהְיוֹת בְּשַׁבָּת מַפְטִירִין °"חָדְשֵׁיכֶם וּמוֹעֲדֵיכֶם שָׂנְאָה נַפְשִׁי הָיוּ עָלַי לָטוֹרַח". *מַאי "הָיוּ עָלַי לָטוֹרַח"? אָמַר הקב"ה: לֹא דַּיָּין לָהֶם לְיִשְׂרָאֵל שֶׁחוֹטְאִין לְפָנַי, אֶלָּא שֶׁמַּטְרִיחִין אוֹתִי לֵידַע אֵיזוֹ גְּזֵירָה קָשָׁה אָבִיא עֲלֵיהֶם. בְּתִשְׁעָה בְּאָב גּוּפֵיהּ מַאי מַפְטְרִינַן? אָמַר רַב: °"אֵיכָה הָיְתָה לְזוֹנָה", מִקְרָא מַאי? תַּנְיָא, אֲחֵרִים אוֹמְרִים: °"וְאִם לֹא תִשְׁמְעוּ לִי". ר' נָתָן בַּר יוֹסֵף אוֹמֵר: °"עַד אָנָה יְנַאֲצוּנִי הָעָם הַזֶּה", וְיֵשׁ אוֹמְרִים °"עַד מָתַי לָעֵדָה הָרָעָה הַזֹּאת". אָמַר אַבַּיֵי: בהָאִידָּנָא נְהוּג עָלְמָא לְמִיקְרֵי °"כִּי תוֹלִיד בָּנִים" וּמַפְטִירִין °"אָסֹף אֲסִיפֵם". § [בַּמַּעֲמָדוֹת] גבְּמַעֲשֵׂה בְרֵאשִׁית וכו'. § מְנָהָנֵי מִילֵּי? א"ר אַמִי: אִלְמָלֵא מַעֲמָדוֹת *לֹא נִתְקַיְּימוּ שָׁמַיִם וָאָרֶץ, שֶׁנֶּאֱמַר °"אִם לֹא בְרִיתִי יוֹמָם וָלָיְלָה חוּקּוֹת שָׁמַיִם וָאָרֶץ לֹא שָׂמְתִּי", וּכְתִיב °"וַיֹּאמַר ה' אֱלֹהִים בַּמָּה אֵדַע כִּי אִירָשֶׁנָּה" אָמַר אַבְרָהָם לִפְנֵי הקב"ה: רבש"ע! שֶׁמָּא ח"ו יִשְׂרָאֵל חוֹטְאִים לְפָנֶיךָ וְאַתָּה עוֹשֶׂה לָהֶם כְּדוֹר הַמַּבּוּל וּכְדוֹר הַפַּלָּגָה? אָמַר לוֹ: לָאו. אָמַר לְפָנָיו: רבש"ע, בַּמָּה אֵדַע? אָמַר לוֹ: "קְחָה לִי עֶגְלָה מְשׁוּלֶּשֶׁת" וגו'. אָמַר לְפָנָיו: רבש"ע, תֵּינַח בִּזְמַן שֶׁבֵּית הַמִּקְדָּשׁ קַיָּים, בִּזְמַן שֶׁאֵין בֵּית הַמִּקְדָּשׁ קַיָּים מַה תְּהֵא עֲלֵיהֶם? אָמַר לוֹ: כְּבָר תִּקַּנְתִּי לָהֶם סֵדֶר קָרְבָּנוֹת, כָּל זְמַן שֶׁקּוֹרְאִין בָּהֶן מַעֲלֶה אֲנִי עֲלֵיהֶן כְּאִילּוּ מַקְרִיבִין לְפָנַי קָרְבָּן, וּמוֹחֵל אֲנִי עַל כָּל עֲוֹנוֹתֵיהֶם. § ד"בְּתַעֲנִיּוֹת בְּרָכוֹת וּקְלָלוֹת הוְאֵין מַפְסִיקִין בַּקְּלָלוֹת". § מה"מ? אָמַר ר' חִיָּיא בַּר גַּמְדָּא אָמַר רַבִּי אַסִי: דְּאָמַר קְרָא °"מוּסַר ה' בְּנִי אַל תִּמְאָס". רֵישׁ לָקִישׁ אָמַר: *לְפִי שֶׁאֵין אוֹמְרִים בְּרָכָה עַל הַפּוּרְעָנוּת. אֶלָּא הֵיכִי עָבֵיד? תָּנָא: כְּשֶׁהוּא מַתְחִיל – מַתְחִיל בְּפָסוּק שֶׁלִּפְנֵיהֶם, וּכְשֶׁהוּא מְסַיֵּים – מְסַיֵּים בְּפָסוּק שֶׁלְּאַחֲרֵיהֶן. אָמַר אַבַּיֵי: ולֹא שָׁנוּ אֶלָּא בַּקְּלָלוֹת שֶׁבְּתוֹרַת כֹּהֲנִים, אֲבָל קְלָלוֹת שֶׁבְּמִשְׁנֵה תוֹרָה – פּוֹסֵק. מַאי טַעְמָא? הַלָּלוּ – בִּלְשׁוֹן רַבִּים אֲמוּרוֹת, וּמֹשֶׁה מִפִּי הַגְּבוּרָה אֲמָרָן. וְהַלָּלוּ – בִּלְשׁוֹן יָחִיד אֲמוּרוֹת, וּמֹשֶׁה מִפִּי עַצְמוֹ אֲמָרָן. לֵוִי בַּר בּוּטֵי הֲוָה קָרֵי וְקָא מְגַמְגֵּם קַמֵּיהּ דְּרַב הוּנָא בַּ"אֲרוּרֵי", אָמַר לוֹ: אַכְּנַפְשָׁךְ, לֹא שָׁנוּ אֶלָּא קְלָלוֹת שֶׁבְּתוֹרַת כֹּהֲנִים, אֲבָל שֶׁבְּמִשְׁנֵה תוֹרָה – פּוֹסֵק. תַּנְיָא, ר' שִׁמְעוֹן בֶּן אֶלְעָזָר אוֹמֵר: זעֶזְרָא תִּיקֵּן לָהֶן לְיִשְׂרָאֵל שֶׁיְּהוּ קוֹרִין קְלָלוֹת שֶׁבְּתוֹרַת כֹּהֲנִים קוֹדֶם עֲצֶרֶת, וְשֶׁבְּמִשְׁנֵה תוֹרָה קוֹדֶם ר"ה. מַאי טַעְמָא? אָמַר אַבַּיֵי וְאִיתֵּימָא רֵישׁ לָקִישׁ: כְּדֵי שֶׁתִּכְלֶה הַשָּׁנָה וְקִלְלוֹתֶיהָ. בִּשְׁלָמָא שֶׁבְּמִשְׁנֵה תוֹרָה אִיכָּא כְּדֵי שֶׁתִּכְלֶה שָׁנָה וְקִלְלוֹתֶיהָ, אֶלָּא שֶׁבְּתוֹרַת כֹּהֲנִים, אַטּוּ עֲצֶרֶת רֹאשׁ הַשָּׁנָה הִיא? אִין, עֲצֶרֶת נַמִּי רֹאשׁ הַשָּׁנָה הִיא, דִּתְנַן: *וּבַעֲצֶרֶת עַל פֵּירוֹת הָאִילָן. תַּנְיָא, *רַבִּי שִׁמְעוֹן בֶּן אֶלְעָזָר אוֹמֵר: אִם יֹאמְרוּ לְךָ זְקֵנִים: "סְתוֹר!" וִילָדִים: "בְּנֵה!" – סְתוֹר *וְאַל תִּבְנֶה, מִפְּנֵי שֶׁסְּתִירַת זְקֵנִים – בִּנְיָן, וּבִנְיַן נְעָרִים – סְתִירָה, וְסִימָן לַדָּבָר: °רְחַבְעָם בֶּן שְׁלֹמֹה. ת"ר: *מָקוֹם שֶׁמַּפְסִיקִין בְּשַׁבָּת שַׁחֲרִית שָׁם קוֹרִין בַּמִּנְחָה, בַּמִּנְחָה – שָׁם קוֹרִין בַּשֵּׁנִי, בַּשֵּׁנִי – שָׁם קוֹרִין בַּחֲמִישִׁי, בַּחֲמִישִׁי – שָׁם קוֹרִין לַשַּׁבָּת הַבָּאָה, דִּבְרֵי ר' מֵאִיר. ר' יְהוּדָה אוֹמֵר: מָקוֹם שֶׁמַּפְסִיקִין בְּשַׁבָּת שַׁחֲרִית – שָׁם קוֹרִין בַּמִּנְחָה וּבַשֵּׁנִי וּבַחֲמִישִׁי וְלַשַּׁבָּת הַבָּאָה. אָמַר רַבִּי זֵירָא: הֲלָכָה חמָקוֹם שֶׁמַּפְסִיקִין בְּשַׁבָּת שַׁחֲרִית – שָׁם קוֹרִין בַּמִּנְחָה וּבַשֵּׁנִי וּבַחֲמִישִׁי וְלַשַּׁבָּת הַבָּאָה. *וְלֵימָא: הֲלָכָה כְּרַבִּי יְהוּדָה! מִשּׁוּם

(ישעיה א) (שם) (ויקרא כו) (במדבר יד) (שם) (דברים כח) (ירמיה ח) (שם לג) (בראשית טו) (משלי ג)

תורה אור

עד אָנָה יְנַאֲצוּנִי וְעַד מָתַי לָעֵדָה הָרָעָה. תַּרְוַויְיהוּ בַּמְרַגְּלִים, וְהֵם חָזְרוּ בט"ב, כִּדְאָמְרִינַן בְּמַסֶּכֶת תַּעֲנִית (דף כט.): מְנָהָנֵי מִילֵּי. מָה עִנְיַן בְּרֵאשִׁית אֵצֶל מַעֲמָדוֹת: בַּמָּה אֵדַע. מַה תֹּאמַר לִי לְלַמְּדָן דָּבָר שֶׁיִּתְכַּפְּרוּ בּוֹ עֲוֹנוֹתֵיהֶן: קְחָה לִי עֶגְלָה מְשׁוּלֶּשֶׁת. כְּלוֹמַר: הַקָּרְבָּנוֹת יְכַפְּרוּ עֲלֵיהֶן: מְנָהָנֵי מִילֵּי. דְּאֵין מַפְסִיקִים בַּקְּלָלוֹת: אַל תִּמְאָס. וְהַמַּפְסִיק בָּהֶן מַרְאֶה עַצְמוֹ שֶׁקָּשֶׁה לוֹ לִקְרוֹת. וּבְמַסֶּכֶת סוֹפְרִים (פי"ב) יָלֵיף לָהּ מִסֵּיפֵיהּ דִּקְרָא "וְאַל תָּקוֹץ בְּתוֹכַחְתּוֹ" – אַל תַּעֲשׂוּ קוֹצִין קוֹצִין, פְּסָקִים פְּסָקִים, לְשׁוֹן קְצִיצָה: מֹשֶׁה מִפִּי הַגְּבוּרָה אֲמָרָן. וְנַעֲשָׂה שָׁלִיחַ לוֹמַר: כָּךְ אָמַר לִי הקב"ה, שֶׁהֲרֵי אֲמוּרִין בִּלְשׁוֹן "וְנָתַתִּי" "וְהִפְקַדְתִּי" "וְשִׁלַּחְתִּי" – מִי שֶׁהַיְכוֹלֶת בְּיָדוֹ לַעֲשׂוֹת. אֲבָל בְּמִשְׁנֵה תוֹרָה כְּתִיב "יַכְּכָה הַשֵּׁם" "יַדְבֵּק ה' בְּךָ" – מֹשֶׁה אֲמָרָן מֵאֵלָיו: אִם תַּעַבְרוּ עַל מִצְוֹתָיו הוּא יַפְקִיד עֲלֵיכֶם: מְגַמְגֵּם. קָרָא אוֹתָן בִּמְרוּצָה וּבְקוֹשִׁי: בַּאֲרוּרֵי. בְּמִשְׁנֵה תוֹרָה: אַכְּנַפְשָׁךְ. אִם רְצוֹנְךָ לְהַפְסִיק פָּסוּק, הוֹאִיל וְאַתָּה קָץ בִּקְרִיאָתָן: קוֹדֶם עֲצֶרֶת. שֶׁהוּא זְמַן קָצִיר וּזְמַן פֵּירוֹת הָאִילָן, כִּדְמְפָרֵשׁ וְאָזֵיל: מִשּׁוּם

ראש חדש אב שחל להיות בשבת מפטירין חדשיכם ומועדיכם שנאה נפשי וגו'. ואין אנו עושין כן, אלא מפטיר בירמיה (ב) "שמעו* דבר ה'" ובשבת שלפני ט"ב "חזון ישעיהו". והטעם – לפי שאנו נוהגין על פי הפסיקתא, לומר ג' דפורענותא קודם תשעה באב. ואלו הן: "דברי ירמיה", "שמעו דבר ה'", "חזון ישעיהו". ובתר תשעה באב שב דנחמתא ותרתי דתיובתא, ואלו הן: "נחמו נחמו" "ותאמר ציון" "עניה סוערה" לבדה, "אנכי אנכי" "רני עקרה" "קומי אורי" "שוש אשיש" "דרשו" "שובה". ולפיכך מקדימין "עניה סוערה" קודם "רני עקרה" דדרך הנחמות להיות הולכות ומשובחות יותר. וסדר זה מתחיל בפנחס, וסימניך: דש"ח נו"ע אר"ק שד"ש. ולעולם "שוש אשיש" ב"אתם נצבים", דהיינו שבת שלפני ר"ה, לפי שהוא סוף הנחמות. ו"דרשו" בצום גדליה, ו"שובה" בשבת שלפני יום הכפורים, וכשיש שבת בין יום הכפורים לסוכות – אז הוי "דרשו" בשבת שלפני יום הכפורים, משום דכתיב ביה "דרשו ה' בהמצאו" – והיינו בימי תשובה, ו"שובה" בין כפור לסוכות, *דכתיב בה "ונתתי לך יורה ומלקוש" וכן "וה' נתן קולו לפני חילו" דמשתעי במים ושייך שפיר לפני סוכות. וזה המנהג לא ישתנה לעולם ע"פ הפסיקתא. וכן פירש ר"ת, ולא כדברי רב החובל ההופך ומבלבל לומר "שובה" קודם כפור, ו"שוש אשיש" בין כפור לסוכות – דאין להפסיק בין השש נחמות לשביעית, אלא כדברי רבינו תם עם ישרים נחתם: "שוש אשיש" – בראשיתו, ו"שובה" – באחריתו. *והא שאין אנו מפטירין חזון בשבת שחל בו ר"ח אב – משום דקיימא לן* דאין אבילות חל אלא בשבוע שחל ט"ב להיות בתוכה. ורב דאמר דמפטיר חזון – סבר דהאבלות חל מיד שנכנס ר"ח, ואין הלכה כן. וכן פירש הר"ר אליעזר ממיץ. ולכך אנו מפטירין "שמעו". וכן אנו נוהגין ע"פ מסכת סופרים* שאנו קורין "ויחל" בתעניות, ובמתניתין אמרינן שקורין ברכות וקללות*:

אין מפסיקין בקללות. וקורין אחד, משום דכתיב "מוסר ה' בני אל תמאס ואל תקוץ בתוכחתו" א"ר אחא: אל תעש התוכחה קוצים קוצים. וא"ר יהושע דסכנין: אני אמרתי "עמו אנכי בצרה" ואם כן אין דין שיברכוני בני על הצרות שלהם, אלא יקרא אחד הכל, ויתחיל(א) בדבר אחר ויסיים בדבר אחר, ואז יוכל לברך תחילה וסוף:

מתחיל בפסוק שלפניהם. לאו דוקא פסוק, דהא יש פרשה, ואין מתחילין ומשיירין בפחות משלשה פסוקים: **משה** מעצמו אמרם. וברוח הקדש:

קללות. שבת"כ קודם עצרת ושבמשנה תורה קודם ראש השנה שאלו בבית המדרש של רבינו נסים: למה מחלקים פרשת נצבים וילך לשנים כשיש ב' שבתות בין ר"ה לסוכות בלא יוה"כ, ואין מחלקין מטות ומסעי שארוכות יותר? והשיב: לפי שב"אתם נצבים" יש קללות שקלל ישראל, ורוצה לסיימם קודם ר"ה. וקשה: שאנו לא מחשבין הקללות שקלל משה ישראל, כדמשמע בפרק "המוכר את הספינה" (ב"ב דף פח: ושם), א"ר לוי: בא וראה שלא כמדת הקב"ה מדת ב"ו, הקב"ה בירך ישראל בכ"ב וקללן בשמנה, ומשה ברכם בשמנה וקללם בעשרים ושתים, וחשיב מ"ואם לא תשמעו" עד ו"אין קונה". משמע בהדיא שעד "אין קונה" הוי מן הקללות, ולא יותר! ועוד קשיא: לפי סברתו אמאי אין קורין "האזינו" קודם ר"ה? שהרי גם שם יש קללות "מזי רעב ולחומי רשף"! לכך נראה לי הטעם שאנו מחלקים אותן – לפי שאנו רוצים להפסיק ולקרות שבת אחת קודם ר"ה בפרשה שלא תהא מדברת בקללות כלל, שלא להסמיך הקללות לר"ה. ומטעם זה אנו קורין "במדבר סיני" קודם עצרת, כדי שלא להסמיך הקללות שב"בחוקותי" לעצרת: ילמדנו של פרשת יתרו: אין אדם רשאי לקרות בתורה עד שיסדיר הפרשה ג' פעמים, שנאמר (איוב כח) "אז ראה ויספרה(ב) הכינה וחקרה" ואחרי כן "ויאמר לאדם". ואסור לסמוך על הבימה, דמה נתינתה מעומד – אף קריאתה מעומד: הלוחות

[ע' תוס' פסחים מ: ד"ה אבל וכו' וקל"ע וע' תרומת הדשן סי' יט]

פד א מיי' פי"ג מהל' תפלה הלכה ד טוש"ע א"ח סימן תכה סעיף א בהג"ה:
פה ב מיי' שם הלכה יח טוש"ע א"ח סימן תקנט סעיף ד בהג"ה:
פו ג מיי' פ"ו מהלכות כלי המקדש הל' ו:
פז ד מיי' פי"ג מהל' תפלה הלכה יח טוא"ח סימן תקעט:
פח ה ו מיי' שם הל' ז טוש"ע א"ח סימן תכח סעיף ו:
פט ז מיי' שם הלכה ב טוש"ע שם סעי' ז:
צ ח מיי' שם הלכה ג סמג עשין יט טוא"ח סימן רלב:

נ"ל וכן וה' נתן כו' דמשתעי במים דכתיב בה יורה ומלקוש ושייך כו'

מהרש"א הגיה וי"א

[תענית כט:]

[פי"ז ה"ז]

[וע"ע תוס' ברכות יח. ד"ה למחר ותוס' פסחים מ: ד"ה אבל]

ר"ה דף טז. [תוספתא ע"ז פ"א]

[שבת קמה:]

תענית ד' כז: ע"ש

בראשית טו

[במס' סופרים פי"ב איתא בזה הלשון אמר ר' לוי אמר הקב"ה אינו דין שיהיו בני מתקללין ואני מתברך]

נדרים מ.

ד"א זוטא פ"ז

מלכים א יב

[תוס' פ"ג מס' סופרים פ"י הלכה ד]

[עי' תוספות מנחות ל: ד"ו ולימא]

רבינו חננאל

היא אין מפסיקין בקללות אלא אחד קורא את כולן שנאמר אל תקוץ בתוכחתו *) מ"ט שאין מפסיקין. שאין אומרים ברכה על הפורענות. היכי עבדינן תנא כשמתחיל מתחיל בפסוק שלפניהם וכשמסיים מסיים בפסוק שלאחריהם ואמר אביי לא שנו אלא בקללות שבתורת כהנים והן אם בחקותי תלכו שנא' בלשון רבים ומשה רבינו מפני הגבורה אמרן אבל שבמשנה תורה פוסק מ"ט דבלשון יחיד אמורות ומשה מפי עצמו אמרן להיכתב. וכן אמר רב הונא ללוי בר בוטא דהוה מגמגם וקורא בארורי דמשנה תורה. א"ל אכנפשך קללות שבמשנה תורה פוסק. ר' שמעון בן אלעזר אומר עזרא תיקן להן לישראל להיות קורין קללות שבתורת כהנים קודם עצרת שהיא ר"ה לדין האילנות דתנן בד' פרקים העולם נידון. ובעצרת על פירות האילן. וקללות שבמשנה תורה קודם ר"ה כדי שתכלה שנה וקללותיה. תניא אם יאמרו לך זקנים סתור וילדים בנה כו'. בשני ובחמישי ובשבת במנחה קורין כסדרן כו'. אמר שמואל מקום שמפסיקין בשבת שחרית

*) נראה דצ"ל ר"ל אומר אין מפסיקין משום שאין אומרים וכו'.

הגהות הב"ח

(א) תוס' ד"ה אין מפסיקין וכו' ויתחיל בברכה ויסיים בברכה ואז יוכל: (ב) ד"ה משה וכו' ראה ויספרה הכינה וגם חקרה ויאמר לאדם:

*משום דאפכי להו. ת"ר: פותח ורואה גולל ומברך וחוזר ופותח וקורא דברי רבי מאיר, רבי יהודה אומר: אפותח ורואה ומברך וקורא. מאי טעמא דרבי מאיר — כדעולא, דאמר עולא: מפני מה אמרו בהקורא בתורה לא יסייע למתורגמן — כדי שלא יאמרו תרגום כתוב בתורה, הכא נמי — כדי שלא יאמרו ברכות כתובין בתורה. ורבי יהודה: תרגום איכא למיטעי, ברכות — ליכא למיטעי. אמר רבי זירא אמר רב מתנה: הלכה, פותח ורואה ומברך וקורא. *ולימא הלכה כר' יהודה! •משום דאפכי להו. אמר ר' זירא אמר רב מתנה: גהלוחות והבימות אין בהן משום *קדושה. *אמר ר' שפטיה אמר ר' יוחנן: דהגולל ספר תורה צריך שיעמידנו על התפר. ואמר ר' שפטיה א"ר יוחנן: ההגולל ספר תורה — גוללו מבחוץ ואין גוללו מבפנים, וכשהוא מהדקו — מהדקו מבפנים, ואינו מהדקו מבחוץ. ואמר ר' שפטיה א"ר יוחנן: עשרה שקראו בתורה — זהגדול שבהם גולל ספר תורה. חהגוללו נוטל שכר כולן, דאמר ר' יהושע בן לוי: עשרה שקראו בתורה — הגולל ספר תורה קיבל שכר כולן. *שכר כולן סלקא דעתך? אלא אימא: קיבל שכר כנגד כולן. ואמר ר' שפטיה אמר ר' יוחנן: •מנין שמשתמשין *בבת קול — שנאמר °"ואזניך תשמענה דבר מאחריך לאמר" (ישעיה ל). והני מילי — דשמע קל גברא במתא, וקל איתתא בדברא. והוא דאמר הין הין, והוא דאמר לאו לאו. ואמר ר' שפטיה אמר ר' יוחנן: כל הקורא בלא נעימה ושונה בלא זמרה — עליו הכתוב אומר °"וגם אני נתתי להם חוקים לא טובים" וגו' (יחזקאל כ). מתקיף לה אביי: משום דלא ידע לבסומי קלא °"משפטים לא יחיו בהם" קרית ביה?! (שם) אלא כדרב משרשיא, דאמר: שני תלמידי חכמים היושבים בעיר אחת ואין נוחין זה את זה בהלכה — עליהם הכתוב אומר "וגם אני נתתי להם חוקים לא טובים ומשפטים לא יחיו בהם". *אמר רבי פרנך אמר רבי יוחנן: טכל האוחז ספר תורה ערום נקבר ערום. ערום סלקא דעתך? אלא אימא: נקבר ערום בלא מצות. בלא מצות סלקא דעתך?! אלא אמר אביי: נקבר ערום בלא אותה מצוה. אמר רבי ינאי בריה דרבי ינאי סבא משמיה דרבי ינאי רבה: ימוטב תיגלל המטפחת ואל יגלל ספר תורה.§ °"וידבר משה את מועדי ה' אל בני ישראל" (ויקרא כג) מצותן שיהיו קורין אותן כל אחד ואחד בזמנו.§ ת"ר: *כמשה תיקן להם לישראל שיהו שואלין ודורשין בענינו של יום, הלכות פסח בפסח, הלכות עצרת בעצרת, הלכות חג בחג.§

הדרן עלך בני העיר וסליקא לה מסכת מגילה

רש"י

משום דאפכי להו. דרבי מאיר לדרבי יהודה, ודרבי יהודה לדרבי מאיר: איכא למיטעי. ואומר תרגום כתוב בתורה, ואתו למיכתב תרגום בתורה: אבל ברכות. הכל יודעין שאין ברכות כתובין בתורה: הלוחות. לא ידעתי מה הן. ויש מפרשין הן העשוין לספרים שלנו שאינן עשוין בגיליון: בימה. שהיו עושין למלך בפרשת המלך, כדאמרינן במסכת סוטה (דף מא.): יעמידנו על התפר. כנגד התפר, שאם רְאוּי להדקו יפה: הגולל ספר תורה. מעניין לעניין, והוא יחיד, וספר תורה מונח לו על ברכיו — גוללו מבחוץ, העמוד שהוא חוזה לו גוללו, ויגול מצד חוץ לצד פנים. שאם יאחוז עמוד הפנימי ויגול לצד החוץ — יתפשט החיצון ויפול לארץ: וכשהוא מהדקו. כשגמר מלגלול ובא להדקו, יאחוז בפנימי ויהדק על החיצון, כדי שלא יכסה הכתב בזרועותיו, שמצוה להראות את [הכתב אל] העם כשמהדקו, במסכת סופרים*: עשרה שקראו. שנאספו וקראו הג' או הז' כחוק היום. ולפי שאין קורין בתורה פחות מעשרה נקט י' שקראו בתורה: משתמשין בבת קול. אם בלבו להתחיל דבר, ושמע קול או הין או לאו — הולך אחריו, ואין כאן משום ניחוש: קל גברא במתא. קול שאינו מצוי הוא, ובת קול באה אליו: והוא דאמר הין הין או לאו לאו. שנכפל ב' פעמים: נעימה. כגון טעמי המקראות: ערום. בלא מטפחת סביב ספר תורה: ואל יגלול ספר תורה. בתוך המטפחת: וידבר משה את מועדי ה' אל בני ישראל משה תיקן להם לישראל שיהו שואלין ודורשין בעניינו של יום הלכות פסח בפסח הלכות עצרת בעצרת. למה הוצרך לכתוב כאן "וידבר משה", וכי כל המצות כולן לא אמרן משה לישראל? מהו "וידבר משה את מועדי ה' אל בני ישראל"? — מלמד שהיה מדבר עמהן הלכות כל מועד ומועד בזמנו, להודיע חוקי האלהים ותורותיו וקבלו וקיימו שכר המצות עליהם ועל בניהם בזה ובבא:

הדרן עלך בני העיר וסליקא לה מסכת מגילה

תוספות

הלוחות והבימות אין בהן משום קדושה. פירש בערוך:* גליוני ספר תורה שלמעלה ושלמטה, ושל בין דף לדף. וקשיא: דהא פרק "כל כתבי" (שבת דף קטז.) תנן בהדיא דמטמאין את הידים! ויש לומר: דהתם ר"ל כל זמן שהן מחוברין בספר תורה, והכא מיירי היכא דגייז. ואכתי קשה: שהרי התם מיבעיא לן היכא דגייזי אי יש בהן קדושה אי לאו, ואמאי לא פשיט ליה מהכא?

גוללו מבחוץ וכשהוא מהדקו מהדקו מבפנים. פר"ח: דקאי אקשר מטפחת, כשקושר מטפחת סביב הס"ת יהא הקשר מבפנים כלפי הכתב, שאם יהיה מאחריו — כשיפתח הספר תורה יהיה צריך להופכו על הכתב להתיר הקשר, ואין זה דרך כבוד. נהגו לומר כשמוליאין ספר תורה הני פסוקי דרחמי "תורת ה' תמימה עדות ה' נאמנה פקודי ה' ישרים מצות ה' ברה" לפי שמתן שכרם בצדם. ואחר כך אומר "גדלו" שיש בו שש תיבות כנגד ששה צעדים של נושאי הארון (שמואל ב ו) (א). ומ' תיבות יש ב"תורת ה' תמימה" — כנגד המ' יום שבהם ניתנה התורה. ואח"כ פותחו למקום שירצה לקרות בו, וקורא כהן. (ב) ולכתחילה הוא גוללו וסותמו קודם שיברך, כדי שלא יאמרו ההמון שהברכות כתובות בו. אבל בדיעבד — אין לחוש, שהרי לא שכיחי עמי הארץ כל כך עתה. אבל לאחר שקרא בו — ודאי צריך לגוללו *קודם שיברך, *כר' יהודה:

גדול שבכולן גולל. לפי שהוא כבודו, וגם לפי שהוא גדול שבכולן — כדאי הוא ליטול שכר כנגד כולם, כדאמר רבי יהושע:

מנין שמשתמשין בבת קול. בירושלמי (שבת פרק "במה אשה") תני: כתיב "לא תנחשו ולא תעוננו", ואף ע"פ שאין ניחוש — יש סימן:

והשונה בלא זמרה. שהיו רגילין לשנות המשניות בזמרה, לפי שהיו שונין אותן על פה, וע"י כך היו נזכרים יותר:

בלא אותה מצוה. י"מ: מצות אחיזה. וקשה: מאי רבותא? פשיטא שאין לו שכר, כיון שלא עשה המצוה כהוגן! לכך פירש ריב"א: בלא אותה מצוה שעשה באותה שעה, שאם אחז ספר תורה ערום וקרא בו — אין לו שכר מן הקריאה, וכן אחזו לגוללו או להגיהו. אבל אחזו במטפחת — "אורך ימים בימינה בשמאלה עושר וכבוד":

הדרן עלך בני העיר וסליקא לה מסכת מגילה

רבינו חננאל

שחרית שם קורין במנחה בשבת ובשני ובחמישי ובשבת הבאה: ת"ר פותח ורואה מברך וקורא דברי ר' יהודה והלכה כמותו. מפני מה אמרו הקורא בתורה לא יסייע למתורגמן. כדי שלא יאמרו תרגום כתוב בתורה. אמר שמואל הלוחות והבימות. פירוש החלק של מעלה ושל מטה ושל בין הדפין של ס"ת אין בהן משום קדושה א) כלומר אם יכלה ויגנז ויחתך החלק שם אין בו משום קדושה. א"ר יוחנן הגולל ספר כו' פירוש שאם יקרע יקרע בתפר. ועוד אמר הגולל ספר כו' פירוש מבחוץ כלומר כשהוא מונח הספר בחיקו הכרך ב) החיצון שם גולל מן הכרך הפנימי. שאם יגלול על הפנימי מן החיצון יפול החיצון לארץ וכשהוא מהדקו מחזיק החיצון ומהדק הפנימי. ואריב"ל י' שקראו בתורה הגולל ס"ת. כלומר המשלים נותנין לו שכר כנגד כולן. וא"ר יוחנן מנין שמשתמשין בבת קול שנאמר ואזניך תשמענה דבר מאחריך וגו' והוא דשמע קל גברא במתא וקל איתתא בדברא והוא דאמר הן הן או לאו לאו. ועוד אמר הקורא בלא נעימה והשונה בלא זמרה. ג) ומתמהינן משום דלא ידע לבסומי קלא אינון חוקים לא טובים ומשפטים לא יחיו בהם. אלא הכי קאמר ב' תלמידי חכמים היושבים בעיר אחת ואינן נוחין זה לזה בהלכה עליהם הכתוב אומר וגם אני נתתי להם חוקים והם לא טובים זה לזה ומשפטים לא יחיו בהם. א"ר יוחנן האוחז ס"ת ערום נקבר ערום. בלא אותה מצוה. א"ר ינאי תיגלל המטפחת ואל יגלל ס"ת כלומר בלא מטפחת. מצוותן שיהיו קורין כל אחד ואחד בזמנו: ת"ר משה תיקן לישראל שיהו שואלין ודורשין הלכות פסח בפסח ועצרת בעצרת והחג בחג: הדרן עלך בני העיר:

א) עי' בתוס' כאן ד"ה הלוחות מה שהקשו על פירוש הערוך שהוא כפירוש רבינו ואמנם לפי מש"כ רבינו דמיירי אם כלה הכתב ונגנז א"ש וכעין זה תירץ הש"ס בשבת קטז בלה שאני ע"ש היטב. ב) אולי צ"ל הכרך החיצון יגלול על הכרך הפנימי שאם יגלול מן הפנימי על החיצון יפול החיצון וכו' וצ"ע בזה. ג) צ"ל עליו הכתוב אומר וגם אני נתתי להם חוקים לא טובים.

עין משפט נר מצוה

[ערך במות]

צא א מיי' פי"ב מהל' תפלה הלכה ה סמג עשין יט טוש"ע א"ח סימן קלט סעיף ד:

צב ב מיי' שם הלכה יא טוש"ע א"ח סימן קמה סעיף א:

צג ג מיי' פ"י מהלכות ס"ת הל' ד טוש"ע א"ח סי' קנד סעי' ז וטוש"ע י"ד סי' רפב סעיף יד:

צד ד מיי' פי"ב מהל' תפלה הל' כד סמג עשין יט טוש"ע א"ח סי' קמז סעיף ג:

צה ה ו מיי' שם טוש"ע שם סעי' ד:

צו ז טוש"ע שם סעיף א:

צז ח מיי' שם הל' יח:

[גי' הרא"ש קדושת ארון ויש בהן קדושת בהכ"נ]

צח ט מיי' פ"י מהל' ס"ת הל' ו טוש"ע שם סעיף א וטוש"ע י"ד סי' רפב סעיף ד:

צט י טוש"ע א"ח סימן קמז סעיף ה:

ק כ מיי' פי"ג מהל' תפלה הלכה ח:

[וכ"ה במס' סופרים פי"ג ה"ח]

[ויש מגיהין צ"ל אפילו כר' יהודה. עיין בקיקיון דיונה]

מסורת הש"ס

גיטין כח. מנחות ל: ועי' קדושין נט:

[ע' תוס' מנחות ל: ד"ה ולימא]

[פ"ג ה"י ופי"ד הי"ד] [מ"ס פ"ג ה"י]

[ברכות מז:]

[פירושו עי' תוספות סנהדרין יא. ד"ה בת קול]

שבת יד. ע"ש [מסכת סופרים פ"ג הל' טז]

ויקרא כג

לעיל ד.

סליקא מסכת מגילה, שבח לרב עלילה, ברכה ותהלה, תפארת וצהלה, ירום קרנו למעלה:

הגהות הב"ח

(א) תום' ד"ה גוללו וכו' ואלכעים תיבות יש בתורת. נ"ב פי' בתורת ה' תמימה עד מלות ה' ברה יש כ' תיבות ובפסוק האל תמים דרכו עד זולתי אלהינו יש ג"כ כ' תיבות: (ב) בא"ד ולכתחלה הוא גוללו. נ"ב אע"ג דהלכה כר' יהודה שאינו מחוייב לגוללו [קודם הברכה היינו] דלא עביד איסור להניח [את הספר] פתוח ולברך אבל אם סותמו ומברך עדיף טפי הלכך לכתחלה כו':

גליון הש"ס

גמ' משום דאפכי להו. גיטין כח ע"א מנחות ל ע"ב: שם מנין שמשתמשין בבת קול. ע' תוי"ט פט"ז מ"ז דיבמות:

The following paragraph is recited three times:

הַדְרָן עֲלָךְ מַסֶּכֶת מְגִלָּה וְהַדְרָךְ עֲלָן, דַּעְתָּן עֲלָךְ מַסֶּכֶת מְגִלָּה וְדַעְתָּךְ עֲלָן, לָא נִתְנְשֵׁי מִנָּךְ מַסֶּכֶת מְגִלָּה וְלָא תִתְנְשֵׁי מִנָּן, לָא בְּעָלְמָא הָדֵין וְלָא בְּעָלְמָא דְאָתֵי.

יְהִי רָצוֹן מִלְּפָנֶיךָ יהוה אֱלֹהֵינוּ וֵאלֹהֵי אֲבוֹתֵינוּ, שֶׁתְּהֵא תוֹרָתְךָ אֻמָּנוּתֵנוּ בָּעוֹלָם הַזֶּה, וּתְהֵא עִמָּנוּ לָעוֹלָם הַבָּא. חֲנִינָא בַּר פַּפָּא, רָמֵי בַּר פַּפָּא, נַחְמָן בַּר פַּפָּא, אֲחַאי בַּר פַּפָּא, אַבָּא מָרִי בַּר פַּפָּא, רַפְרָם בַּר פַּפָּא, רָכִישׁ בַּר פַּפָּא, סוּרְחַב בַּר פַּפָּא, אַדָּא בַּר פַּפָּא, דָּרוּ בַּר פַּפָּא.

הַעֲרֶב נָא יהוה אֱלֹהֵינוּ אֶת דִּבְרֵי תוֹרָתְךָ בְּפִינוּ וּבְפִי עַמְּךָ בֵּית יִשְׂרָאֵל, וְנִהְיֶה אֲנַחְנוּ וְצֶאֱצָאֵינוּ (וְצֶאֱצָאֵי צֶאֱצָאֵינוּ) וְצֶאֱצָאֵי עַמְּךָ בֵּית יִשְׂרָאֵל, כֻּלָּנוּ יוֹדְעֵי שְׁמֶךָ וְלוֹמְדֵי תוֹרָתְךָ לִשְׁמָהּ. (תהלים קיט) מֵאֹיְבַי תְּחַכְּמֵנִי מִצְוֹתֶךָ כִּי לְעוֹלָם הִיא־לִי: יְהִי־לִבִּי תָמִים בְּחֻקֶּיךָ לְמַעַן לֹא אֵבוֹשׁ: לְעוֹלָם לֹא־אֶשְׁכַּח פִּקּוּדֶיךָ כִּי־בָם חִיִּיתָנִי: בָּרוּךְ אַתָּה יהוה לַמְּדֵנִי חֻקֶּיךָ: אָמֵן אָמֵן אָמֵן סֶלָה וָעֶד.

מוֹדִים אֲנַחְנוּ לְפָנֶיךָ יהוה אֱלֹהֵינוּ וֵאלֹהֵי אֲבוֹתֵינוּ שֶׁשַּׂמְתָּ חֶלְקֵנוּ מִיּוֹשְׁבֵי בֵּית הַמִּדְרָשׁ, וְלֹא שַׂמְתָּ חֶלְקֵנוּ מִיּוֹשְׁבֵי קְרָנוֹת. שֶׁאָנוּ מַשְׁכִּימִים וְהֵם מַשְׁכִּימִים, אָנוּ מַשְׁכִּימִים לְדִבְרֵי תוֹרָה, וְהֵם מַשְׁכִּימִים לִדְבָרִים בְּטֵלִים. אָנוּ עֲמֵלִים וְהֵם עֲמֵלִים, אָנוּ עֲמֵלִים וּמְקַבְּלִים שָׂכָר, וְהֵם עֲמֵלִים וְאֵינָם מְקַבְּלִים שָׂכָר. אָנוּ רָצִים וְהֵם רָצִים, אָנוּ רָצִים לְחַיֵּי הָעוֹלָם הַבָּא, וְהֵם רָצִים לִבְאֵר שַׁחַת, שֶׁנֶּאֱמַר: (תהלים נה) וְאַתָּה אֱלֹהִים תּוֹרִדֵם לִבְאֵר שַׁחַת אַנְשֵׁי דָמִים וּמִרְמָה לֹא־יֶחֱצוּ יְמֵיהֶם וַאֲנִי אֶבְטַח־בָּךְ:

יְהִי רָצוֹן מִלְּפָנֶיךָ יהוה אֱלֹהַי, כְּשֵׁם שֶׁעֲזַרְתַּנִי לְסַיֵּם מַסֶּכֶת מְגִלָּה כֵּן תַּעַזְרֵנִי לְהַתְחִיל מַסֶּכְתּוֹת וּסְפָרִים אֲחֵרִים וּלְסַיְּמָם, לִלְמֹד וּלְלַמֵּד לִשְׁמֹר וְלַעֲשׂוֹת וּלְקַיֵּם אֶת כָּל דִּבְרֵי תַלְמוּד תּוֹרָתְךָ בְּאַהֲבָה, וּזְכוּת כָּל הַתַּנָּאִים וְאָמוֹרָאִים וְתַלְמִידֵי חֲכָמִים יַעֲמֹד לִי וּלְזַרְעִי שֶׁלֹּא תָמוּשׁ הַתּוֹרָה מִפִּי וּמִפִּי זַרְעִי וְזֶרַע זַרְעִי עַד עוֹלָם, וְיִתְקַיֵּם בִּי: (משלי ו) בְּהִתְהַלֶּכְךָ תַּנְחֶה אֹתָךְ בְּשָׁכְבְּךָ תִּשְׁמֹר עָלֶיךָ וַהֲקִיצוֹתָ הִיא תְשִׂיחֶךָ: (משלי ט) כִּי־בִי יִרְבּוּ יָמֶיךָ וְיוֹסִיפוּ לְךָ שְׁנוֹת חַיִּים: (משלי ג) אֹרֶךְ יָמִים בִּימִינָהּ בִּשְׂמֹאולָהּ עֹשֶׁר וְכָבוֹד: (תהלים כט) יהוה עֹז לְעַמּוֹ יִתֵּן יהוה יְבָרֵךְ אֶת־עַמּוֹ בַשָּׁלוֹם:

The following paragraph is recited three times:

הַדְרָן We shall return to you, tractate *Megilla,* and your glory is upon us. Our thoughts are upon you, tractate *Megilla,* and your thoughts are upon us. We will not be forgotten from you, tractate *Megilla,* and you will not be forgotten from us; neither in this world nor in the World-to-Come.

יְהִי רָצוֹן May it be Your will, Lord our God and God of our ancestors, that Your Torah will be our avocation in this world and will accompany us to the World-to-Come. Ḥanina bar Pappa, Ramei bar Pappa, Naḥman bar Pappa, Aḥai bar Pappa, Abba Mari bar Pappa, Rafram bar Pappa, Rakhish bar Pappa, Surḥav bar Pappa, Adda bar Pappa, Daru bar Pappa.

הַעֲרֶב נָא Please, Lord our God, make the words of Your Torah sweet in our mouths and in the mouths of Your people, the house of Israel, so that we, our descendants (and their descendants), and the descendants of Your people, the house of Israel, may all know Your name and study Your Torah for its own sake. (*Psalms 119*) Your commandments make me wiser than my enemies, for they are ever with me. Let my heart be undivided in Your statutes, in order that I may not be put to shame. I will never forget Your precepts, for with them You have quickened me. Blessed are You, O Lord; teach me Your statutes. Amen, Amen, Amen, Selah, Forever.

מוֹדִים We give thanks before You, Lord Our God and God of our ancestors, that You have placed our lot among those who sit in the study hall and that you have not given us our portion among those who sit idly on street corners. We rise early and they rise early. We rise early to pursue matters of Torah and they rise early to pursue frivolous matters. We toil and they toil. We toil and receive a reward and they toil and do not receive a reward. We run and they run. We run to the life of the World-to-Come and they run to the pit of destruction, as it is stated: (*Psalms 55*) But You, God, will bring them down into the pit of destruction; men of blood and deceit shall not live out half their days; but as for me, I will trust in You.

יְהִי רָצוֹן May it be Your will, Lord my God, just as you have assisted me in completing tractate *Megilla* so assist me to begin other tractates and books and conclude them to learn and to teach, to observe and to perform, and to fulfill all the teachings of Your Torah with love. And may the merit of all the *tanna'im* and *amora'im* and Torah scholars stand for me and my descendants so that the Torah will not move from my mouth and from the mouths of my descendants and the descendants of my descendants forever. And may the verse: (*Proverbs 6*) When you walk, it shall lead you, when you lie down, it shall watch over you; and when you awaken, it shall talk with you be fulfilled in me. (*Proverbs 9*) For in the Torah your days shall be multiplied, and the years of your life shall be increased. (*Proverbs 3*) Length of days is in her right hand; in her left hand are riches and honor. (*Psalms 29*) May the Lord give strength to His people; the Lord will bless His people with peace.

The following קדיש *requires the presence of a* מנין.

יִתְגַּדַּל וְיִתְקַדַּשׁ שְׁמֵהּ רַבָּא
בְּעָלְמָא דְּהוּא עָתִיד לְאִתְחַדָּתָא
וּלְאַחְיָאָה מֵתַיָּא, וּלְאַסָּקָא יָתְהוֹן לְחַיֵּי עָלְמָא
וּלְמִבְנֵא קַרְתָּא דִירוּשְׁלֵם, וּלְשַׁכְלָלָא הֵיכְלֵהּ בְּגַוַּהּ
וּלְמֶעְקַר פֻּלְחָנָא נֻכְרָאָה מֵאַרְעָא
וּלַאֲתָבָא פֻּלְחָנָא דִשְׁמַיָּא לְאַתְרֵהּ
וְיַמְלִיךְ קֻדְשָׁא בְּרִיךְ הוּא בְּמַלְכוּתֵהּ וִיקָרֵהּ
(נוסח ספרד: וְיַצְמַח פּוּרְקָנֵהּ וִיקָרֵב מְשִׁיחֵהּ)
בְּחַיֵּיכוֹן וּבְיוֹמֵיכוֹן וּבְחַיֵּי דְכָל בֵּית יִשְׂרָאֵל
בַּעֲגָלָא וּבִזְמַן קָרִיב, וְאִמְרוּ אָמֵן.

יְהֵא שְׁמֵהּ רַבָּא מְבָרַךְ לְעָלַם וּלְעָלְמֵי עָלְמַיָּא.

יִתְבָּרַךְ וְיִשְׁתַּבַּח וְיִתְפָּאַר וְיִתְרוֹמַם וְיִתְנַשֵּׂא
וְיִתְהַדָּר וְיִתְעַלֶּה וְיִתְהַלָּל
שְׁמֵהּ דְּקֻדְשָׁא בְּרִיךְ הוּא
לְעֵלָּא מִן כָּל בִּרְכָתָא
/בעשרת ימי תשובה: לְעֵלָּא לְעֵלָּא מִכָּל בִּרְכָתָא/
וְשִׁירָתָא, תֻּשְׁבְּחָתָא וְנֶחֱמָתָא, דַּאֲמִירָן בְּעָלְמָא
וְאִמְרוּ אָמֵן. (קהל: אָמֵן)

עַל יִשְׂרָאֵל וְעַל רַבָּנָן
וְעַל תַּלְמִידֵיהוֹן וְעַל כָּל תַּלְמִידֵי תַלְמִידֵיהוֹן
וְעַל כָּל מָאן דְּעָסְקִין בְּאוֹרַיְתָא
דִּי בְּאַתְרָא (בארץ ישראל: קַדִּישָׁא) הָדֵין, וְדִי בְּכָל אֲתַר וַאֲתַר
יְהֵא לְהוֹן וּלְכוֹן שְׁלָמָא רַבָּא
חִנָּא וְחִסְדָּא, וְרַחֲמֵי, וְחַיֵּי אֲרִיכֵי, וּמְזוֹנֵי רְוִיחֵי
וּפֻרְקָנָא מִן קֳדָם אֲבוּהוֹן דִּי בִשְׁמַיָּא
וְאִמְרוּ אָמֵן.

יְהֵא שְׁלָמָא רַבָּא מִן שְׁמַיָּא
וְחַיִּים (טוֹבִים) עָלֵינוּ וְעַל כָּל יִשְׂרָאֵל
וְאִמְרוּ אָמֵן.

Bow, take three steps back, as if taking leave of the Divine Presence, then bow, first left, then right, then center, while saying:

עֹשֶׂה שָׁלוֹם/ בעשרת ימי תשובה: הַשָּׁלוֹם/ בִּמְרוֹמָיו
הוּא יַעֲשֶׂה בְרַחֲמָיו שָׁלוֹם, עָלֵינוּ וְעַל כָּל יִשְׂרָאֵל
וְאִמְרוּ אָמֵן.

The following Kaddish requires the presence of a minyan.

Magnified and sanctified may His great name be,
in the world that will in future be renewed,
reviving the dead and raising them up to eternal life.
He will rebuild the city of Jerusalem
and in it re-establish His Temple.
He will remove alien worship from the earth
and restore to its place the worship of Heaven.
Then the Holy One, blessed be He,
will reign in His sovereignty and splendor.
May it be in your lifetime and in your days,
(*Nusaḥ Sepharad:* make His salvation flourish,
and hasten His messiah,)
and in the lifetime of all the House of Israel,
swiftly and soon – and say: Amen.

May His great name be blessed for ever and all time.

Blessed and praised,
glorified and exalted,
raised and honored,
uplifted and lauded
be the name of the Holy One,
blessed be He,
beyond any blessing,
song, praise and consolation uttered in the world –
and say: Amen.

To Israel, to the teachers,
their disciples and their disciples' disciples,
and to all who engage in the study of Torah,
in this (*in Israel add:* holy) place or elsewhere,
may there come to them and you great peace,
grace, kindness and compassion,
long life, ample sustenance and deliverance,
from their Father in Heaven –
and say: Amen.

May there be great peace from heaven,
and (good) life for us and all Israel –
and say: Amen.

Bow, take three steps back, as if taking leave of the Divine Presence, then bow, first left, then right, then center, while saying:

May He who makes peace in His high places,
in His compassion make peace for us and all Israel –
and say: Amen.

לוח ספרים ופירושים

רשימת הספרים והפירושים אשר הובאו במסכת מגילה

אבודרהם — לר׳ דוד אבודרהם, פירוש על סידור התפילה.

ר׳ אברהם בן עזרא — פירושו למקרא.

אגודה — לר׳ אברהם זוסלין הכהן מפפד״מ, קיצור חידושי דינים.

אגדות התלמוד — קובץ עתיק של אגדות התלמוד עם ביאור למחבר שלא נודע שמו.

אדרת אליהו — לר׳ עמנואל חי ריקי, חידושים על הש״ס.

אוצר הכבוד — לר׳ טודרוס הלוי, אבולעפיא, פירוש לאגדות הש״ס.

אור זרוע — לרבינו יצחק מוינה, ביאורים לסוגיות התלמוד.

אור חדש — למהר״ל מפראג, ביאור על מגילת אסתר.

אליה רבה — לר׳ אליהו שפירא, ביאור על שולחן ערוך אורח חיים.

אלשיך — לר׳ משה אלשיך, פירוש לתורה (״תורת משה״).

אשל אברהם — לר׳ אברהם דוד מבוטשאטש, ביאורים לשולחן ערוך.

ביאור הלכה — לר׳ ישראל מאיר הכהן, חלק מ״משנה ברורה״.

בה״ג — עיין: הלכות גדולות.

בינה לעיתים — לר׳ יהונתן אייבשיץ, חידושי מסכתות.

בית חדש — לר׳ יואל סירקיש הלוי, פירושו על ספר ה״טורים״. מובא גם מהגהותיו על הש״ס.

בית יוסף — לר׳ יוסף קארו, פירושו על ספר ה״טורים״.

בית פרץ — לר׳ פרץ בן ר׳ משה, חידושים למסכת מגילה.

ברכי יוסף — לר׳ חיים יוסף דוד אזולאי, חידושים לשולחן ערוך.

גאון יעקב — לר׳ יעקב כהנא, חידושי מסכתות.

גאונים — הכוונה בעיקר לדבריהם המובאים ב״אוצר הגאונים״ לר׳ בנימין מנשה לוין.

גבול בנימין — לר׳ בנימין זאב ווינטרניץ, חידושי הלכות.

גל נעול — לר׳ יוסף מעסניג, חידושים על מסכת מגילה.

גנזי המלך — לר׳ ידידיה טיאה וויל, חידושים למסכת מגילה.

גר״א — לגאון ר׳ אליהו מוילנא, בעיקר ביאורו לשולחן ערוך. לעתים גם מהגהותיו לש״ס.

דגן שמים — לר׳ ישראל יונה לנדא, חידושים למסכתות אחדות.

דרכי משה — לר׳ משה איסרליש, פירושו לספר ה״טורים״.

דרשות ראנ״ח — לר׳ אליהו אבן חיים, ספר דרשות.

הכותב — לר׳ יעקב בן חביב, מלקט ״עין יעקב״, פירוש לספרו.

הלכות גדולות (בה״ג) — ספר פסקים שחיבר אחד הגאונים; מיוחס לר׳ יהודאי גאון.

המאור — לרבינו זרחיה הלוי, השגות והוספות לרי״ף.

השגות הראב״ד — לרבינו אברהם בן דוד, השגות והערות ל״יד החזקה״.

זכרון בספר — לר׳ שמואל לייב קוידר, חידושיו למסכת מגילה.

חידושי אגדות הרשב״א — לרבינו שלמה בן אדרת, ליקוט ביאורים לאגדות שונות שבתלמוד.

חכם צבי — לחכם צבי אשכנזי מאמשטרדם, שאלות ותשובות.

חכמת מנוח — לר׳ מנוח ב״ר שמריה, הגהות והערות על הש״ס.

חסדי דוד — לר׳ דוד פארדו, פירוש לתוספתא.

חתם סופר — לר׳ משה סופר, מן השו״ת וחידושים לש״ס ושו״ע, לר׳ משה סופר.

טור, טורים — לר׳ יעקב בן הרא״ש, פסקי הלכות.

טורי אבן — לר׳ אריה ליב (״שאגת אריה״), חידושים למסכתות אחדות.

טורי זהב — לר׳ דוד חריף, פירוש לשולחן ערוך.

יוחסין — לר׳ אברהם זכות על תולדות ישראל.

יערות דבש — לר׳ יונתן אייבשיץ, ספר דרשות.

יפה מראה — לר׳ שמואל אשכנזי יפה, ביאור אגדות מן התלמוד.

יפה ענף — לר שמואל אשכנזי יפה, ביאור למדרש רבה לחמש המגילות.

יפה תואר — לר׳ שמואל יפה אשכנזי, ביאור למדרש רבה

כל בו — ספר הלכות למחבר קדמון אשר לא נודע שמו.

כללי התלמוד — לר׳ בצלאל אשכנזי, ביאור על דרכי התלמוד.

כסף משנה — לר׳ יוסף קארו, פירוש על ה״יד החזקה״.

כף החיים — לר׳ יעקב סופר, פירוש לשולחן ערוך.

לבוש — לר׳ מרדכי יפה, שם כולל לאוסף ספריו.

לחם משנה — לר׳ אברהם די בוטון, פירוש על ה״יד החזקה״.

מאירי — לרבינו מנחם בן שלמה לבית מאיר, ספר ״בית הבחירה״ בעיקר על ההלכה שבתלמוד.

מבי״ט — לר׳ משה בן יוסף טראני, שאלות ותשובות.

מגן אברהם — לר׳ אברהם מגומבין, פירוש על שולחן ערוך אורח חיים.

מהרי״ו — מורנו הרב ר׳ יעקב וויל, שאלות ותשובות.

מהרי״ל — מורנו הרב רבינו יעקב מולין, חידושי הלכה ושאלות ותשובות.

מהר״ל — מורנו הרב ר׳ ליואי מפראג, ספריו, ובעיקר ביאורי אגדות התלמוד.

מהר״ם שיף — לר׳ מאיר שיף, חידושים על התלמוד.

מהרש״א — מורנו הרב ר׳ שמואל אליעזר איידליש, חידושי הלכות ואגדות לתלמוד.

מחזיק ברכה — לר׳ חיים יוסף דוד אזולאי, חידושי הלכות.

מכתם — לרבינו דוד בר׳ לוי, חידושי הלכות.

מלאכת שלמה — לר׳ שלמה עדני, ביאור על המשנה.

מלוא הרועים — לר׳ יעקב צבי יאליש, הגהות והערות לש״ס.

מנות הלוי — לר׳ שלמה אלקבץ, ביאור למגילת אסתר.

מנחת בכורים — לר׳ שמואל אביגדור מקרלין, פירוש לתוספתא.

משחת אהרן — לר׳ אהרן זליג מאוסטראה, חידושי הלכות למסכתות שונות.

משנה ברורה — לר׳ ישראל מאיר הכהן, פירוש לשולחן ערוך.

נודע ביהודה — לר׳ יחזקאל לנדא מפראג, שאלות ותשובות.

נזר הקודש — לר׳ יחיאל מיכל בר׳ עוזיאל, פירוש למדרש רבה.

נמוקי יוסף — לר׳ יוסף חביבא, פירוש להלכות הרי״ף.

ספר הישר — לרבינו תם, על עניינים שונים בתלמוד.

עולת שבת — לר׳ יואל בן שועיב, דרשות על פרשת השבוע.

עטרת זקנים — לר׳ מנחם מענדל אוירבך, פירוש לשולחן ערוך.

עין יעקב — לר׳ יעקב בר׳ יוסף ריישר, פירוש ל״עין יעקב״.

עין יעקב — לר׳ יעקב בן חביב, ליקוט אגדות הש״ס ופירושן.

ערוגת הבושם — לר׳ צבי הירש געץ, חידושים למסכת מגילה.

ערוך — לר׳ נתן בר׳ יחיאל מרומי, המילון התלמודי הראשון.

ערוך השולחן — לר׳ יחיאל מיכאל אפשטיין, קובץ פסקי הלכה.

פורת יוסף — לר׳ יוסף בר׳ צבי מוילנא, חידושים למסכתות בתלמוד.

פירוש המשניות לרמב״ם — פירוש הרמב״ם למשנה, הקרוי ״ספר המאור״.

פני יהושע — לר׳ יעקב יהושע פלק מפרנקפורט, חידושי הש״ס.

פרדס רמונים — לר׳ שם טוב אבן שפרוט. על אגדות הש״ס.

פרי חדש — לר׳ חזקיה דא סילוא, חידושי הלכות.

פרי מגדים — לר׳ יוסף תאומים, פירוש למפרשי השולחן ערוך.

פתח עיניים — לר׳ חיים יוסף דוד אזולאי, ביאור למסכתות הש״ס (בעיקר באגדה).

קול יהודה — לר׳ יהודה מגלוגא, קובץ חידושים מגדולי דורו.

קרבן העדה — לר׳ דוד פרנקל, פירוש לתלמוד הירושלמי.

קרן אורה — לר׳ יצחק בר׳ אהרן קארלין, חידושים למסכתות הש״ס.

רא״ה — רבינו אהרן הלוי, בן דורו של הרשב״א, חידושים.

ראבי״ה — לר׳ אליעזר בר׳ יואל הלוי, פסקי דינים, חידושים ושו״ת.

רא״ש — רבינו אשר, בעיקר פסקי ההלכה שלו לתלמוד, וגם תוספות הרא״ש על כמה מסכתות.

ראש יוסף — לר׳ יוסף בר׳ יעקב מפעטשוב, חידושים על אגדות הש״ס.

ראשון לציון — לר׳ חיים בן עטר, חידושים לכמה מסכתות.

רבינו בחיי — לרבינו בחיי בן אשר, פירוש לתורה (״כד הקמח״).

ר״ג, רגמ״ה — רבינו גרשון מאור הגולה, פירושו לתלמוד.

רדב״ז — לרבינו דוד בן זמרא הכוונה לפירושיו לכמה מספרי הרמב״ם ולספר השאלות ותשובות שלו.

רב האי גאון — בעיקר דברים המובאים משאלות ותשובות וקבצי תורת הגאונים.

רוקח — לרבינו אליעזר מגרמייזא, דינים ודברי מוסר.

רז״ה — רבינו זרחיה הלוי, בעיקר מספר ״המאור״.

ר״ח — רבינו חננאל מקיירואן, פירושו לתלמוד.

ר׳ יונתן — רבינו יהונתן מלוניל, פירוש על הרי״ף.

ר״י בן מיגאש — ר׳ יוסף אבן מיגאש, שאלות ותשובות.

ריא״ז — רבינו ישעיה אור זרוע, פסקי הלכות.

ריא״ף — ר׳ יאשיה פינטו, הכוונה לפירושו על ״עין יעקב״.

ריב״ש — ר׳ יצחק בר ששת, הכוונה לחידושיו.

רי״ד — רבינו ישעיה מטראני, פירושיו למסכתות שונות בתלמוד. וכן ״פסקי הרי״ד״ — פסקיו לפי סדר התלמוד.

ריטב״א — רבינו יום טוב אלאשבילי, הכוונה לחידושיו לש״ס.

ריח דודאים — לר׳ צבי אלימלך שפירא, חידושים למסכת מגילה.

ריעב״ץ — ר׳ יעקב עמדין בר׳ צבי, הגהות על הש״ס.

רי״ף — רבינו יצחק אלפסי, ספר הלכות.

רלב״ח — ר׳ לוי בן חביב, שאלות ותשובות.

רמ״א — ר׳ משה איסרליש, בעיקר חידושים והגהותיו (ספר ה״מפה״) לשולחן ערוך.

רמב״ם — רבינו משה בן מימון, הכוונה לספר ״יד החזקה״, לעתים גם לדבריו ב״פירוש המשניות״.

רמב״ן — רבינו משה בן נחמן, מחידושיו לש״ס, ומפירושו לתורה.

רמ״ע — ר׳ מנחם עזריה מפאנו, בעיקר ספרו ״עשרה מאמרות״ ותשובותיו.

רמת שמואל — לר׳ שמואל הלוי, חידושים לכמה מסכתות.

ר״ן — רבינו נסים, הכוונה בעיקר לפירושו על הרי״ף. כמו כן לספר ״חידושי הר״ן״, המיוחס לו לפי דעות מסויימות.

רב נתן אב הישיבה — פירוש למשנה של אחד מראשי ישיבת ירושלים בתקופת הגאונים.

רב עמרם גאון — הכוונה לסידור קדמון שנערך על ידיו.

ר׳ עקיבא איגר — הערותיו למשנה ולתלמוד, ״דרוש וחידוש״, וגליון הש״ס.

ר״צ חיות — ר׳ צבי חיות, הגהותיו וחידושיו לתלמוד.

רב צמח גאון — מדבריו ב״אוצר הגאונים״ ושאר מקורות.

ר״ש — הוא רבינו שמשון בן אברהם, הכוונה בעיקר לפירושו על סדר זרעים במשנה.

רשב״א — רבינו שלמה בן אברהם בן אדרת, הכוונה בעיקר לחידושיו לש״ס.

רשב״ץ — ר׳ שמעון בן צמח דוראן, שאלות ותשובות.

רש״ל — ר׳ שלמה לוריא, מתוך חידושיו על הש״ס, וספרו ״ים של שלמה״.

רש״ש — ר׳ שמואל שטראשון, הגהותיו על הש״ס.

שאילתות — לרב אחאי גאון, פסקי הלכה מסודרים לפי פרשיות השבועה.

שדי חמד — לר׳ חיים חזקיהו מדיני, פסקי הלכות וחידושים.

שולחן ערוך הרב — לר׳ שניאור זלמן מלאדי, ספר הלכות.

שו״ע — לר׳ יוסף קארו, שולחן ערוך (וחלקיו: אורח חיים, יורה דעה, חושן משפט, אבן העזר).

ש״ך — שפתי כהן, לר׳ שבתי כהן, פירוש לחלקי ה״שולחן ערוך״.

שו״ת בית אפרים — לר׳ אפרים זלמן מרגליות, שאלות ותשובות.

שו״ת מהרי״ט — מורנו הרב ר׳ יום טוב אלגאזי, שאלות ותשובות.

שו״ת פנים מאירות — לר׳ מאיר אייזנשטט, שאלות ותשובות.

שו״ת רדב״ז — לר׳ דוד בן זמרה, שאלות ותשובות.

שו״ת שבות יעקב — לר׳ יעקב בר׳ יוסף ריישר, שאלות ותשובות.

שיירי כנסת גדולה — לר׳ חיים בנבנישתי, אוסף פסקי הלכה.

שני לוחות הברית — לר׳ ישעיהו הלוי הורביץ, ספר מוסר והלכה.

שערי אפרים — לר׳ אפרים זלמן מרגליות, קובץ דינים על קריאת התורה.

שערי תשובה — לר׳ חיים מרדכי מרגליות, קובץ תשובות לפי סדר ה״שולחן ערוך״.

שפת אמת — לר׳ יהודה לייב אלתר, חידושים למסכתות התלמוד.

תוספות הרא״ש — לרבינו אשר פירוש לכמה מסכתות.

תוספות יום טוב — לר׳ יום טוב ליפמן הלר, פירוש למשניות.

תוספות ישנים — מהדורה אחרת של פירוש בעלי התוספות לכמה מסכתות.

תוספתא כפשוטה — לר׳ שאול ליברמן, פירוש לתוספתא.

תורת משה — לר׳ משה סופר (״חתם סופר״), פירוש לתורה.

תפארת ישראל — לר׳ ישראל ליפשיץ, פירוש המשניות.

תפילה למשה אלמושנינו — לר׳ משה אלמושנינו, ספר מוסר והגות.

לוח ראשי תיבות

שהובאו בצורה זו במסכת מגילה

אדר״נ — אבות דר׳ נתן

אה״ע — אבן העזר

אה״ת — אגדות התלמוד

או״ז — אור זרוע

או״ח — אורח חיים

איכ״ר — איכה רבה

אסת״ר — אסתר רבה

א״ר — אליה רבה

אר״י — אדוננו רבינו יצחק

בה״ג — בעל הלכות גדולות

בה״ל — ביאור הלכה

ב״ח — בית חדש

ב״י — בית יוסף

ב״מ — בבא מציעא

במדב״ר — במדבר רבה

ב״ק — בבא קמא

ב״ר — בראשית רבה

גר״א — גאון רבי אליהו (מוילנה)

ד״ה — דיבור המתחיל

דה״י — דברי הימים

ד״מ — דרכי משה

דפו״י — דפוס ישן, דפוסים ישנים

ה׳ — הלכה. כגון: ה״א = הלכה א׳. ה״ב = הלכה ב׳ וכו׳

הג״א — הגהות אשרי

הקב״ה — הקדוש ברוך הוא

ויק״ר — ויקרא רבה

חז״ל — חכמים זכרונם לברכה

חיד״א — חיים יוסף דוד אזולאי

חכ״צ — חכם צבי

חס״ד — חסדי דוד

חת״ס — חתם סופר

טו״א — טורי אבן

יו״ד — יורה דעה

כיו״ב — כיוצא בזה

כצ״ל — כן צריך להיות. כן צריך לומר.

כ״מ — כסף משנה

כפ״ה — כף החיים

כת״י — כתב יד, כתבי יד

כתי״מ — כתב יד מינכן

ל״מ — לחם משנה

מ׳ — משנה. כגון: מ״א = משנה א׳ וכו׳

מ״א — מגן אברהם

מ״ב — משנה ברורה

מבי״ט — משה בן יוסף טראני

מהרי״ן — מורנו הרב רבי יעקב וייל

מהר״ל — מורנו הרב רבי יהודה ליוואי (מפראג)

מהר״ם שיף — מורנו הרב ר׳ מאיר שיף

מהרש״א — מורנו הרב ר׳ שמואל אליעזר (אידליש)

מו״ק — מועד קטן

מלא״ש — מלאכת שלמה

מנ״ב — מנחת ביכורים

מס׳ — מסכת

מע״ש — מעשר שני

נו״ב — נודע ביהודה

נ״ך — נביאים כתובים

נמו״י — נמוקי יוסף

ס׳ — סימן, סעיף.

עה״ש — ערוך השולחן

עה״ת — על התורה

ע״ז — עבודה זרה

עט״ז — עטרת זקנים

ע״י — עין יעקב. על ידי.

עיי״ש — עיין שם

עפ״י — על פי

פ׳ — פרק, פרשה. כגון: פ״א — פרק א׳. פ״א — פרשה א׳ וכו׳.

פיה״מ — פירוש המשניות

פנ״י — פני יהושע

פרדר״א — פרקי דר׳ אליעזר

פר״ח — פרי חדש

צ״ע — צריך עיון

קה״ר — קהלת רבה

ר׳ — ראה. רבי רבינו.

ראב״ד — רבינו אברהם בן דוד

ראבי״ה — רבינו אלעזר בר׳ יואל הלוי

רא״ה — רבינו אהרן הלוי

ראנ״ח — רבי אליהו אבן חיים

רא״ש — רבינו אשר

ר״ג, רגמ״ה — רבינו גרשום מאור הגולה

רדב״ז — ר׳ דוד בן זמרה

ר״י מיגאש — ר׳ יוסף אבן מיגאש

ריב״א — רבינו יצחק בן אשר

רמ״ע — ר׳ מנחם עזריה מפאנו

ר״ה — — ראש השנה

רה״ג — רב האי גאון

רו״ר — רות רבה

רז״ה — רבינו זרחיה הלוי

ר״ח — רבינו חננאל

ריא״ז — רבינו ישעיה אור זרוע

ריא״ף — ר׳ יאשיה פינטו

ריב״ש — רבינו יצחק בר ששת

רי״ד — ר׳ ישעיה דיטראני

ריטב״א — רבינו יום טוב בן אברהם (אלאשבילי)

ריעב״ץ — ר׳ יעקב עמדין בן צבי

רי״ף — ר׳ יצחק אלפסי

רלב״ח — רבי לוי בן חביב

רמ״א — ר׳ משה איסרליש

רמב״ם — רבינו משה בן מיימון

רמב״ן — רבינו משה בן נחמן

ר״נ — רבינו נסים (בן ראובן)

רע״ח ריקי — רבינו עמנואל חי ריקי

רעק״א — ר׳ עקיבא איגר

ר״צ חיות — ר׳ צבי חיות

ר״ש — רבינו שמשון (בן אברהם)

רשב״א — רבינו שלמה בן אברהם בן אדרת

רשב״ם — רבינו שמואל בן מאיר

רשב״ץ — ר׳ שמעון בן צמח

רש״י — רבינו שלמה יצחקי

רש״ל — ר׳ שלמה לוריא

רש״ש — ר׳ שמואל שטראשון

ר״ת — רבינו תם

שה״ר — שיר השירים רבה

שוח״ט — שוחר טוב

שו״ע — שולחן ערוך

שועה״ר — שולחן ערוך הרב

שו״ת — שאלות ותשובות

ש״ך — שפתי כהן

שכנה״ג — שיירי כנסת הגדולה

של״ה — שני לוחות הברית

שמו״ר — שמות רבה

שע״א — שערי אפרים

שפ״א — שפת אמת

ש״ת — שערי תשובה

תוי״ט — תוספות יום טוב

תו״כ — תורת כהנים

תוס׳ — תוספות

תוס׳ הרא״ש — תוספות הרא״ש

תכ״פ — תוספתא כפשוטה

תנדב״א — תנא דבי אליהו

תפא״י — תפארת ישראל